2020

the Next EXIT®

The Most Accurate Interstate Highway Service Guide Ever Printed™

the Next EXIT® will save time, money and frustration.

This tool will help you find services along the USA Interstate Highways like nothing you have ever used.

Restaurants • Gas Stations • Hotels • RV Camping • And Much More

PO Box 888
Garden City, UT 84028
www.theNextExit.com

the Next Exit®

USER GUIDE

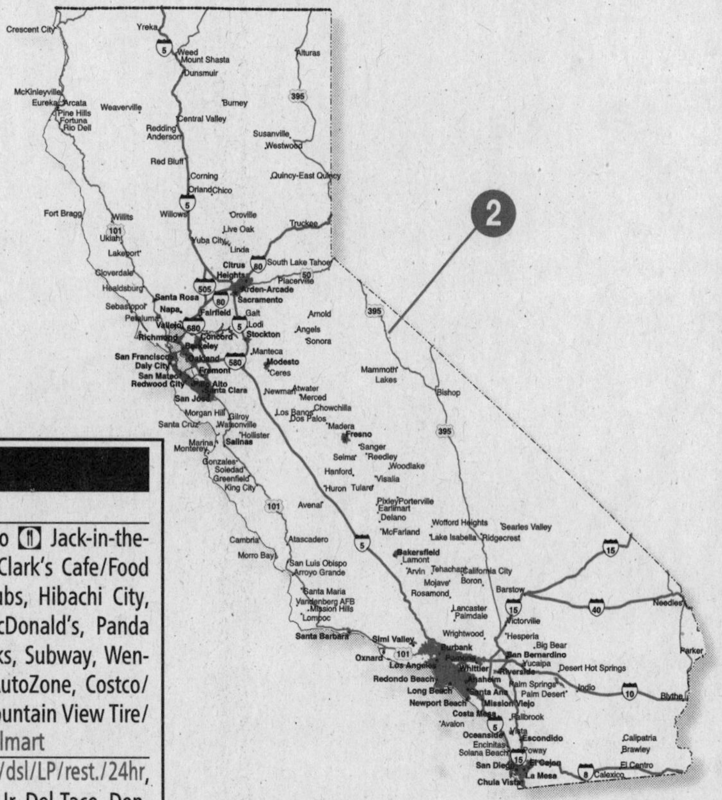

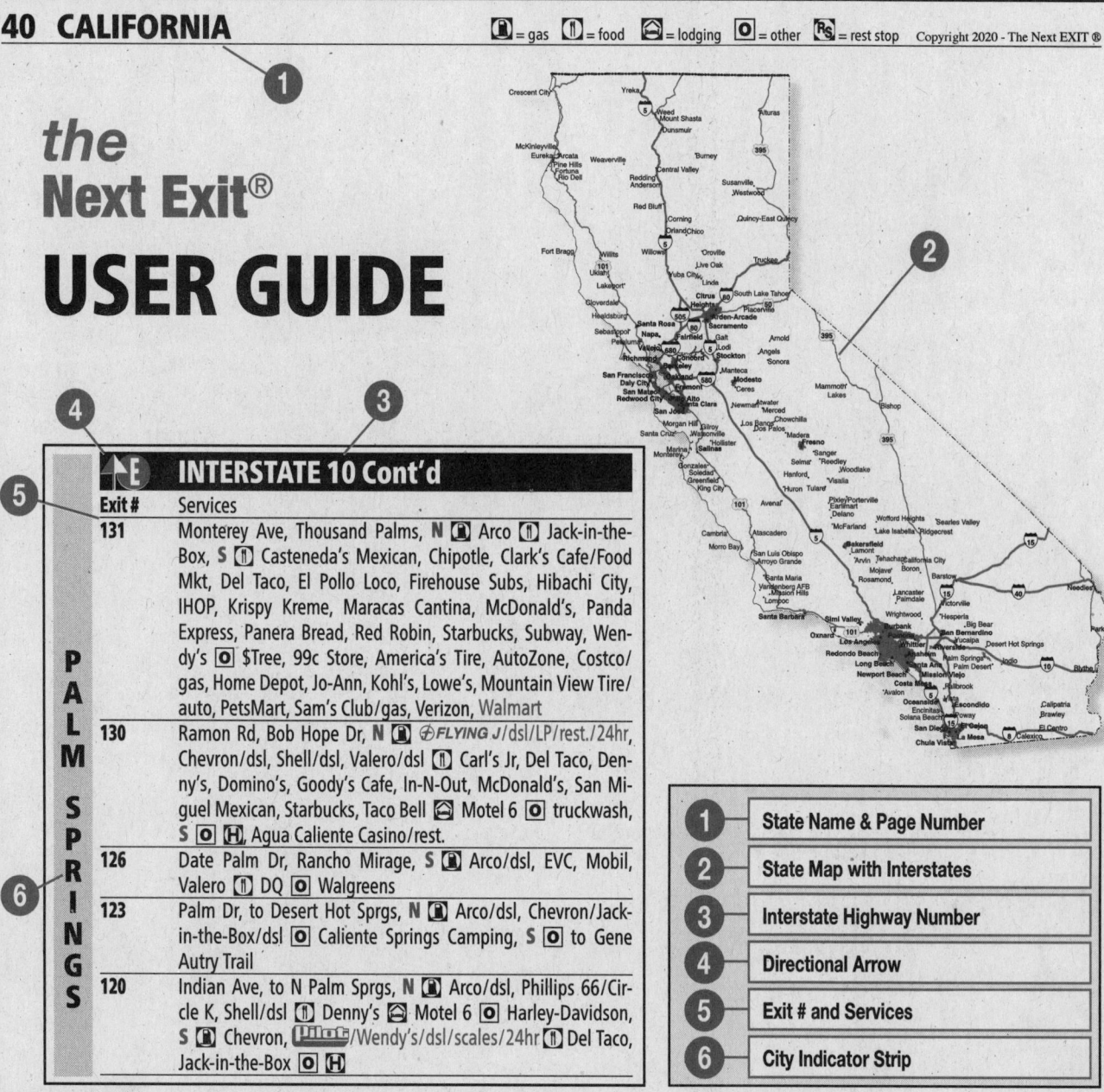

	INTERSTATE 10 Cont'd
Exit #	**Services**
131	Monterey Ave, Thousand Palms, **N** Arco Jack-in-the-Box, **S** Casteneda's Mexican, Chipotle, Clark's Cafe/Food Mkt, Del Taco, El Pollo Loco, Firehouse Subs, Hibachi City, IHOP, Krispy Kreme, Maracas Cantina, McDonald's, Panda Express, Panera Bread, Red Robin, Starbucks, Subway, Wendy's $Tree, 99c Store, America's Tire, AutoZone, Costco/gas, Home Depot, Jo-Ann, Kohl's, Lowe's, Mountain View Tire/auto, PetsMart, Sam's Club/gas, Verizon, Walmart
130	Ramon Rd, Bob Hope Dr, **N** FLYING J/dsl/LP/rest./24hr, Chevron/dsl, Shell/dsl, Valero/dsl Carl's Jr, Del Taco, Denny's, Domino's, Goody's Cafe, In-N-Out, McDonald's, San Miguel Mexican, Starbucks, Taco Bell Motel 6 truckwash, **S** H, Agua Caliente Casino/rest.
126	Date Palm Dr, Rancho Mirage, **S** Arco/dsl, EVC, Mobil, Valero DQ Walgreens
123	Palm Dr, to Desert Hot Sprgs, **N** Arco/dsl, Chevron/Jack-in-the-Box/dsl Caliente Springs Camping, **S** to Gene Autry Trail
120	Indian Ave, to N Palm Sprgs, **N** Arco/dsl, Phillips 66/Circle K, Shell/dsl Denny's Motel 6 Harley-Davidson, **S** Chevron, Pilot/Wendy's/dsl/scales/24hr Del Taco, Jack-in-the-Box H

PALM SPRINGS

1. State Name & Page Number
2. State Map with Interstates
3. Interstate Highway Number
4. Directional Arrow
5. Exit # and Services
6. City Indicator Strip

Exit

Most states number exits by the nearest mile marker(mm). A few states use consecutive numbers, in which case mile markers are given in ( ). Mile markers are the little green vertical signs beside the interstate at one mile intervals which indicate distance from the southern or western border of a state. Odd numbered interstates run north/south, even numbered run east/west.

Services

Services are listed alphabetically by category = **gas** = **food** = **lodging** = **rest stop** = **other** services including camping.

"H" indicates an exit from which a hospital may be accessed, but it may not be close to the exit.

Services located away from the exit may be referred to by "access to," or "to" and a distance may be given.

A directional notation is also given, such as **N**, **S**, **E** or **W**

Directional Arrows

Follow exits DOWN the page if traveling from North to South or East to West, UP the page if traveling South to North or West to East.

Additional copies may be ordered by using the form supplied in the back of this book, or by visiting online at ***www.theNextExit.com***
the Next EXIT, inc. makes no warranty regarding the accuracy of the information contained in this publication. This information is subject to change without notice.

TABLE OF CONTENTS

Abbreviations & Symbols used in the Next EXIT ®

AFB ....Air Force Base
B&B ....Bed&Breakfast
Bfd............Battlefield
CNG..........Compressed Natural Gas
Ctr ....Center
Coll ....College
Cyn ....canyon
dsl.............diesel
$................Dollar
EVC ....Electric Vehicle Charger
LNG ....Liquid Natural Gas
Mem ....Memorial
Mkt ....Market
Mtn ....Mountain
mm ....mile marker
N ....north side of exit
S ....south side of exit
E ....east side of exit
W ....west side of exit

NM............National Monument
NHS ....Nat Hist Site
NWR.........Nat Wildlife Reserve
NF.............National Forest
[H] ....Hospital
[Airport] ....Airport
[Picnic] ....Picnic Tables
NP.............National Park
NRA..........Nat Rec Area
pk ....park
pkwy.........parkway
rest. ....restaurant
nb ....northbound
sb ....southbound
eb ....eastbound
wb.............westbound
SP.............state park
SF ....state forest
Sprs..........springs

st ....street, state
sta ....station
TPK...........Turnpike
USPO ....Post Office
vet ....veterinarian
whse.........warehouse
@..............truckstop (full service)
red print....RV accessible
[Handicapped] ....Handicapped accessible
[Telephone] ....Telephone
[Gas] ....Gas
[Food] ....Food
[Lodging] ....Lodging
[O] ....Other
[RS] ....Rest Stop / Rest Area

More digital options are available at www.theNextExit.com

Tale of the Tickets

Mark Watson – Winter 2020

Late summer in the northern hemisphere is special. Not only do the days and temperature begin to shrink, the sunlight shines in at a different angle, casting the landscape with a softer hue. By autumnal equinox the shadows of evening display a unique slant. Humidity, persistent in August, loosens its grip by September giving way to periods of drier and cooler weather. And the colors? My Goodness! From the northern woods to coastal Carolina or New England to the Rockies, nature shares an extravaganza free for viewing, no ticket needed. The red sumac underbrush by the highways signals that changes are afoot and most importantly, football season is coming!

Drive through any town on a fall Friday night and look for high school stadium lights. Colonies of spectators: students, parents, girlfriends and neighbors, all gather around these buzzing hives of activity in anticipation of a contest. On October Saturdays university towns swell with swarms of the faithful, surging to support the home team. The cheers, pageantry and tail gate; even the air vibrates with excitement. When the warriors take the field, you can feel the hum. I am sorry for anyone who doesn't appreciate football, particularly at the collegiate level.

As autumn wears on, the trees undress even as the green grass lingers; on the gridiron, the better teams emerge. The seasons are great when your team is good, but if your boys reach November undefeated the real fun begins. And if they play the first week of December when conference championships are decided, there is a chance Old Man Winter can be held off nearly to February. Around New Year's Day, four teams meet in three games to decide which is best in all the land. For most folks, attending such an event might happen only once or twice in a lifetime. It is

Continued Next Page

lightning in a bottle and ought to be celebrated. At least that is the way I saw it last year when Clemson made the playoffs.

I pulled away from the Atlantic Ocean early on the morning of December 27th headed for Arlington, Texas and with a little luck, Santa Clara, California. The odometer showed 000114, mostly from test driving. The Farm was right on the way so I breezed by to discover the Stars and Stripes hanging from the pecan tree by only one grommet. Any patriot knows this will not do. A quick fix and I felt better heading west with Old Glory fluttering freely in the rearview mirror.

At the Costco in Augusta, a Georgia Bulldog saw my paw and offered good luck with the Irish but cautioned that the Tigers would struggle against the mighty Alabama Tide. "Doesn't everyone?" I asked. This could have escalated into a skirmish, but I had loftier aspirations this day than growling back at dawgs.

"...we returned to the parking lot and found the CRV missing, towed to a wrecking yard on the rough side of Fort Worth. Nothing says 'welcome to town' like ransoming your car through bullet-proof glass from the tattooed lady in a smoke-filled room."

I ground travel *a lot*, and I mean it. Publishing ***the Next EXIT*** requires that wherever the interstate highways go, there I go, explaining why I seldom drive directly to a destination. Instead of following I-20 straight to Dallas, I bore right at Birmingham and spent the first night near Little Rock, aiming to update I-30 toward AT&T Stadium, which I did on the second day. Courtesy of two $44 airline tickets from Vegas, my son and grandson joined me that evening, increasing our fandom to three generations.

By Saturday morning, game prices stopped falling and began to rise. Unwilling to accept the reality that the Cotton Bowl was more popular than we anticipated, we headed to the stadium to buy tickets "on the street," an exercise I have conducted many times. Imagine our delight when a nice man not only sold them to us but pointed out free parking as well. Think of our dismay when the beautifully mastered tickets would not scan at the gate. A pox on the counterfeiter! A blessing on the Will Call window which issued us standing-room-only passes to help cover our losses!

Everything considered, we had a splendid view of the game and cheered the Tigers to victory.

After $31 worth of chicken tenders we returned to the parking lot and found the CRV missing, towed to a wrecking yard on the rough side of Fort Worth. Nothing says "welcome to town" like ransoming your car through bullet-proof glass from the tattooed lady in a smoke-filled room. After this, we were off to watch what was left of the other semi-final game.

Except for a snowstorm between Albuquerque and Flagstaff, the trip to northern Utah was less eventful. By midweek, I had removed the snow, filled the propane tank and made ready to streak across Nevada toward the biggest game on this stage. It snowed again the morning we left, but another son, his wife and I quickly vanquished Interstate 80, this time pushing the button on valid electronic game tickets near the Humboldt Sink. Everything seemed to be going our way as we wheeled into Reno; the roads were dry and traffic and our moods were light. Then the highway information sign blinked, "I-80 W of Reno closed until further notice."

We did not come this far only to be thwarted by blizzard conditions near Donner Pass. After asking a few questions we decided on US 50 over Spooner

Pass around the south shore of Lake Tahoe. I sat in the all-wheel drive vehicle while the youngsters figured out the tire chains, but with the wind and snow gusting near 30 mph our first attempt failed. We regrouped at Chipotle in Carson City, chained up underneath the protection of a service station canopy and climbed over the mountain. Things were looking better by South Tahoe but then traffic stopped, allowing us to see snow swirling and trees swaying along the road. After moving one mile in three hours we determined to find lodging. A Donner Party TV documentary ran that night, reminding us of what can happen to people caught in a blizzard. We watched, hoping the roads would be better by morning.

They were, and by afternoon we coasted down the western slope of the Sierras, donned our orange tiger paws, added my daughter from UC Davis and began the search for parking in Santa Clara. "$80," said the friendly man, pointing to a spot. "Will we be towed?" I queried. "Of course not," he reassured. And he was right.

Since we were the underdogs, the Tide fans were polite but condescending. By the end of the first quarter, I said to my son, "We can play with these guys." By halftime, I added "we might beat these guys." And we did. After In-N-Out, we breezed back to Davis, exhausted but elated.

Next day, I said goodbye to the children and worked down I-5 toward Los Angeles, turning east on the 210 to avoid the city. A day later I passed the Fiesta Bowl in Phoenix, a venue of past Tiger glory and two days after that whiffed by the Superdome in New Orleans where college football hopes are centered for early 2020. By now, the South Carolina coast was a hard day's drive but achievable in a slightly used Honda. I wrote the mileage down when I arrived, penciling in 008416. Not a bad ticket price, all in all, for a national championship. Go Tigers! ❖

ALABAMA

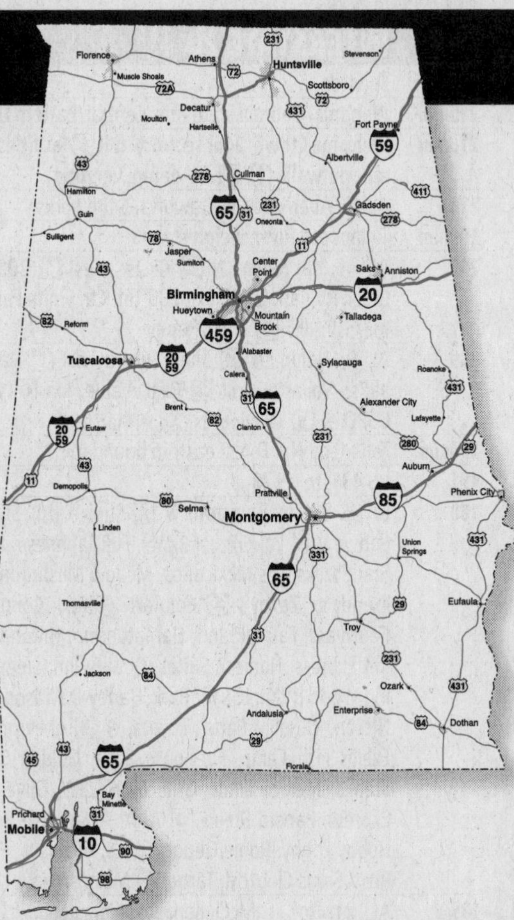

INTERSTATE 10

Exit #	Services
66.5mm	Alabama/Florida state line
66mm	**Welcome Ctr full facilities, litter barrels, petwalk, vending**
53	rd 64, Wilcox Rd, N Marathon/Oasis/Chester's/Stuckey's/Subway/dsl/scales/24hr/@ Riverside RV Park, Styx River Resort, S Chevron/dsl Azalea Acres RV Park, fireworks, Hilltop RV Park (1.5 mi), Wilderness RV Park
49	Rd 68, Baldwin Beach Express, to Gulf Shores, Orange Beach, Gulf SP, S Buc-ee's/dsl
44	AL59, Loxley, N Loves/Arby's/dsl/scales/24hr Bay Inn, S Chevron/dsl, Exxon/dsl, RaceWay/dsl Burger King, Hardee's, McDonald's, Waffle House Loxley Motel (3mi), WindChase Inn to Gulf SP
38	AL 181, Malbis, N CA Dreaming, Chick-fil-A, Cracker Barrel, Half Shell Oyster House, IHOP, Logan's Roadhouse, Marble Slab, McDonald's, Moe's SW Grill, Newk's Eatery, Olive Garden, Panera Bread, Pizza Hut, Poor Mexican, Ruby Tuesday, Sonic, Starbucks, Stix Asian, Taco Bell, Waffle House, Wendy's Best Western, Comfort Inn, Holiday Inn Express, La Quinta $Tree, Advance Parts, Barnes&Noble, Belk, Best Buy, Dillard's, GNC, Goodyear/auto, Michael's, Old Navy, Petsmart, Publix, Ross, Tuesday Morning, Verizon, Walgreens, World Mkt, S Chevron/dsl, Shell/LA Subs, Texaco/dsl Burger King, Don Carlos, Firehouse Subs, Mellow Mushroom, Zaxby's Malbis Motel (1mi), Woodspring Suites AT&T, Honda, Hyundai, Lowe's, Nissan, Sam's Club/gas, Toyota, URGENT CARE, VW
35	US 90, US 98, N Marathon, Shell Beef O'Brady's, China Fun Courtyard, Fairfield Inn Bass Pro Shops, JC Penney, Kohl's, Piggly Wiggly, Rite Aid, to Blakeley SP, USPO, S Exxon/dsl, Shell/dsl Arby's, Bangkok Thai, Boudreaux's Cajun Grill, Burger King, Dickey's BBQ, Domino's, Dragon City Buffet, Dunkin', El Rancho Mexican, Firehouse Subs, Five Guys, Foosackly's Chicken Fingers, Hooters, IHOP, Jubilee Diner, Longhorn Steaks, Los Tacos, Maddio's, McDonald's, Mediterranean Sandwich, O'Charley's, Papa John's, Pizza Hut, S China Rest., Smoothie King, Starbucks, Subway, Taco Bell, Waffle House, Waffle House (2), Zaxby's Comfort Suites, Eastern Shore Motel, Hampton Inn, Hilton Garden, Homewood Suites, Microtel H, $Tree, AT&T, Dick's, Fresh Mkt, GNC, Hobby Lobby, Home Depot, Office Depot, Petco, TJ Maxx
30	US 90/98, Battleship Pkwy, N Blue Gill Rest., Ed's Seafood Shed, Oyster House, S same as 27
27	US 90/98, Battleship Pkwy, Gov't St, S Cafe Del Rio, Felix's Fish Camp, R&R Seafood, Ralph&Kacoo's Seafood to USS Alabama
26b	Water St, Mobile, downtown, N Candlewood Suites, Hampton Inn, Holiday Inn, Quality Inn, Renaissance, to Visitors Ctr
26a	Canal St (from eb), same as 26b
25b	Virginia St, Mobile, N Shell/dsl
25a	Texas St (from wb, no return)
24	Broad St, to Duval St, Mobile, N Chevron/dsl
23	Michigan Ave, N Shell/dsl
22b a	AL 163, Dauphin Island Pkwy, N $General, Family$, S Exxon/Subway, Mobil/dsl Checkers, Hart's Chicken, Kim's Palace, Waffle House $General
20	I-65 N, to Montgomery
17	AL 193, Tillmans Corner, to Dauphin Island, N Firehouse Subs, Five Guys, Golden Corral, IHOP, Moe's SW, Panda Express, Ruby Tuesday, Zaxby's H, AT&T, auto repair, Lowe's, Office Depot, URGENT CARE, Verizon, Walmart/Subway
15b a	US 90, Tillmans Corner, to Mobile, N Chevron, Murphy Express/dsl, RaceWay/dsl Arby's, Aztecas Mexican, Burger King, Domino's, Godfather's, Hooters, KFC, Krystal, Little Caesar's, McDonald's, Papa John's, Popeye's, Russell's BBQ, Shrimp Basket, Subway, Taco Bell, Waffle House Baymont Inn, Best Value Inn, Comfort Suites, Days Inn, EconoLodge, Extended Suites, Hampton Inn, Holiday Inn, Holiday Inn Express, Home 2 Suites, InTown Suites, La Quinta, Motel 6, Quality Inn, Red Roof Inn, Rodeway Inn, Super 8 $General, $Tree, AutoZone, BigLots, Family$, Firestone/auto, Mike's Transmissions, O'Reilly Parts, PepBoys, vet, Walgreens, Winn-Dixie, S Exxon, RaceWay/dsl, Shell/dsl Hardee's, Waffle House Advance Parts, auto repair, B&R Campers, Boutique RV Ctr, Peterbilt, tires, transmissions, USPO, vet
13	to Theodore, N Clark/dsl, Pilot/Wendy's/dsl/scales/24hr, Shell/Subway Burger King, Church's, McDonald's, Waffle House Advance Parts, auto repair, Family$, Greyhound Prk, Rouse's Mkt, transmissions, Walgreens, Walmart Mkt/dsl, S Chevron/dsl Bellingraf Gardens, I-10 Kamping, Paynes RV Park (4mi)
10	rd 39, Bayou La Batre, Dawes, N Waffle House Kenworth
4	AL 188 E, to Grand Bay, N Exxon, Shell/Subway, TA/Dunkin'/Popeye's/Country Pride/dsl/scales/24hr/@ Arby's, McDonald's, Sam's Super Burger, Waffle House $General, Bumper Parts, S Chevron Hardee's Trav-L-Kamp
1mm	**Welcome Ctr eb, full facilities, info, litter barrels, petwalk, RV dump**
0mm	Alabama/Mississippi state line

MOBILE

THEODORE

AL

INTERSTATE 20

Exit #	Services
215mm	Alabama/Georgia state line, Central/Eastern time zone
213mm	**Welcome Ctr wb, 24hr security, full facilities, info, litter barrels, petwalk, , , RV dump, vending**
210	AL 49, Abernathy, N fireworks, S fireworks
209mm	Tallapoosa River, **weigh sta wb**
205	AL 46, to Heflin, N Circle K/dsl 205 Cafe Cane Creek RV Park (2mi), Exit 205 Tire Ctr, Smith Farms, S Chevron/dsl/24hr Truck Repair
199	AL 9, Heflin, N Shell/Subway/dsl Hardee's, McDonald's, Vallarta Grill Best Value Inn Chevrolet, Ford, USPO, S Chevron/dsl, SuperMart/dsl
198mm	Talladega Nat Forest eastern boundary
191	US 431, to US 78

ANNISTON

Exit #	Services
188	to US 78, to Anniston, N Samco/dsl, Shell/dsl, Texaco/Subway/dsl Cracker Barrel, Fuji Japanese, IHOP, KFC, LoneStar Steaks, Los Mexicanos, Mellow Mushroom, Waffle House, Wendy's, Zaxby's Comfort Suites, Country Inn&Suites, Courtyard, Fairfield Inn, Hampton Inn, Hilton Garden, Holiday Inn Express, Home 2 Suites, Quality Inn, Sleep Inn Camping World RV Ctr, GS RV Park, Harley-Davidson, Honda, Lowe's, Nissan, O'Reilly Parts, Toyota, S Chevron/dsl Arby's, Ezell's Fish Camp, Firehouse Subs, Golden Corral, Longhorn Steaks, Mexico Lindo Grill, Moe's SW, Olive Garden, Panda Express, Panera Bread AAA, AT&T, Best Buy, Dick's, GNC, Hobby Lobby, Home Depot, Kohl's, Old Navy, Petsmart, Publix, Ross, Sams Club/dsl, Target, TJ Maxx, Verizon
185	AL 21, to Ft McClellan, to Anniston, N Chevron/dsl, GrubMart/dsl, Shell/dsl, Texaco Applebee's, Arby's, Bojangles, Burger King, Capt D's, China Luck, CiCi's Pizza, Hardee's, HoneyBaked Ham, Jack's Rest., Logan's Roadhouse, Los Mexicanos, McAlister's Deli, McDonald's, O'Charley's, Papa John's, Pizza Hut, Red Lobster, Red Pepper Grill, Shoney's, Sonic, Starbucks, Super Buffet, Taco Bell, Waffle House, Western Sizzlin Best Value Inn, Liberty Inn, Red Carpet Inn $General, Advance Parts, Aldi Foods, BooksAMillion, CVS Drug, Dillard's, Firestone/auto, Ford, JC Penney, Martin's Foods, Rite Aid, S Chevron/dsl, Circle K/dsl/scales, Murphy USA/dsl, RaceWay, Valero/Subway/dsl Chick-fil-A, Jefferson's Rest, Outback Steaks, Waffle House, Wendy's Comfort Inn, EconoLodge, Key West Inn, Motel 6, Super 8 H, $Tree, Cobb Automotive, Walmart
179	AL 202, to US 78, to Munford, Coldwater, N Chevron/Subway/dsl China King, Jack's Rest. $General, Anniston Army Depot, Rite Aid, Winn Dixie, S Marathon/dsl
173	AL 5, Eastaboga, S Sunoco/cafe Mapco/Stuckey's to Speedway/Hall of Fame
168	AL 77, to Talladega, N Exxon/QV/Domino's, Marathon/KFC/Taco Bell, Pilot/dsl/scales/24hr Jack's Rest., Waffle House, S AOC/Burger King, Chevron/Subway/dsl, TA/Popeye's/dsl/scales/24hr McDonald's, MT Grill, Rana's Mexican Comfort Inn, Days Inn, Lincoln Inn Hall of Fame, to Speedway
165	Embry Cross Roads, N Hi-Tech/dsl, Pilot/Subway/dsl/scales/24hr Paradise Island RV Park, S 165 TP/Huddle House/dsl, I-20TrkStp/rest./dsl/scales/24hr Doghouse Grill McCaig Motel
164mm	Coosa River
162	US 78, Riverside, N Safe Harbor RV Park, S Chevron/dsl Best Value Inn/rest

PELL CITY

Exit #	Services
158	US 231, Pell City, N Marathon/dsl, Murphy USA/dsl by's, Azteca Mexican, Buffalo Wild Wings, Chick-fil-A, City N Grill, Cracker Barrel, Golden Rule BBQ, Hwy 55 Cafe, Jad Chinese, Krystal, Wendy's, Zaxby's Comfort Suites, Ham ton Inn, Holiday Inn Express H, $Tree, AT&T, City T Home Depot, URGENT CARE, Walgreens, Walmart/Subw S Shell/dsl, Texaco/dsl, Valero Akita Japanese, Bur King, Dunkin'/Baskin Robbins, Hardee's, Jack's Rest., KFC, Li Caesar's, McDonald's, Pell City Steaks, Pizza Hut, Subway, T Bell, Waffle House Quality Inn $General, AutoZo Chrysler/Dodge/Jeep, CVS Drug, Ford, O'Reilly Parts, Verizo
156	US 78 E, to Pell City, S Chevron/dsl, Shell/dsl
153	US 78, Chula Vista
152	Cook Springs
147	Brompton, N Sunoco, Valero TC/dsl/scales/24hr, S Loves/McDonald's/Subway/dsl/scales/24hr, Valero/dsl/d

LEEDS

Exit #	Services
144	US 411, Leeds, N 76/dsl, RaceWay/dsl, Shell/Su way Arby's, Bojangles, Burger King, Cracker Barrel, Kryst Logan's Roadhouse, Milo's Burgers, Pizza Hut, Ruby Tuesd Waffle House, Wendy's, Zaxby's Best Western+, Co fort Inn, Super 8 $Tree, Publix, Verizon, S Chevr RaceWay/dsl Capt D's, Chick-fil-A, El Cazador Mexic Guadalajara Jalisco Mexican, Hardee's, KFC, Little Caesa McDonald's, Sakura Steaks, Taco Bell, Waffle House D Inn $General, Advance Parts, AT&T, AutoZone, Low O'Reilly Parts, Walgreens, Walmart/Subway
140	US 78, Leeds, N Distinctive Outlets/famous bran S Buc-ee's/dsl, Chevron, Marathon Subway B Value Inn, Hampton Inn Bass Pro Shop
139mm	Cahaba River
136	I-459 S, to Montgomery, Tuscaloosa
135	US 78, Old Leeds Rd, N Shell/dsl B'ham Race Course
133	US 78, to Kilgore Memorial Dr, (wb return at 132), N Ch ron, Exxon/Circle K/dsl Golden Rule BBQ, Hamburger Hea en, Jack's, Krystal, Waffle House Red Roof Inn, Siesta M tel same as 132, S Shell McDonald's Hampt Inn, Holiday Inn Express, Quality Inn Tire Engineers
132b a	US 78, Crestwood Blvd, N Chevron, Exxon/Circle dsl Golden Rule BBQ, Hamburger Heaven, Jack's, Kr tal, Subway, Waffle House Red Roof Inn, Siesta M tel $General, Aamco, O'Reilly Parts, same as 1 S Chevron, Exxon, Marathon/dsl, Murphy Express/d Shell, Texaco/dsl Arby's, Bojangles, Burger King, Capt D Chick-fil-A, Domino's, El Cazador Mexican, Honeybaked Ha IHOP, KFC, King Buffet, Los Arcos Mexican, McDonald's, Mil Burgers, New China Buffet, Olive Garden, Pancho's Mexica Shrimp Basket, Starbucks, Taco Bell, Zaxby's Comfort I Delux Inn, Garden Suites H, $Tree, Advance Parts, A Foods, Burlington Coats, Firestone/auto, Home Depot, Off Depot, PepBoys, Ross, TJ Maxx, Tuesday Morning, URGE CARE, Verizon, Walgreens, Walmart
130b	US 11, 1st Ave, N Chevron, Petro, Sunoco AutoZo Family$, Piggly Wiggly, S Chevron/dsl McDonal Pacific Seafood Relax Inn, Sky Inn
130a	I-59 N, to Gadsden
I-59 S and I-20 W run together from B'ham to Meridian, MS	
129	Airport Blvd, N Ramada , S Mobil, Shell/ Shell/dsl Hardee's, Kabob House Best Inn, Holiday I
128	AL 79, Tallapoosa St, N Circle K/Subway/dsl/scales, She Wings/dsl
126b	31st St, N Shell/dsl, Texaco/dsl McDonald's Fami

E INTERSTATE 20 Cont'd

Exit #	Services
126a	US 31, US 280, 26th St, Carraway Blvd, N [food] Church's, KFC, Rally's
125b	22nd St, N [food] Subway [lodging] Sheraton, Westin
125a	17th St, to downtown
124b a	I-65, S to Montgomery, N to Nashville
123	US 78, Arkadelphia Rd, N [gas] Chevron, Jet-Pep, Pilot/Wendy's/dsl/scales/24hr (0.5mi), Shell/dsl [food] Popeye's [lodging] Days Inn, S [other] [H], to Legion Field
121	Bush Blvd (from wb, no return), Ensley, N [gas] Exxon, Marathon
120	AL 269, 20th St, Ensley Ave, N [gas] Jet-Pep [food] KFC [other] Honda, S [gas] Chevron [other] [H], Toyota
119b	Ave I (from wb)
119a	Lloyd Noland Pwky, N [gas] Chevron/dsl, Sunoco/dsl [food] Burger King, Fairfield Seafood, McDonald's, Subway, S [gas] Mobil, Texaco [other] [H]
118	AL 56, Valley Rd, Fairfield, S [gas] Shell [food] Papa John's [lodging] Best Inn [other] Advance Parts, Home Depot, URGENT CARE
115	Allison-Bonnett Memorial Dr, N [gas] Marathon/dsl, RaceWay/dsl, Shell/dsl [food] Church's, Jack's, Los Reyes, Subway, Zaxby's [other] Advance Parts, O'Reilly Parts, USPO
113	18th Ave, to Hueytown, S [gas] Chevron/dsl/24hr, Marathon [food] McDonald's
112	18th St, 19th St, Bessemer, N [gas] RaceWay/dsl, Shell [food] Jack's Rest. [other] tire/repair, S [gas] Chevron, Sunoco/dsl [food] KFC, Muffaletta's Italian, Rally's, Subway, Sykes BBQ [other] Advance Parts, FMS Drug, Lowe's, NAPA, O'Reilly Parts, Walgreens
110	AL Adventure Pkwy, N [other] Splash Adventure Funpark, S [other] [H]
108	US 11, AL 5 N, Academy Dr, N [gas] Circle K [food] Applebee's, Carnation Buffet, Catfish Cabin, Cracker Barrel, Waffle House [lodging] Best Western, Comfort Inn, Country Inn&Suites, Fairfield Inn, Holiday Inn Express, Quality Inn, Wood Spring Suites [other] Chevrolet, Chrysler/Dodge/Jeep, Nissan, S [gas] Chevron/Church's/dsl, Murphy USA/dsl, Shell [food] Burger King, Domino's, Jade Garden, Little Caesar's, McDonald's, Milo's Burgers, Ruby Tuesday, Sonic, Wendy's, Zaxby's [lodging] Economy Inn, Hampton Inn, Knights Inn, Motel 6 [other] [H], $Tree, BigLots, Ford, PepBoys, to civic ctr, Verizon, Walmart/Subway
106	I-459 N, to Montgomery
104	Rock Mt Lake, S [gas] FLYING J/Subway/dsl/LP/24hr
100	to Abernant, N [gas] Loves/McDonald's/Subway/dsl/scales/24hr, S [gas] Citgo, Marathon, Petro/Valero/Iron Skillet/Popeyes/dsl/scales/24hr/@ [other] $General, Tannehill Ironworks Camping, Tannehill SP (3mi)
97	US 11 S, AL 5 S, to W Blocton, S [gas] Chevron/KFC/dsl, Citgo/dsl, Exxon/Subway/dsl [food] Jack's Rest., La Tortilla Grill [other] Cahaba River NWR
89	Mercedes Dr, N [lodging] Greystone Inn, S [other] Mercedes Auto Plant
86	Vance, to Brookwood, N [gas] Marathon/Huddle House/Subway/dsl, Shell/dsl/rest./24hr
85mm	**[rest stop] both lanes, full [handicapped] facilities, litter barrels, petwalk, [phone], [picnic], RV dump, vending**
79	US 11, University Blvd, Coaling, S [gas] Chevron/dsl, Texaco/dsl
77	Cottondale, N [gas] Chevron/McDonald's, Pilot/Wendy's/dsl/scales/24hr, TA/BP/Taco Bell/dsl/scales/24hr/@ [food] Arby's, Pizza Hut, Ruby Tuesday [lodging] Hampton Inn, Microtel [other] Blue Beacon, Harley Davidson, SpeedCo, USPO, S [other] Chevrolet
76	US 11, E Tuscaloosa, Cottondale, N [gas] Chevron, Marathon, Shell/dsl [food] Burger King, Cracker Barrel, Waffle House [lodging] Centerstone Inn, Howard Johnson, Western Motel, Wingate Inn, Woodspring Suites [other] Sunset 2 RV Park, transmissions,

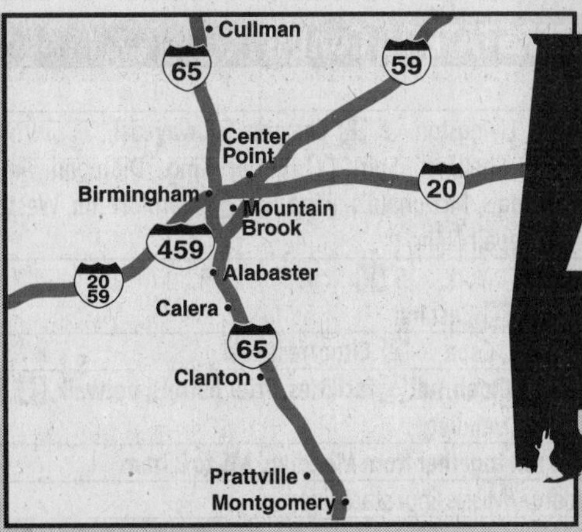

TUSCALOOSA

Exit #	Services
76	Continued S [gas] Pilot/Subway/dsl/scales/24hr, Texaco/dsl [lodging] Rodeway Inn
73	US 82, McFarland Blvd, Tuscaloosa, N [gas] Chevron/dsl, Circle K, RaceWay, Shell [food] Applebee's, Arby's, Buffalo Wild Wings, Burger King, Capt D's, Chick-fil-A, Chipotle, Five Guys, Full Moon BBQ, Jason's Deli, Krystal, Longhorn Steaks, Moe's SW Grill, O'Charley's, Olive Garden, Panera Bread, Popeye's, Red Lobster, Shrimp Basket, Starbucks, TCBY, Waffle House [lodging] Best Value Inn, Best Western, Comfort Suites, Guest Lodge, Holiday Inn Express, Masters Inn [other] [H], $General, Aamco, Advance Parts, AT&T, Barnes&Noble, Belk, Best Buy, CVS Drug, Firestone/auto, Goodyear/auto, Home Depot, JC Penney, Michael's, OK Tire, Old Navy, PepBoys, Rite Aid, Ross, SteinMart, Target, Verizon, vet, S [gas] Jet-Pep/dsl, Marathon [food] Buffet City, Checkers, Cheddar's, Chili's, Hardee's, KFC, Logan's Roadhouse, McDonald's, Papa John's, Pizza Hut, Sonic, Subway, Taco Bell, Taco Casa, Trey Yuen Cinese [lodging] Ambassador Inn, Candlewood Suites, Country Inn&Suites, Days Inn, EconoLodge, La Quinta, Motel 6, Quality Inn, Ramada Inn, Super 8 [other] $General, $Tree, Chrysler/Dodge/Jeep, NAPA, Office Depot, Rite Aid, Sam's Club/gas, TJ Maxx, U-Haul, Walmart/Subway
71b	I-359, Al 69 N, to Tuscaloosa, N [other] [H], to Stillman Coll, U of AL
71a	AL 69 S, to Moundville, S [gas] Chevron, Citgo/dsl, Mapco/Quiznos/dsl, Shell/dsl [food] Arby's, Baumhower's Rest., Chick-fil-A, Costa BBQ, Hooters, IHOP, LoneStar Steaks, OutBack Steaks, Pizza Hut, Ryan's, Waffle House, Wendy's, Zaxby's [lodging] Baymont Inn, Courtyard, Fairfield Inn, Hilton Garden [other] Advance Parts, Goodyear/auto, Kia/Mazda/VW, Lowe's, O'Reilly Parts, PepBoys, to Mound SM, URGENT CARE
68	Northport-Tuscaloosa Western Bypass
64mm	Black Warrior River
62	Fosters, N [gas] Chevron/Subway/dsl [other] $General, Foodland, USPO, vet
52	US 11, US 43, Knoxville, N [gas] Circle K/dsl
45	AL 37, Union, S [gas] Chevron/Subway/dsl, Texaco/dsl [food] South Fork Rest [lodging] Econolodge, Travel Inn [other] Greene Co Greyhound Park
40	AL 14, Eutaw, N [other] to Tom Bevill Lock/Dam, S [gas] Marathon [other] [H]
39mm	**[rest stop] wb, full [handicapped] facilities, litter barrels, petwalk, [phone], [picnic], RV dump, vending**
38mm	**[rest stop] eb, full [handicapped] facilities, litter barrels, petwalk, [phone], [picnic], RV dump, vending**
32	Boligee, N [gas] Marathon/rest./dsl/24hr, S [gas] Chevron/Subway/dsl
27mm	Tenn-Tom Waterway, Tombigbee River
23	rd 20, Epes, to Gainesville

AL

INTERSTATE 20 Cont'd

Exit #	Services
17	AL 28, Livingston, S [gas] Chevron/Subway/dsl, Exxon/L&B/dsl/24hr, Shell/dsl, Spirit [food] Burger King, Diamond Jim's/Mrs Donna's, McDonald's, Pizza Hut [lodging] Comfort Inn, Western Inn [other] repair/24hr
8	AL 17, York, S [gas] Marathon/New Orleans Grill/dsl/scales/@ [lodging] Best Inn
1	to US 80 E, Cuba, S [gas] Citgo/rest./dsl
.5mm	**Welcome Ctr eb, full [handicapped] facilities, litter barrels, petwalk, [phone], [picnic], RV dump, vending**
I-20 E and I-59 N run together from Meridian, MS to B'ham	
0mm	Alabama/Mississippi state line

INTERSTATE 22

Exit #	Services
96	I-65, N to Nashville, S to Birmingham, **I-22 begins/ends.**
93	rd 77
91	rd 105, to Brookside
89	rd 65, to Adamsville, Graysville
87	rd 112, to Graysville
85	US 78, Birmingham
81	rd 45, W Jefferson
78	rd 81, Dora, Sumiton, N [gas] TJ's/dsl
72	rd 61, Cordova
70	rd 22, Cordova, Parish
65	Bevill Ind Pkwy, Jasper, N [lodging] Hampton Inn (3mi) [other] [H], to Walker Co Lake, S [gas] [Love's]/McDonald's/Subway/dsl/scales/24hr [food] Cracker Barrel, Waffle House [lodging] Sleep Inn [other] Buick/Cadillac/Chevrolet/GMC
63	AlL 269, Jasper, Parish, N [gas] Chevron/deli/dsl
61	AL 69, Jasper, Tuscaloosa, N [gas] RJ's [food] Deano's Hickory Pit
57	AL 118 E, Jasper, N [gas] Chevron, Shell/dsl [food] The Barn Rest.
53	to AL 118
52	AL 118, Carbon Hill
46	rd 11, Carbon Hill, Nauvoo, S [gas] Chevron/dsl, Shell
39	AL 13, Natural Bridge, Eldridge
34	AL 233, Glen Allen, Natural Bridge
30	AL 129, Brilliant, Winfield, S [gas] Chevron/deli/dsl, Shell/deli/dsl [food] Huddle House [lodging] Hampton Inn
26	AL 44, Brilliant, Guin, S [lodging] Holiday Inn [other] [H]
22	rd 45
16	US 43, US 278, Hamilton, Guin, S [gas] Shell/deli/dsl
14	Hamilton, N [gas] Texaco/dsl [food] Huddle House [lodging] Days Inn (1mi), EconoLodge (1mi), Keywest Inn
11	AL 17, Hamilton, Sulligent, N [gas] Citgo/dsl [other] [H]
7	Hamilton, Weston, N [other] [H]
3	rd 33
0mm	Alabama/Mississippi State Line

INTERSTATE 59

Exit #	Services
241.5mm	Alabama/Georgia state line, Central/Eastern time zone
241mm	**Welcome Ctr sb, full [handicapped] facilities, litter barrels, petwalk, [phone], [picnic], RV dump, vending**
239	to US 11, Sulphur Springs Rd, E [other] camping
231	AL 40, AL 117, Hammondville, Valley Head, E [other] camping (5mi), DeSoto SP, W [gas] Fuel City
224	49th St, to Ft Payne, W [gas] Mapco
222	US 11, to Ft Payne, 1 mi E [food] Arby's, Hardee's, Jack's Rest., KFC, Krystal, Pizza Hut, SteviB's Pizza, Subway, Toke Thai Grill,
	FT PAYNE
222	Continued Wingstop [lodging] Quality Inn [other] Chevrolet, Foodland/dsl, W [gas] C go/dsl [food] Waffle King
218	AL 35, Ft Payne, E [food] Capt D's, Don Chico Mexican, DQ, Jack Jefferson's Burgers, Little Caesar's, McDonald's, New China, Pa John's, Sonic, Taco Bell, Western Sizzlin, Zaxby's [other] $Gener Advance Parts, Alabama Museum, AutoZone, BigLots, Chry ler/Dodge/Jeep, O'Reilly Parts, URGENT CARE, W [gas] Circ K/dsl, MapCo, Mapco/dsl, Murphy USA/dsl [food] Applebee Burger King, Chick-fil-A, Chow King, Cracker Barrel, Hardee Huddle House, Los Arcos, Ruby Tuesday, Santa Fe Steaks, W fle House [lodging] Days Inn, EconoLodge, Hampton Inn, Holiday I Express [other] [H], $Tree, AT&T, Ford/Lincoln, GNC, Lowe's, Verizo Walgreens, Walmart, Will's Creek RV Park
205	AL 68, Collinsville, E [gas] Delta [food] Jack's Rest. [lodging] Travele Inn [other] to Little River Canyon, Weiss Lake, W [gas] BP/dsl, Ma Co [food] Burger King
188	AL 211, to US 11, Gadsden, E [gas] Jet-Pep [other] Noccalula Fa Camping, W [gas] Marathon/dsl/e85
	GADSDEN
183	US 431, US 278, Gadsden, E [gas] Jet-Pep/dsl, Shell, Texac dsl [food] Waffle House [lodging] Days Inn, HomeLodge, Motel 6, Rod way Inn [other] st police, W [gas] Chevron, Exxon, Jet-Pep [food] KF McDonald's, Pizza Hut, Subway, Taco Bell
182	I-759, to Gadsden
181	AL 77, Rainbow City, to Gadsden, E [gas] Petro/Popeye's/d scales/24hr/@ [food] Jack's [lodging] EconoLodge, W [gas] Circle K/d Murphy Express/dsl [food] Arby's, Bubba Rito's SW Grill, Crack Barrel, Domino's, El Patron, Hardee's, Hector's Kitchen, Luc Wok, McDonald's, Old Mexico Grille, Ruby Tuesday, Subwa Waffle House, Wendy's [lodging] Best Western+, Comfort Suite Fairfield Inn, Hampton Inn, Holiday Inn Express [other] $Gener $Tree, O'Reilly Parts, Walmart/Papa John's
174	to Steele, E [gas] [Love's]/Subway/Chester's/dsl/scales/24 W [gas] Marathon/dsl, Sunoco/Molina's/dsl
168mm	**[rest stop] sb, full [handicapped] facilities, litter barrels, petwalk, [phone], [picnic], RV dum vending**
166	US 231, Whitney, to Ashville, E [gas] BP, Chevron/dsl, W [gas] Te aco/dsl [food] Huddle House, Jack's Rest., Subway
165mm	**[rest stop] nb, full [handicapped] facilities, litter barrels, petwalk, [phone], [picnic], RV dum vending**
156	AL 23, to US 11, Springville, to St Clair Springs, W [gas] Murp USA/dsl, Shell /dsl [food] Azteca's Mexican, Burger King, Chi Stix, KFC, Pizza Hut, Taco Bell, Waffle House, Zaxby's [other] $Tre AT&T, Walmart/Subway
154	AL 174, Springville, to Odenville, E [gas] Exxon/dsl, W [gas] B Subway, Chevron, Citgo, MapCo, Shell/dsl [food] Choppin Blo Rest., Gulf Seafood, Jack's Rest., McDonald's
148	to US 11, Argo, E [gas] Shell [food] Jack's, Subway
143	Mt Olive Church Rd, Deerfoot Pkwy, E [gas] Chevron/dsl/CN Shell/dsl (1mi) [food] Munoz Mexican [other] Publix (1mi)
	TRUSSVILLE
141	to Trussville, Pinson, E [gas] Bama/dsl, Shell/dsl, Texaco/dsl Applebee's,, Cracker Barrel, Guthrie's, McDonald's, Papa John Pizza Hut, Taco Bell, Waffle House, Wendy's [lodging] Comfort Inn, Ho iday Inn Express, Quality Inn [other] Harley-Davidson, W [gas] Che ron, Marathon, Shell/dsl, Texaco [food] Arby's, Buffalo Wild Wing Burger King, Chick-fil-A, Cici's, Costa's Mediterranean, DQ, Ea Buffet, Frontera Grill, Full Moon BBQ, Jack's, Konomi Japanes Krystal, Milo's Burgers, Moe's SW Grill, Momma Goldberg's De Palace Asian, Paul's Hotdogs, Ruby Tuesday, Whataburger, Za by's [other] $Tree, Ace Hardware, Advance Parts, BigLots, CVS Dru GNC, Kohl's, Marshall's, Office Depot, Petsmart, Sam's Club/ga Verizon, vet, Walgreens, Walmart/Subway

INTERSTATE 59 Cont'd

Exit #	Services
137	I-459 S, to Montgomery, Tuscaloosa
134	to AL 75, Roebuck Pkwy, W [gas] BP/Circle K, Chevron, Murphy USA/dsl, Shell/dsl [food] Arby's, Burger King, Chick-fil-A, Crab Barrack, Hardee's, McDonald's, Milo's Burgers, Pizza Hut, Subway, Taco Bell [other] [H], $Tree, Aldi Foods, AT&T, CVS Drug, GNC, Honda, NTB, O'Reilly Parts, URGENT CARE, Vo Tires, Walgreens, Walmart/Burger King
133	4th St, to US 11 (from nb), same as 134, W [food] Papa John's [other] $General, USPO
132	US 11 N, 1st Ave, Esame as 131, W [gas] Chevron, Shell/dsl [food] Krispy Kreme [other] city park
131	Oporto-Madrid Blvd (from nb), E [gas] BP/Subway, Chevron [food] Church's, Little Caesar's [other] CVS Drug, Family$, O'Reilly Parts, same as 132, U-Haul
130	I-20, E to Atlanta, W to Tuscaloosa

I-59 S and I-20 W run together from B'ham to Mississippi. See Alabama Interstate 20, exits 129-1.

INTERSTATE 65

Exit #	Services
366mm	Alabama/Tennessee state line
365	AL 53, to Ardmore, E [lodging] Budget Inn
364mm	**Welcome Ctr sb, full [handicapped] facilities, info, litter barrels, petwalk, [phone], [picnic], RV dump, vending**
361	Elkmont, W [gas] BP/dsl [food] Momma D's Rest. [other] antiques, repair
354	US 31 S, to Athens, W [gas] Chevron/dsl [food] Capt D's, Domino's, Jack's Rest., Little Caesar's, McDonald's, Pizza Hut, Rooster's Cafe, Subway [lodging] Mark Motel [other] [H], $General, Advance Parts, city park, CVS Drug, HomeTown Mkt, Northgate RV Park, Walgreens
351	US 72, to Athens, Huntsville, E [gas] Exxon, RaceWay/dsl, Shell/Subway, Valero/dsl [food] Buffalo Wild Wings, Burger King, Cracker Barrel, Dunkin', Jack's, Las Trejas Mexican, Lawler's BBQ, McDonald's/RV Parking, Taco Bell, Waffle House, Wendy's [lodging] Econolodge, Hampton Inn, Quality Inn, Travel Inn [other] $General, Publix, Russell Stover, Verizon, vet, W [gas] Chevron/dsl, Citgo/dsl, Marathon, Murphy USA [food] Applebee's, Arby's, Bojangle's, Burger King, Catfish Cabin, Chick-fil-A, DQ, Firehouse Subs, Hardee's, IHOP, KFC, Krystal, Logan's Roadhouse, Papa John's, Papa Murphy's, Pizza Hut, Popeye's, Ruby Tuesday, Shoney's, Sonic, Starbucks, Steak-Out, Subway, Zaxby's [lodging] Best Western, Days Inn, Fairfield Inn, Holiday Inn Express, Sleep Inn, Super 8 [other] [H], $General, $Tree, Advance Parts, Aldi Foods, AT&T, Big Lots, Chevrolet, Chrysler/Dodge/Jeep, Ford, Goodyear/auto, Lowe's, O'Reilly Parts, Pepboys, SaveALot Foods, Staples, to Joe Wheeler SP, Tuesday Morning, Walmart
347	Brownsferry Rd, Huntsville, W [gas] Chevron [other] Swan Creek RV Park
340b	I-565, to Alabama Space & Rocket Ctr, to Huntsville
340a	AL 20, to Decatur, W [gas] Chevron/dsl [lodging] Courtyard (7mi), Hampton Inn (7mi), Holiday Inn Express (7mi)
337mm	Tennessee River
334	AL 67, Priceville, to Decatur, E [gas] Marathon/dsl, RaceWay/dsl [food] JW's Steaks [lodging] Days Inn, Super 8 [other] $General, Family$, Foodland, W [gas] Chevron/dsl, Mapco/dsl, Pilot/Subway/Wendy's/dsl/scales/24hr [food] Burger King, DQ, Hardee's, Krystal, McDonald's, Pizza Hut, Taco Bell, Taste of China, Waffle House [lodging] Comfort Inn [other] [H], Johnston RV Ctr, Publix

ATHENS

DECATUR

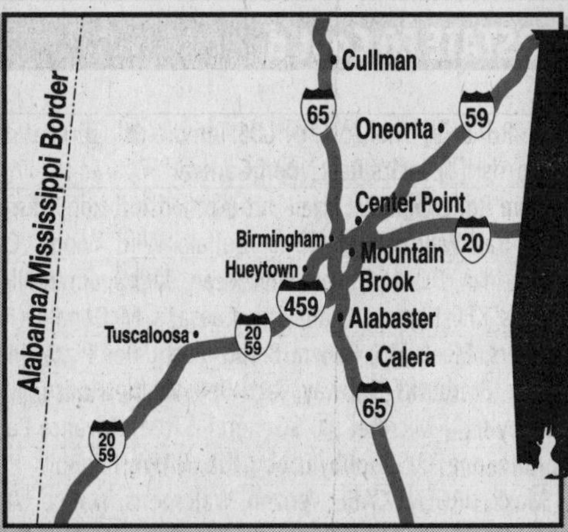

CULLMAN

Exit #	Services
328	AL 36, Hartselle, E [food] Cracker Barrel, W [gas] Chevron/dsl, Cowboys/dsl, Jet-Pep/dsl, Ztrac [food] Huddle House [lodging] Red Roof Inn [other] $General, vet
325	Thompson Rd, to Hartselle
322	AL 55, to US 31, to Falkville, Eva, E [gas] Marathon/Chester's/dsl, W [gas] Chevron, Love's/McDonald's/Subway/dsl/scales/24hr [food] Log Cabin Rest. [other] $General
318	US 31, to Lacon
310	AL 157, Cullman, West Point, E [gas] 76/dsl, Chevron/Popeye's, Conoco/Subway/dsl, Shell/dsl, Texaco/Wendy's/dsl [food] Arby's, Bueno Vista Mexican, Burger King, Cracker Barrel, Denny's, KFC, Lawler's BBQ, Little Caesar's, Logan's Roadhouse, McDonald's, Panda Express, Ruby Tuesday, Taco Bell, Waffle House, Zaxby's [lodging] Best Western, Comfort Suites, Hampton Inn, Holiday Inn Express, La Quinta, Quality Inn, Sleep Inn [other] [H], Buick/GMC, Ford/Lincoln, Verizon, Walmart, W [gas] Exxon/dsl, Marathon/dsl [lodging] Best Value Inn
308	US 278, Cullman, E [lodging] Days Inn [other] Smith Farms, W [gas] Chevron [other] $General, Chrysler/Dodge/Jeep, flea mkt
305	to Al 69
304	AL 69 N, Good Hope, to Cullman, E [gas] Exxon/dsl, Jet-Pep/dsl, Pilot/Wendy's/Dunkin'/dsl/scales/24hts, Shell/dsl/scales [food] Hardee's, Waffle House [lodging] EconoLodge [other] [H], Good Hope Camping, Johnston RV Ctr, W [gas] Jet-Pep [other] $General, to Smith Lake Camping
301mm	**[RS] both lanes, full [handicapped] facilities, litter barrels, petwalk, [phone], [picnic], RV dump, vending**
299	AL 69 S, to Jasper, E [gas] Jet-pep/dsl [other] Millican RV Ctr, repair/tires, W [gas] Chevron/dsl, Petro/Burger King/Popeye's/Papa John'sdsl/scales/24hr, Shell/McDonald's/dsl [food] Jack's Rest., Subway [other] $General
291	AL 91, to Arkadelphia, E [gas] Jet-Pep/dsl [other] Country View RV Park (1mi), W [gas] Shell/dsl/24hr [food] 291 Roadhouse Rest.
291mm	Warrior River
289	to Blount Springs, W [gas] Citgo [other] to Rickwood Caverns SP
287	US 31 N, to Blount Springs, E [gas] Jet-Pep/dsl
284	US 31 S, AL 160 E, Hayden, E [gas] Shamrock/dsl, Sunoco/dsl, Valero Travel Center/dsl [food] Jack's [other] URGENT CARE, W [other] tires
282	AL 140, Warrior, E [gas] Chevron/Subway/dsl, Exxon/McDonald's, Shell/Dunkin'/Little Caesar's/dsl [food] Hardee's, Pizza Hut, Taco Bell, W [gas] Marathon [food] Huddle House
281	US 31, to Warrior
280	to US 31, to Warrior, E [gas] Chevron/dsl [other] vet
279mm	Warrior River
275	to US 31, Morris

= gas = food = lodging = other = rest stop

AL

INTERSTATE 65 Cont'd

Exit #	Services
272	Mt Olive Rd, E Shell/dsl LDS Temple, W Chevron/dsl, Citgo/dsl Jack's Rest. $General
271	Fieldstown Rd, E BP/Circle K, Chevron/dsl, Exxon, Murphy USA/dsl, RaceWay/dsl Arby's, Buffalo Wild Wings, Capt D's, Chick-fil-A, DQ, Habanero's Mexican, Jack's, Jim'n Nick's BBQ, Joel's, KFC, Kumo's Asian, Little Caesar's, McDonald's, Milo's Burgers, Moe's SW, Panera Bread, Pasquales Pizza, Pizza Hut, Sonic, Starbucks, Subway, Taco Bell, Waffle House, Wendy's, Zaxby's Microtel $General, $Tree, Advance Parts, AT&T, AutoZone, CVS, Hobby Lobby, Kia, NAPA, PepBoys, Publix, TJ Maxx, URGENT CARE, Verizon, Walgreens, Walmart/McDonald's, W Shell/dsl Cracker Barrel Best Western
267	Walkers Chapel Rd, to Fultondale, E BP/dsl, Jet-Pep, Murphy Express/dsl, Shell/Subway/dsl Applebee's, Arby's, Bojangles, Burger King, Casa Fiesta, Chick-fil-A, Chili's, Domino's, Firehouse Subs, Five Guys, Fullmoon BBQ, Hardee's, Jack's Rest., Logan's Roadhouse, McDonald's, O'Charley's, Outback Steaks, Shoney's, Stix Asian, Waffle House, Whataburger, Wintzell's Oyster House, Zaxby's Comfort Inn, Comfort Suites, Fairfield Inn, Hampton Inn, Holiday Inn Express, Home 2 Suites, La Quinta $General, AAA, Aldi Foods, AT&T, Best Buy, Books-A-Million, CVS Drug, GNC, JC Penney, Lowe's, O'Reilly Parts, Rite Aid, Ross, Target, URGENT CARE, USPO, Verizon, Volvo/Mack Trucks, Winn-Dixie, W Chevron/dsl
265b	US 31, Fultondale, E Chevron/dsl Days Inn, Econolodge
265a	I-22 W, to Memphis
264	41st Ave, W FLYING J/Denny's/dsl/LP/scales/24hr, LNG
263	33rd Ave, E Chevron/dsl, W Exxon
262b a	16th St, Finley Ave, E Chevron, Marathon/dsl, Sunoco/dsl Kenworth, W Chevron, Fuel City/dsl Capt D's, McDonald's, Popeye's
261b a	I-20/59, E to Gadsden, W to Tuscaloosa
260b a	6th Ave N, E Citgo, Shell, Texaco Mrs Winner's Tourway Inn Chevrolet, Chrysler/Dodge/Jeep, Hyundai, Nissan, Subaru, W Chevron/dsl Tire Pros, to Legion Field
259b a	University Blvd, 4th Ave, 5th Ave, E Chevron/dsl Capt D's, McDonald's, Ted's Cafeteria H, W Chevron/dsl Goodyear
258	Green Springs Ave, E Chevron, Shell, Sunoco/dsl Exotic Wings
256b a	Oxmoor Rd, E Exxon, Marathon, Mobil/dsl, Shell Acapulco Grill, Alfredo's Pizza, Burger King, Domino's, Firehouse Subs, Hunan Rest., KFC, McDonald's, Papa Murphy's, Paw Paw Patch, Popeye's, Purple Onion, San Miguel Mexican, Taco Bell, The Baskits, Zaxby's Howard Johnson $Tree, Aldi Foods, AutoZone, BigLots, Firestone/auto, Food World, Fred's, Midas, Office Depot, Omega Tire Pros, PepBoys, Publix, Tire Engineers, Tuesday Morning, URGENT CARE, Walgreens, Walmart Mkt, W Chevron, Texaco/dsl Hamburger Heaven, Hardee's, Jim'n Nick's BBQ, Waffle House Best Inn, Best Value Inn, Comfort Inn, EconoLodge, Motel 6, Quality Inn, Super 8 Batteries+, Valley Tire, vet
255	Lakeshore Dr, E BP/Circle K H, to Samford U, URGENT CARE, W Chevron, Shell Arby's, Chick-fil-A, Chili's, Costas BBQ, Hooters, IHOP, La Catrina Mexican, Landry's Seafood, McAlister's Deli, McDonald's, Milo's Burger, Moe's SW Grill, Mr Wang's, O'Charley's, Okinawa Grill, Outback Steaks, Starbucks, Subway, Taco Bell, Taco Casa, Wendy's Best Western, Candlewood Suites, Country Inn&Suites, Drury Inn, Extended Stay, Hampton Inn, Hilton Garden, Holiday Inn, La Quinta, Residence Inn,
255	Continued TownePlace Suites $Tree, AT&T, Goodyear/auto, Hob Lobby, Lowe's, Sam's Club/gas, Verizon, Walmart/Subway
254	Alford Ave, Shades Crest Rd, E Chevron vet, W E dsl, Shell/dsl
252	US 31, Montgomery Hwy, E Chevron, Shell, Sunoco, Te co/dsl Arby's, Backyard Burger, Bruster's, Capt D's, Chuc Cheese's, Hardee's, Ichiban Japanese, Milo's Burger, Wa House Baymont Inn, Days Inn H, Aamco, GMC, NA PepBoys, Verizon, vet, Volvo, VW, W Exxon/dsl, Shell/c Sunoco/dsl Burger King, Chick-fil-A, FishMkt Rest., F Moon BBQ, Golden Rule BBQ, Habanero's Mexican, Kris Kreme, Krystal, Mandarin House, McDonald's, Outback Stea Papa John's, Papa Murphy's, Purple Onion, Salvatore's Piz Starbucks, Subway, Waffle House EconoLodge $Tr Acura, Advance Parts, AutoZone, Cadillac, Chevrolet, Chrysl Dodge/Jeep, Firestone, Goodyear/auto, Honda, Hyundai, Transmission, Nissan, Publix, Rite Aid, Staples, TJ Maxx, vet
250	I-459, to US 280
247	rd 17, Valleydale Rd, E BP/Circle K Hardee's, Jefferso Wings Goodyear/auto, Lowe's, W Marathon, Ra Way/dsl, Shell/dsl Arby's, Backyard Burger, IHOP, Mil Burgers, Papa John's, RagTime Café, Subway, Waffle Hou Zapatas Mexican Homewood Suites, InTown Suites, Quinta Publix, Rite Aid, vet, Walgreens
246	AL 119, Cahaba Valley Rd, E to Oak Mtn SP, W Che ron, Circle K/dsl/scales, Murphy USA/dsl, RaceWay/dsl, She dsl Applebee's, Arby's, Burger King, Capt D's, Chick-fil- Cracker Barrel, DQ, Dunkin', Golden Corral, Hooters, John Ray's BBQ, KFC, Krystal, Margarita Grill, McAlister's Deli, M Donald's, Pizza Hut, Purple Onion, Ruby Tuesday, Sonic, Ta Bell, Two Pesos Mexican, TX Roadhouse, Waffle House, We dy's, Whataburger Best Western, Comfort Suites, Fairfie Inn, Hampton Inn, Holiday Inn Express, Quality Inn, Ramac Sleep Inn, Travelodge, Woodspring Suites $Tree, Advar Parts, AutoZone, Firestone/auto, Harley-Davidson, Kia, Mazc NAPA, O'Reilly Parts, Verizon, Walmart
242	rd 52, Pelham, E Chevron/dsl, Exxon/dsl, She dsl Johnny Ray's BBQ, Subway CVS Drug, Publ W Shelby Motel (2mi) H, Good Sam Camping (1mi)
238	US 31, Alabaster, Saginaw, E Murphy USA/dsl -Arby Buffalo Wild Wings, Chick-fil-A, DQ, Firehouse Subs, Full Mo BBQ, Habanero's Mexican, HoneyBaked Ham, Jim'n Nick BBQ, Longhorn Steaks, McDonald's, Mizu Japanese, Moe's S Grill, Momma Goldberg Deli, O'Charley's, Olive Garden, Pan House, Panera Bread, Ruby Tuesday, Starbucks, Steak'n Shak Taco Bell Candlewood Suites $Tree, AT&T, Belk, Be Buy, Books-A-Million, Dick's, GNC, JC Penney, Lowe's, NTB, O Navy, Petsmart, Ross, Target, TJ Maxx, URGENT CARE, Walmar Subway, W Chevron/dsl, Shell/dsl Waffle House, Wh taburger Shelby Motel H
234	Shelby County Airport, E BP/Subway/dsl, W Chevro dsl, Shell/dsl Buick/GMC, Camping World RV Ctr
231	US 31, Saginaw, E GasBoy, Murphy USA/dsl, She dsl Bojangles, Capt D's, Cracker Barrel, Ezell's Catfish Ca in, McDonald's, Milo's Burgers, Pizza Hut, Subway, Taco Be Waffle House, Zaxby's, Zopapan Mexican Hampton In Quality Inn $Tree, AT&T, Burton RV Ctr, Publix, Rolling Hi RV Park, URGENT CARE, Verizon, Walmart/Subway
228	AL 25, to Calera, E Marathon/dsl, Shell/dsl Calera In W Chevron/dsl Little Caesar's, Subway $Genera Family$, to Brierfield Iron Works SP (15mi)

FULTONDALE

BIRMINGHAM

HOOVER

PELHAM

INTERSTATE 65 Cont'd

Exit #	Services
227mm	Buxahatchie Creek
219	Union Grove, Thorsby, E Chevron/dsl, Exxon/Subway/dsl Peach Queen Camping, W Shell/dsl Jack's Rest., Smokey Hollow Rest.
213mm	**both lanes, full facilities, litter barrels, petwalk, , , RV dump, vending**
212	AL 145, Clanton, E Chevron/dsl Nissan, Toyota, W Headco/dsl, Texaco/Subway , Buick/Chevrolet/GMC, Chrysler/Dodge/Jeep, One Big Peach
208	Clanton, E Loves/Arby's/dsl/scales/24hr Higgins Ferry RV Park (8mi), W Exxon/dsl Shoney's Clanton Inn Dandy RV Park/Ctr, Heaton Pecans, KOA
205	US 31, AL 22, to Clanton, E Jet-Pep/dsl/e85, Shell/dsl, Texaco/dsl McDonald's, Waffle House, Whataburger Best Western, Days Inn, Holiday Inn Express, Scottish Inn Peach Park, to Confed Mem Park (9mi), **0-2 mi** W Chevron/dsl, Murphy USA/dsl, Shell/dsl Boomerang's Grill, Burger King, Capt D's, Jack's Rest., KFC, New China Buffet, Papa John's, Pizza Hut, San Marcos Mexican, Subway, Taco Bell, Wendy's, Zaxby's Key West Inn $General, $Tree, auto repair, Durbin Farms Mkt, Verizon, Walmart
200	to Verbena, E Texaco/dsl, W Sunoco
195	Worlds Largest Confederate Flag
186	US 31, Pine Level, E Confederate Mem Park (13mi), W Chevron/dsl, Exxon/dsl, Texaco/Subway/dsl Shann's Kitchen
181	AL 14, to Prattville, E Chevron/dsl, Entec/dsl Jack's, W BP, Circle K, QV, Shell/DQ/dsl Cracker Barrel, Los Toros, McDonald's, Ruby Tuesday, Subway, Waffle House, Wendy's EconoLodge, Hometowne Suites, La Quinta, Quality Inn, Super 8
179	US 82 W, Millbrook, E Chevron/dsl/24hr Country Inn&Suites, Key West Inn, Sleep Inn, Springhill Suites K&K RV Ctr/Park, **0-2 mi** W Liberty/dsl, Murphy Express/dsl, RaceWay/dsl, Shell/dsl Applebee's, Arby's, Beef'O'Brady's, Bruster's, Burger King, Capt. D's, Chappy's Deli, Chick-fil-A, Chipotle, CiCi's Pizza, City Buffet, El Patron, Five Guys, Hardee's, IHOP, Jim'n Nick's BBQ, KFC, Krystal, Las Casitas Mexican, Logan's Roadhouse, Longhorn Steaks, McAlister's Deli, McDonald's, Mellow Mushroom, Mexico Tipico, Moe's SW Grill, O'Charley's, Olive Garden, Outback Steaks, Panda Express, Popeye's, Sonic, Starbucks, Steak'n Shake, Subway, Waffle House, Zaxby's Courtyard, Days Inn, Hampton Inn, Holiday Inn Express, Howard Johnson, Rodeway Inn $General, $Tree, AT&T, AutoZone, Bass Pro Shops, Belk, Best Buy, BigLots, Books-A-Million, Chevrolet, CVS Drug, Firestone/auto, Ford, GNC, Hobby Lobby, Home Depot, JC Penney, Kohl's, Lowe's, Michael's, Office Depot, O'Reilly Parts, PepBoys, Petsmart, Publix, Ross, Target, TJ Maxx, URGENT CARE, Verizon, vet, Walmart
176	AL 143 N (from nb, no return), Millbrook, Coosada
173	AL 152, North Blvd, to US 231
172mm	Alabama River
172	Clay St, Herron St, E Embassy Suites, Hampton Inn, Renaissance Hotel, W Chevron/dsl
171	I-85 N, Day St
170	Fairview Ave, E Citgo/Subway, Sunoco/dsl Church's, McDonald's, Wing Master $General, $Tree, Advance Parts, AutoZone, CVS Drug, Family$, O'Reilly Parts, Piggly Wiggly, Walgreens, W Family$
169	Edgemont Ave (from sb), E Liberty
168	US 80 E, US 82, South Blvd, E Circle K/dsl, Marathon/dsl, TA/Marathon/Country Pride/dsl/24hr/@ Arby's, Burger King, Capt D's, KFC, McDonald's, Pizza Hut, Popeye's, Taco Bell, Waffle House , The Woods RV Park, W Chevron/dsl, RaceWay/dsl DQ, Hardee's, Wendy's Super 8
167	US 80 W, to Selma
164	US 31, Hyundai Blvd, Hope Hull, E Liberty, Saveway/dsl/scales/24hr, Shell/dsl El Amigo Mexican auto repair, Montgomery Camping, W Chevron, Liberty/Subway, Marathon Burger King, Hardee's, McDonald's, Waffle House Comfort Suites, Fairfield Inn, Hampton Inn, Holiday Inn, Motel 6, Quality Inn auto repair
158	to US 31, Tyson, E Loves/Subway/Godfather's/Chester's/dsl/scales/24hr, Shell/DQ/Stuckey's Montgomery South RV Park, W FLYING J/Denny's/dsl/scales/24hr
151	AL 97, to Letohatchee, E Marathon/dsl, W Link
142	AL 185, to Ft Deposit, E Petro+/dsl Priester's Pecans, Subway auto parts, W Chevron
133mm	**s both lanes, full facilities, litter barrels, petwalk, , , RV dump, vending**
130	AL10 E, AL 185, to Greenville, E Chevron/dsl, PaceCar/dsl, Shell Arby's, Capt D's, China Town, Hardee's, KFC, McDonald's, Old Mexico, Papa John's, Pizza Hut, Waffle House, Wendy's Days Inn, Quality Inn $General, Advance Parts, CVS Drug, Fred's Store, O'Reilly Parts, Super Foods, to Sherling Lake Park, Walgreens, W Exxon/Subway/dsl, Mobil, Murphy USA/dsl, Texaco/dsl Bates Turkey Cafe, Burger King, Cracker Barrel, Krystal, Ruby Tuesday, Shoney's, Sonic, Taco Bell, Wintzell's Oyster House Baymont Inn, Best Western, Comfort Inn, Hampton Inn, Holiday Inn Express $Tree, AT&T, Chevrolet, URGENT CARE, Verizon, Walmart/Subway
128	AL 10, to Greenville, E Shell/Smokehouse , W Marathon
114	AL 106, to Georgiana, E Hank Williams Museum, W Chevron, Marathon auto repair
107	rd 7, to Garland
101	to Owassa, E Marathon/dsl, W Gulf/dsl dsl repair, Owassa RV Park
96	AL 83, to Evergreen, E Chevron, Shell Burger King, Hardee's, KFC/Taco Bell, McDonald's, Shoney's, Shrimp Basket, Subway, Waffle House, Wendy's, Zaxby's Sleep Inn , Piggly Wiggly, vet, W Spirit/Subway/dsl EconoLodge, Evergreen Inn, Quality Inn
93	US 84, to Evergreen, E Liberty/dsl, W Loves/Arby's/dsl/scales/24hr, Shell/dsl
89mm	**sb, full facilities, litter barrels, petwalk, , , RV dump, vending**

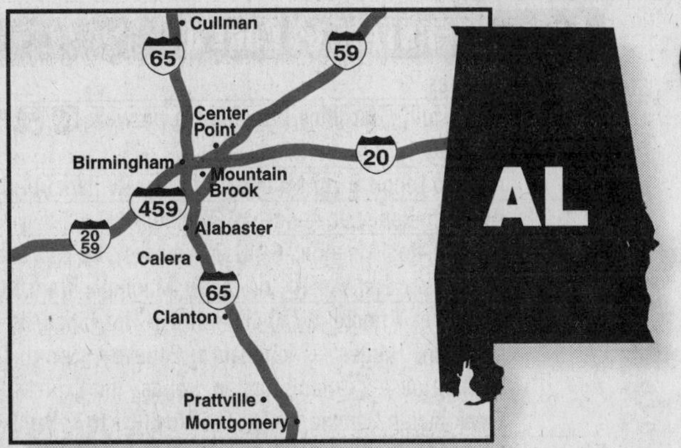

AL

INTERSTATE 65 Cont'd

ATMORE

Exit #	Services
85mm	nb, full facilities, litter barrels, petwalk, , , RV dump, vending
83	AL 6, to Lenox, E Marathon/dsl RV Park (4mi)
77	AL 41, to Range, to Range, W Shell/dsl
69	AL 113, to Flomaton, E Chevron/dsl, Jet-Pep/Subway/dsl, Shell/dsl/scales/24hr dsl repair, Magnolia Branch Camping
57	AL 21, to Atmore, E Chevron/dsl/24hr, Shell/dsl Fairfield Inn, Hardee's, McDonald's, Popeye's, Sonic, Taco Bell, Waffle House Hampton Inn, Holiday Inn Express Wind Creek Indian Gaming, W Shell/dsl to Kelley SP
54	Escambia Cty Rd 1, E Chevron/Subway/dsl to Creek Indian Res, W Shell/diner/dsl $General
45	to Perdido, W Chevron/dsl
37	AL 287, Gulf Shores Pkwy, to Bay Minette, E Marathon/dsl
34	to AL 59, to Bay Minette, Stockton
31	AL 225, to Stockton, E to Blakeley SP, W Shell/Subway/dsl Landing RV Park (2mi)
29mm	Tensaw River
28mm	Middle River
25mm	Mobile River
22	Creola, E River Delta RV Park (1mi)
19	US 43, to Satsuma, E Chevron/dsl/24hr, Pilot/Arby's/dsl/scales/24hr McDonald's, Waffle House La Quinta, W BP/dsl, Chevron/dsl I-65 RV Park (1.5mi)
15	AL 41, E Chevron, Chevron/DQ/dsl China Chef, Church's, Godfather's Pizza, Pizza Hut AT&T, AutoZone, CVS, Family$, O'Reilly Parts, Rite Aid, Rouse's Mkt, Walgreens, W Shell/Circle K, Shell/Subway/dsl $General
13	AL 158, AL 213, to Saraland, E Murphy USA/dsl, Shell/dsl Goldberg's Deli, Krystal, Marble Slab, Rotolo's Pizza, Ruby Tuesday, Waffle House, Whataburger, Wintzell's Oyster House Comfort Suites, Country Inn Suites, Microtel, Motel 6, Quality Inn, Red Lion Inn, Red Roof Inn $Tree, AT&T, URGENT CARE, Walmart/McDonald's, W Exxon/Subway Cracker Barrel Baymont Inn, Fairfield Inn, Hampton Inn, Holiday Inn Express, TownePlace Suites Publix, to Chickasabogue Campground
10	W Lee St, E Shell/Circle K M Star Hotel
9	I-165 S, to I-10 E, to Mobile
8b a	US 45, to Prichard, E Chevron/Circle K/dsl, Texaco/dsl $General, Family$, tires/repair, W 1st Stop, Energize/dsl, Love's/Subway/dsl/scales/24hr, Texaco/dsl, Valero/dsl Burger King, Domino's, Hardee's, McDonald's $General, Advance Parts, CVS Drug, Family$, O'Reilly Parts
5b	US 98, Moffett Rd, E Exxon/dsl, Texaco/dsl BJ's BBQ, Burger King, Church's, McDonald's, Sub King AutoZone, Family$, PepBoys, W Hardee's Super 8 auto repair
5a	Spring Hill Ave, E Burger King, Dreamland BBQ, McDonald's Mr Transmission, PepBoys, W Chevron/dsl, Shell/dsl Hibachi Express, Starbucks, Subway, Waffle House, Zaxby's Extended Stay America, Wingate Inn H
4	Dauphin St, E BP/Circle K/dsl, Shell/dsl Checkers, Chick-fil-A, Cracker Barrel, Krystal, McDonald's, Taco Bell, Taco Bell, Waffle House, Wendy's Comfort Suites, Extended Suites, Red Roof Inn, Rodeway Inn $General, Buick/GMC, FoodChamps, Lowe's, Mercedes, same as 3 & 5a, Walmart/McDonald's, W H
3	Airport Blvd, E Shell Burger King, Cane's, Logan's Roadhouse, Macaroni Grill, McDonald's, Morrison's Cafeteria, Santa Fe Grill, Starbucks, Waffle House, Wendy's Marriott

MOBILE

Exit #	Services
3	Continued $Tree, Acura, Belk, Best Buy, BigLots, Cadillac, Dillar Firestone/auto, Ford, Goodyear/auto, Harley-Davidson, H da, Infiniti, Land Rover, Marshall's, Michaels, Nissan, Old Na Sam's Club/gas, Staples, Target, Verizon, W BudgetZor dsl, Shell/dsl Arby's, Bamboo Japanese, Baumhowe Boiling Pot, Burger King, Carrabba's, Cheddar's, China Doll, C potle, ChuckECheese, Denny's, Dunkin', Firehouse Subs, Go berg's Deli, Honeybaked Ham, Hooters, IHOP, Jason's Deli, L ny's Subs, Los Rancheros Mexican, Marble Slab, Melting P Moe's SW Grill, Newk's Cafe, O'Charley's, Olive Garden, Osa Japanese, Outback Steaks, Panda Express, Panera Bread, P eye's, Red Lobster, Ruby Tuesday, Starbucks, Subway, Taco B Waffle House Ashberry Suites, Baymont Inn, Best Va Inn, Comfort Inn, Courtyard, Drury Inn, EconoLodge, Fairfi Inn, Family Inn, Hampton Inn, Hilton Garden, Holiday I Homewood Suites, InTowne Suites, La Quinta, Motel 6, Qua Inn, Residence Inn, Woodspring Suites H, $General, $Tr AT&T, BooksAMillion, Fresh Mkt Foods, Home Depot, Jo-A Fabrics, Office Depot, PepBoys, Petsmart, Ross, SteinMart, Maxx, to USAL, U-Haul, vet, Walgreens
1b a	US 90, Government Blvd, E Raceway/dsl, She dsl Dickey's BBQ, Firehouse Subs, Five Guys, McA ter's Deli, Newk's Eatery, Panda Buffet, Starbucks, Steal Shake Home 2 Suites, Tru Hilton $Tree, AT&T, Au Porsche/VW, Best Buy, BMW, Chevrolet, Costco/gas, Dick Dodge, Family$, Field&Stream, Hobby Lobby, Kia, Lexus, L coln/Volvo, Mazda, Old Navy, Petco, Ross, Subaru, Toyota, V izon, W Shell/dsl Waffle House
0mm	I-10, E to Pensacola, W to New Orleans. **I-65 begins/ends I-10, exit 20.**

INTERSTATE 85

LANETT

Exit #	Services
80mm	Alabama/Georgia state line, Chattahoochee River
79	US 29, to Lanett, E Murphy USA, Shell/Circle K Arby Burger King, Capt D's, Chuck's BBQ, DQ, Dunkin', KFC, Kryst Little Caesar's, McDonald's, Pizza Hut, San Marcos Mexica Subway, Taco Bell, Waffle House, Wendy's, Wing Stop $General, $Tree, Advance Parts, repair, Verizon, Walma W Exxon/QV, JetPep, RaceWay/dsl Domino's, Jin Ja anese Steaks, Sonic EconoLodge AutoZone, CVS Dru Kroger, O'Reilly Parts, to West Point Lake, vet
78.5mm	**Welcome Ctr sb, full facilities, litter barrels, petwalk, , vending**
77	AL 208, to Huguley, E Jet Pep/Church's/dsl, Shell/Circle dsl Waffle House Quality Inn Chevrolet, Chrysle Dodge/Ford/Lincoln, Ford, W Hampton Inn fireworks
76mm	Eastern/Central time zone
70	AL 388, to Cusseta, E BigCat/dsl, Sunoco/Louie's/ds scales/24hr/@, W fireworks
66	Andrews Rd, to US 29
64	US 29, to Opelika, E Sunoco/dsl, W Tiger/dsl
62	US 280/431, to Opelika, E Chevron/dsl, Eagle/dsl, Mara thon/dsl, Shell/Circle K/Church's/dsl Burger King, Durang Mexican, McDonald's, Subway, Taco Bell, Wasabi Japanes Wok'n Roll Rest. Days Inn, EconoLodge, Motel 6, Quality In Red Carpet Inn, Red Roof Inn $General, W GrubMa JetPep Capt. D's, Cracker Barrel, Sizzlin Steaks, Waff House Comfort Inn, Magnuson Hotel Buick/Chevrole GMC, Chrysler/Dodge/Jeep, Ford, H&W Tire, Harley-Davidso USA Stores/famous brands

INTERSTATE 85 Cont'd

Exit #	Services
60	AL 51, AL 169, to Opelika, E RaceWay/dsl Hardee's $General, W Citgo H, auto repair
58	US 280 W, to Opelika, E Eagle/Guthrie's/dsl Freddy's, Wild Wing Cafe Hampton Inn, Holiday Inn Express, Home 2 Suites, La Quinta golf, W Chevron/Subway/dsl Arby's, Brick Oven Pizza, Buffalo Wild Wings, BurgerFi, Chick-fil-A, Chipotle, El Patron Mexican, Huddle House, Jersey Mike's, Jim Bob's, Logan's Roadhouse, Longhorn Steaks, Marble Slab, McDonald's, Moe's SW Grill, New Tokyo, Newk's Eatery, O'Charley's, Olive Garden, Pyro's Pizza, Sonic, Starbucks, Steak'n Shake, Taziki's, Waffle House, Which Wich?, Zaxby's Fairfield Inn, Microtel, Motel 6 H, AT&T, Best Buy, Books-A-Million, Dick's, Hobby Lobby, Home Depot, Kohl's, Kroger/dsl, Lowe's, Office Depot, Old Navy, PetCo, Ross, Target, TJ Maxx, URGENT CARE, World Mkt
57	Bent Creek Rd, W Exxon, Mapco Baumhower's Victory Grille, Moe's Original BBQ, Shakey's Pizza, Venditori's Italian, Waffle House, Wendy's Hilton Garden, Sleep Inn Sam's Club/gas
51	US 29, to Auburn, E Chevron/dsl, Grub Mart Courtyard, Hampton Inn, Tru $General, Cadillac/Chevrolet, Leisure Time RV Park/Camping, Nissan, to Chewacla SP, Toyota, vet, W Chevron/Subway/dsl, Murphy USA Arby's, Burger King, Dunkin', El Dorado Mexican, Firehouse Subs, Jack's, Jim'n Nick's BBQ, KJ's Fish Camp, Krystal, Little Caesar's, McDonald's, Ozzio's Italian, Philly Connection, Pizza Hut, Ruby Tuesday, Shrimp Basket, Sonic, Taco Bell, Waffle House, Wendy's, Zaxby's Clarion, EconoLodge, Holiday Inn Express, Microtel, Pannie George's Kitchen, Quality Inn, Sleep Inn Advance Parts, Ford/Lincoln, Kia, tires/repair, to Auburn U, URGENT CARE, Walmart, Winn-Dixie
50	Cox Rd
44mm	**both lanes, 24hr security, full facilities, litter barrels, petwalk, , , RV dump, vending**
42	US 80, AL 186 E, Wire Rd, E dsl repair/tires, to Tuskegee NF, W Torch 85/rest./dsl/24hr
38	AL 81, to Tuskegee, E to Tuskegee NHS, Tuskegee University
32	AL 49 N, to Tuskegee, E Sunoco/dsl
26	AL 229 N, to Tallassee, E Chevron/Guthrie's/dsl
22	US 80, to Shorter, E Loves/McDonald's/Subway/dsl/scales/24hr, Petro/rest./dsl/scales/24hr Days Inn Wind Drift RV Park
16	Waugh, to Cecil, E Entec/Circle K/Subway/dsl auto repair
15	AL 108 W, Pike Rd
11	US 80, AL 110, to Mitylene, to Mt Meigs, E BP/dsl, Liberty/dsl, Murphy USA/dsl, Shell/Subway/dsl Anthony's Rest., Bruster's, Burger King, Cracker Barrel, Jose's Grill, Krystal, McDonald's, Milo's, Taco Bell, Top China, Waffle House Candlewood Suites, Comfort Inn, Country Inn&Suites, Fairfield Inn, Holiday Inn Express, Sleep Inn Hobby Lobby, Home Depot, O'Reilly Parts, Walmart/Subway, W Chevron/dsl Microtel
9	AL 271, to AL 110, to Auburn U/Montgomery, E Arby's, BoneFish Grill, Buffalo Wild Wings, Chick-fil-A, Chili's, Chipotle Mexican, Del Taco, Firebirds Grill, Five Guys, Full Moon BBQ, Genghis Grill, Ixtapa Mexican, La Jolla Rest., Moe's SW Grill, Outback Steaks, Panera Bread, Pieology, Red Robin, Ruby Tuesday, Sonic, Starbucks, Taziki's Cafe, Twin Peaks, TX Roadhouse, Wendy's, Zoe's Kitchen Hampton Inn, Staybridge Suites, TownePlace Suites AT&T, Books-A-Million, Costco/gas,

MONTGOMERY

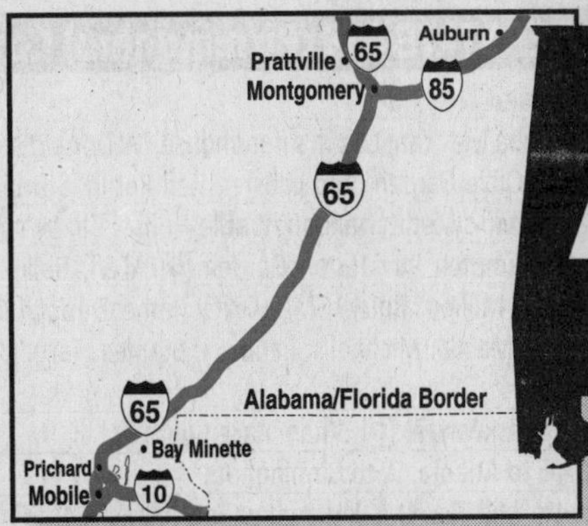

Exit #	Services
9	Continued Dick's, Dillard's, Firestone/auto, Jo-Ann Fabrics, Kohl's, Michael's, Old Navy, Petsmart, Ross, Target, URGENT CARE, Verizon, vet, Whole Foods Mkt, World Mkt, W H
6	US 80, US 231, AL 21, East Blvd, **0-2 mi** E Chevron, Exxon/dsl, RaceWay/dsl, Shell Arby's, Baumhowers Rest., Burger King, Carrabba's, Chick-fil-A, Gangnam Grill, Golden Corral, Hardee's, Jason's Deli, KFC, Longhorn Steaks, Los Cabos, Los Vaqueros Mexican, McDonald's, Ming's Garden, Olive Garden, Piccadilly Cafe, Popeye's, Rock Bottom Cafe, Schlotzsky's, Starbucks, Subway, Sushiyama, Taco Bell, Waffle House, Wendy's, Zaxby's Arlington Lodge, Best Inn, Comfort Inn, Country Inn&Suites, Courtyard, Extended Stay America, Home-Towne Suites, La Quinta, Quality Inn, Quality Roof Inn, Residence Inn, Sleep Inn, Springhill Suites, Wingate Inn, Woodspring Suites $General, $Tree, Acura, Best Buy, Books-A-Million, Family$, Ford/Lincoln, Fresh Mkt Foods, Home Depot, Honda, Hyundai, Lowe's, Office Depot, Pepboys, PetCo, Subaru, TJ Maxx, Tuesday Morning, UHaul, USPO, Walmart/McDonald's, Winn-Dixie, W Chevron, Liberty, Mapco/dsl, Shell Arby's, Capt D's, Hardee's, Hibachi Buffet, IHOP, Jan's Rest., Krispy Kreme, Krystal, McDonald's, Outback Steaks, Red Lobster, Saigon Bistro, Taco Bell, Waffle House Alabama Hotel, Baymont Inn, Comfort Suites, Drury Inn, Express Inn, Motel 6, Ramada Inn $General, Audi/VW, BMW, Buick/Cadillac/GMC, Chevrolet, Chrysler/Dodge/Jeep, Firestone/auto, Infiniti, JC Penney, Kia, Lexus, Mercedes, Nissan, Sam's Club/gas, Toyota, Volvo
4	Perry Hill Rd, E Chappy's Deli, Marco's Pizza Fresh Mkt, W Chevron, Texaco/dsl Hardee's, Subway Hilton Garden, Homewood Suites $General, Express Oil Change
3	Ann St, E Chevron Arby's, Bojangle's, Capt D's, Domino's, KFC, Krystal, McDonald's, Taco Bell, Waffle House, Wendy's, Zaxby's Red Roof Inn Pepboys, W Entec, Murphy USA/dsl, PaceCar, Ztec Burger King, Chick-fil-A, CiCi's Pizza, Hardee's, Popeye's Stay Lodge $Tree, AT&T, Office Depot, O'Reilly Parts, Ross, Verizon, Walmart/Subway
2	Forest Ave, E CVS Drug, W H
1	Court St, Union St, downtown, E Marathon/dsl, W to Ala St U
0mm	**I-85 begins/ends on I-65, exit 171 in Montgomery**

INTERSTATE 459 (Birmingham)

Exit #	Services
33b a	I-59, N to Gadsden, S to Birmingham
32	US 11, Trussville, N Marathon/dsl, S BP/Wendy's, Chevron/dsl, RaceWay/dsl, Shell/dsl Arby's, Bojangles, Burger King, Cajun Steamer, Chili's, China Palace, Coldstone, Dunkin', El Cazador Mexican, Firehouse Subs, Five Guys, Habanero's Rest., Hooters, Jack's Rest., Jim'n Nick's BBQ, KFC,

= gas = food = lodging = other = rest stop

AL

INTERSTATE 459 (Birmingham) Cont'd

BIRMINGHAM

32 Continued
La Bamba Mexican, Logan's Roadhouse, McDonald's, Mizu Japanese, Olive Garden, Red Lobster, Red Robin, Starbucks, Subway, Taziki's Mediterranean, Waffle House, Zaxby's Courtyard, Hampton Inn, Hilton Garden AT&T, Belk, Best Buy, Books-A-Million, Buick/GMC, GNC, Home Depot, JC Penney, Lowe's, Mazda, Michael's, Pepboys, Staples, Target, TJ Maxx, Verizon

31 Derby Parkway, **N** B'ham Race Course

29 I-20, E to Atlanta, W to Birmingham

27 Grants Mill Rd, **N** Hampton Inn Fiat, **S** Chevron/dsl Audi/Porsche, BMW, Chrysler/Dodge/Jeep, Land Rover, Lexus, Mini

23 Liberty Parkway, **S** Billy's Grill, DQ, Taziki's Greek Hilton Garden

19 US 280, Mt Brook, Childersburg, **N** Chevron/dsl CA Pizza Kitchen, Cheesecake Factory, Chuy's Mexican, Flemings Rest., Johnny Rockets, Lime Tex Mex, Macaroni Grill, Panera Bread, PF Chang's, Seasons Grille, Village Tavern, Which Wich?, Zoe's Kitchen AT&T, Barnes&Noble, Belk, Old Navy, Verizon, **0-3 mi S** BP/Circle K, Chevron, Marathon, Shell, Shell Arby's, Asian Rim, Black Pearl Asian, Buffalo Wild Wings, Burger King, Carrabba's, Chick-fil-A, Chili's, Chipotle Mexican, Cracker Barrel, Edgar's Rest., Full Moon BBQ, Jason's Deli, Jimmy John's, Kobe Japanese, Logan's Roadhouse, Longhorn Steaks, McDonald's, Milo's Burgers, Mooyah Burgers, Newk's Eatery, Pablo's, Papa John's, Pappadeaux, Pizza Hut, Schlotzsky's, Starbucks, Steak'n Shake, Subway, Superior Grill, Suriname 280, Taco Bell, Taziki's Greek, Wendy's, Zaxby's Courtyard, Days Inn, Drury Inn, Extended Stay America, Hampton Inn, Hilton, Homewood Suites, Hyatt Place, La Quinta, Marriott, Quality Inn, Residence Inn, SpringHill Suites AT&T, Autozone, Best Buy, CVS Drug, Firestone/auto, Fresh Mkt Foods, Goodyear/auto, Home Depot, Kohl's, NTB, Staples, Target, vet, Walgreens, Winn-Dixie, World Mkt

17 Acton Rd, **N** Shell/dsl Krystal, McDonald's, **S** Comfort Inn

15b a I-65, N to Birmingham, S to Montgomery

HOOVER

13 US 31, Hoover, Pelham, **N** Exxon/dsl, Shell/dsl, Sunc dsl Burger King, Chick-fil-A, Fish Mkt Rest., Full Moon B Golden Rule BBQ, Habanero's, Krispy Kreme, Krystal, McD ald's, Outback Steaks, Papa John's, Purple Onion, Salvat Pizza, Starbucks, Subway Econolodge $Tree, Ac AutoZone, Cadillac, Chevrolet, Firestone/auto, Goodyear/a Honda, Hyundai, Mr Transmission, Nissan, Publix, Rite Aid, ples, TJ Maxx, vet, **S** Exxon, Jet-Pep, Shell/dsl Arb Bonefish Grill, CA Pizza Kitchen, Chick-fil-A, Chipotle Mexic Firebird's Grill, Firehouse Subs, J Alexander's Rest., Jasc Deli, Jim'n Nicks BBQ, La Paz, McDonald's, Moe's BBQ, M SW Grill, Newk's Eatery, Olive Garden, Panera Bread, Pi Hut, Ruby Tuesday, Steak'n Shake, Stix Asian, Sumo Japane Taco Bell, Twin Peaks Rest., Wendy's Courtyard, Days Embassy Suites, Hampton Inn, Hyatt Place, Hyatt Regen Wynfrey Hotel Barnes&Noble, Belk, Best Buy, Costco/g Dick's, GNC, Hancock Fabrics, Home Depot, Infiniti, JC Penn Jo-Ann Fabrics, Macy's, Mercedes, Michael's, NTB, Office pot, PepBoys, Petsmart, Ross, Sam's Club/gas, Tuesday Mo ing, Verizon, Walgreens, World Mkt

10 AL 150, Waverly, **N** Beef o Brady's, Chick-fil-A, Fredd Frontera Mexican Grill, Jimmy John's, McDonald's, St bucks $Tree, Kohl's, Marshall's, PetCo, Sprouts Mkt, Targ URGENT CARE, **S** Circle K/dsl, Shell Hampton Inn, att Place Ford/Lincoln, Publix/deli, Toyota, Walgreens

BESSEMER

6 AL 52, to Bessemer, **N** Shell/dsl, **S** Chevron/dsl, Cir K, Texaco/DQ Arby's, China Wok, Domino's, McDonal Papa John's, Pizza Hut, Railroad Cafe, Subway, Waffle Hou Wendy's Sleep Inn $General, CVS Drug, RV Campi Winn-Dixie

1 AL 18, Bessemer, **N** Exxon/dsl, Shell/Dunkin'/dsl Bu er King, Chick-fil-A, Firehouse Subs, Full Moon BBQ, Hab nero's Mexican, Logan's Roadhouse, McAlister's Deli, Ta Bell AAA, AT&T, GNC, Michaels, Petsmart, Publix, Ro Target, URGENT CARE, **S** Sunoco/dsl Bojangles, Chi King, McDonald's, San Antonio Grill, Subway, Zaxby's A vance Parts, CVS Drug, Meineke, Piggly Wiggly, to Tannehill Verizon

0mm **I-459 begins/ends on I-20/59, exit 106.**

NOTES

ARIZONA

AZ

INTERSTATE 8

Exit #	Services
178b a	I-10, E to Tucson, W to Phoenix, **I-8 begins/ends on I-10, exit 199.**
174	Trekell Rd, to Casa Grande, **2-4 mi N** food, gas, lodging
172	Thornton Rd, to Casa Grande, **5-8 mi N** gas food Francisco Grande Resort, Holiday Inn
171mm	Santa Cruz River
169	Bianco Rd
167	Montgomery Rd
163mm	Santa Rosa Wash
161	Stanfield Rd
151	AZ 84 E, Maricopa Rd, to Stanfield, **S** Saguaro RV Park
151mm	**picnic area wb, , litter barrels**
149mm	**picnic area eb, , litter barrels**
144	Vekol Rd
140	Freeman Rd
119	Butterfield Trail, to AZ 85, I-10, Gila Bend, **3 mi N** Shell/dsl/scales, Shell/Subway/dsl/scales/RV Park/24hr Little Italy, Subway America's Choice Inn, Best Western, Knights Inn, Palms Inn, Space Age/rest. $General
117mm	Sand Tank Wash
115	AZ 85, to Gila Bend, **1-2 mi N** Chevron/dsl, Circle K, Loves/Taco Bell/dsl/scales/24hr, Tesla EVC Burger King, Carl's Jr, McDonald's, Sofia's Mexican Best Western, Palms Inn Family$, NAPA
111	Citrus Valley Rd
106	Paloma Rd
102	Painted Rock Rd, **N** Painted Rock Petroglyph Site (11mi)
87	Aqua Caliente Rd, Sentinel Rd, Sentinel, Hyder, **N** Conde's Gen Store/dsl RV Camping
85mm	**wb, full facilities, litter barrels, petwalk, , , vending**
84mm	**eb, full facilities, litter barrels, petwalk, , , vending**
78	Spot Rd
73	Aztec, **S** Oasis RV Park/dump (4mi)
67	Dateland, **S** Chevron/dsl/24hr Dateland RV Park, Oasis RV Park/dump (2mi)
56mm	**both lanes, full facilities, litter barrels, petwalk, , , vending**
54	Ave 52 E, Mohawk Valley
42	Ave 40 E, to Tacna, **N** Chevron/dsl Jac's Whistlestop Cafe USPO, **S** Shell/Subway/dsl Copper Mtn RV Park
37	Ave 36 E, to Roll
30	Ave 29 E, Wellton, **N** Circle K/dsl Geronimo Mexican Desert Motel Family$, NAPA, Tier Drop RV Park, USPO, **S** Chevron/dsl Dusty's Pizza & Wings, Jack-in-the-Box Microtel
24mm	Ligurta Wash
23mm	Red Top Wash
22mm	**parking area/litter barrels both lanes**
21	Dome Valley, **N** Ligurta Sta Rest./RV park Yuma Proving Ground (16mi)
17mm	**insp sta eb**
15mm	Fortuna Wash
14	Foothills Blvd, **N** Sundance RV Park, **S** Domino's, Foothills Eatery, Jimmy K's auto/RV care/lube ctr, Family$, Foothills RV Park
12	Fortuna Rd, to US95N, **N** Chevron/dsl, FLYING J/Giant/dsl/scales/24hr DayBreakers Cafe, Jack-in-the-Box, Las Palapas

GILA BEND

WELLTON

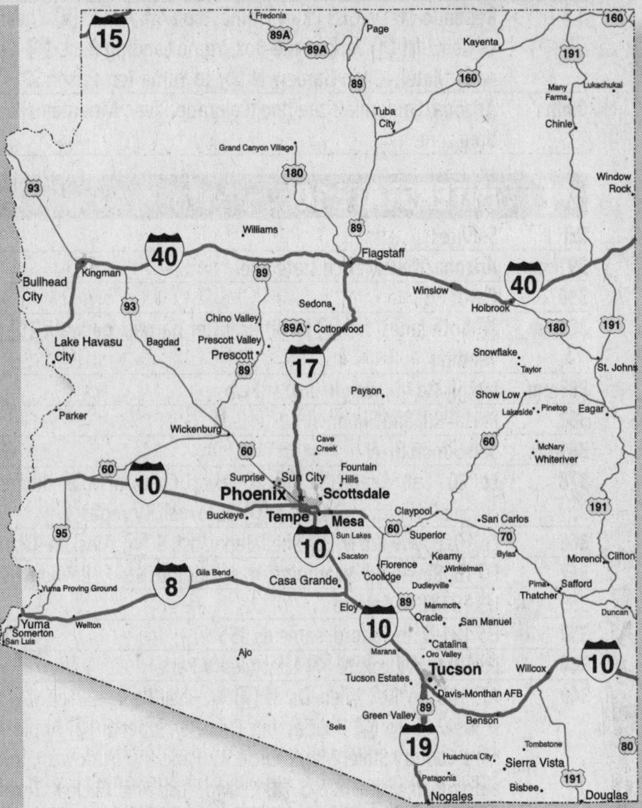

Exit #	Services
12	Continued Tacos, McDonald's, Pizza Hut, Starbucks, Taco Bell Comfort Inn, Courtesy Inn Caravan RV Park, Oasis RV Park, Shangri La RV Park, **S** Chevron/dsl, Mobil/Burger King/dsl A&W/KFC, Applebee's, Carl's Jr, Daboyz Pizza, Denny's, Dunkin', Little Caesar's, Papa John's, Subway Best Western+ $General, $Tree, AutoZone, Big O Tire, CVS Drug, Fry's Foods/dsl, O'Reilly Parts, USPO, Verizon, Walgreens
9	32nd St, to Yuma, **S** Del Taco, Panda Express RV Parks, Verizon, Walmart/McDonald's
7	AZ 195, Araby Rd, **N** Circle K/dsl to AZWU, **S** Chevron/Jack-in-the-Box/dsl, Circle K/dsl RV Parks, RV World
3	AZ 280 S, Ave 3E, **N** Arby's Candlewood Suites, Holiday Inn Express, **S** Loves/Chester's/Subway/dsl/scales/24hr CarQuest, Harley-Davidson, to Marine Corp Air Sta
2	US 95, 16th St, Yuma, **N** Circle K Ah-So Steaks, Black Bear Diner, Buffalo Wild Wings, Chick-fil-A, Chili's, Chipotle Mexican, ChuckeCheese, Coldstone Creamery, Cracker Barrel, Del Taco, Denny's, Famous Dave's BBQ, Five Guys, Freddy's, Hawaiian BBQ, Hooters, In-N-Out, Jack-in-the-Box, Kneaders, Lin's Chinese, Olive Garden, Panda Express, Penny's Diner, Red Lobster, Starbucks, Subway Baymont Inn, Best Western, Days Inn, Fairfield Inn, Hampton Inn, Holiday Inn, Homewood Suites, Hotel Inn & Suites, La Fuente Inn, Motel 6, Shilo Inn, SpringHill Suites, TownePlace Suites, Wingate Inn AT&T, Best Buy, Dillard's, Discount Tire, GNC, JC Penney, Kohl's, Marshall's, Old Navy, PetsMart, Ross, Sam's Club/gas, Target, Verizon, **S** Arco/dsl, Chevron/dsl, Speedway/dsl Applebee's, Burger King, Carl's Jr, Chretin's Mexican, Dunkin', Golden Corral, IHOP, Jack-in-the-Box, McDonald's, Subway, TX Roadhouse, Village Inn Pizza, Wendy's Budgetel, Quality Inn, Radisson, Super 8 BigLots, Family$, Home Depot, Staples

YUMA

[gas] = gas [food] = food [lodging] = lodging [other] = other [rest stop] = rest stop

INTERSTATE 8 Cont'd

Exit #	Services
1.5mm	**weigh sta both lanes**
1	Redondo Ctr Dr, Giss Pkwy, Yuma, **S on 4th Ave E** [gas] Chevron, Circle K/dsl [food] Jack-in-the-Box, Yuma Landing Rest. [lodging] Coronado Motel, Hilton Garden, **N** [other] to Yuma Terr Prison SP
0mm	Arizona/California state line, Colorado River, Mountain/Pacific time zone

INTERSTATE 10

Exit #	Services
391mm	Arizona/New Mexico state line
390	Cavot Rd
389mm	**[rest stop] both lanes, full [handicap] facilities, litter barrels, petwalk, [phone], [picnic], vending**
383mm	**weigh sta eb, weigh/insp sta wb**
382	Portal Rd, San Simon
381mm	San Simon River
378	Lp 10, San Simon, **N** [gas] 4K Trkstp/Chevron/Noble Romans/Quiznos/dsl/scales/24hrs/@ [other] auto/dsl/RV repair
366	Lp 10, Bowie Rd, **N** [gas] Shell/Jerky/dsl, **S** [other] Alaskan RV park
362	Lp 10, Bowie Rd, **N** camping, gas, lodging, **S** to Ft Bowie NHS
355	US 191 N, to Safford
352	US 191 N, to Safford, same as 355
344	Lp 10, to Willcox, **N** [other] Lifestyle RV Park
340	AZ 186, to Rex Allen Dr, **N** [gas] TA/Shell/Popeye's/Subway/dsl/scales/24hr/@ [lodging] Holiday Inn Express, Super 8 [other] Apple Annie's Country Store, Magic Circle RV Park, RV/Truckwash, truck/auto repair, visitor info, **S** [gas] Chevron/dsl/24hr, Circle K, Texaco/dsl [food] Burger King, Carl's Jr, McDonald's, Pizza Hut [lodging] Days Inn, Quality Inn, Rodeway Inn [other] [H], $General, Ace Hardware, auto/tire/RV repair, AutoZone, Beall's, Family$, Grande Vista RV Park, KT's Mkt, Medicine Shoppe, Safeway, to Chiricahua NM, Verizon
336	AZ 186, Willcox, **S** [gas] Chevron/dsl/LP [lodging] Royal Western Lodge [other] Ft Willcox RV Park, Life Style RV Park
331	US 191 S, to Sunsites, Douglas, **S** [other] to Cochise Stronghold
322	Johnson Rd, **S** [gas] Shell/DQ/dsl/gifts
320mm	**[rest stop] both lanes, full [handicap] facilities, litter barrels, petwalk, [phone], [picnic], vending**
318	Triangle T Rd, to Dragoon, **S** [other] Amerind Museum (1mi), camping, lodging
312	Sibyl Rd
309mm	Adams Peak Wash
306	AZ 80, Pomerene Rd, Benson, **1-2 mi S** [gas] Circle K, Shell [food] 86 Cafe [other] CarQuest, El Rio RV Park, Pato Blanco Lakes RV Park, repair, San Pedro RV (2mi)
305mm	San Pedro River
304	Ocotillo St, Benson, **N** [food] Denny's, Dickey's BBQ, Jack-in-the-Box [lodging] Days Inn, Super 8 [other] Benson RV Park, KOA, **S** [gas] Chevron [food] Beijing Chinese, Farmhouse Rest, Galleano's Italian-American, Little Caesar's, Magaly's Mexican, Subway, Wendy's [lodging] Quality Inn, QuarterHorse Inn/RV Park [other] [H], $General, Ace Hardware, Butterfield RV Resort, Dillon RV Ctr, Pardner's RV Park, Safeway, Walmart
303	US 80 (eb only), to Tombstone, Bisbee, **S** [food] Farmhouse Rest., Little Caesar's, Pablo's Steaks, Reb's Rest., Subway [lodging] Quarter Horse Motel/RV Park [other] auto/dsl/repair, Medicine Shoppe, O'Reilly Parts, Pardners RV Park, to Douglas NHL, to Tombstone Courthouse SHP (26mi), Verizon, Walmart
302	AZ 90 S, to Ft Huachuca, Benson, **S** [gas] Love's/Chester's/Subway/dsl/scales/24hr, Shell/dsl [food] KFC/Taco Bell, McDonald's

WILLCOX

BENSON

Exit #	Services
302	Continued [lodging] Comfort Inn, Motel 6 [other] AZ Legends RV Resort, Coch Terrace RV Park, Ft Huachuca NHS (25mi)
299	Skyline Rd
297	Mescal Rd, J-6 Ranch Rd, **N** [gas] Chevron/dsl
292	Empirita Rd
291	Marsh Station Rd
288mm	Cienega Creek
281	AZ 83 S, to Patagonia
279	Colossal Cave Rd, Wentworth Rd, **N** [gas] Chevron/dsl [food] Pizza Co, DQ, Montgomery's Grill [other] to Colossal Caves (7m USPO
275	Houghton Rd, **N** [food] Panda Express [other] Adventure Bound Resort, Discount Tire, to Saguaro NP (10mi), Walmart, **S** [other] fairgrounds (1mi)
273	Rita Rd, **N** [gas] Pilot/Subway/dsl [food] Burger King [lodging] Hamton Inn, **S** [other] fairgrounds
270	Kolb Rd, **S** [other] Bay RV Resort, Voyager RV Resort
269	Wilmot Rd, **N** [gas] Chevron/A&W/dsl [lodging] Travel Inn, **S** [gas] She pizza/subs/dsl
268	Craycroft Rd, **N** [gas] Circle K, Mr T/dsl/LP, Pilot/Subway/Ta Bell/dsl/lp/scales/24hr/@, TTT/rest/dsl/scales/24hr [other] Cra Horse RV Park, Freightliner, truck/RV wash, **S** [other] dsl repair
267	Valencia Rd, **N** [gas] Shell/Jack-in-the-Box [other] Pima Air&Spa Museum, **S** [gas] Valero/dsl [other] [airport]
265	Alvernon Way, **N** [other] Davis-Monthan AFB
264b a	Palo Verde Rd, **N** [gas] Circle K/dsl [food] Denny's, Shell/Wendy' dsl, Waffle House [lodging] Comfort Inn, Crossland Suites, Days In Holiday Inn, Red Roof Inn [other] Camping World RV Resort, Fre dom RV Ctr, **S** [food] Arby's, McDonald's [lodging] Quality Inn, Studio [other] La Mesa RV Ctr, Lazy Days RV Ctr/Resort, Pedata RV Ctr
263b	Kino Pkwy N, **N** [gas] Shell/dsl [food] Culver's, Dave&Buster In-N-Out, Jimmy John's, Starbucks [other] AT&T, Costco/gas, Di count Tire, Verizon, Walmart/Subway
263a	Kino Pkwy S, **N** [other] [H], **S** [gas] Arco/dsl, Shamrock [food] Burg King, KFC, Little Caesar's, Mandarin Buffet, Papa John's, Ta Bell [other] $Tree, AutoZone, Family$, Food City, Fry's Food O'Reilly Parts, to Tucson Intn'l Airport, Walgreens
262	Benson Hwy, Park Ave, **S** [gas] Arco/dsl, Chevron/McDonald' dsl, Circle K/dsl [food] Carl's Jr. [lodging] Best Value Inn, Motel 6, Rod way Inn, Western Inn [other] Mack/Volvo Trucks, USPO
261	6th/4th Ave, **N** [gas] GasCo [food] Little Caesar's, Los Portal [lodging] EconoLodge [other] Discount Tire, Family$, Food City, USP **S** [gas] Circle K/dsl [food] Church's, El Indio, Jack-in-the-Box, Pa da Express, Silver Saddle Steaks, Whataburger [lodging] Lazy 8 M tel [other] Big O Tire, El Super Foods, Family$, Midas, O'Reilly Par
260	I-19 S, to Nogales
259	22nd St, Starr Pass Blvd, **N** [gas] Circle K/dsl, **S** [food] Kettle, Waff House [lodging] Clarion, Regal Inn, Silverbell Inn, Super 8, Travel In
258	Congress St, Broadway St, **N** [gas] Circle K [lodging] Hotel Tusca **S** [food] Carl's Jr [lodging] Days Inn, Howard Johnson, Motel 6, Rive Park Inn, Travelodge
257a	St Mary's Rd, **S** [gas] Shell/dsl [food] Burger King, Church's, Den ny's, Eegee's Cafe, Furr's Cafeteria, Jack-in-the-Box, Litt Caesar's; Whataburger [lodging] Country Inn&Suites, Ramad Ltd. [other] [H], Family$, Food City, Pima Comm Coll
257	Speedway Blvd, **N** [lodging] Best Western, EconoLodge [other] [H], of AZ, Victory Motorcycles, **S** [gas] Arco/dsl [other] museum, Ol Town Tucson
256	Grant Rd, **N** [gas] Circle K [food] auto/dsl repair, Burger King, Jack in-the-Box, Sonic [other] Walgreens, **S** [gas] Circle K, QT/dsl, Shel dsl [food] Arby's, Del Taco, Eegee's Cafe, IHOP, Waffle Hous

TUCSON

INTERSTATE 10 Cont'd

256 Continued
Comfort Inn, Grant Inn, Holiday Inn Express, Super 8
Ace Hardware, Safeway, Walgreens

255 AZ 77 N, to Miracle Mile

254 Prince Rd, N Circle K, Valero/dsl $General, O'Reilly Parts, Walgreens, S golf, Kenworth, Prince of Tucson RV Park

252 El Camino del Cerro, Ruthrauff Rd, N Arco Ruthrauff RV Ctr, S Shell/Jack-in-the-Box/dsl

251 Sunset Rd

250 Orange Grove Rd, N Arco/dsl, Circle K/dsl Burger King, Culver's, Domino's, Firehouse Subs, Golden Corral, Little Caesar's, Subway, Tulioberto's, Wendy's Big O Tire, Costco/gas, diesel repair, Home Depot, Petsmart, South Forty RV Park, Sprouts Mkt, Staples, URGENT CARE, vet

248 Ina Rd, N Chevron/dsl, Circle K/dsl, Shell/dsl Bisbee Breakfast Club, Carl's Jr, ChickeNuevo, Chuy's Mesquite, DQ, Eegee's Cafe, Five Guys, Hooters, Jack-in-the-Box, Jade Garden, Losbetos Cafe, Lupita's Cafe, McDonald's, Miss Saigon, Molinitas Mexican, Papa John's, Peter Piper's Pizza, Pollo Loco, Starbucks, Subway, Taco Bell, Waffle House InTown Suites, Motel 6 $Tree, 99c Store, auto repair, AutoZone, BigLots, CarQuest, CVS Drug, Discount Tire, Firestone/auto, Fry's Foods/dsl, Goodyear/auto, Hancock Fabrics, Lowe's, Michael's, Midas, O'Reilly Parts, PepBoys, Target, U-Haul, Walgreens, S Circle K Denny's, Starbucks Best Western, Red Roof Inn, Travelodge Ace Hardware, Freedom RV Ctr, Harley-Davidson

246 Cortaro Rd, N Circle K/Arby's/dsl, QT/dsl IHOP, Wendy's, S Shell/dsl Boston's Rest, Burger King, Chili's, Chipotle, Chopstix, Cracker Barrel, Dunkin, Eegee's Rest., In-N-Out, Jersey Mike's, Jimmy John's, KFC, Little Caesar's, McDonald's, Nana's Mexican, Native New Yorker, New Town Asian, Panda Express, Starbucks, Subway, Taco Bell, TX Roadhouse Comfort Inn, Days Inn, Holiday Inn Express, La Quinta, Super 8, Village Inn $Tree, access to RV camping, Ace Hardware, AT&T, Batteries+, GNC, Kohl's, O'Reilly Parts, Petco, Ross, TJ Maxx, USPO, Verizon, Walmart/McDonald's

244 Twin Peaks Rd, N Tucson Outlets/famous brands

242 Avra Valley Rd, S , RV camping, Saguaro NP (13mi)

240 Tangerine Rd, to Rillito, N A-A RV Park, S USPO

236 Marana, S Chevron/dsl/LP, Circle K/dsl McDonald's, R&R Pizza auto repair, Family$, Sun RV Park

232 Pinal Air Park Rd, S Pinal Air Park (3mi)

228mm to frontage rd, wb pulloff

226 Red Rock, S USPO

219 Picacho Peak Rd, N Shell/DQ, Shell/Subway/dsl, S Ostrich Ranch, Pichaco Peak RV Park, to Picacho Peak SP

212 Picacho (from wb), S KOA

211b AZ 87 N, AZ 84 W, to Coolidge, S KOA

211a Picacho (from eb), S KOA, state prison

208 Sunshine Blvd, to Eloy, N Pilot/Subway/DQ/dsl/scales/24hr dsl repair, S FLYING J/Denny's/dsl/scales/24hr Blue Beacon

203 Toltec Rd, to Eloy, N Chevron/McDonald's/playplace/24hr, Circle K/dsl Carl's Jr, El Caballito Mexican Best Value Inn, Super 8 Desert Valley RV Park, dsl/tire repair, S Sinclair/dsl, TA/A&W/Taco Bell/dsl/RV dump/24hr/@ Pizza Hut golf, truckwash

200 Sunland Gin Rd, Arizona City, N Petro/Iron Skillet/dsl/scales/24hr/@, Pride/Subway/dsl/24hr Burger King, Eva's Mexican Days Inn, Quality Inn Blue Beacon,

CASA GRANDE

200 Continued
Eagle Truckwash, Las Colinas RV Park, S Loves/Arby's/Baskin-Robbins/dsl/24hr Golden 9 Rest Motel 6 Speedco Lube

199 I-8 W, to Yuma, San Diego

198 AZ 84, to Eloy, Casa Grande, N Robson Ranch Rest./golf (3mi)

194 AZ 287, Florence Blvd, to Casa Grande, N Tesla EVC Buffalo Wild Wings, Cactus Moon Grill, Cane's, Chick-fil-A, Culver's, In-N-Out, Krispy Kreme, Mimi's Cafe, Olive Garden, Rubio's, Subway Dillard's, GNC, JC Penney, Kohl's, Marshall's, Michael's, Petsmart, Ross, Staples, Sunscape RV Park (7mi), Target, Verizon, Walgreens, World Mkt, **0-2 mi S** 76/DQ, Arco/dsl, Chevron/Little Caesars/dsl, Circle K/gas Arby's, Burger King, Carl's Jr, Chili's, China Buffet, Chipotle Mexican, Church's, Coldstone, Cracker Barrel, Del Taco, Denny's, Eegee's, Filiberto's Mexican, Golden Corral, IHOP, Jack-in-the-Box, JB's, Jimmy John's, LJ Silver/Taco Bell, Macayo's Mexican, McDonald's, Panda Express, Papa John's, Papa Murphy's, Peter Piper Pizza, Sonic, Starbucks, Subway, T&M Italian, Wendy's Comfort Inn, Holiday Inn Express, Legacy Suites, Mainstay Suites, Quality Inn, Super 8 H, $Tree, 99cents Store, AT&T, AutoZone, Big Lots, Big O Tire, CVS Drug, Discount Tire, Encore Camping (2mi), Family$, Fiesta Grande RV Resort, Food City, Fry's Food/drug/dsl, Goodyear/auto, Home Depot, Jo-Ann Fabrics, Lowe's, U-Haul, URGENT CARE, Verizon, vet, Walgreens, Walmart/McDonald's

190 McCartney Rd, N to Central AZ Coll, S Circle K/dsl Barro's Pizza (3mi)

185 AZ 387, to Casa Grande, Casa Grande Ruins NM, S Eva's Mexican (6mi) Francisco Grande (6mi), Holiday Inn (6mi) Fry's Food/gas (6mi), hwy patrol, to Casa Grande Ruins NM, Val Vista RV camping (3mi)

183mm **wb, full facilities, litter barrels, petwalk, , vending**

181mm **eb, full facilities, litter barrels, petwalk, , vending**

175 AZ 587 N, Casa Blanca Rd, Chandler, Gilbert, S Chevron/dsl

173mm Gila River

167 Riggs Rd, to Sun Lake, N Shell/dsl Akimel Smoke Shop

164 AZ 347 S, Queen Creek Rd, to Maricopa, N gas to Chandler Airport

162b a Wild Horse Pass Rd, Sundust Rd, N Loves/Arby's/dsl/scales/24hr McDonald's Best Western+ MotorCoach Resort, S Chevron/dsl Sheraton Resort, Wildhorse Pass Hotel/Casino Firebird Sports Park, Gila River Casino, Phoenix Outlets/famous brands

161 AZ 202 E, Pecos Rd

160 Chandler Blvd, to Chandler, N Chevron/dsl, Circle K, Circle K/dsl Can't Stop Smokin' BBQ, Denny's, Filiberto's Mexican,

AZ

INTERSTATE 10 Cont'd

CHANDLER

Exit	Services
160	Continued Marie's Rest., McDonald's, Rudy's BBQ, Sandella's Flatbread Cafe, Starbucks, Subway, US Egg Cafe, Wendy's, Whataburger Comfort Inn, Fairfield Inn, Hampton Inn, Hawthorn Suites, Homewood Suites, Motel 6, Quality Inn, Radisson, Super 8 $Tree, Aamco, ADS Auto Repair, CVS, Firestone/auto, Harley-Davidson, to Compadre Stadium, U-Haul, vet, Walmart Mkt, Williams AFB, S 7-11, Chevron/dsl, Circle K/dsl, Shell/dsl Bell Italian Pizza, Brazilian Bull Steaks, Carl's Jr, Cracker Barrel, Del Taco, Dunkin', Hong Kong Buffet, Jersey Mike's, Qdoba, Spinato's Pizzaria, Starbucks, Tukee's Grille, Waffle House, Wendy's Extended Stay America, Holiday Inn Express, InTown Suites, La Quinta H, AT&T, AutoZone, Discount Tire, Kohl's, URGENT CARE
159	Ray Rd, N Circle K, Shell Buca Italian, Carrabba's, Charleston's Rest., Chipotle Mexican, Fleming's Steaks, Frederico's Mexican, Genghis Grill, Habit Burger, In-N-Out, Jasons Deli, Jimmy John's, Longhorn Steaks, McDonald's, Nabers Rest., Outback Steaks, Paradise Cafe, Pei Wei Asian, Red Lobster, Roy's Hawaiian, Rumbi Grill, Sandbar Mexican, Starbucks, Subway, Tejas, Zoe's Kitchen Courtyard AJ's Fine Foods, Audi, BMW, Chevrolet, Ford, Home Depot, Lexus, Lowe's Whse, Mercedes, PetsMart, Sam's Club/gas, Verizon, S Circle K/dsl Barro's Pizza, Boston Mkt, Chick-Fil-A, Five Guys, Honeybaked Ham, IHOP/24hr, Jack-in-the-Box, Kneaders Cafe, Mellow Mushroom, Mimi's Café, Native Grill, Neo Tokyo, On-the-Border, Peter Piper Pizza, Pizza Hut, Rubio's, Subway, Uncle Bear's Grill, Vincent's Pizza, Wendy's Extended Stay America, Extended Stay America AT&T, auto repair, Barnes&Noble, Best Buy, Fresh&Easy Mkt, Hobby Lobby, JC Penney, Jo-Ann Fabrics, Marshall's, Michael's, PetCo, Ross, Sprouts Mkt, Target, Verizon
158	Warner Rd, N Circle K/dsl, QT Carl's Jr, Dunkin', Forefathers Cheesteaks, Port of Subs, Topical Smoothie Drury Inn Dick's, IKEA, S Circle K/dsl, Minute Mart/dsl AZ Sandwich Co., Burger King, ChuckeCheese, DQ, Hillside Spot Cafe, Macayo's Mexican, McDonald's, Nello's Pizza, Panda Garden, Ruffino's Italian, Taco Bell, Zipp's Grill Ace Hardware, Basha's Foods, Big O Tire, Goodyear/auto, vet
157	Elliot Rd, N Chevron/dsl, QT/dsl, Shell/Circle K/dsl Applebee's, Arby's, Burger King, Crackers Cafe, Crazy Buffet, Fuddrucker's, Jimmy John's, Kabab Palace, Kobe Japanese, McDonald's, Olive Garden, Oregano's Pizza Bistro, Panda Express, Red Robin Rest., Sonic, Starbucks, Subway, Taco Bell, Wendy's, YC Mongolian Grill Days Inn&Suites $Tree, Acura, Buick, Cadillac/GMC, Chrysler/Dodge/Jeep, Costco/gas, Discount Tire, Fiat, Honda, Hyundai, Kia, Mazda, Mini, NAPA, Nissan, PetsMart, Ross, Savers, Staples, Toyota, URGENT CARE, Volvo, Walmart, S Circle K/Dsl, Shell/Circle K/dsl Biscuits, Cactus Jack's, Niros Gyros, Original Burrito, Pacific Gardens Asian, Starbucks, Sub Factory, Subway Clarion, Sheraton auto repair, O'Reilly Parts, Safeway, vet, Walgreens
155	Baseline Rd, Guadalupe, N Circle K/dsl, Shell/Circle K/Popeye's/dsl Carl's Jr, ClaimJumper, Ell Pollo Loco, Joe's Crabshack, KFC, McDonald's, Poliberto's Tacos, Rainforest Cafe, Subway, Taco Bell, Waffle House, Wendy's Best Western, Candlewood Studios, Holiday Inn Express, InnSuites, Ramada, Residence Inn, SpringHill Suites, TownePlace Suites AutoZone, AZ Mills/Famous Brands, CVS Drug, Food City, Home Depot, Marshall's, Parts Authority, Ross, Walgreens, S 7-11, Arco/dsl, QT Aunt Chilada's Mexican, China Town, Denny's, Little Caesar's, Sonic, Subway Fry's Electronics, Fry's Foods, URGENT CARE

PHOENIX

Exit	Services
154	US 60 E, AZ 360, Superstition Frwy, to Mesa, N to Campir World (off Mesa Dr)
153b	Broadway Rd E, N Denny's Comfort Suites, Extended Stay America, La Quinta, Quality Inn, Red Roof Inn, Sheraton to Diablo Stadium, S Chevron/dsl, Shell/Circle Del Taco/24hr Goodcents Deli, Panda Express, Papa John' Pizza Hut, Port of Subs, Taco Bell, Whataburger Country Ir & Suites, Homewood Suites Staples
153a	AZ 143 N, N Denny's Courtyard, Fairfield Inn, Hilto Holiday Inn, La Quinta, Sleep Inn to Diablo Stadium, S same as 153b
152	40th St, N Shell/dsl U Phoenix, S Shell/Circle Burger King, Quiznos
151mm	Salt River
151b a	28th St, 32nd St, University Ave, N Waffle House Dru Inn, Extended Stay America, Hilton Garden, Holiday Inn Expre AZSU, U Phoenix, S Circle K/dsl, QT/dsl McDonald'
150b	24th St E (from wb), N Motel 6 Air Nat Guar S Best Western/rest.
150a	I-17 N, to Flagstaff
149	Buckeye Rd, N Sky Harbor Airport
148	Washington St, Jefferson St, N Chevron/dsl, Shell, Tiemcc dsl Carl's Jr, McDonald's Motel 6, Sterling Hotel Sky Harbor Airport, S Circle K H
147b a	AZ 51 N, AZ 202 E, to Squaw Peak Pkwy
146	16th St (from sb), N Shell/Circle K Filiberto's Mexica S Circle K, Shamrock/dsl Church's, Jack-in-the-Box, Litt Caesar's, Salsita's Mexican H, O'Reilly Parts, Ranch Mkt
145	7th St, N Chicos Tacos, McDonald's, Sonic, Starbuck Subway, Taco Bell, Whataburger H, Safeway Foods, Wa greens, S Circle K, Shell, Sinclair/dsl Jimmy John Holiday Inn Express, Hyatt, Sheraton, Springhill Suite to Chase Field
144	7th Ave, N Circle K Chipotle, Five Guys, Habit Burger, Jersey Mike's, NY Pizza, Peiwei Asian, Potbelly, Starbuck Zoe's Kitchen, S Circle K central bus dist
143c	US 60, 19th Ave (from wb), downtown
143b a	I-17, N to Flagstaff, S to Phoenix
142	27th Ave (from eb, no return), N Comfort Inn
141	35th Ave, N Jack-in-the-Box, Rita's Mexican, S Shel Circle K
140	43rd Ave, N Arco, Circle K/dsl Filberto's Mexican, KFC Little Caesar's, Pizza Hut, Salsita's Mexican, Subway Woodspring Suites AutoZone, Family$, Food City, Fry's Mercado gas, Walgreens
139	51st Ave, N Chevron/dsl, Circle K Burger King, Domino's, El Pollo Loco, McDonald's, Sonic American Inn, Budge Inn, Holiday Inn, Hometowne Suites, InTown Suites, La Quinta Motel 6, Red Roof+, Travelodge Food City, S QT/dsl scales, Shell/dsl Carl's Jr, Filiberto's Mexican, IHOP, Jack-in-the-Box, Port of Subs, Taco Bell Baymont Inn, Comfort Inn Travelers Inn
138	AZ 202, S Liberty/Chester's/dsl/24hr Waffle House Blue Beacon/scales
137	67th Ave, N Circle K/dsl, Mobil/dsl, QT/dsl Church's Dunkin', S FLYING J/Denny's/dsl/LP/24hr, Circle K/ds Jack-in-the-Box
136	75th Ave, N Chevron/dsl, Circle K Applebee's, Chili's CiCi's Pizza, Denny's, Filiberto's, Hawaiian BBQ, Hooters, IHOP Lin's Buffet, Longhorn Steaks, McDonald's, Olive Garden, Red Lobster, Starbucks, Subway, Taco Bell, TX Roadhouse, Wendy's Whataburger, Wing Stop $Tree, AT&T, Big Lots, Big O Tire

INTERSTATE 10 Cont'd

PHOENIX

136	Continued Dillard's, GNC, Home Depot, La Mesa RV Ctr, Lowe's, Ross, Target, URGENT CARE, Walmart, S Arco
135	83rd Ave, N Circle K, QT/dsl Burger King, Jack-in-the-Box, Waffle House Best Western, Premier Inn, Victory Inn Sam's Club/gas
134	91st Ave, Tolleson, N Circle K/dsl
133b	Lp 101 N
133a	99th Ave, N Chevron/Dunkin'/dsl Blaze Pizza, Cafe Rio, Cafe Zupas, Cane's, Carrabba's, Chick-fil-A, China City, Chipotle Mexican, ClaimJumper, Coldstone, Dickey's BBQ, El Pollo Loco, Firehouse Subs, Habit Burger, HoneyBaked Ham, Island's Burgers, Jack-in the-Box, Jamba Juice, Jersey Mike's, Jimmy John's, Kneaders Cafe, McDonald's, Native Grill, Panda Express, Panera Bread, Peter Piper Pizza, Pieology, Pita Kitchen, Portillo's Hot Dogs, Potbelly, Red Robin, Rubio's, Smashburger, Starbucks, Subway, Taco Bell, Tokyo Joe's, Village Inn, Waba Grill Courtyard Best Buy, Costco/gas, Discount Tire, GNC, Hobby Lobby, Marshall's, Old Navy, PetCo, Ross, Tuesday Morning, URGENT CARE, Verizon, S Pilot/Subway/Wendy's/dsl/scales/24hr CarMax, Chevrolet
132	107th Ave, N Walgreens, S EVC Camping World RV Ctr, Chrysler/Jeep, Dodge/Ram, Fiat, Honda, Hyundai, Kia, Mazda, Nissan, Toyota, VW
131	Avondale Blvd, to Cashion, N Circle K/dsl, S Culver's, Jack-in-the-Box, Panda Express Hilton Garden, Homewood Suites CVS Drug, to ISM Raceway
129	Dysart Rd, to Avondale, N Chevron/dsl, Shell/Circle K/dsl Buffalo Wild Wings, Chick-fil-A, ChuckECheese, El Pollo Loco, Fiesta Mexican, Fired Pie, In-N-Out, Jack-in-the-Box/24hr, Jersey Mike's, Manuel's Mexican, Mimi's Cafe, Nakama Japanese, NYPD Pizza, Ono Hawaiian BBQ, Panda Express, Pei Wei Asian, Starbucks, Subway, Taco Bell, Tomo Japanese Holiday Inn $Tree, AT&T, AutoZone, Discount Tire, Fry's Foods, JC Penney, Jo-Ann Fabrics, Kohl's, Lowe's, PetsMart, Sprouts Mkt, Verizon, vet, Walmart, S QT/dsl Black Bear Diner, Del Taco, Golden Corral, IHOP, KFC, Krispy Kreme, McDonald's, Peter Piper Pizza, Pizza Hut, Red Dragon, Subway, Waffle House, Whataburger Quality Inn, Super 8 Brakemasters, Food City, Home Depot, Pepboys, S&S Tire/repair, Sam's Club/gas, Walgreens
128	Litchfield Rd, N Circle K/dsl Applebee's, Black Angus Steaks, Chili's, Chipotle Mexican, Cracker Barrel, Denny's, Five Guys, Freddy's Steakburger, Gus' NY Pizza, Hayashi Japanese, Haymaker, Jimmy John's, Macaroni Grill, Macayo's Mexican, McDonald's, MOD Pizza, Raul&Theresa's Mexican, Starbucks, Subway, Wendy's, Wildflower Bread Co. Hampton Inn, Red Lion Inn, Residence Inn H, Barnes&Noble, Best Buy, Michael's, Ross, Target, to Luke AFB, URGENT CARE, Wigwam Resort/rest (3mi), S Circle K/dsl Angry Crab Shack, Arby's, Burger King, Little Caesar's, Ramiro's Mexican, Rudy's BBQ, Schlotsky's, Taco Bell Best Western, TownePlace Suites AutoZone, BigLots, Buick/GMC, Ford, O'Reilly Parts
127	Bullard Ave, N PF Chang's, Red Robin
126	PebbleCreek Pkwy, to Estrella Park, N Ah-So Steaks, Arriba Mexican, Barro's Pizza, Burger King, Del Taco, Jamba Juice, Native Grill, Olive Garden, Oregano's Pizza, Panera Bread, Popeye's, Red Lobster, Rubio's, Starbucks, Taco Bell, TX Roadhouse $Tree, Cal Ranch, Firestone/auto, GNC, Old Navy, PetCo, Staples, TJ Maxx, Walgreens, S QT/dsl Augie's Grill, Baskin Robbins, Filiberto's Mexican, Jack-in-the-Box,

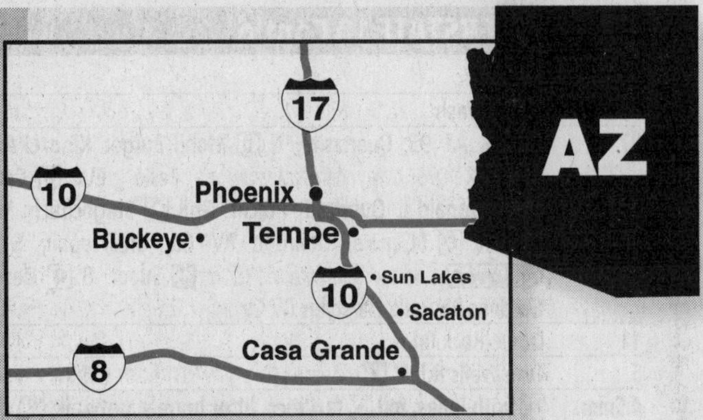

126	Continued Jimmy John's, Marco's Pizza, McDonald's, Panda Express, Pizza Hut, Robeks Juice, Sammy's Burgers, Senor Taco, Starbucks, Subway, Yan's Chinese Comfort Suites Ace Hardware, Fletcher Tire, Safeway Foods/dsl, URGENT CARE, Verizon, vet, Walgreens, Walmart
125	Sarival Ave, Cotton Lane (from wb)
125mm	Roosevelt Canal
124	AZ 303
123	Citrus Rd, to Cotton Ln, S Destiny RV Park, UHaul
122	Perryville Rd
121	Jackrabbit Trail, N Chevron/dsl $General, S Circle K/dsl CarQuest
120	Verrado Way, N Shell/dsl Culver's, Starbucks Verizon
117	Watson Rd, S Circle K/dsl Carl's Jr, Chipotle Mexican, Cracker Barrel, Denny's, Dunkin', El Pollo Loco, Federico's Mexican, Firehouse Subs, Jack-in-the-Box, Jimmy John's, KFC, Little Caesar's, McDonald's, Palermo's Pizza, Panda Express, Papa John's, Peter Piper Pizza, Subway, Taco Bell, Wendy's Holiday Inn Express $Tree, AT&T, AutoZone, Discount Tire, Fletcher's Tire, Fry's Foods/dsl, Lowe's, PetsMart, URGENT CARE, Verizon, vet, Walgreens, Walmart/McDonald's
114	Miller Rd, to Buckeye, S Chevron/Sam's Deli/dsl/e85/LP/24hr, Loves/Chester's/Subway/dsl/scales/24hr, QT/dsl Burger King Days Inn Ford, Leaf Verde RV Park
112	AZ 85, to I-8, Gila Bend
109	Sun Valley Pkwy, Palo Verde Rd
104mm	Hassayampa River
103	339th Ave, S TA/Country Pride/Pizza Hut/Shell/Subway/Taco Bell/dsl/scales/LP/24hr/@ truckwash
98	Wintersburg Rd
97mm	Coyote Wash
95.5mm	Old Camp Wash
94	411th Ave, Tonopah, S Chevron/dsl, Mobil/dsl, Pilot/Subway/dsl/LP/24hr Tonopah Rest. Saddle Mtn RV Park, USPO
86mm	**Rs both lanes, full facilities, litter barrels, petwalk, vending**
81	Salome Rd, Harquahala Valley Rd
69	Ave 75E
53	Hovatter Rd
52mm	**Rs both lanes, full facilities, litter barrels, petwalk, vending**
45	Vicksburg Rd, N Pilot/Subway/dsl/scales/LP/24hr, S Pride/Pizza Hut/dsl/scales/24hr J&K repair/towing, Kofa NWR, RV Park, tires
31	US 60 E, to Wickenburg, 12 mi N camping, food
26	Gold Nugget Rd
19	Quartzsite, to US 95, Yuma, N 76/dsl, Arco/dsl, Chevron/dsl Taco Mio Family$, Roadrunner Foods, RV camping

= gas = food = lodging = other = rest stop

AZ

QUARTZSITE

INTERSTATE 10 Cont'd

Exit #	Services
18mm	Tyson Wash
17	US 95, AZ 95, Quartzsite, N Mobil/Burger King/LP/dsl, Pilot/DQ/Subway/dsl/scales/24hr, Tesla EVC Carl's Jr, McDonald's, Quartzsite Yacht Grill Stagecoach Motel/rest. $General, Johnson RV Ctr, tires/repair, S Loves/Chester's/Subway/dsl/24hr Super 8 Desert Gardens RV Park, Lifestyles RV Ctr
11	Dome Rock Rd
5	Tom Wells Rd, N Chevron/Subway/dsl/scales/24hr
4.5mm	**both lanes, full facilities, litter barrels, petwalk, , , vending**
3.5mm	**AZ Port of Entry, weigh st**
1	Ehrenberg, to Parker, N 76/dsl, Texaco Family$, RV Resorts, S FLYING J/Wendy's/dsl/LP/scales/lube/repair/tires/24hr Best Western
0mm	Arizona/California state line, Colorado River, mountain/pacific time zone

INTERSTATE 15

Exit #	Services
29.5mm	Arizona/Utah state line
27	Black Rock Rd
21mm	turnout sb
18	Cedar Pocket, S parking area, Virgin River Canyon RA/camping
16mm	**truck parking both lanes**
15mm	**truck parking nb**
14mm	**truck parking nb**
10mm	**truck parking nb**
9	Desert Springs
8.5mm	Virgin River
8	Littlefield, Beaver Dam, E RV park, **1 mi** W camping, food, gas/dsl, lodging
0mm	Arizona/Nevada state line, mountain/pacific time zone

FLAGSTAFF

CAMP VERDE

INTERSTATE 17

Exit #	Services
341	McConnell Dr, **I-17 begins/ends**, N Chevron/dsl, Circle K, Conoco/dsl, Giant/dsl, Mobil/dsl, Phillips 66/Wendy's/dsl, Shell Arby's, August Moon Chinese, Baskin-Robbins, Buffalo Wild Wings, Burger King, Buster's Rest., Cafe Rio, Cafe Rio, Cane's, Carl's Jr, Chick-fil-A, Chili's, China Garden, Chipotle Mexican, Coco's, Coldstone, Del Taco, Denny's, Domino's, DQ, Dunkin', Five Guys, Freddy's Steakburgers, IHOP, Jack-in-the-Box, Jimmy John's, KFC, Little Caesar's, McDonald's, Native Grill, Ni Marco's Pizza, Olive Garden, Panda Express, Papa John's, Papa Murphy's, Peter Piper Pizza, Picazzo's Pizza, Pizza Hut, Quiznos, Red Lobster, Sizzler, Starbucks, Subway, Taco Bell Baymont Inn, Best Inn, Budget Inn, Canyon Inn, Comfort Inn, Courtyard, Days Inn, Drury Inn, EconoLodge, EconoLodge, Embassy Suites, GreenTree Inn, Hampton Inn, Hilton Garden, Knights Inn, La Quinta, Motel 6, Quality Inn, Sleep Inn, SpringHill Suites, Super 8 H, $Tree, AT&T, Barnes&Noble, Basha's Foods, Discount Tire, Jo-Ann Crafts, Kohl's, Michael's, O'Reilly Parts, Petsmart, Ross, Safeway, Sprouts Mkt, Staples, Target, Verizon, Walgreens, Walmart
340b a	I-40, E to Gallup, W to Kingman
339	Lake Mary Rd (from nb), Mormon Lake, E Circle K/dsl AZ Mtn Inn access to same as 341
337	AZ 89A S, to Sedona, Ft Tuthill RA, W camping
333	Kachina Blvd, Mountainaire Rd, E Mountainaire Rest. (1 Abineau B&B, W Shell/Subway/dsl county park
331	Kelly Canyon Rd
328	Newman Park Rd
326	Willard Springs Rd
322	Pinewood Rd, to Munds Park, E Shell/dsl, Woody's/ Lone Pine Rest. golf, Motel in the Pines, W Chevron/dsl Munds RV Park
322mm	Munds Canyon
320	Schnebly Hill Rd
317	Fox Ranch Rd
316mm	Woods Canyon
315	Rocky Park Rd
313mm	scenic view sb, litter barrels
306	Stoneman Lake Rd
300mm	**runaway truck ramp sb**
298	AZ 179, to Sedona, Oak Creek Canyon, **7-15 mi** W Burger King, Cowboy Club Rest., Joey's Bistro Belrock Inn, Diamond Resort, Hilton, La Quinta, Radisson/cafe, Wildflow Inn Rancho Sedona RV Park
297mm	**both lanes, full facilities, litter barrels, petwalk, , vending**
293mm	Dry Beaver Creek
293	Cornville Rd, McGuireville Rd, to Rimrock, E McGuireville Nikki's Grill, W 76/dsl, Conoco/Beaver Hollow dsl El Patio Grill
289	Middle Verde Rd, Camp Verde, E Chevron/dsl Son The Gathering Rest. Cliff Castle Hotel/casino/rest. Montezuma Castle NM, W Distant Drums RV Park
288mm	Verde River
287	AZ 260, to AZ 89A, Cottonwood, Payson, E Shell/Subway/dsl RV dump/LP/24hr Burger King, Carl's Jr, Denny's, DQ, Gabriela's Mexican, Los Betos Mexican, McDonald's, Starbucks, Taco Bell Comfort Inn, Days Inn, Super 8 Territorial RV Pa (1mi), Trails End RV Park, Zane Grane RV Park (9mi), W Chevron/Wendy's/dsl/24hr RV camping, to Jerome SP
285	Camp Verde, Gen Crook Tr, **3 mi** E Rio Verde Mexican Territorial Town Inn to Ft Verde SP, Trail End R Park, Zane Gray RV Park (9mi)
281mm	safety pullout area nb
278	AZ 169, Cherry Rd, to Prescott
269mm	Ash Creek
268	Dugas Rd, Orme Rd
265.5mm	Agua Fria River
263b a	AZ 69 N, Cordes Jct Rd (262 from nb), to Prescott, E Chevron, Shell/Noble Roman's/Subway/dsl/LP/24hr Cafe Char McDonald's Cordes Jct Motel/RV Park Family$
259	Bloody Basin Rd, to Crown King, Horse Thief Basin RA
256	Badger Springs Rd
252	**Sunset Point, /scenic view both lanes, full facilities, , litter barrels, , vending**
248	Bumble Bee, W Horsethief Basin RA
244	Squaw Valley Rd, Black Canyon City, E Chilleen's on 1 BBQ/Steaks, W Shell Beni's Pizza Mountai Breeze Motel Bradshaw Mtn RV Resort (2mi), Family$
243.5mm	Agua Fria River
242	Rock Springs, Black Canyon City, E KOA (1mi), W 76 dsl, Shell Beni's Pizza, Rock Springs Cafe Bradshaw Mtn RV Resort, Mtn Breeze Motel Ron's Mkt
239.5mm	Little Squaw Creek
239mm	Moore's Gulch
236	Table Mesa Rd

INTERSTATE 17 Cont'd

Exit #	Services
232	New River, E RoadRunner Rest.
231.5mm	New River
229	Anthem Way, Desert Hills Rd, E Circle K Hungry Howie's, McDonald's, Pizza Hut, Rosati's Pizza, Starbucks, Subway, Taco Bell, Wendy's CVS Drug, Safeway, URGENT CARE, W Chevron/dsl, Circle K/dsl Del Taco, Denny's, Fresca's Mexican, Subway Hampton Inn $Store, Anthem Outlets/famous brands/food court, Discount Tire, Harley-Davidson, Meineke, O'Reilly Parts, Tobias Auto, U-Haul, Walmart
227	Daisy Mtn Dr, E Circle K/dsl Cafe Provence, Domino's, Jack-in-the-Box, Roberto's Mexican, Starbucks, Streets of NY Deli, Streets of NY Deli, Subway CVS Drug, Fry's Foods, GNC, Verizon, vet
227mm	Dead Man Wash
225	Pioneer Rd, W Pioneer AZ Museum, Pioneer RV Park
223	AZ 74, Carefree Hwy, to Wickenburg, E Chevron AZool Grill, Chili's, Denny's, Good Egg Cafe, In-N-Out, McDonald's, Ray's Pizza, Starbucks, Subway, Taco Bell Albertson's/Osco, GNC, Home Depot, Kohl's, Staples, W Cibola Vista Camping (11mi)
222	Dove Valley
221	AZ 303, Senora Desert Dr
220	Dixileta (from nb)
219	Jomax Rd
218	Happy Valley Rd, E Circle K/dsl, Shell Applebee's, Bajio, Buffalo Wild Wings, Burger King, Carl's Jr, Chipotle Mexican, Coldstone, IHOP, Jack-in-the-Box, Jersey Mike's Subs, Joey's Hotdogs, Johnny Rocket's, L&L Hawaiian BBQ, Logan's Roadhouse, Mellow Mushroom Pizza, Olive Garden, Panda Express, Paradise Cafe, PF Chang's, Rays Pizza, Red Robin, Sauce Pizza, Shane's Ribshack, Smash Burger, Starbucks, Subway, TGIFriday's, Zupas Courtyard, Hampton Inn, Homewood Suites, Residence Inn $Tree, Barnes&Noble, Best Buy, Big O Tire, Dick's, Lowe's, Old Navy, O'Reilly Parts, PetCo, Ross, Staples, TJ Maxx, Verizon, vet, Walmart, World Mkt, W to Meg&DeLyle's
217	Pinnacle Peak Rd, E Drury Inn, Hilton Garden Phoenix RV Park
215a	Rose Garden Ln, same as 215b
215b	Deer Valley Rd, E Shell/Circle K Arby's, Armando's Mexican, Culvers, Dunkin', Jack-in-the-Box, McDonald's, Sonic, Subway, Taco Bell, Wendy's Little Dealer RV Ctr, W Arco/dsl, Circle K/dsl Cracker Barrel, Denny's, Times Square Italian, Waffle House Days Inn, Extended Stay America H, U-Haul
214c	AZ 101 loop
214b	Yorkshire Dr, W 7-11 Chick-fil-A, Chili's, Chipotle, In-N-Out, Jack-in-the-Box, Jimmy John's, Macaroni Grill, Pizza Hut, Wendy's Budget Suites H, AT&T, Costco/gas, Michael's, Petsmart, Ross, Target
214a	Union Hills Dr, E Circle K/dsl, Valero, W Arco/dsl Comfort Inn, Sleep Inn, Studio 6
212b a	Bell Rd, Scottsdale, to Sun City, E Chevron/dsl, Circle K, QT, Shell/dsl Big Apple Rest., Caramba Mexican, IHOP, Jack-in-the-Box, LJ Silver, Manuel's Mexican, McDonald's, Schlotzsky's, Shenanigan's Grill, Waffle House Fairfield Inn, Motel 6, Super 8 Big O Tire, Chevrolet, Chrysler/Jeep/Dodge, Discount Tire, Fiat, Ford, Honda, Hyundai, Kohl's, Lincoln, Mazda, Nissan, O'Reilly Parts, Sam's Club/gas, Toyota, U-Haul, Volvo, Walmart, W Applebee's, Denny's, Native New Yorker, US Egg Breakfast Red Roof Inn Fry's Foods/dsl

SCOTTSDALE

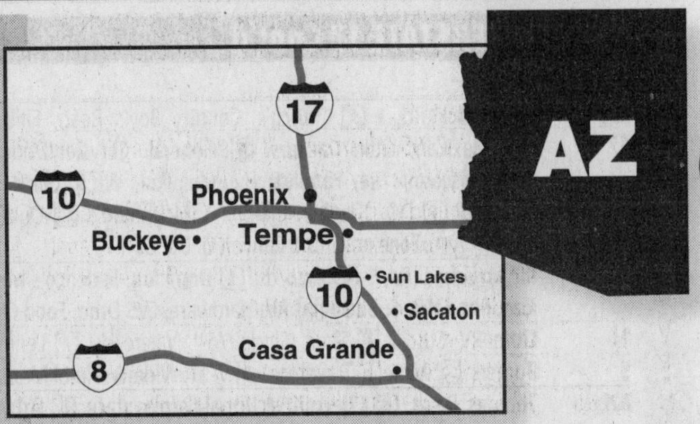

Exit #	Services
211	Greenway Rd, E Embassy Suites, La Quinta 7-11
210	Thunderbird Rd, E Circle K/dsl, Valero/dsl/LP Asian Cafe, Barro's Pizza, Hong Kong Chinese, Jack-in-the-Box, Macayo's Mexican, Pizza Hut/Taco Bell, Subway, Wendy's CVS Drug, Home Depot, Walgreens, W Jamba Juice, McDonald's, Port of Subs, Whataburger Travelodge Best Buy, Fry's Electronics, Lowe's
209	Cactus Rd, W 7-11, Chevron/dsl, QT/dsl China Harvest, Tuliaberto's Mexican Holiday Inn
208	Peoria Ave, E Fajita's, First Watch Cafe, Native Grill, Outback Steaks, Pappadeaux, Sweet Tomatoes Candlewood Suites, Comfort Suites, Crowne Plaza, Extended Stay America, Homewood Suites, Hyatt Place, W QT/dsl Black Angus, Buffalo Wild Wings, Burger King, Cane's, Chili's, Chipotle Mexican, Coldstone, Culvers, Fat Burger, Filiberto's Mexican, Hibachi Grill, Hooters, In-N-Out, Jason's Deli, Longhorn Steaks, Mi Pueblo, Mimi's Cafe, Mongolian BBQ, Old Country Buffet, Olive Garden, Peter Piper Pizza, Red Lobster, Sizzler, Souper Salad, Starbucks, Subway, TX Roadhouse, Wendy's Metro Plaza, Premier Inn $Tree, AT&T, Barnes&Noble, Dillard's, Discount Tire, Firestone/auto, Macy's, Michael's, PetCo, Petsmart, Ross, Staples, Tire Pros/repair, URGENT CARE, Verizon
208.5mm	Arizona Canal
207	Dunlap Ave, E Circle K, Shell/dsl Blimpie, Domino's, Fajitas, First Watch Cafe, Fuddrucker's, Jack-in-the-Box, Native Grill, Outback Steaks, Steaken Burger, Subway, Sweet Tomatoes, Wong's Comfort Suites, Courtyard, Mainstay Suites, Sheraton, SpringHill Suites, TownPlace Suites Aamco, CVS Drug, URGENT CARE, W Chevron/dsl Bobby-Q's Rest., Denny's, Schlotzsky's, Subway Woodspring Suites Midas, repair, U-Haul
206	Northern Ave, E Circle K/dsl, Shell/dsl Boston Mkt, Burger King, Del Taco, Denny's, Dunkin', El Pollo Loco, Gyros House, IHOP, Los Compadres, McDonald's, Papa John's, Pizza Hut, Starbucks, Subway, Uncle Tony's Pizza Best Western Albertson's/Osco, AutoZone, Sprouts Mkt, URGENT CARE, Walgreens, W Arco, QT DQ Motel 6, Residence Inn, Super 8 $General, auto repair, vet
205	Glendale Ave, E 7-11, QT Pizza Patron, Subway Ace Hardware, Fry's Foods/dsl, repair, transmissions, vet, W Circle K/dsl Jack-in-the-Box, Lenny's Burger 7-11, O'Reilly Parts, to Luke AFB, Walgreens
204	Bethany Home Rd, E Arco, Chevron/dsl, Shell/Church's/dsl Carl's Jr, Dunkin', KFC, Mandarin Buffet, McDonald's, Papa Joe's, Pizza Hut/Taco Bell, Subway, Tulioberto's Mexican, Whataburger H, $Tree, BigLots, Costco/gas, JC Penney, Petsmart, Ross, Target, URGENT CARE, Walgreens, Walmart, W Shell, Valero Burger King, Familia Lorito, Great Dragon Knights Inn auto repair, Food City, Jiffy Lube, Savers

PHOENIX

= gas = food = lodging = other = rest stop

AZ

INTERSTATE 17 Cont'd

PHOENIX

Exit #	Services
203	Camelback Rd, E Church's, Country Boy's Rest., Filiberto's Mexican, Little Caesars $General, Chrysler/Dodge/Jeep, Discount Tire, Family$, Hyundai, Kia, W Circle K/dsl, QT DQ, Jack-in-the-Box, McDonald's Quality Inn AutoZone, to Grand Canyon U, USPO
202	Indian School Rd, E Arco/dsl Domino's, Federico's Mexican, Pizza Hut, Subway Ace Hardware, CVS Drug, Food City, Little RV Ctr, W Shell, Sinclair/dsl, Valero/dsl Lenny's Burgers Motel 6, Travel Inn 7-11, Wide World of Maps
201	Thomas Rd, E Chevron/McDonald's/playplace Arby's, Denny's, Dunkin', Jack-in-the-Box, Starbucks Days Inn, La Quinta Circle K, W Carl's Jr, Subway NAPA
200b	McDowell Rd, Van Buren, E Purcell's Tire, W Knights Inn
200a	I-10, W to LA, E to Phoenix
199b	Jefferson St (from sb), Adams St (from nb), Van Buren St (from nb), E Circle K Jack-in-the-Box to st capitol, W Circle K/gas La Canasta Mexican Penny Pincher Parts, PepBoys
199a	Grant St
198	Buckeye Rd (from nb)
197	US 60, 19th Ave, Durango St, E Jack-in-the-Box, to St Capitol, Whataburger $General, AutoZone
196	7th St, Central Ave, W Shell/dsl
195b	7th St, Central Ave, E Circle K/dsl Jack-in-the-Box, McDonald's, Taco Bell EZ 8 Motel H, NAPA Care
195a	16th St (from sb, no EZ return), E Shell/Subway/dsl Burger King to Sky Harbor Airport
194	I-10 W, to AZ 151, to Sky Harbor Airport

I-17 begins/ends on I-10, exit 150a.

INTERSTATE 19

TUCSON

Exit #	Services
	I-19 uses kilometers (km)
101b a	I-10, E to El Paso, W to Phoenix. **I-19 begins/ends on I-10, exit 260.**
99	AZ 86, Ajo Way, E Circle K, Speedway Eegee's Cafe, Hamburger Stand, Peter Piper Pizza, Pizza Hut, Subway, Taco Bell H, $Tree, Fry's Foods, Goodyear/auto, U-Haul, URGENT CARE, vet, Walgreens, W QT/dsl, Shell/dsl Burger King, Church's, Little Caesar's, Los Betos Mexican, McDonald's $General, city park, Family$, Food City, Jiffy Lube, museum, to Old Tucson
98	Irvington Rd, E Arco/dsl TX Roadhouse AutoZone, W Circle K/dsl, Speedway Buffalo Wild Wings, Chick-fil-A, China Olive Buffet, Chipotle, Firehouse Subs, Five Guys, McDonald's, MOD Pizza, Olive Garden, Panda Express, Peter Piper Pizza, Red Lobster, Starbucks, Subway, Taco Bell $Tree, AT&T, Best Buy, Discount Tire, Family$, Food City, GNC, Home Depot, JC Penney, Marshall's, Michael's, Old Navy, Petsmart, Ross, Target, Verizon
95b a	Valencia Rd, E Circle K, Speedway Chickenuevo, Church's, Donut Wheel, Eegee's Cafe, Jack-in-the-Box, Little Caesar's, McDonald's, Peter Piper Pizza, Sonic, Subway, Whataburger, Yokohama Asian $Tree, AutoZone, Brake Masters, Family$, Food City, Jiffy Lube, Midas, O'Reilly Parts, to ✈, USPO, Walgreens, W Circle K/dsl, QT/dsl Arby's, Blake's, Burger King, Carl's Jr, Casa Valencia, Chili's, China Dragon, Denny's, DQ, Dunkin', El Taco Tote, Golden Corral, Grand Buffet, Hamburger Stand, Little Caesar's, Papa John's, Papa Murphy's, Pizza Hut, Subway, Taco Bell, Wendy's 99c Store, Big O Tire, BigLots, CVS Drug, Lowe's, repair, transmissions, URGENT CARE, Walgreens, Walmart
92	San Xavier Rd, W to San Xavier Mission (2mi)
91.5km	Santa Cruz River
87	Papago Rd
80	Pima Mine Rd, E Agave Rest., Diamond Casino
75	Helmut Peak Rd, to Sahuarita, E Fry's Fuel, Speedway/dsl/e Dunkin'/Baskin Robbins, EVC, McDonald's, Panda Expre Starbucks, Subway, Taco Bell Fry's Foods/drug, USPO, vet

GREEN VALLEY

Exit #	Services
69	US 89 N, Duval Mine Rd., Green Valley, E 50's Diner, Ca Jr., Culver's, Denny's, Little Caesar's, Panda House, Pizza H Rigoberto's, Subway $Tree, 99c Store, Ace Hardware, Aut Zone, BigLots, Fletcher's Repair, Jo-Ann Fabrics, O'Reilly Par Petco, Ross, Verizon, Walgreens, Walmart/Subway, W Cir K Arby's, Burger King, Domino's, DQ, Jerry Bob's Res Manuel's Mexican, Papa John's, Starbucks, Taco Bell Vag bond Inn Big O Tire, Ford/Hyundai, Green Valley RV Reso Safeway/dsl, Titan Missile Museum, URGENT CARE, vet
65	Esperanza Blvd, to Green Valley, E Shell/repair/d W AZ Family Rest., El Rodeo Mexican Best Wester rest., Comfort Inn Ace Hardware, Walgreens
63	Continental Rd, Green Valley, E Quail Creek Rest. (7m golf, San Ignacio Golf Club/rest., USPO, W Chevro HotStuff Pizza KFC, McDonald's, Starbucks CVS Dru repair/tires, Safeway, to Madera Cyn RA, TrueValue, Verizo Walgreens
56	Canoa Rd, W Canoa Resort

AMADO

Exit #	Services
54km	**both lanes, full facilities, litter barrels, petwalk, vending**
48	Arivaca Rd, Amado, **2-3 mi** E Amado Inn DeAnza F Resort (2mi), Mtn View RV Park, W Cow Palace Rest., Lon horn Grill $General, Amado Mkt/gas
42	Agua Linda Rd, to Amado, E Mtn View RV Park
40	Chavez Siding Rd, Tubac, E Tubac Golf Resort
34	Tubac, E El Mercado Elvira's Cafe, Habaneros Mexica Italian Peasant, Tubac Deli, Tubac Jack's Rest. to Tubac Pr sidio SP, Tubac Golf Resort, Tubac Mkt, USPO
29	Carmen, Tumacacori, E to Tumacacori Nat Hist Park, foo gas, lodging
25	Palo Parado Rd
22	Pec Canyon Rd

NOGALES

Exit #	Services
17	Rio Rico Dr, Calabasas Rd, E Esplendor Resort, W Chev ron/dsl/LP Hua Mei Chinese, Nickles Diner, Su way IGA Foods, USPO, vet
12	AZ 289, to Ruby Rd, E Pilot/Wendy's/dsl/scales/24h W to Pena Blanca Lake RA
8	AZ 82 (exits left from sb, no return), Nogales, E Circl K Mi Casa RV Park
4	AZ 189 S, Mariposa Rd, Nogales, E 76, FasTrip/d Chuyitos Hotdogs, City Salads, Dragon Buffet, Exquisit Mexican, Jack-in-the-Box, KFC, Little Caesar's, McDonald's Panda Express, Pizza Pollis, Subway, Tacos & Taros, Tito Pizza Mariposa Hotel $Tree, AutoZone, Buick/GMC Chevrolet, Ford, GNC, Hobby Lobby, Home Depot, JC Pen ney, Marshall's, O'Reilly Parts, Petsmart, Ross, Safeway, Wal greens, Walmart/McDonald's (N Grand Ave), W Circle K/ds Carl's Jr, IHOP Best Western, Candlewood Suites, Holi day Inn Express Mexico Insurance
1b	Western Ave, Nogales
1a	International St
0km	**I-19 begins/ends in Nogales,** Arizona/Mexico Border, **1/2 m** N Circle K, Jr's Fuel Depot/dsl, Shell Church's, Denny's Jack-in-the-Box, McDonald's, Peter Piper Pizza, Pizza Hut, Sub way AutoZone, CarQuest, Family$, Food City, museum NAPA, O'Reilly Parts, PepBoys

INTERSTATE 40

Exit #	Services
359.5mm	Arizona/New Mexico state line
359	Grants Rd, to Lupton, **N Welcome Ctr/[rest stop] both lanes, full [handicap] facilities, litter barrels, petwalk, [phone], [RV dump],** [gas] Speedy's/dsl/rest./24hr [other] Tee Pee Trading Post/rest., YellowHorse Indian Gifts,
357	AZ 12 N, Lupton, to Window Rock, **N** [other] USPO
354	Hawthorne Rd
351	Allentown Rd, **N** [other] Chee's Indian Store, Indian City Gifts
348	St Anselm Rd, Houck, **N** [other] Ft Courage Food/gifts
347.5mm	Black Creek
346	Pine Springs Rd
345mm	Box Canyon
344mm	Querino Wash
343	Querino Rd
341	Ortega Rd, Cedar Point, **N** [gas] Armco/gas/gifts
340.5mm	**insp/weigh sta both lanes**
339	US 191 S, to St Johns, **S** [gas] Conoco/dsl [other] Family$, RV Park, USPO
333	US 191 N, Chambers, **N** [other] to Hubbell Trading Post NHS, USPO, **S** [gas] Mobil/dsl [lodging] Days Inn/rest.
330	McCarrell Rd
325	Navajo, **S** [gas] Shell/Subway/Navajo Trading Post/dsl/24hr
323mm	Crazy Creek
320	Pinta Rd
316mm	Dead River
311	Painted Desert, **N** [gas] Painted Desert/dsl [other] Painted Desert, Petrified Forest NP
303	Adamana Rd, **N** [other] Stewarts/gifts, **S** [other] Painted Desert Indian Ctr
302.5mm	Big Lithodendron Wash
301mm	Little Lithodendron Wash
300	Goodwater
299mm	Twin Wash
294	Sun Valley Rd, **N** [lodging] Root 66 RV camping, **S** [other] Knife City
292	AZ 77 N, to Keams Canyon, **N** [gas] Conoco/Burger King/dsl/24hr [other] dsl repair
289	Lp 40, Holbrook, **N** [gas] Chevron/dsl, Hatch's/dsl [food] Denny's, Mesa Rest. [lodging] Best Western, Days Inn, EconoLodge, Howard Johnson, Motel 6, Quality Inn, Sahara Inn, Travelodge [other] Goodyear
286	Navajo Blvd, Holbrook, **N** [gas] 76/dsl, Circle K, Maverik/dsl [food] Aliberto's Mexican, Burger King, Carl's Jr, Hilltop Cafe, McDonald's, Taco Bell, Tom & Suzie's [lodging] 66 Motel, Lexington Inn, Super 8 [other] $General, KOA, OK RV Park, O'Reilly Parts, Econolodge, Taco Bell, **S** [gas] Chevron/dsl, Fuel Express/dsl, MiniMart/gas, Speedy Dsl [food] DQ, Rte 66 Cafe [lodging] Best Value, El Rancho Motel/rest., Knights Inn [other] [H], Dodge/Ford/Lincoln, museum, rockshops, Scotty & Son Repair, SW Transmissions, Little Caesars
285	US 180 E, AZ 77 S, Holbrook, **1 mi S [rest stop], [RV dump], litter barrels,** [gas] Giant/dsl [food] Butterfield Steaks [lodging] Economy Inn, Globetrotter Hotel, Wigwam Motel [other] Best Hardware, Family$, Safeway, to Petrified Forest NP
284mm	Leroux Wash
283	Perkins Valley Rd, Golf Course Rd, **S** [gas] TA/Shell/Popeyes/dsl/scales/24hr/@
280	Hunt Rd, Geronimo Rd, **N** [other] Geronimo Trading Post
277	Lp 40, Joseph City, **N** [gas] Loves/Chester's/Subway/scales/dsl/24hr, **S** [other] RV camping, to Cholla Lake CP

CHAMBERS

HOLBROOK

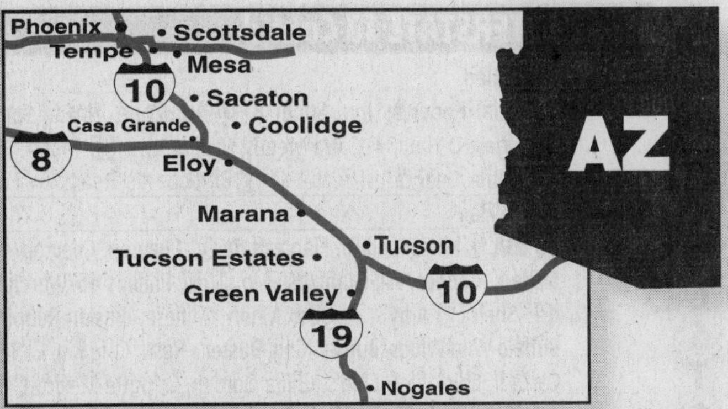

Exit #	Services
274	Lp 40, Joseph City, **N** food, gas, lodging, RV camping
269	Jackrabbit Rd, **S** [other] Jackrabbit Trading Post
264	Hibbard Rd
257	AZ 87 N, to Second Mesa, **N** [other] camping, to Homolovi Ruins SP, **S** [other] trading post
256.5mm	Little Colorado River
255	Lp 40, Winslow, **N** [gas] Winslow Fuel/dsl [food] Mi Pueblo Mexican [lodging] Best Western+ [other] Take-A-Rest RV Park, **S** [rest stop], [gas] FLYING J/Denny's/dsl/LNG/scales/RV Dump/24hr [food] Sonic [other] Chrysler/Dodge/Jeep, Nissan
253	N Park Dr, Winslow, **N** [gas] Chevron, Maverik/dsl [food] Capt Tony's Pizza, Pizza Hut [other] $General, Ford, O'Reilly Parts, tires/lube, Walmart/Subway, AutoZone, Carl's Jr, **S** [food] Alfonso's Mexican, LJ Silver/Taco Bell, McDonald's, Subway [lodging] Motel 6, Quality Inn, Travelodge [other] [H], Family$, NAPA, Safeway, China Town
252	AZ 87 S, Winslow, **S** [gas] 76/dsl [food] Entre Chinese [lodging] EconoLodge, Rodeway Inn
245	AZ 99, Leupp Corner
239	Meteor City Rd, Red Gap Ranch Rd, **S** [other] to Meteor Crater
235mm	**[rest stop] both lanes, full [handicap] facilities, info, litter barrels, petwalk, [phone], [RV dump]**
233	Meteor Crater Rd, **S** [gas] Mobil/Meteor Crater RV Park/dump [other] to Meteor Crater NL
230	Two Guns
229.5mm	Canyon Diablo
225	Buffalo Range Rd
219	Twin Arrows, **N** [other] Twin Arrows Resort/Casino
218.5mm	Padre Canyon
211	Winona, **N** [gas] Shell/dsl/repair
207	Cosnino Rd
204	to Walnut Canyon NM
201	US 89, Flagstaff, to Page, **N** [gas] 76/Express Stop/dsl, Chevron/dsl, Circle K/dsl, Maverik/dsl, Shell, VP/dsl [food] Burger King, Del Taco, Denny's, Jack-in-the-Box, LJ Silver/Taco Bell, McDonald's, Pizza Hut, Sizzler, Village Inn, Wendy's [lodging] Best Western, Country Inn Suites, Days Inn, Howard Johnson, Mtn View Inn, Super 8, Travelodge [other] [H], auto repair, Best Buy, Chrysler/Dodge/Jeep/Fiat, CVS Drug, Dillard's, Discount Tire, Evert's RV Center, Family$, Family$, Home Depot, Honda, JC Penney, KOA, Marshall's, Nissan/Subaru, Old Navy, O'Reilly Parts, Pepboys, PetCo, Safeway/dsl, Toyota, Tuesday Morning, VW, World Mkt, **S** [gas] Mobil/dsl, Shell/dsl [food] Oregano's Pizza [lodging] Fairfield Inn, Hampton Inn, Sonesta Suites, Wyndham Resort
198	Butler Ave, Flagstaff, **N** [gas] Chevron, Conoco/dsl, Shell [food] Burger King, Country Host Rest., Cracker Barrel, Culver's, Denny's, McDonald's, Outback Steaks, Sonic, Starbucks, Subway, Taco Bell, Texas Roadhouse [lodging] Comfort Inn, Holiday Inn Express, Howard Johnson, La Quinta, Motel 6, Quality Inn,

WINSLOW

AZ

INTERSTATE 40 Cont'd

FLAGSTAFF

198 Continued
Ramada, Rodeway Inn, Super 8 AutoZone, NAPA, Sam's Club/gas, U-Haul, vet, Walgreens, Walmart, S Mobil, Sinclair/Little America/dsl/motel/@ Black Bart's Steaks/RV Park

197.5mm Rio de Flag

195b US 89A N, McConnell Dr, Flagstaff, N Chevron, Chevron/dsl, Circle K, Conoco/dsl, Giant/dsl, Mobil/dsl, Phillips 66/Wendy's/dsl, Shell Arby's, August Moon Chinese, Baskin-Robbins, Buffalo Wild Wings, Burger King, Buster's Rest., Cafe Rio, Cane's, Carl's Jr, Chick-fil-A, Chili's, China Garden, Chipotle Mexican, Coco's, Coldstone, Country Host Rest., Del Taco, Denny's, Domino's, DQ, Dunkin', Five Guys, Freddy's Steakburgers, IHOP, Jack-in-the-Box, Jimmy John's, Little Caesar's, McDonald's, Native Grill, Ni Marco's Pizza, Olive Garden, Panda Express, Papa John's, Papa Murphy's, Peter Piper Pizza, Picazzo's Pizza, Pizza Hut, Quiznos, Red Lobster, Sizzler, SmashBurger, Starbucks, Subway, Taco Bell Baymont Inn, Best Inn, Budget Inn, Canyon Inn, Comfort Inn, Courtyard, Days Inn, Drury Inn, EconoLodge, Embassy Suites, GreenTree Inn, Hampton Inn, Hilton Garden, Howard Johnson, Knights Inn, La Quinta, Motel 6, Quality Inn, Sleep Inn, SpringHill Suites, Super 8 (H), $Tree, AT&T, Barnes&Noble, Basha's Foods, Discount Tire, GNC, Jo-Ann Crafts, Kohl's, Michael's, Natural Grocers, O'Reilly Parts, Petsmart, Ross, Safeway, Sprouts Mkt, Staples, Target, Verizon, Walgreens, Walmart

195a I-17 S, AZ 89A S, to Phoenix

192 Flagstaff Ranch Rd

191 Lp 40, to Grand Canyon, Flagstaff, **5 mi** N Chevron, Maverik Budget Host, DoubleTree, Super 8 Home Depot, Kia, Kit Carson RV Park, O'Reilly Parts, vet, Woody Mtn Camping

190 A-1 Mountain Rd

189.5mm Arizona Divide, elevation 7335

185 Transwestern Rd, Bellemont, N Pilot/McDonald's/Subway/dsl/scales/24hr/@ Days Inn, S Harley-Davidson/Roadside Grill, Rte 66 RV Ctr

178 Parks Rd, N Texaco/dsl USPO

171 Pittman Valley Rd, Deer Farm Rd, S Mountain Ranch Resort

167 Garland Prairie Rd, Circle Pines Rd, N KOA

165 AZ 64, to Williams, Grand Canyon, N 76 (8mi), Shell/dsl (4mi) KOA (4mi), to Grand Canyon, S Super 8 (1mi)

WILLIAMS

163 same as 161, Williams, N Chevron/dsl, Loves/Arby's/dsl/scales/24hr Quality Inn Canyon Gateway RV Park, S Circle K, Mobil/dsl, Mustang/dsl, Shell/dsl Jack-in-the-Box, KFC/Taco Bell, McDonald's, Old Town Rest., Pancho's Mexican, Pine Country Rest., Pizza Hut, Red Garter Rest, Rod's Steaks, Rte 66 Diner, Twisters Soda Fountain Canyon Motel/RV Park, EconoLodge, El Rancho Motel, Grand Canyon Railway Hotel, Howard Johnson, Knights Inn, Mountainside Motel, Ramada Inn, Rodeway Inn, Rodeway Inn, The Lodge Motel, Travelodge $General, USPO

161 Lp 40, Golf Course Dr, Williams, N RV camping, **0-3 mi** S Circle K, Conoco/dsl/LP, Shell Buffalo Pointe Inn, DQ, Jessica's Rest., Maria's Tacos AZ Motel, Best Value, Best Western, Budget Host, Canyon Country Inn, Comfort Inn, Days Inn, Grand Canyon Hotel, Highlander Motel, Motel 6, Western Motel (H), Family$, Safeway, to Grand Canyon Railway

157 Devil Dog Rd

155.5mm **safety pullout wb, litter barrels**

151 Welch Rd

149 Monte Carlo Rd, N dsl repair

148 County Line Rd

SELIGMAN

146 AZ 89, to Prescott, Ash Fork, N Mobil/dsl, Shell/dsl Lu Belle's BBQ, Ranch House Cafe Ash Fork Inn Family$

144 Ash Fork, N Ash Fork Inn Grand Canyon RV Park, museum/info, USPO, S Shell/Piccadilly's/dsl, Texaco/dsl/ Park auto/RV repair

139 Crookton Rd, to Rte 66

123 Lp 40, to Rte 66, to Grand Canyon Caverns, (same as 121), Seligman, N Chevron/A&W, Shell/dsl Copper Cart Ca Lilo's Rest., Pizza Joint, Snow Cap Burgers Canyon Lodg Deluxe Inn, Stagecoach 66 Motel, Supai Motel KOA (1m repair, USPO, S Chevron/Subway/dsl

121 Lp 40, to Rte 66, same as 123, Seligman, N Chevron/A& Phillips 66/dsl Copper Cart Cafe, Lilo's Rest., Roadk Cafe Canyon Lodge, Route 66 Motel/pizza, Supai M tel KOA (1mi), repair, to Grand Canyon Caverns, USPO

109 Anvil Rock Rd

108mm Markham Wash

103 Jolly Rd

96 Cross Mountain Rd

91 Fort Rock Rd

87 Willows Ranch Rd

86mm Willow Creek

79 Silver Springs Rd

75.5mm Big Sandy Wash

73.5mm Peacock Wash

71 US 93 S, to Wickenburg, Phoenix

66 Blake Ranch Rd, N Petro/Iron Skillet/dsl/scales/24hr/ Blake Ranch RV Park, SpeedCo Lube

60mm Frees Wash

59 DW Ranch Rd, N Loves/Chester's/Subway/dsl/scales 24hr truckwash, S Hualapai Mtn Park (9mi)

57mm Rattlesnake Wash

KINGMAN

53 AZ 66, Andy Devine Ave, to Kingman, N FLYING J/Denny's/dsl/LP/scales/24hr, Chevron/dsl, Maverik/dsl, Terrible's dsl, Texaco/dsl Arby's, Burger King, Denny's, Jack-in-the Box, McDonald's, Pizza Hut, Taco Bell Days Inn, Knigh Inn, Motel 6, Red Roof Inn, Super 8, Travelodge $Gene al, Basha's Foods, Blue Beacon, dsl/tire repair, Freightline Harley-Davidson, KOA (1mi), S Mobil/dsl, Shell/dsl/re pair JB's, Oyster's Mexican, Sonic Best Western+, Cla ion, Days Inn, High Desert Inn, Holiday Inn Express, Ramad Inn, Rodeway Inn, Rte 66 Motel, SpringHill Suites Chrysler Dodge/Jeep, Kia, NAPA, Sunrise RV Park, Uptown Drug

51 Stockton Hill Rd, Kingman, N Arco/dsl, Chevron, Circle K dsl Carl's Jr, Chili's, Chipotle Mexican, Cracker Barrel, De Taco, Domino's, Dunkin', Five Guys, Golden Corral, IHOP, In-N Out, Jimmy John's, KFC, Lin's Little China, McDonald's, Panda Ex press, Papa John's, Papa Murphy, Plaza Bonita, Sonic, Starbucks Subway, Taco Bell Hampton Inn, La Quinta (H), $Gener al, $Tree, AutoZone, AZ RV Depot/repair, BigLots, BrakeMasters Buick/Chevrolet, CVS Drug, Discount Tire, Ford/Lincoln, Hom Depot, Honda, Hyundai, O'Reilly Parts, PetCo, Petsmart, Ross Safeway/gas, Smith's Foods/dsl, Staples, Superior Tire, True Value, Valvoline, Verizon, vet, Walgreens, Walmart, S Circl K DQ, Little Caesar's, Pizza Hut Home 2 Suites 99 Store, CarQuest, JC Penney, Safeway/dsl

48 US 93 N, Beale St, Kingman, N 76/Little Caesar's/dsl, Chevron/dsl, Diesel, Mobil/dsl, Shell/dsl, TA/Country Pride/Popeye's dsl/scales/24hr/@, USA/Subway/dsl, Woody's Wendy' Economy Inn, Tristate Inn Best Tire Pros, S Chevron Tacos/dsl, Tesla EVC Calico's Rest., Carl's Jr, Frederico's A Inn, Motel 6 city park, Ft Beale RV Park, Mohave Museum

AZ
AR

INTERSTATE 40 Cont'd

Exit #	Services
46.5mm	Holy Moses Wash
44	AZ 66, Oatman Hwy, McConnico, to Rte 66, S Crazy Fred's/café/dsl Canyon West RV Camping (3mi), truckwash
40.5mm	Griffith Wash
37	Griffith Rd
35mm	Black Rock Wash
32mm	Walnut Creek
28	Old Trails Rd
26	Proving Ground Rd, S AZ Proving Grounds
25	Alamo Rd, to Yucca, N USPO
23mm	both lanes, full facilities, litter barrels, petwalk, vending
21mm	Flat Top Wash
20	Santa Fe Ranch Rd
18.5mm	Illavar Wash
15mm	Buck Mtn Wash
13.5mm	Franconia Wash, Franconia Wash
13	Franconia Rd
9	AZ 95 S, to Lake Havasu City, Parker, London Br, S Chevron/dsl, Loves/Carl's Jr/Subway/dsl/scales/24hr, Pilot/Wendy's/dsl/scales/24hr Havasu RV Park, Prospectors RV Resort
4mm	**weigh sta both lanes**
2	Needle Mtn Rd
1	Topock Rd, to Bullhead City, Oatman, N camping, food, gas, to Havasu NWR
0mm	Arizona/California state line, Colorado River, Mountain/Pacific time zone

ARKANSAS

INTERSTATE 30

Exit #	Services
	I-30 begins/ends on I-40, exit 153b.
143b a	I-40, E to Memphis, W to Ft Smith
142	15th St, S Super Stop/dsl
141b	US 70, Broadway St, downtown, N Exxon, U.S. Fuel Burger King U-Haul, Verizon Arena, S Phillips 66, Valero/dsl McDonald's, Popeye's, Shark's, Taco Bell, Wendy's Econolodge Family$
141mm	Arkansas River
141a	AR 10, Cantrell Rd, Markham St (from wb), W to downtown
140	9th St, 6th St, downtown, N Shell, SuperStop Pizza Hut Holiday Inn USPO, S SuperStop Comfort Inn
139b	I-630, downtown
139a	AR 365, Roosevelt Rd, N Exxon Sim's BBQ AutoZone, O'Reilly Parts, S Shell $Tree, Family$, Kroger
138b	I-530 S, US 167 S, US 65 S, to Pine Bluff
138a	I-440 E, to Memphis, S
135	W 65th St, N Exxon/dsl, Shell/dsl, Valero/dsl Baymont Inn, S Rodeway Inn
134	Scott Hamilton Dr, S Exxon/dsl Best Value Inn, Motel 6
133	Geyer Springs Rd, N Exxon, Hess, Mobil Church's, Sims BBQ, Subway, S Citgo, Phillips 66, Shell Arby's, El Chico, KFC, Little Caesar's, McDonald's, Rally's, Sonic, Taco Bell, Waffle House Days Inn, Quality Inn, Red Roof Inn, Rest Inn CVS Drug, Family$, Goodyear/auto, Kroger/gas, Walgreens
132	US 70b, University Ave, N RaceWay/dsl, SuperStop, Valero Best Value Inn, S Kum&Go/dsl O'Reilly Parts
131	McDaniel Dr, N U-Haul, S Economy Inn, Super 7 Inn Crain RV Ctr
130	AR 338, Baseline Rd, Mabelvale, N Cimarron Inn, EconoLodge Harley-Davidson, S Murphy Express/dsl, Shell/dsl Asian Buffet, McDonald's, Pizza Hut, Popeye's, Sonic, Taco Bueno, Wendy's $Tree, Chevrolet, Crain RV Ctr, GNC, Home Depot, URGENT CARE, Walmart/Subway
129	I-430 N

LITTLE ROCK

MABELVALE

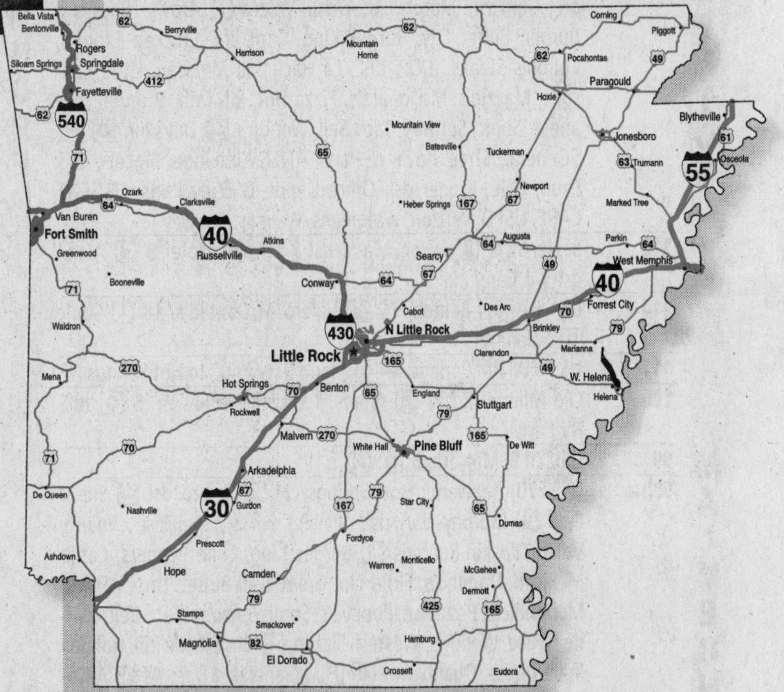

MABELVALE

Exit #	Services
128	Otter Creek Rd, Mabelvale West, N Loves/Hardee's/Subway/dsl/scales/24hr Chick-fil-A, David's Burger, Hooters, Saltgrass Steaks AT&T, Bass Pro Shop, Cavender's, Little Rock Outlets/famous brands, S Exxon/dsl Super 8 $General, Purcell Tire/auto
126	AR 111, County Line Rd, Alexander, N Shell/dsl, S Citgo/Subway Cherokee RV Park/dump (4mi)
123	AR 183, Reynolds Rd, to Bryant, Bauxite, N Murphy USA/dsl, Shell Arby's, Burger King, Casa Mexicana, Cracker Barrel, David's Burgers, Dickey's BBQ, Domino's, Firehouse Subs, IHOP, KFC, Papa John's, Pizza Hut, Popeye's, Subway, Ta Molly's, Waffle House, Whole Hog Cafe Best Value Inn, Comfort Inn, Country Inn Suites, Econolodge, Hampton Inn, Hometown Hotel, La Quinta $Tree, AT&T, AutoZone, CVS Drug, Tire Pros, vet, Walgreens, Walmart/Subway, S Exxon/dsl, Kum&Go/dsl/e85, Mapco/dsl/e85, Valero/dsl Bryant Cafe, Chick-fil-A, Dunkin', Little Caesar's, Logan's Roadhouse,

= gas = food = lodging = other = rest stop

INTERSTATE 30 Cont'd

Exit	Services
123	Continued McDonald's, Mi Ranchito, Sonic, Taco Bell, Wendy's, Zaxby's Super 8 $General, Family$, Food Giant, Lowe's, O'Reilly Parts, USPO, vet
121	Alcoa Rd, N EZ Go, Pilot/Subway/dsl/scales/24hr/@ DQ, Freddy's, McDonald's, Pie Five, Red Robin, Slim Chickens, Sonic, Taco Bueno, Tacos 4Life, TX Roadhouse, Zaxby's Chrysler/Dodge/Jeep, Discount Tire, Fiat, Firestone/auto, Hobby Lobby, Infinity, Kroger/dsl, Nissan, Petsmart, TJ Maxx, Tuesday Morning, S Buffalo Wild Wings, Chili's, McAlister's Deli, Moe's SW Grill, Sakura Japanese, Starbucks, Subway Holiday Inn Express AT&T, Buick/GMC, GNC, Kohl's, PetCo, Target, Verizon
118	Congo Rd, N Applebee's, Brown's Rest., Domino's, Gino's Grill Fairfield Inn, Relax Inn Chevrolet, Home Depot, Williams Tire, S Exxon, Kum&Go/dsl/e85 Burger King, Popeye's Days Inn Ford, I-30 Travel Park, RV City, USPO
117	US 64, AR 5, AR 35, N Shell Papa John's, Waffle House Best Western, EconoLodge, Rodeway Inn, S Exxon, Gulf/dsl, Murphy USA/dsl, Valero Arby's, Backyard Burger, Buffet City, Burger King, Capt D's, Chicken Express, Colton's Steaks, IHOP, KFC, La Hacienda Mexican, Little Caesar's, Mazzio's, McDonald's, Pizza Hut, Rib Crib, Samurai Japanese, Sonic, Subway, Taco Bell, Wendy's Days Inn H, $General, $Tree, Advance Parts, AT&T, AutoZone, BigLots, CVS Drug, GNC, Kroger/dsl, Office Depot, O'Reilly Parts, URGENT CARE, USPO, Verizon, Walgreens, Walmart/Subway
116	Sevier St, N Exxon, Mac's/dsl Troutt Motel, S Alon/dsl Capri Inn
114	US 67 S, Benton, S Valero/McDonald's/dsl Sonic $General
111	US 70 W, Hot Springs, N Cloud 9 RV Park, to Hot Springs NP
106	Old Military Rd, N Alon/JJ's Rest./dsl/scales/@, S JB'S RV Park
99	US 270 E, Malvern, S H
98b a	US 270, Malvern, Hot Springs, N Valero/dsl Super 8, S Murphy USA/dsl, Phillips 66/dsl, Shell/dsl, Valero, Valero/Baskin-Robbins Burger King, Chile Peppers, Cotija Mexican, Domino's, El Parian, Great Wall Buffet, Larry's Pizza, McDonald's, Pizza Hut, Popeye's, Sonic, Subway, Taco Bell, Waffle House, Wendy's, Western Sizzlin Best Value Inn, Holiday Inn Express, Quality Inn H, $General, $Tree, AT&T, AutoZone, Chevrolet, Chrysler/Dodge/Jeep, city park, Ford, O'Reilly Parts, USPO, Verizon, Walmart/Subway
97	AR 84, AR 171, N Lake Catherine SP, RV camping
93mm	**(both lanes exit left), full facilities, litter barrels, petwalk, vending**
91	AR 84, Social Hill
83	AR 283, Friendship, S Valero/dsl
78	AR 7, Caddo Valley, N Pilot/PJ Fresh Deli/dsl/scales/24hr, Shell/dsl Cracker Barrel, Flying Burger Holiday Inn Express Arkadelphia RV Park, De Gray SP, to Hot Springs NP, S Exxon/Subway/dsl, Valero Fat Boys Cafe, McDonald's, Taco Bell, Waffle House Best Value Inn, Comfort Inn, EconoLodge, Economy Inn, Hampton Inn, Motel 6, Quality Inn, Super 8
73	AR 8, AR 26, AR 51, Arkadelphia, N Phillips 66/dsl, Shell/Stuckey's Allen's BBQ, Chicken Express, Domino's, Great Wall Buffet, McDonald's, Wendy's, Western Sizzlin $Tree, to Crater of Diamond SP, Verizon, Walmart/Subway, S Exxon/dsl, Shell Andy's Rest., Big Cheese Pizza, Burger King,
73	Continued Dunkin/Baskin Robbins, Great Wok, Little Caesar's, Ranch Mexican, Subway H, $General, Ace Hardware, AT&T, AutoZone, Brookshire Foods, O'Reilly Parts, vet, Walgreens
69	AR 26 E, Gum Springs
63	AR 53, Gurdon, N South Fork Trkstp/Citgo/rest./dsl Southfork Inn, S Phillips 66/dsl to White Oak Lake SP
56mm	**both lanes, full facilities, litter barrels, petwalk, vending, vending**
54	AR 51, Gurdon, Okolona
46	AR 19, Prescott, N Phillips 66/cafe/dsl/24hr Crater of Diamonds SP (31mi), S Love's/Hardee's/dsl/scales/24 Casa Carlos Mexican
44	AR 24, Prescott, N TA/Country Pride/Subway/Taco Bell/dsl/scales/24hr/@, S Norman's 44 Trkstp/rest/dsl/scales/@ Best Value Inn to S Ark U, truckwash
36	AR 299, to Emmett
31	AR 29, Hope, N SuperStop/dsl Relax Inn, Village Inn/RV park st police, S Exxon/dsl, Valero/dsl KFC Best Value Inn H
30	AR 4, Hope, N EVC, Murphy USA/dsl, Shell/dsl Del Loco Gringos Best Western, Hampton Inn, Holiday Inn Express, Super 8 Millwood SP, Old Washington Hist SP, Verizon, Walmart/Subway, S Exxon/Baskin-Robbins/Wendy's, Valero Amigo Juan Mexican, Big Jake's BBQ, Burger King, Chicken Express, Little Caesar's, McDonald's, Pizza Hut, Sonic, Subway, Taco Bell, Waffle House Motel 6 H, $Tree, AT&T, AutoZone, Buick/Chevrolet/GMC, Bumper Parts, Ford, Fred's, O'Reilly Parts, Super 1 Foods/gas, Walgreens
26mm	**weigh sta both lanes**
18	rd 355, Fulton, N Red River Trkstp/dsl
17mm	Red River
12	US 67 (from eb), Fulton
7mm	**Welcome Ctr eb, full facilities, info, litter barrels, petwalk, vending**
7	AR 108, Mandeville, N FLYING J/Denny's/dsl/LP/24 Sunrise RV Park truckwash
3	I-49, N to Ft Smith, S to Shreveport
2	Four States Fair Pkwy, Texarkana, N RoadRunner/dsl, Shell Circle K/dsl, S Camp I-30 Trkstp Ferguson Fairpark, Nick's RV Ctr
1	US 71, Jefferson Ave, Texarkana, N Best Western+, Comfort Suites, Hampton Inn, Holiday Inn, Holiday Inn Express KO, S Country Host Inn
0mm	Arkansas/Texas State line

BENTON · MALVERN · ARKADELPHIA · HOPE

INTERSTATE 40

Exit #	Services
285mm	Arkansas/Tennessee state line, Mississippi River
284mm	**weigh sta wb**
281	AR 131, S to Mound City
280	Club Rd, Southland Dr, N Blu/dsl/LNG/24hr, Pilot/Wendy's/dsl, S FLYING J/Denny's/dsl/LP/24hr, Love's Subway/dsl, Petro/Iron Skillet/dsl/24hr/@ KFC/Taco Bell, McDonald's Best Western, Deluxe Inn, Express Inn, Super 8 Blue Beacon, SpeedCo Lube
279b	I-55 S (from eb)
279a	Ingram Blvd, N Margaritas Mexican Days Inn, Homegate Inn, Knights Inn, Red Roof Inn Ford, Southland Racetrack, S Citgo/dsl, Phillips 66, Shell /dsl Cross Creek Rest., Waffle House Best Value Inn, Clarion, EconoLodge, Hampshire Inn, Motel 6, Ramada, Relax Inn

WEST MEMPHIS

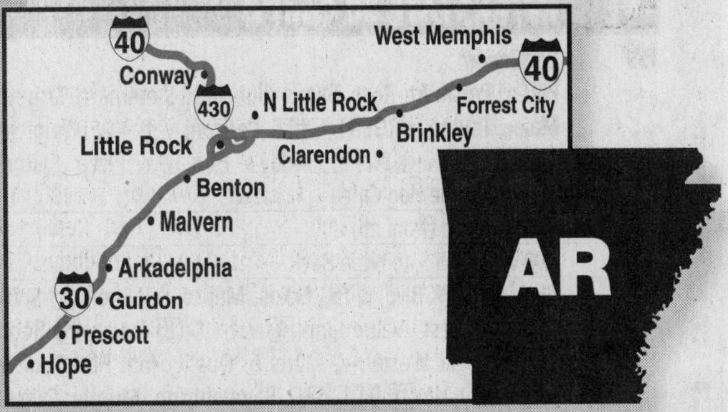

AR

E INTERSTATE 40 Cont'd

Exit #	Services
278	AR 77, 7th St, Missouri St, **N Welcome Ctr/[RS], full [handicap] facilities, [picnic], litter barrels, petwalk** [gas] Shell/dsl, **S on Missouri** [gas] Exxon, MapCo, Phillips 66/dsl, Shell [food] Applebee's, Burger King, Cracker Barrel, Domino's, Krystal, Lenny's Subs, Little Caesar's, McDonald's, Papa John's, Pizza Hut, Popeye's, Shoney's, Subway, Taco Bell, Wendy's [lodging] Comfort Suites, Extend Suites, Holiday Inn Express [other] [H], $Tree, Goodyear/auto, Kroger/dsl, Walgreens, Walmart
277	I-55 N, to Jonesboro
276	AR 77, Rich Rd, to Missouri St (from eb, same as 278), **S** [gas] Exxon, MapCo, Murphy Express/dsl, Phillips 66/dsl, Shell [food] Applebee's, Burger King, Domino's, Fusion Buffet, Krystal, Lenny's Subs, Little Caesar's, McDonald's, Mi Pueblo Mexican, Papa John's, Pizza Hut, Popeye's, Shoney's, Subway, Taco Bell, Wendy's [lodging] Extend Suites [other] [H], $Tree, AT&T, Family$, Goodyear/auto, Kroger/dsl, Walgreens, Walmart
275	AR 118, Airport Rd, **S** [gas] Shell/DQ/dsl [food] Huddle House [other] city park, URGENT CARE
274mm	**weigh sta eb, parking area wb**
271	AR 147, to Blue Lake, **S** [gas] Exxon/Chester's/dsl, Valero/dsl [other] tires, to Horseshoe Lake
265	US 79, AR 218, to Hughes
260	AR 149, to Earle, **N** [gas] Citgo/Subway, TA/Country Pride/Burger King/Taco Bell/dsl/scales/24hr/@, Valero/dsl [lodging] Relax Inn [other] Shell Lake Camping, **S** [gas] Citgo [other] dsl repair
256	AR 75, to Parkin, Parkin Archeological Park (12mi)
247	AR 38 E, to Widener
245mm	St Francis River
243mm	**[RS] wb, full [handicap] facilities, litter barrels, petwalk, [phone], [picnic], vending**
242	AR 284, Crowley's Ridge Rd, **N** [other] [H], to Village Creek SP
241b a	AR 1, Forrest City, **N** [gas] Citgo/DQ/dsl, Shell/Popeye's/dsl [food] Don Jose Mexican, HoHo Chinese, Wendy's [lodging] Best Value, Comfort Suites, Days Inn, Econolodge, Hampton Inn, Holiday Inn Express, Luxury Inn, Super 8 [other] st police, **S** [gas] Citgo/dsl, Exxon/dsl, Murphy USA/dsl, Shell/dsl [food] Burger King, Domino's, Dragon China, Iguanas Mexican, KFC, McDonald's, Ole Sawmill Cafe, Pizza Hut, Sonic, Subway, Taco Bell, Waffle House [lodging] Quality Inn, Red Roof Inn [other] $Tree, AT&T, Food Giant, Fred's, O'Reilly Parts, Save-A-Lot Foods, Verizon, Walgreens, Walmart
239	AR 1, to Wynne, Marianna
235mm	**[RS] eb, full [handicap] facilities, litter barrels, petwalk, [phone], [picnic], vending**
234mm	L'Anguille River
233	AR 261, Palestine, **N** [gas] Loves/Chester's/Subway/dsl/scales/24hr [lodging] Rest Inn, **S** [gas] Exxon/dsl
221	AR 78, Wheatley, **N** [gas] SweetPea/dsl/repair, **S** [gas] MapCo/Subway/dsl, Valero/Pitstop/diner/dsl
216	US 49, AR 17, Brinkley, **N** [gas] Citgo, Mobil/dsl [lodging] Best Inn, Days Inn, EconoLodge, Super8/RV Park, Sure Stay [other] dsl repair, KFC/Taco Bell, Los Piños Mexican, **S** [gas] Exxon/Baskin-Robbins/dsl, Shell, Victory/dsl [food] Gene's BBQ, McDonald's, New China, Pizza Hut, Sonic, Subway, Waffle House [lodging] Heritage Inn/RV Park [other] $General, AT&T, Family$, Fred's, Kroger, O'Reilly Parts
205mm	Cache River
202	AR 33, to Biscoe
200mm	White River
199mm	**[RS] both lanes, full [handicap] facilities, litter barrels, no [phone], [picnic], vending**
193	AR 11, to Hazen, **N** [gas] Exxon/Chester's/dsl [other] Lower White River RV Park, **S** [gas] Citgo/dsl, Loves/Carl's Jr/dsl/scales/24hr [food] El Amigo Mexican [lodging] Super 8, Travel Inn
183	AR 13, Carlisle, **S** [gas] Citgo, Conoco/dsl, Exxon/Subway/dsl, Valero/dsl [food] Nick's BBQ, Pizza 'N More, Sonic [lodging] Days Inn [other] $General
175	AR 31, Lonoke, **N** [gas] Phillips 66, Valero/dsl [food] Burger King, Marachi Mexican, McDonald's, Waffle House [lodging] Best Western, Days Inn, Economy Inn, Hampton Inn, Holiday Inn Express [other] AT&T, Verizon, Walmart, **S** [gas] Shell/Subway [food] KFC/Taco Bell, Pizza Hut, Sonic [lodging] Perry's Motel [other] $Tree, $General, Goodyear/auto, O'Reilly Parts, vet
173	AR 89, Lonoke
169	AR 15, Remington Rd
165	Kerr Rd
161	AR 391, Galloway, **N** [gas] Loves/Chester's/subs/dsl/scales/24hr [other] Camping World RV Ctr, **S** [gas] IA-80 TruckOMat/dsl/scales, LNG, Petro/Iron Skillet/dsl/scales/24hr/@, Pilot/Subway/Pizza Hut/dsl/scales/24hr [lodging] Days Inn [other] Blue Beacon, dsl repair, Freightliner, Southern Tire Mart, SpeedCo, Burger King
159	I-440 W, **S** [airport]
157	AR 161, to US 70, **N** [gas] Exxon/dsl, **S** [gas] Hess, Mobil/dsl, Shell/dsl, Valero/dsl [food] Burger King, McDonald's, Sonic, Taco Bell [lodging] Days Inn, EconoLodge, Quality Inn, Red Roof Inn, Rest Inn, Super 8 [other] Family$
156	Springhill Dr, **N** [gas] Kum&Go/dsl, Mapco/dsl, Murphy USA/dsl [food] Cracker Barrel [lodging] Candlewood Suites, Fairfield Inn, Hilton Garden, Holiday Inn Express, Residence Inn, Walmart
155	US 67 N, US 167, to Jacksonville (exits left from eb), Little Rock AFB, **0-3 mi N on US 167/McCain Blvd** [gas] Murphy USA/dsl, Phillips 66/dsl, Shell, Valero/dsl [food] Arby's, Bar Louie, BJ's Rest., Buffalo Wild Wings, Burger King, Cactus Jacks, Carino's Italian, Chick-fil-A, Chili's, ChuckECheese's, Chuy's TexMex, CiCi's Pizza, Corky's BBQ, David's Burgers, Dixie Cafe, El Porton Mexican, Firehouse Subs, Five Guys, Fox & Hound, Golden Corral, Hog Wild Cafe, Hooters, IHOP, Jason's Deli, Jimmy John's, Kanpai Japanese, McDonald's, Newk's Eatery, Old Chicago Pizza, Olive Garden, On-the-Border, Outback Steaks, Panera Bread, Pizza Hut, Popeyes, Rally's, Red Lobster, Saddle Creek Grill, Sonic, Subway, Super King Buffet, Taco Bell, Taziki's Mediterranean, TGIFriday's, TX Roadhouse, US Pizza, Waffle House, Wendy's [lodging] Candlewood Suites, Comfort Inn, Courtyard, Hampton Inn, Hilton Garden, Holiday Inn Express, La Quinta, Motel 6, Super 8 [other] [H], $Tree, Aamco, AT&T, Barnes&Noble, Best Buy, BigLots, Books-A-Million, Buick/GMC, Chevrolet, Chrysler/Dodge/Jeep, Dillard's, Firestone/auto, Ford, Home Depot, Honda, Hyundai, JC Penney, Jo-Ann, Kia, Kroger, Lincoln, Lowe's, Mazda, Michael's, Nissan, Office Depot, PepBoys,

FORREST CITY

BRINKLEY

LONOKE

LITTLE ROCK

AR

LITTLE ROCK

CONWAY

INTERSTATE 40 Cont'd

155	Continued PetCo, Petsmart, Ross, Sam's Club/gas, Steinmart, Target, TJ Maxx, Toyota, URGENT CARE, Verizon, vet, VW, Walgreens, Walmart/Subway, Dick's, Freddy's, Hideaway Pizza, Saltgrass Steaks, Whole Hog Cafe
154	to Lakewood (from eb)
153b	I-30 W, US 65 S, to Little Rock
153a	AR 107 N, JFK Blvd, N Exxon, Mapco/dsl, Shell Schlotzsky's Best Value Inn vet, S Exxon Bogie's Grill Best Western+, Motel 6, Quality Inn, Red Roof Inn, Super Stay Inn H, USPO, Baymont Inn, Murphy Express/dsl, Taco Bueno
152	AR 365, AR 176, Camp Pike Rd, Levy, N Exxon, Shell Burger King, KFC, Little Caesar's, McDonald's, Mexico Chiquito, Pizza Hut, Señor Tequila, Sonic, Subway, Taco Bell, US Pizza, Waffle House $General, AutoZone, Family$, Kroger/gas, O'Reilly Parts, S Shell Chicken King H, Family$, Save a Lot
150	AR 176, Burns Park, Camp Robinson, S camping, info
148	AR 100, Crystal Hill Rd, N Shell, S Citgo/dsl, Exxon/dsl KOA
147	I-430 S, to Texarkana
142	AR 365, to Morgan, N Shamrock, Valero/dsl Razorback Inn Bumper Parts, Trails End RV Park, S Kum&Go/dsl, Shell/dsl KFC, McDonald's, Razorback Pizza, Smokeshack BBQ, Subway, Waffle House Best Value Inn, Holiday Inn Express, Quality Inn $General, Autozone
135	AR 365, AR 89, Mayflower, N Hess/dsl, S Exxon/dsl, Valero Sonic, Subway $General, Harp's Mkt
134mm	**truck parking both lanes**
132	Baker-Wills Pkwy, S VP Fuel
129	US 65B, AR 286, Conway, N Sam's Club/dsl On the Border $Tree, AT&T, BAM!, Buick/GMC, Kia, Michael's, Petco, Ross, David's Burgers, Hideaway Pizza, Red Robin, Rita's Custard, Subway, S Exxon/dsl, MapCo/dsl Subway H, Chevrolet, Chrysler/Dodge/Jeep, Honda, st police, to Toad Suck SP, Toyota, Burge's Cafe, Meineke, URGENT CARE
127	US 64, Conway, N Gulf/dsl, Shell, Valero/dsl Arby's, Buffalo Wild Wings, Chick-fil-A, Chili's, Chipotle, Freddy's, Golden Corral, Las Palmas Mexican, Logan's Roadhouse, Mulan's Buffet, Popeye's, Sonic, Starbucks, Subway, TGIFriday's, Waffle House Best Value Inn, Best Western, Comfort Suites, Country Inn&Suites, Days Inn, Hampton Inn, Hilton Garden, Home 2 Suites $General, AT&T, Belk, Best Buy, Dick's, Firestone/auto, Ford, GNC, Goodyear/auto, Harley-Davidson, Home Depot, Hyundai, Kohl's, Moix RV Ctr, NAPA, Nissan, Old Navy, O'Reilly Parts, Petsmart, repair/transmissions, Staples, Target, TJ Maxx, to Lester Flatt Park, Verizon, vet, Blaze Pizza, S RaceWay, Shell/dsl, Valero/dsl Burger King, Church's, Colton's Steaks, Dunkin'/Baskin Robbins, Jimmy John's, LJ Silver, McDonald's, Rally's, Saigon Rest., Taco Bell, Tacos 4 Life, Taziki's Mediterranean, Wendy's, Whole Hog Cafe Kings Inn AutoZone, BigLots, Family$, Fred's Drugs, Hobby Lobby, Kroger/gas, tires, Walgreens, Captain Hook's, CVS
125	US 65, Conway, N Conoco/dsl, Exxon/Subway/dsl China Town, Cracker Barrel, El Acapulco Mexican, McDonald's, MktPlace Deli Quality Inn $Tree, JC Penney, Office Depot, S Citgo, CNG, Horton's, Mobil/dsl, Murphy USA/dsl Burger King, Cast Iron Skillet, CiCi's Pizza, David's Burgers, Dixie Cafe, Firehouse Subs, Fuji Steaks, IHOP, Los Potrillos

MORRILTON

RUSSELLVILLE

125	Continued Mexican, McAlister's Deli, Mexico Chiquito, New China, O back Steaks, Panera Bread, Ruby Tuesday, Russo's Italian Kit en, Sonic, Starbucks, Subway, Waffle House, Wendy's C dlewood Suites, Comfort Inn, Fairfield Inn, Holiday Inn Expre Howard Johnson, La Quinta, Microtel, Motel 6, Super 8 Advance Parts, AT&T, Lowe's, tires, Walmart
124	AR 25 N, to Conway, S Alon/Hess/dsl, Kum&Go/dsl D KFC, Popeye's H, vet
120mm	Cadron River
117	to Menifee
112	AR 92, Plumerville, N Exxon/dsl, S Country Store/ USPO
108	AR 9, Morrilton, N Ford/Lincoln, S Murphy USA, She Pizza Pro/dsl, Valero Chop Stix, Colton's Steaks, Harde Mama DeLuca's Pizza, McDonald's, Ortega's Mexican, Piz Hut, Sonic, Subway, Taco Bell, Waffle House, Wendy's H iday Inn Express, Super 8 H, $General, Ace Hardwa AT&T, Chrysler/Dodge/Jeep, Kroger, NAPA, to Petit Jean (21mi), Verizon, vet, Walmart, AutoZone, Blue Diamond Cafe
107	AR 95, Morrilton, N Sunoco/dsl Best Value I I-40/107 RV Park, S Loves/Subway/dsl/24 Morrilton Drive Inn, Yesterdays Rest. Days I Bumper Parts
101	Blackwell, N Blackwell TrkStp/Citgo/Domino's/diner/d scales/24hr Utility Trailer Sales
94	AR 105, Atkins, N Exxon/Subway/dsl, VP/McDonald's/ El Parian Mexican, Sonic $General, S Casey's/ Cash Saver Foods
88	Pottsville, S $General, truck repair/wash
84	US 64, AR 331, Russellville, N FLYING J/Denny's/d scales/LP/24hr, Shell/dsl Ivys Cove RV Retreat, S Ph lips 66, Pilot/Subway/Wendy's/dsl/scales Chick-fil-A, Ci's Pizza, Hardee's, McDonald's, Mulan's Buffet, Sonic, Waf House Comfort Inn, Quality Inn H, $Tree, AT&T, Be Buick/Chevrolet/GMC, Chrysler/Dodge/Jeep, GNC, Hobby Lo by, Hyundai, JC Penney, Lowe's, Nissan, Petsmart, Ross, St ples, TJ Maxx, Toyota, USPO
83	AK 326, Weir Rd, S Phillips 66/dsl, Walmart Gas/dsl Bu falo Wild Wings, DQ, McAlisters Deli, Popeye's, Starbuck Steak'n Shake, Subway, Sumo, Taco Bell, Taco John's Con fort Inn $General, AutoZone, Firestone/auto, Ford/Lincol Mazda, NAPA, O'Reilly Parts, Verizon, Walmart/McDonald Zaxby's, Chili's
81	AR 7, Russellville, N SuperStop/dsl CJ's Bur ers Motel 6 $General, Outdoor RV Ctr/Park, Courtyar S Exxon/dsl, Phillips 66/dsl, Shell Arby's, Burger Kin Cagle's Mill Rest., Colton's Steaks, Cracker Barrel, Dixie Caf Firehouse Subs, IHOP, La Huerta Mexican, New China, Ru Tuesday, Subway, Waffle House Best Value, Best Wester Clarion, Days Inn, Econolodge, Fairfield Inn, Hampton Inn, L Quinta, Super 8 RV camping, to Lake Dardanelle SP
80mm	Dardanelle Reservoir
78	US 64, Russellville, S Darrell's Mkt Fat Daddy's BB H, Mission RV Park, to Lake Dardanelle SP
74	AR 333, London
72mm	**wb, full facilities, litter barrels, petwalk, , vendi**
70mm	overlook wb, litter barrels
68mm	**eb, full facilities, litter barrels, petwalk, , vendi**
67	AR 315, Knoxville, S USPO
64	US 64, Clarksville, Lamar, S Valero/dsl Dad's Dream R Park

INTERSTATE 40 Cont'd

Exit #	Services
58	AR 21, AR 103, Clarksville, N Casey's/dsl, Shell, Valero Emerald Dragon Chinese, KFC, La Chiquita Mexican, McDonald's, Pizza Hut, Subway, Taco Bell, Waffle House Best Western, Executive Inn, Quality Inn, Super 8 H, $General, Buick/Chevrolet, S Murphy USA/dsl Arby's, China Fun, Wendy's $Tree, AT&T, Chrysler/Dodge/Jeep, Ford, Walmart/Subway
57	AR 109, Clarksville, N Fuel Stop/dsl Sonic, Subway Family$, Harp's Mkt, S Shell/Steak'n Shake/dsl Truckwash, TrueValue
55	US 64, AR 109, Clarksville, N Hardee's, Kountry Kitchen Grille Hampton Inn, Holiday Inn Express, Sunset Inn, S Valero/AutoTruck/dsl st police
47	AR 164, Coal Hill
41	AR 186, Altus, N Swiss Family Rest., S Wiederkehr Rest. (4mi) winery (4mi)
37	AR 219, Ozark, S Love's/Subway/dsl/scales/24hr, Valero/McDonald's/dsl KFC/Taco Bell Best Value Inn H
36mm	**both lanes, full facilities, litter barrels, petwalk,**
35	AR 23, Ozark, N Valero/Red Hog BBQ/dsl/scales Hillbilly Hideout Rest, **3 mi** S Oxford Inn, Ozark Inn H, Aux Arc Park (5mi), to Mt Magazine SP (20 mi)
24	AR 215, Mulberry, S Vine Prairie Park
20	Dyer, N Short Stop/dsl, S Phillips 66/dsl, Shell/dsl Mill Creek Inn
13	US 71 N, to Fayetteville, N Shell, Sunoco/dsl Burger King, Catfish Hole, China Fun, Cracker Barrel, KFC, La Fiesta Mexican, Pizza Parlor, Subway, Taco Bell Quality Inn $General, Crabtree RV Ctr/Park, KOA (2mi), Lake Ft Smith SP, O'Reilly Parts, to U of AR, Bumper Parts, Hog Pizza, S Murphy USA/dsl, Valero/dsl, Workman's Braum's, Geno's Pizza, McDonald's, Pizza Hut, Sonic Days Inn AT&T, Coleman Drug, Harp's Foods, Shoppers Value Foods, Walgreens, Walmart, $Tree
12	I-49 N, to Fayetteville, N to Lake Ft Smith SP
9mm	**weigh sta both lanes**
7	I-540 S, US 71 S, to Ft Smith, Van Buren, S H
5	AR 59, Van Buren, N Citgo/dsl, Murphy USA/dsl, VP Fuels Arby's, Burger King, Chili's, Domino's, Firehouse Subs, Golden Wok, La Fiesta Mexican, Little Caesar's, McDonald's, Starbucks, Zaxby's Best Western, Hampton Inn $Tree, Advance Parts, AT&T, CVS Drug, Lowe's, NAPA, USPO, Verizon, Walmart/Subway, Aldi, Tropical Cafe, S Casey's/dsl, Shell/dsl Braum's, Geno's Pizza, KFC/Taco Bell, La Fresas Mexican, Sonic, Subway, Waffle House, Wendy's Holiday Inn Express, Sleep Inn, Super 8 $General, Grizzle Tire, Outdoor RV Park, Shoppers Value Foods, truckwash, vet, Walgreens, Colton's Steaks, Frank's Italian
3	Lee Creek Rd, N Shell/dsl Park Ridge Camping
2.5mm	**Welcome Ctr eb, full facilities, info, litter barrels, petwalk, , vending**
1	to Ft Smith (from wb), Dora
0mm	**Arkansas/Oklahoma state line**

INTERSTATE 49 (Fayetteville)

Exit #	Services
93	US 71B, Bentonville, **I-49 begins/ends on US 71 N.**
88	AR 72, Bentonville, Pea Ridge, E Casey's River Grille Comfort Inn, Courtyard, W Kum&Go/dsl, Shell/dsl Smokin' Joe's Ribs Walmart Visitors Ctr

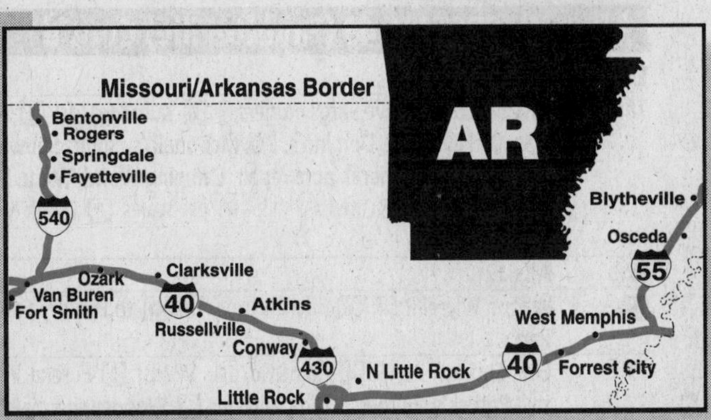

BENTONVILLE

Exit #	Services
87	8th St
86	US 62, AR 102, Bentonville, Rogers, E EVC TownePlace Suites Pea Ridge NMP, Sam's Club/gas, Walmart Mkt, W Shell/dsl Arby's, Dunkin', McDonald's, Sonic, Subway, Taco Bell Woodspring Suites
85	US 71B, AR 12, Bentonville, Rogers, E Conoco/dsl Abuelo's, Applebee's, Arby's, Boar's Nest, Cane's, Carino's Italian, Chick-fil-A, Chili's, Colton's Steaks, Freddy's Burgers, IHOP, Logan's Roadhouse, McDonald's, Napoli's Pizza, On-the-Border, Outback Steaks, Quiznos, Red Robin, Rick's Café, Sonic, Starbucks, Tokyo House, Zoe's Kitchen Candlewood Suites, Country Inn&Suites, Fairfield Inn, Hampton Inn, Homewood Suites, Hyatt Place, Mainstay Suites, Residence Inn AT&T, Barnes&Noble, Belk, Firestone/auto, Jo-Ann, Kohl's, Lowe's, Marshall's, Office Depot, PetCo, Prairie Creek SP, Ross, Staples, Verizon, W Kum&Go/dsl, Murphy Express/dsl, Shell Azul Tequila Mexican, Braum's, Buffalo Wild Wings, Chipotle, Cracker Barrel, Denny's, Firehouse Subs, HoneyBaked Ham, Jimmy John's, Joe's Italian, Jonny Brusco's Pizza, Krispy Kreme, Lenny's Subs, Lin's Garden, Mama Fu's Asian, McAlister's Deli, Panera Bread, Shogun Japanese, Smashburger, Starbucks, Subway, Taco Bueno, Taziki's Mediterranean Cafe, Village Inn, Waffle House, Whole Hog Cafe, Zaxby's Best Western+, Comfort Suites, Days Inn, DoubleTree Hotel, EconoLodge, Element Westin, Hilton Garden, Holiday Inn Express, La Quinta, Microtel, Red Roof Inn, Sheraton, SpringHill Suites, Super 8 H, BMW, Buick/GMC, Cadillac, Chevrolet, Christian Bros Auto, Chrysler/Dodge/Jeep, Honda, Hyundai, Kia, Mazda, Mercedes, Nissan, Toyota, URGENT CARE
83	AR 94 E, Pinnacle Hills Pkway, E Phillips 66 After 5 Grill, Bariola's Pizza, ChuckECheese's, Dickey's BBQ, Firehouse Subs, Five Guys, Jimmy John's, Mojitos Mexican, Olive Garden, Panda Express, Qdoba, Red Lobster, Slim Chickens, Starbucks, Steak'n Shake, Taco Bell H, Home Depot, Horse Shoe Bend Park, URGENT CARE, Walgreens, W Bonefish Grill, Carraba's, Coldstone, Crabby's Seafood Grill, Grub's Grille, Ruth's Chris Steaks, Subway, The Egg&I, Theo's, Tropical Smoothie ALoft, Embassy Suites, Holiday Inn, Staybridge Suites
82	Promenade Blvd, E Fish City Grill, Longhorn Steaks, Mimi's Cafe, PF Chang's, Twin Peaks Courtyard H, AT&T, Bass Pro Shops, Best Buy, Dillard's, Fresh Mkt, GNC, Gordman's, JC Penney, Old Navy, Petsmart, Target, TJMaxx, Verizon, W Chick-fil-A, Chuy's Mexican, Newk's Eatery, Pei Wei, Tacos 4 Life Walmart Mkt/dsl
81	Pleasant Grove Rd, E Murphy USA/dsl Backyard Burger, Chick-fil-A, Golden Corral, Gusano's Pizzaria, McDonald's, Moe's SW, Old Chicago, Papa Murphy's, Starbucks, Subway, Taco Bueno, Whataburger Burlington, Cavender's, Duluth Trading, Firestone/auto, Walgreens, Walmart, W Casey's/dsl

AR

= gas = food = lodging = other = rest stop

AR

INTERSTATE 49 (Fayetteville) Cont'd

SPRINGDALE

FAYETTEVILLE

Exit #	Services
78	AR 264, Lowell, Cave Sprgs, Rogers, E Kum&Go/dsl Arby's, Dickey's BBQ, Domino's, DQ, McDonald's, Sonic, Subway, Taco Bell $General, auto repair, Camping World RV Ctr, Super 8, W Kum&Go/dsl, Phillips 66/dsl/scales Ozark Mtn Grill
77	AR 612
76	Wagon Wheel Rd, E Shell/Subway/dsl to Hickory Creek Park
73	Elm Springs Rd, E Kum&Go/dsl, VP/dsl Eureka Pizza, Patrick's Burgers, Whataburger Woodspring Suites Chevrolet, Family$, W Shell/dsl, Walmart/dsl McDonald's, MJ Pizzaria, Panda Express H, URGENT CARE, Walmart
72mm	**weigh sta nb**
72	US 412, Springdale, Siloam Springs, E Citgo/dsl, Kum&Go/dsl, Phillips 66 Angus Jack's Burgers, Applebee's, Braum's, Cotton Patch Cafe, Denny's, Golden Dragon Buffet, Jimmy John's, Little Caesar's, McDonald's, Mkt Place Rest., Sonic, Subway, Sunset Grill, Taco Bell, Waffle House, Wendy's, Western Sizzlin DoubleTree Hotel, Extended Stay America, Fairfield Inn, Hampton Inn, Holiday Inn, Home 2 Suites, La Quinta, Quality Inn, Residence Inn, Royal Inn, Sleep Inn, Super 8 AT&T, Big O Tire, Harp's Mkt, Kenworth/Volvo Trucks, Lowe's, Office Depot, O'Reilly Parts, URGENT CARE, Verizon, Walgreens, W Casey's/dsl, Murphy Express/dsl, Pilot/Burger King/dsl/scales/24hr Arby's, Buffalo Wild Wings, Cracker Barrel, Domino's, Flying Burrito, Freddy's, McDonald's, Pizza Hut, Popeye's, Rib Crib, Slim Chickens, Subway, Taco Bueno, Tacos 4 Life, Tropical Smoothie Buick/GMC, Harp's Mkt/dsl, Hobby Lobby, NW RV Ctr, Sam's Club/dsl
71mm	**weigh sta sb**
70	Don Tyson Pkwy, E Casey's/dsl, Walmart/dsl Walmart Mkt
69	Johnson Mill Blvd, Johnson, E Inn at the Mill Rest. Inn at the Mill, TownePlace Suites
67	US 71B, Fayetteville, E H
66	AR 112, Garland Ave, E Phillips 66/dsl, W Acura, Chevrolet, Honda, Hyundai, Sam's Club/dsl, Toyota
65	Porter Rd, W Subaru
64	AR 16 W, AR 112 E, Wedington Dr, W Citgo/McDonald's/dsl, Murphy Express/dsl Dickey's BBQ, El Matador Mexican, Freddy's, Gusano's Pizza, IHOP, Marco's Pizza, Sonic, Starbucks, Subway, Taco Bell Comfort Inn, Hilton Garden, Holiday Inn Express, Homewood Suites AT&T, Harp's Food/gas, Walmart Mkt
62	US 62, AR 180, Farmington, E Citgo, Shell/dsl Andy's Custard, Arby's, Braum's, Burger King, Cane's, Chick-fil-A, DQ, Ginger Rice&Noodle, KFC, McDonald's, Mexico Viejo, Panda Express, Pieology, Popeye's, Slim Chickens, Sonic, Starbucks, Subway, Taco Bell, Taco Bueno, Thai Wok, Waffle House, Wendy's, Whataburger, Zaxby's Best Western, Candlewood Suites, EconoLodge Bumper Parts, W Murphy USA/dsl Firehouse Subs, Jimmy's Egg, King Burrito, Papa Murphy's, Pavilion Buffet, Serrano's Baymont Inn, Days Inn, Hampton Inn, Regency 7 Motel, Super 8, Woodspring Suites $Tree, Aldi Foods, AT&T, AutoZone, Big O Tire, Lowe's, Verizon, Walgreens, Walmart/McDonald's
61	US 71 (from sb), to Boston Mtn Scenic Lp
60	AR 112, AR 265, Razorback Rd, E Staybridge Suites Southgate RV Park, to U of AR
58	Greenland, W Phillips 66/McDonalds/dsl/scales/24hr Sc
53	AR 170, West Fork, E Harp's/dsl Harp's Mkt, W Creek RV Resort (4mi), W to Devils Den SP
45	AR 74, Winslow, W to Devils Den SP
41mm	Bobby Hopper Tunnel
34	AR 282, to US 71, Chester, W USPO
29	AR 282, to US 71, Mountainburg, **1 mi** E $General, to La Ft Smith SP
24	AR 282, to US 71, Rudy, E Loves/Chester's/Subw dsl/scales/24hr, Phillips 66/dsl Red Hog Cafe Bos Mtns Scenic Lp, KOA
21	Collum Ln
20	to I-40 (from sb). **I-49 N begins/ends on I-40, exit 12.**

INTERSTATE 49 (Texarkana)

Exit #	Services
42	**I-49 (Texarkana) begins/ends on US 59.**
41	Sanderson Ln
37b a	I-30, E to Little Rock, W to Dallas
35	Arkansas Blvd, Four States Pkwy, E fairgroun W $General
32	US 82, 19th St, 9th St, E Shell/dsl, Valero/dsl Subw TA Molly's Mexican $General, CashSaver
31	AR 196, Genoa Rd
29b a	US 71, Texarkana, US 59, to Houston, W Shell/dsl
26	AR 237
24	Rd 10, Ferguson
18	N Fouke Rd
16	US 71, Fouke
6	Rd 197, Spruell Rd
4	US 71, Doddridge
0mm	Arkansas/Louisiana state line

INTERSTATE 55

BLYTHEVILLE

Exit #	Services
72mm	Arkansas/Missouri state line
72	State Line Rd, **weigh sta sb**
71	AR 150, Yarbro
68mm	**Welcome Ctr sb, full facilities, litter barrels, petwalk,**
67	AR 18, Blytheville, E Mobil/dsl, Murphy Express/ Burger King, Hardee's, Las Brisas Mexican, Waffle Inn, Za by's Best Value Inn, Days Inn/RV park Chrysler/Dodg Jeep, Lowe's, Verizon, Walmart/Subway, W Citgo/dsl, Ph lips 66/dsl; Shell El Puerto Mexican, GreatWall Chines Grecian Steaks, Little Caesar's, McDonald's, Olympia Stea Perkins, Pizza Hut, Pizza Inn, Sonic, Subway, Taco Bell, Wend Comfort Inn, Fairview Suites, Hampton Inn, Holiday In Quality Inn, Super 8 H, AT&T, AutoZone, Bumper Par Family$, Ford/Nissan
63	US 61, to Blytheville, E Loves/IHOP/Chester's/God ther's/dsl/scales/24hr Shearins RV Park (2mi), W C go/McDonald's/dsl, Dodge's Store/dsl, Exxon/Baskin-Robbin Chester's/Pizza Hut/dsl Deerfield Inn, Relax Inn truckwash
57	AR 148, Burdette, E NE AR Coll
53	AR 158, Victoria, Luxora
48	AR 140, to Osceola, E Shell/Baskin-Robbins/Chester's/ McDonald's (3mi), Pizza Inn (3mi), Sonic (3mi), Subway mi) Days Inn, Deerfield Inn, EconoLodge H, Hudd House, Mamma Mia's
45mm	**truck parking nb, litter barrels**
44	AR 181, Keiser

INTERSTATE 55 Cont'd

Exit #	Services
41	AR 14, Marie, E to Hampson SP/museum
36	AR 181, to Wilson, Bassett
35mm	**truck parking sb, litter barrels**
34	AR 118, Joiner
23b a	US 63, AR 77, to Marked Tree, Jonesboro, ASU, E Citgo/chicken/pizza
21	AR 42, Turrell, W Valero/pizza/dsl/scales/24hr
17	AR 50, to Jericho
14	rd 4, to Jericho, E Citgo/dsl/scales/24hr, W Citgo/Stuckey's Chevrolet, KOA
10	US 64 W, Marion, E Citgo/Baskin-Robbins/Subway/scales, Shell/McDonald's KFC/Taco Bell, Sonic, Tops BBQ, Wendy's Comfort Inn, Hallmarc Inn $General, Family$, Mkt Place Foods, USPO, W Exxon/dsl, Shamrock Andrey Grill, Burger King, Colton's Steaks, Mi Pueblo, Tropical Cafe, Zaxby's Best Value Inn, Fairfield Inn, Hampton Inn, Journey Inn AutoZone, to Parkin SP (23mi)
9mm	**truck parking nb, weigh sta sb**
8	I-40 W, to Little Rock

I-55 and I-40 run together 3 mi. See I-40, exits 278-279b.

Exit #	Services
5	(279 a from I-40) Ingram Blvd, E **Welcome Ctr/, full facilities, , litter barrels, petwalk,** Margaritas Mexican Days Inn, Homegate Inn, Knights Inn, Red Roof Inn Ford, Southland Racetrack, W Citgo/dsl, Phillips/dsl, Shell/dsl Cross Creek Rest., Waffle House Best Value Inn, Clarion Inn, EconoLodge, Hampshire Inn, Motel 6, Ramada, Relax Inn
4	King Dr, Southland Dr, E FLYING J/Denny's/dsl/LP/scales/RV dump, LNG, Love's/Subway/dsl/scales/ @, Petro/Iron Skillet/rest./dsl/24hr/@, Pilot/Subway/Wendy's/dsl/scales/24hr, Valero/dsl KFC/Taco Bell, McDonald's Best Western, Deluxe Inn, Express Inn, Super 8 Blue Beacon, SpeedCo Lube, W Pancho's Mexican Sunset Inn
3b a	US 70, Broadway Blvd, AR 131, Mound City Rd (exits left from nb), W Budget Inn
2mm	**weigh sta nb**
1	Bridgeport Rd
0mm	Arkansas/Tennessee state line, Mississippi River

INTERSTATE 430 (Little Rock)

Exit #	Services
13b a	I-40. **I-430 begins/ends on I-40, exit 147.**
12	AR 100, Maumelle, W Kum&Go/dsl/e85 NAPA, O'Reilly Parts, vet
10mm	Arkansas River
9	AR 10, Cantrell Rd, W Maumelle Park, Pinnacle Mtn SP
8	Rodney Parham Rd, E Conoco/dsl, Kroger/dsl, Phillips 66/dsl, Shell Arby's, Baskin-Robbins, Dunkin', Firehouse Subs, McDonald's, Mt Fuji Japanese, Sonic, Starbucks, Subway, Taco Bell, Terri Lynn's BBQ, Tropical Smoothie Cafe, US Pizza La Quinta $General, AAA, Advance Parts, AutoZone, Drug Emporium, get, Kroger, TJ Maxx, Walgreens, W Exxon Burger King, Chili's, Dixie Cafe, Domino's, Franke's Café, Marco's Pizza, Olive Garden, Ponchito's Mexican, Shorty Small's Ribs, Starbucks, Wendy's Best Western Audi, Cadillac, Firestone/auto, GNC, vet, Volvo
6b	Kanis Rd, Markham St, to downtown, E Shell Burger King, Kroger, Red Lobster, Subway Candlewood Suites, Comfort Inn, Motel 6, SpringHill Suites Burlington Coats, Ross, W Exxon/dsl Applebee's, Bobby's Country Cookin',

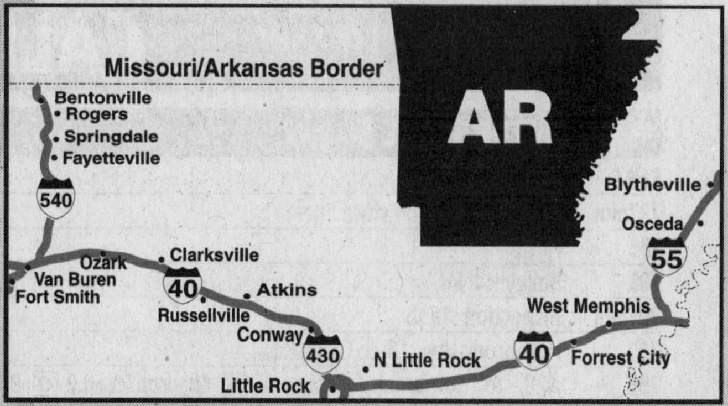

LITTLE ROCK

Exit #	Services
6b	Continued Butcher Shop Steaks, Cactus Jack's, Chi Rest., Church's, Denny's, Famous Dave's BBQ, IHOP, Jason's Deli, KFC, Khalil's Grill, Kobe Japanese, Lenny's Subs, Macaroni Grill, McAlister's Deli, McDonald's, Mexico Cafe, Mimi's Cafe, On-the-Border, Outback Steaks, PF Chang's, Pizza Hut, Popeye's, Purple Cow, Shotgun Dan's Pizza, Slim Chickens, Sonic, Starbucks, Taco Bell, Tokyo House, Twin Peaks, Waffle House, Wendy's, West End Steaks, Whole Foods Mkt Courtyard, Crowne Plaza, Embassy Suites, Extended Stay America, Holiday Inn, La Quinta, Ramada Ltd $Tree, AT&T, Barnes&Noble, Best Buy, Michael's, Office Depot, PetsMart, Sam's Club/gas, Verizon, Walmart
6a	I-630, E to Little Rock, E H
5	Kanis Rd, Shackleford Rd, E Arby's, BJ's Rest., ChuckE-Cheese, Copeland's Rest., Cracker Barrel, Longhorn Steaks, Panda Garden, Samurai Steaks, TX Roadhouse, Zangna Thai Comfort Suites, Home 2 Suites, La Quinta, Towneplace Suites AT&T, Gordman's, JC Penney, Jo-Ann, Verizon, Walmart/Subway, W Shell Dunkin', Krispy Kreme, Mooyah Burger, Panera Bread Extended Stay America, Hampton Inn, Hilton Garden, Residence Inn, Wingate Inn H, Lexus
4	AR 300, Col Glenn Rd, E American Pie Pizza, Subway, Wendy's Holiday Inn Express, Woodspring Suites Hotel Toyota, W Valero/Burger King/dsl Sonic BMW, Chrysler/Dodge/Jeep, Ford, Honda, Hyundai, Infiniti, Jaguar, Land Rover, Mazda, Mercedes, Nissan, Subaru, VW
1	AR 5, Stagecoach Rd, W Mapco/dsl/e85, Phillips 66, Valero/Domino's Down Home Rest., Subway $General, CBI Tires, Walgreens

I-430 begins/ends on I-30, exit 129.

INTERSTATE 440 (Little Rock)

Exit #	Services
11	**I-440 begins/ends on I-40, exit 159.**
10	US 70, W Peterbilt
8	Faulkner Lake Rd
7	US 165, to England, S Valero/dsl Agricultural Museum, Toltec Mounds SP, Willow Beach SP
6mm	Arkansas River
5	Fourche Dam Pike, LR Riverport, N Exxon/dsl, Shell/Subway McDonald's Travelodge Kenworth, S Phillips 66/dsl, Valero/dslΔ
4	Lindsey Rd
3	Bankhead Dr, N Comfort Inn LR Airport, S Valero Boston's Rest., Waffle House Days Inn, Holiday Inn, Holiday Inn Express
1	AR 365, Springer Blvd, S Little Rock Ntl Cemetery
0mm	**I-440 begins/ends on I-30, exit 138.**

CA

CALIFORNIA

INTERSTATE 5

Exit #	Services
797mm	California/Oregon state line
796	Hilt
793	Bailey Hill Rd
791mm	**inspection sta sb**
790	Hornbrook Hwy, Ditch Creek Rd
789	A28, to Hornbrook, Henley, E Chevron/dsl/LP Blue Heron RV Park/rest., to Iron Gate RA
786	CA 96, Klamath River Hwy, W **both lanes, full facilities, info, litter barrels, petwalk,** , , to Klamath River RA
782mm	Anderson Summit, elevation 3067
780mm	vista point sb
779mm	Shasta River
776	Yreka, Montague, E Holiday Inn Express Yreka RV Park, W Mobil/dsl Casa Ramos Mexican, J&D Diner, Puerto Vallarta Mtn View Inn, Super 8 Grocery Outlet
775	Miner St, Central Yreka, W 76/dsl, Chevron/dsl Grandma's House, Poor George's, RoundTable Pizza, Subway Best Western, Budget Inn, EconoLodge, Klamath Motel, Relax Inn, Rodeway Inn, Yreka Motel H, Ace Hardware, Baxter Parts, CarQuest, Dunn Automotive, museum, NAPA, Rite Aid, USPO
773	CA 3, to Ft Jones, Etna, E Les Schwab, tires, Trailer Haven RV Park, W Shell/dsl, Valero/dsl BlackBear Diner, Burger King, Carl's Jr, Jefferson's Roadhouse, KFC, McDonald's, Starbucks, Subway, Taco Bell Baymont Inn, Comfort Inn, Motel 6 H, $Tree, AAA, AT&T, AutoZone, CHP, Ford, JC Penney, O'Reilly Parts, Raley's Foods, Verizon, Walmart
770	Shamrock Rd, Easy St, W Beacon/LP, Fuel 24/7/dsl RV camping
766	A12, to Gazelle, Grenada, E Shell/dsl, W Chevron/dsl/24hr RV camping
759	Louie Rd
753	Weed Airport Rd, **both lanes, full facilities, litter barrels, petwalk,** ,
751	Stewart Springs Rd, Edgewood, E Lake Shasta RA/RV camp (2mi), W RV camp (7mi)
748	to US 97, to Klamath Falls, Weed, E Chevron, Shell/dsl, Spirit/dsl Ellie's Cafe, Pizza Factory, Subway Hi-Lo Motel/rest., Motel 6, Summit Inn, Townhouse Motel auto repair, golf, NAPA, Ray's Foods, RV camping
747	Central Weed, E auto repair, same as 748, W Coll of Siskiyou
745	S Weed Blvd, E Chevron/dsl, Pilot/Subway/dsl/scales/24hr, Shell/dsl Burger King, Dos Amigos Mexican, McDonald's/RV parking, Starbucks, Taco Bell Comfort Inn, Quality Inn, Sis-Q Inn Friendly RV Park, Grocery Outlet
743	Summit Dr, Truck Village Dr
742mm	Black Butte Summit, elevation 3912
741	Abrams Lake Rd, W Abrams Lake RV Park
740	Mt Shasta City (from sb), E Pacific Pride/dsl/LP, Shell/dsl/CFN Cold Creek Inn KOA, repair, vet
738	Central Mt Shasta, E 76/dsl, Chevron/dsl, Shell/dsl/LP BlackBear Diner, Burger King, KFC/Taco Bell, RoundTable Pizza, Subway Best Western/Treehouse Rest., Mt Shasta Inn, Travel Inn H, Best Hardware, NAPA, O'Reilly Parts, Ray's Foods, Rite Aid, USPO, visitors info, W Lake Siskiyou RV Park, Mt Shasta Resort/rest., Sisson Museum

YREKA

WEED

MT SHASTA

Exit #	Services
737	Mt Shasta City (from nb), E Casa Ramos, LaiLai Chin Lily's Rest., Piemont Italian, Wayside Grill Alpine Loc Choice Inn, Evergreen Lodge, Swiss Holiday Lodge Cloud RV Park, same as 738
736	CA 89, to McCloud, to Reno, E Swiss Holiday Lodge
735mm	**weigh sta sb**
734	Mott Rd, to Dunsmuir
732	Dunsmuir Ave, Siskiyou Ave, E Penny's Diner T elodge, W Chevron/dsl Acorn Inn, Cedar Lodge
730	Central Dunsmuir, E Burger Barn, Cornerstone Cafe, Du muir Brewery Rest., Pizza Factory Dunsmuir Inn, Hotel D smuir/Rest Dunsmuir Mkt, True Value, USPO, W Ch ron/dsl/LP Hitching Post, Wild Land Burgers C Springs Motel city park
729	Dunsmuir (from nb), E Manfredi's/deli/dsl auto re Dunsmuir Lodge to hist dist
728	Crag View Dr, Dunsmuir, Railroad Park Rd, W Railroad P Motel/RV Park
727	Crag View Dr (from nb), RV Camping
726	Soda Creek Rd, to Pacific Crest Trail
724	Castella, W Chevron/dsl Castle Crags SP, RV camp USPO
723mm	vista point nb
723	Sweetbrier Ave
721	Conant Rd
720	Flume Creek Rd
718	Sims Rd, W RV camping
714	Gibson Rd
712	Pollard Flat, E Pollard Flat/dsl/LP Pollard Flat Diner
710	Slate Creek Rd, La Moine
707	Delta Rd, Dog Creek Rd, to Vollmers
705mm	**sb, full facilities, litter barrels,** ,
704	Riverview Dr, E Klondike Diner Lakehead Lodge Camping
702	Antlers Rd, Lakeshore Dr, to Lakehead, E Chevron/S way/dsl Antlers RV Park, Lakehead Camping, Neu Lo Motel auto repair, USPO, W Texaco/dsl Allys Rest., Bass Hole Rest. Lakeshore Mkt, Shasta Lake Mo RV Villa RV Park
698	Salt Creek Rd, Gilman Rd, W Salt Creek Resort/RV P Trail In RV Park
695	Shasta Caverns Rd, to O'Brien
694mm	**nb, full facilities, litter barrels, petwalk,** ,
693	Packers Bay Rd (from sb)
692	Turntable Bay Rd
690	Bridge Bay Rd, W Tail of a Whale Rest. Bridge Bay M
689	Fawndale Rd, Wonderland Blvd, E Fawndale Lodge, Fa dale Oaks RV Park, W Wonderland RV Park
687	Wonderland Blvd, Mountain Gate, E Chevron/dsl/LP Fogata Mountain Gate RV Park, Ranger Sta, W Sh dsl/LP
685	CA 151, Shasta Dam Blvd, Project City, Central Va W 76/Circle K/dsl, Shell/Burger King/dsl/LP, Vale dsl McDonald's, Pizza Factory, Taco Shop Shasta D Motel NAPA, Rite Aid, Sentry Foods, USPO, vet
684	Pine Grove Ave, W Valero/dsl/LP
682	Oasis Rd, E CA RV Ctr, Peterbilt, W Arco, Shell/S way/dsl CHP, Towtally RV Ctr, U-Haul

DUNSMUIR

INTERSTATE 5 Cont'd

Exit #	Services
681b	(from sb, no re-entry) CA 273, Market St, Johnson Rd, to Central Redding, W [other] [H]
681a	Twin View Blvd, E [gas] Chevron/dsl [lodging] Motel 6, Ramada Ltd [other] Harley-Davidson, W [gas] Pacific Pride/dsl [food] El Zarape [lodging] Best Western+, Comfort Suites, Fairfield Inn
680	CA 299E, **1/2 mi** W [gas] Arco, Chevron/dsl [food] A&W/KFC, Carl's Jr, Giant Burger, Little Caesar's, McDonald's, Papa Murphy's, Popeye's, RoundTable Pizza, Starbucks, Subway [other] AutoZone, O'Reilly Parts, Raley's Foods, Redding RV Camp, Redding RV Park, transmissions, Twin View RV Park, Walgreens
678	CA 299 W, CA 44, to Eureka, Redding, Burney, E **between Hilltop & Churncreek** [gas] Chevron/dsl, Shell [food] Applebee's, Carl's Jr, Casa Ramos, Chipotle Mexican, ChuckeCheese, Coldstone, Famous Dave's, Five Guys, Five Thai's, In-N-Out, Jack-in-the-Box, Jamba Juice, Jersey Mike's, Mazatlan Grill, McDonald's, MOD Pizza, Olive Garden, Outback Steaks, Panda Express, Panda Express, Red Lobster, Red Robin, Starbucks, Subway, Taco Bell [lodging] Motel 6, Red Lion Inn [other] AT&T, Barnes&Noble, Best Buy, BigLots, Costco, Dick's, FoodMaxx, Home Depot, JC Penney, Jo-Ann, Kohl's, Macy's, Michael's, Old Navy, O'Reilly Parts, PetCo, Petsmart, Schwab Tire, Target, TJ Maxx, Trader Joe's, Verizon, Walmart/McDonald's, WinCo Foods, World Mkt

REDDING

677	Cypress Ave, Hilltop Dr, Redding, E [gas] Chevron/dsl, Shell/dsl, Valero/dsl, Valero/dsl [food] Black Bear Diner, Burger King, Carl's Jr, Cattlemen's Rest., Coldstone, Del Taco, Denny's, Domino's, Gibbs Grille, Grand Buffet, IHOP, Jack-in-the-Box, KFC, Little Caesar's, Logan's Roadhouse, Marie Callender's, McDonald's, Papa Murphy's, Pizza Hut, Popeye's, Starbucks, Subway, Taco Bell, Togo's, Wendy's [lodging] Baymont Inn, Best Western+, Comfort Inn, Hampton Inn, Holiday Inn, La Quinta, Oxford Suites, Quality Inn, TownePlace Suites [other] 99c Store, AutoZone, Buick/Cadillac/GMC, Chevron/dsl, CVS Drug, Lowe's, Rite Aid, Ross, Safeway/gas, vet, Walgreens, W [gas] 76, Chevron/dsl, Mobil/dsl [food] Burrito Bandito, CA Cattle Rest., Denny's, Humble Joe's Chophouse, Lumberjack's Rest., RoundTable Pizza, Subway [lodging] Motel 6, Red Lion Inn, Vagabond Inn [other] America's Tire, Big O Tire, Chevrolet, Dodge, Ford/Lincoln, Honda, Kia, Nissan, Office Depot, Subaru, Toyota, U-Haul, URGENT CARE
675	Bechelli Lane, Churn Creek Rd, E [gas] Arco/dsl, Chevron/dsl, Valero [lodging] Super 8, W [gas] Chevron/Burger King/dsl [lodging] Hilton Garden

ANDERSON

673	Knighton Rd, E [gas] TA/Country Pride/Pizza Hut/Popeye's/dsl/LP/scales/24hr/@, W [other] JGW RV Park (3mi), Sacramento River RV Park (3mi)
670	Riverside Ave, E [food] Woodside Grill [lodging] Gaia Hotel, W [other] Camping World RV Ctr
668	Balls Ferry Rd, Anderson, E [gas] Shell/dsl, Valero/dsl [food] A&W/KFC, Burger King, Joe's Chophouse, Little Caesar's, McDonald's, Papa Murphy's, Peacock Chinese, Popeye's, Puerto Vallarta Mexican, RoundTable Pizza, Starbucks, Subway, Taco Bell [lodging] Best Western, Motel 6 [other] $Tree, Les Schwab Tire, NAPA, Rite Aid, Safeway/dsl, W [food] Players Pizza [other] O'Reilly Parts
667	CA 273, Factory Outlet Blvd, E [other] vet, W [gas] Arco/dsl, Chevron/dsl, Shell/dsl [food] Arby's, Jack-in-the-Box, Mary's Pizza, Panda Express, Sonic, Starbucks, Westside Pizza [lodging] Baymont Inn [other] $Tree, AT&T, Grocery Outlet, Shasta Outlets/famous brands, Tire Pros, Verizon, Walmart/Subway

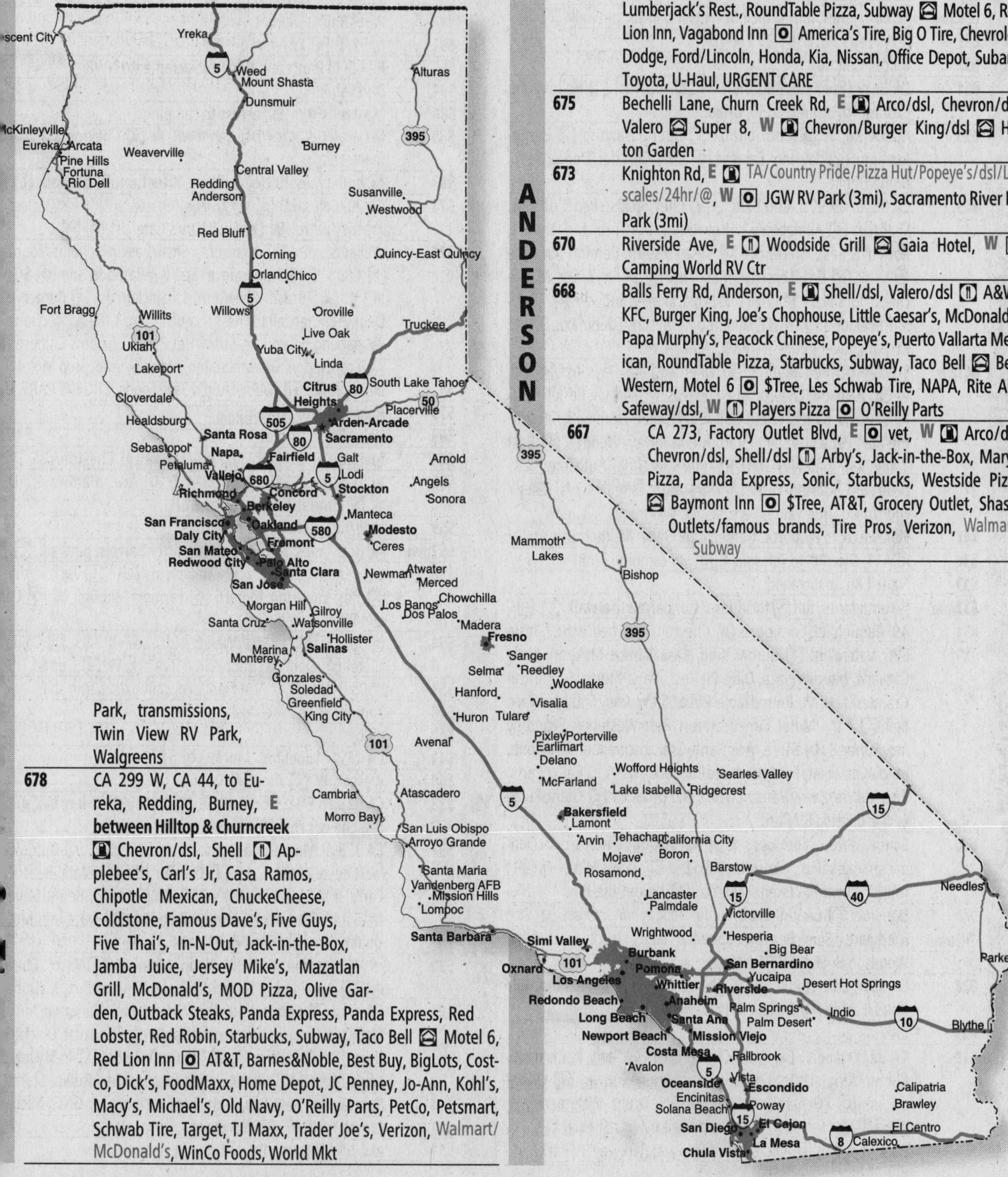

INTERSTATE 5 Cont'd

Exit #	Services
665	(from sb) Cottonwood, E Alamo Motel/RV park, Travelers Motel/RV Park
664	Gas Point Rd, to Balls Ferry, E Chevron/dsl/LP, Speedway/dsl Alamo Motel, Travelers Motel Alamo RV Park, auto repair, W Holiday/dsl, Sunshine/dsl Eagles Nest Pizza, Subway Ace Hardware, Holiday Foods, vet
662	Bowman Rd, to Cottonwood, E Chevron/dsl/24hr
660mm	**weigh sta both lanes**
659	Snively Rd, Auction Yard Rd, (Sunset Hills Dr from nb)
657	Hooker Creek Rd, Auction Yard Rd
656mm	**both lanes, full facilities, litter barrels, petwalk,**
653	Jellys Ferry Rd, E RV Park/LP
652	Wilcox Golf Rd
651	CA 36W (from sb), Red Bluff, W Arco/dsl Holiday Inn Express same as 650, UHaul
650	Adobe Rd, W Chevron/dsl Burrito Bandito Hampton Inn, Holiday Inn Express CHP, Chrysler/Dodge/Jeep, Home Depot
649	CA 36, to CA 99 S, Red Bluff, E Chevron/dsl, Red Bluff Gas, Shell/dsl Applebee's, Burger King, Del Taco, McDonald's, Rockin' R Rest., Starbucks Best Western, Comfort Inn, Motel 6, W Gas4Less/dsl, Mobil/dsl Denny's, Los Mariachis, Luigi's Pizza, RoundTable Pizza, Shari's, Subway Super 8, Travelodge AT&T, Durango RV Resort, Foodmaxx, O'Nite RV Park, River's Edge RV Park, Verizon, vet
647a b	S Main St, Red Bluff, E Valero/dsl Days Inn H, W Arco/dsl, Chevron/dsl, Shell/dsl Arby's, Baskin-Robbins, China Buffet, China Doll, Cozy Diner, Domino's, Jack-in-the-Box, Papa Murphy's, Starbucks, Subway, Wendy's Best Value Inn, Gateway Inn, Triangle Motel AutoZone, CVS Drug, GNC, Grocery Outlet, I-5 Tire/auto, O'Reilly Parts, Raley's Food/drug, True Value, Verizon, vet, Walgreens, Walmart
642	Flores Ave, to Proberta, Gerber, **1 mi** E Walmart Dist Ctr
636	rd A11, Gyle Rd, to Tehama, E RV camping (7mi)
633	Finnell Rd, to Richfield
632mm	**both lanes, full facilities, litter barrels, petwalk,**
631	A9, Corning Rd, Corning, E Chevron/dsl, Shell/dsl/LP, Tesla EVC, Valero/dsl Burger King, Casa Ramos Mexican, Little Caesar's, Marco's Pizza, Olive Pit Rest., Papa Murphy's, Rancho Grande Mexican, RoundTable Pizza, Starbucks, Subway, Taco Bell 7 Inn Motel, American Inn, Best Western+, Economy Inn, Super 8 $Tree, Ace Hardware, auto repair, AutoZone, Buick/Chevrolet, Ford, Heritage RV Park, NAPA, O'Reilly Parts, Rite Aid, Safeway, Verizon, West End Drug, W Giant Burger Corning RV Park
630	South Ave, Corning, E Loves/Denny's/dsl/LP/RV dump/scales/24hr, Petro/Iron Skillet/dsl/scales/24hr/ @, TA/Arby's/Subway/dsl/scales/24hr/@ Jack-in-the-Box, McDonald's CA Inn, Econolodge, Holiday Inn Express Ace Hardware, Blue Beacon, SpeedCo Lube, truck wash/lube, Woodson Br SRA/RV Park (6mi)
628	CA 99W, Liberal Ave, W Chevron/dsl/24hr Rolling Hills Hotel/Casino Rolling Hills RV Park
621	CA 7
619	CA 32, Orland, E Arco, Chevron/dsl Berry Patch Rest., Burger King, Little Caesar's, Starbucks, Subway Orlanda Inn $General, AutoZone, CVS Drug, Walgreens, W Pilot/Wendy's/PJ Fresh/dsl/scales/24hr, Shell/dsl I-5 Cafe, Taco Bell Old Orchard RV Park, Parkway RV Park
618	CA 16, E Shell/dsl El Potrero Mexican Orland $Tree, Grocery Outlet
614	CA 27
610	Artois
608mm	**both lanes, full facilities, litter barrels, petwalk,** RV dump
607	CA 39, Blue Gum Rd, Bayliss, **2 mi** E Blue Gum Motel
603	CA 162, to Oroville, Willows, E Arco, Chevron, Shell/ Black Bear Diner, Burger King, Casa Ramos, KFC, La C cada Mexican, McDonald's, RoundTable Pizza, Starbucks, S way, Taco Bell, Wong's Chinese Baymont Inn, Best W ern/RV parking, Holiday Inn Express, Motel 6, Super 8 $Tree, CHP, O'Reilly Parts, W Nancy's Café/24hr Park (8mi), Walmart
601	rd 57, E Chevron/dsl/24hr
595	Rd 68, to Princeton, E to Sacramento NWR
591	Delevan Rd
588	Maxwell (from sb), access to camping
586	Maxwell Rd, E Delevan NWR, W Chevron Maxv Inn/rest.
583	**both lanes, full facilities, litter barrels, petwalk,**
578	CA 20, Colusa, E Loves/Chester's/IHOP/dsl/scales/2 hwy patrol, W Shell/Orv's Cafe/dsl H
577	Williams, E Arco/dsl, Shell/Baskin-Robbins/Togo's Carl's Jr, Subway, Taco Bell Ramada Inn $Ge al, W 76/dsl, Chevron/dsl, Sinclair/dsl Burger K Denny's, Granzella's Rest., Louis Cairo's Rest., McDonal RV parking, Starbucks, Straw Hat Pizza, Williams Chinese R Econolodge, Granzella's Inn, Motel 6, StageStop Motel, T elers Inn H, NAPA, Shop'n Save Foods, URGENT CARE, U
575	Husted Rd, to Williams
569	Hahn Rd, to Grimes
567	frontage rd (from nb), to Arbuckle, W Chevron/dsl
566	to College City, Arbuckle, E Ace Hardware, US W Sinclair/dsl $General
559	Yolo/Colusa County Line Rd
557mm	**both lanes, full facilities, litter barrels, petwalk,**
556	E4, Dunnigan, E Chevron/dsl/LP Jack-in-the- Best Value Inn, Motel 6 Farmers Mkt Deli, W Ca er's RV Park/golf (1mi)
554	rd 8, E Pilot/Wendy's/dsl/scales/24hr Califo Motel Denny's, HappyTime RV Park, W United TP/
553	I-505 (from sb), to San Francisco, callboxes begin sb
548	Zamora, E Shell/dsl
542	Yolo
541	CA 16W, Woodland, **3 mi** W H
540	West St, W Arco Denny's
538	CA 113 N, E St, Woodland, E Valley Oaks Inn, W C dsl, Chevron/dsl Best Western
537	CA 113 S, Main St, to Davis (same as 536), E Buick/Ca lac/Chevrolet/GMC, W Chevron/dsl Black Bear Di Carl's Jr, Denny's, Dickey's BBQ, McDonald's, RoundTable za, Sonic, Starbucks, Subway, Taco Bell Days Inn, Mote Quality Inn $Tree, Food4Less
536	rd 102 (same as 537) **E on Main St** Arco, Chevr dsl Applebee's, Burger King, Jack-in-the-Box, McDona Subway Comfort Suites, Fairfield Inn, Hampton Inn, iday Inn Express America's Tire, Chevrolet/Buick/G Home Depot, Walmart, W Circle K/dsl In-N-Out, boy's Tacos, MOD Pizza, Panda Express, Red Robin, Starbu Subway Best Buy, Best Buy, Costco/gas, GNC, Micha Target, URGENT CARE, Verizon
531	rd 22, W Sacramento

RED BLUFF

CORNING

WILLIAMS

WOODLAND

CA

INTERSTATE 5 Cont'd

Exit #	Services
530mm	Sacramento River
529mm	sb, full facilities, litter barrels, petwalk
528	Airport Rd, E Arco
525b	CA 99, to CA 70, to Marysville, Yuba City
525a	Del Paso Rd, E Chevron A&W/KFC, BurgerIM, Chick-en'n Waffles, Denny's, IHOP, In-N-Out, Jack-in-the-box, Jersey Mike's, Jimmy John's, Malabar Rest., Panda Express, Panera Bread, Papa Murphy's, Pizza Guys, Sizzler, Sizzler, Taco Bell Hampton Inn, Hilton Garden, Holiday Inn Express, Homewood Suites Rite Aid, Safeway Foods/dsl, W Subway Sheraton Four Points Walgreens
524	Arena Blvd, E Huckleberry's, Papa John's, Subway Sleep Train Arena, W Panda Garden, RoundTable Pizza, Starbucks Jimboy's Tacos Bel-Air Food/Drug/dsl
522	I-80, E to Reno, W to San Francisco
521b	W El Camino Ave (from nb, no return), West El Camino, W Shell/dsl Carl's Jr, Jack-in-the-Box, Jamba Juice, Starbucks, Subway, Togo's/Baskin-Robbins Courtyard, Hilton Garden, Residence Inn, SpringHill Suites
521a	Garden Hwy, W Courtyard
520	Richards Blvd, E Chevron/dsl Denny's, McDonald's Governor's Inn, Hawthorn Suites, Surestay+, W Arco, Shell Nena's Mexican Best Western, Comfort Suites, Days Inn, La Quinta, Motel 6 waterfront park
519b	J St, Old Sacramento, E Holiday Inn, Vagabond Inn, W Embassy Suites Railroad Museum
519a	Q St, downtown, Sacramento, W Embassy Suites, to st capitol
518	US 50, CA 99, Broadway, E services downtown
516	Sutterville Rd, E 76/dsl, Chevron/dsl La Bou Cafe, Macau Cafe Sprouts Mkt, Wm Land Park, zoo
515	Fruitridge Rd, Seamas Rd
514	43rd Ave, Riverside Blvd (from sb), E 76/7-11
513	Florin Rd, E Arco, Chevron/dsl Carl's Jr, RoundTable Pizza, Starbucks $Tree, Bel Air Foods, CVS Drug, O'Reilly Parts, W Burger King, JimBoy's Tacos, L&L Hawaiian BBQ, Panda Garden, Shari's, Starbucks, Subway, Wingstop Marshall's, Nugget Mkt, Petco, Rite Aid
512	CA 160, Pocket Rd, Meadowview Rd, to Freeport, E Chevron/dsl, Shell/dsl Baskin Robbins/Togo's, IHOP, KFC, McDonald's, Starbucks, Wendy's AT&T, Home Depot, Schwab Tire, Staples, vet, Walgreens
510	Cosumnes River Blvd, E Chick-fil-A, Chipotle, El Pollo Loco, Habit Burger, In-N-Out, Jamba Juice, Jersey Mike's, Noodles, Panda Express, Panera Bread, Pieology, Starbucks AT&T, Dick's, GNC, Hobby Lobby, Old Navy, Petsmart, Ross, Verizon, Walmart
508	Laguna Blvd, E 76/Circle K/dsl/LP, Chevron/Taco Bell/dsl, Shell A&W/KFC, Starbucks, Subway, Wendy's Extended Stay America, Hampton Inn Jiffy Lube, Laguna Auto Repair, U-Haul
506	Elk Grove Blvd, E Arco/dsl, Chevron/dsl, Shell/dsl Carl's Jr, Flaming Grill Burger, Pete's Grill, Wasabi Grill Holiday Inn Express vet
504	Hood Franklin Rd
498	Twin Cities Rd, to Walnut Grove
493	Walnut Grove Rd, Thornton, E CFN/dsl, Chevron/Subway/dsl
490	Peltier Rd
487	Turner Rd
485	CA 12, Lodi, E FLYING J/Denny's/Subway/dsl/scales/24hr, Arco/dsl, Chevron/dsl, Loves/Arby's/dsl/scales/24hr,

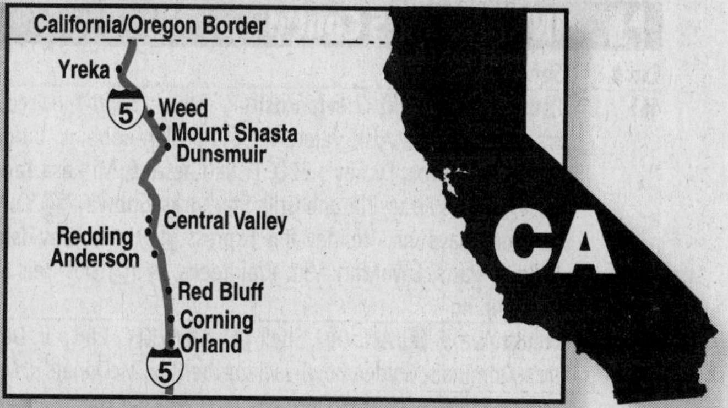

CA

STOCKTON

Exit #	Services
485	Continued Shell/dsl, Sinclair/Rocky's Rest./dsl/scales/24hr Burger King, Carl's Jr, McDonald's, Starbucks, Tortilla Flats Best Western, Microtel Blue Beacon, Flag City RV Resort, Profleet Truck-lube, W KOA (5mi)
481	Eight Mile Rd, W Arco/dsl, Chevron/Jack-in-the-Box/dsl Baskin-Robbins, Chipotle, El Pollo Loco, GK Mongolian BBQ, Hawaiian BBQ, Jamba Juice, McDonald's, MooMoo's Burgers, Panda Express, Panera Bread, RoundTable Pizza, Sonic, Starbucks, Subway, Sugar Mediterranean, Wendy's $Tree, AAA, AT&T, Jo-Ann Fabrics, Kohl's, Lowe's, Mercedes, Petsmart, Ross, Target, Verizon, Walmart/McDonald's, World Mkt
478	Hammer Lane, Stockton, E 76/dsl, Arco Adalberto's Mexican, Carl's Jr, KFC, Little Caesar's, McDonald's, Subway AutoZone, Food Source, Walgreens, W Chevron/dsl, QuikStop Jack-in-the-Box, Nations Burger, Taco Bell
477	Benjamin Holt Dr, Stockton, E Arco, Chevron/dsl Pizza Guys Motel 6 QwikStop, W 7-11 Eddie's Pizza, Lumber Jack's Rest., Lyon's Rest., Mandarin Villa, McDonald's, Starbucks, Subway/TCBY Ace Hardware, Marina Foods, vet
476	March Lane, Stockton, E 7-11 Applebee's, Carl's Jr, Chick-fil-A, Denny's, Domino's, El Torito, Jack-in-the-Box, McDonald's, Olive Garden, Red Lobster, Taco Bell, Toot Sweets Bakery, Wendy's Hilton, Motel 6 CVS Drug, Marshall's, SMart Foods, W 76/dsl Habit Burger, IHOP, In-N-Out, Jamba Juice, Krispy Kreme, RoundTable Pizza, Starbucks, Subway, Wong's Chinese Courtyard, Extended Stay America, La Quinta, Residence Inn Home Depot
475	Alpine Ave, Country Club Blvd, same as 474 b
474b	Country Club Blvd (from nb), E Mobil/dsl, W 7-11, Shell/dsl Mtn Mike's Pizza, Papa Murphy's, Subway BigLots, Safeway/gas
474a	Monte Diablo Ave
473	Pershing Ave (from nb), W Arco Red Roof Inn
472	CA 4 E, to CA 99, Fresno Ave, downtown
471	CA 4 W, Charter Way, E Arco, Chevron/dsl, Shell Burger King, Denny's, Little Caesar's, McDonald's $General Mkt, O'Reilly Parts, W 76/dsl/scales/24hr, Valero/Subway Carl Jr, Jack-in-the-Box, Taco Bell Motel 6 Les Schwab Tire, truck repair
470	8th St, Stockton, W CA Stop/dsl, Shell/dsl I-5 Inn
469	Downing Ave, W China Express, Louie's Chinese, Mtn Mike's Pizza, Papa Murphy's, Subway $Tree, AutoZone, Food4Less/gas
468	French Camp, E 76/Togo's/dsl Pan Pacific RV Ctr, W H
467b	Mathews Rd, E J&L Mkt/dsl tires/repair, W H
467a	El Dorado St (from nb)
465	Roth Rd, Sharpe Depot, E FL/dsl, FLYING J/PJ Fresh/dsl/scales/24hr Freightliner, Kenworth, truck/rv repair

[gas] = gas [food] = food [lodging] = lodging [other] = other [Rs] = rest stop Copyright 2020 - The Next EXI

INTERSTATE 5 Cont'd

WESTLEY

Exit #	Services
463	Lathrop Rd, E Chevron/dsl/LP, Joe's Trkstp/Togo's/dsl/scales, PowerMart/dsl, Valero/dsl Baskin-Robbins, Burger King, China Wok, Dickey's BBQ, Little Caesar's, Mi Kasa Japanese, Milan's Pizza, Platano Grill, Starbucks, Subway Comfort Inn, Days Inn, Holiday Inn Express Harley-Davidson, O'Reilly Parts, SaveMart Mkt, Walgreens, W Dos Reis CP, RV camping
462	Louise Ave, E Arco/dsl, Shell A&W/KFC, Carl's Jr, Denny's, Domino's, Golden Bowl, Jack-in-the-Box, McDonald's, Mtn Mike's Pizza, Popeye's, Quiznos, Taco Bell Hampton Inn, Quality Inn, W Mossdale CP, Target
461	CA 120, to Sonora, Manteca, E Oakwood Lake Resort Camping, to Yosemite
460	Mossdale Rd, E Chevron/dsl, W fruit stand/cafe
458b	I-205, to Oakland (from sb, no return)
458a	11th St, to Tracy, Defense Depot, 2 mi W gas/dsl/food
457	Kasson Rd, to Tracy, W Valley Pacific/dsl
452	CA 33 S, Vernalis
449b a	CA 132, to Modesto, E The Orchard Campground
446	I-580 (from nb, exits left, no return)
445mm	full facilities, litter barrels, petwalk, RV dump, Westley Rest Area both lanes
441	Ingram Creek, Howard Rd, Westley, E 76/dsl, Chevron/dsl, Joe's Trvl Plaza/Denny's/dsl/scales/24hr, Westley Triangle TruckStp/dsl Carl's Jr, McDonald's, Subway Days Inn, EconoLodge, Holiday Inn Express, Motel 6, W Shell/dsl truck repair
434	Sperry Ave, Del Puerto, Patterson, E 76/Subway/dsl, Arco/dsl, Chevron, FLYING J/Wendy's/PJ Fresh/dsl/scales/24hr, Mobil/dsl, Valero/dsl A&W/KFC, Apricot Wood BBQ, Carl's Jr, Denny's, El Rosal Mexican, Golden Lion Chinese, Jack-in-the-Box, Pizza Factory, Starbucks Best Western+, Hampton Inn Kit Fox RV Park
430mm	vista point nb
428	Fink Rd, Crow's Landing
423	Stuhr Rd, Newman, 5 mi E food, lodging, RV camping
422mm	vista point sb
418	CA 140E, Gustine, E Chevron/dsl, Sinclair/dsl
409	weigh sta both lanes
407	CA 33, Santa Nella, E Arco, Loves/Del Taco/dsl/scales/24hr, TA/Shell/Country Pride/Popeye's/dsl/scales/24hr/@ Andersen's Rest., Carl's Jr, Subway, Wendy's Best Western/Andersen's, Quality Inn, W 76/dsl, Chevron, Rotten Robbie/dsl/scales, Valero/Circle K/dsl Denny's, In-N-Out, McDonald's, Panda Express, Pizza Factory, Starbucks, Taco Bell Hotel Mission de Oro, Motel 6 Santa Nella RV Park
403b a	CA 152, Los Banos, 6 mi E H, 1 mi W Petro/Shell/diner/dsl/24hr Motel 6 KOA
391	CA 165N, Mercy Springs Rd, E H, W Shell
388	vista point (from nb)
386mm	Rs both lanes, full facilities, litter barrels, petwalk
385	Nees Ave, to Firebaugh, W Chevron/CFN/Subway/dsl/scales
379	Shields Ave, to Mendota
372	Russell Ave
368	Panoche Rd, W 76/dsl, Chevron/McDonald's, Mobil/Wayback Burger/dsl, Shell/dsl, Valero/dsl Subway Best Western country store
365	Manning Ave, to San Joaquin
357	Kamm Ave
349	CA 33 N, Derrick Ave

SANTA NELLA

BUTTONWILLOW

Exit #	Services
337	CA 33 S, CA 145 N, to Coalinga
334	CA 198, to Lemoore, Huron, E Shell/Subway/dsl/24hr, Te EVC Harris Ranch Inn/rest., W 76/dsl, Arco/dsl, Ch ron/dsl, Valero/Subway/dsl Burger King, Carl's Jr, D ny's, McDonald's, Taco Bell Best Western, Motel 6, Tr elodge H, auto repair
325	Jayne Ave, to Coalinga, W Shell/Baja Fresh/dsl, Val Sommerville RV Park/LP H
320mm	Rs both lanes, full facilities, litter barrels, petwalk
319	CA 269, Lassen Ave, to Avenal, W Hillcrest TP/76/Subw dsl/scales/24hr
309	CA 41, Kettleman City, E 76/Subway/TCBY, CFN/dsl, Ch ron/McDonald's, Mobil/Starbucks/dsl/24hr, Shell/Baja Fre dsl, Tesla EVC, Valero/dsl Carl's Jr, Denny's, In-N-Out, Ja in-the-Box, Little Caesar's, Pizza Hut/Taco Bell, Wienerschni Best Western, Quality Inn Bravo Farms Mercantile
305	Utica Ave
288	Twisselman Rd
278	CA 46, Lost Hills, E Buford Star Mart/dsl/LP to Kern NW W 76/Quiznos, Arco/DQ/dsl, Chevron/dsl, Love Arby's/dsl/scales/24hr, Mobil/McDonald's/dsl/LP, Pilo Wendy's/dsl/scales/24hr, Shell/Pizza Hut/Subway/Taco B dsl, Valero/7-11/dsl Carl's Jr, Denny's, Jack-in-the- Days Inn, Motel 6 KOA, Royal Truck Wash/lube
268	Lerdo Hwy, to Shafter
262	7th Standard Rd, Rowlee Rd, to Buttonwillow
259mm	Buttonwillow Rest Area both lanes, full facilities, litter b rels, petwalk
257	CA 58, to Bakersfield, Buttonwillow, E 76/Circle K/Quizn dsl, Arco/dsl, Chevron/dsl, Shell/dsl, Speedy Fuel/dsl/wash, Mobil/Pizza Hut/Taco Bell/dsl/scales/24hr/@ Carl's Jr, Donald's, Starbucks, Subway, Tita's Mexican, Willow Ra BBQ California Inn, Buttonwillow Inn, Motel 6, Vagab Inn Castro's Tire/Truckwash, W Valero/dsl
253	Stockdale Hwy, E Chevron/Subway/dsl, Shell/dsl/2 IHOP, Jack-in-the-Box Best Western, Vagabond W Tule Elk St Reserve
246	CA 43, to Taft, Maricopa, to Buena Vista RA
244	CA 119, to Pumpkin Center, E Mobil/dsl, W Arco/ scales, Chevron/dsl/LP
239	CA 223, Bear Mtn Blvd, to Arvin, E Bear Mtn RV Res W RV camping, to Buena Vista RA
234	Old River Rd
228	Copus Rd, E Murray Farms Mkt
225	CA 166, to Mettler, W Chevron/Subway/dsl
221	I-5 and CA 99 (from nb, exits left, no return)
219b a	Laval Rd, Wheeler Ridge, E Shell/dsl, TA/Shell/Popey Subway/scales/@ Baja Fresh, Black Bear Diner, Bu King, Carl's Jr, Habit Burger, Pieology, Pizza Hut, Starbu Taco Bell Hampton Inn, Microtel Blue Beacon, Te Outlets/famous brands, W 76/Subway/dsl, Mobil/ Petro/Iron Skillet/Subway/dsl/scales/24hr/@, Tesla EVC by's, Baskin-Robbins, Chipotle Mexican, Del Taco, Denn Firehouse, In-N-Out, McDonald's, Panda Express, Starbu Wendy's Best Western
218	truck weigh sta sb
215	Grapevine, E Valero/dsl Denny's, Jack-in-the- W Shell/dsl Don Perico Grill Days Inn
210	Ft Tejon Rd, W to Ft Tejon Hist SP, towing/repair
209mm	brake check area nb
207	Lebec Rd, W antiques, towing, USPO

FT TEJON

INTERSTATE 5 Cont'd

Exit #	Services
206mm	**both lanes, full facilities, petwalk, , litter barrels, vending**
205	Frazier Mtn Park Rd, **W** FLYING J/dsl/LP/24hr/@, Arco, Arco/dsl, Chevron/dsl, Mobil/Subway/dsl/24hr Jack-in-the-Box, Los Pinos Mexican Holiday Inn Express, Motel 6 auto repair/towing, Carquest, to Mt Pinos RA
204	Tejon Pass, elev 4144, **truck brake insp sb**
202	Gorman Rd, to Hungry Valley, **E** 76/dsl, Chevron/dsl/LP Carl's Jr, El Grullense, Ranch House Rest. Motel 6, **W** Shell/dsl McDonald's auto repair
199	CA 138 E, Lancaster Rd, to Palmdale
198b a	Quail Lake Rd, CA 138 E (from nb)
195	Smokey Bear Rd, Pyramid Lake, **E** Pyramid Lake RV Park
191	Vista del Lago Rd, **W** visitors ctr
186mm	**brake inspection area sb, motorist callboxes begin sb**
184mm	**brake check sb**
183	Templin Hwy, **W** Ranger Sta, RV camping
176b a	Lake Hughes Rd, Parker Rd, Castaic, **E** 7-11, Arco/dsl, Castaic Trkstp/dsl/24hr, Pilot/PJ Fresh/dsl/scales/24hr/@, Shell/dsl Cajun Chicken, Carl's Jr, Denny's, Domino's, El Pollo Loco, Fosters Freeze, McDonald's, Mike's Diner, Panda Express, Pizza Factory, Red Dot Pizza, Starbucks, Subway, Waba Grill, Wok's Chinese Days Inn, Rodeway Inn $Tree, Benny's Tire/repair, Castaic Inn, Castaic Lake RV Park, O'Reilly Parts, to Castaic Lake, vet, **W** 76/repair, Chargepoint EVC, Mobil Jack-in-the-Box, Taco Bell auto repair, Walgreens
173	Hasley Canyon Rd, **W** Pizza Hut, Subway Ralph's Foods
172	CA 126 W, to Ventura, **E** Courtyard, Embassy Suites
171mm	**weigh sta nb**
171	Rye Canyon Rd (from sb), **W** Arco/dsl, Conserv/dsl Del Taco, Jack-in-the-Box, Jimmy Dean's, Starbucks, Tommy's Burgers Six Flags
170	CA 126 E, Magic Mtn Pkwy, Saugus, **E** Azul Tequila Mexican, Denny's, Rustic Eatery, Sam's Grille, Starbucks Best Western/rest., Holiday Inn Express, **W** Chevron/dsl, Shell/dsl Coffee Bean, McDonald's, Red Lobster, Wendy's Hilton Garden Six Flags of CA
169	Valencia Blvd, **W** Fat Burger, Magic Pizza, Panda Express, Robeks, Starbucks, Subway Verizon
168	McBean Pkwy, **E** H, **W** Cabo Cabana, Chili's, ChuckeCheese, ClaimJumper, Jamba Juice, Jersey Mikes Subs, Mama Mia Italian, MOD Pizza, Pick Up Stix, Starbucks, Subway, Urbane Cafe Michael's, Old Navy, Verizon, Vons Foods, WorldMkt
167	Lyons Ave, Pico Canyon Rd, **E** 76/Circle K/dsl, Chevron/dsl, Shell/dsl Burger King, Wendy's, **W** Arco, Shell/dsl Cabo Cabana, Carl's Jr, Chuy's, Coco's, Del Taco, Denny's, El Pollo Loco, Fortune Express Chinese, IHOP, In-N-Out, Jack-in-the-Box, Jersey Mike's, McDonald's, Outback Steaks, Spumoni Italian, Taco Bell, Wood Ranch BBQ, Yamato Japanese Comfort Suites, Extended Stay America, Fairfield Inn, Hampton Inn, La Quinta, Residence Inn AT&T, Camping World RV Ctr, GNC, Jiffy Lube, Marshall's, Old Navy, Petsmart, Ralph's Foods, Ross, Staples, SteinMart, Walmart/McDonald's
166	Calgrove Blvd
162	CA 14 N, to Palmdale
161b	Balboa Blvd (from sb)
160a	I-210, to San Fernando, Pasadena
159	Roxford St, Sylmar, **E** Chevron/dsl, Mobil/dsl Denny's/24hr, McDonald's Good Nite Inn, Motel 6

ARLETA

SUN VALLEY

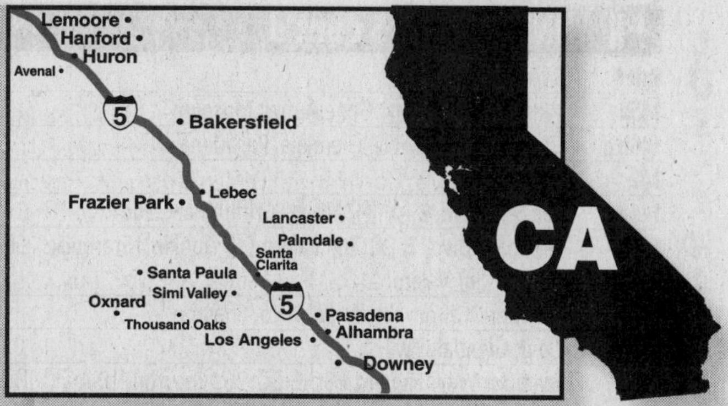

Exit #	Services
158	I-405 S (from sb, no return)
157b a	SF Mission Blvd, Brand Blvd, **E** 76, Arco, Chevron/dsl, Mobil/dsl, Shell Carl's Jr, In-N-Out, Little Caesar's, New Asia, Pollo Gordo, Popeye's, Subway, Taco Bell, Winchell's H, Honda, Rite Aid, Vallarta Mkt
156b	CA 118
156a	Paxton St, Brand Ave (from nb), **E** G&M/dsl 7-11
155b	Van Nuys Blvd (no EZ nb return), **E** Arco Jack-in-the-Box, KFC/LJ Silver, McDonald's, Pizza Hut, Popeye's Discount Parts, USPO, **W** Domino's auto repair
155a	Terra Bella St (from nb), **E** USA
154	Osborne St, to Arleta, **E** Arco, Chevron/dsl AutoZone, BigLots, Food4Less, Ross, Target, **W** 76, Mobil/Burger King 7-11
153b	CA 170 (from sb), to Hollywood
152a	Sheldon St, **E** Big Jim's Rest. H, auto repair, Big O Parts
152	Lankershim Blvd, Tuxford, **E** Superfine/dsl/scales
151	Penrose St
150b	Sunland Blvd, Sun Valley, **E** 76/dsl, Mobil Acapulco Rest., Carl's Jr, El Pollo Loco, Old Time Burger, Papa John's, Quiznos, Subway, Town Café, Yoshinoya Economy Inn $Tree, 7-11, Grocery Outlet, Sunland Produce, **W** Chevron/7-11, Shell McDonald's, Starbucks
150a	GlenOaks Blvd (from nb), **E** Arco/dsl Willows Motel
149	Hollywood Way, **W** Shell/dsl , U-Haul
148	Buena Vista St, **E** Hampton Inn, **W** 76/dsl Jack-in-the-Box Quality Inn, Ramada Inn
147	Scott Rd, to Burbank, **E** Sevan/dsl, **W** HomeTown Buffet, Jamba Juice, Krispy Kreme, Olive Garden, Outback Steaks, Panda Express, Sharky's Mexican, Starbucks, Wendy's Courtyard, Extended Stay America Best Buy, Lowe's, Marshall's, Michael's, REI, Staples, Target, Verizon
146b	Burbank Blvd, **E** 76/repair Baskin-Robbins, Buffalo Wild Wings, CA Pizza Kitchen, Carl's Jr, Chevy's Mexican, Chipotle, ChuckECheese's, Corner Cafe, El Pollo Loco, Harry's Rest., Hooters, IHOP, In-N-Out, Islands Burger, Jersey Mike's, McDonald's, Pizza Hut, Popeye's, Robek's Juice, Shakey's Pizza, Starbucks, Starbucks, Subway, Taco Bell, Tommy's Burgers, Yoshinoya, Zankou Chicken Barnes&Noble, CVS Drug, IKEA, Macy's, Office Depot, Old Navy, Ralph's Foods, Ross, Sprouts Mkt, **W** McDonald's, Subway Costco/gas, Discount Tire, Walmart
146a	Olive Ave, Verdugo, **E** BJ's Rest., Black Angus Holiday Inn USPO, **W** H, 7-11, Chevrolet, Metro RV Ctr
145b	Alameda Ave, **E** Chevron Baskin-Robbins/Togo's, Habit Burger, Starbucks CarMax, CVS Drug, Home Depot, IKEA, Ralph's Foods, Trader Joes, Walgreens, **W** 76/dsl, Arco, Shell Burbank Inn U-Haul

= gas = food = lodging = other = rest stop

CA

LOS ANGELES AREA

INTERSTATE 5 Cont'd

Exit #	Services
145a	Western Ave, W Gene Autrey Museum
144b a	CA 134, Ventura Fwy, Glendale, Pasadena
142	Colorado St
141a	Los Feliz Blvd, E H, W Griffith Park, zoo
140b	Glendale Blvd, E 76, Valero Dunkin', Starbucks, Subway, W Valero
140a	Fletcher Dr (from sb), W Arco, Chevron
139b a	CA 2, Glendale Fwy
138	Stadium Way, Figueroa St, E 76, Chevron, USA IHOP, McDonald's Home Depot, W to Dodger Stadium
137b a	CA 2, Glendale Fwy, W 76
136b	Broadway St (from sb), W 76
136a	Main St, E 76, Chevron/24hr Chinatown Express, Jack-in-the-Box, McDonald's H
135c	I-10 W (from nb), Mission Rd (from sb), E Jack-in-the-Box, McDonald's H, W 76/dsl
135b	Cesar Chavez Ave, W H
135a	4th St, Soto St, E Sinclair/dsl city park, W 76/dsl
134b	Ca 60 E (from sb), Soto St (from nb)
134a	CA 60 W, Santa Monica Fwy
133	Euclid Ave (from sb), Grand Vista (from nb), W Mobil
132	Calzona St, Indiana St, E Arco/dsl
131b	Indiana St (from nb), E Arco/dsl, Valero/dsl
131a	Olympic Blvd, E H, W Jack-in-the-Box, King Taco
130c b	I-710 (exits left from nb), to Long Beach, Eastern Ave, E McDonald's
130a	Triggs St (from sb), E outlet W Denny's/24hr Destiny Inn
129	Atlantic Blvd N, Eastern Ave (from sb), E Carl's Jr, Chipotle, Panda Express, Starbucks, Subway Doubletree Hyundai, outlets/famous brands, W Denny's, Steven's Steaks
128b	Washington Blvd, Commerce, E Chevron/dsl/repair/ 24hr McDonald's Crowne Plaza Hotel/casino, Doubletree Costco/gas, outlets/famous brands, W Arco Del Taco, Subway
128a	Garfield Blvd, E Crown Plaza/casino Home Depot, Office Depot, W 76
126b	Slauson Ave, Montebello, E Shell/dsl, Valero/dsl Mollie's Burger, Ozzie's Diner, Starbucks Quality Inn, Travelodge, W Arco Denny's Motel 6, Ramada Inn
126a	Paramount Blvd, Downey, E Shell/Jack-in-the-Box/dsl
125	CA 19 S, Lakewood Blvd, Rosemead Blvd, E Arco, Mobil Arthurs Cafe, Sam's Burgers, Starbucks EconoLodge, Guesthouse Inn, W Chris&Pitt's BBQ, Golden Corral, McDonald's, Subway, Taco Bell, Toppings Pizza Ralph's Foods
124	I-605
123	Florence Ave, to Downey, E Mobil, W Honda, repair
122	Imperial Hwy, Pioneer Blvd, E Chevron Applebee's, Habit Burgers, IHOP, Jack-in-the-Box, Jimmy John's, McDonald's, Panda Express, Pizza Hut, Subway, Wendy's, Wood Grill Buffet O'Reilly Parts, Rite Aid, Target, USPO, W 7-11 Alberts Mexican, Denny's, Panda King, Pizza Hut, Rally's, Shakey's Pizza, Wienerschnitzel Imperial Inn, Keystone Motel, Motel 6 Toyota, Walmart
121	San Antonio Dr, to Norwalk Blvd, E IHOP, Jack-in-the-Box, McDonald's, Outback Steaks, Starbucks, Wood Grill Buffet Doubletree Inn Rite Aid, Target, W Shell auto repair
120b	Firestone Blvd (exits left from nb)

NORWALK

ANAHEIM

Exit #	Services
120a	Rosecrans Ave, E 76/7-11/dsl Casa Adelita, Ji Burgers, KFC, Little Caesar's, Starbucks, Subway W Arco/24hr Guesthouse Inn El Monte RV Ctr
119	Carmenita Rd, Buena Park, E Arco Burger King F Trucks, Lowe's, W Galaxy Burgers Budget Inn, Dyna Suites
118	Valley View Blvd, E Arco/dsl In-N-Out, Northwo Inn, Starbucks, Subway, Wendy's Extended Stay Amer Holiday Inn Select, Residence Inn, W Thompson's RV Ct Camping World
117	Artesia Blvd, Knott Ave, E Chevron Extended S America CarMax, W Knotts Berry Farm, to Camp World RV Ctr
116	CA 39, Beach Blvd, E Chevron Travelodge BM Buick/GMC, CarMax, Chevrolet, Honda, Mercedes, Nissan, Te Toyota, W Chevron Arby's, Black Angus, Denny's, F druckers, KFC, Pizza Hut, Subway, Wendy's Hilton, Holi Inn H, Stater Bros, Target, to Knotts Berry Farm, Verizon
115	Manchester (from nb), same as 116
114b	CA 91 E, Riverside Fwy, E to
114a	Magnolia Ave, Orangethorpe Ave, E Mobil/dsl Bu King, Burger Town, Taco Bell 7-11, Harley-Davidson
113c	CA 91 W (from nb)
113b a	Brookhurst St, LaPalma, E Chevron/dsl Subw W Arco, Texaco/dsl Burger King, Carl's Jr, S bucks Home Depot, Staples
112	Euclid St, E Arco Happy Dragon, IHOP, Marie Cal der's, McDonald's, Rubio's, Starbucks, Subway, Taco Bell, W dy's AAA, El Super, GNC, Old Navy, PetCo, Ross, TJ Ma Verizon, Walmart, W 76, Mobil Charley's Subs, D ny's, KFC/LJ Silver, Subway, Wok Experience Aldi Foo Target, Verizon
111	Lincoln Ave, to Anaheim, E La Villa Mexican, Ruby's Di Starbucks vet
110b	Ball Rd (from sb), E 7-11, Chevron/dsl, Shell Bu King, Carolina's Italian, El Pollo Loco, KFC, McDonald's, Shak Pizza, Starbucks, Subway, Taco Bell Best Value Inn, D Inn, Frontier Inn, Sheraton Anaheim RV, Traveler's W RV Park, W Arco/24hr, Shell/dsl Best Western, Bud Inn, Holiday Inn, Majestic Garden Hotel, Staybridge Suites, per 8, Travelodge Disneyland, USPO
110a	Harbor Blvd, E Chevron, Shell Shakey's Pizza, Starbu Taco Bell Days Inn, Frontier, Ramada Anaheim Ha RV Park, **0-2 mi** W Captain Kidd's, Coldstone, Dennys, IH McDonald's, Mimi's Cafe, Mortons Steaks, Panera Bread, T Roma's Anaheim Resort, Best Western+, Camelot Inn, Ca Cane Inn, Castle Inn Suites, Clarion, Courtyard, Del Sol Inn, F field Inn, Hampton Inn, Hilton Garden, Howard Johnson, H House, ParkVue Inn, Portofino Inn, Ramada Inn, Red Lion, Sh aton, Travelodge, Tropicana Inn multiple hotels & rest rants, same as 109, to Disneyland
109	Katella Ave, Disney Way, E Arco Baskin-Robbins, Ca Jr, Denny's, McDonald's, Panda Express, Starbucks, Subway, go's TownePlace Suites Angels Stadium, W Ch ron Bubba Gump Shrimp, CA Pizza Kitchen, Cheesec Factory, McCormick&Schmick, PF Chang's, Roy Roy's, S way Best Value Inn, Cambria, Comfort Inn, Desert Pa Suites, Extended Stay America, Hilton, Hotel Indigo, H House, Kings Inn, Little Boy Blue, Marriott, Peacock Suites, mada Inn, Residence Inn, Riviera Motel, SpringHill Suites, S bridge Suites, Worldmark, Wyndham Garden 7-11, CVS Disneyland

INTERSTATE 5 Cont'd

Exit #	Services
107c	St Coll Blvd, City Drive, E Del Taco Embassy Suites, W Alo Hotel, Ayres Hotel, Doubletree Hotel
107b a	CA 57 N, Chapman Ave, E Burger King, Del Taco, Denny's, Jack-in-the-Box, Waba Grill Motel 6, W Chevron Krispy Kreme, Lucille's BBQ, Starbucks, Taco Bell, Wendy's Ayres Inn, DoubleTree H, Best Buy
106	CA 22 W (from nb), Garden Grove Fwy, Bristol St
105b	N Broadway, Main St, E 7-11 Baskin-Robbins, CA Pizza Kitchen, Carl's Jr, Chipotle, Corner Bakery Cafe, Habit Burgers, Jamba Juice, Olive Garden, Papa Johns, Polly's Café, Rubio's Grill, Starbucks, Subway, Taco Bell, Togo's Days Inn, Red Roof Inn H, Barnes&Noble, CVS Drug, JC Penney, Macy's, Staples, Verizon, W Golden West Motel, Travel Inn Bowers Museum
105a	17th St, E 76/dsl/24hr Hometown Buffet, IHOP, McDonald's Chevrolet, CVS Drug, same as 104b, Walgreens, W Chevron YumYum Donuts 7-11
104b	Santa Ana Blvd, Grand Ave, E Gavilan, Hometown Buffet, IHOP, KFC/LJ Silver, Marie Callender, McDonald's, Popeye's, Starbucks, Subway, Taco Bell, Taco Sinaloa, Waba Grill $Tree, AT&T, CVS Drug, O'Reilly Parts, Target, vet, Walgreens, W Kia
104a	(103c from nb), 4th St, 1st St, to CA 55 N, E Chevron, Shell, US Gas Del Taco
103b	CA 55 S, to Newport Beach
103a	CA 55 N (from nb), to Riverside
102	Newport Ave (from sb), E Arby's, Jack-in-the-Box, W Arco Carl's Jr, Domino's, Little Caesar's American Tire Depot
101b	Red Hill Ave, E Mobil/dsl, Shell/repair Del Taco, Denny's, Starbucks, Wendy's Key Inn BigLots, U-Haul, W Arco/24hr, Chevron/24hr, Valero Pizza Shack, Taco Bell 7-11, Stater Bros
101a	Tustin Ranch Rd, E McDonald's Acura, Buick/GMC, Cadillac, Chrysler/Dodge/Jeep, Costco, Ford/Lincoln, Hyundai, Infiniti, Lexus, Mazda, Nissan, Toyota
100	Jamboree Rd, E Shell Baja Fresh, BJ's Rest., Boston Mkt, Burger King, CA Pizza, Carl's Jr, Chick-fil-A, Corner Bakery, Daphne's Greek, DQ, El Pollo Loco, In-N-Out, Islands Burger, Lazy Dog Cafe, Macaroni Grill, Miguel's Mexican, Panda Express, Panera Bread, Pick-up Stix, Rubio's, Starbucks, Subway, Taco Bell, Taco Rosa AAA, AT&T, Barnes&Noble, Best Buy, Costco, Dick's, Home Depot, Old Navy, Petsmart, Ralph's Foods, REI, Rite Aid, Ross, Sprouts Mkt, Target, TJ Maxx, Verizon
99	Culver Dr, E Shell/24hr vet, W Buffalo Wild Wings, Domino's
97	Jeffrey Rd, E Arco Baskin-Robbins, Juice-it-Up, Starbucks, Subway Albertson's, Kohl's, W 76/dsl China Garden, Thai Cafe 99 Ranch Mkt, vet
96	Sand Canyon Ave, Old Towne, W 76/dsl Denny's, Jack-in-the-Box, Knowlwood Burgers La Quinta H
95	CA 133 (toll), Laguna Fwy, N to Riverside, S Laguna Beach
94b	Alton Pkwy, E Shell/Subway/dsl Carl's Jr, Starbucks Extended Stay America Costco/gas, Office Depot, Walmart, W Brio, CA Pizza, Capital Grill, Cheesecake Factory, Chipotle Mexican, Dave&Buster's, Johnny Rockets, Panda Express, PF Chang's, Pieology, Ruby's Diner, Starbucks, Wahoo's Fish Tacos, Wood Ranch, Yardhouse Rest. Doubletree Inn Barnes&Noble, Nordstrom, Old Navy, Target
94a	I-405 N (from nb)

LAGUNA HILLS

MISSION VIEJO

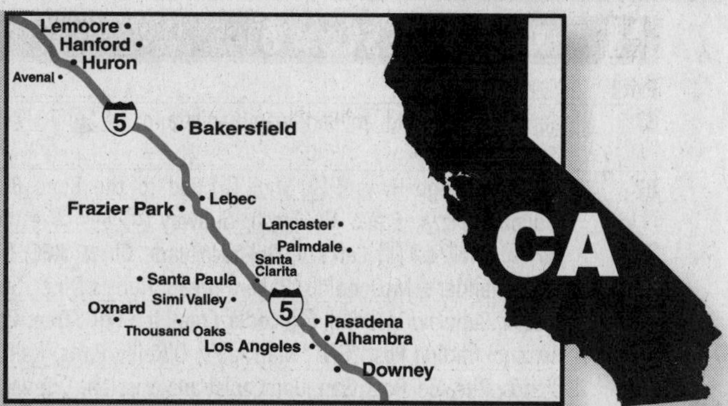

CA

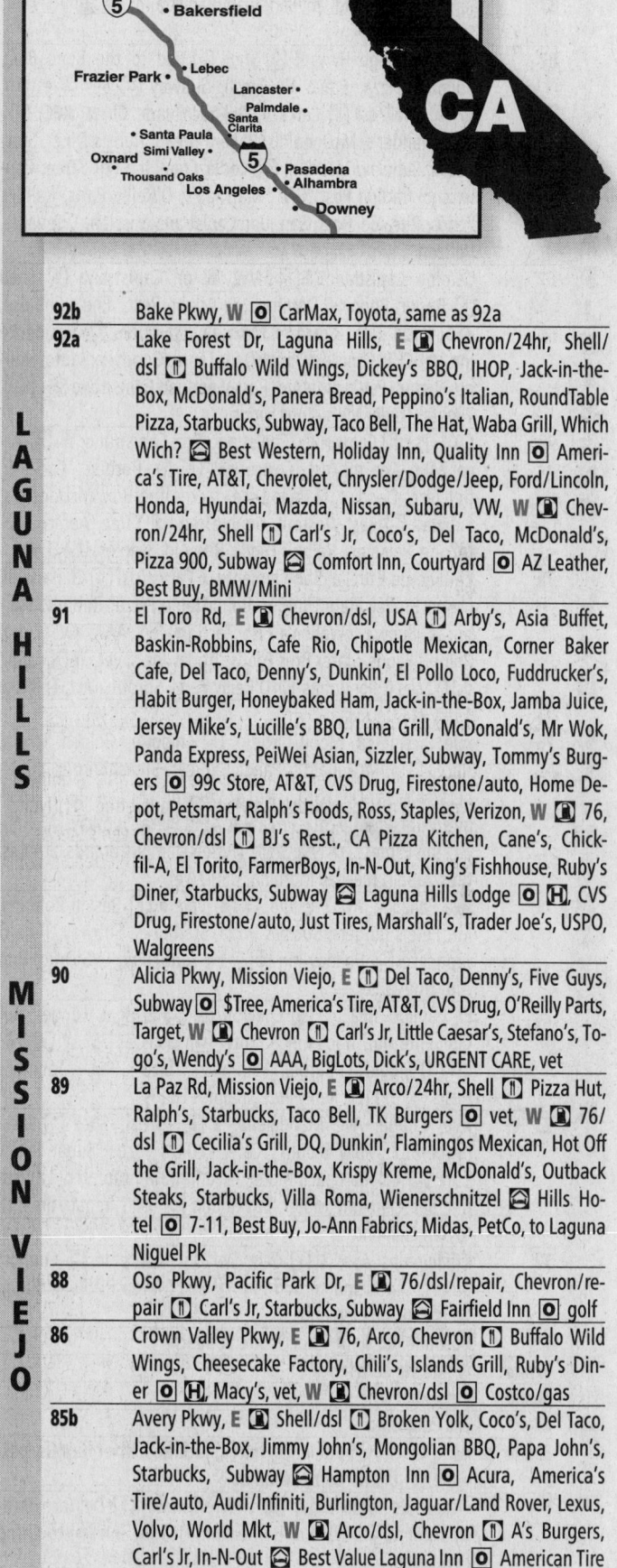

Exit #	Services
92b	Bake Pkwy, W CarMax, Toyota, same as 92a
92a	Lake Forest Dr, Laguna Hills, E Chevron/24hr, Shell/dsl Buffalo Wild Wings, Dickey's BBQ, IHOP, Jack-in-the-Box, McDonald's, Panera Bread, Peppino's Italian, RoundTable Pizza, Starbucks, Subway, Taco Bell, The Hat, Waba Grill, Which Wich? Best Western, Holiday Inn, Quality Inn America's Tire, AT&T, Chevrolet, Chrysler/Dodge/Jeep, Ford/Lincoln, Honda, Hyundai, Mazda, Nissan, Subaru, VW, W Chevron/24hr, Shell Carl's Jr, Coco's, Del Taco, McDonald's, Pizza 900, Subway Comfort Inn, Courtyard AZ Leather, Best Buy, BMW/Mini
91	El Toro Rd, E Chevron/dsl, USA Arby's, Asia Buffet, Baskin-Robbins, Cafe Rio, Chipotle Mexican, Corner Baker Cafe, Del Taco, Denny's, Dunkin', El Pollo Loco, Fuddrucker's, Habit Burger, Honeybaked Ham, Jack-in-the-Box, Jamba Juice, Jersey Mike's, Lucille's BBQ, Luna Grill, McDonald's, Mr Wok, Panda Express, PeiWei Asian, Sizzler, Subway, Tommy's Burgers 99c Store, AT&T, CVS Drug, Firestone/auto, Home Depot, Petsmart, Ralph's Foods, Ross, Staples, Verizon, W 76, Chevron/dsl BJ's Rest., CA Pizza Kitchen, Cane's, Chick-fil-A, El Torito, FarmerBoys, In-N-Out, King's Fishhouse, Ruby's Diner, Starbucks, Subway Laguna Hills Lodge H, CVS Drug, Firestone/auto, Just Tires, Marshall's, Trader Joe's, USPO, Walgreens
90	Alicia Pkwy, Mission Viejo, E Del Taco, Denny's, Five Guys, Subway $Tree, America's Tire, AT&T, CVS Drug, O'Reilly Parts, Target, W Chevron Carl's Jr, Little Caesar's, Stefano's, Togo's, Wendy's AAA, BigLots, Dick's, URGENT CARE, vet
89	La Paz Rd, Mission Viejo, E Arco/24hr, Shell Pizza Hut, Ralph's, Starbucks, Taco Bell, TK Burgers vet, W 76/dsl Cecilia's Grill, DQ, Dunkin', Flamingos Mexican, Hot Off the Grill, Jack-in-the-Box, Krispy Kreme, McDonald's, Outback Steaks, Starbucks, Villa Roma, Wienerschnitzel Hills Hotel 7-11, Best Buy, Jo-Ann Fabrics, Midas, PetCo, to Laguna Niguel Pk
88	Oso Pkwy, Pacific Park Dr, E 76/dsl/repair, Chevron/repair Carl's Jr, Starbucks, Subway Fairfield Inn golf
86	Crown Valley Pkwy, E 76, Arco, Chevron Buffalo Wild Wings, Cheesecake Factory, Chili's, Islands Grill, Ruby's Diner H, Macy's, vet, W Chevron/dsl Costco/gas
85b	Avery Pkwy, E Shell/dsl Broken Yolk, Coco's, Del Taco, Jack-in-the-Box, Jimmy John's, Mongolian BBQ, Papa John's, Starbucks, Subway Hampton Inn Acura, America's Tire/auto, Audi/Infiniti, Burlington, Jaguar/Land Rover, Lexus, Volvo, World Mkt, W Arco/dsl, Chevron A's Burgers, Carl's Jr, In-N-Out Best Value Laguna Inn American Tire Depot, Cadillac/GMC, Costco/gas, Hyundai, Mercedes
85a	CA 73 N (toll)

CA

INTERSTATE 5 Cont'd

CAPISTRANO

Exit #	Services
83	Junipero Serra Rd, to San Juan Capistrano, W 76/7-11, Shell
82	CA 74, Ortego Hwy, E Shell Bad to the Bone BBQ, Ballpark Pizza, Bravo CA Fresh, Subway Best Western, W Shell/dsl Carl's Jr, Del Taco, Jade China, KFC, Marie Callender's, McDonald's, Panera Bread, Ruby's Diner, Starbucks, Subway, Taco Bell Cedar Creek Inn $Tree, Capistrano Trading Post, GNC, Marshall's, O'Reilly Parts, Ralph's Foods, Rite Aid, Ross, San Juan Capistrano Mission, TrueValue, Verizon
81	Camino Capistrano, E VW, W **on Capistrano** Shell Baskin Robbins, Domino's, El Adobe Rest., Eng's Chinese, KFC, Pizza Hut, Ricardo's Mexican, Starbucks Residence Inn CHP, Chrysler/Dodge/Jeep, Ford, Goodyear/auto, Honda, Nissan, PetCo, Rite Aid, Ross, San Juan Capistrano SP (1mi), Toyota, Trader Joe's, Vons Foods
79	CA 1, Pacific Coast Hwy, Capistrano Bch, Capistrano, W Arco/24hr, Chevron/dsl, Costco/gas A's Burgers, Carl's Jr, Del Taco, Denny's, El Pollo Loco, Jack-in-the-Box, McDonald's, Subway Best Western, DoubleTree $Tree, Aamco, AutoZone, Petsmart, Ralph's Foods, Rite Aid, Staples, USPO, vet

SAN CLEMENTE

Exit #	Services
78	Camino de Estrella, San Clemente, E 76/dsl China Well, Flame Broiler, Habit Burger, RoundTable Pizza, Rubio's, Starbucks, Subway, Wahoo's Fish Taco H, AAA, CVS Drug, Ralph's Foods, Stater Bros Foods, Trader Joe's, vet, W USA/dsl Las Golondrinas O'Reilly Parts, Sprouts Mkt, TJ Maxx
77	Ave Vista Hermosa
76	Ave Pico, E Mobil/Circle K Chipotle, Golden Spoon, Juice it Up, McDonald's, Panda Express, SmashBurger Albertson's/Sav-On, GNC, W Chevron Del Taco, Denny's/24hr, Pick-up-Stix, Pizza Hut, Stuft Pizza, Subway Holiday Inn Express 99c Store, Outlets/famous brands, Staples, tires/repair, Tuesday Morning, USPO, vet
75	Ave Palizada, Ave Presidio, W Valero Baskin-Robbins, Mr. Pete's Burgers, Sonny's Pizza, Starbucks, Subway, Taka-O Japanese Holiday Inn 7-11, AutoZone, CVS Drug, Rite Aid, TrueValue
74	El Camino Real, E Chevron/dsl Budget Lodge, San Clemente Inn, Tradewinds Motel same as 75, W 76/dsl Biggie's Burger, Subway, Taco Bell, Tommy's Rest. 7-11, O'Reilly Parts, Ralph's Foods
73	Ave Calafia, Ave Magdalena, E 76/dsl, Shell Jack-in-the-Box, Molly Bloom's Cafe, Pedro's Tacos, Sugar Shack Cafe Calafia Beach Motel, C-Vu Inn, Hampton Inn, LaVista Inn, San Clemente Motel, Travelodge 7-11, repair/tires, W to San Clemente SP
72	Cristianitios Ave, E Cafe Del Sol, Carl's Jr. Comfort Suites, San Clemente Surf Inn San Mateo RV Park/dump, W to San Clemente SP
71	Basilone Rd, W San Onofre St Beach
67mm	**weigh sta both lanes**
66mm	viewpoint sb
62	Las Pulgas Rd
59mm	**Aliso Creek both lanes, full facilities, litter barrels, petwalk, , , RV dump, vending**
54c	Oceanside Harbor Dr, W Chevron, Mobil Del Taco, Denny's/24hr Days Inn, Harbor Inn, Holiday Inn to Camp Pendleton
54b	Hill St (from sb), to Oceanside, W Chevron, Mobil Denny's, In-N-Out Days Inn, Holiday Inn, Rodeway Inn

OCEANSIDE

Exit #	Services
54a	CA 76 E, Coast Hwy
53	Mission Ave, Oceanside, E 7-11/dsl, Arco/24hr, Mo dsl Alberto's Mexican, Arby's, Armando's Tacos, Arm do's Tacos, Burger King, Jack-in-the-Box, KFC, McDonal Starbucks Ramada, Travelodge Bussy's Automot CarQuest, El Super Mkt, W El Pollo Loco, Panda Expr Subway, Wendy's 99c Store, AutoZone, Walmart Mkt
52	Oceanside Blvd, E Arco Alberto's Mexican, IHOP, Donald's, Pizza Hut, Starbucks, Subway, Taco Bell, Wie schnitzel $Tree, CVS Drug, Frazier Farms Mkt, W C dsl Best Western
51c	Cassidy St (from sb)
51b	CA 78, Vista Way, Escondido, E Chevron/dsl, Shell plebee's, Boston Mkt, Buffalo Wild Wings, Burger King, Ca Jr, Cheesecake Factory, Chili's, Chipotle, ChuckECheese's, D e&Buster's, Domino's, Islands Rest., Jersey Mike's, Maca Grill, McDonald's, Mimi's Café, Olive Garden, Outback Ste QuikWok, Red Lobster, Rubio's, Starbucks, Subway, TX Ro house $Tree, Best Buy, CVS Drug, Dick's, Firestone/a JC Penney, Macy's, Marshall's, Michael's, PetCo, Sprouts M Staples, Stater Bros Foods, Target, Tuesday Morning, Veriz Vons Foods, Walmart, World Mkt, W Hunter Steaks
51a	Las Flores Dr

CARLSBAD

Exit #	Services
50	Elm Ave, Carlsbad Village Dr, E Shell Lotus Thai Bis W 7-11 Al's Cafe, Carl's Jr, Denny's/24hr, Jack-in- Box, KFC/Taco Bell, Mikko Japanese, Subway Exten Stay America, Motel 6 Albertson's, TrueValue
49	Tamarack Ave, E 76/dsl, Chevron Village Kitc Days Inn Rite Aid, Vons Foods, W Arco Stag&l Grille
48	Cannon Rd, Car Country Carlsbad, E Acura, Buick/GMC dillac, Chevrolet, Chrysler/Dodge/Jeep, Ford, Honda, Kia, us, Lincoln, Mazda, Mercedes, VW, W West Mart V Steak&Seafood Hyatt House, West Inn
47	Carlsbad Blvd, Palomar Airport Rd, E 7-11, Chevron, bil/dsl BJ's Rest., Carl's Jr, Corner Bakery Cafe, Isla Burgers, Kings Fish House, Panda Express, PF Chang's, Ru Diner, SeaFire Rest., Starbucks, Strauss Brewery Rest., Subv Taco Bell Carlsbad by the Sea, Motel 6 AT&T, Carls Ranch/Flower Fields, Chrysler/Dodge/Jeep, Costco/gas, F GNC, outlet W Shell/dsl In-N-Out, McDonald's, guel's Mexican, Pisco Rotisserie Hilton Garden S Ca bad St Bch
45	Poinsettia Lane, W Shell/dsl Benihana, El Pollo L Jack-in-the-Box, Pick-Up Stix, Starbucks, Subway Holi Inn Express, La Quinta, Motel 6, Ramada Ace Hardw Porsche/Volvo, Ralph's Foods, Rite Aid

ENCINITAS

Exit #	Services
44	La Costa Ave, E vista point, W Chevron/dsl
43	Leucadia Blvd, E Quality Inn, W Shell/service S bucks
42b	Encinitas Blvd, E Chevron/dsl, Mobil, Valero Ho Baked Ham, In-N-Out, Oggi's Pizza CVS Drug, NAPA, Pe to Quail Botanical Gardens, vet, W Shell Denny's, L Caesar's, Subway, Wendy's Best Western/rest., Days In
41a	Santa Fe Dr, to Encinitas, E Shell Carl's Jr, El No to 7-11, W Domino's, Schooner Pizza H, Rite vet, Vons Foods
40	Birmingham Dr, E Chevron, Valero El Pueblo day Inn Express, W Arco
39mm	viewpoint sb
39	Manchester Ave, E to MiraCosta College

N INTERSTATE 5 Cont'd

Exit #	Services
37	Lomas Santa Fe Dr, Solana Bch, E Baskin-Robbins, Habit Burger, Jersey Mike's, Pizza Nova, Samurai Rest., Starbucks Vons Foods, We-R-Fabrics, W Mobil Carl's Jr, Jamba Juice, Panda Express, Panera Bread, Starbucks AT&T, CVS Drug, Discount Tire, GNC, Marshall's, Sprouts Mkt, Staples
36	Via de La Valle, Del Mar, E Chevron, Mobil Chipotle, Coffee Bean, McDonald's, Milton's Deli, Taste of Thai, Urban Pizza Albertson's/SavOn, Gelson's Mkt, PetCo, Verizon, Whole Foods Mkt, W Arco/24hr, Shell/dsl Denny's, FishMkt Rest., Red Tracton's Rest. Hilton racetrack
34	Del Mar Heights Rd, E Shell/dsl, W 7-11 Broken Yolk Cafe, Bushfire Kitchen, Jack-in-the-Box, Jersey Mike's, Starbucks AAA, CVS Drug, vet, Vons Foods
33	Carmel Mtn Rd, E Arco, Shell/repair Ruth's Chris, Taco Bell, Tio Leo's Mexican DoubleTree Hotel, Hampton Inn, Marriott, Residence Inn
32	CA 56 E, Carmel Valley Rd
31	I-805 (from sb)
30	Sorrento Valley Rd
29	Genesee Ave, E H
28b	La Jolla Village Dr, E Embassy Suites, Hyatt, Marriott H, to LDS Temple, W Mobil/dsl BJ's Rest., CA Pizza Kitchen, Chipotle Mexican, Dominos, Flame Broiler, Islands Burgers, Jamba Juice, Mrs Gooch's, RockBottom Café, Rubio's, Starbucks Sheraton AT&T, Best Buy, CVS Drug, Marshall's, PetsMart, Ralph's Foods, Ross, Trader Joe's, Verizon, Whole Foods Mkt
28a	Nobel Dr (from nb), E Hyatt LDS Temple, W same as 28b
27	Gilman Dr, La Jolla Colony Dr
26b	CA 52 E
26a	La Jolla Rd (from nb)
23b	CA 274, Balboa Ave, E Del Taco, Starbucks H, Costco/gas, W 7-11, 76/repair In-N-Out, McDonald's, Rubio's, Sonic, Wienerschnitzel Holiday Inn Express, La Quinta, Red Roof Inn, San Diego Motel Discount Tire, Ford, Mission Bay Pk, Nissan, Toyota
23a	Grand Ave, Garnet Ave, same as 23b
22	Clairemont Dr, Mission Bay Dr, E Shell, USA Best Western Chevrolet, VW, W to Sea World Dr
21	Sea World Dr, Tecolote Dr, E Shell Seaside Inn Aamco, Circle K, PetCo, W Hilton Old Town SP, Seaworld
20	I-8, W to Nimitz Blvd, E to El Centro, CA 209 S (from sb), to Rosecrans St
19	Old Town Ave, E Arco, Shell Courtyard, La Quinta
18b	Washington St, E Holiday Inn Express
18a	Pacific Hwy Viaduct, Kettner St
17b	India St, Front St, Sassafras St, E Mobil, W
17a	Hawthorn St, Front St, E H, W Mobil/dsl Motel 6, Sheraton
16b	6th Ave, downtown
16a	CA 163 N, 10th St, E H, AeroSpace Museum, W Shell Burger King, Del Taco, Jack-in-the-Box, McDonald's Days Inn, Downtown Lodge, El Cortez Motel, Holiday Inn, Marriott
15c b	CA 94 E (from nb), Pershing Dr, B St, W civic ctr
15a	CA 94 E, J St, Imperial Ave (from sb),
14b	Cesar Chavez Pkwy
14a	CA 75, to Coronado, W **toll rd to Coronado**
13b	National Ave SD, 28th St, E Jack-in-the-Box, Little Caesar's, Panda Express, Starbucks, Subway AutoZone,

SAN DIEGO AREA

SAN YSIDRO

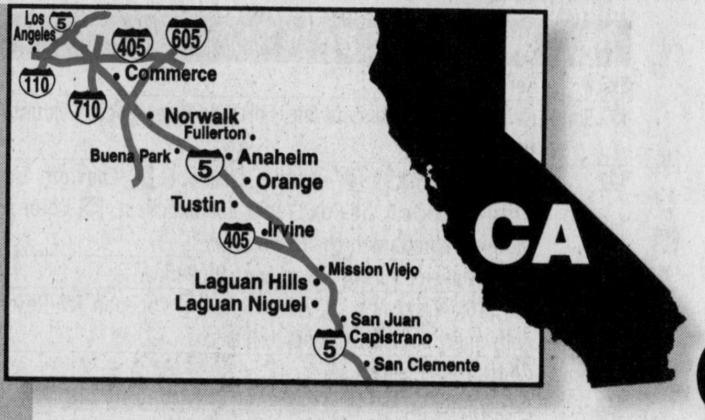

CA

Exit #	Services
13b	Continued W Shell Burger King, Del Taco, El Pollo Loco, McDonald's
13a	CA 15 N, to Riverside
12	Main St, National City
11b	8th St, National City, E Arco Jack-in-the-Box Cassia Hotel, Howard Johnson, National City Inn, Ramada Inn, Rodeway Inn
11a	Harbor Dr, Civic Center Dr
10	Bay Marina, 24th St, Mile of Cars Way, E Chick-fil-A, Chipotle, Denny's, Freddy's, In-N-Out, Jersey Mike's, Starbucks, W Best Western+
9	CA 54 E
8b	E St, Chula Vista, E Arco, Black Angus, Denny's, Taco Bell Days Inn, Motel 6, W GoodNite Inn
8a	H St
7b	J St (from sb)
7a	L St, E 76, Shell/dsl China Vista Inn NAPA
6	Palomar St, E Arco Carl's Jr., DQ, HomeTown Buffet, IHOP, KFC, Little Caesar's, McDonald's, Panda Express, Starbucks, Subway Palomar Inn $Tree, 7-11, Costco/gas, Food4Less, Jack-in-the-Box, Michael's, Office Depot, Petco, Ross, Target, Walmart, Yoshinoya, W Valero
5b	Main St, to Imperial Beach, E Arco
5a	CA 75 (from sb), Palm Ave, to Imperial Beach, E Arco, USA Armando's Mexican, Papa John's, Starbucks 7-11, Discount Tire, Soto's Transmissions, W 7-11, 76, Arco, Shell Boll Weevil Diner, Burger King, Carl's Jr, Coldstone Creamery, IHOP, McDonald's, Rally's, Subway, Wienerschnitzel Prime Inn, Super 8 99c Store, AutoZone, CVS Drug, GNC, Home Depot, Von's Foods, Walmart
4	Coronado Ave (from sb), E Chevron/service, Shell/service Taco Bell EZ 8 Motel 7-11, W Arco, Hollister/dsl Denny's Motel 6 to Border Field SP
3	CA 905, Tocayo Ave, W 7-11
2	Dairy Mart Rd, E Arco/24hr Burger King, Carl's Jr, Coco's, KFC, McDonald's Best Western Pacifica RV Resort, W Quality Inn
1b	Via de San Ysidro, W Chevron, Mobil/dsl Denny's Knights/RV park, Motel 6, Travelodge
1a	I-805 N (from nb), Camino de la Plaza (from sb), E Burger King, Jack-in-the-Box, KFC, McDonald's, Subway Holiday Motel AutoZone, W Achiato Mexican, IHOP, Iron Wok, McDonald's, Starbucks, Sunrise Buffet $Tree, Baja Duty-Free, border parking, factory outlet, Marshall's, Old Navy, Ross, TJ Maxx

California state line, US/Mexico Border, customs, **I-5 begins/ends.**

CA

INTERSTATE 8

YUMA

Exit #	Services
172.5mm	California/Arizona state line, Colorado River, Pacific/Mountain time zone
172	4th Ave, Yuma, N [other] Paradise Casino, S [gas] Chevron, Circle K/dsl [food] Jack-in-the-Box, Yuma Landing Rest. [lodging] Coronado Motel, Hilton Garden [other] to Yuma SP
170	Winterhaven Dr, S [other] Rivers Edge RV Park
166	CA 186, Algodones Rd, Andrade, S [other] Cocopah RV Resort/golf, Quechan Hotel/Casino, to Mexico
165mm	CA Insp/weigh sta
164	Sidewinder Rd, N [other] st patrol, S [gas] Chevron/LP/dsl [other] Pilot Knob RV Park
159	CA 34, Ogilby Rd, to Blythe
156	Grays Well Rd, N Imperial Dunes RA
155mm	**[rest stop] both lanes (exits left), full facilities, litter barrels, petwalk, [picnic]**
151	Gordons Well
146	Brock Research Ctr Rd
143	CA 98, to Calexico, Midway Well
131	CA 115, VanDerLinden Rd, to Holtville, **5 mi** N [other] food, gas, lodging, RV camping
128	Bonds Corner Rd
125	CA 7 S, Orchard Rd, Holtville, **4 mi** N [other] food, gas/dsl
120	Bowker Rd
118b a	CA 111, to Calexico, N [other] Country Life RV Park
116	Dogwood Rd, S [gas] Arco/dsl, Tesla EVC [food] Buffalo Wild Wings, Burger King, Carino's, Chili's, ChuckeCheese, Denny's, Famous Dave's BBQ, Fortune Garden, Jack-in-the-Box, Olive Garden, Sombrero Mexican, Starbucks, Subway [lodging] Fairfield Inn, Hampton Inn, TownePlace Suites [other] $Tree, 99c, AT&T, Best Buy, Dillard's, Discount Tire, JC Penney, Kohl's, Macy's, Marshall's, Michael's, PetCo, Ross, Staples
115	CA 86, 4th St, El Centro, N [gas] 7-11/dsl, Arco/dsl, Chevron/dsl, FillCo/dsl, Shell/dsl [food] Carl's Jr, Exotic Thai, Jack-in-the-Box, Las Palmitas Tacos, Lucky Chinese, McDonald's [lodging] Holiday Inn Express, Motel 6 [other] Family$, O'Reilly Parts, U-Haul, S [gas] 7-11/Subway, Mobil/dsl/scales [food] Habit Burger, IHOP, In-N-Out, Johnny's Burritos, Korean BBQ, Panda Express, Starbucks, Taco Bell [lodging] Best Value Inn, Best Western, Comfort Inn, Mainstay Inn [other] AutoZone, Buick/Chevrolet/GMC/Cadillac, Desert Trails RV Park, Home Depot, Honda, Hyundai
114	Imperial Ave, El Centro, **0-3 mi** N [gas] 7-11/dsl, Arco, Chevron/dsl, USA/dsl [food] Applebee's, Broken Yolk Cafe, Burrito Factory, Carl's Jr, Carrow's, Church's, Coldstone, Del Taco, Denny's, Domino's, El Pollo Loco, Farmer Boys, Hamburger Stand, Jack-in-the-Box, Jack-in-the-Box, KFC, La Resaca, Little Caesar's, McDonald's, Papa John's, Pizza Hut, Rally's, Sizzler, Sonic, Starbucks, Subway, Taco Bell, Wendy's [lodging] Crown Motel, Days Inn, Quality Inn, Super 8, Travelodge/RV Park, Value Inn [other] [H], $General Mkt, $Tree, 99c Store, Aldi Foods, Chrysler/Dodge/Jeep, Costco/gas, CVS Drug, Discount Tire, Food4Less, Ford, Goodyear/auto, Jo-Ann, Kia, Lowe's, Nissan, O'Reilly Parts, PepBoys, Petsmart, Rite Aid, Ross, st patrol, Target, Toyota, Verizon, Von's Foods, VW, Walgreens, Walmart
111	Forrester Rd, to Westmorland
108mm	**Sunbeam Rest Area both lanes, full [handicap] facilities, litter barrels, petwalk, [phone], [picnic], RV dump**
107	Drew Rd, Seeley, N [other] Sunbeam RV Park, to Sunbeam Lake, S [other] Rio Bend RV Park
101	Dunaway Rd, elev 0 ft, Imperial Valley, N [other] st prison

EL CENTRO

89	Imperial Hwy, CA 98, Ocotillo, N [other] Red Feathers Mkt/C RV camping, USPO, S [gas] Chevron/dsl [other] Desert Museum
87	CA 98 (from eb), to Calexico
81mm	runaway truck ramp eb
80	Mountain Springs Rd
77	In-ko-pah Park Rd, N [phone], towing
75mm	**brake insp area eb**
73	Jacumba, S [gas] Chevron/dsl, Shell/Subway/dsl/24hr
65	CA 94, Boulevard, to Campo, S [gas] MtnTop/dsl [food] Manz ta Diner [lodging] Back Country Inn [other] to McCain Valley RA (7 USPO
63mm	Tecate Divide, elev 4140 ft
62mm	Crestwood Summit, elev 4190 ft
61	Crestwood Rd, Live Oak Springs, S [gas] Golden Acorn Trkstp sino/dsl [other] info
54	Kitchen Creek Rd, Cameron Station, S food, RV camping
51	rd 1, Buckman Spgs Rd, to Lake Morena, **[rest stop] both lanes, [handicap] facilities, litter barrels, petwalk, [phone], [picnic],** S food, gas/ds Lake Morena CP (7mi), lodging, Potrero CP (19mi), RV cam RV dump
48	**insp sta wb**
47	rd 1, Sunrise Hwy, Laguna Summit, elev 4055 ft, N to La Mtn RA
45	Pine Valley, Julian, N [food] Frosty Burger, Major's Diner [lodging] Valley Inn [other] city park, Mtn Mkt, Pine Valley/gas, to Cuya ca Rancho SP, USPO, vet
44mm	Pine Valley Creek
42mm	elev 4000 ft
40	CA 79, Japatul Rd, Descanso, N [food] Descanso Rest. Cuyamaca Rancho SP
37mm	vista point eb, elev 3000 ft
36	E Willows, N [other] Alpine Sprs RV Park, casino, Viejas Indiar
33	W Willows Rd, to Alpine, same as 36, N [other] Alpine Spr Park, casino, Viejas Outlets/famous brands, S [other] ranger s
31mm	elev 2000 ft
30	Tavern Rd, to Alpine, N [gas] Chevron/dsl, Shell/dsl, S [gas] lips 66/Circle K, Tesla EVC [food] American Grill, Carl's Jr, G Village Grill, La Carreta, Little Caesar's, Mananas Mexican, M iterraneo Grill, Panda Machi Chinese [lodging] Ayre's Lodge [other] Hardware, CVS Drug, Rite Aid
27	Dunbar Lane, Harbison Canyon, N [other] Flinn Sprgs CP, RV cam
25mm	elev 1000 ft
24mm	[phone]
23	Lake Jennings Pk Rd, Lakeside, N [gas] Mobil/Jac the-Box/dsl/24hr, to Lake Jennings CP [other] RV cam S [gas] 7-11 [food] Burger King, Marechiaro's Pizza
22	Los Coches Rd, Lakeside, N [gas] 7-11, Eagle/dsl/LP, County Gas [food] Albert's Mexican, Giant Pizza, Laposta M can [other] RV camping/dump, S [gas] Shell/dsl [food] Denny's, Donald's, Panda Express, Subway, Taco Bell [other] Walmart
20b	Greenfield Dr, to Crest, N [gas] Chevron/dsl, Sky dsl [food] Jack-in-the-Box, Janet's Cafe, Marieta's Mexican, Donald's, Panchos Tacos, Subway [other] 7-11, 99c Store, Al son's, auto repair, AutoZone, Ford, RV camping, st patrol GENT CARE, vet, S [gas] Mobil/dsl/LP
20a	E Main St (from wb, no EZ return), N [lodging] Budget Inn [other] Vacationer RV Park, S [gas] Arco [other] Combs RV Ctr
19	2nd St, CA 54, El Cajon, N [gas] Arco, Chevron/dsl, Phillips dsl [food] Marechiaro's Italian, Pancake House [other] CVS Genie Auto Ctr, USPO, S [gas] Gas Depot, Golden State Shell [food] Arby's, Baskin-Robbins, Carl's Jr, Chipotle, El Cha El Compadre Tacos, IHOP, Jack-in-the-Box, Jamba Juice,

LAKESIDE

INTERSTATE 8 Cont'd

19 Continued
Little Caesar's, McDonald's, Popeye's, Starbucks, Subway, Taco Bell, Wing Stop, Wings n Things Best Value Inn $Tree, 7-11, CarQuest, Firestone/auto, Grocery Outlet, Jiffy Lube, Pep-Boys, PetCo, Sprouts Mkt, Walgreens, Walmart Mkt

18 Mollison Ave, El Cajon, N Chevron Denny's, Starbucks Best Western, Days Inn, Quality Inn, S Arco, QuickTrip/dsl Los Garcia's EconoLodge

17c Magnolia Ave, CA 67 (from wb), to Santee, N Arco Black Angus Steaks, Del Taco, El Pollo Loco, Jack-in-the-Box, Jersey Mike's, Panda Express, Starbucks AT&T, Food4Less, Target, S EVC, Shell/service/dsl Panda Express, Perry's Cafe, Rubio's, Super Buffet Courtyard, Motel 6, Super 8 Nudo's Drug, Ross

17b CA 67 (from eb), same as 17 a&c

17a Johnson Ave (from eb), N EVC Applebee's, Black Bear Diner, Boston Mkt, Burger King, Carl's Jr, Dunkin', Five Guys, Fuerte's NY, Hacienda Mexican, In-N-Out, Jamba Juice, KFC, Little Caesar's, LJ Silver, McDonald's, New Century Buffet, O's American Kitchen, Panera Bread, Rubio's, Subway $Tree, Best Buy, CVS Drug, Dick's, Home Depot, Honda, JC Penney, Lexus, Macy's, Marshall's, Mercedes, Office Depot, PetsMart, Subaru, Tire Choice/auto, Toyota, Walmart, S Aamco, Kia, Mazda, vet

16 Main St, N Arco Denny's, Sombrero Mexican Relax Inn 7-11, S Chevron/dsl, Super Star brakes/transmissions, Nissan

15 El Cajon Blvd (from eb), N Rodeway Inn, S 76/dsl Wrangler BBQ BMW

14c Severin Dr, Fuerte Dr (from wb), N Shell/dsl, Tesla EVC Anthony's Fish Grotto, Charcoal House Rest., La Casa Blanca Best Western+, S Brigantine Seafood Rest.

14b a CA 125, to CA 94

13b Jackson Dr, Grossmont Blvd, N Chevron BJ's Rest., Casa de Pico, Chili's, ChuckeCheese, ClaimJumper, Fuddrucker's, Olive Garden, Panda Express, Panera Bread, Red Lobster, Starbucks, Vallarta Express H, $Tree, Best Buy, CVS Drug, Macy's, Office Depot, O'Reilly Parts, Petco, Target, USPO, Verizon, vet, Walmart, World Mkt, S Phillips 66/Circle K Honeybaked Ham, Jack-in-the-Box, Jersey Mike's Discount Tire, Ford, Hobby Lobby, Hyundai, Ross, Walmart Mkt

13a Spring St (from eb), El Cajon Blvd (from wb), S El Pollo Loco, El Torito, Starbucks, Subway Hitching Post 99c Store, AutoZone

12 Fletcher Pkwy, to La Mesa, N Shell/dsl Carl's Jr, Chick-fil-A, Chipotle Mexican, Habit Burger, McDonald's, Pick Up Stix Heritage Inn, Holiday Inn 7-11, Costco, S El Torito, Starbucks, Subway Motel 6 99c Store, Chevrolet, San Diego RV Resort

11 70th St, Lake Murray Blvd, N Shell/dsl Subway, S Shell/7-11/dsl Akin's Deli, Denny's, Marie Callender's H, auto repair, URGENT CARE

10 College Ave, N Chevron/dsl Windmill Farms Mkt, S H, to SDSU

9 Waring Rd, N Days Inn, Rodeway Inn

8 Fairmount Ave (7 from eb), to Mission Gorge Rd, N 7-11, Arco/dsl, Mobil, Sky/dsl Black Angus, Carl's Jr, Chili's, Denny's, El Pollo Loco, Jack-in-the-Box, Jamba Juice, Jersey Mike's, McDonald's, Rolando's Tacos, Rubio's, Sombrero Mexican, Starbucks, Subway, Szechuan Chinese, Taco Fiesta, Wendy's H, AutoZone, CVS Drug, Discount Tire, Home Depot, Honda, Rite Aid, Toyota, Tuesday Morning, Vons Foods

SAN DIEGO AREA POINT LOMA

7b a I-15 N, CA 15 S, to 40th St

6b I-805, N to LA, S to Chula Vista

6a Texas St, Qualcomm Way, same as 5, N Dave&Buster's

5 Mission Ctr Rd, N Chevron, EVC Broken Yolk Cafe, Buffalo Wild Wings, Chipotle Mexican, Corner Cafe, El Pollo Loco, Habit Burger, Hooters, In-N-Out, King's Fish House, Lazy Dog Rest., Mimi's Cafe, On The Border, Outback Steaks, Panda Express, Pei Wei, Pick-Up Stix, Robek Juice, Rubio's, Sammy's Woodfired Pizza, Starbucks, Subway, Taco Bell Marriott, Springhill Suites AT&T, Best Buy, Chevrolet, Lincoln, Marshall's, Michael's, Nordstrom Rack, Old Navy, Staples, Target, Trader Joe's, S Benihana, Denny's, Fuji Japanese, Wendy's Hilton, Homewood Suites, La Quinta, Quality Suites, Sheraton Buick/GMC/Cadillac, Chrysler/Dodge/Jeep, Mazda

4c b CA 163, Cabrillo Frwy, S to downtown, zoo

4a Hotel Circle Dr (from eb), CA 163 (from wb)

3a Hotel Circle, Taylor St, N Hunter Steaks Comfort Suites, Crowne Plaza, Handlery Hotel, Motel 6, Town&Country Motel golf, S Tesla EVC Best Western, Candlewood Suites, Courtyard, Days Hotel, DoubleTree Inn, Extended Stay America, Hampton Inn, Holiday Inn Express, Homewood Suites, Hotel Iris, Howard Johnson, King's Inn/rest., Quality Inn, Residence Inn, Super 8 vet

2c Morena Blvd (from wb)

2b I-5, N to LA, S to San Diego

2a Rosecrans St (from wb), CA 209, S Shell Chipotle Mexican, ChuckECheese, Del Taco, Denny's, In-N-Out, Panda Express, Starbucks, Subway Goodnite Inn, Sheraton Staples

1 W Mission Bay Blvd, Sports Arena Blvd (from wb), N to SeaWorld, S Arby's, Buffalo Wild Wings, Chick-fil-A, Chili's, Denny's, Jack-in-the-Box, McDonald's, Phil's BBQ, Red Lobster, Wendy's Green World Inn, Holiday Inn Express, Wyndham Garden Dick's, Home Depot, Ralph's, Target, U-Haul, Von's

0mm **I-8 begins/ends on Sunset Cliffs Blvd, 1/4 mi W** Phillips 66, Shell/repair Jack-in-the-Box, Kaiserhof Cafe, N Mission Bay Park

INTERSTATE 10

Exit #	Services
245mm	California/Arizona state line, Colorado River, pacific/mountain time zone
244mm	**inspection sta wb**
243	Riviera Dr, S The Cove RV Park
241	US 95, Intake Blvd, to Needles, Blythe, N Mobil/dsl, Shell/Baja Fresh/dsl Steaks'n Cakes Rest. Magnuson Motel, Relax Inn auto/RV repair/24hr, Burton's RV Park, S Hampton Inn McIntyre Park

CA

INTERSTATE 10 Cont'd

BLYTHE

Exit #	Services
240	7th St, N EZ Mart, Valero/dsl China Garden, Little Caesar's, Starbucks Blue Line Motel, Budget Inn, Knights Inn, Motel 6 $General, Albertson's, AutoZone, Ford, repair, Rite Aid, S Buick/Chevrolet, Chrysler/Dodge/Jeep
239	Lovekin Blvd, Blythe, N Mobil/dsl, Shell/Quiznos Carl's Jr, Del Taco, Domino's, Jack-in-the-Box, McDonald's, Popeye's, Sizzler, Starbucks Best Western, Clarion, Emerald Inn, Red Roof Inn, Regency Inn H, $Tree, Ace Hardware, Goodyear/auto, O'Reilly Parts, Verizon, S Chevron/dsl, R/dsl/24hr, Valero/Circle K, VP/dsl Ampola Mexican, Burger King, Denny's, Pizza Studio, Subway, Taco Bell Comfort Suites, Motel 6, Quality Inn, Super 8 city park
236	CA 78, Neighbours Blvd, to Ripley, N Valero/dsl, S to Cibola NWR
232	Mesa Dr, N BB TC/scales/24hr/@, Valero/dsl
231	**weigh sta wb**
222mm	Wileys Well Rd, N **both lanes, full facilities, litter barrels, petwalk**, S to st prison
217	Ford Dry Lake Rd
201	Corn Springs Rd
192	CA 177, Rice Rd, to Lake Tamarisk, N camping, USPO
189	Eagle Mtn Rd
182	Red Cloud Rd
177	Hayfield Rd
173	Chiriaco Summit, N Chevron/Foster's Freeze/dsl/24hr Chiriaco Rest. camping, Patton Museum, truck/tire repair
168	to Twentynine Palms, to Mecca, Joshua Tree NM
162	frontage rd
159mm	**Cactus City Rest Area both lanes, full facilities, litter barrels, petwalk,**
147mm	0 ft elevation
146	Dillon Rd, to CA 86, to CA 111 S, Coachella, N Chevron, Loves/Carl's Jr/dsl/24hr Del Taco, S Chevron, TA/Shell/Country Pride/Taco Bell/dsl/24hr/@ Santiago's Mexican Spotlight Casino, truckwash

INDIO

Exit #	Services
145	CA 86 S (from eb)
144	CA 111 N, CA 86 S, Indio, N Arco/dsl Holiday Inn Express, Quality Inn Fantasy Sprgs Casino/Hotel/Cafe, Indio Sprgs RV Park
143	Jackson St, Indio, N Arco/dsl Carl's Jr, Domino's, Dunkin', IHOP, KFC, McDonald's, Panda Express, Starbucks, Subway, Taco Bell Fairfield Inn $Tree, AT&T, AutoZone, BigLots, CVS Drug, GNC, Home Depot, Marshall's, PetCo, Ramona Tire/auto, Ross, Verizon, Walgreens, WinCo Foods, S 7-11
142	Monroe St, Central Indio, N Circle K/dsl Starbucks Walmart, S Circle K, Mobil/dsl/LP, Phillips 66/dsl Mexicali Cafe, Subway, Taco Jalisco Days Inn $General
139	Jefferson St, Indio Blvd, N hwy patrol, Shadow Hills RV Resort
137	Washington St, Country Club Dr, to Indian Wells, N Arco, Chevron/dsl, EVC Burger King, Coco's, Del Taco, Legends & Icons Grill, Mario's Italian, McDonald's, Papa John's, Popeye's, Starbucks, Taco Bell, Winchell's Comfort Suites, Motel 6 Buick/GMC, Chrysler/Dodge/Jeep, Ford, Holland RV Ctr, Honda, Palm Springs RV Park, Rite Aid, Stater Bros, Toyota, TrueValue, VW, Walgreens, S 76, Mobil/Circle K Carl's Jr, China Wok, Domino's, Goody's Cafe, La Casita Mexican, Pizza Hut, Subway, TJ's Steaks, Victor's Mexican, Wendy's Firestone/auto, Goodyear/auto

PALM SPRINGS

Exit #	Services
134	Cook St, to Indian Wells, S Arco, Mobil/Circle K/dsl plebee's, Billy Q's, Buccatini, Carl's Jr, Castenada's Mexi Firehouse Grill, Jack-in-the-Box, Pueblo Viejo Grill, Starbu Subway Courtyard, Fairfield Inn, Hampton Inn, Homew Suites, Residence Inn vet
131	Monterey Ave, Thousand Palms, N Arco Jack-in-Box, S Casteneda's Mexican, Chipotle, Clark's Cafe/F Mkt, Del Taco, El Pollo Loco, Firehouse Subs, Hibachi IHOP, Krispy Kreme, Maracas Cantina, McDonald's, Pa Express, Panera Bread, Red Robin, Starbucks, Subway, W dy's $Tree, 99c Store, America's Tire, AutoZone, Cost gas, Home Depot, Jo-Ann, Kohl's, Lowe's, Mountain View T auto, PetsMart, Sam's Club/gas, Verizon, Walmart
130	Ramon Rd, Bob Hope Dr, N FLYING J/dsl/LP/rest./2 Chevron/dsl, Shell/dsl, Valero/dsl Carl's Jr, Del Taco, D ny's, Domino's, Goody's Cafe, In-N-Out, McDonald's, San guel Mexican, Starbucks, Taco Bell Motel 6 truckw S H, Agua Caliente Casino/rest.
126	Date Palm Dr, Rancho Mirage, S Arco/dsl, EVC, Mobil, V ro DQ Walgreens
123	Palm Dr, to Desert Hot Sprgs, N Arco/dsl, Chevron/J in-the-Box/dsl Caliente Springs Camping, S to G Autry Trail
120	Indian Ave, to N Palm Sprgs, N Arco/dsl, Phillips 66/ cle K, Shell/dsl Denny's Motel 6 Harley-David S Chevron, Pilot/Wendy's/dsl/scales/24hr Del T Jack-in-the-Box H
117	CA 62, to Yucca Valley, Twentynine Palms, to Joshua Tree N
114	Whitewater, many windmills
113mm	**both lanes, full facilities, litter barrels,**
112	CA 111 (from eb), to Palm Springs
110	Haugeen-Lehmann
106	Main St, to Cabazon, N Shell/dsl Burger King, S 76/Circle K/dsl $General
104	Cabazon, same as 103
103	Fields Rd, N Chevron, Morongo/dsl, Tesla EVC Blaze za, Chipotle, Coldstone, In-N-Out, Jersey Mike's, McDona Panda Express, Ruby's Diner, Starbucks, Taco Bell Ha Fruit Orchards, Morongo Reservation/casino, Premium Outl famous brands
102.5mm	**Banning weigh sta both lanes**

BANNING

Exit #	Services
102	Ramsey St (from wb)
101	Hargrave St, Banning, N Arco/dsl, Mobil/Church's C suelo's Mexican Country Inn, Stagecoach Motel tir
100	CA 243, 8th St, Banning, N Chevron/dsl IHOP, Jack the-Box, Subway Rite Aid
99	22nd St, to Ramsey St, N Arco/dsl, Shell/dsl Carl' Del Taco, KFC, Little Caesar's, Los Victor's, McDonald's, P Hut, Russo's Italian, Sizzler, Starbucks, Taco Bell, Wall nese Days Inn, Travelodge $General, Banning RV Family$, Goodyear/auto
98	Sunset Ave, Banning, N Chevron/dsl Domin Gramma's Kitchen, Gus Jr #7 Burger Holiday Inn Exp $Tree, AutoZone, Boyd's RV Ctr, Buick/Chevrolet/GMC pair, Rio Ranch Mkt, vet
96	Highland Springs Ave, N Arco, Chevron/dsl, Shell/dsl plebee's, Burger King, Denny's, FarmHouse Rest., Guy's Ital Jack-in-the-Box, Little Caesar's, Papa John's, Subway, Thai chid, Wendy's Hampton Inn H, Best Hardware, Fo 4Less, Stater Bros Foods, Walgreens, S Mobil C Jr, Chili's, Dickey's BBQ, El Pollo Loco, FarmerBoys, Fireho Subs, Good China, La Casita, McDonald's, Panda Exp

INTERSTATE 10 Cont'd

96 Continued
Panera Bread, Patsy's Country Kitchen, Sonic, Starbucks, Taco Bell, Waba Grill, Wienerschnitzel, Wingstop $Tree, Albertson's, Aldi, Best Buy, GNC, Hobby Lobby, Home Depot, hwy patrol, Kohl's, Marshall's, PetCo, Ramona Tire/auto, Rite Aid, Rite Aid, Ross, Verizon, Walmart/Subway

95 Pennsylvania Ave (from wb), Beaumont, N Country Jct Rest., Marla's Rest. Rodeway Inn AutoZone, Meineke, Miller RV Ctr

94 CA 79, Beaumont, N 76/dsl, USA Baker's DriveThru, Casa Palacios, Juan Pollo, McDonald's, Popeye's, YumYum Donuts Best Value Inn, Motel 6 Family$, NAPA, O'Reilly Parts, S Arco/dsl, Chevron/dsl, Shell/Circle K/dsl Del Taco, Denny's, Jack-in-the-Box, Subway vet

93 CA 60 W, to Riverside

92 San Timoteo Canyon Rd, Oak Valley Pkwy, N Chevron/dsl Sand Trap Grill, Subway Holiday Inn Express golf, Rite Aid, S golf

91mm **wb, full facilities, litter barrels, petwalk,**

90 Cherry Valley Blvd, N truck/tire repair

89 Singleton Rd (from wb), to Calimesa

88 Calimesa Blvd, N Arco/dsl, Chevron/dsl, Shell/dsl Best Wok, Burger King, Carl's Jr, Denny's, McDonald's, NY Pizzaria, Starbucks, Subway, Taco Bell Calimesa Inn $Tree, Stater Bros Foods, Walgreens, S Big Boy, Jack-in-the-Box

87 County Line Rd, to Yucaipa, N FasTrip/dsl, Shell/dsl Baker's DriveThru, Del Taco Best Value $General, 99c Store, USPO, vet

86mm **Wildwood Rest Area eb, full facilities, litter barrels, petwalk,**

85 Live Oak Canyon Rd, Oak Glen, N Arco/dsl

83 Yucaipa Blvd, N Arco/dsl, Chevron/dsl, Mobil Baker's DriveThru, Corky's Kitchen, In-N-Out, Starbucks, S Subway

82 Wabash Ave (from wb)

81 Redlands Blvd, Ford St, S Phillips 66 Starbucks

80 Cypress Ave, University St, N to U of Redlands, S

79b a CA 38, 6th St, Orange St, Redlands, N Arco, Chevron Domino's Budget Inn, Stardust Motel Stater Bros Foods, S Phillips 66, Shell Chipotle Mexican, Corner Cafe, Eureka Burger, Jersey Mike's, Las Fuentes Mexican, Phoenicia Greek, Pieology, Rubio's, Starbucks Firestone/auto, Office Depot, O'Reilly Parts, Sprouts Mkt, Trader Joe's, Verizon, Von's Foods

77c (77b from wb) Tennessee St, N 7-11 Jack-in-the-Box, Shakey's Pizza Home Depot, Toyota, S Shell Arby's, Bakers DriveThru, Burger King, Carl's Jr, Coco's, El Burrito, El Pollo Loco, Papa John's, Subway, Taco Bell Ayers Hotel, Comfort Suites, Dynasty Suites, Motel 6 American Tire Depot, Ford, USPO, vet

77b (77c from wb) CA 210, to Highlands

77a Alabama St, N Phillips 66/Circle K/dsl Buffet Star, Cafe Rio, Chick-fil-A, Chili's, Chipotle, Coldstone Creamery, Denny's, Famous Dave's BBQ, Farmer Boys, Five Guys, Habit Burger, Hawaiian BBQ, Jamba Juice, Jersey Mike's, Jimmy John's, Macaroni Grill, Magic Wok, MOD Pizza, Noodle 21 Asian, Red Robin, Starbucks, Subway, Tom's Burgers Best Value Inn, Motel 7 West, Super 8 Barnes&Noble, GNC, Hobby Lobby, JC Penney, Jo-Ann Superstore, Kohl's, Marshall's, Michael's, PetCo, Ross, Target, Tuesday Morning, U-Haul, Verizon, World Mkt, S Chevron, Shell Del Taco, IHOP, McDonald's, Mr Taco, Nick's Burgers, Old Spaghetti Factory, Pizza Hut Country

SAN BERNARDINO

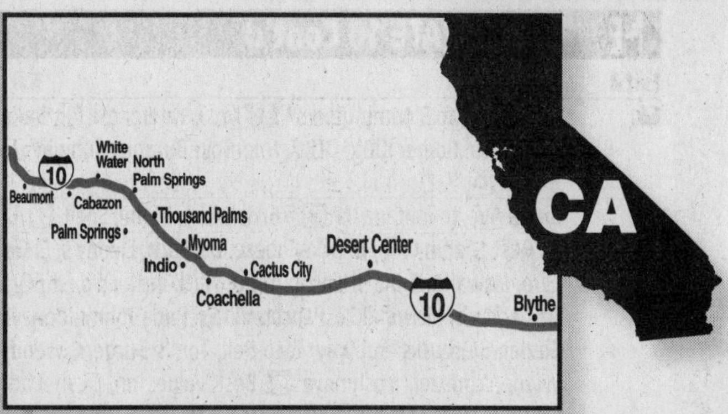

77a Continued
Inn&Suites, GoodNite Inn $Tree, 7-11, 99c Store, BigLots, Chevrolet, CVS Drug, Discount Tire, Goodyear/auto, Lowe's, Midas, Nissan, PepBoys

76 California St, N Mill Creek Rest. funpark, museum, S Arco, EVC, Shell/LP/dsl Applebee's, Bravo Burger, Jack-in-the-Box, Jose's Mexican, Little Caesar's, Panda Express, Red Chili Szechuan, Subway, Wendy's, Wienerschnitzel AT&T, AutoZone, Food4Less, Mission RV Park, Walmart

75 Mountain View Ave, Loma Linda, N Valero/dsl, S Shell/Circle K/dsl Alberto's Mexican, Domino's, FarmerBoys Burgers, Subway

74 Tippecanoe Ave, Anderson St, N BJ's Rest., Cane's, Chipotle Mexican, El Pollo Loco, Hawaiian BBQ, In-N-Out, Jack-in-the-Box, Jamba Juice, Jimmy John's, Panera Bread, Pick-Up Stix, Pollo Campero, Starbucks, Subway, Tasty Goody Fairfield Inn, Hampton Inn, Homewood Suites, Residence Inn Best Buy, Costco/gas, Sam's Club/gas, Staples, Verizon, S Phillips 66/dsl Baker's DriveThru, Del Taco, HomeTown Buffet, KFC, Napoli Italian, Waba Grill auto repair, Honda, Hyundai, to Loma Linda U

73b a Waterman Ave, N Chevron, G&M/dsl Baja Fresh, Black Angus, Buffalo Wild Wings, Chili's, ChuckeCheese, ClaimJumper, Cutting Board Rest., El Torito, Five Guys, Golden Corral, IHOP, King Buffet, Lotus Garden Chinese, Mimi's Café, Olive Garden, Outback Steaks, Panda Express, Red Lobster, Sizzler, Souplantation, Star Crab, Subway, TGIFriday's Days Inn, DoubleTree, Hilton Garden, La Quinta, Quality Inn, Super 8, SureStay+ 7-11, Aldi Foods, Home Depot, Office Depot, PetsMart, S Arco Burger King, Carl's Jr, Gus Jr Burger #8, McDonald's, Popeye's, Starbucks Motel 6 Camping World RV Ctr, El Monte RV Ctr, repair

72 I-215, CA 91

71 Mt Vernon Ave, Sperry Ave, N 7-11, Trkstp/dsl/LP Alberto's Mexican Colony Inn, Colton Motel, Comfort Inn repair

70b 9th St, N Mobil Denny's, Domino's, McDonald's, P&G Burgers, Starbucks, Subway Best Western+ NAPA, Stater Bros Foods, USPO

70a Rancho Ave, N Del Taco, Jack-in-the-Box, KFC/Taco Bell, Wienerschnitzel

69 Pepper Dr, N Arco/Chelo's/dsl, Chevron Baker's Drive-Thru

68 Riverside Ave, to Rialto, N Chevron/dsl, EVC, I-10 Trkstp/dsl/scales, USA Burger King, Burger King, Coco's, El Pollo Loco, HomeTown Buffet, Jack-in-the-Box, McDonald's, Panda Express, Starbucks, Subway, Taco Joe's American Inn, Days Inn, Welcome Inn American Tire Depot, dsl repair, Pepboys, Walmart, S Shell/Circle K/dsl

CA

= gas = food = lodging = other = rest stop

CA

INTERSTATE 10 Cont'd

ONTARIO

Exit #	Services
66	Cedar Ave, to Bloomington, N Arco, Valero/dsl Baker's DriveThru, Burger King, DQ, FarmerBoys Burgers, Subway, Taco Bell, S 7-11
64	Sierra Ave, to Fontana, N 76/dsl, Arco, Mobil, Shell Billy J's Rest., Cajun Crab, ChuckeCheese, Del Taco, Denny's, El Gallo Giro, Hawaiian BBQ, IHOP, In-N-Out, Jack-in-the-Box, KFC, Little Caesar's, McDonald's, Pancho Villa's, Papa John's, Popeye's, Sizzler, Starbucks, Subway, Taco Bell, Tom's Burgers, Wendy's, Wienerschnitzel, Yoshinoya Best Value Inn, EconoLodge, Motel 6, Valley Motel H, $Tree, American Tire Depot, AutoZone, BigLots, Cardenas Foods, CVS Drug, Food4Less, GNC, PepBoys, Rite Aid, Stater Bros Foods, Verizon, S Chevron/dsl Brandon's Diner, Chipotle, Circle K, Del Taco, Five Guys, National Buffet, Pizza Hut, Shakey's Pizza, Starbucks, Subway, Tasty Goody Hilton Garden AutoZone, O'Reilly Parts, Ross, Target, TJ Maxx
63	Citrus Ave, N Baker's DriveThru, Subway Ford, S 7-11/dsl, Arco/dsl
61	Cherry Ave, N Arco, Chevron, Fontana Trkstp/dsl/24hr, One Stop/dsl Carl's Jr, Del Taco, Jack-in-the-Box Mack/Volvo, truck sales, S 3 Sisters Trkstp/dsl/@, North American Trkstp/dsl, Phillips 66/Circle K Farmer Boy's Rest., La Chiquita Peterbilt
59	Etiwanda Ave, Valley Blvd
58b a	I-15, N to Barstow, S to San Diego
57	Milliken Ave, N 76/dsl, Arco/24hr, Chevron, Mobil/Cherony's/dsl, Shell Applebee's, Baja Fresh, BJ's Rest., Burger King, Carl's Jr, Chevy's Mexican, Chick-fil-A, Chipotle, Dave&Buster's, Del Taco, Denny's, El Pollo Loco, Famous Dave's BBQ, Fat Burger, Fourth and Mill, Fuddrucker's, Hooters, IHOP, In-n-Out, Jack-in-the-Box, Jamba Juice, Jersey Mike's, KFC, Krispy Kreme, McDonald's, Mkt Broiler, New York Grill, Olive Garden, Outback Steaks, Panda Express, Panera Bread, Rain Forest Cafe, Ramona's Mexican, Red Lobster, Rubio's, Sonic, Starbucks, Subway, Taco Bell, Tokyo Wako, Wendy's, Wienerschnitzel Ayre's Suites, Country Inn&Suites, Courtyard, Hampton Inn, Hilton Garden, Holiday Inn Express, Homewood Suites, Hyatt Place, TownePlace Suites $Tree, America's Tire, Carmax, Costco/gas, Jo-Ann Fabrics, Kohl's, Marshall's, Ontario Mills Mall, Petsmart, Ross, Sam's Club/gas, Staples, Target, Verizon, S TA/Shell/Pizza Hut/Subway/Taco Bell/dsl/rest./24hr/@ Rodeway Inn
56	Haven Ave, Rancho Cucamonga, N Mobil Benihana, Black Angus, El Torito, Five Star Pizza, Hamburger Mary's Aloft Hotel, Best Western, Extended Stay America, La Quinta, Ontario Airport Hotel, Ontario Grand Inn, S Panda Chinese, TGIFriday's Embassy Suites, Fairfield Inn
55b a	Holt Blvd, to Archibald Ave, N Arco, Mobil/dsl Baker's Drive-thru, Burgertown USA, Joey's Pizza, Starbucks, Subway, Weinerschnitzel
54	Vineyard Ave, N 76/Circle K Carl's Jr, Del Taco, El Pollo Loco, Great China, Pizza Hut/Taco Bell, Popeye's, Rocky's Pizza, Subway AutoZone, Rite Aid, Stater Bros Foods, S 76/dsl, Mobil, Quick Gas/dsl Denny's, In-N-Out, Jack-in-the-Box, Marie Callenders, Porter's Steaks, Rossa's Italian, Spires Rest., Starbucks, Subway, Wendy's, Yoshinoya Japanese Azure Suites, Best Western, Comfort Suites, DoubleTree Inn, Folk Inn, Holiday Inn, Motel 6, Ontario Airport Inn, Quality Inn, Ramada Inn, Red Roof Inn, Residence Inn, Sheraton Buick/Cadillac/Chevrolet/GMC, to Airport, USPO

MONTCLAIR

COVINA

Exit #	Services
53	San Bernardino Ave, 4th St, to Ontario, N 7-11, A Shell Carl's Jr, Domino's, Golden Corral, Jack-in-Box EconoLodge, Motel 6, S Arco/24hr, Chevron, tario Fuel/dsl Denny's, Little Caesar's, McDonald's, way, YumYum Donuts Days Inn, Travelodge city pa
51	CA 83, Euclid Ave, to Ontario, Upland, N H
50	Mountain Ave, to Mt Baldy, N Chevron, Mobil/Circle K, Shell/dsl Corky's Kitchen, Dunkin', El Torito, Hawaiian HoneyBaked Ham, Panda Express, Subway, Wendy's S 8 $Tree, AT&T, CVS Drug, GNC, Hobby Lobby, Home De Michaels, Staples, S 76/dsl Carl's Jr, Casa Jime Chopstix, Coldstone, Juice it Up, Starbucks, Wingnuts Walmart/Subway
49	Central Ave, to Montclair, N Carl's Jr., Chipotle Mexica Pollo Loco, Gen Korean BBQ, John's Incredible Pizza, McD ald's, Panda Garden Buffet, Paradise Buffet, Pizza Hut, Rodri Mexican, Starbucks, Subway, Taco Bell, Waba Grill $T 99c Store, America's Tire, AutoZone, Barnes&Noble, Best Firestone/auto, Giant RV Ctr, Harley-Davidson, JC Penney, Tires, Macy's, PepBoys, PetCo, Ross, same as 48, Target, S Chevron, USA Dickey's BBQ, Fulin Chinese, Jack the-Box, Jersey Mike's, Starbucks, Subway, Tommy's Burg Wienerschnitzel 7-11, Acura/Honda/Infiniti/Nissan, A Costco/gas, Stater Bros
48	Monte Vista, N Acapulco Mexican, Applebee's, B Angus, Chilis, Elephant Bar Rest., Olive Garden, Red ster Macy's, Nordstrom's, same as 49, S H
47	Indian Hill Blvd, to Claremont, N Shell/dsl Cafe Claremont Lodge, Knights Inn, S 76/dsl, Chev McDonald's Carl's Jr, Chipotle, Denny's, In-N-Out, No Rest., Popeye's, RoundTable Pizza, Starbucks, Subway tel 6 Hyundai, Toyota, Verizon
46	Towne Ave, N 7-11, Chevron/dsl Jack-in-the-Box
45b	Garey Ave, to Pomona, N USA/dsl H, vet, S Ch ron, Shell/dsl Del Taco
45	White Ave, Garey Ave, to Pomona
44	(43 from eb)Dudley St, Fairplex Dr, N Arco/dsl C Palm, Denny's LemonTree Motel, S Chevron/ Jack-in-the-Box, McDonald's, Starbucks 7-11
42b	CA 71 S (from eb), to Corona
42a	to I-210, CA 57 S
41	Kellogg Dr, S to Cal Poly Inst
40	Via Verde
38b	Holt Ave, to Covina, N Hamiltons Steaks Vanllee Su
38a	Grand Ave, N 76, Arco/dsl Denny's, Misky Misky P ana Best Western+ 7-11
37b	Barranca St, Grand Ave, N BJ's Rest., Carl's Jr, Ch Chipotle Mexican, El Torito, Habit Burgers, Hawaiian B Hooters, Islands Rest., Marie Callender, Mariposa Mexi Pacific Fish Grill, Starbucks, Waba Grill Fairfield Inn, Ha ton Inn, Holiday Inn $Tree, Albertsons, CVS Drug, Di Hobby Lobby, IKEA, Marshalls, Petsmart, Ross, Target, Veri S In-N-Out, McDonald's 5 Star Inn, Days Inn, sam 37a
37a	Citrus Ave, to Covina, N Chevron Buffalo Wild Wi Burger King, Del Taco, IHOP, Jack-in-the-Box, Jersey Mik Millie's Rest., Starbucks, Subway, TGIFriday's, Yum Yum nuts Acura, Albertsons, AT&T, Baja Ranch Foods, Bu GMC, Chevrolet, CVS Drug, Kia, Marshall's, Nissan, Office pot, VW, Walmart, S 76/7-11 Classic Burger Ca lac, same as 37b

INTERSTATE 10 Cont'd

Exit #	Services
36	CA 39, Azusa Ave, to Covina, N 76/dsl, Arco/24hr Denny's, Green Field Brazillian, McDonald's, Norm's Rest., Papa John's, Subway $Tree, American Tire Depot, BigLots, Chrysler/Dodge/Jeep, CVS Drug, Food4Less, Stater Bros, S Mobil, Shell/dsl Audi, Ford, Honda, Mercedes, Toyota
35	Vincent Ave, Glendora Ave, N Chevron auto repair, S Blaze Pizza, Chipotle, Five Guys, Gen Korean BBQ, Jamba Juice, Lazy Dog Rest., Lucille's BBQ, Mikomi Japanese, Panera Bread, Pizza Hut, Red Robin, Starbucks, Subway, Weinerschnitzel Best Buy, Firestone/auto, JC Penney, Macy's, Michael's, USPO, Verizon
34	Pacific Ave, N 76, S Shell H, Discount Tire, same as 35
33	Puente Ave, N Chevron Denny's, Farmer Boy's, Guadalajara Grill, McDonald's, Panda Express, Sizzler, Starbucks Courtyard, Motel 6 AT&T, Home Depot, Verizon, Walmart, S Jack-in-the-Box Regency Inn Harley-Davidson
32b	Francisquito Ave, to La Puente, N Valero, S Carl's Jr, In-N-Out, Wienerschnitzel Grand Park Inn hwy patrol
32a	Baldwin Pk Blvd, N Chevron/McDonald's IHOP, Jack-in-the-Box, Papa Johns, Pizza Hut/Taco Bell, Starbucks, Subway, Wendy's, Yum Yum Donuts CVS Drug, Food4Less, Target, transmissions, S H
31c	(31b from wb) Frazier St, N 7-11
31b a	(31a from wb) I-605 N/S, to Long Beach
30	Garvey Ave, S Rte 66
29b	Valley Blvd, Peck Rd, N Chevron Baskin-Robbins, Burger King, Carl's Jr., Denny's, Jamba Juice, KFC, Papa Johns, Shakey's Pizza, Subway, Taco Bell, Yoshinoya Motel 6 Honda, Hyundai, Lexus, Nissan, Toyota, Walgreens, S McDonald's, Tommy's Burgers, Waba Grill
29a	S Peck Rd (from eb)
28	Santa Anita Ave, to El Monte, S 76/dsl 7-11, vet
27	Baldwin Avenue, Temple City Blvd, S Arco/24hr Denny's, same as 26b a
26b	CA 19, Rosemead Blvd, Pasadena, N Habit Burger, Chipotle, Coldstone, IHOP, Jamba Juice, Starbucks, Subway $Tree, GNC, Office Depot, Target, S Del Taco, Jack-in-the-Box, Starbucks
26a	Walnut Grove Ave
25b	San Gabriel Blvd, N Shell Carl's Jr, Popeye's, Taco Bell Budget Inn, S 7-11
25a	Del Mar Ave, to San Gabriel, N Mobil auto repair, S Shell/dsl, USA Travelodge
24	New Ave, to Monterey Park, N KFC, to Mission San Gabriel
23b	Garfield Ave, to Alhambra, S 76, Arco Grand Inn H, auto repair
23a	Atlantic Blvd, Monterey Park, N Pizza Hut, Popeye's, Starbucks H, S Courtyard, Monterey Park Inn Ralph's Foods
22	Fremont Ave, N H, S Papa Johns, Subway 7-11
21	I-710, Long Beach Fwy, Eastern Ave (from wb)
20b a	Eastern Ave, City Terrace Dr, S Chevron/service, Mobil Burger King, McDonald's
19c	Soto St (from wb), N Chevron/dsl H, city park, S 76, Mobil

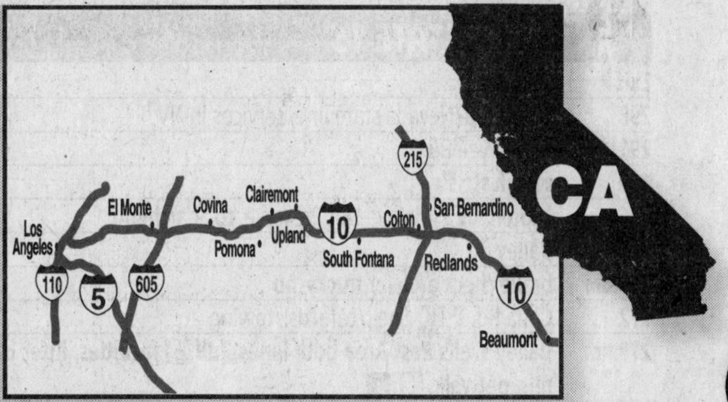

LOS ANGELES AREA

Exit #	Services
19b	I-5 (from wb), US 101 S, N to Burbank, S to San Diego
19a	State St, N H
17	I-5 N
16b	I-5 S (from eb)
16a	Santa Fe Ave, San Mateo St, S 76/dsl, Mobil industrial area, Penske Trucks
15b	Alameda St, N 76/dsl Jack-in-the-Box, to downtown, S industrial area
15a	Central Ave, N Shell/repair, S Shell
14b	San Pedro Blvd, S industrial
14a	LA St, N conv ctr, S El Pollo Loco, McDonald's 99c Store, O'Reilly Parts, Rite Aid, URGENT CARE
13	I-110, Harbor Fwy
12	Hoover St, Vermont Ave, N Chevron Burger King, McDonald's, Subway AutoZone, CVS Drug, PepBoys, S 76, Chevron Jack-in-the-Box, Papa Johns, Yoshinoya Ralph's Foods
11	Normandie Ave, Western Ave
10	Arlington Ave, N 76, Chevron
9	Crenshaw Blvd, N Mobil, S 76, Chevron El Pollo Loco, McDonald's, Subway, Taco Bell, Yoshinoya U-Haul
8	La Brea Ave, N Valero/dsl USPO, S Chevron AutoZone
7b	Washington Blvd, Fairfax Ave, S Mobil, same as 8
7a	La Cienega Blvd, Venice Ave (from wb), N Chevron/24hr, Mobil Carl's Jr., Del Taco Aamco, Firestone/auto, S Subway
6	Robertson Blvd, Culver City, N Chevron/dsl, Valero Domino's, Taco Bell EZ Lube, S Del Taco
5	National Blvd, N Papa John's, Starbucks, Subway, Taco+ Rite Aid, Von's Foods, S Arco
4	Overland Ave, S Mobil/dsl

SANTA MONICA

Exit #	Services
3b a	I-405, N to Sacramento, S to Long Beach
2c b	Bundy Dr, N Chevron, Shell/dsl Taco Bell Cadillac/GMC, Staples
2a	Centinela Ave, to Santa Monica, N Taco Bell, S McDonald's, Trader Joe's Travelodge
1c	20th St (from wb), Cloverfield Blvd, 26th St (from wb), N 76/dsl, Chevron, Shell/repair H
1b	Lincoln Blvd, CA 1 S, N Denny's, McDonald's, Starbucks BrakeMasters, Toyota, Tuesday Morning, USPO, Vons Foods, S Chevron/dsl, Shell Dominos, Jack-in-the-Box, Subway Doubletree Suites 7-11, Firestone/auto, U-Haul
1a	4th, 5th, (from wb)
0	Santa Monica Blvd, to beaches, **I-10 begins/ends on CA 1.**

CA

INTERSTATE 15

Exit #	Services
298	California/Nevada state line, services in NV
291	Yates Well Rd
289	**weigh sta sb**
286	Nipton Rd, E Mojave Nat Preserve, to Searchlight
281	Bailey Rd
276mm	**brake check area for trucks, nb**
272	Cima Rd, E Shell/cafe/dsl/towing
270mm	**Valley Wells Rest Area both lanes, full facilities, litter barrels, petwalk,**
265	Halloran Summit Rd
259	Halloran Springs Rd
248	to Baker (from sb), same as 246

BAKER

Exit #	Services
246	CA 127, Kel-Baker Rd, Baker, to Death Valley, W Tesla EVC, 76/dsl, Arco, Chevron/Subway/Fatburger/Pizza Hut/dsl, Chevron/Taco Bell, Shell/DQ/dsl, Shell/Jack-in-the-Box/dsl, Valero, Valero/A&W/Pizza Hut/Subway/dsl Arby's, Burger King, Carl's Jr, Del Taco, Denny's, Mad Greek Café BunBoy Hotel, Santa Fe Motel Alien Fresh Jerky, Baker Mkt Foods, Country Store, repair, USPO, World's Tallest Thermometer
245	to Baker (from nb), same as 246
239	Zzyzx Rd
233	Rasor Rd, E Shell/Rasor Sta/dsl/towing/24hr
230	Basin Rd
221	Afton Rd, to Dunn, W Mini Mkt
217mm	**both lanes, full facilities, litter barrels, petwalk,**
213	Field Rd
206	Harvard Rd, to Newberry Springs
198	Minneola Rd, W Cali Burger, Shell/dsl
197mm	**agricultural insp sta sb**
196	Yermo Rd, Yermo
194	Calico Rd, E Eddie World/dsl, Tesla EVC
191	Ghost Town Rd, E Arco/24hr, Mohsen Oil Trkstp/dsl/24hr Jack-in-the-Box, Peggy Sue's 50s Diner, Penny's Diner Baymont Inn, W Chevron/dsl, Shell/Subway/dsl/24hr Calico GhostTown (3mi), KOA
189	Ft Irwin Rd
186	CA 58 W, to Bakersfield

BARSTOW

Exit #	Services
184	E Main, Barstow, Montera Rd (from eb), to I-40, E Phillips 66/dsl Grill It, McDonald's, Mega Tom's Burgers, Panda Express, Popeye's, Starbucks, Subway Arco, Best Western, Travelodge Walmart, W Chevron, Circle K, EVC, Mobil/dsl, USA/dsl Alberto's, Burger King, Carl's Jr, China Town Buffet, Del Taco, Denny's, Di Napoli's Italian, IHOP, Jack-in-the-Box, Jenny's Grill, Little Caesar's, Rigoberto's, Wienerschnitzel Astro Budget Motel, Best Motel, Budget Inn, CA Inn, Days Inn, Desert Inn, EconoLodge, Economy Inn, Motel 6, Quality Inn/rest., Ramada Inn, Rodeway Inn, Super 8 $Tree, 99c Store, AutoZone, O'Reilly Parts, U-Haul/LP
184a	I-40 E (from nb), **I-40 begins/ends.**
183	CA 247, Barstow Rd, E Circle K, Valero/7-11/dsl Jimenez Mexican, Pizza Hut, Subway $General, Rite Aid, W Food-4Less/dsl, Shell H, Food4Less, Marshall's, Mojave River Valley Museum, st patrol
181	L St, W Main, Barstow, W Arco/dsl, Chevron, USA Foster's Freeze Baymont Inn Firestone/auto, Home Depot, NAPA, tires/towing
179	CA 58, to Bakersfield
178	Lenwood, to Barstow, E FLYING J/Denny's/dsl/24hr, 76/dsl, Arco/dsl, Chevron, Shell/dsl, Valero Arby's, Big Boy,
178	Continued Burger King, Carl's Jr, Chili's, Chipotle Mexican, Del Taco, D ny's, El Pollo Loco, Fatburger, Habit Burger, IHOP, In-N-C Jack-in-the-Box, Jersey Mike's, Oggi's, Panda Express, Par Bread, Starbucks, Subway, Tommy's Burgers Ayres Ho Comfort Suites, Hampton Inn, Holiday Inn Express B Beacon, Old Navy, Tanger Outlet/famous brands/food ct, W Loves/Chester's/Godfather's/dsl/scales/24hr/@, Pilo Subway/dsl/scales/24hr, TA/Shell/Country Fare/Subway/ scales/24hr/@ McDonald's Days Inn repair, tru wash, Zippy Lube
175	Outlet Ctr Dr, Sidewinder Rd
169	Hodge Rd
165	Wild Wash Rd
161	Dale Evans Pkwy, to Apple Valley
157	Stoddard Wells Rd, to Bell Mtn
154	Stoddard Wells Rd, to Bell Mtn, E Shady Oasis Camping. W 76/dsl, Mobil Franky's Diner Motel 6, Que Motel
153.5mm	Mojave River

VICTORVILLE

Exit #	Services
153b	E St
153a	CA 18 E, D St, to Apple Valley, E Arco H, repair, W Arco/Subway/dsl
151b	Mojave Dr, Victorville, E Mobil/dsl Rodeway W Valero/dsl Economy Inn, Sunset Inn
151a	La Paz Dr, Roy Rogers Dr, E Chevron, Shell/dsl Bu King, Carl's Jr, El Pollo Loco, HomeTown Buffet, IHOP, Jack the-Box, McDonald's, Wendy's, Wienerschnitzel $Gene $Tree, 99c Store, AutoZone, BigLots, Costco/gas, Fiat, Fo 4Less, Goodyear/auto, Harley-Davidson, Pepboys, Rite A Toyota, W Arco Carl's Jr, Dickey's BBQ, Domin Farmer Boys, Golden ChopStix, Hawaiian BBQ, In-N-Out, P da Express, Papa John's, Starbucks, Subway Americas T Buick/GMC, Chrysler/Dodge/Jeep, Home Depot, Honda, Nissan, Stater Bros, Verizon, Walgreens, WinCo Foods
150	CA 18 W, Palmdale Rd, Victorville, E Baker's Drive-T Burger King, Denny's, KFC, Richie's Diner Greentree Red Roof Inn, W 76/dsl, Arco, Circle K Coco's, Del Ta House of Joy, La Casita Mexican, McDonald's, Pizza Hut, Ra Mexican, Starbucks, Subway, Taco Bell, Tom's Rest. Bud Inn, Days Inn, Holiday Inn H, $General, Aamco, AutoZo CVS Drug, Ford, Hyundai, Kamper's Korner RV, Mazda, Targ Town&Country Tire, vet
148	La Mesa Rd, Nisquali Rd, E Red Roof Inn, W Baskin-R bins, Buffalo's, ChuckeCheese, Fatburger AT&T, Petsma
147	Bear Valley Rd, to Lucerne Valley, 0-2 mi E 76/Circle K Arco, Chevron, Mobil Arby's, Baker's Drive-Thru, Burger K Carl's Jr, Del Taco, Dragon Express, John's Pizza, KFC, Los Alaza Mexican, Los Toritos, Marie Callender's, McDonald's, Panda press, Red Robin, Starbucks, Steak'n Shake, Steer'n Stein, Ta Mexico, Wienerschnitzel Best Value Inn, Comfort Su Day&Night Inn, EconoLodge, Extended Stay, Extended Stu Hotel, La Quinta, Travelodge Affordable RV Ctr, Ameri Tire, AutoZone, Firestone/auto, Home Depot, Michael's, O'R Parts, Range RV, Rite Aid, Scandia Funpark, Tire Depot, Valla Foods, vet, Walmart/McDonald's/auto, W 76/Circle K, A Chevron/dsl, Valero/dsl Applebee's, Archibald's Drive-T Baja Fresh, Carino's, Chili's, Chipotle Mexican, Cracker Ba Del Taco, El Pollo Loco, El Tio Pepe Mexican, Farmer Boy's Re Freddy's Custard, Giuseppe's, Jack-in-the-Box, Little Caes McDonald's, Mimi's Cafe, Olive Garden, Outback Steaks, Pan Villa's, Red Lobster, RoadHouse Grill, Sonic, Starbucks, Subw

INTERSTATE 15 Cont'd

147 Continued
Tokyo Steaks, Wendy's Hawthorn Suites 99c Store, AAA, Barnes&Noble, Best Buy, CVS Drug, Dick's, Goodyear/auto, Hobby Lobby, JC Penney, Kohl's, Lowe's, Macy's, Rite Aid, Stater Bros., Verizon, Walgreens, Walmart

143 Main St, to Hesperia, Phelan, **E** Chevron/dsl, Mobil/Alberto's, Shell/Popeye's/dsl Arby's, Burger King, Chipotle, Del Taco, Denny's, IHOP, In-N-Out, Jack-in-the-Box, Panda Express, Quiznos, Starbucks Courtyard, SpringHill Suites Walmart/Subway, **W** 76/dsl, Arco/dsl Baker's Drive-thru, FarmerBoys, Five Guys, Golden Corral, Subway, Waba Grill Holiday Inn Express, Motel 6 Desert Willow RV Park, GNC, Jo-Ann Fabrics, Marshall's, Ross, SuperTarget, URGENT CARE, Verizon

141 US 395, Joshua St, Adelanto, **W** Arco/dsl, Pilot/Wendy's/dsl/scales/24hr Outpost Café repair, RV supply ctr, truck/RV wash, Zippy Lube

140 Ranchero Rd

138 Oak Hill Rd, **E** Chevron/dsl Summit Inn Café, **W** Oak Hills RV Village/LP

137mm **brake check sb**, Cajon Summit, elevation 4260

131 CA 138, to Palmdale, Silverwood Lake, **E** Chevron McDonald's Silverwood SRA, **W** 76/Circle K/Del Taco/LP, Shell/Subway/dsl/LP Best Western

130mm elevation 3000, **weigh sta both lanes**

129 Cleghorn Rd

124 Kenwood Ave

123 I-215 S, to San Bernardino, **E** Arco to Glen Helen Park

122 Glen Helen Parkway

119 Sierra Ave, **W** Arco/dsl, Chevron/dsl, Shell/Del Taco/dsl, Valero/dsl Jack-in-the-Box, McDonalds to Lytle Creek RA

118 Duncan Canyon Rd

116 Summit Ave, **E** 7-11, Chevron Chili's, Coldstone, Del Taco, El Ranchero, Five Guys, Hawaiian BBQ, Jack-in-the-Box, Juice It Up, Little Caesar's, Panera Bread, Quiznos, Roundtable Pizza, Starbucks, Subway, Taco Bell, Wendy's $Tree, CVS Drug, GNC, Kohl's, Marshall's, Michael's, Petsmart, Ross, Staples, Stater Bros, Target, Verizon

115b a CA 210, Highland Ave, **E** to Lake Arrowhead

113 Base Line Rd, **E** USA Denny's, Jack-in-the-Box, Logans Roadhouse, Pizza Hut, Rosa Maria's, Starbucks Comfort Inn

112 CA 66, Foothill Blvd, **E** Chevron Asia Buffet, ClaimJumper, Golden Spoon, In-N-Out, Panda Express, Subway, Taco Bell, Wienerschnitzel $City, Food4Less, Jiffy Lube, Walmart, **1-2 mi W** 76/dsl, Chevron/dsl Baker's, Buffalo Wild Wings, Carino's, Cheesecake Factory, Chick-fil-A, Chipotle Mexican, Del Taco, Denny's, El Pollo Loco, El Torito, Flemings Steaks, Islamadora Fish Co, Jack-in-the-Box, Joe's Crab Shack, Johnny Rockets, Kings Fishouse, Lucille's BBQ, Old Spagetti Factory, Paisano's Rest., PF Chang's, Popeyes, Red Robin, Richie's Diner, Shakey's Pizza, Starbucks, TGIFriday's, The Hat Grill, Wendy's Sheraton 4 Points AT&T, AutoZone, Bass Pro Shops, Best Buy, Fresh&Easy Mkt, Home Depot, JC Penney, Macy's, Office Depot, Sears Grand

110 4th St, **E** Arco/dsl Baker's, Subway, **W** 76/dsl, Arco, Chevron/Alberto's Mexican/dsl, Shell/dsl Applebee's, Arby's, Baja Fresh, Baskin-Robbins, BJ's Rest., Boston's, Burger King, Carl's Jr, Chevy's Mexican, Chick-fil-A, Chipotle, Chop Sticks, Coco's, Daphne's Greek, Del Taco, Denny's, El Pollo Loco, Famous Dave's BBQ, Fat Burger, Fuddruckers, Hooters, IHOP, In-N-Out, Jack-in-the-Box, Jamba Juice, Juice It Up, KFC, Krispy Kreme, Lazy Dog Cafe, McDonald's, Mkt Broiler, New City Buffet, NY Grill,

ONTARIO

NORCO

CA

110 Continued
Olive Garden, Outback Steaks, Panera Bread, Rain Forest Cafe, Red Brick Pizza, Red Lobster, Rubio's, Sonic, Starbucks, Subway, Tokyo Tokyo, Wendy's, Wienerschnitzel, Wing Place Ayre's Suites, Country Inn&Suites, Courtyard, Hampton Inn, Hilton Garden, Holiday Inn Express, Homewood Suites, Hyatt Place, TownePlace Suites $Tree, America's Tire, Costco/gas, JC Penney, Jo-Ann Fabrics, Kohl's, Marshall's, Ontario Mills Mall, Petsmart, Sam's Club/gas, Staples, Target, Tire Pros, Verizon

109b a I-10, E to San Bernardino, W to LA

108 Jurupa St, **E** Chevron/dsl Burger King, Del Taco, El Gran Burrito, Starbucks, Subway Affordable RV, BMW, Chrysler/Dodge/Jeep, Family RV Ctr, Fiat, Honda, Hyundai, Lexus, Mazda, Mini, Nissan, Subaru, Toyota, Volvo, VW, **W** Arco Carl's Jr Ford, Kia, Scandia funpark

106 CA 60, E to Riverside, W to LA

105 Cantu-Galleano Ranch Rd

103 Limonite Ave, **E** Asado Grill, Carl's Jr, Del Taco, Denny's, Five Guys, Hawaiian BBQ, Jamba Juice, Subway Lowe's, Michael's, PetCo, Ross, **W** Chevron Applebee's, Blaze Pizza, Buffalo Wild Wings, Carino's, Chipotle, Coldstone, Dickey's BBQ, Domino's, Farmer Boys, Habit Burger, Jersey Mike's, Juice it Up, Little Caesar's, McDonald's, On-the-Border, Pacific Fish Grill, Panda Express, Panera Bread, Pick Up Stix, Starbucks, Subway, Taco Bell, Tutti Frutti Yogurt, Wendy's AT&T, Best Buy, GNC, Home Depot, Kohl's, Nestle Tollhouse, Petsmart, Ralph's Foods/gas, Staples, Target, TJ Maxx, Verizon, Vons Foods/gas, Walgreens

100 6th St, Norco Dr, Old Town Norco, **E** 76/dsl, Chevron Jack-in-the-Box, McDonald's Rite Aid, **W** Arco, Valero/dsl Big Boy, Norco's Burgers, Starbucks, Wienerschnitzel Fairfield Inn Brake Masters, Jiffy Lube, USPO, vet

98 2nd St, **W** Mobil, Shell/dsl, Thrifty Baja Fish Tacos, Burger Basket, Burger King, Carl's Jr, Del Taco, In-N-Out, Pancake House, Pizza Hut, Polly's Cafe, Subway $Tree, 7-11, Ace Hardware, Chrysler/Dodge/Jeep, Ford, Norco Tires, Schwab Tire, Stater Bros

97 Yuma Dr, Hidden Valley Pkwy, **E** 7-11 Chick-fil-A, Hot Dog Shoppe, Marco's Pizza, Shogun Japanese, Starbucks, Starbucks, Subway, Waba Grill Kohl's, Stater Bros, **W** 76/dsl, Chevron, Shell/dsl Alberto's Mexican, Burger City Grill, Carl's Jr, Chipotle, Denny's, Domino's, Fantastic Cafe, Five Guys, Hawaiian BBQ, Hickory Joe's BBQ, Jack-in-the-Box, Jamba Juice, Jersey Mike's, Jimmy John's, KFC, McDonald's, Miguel's Jr, Papa John's, Pieology, Popeye's, Rodrigo's Mexican, Rubio's, Taco Bell, Wahoos Fish Taco Hampton Inn, Howard Johnson Express America's Tire, AT&T, AutoZone, BigLots, GNC, Hobby Lobby, O'Reilly Parts, Staples, Target, URGENT CARE, Verizon, Walgreens, Walgreens, Winco

CA

INTERSTATE 15 Cont'd

EL CERRITO / LAKE ELSINORE / MURRIETA

Exit #	Services
96b a	CA 91, to Riverside, beaches
95	Magnolia Ave, **E** [gas] Chevron/Jack-in-the-Box/dsl [food] Islands Burgers, Shamrock's Grill [lodging] Residence Inn [other] AAA, Lowe's, Office Depot, **W** [gas] Mobil/Circle K, Shell [food] Baskin-Robbins, Broken Yolk, Coco's, Jersey's Pizza, Little Caesar's, McDonald's, Sizzler, Subway, Waba Grill [lodging] Holiday Inn Express [other] $Tree, AT&T, CVS Drug, El Super Mkt, O'Reilly Parts, Sonic, Stater Bros Foods
93	Ontario Ave, to El Cerrito, **E** [gas] Shell/dsl [food] Sombrero Mexican, Starbucks [other] Mtn View Tire, vet, **W** [gas] 76/Circle K, Arco, Chevron [food] Chipotle, Chopstix, Del Taco, Denny's, El Pollo Loco, Hawaiian BBQ, In-N-Out, Jack-in-the-Box, Jersey Mike's, Juice It Up, KFC, Magic Wok, McDonald's, Miguel's Jr, Papa John's, Pieology, Porky's Pizza, Rubio's, SpringHill Suites, Subway, Taco Bell, Tommy's Burgers, Wienerschnitzel [other] Albertson's/Sav-On, America's Tire, AutoZone, CVS Drug, Home Depot, Sam's Club/gas, USPO, Walmart
92	El Cerrito Rd
91	Cajalco Rd, **E** [food] BJ's Rest., Buffalo Wild Wings, Chick-fil-A, Chili's, Chipotle, Five Guys, Jamba Juice, King's Fish House, Macaroni Grill, Panera Bread, Rock Brews Rest., Starbucks, Wendy's [other] AT&T, Barnes&Noble, Best Buy, Kohl's, Marshall's, Michael's, Old Navy, PetCo, Ross, See's Candies, Staples, Target, Verizon, World Mkt, **W** [gas] Mobil/dsl [food] Jack-in-the-Box, NY Pizza, Subway [other] Stater Bros, vet
90	Weirick Rd, Dos Lagos Dr, **E** [gas] Arco/dsl [food] Citrus City Grille, Fatburger, Miguel's, Tap's Rest., TGIFriday's, Wood Ranch BBQ [lodging] Staybridge Suites [other] 7 Oaks Gen Store, Trader Joe's
88	Temescal Cyn Rd, Glen Ivy, **E** [gas] Shell, **W** [gas] Arco/dsl [food] Carl's Jr, Tom's Farms/BBQ
85	Indian Truck Trail, **W** [food] Pizza Hut, Starbucks, Subway [other] CVS Drug, Von's Foods/dsl
81	Lake St
78	Nichols Rd, **W** [gas] Arco/dsl [other] Outlets/famous brands
77	CA 74, Central Ave, Lake Elsinore, **E** [gas] Arco, Chevron, Mobil/Circle K/dsl [food] Archibald's, Burger King, Chili's, Del Taco, Dickey's BBQ, Douglas Burgers, Golden Corral, Hawaiian BBQ, Juice It Up, Panda Express, Submarina, Taco Del Mar, Tom's ChiliBurgers, Wendy's [other] $Tree, AT&T, Costco/gas, Lowe's, Petsmart, Staples, Valvoline, **W** [food] El Pollo Loco, Farmer Boys, Golden Chop Stix, IHOP, McDonald's, Papa John's, Starbucks, Subway, Wienerschnitzel [other] 99c Store, Aldi Foods, Home Depot, Marshall's, PetCo, Target, Verizon, Walgreens
75	Main St, Lake Elsinore, **W** [gas] Main St Gas/dsl [other] 7-11, tires/repair
73	Railroad Cyn Rd, to Lake Elsinore, **E** [gas] 76/7-11, Shell/Circle K/dsl [food] Alberto's Mexican, Denny's, El Pollo Loco, In-N-Out, KFC, Peony Chinese, Starbucks [lodging] Holiday Inn Express [other] GNC, Jiffy Lube, O'Reilly Parts, URGENT CARE, Verizon, vet, Von's Foods, Walmart/McDonald's, **W** [gas] Arco, Chevron, Mobil/Circle K/dsl [food] Annie's Cafe, Cafe China, Carl's Jr, Del Taco, Don Jose's Mexican, King Kabob, McDonald's, Pizza Hut, Sizzler, Subway, Taco Bell, Vincenzo's [lodging] Best Western+, Quality Inn, Travel Inn [other] $Tree, 7-11, AutoZone, BigLots, Buick/GMC, Chevrolet, CVS Drug, Express Tire/auto, Firestone/auto, Ford, Stater Bros, vet, Walgreens
71	Bundy Cyn Rd, **E** [gas] Shell/Circle K, **W** [gas] Arco [food] Jack-in-the-Box
69	Baxter Rd
68	Clinton Keith Rd, **E** [gas] Chevron/dsl, USA [food] Denny's, Golden Spoon, Los Jilbetos Tacos, Los Reyes Grill, McDonald's, Panda

Exit #	Services
68	Continued Express, Starbucks, Subway [other] [hospital], Ace Hardware, Albertso Sav-on, **W** [gas] 7-11, Arco/dsl [food] Del Taco, Jack-in-the- Stadium Pizza, Starbucks, Tresino's Italian, Yellow Basket Bu ers [other] Baron's Mkt, Rite Aid, Stater Bros
65	California Oaks Rd, Kalmia St, **E** [gas] 76/Circle K/dsl, Chev Shell/7-11/dsl [food] Burger King, Carl's Jr, Chili's, Chipotle, Jade Chinese, Jamba Juice, Jersey's Pizza, Jimenez Mexi KFC, Little Caesar's, McDonald's, Papa John's, Starbucks, S way, Wings'N Things [lodging] Comfort Inn [other] $Tree, Albertso Sav-On, AutoZone, Express Tire, O'Reilly Parts, Rite Aid, get, Tuesday Morning, vet, Walgreens, **W** [gas] Arco/dsl, Ch ron [food] Applebee's, Chick-fil-A, Farmer Boys, Jack-in-the-E Juice it Up, Pick Up Stix, Sizzlin Steer, Taco Bell [other] Ameri Tire, Giant RV Ctr, Kohl's, Lowe's, Office Depot, PetCo
64	Murrieta Hot Springs Rd, to I-215, **E** [gas] 7-11, Shell/dsl [food] falo Wild Wings, Carl's Jr, El Pollo Loco, Hungry Bull, Rich Diner, Rubio's, Sizzler, Starbucks, Wendy's [other] Ralph's Foo Rite Aid, Ross, Sam's Club/gas, Walgreens, **W** [gas] 7-11, Sh Popeye's/dsl [food] Arby's, Chuy's, Coldstone, Denny's, IH Jersey Mike's Subs, McDonald's, Panda Express, Starbu Subway, Tom's Burgers, Wienerschnitzel [other] 99c Store, A American Tire Depot, AT&T, Best Buy, BigLots, CarMax, Ho Depot, Petsmart, Staples, Walmart/McDonald's
63	I-215 N (from nb), to Riverside
62	French Valley Pkwy (from sb, no return), **W** [food] Los bos [other] BMW, O'Reilly Parts, VW
61	CA 79 N, Winchester Rd, **E** [gas] 76/dsl, Chevron [food] Baja Fre Baskin-Robbins/Togo's, BF Greek Rest., BJ's Rest., Burger Ki CA Pizza Kitchen, Chick-fil-A, Chipotle Mexican, Coldsto Corner Cafe, Del Taco, Dickey's BBQ, El Torito, Famous Da Fatburger, Five Guys, Freebirds Burrito, Harry's Grill, Hometo Buffet, Islands Burgers, Jamba Juice, Lazy Dog Cafe, Luci BBQ, Macaroni Grill, McDonald's, Mimi's Cafe, Ming's, O Garden, Outback Steaks, Panda Express, Panera Bread, Chang's, Red Ginger Chinese, Red Lobster, Red Robin, Shak Pizza, Shogun Chinese, Souplantation, Starbucks, Subw Taco Bell, TGIFriday's, Tilted Kilt, Wahoo's, Yellow Basket Ha burgers [other] $Tree, 99c Store, America's Tire, AT&T, AutoZo Barnes&Noble, Costco/gas, CVS Drug, Express Tire, Express T Food4Less, GNC, Hobby Lobby, Hyundai, JC Penney, Jo-Ann F rics, Lowe's, Macy's, Nissan, Office Depot, Old Navy, PepB PetCo, Ramona Tire, Roots Mkt, See's Candies, TJ Maxx, Tra Joe's, Verizon, WinCo Foods, World Mkt, **W** [gas] Arco, Chevr dsl [food] Arby's, Banzai Japanese, Chin's Gourmet Chinese, Taco, El Pollo Loco, Farmer Boys, In-N-Out, Jack-in-the-Box, sy's Country Kitchen, Serrano's Grill, Starbucks, Subway, Su China, Tacos El Gallo, Vail Ranch Steakhouse, Wendy's [lodging] B Western, Extended Stay America, Fairfield Inn, Holiday Inn press, La Quinta, Quality Inn [other] NAPA, Richardson's RV Ct patrol, tires/repair, vet
59	Rancho California Rd, **E** [gas] Arco, Mobil/Circle K/dsl, Sh dsl [food] Black Angus, Chili's, ClaimJumper, Del Taco, Gol Spoon, Jilberto's Mexican, Little Caesar's, Marie Callend Pat&Oscar's Rest., Peony Chinese, Pizza Hut, RoundTable Piz Rubio's, Starbucks, Subway, Times Square NY Pizza [lodging] Emb sy Suites [other] BigLots, CVS Drug, Ford, Mazda, Michael's, Suba Target, URGENT CARE, Verizon, vet, Von's Foods, **W** [gas] 76/Ci K/dsl, Chevron [food] Alberto's Mexican, Denny's, McDonald's, Kabob Grill, Penfold's Cafe, Rosa's Café, Starbucks, Vince's S ghetti [lodging] Hampton Inn, Motel 6, Rancho California Inn, Ro way Inn, SpringHill Suites [other] to Old Town Temecula, USPO

INTERSTATE 15 Cont'd

Exit #	Services
58	CA 79 S, to Indio, Temecula, E Mobil/Circle K/dsl, Valero/Circle K/dsl Carl's Jr, Del Taco, Domino's, Domino's, Francesca's Italian, Golden Bowl Asian, In-N-Out, Los Jilberto's, Starbucks, Utopizza, Wing-n-Things 7-11, Ace Hardware, America's Tire, CVS Drug, Valvoline, W Arco, Shell/dsl Baskin-Robbins, Eldorado Mexican, Garage Rest., Hungry Howie's, Leinzo Charro Mexican, Wienerschnitzel Ramada Inn Express Tire, Harley-Davidson
55mm	check sta nb
54	Rainbow Valley Blvd, 2 mi E gas food, W CA Insp Sta
51	Mission Rd, to Fallbrook, W H
46	CA 76, to Oceanside, Pala, E RV camp, W Mobil/Circle K McGrath's Grill Quality Inn Pala Meas Mkt
44mm	San Luis Rey River
43	Old Hwy 395
41	Gopher Canyon Rd, Old Castle Rd, 1 mi E Welk Resort RV camping
37	Deer Springs Rd, Mountain Meadow Rd, W Arco
34	Centre City Pkwy (from sb)
33	El Norte Pkwy, E Arco, Shell/dsl Arby's, DQ, IHOP, Papa John's, Starbucks Best Western CVS Drug, Express Tire/auto repair, RV Resort, vet, Von's Foods, W 76/7-11/dsl, Circle K Jack-in-the-Box, Killer Pizza, Rita's Custard, Subway, Wendy's vet, Von's Foods
32	CA 78, to Oceanside
31	Valley Pkwy, E Arco Chili's, ChuckeCheese, Cocina del Charro, Firehouse Subs, McDonald's, Olive Garden, Panda Express, Rock'N Jenny's Subs, Thai Kitchen H, Barnes&Noble, Meineke, Michael's, PetCo, URGENT CARE, W Express Applebee's, Burger King, Carl's Jr, Chipotle Mexican, Coco's, Del Taco, El Pollo Loco, Five Guys, In-N-Out, Jamba Juice, Mike's BBQ, Panera Bread, Pick Up Stix, Port of Subs, Primo's Mexican, Soup Plantation, Starbucks, Subway, Wendy's Comfort Inn, Holiday Inn Express 7-11, Albertson's, AT&T, BigLots, CVS Drug, Dick's, GNC, Home Depot, Lexus, Ross, Staples, Target, TJ Maxx, Verizon, World Mkt
30	9th Ave, Auto Parkway, E Infiniti, Mercedes, W same as 31
29	Felicita Rd
28	Centre City Pkwy (from nb, no return), E Center City Café Escondido Lodge vet
27	Via Rancho Pkwy, to Escondido, E Chevron/dsl, Shell BJ's Rest., Cheesecake Factory, Macaroni Grill, On-the-Border, Panera Bread, Red Robin JC Penney, Macy's, Nordstrom, San Diego Animal Park, Target, W Shell/Quiznos/dsl McDonald's, Starbucks, Subway Verizon
26	W Bernardo Dr, to Highland Valley Rd, Palmerado Rd
24	Rancho Bernardo Rd, to Lake Poway, E Arco, Mobil/Circle K Chef Chin, Cojita's Taco, Pizza Hut, Soup Plantation, Starbucks, Stirfresh, Sub Marina, Subway Hilton Garden AT&T, Barons Mkt, GNC, Von's Foods, W 76/Circle K, Chevron/7-11 Elephant Bar Rest., Starbucks Holiday Inn Express, Radisson
23	Bernardo Ctr Dr, E Chevron Burger King, Carl's Jr, Coco's, Denny's, Hibachi Buffet, Jack-in-the-Box, Little Caesar's, McDonald's, Quiznos, Robeks Juice, RoundTable Pizza, Rubio's 7-11, CVS Drug, Express Tire/auto, Firestone/auto, vet
22	Camino del Norte
21	Carmel Mtn Rd, E Chevron, Shell/dsl Athens Greek, Baskin-Robbins, Boston Mkt, Broken Yolk Cafe, CA Pizza Kitchen, Carl's Jr, Chick-fil-A, China Fun, Chipotle Mexican,

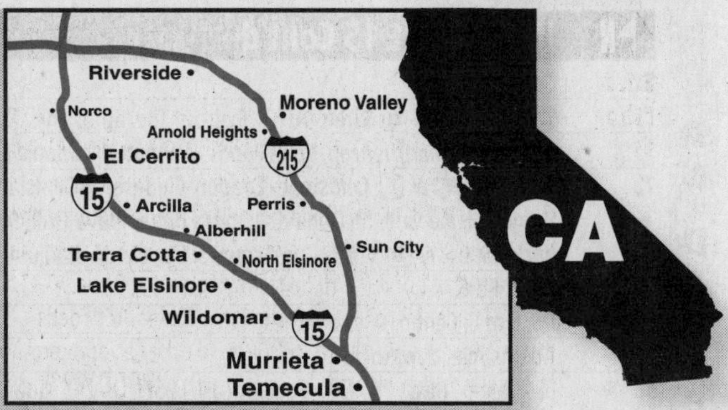

CARMEL MTN

MIRA MESA

Exit #	Services
21	Continued ClaimJumper, DQ Orange Julius, El Pollo Loco, Habit Burgers, In-N-Out, Islands Burgers, Jamba Juice, Little Tokyo, Marie Callender's, McDonald's, Olive Garden, O's American Kitchen, Panda Express, Panera Bread, Rubio's, Sombrero Mexican, Subway, Taco Bell, TGIFriday's, Wendy's, Which Wich? Residence Inn AT&T, Barnes&Noble, Best Buy, Costco/gas, GNC, Home Depot, Marshall's, Michael's, PetCo, Ralph's Foods, Rite Aid, Ross, Sears Outlet, See's Candies, Sprouts Mkt, Staples, TJ Maxx, Trader Joe's, USPO, Valvoline, Verizon, W Chevron Jack-in-the-Box, Starbucks 7-11, Albertson's, Big O Tire, Office Depot
19	CA 56 W, Ted Williams Pkwy
18	Rancho Penasquitos Blvd, Poway Rd, E Arco Alvero's Mexican, Papa John's AAA, W 76/dsl, Mobil/dsl IHOP, McDonald's, Mi Ranchito Mexican, MXN Cafe, NY Pizza, Starbucks, Subway La Quinta 7-11
17	Mercy Rd, Scripps Poway Pkwy, E USA/dsl Chili's, Wendy's, Yanni's Grill Residence Inn, SpringHill Suites, W Chevron KFC, Que Pasa Mexican, Starbucks
16	Mira Mesa Blvd, to Lake Miramar, E Bruski Burgers, ChuckeCheese, Denny's, Filippi's Pizza, Filippi's Pizza, Gyu-Kaku Japanese, Lucio's Mexican, Nok Thai, Pizza Hut, Shozen BBQ Comfort Suites, Holiday Inn Express Trader Joe's, USPO, W Arco, Shell Applebee's, Arby's, Buca Italian, Coldstone, El Patron, In-N-Out, Islands Burgers, Jack-in-the-Box, Jamba Juice, Jersey Mike's Subs, McDonald's, Mimi's Café, MXN Mexican, On the Border, Panera Bread, Pick Up Stix, Popeye's, Rubio's, Starbucks, Subway, Wings n Things Albertson's/Sav-On, AutoZone, Barnes&Noble, Best Buy, BigLots, CVS Drug, Discount Tire, GNC, Home Depot, Old Navy, Ralph's Foods, Rite Aid, Ross, USPO, Verizon
15	Carroll Canyon Rd, to Miramar College, E Carl's Jr, Subway
14	Pomerado Rd, Miramar Rd, W Chevron/dsl, Mobil, Shell/dsl, USA/dsl Carl's Jr, Chin's Rest., IHOP, Rice King, Subway Best Western, Holiday Inn, Quality Inn Audi/Porsche, aviation museum, Land Rover, vet
13	Miramar Way, US Naval Air Station
12	CA 163 S (from sb), to San Diego
11	to CA 52
10	Clairemont Mesa Blvd, W Boll Weevil Rest., Carl's Jr, China Express, Giovanni's, Giovanni's Pizza, Jack-in-the-Box, Jersey Mike's, La Salsa, McDonald's, Panda Express, Primo's Mexican, Robeks, Rubio's, Spice House Cafe, Starbucks, Subway, Sunny Donuts, Taco Bell, Taco Bell, Togo's, Wendy's 7-11, vet
9	CA 274, Balboa Ave
8	Aero Dr, W Arco, Chevron/dsl Baskin-Robbins/Togo's, Jack-in-the-Box, McDonald's, Papa John's, Pick Up Stix, Rubio's, Sizzler, SmashBurger, Starbucks, Submarina, Subway, Taco Bell

CA

INTERSTATE 15 Cont'd

SAN DIEGO AREA

8	Continued Holiday Inn $Tree, AT&T, Express Tire/auto, Fry's Electronics, Petsmart, Verizon, Von's Foods, Walmart/McDonald's
7b	Friars Rd W, W Coldstone, Dragon Chinese, IHOP, Islands Burgers, Luna Grill, McDonald's, Oggi's Pizza, Playa Grill, Starbucks, Subway Costco/gas, Lowe's, San Diego Stadium
7a	Friars Rd E
6b	I-8, E to El Centro, W to beaches
6a	Adams Ave, downtown
5b	El Cajon Blvd, E Pearson/dsl/E85/NG Subway Carquest, Ford, W Chevron/dsl, United Oil Church's PepBoys
5a	University Ave, E Chevron/dsl Burger King, Jack-in-the-Box
3	I-805, N to I-5, S to San Ysidro
2b	(2c from nb) CA 94 W, downtown
2a	Market St, E Costco/gas
1c	National Ave, Ocean View Blvd
1b	(from sb) I-5 S, to Chula Vista
1a	(from sb) I-5 N. **I-15 begins/ends on I-5.**

INTERSTATE 40

NEEDLES

Exit #	Services
155	California/Arizona state line, Colorado River, pacific/mountain time zone
153	Park Moabi Rd, to Rte 66, N boating, camping
149mm	insp both lanes
148	5 Mile Rd, to Topock, Rte 66 (from eb)
144	US 95 S, E Broadway, Needles, N Chevron/dsl/24hr, Mobil, Shell/dsl/LP Domino's AutoZone, Harris Repair/towing, Rite Aid
142	J St, Needles, N American/dsl Jack-in-the-Box, McDonald's Quality Inn Big O Tire, NAPA, S Days Inn, Motel 6 H
141	W Broadway, River Rd, Needles, N Porky's BBQ, River City Pizza Best Motel, Desert Mirage Inn, River Valley Motel, S Chevron/Circle K/dsl, Mobil/dsl, Shell/DQ/Subway/dsl, Tesla EVC Carl's Jr, Giggling Cactus, Panda Garden, Wagon Wheel Rest. Best Western, Budget Inn, Red Roof Inn, Rio Del Sol Inn auto/RV/tire/repair
139	River Rd Cutoff (from eb), N Desert View RV Park, KOA, Hist Rte 66, rec area
133	US 95 N, to Searchlight, to Rte 66
120	Water Rd
115	Mountain Springs Rd, Mountain Springs Summit, elev 2770, elev 2770, High Springs Summit
107	Goffs Rd, Essex, N Hi Sahara Oasis/dsl/snacks, Hist Rte 66
106mm	**both lanes, full facilities, litter barrels, petwalk,**
100	Essex Rd, Essex, N Mitchell Caverns, to Providence Mtn SP
78	Kelbaker Rd, to Amboy, E Mojave Nat Preserve, Kelso, S Hist Rte 66
50	Ludlow, N 76/DQ, S Chevron/dsl Ludlow Cafe Ludlow Motel
33	Hector Rd, to Hist Rte 66
28mm	**both lanes, full facilities, litter barrels, petwalk,**
23	Ft Cady Rd, to Newberry Spgs, N Mobil/Circle K/dsl, S Newberry Mtn RV Park
18	Newberry Springs, N Chevron/dsl/24hr, S Shell/Subway/dsl/LP
12	Barstow-Daggett Airport, N
7	Daggett, N RV camping (2mi), to Calico Ghost Town

BARSTOW

5	Nebo St (from eb), to Hist Rte 66
2	USMC Logistics Base, N Desert Rat RV Park
1	E Main St, Montara Rd, Barstow, **1 mi** N Chevron, Ci K/dsl, EVC, Mobil/dsl, Phillips 66/dsl, USA/dsl Alber Mexican, Burger King, Carl's Jr, China Town Buffet, Del Ta Denny's, Di Napoli's Italian, Grill It, IHOP, Jack-in-the-Box, J ny's Grill, Little Caesar's, McDonald's, Panda Express, Popey Rigoberto's, Starbucks, Subway, Taco Bell, Tom's Burgers, W nerschnitzel Astro Budget Motel, Best Motel, Best Weste Budget Inn, CA Inn, Days Inn, Desert Inn, EconoLodge, Eco my Inn, Motel 6, Quality Inn/rest., Ramada Inn, Rodeway Super 8, Travelodge $Tree, 99c Store, AutoZone, O'Re Parts, U-Haul/LP, S Arco Walmart/McDonald's
0mm	**I-40 begins/ends on I-15 in Barstow.**

INTERSTATE 80

TRUCKEE

Exit #	Services
208	California/Nevada state line
201	Farad
199	Floristan
194	Hirschdale Rd, N Stampede Dam, to Boca Dam, S RV Park
191	**(from wb), inspection sta, weigh sta**
190	Overland Trail
188	CA 89 N, CA 267, to N Shore Lake Tahoe, N Coachland Park, USFS, S same as 186
186	Central Truckee (no eb return), S 76/dsl, Beacon Bu er Me, Casa Baeza Mexican, El Toro Bravo Mexican, Jax Truc Diner, Marg's Taco Bistro, Wagon Train Café Hilltop Lod Truckee Hotel **CA Welcome Ctr**
185	CA 89 S, to N Lake Tahoe, N DQ, Golden Rotisserie, Pa Express, Port of Subs, RoundTable Pizza, Starbucks, Zano's Pi H, 7-11, Ace Hardware, NAPA, New Moon Natural Foo Rite Aid, Safeway Foods, URGENT CARE, Verizon, S Sh dsl McDonald's, Pizzaria, Starbucks, Subway auto pair, CVS Drug, O'Reilly Parts, SaveMart Foods, to Squaw Va
184	Donner Pass Rd, Truckee, N Shell/dsl La Bamba Me can, Smokey's Kitchen Sunset Inn vet, S Chevr dsl Taco Bell Truckee Donner Lodge chain serv RV camp/dump, to Donner SP
181mm	vista point both lanes
180	Donner Lake (from wb), S Donner Lake Village Resort
177mm	Donner Summit, elev 7239, **both lanes, full facilities, ter barrels, petwalk, , view area**
176	Castle Park, Boreal Ridge Rd, S Boreal Inn/rest. Pac Crest Trailhead, skiing
174	Soda Springs, Norden, S Sugar Bowl/dsl Summit R Donner Summit Lodge chain services
171	Kingvale, S Shell
168	Rainbow Rd, to Big Bend, S Rainbow Lodge/rest. camping
166	Big Bend (from eb)
165	Cisco Grove, N RV camp/dump, skiing, snowmobili S Chevron/dsl/24hr Subway chain services
164	Eagle Lakes Rd
161	CA 20 W, to Nevada City, Grass Valley
160	Yuba Gap, S boating, camping, , skiing, snowpar
158	Laing Rd, S Sierra Woods Lodge/café USPO
157mm	brake check area, wb
158a	Emigrant Gap (from eb), S Sierra Woods Lodg café USPO
156	Nyack Rd, Emigrant Gap, S Shell/Burger King/dsl Nya Café USPO

INTERSTATE 80 Cont'd

Exit #	Services
156mm	**brake check area**
155	Blue Canyon
150	Drum Forebay
148b	Baxter, N [other] chainup services, food, [phone], RV camping
148a	Crystal Springs
146	Alta
145	Dutch Flat, N [food] Monte Vista Rest., S [gas] 76/dsl [other] chainup services, Dutch Flat RV Resort, hwy patrol
144	Gold Run (from wb), N chainup, food, gas/dsl, [phone]
143mm	**[rest stop] both lanes, full [handicapped] facilities, litter barrels, petwalk, [phone], [picnic]**
143	Magra Rd, Gold Run, N chainup services
140	Magra Rd, Rollins Lake Rd, Secret Town Rd
139	Rollins Lake Road (from wb), RV camping
135	CA 174, to Grass Valley, Colfax, N [gas] 76/dsl, Beacon/dsl [food] McDonald's, Pizza Factory, Starbucks, Taco Bell, TJ's Roadhouse [lodging] Colfax Motel [other] $General, NAPA, Sierra Mkt Foods, S [gas] Chevron/dsl, Valero/dsl [food] Shang Garden Chinese, Subway
133	Canyon Way, to Colfax, S [food] Dine'n Dash Cafe [other] Chevrolet, Plaza Tire
131	Cross Rd, to Weimar
130	W Paoli Lane, to Weimar, S [gas] Weimar Store/dsl
129	Heather Glen, elev 2000 ft
128	Applegate, N [gas] Valero/dsl/LP [other] chainup services
125	Clipper Gap, Meadow Vista
124	Dry Creek Rd
123	Bell Rd
122	Foresthill Rd, Ravine Rd, Auburn, N [lodging] Marriott, S [food] Awful Annie's Rest., Burger King, Ikeda's Cafe, Sizzler, Starbucks, Subway [lodging] Best Western, Rodeway Inn [other] same as 121
121	Lincolnway (from eb), Auburn, N [gas] Mobil, Mobil/dsl, Valero/dsl [food] JimBoy's Tacos, Starbucks, Taco Bell, Wienerschnitzel [lodging] Red Lion Inn, Foothills Motel, Motel 6, Super 8, S [gas] Arco, Auburn/dsl, Chevron/dsl, Gas&Shop, Shell/dsl [food] Awful Annie's Rest., Black Bear Diner, Burger King, Burrito Shop, Carl's Jr, Hawaiian BBQ, Jack-in-the-Box, Joe Caribe Bistro, KFC, McDonald's, Pete's Grill, Sierra Grill, Sizzler, Starbucks, Subway [lodging] Best Western, Rodeway Inn [other] Ikeda's Cafe, Raley's Foods, Verizon
120	Russell Ave (from wb), same as 121, to Lincolnway from eb
119c	Elm Ave, Auburn, N [gas] 76/dsl, Shell/dsl [food] Burger&Cream, Roundtable Pizza, Starbucks [lodging] Holiday Inn [other] CVS Drug, Grocery Outlet, Rite Aid, SaveMart Foods, Staples, Verizon
119b	CA 49, to Grass Valley, Auburn, N [gas] 76/dsl, Shell/dsl [food] In-N-Out [lodging] Holiday Inn [other] RV Connection, Staples
119a	Maple St, Nevada St, Old Town Auburn, S [gas] Valero [food] Cafe Delicias, Tio Pepe Mexican [other] USPO
118	Ophir Rd (from wb)
116	CA 193, to Lincoln
115	Indian Hill Rd, Newcastle, N [other] transmissions, USPO, S [gas] Mobil/dsl, Valero/dsl [food] Denny's [other] CHP
112	Penryn, N [gas] 76/dsl, Chevron/dsl [food] Subway
110	Horseshoe Bar Rd, to Loomis, N [food] Burger King, RoundTable Pizza, Starbucks, Taco Bell [other] Raley's Food
109	Sierra College Blvd, N [gas] 7-11/dsl, Arco/dsl, Chevron/McDonald's/dsl [food] Blast Pizza, Carl's Jr, Chipotle, Mooyah Burger, Noodles&Co, Panera Bread, Subway [other] Camping World RV Ctr, GNC, Rocklin RV Ctr, Ross, Steinmart, Target, Tesla, Verizon, S [gas] Shell/dsl [food] Dickey's BBQ, In-N-Out, Jimboy's Tacos, Mod Pizza, Panda Express, Starbucks, Wing Stop [other] AT&T, Bass Pro Shop, Petsmart, TJ Maxx, Walmart

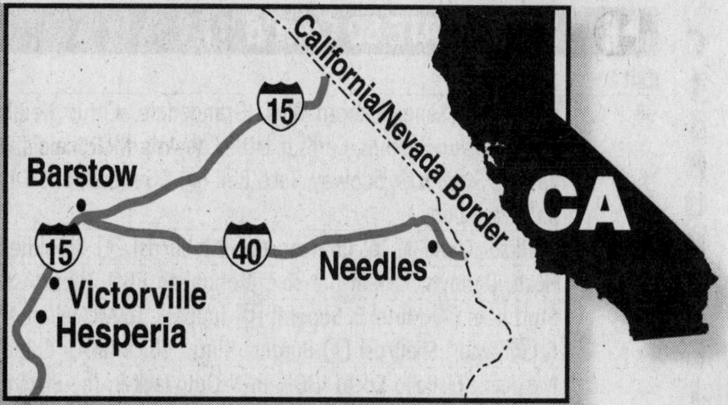

CA

ROCKLIN

CITRUS HEIGHTS

Exit #	Services
108	Rocklin Rd, N [gas] Valero/dsl [food] A&W/KFC, Adalberto's Mexican, Arby's, Baskin-Robbins, Denny's, Golden Dragon, Jack-in-the-Box, Jamba Juice, Koja Kitchen, Milo's, Papa Murphy's, RoundTable Pizza, Starbucks, Subway, Taco Bell [lodging] Comfort Inn, Days Inn, SureStay Inn [other] CVS Drug, GNC, Land Rover, Mercedes, Porsche, Safeway Foods, S [gas] Arco [food] Little Caesar's [lodging] Rocklin Park Hotel [other] vet
106	CA 65, to Lincoln, Marysville, **1 mi N on Stanford Ranch Rd** [gas] 76, Arco, Shell [food] Black Bear Diner, Carl's Jr, Cheesecake Factory, Chipotle, IHOP, Jack-in-the-Box, KFC, McDonald's, Olive Garden, On-the-Border, PF Changs, Ruth's Chris Steaks, TGIFriday [lodging] Courtyard, Holiday Inn Express, Homewood Suites, Hyatt Place [other] AutoZone, Barnes&Noble, Best Buy, Costco/dsl, JC Penney, Macy's, Marshall's, Michael's, Nordstrom's, Old Navy, Ross, Sprouts Mkt, Staples
105b	Taylor Rd, to Rocklin (from eb), N [food] Cattlemen's Rest., S [gas] 76/Burger King/dsl, Chevron [food] Islands Burgers, Subway, Tahoe Joe's [lodging] Courtyard, Fairfield Inn, Hilton Garden, Holiday Inn Express, Larkspur Suites, Residence Inn [other] [H], funpark
105a	Atlantic St, Eureka Rd, S [gas] 76/7-11/dsl, Shell/Circle K [food] Brookfield's Rest., Chicago Fire Rest., In-N-Out, Taco Bell, Wendy's [other] [H], Acura, America'sTire, Buick/GMC, Carmax, Chevrolet, Chrysler/Dodge/Jeep, Fiat, Ford, Home Depot, Honda, Hyundai, Infiniti, Kia, Lexus, Mazda, Nissan, Petsmart, Subaru, Target, Toyota, VW
103b a	Douglas Blvd, N [gas] 76/dsl, Arco/dsl, Chevron/7-11, Shell/dsl [food] Burger King, Carolina's Mexican, Claim Jumper, McDonald's, Mongolian BBQ, Popeye's, Starbucks, Subway [lodging] Best Western, Extended Stay America, Heritage Inn [other] $Tree, Ace Hardware, Autozone, Big O Tire, BigLots, BrakeMasters, Goodyear, Grocery Outlet, Midas, O'Reilly Parts, Rite Aid, Trader Joe's, S [food] Carl's Jr, Chevy's, Del Taco, Denny's, Jack-in-the-Box, Lorenzo's Mexican, Outback Steaks, Panera Bread, Rubio's, Sizzler, Subway [lodging] Best Western, Hampton Inn [other] [H], Fry's Electronics, Hobby Lobby, Office Depot, Ross, Target
102	Riverside Ave, Auburn Blvd, to Roseville, N [gas] Arco/dsl, Chevron/dsl [food] Starbucks [other] auto repair, Meineke, S [gas] Chevron/7-11, Shell, Towne Mart [food] Back 40 TX BBQ, Baskin-Robbins, CA Burgers, Jack-in-the-Box, Subway [other] $General, auto repair, AutoZone, BMW Motorcycles, Camping World RV Ctr, NAPA, Schwab Tire
100	Antelope Rd, to Citrus Heights, N [gas] [food] Carl's Jr, Extreme Hummus, Giant Pizza, McDonald's, Papa Murphy's, Popeye's, RoundTable Pizza, Subway, Taco Bell, Wendy's [other] $Tree, 7-11, O'Reilly Parts, Raley's Foods, vet
100mm	**weigh sta both lanes**

CA

CITRUS HEIGHTS

SACRAMENTO

INTERSTATE 80 Cont'd

Exit #	Services
98	Greenback Lane, Elkhorn Blvd, Orangedale, Citrus Heights, N Baskin Robbins, Carl's Jr, Little Caesar's, McDonald's, Pizza Hut, Starbucks, Subway, Taco Bell $General, CVS Drug, Safeway Foods
96	Madison Ave, N Chevron/dsl, Mobil/dsl Brookfield's Rest., Denny's, Jack-in-the-Box, Mongolian BBQ, Ninja Asian, Starbucks Motel 6, Super 8 funpark, to McClellan AFB, S Arco, Shell/dsl Burger King, Chick-fil-A, Chipotle Mexican, El Pollo Loco, IHOP, In-N-Out, Jack-in-the-Box, McDonald's, Panda Express, Starbucks, Subway, Wienerschnitzel Crowne Plaza, La Quinta 7-11, Acura, AT&T, Chevrolet, Firestone/auto, Ford, Office Depot, PepBoys, Schwab Tire, Target, Verizon, Volvo, Walgreens
95	CA 99 S
94b	Auburn Blvd
94a	Watt Ave, N 76/dsl, Arco Carl's Jr, Del Taco, Golden Corral, Jack-in-the-Box, KFC, McDonald's, Panda Express, Starbucks, Subway, Taco Bell Best Value Inn $Tree, Firestone/auto, McClellan AFB, Walmart, S 76/dsl, Arco, Chevron, Shell Denny's, Jimboy's Tacos, Quiznos, Starbucks, Wendy's Red Roof Inn AutoZone, Grocery Outlet
93	Longview Dr
92	Winters St
91	Raley Blvd, Marysville Blvd, to Rio Linda, N Arco, Chevron/dsl, S $General, Hooten Tires, USPO, Valley Tire, Viva Mkt
90	Norwood Ave, N Arco/Jack-in-the-Box, Valero Little Caesar's, McDonald's, RoundTable Pizza, Starbucks, Subway Rite Aid, Viva Foods, Walgreens, S $General
89	Northgate Blvd, Sacramento, N Cilantro's Mexican, L&L Hawaiian BBQ, Subway Fry's Electronics, S Arco, Shell, Valero/Circle K 524 Mexican, Carl's Jr, Classic Burgers, El Pollo Loco, IHOP, KFC, LampPost Pizza, LJ Silver, McDonald's/playplace, Subway, Taco Bell Econolodge, Extended Stay America $Tree, Foodsco Foods, O'Reilly Parts, PepBoys, Schwab Tire
88	Truxel Rd, N Chevron/McDonald's, Shell/dsl Applebee's, BJ's Rest, Buffalo Wild Wings, Casa Ramos, Chili's, Chipotle Mexican, Del Taco, Firehouse Subs, Hooters, In-N-Out, Logan's Roadhouse, On the Border, Panda Express, Panera Bread, Rubio's, Sandwich Spot, Starbucks, Subway, Tokyo Steakhouse Staybridge Suites AT&T, Barnes&Noble, Best Buy, GNC, Home Depot, Michael's, Old Navy, Petsmart, Power Balance Pavilion, Ross, See's Candies, Staples, Target, TJ Maxx, Verizon, Walmart, World Mkt
86	I-5, N to Redding, S to Sacramento, to CA 99 N
85	W El Camino, N 49er Trkstp/Silver Skillet/dsl/scales/24hr/@, Chevron/Subway/dsl/24hr Black Bear Diner, Burger King Fairfield Inn, Super 8, S Arco
83	Reed Ave, N Chevron/dsl Jack-in-the-Box, Panda Express, Starbucks, Subway Extended Stay America, Hampton Inn, Spring Hill Suites, S Arco/24hr, Shell/McDonald's/dsl Burger King, Chipotle, Five Guys, IHOP, In-N-Out, Taco Bell America's Tire, Firestone/auto, GNC, Home Depot, IKEA, Petco, Ross, Walmart
82	US 50 E, W Sacramento
81	Enterprise Blvd, W Capitol Ave, W Sacramento, N Arco/dsl, Chevron Granada Inn, S 7-11 Eppie's Diner, Starbucks, Subway KOA
78	Rd 32A, E Chiles Rd, S Fruit Stand

DAVIS

VACAVILLE

Exit #	Services
75	Mace Blvd, N Arco Target, TJ Maxx, to Mace Ra[...] Verizon, S Chevron/dsl, Gas&Shop/dsl, Sinclair/dsl, V[...]ro/dsl Cindy's Rest., Domino's, McDonald's, Starbu[...] Subway, Taco Bell Days Inn, Motel 6 American R[...] RV Ctr, Chevrolet, Chrysler/Dodge/Jeep, Honda, Kia, La M[...] RV Ctr, Nissan, Nugget Mkt Foods, Toyota
73	Olive Dr (from wb, no EZ return)
72b a	Richards Blvd, Davis, N Shell In-N-Out, Red Burger University Park Inn NAPA, S Chev[...] dsl Applebee's, Carl's Jr, IHOP, KFC, Starbucks Holi[...] Inn Express, La Quinta Jiffy Lube, O'Reilly Parts
71	to UC Davis
70	CA 113 N, to Woodland, N H
69	Kidwell Rd
67	Pedrick Rd, N 76/LP, Chevron/dsl/24hr produce
66b	Milk Farm Rd (from wb)
66a	CA 113 S, Currey Rd, to Dixon, S Chevron/dsl, Shell/[...] Valero/Popeye's/dsl Cattlemen's Rest., Jack-in-the-[...] La Cocina, Papa Murphy's, Subway, Wendy's Country Suites Schwab Tires, Walmart
64	Pitt School Rd, to Dixon, S Chevron/24hr, Valero/2[...] Arby's, Asian Garden, Baskin Robbins, Burger King, Ca[...] China, Denny's, IHOP, Little Caesar's, Maria's Mexican, Ma[...] Pizza, McDonald's, Pizza Guys, Solano Bakery, Starbucks, S[...]way, Taco Bell Best Western+, Motel 6 Safeway/dsl
63	Dixon Ave, Midway Rd, N Truck Stp/dsl, S A[...] LP/lube, Chevron/dsl Alheli's Drive Thru, Carl's Jr, Taco Super 8 Dixon Fruit Mkt
60	Midway Rd, Lewis Rd, Elmyra, N Produce Mkt, RV camp (3mi)
59	Meridian Rd, Weber Rd
57	Leisure Town Rd, N H, Camping World, S 76/[...] Donald's, Arco, Chevron/dsl, QuikStop Black Oak R[...] Clay Oven Grill, Hideaway Grill, Jack-in-the-Box, King's Bu[...] Popeye's, Starbucks, Subway, Taco Bell Comfort Suites, [...]tended Stay America, Fairfield Inn, Holiday Inn Express, M[...] 6, Quality Inn, Residence Inn Buick/GMC, Chevrolet, Ch[...]ler/Dodge/Jeep, Harley-Davidson, Home Depot, Honda, Ko[...] Mazda, Nissan, Toyota, VW
56	I-505 N, to Winters
55	Nut Tree Pkwy, Monte Vista Dr, Allison Dr, N 7-11, 76/[...]cle K, Chevron Boudin SF Sourdough, Buckhorn BBQ, [...]falo Wild Wings, Burger King, Chipotle, Denny's, El Pollo Lo[...] Fenton's Creamery, Firehouse Subs, Five Guys, Food Court, H[...]it Burger, Hawaiian BBQ, Hisui Japanese, IHOP, Jamba Ju[...] Krispy Kreme, McDonald's, Murillo's Mexican, Nations Bur[...] Noodles&Co, Panda Express, Panera Bread, Pelayo's Mexic[...] Pieology Pizza, Round Table Pizza, Rubio's, Starbucks, Subw[...] Taco Bell, Wendy's, Yen King Chinese Best Value Inn, B[...] Western, Super 8 America's Tire, Best Buy, Big O Tire, [...] Drug, Firestone/auto, Lowe's Whse, Michael's, Nugget Foo[...] Old Navy, Petsmart, See's Candies, U-Haul, Verizon, World M[...] S Arco/24hr, Chevron/24hr Applebee's, BJ's Grill, Bl[...] Oak Rest., Carl's Jr, Chick-fil-A, Chili's, Coldstone Cream[...] Dickey's BBQ, Favela's Mexican Grill, Freebirds Burrito, Groc[...] Outlet, Home Towne Buffet, In-N-Out, Jack-in-the-Box, Jam[...] Juice, Mel's Diner, Olive Garden, Popeye's, Red Robin, S[...]bucks, Starbucks, String's Italian, Subway, Tahoe Joe's Stea[...] Togo's Comfort Suites, Courtyard, Fairfield Inn, Holiday Express, Motel 6, Residence Inn H, GMC, GNC, Jo-Ann F[...]rics, Marshall's, PetCo, Ross, Safeway, Sam's Club/dsl, Stap[...] Target, Vacaville Stores/famous brands, Walmart/McDonald'[...]

INTERSTATE 80 Cont'd

Exit #	Services
54b	Mason St, Peabody Rd, N Chevron/7-11, Conservative Fuel/dsl Hampton Inn CVS Drug, NAPA, O'Reilly Parts, Schwab Tire, S Shell Carl's Jr, Domino's, Starbucks, Subway $Tree, 7-11, Costco/gas
54a	Davis St, N Chevron/McDonald's Outback Steaks Hampton Inn, S DQ, Sonic repair, WinCo Foods
53	Merchant St, Alamo Dr, N Chevron, Merchant/dsl, Shell/dsl Baldo's Mexican, Baskin-Robbins, Black Bear Diner, RoundTable Pizza, Tony's Rest. Alamo Inn BigLots, S 76/dsl Jack-in-the-Box, KFC, McDonald's, Pizza Hut, Rita's Custard, Starbucks, Subway Walmart Mkt
52	Cherry Glen Rd (from wb)
51b	Pena Adobe Rd, S Ranch Hotel
51a	Lagoon Valley Rd, Cherry Glen
48	N Texas St, Fairfield, S Arco/24hr, Chevron/dsl, Shell El Pollo Loco, Jim Boy's Tacos, McDonald's, Panda Express, RoundTable Pizza, Starbucks, Subway, Texas Roadhouse Best Value Inn CVS, Lowe's, Raley's Foods
47	Waterman Blvd, N Dynasty Chinese, RoundTable Pizza, Starbucks, Subway Chevrolet/Subaru, Safeway, to Austin's Place, S museum, to Travis AFB
45	Travis Blvd, Fairfield, N Arco/24hr, Chevron Baskin-Robbins, Burger King, Denny's, Domino's, Huckleberry's Cafe, In-N-Out, McDonald's, Peking Rest., Subway, Taco Bell, To-go's Courtyard, Motel 6 $Tree, CHP, Meineke, PetCo, Raley's Foods, S 76/dsl Buffalo Wild Wings, Carino's Italian, Chevy's Mexican, Chick-fil-A, Chipotle Mexican, Coldstone, Five Guys, Fuddrucker's, HomeTown Buffet, Jamba Juice, Mimi's Café, Panda Express, Panera Bread, Pieology, Red Lobster, Red Robin, Rubio's, Starbucks, Subway, Wing Stop Hilton Garden H, AT&T, Barnes&Noble, Best Buy, Firestone/auto, JC Penney, Macy's, Michael's, Ross, Trader Joe's, Verizon
44	W Texas St, same as 45, Fairfield, N A&A/dsl, KwikServ/dsl ChuckeCheese, Gordito's Mexican, Popeye's, Starbucks Extended Stay America Staples, S Valero/dsl Baldo's Mexican, McDonald's, Paleyo's Mexican 99c Store, Acura/Honda, CarMax, Chrysler/Jeep/Dodge, Ford/Lincoln, Home Depot, Hyundai, Infiniti, Mercedes, Nissan, O'Reilly Parts, Target, Toyota, VW, Walgreens
43	CA 12 E, Abernathy Rd, Suisun City, S Budweiser Plant, Walmart
42mm	weigh sta both lanes
41	Suisan Valley Rd, N Homewood Suites, Staybridge Suites, S 7-11, 76, Chevron/dsl, Shell/dsl, Valero/dsl Arby's, Burger King, Carl's Jr, Cenario's Pizza, Del Taco, Denny's, Green Bamboo, Jack-in-the-Box, Jersey Mike's, McDonald's, Starbucks, Straw Hat Pizza, Subway, Taco Bell, Wendy's Best Western, Comfort Inn, Fairfield Inn, La Quinta, Motel 6, Travelodge Fairfield RV Ctr, Scandia FunCtr, vet
40	I-680 (from wb)
39b	Green Valley Rd, I-680 (from eb), N Happy Garden, Hawaiian BBQ, Hinata, Peloyas Mexican, RoundTable Pizza, Starbucks, Subway Homewood Suites, Staybridge Suites Costco/gas, CVS, Safeway, TJ Maxx, S Arco Kia
39a	Red Top Rd, N Chevron Jack-in-the-Box
36	American Canyon Rd
34mm	wb, full facilities, info, litter barrels, petwalk, vista parking

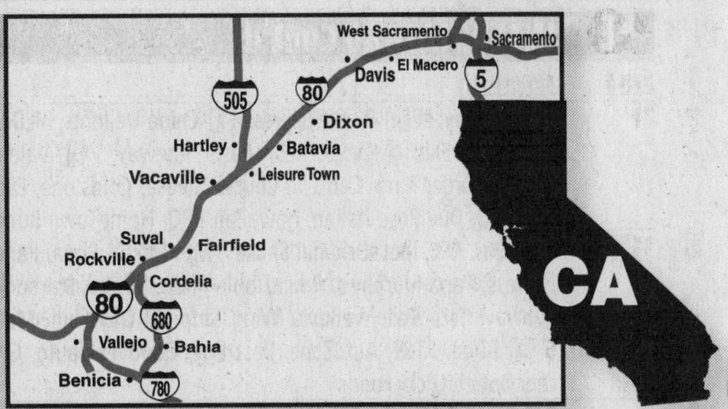

CA

VALLEJO

Exit #	Services
33b a	CA 37, to San Rafael, Columbus Pkwy, N Chevron/dsl, Valero/dsl Baskin-Robbins, Carl's Jr. Best Western, Courtyard funpark, S same as 32
32	Redwood St, to Vallejo, N Chevron Denny's, Panda Garden Best Value Inn, Motel 6 H, S Shell, Valero Applebee's, Black Angus, Black Bear Diner, Chevy's Mexican, Chick-fil-A, Chipotle, Coldstone, Habit Burger, IHOP, Jamba Juice, Jimmy John's, Little Caesar's, McDonald's, Mtn. Mike's Pizza, Olive Garden, Panda Express, Papa Murphy's, Red Lobster, Rubio's, Starbucks, Subway, Taco Bell, Wendy's, Wing Stop Comfort Inn, Ramada Inn $Tree, AT&T, AutoZone, Best Buy, Cadillac/Chevrolet, Chrysler/Dodge/Jeep, Costco/gas, CVS, Home Depot, Honda, Hyundai, Kohl's, Lowe's, Marshall's, Mazda, Michael's, PepBoys, PetCo, Ross, Safeway, Target, Toyota, Verizon, vet
31b	Tennessee St, to Vallejo, S Flyers, Valero/dsl Jack-in-the-Box, Pizza Guys Great Western Inn, Howard Johnson Grocery Outlet, USPO
31a	Solano Ave, Springs Rd, N Burger King, Church's, Subway, Szechuan, Taco Bell Rodeway Inn, Super 8 Mi Pueblo Mkt, Rite Aid, U-Haul, S Chevron, Grand Gas, QuikStop DQ, McDonald's, Pizza Hut, Subway Express Inn Island Pacific Foods, O'Reilly Parts
30c	Georgia St, Central Vallejo, N Safeway/gas, S Chevron/Starbucks/dsl McDonald's California Motel
30b	Benicia Rd (from wb), S Chevron/dsl McDonald's, Starbucks
30a	I-780, to Martinez
29b	Magazine St, Vallejo, N Gas&Shop/dsl Starbucks, Subway 7 Motel, Economy Inn, El Rancho Tradewinds RV Park, S McDonald's Travel Inn 7-11
29a	CA 29, Maritime Academy Dr, Vallejo, N 5 Star Gas, Chevron/dsl Motel 6
28mm	pay toll from eb, toll plaza
27	Pomona Rd, Crockett, N Dead Fish Seafood, vista point
26	Cummings Skyway, to CA 4 (from wb), to Martinez
24	Willow Ave, to Rodeo, N Straw Hat Pizza, Subway Safeway, USPO, S 76/dsl Burger King, Mazatlan, Mtn Mike's Pizza, Starbucks, Willow Garden Chinese
23	CA 4, to Stockton, Hercules, N Shell Extreme Pizza, Jack-in-the-Box, Starbucks, S Dragon Terrace, McDonald's, RoundTable Pizza, Subway, Taco Bell BigLots, Home Depot, Lucky Foods, Rite Aid
22	Pinole Valley Rd, S Arco/24hr, Chevron/dsl Chipotle, Five Guys, Jack-in-the-Box, Jamba Juice, Krispy Kreme, Mod Pizza, Red Onion Rest., Subway 7-11, Trader Joe's, Walgreens

[gas] = gas [food] = food [lodging] = lodging [other] = other [Rs] = rest stop

CA

E INTERSTATE 80 Cont'd

RICHMOND / EL CERRITO / BERKELEY

Exit #	Services
21	Appian Way, N [gas] Pinole Express [food] China Delights, McDonald's, Pizza Hut [other] CVS, O'Reilly Parts, Safeway, S [gas] Valero/dsl [food] Burger King, Carl's Jr, ChuckECheese, Coldstone, Dickey's BBQ, Due Rose Italian, Hawaiian BBQ, HomeTown Buffet, In-N-Out, KFC, Mel'sOriginal Shakes, Mtn Mike's Pizza, Panda Express, Papa Murphy's, RoundTable Pizza, Sizzler, Starbucks, Subway, Taco Bell, Wendy's, Wing Stop [lodging] Days Inn, Motel 6 [other] $Tree, AT&T, AutoZone, Best Buy, Goodyear/auto, Grocery Outlet, Lucky Foods
20	Richmond Pkwy, to I-580 W, N [gas] Chevron/dsl [food] IHOP, McDonald's, Me&Ed's Pizza, Subway [other] 99c Store, Buick/GMC, Chrysler/Dodge/Jeep, Ford, Hyundai, Kia, Nissan, Ross, Toyota, VW, S [gas] Shell/dsl [food] Applebee's, Cheese Steak, In-N-Out, Mel's Original Shakes, Outback Steaks, Panda Express, Panera Bread, RoundTable Pizza [other] FoodMaxx, Michael's, O'Reilly Parts, Petsmart, Staples, Target, TJ Maxx
19b	Hilltop Dr, to Richmond, N [gas] Chevron [food] Chevy's Mexican [lodging] Courtyard, Extended Stay America [other] Firestone/auto, Macy's, Walmart, S [gas] Hilltop Fuel/dsl
19a	El Portal Dr, to San Pablo, S [gas] Shell [food] McDonalds, Mtn. Mike's Pizza, Starbucks, Subway [other] Raley's Foods, vet, Walgreens
18	San Pablo Dam Rd, N [gas] Chevron [food] Burger King, Denny's, El Pollo Loco, Empire Buffet, Jack-in-the-Box, Jamba Juice, Nations Burgers, Pizza Guys, Popeye's, RoundTable Pizza, Starbucks, Subway, Taco Bell [lodging] Holiday Inn Express [other] [H], $Tree, AutoZone, Big Lots, FoodMaxx, Ross, Walgreens
17	Macdonald Ave (from eb), McBryde Ave (from wb), Richmond, N [gas] Arco/24hr [food] Burger King, S [gas] Chevron/24hr [food] Wendy's [other] auto repair
16	San Pablo Ave, to Richmond, San Pablo, S [gas] Chevron [food] KFC, LJ Silver, Subway, Wendy's
15	Cutting Blvd, Potrero St, to I-580 Br (from wb), to El Cerrito, N [gas] Arco [food] Panda Express [other] Target, S [gas] Valero/dsl [food] Church's, Denny's, IHOP, Jack-in-the-Box, McDonald's, Starbucks, Trevino's Mexican [other] $Tree, Home Depot, Honda, Safeway, Staples, Walgreens
14b	Carlson Blvd, El Cerrito, N [gas] KwikServ [lodging] 40 Flags Motel, S [lodging] Best Value Inn
14a	Central Ave, El Cerrito, S [gas] 76, Shell/dsl, Valero [food] Burger King, Chipotle, KFC, Nations Burgers
13	to I-580 (from eb), Albany
12	Gilman St, to Berkeley, N [other] Golden Gate Fields Racetrack, S [other] Target
11	University Ave, to Berkeley, S [gas] Element/dsl, 76, Econo Gas [lodging] La Quinta [other] to UC Berkeley
10	CA 13, to Ashby Ave
9	Powell St, Emeryville, N [gas] Shell [food] Chevy's Mexican [lodging] Hilton Garden, S [gas] [food] Black Bear Diner, Burger King, CA Pizza Kitchen, Denny's, Jamba Juice, PF Chang's, Starbucks, Togo's [lodging] Courtyard, Hyatt House, Sheraton [other] Barnes&Noble, Marshall's, Old Navy, Petco, Ross, Trader Joe's
8c b	Oakland, to I-880, I-580
8a	W Grand Ave, Maritime St
7mm	**toll plaza wb**
5mm	SF Bay
4a	Treasure Island (exits left)
2c b	Fremont St, Harrison St, Embarcadero (from wb)
2a	4th st (from eb), S [gas] Shell
1	9th st, Civic Ctr, downtown SF
1b a	**I-80 begins/ends on US 101 in SF.**

E INTERSTATE 110 (Los Angeles)

LA AREA

Exit #	Services
21	**I-110 begins/ends on I-10.**
20c	Adams Blvd, E [gas] Chevron [other] Audi, Chrysler/Dodge/J LA Convention Ctr., Mercedes, Nissan, Office Depot, VW
20b	37th St, Exposition Blvd, W [gas] Chevron/McDonald's [lodging] Ra son [other] Chevrolet
20a	MLK Blvd, Expo Park, W [gas] Chevron [food] McDonald's, Subw
19b	Vernon Ave, E [gas] Mobil [food] Tacos El Gavilan, W [gas] 76/2 Shell [food] Burger King, Jack-in-the-Box, Tom's Burger [other] Aid, Ross
18b	Slauson Ave, E [gas] Mobil, W [gas] 76
18a	Gage Blvd, E [gas] Arco [food] Church's, Hercules Burgers
17	Florence Ave, E [gas] Shell [food] Jack-in-the-Box, W [gas] Chev Valero [food] Burger King, Little Caesar's, McDonald's, Pizza Subway
16	Manchester Ave, E [gas] Arco [food] El Pollo Loco, Little C sar's, McDonald's, Subway, Winchell's [other] AutoZone, W [food] Church's, Jack-in-the-Box, Popeye's, Tam's Burgers
15	Century Blvd, E [gas] Arco, Shell/Subway/dsl [food] Burger K McDonald's, W [gas] 76/dsl
14b	Imperial Hwy, W [gas] Chevron/dsl [food] Jack-in-the-Box, McDona
14a	I-105
13	El Segundo Blvd, E [food] Taco Bell, W [gas] Shell
12	Rosecrans Ave, E [gas] Arco/24hr, Valero, W [gas] Chevron/ Donald's, Sinclair [food] Jack-in-the-Box, KFC/LJ Silver, Pizza Popeye's, Subway, Yoshinoya [other] 7-11, casino
11	Redondo Beach Blvd, E [food] McDonald's, W [gas] M bil [food] FarmerBoys, Subway [other] [H], casino, Ross, Staples
10b a	CA 91, 190th St, W [gas] Arco [food] Jack-in-the-Box, Krispy Kre McDonald's, Subway, Taco Bell [other] Food4Less, Ranch M Sam's Club
9	I-405, San Diego Fwy
8	Torrance Blvd, Del Amo, E [food] Burger King, Chile Verde, S bucks, Waba Grill, W [gas] Mobil, Shell/Subway/dsl
7b	Carson St, E [food] KFC [lodging] Cali Inn [other] vet, W [gas] Harbor F Shell [food] Carl's Jr., FatBurger, In-N-Out, Jack-in-the-Box, Paisas Mexican, McDonalds, Pizza Hut, Starbucks, Subw Wienerschnitzel [other] [H], Autozone, Bella Vida Drug, Num Uno Mkt, O'Reilly Parts, Rite Aid
5	Sepulveda Blvd, E [food] McDonald's, Starbucks [other] Albertso Home Depot, Staples, Target, W [gas] Arco/24hr, Chevron, M bil/dsl [food] Burger King, Carl's Jr, McDonald's, Popeye's, St bucks, Subway, Taco Bell [lodging] Motel 6 [other] $Tree, 99c Sto AT&T, Big Lots, Food4Less, Ross
4	CA 1, Pacific Coast Hwy, E [gas] Arco [food] Jack-in-the-Box, za Hut, Wienerschnitzel [other] $Tree, W [gas] 76, Mobil, Unit dsl [food] Del Taco, Denny's, El Pollo Loco, Subway [lodging] Best We ern [other] [H], PepBoys, Rite Aid, transmissions
3b	Anaheim St, E [gas] [food] Dunkin'
3a	C St
1b	Channel St, W [gas] Arco, Chevron [food] Big Nick's Pizza, Lar Hamburgers [other] 7-11, Home Depot, Target
1a	CA 47, Gaffey Ave
0mm	**I-110 begins/ends.**

N INTERSTATE 205 (Tracy)

Exit #	Services
12	**I-205 begins wb, ends eb, accesses I-5 nb.**
9	MacArthur Dr, Tracy, S [gas] Chevron/Jack-in-the-Box/Subw dsl [other] Tracy Outlet Ctr/famous brands

INTERSTATE 205 (Tracy) Cont'd

Exit #	Services
8	Tracy Blvd, Tracy, N 76/Mean Gene's Burger/dsl, Chevron, Shell/dsl Denny's Holiday Inn Express, Motel 6, S Arco Arby's, Burger King, In-N-Out, Lyon's Rest., McDonald's, Milano Pizza, Nations Burgers, Pizza Guys, Starbucks, Straw Hat Pizza, Subway, Wendy's Best Western, Microtel, Quality Inn H, CHP, CVS Drug, Mi Pueblo Mkt, O'Reilly Parts
6	Grant Line Rd, Antioch, N Chevron/dsl Applebee's, Buffalo Wild Wings, Burger King, Dickey's BBQ, Famous Dave's BBQ, Five Guys, Golden Corral, Hometown Buffet, IHOP, Jamba Juice, Olive Garden, Panda Express, Red Robin, RoundTable Pizza, Rubio's, Sonic, Squeeze Inn Burger, Starbucks, Strings Italian, Subway, Taco Bell, TX Roadhouse, Wienerschnitzel Extended Stay America, Fairfield Inn, Hampton Inn America's Tire, AT&T, Barnes&Noble, Best Buy, Chevrolet, Chrysler/Dodge/Jeep, Costco/gas, Ford, Home Depot, Honda, Hyundai, JC Penney, Les Schwab Tire, Macy's, Marshall's, Michael's, Nissan, Petsmart, Ross, See's Candies, Staples, Target, Toyota, Verizon, VW, Walmart/McDonald's/auto, WinCo Foods, World Mkt, World Mkt, S 7-11, 76/Subway/dsl, Arco, Shell/dsl A&W/KFC, Black Bear Diner, Carl's Jr, Chili's, Hawaiian BBQ, Mtn Mike's Pizza, Popeye's Rite Aid
4	11th St (from eb), to Tracy, Defense Depot
2	Mtn House Pkwy, to I-580 E
0mm	**I-205 begins eb/ends wb, accesses I-580 wb.**

INTERSTATE 210 (Pasadena)

Exit #	Services
85a	**I-210 begins/ends on I-10, exit 77.**
84	San Bernardino Ave, W Habit Burger Hobby Lobby, Old Navy, Ross, TJ Maxx
83	W 5th St, Greenspot Rd, E Chevron/dsl Del Taco, Dickey's BBQ, In-N-Out, Subway, Waba Grill AT&T, Lowe's, Staples
82	Base Line Rd, E Arco, Valero Carl's Jr, KFC/Taco Bell, McDonald's, Subway, Wendy's Albertson's, CVS Drug, Walgreens, W 76/dsl Baker's, Popeye's, Starbucks AutoZone, CVS Drug, Family$
81	CA 330 N, to Big Bear
79	Highland Ave, N Chevron/Subway, Shell/dsl Baker's, Coco's, IHOP, Taco Bell, Wienerschnitzel/Tastee Freez, S Del Taco, El Pollo Loco, KFC $Tree, 99c Store, O'Reilly Parts, Rite Aid, Target, Walmart Mkt
78	Del Rosa Ave, N 7-11, Shell Del Taco, S Circle K, Exxon, Valero Jack-in-the-Box, McDonald's CVS Drug, Stater Bros, Walgreens
76	Waterman Ave, S Mobil/7-11/dsl H
75	CA 259 (from wb), H St
74	I-215 N to Barstow S to San Bernardino
73	State St, University Pkwy, N American, USA $General
71	Riverside Ave, N Chevron Carl's Jr, Del Taco, Panda Paradise, Starbucks, Subway GNC, Ralph's Foods, Rite Aid, Verizon, Walgreens, S Arco Chipotle, In-N-Out, Jack-in-the-Box 7-11, URGENT CARE
70	Ayala Dr, S city park
68	Alder Ave, N Arco/Subway/dsl
67	Sierra Ave, N Applebee's, Boston's, Carl's Jr, Dickie's BBQ, El Pollo Loco, Jamba Juice, McDonald's, Mimi's Cafe, Panda Express, Papa Murphy's, Pizza Hut, Starbucks, Subway, Tio's Mexican, Waba Grill 7-11, $Tree, Costco/gas, Jo-Ann, Lowe's Whse,

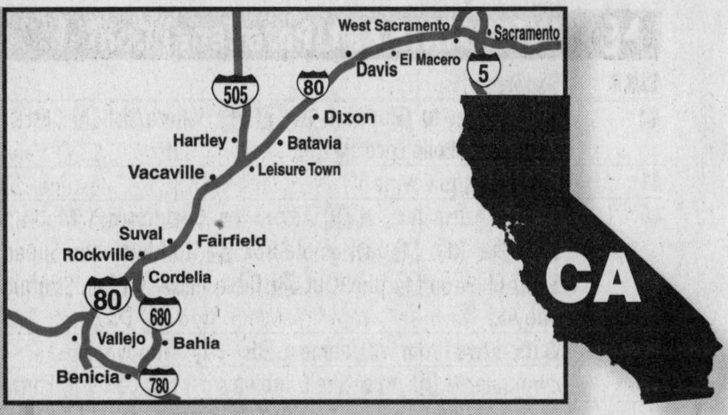

CA

SAN DIMAS

Exit #	Services
67	Continued Petco, Schwab Tire, Verizon, S Burgerim Burgers, Cane's Chevrolet, Honda, Nissan, Sprouts Mkt
66	Citrus Ave, N El Ranchero, FarmerBoys Rest., Jimmy John's, Juice It Up, Pick Up Stix, Popeye's, Red Brick Pizza, Taco Bell America's Tire, AutoZone, Home Depot, Ralph's Foods, Walgreens, S Arco/dsl
64	Cherry Ave
63	I-15 N to Barstow, S to San Diego
62	Day Creek Blvd, S Arco/dsl, Shell Chinese Food, Jack-in-the-Box, Starbucks, Subway, Wendy's Ralph's Foods
60	Milliken Ave, S Mobil/Circle K/dsl Subway, Taco Bell $Tre, Albertsons, CVS Drug, Verizon, vet
59	Haven Ave, N 7-11, 76, Mobil Corky's Kitchen, Del Taco, Domino's, Jack-in-the-Box, McDonald's, Subway, Tio's Mexican Trader Joe's, vet, Vons Foods, Walgreens
58	Archibald Ave, S Bamboo Garden, Barboni's Pizza, Carl's Jr Stater Bros, vet
57	Carnelion St, S Baskin-Robbins, Del Taco, El Ranchero Mexican, Juice It Up, Papa John's, Starbucks, Subway Rite Aid, Vons Foods, Walgreens
56	Campus Ave, N Arco/dsl In-N-Out, S Carl's Jr, Chick-fil-A, Chili's, Chipotle, El Pollo Loco, Golden Spoon Yogurt, Habit Burger, Hawaiian BBQ, Jersey Mike's, Magic Wok, Panera Bread, Pick Up Stix, Pieology Pizza, Qdoba Mexican, Starbucks, Subway, Which Wich? AT&T, Dick's, GNC, Goodyear/auto, Haggen Mkt, Home Depot, Kohl's, Office Depot, Petsmart, Target, TJ Maxx, Verizon
54	Mtn Ave, Mount Balde
52	Baseline Rd, S Corky's Kitchen, Jersey Mike's, MOD Pizza, Starbucks, Waba Grill CVS Drug, Whole Foods Mkt
50	Towne Ave
48	Fruit St, Via Verde, S Shell Chipotle, El Pollo Loco, In-N-Out, Jersey Mike's, Jimmy John's, McDonald's, Myabi Japanese, Panda Express, Panera Bread, Pizza Hut, Round Table Pizza, Rubio's Grill, Starbucks, Subway Kohl's, Marshall's, Staples, Target, U of LaVerne, vet
47	Foothill Blvd, LaVerne, N Mobil Mr D's, S 76/dsl IHOP, Jack-in-the-Box, Starbucks, The Grill House, To-go's GNC
46	San Dimas Ave, San Dimas, N San Dimas Canyon CP
45	CA 57 S
44	Lone Hill Ave, Santa Ana, N Panda Express, S Chevron Baja Fresh, Chili's, Chipotle, Coco's, Corner Bakery Cafe, In-N-Out, Olive Garden, Subway, Wendy's Barnes&Noble, Best Buy, Chevrolet, Chrysler/Dodge/Jeep, Costco/gas, Ford, Home Depot, Hyundai, Kohl's, Old Navy, Petsmart, Sam's Club/gas, Staples, Toyota, Verizon, Walmart/auto
43	Sunflower Ave

= gas = food = lodging = other = rest stop

CA

INTERSTATE 210 (Pasadena) Cont'd

Exit #	Services
42	Grand Ave, to Glendora, N 76, Valero/dsl Carl's Jr, Denny's, El Pollo Loco H
41	Citrus Ave, to Covina
40	CA 39, Azusa Ave, N Arco/24hr, Chevron/dsl, Mobil/dsl, Shell/Del Taco Jack-in-the-Box Rodeway Inn, Super 8, S Chevron In-N-Out Best Value 7-11, Family$, Rite Aid
39	Vernon Ave (from wb), same as 38
38	Irwindale, N Arco, Shell/Subway/dsl Carl's Jr, Farmer-Boys Rest., McDonald's, Taco Bell Costco/gas
36b	Mt Olive Dr, N Mobil/dsl Subway CVS, Fresh&Easy Mkt
36a	I-605 S
35b a	Mountain Ave, N Arco, Chevron Del Taco, Denny's, Old Spaghetti Factory, Qdoba, Sonic, Taco Bell, Tommy's Hamburgers, Wienerschnitzel Oak Park Motel Best Buy, BMW/Mini, Buick/Chevrolet, CarMax, Chrysler/Dodge/Jeep, Fiat, Ford, Goodyear/auto, Honda, Infiniti, Mazda, Staples, Subaru, Target, Walgreens, S IHOP, Panda Express, Subway Home Depot, Ross, Verizon, Walmart/McDonald's
34	Myrtle Ave, S 76, Chevron/dsl Jack-in-the-Box
33	Huntington Dr, Monrovia, N Shell/dsl Applebee's, Black Angus, Burger King, Chili's, Chipotle, ChuckeCheese, Domenico's Italian, Domino's, Jack-in-the-Box, Jersey Mike's, Jimmy John's, LeRoy's Rest., McDonald's, Mimi's Cafe, Panda Express, Panera Bread, Papa Murphy's, Popeye's, RoundTable Pizza, Rubio's, Smashburger, Starbucks Courtyard Baja Ranch Foods, GNC, Kohl's, Marshall's, Pepboy's, Petsmart, Rite Aid, Sprouts Mkt, Trader Joe's, vet, Walgreens, S Baja Fresh, BJ's Grill, Capistrano's, Capital Seafood, ClaimJumper, Derby Rest., Golden Dragon, Olive Garden, Outback Steaks, Pieology, Red Lobster, Robeks Juice, Soup Plantation, Starbucks, Subway, Taisho Rest., Togo's, Tokyo Wako, Zen Buffet DoubleTree, Embassy Suites, Extended Stay America, Extended Stay America (2), Hampton Inn, Hilton Garden, Oak-Tree Inn, Residence Inn, SpringHill Suites Verizon
32	Santa Anita Ave, Arcadia, N 76, Arco McDonald's, Pizza Hut, Subway Ralph's Foods, Rite Aid, Walgreens, S Chevron/dsl In-N-Out carwash, vet
31	Baldwin Ave, to Sierra Madre
30b a	Rosemead Blvd, N 76/dsl, Arco Baskin Robbins, ChuckeCheese, Corner Bakery Cafe, Del Taco, Habit Burger, Island Burger, Jamba Juice, Panda Express, Panera Bread, Pick Up Stix, Starbucks, Subway AT&T, CVS Drug, Marshall's, Ralph's Foods, Rite Aid, Toyota, Verizon, Whole Foods Mkt, S Coco's, Jack-in-the-Box Best Value Inn, Best Western Big O Tires, Sprouts Mkt, Staples, World Mkt
29b a	San Gabriel Blvd, Madre St, N Chipotle Mexican, El Torito, Pizza Rey, Starbucks, Togo's Best Buy, Dick's, Old Navy, Petsmart, Ross, S Subway Best Western, Holiday Inn Express, Hotel La Reve Buick/Chevrolet/GMC, Cadillac, Land Rover Staples, Target
28	Altadena Dr, Sierra Madre, S Chevron, Mobil Just Tires
27b	Allen
27a	Hill Ave
26	Lake Ave, N Mobil/Circle K/dsl AutoZone
25b	CA 134, to Ventura
25a	Del Mar Blvd, CA Blvd, CO Blvd (exits left from eb)
24	Mountain St
23	Lincoln Ave, S Lincoln Motel tire service
22b	Arroyo Blvd, N Jack-in-the-Box, S to Rose Bowl
22a	Berkshire Ave, Oak Grove Dr
21	Gould Ave, S Arco, Chevron McDonald's, RoundTa Pizza, Subway, Trader Joe's Firestone/auto, Just Tires, Canada Automotive, Petco, Ralph's Foods
20	CA 2, Angeles Crest Hwy, S 76, Shell
19	CA 2, Glendale Fwy, S H
18	Ocean View Blvd, to Montrose
17b a	Pennsylvania Ave, La Crescenta Ave, La Crescenta, N Shell/7-11, Valero Baja Fresh, Burger King, Domino's, Lit Caesar's, Starbucks, Subway, Togo's, Wienerschnitzel fice Depot, O'Reilly Parts, Ralph's Foods, Rite Aid, Toyo USPO, Verizon, vet, Vons Foods, Walgreens, S Garde Mkt/deli
16	Lowell Ave
14	La Tuna Cyn Rd
11	Sunland Blvd, Tujunga, N Chevron, Mobil/dsl, Shell co's, Jack-in-the-Box, Panda Express, Pizza Hut, Starbuc Subway, Yum Yum Donuts 7-11, city park, O'Reilly Pa Ralph's Foods, Rite Aid, Verizon
9	Wheatland Ave
8	Osborne St, Lakeview Terrace, N Ranch Side Cafe 7-
6a	Paxton St
6b	CA 118
5	Maclay St, to San Fernando, S 76/dsl, Chevron El Po Loco, KFC, McDonald's, Quizno's, Subway, Taco Bell Ho Depot, Office Depot
4	Hubbard St, N Chevron Denny's, Yum Yum D nuts 99c Store, AutoZone, Fresh&Easy, S Mobil/c Shell El Caporal Mexican, Jack-in-the-Box, Shakey's Piz Starbucks, Subway USPO, Von's Foods
3	Polk St, S Arco, Chevron/dsl KFC H, 7-11
2	Roxford St, N Arco/dsl Fresh&Fast Mexican H, fy Lube, S Travelodge
1c	Yarnell St
1b a	**I-210 begins/ends on I-5, exit 160.**

MONROVIA

PASADENA

INTERSTATE 215 (Riverside)

Exit #	Services
55	**I-215 begins/ends on I-15.**
54	Devore, E Arco/dsl, Shell, W Tony's Diner
50	Palm Ave, Kendall Dr, E 7-11, Arco Albertacos, Burg King, Mi Cocina Mexican, Starbucks, Subway, W Denny's
48	University Pkwy, E 76/Circle K, Chevron/dsl Alberto Baskin Robbins/Togo's, Carl's Jr, Del Taco, Domino's, IHOP, K Little Caesar's, McDonald's, Papa John's, Starbucks, Subw Wienerschnitzel AT&T, Jiffy Lube, Ralph's Foods, Stapl W Arco, Mobil/dsl/LP Don Martin Grill, Jack-in-the-B Taco Bell Days Inn, Motel 6 Verizon, Walmart/Subway
46c a	CA 210, Redlands, to Pasadena, E golf, W golf
46b	Highland Ave
45a	CA 210 E, Highlands
45	Baseline Rd, E 76, Arco
44a	CA 66 W, 5th St, E In-N-Out Best Value Inn, Coun Inn, Golden Star Inn, Leisure Inn, Rodeway Inn
43	2nd St, Civic Ctr, E Chevron/dsl Del Taco, Honeybak Ham, In-N-Out, McDonald's, Starbucks, Subway, Taco B Best Value Inn $Tree, Food4Less, Ford, Marshall's, Ros
42b	Mill St, E Carl's Jr, Jack-in-the-Box AutoZone, Shell Yum-yum Donuts
42a	Inland Ctr Dr, E Chevron/dsl Carl's Jr, Jack-in-th Box, Wienerschnitzel AutoZone, Macy's, O'Reilly Par W Arco/dsl

SAN BERNARDINO

INTERSTATE 215 (Riverside) Cont'd

Exit #	Services
41	Orange Show Rd, E 76/dsl, World Burger Mania, ChuckECheese, Jose's Mexican, Subway, Sundowners Rest., Viva Villa Grill Knights Inn, Orange Show Inn 7-11, 99c Store, BigLots, Chrysler/Dodge/Jeep, Firestone/auto, Kelly Tire, Target, W AT&T, Kia, Mitsubishi, Nissan, Subaru, Toyota, VW
40b a	I-10, E to Palm Springs, W to LA
39	Washington St, Mt Vernon Ave, E 5 Point/repair, 76/Circle K, Arco Baker's Drive-Thru, China Town, DQ, George's Burgers, Siquio's Mexican, Starbucks, Taco Joe's Colton Inn BigLots, Goodyear/auto, Jiffy Lube, W Buffet Star, Carl's Jr, Church's, Del Taco, Denny's, Graziano's Pizza, Jack-in-the-Box, McDonald's, Starbucks, Subway, Taco Patron Red Tile Inn 99c Store, GNC, multiple RV dealers, Ross, Walmart/auto
38	Barton Rd, E Arco, Shell/Circle K/dsl Miguel's Mexican, Quiznos AutoZone, Stater Bros., W Demetri's Burgers vet
37	La Cadena Dr, (Iowa Ave from sb), E Shell/dsl Jack-in-the-Box Holiday Inn Express
36	Center St, to Highgrove, E Chevron/Subway/dsl, W Valero/dsl
35	Columbia Ave, E Arco/dsl, W Circle K
34b a	CA 91, CA 60, Main St, Riverside, to beach cities
33	Blaine St, 3rd St, E 76, Shell, Valero Baker's Drive-Thru, Jack-in-the-Box, Starbucks Stater Bros., Valvoline
32	University Ave, Riverside, W Mobil/dsl, Shell, Thrifty Canton Chinese, Carl's Jr, Coco's, Denny's, Domino's, Fatburger, Gus Jr, IHOP, Jack-in-the-Box, Jersey Mike's, Little Caesar's, Mandarin Chinese, Papa John's, Pizza Hut, Rubio's, Santana's Mexican, Shakey's Pizza, Starbucks, Subway, Taco Bell, Wienerschnitzel Comfort Inn, Courtyard, Motel 6 $Tree, AT&T, Food4Less, O'Reilly Parts, Rite Aid, USPO, Walgreens
31	MLK Blvd, El Cerrito
30b	Central Ave, Watkins Dr
30a	Fair Isle Dr, Box Springs, E Marjon RV Ctr, W 76/Circle K/Subway/dsl Jack-in-the-Box Ford, Nissan
29	CA 60 E, to Indio, E Arco, Shell/dsl Applebee's, Baffalo Wild Wings, Baker's Drive-Thru, BJ's Rest., Burger Boss, Carl's Jr, Chick-fil-A, Chili's, Chipotle Mexican, El Pollo Loco, Five Guys, Golden Chop Stix, Hawaiian BBQ, Home Town Buffet, Hooters, Jamba Juice, Jason's Deli, Jersey Mike's, John's Pizza, McDonald's, Miguel's Mexican, Mimi's Cafe, Olive Garden, Outback Steaks, Panda Express, Panera Bread, Portillo's Hot Dogs, Round Table Pizza, Rubio's, Starbucks, Subway, Waba Grill, Wendy's, Wienerschnitzel Ayres Hotel, Hampton Inn $Tree, 99c Store, Best Buy, Costco/gas, JC Penney, Jo-Ann Fabrics, Lowe's, Macy's, Marshall's, Michael's, Old Navy, PetCo, Petsmart, Ross, Staples, Target, TJ Maxx, Verizon, Walmart, WinCo Foods, World Mkt
28	Eucalyptus Ave, Eastridge Ave, E Bravo Burgers, Hooters Sam's Club/gas, Target, Walmart, same as 29
27b	(27c from sb) Alessandro Blvd, E Arco/dsl auto repair, Big O Tire, W Chevron Farmer Boys
27a	Cactus Ave to March ARB, E 76/Circle K/dsl, Chevron/dsl Carl's Jr, Gus Jr
25	Van Buren Blvd, E March Field Museum, W Riverside Nat Cem
23	Harley Knox Blvd
22	Ramona Expswy, E Arco, Chevron/dsl, Mobil/Circle K, Shell/Subway/dsl Farmer Boys, Harry's Cafe, McDonald's, Papa John's, Starbucks, Subway, Valentino's Pizza, W

PERRIS

Exit #	Services
22	Continued 76/Circle K/dsl/LP, Arco/dsl/scales/24hr Jack-in-the-Box
19	Nuevo Rd, E Arco, Chevron/dsl, Mobil/Circle K Baskin-Robbins, Burger King, Carl's Jr, China Palace, Del Taco, El Pollo Loco, IHOP, Jenny's Rest., McDonald's, Pizza Hut, Sizzler, Starbucks, Subway AutoZone, Food4Less, GNC, Rite Aid, Stater Bros Foods, Walmart
17	CA 74 W, 4th St, to Perris, Lake Elsinore, E Shell, W Chevron Del Taco, Denny's, Jack-in-the-Box, Jimenez Mexican, Little Caesar's, Popeye's Holiday Inn Express AutoZone, Chrysler/Dodge/Jeep/Kia
15	CA 74 E, Hemet, E Jack-in-the-Box Sun Leisure Motel
14	Ethanac Rd, E KFC/Taco Bell Richardson's RV, W 76/dsl, Circle K/dsl Carl's Jr, Del Taco, Ono Hawaiian BBQ, Starbucks, Subway Home Depot, Just Tires, Verizon, WinCo Foods
12	McCall Blvd, Sun City, E Valero/dsl Wendy's Best Value Inn, Motel 6 H, W Chevron/dsl, United Oil Coco's, Domino's, McDonald's, Papa Murphy's, Santana's Mexican, Subway $Tree, Rite Aid, Stater Bros, Von's Foods, Walgreens
10	Newport Rd, Quail Valley, E Shell/Del Taco/dsl Cathay Chinese, Jack-in-the-Box, Papa John's, Subway, Taco Bell $Tree, AutoZone, GNC, Ralph's Foods, Ross, vet, W Circle K/dsl Applebee's, Baskin-Robbins, BJ's Rest., Chipotle Mexican, In-N-Out, Miguel's Mexican, NY Pizza, Panda Express, Panera Bread, Red Robin, Starbucks, Subway, TX Roadhouse, Yellow Basket Cafe AT&T, Best Buy, CVS Drug, Kohl's, Lowe's, Michael's, Old Navy, PetCo, Staples, SuperTarget, TJ Maxx, URGENT CARE, Verizon, vet
7	Scott Rd, E 7-11, Arco/dsl Carl's Jr, Del Taco, Jack-in-the-Box, Submarina, Subway, Wood Rock Fire Pizza Albertson's/SavOn, Verizon, vet, Walgreens, W Marco's Pizza
4	Clinton Keith Rd, W Arco/dsl Del Taco, Jersey Mike's, Juice It Up, Starbucks, Subway Mtn View Tire, Target, URGENT CARE, Verizon, Walgreens
2	Los Alamos, E Shell Board'z Grill, Cojito's Mexican, In-N-Out, Miguel's Jr Mexican, Peony Chinese, Starbucks, Taco Bell USPO, W Mobil/Circle K/dsl ChuckeCheese, Jack-in-the-Box, McDonald's, Pizza Hut, Starbucks, Subway, TJ's Pizza CVS Drug, Stater Bros., vet
1	Murrieta Hot Springs, E 7-11, Shell/dsl Alberto's Mexican, Buffalo Wild Wings, Carl's Jr, El Pollo Loco, Habit Burger, Hungry Bull, Richie's Diner, Rubio's, Sizzler, Starbucks, Submarina, Wendy's $Tree, Dick's, Ralph's Foods, Rite Aid, Ross, Sam's Club/gas, Verizon, vet, Walgreens, W Richie's Diner, Starbucks
0mm	**I-215 begins/ends on I-15.**

MURRIETA

= gas = food = lodging = other = rest stop

INTERSTATE 280 (Bay Area)

SAN FRANCISCO

Exit #	Services
58	I-280 begins/ends, 4th St, N Whole Foods Mkt, S Shell
57	7th St, to I-80, downtown
56	Mariposa St, downtown
55	Army St, Port of SF
54	US 101 S, Alemany Blvd, Mission St, E Shell
52	San Jose Ave, Bosworth St (from nb, no return)
51	Geneva Ave
50	CA 1, 19th Ave, W Chevron SFSU, to Bay Bridge
49	Daly City, Daly City, E 76/dsl/LP, Flyers Toyota, Walgreens, W 76, Arco Carl's Jr, Domino's, IHOP, In-N-Out, Krispy Kreme, McDonald's, Val's Rest. Hampton Inn
47a	Serramonte Blvd, Daly City (from sb), same as 47b
47b	CA 1, Mission St (from nb), Pacifica, E Chipotle, Hawaiian BBQ, Popeye's, RoundTable Pizza, Sizzler, Starbucks H, $Tree, Chevrolet, Chrysler/Jeep/Dodge, Ford, Fresh Choice Foods, Hyundai, Lexus, Michael's, Nissan, Target, Verizon, VW/Subaru, W JC Penney, Target
46	Hickey Blvd, Colma, E Chevron/dsl, Shell/dsl, W Shell/dsl/24hr Boston Mkt, Celia's Rest., Habit Burger, Koi Palace, Max's Filipino, Moonstar, Outback Steaks, Panera Bread, Pieology 7-11, AT&T, CVS, Petsmart, Ross, Sprouts Mkt, Target
45	Avalon Dr (from sb), Westborough, W Arco/24hr, Valero/dsl Five Guys, McDonald's, Subway, Take One Pizza AT&T, Pacific Mkt, Safeway, Skyline Coll, Walgreens/24hr
44	(from nb), W same as 45
43b	I-380 E, to US 101, to SF Airport
43a	San Bruno Ave, Sneath Ave, E Au's Kitchen, Baskin-Robbins, Cafe Grillades, Carl's Jr, Extreme Pizza, Jamba Juice, Nueve Mexican, Pasta Pomodoro, Starbucks CVS, GNC, Mollie Stones Mkt, W 76, Chevron, Kwik Serv Shari's 7-11
42	Crystal Springs (from sb), E county park
41	CA 35 N, Skyline Blvd (from wb, no EZ return), to Pacifica, **1 mi** W Chevron
40	Millbrae Ave, Millbrae, E Chevron
39	Trousdale Dr, to Burlingame, E H
36	Black Mtn Rd, Hayne Rd, W vista point, golf
36mm	**Crystal Springs wb, full facilities, litter barrels, petwalk, picnic table**
35	CA 35, CA 92W (from eb), to Half Moon Bay
34	Bunker Hill Dr
33	CA 92, to Half Moon Bay, San Mateo
32mm	vista point both lanes
29	Edgewood Rd, Canada Rd, to San Carlos, E H
27	Farm Hill Blvd, E Cañada Coll
25	CA 84, Woodside Rd, Redwood City, **1 mi** W Chevron/dsl Buck's Rest., Firehouse Bistro Robert's Mkt, USPO
24	Sand Hill Rd, Menlo Park, **1 mi** E Shell Starbucks CVS, Safeway
22	Alpine Rd, Portola Valley, E H, W Shell/autocare Amigos Grill, Lobster Shack Bianchi's Mkt
20	Page Mill Rd, to Palo Alto, E H, to Stanford U
16	El Monte Rd, Moody Rd
15	Magdalena Ave
13	Foothill Expswy, Grant Rd, E Chevron/24hr Red Pepper Grill, Starbucks, Subway Rite Aid, Trader Joe's, Verizon, W to Rancho San Antonio CP
12b a	CA 85, N to Mtn View, S to Gilroy

SAN JOSE

Exit #	Services
11	Saratoga, Cupertino, Sunnyvale, E Chevron/dsl potle, Starbucks Cupertino Inn Goodyear/auto, chael's, Rite Aid, Ross, Safeway, SteinMart, W 76, Ch ron, Valero BJ's Rest., Outback Steaks, Starbucks, Wi BBQ Aloft, Juniper Hotel Apple Computer HQ, Spro Mkt
10	Wolfe Rd, E Arco/24hr Mod Pizza, Panchero's, S bucks Courtyard, Hilton Garden Ranch Mkt, W Alexander Steaks, Benihana, Vallco Dynasty Chin FreshChoice Foods, JC Penney, Vallco Fashion Park
9	Lawrence Expswy, Stevens Creek Blvd (from eb), N Pollo Loco, McDonald's, Panda Express, Starbucks AT Marshall's, Nissan, Safeway, Verizon, S Rotten Robb Shell IHOP, Subway Woodcrest Hotel 7-11
7	Saratoga Ave, N Arco/24hr, Chevron/24hr Bur King, Happi House, Harry's Hofbrau, Lion Foods, McDonal Starbucks, Subway, Taco Bell, Togo's TownePlace Sui 7-11, Chevrolet, Ford, PepBoys, Walmart Mkt, S Shell, Valero Applebee's, Lyon's Rest. Sheraton
5c	Winchester Blvd, Campbell Ave (from eb)
5b	CA 17 S, to Santa Cruz, I-880 N, to San Jose
5a	Leigh Ave, Bascom Ave
4	Meridian St (from eb), N Big Lots, FoodMaxx, Har Davidson, S Chevron Subway 7-11
3b	Bird Ave, Race St, N Chevron
3a	CA 87, N Hilton, Marriott, Westin
2	7th St, to CA 82, N conv ctr
1	10th St, 11th St, N 7-11, to San Jose St U
0mm	**I-280 begins/ends on US 101.**

INTERSTATE 405 (Los Angeles)

LOS ANGELES AREA

Exit #	Services
73	I-5, N to Sacramento, I-5, S to LA.
72	Rinaldi St, Sepulveda, E Chevron/dsl Arby's, McDo ald's, Presidente Mexican, Starbucks, Subway H, Niss Toyota, W Shell Best Value Inn
71	CA 118 W, Simi Valley
70	Devonshire St, Granada Hills, E 76, Arco, Sincla dsl Mandarin Island, Millie's Rest., Papa John's, Saf Room Rest, Starbucks, Subway Rite Aid, Verizon, Vo Foods
69	Nordhoff St, E Mobil/dsl China Wok, Coldstone, D Taco, KFC, Panda Express, Pollo Campero, Starbucks, Su way Hillcrest Inn 7-11, Marshalls, Vallarta Foods, W greens, W 76/dsl, Arco Jack-in-the-Box, Pizza Hut
68	Roscoe Blvd, to Panorama City, E 76/dsl, Shell Burg King, Denny's, Horseless Carriage Rest., Jack-in-the-Box, Kou try Folks Rest., Little Caesar's, McDonald's, Panda Express, Ta Bell, Yoshinoya Holiday Inn Express 7-11, AutoZon Ford, Jaguar/Volvo, Lincoln, U-Haul, W Chevron/dsl, She dsl Tommy's Burgers Motel 6
66	Sherman Blvd, Reseda, E Chevron, Mobil/LP McDo ald's, Starbucks Motel 6 H, BigLots, CVS Drug, Jor Foods, W 76/dsl/24hr Taco Bell USPO
65	Victory Blvd, Van Nuys, E Carl's Jr, El Pollo Loco, Fatburg er, Jack-in-the-Box, Subway, Wendy's H, Costco/ga CVS Drug, El Monte RV Ctr, Office Depot, PepBoys, Staple W Arco/24hr
64	Burbank Blvd, E Chevron, Shell Denny's, Zankou Chic en Best Western, Hampton Inn Target
63b	US 101, Ventura Fwy

INTERSTATE 405 (Los Angeles) Cont'd

Exit #	Services
63a	Ventura Blvd (from nb), E [gas] Mobil [food] Cheesecake Factory, El Pollo Loco, PF Chang's [other] Whole Foods Mkt, W [gas] [food] Ameci Pizza, CA Chicken Cafe, Corner Bakery Cafe, IHOP, McDonald's [lodging] Courtyard, Valley Inn
63a	Valley Vista Blvd (from sb)
61	Mulholland Dr, Skirvall Dr
59	Sepulveda Blvd, Getty Ctr Dr, W [other] to Getty Ctr
57	Sunset Blvd, Morega Dr, E [gas] 76/dsl, Chevron/24hr [other] to UCLA, W [lodging] Luxe Hotel
56	Waterford St, Montana Ave (from nb)
55c b	Wilshire Blvd, E [other] [H], downtown
55a	CA 2, Santa Monica Blvd, E [gas] Chevron, Mobil, Mobil, Shell [food] Coffee Bean, Del Taco, Fatburger, Jack-in-the-Box, Jamba Juice, Jin Jiang Chinese, Starbucks [other] 7-11, LDS Temple, Porsche, Staples, Tesla, W [gas] 76, Chevron/dsl [food] Subway [lodging] Holiday Inn Express [other] vet
54	Olympic Blvd, Peco Blvd, E [gas] Mobil [food] Islands Burgers, Starbucks, Subway [other] USPO, W [food] Big Tomy's Rest. [other] Best Buy, Marshall's, Michael's, Petsmart
53	I-10, Santa Monica Fwy
52	Venice Blvd, E [gas] Chevron/service, Shell/dsl [food] Carl's Jr, Subway [lodging] Ramada [other] 7-11, **services W on Sepulveda** [gas] SP/dsl [food] FatBurger
51	Culver Blvd, Washington Blvd, E [food] Dear John's Café, Domino's, Taco Bell [other] vet, W [gas] 76/repair, CIC Gas
50b	CA 90, Slauson Ave, to Marina del Rey, E [gas] Arco/24hr [food] Del Taco, El Pollo Loco, HoneyBaked Ham, Shakey's Pizza, Winchell's [other] $Tree, BigLots, Goodyear/auto, Just Tires, Office Depot, Old Navy
50a	Jefferson Blvd (from sb), E [food] Coco's, Jack-in-the-Box [other] PetsMart, Rite Aid, Target, W to LA Airport
49	Howard Hughes Pkwy, to Centinela Ave, E [gas] Chevron/dsl, Mobil/dsl [food] BJ's Brewhouse, Five Guys, Lucille's BBQ, Qdoba, Sizzler, Subway [lodging] Courtyard, Sheraton [other] Best Buy, CVS Drug, Ford, Honda, JC Penney, Macy's, Marshall's, Target, Tesla, W [gas] Chevron [food] Buffalo Wild Wings, Chick-fil-A, Chuy's Mexican, Dinah's Rest., Habuki Japanese, Islands Burgers, Starbucks [lodging] Extended Stay America [other] Howard Hughes Ctr, Nordstrom
48	La Tijera Blvd, E [gas] Mobil/sl [food] Burger King, ChuckeCheese, El Pollo Loco, Jamba Juice, KFC, McDonald's, Starbucks, Subway, Taco Bell, TGIFriday's [lodging] Best Western [other] 99c Store, CVS Drug, Ralph's Foods, Ross, Vons Foods, W [gas] 76, Arco [food] Wendy's [other] USPO
47	CA 42, Manchester Ave, Inglewood, E [gas] 76/Circle K/dsl/24hr [food] Carl's Jr, Subway [lodging] Best Western, Economy Inn [other] 7-11, W [gas] 76, Arco, Mobil/7-11, Shell [food] Arby's, Burger King, Denny's, El Pollo Loco, Jack-in-the-Box, Subway [lodging] Days Inn [other] CarMax, Home Depot
46	Century Blvd, E [food] El Pollo Loco, Hawaiian BBQ, Little Caesar's, Panda Express, Rally's [lodging] Best Western, Motel 6, Quality Inn, Tivoli Hotel [other] 7-11, W [gas] 76, Arco/24hr, Chevron/dsl, Shell [food] Carl's Jr, Denny's, McDonald's, Taco Bell [lodging] Crowne Plaza, Embassy Suites, Hilton, Holiday Inn, La Quinta, Marriott, Residence Inn, Travelodge, Westin Hotel [other] to LAX
45	I-105, Imperial Hwy, E [gas] 76/dsl, Shell, Valero [food] El Pollo Loco, Jack-in-the-Box, McDonald's, Starbucks [lodging] Best Value Inn, Candlewood Suites, Hampton Inn, Holiday Inn Express
44	El Segundo Blvd, to El Segundo, E [gas] 76, Chevron/dsl, Thrifty [food] Burger King, Cougars Burgers, Jack-in-the-Box,

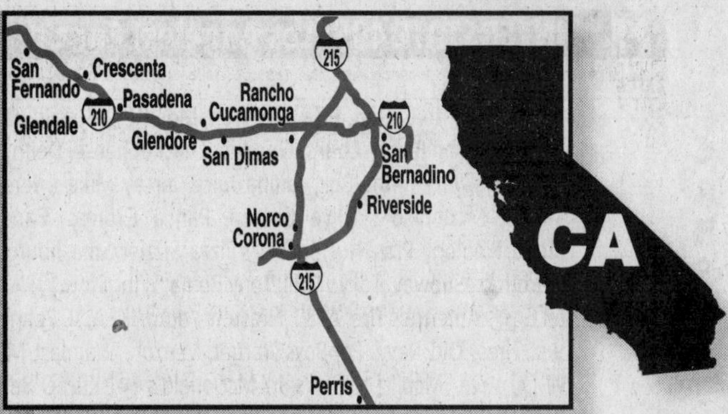

HAWTHORNE

TORRANCE

Exit #	Services
44	Continued Subway [lodging] El Segundo Inn [other] transmissions, W [food] Denny's [lodging] Ramada Inn
43b a	Rosecrans Ave, to Manhattan Beach, E [gas] 76, Shell [food] Denny's, El Pollo Loco, Pizza Hut, Starbucks, Subway, Waba Grill [other] Best Buy, CVS Drug, Food4Less, Ford/Lincoln, Home Depot, Marshall's, Michael's, Ross, TJ Maxx, Verizon, Walmart Mkt, W [gas] Arco [food] Blaze Pizza, Cafe Rio, Carl's Jr, Chipotle Mexican, Coffee Bean, Flemings Rest., Hawaiian BBQ, Houston's, Jamba Juice, Luigi's Rest., McDonald's, Robeks Juice, Sansai Japanese, Starbucks, Subway [lodging] Ayres Hotel, Hyatt, SpringHill Suites, TownePlace Suites [other] REI, AT&T, Barnes&Noble, Costco/gas, CVS Drug, Office Depot, Old Navy, Porsche, Subaru, Trader Joe's, VW
42b	Inglewood Ave, E [gas] Arco, Shell [food] Del Taco, Denny's, Domino's, In-N-Out, Panda Wok [other] CVS Drug, Marshall's, PetCo, Vons Foods, Walmart Mkt, W [gas] Chevron/dsl, Chevron/dsl (2) [food] Chile Verde Mexican, Subway [other] 99c Store, repair
42a	CA 107, Hawthorne Blvd, E [gas] Chevron [food] Carl's Jr, Jack-in-the-Box, McDonald's, Panda Express, Papa John's, Spires Rest., Starbucks, Wendy's, Wienerschnitzel [lodging] Baymont Inn, Best Western, Days Inn [other] 99c Store, CVS Drug, El Super Foods, O'Reilly Parts, PepBoys, vet, W [gas] Arco/24hr, USA/dsl [food] Boston Mkt, Del Taco, Sizzler, Starbucks, Subway, Taco Bell, Yoshinoya [other] AutoZone, Macy's, Nordstom, Walgreens
40b	Redondo Beach Blvd (no EZ sb return), Hermosa Beach, E [gas] 76, Arco/24hr [food] ChuckeCheese, Jack-in-the-Box [other] golf, W [food] Coldstone, RoundTable Pizza, Starbucks [other] $Tree, AutoZone, CVS Drug, Walgreens
40a	CA 91 E, Artesia Blvd, to Torrance, W [gas] Chevron [other] Carl's Jr, Starbucks, YumYum Donuts
39	Crenshaw Blvd, to Torrance, E [gas] Arco/24hr, Shell [food] Coffee Bean, El Pollo Loco, McDonald's [other] USPO, W [gas] Shell/Subway/dsl [other] Jiffy Lube
38b	Western Ave, to Torrance, E [gas] 76/dsl, Arco, Chevron [food] Chipotle, Del Taco, Denny's, In-N-Out, Jersey Mike's, Local Place, Panda Express, Papa John's, Quiznos, Starbucks, Wendy's [lodging] Dynasty Inn [other] Albertson's/Sav-On, AT&T, GNC, Toyota, W [gas] Mobil [lodging] Courtyard
38a	Normandie Ave, to Gardena, E [lodging] Travelodge, W [gas] Shell/dsl [food] Carl's Jr, Hong Kong Cafe, On + On Asian, Pizza Hut/Taco Bell, Quiznos, Starbucks, Subway, Wienerschnitzel [lodging] Extended Stay America [other] $Tree, AT&T, AutoZone, Office Depot, Walmart
37b	Vermont Ave (from sb), E [food] Paradise Rest., W [lodging] Holiday Inn
37a	I-110, Harbor Fwy
36	Main St (from nb)
36mm	**weigh sta both lanes**

INTERSTATE 405 (Los Angeles) Cont'd

CARSON

Exit #	Services
35	Avalon Blvd, to Carson, E Chevron, Mobil Buffalo Wild Wings, Carson Buffet, Chili's, Chipotle, ChuckeCheese, Denny's, Five Guys, Jack-in-the-Box, Jamba Juice, Jersey Mike's, Jersey Mike's, McDonald's, Olive Garden, Panda Express, Panera Bread, Pieology, Pizza Hut, Shakey's Pizza, Sizzler, Smashburger, Starbucks, Subway, Tokyo Grill, Tony Roma, WingStop Motel 6 America's Tire, AT&T, Firestone/auto, IKEA, JC Penney, Just Tires, Old Navy, PepBoys, Target, Verizon, Walmart Mkt, W Arco, Mobil Carl's Jr, McDonald's Kia, O'Reilly Parts, Ralph's Foods, USPO
34	Carson St, to Carson, E EconoLodge, W 76/dsl, Mobil Carl's Jr, Jack-in-the-Box, Subway DoubleTree Inn
33b	Wilmington Ave, E Shell/dsl Carson Burgers, W Chevron/Jack-in-the-Box/dsl, Shell/Subway/dsl Del Taco, Spires Rest. Chevrolet/Hyundai, Honda, Nissan, Toyota
33a	Alameda St
32d	Santa Fe Ave (from nb), E SC Fuels, W 76, Chevron/24hr, Oasis/dsl Fantastic Burgers, Tom's Burgers
32c b	I-710, Long Beach Fwy
32a	Pacific Ave (from sb)
30b	Long Beach Blvd, E Arco/dsl Subway 7-11, W United H
30a	Atlantic Blvd, E Arby's, Carl's Jr, Denny's/24hr, El Torito, Jack-in-the-Box, Polly's Cafe CVS Drug, Staples, Target, vet, Walgreens, W Applebee's, Chipotle, In-N-Out, Starbucks H, $Tree, Home Depot, PetCo, Ross
29c	Orange Ave (from sb)
29b a	Cherry Ave, to Signal Hill, E Mobil/dsl Fantastic Burgers Ford, Lincoln, Mazda, W 76/dsl America's Tire, Best Buy, Buick/GMC, Cadillac, Chrysler/Dodge/Jeep, Costco/gas, Home Depot, Honda, Mercedes, Mini, Nissan
27	CA 19, Lakewood Blvd, E Marriott, W Chevron, Shell Spires Rest., Subway Extended Stay America, Holiday Inn, Residence Inn H, Goodyear/auto, Verizon
26b	Bellflower Blvd, E Burger King, Carl's Jr, Denny's, Jamba Juice, KFC, Papa John's, Starbucks, Subway, Togo's Ford, Lowe's, Verizon, W Chevron, Mobil/dsl Hof's Hut, IHOP, McDonald's, Pick-Up Stix, Pieology, Wendy's H, AT&T, BigLots, CVS Drug, Goodyear/auto, See's Candies, Target, TJ Maxx, Trader Joe's, USPO
26a	Woodruff Ave (from nb)
25	Palo Verde Ave, W Del Taco, Domino's, Starbucks, Subway, Taco Bell
24b	Studebaker Rd (from sb)
24a	I-605 N
23	CA 22 W, 7th St, to Long Beach
22	Seal Beach Blvd, Los Alamitos Blvd, E 76/dsl, Chevron/repair/24hr, Mobil/dsl Baja Fresh, CA Pizza Kitchen Daphne's Greek, Chick-fil-A, Chipotle, Hot Off the Grill, In-N-Out, Islands Burgers, Jamba Juice, Kobe Japanese, Macaroni Grill, Marie Callenders, Peiwei Asian, Pick-Up Stix, Rubio's, Spaghettini Grill, Starbucks, Subway Ayres Hotel AT&T, CVS Drug, GNC, Kohl's, Marshall's, Ralph's Foods, Sprouts Mkt, Staples, Target, Verizon, **1 mi W** 76/dsl, Chevron Carl's Jr, Del Taco, Denny's, Domino's Hampton Inn
21	CA 22 E, Garden Grove Fwy, Valley View St, E Dillon RV Ctr
19	Westminster Ave, to Springdale St, E 76/dsl, USA Café Westminster, Carl's Jr, Chipotle, In-N-Out, KFC, McDonald's, Pizza Hut, Popeye's Motel 6, Quality Inn $Tree, 7-11, Albertson's, America's Tire, AutoZone, BigLots, Home Depot,

CA

Exit #	Services
19	Continued O'Reilly Parts, Rite Aid, Ross, W 76/dsl, Chevr dsl/24hr Ranchito Mkt, Starbucks, Subway Best We ern, Courtyard Inn
18	Bolsa Ave, Golden West St, W Mobil/dsl Del Taco Torito, Jack-in-the-Box, Outback Steaks, Rodrigo's Mexic Starbucks, TGIFriday, Wendy's $Tree, CVS Drug, JC Penn Jo-Ann Fabrics, Jons Foods, Macy's, Target
16	CA 39, Beach Blvd, to Huntington Bch, E Chevron Ja in-the-Box, Subway Hotel 39 H, Infiniti, PepBo Toyota, U-Haul, W Mobil/service Arby's, BJ's Re Buca Italian, Burger King, CA Pizza Kitchen, Cheesecake F tory, Chick-fil-A, Chipotle Mexican, Islands Burgers, Jack-the-Box, Macaroni Grill, Marie Callender's, McDonald's, Pa ra Bread, Starbucks, Subway Comfort Suites, Spring Suites AT&T, Barnes&Noble, Chrysler/Dodge/Jeep, Cost gas, Firestone/auto, Kohl's, Old Navy, REI, See's Candies, S ples, Target, Verizon, Whole Foods Mkt
15b a	Magnolia St, Warner Ave, E Del Taco, Mel's Diner, Sizz W Chevron, Mobil/Circle K Magnolia Café, Qua Trang Rest., Starbucks, Tommy's Burgers, Winchell's Mo 6 7-11, Aldi Foods, CVS Drug, Tuesday Morning
14	Brookhurst St, Fountain Valley, E Arco/24hr, Chevron, M bil, Shell Carl's Jr, Del Taco, KFC, Sabrosada Mexican, Ta Bell Ayres Inn, Courtyard, Residence Inn Sam's Clu gas, Thompson's RV Ctr, W Arco, Berri Bros/dsl, She dsl, USA/dsl Applebee's, Black Angus, ClaimJump Coldstone, Corner Bakery Cafe, Dickey's BBQ, Dunkin', Islan Burgers, Jamba Juice, Jersey Mike's, Mandarin Chinese, Mim Cafe, Pick Up Stix, Rubio's, Starbucks, Subway, Wendy's Albertson's, Office Depot, Ralph's Foods, Rite Aid, TJ Maxx, V izon, vet
12	Euclid Ave, E Tesla EVC Cancun Fresh, Coffee Bea FlameBroiler, Jimmy John's, McDonald's, Panda Express, Sc plantation, Starbucks, Subway, Taco Bell H, $Tree, Costc gas, PetsMart, Ross, Tire Whse
11b	Harbor Blvd, to Costa Mesa, E Hooters La Quin W Arco, Chevron, Mobil Cane's, Chick-fil-A, Denny El Pollo Loco, Five Guys, Flame Broiler, IHOP, In-N-Out, Jack-i the-Box, McDonald's, Panera Bread, Sonic, Starbucks, Subwa Taco Bell Motel 6, Super 8, Vagabond Inn Acura, A toZone, CarMax, Chevrolet, Chrysler/Dodge/Jeep, Honda, Ni san, Rite Aid, Sprouts Mkt, Target, Vons Foods
11a	Fairview Rd, E Starbucks Best Buy, Marshall's, O Navy, Verizon, W 76, Chevron, Shell Del Taco, Jack-i the-Box, Round Table Pizza CVS Drug, O'Reilly Parts, Stat Bros
10	CA 73, to CA 55 S (from sb), Corona del Mar, Newport Beach
9b	Bristol St, E Chevron/dsl Antonello's Italian, Baskin-Ro bins, Boudin SF Cafe, Buffalo Wild Wings, Capital Grill, Chic fil-A, China Olive, Chipotle Mexican, ClaimJumper, Corner Ba ery, In-N-Out, Jack-in-the-Box, Maggiano's Rest., McDonald Morton's Steaks, Pizza Hut, Red Robin, Starbucks, Subway, TG Friday Marriott Suites, Westin Hotel $Tree, AT&T, B gLots, Bloomingdale's, CVS Drug, Firestone/auto, GNC, Macy Michael's, PetCo, Rite Aid, Staples, Trader Joe's, Vons Food W 76/Circle K/dsl, Chevron/dsl Del Taco, El Pollo Loc Subway, Wahoo's Fish Taco Crowne Plaza, Hilton 7-1 PepBoys, vet
9a	CA 55, Costa Mesa Fwy, to Newport Bch, Riverside
8	MacArthur Blvd, E Chevron, Mobil/Subway Carl's J Jersey Mike's, McDonald's, Starbucks Embassy Suites

COSTA MESA

INTERSTATE 405 (Los Angeles) Cont'd

8	Continued Homewood Suites, W Chevron El Torito, Gulliver's Ribs, IHOP Atrium Hotel, Hilton, to
7	Jamboree Rd, Irvine, E Shell Andrei's Rest., Del Taco, Soup Plantation Courtyard, Hotel Irvine, Hyatt, Residence Inn, W Houston's, Melting Pot, North Italia, Panini Cafe, Ruth's Chris Steaks, Starbucks, Subway, Wahoo's Fish Taco, Which Wich? Marriott Verizon
5	Culver Dr, W Alfie's Gas, Chevron/dsl Carl's Jr, Subway Ace Hardware, Rite Aid, Wholesome Choice Mkt
4	Jeffrey Rd, University Dr, E Chevron, Mobil/Circle K CA Pizza Kitchen, El Pollo Loco, Golden Spoon, I Can Korean BBQ, McDonald's, Mooyah Burgers, Olive's Branch, Pick-Up Stix, Pizza 90, Square One Pizza, Starbucks, Togo's H, CVS Drug, Gelson's Mkt, Ralph's Foods, Verizon, Walgreens, W Mobil/dsl Korean House, Subway vet, ZionMart
3	Sand Canyon Ave, E H, URGENT CARE, W Arco/dsl Johnny's NY Pizza, Sharkey's Mexican, Starbucks, Subway, Thai Bamboo, Thai Bamboo, Two Left Forks Albertson's, CVS Drug, vet
2	CA 133, to Laguna Beach, E Courtyard, DoubleTree Inn
1c	Irvine Center Dr, E Cheesecake Factory, Chipotle Mexican, Dave&Buster's, Panda Express, PF Chang's, Pieology, Wahoo's Fish Tacos Barnes&Noble, Macy's, Nordstrom, Target, W 7-11 Burger King, Puesto Mexican, Starbucks, Togo's Big O Tire, URGENT CARE, Whole Foods Mkt
1b	Bake Pkwy, W Carmax, Toyota
1a	Lake Forest
0mm	**I-405 begins/ends on I-5, exit 132.**

INTERSTATE 505 (Winters)

Exit #	Services
33	**I-5. I-505 begins/ends on I-5.**
31	CR 12A
28	CR 14, Zamora
24	CR 19
21	CA 16, to Esparto, Woodland, W Guy's Food/fuel La Plazita
17	CR 27
15	CR 29A
11	CA 128 W, Russell Blvd, W Arco/Burger King/dsl, Chevron/24hr RoundTable Pizza, Starbucks, Subway, Taco Bell $General, Lorenzo's Mkt
10	Putah Creek Rd, no crossoversame as 11
6	Allendale Rd
3	Midway Rd, E RV camping
1c	Vaca Valley Pkwy, E H, W Vaca Valley TC/Chevron/Blimpie/dsl Burger King
1b	I-80 E. I-505 begins/ends on I-80.

INTERSTATE 580 (Bay Area)

Exit #	Services
79	**I-580 begins/ends, accesses I-5 sb.**
76b a	CA 132, Chrisman Rd, to Modesto, E 76/dsl RV camping (5mi)
72	Corral Hollow Rd
67	Patterson Pass Rd, E Subway, W Shell/7-11/dsl
65	I-205 (from eb), to Tracy
63	Grant Line Rd, to Byron

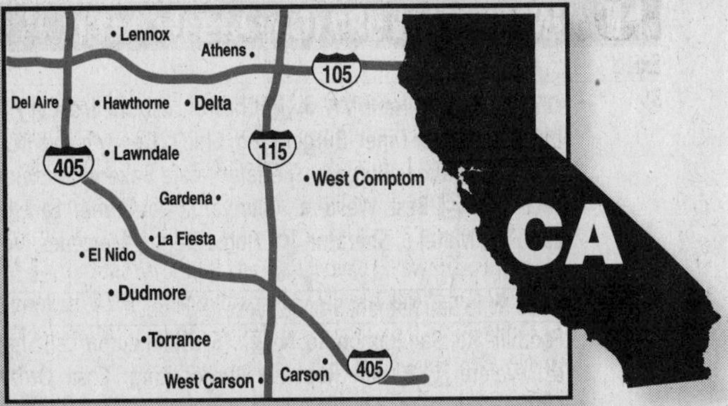

59	N Flynn Rd, Altamont Pass, elevation 1009, S Brake Check Area, many wind-turbines
57	N Greenville Rd, Laughlin Rd, Altamont Pass Rd, to Livermore Lab, S 76/7-11/dsl Best Western, La Quinta Harley-Davidson
56mm	**weigh sta both lanes**
55	Vasco Rd, to Brentwood, N 7-11, Arco, Chevron/dsl, Gas&Shop/dsl, QuikStop/dsl A&W/KFC, Country Waffles, McDonald's, Wienerschnitzel/Tastee Freez Toyota, S 7-11, Valero/dsl Jack-in-the-Box, Taco Bell Quality Inn

LIVERMORE

54	CA 84, 1st St, Springtown Blvd, Livermore, N Chevron/dsl Zpizza DoubleTree, Motel 6, Springtown Inn 7-11, S 76, Chevron, Shell, Valero/Circle K Applebee's, Burger King, Chili's, Chipotle, IHOP, Jamba Juice, McDonald's, Panda Express, Panera Bread, Peking Chinese, Starbucks, Subway, Taco Bell, Togo's America's Tire, Big Lots, CVS Drug, GNC, Lowe's Whse, Petco, Ross, Safeway/gas, Target, TJ Maxx, vet
52	N Livermore Ave, S 7-11, Chevron Baja Fresh, Coldstone, Denica's Kitchen, In-N-Out, Jack-in-the-Box, Popeye's, Quizno's, String's Italian Hawthorn Suites AT&T, Home Depot, Honda, Kohl's, Schwab Tire, Subaru, USPO, Walmart/Subway
51	Portola Ave, Livermore (no EZ eb return), S Ford/Lincoln
50	Airway Blvd, Collier Canyon Rd, Livermore, N Chevron/dsl Wendy's Comfort Inn, Courtyard, Hampton Inn, Hilton Garden, Holiday Inn Express, Residence Inn Costco/gas, S Carl's Jr, Cattlemen's Rest., Cholula's, Starbucks, Subway Extended Stay America 7-11
48	El Charro Rd, O'Fallon Rd, N Chevron/dsl BJ's Rest., Fresh Pixx, Jersey Mike's, Panera Bread, Starbucks Dick's, Target, S Chrysler/Dodge/Jeep, SF Outlets/famous brands
47	Santa Rita Rd, Tassajara Rd, N Baja Fresh, Buffalo Wild Wings, Coco Cabana Buick/GMC, GNC, Kia, Lowe's, Safeway, S Shell McDonald's, Ozora Steaks, Pizza Guys, Subway $Tree, Acura, AutoZone, BMW/Mini, Chevrolet/Cadillac, CVS Drug, Goodyear/auto, Lexus, Ranch Mkt, Trader Joe's

PLEASANTON

46	Hacienda Dr, Pleasanton, N Shell Applebee's, Black Angus, Chipotle, Five Guys, Fuddruckers, Habit Burger, Lazy Dog Rest., Mimi's Cafe, On-the-Border, Papa John's, Quiznos, Starbucks, Urban Plates Hyatt Place Barnes&Noble, Best Buy, Old Navy, TJ Maxx, Toyota, Verizon, Whole Foods Mkt, S Red Robin, Subway H, Kohl's, Walmart/McDonald's
45	Hopyard Rd, Pleasanton, N 76, Chevron/dsl, Shell/dsl IHOP, Subway La Quinta America's Tire, El Monte RV Ctr, Fiat, Honda, Hyundai, Mazda, Nissan, Office Depot,

CA

INTERSTATE 580 (Bay Area) Cont'd

CASTRO VALLEY / OAKLAND AREA

45	Continued O'Reilly Parts, U-Haul, VW, S Chevron/dsl, Shell/dsl Arby's, Black Bear Diner, Burger King, Chili's, Denny's, Faz Rest., In-N-Out, Nations Burgers, Specialty's Cafe Bakery, Starbucks, Taco Bell Best Western, Courtyard, Doubltree, Larkspur Landing, Motel 6, Sheraton Home Depot, Mercedes, Verizon
44b	I-680, N to San Ramon, S to San Jose
44a	Foothills Rd, San Ramon Rd, N 76/dsl, Chevron/dsl, Shell/dsl, Valero Baskin Robbins, Burger King, Casa Orozco, Chipotle Mexican, ChuckeCheese, Country Waffles, Elephant Bar Rest., Frankie Johnnie & Luigi's Too, Freebirds Burrito, Habit Burger, Hana Japan, Hooters, Korean BBQ, McNamara's Steaks, Outback Steaks, Panda Express, Panera Bread, Popeye's, RoundTable Pizza, Starbucks, Subway, Togo's Holiday Inn $Tree, Big Lots, CVS Drug, Hobby Lobby, JoAnn, Marshall's, Michael's, O'Reilly Parts, PetCo, PetsMart, Ranch Mkt Foods, REI, Ross, Safeway/gas, Sprouts, Target, S Baja Fresh, CA Pizza Kitchen, Cheesecake Factory, PF Chang's Marriott, Residence Inn, Sheraton JC Penney, Macy's, Nordstrom, Sears
39	Eden Canyon Rd, Palomares Rd, S rodeo park
37	Center St, Crow Canyon Rd, N Dickey's BBQ, Panda Express, Subway GNC, Petco, Rite Aid, Safeway, S 76/dsl, Chevron/dsl, same as 35
36	Redwood Rd, Castro Valley, N 76/dsl, Chevron/dsl Burger King, Chipotle Mexican, KFC, McDonald's, Round Table Pizza, Starbucks, Taco Bell, Wendy's Comfort Suites, Holiday Inn Express CVS, Goodyear, Lucky Foods, Rite Aid, Safeway, Walgreens
34	I-238 W, to I-880, CA 238, W off I-238 Jack-in-the Box 99c Store
33	164th Ave, Miramar Ave, E Chevron/dsl, National Fairmont Inn
32	150th Ave, Fairmont, E H, W 76/dsl, Mash/dsl, Shell Arby's, Burger King, Chili's, Denny's, Jamba Juice, Starbucks, Subway, Tito's Cafe $Tree, CVS, Goodyear, Kohl's, Lucky Foods, Michael's, Old Navy, Pepboys, Ross, Staples, Target
31	Grand Ave (from sb), Dutton Ave, W Valero Rite Aid
30	106th Ave, Foothill Blvd, MacArthur Blvd, W Arco
29	98th Ave, Golf Links Rd, E Shell Oakland Zoo, W 76/dsl, Valero
27b	Keller Ave, Mtn Blvd, E repair
27a	Edwards Ave (from sb, no EZ return), E US Naval Hospital
26b	Seminary Rd, E Observatory/Planetarium, W Seminary
26a	CA 13, Warren Fwy, to Berkeley (from eb)
25b a	High St, to MacArthur Blvd, E Razzo's Pizza, Subway O'Reilly Parts, USPO, vet, W Valero Walgreens
24	35th Ave (no EZ sb return), E Chevron Taco Bell, W Energy, QuikStop
23	Coolidge Ave, Fruitvale, E Shell/dsl Little Caesar's, McDonald's, Subway CVS, Farmer Joe's
22	Park Blvd, W Arco H
21b	Grand Ave, Lake Shore, E 76/24hr, Chevron/dsl Chipotle, KFC, Subway CVS, Trader Joe's, USPO, Walgreens
21a	Harrison St, Oakland Ave, E Quikstop, W Honda
19d c	CA 24 E, I-980 W, to Oakland
19b	West St, San Pablo Ave, E Panera Bread Extended Stay America Best Buy, Home Depot, Michael's, Office Depot, Safeway, Target

OAKLAND AREA

19a	I-80 W
18c	Market St, to San Pablo Ave, downtown
18b	Powell St, Emeryville, E Burger King, CA za Kitchen, Denny's, Elephant Bar/Grill, Jamba Juice, Chang's, Starbucks, Togo's Courtyard, Sheraton, Wc fin Suites Barnes&Noble, Old Navy, Ross, Trader Jo W Shell Chevy's Mexican Hilton Garden
18a	CA 13, Ashby Ave, Bay St, same as 18b
17	University Ave, Berkeley, E 76, University Gas La Q ta to UC Berkeley
16	Gilman St, E Golden Gate Fields Race Track, W Targ
13	Albany St, Buchanan St (from eb)
12	Central Ave (from eb), El Cerrito, E Shell/dsl, Val W Costco/gas
11	Bayview Ave, Carlson Blvd
10b	Regatta Blvd, E Golden Gate/dsl
10a	S 23rd St, Marina Bay Pkwy, E Subway, W Arti Kitchen CVS
9	Harbour Way, Cutting Blvd, E Arco, W Burger King
8	Canal Blvd, Garrard Blvd, W Chevron/dsl Days Inn, M rina Inn Suites
7b	Castro St, to I-80 E, Point Richmond, downtown industrial
7a	Western Drive (from wb), Point Molate
5mm	Richmond-San Rafael Toll Bridge
2a	Francis Drake Blvd, to US 101 S, E Extended Stay Ame ca BMW, Home Depot, Honda
1b	Francisco Blvd, San Rafael, E 76, Beacon, Circle K Bu er King, La Croissant Motel 6, Travelodge Mazda, ti U-Haul, W Subway $Tree, Office Depot, to San Que tin, USPO
1a	US 101 N to San Rafael, **I-580 begins/ends on US 101.**

INTERSTATE 605 (Los Angeles)

Exit #	Services
27c	**I-605 begins/ends.** Huntington Dr. Mobil/dsl Subw CVS Drug, Fresh&Easy Foods
27	I-210
26	Arrow Hwy, Live Oak, E Santa Fe Dam, W Irwinda Speedway
24	Lower Azusa Rd, LA St
23	Ramona Blvd, E Mobil Del Taco/24hr
22	I-10, E to San Bernardino, W to LA
21	Valley Blvd, to Industry, E 76, Chevron/Chester's/Subwa dsl Taco Nazo, Winchell's Donuts Valley Inn
19	CA 60, Pamona Fwy
18	Peck Rd, E Shell, W Ford Trucks
17	RoseHills Rd
16	Beverly Blvd
15	Whittier Blvd, E 76/dsl Carl's Jr, Taco Bell, YumYu Donuts GoodNite Inn 7-11, W Arco, Shell Pi za Hut, Shakey's Pizza, Starbucks, Subway, Tommy's Burge Howard Johnson AutoZone, Rite Aid
14	Washington Blvd, to Pico Rivera, E Firestone/auto
13	Slauson Ave, E Arco, Mobil Denny's Motel 6
12	Telegraph Rd, to Santa Fe Springs, E 76, Chevron D Taco, Jack-in-the-Box, Jersey Mike's, KFC, Subway, Yoshinoy W Arco/dsl
12mm	I-5
11	Florence Ave, to Downey, E Arco Honda
10	Firestone Blvd, E ChuckeCheese, KFC, McDonald' Sam's Burgers, Starbucks, Subway, Waba Grill Be Western 99c Store, Audi/BMW/Porsche, Costco/ga

INTERSTATE 605 (Los Angeles) Cont'd

10	Continued CVS Drug, Food4Less, Verizon, Walgreens, W Chevron/repair Starbucks Chrysler/Dodge/Jeep, Office Depot, Target
8	I-105, Imperial Hwy, E Chevron Domino's, KFC, LJ Silver, McDonald's, Taco Bell CVS Drug, Food4Less, W Arco
9	Rosecrans Ave, to Norwalk, E Chevron, Mobil Little Caesar's, McDonald's, Pizza Hut, Starbucks, Subway H, Walgreens, W Motel 6 7-11
7	Alondra Blvd, E 7-11, Chevron Frantone's Rest., In-N-Out, KFC, RC Burgers CVS Drug, Home Depot, Staples, W Shell Del Taco
6	CA 91
5	South St, E Baja Fresh, BJ's Rest., Blaze Pizza, Buffalo Wild Wings, CA Pizza Kitchen, Carl's Jr, Cheesecake Factory, Chick-fil-A, Coco's, Coldstone, DQ, Five Guys, Four Seasons Buffet, Gen Korean BBQ, Jamba Juice, Lazy Dog Cafe, Lucille's BBQ, Olive Garden, Panda Express, Panera Bread, Panera Bread, Peking Wok, Starbucks Aldi Foods, AT&T, Dick's, Firestone/auto, Macy's, Nordstrom's, Target, Verizon, W Shell/service, Valero Acura, Buick/GMC, Chevrolet, Chrysler/Dodge/Jeep, Ford, Honda, Hyundai, Infiniti, Kia, Land Rover, Lexus, Mazda, Nissan, Toyota, VW
4	Del Amo Blvd, to Cerritos, E Del Taco, Loft Hawaiian, Omega Burgers, Starbucks
3	Carson St, E Little Caesar's, McDonald's, Popeye's, Starbucks, Subway, Wienerschnitzel Lakewood Inn 7-11, CVS Drug, Food4Less, O'Reilly Parts, W Chevron/Subway/dsl, Sam's Club Gas Carl's Jr, Chick-fil-A, Del Taco, Denny's, El Pollo Loco, El Torito, In-N-Out, Island's Burgers, Jack-in-the-Box, Lucille's BBQ, Panda Express, Roadhouse Grill, Starbucks, SuperMex, TGIFriday's America's Tire, Barnes&Noble, Lowe's, Michael's, Old Navy, Petsmart, Ross, Sam's Club, Verizon, Walmart/auto
1	Katella Ave, Willow St, E Shell Madera's Steaks, McDonald's, Polly's Cafe, Starbucks H, CVS Drug, W Eldorado Regional Park
0mm	**I-605 begins/ends on I-405.**

INTERSTATE 680 (Bay Area)

Exit #	Services
71b a	I-80 E, to Sacramento, W to Oakland, **I-680 begins/ends on I-80.**
70	Green Valley Rd (from eb), Cordelia, W Kia, N Arco Costco/gas, CVS, Safeway
68	Gold Hill Rd, W Chevron/dsl
65	Marshview Rd
63	Parish Rd
61	Lake Herman Rd, E Texaco/Jack-in-the-Box/dsl, W Chevron/Carl's Jr/dsl/24hr, Gas City/dsl vista point
60	Bayshore Rd, industrial park
58	I-780, to Benicia, **toll plaza**
56	Marina Vista, to Martinez
55mm	Martinez-Benicia Toll Br
54	Pacheco Blvd, Arthur Rd, Concord, W Chevron/dsl, Shell/dsl
53	CA 4 E to Pittsburg, W to Richmond, Pittsburg
52	CA 4 E, Concord, Pacheco, E Blaze Pizza, Buffalo Wild Wings, Habit Burger, Hometown Buffet, Jimmy John's, Noodles&Co, Starbucks, Subway, Taco Bell Clarion, Crowne Plaza Ford/Lincoln, Home Depot, Hyundai, Infiniti/VW, Kia,

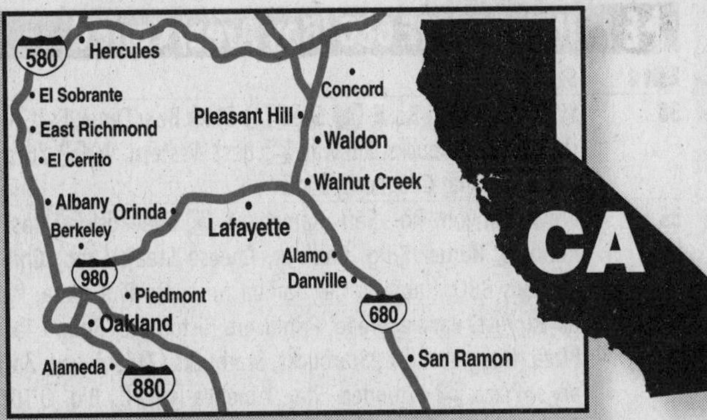

CONCORD

WALNUT CRK

52	Continued Petco, Sam's Club, Seafood City Mkt, Toyota, Trader Joe's, USPO, W Grand Gas, Shell/24hr, Valero/dsl A&W/KFC, Burger King, Denny's, In-N-Out, Lucille's BBQ, McDonald's, Round Table Pizza, Taco Bell, Wendy's AutoZone, Firestone/auto, Harley Davidson, Nordstrom's, O'Reilly Parts, Pepboys, Ross, Safeway/dsl, Schwab Tire, Target
51	Willow Pass Rd, Taylor Blvd, E Benihana Rest., Claim Jumper, Denny's, Elephant Bar Rest., Fuddruckers, Jamba Juice, Krispy Kreme, Lazy Dog Rest., Lin's Buffet, Panera Bread Hilton Hobby Lobby, Old Navy, REI, Willows Shopping Ctr, World Mkt, W Baja Fresh, Red Robin, Tahoe Joe's Steaks JC Penney, Macy's, See's Candies, URGENT CARE
50	CA 242 (from nb), to Concord
49b	Monument Blvd, Gregory Lane (from sb), E 76/dsl Country Waffles, Hawaiian BBQ, Panda Express, Pieology, Rubio's, Starbucks, Wing Stop $Tree, AT&T, Dick's, Kohl's, Marshall's, W Chevron/dsl Boston Mkt, Chipotle, Corner Bakery Cafe, Five Guys, Jack-in-the-Box, Jack's Rest., Jamba Juice, McDonald's, Mtn Mike's Pizza, Nations Burgers, Original Pancakes, Pizza Hut, Starbucks, Subway, Sweet Tomatoes, Taco Bell Courtyard, Hyatt Big O Tire, Grocery Outlet, Michael's, Rite Aid, Ross, Safeway Foods, Staples, Tuesday Morning
49a	Contra Costa Blvd (from nb)
48	Treat Blvd, Geary Rd, E Chevron Back 40 BBQ, Heavenly Cafe, Starbucks, Subway Embassy Suites, Extended Stay America 7-11, Best Buy, Office Depot, W Chevron, Shell Black Angus, Chick-fil-A, Freebirds Burrito, Habit Burger, IHOP, Jimmy John's, Starbucks, Wendy's, Yan's China Bistro Volvo, Walgreens
47	N Main St, to Walnut Creek, E Chevron Fuddrucker's, Jack-in-the-Box, Taco Bell Marriott, Motel 6 Cadillac, Chrysler/Dodge/Jeep, Honda, Jaguar, Land Rover, Mercedes, Nissan, Target, VW, W 76/7-11/dsl/24hr Domino's Holiday Inn Express NAPA, Porsche, Subaru
46b	Ygnacio Valley Rd
46a	SR-24 W
45b	Olympic Blvd, Oakland
45a	S Main St, Walnut Creek, E H
44	Rudgear (from nb)
43	Livorna Rd
42b a	Stone Valley Rd, Alamo, W Chevron/dsl, Shell/dsl Alamo Grill, Don Jose's, Panera Bread, Papa Murphy's, Round Table Pizza, Starbucks, Subway, Taco Bell, Xenia's CVS, Rite Aid, Safeway, USPO, vet
41	El Pintado Rd, Danville
40	El Cerro Blvd
39	Diablo Rd, Danville, E Chevron China Gourmet, Taco Bell Mt Diablo SP (12mi), W Valero

INTERSTATE 680 (Bay Area) Cont'd

SAN RAMON

Exit #	Services
38	Sycamore Valley Rd, E Shell Black Bear Diner, Esin, Maria Maria, Starbucks, Subway Best Western, W 76/dsl, Valero/dsl CVS, Lucky Foods
36	Crow Canyon Rd, San Ramon, E Shell/dsl Baskin Robbins, Burger King, Carl's Jr, Cheese Steak Shop, Chili's, Dickey's BBQ, Habit Burger, Jamba Juice, On Fire Pizza, Panda Express, Panera Bread, Primavera Ristorante, Round Table Pizza, Ruggie's Rest., Starbucks, Starbucks (2), Subway, Zachary's Pizza Extended Stay America H, Big O Tire, Costco, GNC, Marshall's, Office Depot, PetCo, Rite Aid, Sea's Candies, Sprouts, W 76, Chevron/dsl, Shell/autocare, Valero Chipotle Mexican, Giuseppe's Italian, In-N-Out, McDonald's, Nation's Burger's, Subway, Taco Bell, Togo's Hyatt House Hotel 7-11, CVS Drug, Home Depot, Safeway, Staples, Verizon, vet
34	Bollinger Canyon Rd, E Valero Baja Fresh, Buffalo Wild Wings, Izzy's Steaks, Jimmy John's, Pasta Pomodoro Marriott, Residence Inn AT&T, CVS Drug, Target, Whole Foods Mkt, W Chevron/dsl Chevy's Mexican, Clementine's Grill Courtyard, Extended Stay America
31	Alcosta Blvd, to Dublin, E 76/dsl 7-11, W Chevron, Shell/dsl DQ, McDonalds, Papa Murphy's, Peking Delight, Subway, Taco Bell Lucky Foods, Walgreens
30	I-580, W to Oakland, E to Tracy
29	Stoneridge, Dublin, E DoubleTree, W Baja Fresh, Cheesecake Factory, PF Chang's, Taco Bell Sheraton JC Penney, Macy's, Nordstrom, Sears
26	Bernal Ave, Pleasanton, E Chevron/Jack-in-the-Box/dsl Dickey's BBQ, Habit Burger, Jamba Juice, Jersey Mike's, Lindo's Mexican, Panda Express, Round Table Pizza, Starbucks, Subway CVS, Safeway/dsl
25	Sunol Blvd, Pleasanton
21b a	CA 84, Calvaras Rd, Sunol, W to Dumbarton Bridge
20	Andrade Rd, Sheridan Rd (from sb), E Sunol Super Stp/dsl
19mm	**weigh sta nb**
19	Sheridan Rd (from nb)
18	Vargas Rd
16	CA 238, Mission Blvd, to Hayward, E Shell McDonald's, W H
15	Washington Blvd, Irvington Dist, E QuikStop
14	Durham Rd, to Auto Mall Pkwy, W 76/Subway/24hr, Jack-in-the-Box Fry's Electronics, Home Depot, Walmart
12	CA 262, Mission Blvd, to I-880, Warm Springs Dist, W 76, Valero Burger King, Carl's Jr, Denny's, Jack-in-the-Box, KFC, RoundTable Pizza, Subway, Taco Bell Extended Stay America, Motel 6 CVS, Ross, Safeway
10	Scott Creek Rd
9	Jacklin Rd, E Bonfare Mkt, W Shell/dsl
8	CA 237, Calaveras Blvd, Milpitas, E 76, Shell/repair King Wah, Round Table Pizza, Shabu House, Starbucks, Subway Executive Inn 7-11, Oceans SuperMkt, W Shell El Torito, Giorgio's Italian, IHOP, Jamba Juice, McDonald's, Mtn Mike's Pizza, Panda Express, Red Lobster, Starbucks, Subway Embassy Suites, Extended Stay America CVS, Safeway, Staples
6	Landess Ave, Montague Expswy, E 76, Arco, Chevron Burger King, Jack-in-the-Box, McDonald's, Starbucks, Subway, Taco Bell, Togo's Firestone/auto, Lucky Foods, Rite Aid, Target, vet, Walgreens

FREMONT

SAN JOSE

Exit #	Services
5	Capitol Ave, Hostetter Ave, E Shell Carl's Jr, Popeye's Lucky Foods, W 7-11
4	Berryessa Rd, E Arco/24hr, Shell/dsl Denny's, L Sandwiches, McDonald's, Round Table Pizza, Starbucks, T Bell $Tree, AutoZone, CVS, Safeway
2b	McKee Rd, E 76, Chevron, Shell/dsl Burger King, Chipotle, HomeTown Buffet, Jamba Juice, Panda Express, Popeye's, Starbucks, Togo's, Wienerschnitzel, Wingstop $Tree, GNC, Grocery Outlet, Marshall's, Mi Pueblo Mkt, Ross, Targ Walgreens, W World Gas Baskin-Robbins, Lee's Sandwiches, McDonald's, RoundTable Pizza, Subway, Wendy's, Yum Donuts H, Kohl's
2a	Alum Rock Ave, E Shell/dsl/24hr Jack-in-the-Box, Taco Bell, W Chevron, Valero Carl's Jr AutoZone
1d	Capitol Expswy
1c	King Rd, Jackson Ave (from nb), E L&D Gas, Shell El Pollo Loco, Jack-in-the-Box, Kings Burger, Starbucks, Subway Tropicana Buffet AT&T, Target, Verizon, Walgreens
1b	US 101, to LA, SF
1a	(exits left from sb) **I-680 begins/ends on I-280.**

INTERSTATE 710 (Los Angeles)

LA AREA

Exit #	Services
23	**I-710 begins/ends on Valley Blvd.** E Arco
22b a	I-10
20c	Chavez Ave
20b	CA 60, Pamona Fwy, E King Taco, Monterey Hill Re W Shell AutoZone
20a	3rd St
19	Whittier Blvd, Olympic Blvd, W McDonald's
17b	Washington Blvd, Commerce, W Commerce Trkstp/dsl/res
17a	Bandini Blvd, Atlantic Blvd, industrial
15	Florence Ave, E Alfredo's Mexican, Applebee's, Coldstone, Dunkin', El Pollo Loco, IHOP, Jack-in-the-Box, KFC, Little Caesar's, McDonald's, Panda Express, Starbucks, Subway, Taco Bell Quality Inn $Tree, casino, Food4Less, Marshall Rite Aid, Ross, W Chevron
13	CA 42, Firestone Blvd, E Arco Burger King, Denny Golden Bowl, Hooters, McDonald's, Panda Express, Starbuc Subway Guesthouse Inn El Super Foods, Ford, GN Sam's Club, Target
12b a	Imperial Hwy, E GM/dsl Carl's Jr., El Pollo Loco, Subway, W 76, Arco, Chevron/dsl Church's, KFC, McDonald's, Panda Express, Starbucks, Subway, Taco Bell, Wienerschnitzel, Winchell's AutoZone, El Super Mkt, Manny Repair, Walgreens
11b a	I-105
10	Rosecrans Ave
9b a	Alondra Ave, E Chevron/dsl Jack-in-the-Box Home Depot
8b a	CA 91
7b a	Long Beach Blvd, E 76/dsl, Chevron, Mobil, Sinclair Cortez Mexican, McDonald's, Sizzler CVS Drug, W Arco/24hr Jack-in-the-Box, Subway Luxury Inn
6	Del Amo Blvd
4	I-405, San Diego Freeway
3b a	Willow St, E Arco, Chevron/dsl Baskin-Robbins, Domino's, Pizza Hut, Wienerschnitzel Albertson's, Walgreen W 76, Arco KFC, Popeye's AutoZone
2	CA 1, Pacific Coast Hwy, E 76/dsl, Arco/mart, Chevron, Mobil Hong Kong Express, KFC, McDonald's Best Western, LaMirageInn, TravelEagleInn RanchMkt, W 76/service

INTERSTATE 710 (Los Angeles) Cont'd

2	Continued PCH Trkstp/dsl, Shell/Carl's Jr/dsl [food] Alberto's Mexican, Golden Star Rest., Jack-in-the-Box, McDonald's, Taco Bell, Tom's Burgers, Winchell's [lodging] Hiland Motel, SeaBreeze Motel
1d	Anaheim St, W [other] auto repair
1c	Ahjoreline Dr, Piers B, C, D, E, Pico Ave
1b	Pico Ave, Piers F-J, Queen Mary
1a	Harbor Scenic Dr, Piers S, T, Terminal Island, E [lodging] Hilton

I-710 begins/ends in Long Beach.

INTERSTATE 780 (Vallejo)

Exit #	Services
7	**I-780 begins/ends on I-680.**
6	E 5th St, Benicia, N [gas] Fast&Easy, S [gas] 7-11, 76/dsl [food] China Garden [lodging] Holiday Inn Express [other] Big O Tire, repair
5	E 2nd St, Central Benicia, N [gas] Valero/dsl [lodging] Best Western, S [food] Kimono Steaks, McDonald's, Nations Burger, Subway
4	Southampton Rd, Benicia, N [food] Burger King, Ensenada Mexican, Huckleberry's, Jamba Juice, Panda Express, RoundTable Pizza, Starbucks, Subway [other] $Tree, Ace Hardware, AT&T, Raley's Foods
3b	Military West
3a	Columbus Pkwy, N [gas] Chevron/dsl [food] Burger King, McDonald's, Mtn Mike's Pizza, Napoli Pizza, Papa Murphy's, Starbucks, Subway [other] CVS, Jiffy Lube, S to Benicia RA
1d	Glen Cove Pkwy, N [other] Hwy Patrol, S [food] Domino's, J's Garden, Subway [other] GNC, Safeway
1c	Cedar St
1b a	**I-780 begins/ends on I-80.**

INTERSTATE 805 (San Diego)

Exit #	Services
28mm	I-5 (from nb), **I-805 begins/ends on I-5.**
27.5	CA 56 E (from nb)
27	Sorrento Valley Rd, Mira Mesa Blvd
26	Vista Sorrento Pkwy, E [gas] Mobil/dsl [food] Chili's, Flame Broiler, Jamba Juice, McDonald's, Quizno's, Rubio's, Starbucks, Subway [lodging] Country Inn, Courtyard, Extended Stay America, Holiday Inn Express, Hyatt House [other] Staples
25b a	La Jolla Village Dr, Miramar Rd, **1 mi E** [gas] 76/dsl [other] Discount Tire, Firestone, W [food] Corner Cafe, Cozymel's Cantina, Donovan's Grill, Harry's Grill, PF Chang's, Seasons Fresh Grill [lodging] Embassy Suites, Marriott [other] [H], Macy's, Nordstom's, Sears
24	Governor Dr
23	CA 52
22	Clairemont Mesa Blvd, E [gas] 7-11/dsl, Chevron/dsl, Mega/Subway/dsl, Shell [food] Arby's, Burger King, Carl's Jr, Chipotle Mexican, Coco's, Godfather Rest., Jersey Mike's, McDonald's, Rubio's Grill, Souplantation, Starbucks, Subway, Tommy's Burgers [other] Food4Less, Ford/Kia, Nissan, Ranch Mkt, Verizon, Walmart, W [gas] Gas [food] Buga Korean BBQ, Subway [lodging] Best Western, CA Suites, Motel 6
21	CA 274, Balboa Ave, E [gas] 7-11, 76, Arco/dsl, Chevron/dsl [food] Applebee's, Islands Burger, Jack-in-the-Box [other] CarMax, Chevrolet, Chrysler/Dodge/Jeep, Jaguar, VW
20	CA 163 N, to Escondido
20a	Mesa College Dr, Kearney Villa Rd, W [other] [H]
18	Murray Ridge Rd, to Phyllis Place
17b	I-8, E to El Centro, W to beaches

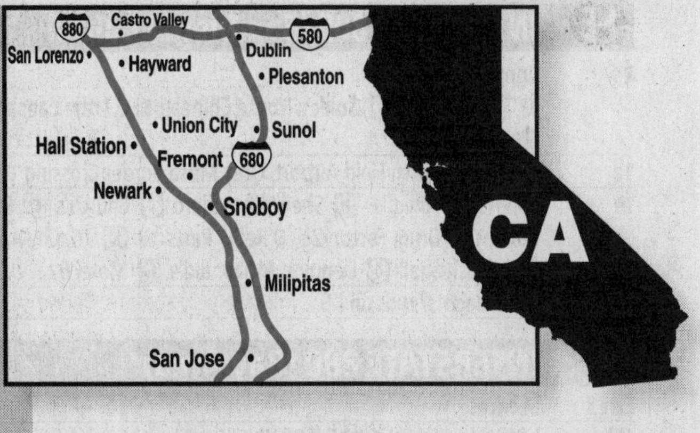

SAN DIEGO AREA

16	El Cajon Blvd, E [gas] Arco, Ultra [other] Pancho Villa Mkt, W [gas] [food] Carl's Jr, Jack-in-the-Box, Rudford's Rest., Subway, Wendy's [other] O'Reilly Parts
15	University Ave, E [gas] Chevron [food] Subway, W [gas] 76/dsl, USA/dsl [food] Starbucks [other] CVS Drug, Fresh&Easy Mkt, Walgreens
14	CA 15 N, 40th St, to I-15
13b	Home Ave, MLK Ave
13a	CA 94
12b	Market St
12a	Imperial Ave, E [gas] Homeland Gas/dsl, United, W [food] Asia Wok, Cojita's Taco, Domino's, KFC/LJ Silver, Sizzler, Subway [other] 99c Store, Home Depot
11b	47th St
11a	43rd St, W [food] Giant Pizza, Jack-in-the-Box, Subway [other] AutoZone, CVS Drug, Northgate Mkt
10	Plaza Blvd, National City, E [food] Chow King, McDonald's, Pizza Hut, Popeye's, Starbucks, Subway, Winchell's [other] [H], AutoZone, Firestone/auto, Vallarta Foods, vet, Walgreens, Well's Drug, W [gas] USA [food] Bistro City Chinese, Carl's Jr, Family House Rest., IHOP, Jubilee Chicken/burgers, Little Caesar's, Papa John's, Subway, Wings n Things [lodging] Holiday Inn Express, Motel 6, Stardust Inn [other] AT&T, Big Lots, CVS Drug, Discount Tire, Firestone/auto, Jo-Ann Fabrics, O'Reilly Parts, Walmart
9	Sweetwater Rd, E [food] Applebee's, Outback Steaks [lodging] Sweetwater Inn [other] 7-11, JC Penney, Macy's, W [gas] Chevron/7-11/dsl [food] Ben's Rest., Carl's Jr, Denny's, Hanaoka Japanese, Mike's NY Pizza, Pizza Hut, Pizza Hut, Starbucks, Subway, Taco Bell [other] CVS Drug, Food4Less, Goodyear/auto, Staples
8	CA 54
7c	E St, Bonita Rd, **E on Bonita Plaza Rd** [food] Applebee's, El Torito, Outback Steaks, Red Robin, Starbucks, Subway [other] JC Penney, Macy's, Target, W [gas] Chevron/dsl, Circle K, Shell/dsl [food] Burger King, Denny's, La Tequila Mexican [lodging] Comfort Inn, La Quinta
7b a	H St, E [gas] Shell [food] China China, Coldstone, Daphne's CA Greek, D'Lish Pizza, Honeybaked, Jack-in-the-Box, Robeks Juice, Subway, Taco Bell [other] CVS Drug, Marshall's, Vons Foods, W [food] Caffe Tazza
6	L St, Telegraph Canyon Rd, E [gas] Arco/dsl [food] Little Caesar's, Mandarin Canyon, McDonald's, Starbucks, Subway [other] [H], Olympic Training Ctr, Rite Aid, vet, Von's Foods, W [gas] 76/Circle K/dsl, USA [food] Canada Steakburger [other] 7-11
4	Orange Ave, E [lodging] Olympic Training Ctr
3	Main St, Otay Valley Rd, E [gas] Shell/dsl [food] Panda Express, Souplantation [other] Ford/Kia, Honda, Kohl's, Nissan, PetsMart, Staples, Toyota, W [gas] Circle K/dsl [lodging] Best Western
2	Palm Ave, E [gas] Arco, Chevron [food] Carl's Jr, Hometown Buffet, Starbucks, Subway, Taco Bell [other] AT&T, Home Depot, Meineke, Tire Pros, USPO, Von's Foods, Walmart/McDonald's,

CA

INTERSTATE 805 (San Diego) Cont'd

2	Continued W Chevron Golden House Chinese, KFC, Little Caesar's, McDonald's
1b	CA 905, E Brown Field Airport, Otay Mesa Border Crossing
1a	San Ysidro Blvd, E Shell/dsl, Valero Church's 99c Store, CVS Drug, Factory2U, O'Reilly Parts, W 76, Chevron, Mobil/dsl, Shell Denny's, McDonald's Motel 6
0	I-805 begins/ends on I-5.

INTERSTATE 880 (Bay Area)

OAKLAND AREA

Exit #	Services
46b a	I-80 W (exits left). I-80 E/580 W.
44	7th St, Grand Ave, downtown
42b a	Broadway St, E KFC, McDonald's Marriott, W Jack London Inn to Jack London Square
41a	Oak St, Lakeside Dr, downtown
40	5th Ave, Embarcadero, E Burger King, W Starbucks, Subway Best Western, Executive Inn, Homewood Suites, Motel 6
39b a	29th Ave, 23rd Ave, to Fruitvale, E Shell Boston Mkt, DonutStar, Popeye's, Starbucks AT&T, AutoZone, Food-Maxx, W 7-11
38	High St, to Alameda, E Mash/dsl Bay Breeze Inn, Coliseum Motel, W Shell/dsl McDonald's Home Depot
37	66th Ave, Zhone Way, E coliseum
36	Hegenberger Rd, E Arco/24hr, Shell/dsl Burger King, Chubby Freeze, Denny's, Jack-in-the-Box/24hr, McDonald's, Taco Bell Comfort Inn, Day's Hotel, La Quinta, Motel 6, Quality Inn Freightliner, GMC/Volvo, W 76/dsl, Chevron/Del Taco/dsl, Shell Black Bear Diner, Chipotle, Francesco's Rest., In-N-Out, Jamba Juice, Panda Express, Red Brick Pizza, Starbucks, Subway, Subway, Wing Stop Best Western, Courtyard, Econolodge, Hilton, Holiday Inn, Holiday Inn Express, Red Lion Harley-Davidson, Infiniti, Lexus, to Oakland Airport, Toyota
35	98th Ave, W
34	Davis St, W Shell/Burger King Hawaiian BBQ, Togo's $Tree, Costco/gas, Home Depot, Office Depot, See's Candy, Verizon, Walmart/McDonald's
33b a	Marina Blvd, E Chevron/dsl, Valero Jack-in-the-Box, La Salsa Mexican, Panda Express, Pieology, Starbucks, Taco Bell Chevrolet, Ford/Lincoln, Honda, Hyundai, Kia, Marshall's, Nissan, Nordstrom's, Volvo, W Flyers/dsl A&W/KFC, Denny's
32	Washington Ave (from nb), Lewelling Blvd (from sb), W 76/dsl, Arco, Chevron Jack-in-the-Box, McDonald's, Mtn Mike's Pizza, Papa Murphy's, Subway Nimitz Motel 99c Store, Big O Tire, CVS, Food Maxx, GNC, Jo-Ann, Safeway, same as 30, Walgreens/24hr
31	I-238 (from sb), to I-580, Castro Valley
30	Hesperian Blvd, E National In-N-Out, Starbucks, Taco Bell O'Reilly Parts, Walmart/Subway, Wheel Works, W 76, Arco, Chevron Black Angus, Peking Garden, Round Table Pizza Hilton Garden, Nimitz Inn 99c Store, CVS, Food Maxx, Lucky Foods, same as 32, USPO
29	A St, San Lorenzo, E 880/dsl/e85 McDonald's Best Western Costco, tires/repair, W 76/7-11/dsl, Valero/dsl Burger King, Chef Ming, Five Guys, Hawaiian BBQ, Jamba Juice, Pizza Hut, Rigatoni's Italian, Starbucks, Subway Days Inn, La Quinta, Rodeway Inn $Tree, Home Depot, Mi Pueblo Foods, Target

FREMONT

28	Winton Ave, W Chevron Applebee's, Buffalo W Wings, Coldstone, Elephant Grill, Famous Dave's BBQ, waiian BBQ, Hometown Buffet, Olive Garden, Panda Expr Panera Bread, Sizzler, Subway Dick's, Firestone/a Goodyear/auto, JC Penney, Macy's, O'Reilly Parts, Ross, Veri
27	CA 92, Jackson St, E 76/dsl, Valero Asian Wok, Haw ian BBQ, Mtn Mike's Pizza, Nations Burgers, Papa John's, P eye's, Round Table Pizza, Starbucks, Subway, Taco Bell 7- CVS, Grocery Outlet, Lucky Foods, Safeway, Walgreens, W Mateo Br
26	Tennyson Rd, E 76, All Star dsl, Shell Jack-in-the-B KFC O'Reilly Parts, Walgreens, W
25	Industrial Pkwy (from sb), E Golden Gate/dsl, Industri dsl Fuzhou Kitchen, Starbucks, Straw Hat Pizza, Subw W Pheonix Lodge
24	Whipple Rd, Dyer St, E 76/dsl, Chevron/dsl/24hr Co try Waffles, Denny's, Hawaiian BBQ, McDonald's, Par Express, Starbucks, Subway, Taco Bell, Wing Stop B Value Inn, Motel 6 FoodMaxx, Home Depot, PepBo Target, W Shell Andersen Baker a Cafe, Applebe Baskin-Robbins, Buckhorn Grill, Buffalo Wild Wings, Chev Mexican, Chili's, Chipotle, Coldstone, Fuddrucker's, IHOP, In-Out, Jamba Juice, Jollibee, Krispy Kreme, La Salsa Mexican, M Mike's Pizza, Pasta Pormadora, Starbucks, Texas Roadhou TGIFriday, Togo's, Tomatina Italian Extended Stay Ame ca, Hampton Inn, Holiday Inn Express AT&T, Best Buy, GM Lowe's Whse, Lucky Foods, Michael's, PetCo, Tuesday Morni Verizon, Walmart
23	Alvarado-Niles Rd, E Shell Crowne Plaza 7- W Shell Burger King Walmart, (same as 24)
22	Alvarado Blvd, Fremont Blvd, E Fortune Kitchen, Su way Motel 6 Lucky Foods
21	CA 84 W, Decoto Rd to Dumbarton Br, E 7-11 McDo ald's Walgreens
19	CA 84 E, Thornton Ave, Newark, E U-Haul, W Chevro dsl, Shell Carl's Jr, KFC, Mtn Mike's Pizza, My Cafe, Rou Table Pizza, Subway, Taco Bell 7-11, BigLots, Home Depo
17	Mowry Ave, Fremont, E 76/Circle K, Chevron/dsl, QuikSto Valero Applebee's, Chick-fil-A, Denny's, Olive Garden, Pa Murphy's, Starbucks, Subway Best Western, Extended St America, Residence Inn H, Lucky Foods, W A by's, BJ's Rest., Bombay Garden, Jack-in-the-Box, Little Ca sar's, McDonald's, Papa John's, Ray's Chinese, Ray's Crabshac Red Robin, Subway, Taco Bell Chase Suites, Comfort Inn, 8 Motel, Homewood Suites, Towneplace Suites Chrysle Dodge/Jeep, Firestone/auto, Ford, JC Penney, Jiffy Lube, Lic Mkt, Macy's, Mazda, Target, VW
16	Stevenson Blvd, E Arco/dsl, Shell Jack-in-the-Box, Ou back Steaks $Tree, W Chevron Carl's Jr, Chuck Cheese, Isla Filipino, Nijo Castle Japanese, Starbucks, Subwa World Gourmet Buffet Doubletree Fiat, Ford, Walmar
15	Auto Mall Pkwy, E Arco, Chevron/dsl, W She dsl Applebee's, Asian Pearl, Bennigan's, Blaze Pizza, Bu falo Wild Wings, Chick-fil-A, Chipotle, ClaimJumper, Coldston Dickey's BBQ, Dog Haus, Firehouse Subs, Five Guys, Habit Bur er, Hawaiian BBQ, In-N-Out, Jamba Juice, Krispy Kreme, MilkCo Cafe, Mkt Broiler, Panchero's, Panda Express, Panera Bread, P Chang's, Rubio's, Starbucks, Subway, Wendy's, Which Wich Wing Stop Holiday Inn Express Acura, AT&T, BMV Buick/GMC/Cadillac, Chevrolet, Costco/gas, Dick's, Honda, Jo Ann Fabrics, Kia, Kohl's, Lexus, Lowe's Whse, Mercedes, Nissa Nordstrom's, Old Navy, Target, TJ Maxx, Toyota, Verizon, Volvo

INTERSTATE 880 (Bay Area) Cont'd

Exit #	Services
14mm	**weigh sta both lanes**
13	Fremont Blvd, Irving Dist, W Chevron/Subway McDonald's Extended Stay America, GoodNite Inn, La Quinta, Marriott
13a	Gateway Blvd (from nb), E Comfort Inn
12	Mission Blvd, E Burger King, Carl's Jr, Denny's, Jack-in-the-Box, KFC, Subway, Taco Bell Comfort Inn CVS, Safeway, to I-680, W Courtyard, Hampton Inn, Hyatt Place
10	Dixon Landing Rd, E McDonald's Residence Inn 7-11
8b	CA 237, Alviso Rd, Calaveras Rd, to McCarthy Rd, Milpitas, E 76/7-11/dsl, Arco Black Bear Diner, Burger King, Chili's, Denny's, King Egg Roll, Lee's Sandwiches, Milpitas Buffet Best Western, Chili Palace, Days Inn, Heritage Inn 7-11, BigLots, Grocery Outlet, O'Reilly Parts, Walgreens, W Applebee's, Black Angus, Happi House, In-N-Out, Macaroni Grill, McDonald's, On the Border, Starbucks, Subway, Taco Bell, Togo's Crowne Plaza, Extended Stay America, Hampton Inn, Hilton Garden, Larkspur Landing Hotel, Staybridge Suites $Tree, AT&T, Best Buy, Chevron, GNC, Michael's, Petsmart, RanchMkt Foods, Ross, Verizon, Walmart/McDonald's/auto
8a	Great Mall Parkway, Tasman Dr, E Honda, Toyota
7	Montague Expswy, E Shell/dsl, Valero Carl's Jr, Jack-in-the-Box Quality Inn U-Haul, W Chevron/dsl Beverly Heritage Hotel, Sheraton
5	Brokaw Rd, W America's Tire, CHP, Ford Trucks, Fry's Electronics
4d	Gish Rd (nb only), W auto/dsl repair/transmissions
4c b	US 101, N to San Francisco, S to LA
4a	1st St, E Chevron/dsl, Shell/repair Subway, W Cathay Chinese, Denny's/24hr, Genji Japanese Caravelle

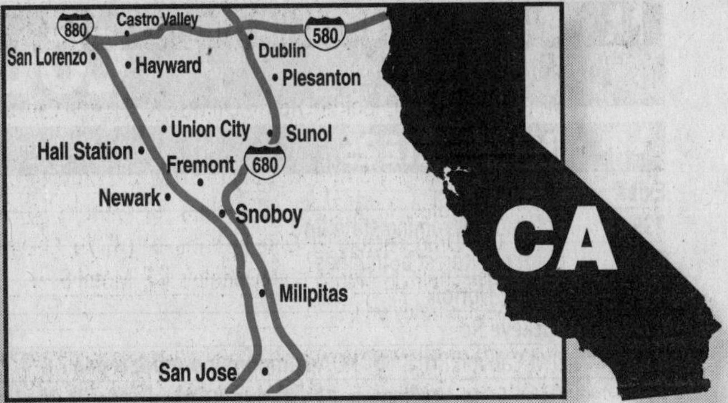

Exit #	Services
4a	Continued Inn, Comfort Suites, Country Inn Suites, Days Inn, Extended Stay America, EZ 8 Motel, Holiday Inn, Residence Inn, Springhill Suites, Vagabond Inn, Wyndham Garden 7-11
3	Coleman St, E Valero/dsl, W Chevron/dsl Chipotle, In-N-Out, Mod Pizza, Smoking PIG BBQ, Starbucks, Which Wich? , Staples
2	CA 82, The Alameda, W Shell/repair Bill's Cafe, Round Table Pizza, Starbucks, Subway, Taco Bell Best Western, Santa Clara Inn, St. Francis Hotel, Sterling Motel, Valley Inn Safeway, Santa Clara U
1d	Bascom Ave, to Santa Clara, W Rotten Robbie/dsl, Valero Burger King
1c	Stevens Creek Blvd, San Carlos St, E Valero/dsl, Valley/dsl The Row Hotel H, W Arby's, CheeseCake Factory, Jack-in-the-Box, Yard House 7-11, Audi/VW, Best Buy, Chevrolet, CVS, Ford, Goodyear/auto, Kia, Lexus, Macy's, Nordstrom's, Old Navy, Safeway, Subaru
1b	**I-280. I-880 begins/ends on I-280.**
1a	Ca 17 to Santa Cruz.

NOTES

 = gas = food = lodging = other = rest stop

COLORADO

CO

INTERSTATE 25

FT COLLINS

Exit #	Services
299	Colorado/Wyoming state line
296	point of interest both lanes
293	to Carr, Norfolk
288	Buckeye Rd
281	Owl Canyon Rd, E KOA Campground, truck repair
278	CO 1 S, to Wellington, W Kum&Go/dsl, Loaf'N Jug/dsl, Shell/dsl Burger King, Domino's, McDonald's, Subway, Taco Bell, Taco John's Days Inn Family$, Ridley's Mkt, USPO, vet
271	Mountain Vista Dr, W Budweiser Brewery
269b a	CO 14, to US 87, Ft Collins, E Maverick/dsl McDonald's Best Value Inn, W Shell/dsl Denny's, Hacienda Real, Waffle House 9 Motel, Comfort Inn, Days Inn, EconoLodge, La Quinta, Motel 6, Red Lion Inn, Rodeway Inn, Super 8 to CO St U, vet
268	Prospect Rd, to Ft Collins, W H, **Welcome Ctr/ both lanes, full facilities, litter barrels, , petwalk**
267mm	**weigh sta both lanes**
266mm	E st patrol
265	Harmony Rd, Timnath, E Murphy USA/dsl Chick-fil-A, Freddy's, Starbucks, Taco Bell, Wendy's Costco/dsl, Schwab Tires, Walmart/Subway, **2-3 mi** W Sinclair/dsl Austin's Grill, BJ's Rest., Carrabba's, Chipotle, Famous Dave's, Firehouse Subs, Five Guys, HuHot, IHOP, Jersey Mike's, Macaroni Grill, McAlister's Deli, Old Chicago, Outback Steaks, Panera Bread, Papa John's, Potbelly, Qdoba, Red Robin, Rustic Oven, SmashBurger, Sprouts Mkt, Starbucks, Subway, Texas Roadhouse, Tom+Chee, Village Inn, Wahoo's, Which Wich? Cambria Suites, Comfort Suites, Courtyard, Fairfield Inn, Hampton Inn, Hilton Garden, Holiday Inn Express, Home 2 Suites, Homewood Suites, Residence Inn H, AT&T, Kohl's, Lowe's, Office Depot, Safeway/gas, Sam's Club, Staples, Target, Verizon, Walgreens, World Mkt
262	CO 392 E, to Windsor, E 7-11/dsl, Shell/Subway/dsl Arby's, Pueblo Viejo, Taco John's AmericInn vet, W Powder River RV Ctr
259	Crossroads Blvd, E 7-11/dsl, Kum&Go/dsl, Shell/dsl Boot Grill, Carl's Jr, Nordy's, Palomino Mexican, Perkins, Qdoba Mexican, Subway My Place, Candlewood Suites, Embassy Suites, Holiday Inn Express, Microtel, Woodspring Suites, W Hooters BMW, Buick/GMC, CarMax, Chevrolet, Harley-Davidson, Hyundai, Mercedes, Mini, Subaru, to
257b a	US 34, to Loveland, E 7-11/dsl, Shell/dsl Bent Fork Grill, Biaggi Italian, BoneFish Grill, Culver's, East Coast Pizza, On-the-Border, PF Chang's, Qdoba, Red Robin, Rock Bottom Rest., Starbucks AT&T, Barnes&Noble, Best Buy, Dick's, GNC, Macy's, See's Candies, Verizon, W Conoco/dsl Buffalo Wild Wings, Carino's Italian, Chick-fil-A, Chili's, Chipotle Mexican, Cracker Barrel, IHOP, Jimmy John's, KFC/Taco Bell, LoneStar Steaks, McDonald's, Mimi's Cafe, Noodles&Co, Old Chicago, Panera Bread, Starbucks, Subway, Wendy's Best Western+, Fairfield Inn, Hampton Inn, Residence Inn H, Jo-Ann Fabrics, Loveland Outlets/famous brands, Loveland RV Resort, Marshall's, museum, Old Navy, Petsmart, Ross, Sportsman's Whse, Staples, Target, to Rocky Mtn NP
255	CO 402 W, to Loveland

LOVELAND

LONGMONT

Exit #	Services
254	to CO 60 W, to Campion, E Johnson's Corner/Sinclair/ca dsl/scales/motel/24hr Budget Host Lazydays RV C retreat
252	CO 60 E, to Johnstown, Milliken, W Loaf'n Jug/Subway/
250	CO 56 W, to Berthoud, W Love's/Subway/Taco Joh dsl/scales/24hr to Carter Lake
245	to Mead
243	CO 66, to Longmont, Platteville, E Conoco/dsl, Kum&C dsl, Shell/7-11 Rancheros Rest., Red Rooster Re Camping World/K&C RV Ctr, tires, vet, W to Estes Pa to Rocky Mtn NP
241mm	St Vrain River
240	CO 119, to Longmont, E Murphy Express/dsl, Shell/7-1 dsl Burger King, Carl's Jr, Del Taco, Good Times Grill, K Pizza Hut, Popeye's, Qdoba, Starbucks, Wendy's Best We ern, Comfort Suites, Woodspring Suites Century RV C Home Depot, Kia, Lexus, Toyota, Transwest RV Ctr, Veriz W 7-11/Subway/dsl, Phillips 66/dsl/scales/24hr, Shell/Ci K/dsl Arby's, McDonald's, Taco Bell, Waffle House Inn, Best Value Inn, Quality Inn, Super 8, Travelodge mu um, to Barbour Ponds SP, truckwash, Valley Camper RV Ctr
235	CO 52, Dacono, E Kum&Go/dsl Burger King Fo Infiniti, W Conoco/dsl/LP McDonald's, Pepper Ja Grille, Starbucks, Subway Harley-Davidson, to Eldora Area
232	to Erie, Dacono
229	CO 7, to Lafayette, Brighton, E Buffalo Wild Wings, Chi fil-A, Chili's, Famous Dave's BBQ, Goodtimes Burgers, Gunth Toody's, La Fogata, Starbucks, Subway, Village Inn AT Costco/gas, Dick's, Home Depot, Petsmart, Sears Grand, W Murphy Express/dsl Sonic, Wendy's King's Sooper/dsl
228	E-470 **(tollway)**, to Limon
226	144th Ave, E Murphy Express/dsl Arby's, Cuba Cub Firehouse Subs, Five Guys, Freddy's, Freddy's, Panda Express, Po belly, Wendy's Candlewood Suites, Hilton Garden Cab la's, Hobby Lobby, Steinmart, W HuHot Mongolian, Mim Cafe, Mooyah Burgers, Panera Bread, Red Robin, Rusty Buck Starbucks, Which Wich? H, $Tree, AT&T, JC Penney, Macy Marshall's, Old Navy, REI, Ross, Staples, Target, Verizon
225	136th Ave, E Kum&Go/dsl Denver Outlets/famo brands, W Valero/dsl Big Burrito, Carl's Jr, KFC/ Silver, Starbucks, Subway Advance Parts, Firestone/aut Lowe's, URGENT CARE, Walmart/McDonald's
223	CO 128, 120th Ave, to Broomfield, E Conoco, Valero/d Applebee's, Bad Daddy's Burger Bar, Burger King, Café Ri Chick-fil-A, Chipotle Mexican, Coldstone, Fazoli's, First Wat Cafe, Jimmy John's, Jim'N Nick's BBQ, Krispy Kreme, LoneSt Steaks, Longhorn Steaks, McDonald's, Olive Garden, Outba Steaks, Panda Express, Panera Bread, Smashburger, Soni Starbucks, Subway, Taziki's Cafe, Tequila's Mexican, TGIF day's DoubleTree, EconoLodge, Hampton Inn, Holiday In Express, Ramada Inn $Tree, Albertson's, AT&T, Barnes&N ble, Big O Tire, Brakes+, CarQuest, Discount Tire, GNC, Meinek Michael's, O'Reilly Parts, PetCo, Sprouts Mkt, Target, Tires- Verizon, vet, Walgreens, W Conoco/dsl, Shell/Circle K/Po eye's/dsl, Valero/dsl CB Potts Rest., Chili's, Cracker Barre DQ, Hooters, Laguna's Mexican, Perkins, Qdoba, Starbucks, Su way, Village Inn Rest., Wendy's Comfort Suites, Cottonwoo Suites, Extended Stay America, Fairfield Inn, La Quinta, Super 8

BROOMFIELD

INTERSTATE 25 Cont'd

Exit #	Services
221	104th Ave, to Northglenn, E Conoco, Shell Buffalo Wild Wings, Burger King, CiCi's Pizza, Denny's, DQ, Firehouse Subs, Old Chicago, Qdoba, Subway, Texas Roadhouse GNC, Home Depot, King's Soopers, Tires+, Walgreens, W 7-11, Shell/Circle K/dsl Applebee's, Atlanta Bread, Blackeyed Pea, Cinzzetti's Italian, GoodTimes Burger, Gunther Toody's, McDonald's, Seoul BBQ, Starbucks, Taco Bell, The Armadillo Best Buy, Fiat, Firestone/auto, Ford, Goodyear/auto, Hyundai, Jo-Ann Fabrics, Lowe's, Marshalls, Office Depot, Petsmart, Ross, Sheplar's
220	Thornton Pkwy, E Golden Corral, Rico Pollo AT&T, Hobby Lobby, Sam's Club/gas, Thornton Civic Ctr, Walmart/McDonald's, W Shell, Valero/dsl, Western/dsl Subway
219	84th Ave, to Federal Way, E Shell/dsl, Valero/dsl Arby's, McDonald's, Quiznos, Sonic, Starbucks, Subway, Taco Bell, Taco Star, Waffle House O'Reilly Parts, W Econogas, Valero/dsl Burger King, DQ, El Fogon, McDonald's, Popeye's, Santiago's Mexican, Village Inn Rest. Motel 6 AutoZone, CarQuest, Discount Tire, Meineke, Save-A-Lot, vet
217	US 36 W (exits left from nb), to Boulder, W Ammco Subway Chevrolet, Toyota
216b a	I-76 E, to I-270 E
215	58th Ave, E Burger King, McDonald's, Steak Escape, Subway, Wendy's Comfort Inn URGENT CARE, W Conoco/dsl, Shamrock/dsl Super 8 O'Reilly Parts
214c	48th Ave, E coliseum, W Village Inn Rest. Clarion, Quality Inn
214b a	I-70, E to Limon, W to Grand Junction
213	Park Ave, W 38th Ave, 23rd St, downtown, E Conoco Domino's, McDonald's, Starbucks La Quinta, W Town&Country Motel
212c	20th St, downtown, Denver
212b a	Speer Blvd, E museum, downtown, W Conoco/dsl, Shell/dsl Starbucks, Subway Hampton Inn, Ramada, Residence Inn, Super 8 AutoZone, Walgreens
211	23rd Ave, E funpark
210c	CO 33 (from nb)
210b	US 40 W, Colfax Ave, W Denny's, KFC Ramada Inn/rest. Mile High Stadium
210a	US 40 E, Colfax Ave, E civic center, U-Haul, downtown
209c	8th Ave
209b	6th Ave W, US 6, W Shell/dsl
209a	6th Ave E, downtown, Denver
208	CO 26, Alameda Ave (from sb), E Shamrock/dsl Burger King, Denny's Home Depot, same as 207b, W Conoco/dsl
207b	US 85 S, Santa Fe Dr, same as 208
207a	Broadway, Lincoln St, E Griff's Burgers USPO
206b	Washington St, Emerson St, E Whole Foods Mkt, W
206a	Downing St (from nb)
205b a	University Blvd, W to U of Denver

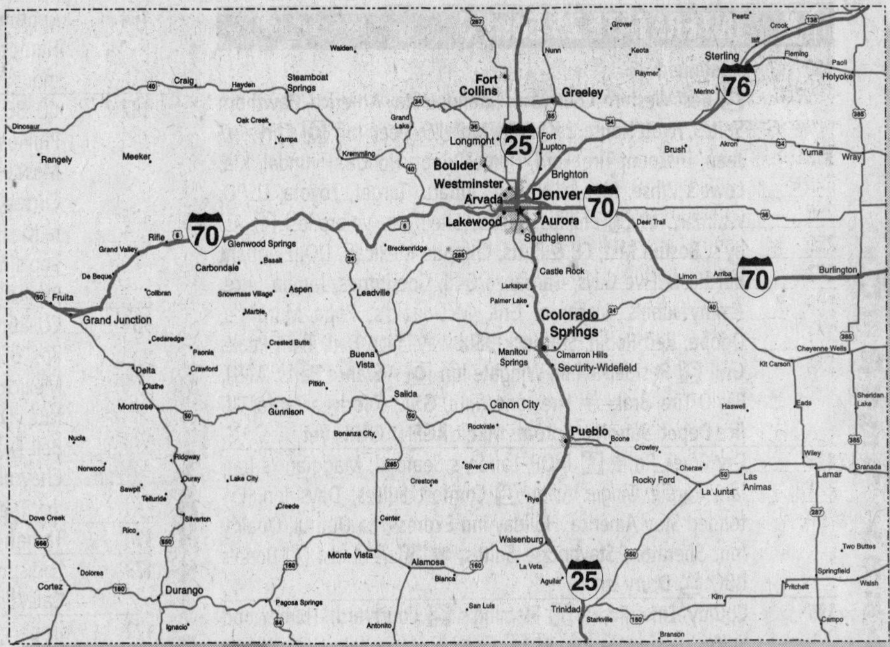

Exit #	Services
204	CO 2, Colorado Blvd, E Conoco/dsl, Loaf'n Jug, Shamrock, Shell/Circle K Arby's, Black Eyed Pea, Chili's, Domino's, GoodTimes Grill, Hacienda Colorado, IHOP, Jimmy John's, McDonald's, Noodles&Co, Old Chicago Pizza, Pizza Hut, Qdoba, Smashburger, Starbucks, Subway, Taco Bell, Tokyo Joe's, Village Inn Rest., Wahoo's, Whole Foods Mkt Belcaro Motel, Courtyard, Fairfield Inn, Hampton Inn Barnes&Noble, Best Buy, Chevrolet, Home Depot, Mercedes/BMW, Petco, Ross, Safeway Foods, Staples, vet, VW, Walgreens, W Conoco A&W/KFC, Dave&Buster's, McDonald's, Pei Wei, Perkins, Which Wich La Quinta Natural Grocers, Office Depot, USPO
203	Evans Ave, E Rockies Inn, W Cameron Motel Ford
202	Yale Ave, W BeauJo's CO Pizza, Chipotle Mexican GNC, King's Sooper, Michaels, Petsmart
201	US 285, CO 30, Hampden Ave, to Englewood, Aurora, E Conoco/Circle K/LP, Shamrock, Shell Chick-fil-A, Chipotle Mexican, Coldstone, Domino's, Firehouse Subs, Jimmy John's, McDonald's, Noodles&Co, NY Deli, Panera Bread, Qdoba, Smashburger, Starbucks, Subway, Wahoos Fish Taco, Zanitas Mexican Embassy Suites Discount Tire, King's Sooper/dsl, Omaha Steaks, Petco, Target, URGENT CARE, Verizon, vet, Walgreens, Whole Food Mkt, W Conoco/7-11 Burger King, Starbucks Safeway
200	I-225 N, to I-70
199	CO 88, Belleview Ave, to Littleton, E Baker St Grill, Chipotle Mexican, Cool River Cafe, Fiocchi's Pizzeria, Fornaio Rest., Garcia's Mexican, Great Northern Rest., Noodles&Co, Pancake House, Panera Bread, Qdoba, Starbucks, Wendy's, Which Wich? Hampton Inn, Hilton Garden, Hyatt Place, Marriott, W Conoco, Shamrock McDonald's, Pappadeaux Café, Pizza Hut/Taco Bell Extended Stay Am, Extended Stay America Lexus
198	Orchard Rd, E Del Frisco's Steaks Shepler's, W Shell/Circle K/dsl Subway DoubleTree vet
197	Arapahoe Blvd, E Conoco/dsl, Shell/Circle K/dsl A&W/KFC, Bros BBQ, Burger King, Chick-fil-A, Del Taco, Dickie's BBQ, Domino's, El Parral, El Tapatio Mexican, Gunther Toody's Rest., Hoong's Palace, McDonald's, Outback Steaks, Pat's Cheesesteak, Pizza Hut, Qdoba, Schlotsky's, Smashburger, Sonic, Starbucks, Subway, Volcano Chinese, Wendy's

CO

= gas = food = lodging = other = rest stop

CO

DENVER AREA

INTERSTATE 25 Cont'd

197 Continued
Best Western, Courtyard, Extended Stay America, Hawthorn Suites, Hyatt House, LaQuinta, Motel 6, Sleep Inn Chrysler/Jeep, Discount Tire, Ford, Home Depot, Honda, Hyundai, Kia, Lowe's Whse, Mazda, Nissan, Subaru, Target, Toyota, USPO, Walmart, **W** Phillips 66/dsl, Shell/dsl, Valero/dsl Arby's, Boston Mkt, CB & Potts, Chipotle Mexican, DQ, Elephant Bar Rest., Five Guys, Garbanzo Grill, Goodtimes, Jamba Juice, Jimmy John's, Macaroni Grill, McDonald's, Papa Murphy's, Qdoba, Red Robin, Starbucks, Subway, Taco Bell, Twin Peaks Grill Residence Inn, Wingate Inn Advance Parts, AT&T, Big O Tire, Brakes+, Firestone/auto, GNC, Goodyear/auto, Office Depot, Safeway, Sprouts Mkt, URGENT CARE, vet

196 Dry Creek Rd, **E** IHOP, Landry's Seafood, Maggiano's Italian, Purple Ginger Asian Comfort Suites, Days Inn, Extended Stay America, Holiday Inn Express, La Quinta, Quality Inn, Sheraton, Staybridge Suites, **W** 7-11/dsl Bono's BBQ Drury Inn

195 County Line Rd, **E** Fleming's Courtyard, Homewood Suites, Residence Inn, **W** Conoco Buffalo Wild Wings, Burger King, CA Pizza Kitchen, Chick-fil-A, Chipotle Mexican, Earl's Kitchen, Firehouse Subs, Genghis Grill, J Alexander's, Jason's Deli, Panda Express, PF Changs, Red Lobster, Red Robin, Rock Bottom Brewery/Cafe, Smashburger, Starbucks, TGIFriday's, Thai Basil, Tokyo Joe's Hyatt Place AT&T, Barnes&Noble, Best Buy, Costco/gas, Dick's, Dillard's, Home Depot, JC Penney, Jo-Ann Fabrics, Macy's, Marshall's, Michaels, Nordstrom, Old Navy, PetsMart, REI, Ross, Verizon

194 CO 470 W, CO 470 E (tollway)

193 Lincoln Ave, to Parker, **E** 7-11/dsl, Conoco, Valero/dsl Carl's Jr, Hacienda Colorado, Starbucks, Subway Candlewood Suites, Hilton Garden, **W** Conoco/dsl Chili's, Chipotle Mexican, Firehouse Subs, Five Guys, Garbanzo Grill, Heidi's, KFC, McDonald's, Noodles&Co, Papa John's, Papa Murphy's, Pizza Hut/Taco Bell, Qdoba, Starbucks, Subway Hampton Inn, Marriott H, Discount Tire, GNC, Safeway, Sprouts Mkt, Target

192 Ridgegate Pkwy, **W** TownePlace Suites H, Cabela's

191 no services

190 Surrey Ridge, Surrey Ridge

188 Castle Pines Pkwy, **W** Conoco/dsl, Shell/Circle K/Taco Bell/dsl La Dolce Vita, Las Fajitas Mexican, Papa John's, Papa Murphy's, Starbucks, Subway, Wendy's Big O Tires, Discount Tire, King's Sooper/dsl, Safeway, URGENT CARE, vet, Wlagreens

CASTLE ROCK

187 Happy Canyon Rd, **W** **services 2 mi**

185 Castle Rock Pkwy, **W** Phillips 66/7-11 Del Taco Petco, Sam's Club/dsl, TJ Maxx, Verizon

184 Founders Pkwy, Meadows Pkwy, to Castle Rock, **E** Conoco/dsl, Shell/Circle K/dsl A&W/KFC, Applebee's, Baskin-Robbins, Canes, Chick-fil-A, Chipotle Mexican, Coldstone, Five Guys, Goodtimes Grill, Jimmy John's, Little Caesar's, Noodles&Co, Outback Steaks, Panera Bread, Parry's Pizza, Qdoba, Red Robin, Sonic, Starbucks, Subway, Taco Bell, Wendy's $Tree, Advance Parts, AT&T, Brakes+, Discount Tire, Firestone/auto, GNC, Goodyear/auto, Grease Monkey, Home Depot, Just Brakes, King's Sooper, Kohl's, Michael's, Natural Grocers, Office Depot, O'Reilly Parts, Petsmart, Sprouts Mkt, Target, Verizon, vet, Walgreens, Walmart, **W** Loaf'n Jug/dsl Arby's, Blackeyed Pea, Cafe Rio, Chili's, Food Court, Freddy's Steakburger, IHOP, McDonald's, MOD Pizza, Popeye's, Potbelly, Rockyard Grill, Smashburger Best Western+, Comfort Suites, Days Inn,

184 Continued
Hampton Inn, Holiday Inn Express Castle Rock Outlet/famous brands, King's Sooper/dsl, Lowe's, Midas, st patrol

182 CO 86, Castle Rock, Franktown, **E** 7-11/dsl, Conoco/d Phillips 66/dsl Augustine Grill, B&B Cafe, Castle Cafe, Meson Mexican Castle Pines Motel vet, **W** She Circle K/dsl, Valero/dsl Burger King, Domino's, Guadalajara Mexican, Jack-in-the-Box, McDonald's, Old West BBQ, Santiago's Mexican, Village Inn, Waffle House, Wendy's Cas Inn, LaQuinta, Super 8 NAPA

181 CO 86, Wilcox St, Plum Creek Pkwy, Castle Rock, **E** Phillips 66, Valero/dsl, Western/dsl Blimpie, DQ, El Mes Mexican, Jimmy John's, Papa John's, Papa Murphy's, Piz Hut, Quiznos, Starbucks, Stumpy's Pizzaria, Subway, Ta Bell Castle Rock Motel AutoZone, Big O Tire, Buic Chevrolet/GMC, Chrysler/Dodge/Jeep, Ford, Midas, Safewa dsl, Tuesday Morning, URGENT CARE, USPO, Walgreens

LARKSPUR

174 Tomah Rd, **W** Yogi Bear's Campground

173 Larkspur (from sb, no return), **3 mi** **W** Conoco/Larksp Cafe/dsl/

172 Upper Lake Gulch Rd, Larkspur, **2 mi** **W** Conoc dsl/ Larkspur Pizza Cafe, Spur Grill USPO

167 Greenland

163 County Line Rd

162.5mm elev 7352, Monument Hill

162mm **weigh sta both lanes**

161 CO 105, Woodmoor Dr, **E** Kum&Go/dsl, Sinclair/dsl Margaritas Mexican, Jimmy John's, Papa John's Ram da/Sundance Mtn Lodge/rest. CO Hts RV Park (2mi), v **W** 7-11, Phillips 66/dsl Arby's, Domino's, La Ca Fiesta New Mexican, McDonald's, Rosie's Diner, Starbuc Subway, Taco Bell, Village Inn Big O Tire, Natural Groce Safeway/dsl, USPO, Walgreens

158 Baptist Rd, **E** Murphy USA/dsl, Shell/Circle K/Popeye' dsl/24hr Borriello Bros. Pizza, Carlos Miguel's, Chili Coldstone, Freddy's Steakburgers, McDonald's, Mexican Gr Papa Murphy's, Qdoba, Subway, TX Roadhouse Fairfie Inn Advance Parts, AutoZone, Christian Bros. Auto, Di count Tire, GNC, Home Depot, Jiffy Lube, King's Sooper, Kohl Natural Grocers, O'Reilly Parts, Petsmart, Staples, URGEN CARE, Verizon, Walgreens, Walmart/Subway, **W** Pilot Arby's/dsl/scales/24hr, Shamrock/dsl/scales

156b N Entrance to USAF Academy, **E** Loaf'n Jug/Subwa dsl Bourbon Bros Kitchen, C B & Potts Rest., Costa Vid Jimmy John's, Kneaders Cafe, Wendy's AT&T, Bass P Shops, **W** visitors center

156a Gleneagle Dr, **E** mining museum

153 InterQuest Pkwy, **E** Kum&Go/dsl Cheddar's, CO M Brewery/rest., Dickey's BBQ, Freddy's, Jersey Mike's, Starbuck Taco Bell, Zoup! Drury Inn, Hampton Inn, Residence Inn

152 scenic overlook on sb

151 Briargate Pkwy, **E** 7-11 Biaggi's, CA Pizza Kitchen, Ga banzo Grill, Marco's Pizza, Panera Bread, PF Changs, Qdob Salsa Brava Mexican, Starbucks, Ted's MT Grill Hilton Ga den, Homewood Suites AT&T, to Black Forest

150b a CO 83, Academy Blvd, **E** Shamrock/dsl, Shell/Circle K/d A&W, Amanda's Fonda, Applebee's, Baskin-Robbins, Buff lo Wild Wings, Burger King, Chick-fil-A, Chipotle Mexican, Col stone, Cracker Barrel, Crave Burgers, Culver's, Del Taco, Denny Drifters Hamburgers, Egg&I Café, Elephant Bar Rest., Extrem Pizza, Famous Dave's, Firehouse Subs, Five Guys, HuHot Mo golian, IHOP, Jason's Deli, Jimmy John's, KFC, McDonald

INTERSTATE 25 Cont'd

150b a Continued
Mimi's Café, Noodles&Co, Olive Garden, On-the-Border, Panera Bread, Pei Wei, Qdoba, Red Robin, Salt Grass Steaks, Schlotzsky's, Sonic, Starbucks, Steak'n Shake, Subway, Tokyo Joe's Grill, Wendy's Academy Hotel, Comfort Suites, Days Inn, Drury Inn, EconoLodge, Howard Johnson, Super 8 $Tree, Advance Parts, AT&T, Barnes&Noble, Best Buy, Chevrolet, Dick's, Dillard's, Firestone/auto, Ford, Hobby Lobby, Home Depot, Hyundai, JC Penney, Kia, King's Sooper, Macy's, Marshall's, Michael's, Midas, Natural Grocers, Old Navy, O'Reilly Parts, PepBoys, Petsmart, REI, Ross, Sam's Club/gas, to Peterson AFB, URGENT CARE, Verizon, VW, Walmart/Subway, Whole Foods Mkt, **W** S Entrance to USAF Academy

149 Woodmen Rd, **E** Carl's Jr, Carraba's Nissan, **W** Shell/Circle K/dsl Hooters, Old Chicago Pizza, Outback Steaks, TGIFriday's Comfort Inn, Embassy Suites, Fairfield Inn, Hampton Inn, Holiday Inn Express, Microtel, Staybridge Suites

148 Corporate Ctr Dr, Nevada Ave, **E** BJ's Rest., Bonefish Grill, Chipotle Mexican, Hacienda Colorado, Noodles&Co, Panera Bread, Pita Pit, Smashburger, Tokyo Joe's Grill, Which Wich? The Lodges BMW, Costco/gas, Harley-Davidson, Kohl's, Lowe's, Petco, SteinMart, Trader Joe's, **W** Shell/Circle K Crestwood Suites, Extended Stay America, Hyatt House, Marriott to Rodeo Hall of Fame

146 Garden of the Gods Rd, **E** Conoco/7-11, Shell/Circle K/dsl Carl's Jr, Caspian Cafe, Drifter's Burgers, McDonald's Best Value Inn, La Quinta Aamco, **W** Conoco/7-11, Exxon/dsl, Phillips 66/Circle K, Shamrock/dsl Applebee's, Arby's, Arceo's Mexican, Blackeyed Pea, Chick-fil-A, Freddy's Steakburgers, Jimmy John's, Mollica's Italian, Sonic, Souper Salad, Subway, Taco Bell, Taco Bueno, Village Inn, Wendy's Days Inn, Hyatt Place, Quality Inn, Super 8 $Tree, AutoZone, Discount Tire, to Garden of Gods, vet

145 CO 38 E, Fillmore St, **E** Conoco/7-11, Shamrock/dsl, Western/dsl Arby's, Burger King, Carl's Jr, DQ, Lucky Dragon, McDonald's, Subway, Taco Bell Budget Host H, Advance Parts, Walgreens, **W** Kum&Go/dsl Waffle House Best Western+, Motel 6, Super 8

144 Fontanero St

143 Uintah St, **E** 7-11 Uintah Fine Arts Ctr

142 Bijou St, Bus Dist, **E** The Antlers Hotel Firestone/auto, visitor info, **W** Denny's Clarion, Holiday Inn Express, Quality Inn

141 US 24 W, Cimarron St, to Manitou Springs, **W** Shell/7-11/dsl, Sinclair/dsl Arby's, Capt D's, La Casita Mexican, McDonald's, Popeye's, Sonic, TX Roadhouse Acura, Audi, AutoZone, Brakes+, Buick/GMC, Cadillac, Chevrolet, Chrysler/Dodge/Jeep, Discount Tire, Ford, Grease Monkey, Hobby Lobby, Hyundai, Infiniti, Kia, Land Rover/Jaguar, Lexus, Lincoln, Mazda, Meineke, Mercedes, NAPA, Office Depot, Porsche, Subaru, to Pikes Peak, Toyota, Volvo, VW, Walmart/McDonald's

140b US 85 S, Tejon St, **E** Peerless Tires, **W** Conoco/dsl access to same as 141

140a Nevada Ave, **E** Kum & Go/dsl Chateau Motel, Howard Johnson repair, **W** 7-11, Shamrock Arceo's Mexican, Burger King, China Kitchen, Chipotle Mexican, IHOP, KFC, McDonald's, Noodles&Co, On the Border, Panda Express, Panera Bread, Rancho Alegre Mexican, Red Robin, Schlotzsky's, Starbucks, Subway, Taco Bell, Taco Express, Wendy's Rodeway Inn, Sunsprings Motel, Travel Star Inn $Tree, access to auto dealers at 141, Big O Tire, Family$, Michael's, Midas, Natural Grocers,

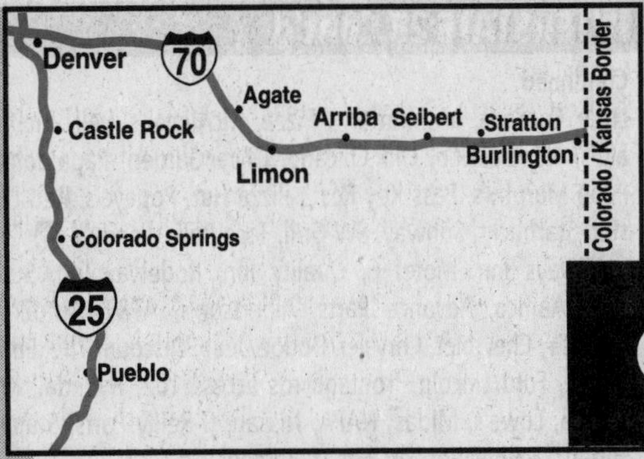

CO

140a Continued
Office Depot, O'Reilly Parts, Petsmart, Ross, Safeway Foods, Tuesday Morning, Walgreens

139 US 24 E, to Lyman, Peterson AFB

138 CO 29, Circle Dr, **E** Conoco, Shell/Circle K/dsl McDonald's Days Inn, Hotel Elegante, Super 8 , Kohl's, URGENT CARE, zoo, **W** 7-11 Arby's, Buffalo Wild Wings, Burger King, Carl's Jr, Carrabba's, Chili's, ChuckeCheese, Culver's, Denny's, Fazoli's, Flatiron Grill, Macaroni Grill, Outback Steaks, Smoothie King, Subway, Village Inn Best Western, Comfort Inn, Courtyard, DoubleTree Hotel, Fairfield Inn, Hampton Inn, La Quinta, Residence Inn AT&T, GNC, PetCo, Target

135 CO 83, Academy Blvd, **E** to , **W** Freddy's, Jersey Mike's, MOD Pizza, Qdoba, Starbucks Ft Carson, Sam's Club/dsl, to Cheyenne Mtn SP, Verizon, Walmart/Subway

132 CO 16, Wide Field Security, **E** Loves/Subway/dsl Microtel Camping World RV Ctr, KOA

128 to US 85 N, Fountain, Security, **E** 7-11, Loaf'n Jug/Subway/dsl Family$, USPO, **W** Tomahawk/Exxon/rest./dsl/24hr/@ Fountain Inn, Super 8 Freightliner

125 Ray Nixon Rd

123 no services

122 to Pikes Peak Meadows, **W** Pikes Peak Intn'l Raceway

119 Rancho Colorado Blvd, Midway

116 county line rd

115mm **nb, full facilities, litter barrels, petwalk,**

114 Young Hollow

112mm **sb, full facilities, litter barrels, petwalk,**

110 Pinon, **W** Maggie's Farm/dsl

108 Purcell Blvd, Bragdon, **E** racetrack, **W** KOA

106 Porter Draw

104 Eden, **W** Loves/Chester's/Subway/dsl/scales/24hr Peterbilt

PUEBLO

102 Eagleridge Blvd, **E** Loaf'n Jug/dsl Burger King, Subway, TX Roadhouse Candlewood Suites, Holiday Inn Express Big O Tire, Home Depot, Sam's Club/gas, **W** Conoco/dsl Buffalo Wild Wings, Cactus Flower Mexican, Chili's, Cracker Barrel, IHOP, Mexican Grill, Starbucks, Village Inn, Wonderful Bistro Best Western, Comfort Inn, EconoLodge, Hampton Inn, La Quinta, Ramada, Wingate Inn Best Buy, Cavender's Boots, Dick's, frontage rds access 101, Harley-Davidson, Kohl's, Old Navy, PetCo

101 US 50 W, Pueblo, **E** Capt D's, Coldstone, Country Buffet, Margaritas Mexican, Ruby Tuesday, Souper Salad Baymont Inn Barnes&Noble, CO Tire, Dillard's, JC Penney, Jo-Ann, Petsmart, Ross, Target, TJ Maxx, U-Haul, Verizon, Walmart/Subway, **W** Conoco/7-11, Loaf'n Jug/dsl, Shell/dsl, Valero/dsl Applebee's, Arby's, Arriba Mexican, Blackeyed Pea, Carl's Jr, China Rest., Chipotle Mexican, Country Kitchen, DJ's Steaks, Domino's, DQ, Fazoli's, Golden Corral, Jack-in-the-Box,

CO

INTERSTATE 25 Cont'd

101	Continued Little Caesar's, Manhattan's Pizza, McAlister's Deli, McDonald's, Noodles&Co, Old Chicago, Olive Garden, Papa John's, Papa Murphy's, Pass Key Rest., Pizza Hut, Popeye's, Red Lobster, Starbucks, Subway, SW Grill, Taco Bell, Wendy's Clarion, Days Inn, Motel 6, Quality Inn, Rodeway Inn, Super 8 Aamco, Advance Parts, Albertson's, AT&T, AutoZone, Brakes+, Chevrolet, Chrysler/Dodge/Jeep, Discount Tire, EmergiCare, Ford/Lincoln, frontage rds access 102, Hyundai, Kia/Mazda, Lowe's, Midas, NAPA, Nissan, O'Reilly Parts, Staples, Subaru, Toyota, Verizon, vet, Walgreens
100b	29th St, Pueblo, **E** Country Buffet, Mongolian Grill $Tree, Car Dr, Hobby Lobby, King's Sooper Foods, Natural Grocers, Peerless Tires, Tuesday Morning, **W** Conoco Sonic USA Motel Family$, Grease Monkey, Safeway
100a	US 50 E, to La Junta, **E** Loaf'n Jug/dsl, Shell Little Caesar's, McDonald's, Pizza Hut, Wendy's Advance Parts, AutoZone, Belmont Tire/repair, Family$, Save-A-Lot Foods, Walgreens
99b a	Santa Fe Ave, 13th St, downtown, **W** Subway, Taco Bell, Wendy's Bramble Tree Inn, Travelers Motel H, Buick/Cadillac/GMC, CarQuest, Honda
98b	CO 96, 1st St, Union Ave Hist Dist, Pueblo, **W** Loaf'n Jug/dsl Carl's Jr Courtyard
98a	US 50E bus, to La Junta, **W** Sonic
97b	Abriendo Ave
97a	Central Ave, **W** Alta/dsl McDonald's $General
96	Indiana Ave, **W** H
95	Illinois Ave (from sb), **W** to dogtrack
94	CO 45 N, Pueblo Blvd, **W** Loaf'n Jug/dsl, Western/dsl Subway, Taco Bell Hampton Inn, Microtel Forts RV Park, to Lake Pueblo SP
91	Stem Beach
88	Burnt Mill Rd
87	Verde Rd
83	no services
77	Hatchet Ranch Rd, Cedarwood
74	CO 165 W, Colo City, **E** Shamrock/deli/dsl/24hr Obie's BBQ KOA, **W** **both lanes full facilities, litter barrels, petwalk**, , vending, Sinclair/Subway/dsl Max's Place Days Inn/rest.
71	Graneros Rd
67	to Apache
64	Lascar Rd
60	Huerfano
59	Butte Rd
56	Redrock Rd
55	Airport Rd
52	CO 69 W, to Alamosa, Walsenburg, **W** Conoco/dsl, Loaf'n Jug/dsl (2mi), TA/Phillips 66/A&W/dsl Carl's Jr (2mi), George's Rest., KFC/Taco Bell, Subway (2mi) Best Western, Budget Host/RV Park Country Host RV Park, Dakota RV Park/camping, Family$ (2mi), San Luis Valley, to Great Sand Dunes NM
50	CO 10 E, to La Junta, **W** H
49	Lp 25, to US 160 W, Walsenburg, **1 mi W** Loaf'n Jug/dsl Carl's Jr., Subway Lathrop SP, to Cuchara Ski Valley
42	Rouse Rd, to Pryor
41	Rugby Rd
34	Aguilar
30	Aguilar Rd, **W** Green Earth RV Park

27	Ludlow, **W** Ludlow Memorial
23	Hoehne Rd
18	El Moro Rd, **W** **both lanes, full facilities, litter barre petwalk**,
15	US 350 E, Goddard Ave, **E** Burger King, Pizza Hut Sup 8 H, Art Cartopia Museum, AutoZone, Big R Ranch Sto Family$, **W** Shell/dsl Frontier Motel/café
14	Commercial St, downtown, Trinidad, same as 13b
13b	Main St, Trinidad, **E CO Welcome Ctr,** Exxon/dsl KF Taco Bell, McDonald's, Sonic Days Inn CarQuest, Safeway Foods/dsl, Trinidad Motor Inn, **W** Conoco/ Monument Lake, to Trinidad Lake
13a	Santa Fe Trail, Trinidad, **E** RV camping
11	Starkville, **E** Shell/Wendy's/dsl/24hr Tequila's Mexic Budget Host/RVPark, Holiday Inn, Rodeway Inn Su mit RV Park, to Santa Fe Trail, weigh/check sta, **W** La Qu ta, Quality Inn/rest Big O Tire, Grease Monkey, O'Rei Parts, Walmart
8	Springcreek
6	Gallinas
2	Wootten
1mm	scenic area pulloff nb
0mm	Colorado/New Mexico state line, Raton Pass, elev 7834, **wei sta sb**

INTERSTATE 70

Exit #	Services
450mm	Colorado/Kansas state line
438	US 24, Rose Ave, Burlington, **N** Hi-Lo Motel, Sloan's Mo H, $General, Bomgaars, Buick/Cadillac/Chevrolet/GM CarQuest, Family$, Ford/Lincoln, NAPA, O'Reilly Parts, Outba RV Park, Safeway Foods, **S** Sinclair/Reynaldo's Mexica dsl/24hr truck repair
437.5mm	**Welcome Ctr wb, full facilities, historical site, info, litter ba rels, petwalk**, ,
437	US 385, Burlington, **N** Conoco/dsl, Phillips 66/dsl A by's, Burger King, Dish Room, McDonald's, Pizza Hut, Subw Burlington Inn, Burlington Stay Inn, Chaparral Motel, Qu ity Inn, Western Motel H, **S** Loves/Carl's Jr/d scales/24hr/@ Best Western+, Fairfield Inn, Woodspri Suites
429	Bethune
419	CO 57, Stratton, **N** Cenex/dsl, Conoco/dsl Dairy Tre Claremont Inn/café, Rodeway Inn Marshall Ash Villa Camping, Trails End Camping
412	Vona, **1/2 mi N** gas,
405	CO 59, Seibert, **N** Shady Grove Camping/RV dum **S** Conoco/dsl tire repair
395	Flagler, **N** Loaf'N Jug/dsl I-70 Diner, Subway L tle England Motel Flagler SWA, G&B RV camping, NAP **S** Cenex/dsl golf
383	Arriba, **N** DJ/café/dsl motel, **S** **both lanes full f cilities, litter barrels, petwalk**, , **point of interest**, RV cam ing
376	Bovina
371	Genoa, **N** food, gas, , point of interest, **S** H
363	US 24, US 40, US 287, to CO 71, to Hugo, Limon, **13 mi S**
361	CO 71, Limon, **N** Ace Hardware, **S** Shell/Wendy's/d Sinclair/dsl Golden China, Pizza Hut 1st Inn Gold, Co ote Motel KOA, RV camping, st patrol
360.5mm	**weigh/check sta both lanes**

INTERSTATE 70 Cont'd

Exit #	Services
359	to US 24, to CO 71, Limon, N FLYING J/IHOP/dsl/scales/LP/24hr La Quinta dsl repair, RV camping, S Qwest/dsl, Sinclair/dsl, TA/Phillips 66/Subway/Country Pride/dsl/scales/24hr/@ Arby's, McDonald's, Oscar's Grill, Taco Bell Baymont Inn, Comfort Inn, EconoLodge, Holiday Inn Express, Microtel, Quality Inn, Super 8 Chrysler/Dodge/Jeep
354	no services
352	CO 86 W, to Kiowa
348	to Cedar Point
340	Agate, 1/4 mi S gas/dsl,
336	to Lowland
332mm	wb, full facilities, info, litter barrels, petwalk, , vending
328	to Deer Trail, N Phillips/dsl, S Shell/dsl USPO
325mm	East Bijou Creek
323.5mm	Middle Bijou Creek
322	to Peoria
316	US 36 E, Byers, N Sinclair/dsl Budget Host Thriftway Foods/Drug, S Tri Valley Country Burger Rest. USPO
310	Strasburg, N Conoco/dsl Coronas Mexican, KT's BBQ, Patio Cafe, Subway Country Gardens RV Camping (3mi), dsl/auto repair, KOA, NAPA, USPO, vet, Western Hardware
306	Kiowa, Bennett
305	Kiowa (from eb)
304	CO 79 N, Bennett, N Conoco/Hotstuff Pizza/dsl, Loves/McDonald's/dsl/scales/24hr Carl's Jr, China Kitchen, High Plains Diner, Starbucks, Subway, Taco Bell Family$, King Soopers Foods/dsl, O'Reilly Parts, USPO, S Ace Hardware
299	CO 36, Manila Rd, S Shamrock/dsl
295	Lp 70, Watkins, N Shell/Tomahawk/rest/dsl/24hr/@ Biscuit's Cafe, Lulu's Cafe Country Manor Motel USPO
292	CO 36, Airpark Rd
289	E-470 Tollway, 120th Ave, CO Springs
288	US 287, US 40, Lp 70, Colfax Ave (exits left from wb)
286	CO 32, Tower Rd, N Murphy Express/dsl Chick-fil-A, Chili's, Chipotle Mexican, Del Taco, DQ, Firehouse Subs, McAlister's Deli, Noodles&Co, Panda Express, Starbucks, Wendy's $Tree, AT&T, Best Buy, Brakes+, Discount Tire, GNC, Home Depot, Les Schwab Tire, Office Depot, O'Reilly Parts, PetCo, Verizon, Walmart/Subway
285	Airport Blvd, N Denver Int Airport, S FLYING J/Denny's/dsl/scales/24hr, Conoco/McDonald's/dsl Comfort Inn, Quality Inn Harley-Davidson
284	I-225 N (from eb)
283	Chambers Rd, N Conoco, Shell/Circle K/Popeye's A&W/KFC, Anthony's Pizza, Applebees, Chicago Grill, Jimmy John's, LJ Silver/Taco Bell, Outback Steaks, Pizza Hut, Qdoba, Sonic, Subway, Ted's MT Grill, Urban Sombrero, Wendy's, Zume Asian A Loft, Cambria Suites, Country Inn&Suites, Crowne Plaza, Econolodge, Hampton Inn, Hilton Garden, Homewood Suites, Hyatt Place, Marriott, Residence Inn, TownePlace Suites, Woolley's Suites Tires+, U-haul, S Shamrock Burger King, Jack-in-the-Box Crossland Suites, Woodspring Suites RV America, URGENT CARE
282	I-225 S, to Colorado Springs
281	Peoria St, N 7-11, Conoco/dsl, Shell/dsl Ajua Mexican, Burger King, Del Taco, Domino's, GoodTimes Burgers, McDonald's, Peoria Grill, Quizno's, Starbucks, Subway Holiday Inn Express, La Quinta, Rodeway Inn, Timbers Motel Big O Tire,

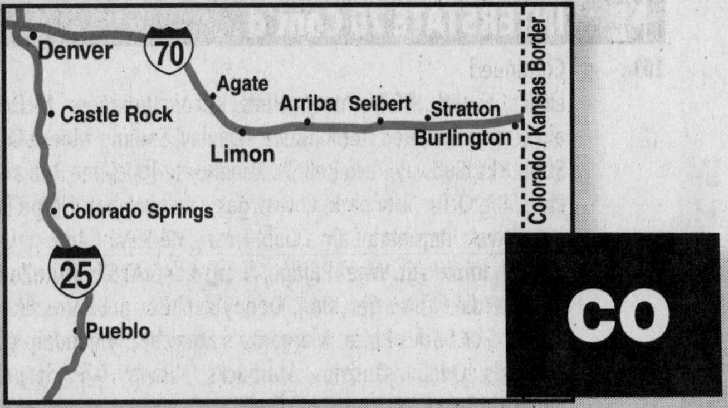

DENVER AREA

Exit #	Services
281	Continued Family$, S Phillips 66/dsl, Shamrock/dsl Bennett's BBQ, Denny's, Ho Mei Chinese, Taco Bell, Taco Mex Motel 6, Rodeway Inn, Star Hotel, Stay Inn auto/RV repair, Goodyear/auto
280	Havana St, N Embassy Suites
279b	Central Ave, N Drury Inn, Residence Inn
279	I-270 W, US 36 W (from wb), to Ft Collins, Boulder
278	CO 35, Quebec St, N Sapp Bros/Sinclair/Subway/dsl/@, TA/dsl/rest./24hr/@ Bar Louie, Coldstone, Del Taco, Islamorada Fish Co, Jim'n Nick's BBQ, La Sandia Cantina, Marco's Pizza, Olive Garden, Qdoba, Red Lobster, Red Robin, Starbucks, Subway, TGIFriday's, TX Roadhouse, Wahoo's, Which Wich? Best Inn, Comfort Inn, Staybridge Suites Bass Pro Shops, JC Penney, Macys, Old Navy, Super Target, S Walmart Gas Arby's, Buffalo Wild Wings, Country Buffet, Famous Dave's BBQ, IHOP, Jimmy John's, La Mariposa, McDonald's, Panda Express, Panera Bread, Papa John's, Smashburger, Sonic, Subway Best Western, Courtyard, DoubleTree Hilton, DoubleTree Hotel, Holiday Inn, Renaissance Inn, Super 8 AT&T, GNC, Home Depot, Office Depot, Petsmart, Ross, Sam's Club, Tires+, Walgreens, Walmart/Subway
277	to Dahlia St, Holly St, Monaco St, frontage rd
276b	US 6 E, US 85 N, CO 2, Colorado Blvd, S Conoco/Subway/dsl Carl's Jr, Domino's, KT'S BBQ, Starbucks
276a	Vasquez Ave, N Pilot/Wendy's/dsl/scales/24hr Western Inn Blue Beacon, Ford Trucks, Peterbilt, S 7-11 Burger King
275c	York St (from eb)
275b	CO 265, Brighton Blvd, Coliseum, N 7-11
275a	Washington St (from wb), N 7-11 Pizza Hut, S Conoco/dsl McDonald's
274b a	I-25, N to Cheyenne, S to Colorado Springs
273	Pecos St, N Conoco/7-11/dsl Family$, SavALot Foods, S 7-11 Quiznos Autocare
272	US 287, Federal Blvd, N Phillips 66/dsl, Sinclair Burger King, Goodtimes Burgers, Little Caesar's, McCoy's Rest., McDonald's, Pizza Hut, Rico Pollo, Subway, Taco Bell, Village Inn, Wendy's, Winchell's Motel 6 $Tree, 7-11, Advance Parts, Family$, tires, S Conoco/Mkt/dsl El Padrino Mexican, Popeye's, Starbucks Travelers Inn
271b	Lowell Blvd, Tennyson St (from wb)
271a	CO 95, S funpark
270	Sheridan Blvd, N Shell/dsl, S Murphy Express/dsl El Paraiso Mexican, Grammy's Pizza Family$, Firestone/auto, fun park, Schwab Tire, Walmart
269b	I-76 E (from eb), to Ft Morgan, Ft Collins
269a	CO 121, Wadsworth Blvd, N 7-11, Conoco, Shell/dsl Anthony's Pizza, Applebee's, BeauJo's, Bennet's BBQ, Chick-fil-A, Chipotle Mexican, Coldstone, Country Buffet, El Tapatio Mexican, F

CO

CO

INTERSTATE 70 Cont'd

WHEAT RIDGE

269a Continued
azoli's, HuHot, IHOP, Jimmy John's, Kukoro Japanese, McDonald's/playplace, Red Robin, Ruby Tuesday, Smiling Moose Deli, Starbucks, Subway, Taco Bell, TX Roadhouse $Tree, Advance Parts, Big O Tire, city park, Costco/gas, Discount Tire, Home Depot, Lowe's, Petsmart, Sam's Club, Tires+, URGENT CARE

267 CO 391, Kipling St, Wheat Ridge, N Conoco, Shell/Carl's Jr/Circle K/dsl Burger King, Denny's, Einstein Bros, Jack-in-the-Box, Lil Nick's Pizza, Margarita's Mexican, Panda Express, Popeye's, Qdoba, Quiznos, Starbucks, Subway American Inn, Motel 6 7-11, AT&T, Cadillac/Chevrolet, GNC, NAPA, Natural Grocers, repair, Target, Verizon, vet, S Conoco/Mkt/dsl, Shell Taco Bell, Three Agaves Mexican, Village Inn, Winchell's Affordable Inn, Best Value Inn, Comfort Inn, Holiday Inn Express, Super 8 Ketelesen RV Ctr

266 CO 72, W 44th Ave, Ward Rd, Wheat Ridge, N Conoco/dsl transmissions, S TA/Country Pride/dsl/scales/24hr/@, Valero/dsl Howard Johnson Trailer Source RV Ctr

265 CO 58 W (from wb), to Golden, Central City

264 Youngfield St, W 32nd Ave, N Phillips 66/mkt Denny's, GoodTimes Burgers La Quinta, S Abrusci's Italian, Chili's, Chipotle, DQ, McDonald's, Noodles&Co, Pizza Hut, Pizza Hut/Taco Bell, Qdoba, SmashBurger, Starbucks, Subway Four Seasons RV Ctr, King's Sooper/24hr, Petsmart, Tuesday Morning, Walgreens, Walmart/Subway

263 Denver West Blvd, N Marriott/rest., S Coldstone, Freddy's, Jamba Juice, Keg Steaks, Macaroni Grill, Mimi's Cafe, Noodles&Co, Olive Garden, Qdoba, Twin Peaks Barnes&Noble, Best Buy, Old Navy, same as 262, Whole Foods Mkt

LAKEWOOD

262 US 40 E, W Colfax, Lakewood, N Sinclair/dsl El Señor Sol Mexican, Jack-in-the-Box, Lil' Ricci's Cafe, Subway Hampton Inn, Holiday Inn Express Buick/GMC, Camping World RV Ctr, Chrysler/Jeep, Dodge, Home Depot, Honda, Hyundai, Kohl's, PetCo, Staples, Subaru, transmissions, U-Haul, vet, S Shell/Circle K/dsl/LP Bonefish Grill, Cafe Rio, Carrabba's, Chick-fil-A, Chipotle Mexican, Five Guys, Garbanzo Grill, Jamba Juice, Jimmy John's, Mimi's Cafe, Mod Mkt Eatery, Native Foods Cafe, On-the-Border, Outback Steaks, Panera Bread, Pei Wei Asian, Pieology, Wendy's, Which Wich?, Yard House Courtyard, Days Inn/rest., Mtn View Inn, Residence Inn Chevrolet, Lexus, Marshall's, Old Navy, same as 263, Target, Toyota, Verizon, World Mkt

261 US 6 E (from eb), W 6th Ave, to Denver

260 CO 470, to Colo Springs

259 CO 26, Golden, N Shamrock/dsl Hampton Inn (2mi), Holiday Inn Express (2mi) Heritage Sq Funpark, S Music Hall, to Red Rocks SP

257mm **runaway truck ramp eb**

256 Lookout Mtn, N to Buffalo Bill's Grave

254 Genesee, Lookout Mtn, N to Buffalo Bill's Grave, S Conoco/Genesee Store Chart House Rest., Guido's Pizza, Hideaway Cafe vet

253 Chief Hosa, S RV Camping,

252 (251 from eb), CO 74, Evergreen Pkwy, S Phillips 66 El Señor Sol, Illegal Burger, McDonald's, Qdoba, Starbucks Comfort Suites Big O Tire, Echo Mtn Ski Area, Home Depot, King Sooper (2mi), Walmart/Subway

248 (247 from eb), Beaver Brook, Floyd Hill, S antiques

244 US 6, to CO 119, to Golden, Central City, Eldora Ski Area

243 Hidden Valley, N Valero/dsl

242mm tunnel

IDAHO SPRINGS

241b a rd 314, Idaho Springs West, N Phillips 66/McDonal dsl, Shell/dsl, Sinclair, Western/dsl/e85 Carl's Jr, Che Blossom Chinese, Marion's Rest., Picci's Pizzaria, Smokin' Ya BBQ, Starbucks, Subway, Wildfire Rest. 6&40 Motel, A Inn, Columbine Inn, H&H Motel, Idaho Springs Hotel, JC M tel CarQuest, Safeway Foods/Drug, USPO

240 CO 103, Mt Evans, N Kum&Go/dsl, Shell/dsl, Sincla dsl 2 Bros Deli, Azteca Mexican, Beaujo's Pizza, Buff Rest., Jiggie's Cafe, Main St Rest., Tommy Knocker Grill, W Winds Cafe same as 241, vet, S to Mt Evans

239 Idaho Springs, S camping

238 Fall River Rd, to St Mary's Glacier

235 Dumont (from wb)

234 Downeyville, Dumont, N Sinclair/Subway/dsl Starbuc Taco Bell ski rentals, S **weigh sta both lanes**

233 Lawson (from eb)

232 US 40 W, to Empire, N Rocky Mtn NP, to Berthoud Pa Winterpark/Sol Vista ski areas

228 Georgetown, S Exxon/Subway/dsl, Shell/dsl, Valero/ Blue Sky Cafe, Mountain Buzz Cafe Best Value Inn, Ch teau Chamonix Family$, visitors ctr

226.5mm scenic overlook eb

226 Georgetown, Silver Plume Hist Dist, N repair

221 Bakerville

220mm Arapahoe NF eastern boundary

219 **parking area (eb only)**

218 no services

216 US 6 W, Loveland Valley, Loveland Basin, ski areas

214mm Eisenhower/Johnson Tunnel, elev 11013

213mm **parking area eb**

SILVERTHORNE

205 US 6 E, CO 9 N, Dillon, Silverthorne, N 7-11, Kum&Go/ Shell/7-11/dsl, Sinclair/dsl, Tesla EVC Cafe Toro, Chipo Mexican, Dominos, Mint Cafe, Mtn Lyon Café, Murphy's Cafe, C Chicago, Quiznos, Wendy's, Which Wich? 1st Interstate I Days Inn, La Quinta, Luxury Suites, Quality Inn, Silver Inn A toZone, Buick/Cadillac/Chevrolet/GMC, CarQuest, Chrysl Dodge/Jeep, Ford, Lowe's, Murdoch's, Outlets/famous bran Subaru, Target, TrueValue, S Conoco, Shell/dsl Arby Bamboo Garden, Blue Moon Deli, Burger King, Chimayo Burri Dam Brewery/Rest., DQ, Fiesta Mexican, Jimmy John's, McDo ald's, Nick'n Willy's Pizza, Noodles&Co, Nozawa Japanese, Piz Hut, Qdoba, Red Mtn Grill, Ruby Tuesday, SmashBurger, Smili Moose Cafe, Starbucks, Subway, Sunshine Cafe Comf Suites, Dillon Inn, Hampton Inn, Super 8 AT&T, City M Foods/gas, GNC, Natural Grocers, Outlets/famous brands, Pet Tuesday Morning, Verizon, vet, Walgreens

203.5mm scenic overlook both lanes

FRISCO

203 CO 9 S, to Breckenridge, Frisco, S 7-11, Conoco/Wendy dsl, Shell/dsl, Valero/dsl Hacienda Real Mexican, K Q4U BBQ, Rio Grande Mexican, Spinelli's Pizza/Subs, Spo ing News Grill, Starbucks, Subway, Szechuan Chinese, Ta Bell Alpine Inn, Baymont Inn, Holiday Inn, Ramada L Summit Inn Big O Tire, Meadow Creek Tire/auto, NAPA, Resort (6mi), Safeway Foods, to Breckenridge Ski Area, Verizo Walmart, Whole Foods Mkt

201 Main St, Frisco, S Loaf N' Jug Backcountry Brew Pu Bagali's Italian, Blue Spruce Inn, Boatyard Pizzaria, Butte horn Cafe, Frisco Emporium, Greco's Pastaria, Log Cabin Ca Lost Cajun Rest., Moosejaw Cafe, Rainbow Ct Rest. Fris Lodge, Hotel Frisco, Snowshoe Motel museum/visitor in RV camping, to Breckenridge Ski Area, USPO

198 Officers Gulch, emergency callbox

INTERSTATE 70 Cont'd

Exit #	Services
196mm	scenic area (wb only)
195	CO 91 S, to Leadville, 1 mi S Conoco/dsl Healthy Tomato Deli Copper Lodging to Copper Mtn Ski Resort
190	**S both lanes, full facilities, litter barrels,**
189mm	elev 10662 ft, **parking area both lanes,** Vail Pass Summit
180	Vail East Entrance, **S services 3-4 mi**
176	Vail, **S** H, ski info/lodging
173	Vail Ski Area, **N** Phillips 66, Shell/dsl Casa Mexico, May Palace, McDonald's, Old Forge Pizza, Qdoba, Subway, Westside Cafe Holiday Inn Ace Hardware, City Mkt Foods/deli, Safeway Food/Drug, USPO, **S** Conoco/dsl/LP Marriott/Streamside Hotel
171	US 6 W, US 24 E, to Minturn, Leadville, **N** Ski Cooper ski area, **2 mi S** Shell Magusto's Italian, Minturn Steaks Minturn Inn RV Camping, USPO
169	Eaglevale, (from wb), no return
168	William J. Post Blvd, **S** Castle Peak Grill Home Depot, Verizon, Walmart/McDonald's
167	Avon, **N** Exxon/7-11/dsl, Shell Northside Kitchen vet, **S** Boxcar Rest., Burger King, Domino's, Fiesta Jalisco Mexican, Gondola Pizza, Montana's Smokehouse, Pazzo's Pizza, Starbucks, Subway Avon Ctr Lodge, Christie Lodge, Comfort Inn, Sheraton, Westin City Mkt/drugs, GNC, ski info, to Beaver Creek/Arrowhead Ski, URGENT CARE, USPO, Walgreens
163	Edwards, **S both lanes, full facilities, litter barrel, RV dump** Conoco/dsl, Shell/Wendy's/dsl Cafe Milano, Dive Cafe, East Asian, Fiestas Cafe, Gashouse Rest., Gore Range Brewery, Henry's Chinese, Main St Grill, Marble Slab Creamery, Marko's Pizza, Old Forge Pizza, Smiling Moose, Starbucks, Subway, Zino's Italian Riverwalk Inn AT&T, to Arrowhead Ski Area, USPO, Village Mkt
162mm	scenic area eb
159mm	Eagle River
157	CO 131 N, Wolcott, **N** to Steamboat Ski Area
147	Eagle, **N** Kum&Go/dsl Burger King, Roberto's Italian, Starbucks AmericInn, Comfort Inn, Holiday Inn Express AT&T, City Mkt Foods, **S both lanes, full facilities, info,** Conoco/dsl, Shell/dsl, Sinclair/Subway/dsl Eagle Diner, Gourmet China, Grand Ave Grill, Moe's Original BBQ, Pazzo's Pizzaria, Primavera Mexican, Taco Bell, Wendy's Best Western, Eagle Lodge&Suites, Hawthorn Suites AutoZone (3mi), Costco/dsl (3mi), USPO, vet
140	Gypsum, **S** Conoco, Kum&Go/dsl, Shell/dsl Asian Fusion, Buffalo Grill, Gypsum Grill, Ridley's Mkt, Tu Casa Mexican Family$, O'Reilly Parts, River Dance Resort camping, USPO
134mm	Colorado River
133	Dotsero, **N** River Dance RV Camping (3mi)
129	Bair Ranch, **S both lanes, full facilities, litter barrels, petwalk,**
128.5mm	**parking area eb**
127mm	tunnel wb
125mm	tunnel
125	to Hanging Lake (no return eb)
123	Shoshone (no return eb)
122.5mm	exit to river (no return eb)
121	to Hanging Lake, Grizzly Creek, **S both lanes, full facilities, litter barrels,**
119	No Name, **both lanes, full facilities, rafting, RV camping**
118mm	tunnel

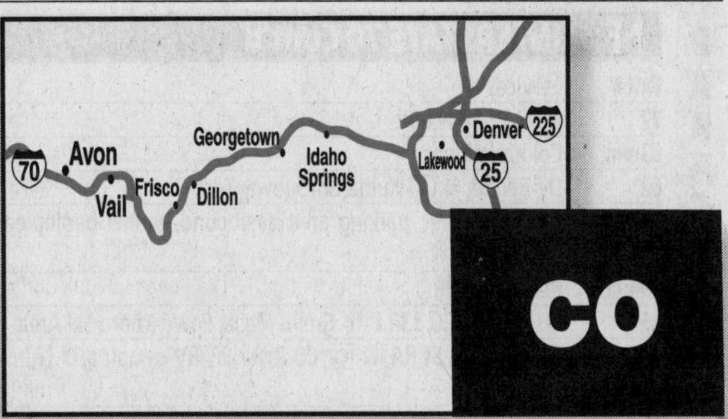

GLENWOOD SPGS

Exit #	Services
116	CO 82 E, to Aspen, Glenwood Springs, **N** Kum&Go/dsl, Shell/dsl Chomp's Rest., Fiesta Guadalajara, KFC, Qdoba, Subway, Tequilas Rest., Village Inn Best Western, Glenwood Springs Inn, Hampton Inn, Holiday Inn Express, Hotel Colorado, Hotel Glenwood Springs, La Quinta, Silver Spruce Motel, Starlight Motel Hot Springs Bath, Land Rover, **0-2 mi S** Conoco, Phillips 66/dsl, Shamrock/dsl, Shell, Sinclair 19th St Diner, Chang Thai Cuisine, China Town, Domino's, Jimmy John's, McDonald's, Pizza Hut, Starbucks, Subway, Taco Bell, Taipei Japanese, Wendy's Caravan Inn, Cedar Lodge, Frontier Lodge, Hotel Denver H, 7-11, Alpine Tire, AutoZone, B.Thornal DDS, Chrysler/Dodge/Jeep, City Mkt Foods, city park, Midas, NAPA, Office Depot, Rite Aid, Safeway Foods, to Ski Sunlight, USPO, Walmart
114	W Glenwood Springs, **N** 7-11, Exxon/Arby's/dsl, Shell/dsl Culver's, Jilberito's Mexican, Rte 6 Grill House, Vicco's Charcoal Burger Affordable Inn, Hanging Lake Inn, Ponderosa Motel, Red Mtn Inn, Rodeway Inn Big O Tire, Carquest, Chevrolet, Discount Tire, Ford, Honda, O'Reilly Parts, Ross, Subaru, Toyota, Verizon, **S** Kum&Go/DQ/dsl Chili's, Moe's SW Grill, Russo's Pizza, Starbucks, Zheng Asian Courtyard, Glenwood Suites, Quality Inn, Residence Inn AT&T, Audi/VW, Harley-Davidson, Lowe's, Natural Grocers, PetCo, Target, URGENT CARE, Verizon
111	South Canyon
109	Canyon Creek
108mm	**parking area both lanes**
105	New Castle, **N** Conoco/dsl, Kum&Go/dsl Hong's Garden, McDonald's, New Castle Diner, Subway Econolodge City Mkt Foods/deli, Elk Creek Campground (4mi), **S** Best Hardware
97	Silt, **N** Kum&Go/dsl, Sinclair/dsl, Tim's/dsl Brickhouse Italian Red River Inn $General, to Harvey Gap SP, **S** Holiday Inn Express Heron's Nest RV Park, KOA
94	Garfield County Airport Rd
90	CO 13 N, Rifle, **N both lanes, full facilities, litter barrels, NF Info, RV dump,** Conoco/dsl, Kum&Go/dsl, Phillips 66/dsl, Shell Dickey's BBQ Gateway Lodge Rifle Gap SP (10mi), USPO, **S** Kum&Go/dsl, Phillips 66/Subway/dsl Burger King, Domino's, Little Caesar's, McDonald's/playplace, Rib City Grill, Sonic, Starbucks, Subway, Taco Bell Comfort Inn, Hampton Inn, La Quinta, Rodeway Inn H, AutoZone, O'Reilly Parts, Verizon, Walmart/Subway
87	to CO 13, West Rifle
81	Rulison
75	Parachute, **N both lanes, full facilities, info, litter barrels, petwalk,** CNG, Shell/Wienerschnizel/dsl, Sinclair/dsl El Tapatio Mexican, Hong's Garden Chinese, Outlaws Rest., Subway Comfort Inn, Parachute Inn NAPA, USPO, vet, **S** Phillips 66/Domino's/dsl, Shell/Wendy's/dsl Candlewood Suites, Days Inn Family$, RV Park (4mi)

RIFLE

= gas = food = lodging = other = rest stop

CO

PARACHUTE

INTERSTATE 70 Cont'd

Exit #	Services
72	US 6, W Parachute
63mm	Colorado River
62	De Beque, N Kum&Go/Subway/dsl
50mm	Colorado River, parking area eastbound, tunnel begins eastbound
49mm	Plateau Creek
49	CO 65 S, to CO 330 E, to Grand Mesa, Powderhorn Ski Area
47	Island Acres St RA, N CO River SP, RV camping, S Exxon/rest./dsl
46	Cameo
44	Lp 70 W, to Palisade, **3 mi S** food, gas, lodging
43.5mm	Colorado River
42	US 6, Palisade, S Golden Gate/dsl Wine Country Inn Fruitstand/store, wineries
37	to US 6, to US 50 S, Clifton, Grand Jct, **0-1 mi S** Conoco/dsl, Maverik/dsl, Shamrock/dsl, Shell/dsl, Sinclair/dsl Burger King, Chin Chin Oriental, China Jade, Denny's, Dos Hombres, Enzo's Pizza, Jimmy John's, KFC, Little Caesar's, McDonald's/playplace, Papa John's, Papa Murphy's, Pizza Hut, Qdoba, Sonic, Starbucks, Starvin Arvin's Steaks, Subway, Taco Bell, Taco John's, Wendy's Best Western Ace Hardware, AutoZone, City Mkt Food/dsl, Family$, GNC, Murdoch's Store, O'Reilly Parts, repair, RV Ranch, URGENT CARE, USPO, vet, Walgreens, Walmart/gas (2mi)

GRAND JCT

Exit #	Services
31	Horizon Dr, Grand Jct, N Shell/dsl Pantuso Mexican, Peppers Rest., Tepanyaki Rest., Village Inn, Wendy's Best Value Inn, Clarion, Comfort Inn, Courtyard, Econolodge, Grand Vista Hotel, Holiday Inn, La Quinta, Motel 6, Ramada Inn, Residence Inn Harley-Davidson, Zarlingo's Repair, S Exxon/Subway/dsl, Shell/dsl Applebee's, Aztecas, Burger King/playland, Denny's, Enzo's Pizza, Freddy's, Good Pastures Rest., Nick'n Willy's Pizza, Sang Garden, Starbucks, Taco Bell Days Inn, Doubletree Hotel, Mesa Inn, Quality Inn, Rodeway Inn, Super 8, Super 8, Travelodge H, CO NM, golf, Safeway Food/drug/gas, Shop'n Save, to Mesa St Coll, visitors ctr
28	Redlands Pkwy, 24 Rd, N Kenworth, **0-2 mi S** Candlewood Suites, Woodspring Suites city park, same as 26, Subaru, VW
26	US 6, US 50, Grand Jct, N Loves/Carl's Jr/dsl/scales/Lp/24hr, Pilot/PJ Fresh/dsl/scales/24hr Hyundai, Jct W RV Park, **0-4 mi S** TA/Conoco/A&W/dsl Boston's Grill, Buffalo Wild Wings, Burger King, Cafe Rio, Chick-fil-A, Chili's, Chipotle Mexican, ChuckeCheese, Citrolas Italian, Coldstone, Costa Vida, Del Taco, Famous Dave's BBQ, Genghis Grill, Golden Corral, Grand Buffet, Honeybaked Ham, IHOP, Jimmy John's, McDonald's/playplace, Mi Mexico, Noodles&Co, Olive Garden, Outback Steaks, Papa Murphys, Qdoba, Red Lobster, Red Robin, Schlotzky's, Sonic, Starbucks, Subway, Taco Bell, Tequila's, Wendy's, Which Wich? Holiday Inn Express, Red Roof Inn $Tree, AT&T, AutoZone, Barnes&Noble, Best Buy, Big O Tire, Buick/Chevrolet, Cabela's, Chrysler/Dodge/Jeep, City Mkt/dsl, Ford, Freightliner, Hobby Lobby, Home Depot, JC Penney, Kohl's, Lowe's, Michael's, Mobile City RV Park, Natural Grocers, Nissan, Office Depot, Old Navy, PetCo, Petsmart, Ross, Sam's Club/dsl, Scott RV Ctr, Sprouts Mkt, Target, TJ Maxx, Toyota, Verizon, Walmart/McDonald's

FRUITA

Exit #	Services
19	US 6, CO 340, Fruita, N Conoco/dsl Burger King, Munchie's Burgers/Pizza Balanced Rock Motel H, City Mkt Foods/deli/24hr, city park, NAPA, USPO, Walgreens, **S Welcome Ctr, full facilities, litter barrels, petwalk,**
19	Continued RV dump Exxon/Quiznos/dsl/24hr, LNG, Shell/Wend dsl/24hr DQ, Dragon Treasure Chinese, El Tapatio Mexic FeedLot Rest., Jimmy John's, McDonald's/playplace, Pab Pizza, Rib City Grill, Starbucks, Subway, Taco Bell Com Inn, La Quinta, Super 8 dinosaur museum, Monument Park, Peterbilt/Volvo, to CO NM, vet
17mm	Colorado River
15	CO 139 N, to Loma, Rangely, N gas/dsl, to Highline Lake SP
14.5mm	**weigh/check sta both lanes**
11	Mack, **2-3 mi N** food, gas/dsl
2	Rabbit Valley, N to Trail Through Time
0mm	Colorado/Utah state line

INTERSTATE 76

Exit #	Services
185mm	**I-76 begins/ends on NE I-80, exit 102.**
184mm	Colorado/Nebraska state line
180	US 385, Julesburg, N **Welcome Ctr/ both lanes, full fa ities, info, RV dump, RV dump,** Shell Subway B get Host H, S Conoco/dsl
172	Ovid
165	CO 59, to Haxtun, Sedgewick, N Lucy's Cafe
155	Red Lion Rd
149	CO 55, to Fleming, Crook, S Sinclair/dsl/café
141	Proctor
134	Iliff

STERLING

Exit #	Services
125	US 6, Sterling, **0-3 mi** N **both lanes (full facilities, litter barrels, petwalk, vending, RV dump,** Cenex/dsl, dsl Arby's, Bamboo Garden, Burger King, Domino's, Jimmy John's, Little Caesar's, McDonald's, Papa Murph Pizza Hut, Sonic, Subway, Taco Bell, Taco John's, Village I Wendy's 1st Interstate Inn, Best Western, Holiday Inn press H, $Tree, AutoZone, Bomgaars, Buick/Chevro Chrysler/Dodge/Jeep, Family Food Mkt, Ford/Lincoln, Home pot, museum, N Sterling SP, NAPA, O'Reilly Parts, st patrol, US Verizon, vet, Walgreens, Walmart, S Reata/dsl Bud Inn, Quality Inn, Ramada Inn, Super 8 RV Camping
115	CO 63, Atwood, N Sinclair/dsl H
102	Merino
95	Hillrose
92	to US 6 E, to US 34, CO 71 S
90b a	CO 71 N, to US 34, Brush, N Brush Trkstp/Shell/S way/dsl/24hr, Tesla EVC China Dragon, Pizza H Wendy's Rodeway Inn, S Conoco/dsl McDo ald's Microtel
89	Hospital Rd, S Loves/Carl's Jr/dsl/scales/24hr golf
86	Dodd Bridge Rd

FT MORGAN

Exit #	Services
82	Barlow Rd, N The Mav Grill Best Western+, Comf Inn, Rodeway Inn Silver Spur Camping, S Reata/d scales Burger King Fairfield Inn $Tree, Walma Subway
80	CO 52, Ft Morgan, N City Park, Golf, RV Camping, S Co oco/dsl, Conoco/dsl, Maverik/dsl, Sinclair/dsl Arby's, D McDonald's, Sonic, Subway, Taco Bell, Taco John's, Wonder House Chinese Hampton Inn, Sands Inn, Super 8 AutoZone, Family$, Toyota, Verizon, Walgreens
79	CO 144, to Weldona, (no wb return)
75	US 34 E, to Ft Morgan, S Shell/pizza/dsl Emb Rest. Baymont Inn GS RV Park, st patrol
74.5mm	**weigh sta both lanes**

INTERSTATE 76 Cont'd

Exit #	Services
73	Long Bridge Rd
66b	US 34 W (from wb), to Greeley
66a	CO 39, CO 52, to Goodrich, N Shamrock/dsl RV Camping, to Jackson Lake SP, S **both lanes, full facilities, litter barrels, petwalk, vending,** Sinclair/cafe/dsl/e-85
64	Wiggins
60	to CO 144 E, to Orchard
57	rd 91
49	Painter Rd (from wb)
48	to Roggen, N Conoco/dsl, S USPO
39	Keenesburg, S Shell/dsl Deno's Rest. Keene Motel Family$, Tim's Car Clinic
34	Kersey Rd
31	CO 52, Hudson, N Loves/Subway/Carl's Jr/scales/24hr/dsl Best Western+, S Conoco/dsl, Shell/dsl Pepper Pod Rest. Pepper Pod Camping, USPO
25	CO 7, Lochbuie, N Shell/dsl
22	Bromley, N Circle K/dsl KFC/LJ Silver, Wendy's Hampton Inn (4mi) H, Lowe's, S Kum&Go/dsl/e85 Barr Lake SP, Freightliner
21	144th Ave, Eagle Blvd, N Arby's, Buffalo Wild Wings, Chick-fil-A, Chili's, McDonald's, Old Chicago, Panda Express, Red Robin, Subway, Taco Bell Candlewood Suites, Comfort Suites, Holiday Inn Express H, $Tree, AT&T, Dick's, GNC, Hobby Lobby, Home Depot, JC Penney, Kohl's, Michael's, Office Depot, Petsmart, Ross, Target, Verizon
20	136th Ave, N Barr Lake RV Park, same as 21
18	**E-470 tollway**, to Limon (from wb)
16	CO 2, Sable Blvd, Commerce City, N to Denver Airport
12	US 85 N, to Brighton (exits left from eb), Greeley
11	96th Ave, N dsl repair, S Buick/GMC
10	88th Ave, N Shell/dsl La Quinta, Super 8, S flea mkt
9	US 6 W, US 85 S (no EZ wb return), Commerce City, S Shell/dsl st patrol, transmissions
8	CO 224, 74th Ave (no EZ eb return), **1 mi N** NAPA
6b a	I-270 E, to Limon, to ✈, to I-25 N
5	I-25, N to Ft Collins, S to Colo Springs
4	Pecos St
3	US 287, Federal Blvd, N Shamrock/dsl, S Advance Parts, vet
1b	CO 95, Sheridan Blvd
1a	CO 121, Wadsworth Blvd, N 7-11/gas, EVC, Exxon, Shell/dsl Anthony's Pizza, Applebee's, BeauJo's, Bennet's BBQ, Chick-fil-A, Chipotle Mexican, Coldstone Creamery, Country Buffet, El Tapatio Mexican, Fazoli's, HuHot, IHOP, Jimmy John's, Kukoro Japanese, McDonald's/playplace, Red Robin, Ruby Tuesday, Smiling Moose, Starbucks, Subway, Taco Bell, TX Roadhouse $Tree, Advance Parts, Big O Tire, Costco/gas, Discount Tire, Home Depot, Lowe's Whse, Petsmart, Sam's Club, Tires+, URGENT CARE

I-76 begins/ends on I-70, exit 269b.

INTERSTATE 225 (Denver)

Exit #	Services
12b a	I-70, W to Denver, E to Limon
10	US 40, US 287, Colfax Ave, E Conoco/dsl, Shell/dsl, Sinclair Burger King, Del Taco, Domino's, DQ, El Pelicano Seafood, KFC, McDonald's, Pizza Hut/Taco Bell, Popeye's, Starbucks, Subway, Village Inn, Wendy's 7-11, Aamco, Advance Parts, Chevrolet, Family$, King's Sooper/gas, NAPA,

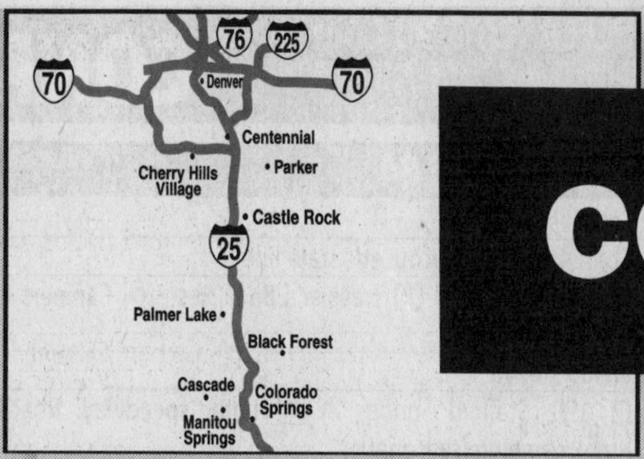

CO

DENVER

Exit #	Services
10	Continued Walgreens, W Conoco/dsl, Shamrock/dsl Caribou Coffee, Chipotle Mexican, Noodles&Co, Panera Bread, Smashburger, Which Wich? SpringHill Suites H, U-Haul
9	Co 30, 6th Ave, E Conoco/dsl Denny's Travelodge, Woodspring Suites, W Shell/dsl H
8	Alameda Ave, E Valero/dsl Atlanta Bread, BJ's Rest., Chick-fil-A, Chili's, Coldstone, FatBurger, Jamba Juice, Jimmy John's, L&L BBQ, Macaroni Grill, Mimi's Cafe, Panda Express, Sabor Mexican, Starbucks, TGIFriday, Wingstop AT&T, Barnes&Noble, Dillards, Hobby Lobby, JC Penney, Macy's, Michael's, Petsmart, Ross, Super Target, W Conoco/dsl, Shell/Circle K $Tree
7	Mississippi Ave, Alameda Ave, E Arby's, Burger King, Chubby's Mexican, ChuckeCheese, CiCi's, Fazoli's, Guadalajara Mexican, McAlister's Deli, Schlotsky's, Sonic, Starbucks, Subway, Tokyo Joe's, Village Inn Best Western, Holiday Inn Express, La Quinta Best Buy, Burlington Coats, Home Depot, JoAnn Fabrics, Sam's Club/gas, Tires +, Verizon, Walmart, W IHOP, McDonald's, Mirage Rest., Senor Ric's, Waffle House 7-11, AutoZone, Pepboys
5	Iliff Ave, E 7-11 Ajuua Mexican, Applebee's, Boston Mkt, Carrabba's, Hibachi Japanese, Joe's Crabshack, Outback Steaks, Real de Minas Mexican, Rosie's Diner, Ruby Tuesday, Sweet Tomatoes, TX Roadhouse Comfort Inn, Crestwood Suites, Extended Stay America, Extended Stay America (2), Fairfield Inn, Motel 6, W Conoco Dragon Boat, Legends Grill, Subway DoubleTree 7-11
4	CO 83, Parker Rd, E Radisson Cherry Creek SP, W Shell/dsl Big Burrito, DQ, Little Caesar's, Popeye's, Starbucks, Subway, Taco Bell, Wendy's $Tree, 7-11, Firestone/auto, King Sooper/dsl
2b	Yosemite St
2	DTC Blvd, Tamarac St, W Conoco/7-11 Fel Fel Mediterranean, La Fogata Mexican, Sonic, South Garden Chinese, Subway $Tree, Goodyear/auto
1b a	**I-25. I-225 begins/ends on I-25, exit 200.**

INTERSTATE 270 (Denver)

Exit #	Services
4	I-70
3	N TA/Burger King/Country Pride/Popeye's/Pizza Hut/dsl/24hr/@, S Sapp Bros/Sinclair/Subway/dsl/@
2b a	US 85, CO 2, Vasquez Ave, N Arby's, Carls Jr, Chipotle Mexican, Jack-in-the-Box, KFC/LJ Silver, McDonald's, Taco Bell, Wendy's TDS Tire, Walgreens, Walmart
1b	York St
1a	I-76 E, to Ft Morgan
1c	I-25 S, to Denver

CO

= gas = food = lodging = other = rest stop

CONNECTICUT

CT

INTERSTATE 84

Exit #	Services
98mm	Connecticut/Massachusetts state line
74 (97)	CT 171, Holland, S Traveler's Book Rest. Campers Inn RV Ctr
95mm	**weigh sta wb**
73 (95)	CT 190, Stafford Springs, N motor speedway, Roaring Brook camping (seasonal)
72 (93)	CT 89, Westford, N Ashford Motel, Roaring Brook camping (seasonal)
71 (88)	CT 320, Ruby Rd, S TA/Shell/Burger King/Country Pride/dsl/scales/24hr/@ Dunkin' Rodeway Inn
70 (86)	CT 32, Willington, N H, Wilderness Lake Camping, S Mobil/dsl, Sunoco/dsl
85mm	**both lanes, campers, full facilities, info, litter barrels, petwalk, , vending**
69 (83)	CT 74, to US 44, Willington, S food, gas, , RV camping, st police
68 (81)	CT 195, Tolland, N Gulf/dsl, Mobil Dunkin', Papa T's Rest., Subway NAPA, S Citgo Camille's Pizza, Lee's Garden Big Y Foods, Verizon, vet
67 (77)	CT 31, Rockville, N Mobil, Shell/dsl Beni's Grill, Burger King, China Taste, Dunkin', McDonald's, Subway H, S Nathan Hale Mon
66 (76)	Tunnel Rd, Vernon
65 (75)	CT 30, Vernon Ctr, N Cumberland/dsl, Mobil/dsl, Shell Brick Oven Pizza, Burger King, Donuts', KFC, Oki Asian, Rein's Deli, Simply Thai, Vernon Diner, Wang's Buffet Days Inn, Red Roof Inn Firestone/auto, Meineke, Stop&Shop/gas
64 (74)	Vernon Ctr, N Sunoco 99 Rest., Angellino's Italian, Anthony's Pizza, D'angelo's, Denny's, Dunkin', Friendly's, McDonald's, Moe's SW, Rita's Custard, Starbucks, Taco Bell, Wendy's, Wood'n Tap Holiday Inn Express $Tree, AutoZone, CVS Drug, GNC, Goodyear/auto, Staples, TJ Maxx, vet, S Motel 6 Chevrolet, VW
63 (72)	CT 30, CT 83, same as 62, Manchester, S Windsor, N Azteca Mexican, BurgerIM, Chipotle Mexican, Dunkin', HomeTown Buffet, IHOP, Longhorn Steaks, McDonald's, Outback Steaks, Panera Bread, Red Robin, Smashburger, Starbucks, Subway, TGIFriday's Courtyard, Residence Inn AT&T, Best Buy, Marshall's, PetCo, Verizon, Walgreens, Walmart, S Best, BP/dsl, EVC, Shell/dsl, Sunoco/dsl, Xtra Shea's Pizzaria Best Value Inn, Extended Stay America, Motel 6 H, Big Y Mkt, Hyundai, Kohl's, Nissan, Subaru, Toyota, U-Haul, USPO
62 (71)	Buckland St, same as 63, N Mobil/Dunkin'/dsl, Tesla EVC Artisanal Burger, Boston Mkt, Burton's Grill, Chili's, Dave&Buster's, Five Guys, Friendly's, Hooters, Jersey Mike's, Maggie McFly's, Market Grille, Moe's SW Grill, Olive Garden, Panera Bread, Sakura Garden, Starbucks, Taco Bell, Ted's MT Grill Fairfield Inn, Hampton Inn, Homewood Suites $Tree, Barnes&Noble, BigLots, Dick's, Hobby Lobby, Home Depot, JC Penney, Jo-Ann Fabrics, LL Bean, Lowe's, Macy's, Michael's, Old Navy, PetsMart, Target, Town Fair Tire, Trader Joe's, Verizon, S Shell/dsl Buffalo Wild Wings, Burger Fi, ChuckeCheese, EVC, Golden Dragon, Joey Garlic's, Kobe Asian, McDonald's, Sonic, Subway, TX Roadhouse, Wendy's BJ's Whse/gas, Firestone/auto, GNC, Honda, USPO
61 (70)	I-291 W, to Windsor

VERNON CTR

WINDSOR

HARTFORD

Exit #	Services
60 (69)	US 6, US 44, Burnside Ave (from eb)
59 (68)	I-384 E, Manchester
58 (67)	Roberts St, Burnside Ave, N Margaritas Grill, Nolita Ri... rante Comfort Inn, S Mobil, Sunoco Dunkin', Qu... Pizza, Taco Bell Cabela's, vet
57 (66)	CT 15 S, to I-91 S, Charter Oak Br
56 (65)	Governor St, E Hartford, S
55 (64)	CT 2 E, New London, downtown
54 (63)	Old State House, N Audi, Chevrolet, Chrysler/Dodge/Je... Ford, Kia, Lexus, Lincoln, S Hampton Inn
53 (62)	CT Blvd (from eb), S Holiday Inn
52 (61)	W Main St (from eb), downtown
51 (60)	I-91 N, to Springfield
50 (59.8)	to I-91 S (from wb), N Red Lion, S Hilton, Residence
48 (59.5)	Asylum St, downtown, N Red Lion, S Capitol Hc... Homewood Suites H
47 (59)	Sigourney St, downtown, N Hartford Seminary, Mark Tw... House
46 (58)	Sisson St, downtown (from wb, exits left), N UConn ... School
45 (57)	Flatbush Ave (from wb, exits left)
44 (56.5)	Prospect Ave, N Mobil, Shell/dsl Burger King, Golc... Diner, Hibachi Grill, McDonald's, Prospect Pizza, Wen... ShopRite Foods
43 (56)	Park Rd, W Hartford, N to St Joseph Coll
42 (55)	Trout Brk Dr (exits left from wb), to Elmwood
41 (54)	S Main St, Elmwood, N American School for the Deaf
40 (53)	CT 71, New Britain Ave, S Sunoco/dsl, Tesla EVC ... Grille, Burger King, CA Pizza, Chili's, China Pan, Chipotle M... can, McDonald's, Olive Garden, Panera Bread, PF Chang's, ... Robin, Starbucks, Subway, Wendy's Courtyard A... Barnes&Noble, Best Buy, Costco/dsl, JC Penney, Macy's, ... chael's, Nordstrom, Old Navy, PetCo, Target, TJ Maxx, Tra... Joe's, Verizon
39a (52)	CT 9 S, to New Britain, Newington, S H
39 (51.5)	CT 4, (exits left from eb), Farmington, N H
38 (51)	US 6 W (from wb), same as 37, Bristol
37 (50)	Fienemann Rd, to US 6 W, N Dunkin', Subway Har... ton Inn, Marriott, S Noble/Dunkin'/dsl Extended ... America
36 (49)	Slater Rd (exits left from eb), S H
35 (48)	CT 72, to CT 9 (exits left from both lanes), New Britain, S
34 (47)	CT 372, Crooked St, N EVC, Gulf/dsl, Sunoco Applebe... Friendly's, McDonald's, Starbucks, Taco Bell/LJ Silver, Wen... Fairfield Inn $Tree, AT&T, Big Y Mkt, Dick's, Ford/... coln, Kohl's, Lowe's, Marshall's, Old Navy, Petsmart, VW
33 (46)	CT 72 W, to Bristol (exits left from eb)
32 (45)	Ct 10, Queen St, Southington, N Cumberland Farms, Ex... Shell/dsl Buffalo Wild Wings, Burger King, Chick-fil-A, Chi... Chipotle, D'angelo, Denny's, Dunkin', Gobi Mongolian, IH... JD's Rest., KFC, Luen Hop Chinese, McDonald's, Moe's SW G... Noodles&Co, Outback Steaks, Puerto Vallarta, Smashbur... Starbucks, Subway, Taco Bell, Vivaldi Pizza Motel 6 ... $Tree, 7-11, Aldi, AutoZone, BJ's/gas, CVS Drug, GNC, Hc... Depot, Jo-Ann, O'Reilly Parts, PetCo, ShopRite Foods, Staples... Maxx, TownFair Tire, Verizon, S Gulf, Mobil, Sunoco A... gos Italian, Dunkin', Eddie's Sombrero, Friendly's, Nardelli's C... Noble Japanese, Panera Bread, Rita's Custard, Subway, To... Japanese, Wendy's, Wood'n Tap Grill Days Inn, Holiday

SOUTHINGTON

INTERSTATE 84 Cont'd

32 (45)	Continued Express Advance Parts, AT&T, Firestone/auto, Midas, Monro, PriceChopper Foods, URGENT CARE, Walmart
31 (44)	CT 229, West St, N EVC, Mobil/dsl, Sunoco/dsl Chip's, Dunkin', Popeye's, Starbucks Courtyard, Homewood Suites Lowe's, Michael's, Target, S Citgo, Gulf/dsl Dunkin', Giovanni's Pizza, Subway Residence Inn
30 (43)	Marion Ave, W Main, Southington, N ski area, S Mobil/dsl H
29 (42)	CT 10, from wb, exits left, Milldale (exits left from wb)
41.5mm	**eb, full facilities, info, litter barrels, petwalk,**
28 (41)	CT 322, Marion, S Fleet/dsl, Mobil, TA/Popeye's/Taco Bell/dsl/scales/24hr/@ Blimpie, Burger King, DQ, Dunkin', Manor Inn Rest., Subway, Young Young Chinese Comfort Suites, EconoLodge Home Depot
27 (40)	I-691 E, to Meriden
26 (38)	CT 70, to Cheshire, N Blackie's Cafe
25a (37)	Austin Rd, N Winzz/dsl Asian Garden, Subway, Tiramisu Italian Costco/gas, Kohl's
25 (36)	Harper's Ferry Rd, Reed Dr, Scott Rd, E Main St, N Mobil/dsl Dunkin' AT&T, NAPA, S Burger King, Dunkin', Golden Wok, McDonald's, Nino's Rest., Subway, TX Roadhouse Quality Inn Aldi Foods, BJ's Whse/gas, Cadillac/Chevrolet, CVS Drug, Super Stop&Shop/gas
23 (33.5)	CT 69, Hamilton Ave, N Buffalo Wild Wings, Chili's, IHOP, McDonald's, Olive Garden, TGIFriday's H, Barnes&Noble, JC Penney, Macy's, Michael's, Petco, Save-a-Lot Foods, TJ Maxx, S Shell Dunkin'
22 (33)	Baldwin St, same as 23, Waterbury, N Gulf Courtyard H, USPO
21 (33)	Meadow St, Banks St, N 7-11, S Exxon/dsl Home Depot, PetsMart
20 (32)	CT 8 N (exits left from eb), to Torrington
19 (32)	CT 8 S (exits left from wb), to Bridgeport
18 (32)	W Main, Highland Ave, N ProFuel/dsl Dunkin', Lena's Deli, Starbucks, Subway, Wayback Burger Hampton Inn H, CVS Drug
17 (30)	CT 63, CT 64, to Watertown, Naugatuck, N Maggie McFly's Rest., S Mobil/dsl Dunkin', Leo's Rest., Maples Rest., Subway
16 (25)	CT 188, to Middlebury, N Mobil Patty's Pantry Deli Crowne Plaza
15 (22)	US 6 E, CT 67, Southbury, N Citgo/deli, Mobil, Shell/repair Dunkin', McDonald's, Panera Bread, Subway Heritage Hotel AT&T, Stop&Shop, TJ Maxx, Verizon, S to Kettletown SP
14 (20)	CT 172, to S Britain, N Mobil Dunkin', Maggie McFly's, S st police
20mm	motorist callboxes begin eb, end wb
13 (19)	River Rd (from eb), to Southbury
11 (16)	CT 34, to New Haven
10 (15)	US 6 W, Newtown, N Fig's Rest., Foundry Kitchen, Subway, Villa Rest., S Citgo/dsl, Mobil/dsl Blue Colony Diner, Pizza Palace, Starbucks
9 (11)	CT 25, to Hawleyville, N USPO

DANBURY

8 (8)	Newtown Rd, N Global, Mobil/dsl Applebee's, Dunkin', Outback Steaks La Quinta, Quality Inn Best Buy, Harley-Davidson, Lowe's, Volvo, S Shell/dsl, Sunoco 99 Rest., Black Angus, Boston Mkt, Burger King, Chili's, Denny's, Dunkin', Ichiro Steaks, Little Caesar's, McDonald's, Popeye's, Puerto Vallarta, Rizzuto's, Starbucks, Subway, Taco Bell, TX Roadhouse, Wayback Burger Best Western, Courtyard, Days Inn, Hampton Inn, Holiday Inn/rest., Microtel $Tree, Aldi Foods, Marshall's, Staples, Stop&Shop, Subaru, Target, TJ Maxx, Town Fair Tire, Verizon, Walmart/Subway
7 (7)	US 7N/202E, to Brookfield (exits left from eb), New Milford **1 mi N on Federal Rd** Irving, Mobil, Sunoco Arby's, Burger King, Chick-fil-A, Dunkin', Five Guys, Jersey Mike's, KFC, McDonald's, Moe's SW, Panera Bread, Starbucks, Wendy's AT&T, Bj's Whse/gas, Costco/gas, CVS Drug, Firestone/auto, Ford, GNC, Home Depot, Jo-Ann Fabrics, Kohl's, Michael's, Petco, ShopRite Foods, Stew Leonards, Town Fair Tire, Toyota, Verizon, Walgreens
6 (6)	CT 37 (from wb), New Fairfield, N Gulf Burger King, Castello's Italian, Dunkin', Elmer's Diner, Grand Century Buffet, McDonald's, Moon Star Chinese, Starbucks $Tree, CVS Drug, Rite Aid, S Shell KFC
5 (5)	CT 37, CT 39, CT 53, Danbury, N Exxon/dsl, Shell Best Value Inn, S Mobil Dunkin', Taco Bell H, to Putnam SP
4 (4)	US 6 W/202 W, Lake Ave, N Gulf/dsl, Orbit/dsl, Shell/dsl Dunkin', McDonald's Ethan Allen Hotel, Maron Hotel, Super 8 CVS Drug, Stop&Shop Foods, S Chuck's Steaks Residence Inn, to mall
3 (3)	US 7 S (exits left from wb), to Norwalk, S EVC, Mobil/Burger King/dsl, Tesla EVC Agave Mexican, Brio Grille, Buffalo Wild Wings, Cheesecake Factory, Chipotle, Coldstone, Olive Garden, Panera Bread, Red Lobster AT&T, Barnes&Noble, Dick's, JC Penney, LL Bean, Lord&Taylor, Macy's, Petco, Whole Foods Mkt
2b a (1)	US 6, US 202, Mill Plain Rd, N Mobil/dsl Chipotle, Rosy Tomorrows, Starbucks, Tuscanero's Pizza Hilton Garden, Holiday Inn Express Rite Aid, Staples, Trader Joe's, S **Welcome Ctr/weigh sta, full facilities, info, , litter barrels, petwalk,** Crowne Plaza, Hotel Zero Degrees, SpringHill Suites to Old Ridgebury
1 (0)	Saw Mill Rd, N Hilton Garden, Holiday Inn Express, Maron Hotel
0mm	Connecticut/New York state line

CT

= gas = food = lodging = other = rest stop

INTERSTATE 91

Exit #	Services
58mm	Connecticut/Massachusetts state line
49 (57)	US 5, to Longmeadow, MA, E Pride/dsl Dunkin', McDonald's Holiday Inn Meineke, repair, W Sunoco/dsl Baco's Pizza, Cloverleaf Café, DQ, Dunkin', Pizza Palace $General, Chrysler/Dodge
48 (56)	CT 220, Elm St (same as 47), E Mobil/Dunkin'/dsl Burger King, Denny's, Dunkin', Figaro, First Wok, Friendly's, Jason's Seafood, McDonald's, Outback Steaks, Panera Bread, Starbucks, TGIFriday's, Wendy's $Tree, AutoZone, Best Buy, Costco/gas, Dick's, Firestone/auto, Home Depot, Honda, Hyundai, Jo-Ann Fabrics, Kohl's, Nissan, Target, TownFair Tire, Toyota, USPO, VW
47 (55)	CT 190, to Hazardville (same as 48), E 99 Rest., Acapulcos Mexican, Cheng's Garden, Chick-fil-A, Chipotle, D'angelo, Dunkin', Longhorn Steaks, McDonald's, Moe's SW Grill, Olive Garden, Red Robin, Starbucks, Subway, Taco Bell Hampton Inn, Motel 6, Red Roof Inn H, Advance Parts, Aldi Foods, AT&T, Barnes&Noble, Big Y Foods, CVS Drug, Ford, Marshall's, Michael's, NAPA, Old Navy, PetCo, Petsmart, Rite Aid, ShopRite, Staples, Stop&Shop/gas, Suburban Tire/auto, URGENT CARE, Verizon, Walgreens
46 (53)	US 5, King St, to Enfield, E Mobil Astro's Rest., W Enfield Inn
45 (51)	CT 140, Warehouse Point, E Shell Burger King, Chen's Chinese, Cracker Barrel, Dunkin', Sofia's Rest., Subway, Wayback Burgers Comfort Inn to Trolley Museum, W Sunoco/dsl Rodeway Inn Advance Parts
44 (50)	US 5 S, to E Windsor, E Sunoco/dsl Big Y Mkt, Dunkin', Elizabeth's Rest., KFC, Taco Bell, Wendy's Baymont Inn Walmart
49mm	Connecticut River
42 (48)	CT 159, Windsor Locks, E Longview RV Ctr, W same as 41
41 (47)	Center St (exits with 39), W Ad's Pizzaria HillPoint Hotel
40 (46.5)	CT 20, W , Old New-Gate Prison
39 (46)	Kennedy Rd (exits with 41), Community Rd, E vet, W Shell/Dunkin'/dsl Char Koon, Chili's, Starbucks $Tree, AT&T, GNC, PetCo, Stop&Shop Foods, Target
38 (45)	CT 75, to Poquonock, Windsor Area, E Mobil/Circle K/dsl Asian Bistro, Buffalo Wild Wings, Dunkin', Moe's SW, Pizzarama, Subway PriceChopper Foods, to Ellsworth Homestead, W The Bistro Courtyard, Hilton Garden, Hyatt House Suites, Marriott
37 (44)	CT 305, Bloomfield Ave, Windsor Ctr, E Mobil/dsl McDonald's, W Sunoco Residence Inn
36 (43)	CT 178, Park Ave, to W Hartford
35b (41)	CT 218, to Bloomfield, to S Windsor, E food, gas/dsl
35a	I-291 E, to Manchester
34 (40)	CT 159, Windsor Ave, E Sunoco/dsl, W Citgo/dsl RanchHouse Rest. H
33 (39)	Jennings Rd, Weston St, E Tesla EVC Cadillac, Fiat, Jaguar, VW, W Mobil/dsl Burger King, Dunkin', McDonald's, Subway Super 8, Travel Inn CarMax, Honda, Hyundai, Infiniti, Mazda, Mercedes, Midas, Nissan, Subaru, Toyota
32b (38)	Trumbull St (exits left from nb), W Hilton, Red Lion H, Goodyear, to downtown
32a	(exit 30 from sb), I-84 W
29b (37)	I-84 E, Hartford
29a (36.5)	US 5 N, CT 15 N (exits left from nb), W H, capitol, civic ctr, downtown

WINDSOR AREA

Exit #	Services
28 (36)	US 5, CT 15 S (from nb), W Citgo Burger King, Dur Wendy's
27 (35)	Brainerd Rd, Airport Rd, E Mobil/Dunkin'/Subway, Shell/Dunkin'/dsl McDonald's, USS Chowder Pot Western, Days Inn Regional Mkt
26 (33.5)	Marsh St, W CT MVD, Silas Deane House, Webb House
25 (33)	CT 3, Glastonbury, Wethersfield
24 (32)	CT 99, Rocky Hill, Wethersfield, E Phillips 66/dsl garve Grill, Chuck's Steaks, Dakota Steaks, Dunkin', McI ald's, On-the-Border, Rita's Custard, Rockyhill Pizza, Sayb Seafood, Subway Holiday Inn Express, Howard John Super 8 Aldi Foods, Kohl's, Meineke, Monro, W bil, Shell/dsl, Valero/dsl Buffalo Wild Wings, Burger K Chip's Rest., Chipotle, D'Angelo, Denny's, Friendly's, Ginza sine, KFC, Panera Bread, Red Lobster, Sake Japanese, So Pizzaria, Starbucks, Subway, Townline Diner, Wendy's, W n-Tap Grill Comfort Inn, Motel 6 $Tree, AT&T, CVS D Goodyear/auto, Marshall's, Stop&Shop, TJMaxx, TownFair Verizon, Walgreens, Walmart/Subway
23 (29)	to CT 3, West St, Rocky Hill, Vet Home, E Sheraton Dinosaur SP, W Cumberland Farms/dsl, Exxon/dsl, bil DeNovellis, Michelangeo's Pizza, Starbucks, way Residence Inn Westside Mktplace
22 (27)	CT 9, to New Britain, Middletown
21 (26)	CT 372, to Berlin, Cromwell, E Sunoco/dsl/repair Q ity Inn, Red Lion Inn Krauszer's Foods, Lowe's, W go/Subway/dsl, Mobil/dsl Baci Grill, Burger King, Ch Cromwell Diner, Dunkin', McDonald's, Mizzu Asian, Na li's Courtyard, Super 8 Firestone/auto, PriceRite Fo URGENT CARE, Verizon, vet, Walmart
20 (23)	Country Club Rd, Middle St
22mm	**/weigh sta nb, full facilities, info, litter barrels, petw , RV dump, vending**
19 (21)	Baldwin Ave (from sb)
18 (20.5)	I-691 W, to Marion, access to same as 16 & 17, ski area
17 (20)	CT 15 N (from sb), to I-691, CT 66 E, Meriden
16 (19)	CT 15, E Main St, E Gulf/dsl, Mobil/dsl, Valero An can Steaks, Gianni's Rest., Huxley's Cafe, Kings Garden Chir Olympos Diner, Subway Extended Stay America, Hawt Inn, Red Roof Inn, The Meridan Inn, W Gulf/repair, S dsl Boston Mkt, Boston Mkt, Burger King, Dunkin', KFC, Dairy Bar, Little Caesar's, McDonald's, Nardelli's, Subway, Bell, Wayback Burgers, Wendy's Comfort Inn H, Drug, Hancock's Drug, Walgreens
15 (16)	CT 68, to Durham, E Hilton Garden golf, W C yard, Fairfield Inn, Homewood Suites
15mm	**sb, full facilities, info, litter barrels, petwalk, ,**
14 (12)	CT 150 (no EZ return), Woodhouse Ave, Wallingford
13 (10)	US 5 (exits left from nb), Wallingford, **services 2 mi W o** 5, to Wharton Brook SP
12 (9)	US 5, Washington Ave, E Exxon, Sunoco, Valero ton Mkt, Burger King, D'angelo's, DQ, Dunkin', McDona Popeye's, Starbucks, Subway CVS Drug, Stop&Shop F Town Fair Tire, USPO, Verizon, Walgreens, W BP, bil, Shell/dsl Arby's, Athena II Diner, Dunkin', Out Steaks Best Western+/Harry's Grill Advance P BigY Foods/drug, vet
11 (7)	CT 22 (from nb), North Haven, same as 12
10 (6)	CT 40, to Cheshire, Hamden
9 (5)	Montowese Ave, W Gulf/dsl, Sunoco Buffalo Wings, Chick-fil-A, Dunkin', Friendly's, Longhorn Steaks, Mc ald's, Olive Garden, Panera Bread, Red Lobster, Ruby Tues

ROCKY HILL

WALLINGFORD

INTERSTATE 91 Cont'd

9 (5)	Continued Subway, Wendy's $Tree, AT&T, Barnes&Noble, Best Buy, BigLots, BJ's Whse/gas, CVS, Dick's, GNC, Home Depot, Michael's, Nissan/Jeep, PetCo, Petsmart, Target, TJMaxx, URGENT CARE, Verizon
8 (4)	CT 17, CT 80, Middletown Ave, E 7-11, Global/dsl, Mercury/dsl, Shell 91 Diner, Burger King, Dunkin', KFC, McDonald's, Popeye's, Seasons, Taco Bell Days Inn Advance Parts, Aldi Foods, AutoZone, Lowe's, vet, Walgreens, Walmart/Subway
7 (3)	Ferry St (from sb), Fair Haven, W Exxon/dsl NAPA
6 (2.5)	Willow St (exits left from nb), Blatchley Ave, E repair
5 (2)	US 5 (from nb), State St, Fair Haven
4 (1.5)	State St (from sb), downtown
3 (1)	Trumbull St, downtown, W Peabody Museum
2 (.5)	Hamilton St, downtown, New Haven
1 (.3)	CT 34W (from sb), New Haven, W H, downtown

I-91 begins/ends on I-95, exit 48.

INTERSTATE 95

Exit #	Services
94mm	Connecticut/Rhode Island state line
93 (111)	CT 216, Clarks Falls, E Citgo/dsl/repair Subway, to Burlingame SP $General, W Mobil/dsl, Pilot/Shell/Stuckey's/Sbarro's/dsl/scales/24hr Dunkin' Budget Inn, Stardust Motel
92 (107)	CT 2, CT 49 (no EZ nb return), **sb, full facilities**, Pawcatuck, E Shell Dunkin', McDonald's La Quinta H, Stop&Shop, W Cedar Park Suites FoxWoods (8mi), KOA
91 (103)	CT 234, N Main St, to Stonington, E H
90 (101)	CT 27, Mystic, E Shell/Domino's/Dunkin/dsl, Tesla EVC Friendly's, Go Fish, McDonald's, Mystic Diner, Peking Tokyo, Starbucks, Steak Loft Hilton, Holiday Inn Express, Howard Johnson, Hyatt Place, Rodeway Inn aquarium, Mystic Outlet Shops, W Mobil/Subway/dsl Cristo's Pizza, Dunkin', Frank's Grille Days Inn, Hampton Inn, Mystic River Inn, Quality Inn, Residence Inn Chevrolet, Chrysler/Dodge/Jeep, Ford, TrueValue, VW
89mm	Mystic River, scenic overlook nb, scenic overlook
89 (99)	CT 614, Mystic St, Allyn St, W camping (seasonal)
88 (98)	CT 117, to Noank, E , W Octagon Steaks, Starbucks Marriott
87 (97)	Sharp Hwy (exits left from sb), Groton, E Applebee's Hampton Inn , to Griswold SP
86 (96)	rd 184 (exits left from nb), Groton, E 99 Rest., Applebee's, Olio Rest. Hampton Inn, Motel 6, Rodeway Inn Walgreens, W Gulf/dsl, Mobil/dsl, Shell/dsl, Xpress Fuel Chinese Kitchen, Domino's, Dunkin', Five Guys, Flanagan's Diner, Groton Rest., KFC, Moe's SW, Panera Bread, Pick Pockets Deli, Subway, Taco Bell Days Inn, Groton Inn, Hilton Garden, Ramada, Super 8 Advance Parts, GNC, Honda, Kia, Kohl's, Midas, Stop&Shop, to US Sub Base, Verizon
85 (95)	US 1 N, Groton, downtown, E Norms Diner Sleep Inn
84 (94)	CT 32 (from sb), New London, downtown
83 (92)	CT 32, New London, E to Long Island Ferry
82a (90.5)	frontage rd, same as 82, New London, E Mobil/dsl Denny's, TX Roadhouse Advance Parts, AutoZone, Goodyear/auto, NSA Foods, Staples, TownFair Tire, W Sunoco Chili's, Outback Steaks, Panda Buffet Clarion, Red Roof Inn, SpringHill Suites Marshall's, Petsmart, ShopRite Foods

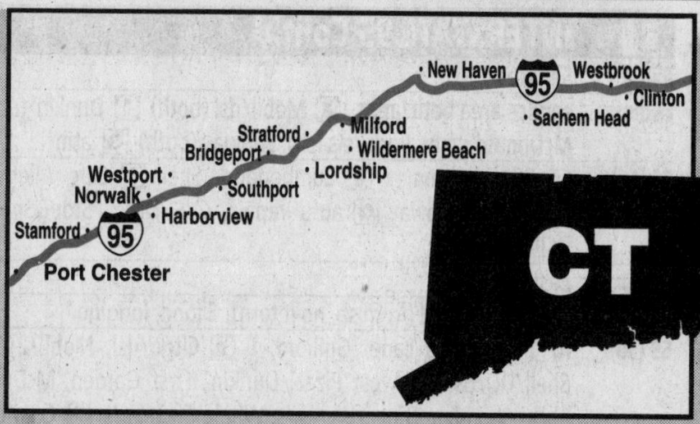

NEW LONDON

NIANTIC

82 (90)	CT 85, to I-395 N, New London, W Mobil/Dunkin' Buffalo Wild Wings, Coldstone, Jersey Mike's, Longhorn Steaks, Moe's SW, Olive Garden, Panera Bread, Ruby Tuesday, Smashburger, Starbucks, Subway BAM, Best Buy, Dick's, Home Depot, JC Penney, Macy's, Michael's, PetCo, Target, Verizon
90mm	weigh sta both directions
81 (89.5)	Cross Road, W Rodeway Inn $Tree, BJ's Whse/gas, Lowe's, Walmart/McDonald's
80 (89.3)	Oil Mill Rd (from sb), W Rodeway Inn
76 (89)	I-395 N (from nb, exits left), to Norwich
75 (88)	US 1, to Waterford
74 (87)	rd 161, to Flanders, Niantic, E Citgo/dsl, Mobil, Niantic/dsl/repair Burger King, Country Gourmet, Dunkin', Illiano's Grill, Starbucks Days Inn, Motel 6, Niantic Inn, Sleep Inn Ford, Monro Automotive, Stop&Shop/gas, Verizon, W Shell Flanders Seafood, King Garden, McDonald's, Osaka Japanese, Shack Rest., Smokey O'Grady's BBQ, Subway, Yummy Yummy Pizza CVS Drug, Tri Town Foods, TrueValue, Walgreens
74mm	**sb, full facilities, st police**
73 (86)	Society Rd
72 (84)	to Rocky Neck SP, **2 mi** E food, lodging, RV camping, to Rocky Neck SP
71 (83)	4 Mile Rd, River Rd, to Rocky Neck SP, **1 mi** E KOA (seasonal), beaches
70 (80)	US 1, CT 156, Old Lyme, W Shell/dsl Dock 11 Cafe, Dunkin', Subway Old Lyme Inn/dining Big Y Foods, Griswold Museum, Rite Aid, USPO, vet
69 (77)	US 1, CT 9 N, to Hartford, W Otter Cove Quality Inn
68 (76.5)	US 1 S, Old Saybrook, E Mobil, Shell/dsl Cloud 9 Deli, Mystic Mkt Kitchen, W Buick/GMC, Chevrolet, Chrysler/Dodge/Jeep, Hyundai, Kia, Nissan, VW
67 (76)	CT 154, Elm St (no EZ sb return), Old Saybrook, E same as 68
66 (75)	to US 1, Spencer Plain Rd, E Citgo/dsl Alforno Trattoria, Cuckoo's Nest Mexican, Dunkin', Five Guys, Sal's Pizza, Samurai Japanese, Wayback Burgers EconoLodge, Saybrook Motel, Super 8 Big Y Mkt, Kohl's, NAPA, transmissions, URGENT CARE, vet
65 (73)	rd 153, Westbrook, E Mobil/Dunkin', Valero Cafe Routier, Cristy's Rest., Denny's Honda, H, Old Navy, Toyota, USPO, Walgreens, Westbrook Outlets/famous brands
64 (70)	rd 145, Horse Hill Rd, Clinton
63 (68)	CT 81, Clinton, E Shell, Shell/dsl/LP, Sunoco/dsl Chester's BBQ, Chips Rest., McDonald's, Subway CVS Drug, USPO, vet, W Coldstone, Dunkin' AT&T, Clinton Crossing Premium Outlets/famous brands, PetCo
62 (67)	E beaches, RV camping, to Hammonasset SP

INTERSTATE 95 Cont'd

MADISON

Exit #	Services
66mm	**service area both lanes,** Mobil/dsl (both) Dunkin' (nb), McDonald's (sb), Popeye's (sb), Subway (both) atm
61 (64)	CT 79, Madison, E Cumberland, Shell Cafe Allegre, Starbucks, Subway auto repair, CVS Drug, Stop&Shop, USPO, Verizon
61mm	East River
60 (63.5)	Mungertown Rd (from sb, no return), E food, lodging
59 (60)	rd 146, Goose Lane, Guilford, E Citgo/dsl, Mobil/24hr, Shell/DQ/dsl Avest Pizza, Dunkin', First Garden, McDonald's, Shoreline Diner, Wendy's, Whole Enchilada Comfort Inn, Tower Motel $Tree, Big Y Foods, NAPA, transmissions, Verizon, Walmart
58 (59)	CT 77, Guilford, E on US 1 Gulf/dsl, Mobil, Wave/dsl, Xpress Dunkin' CVS Drug, to Henry Whitfield Museum, Walgreens, W on US 1 vet
57 (58)	US 1, Guilford, E Shell/Dunkin'/dsl, W Fresh Mkt, Michael's, Petco, Verizon, vet
56 (55)	rd 146, to Stony Creek, E Rodeway Inn, W Mobil, Shell/dsl, TA/Popeye's/Starbucks/Subway/dsl/scales/24hr/@ 56 Diner, Dunkin', USS Chowderpot American Inn, Baymont Inn Freightliner, Stop&Shop Foods

BRANFORD

Exit #	Services
55 (54)	US 1, E Branford/repair, Cumberland, Shell/dsl Carson's Rest., Dunkin', Hornet's Nest Deli, Lynn's Rest., Marco Pizzaria Holiday Inn Express, Motel 6 Ford, vet, Walgreens, W Gulf, Mobil/Dunkin'/dsl Brother's Deli, Cafe Fiore, Gourmet Wok, Parthenon Diner Days Inn
54 (53)	Cedar St, Branford, E Mobil, Stop&Shop Gas Dragon East Chinese, Dunkin', La Luna Ristorante Kia, Staples, Subaru, W Krauszer's Foods, NAPA
52mm	**service area both lanes,** Mobil/dsl (both) Dunkin' (sb), McDonald's (nb), Subway (nb)
52 (50)	rd 100, North High St, E to Trolley Museum
51 (49.5)	US 1, Easthaven, E Sunoco, Valero/dsl, Xpress/dsl Boston Mkt, Chili's, Dunkin' Quality Inn $Tree, Big Lots, Chevrolet, Hobby Lobby, Lexus, TJ Maxx, W Golden Dragon, Wendy's AutoZone, CarMax, Home Depot, Hyundai
50 (49)	Woodward Ave (from nb), E Shell Ft Nathan Hale, US Naval/Marine Reserve

NEW HAVEN

Exit #	Services
49 (48.5)	Stiles St (from nb)
48 (48)	I-91 N, to Hartford
47 (47.5)	CT 34, New Haven, W Mobil/Dunkin'/dsl Brazi's Italian, Greek Olive Diner La Quinta Ikea, Long Wharf Theater, same as 46
46 (47)	Long Wharf Dr, Sargent Dr, E Lenny & Joe's Rest., W Mobil/Dunkin'/dsl Brazi's Italian, Greek Olive Diner La Quinta Ikea, Long Wharf Theater
44 (46)	CT 10 (from nb), Kimberly Ave, E Super 8, W DQ, Dunkin', McDonald's, Popeye's, Townhouse Pizza same as 45
43 (45)	CT 122, 1st Ave (no EZ return), West Haven, W 1st Fuel/dsl, Xtra H, NAPA, to U of New Haven, vet
42 (44)	CT 162, Saw Mill Rd, E Mobil/Dunkin' EconoLodge, W Shell Chipotle, Denny's, Dunkin', McDonald's, Starbucks, Subway, TX Roadhouse Best Western, Hampton Inn Aldi Foods, Firestone/auto, Walmart/Subway
41 (42)	Marsh Hill Rd, to Orange, E Homewood Suites, W Outback Steaks Courtyard
41mm	service area both lanes, Mobil/dsl, Tesla EVC Dunkin', McDonald's, Panda Express
40 (40)	Old Gate Lane, Woodmont Rd, E Citgo/dsl, Pilot/Wendy's/dsl/scales/24hr, Shell, Sunoco Cracker Barrel, Duchess Rest.,

MILFORD

Exit #	Services
40 (40)	Continued Dunkin', Gipper's Rest., Popeye's Hilton Garden, Holiday Express, Hyatt Place, Mayflower Motel, Milford Inn Mid
39 (39)	US 1, to Milford, E Cumberland Farms/dsl A nian Diner, Dunkin', Hooters, Mama Teresa's, Mexico co Howard Johnson, Super 8 $Tree, CVS Drug, F tone/auto, Mazda/Volvo, ShopRite Foods, vet, Walgreens US 1, W Mobil, Tesla EVC Boston Mkt, Buffalo Wings, Burger King, Chili's, Chipotle Mexican, DiBella S Domino's, Dunkin', Golden Corral, HoneyBaked Ham, Donald's, Panera Bread, Rustica Rest., Smashburger, S Starbucks, Subway, Taco Bell Acura, Advance Parts, A Barnes&Noble, BigLots, Chrysler/Dodge/Jeep, Costco/ Dick's, Jo-Ann Fabrics, Macy's, Marshall's, Michael's, Old N PetCo, Rite Aid, Shop&Shop/gas, Staples, Target, TownFair Walmart/Subway, Whole Foods Mkt
38 (38)	CT 15, Merritt Pkwy, Cross Pkwy
37 (37.5)	High St (no ez nb return), E Citgo, Gulf way 7-11, Toyota, vet
36	Plains Rd, E Cumberland Farms, EVC, Mobil Dun Gusto Italian Hampton Inn Aldi Foods
35 (37)	Bic Dr, School House Rd, E EVC Wendy's M 6 AutoZone, Chevrolet, CVS Drug, Dennis' Parts, Ford/ coln, Honda, Land Rover, Nissan, Stop&Shop Foods/gas, S ru, Walgreens, W Red Roof Inn, Residence Inn, Spring Suites
34 (34)	US 1, Milford, E on US 1 Dunkin', McDonald's, Ming F Chinese, Subway, Taco Bell Devon Motel $Tree, Hy dai, Walgreens
33 (33.5)	US 1 (from nb, no EZ return), CT 110, Ferry Blvd, E S dsl, Sunoco/dsl Boathouse Cantina Grill, Danny's D In, Riverview Bistro, Subway $Tree, BJ's Whse, Pe W EVC 99 Rest., McDonald's, Popeye's, Villa za Home Depot, Marshall's, ShopRite Foods, Stop&Sh dsl, USPO, Walmart/Subway
32 (33)	W Broad St, Stratford, E Sunoco/dsl, W G dsl Acropolis Pizza, Dunkin'
31 (32)	South Ave, Honeyspot Rd, E Gulf HoneySpot M Quality Suites NAPA, W Citgo/dsl TownFair Ti
30 (31.5)	Lordship Blvd, Surf Ave, E Gulf/dsl, Shell/dsl Dur URGENT CARE, W Massey/dsl
29 (31)	rd 130, Stratford Ave, Seaview Ave, same as 28, W H
28 (30)	CT 113, E Main St, Pembrook St, E EVC Chipotle, S bucks, Uncle Buck's Grill Bass Pro Shop
27 (29.5)	Lafayette Blvd, downtown, W Dunkin' H, Bar Museum
27a (29)	CT 25, CT 8, to Waterbury
26 (28)	Wordin Ave
25 (27)	CT 130 (from sb, no EZ return), State St, Commerce Dr, Fair Ave, E Audi, Infiniti, Mercedes, Porsche, USPO, W Donald's
24 (26.5)	Black Rock Tpk, E Blackrock Oyster Bar, Fairfield za, Rio Bravo, Sweet Basil Best Western+ A BJ's Whse/Subway, Lexus, Porsche, Staples, USPO, Ver W Gulf Firestone/auto, Nissan
23 (26)	US 1, Kings Hwy, E EVC, Sunoco/dsl Chipotle, Guys CVS Drug, Home Depot, Petco, Whole Foods Mkt
22 (24)	Round Hill Rd, N Benson Rd
23.5mm	**service area both lanes,** Mobil/dsl Dunkin', McD ald's, Qdoba, Subway

CT

INTERSTATE 95 Cont'd

Exit #	Services
21 (23)	Mill Plain Rd, E Citgo/dsl, Mobil/dsl Avellino's Italian, DQ, Geronimo SW Grill, Rawley's Drive-In, Shu Chinese, Starbucks, Subway, Tequila Revolucion Hemlock Hardware, Hyundai, Rite Aid
20 (22)	Bronson Rd (from sb)
19 (21)	US 1, Center St, W Exxon, Shell, Shell/7-11/dsl Athena Diner, Baskin-Robbins/Dunkin', Border Grill, Panera Bread, Shake Shack, Starbucks, Subway Westport Inn Balducci's Mkt, Honda, Michael's, Stop&Shop, TownFair Tire
18 (20)	to Westport, E beaches, Sherwood Island SP, **1 mi W on US 1** Gulf Angelina's Trattoria, Five Guys, Fresh Mkt, Little Barn, McDonald's, Sakura Japanese, Sherwood Diner, Starbucks Barnes&Noble, Marshall's, Toyota, URGENT CARE, vet, Walgreens
17 (18)	CT 33, rd 136, Westport
16 (17)	E Norwalk, E Citgo, Mobil/Dunkin'/dsl, Shell/dsl Baskin-Robbins, Mike's Deli, Penny's Diner, Subway Rite Aid
15 (16)	US 7, to Danbury, Norwalk
14 (15)	US 1, CT Ave, S Norwalk, E Shell Walgreens, W Exxon, Global, Shell Burger King, Dunkin', Post Road Diner, Silver Star Diner, Starbucks, Subway, Wendy's H, $Tree, Best Buy, CVS Drug, GNC, Kohl's, Petsmart, REI, same as 13, ShopRite Foods, Stop&Shop, TJ Maxx, TownFair Tire
13 (13)	US 1 (no EZ return), Post Rd, Norwalk, W EVC, Mobil, Shell, Sunoco American Steaks, Bertucci's, Blue Wave Taco, Chipotle Mexican, Darien Diner, Driftwood Diner, KFC, McDonald's DoubleTree AT&T, Costco, Home Depot, Mini, same as 14, vet, Walmart
12.5mm	**service area nb,** Mobil/dsl, Tesla EVC McDonald's, Sbarro's, Subway, Taco Bell
12 (12)	rd 136, Tokeneke Rd (from nb, no return), W SoNo Cafe
11 (11)	US 1, Darien, E EVC, EVC, Exxon Shake Shack Chevrolet, Land Rover/Jaguar, repair, vet, W Gulf Dunkin' BMW, CVS, Whole Foods Mkt
10 (10)	Noroton, W Mobil, Shell Jake's Place, Subway vet
9.5mm	**service area sb,** Mobil/dsl, Tesla EVC Chipotle, Dunkin', McDonald's, Subway
9 (9)	US 1, rd 106, Glenbrook, E Red Carpet Inn, W Gulf Dunkin', McDonald's, Subway Advance Parts, Meineke
8 (8)	Atlantic Ave, Elm St, E Sunoco Dunkin', W Marriott H
7 (7)	CT 137, Atlantic Ave, W Capital Grille Hampton Inn, Marriott Barnes&Noble, same as 8
6 (6)	Harvard Ave, West Ave, E Stamford Diner, Starbucks La Quinta Advance Parts, Petsmart, Subaru, USPO, W Shell Super 8 H
5 (5)	US 1, Riverside, Old Greenwich, W BP, Mobil, Shell Boston Mkt, Chipotle, Corner Deli, McDonald's, Starbucks, Taco Bell, Valbella Ristorante Hyatt Regency Acme Mkt, CVS Drug, GNC, Staples, USPO, Walgreens
4 (4)	Indian Field Rd, Cos Cob, W Bush-Holley House Museum
3 (3)	Arch St, Greenwich, E Bruce Museum, W Shell H, Cadillac, Lexus
2mm	**weigh sta nb**
2 (1)	Delavan Ave, Byram
0mm	Connecticut/New York state line

PUTNAM

PLAINFIELD

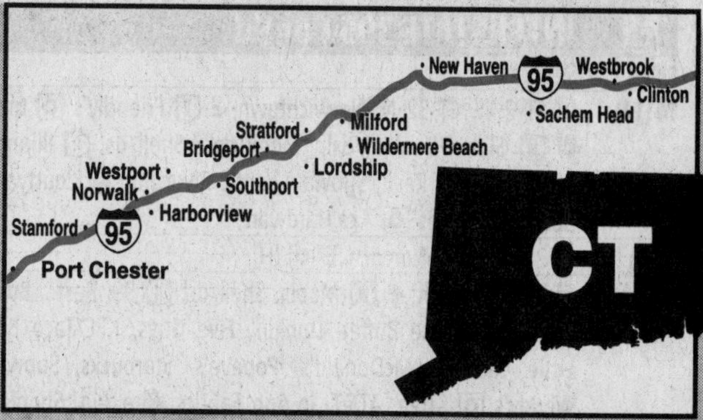

INTERSTATE 395

Exit #	Services
55.5mm	Connecticut/Massachusetts state line
53 (54)	E Thompson, to Wilsonville
50 (50)	rd 200, N Grosvenor Dale, W W Thompson Lake Camping (seasonal)
49 (49)	to CT 12 (from nb, exits left), Grosvenor Dale
47 (47)	US 44, to E Putnam, E Dunkin', Empire Buffet, McDonald's, Subway, Wendy's $Tree, Advance Parts, CVS Drug, Giant Pizza, GNC, Stop&Shop/gas, W Citgo/dsl/repair, Mobil AutoZone, Walmart/Subway
46 (46)	to CT 12, Putnam, W Best Value Inn H
45 (45)	Kennedy Dr, to Putnam, E Ford, W H
43 (43)	Ballouville, W Comfort Inn
41 (41)	CT 101, to Dayville, E Gulf, Shell/dsl Burger King, China Garden, Dayville Mexican, Domino's, Dunkin', Subway, Yamato Japanese, Zip's Diner Budget Inn $General, $Tree, Aldi Foods, Kohl's, O'Reilly Parts, Town Fair Tire, Walgreens, W Mobil/Taco Bell/dsl, Shell/dsl 99 Rest., Dunkin', McDonald's, Railside Tavern AT&T, city park, GNC, Lowe's, Michael's, PetCo, Staples, Stop&Shop, Target, TJ Maxx, Verizon
38 (39)	to S Killingly, W Dunkin', Giant Pizza st police
37 (38)	US 6 W, to Danielson, to Quinebaug Valley Coll
35 (36)	to US 6 E (from nb), to Providence
35mm	**both lanes, full facilities,** Mobil/dsl Dunkin', Subway
32 (32)	CT 14, to Sterling, Central Village, E Cumberland, T&S/repair Edi's Place, Pizza Pizzaz RV camping, USPO, Walgreens, W Citgo, Valero/dsl Dunkin', Frank O's Pizza, Subway Knights Inn $General, transmissions
29 (30)	CT 14A to Plainfield, W Mobil
28 (28)	Lathrop Rd, to Plainfield, E Shell/Domino's/dsl Dunkin', HongKong Star Chinese, Subway, Wendy's La Quinta, Quality Inn Big Y Foods, Ford, Hyundai/VW, Mazda, W Ardmore Fuel, Sunoco/dsl Bakers Dozen Cafe, McDonald's, Mr Z's Rest. Advance Parts, CVS Drug
24 (24)	rd 201, Hopeville, E Hopeville Pond SP, RV camping
22 (23)	CT 164, CT 138, to Pachaug, Preston, E Exxon/Petro Max/Dunkin'/dsl $Tree, Campers World, W AmericInn
21 (21)	CT 12, Jewett City, E Chili's, Panera Bread, Ruby Tuesday, Starbucks Aldi Foods, AT&T, Dick's, GNC, Home Depot, Kohl's, Lowe's, PetCo, Target, Verizon, Walmart/Dunkin', W Mobil/Dunkin'/dsl, Shell/dsl McDonald's Val-U Foods, vet
19a (20)	CT 169 (from nb), Lisbon, E Hidden Acres RV camping
18 (18)	rd 97, Taftville, E Shell/dsl, W 7-11/dsl

NORWICHTOWN

CT

N INTERSTATE 395 Cont'd

Exit #	Services
14 (14)	to CT 2 W, CT 32 N, Norwichtown, **E** [food] Friendly's [other] tires, **W** [gas] Global/Dunkin'/dsl, Mobil/dsl, Shell/dsl [food] Illiano's Grill, Prime 82 Rest., Subway, Yantic River Inn [lodging] Courtyard, Rosemont Suites [other] Ace Hardware
13b a (14)	CT 2 E, CT 32 S, Norwich, **E** [other] [H]
11 (12)	CT 82, Norwich, **E** [gas] Mobil, Shell/dsl [food] 99 Rest., Burger King, Chinese Buffet, Dunkin', Five Guys, KFC/Taco Bell, Little Caesar's, McDonald's, Popeye's, Starbucks, Subway, Wendy's [other] $Tree, AT&T, Jo-Ann Fabrics, Rite Aid, ShopRite Foods, Staples, TJ Maxx, TownFair Tire, Verizon, **W** [lodging] Holiday Inn [other] Big Y Foods, Walmart
9a (10)	CT 2A E, to Ledyard, to Pequot Res
8.5mm	**service plaza sb,** [gas] Mobil/dsl (sb) [food] Dunkin' (sb), Subway (sb) [other] st police (nb)
6 (6)	rd 163, to Uncasville, Montville, **1 mi E** [gas] Mobil/dsl [food] Dunkin', Friendly Pizza, McDonald's [other] repair
5 (5)	CT 32 (from sb, exits left), to New London, RI Beaches
2 (2)	CT 85, to I-95 N, Colchester, **1/2 mi E** [gas] Dunkin', Shell/dsl [lodging] Oakdell Motel

I-95. I-395 begins/ends on I-95, exit 76.

E INTERSTATE 691

Exit #	Services
	I-691 begins/ends on I-91.
12 (12)	Preston Ave
11 (11)	I-91 N, to Hartford
10 (11)	I-91 S, to New Haven, CT 15 S, W Cross Pkwy
9	Berlin Tpk
8 (10)	US 5, Broad St, **N** [gas] HH Gas, Irving, Shell/dsl [food] DQ, G met Chinese Kitchen
7 (9)	downtown (no ez wb return), Meriden (from wb)
6 (8)	Lewis Ave (from wb, no EZ return), to CT 71, **N** [food] Ruby Tu day [other] [H], Best Buy, Dick's, Macy's, Old Navy, Target, TJ Ma **S** [gas] 7-11 [food] Subway
5 (7)	CT 71, to Chamberlain Hill (from eb, no EZ return), **N** [other] Best Buy, Target, **S** [gas] 7-11/gas [food] Subway
4 (4)	CT 322, W Main St (no re-entry from eb), **N** [gas] Su co [food] Dunkin', Hubbard Park Pizza [other] [H]
3mm	Quinnipiac River
3 (1)	CT 10, to Cheshire, Southington, **N** [food] Sam's Clams Rest., ny's Rest.
2 (0)	I-84 E, to Hartford
1 (0)	I-84 W, to Waterbury

I-691 begins/ends on I-84.

NOTES

DELAWARE

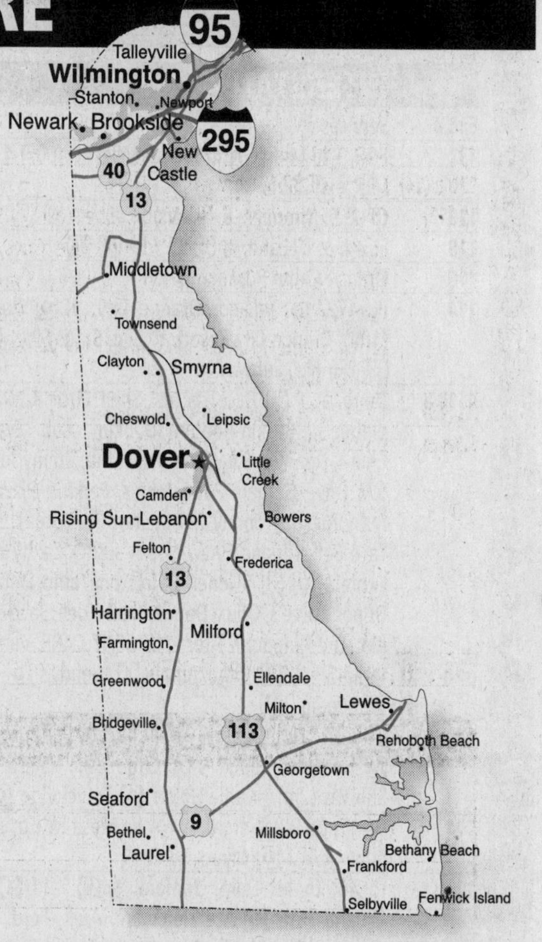

INTERSTATE 95

Exit #	Services
23mm	Delaware/Pennsylvania state line, motorist callboxes for 23 miles sb
11(22)	to I-495 S, DE 92, Naamans Rd, E $General, Burlington Coats, Goodyear/auto, Jo-Ann Fabrics, SaveALot, WaWa, W Shell/Circle K/dsl, WaWa/dsl KFC/Taco Bell Crowne Plaza CVS Drug, Home Depot, Rite Aid
10(21)	Harvey Rd (no nb return)
9(19)	DE 3, to Marsh Rd, E Dunkin' Rockwood Museum, st police, to Bellevue SP
8b a(17)	US 202, Concord Pike, to Wilmington, E Home Depot, to Brandywine Park
7b a(16)	DE 52, Delaware Ave
6(15)	DE 4, MLK Blvd, E Joe's Crabshack, McDonald's AAA, Fresh Grocer Foods, Rite Aid, W Liberty Family$
5c(12)	I-495 N, to Wilmington, to DE Mem Bridge
5b a(11)	DE 141, to US 202, to New Castle, Newport, E Sheraton
4b a(8)	DE 1, DE 7, to Christiana, E Bahama Breeze, Brio Tuscan Grille, CA Pizza Kitchen, Cheesecake Factory, Don Pablo, Foodcourt, JB Dawson's Rest., Panera Bread, Ted's MT Grill Barnes&Noble, Cabela's, Costco, Dick's, JC Penney, Macy's, Michael's, Nordstrom, PetCo, Target, W Applebee's, Dunkin', Firebird's Grill, Fuddrucker's, Jimmy John's, Marble Slab Creamery, Michael's Rest., Olive Garden, Red Lobster Country Inn&Suites, Courtyard, Days Inn, Extended Stay America, Hampton Inn, Hilton, Quality Inn, Red Roof Inn H, AAA, Best Buy, casino/racetrack, Home Depot, Petsmart, TJ Maxx, Verizon
3b a(6)	DE 273, to Newark, Dover, E BP, Exxon/dsl Bertucci's, Bob Evans, Boston Mkt, Ciao Pizza, Famous Dave's BBQ, Olive Grill Italian, Red Robin, Shell Hammer's Grille, Wendy's Ramada Inn, Residence Inn, Sheraton, Staybridge Suites, TownePlace Suites Acme Foods, Boscov's, Jo-Ann Fabrics, Old Navy, Staples, Walgreens, W Getty, Shell/dsl Denny's, Dunkin' Comfort Inn, Holiday Inn Express, Motel 6 7-11
5mm	**service area both lanes (exits left from both lanes),** Sunoco/dsl Baja Fresh, Burger King, Famiglia, Popeye's, Starbucks info
1b a(3)	DE 896, to Newark, to U of DE, Middletown, W Exxon, Shell/dsl, Sunoco Boston Mkt, China Garden, Dunkin', Friendly's, Jersey Mike's, Malin's Deli, Mario's Pizza, McDonald's, TGIFriday's Baymont Inn, Candlewood Suites, Embassy Suites, Homewood Suites, Red Roof Inn, Rodeway Inn DE Tire Ctr
1mm	**toll booth,** st police
0mm	Delaware/Maryland state line, motorist callboxes for 23 miles nb

INTERSTATE 295 (Wilmington)

Exit #	Services
15mm	Delaware/New Jersey state line, Delaware River, Delaware Memorial Bridge
14.5mm	**toll plaza**
14	DE 9, New Castle Ave, to Wilmington, E Giovanni's Cafe Advance Parts, CVS Drug, Family$, Firestone/auto, Harley-Davidson/rest., Rite Aid, Super G Foods, W Shell, Super/dsl Dunkin', McDonald's Best Night Inn, Budget Inn, SuperLodge
13	US 13, US 40, to New Castle, E BP, Shell/dsl, Speedway/dsl, Sunoco/dsl, WaWa Applebee's, Arby's, Arner's Rest, Burger King, Checkers, DogHouse, Dove Diner, Dunkin', Hooters, IHOP, KFC, Krispy Kreme, Little Caesar's, McDonald's, Popeye's, Season's Pizza, Taco Bell, TGIFriday's, Wendy's Quality Inn, Super 8 $General, $Tree, Acura, AutoZone, Big Lots, BJ's Whse/gas, Chevrolet, Chrysler/Jeep/Dodge, Cottman Transmissions, Fiat, Ford, GNC, Home Depot, Hyundai, Lincoln, Mazda, Nissan, PepBoys, repair, Ross, Save-a-Lot, Staples, Toyota, URGENT CARE, Verizon, Walgreens, Walmart, W WaWa/dsl Dunkin' Clarion, Fairfield Inn Ford Trucks, Lowe's
12	I-495, US 202, N to Wilmington

I-295 begins/ends on I-95.

WILMINGTON

INTERSTATE 495

Exit #	Services
11mm	**I-95 N. I-495 begins/ends on I-95.**
5(10)	US 13, Phila Pike, Claymont, W BP, Exxon/dsl, Sunoco/dsl, WaWa/dsl Arby's, Boston Mkt, Burger King, Dunkin', McDonald's Milan Motel Aamco, Family$, Food Lion, USPO
4(5)	US 13, rd 3, Edgemoor Rd, to Fox Point Park
3(4)	12th St
2(3)	rd 9A, Terminal Ave, Port of Wilmington
1(1)	US 13, E WaWa/dsl Dunkin' Clarion Ford Trucks, Lowe's
0mm	**I-95 S. I-495 begins/ends on I-95.**

FL

FLORIDA

INTERSTATE 4

DELTONA

Exit #	Services
132	I-95, S to Miami, N to Jacksonville, FL 400. **I-4 begins/ends on I-95, exit 260b.**
129	to US 92 (from eb, exits left)
118	FL 44, to DeLand, N BP/dsl H
116	Orange Camp Rd, Lake Helen
114	FL 472, to DeLand, Orange City, N Clark Campground (1mi), Orange City Resort, to Blue Sprgs SP, S RaceTrac/dsl Dunkin', Subway
111b a	Deltona, N RaceTrac/dsl, Shell/Circle K, Wawa/dsl Applebee's, Baskin-Robbins/Dunkin', Bob Evans, Chick-fil-A, Chili's, Denny's, Five Guys, Fujiyama, Jimmy John's, KFC, Moe's SW, Olive Garden, Papa John's, Perkins, Pizza Hut, Popeye's, Ruby Tuesday, Sonny's BBQ, Starbucks, Steak'n Shake, Subway, Taco Bell, Tijuana Flats, Woody's BBQ, Zaxby's Holiday Inn Express H, $General, Firestone/auto, Hobby Lobby, Home Depot, Lowe's, Office Depot, Publix/deli, Save-A-Lot Foods, Target, Tire Kingdom, Tires+, URGENT CARE, Verizon, Walgreens, Walmart, S Citgo/repair Wendy's Family$, Publix, Walgreens
108	Dirksen Dr, DeBary, Deltona, N Burger King, IHOP Hampton Inn, S Citgo/dsl, Valero McDonald's, Subway (2mi), Waffle House Travelodge Publix (2mi)
104	US 17, US 92, Sanford, N La Mesa RV Ctr, S Marathon/ Subway/dsl Myers RV Ctr
101c	rd 46, to Mt Dora, Sanford, N 7-11 IHOP, Subway, Tijuana Flats Ace Hardware, Audi, Ford, vet, S 7-11, Chevron/dsl, Mobil, Murphy USA/dsl, RaceTrac/dsl, Shell/dsl Buffalo Wild Wings, Burger King, Carrabba's, Cheddar's, Chianti's Pizza, Chipotle, Cracker Barrel, Don Pablo, Dunkin', El Paso Mexican, Firehouse Subs, Habaneros, Honeybaked Ham, Hooters, Joe's Crabshack, LJ Silver/Taco Bell, Logan's Roadhouse, Longhorn Steaks, McDonald's, Mellow Mushroom, Olive Garden, Orlando Alehouse, Outback Steaks, Panda Express, Panera Bread, PDQ Grill, Pollo Tropical, Red Lobster, Red Robin, Rte 46 Smokehouse, Smokey Bones BBQ, Steak'n Shake, Subway, Wendy's Comfort Inn, SpringHill Suites H, $Tree, Aldi Foods, AT&T, Beall's, Best Buy, Big Lots, BJ's Whse/gas, Books-A-Million, Chrysler/Dodge/Jeep, CVS Drug, Dick's, Dillard's, GNC, Goodyear/auto, Harley-Davidson, JC Penney, Jo-Ann Fabrics, Macy's, Marshall's, Michael's, Old Navy, PetCo, Ross, Target, Tire Kingdom, Tuesday Morning, Tuffy Auto, URGENT CARE, Verizon, Walmart, World Mkt
101a b	rd 46a, FL 417 (**toll**), FL 46, Sanford, Heathrow, N Applebee's, Coldstone, Crisper's, Duffy's Grill, F&D Cafe, FishBones, Friendly Confines Grill, McDonald's, Moe's SW Grill, Papa Joe's Pizza, Ruth's Chris Steaks, Shula's 347 Grill, Subway, Terra Mia Pizza Hampton Inn, Marriott, Residence Inn, Westin Publix, URGENT CARE, Walgreens, S Giovanni's, Jersey Mike's, Marco's Pizza, Smokey Joe's BBQ 7-11, Acura, CarMax, CVS Drug, Honda, Infiniti, Kohl's, Mercedes, Publix, Sam's Club/gas, Toyota
98	Lake Mary Blvd, Heathrow, N Shell Casey's Grill, Luigino's Italian, Panera Bread, RW Blue Grill, Stonewood Grill, Subway Courtyard, Hyatt Place CVS Drug, Walgreens, Winn-Dixie, S 7-11, BP/24hr, Marathon/Kangaroo/dsl, Mobil/dsl Arby's, Baskin-Robbins/Dunkin', Bob Evans,

HEATHROW

98	Continued Boston Mkt, Burger Fi, Burger King, Chick-fil-A, Chili's, C na King, Chipotle Mexican, Chop Stix, Domino's, Dunk Firehouse Subs, Fred's Mkt, Jason's Deli, Jimmy John's, K Longhorn Steaks, Marble Slab, McDonald's, Mikado Japane Noodles&Co, Panera Bread, Papa Joe's Pizza, Papa John's, P Murphy's, Starbucks, Steak'n Shake, Subway, Taco Bell, Ti Kilt, Wendy's, Which Wich? Candlewood Suites, Exte ed Stay America, Hilton Garden, Homewood Suites, La Qu ta Advance Parts, AT&T, Fresh Mkt, GNC, Goodyear/a Home Depot, Office Depot, Petsmart, Publix, Ross, Stap Target, Tires+, TJ Maxx, USPO, Verizon, Walgreens
95mm	**both lanes, 24hr security, full facilities, litter barrels, walk, , vending**
94	FL 434, to Winter Springs, Longwood, N 7-11, Chev Mobil/7-11/dsl Burger King, China Gate, FirstWatch C Imperial Dynasty, Jimmy John's, Kobe Japanese, Melting Rest., Mykonos Greek, Panera Bread, Papa Joe's Pizza, S bucks, Starbucks, Tijuana Flats, Wendy's CVS Drug, Pub vet, S Bonefish Grill, Boston Mkt, Carmela's Rest., Pick NY, Smokehouse H

ALTAMONTE SPGS

92	FL 436, Altamonte Springs, N 7-11, Chevron/dsl, Sh Circle K/dsl Boston Mkt, Checkers, Chick-fil-A, Chip Mexican, ChuckeCheese, Cracker Barrel, Kobe Japanese, L Caesar's, Longhorn Steaks, McDonald's, Olive Garden, kins, Pollo Tropical, Popeye's, Red Lobster, Sweet Tomat Taco Bell, Twin Peaks, Waffle House, WingHouse Days Hampton Inn, Howard Johnson, Quality Inn, Ramada, R ington Inn, Residence Inn, SpringHill Suites Best Buy, Drug, Family$, Firestone/auto, O'Reilly Parts, Tire Kingd U-Haul, URGENT CARE, Walgreens, S BP/Circle K, Chev Mobil/dsl, Speedway/dsl Bahama Breeze, Burger K Chili's, Coldstone, Denny's, Duffy's Grill, Dunkin', Five Guys, son's Deli, Moe's SW Grill, Orlando Alehouse, Panda Expr Pei Wei, Starbucks, Steak'n Shake, Subway, Wendy's bassy Suites, Extended Stay America, Hilton H, Adva Parts, Albertson's, AT&T, Barnes&Noble, CVS Drug, Dillard's Penney, Marshall's, PetCo, Publix, Ross, Whole Foods Mkt
90b a	FL 414, Maitland Blvd, N 7-11 Applebee's, Chick-f Oak Grill, Wendy's Extended Stay America, Extended America (2), Homewood Suites, Sheraton, S Maitland Ar
88	FL 423, Lee Rd, N 7-11 Christner's Rest., IHOP, L Caesar's, LJ Silver/Taco Bell, McDonald's, Popeye's, Sh Rest., Wild Rice Buffet Europe Inn, InTown Suites, Mot Quality Inn Advance Parts, Family$, Firestone/auto, H Depot, O'Reilly Parts, VW, S Chevron/dsl, Sunoco D ny's Aamco, BMW
87	FL 426, Fairbanks Ave (no eb re-entry), N Speedw Dunkin'/dsl
86	Par St (from eb, no re-entry), S Shell/Circle K
85	Princeton St, S 7-11 Wendy's Comfort Suites
84	FL 50, Colonial Dr, Ivanhoe Blvd, N Crowne Plaza
83b	US 17, US 92, FL 50, Amelia St (from eb), N Crowne Pla
83a	FL 526 (from eb), Robinson St
83	South St (from wb), downtown
82c	Anderson St E, Church St Sta Hist Dist, downtown
82b	Gore Ave (from wb), S H, downtown
82a	FL 408 (**toll**), to FL 526
81b c	Kaley Ave, S Mobil H

INTERSTATE 4 Cont'd

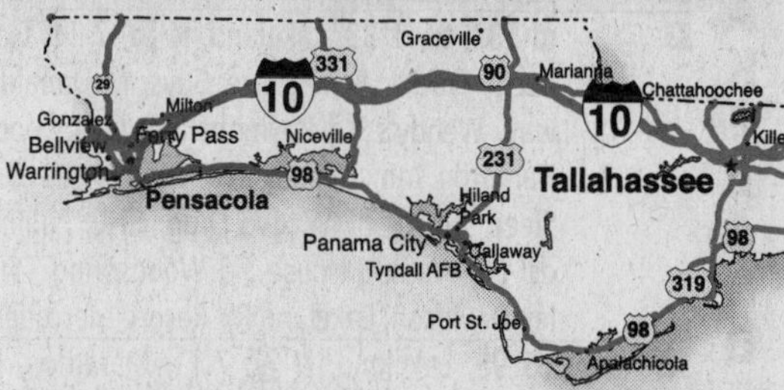

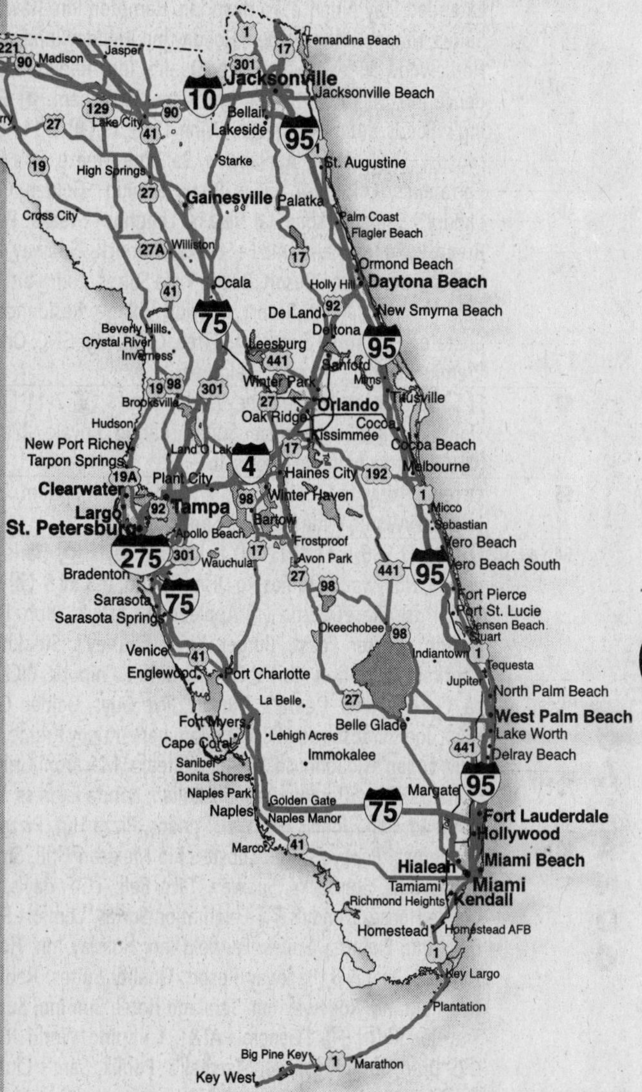

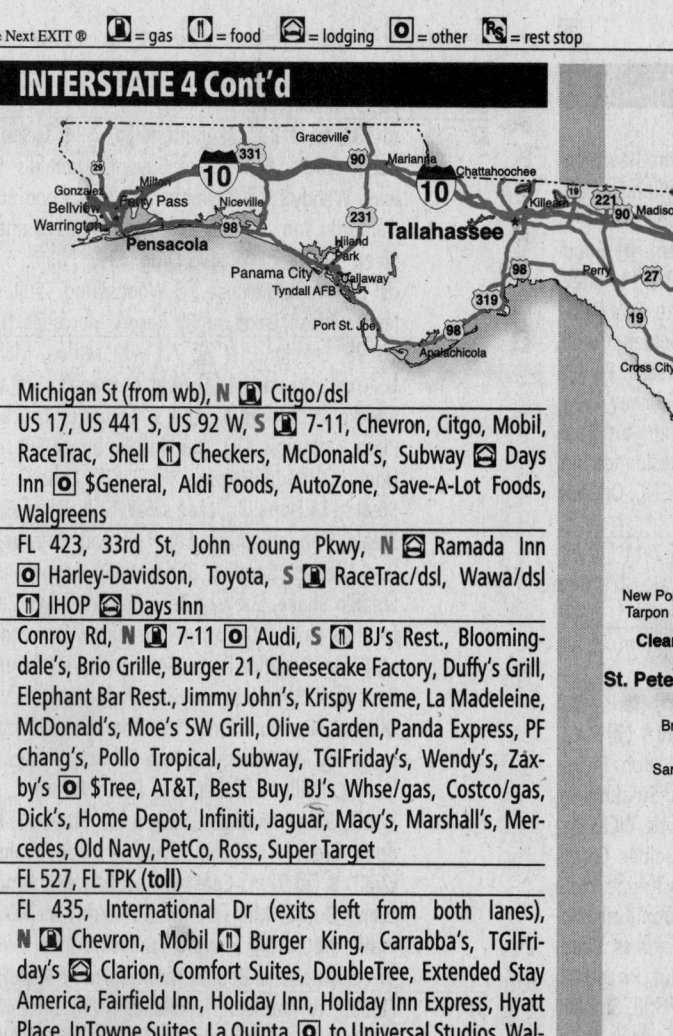

81a	Michigan St (from wb), **N** [gas] Citgo/dsl
80b a	US 17, US 441 S, US 92 W, **S** [gas] 7-11, Chevron, Citgo, Mobil, RaceTrac, Shell [food] Checkers, McDonald's, Subway [lodging] Days Inn [other] $General, Aldi Foods, AutoZone, Save-A-Lot Foods, Walgreens
79	FL 423, 33rd St, John Young Pkwy, **N** [lodging] Ramada Inn [other] Harley-Davidson, Toyota, **S** [gas] RaceTrac/dsl, Wawa/dsl [food] IHOP [lodging] Days Inn
78	Conroy Rd, **N** [gas] 7-11 [other] Audi, **S** [food] BJ's Rest., Bloomingdale's, Brio Grille, Burger 21, Cheesecake Factory, Duffy's Grill, Elephant Bar Rest., Jimmy John's, Krispy Kreme, La Madeleine, McDonald's, Moe's SW Grill, Olive Garden, Panda Express, PF Chang's, Pollo Tropical, Subway, TGIFriday's, Wendy's, Zaxby's [other] $Tree, AT&T, Best Buy, BJ's Whse/gas, Costco/gas, Dick's, Home Depot, Infiniti, Jaguar, Macy's, Marshall's, Mercedes, Old Navy, PetCo, Ross, Super Target
77	FL 527, FL TPK (**toll**)
75b a	FL 435, International Dr (exits left from both lanes), **N** [gas] Chevron, Mobil [food] Burger King, Carrabba's, TGIFriday's [lodging] Clarion, Comfort Suites, DoubleTree, Extended Stay America, Fairfield Inn, Holiday Inn, Holiday Inn Express, Hyatt Place, InTowne Suites, La Quinta [other] to Universal Studios, Walgreens, **S** [gas] 7-11, Chevron/dsl, Speedway/dsl [food] Black Angus Steaks, Burger King, Del Taco, Denny's, IHOP, Red Lobster, Sonic, Subway, Sweet Tomatoes [lodging] Best Western, Day Inn, Hampton Inn, Hilton Garden, Homewood Suites, International Palms Inn, La Quinta, Motel 6, multiple hotels & resorts, Sheraton, Sunsol Hotel, Super 8 [other] Artegon/famous Brands, Bass Pro Shops, Walgreens
74b	**N** [other] Universal Studios (from wb)
74a	FL 482, Sand Lake Rd, **N** [gas] 7-11, Chevron [food] Chick-fil-A, Dunkin a Donuts, Fresca Italian, McDonald's, O'Charley's, Pei Wei, Wendy's, Zoe's Kitchen [lodging] Drury Inn [other] [H], $Tree, GNC, Michael's, Publix, Tire Kingdom, Walgreens, Walmart/McDonald's, Whole Food Mkt, **S** [gas] BP/Circle K/dsl, Shell/Circle K/dsl [food] Bahama Breeze, BJ's Rest., Boston Lobster, Brickhouse Grill, Buffalo Wild Wings, Burger King, Capital Grille, Carrabba's, Charley's Steaks, Checkers, Chili's, China Jade, ChuckECheese, Chuy's Mexican, CiCi's Pizza, Coldstone, Dave&Buster's, Del Frisco's, Denny's, Domino's, Don Pablo's, Fish Bones Rest., Friendly's, Golden Corral, Hooters, IHOP, Joe's Crabshack, Kobe Japanese, Longhorn Steaks, Maggiano's, McDonald's, Miller's Alehouse, Ming Court, Olive Garden, Outback Steaks, Panda Express, Perkins, Pizza Hut, Ponderosa, Popeye's, Red Robin, Senor Frogs, Subway, TGIFriday's, Tommy Bahama's, Tony Roma, Twin Peaks, Uno, Vito's Chophouse, Yardhouse [lodging] Avanti Resort, Best Western, Castle Hotel, Comfort Inn, Courtyard, Crowne Plaza, EconoLodge, Embassy Suites, Extended Stay America, Fairfield Inn, Hampton Inn, Hampton Inn (2), Holiday Inn Express, Homewood Suites, Hyatt Place, Hyatt Regency, La Quinta, La Quinta (2), Ramada Inn, Residence Inn, Rosen Suites, Sonesta Suites, Springhill Suites, Wyndham Resort [other] Harley-Davidson, Ripley's Believe-it-or-not!, Walgreens

ORLANDO

72	FL 528 E (**toll**, no eb re-entry), to Cape Canaveral, **N** [other] USPO, **S** [lodging] Hilton [other] to [airport]
71	Central FL Pkwy (from eb no re-entry), **S** [gas] 7-11/dsl, Chevron, Wawa/dsl [food] Bonefish Grill, Buffalo Wild Wings, KFC, McDonald's, Mellow Mushroom, Panera Bread, Starbucks, Taco Bell, TGIFridays, Wendy's [lodging] Fairfield Inn, Hampton Inn, Hilton Garden, Renaissance Resort, Residence Inn, Springhill Suites, to SeaWorld [other] CVS, Publix, Walgreens
68	FL 535, Lake Buena Vista, **N** [gas] 7-11, Mobil/dsl, Shell/Circle K/dsl [food] AleHouse, Black Angus Steaks, Black Fire Brazilian Steaks, Buffalo Wild Wings, Burger King, Chevy's Mexican, Chili's, China Buffet, CiCi's Pizza, Denny's, Domino's, Dragon Super Buffet, Dunkin', El Patron, Firehouse Subs, Flipper's Pizzaria, Fuddrucker's, Giordano's, Hooters, IHOP, Jamba Juice, Joe's Crabshack, Johnnie's Rest., Kobe Japanese, Macaroni Grill, McDonald's, Noodles&Co, Olive Garden, Papa John's, Perkins, Pizza Hut, Qdoba, Red Lobster, Seadog Brewing, Shoney's, Sofrito Latin Cafe, Steak'n Shake, Subway, Sweet Tomatoes, Taco Bell, TGIFriday's, The Knife Argentinian Steaks, Tom+Chee, Uno, Waffle House [lodging] B Resort, Clarion, Comfort Inn, Courtyard, Delta Orlando, DoubleTree, Embassy Suites,

FL

INTERSTATE 4 Cont'd

ORLANDO

68 Continued
Extended Stay America, Fairfield Inn, Hampton Inn, Hawthorn Suites, Hilton, Hilton Garden, Holiday Inn, Holiday Inn Express, Homewood Suites, Hyatt Place, Quality Inn, Radisson, Residence Inn, Sheraton, StayBridge Suites, Wyndham Gooding's Foods/drug, Walgreens, Winn Dixie, **S** 7-11, Chevron/dsl, Shell/dsl Applebee's, Bahama Breeze, BJ's Rest., Carrabba's, Chick-fil-A, CiCi's Pizza, Dunkin', Golden Corral, Landry's Seafood, LoneStar Steaks, Longhorn Steaks, Panera Bread, Pollo Tropical, Santa Fe Steaks, Starbucks, Subway, Wendy's Blue Heron Resort, Buena Vista Suites, Courtyard, Fairfield Inn, Holiday Inn Resort, Marriott Village, Residence Inn, Sheraton, SpringHill Suites $Tree, CVS Drug, GNC, Orlando Premium Outlets, Verizon, Walgreens

67 Fl 536, to Epcot, **N** DisneyWorld, **1 mi S** 7-11 Fusion Rest. Buena Vista Suites, Caribe Royale, Marriott CVS Drug, multiple resorts, to

65 Osceola Pkwy, to FL 417 (**toll**), **N** Animal Kingdom, Epcot, to DisneyWorld, Wide World of Sports

64b a US 192, FL 536, to FL 417 (**toll**), to Kissimmee, **N** Harley-Davidson, Hollywood Studios, to DisneyWorld, **0-3 mi S** 7-11, Mobil/dsl, RaceTrac/dsl Applebee's, Arby's, Bob Evans, Boston Lobster Feast, Burger King, Charley's Steakhouse, Checkers, Chick-fil-A, Chili's, Chinese Buffet, Chipotle, CiCi's Pizza, Cracker Barrel, Denny's, Dunkin', Five Guys, Golden Corral, IHOP, Joe's Crabshack, KFC, Kobe Japanese, Krispy Kreme, Little Italy, Logan's Roadhouse, Longhorn Steaks, Macaroni Grill, McDonald's, Olive Garden, Pacino's Italian, Panda Express, Panera Bread, Papa John's, Pei Wei, Perkins, Pizza Hut, Pizza Hut, Ponderosa, Popeye's, Red Lobster, Rio Mexican Grill, Smokey Bones BBQ, Starbucks, Subway, Taco Bell, TGIFriday's, Uno, Waffle House, Wendy's Celebration Suites, Comfort Suites, Days Inn, Embassy Suites, Fairfield Inn, Holiday Inn, Howard Johnson, Motel 6, Parkway Resort, Quality Suites, Radisson, Red Roof Inn, Rodeway Inn, Seralago Hotel, Sun Inn, Super 8, Travelodge H, $General, AT&T, Camping World RV Ctr, CVS Drug, Jo-Ann Fabrics, Marshall's, Publix, Sam's Club/dsl, Target, USPO, Walgreens

62 FL 417 (**toll**, from eb), World Dr, Celebration, **N** to DisneyWorld, **S** to

60 Fl 429 N (**toll**), Apopka

58 FL 532, to Kissimmee, **N** 7-11, BP/Circle K/dsl Chili's, China One, Dunkin', McDonald's, Pizzaria, Subway, Wendy's Championship Gate Resort Publix, Walgreens, **S** Reunion Resort (2mi)

55 US 27, to Haines City, **N** 7-11, Chevron/dsl, Loves/Arby's/dsl/scales/24hr, Sunoco/dsl Burger King, Cracker Barrel, Denny's, McDonald's, Waffle House, Wendy's Comfort Inn, Hampton Inn, Holiday Inn Express, Quality Inn FL Camp Inn (5mi), Ford, **S** 7-11, Marathon/dsl, RaceTrac/dsl, Wawa/dsl Bob Evans, CiCi's Pizza, Davenport's Ale House, Grand China, Perkins, Popeye's, Sake Steaks, Subway, Taco Bell Days Inn, Ramada Inn H, $Tree, AT&T, Best Buy, Books-A-Million, Deer Creek RV Resort, Dick's, Family$, GNC, JC Penney, KOA, Michael's, Petsmart, Ross, Staples, Target, Theme World RV Park, to Cypress Gardens, tourist info

48 rd 557, to Winter Haven, Lake Alfred, **S** Marathon/dsl

46mm **both lanes, 24hr security, full facilities, litter barrels, petwalk, , , vending**

44 FL 559, to Auburndale, **S** Loves/Arby's/dsl/scales/24hr, Shell/Subway/dsl/scales/24hr

LAKELAND

41 FL 570 W **toll**, Auburndale, Lakeland

38 FL 33, to Lakeland, Polk City

33 rd 582, to FL 33, Lakeland, **N** 7-11, Exxon/dsl Ap bee's, Cracker Barrel, Five Guys, McDonald's, Starbucks, way, Wendy's Baymont Inn, Crestwood Suites, Days Hampton Inn, Holiday Inn Express, La Quinta, Quality Sleep Inn BMW, CVS Drug, GNC, Publix, **S** Marat dsl Waffle House Woodspring Suites H, ley-Davidson, Lakeland RV Resort, Mercedes, Nissan

32 US 98, Lakeland, **N** 7-11, Marathon, Mobil/dsl, Mu USA/dsl, Wawa/dsl Beef o' Brady's, Buffalo Wild W Checkers, Chick-fil-A, Chili's, Chipotle, ChuckeCheese, C Pizza, Domino's, DQ, Dunkin', Firehouse Subs, Golden Co Hooters, Hungry Howie's, IHOP, KFC, Little Caesar's, Long Steaks, McDonald's, Moe's SW Grill, Olive Garden, Out Steaks, Panda Express, Panera Bread, Papa John's, Pizza Red Lobster, Smokey Bones BBQ, Sonny's BBQ, Starb Steak'n Shake, Subway, Taco Bell, Wendy's, Zaxby's C fort Inn, La Quinta, TownPlace Suites, Travelodge $Ge al, $Tree, Advance Parts, Aldi Foods, AT&T, AutoZone, Be Best Buy, Big Lots, Chrysler/Dodge/Jeep, CVS Drug, D Dillard's, Discount Tire, Firestone/auto, Goodyear/auto, by Lobby, JC Penney, JoAnn Fabrics, Lowe's, Michael's, Navy, O'Reilly Parts, PepBoys, PetCo, Petsmart, Publix, Ross World, Sam's Club/gas, Save a Lot, Staples, Target, Tire K dom, Tires+, TJ Maxx, Toyota, Verizon, Walgreens, Wal (2mi), **S** 7-11, Coastal, RaceTrac/dsl, Sunoco/dsl Evans, Burger King, Denny's, Dunkin', McDonald's, Pope Waffle House Howard Johnson, Motel 6, Ramada $Tree, AutoZone, Beall's, Family$, Home Depot, NAPA, U-H

31 FL 539, to Kathleen, Lakeland, **N** Circle K/dsl, Mara Romeo's Pizza, Subway, Wendy's Publix/dsl, greens, **S** hist dist

28 FL 546, to US 92, Memorial Blvd, Lakeland (from eb re-en **S** Citgo, Shell/Circle K/dsl, Sunoco/dsl Hardee's

27 FL 570 E **toll**, Lakeland

25 County Line Rd, **S** Mobil/dsl, Shell/Circle K/Subway Donald's, Wendy's Fairfield Inn FL Air Museum

22 FL 553, Park Rd, Plant City, **N** Smokin Aces BBQ C rolet, **S** Shell/Circle K/Subway Arby's, Burger K Denny's, Popeye's Comfort Inn, Holiday Inn Express

21 FL 39, Alexander St, to Zephyrhills, Plant Cityon FL 39, **S** dsl, Mobil/dsl Knights Inn, Red Rose Inn/rest.

19 FL 566, to Thonotosassa, **N** Marathon/dsl, **S** Race dsl, Wawa/dsl Applebee's, BuddyFreddy's Rest., Bu King, Carrabba's, Lin's Chinese, Little Caesar's, McDonald's Casa, OutBack Steaks, Pizza Hut/Taco Bell, Sonny's BBQ, bucks, Subway, Waffle House Hampton Inn H, $ eral, AT&T, GNC, Publix, Walgreens

17 Branch Forbes Rd, **N** Citgo/dsl, Marathon/dsl Dino World, **S** BP, Citgo/dsl, Shell/Circle K/Subway/dsl vance Parts, AutoZone

MANGO

14 McIntosh Rd, **N** BP/dsl Camping World RV Ctr, W ward RV Park (2mi), **S** 7-11/dsl, Marathon/dsl, Race dsl, Speedway/dsl Burger King, McDonald's/play East Tampa RV Park, General RV Ctr, Tampa RV Ctr

12mm **weigh sta both lanes**

10 rd 579, Mango, Thonotosassa, **N** FLYING J/Denny's LP/scales/24hr, Sunoco, TA/Arby's/Popeye's/dsl/scales/24h Bob Evans, Cracker Barrel Country Inn&Suites, Ha ton Inn Ford/Lincoln, Hillsboro River SP, Lazy Day's RV

INTERSTATE 4 Cont'd

10 Continued
Resort, S Shell/Circle K/dsl Hardee's, Subway, Wendy's Masters Inn

9 I-75, N to Ocala, S to Naples

7 US 92W, to US 301, Hillsborough Ave, N Mobil/dsl, Mobil/rest./dsl/scales/24hr, Wawa/dsl Waffle House Hard Rock Hotel/casino, S BP, Speedway/Dunkin'/dsl, Wawa/dsl Five Guys, WingHouse Comfort Suites, Holiday Inn Express, La Quinta, Red Roof Inn FL Expo Fair

6 Orient Rd (from eb)

5 FL 574, MLK Blvd, N McDonald's truck/rv wash, S BP, Mobil, Sunoco/Subway Wendy's Fairfield Inn Kenworth

3 US 41, 50th St, Columbus Dr (exits left from eb), N Chevron/dsl, Shell/Subway/dsl Days Inn, Quality Inn $General, to Busch Gardens, S Marathon/dsl, Sunoco/Circle K/dsl Burger King, Checkers, Church's, KFC, McDonald's, Salem's Subs, Subway, Taco Bell Rodeway Inn Advance Parts, Family$, Save-A-Lot, URGENT CARE

1 FL 585, 22nd, 21st St, Port of Tampa, S Sunoco Burger King, McDonald's museum

I-4 begins/ends on I-275, exit 45b.

INTERSTATE 10

Exit # Services

363mm **I-10 begins/ends on I-95, exit 351b.**

362 Stockton St, to Riverside, S BP, Gate H

361 US 17 S (from wb)

360 FL 129, McDuff Ave, S Sunoco Popeye's

359 Luna St, to Lenox Ave (from wb)

358 FL 111, Cassat Ave, N Shell/Subway/dsl, Sunoco/Godfather's/Quiznos/dsl Burger King, McDonald's, Popeye's AutoZone, S BP/dsl, RaceWay/dsl Baskin-Robbins/Dunkin', Domino's, Krispy Kreme, Pizza Hut, Royal Buffet, Taco Bell, Wendy's Advance Parts, Discount Tire, Lowe's, Walgreens

357 FL 103, Lane Ave, N CNG, Speedway/dsl Andy's Sandwiches Knights Inn, Stars Rest Inn, S BP, Shell/dsl Applebee's, Bono's BBQ, Cross Creek Steaks, Hardee's, KFC, Lee's Dragon, McDonald's Diamond Inn, Sleep Inn CVS Drug, Firestone/auto, Home Depot, Office Depot, PepBoys

356 I-295, N to Savannah, S to St Augustine

355 Marietta, N Flash, S Speedway/Dunkin'/dsl Domino's

354 Hammond Blvd

351 FL 115, Chaffee Rd, to Cecil Fields, N Kangaroo/dsl $General, Campers RV Ctr, S Shell/Subway/dsl, Valero Cracker Barrel, King Wok, McDonald's, Mr Chubby's Wings, Perard's Italian, Subway, Wendy's Best Western, Fairfield Inn, Hampton Inn, Holiday Inn Express Family$, Winn-Dixie

350 FL 23, Cecil Commerce Ctr Pkwy

343 US 301, to Starke, Baldwin, S Pilot/Subway/dsl/scales/24hr, TA/Shell/Arby's/dsl/scales/24hr/@, Valero Burger King, McDonald's, Waffle House Red Roof Inn

336 FL 228, to Maxville, Macclenny, N Murphy USA/dsl Starbucks H, fireworks, GNC, Walmart/Subway

335 FL 121, to Lake Butler, Macclenny, N Mobil, Shell/dsl China Dragon, Crystal River Seafood, Domino's, Firehouse Subs, Hardee's, KFC, Krystal, McDonald's, Pier 6, Pizza Hut, Subway, Taco Bell, Waffle House, Wendy's, Woody's BBQ,

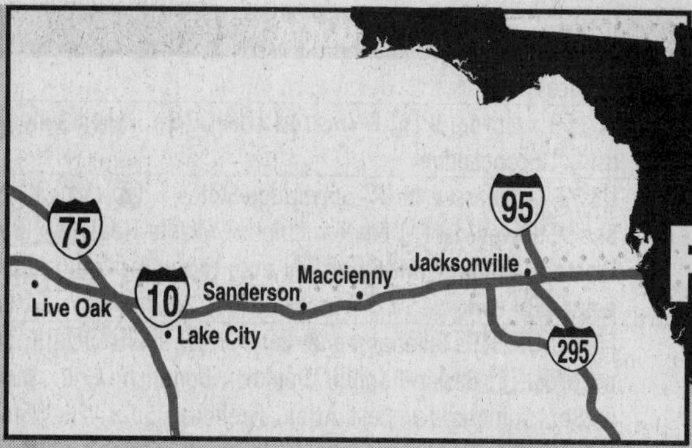

LAKE CITY LIVE OAK

335 Continued
Zaxby's Motel 6 H, $General, $Tree, Advance Parts, AutoZone, Save-A-Lot Foods, USPO, Verizon, vet, Walgreens, Winn-Dixie, S Exxon/dsl, RaceWay/dsl Burger King, China Buffet, San Jose Mexican EconoLodge, Travelodge

333 rd 125, Glen Saint Mary, N Citgo/dsl/e85

327 rd 229, to Raiford, Sanderson

324 US 90, to Olustee, Sanderson, S Mobil/dsl, Osceola NF, to Olustee Bfd

318mm **both lanes, 24hr security, full facilities, litter barrels, petwalk, vending**

303 US 441, Lake City, N Chevron/dsl Lake City Camping (1mi), Lake City RV Resort, S Shell/dsl, Sunoco/dsl Huddle House Days Inn H

301 US 41, to Lake City, N Marathon/Busy Bee/dsl to Stephen Foster Ctr, S H

296b a I-75, N to Valdosta, S to Tampa

294mm **both lanes, 24hr security, full facilities, litter barrels, petwalk, vending**

292 rd 137, to Wellborn

283 US 129, to Live Oak, N Busy Bee/Burger King/Dunkin'/dsl/24hr, to Boys Ranch, S BP, Chevron/dsl, Exxon/dsl, Murphy USA/dsl, Shell/dsl China Buffet, Hungry Howie's, Krystal, McDonald's, Subway, Taco Bell, Waffle House, Wendy's, Zaxby's EconoLodge, Holiday Inn Express, Quality Inn H, $Tree, GNC, Lowe's, Verizon, Walmart

275 US 90, Live Oak, N to Suwannee River SP, S H

271mm **truck insp sta both lanes**

269mm Suwannee River

265mm **both lanes, 24hr security, full facilities, litter barrels, petwalk, vending**

264mm **weigh sta both lanes**

262 rd 255, Lee, N to Suwannee River SP, S Jimmy's/Chevron/Red Onion Grill/dsl/scales/24hr/@, Loves/Arby's/dsl/scales/24hr

258 FL 53, N Chevron/McDonald's/dsl, Mobil/DQ/Subway/Wendy's/dsl/scales/24hr Denny's, Waffle House Best Western, Days Inn, Super 8 H, S Deerwood Inn Jellystone Camping, Madison Camping

251 FL 14, to Madison, N Mobil/Arby's/24hr H

241 US 221, Greenville, N Mobil/DQ

234mm **both lanes, 24hr security, full facilities, litter barrels, petwalk**

233 rd 257, Aucilla, N Shell/dsl

225 US 19, to Monticello, N Camper's World Camping, S Chevron/McDonald's/dsl, Mobil/Arby's/dsl, Sunoco/dsl Days Inn, Super 8 A Stones Throw RV Park, KOA

FL

INTERSTATE 10 Cont'd

TALLAHASSEE

Exit #	Services
217	FL 59, Lloyd, S BP/rest/dsl/scales/24hr, Shell/Subway/dsl EconoLodge
209b a	US 90, Tallahassee, N Staybridge Suites, S Circle K/dsl, Shell/Subway/dsl Eastern Chinese, Waffle House Best Western, Country Inn&Suites auto museum, Publix, Tallahassee RV Park
203	FL 61, US 319, Tallahassee, N BP/dsl, Shell/Circle K, Sunoco/dsl Baskin-Robbins/Dunkin', Bonefish Grill, Burger Bar, Chipotle, Far East Asian, Firehouse Subs, Five Guys, Hungry Howie's, Jimmy John's, McDonald's, Moe's SW Grill, Newk's Eatery, Panda Buffet, Panera Bread, Pepper's Cantina, Popeye's, Shogun Japanese, Smashburger, Sonny's BBQ, Starbucks, Subway, Taco Bell, Trader Joe's, Waffle House, Wendy's, Which Wich? $Tree, AT&T, Books-A-Million, CVS Drug, Discount Tire, Fresh Mkt Foods, GNC, Hobby Lobby, Petco, Publix, SteinMart, SuperLube, TJ Maxx, Walgreens, Walmart (3mi), S Citgo, Marathon/dsl Carrabba's, Chick-fil-A, McDonald's, Osaka Japanese, Outback Steaks, Steak'n Shake, Subway, Ted's MT Grill, TGIFriday's, TX Roadhouse, Village Inn, Zaxby's Courtyard, Extended Stay America, Hampton Inn, Hilton Garden, Holiday Inn Express, Mainstay Suites, Residence Inn H, Advance Parts, Goodyear/auto, Home Depot, Infiniti, Office Depot, O'Reilly Parts, Petsmart, U-Haul, URGENT CARE
199	US 27, Tallahassee, N Chevron/dsl, Kangaroo/dsl, McKenzie/dsl Burger King, Domino's, McDonald's, Papa John's, Pizza Hut, Starbucks, Subway, Taco Bell, Waffle House Baymont Inn, Baymont Inn, Best Western, Country Inn&Suites, Fairfield Inn, Holiday Inn, Microtel, Quality Inn $General, Ace Hardware, Advance Parts, AutoZone, Big Oak RV Park (2mi), CVS Drug, Family$, USPO, vet, Walgreens, Walmart, Winn-Dixie, S Chevron/dsl, Shell, Shell/Circle K Arby's, Boston Mkt, Chick-fil-A, China Buffet, ChuckECheese, Cracker Barrel, Crystal River Seafood, Denny's, DQ, Dunkin', El Jalisco, Firehouse Subs, Golden Corral, Guthrie's, Hardee's, Hooters, IHOP, Kacey's Rest, Krispy Kreme, Little Caesar's, Longhorn Steaks, McDonald's, Melting Pot, Papa John's, Red Lobster, Sonic, Sonny's BBQ, Starbucks, Subway, Wendy's, Whataburger, Zaxby's EconoLodge, Howard Johnson, La Quinta, Motel 6, Red Roof Inn, Rodeway Inn, Suburban Hotel, Travelodge, Wingate Advance Parts, AT&T, AutoZone, Barnes&Noble, Belk, city park, CVS Drug, PepBoys, Publix, Ross, Staples, Sun Tire, Tuffy Auto, U-Haul, Verizon, vet, Walgreens
196	FL 263, Tallahassee, S Chevron/dsl, Inland/dsl, Murphy USA/dsl, Shell/dsl, Stop'n Save Gas Applebee's, DQ, Dunkin', Firehouse Subs, KFC, McDonald's, Sonic, Steak'n Shake, Subway, Taco Bell, Waffle House, Wendy's, Zaxby's Sleep Inn $Tree, Advance Parts, , AutoZone, Chrysler/Dodge/Jeep, Harley-Davidson, Home Depot, Hyundai, Lowe's, Mazda, Office Depot, Toyota, Verizon, Walgreens, Walmart
194mm	**both lanes, 24hr security, full facilities, litter barrels, petwalk, , , vending**

QUINCY

Exit #	Services
192	US 90, to Tallahassee, Quincy, N FLYING J/Denny's/dsl/LP/scales/24hr, BP Comfort Inn, Howard Johnson Camping World RV Ctr (2mi), S Pilot/Subway/dsl/scales/24hr Waffle House Best Western
181	FL 267, Quincy, 1 mi N Murphy USA/dsl Domino's, Mayflower Chinese H, Walmart, S BP/dsl, Citgo/dsl Hampton Inn, Holiday Inn Express, Parkway Inn, to Lake Talquin SF
174	FL 12, to Greensboro, N Marathon/dsl, Shell/Burger King/dsl
166	rd 270A, Chattahoochee, N to Lake Seminole, S S dsl to Torreya SP, Triple C RV Park (1mi)
161mm	**both lanes, 24hr security, full facilities, litter barrels, walk, , , vending**
160mm	Apalachicola River, central/eastern time zone
158	rd 286, Sneads, N Lake Seminole, to Three Rivers SP
155mm	**weigh sta both lanes**
152	FL 69, to Grand Ridge, Blountstown, N Exxon/dsl, M thon/dsl
142	FL 71, to Marianna, Oakdale, N Murphy USA/dsl, Arby's/dsl/scales/24hr Beef'O'Brady's, Burger King, house Subs, Hong Kong Chinese, Pizza Hut, PoFolks, Ruby T day, San Marco's Mexican, Sonny's BBQ, Waffle House C fort Inn, Days Inn, Econolodge, Fairfield Inn, Marianna Microtel, Quality Inn, Super 8 H, $Tree, AT&T, Lowe's, Caverns SP (8mi), Verizon, Walmart/Subway, S Chevron TA/Pizza Hut/Popeye's/Taco Bell/dsl/scales/24hr/@ Dic BBQ, DQ, McDonald's Best Value Inn Dove Rest RV
136	FL 276, to Marianna, N to FL Caverns SP (8mi)
133mm	**both lanes, 24hr security, full facilities, litter barrels, walk, , **

CHIPLEY

Exit #	Services
130	US 231, Cottondale, N Chevron, Sunoco/dsl Hard Subway, S Loves/Chester's/McDonald's/dsl/sc 24hr/@
120	FL 77, to Panama City, Chipley, N Exxon/Burger K Stuckey's, Marathon/dsl, Murphy USA/dsl, Shell/dsl gel's Buffet, Arby's, Cancun Mexican, Dunkin', Hardee's, Hu Howie's, JinJin Chinese, KFC, McDonald's, Pizza Hut, Sonic, way, Waffle House, Wendy's Comfort Inn, Days Inn/ Executive Inn, Quality Inn, Super 8 H, $General, $ Advance Parts, Brickyard Mkt, NAPA, O'Reilly Parts, Ve Walmart, S Falling Water SP
112	FL 79, Bonifay, N Chevron, Shell/dsl, Tom Thu dsl Burger King, Cancun Mexican, Castaway Cafe, H ee's, Hungry Howie, McDonald's, Pizza Hut, Subway, W House Bonifay Inn, Holiday Inn Express, Tivoli Inn FL Springs RV Camping, Fred's, S Panama City Beach
104	rd 279, Caryville
96	FL 81, Ponce de Leon, N $General, to Ponce de Leon Vortex Spring Camping (5mi), S **both lanes, full facil , , litter barrels, petwalk, 24hr security,** Shell/ds noco, Sunoco/Subway/dsl Ponce de Leon Motel
85	US 331, De Funiak Springs, N Murphy USA/dsl, Sun dsl Arby's, Beef O'Brady's, Burger King, Hungry How McLain's Steaks, Pizza Hut, Sonic, Subway, Taco Bell, W House Econolodge, Regency Inn, Sundown Inn, S 8 $General, $Tree, AT&T, Buick/Chevrolet, Lowe's, zon, Walgreens, Walmart, winery, Winn-Dixie, S Su Sunoco/dsl, Sunoco/dsl KFC, McDonald's, Whatab er Best Western H
70	FL 285, to Ft Walton Bch, Eglin AFB, N Loves Donald's/Subway/dsl/scales24hr, RaceWay/dsl Sleep I-10 Truck Ctr, S Econolodge Dixie RV Ctr
60mm	**both lanes, 24hr security, full facilities, litter barrels, walk, , , vending**
56	FL 85, Crestview, Eglin AFB, N BP/dsl, Mobil/Chest dsl Applebee's, Beef O'Brady's, Burger King, Capt D's, na 1, Dunkin', Firehouse Subs, Golden Asian, Hungry Hov Hunon Chinese, Krystal, Lenny's Subs, McDonald's, Mia's Ita Panera Bread, Papa Murphy's, Ryan's, Sonic, Starbucks, Bell Country Inn&Suites, EconoLodge H, $Ger

FL

INTERSTATE 10 Cont'd

56	Continued Advance Parts, AT&T, AutoZone, BigLots, GNC, Lowe's, Publix, Staples, URGENT CARE, Verizon, Walgreens, Walmart, **S** Exxon/dsl, Tom Thumb/dsl Arby's, Cracker Barrel, Hardee's, Hooters, LaRumba Mexican, Waffle House, Wendy's, Whataburger, Zaxby's Baymont Inn, Best Value Inn, Comfort Inn, Holiday Inn Express, Quality Inn, Super 8 Buick/GMC, Chevrolet, Chrysler/Dodge/Jeep, Ford, Stay Suites
45	rd 189, to US 90, Holt, **N** Marathon (1mi) Eagle's Landing RV Park, to Blackwater River SP, **S** River's Edge RV Park (1mi)
31	FL 87, to Ft Walton Beach, Milton, **N** Exxon/dsl Waffle House Holiday Inn Express Blackwater River SP, KOA, **S** BP, Shell/dsl Blackwater Inn, Milton Inn
31mm	**both lanes, 24hr security, full facilities, litter barrels, petwalk,**
28	rd 89, Milton, **N** H
27mm	Blackwater River
26	rd 191, Bagdad, Milton, **N** Shell/Circle K/dsl H, $General, **S** Chevron/DQ/Stuckey's Pelican Palms RV Park
22	N FL 281, Avalon Blvd, **N** RaceWay/dsl, Tom Thumb McDonald's, **S** Shell/Circle K/Subway/dsl Waffle House Red Roof Inn Avalon Landing RV Park (3mi)
18mm	Escambia Bay
17	US 90, Pensacola, **N** Marathon/dsl, **S** Exxon/DQ Quality Inn/rest.
13	FL 291, to US 90, Pensacola, **N** Exxon, Shell/dsl Arby's, Capt D's, Denny's, La Hacienda Mexican, McDonald's, Santino's Cafe, Subway, Taco Bell, Waffle House Comfort Inn, Days Inn, Holiday Inn, La Quinta H, $Tree, CVS Drug, Ross, U-Haul, Walgreens, **S** Cheddar's, ChuckECheese, Dickey's BBQ, Egg&I Cafe, Fazoli's, HoneyBaked Ham, Jimmy John's, Moe's SW, O'Charley's, Shrimp Basket Rest, TX Roadhouse, Waffle House, Wendy's, Whataburger Baymont Inn, Best Value Inn, Courtyard, Econolodge, Extended Stay America, Fairfield Inn, Hampton Inn, Mainstay Suites, Red Roof Inn, Springhill Suites, Super 6 Inn, TownePlace Suites $General, Big Lots, Books-A-Million, Firestone/auto, GNC, Hobby Lobby, JC Penney, Jo-Ann Fabrics, Mr Transmission, PepBoys, Petsmart, TJ Maxx, Tuesday Morning, U-Haul, Verizon
12	I-110, to Pensacola, Hist Dist, Islands Nat Seashore
10b a	US 29, Pensacola, **N** Kangaroo/dsl/scales, Murphy USA/dsl Church's, Hardee's, Ryan's, Sonic $Tree, Advance Parts, AT&T, AutoZone, Carpenter's RV Ctr, GNC, Office Depot, O'Reilly Parts, Tires+, Walmart, **0-2 mi S** RaceWay/dsl, Shell/Circle K, Tom Thumb 3D Burgers, Capt D's, IHOP, McDonald's, Pizza Hut, Smokey's BBQ, Subway, Waffle House, Wendy's, Whataburger Best Value Inn, Executive Inn, Key West Inn, Luxury Suites, Magnuson Hotel, Motel 6, Pensacola Inn $General, Buick/Cadillac/GMC, Chevrolet, Chrysler/Dodge/Jeep, Ford, funpark, Harley-Davidson, Honda, Hyundai, Kia, Lincoln, Mazda, NAPA Autocare, Nissan, Subaru, Toyota
7b a	Fl 297, Pine Forest Rd, **N** Chevron Beef'O'Brady's, Starbucks, Wendy's Best Western, Garden Inn, Quality Inn, Woodspring Suites Publix, transmissions, Walmart Mkt, **S** Raceway/dsl, Shell, Tom Thumb Burger King, Cracker Barrel, Hardee's, McDonald's, Ruby Tuesday, Sonny's BBQ, Subway, Waffle House, Wayne's Diner Country Inn&Suites, Days Inn, Econolodge, Hampton Inn, Holiday Inn Express, Red Roof Inn Big Lagoon SRA (12mi)

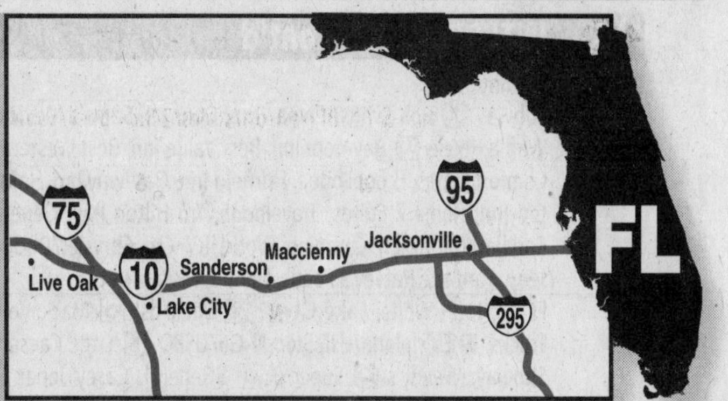

5	US 90 A, **N** Shell/Circle K, Shell/dsl Beef'O Brady's, Hot Head Burrito, Jersey Mike's, Ollie's Grill, Papa Murphy's, Starbucks, Wendy's AT&T, Publix/gas, Verizon, Walgreens, **S** Leisure Lakes Camping
4mm	**Welcome Ctr eb, 24hr security, full facilities, info, litter barrels, petwalk, , vending, wi-fi**
3mm	**weigh sta both lanes**
1mm	**inspection sta eb**
0mm	Florida/Alabama state line, Perdido River

LAKE CITY

FL

INTERSTATE 75

Exit #	Services
471mm	Florida/Georgia state line
469mm	**Welcome Ctr sb, full facilities, info, litter barrels, petwalk, , vending**
467	FL 143, Jennings, **W** Marathon/dsl N Florida Inn fireworks, Jennings Camping
460	FL 6, Jasper, **E** Indian River Fruit/gas, Marathon/Burger King/dsl, Marathon/Huddle House/dsl Budget Inn, **W** Pilot/Subway/dsl/scales/24hr, Shell/dsl, Sunoco/dsl American Inn Suwanee River SP
451	US 129, Jasper, Live Oak, **E** Loves/Arby's/dsl/scales/24hr, Mobil/DQ/Subway/dsl, **W** Marathon/Wendy's/dsl Suwanee Music Park (4mi), to FL Boys Ranch
448mm	**weigh sta both lanes**
446mm	**insp sta both lanes**
443mm	Historic Suwanee River
439	to FL 136, White Springs, Live Oak, **E** Gate/dsl/e-85, Shell/dsl McDonald's Suwanee RV Camping (4mi), to S Foster Ctr, **W** Best Value Inn
435	I-10, E to Jacksonville, W to Tallahassee
427	US 90, to Live Oak, Lake City, **E** Chevron/dsl, Exxon, Murphy USA/dsl, Shell/dsl, Tesla EVC Arby's, Bojangles, Buffalo Wild Wings, Burger King, Cedar River Seafood, Chick-fil-A, CiCi's, Cracker Barrel, Domino's, DQ, Dunkin', El Potro, Elliano's Coffee, Firehouse Subs, Five Guys, Gondolier Italian, Hardee's, IHOP, Jersey Mike's, Krystal, Longhorn Steaks, McDonald's, Moe's SW Grill, Neapolitan Pizza, Ole Times Buffet, Olive Garden, Panda Express, Panera Bread, Papa John's, Red Lobster, Ruby Tuesday, Sonny's BBQ, Starbucks, Steak'n Shake, Subway, Taco Bell, TX Roadhouse, Waffle House, Wendy's, Zaxby's Best Inn, Cypress Inn, Days Inn, Driftwood Inn, Holiday Inn, Quality Inn, Ramada Ltd, Rodeway Inn H, $Tree, Advance Parts, Aldi Foods, AT&T, AutoZone, Belk, BigLots, CVS Drug, Discount Tire, Ford/Lincoln, Hobby Lobby, Home Depot, Inn&Out RV Park, JC Penney, Kia, Lowe's, Michael's, Petsmart, Publix, Tire Kingdom, TireMart, TJ Maxx, Toyota, Verizon, Walgreens, Walmart, **W** Chevron/dsl, Circle K/dsl, Marathon/

INTERSTATE 75 Cont'd

LAKE CITY

427 Continued
Subway [food] Bob Evans, China One, Denny's, Salsa's Mexican, Waffle House [lodging] Baymont Inn, Best Value Inn, Best Western+, Comfort Suites, EconoLodge, Fairfield Inn, Gateway Inn, Hampton Inn, Home 2 Suites, Travelodge, Tru Hilton [other] $General, Cadillac/Chevrolet, Camping World RV Ctr, Chrysler/Dodge/Jeep, Family$, Harvey's Foods, Honda, Nissan, vet

423 FL 47, to Ft White, Lake City, E [gas] Shell/dsl [other] Mack/Volvo Trucks, W [gas] Inland/dsl, Stop-N-Go/USPO [food] Little Caesar's, Subway, Wendy's [lodging] Super 8 [other] $General, Casey Jones RV Park, Freightliner

414 US 41, US 441, to Lake City, High Springs, E [gas] Chevron/dsl, Exxon, Pitstop [lodging] Traveler's Inn [other] $General, W [gas] Marathon/dsl, Shell/Wendy's/dsl [food] Country Skillet, Subway [other] antiques, to O'Leno SP (5 mi)

413mm **[RS] both lanes, 24hr security, full [handicapped] facilities, litter barrels, petwalk, [phone], [picnic], vending**

409mm Santa Fe River

404 rd 236, to High Springs, E [gas] Chevron/fruits/gifts, Citgo/dsl, Marathon, W [other] High Springs Camping

399 US 441, to High Sprs, Alachua, E [gas] BP, Kangaroo [food] Domino's, El Toro, McDonald's, Mi Apa Latin Cafe, Moe's SW Grill, NY Pizza, Pizza Hut, Sonny's BBQ, Subway, Taco Bell, Waffle House [lodging] EconoLodge, Quality Inn [other] $General, Advance Parts, AT&T, AutoZone, CVS Drug, Family$, Hitchcock's Foods, Lowe's, Traveler's Campground (1mi), Verizon, vet, Walgreens, W [gas] Exxon/Kangeroo, Kangaroo/Wendy's, Mobil/Dunkin'/dsl, RaceWay/dsl [food] Hungry Howie's, Zaxby's [lodging] Best Value Inn, Royal Inn [other] Publix

FL

GAINESVILLE

390 FL 222, to Gainesville, E [gas] Circle K/Subway/dsl, Marathon/McDonald's/dsl, Valero/dsl [food] Burger King, Chan's Chinese, Pomodoro Cafe, Sonny's BBQ, Wendy's [other] Publix, Walgreens, W [gas] Shell/DQ/Dunkin'/dsl [food] Wahoo Grill [lodging] Best Western [other] Harley-Davidson, vet

387 FL 26, to Newberry, Gainesville, E [gas] Chevron/dsl, Shell/dsl, Sunoco [food] BJ's Rest., Bono's BBQ, Boston Mkt, Buffalo Wild Wings, Burger King, Dunkin', FoodCourt, HoneyBaked Ham, Jason's Deli, McAlister's Deli, McDonald's, Ocean Buffet, Panda Express, Panera Bread, Perkins, Red Lobster, Red Robin, Ruby Tuesday, Starbucks, Subway, Wendy's [lodging] La Quinta [other] [H], AT&T, Belk, Books-A-Million, Dillard's, Hobby Lobby, JC Penney, Office Depot, PetCo, to UF, Verizon, W [gas] BP, Chevron/dsl, Exxon/dsl, Marathon/dsl [food] Applebee's, Hardee's, Krystal, Moe's SW Grill, Napolatanos Rest., Peppers Mexican, Pizza Hut, Taco Bell, Waffle House [lodging] Baymont Inn, Best Value Inn, Days Inn, EconoLodge, TownePlace Suites [other] $Tree, Advance Parts, Goodyear/auto, Home Depot, PepBoys, Publix, tires/repair, TJ Maxx, vet, Walgreens

384 FL 24, to Archer, Gainesville, E [gas] Exxon/dsl, Shell, Valero/dsl [food] Arby's, Asian Wok, Blaze Pizza, BoneFish Grill, Burger King, BurgerFi, Carrabba's, Chick-fil-A, Chili's, Chipotle Mexican, Chuy's Mexican, CiCi's Pizza, Coldstone, Domino's, DQ, Firehouse Subs, Five Guys, Gainesville Alehouse, Hungry Howie's, KFC, McAlister's Deli, McDonald's, Moe's SW Grill, Olive Garden, Outback Steaks, Panda Express, Panera Bread, Panera Bread, Papa John's, Pizza Hut, Pollo Tropical, Sonny's BBQ, Starbucks, Steak'n Shake, Subway, Taco Bell, TGIFriday's, Tijuana Flats, TX Roadhouse, Waffle House, Wendy's, Wing House, Zaxby's, Zoe's Kitchen [lodging] Comfort Inn, Courtyard, Extended Stay America, Hampton Inn, Hilton Garden, Homewood Suites, Motel 6, Red Roof Inn, Residence Inn, Sleep Inn, SpringHill Suites,

GAINESVILLE

384 Continued
Super 8, The Lodge [other] $Tree, AT&T, AutoZone, Best CVS Drug, Discount Tire, Firestone/auto, GNC, Jo-Ann, Kc Lowe's, Michael's, Old Navy, Petsmart, Publix, Publix, Target, Trader Joe's, Tuesday Morning, Verizon, Walgre Walmart, W [gas] Marathon/dsl [food] Cracker Barrel [lodging] Co Inn&Suites, Holiday Inn Express [other] to Bear Museum

382 FL 121, to Williston, Gainesville, E [gas] Marathon/dsl, bil/dsl [food] First Wok, Little Caesar's, McDonald's, way [other] Publix, USPO, W [gas] Chevron/dsl, Circle K/dsl, S dsl [food] 43rd St Deli [lodging] Quality Inn, Rodeway Inn, Woods Suites [other] Fred Bear Museum

381mm **[RS] both lanes, 24hr security, full [handicapped] facilities, litter barrels, walk, [phone], [picnic], vending**

374 rd 234, Micanopy, E [gas] BP, Chevron/dsl [other] antiques Paynes Prairie SP, W [lodging] Micanopy Inn [other] repair

368 rd 318, Orange Lake, E [gas] Jim's/BBQ, Petro/BP/Iron Sk dsl/scales/24hr/@ [food] Wendy's [other] Grand Lake RV Park (3 W [other] Ocala N RV Camping

358 FL 326, E [gas] Marathon/McDonald's/dsl, Pilot/Arby's scales/24hr, Pilot/Wendy's/dsl/scales/24hr, Sunoco/FL rus Ctr/dsl [other] auto/truck repair, Freightliner, W [gas] Lo /Chester's/Subway/dsl/scales/24hr, Shell/Circle K/dsl [food] DQ

OCALA

354 US 27, to Silver Springs, Ocala, E [gas] Marathon/dsl, R Trac/dsl [food] Burger King, Rascal's BBQ [lodging] Golden Palms W [gas] BP/dsl, Chevron/dsl, Shell/dsl [food] Blanca's Cafe, C Taste, CiCi's, Darrell's Diner, McDonald's, Pizza Hut, Roma ian, Subway [lodging] Budget Host, Comfort Suites, Days Inn, ard Johnson, Motel 6 [other] $General, $Tree, AT&T, Family$, Nelson's Trailers, Oaktree Village Camping, Publix, Walgre Winn-Dixie

352 FL 40, to Silver Springs, Ocala, E [gas] Chevron/dsl, Mobil cle K/dsl, RaceTrac/dsl, Sunoco/dsl, Valero/dsl [food] Dun McDonald's, Subway, Taco Bell, Waffle House, Wendy's, by's [lodging] Days Inn/café, Motor Inn/RV [other] Family$, to S River SP (8mi), W [gas] Shell/dsl [food] Burger King, Denny's, fle House [lodging] Red Roof Inn, Super 8 [other] Holiday Trav-L Pa

350 FL 200, to Hernando, Ocala, **0-2 mi** E [gas] BP/dsl, Citgo/dsl, aco/dsl [food] Applebee's, Arby's, Black Bear Smokehouse, Evans, Boston Mkt, Burger King, Carrabba's, Checkers, C fil-A, Chili's, Chipotle, ChuckECheese, Cody's Roadhouse, C stone, Crisper's, Domino's, El Toreo Mexican, Firehouse S Five Guys, Freddy's, Golden Corral, Hardee's, Hungry How Jersey Mike's, Jimmy John's, Krystal, Lee's Chicken, Log Roadhouse, Maddio's Pizza, McDonald's, Moe's SW Grill, O Buffet, Olive Garden, Outback Steaks, Panda Express, Pa Bread, Papa John's, Papa Murphy's, PDQ Grill, Pizza Hut, Lobster, Ruby Tuesday, Smoothie King, Sonic, Sonny's Starbucks, Stevie B's Pizza, Subway, Taco Bell, Wendy's, my House, Zaxby's [lodging] Country Inn&Suites, Hilton, La Qui Quality Inn [other] [H], $Tree, Acura, Advance Parts, Aldi Fo Belk, Best Buy, Chevrolet, CVS Drug, Discount Tire, Goody auto, Hobby Lobby, Home Depot, Honda, Hyundai, JC ney, Jo-Ann Fabrics, Kia, Lowe's, Macy's, Mazda, Micha Nissan, Office Depot, O'Reilly Parts, PepBoys, Petsmart, F Staples, Target, Tire Kingdom, TJ Maxx, Toyota, Tuesday M ing, Tuffy Auto, URGENT CARE, Verizon, Walgreens, Waln W [gas] Marathon, RaceTrac/dsl, Tesla EVC, Valero/Kanga WaWa/dsl [food] Bonefish Grill, Burger King, Cheddar's, Cra Barrel, Crazy Cucumber, Dunkin', Edo Japanese, Gator's D side, KFC, Las Margaritas, McAlister's Deli, McDonald's, Mi Cafe, Panera Bread, Starbucks, Steak'n Shake, Tijuana F

INTERSTATE 75 Cont'd

350 Continued
Waffle House, Yamato Japanese [lodging] Best Western, Courtyard, Fairfield Inn, Hampton Inn, Holiday Inn, Homewood Suites, Residence Inn [other] [H], AT&T, Barnes&Noble, BMW, Buick/GMC, Cadillac, Dick's, Dillard's, Kohl's, Ocala RV Park, Old Navy, PetCo, Porsche, Sam's Club/gas, Tires+, Verizon, vet, VW, Walgreens

346mm **[RS] both lanes, 24hr security, full [handicapped] facilities, litter barrels, petwalk, [phone], [picnic], vending**

341 rd 484, to Belleview, E [gas] Exxon/dsl, Marathon/fruit, RaceTrac/dsl, Shell/dsl [food] Baskin-Robbins/Dunkin', Cracker Barrel, KFC/Taco Bell, Sonny's BBQ, Zaxby's [lodging] Microtel, Sleep Inn [other] drag racing museum, FL Citrus Ctr, W [gas] Pilot/DQ/Wendy's/dsl/scales/24hr [food] McDonald's, Subway, Waffle House [lodging] Hampton Inn [other] Ocala Sun RV Resort, outlets

338mm **weigh sta both lanes**

329 FL 44, to Inverness, Wildwood, E [gas] Marathon/dsl, Pilot/Steak'n Shake/dsl/scales/24hr, Sunoco [food] Burger King, McDonald's, Waffle House, Wendy's [other] FL Citrus Ctr, KOA, W [gas] Citgo/dsl/repair/24hr, Pilot/dsl/scales/24hr, TA/BP/Pizza Hut/Popeye's/Subway/dsl/scales/24hr/@ [food] IHOP, KFC [lodging] Budget Inn, Days Inn, Motel 6 [other] truck repair, truckwash

328 FL TPK (from sb), to Orlando

321 rd 470, to Sumterville, Lake Panasoffkee, E [gas] Spirit/deli/dsl/scales/24hr [other] Coleman Correctional, W [gas] Chevron/Circle K/dsl, Mobil/Hardee's/Subway/dsl [other] Countryside RV Park, KOA

314 FL 48, to Bushnell, E [gas] Citgo, Murphy USA/dsl, Shell/Circle K/Subway [food] Hong Kong Chinese, KFC/Taco Bell, Little Caesar's, McDonald's, Wendy's [lodging] Bushnell Inn [other] $Tree, AutoZone, BlueBerry Hill RV Camp, Red Oaks Camp (1mi), to Dade Bfd HS, Verizon, vet, Walmart, W [gas] Love's/Arby's/dsl/scales/24hr, Sunoco/dsl [food] Beef'O'Brady's, Sonny's BBQ [lodging] Microtel [other] Flagship RV Ctr

309 rd 476, to Webster, E [other] Breezy Oaks RV Park (1mi), Sumter Oaks RV Park (1mi)

307mm **[RS] both lanes, 24hr security, coffee, full [handicapped] facilities, litter barrels, petwalk, [phone], [picnic], vending**

301 US 98, FL 50, to Dade City, E [gas] RaceTrac/dsl [food] Beef'O'Brady's, Cracker Barrel, Dunkin', McDonald's, Monticello's Pizzaria, Subway, Taco Bell, Waffle House, Wendy's [lodging] Days Inn, Holiday Inn Express [other] $General, Advance Parts, Winn-Dixie, W [food] Burger King [lodging] Hampton Inn, Microtel, Quality Inn [other] [H]

293 rd 41, to Dade City, E [gas] Citgo (2mi) [other] to Sertoma Youth Ranch, W [other] Travelers Rest Resort RV Park (3mi)

285 FL 52, to Dade City, New Port Richey, E [gas] FLYING J/Denny's/dsl/LP/scales/24hr [other] [H], Blue Beacon

279 FL 54, to Land O' Lakes, Zephyrhills, E [gas] Speedway/Dunkin'/dsl [food] Applebee's, Burger King, Chili's, China Wok, City Grill, Gonna China, Las Vallartas, Papa's John's, Pizza Hut/Taco Bell, Sonny's BBQ, Subway, Waffle House, Wendy's [other] Ace Hardware, Advance Parts, Beall's, Fiat, Ford, Happy Days RV Camping (9mi), Kia, Leasure Days RV Park (7mi), Nissan, Publix, Ralph's RV Camping (7mi), to Hillsborough River SP (18mi), Toyota, Walgreens, Walmart, W [gas] 7-11, Marathon, Mobil/Dunkin', Shell/Circle K/dsl [food] Beef'O'Brady's, ChuckeCheese, Cody's Roadhouse, Cracker Barrel, DQ, Hardee's, Hungry Howie's, Marco's Pizza, McDonald's, Outback Steaks, Winghouse [lodging] Best Western, EconoLodge, Rodeway Inn, Sleep Inn [other] $General, $Tree, Advance Parts, Best Buy, Chevrolet, CVS Drug, Dick's, GNC, Goodyear/auto, Honda, Hyundai, Mazda, Michael's, Old Navy, Petsmart, Quail Run RV Camping,

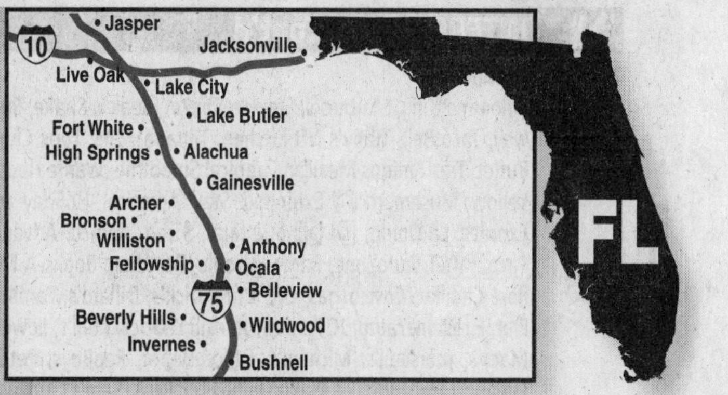

279 Continued
Ross, Tire Kingdom, TJ Maxx, Tuffy Auto, URGENT CARE, Verizon, Winn Dixie

277mm **[RS] both lanes, 24hr security, full [handicapped] facilities, litter barrels, petwalk, [phone], [picnic], vending**

275 FL 56, Land O Lakes, Tarpon Springs, E [gas] BP/Dunkin'/dsl, Gate/dsl, RaceTrac/dsl [food] Buffalo Wild Wings, TX Roadhouse [lodging] Hampton Inn, Holiday Inn Express [other] Mercedes, Mini, Publix (2mi), vet, W [gas] Shell/dsl [food] Abuelo's, Culver's [other] Tampa Outlets/famous brands, Walgreens

274 I-275 (from sb), to Tampa, St Petersburg

TAMPA

270 rd 581, Bruce B Downs Blvd, E [gas] 7-11, Mobil, Shell/Circle K/Taco Bell/dsl, Speedway/dsl [food] Baskin-Robbins/Dunkin', Boston Mkt, Chick-fil-A, Chili's, Chipotle, Coldstone, DQ, Glory Days Grill, Jimmy John's, Kobe Japanese, Kobe Japanese, Liang's Asian Bistro, McDonald's, Moe's SW Grill, Panera Bread, Papa John's, Pizza Hut, Ruby Tuesday, Senor T's, Starbucks, Steak'n Shake, Subway, TGIFriday's, Tijuana Flats, Wendy's [lodging] Holiday Inn Express, La Quinta [other] AT&T, Best Buy, CVS Drug, GNC, Home Depot, Kauffman Tire, Michael's, Publix, Tires+, Verizon, vet, Walgreens, Walmart/Subway, W [gas] 7-11 [food] McDonald's, Olive Garden, Red Lobster, Stonewood Grill [lodging] SpringHill Suites [other] $Tree, BJ's Whse/Subway/gas, CVS Drug, Jo-Ann Fabrics, Lowe's, Petsmart, Ross, Staples, USPO

266 rd 582A, Fletcher Ave, W [gas] Shell/Circle K/dsl [food] Baskin-Robbins/Dunkin', Bob Evans, Lenny's Subs, Starbucks, Wendy's [lodging] Courtyard, Extended Stay America, Fairfield Inn, Hampton Inn, Hilton Garden, Holiday Inn Express, Residence Inn, Sleep Inn, Sleep Inn [other] [H]

265 FL 582, Fowler Ave, Temple Terrace, E [other] flea mkt, Happy Traveler RV Park, W [gas] Marathon, Sunoco, Value/dsl [food] IHOP, Marco's Pizza [lodging] Ramada Inn [other] to Busch Gardens, to USF

261 I-4, W to Tampa, E to Orlando

260b a FL 574, to Mango, Tampa, E [gas] Citgo/dsl, Mobil, Shell/Circle K/Subway [food] Baskin-Robbins/Dunkin', China Wok, Domino's, Waffle House [other] Walgreens, Winn Dixie, W [gas] Citgo, Mobil [lodging] Quality Inn, Residence Inn, Sheraton, Staybridge Suites [other] Family$

257 FL 60, Brandon, E [gas] Mobil (2), Mobil/dsl, Shell/Circle K, Tesla EVC, WaWa/dsl [food] Bahama Breeze, Boston Mkt, Brandon Ale House, Buffalo Wild Wings, Checkers, Cheddar's, Cheesecake Factory, Chick-fil-A, Chili's, Chipotle, ChuckECheese, Corner Bakery Cafe, Denny's, Dunkin', Firehouse Subs, Firehouse Subs, Five Guys, Ford's Garage, Honeybaked Ham, Hungry Howie's, Jimmy John's, KFC, Kobe Japanese, Krispy Kreme, Little Caesar's, LJ Silver, Longhorn Steaks, Macaroni Grill, McDonald's, McDonald's (2), Mission BBQ, Moe's SW Grill, Olive Garden, Outback Steaks, Panda Express, Panera Bread, Papa John's, Popeye's, Portillo's, Qdoba, Red Lobster, Smokey Bones BBQ,

FL

BRANDON

INTERSTATE 75 Cont'd

257 Continued
Smoothie King, Starbucks, Steak'n Shake, Steak'n Shake, Subway, Taco Bell, Tibby's NO Kitchen, Tijuana Flats, Tops China Buffet, Tres Amigos Mexican, Tropical Smoothie, Waffle House, Yellow Mushroom Extended Stay America, Holiday Inn Express, La Quinta $General, $Tree, Aamco, Advance Parts, AT&T, AutoZone, Barnes&Noble, Best Buy, Books-A-Million, Cadillac, Costco/gas, CVS Drug, Dick's, Dillard's, Family$, Fiat, Firestone/auto, JC Penney, Jo-Ann Fabrics, Kohl's, Lowe's, Macy's, Marshall's, Michael's, Office Depot, PepBoys, PetCo, Petsmart, Petsmart (2), Publix, Publix (2), Ross, Sam's Club/gas, Staples, Target, Tires+, TJ Maxx, Verizon, Walgreens, Walmart, **W** Citgo/dsl, Marathon, Shell Bob Evans, Burger King, Hooters, McDonald's, Sonny's BBQ, Subway, Sweet Tomatoes, Wendy's Clarion, Comfort Suites, Country Inn&Suites, Courtyard, Embassy Suites, Fairfield Inn, Homewood Suites, La Quinta, Motel 6, Red Roof Inn, SpringHill Suites Bass Pro Shops, Buick/GMC, Chevrolet, Chrysler/Dodge/Jeep, Ford, Harley-Davidson, Home Depot, Honda, Hyundai, Kia, Mazda, Nissan, Office Depot, Toyota, VW

256 FL 618 W (**toll**), to Tampa

254 US 301, Riverview, **E** Thornton's/dsl, WaWa/dsl Panda Express, Steak'n Shake CVS Drug, Firestone/auto, Home Depot, Target, **W** 7-11/dsl China 1, Crazy Cafe, Dunkin', McDonald's, Pizza Hut, Smokin' Pig BBQ, Starbucks, Subway Hilton Garden GNC, Publix

250 Gibsonton Dr, Riverview, **E** 7-11/dsl, RaceWay/dsl, Victory Lane/dsl, WaWa/dsl Beef'O'Brady's, Burger King, DQ, Hungry Howie's, Jola Pizza, Little Caesar's, McDonald's, New China, Pizza Hut, Ruby Tuesday, Subway, Taco Bell, Wendy's $Tree, Alafia River RV Resort, Beall's, CVS Drug, Family$, Hidden River RV Resort (4mi), Lowe's, Save-a-Lot, USPO, Walgreens, **W** Murphy USA/dsl Walmart/McDonald's

246 rd 672, Big Bend Rd, Apollo Bch, **E** 7-11, Speedway/dsl, Thornton's/dsl Applebee's, Beef'O'Brady's, Buffalo Wild Wings, Burger King, China Taste, DQ, East Coast Pizza, Firehouse Subs, First Watch Cafe, Little Caesar's, McDonald's, Mi Casa, Panera Bread, Papa John's, PDQ Cafe, Pita's, Pizza Hut, Popeye's, Qdoba, Sakura Japanese, Sonic, Starbucks, Subway, Taco Bell, Tijuana Flats, Village Inn, Wendy's $General, $Tree, Ace Hardware, Advance Parts, AT&T, AutoZone, Beall's, Dunkin', Firestone/auto, GNC, Goodyear/auto, H, Kauffman Tire, Marshall's, Publix, Sam's Club/gas, Tire Choice, Tuffy Auto, URGENT CARE, Verizon, vet, Walgreens, Walmart Mkt, WaWa/dsl, Winn Dixie, **W** Shell/Circle K/Dunkin'/dsl

240b a FL 674, Sun City Ctr, Ruskin, **E** Shell Beef'O'Brady's, Bob Evans, BubbaQue's BBQ, Burger King, Checkers, China Star, Denny's, Dunkin', Hungry Howie's, Little Caesar's, Pizza Hut, Popeye's, Sonny's BBQ, Subway, Taco Bell, Wendy's Comfort Inn H, AT&T, Beall's, GNC, Home Depot, to Little Manatee River SP, Verizon, **W** Circle K/dsl, Marathon/dsl, RaceTrac/dsl China Wok, KFC, McDonald's Ruskin Inn $General, auto repair, BigLots, NAPA, SunLake RV Resort (1mi)

237mm **both lanes, 24hr security, full facilities, litter barrels, petwalk, , , vending**

229 rd 683, Moccasin Wallow Rd, to Parrish, **E** Little Manatee Sprs SRA (10mi), **W** Circle K, Fiesta Grove RV Park (3mi), Frog Creek RV Park (3mi), Terra Ceia RV Village (2mi), Winterset RV Park (3mi)

228 I-275 N, to St Petersburg

FL

BRADENTON

224 US 301, to Bradenton, Ellenton, **E** Mobil, Shell/Circl dsl Applebee's, Checkers, Chili's, Dunkin', Hungry How King's Wok, McDonald's, Peach's Rest., Ruby Tuesday, Sub Taco Bell, Wendy's, Winghouse, Woody's River Grill Ha ton Inn, Sleep Inn $General, $Tree, Ace Hardware, Be Ellenton Outlets/famous brands, GNC, TJ Maxx, U Walgreens, **W** Pilot/dsl Anna Maria's, W House Red Roof Inn, Super 8

223 Manatee River

220b a FL 64, to Zolfo Springs, Bradenton, **E** Lake Manatee **W** Citgo/dsl, Marathon/dsl, RaceTrac/dsl, Shell/Circl dsl Burger King, Cracker Barrel, Dunkin', IHOP, KFC/LJ S McDonald's, Sonny's BBQ, Starbucks, Subway, Waffle Ho Wendy's Best Value Inn, Best Western+, Days Inn, M 6, Quality Inn, Sunrise Inn H, Encore RV Resort (1mi), zeny's RV Ctr, Harley-Davidson, Toyota, Walmart

217b a FL 70, to Arcadia, **E** Speedway/dsl Burger King, ver's, Hungry Howie's, Jersey Mike's, Menchie's, PDQ Cafe Roadhouse, Wasabi Foods Holiday Inn Express Tire Choice/auto, Walmart/Subway, **W** 7-11/dsl, Marat Dunkin'/dsl, RaceTrac/dsl, Shell/Circle K Applebee's, Evans, Bogey's Rest., Boneyard BBQ, Chick-fil-A, DQ, Fred Gecko's Grill, Jimmy John's, LJ Silver/Taco Bell, McDona Papa John's, Rice Bowl, Starbucks, Subway Country I Suites $Tree, Beall's, CVS Drug, Lowe's, Pleasant Lake Resort, Publix, Tire Kingdom, Tires+, Tuffy Auto, Verizon

SARASOTA

213 University Parkway, to Sarasota, **E** Mobil/Subw dsl Alamo Steaks, Broken Egg Cafe, Chili's, First W Cafe, Little Greek, Pizza Hut Fairfield Inn, Holiday Hyatt Place H, GNC, Publix, URGENT CARE, Walgre **W** WaWa/dsl Apollonian Mediterranean, Blaze P BoneFish Grill, Brio, Buffalo Wild Wings, BurgerFi, Capital G Carrabba's, Cheesecake Factory, Chicken Kitchen, Chip Mexican, Daily Eats, Five Guys, Jason's Deli, Jersey Mike's S Jimmy John's, Kumo Japanese, Moe's SW Grill, Newk's Ea Panera Bread, Pei Wei, Ruby Tuesday, Seasons Rest., Selm Rest., Starbucks, Stonewood Grill, Subway, Sweet Tomat Tijuana Flats, Tom+Chee, Valentino's, Wendy's, Zoe's K en Homewood Suites, Courtyard, Hampton Inn $T AT&T, Best Buy, BJ's Whse/gas, CVS Drug, Dillard's, Fresh Foods, Home Depot, Jo-Ann Fabrics, Kohl's, Macy's, Marsh Michael's, Old Navy, PetCo, Ross, Staples, SteinMart, Targe Maxx, to Ringling Museum, Verizon, vet, Whole Foods Mkt

210 FL 780, Fruitville Rd, Sarasota, **E** Sun-N-Fun RV Park (1 **W** Marathon/dsl, Mobil/7-11/dsl, RaceTrac/dsl, S dsl Applebee's, Bob Evans, Burger King, Checkers, C fil-A, Chipotle, Culver's, Daruma Japanese, Dunkin', Fireh Subs, Five Guys, Gecko's Grill, Gonzalez Asian, Jersey Mi Jets Pizza, Longhorn Steaks, McDonald's, Perkins, Ping's nese, Pollo Tropical, Rodizio Grill, Starbucks, Subway, S Buffet, Taco Bell Homewood Suites (2mi), La Quinta, M stay Suites, Sleep Inn $Tree, Advance Parts, AT&T, Drug, GNC, Lowe's, Office Depot, Publix, Sam's Club, Tar Tire Kingdom, Winn-Dixie

207 FL 758, Sarasota, **E** RaceTrac/dsl, **W** BP/Subway/ Marathon/Dunkin'/Subway Arby's, Chili's, Domino's, Watch Cafe, Jimmy John's, Joey D's Eatery, McDonald's, Par Bread, Pizza Hut, Sarasota Alehouse, Starbucks, Steak'n Sh Taco Bell Hampton Inn H, Beall's, Home Depot, P lix, to Selby Botanical Gardens (8mi), Verizon, vet, Walgre Walmart

INTERSTATE 75 Cont'd

Exit #	Services
205	FL 72, to Arcadia, Sarasota, E Myakka River SP (9mi), W 7-11/dsl, Marathon/Jimmy John's/dsl, Mobil/7-11/dsl, Shell/Circle K Applebee's, Burger King, Chick-fil-A, Dunkin', Gecko's Grill, McDonald's, Starbucks, Subway, Waffle House, Wendy's Days Inn, Holiday Inn Express, Quality Inn Acura, Audi, Beall's, BMW, CVS Drug, Infiniti, Jaguar, Land Rover, Lexus, Mercedes/Smart, O'Reilly Parts, Publix, Tire Kingdom, Turtle Beach Camping (8mi), USPO, vet, Walgreens, Walmart Mkt, Windward Isle RV Park
200	FL 681 S (from sb), to Venice, Osprey, Gulf Bchs
195	Laurel Rd, Nokomis, E Shell/USPO/dsl Subway, W Encore RV Park (2mi), Scherer SP (6mi)
193	Jaracanda Blvd, Venice, W RaceTrac/dsl, Shell, Speedway/dsl, WaWa/dsl BrewBurgers, China Taste, Cracker Barrel, Culver's, Dunkin', McDonald's, Ping's Chinese, Tomatillo's Best Western+, Fairfield Inn, Holiday Inn Express CVS Drug, Publix, Verizon
191	rd 777, Venice Rd, to Englewood, W Encore RV Park (3mi), KOA (6mi), to Myakka SF (9mi)
182	rd 771, Sumter Blvd, to North Port
179	rd 779, Toledo Blade Blvd, North Port, W Mobil/Subway/dsl, Shell//dsl Burger King Publix
170	rd 769, to Arcadia, Port Charlotte, E 7-11/dsl, Murphy USA/dsl, RaceTrac/dsl Applebee's, Culver's Hampton Inn, Holiday Inn Express Lettuce Lake Camping (7mi), Riverside Camping (5mi), Walmart, W Mobil/Circle K/DQ/dsl, Shell/Circle K/Dunkin', Speedway/dsl Burger King, Cracker Barrel, Domino's, DQ, Golden China, Jets Pizza, McDonald's, Papa John's, Pizza Hut, Starbucks, Subway, Taco Bell, Top China, Waffle House, Wendy's Country Inn&Suites, La Quinta, Sleep Inn H, $General, $Tree, Ace Hardware, Advance Parts, Beall's, CVS Drug, Publix, vet, Walgreens, Winn-Dixie
167	rd 776, Port Charlotte
164	US 17, Punta Gorda, Arcadia, E 7-11/dsl, RaceWay/dsl, Shell/Circle K/dsl King House Chinese, RV camping, Subway, vet $General, Winn-Dixie, W Fisherman's Village Rest. (2mi) H
161	rd 768, Punta Gorda, W Marathon/DQ, Murphy USA/**dsl**, Pilot/Arby's/dsl/scales/24hr, Shell/dsl Burger King, McDonald's, Pizza Hut, Subway, Waffle House, Wendy's Best Value Inn, Holiday Inn Express, Knights Inn Encore RV Park (2mi), Walmart
160mm	**weigh sta both lanes**
158	rd 762, Tropical Gulf Acres, Tuckers Grade, E Babcock-Wells Wildlife Mgt Area
143	FL 78, to Cape Coral, N Ft Myers, E Marathon/dsl Seminole Camping (1mi), Up River Camping, W Loves/Subway/Wendy's/dsl/scales/24hr Encore RV Camping
141	FL 80, Palm Bch Blvd, Ft Myers, E Marathon, Sunoco/dsl Cracker Barrel, Waffle House Comfort Inn, Woodspring Suites, W Gulf, Mobil, Speedway/Dunkin'/dsl Domino's, Hardee's, KFC, Papa John's, Popeye's, Subway, Taco Bell $General, BigLots, CVS Drug, Family$, North Trail RV Ctr, Save-A-Lot, USPO, vet
139	Luckett Rd, Ft Myers, E Camping World RV Service/supplies, Cypress Woods RV Resort, W Pilot/Subway/dsl/scales/24hr/@
138	FL 82, to Lehigh Acres, Ft Myers, E 7-11/dsl Hyatt Place, W Mobil/dsl, RaceTrac/dsl, Sunoco/dsl Peterbilt

FT MYERS CAPE CORAL ESTERO

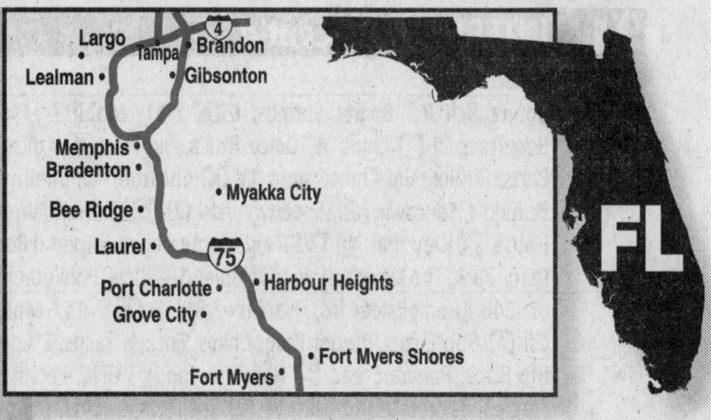

Exit #	Services
136	FL 884, Colonial Blvd, Ft Myers, E 7-11/dsl Bajio, Bella Mozzarella, Buffalo Wild Wings, Domino's, Firehouse Subs, Five Guys, McAlister's Deli, Moe's SW, Pizza Hut, Starbucks, Subway Candlewood Suites, Holiday Inn Express GNC, Home Depot, PetCo, Ross, Staples, Target, Winn Dixie, W 7-11/dsl, Marathon/dsl, Murphy USA/dsl, RaceTrac/dsl, Shell/Circle K/dsl Applebee's, Bellacino's, Bob Evans, Burger King, Chick-fil-A, Chili's, China King, Chipotle, Culver's, Dickey's BBQ, Dunkin', First Watch Cafe, Golden Corral, LJ Silver/Taco Bell, McDonald's, Panda Express, Pollo Tropical, Steak'n Shake, Subway, Tijuana Flats, Tropical Cafe, TX Roadhouse Woodspring Suites H, $Tree, AT&T, Beall's, BJ's Whse/gas, Hobby Lobby, Kohl's, Lowe's, Petsmart, Publix, Tire Choice/auto, Verizon, Walmart/McDonald's
131	rd 876, Daniels Pkwy, to Cape Coral, E **both lanes, full facilities, vending, litter barrels, petwalk, 24hr security,** RaceTrac/dsl, Shell/Subway/dsl Cracker Barrel, Fat Katz Comfort Inn, Dsys Inn, Sheraton Audi, CVS Drug, Harley Davidson, Porsche, W 7-11, RaceTrac/dsl, Shell/Circle K/dsl, Speedway/Dunkin'/dsl Arby's, Beef'O'Brady's, Burger King, Denny's, DQ, La Grotia, McDonald's, New China, Papa John's, Sports Page Grill, Starbucks, Subway, Taco Bell, Two Meatballs Italian, Waffle House, Wendy's Baymont Inn, Best Western, Hampton Inn, La Quinta, Quality Inn, SpringHill Suites, Travelodge H, AT&T, CVS Drug, Publix, Tire Choice/auto, Tuffy Auto, Walgreens
128	Alico Rd, San Carlos Park, E 7-11 Arby's, Aurelio's Pizza, BJ's Rest., BurgerFi, Carrabba's, Cheddar's, Chick-fil-A, Chili's, Chipotle, Connor's Steaks, Culver's, Famous Dave's BBQ, First Watch Cafe, Jason's Deli, Jimmy John's, Longhorn Steaks, McDonald's, Miller's Alehouse, Moe's SW Grill, Olive Garden, Outback Steaks, Panera Bread, PDQ Cafe, Pei Wei, PF Chang's, Pincher's Crabshack, Pita Pit, Pollo Tropical, Red Robin, Rita's, Starbucks, Subway, Taco Bell, Tijuana Flats, Twin Peaks, Zaxby's Courtyard, Drury Inn, Hilton Garden, Holiday Inn, Homewood Suites, Residence Inn $Tree, AT&T, Bass Pro Shop/Islamorada Fish Co, Belk, Best Buy, Costco/gas, Dick's, GNC, JC Penney, Jo-Ann Fabrics, Marshall's, PetCo, Ross, Staples, Target, Verizon, W 7-11/dsl, Marathon/Dunkin'/dsl, RaceTrac/dsl Family$
123	rd 850, Corkscrew Rd, Estero, E Marathon/7-11/dsl, Shell/Dunkin'/dsl Beef'O'Brady's, China Gourmet, Duffy's Grill, Dunkin', Ford's Garage, Marsala's Italian, McDonald's, Naples Flat Bread, Perkins, Subway, Wasabi Steaks CVS Drug, GNC, Johnson Tire/auto, Miramar Outlet/famous brands, Publix, W 7-11, Mobil/dsl, Speedway/Dunkin'/dsl Applebee's, Arby's, Culver's, Rib City, Ruby Tuesday Embassy Suites, Hampton Inn Chevrolet, Koreshan SHS (2mi), Lowe's, Tire Choice/auto, Woodsmoke RV Park (4mi)

FL

INTERSTATE 75 Cont'd

NAPLES

Exit #	Services
116	Bonita Bch Rd, Bonita Springs, E 7-11, Mobil/7-11/dsl, RaceTrac/dsl China A, Dolce Rita's, Subway Advance Parts, Publix, Tire Choice/auto, W Chevron/dsl, Shell/McDonald's, Speedway/dsl, Speedway/dsl (2) Culver's, Waffle House Days Inn CVS Drug, Home Depot, Imperial Bonita RV Park, Tire Kingdom, to Lovers Key SP (11mi), Walgreens
111	rd 846, Immokalee Rd, Naples Park, E 7-11, Mobil/dsl Bob Evans, Burger King, Chili's, Fuzzy's Tacos, L'Appetito Pizza, Panera Bread Hampton Inn GNC, Petsmart, Staples, Target, World Mkt, W Shell/Circle K/dsl McDonald's, Skillets, Subway H, Publix, to Delnor-Wiggins SP, Verizon, Walmart
107	rd 896, Pinebridge Rd, Naples, E BP/McDonald's/dsl China Garden, Giovanni Ristorante, Subway, Tropical Smoothie H, Publix, vet, Walgreens, W RaceTrac/dsl, Shell/Circle K/dsl Burger King, Five Guys, Hooters, IHOP, Napoli Pizza, Perkins, Senor Tequilas, Sophia's Rest., Starbucks, Waffle House Best Western, Hawthorn Suites, Spinnaker Inn Harley-Davidson, Johnson Tire/auto, Nissan, URGENT CARE, vet
105	rd 886, to Golden Gate Pkwy, Golden Gate, E Subway CVS Drug, W to , zoo
101	rd 951, to FL 84, to Naples, E Shell/Subway/dsl Fairfield Inn, SpringHill Suites, Woodspring Suites H, W Marathon/Subway/dsl, Mobil/Subway/dsl, Shell/dsl Chili's, China Dragon, Cracker Barrel, Dunkin', McDonald's, Taco Bell, Waffle House Comfort Inn, Holiday Inn Express, La Quinta, Super 8 $Tree, AT&T, Club Naples RV Resort, KOA (7mi), vet, Walmart
100mm	toll plaza eb
80	FL 29, to Everglade City, Immokalee, W Big Cypress NR, Everglades NP, Smallwoods Store
71mm	Big Cypress Nat Preserve, hiking, no security
63mm	**W both lanes, 24hr security, full facilities, litter barrels, petwalk, , , vending**
49	rd 833, Snake Rd, Big Cypress Indian Reservation, E Miccosukee Service Plaza/deli/dsl museum, swamp safari
41mm	**rec area eb, litter barrels,**
38mm	**rec area wb, litter barrels,**
35mm	**W /rec area both lanes, 24hr security, full facilities, litter barrels, petwalk, , , vending**
32mm	**rec area both lanes, litter barrels,**
25mm	motorist callboxes begin/end, **toll plaza** wb
23	US 27, FL 25, Miami, South Bay
22	FL 84 W, NW 196th, Glades Pkwy, W Publix, same as 21
21	FL 84 W (from nb), Indian Trace, W Exxon/dsl, Shell Las Rikuras, McDonald's, Papa John's, Spain's Cuisine CVS Drug
19	I-595 E, FL 869 **(toll)**, Sawgrass Expswy
15	Royal Palm Blvd, Weston, Bonaventure, W Chevron, Mobil BurgerFi, Carolina Ale House, Flanigan's Rest, La Granja, Los Verdes, Lucille's Cafe, Moon Thai, Offerdahl's Grill, Pollo Tropical, Subway, Wendy's Comfort Suites, Courtyard, Residence Inn H, Meineke, Tires+, USPO, VW
13b a	Griffin Rd, E Shell/dsl, Usave/dsl Burger King, Donato's Rest., DQ, Outback Steaks, Waffle House Goodyear/auto, LDS Temple, Porsche, Publix, vet, W 7-11/dsl, Tom Thumb/dsl Anthony's Pizza, Aprezo 2 Venezuelan, Bone Fish Grill, Chick-fil-A, Chili's, Chipotle, Coldstone, Domino's, Dunkin', HoneyBaked Ham, Jimmy John's, McDonald's, Panera Bread, Pei Wei, Pizza Heaven, Starbucks, Weston Diner

FL

MIAMI

13b a	Continued AT&T, Fiat, Home Depot, Honda, Hyundai, Nissan/Vo Office Depot, Publix, Toyota, vet, Walgreens
11b a	Sheridan St, E Chevron Cracker Barrel, Wen Hampton Inn, Holiday Inn Express Audi, BMW, H (3 Piccolo Park, W Shell/dsl China One, Coldstone, Li Caesar's, McDonald's, Original Pancake House, Piola Pi Romeus Cuban, Starbucks, Subway, TGIFriday's Firesto auto, Lowe's, Publix, URGENT CARE, Verizon, vet, Walgreen
9b a	FL 820, Pine Blvd, Hollywood Blvd, E Marath Shell BJ's Rest., Boston Mkt, Brimstone Woodfire G Brio Italian, Cheesecake Factory, Chick-fil-A, Chili's, First Wa Cafe, Fuddrucker's, Habit Burger, Havana 1957, HoneyBa Ham, Jason's Deli, La Granja, Lime Mexican Grill, McDona Sal's Italian, Sergio's Grill, Starbucks, Subway, The Pub, Tiju Flats, Twin Peaks, Village Tavern, Wendys H, Barnes& ble, BJ's Whse/gas, Chrysler/Dodge/Jeep, Dick's, Merce Old Navy, Petsmart, Publix, Trader Joe's, USPO, Verizon, W greens, Walmart, W Chevron/dsl, Marathon/dsl, M bil Burger King, BurgerFi, Chipotle Mexican, Corner Ba Cafe, Dickey's BBQ, Firehouse Subs, KFC/Taco Bell, La Gra Las Vegas Cuban, Marco's Pizza, Mazda Mediterranean, Pa Express, Sal's Italian, SmashBurger, Starbucks, Sweet To toes, Wasabi, Wendy's, Wingstop $Tree, Acura, Adva Parts, AT&T, AutoZone, Costco/gas, CVS Drug, GNC, Le Petco, Publix, Ross, Sedano's Foods, Subaru, Tires+, TJ Ma Tuesday Morning, vet, Walgreens, Whole Foods Mkt
7b a	Miramar Pkwy, E Chevron Baskin-Robbins/Dun Blue Ginger Rest., Jimmy John's, La Carreta, McDonald's, P John's, Pollo Tropical, Sal's Italian, Starbucks, Subway, Tij na Flats, Wendy's Courtyard, Hilton Garden, Reside Inn, Wingate Inn $Tree, Publix, USPO, vet, Walgree W Mobil, Shell Anthony's Pizza, Benihana, Ch fil-A, Chili's, Chipotle, Coldstone, Jersey Mike's, McDona Orient Chef, Panera Bread, Primo's Pizza, Starbucks, Subw TX Roadhouse H, city park, CVS Drug, GNC, Home De Marshall's, Ross, SuperTarget, Verizon, Winn-Dixie
5	to FL 821 (from sb), FL TPK **(toll)**
4	FL 860, NW 186th, Miami Gardens Dr, E Chevron, M bil Carrabba's, Dunkin', McDonald's, Subway AT CVS Drug, GNC, Publix/deli, Sedanos Foods, vet
2	NW 138th, Graham Dairy Rd, W Mobil, Shell/dsl Ch Casa, China Wok, IHOP, Latin Cuban Cafe, Little Caesar's, Donald's, Pollo Tropical, Starbucks, Subway, Wendy's $G eral, Aldi Foods, AT&T, GNC, Publix, Ross, vet, Walgreens
1b a	**I-75 begins/ends on FL 826, Palmetto Expswy,** multiple vices on FL 826.

INTERSTATE 95

Exit #	Services
382mm	Florida/Georgia state line, St Marys River
381mm	**inspection sta both lanes**
380	US 17, to Yulee, Kingsland, E Osprey RV Park, W Shell
378mm	**Welcome Ctr sb, 24hr security, full facilities, litter bar petwalk, , , vending**
376mm	**weigh sta both lanes**
373	FL 200, FL A1A, to Yulee, Callahan, Fernandina Bch, E Fla Krystal, Marathon/dsl, RaceWay/dsl Burger King, DQ, K McDonald's, Wendy's Best Western, Comfort Inn, Holi Inn Express to Ft Clinch SP (16mi), W BP/Subway/ Flash/dsl

INTERSTATE 95 Cont'd

Exit #	Services
366	Pecan Park Rd, E Love's/Chester's/Subway/dsl/scales/24hr, W Flea&Farmer's Mkt, Pecan Park RV Camping
363b a	Duval Rd, E Mobil/7-11/dsl Arby's, BJ's Rest., Blaze Pizza, Boston's, Buffalo Wild Wings, Buffalo's Philly, Carrabba's, Chick-fil-A, Chili's, Chipotle, Coldstone, Cracker Barrel, Firehouse Subs, Five Guys, Green Papaya, Hardee's, Jimmy John's, Logan's Roadhouse, McDonald's, Mellow Mushroom Pizza, Moe's SW Grill, Newk's Eatery, Olive Garden, Outback Steaks, Panda Express, Panera Bread, Pollo Tropical, Red Lobster, Starbucks, Sticky Fingers, Subway, Taco Bell, Wasabi, Wendy's A Loft $Tree, AT&T, AutoZone, Best Buy, Dick's, Discount Tire, GNC, Goodyear/auto, Hobby Lobby, Lowe's, Marshall's, Michael's, Old Navy, Petsmart, Ross, Tire Kingdom, URGENT CARE, Verizon, Walgreens, Walmart/Subway, W BP/dsl, Flash/dsl, Sunoco/Subway, Valero/dsl Denny's, Longhorn Steaks, Millhouse Steaks, Ruby Tuesday, Waffle House, Zaxby's Airport Inn, Best Airport Inn, Comfort Suites, Courtyard, Crowne Plaza, Days Inn, Econolodge, Fairfield Inn, Hampton Inn, Hilton Garden, Holiday Inn Express, Hyatt Place, Jacksonville Plaza Hotel, Microtel, Red Roof Inn, Residence Inn, SpringHill Suites, Travelodge , Gore's RV Ctr
362b a	I-295 S, FL 9A, to Blount Island, Jacksonville
360	FL 104, Dunn Ave, Busch Dr, E Gate/dsl Hardee's, Waffle House Woodspring Suites NAPA, Sam's Club/gas, USPO, W BP/dsl, Chevron/dsl, Marathon/dsl, Shell/dsl, Sunoco, Valero Arby's, Burger King, Capt D's, Chan's Chinese, Checker's, China Buffet, CiCi's, Country Cabin Rest., Dunkin', Firehouse Subs, KFC, Krystal, Little Caesar's, McDonald's, New China, Papa Murphy's, Pizza Hut, Popeye's, Sonny's BBQ, Starbucks, Subway, Taco Bell, Wendy's Knights Inn, Motel 6, River City Inn $Tree, Aamco, Advance Parts, Camping World RV Ctr, CVS Drug, Family$, PepBoys, Publix, Tires+, Walgreens
358b a	FL 105, Broward Rd, Heckscher Dr, E zoo, W BP/dsl
357mm	Trout River
357	FL 111, Edgewood Ave, W BP/dsl, Texaco/dsl
356b a	Fl 115, FL 117, Lem Turner Rd, Norwood Ave, E Hardee's, W BP/dsl, RaceWay/dsl, Shell, Speedway/Dunkin' Burger King, Checker's, Golden EggRoll, Ho-Ho Chinese, Krystal, Popeye's, Subway, Taco Bell Advance Parts, King Tires, Save-A-Lot, Walgreens
355	Golfair Blvd, E Shell, W Chevron/dsl, RaceWay/dsl
354b a	US 1, 20th St, to Jacksonville, to AmTrak, MLK Pkwy
353d	FL 114, to 8th St, E McDonald's H, Walgreens
353c	US 23 N, Kings Rd, downtown
353b	US 90A, Union St, Sports Complex, downtown
353a	Church St, Myrtle Ave, Forsythe St, downtown
352d	I-10 W, Stockton St (from sb), Lake City
352c	Monroe St (from nb), downtown
352b a	Myrtle Ave (from nb), downtown
351d	Stockton St, W H, downtown
351c	Margaret St, downtown
351b	I-10 W, to Tallahassee
351a	Park St, College St, H, to downtown
351mm	St Johns River
350b	FL 13, San Marco Blvd, E H
350a	Prudential Dr, Main St, Riverside Ave (from nb), to downtown, E Extended Stay America, Hampton Inn, W Panera Bread Hilton Garden, Homewood Suites
349	US 90 E (from sb), to beaches, W Shell/dsl Scottish Inn, downtown

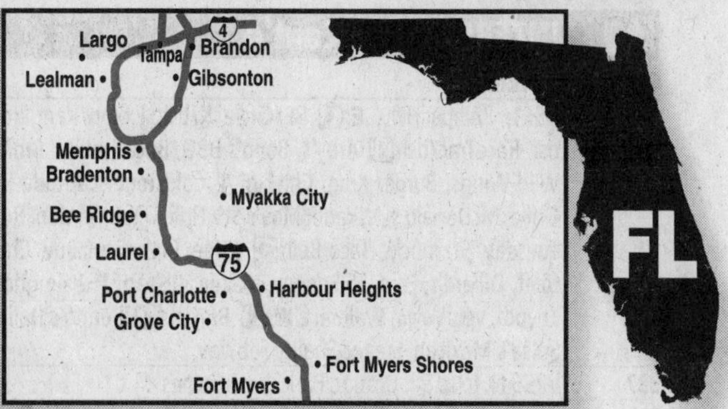

JACKSONVILLE

Exit #	Services
348	US 1 S (from sb), Philips Hwy, W Scottish Inn, Super 8
347	US 1A, FL 126, Emerson St, E Chevron/dsl, Shell Hot Wok Advance Parts, Family$, O'Reilly Parts, W BP/dsl, Gate, Gate/dsl, Speedway/dsl Dunkin', McDonald's, Taco Bell Emerson Inn Chevrolet, Goodyear/auto
346b a	FL 109, University Blvd, E BP, Shell, Speedway/dsl, Sunoco/dsl Baldino's Subs, Capt D's, Checkers, DQ, Firehouse Subs, Happy Garden Chinese, Hungry Howie's, Korean BBQ, Krystal, Pizza Hut, Subway, Ying's Chinese, Zaxby's H, Ace Hardware, CVS Drug, Family$, Fresh Fields Mkt, Meineke, NAPA, Sun Tire, Tires+, Tires+, Winn-Dixie, W BP/dsl, RaceTrac/dsl Baskin-Robbins/Dunkin', Burger King, Famous Amos, KFC, Krispy Kreme, McDonald's, Papa John's, Sonny's BBQ, Taco Bell, Wendy's, Whataburger Days Inn, Econolodge, Super 8 $Tree, auto repair, AutoZone, Family$, TJ Maxx, U-Haul
345	FL 109, University Blvd (from nb), E Gate/dsl/24hr, Mobil/Subway/dsl, Speedway/dsl Bono's BBQ, Parisian Sandwich, Vino's Pizza H
344	FL 202, Butler Blvd, E Gate/dsl Dave&Buster's Best Western, Candlewood Suites, Country Inn Suites, Extended Stay America, Holiday Inn Express, Marriott, Radisson H, USPO, W BP/dsl, Shell, Texaco/dsl Applebee's, Baskin-Robbins/Dunkin', Chick-fil-A, Cracker Barrel, Jimmy John's, McDonald's, Sonic, Starbucks, Waffle House, Wendy's, Whataburger/24hr, Zaxby's Baymont Inn, Courtyard, Extended Stay America, Extended Stay America (2), Fairfield Inn, Hampton Inn, Hometown Inn, La Quinta, Red Roof Inn, TownePlace Suites
341	FL 152, Baymeadows Rd, E BP/dsl, Gate/dsl, Shell/dsl Arby's, Chili's, Four Rivers Smokehouse, Hardee's, Jimmy John's, Krystal, Panda Express, Subway Comfort Suites, Embassy Suites, Extended Stay America, Ramada Inn Advance Parts, Autozone, Publix, Tires+, Walgreens, W Mobil/Kangaroo, Shell Al's Pizza, Denny's, Dunkin', Firehouse Subs, Gator's Dockside, IHOP, Jersey Mike's, KFC, Larry's Subs, Little Caesar's, McDonald's, Pagoda Chinese, Red Lobster, Taco Bell, Waffle House, Wendy's, Woody's BBQ Best Inn, Days Inn, Hawthorn Suites, InTown Suites, Knights Inn, La Quinta, Motel 6, Quality Inn, Residence Inn, Sheraton, Suburban Inn $Tree, AT&T, BJ's Whse/gas, CVS Drug, Discount Tire, Harley-Davidson, Lowe's, Office Depot, Pepboys, Verizon
340	FL 115, Southside Blvd (from nb), E on FL 115 Marathon/Kangaroo Five Guys, Fusion Buffet, Longhorn Steaks, Newk's Eatery Aldi, AT&T, Home Depot, Michael's, Petsmart, same as 339, Target

= gas = food = lodging = other = rest stop

INTERSTATE 95 Cont'd

Exit #	Services
339	US 1, Philips Hwy, E BP/Circle K/dsl, Exxon/Kangaroo/dsl, RaceTrac/dsl Arby's, Bono's BBQ, Buca Italian, Buffalo Wild Wings, Burger King, Chick-fil-A, Coldstone, Latitude 360 Grille, McDonald's, Mikado, Moe's SW Grill, Olive Garden, Ruby Tuesday, Starbucks, Taco Bell $Tree, Belk, Best Buy, Chevrolet, Dillard's, Ford, JC Penney, Mazda, Nissan, Tire Kingdom, Toyota, vet, Volvo, Walmart, W BP/dsl Benito's Italian, Salsa's Mexican, Steak&Shake, Subway
337	I-295 N, to rd 9a, Orange Park, Jax Beaches
335	Old St Augustine Rd, E Applebee's, Starbucks Courtyard H, W Gate/dsl, Shell/dsl Bamboo Wok, Bono's BBQ, Brooklyn Pizza, Chili's, Chipotle, Daruma Steaks, Dunkin', Five Guys, Hurricane Grill, Jersey Mike's, McDonald's, Moe's SW, Panda Express, Panera Bread, PDQ Cafe, Pei Wei, Pollo Tropical, Subway, Tijuana Flats, Wendy's, Zaxby's, Zoe's Kitchen Hampton Inn, Residence Inn AT&T, GNC, Goodyear/auto, Kohl's, Publix, Verizon, vet, Walgreens
333	FL 9b, to US 1, I-295, N Jacksonville Beaches
331mm	**both lanes, 24hr security, full facilities, litter barrels, petwalk, , vending**
329	rd 210, Green Cove Springs, Ponte Vedra Beach, E Pilot/McDonald's/dsl/scales/24hr, Sunoco/fruit, TA/Mobil/Subway/dsl/scales/24hr/@ Waffle House, W Circle K/dsl, Mobil/Subway/dsl/USPO, Shell/dsl Burger King, China Wok, Domino's, Dunkin', Firehouse Subs, Jenk's Pizza, Los Portales, Papa John's, Starbucks, Tropical Smoothie, Yummy Asian AT&T, CVS Drug, fireworks, Goodyear/auto, vet, Winn-Dixie
323	International Golf Pkwy, E BP/dsl/USPO, Shell/Subway/dsl St Augustine Suites, W Cino's Pizza, King Wok, Village Grill/Subs Renaissance Resort vet, World Golf Village
318	FL 16, Green Cove Sprgs, St Augustine, E Chevron/DQ/dsl, Gate/dsl/fruit, Mobil/Kangaroo/dsl, Shell/dsl Burger King, Dunkin', Krystal, McDonald's, NY Diner, Starbucks, Subway Comfort Inn, Courtyard, Fairfield Inn, Holiday Inn Express, La Quinta, Quality Inn, St Augustine Motel Cadillac, Camping World RV Ctr, Ford/Lincoln, Gore's RV Ctr, St Augustine Outlets/Famous Brands, W Exxon, RaceTrac/dsl Cracker Barrel, Denny's, Giovanni's Italian, IHOP, KFC, Lemongrass Asian, Ruby Tuesday, Sonny's BBQ, Taco Bell, Wendy's Best Western, Days Inn, Hampton Inn, Howard Johnson, Scottish Inn, Super 8, Wingate Inn Discount Tire, funpark, St Augustine Outlets
311	FL 207, St Augustine, E BP/Subway/dsl, RaceTrac/dsl Burger King, Dunkin' H, flea mkt, Indian Forest RV Park (2mi), KOA (7mi), St Johns RV Park, to Anastasia SP, W Quality Inn
305	FL 206, to Hastings, Crescent Beach, E FLYING J/Denny's/Subway/dsl/LP/scales/24hr to Ft Matanzas NM, truck repair, W truck repair
302mm	**both lanes, 24hr security, full facilities, litter barrels, petwalk, , vending**
298	US 1, to St Augustine, E BP/dsl, Indian River Fruit, Marathon to Faver-Dykes SP, W Mobil/DQ/dsl, Sunoco/dsl
293	Matanzas Woods Pky
289	to FL A1A (toll br), to Palm Coast, E Exxon, Mobil/7-11, RaceTrac/dsl, Shell Anthony's Pizza, China Express, Cracker Barrel, Denny's, Dunkin', Grand China, Hungry Howie's, KFC, McDonald's, Metro Diner, Salsa's Mexican, Starbucks, Wendy's Best Western, Fairfield Inn, Microtel, Red Roof Inn
289	Continued Beall's, CVS Drug, Publix, Staples, Walgreens, W go, Exxon, Exxon/Kangaroo/dsl, Kangaroo/dsl, S dsl Baskin-Robbins/Dunkin', Bob Evans, Bruster's, rabba's, Chick-fil-A, China King, China One, Golden C Houligan's, Joe's NY Pizza, McDonald's, Nathan's Cafe, back Steaks, Ruby Tuesday, Sakura Japanese, Sonny's Steak'n Shake, Subway, Taco Bell, Wendy's, Zaxby's Inn $General, $Tree, Advance Parts, AutoZone, Be Belk, CVS Drug, Ford, GNC, Home Depot, Kohl's, Lowe's, Pu Tire Kingdom, Tuffy Auto, USPO, Verizon, Walgreens, Waln Winn-Dixie
286mm	**weigh sta both lanes**
284	FL 100, to Bunnell, Flagler Beach, E Mobil/dsl, S dsl Burger King, Domino's, Joe's Pizza, McDonald's, ental Garden, Subway, Woody's BBQ Hampton Inn, iday Inn Express Ace Hardware, Winn-Dixie, W terstate 100 McDonald's, Panda Express, Pizza Subway Hilton Garden H, $Tree, AT&T, Chevr Chrysler/Dodge/Jeep, Dunkin', Michael's, Olive Garden, Pa Bread, Petsmart, Ross, Target, TJ Maxx, Verizon
278	Old Dixie Hwy, E 7-11 King Chinese, Mezza Pizza Bulow RV Park (3mi), Publix, to Tomoka SP, W BP/dsl Holiday Travel Park, vet
273	US 1, E Mobil, RaceTrac/dsl McDonald's, Waffle H La Quinta, Motel 6 fruit/fireworks, Giant Rec RV W Exxon/Burger King, Loves/Arby's/dsl/scales/ Daytona Pig Stand BBQ, DQ, Houligan's Days Econolodge, Howard Johnson, Scottish Inn, Super 8 En RV Park, Harley-Davidson
268	FL 40, Ormond Beach, E Speedway/dsl, Sunoco/dsl, V ro/dsl Agave Cantina, Applebee's, Boston Mkt, Chick-f Chili's, Chipotle, Denny's, Dustin's BBQ, Houligan's, Je Mike's, Mama Mia's Pizza, Panera Bread, Papa John's, Pie F Red Bowl, Starbucks, Steak'n Shake, Subway, Taco Bell, Tak Steaks, Wendy's, Wok&Roll Sleep Inn H, $Gene $Tree, Beall's, Discount Tire, GNC, Love Whole Foods, Low Petco, Publix, Ross, Tire Kingdom, to Tomoka SP, USPO, Walmart, W 7-11, BP/Dunkin', Citgo/dsl, RaceTrac/ Texaco Cantina Mezcal, Cracker Barrel, Little Italy, McD ald's Baymont Inn, Hampton Inn Walgreens
265	LPGA Blvd, Holly Hill, Daytona Beach, E 7-11, Shell/C K/Dunkin'/dsl Vince Carter Rest., Wendy's CVS D Tanger Outlets/famous brands, W Holiday Inn B Chrysler/Dodge/Jeep, Fiat, Ford, Infiniti, Lincoln, Mazda, M cedes, Mini, Nissan, VW
261b a	US 92, to DeLand, Daytona Bch, E 7-11, Citgo/dsl, R Way/dsl, Speedway/Dunkin'/dsl, Sunoco/dsl Applebe Asian Grill, Bahama Breeze, Bahama Breeze, BJ's Rest., Evans, Buffalo Wild Wings, Burger King, Burger King, Bu King, Carrabba's, Checkers, Cheddar's, Cheddar's, Chick-f Chili's, Chipotle Mexican, Cracker Barrel, Daytona Ale Ho Firehouse Subs, Five Guys, Honeybaked Ham, Honeyba Ham, Hooters, IHOP, Jersey Mike's Subs, Jimmy John's, K tal, Krystal, Longhorn Steaks, McDonald's, Olive Garden, back Steaks, Panda Express, Panda Express, Panera Br Red Lobster, Ruby Tuesday, Smoke Shack BBQ, Starbucks, S bucks, Subway, Taco Bell, Tijuana Flats, Waffle House, W dy's, Winghouse Best Western, Best Western, Courty Courtyard, Extended Stay America, Extended Stay Amer Hampton Inn, Hilton Garden, Holiday Inn Express, Homew Suites, La Quinta, Quality Inn, Residence Inn H, $T

ST AUGUSTINE

PALM COAST

ORMOND BEACH

DAYTONA

FL

INTERSTATE 95 Cont'd

261b a Continued
AT&T, Barnes&Noble, Bass Pro Shops, Beall's, Best Buy, BigLots, Books-A-Million, Dick's, Dillard's, Firestone/auto, Hobby Lobby, Home Depot, JC Penney, Jo-Ann Fabrics, Macy's, Michael's, Old Navy, PepBoys, Petsmart, Staples, SteinMart, Target, TJMaxx, to Daytona Racetrack, Tuesday Morning, Verizon, World Mkt, **W** BP/dsl, RaceTrack/dsl McDonald's Days Inn, Motel 6 flea mkt, KOA

260b a I-4, to Orlando, FL 400 E, to S Daytona, **E** RaceTrac/dsl/e85, Shell/Circle K/dsl

256 FL 421, to Port Orange, **E** BP, Murphy USA/dsl, Shell/dsl, WaWa/dsl Applebee's, Bob Evans, Boston Mkt, Burger King, Chicken Salad Chick, Chick-fil-A, Chili's, Chipotle, Culver's, Daily Grind Burgers, Denny's, Domino's, Dustin's BBQ, Golden Corral, Houligan's, KFC, McDonald's, Mellow Mushroom, Moe's SW, Monterrey Grill, Panera Bread, Papa John's, Pollo Tropical, Red Bowl Asian, Smoothie King, Sonny's BBQ, Starbucks, Stonewood Grill, TGIFriday's, Tijuana Flats Country Inn&Suites, La Quinta BigLots, BJ's/gas, CVS Drug, Daytona Beach RV Park, Home Depot, Lowe's, Save-a-Lot, Super Target, Tuffy Auto, Verizon, vet, Walgreens, Walmart, **W** 7-11/dsl, Marathon/dsl China Chef, ChuckECheese, Coldstone, Five Guys, Luigi's Pizzaria, Malibu Beach Grill, McDonald's, Olive Garden, Panda Express, Popeye's, Red Robin, Subway, Takara Steaks, TX Roadhouse, Waffle House, Wendy's $Tree, AT&T, Belk, Firestone/auto, GNC, Kohl's, Love Whole Foods, Marshall's, Michael's, PetCo, Publix, Walgreens

249b a FL 44, to De Land, New Smyrna Beach, **E** New Smyrna RV Camp (3mi), **W** Chevron/dsl McDonald's Walmart/Subway

244 FL 442, to Edgewater, **E** Marathon/dsl truck repair

231 rd 5A, Scottsmoor, **E** BP/Stuckey's/dsl Crystal Lake RV Park

227mm sb, 24hr security, full facilities, litter barrels, petwalk, vending

225mm nb, 24hr security, full facilities, litter barrels, petwalk, vending

223 FL 46, Mims, **E** McDonald's, **W** BP, Chevron/dsl $General, KOA/LP, Seasons RV Park

220 FL 406, Titusville, **E** BP/dsl, Shell/Hungry Howie's/dsl Beef O'Brady's, First Wok, Kelsey's Pizza, McDonald's, Subway, Valentino's Rest., Wendy's Executive Garden Inn H, $General, $Tree, Advance Parts, GNC, O'Reilly Parts, Publix, Tires+, to Canaveral Nat Seashore, Walgreens

215 FL 50, to Orlando, Titusville, **E** BP/KFC/dsl, Chevron/Subway/dsl, Exxon/Circle K, Murphy USA/dsl, Shell/Dunkin'/dsl Burger King, Denny's, Durango Steaks, McDonald's, Panda Express, Sonny's BBQ, Starbucks, Taco Bell, Waffle House, Wendy's Best Western, Ramada Inn Aldi Foods, AT&T, Ford, GNC, Home Depot, Lowe's, Marshall's, Pepboys, PetCo, Staples, Target, Tire Kingdom, to Kennedy Space Ctr, Walmart, **W** Cracker Barrel, IHOP Days Inn, Fairfield Inn, Hampton Inn, Holiday Inn, Quality Inn Christmas RV Park (8mi), Great Outdoors RV/golf Resort

212 FL 407, to FL 528 **toll** (no re-entry sb)

208 Port St John

205 FL 528 (**toll** 528), to Cape Canaveral & Cape Port AFS, City Point

202 FL 524, Cocoa, **E** FLYING J/Wendy's/dsl/scales/24hr, Shell/dsl Museum of History&Science, **W** BP/dsl Days Inn

MELBOURNE PALM BAY

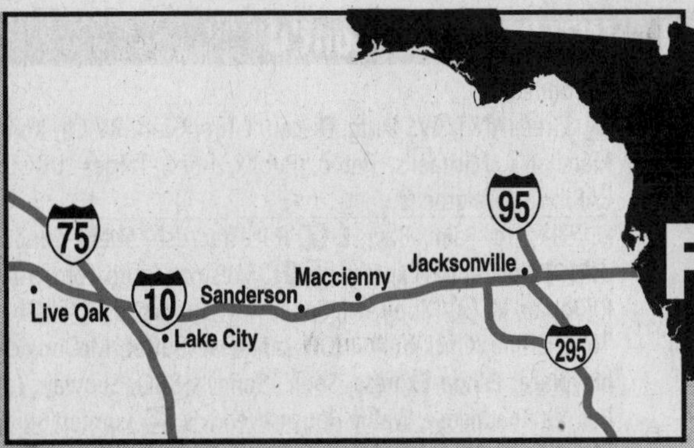

201 FL 520, to Cocoa Bch, Cocoa, **E** BP/dsl, Exxon/Circle K, Pilot/Subway/dsl/scales/24hr IHOP, Waffle House Best Western, Budget Inn H, fireworks, Sams Club/gas, **W** Chevron/dsl, Shell/Burger King, Sunoco/dsl McDonald's Holiday Inn Express Camping World RV Ctr

195 FL 519, Fiske Blvd, **E** 7-11, Mobil/dsl Baci Pizza, Ruby Tuesday Swiss Inn H, Discount Tire, Lowe's, Space Coast RV Park

193 Viera Blvd, **E** Brooklyn Pizza, Long Doggers Earth Fare Mkt, Walgreens, **W** Mobil/pizza Dunkin', El Leoncito, Kimbo Chinese, McDonald's, Publix, Slow&Low BBQ, Vincinos Pizza

191 rd 509, to Satellite Beach, Viera, **E** 7-11, BP, Speedway/dsl, Sunoco/dsl Bob Evans, Carrabba's, Chick-fil-A, Domino's, DQ, Firehouse Subs, Jimmy John's, McDonald's, Papa John's, Perkins, Pizza Hut/Taco Bell, Sonny's BBQ, Subway, Uno Grill, Wendy's Hampton Inn, Holiday Inn AT&T, CVS Drug, Publix, Tires+, to Patrick AFB, Tuffy Auto, URGENT CARE, Walgreens, zoo, **W** Murphy USA/dsl, Shell/dsl Asian Wok, Bonefish Grill, Buffalo Wild Wings, Burger King, Chili's, Chipotle, Coldstone, Cracker Barrel, Five Guys, Longhorn Steaks, Melting Pot, Moe's SW Grill, Outback Steaks, Panera Bread, Pizza Gallery, Pollo Tropical, Starbucks, Steak'nShake, Subway, Tijuana Flats, Which Wich? La Quinta H, $Tree, AT&T, Belk, Books-A-Million, GNC, Hobby Lobby, Kohl's, Lexus, Michael's, Office Depot, Old Navy, PetCo, Petsmart, Ross, SuperTarget, Tire Kingdom, TJ Maxx, Verizon, Walmart/McDonald's, World Mkt

188 FL 404, Patrick AFB, Satellite Beach

183 FL 518, Melbourne, Indian Harbour Beach, **E** 7-11, BP/dsl, Marathon/Dunkin', RaceTrac/dsl, WaWa/dsl H, art museum, AT&T, **W** Flea Mkt

180 US 192, to Melbourne, **E** BP/dsl, Cumberland/dsl, Mobil/dsl, RaceTrac/dsl, Shell/Circle K, Sunoco/dsl ChuckECheese, Denny's, Dunkin', Waffle House Best Value Inn, Budget Inn, Days Inn, Fairfield Inn, Hampton Inn, Holiday Inn Express, La Quinta, Melbourne Suites, Woodspring Suites H, Ace Hardware, fireworks, Lowe's, Sam's Club/gas, Subaru, Volvo

176 rd 516, to Palm Bay, **E** 7-11, BP/Circle K/dsl, Murphy USA/dsl, Pro Energy, RaceTrac/dsl Baskin Robbins/Dunkin', Chick-fil-A, Cracker Barrel, Denny's, Golden Corral, Popeye's, Starbucks, Tijuana Flats Hampton Inn, Quality Inn Aldi Foods, Bass Pro Shops, BJ's Whse/gas, GNC, Harley-Davidson, Office Depot, Verizon, Walgreens, Walmart, **W** 7-11, Mobil/dsl, Shell Buffalo Wild Wings, Burger King, Firehouse Subs, Five Guys, Long Doggers, Longhorn Steaks, McDonald's, Michelli's Pizzeria, Moe's SW Grill, Panda Express, Panera Bread, Pollo Tropical, Subway, Wendy's

FL

[gas icon] = gas [food icon] = food [lodging icon] = lodging [other icon] = other [RS] = rest stop

PALM BAY

INTERSTATE 95 Cont'd

176	Continued
	$Tree, AT&T, CVS Drug, Discount Tire, Giant RV Ctr, Kohl's, Marshall's, Michael's, PetCo, Publix, Ross, Target, URGENT CARE, vet, Walgreens
173	FL 514, to Palm Bay, **E** RaceTrac/dsl, Shell, Sunoco/dsl Holiday Inn Express H, Firestone/auto, Ford, truck/RV repair, **W** Mobil/dsl, Speedway, Sunoco/dsl Arby's, Burger King, Chick-fil-A, IHOP, Japanese Buffet, McDonald's/playplace, Panda Express, Sonic, Sonny's BBQ, Subway, Taco Bell, TX Roadhouse, Waffle House, Wendy's Comfort Suites, Motel 6 $General, Advance Parts, CVS Drug, Gatto's Tire/auto, Home Depot, Lowe's, Publix, Tire Kingdom, URGENT CARE, USPO, Verizon, Walgreens, Walmart
168mm	**both lanes, 24hr security, full facilities, litter barrels, petwalk, C, vending**
166	St John's Heritage Pkwy
156	rd 512, to Sebastian, Fellsmere, **E** BP/DQ/Stuckey's/dsl, Chevron/McDonald's, RaceWay/dsl H, Encore RV Park, Sebastian Inlet SRA, **W** St Sebastian SP
147	FL 60, Osceola Blvd, **E** 7-11, BP/dsl, Citgo/dsl, Mobil/dsl, Sunoco, TA/BP/Popeye's/Subway/dsl/scales/24hr/@, Valero/dsl, WaWa/dsl Dunkin', IHOP, McDonald's, Wendy's Comfort Suites, Howard Johnson, Motel 6, Vero Beach Resort, Vero Beach Suites H, Hyundai, USPO, vet, **W** Shell/dsl Cracker Barrel, McDonald's, Steak'n Shake Country Inn&Suites, Hampton Inn, Holiday Inn Express Vero Beach Outlets/famous brands
138	FL 614, Indrio Rd, **3 mi E** Oceanographic Institute
133mm	**both lanes, 24hr security, full facilities, litter barrels, petwalk, C, vending**
131b a	FL 68, Orange Ave, **E** H, to Ft Pierce SP, **W** FLYING J/Denny's/Subway/dsl/LP/scales/24hr, Loves/Hardee's/dsl/scales/24hr Blue Beacon
129	FL 70, to Okeechobee, **E** Citgo, Murphy USA, RaceTrac/dsl, Shell, Sunoco/dsl Applebee's, Cowboys BBQ, Golden Corral, Sonic, Waffle House H, $General, $Tree, Advance Parts, AT&T, Firestone/auto, Home Depot, URGENT CARE, Walgreens, Walmart/Subway, **W** Citgo, Loves/Arby's/dsl/24hr/@, Marathon/scales/dsl, Mobil/Dunkin'/Subway, Pilot/McDonald's/dsl/scales/24hr Burger King, Cracker Barrel, Golden Bear Rest., KFC, La Granja, LJ Silver, McDonald's, Red Lobster, Steak'n Shake, Subway, Waffle House, Wendy's Best Value Inn, Comfort Suites, Days Inn, Fairfield Inn, Hampton Inn, Holiday Inn Express, La Quinta, Motel 6, Quality Inn, Rodeway Inn, Sleep Inn to FL TPK, Treasure Coast RV Park
126	rd 712, Midway Rd, **E** Marathon/Subway/dsl
121	St Lucie West Blvd, **E** 7-11, Mobil/Dunkin', Murphy USA/dsl, Shell/Subway/dsl Arby's, Bob Evans, Burger King, Carrabba's, Cheddar's, Chili's, Chipotle Mexican, First Watch, Five Guys, Frank&Al's Pizza, Friendly's, Hokkaido, Jersey Mike's, Jimmy John's, KFC, Little Caesar's, McDonald's, Moe's SW Grill, Outback Steaks, Panda Express, Panera Bread, Pollo Tropical, Ruby Tuesday, Starbucks, Subway, Taco Bell, TGIFriday's, Tijuana Flats, Wendy's Hampton Inn, Holiday Inn Express, Residence Inn, SpringHill Suites, TownePlace Suites $Tree, AT&T, Beall's, CVS Drug, GNC, Outdoor Resorts Camping (2mi), PetCo, Publix/deli, Ross, Staples, SteinMart, Tire Kingdom, Tires+, URGENT CARE, USPO, Verizon, Walgreens, Walmart, **W** Chevron/dsl Hilton Garden, MainStay Suites, Sheraton Resort, Sleep Inn PGA Village
120	Crosstown Pkwy

OKEECHOBEE

FL

118	Gatlin Blvd, to Port St Lucie, **E** BP/dsl, Chevron/Dun Subway/dsl, Mobil/Dunkin', RaceTrac, Sunoco/e85 Donald's, Taco Bell, Wendy's AutoZone, Bass Pro Sh Home Depot, Sam's Club/gas, Tire Kingdom, Tires+, vet, greens, Walmart, **W** WaWa/dsl Culver's, Long Steaks, McDonald's, Olive Garden, Panda Express, Pa Bread, Recovery Grill, Subway, Tropical Smoothie Ho wood Suites H, AT&T, GNC, Michael's, Old Navy, Petsm Publix, Target, TJ Maxx
114	Becker Rd
112mm	**weigh sta sb**
110	FL 714, to Martin Hwy, Palm City, **E** H
106mm	**both lanes, 24hr security, full facilities, litter barrels, walk, C, vending**
102	Rd 713, High Meadow Ave, Palm City
101	FL 76, to Stuart, Indiantown, **E** Chevron/dsl, Race dsl, Sunoco/dsl Popeye's, Baskin-Robbins/Dunkin', C er Barrel, La Forchetta Pizza, McDonald's, Wendy's Co yard, Holiday Inn Express H, city park, Publix, Walgre **W** Marathon/DQ/dsl, Mobil/dsl
96	rd 708, to Hobe Sound, **E** Dickinson SP (11mi), RV cam
92mm	**weigh sta nb**
87b a	FL 706, to Okeechobee, Jupiter, **E** Citgo, Mobil/dsl, Sh dsl, Sunoco Cheeseburgers&More, Chipotle, Domi Duffy's Rest., Dunkin', First Watch Cafe, Five Guys, Giusepp Hurricane Grill, IHOP, Jersey Mike's Subs, KFC, McDona Panera Bread, Park Ave Grill, Pollo Tropical, Rancho Chico, bucks, Subway, Taco Bell, Tijuana Flats, Tomato Pie, Vi Pizza, YumYum Comfort Inn, Fairfield Inn H, Adva Parts, AT&T, BMW, GNC, Home Depot, PepBoys, Petsm Publix, Tire Kingdom, to Dickinson SP, URGENT CARE, vet, greens, Walmart, Winn-Dixie, **W** Sunoco CVS Drug FL TPK
83	Donald Ross Rd, **E** Marathon/Subway, Shell/deli Donald's Hampton Inn (3mi), Holiday Inn Express (3 Homewood Suites H, AT&T, CVS Drug, Publix, stadi Walgreens
79c	FL 809 S (from sb), Military Tr, **W** same services as 79b, t TPK
79a b	FL 786, PGA Blvd, **E** Shell/dsl Chili's, Moe's SW, Y house Rest. Hilton Garden, Marriott H, Best Michael's, PetCo, Publix, Whole Foods Mkt, **W** Shell Blaze Pizza, Bonefish Grill, Chipotle Mexican, J Alexand Outback Steaks, Panera Bread, Starbucks, Three Forks DoubleTree Hotel, Embassy Suites CVS Drug, Publix
77	Northlake Blvd, to W Palm Bch, **E** Shell/dsl, Spe way Applebee's, Arby's, Burger King, Checkers, Chick-f Giovanni's Rest., Habit Burger, Jersey Mike's, Jimmy John's Granja, McDonald's, Miami Subs, Panera Bread, Pollo Trop Starbucks, Taco Bell H, $Tree, AT&T, Buick/Chevro GMC, Chrysler/Dodge/Jeep, Costco, CVS Drug, Ford, Ford, H by Lobby, Home Depot, Hyundai, Jo-Ann, Kia, Lowe's, PepB Ross, Staples, Target, vet, VW, Walgreens, **W** Chev Mobil/dsl, Shell, Sunoco/dsl Duffy's Grill, Dunkin', Orig Pancakes, Papa John's, Pizza Hut, Subway, Wendy's of America Advance Parts, CVS Drug, Publix, Tires+, Winn-Dixie
76	FL 708, Blue Heron Blvd, **E** Marathon/dsl, Shell/WaWa/dsl Wendy's Travelodge Honda, Niss **W** 7-11/dsl, Chevron/dsl, Cumberland Farms, Marath Subway/dsl, RaceTrac/dsl Burger King, Denny's, McDonald's Super 8

W PALM BEACH

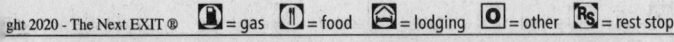

INTERSTATE 95 Cont'd

Exit #	Services
74	FL 702, 45th St, **E** [gas] 7-11/dsl [food] Burger King, IHOP [lodging] Days Inn [other] [H], Cadillac, URGENT CARE, Walgreens, **W** [gas] RaceTrac/dsl [food] Cracker Barrel, McDonald's, Pollo Tropical, Subway, Taco Bell, Wendy's [lodging] Courtyard, Extended Stay America, Holiday Inn Express, Homewood Suites, Red Roof Inn, Residence Inn, SpringHill Suites [other] FoodTown, Harley-Davidson, Sams Club/gas, Walmart
71	Lake Blvd, Palm Beach, **E** [gas] Marathon/Dunkin'/dsl [food] BJ's Rest., McDonald's, Pei Wei, Red Robin, Starbucks [lodging] Best Western, Hawthorn Suites [other] [H], Best Buy, Home Depot, Old Navy, Petsmart, Ross, Target, TJ Maxx, Whole Foods Mkt, **W** [gas] Texaco/dsl, Valero [food] Chick-fil-A, Chipotle Mexican, Dunkin', Hooters, Raindancer Steaks, Red Lobster, Sweet Tomatoes, Tijuana Flats, Twin Peaks [lodging] La Quinta, Ramada [other] URGENT CARE, vet, Walgreens
70b a	FL 704, Okeechobee Blvd, **E** [food] Ruth's Chris Steaks [lodging] Hilton, Marriott, **W** [gas] BP/dsl, Chevron/dsl, Mobil/dsl, Shell, Speedway, Valero/dsl [food] Arby's, Burger King, Checkers, ChuckECheese, Denny's, Firehouse Grill, IHOP, McDonald's, PDQ Cafe, Pizza Hut, Pollo Tropical, Starbucks, Subway, Taco Bell [other] $Tree, Advance Parts, Aldi Foods, AT&T, Audi/Porsche, BMW/Mini, Chevrolet, Firestone/auto, GNC, Hyundai, Mercedes, Michael's, Office Depot, Staples, Verizon, VW
69b	**W** [other] to [airport]
69a	Belvedere Rd, **W** [gas] BP, Shell, WaWa/dsl [food] Burger King, IHOP, Wendy's [lodging] Courtyard, DoubleTree, Embassy Suites, Hampton Inn, Hilton Garden, Holiday Inn/rest., Stay Inn, Studio 6
68	US 98, Southern Blvd, **E** [gas] Coastal, W Palm Gas [food] Subway [other] CVS Drug, Publix, **W** [lodging] Hilton
66	Forest Hill Blvd, **W** [gas] Chevron/dsl, Sunoco [food] Dunkin' [other] Advance Parts
64	10th Ave N, **W** [gas] Citgo, Marathon/Circle K/dsl, Mobil/dsl, Murphy USA/dsl [food] Chili's, Dunkin', Flanigan's Grill, Taco Bell, Wendy's [lodging] Woodspring Suites [other] CVS Drug, Ford, President Foods, Ross, Tires+, Walgreens, Walmart/Subway
63	6th Ave S, **W** [other] [H]
61	FL 812, Lantana Rd, **E** [gas] Shell [food] Domino's, Dunkin', KFC, Little Caesar's, McDonald's, Riggins Crabhouse, Subway [lodging] Motel 6 [other] $General, 7-11, Ace Hardware, AutoZone, CVS Drug, Publix, **W** [other] [H], Costco/gas
60	Hypoluxo Rd, **E** [gas] Chevron/dsl, Mobil/dsl, RaceTrac/dsl, Shell/dsl [food] Popeye's, Subway, Taco Bell, Wendy's [lodging] Comfort Inn, Holiday Inn Express, Super 8 [other] Family$, NAPA, Tire Kingdom, Tire Pros, Tires+, Winn-Dixie, **W** [gas] Valero/dsl [food] Anchor Inn Rest. [other] Advance Parts
59	Gateway Blvd, **W** [gas] Mobil/7-11/dsl [food] Bonefish Grill, Boynton Alehouse, BurgerFi, Carrabba's, Chili's, Egg&I Cafe, Firehouse Subs, Golden Phoenix Chinese, McDonald's, PizzaRox, Starbucks, Subway, Tropical Smoothie [lodging] Hampton Inn, TownePlace Suites [other] $Tree, AT&T, CarMax, CVS Drug, Kohl's, Publix, Ross, Tuesday Morning, vet
57	FL 804, Boynton Bch Blvd, **E** [gas] Marathon/dsl [food] KFC [lodging] Boynton Beach Inn [other] [H], USPO, **W** [gas] BP, Chevron/dsl, Mobil, Shell [food] Applebee's, Burger King, Checkers, Chick-Fil-A, Dunkin', Golden Corral, KFC, La Brasa, Little Caesar's, Olive Garden, Sonic, Starbucks, Steak'n Shake, Subway, TGIFriday's, Tijuana Flats, TX Roadhouse, Wendy's [other] $Tree, 7-11, Barnes&Noble, BJ's Whse/gas, CVS Drug, Dick's, GNC, Office Depot, Old Navy, PetCo, Petsmart, Publix, SteinMart, TJ Maxx, USPO, vet, Walgreens, Walmart

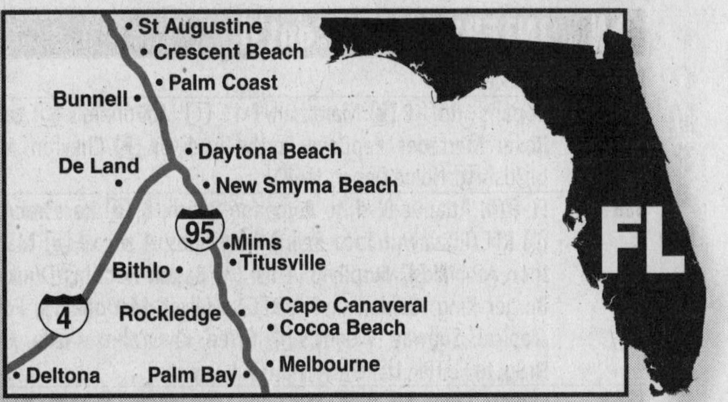

Exit #	Services
56	Woolbright Rd, **E** [gas] Shell [food] McDonald's, Panera Bread, Smashburger, Subway, Tijuana Flats, Wendy's [other] [H], 7-11, GNC, Jo-Ann Fabrics, Publix, vet, Walgreens, **W** [gas] Marathon/McDonald's, RaceTrac/dsl [food] Burger King, Cracker Barrel, Dunkin' [other] Advance Parts, Home Depot, Lowe's, Staples, Walgreens
52b a	FL 806, Atlantic Ave, **W** [gas] Chevron/dsl, Shell/dsl [food] Dunkin', Sandwich Man, Silver Wok, Subway [other] [H], Tires+, transmissions, Verizon, vet, Walgreens
51	rd 782, Linton Blvd, **E** [gas] Shell [food] Arby's, Chick-fil-A, Chipotle Mexican, DQ, Duffy's Grill, Five Guys, KFC, McDonald's, Outback Steaks, Pollo Tropical, Starbucks, Steak'n Shake, Subway, Taco Bell, Tijuana Flats, Wendy's [other] $Tree, AT&T, Chevrolet, Ford, Home Depot, Marshall's, Mercedes, Michael's, Petsmart, Publix, Ross, Target, Tire Kingdom, TJ Maxx, **W** [gas] Shell [food] Dunkin', Little Caesar's [other] [H], AutoZone, URGENT CARE
50	Congress Ave, **W** [gas] Mobil [lodging] Hilton Garden, Residence Inn [other] Costco/gas
48b a	FL 794, Yamato Rd, **E** [gas] Mobil [food] Panera Bread [other] CVS Drug, **W** [gas] BP/dsl, Mobil [food] Blue Fin, Dunkin', Jersey Mike's Subs, Jimmy John's, McDonald's, Miller's Alehouse, Sal's Italian, Starbucks, The Grille, Wendy's [lodging] Embassy Suites, Hampton Inn, Ramada, SpringHill Suites, TownePlace Suites
45	FL 808, Glades Rd, **E** [gas] Mobil/dsl [food] J Alexander's Rest., Jamba Juice, PF Chang's [lodging] Fairfield Inn [other] Barnes&Noble, CVS Drug, Whole Foods Mkt, **W** [gas] Marathon [food] Brewzzi Cafe, Brio Italian Grill, CA Pizza Kitchen, Capital Grille, Cheesecake Factory, Chili's, Chipotle Mexican, Farmer's Table, Hooters, Houston's Rest., Madison's Grill, Maggiano's Italian, Moe's SW Grill, Morton Steaks, Season's Rest., Starbucks [lodging] Courtyard, Marriott, Renaissance, Wyndham Garden [other] Publix
44	Palmetto Park Rd, **E** [gas] Valero/dsl [food] Denny's, Dunkin', Subway, Taco Bell, Tomasso's Pizza [other] Publix, USPO
42b a	FL 810, Hillsboro Blvd, **E** [gas] Marathon, Shell/dsl [food] Dunkin', Hook Fish&Chicken, McDonald's, Popeye's, Wendy's [lodging] Doubletree, Hampton Inn, La Quinta [other] Advance Parts, **W** [gas] Chevron/dsl, Mobil/dsl, WaWa/dsl [food] Checkers, Dunkin', Subway [lodging] La Quinta [other] CVS Drug, Home Depot, Walgreens
41	FL 869 (**toll**), SW 10th, to I-75, **E** [gas] Mobil/7-11 [food] Cracker Barrel, Pizza Express [lodging] Extended Stay America, Woodspring Suites, **W** [lodging] Best Western+, Quality Suites
39	FL 834, Sample Rd, **E** [gas] Marathon/dsl, Shell/dsl, Speedway/dsl [food] Taco Bell [other] [H], $General, AutoZone, Save-A-Lot, U-Haul, **W** [gas] Chevron, Citgo/dsl, Mobil, Mobil/dsl, Solo/dsl, Sunoco/dsl, WaWa/dsl [food] Burger King, Checkers, IHOP, La Granja, McDonald's, Miami Subs, Subway [other] CarMax, Costco/gas, CVS Drug, Family$, Seabra Foods, vet

FL

FL

INTERSTATE 95 Cont'd

POMPANO BEACH

Exit #	Services
38b a	Copans Rd, E Marathon/7-11 McDonald's Land Rover, Mercedes, PepBoys, Porche/Audi, W Chevron, Mobil/dsl Home Depot, NAPA
36b a	FL 814, Atlantic Blvd, to Pompano Beach, E RaceTrac/dsl KFC/Pizza Hut/Taco Bell, Miami Subs, 1 mi W Marathon, Mobil/dsl, Murphy USA/dsl Baskin-Robbins/Dunkin', Burger King, Golden Corral, KFC/LJ Silver, McDonald's, Pollo Tropical, Subway, Wendy's $Tree, Chevrolet/Mazda, CVS Drug, to FL TPK, USPO, Walmart/Subway
33b a	Cypress Creek Rd, E Marathon, Speedway Duffy's Diner, Subway Extended Stay America, Hampton Inn, Westin Hotel 7-11, W Shell/repair Arby's, Blaze Pizza, Burger Freak, Burger King, Carlucci's Italian, Chili's, Five Guys, Hooters, Jersey Mike's, Jimmy John's, Longhorn Steaks, McDonald's, Moonlite Diner, Starbucks, Subway, Sweet Tomatoes, Wendy's Courtyard, La Quinta, Marriott, Sheraton Suites AT&T, GNC, Jaguar, Office Depot, Tires+, URGENT CARE

FT LAUDERDALE

Exit #	Services
32	FL 870, Commercial Blvd, Lauderdale by the Sea, Lauderhill, E Subway, W Chevron, Circle K, Mobil/dsl, Shell, Sunoco/dsl Dunkin', KFC, McDonald's, Miami Subs, Waffle House Best Western, Holiday Inn Express, Universal Palms Motel Advance Parts, auto repair, BJ's Whse/gas
31b a	FL 816, Oakland Park Blvd, E 7-11, Chevron, Mobil/dsl Burger King, Denny's, Dunkin', Little Caesar's, McDonald's, Miami Subs, Subway, Wendy's Lowe's, Publix, Walgreens, W Chevron/dsl, Exxon, RaceTrac/dsl, Shell, Valero Baskin-Robbins/Dunkin', Burger King, Checkers, KFC, Subway Days Inn $General, Home Depot, Toyota, USPO, Walgreens
29b a	FL 838, Sunrise Blvd, E Marathon/dsl, Mobil/dsl, Shell, Sunoco/dsl/e85 Burger King, Miami Subs, Popeye's Advance Parts, auto repair/tires, AutoZone, Family$, to Birch SP, W BP, Exxon/dsl, Marathon, Shell, Valero China Bowl, Church's, Dunkin', KFC, McDonald's, Snapper's Fish&Chicken, Subway H, Family$
27	FL 842, Broward Blvd, Ft Lauderdale, E Marathon Burger King, Dunkin Days Inn H, Walgreens, W RaceTrac/dsl, WaWa/dsl Charley's, Checkers, Chen's, Chipotle, McDonald's Verizon, Walmart/Burger King
26	I-595 (from sb), FL 736 (from nb), Davie Blvd, E to
25	FL 84, E 7-11, Marathon, Marathon/dsl, RaceTrac/dsl, Sunoco/dsl, Texaco Dunkin', Li'l Red's BBQ, McDonald's, Ruby Chinese, Subway, Wendy's Best Western, Candlewood Suites, Hampton Inn, Holiday Inn Express, Motel 6, Sky Motel $Tree, BigLots, Firestone/auto, U-Haul, Walgreens, Winn-Dixie, W Ramada Inn, Red Carpet Inn, Rodeway Inn
24	I-595 (from nb), to I-75, E to
23	FL 818, Griffin Rd, E Ft Lauderdale Hotel, W Mobil Dunkin', Subway, Wendy's Courtyard, Fairfield Inn, Homewood Suites, Residence Inn Bass Pro Shops, Publix
22	FL 848, Stirling Rd, Cooper City, E Mobil/Dunkin'/dsl AleHouse Grill, Burger King, Chipotle Mexican, Dave&Buster's, Firehouse Subs, McDonald's, Moonlite Diner, Red Lobster, Sal's Italian, Subway, Sweet Tomatoes, Taco Bell, TGIFriday's, Wendy's, Yum Berry Yogurt Hampton Inn, Hilton Garden, Hyatt House, Hyatt Place, La Quinta, Quality Inn, SpringHill Suites Advance Parts, BJ's Whse, GNC, Home Depot, Marshall's, Michael's, Old Navy, Petsmart, Ross, to Lloyd SP, Verizon, W Las Vegas Cuban, Subway Best Western, Cambria Suites, Comfort Suites, Home 2 Suites CVS Drug, PepBoys, Tire Kingdom, vet, Walgreens

HOLLYWOOD

Exit #	Services
21	FL 822, Sheridan St, E Chevron/dsl, Cumberland Fa gas, Marathon/Dunkin'/dsl Domino's, W Shell ny's, McDonald's Days Inn, Holiday Inn
20	FL 820, Hollywood Blvd, E Shell IHOP, Miami Hollywood Gateway Inn Goodyear/auto, U-Haul, ve Chevron/dsl, Marathon Boston Mkt, Burgers&Sha China Hollywood, Coldstone, McDonald's, Offerdahl's Starbucks, Subway, Taco Bell, Waffle Works, Wendy's Publix, Target, Walgreens
19	FL 824, Pembroke Rd, E Orion/dsl, Shell Fam W Mobil/dsl
18	FL 858, Hallandale Bch Blvd, E 7-11, Exxon, Baskin-Robbins/Dunkin', Burger King, Denny's, IHOP, La Granja, Little Caesar's, McDonald's, Miami Subs, Pollo T ical, Subway, Taco Bell, Wendy's, Won Ton Garden Western+ Family$, Goodyear/auto, Tire Kingdom, Walgreens, Winn-Dixie, W Mobil/dsl, RaceTrac/dsl Advance Parts
16	Ives Dairy Rd, E H, W Marathon/7-11 Subwa
14	FL 860, Miami Gardens Dr, N Miami Beach, E H, Oleta er SRA, W Shell/dsl, Valero/dsl
12c	US 441, FL 826, FL TPK, FL 9, E 7-11, Chevron, Ex dsl, Marathon/dsl, Marathon/dsl, Speedway, Valero Baskin-Robbins/Dunkin', Burger King, La Granja, Donald's, Starbucks, Subway, Taco Bell/Pizza Hut, Wen Rodeway Inn H, PepBoys, Toyota
12b	US 441 (from nb), same as 12c
12a	FL 868 (from nb), FL TPK N
11	NW 151st (from nb), W Sunoco/dsl McDonald's vance Parts, Winn-Dixie
10b	FL 916, NW 135th, Opa-Locka Blvd, W Chevron, Mobil Checkers, Pizza Hut, Subway
10a	NW 125th, N Miami, Bal Harbour, W Shell Burger K Wendy's $General
9	NW 119th (from nb), W 7-11/dsl, Marathon/McDona KFC, Pollo Tropical, Popeye's Advance Parts, AutoZ CVS Drug, Family$, Walgreens, Winn-Dixie
8b	FL 932, NW 103rd, E Chevron, Shell 7-11, W Su co, Sunshine/dsl $General, Baskin-Robbins/Dunkin', Br Foods
8a	NW 95th, E Chevron, W 7-11/dsl, CR/dsl, Mobil McDonald's H, Advance Parts, Walgreens
7	FL 934, NW 81st, NW 79th, E Chevron/dsl, Valero/ W Sunoco Checkers
6b	NW 69th (from sb)
6a	FL 944, NW 62nd, NW 54th, W China Town, McDona Subway Family$, Presidente Mkt, Walgreens

MIAMI

Exit #	Services
4b a	I-195 E, FL 112 W (**toll**), Miami Beach, E downtown, W
3b	NW 8th St (from sb)
3a	FL 836 W (**toll**) (exits left from nb), W H, to
2d	I-395 E (exits left from sb), to Miami Beach
2c	NW 8th, NW 14th (from sb), Miami Ave, E Port of Miam
2b	NW 2nd (from nb), downtown Miami
2a	US 1 (exits left from sb), Biscayne Blvd, downtown Miami
1b	US 41, SW 7th, SW 8th, Brickell Ave, E Chevron, Ci Burger King, Graziano's, McDonald's, Pepper's Mexi Grill, Subway, Wendy's Extended Stay America, Hamp Inn CVS Drug, GNC, Publix, W Shell Papa John's
1a	SW 25th (from sb), downtown, to Rickenbacker Causew E to Baggs SRA
0mm	**I-95 begins/ends on US 1. 1 mi S Mobil**

INTERSTATE 275 (Tampa)

Exit #	Services
59mm	I-275 begins/ends on I-75, exit 274.
53	Bearss Ave, E [gas] Citgo/dsl, Wawa/dsl [food] Culver's [other] Carmax, Walmart, W [gas] BP, Chevron/dsl, Marathon/Dunkin', RaceTrac/dsl, Shell/dsl [food] Burger King, IHOP, McDonald's, Popeye's, Subway [lodging] Vista Inn [other] Aldi Foods, BigLots, CVS Drug, GNC, Ross
52	Fletcher Ave, E [gas] Citgo/dsl, Marathon, Mobil/dsl, RaceTrac/dsl, Speedway, Sunoco, Wawa/dsl [food] Arby's, Bruno's Pizza, Church's, DQ, Krystal, McDonald's, Popeye's [lodging] Days Inn [other] [H], Aldi Foods, Family$, to USF, Toyota, Walmart, W [gas] Citgo, Marathon, Mobil [lodging] Super 8 [other] Cadillac, Family$, Jaguar, Save-A-Lot
51	FL 582, Fowler Ave, E [gas] Citgo/dsl, Marathon/dsl, Mobil/dsl, Shell/Circle K [food] A&W/LJ Silver, Burger King, Chili's, Chipotle Mexican, Denny's, Firehouse Subs, Five Guys, Jason's Deli, Jimmy John's, KFC, Longhorn Steaks, McDonald's, Panda Express, Pizza Hut, Shell Rest., Sonic, Starbucks, Steak'n Shake, Subway, Taco Bell, TGIFriday's, Waffle House, Wendy's [lodging] Clarion, Embassy Suites, Holiday Inn, Hyatt Place, La Quinta, Wingate Inn [other] $General, $Tree, Advance Parts, AT&T, CVS Drug, O'Reilly Parts, Verizon, Walgreens, Winn Dixie, W [lodging] Rodeway Inn [other] Audi, BMW, Chevrolet, NAPA, Porsche, VW
50	FL 580, Busch Blvd, E [gas] Citgo, Marathon [food] Burger King, McDonald's, Olive Garden, Popeye's, Red Lobster, Subway, Taco Bell [lodging] Hampton Inn, Holiday Inn Express, La Quinta, Red Roof Inn [other] $General, Advance Parts, AutoZone, Busch Gardens, Family$, Walgreens, W [food] Burger King [other] $Tree, Advançe Parts, CVS Drug, Family$, Firestone/auto, Home Depot, Walmart Mkt
49	Bird Ave (from nb), E [other] Family$, W [food] Checkers, KFC, Krispy Kreme, McDonald's, Subway, Wendy's [other] $General, Save-A-Lot
48	Sligh Ave, E [gas] Marathon, Sunoco [other] USPO, W [other] zoo
47b a	US 92, to US 41 S, Hillsborough Ave, E [gas] Marathon, Mobil/dsl, Shell/Circle K [food] Burger King, Checkers, McDonald's, Popeye's, Subway, Taco Bell, Wendy's [other] Advance Parts, Ross, vet, Walgreens, Walmart, W [gas] BP, Shell/Circle K [food] Papa John's, Starbucks [lodging] Dutch Motel
46b	FL 574, MLK Blvd, E [gas] [other] Advance Parts, Walgreens, Winn Dixie, W [gas] Chevron/dsl [food] McDonald's [other] [H]
46a	Floribraska Ave (from sb, no return)
45b	I-4 E, to Orlando, I-75
45a	Jefferson St, downtown E
44	Ashley Dr, Tampa St, downtown W
42	Howard Ave, Armenia Ave, W [gas] Marathon/dsl [food] Popeye's
41c	Himes Ave (from sb), W [other] RJ Stadium
41b a	US 92, Dale Mabry Blvd, E [gas] Marathon, Marathon (2), Mobil/dsl, Shell/Circle K, Wawa/dsl [food] Brickhouse Grill, Burger King, Carrabba's, Chick-Fil-A, Crispers, Don Pan Cuban, Donatello Italian, Grill 116, IHOP, J.Alexanders Rest, Jersey Mike's Subs, Little Caesar's, Pei Wei, Pizza Hut, Ruby Tuesday, Shells Rest., Starbucks, Subway, Village Inn [lodging] Best Western, Courtyard, Quality Inn, Tahitian Inn/cafe [other] AT&T, Barnes&Noble, CVS Drug, Office Depot, Publix, Tire Kingdom, to MacDill AFB, Trader Joe's, Verizon, W [gas] Marathon/Dunkin' [food] Burger King, Chili's, China 1, Chipotle, Denny's, Jimmy John's, Joe's Pizza, McDonald's, Moe's SW Grill, Sonic, Starbucks, Subway, Sweet Tomatoes, Wendy's [lodging] Fairfield Inn, Hilton, Howard Johnson, Residence Inn [other] Best Buy, Chrysler/Dodge/Jeep,

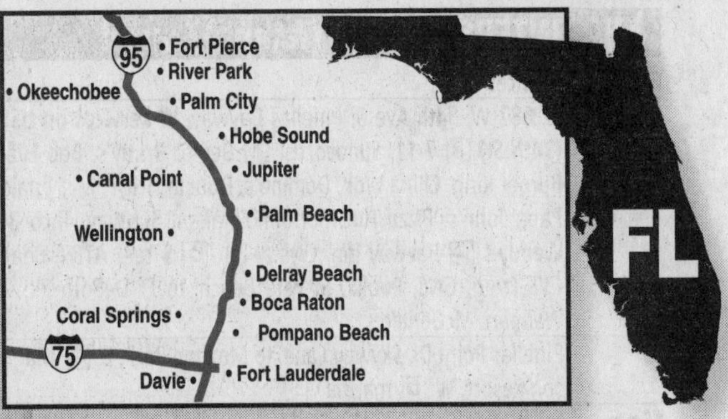

Exit #	Services
41b a	Continued Family$, Home Depot, Honda, Petsmart, Staples, Target, to RJ Stadium, Walmart, Whole Foods Mkt, Winn Dixie
40b	Lois Ave, W [gas] Marathon/dsl [food] Charley's Rest. [lodging] DoubleTree Hotel, Sheraton
40a	FL 587, Westshore Blvd, E [gas] BP, Chevron/dsl, Citgo/Subway [food] Burger King, Chipotle Mexican, Gogo's Greek, Jimmy John's, Maggiano's Rest., McDonald's, Panera Bread, PF Chang's, Season's Grill, Starbucks, Taco Bell, Waffle House [lodging] Crowne Plaza, Embassy Suites [other] Firestone, JC Penney, Macy's, Old Navy, PetCo, Walgreens, W [gas] Shell/Subway [food] Blue Water Grill [lodging] Hampton Inn, Holiday Inn, Marriott, Ramada Inn, SpringHill Suites
39b a	FL 60 W, W [other] to [airport]
32	Fl 687 S, 4th St N, to US 92 (no sb re-entry)
31b a	9th St N, MLK St N (exits left from sb), [other] [airport], info
30	FL 686, Roosevelt Blvd, 0-2 mi W [gas] Rally [food] Bascom's Chophouse, Burger King, Chil-fil-A, Cracker Barrel, Mamma Mia's, McDonald's, Starbucks, Subway, Taco Bell, Wendy's [lodging] Comfort Inn, Courtyard, Extended Stay America, Fairfield Inn, Hampton Inn, Holiday Inn, La Quinta, Marriott, Quality Inn, Red Roof Inn, Sleep Inn, SpringHill Suites, Super 8 [other] CVS Drug, Publix
28	FL 694 W, Gandy Blvd, Indian Shores, 0-2 mi W [gas] Citgo, Murphy USA/dsl, Speedway/dsl, WaWa/dsl [food] Applebee's, BJ's Brewhouse, Bob Evans, Buffalo Wild Wings, Burger King, Cheddar's, Chick-fil-A, Chili's, Chipotle, Coldstone, Dunkin', Firehouse Subs, Five Guys, IHOP, McDonald's, Moe's SW, Panda Express, Panera Bread, Pizza Hut/Taco Bell, Pollo Tropical, Sonny's BBQ, Starbucks, Subway, Wendy's [lodging] La Quinta [other] $Tree, Bentley, BMW, Cadillac, GNC, Home Depot, Honda, Marshall's, Michael's, Office Depot, PetCo, Publix, Rolls Royce, Target, U-Haul, Walgreens, Walmart

ST PETERSBURG

Exit #	Services
26b a	54th Ave N, E [food] Cracker Barrel [lodging] Comfort Inn, Holiday Inn Express, W [gas] RaceTrac/dsl [food] Waffle House [lodging] Knights Inn [other] [H], Harley-Davidson, NAPA
25	38th Ave N, to beaches, W [gas] Citgo/dsl, Wawa/dsl [food] Burger King, Hardee's [other] Subaru, VW, Walgreens
24	22nd Ave N, W [gas] Citgo/dsl, RaceTrac/dsl, Wawa/dsl [food] Dunkin', Little Caesar's [other] Advance Parts, Home Depot, Lowe's
23b	FL 595, 5th Ave N, E [other] [H]
23a	I-375, E [other] The Pier, Waterfront, downtown
22	I-175 E, Tropicana Field, E [other] [H]
21	28th St S, downtown
20	31st Ave (from nb), downtown
19	22nd Ave S, Gulfport, W [gas] Chevron, Citgo, Shell/dsl [food] Church's, KFC [other] Family$
18	26th Ave S (from nb)

FL

INTERSTATE 275 (Tampa) Cont'd

Exit #	Services
17	FL 682 W, 54th Ave S, Pinellas Bayway, **W services on US 19 (34th St)** 7-11, Sunoco/dsl Beef'O'Brady's, Bob Evans, Burger King, China Wok, Domino's, Dunkin', IHOP, McDonald's, Papa John's, Pizza Hut, Portofino Italian, Subway, Taco Bell, Wendy's Bayway Inn, Crystal Inn $Tree, AT&T, Beall's, CVS Drug, GNC, Publix, St Pete Beach, to Ft DeSoto Pk, vet, Walmart/McDonald's
16	Pinellas Point Dr, Skyway Lane, to Maximo Park, **E** Magnuson Resort, **W** marina
16mm	**toll plaza sb**
13mm	N Skyway Fishing Pier, **W both lanes, full facilities, litter barrels, petwalk, , , vending**
10mm	Tampa Bay
7mm	S Skyway Fishing Pier, **E both lanes, full facilities, litter barrels, petwalk, , , vending**
6mm	**toll plaza nb**
5	US 19, Palmetto, Bradenton
2	US 41, (last nb exit before toll), Palmetto, Bradenton, **E** Circle K, Fiesta Grove RV Resort, Frog Creek Campground, Terra Ceia Village Campground, Winterset RV Resort, **W** Shell/DQ/Subway/dsl
0mm	**I-275 begins/ends on I-75, exit 228.**

INTERSTATE 295 (Jacksonville)

JACKSONVILLE

Exit #	Services
61b a	**I-295 begins/ends on I-95, exit 337.**
60	US 1, Philips Hwy, **E** RaceTrac/dsl Buick/GMC, Honda, Toyota, VW, **W** BP/dsl Chevrolet, Ford, Mazda, Nissan, Tire Kingdom, Volvo
58	FL 9b (from sb)
56	FL 152, Baymeadows Rd, **E** Gate/dsl McDonald's Holiday Inn Chrysler/Dodge/Jeep, Fiat, **W** Shell Carrabba's, China Wok, Hurricane Grill, Outback Steaks, Sticky Fingers, Tequila's Mexican, Tony D's Pizza, Wendy's Hampton Inn Publix, SteinMart, URGENT CARE, Walgreens, Winn Dixie
54	Gate Pkwy, **W** Melting Pot, Otaki Japanese Steaks
53	FL 202, Butler Blvd, **1 mi W on Gate Pkwy** Shell/dsl Arby's, Bahama Breeze, BJ's Rest, Bono's BBQ, Brio Grille, Burger-Fi, Cantina Laredo, Capital Grill, Cheesecake Factory, Chick-fil-A, Chipotle Mexican, Cooper's Hawk, J Alexander's, Maggiano's Italian, McDonald's, Mimi's Cafe, Moxie Kitchen, Ovinte, Panda Express, Panera Bread, Pei Wei, PF Chang's, Pollo Tropical, Seasons Rest, Ted's MT Grill, Wasabi, Wendy's, Zaxby's, Zoe's Kitchen Sheraton $Tree, AT&T, Barnes&Noble, Best Buy, Costco, CVS Drug, Dick's, Dillard's, Jo-Ann, Nordstrom, Old Navy, Petsmart, REI, Ross, Staples, Target, Verizon
52	U of NF Dr, Town Center Pkwy, same as 53
51	US 90, Beach Blvd, **E** Burger King, Dunkin', Jimmy John's, **W** Shell Arby's, Checkers, McDonald's, Pizza Hut, Sonic, Taco Bell InTown Suites $Tree, Advance Parts, Sam's Club/gas, USPO, vet, Walgreens, Winn-Dixie
49	St John's Bluff Rd (from nb), **E** BP, Shell Papa John's Holiday Inn Express, InTown Suites $Tree, Nissan, O'Reilly Parts
48	FL 10, to Atlantic Blvd
47	Monument Rd, **E** Marathon/Kangaroo/dsl Domino's, Hong Kong Chinese, Mudville Grille vet, **W** Gate/dsl Ruby Tuesday Courtyard, Hampton Inn Walmart/McDonald's
46	FL 116 E, Wonderwood Connector, Merrill Rd, **E** Car wood Suites, **W** Woodspring Suites
44mm	St John's River
41	FL 105, Heckscher Dr, Zoo Pkwy, **E** Gate/dsl, **W** Va Kangaroo/dsl Wendy's Holiday Inn Express zoo
40	Alta Dr, **E** Molly Brown's Grill, Viva Mexican
37	Pulaski Rd, **E** Marathon/Kangaroo/dsl
36	US 17, Main St, **E** Kangaroo/dsl DQ, McDona Winn-Dixie, **W** Subway
35b a	I-95, S to Jacksonville, N to Savannah
33	Duval Rd, **W**
32	FL 115, Lem Turner Rd, **E** 7-11/dsl Burger King, na Wok, McDonald's (1mi), Subway, Waffle House, Wen $Tree, Home Depot, Walmart/McDonald's, **W** Flami Lake RV Resort, Lakeside Cabins/RV Park
30	FL 104, Dunn Ave, **E** 7-11/dsl, Gate/dsl, Shell (1mi), Va (1mi) McDonald's (1mi), **W** Big Tree RV Park
28b a	US 1, US 23, to Callahan, Jacksonville, **E** Kangaroo **W** auto repair, BP/DQ/dsl, RaceTrak/dsl Wen **S** Valero/Kangaroo/Subway/dsl
25	Pritchard Rd, **W** Kangaroo/Subway/deli/dsl/24hr
22	Commonwealth Ave, **E** BP/dsl Burger King, H ee's, Waffle House, Zaxby's Quality Inn dogtr **W** Wendy's Comfort Suites, Country Inn&Suites
21b a	I-10, W to Tallahassee, E to Jacksonville
19	FL 228, Normandy Blvd, **E** BP/dsl, Murphy U dsl Burger King, Capt D's, El Potro, Firehouse Subs, G en Corral, Hot Wok, McDonald's, Panda Express, Papa Joh Sonic, Waffle House, Wendy's $Tree, AT&T, CVS Drug, S A-Lot, Walgreens, Walmart, **W** BP, RaceTrac/dsl, Shell/ Speedway/dsl Famous Amos, Golden China, Harde KFC, Larry's Subs, McDonald's, Pizza Hut, Popeye's, Sam's S food Rest., Whataburger Advance Parts, CVS Drug, Fa ly$, Publix, Walgreens, Winn-Dixie
17	FL 208, Wilson Blvd, **E** 7-11/dsl, BP/Subway/dsl, Spe way/Dunkin'/dsl China Wok, Hardee's $General, vance Parts, FL RV Ctr, Walmart Mkt, **W** Kangaroo
16	FL 134, 103rd St, Cecil Field, **E** BP/dsl, Gate/dsl, Mur Express/dsl, RaceTrac/dsl, Speedway Applebee's, C D's, Firehouse Subs, Krispy Kreme, Krystal, Papa John's, Pi Hut, Popeye's, Sonic, Wendy's, Ying's Chinese Hospita Inn $General, $Tree, Advance Parts, AT&T, CVS Drug, G Goodyear/auto, NAPA, Save-A-Lot Foods, Tires+, U-Haul, GENT CARE, Walmart/McDonald's, **W** BP/dsl, Exxon/ Shell Burger King, DQ, Dunkin', IHOP, KFC, Little Caesa McDonald's, Subway, Taco Bell, Waffle House Aamco, toZone, Family$, Goodyear/auto, O'Reilly Parts, Publix, Tires, vet, Walgreens
12	FL 21, Blanding Blvd, **E** BP, RaceTrac/dsl, Speedw Dunkin'/dsl, Texaco Burger King, Dunkin', Larry's Su McDonald's, Pizza Hut, Subway $General, Acura, Au Best Buy, BMW, Buick/GMC, Cadillac, CarMax, Chrysl Dodge/Jeep, CVS Drug, Fiat, Ford, Honda, Hyundai, Infin Lexus, Lincoln, Mazda, Mercedes/Smart, Nissan, Office Dep Subaru, U-Haul, USPO, VW, Walgreens, **W** BP, Carrabb Marathon/Kangaroo/dsl, Shell Applebee's, Arby's, B falo Wild Wings, Burger King, Chick-fil-A, Chili's, China B fet, Chipotle Mexican, ChuckeCheese, Denny's, Dick's Win Firehouse Subs, Five Guys, HoneyBaked Ham, Hooters, K Krystal, Kyodai Steaks, Longhorn Steaks, Mission BBQ, Ol Garden, Orange Park Ale House, Outback Steaks, Panda press, Panera Bread, Papa John's, Red Lobster, Ruby Tuesd

INTERSTATE 295 (Jacksonville) Cont'd

12 Continued
Starbucks, Steak'n Shake, Sweet Tomatoes, Taco Bell, Ted's MT Grill, TGIFriday's, Thai Garden, Wendy's [lodging] Country Inn Suites, La Quinta, Motel 6, Quality Inn, Red Roof Inn, Super 8 [other] H, $Tree, AT&T, Belk, Books-A-Million, Dick's, Dillard's, Discount Tire, Firestone/auto, Goodyear/auto, Home Depot, JC Penney, Jo-Ann Fabrics, Michael's, O'Reilly Parts, PepBoys, Petsmart, Publix, Sam's Club/gas, Tires+, TJMaxx, Toyota, Verizon, Walgreens, Walmart/dsl

10 US 17, FL 15, Roosevelt Blvd, Orange Park, **E** [lodging] Best Western, **W** [gas] BP/dsl, Chevron/dsl, RaceTrac/dsl, Speedway/dsl [food] Aron's Pizza, Cracker Barrel, Dunkin', Four Rivers Smokehouse, Krystal, McDonald's, Subway, Waffle House, Wendy's [lodging] Courtyard, Days Inn, Fairfield Inn, Hampton Inn, Hilton Garden, Holiday Inn, Rodeway Inn [other] H, $Tree, CVS Drug, General RV Ctr, Harley-Davidson, Sun Tire, vet, Winn-Dixie

7mm St Johns River, Buckman Br

5b a FL13, San Jose Blvd, **E** [gas] Speedway/dsl, Valero/DQ/dsl [food] Arby's, Bob Evans, Bono's BBQ, Carrabba's, Chick-fil-A, Crystal River Seafood, Dickey's BBQ, Domino's, Famous Amos, Firehouse Subs, Five Guys, HoneyBaked Ham, Krystal, McDonald's, Outback Steaks, Popeye's, Red Elephant Pizza, Smoothie King,

5b a Continued
Starbucks, Steak'n Shake, The Loop Pizza, Village Inn, Which Wich?, Zaxby's [lodging] La Quinta, Ramada Inn [other] Aamco, Advance Parts, BigLots, CVS Drug, Firestone/auto, Office Depot, PepBoys, Publix, Save-A-Lot, Sun Tire, Target, Tire Kingdom, Tires+, URGENT CARE, Verizon, Whole Foods Mkt, **W** [gas] BP, Citgo, Shell [food] Al's Pizza, Bonefish Grill, Bruster's, Chili's, Chipotle Mexican, Dunkin', Golden Corral, Hardee's, Jimmy John's, Krispy Kreme, Mama Fu's, Mandarin Ale House, McDonald's, Moe's SW Grill, Newk's Eatery, Osaka Grill, Panera Bread, Papa John's, Papa Murphy's, Pizza Hut, Pollo Tropical, Starbucks, Subway, Taco Bell, Tree Steakhouse [other] $Tree, Advance Parts, AT&T, AutoZone, Barnes&Noble, Goodyear/auto, Marshall's, Michael's, NAPA, PetCo, Publix, Staples, SteinMart, Tire Kingdom, TJ Maxx, U-Haul, vet, Walgreens, Walmart, Winn-Dixie, World Mkt

3 Old St Augustine Rd, **E** [gas] BP/dsl, Shell/dsl [food] Burger King, Little Caesar's, Little China, McDonald's, Pizza Hut, Salento Steaks, St Mary's Seafood, Taco Bell, Wendy's [lodging] Holiday Inn Express [other] $General, $Tree, CVS Drug, GNC, Hobby Lobby, Publix/deli, Winn-Dixie, **W** [gas] Gate/dsl, Marathon/Kangaroo/dsl [food] Firehouse Subs, KFC, Rosy's Mexican, Subway, Vino's Pizza [other] Lowe's, vet, Walgreens

FL

NOTES

GEORGIA

INTERSTATE 16

	Exit #	Services
	167b a	W Broad, Montgomery St, **I-16 begins/ends in Savannah.**, Savannah, **0-1 mi N** [gas] Chevron, Enmarket, Parker's [lodging] Best Western, Courtyard, DoubleTree, Fairfield Inn, Hampton Inn, Hilton Garden, Holiday Inn, Quality Inn, Residence Inn, Springhill Suites, **S** [food] Burger King, Popeye's, Wendy's [other] Family$
	166	US 17, Gwinnet St, Savannah, Savannah Visitors Ctr
	165	GA 204, 37th St (from eb), to Ft Pulaski NM, **N** [other] Savannah College
	164b a	I-516, US 80, US 17, GA 21
	162	Chatham Pkwy, **S** [gas] Shell/dsl [food] Kan Pai Japanese, Larry's Subs, Nicky's Pizza, Sunrise Rest. [other] Acura, Chrysler/Dodge/Jeep, Kia, Lexus, Subaru, Toyota
	160	GA 307, Dean Forest Rd, **N** [gas] Parker's/dsl, Pilot/Subway/dsl/scales, Shell/dsl [food] Ronnie's Rest., Waffle House
	157b a	I-95, S to Jacksonville, N to Florence
	155	Pooler Pkwy, **N** [gas] EnMarket/dsl, Murphy USA/dsl [food] Jalapeno's Mexican, Papa John's, Subway, Wasabi Fusion [other] Lowe's, Savannah Tire, to Airport, Verizon, **S** [gas] BP/dsl, Parker's/dsl
	152	GA 17, to Bloomingdale
	148	Old River Rd, to US 80
	144mm	**weigh sta both lanes**
	143	US 280, to US 80, **S** [gas] BP/Subway/dsl, Marathon/dsl
	137	GA 119, to Pembroke, Ft Stewart
	132	Ash Branch Church Rd
	127	GA 67, to Pembroke, Ft Stewart, **N** [gas] BP/dsl, EnMarket/dsl [food] Sallie Mae's Kitchen [other] antiques
	116	US 25/301, to Statesboro, **N** [gas] Chevron/PoJo Diner/dsl/scales/24hr [other] Magnolia Springs SP (45 mi), to GA Southern U, **S** [lodging] Patriot Inn
	111	Pulaski-Excelsior Rd, **S** [gas] Citgo/Grady's Grill/dsl [other] Beaver Run RV Park, tires/repair
METTER	104	GA 22, GA 121, Metter, **N** [gas] BP/dsl/scales/24hr, Enmark, EVC, Parker's/dsl, Shell/dsl [food] Bevrick's Grille, Burger King, DQ, El Mariachi, Jomax BBQ, KFC/Taco Bell, McDonald's, Papa Buck's BBQ, Pizza Hut, Shogun, Subway, Waffle House, Zaxby's [lodging] American Inn, Days Inn, Econo Inn, Garden Inn [other] (H), Chevrolet, info, O'Reilly Parts, to Smith SP, Walgreens, **S** [gas] Chevron/dsl, Marathon/dsl [other] Ford
	101mm	Canoochee River
	98	GA 57, to Stillmore, **S** [gas] BP/dsl/24hr, Chevron/dsl [other] to Altahama SP
	90	US 1, to Swainsboro, **N** [gas] Chevron/Subway/dsl, Marathon/dsl
	88mm	Ohoopee River
	84	GA 297, to Vidalia, **N** [other] truck sales
	78	US 221, GA 56, to Swainsboro
	71	GA 15, GA 78, to Soperton, **N** [gas] Chevron/dsl
	67	GA 29, to Soperton, **S** [gas] Marathon/dsl [food] Huddle House
	58	GA 199, Old River Rd, East Dublin
	56mm	Oconee River
DUBLIN	54	GA 19, to Dublin, **S** [gas] Chevron/dsl/24hr
	51	US 441, US 319, to Dublin, **N** [gas] BP/Subway/dsl, EVC, Exxon/dsl, Flash/gas, Pilot/dsl/scales/24hr [food] Arby's, Asian Buffet, Burger King, KFC, King's Inn/rest., McDonald's, Ruby Tuesday, Salsa's Mexican, Taco Bell, Wendy's [lodging] Baymont Inn, Days Inn, Holiday Inn Express, Motel 6, Quality Inn, Relax Inn, Super 8 [other] (H), $General, Chrysler/Dodge/Jeep, Steve's RV,
	51	Continued **S** [gas] Chevron/dsl, Tesla EVC [food] Cracker Barrel, Longh Steaks, Waffle House, Zaxby's [lodging] Fairfield Inn, Hampton La Quinta [other] to Little Ocmulgee SP, visitor ctr
	49	GA 257, to Dublin, Dexter, **N** [gas] Friendly Gus/dsl [other] (H), H eysuckle Farm RV Park, **S** [gas] Loves/Chester's/Subw dsl/scales/24hr
	46mm	**[rest stop] wb, full (handicapped) facilities, litter barrels, petwalk, (phone), (picnic), dump, vending**
	44mm	**[rest stop] eb, full (handicapped) facilities, litter barrels, petwalk, (phone), (picnic), RV du vending**
	42	GA 338, to Dudley
	39	GA 26, to Cochran, Montrose
	32	GA 112, Allentown, **S** [gas] Chevron/dsl
	27	GA 358, to Danville
	24	GA 96, to Jeffersonville, **N** [gas] Marathon/dsl, **S** [gas] Exxon/Hu House/dsl/24hr [lodging] Suburban Inn [other] museum, to Robins AFB
OCMULGEE	18	Bullard Rd, to Jeffersonville, Bullard
	12	Sgoda Rd, Huber, **N** [gas] Marathon/dsl
	6	US 23, US 129A, East Blvd, Ocmulgee, **N** [gas] Shell/Circle K/ Texaco/dsl [food] McDonald's, Waffle House [other] GA Forestry to (airport), **S** [gas] Chevron/Huddle House/dsl/scales/24hr, Frien Gus [food] Subway
	2	US 80, GA 87, MLK Jr Blvd, **N** [lodging] Marriott [other] (H), conv ctr, mulgee NM, **S** [gas] Marathon/dsl [other] to Hist Dist
	1b	GA 22, to US 129, GA 49, 2nd St (from wb), **S** [other] (H)
MACON	1a	US 23, Gray Hwy (from eb), **N** [gas] Exxon, Flash/dsl, Valero [food] by's, Bojangles, Burger King, Chen's Wok, DQ, El Sombrero M ican, Fincher's BBQ, Hardee's, Hong Kong Express, Krispy Kre Krystal, McDonald's, Nu-Way Weiners, Papa John's, Subway, T Bell, Wendy's [other] (H), Attaway Tire, CVS Drug, Family$, Kro O'Reilly Parts, U-Haul, Walgreens, **S** [gas] Jumbo's, Sunoco/dsl Burger King, Checker's, Krystal, Pizza Hut, Waffle House, Zaxby
	0mm	I-75, S to Valdosta, N to Atlanta. **I-16 begins/ends on I-75, e 165 in Macon.**

INTERSTATE 20

	Exit #	Services
	202mm	Georgia/South Carolina state line, Savannah River
	201mm	**Welcome Ctr wb, full (handicapped) facilities, litter barrels, petwalk, (phone), (picnic), vending**
	200	GA 104, Riverwatch Pkwy, Augusta, **N** [gas] Pilot/Wendy dsl/scales/24hr [food] Waffle House [lodging] Baymont Inn, Cand wood Suites, Comfort Suites, Ecco Suites, Microtel, Quality I Sleep Inn, Woodspring Suites [other] Freightliner, **S** [other] Cabela Costco/gas, $Tree
AUGUSTA	199	GA 28, Washington Rd, Augusta, **0-3 mi N** [gas] BP, RaceW Shell/Circle K, Sprint [food] Applebee's, Baskin-Robbins/Dunk Burger King, CA Dreaming, Capt D's, Checkers, Chick-fil- Denny's, Domino's, DQ, Fujiyama Japanese, Krystal, Longho Steaks, McDonald's, Mi Rancho Mexican, Piccadilly, Pizza H Rhinehart's Seafood, Starbucks, Steakout, Veracruz Mexica Waffle House, Wife Saver Rest, Wild Wing Cafe [lodging] Claric Courtyard, Econolodge, Hampton Inn, Hilton Garden, Holiday I Express, Homewood Suites, La Quinta, Masters Inn, Scottish In Sheraton, Sunset Inn, Super 8, Travelodge [other] $Tree, AutoZor Buick/GMC, Chevrolet, Chrysler/Dodge/Jeep, Hyundai, Infi ti, Lexus, Mercedes, NAPA, Nissan, Toyota, Tuesday Mornir

GA

INTERSTATE 20 Cont'd

199 Continued
S [gas] BP, Circle K/dsl, Shell/Circle K/dsl [food] Arby's, BoneFish Grill, Carrabba's, Crazy Turk's Pizza, Five Guys, HoneyBaked Ham, Hooters, Krispy Kreme, McDonald's, Moe's SW Grill, New Peking, Olive Garden, Outback Steaks, Red Lobster, Roadrunner Cafe, Shangri La, Straw Hat Pizza, Subway, Taco Bell, T-Bonz Steaks, Teresa's Mexican, TGIFriday's, Thai Jong Rest., TX Roadhouse, Vallarta Mexican, Waffle House, Wendy's, Zaxby's [lodging] Best Western, Country Inn&Suites, Knights Inn, Magnolia Inn, Motel 6, Parkway Inn, Staybridge Suites, Westbank Inn [other] $Tree, AT&T, CVS Drug, Firestone/auto, Fresh Mkt Foods, Goodyear/auto, Kroger/dsl, Midas, PepBoys, Publix, SteinMart, Tire Kingdom, Verizon, Walgreens, Whole Food Mkt

196b GA 232 W, N [gas] Enmark, Murphy Express/dsl [food] Checkers, Golden Corral, Krystal, Salsa's Grill, Stevi B's Pizza [lodging] Baymont Inn, Travel Inn [other] Aldi Foods, Discount Tire, GNC, Home Depot, Lowe's, NTB, O'Reilly Parts, Sam's Club/dsl, URGENT CARE, Walgreens, Walmart, Sprouts Mkt

196a I-520, Bobby Jones Fwy, S [food] Atlanta Bread Co, Buffalo Wild Wings, Carolina Alehouse, Chick-fil-A, Chili's, Dunkin', Genghis Grill, Logan's Roadhouse, Macaroni Grill, McDonald's, O'Charley's, Panera Bread, Starbucks, Sticky Fingers, Subway, Waffle House [lodging] DoubleTree Hotel [other] [H], Best Buy, Hobby Lobby, Michael's, Office Depot, Old Navy, Petsmart, Rite Aid, Staples, Target, Tires+, to [airport], Verizon, vet

195 Wheeler Rd, N [gas] Sprint [food] Barnyard Burgers [lodging] Hyatt Place [other] CarMax, S [gas] Shell/Circle K/Blimpie [food] Guiseppe's Pizza, Sonic [lodging] Days Inn [other] [H], BP/dsl, Harley-Davidson, Rite Aid, URGENT CARE

194 GA 383, Belair Rd, to Evans, N [gas] Shell/Circle K/dsl, Sprint [food] Bojangles, Burger King, Hungry Howie's, Popeye's, Sun Kwong Chinese, Taco Bell, Waffle House, Wendy's [lodging] GA Inn [other] Family$, Food Lion, Fun Park, S [gas] BP/DQ/dsl, Fuel Express, Pilot/Subway/dsl/scales/24hr [food] Cookout, Cracker Barrel, McDonald"s, Steak'n Shake, Waffle House [lodging] Augusta Inn, Best Suites, Best Value Inn, Best Western, Comfort Inn, Hampton Inn, Hawthorn Suites, Holiday Inn, Howard Johnson, Quality Inn, Red Roof Inn, Super 8, Wingate Inn [other] Goodyear/auto, Kenworth

190 GA 388, to Grovetown, N [gas] TPS/dsl/scales/24hr [food] Waffle House, S [gas] Murphy Express/dsl [food] Applebee's, Arby's, Chick-fil-A, Culver's, Jersey Mike's, Mi Rancho [lodging] Home 2 Suites [other] AT&T, Verizon, Walmart

189mm **weigh sta both lanes**

183 US 221, to Harlem, Appling, N [other] Cushman RV Ctr, S [gas] Exxon/dsl [other] to Laurel&Hardy Museum

182mm **[RS] both lanes, full [handicapped] facilities, litter barrels, petwalk, [phone], [picnic], RV dump, vending**

175 GA 150, N [gas] Chevron/rest/dsl/24hr [lodging] Express Inn [other] to Mistletoe SP

172 US 78, GA 17, Thomson, N [gas] Loves/Chester's/Subway/dsl/scales/24hr [food] Waffle House [other] Chrysler/Dodge/Jeep, S [gas] Circle K/dsl, Citgo/DQ/dsl, M&A/dsl, Marathon/dsl, RaceWay/dsl [food] Arby's, Bojangles, Burger King, Checkers, Chick-fil-A, Domino's, Habaneros Mexican, Kiosco Mexican, Krystal, LJ Silver, Lucky Chinese, McDonald's, MingWah Chinese, Pizza Hut, Popeye's, Ryan's, Taco Bell, Waffle House, Wendy's, Zaxby's [lodging] Comfort Inn, EconoLodge, Hampton Inn, Rodeway Inn, White Columns Inn [other] [H], $General, Advance Parts, AutoZone, Bi-Lo, Family$, O'Reilly Parts, URGENT CARE, Verizon, Walgreens

THOMSON

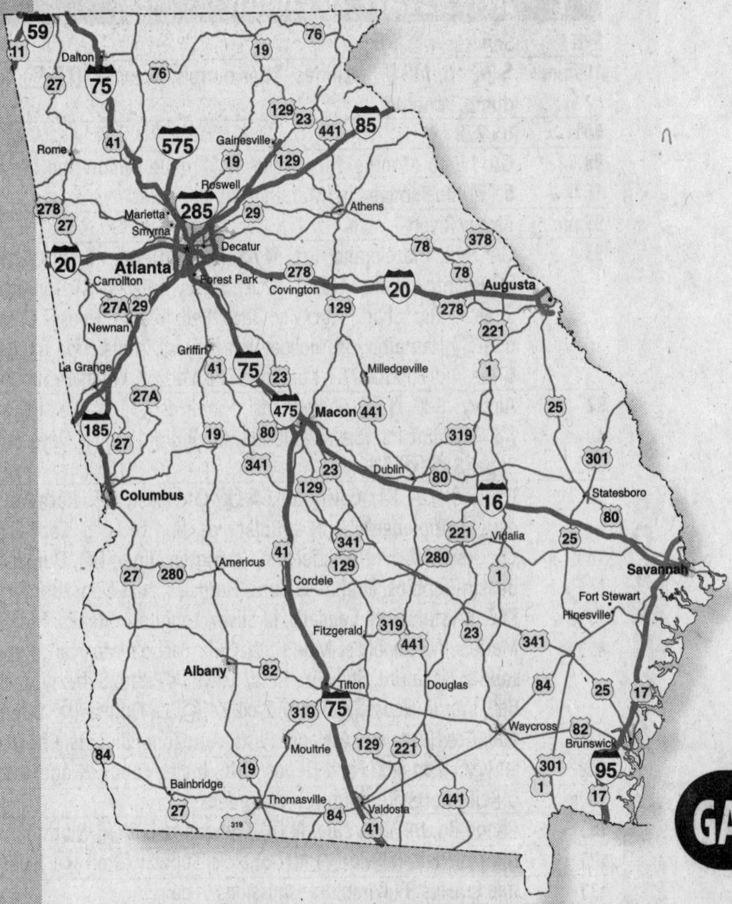

MADISON

169 Thomson

165 GA 80, Camak

160 E Cadley Rd, Norwood

154 US 278, GA 12, Barnett

148 GA 22, Crawfordville, N [gas] [other] to Stephens SP

138 GA 77, GA 15, Siloam, N [gas] FLYING J/Denny's/dsl/LP/scales/24hr, S [gas] Chevron/dsl

130 GA 44, Greensboro, N [gas] BP/dsl, Valero/Subway [food] DQ, McDonald's, Pizza Hut, Waffle House, Wendy's, Zaxby's [lodging] Holiday Lodge, Quality Inn [other] $General, Buick/Chevrolet, Greensboro Tire/repair, S [gas] Chevron/dsl [other] [H], Home Depot/gas

121 to Lake Oconee, Buckhead, S [gas] Chevron/dsl [other] Museum of Art (3mi)

114 US 441, US 129, to Madison, N [gas] Chevron/Subway/dsl, Citgo/dsl, Pilot/Huddle House/dsl/scales/24hr, RaceWay/dsl [food] Arby's, Burger King, Chick-fil-A, Cracker Barrel, Hong Kong Buffet, KFC, Krystal, McDonald's, Pachos Mexican, Pizza Hut, Steak'n Shake, Taco Bell, Waffle House, Wendy's, Zaxby's [lodging] Comfort Inn, Hampton Inn, Quality Inn [other] [H], $General, $Tree, Advance Parts, AutoZone, Ingles Foods/gas, Lowe's, O'Reilly Parts, Rite Aid, Verizon, Walmart, S [gas] Flash/dsl, Shell, TA/BP/Country Pride/Popeye's/dsl/scales/24hr/@ [food] Waffle House [lodging] Deerfield Inn, Holiday Inn Express, Super 8, Wingate Inn [other] Country Boys RV Park (1mi), truckwash/service

113 GA 83, Madison, N [gas] BP/dsl [other] [H], st patrol, S [gas] Exxon/dsl

108mm **N [RS] wb, full [handicapped] facilities, litter barrels, petwalk, [phone], [picnic], RV dump, vending**

105 Rutledge, Newborn, N [gas] Valero/pizza/dsl [other] Hard Labor Creek SP

GA

INTERSTATE 20 Cont'd

COVINGTON

Exit #	Services
103mm	**S eb, full facilities, litter barrels, petwalk, RV dump, vending**
101	US 278
98	GA 11, to Monroe, Monticello, N Blue Willow Inn (4mi), S BP/Blimpie/dsl, Marathon
95mm	Alcovy River
93	GA 142, Hazelbrand Rd, N Home Depot, S QT/dsl Bullrito's Cafe, Chili's, IHOP, Jersey Mike's, McDonald's, Shane's Rib Shack, Subway, Taco Bell, Waffle House, Wendy's Hampton Inn, Holiday Inn Express, Travelodge H, $Tree, Aldi Foods, AT&T, Kauffman Tire, Verizon, Walmart/Subway
92	Alcovy Rd, N Chevron/dsl, Shell/dsl Waffle House Baymont Inn, Best Value Inn, Covington Lodge, Days Inn, Super 8, S H
90	US 278, GA 81, Covington, S Citgo/dsl, QT, RaceWay/dsl Applebee's, Arby's, Bojangles, Burrito Loco, Capt D's, Checkers, Chick-fil-A, Church's, Covington Diner, DQ, Dunkin'/Baskin-Robbins, Firehouse Subs, Hardee's, Just Dogs/Burgers, KFC, Krystal, Little Caesar's, LJ Silver, Longhorn Steaks, Mama Maria's, McDonald's, Moe's SW Grill, Pacho's Mexican, Papa John's, Pizza Hut, Stalvey's Rest., Stevi B's Pizza, Subway, Taco Bell, Waffle House, Wendy's, Zaxby's La Quinta $General, Ace Hardware, Advance Parts, AutoZone, BigLots, Chevrolet, CVS, Family$, Food Depot, GNC, Ingles Foods, Kroger/dsl, O'Reilly Parts, Rite Aid, vet, Walgreens
88	Almon Rd, to Porterdale, N Chevron/dsl, S Marathon/Dunkin'/deli, Texaco McDonald's, Subway (2mi) Riverside Estates RV Camp, transmissions/repair
84	GA 162, Salem Rd, to Pace, N BJ's Whse/gas, Marathon/dsl Chrysler/Dodge/Jeep, S Citgo, QT, RaceWay/dsl, Shell/dsl Baskin-Robbins, Burger King, Dunkin', Hardee's, KFC, Los Bravos Mexican, McDonald's, Quiznos, Subway, Taco Bell, Waffle House, Wendy's Advance Parts, Family$, Food Depot, Ingles/gas, Olympic Auto, O'Reilly Parts, PepBoys, Rite Aid

CONYERS

Exit #	Services
82	GA 138, GA 20, Conyers, N BP/dsl, QT Applebee's, Bruster's, Chili's, ChuckECheese, Coldstone, Cracker Barrel, Don Tello's, Golden Corral, IHOP, O'Charley's, Outback Steaks, Red Lobster, Sonic, Subway Country Inn&Suites, Days Inn, Hampton Inn, Holiday Inn Express, Jameson Inn, La Quinta AT&T, Belk, Chevrolet/Buick/GMC, Courtyard, Ford, Harley-Davidson, Home Depot, Jo-Ann, Kohl's, Michael's, Office Depot, Old Navy, Petsmart, Staples, Tires+, TJ Maxx, U-Haul, Walmart, S Chevron, Shell/dsl Blimpie, Burger King, Capt D's, Checkers, Chick-fil-A, CiCi's Pizza, Dunkin'/Baskin-Robbins, Firehouse Subs, Folk's Rest., Frontera Mexican, Grand Buffet, HoneyBaked Ham, Hooters, Jim'n Nick's BBQ, KFC, Krystal, Little Caesar's, Mandarin Garden, McDonald's, Mellow Mushroom, Milano Cafe, Moe's SW Grill, Panda Express, Panera Bread, Piccadilly Cafe, Popeye's, Ruby Tuesday, Silver Dragon, Sonny's BBQ, Starbucks, Subway, Taco Bell, Waffle House Microtel $General, $Tree, Aldi Foods, BigLots, Discount Tire, Firestone/auto, GNC, Goodyear/auto, Hobby Lobby, Honda, Hyundai, Kauffman Tire, Kroger/gas, NTB, PepBoys, Publix, Ross, Target, USPO, Verizon, Walgreens
80	West Ave, Conyers, N Shell/dsl, Valero/dsl Domino's, DQ, Subway, Waffle House Best Value Inn, Motel 6 Conyers Drug, Family$, Meineke, Piggly Wiggly, S QT/dsl, Texaco/dsl Fish House, Longhorn Steaks, McDonald's Comfort Inn Nissan, vet
79mm	parking area eb

LITHONIA

Exit #	Services
78	Sigman Rd, N Shell/dsl, Texaco Waffle House
75	US 278, GA 124, Turner Hill Rd, N BP/dsl, Citgo, S Applebee's, Arizona's, Bruster's, Buffalo Wild Wi Chicken&Waffles, Chick-fil-A, Chili's, Don Tello's Mexican, F house Subs, Grand China, IHOP, Kampai's Steaks, McDona Olive Garden, Panera Bread, Smokey Bones BBQ, Steak n'Sh Steak'n Shake, Subway, Taco Bell, TGIFriday, Zaxby's C fort Inn, Comfort Suites, Fairfield Inn, Hilton Garden, Holi Inn Express, Hyatt Place $Tree, AT&T, Big Lots, Dillard's Penney, Kia, Kohl's, Macy's, Marshalls, PetCo, Rite Aid, R Staples, Target, Tires+, Toyota, Verizon, Walmart
74	Evans Mill Rd, GA 124, Lithonia, N BP/Circle K, Chev Shell Capt D's, McDonald's, Pizza Hut, SoulFood R Subway, Wendy's Advance Parts, CVS Drug, O'Reilly Pa S Citgo/dsl Da-Bomb Wings/Seafood, DQ, Dudl Rest., Krystal, Waffle House Microtel $General
71	Hillandale Dr, Farrington Rd, Panola Rd, N QT/dsl, Sh dsl Burger King, Checkers, KFC, McDonald's, Rib T Waffle House, Wings&Philly Budgetel, Quality Inn, Su 8 Family$, S BP/dsl, Citgo, Murphy USA/dsl, Sh dsl Dunkin', IHOP, Marco's Pizza, New China, Popey Ruby Tuesday, Subway, Taco Bell/LJ Silver, Town Wings, W dy's Red Roof Inn Lowe's, Publix, Tires+, Verizon, V greens, Walmart/McDonald's
68	Wesley Chapel Rd, Snapfinger Rd, N Capt D's, Check Chick-fil-A, China Cafeteria, Church's, Dunkin', KFC, Little C sar's, New China, Subway, Taco Bell, Waffle House Ec omy Inn $General, DJ's Repair, Home Depot, Kro NTB, S Chevron/dsl, Mobil, QT, Shell/dsl Dragon C nese, JJ's Fish& Chicken, McDonald's, Popeye's Super Family$, USPO
67b a	I-285, S to Macon, N to Greenville
66	Columbia Dr (from eb, no return), N Chevron
65	GA 155, Candler Rd, to Decatur, N Chevron, Citgo, Ma thon/dsl Pizza Hut, Popeye's, Red Lobster, Wendy's B Value Inn CVS Drug, U-Haul, S BP, Chevron, Shell/ Texaco Baskin-Robbins/Dunkin', Burger King, Check Church's, DQ, KFC, McDonald's, Subway, Taco Bell, Waffle K Country Hearth Inn BigLots, Firestone/auto, Macy's

ATLANTA AREA

Exit #	Services
63	Gresham Rd, N Chevron, Citgo/dsl American D Walmart/Subway, S Citgo, Marathon, Shell, Texaco/ Church's
62	Flat Shoals Rd (from eb, no return)
61b	GA 260, Glenwood Ave, N Chevron, Texaco/dsl
61a	Maynard Terrace (from eb, no return)
60b a	US 23, Moreland Ave, N Texaco, Valero Atlanta Mo Advance Parts, S Citgo/dsl, Shell Checkers, Kryst LJ Silver, McDonald's, Wendy's
59b	Memorial Dr, Glenwood Ave (from eb)
59a	Cyclorama, N Chevron/Blimpie/dsl MLK Site, S B Subway Confederate Ave Complex, CVS
58b	Hill St (from wb, no return), N Shell Mrs. Winners
58a	Capitol St (from wb, no return), N to GA Dome, S Capital In downtown
57	I-75/85
56b	Windsor St (from eb)
56a	US 19, US 29, McDaniel St (eb only), N Chevron/dsl
55b	Lee St (from wb), Ft McPherson, S Exxon, Shell Church Popeye's, Taco Bell, West Inn Food Court $Family, Maxwa Sav-A-Lot
55a	Lowery Blvd, S Exxon/dsl, Shell Church's, Popeye Taco Bell, West Inn Food Court Family$, Maxway, Sav-A-L

GA

INTERSTATE 20 Cont'd

Exit #	Services
54	Langhorn St (from wb), to Cascade Rd
53	MLK Dr, to GA 139, N Chevron, Shell/dsl, S Texaco/dsl auto repair
52b a	GA 280, Holmes Dr, High Tower Rd, S Chevron Hong Kong Chinese, McDonald's, Wendy's AutoZone, CVS Drug, Family$
51b a	I-285, S to Montgomery, N to Chattanooga
49	GA 70, Fulton Ind Blvd, N Citgo/dsl, Shamrock/dsl Wendy's Budgetel, Days Inn , S BP/dsl, Chevron/dsl, Texaco/dsl, Valero Grand Buffet, McDonald's, Waffle House Fairview Inn, Red Roof Inn U-Haul
48mm	Chattahoochee River
47	Six Flags Pkwy (from wb), N EconoLodge, S Knights Inn, Sleep Inn, Wingate Inn Six Flags Funpark
46b a	Riverside Parkway, N Citgo/Church's, Marathon, QT/dsl Hong Kong Buffet, Waffle House Super 8 Family$, S Texaco Wendy's Knights Inn, Sleep Inn, Wingate Inn Six Flags Funpark
44	GA 6, Thornton Rd, to Lithia Springs, N BP, QT, RaceTrac/dsl, Shell/dsl, Valero Applebee's, BBQ House, Bojangles, Burger King, Chick-fil-A, Church's, Domino's, Firehouse Subs, Golden Dragon Chinese, Hardee's, IHOP, KFC, Krystal, McDonald's, Olive Tree Rest., Popeye's, Ruby Tuesday, Shoney's, Sonic, Subway, Taco Bell, Waffle House, Wendy's, Zaxby's Budget Inn, Holiday Inn Express, InTowne Suites, Quality Inn $General, AT&T, Atlanta West Camping (2mi), Autozone, Carmax, Chevrolet, Ford, Harley Davidson, Home Depot, Honda, Hyundai, Kroger/gas, Midas, Nissan, Office Depot, Tires+, Verizon, vet, VW, Walgreens, S Shell Bei Jin China, Cracker Barrel, Fiesta Mexican Candlewood Suites, Country Inn&Suites, Courtyard, Fairfield Inn, Hampton Inn, Hilton Garden, Motel 6, SpringHill Suites Chrysler/Dodge/Jeep, Kia, to Sweetwater Creek SP, Toyota, Walmart
42mm	**weigh sta eb**
41	Lee Rd, to Lithia Springs, N Marathon/dsl
37	GA 92, to Douglasville, N RaceTrac/dsl, Shell/dsl Blimpie, Checker's, Chick-fil-A, Church's, DQ, Kenny's Rest., Krystal, Longhorn Steaks, Martin's Rest., McDonald's, Pizza Hut, Popeye's, Subway, Taco Bell, Waffle House, Wendy's Best Value Inn, Comfort Inn, Days Inn, EconoLodge, Quality Inn, Ramada Ltd, Royal Inn H, AutoZone, CVS Drug, Family$, Kroger/dsl, NAPA, O'Reilly Parts, Tires+, Walgreens, S Chevron/dsl, QT, Texaco/dsl Domino's, Waffle House $General, Aamco, Advance Parts, Ingles Foods
36	Chapel Hill Rd, N H, S QT, Shell/dsl Arby's, Carrabba's, China Garden, Coldstone, Daruma, Five Guys, Joe's Crabshack, Johnny's Subs, Logan's Roadhouse, McDonald's, O'Charley's, Olive Garden, Outback Steaks, Panda Express, Provino's Italian, Shane's Rib Shack, Starbucks, Subway, TX Roadhouse, Waffle House Hampton Inn $Tree, Aldi Foods, Belk, BigLots, Dillard's, Discount Tire, Firestone/auto, Hobby Lobby, JC Penney, Kohl's, Macy's, Marshall's, Michael's, Old Navy, Petsmart, Rite Aid, Ross, Target, Verizon
34	GA 5, to Douglasville, N RaceTrac/dsl, Texaco/dsl Atlantic Grill, Cracker Barrel, Stevie B's Pizza, Waffle House, Williamson Bros BBQ, Zaxby's Holiday Inn Express, La Quinta, Sleep Inn $Tree, Kauffman Tires, Sam's Club, URGENT CARE, Walmart, S Chevron/dsl, Circle K, Shell/dsl Applebee's, Bruster's, Buffalo Wild Wings, Burger King, Chick-fil-A, ChuckECheese, DQ, Dunkin', El Tio Mexican, Fiesta Mexican, Folk's Rest.,

DOUGLASVILLE

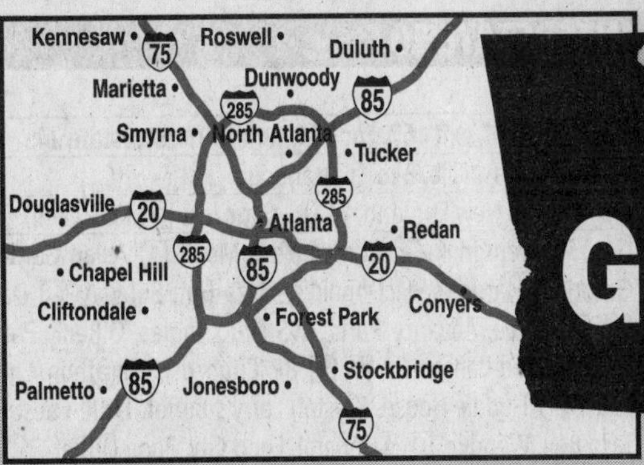

Exit #	Services
34	Continued Golden Corral, HoneyBaked Ham, IHOP, KFC, King Buffet, Krystal, La Salsa, LJ Silver, McDonald's, Moe's SW Grill, Monterrey Mexican, Papa John's, Pizza Buffet, Popeyes, Quiznos, Red Lobster, Seabreeze Seafood, S'more BBQ, Sonic, Steak'n Shake, Subway, Taco Bell, Taco Mac, Waffle House, Wasabi Japanese, Wendy's InTown Suites Advance Parts, AT&T, Batteries+, Best Buy, Goodyear/auto, Home Depot, Jo-Ann Crafts, Kroger/dsl, Lowe's, Meineke, NTB, Office Depot, O'Reilly Parts, PepBoys, Publix, Tuesday Morning, U-Haul, vet, Walgreens
30	Post Rd, S Shell/dsl
26	Liberty Rd, Villa Rica, N Shell/dsl, Swifty/dsl China Wok, Johnny's Pizza, McDonald's, Mex-Grill, Olive Tree Rest., Subway, Sumo Japanese, Waffle House H, $General, Publix, vet, Walgreens, S Chevron, Pilot/Subway/dsl/scales/24hr American Inn
24	GA 101, GA 61, Villa Rica, N BP/dsl, RaceTrac/dsl, Shell/dsl Arby's, Chick-fil-A, Hardee's, KFC/Taco Bell, Krystal, Lin's Garden Chinese, McDonald's, Pizza Hut, Romero's Italian, Sonic, Stix Grill, Subway, Waffle House, Wendy's Comfort Inn, Days Inn, EconoLodge, Super 8 H, Advance Parts, AT&T, AutoZone, CVS Drug, Ingles Foods, Rite Aid, Walgreens, S QT, Shell/dsl Bojangles, Burger King, Capt D's, Domino's, El Ranchito Mexican, O'Charley's, Papa John's, Waffle House, Zaxby's $Tree, Chevrolet, GNC, Home Depot, to W GA Coll, URGENT CARE, Verizon, Walmart/Subway
21mm	Little Tallapoosa River
19	GA 113, Temple, N FLYING J/dsl/scales/24hr, Pilot/Subway/Wendy's/dsl/scales/24hr/@ El Tapatio's, Fortune Star Chinese, Hardee's, McDonald's, Temple Pizza, Waffle House Ingles Foods/gas
15mm	**weigh sta wb**
11	US 27, Bremen, Bowdon, N Chevron/dsl, Marathon/dsl, Murphy USA/dsl, Valero/Domino's/dsl Arby's, Capt D's, Checker's, Chopsticks Chinese, Cracker Barrel, Jack's, Juanito's, KFC/Taco Bell, Little Caesar's, McDonald's, Papa John's, Subway, Waffle House, Wendy's, Zaxby's Hampton Inn, Holiday Inn Express, Microtel, Motel 6, Quality Inn H, $General, Advance Parts, Ford, Ingles Foods/gas, URGENT CARE, Verizon, Walmart/McDonald's, S BP/dsl, Circle K/dsl John Tanner SP
9	Waco Rd, N Loves/Chesters/Subway/dsl/scales/24hr Jellystone RV Park (2mi)
5	GA 100, Tallapoosa, N Exxon/dsl, Robinson's/dsl/24hr Waffle House Big Oak RV park, S Newborn TrkStp/rest/dsl/24hr/@, Pilot/KFC/Taco Bell/dsl/scales/24hr, Robinson/Subway DQ, GA Diner Super 8 to John Tanner SP, truck repair/wash
1mm	**Welcome Ctr eb, full facilities, litter barrels, petwalk, , , vending**
0mm	Georgia/Alabama state line, Eastern/Central time zone

VILLA RICA

BREMEN

GA

= gas = food = lodging = other = rest stop

INTERSTATE 59

TRENTON

Exit #	Services
I-59 begins/ends on I-24, exit 167. For I-24, turn to TN Interstate 24.	
20mm	I-24, W to Nashville, E to Chattanooga
17	Slygo Rd, to New England, W Citgo/dsl KOA (2mi)
11	GA 136, Trenton, E Chevron/dsl, Mobil Asian Garden, Guthrie's, Hardee's, McDonald's, Pizza Hut, Subway Days Inn $Tree, Advance Parts, CVS Drug, Ingles, O'Reilly Parts, to Cloudland Canyon SP, W BP, Citgo/dsl, Marathon/Circle K/dsl Huddle House, Krystal, Larry's Buffet, Little Caesar's, Taco Bell, Wendy's $General, Food City, Food Outlet
4	Rising Fawn, E Marathon, W BP/dsl, Pilot/Subway/dsl/scales/24hr camping
0mm	Georgia/Alabama state line, eastern/central time zone

INTERSTATE 75

DALTON

Exit #	Services
355mm	Georgia/Tennessee state line
354mm	Chickamauga Creek
353	GA 146, Rossville, E Marathon Cloud Springs Lodge, W BP/Subway/dsl, Shell/dsl Cabela's, Costco/gas
352mm	**Welcome Ctr sb, full facilities, info, litter barrels, petwalk, vending**
350	GA 2, Bfd Pkwy, to Ft Oglethorpe, E Chevron/dsl/24hr, Mobil/Circle K/dsl Farm to Fork Hampton Inn, Hometown Inn, Springhill Suites, W RaceTrac/dsl, Shell Subway H, Battleground Camping, to Chickamauga NP
348	GA 151, Ringgold, E BP/Circle K/dsl, Mapco Cracker Barrel, Hardee's, KFC, Little Caesar's, McDonald's, Pizza Hut, Sonic, Subway, Taco Bell, Waffle House Holiday Inn Express, Super 8, Tru Hilton $General, Advance Parts, AutoZone, Chevrolet, CVS Drug, Hyundai, Ingles, vet, Walgreens, W Exxon/dsl Arby's, Bojangles, Burger King, Domino's, Guthrie's, Krystal, New China, Wendy's Ace Hardware, Chrysler/Dodge/Jeep, Dunlap RV Ctr, Family$, Food Lion, Northgate RV Ctr, Peterbilt, truck repair
345	US 41, US 76, Ringgold, E BP, W Circle/Subway/dsl/scales/24hr, Cochran's TP/rest./dsl/scales/24hr/@, Shell Waffle House
343mm	**weigh sta both lanes**
341	GA 201, to Varnell, Tunnel Hill, W BP/Mapco carpet outlets
336	US 41, US 76, Dalton, Rocky Face, E Mapco, Murphy USA/dsl, RaceTrac/dsl Burger King, Checkers, Mr Biscuit, Waffle House H, Ford/Lincoln, Home Depot, Kohl's, PetCo, Verizon, Walmart/Subway, W BP/dsl, Victory Fuels Los Pablos, Wendy's Baymont Inn, carpet outlets, Econolodge, Guest Inn, Motel 6, Staylodge
333	GA 52, Dalton, E BP/dsl, RaceTrac/dsl, Sexton's/dsl Applebee's, Bruster's, Burger King, Chick-fil-A, CiCi's Pizza, Cracker Barrel, Five Guys, Fuji Japanese, IHOP, Jersey Mike's Subs, KFC, Krispy Kreme, Las Palmas Mexican, Longhorn Steaks, McDonald's, Outback Steaks, Panda Express, Panera Bread, Pizza Hut, Schlotzsky's, Shoney's, Sonic, Starbucks, Steak'n Shake, Subway, Taco Bell, Waffle House Days Inn, Hampton Inn, Holiday Inn Express, Red Roof Inn, Super 8 $Tree, AT&T, BigLots, Chevrolet, Chrysler/Dodge/Jeep, Food City, Harley-Davidson, Kroger/dsl, Petsmart, TJ Maxx, Tuesday Morning, Walgreens, W Bojangles, Chili's, Red Lobster, Zaxby's Comfort Inn, Country Inn Suites, Courtyard, Hilton Garden, Holiday Inn Express,

RESACA · CALHOUN · ADAIRSVILLE

Exit #	Services
333	Continued Howard Johnson, La Quinta, Quality Inn, Super 8 NW Trade/Conv Ctr
328	GA 3, to US 41, E BP/Circle K/dsl, Pilot/Arby's/scales/24hr Waffle House, Wendy's Best Value W carpet outlets
326	Carbondale Rd, E LNG, Pilot/McDonald's/Subway/scales, W BP
320	GA 136, to Lafayette, Resaca, E Flying J/Denny's/LP/24hr Dollar General Mkt, truck repair/parts
319mm	**Oostanaula River, sb, full facilities, litter barrels, walk, vending**
318	US 41, Resaca, E Pilot/DQ/Wendy's/Dunkin'/sca dsl/24hr Hardee's Rodeway Inn, W Marath Shell/dsl Chuckwagon Rest. Best Inn, Budget Duffy's Motel, Executive Inn
317	GA 225, to Chatsworth, E New Echota HS, Vann House W BP/Circle K Express Inn
315	GA 156, Redbud Rd, to Calhoun, E Subway, Waffle Ho AOK Camping (2mi), Food Lion, W BP/dsl, Liberty by's, Shoney's Quality Inn H, URGENT CARE, Walgre
312	GA 53, to Calhoun, E Shell/dsl Applebee's, Cracker Ba Longhorn Steaks, Wendy's Country Inn&Suites, EconoLoc Fairfield Inn, La Quinta Calhoun Outlets/famous bra W BP/Arby's, Circle K, Exxon/dsl, Murphy USA, RaceT dsl, Shell Bojangles, Burger King, Capt D's, Checkers, Ch fil-A, China Palace, DQ, Dunkin', El Nopal Mexican, Five G Gondolier Pizza, Hardee's, Hibachi Buffet, Huddle House, IH KFC, Krystal, Little Caesar's, McDonald's, Panda Express, P eye's, Ruby Tuesday, Starbucks, Subway, Taco Bell, Tokyo Stea Waffle House, Zaxby's Baymont Inn, Motel 6, Red Roof Scottish Inn, Super 8 $General, Advance Parts, Aldi Foo AT&T, AutoZone, GNC, Goodyear/auto, Home Depot, Kroger/ NAPA, Office Depot, Verizon, vet, Walmart
310	Union Grove Rd, E Loves/Burger King/dsl/scales/24
308mm	**nb, full facilities, litter barrels, petwalk, vendi**
306	GA 140, Adairsville, E Click/dsl, Patty's Tkstp/rest./ QT/dsl/scales/24hrs, Valero/dsl Cracker Barrel, Wend Hampton Inn truck repair, W BP/dsl, Chevron/ Shell/dsl Burger King, Hardee's, McDonald's, Subway, Ta Bell, Waffle House, Zaxby's Magnuson Hotel, Oyo Ho Quality Inn Advance Parts, AutoZone, Family$, Food Li Harvest Moon RV Park
296	Cassville-White Rd, E Pilot/McDonald's/Subway/d scales, TA/BP/Burger King/Pizza Hut/Popeye's/Taco Bell/d scales/24hr/@, Texaco/dsl Baymont Inn truckwash, W Chevron, Citgo/dsl, Marathon/dsl Country Hearth Inn K
293	US 411, to White, E Sunoco/dsl, Texaco/dsl Quality Inn, Chevron/dsl, Marathon, Tesla EVC, Valero/Subway Waf House Motel 6 Harley-Davidson, mineral museum
290	GA 20, to Rome, E Chevron/dsl, Circle K/dsl, Exxon/Subwa dsl Arby's, Fire it Up BBQ, McDonald's, Wendy's Be Value Inn, Best Western, Country Inn Suites, EconoLodge, M tel 6, Red Roof Inn, Super 8, W Murphy USA (1.5mi), She dsl, Texaco/dsl Cracker Barrel, Shoney's, Waffle House, Za by's Days Inn, Hampton Inn, Holiday Inn Express $Tree, Lowe's, Walgreens, Walmart/McDonald's
288	GA 113, Cartersville, 0-2 mi W Exxon/Circle K/dsl, Rac Trac/dsl, Shell/dsl Applebee's, Bojangles, Bruster's, Burg King, Chick-Fil-A, Chili's, CiCi's, Firehouse Subs, Five Guys, Fre dy's, Gondolier Pizza, IHOP, KFC, Krystal, Larry's Subs, Longho Steaks, McDonald's, McDonald's, Ming Moon, Moe's SW Gr

GA

INTERSTATE 75 Cont'd

288 Continued
Papa John's, Red Lobster, Shane's Ribshack, Starbucks, Steak'n Shake, Subway, Taco Bell, Waffle House, Wendy's, Willy's Mexicana Fairfield Inn, Hilton Garden, Home 2 Suites, Knights Inn $General, $Tree, AT&T, Belk, Big Lots, Chrysler/Dodge/Jeep, Discount Tire, GNC, Hobby Lobby, Honda, Kohl's, O'Reilly Parts, Petsmart, Publix, Staples, Target, TJ Maxx, to Etowah Indian Mounds (6mi), USPO, Verizon

286mm Etowah River

285 Emerson, **E** Sunoco Red Top Mtn Lodge to Red Top Mtn SP, **W** to Allatoona Dam

283 Allatoona Rd, Emerson, **W** Loves/McDonald's/Subway/dsl/scales/24hr Arby's, Chick-fil-A, Starbucks, Taco Bell, Tokyo Steaks, Wendy's Hampton Inn, MainStay Suites, Sleep Inn

280mm Allatoona Lake

278 Glade Rd, to Acworth, **E** Exxon/Circle K/dsl, Shell Best Value McKinney Camping (3mi), to Glade Marina, **W** RaceTrac/dsl Bojangles, KFC, Krystal, Papa John's, Pizza Hut, Taco Bell, Waffle House Red Roof Inn AutoZone, Ingles/cafe, O'Reilly Parts

277 GA 92, Acworth, **E** BP/Dunkin'/dsl, RaceTrac/dsl Hardee's, Shoney's, Waffle House Comfort Inn, Days Inn, Holiday Inn Express Cabela's, **W** Chevron/dsl, Shell/DQ/dsl Arby's, Bamboo Garden, China Chef, Domino's, La Bamba Mexican, McDonald's, Sonic, Subway, Waffle House, Wendy's, Zaxby's Best Western, Deerfield Lodge, Econolodge, Fairfield Inn, Quality Inn, Super 8 $General, Advance Parts, CVS Drug, Family$, Goodyear/auto, Publix, Walgreens

273 Wade Green Rd, **E** BP/dsl, RaceTrac/dsl Arby's, Burger King, Coldstone, Dunkin', Firehouse Subs, Happy Panda, Las Palmas Mexican, Marco's Pizza, McDonald's, Papa John's, QT/dsl, Subway, Taco Bell, Waffle House Red Roof Inn, Sleep Inn $Tree, BigLots, GNC, O'Reilly Parts, Pepboys, Publix, Tires+, **W** Shell, Texaco/dsl Bojangles, Johnny's Pizza/Subs, Mandarin Cafe, Starbucks, Wendy's, Wing Zone Home Depot, Kroger/gas, Mavis Tire, Verizon, Walgreens

271 Chastain Rd, to I-575 N, **E** Chevron/Circle K, Tesla EVC Chick-Fil-A, Chipotle, Cookout, Cracker Barrel, Del Taco, Dunkin'/Baskin Robbins, Five Guys, O'Charley's, Panda Express, Panera Bread, Ruth's Chris Steaks, Starbucks, Taco Mac, Taziki's, Tin Lizzy Cantina, Willy's Mexicana, Zaxby's Comfort Suites, Embassy Suites, Fairfield Inn, Hampton Inn, Kennesaw Inn, Residence Inn, **W** Shell/dsl, Swifty Save Gas/Blimpie Arby's, Burger King, Jimmy John's, Mellow Mushroom, Taco Bell, Waffle House, Wendy's Baymont Inn, InTown Suites, SpringHill Suites museum

269 to US 41, to Marietta, **E** EVC, Shell/dsl Anchor Grill, Applebee's, Honey Baked Ham, J Christopher's, Jimmy John's, McDonald's, Olive Garden, Penang Malaysian, Provino's, Red Lobster, Shogun Japanese, Smoothie King, Starbucks, Subway, Twin Peaks Comfort Inn, Country Inn Suites, Holiday Inn Express, Red Roof Inn Belk, Firestone/auto, Home Depot, JC Penney, Macy's, Marshall's, Midas, Pepboys, TJ Maxx, Verizon, **W** BP/dsl, Chevron, Tesla EVC Bahama Breeze, Burger King, Carrabbas, Chick-fil-A, Chili's, Chipotle, ChuckeCheese, Chuy's Mexican, Coldstone, Copeland's Grill, Golden Corral, Jason's Deli, Jersey Mike's, Longhorn Steaks, Melting Pot, On-the-Border, Outback Steaks, Panera Bread, Rafferty's, Sivas Tavern, Starbucks, Steak'n Shake, Sweet Tomato, Ted's MT Steaks, TGIFriday, Willy's Mexicana Courtyard, Day's Inn, Hampton Inn,

MARIETTA

SMYRNA

ATLANTA

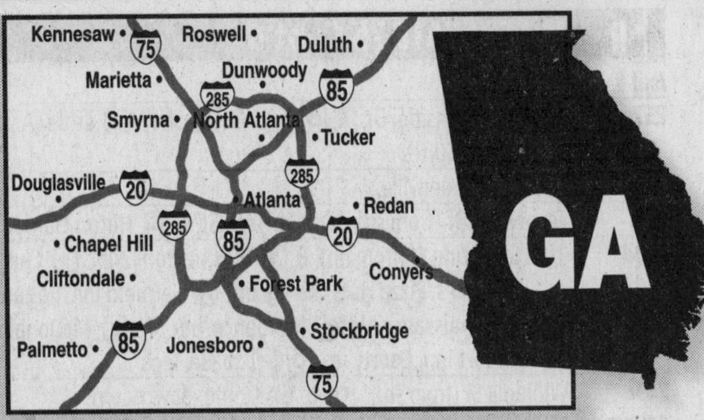

269 Continued
Hilton Garden, Homewood Suites, La Quinta, Quality Inn Aldi Foods, Best Buy, Buick/GMC, CarMax, Chevrolet, Costco/gas, Dick's, Ford/Lincoln, Jo-Ann Fabrics, Kia, Michael's, Nissan, NTB, Old Navy, PetsMart, REI, Subaru, Target, to Kennesaw Mtn NP, Toyota, VW

268 I-575 N, GA 5 N, to Canton

267b a GA 5 N, to US 41, Marietta

265 GA120, N Marietta Pkwy, **W** Chevron/dsl, Shell/dsl Days Inn Advance Parts, Family$, Office Depot, O'Reilly Parts

263 GA 120, to Roswell, **E** Chevron, QT, Shell, **W** Applebee's, China Kitchen, DQ, Haveli Rest., Piccadilly's, Subway, Tasty China Econolodge, Ltd Suites, Radisson, Super 8, Wyndham Garden repair, U-Haul

261 GA 280, Delk Rd, to Dobbins AFB, **E** Chevron/dsl, RaceTrac/dsl, Shell, Shell/Subway/dsl Delray Diner, Hardee's, KFC/Taco Bell, Little Caesar's, Marco's Pizza, McDonald's, Ruby Tuesday, Waffle House Courtyard, Drury Inn, Motel 6, Ramada, Rodeway Inn Kroger, **W** BP, Chevron/dsl Bojangles, Cracker Barrel, Dave&Busters Baymont Inn, Days Inn, Economy Hotel, Holiday Inn Express, Quality Inn

260 Windy Hill Rd, to Smyrna, **E** BP/dsl Boston Mkt, Jersey Mike's Subs, Mellow Mushroom, Pappadeaux Seafood, Pappasito's Cantina, Schlotzsky's, Subway Best Western, Country Hearth Inn, Extended Stay America, Extended Stay America (2), Hilton Garden, Hyatt Regency, Marriott CVS Drug, USPO, **W** Chevron, Conoco, Shell, Texaco/dsl Chick-fil-A, McDonald's, Panda Express, Popeye's, Starbucks, Waffle House, Wendy's Comfort Inn, Country Inn&Suites, Courtyard, Days Inn, DoubleTree, Masters Inn, Motel 6, Red Roof Inn H, Target

259b a I-285, W to Birmingham, E to Greenville, Montgomery

258 Cumberland Pkwy, **E** Hyatt House, **W** Chick-fil-A, Chipotle Mexican, Copeland's Rest., Firehouse Subs, Hooters, Longhorn Steaks, Moe's SW Grill, Shane's Ribshack, Subway Homewood Suites Kroger

257mm Chattahoochee River

256 to US 41, Northside Pkwy

255 US 41, W Paces Ferry Rd, **E** Chevron, Shell/dsl Blue Ridge Grill, Chick-fil-A, Flying Biscuit Cafe, Houston's Rest., McDonald's, OK Café, Pero's Pizza, Smoothie King, Starbucks, Steak'n Shake, Willy's Mexicana H, Ace Hardware, CVS Drug, Publix, Whole Foods Mkt, **W** Exxon

254 Moores Mill Rd

252b Howell Mill Rd, **E** Shell/auto Chick-fil-A, Chipotle, Domino's, Jersey Mike's, McDonald's, Willy's Mexicana Goodyear/auto, Publix, USPO, Walgreens, **W** Shell Arby's, Chin Chin Chinese, Dunkin', La Parrilla Mexican, Starbucks, Subway, Taco Bell, Waffle House, Wendy's Ace Hardware, Firestone/auto, GNC, Kroger, NTB, Office Depot, Petsmart, TJ Maxx, Verizon, Walmart

GA

ARIETTA

[gas] = gas [food] = food [lodging] = lodging [other] = other [rest stop] = rest stop

INTERSTATE 75 Cont'd

ATLANTA

Exit #	Services
252a	US 41, Northside Dr, E [other] [H], W [gas] Shell [food] Little Azio's [lodging] InTown Suites
251	I-85 N, to Greenville
250	Techwood Dr (from sb), 10th St, 14th St, E [lodging] Hilton Garden
249d	10th St, Spring St (from nb), E [gas] BP, Chevron/24hr [food] Checker's, Domino's, Pizza Hut, The Varsity [lodging] Fairfield Inn, Regency Suites, Renaissance Hotel, Residence Inn, W [food] McDonald's [lodging] Comfort Inn, Courtyard [other] [H], to GA Tech
249c	Williams St (from sb), [other] to GA Dome, downtown
249b	Pine St, Peachtree St (from nb), downtown, W [lodging] Hilton, Marriott
249a	Courtland St (from sb), downtown, W [lodging] Hilton, Marriott [other] GA St U
248d	Piedmont Ave, Butler St (from sb), downtown, W [lodging] Courtyard, Fairfield Inn, Radisson [other] [H], Ford, MLK NHS
248c	GA 10 E, Intn'l Blvd, downtown, W [lodging] Hilton, Holiday Inn, Marriott Marquis, Radisson
248b	Edgewood Ave (from nb), W [other] [H], downtown, hotels
248a	MLK Dr (from sb), W st capitol, to Underground Atlanta
247	I-20, E to Augusta, W to Birmingham
246	Georgia Ave, Fulton St, E [lodging] Comfort Inn, Country Inn& Suites, Holiday Inn [other] stadium, W [gas] [food] KFC [other] GSU, to Coliseum
245	Ormond St, Abernathy Blvd, E [lodging] Comfort Inn, Country Inn& Suites [other] stadium, W [other] st capitol
244	University Ave, E [gas] Chevron, Exxon [other] NAPA, W [food] Mrs Winner's
243	GA 166, Lakewood Fwy, to East Point
242	I-85 S, [other] to [airport]
241	Cleveland Ave, E [gas] BP, Chevron/Subway/dsl [food] Checkers, Church's, McDonald's [other] Advance Parts, W [gas] Citgo/dsl, ExpressZone, Marathon [food] Ameican Deli, Burger King, Krystal, Papa John's [lodging] American Inn [other] $Tree, AutoZone, Big Lots, CVS Drug, Family$, Kroger, Walgreens
239	US 19, US 41, E [gas] Chevron/dsl [food] Waffle House [other] USPO, W [gas] Texaco [food] Chick-fil-A, IHOP, McDonald's, Wendy's [lodging] Best Western [other] to [airport]
238b a	I-285 around Atlanta
237a	GA 85 S (from sb)
237	GA 331, Forest Parkway, E [gas] BP, Chevron/dsl, Shell/McDonald's, SunPetro/dsl [food] Burger King, Mr Taco, Subway, Waffle House [lodging] Econolodge [other] Farmer's Mkt, W [gas] BP, Exxon/Subway/dsl [food] Quizno's [lodging] Atlanta Inn, Ramada Ltd [other] Lee Tires/repair
235	US 19, US 41, GA 3, Jonesboro, E [gas] Chevron/dsl, Circle K/Subway/dsl, Texaco/dsl [lodging] Super 8, Travelodge, W [gas] Chevron/dsl, Citgo, Texaco/dsl [food] Applebee's, Burger King, Checkers, ChuckeCheese, Dunkin', Hibachi Grill, Hooters, Little Caesar's, McDonald's, Popeye's, Red Lobster, Waffle House, Zaxby's [lodging] Amercan Inn, Econolodge, Motel 6 [other] [H], $General, $Tree, Little Giant Farmers Mkt, Office Depot, O'Reilly Parts

MORROW

Exit #	Services
233	GA 54, Morrow, E [gas] BP/dsl, Citgo, Gulf [food] Cookout, Cracker Barrel, IHOP, Krystal, Taco Bell, Waffle House, Wendy's [lodging] Best Western, Comfort Suites, Days Inn, Drury Inn, Red Roof Inn [other] Walmart, W [gas] Chevron/dsl, Exxon/dsl, QT/dsl [food] China Café, Golden Buddha, KFC, Lenny's Subs, Olive Garden, Subway, Three$ Cafe, Waffle House, Wendy's [lodging] Hampton Inn, Quality Inn [other] Acura, Buick/GMC/Mazda, Burlington Coats, Cadillac, Costco/gas, Fiat, Harley-Davidson, Kia, Macy's, Nissan, Sam's Club/gas, TJ Maxx, Toyota
231	Mt Zion Blvd, E [gas] [other] Chrysler/Dodge/Jeep, Ford/Linc Honda, W [gas] BP/Circle K/Subway/dsl, Chevron, Texa dsl [food] Arby's, Atlanta Bread, Bruster's, Burger King, Car ba's, Chili's, China King, Chipotle, City Cafe Diner, Joe's C shack, Longhorn Steaks, McDonald's, Moe's SW Grill, Mo- Wings, Panda Express, Papa John's, Pizza Hut, Skyboxx R Steak'n Shake, Taco Bell, TGIFriday, Truett's Rest., Wa House, Wendy's, Wok Asian, Zaxby's [lodging] Best Value Inn, Co try Inn&Suites, Extended Stay America, Sun Suites [other] AT Barnes & Noble, Best Buy, Home Depot, NTB, Petsmart, Pub Ross, Verizon

JONESBORO

Exit #	Services
228	GA 54, GA 138, Jonesboro, E [gas] Raceway/dsl [food] Applebe Broadway Diner, Chick-fil-A, Frontera Mexican, Golden Co Honeybaked Ham, IHOP, Krystal, Marco's Pizza, O'Charle Piccadilly's, Stevi B's Pizza, Subway, Taco Mac, Tokyo Seafo Waffle House, Wing Nuts [lodging] Comfort Inn, Day's Inn, Exp Inn, Hampton Inn, Holiday Inn, La Quinta, Red Roof Inn [other] Kroger/dsl, Lowes Whse, Office Depot, Tires+, URGE CARE, Verizon, W [gas] Marathon, Mobil, Raceway/Wendy dsl [food] Dragon Garden Chinese, McDonald's, Ranchero's Me can [lodging] Fairfield Inn [other] CarMax, CVS Drug, Kohl's
227	I-675 N, to I-285 E (from nb)
224	Hudson Bridge Rd, E [gas] Shell/dsl, Texaco/dsl [food] Chick-fi China Wok, DQ, Italian Oven, Johnny's NY Pizza, KFC, La cienda, Outback Steaks, Pueblo Mio, Serafino Itlian, St bucks, Sticky Cactus Mexican, Subway, Waffle House, W dy's [lodging] Quality Inn [other] [H], Kauffman Tire, Publix, Rite A Walgreens, W [gas] Murphy USA/dsl, QT [food] Arby's, China Ca Firehouse Subs, McDonald's, Mellow Mushroom, Taco B Zaxby's [lodging] Super 8 [other] $Tree, AT&T, AutoZone, Discount T GNC, Verizon, Walmart
222	Jodeco Rd, E [gas] Citgo, Shell, Texaco [food] Hardee's, W [food] F teenth St Pizza [other] Atlanta So. RV Camping
221	Jonesboro Rd, E [gas] QT/dsl, Shell/dsl [other] Kauffman Ti Kroger/gas (2mi), W [food] American Deli, Arby's, Burger Ki Cheddar's, Chili's, Firehouse Subs, Golden Corral, Hong Ko Cafe, Hooters, La Parrilla, Logan's Roadhouse, Longhorn Stea Marble Slab Creamery, McDonald's, Mike's Burger, O'Charley Olive Garden, Red Lobster, Rocky's Pizza, Starbucks, Subw Truett's Grill, Wendy's, Wild Wing Cafe, Yuki Hibachi [lodging] Cou yard, Fairfield Inn, Home 2 Suites [other] AT&T, AutoZone, Be Best Buy, Books-A-Million, Dick's, Home Depot, Marshall Michael's, Old Navy, PetsMart, Ross, Sam's Club/gas, Staple Target, Verizon

MCDONOUGH

Exit #	Services
218	GA 20, GA 81, McDonough, E [gas] BP/dsl, Murphy USA/d QT, Texaco [food] American Deli, Applebee's, Arby's, Burger Ki China King, China Star, Cracker Barrel, DQ, IHOP, KFC, Maritza Frank's Rest., McDonald's, Mesquite Mexican, Moe's SW Gri Montego Bay Cafe, OB's BBQ, Pizza Hut, Popeye's, Ruby Tue day, Sakura Hibachi, South Side Diner, Taco Bell, Three $ Caf Waffle House, Zaxby's [lodging] Baymont Inn, Best Western, Econ my Inn, Howard Johnson, Super 8 [other] $General, $Tree, Aamc Discount Tire, Goodyear, Lowe's Whse, Office Depot, Rite Ai URGENT CARE, Walmart, W [gas] RaceTrac/dsl, Shell [food] Chic fil-A, Dunkin', El Agade Mexican, Firehouse Subs, Folks Res Freddy's, Hardee's, Ichiban Express, Jimmy John's, Starbuck Subway, Waffle House [lodging] Comfort Suites, Econolodge, Fa Bridge Inn, Hampton Inn, Hilton Garden, Holiday Inn Expres Motel 6 [other] Advance Parts, AT&T, Hobby Lobby, Honda, JC Pe ney, Kia, Kohl's, NTB, TJ Maxx, Toyota, Verizon
216	GA 155, McDonough, Blacksville, E [gas] Shell/dsl, Sunoc [food] Honk Kong Express, Sonic [lodging] Best Value, Day's In

GA

INTERSTATE 75 Cont'd

216 Continued
Rodeway Inn Chevrolet/Buick/GMC, Ford, GMC, Hyundai, Tire South, **W** BP, Chevron, Citgo/dsl/24hr, Exxon/dsl, QT Bass BBQ, Da Vinci's Pizza, El Jimador, Graffiti's Oizza, Krystal, Kuma Japanese, Steve's Cafe, Subway, Waffle House Country Inn&Suites, Quality Inn, Sleep Inn

212 to US 23, Locust Grove, **E** BP/McDonald's/dsl, Chevron/Burger King, Marathon/Quizno's, Murphy USA/dsl, QT/dsl, Shell/dsl American Deli, Capt D's, Denny's, Hamburger Mike's, IHOP, KFC/Taco Bell, Koji Japanese, Little Caesar's, Pizza Hut, San Diego Mexican, Shane's Ribshack, Subway, Sunrise China, Waffle House, Wendy's, Zaxby's Executive Inn, La Quinta, Ramada, Red Roof Inn $Tree, Advance Parts, AT&T, Ingles/gas, NapaCare, Tanger Outlet/famous brands, Verizon, Walmart, **W** Exxon/dsl, Shell/DQ/dsl Subway Comfort Suites, Scottish Inn, Sundown Lodge, Super 8 Bumper Parts

205 GA 16, to Griffin, Jackson, **E** BP, **W** Chevron/Subway/dsl Hogfather's BBQ Forest Glen RV Park

201 GA 36, to Jackson, Barnesville, **E** Loves/McDonald's/dsl/grill/scales/24hr, Pilot/DQ/Wendy's/dsl/scales/24hr/@, TA/Subway/Taco Bell/dsl/scales/24hr/@ Blue Beacon, **W** FLYING J/Denny's/dsl/LP/24hr, BP/dsl Waffle House Speedco Lube, truckwash

198 Highfalls Rd, **E** Exxon (1mi) High Falls BBQ High Falls Lodge High Falls SP, HighFalls RV Park (1mi)

193 Johnstonville Rd, **W** Marathon/dsl

190mm **weigh sta both lanes**

188 GA 42, **E** Shell Budget Inn, Hill Top Garden Inn RV camping, to Indian Springs SP

187 GA 83, Forsyth, **E** Econolodge, Regency Inn KOA, **W** Citgo/dsl, Exxon/Circle K, Marathon, Shell, Valero/dsl Burger King, Capt D's, DQ, Hardee's, McDonald's, Subway, Taco Bell, Waffle House, Wendy's Day's Inn $Tree, Advance Parts, Family$, Freshway Foods, O'Reilly Parts, Verizon, Walmart/dsl

186 Tift College Dr, Juliette Rd, Forsyth, **E** Jarrell Plantation HS (18mi), KOA, **W** BP/dsl, Chevron/dsl, Marathon Waffle House Holiday Inn Express, Motel 6, Super 8 H, CVS Drug, Ingles/Deli

185 GA 18, **E** L&D RV Park (2mi), **W** Exxon/Circle K, Shell/dsl Shoney's Comfort Inn Ford, st patrol

181 Rumble Rd, to Smarr, **E** BP/dsl

179mm **sb, full facilities, litter barrels, petwalk, , , vending**

177 I-475 S around Macon (from sb)

175 Pate Rd, Bolingbroke (from nb, no re-entry)

172 Bass Rd, **E** McDonald's, Zaxby's Bass Pro Shop, **W** Citgo/dsl, Flash/DQ/dsl Chick-fil-A, Genghis Grill, Homewood Suites, Magarita's Mexican, Mellow Mushroom, Natalia's Rest., Subway, Taco Bell, Zheng's Wok Microtel, Woodspring Suites CVS, Publix, to Museum of Arts&Sciences

171 US 23, to GA 87, Riverside Dr, **E** BP, Marathon/dsl Barbarito's Cantina, Bonefish Grill, Buca Italian, Chili's, Firehouse Subs, GA Bob's BBQ, Jersey Mike's, La Parrilla, TX Roadhouse, Wild Wing Cafe SpringHill Suites Acura, AT&T, Barnes & Noble, Belk, BMW, Dick's, Dillard's, GNC, Hobby Lobby, Jo-Ann, Mercedes, Petsmart, Subaru, Verizon, Volvo, **W** Lexus, Toyota

169 to US 23, Arkwright Dr, **E** Shell/Circle K/24hr Carrabba's, Logan's Roadhouse, Outback Steaks, Waffle House, Wager's Grill Candlewood Suites, Comfort Inn, Country Inn & Suites, Courtyard, Fairfield Inn, Hampton Inn, Holiday Inn,

FORSYTH

MACON

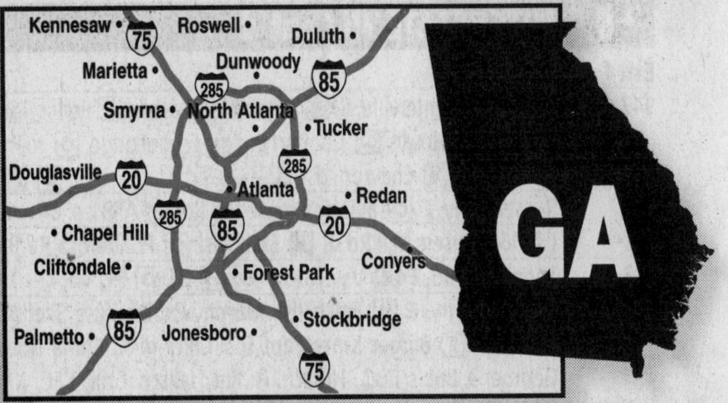

169 Continued
Home 2 Suites, La Quinta, Red Roof Inn, Residence Inn, Sleep Inn Buick/Cadillac/GMC, **W** Chevron/dsl, Marathon/dsl Arby's, Buffalo Wild Wings, Burger King, Cheddar's, Chick-fil-A, Chipotle, Cracker Barrel, Dunkin', Five Guys, Guitarras Mexican, Hooters, IHOP, Joy's Buffet, KFC, Krystal, Little Caesar's, Longhorn Steaks, Mandarin Chinese, McDonald's, Panda Express, Panera Bread, Papa John's, Starbucks, Steak'n Shake, Steve B's Pizza, Subway, Taco Bell, Waffle House, Wendy's Baymont Inn, Budgetel, Days Inn, Extended Stay America, Quality Inn, Rodeway Inn, Travelodge, Wingate Inn H, $General, $Tree, Ace Hardware, Chrysler/Jeep/Dodge, GNC, Goodyear/auto, Hyundai, Kia, Kroger/dsl, Mazda, O'Reilly Parts, Publix, Tuesday Morning

167 GA 247, Pierce Ave, **E** United Inn, **W** Exxon, Fastrip/dsl, Shell/Circle K/dsl, Shell/dsl Applebee's, Loco's Grill, Marco's Pizza, Metropolis Mediterranean, S&S Cafeteria, Shogun Japanese, SteakOut, Waffle House Best Western/rest., Holiday Inn Express, Howard Johnson, Magnuson Hotel, Palmtree Extended Stay Firestone/auto, Rite Aid

165 I-16 E, to Savannah

164 US 41, GA 19, Forsyth Ave, Macon, **E** Sid's Rest. H, hist dist, **W** Citgo/dsl museum

163 GA 74 W, Mercer U Dr, **E** Hilton Garden to Mercer U, **W** Citgo

162 US 80, GA 22, Eisenhower Pkwy, **W** Citgo/dsl, Lo-lo Gas, Sunoco/dsl Burger King, Capt D's, Checker's, Krispy Kreme, Krystal, McDonald's, Mrs Winners, Overtyme Grill, Subway, Wendy's InTown Suites $Tree, O'Reilly Parts, PepBoys, Save-A-Lot Foods, Walgreens

160 US 41, GA 247, Pio Nono Ave, **E** Flash/dsl, RaceWay/Dunkin'/dsl Waffle House, **W** BP, Enmark/dsl Arby's, DQ, KFC, McDonald's, Subway, Waffle House $General, Advance Parts, Family$, O'Reilly Parts, Piggly Wiggly, Raffield Tire, Roses

156 I-475 N around Macon (from nb)

155 Hartley Br Rd, **E** Shell/KFC/dsl Domino's, Subway, Waffle House, Wendy's Kroger/dsl, Verizon, **W** Citgo/dsl, Flash/DQ/dsl McDonald's, Zaxby's Best Value Inn Advance Parts, CVS Drug

153 Sardis Church Rd, **E** Citgo/dsl

149 GA 49, Byron, **E** Chevron/dsl, Shell/dsl Burger King, Casa Mexico, Denny's, GA Bob's BBQ, Krystal, Marco's Pizza, McDonald's, Pizza Hut, Subway, Waffle House, Wendy's, Zaxby's Best Western, Comfort Suites, Holiday Inn Express, Super 8 Campers Inn RV Ctr, Mid-State RV Ctr, Peach Stores/famous brands, **W** Citgo/dsl/24hr, Flash/dsl, Marathon/dsl, RaceWay/dsl, Texaco/dsl DQ, Hardee's, Hudson's BBQ, Waffle House Budget Inn, Days Inn, EconoLodge, Quality Inn $General, Advance Parts, Bumper Parts, Camping World RV Ctr, Chevrolet, Ford, Interstate RV Ctr/park, O'Reilly Parts, Verizon

GA

= gas = food = lodging = other = rest stop

INTERSTATE 75 Cont'd

Exit #	Services
146	GA 247, to Centerville, E Exxon/dsl, Flash/dsl, Shell Subway, Waffle House Comfort Lodge, EconoLodge to Robins AFB, W Chevron/dsl, Pilot/Arby's/dsl/24hr H
144	Russel Pkwy, E aviation museum, Robins AFB
142	GA 96, Housers Mill Rd, E Shell/dsl Ponderosa RV Park
138	Thompson Rd, E Valero/dsl H, W
136	US 341, Perry, E Flash/dsl, Murphy Express/dsl, Shell/Circle K/dsl Burger King, Capt D's, Chick-fil-A, China House, George & Bob's BBQ, Hibachi Buffet, Jalisco Grill, KFC, Krystal, Little Caesar's, Longhorn Steaks, McDonald's, Pizza Hut, Red Lobster, Sonny's BBQ, Steamers Seafood, Subway, Taco Bell, Waffle House, Wendy's, Zaxby's Great Inn, Hampton Inn, Howard Johnson, Jameson Inn, Motel 6, Rodeway Inn, Super 8 H, $General, $Tree, Ace Hardware, Advance Parts, Boland's RV Park, GNC, Kroger/dsl, NAPA, Verizon, Walmart, W Shell/Circle K/dsl Applebee's, Grill Master BBQ Days Inn, EconoLodge, Hardee's, Holiday Inn Express, Knights Inn, Passport Inn, Quality Inn, Ramada Inn Crossroads Travel Oark
135	US 41, GA 127, Perry, E Chevron/dsl, Flash/dsl, Flash/dsl (2), Shell, Texaco/dsl Cracker Barrel, DQ, Subway, Waffle House Best Western, Budget Inn, Comfort Inn, Relax Inn, Travelodge Chrysler/Dodge/Jeep, GA Nat Fair, Kia, W Fair Harbor RV Park, st patrol
134	South Perry Pkwy, W Microtel Buick/Chevrolet/GMC, Ford
127	GA 26, Henderson, E Twin Oaks Camping, W Shell/dsl
122	GA 230, Unadilla, E Chevron/dsl Chevrolet/Ford
121	US 41, Unadilla, E Borum/repair, Flash/DQ/dsl Subway Scottish Inn $General, Family$, Firestone, Piggly Wiggly, Southern Trails RV Resort, USPO, W Citgo/rest./dsl/scales/24hr
118mm	**sb, full facilities, litter barrels, petwalk, , RV dump, vending**
117	to US 41, Pinehurst, W GasnGo/Subway/dsl
112	GA 27, Vienna
109	GA 215, Vienna, E Pilot/McDonalds/dsl/scales/24hr, W Shell/dsl, Sunoco Popeye's Executive Inn $General Mkt, Cotton Museum
108mm	**nb, full facilities, litter barrels, petwalk, , RV dump, vending**
104	Farmers Mkt Rd, Cordele
102	GA 257, Cordele, E Sunoco/dsl, W Smoothie's BBQ H
101	US 280, GA 90, Cordele, E BP/dsl, Pilot/Arby's/dsl/scales/24hr, Shell Denny's, Golden Corral, Waffle House Fairfield Inn, Holiday Inn Express, Motel 6, Ramada Inn Ford, st patrol, W Flash/dsl, Gas'n Go, Sunoco, VP/Subway Burger King, Capt D's, Chick-fil-A, Cracker Barrel, DQ, Hachi Japanese Grill, Hardee's, KFC, Krystal, Little Caesar's, Los Compadres, McDonald's, New China, Pizza Hut, Sonic, Subway, Taco Bell, TJ's Rest, Wendy's, Zaxby's Ashburn Inn, Athens 8 Motel, Baymont Inn, Best Western, EconoLodge, Hampton Inn, Quality Inn, Travelodge $General, $Tree, Advance Parts, AT&T, AutoZone, Belk, Harvey's Foods, Home Depot, J Carter HS, Kauffman Tire, O'Reilly Parts, Save-A-Lot, to Veterans Mem SP, Verizon, Walgreens, Walmart
99	GA 300, GA/FL Pkwy, E Marathon/DQ/dsl, W Waffle House Comfort Inn to Chehaw SP
97	to GA 33, Wenona, E Cordele RV Park, dsl rep W KOA, truckwash
92	Arabi, E Shell/Plantation House, W Southern Gates Park
85mm	**nb, full facilities, litter barrels, petwalk, , , vend**
84	GA 159, Ashburn, W Chevron/DQ/Blimpie/dsl/24hr A burn Inn/RV Park
82	GA 107, GA 112, Ashburn, W BP, Shell Carroll's S sage & Country Store/RV Park, KFC, McDonald's, Pizza Shoney's, Subway, Waffle House, Zaxby's Best West Days Inn, Holiday Inn Express, Super 8 Buick/Chevro GMC, O'Reilly Parts, O'Reilly Parts, Piggly Wiggly, Rite Aid Chehaw SP
80	Bussey Rd, Sycamore, W Allen's Tires
78	GA 32, Sycamore, E to Jefferson Davis Mem Pk (14mi)
76mm	**sb, full facilities, litter barrels, petwalk, , , vendi**
75	Inaha Rd
71	Willis Still Rd, Sunsweet, W Citgo/dsl
69	Chula-Brookfield Rd, E Sunoco/dsl
66	Brighton Rd
64	US 41, Tifton, E BP/dsl Waffle House H, $Gene Harvey's Foods, W Shell
63b	8th St, Tifton, E Flash/dsl/e85 El Patron, Fireho Subs Jo-Ann, Publix, TJ Maxx, W Pit Stop BBQ Museum of Agriculture
63a	2nd St, Tifton, E BP/dsl, Marathon Arby's, As Xpress, Barberito's, Checkers, El Metate, JoJo's Rest., K Krystal, McDonald's, Pizza Hut, Red Lobster, Subway, S cheros Grill, Taco Bell, Waffle House EconoLodge, Su 8 $General, $Tree, Big Lots, W Bob's/dsl El Ca dore Mexican Motel 6, Quality Inn
62	US 82, to US 319, Tifton, E Flash/dsl Applebee's, jangles, Charles Seafood, Chili's, Cracker Barrel, DQ, Golden C ral, Hardee's, King Buffet, Logan's Roadhouse, Ole Times B fet, Sonic, Tokyo Japanese, Waffle House, Zaxby's Comf Inn, Country Inn&Suites, Fairfield Inn, Hampton Inn, Holiday Express, Microtel $Tree, Advance Parts, AutoZone, BigLo Chrysler/Dodge/Jeep, Family$, Ford/Lincoln, NAPA, O'Re Parts, Pecan Outlet, Save-A-Lot, Staples, W EZ Mart, Flas dsl, Murphy USA/dsl, Shell/dsl, Tesla EVC Buffalo W Wings, Burger King, Capt D's, Chick-fil-A, Cookout, HogBor BBQ, Little Caesar's, Longhorn Steaks, McDonald's, Oishi Ja anese, Olive Garden, Panera Bread, Pizza Hut, Ruby Tuesd Starbucks, Taco Bell, Waffle House, Wendy's Days Inn, H ton Garden $General, AT&T, Chevrolet, Hobby Lobby, Ho da, Lowe's, Toyota, URGENT CARE, Verizon, Walmart/Subway
61	Omega Rd, E Nissan, W Shell/Waffle King/pizza/dsl/24 Howard Johnson Harley-Davidson, Pines RV Park
60	Central Ave, Tifton, E Chevron Dragon 1 Chines W Pilot/Steak'n Shake/Subway/dsl/scales/24hr Bl Beacon, KOA
59	Southwell Blvd, to US 41, Tifton, E Loves/Hardee's/d scales/24hr
55	to Eldorado, Omega, E Shell/Magnolia Plantation/dsl
49	Kinard Br Rd, Lenox, E Dixie/dsl Lenox Inn, W B dsl/24hr, Chevron
47mm	**both lanes, full facilities, litter barrels, petwalk, , vending**
45	Barneyville Rd
41	Rountree Br Rd, E Citgo, W to Reed Bingham SP
39	GA 37, Adel, Moultrie, E Citgo/dsl, Dixie Gas, McDonald' QuickGas DQ, Hardee's, Subway, Waffle House Super

PERRY CORDELE ASHBURN TIFTON GA

INTERSTATE 75 Cont'd

39	Continued Zaxby's H, $General, $Tree, Ace Hardware, Advance Parts, Family$, O'Reilly Parts, Piggly Wiggly, Rite Aid, W BP, Citgo/Huddle House/dsl/scales, Shell Burger King, Capt D's, Don Julio's, Taco Bell, Wendy's, Western Sizzlin Hampton Inn to Reed Bingham SP, Verizon, Walmart
37	Adel, E Liberty/dsl GMC
32	Old Coffee Rd, Cecil, E Citgo/dsl Stagecoach Inn, W Chevron/dsl Cecil Bay RV Park
29	US 41 N, GA 122, Hahira, Sheriff's Boys Ranch, E Down Home Pizza, Harvey's Mkt, Huddle House NAPA, vet, W Citgo/dsl, Shell/Big Foot/cafe/dsl/24hr Hahira Inn
23mm	**weigh sta both lanes**
22	US 41 S, to Valdosta, E BP, Shell/Subway/dsl Waffle House Best Western+ H, Buick/Chevrolet/GMC, Mazda, W Citgo/dsl Burger King Howard Johnson Valdosta Oaks RV Park
18	GA 133, Valdosta, E Flash, Mobil, Tesla EVC Applebee's, Arby's, Beijing Cafe, Buffalo Wild Wings, Burger King, Chick-fil-A, Chili's, Chow Town, CiCi's Pizza, Cookout, Cracker Barrel, Crystal River Seafood, Denny's, Dick's Wings, El Toreo, Fazoli's, Firehouse Subs, Five Guys, Honeybaked Ham, Hooters, KFC, Krystal, Little Caesar's, Longhorn Steaks, McDonald's, Mellow Mushroom, Ole Times Country Buffet, Olive Garden, Outback Steaks, Panda Express, Panera Bread, Red Lobster, Sonny's BBQ, Starbucks, Steak'n Shake, Subway, Taco Bell, TX Roadhouse, Waffle House, Wendy's, Zaxby's Baymont Inn, Candlewood Suites, Comfort Suites, Country Inn&Suites, Courtyard, Drury Inn, Hilton Garden, Holiday Inn Express, InTown Suites, La Quinta, Motel 6, Oyo Hotel, Quality Inn $Tree, AT&T, Belk, Best Buy, Books-A-Million, Discount Tire, Family$, Goodyear/auto, Hobby Lobby, Home Depot, JC Penney, Kohl's, Lowe's, Michael's, Old Navy, Petsmart, Publix, Ross, Target, TJ Maxx, URGENT CARE, Verizon, Walgreens, W BP/dsl, RaceWay/dsl Days Inn, EconoLodge, Sleep Inn, Super 8 River Park Camping, Toyota
16	US 84, US 221, GA 94, Valdosta, E BP/dsl, Exxon/dsl, Murphy Express/dsl, Shell/dsl, Sunoco Aligatou Japanese, Bojangles, Bubba Jax Crab Shack, Burger King, Cajun Wild Crab, Cheddar's, IHOP, McDonald's, Pizza Hut, Sonic, Waffle House, Wendy's Comfort Inn, Days Inn, Fairfield Inn, Hampton Inn, Holiday Inn, Motel 6, Super 8, Super Value Inn Sam's Club/gas, Walmart/Subway, W Citgo/dsl/24hr, Sunstop/Moe's SW/dsl Austin's Steaks Briarwood Inn, Kinderlou Inn, Oyo Inn
13	Old Clyattville Rd, Valdosta, W Wild Adventures Park
11	GA 31, Valdosta, E LNG, Pilot/Dunkin'/dsl/scales/24hr, Pilot/Subway/dsl/24hr/@ Waffle House Travelers Inn truckwash, W Quick Gas $General
5	GA 376, to Lake Park, E Flash Foods/Stuckey's/dsl, RaceWay/dsl, Shell Chick-fil-A, Cowboys Grill, Domino's, Farmhouse Rest., Krystal, Lin's Garden Chinese, Rodeo Mexican, Subway, Taco Bell, Waffle House, Zaxby's Lake Park Express, Motel 6 $Tree, antiques, Day Bros RV Ctr, Eagles Roost Camping, Family$, Horizon RV Ctr, USPO, Winn-Dixie, W Exxon/dsl Cracker Barrel, McDonald's, Pizza Hut, Wendy's Best Value Inn, Days Inn, Hampton Inn, Holiday Inn Express, Travelodge Camping World RV Ctr, Lake Park Camping
3mm	**Welcome Ctr nb, full facilities, litter barrels, petwalk, vending**

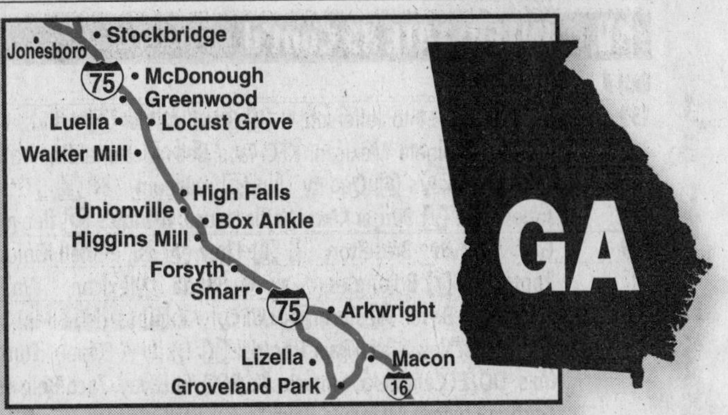

2	Lake Park, Bellville, E TA/BP/Arby's/dsl/scales/24hr/@ SpeedCo, W FLYING J/Denny's/Subway/dsl/LP/scales/24hr Stay Inn Suites lube/tires/wash
0mm	Georgia/Florida state line

INTERSTATE 85

Exit #	Services
179mm	Georgia/South Carolina state line, Tugaloo River, Lake Hartwell
177	GA 77 S, to Hartwell, E BP/gifts/dsl Dad's Grill to Hart SP, W Tugaloo SP
176mm	**Welcome Ctr sb, full facilities, info, litter barrels, petwalk, vending**
173	GA 17, to Lavonia, E Raceway/dsl Bojangles, Cracker Barrel, La Cabana Mexican, McDonald's, Subway, Taco Bell, Waffle House Days Inn, EconoLodge, Rodeway Inn $General, Lavonia Foods, Rite Aid, W Exxon/dsl Burger King, Chic, DQ, Hardee's, J Peters Grill, Pizza Hut, Shoney's, Zaxby's Hampton Inn, Holiday Inn Express, Super 8 Chrysler/Dodge/Jeep, Ford, to Tugaloo SP
171mm	**weigh sta nb**
169mm	**weigh sta sb**
166	GA 106, to Carnesville, Toccoa, E Exxon/dsl, Pilot/Dunkin'/DQ/Wendy's/dsl/scales/24hr Little Caesar's, W Echo Trkstp/Chevron/Echo Rest./dsl/scales/24hr
164	GA 320, to Carnesville
160	GA 51, to Homer, E Marathon/Subway/dsl/24hr to Russell SP, Ty Cobb Museum, Victoria Bryant SP, W FLYING J/dsl/24hr, Petro/BP/Iron Skillet/dsl/scales/24hr/@ Blue Beacon
154	GA 63, Martin Br Rd
149	US 441, GA 15, to Commerce, Homer, E EVC, Murphy USA, QT/dsl, TA/Shell/Country Pride/dsl/scales/24hr/@ Bojangles, Capt D's, Grand Buffet, Koji Japanese, Krispy Kreme, Little Caesar's, Longhorn Steaks, Outback Steaks, Papa John's, Sonny's BBQ, Taco Bell, Waffle House, Zaxby's Days Inn, Hampton Inn, Red Roof Inn, Scottish Inn H, $General, $Tree, AT&T, Chrysler/Dodge/Jeep, Funopolis, GNC, O'Reilly Parts, URGENT CARE, Walmart/Subway, W BP/Krystal/dsl, Petro Express/dsl, RaceTrac/dsl Applebee's, Arby's, Burger King, Chick-fil-A, Cracker Barrel, Culver's, DQ, Five Guys, Hawg Wild BBQ, La Hacienda, McDonald's, Pizza Hut, Popeye's, Ruby Tuesday, Ryan's, Sonic, Starbucks, Subway, Wendy's Best Western, Comfort Suites, Country Inn&Suites, Fairfield Inn, Holiday Inn Express, Howard Johnson, Motel 6, Quality Inn, Super 8, Travelodge Home Depot, Pritchett Tires, Tanger Outlet/famous brands, Verizon
147	GA 98, to Commerce, E Citgo/dsl, Loves/Dunkin'/dsl/24hr H, W Chevron
140	GA 82, Dry Pond Rd, E Circle K Trkstp/dsl/scales Freightliner, W Truck Repair

LAVONIA

COMMERCE

GA

= gas = food = lodging = other = rest stop

INTERSTATE 85 Cont'd

JEFFERSON

Exit #	Services
137	US 129, GA 11 to Jefferson, E RaceTrac/dsl Arby's, Bojangles, El Jinete Mexican, KFC/Taco Bell, McDonald's, Waffle House, Zaxby's Quality Inn museum, W QT/dsl/scales/24hr Burger King, Waffle House, Wendy's flea mkt
129	GA 53, to Braselton, E Chevron/dsl, Shell/Golden Pantry/dsl Bojangles, La Hacienda Mexican, Waffle House Best Western USPO, W Pilot/McDonald's/dsl/scales/24hr, RaceTrac/dsl Cracker Barrel, Domino's, DQ, El Centinela, Stonewall's BBQ, Subway, Taco Bell, Tea Garden Chinese, Wendy's, Zaxby's Fairfield Inn
126	GA 211, to Chestnut Mtn, E Circle K/Burger King/dsl, RaceTrac/dsl, Shell/dsl Subway, Waffle House Country Inn&Suites, Holiday Inn Express, W BP/dsl, EVC Chateau Elan Winery/rest., China Garden, Papa John's Baymont Inn, Hampton Inn Publix, Verizon, vet
120	to GA 124, Hamilton Mill Rd, E BP, QT/dsl Arby's, Buffalo's Café, Burger King, Caprese Rest., Firehouse Subs, Five Guys, McDonald's, Moe's SW Grill, Riverside Pizza, Starbucks, Wendy's, Zaxby's Aldi Foods, auto repair, Home Depot, Kohl's, Publix/Deli, RV World of GA (1mi), vet, W Chevron, EVC, Murphy USA/dsl, Shell/dsl Barberito's, Chick-fil-A, Chili's, Dunkin', El Molcajate, Hardee's, Italy's Pizza, Krystal, Little Caesar's, Taco Bell $Tree, Advance Parts, AT&T, CVS Drug, O'Reilly Parts, Tires+, USPO, Verizon, Walmart/Subway
115	GA 20, to Buford Dam, E Waffle House Pepboys, W Arby's, Atlanta Bread, Bonefish Grill, Bruster's, Burger 21, Burger King, Cheesecake Factory, Chick-fil-A, Chili's, Chipotle, ChuckeCheese, East Coast Wings, Einstein's Bagels, Firehouse Subs, Genghis Grill, Honeybaked Ham, Kani House, Krispy Kreme, Longhorn Steaks, Macaroni Grill, Maddio's Pizza, McDonald's, Mimi's Cafe, Moe's SW Grill, O'Charley's, Olive Garden, On-the-Border, Panda Express, Panera Bread, PF Chang's, Provino's Italian, Red Lobster, Shogun Japanese, Sonny's BBQ, Starbucks, Steak n' Shake, Subway, Taco Mac, Ted's MT Grill, TGIFriday's, Tilted Kilt, Waffle House, Wendy's, Which Wich? Country Inn&Suites, Courtyard, Hampton Inn, SpringHill Suites, Wingate Inn $Tree, AT&T, Barnes&Noble, Belk, Best Buy, Buick/GMC, Costco/gas, Dick's, Dillard's, Discount Tire, Fiat, Firestone/auto, Honda, Hyundai, JC Penney, Lowe's, Macy's, Marshall's, Mazda, Michael's, Nissan, Nordstrom Rack, PetCo, Petsmart, REI, Ross, Sam's Club/gas, Staples, SteinMart, Target, TJ Maxx, to Lake Lanier Islands, Toyota, Tuesday Morning, Verizon, Von Maur, VW, Walmart
113	I-985 N (from nb), to Gainesville
111	GA 317, to Suwanee, E BP/dsl, Valero/dsl Applebee's, Arby's, Checker's, Chick-fil-A, Cracker Barrel, Dunkin', Orient Garden, Outback Steaks, Philly Connection, Pizza Hut, Schlotsky's, Subway, Taco Bell, Waffle House, Wendy's Comfort Suites, Courtyard, Fairfield Inn, Motel 6, Quality Inn, Sun Suites CVS Drug, GNC, O'Reilly Parts, W Chevron/dsl, Murphy USA/dsl, QT/dsl, Raceway/dsl, Shell Dunkin', Greek Island, HoneyBaked Ham, IHOP, Jimmy John's, KFC, McDonald's, Moe's SW Grill, Sonic, Subway, Taco Mac Red Roof Inn, Super 8 $Tree, Advance Parts, AT&T, Lowe's, Office Depot, Walmart
109	Old Peachtree Rd, E McAlister's, McDonald's, Mi Casa Mexican Hampton Inn, Homewood Suites Bass Pro Shops, Publix, W Arena Tavern, Carrabba's, Chick-fil-A, China Delight, Firehouse Subs, Five Guys, Jim&Nicks BBQ, Starbucks, Subway, Tilted Kilt, Waffle House Hilton Garden, Holiday Inn, Residence Inn Home Depot

SUWANEE

DULUTH

ATLANTA AREA

Exit #	Services
108	Sugarloaf Pkwy (from nb), E Hampton Inn, Homew Suites, W Carrabba's, Chick-fil-A, Tin Lizzy Cantina ton Garden, Holiday Inn Gwinnett Civic Ctr
107	GA 120, to GA 316 E, Athens, E Shell Burger King, rino's, Dave&Busters, Dunkin', Subway, Zaxby's Bass Shops, Books-a-Million, Burlington Coats, Discount Tire, Aid, Ross, Saks 5th Ave, Suburban Tire, W BP/dsl, Ch ron Bojangles, China Gate, McDonald's, Subway, Wa House La Quinta, Suburban Lodge
106	Boggs Rd (from sb, no return), Duluth, W dsl/24hr Mercedes
104	Pleasant Hill Rd, E Chevron/e85, QT/dsl, Shell/dsl, Vale dsl Bahama Breeze, Burger King, Chick-fil-A, Costas Nay itas, Don Pedro Mexican, East Pearl, Fung Mei Chinese, Diner, Golden House, Joe's Crabshack, McDonald's, Popey Schlotsky's, Stevi B's Pizza, Subway, Super Buffet, TGIFrida Waffle House, Wendy's Best Western, Candlewood Sui Comfort Suites, Fairfield Inn, Hampton Inn Suites, Holi Inn Express, Residence Inn, Sonesta $General, $Tree, vance Parts, Best Buy, Family$, Home Depot, Publix, URGE CARE, Walgreens, W BP/Dunkin'/dsl, Chevron/dsl, Va ro/dsl Applebee's, Arby's, Barnacle's, Bruster's, Bur King, Checker's, Chili's, Chipotle Mexican, Hooters, IHOP, Ji my John's, KFC, Krispy Kreme, McDonald's, Melting Pot, O Garden, On the Border, Panda Express, Red Lobster, Starbuc Steak'n Shake, Subway, Taco Bell, Wendy's Courtyard, tended Stay America, Haven Hotel, Hyatt Place, Quality I Wingate Inn, Wyndham Garden AT&T, Audi, Batterie Belk, BMW, Buick/GMC, Firestone/auto, Ford, Fry's Electroni Goodyear/auto, Honda, Hyundai, Infiniti, JC Penney, Jo-A Fabrics, Kia, Macy's, Marshall's, Nissan, PetCo, Rite Aid, S ples, Subaru, TJ Maxx, Toyota, Verizon
103	Steve Reynolds Blvd (from nb, no return), W Q dsl, Shell Dave&Buster's, Waffle House InTow Suites $Tree, Big Lots, Costco/gas, Kohl's, Petsmart, sar as 104, Sam's Club
102	GA 378, Beaver Ruin Rd, E QT, Shell/dsl, Valero/ Subway, W Citgo
101	Lilburn Rd, E QT, Shell/dsl Blimpie, Bruster's, Bur er King, Domino's, Hong Kong Buffet, Jimmy John's, KF Krystal, McDonald's/playplace, Starbucks, Taco Bell, Waf House Guesthouse Inn, InTown Suites, Super 8 Jon RV Park, W Chevron, Marathon/dsl, QT Arby's, Chi Panda, El Taco Veloz, Papa John's, Pizza Plaza, Subway, Wa fle House, Wendy's Knights Inn, Red Roof Inn CarMa Chrysler/Dodge/Jeep, Lowe's
99	GA 140, Jimmy Carter Blvd, E Shell/dsl Checker Chick-fil-A, Cracker Barrel, Denny's, Dunkin', McDonald Papa John's, Pollo Campero, Subway, Taco Bell Congre Suites, Courtyard, Horizon Inn, La Quinta, Motel 6, Rite4 Inn Advance Parts, Aldi Foods, Family$, U-Haul, Walgreer W Chevron/dsl, QT/dsl, Valero/dsl Hibachi Grill, Ho Kong Buffet, Pappadeaux Steak/seafood, Sonic, Waffle Hous Wendy's Country Inn&Suites, Days Inn, Microtel, Rodew Inn AutoZone, CarQuest, NTB, O'Reilly Parts, PepBoys
96	Pleasantdale Rd, Northcrest Rd, E Burger King, Pleasar dale Chinese, W Exxon/dsl, QT/dsl Subway Atla ta Lodge
95	I-285
94	Chamblee-Tucker Rd, E Chevron/Subway/dsl, Shell/d to Mercer U, W QT/dsl DQ, Waffle House Mot 6, Super 8

GA

INTERSTATE 85 Cont'd

Exit #	Services
93	Shallowford Rd, to Doraville, E Shell Hop Shing Chinese, Marco's Pizza, Subway Publix, U-Haul, W Shell/dsl Quality Inn
91	US 23, GA 155, Clairmont Rd, E Chevron/dsl, QT/dsl IHOP, Mo's Pizza, Popeye's repair, URGENT CARE, W McDonald's, Waffle House Extended Stay America, Holiday Inn Express, Marriott NTB, Sam's Club/dsl
89	GA 42, N Druid Hills, E Chevron/Subway/dsl, QT, Shell/dsl Arby's, Boston Mkt, Burger King, Chick-fil-A, El Torero, Fortune Cookie, Grub Burger, Jersey Mike's, McDonald's, Moe's SW Grill, Newk's Eatery, Panera Bread, Penn Sta Subs, Piccadilly's, Starbucks, Taco Bell, Tin Roof Cantina, Willy's Mexicana, Zoe's Kitchen Courtyard $Tree, Firestone/auto, GNC, Target, Walgreens, W Chevron/dsl, Exxon/dsl, Shell HoneyBaked Ham, Krystal, McDonald's, Waffle House DoubleTree, Hampton Inn, Red Roof Inn CVS Drug, Just Brakes
88	Lenox Rd, GA 400 N, Cheshire Br Rd (from sb), E Valero/dsl McDonald's La Quinta
87	GA 400 N (from nb)
86	GA 13 S, Peachtree St, E BP, Chevron Papa John's, Wendy's Intown Inn Sprouts Mkt, vet
85	I-75 N, to Marietta, Chattanooga
84	Techwood Dr, 14th St, E BP, Shell CheeseSteaks, La Bamba Mexican, Thai Cuisine, VVV Ristorante Italiano Best Western, Hampton Inn, Marriott, Sheraton, Travelodge Woodruff Arts Ctr, W Blimpie Courtyard, Knights Inn CVS Drug, Dillard's, Office Depot, to Georgia Tech
77	I-75 S
76	Cleveland Ave, E Citgo/dsl Burger King, Papa John's H, $Tree, AutoZone, BigLots, CVS Drug, Family$, Kroger, Walgreens, W Shell/dsl, Texaco/dsl Chick-fil-A, Church's CVS, O'Reilly Parts
75	Sylvan Rd, E Shell/dsl
74	Loop Rd, Aviation Commercial Center
73b a	Virginia Ave, E Citgo/dsl Jimmy John's, Jonny's Pizza, Landmark Diner, Malone's Grill, McDonald's, Pizza Hut, Ruby Tuesday, Schlotsky's, Spondivit's Rest., Waffle House, Wendy's, Willy's Mexican Courtyard, Drury Inn, Hilton, Motel 6, Renaissance Hotel, Residence Inn, W Chevron/Subway, Shell Arby's, BBQ Kitchen, Blimpie, Giovanna's Italian, Happy Buddha Chinese, KFC, La Fiesta Mexican, Waffle House Country Inn&Suites, Crowne Plaza, DoubleTree, EconoLodge, Fairfield Inn, Hampton Inn, Hilton Garden, Holiday Inn, Homewood Suites, Hyatt Place, Palms Hotel, Staybridge Inn, Wellesley Inn
72	Camp Creek Pkwy
71	Riverdale Rd, Atlanta Airport, E Ruby Tuesday Courtyard, Fairfield Inn, Hampton Inn, Holiday Inn, Hyatt Place, La Quinta, Microtel, Sheraton/grill, Sleep Inn, Super 8, W Days Inn, Embassy Suites, Hilton Garden, Holiday Inn Express, Marriott, Westin Hotel
70	I-85 (from sb)
69	GA 14, GA 279, E Chevron/dsl, Citgo, Exxon/dsl, Valero Blimpie, Bojangles, Burger King, Checker's, China Cafe, Church's, Cozumel, KFC, Krystal, McDonald's, Piccadilly Cafeteria, Subway, Taco Bell, Waffle House, Wendy's Comfort Inn, Days Inn, Quality Inn, Super 8, Travelodge, Windsor Atl Hotel AutoZone, Family$, U-Haul, URGENT CARE, W Chevron/dsl, Texaco Waffle House EconoLodge

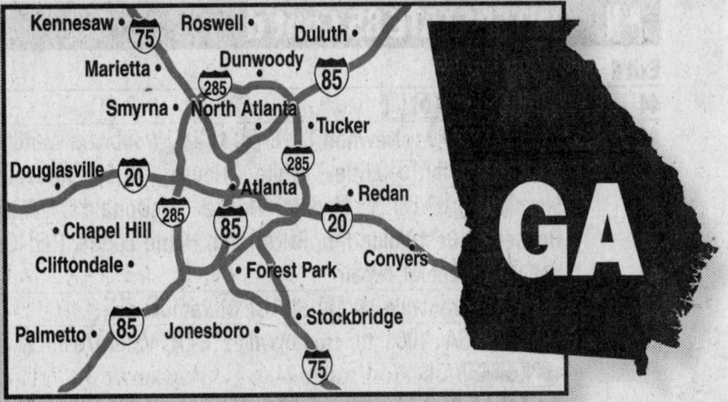

FAIRBURN

NEWNAN

Exit #	Services
68	I-285 Atlanta Perimeter (from nb)
66	Flat Shoals Rd, W BP, Chevron/dsl/24hr, Shell/Blimpie King's Rest., Waffle House Motel 6
64	GA 138, to Union City, E BP/dsl, RaceTrac/dsl Waffle House EconoLodge, Western Inn BMW/Mini, Chevrolet, Chrysler/Dodge/Jeep, CVS Drug, Ford/Lincoln, Honda, Infiniti, Kia/Nissan, Lexus, Toyota, VW, W Chevron/dsl, QT, Shell/dsl Arby's, Burger King, Capt D's, China Garden, China King, Corner Cafe, Dunkin', IHOP, KFC, Krystal, McDonald's, Papa John's, Pizza Hut, Sonic, Southern Grill, Subway, Taco Bell, Wendy's, Zaxby's Best Western, Comfort Inn, Country Hearth Inn, Garden Inn, La Quinta, Magnuson Hotel, Microtel $Tree, Advance Parts, AT&T, BigLots, Firestone/auto, Kroger/dsl, NTB, O'Reilly Parts, PepBoys, vet, Walgreens, Walmart/Subway
61	GA 74, to Fairburn, E BP/Huddle House/dsl/scales/24hr, QT/dsl, RaceWay/dsl, Shell Bojangle's, Chick-fil-A, Cracker Barrel, Dunkin', Hardee's, Krystal, Marco's Pizza, McDonald's, Starbucks, Taco Bell, Waffle House, Wendy's, Zaxby's Best Western+, Country Inn&Suites, Fairfield Inn, Hampton Inn, Holiday Inn Express, Wingate Inn Fairburn Tires, vet, W Chevron/dsl, Sun Petro/dsl Efficiency Motel
56	Collinsworth Rd, W Marathon/dsl, Shell Frank's Rest. South Oaks Camping
51	GA 154, to Sharpsburg, E Marathon/dsl, Texaco/Subway/dsl Hardee's, W Chevron/dsl, Shell/Circle K/dsl Waffle House
47	GA 34, to Newnan, E Chevron/dsl, Marathon/Subway/dsl, QT, Shell/dsl Applebee's, Arby's, Asian Chef, Capt D's, Chin Chin, Chipotle, Dunkin', Fried Tomato Buffet, Hooters, La Hacienda, Longhorn Steaks, Marco's Pizza, Moe's SW Grill, Panda Express, Red Lobster, Ruby Tuesday, Sprayberry's BBQ, Starbucks, Steak'n Shake, Stevi B's Pizza, TX Roadhouse, Waffle House, Wendy's Country Inn&Suites, Hampton Inn, Quality Inn, Springhill Suites H, Aldi Foods, GNC, Goodyear/auto, Hobby Lobby, Home Depot, Jo-Ann, Kauffman Tire, Kohl's, Lowe's, Petsmart, Ross, Walmart/McDonald's, W RaceTrac/dsl Burger King, Checkers, Chick-fil-A, Coldstone, Cracker Barrel, Firehouse Subs, Five Guys, Goldberg's Deli, Golden Corral, HoneyBaked Ham, IHOP, Jimmy John's, KFC, Krystal, La Parrilla Mexican, Newk's Cafe, O'Charley's, Olive Garden, Panera Bread, Red Robin, Rockback Pizza, Shane's BBQ, Shoney's, Starbucks, Taco Bell, Taco Mac, Thai Heaven, Tokyo Japanese, Yogli Mogli, Zaxby's Best Western, Comfort Inn, La Quinta, Motel 6, Newnan Inn $General, $Tree, AT&T, Barnes&Noble, Belk, Best Buy, BigLots, BJ's Whse/gas, Buick/Cadillac/GMC, Chevrolet, Dick's, Dillards, Ford/Lincoln, Hyundai, JC Penney, Michael's, Office Depot, Old Navy, Publix, Target, Tires+, TJ Maxx, Toyota, Verizon, vet, Walgreens

GA

LAGRANGE

INTERSTATE 85 Cont'd

Exit #	Services
44	Poplar Rd, E
41	US 27/29, Newnan, E Pilot/Subway/Wendy's/dsl/scales/24hr Little White House NHS, Roosevelt SP, W BP/dsl Huddle House, McDonald's, Waffle House Best Value Inn, Falcon Inn, Home Lodge, Red Carpet $General, repair
35	US 29, to Grantville, W BP/dsl, Marathon/dsl
28	GA 54, GA 100, to Hogansville, E Valero/dsl, W Loves/Arby's/dsl/scales/24hr, Marathon/dsl, Shell/dsl McDonald's, Roger's BBQ, Subway, Waffle House, Wendy's, Wendy's Garden Inn, Woodstream Inn Ingles
23mm	Beech Creek
22mm	**weigh sta both lanes**
21	I-185 S, to Columbus
18	GA 109, to Mountville, E Marathon/Domino's Rodeway Inn, Wingate Inn Little White House HS, to FDR SP, W BP/dsl, Exxon/Circle K/dsl, Mobil/dsl, RaceTrac/dsl, Shell/dsl, Valero Applebee's, Banzai Japanese, Burger King, Chick-fil-A, Cracker Barrel, Firehouse Subs, IHOP, Juanito's Mexican, Longhorn Steaks, Los Nopales, McDonald's, Mi Casa Mexican, Moe's SW Grill, Starbucks, Subway, Waffle House, Wendy's, Zaxby's Baymont Inn, Comfort Inn, Holiday Inn Express, La Quinta, Lafayette Garden Inn, Quality Inn, Super 8 AT&T, Belk, Chrysler/Dodge/Jeep, Ford/Lincoln, Hobby Lobby, Home Depot, Honda, Hyundai, JC Penney, TJ Maxx, Verizon
14	US 27, to La Grange, W Exxon, Marathon, Shell/Summit/dsl Waffle House Hampton Inn
13	GA 219, to La Grange, E Exxon/dsl/scales/24hr Waffle House EconoLodge, W Pilot/Subway/dsl/scales/24hr Arbys, McDonald's, Wendy's Great Wolf Lodge, Home 2 Suites
10mm	Long Cane Creek
6	Kia Blvd, W Kia Plant
2	GA 18, to West Point, E Chevron/dsl, Shell/Summit/dsl Best Value, W BP/dsl Subway (1.5) camping, to West Point Lake
.5mm	**Welcome Ctr nb, full facilities, litter barrels, petwalk, , , vending**
0mm	Georgia/Alabama state line, Chattahoochee River

SAVANNAH

INTERSTATE 95

Exit #	Services
113mm	Georgia/South Carolina state line, Savannah River
111mm	**Welcome Ctr/weigh sta sb, full facilities, info, litter barrels, petwalk, , , vending**
109	GA 21, to Savannah, Pt Wentworth, Rincon, E Enmark/dsl, Pilot/McDonald's/Subway/dsl/scales/24hr Waffle House Best Western, Country Inn&Suites, Hampton Inn, Mulberry Grove Inn Freightliner, W Flash/dsl, Murphy Express/dsl, Shell/Circle K/Blimpie/dsl Bojangles, Dunkin', El Ranchito, Happy Wok, Island Grill, Port Side Seafood, Sweet Tea Grill, Wendy's, Zaxby's Comfort Suites, Days Inn, Holiday Inn Express, Palm Extended Stay, Quality Inn, Savannah Inn, Sleep Inn, Super 8 CVS Drug, Family$, Food Lion, Whispering Pines RV Park (3mi)
107mm	Augustine Creek
106	Jimmy DeLoach Pkwy
104	Savannah Airport, E BP, Shell/Wendy's/dsl Sam Sneed's Grill, Waffle House, Waffle House Candlewood Suites,
104	Continued Comfort Suites, Country Inn&Suites, DoubleTree, Fairfield Hampton Inn, Hilton Garden, Holiday Inn Express, Hyatt P SpringHill Suites, Staybridge Suites, TownePlace Suites, W gate Inn to , W Murphy USA, Parkers/dsl, Shell/S way Applebee's, Arby's, Buffalo Wild Wings, Chedd Chick-fil-A, Chili's, Chipotle, CookOut, DQ, Fatz Cafe, Fireho Subs, Five Guys, Hilliard's Rest., IHOP, Jalapeños, Jersey Mi Jimmy John's, Krystal, Little Caesar's, Logan's Roadho Longhorn Steaks, McAlister's Deli, McDonald's, Mellow M room, Moe's SW, Olive Garden, Panda Express, Panera Br Ruby Tuesday, Shane's Rib Shack, Sonic, Starbucks, Ste Shake, TX Roadhouse, Wild Wing Cafe, Zaxby's Em sy Suites, Holiday Inn, Red Roof Inn, Residence Inn A Chevrolet, Dick's, GNC, Goodyear, Hobby Lobby, Home De Michael's, Petsmart, Publix, Ross, Sam's Club/gas, Savan Tire, Tanger Outlets/famous brands, TJ Maxx, URGENT CA Verizon, Walmart/McDonald's
102	US 80, to Garden City, E El Cheapos/Baldinos Subs, market/dsl, Flash/dsl Bojangles, Cracker Barrel, Dick BBQ, Guerrero Mexican, Hiranos Steaks, Jersey Style Subs, K Krystal, Larry's Subs, Los Bravos Mexican, McDonald's, Pek Chinese, Spanky's, Subway, Taco Bell, Waffle House B Western, Microtel, Motel 6, Quality Inn, Travelodge Ca ing World RV Ctr, Family$, Food Lion, museum, to Ft Pula NM, W Gate/dsl, Marathon, Shell Burger King, Do no's, El Potro Mexican, Hardee's, Italian Pizza, Pizza Hut, W dy's, Western Sizzlin EconoLodge, Holiday Inn, La Qui Magnolia Inn, Ramada, Sleep Inn $General
99b a	I-16, W to Macon, E to Savannah
94	GA 204, to Savannah, Pembroke, E 76/dsl/e85, BP/ Exxon, Murphy USA/dsl (2mi), Shell/dsl Applebee's, Cra er Barrel, Denny's, Hardee's, Houlihan's, IHOP, McDonal Perkins, Ruby Tuesday, Sonic Baymont Inn, Best Inn, B Western, Clarion, Comfort Suites, Country Inn Suites, Days I EconoLodge, Fairfield Inn, Hampton Inn, Holiday Inn, Holiday Express, Howard Johnson, La Quinta, Quality Inn, Red Roof I San's Boutique Hotel, Scottish Inn, Sleep Inn, SpringHill Suit Super 8, Travelodge , Factory Stores/Famous Bra GNC, Walmart (2mi), W Chevron/dsl, Sunoco Hoote Shellhouse Rest, Subway, Waffle House Motel 6, Rodew Inn Harley-Davidson, Indian Motorcycles, Savannah Oa RV Park (2mi)
91mm	Ogeechee River
90	GA 144, Old Clyde Rd, to Ft Stewart, Richmond Hill SP, E E on/dsl, Parkers DQ, Jalapeno's, Pizza Hut, Subway, Z by's AT&T, Kroger/deli/dsl, URGENT CARE, Verizon, W Loves/McDonald's/dsl/scales/24hr, Marathon/dsl C re's RV Ctr
87	US 17, to Coastal Hwy, Richmond Hill, E BP/Subway, Ch ron/dsl, RaceWay/dsl China 1, Denny's, Domino's, Fuji Ja anese, Molly McPherson's Grill, Papa Murphy's, Smokin' Pig BB Southern Image Rest., Steamer's Rest., Waffle House Da Inn, Motel 6, Royal Inn, Scottish Inn, Travelodge Food Li URGENT CARE, W McDonald's, Shell/dsl, Sunoco/dsl, T BP/Pizza Hut/Popeye's/dsl/scales/24hr/@ Arby's, KFC/Ta Bell, Waffle House, Wendy's Best Western+, EconoLodg Fairfield Inn, Hampton Inn, Holiday Inn Express, Quality In Super 8 KOA
85mm	Elbow Swamp
80mm	Jerico River

INTERSTATE 95 Cont'd

Exit #	Services
76	US 84, GA 38, to Midway, Sunbury, E hist sites, W Gulf/McDonald's/dsl, Parker's/dsl, Shell/dsl/scales Huddle House, Smokin' Pig BBQ
67	US 17, Coastal Hwy, to S Newport, E BP/Subway/dsl, Citgo/dsl, El Cheapo, Shell/McDonald's Jones BBQ Harris Neck NWR, W Texaco
58	GA 99, GA 57, Townsend Rd, Eulonia, E BP/dsl, Citgo $General, USPO, W Exxon/dsl, Shell/Stuckey's/dsl, Snappy Huddle House Motel 6 Lake Harmony RV Park, McIntosh Lake RV Park
55mm	**weigh sta both lanes**
49	GA 251, to Darien, E Mobil/dsl DQ, McDonald's, Waffle House Ford, Inland Harbor RV Park, W BP/dsl/scales, Parker's Burger King, KFC/Taco Bell, Ruby Tuesday, Wendy's Days Inn, Econolodge, Hampton Inn, Quality Inn, Super 8
47mm	Darien River
46.5mm	Butler River
46mm	Champney River
45mm	Altamaha River
42	GA 99, E to Hofwyl Plantation HS
41mm	**sb, full facilities, info, litter barrels, petwalk, , , vending**
38	US 17, GA 25, N Golden Isles Pkwy, Brunswick, E RaceTrac/dsl McDonald's, Millhouse Steaks Comfort Suites, Country Inn&Suites, Embassy Suites (2mi), Fairfield Inn, Holiday Inn, Microtel , Nissan, W Flash, Marathon/dsl, Parker's, Shell/dsl China Town, Denny's, Huddle House, Subway, Toucan's, Waffle House Best Western+, Courtyard, EconoLodge, Guest Cottage Motel, Hampton Inn, Quality Inn, Sleep Inn $General, Family$, Harley-Davidson, Toyota, Winn Dixie
36b a	US 25, US 341, to Jesup, Brunswick, E Chevron/Subway/dsl, Exxon/dsl, RaceWay/dsl Burger King, Cracker Barrel, IHOP, KFC, Krystal, McDonald's, Pizza Hut, Starbucks, Taco Bell, Waffle House, Wendy's Days Inn, Jameson Inn, La Quinta, Motel 6, Red Roof Inn, Tropical Inn Jack's Tires, W Parker's/dsl, Shell/dsl Capt Joe's Seafood, China Buffet, Huddle House, Larry's Subs, Sonny's BBQ, Waffle House Clarion, Comfort Inn, Economy Inn, Magnuson Inn, Ramada Inn, Stay Express, Super 8 $General, Advance Parts, AutoZone, CVS Drug, Family$, Fred's, URGENT CARE, Winn-Dixie
33mm	Turtle River
30mm	S Brunswick River
29	US 17, US 82, GA 520, S GA Pkwy, Brunswick, E Exxon/dsl, Flash, Love's/Godfather's/Subway/Chester's/dsl/scales/24hr, Mobil/dsl Bubba Jack's Crab Shack, Huddle House, Krystal, McDonald's, Zaxby's Comfort Suites Blue Beacon, SpeedCo, W FLYING J/Denny's/dsl/LP/scales/24hr, Shell/Dunkin'/dsl, TA/BP/Burger King/Starbucks/Subway/dsl/24hr Domino's, Larry's Subs, Waffle House, Zachry's Rest EconoLodge, Motel 6, Super 8 $General, Family$, Golden Isles Camping, TA Truck Service, Winn Dixie
27.5mm	Little Satilla River
26	Dover Bluff Rd, E Mobil/Stuckey's/dsl
22	Horse Stamp Church Rd
21mm	White Oak Creek
19mm	Canoe Swamp
15mm	Satilla River

BRUNSWICK

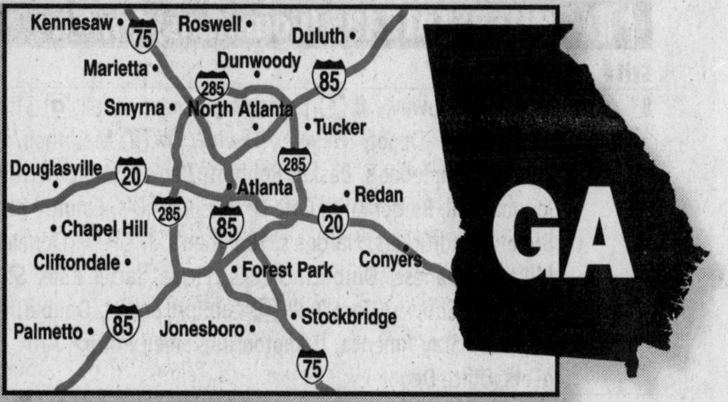

ST MARYS

Exit #	Services
14	GA 25, to Woodbine, W Chevron/Sunshine/rest/dsl/scales/24hr Stardust Motel (3mi)
7	Harrietts Bluff Rd, E Flash/dsl, Shell/Subway, W BP/dsl Walkabout Camping/RV Park
6.5mm	Crooked River
6	Laurel Island Pkwy, E Gtrac Express/dsl, Shell/Chester's/dsl
3	GA 40, Kingsland, to St Marys, E Chevron, El Cheapo/dsl, Flash/dsl, Mobil, Murphy USA/dsl, Shell/Subway, Sunoco Angelo's Italian, Applebee's, Burger King, Capt D's, Chick-fil-A, DQ, Dunkin', Firehouse Subs, KFC, Little Caesar's, Longhorn Steaks, McDonald's, OPS Kitchen, Papa John's, Ruby Tuesday, Sonny's BBQ, Taco Bell, Waffle House, Wendy's, Zaxby's Best Western, Comfort Suites, Country Inn&Suites, Days Inn, Fairfield Inn, Hawthorn Suites, Magnolia Inn, Microtel, Motel 6, Quality Inn, Red Roof Inn, Rodeway Inn, Sleep Inn , $Tree, Buick/Chevrolet, Chrysler/Dodge/Jeep, CVS Drug, Ford, GNC, Lowe's, NAPA, Publix, Tire Kingdom, to Crooked River SP, to Submarine Base, URGENT CARE, Verizon, Walgreens, Walmart, Winn-Dixie, W **Welcome Ctr/info**, Flash/dsl, Petro/Popeye's/dsl/scales/24hr/@, RaceWay/dsl, Shell/dsl Cracker Barrel, Denny's, Domino's, IHOP, Millhouse Steaks, Waffle House Baymont Inn, EconoLodge, Hampton Inn, La Quinta, Springfield Suites, Travelers Inn Ace Hardware, Advance Parts, Fred's, Kiki RV Park
1	St Marys Rd, to Cumberland Is Nat Seashore, E **Welcome Ctr nb, full facilities, , vending, , litter barrels, petwalk,** Pilot/Subway/PJ Fresh/dsl/scales/24hr, Shell/dsl W BP/dsl, Chevron/dsl, Pilot/Dunkin'/Wendy's/dsl/scales/24hr Little Pearl's Bistro Country Oaks RV Park, KOA
0mm	Georgia/Florida state line, St Marys River

INTERSTATE 185 (Columbus)

Exit #	Services
48	**I-85. I-185 begins/ends on I-85.**
46	Big Springs Rd, E Shell/dsl, W tires
42	US 27, Pine Mountain, E Marathon/dsl, Summit/dsl Waffle House Little White House HS, Pine Mtn Camping, to Callaway Gardens
34	GA 18, to West Point, E to Callaway Gardens
30	Hopewell Church Rd, Whitesville, W Shell/dsl $General
25	GA 116, to Hamilton, W RV camping
19	GA 315, Mulberry Grove, W Chevron/dsl/24hr
14	Smith Rd
12	Williams Rd, W **Welcome Ctr/rest rooms** Chevron, Summit/dsl Country Inn&Suites, Microtel
10	US 80, GA 22, to Phenix City, W Springer Opera House

GA

INTERSTATE 185 (Columbus) Cont'd

COLUMBUS

Exit #	Services
8	Airport Thruway, E Bojangles, Great Wall $Tree, GNC, Home Depot, Walmart/Subway, W Marathon/dsl, Shell Applebee's, Baskin Robbins, Ben's Chophouse, Blue Iguana Grill, Burger King, Cafe Le Rue, Capt D's, Country Road Buffet, Fuddruckers, Hardee's, Houlihan's, IHOP, McDonald's, Mikata Japanese, Outback Steaks, Pickle Barrel Cafe, Stevi B's Pizza, Subway, Taco Bell Comfort Suites, DoubleTree, Extended Stay America, Hampton Inn, Sleep Inn AAA, BigLots, Office Depot
7	45th St, Manchester Expswy, E Applebee's, Burger King, Carino's Italian, Krystal, Ruby Tuesday Courtyard, La Quinta, Super 8 Best Buy, Cadillac/Chevrolet, Dillard's, JC Penney, Macy's, W BP/dsl, Chevron/dsl, Circle K/dsl, Marathon Arby's, Chick-fil-A, China Express, Dunkin', Goldberg's Deli, Golden Corral, Jimmy John's, KFC, Little Caesar's, Logan's Roadhouse, Lucky China, McDonald's, Pizza Hut, Ryan's, Shogun Japanese, Sonic, Starbucks, SteakOut, Subway, Waffle House Fairfield Inn, Holiday Inn, TownePlace Suites H, $General, Advance Parts, Big T Tire/repair, Civil War Naval Museum, Midas, Mr Transmission
6	GA 22, Macon Rd, E Chevron/dsl, Circle K/dsl Bruster's, Burger King, DQ, Little Caesar's, Taco Bell, Waffle House Best Western, Comfort Inn, Days Inn $General, Rite Aid, U-Haul, vet, Walgreens, W Chevron/dsl, Shell/dsl American Deli, Capt D's, ChuckeCheese, Cici's, Country's BBQ, Denny's, Dunkin'/Baskin Robbins, Firehouse Subs, Jimmy John's, Longhorn Steaks, McDonald's, Subway, Zaxby's Efficiency Lodge, La Quinta AT&T, CVS Drug, Fred's, GNC, Goodyear/auto, Publix, TJ Maxx, Tuesday Morning, Verizon
4	Buena Vista Rd, E BP, Circle K, Solo Burger King, Capt D's, Checkers, Church's, Krystal, McDonald's, Papa John's, Pizza Hut, Subway, Taco Bell, Waffle House, Zaxby's $Tree, AutoZone, Family$, Firestone/auto, Goodyear/auto, O'Reilly Parts, Rainbow Foods, repair, USPO, vet, Walgreens, Walmart, Winn-Dixie, W Marathon
3	St Marys Rd, E Domino's Microtel Family$, W FuelTech/dsl, Shell/dsl Hardee's, Shark Seafood/Chicken $General, Ace Hardware, Piggly Wiggly
1b a	US 27, US 280, Victory Dr, 0-3 mi W Chevron/dsl, Circle K, Liberty, RaceWay/dsl Burger King, Capt D's, Checkers, Krystal, McDonald's, Papa John's, Sonic, Subway, Taco Bell, Waffle House, Wendy's Candlewood Suites, Columbus Inn, EconoLodge, Holiday Inn Express, Motel 6, Suburban Lodge $General, Advance Parts, AutoZone, CVS Drug, Family$, O'Reilly Parts, Piggly Wiggly, Verizon
0mm	**I-185 begins/ends on Victory Dr**

GA

INTERSTATE 285 (Atlanta)

ATLANTA AREA

Exit #	Services
62	GA 279, S Fulton Hwy, Old Nat Hwy, N Chevron/dsl, Texaco Waffle House Econolodge, S Chevron, Citgo, Exxon, Shell, Valero American Deli, Blimpie, Bojangles, Burger King, Checker's, China Cafeteria, Church's, Cozumel Mexican, KFC, Krystal, McDonald's, Piccadilly Cafeteria, Subway, Taco Bell, Waffle House, Wendy's Baymont Inn, Day's Inn, Quality Inn, Super 8, Travelodge, Windsor Atl Hotel AutoZone, Family$, Midas, O'Reilly Parts, U-Haul
61	I-85, N to Atlanta, S to Montgomery
60	GA 139, Riverdale Rd, N Fairfield Inn (2mi), Micro (2mi), Wingate Inn (2mi), S QT/dsl, Shell/dsl, Vale dsl Checkers, Church's, McDonald's, Papa John's, Wa House Best Western, Day's Inn, Quality Hotel $General, Advance Parts, Family$
59	Clark Howell Hwy, N air cargo
58	I-75, N to Atlanta, S to Macon (from eb), to US 19, US 41, Hapeville, S BP/dsl, Citgo/dsl, Exxon/dsl Americ Deli, Jimmy John's, Subway, Tijuana Joe's, Waffle House, Wendy's Home Lodge Motel
55	GA 54, Jonesboro Rd, N Super 8, S BP/dsl, Citg dsl, Shell/dsl, Texaco/dsl DaiLai Vietnamese, McDonal Family$, Home Depot, repair
53	US 23, Moreland Ave, to Ft Gillem, N BP/dsl, Citg dsl, S Chevron/dsl, Citgo Wendy's EconoLod USPO
52	I-675, S to Macon
51	Bouldercrest Rd, N BP, Pilot/Wendy's/dsl/24 Checkers, Domino's, Hardee's, KFC, WK Wings Famil Wayfield Foods, S Exxon/dsl, Shell/Blimpie/dsl, Texaco/
48	GA 155, Flat Shoals Rd, Candler Rd, N BP, Chevron, Citg dsl, Shell/dsl, Texaco/dsl Burger King, Checkers, Church DQ, Dunkin'/BR, KFC, McDonald's, Taco Bell, Waffle King, V Wings Gulf American Inn BigLots, Macy's, S C go, QT, Texaco/dsl Burger King, China One, Sonic, Su way Family$
46b a	I-20, E to Augusta, W to Atlanta
44	GA 260, Glenwood Rd, E Sunoco/dsl EconoLod W Exxon/dsl, Texaco/dsl, Valero/dsl
43	US 278, Covington Hwy, E Chevron/Subway, Texac dsl Waffle House U-Haul, W Mystik/dsl, QT, Rac Trac/dsl, Texaco/dsl HoneyBaked Ham, Wendy's Be Inn Advance Parts, Family$
42	(from nb), Marta Station
41	GA 10, Memorial Dr, Avondale Estates, E Citgo, My tik Applebee's, Baskin-Robbins/Dunkin', Burger Kir Church's, Domino's, IHOP, Pancake House, Pizza Hut, Subwa Taco Bell, Waffle House, Wendy's Best Value Inn, Budget United Suites $Tree, Advance Parts, Atl Tires, AutoZor Family$, Firestone/auto, GNC, Office Depo, Ross, transm sions, U-Haul, USPO, Walgreens
40	Church St, to Clarkston, E Chevron, Marathon/dsl, Texa auto repair, W H
39b a	US 78, to Athens, Decatu
38	US 29, Lawrenceville Hwy, E Citgo, QT/dsl, RaceTra dsl Bojangle's, Waffle House Best Value Inn, Knigh Inn H, W Citgo/dsl Bruster's Masters In Motel 6 AutoZone, CVS Drug
37	GA 236, to LaVista, Tucker, E Chevron/dsl, Exxon Chec ers, Folks Rest., Hudson Grille, IHOP, O'Charley's, Piccad ly's, Pollo Tropical, Waffle House Comfort Suites, Da Inn DeKalb Tire/auto, Firestone/auto, Target, W B Domino's, Chevron, Shell/dsl Blue Ribbon Grill, Capt D Chick-fil-A, Chipotle, Coco Cabana Cuban, Dunkin', Eduardo Mexican, HoneyBaked Ham, Jason's Deli, Kacey's Rest., Ko Steaks, Lucky Key Chinese, Maddio's Pizza, Marlow's Taver McDonald's, Mellow Mushroom, Moe's SW, Monterrey Mex can, Panda Express, Panera Bread, Pizza Hut, Popeye's, R Lobster, Starbucks, Subway Courtyard, DoubleTree, Holid Inn, Quality Inn $Tree, Aldi Foods, AT&T, Best Buy, Goo year/auto, JC Penney, Kohl's, Kroger, Michael's, Office Dep Petsmart, Publix, TJ Maxx, Verizon

INTERSTATE 285 (Atlanta) Cont'd

Exit #	Services
36	Northlake Pkwy (from sb, no return)
34	Chamblee-Tucker Rd, E Texaco/dsl $3 Cafe, China Star, Galaxy Diner, Hunan Inn, Jersey Mike's Subs, KFC/Taco Bell, Moe's SW Grill, Wendy's Advance Parts, Goodyear/auto, Kroger, Rite Aid, USPO, W Citgo, Shell McDonald's, Subway BigLots, vet
33b a	I-85, N to Greenville, S to Atlanta
32	US 23, Buford Hwy, to Doraville, E BP/dsl Baldino's Subs, Bojangle's, Burger King/playland, Checkers, Chick-fil-A, McDonald's, Waffle House, White Windmill Café, Zaxby's Advance Parts, Firestone/auto, Marshalls, PepBoys, W Citgo, QT/dsl McDonald's, Monterrey Mexican, Subway, Waffle House Clarion $Tree, Aamco, Meineke
31b a	GA 141, Peachtree Ind, to Chamblee, W Arby's, Baskin-Robbins/Dunkin', Chick-fil-A, IHOP, McDonald's, Pizza Hut, Subway, Wendy's Acura, Advance Parts, AT&T, Audi, Brandsmart, Buick/GMC, Chevrolet, Chrysler/Dodge/Jeep, CVS Drug, Firestone/auto, Ford, Honda, Hyundai, Infiniti, Kia, Lexus, Mazda, Mini, Nissan, Office Depot, Porsche, Toyota, VW, Walgreens
30	Chamblee-Dunwoody Rd, N Shallowford Rd, to N Peachtree Rd, N BP/dsl, BP/Dunkin', Shell, Texaco/dsl Bagel&Co. Deli, Burger King, Marco's Pizza, McDonald's, Starbucks, Subway, Takorea, Waffle House Kroger, Tuesday Morning, S Exxon/dsl, Mobil, Shell, Texaco/dsl, Valero La Botana Mexican, Mad Italian Rest., Papa John's, Taco Bell, Wendy's, Wild Ginger Thai Residence Inn
29	Ashford-Dunwoody Rd, N Exxon/Subway Brio Tuscan, Broken Egg, CA Pizza Kitchen, Capital Grille, Cheesecake Factory, Chick-fil-A, Chili's, Corner Bakery&Cafe, Fogo de Chao, J. Alexander's, Jason's Deli, Maddio's Pizza, Maggiano's Little Italy, McDonald's, McKendrick Steaks, Memphis BBQ, Newk's Eatery, Olive Garden, PF Chang's, Popeye's, Schlotzsky's, Seasons 32 Grill, Starbucks, Wild Wing Cafe Crowne Plaza, Hampton Inn Barnes&Noble, Best Buy, Dillard's, Hobby Lobby, Macy's, Marshalls, Nordstrom, Old Navy, USPO, Walmart, S Hilton Garden
28	Peachtree-Dunwoody Rd (no EZ return wb), N Arby's, Chuy's Mexican, Domino's, Five Guys, Panera Bread, Subway, Uncle Julio's Mexican, Willy's Mexican Comfort Suites, Courtyard, Extended Stay America, Extended Stay America (2), Fairfield Inn, Hampton Inn, Hilton Suites, Holiday Inn Express, La Quinta, Marriott, Microtel, Residence Inn, Sheraton, Westin Costco/gas, GNC, Home Depot, Publix, Rite Aid, Ross, Target, TJ Maxx, S H
27	US 19 N, GA 400, 2 mi N LDS Temple
26	Glenridge Dr (from eb), Johnson Ferry Rd
25	US 19 S, Roswell Rd, Sandy Springs, N BP, Shell/dsl, Shell/dsl Andres Mexican, Bobbys Burgers, Boston Mkt, Burger King, Chick-fil-A, Chipotle Mexican, Domino's, Dunkin', Egg Harbor Café, El Azteca Mexican, Firehouse Subs, Five Guys, Hudson Grille, IHOP, Jimmy John's, Longhorn Steaks, Maya Steaks, McDonald's, Mellow Mushroom, Moe's SW Grill, Pizza Hut, Roasters, Starbucks, Steak'n Shake, Subway, Taco Bell, Waffle House, Wendy's, Willy's Mexican, Zaxby's Comfort Inn $Tree, Aldi Foods, AT&T, CVS Drug, DeKalb Tire, Lowe's, Marshalls, Mr Tire, NAPA AutoCare, Office Depot, PepBoys, PetCo, Publix, Target, Toyota, Trader Joe's, Tuesday Morning, URGENT CARE, Verizon, Walgreens, Whole Foods Mkt, S Chevron/dsl, Citgo, Shell Barberitos, El Taco Veloz, Five Seasons Rest., Marlow's

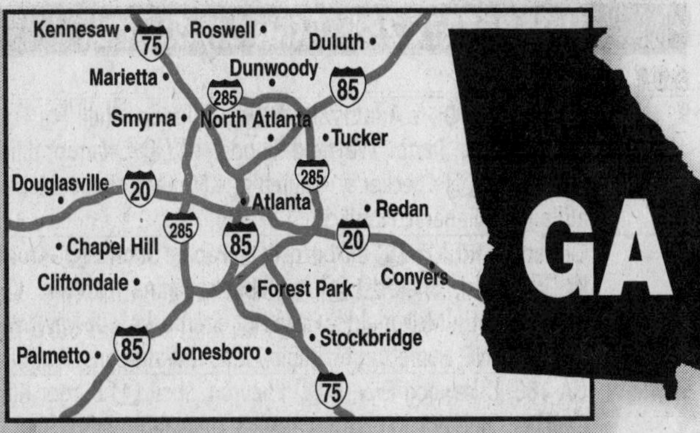

ATLANTA AREA

Exit #	Services
25	Continued Tavern, Panda Express, Starbucks, Taco Mac Publix, Staples, Target, URGENT CARE
24	Riverside Dr
22	New Northside Dr, to Powers Ferry Rd, N Shell/Subway/dsl Extended Stay America, S BP, Chevron/dsl McDonald's, Ray's Rest., Rio Bravo, Subway, Waffle House Wyndham CVS Drug, Publix, vet
21	(from wb), N Chevron Harry's Pizza, Homestead Village Extended Stay America BMW/Mini
20	I-75, N to Chattanooga, S to Atlanta (from wb), to US 41 N
19	US 41, Cobb Pkwy, to Dobbins AFB, N BP/dsl, Marathon, QT Applebee's, Bruster's, Burger King, Carrabba's, Chucke-Cheese, Del Taco, Dunkin', IHOP, Jade Palace, KFC, McDonald's, Olive Garden, Panda Express, Papa John's, Red Lobster, Scalini's Italian, Subway, Taco Bell, Thompson Bros BBQ, Waffle House, Wendy's, Zaxby's DoubleTree, Extended Stay America, Hampton Inn, Holiday Inn Express, Hyatt, Residence Inn, Wingate Inn $Tree, Aldi Foods, Best Buy, Braves Stadium, Cadillac, Chevrolet, Discount Tire, Honda, Hyundai, Kia, Lexus, Marshall's, Michael's, NTB, Office Depot, PetsMart, Ross, Target, Verizon, Walgreens, S Buffalo Wild Wings, Cheesecake Factory, Chick-fil-A, Chipotle Mexican, Corner Bakery Cafe, Firehouse Subs, Hooters, Jason's Deli, Longhorn Steaks, Maggiano's Italian, PF Chang's, Pizza Hut, Pollo Tropical, Schlotsky's, Stoney River Steaks, Subway, Tilted Kilt, Zoe's Kitchen Courtyard, Hampton Inn, Homewood Suites, Renaissance, Sheraton Suites AT&T, Barnes&Noble, Costco/gas, Macy's, Old Navy, USPO
18	Paces Ferry Rd, to Vinings, N Panera Bread Fairfield Inn, La Quinta, S QT/24hr Chick-fil-A, Starbucks, Subway, Willy's Grill Extended Stay America Goodyear/auto, Home Depot, Publix, Verizon
16	S Atlanta Rd, to Smyrna, N Five Guys, Waffle House Days Inn H, S Chevron/Subway/dsl, Shell/dsl Jersey Mike's Kroger
15	GA 280, S Cobb Dr, E Araamda U-Haul, W BP/dsl, Mobil, RaceTrac/dsl, Shell Arby's, Chick-fil-A, China Cafe, Dunkin', IHOP, Jimmy John's, Krystal, McDonald's, Subway, Taco Bell, Zaxby's Baymont Inn, Comfort Inn, Country Inn Suites, Knight's Inn, Sun Suites
14mm	Chattahoochee River
13	Bolton Rd (from nb)
12	US 78, US 278, Bankhead Hwy, E Petro/Iron Skillet/dsl/scales/24hr/@, Shell/dsl/24hr, Valero/dsl Burger King Blue Beacon, W BP, Texaco
10b a	I-20, W to Birmingham, E to Atlanta (exits left from nb), W to Six Flags

 = gas = food = lodging = other = rest stop

INTERSTATE 285 (Atlanta) Cont'd

Exit #	Services
9	GA 139, MLK Dr, to Adamsville, E Quikmart, Shell Family$, O'Reilly Parts, Wayfield Foods, W Chevron, Shell, Texaco/dsl Checker's, Church's, KFC/Taco Bell, McDonald's $General, Family$
7	Cascade Rd, E Exxon/dsl Papa John's Kroger, W BP/dsl, Shell/dsl Applebee's, China Express, KFC, Little Caesar's, McDonald's, Pizza Hut, Starbucks, Subway, Wendy's GNC, Home Depot, Publix, Tires+, Walgreens, Walmart
5b a	GA 166, Lakewood Fwy, E Chevron, Shell Burger King, Capt D's, Checker's, KFC, Little Caesar's, Subway, Wendy's CVS Drug, Firestone, Goodyear/auto, Kroger, Macy's, W BP, RaceWay/dsl, Shell/dsl, Texaco/dsl, Valero Church's Deluxe Inn AutoZone, Family$, O'Reilly Parts
2	Camp Creek Pkwy, to ✈, E Exxon/dsl, Texaco Checker's, Church's, McDonald's, W RaceTrac/dsl American Deli, Bruster's, Carino's, Chick-fil-A, Chili's, China 1, Five Guys, Jason's Deli, LongHorn Steaks, Moe's SW, Panda Express, Papa John's, Popeyes, Red Lobster, Ruby Tuesday, Starbucks, Taco Bell, TGIFriday, Wendys, Zaxby's Courtyard, Hampton Inn, Holiday Inn Express $Tree, AT&T, Barnes&Noble, BJ's Whse/gas, Lowes Whse, Marshall's, Old Navy, PetsMart, Publix, Ross, Staples, Target, TJ Maxx, Verizon, Walgreens
1	Washington Rd, E Texaco/dsl, W Chevron/dsl

INTERSTATE 475 (Macon)

Exit #	Services
16mm	**I-475 begins/ends on I-75, exit 177.**
15	US 41, Bolingbroke, 1 mi E Exxon/dsl/LP, Marathon/dsl
9	Zebulon Rd, E Marathon/dsl, Shell/Circle K/24hr Applebee's, Buffalo's Café, Chick-fil-A, Johnny's NY Pizz, Krystal, Macon Pizza Co, Margarita's Mexican, McAlister's Deli, McDonald's, Moe's SW, NU Way Wieners, Papa John's, Pizza Hut, Sonic, Subway, Taco Bell, Taki Japanese, Tutti Frutti, Waffle House, Wendy's Baymont Inn, Comfort Suites, Fairfield Inn, Sleep Inn H, Goodyear/auto, Kohl's, Kroger/dsl, Lowe's, URGENT CARE, USPO, Verizon, Walgreens, Walmart/Subway, W Marathon/dsl, Sunoco/dsl Marco's Pizza, Polly's Cafe, Zaxby's Advance Parts, CVS Drug
8mm	**nb, full facilities, litter barrels, petwalk, vending**
5	GA 74, Macon, E RaceWay/dsl Waffle House Harley-Davidson, to Mercer U, W Flash/Subway/dsl, Texaco/Church's/dsl Capt D's A1 Economy $General, Tires+, to Lake Tobesofkee, vet
3	US 80, Macon, **0-2 mi** E Marathon/dsl, Murphy USA/dsl, RaceWay, Shell/Circle K/Subway Aldi Foods, Applebee's, Burger King, Chick-fil-A, China Buffet, Cracker Barrel, DQ, Firehouse Subs, Golden Corral, JL's BBQ, Margarita's Mexican, McAlister's Deli, McDonald's, Papa John's, S&S Cafeteria, Silver Bay Seafood, Smokin' Pig BBQ, Taco Bell, Waffle House, Zaxby's Best Inn, Best Western, Bridgeview Inn, Comfort Suites, Days Inn, Discovery Inn, EconoLodge, Hampton Inn, Holiday Inn Express, La Quinta, Motel 6, Quality Inn, Ramada Inn, Red Roof Inn, Super 8, Woodspring Suites $Tree, AT&T, Best Buy, BigLots, CVS Drug, Dick's, Discount Tire, Firestone/auto, GNC, Home Depot, Honda, Kroger/gas, Lowe's, Macy's, Marshall's, Michael's, Nissan, Office Depot, Old Navy, Petsmart, Ross, Sam's Club/gas, Staples, Target, Verizon, vet, VW, Walmart/Subway, W Shell/Circle K, Sunoco/dsl Burger King Best Value Inn, Windsor Economy Inn
1	Hartley Bridge Rd, same as I-75 exit 156
0mm	**I-475 begins/ends on I-75, exit 156.**

MACON

CANTON

INTERSTATE 575

Exit #	Services
30mm	**I-575 begins/ends on GA 5/515.**
27	GA 5, Howell Br, to Ball Ground
24	Airport Dr
20	GA 5, to Canton, E Bojangles, Buffalo's Cafe, Cas Rest., Chick-fil-A, Dos Margaritas Mexican, Jin's Buffet, S B's Pizza, Waffle Wouse, Wendy's Econolodge, Homest Inn, Motel 6 AT&T, Chevrolet, Chrysler/Dodge/Jeep, G Toyota, Verizon, Walmart, W RaceTrac/dsl, Shell/Subw Texaco/dsl Applebee's, Arby's, Cracker Barrel, Five G Honeybaked Ham, Longhorn Steaks, McDonald's, O'Charle Okinawa Steaks, Outback Steaks, Panda Express, Provino's, Lobster, Seven Tequilas Mexican, Starbucks, Zaxby's B Western, Hampton Inn, Holiday Inn Express H, Belk, Ho Depot, Michaels, Publix, Ross
19	GA 20 E, Canton, E Bobby's Burgers, Chick-fil-A, Chipo IHOP, Jimmy John's, La Parrilla Mexican, Maddio's Pizza, Donald's, Olive Garden, Starbucks, Subway, Taco Mac, Wa House, Which Wich?, Zaxby's Best Buy, BooksAMilli Dick's, Goodyear/auto, Kohl's, Lowe's, NTB, Petsmart, Targ TJ Maxx
17	GA 140, to Roswell (from sb), Canton
16	GA 20, GA 140, W Citgo, RaceTrac/dsl Burger Ki KFC, Mandarin House, Papa John's, Subway, Taco Bell, Wa House $General, Advance Parts, Rite Aid
14	Holly Springs, E Texaco/dsl Domino's, Ichiban Buf Las Palmas Mexican, Pizza Hut Pinecrest Motel Walmart/Subway, W Chevron, Shell/dsl Dunkin', Go en China, McDonald's, Subway, Taste of Italy, Viva Mexi Wendy's, Zaxby's Autozone, Family$, Kauffman Tire, K ger/dsl, Publix, Verizon, Walgreens
11	Sixes Rd, E Chevron/dsl, QT Shane's Ribshack, Z by's Home Depot, Verizon
9	Ridgewalk Pkwy, E Applebee's, Chick-fil-A, Five Guys, Donald's, Panda Express outlets/famous brands
8	Towne Lake Pkwy, to Woodstock, E Shell/dsl Subw Waffle House Ford, W Phillips 66, QT Chili's, Lo horn Steaks Tuesday Morning, Walgreens
7	GA 92, Woodstock, E Chevron, QT Arby's, Bubba Rest., Burger King, Capt D's, Checker's, Chick-fil-A, Chin Ch Del Taco, DQ, Dunkin', Firehouse Subs, Folk's Kitchen, H eybaked Ham, Maddio's Pizza, McDonald's, Moe's SW G O'Charley's, Resturante Mexico, Ruby Tuesday, Starbuc Stevi B's Pizza, Subway, Taco Bell, Waffle House Comf Suites, Hampton Inn, InTown Suite Camping World, Fi stone/auto, Goodyear/auto, W Texaco/dsl Hacien Vieja Mexican, IHOP, Jimmy John's, Schlotzky's, Steak'n Sha Taco Mac Microtel AT&T, Atlanta Bread, Big Lots, B Whse/gas, Discount Tire, GNC, Home Depot, Honda, Koh Lowe's Whse, Old Navy, Petsmart, Target, Verizon
4	Bells Ferry Rd, W QT, RaceTrac/dsl, Shell/dsl Arby Burger King, Dunkin', Pizza Hut, Ralph's Grill, Subway, Wa House Pepboys, Publix, Walgreens
3	Chastain Rd, to I-75 N, W Chevron CA Dreami Cookout, Cracker Barrel, Del Taco, Firehouse Subs, Five Gu Los Reyes, Maddio's Pizza, Marlow's Tavern, O'Charley's, Pa da Express, Papa's Cuban, Ruth's Chris Steks, Starbucks, Ta Mac Best Western, Comfort Suites, Embassy Suites, Fairfi Inn, Residence Inn, Springhill Suites to Kennesaw St Coll

WOODSTOCK

GA

INTERSTATE 575 Cont'd

Exit #	Services
1	Barrett Pkwy, to I-75 N, US 41, **E** [gas] Murphy USA/dsl, QT [food] Buffalo Wild Wings, Burger King, Cheeseburger Bobby's, Fuego Tortillo, Pacific Buffet, Starbucks, Texas Roadhouse, Twisted Kitchen, Waffle House, Wendy's, Zaxby's [other] $Tree, AT&T, Barnes&Noble, CVS Drug, Mavis Tire, Petco, Publix, Ross, SteinMart, Tuesday Morning, Walmart/Subway, **W** [gas] Shell/dsl [food] Anchor Grill, Applebee's, Honeybaked Ham, Jimmy John's, McDonald's, Olive Garden, Provino's Italian, Red Lobster, Shogun Japanese, Starbucks, Subway, Twin Peaks [lodging] Comfort Inn, Country Inn&Suites, Holiday Inn Express, Red Roof Inn [other] Belk, Firestone/auto, Home Depot, Marshall's, Midas, Pepboys, TJ Maxx, Verizon
0mm	**I-575 begins/ends on I-75, exit 268.**

INTERSTATE 675

Exit #	Services
10mm	I-285 W, to Atlanta Airport, E to Augusta. **I-675 begins/ends on I-285, exit 52.**
7	Anvil Block Rd, Ft Gillem, **E** [gas] Chevron/dsl [food] Waffle House, Wendy's [other] $Tree, Walmart/Subway, **W** [gas] Exxon/dsl
5	Forest Pkwy, **E** [gas] Texaco/dsl, **W** [gas] BP/dsl, QT/dsl/scales, Texaco/dsl [food] McDonald's, Waffle House
2	US 23, GA 42, **E** [gas] BP, Texaco, Valero/Subway/dsl [food] El Granero Mexican, **W** [gas] Chevron/dsl, Citgo [food] Waffle House [other] Family$, Food Depot, GoodTime/auto, Rite Aid, USPO
1	GA 138, to I-75 N, Stockbridge, **E** [gas] Citgo/dsl, Exxon/dsl, Murphy USA/dsl, QT, Sunoco/dsl [food] Burger King, Capt D's, Checker's, Church's Chicken, DQ, Dunkin', Golden Corral, Hibachi Buffet, KFC, Krispy Kreme, Little Caesar's, McDonald's, Olympia Pizza, Papa John's, Popeye's, Taco Bell, Waffle House, Wendy's, Zaxby's [lodging] Best Value, Econolodge, Knights Inn, Magnolia Inn, Quality Inn, Sleep Inn, Stay Inn, Stockbridge Inn [other] $General, $Tree, Advance Parts, Aldi Foods, BigLots, CVS Drug, Goodyear/auto, NAPA, Pepboys, Walmart, **W** [gas] Raceway/dsl [food] Applebee's, Broadway Diner, Chick-fil-A, Frontera Mexican, Honeybaked Ham, IHOP, Krystal, O'Charley's, Piccadilly's, Subway, Taco Mac, Tokyo Seafood, Waffle House [lodging] Comfort Inn, Day's Inn, Express Inn, Hampton Inn, Holiday Inn, La Quinta, Red Roof Inn [other] Kroger/dsl, Lowes Whse, Office Depot, Tires+, URGENT CARE, Verizon
0mm	**I-675 begins/ends on I-75, exit 227.**

GAINESVILLE

INTERSTATE 985 (Gainesville)

Exit #	Services
24.5	**I-985 begins/ends on US 23, 25mm.**
24	to US 129 N, GA 369 W, Gainesville, **N** [gas] QT/dsl [food] McDonald's, Papa John's, Taco Bell [other] [H], Autozone, Kroger/dsl, **S** [gas] BP/dsl, Chevron/dsl [food] Double B Burger, Rabbittown Cafe, Subway
22	GA 11, Gainesville, **N** [gas] QT/dsl, Shell/dsl [food] Burger King, **S** [gas] Chevron/dsl, Shell/dsl [food] Waffle House [lodging] Motel 6 [other] $General
20	GA 60, GA 53, Gainesville, **N** [gas] RaceTrac/dsl, **S** [gas] Kangaroo/Subway/dsl [food] Waffle House
17	GA 13, Gainesville
16	GA 53, Oakwood, **N** [food] Arby's, Burger King, Capt D's, DQ, Dunkin', El Sombrero Mexican, Firehouse Subs, Hardee's, KFC, McDonald's, Napoli's Pizza, Pizza Hut, Steak'n Shake, Taco Bell, Waffle House, Zaxby's [lodging] Best Western, Jameson Inn [other] $Tree, Aldi Foods, Camping World RV Ctr, Chrysler/Dodge/Jeep, Sam's Club/dsl, Walmart/Subway, **S** [gas] QT/dsl [food] Buffalo's Cafe, Chick-Fil-A, Krystal, La Parilla Mexican, Sonic, Sonny's BBQ, Subway, Waffle House, Wendy's [lodging] Quality Inn [other] Ace Hardware, AutoZone, Kauffman Tire, O'Reilly Parts, Publix, Slack Parts, Toyota, Walgreens
12	Spout Springs Rd, Flowery Branch, **N** [gas] Exxon/dsl, **S** [gas] Chevron/dsl, Marathon/Subway/dsl [food] Burger&Shake, Chick-fil-A, Chili's, China Garden, CrossRoads Grill, Domino's, El Sombrero Mexican, Firehouse Subs, Little Caesar's, Napoli's Pizza, Shane's Ribshack, Shogun Japanese [lodging] Hampton Inn [other] AT&T, GNC, Home Depot, Kohl's, Petsmart, Publix, Rite Aid, Ross, Target, TJ Maxx, Verizon, Walgreens
8	GA 347, Friendship Rd, Lake Lanier, **N** [gas] Chevron/dsl, QT/dsl, Shell/dsl [food] Blimpie, Burger King, Cracker Barrel, McDonald's, Mykonos Cafe, Shoney's, Subway, Vinny's NY Grill, Waffle House, Wendy's, Zaxby's [lodging] Holiday Inn Express [other] $General, Advance parts, Family$, O'Reilly Parts, Publix, URGENT CARE, Verizon, vet, **S** [other] Camper City RV Ctr, Harley Davidson
4	US 23 S, GA 20, Buford, **N** [gas] QT, Shell/dsl [food] Arby's, Bojangles, Burger King, Capt D's, Golden Buddah, Golden Corral, Hardee's, IHOP, KFC, McDonald's, Pizza Hut, Subway, Taco Bell, Waffle House, Wendy's, Zaxby's [lodging] Best Value Inn, Holiday Inn Express [other] Ace Hardware, Chrysler/Dodge/Jeep, Hobby Lobby, Home Depot, Kia, NAPA Autocare, NTB, O'Reilly Parts, **S** [gas] Chevron/dsl, Exxon/dsl, Mtn Express/dsl [food] Asia Buffet, Sonny's BBQ, Stevi B's Pizza, Viva Mexico [other] $Tree, Firestone/auto, Honda, Kauffman Tire, Lowes Whse, Walmart
0mm	**I-985 begins/ends on I-85.**

GA

NOTES

= gas = food = lodging = other = rest stop

IDAHO

INTERSTATE 15

DUBOIS

Exit #	Services
196mm	Idaho/Montana state line, Monida Pass, continental divide, elev 6870
190	Humphrey
184	Stoddard Creek Area, E Historical Site, RV camping, W Stoddard Creek Camping
180	Spencer, E Opal Country Café/gas High Country Opal Store, W Spencer Grill/RV Park
172	no service
167	ID 22, Dubois, E **both lanes, full facilities, litter barrels, petwalk, , picnic table,** Phillips 66/dsl city park, USPO, W Nez Pearce Tr, to Craters NM
150	Hamer, E Ron's Tire, USPO, W Camus NWR
143	ID 33, ID 28, to Mud Lake, Rexburg, W Sacajawea Hist Bywy, **weigh sta both lanes**
142mm	hist site, roadside parking
135	ID 48, Roberts, E Exxon/cafe/dsl/LP city park
128	Osgood Area, E Osgood/dsl camping (6mi)
119	US 20 E, to Rexburg, Idaho Falls, E **on Lindsay** Sinclair/dsl Denny's, Jaker's Steaks, Outback Steaks, Sandpiper Rest. Best Western+, Fairbridge Inn, Hampton Inn, Hilton Garden, LeRitz Hotel, Motel 6, Quality Inn, Safari Inn, Shilo Inn/rest., Super 8, Tru Hilton LDS Temple, same as 118, Snake River RV Park/camping, W Sinclair/dsl
118	US 20, Broadway St, Idaho Falls, E Phillips 66/dsl, Walmart/dsl Applebee's, Arctic Circle, Buffalo Wild Wings, Carl's Jr, Cedric's Rest., Chili's, Culver's, Domino's, Famous Dave's BBQ, Jimmy John's, MacKenzie River Grill, Olive Garden, Panda Express, Shari's Rest., Smitty's Pancakes, Starbucks, Wendy's Candlewood Suites, Fairfield Inn, Hampton Inn, Hilton Garden, Residence Inn, SpringHill Suites H, Candy Jct, Ford, Harley-Davidson, LDS Temple, same as 119, tires, URGENT CARE, Verizon, Walmart/Subway, W Exxon/dsl, Phillips 66/dsl, Sinclair/McDonald's Arby's, Burger King, Fiesta Ole, Five Buck Pizza, Hong Kong Rest., Jack-in-the-Box, Los Adalaberto's Mexican, O'Brady's, Papa Murphy's, Pizza Hut, Subway Comfort Inn, Motel 6, Motel West Albertsons, AutoZone, Camping World RV Ctr, O'Reilly Parts, Walgreens
116	US 26, Sunnyside Rd, Ammon, Jackson, E H, BMW, Chevrolet, Honda, Sunnyside Acres RV Park, Toyota, VW, W Exxon/diesel DoubleDown Grill Sleep Inn
113	US 26, to Idaho Falls, Jackson, E Blu LNG/dsl, Chevron/Burger King/dsl, FLYING J/Subway/dsl/24hr/@, Loves/McDonald's/dsl/scales/24hr Subway H, Jack's Tires, Peterbilt
108	Shelley, Firth Area, **1 mi** E RV Park/dump
101mm	**both lanes, full facilities, geological site, litter barrels, petwalk, ,**
98	Rose-Firth Area
94.5mm	Snake River
93	US 26, ID 39, Blackfoot, E Chevron/Jimmy John's/dsl, Maverik/dsl, Sinclair/Stinker/dsl Arby's, Burger King, Domino's, Homestead Rest., Hong Kong Garden, Little Caesar's, McDonald's, Papa Murphy's, Pizza Hut, Roberto's Mexican, Subway, Taco Bell, Taco Time, Wendy's Best Western, Super 8 $Tree, AutoZone, Bealls, Chrysler/Dodge/Ford/Jeep, city park,

IDAHO FALLS

BLACKFOOT

POCATELLO

Exit #	Services
93	Continued Kesler's Foods, O'Reilly Parts, Point S Auto, Ridley's M Schwab Tire, URGENT CARE, Verizon, Walgreens, Walmart/S way, W Sinclair/A&W/dsl Riverside Boot/saddles (4mi)
90.5mm	Blackfoot River
89	US 91, S Blackfoot, W Sinclair/Sage Cafe/dsl
80	Ft Hall, W Phillips 66/rest./dsl/casino Shoshone B nock Hotel/casino
72	I-86 W, to Twin Falls
71	Pocatello Creek Rd, Pocatello, E Chevron/Burger Ki dsl, Phillips 66/dsl, Shell/dsl Applebee's, Jack-in-the B Perkins, Sandpiper Rest., Subway Best Western, Clari La Quinta, Quality Inn, Red Lion Inn, Super 8 KOA (1r **0-2 mi** W Exxon, Maverik/dsl Arby's, Bamboo Gard Butter Burr's Lickety Split, Butter Burr's Rest., Café Rio, Ca Jr, Changs Garden Chinese, Coldstone, El Caporal, Gold Corral, Jamba Juice, KFC, Mandarin House, McDonald's, Pa Murphy's, Ridley's Mkt, Senor Iguana's Mexican, Sizzler, So Starbucks, Subway, Taco Bell, Taco Time, Thai Kitchen, Wend Winger's $Tree, Advance Parts, AutoZone, BigLots, Bui GMC, Chevrolet, Fred Meyer/dsl, Harley-Davidson, Hyun O'Reilly Parts, Subaru, Tuesday Morning, Walgreens, Wir Foods
69	Clark St, Pocatello, E Chevron/cafe/dsl, Maverik/dsl, S clair/Arctic Circle/dsl Jakers Grill Hampton Inn, H day Inn Express, TownePlace Suites H, W museum, ID St U
67	US 30/91, 5th St, Pocatello, E Exxon/dsl, **1-2 mi** W Ch ron/dsl, Shell/dsl Elmer's Dining, Goody's Deli, Jim John's, McDonald's, Pizza Hut, Subway, Taco Bell Rodev Inn, Thunderbird Motel H, city park, info, museum, C Fort Hall, RV dump
63	Portneuf Area, W RV camp/dump, to Mink Creek RA
59mm	**weigh sta both lanes**
58	Inkom (from sb), **1/2 mi** W Sinclair/café/dsl Bishara Mkt, Pebble Creek Ski Area, repair, USPO
57	Inkom (from nb), same as 58
47	US 30, to Lava Hot Springs, McCammon, E FLYING J/d scales/LP/RV dump/24hr, Chevron/A&W/Taco Time/dsl Su way Lava Hot Springs RA, McCammon RV Park, to KOA
44	Lp 15, Jenson Rd, McCammon, E access to food
40	Arimo, E USPO
36	US 91, Virginia
31	ID 40, to Downey, Preston, E Shell/Flags West/café/dsl/m tel/24hr/@ Downata Hot Springs RV camping (6mi)
25mm	**sb, full facilities, litter barrels, petwalk, ,**
24.5mm	Malad Summit, elevation 5574
22	to Devil Creek Reservoir, E RV camping
17	ID 36, to Weston, to Preston
13	ID 38, Malad City, W Chevron/Burger King, Chevron/d Phillips 66/café/dsl Me&Lou's Rest., Pines Rest., Sperov BBQ, Subway Village Inn Motel H, 3R's Tire, Family pioneer museum, repair, RV dump
7mm	**Welcome Ctr nb, full facilities, info, litter barrels, petwa , , vending**
3	to Samaria, Woodruff
0mm	Idaho/Utah state line

ID

INTERSTATE 84

Exit #	Services
275mm	Idaho/Utah state line
270mm	**[RS] both lanes, full [accessible] facilities, geological site, litter barrels, petwalk, [phone], [picnic]**
263	Juniper Rd
257mm	Sweetzer Summit, elev 5530
254	Sweetzer Rd
245	Sublett Rd, to Malta, **N** [gas] Sublett/dsl/café
237	Idahome Rd
234mm	Raft River
229mm	**[RS]/weigh sta both lanes, full [accessible] facilities, litter barrels, petwalk, [phone], [picnic]**
228	ID 81, Yale Rd, to Declo
222	I-86, US 30, E to Pocatello
216	ID 77, ID 25, to Declo, **N** [gas] Phillips 66/Food Court/dsl [other] [H], to Walcott SP, Village of Trees RV Park, **S** [gas] Sinclair/Pit Stop Grill/dsl
215mm	Snake River
211	ID 24, Heyburn, Burley, **N** [gas] Sinclair/A&W/café/dsl [food] Wayside Cafe [lodging] Tops Motel [other] [H], Country RV Village/park, **S** [gas] Loves/Carl's Jr./dsl/scales/24hr [other] Riverside RV Park, truck repair, truck wash
208	ID 27, Burley, **N** [gas] Phillips 66/dsl [food] Conner's Cafe [lodging] Super 8 [other] Kenworth, **S** [gas] Chevron/Subway/dsl/24hr, Maverik/dsl, Shell/dsl, Sinclair/dsl [food] Aguila's Mexican, Arby's, Burger King, Denny's, El Caporal, Guadalajara Mexican, Jack-in-the-Box, KFC, Little Caesar's, McDonald's, Morey's Steaks, Perkins, Taco Bell, Wendy's [lodging] Best Western+, Budget Motel, Fairfield Inn [other] [H], $Tree, Beall's, Buick/GMC, Cal Ranch Store, CarQuest, Chrysler/Dodge/Jeep, Commercial Tire, NAPA, O'Reilly Parts, to Snake River RA, URGENT CARE, Verizon, Walmart
201	ID 25, Kasota Rd, to Paul, **N** [other] Kasota RV Park
194	ID 25, to Hazelton
188	Valley Rd, to Eden
182	ID 50, to Kimberly, Twin Falls, **N** [gas] Sinclair/dsl [other] Gary's RV Ctr/park/dump, **S** [gas] Shell/Blimpie/Taco Time/dsl/scales/24hr/@ [food] Garden of Eden Cafe [lodging] Amber Inn [other] [H], auto/truck/rv repair, to Shoshone Falls scenic attraction
173	US 93, Twin Falls, **N** [gas] FLYING J/dsl/LP/24hr/@, Phillips 66/dsl [food] Subway [lodging] Comfort Inn, Red Lion Inn [other] Blue Beacon, Freightliner, KOA (1mi), to Sun Valley, **5 mi S** [gas] Chevron/Subway/dsl, Maverik/dsl, Phillips 66/dsl, Shell/dsl, Sinclair, Walmart Fuel/dsl [food] Applebee's, Arby's, Arctic Circle, Baskin-Robbins, Blaze Pizza, Buffalo Wild Wings, Burger King, Cafe Rio, Carino's, Chick-fil-A, Chili's, Coldstone, Costa Vida, Culver's, Denny's, Dickey's BBQ, DQ, Five Guys, Golden Corral, Habit Burger, Idaho Joe's, IHOP, IHOP, Jack-in-the-Box, Jakers Grill, Jamba Juice, Jimmy John's, KFC, La Fiesta, Mandarin Chinese, McDonald's, Noodles&Co, Outback Steaks, Panda Express, Papa John's, Papa Murphy's, Perkins, Pizza Hut, River Rock Grill, Shari's, Sizzler, Sonic, Starbucks, Subway, Taco Bell, Tomato's Italian, Wendy's, Wok In Grill [lodging] Best Western, Fairfield Inn, Hampton Inn, Hilton Garden, Holiday Inn Express, La Quinta, Motel 6, Quality Inn, Red Lion, Super 8 [other] [H], $Tree, AT&T, AutoZone, Barnes&Noble, Best Buy, Buick/GMC, Chevrolet, Chrysler/Dodge/Jeep, Coll of S ID, Commercial Tire, Costco/gas, Dick's, Ford/Lincoln, Fred Meyer/dsl, Home Depot, Honda, Hyundai, JC Penney, Jo-Ann Fabrics, LDS Temple, Les Schwab Tire, Lowe's, Mazda/VW, Michael's, Nissan, Old Navy, O'Reilly Parts, Petco, Petsmart, Point S Automotive, Ross,

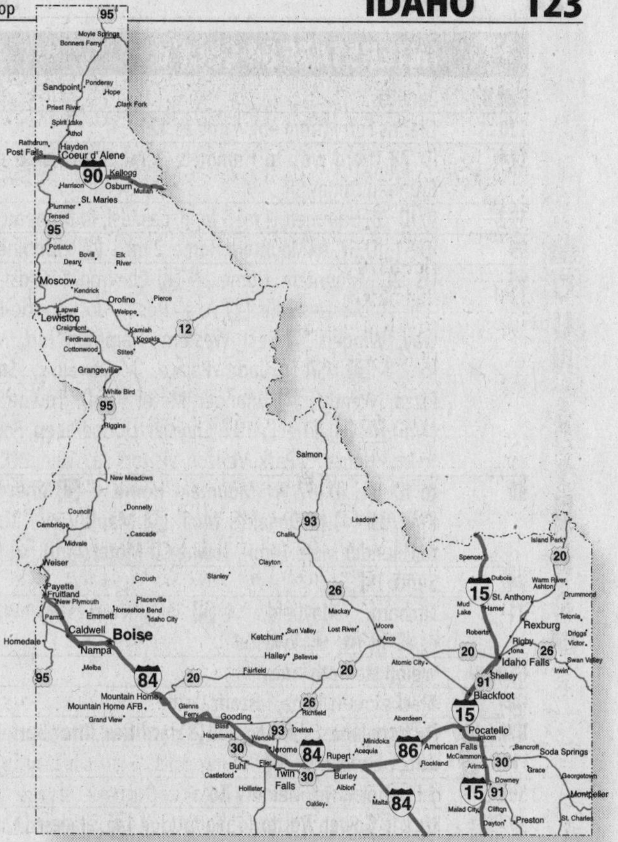

JEROME

Exit #	Services
173	Continued Sportsmans Whse, Target, TJ Maxx, Verizon, visitors ctr, Walgreens, Walmart/Subway, WinCo Foods
171mm	**[RS]/weigh sta eb, full [accessible] facilities, litter barrels, petwalk, [phone], [picnic], vending**
168	ID 79, to Jerome, **N** [gas] Blu/LNG/dsl, Chevron/dsl/24hr, Shell/Wendy's/dsl, Tesoro/dsl [food] Burger King, Domino's, DQ, Garibaldi's Mexican, Little Caesar's, McDonald's, Pizza Hut [lodging] Best Western, Crest Motel, Holiday Motel [other] [H], $Tree, AutoZone, Brockman RV Ctr, Family$, Les Schwab Tire, NAPA, O'Reilly Parts, Verizon, Walmart/Subway, **S** [food] Subway [other] Chevrolet
165	ID 25, Jerome, **N** [gas] Sinclair/dsl [lodging] Holiday Motel (1mi) [other] [H], RV camping/dump, vet
157	ID 46, Wendell, **1 mi N** [food] Subway [other] [H], CarQuest, Family$, Intermountain RV Park, **S** [gas] Phillips 66/dsl [food] Farmhouse Rest.
155	ID 46, to Wendell, **N** [other] Intermountain RV Camp/ctr
147	to Tuttle, **S** [other] High Adventure RV Park/cafe, to Malad Gorge SP
146mm	Malad River
141	US 26, to US 30, Gooding, **N** [other] [H], **S** [gas] Phillips 66/café/dsl, Sinclair/dsl [lodging] Amber Inn, Hagerman Inn (9mi) [other] Hagerman RV Village (8mi)
137	Lp 84, to US 30, to Pioneer Road, Bliss, **2 mi S** [gas] Sinclair/Stinker/dsl/24hr [other] camping
133mm	**[RS] both lane, full [accessible] facilities, info, litter barrels, petwalk, [phone], [picnic]**
129	King Hill
128mm	Snake River
125	Paradise Valley
122mm	Snake River
121	Glenns Ferry, **1 mi S** [gas] Sinclair/dsl, Veltex/dsl [lodging] Hansen Motel/cafe, Redford Motel [other] Carmela Winery/rest., Family$, fudge factory, NAPA, tires, to 3 Island SP, Trails Break RV camp/dump

ID

INTERSTATE 84 Cont'd

MOUNTAIN HOME

Exit #	Services
120	Glenns Ferry (from eb), same as 121
114	ID 78 (from wb), to Hammett, **1 mi S** access to gas/dsl, to Bruneau Dunes SP
112	to ID 78, Hammett, **1 mi S** food, gas/dsl, to Bruneau Dunes SP
99	ID 51, ID 67, to Mountain Home, **2 mi S** camping
95	US 20, Mountain Home, **N** Chevron/KFC/dsl, Pilot/Arby's/dsl/scales/24hr AJ's Rest., Jack-in-the-Box, Subway, Wingers Best Western, Hampton Inn, Mtn Home Inn, **S** USA Jade Palace, McDonald's, Smoky Mtn Pizza, Wendy's Hilander Motel (1mi), Towne Ctr Motel (1mi) H, $Tree, AT&T, Chrysler/Dodge/Jeep, Ford/Lincoln, to Mtn Home RV Park, Verizon, visitors ctr, Walmart/Subway
90	to ID 51, ID 67, W Mountain Home, **S** Chevron/Burger King/dsl McDonald's (4mi) Maple Cove Motel (4mi), to Hilander Motel (4mi), Towne Ctr Motel (4mi) KOA
74	Simco Rd
71	Orchard, Mayfield, **S** Sinclair/rest./StageStop Motel/dsl/24hr truckwash
66mm	**weigh sta both lanes**
64	Blacks Creek, Kuna, historical site
62mm	**both lanes, vending, full facilities, litter barrels, OR Trail info, petwalk**

BOISE

Exit #	Services
59b a	S Eisenman Rd, Memory Rd
57	ID 21, Gowen Rd, to Idaho City, **N** Sinclair Domino's, Jack-in-the-Box, McDonald's, Quiznos, Subway, Taco Del Mar Best Western/NW Lodge Albertsons/Sav-On, Peterbilt, to Micron, **S** Chevron/dsl Burger King, Food-Court Boise Stores/famous brands, ID Ice World
54	US 20/26, Broadway Ave, Boise, **N** FLYING J/dsl/LP/24hr, Chevron/dsl, Fred Meyer/dsl, Shell/dsl A&W/KFC, Arby's, Fiesta Mexican, IHOP, Jack-in-the-Box, Mongolian Noodles, Pizza Pie Cafe, Port Of Subs, Sonic Courtyard (3mi) Big O Tire, Firestone/auto, Fred Meyer, Goodyear/auto, Home Depot, Jo-Ann Fabrics, O'Reilly Parts, PetCo, Ross, to Boise St U, vet, Walgreens, **S** TA/Country Pride/Taco Bell/Subway/dsl/24hr/@ Red Lion Inn Bretz RV Ctr, Kenworth, Mtn View RV Park
53	Vista Ave, Boise, **N** Shell/dsl, Texaco/dsl Applebee's, Pizza Hut Comfort Inn, Comfort Suites, Extended Stay America, Fairfield Inn, Hampton Inn, Holiday Inn/rest., La Quinta, Super 8, Wyndham Garden museums, st capitol, st police, zoo, **S** Chevron/dsl Denny's, Kopper Kitchen Best Western, InnAmerica, Motel 6, Quality Inn, Rodeway Inn
52	Orchard St, Boise, **N** Maverik/dsl, Shell/dsl Subway BMW Motorcycles, Fiat, GMC
50b a	Cole Rd, Overland Rd, **N** Chevron/dsl, Shell, Sinclair Cancun Mexican, Cobby's Sandwiches, Eddie's Rest., McDonald's, Outback Steaks, Pizza Hut, Subway, Taco Bell, Taco Time Grocery Outlet, LDS Temple, transmissions, **S** Phillips 66/dsl, Shell/dsl A&W/KFC, Black Bear Diner, Burger King, Carino's, Carl's Jr, Chapala Mexican, Chuck-a-Rama, Cracker Barrel, Del Taco, Goodwood BBQ, Jimmy John's, Lucky Palace Chinese, McGrath's FishHouse, Nato's Mexican, On the Border, Panda Express, Papa John's, Sonic, Starbucks, Tucano's Brazilian Grill, Twin Peaks Hampton Inn, Hilton Garden, Homewood Suites, Howard Johnson's, Oxford Suites Commercial Tire, Costco/gas, Dillon RV Ctr, Discount Tire, Einstein Oilery, Les Schwab Tire, Lowe's, Meineke, USPO, Verizon, vet, Walmart/McDonald's

EAGLE

Exit #	Services
49	I-184 (exits left from eb), to W Boise, **N** H
46	ID 55, Eagle, **N** Chevron/McDonald's/dsl Buffalo W Wings, Del Taco, Ling&Louie's, Los Beto's, Mi Casa, Sma Burger, Starbucks, Subway Hampton Inn, Holiday Inn press, La Quinta H, **S** Chevron/dsl Beef'O'Brady Chicago Connection, Dickey's BBQ, Dutch Bros Coffee, Hap Teriyaki, Jack-in-the-Box, Jimmy John's, Joy Garden, Pan Garden, Pita Pit, Qdoba, Rudy's Grill, Sakana Japanese, Su way, Taco Bell, TCBY, The Griddle Candlewood Suit Courtyard, TownePlace Suites, Tru AAA, Harley-Davids Indian Motorcycles, URGENT CARE, vet
44	ID 69, Meridian, **N** Chevron/dsl, Maverik/dsl, Sincl 50's Cafe, A&W/KFC, China Wok, DQ, Jimmy John's, M Donald's, Panda Express, Pizza Hut, Shari's, Starbucks, Su way, Taco Bell, Taco Time, Wendy's Best Western+, M tel 6 AT&T, Home Depot, Johnny's Autocare, Les Schw Tire, Sierra Trading Post, Verizon, WinCo Foods, **S** She dsl Starbucks, Carl's Jr, JB's, Papa John's Mr Sandm Inn Camping World RV Ctr, Ford, Lowe's, O'Reilly Pa Walgreens, Walmart, waterpark

NAMPA

Exit #	Services
42	Ten Mile Rd
38	Garrity Blvd, Nampa, **N** Chevron/dsl, Walmart G dsl Dutch Bros Coffee, Jack-in-the-Box, Los Betos, Port Subs, Sonic Hampton Inn, Home 2 Suites Buick/GM Cadillac/Chevrolet, Chrysler/Dodge/Jeep, Ford, Hyundai, Inf iti, Kia, Nissan, Toyota, Walmart/Subway, **S** Phillips 66/ Shell/dsl Fiesta Guadalajara, Jimmy John's, McDonal Panda Express, Papa Murphy's, Pizza Hut, Popeye's, Starbuc Subway, Taco Bell, Wendy's Holiday Inn Express Freddy's, Garrity RV Park, JC Penney, Verizon, War Hawk Mu um, Winco Foods
36	Franklin Blvd, Nampa, **N** Blu/LNG/dsl, Maver dsl Jack-in-the-Box Shilo Inn/rest., **S** Chevron/ Shell/Subway/dsl/RV dump/scales/4hr Sleep Inn Bretz RV Ctr, Freightliner, Honda, Mason Cr RV Park
35	ID 55, Nampa, **S** Maverik/dsl, Shell/dsl Denn Nampa Inn, Rodeway Inn, Super 8
33b a	ID 55 S, Midland Blvd, Marcine, **N** Blaze Pizza, Chick-fil Cracker Barrel, Dickey's BBQ, Habit Burger, McDonald's, Ol Garden, Panera Bread, Qdoba Mexican, Sonic, Subway, TGI day's, Winger's Fairfield Inn, Holiday Inn AT&T, Best B Costco/gas, Dick's, Discount Tire, Gordmans, Hobby Lobby, Kohl's, Michael's, Old Navy, PetCo, Petsmart, Sportsmans Wh Target, TJ Maxx, Verizon, World Mkt, **S** Shell/dsl App bee's, Arby's, Baskin-Robbins, Blimpie, Buffalo Wild Wings, Ca Jr, Chipotle, Coldstone, Costa Vida, DQ, Golden Corral, IHOP, Ja in-the-Box, Jade Garden, Jalapeno's Grill, Jimmy John's, Mon lian BBQ, Outback Steaks, Papa Murphy's, Pizza Hut, Red Rob Shari's Rest, Smashburger, Smokey Mtn Grill, Starbucks, Subw Taco Bell, TX Roadhouse, Wendy's, Zupas Kitchen $T Home Depot, Jo-Ann Fabrics, Lowe's, Nampa Tire, NAPA, Po S Automotive, Ross, Savers, Staples, U-Haul, Verizon, Verizon vet, Walgreens, WinCo Foods

CALDWELL

Exit #	Services
29	US 20/26, Franklin Rd, Caldwell, **N** FLYING J/Denny dsl/LP/scales/24hr Ambassador RV camping, RV dum **S** Sage/Sinclair/cafe/dsl/24hr Burger King, Du Bros Best Western+, La Quinta
28	10th Ave, Caldwell, **N** Maverik/dsl city park, U-Ha **S** Chevron/dsl, Shell/dsl Carl's Jr, Fiesta Mexican, Ja in-the-Box, Mr V's Rest., Pizza Hut, Subway, Wendy's AutoZone, Point S Automotive, Walgreens
27	ID 19, to Wilder, **1 mi S** Chevron/dsl visitor info

ID

INTERSTATE 84 Cont'd

Exit #	Services
26.5mm	Boise River
26	US 20/26, to Notus, N Caldwell Campground, S Sinclair/dsl RV Resort
25	ID 44, Middleton, N Sinclair/dsl 44 Burgers/shakes, S Insp sta eb
17	Sand Hollow, N Sinclair/Sand Hollow Café/dsl Country Corners RV Park
13	Black Canyon Jct, S Sinclair/rest./motel/dsl/scales/24hr
9	US 30, to New Plymouth
3	US 95, Fruitland, N Chevron/A&W/dsl Neat Retreat RV Park (5mi), to Hell's Cyn RA (26mi)
1mm	**Welcome Ctr eb, full facilities, info, litter barrels, petwalk,**
0mm	Idaho/Oregon state line, Snake River

INTERSTATE 86

Exit #	Services
63b a	I-15, N to Butte, S to SLC. **I-86 begins/ends on I-15, exit 72.**
61	US 91, Yellowstone Ave, Pocatello, N Exxon, Maverik/dsl, Shell/dsl Arby's, Arctic Circle, Burger King, Chapala Mexican, Domino's, Five Mile Café, Jack-in-the-Box, Lei's BBQ, Papa Murphy's, Subway, Tres Hermanos, Wendy's Motel 6, Travelodge $Tree, AutoZone, Bargain Tire, Crossroads RV Ctr, Family$, O'Reilly Parts, Smith's Foods/dsl, vet, S Exxon/dsl, Phillips 66/dsl Buffalo Wild Wings, Chili's, Costa Vida, Denny's, Firehouse Subs, Five Guys, Freddy's, Great Wall, IHOP, Jimmy John's, MacKenzie River Grill, McDonald's, Noodles&Co, Panda Express, Panera Bread, Pizza Hut, Pizza Pie Café, Popeye's, Red Lobster, Red Robin, Starbucks, TX Roadhouse AT&T, Cal Ranch Store, Chrysler/Dodge/Jeep, Costco/gas, Dick's, Discount Tire, Ford/Lincoln, Hobby Lobby, Home Depot, Honda, JC Penney, Jo-Ann Fabrics, Kia, Lowe's, NAPA, Nissan, PetCo, Petsmart, Ross, Schwab Tire, TJ Maxx, Toyota, Verizon, Walgreens, Walmart
58.5mm	Portneuf River
58	US 30, W Pocatello, N Batise Springs RV Park/dump (1mi-seasonal)
56	N Pocatello Reg Airport, S Sinclair/dsl/24hr
52	Arbon Valley, S Phillips 66/Bannock Peak/dsl casino
51mm	Bannock Creek
49	Rainbow Rd
44	Seagull Bay
40	ID 39, American Falls, N Sinclair/dsl (1mi), Texaco Pizza Hut, Subway, Tres Hermanos Mexican American Motel H, auto repair, Family$ (1mi), Jiffy Lube, NAPA, Schwab Tire, to Am Falls RA, Willow Bay RV Park/dump, S Hillview Motel
36	ID 37, to Rockland, American Falls, 2 mi N Shell/dsl Falls Motel H, 2 mi S Indian Springs RV Resort
33	Neeley Area
31mm	**wb, full facilities, hist site, litter barrel, petwalk, , picnic table, vending**
28	N Register Rock Hist Site, RV camping/dump, to Massacre Rock SP
21	Coldwater Area
19mm	**eb, full facilities, hist site, litter barrel, petwalk, , picnic table, vending**
15	Raft River Area
1	I-84 E, to Ogden. **I-86 begins/ends on I-84, exit 222.**

WALLACE KELLOGG

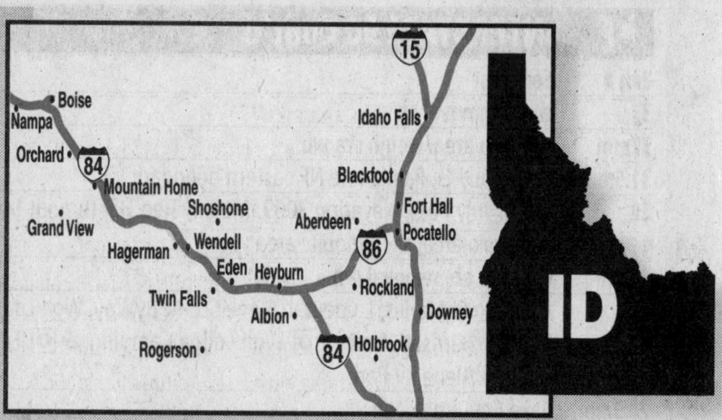

INTERSTATE 90

Exit #	Services
74mm	Idaho/Montana state line, Pacific/Central time zone, Lookout Pass elev 4680
73mm	scenic area/hist site wb
72mm	scenic area/hist site eb
71mm	**runaway truck ramp wb**
70mm	**runaway truck ramp wb**
69	Lp 90, Mullan, N Sinclair/dsl Mullan Trail grocery/RV Park, museum, USPO
68	Lp 90 (from eb), Mullan, same as 69
67	Morning District, Morning District
66	Gold Creek (from eb)
65	Compressor District
64	Golconda District
62	ID 4, Wallace, S Conoco Pizza Factory, Smokehouse Rest. Brooks Hotel, Stardust Motel Harvest Foods, museum, Wallace RV Park
61	Lp 90, Wallace, S Conoco/dsl Pizza Factory, Smokehouse Rest., Trailside Cafe Brooks Hotel/rest., Wallace Inn auto repair, info ctr, same as 62
60	Lp 90, Silverton, S RV camping
57	Lp 90, Osburn, S 76/dsl Blue Anchor RV Park, Stein's Foods, USPO
54	Big Creek, N hist site
51	Lp 90, Division St, Kellogg, N Conoco/dsl Trail Motel H, Bender Drug, Buick/Cadillac/Chevrolet/GMC, Chrysler/Dodge/Jeep, Schwab Tire, Stein's Foods, vet, S Moose Creek Grill USPO
50	Hill St (from eb), Kellogg, N Humdinger Drive-In Trail Motel Ace Hardware, Benzer Drug, NAPA, Stein's Foods, tires, S Conoco/dsl museum, Silver Mtn Ski/summer resort/rec area, Yoke's Foods
49	Bunker Ave, N Conoco/dsl McDonald's, Sam's Drive-In, Subway Silverhorn Motel/rest. H, S Noah's Canteen, Silver Mtn Rest. Fairbridge Inn, Morning Star Lodge city park, museum, RV dump, Silver Mtn RA
48	Smelterville, S Dave Smith Tire, O'Reilly Parts, USPO, Walmart
45	Pinehurst, S Chevron/dsl/repair, Conoco/dsl By-the-way Camping, Harvest Foods, TrueValue, USPO
43	Kingston, N Conoco/dsl, S Exxon/dsl/rv dump, USPO
40	Cataldo, N Timbers Roadhouse, USPO, S RV Park
39.5mm	Coeur d' Alene River
39	Cataldo Mission, S Nat Hist Landmark, Old Mission SP
34	ID 3, to St Maries, Rose Lake, S Conoco/dsl, Rose Lake/dsl Rose Lake Cafe White Pines Scenic Rte

ID

INTERSTATE 90 Cont'd

COUER d' ALENE

Exit #	Services
33	**chain removal eb**
32mm	**chainup area/weigh sta wb**
31.5mm	4th of July Cr, Panhandle NF eastern boundary
28	4th of July Pass, elevation 3069, Mullen Tree HS, turnout both lanes, ski area, snowmobile area
24mm	**chainup eb, removal wb**
22	ID 97, to St Maries, L Coeur d' Alene Scenic ByWay, Wolf Lodge District, Harrison, **1 mi N** Wolf Lodge Camping, **S** Lake Coeur d'Alene RV Park
20.5mm	Lake Coeur d' Alene
17	Mullan Trail Rd
15	Lp 90, Sherman Ave, Coeur d' Alene, **N** forest info, Lake Coeur D' Alene RA/HS, **S** Chevron, Exxon/dsl, Mobil/dsl/LP Jimmy's Cafe, Michael D's Eatery, Moontime Cafe, O'Shay's Rest., Roger's Burgers, Zip's Rest. Baymont Inn, BudgetSaver Motel, El Rancho Motel, Flaming Motel, Holiday Motel, Japan House Suites, State Motel, Two Lakes Motel auto repair, Harvest Foods, tourist info
14	15th St, Coeur d' Alene, **S** TAJ Mart Jordon's Grocery
13	4th St, Coeur d' Alene, **N** A&D/dsl Atilano's Mexican, Baskin Robbins, Carl's Jr, Davis Donuts, Denny's, DQ, IHOP, Jimmy John's, Little Caesar's, Original Mongolian BBQ, Panda Express, Starbucks, Subway, Taco Time, Wendy's Ramada Inn AutoZone, BigLots, Costco/gas, NAPA, same as 12, Schwab Tire, Verizon, **S** Exxon/dsl Thai Bamboo Maserati/Alfa Romeo
12	US 95, to Sandpoint, Moscow, **N** Exxon/dsl, Holiday/dsl, Mobil/dsl, Walmart/dsl Applebee's, Arby's, Buffalo Wild Wings, Cafe Rio, Chili's, China Town, Del Taco, Elmer's, Golden Corral, JB's Rest., Jimmy John's, MacKenzie River Pizza, McDonald's, Olive Garden, Panda Express, Panera Bread, Pizza Hut, Red Lobster, Taco Bell, Tomato St., TX Roadhouse Best Western+, Comfort Suites, Fairbridge Inn, Motel 6, Quality Inn, Super 8 $Tree, Advance Parts, Albertson's, AT&T, Best Buy, Blue Dog RV, Buick/GMC, Cadillac, Combs RV, Discount Tire, Ford/Subaru, Fred Meyer/dsl, Grocery Outlet, Home Depot, JC Penney, Jo-Ann Fabrics, Kia, Kohl's, Michael's, Natural Grocers, O'Reilly Parts, PetCo, Ross, Safeway/dsl, Super 1 Foods, Target, TireRama, TJ Maxx, Toyota, Tuesday Morning, U-Haul, URGENT CARE, Verizon, Walgreens, Walmart/Subway, **S** Conoco/dsl, Mobil Asian Twist, Jack-in-the-Box, Jamba Juice, Papa Murphy's, Qdoba Mexican, Shari's, Starbucks La Quinta H, Albertson's, AT&T, GNC, Rite Aid, same as 13, Staples
11	Northwest Blvd, **N** Conoco/dsl Cracker Barrel, Firehouse Subs, Jack-in-the-Box, MOD Pizza, Subway, Sweet Burrito, Thai Express Lowe's, WinCo Foods, **S** Exxon/dsl, SpeeDee Anthony's, Azteca Mexican, Bullman's Woodfired Pizza, Coldstone, Ipanema Brazilian, Martino Tuscan, McDonald's, Outback Steaks, Red Robin, SF Sourdough, Starbucks Days Inn, Hampton Inn, Holiday Inn Express, Springhill Suites, Staybridge Suites H, Honda, Riverwalk RV Park, Verizon
8.5mm	**Welcome Ctr/weigh sta eb, both lanes, full facilities, info, litter barrels, petwalk,**
7	ID 41, to Rathdrum, Spirit Lake, **N** 76/dsl Burger King, Del Taco, Domino's, NY Pizza, Papa Murphy's, Pita Pit, Popeye's, Sonic, Starbucks, Subway, Wendy's $Tree, AT&T, auto repair, Chevrolet, Chrysler/Dodge/Jeep, Couer d'Alene RV Park, Hyundai, Nissan, VW, Walmart/Subway, **S** Chevron/dsl, Coleman/dsl A&W/KFC, Capone's Grill, DQ Quality Inn Robins RV Ctr, truck repair, Verizon, vet

ID

POST FALLS

Exit #	Services
6	Seltice Way, **N** 7-11 La Cabana Mexican, Paul Bun Burgers, Pizza Hut NAPA, Super 1 Foods, Walgree **S** 76/dsl/LP Denny's, Dueling Irons Cafe, Fuki Ja nese, Little Caesar's, McDonald's, Old European Cafe, Ran Viejo Mexican, Taco Bell, Timbers Rest. Ace Hardw O'Reilly Parts, TireRama, USPO, vet, Yoke's Foods
5	Lp 90, Spokane St, Treaty Rock HS, **N** 76/dsl, Exx dsl Corner Cafe, Golden Dragon, Hunter's Rest., P John's, Rob's Seafood/burgers, Subway, WhiteHouse AutoZone, Blue Dog RV Ctr, Meineke, Perfection Tire/rep Schwab Tire, **S** Handy Mart/Pacific Pride/dsl Red Inn visitors ctr
2	Pleasant View Rd, **N** FLYING J/Conoco/Subway/dsl scales/24hr, Exxon/dsl, Loves/Carl's Jr/dsl/scales/24hr McDonald's, Toro Viejo Mexican Sure Stay Inn+ truckwash, Suntree RV Park, **S** Exxon/dsl Zip's Dr in Riverbend Inn, Sleep Inn dogtrack
1	Beck Rd, **N** Panda Express Cabela's, Walmart/Subw **S** greyhound track
0mm	Idaho/Washington state line

INTERSTATE 184 (Boise)

BOISE

Exit #	Services
6mm	**I-184 begins/ends on 13th St**, downtown, Shell Bo fish Grill, Chandler's Steaks, Five Guys, PF Chang's Ha ton Inn, Safari Inn, The Grove Office Depot, USPO
5	River St (from eb), **W** Chevron McDonald's Red L
4.5mm	Boise River
3	Fairview Ave, to US 20/26 E, **W** Joe's Crabshack, Tepar ki Japanese Boise Inn, Cottonwood Suites, Riverside tel Commercial Tire
2	Curtis Rd, to Garden City, **E** Shell H
1b a	Cole Rd, Franklin Rd, **E** Chevron/Subway/dsl Ac Chrysler/Dodge/Jeep, Honda, Jaguar, Land Rover, Merce Volvo, **W** Chevron/dsl, Sinclair/dsl Applebee's, C Ole, Cafe Rio, Carl's Jr, Cheesecake Factory, Chick-fil-A, Chi Chipotle, Dave&Buster's, Fujiyama Japanese, Golden ral, IHOP, Jalapeno's, McDonald's, Noodles&Co, Old Chic Pizza, Olive Garden, Port of Subs, Quiznos, Red Lobster, Robin, Rumbi Island Grill, Shari's, Sizzler, Smash Burger, S bucks, Wendy's Candlewood Suites, La Quinta, Reside Inn AT&T, AT&T, Audi/VW, Best Buy, Cabela's, Dick's, lard's, JC Penney, Kohl's, Macy's, Michael's, Old Navy, Pe Petsmart, REI, Ross, Target, TJ Maxx, Tuesday Morning, Veri
0mm	**I-184 begins/ends on I-84, exit 49.**

NOTES

ILLINOIS

INTERSTATE 24

Exit #	Services
38mm	Illinois/Kentucky state line, Ohio River
37	US 45, Metropolis, N [rest stop] **both lanes, full [handicapped] facilities, info, litter barrels, petwalk, [picnic], vending**, S [gas] BP/Quiznos/dsl [food] Bill's BBQ, China House, El Tequila, Huddle House, McDonald's, Pizza Hut, Sonic [lodging] Best Value Inn, Holiday Inn Express, Motel 6, Quality Inn, Super 8 [other] [H], $General, Buick/Chrysler/Dodge/GMC/Jeep, camping, Chevrolet, Ft Massac SP, O'Reilly Parts, Plaza Tire, to Riverboat Casino
27	to New Columbia, Big Bay
16	IL 146, Vienna, S [gas] BP/dsl, Citgo/dsl, FastStop [food] DQ, McDonald's, Smokin Daddy's Grill, Subway, Vienna Diner [lodging] Hotel 7 [other] vet
14	US 45, Vienna, S [other] camping
7	to Goreville, Tunnel Hill, N [other] winery (7mi), S [other] camping, to Ferne Clyffe SP
1	I-57, N to Chicago, S to Memphis. **I-24 begins/ends on I-57, exit 44.**

INTERSTATE 39

Exit #	Services
122.5	**I-39 and I-90 run together into Wisconsin. See Illinois Interstate 90, exits 15mm-1.**
122b a	US 20 E, Harrison Ave, to Belvidere (last nb exit before toll rd), W [gas] Fas Fuel/Subway/dsl, Mobil, Tesla EVC [food] Arby's, Bergner's, Burger King, DQ, Granite City Rest., Lung Fung, Rosati's, Rosati's Pizza, Sonic, Taco Bell, TGIFriday's [other] Barnes&Noble, BMW, Buick/Chevrolet/GMC, Collier RV Ctr, Goodyear/auto, Harley-Davidson, JC Penney, Macy's, Menards, Schnuck's Foods/gas, Tires+, vet, VW, Walgreens
119	US 20 W, Alpine Rd, to Rockford
116.5mm	Kishwaukee River
115	Baxter Rd, E [gas] Shell/Subway/dsl/scales/24hr/@
111	IL 72, to Monroe Center, E [gas] BP/Sunrise Family Rest./dsl/24hr, Marathon (1mi)
104	IL 64, to Oregon, Sycamore, W [food] Grubsteakers Rest/truck parking (2mi)
99	IL 38, to De Kalb, Rochelle, 0-2 mi W [gas] Murphy USA/dsl, Murphy USA/dsl, Petro/Iron Skillet/dsl/scales/RV Dump/@, Phillips 66/Circle K/dsl, Road Ranger/Pilot/Subway/dsl/scales/24hr, Shell/dsl [food] Arby's, Butterfly Rest, China Wok, Culver's, Dunkin', Jimmy John's, Little Caesar's, McDonald's, New China, Pizza Hut, Subway, Taco Bell, Wendy's [lodging] Comfort Inn, Country Hearth Inn, Holiday Inn Express, Super 8 [other] [H], $General, $Tree, Blue Beacon, GNC, O'Reilly Parts, Sullivan's Foods, Verizon, Walgreens, Walmart
97b a	I-88 tollway, to Moline, Rock Island, Chicago
93	Steward
87	US 30, to Sterling, Rock Falls, E [other] to Shabbona Lake SP, W [other] Yogi Bear Camping (16mi)
84.5mm	[rest stop] **both lanes, full [handicapped] facilities, litter barrels, petwalk, [phone], [picnic], playground, vending**
82	Paw Paw, 3 mi E [gas] Casey's (3mi), W many wind turbines
72	US 34, to Mendota, Earlville, W [gas] BP/Cindy's/dsl/scales/24hr, Road Ranger/Pilot/Subway/dsl/scales/24hr [food] KFC/Taco Bell, McDonald's [lodging] Quality Inn, Super 8/truck parking [other] [H]
67.5mm	Little Vermilion River
66	US 52, Troy Grove, E [other] KOA (6mi)
62.5mm	Tomahawk Creek
59b a	I-80, E to Chicago, W to Des Moines
57	US 6, to Peru, La Salle, 1-2 mi W [gas] Casey's [lodging] Daniel's Motel [other] city park
56mm	Illinois River, Abraham Lincoln Mem Bridge
54	Oglesby, E [gas] BP/dsl, Casey's, Phillips 66/dsl, Shell [food] Burger King, Delaney's Rest., KFC/Taco Bell, McDonald's, Root Beer Stand, Subway [lodging] Best Western, Days Inn [other] Starved Rock SP, W [gas] Love's/Hardee's/dsl/scales/24hr
52	IL 251, to La Salle, Peru
51	IL 71, to Hennepin, Oglesby
48	Tonica, E [gas] Casey's [other] city park
41	IL 18, to Streator, Henry
35	IL 17, to Wenona, Lacon, E [gas] BP/dsl, Casey's (2mi), Shell/Burger King/dsl/RV dump [food] Subway [lodging] Best Value Inn/truck parking
27	to Minonk, E [gas] Casey's (2mi), Pilot/Road Ranger/Subway/Woody's Rest./dsl/24hr [lodging] Motel 6 [other] NAPA
22	IL 116, to Peoria, Benson
14	US 24, to El Paso, Peoria, E [gas] BP/Subway/dsl/24hr, Casey's/dsl, Freedom/dsl [food] DQ, Hardee's, McDonald's, Woody's Family Rest. [lodging] Days Inn [other] Buick/Chevrolet/GMC, city park, Ford, IGA Foods, USPO, W [food] Monical's Pizza [lodging] Super 8 [other] $General, Hickory Hill Camping (4mi), PROMPT CARE
9mm	Mackinaw River
8	IL 251, Lake Bloomington Rd, E [other] Lake Bloomington, W [other] Evergreen Lake, to Comlara Park
5	Hudson, 1 mi E [gas] Casey's/dsl
2	US 51 bus, Bloomington, Normal
0mm	**I-39 begins/ends on I-55, exit 164.**

OGLESBY

IL

INTERSTATE 55

CHICAGO AREA

Exit #	Services
295mm	**I-55 begins/ends on US 41**, Lakeshore Dr, in Chicago.
293a	to Cermak Rd (from nb)
292	I-90/94, W to Chicago, E to Indiana
290	Damen Ave, Ashland Ave (no EZ nb return), E Marathon, Shell Starbucks Target
289	to California Ave (no EZ nb return), E Marathon, Pilot/Road Ranger/Subway/dsl, Thornton's/dsl
288	Kedzie Ave, (from sb no ez return), E Citgo
287	Pulaski Rd, E BP/dsl, Shell Burger King, Domino's, Dunkin', Subway, Wendy's Advance Parts, Aldi Foods, AT&T, Dodge, Honda, Marshall's, Michael's, Pete's Mkt, Petsmart, Ross, Target, Walgreens
286	IL 50, Cicero Ave, E BP, Mobil/dsl, Shell/dsl Dunkin', McDonald's, Starbucks, Subway AutoZone, O'Reilly Parts, to
285	Central Ave, E BP/dsl, Grand Prix/Dunkin', Minuteman/Dunkin' Burger King, Donald's HotDogs
283	IL 43, Harlem Ave, E Shell Baskin-Robbins/Dunkin', Burger King, Domino's, Little Caesar's, Portillo HotDogs, Potbelly's, Subway Aldi Foods, AT&T, AutoZone, Fannie May Candies, Walgreens
282b a	IL 171, 1st Ave, W Brookfield Zoo
279b	US 12, US 20, US 45, La Grange Rd, **0-2 mi** W BP, Mobil, Shell/Circle K Andy's Custard, Applebee's, Arby's, Baskin-Robbins/Dunkin', Boston Mkt, Burger King, Chick-fil-A, Cocula Rest., Dragon Buffet, Dunkin', Hooters, JC Georges Rest., Jimmy John's, Ledo's Pizza, LoneStar Steaks, McDonald's, Nonno's Pizza, Panda Express, Pizza Hut, Popeye's, Starbucks, Subway, Taco Bell, Taco Tico, Time Out Grill, TX Roadhouse, Via Bella, Wendy's, White Castle Best Western+, Holiday Inn $Tree, Aldi Foods, Best Buy, Buick/Cadillac/GMC, Chevrolet, Chrysler/Dodge/Jeep, Discount Tire, Firestone/auto, Ford, GNC, Harley Davidson, Home Depot, Honda, Jo-Ann Fabrics, Kohl's, Mazda, Menards, NAPA, Nissan, NTB, O'Reilly Parts, PepBoys, PetCo, Petsmart, Sam's Club/gas, Subaru, Target, Toyota, Verizon, VW, Walmart
279a	La Grange Rd, **to I-294 toll**, S to Indiana
277b	**I-294 toll** (from nb), S to Indiana
277a	**I-294 toll**, N to Wisconsin
276c	Joliet Rd (from nb)
276b a	County Line Rd, E Capri Rest., China King, Ciazza's Grill, Cooper's Hawk, Eddie Merlot's, Patti's Sunrise Cafe, Starbucks, Subway, Topaz Rest. Extended Stay America, Marriott, Quality Inn Tuesday Morning, W SpringHill Suites
274	IL 83, Kingery Rd, E Shell, W BP/dsl, Mobil/dsl, Shell Bakers Square, Buffalo Wild Wings, Chick-fil-A, Chipotle Mexican, Denny's, Dunkin', Jamba Juice, Jimmy John's, MOD Pizza, Panera Bread, Papa John's, Patio BBQ, Portillo's HotDogs, Potbelly's Rest., Starbucks, Wendy's Econolodge, Holiday Inn, La Quinta, Red Roof Inn Ford/KIA, GNC, Marshall's, Marshall's, Michael's, Staples, Target, Verizon
273b a	Cass Ave, W Shell Al Chile Mexican, Chuck's Rest., Rosati's Pizza, Uncle Mao's Chinese
271b a	Lemont Rd, E Extended Stay America, W Shell
269	**I-355 toll**, to W Suburbs
268	(from sb only), Joliet, same as 267
267	IL 53, Bolingbrook, E 55 Trkstp/rest./dsl/scales/24hr/@, BP/dsl McDonald's Ramada Ltd, Super 8 Chevrolet, W Shell/Circle K, Speedway/dsl Burger King, Cheddar's,

BOLINGBROOK

JOLIET

Exit #	Services
267	Continued Denny's, Dunkin', El Burrito Loco, Family Square Rest., Go Chopsticks, Golden Corral, McDonald's, Popeye's, Starbu Subway, Wendy's, White Castle Hampton Inn, Hilton den, Holiday Inn, Quality Inn, Residence Inn, SpringHill Su $Tree, Aldi Foods, Fiesta Mkt, NAPA, Tony's Mkt, U-H Walgreens, Walmart
266mm	**weigh sta both lanes**
263	Weber Rd, E 7-11, BP/dsl, Speedway/Dunkin'/dsl Burger King, Burrito's, Culver's, Doc Watson's Smokeho KFC, Little China, McDonald's, Michael's Pizza, Popeye's, Sub Todake Steaks, White Castle Days Inn, Holiday Inn Expres Ace Hardware, BB Rest., Discount Tire, GNC, Reba's Automo Walgreens, W Mobil/Jimmy John's/dsl, Shell/Circle K by's, Cracker Barrel, Wendy's Comfort Inn, Country Inn&Su Extended Stay America, Woodspring Suites
261	IL 126 (from sb), to Plainfield
257	US 30, to Joliet, Aurora, E Shell/Circle K Antho Rest., Applebee's, Baskin-Robbins/Dunkin', Burger King, Ch tle, ChuckeCheese, Denny's, Diamand's Rest., Five Guys, F Thyme Mkt, Hooters, LoneStar Steaks, McDonald's, Outb Steaks, Panera Bread, Red Lobster, Steak'n Shake, Subway, Bell, TGIFriday's, TX Roadhouse, Wendy's Best Weste Comfort Inn, Fairfield Inn, Hampton Inn, Home 2 Suites, M 6, Super 8 $Tree, Aldi Foods, AT&T, AutoZone, Barnes& ble, Best Buy, Dick's, Discount Tire, Firestone/auto, H Depot, Honda, JC Penney, Jo-Ann Fabrics, Macy's, Micha NTB, Old Navy, Petsmart, Ross, Target, Verizon, W Mc dsl Blue's BBQ, Luigi's Pizza Chevrolet, Ford
253b a	US 52, Jefferson St, Joliet, E Citgo/dsl, Mobil/dsl, S Joe's Rest., McDonald's Best Western, Econolo Elk's Motel, La Quinta, Wingate Inn H, Ford, F dom Automotive, Freightliner, Harley-Davidson, Rick's RV W BP/dsl, Shell Burger King, Casa Maya, DQ, Ros Pizza, Starbucks, Subway 7-11, Chrysler/Dodge/Jeep, el-Osco, vet
251	IL 59 (from nb), to Shorewood, access to same as 253 W
250b a	I-80, W to Iowa, E to Toledo
248	US 6, Joliet, E Pilot/Dunkin'/Subway/dsl/24hr, Spe way/dsl Taco Burrito King, W BP/McDonald's, Th ton's/dsl/scales
247	Bluff Rd
245mm	Des Plaines River
244	Arsenal Rd, E Exxon/Mobil Refinery
241	to Wilmington
241mm	Kankakee River
240	Lorenzo Rd, E BP/dsl, W Mobil/pizza/dsl/scales/2 Petro/Shell/Iron Skillet/dsl/scales/24hr/@ Knights Inn
238	IL 129 S, to Wilmington (from nb), Braidwood
236	IL 113, Coal City, E EZ Living RV Ctr, Fossil Rock Camp W Casey's, Shell/DQ/dsl KFC/Taco Bell, Little Caes Los 3 Burritos, WhistleStop Cafe
233	Reed Rd, E Marathon/dsl Jones-sez BBQ
227	IL 53, Gardner, E Casey's Gardner Rest., Sub $General, truck/tire repair, W BP/dsl
220	IL 47, Dwight, E BP/Burger King/dsl, Loves/H ee's/dsl/scales/24hr, Marathon/Circle K/dsl/24hr Ar Dwight Chinese, Dwight Pizza, McDonald's, Pete's Rest., S way Classic Motel, Super 8
217	IL 17, Dwight, E Casey's, Shell/Circle K/dsl/24hr DQ, 66 Rest. Ace Hardware, CVS Drug, Family$, NAPA
213mm	Mazon River

IL

INTERSTATE 55 Cont'd

Exit #	Services
209	Odell, E USPO
201	IL 23, Pontiac, 0-3 mi E DQ, La Mex 4H RV Camp (seasonal) RV Ctr, Pontiac RV Ctr, W truck repair
198mm	Vermilion River
197	IL 116, Pontiac, E BP/dsl, Shell/dsl, Thornton's/dsl Arby's, Baby Bull's Rest., Burger King, Cafe Fontana, Dunkin', KFC, LJ Silver, McDonald's, Monical's Pizza, Pizza Hut, Subway, Taco Bell, Wendy's Best Western, Hampton Inn, Quality Inn, Super 8 $General, $Tree, Advance Parts, Aldi Foods, AT&T, AutoZone, Big R Store, Buick/Chevrolet/Cadillac/GMC, Chrysler/Dodge/Jeep/Lincoln, Firestone/auto, Lincoln, Verizon, Walgreens, Walmart/Subway, W Mobil/dsl
193mm	**both lanes, full facilities, litter barrels, petwalk, , vending**
187	US 24, Chenoa, E Casey's/dsl, Phillips 66/McDonald's/dsl, Shell/Subway/dsl Best Value Inn, Chenoa Family Rest.
179mm	Des Plaines River
178	Lexington, E BP/McDonalds/dsl, Freedom/dsl Subway $General, W Chevrolet
178mm	Mackinaw River
171	Towanda, E FastStop/dsl
167	Lp 55 S Veterans Pkwy, to Normal, 0-3 mi E BP/Circle K, Marathon/Circle K/dsl Alexander's Steaks, Applebee's, Bandana's BBQ, Biaggi's Ristorante, Bob Evans, Burger King, Carlos O'Kelly's, Chick-fil-A, Chili's, Chipotle Mexican, Chucke-Cheese, Coldstone, Destihl Rest., DQ, Fazoli's, Fiesta Ranchera Mexican, FlatTop Grill, Hardee's, IHOP, Jason's Deli, Jimmy John's, Jimmy John's (2), Krispy Kreme, Logan's Roadhouse, Lonestar Steaks, McDonald's, Monical's Pizza, Noodles&Co, Olive Garden, Outback Steaks, Panda Express, Panera Bread, Papa John's, Pizza Hut, Pizza Ranch, Popeye's, Portillo's, Potbelly, Qdoba Mexican, Red Lobster, Red Robin, Schlotzsky's, Smashburger, Sonic, Starbucks, Steak'n Shake, Subway, Taco Bell, Tony Roma's, Wendy's, Wild Berries Rest. Baymont Inn, Candlewood Suites, Chateau, Comfort Suites, Courtyard, Hampton Inn, Holiday Inn Express, Motel 6, Quality Inn, Super 8 , $Tree, Advance Parts, Aldi Foods, AT&T, AutoZone, Barnes&Noble, Best Buy, CVS Drug, Dick's, Fresh Mkt, GNC, Goodyear/auto, Gordman's, Hobby Lobby, Home Depot, Honda, Hyundai, HyVee, Jewel-Osco, Jo-Ann Fabrics, Kohl's, Kroger/dsl, Lowe's, Meijer/dsl, Meineke, Menards, Michael's, Midas, Office Depot, Old Navy, O'Reilly Parts, PetCo, Sam's Club/gas, Schnuck's Foods, Target, TJ Maxx, to , Tuesday Morning, Tuffy, Verizon, Von Maur, Walgreens, Walmart/Subway
165b a	US 51 bus, to Bloomington, E BP/Circle K, Mobil/Arby's/dsl, Qik-n-EZ, Shell/Burger King/dsl Denny's, Dunkin', McDonald's, Moe's SW Grill, Rosati's Pizza, Smoothie King, Starbucks, Steak'n Shake, Subway, Uncle Tom's Pancakes, Wendy's Baymont Inn, Motel 6, Radisson, Super 8 , $General, $Tree, Discount Tire, Schnuck's Foods, to Ill St U, Verizon, Walgreens, W dsl repair
164	I-39, US 51, N to Peru
163	I-74 W, to Peoria
160b a	US 150, IL 9, Market St, Bloomington, E BP/Circle K, Freedom/dsl, Pilot/Wendy's/dsl/scales/24hr, Shell/repair, TA/Country Pride/dsl/scales/24hr/@ Arby's, Cracker Barrel, Culver's, KFC, McDonald's, Popeye's, Subway, Taco Bell Days Inn, EconoLodge, Hawthorn Suites, Quality Inn, Quality Suites, Red Roof Inn , Advance Parts, Blue Beacon, Family$, Peterbilt, W Marathon/Circle K/dsl, Murphy USA/dsl Bob

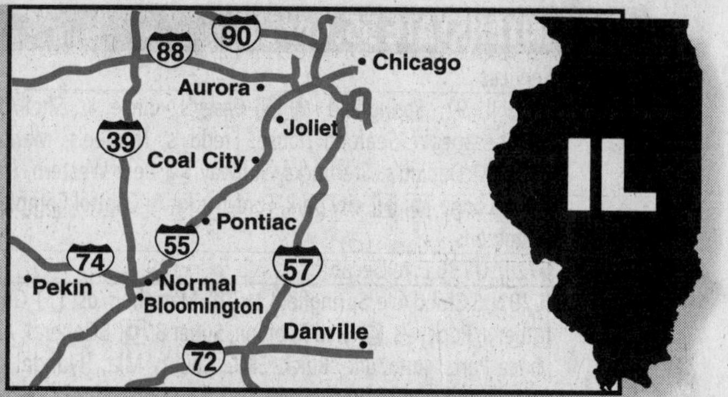

Exit #	Services
160b a	Continued Evans, Fiesta Ranchera Mexican, Steak'n Shake/24hr Comfort Suites, Country Inn&Suites, Fairfield Inn, Hampton Inn, Holiday Inn Express, Ramada Ltd Aldi Foods, Farm&Fleet, Walmart
157b	Lp 55 N, Veterans Pkwy, Bloomington, E , to
157a	I-74 E, to Indianapolis, US 51 to Decatur
154	Shirley
149	**W both lanes, full facilities, litter barrels, petwalk, , playground, vending**
145	US 136, E Quality RV Ctr, W Dixie/Pilot/Road Ranger/Subway/dsl/scales/24hr, Mobil/dsl McDonald's, Rte 66 Drive Thru Super 8
140	Atlanta, E RV camping (3mi), W Casey's/dsl Country-Aire Rest. Atlanta Inn $General, NAPA
133	Lp 55, Lincoln, 2 mi E , Camp-A-While Camping
127	I-155 N, to Peoria
126	IL 10, IL 121 S, Lincoln, 0-2 mi E BP/Arby's/dsl/24hr, Casey's/dsl, Thornton's/Pilot/dsl/scales/24hr Bonanza Steaks, Burger King, Cracker Barrel, Culver's, Daphne's Rest., DQ, Dunkin', El Mazatlan Mexican, Hardee's, McDonald's, Pizza Hut, Rio Grande Grill, Steak'n Shake, Subway, Taco Bell, Wendy's EconoLodge, Hampton Inn, Holiday Inn Express, Super 8 , $General, $Tree, Aldi Foods, AT&T, AutoZone, Chrysler/Dodge/Jeep, CVS Drug, Ford/Lincoln, Kroger, O'Reilly Parts, Russell Stover, Verizon, Walgreens, Walmart/Subway
123	Lp 55, to Lincoln, E
119	Broadwell
115	Elkhart
109	IL 123, Williamsville, E Casey's Subway, W Loves/McDonalds/dsl/scales/24hr Huddle House New Salem SHS
107mm	**weigh sta sb**
105	Lp 55, to Sherman, W Casey's Cancun Mexican, China King, Fairlane Diner, Fire&Ale Grill, Ricco's Pizza, Sam's Too Pizza, Subway Conv Ctr, County Mkt Foods, hist sites, Military Museum, repair, Riverside Park Campground, Verizon, vet, Walgreens
103mm	**sb, full facilities, litter barrels, petwalk, , vending**
102mm	Sangamon River
102mm	**nb, full facilities, litter barrels, petwalk, , vending**
100b	IL 54, Sangamon Ave, Springfield, W BP/Circle K, Marathon/Circle K, Murphy USA/dsl, Shell/dsl Arby's, Buffalo Wild Wings, Burger King, Culver's, DQ, Hickory River BBQ, Jimmy John's, McDonald's, Panda Express, Parkway Cafe, Penn Sta Subs, Sonic, Steak'n Shake, Taco Bell, Thai Basil, Wendy's, Wings Etc, Xochimilco Mexican, Yummy House Northfield Suites, Ramada , Aldi Foods, AT&T, GNC, Harley-Davidson, Lowe's, Menards, to Vet Mem, Verizon, Walmart/Subway
100a	Il 54, E to Clinton, E Road Ranger/Pilot/Subway/dsl/scales/24hr Kenworth/Ryder/Volvo, truckwash

LINCOLN

IL

= gas = food = lodging = other = rest stop

INTERSTATE 55 Cont'd

SPRINGFIELD

Exit #	Services
98b	I-72, IL 97, Springfield, W Casey's, Circle K, Shell/dsl Chesapeake Seafood House, Freddy's, Hardee's, Mario's Pizza, McDonald's, Starbucks, Subway Best Western, Lincoln's Lodge H, city park, Ford Trucks, to Capitol Complex, Walgreens
98a	I-72 E, US 36 E, to Decatur
96b a	IL 29 N, S Grand Ave, Springfield, W Marathon/dsl Godfather's, Popeye's Red Roof Inn, Super 8 $General, Advance Parts, AutoZone, Buick/GMC, County Mkt, Hyundai, JC Penney, museum, O'Reilly Parts
94	Stevenson Dr, Springfield, E KOA (7mi), W Circle K/dsl, Shell/dsl, Subway Applebee's, Arby's, Blue Margaritas, Bob Evans, Cancun Mexican, Dew Chili, Gallina Pizza, Hardee's, Hooters, IHOP, La Fiesta Mexican, LJ Silver, McAlister's Deli, McDonald's, Panera Bread, Papa John's, Red Lobster, Smokey Bones BBQ, Steak'n Shake, Taste of Thai Candlewood Suites, Comfort Suites, Country Inn Suites, Crowne Plaza, Drury Inn, Hilton Garden, Holiday Inn Express, Microtel, Residence Inn, Wingate Inn $General, auto repair, BigLots, CVS Drug, GNC, Walgreens
92b a	I-72 W, US 36 W, 6th St, Springfield, W Marathon/dsl, Thornton's Arby's, Burger King, Chadito's Tacos, Cozy Drive In, Golden Corral, Jimmy John's, KFC, Marco's Pizza, McDonald's, Pizza Hut, Pizza Ranch, Sgt. Pepper's Cafe, Starbucks, Subway, Taco Bell Comfort Inn, La Quinta, Route 66 H, Aldi, AT&T, AutoZone, CarX, County Mkt Foods, Mazda, Walgreens, Walmart/McDonald's
90	Toronto Rd, E Qik-n-EZ/Wendy's/dsl, Shell/Circle K Antonio's Pizza, China Express, Cracker Barrel, Head West Subs, Hen House, McDonald's, Subway, Taco Bell Baymont Inn, Day's Inn, Motel 6, W Pilot/Road Ranger/dsl/24hr
89mm	Lake Springfield
88	E Lake Dr, Chatham, E KOA, to Lincoln Mem Garden/Nature Ctr, W JJ RV Park/camping (2mi)
83	Glenarm, W JJ RV Park/camping (4mi)
82	IL 104, to Pawnee, E to Sangchris Lake SP, W Mobil/Auburn Trvl Ctr/Subway/scales/dsl/rest/24hr Toni's Cafe antiques/crafts
80	Hist 66, Divernon, W antiques
72	Farmersville, W Phillips 66/Subway/dsl/24hr, Shell
65mm	**both lanes, full facilities, litter barrels, petwalk, playground, vending**
63	IL 48, IL 127, to Raymond
60	IL 108, to Carlinville, E Kamper Kampanion RV Park, W Shell/dsl/LP/café Magnuson Grand Hotel/cafe antiques, to Blackburn Coll
56mm	**weigh sta nb**
52	IL 16, Hist 66, Litchfield, E BP, Casey's, Faststop/deli/dsl/scales, Murphy USA/dsl, Phillips 66/Jack-in-the-Box/dsl, Shell A&W/LJ Silver, Arby's, Ariston Café, Burger King, China Town, Denny's, DQ, El Rancherito Mexican, Huddle House, Jimmy John's, Jubelt's Rest., KFC, Maverick Steaks, McDonald's, Pizza Hut, Ruby Tuesday, Subway, Taco Bell, Wendy's Best Value Inn, Hampton Inn, Holiday Inn Express, Quality Inn, Super 8 H, $General, $Tree, Aldi Foods, AT&T, Buick/Cadillac/Chevrolet/GMC, Ford, Goodyear/auto, IGA Foods, NAPA, O'Reilly Parts, Rte 66 Museum, Verizon, vet, Walgreens, Walmart/Subway, W st police
44	IL 138, to Benld, Mt Olive, E Crossroads Diner, Rte 138 Cafe Mother Jones Mon
41	to Staunton, E Country Classic Cars, W Casey's DQ Super 8 H, $General, Chrysler/Dodge/Jeep

LITCHFIELD

COLLINSVILLE

Exit #	Services
37	Livingston, New Douglas, W Shell/dsl Gasper Café Country Inn/cafe AutoCare, IGA Foods, USPO
33	IL 4, to Staunton, Worden
30	IL 140, Hamel, E Love's/McDonald's/Subway/scales/24hr Innkeeper Motel, W Shell Weezy's
28mm	**both lanes, full facilities, litter barrels, petwalk, vending**
23	IL 143, Edwardsville, E Phillips 66/dsl
20b	I-270 W, to Kansas City
20a	I-70 E, to Indianapolis
I-55 S and I-70 W run together 18 mi.	
18	IL 162, to Troy, E Casey's/dsl, Phillips 66/Circle K Pilot/Arby's/dsl/scales/24hr, TA/BP/Country Pride/scales/24hr/@, ZX Alfonzo's Pizza, Burger King, China K Domino's, DQ, Dunkin', El Potro Mexican, Jack-in-the-Box, tle Caesar's, McDonald's/playplace, Pizza Hut, Subway $General, Ace Hardware, O'Reilly Parts, Schuette's Mkt, Sp co, truckwash, USPO, vet, Walgreens, W Cracker Ba Fire'n Smoke Kitchen, Joe's Pizza, Taco Bell Best Wes Holiday Inn Express, Motel 6, Red Roof Inn, Super 8 Frei liner, Verizon
17	US 40 E, to Troy, to St Jacob
15b a	IL 159, Maryville, Collinsville, 0-2 mi E Phillips 66/Circl dsl, VP/dsl, Zx Gas Asia Garden, Carisillo's Mexican, McDonald's, Sonic, Subway $General, Advance Parts, Foods, AutoZone, CVS Drug, Ford/Lincoln, O'Reilly Parts, Walgreens, W Loyalty Inn
14mm	**weigh sta sb**
11	IL 157, Collinsville, E Casey's A&W/LJ Silver, Den Golden Corral, Little Caesar's, McDonald's, Penn Sta Subs, C ba Mexican, St Louis Bread Co, Starbucks, Waffle House, W dy's Best Value Inn AT&T, Dobbs Tire, Gateway RV GNC, Home Depot, Midas, Verizon, Walgreens, Walmart/ way, W Motomart/dsl/24hr Applebee's, Arby's, dana's BBQ, Bob Evans, Burger King, Colton's Steaks, Culv DQ, Jimmy John's, Pizza Hut, Porter's Steaks, Ruby Tues Steak'n Shake, White Castle/24hr, Zapata's Mexican C fort Inn, Days Inn, DoubleTree Inn, Drury Inn, Fairfield Hampton Inn, La Quinta, Super 8 Buick/GMC, st police
10	I-255, S to Memphis, N to I-270
9	Black Lane (from nb, no return), E Fairmount RaceTrack
6	IL 111, Great River Rd, Fairmont City, E Exxon R Inn, Royal Budget Inn auto repair, W Horseshoe SP
4b a	IL 203, Granite City, E BP/dsl Western Inn, W Pilot/Subway/Taco Bell/dsl/scales/24hr/@ Gateway Raceway
3c	Exchange Ave
3b	I-70 W, to KC
3a	I-64 E, IL 3 N, St Clair Ave
2b	3rd St
2a	M L King Bridge, to downtown E St Louis
1	IL 3, to Sauget (from sb)
I-55 N and I-70 E run together 18 mi	
0mm	Illinois/Missouri state line, Mississippi River

INTERSTATE 57

Exit #	Services
358mm	I-94 E to Indiana, **I-57 begins/ends on I-94, exit 63 in Chica**
357	IL 1, Halsted St, E BP, Gulf/dsl auto repair, W Sl Dunkin', Supersave McDonald's, Shark's
355	111th St, Monterey Ave, W BP, Citgo
354	119th St, W Citgo/Dunkin' Chili's, Panda Express, way $Tree, AT&T, GNC, Jewel-Osco, PetCo, Pizza Hut

IL

INTERSTATE 57 Cont'd

Exit #	Services
353	127th St, Burr Oak Ave, E Citgo, GoLo, Shell Burger King, Dillinger's Drive-In, Dunkin', McDonald's, Wendy's Days Inn, M Hotel, Plaza Inn Ace Hardware, Advance Parts, Family$, Walgreens, W BP, Citgo/dsl Egg Shack H, JJ Fish&Chicken
352mm	Calumet Sag Channel
350	IL 83, 147th St, Sibley Blvd, E Marathon/dsl Checkers, Domino's, Harold's Chicken, McDonald's, Subway $General, Aldi Foods, Family$, O'Reilly Parts, W USPO
349	I-294 (from nb)
348	US 6, 159th St, E BP/dsl, Clark, Marathon/dsl Baskin-Robbins/Dunkin', Burger King, McDonald's, Popeye's, Subway, Taco Bell, White Castle $Tree, AutoZone, U-Haul, W Shell/dsl
346	167th St, Cicero Ave, to IL 50, E BP, Shell/dsl, Tesla EVC Baskin-Robbins/Dunkin', Harold's Chicken, Kenny's Ribs, McDonald's, Panda Express, Pizza Hut, Shark's Fish&Chicken, Sonic, Starbucks, Wendy's Best Western GNC, Walmart/Subway, W Shell 7-11
345b a	I-80, W to Iowa, E to Indiana, to I-294 N **toll** to Wisconsin
342	Vollmer Rd, E Shell/Circle K/dsl H
340b a	US 30, Lincoln Hwy, Matteson, E BP, Marathon/dsl A Fusion Asian, A&W/LJ Silver, Bar Louie, Bocce's Grill, Burger King, Chipotle, ChuckeCheese, Culver's, Dunkin', Dusties Buffet, Five Guys, Fuddrucker's, Giordano's, Harold's Chicken, IHOP, Jimmy John's, KFC, McDonald's, Olive Garden, Panda Express, Panera Bread, Pepe's, Perros Bros Gyros, Pizza Hut, Potbelly, Red Lobster, Rosati's, Shark's, Starbucks, Subway, White Castle Comfort Inn, Country Inn&Suites, Hampton Inn, Holiday Inn, Quality Inn $Tree, Aldi Foods, Best Buy, Chrysler/Dodge/Jeep, Discount Tire, Firestone/auto, GNC, Home Depot, JC Penney, Marshall's, Menards, NTB, PepBoys, Petsmart, Ross, USPO, Verizon, Walgreens, W Buick/Cadillac/GMC, Ford/Lincoln, Honda, Hyundai, Kia, Nissan, Toyota, Walgreens
339	Sauk Trail, to Richton Park, E BP/dsl, Marathon/dsl Blue Sharks, Domino's, McDonald's Family$, Walgreens, W Walmart/dsl
337	Stuenkel Rd
335	Monee, E BP/Dunkin'/Subway/dsl, Petro/Iron Skillet/dsl/e85/scales/24hr/@, Pilot/McDonald's/dsl/scales/24hr Burger King, Culver's, KFC/Taco Bell, Lucky Burrito, Pizza Hut, Schoops Rest. Country Host Motel, Quality Inn, Red Roof Inn, Super 8 Advance Parts, Blue Beacon
332mm	**Prairie View Rest Area both lanes, full facilities, info, litter barrels, petwalk, , , vending**
330mm	**weigh sta both lanes**
327	to Peotone, E Casey's, Circle K McDonald's/RV parking
322	Manteno, E BP/McDonald's/dsl, Casey's/dsl, Phillips 66/Subway DQ, Jimmy John's, KFC/Taco Bell, Monical's Pizza, Pizza Hut, Wendy's Country Inn&Suites, Howard Johnson Harley-Davidson, vet, W BP/Dunkin'/dsl
320	E. 6000N Rd
315	IL 50, Bradley, E Circle K/Burger King, EVC, F&F Buffalo Wild Wings, Chipotle, Cracker Barrel, Firehouse Subs, Five Guys, Jimmy John's, KanSai Japanese, McDonald's, Noodles&Co, Olive Garden, Panera Bread, Red Lobster, Starbucks, Taco Bell, TGIFriday's, Tucci's Rest., White Castle Comfort Inn, Fairfield Inn, Hampton Inn, Holiday Inn Express, Magnuson Aldi, AT&T, Barnes&Noble, Best Buy, Chrysler/Dodge/Jeep, Dick's, Discount Tire, GNC, JC Penney, Kohl's, Marshall's, Michael's, PetCo,

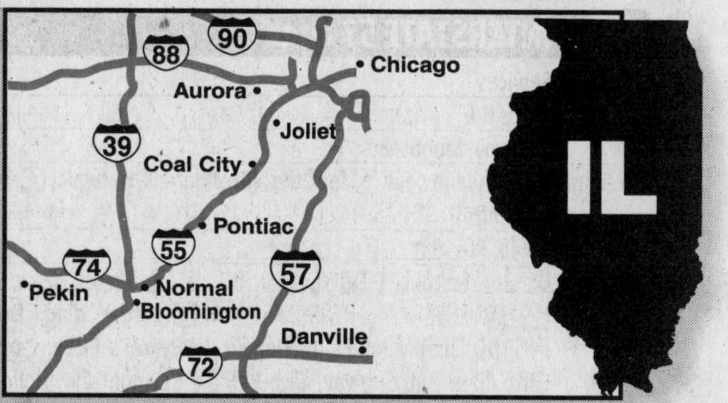

KANKAKEE

Exit #	Services
315	Continued Petsmart, Ross, Staples, Target, Verizon, Walmart/Subway, W BP/dsl, Circle K/dsl, CircleK/dsl, Speedway/dsl Applebee's, Arby's, Bakers Square, Checkers, Coyote Canyon, Denny's, IHOP, Mancino's Pizza, McDonald's, Oberweis Ice Cream, Panda Express, Steak'n Shake, Subway, Texas Roadhouse, Wendy's Quality Inn, Super 8 $Tree, AT&T, Bradley RV Ctr, Buick/GMC, Chevrolet, Hobby Lobby, Honda, Hyundai, JoAnn Fabrics, Kia, Lowe's, Menards, Nissan, O'Reilly, to Kankakee River SP, URGENT CARE, Verizon, vet
312	IL 17, Kankakee, W BP/dsl, Circle K, Marathon/dsl McDonald's, PoorBoy Rest. H, $ General, Advance Parts, Family$
310.5mm	Kankakee River
308	US 45, US 52, to Kankakee, E Loves/Arby's/dsl/scales/24hr , KOA (3mi), W Murphy USA, Speedway/Dunkin'/Subway/dsl El Mexicano, KFC/Taco Bell Fairview Motel, Hilton Garden $Tree, Aldi Foods, Walmart/Subway
302	Chebanse, W truck repair
297	Clifton, W Phillips 66/Circle K/DQ/dsl $General
293	IL 116, Ashkum, E BP/Subway/dsl st police, tires, W Beans and Barley
283	US 24, IL 54, Gilman, E K&H Trkstp/BP/dsl/scales/24hr/@, Mobil/dsl, Pilot/Denny's/dsl/scales/24hr Burger King, DQ, McDonald's, Monical's Pizza Motel 6, Super 8, W BP/dsl
280	IL 54, Onarga, E Casey's, Phillips 66 USPO, W Lake Arrowhead RV camping
272	to Roberts, Buckley
268.5mm	**both lanes, full facilities, litter barrels, petwalk, , , vending**
261	IL 9, Paxton, **0-1 mi** E Casey's, Phillips 66/dsl Hardee's, Monical's Pizza, Pizza Palace, Subway Buick/Cadillac/Chevrolet/GMC, IGA Foods, NAPA, TrueValue, USPO, W Phillips/dsl Country House Rest. Cobblestone Inn, Paxton Inn
250	US 136, Rantoul, **0-1 mi** E BP/Circle K, Casey's/dsl, Circle K/dsl Arby's, Burger King, Dunkin', McDonald's, Monical's Pizza, Papa John's, Red Wheel Rest., Subway Heritage Inn, Holiday Inn Express, Knights Inn, Super 8 $General, Chrysler/Dodge/Jeep, Ford, NAPA, vet, Walgreens, Walmart
240	Market St, E Road Ranger/Pilot/McDonald's/dsl/scales Kenworth/Volvo, truck/tire repair, W D&W Lake Camping/RV Park
238	Olympian Dr, to Champaign, W Circle K/dsl DQ Microtel RV/dsl repair
237b a	I-74, W to Peoria, E to Urbana
235b	I-72 W, to Decatur
235a	University Ave, to Champaign, E H, U of Ill

RANTOUL

= gas = food = lodging = other = rest stop

INTERSTATE 57 Cont'd

Exit #	Services
232	Curtis Rd
229	to Savoy, Monticello
221.5mm	**both lanes, full facilities, litter barrels, petwalk, , , vending**
220	US 45, Pesotum, E st police
212	US 36, Tuscola, E FuelMart/dsl, W BP/dsl, Circle K, Pilot/Road Ranger/dsl/scales/24hr Burger King, Denny's, DQ, Jimmy John's, McDonald's, Monical's Pizza, Pantry Cafe, Pizza Hut, Subway, Taco Bell Baymont Inn, Holiday Inn Express, Super 8 $General, Ford, IGA Foods, O'Reilly Parts, Tuscola Outlets/Famous Brands, Verizon
203	IL 133, Arcola, E Best Western+, W Phillips 66/Subway/dsl, Sunrise/dsl DQ, El Toro Mexican, Hen House, McDonald's, Monical's Pizza Arcola Inn, Quality Inn $General, city park, NAPA, vet
192	CtyRd 1000 N, Rd 18
190b a	IL 16, to Mattoon, E BP/dsl H, Fox Ridge SP, to E IL U, W Huck's, Murphy USA/dsl, Phillips 66/Subway/dsl A&W/LJ Silver, Alamo Steaks, Arby's, Buffalo Wild Wings, China Wok, Cracker Barrel, Denny's, Domino's, Don Sol Mexican, DQ, El Vaquero Mexican, Freddy's, Japanese Steaks, Jimmy John's, KFC, Lee's Chicken, McDonald's, McHugh's, Papa Murphy, QQ Buffet, Stadium Grill, Starbucks, Steak'n Shake, Taco Bell, Wendy's Baymont Inn, Comfort Suites, Hampton Inn, Holiday Inn Express, Suite Dreams, Super 8 $General, $Tree, Aldi Foods, AT&T, BigLots, CVS Drug, GNC, Home Depot, JC Penney, JoAnn, O'Reilly Parts, Petsmart, Verizon, Walgreens, Walmart/Subway
184	US 45, IL 121, to Mattoon, E Phillips 66/Subway/dsl, W McDonald's Motel 6, Quality Inn to Lake Shelbyville
177	US 45, Neoga, E FuelMart/Subway/dsl/e-85 NAPA, W Casey's/dsl (1mi) $General
166.5mm	**both lanes, full facilities, litter barrels, petwalk, , , vending**
163	I-70 E, to Indianapolis
I-57 S and I-70 W run together 6 mi.	
162	US 45, Effingham, E Motomart Harley-Davidson, W Pilot/McDonald's/dsl/scales/24hr Subway Camp Lakewood (2mi), truck repair
160	IL 33, IL 32, Effingham, E Domino's, Jimmy John's, McAlister's Deli, Papa John's, Pizza Hut Best Western, Fairfield Inn, Quality Inn H, $General, Aldi Foods, AutoZone, Save-a-Lot, Verizon, vet, W FLYING J/Denny's/dsl/LP/scales/24hr, Murphy USA/dsl, Phillips 66/dsl, TA/Popeye's/dsl/@ Arby's, Buffalo Wild Wings, Burger King, Chili's, Chipotle, Cracker Barrel, Denny's, El Rancherito Mexican, Fujiyama Steaks, KFC, LJ Silver, McDonald's, Panda Express, Panera Bread, Starbucks, Steak'n Shake, Taco Bell, TGIFriday's, Wendy's Country Inn&Suites, Days Inn, Hampton Inn, Holiday Inn, La Quinta, Super 8 $Tree, AT&T, Blue Beacon, Camp Lakewood RV Park, Ford/Lincoln, Hodgson Mill Mercantile, Kohl's, Menards, Peterbilt, SpeedCo, Verizon, Walmart/Subway
159	US 40, Effingham, E Phillips 66/dsl, Speedway/Speedy's Cafe/dsl/24hr China Buffet, Culver's, Hardee's, Little Caesar's, Niemerg's Rest, Subway Abe Lincoln Motel, Best Value Inn, Comfort Suites, EconoLodge, Lexington Inn Honda, O'Reilly Parts, tires/repair, Walgreens, W Petro/Iron Skillet/dsl/24hr/@ Baymont Inn Blue Beacon, Freightliner
I-57 N and I-70 E run together 6 mi.	

MATTOON

EFFINGHAM

IL

Exit #	Services
157	I-70 W, to St Louis
151	Watson, 5 mi E Percival Springs RV Park
150mm	Little Wabash River, Little Wabash River
145	Edgewood, E Phillips 66/dsl city park
135	IL 185, Farina, E Shell/Subway/dsl $General, Ford
127	to Kinmundy, Patoka
116	US 50, Salem, E Circle K/dsl, Huck's/dsl, Motomart, EVC Burger King, China King, Denny's, Domino's, H ee's, La Cocina Mexican, McDonald's, Pizza Hut, Pizza Subway, Taco Bell, Village Garden, Wendy's Holiday Express H, $General, AutoZone, Chrysler/Dodge/ CVS Drug, GMC, NAPA, O'Reilly Parts, Save-A-Lot, to Forbe USPO, Verizon, W Murphy USA/dsl, Phillips 66/dsl plebee's, Arby's, El Rancherito, KFC, Mi Pueblo Days Quality Inn, Super 8 $Tree, AT&T, Buick/Chevrolet, Ca Lake (23mi), Ford, Salem Tires, Walmart
114mm	**both lanes, full facilities, litter barrels, petwalk, playground, vending**
109	IL 161, to Centralia, W Biggie's General Store/cafe/dsl
103	Dix, E Phillips 66/dsl Red Carpet Inn
96	I-64 W, to St Louis
95	IL 15, Mt Vernon, E Circle K/dsl, Hucks Agave Mex Asian Buffet, Bandana's BBQ, Domino's, El Rancherito Mex Fazoli's, Hardee's, KFC, Little Caesar's, LJ Silver, McAlister's McDonald's, Moe's SW Grill, Panda Express, Panera Bread, za Hut, Starbucks, Steak'n Shake, Subway, Taco Bell, The G Waffle Co, Wendy's Best Value Inn, Comfort Suites, Drury Motel 6, Super 8 H, AT&T, AutoZone, Big Lots, Chevr Cadillac, CVS Drug, Harley-Davidson, Hobby Lobby, JC Pe Kroger/dsl, Midas, O'Reilly Parts, Plaza Tire, Prompt Care, Verizon, Walgreens, W Circle K/dsl, FLYING J/Hucks/ dle House/dsl/scales/24hr, Pilot/Denny's/dsl/scales/24hr, Country Pride/Popeye's/dsl/24hr/@, Tesla EVC Applebee's by's, Bob Evans, Buffalo Wild Wings, Burger King, Chili's, Cr Barrel, Double Overtime Grill, Jimmy John's, McDonald's, Ry Sonic, Subway Days Inn, Doubletree, Fairfield Inn, Ham Inn, Holiday Inn Express, Quality Inn $Tree, Archway RV Buick/GMC, Freightliner, Kohl's, Lowe's, NAPA, Staples, To truckwash, Walmart
94	Veteran's Memorial Dr, E Phillips 66/dsl Cul H, W Menards
92	I-64 E, to Louisville
83	Ina, E Love's/McDonald's/dsl/scales Uncle BBQ tire/trailer repair, W to Rend Lake Coll
79mm	**sb, full facilities, info, litter barrels, petwalk, , playground, vending**
77	IL 154, to Whittington, E Phillips 66/dsl Surestay Whittington Woods RV Park, W Seasons at Rend Lodge/rest. golf, to Rend Lake, Wayne Fitzgerrell SP
74mm	**nb, full facilities, litter barrels, petwalk, , , ground, vending**
71	IL 14, Benton, E Arby's, Hardee's, KFC/Taco Bell, Pizza Country Hearth Inn, Gray Plaza Motel, Phillips 66/dsl AutoZone, CVS Drug, KOA (1.5mi), O'Reilly Parts, Plaza W Casey's/dsl, Circle K/dsl, Murphy USA/dsl A bee's, Burger King, McDonald's, Subway $Tree, AT& Rend Lake, Verizon, Walmart
65	IL 149, W Frankfort, E Circle K/dsl, ROC/dsl C Star, Dixie Cream Deli, Don Luna Mexican, Hardee's, La ta Mexican, LJ Silver, Mike's Drive-In, Opie's Rest., Sonic, way Gray Plaza Motel CVS Drug, NAPA, W Casey's

SALEM

MT VERNON

BENTON

INTERSTATE 57 Cont'd

65	Continued Phillips 66/dsl Bonnie's Cafe, McDonald's, Taco Bell Best Value Inn $General, $Tree, Buick/Chevrolet/GMC, Chrysler/Dodge/Jeep, Kroger
59	to Herrin, Johnston City, E ROC/dsl/e85, Stuckey's/dsl, ZX/dsl DQ, McDonald's, Subway $General, Bandy Drug, camping (2mi), W H, camping (4mi)
54b a	IL 13, Marion, E Circle K/dsl Arby's, Fazoli's, Hardee's, KFC, La Fiesta Mexican, Little Caesar's, LJ Silver, Papa John's, Pizza Hut, Subway, Tequila's Mexican, Wendy's Best Value Inn, EconoLodge $General, Advance Parts, Aldi Foods, AutoZone, Ford/Hyundai/Lincoln, Kroger/gas, Plaza Tire, USPO, Walgreens, W Huck's/dsl, Phillips 66/dsl, Pilot/Subway/dsl/scales/24hr 17th St Grill, Applebee's, Backyard Burger, Bob Evans, Buffalo Wild Wings, Burger King, Culver's, Don Sol Mexican, Freddy's, Hong Kong BBQ, IHOP, Jimmy John's, Krispy Kreme, Logan's Roadhouse, Mackie's Pizza, McAlister's Deli, McDonald's, O'Charley's, Panda Express, Panera Bread, Red Lobster, Sonic, Starbucks, Steak'n Shake, Taco Bell, Wok'n Roll Buffet Comfort Inn, Country Inn&Suites, Drury Inn, Fairfield Inn, Hampton Inn, Holiday Inn Express, Super 8 H, $Tree, AT&T, Buick/Chevrolet/GMC, Chrysler/Dodge/Jeep, Dillard's, GNC, Harley-Davidson, Home Depot, Honda, Menards, Mercedes, Nissan, Sam's Club/gas, Subaru, Target, Toyota, Verizon, Walmart/Subway
53	Main St, Marion, E Casey's/dsl DQ H, Marion Camping/RV Park, NAPA, W Motomart Cracker Barrel, HideOut Steaks, Huddle House Baymont Inn, Best Western, Quality Inn
47mm	**weigh sta both lanes**
45	IL 148, **1 mi** E Marathon/dsl Lake Tree Inn camping, vet, W dsl repair
44	I-24 E to Nashville
40	Goreville Rd, E camping, Ferne Clyffe SP, scenic overlook
36	Lick Creek Rd, W vineyards
32mm	**Trail of Tears Rest Area both lanes, full facilities, info, litter barrels, petwalk, playground, vending**
30	IL 146, Anna, Vienna, W H, auto/RV repair
25	US 51 N (from nb, exits left), to Carbondale
24	Dongola Rd, W BP/dsl $General
18	Ullin Rd, W Fast Stop/dsl EEE BBQ Best Value Inn Chevrolet, st police
8	Mounds Rd, to Mound City, E Huckleberry's Rest.
1	IL 3, to US 51, Cairo, E Quality Inn $General, camping, Mound City Nat Cem (4mi), W camping
0mm	Illinois/Missouri state line, Mississippi River

INTERSTATE 64

Exit #	Services
131.5mm	Illinois/Indiana state line, Wabash River
131mm	**Skeeter Mtn Welcome Ctr wb, full facilities, litter barrels, petwalk, vending**
130	IL 1, to Grayville, N Casey's (2mi), Road Ranger/dsl/scales/24hr Guadalajara Mexican, Subway Super 8, Windsor Oaks Inn/rest. Beall Woods SP (10mi)
124mm	Little Wabash River
117	Burnt Prairie, S CountryMark/dsl ChuckWagon Charlie's Café antiques
110	US 45, Mill Shoals
100	IL 242, to Wayne City, N Citgo/dsl

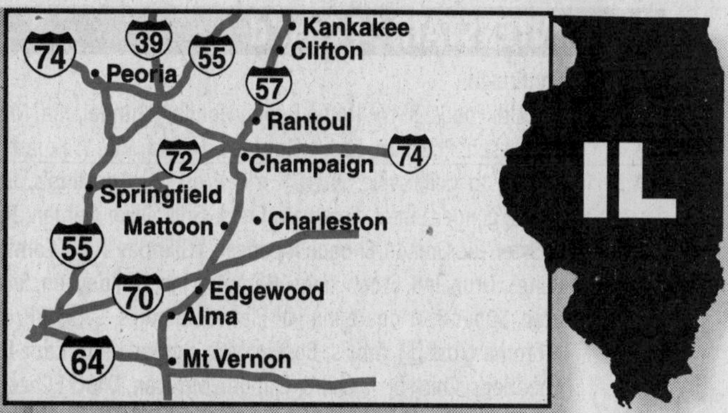

89	to Belle Rive, Bluford
86mm	**wb, full facilities, litter barrels, petwalk, vending**
82.5mm	**eb, full facilities, litter barrels, petwalk, vending**
80	IL 37, to Mt Vernon, **2 mi** N Hucks/dsl/24hr, Phillips 66/Circle K/Burger King/dsl $General
78	I-57, S to Memphis, N to Chicago
I-64 and I-57 run together 5 mi. See I-57, exits 95-94	
73	I-57, N to Chicago, S to Memphis
69	Woodlawn
61	US 51, to Centralia, Richview
50	IL 127, to Nashville, N to Carlyle Lake, S BP/dsl, Citgo/dsl/e85/rest., Little Nashville/Conoco/rest/dsl/scales/24hr McDonald's Best Western H
41	IL 177, Okawville, S Road Ranger/dsl/24hr Burger King, DQ, Subway Original Springs Motel, Super 8 $General, tires/repair, USPO
37mm	Kaskaskia River
34	to Albers, **3 mi** N Casey's
27	IL 161, New Baden, N Casey's/dsl, Shell/dsl A Fine Swine BBQ, China King, Good Ol Days Rest., McDonald's, Subway $General, S Loves/Hardee's/dsl/scales/24hr
25mm	**both lanes, full facilities, info, litter barrels, petwalk, vending**
23	IL 4, to Mascoutah, N Phillips 66/Huddle House/dsl/RV dump Domino's Best Western+, S
21	Rieder Rd
19b a	US 50, IL 158, N Motomart/dsl Subway Super 8 H, S to Scott AFB
18mm	**weigh sta eb**
16	to O'Fallon, Shiloh, N Bella Milano, Dewey's Pizza, Lion's Choice, Sonic, Sugarfire Smokehouse, The Egg & I Hampton Inn, Hilton Garden, TownePlace Suites CVS Drug, Harley-Davidson, H, URGENT CARE, S Motomart/dsl 54th St. Grille, Applebee's, Arby's, Aroy Thai, Buffalo Wild Wings, China King, Coldstone, Cracker Barrel, Freddy's, Golden Corral, Hop House Rest., Jersey Mike's, Jimmy John's, La Casa Mexicana, Little Caesar's, McAlister's Deli, McDonald's, Noodles&Co, Qdoba, St. Louis Bread Co., Starbucks, Subway, TX Roadhouse, White Castle Drury Inn, Holiday Inn Express $Tree, AT&T, Carmax, Dierbergs Foods, Dobb's Tire, GNC, Menard's, Michael's, Target, vet
14	O'Fallon, N Circle K/dsl, Motomart, Shell/dsl IHOP, Steak'n Shake, Subway Best Western, Extended Stay America, HomeTowne Suites, La Quinta, Sleep Inn Cadillac, Chevrolet, Ford, O'Reilly Parts, S Chevy's Mexican, Culver's, Hardee's, Jack-in-the-Box, KFC, McDonald's, O'Charley's, Panda Express, Papa Murphy's, Sake Grill, Starbucks, Syberg's Rest., Taco Bell Baymont Inn, Candlewood Suites, Quality Inn

O'FALLON

IL

INTERSTATE 64 Cont'd

COLLINSVILLE

14 Continued
Aldi Foods, BMW, Home Depot, Honda, Hyundai, Kia, Mazda, Nissan, Petsmart, Sam's Club/gas, Toyota, VW, Walmart

12 IL 159, to Collinsville, N Circle K/dsl Agostino's, Bob Evans, Ginger Buffet, Lotawata Creek Grill, Olive Garden, Red Lobster, Rio Grande, Shogun Japanese, TGIFriday's Comfort Suites, Drury Inn, EconoLodge, Hampton Inn, Holiday Inn, Sheraton, Super 8, Wingate Inn Fiat, Gordman's, S BP/dsl, Motomart/dsl Arby's, Boston Mkt, Burger King, Capt D's, Cheddar's, Chick-fil-A, Chili's, Chipotle Mexican, ChuckECheese, Domino's, Dunkin', Fazoli's, Firehouse Subs, Five Guys, Honeybaked Ham, Hooters, Imo's Pizza, Jimmy John's, Krispy Kreme, Little Caesar's, LJ Silver, Longhorn Steaks, McAlister's Deli, McDonald's, Popeye's, Red Robin, Ruby Tuesday, St. Louis Bread, Subway, Taco Bell, Wasabi, Wendy's, White Castle $General, $Tree, Aamco, Aldi Foods, AT&T, Barnes&Noble, Best Buy, BigLots, Burlington Coats, CarX, Dick's, Dillard's, Dobb's Tire, Firestone/auto, Fresh Thyme Mkt, Hobby Lobby, JC Penney, JoAnn Fabrics, Kohl's, Lowe's, Macy's, Marshall's, Meineke, Midas, NTB, Old Navy, O'Reilly Parts, PetCo, Ross, Russell Stover, Schnuck's Foods, TJ Maxx, Verizon, vet, Walgreens

9 IL 157, to Caseyville, N Gulf/Subway, Huck's/dsl Hardee's Western Inn, S Cracker Barrel, Domino's, DQ, McDonald's, Taco Bell Best Inn, Fairbridge Inn, Motel 6, Quality Inn

7 I-255, S to Memphis, N to Chicago

6 IL 111, Kingshighway, N BP, Crown Church's, Ray's Rest.

5 25th St

4 15th St, Baugh

3 I-55 N, I-70 E, IL 3 N, to St Clair Ave, to stockyards

2b a 3rd St, S gas

1 IL 3 S, 13th St, E St Louis, N Casino Queen

0mm Illinois/Missouri state line, Mississippi River

IL

INTERSTATE 70

Exit #	Services
156mm	Illinois/Indiana state line
154	US 40 W
151mm	**weigh sta wb**
149mm	**wb, full facilities, info, litter barrels, petwalk, , , vending**
147	IL 1, Marshall, N Pilot/Road Ranger/Church's/dsl/scales/24hr Crossroads Rest., S Casey's (1mi), DQ, Marathon/Arby's/dsl, Phillips 66/dsl Burger King, Los Tres Caminos, McDonald's, Pizza Hut, Sam's Steaks, Subway, Wendy's Lincoln Suites, Relax Inn, Super 8 antiques, Ford, Lincoln Trail SP, Walmart
136	to Martinsville, S Phillips 66/dsl/24hr
134.5mm	N Fork Embarras River
129	IL 49, Casey, N KOA (seasonal), RV service, S Casey's, DQ, Marathon/Circle K/dsl, Phillips 66/dsl Hacienda Mexican, McDonald's, Pizza Hut, Subway Days Inn $General, IGA Foods
119	IL 130, Greenup, S Casey's/dsl, Loves/Chester's/IHOP/dsl/scales/24hr, Phillips 66/dsl Backyard BBQ, DQ, Subway Budget Host, Greenup Motel $General, hist sites, NAPA
105	Montrose, N Spring Creek Camping (1mi), S BP/dsl, Phillips/dsl Fairview Inn
98	I-57, N to Chicago.

VANDALIA

I-70 and I-57 run together 6 mi. See I-57, 159-162.

92	I-57, S to Mt Vernon
91mm	Little Wabash River
87mm	**both lanes, full facilities, info, litter barrels, petwalk, , playground, RV dump, vending**
82	IL 128, Altamont, N Casey's/dsl, Phillips 66/Subw dsl/24hr Dairy Bar, Joe's Pizza/pasta, McDonald's tamont Motel, Cobblestone Inn $General, city p S Relax Inn
76	US 40, St Elmo, N Casey's Waldorf Motel Tim line Camping (2mi)
71mm	**weigh sta eb**
68	US 40, Brownstown, N Okaw Valley Kamping, S t repair
63.5mm	Kaskaskia River
63	US 51, Vandalia, N Chuck Wagon Cafe, LJ Silver Value Inn, S Casey's, Phillips 66, Phillips 66/Bu King/24hr Arby's, China Gate, DQ, McDonald's, Pizza Rancho Nuevo Mexican, Sonic, Subway, Wendy's Econ Inn, Jay's Inn , Aldi Foods, city park, County Mkt Fo hist site
61	US 40, Vandalia, N Fast Stop/Denny's/dsl/scales/2 S Murphy USA/dsl China King, Embers Pizza, Hu House, KFC/Taco Bell, Ponderosa Holiday Inn Express, mada $Tree, AT&T, AutoZone, Verizon, Walmart
52	US 40, Mulberry Grove, N Casey's/dsl Timber Camp-In (2mi), S Cedar Brook Camping (1mi)
45	IL 127, Greenville, N Loves/Subway/dsl/scales/2 Shell/dsl Chang's Buffet, Domino's, Huddle House, KFC/ Bell, Los Amigos, Lu-Bob's Rest., McDonald's EconoLo Red Carpet Inn, Super 8 , S Comfort Inn An can Farm Heritage Museum, RV Service, to Carlyle Lake
41	US 40 E, to Greenville
36	US 40 E, Pocahontas, S BP/dsl, Phillips 66/dsl derburk's Grill Lighthouse Lodge, Powhatan Motel/ Tahoe Motel truck/tire repair
30	US 40, IL 143, to Highland, S Shell/dsl/wifi Springs Café , Tomahawk RV Park (7mi)
26.5mm	**Silver Lake both lanes, full facilities, litter barrels, walk, , , vending**
24	IL 143, Marine, 4 mi S
21	IL 4, Troy
15b a	I-55, N to Chicago, S to St Louis, I-270 W to Kansas City.

I-70 and I-55 run together 18 mi. See I-55, exits 1-18.

19mm	motorist callboxes begin wb every 1/2mile
0mm	Illinois/Missouri state line, Mississippi River

INTERSTATE 72

URBANA

Exit #	Services
183mm	**I-72 begins/ends, E** Gas Depot, Thornton's/dsl Ar Burger King, Dunkin', Garcia's Pizza, Jets Pizza, Jimmy Jo KFC, La Bamba Mexican, McDonald's, Monical's Pizza, Orig Pancakes, Papa John's, Pizza Hut, Sonic, Subway, Taco Bel Roadhouse $General, Advance Parts, AutoZone, Big CVS Drug, O'Reilly Parts, Schnuck's Foods/e85, ValuCheck Walgreens
182b a	I-57, N to Chicago, S to Memphis, to I-74
176	IL 47, to Mahomet
172	IL 10, Lodge, Seymour
169	White Heath Rd

INTERSTATE 72 Cont'd

Exit #	Services
166	IL 105 W, Market St, **N** [other] [H], Ford, **S** [gas] Circle K/dsl [food] Red Wheel Rest. [lodging] Best Western, Foster Inn [other] city park, railway museum
165mm	Sangamon River
164	Bridge St, **1 mi S** [gas] Circle K/dsl [food] DQ, Golden Kitchen, Hardee's, McDonald's, Monical's Pizza, Pizza Hut, Subway [other] [H], $General, Buick/Chevrolet, Chrysler/Dodge/Jeep, USPO, vet
156	IL 48, to Weldon, Cisco, **N** [other] Friends Creek Camping (may-oct) (3mi)
153mm	**[rest stop] both lanes, full [handicapped] facilities, litter barrels, petwalk, [phone], [picnic], vending**
152mm	Friends Creek
150	Argenta
144	IL 48, Oreana, **S** [gas] Pilot/McDonald's/Subway/dsl/scales/24hr [lodging] Sleep Inn [other] [H], Chrysler/Dodge/Jeep, Honda, Hyundai, Pressley RV Ctr (3mi)
141b a	US 51, Decatur, **N** [gas] Casey's/dsl, Circle K [food] Applebee's, Buffalo Wild Wings, Burger Theory, Cheddar's, Cracker Barrel, McDonald's, Panda Express, Penn Sta Subs, Pizza Hut, Red Lobster, Steak'n Shake, Subway, Taco Bell, TX Roadhouse [lodging] Baymont Inn, Country Inn&Suites, EconoLodge, Fairfield Inn, Hampton Inn, Homewood Suites, Quality Inn, Ramada Ltd, Residence Inn [other] $Tree, AT&T, Best Buy, Buick/Cadillac/GMC, GNC, Harley-Davidson, Hobby Lobby, Kohl's, Lowe's, Menards, Petsmart, Ross, Staples, TJ Maxx, Verizon, Von Maur, **S** [food] Arby's, Burger King, El Rodeo Mexican, Fuji Japanese, La Fondita, Monical's Pizza, Olive Garden, Panera Bread, Papa Murphy's, Starbucks [other] [H], Jo-Ann Fabrics, Sam's Club, Target, Verizon, Walgreens, Walmart/Subway
138	IL 121, Decatur, **S** [gas] Loves/Hardee's/dsl/scales24hr [other] [H]
133b a	US 36 E, US 51, Decatur, **S** [gas] Shell/Subway/dsl [lodging] Best Value Inn, Decatur Hotel/rest.
128	Niantic
122	to Mt Auburn, Illiopolis, **N** [gas] FastStop/dsl [other] $General
114	Buffalo, Mechanicsburg, **2 mi S** [gas] Gas Depot/dsl [other] USPO
108	Riverton, Dawson
107mm	Sangamon River
104	Camp Butler, **2 mi N** [other] golf
103b a	I-55, IL 97.

I-72 and I-55 run together 6 mi. See I-55, exits 92-98.

Exit #	Services
97b a	6th St, I-55 S, Loop 55 N (from eb), 6th St, I-55 S, **N** [gas] Road Ranger [food] Golden Corral, McDonald's, Pizza Ranch [lodging] Comfort Inn, La Quinta, Rte 66 [other] Aldi Foods, Lincoln, Mazda, Walmart
96	MacArthur Blvd, **N** [gas] Tesla EVC [food] Engrained Brewing Co [lodging] Springhill Suites [other] Scheels
93	IL 4, Springfield, **N** [gas] Hucks, Thorntons/dsl [food] Applebee's, Arby's, Bakers Square, Burger King, Casa Real, Chick-fil-A, Chili's, Chipotle Mexican, Cooper's Hawk Rest., Dew's Chili, Five Guys, Indigo, Jersey Mike's, Jimmy John's, Kiku Japanese, Longhorn Steaks, Los Rancheros Mexican, McDonald's, Noodles&Co, Olive Garden, Outback Steaks, Panda Express, Panera Bread, Pasta House, Penn Sta Subs, Popeye's, Qdoba, Red Robin, Sonic, Starbucks, Subway, Taco Bell, TGIFriday's, TX Roadhouse, Wendy's [lodging] Courtyard, Fairfield Inn, Quality Inn, Sleep Inn [other] Aldi Foods, AT&T, Barnes&Noble, Best Buy, Big Lots, County Mkt Foods, Dick's, Discount Tire, Fannie May, Gordman's, Hobby Lobby, Jo-Ann Fabrics, Kohl's, Lowe's, Macy's, Marshall's, Michael's, Office Depot, Old Navy, PetCo, Petsmart, Ross, Sam's Club/gas, Target, TJ Maxx, Verizon, Walgreens, Walmart, **S** [gas] Meijer/dsl/e85

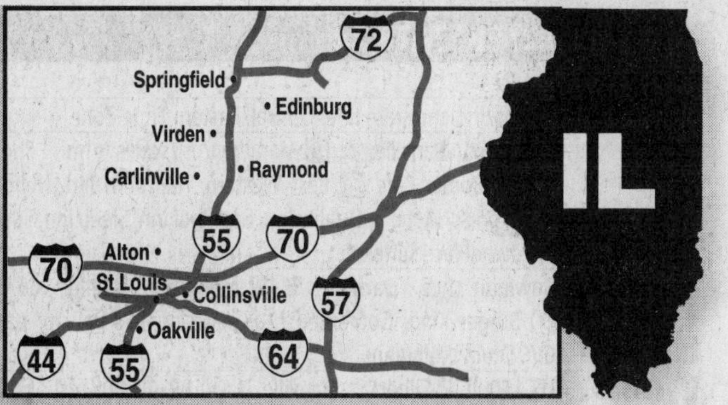

Exit #	Services
93	Continued [food] Bob Evans, Monical's Pizza, Steak'n Shake [lodging] Hampton Inn, Staybridge Suites [other] Cadillac, CarMax, Chevrolet, Chrysler/Jeep, Fiat, Ford, Honda, Menards
91	Wabash Ave, to Springfield, **N** [gas] Qik-n- EZ/dsl [food] Bella Milano, Buffalo Wild Wings, Culver's, Freddy's, IHOP, McDonald's, Mimosa Thai, Papa Frank's Italian [other] Audi/VW, Dodge/Ram, Kia/Subaru, Nissan, Toyota, **S** [other] Colmans RV Ctr
82	New Berlin, **S** [gas] Pilot/Road Ranger/Subway/dsl [other] $General
76	IL 123, to Ashland, Alexander
68	to IL 104, to Jacksonville, **2 mi N** [gas] Casey's/dsl, Circle K [other] [H]
64	US 67, to Jacksonville, **2 mi N** [gas] Circle K/dsl, FastStop/dsl, Loves/IHOP/dsl/scales/24hr, Qik-n-EZ/Subway/dsl [food] KFC, Little Caesar's, McDonald's [lodging] Baymont Inn, Comfort Inn, Holiday Inn Express, Sleep Inn [other] [H], $General, CVS Drug, Family$, Hopper RV Ctr, Walgreens
60	to US 67 N, to Jacksonville, **6 mi N on IL 104** [other] [H], food, gas, lodging
52	to IL 106, Winchester, **N** [other] golf, **2 mi S** food, gas, lodging
46	IL 100, to Bluffs
42mm	Illinois River
35	US 54, IL 107, to Pittsfield, Griggsville, **4 mi N** food, gas, lodging, **S** [other] [H], Jellystone Camping (6mi), st police
31	to Pittsfield, New Salem, **5 mi S** [other] [H], Jellystone Camping, food, gas, lodging
20	IL 106, Barry, **S** [gas] FastStop/dsl/24hr, Shell/dsl [food] Wendy's [lodging] Ice House Inn [other] $General
10	IL 96, to Payson, Hull
4a	I-172, N to Quincy
1	IL 106, to Hull
0mm	Illinois/Missouri state line, Mississippi River.

Exits 157 & 156 are in Missouri.

Exit #	Services
157	to Hannibal, MO 179, **S** [gas] Ayerco, BP, Pickadilly, Shell/dsl [food] Mark Twain Dinette, Subway [lodging] Best Way Inn, Best Western, Country Hearth Inn, Hotel Mark Twain [other] auto repair, visitor info
156	US 61, New London, Palmyra. **I-72 begins/ends in Hannibal, MO on US 61. N** [gas] BP, Casey's/dsl, Murphy USA/dsl [food] Arby's, Burger King, Country Kitchen, Domino's, Gabriella's Mexican, LJ Silver, McDonald's, Mi Mexico, Pizza Hut, Royal Garden, Rustic Oak Grill, Saints Ave Steaks, Sonic, Subway, Taco Bell [other] $General, $Tree, Aldi Foods, BigLots, Ford, JC Penney, Lowe's, Walmart, **0-2 mi S** [gas] Ayerco, Shell/dsl [food] Cassano's Subs, China King, DQ, Gran Rio Mexican, Hardee's, Jimmy John's, KFC, Little Caesar's, Logue's Rest, Wendy's [lodging] Comfort Inn, Days Inn, Economy Inn, Hannibal Inn, Motel 6, Super 8 [other] $General, AT&T, AutoZone, Buick/Chevrolet, Chrysler/Dodge/Jeep, County Mkt Foods, CVS Drug, O'Reilly Parts, Walgreens

INTERSTATE 74

DANVILLE

Exit #	Services
221mm	Illinois/Indiana state line, Central/Eastern Time Zone
220	Lynch Rd, Danville, N Marathon/dsl/scales (1mi), Shell/dsl Border Cafe Best Western, Hampton Inn, Holiday Inn Express, Motel 6, Quality Inn, Red Roof Inn, Sleep Inn, Super 8, TownePlace Suites
216	Bowman Ave, Danville, N Mobil/dsl, Phillips 66/dsl Burger King, Godfather's, KFC, McDonald's city park, CVS Drug, Walgreens
215b a	US 150, IL 1, Gilbert St, Danville, N BP/Circle K/dsl Arby's, El Toro, La Potosina, LJ Silver, McDonald's, Pizza Hut, Steak'n Shake, Subway, Taco Bell Best Western, Days Inn H, Aldi Foods, BigLots, S Casey's/dsl, Marathon/Circle K/dsl, Marathon/dsl Burger King, Green Jade Chinese, Mike's Grill, Monical's Pizza, Rich's Rest. $General, $Tree, AutoZone, Big R, Buick/Chevrolet/GMC, County Mkt, Family$, Forest Glen Preserve Camping (11mi), Toyota
214	G St, Tilton
210	US 150, MLK Dr, 2 mi N Marathon Little Nugget Steaks H, to Kickapoo SP
206	Oakwood, N Loves/Hardee's/dsl/scales/24hr, S Casey's (1mi), Phillips 66/Subway/dsl/scales, Pilot/PJ Fresh/dsl/scales/24hr McDonald's $General
200	IL 49 N, to Rankin
197	IL 49 S, Ogden, S Phillips 66/Godfather's/dsl Rich's Rest. city park
192	St Joseph, S Casey's, Shell/dsl DQ, Monical's Pizza, Subway antiques
185	IL 130, University Ave
184	US 45, Cunningham Ave, Urbana, N F&F Hyundai, Kia, Mazda, Toyota, VW, S Marathon/Circle K/Subway/dsl, Shell/dsl Arby's, Cracker Barrel, Hickory River BBQ, McDonald's, Steak'n Shake, Toro Loco, Wendy's Eastland Suites, Motel 6 $General, auto repair, vet
183	Lincoln Ave, Urbana, S Circle K/dsl, Marathon/Circle K/dsl Urbana Garden Rest. Comfort Suites, Holiday Inn Express, Knights Inn, Ramada Inn, Sleep Inn, Wyndham Garden H, Harley-Davidson, to U of IL
182	Neil St (same as 181), Champaign, N Alexander's Steaks, Bob Evans, Buca Italian, Food Court, McDonald's, Old Chicago, Olive Garden, Panera Bread, Taco Bell, TGIFriday's, Za's Italian Baymont Inn, La Quinta, Quality Inn, Red Roof Inn, Super 8 Barnes&Noble, Bergner's, Cadillac/Chevrolet, Chrysler/Dodge/Jeep, Dick's, Field&Stream, Gordman's, Hobby Lobby, Kohl's, Macy's, Mercedes/Volvo, Office Depot, TJ Maxx, Tuesday Morning, Verizon, S Mobil/Circle K
181	Prospect Ave (same as 182), Champaign, N Murphy USA/dsl Applebee's, Best Wok, Blaze Pizza, Buffalo Wild Wings, Burger King, Chili's, Chipotle, Culver's, Denny's, Denny's, Fazoli's, Firehouse Subs, Five Guys, HuHot Mongolian, Longhorn Steaks, O'Charley's, Oishi Asian, Outback Steaks, Panda Express, Penn Sta Subs, Portillo's, Red Lobster, Ruby Tuesday, Starbucks, Steak'n Shake, Subway, Super Niro's Gyros, Super Niro's Gyros, Wendy's Candlewood Suites, Country Inn&Suites, Courtyard, Drury Inn, Extended Stay America, Fairfield Inn, Quality Inn, Residence Inn, Residence Inn, Wingate Inn, Woodspring Suites $Tree, Advance Parts, Aldi Foods, AT&T, Best Buy, Ford/Lincoln, Ford/Lincoln, Jo-Ann, Jo-Ann, Lowe's, Meijer/dsl, Menards, Michael's, Nissan, Nissan, Petsmart,

CHAMPAIGN

IL

BLOOMINGTON

Exit #	Services
181	Continued Sam's Club/gas, Staples, Target, Tires+, Verizon, Walmart/way, S Marathon/Circle K, Mobil/Jimmy John's, Phillips dsl, Shell/dsl Arby's, Dos Reales Mexican, Dunkin', LJ Si McDonald's, Popeye's Best Value Inn, Days Inn $eral, CarX, Home Depot, NAPA, Tire Barn, Walgreens
179b a	I-57, N to Chicago, S to Memphis
174	Lake of the Woods Rd, Prairieview Rd, N BP, Casey's, M Circle K/dsl $General, auto repair, Lake of the Woods SP Cup RV Park, S Marathon/Subway/dsl McDonald'
172	IL 47, Mahomet, N R&S RV Sales, S Exxon/Domir dsl, Mobil/dsl Arby's, Azteca, DQ, El Toro Mexican, House Rest., Los Zerapes, Monical's Pizza, Peking House, way, The Wok Heritage Inn Ace Hardware, CVS D IGA Foods, NAPA, Walgreens
166	Mansfield, S Phillips 66/dsl Mansfield Gen. St Rest.
159	IL 54, Farmer City, S Casey's/dsl, Huck's/Godfather's Imo's Cafe, Subway Budget Motel, Days Inn $eral, NAPA, to Clinton Lake RA, USPO
156mm	**both lanes, full facilities, litter larrels, petwalk, playground, vending**
152	US 136, to Heyworth
149	Le Roy, N Casey's/dsl, Loves/Arby's/dsl/scales/ Jack's Cafe, McDonald's, Roma Pizza, Subway day Inn Express $General, IGA Foods, NAPA, to Mor View SP, TrueValue, S Shell/Woody's Rest./dsl/scales/ Days Inn camping, Clinton Lake
142	Downs, N Mobil/Pizza/Subs/dsl/24hr USPO
135	US 51, Bloomington, N Huck's/dsl, Mobil/Circle K McDonald's, Pizza Hut $General, S BP/dsl
134b[157]	Veterans Pkwy, to Bloomington, N H, to
134a	I-55, N to Chicago, S to St Louis, I-74 E
I-74 and I-55 run together 6 mi. See I-55, exits 157b-160b a.	
127[163]	I-55, N to Chicago, S to St Louis, I-74 W to Peoria
125	US 150, to Bloomington, Mitsubishi Motorway
123mm	**weigh sta wb**
122mm	**weigh sta eb**
120	Carlock, N BP/dsl/repair Carlock Rest., S K Komfort Camping (Apr-Oct)
114.5mm	**both lanes, full facilities, litter barrels, petwalk, vending**
113.5mm	Mackinaw River
112	IL 117, Goodfield, N Shell/Subway/dsl Busy Co Rest. Eureka Coll, Jellystone Camping (1mi), Reagan H to Timberline RA, USPO
102b a	Morton, N Mobil/Arby's/dsl/scales/24hr Baskin ins/Dunkin', Burger King, Cracker Barrel, Culver's, Ste Shake, Taco Bell Baymont Inn, Best Value Inn, Days Holiday Inn Express, Park Inn, Quality Inn Chrysler/Do Jeep, Farm&Fleet, Freightliner, Walmart/Subway, S Circle K, Casey's/dsl, Marathon/Circle K, Subway C Dragon, Domino's, Great Harvest Bread Co, Jimmy John's Fiesta, Lin's Buffet, McDonald's, Monical's Pizza, Pizza Hut, za Ranch $Tree, Buick/GMC, CVS Drug, Ford, Kroger O'Reilly Parts, Verizon
101	I-155 S, to Lincoln
99	I-474 W,
98	Pinecrest Dr
96	95c (from eb), US 150, IL 8, E Washington St, E Pe N Fast Stop/dsl Subway, Super Gyros Super 8 O'Reilly Parts

INTERSTATE 74 Cont'd

Exit #	Services
95b	(from eb) IL 116, to Metamora
95a	N Main St, Peoria, N Shell/dsl Burger King Hampton Inn, Paradice Hotel/Casino, S BP/Circle K A&W/LJ Silver, Bob Evans, Chick-fil-A, Chipotle Mexican, Firehouse Pizza, Hardee's, IHOP, Jason's Deli, Jersey Mike's, Jimmy John's, Johnny's Italian Steaks, McDonald's, Moe's SW, Noodles&Co, Panda Express, Papa Murphy's, Pizza Hut, Popeye's, Potbelly, Red Robin, Subway, Taco Bell, Tequilas Grill, Wendy's Best Value Inn, Best Western+, Fairfield Inn, Holiday Inn $Tree, Advance Parts, Aldi Foods, AT&T, Costco/gas, CVS Drug, GNC, Goodyear/auto, Gordman's, Kohl's, Kroger, Ross, Target, Verizon, Walgreens
94	IL 40, RiverFront Dr, S Hucks/Godfather's/dsl Arby's, Buffalo Wild Wings, Chili's, Culver's, Granite City Grill, Logan's Roadhouse, Lorena's Mexican, Panera Bread, Papa John's, Qdoba Mexican, Shogun, Slim Chickens, Steak'n Shake, TX Roadhouse, Uncle Buck's Grill Embassy Suites, Holiday Inn Express Bass Pro Shop, Lowe's, PetsMart, Verizon, Walmart/Subway
93.5mm	Illinois River
93b	US 24, IL 29, Peoria, N BP, S Mark Twain Hotel civic ctr
93a	Jefferson St, Peoria, N BP, S Two 25 Grill Mark Twain Hotel, Marriott, Sheraton to civic ctr
92b	Glendale Ave, Peoria, S H, downtown
92a	IL 40 N, Knoxville Ave, Peoria, S Sheraton H
91	University St, Peoria
90	Gale Ave, Peoria, S Marathon to Bradley U, $General
89	US 150, War Memorial Dr, Peoria, N on War Memorial BP/Circle K, Marathon/dsl Burger King, Dunkin', Golden Corral, IHOP, McDonald's, Papa Murphy's, Perkins, Popeye's, Steak'n Shake, Wendy's Baymont Inn, Comfort Suites, Courtyard, EconoLodge, Extended Stay America, Quality Inn, Red Roof Inn, Residence Inn, Super 8 Aldi Foods, AT&T, AutoZone, Barnes&Noble, Best Buy, Chevrolet/Cadillac, Hobby Lobby, Lowe's, Midas, NAPA, PetsMart, Target, Tires+, U-Haul, vet, Walgreens, Walmart/Subway
88	to US 150, War Memorial Dr, N Shell Arby's, Avanti's Rest., Baskin Robins/Dunkin', Biaggi's, Chick-fil-A, Chipotle, ChuckECheese, Firehouse Subs, Five Guys, Panda Express, Panera Bread, Portillo's, Red Lobster, Sonic Motel 6, SpringHill Suites $Tree, JC Penney, Michael's, Ross, Verizon, Walgreens
87b a	I-474 E, IL 6, N to Chillicothe, S
82	Edwards Rd, Kickapoo, N Mobil/dsl/service, Shell/Subway/dsl Jubilee Café to Jubilee Coll SP, S USPO, Wildlife Prairie SP
75	Brimfield, Oak Hill, N Casey's/dsl
71	to IL 78, to Canton, Elmwood
62mm	**both lanes, full facilities, litter barrels, petwalk, vending**
61.5mm	Spoon River
54	US 150, IL 97, Lewistown, N TravL Park Camping (1mi), S Mobil/dsl (2mi) Alfano's Pizza (2mi)
51	Knoxville, S BP/dsl, Love's/Subway/Chester's/dsl/scales/24hr, Phillips 66/Charley's Subs/dsl/scales Hardee's, McDonald's Best Value Inn
48b a	E Galesburg, Galesburg, N Best Western Harley-Davidson, S BP/Circle K/dsl, HyVee/dsl, Phillps 66/Beck's/dsl DQ, Hardee's, Jalisco Mexican, KFC, Marco's Pizza, McDonald's, Pizza Hut, Subway, Taco Bell Baymont Inn, Holiday Inn Express Family$, HyVee Foods, Lincoln-Douglas Debates, Sav-A-Lot Foods, to Sandburg Birthplace, Walgreens

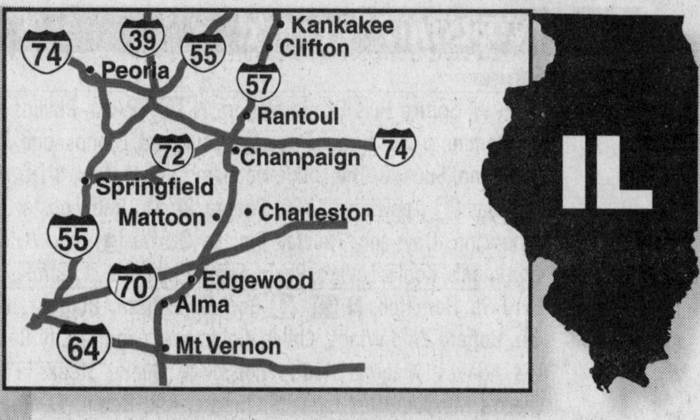

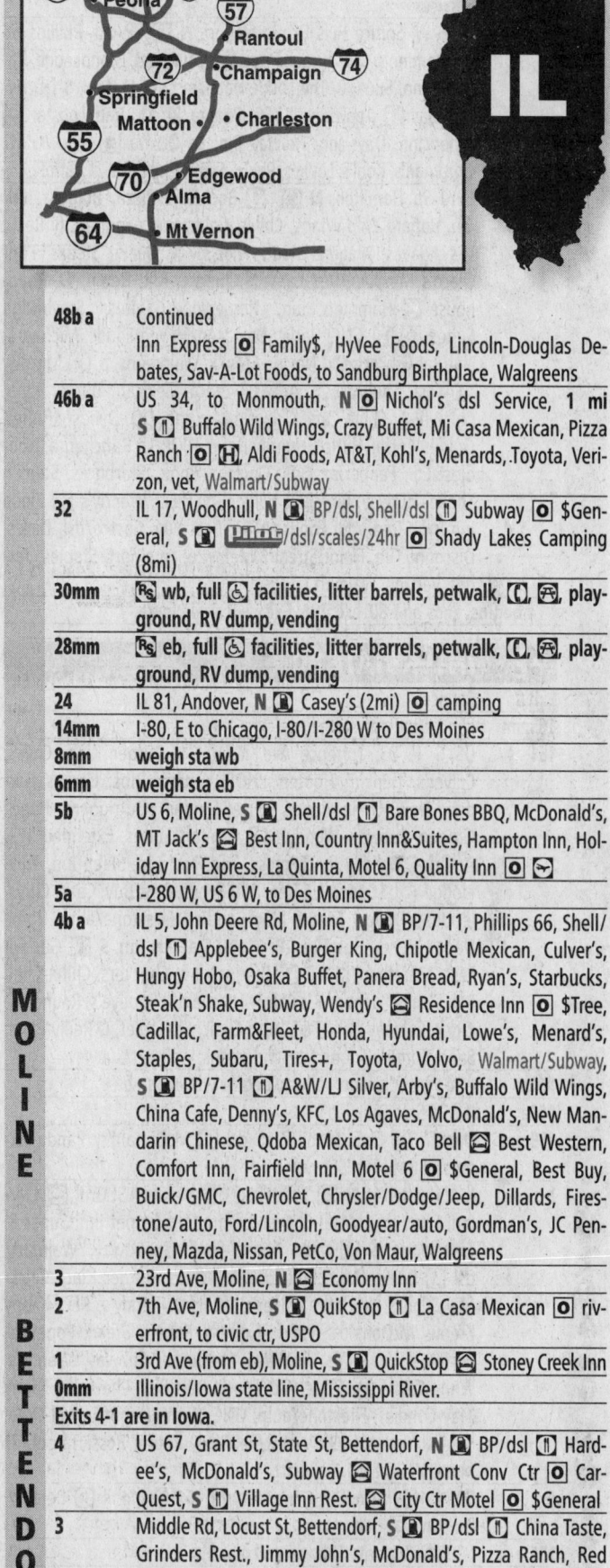

Exit #	Services
48b a	Continued
46b a	US 34, to Monmouth, N Nichol's dsl Service, 1 mi S Buffalo Wild Wings, Crazy Buffet, Mi Casa Mexican, Pizza Ranch H, Aldi Foods, AT&T, Kohl's, Menards, Toyota, Verizon, vet, Walmart/Subway
32	IL 17, Woodhull, N BP/dsl, Shell/dsl Subway $General, S Pilot/dsl/scales/24hr Shady Lakes Camping (8mi)
30mm	**wb, full facilities, litter barrels, petwalk, playground, RV dump, vending**
28mm	**eb, full facilities, litter barrels, petwalk, playground, RV dump, vending**
24	IL 81, Andover, N Casey's (2mi) camping
14mm	I-80, E to Chicago, I-80/I-280 W to Des Moines
8mm	**weigh sta wb**
6mm	**weigh sta eb**
5b	US 6, Moline, S Shell/dsl Bare Bones BBQ, McDonald's, MT Jack's Best Inn, Country Inn&Suites, Hampton Inn, Holiday Inn Express, La Quinta, Motel 6, Quality Inn
5a	I-280 W, US 6 W, to Des Moines
4b a	IL 5, John Deere Rd, Moline, N BP/7-11, Phillips 66, Shell/dsl Applebee's, Burger King, Chipotle Mexican, Culver's, Hungy Hobo, Osaka Buffet, Panera Bread, Ryan's, Starbucks, Steak'n Shake, Subway, Wendy's Residence Inn $Tree, Cadillac, Farm&Fleet, Honda, Hyundai, Lowe's, Menard's, Staples, Subaru, Tires+, Toyota, Volvo, Walmart/Subway, S BP/7-11 A&W/LJ Silver, Arby's, Buffalo Wild Wings, China Cafe, Denny's, KFC, Los Agaves, McDonald's, New Mandarin Chinese, Qdoba Mexican, Taco Bell Best Western, Comfort Inn, Fairfield Inn, Motel 6 $General, Best Buy, Buick/GMC, Chevrolet, Chrysler/Dodge/Jeep, Dillards, Firestone/auto, Ford/Lincoln, Goodyear/auto, Gordman's, JC Penney, Mazda, Nissan, PetCo, Von Maur, Walgreens
3	23rd Ave, Moline, N Economy Inn
2	7th Ave, Moline, S QuikStop La Casa Mexican riverfront, to civic ctr, USPO
1	3rd Ave (from eb), Moline, S QuickStop Stoney Creek Inn
0mm	Illinois/Iowa state line, Mississippi River.
Exits 4-1 are in Iowa.	
4	US 67, Grant St, State St, Bettendorf, N BP/dsl Hardee's, McDonald's, Subway Waterfront Conv Ctr Car-Quest, S Village Inn Rest. City Ctr Motel $General
3	Middle Rd, Locust St, Bettendorf, S BP/dsl China Taste, Grinders Rest., Jimmy John's, McDonald's, Pizza Ranch, Red Ginger Asian, Starbucks, Subway Hilton Garden H, AT&T, Burlington Coats, Hobby Lobby, Home Depot, Marshall's, Schuck's Foods, Verizon, Walgreens

MOLINE

BETTENDORF

INTERSTATE 74 Cont'd

Exit #	Services
2	US 6 W, Spruce Hills Dr, Bettendorf, N BP/dsl, Phillips 66 Domino's, Old Chicago Pizza Courtyard, EconoLodge, Ramada Inn, Super 8, The Lodge Hotel/rest. U-Haul, S Hy-vee Gas Applebee's, KFC, Panera Bread, Red Lobster AmericInn, Days Inn, Holiday Inn, La Quinta Buick/GMC, Gordman's, Kohl's, Lowe's, PetCo, Sam's Club/gas, st patrol
1	53rd St, Hamilton, N Bad Boyz Pizza, Biaggi's Italian, Buffalo Wild Wings, Chili's, Coldstone, Granite City Rest., Los Agaves, Maggie Moo's, Moe's SW, Osaka Steaks, Panchero's Mexican, Red Lantern Chinese, Red Robin, TX Roadhouse Hampton Inn, Homewood Suites, Staybridge Suites H, GNC, Harley-Davidson, HyVee Foods, Michael's, Natural Grocers, Old Navy, TJ Maxx, Walgreens, S Murphy USA/dsl, Shell/dsl Arby's, Azteca Mexican, Burger King, Chick-fil-A, China Cafe, Chipotle Mexican, DQ, Dynasty Buffet, Golden Corral, HuHot, Hungry Hobo, IHOP, La Rancherita, Noodles&Co., PepperJax Grill, Quiznos, Sonic, Starbucks, Steak'n Shake, Subway, Taco Bell, Village Inn Rest., Wendy's Sleep Inn $Tree, Aldi Foods, AT&T, Best Buy, Costco/dsl, Dick's, Discount Tire, Field&Stream, Meineke, PetsMart, Staples, Target, Verizon, Walmart

I-74 begins/ends on I-80, exit 298. Exits 1-4 are in Iowa.

INTERSTATE 80

CHICAGO AREA

Exit #	Services
163mm	Illinois/Indiana state line
161	US 6, IL 83, Torrence Ave, N Burger King, Chili's, Culver's, Dunkin', Hooters, IHOP, Kenny's Ribs, Liang's Garden, New China Buffet, Olive Garden, Outriggers, Ranch Grande, Subway, Wendy's Comfort Suites, Extended Stay America, Holiday Inn Express, Red Roof Inn, Sleep Inn, Travelodge $General, $Tree, Aldi Foods, Best Buy, CarX, Chrysler/Jeep/Dodge, Fannie May Candies, Firestone/auto, Home Depot, Honda, JustTires, PepBoys, Starway Inn, S Gas For Less, Marathon, Mobil Burger King, Checkers, China Chef, DQ, Dunkin', Johnny K's Cafe, McDonald's, Popeye's, Round the Clock, Subway AT&T, Auto Clinic, Chevrolet, O'Reilly Parts, Saab, SunRise Foods, vet, Walgreens, Walmart/Subway
160b	I-94 W, to Chicago, **tollway begins wb, ends eb**
160a	IL 394 S, to Danville
159mm	Oasis, EVC, Mobil/7-11/dsl McDonald's, Panda Express, Starbucks, Subway
2	IL 1, Halsted St, N Quick Fuel Maxwell St Grill Clarion, Days Inn, Motel 6, Quality Inn, Red Carpet Inn, Super 8, Travelodge, S Delta Sonic, Shell, Speedway, Walmart/dsl Boston Mkt, Buffalo Wild Wings, Burger King, Chick-fil-A, Chili's, Chipotle, Culver's, Dunkin', Freddy's, KFC, Krispy Kreme, McDonald's, Panda Express, Panera Bread, Popeye's, Portillo's Hot Dogs, Potbelly, Starbucks, Subway, Wendy's, White Castle $Tree, Aldi Foods, Best Buy, Chevrolet, Fanny May Candies, Firestone/auto, GNC, Home Depot, Jewel-Osco, Kohl's, Menards, Old Navy, PepBoys, PetCo, Ross, Target, TJ Maxx, Walgreens, Walmart
4	Dixie Hwy (from eb, no return), S Mobil Belagio, Dunkin' golf
155	I-294 N, Tri-State Tollway, **toll plaza**
154	Kedzie Ave (from eb, no return), N Speedway, S H
151b a	I-57 (exits left from both directions), N to Chicago, S to Memphis
148b a	IL 43, Harlem Ave, N Speedway/dsl Buffalo Wings, Burger King, Cracker Barrel, Culver's, Dunkin', Ham of Japan, Joy Yee Asian, Pop's Italian Beef, Side Street Tav Tin Fish Grill, Wendy's Comfort Suites, Fairfield Inn, Ha ton Inn, Holiday Inn, La Quinta, Sleep Inn, Wingate Inn, Wo spring Suites AT&T, Tinley Park Convention Center, Veri S EVC Arby's, Panera Bread, Subway, Taco Bell, TG day's ampitheater, Best Buy, CarMax, Dick's, GNC, Ko Michael's, Old Navy, PetsMart, Ross, SuperTarget, TJ Maxx
147.5mm	**weigh sta wb**
145b a	US 45, 96th Ave, N Arby's, Arrenello's Pizza, Baskin-R bins/Dunkin', Tokyo Steaks, TX Roadhouse Country n&Suites, Hilton Garden Harley-Davidson, vet, **0-2** S BP, Shell/Circle K/dsl/24hr Beggar's Pizza, Chipo Denny's, Doc's Smokehouse, Domino's, DQ, Legends, Min Ribs, Mobil, Rising Sun Chinese, Starbucks, Stoney Pt Grill, S way, Wendy's, White Castle Super 8 Firestone/a repair, vet
143mm	**weigh sta eb**
140	SW Hwy, **I-355 N Tollway**, US 6 S, N H
137	US 30, New Lenox, N Williamson's Rest., S Shell/Ci K/dsl, Speedway/dsl Al's Hotdogs, Beggar's Pizza, Buf Wild Wings, Burger King, Keys's Chophouse, KFC, McDona Paisano's Pizza, Subway, Taco Bell Ace Hardware, Go year/auto, Jewel-Osco/dsl, Walgreens
134	Briggs St, N Speedway, S Mobil/dsl, Shell/dsl M tin Camping
133	Richards St
132b a	US 52, IL 53, Chicago St, N BP, Shell Dunkin', Shark Chicken
131.5mm	Des Plaines River
131	US 6, Meadow Ave, N to Riverboat Casino
130b a	IL 7, Larkin Ave, N Delta Sonic/dsl, Marathon/24hr, bil/CircleK/dsl, Shell, Speedway Baskin-Robbins/Dun Bob Evans, Boston Mkt, Burger King, Checkers, Culver's, JJ Fish&Chicken, KFC, Little Caesar's, McDonald's, Subw Taco Bell, Wendy's, White Castle Budget Inn, Clarion, liet Inn, Motel 6, Quality Inn, Red Roof Inn H, 7-11, AT auto repair, Cadillac/Chevrolet, Discount Tire, Goodyear/a Meineke, Pepboys, Sam's Club/gas, to U of St Francis, US S Mobil/dsl
127	Houbolt Rd, to Joliet, N 7-11, BP/deli Burger Ki Burger Theory, China Kitchen, Cracker Barrel, Dunkin', ros Sports Grill, Jimmy John's, Jimmy K's, McDonald's, S way Comfort Inn, Fairfield Inn, Hampton Inn, Holiday TownePlace Suites Riverboat Casino
126b a	I-55, N to Chicago, S to St Louis
125.5mm	Du Page River
122	Minooka, N Circle K/dsl, S BP, Pilot/Arby's/sca dsl/24hr 2-Fers Pizza, Baskin-Robbins/Dunkin', McD ald's, Rosati's Pizza, Subway, Taco Bell, Wendy's, Wi Etc Hampton Inn, TownePlace Suites $General, 7-1
119mm	**wb, full facilities, litter barrels, petwalk, , , p ground, vending**
117mm	**eb, full facilities, litter barrels, petwalk, , , p ground, vending**
116	Brisbin Rd, CR 3000 E
112	IL 47, Morris, N Citgo/dsl, Pilot/Subway/dsl/scales/2 TA/BP/RPlace/scales/dsl/24hr/@ Bellacino's, Chili's, IH Comfort Inn, Days Inn, Holiday Inn Express, Quality $General, Menards, S BP/dsl, Circle K/dsl, Shell falo Wild Wings, Burger King, Culver's, DQ, Dunkin', Hong K

MORRIS

IL

INTERSTATE 80 Cont'd

112	Continued Chinese, KFC/LJ Silver, Maria's Ristorante, McDonald's, Morris Diner, Pizza Hut, Rosati's Pizza, Sherwood Oaks Rest., Subway, Taco Bell, Wendy's [lodging] Park Motel, Super 8 [other] H, $Tree, Aldi Foods, AT&T, AutoZone, Big R Store, Buick/Cadillac/Chevrolet, Chrysler/Dodge/Jeep, Fisher Parts, Ford, GMC, GNC, Jewel-Osco, to Stratton SP, transmissions/repair, Verizon, Walgreens, Walmart/Subway
105	to Seneca
97	to Marseilles, S [gas] Shell/dsl [other] Four Star Camping (5mi), Glenwood Camping (4mi), to Illini SP
93	IL 71, Ottawa, N [gas] Pilot/Road Ranger/Subway/dsl/scales/24hr, Shell/rest./dsl, S [food] Hank's Farm Rest., New Chiam [other] H
92.5mm	Fox River
90	IL 23, Ottawa, N [gas] BP/Subway [food] Arby's, Cracker Barrel, Fondita Mexican, Rosati's Pizza, Taco Bell [lodging] Comfort Inn, Hampton Inn [other] AT&T, F&F, GNC, Honda, Toyota, Verizon, Walmart/McDonald's, S [gas] BP/dsl/LP, Thornton's/dsl [food] China Inn, Culver's, DQ, Dunkin', Hardee's, KFC/LJ Silver, Sunfield Rest. [lodging] Fairfield Inn, Holiday Inn Express, Quality Inn, Super 8, Surrey Motel [other] H, $Tree, Aldi Foods, Ford/Lincoln/Kia, Harley-Davidson, Kroger, O'Reilly Parts, USPO, Verizon
81	IL 178, Utica, N [gas] Love's/McDonald's/Subway/dsl/scales/24hr [other] KOA (2mi), S [gas] Casey's/dsl, Shell/Jimmy Johns/dsl [other] repair, to Starved Rock SP, visitor info
79b a	I-39, US 51, N to Rockford, S to Bloomington
77.5mm	Little Vermilion River
77	IL 351, La Salle, S [gas] Flying J/Denny's/dsl/scales/24hr [food] UpTown Grill (3mi) [lodging] Daniels Motel (1mi) [other] st police
75	IL 251, Peru, N [gas] Mobil, Shell/rest./dsl/24hr [food] Arby's, Four Star Rest., McDonald's, Olive Garden, Starbucks, Taco Bell [lodging] Holiday Inn Express, Quality Inn, Super 8 [other] Kohl's, Petsmart, Walmart/Dunkin', S [gas] BP, Shell, Tesla EVC [food] Applebee's, Buffalo Wild Wings, Burger King, Culver's, DQ, IHOP, Jalepeno's Mexican, Jersey Mike's, Jimmy John's, Master Buffet, McDonald's, Pizza Hut, Red Lobster, Steak'n Shake, Subway, Wendy's [lodging] Fairfield Inn, Hampton Inn, La Quinta [other] H, $Tree, Advance Parts, Aldi Foods, AT&T, AutoZone, BigLots, Buick/GMC, Chevrolet, Chrysler/Dodge/Jeep, CVS Drug, Ford/Hyundai/Lincoln, Goodyear/auto, Hobby Lobby, Home Depot, HyVee Food/dsl, Jo-Ann Fabrics, Marshall's, Menards, Mercedes, Midas, NAPA, Nissan, O'Reilly Parts, Staples, Target, Verizon, Walgreens
73	Plank Rd, N [gas] Sapp Bros/Burger King/Subway/dsl/scales/@, Speedway/Speedway Cafe/dsl [food] Big Apple Rest. [other] Mack Trucks
70	IL 89, to Ladd, N [gas] Casey's, S [lodging] Spring Valley Motel [other] H, golf
61	I-180, to Hennepin
56	IL 26, Princeton, N [gas] Road Ranger/Pilot/scales/dsl/@ [lodging] Super 8, S [gas] BP/Beck's/dsl, Casey's, Shell/dsl [food] Big Apple Rest., Burger King, Coffee Cup Rest., Culver's, McDonald's, Subway, Wendy's [lodging] AmericInn, Days Inn, EconoLodge [other] H, $General, AutoZone, Buick/Cadillac/Chevrolet, O'Reilly Parts, Sullivan's Food/gas/e85, vet, Walmart
51mm	**[RS] both lanes, full [handicap] facilities, litter barrels, petwalk, [phone], [picnic], playground, RV dump, vending**
45	IL 40, N [other] antiques, to Ronald Reagan Birthplace (21mi), S [other] Hennepin Canal SP
44mm	Hennepin Canal

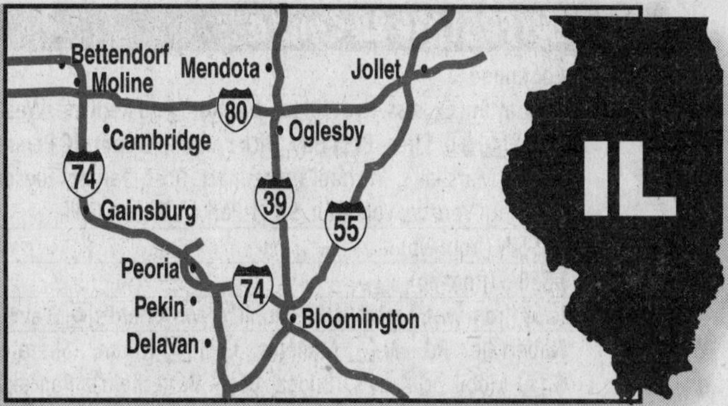

GENESEO

33	IL 78, to Kewanee, Annawan, N [gas] Shabbona RV Ctr/Camp (3mi), S [gas] Cenex/dsl, FS/dsl/e85, Shell/Subway/dsl [lodging] Best Western [other] to Johnson-Sauk Tr SP
27	to US 6, Atkinson, N [gas] Casey's (1mi), Love's/Chester's/Godfathers's/Subway/dsl/scales24hr
19	IL 82, Geneseo, N [gas] BP/dsl, Casey's/dsl [food] Culver's, DQ, Happy Joe's Pizza, Hardee's, McDonald's, New China, Pizza Hut, Subway, Sweet Pea's Grill [lodging] Best Western [other] H, $General, Ford, SaveALot Foods, Verizon, Walgreens, Walmart, S [food] Los Ranchitos Mexican
10	I-74, I-280, W to Moline, E to Peoria
9	US 6, to Geneseo, N [food] Lavender Crest Winery/Cafe, S [other] Niabi Zoo
7	Colona, N [gas] Shell/dsl
5mm	Rock River
4a	IL 5, IL 92, W to Silvis, S [other] Lundeen's Camping
4b	I-88, IL 92, E to Rock Falls
2mm	**weigh sta both lanes**
1.5mm	**Welcome Ctr eb, full [handicap] facilities, info, litter barrels, petwalk, [phone], [picnic], scenic overlook**
1	IL 84, 20th St, Great River Rd, E Moline, N [gas] BP/dsl [food] Bros Rest. [other] The Great River Rd, 3 mi S [other] camping
0mm	Illinois/Iowa state line, Mississippi River

INTERSTATE 88

OAKBROOK

Exit #	Services
139.5mm	**I-88 begins/ends on I-290.**
139	I-294, S to Indiana, N to Milwaukee
138mm	**toll plaza**
137	IL 83 N, Cermak Rd, N [food] Cheesecake Factory, Clubhouse Rest., Ditka's Rest., McDonald's [lodging] Marriott [other] Barnes&Noble, Lord&Taylor, Macy's, Nieman-Marcus
136	IL 83 S, Midwest Rd (from eb), N [gas] Shell/Circle K [food] Chipotle Mexican, Denny's, Devon Steaks, Giordano's Rest., Jamba Juice, Jimmy John's, McDonalds, Noodles&Co, Redstone Grill, Starbucks, Subway, Twin Peaks, Which Wich? [lodging] Courtyard, Holiday Inn, La Quinta, Staybridge [other] AT&T, Big Lots, Costco/gas, Home Depot, Nordstrom's, Old Navy, REI, TJ Maxx, Walgreens, World Mkt
134	Highland Ave (no EZ wb return), N [food] Barbokoa, Benihana, Brick House, Brio Grille, Buca Italian, Burger King, Capital Grille, Chama Guacha Brazilian, Champps Grill, Chick-fil-A, Chipotle, Claimjumper Rest., Fuddruckers, Harry Caray's, Honey-Jam Cafe, Hooters, Kona Grill, Kyoto, McCormick & Schmick's, Melting Pot, Miller's Rest., Noodles&Co, Olive Garden, Olive Therapy Pizza, Panera Bread, PF Chang's, Portillo's Hotdogs, Potbelly, Red Lobster, Rockbottom Brewery, Ruby Tuesday, Starbucks, Starbucks, Subway, TGIFriday's, Tom&Eddie's Burgers, Uncle Julio's [lodging] Comfort Inn, Embassy Suites, Extended Stay America,

INTERSTATE 88 Cont'd

NAPERVILLE

134	Continued Holiday Inn Express, Hyatt Place, Marriott, Red Roof Inn, Westin Hotel H, $Tree, Best Buy, Dick's, Home Depot, JC Penney, Kohl's, Marshall's, Michael's, Petsmart, Ross, Target, Tuesday Morning, Verizon, Vonmaur, **S** Parkers Ocean Grill
132	I-355 N (from wb)
131	I-355 S (from eb)
130	IL 53 (from wb), **1 mi N** BP, Mobil McDonald's Walmart
127	Naperville Rd, **N** Mullen's Grill Hilton, Sheraton, **S** Mobil Arby's, Buona Beef, Butterfield's Pancakes, Chipotle, Coopers Hawk, Fogo de Chao Brazilian, Granite City, HoneyBaked Ham, Jason's Deli, Maggiano's, McDonald's, Ming Hin, Morton's Steaks, Paisan's Pizza, Panera Bread, Pizza Hut, Subway, Tom & Eddie's Burgers, Uncle Julio's, Wendy's, White Chocolate Grill Best Western, Country Inn & Suites, Courtyard, Embassy Suites, Extended Stay America, Fairfield Inn, Hampton Inn, Marriott, Motel 6, Regency Inn $Tree, CVS, Staples, Subaru
125	Winfield Rd, **N** BP, Mobil Hyatt House, Hyatt Place, Resedence Inn H, Walgreens, **S** Buffalo Wild Wings, CA Pizza Kitchen, Chipotle Mexican, Corner Bakery Cafe, Eddie Merlot, Masala, McDonald's, Potbelly, Red Robin, Rockbottom Brewery, Starbucks, Twin Peaks, Zoup Hilton Garden, Springhill Suites SuperTarget
123	IL 59, **N** Speedway/dsl CarMax, **S** BP/Domino's, Delta Sonic, Speedway Baskin Robbins/Dunkin', Cracker Barrel, Firehouse Subs, Jimmy John's, McDonald's, Oberweis, Starbucks, Subway, TX Roadhouse, Wendy's Extended Stay America, Fairfield Inn, Red Roof Inn, Sleep Inn, Towneplace Suites $Tree, 7-11, CVS Drug
119	Farnsworth Ave, **N** BP, Shell, Thornton's/dislike Chipotle, McDonald's, Noodles&Co, Panera Bread, Papa Bear Rest., Quizno's, Sonic, Starbucks Fox Valley Inn, Motel 6 Advance Parts, AT&T, Firestone/auto, GNC, Premium Outlets/Famous Brands, Verizon, Walgreens, Walmart/Subway, **S** Marathon, Moble, Shell, Speedway Baskin-Robbins/Dunkin', Goody's, Little Caesar's, McDonald's, Mike&Denise's Pizza, Subway, Taco Bell $General, 7-11, AutoZone, Family$, Walgreens
118mm	**toll plaza**
117	IL 31, IL 56, to Aurora, Batavia, **N** BP/dsl A&W 7-11, **S** Mobil, Speedway/dsl, Thornton's/dsl Baskin-Robbins/Dunkin', Burger King, Culver's, Denny's, McDonald's, Nikarry's, Popeye's, Subway, Taco Bell, Wendy's, White Castle Baymont Inn H, $General, $Tree, Ace Hardware, Advance Parts, AutoZone, Cermak Foods, Family$, Firestone, GNC, O'Reilly Parts, Ross, U-Haul, Walgreens
115	Orchard Rd, **N** Dunkin', McDonald's, Subway $Tree, Best Buy, Chrysler/Dodge/Jeep, Ford/Lincoln, Hyundai, JC Penney, Kia, Michaels, Nissan, PetCo, Subaru, Target, Verizon, Woodman's/dsl, **0-2 mi S** 7-11 Arby's, Buffalo Wild Wings, Chili's, Chipotle, IHOP, Jimmy John's, Panera Bread, Papa Saverio's, Pizza Hut, Starbucks, Wendy's Candlewood Suites, Hampton Inn, Holiday Inn AT&T, CVS Drug, Discount Tire, Home Depot, Office Depot
114	IL 56W, to US 30 (from wb, no EZ return), to Sugar Grove
109	IL 47 (from eb), Elburn
94	Peace Rd, to IL 38, **N** H
93mm	**Dekalb Oasis/24hr both lanes,** Mobil/dsl McDonald's, Panda Express, Starbucks, Subway

DEKALB

92	IL 38, IL 23, Annie Glidden Rd, to DeKalb, **2-3 mi N** Road Ranger/dsl, Shell Baskin-Robbins, Burger King, Chipotle Mexican, Culver's, Dunkin', Fatty's, Happy Wok Chin IHOP, Jct Rest., Jersey Mike's, McDonald's, Miki MOto, Mo Eatery, Panda Express, Papa John's, Pizza Hut, Pizza Pros, Pizza Villa, Potbelly, Starbucks, Subway, Taco Bell, Tom&Jer Topper's Pizza Baymont Inn, Hampton Inn, Red Roof Super 8 CVS, Ford, Illini Tire, Schnuck's Food/Drug, to U, Walgreens
86mm	**toll plaza**
78	I-39, US 51, S to Bloomington, N to Rockford
76	IL 251, Rochelle, **N** BP/dsl, Casey's, Shell H, F tires/repair, **S** Loves/Hardee's/dsl/scales/24hr
56mm	**toll plaza**

DIXON

54	IL 26, Dixon, **N** Murphy USA/dsl, Pilot/Road Ran dsl/24hrs Hardee's, Las Palmas, Panda Chinese, P Hut Comfort Inn, Super 8 H, $Tree, Aldi, GNC, to J Deere HS, to Ronald Reagan Birthplace, to St Parks, URG CARE, Verizon, Walmart
44	US 30 (last free exit eb), **N** Leisure lake RV Ctr (2mi), fo gas, lodging
41	IL 40, to Sterling, Rock Falls, **1-2 mi N** Mobil/ Shell American Grill, Arby's, Arthur's Deli, Burger K Candlelight Rest., Culver's, Gazi's Rest., Hardee's, Jim John's, McDonald's/playplace, Perna's Pizza, Pizza Hut, Apple Rest., Subway Country Inn&Suites, Days Inn, Hol Inn Express, Super 8 H, $General, AutoZone, Harley-vidson, O'Reilly Parts, Sav-a-Lot, Verizon, Walgreens, Walm
36	to US 30, Rock Falls, Sterling
26	IL 78, to Prophetstown, Morrison, **N** to Morrison-Rockw SP

E MOLINE

18	to Albany, Erie
10	to Port Byron, Hillsdale, **S** Phillips 66/dsl, Shell/Subw scales/dsl/24hr
6	IL 92 E, to Joslin, **N** Jammerz Roadhouse (2mi), **S** S set Lake Camping (1mi)
2	Former IL 2
1b a	I-80, W to Des Moines, E to Chicago
0mm	IL 5, IL 92, W to Silvis, Lundeen's Camping, to Quad City Dov

I-88 begins/ends on I-80, exit 4b.

INTERSTATE 90

Exit #	Services
0mm	Illinois/Indiana state line, **Chicago Skyway Toll Rd begins/e**
1mm	US 12, US 20, 106th St, Indianapolis Blvd, **N** bil Burger King, Starbucks, Taco Bell Aldi Foods, toZone, casino, Jewel-Osco, **S** Citgo Beggars Pi McDonald's auto repair
2.5mm	Skyway Oasis McDonald's **toll plaza**
3mm	87th St (from wb)
4mm	79th St, services on 79th St and Stoney Island Ave
5.5mm	73rd St (from wb)
6mm	State St (from wb), **S** Citgo
7mm	I-94 N (mile markers decrease to IN state line)

I-90 E and I-94 E run together. See I-94, exits 43b - 59a.

84	I-94 W, Lawrence Ave, **N** BP/dsl
83b a	Foster Ave (from wb), **N** Elly's Pancakes, S way Advance Parts, Firestone/auto, Walgreens
82c	Austin Ave, to Foster Ave
82b	Byrn-Mawr (from wb)
82a	Nagle Ave
81b	Sayre Ave (from wb)

INTERSTATE 90 Cont'd

Exit #	Services
81a	IL 43, Harlem Ave, S Gas Depot, Shell Dunkin', Popeye's, Sally's Pancakes, Wendy's $Tree, AutoZone
80	Canfield Rd (from wb), N Walgreens
79b a	IL 171 S, Cumberland Ave (from wb), N 7-11, Mobil Al's Burgers, Dunkin'/Baskin Robbins, Hooters, McDonald's, Nancy's Pizza, Outback Steaks Marriott, SpringHill Suites, Westin Hotel Hampton Inn, Mariano's Mkt, S Bar Louie's, Starbucks Holiday Inn, Hyatt, Renaissance
78	I-294, I-190 W, N Mobil McDonald's Hampton Inn, Westin, S Hyatt to O'Hare Airport
76	IL 72, Lee St (from wb), N Buona, Chili's, Chipotle, Culver's, IHOP, Jimmy John's, Longhorn Steaks, Panda Express, Steak'n Shake, Subway Extended Stay America, Radisson, Residence Inn Target, S McDonald's Best Western, Holiday Inn Express, Holiday Inn Select, Sheraton Gateway
73	Elmhurst Rd (from wb), S Shell Burger King, McDonald's, Subway, White Castle Best Western, Days Inn, InTowne Suites, La Quinta, Motel 6, Super 8, Wyndham Garden
70	Arlington Hts Rd, S Mobil, Shell Subway Sheraton Chevrolet, N on Algonquin BP/dsl, Shell/dsl Arby's, Buona Beef, Chef Ping, Chipotle Mexican, Coopers Hawk, Denny's, Five Guys, Honey Baked Ham, Jimmy Johns, McDonald's, Noodles&Co, Panda Express, Panera Bread, Pie Five, Potbelly's, Steak'n Shake Comfort Inn, Courtyard, DoubleTree, Holiday Inn Express, Red Roof Inn, Wingate Inn AT&T, GNC, Lowe's Whse, Meijer/dsl, NTB, Staples, vet, Walmart
68	I-290, IL 53, **N on Algonquin,** Embassy Suites, Holiday Inn, Holiday Inn Express, Renaissance Inn, **1 mi S on Golf Rd** CA Pizza Kitchen, Cheesecake Factory, Chevy's Mexican, Hooters, Joe's Crabshack, Longhorn Steaks, Maggiano's, Olive Garden, Panera Bread, Qdoba, Red Robin, Starbucks, Subway, TGI Friday's, Uno Extended Stay America, Hyatt, Residence Inn AT&T, Costco/gas, Firestone/auto, JC Penney, Lord&Taylor, Macy's, Marshall's, Michael's, Nordstrom, Old Navy, Petsmart, Trader Joe's
65	Roselle Rd (from wb, no return), N Medieval Times Funpark, S Mobil Boston Mkt, Chipotle Mexican, Denny's, Fox&Hound, Jimmy John's, KFC, McDonald's, Melting Pot, Outback Steaks, Panda Express, Papa John's, Subway, Taco Bell, Wendy's Country Inn&Suites, Extended Stay America, Extended Stay America (2), Holiday Inn Express, Radisson 7-11, Buick/GMC, Carmax, Chrysler/Dodge/Jeep, Fiat, Firestone/auto, Jewel-Osco, Mazda, Office Depot, O'Reilly Parts, PetCo, TJ Maxx, Walgreens
62	Barrington Rd (from wb), N Apple Villa Pancake House, Gino's East, Hunan Beijing, Jersey's Grill, Jimmy John's, Lucky Monk Hilton Garden vet, S BP, Mobil/dsl Buona Beef, Burger King, Chili's, Domino's, IHOP, Macaroni Grill, McDonald's, Moretti's, Starbucks, Steak'n Shake, Subway, Sweet Caroline's Hampton Inn, Hawthorn Suites, Hyatt Place, La Quinta, Quality Inn, Red Roof Inn U-Haul
59	IL 59, N Buffalo Wild Wings, Chipotle Mexican, Claim Jumper Rest., Cooper's Hawk Rest., Culver's, Dunkin', Firehouse Subs, Jersey Mike's, Jimmy John's, Moe's SW Grill, Noodles&Co, Panda Express, Panera Bread, Potbelly, Red Robin, Rookie's Grill, Ruth's Chris Steaks, Starbucks, Subway, Which Wich? Marriott Cabela's, CVS Drug, Duluth Trading, GNC, Petsmart, Ross, Target, TJ Maxx, Verizon, World Mkt
58	Beverly Rd (from wb)

ELGIN

ROCKFORD

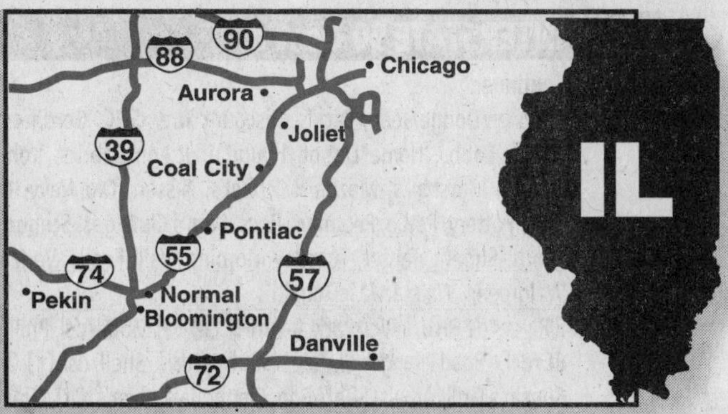

Exit #	Services
56	IL 25, N Lexington Inn, S BP/dsl, Shell/dsl, Speedway/dsl Arby's, Baker Hill Pancakes, Subway, Wendy's Advance Parts, city park, NAPA AutoCare
54b a	IL 31, N BP, Thornton's Alexander's Rest., Baskin-Robbins/Dunkin' Courtyard, Hampton Inn, Holiday Inn, Quality Inn, Super 8, TownePlace Suites
53.5mm	**Elgin Toll Plaza,**
52	Randall Rd, N Shell Big Sammy's Hot Dogs, Burnt Toast, Cafe Roma, DQ, Jimmy John's, Jimmy's Charhouse, Mr Wok, Panera Bread, Rookies Grill, Starbucks, Village Pizza Comfort Suites, Country Inn&Suites Honda, VW, S 7-11 Candlewood Suites H, Subaru
46	IL 47, to Woodstock, N Ford, General RV Ctr, Huntley Outlets/famous brands
42	US 20, Marengo, N Citgo/Mexican Grill/dsl/scales/24hr, Loves/Arby's/dsl/scales/24hr, Pilot/Road Ranger/Subway/dsl/scales/24hr, Speedway/Speedy's Cafe/dsl/24hr, TA/BP/Country Pride/Burger King/Popeye's/dsl/scales/24hr/@ McDonald's, Wendy's Super 8 access to services at exit 46 (6mi), Ford, Huntley Outlets, to museums
38mm	**Marengo Toll Plaza (from eb)**
25	Genoa Rd, to Belvidere, N Murphy USA/dsl Applebee's, Rosati's Pizza, Starbucks, Subway Verizon, Walmart/Dunkin'
24mm	**Belvidere Oasis both lanes,** Mobil/7-11/dsl/24hr Food Court, McDonald's, Panda Express, Sbarro, Starbucks, Subway
20	Irene Rd
18mm	Kishwaukee River
17mm	I-39 S, US 20, US 51, to Rockford, S funpark
15	US 20, State St, N Mobil/dsl, Phillips 66/Subway/dsl Cracker Barrel Baymont Inn, Clocktower Resort, Days Inn, **0-2 mi S** FasFuel/dsl, Mobil/dsl Applebee's, Buffalo Wild Wings, Burger King, Chick-fil-A, Chili's, Chipotle Mexican, City Buffet, Coldstone, Culver's, Denny's, Dos Reales, Fiesta Cancun, Five Guys, Gerry's Pizza, Giovanni's Rest., Hoffman House Rest., Hooters, IHOP, Jason's Deli, Jersey Mike's, Jimmy John's, KFC/LJ Silver, Lino's Italian, LoneStar Steaks, Longhorn Steaks, Machine Shed Rest, McDonald's, Noodles&Co, Old Chicago Grill, Olive Garden, Outback Steaks, Panda Express, Panera Bread, Panino's Drive-Thru, Perkins, Pizza Hut/Taco Bell, PotBelly, Red Lobster, Red Robin, Ruby Tuesday, Starbucks, Steak'n Shake, Stone Eagle Tavern, Subway, ThunderBay Grille, TX Roadhouse, Wendy's Candlewood Suites, Comfort Inn, Courtyard, Extended Stay America, Fairfield Inn, Hampton Inn, Hilton Garden, Holiday Inn, Motel 6, Quality Suites, Radisson, Red Roof Inn, Residence Inn, Sleep Inn, Staybridge Suites, Super 8 H, $Tree, Advance Parts, Aldi Foods, AT&T, Best Buy, BigLots, Burlington Coats, Cadillac,

IL

INTERSTATE 90 Cont'd

15	Continued Chrysler/Dodge/Jeep, Dick's, Discount Tire, GNC, Gordman's, Hobby Lobby, Home Depot, Hyundai, JoAnn Fabrics, Kohl's, Lowe's, Marshall's, Mazda, Michael's, Nissan, Old Navy, Old Time Pottery, PetCo, Petsmart, Ross, Sam's Club/gas, Schnuck's Foods, Subaru, Target, Tuesday Morning, Valli Foods, Verizon, Walgreens, Walmart/McDonald's
12	E Riverside Blvd, Loves Park, **0-2 mi S** BP, Mobil/dsl, Phillips 66/dsl, Road Ranger/Pilot/Subway/dsl, Shell/dsl 2nd Cousin's Grill, Arby's, BeefARoo, Ciaobella, Culver's, DQ, Greenfire Rest., India House, Japanese Express, KFC, McDonald's, RBI Rest., Rosatti's Pizza, Sam's Ristorante, Singapore Grill, Subway, Taco Bell, Wendy's Holiday Inn Express, Quality Inn Audi/Honda/Mercedes, Autowerks, Farm&Fleet, funpark, Lexus, to Rock Cut SP, Toyota, Tuffy Auto, Walgreens
8	Il 173, **S** to Rock Cut SP
3.5mm	**S Beloit Toll Plaza**
3	Rockton Rd, **S** Loves/Hardee's/dsl/scales/24hr
1.5mm	**Welcome Ctr/ eb, full facilities, info, litter barrels, petwalk, , , playground, RV dump**
1	US 51 N, IL 75 W, S Beloit, **N** Road Ranger/McDonald's/dsl, **S** FLYING J/Denny's/dsl/scales/24hr, Road Ranger/Pilot/Subway/dsl/E85/scales/24hr Best Western, Tollway Inn Finnegan's RV Ctr
0mm	Illinois/Wisconsin state line

INTERSTATE 94

Exit #	Services
77mm	Illinois/Indiana state line
I-94 and I-80 run together 3 mi. See I-80, exit 161.	
74[160]b	I-80/I-294 W
74a	IL 394 S, to Danville
73b a	US 6,159th St, **N** Loves/Hardee's/dsl/scales/24hr, Mobil Applebee's, Buffalo Wild Wings, Continental Rest., Denny's, Outback Steaks, Panda Express, Sonic, Starbucks, Taco Bell, Tilly's, White Castle BigLots, Cadillac, Goodyear Commercial Tire, Hyundai, JC Penney, Kia, Lincoln, Macy's, Marshall's, Nissan, PetCo, Ross, Sam's Club, Toyota, USPO, vet, **S** BP, Marathon Checkers, Harold's Chicken, Little Caesar's, McDonald's, Papa John's, Popeye's, Shark's, Subway Holland Inn Aldi Foods, Family$, Jewel-Osco, O'Reilly Parts, Stanfa Tire/repair
71b a	Sibley Blvd, **N** BP/dsl, Citgo, Mobil/dsl McDonald's, Nick's Gyros, Popeye's, Shark's, Subway Baymont Inn $Tree, Family$, Pete's Mkt, **S** Circle K/Checkers/dsl, Marathon/dsl, Shell Baskin-Robbins/Dunkin', Burger King, KFC, Taco Bell, Wendy's, White Castle Best Motel $General, Advance Parts, AutoZone, Family$, Food4Less/gas, Menards, Walgreens
70b a	Dolton
69	Beaubien Woods (from eb), Beaubien Woods Forest Preserve
68b a	130th St
66b	115th St, **S** McDonald's
66a	111th Ave, **S** Citgo/dsl, Shell H, $Tree, Firestone/auto, Ross, Walmart
65	103rd Ave, Stony Island Ave
63	I-57 S (exits left from wb)
62	Wentworth Ave (from eb), **N** Citgo Burger King, KFC, **S** McDonald's
61b	87th St, **N** BP, Shell/dsl Burger King, McDonald's, S Starbucks, Subway $Tree, AutoZone, Burlington Co Food4Less, Home Depot, Jewel-Osco, Marshall's, O'Reilly Pa Staples, Verizon
61a	83rd St (from eb), **N** Shell Subway st police
60c	79th St, **N** Mobil, Shell Walgreens, **S** Falcon Church's, Subway
60b	76th St, **N** BP, Mobil, Shell Walgreens, **S** KFC, Pope
60a	75th St (from eb), **N** BP, Shell Aldi Foods, **S** Popeye's
59c	71st St, **N** BP, **S** McDonald's
59a	I-90 E, to Indiana Toll Rd
58b	63rd St (from eb), **N** BP, **S** Mobil
58a	I-94 divides into local and express, 59th St, **S** Mobil
57b	Garfield Blvd, **N** Checker's Family$, Walgreens, **S** Citgo, Mobil, Shell/24hr Wendy's
57a	51st St
56b	47th St (from eb)
56a	43rd St, **S** BP/Subway/dsl, Citgo/dsl
55b	Pershing Rd
55a	35th St, **S** to New Comiskey Park
54	31st St
53c	I-55, Stevenson Pkwy, N to downtown, Lakeshore Dr
53b	I-55, Stevenson Pkwy, S to St Louis
52c	18th St (from eb), **N** Whole Foods
52b	Roosevelt Rd, Taylor St (from wb), **N** Citgo Chipotle Best Buy, Home Depot, Walgreens, Whole Foods Mkt
52a	Taylor St, Roosevelt Rd (from eb), **N** Citgo
51h-i	I-290 W, to W Suburbs
51g	E Jackson Blvd, downtown
51f	W Adams St, downtown
51e	Monroe St (from eb), downtown, **S** Crowne Plaza Walgreens, Whole Foods
51d	Madison St (from eb), **S** Crowne Plaza Walgree Whole Foods, downtown
51c	E Washington Blvd, downtown
51b	W Randolph St, downtown
51a	Lake St (from wb)
50b	E Ohio St, **S** Marathon, downtown
50a	Ogden Ave
49b a	Augusta Blvd, Division St, **N** Acura, Lexus, Merced **S** BP, Shell
48b	IL 64, North Ave, **N** BP, **S** Mercedes
48a	Armitage Ave, **N** Best Buy, Kohl's, Lexus, **S** Sl Jaguar, Land Rover, Volvo
47c b	Damen Ave, **N** car/vanwash
47a	Western Ave, Fullerton Ave, **N** Mobil Burger Ki Dunkin', Popeye's, Starbucks, Subway Costco/gas, Ho Depot, Jo-Ann Fabrics, Pepboys, Petsmart, Staples, Tar **S** Marathon
46b a	Diversey Ave, California Ave, **S** IHOP/24hr, P eye's Walgreens
45c	Belmont Ave
45b	Kimball Ave, **N** Marathon/dsl CVS Drug, Home Depo Shell Dunkin', Subway Aldi Foods, Best Buy, Walgree
45a	Addison St
44b	Pulaski Ave, Irving Park Rd, **N** Mobil/Subway, Shell/dsl
44a	IL 19, Keeler Ave, Irving Park Rd, **N** Mobil/Subway, Sh dsl to Wrigley Field
43c	Montrose Ave
43b	I-90 W
43a	Wilson Ave

CHICAGO AREA

IL

INTERSTATE 94 Cont'd

Exit #	Services
42	W Foster Ave (from wb), S Marathon/service, Mobil Subway
41mm	Chicago River, N Branch
41c	IL 50 S, to Cicero, to I-90 W
41b a	US 14, Peterson Ave, N Whole Foods Mkt
39b a	Touhy Ave, N BP/dsl, Shell/Circle K Cassidy Tire, Toyota, S BP, Citgo, Mobil, Shell Bar Louie's, Baskin-Robbins/Dunkin', Brickhouse Rest., Buffalo Wild Wings, Burger King, Chili's, Chipotle Mexican, ChuckeCheese, Corner Bakery Cafe, Jersey Mike's, Jimmy John's, McDonald's, Noodles&Co, Outback Steaks, Panda Express, Penn Sta Subs, Red Robin, Sander's Rest., Shallot's Bistro, Starbucks, Subway, Tilted Kilt Holiday Inn Barnes&Noble, Best Buy, Dick's, Fresh Farms Mkt, GNC, Jewel-Osco, Michael's, Nissan, PepBoys, Petsmart, Ross, Tuesday Morning, vet, Walgreens, Walmart
37b a	IL 58, Dempster St, N Shell Panda Express, Subway, S BP/dsl, Shell Pizza Hut Midas
35	Old Orchard Rd, N BP, Shell Bloomingdale's, Buffalo Wild Wings, CA Pizza Kitchen, CheeseCake Factory, H, Lord&Taylor, Macy's, Nissan, Nordstrom's, S Ruby Tuesday Extended Stay America, Hampton Inn, Residence Inn
34c b	E Lake Ave, N BP/dsl Corner Bakery Cafe, Five Guys, Panda Express, Starbucks, Subway Fresh Mkt Foods, GNC, Walgreens, S Shell DQ, Jimmy John's, Starbucks auto repair
34a	US 41 S, Skokie Rd (from eb)
33b a	Willow Rd, S Shell Dunkin', Starbucks Mariano's Mkt, USPO, Walgreens
31	E Tower Rd, S BMW, Carmax, Infiniti, Land Rover, Mercedes, Toyota, vet, Volvo
30b a	Dundee Rd (from wb, no EZ return), S Citgo/dsl Barnaby's Rest., Chipotle, Morton's Steaks, Noodles&Co, Panera Bread, Potbelly, Roti Mediterranean, Ruth's Chris Steaks, Starbucks Renaissance Mariano's Mkt
29	US 41, to Waukegan, to Tri-state tollway
28	IL 43, Waukegan Rd (from eb), N BP, Shell Dunkin'/Baskin Robbins, Mod Pizza, Noodles&Co, Starbucks Courtyard, Embassy Suites, Red Roof Inn Hobby Lobby, Home Depot, Jewel-Osco, Just Tires
25	I-294 S, Lake-Cook Rd (from sb), E Embassy Suites, Hyatt, W J Alexander's Rest.
24	Deerfield Rd (from nb), W Mobil Marriott Suites
21	IL 22, Half Day Rd, E Leaf Cafe La Quinta, W Homewood Suites
19	IL 60, Town Line Rd, E H, W Hilton Garden, Residence Inn Costco/gas
18mm	**Lake Forest Oasis both lanes,** Mobil/7-11/dsl KFC/Taco Bell, McDonald's, Panda Express, Starbucks, Subway info
16mm	IL 176, Rockland Rd (no nb re-entry), E Harley-Davidson, to Lamb's Farm
14mm	IL 137, Buckley Rd, E Chicago Med School, to VA H
11mm	IL 120 E, Belvidere Rd (no nb re-entry), E H
10mm	IL 21, Milwaukee Ave (from eb, no eb re-entry), E H, Six Flags
8mm	IL 132, Grand Ave, E Speedway/dsl Baskin-Robbins/Dunkin', Burger King, ChuckeCheese, Cracker Barrel, Cravings Red Hots, Culver's, Golden Corral, Ichibahn, IHOP, Jimmy John's, Joe's Crabshack, KFC/LJ Silver, Mama K's Zpizza, McDonald's, Oberweiss, Old Chicago Red Hots, Olive Garden, Outback

GURNEE

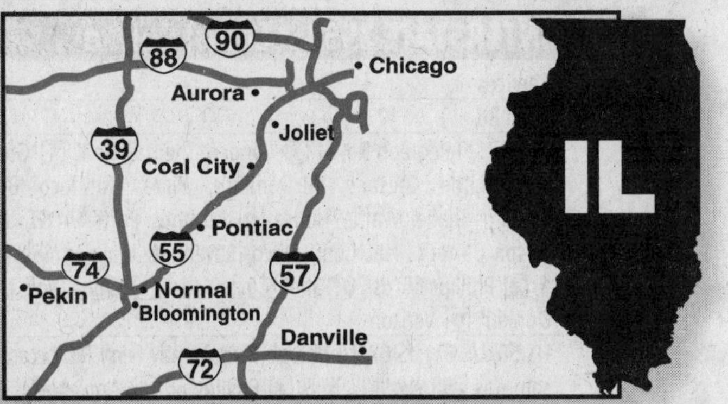

Exit #	Services
8mm	Continued Steaks, Rosati's Pizza, Starbucks, Subway Baymont Inn, Country Inn&Suites, Extended Stay America, Hampton Inn, Key Lime Cove Resort, La Quinta, Super 8 Six Flags Park, 0-2 mi W Shell/Circle K Bakers Square, Boston Mkt, Buffalo Wild Wings, Chili's, Chipotle Mexican, Denny's, Five Guys, Giordano's Pizza, Jersey Mike's Subs, Jimano's Pizza, LoneStar Steaks, McDonald's, Noodles&Co, Panda Express, Panera Bread, Penn Sta Subs, Pizza Hut, Portillo's, Potbelly's, Red Lobster, Red Robin, Ruby Tuesday, Starbucks, Steak'n Shake, Taco Bell, TGIFriday's, Uno Grill, Wendy's, White Castle Comfort Inn, Fairfield Inn, Holiday Inn $Tree, AT&T, AutoZone, Bass Pro Shops, Best Buy, Buick/GMC, Chrysler/Dodge/Jeep, Goodyear, Gurnee Mills Outlet Mall/famous brands, Home Depot, Honda, Hyundai, Jewel-Osco, Kohl's, Macy's, Mariano's Mkt, Marshall's, Menards, Michael's, Old Navy, Petsmart, Ross, Sam's Club, Target, TJ Maxx, Tuesday Morning, Verizon, VW, Walgreens, Walmart
5mm	**Waukegan toll plaza**
2	IL 173 (from nb, no return), Rosecrans Ave, E to IL Beach SP
1b	US 41 S, to Waukegan (from sb)
1a	Russell Rd, E I-94 RV Ctr, W Citgo/dsl/scales, TA/Country Pride/dsl/scales/24hr/@ Peterbilt
0mm	Illinois/Wisconsin state line

INTERSTATE 255 (St Louis)

Exit #	Services
	I-255 begins/ends on I-270, exit 7.
30	I-270, W to Kansas City, E to Indianapolis
29	IL 162, to Glen Carbon, to Pontoon Beach, Granite City
26	Horseshoe Lake Rd, E st police
25b a	I-55/I-70, W to St Louis, E to Chicago, Indianapolis
24	Collinsville Rd, E Jack-in-the-Box Shop'n Save, W Fairmount Racetrack
20	I-64, US 50, W to St Louis, E to Louisville. **Services 1 mi E off I-64, exit 9.**
19	State St, E St Louis, E Western Inn, W Holten SP
17b a	IL 15, E St Louis, to Belleville, Centreville, E FLYING J/Denny's/dsl/scales/24hr, W Phillips 66 auto repair
15	Mousette Lane, E H, W Peterbilt
13	IL 157, to Cahokia, E Phillips 66, W BP, MotoMart Capt D's, China Express, Classic K Burgers, Domino's, Hardee's, KFC, Little Caesar's, McDonald's, Pizza Hut, Rally's, Subway, Taco Bell, White Castle Comfort Inn $General, $Tree, Advance Parts, Aldi Foods, AutoZone, Dobb's Tires, Family$, Schnuck's, Shop'n Save Foods, Walgreens, Walmart
10	IL 3 N, to Cahokia, E St Louis, W Fuelmart/Subway/dsl
9	to Dupo, W Hucks
6	IL 3 S, to Columbia (exits left from sb), E Phillips 66, Shell/dsl/24hr Hampton Inn (2mi) Chevrolet
4mm	Missouri/Illinois state line, Mississippi River

INTERSTATE 255 (St Louis) Cont'd

Exit #	Services
3	Koch Rd
2	MO 231, Telegraph Rd, **N** Conoco, Shell/Circle K Great Wall, Little Caesar's, McDonald's, Pizza Hut/Taco Bell, Steak'n Shake, Waffle House Advance Parts, AT&T, Jefferson Barracks Nat Cem, Petco, SaveALot, Walmart/Subway, **S** Phillips 66/dsl, QT, Shell/Circle K/dsl China Wok, DQ, Dunkin' Verizon
1d c	US 50, US 61, US 67, Lindbergh Blvd, Lemay Ferry Rd, accesses same as I-55 exit 197 E, **N** Phillips 66 Applebee's, Arby's, Buffalo Wild Wings, ChuckeCheese, CiCi's Pizza, Dillard's, Hometown Buffet, HoneyBaked Ham, Hooters, IHOP, Imo's Pizza, Krispy Kreme, McAlister's Deli, Noodles&Co, Penn Sta Subs, Qdoba Mexican, Starbucks, Steak'n Shake, Subway, Taco Bell, Tucker's Place, Wendy's Holiday Inn AT&T, Best Buy, Chrysler/Dodge/Jeep, Costco/gas, CVS Drug, Dick's, Ford/Lincoln, Home Depot, JC Penney, Macy's, Marshall's, NTB, Verizon, vet, **S** Phillips 66 Jack-in-the-Box, Jimmy John's, McDonald's, Rich & Charlie's Italian, White Castle $General, $Tree, BigLots, Firestone, Old Navy, Petsmart, Sam's Club/gas, Walgreens
1b a	I-55 S to Memphis, N to St Louis.
I-255 begins/ends on I-55, exit 196.	

INTERSTATE 270

See Missouri Interstate 270 (St Louis)

INTERSTATE 294 (Chicago)

Exit #	Services
I-294 begins/ends on I-94, exit 71.	
I-294 & I-80 run together 5 mi. See I-80, exits 155-160.	
39.5mm	**toll booth eb**
5mm	I-80 W, access to I-57
5.5mm	167th St, **toll booth,**
6mm	US 6, 159th St, **E** Citgo, Exxon/dsl, Marathon, Mobil/dsl, Shell/dsl $Tree, AutoZone, Family$, **W** BP/dsl Baskin-Robbins/Dunkin', Burger King, McDonald's, Popeye's, Subway, Taco Bell, White Castle Chicago Inn&Suites $Tree, AutoZone, U-Haul, Walgreens
11mm	Cal Sag Channel
12mm	IL 50, Cicero Ave, **E** BP, Shell/dsl Dunkin', Subway, White Castle Home Depot, O'Reilly Parts, **W** BP, Shell/dsl Applebee's, Boston Mkt, Chipotle, Culver's, IHOP, Lone Star Steaks, Panda Express, Pizza Hut, Popeye's, Portillo's Dogs, Potbelly, Starbucks, Subway Baymont Inn, Days Inn, DoubleTree, Holiday Inn Express AT&T, Best Buy, GNC, Jo-Ann, Kohl's, NTB, PepBoys, Petsmart, Ross, Target, TJ Maxx, Ultra Foods, Walgreens, Walmart/Subway
18mm	US 12/20, 95th St, **E** Marathon Buffalo Wild Wings, Chick-fil-A, Starbucks, TX Corral H, CarMax, Discount Tire, Mazda, **W** 7-11, BP, Shell, Speedway/dsl Arby's, Baskin-Robbins, Burger King, Denny's, Dunkin', Jimmy John's, Les Bros Rest., McDonald's, Papa John's, Prime Time Rest., Subway, Taco Bell, The Pit Ribhouse, Wendy's Motel 6 $Tree, AutoZone, Jewel-Osco, Walgreens
20mm	**toll booth,**
22mm	75th St, Willow Springs Rd
23mm	I-55, Wolf Rd, to Hawthorne Park
25mm	**Hinsdale Oasis both lanes,** Mobil/7-11/dsl KFC/Taco Bell, McDonald's, McDonald's, Panda Express, Sbarro, Subway
28mm	US 34, Ogden Ave, **E** zoo, **W** BP, Shell/deli Dun McDonald's, Starbucks H, Ferrari/Maserati, Firestc auto, LandRover, Whole Foods Mkt
28.5mm	Cermak Rd (from sb, no return)
29mm	**I-88 tollway**
30mm	**toll booth,**
31mm	IL 38, Roosevelt Rd (no EZ nb return), **E** Shell/dsl side Manor Motel vet
32mm	I-290 W, to Rockford (from nb)
34mm	I-290 (from sb), to Rockford
38mm	**O'Hare Oasis both lanes,** Mobil/7-11/dsl KFC, McD ald's, Panda Express, Sbarro, Starbucks, Subway, Taco Bell, T
39mm	IL 19 W (from sb), Irving Park Rd, **E** Citgo, Marath dsl, Shell/dsl Dunkin', McDonald's, Starbucks, Subv Wendy's Comfort Suites 7-11, Aldi Foods, Walgre **W** BP/Subway/desk Mirage Rest. Candlew Suites, Hampton Inn, Sheraton
40mm	I-190 W, **E** Mobil Basil's Kitchen, McDonald's, S bucks Courtyard, Doubletree, Embassy Suites, Hamp Inn, Hilton, Hilton Garden, Holiday Inn, Hyatt, Hyatt Rege Marriott, Rosemont Suites, Westin
41mm	**toll booth,**
42mm	Touhy Ave, **W** Mobil/service Tiffany's Rest. C fort Inn, Radisson
43mm	Des Plaines River
44mm	Dempster St (from nb, no return), **E** Wendy's H, Drug, **W** Dunkin', Subway
46mm	IL 58, Golf Rd, **E** Mobil/Dunkin'/dsl, Shell/Subway Omega Rest. Wyndham CVS Drug, Golf Mill M Meijer, Meineke, Target, **W** H
49mm	Willow Rd, **W** BP/Subway/dsl Chipotle, Jimmy Joh McDonald's, Pie Five Pizza, Starbucks, TGIFriday's E Western, Country Inn Suites, Courtyard, Motel 6 CVS D Mariano's Mkt
53mm	Lake Cook Rd (no nb re-entry), **E** Embassy Suites, Hy **W** J Alexander's
I-294 begins/ends on I-94.	

INTERSTATE 355 (Illinois)

Exit #	Services
31mm	**I-355 begins/end on I-290.**
30	US 20, W Lake St, **E** Marathon, Mobil/dsl Baskin-R bins/Dunkin', Burger King, Chipotle, Culver's, Famous Da BBQ, Firehouse Subs, IHOP, Jimmy John's, La Hacienda M can, Panda Express, Panera Bread, Ristorante de Marco's, S bucks Hampton Inn Midas, Sam's Club/gas, Veriz Walmart/Subway, **W** Shell Dave&Buster's, Venuti's R
29	Army Trail Rd, **E** Mobil/dsl, Shell/dsl Serino's D **W** BP/dsl, Mobil/dsl Hilton Garden
27	IL 64, E North Ave, **E** BP/Subway/dsl, Burger King, Cc fort Suites, Fairfield Inn, McDonald's, Shell/Circle K, Thc ton's/dsl Jimmy John's, **W** Speedway/dsl Rar da Art's RV Ctr, Suburban Tire/auto
24	Roosevelt, **E** Mobil Dunkin', Subway Crowne za Cadillac, Mariano's Mkt, Toyota, **W** Jimmy Joh NAPA, Pete's Mkt
22	IL 56, Butterfield Rd, **E** Arby's, Brick House Rest., Bur King, Chama Gaucha Brazilian, Chipotle Mexican, Fuddrucke Hooters, Melting Pot, Olive Garden, Panera Bread, Portillo's, F Lobster, Ruby Tuesday, Starbucks, Subway, Zoup! Com Inn, Extended Stay America, Holiday Inn Express, Marriott, F Roof Inn $Tree, Best Buy, Kohl's, Michael's, Petsmart, Rc

IL

CHICAGO AREA

N INTERSTATE 355 (Illinois) Cont'd

22	Continued Verizon, **W** [food] Carlucci Italian [lodging] DoubleTree Suites [other] 7-11, Home Depot
20mm	**I-88 E/I-355 run together**
19	US 34, Ogden Ave, **E** [gas] Shell [food] Culver's, Jimmy John's, McDonald's [lodging] InTown Suites [other] AT&T, Buick/GMC, Chrysler/Dodge/Jeep, Ford, **W** [food] Baskin-Robbins/Dunkin' [lodging] Extended Stay America [other] Chevrolet, Speedway/dsl, vet
18	Maple Ave, **1 mi W** [gas] BP, Mobil, Shell/Circle K [food] KFC/Taco Bell, McDonald's [other] Jewel Osco, Walgreens
16	63rd St, Hobson Rd, **E** [gas] Mobil/dsl, Thornton's/McDonald's/dsl [food] Steven's Rest, Subway [other] AutoZone, Familia Fresh Mkt, GNC, Target, Walgreens
15	W 75th St, **E** [gas] Mobil [food] Arby's, Bakers Square Rest [other] Hobby Lobby, Home Depot, Sam's Club/gas, **W** [gas] Marathon [food] Dunkin-Donuts, El Burro Loco, McDonald's, Pizza Italiano [other] Jewel-Osco
14	87th St, Baughton Rd, **E** [gas] BP, Shell [food] Al's Pizza, Dunkin-Donuts, McDonald's, Oberweiss, Subway, Wendy's [other] Costco/gas, CVS Drug, **W** [gas] Mobil [food] Bar Louie, Buffalo Wild Wings, Famous Dave's BBQ, Five Guys, IHOP, Jimmy John's, Longhorn Steaks, Panda Express, Panera Bread, Potbelly, Starbucks, Ted's MT Grill [lodging] ALoft [other] AT&T, Barnes&Noble, Bass Pro Shops, Discount Tire, IKEA, Macy's, Meijer/gas, Verizon, Walgreens
12	I-55
8	127th St, **E** [food] Burger King, Jimmy John's, KFC, McDonald's, Starbucks, Subway, Taco Bell [other] Aldi Foods, AT&T, Firestone/auto, Jewel-Osco, Jiffy Lube, Pepper's Autocare, USPO, Verizon, Walgreens
6	IL 171, Archer Ave, 143rd St, **E** [other] Kohl's, Target, vet
4	159th Ave, IL 7, Orland Park, Homer Glen, **E** [gas] Citgo/dsl, **W** [gas] URGENT CARE
3mm	**toll booth both directions**
1	US 6, **E** [gas] Rte 6 Food'n Fuel/Dunkin'/dsl, **W** [other] H
0mm	I-80 E, W, **I-355 begins/ends on I-80 exit 140.**

PEORIA

E INTERSTATE 474 (Peoria)

Exit #	Services
15	I-74, E to Bloomington, W to Peoria
9	IL 29, E Peoria, to Pekin, **N** [gas] Shell/Arby's/dsl, Thornton's [food] DQ, Driftwood Pizza, Taco John's [other] $General, Riverboat Casino (6mi), **S** [gas] BP/Subway/dsl, Casey's [food] Denny's, Domino's, Lian Wang, McDonald's, Rosati's Pizza [other] Chrysler/Dodge/Jeep, Toyota
8mm	Illinois River
6b a	US 24, Adams St, Bartonville, **S** [gas] BP/dsl, Mobil/dsl [food] Hardee's, KFC, McDonald's, Tyroni's Café
5	Airport Rd, **S** [gas] Mobil/e85/dsl [other] [airport]
3a	to IL 116, Farmington, **S** [other] Wildlife Prairie Park
0b a	I-74, W to Moline, E to Peoria.

I-474 begins/ends on I-74, exit 87.

INDIANA

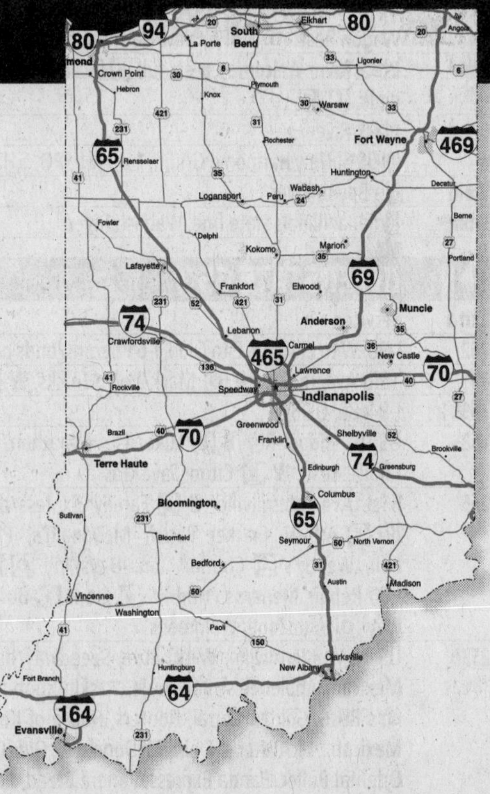

E INTERSTATE 64

Exit #	Services
124mm	Indiana/Kentucky state line, Ohio River
123	IN 62 E, New Albany, **N** [gas] Marathon/dsl, Shell/Circle K [food] DQ [other] H, Family$, Firestone/auto, Save-A-Lot, **S** [gas] Shell/Circle K, Valero [food] Daisy's Cafeteria, Subway, Waffle House [lodging] Best Western, Holiday Inn Express
121	I-265 E, to I-65 (exits left from eb), **N** access to H
119	US 150 W, to Greenville, **N** [gas] Marathon [food] Bean St Cafe, Bearno's Buffet, Beef O'Brady's, Chillburger, China Cafe, Domino's, DQ, El Nopal, McDonald's, Papa John's, Sam's Family Rest., Subway, Taco Bell, Tumbleweed SW Grill [other] AutoZone, JayC Foods, Rite Aid, URGENT CARE, Walgreens
118	IN 62, IN 64W, to Georgetown, **N** [gas] Marathon/dsl/24hr, Shell/Circle K [food] Korner Kitchen, McDonald's [lodging] Red Roof Inn [other] CashSaver Foods, Mr. Hardware, **S** [gas] Marathon/dsl
115mm	**Welcome Ctr wb, full [handicapped] facilities, litter barrels, [phone], [picnic], vending**
113	to Lanesville
105	IN 135, to Corydon, **N** [gas] Marathon/dsl, Shell [food] Big Boy [lodging] Comfort Inn, **S** [gas] 5 Star, BP/dsl [food] Alberto's Italian, Arby's, Beef O'Brady's, Burger King, Cracker Barrel, Culver's, Domino's, DQ, El Nopal Mexican, Hong Kong Buffet, Jimmy John's, KFC, Lee's Chicken, LJ Silver, McDonald's, O'Charley's, Papa John's, Papa Murphy's, Pizza Hut, Ryan's, Subway, Taco Bell, Waffle House, Wendy's, White Castle [lodging] Baymont Inn, Hampton Inn, Holiday Inn Express, Super 8 [other] H, $Tree, Advance Parts, AT&T, AutoZone, Big O Tire, Buick/Chevrolet, Chrysler/Dodge/Jeep, CVS Drug, Family$, Ford, Verizon, Walgreens, Walmart/Subway
100mm	Blue River
97mm	**parking area both lanes**
92	IN 66, Carefree, **N** [other] Marengo Caves, **S** [gas] Marathon/dsl/rest./24hr, Pilot/Subway/dsl/scales/24hr [food] Big Dadd's Rest., Country Style Rest. [lodging] Red Carpet Inn [other] Carefree Truckwash, Harrison Crawford SF, repair, to Wyandotte Caves
88mm	Hoosier Nat Forest eastern boundary
86	IN 37, to Sulphur, **N** to Patoka Lake, **S** food, gas, scenic route

IL IN

INTERSTATE 64 Cont'd

Exit #	Services
79	IN 37, to Tell City, St Croix, S Marathon/Subshop/pizza/dsl to Hoosier NF, to OH River Br
76mm	Anderson River
72	IN 145, to Birdseye, N to Patoka Lake, S St Meinrad Coll, winery (2mi), gas
63	IN 162, to Ferdinand, N Sunoco/dsl China Garden, McDonald's, Subway, Taco Bell, Wendy's Comfort Inn, Red Roof Inn CVS Drug, Ferdinand SF, S Lake Rudolph RV Camping (8mi)
58mm	**both lanes, full facilities, info, litter barrels, , vending**
57	US 231, to Dale, Huntingburg, N H, S Chuckles/dsl Denny's, Wendy's Baymont Inn, Motel 6 Lincoln Boyhood Home, Lincoln SP
54	IN 161, to Holland, Tennyson
39	IN 61, Lynnville, N Marathon Monterrey Mexican USPO
32mm	N Wabash & Erie Canal
29b a	I-69 N, IN 57 N&S, to Evansville
25b a	US 41, to Evansville, N FLYING J/Denny's/dsl/scales/24hr, Loves/Wendy's/dsl/24hr, Pilot/Subway/Taco Bell/dsl/24hr Baymont Inn Blue Beacon, truck repair/lube, S Marathon/dsl Arby's, Denny's, McDonald's, Stoll's Amish Rest. Holiday Inn Express, Quality Inn, Red Roof Inn, Super 8 st police, to U S IN
18	IN 65, to Cynthiana, S Motomart/dsl/24hr
12	IN 165, Poseyville, S CountryMark/Subway/dsl Red Wagon Rest. NAPA, New Harmonie Hist Area/SP
7mm	**Black River Welcome Ctr eb, full facilities, litter barrels, petwalk, ,**
5mm	Black River
4	IN 69 S, New Harmony, Griffin, **1 mi N** USPO, **S** Harmony St Park
2mm	Big Bayou River
0mm	Indiana/Illinois state line, Wabash River

IN

INTERSTATE 65

Exit #	Services
262	I-90, W to Chicago, E to Ohio, **I-65 begins/ends on US 12, US 20.**
261	15th Ave, to Gary, E Mack/Volvo Trucks, W Citgo
259b a	I-94/80, US 6W
258	US 6, Ridge Rd, E Luke/dsl, Marathon/dsl Diner's Choice Rest., W Citgo, Save Gas
255	61st Ave, Merrillville, E Family Express/dsl, Speedway/dsl Arby's, Cracker Barrel, McDonald's, Pizza Hut/Taco Bell, Wendy's Comfort Inn, Days Inn H, Chevrolet, I-65 Repair, Menards, **1 mi W** Clark Burger King, Subway AutoZone, Walgreens
253b	US 30 W, Merrillville, W Blue, Speedway/dsl Abuelo's Mexican, Applebee's, Bar Louie, Baskin-Robbins/Dunkin', Gino's Rest., Golden Corral, Hooters, House of Kobe, La Carreta Mexican, McAlister's Deli, McDonald's, Old Chicago Pizza, Oriental Buffet, Panda Express, Panera Bread, Pepe's Mexican, Pizza Hut, Portillo's Hot Dogs, Qdoba, Starbucks, Steak'n Shake, Subway, TX Corral Steaks, Wendy's, White Castle Baymont Inn, Clarion, Fairfield Inn, Hampton Inn, Knights Inn, Microtel, Red Roof Inn, Residence Inn H, $Tree, Acura, Aldi Foods, Buick/GMC, Cadillac, CarX, Chrysler/Dodge/Jeep, CVS Drug, Discount Tire, Fanny May Candies, Ford/Lincoln, Hyundai, Infiniti, Meijer/dsl, Midas, NTB, Old Time Pottery, Subaru, U-Haul, USPO, Verizon, Walgreens
253a	US 30 E, E BP/Luke/dsl, Speedway/dsl Bakers Squ BC Osaka, Bob Evans, Buffalo Wild Wings, Chick-fil-A, Ch Chipotle Mexican, ChuckeCheese, Culver's, Dunkin', Fireho Subs, IHOP, Jimmy John's, KFC/LJ Silver, Longhorn Steaks, Donald's, Olive Garden, Outback Steaks, Popeye's, Potb Red Lobster, Red Robin, Sheffield's Rest., Starbucks, Starbu (2), Taco Bell, TGIFriday's, Wendy's Best Value Inn, Western, Candlewood Suites, Comfort Suites, Country In Suites, Economy Inn, Extended Stay America, Hilton Garc Home 2 Suites, La Quinta, Motel 6, Quality Inn, Staybri Suites, Super 8, Woodspring Suites AT&T, Audi/VW, A Zone, Best Buy, BigLots, Carmax, Costco/gas, Dick's, Firesto auto, Hobby Lobby, Home Depot, Honda, JC Penney, Jo-A Kia, Kohl's, Lowe's, Macy's, Michael's, Nissan, Office Depot, Navy, PetCo, Petsmart, Ross, Sam's Club/gas, Target, Tire B TJ Maxx, Toyota, Tuesday Morning, vet, Walmart/McDonal
249	109th Ave, W Speedway/dsl Buffalo Wild Wings, Ch Garden, Culver's, Dunkin', Golden Apple Rest., Jimmy John's Quesadilla, Marco's Pizza, Rosati's Pizza $Tree, Aldi, G Verizon, Walgreens
247	US 231, Crown Point, W Family Express H
241mm	**weigh sta sb**
240	IN 2, Lowell, E FLYING J/Denny's/dsl/24hr/@, Pilot Wendy's/dsl/scales/24hr Arby's, McDonald's, S way Comfort Inn, Super 8 truck repair, truck wa W st police
234mm	Kankakee River
231mm	**both lanes, full facilities, info, litter barrels, petwalk, , vending**
230	IN 10, Roselawn, E Loves/Arby's/dsl/scales/24hr, BP/Country Pride/dsl/scales/24hr/@, W Family Expre e85, Marathon/Subway China Wok, J&J Pizza, Sycam Drive-In $General, CVS Drug, Lake Holiday Camping, Lake Camping, SaveALot, TrueValue
220	IN 14, Winamac, W BP/dsl, CNG Tesla EVC F Oaks Farms Store
215	IN 114, Rensselaer, E Family Express/dsl/e85/24hr by's, DQ, KFC, McDonald's, Taco Bell Baymont Inn, Co fort Suites, Interstate Motel H, W Marathon/Trail T Rest./dsl/24hr Burger King Economy Inn firewo tires/repair/towing/24hr
212mm	Iroquois River
205	US 231, Remington, E Crazy D/dsl H, to St Joseph's C
201	US 24/231, Remington, E Caboose Lake RV Camping, W Family Express/dsl, Petro/Shell/Iron Skillet/dsl/scales/24hr Pilot/Subway/dsl/scales/24hr KFC, McDonald's S set Inn, Super 8
196mm	**both lanes, full facilities, info, litter barrels, petwalk, , vending**
193	US 231, to Chalmers, E Marathon/DQ
188	IN 18, to Brookston, Fowler, many windmills
178	IN 43, W Lafayette, E Phillips 66/Subway/dsl, Speedw Taco Bell McDonald's, Wendy's museum, st police, Tippecanoe Bfd, W to Purdue U
176mm	Wabash River
175	IN 25, Lafayette, E Family Express/dsl/e85, Marathon/ W H
172	IN 26, Lafayette, E Tesla EVC Cracker Barrel, Dunkin', El Rodeo, Fox's Pizza, Starbucks, Steak'n Shake, S way, White Castle Baymont Inn, Candlewood Suites, Co fort Inn, Comfort Suites, Days Inn, La Quinta, Motel 6, Tow Place Suites Meijer/dsl/e85, visitor's ctr, W Luke/

MERRILLVILLE

LAFAYETTE

INTERSTATE 65 Cont'd

172 Continued
Shell/Circle K/dsl, Speedway/dsl, Tesla EVC, Tesla EVC Arby's, Bob Evans, Burger King, Cheddar's, Chick-fil-A, Chili's, Chipotle, ChuckeCheese, Coldstone, Culver's, Denny's, Fazoli's, Firehouse Subs, Golden Corral, Grindstone Charlie's, HuHot, IHOP, Jets Pizza, Jimmy John's, KFC, Logan's Roadhouse, Longhorn Steaks, McAlister's Deli, McDonald's, Moe's SW Grill, Mtn Jack's, Noodles&Co, Olive Garden, Outback Steaks, Panera Bread, Pizza Hut, Qdoba, Red Lobster, Sonic, Spageddie's, Starbucks, Steak'n Shake, Subway, Taco Bell, TGIFriday's Courtyard, Doubletree, EconoLodge, Fairfield Inn, Hampton Inn, Holiday Inn Express, Home 2 Suites, Homewood Suites, Quality Inn, Red Roof Inn, Residence Inn, Super 8, Travelodge H, $General, $Tree, Aamco, Chevrolet, CVS Drug, Discount Tire, Fresh Thyme Mkt, Gordman's, Harley Davidson, Hobby Lobby, Home Depot, Hyundai, Lowe's, Nissan, Office Depot, Sam's Club/gas, Target, TJ Maxx, to Purdue U, Toyota, USPO, Verizon, vet, Walgreens, Walmart/Subway

168 IN 38, IN 25 S, Dayton, E BP/Subway, CNG, Shell/Circle K/dsl

158 IN 28, to Frankfort, E BP/Subway/dsl Mack/Volvo, 2 mi W Lincoln Lodge Motel

150mm **sb, full facilities, info, litter barrels, petwalk, vending**

148mm **nb, full facilities, info, litter barrels, petwalk, vending**

146 IN 47, Thorntown, W camping

141 US 52 W (exits left from sb), Lafayette Ave, E H

140 IN 32, Lebanon, E BP/repair, Marathon/dsl Denny's, McDonald's, White Castle Quality Inn H, AutoZone, Goodyear/auto, Menards, O'Reilly Parts, Pomp's Tires, W McClure/dsl/e85, Shell Arby's, Flapjacks Pancakes, KFC, Steak'n Shake, Subway, Taco Bell Best Value Inn, EconoLodge, Holiday Inn Express, Motel 6 truckwash

139 IN 39, Lebanon, E Speedway/dsl Penn Sta Subs, Starbucks, Wendy's $General, W FLYING J/Huddle House/dsl/LP/scales/24hr Donaldson's Chocolates

138 to US 52, Lebanon, E BP/dsl

133 IN 267, Whitestown, W Loves/McDonald's/Subway/dsl/scales/24hr

130 IN 334, Zionsville, E Marathon/Fazoli's/dsl, Shell/Circle K/Subway/dsl, Tesla EVC Buffalo Wild Wings, Burger King, City BBQ, Cracker Barrel, Dunkin', El Rodeo Mexican, Flamme Burger, Flapjacks Pancakes, Fox's Pizza, McAlister's Deli, McDonald's, Panda Express, Panera Bread, Qdoba, Starbucks, Taco Bell, Wendy's, Which Wich? Hampton Inn, Holiday Inn Express, Woodspring Suites H, AT&T, CVS Drug, Lowe's, Meijer/dsl, Petco, Ross, TJ Maxx, Toyota, Verizon, vet, W TA/BP/Popeye's/dsl/scales/24hr/@

129 I-865 E, to I-465 E, US 52 E (from sb)

126mm Fishback Creek

124 71st St, 1 mi E Hot Box Pizza, Starbucks, Steak'n Shake, Subway Best Western+, Candlewood Suites, Courtyard, Hampton Inn, Hilton Garden, Holiday Inn Express, Residence Inn, W Eagle Creek Park

123 I-465 S, S to

121 Lafayette Rd, same as 119 W, E Speedway (2), Speedway/dsl Quality Inn, W Shell/Circle K Arby's, Church's, Fazoli's, La Bamba Burritos Executive Inn H, $Tree, Aldi Foods, AT&T, Batteries+Bulbs, Best Buy, Discount Tire, Family$, GNC, Hyundai, Kia, Mazda, Nissan, PepBoys, SaveALot, Tire Barn, Walmart/Subway

INDIANAPOLIS AREA

GREENWOOD

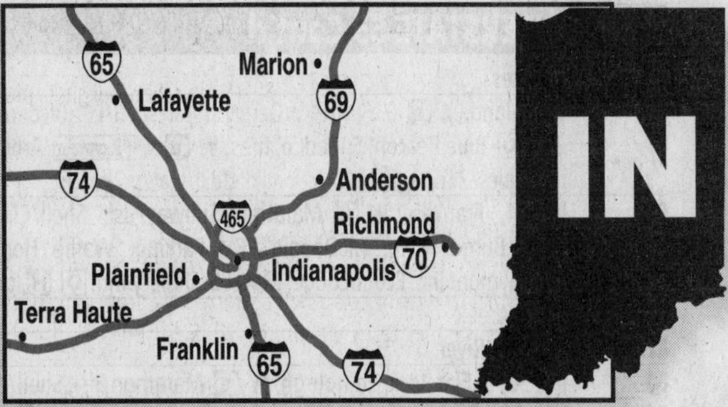

119 38th St (no nb return), same as 121, Dodge, W Phillips 66, Speedway/dsl KFC, McDonald's, Papa John's, Pizza Hut, Red Lobster, Taco Bell Advance Parts, Aldi Foods, Best Buy, Chevrolet, Hyundai, Meijer/dsl, Tires+

117.5mm White River

117 MLK St (from sb), W Marathon/dsl

116 29th St, 30th St (from nb), W Marian Coll

115 21st St, E Shell/Circle K H, W museums, zoo

114 MLK St, West St, downtown

113 US 31, IN 37, Meridian St, to downtown, E H

112a I-70 E, to Columbus

111 Market St, Michigan St, Ohio St, E Hardee's museum, W City Market

110b I-70 W, to St Louis

110a Prospect St, Morris St, East St

109 Raymond St, E H, W BP, Speedway/dsl Little Caesar's, White Castle CVS Drug, Family$, Safeway

107 Keystone Ave, E Mystick Best Value Inn H, W Phillips 66/dsl, Speedway/dsl, Valero Big Kahuna Pizza, Burger King, Denny's, DQ, McDonald's, Subway, Wendy's Comfort Inn $General, U of Indianapolis, Walmart Mkt

106 I-465 and I-74

103 Southport Rd, E BP/McDonald's, Shell/Circle K Arby's, Chicago Grill, Chick-fil-A, Hardee's, Hotbox Pizza, Jersey Mike's, Jimmy John's, Leonardo's Mexican, Longhorn Steaks, Monical's Pizza, Mr Wok, Noble Roman's, O'Charley's, Panda Express, Panera Bread, Penn Sta Subs, Pizza Hut, Qdoba, Rally's Aldi Foods, AT&T, Firestone/auto, Harley-Davidson, Home Depot, Kohl's, Meijer/dsl/e85, Menards, Staples, Target, W EVC, Marathon/Circle K, Phillips 66, Speedway/dsl Bob Evans, Burger King, Carrabba's, Cheeseburger Paradise, Cracker Barrel, McDonald's, Stacked Pickle, Starbucks, Steak'n Shake, Subway, TX Roadhouse, Waffle House, Wendy's Baymont Inn, Comfort Suites, Country Inn&Suites, Courtyard, Fairfield Inn, Hampton Inn, Motel 6, Quality Inn, Super 8 H

101 CountyLine Rd, E Candlewood Suites, W Murphy USA/dsl, Shell/Circle K/dsl Buffalo Wild Wings, Cheddar's, Culver's, El Meson Mexican, Freddy's, Leon Mexican, Lindo Mexico, McAlister's Deli, Newk's Eatery, Popeye's, Primanti Bros, Sonic, Taco Bell, Tokyo Buffet, Zaxby's Hilton Garden, Holiday Inn Express, Home 2 Suites, Residence Inn, Woodspring Suites H, Costco/dsl, Kroger/dsl, Verizon, Walmart/Subway

99 Greenwood, E Road Ranger/Pilot/Subway/dsl/scales/24hr, W Marathon, Shell/Circle K Arby's, China Wok, Denny's, Main St Grille, McDonald's, Papa John's, Puerto Vallarta, Starbucks, Subway, Taco Bell, Waffle House, White Castle InTown Suites, La Quinta, Red Carpet Inn, Red Roof Inn H, Camping World RV Ctr, Sam's Club, vet

97 Worthsville Rd, W Circle K/dsl

IN

[gas] = gas [food] = food [lodging] = lodging [other] = other [RS] = rest stop Copyright 2020 - The Next EX

INTERSTATE 65 Cont'd

Exit #	Services
95	Whiteland, E [gas] FLYING J/Denny's/scales/dsl/LP/RV dump/24hr [other] Blue Beacon, SpeedCo, tires, W [gas] Love's/Arby's/dsl/scales/24hr, Pilot/McDonald's/dsl/scales/24hr/@
90	IN 44, Franklin, W [gas] Marathon/Subway/dsl, Shell/Circle K [food] Burger King, McDonald's/RV Parking, Waffle House [lodging] Baymont Inn, EconoLodge, Motel 6, Quality Inn [other] [H], golf
85mm	Sugar Creek
82mm	Big Blue River
80	IN 252, to Flat Rock, Edinburgh, W [gas] Marathon/dsl, Shell/dsl
76b a	US 31, Taylorsville, E [gas] Shell/Circle K/dsl, Speedway/dsl [food] A&W/KFC, Burger King, El Toreo Mexican, Waffle House [lodging] Red Roof Inn [other] [H], $ General, Toyota, W [gas] EVC, Get-Go/dsl, Marathon, Thornton's/café/dsl [food] Applebee's, Arby's, Cracker Barrel, Hardee's, Max&Erma's, McDonald's, MT Mikes, Ruby Tuesday, Snappy Tomato Pizza, Subway, Taco Bell [lodging] Best Western, Comfort Inn, Hampton Inn, Hilton Garden, Holiday Inn Express [other] antiques, Express Outlets/famous brands, Goodyear, Harley-Davidson, repair
73mm	**[RS] both lanes, full [handicapped] facilities, info, litter barrels, petwalk, [phone], [picnic], vending**
68mm	Driftwood River
68	IN 46, Columbus, E [gas] Shell/Circle K, Speedway/dsl [food] Buffalo Wild Wings, Burger King, Culver's, IHOP, Jimmy John's, Lincoln Sq Rest., McAlister's Deli, McDonald's, Panda Express, RuYi Asian, Starbucks, Subway, TX Roadhouse, Waffle House, Wendy's [lodging] Fairfield Inn, Holiday Inn, Sleep Inn, Super 8 [other] [H], AutoZone, Belle Tire, Chevrolet, Menards, Sam's Club/gas, Verizon, Walgreens, Walmart/Subway, W [gas] [food] Arby's, Bob Evans, Chicago's Pizza, El Nopal Mexican, Freddy's, Marco's Pizza, Noble Roman's, Papa John's, Papa's Grill, Taco Bell [lodging] Courtyard, Days Inn, EconoLodge, La Quinta, Residence Inn [other] $General, CVS Drug, Jay-C Foods, to Brown Co SP, vet
64	IN 58, Walesboro, W [gas] Circle K/dsl, GetGo/dsl
55	IN 11, to Jonesville, Seymour
54mm	White River
51mm	**weigh sta both lanes**
50b a	US 50, Seymour, E [gas] Circle K/dsl, Sunshine Cafe/Waffle House, TA/BP/Country Pride/dsl/24hr/@ [food] McDonald's [lodging] Allstate Inn, Days Inn, EconoLodge, Economy Inn, Motel 6, Travelodge, W [gas] Circle K/dsl, Murphy USA/dsl, Shell/Circle K/dsl, Speedway/dsl [food] Applebee's, Arby's, Bonanza, Buffalo Wild Wings, Buffet China, Burger King, Capt D's, Chili's, Cracker Barrel, Domino's, DQ, El Nopal Mexican, Freddy's, Hardee's, KFC, Little Caesar's, McDonalds, Papa John's, Pizza Hut, Popeye's, Rally's, Steak'n Shake, Subway, Taco Bell, Wendy's, White Castle [lodging] Fairfield Inn, Hampton Inn, Holiday Inn Express, Knights Inn, Quality Inn [other] [H], $General, $Tree, Advance Parts, Aldi Foods, AT&T, AutoZone, BigLots, Buick/Cadillac/Chevrolet/GMC, Chrysler/Dodge/Jeep, CVS Drug, Ford, GNC, Home Depot, Jay-C Foods, JC Penney, O'Reilly Parts, Verizon, Walgreens, Walmart/Subway
41	IN 250, Uniontown, E [other] tires, W [gas] Marathon/dsl
36	US 31, Crothersville, E [other] tires, W [gas] Marathon/dsl
34a b	IN 256, Austin, E [gas] Shell/Circle K [other] Clifty Falls SP, to Hardy Lake, W [gas] Fuelmart/dsl/scales, Sunoco/Huddle House/dsl
29b a	IN 56, to Salem, Scottsburg, E [gas] MotoMart/dsl, Speedway/dsl, Sunoco [food] Burger King, China Wind, Cracker Barrel, Denny's, Domino's, First Wok, KFC, Papa John's, Ponderosa, Popeye's, Sonic, Subway, Taco Bell [lodging] Holiday Inn Express, Mariann Inn [other] [H], Ace Hardware, Advance Parts, AutoZone, CVS Drug, O'Reilly Parts, W [gas] Circle K, Murphy USA [food] Arby's,
29b a	Continued Chillers, LJ Silver, McDonald's, Pizza Hut, Puerto Vallarta, Ro... house USA, Waffle House, Wendy's [lodging] Hampton Inn, Qua... Inn, Red Roof Inn [other] Big O Tire, Buick/Chevrolet, Jellyst... Camping (4mi), Verizon, Walmart/Subway
22mm	**[RS] both lanes, full [handicapped] facilities, info, litter barrels, petwalk, [picnic], vending**
19	IN 160, Henryville, E [gas] Circle K, Marathon/Subway/... [other] $General, USPO
16	Memphis Rd, Memphis, E [gas] Love's/McDonald's/Sub... way/dsl/scales/24hr, W [gas] Pilot/Arby's/dsl/scales/24h... [other] Customers First RV Ctr
9	IN 311, to New Albany, Sellersburg, E [gas] Circle K, Su... co [food] Arby's, Cracker Barrel, DQ, Waffle House [lodging] D... Inn, Ramada Inn [other] Carmerica/repair, Ford, O'Reilly Pa... W [gas] Circle K [food] Burger King, El Nopal Mexican, McDonal... Taco Bell [lodging] Quality Inn
7	IN 60, Hamburg, E [gas] BP/dsl, W [food] Cricket's Cafe, KFC/Pi... Hut [lodging] Travelodge
6b a	I-265 W, to I-64 W, IN 265 E, New Albany
5	Veterans Parkway, E [gas] Marathon/dsl [food] Boombozz ... za, Bubba's BBQ, Culver's, Krispy Kreme, Popeye's, W... Eggs [other] [H], AT&T, Hobby Lobby, Menards, Tire Discount... W [food] Buffalo Wild Wings, Cheddar's, Chick-fil-A, Chuy's M... ican, DQ, First Watch, IHOP, Jimmy John's, Kansai, Longh... Steaks, McAlister's Deli, Mission BBQ, Olive Garden, Outb... Steaks, Panda Express, Panera Bread, Papa Murphy's, Pizza H... Qdoba, Red Robin, Storming Crab, Subway, Taco Bell [lodging] C... dlewood Suites, Home 2 Suites, Suburban Inn [other] Bass ... Shops, Best Buy, Buick/Chevrolet/GMC, Lowe's, Michael's, ... Navy, Old Time Pottery, Petsmart, Ross, Sam's Club/gas, S... ples, Target, Verizon, Walgreens, Walmart/Subway
4	US 31 N, IN 131 S, Clarksville, New Albany, E [gas] Tho... tons/dsl [food] Momma's Pizza, White Castle [lodging] Woodspr... Suites [other] Raben Tire, W [gas] Speedway/dsl [food] Applebe... Arby's, Bob Evans, Burger King, Capt D's, Chili's, China Buf... ChuckeCheese, Denny's, Fazoli's, Golden Corral, Hooters, LJ ... ver, Logan's Roadhouse, McDonald's, Mr Gatti's, Outback Stea... Papa John's, Rally's, Red Lobster, Senor Iguana, Steak'n Sha... TX Roadhouse, Wendy's, Zesto [lodging] Best Western, Candlewo... Suites, Hampton Inn, Suburban Lodge [other] $Tree, AT&T, Au... Zone, BigLots, Books-A-Million, CVS Drug, Dick's, Dillard's, D... count Tire, Ford, Home Depot, Honda, JC Penney, Jo-Ann Fabr... Kia, Kroger/gas, Nissan, O'Reilly Parts, PepBoys, TJ Maxx, To... ery Tire/auto, Toyota, Tuesday Morning, USPO, VW, Walgreen...
2	Eastern Blvd, Clarksville, E [lodging] Days Inn, Quality Suites, R... Carpet, Value Inn [other] [H], U-Haul, W [gas] Circle K [lodging] Best In...
1	US 31 S, IN 62, Stansifer Ave, E [gas] Thornton's/dsl [food] D... Subway [other] [H], $General, Advance Parts, CVS Drug, W... greens, W [lodging] Radisson [other] Stinnett RV Ctr
0	Jeffersonville, E [gas] Thornton's/dsl [food] Hardee's [other] [H], Chr... ler/Jeep/Dodge, CVS Drug, Hyundai, to Falls of OH SP, W... greens, W [food] Hooters, Kingfish Rest., Kobe [lodging] Fairfield I... Hawthorn Suites, Sheraton
0mm	Indiana/Kentucky state line, Ohio River

COLUMBUS

SEYMOUR

SCOTTSBURG

CLARKSVILLE

IN

INTERSTATE 69

Exit #	Services
358mm	Indiana/Michigan state line
357	Lake George Rd, to IN 120, Fremont, Lake James, E [gas] Petro/I... Skillet/dsl/LP/scales/24hr/@ [other] Freightliner/Western Star Tru... Repair, Kenworth, W [gas] Marathon/dsl, Pilot/Wendy's/d... scales/24hr, Shell/Subway/dsl [food] McDonald's, Red Arrow Re...

INTERSTATE 69 Cont'd

357 Continued
Holiday Inn Express, Redwood Inn Freemont Outlets/Famous Brands, GNC, Jellystone Camping (5mi), to Pokagon SP

356 I-80/90 Toll Rd, E to Toledo, W to Chicago

354 IN 127, to IN 120, IN 727, Fremont, Orland, **E** Tesla EVC American Inn, Comfort Inn, Quality Inn, Ramada, Travelers Inn golf, **W** Marathon/dsl Holiday Inn Express Freemont Outlets/Famous Brands, Jellystone Camping (4mi), to Pokagon SP

350 rd 200 W, to Lake James, Crooked Lake, **E** Sunoco/dsl fireworks, **W** Marathon, Sunoco/Subway Caruso's Rest., Tasty Pizza Marine Ctr

348 US 20, to Angola, Lagrange, **E** Marathon/Subway/dsl, Speedway/Taco Bell/dsl McDonald's Happy Acres Camping (1mi), University Inn (2mi) H, **W** Loves/Hardee's/dsl/scales/24hr KOA (2mi)

345mm Pigeon Creek

344mm **sb, full facilities, info, litter barrels, petwalk, vending**

340 IN 4, to Hamilton, Ashley, Hudson, **1 mi W** Marathon/Subway/dsl

334 US 6, to Waterloo, Kendallville, **E** Subway $General, **W** BP/dsl, Marathon/dsl/24hr Kathy's Kountry Kitchen

329 IN 8, to Garrett, Auburn, **E** BP, Lassus, Speedway/dsl, Speedway/dsl (2) Applebee's, Arby's, Burger King, Culver's, DQ, Jimmy John's, KFC, Little Caesar's, McDonald's, Papa John's, Peking Buffet, Penguin Point Rest., Pizza Hut, Richard's Rest., Starbucks, Steak'n Shake, Subway, Taco Bell, Wendy's Auburn Inn, Baymont Inn, Comfort Suites, Days Inn, Red Roof Inn, Wingate Inn H, $General, $Tree, Advance Parts, Aldi Foods, AT&T, AutoZone, Buick/Chevrolet/RV Ctr, Chrysler/Dodge/Jeep, CVS Drug, Davis RV Ctr, Ford, GNC, Kroger/dsl, Monro, Save A Lot, Walmart/Subway, **W** Marathon/dsl Buffalo Wild Wings, Cebolla's Mexican, Cracker Barrel, Paradise Buffet, Subway Hampton Inn, Holiday Inn Express Home Depot, Verizon

326 rd 11A, to Garrett, Auburn, **E** Auction Park, **W** Fireside Camping

324mm **nb, full facilities, info, litter barrels, vending**

317 Union Chapel Rd, **E** H

316 IN 1 N, Dupont Rd, **E** Lassus/Elmo's/dsl, Phillips 66/Burger King Arby's, Arcos Mexicano, Culver's, Taco Bell Comfort Suites, Hampton Inn, Holiday Inn Express H, **W** Speedway/dsl Bagger Dave's Burgers, Bob Evans, Domino's, Jimmy John's, McDonald's, Panera Bread, Pine Valley Grill, Starbucks, Trolley Grill Baymont Inn, La Quinta

315 I-469, US 30 E, **W** Woodspring Suites

312b a Coldwater Rd, **E** BP/dsl, Marathon, Sunoco Agaves Mexican, Arby's, Bill's Smokehouse, Buffalo Wings & Rings, Chili's, Cork'N Cleaver, Firehouse Subs, Hall's Factory Rest., IHOP, Jimmy John's, Koto Japanese, Mister Coney, Papa John's, Rally's, Red Lobster, Subway, Taco Bell, Wendy's, Wu's Fine Chinese Hyatt Place, Ramada Plaza $Tree, Aldi Foods, Dick's, Hobby Lobby, Hyundai, JoAnn Fabrics, O'Reilly Parts, PetCo, Tuesday Morning, U-Haul, Walmart/Subway, **W** Marathon Salsa Grille

311b a US 27 S, IN 3 N, **E** Shell/dsl, Sunoco/dsl Arby's, BJ's Rest., Cheddar's, Chick-fil-A, ChuckECheese's, DQ, Fazoli's, Golden Corral, Hall's Rest., Longhorn Steaks, McDonald's, Olive Garden, Starbucks, TGIFriday's, Tim Horton's Candlewood Suites, Hawthorn Suites, TownePlace Suites, Tru Hilton

FT WAYNE

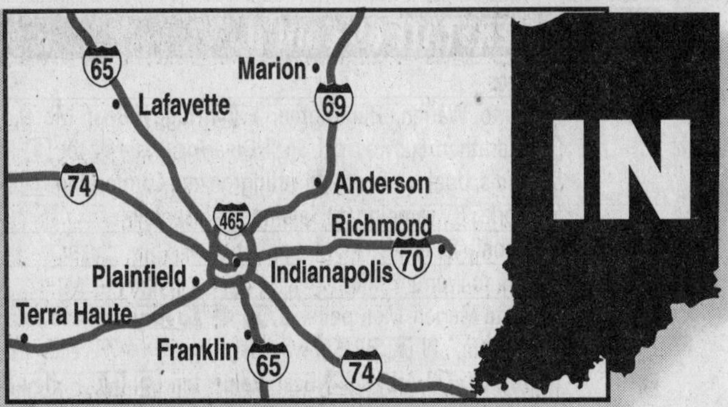

311b a Continued
Barnes&Noble, Chevrolet, Chrysler/Dodge/Jeep, Costco/gas, Discount Tire, Fiat, Ford/Lincoln, Honda, Infiniti, JC Penney, Macy's, Nissan, Subaru, Toyota, Verizon, **W** BP/dsl, Lassus/Elmo's Pizza/dsl, Marathon/dsl Applebee's, Burger King, Chipotle, Cracker Barrel, Culver's, Hardee's, IHOP, Logan's Roadhouse, McDonald's, Panda Express, Sapporo Japanese, Starbucks, Subway, Taco Bell, TX Roadhouse Best Value Inn, Best Western+, Comfort Inn, Days Inn, EconoLodge, Extended Stay America, Fairfield Inn, Fairfield Inn, Guesthouse Motel, Hampton Inn, Quality Inn, Travelodge, Wyndham Garden Belle Tire, CVS Drug, Home Depot, Lowe's, Meijer/dsl/e85, Sam's Club/gas, VW

309b a US 33, Goshen Rd, Ft Wayne, **E** Phillips 66/dsl, Pilot/dsl/scales/24hr, Shell Liberty Diner, McDonald's Ft Wayne Inn, Knights Inn, Motel 6, Red Roof Inn, Rodeway Inn, Travel Inn H, auto/dsl repair, Blue Beacon, NAPA

305b a IN 14 W, Ft Wayne, **E** Lassus, Murphy USA, Shell/Subway/dsl, Speedway/Speedy's Cafe/dsl Arby's, Biaggi's, Chick-fil-A, Chipotle Mexican, Coldstone, Domino's, Eddy Merlot Rest., Firehouse Subs, Flat Top Grill, Great Wall Buffet, Little Caesar's, Logan's Roadhouse, McAlister's Deli, Noodles&Co., O'Charley's, Panda Express, Panera Bread, Penn Sta Subs, Smokey Bones BBQ, Starbucks, Steak'n Shake, Subway, Taco Bell, Tuscanos Brazilian, Wendy's Klopfenstein Suites H, $General, $Tree, Acura, Advance Parts, Audi/Porsche, Barnes&Noble, Belle Tire, Best Buy, BigLots, BMW, Buick/GMC, Cadillac, Chevrolet, Chrysler/Dodge/Jeep, Dick's, Ford/Lincoln, Gordman's, Harley-Davidson, Kia, Kohl's, Lexus, Lowe's, Marshall's, Mazda, McMahon's Tire/auto, Meijer/dsl, Menards, Michael's, NAPA, Old Navy, Petsmart, Target, to St Francis U, Toyota, Tuesday Morning, Verizon, vet, Volvo, Walmart/Subway

302 US 24, to Jefferson Blvd, Ft Wayne, **E** Subway (1mi), Taco Bell (1mi) Extended Stay America, Fairfield Inn, Hampton Inn, Residence Inn H, IN Wesleyan Ft Wayne, **W** Lassus, Marathon/dsl Applebee's, Arby's, Bob Evans, Buffalo Wild Wings, Coventry Tavern Rest., McDonald's, Naked Chopstix, Outback Steaks, Pizza Hut, Salsa Grille, Sara's Rest., Starbucks, Wendy's, Zesto Drive-In Best Western, Comfort Suites, Hilton Garden, Holiday Inn Express, Homewood Suites, Staybridge Suites Kroger/dsl, Meineke, st police, Walgreens

299 Lower Huntington Rd, **E** to

296b a I-469, US 24 E, US 33 S, **E** to

286 US 224, to Huntington, Markle, **E** Marathon/dsl, Phillips 66/Subway/dsl, Sunoco/dsl DQ Guesthouse Inn, Heritage Place Inn H, repair/tires, **W** Roush Lake, to Huntington Reservoir

280mm **weigh sta sb/parking area nb**

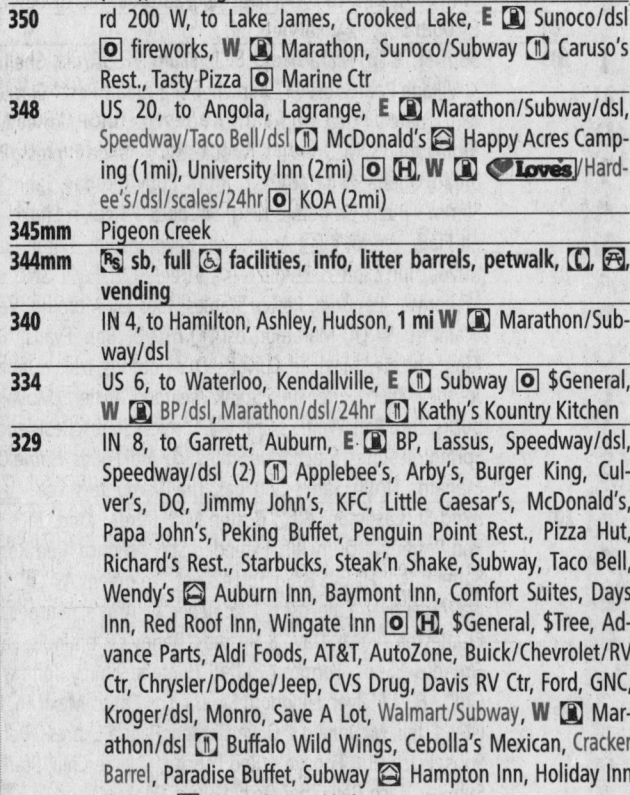

IN

INTERSTATE 69 Cont'd

ANDERSON

Exit #	Services
278	IN 5, to Warren, Huntington, E Huggy Bear Motel, W Marathon/Subway/dsl, Shell/Diner/dsl/scales/24hr McDonald's, Ugalde's Rest. Arlington Inn, Comfort Inn fireworks, RV camping, to Salamonie Reservoir
276mm	Salamonie River
273	IN 218, to Warren
264	IN 18, to Marion, Montpelier, E Loves/McDonalds/dsl/scales/24hr, W BP/Subway/dsl, FLYING J/Wendy's/dsl/scales/24hr Arby's Best Value Inn Harley-Davidson, Ram
260mm	Walnut Creek
259	US 35 N, IN 22, to Upland, E Shell/Subway Burger King, Casa Grande Mexican, China 1, Cracker Barrel Best Western+, Super 8 Mar-Brook Camping, Taylor U, W Marathon/dsl, McClure Trkstp/dsl/24hr, Phillips 66/dsl Hardee's, Starbucks, Taco Bell Holiday Inn Express to IN Wesleyan
255	IN 26, to Fairmount
250mm	**both lanes, full facilities, info, litter barrels, pet walk, , vending**
245	US 35 S, IN 28, to Alexandria, Albany, E Petro/Shell/Iron Skillet/Subway/dsl/scales/24hr/@ RV Camping
241	IN 332, to Muncie, Frankton, E BP/Subway/dsl , to Ball St U
234	IN 67, to IN 32, Chesterfield, Daleville, E Pilot/Subway/dsl/scales/24hr, Shell Arby's, Pizza Hut, Smokehouse BBQ, Taco Bell, Waffle House, White Castle Budget Inn , W McClure/dsl/e85, Pilot/Denny's/dsl/scales/24hr, Speedway/dsl McDonald's, Subway, Wendy's Travel Inn Timberline Valley Camping (3mi)
226	IN 9, IN 109, to Anderson, E A&W/KFC, Culver's, Golden Corral, MT Mike's Fairfield Inn, Hampton Inn, Holiday Inn Express, Quality Inn, Red Roof Inn Belle Tire, Meijer/dsl, Menards, visitors ctr, W BP, Marathon/dsl, Speedway/dsl Applebee's, Arby's, Bob Evans, Buffalo Wild Wings, Burger King, Cracker Barrel, Fazoli's, IHOP, Jimmy John's, McDonald's, Olive Garden, Panda Express, Panera Bread, Papa Murphy's, Payless Mkt/dsl, Penn Sta Subs, Perkins, Pizza Hut, Ponderosa, Popeye's, Qdoba, Red Lobster, Riviera Maya, Ruby Tuesday, Starbucks, Steak'n Shake, Subway, Taco Bell, TX Roadhouse, Waffle House, Wendy's, White Castle Baymont Inn, Best Value Inn, Best Western+, Comfort Inn, Days Inn, Motel 6 , $Tree, AT&T, Big Lots, Cadillac/Chevrolet, Chrysler/Dodge/Jeep, GNC, Hobby Lobby, Honda, Kohl's, Marshall's, Nissan, O'Reilly Parts, Petsmart, Tire Barn, to Anderson U, to Mounds SP, Verizon, vet, Walmart/Subway
222	IN 9, IN 67, to Anderson, W Speedway/dsl Skyline Chili
219	IN 38, Pendleton, E Ricker's/dsl Burger King, McDonald's, Subway, W Pine Lakes Camping
214	IN 13, to Lapel, E BP/dsl, Loves/McDonald's/dsl/scales24hr Waffle House, W Pilot/Subway/dsl/scales/24hr camping
210	IN 238, to Noblesville, Fortville, E BP/dsl Arby's, Culver's, DQ, Starbucks, Subway, Taco Bell, Wendy's , W EVC, Shell/dsl Aspen Grill, BJ's Rest., Chick-fil-A, Chuy's, Coldstone, Famous Dave's, Five Guys, Fresh to Order Cafe, Houlihan's, McAlister's Deli, McDonald's, Olive Garden, Panda Express, Perkins, Potbelly, Qdoba, Red Robin, Stone Creek Rest., Tuscano's Cambria Suites, Embassy Suites, Holiday Inn Express $Tree, AT&T, Cabela's, CVS Drug,

IN

INDIANAPOLIS AREA

Exit #	Services
210	Continued Dick's, Duluth Trading, Earth Fare Foods, Firestone/auto, Penney, Old Navy, Sleepy Bear Camping, Steinmart, Verizon
205	IN 37 N, 116th St, to Noblesville, Fishers, E Bent C Asian, Penn Sta Subs, Sunrise Cafe Kroger, W Sh Circle K, Speedway Brixx Pizzaria, Five Guys, Handel's Cream, Happy Dragon, Jet's Pizza, Marco's Pizza, McAlist Deli, McDonald's, Moe's SW Grill, O'Charley's, Original P cakes, Pure Eatery, Qdoba, Starbucks, Steak'n Shake, Subw Verde Mexican, Wendy's, Wild Ginger Asian Hamp Inn AT&T, CVS Drug, Firestone/auto, Target, URGENT CA
204	E 106th St, W Fairfield Inn
203	96th St, E Marathon/dsl (2), Murphy USA/dsl, Shell/Ci K, Village Pantry/dsl Applebee's, Bubba's Rest., Cracker B rel, Donato's Pizza, Dunkin', Hot Box Pizza, IHOP, Jersey Mik Jimmy John's, McDonald's, Noodles&Co., Panda Express, Pan Bread, Qdoba, Red Habanero, Rita's, Ruby Tuesday, Sahm's G Slimm's Pizza, Smoothie King, Starbucks, Steak'n Shake, Tij na Flats, Wendy's AmericInn, Baymont Inn, Hilton Gard Holiday Inn Express, Studio 6 $Tree, AT&T, Fry's, GNC, Koh Meijer/dsl, PepBoys, PetCo, Staples, Tuesday Morning, Veriz Walmart, W Marathon/dsl Arby's, Bob Evans, Bur King, Chicotes Mexican, Culver's, DJ's Hotdogs, Izakya Japane Journey Rest., Peterson's Steaks/seafood, Riviera Maya, St bucks, Taco Bell, Wolfie's Grill Comfort Suites, Residence I SpringHill Suites, Staybridge Suites Aldi Foods, Home Dep Menards, NAPA, Sam's Club/gas, Tire Discounters, vet
201	82nd St, Castleton, E Boston Mkt, Burger King, Jet's Piz Red Robin Drury Inn, Extended Stay America, Red Roof I Super 8 , CVS Drug, Lowe's, vet, Walgreens, W Spe way/Speedy's Cafe/dsl Applebee's, Arby's, Burger Ki Charleston's Rest., Dave & Buster's, Denny's, Domino's, Fazol Firehouse Subs, Formosa Buffet, Hooters, Jimmy John's, Jo Grill, KFC, LJ Silver, Longhorn Steaks, Los Cabos Mexican, Mc ister's Deli, McDonald's, Olive Garden, Panda Express, Penn S Subs, Pizza Hut, Popeye's, Red Lobster, Skyline Chili, Starbuc Subway, Taco Bell, Thai Orchid, Twin Peaks, Wendy's Ca dlewood Suites, Days Inn, Hampton Inn, Suburban Suites, S estay+ Aamco, Advance Parts, AutoZone, Best Buy, Ca Dick's, Discount Tire, Firestone/auto, fireworks, Goodyear/au JC Penney, Macy's, Midas, O'Reilly Parts, Tire Barn
200mm	I-465 around Indianapolis. **I-69 begins/ends on I-465, exit 3 at Indianapolis.**

INTERSTATE 70

RICHMOND

Exit #	Services
156.5mm	Indiana/Ohio state line, **weigh sta**
156b a	US 40 E, Richmond, N Petro/BP/Iron Skillet/dsl/24hr/ Fairfield Inn Blue Beacon, S Murphy USA/dsl, She dsl, Speedway/dsl, Sunoco A&W/LJ Silver, Applebee's, A by's, Big Boy, Buffalo Wild Wings, Buffalo Wings&Rings, Burg King, Chili's, Chipotle Mexican, Cracker Barrel, El Rodeo Me ican, Fazoli's, Galo's Italian, Golden Corral, IHOP, Jade Hou Chinese, Jimmy John's, KFC, McAlister's Deli, McDonald's, M Cafeteria, O'Charley's, Olive Garden, Papa Murphy's, Pizza H Rally's, Red Lobster, Starbucks, Steak'n Shake, Subway, Ta Bell, TX Roadhouse, Yamato Japanese Best Western, Da Inn, EconoLodge, Hampton Inn, Holiday Inn, Motel 6, Quali Inn $General, $Tree, Advance Parts, Aldi Foods, AT&T, Be Buy, Big Lots, Buick/GMC, Chevrolet, Chrysler/Dodge/Jee Dick's, Dillard's, Firestone/auto, Ford, Hobby Lobby, JC Penne Jo-Ann Fabrics, Kohl's, Kroger/dsl, Lowe's, Menards, O'Rei

INTERSTATE 70 Cont'd

156b a Continued
Parts, Save-A-Lot Foods, Tires+, TJ Maxx, Toyota/Nissan, U-Haul, Verizon, Walgreens, Walmart/Subway

153 IN 227, to Whitewater, Richmond, 2 mi N Grandpa's Farm RV Park (seasonal), KOA

151b a US 27, to Chester, Richmond, N Fricker's Rest. Honda, KOA, S Shell Bob Evans, Burger Time, Carver's Rest., El Bronco Mexican, Hardee's, McDonald's, Subway, Taco Bell, Wendy's Comfort Inn, Red Roof Inn H, CVS Drug, Harley-Davidson, Meijer/dsl/E85

149b a US 35, IN 38, to Muncie, N Loves/Hardee's/dsl/scales/24hr, S Shell/dsl Camping World RV Ctr

148mm **weigh sta wb**

145 Centerville, N Marathon/DQ/Godfather's/dsl Super 8 Goodyear/truck repair, S Warm Glow Candles/cafe

145mm Nolands Fork Creek

144mm **wb, full facilities, info, litter barrels, petwalk, vending**

141mm Greens Fork River

137 IN 1, to Hagerstown, Connersville, N Amish Cheese, S BP/Arby's/dsl/24hr, Shell/Burger King, Speedway/dsl/e85 McDonald's

131 Wilbur Wright Rd, New Lisbon, S Shell/Pizza Hut/Taco Bell/dsl/scales/24hr/@ New Lisbon RV park

126mm Flatrock River

123 IN 3, to New Castle, Spiceland, N All American Inn (3mi), Holiday Inn Express (3mi) H, S FLYING J/Denny's/Subway/dsl/LP/scales/24hr, Mr Fuel/rest./dsl/scales/24hr Montgomery's Steaks tires/repair

117mm Big Blue River

115 IN 109, to Knightstown, Wilkinson, N Loves/McDonald's/Subway/dsl/scales/24hr, Speedway/rest./dsl/scales/24hr Burger King Jellystone Camping

107mm **both lanes, full facilities, litter barrels, petwalk, vending**

104 IN 9, Greenfield, Maxwell, N Speedway/dsl, S Circle K/dsl, Murphy USA/dsl, Shell/Circle K, Speedway/dsl Applebee's, Arby's, Bamboo Garden, Bob Evans, Buffalo Wild Wings, Burger King, Chicago's Pizza, China Inn, Cracker Barrel, Culver's, Firehouse Subs, Hardee's, Jimmy John's, KFC, Little Caesar's, McDonald's, Mi Casa Mexican, MT Mike's Steaks, O'Charley's, Papa John's, Papa Murphy's, Penn Sta Subs, Pizza Hut, Ponderosa, Popeye's, Qdoba, Starbucks, Steak'n Shake, Subway, Taco Bell, Waffle House, Wasabi, Wendy's, White Castle Comfort Inn, Country Inn&Suites, Fairfield Inn, Greenfield Inn, Hampton Inn, Holiday Inn Express, Quality Inn, Super 8 H, $General, $Tree, Advance Parts, Aldi Foods, AutoZone, Big Lots, CVS Drug, GNC, Home Depot, Kohl's, Kroger/dsl, Petsmart, Verizon, Walgreens, Walmart

96 Mt Comfort Rd, N Pilot/Pizza Hut/dsl/scales/24hr, Speedway/Subway/dsl Burger King, Wendy's, S Shell/Circle K McDonald's KOA (seasonal), Mt Comfort RV Ctr

91 Post Rd, to Ft Harrison, N Mobil/Circle K Cracker Barrel, Denny's, Outback Steaks, Steak'n Shake, Wendy's InTown Suites, La Quinta Lowe's, st police, S Admiral, BP/dsl, Shell/dsl, Speedway Hardee's, Jack-in-the-Box, KFC/Taco Bell, Little Caesar's, Waffle House Country Hearth Inn, Days Inn CVS Drug, Family$, Home Depot

90 I-465 (from wb)

89 Shadeland Ave, I-465 (from eb), N Marathon/dsl Bob Evans Baymont Inn, Comfort Inn, Holiday Inn Express,

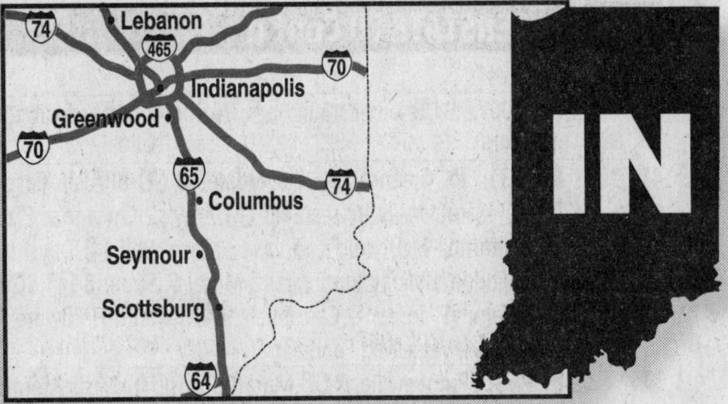

INDIANAPOLIS AREA

89 Continued
Welcome Inn Toyota, U-Haul, S Admiral/dsl, Circle K, Exxon/dsl, Marathon, Speedway/dsl Arby's, Burger King, Damon's, Domino's, Four Seasons Diner, Jimmy John's, Lincoln Sq Rest., McDonald's, Papa John's, Penn Sta Subs, Rally's, Red Lobster, Starbucks, Subway, Taco Bell, TX Roadhouse, Wendy's Always Inn, Best Value Inn, Candlewood Suites, Delta Hotel, Express Inn, Fairfield Inn, Marriott, Quality Inn $General, CarX, Chevrolet, Chrysler/Dodge/Jeep, CVS Drug, Honda, Kia, Kroger/gas, Mazda, Nissan

87 Emerson Ave, N BP/McDonald's, Speedway/dsl, S Shell H

85b a Rural St, Keystone Ave, N Shell Church's fairgrounds, S Shell/dsl

83b(112) I-65 N, to Chicago

83a(111) Michigan St, Market St, S Hardee's, downtown

80(110a) I-65 S, to Louisville

79b Illinois St, McCarty St, downtown

79a West St, N Speedway/dsl Holiday Inn, Holiday Inn Express, Hyatt, JW Marriott, Staybridge Suites H, Govt Ctr, Lucas Oil Stadium, zoo

78 Harding St, to downtown, S Marathon/Subway Wendy's

77 Holt Rd, N Phillips 66/dsl Rally's, Steak'n Shake, S Speedway/Speedy's Cafe/dsl McDonald's

75 Airport Expswy, to Raymond St (no EZ wb return), N Marathon/dsl, Speedway/dsl Indy's Rest., Jimmy John's, Library Rest., Subway, Waffle House Candlewood Suites, Courtyard, Extended Stay America, Fairfield Inn, Hyatt Place, La Quinta, Ramada, Red Roof Inn, Residence Inn, Super 8, Wyndham NAPA, to

73b a I-465 N/S, I-74 E/W

69 (only from eb) to I-74 E, to I-465 S

68 Six Points Rd, N , S Mobil/dsl Burger Theory, Subway Hampton Inn, Hilton Garden, Holiday Inn, Home 2 Suites

66 IN 267, to Plainfield, Mooresville, N Blu/dsl, BP, Shell/Circle K, Speedway/dsl, Thornton's/dsl Arby's, Bob Evans, Burger King, Coachman Rest., Cracker Barrel, Golden Corral, McDonald's, Narita Japanese, Nonna's Italian, Steak'n Shake, Subway, Taco Bell, Waffle House, White Castle Baymont Inn, Best Western+, Budget Inn, Comfort Inn, Days Inn, Embassy Suites, Hampton Inn, Holiday Inn Express, Homewood Suites, Indianapolis Airport Suites, La Quinta, Quality Inn, Staybridge Suites, Super 8, Wingate Inn, Woodspring Suites Buick/GMC, Chateau Thomas Winery, Harley-Davidson

65mm **both lanes, full facilities, info, litter barrels, petwalk, vending**

59 IN 39, to Belleville, N Loves/McDonald's/Subway/dsl/scales/24hr, S TA/Country Pride/dsl/scales/24hr/@, truckwash

INTERSTATE 70 Cont'd

Exit #	Services
51	rd 1100W, S Koger's/Sunoco/dsl/rest./24hr repair/towing/24hr
41	US 231, to Greencastle, Cloverdale, S BP/dsl, Casey's (2mi), Marathon/dsl/scales/24hr Arby's, Chicago's Pizza, El Cantarito, McDonald's, Subway, Taco Bell Days Inn, EconoLodge, Holiday Inn Express, Motel 6, Super 8 $General, Family$, Jordan's Carcare, NAPA, Taylor's Hardware, to Lieber SRA, Value Mkt Foods
37	IN 243, to Putnamville, S Marathon/dsl Misty Morning Campground (4mi), to Lieber SRA
23	IN 59, to Brazil, N Pilot/McDonald's/Subway/dsl/scales/24hr, Speedway/dsl H, truck repair, S BP/dsl, Petro/Iron Skillet/dsl/scales/24hr/@, Road Ranger/Pilot/Subway/dsl/scales Burger King, Family Table Rest. Best Western+, Travelodge
15mm	Honey Creek
11	IN 46, Terre Haute, N Pilot/Subway/dsl/scales/24hr, Thornton/dsl Arby's, Burger King, McDonald's, Monical's Pizza, Real Hacienda, Sonic, Taco Bell Holiday Inn Express, Home 2 Suites $Tree, Aldi Foods, GNC, Meijer/dsl, Verizon, Walmart, S KOA
7	US 41, US 150, Terre Haute, N Casey's/dsl, Marathon/dsl, Sunoco/dsl, Thornton's/dsl Applebee's, Bandana's BBQ, Bob Evans, Coyote's Mexican Hacienda, Cracker Barrel, Dunkin', East Star Buffet, Fazoli's, IHOP, Moe's SW Grill, NewDay Cafe, Pizza Hut, Real Hacienda Mexican, Starbucks, Steak'n Shake, Tokyo Japanese, TX Roadhouse Comfort Suites, Days Inn, Drury Inn, Fairfield Inn, La Quinta, PearTree Inn, Super 8 AT&T, AutoZone, Chrysler/Jeep, O'Reilly Parts, URGENT CARE, S Speedway/dsl, Thornton's/dsl Arby's, Baskin-Robbins, Buffalo Wild Wings, Burger King, Cheddar's, Chick-fil-A, Chili's, Denny's, DQ, Five Guys, Fuddrucker's, Golden Corral, Hardee's, Jimmy John's, KFC, LJ Silver, Longhorn Steaks, Los Tres Caminos, McDonald's, Monical's Pizza, Olive Garden, Outback Steaks, Panda Express, Panda Garden, Panera Bread, Papa John's, Penn Sta Subs, Popeye's, Qdoba, Rally's, Red Lobster, Ruby Tuesday, Starbucks, Subway, Taco Bell, TGIFriday's, Wendy's, White Castle Hampton Inn, Holiday Inn, Motel 6, SpringHill Suites H, $Tree, Aldi Foods, AT&T, Best Buy, Big O Tire, BigLots, BooksAMillion, Buick/Cadillac/GMC, Burlington Coats, Chevrolet, Dodge, Ford, Fresh Thyme Mkt, Goodyear/auto, Harley-Davidson, Hobby Lobby, Hyundai, JC Penney, Jo-Ann Fabrics, Kohl's, Kroger/dsl, Lowe's, NAPA, Nissan, Old Navy, Petsmart, Ross, Sam's Club/gas, Staples, Tire Barn, TJ Maxx, Verizon, Walgreens, Walmart
5.5mm	Wabash River
3	Darwin Rd, W Terre Haute, N to St Mary of-the-Woods Coll
1.5mm	**Welcome Ctr eb, full facilities, info, litter barrels, petwalk, vending**
1	US 40 E (from eb, exits left), to Terre Haute, W Terre Haute
.5mm	**weigh sta eb**
0mm	Indiana/Illinois state line

TERRE HAUTE

IN

INTERSTATE 74

Exit #	Services
171.5mm	Indiana/Ohio state line
171mm	**weigh sta wb**
169	US 52 W, to Brookville, S Chevrolet
168.5mm	Whitewater River
164	IN 1, St Leon, N Shell/Subway/dsl, Sunoco/Pizza/ S BP/Blimpie/dsl Skyline Chili
156	IN 101, to Sunman, Milan, S BP/dsl KOA (2mi)
152mm	**both lanes, full facilities, litter barrels, petwalk, vending**
149	IN 229, to Oldenburg, Batesville, N Marathon, Shell China Buffet, McDonald's, Pizza Hut, Pizza King, Subw Toros Mexican, Wendy's Hampton Inn $General, vance Parts, Kroger/dsl, URGENT CARE, Verizon, S by's, DQ, KFC/Taco Bell, La Rosa's Pizza, Skyline Chili, Stea Shake Quality Inn H, CVS Drug, O'Reilly Parts
143	to IN 46, New Point, N Petro/Iron Skillet/Subway/scales/24hr/@, S Hwy 46 Inn
134b a	IN 3, to Rushville, Greensburg, S BP/dsl, Marathon/D Subway, Speedway/dsl A&W, Arby's, Big Boy, Buff Wings&Rings, Burger King, Chili's, El Chile Poblano, El Re ro Mexican, Great Wall Buffet, Jimmy John's, KFC/LJ Silv Lincoln St Grill, Little Caesar's, McDonald's, Papa John's, Pi Hut, Taco Bell, Waffle House, Wendy's Baymont Inn, H day Inn Express, Quality Inn $General, $Tree, Aldi Foo AT&T, AutoZone, Buick/Chevrolet, Chrysler/Dodge/Jeep, C Drug, Ford, GNC, O'Reilly Parts, TrueValue, Verizon, Walgree Walmart/Subway
132	US 421, to Greensburg, S BP/dsl, CNG Hampton I Holiday Inn Express (2mi)
130mm	Clifty Creek
123	Saint Paul, S Love's/McDonald's/Subway/dsl/scal 24hr repair
119	IN 244 E, to Milroy
116	IN 44, to Shelbyville, Rushville, N Marathon/Circle K/ S BP/dsl, Country Mark/dsl, Marathon, Murphy USA/ Sunoco/dsl Agustin's Mexican, Applebee's, Arby's, Bella no's, Bob Evans, Buffalo Wild Wings, Burger King, China W Cholula Mexican, Denny's, Domino's, DQ, Dunkin', Fazol Jimmy John's, KFC, King Buffet, McDonald's, Papa John's, Pe Sta Subs, Pizza Hut, Rally's, Starbucks, Subway, Taco Bell, We dy's, White Castle Quality Inn H, $General, $Tree, A Hardware, Advance Parts, Aldi Foods, AT&T, AutoZone, BigLo Chevrolet, Ford, GNC, Kroger/dsl, Midas, O'Reilly Parts, Ve zon, Walgreens, Walmart/Subway
115mm	Little Blue River
113mm	Big Blue River
113	IN 9, to Shelbyville, N Speedway/dsl Cracker Barrel, Corral, Wendy's, S Shell, Shell/Circle K/Subway/dsl M Donald's, Waffle House Comfort Inn, EconoLodge, Hampton Inn, Holiday Inn Express, Super 8 H
109	Fairland Rd, N Pilot/McDonald's/dsl/scales/24hr diana Downs/casino, S Brownie's Marine
103	London Rd, to Boggstown
102mm	Big Sugar Creek
101	Pleasant View Rd, N Country Mark/dsl/repair
99	Acton Rd
96	Post Rd, N Marathon/Subway/dsl/24hr McDonald S Shell/Circle K/dsl Taco Bell, Wendy's Chevrolet
94b a	I-465/I-74 W, I-465 N, US 421 N.

I-74 and I-465 run together 21 miles. See I-495, exits 2-16, and 52-53.

Exit #	Services
73b	I-465 N, access to same services as 16a on I-465
73a	I-465 S, I-74 E
71mm	Eagle Creek
68	Ronald Reagan Pkwy, N H
66	IN 267, Brownsburg, N Citgo/dsl, Shell/Circle K Applebee's, Asia Wok, Buffalo Wild Wings, Dunkin', Papa's Pizzari

GREENSBURG

SHELBYVILLE

INTERSTATE 74 Cont'd

66	Continued Starbucks, Steak'n Shake, Subway, Tequila Mexican Hampton Inn, Quality Inn Big O Tire, Midas, **S** BP/dsl, Speedway/dsl Arby's, Bob Evans, Burger King, China's Best, Elegance Rest., Firehouse Subs, Five Guys, HoWah, IHOP, Jimmy John's, KFC, Little Caesar's, McAlister's Deli, McDonald's, Mediterranean Pizza, Papa Murphy's, Penn Sta Subs, Qdoba, Starbucks, Taco Bell, The Toros Mexican, Wendy's, White Castle Comfort Suites, Super 8 AT&T, Firestone/auto, Ford, GNC, Kohl's, Kroger/gas, Lowe's, O'Reilly Parts, USPO, Verizon, Walmart/Subway
61	to Pittsboro, **S** Loves/Godfather's/Subway/dsl/scales/24hr
58	IN 39, to Lebanon, Lizton, **S** Sunoco/dsl/e85 $General
57mm	**both lanes, full facilities, litter barrels, petwalk, , vending**
52	IN 75, to Advance, Jamestown, **2 mi S** camping, food, gas
39	IN 32, to Crawfordsville, **S** Pilot/Subway/dsl/scales/24hr
34	US 231, to Linden, **S** Marathon/dsl, McClure/dsl, Mobil/Circle K, Speedway, Sunoco/dsl Cracker Barrel, McDonald's, Subway Best Western+, Comfort Inn, Hampton Inn, Holiday Inn Express, Knights Inn, Motel 6, Rodeway Inn, Super 8 H, KOA (1mi), Sugar Creek Campground (4mi)
25	IN 25, to Wingate, Waynetown
15	US 41, to Attica, Veedersburg, **1 mi S** Casey's/dsl, Marathon/dsl, Valero/Subway Apple Tree Diner camping, Family$, to Turkey Run SP
8	Covington, **N** Marathon/dsl, Valero/dsl Benjamin's, Overpass Pizza fireworks
7mm	Wabash River
4	IN 63, to Newport, **N** Pilot/Arby's/dsl/scales/24hr Beefhouse Rest.
1mm	**Welcome Ctr eb, full facilities, info, litter barrels, petwalk, , , vending**
0mm	Indiana/Illinois state line, Eastern/Central Time Zone

INTERSTATE 80/90

Exit #	Services
157mm	Indiana/Ohio state line
153mm	**toll plaza, litter barrels**
144	I-69, US 27, Angola, Ft Wayne, **N** Petro/Iron Skillet/dsl/scales/24hr/@, Pilot/Wendy's/dsl/scales, Shell/Subway/dsl McDonald's, Red Arrow Rest. Redwood Inn Freightliner/Western Star/truck repair, services on IN 120, **S** Marathon/dsl Comfort Inn, Holiday Inn Express, Quality Inn, Travelers Inn Freemont Outlet Shops/famous brands, GNC, golf/rest, Jellystone Camping (5mi), to Pokagon SP
131.5mm	Fawn River
126mm	**Ernie Pyle TP both lanes,** Sunoco/dsl Popeye's, Starbucks RV dump
121	IN 9, to Lagrange, Howe, **2 mi N** Marathon, Murphy USA/dsl, Speedway/dsl Applebee's, Buffalo Wild Wings, Burger King, Culver's, Fiesta Mexican, Golden Buddha, Hot'n Now, KFC, King Dragon, Little Caesar's, McDonald's, Pizza Hut, Subway, Taco Bell, Wendy's American Inn, Best Western+, Hampton Inn, Travel Inn, Travelodge $Tree, AT&T, CarQuest, Family$, Ford, GNC, H (4mi), Kroger, Meijer/dsl, Rite Aid, Walgreens, Walmart/Subway, **S** Marathon/dsl Holiday Inn Express, Super 8 H (8mi)

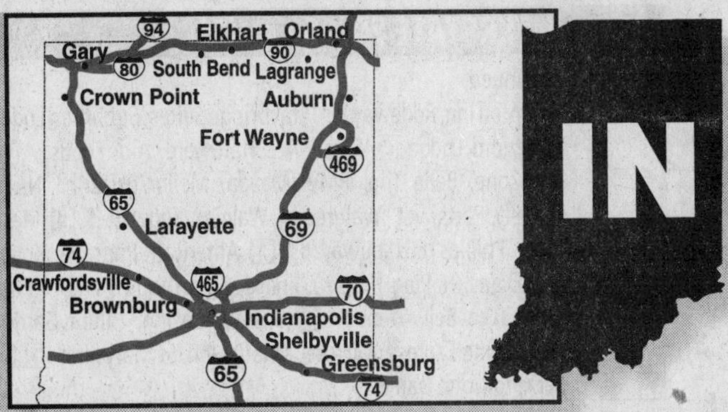

ELKHART

MISHAWAKA

120mm	Fawn River
108mm	**trucks only both lanes**
107	US 131, IN 13, to Middlebury, Constantine, **0-3 mi N** Marathon/dsl, Speedway/dsl Country Table Rest., McDonald's Patchwork Quilt Inn, Plaza Motel $General, **1 mi S** BP/dsl Yup's DairyLand McKenzie House B&B Dollar General, Eby's Pines RV Park, KOA (apr-nov)
101	IN 15, to Goshen, Bristol, **0-2 mi S** Mobil/7-11, Speedway/dsl Subway Eby's Pines Camping (3mi), USPO
96	Rd 1, E Elkhart, **2 mi S** BP/dsl, Marathon, Mobil/7-11 Arby's, China Star, DQ, McDonald's, Subway, Taco Bell Ace Hardware, RV/MH Hall of Fame
92	IN 19, to Elkhart, **N** Marathon, Mobil/7-11/dsl, Phillips 66/Subway/dsl Chubby Trout, Cracker Barrel, Perkins, Steak'n Shake Best Western, Candlewood Suites, Comfort Suites, Country Inn&Suites, Diplomat Motel, EconoLodge, Fairfield Inn, Fairway Inn, Hampton Inn, Hilton Garden, La Quinta, Microtel, Quality Inn, Sheraton, Sleep Inn, Staybridge Suites, Turnpike Motel $General, Aldi Foods, CVS Drug, Elkhart Campground (1mi), Martin's Foods, Montana RV Ctr, Walgreens, **0-2 mi S** Exxon, Marathon/dsl, Speedway/dsl Arby's, Buffalo Wild Wings, Burger King, Callahan's, Culver's, DQ, Dunkin', El Camino Real, Jets Pizza, Jimmy John's, KFC, King Wha Chinese, LJ Silver, Marco's Pizza, McDonald's, MOD Pizza, Noodles&Co, North Garden Buffet, Olive Garden, Panda Express, Papa John's, Penn Sta Subs, Pizza Hut, Qdoba, Red Lobster, Subway, Taco Bell, TX Roadhouse, Wendy's, Wings Etc. Baymont Inn, Budget Inn, Daylite Inn, Garden Inn, Red Roof Inn, Super 8 H, $Tree, Advance Parts, AT&T, AutoZone, Belle Tire, CarQuest, Family$, Honda, Indian Motorcycles, Lowe's, Menards, O'Reilly Parts, Petsmart, Ross, Verizon, Walmart/Subway
91mm	Christiana Creek
90mm	**Schricker TP both directions,** Sunoco/7-11/dsl Starbucks RV Dump, Z Mkt
83	to Mishawaka, **N** BP/dsl, Phillips 66/dsl, Phillips 66/Subway/dsl Applebee's, Bar Louie, Five Guys, Granite City Grill, Longhorn Steaks, Olive Garden, Starbucks, Subway, Wendy's Best Western+, Country Inn&Suites, Fairfield Inn, Hampton Inn, Holiday Inn Express, Quality Inn Barnes&Noble, Best Buy, Costco/dsl, CVS Drug, JC Penney, KOA (mar-nov), Macy's, Martin's Foods/gas, Menards, Ross, Target, Verizon, Walgreens, **S** H
77	US 33, US 31B, IN 933, South Bend, **2 mi N on frtge rd** Admiral, Mobil/dsl, Murphy USA/dsl Arby's, Burger King, DQ, Dunkin', Fazoli's, Hacienda Mexican, Jimmy John's, Jimmy John's, KFC, Little Caesar's, Marco's Pizza, McDonald's, McDonald's, Papa John's, Pizza Hut, Ponderosa, Sonic, Starbucks, Steak'n Shake, Subway, The Farmhouse Comfort Suites,

= gas = food = lodging = other = rest stop

E INTERSTATE 80/90 Cont'd

SOUTH BEND

77	Continued Hampton Inn, Rodeway Inn, Staybridge Suites, Suburban Lodge, Waterford Lodge $Tree, Ace Hardware, Aldi Foods, AT&T, AutoZone, Belle Tire, BMW/Mazda, Meijer/dsl/24hr, NAPA, O'Reilly Parts, vet, Walgreens, Walmart/Subway, **S** Marathon, Phillips 66/Subway/dsl American Pancake House, Bob Evans, HoPing House Chinese, King Gyros, Perkins, Pizza King, Taco Bell, Wendy's Best Value Inn, Hilton Garden, Holiday Inn Express, Microtel, Quality Inn, St Marys Inn H, CarX, to Notre Dame
76mm	St Joseph River
72	US 31, to Niles, South Bend, **N** Pilot/Subway/dsl/scales/24hr, Speedway/Subway/dsl Chivo's Pizza, El Arriero, Taco Bell Super 8, **S** , to Potato Creek SP (20mi)
62mm	Eastern Time Zone/Central Time Zone
56mm	**TP both lanes,** Sunoco/dsl Burger King, Starbucks
49	IN 39, to La Porte, **N** Hampton Inn, **3 mi S** Family Express, Phillips 66/dsl DQ, El Bracero Mexican Best Western+, Blue Heron Inn, Cassidy Inn & RV, Holiday Inn Express, Travelodge
39	US 421, to Michigan City, Westville, **S** Purdue U North Cent
38mm	**trucks only both lanes, litter barrels**
31	IN 49, to Chesterton, Valparaiso, **N** Family Express/dsl, Phillips 66, Speedway/dsl AJ's Pizza, Bob Evans, Clock Rest., Culver's, Subway Hilton Garden CVS Drug, Dean's Tire/auto, Sand Creek RV Park (3mi, Apr-Oct), Strack&Van Til Mkt, to IN Dunes Nat Lakeshore, **S** Hampton Inn (8mi), Super 8 (8mi)
24mm	**toll plaza**

PORTAGE

23	Portage, Port of Indiana, **0-2 mi N** Luke, Marathon Denny's, Mark's Grill Baymont Inn, Best Western+, Country Inn&Suites, Days Inn, Hampton Inn, Quality Inn, Rodeway Inn, Super 8, **S** BP, Speedway/dsl Burger King, CiCi's Pizza, DQ, Dunkin', Jimmy John's, KFC, Little Caesar's, McDonald's, Rosewood Rest., Subway, Wendy's Ace Hardware, Advance Parts, AutoZone, Family$, GNC, O'Reilly Parts, USPO, Walgreens
22mm	**TP both lanes,** Sunoco/dsl Ladson Grill
21mm	**I-90 and I-80 run together eb, separate wb. I-80 runs with I-94 wb. For I-80 exits 1 through 15, see Indiana Interstate 94.**
21	I-94 E to Detroit, I-80/94 W, US 6, IN 51, Lake Station, **S** FLYING J/Denny's/dsl/scales/24hr/@, Mr Fuel/dsl/scales/24hr, Pilot/Road Ranger/Subway/dsl/scales, TA/BP/Popeye's/dsl/scales/24hr/@ Blue Beacon, Blue Beacon
17	I-65 S, US 12, US 20, Dunes Hwy, to Indianapolis
14b	IN 53, to Gary, Broadway, **S** Citgo
14a	Grant St, to Gary, **S** H
10	IN 912, Cline Ave, to Gary, **N** , casino
5	US 41, Calumet Ave, to Hammond, **S** GoLo, Nice'n Easy, Speedway/dsl Aurelio's Pizza, Dunkin', Gorditas, Johnel's Rest., KFC, McDonald's, Subway, Taco Bell, White Castle EconoLodge, Ramada Inn, Super 8 Aldi Foods, AutoZone, O'Reilly Parts, Walgreens
3	IN 912, Cline Ave, to Hammond, **N** to Gary Reg Airport, **S** Shell
1.5mm	**toll plaza**
1mm	US 12, US 20, 106th St, Indianapolis Blvd, **N** BP, Citgo/Dunkin', Luke/dsl IHOP, Popeye's, Starbucks $Tree, AT&T, casino, Ross, Walmart, **S** Burger King, KFC, McDonald's, Pizza Hut, Subway Aldi Foods, O'Reilly Parts
0mm	Indiana/Illinois state line

IN

E INTERSTATE 94

MI CITY

Exit #	Services
46mm	Indiana/Michigan state line
43mm	**Welcome Ctr wb, full facilities, info, litter barrels, petw , vending**
40b a	US 20, US 35, to Michigan City, **N** H, **S** Speedway/
34b a	US 421, to Michigan City, **N** BP/dsl, Family Express/ Marathon, Speedway/dsl, Speedway/White Castle/dsl by's, Baskin-Robbins/Dunkin', Buffalo Wild Wings, Burger K Chili's, Chipotle, Crawford's Eatery, Culver's, Denny's, El Bra Mexican, Five Guys, Hardee's, IHOP, Jimmy John's, KFC, LJ Si McDonald's, Olive Garden, Panda Express, Panera Bread, P Hut, Popeye's, Red Lobster, Sake Asian Fusion, Schoop's R Sonic, Sophia's Pancakes, Starbucks, Subway, Taco Bell, TX Co Wendy's ABC Motel, Baymont Inn, Comfort Suites, Countr n&Suites, Dunes Inn, Hampton Inn, Holiday Inn Express, MI Inn, Microtel, Quality Inn, Red Roof Inn, Super 8, Travel Inn $General, $Tree, Advance Parts, Aldi Foods, AT&T, AutoZ Belle Tire, BigLots, Discount Tire, Family$, Fannie May Canc Ford/Lincoln, GNC, Hobby Lobby, Jo-Ann Fabrics, Kohl's, Lov Meijer/dsl, Menards, Midas, Petsmart, Ross, Save-a-Lot, TJ M Verizon, Walgreens, Walmart/Subway, **S** Speedway/Subv dsl/scales/24hr Buick/Chevrolet/GMC, Harley-Davidson
29mm	**weigh sta both lanes**

CHESTERTON

26b a	IN 49, to Valparaiso, Chesterton, **N** to IN Dunes **S** BP/White Castle, Speedway/dsl A&W/KFC, by's, Burger King, Domino's, DQ, Dunkin', El Salto Mexic Gelsosomo's Pizza, Gino's Grill, Happy Wok, Jimmy Joh Lemon Tree Grill, Little Caesar's, McDonald's, Papa Joh Pizza Hut, Subway, Taco Bell, Tao Chen's, Third Coast C Wendy's Best Western, EconoLodge, Hilton Garden (3r Lakeside Inn, Quality Inn H, Advance Parts, AutoZo Jewel-Osco, Sand Cr Camping (5mi), Verizon, Walgreens
22b a	US 20, Burns Harbor, **N** Shell/Subway/dsl/scales/LP, TA/ Country Pride/Pizza Hut/Popeye's/Taco Bell/dsl/scales/24hr Comfort Inn fireworks, **S** Luke/dsl, Pilot/McD ald's/Subway/dsl/scales/24hr Camp-Land RV Ctr, Chevro fireworks, Ford, Kia, Nissan, repair, Toyota
19	IN 249, to Port of IN, Portage, **N** Family Express/d e85 DQ, El Salto, Hooters, Longhorn Steaks, McDonal Quaker Steak&Lube, Starbucks, Subway, Taco Bell fordable Suites, Country Inn&Suites Bass Pro Sho **S** Luke, Marathon/dsl Denny's, Dunkin', Shenaniga Grill Best Western+, Days Inn, Hampton Inn, Holiday Express, Rodeway Inn, Super 8, Travel Inn
16	access to I-80/90 **toll** road E, I-90 **toll** road W, IN 51N, Ripley same as 15b&a
I-94/I-80 run together wb.	
15b	US 6W, IN 51, **N** FLYING J/Denny's/dsl/scales/24hr/@, Fuel/dsl/scales/24hr, TA/BP/Popeye's/Subway/dsl/scales/24 @ Wing Wah Blue Beacon, Blue Beacon
15a	US 6E, IN 51S, to US 20, **S** GoLo, Road Ranger/Pilot/S way/dsl/scales/24hr, Shell/Luke Burger King, DQ, Dunki LJ Silver, Papa John's, Ruben's Café, Wendy's Ace Ha ware, Walgreens
13	Central Ave (from eb)
12b	I-65 N, to Gary and **toll** road
12a	I-65 S (from wb), to Indianapolis
11	I-65 S (from eb)
10b a	IN 53, Broadway, **N** Clark Tommy's Philly Steak, **S** GoLo Checkers, DQ

INTERSTATE 94 Cont'd

GARY AREA

Exit #	Services
9	Grant St, N Clark $General, $Tree, Advance Parts, County Mkt Foods/gas, Walgreens, S Citgo, Love's/Denny's/dsl/scales/LP/24hr/@, Petro/Iron Skillet/Pizza Hut/dsl/scales/24hr, Speedway/dsl Burger King, Dunkin', McDonald's, Subway $Tree, Aldi Foods, AutoZone, Firestone/auto, Midas
6	Burr St, N Pilot/Subway/dsl/scales/24hr/@, TA/Country Pride/Pizza Hut/Taco Bell/dsl/scales/24hr/@ J&J Fish & Chicken, Philly Steaks, Rico's Pizza SpeedCo, S GoLo, Mr Fuel/dsl/24hr
5	IN 912, Cline Ave, S BP, Speedway/dsl Arby's, Culver's, DQ, Dunkin', Jedi's Garden Rest., KFC, McDonald's, Pizza Hut, Popeye's, Subway, Taco Bell, Wendy's, White Castle Best Western, Hometowne Lodge, Motel 6 $Tree, Family$, Fannie May Candies
3	Kennedy Ave, N GoLo, Speedway Burger King, Domino's, Dunkin'/Baskin Robbins, McDonald's repair, Walgreens, S IN Welcome Ctr, Sixers Buffalo Wild Wings, Cracker Barrel, Squigi's Pizza, Subway, Wendy's Courtyard, Fairfield Inn, Hampton Inn, Holiday Inn Express, Residence Inn USPO
2	US 41S, IN 152N, Indianapolis Blvd, N GoLo, Luke, SavAStop Dunkin', House Of Pizza, Papa John's, Pepe's Mexican, Petros Rest., Pizza Hut, Popeye's, Rally's, Schoop's Burgers, Subway, Taco Bell, Wendy's, Wheel Rest. CarX, Chevrolet, Family$, Midas, vet, S Pilot/dsl/scales/24hr JJ Fish, Starbucks, White Castle Comfort Inn Aldi Foods, Cabela's, Walmart/Subway
1	US 41N, Calumet Ave, N Speedway/dsl Baskin-Robbins/Dunkin' Walgreens, S BP, CT Fuel, GoLo, Marathon Arby's, Baskin-Robbins/Dunkin', Boston Mkt, Burger King, Canton House Chinese, Chipotle, Edwardo's Pizza, Five Guys, Fortune House, Munster Gyros, Panera Bread, Pizza Hut, Subway, Taco Bell, Wendy's $Tree, AT&T, Jewel-Osco, Staples, Target, URGENT CARE, Verizon
0mm	Indiana/Illinois state line

INTERSTATE 465 (Indianapolis)

INDIANAPOLIS AREA

Exit #	Services
	I-465 loops around Indianapolis. Exit numbers begin/end on I-65, exit 106.
53b a	I-65 N to Indianapolis, S to Louisville
52	Emerson Ave, N BP/dsl, Marathon, Shell/Circle K, Speedway/dsl Burger King, Domino's, El Mariachi, KFC, LJ Silver, Subway, Taco Bell, Waffle House Motel 6 H, $General, S Murphy USA/dsl, Speedway/dsl Arby's, Bamboo House, China Buffet, DJ's Hotdogs, DQ, Egg Roll, El Puerto Mexican, Fazoli's, Firehouse Subs, Fujiyama, Hardee's, Jets Pizza, Jimmy John's, Little Caesar's, McDonald's, Papa John's, Papa Murphy's, Pizza Hut, Ponderosa, Rally's, Starbucks, Steak'n Shake, Subway, Taco Bell, Wendy's, White Castle Holiday Inn Express, La Quinta, Red Roof Inn, Super 8 $Tree, Advance Parts, AT&T, AutoZone, CarX, GNC, Goodyear/auto, Kroger/dsl, Lowe's Whse, Meineke, O'Reilly Parts, Verizon, vet, Walgreens, Walmart/Subway
	I-74 W and I-465 S run together around S Indianapolis 21 miles.
49	I-74 E, US 421 S
48	Shadeland Ave (from nb)
47	US 52 E, Brookville Rd, E Marathon, Speedway/dsl Bugsy's Grill, Burger King, McDonald's, Subway, Taco Bell Baymont Inn CVS Drug, Family$, vet

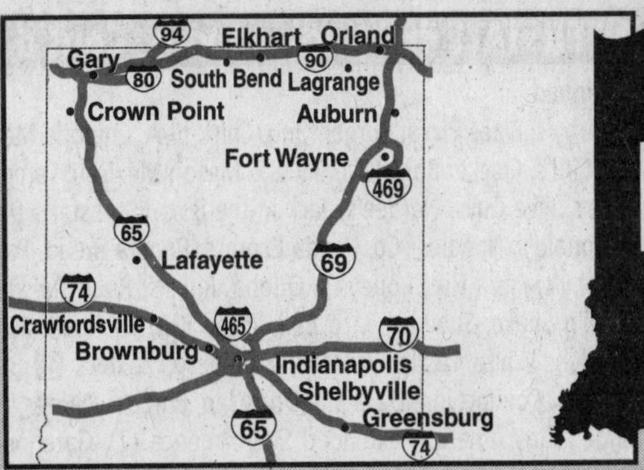

INDIANAPOLIS AREA

Exit #	Services
46	US 40, Washington St, E Marathon, Phillips 66, Shell/dsl, Speedway/dsl Arby's, Blueberry Hill Pancakes, Church's, LJ Silver, Olive Garden, Skyline Chili, Steak'n Shake, Yen Ching Chinese $General, Advance Parts, AutoZone, Ford, Meineke, O'Reilly Parts, W Thornton's/dsl Applebee's, Bob Evans, Fazoli's, McDonald's, Subway Comfort Stay Buick/GMC, Hyundai, PepBoys
44b	I-70 E, to Columbus
44a	I-70 W, to Indianapolis
42	US 36, IN 67 N, Pendleton Pike, E Cafe Heidelberg, Chile Verde, Hardee's, Papa's Rest., Popeye's, Skillet Rest., Wendy's $General, $Tree, Menards, Save-A-Lot Foods, U-Haul, W GetGo/dsl, Speedway/dsl, Thornton's/dsl Arby's, Domino's, Dunkin', KFC, LJ Silver, Los Rancheros, McDonald's, Rally's, Subway, Taco Bell, Waffle House, White Castle H, Advance Parts, Aldi Foods, CVS Drug, Family$, Meineke, Menards, O'Reilly Parts
40	56th St, Shadeland Ave, E Marathon, to Ft Harrison SP
37b a	I-69, N to Ft Wayne, IN 37, E H, W services on frontage rds
35	Allisonville Rd, N Bravo Italian, Buca Italian, Buffalo Wild Wings, Dave&Buster's, Hardee's, MCL Cafeteria, Melting Pot, On-the-Border, Outback Steaks Courtyard Costco/gas, Firestone/auto, JC Penney, Jo-Ann Fabrics, Macy's, REI, Van Maur, S Shell, Speedway/dsl Chipotle, ChuckeCheese, Five Guys, Noodles&Co, Panera Bread, Papa John's, Pie Five, Qdoba, White Castle Quality Inn $Tree, Michael's, Petsmart, Ross, TJ Maxx, Trader Joe's
33	IN 431, Keystone Ave, N BP/McDonald's, Marathon/dsl Bob Evans, Coopers Hawk, Steak'n Shake Acura, BMW/Mini, Chevrolet, Fiat, Ford, Harley-Davidson, Honda, Hyundai, Infiniti, Kia, Mercedes, Nissan, Porsche, Subaru, Toyota, S Benihana, Champp's, Cheesecake Factory, Chipotle, Fleming's Steaks, LePeep Rest., Maggiano's, McAlister's Deli, PF Chang's, Pizza Hut, Ruth Chris Steaks, Seasons 52, Starbucks, Sullivan's Steaks, TGIFriday's Hyatt Place, Marriott, Sheraton Kohl's, Nordstrom's
31	US 31, Meridian St, N Comfort Inn, Courtyard, Holiday Inn H, S Marathon/DQ/dsl, Shell/Circle K/dsl Another Broken Egg Cafe, Arby's, Firebirds Grill, Granite City, McAlister's Deli, McDonald's, Paradise Cafe Bakery, Starbucks Drury Inn
27	US 421 N, Michigan Rd, N Marathon, Speedway/dsl Applebee's, Burger King, DQ, HoneyBaked Ham, Jimmy John's, KFC/Taco Bell, McDonald's, Olive Garden, Outback Steaks, Red Robin, Subway, Wendy's Holiday Inn Express, Red Roof Inn AutoZone, Best Buy, Buick/GMC, Chevrolet, Chrysler/Dodge/Jeep, Home Depot, Kohl's, Marshall's, PetCo, Target, Walgreens, S Citgo/dsl, Marathon, Shell/Circle K

IN

= gas = food = lodging = other = rest stop

INTERSTATE 465 (Indianapolis) Cont'd

INDIANAPOLIS AREA

IN

27	Continued Arby's, Blaze Pizza, Burger King, Chick-fil-A, Chipotle Mexican, CiCi's, Cracker Barrel, Denny's, El Meson Mexican, Famous Dave's, Five Guys, Hardee's, Jack-in-the-Box, McAlister's Deli, McDonald's, Noodles&Co, Panda Express, Panera Bread, Papa Murphy's, Pizza Hut, Popeye's, Qdoba, Rally's, Ruby Tuesday, Steak'n Shake, Subway, Taco Bell, Tilted Kilt, TX Roadhouse, Wendy's, White Castle, Yen Ching Chinese, Zaxby's Best Western, Comfort Inn, Days Inn, Drury Inn, Embassy Suites, Extended Stay America, Extended Stay America (2), Gatehouse Suites, Homewood Suites, InTown Suites, La Quinta, Motel 6, Quality Inn, Rodeway Inn $General, $Tree, Aamco, Aldi Foods, BigLots, Costco/gas, Discount Tire, Firestone, GNC, JC Penney, Lowe's Whse, Office Depot, Staples, Walgreens, Walmart
25	I-865 W, I-465 N to Chicago
23	86th St, E BP, Speedway/dsl Abuelo's, Arby's, Chili's, Coldstone, DiBella Subs, Jimmy John's, Longhorn Steaks, Macaroni Grill, Monical's Pizza, Noodles&Co, Panera Bread, Qdoba, Starbucks, Subway, Taco Bell, Ted's MT Grill, Tom+Chee, Traders Mill Grill, Wendy's Extended Stay America, Fairfield Inn, InTown Suites H, AT&T, Big-O Tires, BooksAMillion, Dick's, Michael's, Old Navy, Petsmart
21	71st St, E BP/dsl Chef Mike's, Hardee's, McDonald's, Steak'n Shake, Subway Candlewood Suites, Clarion Inn, Courtyard, Hampton Inn, Holiday Inn Express, TownePlace Suites, W Gatsby's, Hotbox Pizza, Jimmy John's, LePeep, Starbucks Hilton Garden, Residence Inn, Wingate Inn
20	I-65, N to Chicago, S to Indianapolis
19	56th St (from nb), E Marathon, Speedway/dsl
17	38th St, E BP, Marathon/dsl, Shell/Circle K, Speedway DQ, El Maguey Mexican, Golden Corral, Jack-in-the-Box, Little Caesar's, Red Lobster, Steak'n Shake, Subway, White Castle $General, $Tree, AutoZone, Chevrolet, CVS Drug, Family$, Home Depot, Meijer, O'Reilly Parts, W Arby's, Burger King, Chili's, Cracker Barrel, IHOP, Jersey Mike's, McDonald's, Taco Bell, TGIFriday's Baymont Inn Target

I-74 W and I-465 S run together around S Indianapolis 21 miles.

16b	I-74 W, to Peoria
16a	US 136, to Speedway, E Circle K, Shell/Circle K, Thornton's/dsl Applebee's, Arby's, Buffalo Wild Wings, Burger King, Chicago's Pizza, Chipotle, Denny's, El Rodeo, Firehouse Subs, Grindstone Charley's, Hardee's, Jimmy John's, KFC, LJ Silver, McDonald's, Papa Murphy's, Pizza Hut, Starbucks, Subway, Taco Bell, White Castle $Inn, Courtyard $General, $Tree, Advance Parts, AT&T, Big Lots, CarX, CVS Drug, Firestone/auto, GNC, Goodyear/auto, Kohl's, Kroger/dsl, PetCo, TJ Maxx, Tuesday Morning, Verizon, W BP/dsl Clarion
14b a	10th St, E Peking Chinese, Penn Sta, Pizza Hut, Wendy's H, Lowe's Whse, Walmart Mkt, W Shell/Circle K, Speedway/dsl Arby's, Fazoli's, Flapjacks, Marco's Pizza, McDonald's, Rally's, Starbucks, Taco Bell CVS Drug, Walgreens
13b a	US 36, Rockville Rd, E Mobil Kazablanka Grill Holiday Inn Express, Microtel, Motel 6, Wingate Inn Sam's Club, W Speedway/dsl Bob Evans Best Western
12b a	US 40 E, Washington St, E BP/dsl Burger King, China Inn, Church's, Fazoli's, McDonald's, Papa John's, Pizza Hut, Taco Bell, Wendy's, White Castle $General, $Tree, $Tree, Ace Hardware, Advance Parts, AutoZone, CVS Drug, Family$, Kroger/gas, O'Reilly Parts, Speedway Parts, U-Haul, vet,
12b a	Continued W Circle K/dsl, Phillips 66/dsl, Thornton's/dsl Arb Hardee's, Jimmy John's, LJ Silver, McDonald's, Steak'n Sh Subway Regal 8 Inn $General, CarX, Goodyear/a Save-A-Lot Foods
11b a	Sam Jones Expwy, E Marathon/dsl, Speedway/dsl dy's Rest., Jimmy John's, Library Rest., Subway, Wa House Candlewood Suites, Courtyard, Extended S America, Fairfield Inn, Hyatt Place, La Quinta, Quality Inn, mada Inn, Residence Inn, Super 8, Wyndham, W Crow Plaza, Radisson
9b a	I-70, E to Indianapolis, W to Terre Haute
8	IN 67 S, Kentucky Ave, E Phillips 66/dsl H, W McDonald's/dsl, Shell/Subway/dsl, Speedway/dsl Bu er King, Culver's, Denny's, KFC, Rally's Country In Suites Walmart Mkt
7	Mann Rd (from wb), E H
4	IN 37 S, Harding St, N Mr Fuel/dsl/scales, Pilot/Subw dsl/scales/24hr Omelette Shoppe Best Inn, Qua Inn H, Blue Beacon, S FLYING J/Arby's/PJ Fresh/c LP/scales/24hr/@, Marathon Hardee's, McDonald's, Ta Bell, Waffle House, White Castle Knight's Inn Freig liner, SpeedCo, TruckoMat/scales
2b a	US 31, IN 37, N BP/dsl, Marathon/Dunkin'/dsl Arb China Garden, CiCi's, Domino's, El Azabache, Golden Wok, K King Gyros, Little Caesar's, LJ Silver, MCL Cafeteria, Penn Subs, Pizza Hut, Qdoba, Steak'n Shake, White Castle $G eral, $Tree, Advance Parts, Aldi Foods, AT&T, AutoZone, C Quest, Family$, Firestone/auto, GNC, Kroger/gas, Marsha Meineke, Midas, Save-A-Lot, U-Haul, S BP/dsl, Speedw dsl 8 Lucky Buffet, Bob Evans, El Jalapeño, McDonald's, R Lobster, Subway, Taco Bell, Wendy's Comfort Inn, Holiday Express, Indy Lodge, Super 8, Travel Inn CVS Drug, Walgree
53b a	I-65 N to Indianapolis, S to Louisville

I-465 loops around Indianapolis. Exit numbers begin/end on I-65, exit 1

INTERSTATE 469 (Ft Wayne)

Exit #	Services
31c b a	I-69, US 27 S, Auburn Road. **I-469 begins/ends.**
29mm	St Joseph River
29b a	Maplecrest Rd, W Lassus/DQ/Subway/dsl, Marathon/ds
25	IN 37, to Ft Wayne, W Murphy USA/dsl Agaves Me ican, Antonio's Pizza, Applebee's, Arby's, Bob Evans, Buff lo Wild Wings, Cracker Barrel, DQ, Starbucks, Steak'n Shak Subway, Wendy's, Wings Etc, Zianos Italian AT&T, Di count Tire, Kohl's, Marshall's, Meijer/dsl, Menards, Michael Petsmart, Verizon, Walgreens, Walmart/McDonald's
21	US 24 E
19b a	US 30 E, to Ft Wayne, E FLYING J/Huddle House/Su way/dsl/LP/scales/24hr, Sunoco/Taco Bell/dsl Freigh liner, Mack/Volvo, Peterbilt, truck/tire repair, W Ma athon Mancino's Grinders, Richard's Rest., Zes Drive-In Holiday Inn Express $General
17	Minnich Rd
15	Tillman Rd
13	Marion Center Rd
11	US 27, US 33 S, to Decatur, Ft Wayne, E Shell/Subway/ds
10.5mm	St Marys River
9	Winchester Rd
6	IN 1, to Bluffton, Ft Wayne, W to
2	Indianapolis Rd, W to
1	Lafayette Ctr Rd

IOWA

INTERSTATE 29

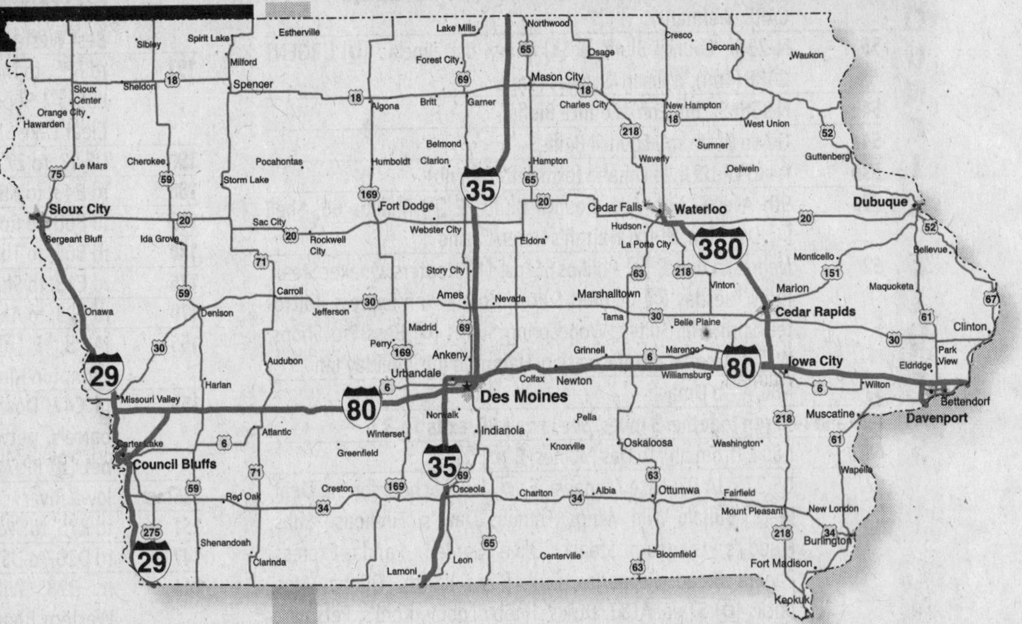

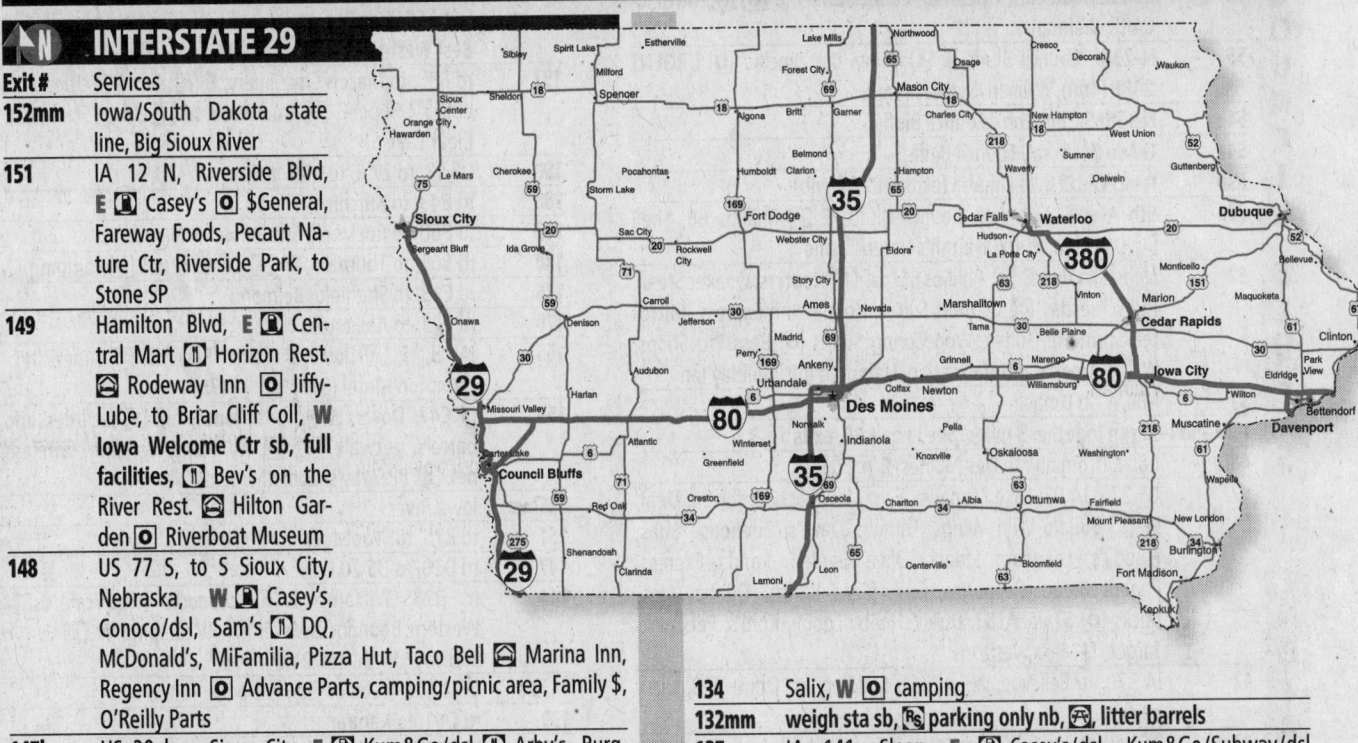

Exit #	Services
152mm	Iowa/South Dakota state line, Big Sioux River
151	IA 12 N, Riverside Blvd, **E** Casey's $General, Fareway Foods, Pecaut Nature Ctr, Riverside Park, to Stone SP
149	Hamilton Blvd, **E** Central Mart Horizon Rest. Rodeway Inn Jiffy-Lube, to Briar Cliff Coll, **W Iowa Welcome Ctr sb, full facilities,** Bev's on the River Rest. Hilton Garden Riverboat Museum
148	US 77 S, to S Sioux City, Nebraska, **W** Casey's, Conoco/dsl, Sam's DQ, McDonald's, MiFamilia, Pizza Hut, Taco Bell Marina Inn, Regency Inn Advance Parts, camping/picnic area, Family $, O'Reilly Parts
147b	US 20 bus, Sioux City, **E** Kum&Go/dsl Arby's, Burger King, Chili's, Famous Dave's BBQ, Hardee's, IHOP, Perkins Holiday Inn, Ramada, Stoney Creek Inn H, Chevrolet, USPO, Walgreens
147a	Floyd Blvd, **E** Sinclair/dsl Home Depot
146.5mm	Floyd River
144b	I-129 W, US 20 W, US 75 S
144a	US 20 E, US 75 N, to Ft Dodge, **1 mi E on Lakeport Rd** Casey's A&W/LJ Silver, Applebee's, Buffalo Wild Wings, Burger King, Chick-fil-A, Chipotle, ChuckeCheese, Firehouse Subs, Golden Corral, Hardee's, HuHot Chinese, Iron Hill Grill, Japanese Steaks, Jimmy John's, McDonald's, Mr Stirfry, Old Chicago, Olive Garden, Outback Steaks, Panda Express, Panera Bread, Qdoba, Red Lobster, Red Robin, Starbucks, TX Roadhouse Candlewood Suites, Comfort Inn, Fairfield Inn, Hampton Inn, Holiday Inn Express, Quality Inn Barnes&Noble, Best Buy, Buick/Honda, Fareway Mkt, Gordman's, Hobby Lobby, Hy-Vee Foods/gas, JC Penney, Jiffy Lube, Kohl's, Lowe's, Marshall's, Michael's, Old Navy, Petsmart, Scheel's, Staples, Target, URGENT CARE, Verizon
143	US 75 N, Singing Hills Blvd, **E** Cenex/dsl, Murphy USA/dsl, Pilot/Burger King/Subway/dsl/scales/24hr China Buffet, Culver's, Four Bros Grill, Hunan Palace, KFC, McDonald's, Pizza Hut, Taco Bell, Taco John's AmericInn, Days Inn, Victorian Inn $Tree, AT&T, Buick/Cadillac/GMC, Ford/Lincoln, Kia, Mazda, Nissan, Sam's Club/gas, Sgt Floyd Mon, Subaru, Toyota, URGENT CARE, VW, Walmart/Subway, **W** Loves/Subway/dsl/scales/24hr/@ Wendy's Super 8 Peterbilt, truckwash/repair
141	D38, Sioux Gateway Airport, **E** Cenex, Shell/dsl Aggies Rest., Pizza Ranch, Subway DeSoto Inn $General, **W** Travelodge , museum
139mm	**both lanes, full facilities, info, litter barrels, , , RV dump, wireless internet**
135	Port Neal Landing
134	Salix, **W** camping
132mm	**weigh sta sb, parking only nb, , litter barrels**
127	IA 141, Sloan, **E** Casey's/dsl, Kum&Go/Subway/dsl Homestead Inn, WinnaVegas Inn RV Park, **W** Pony Express (3mi) to Winnebago Indian Res/hotel/casino (3mi)
120	to Whiting, **W** camping
112	IA 175, Onawa, **E** Cenex/dsl, Conoco/Subway/dsl DQ, McDonald's, Michael's Rest. Super 8 H, NAPA, On-Ur-Wa RV Park, repair, **2 mi W** Keel Boat Exhibit, KOA, Lewis&-Clark SP
110mm	**both lanes, full facilities, info, litter barrels, petwalk, , , RV dump, wireless internet**
105	E60, Blencoe
96mm	Little Sioux River
95	F 20, Little Sioux, **E** gas Loess Hills SF (9mi), **W** Woodland RV Park
92mm	Soldier River
91.5mm	**both lanes, parking only, litter barrels**
89	IA 127, Mondamin, **1 mi E** Jiffy Mart/dsl
82	F50, Modale, **1 mi W** Heartland/dsl
79mm	**both lanes, full facilities, info, litter barrels, , , RV dump, wireless internet**
75	US 30, Missouri Valley, **E Iowa Welcome Ctr** (5mi), Shell/dsl/24hr Arby's, McDonald's, Penny's Diner, Subway Oaktree Inn H (2mi), to Steamboat Exhibit, **W** Cenex/dsl, PetroMart/dsl Burger King, Taco John's, The Edge Rest. Best Value Inn, DeSoto Inn, Rath Inn Buick/Chevrolet
72.5mm	Boyer River
72	IA 362, Loveland, **E** Desoto/dsl, **W** to Wilson Island SP (6mi)
71	I-680 E, to Des Moines
I-29 S & I-680 W run together 10 mi.	
66	Honey Creek, **W** RV Camping
61b	I-680 W, to N Omaha, **W** Mormon Trail Ctr
I-29 N & I-680 E run together 10 mi.	
61a	IA 988, to Crescent, **E** Casey's/dsl

MO VALLEY

IA

= gas = food = lodging = other = rest stop

INTERSTATE 29 Cont'd

COUNCIL BLUFFS

Exit #	Services
56	IA 192 S (sb only, exits left), Council Bluffs, E (H), URGENT CARE, Walmart
55	N 25th, Council Bluffs, E Cenex/dsl, Sinclair URGENT CARE (1mi), Walmart/Subway (1mi)
54b	N 35th St (from nb), Council Bluffs
54a	G Ave (from sb), Council Bluffs
53b	I-480 W, US 6, to Omaha (exits left from nb)
53a	9th Ave, S 37th Ave, Council Bluffs, E Phillips 66, Shell Days Inn, W Harrah's Hotel/Casino
52	Nebraska Ave, E Phillips 66/dsl Hooters, Quaker Steak, Ruby Tuesday Comfort Suites, Holiday Inn Express, Microtel, SpringHill Suites, Woodspring Suites Bass Pro Shops, W AmeriStar Hotel/casino, Hampton Inn, Holiday Inn
51	I-80 W, to Omaha
I-29 and I-80 run together 3 miles. See Iowa I-80, exits 1b-3.	
48	I-80 E (from nb), to Des Moines, E (H)
47	US 275, IA 92, Lake Manawa, E Iowa School for the Deaf, W Buffalo Wild Wings, Famous Dave's, Firehouse Subs, Freddy's, Longhorn Steaks, Olive Garden, Panda Express, Panera Bread, Pepperjax Grill, Pizza Ranch, Qdoba, Starbucks $Tree, AT&T, Dick's, Hobby Lobby, Kohl's, Petsmart, Target, TJ Maxx, Verizon
42	IA 370, to Bellevue, W K&B Saddlery, to Offutt AFB, truck parts
38mm	**both lanes, full facilities, info, litter barrels, petwalk, , , RV dump, wireless internet**
35	US 34 E, to Glenwood, E McDonalds (4mi) Western Inn (4mi) RV Park, W BP/rest/dsl, Loves/Subway/dsl/scales/24hr Bluff View Motel Harley-Davidson
32	US 34 W, Pacific Jct, to Plattsmouth
24	L31, to Tabor, Bartletts
20	IA 145, Thurmans
15	J26, Percival, **1-2 mi E** gas/dsl
11.5mm	**weigh sta nb**
10	IA 2, to Nebraska City, Sidney, E to Waubonsie SP (5mi), W Cenex/Godfathers/dsl/E85, Pilot/Subway/dsl/scales/24hr, Sapp Bros/Apple Barrel Rest/dsl/scales/24hr Wendy's Motel 6, Super 8 antiques, dsl/tire repair, IA Info, Lewis&Clark Ctr (3mi), to Arbor Lodge SP, Victorian Acres RV Park (3mi)
1	IA 333, Hamburg, **1 mi E** Casey's/dsl Blue Moon Grill Hamburg Inn (H), NAPA, Stoner Soda Fountain
0mm	Iowa/Missouri state line

IA

INTERSTATE 35

CLEAR LAKE

Exit #	Services
219mm	Iowa/Minnesota state line
214	rd 105, to Northwood, Lake Mills, E Royal Motel (7mi), W **Welcome Ctr both lanes, full facilities, litter barrels, petwalk, , RV dump, vending, wireless internet** BP/Burger King/dsl, Kum&Go/dsl Country Inn&Suites, Holiday Inn Express casino
212mm	**weigh sta sb, nb, , litter barrels**
208	rd A38, to Joice, Kensett, windmills
203	IA 9, to Manly, Forest City, W to Pilot Knob SP
202mm	Winnebago River
197	rd B20, **8 mi E** Lime Creek Nature Ctr
196mm	**both lanes, litter barrels, parking only**
194	US 18, to Mason City, Clear Lake, E Kwik Star/dsl/ Chevrolet, Freightliner, (H) (8mi), W Casey's/dsl, Kum& dsl, Pilot/Subway/dsl/scales Arby's, Bennigan's, Culv DQ, KFC/Taco Bell, McDonald's, Perkins, Wendy's Americ Best Western, Best Western, Microtel Ford
193	rd B35, to Mason City, Emery, E Kum&Go/Taco John's/ e85 Super 8 truckwash, W Seven Stars Rest. Clear Lake SP
190	US 18, rd 27 E, to Mason City
188	rd B43, to Burchinal
182	rd B60, to Rockwell, Swaledale
180	rd B65, to Thornton, W Cenex (2mi) camping
176	rd C13, to Sheffield, Belmond
170	rd C25, to Alexander
165	IA 3, E Dudley's Corner/Rest./dsl AmericInn (9 Hampton Motel (9mi) (H) (7mi)
159	rd C47, Dows, W **both lanes, full facilities info, li barrels, petwalk, , , RV dump, vending, wireless in net** BP/Arby's/Godfather's/dsl/24hr
155mm	Iowa River
151	rd R75, to Woolstock
147	rd D20, to US 20 E
144	rd D25, Williams, E Boondocks Trkstp/cafe/dsl B Western, Boondocks Motel RV camping, W FLYING Subway/dsl/scales/24hr
142b a	US 20, to Webster City, Ft Dodge
139	rd D41, to Kamrar
133	IA 175, to Jewell, Ellsworth, W Kum&Go/Subway/ Loves/rest./dsl/scales/24hr
128	rd D65, to Stanhope, Randall, **5 mi W** Little Wall Lake Pk
124	rd 115, Story City, W Casey's, Kum&Go/dsl DQ, KF Taco Bell, McDonald's, Pizza Ranch, Royal Cafe, Subw Comfort Inn, Super 8, Viking Motel/rest antiques, Fo Goodlife RV Ctr, VF Factory Stores/famous brands, Whisperi Oaks Camping
123	rd E18, to Roland, McCallsburg
121mm	prairie area sb
120mm	**nb, full facilities, info, litter barrels, , , RV dum scenic prairie area sb, vending, wireless internet**
119mm	**sb, full facilities, litter barrels, , , RV dump, vendin wireless internet**
116	rd E29, to Story, **2 mi W** Story Co Conservation Ctr
113	13th St, Ames, W Kum&Go/Burger King/dsl/E-85, Philli 66/Arby's Burger King, Jimmy John's, Pizza Ranch Ho iday Inn Express, Quality Inn (H), Harley-Davidson, ISU, USDA Vet Labs
111b a	US 30, to Nevada, Ames, E Twin Acres Campground (11m W Kum&Go/DQ/Subway/dsl El Azteca Mexican Ar ericInn, Baymont Inn, Country Inn&Suites, EconoLodge, Fa field Inn, Hampton Inn, Microtel, Red Roof, Super 8, Town Place Suites Chrysler/Dodge/Jeep, to IA St U
109mm	S Skunk River
106mm	**weigh sta sb, nb, no restrooms**
102	IA 210, to Slater, **3 mi W** Subway
100mm	**both lanes, full facilities, , litter barrels, petwalk**
96	to Elkhart, W to Big Creek SP (11mi), Saylorville Lake
94	NE 36th St, Ankeny, W Kum&Go/dsl Subway
92	1st St, Ankeny, W Kum&Go, QT Applebee's, Arby' Burger King, Cazador Mexican, Fazoli's, Guadalajara Mexica KFC, Subway, Tokyo Steaks, Village Inn Days Inn, Fairfie Inn, Quality Inn, Ramada, Super 8 Goodyear/auto, O'Reil Parts, Tires+

AMES

ANKENY

INTERSTATE 35 Cont'd

Exit #	Services
90	IA 160, Ankeny, E [gas] Casey's/dsl [food] Outback Steaks, Waterfront Seafood [lodging] AmericInn, Comfort Inn, Country Inn&Suites, Courtyard, Holiday Inn Express, Homewood Suites [other] Buick/GMC, W [gas] Casey's 2, Casey's/dsl, MurphyUSA/dsl [food] B-bops Rest., Buffalo Wild Wings, Burger King, Chick-fil-A, Chili's, China Buffet, Chipotle, Culver's, Fuzzy's Tacos, HuHot Chinese, IHOP, Jimmy John's, Los Charro, Maid Rite, Marble Slab, McDonald's, Noodles&Co, Okoboji, Old Chicago, Olive Garden, Panchero's Mexican, Panda Express, Panera Bread, Pepperjax, Perkins, Starbucks, Subway, Taco Bell, Tasty Tacos, Wendy's [other] AT&T, Best Buy, Big O Tires, Chevrolet, Chrysler/Dodge/Jeep, Duluth Trading, Ford, GNC, Home Depot, Jo-Ann Fabrics, Kohl's, Menards, Michael's, Petsmart, Staples, Target, TJ Maxx, to Saylorville Lake (5mi), Tuesday Morning, Tuffy Auto, Verizon, Walgreens, Walmart/Subway
89	Corporate Woods Dr, E [lodging] Hampton Inn, W [lodging] Woodspring Suites [other] F&F/dsl, Sam's Club/dsl
87b a	I-235, I-35 and I-80
I-35 and I-80 run together 14 mi around NW Des Moines. See I-80, exits 124-136.	
72b	I-80 W
72a	I-235 E, to Des Moines
70	Civic Pkwy, Mills, E [gas] Kum&Go/McDonald's [food] Fire Creek Grill, Legend's Grill, Quiznos, Starbucks [other] Hy-Vee Foods/gas, Verizon, vet, Walgreens, W [gas] Casey's/dsl [food] Applebee's, Bar Louie, BoneFish Grill, Bravo Italiana, Buffalo Wild Wings, Caribou Coffee, Cheesecake Factory, Chick-fil-A, Draught House 50, Fleming's Rest., Fuddruckers, Iron Wok, Jimmy John's, Joe's Crabshack, Johnny's Italian Steaks, Joseph's Steaks, Monterrey Mexican, Noodles&Co, On-the-Border, Panda Express, Panera Bread, PF Chang's, Red Robin, Tasty Tacos, Wellman's Grill [lodging] Courtyard, Drury Inn, Hilton Garden, Holiday Inn, Residence Inn [other] [H], $Tree, Aldi Foods, Barnes&Noble, Best Buy, Costco/gas, Dick's, Dillards, Firestone/auto, Kohl's, Lowe's, Old Navy, PetCo, Scheel's Sports, Target, TJ Maxx, Trader Joe's, Verizon, Walmart
69b a	Grand Ave, W Des Moines
68.5mm	Racoon River
68	IA 5, 7 mi E [other] to [airport], to Walnut Woods SP
65	G14, to Norwalk, Cumming, W [other] John Wayne Birthplace (14mi), Madison Co Museum (14mi)
61mm	North River
56	IA 92, to Indianola, Winterset, W [other] Good Life RV Ctr
56mm	Middle River
53mm	**[RS] nb, litter barrels, no restrooms**
52	G50, St Charles, St Marys, W [gas] Casey's/dsl [other] John Wayne Birthplace (14mi), museum (14mi)
51mm	**[RS] sb, litter barrels, no restrooms**
47	rd G64, to Truro, W [gas] Kum&Go (4mi)
45.5mm	South River
43	rd 207, New Virginia, E [gas] Kum&Go/Subway/dsl
36	rd 152, to US 69, 3 mi E [lodging] Blue Haven Motel, Evergreen Inn, W [other] st patrol
34	Clay St, Osceola, W [gas] Pilot/Subway/dsl/scales/24hr [other] Lakeside Casino Resort/camping
33	US 34, Osceola, E [gas] Casey's/dsl/scales [food] McDonald's, Pizza Hut, Subway [lodging] Best Value Inn, Quality Inn, Super 8 [other] [H], Ford, Goodyear, Hy-Vee Foods, O'Reilly Parts, W [gas] BP/Arby's/dsl [food] KFC/Taco Bell [lodging] AmericInn [other] Harley-Davidson, Walmart

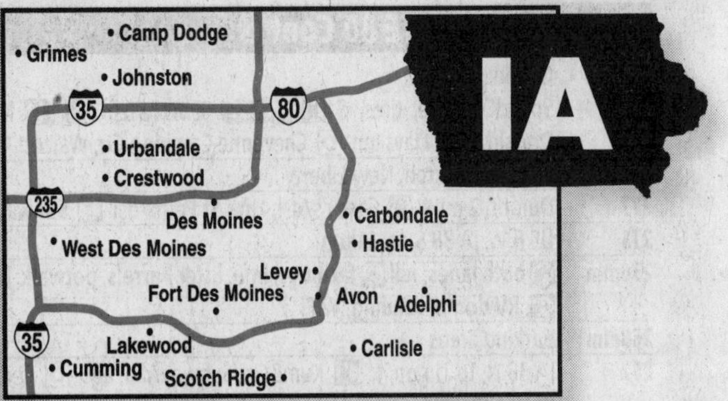

Exit #	Services
32mm	**[RS] both lanes, full [handicapped] facilities, litter barrels, petwalk, [phone], [picnic], RV dump, vending, wireless internet**
31mm	parking area sb, weigh sta nb
29	rd H45
22	rd J14, Van Wert
18	rd J20, to Grand River
12	rd 2, Decatur City, Leon, 5 mi E [gas] Shell/dsl [lodging] Little River Motel (5mi) [other] [H]
7.5mm	Grand River
7mm	**[RS] both lanes, full [handicapped] facilities, info, litter barrels, petwalk, [phone], [picnic], RV dump, vending, wireless internet**
4	US 69, to Davis City, Lamoni, E to 9 Eagles SP (10mi), W IA Welcome Ctr [gas] Casey's (2mi), Kum&Go/dsl/e85 [food] Maid-Rite Cafe, Pizza Hut (2mi), QC Rest., Subway (2mi) [lodging] Chief Lamoni Motel, Super 8 [other] auto/truck repair
0mm	Iowa/Missouri state line

INTERSTATE 80

Exit #	Services
307mm	Iowa/Illinois state line, Mississippi River
306	US 67, to Le Claire, N [gas] BP/A&W (2mi), Shell/dsl [food] Bierstube Grill, Hungry Hobo, McDonald's, Pizza Hut, Steventon's Rest., Subway [lodging] Comfort Inn, Holiday Inn Express, Super 8 [other] Buffalo Bill Museum, Slagles Foods, S [gas] BP (2mi)
301	Middle Rd, to Bettendorf
300mm	**[RS] both lanes, full [handicapped] facilities, litter barrels, petwalk, [phone], [picnic], RV dump, vending, WiFi**
298	I-74 E, to Peoria, S [other] st patrol, to [H]
295b a	US 61, Brady St, to Davenport, N [gas] BP/dsl [other] Fiat, to Scott CP, 0-2 mi S [gas] BP, KwikStar/dsl, Shell [food] Burger King, Cracker Barrel, Happy Joe's Pizza, Hardee's, Hooters, Los Agaves Mexican, McDonald's, Mo Brady's Steaks, Olive Garden, Papa John's, ThunderBay Grille, Village Inn Rest. [lodging] Baymont Inn, Best Western+, Casa Loma Suites, Clarion, Country Inn&Suites, Motel 6, Quad City Inn, Quality Inn, Residence Inn, Super 8, Travelodge, Wickliffe Inn [other] $General, AutoZone, CarQuest, Firestone/auto, Honda, Hyundai, JC Penney, Lexus, Menards, Nissan, Tires+, Toyota, US Adventures RV Ctr, vet, Von Maur, VW
292	IA 130 W, Northwest Blvd, N [gas] FLYING J/Denny's/dsl/LP/scales/24hr, Loves/Arby's/dsl/scales/24hr [lodging] Comfort Inn [other] Farm&Fleet, Interstate RV Park (1mi), Peterbilt, truckwash, S [gas] BP/McDonald's/dsl, Shell [food] Machine Shed Rest. [lodging] Days Inn [other] Freightliner
290	I-280 E, to Rock Island
284	Y40, to Walcott, N [gas] Pilot/Arby's/dsl/24hr/scales, TA/IA 80/BP/DQ/Pizza Hut/Taco Bell/Wendy's/dsl/scales/24hr/@ [food] Checkered Flag Grille, Gramma's Rest. [lodging] Comfort Inn [other] Blue Beacon, IA 80 Trucking Museum, IA 80 Truck-o-Mat,

INTERSTATE 80 Cont'd

IOWA CITY

284 Continued SpeedCo Lube, tires, **S** Pilot/Subway/dsl/24hr McDonald's Days Inn Cheyenne Camping Ctr, Walcott CP

280 Y30, to Stockton, New Liberty

277 Durant, **2 mi S** Casey's/dsl, Fifth St Petro/dsl Subway

271 US 6 W, IA 38 S, to Wilton

270mm **both lanes, full facilities, info, litter barrels, petwalk, RV dump, vending, WiFi**

268mm parking areas

267 IA 38 N, to Tipton, **N** Kum&Go/Subway/dsl/e85 Cedar River Camping

266mm Cedar River

265 to Atalissa, **S** Pilot/dsl only/scales/24hr

259 to West Liberty, Springdale, **S** BP/dsl EconoLodge Little Bear Camping

254 X30, West Branch, **N** BP/Quiznos/dsl, Casey's Hoover NHS, Jack&Jill Foods, USPO, **S** Kum&Go Casa Tequila Mexican, McDonald's Days Inn Chrysler/Dodge/Jeep

249 Herbert Hoover Hwy, **N** winery (2mi), **S** Wildwood Smokehouse golf

246 IA 1, Dodge St, **N** BP/Subway/dsl Jimmy John's, Joensy's Clarion URGENT CARE, **S** Sinclair Bob's Pizza Travelodge

244 Dubuque St, Iowa City, **N** Coralville Lake, **S** H, museum, to Old Capitol

242 to Coralville, **N** Twelve 01 Kitchen Hampton Inn, Radisson, **S** BP, Kum&Go/dsl 30 Hop Cafe, Applebee's, Arby's, Back Pocket Brewing, Bandana's BBQ, Burger King, Casa Azul, DQ, Dunkin', Edge Water Grill, Hardee's, IA Riverpower Rest., McDonald's, Milio's Sandwiches, Mondo's Cafe, Monica's Rest., Old Chicago Grill, Panera Bread, Papa John's, Peking Buffet, Perkins, Sparti's Gyros, Subway, Taco John's, Wig&Pen Rest. Baymont Inn, Best Western, Big Ten Inn, Comfort Inn, Heartland Inn, Homewood Suites, IA Lodge, Marriott, Quality Inn, Super 7, Super 8 H, auto repair, vet, Von Maur, Walgreens

240 IA 965, to US 6, Coralville, N Liberty, **N** BP, Casey's/dsl Buffalo Wild Wings, Cheddar's, Culver's, Jimmy John's, La Cava Mexican, McDonald's, Steak'n Shake, TX Roadhouse, Village Inn, Wendy's AmericInn, Country Inn&Suites, Suburban Lodge Colony Country Camping (3mi), Costco/gas, Gordman's, Harley-Davidson, Kohl's, Michael's, PetCo, TJ Maxx, URGENT CARE, Walgreens, Walmart/Subway, **S** Casey's/dsl Caribou Coffee, Chili's, Coldstone, Food Court, Huhot Mongolian, IHOP, Jimmy John's, Longhorn Steaks, Mellow Mushroom, Noodles&Co, Olive Garden, Panchero's Mexican, Papa Murphy's, Pizza Hut, Red Lobster, Starbucks, Taste of China, Which Wich? Comfort Suites, Holiday Inn Express, Residence Inn Ace Hardware, Advance Parts, Barnes&Noble, Best Buy, Dillard's, Discount Tire, Hobby Lobby, HyVee Foods/dsl, JC Penney, Lowe's, Old Navy, Scheel's Sports, Target, Tires+, U-Haul, Verizon

239b I-380 N, US 218 N, to Cedar Rapids

239a US 218 S

237 Tiffin, **N** Kum&Go/Subway/dsl Jon's Rest (1mi) (seasonal), **S** Sun& Fun RV Ctr

236mm **both lanes, full facilities, litter barrels, petwalk, RV dump, vending, wireless internet**

230 W38, to Oxford, **N** Sleepy Hollow Camping, **S** Kalona Village Museum (15mi)

225 US 151 N, W21 S, **N** Heritage Inn, to Amana Colonies, **S** Casey's 7 Villages Rest., MaidRite Cafe Motel 6, Ramada

IA

220 IA 149 S, V77 N, to Williamsburg, **N** BP, Casey's/Landma Rest./dsl Arby's, McDonald's, Subway Cozy House I Crest Motel, Super 8 factory outlets/famous brands, G Old Navy, **S** Days Inn $General, Williamsburg Tire/au

216 to Marengo, **N** Kum&Go/Subway/dsl H (8mi)

211 to Ladora, Millersburg, **S** Lake IA Park (5mi)

208mm **both lanes, full facilities, litter barrels, petwalk, RV dump, vending, wireless internet**

205 to Victor

201 IA 21, to Deep River, **N** Pilot/Subway/dsl/scales/24 Pleasant Stay Inn, **S** KwikStar/Denny's/dsl/scales/24hr/ truck repair

197 to Brooklyn, **N** TA/Country Pride/Dunkin'/dsl/scales/24hr/

191 US 63, to Montezuma, **S** to Diamond Lake SP (9mi)

182 IA 146, to Grinnell, **0-2 mi N** Casey's, Kum&Go/Subwa dsl/24hr Casa Margaritas, Grinnell Steakhouse, KFC/Ta Bell, McDonald's, Pizza Ranch Best Western, Comfort I Country Inn, Quality Inn, Super 8 $General, Ace Hardwa Buick/Chevrolet/GMC, Chrysler/Dodge/Jeep, H (4mi), HyV Foods, O'Reilly Parts, Verizon, vet, Walmart

180mm **both lanes, full facilities, litter barrels, petwalk, playground, RV dump (eb) wireless internet, vending, weath info**

179 IA 124, to Oakland Acres, Lynnville

175mm N Skunk River

NEWTON

173 IA 224, Kellogg, **N** Phillips 66/Best Burger/dsl/24hr K logg RV Park, Rock Creek SP (9mi), **S** Pella Museum

168 SE Beltline Dr, to Newton, **1 mi N** Casey's/dsl, Murp USA/dsl Arby's, Taco John's $Tree, KOA (seasona Walmart, **S** Love's/Chester's/McDonald's/dsl/scale Valero/dsl AmericInn, Boulders Inn Iowa Speedway

164 US 6, IA 14, Newton, **N** Casey's/dsl, Phillips 66/Subwa dsl Culver's, KFC/Taco Bell, MT Mikes, Okoboji Grill, Pe kins, Pizza Ranch Days Inn, EconoLodge, Quality Inn, Sup 8 H, museum, **S** Best Value Inn Cadillac/Chevr let, Chrysler/Jeep/Dodge, Ford/Lincoln, to Lake Red Rock

159 F48, to Jasper, Baxter

155 IA 117, Colfax, **N** BP/McDonald's/dsl Subway Co fax Inn, Microtel truck repair, **S** Casey's, Kum&Go/pi za/dsl/e85/24hr

153mm S Skunk River

151 **weigh sta wb**

149 Mitchellville

148mm **both lanes, full facilities, litter barrels, petwalk, RV dump, vending, wireless internet**

143 Altoona, Bondurant, **S** Casey's/dsl, Kum&Go/dsl Hamp ton Inn, Holiday Inn Express RV One Ctr

142b a US 65, Hubble Ave, Des Moines, **S** BP, FLYING J/Max Diner/dsl/scales/24hr/@, Git'n Go Bianchi Boys Pizz Big Steer Rest., Burger King, Culver's, Jethro's BBQ, KFC/Tac Bell, McDonald's/playplace, Perkins, Pizza Hut, Subway, Tac John's Adventureland Inn, Best Western+, Comfort In Motel 6, My Place, Quality Inn Adventureland Funpar Blue Beacon, camping, casino, Freightliner, Peterbilt

141 US 6 W, US 65 S, Pleasant Hill, Des Moines, **S** Uncle Buck' Grill Bass Pro Shops

137b a I-35 N, I-235 S, to Des Moines

I-80 W and I-35 S run together 14 mi.

136 US 69, E 14th St, Camp Sunnyside, **N** BP/dsl, Casey's Bo nanza Steaks, MT Mikes Budget Inn, Motel 6, Quality Inn Rodeway Inn Allied Tire, antiques, Volvo, **0-1 mi S** Ca sey's/dsl, QT/Burger King/dsl/scales/24hr, Star Gas Arby's

INTERSTATE 80 Cont'd

136 Continued
Fazoli's, Hardee's, KFC, McDonald's, Papa Murphy's, Pueblo Viejo Mexican, Subway, Taco Bell, Taco John's, Village Inn, Wendy's Baymont Inn, Travelodge $General, Advance Parts, Aldi Foods, AutoZone, CarX, Family$, O'Reilly Parts, Tires+, TruckLube, USPO

135 IA 415, 2nd Ave, Polk City, N Kum&Go/dsl Smokey D's BBQ antiques, Harley-Davidson, Ryder Trucks, S Git'n Go, QT, Shop&Save Earl's Tire, NAPA, st patrol

133mm Des Moines River

131 IA 28 S, NW 58th St, N Casey's, QT Bandit Burrito, Chopsticks, DQ, El Mariachi Mexican, Greenbriar Rest., Jimmy John's, Pagliai's Pizza, Panera Bread, Sonic, Subway, VanDee's Icecream/Sandwiches AmericInn Ace Hardware, Acura, Audi/VW, Goodyear/auto, Hy-Vee Food/dsl, USPO, vet, S BP/dsl/LP/24hr, Casey's, QT Applebee's, Arby's, Bamboo Buffet, Bennigan's, Buffalo Wild Wings, Burger King, Carlos O'Kelly's, Chipotle Mexican, Cici's Pizza, Dunkin', Famous Dave's BBQ, Fazoli's, Hardee's, IHOP, Jimmy John's, KFC, McDonald's, Noodles&Co, Old Chicago, Panda Express, Perfect Taco, Perkins, Pita Pit, Popeye's, Starbucks, Subway, Taco John's, Wendy's Days Inn, EconoLodge, Holiday Inn, Quality Inn, Ramada/Rest., Super 8 $Tree, Advance Parts, AT&T, Big Lots, BigLots, CarX, Chevrolet, Dahl's Food/Fuel, Firestone/auto, Ford, Goodyear/auto, Hobby Lobby, Kia, Kohl's, NAPA, Nissan, Office Depot, Old Navy, PriceChopper, Staples, Target, Toyota, URGENT CARE, Verizon, vet

129 NW 86th St, Camp Dodge, N Kum&Go Burger King, Legends Grill, McDonald's, Okoboji Grill, Panchero's Mexican, Planet Sub, Starbucks, TX Roadhouse, Village Inn Hilton Garden, Stoney Creek Inn, TownePlace Suites Dahl's Foods, Verizon, S Casey's, Kum&Go/dsl Arby's, B-Bops Burgers, Culver's, Friedrich's Coffee, Overtime Grill, Papa Murphy's, Pizza Ranch, Ruby Tuesday, Subway, Viva La Bamba Fairfield Inn, Hampton Inn, Holiday Inn Express, Microtel Walgreens

128 NW 100th St

127 IA 141 W, Grimes, N BP/dsl, QT/dsl MaidRite Cafe, McCoy's Grill, Subway to Saylorville Lake, Toyota, S Kum&Go/dsl/e85 McDonald's, Quiznos Firestone/auto, Home Depot, Target

126 Douglas Ave, Urbandale, E Casey's/dsl EconoLodge, Extended Stay America Chevrolet, W Kum&Go/dsl, Pilot/Subway/dsl/scales/24hr/@ Mama Lacona's

125 US 6, Hickman Rd, E IA Machine Shed Rest., Starbucks, Subway Clive Hotel, Hotel Renovo, Sleep Inn CarMax, Fiat, Honda, Hyundai, to Living History Farms, W Kum&Go/dsl, Loves/Denny's/dsl/scales/LP/24hr Chrysler/Dodge/Jeep, Menards

124 (72c from I-35 nb), University Ave, E Git'n Go/dsl Applebee's, Bakers Square, Chili's, Chuck-fil-A, Huhot Mongolian, Jason's Deli, KFC, Little Caesars, McDonald's, Mi Mexico, Mi Mexico, Outback Steaks, Qdoba Mexican, RockBottom Rest./brewery, Starbucks, TCBY, Twin Peaks, Wobbly Boots BBQ Courtyard, Days Inn, Sheraton, Sterling Suites, Super 8, Wildwood Lodge AT&T, Barnes&Noble, Best Buy, Home Depot, Kohl's, Lowe's, Marshall's, Office Depot, Petsmart, Target, Verizon, Whole Foods Mkt, World Mkt, W Kum&Go/Burger King, QT Biaggi's Rest, Caribou Coffee, Cracker Barrel, El Rodeo Mexican, Jersey Mike's, Other Place Grill, Panera Bread, Red Rossa Pizza, Wendy's, Z'Marik's Cafe Best Western, Country Inn&Suites, La Quinta H, Granite City Food, Walgreens

DES MOINES

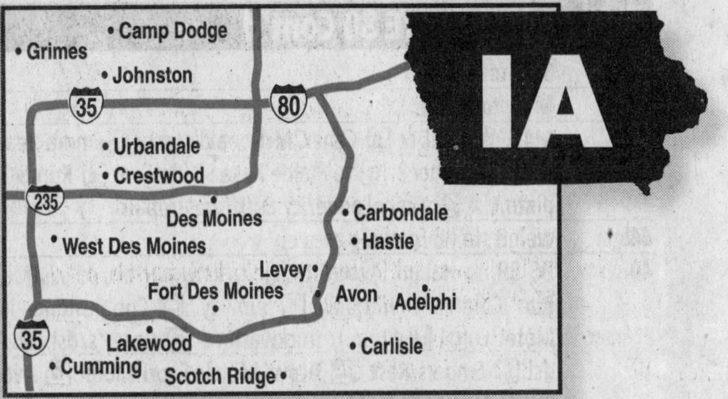

I-80 E and I-35 N run together 14 mi.

123b a I-80/I-35 N, I-35 S to Kansas City, I-235 to Des Moines

122 (from eb)60th St, W Des Moines, N H, same as 121

121 74th St, W Des Moines, N Biaggi's Rest., Panera Bread, Red Rossa Pizza Hampton Inn, Staybridge Suites H, Granite City Foods, HyVee Food/gas, Walgreens, S Kum&Go/Subway Arby's, Burger King, Culver's, McDonald's, Perkins, Quiznos, Taco John's Candlewood Suites, Fairfield Inn, Marriott, Motel 6, SpringHill Suites, vet

118 Grand Prairie Pky, N Kum&Go/dsl

117 R22, Booneville, Waukee, N Kum&Go/dsl/e85 Organic Farm Rest. Timberline Camping (2mi), S Rube's Steaks, Waveland Rest. (2mi)

115mm **weigh sta eb**

113 R16, Van Meter, 1 mi S Casey's Veteran's Cemetary

112mm N Racoon River

111mm Middle Racoon River

110 US 169, to Adel, DeSoto, N camping (6mi), S Casey's/dsl, Kum&Go/dsl/e85 Countryside Inn, Edgetowner Motel $General, John Wayne Birthplace (14mi), USPO

106 F90, P58, N KOA (apr-oct)

104 P57, Earlham, S Casey's (1mi)

100 US 6, to Redfield, Dexter, N Casey's (2mi) Drew's Chocolate (2mi)

97 P48, to Dexter, N camping, Casey's (2mi)

93 P28, Stuart, N Casey's/dsl/scales, Kum&Go/dsl/e85 Burger King, McDonald's/playplace, Subway AmericInn, Best Value Inn $General, Chevrolet, city park, Hometown Foods, S Phillips 66/dsl Country Kitchen Economy Inn NAPA

88 P20, Menlo

86 IA 25, to Greenfield, Guthrie Ctr, N to Spring Brook SP, S Hospital (13mi)

85mm Middle River

83 N77, Casey, 1 mi N Kum&Go camping

80.5mm **both lanes, full facilities, litter barrels, petwalk, RV dump, vending, wireless internet**

76 IA 925, N54, Adair, N Casey's/dsl, Kum&Go/Subway/dsl Chuck Wagon Rest. Adair Budget Inn, Super 8 camping, city park

75 G30, to Adair

70 IA 148 S, Anita, S to Lake Anita SP (6mi)

64 N28, to Wiota

61mm E Nishnabotna River

60 US 6, US 71, to Atlantic, Lorah, S Conoco/dsl/24hr Sunset Inn

57 N16, to Atlantic, N Nelsen RV Ctr, S H (7mi)

54 IA 173, to Elk Horn, 6 mi N **Welcome Ctr/wifi**, Tivoli Inn Windmill Museum

IA

INTERSTATE 80 Cont'd

COUNCIL BLUFFS

Exit #	Services
51	M56, to Marne
46	M47, Walnut, N Cenex/McDonald's/dsl Emma Jean's Rest. Super 8 to Prairie Rose SP (8mi), S Kum&Go/pizza/dsl EconoLodge/RV Park, tires/repair
44mm	**weigh sta wb/parking area eb**
40	US 59, to Harlan, Avoca, N FLYING J/Taco John's/Maid-Rite Cafe/dsl/24hr/scales Subway Cobblestone Inn, Motel 6 H (12mi), truckwash, S Casey's/dsl, Shell/dsl Embers Rest. Acova Motel, Capri Motel Avoca Foods, Farmall-Land Museum (seasonal), Nishna Museum
39.5mm	W Nishnabotna River
34	M16, Shelby, N BP/rest./dsl/e85, Shell/Cornstalk Cafe/dsl DQ, Godfather's Shelby Country Inn/RV Park, S Love's/McDonald's/Chester's/dsl/scales/24hr
32mm	**both lanes, parking only**
29	L66, to Minden, S Casey's/dsl Midtown Motel (2mi) winery (4mi)
27	I-680 W, to N Omaha
23	IA 244, L55, Neola, S Kum&Go/dsl/e85 camping, to Arrowhead Park
20mm	**Welcome Ctr eb/ wb, full facilities, litter barrels, petwalk, RV dump, vending, Wireless Internet**
17	G30, Underwood, N Cenex/Subway/dsl/24hr Underwood Motel truck/tire repair
8	US 6, Council Bluffs, N Casey's/dsl (1mi) $General, H (3mi), S st patrol
5	Madison Ave, Council Bluffs, N BP/dsl Burger King, FoodCourt, Great Wall Chinese, KFC, McDonald's, Papa Murphy's, Starbucks, Subway AmericInn HyVee Foods/drug, Verizon, Walgreens, S Phillips 66 DQ, Village Inn Rest. Western Inn Family Fare Mkt
4	I-29 S, to Kansas City
3	IA 192 N, Council Bluffs, N to Hist Dodge House, S Casey's/dsl, Shell/dsl, TA/Valero/Country Pride/dsl/scales/24hr/@ Applebee's, Beijing Rest., Burger King, Cracker Barrel, Dickey's BBQ, DQ, Fazoli's, Golden Corral, Hardee's, Huhot Mongolian, Jimmy John's, La Mesa Mexican, LJ Silver, McDonald's, Perkins, Red Lobster, Subway, Taco Bell Days Inn, Fairfield Inn, Motel 6, Red Roof Inn Advance Parts, Aldi Foods, Best Buy, Buick/GMC, Cadillac/Chevrolet, Chrysler/Dodge/Jeep, Ford, Freightliner, Gordman's, Home Depot, Hyundai/Subaru, Kia, Menards, Nissan, Outdoor Recreation RV, Sam's Club/gas, truck/dsl repair, U-Haul, Walmart/Subway
1b	S 24th St, Council Bluffs, N BP, Casey's, Pilot/Arby's/scales/dsl/24hr, Sapp Bros/Burger King/dsl Famous Dave's BBQ, Hooters, Quaker Steak&Lube, Ruby Tuesday, Uncle Buck's American Inn, Best Western, Country Inn&Suites, Hilton Garden, Holiday Inn Express, Microtel, SpringHill Suites, Super 8 Bass Pro Shop, Blue Beacon, Camping World RV Ctr, casino, Horseshoe RV Park, Peterbilt, SpeedCo, S **Welcome Ctr, full facilities,** Culver's, TX Roadhouse JC Penney, PetCo
1a	I-29 N, to Sioux City
0mm	Iowa/Nebraska state line, Missouri River

IA

INTERSTATE 235 (Des Moines)

DES MOINES

Exit #	Services
15	I-80, E to Davenports
12	US 6, E Euclid Ave, E Casey's Burger King, Dragon House Chinese, Papa John's, Perkins, Tasty Tacos $Tree, HyVee Foods/drug, Walgreens, W QT/dsl Midas, NAPA
11	Guthrie Ave, W Kum&Go/dsl CarQuest
10b a	IA 163 W, E University Ave, Easton Drs
9	US 65/69, E 14th, E 15th, N Subway Walgree S QT McDonald's, Quiznos, Tasty Tacos H, st ca tol, URGENT CARE, zoo
8b	E 6th St, Penn Ave (from wb), N H
8a	3rd St, 5th Ave, N Holiday Inn H, S Emba Suites, Marriott, Quality Inn Conv Ctr
7	Keo Ways
6	MLK Blvd/31st St, N Drake U, S , Governor's M sion
5b	42nd St, Science & Art Ctr, N Git'n Go Pa John's Drake Automotive
5a	56th St (from wb), N golf
4	IA 28, 63rd St, to Windsor Heights, S Historic Valley Jct,
3	8th St, W Des Moines, N Kum&Go B-Bop's Café, Bu er King, Papa Murphy's, Starbucks HyVee Foods, Pet Sam's Club/gas, Walmart/Subway, S BP, Kum&Go/d e85 Dunkin', Jimmy John's, Lemon Grass Thai, Tacos A dreas Days Inn
2	22nd St, 24th St, W Des Moines, N BP, Casey's/c Kum&Go/dsl, QT/dsl Arby's, ChuckeCheese, Culver's, mous Dave's BBQ, Hardee's, Hibachi Buffet, Jethro's BBQ, M Donald's, SmashBurger, Taco Bell, Village Inn $Tree, Ca Firestone/auto, Gordman's, Meineke, Michael's, Midas, W greens
1b	Valley West Dr, W Des Moines, N BP/dsl Chipotle Me ican, Cozy Cafe, Hamilton's Rest., Hurricane Grill, Jimmy Johr La Hacienda, Noodles&Co, Olive Garden, Panda Express, Par ra Bread, Red Lobster, Subway Valley West Inn AT& Best Buy, Home Depot, HyVee Foods, JC Penney, Marshall Target, Von Maur, Whole Foods Mkt

I-235 begins/ends on I-80, exit 123.

INTERSTATE 280 (Davenport)

Exit #	Services
18b a	I-74, US 6, Moline, S Shell/dsl Bare Bones BBQ, M Donald's, MT Jack's Best Inn, Country Inn&Suites, Hampt Inn, Holiday Inn Express, La Quinta, Motel 6, Quality Inn
15	Airport Rd, Milan, 1 mi N Hardee's, MaidRite Café, McDo ald's, Subway auto repair, Buick/Chevrolet, Firestone
11b a	IL 92, to Andalusia, Rock Island, S Jumer's Hotel/casin rest. KOA Camping
9.5mm	Iowa/Illinois state line, Mississippi River
8	rd 22, Rockingham Rd, to Buffalos
6	US 61, W River Dr, to Muscatine, W camping, ...gas
4	Locust St, rd F65, 160th St, E H, St Ambrose U, to Palm Coll, W Shell/Subway/dsl
1	US 6 E, IA 927, Kimberly Rd, to Walcott, 3 mi E Murp USA/dsl Applebee's, Culver's, Harlan's Rest., Steak Shake, Subway, Wendy's Discount Tire, GNC, Walmart

I-280 begins/ends on I-80, exit 290.

INTERSTATE 380 (Cedar Rapids)

WATERLOO

Exit #	Services
73mm	**I-380 begins/ends on US 218, 73mm in Waterloo. E** BP/d W Clark Pizza Hut
72	San Marnan Dr, W Casey's, Kwik Star/Dallas/e85 A&W LJ Silver, Applebee's, Burger King, Carlos O'Kelly's, Chick-fil-A DQ, Freddie's, Hardee's, IHOP, Jimmy John's, Little Ceasar Lone Star, Longhorn Steaks, McDonald's, Noodles&Co, Oliv Garden, Panchero's, Panda Express, Panera Bread, Red Lobste

INTERSTATE 380 (Cedar Rapids) Cont'd

Exit	Services
72	Continued Starbucks, Subway, Taco Bell, Taco John's, Tokyo Bay, Wendy's [lodging] Baymont Inn, Candlewoods Suites, Comfort Inn, Country Inn&Suites, Days Inn, Fairfield Inn, Hampton Inn, Holiday Inn Express, Motel 6, Super 8 [other] Advance Parts, Aldi Foods, AT&T, Barnes & Noble, Best Buy, Chevrolet, Chrysler/Dodge/Jeep, CVS Drug, Dick's, Dillards, Ford, Gordman's, Hobby Lobby, Home Depot, HyVee Foods, Jo-Ann Fabrics, KIA, Menards, PetCo, PetsMart, Staples, Target, Tires+, TJ Maxx, Verizon, Walmart
71	I-380, US 20, IA 27, Cedar Rapids, Cedar Falls, Dubuque, **W on US 18** [lodging] Isle Hotel/Casino
70	River Forest Rd
68	Elk Run Heights, Evansdale Dr, **E** [gas] FLYING J/Denny's/dsl/scales/24hr, Pilot/RR/Junie's/Subway/dsl/scales/24hr/@ [food] Arby's, McDonald's [lodging] Days Inn [other] Freightliner, Paine's RV Ctr, truckwash/repair
66	Gilbertville, Raymond
65	US 20 E, Dubuque
62	rd d-38, Gilbertville
55	rd v-65, Jesup, La Port, **W** [other] Hickory Hills Park, McFarlane Park
54mm	**weigh sta sb**
51mm	**weigh sta nb**
49	rd d-48, Brandon, **1 mi W** food, gas
43	IA 150, Independence, Vinton, **E** [gas] Casey's/dsl [lodging] Urbana Inn Suites [other] truckwash
41	Urbana, **E** [other] Lazy Acres RV Park, **W** [gas] Casey's/dsl [other] $General
35	rd w-36, Center Point, **E** [gas] BP, Casey's, Sinclair/McDonald's/Subway/dsl/scales/24hr [other] $General, Chrysler/Dodge/Jeep/Ford, **W** [other] Pleasant Creek SRA (5mi)
28	rd e-34, Robins, Toddville, **E** [gas] BP/dsl, **W** [other] Wickiup Outdoor Learning Ctr (5mi)
25	Boyson Rd, Hiawatha, **E** [gas] Casey's [food] Culver's [other] Buick/GMC/Cadillac, Ketelsen RV Ctr, Kia, Nissan, Subaru, **W** [gas] BP [other] Toyota/Mazda
24	IA 100, Blairs Ferry Rd, **E** [gas] KwikShop/dsl [food] Buffalo Wild Wings, Domino's, Hardee's, KFC, Las Glorias Mexican, McDonald's, Scott Family Rest., Wendy's [lodging] Comfort Inn, Country Inn&Suites, Days Inn, Residence Inn [other] Advance Parts, Chrysler/Dodge/Jeep, CVS Drug, Honda, O'Reilly Parts, Target,

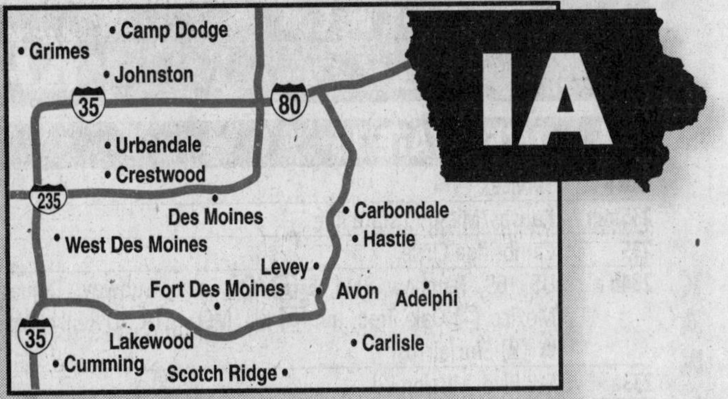

CEDAR RAPIDS

Exit	Services
24	Continued **W** [gas] Fas Fuel [food] Adelitas Mexican, Arby's, Burger King, Dunkin' Donuts, Freddy's, Pizza Hut, Starbucks, Subway, Taco Bell [other] Aldi Foods, AutoZone, GNC, Lowe's, Sam's Club/gas, Walmart
22	Glass Rd, 32nd St, **E** [gas] KwikShop/dsl [food] Papa Johns
21	H St, Cedar Rapids, downtown
20b	7th St E, Cedar Rapids, **E** [other] [H], downtown
20a	US 151 Bus, **E** [lodging] DoubleTree
19b	1st Ave W, **W** [other] NAPA
18	Wilson Ave, [other] museums
17	33rd ave SW, Hawkeye Downs, **W** [gas] Casey's, Casey's/dsl (2) [food] Burger King, Cancun, McDonald's, Taco Bell, Wendy's [lodging] Clarion, Econolodge, Economy Inn, Fairfield Inn, Hampton Inn, Holiday Inn Express, Hometown Inn, Motel 6, Quality Inn, Red Roof Inn, Residence Inn, Super 8, Super 8
16	US 30 W, US 151 S, US 218 N, Tama
13	Ely, **E** [gas] Pilot/Arby's/dsl/scales/24hr, **W** [gas] Casey's/A&W/dsl, Casey's/dsl/scales, Kwik Star/dsl/e85 [food] McDonald's, Subway [lodging] AmericInn, Country Inn&Suites [other]
12mm	**[Rs] both lanes, littler barrels, petwalk, [phone], [picnic], RV Dump, vending, wireless internet**
10	rd f-12, Shueyville, Swisher, **E** [gas] BP/dsl [other] Lake Mcbride SP, **W** [other] Amana Colonies
8mm	Iowa River
4	rd f-28, North Liberty, **E** [gas] Casey's/Blimpie, Kum&Go/dsl/e85 [lodging] Sleep Inn [other] Colony Country RV Park (5mi)
0b a	I-80 E to Iowa City, W to Des Moines, **I-380 begins/ends on I-80.**

NOTES

= gas = food = lodging = other = rest stop

KANSAS

INTERSTATE 35

KANSAS CITY AREA

Exit #	Services
235mm	Kansas/Missouri state line
235	Cambridge Circle
234b a	US 169, Rainbow Blvd, E Sonic, Subway, Taqueria Mexico Oak Tree Inn KU MED CTR, O'Reilly Parts, W Sinclair/dsl
233a	SW Blvd, Mission Rd
233b	37th Ave (from sb)
232b	US 69 N, E Phillips 66/dsl, QT Burger King, China Star, Cici's, McDonald's, Subway, Taco Bell Aldi Foods, Lowe's, Price Chopper, Walgreens, Walmart
232a	Lamar Ave, E Wood Spring Suites
231b a	I-635 (exits left from sb)
230	Antioch Rd (from sb)
229	Johnson Dr, E QT/dsl Chili's, China Garden, Jack-in-the-Box, Jimmy John's, McDonald's, Starbucks, Subway, Taco Bell AT&T, Dick's, GNC, Hen House Mkt, Hobby Lobby, Home Depot, IKEA, Marshall's, Old Navy, Petsmart, Verizon, Walgreens, W Cenex/dsl
228b	US 56 E, US 69, Shawnee Mission Pkwy, E Shell Caribou Coffee, Denny's, Krispy Kreme Drury Inn, Extended Stay America, Super 8 BMW/Mini, W A&W, Arby's, LJ Silver, McAlister's Deli, Panera Bread, Pizza Hut, Subway AutoZone, Discount Tire, Famil$, Firestone/auto, Ford, Goodyear/auto, Jo-Ann Fabrics, O'Reilly Parts, Russell Stover, Walgreens
228a	67th St, E Quality Inn CarMax, W Phillips 66/dsl Hyundai, Infiniti, Jaguar, Land Rover, Lexus, Maserati, Mercedes, Porsche Smart, Toyota
227	75th St, E McDonald's Extended Stay America H, Acura, Audi, Walmart, W QT/dsl Domino's, Sonic, Starbucks, Subway, Taco Bell, Wendy's Hampton Inn Hyundai, URGENT CARE
225b	US 69 S (from sb), Overland Pkwy
225a	87th St, E Green Mill Rest, Wendy's Holiday Inn, W Phillips 66/dsl Dunkin', Taco Bell, Zarda BBQ
224	95th St, E Applebee's, BD Mongolian BBQ, Burger King, Cheddar's, Chick-fil-A, Chipotle Mexican, Five Guys, Houlihan's, Jimmy John's, KFC, McDonald's, Noodles&Co, On-the-Border, Outback Steaks, Panda Express, Pie Five, Subway, Taco Bell, Winstead's Cafe, Zoe's Kitchen Crossland Suites, Crowne Plaza, La Quinta, Motel 6, Quality Inn, Super 8 H, Advance Parts, Barnes&Noble, Best Buy, Dillard's, Firestone/auto, Hobby Lobby, JC Penney, Kohl's, Macy's, Nordstrom, Office Depot, PetCo, Ross, Sam's Club/gas, Target, Verizon, W Phillips 66 Mi Ranchito Costco/gas, O'Reilly Parts, U-Haul
222b a	I-435 W & E
220	119th St, E Conoco/7-11, Phillips 66, Phillips 66/dsl A&W, Buffalo Wild Wings, Burger King, Chick-fil-A, Chipotle Mexican, Chuy's, Coldstone, Cracker Barrel, Firehouse Subs, Five Guys, Five Guys, Freddy's, Granite City Cafe, Hira's Steak, IHOP, Jimmy John's, KC Joe's BBQ, KC Super Buffet, LJ Silver, Master Wok, McDonald's, Mr Gyros Greek, Noodles&Co, Old Chicago, Olive Garden, Panda Express, Panera Bread, Papa Murphy's, Pei Wei, Penn Sta Subs, Pie Five, Planet Sub, Popeye's, Red Lobster, Schlotzsky's, Smashburger, Starbucks, Steak'n Shake, Subway, Taco Bell, Twin Peaks, TX Roadhouse, Wendy's, Zaxby's, Zoe's Kitchen Fairfield Inn, Hampton Inn,

OLATHE

OTTAWA

Exit #	Services
220	Continued Hilton Garden, Holiday Inn Express, Residence Inn, W Spring Suites AT&T, Best Buy, Chrysler/Dodge/Jeep, Dic Fiat, GNC, Goodyear/auto, Home Depot, Honda, Marsha Michael's, Natural Grocers, NTB, Old Navy, Petsmart, R Target, U-Haul, Verizon, Whole Foods Mkt, W Houliha Jason's Deli, Longhorn Steaks, Starbucks Bass Pro Shop
218	135th, Santa Fe St, Olathe, E Phillips 66/dsl Ap bee's, Burger King, Chapala Mexican, China Buffet, Churc McDonald's, Other Place Grill, Papa John's, Perkins, Pizza Sheridan's Custard, Subway, Taco Bell $General, $Tr Ace Hardware, Aldi Foods, AutoZone, BigLots, Discount Foc Ford/Lincoln, GNC, Hobby Lobby, Kohl's, Midas, Office Dep vet, W Domino's, KFC, McDonald's, Subway, Ta Bell, Waffle House Rodeway Inn Aamco, Adva Parts, Buick/GMC, Chevrolet, Harley-Davidson, Hyundai, K Meineke, Nissan, O'Reilly Parts, Subaru, Toyota, VW
217	Old Hwy 56 (from sb), same as 215
215	US 169 S, KS 7, Olathe, E Phillips 66/dsl, QT/dsl Chip le Mexican, IHOP, Jimmy John's, MOD Pizza, Panera Bread, R Robin Candlewood Suites, Quality Inn Aldi Foods, D count Tire, GNC, Home Depot, Jiffy Lube, NTB, Target, W Ph lips 66/dsl/scales/24hr 54th St Grill, Chili's, McDonald's, Ta Bell, Wendy's Best Western, Days Inn, Econolodge, La Qu ta, Motel 6 H, Burlington Coats, Mazda
214	Lone Elm Rd, 159th St
213mm	**weigh sta both lanes**
210	US 56 W, Gardner, W Phillips 66/dsl, QT/dsl Arby Burger King, KFC, McDonald's, Perkins, Pizza Hut, Sonic, Su way, Taco Bell, Waffle House Super 8 AutoZone, Pr Chopper, Walgreens, Walmart
207	US 56 E, Gardner Rd, E Olathe RV Ctr, W Phillips 6 dsl, Phillips 66/dsl (2)
205	Homestead Lane
202	Edgerton
198	KS 33, to Wellsville, W food, gas
193	Tennessee Rd, Baldwin
188	US 59 N, to Lawrence
187	KS 68, Ottawa, W Phillips 66/dsl Central RV Ctr, Mi west RV Ctr
185	15th St, Ottawa
183	US 59, Ottawa, E Loves/Hardee's/dsl/scales/24h W BP, Ottawa/dsl, Phillips 66/dsl Applebee's, Burg King, Freddy's, McDonald's, Nagoya Japanese, Old 56 Res Pizza Hut, Sirloin Stockade, Taco Bell, Wendy's Best Wes ern, Comfort Inn, Days Inn, EconoLodge, Super 8 H, $Ge eral, $Tree, Advance Parts, Ford, Walmart
182b a	US 50, Eisenhower Rd, Ottawa
176	Homewood, W RV camping
175mm	**both lanes, full facilities, litter barrels, petwalk, RV dump, vending, wireless internet**
170	KS 273, Williamsburg, W Gas&Food
162	KS 31 S, Waverly
160	KS 31 N, Melvern
155	US 75, Burlington, Melvern Lake, E Conoco/Subway/dsl, TA Shell/Wendy's/dsl/scales/24hr/@ Wyatt Earp Inn dsl repa
148	KS 131, Lebo, E Casey's, Cenex/dsl Universal In $General, W to Melvern Lake
141	KS 130, Neosho Rapids, E NWR (8mi)
138	County Rd U

KS

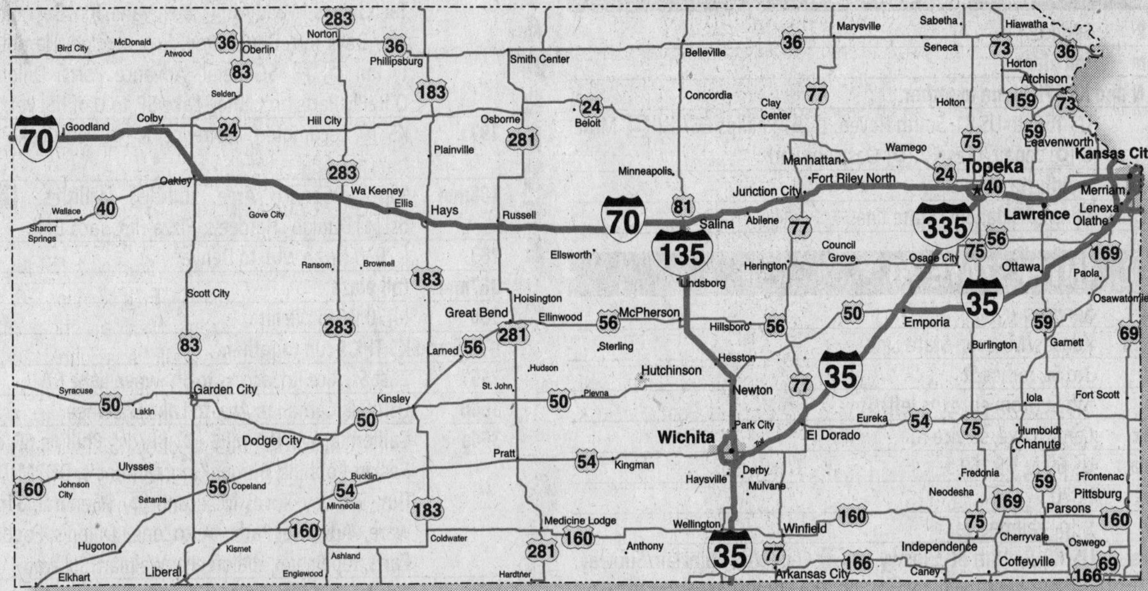

INTERSTATE 35 Cont'd

Exit #	Services
135	County Rd R1, W Dieker RV Ctr, RV camping/
133	US 50 W, 6th Ave, Emporia, 1-3 mi E Casey's Budget Host
131	KS 57, KS 99, Burlingame Rd, E Phillips 66/Circle K/dsl Goodcents Subs, Hardee's Dillon's Food, repair, Tire Pros
130	KS 99, Merchant St, E Phillips 66/dsl Subway CVS Drug, Emporia SU, Lyon Co Museum
128	Industrial Rd, E Arby's, Bruff's Steaks, Burger King, China Buffet, Gambino's Pizza, Ichiban Japanese, Spangles, Subway EconoLodge, Knights Inn, Motel 6 H, $General, Aldi Foods, AT&T, JC Penney, Walgreens, W Phillips 66/WhichWich?/dsl Applebee's, Braum's, Domino's, IHOP, KFC, McDonald's, MT Mike's Steaks, Pizza Hut, Pizza Ranch, Planet Sub, Starbucks, Taco Bell Candlewood Suites, Comfort Inn, Hampton Inn, Holiday Inn Express, La Quinta, Quality Inn $Tree, Staples, Verizon, Walmart/Subway
127c	KS Tpk, I-335 N, to Topeka
127b a	US 50, KS 57, Newton, E FLYING J/Huddle House/dsl/LP/scales/24hr, Casey's/dsl Arby's, China Buffet, Papa John's Best Inn, Best Western/rest., Days Inn, Rodeway Inn, Super 8 Buick/Chevrolet, Chrysler/Dodge/Jeep, dsl repair, Ford/Lincoln, Kenworth, NAPA, Nissan, PriceChopper Foods, Tires-4Less, Toyota, W Emporia RV Park
127mm	I-35 and I-335 KS Tpk, I-35 S and KS tpk S run together, **toll plaza**
I-35 S and KS Tpk S run together.	
125mm	Cottonwood River
111	Cattle Pens
97.5mm	**Matfield Green Service Area (both lanes exit left),** Phillips 66/dsl Hardee's/Dunkin'
92	KS 177, Cassoday, E Fuel'n Service,
76	US 77, El Dorado N, 3 mi E Casey's, Phillips 66/dsl Pizza Hut, Taco Bell Stardust Motel $General, Ace Hardware, city park, Dillon's Foods/dsl, El Dorado SP, Walgreens
71	KS 254, KS 196, El Dorado, E Casey's/dsl, Phillips 66/dsl, QT/dsl Arbys, Braum's, Burger King, Domino's, Freddy's, Gambino's Pizza, Hog Wild BBQ, Jimmy's Egg, KFC, LJ Silver, McDonald's, Pizza Hut, Sonic, Spangles, Subway Days Inn, Holiday Inn Express, Motel 6, Red Coach Inn, Sunset Inn, Super 8 H,
71	Continued $General, AutoZone, Buick/Cadillac, Bumper Parts, Deer Grove RV Park, KS Oil Museum, O'Reilly Parts, Verizon, Walmart
65mm	**Towanda Service Area (both lanes exit left),** Phillips 66/dsl Hardee's/Dunkin'
62mm	Whitewater River
57	21st St, Andover, W golf,

WICHITA

Exit #	Services
53	KS 96, Wichita
50	US 54, Kellogg Ave, **W on Kellogg** Beijing Bistro, BJ's Rest., Bubba's Rest., Burger King, Carlos Kelly's, Chipotle Mexican, Denny's, Firehouse Subs, Golden Corral, Green Mill Rest., IHOP, LJ Silver, Logan's Roadhouse, Longhorn Steaks, McDonald's, Noodles&Co, Old Chicago Pizza, Panda Express, Red Lobster, Subway, Taco Bell Best Western, Comfort Inn, Days Inn, Extended Stay America, Fairfield Inn, Hampton Inn, Hawthorn Suites, Holiday Inn, La Quinta, Marriott, Motel 6, Super 8 $Tree, Acura, AT&T, AT&T, Bosley Tires, Cadillac/Chevrolet, CarMax, CarQuest, Chrysler/Dodge/Jeep, Costco/dsl, Dillard's, Fiat, Firestone/auto, Ford, Honda, Infiniti, JC Penney, Lincoln, Lowe's, Mazda, Michael's, Nissan, Petsmart, Ross, Subaru, TJ Maxx, Toyota, USPO, Verizon, Von Maur, VW, Walmart/Subway
45	KS 15, Wichita, E Spirit Aero Systems
44.5mm	Arkansas River
42	47th St, I-135, to I-235, Wichita, W QT/dsl Applebee's, Arby's, Braum's, Burger King, Carlos O'Kelly's, Domino's, Godfather's, Goodcents Subs, Heritage Rest., Hog Wild BBQ, IHOP, KFC, Little Caesar's, LJ Silver, McDonald's, New China, Pizza Hut, Spangles Rest., Subway, Taco Bell Best Western, Days Inn, Holiday Inn Express, Quality Inn, Springfield Inn, Super 8, Woodspring Suites $General, $Tree, Air Capital RV Park, Dillon's Foods/dsl, O'Reilly Parts, Verizon
39	US 81, Haysville, W JumpStart Sonic, Subway Express Inn, Sleep Inn
33	KS 53, Mulvane, E Mulvane Hist Museum, W Hampton Inn, Kansas Star Casino/Hotel Wyldewood Winery
26mm	**Belle Plaine Service Area (both lanes exit left),** Phillips 66/dsl McDonald's
19	US 160, Wellington, 3 mi W KFC, McDonald's, Penny's Diner OakTree Inn KOA

KS

INTERSTATE 35 Cont'd

Exit #	Services
17mm	**toll plaza**
I-35 N and KS TPK N run together.	
4	US 166, to US 81, South Haven, E Phillips 66/dsl Motel 6 repair/tires, W Oasis RV Park
1.5mm	**weigh sta nb**
0mm	Kansas/Oklahoma state line

INTERSTATE 70

KANSAS CITY

Exit #	Services
424mm	Kansas/Missouri State Line
423b	3rd St, James St
423a	5th St (from eb, exits left)
422d c	Central Ave, service rd
422b a	US 69 N, US 169 S
421b	I-670
421a	S railroad yard
420b a	US 69 S, 18th St Expswy, N Cenex/dsl, Sinclair/Subway/dsl China Town, Jack-in-the-Box, Tapatio Mexican GNC, SunFresh Foods
419	38th St, Park Dr, access to 10 motels
418b	I-635 N (eb only)
418a	I-635 S
417	57th St
415a	KS 32 E (from eb)
415b	to US 24 W, State Ave, Kansas Cityon US 24, N Papa John's, Taco Bell Gables Motel Lowe's
414mm	**parking area both lanes, vehicle insp sta wb**
414	78th St, **N on US 24** Phillips 66, QT/dsl Arby's, Burger King, Capt D's, Domino's, Hardee's, KFC, Krispy Kreme, Lucky Chinese, McDonald's, Papa John's, Papa Murphy's, Sonic, Subway, Taco Bell, Wendy's Days Inn H, $Tree, Advance Parts, BigLots, Buick/GMC, CVS Drug, Firestone/auto, Marshall's, O'Reilly Parts, Petsmart, PriceChopper Foods, SavALot, Tires+, Walgreens, XPress/auto/tire, S American Motel, Comfort Inn
411b	I-435 N, to KCI Airport, access to Woodlands Racetrack
411a	I-435 S
410	110th St, N Chateau Avalon, Great Wolf Lodge Cabela's, KS Speedway
225mm	**I-70 W and KS TPK W run together.**
224	KS 7, to US 73 (last free exit wb before KS TPK), Bonner Springs, Leavenworth, N Phillips 66/7-11/dsl, QT/dsl El Potro Mexican, KFC/Taco Bell, Waffle House Holiday Inn Express, Super 8 museum, S Arby's, Burger King, Goodcents Subs, Lin's Chinese, McDonald's, Papa Murphy's, Pizza Hut, Taco John's $Tree, Ace Hardware, AutoZone, Cottonwood RV Camp, Nachbar Automotive, PriceChopper Foods, Walgreens, Walmart/Subway
217mm	**toll booth**
212	Eudora, Tonganoxie
209mm	**Lawrence Service Area (both lanes exit left) full facilities,** Phillips 66/dsl McDonald's
204	US 24, US 59, to E Lawrence, S Cenex/dsl, Phillips 66/Subway Burger King Motel 6, SpringHill Suites (1mi) $General, O'Reilly Parts
203mm	Kansas River
202	US 59 S, to W Lawrence, **S on US 40** Conoco, Phillips 66/dsl, Zarco/dsl Burger King, Domino's, Dunkin', Jimmy John's, Kobe Japanese, McDonald's, Sonic, Subway, Taco Bell,

BONNER SPGS

LAWRENCE

Exit #	Services
202	Continued Taco John's, Wendy's Best Value Inn, Baymont Inn, Comf Inn, Days Inn, DoubleTree, EconoLodge, Hampton Inn, Qu ty Inn H, $General, Advance Parts, Dillon's Foods/g O'Reilly Parts, to Clinton Lake SP, to U of KS, vet, Walgreens
197	KS 10, Lecompton, Lawrence, N Perry Lake SP, S Cl ton Lake SP
188mm	**Topeka Service Area, full facilities,** Phillips 6 dsl Dunkin', Hardee's, Pizza Hut, Taco Bell
183	I-70 W (from wb), to Denver
367mm	**toll plaza**
366	I-470 W, to Wichita
I-70 E and KS TPK E run together.	
365	21st St, Rice Rd, access to Shawnee Lake RA
364b	US 40 E, Carnahan Ave, to Lake Shawnee
364a	California Ave, **0-1 mi S** BP/dsl, Phillips 66/dsl Arby Baskin-Robbins, Burger King, Domino's, DQ, McDonald's, Piz Hut, Subway, Tacos Mexicano $General, $Tree, Ace Ha ware, Advance Parts, AutoZone, Dillon's Food/gas, O'Re Parts, repair, vet, Walgreens, Walmart/Subway
363	Adams St, S Phillips 66/dsl
362c	10th Ave (from wb), N Ramada Inn, S st capitol
362b a	to 8th Ave, N Ramada, S to St Capitol, downtown
361b	3rd St, Monroe St
361a	1st Ave, S Ryder
359	MacVicar Ave, S H, Kenworth
358b a	Gage Blvd
357b a	Fairlawn Rd, 6th Ave, S Phillips 66, Valero/dsl B Western, Motel 6 $General, NAPACare, vet
356b a	Wanamaker Rd, N Red Robin Hyatt Place KS M seum of History, S BP, Murphy Express/dsl, Phillips 6 dsl Applebee's, Arby's, Buffalo Wild Wings, Burger Kir Chick-fil-A, Chili's, Chipotle Mexican, ChuckECheese, CiC Pizza, Coldstone, Cracker Barrel, Denny's, Five Guys, Fredd Steakburgers, Golden Corral, Hardee's, Hooters, HuHot C nese, IHOP, Jason's Deli, Jersey Mike's Subs, Jimmy John's, Jo Pepper's, Longhorn Steaks, McAlister's, McDonald's, Noodles Co, Old Chicago, Olive Garden, On-the-Border, Panda Expre Panera Bread, Papa John's, Perkins, Pie Five Pizza, Pizza H Qdoba, Red Lobster, Sonic, Spangles, Starbucks, Steak'n Sha Taco Bell, Taco John's, TX Roadhouse, Wendy's Baymo Inn, Candlewood Suites, Clubhouse Inn, Comfort Suites, Cou try Inn&Suites, Courtyard, Days Inn, Econolodge, Fairfield Ir Hampton Inn, Hilton Garden, Holiday Inn Express, Homewo Suites, Quality Inn, Relax Inn, Residence Inn, Sleep Inn, Sup 8, Woodspring Suites $Tree, AAA, Aldi Foods, AT&T, A toZone, Barnes&Noble, Best Buy, Dick's, Dillard's, Goodyea auto, Hobby Lobby, Home Depot, JC Penney, Jo-Ann, Koh Lowe's, Menards, Michael's, Natural Grocers, Old Navy, PetC Sam's Club/gas, Target, TJ Maxx, Tuesday Morning, URGE CARE, Verizon, Walmart/Subway
355	I-470 E, US 75 S, to VA MED CTR, Topeka, **1 mi S** same as 35 air museum
353	KS 4 W, to Auburn Rd
351	frontage rd (from eb), Mission Creek
350	Valencia Rd
347	West Union Rd
346	Carlson Rd, to Rossville, Willard
343	Ranch Rd
342	Keene-Eskridge Rd, access to Lake Wabaunsee
341	KS 30, Maple Hill, S 24-7/Subway/café/dsl/RV dump
338	Vera Rd, S Valero/Baskin-Robbins/dsl

TOPEKA

E INTERSTATE 70 Cont'd

Exit #	Services
336mm	**[rest stop] (exits left from both lanes), full [handicapped] facilities, litter barrels, petwalk, [phone], [picnic], RV parking, wireless internet**
335	Snokomo Rd, Paxico, Skyline Mill Creek Scenic Drive
333	KS 138, Paxico, **N** [other] Mill Creek RV Park, winery
332	Spring Creek Rd
330	KS 185, to McFarland
329mm	**weigh sta both lanes**
328	KS 99, to Alma, **S** Wabaunsee Co Museum
324	Wabaunsee Rd, **N** [other] Grandma Horners Store&Factory
322	Tallgrass Rd
318	frontage rd
316	Deep Creek Rd
313	KS 177, to Manhattan, 8 mi **N** [gas] Phillips 66 [food] Chili's, IHOP, Longhorn Steaks, McAlister's Deli, McDonald's, Olive Garden, Sonic, Taco Bell, TX Roadhouse, Wendy's [lodging] Best Western, Candlewood Suites, Comfort Inn, Fairfield Inn, Hampton Inn, Hilton Garden, Motel 6, Quality Inn, Super 8 [other] Aldi Foods, JC Penney, to KSU, Walmart/Subway
311	Moritz Rd
310mm	**[rest stop] both lanes, full [handicapped] facilities, litter barrels, petwalk, [phone], [picnic], RV dump**
307	McDowell Creek Rd, scenic river rd to Manhattan
304	Humboldt Creek Rd
303	KS 18 E, to Ogden, Manhattan, **N** [other] to KSU
301	Marshall Field, **N** [other] Cavalry Museum, Custer's House, KS Terr Capitol, to Ft Riley
300	US 40, KS 57, Council Grove, **S** hist church
299	Flinthills Blvd, to Jct City, Ft Riley, **N** [gas] Cenex/dsl [food] Stacy's Rest. [lodging] EconoLodge, Grandview Plaza Inn, Great Western Inn
298	Chestnut St, to Jct City, Ft Riley, **N** [gas] Shell/dsl/24hr [food] Arby's, Cracker Barrel, Family Buffet, Freddy's Steakburgers, JC's BBQ, La Fiesta, Pizza Hut, Qdoba, Starbucks, Taco Bell, Tokyo Steaks [lodging] Best Western, Candlewood Suites, Comfort Inn, Courtyard, Quality Inn [other] $General, $Tree, CVS Drug, Verizon, Walmart/Subway
296	US 40, Washington St, Junction City, **N** [gas] Casey's, Cenex/dsl, Phillips 66, Shell/dsl [food] IHOP, McDonald's, Munson's Prime, Peking Chinese, Sonic, Subway [lodging] Budget Host/RV park, Express Inn, Hampton Inn, Jct City Inn, Super 8, Woodspring Suites [other] Cadillac/Chevrolet, Haas Tire, Harley-Davidson, vet
295	US 77, KS 18 W, Marysville, to Milford Lake, **N** [gas] Sapp Bros/A&W/dsl/24hr [lodging] Motel 6 [other] [H], Ford/Lincoln/Kia/Chrysler/Dodge/Jeep, RV Ctr, **S** [other] Owls Nest Camping, truckwash
290	Milford Lake Rd
286	KS 206, Chapman, **S** [gas] Casey's/dsl, Cenex/dsl [other] $General, Chapman Creek RV Park, KS Auto Racing Museum
281	KS 43, to Enterprise, **N** [gas] Phillips 66/dsl [other] 4 Seasons RV Ctr/Park
277	Jeep Rd
275	KS 15, to Clay Ctr, Abilene, **N** [lodging] Brookville Hotel/rest., Holiday Inn Express, **S** [gas] 24-7/Arby's/dsl, KwikShop, Sips [food] Burger King, M&R Grill, McDonald's, Pizza Hut, Sonic, Subway [lodging] Budget Inn, Super 8 [other] [H], $General, Auburn Drug, AutoZone, Buick/Cadillac/Chevrolet, CountryMart Foods, O'Reilly Parts, to Eisenhower Museum
272	Fair Rd, to Talmage, **S** [gas] Love's/Hardee's/dsl/scales/24hr [other] Russell Stover Candies
266	KS 221, Solomon
265mm	**[rest stop] both lanes, full [handicapped] facilities, litter barrels, petwalk, [phone], [picnic], RV dump, vending**

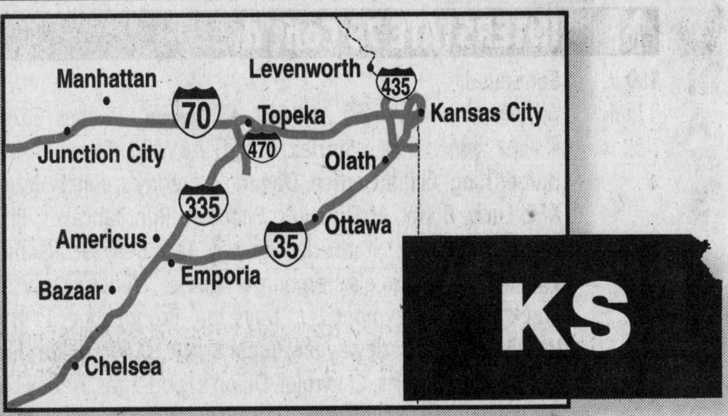

SALINA

RUSSELL

HAYS

Exit #	Services
264mm	Solomon River
260	Niles Rd, New Cambria
253mm	Saline River
253	Ohio St, **N** [other] RV park, **S** [gas] FLYING J/Huddle House/dsl/LP/scales/24hr, LNG [other] [H], Harley-Davidson, Kenworth
252	KS 143, 9th St, Salina, **N** [gas] 24-7/Subway/dsl/24hr, Petro/Shell/Starbucks/Popeye's/dsl/24hr/@ [food] IHOP, Iron Skillet, McDonald's [lodging] Days Inn, Holiday Inn Express, La Quinta, Motel 6, Red Carpet, Rodeway Inn, Super 8 [other] Blue Beacon, dsl repair, Freightliner, KOA, **S** [gas] Pilot/dsl/scales/24hr/@ [lodging] Comfort Inn, EconoLodge
250b a	I-135, US 81, N to Concordia, S to Wichita
249	Halstead Rd, to Trenton
244	Hedville, **S** [gas] Phillips 66/dsl [other] Rolling Hills Park (2mi)
238	to Brookville, Glendale, Tescott
233	290th Rd, Juniata
225	KS 156, to Ellsworth, **S** [gas] D&S/dsl [other] Ft Harker Museum, Ft Larned HS
224mm	**[rest stop] both lanes, full [handicapped] facilities, litter barrels, petwalk, [phone], [picnic], RV dump**
221	KS 14 N, to Lincoln
219	KS 14 S, to Ellsworth, **S** [gas] Conoco/dsl
216	to Vesper
209	to Sylvan Grove
206	KS 232, Wilson, **N** [gas] Travel Shoppe/rest. [other] Wilson Lake (6mi), **S** [other] RV camping
199	Dorrance, **N** [other] to Wilson Lake, **S** [gas] Agco/dsl/food
193	Bunker Hill Rd, **N** [gas] Conoco/Sunmart/pizza/dsl/24hr, to Wilson Lake WA
189	US 40 bus, Pioneer Rd, Russell
187mm	**parking area both lanes, [picnic], litter barrels**
184	US 281, Russell, **N** [gas] 24-7/dsl, Cenex/Fossil Sta./dsl [food] A&W, McDonald's, Meridy's Rest., Pizza Hut, Sonic, Subway [lodging] Days Inn, Fossil Creek Hotel, Quality Inn, Russell's Inn [other] [H], $General, Bumper Parts, CarQuest, Fossil Creek RV Park, JJJ RV Park, Klema Mkt, st patrol
180	Balta Rd, to Russell
175	Gorham, 1 mi **N** [gas] Co-Op/dsl
172	Walker Ave
168	KS 255, to Victoria, **S** [gas] 255 Diner/dsl [other] to Cathedral of the Plains
163	Toulon Ave
161	Commerce Parkway, **S** [other] Volvo/Mack Trucks
159	US 183, Hays, **N** [gas] Cenex/Taco Grande/dsl, EVC, Qwest/dsl [food] Applebee's, IHOP, Old Chicago, Pasta Jay's, Sims BBQ, Wendy's [lodging] Best Western+, Comfort Inn, Fairfield Inn, Hampton Inn, Holiday Inn Express, Sleep Inn, TownePlace Suites [other] AT&T, Chrysler/Dodge/Jeep, Ford/Lincoln, Harley-Davidson, Home Depot, Tesla EVC, Toyota, Verizon,

KS

INTERSTATE 70 Cont'd

HAYS

159	Continued Walmart/Subway, S 24-7/dsl, Loves, Phillips 66/dsl, Phillips 66/dsl/24hr, Sinclair/dsl A&W/LJ Silver, Arby's, Burger King, China Garden, Domino's, Freddy's, Jimmy John's, KFC, Lucky Buffet, McDonald's, Pheasant Run Pancakes, Pizza Hut, Qdoba, Sonic, Starbucks, Subway, Taco Bell, Taco Grande, Thirsty's Grill, Vernie's Hamburger House, Wendy's, Whiskey Creek Grill Baymont Inn, Days Inn, EconoLodge, Ft Hays Inn, Quality Inn, Rodeway Inn, Super 8 H, $Tree, Ace Hardware, Advance Parts, Chevrolet, Dillon's Foods/gas, Hobby Lobby, JC Penney, O'Reilly Parts, Tires 4 Less, Verizon, Walgreens
157	US 183 S byp, to Hays, N Peterbilt, S museum, st patrol, to Ft Hays St U, tourist info
153	Yocemento Ave
145	KS 247 S, Ellis, S Casey's, Loves/DQ/Subway/dsl/scales/24hr Cancun Mexican Days Inn Railroad Museum, RV camping, to Chrysler Museum, USPO
140	Riga Rd
135	KS 147, Ogallah, N Frontier Selfserve/dsl, S to Cedar Bluff SP (13mi)
132mm	**both lanes, full facilities, litter barrels, petwalk, RV dump**
128	US 283 N, WaKeeney, N Super 8
127	US 283 S, WaKeeney, N Jake & Chet's Cafe, Pizza Hut, Tropical Mexican Best Western+, KS Kountry Inn $General, S 24-7/McDonald's/dsl/24hr, Conoco/Subway/dsl EconoLodge antiques, auto repair, KOA
120	Voda Rd
115	KS 198 N, Banner Rd, Collyer
107	KS 212, Castle Rock Rd, Quinter, N Sinclair/dsl First Inn/rest. H, $General, Cobblestone Inn, S Conoco/dsl/24hr DQ, Pizza Sta
99	KS 211, Park, 1 mi N Sinclair/dsl
97mm	**both lanes, full facilities, litter barrels, petwalk, RV dump, vending**
95	KS 23 N, to Hoxie
93	KS 23, Grainfield, N Sinclair/dsl
85	KS 216, Grinnell
79	Campus Rd
76	US 40, to Oakley, S TA/Shell/Buckhorn Rest./Subway/dsl/e-85/scales/24hr/@ Rodeway Inn, Sleep Inn H, Blue Beacon, Fick Museum
70	US 83, to Oakley, N Free Breakfast Inn, S Cenex/dsl Colonial Steaks H, antiques, Fick Museum, High-Plains RV Park
62	rd K, Mingo, S gas/dsl/
54	Country Club Dr, Colby, N LNG, Pilot/Subway/dsl/scales/24hr Hampton Inn H, truck/dsl repair
53	KS 25, Colby, N 24-7/Subway/dsl Arby's, Burger King, China Buffet, Jimmy John's, McDonald's, MT Mike's Steaks, Pizza Hut, Sonic, Subway, Taco John's Days Inn, Holiday Inn Express, Motel 6, Quality Inn, Sleep Inn, Super 8 H, $General, Dillon's Foods/dsl, dsl repair, Ford/Lincoln, Haas Tire, O'Reilly Parts, Prairie Museum, Quilt Cabin, RV park/antiques, visitors ctr, Walmart, S Petro/Phillips 66/scales/dsl/@ City Limits Grill, Qdoba, Quiznos, Starbucks, Village Inn American Inn, Comfort Inn Chrysler/Dodge/Jeep, truck repair
48.5mm	**both lanes, full facilities, litter barrels, petwalk, RV park/dump, vending**
45	US 24 E, Levant

ELLIS — WAKEENEY — COLBY

GOODLAND

36	KS 184, Brewster, N Fuel Depot/dsl
35.5mm	Mountain/Central time zone
27	KS 253, Edson
19	US 24, Goodland, N Pizza Hut $General, High Pla Museum, KOA, NAPA
17	US 24, KS 27, Goodland, N Cenex/dsl, Conoco, Phillips 6 dsl DQ, McDonald's, Reynaldo's Mexican, Sonic, Subw Taco John's Best Value Inn, Econolodge, Motel 6, Qua Inn, Super 8 H, CarQuest/Firestone, Chevrolet/GMC, Fo Walmart, S 24-7/dsl/scales Steak'n Shake Holi Inn Express Mid-America Camping, Tesla EVP
12	rd 14, Caruso
9	rd 11, Ruleton
7.5mm	**Welcome Ctr eb/ wb, full facilities, info, litter barr petwalk, , RV dump, vending, wireless internet**
1	KS 267, Kanorado, N food, gas
.5mm	**weigh sta eb**
0mm	Kansas/Colorado State Line

INTERSTATE 135 (Wichita)

SALINA

Exit #	Services
95b a	I-70, E to KS City, W to Denver, US 81 N. **I-135 begins/ends I-70, exit 250.**
93	KS 140, State St, Salina, E art ctr, museum
92	Crawford St, E 24-7/dsl, KwikShop, Shell, Sinclair by's, Braum's, Cotijas Mexican, Great Wall Chinese, Gutier Mexican, Hickory Hut BBQ, Jim's Chicken, KFC, La Casita, Hacienda, McDonald's, Russell's Rest., Spangles, Subway, Ta Bell, Western Sizzlin Ambassador Hotel, AmericInn, B mont Inn, Days Inn, Econolodge, Value Inn&Suites $Ge eral, $Tree, Advance Parts, Dillon's Foods, Kansas La Tires, NAPA, O'Reilly Parts, Walgreens, W Phillips 6 dsl Quality Inn
90	Magnolia Rd, E Casey's, Phillips 66/dsl Buffalo W Wings, Burger King, Carlos O'Kelly's, Chick-fil-A, Chili's, C ote Canyon Café, Domino's, Freddy's Burgers, Goodce Subs, Hog Wild BBQ, Hong Kong Buffet, IHOP, Jalisco Mexica Longhorn Steaks, Marco's Pizza, McDonald's, Papa Murphy Qdoba, Schlotzsky's, Sonic, Spangles, Starbucks, Subway, Ta Bell Best Value Inn, Candlewood Suites $Gene $Tree, Aldi Foods, AT&T, AutoZone, BigLots, Cadillac/Chev let, Dick's, Dillard's, Dillon's Foods/dsl, Hobby Lobby, Hon JC Penney, Jo-Ann Fabrics, Kohl's, Marshall's, Old Navy, O'Re ly Parts, PetCo, Ross, Subaru, Toyota, Verizon, W Cene dsl Menard's
89	Schilling Rd, E KwikShop/dsl Applebee's, Daima Steaks, Five Guys, Olive Garden, Pizza Hut, Red Lobster, F Crib BBQ, Taco John's, Tucson's Steaks, Wendy's Coun Inn&Suites, Courtyard, Hampton Inn, Hilton Garden, H day Inn Lowe's, Sam's Club/gas, Target, URGENT CA Walmart/Subway, W Casey's Best Western, Comf Suites, Super 8
88	Water Well Rd, E Sleep Inn Chrysler/Dodge/Jeep, Fo Nissan
86	KS 104, Mentor, Smolan
82	KS 4, Falun Rd, Assaria, E RV Camping
78	KS 4 W, Lindsborg, W to Sandz Gallery/Museum
72	Lindsborg, 4 mi E Maxwell WR, McPherson St Fishing La W H, camping, food, gas, lodging, museum
68mm	**(both lanes exit left), full facilities, litter barrels petwa , RV dump**
65	Pawnee Rd

KS

INTERSTATE 135 (Wichita) Cont'd

Exit #	Services
62	Mohawk Rd
60	US 56, McPherson, Marion, E [gas] Loves/Hardee's/dsl/LP/scales/24hr, W [gas] 24/7/Burger King/dsl, Phillips 66/dsl [food] Applebee's, Arby's, Braum's, Freddy's Burgers, Golden Dragon Chinese, KFC/LJ Silver, La Fiesta Mexican, McDonald's, MT Mike's, Perkins, Pizza Hut, Subway, Taco Bell, Taco John's, Woodie's BBQ [lodging] Best Western, Days Inn, EconoLodge, Fairfield Inn, Hampton Inn, Holiday Inn Express, Knights Inn [other] [H], AutoZone, Buick/Cadillac/GMC, Chrysler/Dodge/Jeep, Ford, Walgreens, Walmart
58	US 81, KS 61, to Hutchinson, McPherson
54	18th Ave, Comanche Rd, Elyria
48	KS 260 E, Moundridge, **2 mi W** gas
46	KS 260 W, Moundridge, **2 mi W** [other] truck repair, food, gas
40	Lincoln Blvd, Hesston, E [food] Panda Kitchen [lodging] AmericInn [other] Cottonwood Grove RV Camping, W [gas] Casey's/dsl/24hr [food] El Cerrito Grill, Lincoln Perk Coffee, Pizza Hut, Sonic, Subway [lodging] Best Value Inn [other] city park
34	KS 15, N Newton, to Abilene, KS 15, E [other] RV camping, W [food] Papa John's (1mi), Subway (1mi), Taco Bell (1mi) [other] Kauffman Museum
33	US 50 E, to Peabody (from nb)
31	1st St, Broadway St, E [gas] LoneStar/dsl, Newell TC/dsl/@ [food] Applebee's, CJ's Rest., KFC [lodging] Days Inn, Holiday Inn Express, Newton Inn [other] Cadillac/Chevrolet, Chrysler/Dodge/Jeep, Ford/Lincoln, W [food] Braum's, MT Mike's [lodging] Comfort Inn, Red Coach Inn
30	US 50 W, KS 15 (exits left from nb), to Hutchinson, Newton, W [gas] KwikShop/dsl [food] Arby's, Panda Kitchen, Papa Murphy's, Pizza Hut, Sonic, Subway [other] [H], $Tree, AutoZone, Buick/GMC, Dillon's Foods, R Tires, Verizon, Walmart
28	SE 36th St, W [gas] Phillips 66/dsl [food] Burger King [other] Chisholm Trail Outlets/famous brands
25	KS 196, to Whitewater, El Dorado
23mm	**[RS] both lanes, full [handicapped] facilities, litter barrels, petwalk, [phone], [picnic], RV dump, vending**
22	125th St
19	101st St, W [other] RV camping
17	85th St, Valley Ctr
16	77th St, E [lodging] Motel 6 [other] Wichita Greyhound Park
14	61st St, E [gas] QT/dsl [food] Applebee's, Chopstix, Cracker Barrel, Pizza Hut, Spangles Rest., Subway, Taco Bell, Wendy's [lodging] Red Roof Inn [other] Chevrolet, W [gas] Phillips 66/dsl [food] KFC, McDonald's [lodging] Quality Inn, Super 8 [other] Goodyear/auto

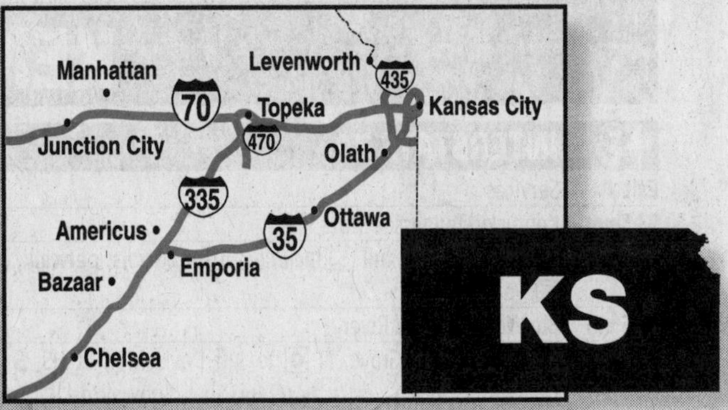

WICHITA

Exit #	Services
13	53rd St, E [other] Freightliner, Harley-Davidson, Volvo/Mack Trucks, W [gas] Phillips 66/dsl [food] Arby's, Country Kitchen [lodging] Best Western, Days Inn
11b	I-235 W, KS 96, to Hutchinson
11a	KS 254, to El Dorado
10b	29th St, Hydraulic Ave
10a	KS 96 E
9	21st St, E [gas] Valero [food] Sonic [other] $General, Wichita St U
8	13th St, E [other] $General, W [food] Pig In Pig Out BBQ
7b	8th St, 9th St, Central Ave., E [other] School of Medicine
7a	downtown
6b	1st St, 2nd St, downtown
5b	US 54, US 400, Kellogg Ave, E [gas] QT/dsl
5a	Lincoln St, E [food] DQ, W [gas] QT/dsl
4	Harry St, **1 mi** E [food] Arby's, Bionic Burger, Burger King, Denny's, Hardee's, Jimmy's Egg, LA Fried Chicken, Little Caesar's, McDonald's, NuWay Drive-Thru, Poblano Mexican, Shanghai Chinese, Spangles Rest., Subway, Taco Bell, Wendy's [other] [H], BigLots, CVS Drug, Firestone/auto, Goodyear/auto, W [gas] BD-C/dsl
3	Pawnee Ave, E [gas] [other] Family$, O'Reilly Parts, W [gas] Jumpstart/dsl [food] Burger King, Pizza Hut, Spangles [other] $General, AutoZone
2	Hydraulic Ave, E [gas] KwikShop, W [food] McDonald's, Subway
2mm	Arkansas River
1c	I-235 N, **2 mi** W [lodging] Hilton
1b a	US 81 S, 47th St, E [gas] QT/dsl [lodging] Days Inn, Holiday Inn Express, Quality Inn, Super 8, W [food] Applebee's, Arby's, Braum's, Burger King, Carlos O'Kelly's, Domino's, Godfather's, Goodcents Subs, Heritage Rest., Hog Wild BBQ, IHOP, KFC, Little Caesar's, LJ Silver, McDonald's, New China, Pizza Hut, Spangles Rest., Subway, Taco Bell [lodging] Best Western, Springfield Inn, Woodspring Suites [other] $General, $Tree, Air Capital RV Park, Dillon's Foods/dsl, O'Reilly Parts, Verizon

I-135 begins/ends on I-35, exit 42.

NOTES

KENTUCKY

INTERSTATE 24

Exit #	Services
93.5mm	Kentucky/Tennessee state line
93mm	**Welcome Ctr wb, full facilities, litter barrels, petwalk, , , vending**
91.5mm	Big West Fork Red River
89	KY 115, to Oak Grove, N to Jeff Davis Mon St HS, S Pilot/McDonald's/dsl/scales/24hr, Shell/Subway/dsl truck repair
86	US 41A, to Ft Campbell, Pennyrile Pkwy, Hopkinsville, N Marathon/Chester's/dsl/scales/24hr, S FLYING J/Denny's/dsl/LP/scales/24hr, Exxon/dsl, Pilot/Subway/Wendy's/dsl/scales/24hr McDonald's, Waffle House Candlewood Suites, Days Inn, Holiday Inn Express, Oak Grove Inn, Quality Inn, Sleep Inn H, truck wash
81	Pennyrile Pky N, to Hopkinsville
79mm	Little River
73	KY 117, to Gracey, Newstead
65	US 68, KY 80, to Cadiz, S BP/dsl, Marathon/dsl, Shell/dsl Cracker Barrel, Harper House Rest., KFC, McDonald's, Subway, Taco Bell, Triplets BBQ, Wendy's Knights Inn, Quality Inn, Red Roof Inn, Super 7 Inn H, Chevrolet, golf, to NRA
56	KY 139, to Cadiz, Princeton, S Marathon/dsl KOA (9mi), NRA
47mm	Lake Barkley
45	KY 293, to Princeton, Saratoga, S Marathon/dsl Mineral Mound SP, RV Camping, to KY St Penitentiary
42	I-69 N, to W KY Pkwy, Elizabethtown
40	US 62, US 641, Kuttawa, Eddyville, N Regency Inn (2mi), Relax Inn Mineral Mound SP, S BP/Wendy's/dsl/24hr, Exxon, Pilot/Huck's/Godfather's/dsl/scales/24hr Huddle House, SW Grill Days Inn, Hampton Inn KY Lake Rec Areas, to Lake Barkley
36mm	**weigh sta both lanes**
34mm	Cumberland River
31	KY 453, to Grand Rivers, Smithland, N BP/dsl Patti's Inn, S Marathon/dsl Miss Scarlett's Green Turtle Resort (3mi), Lighthouse Landing Resort, Motel 6 Exit 31 RV Park, NRA
29mm	Tennessee River
27	US 62, to KY Dam, Calvert City, N BP/dsl, Marathon/dsl Cracker Barrel, DQ, Mama D's Italian, McDonald's, Waffle House Days Inn, KY Dam Motel, Super 8 Cypress Lakes Camp, Freightliner, KOA, O'Reilly Parts, vet, S Love's/Arby's/dsl/scales/24hr Subway Econolodge
25b a	I-69 S, Carroll/Purchase Pkwy, to Calvert City, N services 1 mi S to KY Lake RA
16	US 68, to Paducah, S BP/Southern Pride/Subway/dsl/scales/24hr flea mkt
11	rd 1954, Husband Rd, to Paducah, N BP/dsl, FiveStar/dsl Best Western Duck Creek RV Park, S Harley-Davidson
7	US 45, US 62, to Paducah, N FiveStar/dsl Burger King, Taco Bell H, S **Welcome Ctr both lanes, full facilities, litter barrels, petwalk, , , vending,** BP, Marathon/dsl Arby's, Backyard Burger, Chong's Chinese, Domino's, Hardee's, KFC, Los Amigo's Mexican, McDonald's, Papa John's, Popeye's, Sonic, Subway, Waffle House, Wendy's Travelers Inn AT&T, Banks Mkt/gas, CVS Drug, Family$, O'Reilly Parts, Plaza Tires, Verizon

PADUCAH

Exit #	Services
4	US 60, to Paducah, N BP, Exxon/dsl Applebee's, B Evans, Burger King, McDonald's, O'Charley's, Outback Stea Rafferty's Auburn Place, Candlewood Suites, Comfort n&Suites, Courtyard, Days Inn, Drury Inn, Fairfield Inn, Han ton Inn, Holiday Inn Express, Homewood Suites, La Quin Residence Inn, Westowne Inn Toyota, S BP, Murp USA/dsl Arby's, Buffalo Wild Wings, Capt D's, Chick-fi Chong's Chinese, ChuckeCheese, Cracker Barrel, Culver's, Do no's, Fazoli's, Firehouse Subs, Five Guys, Hardee's, IHOP, Jim John's, La Juicy Seafood, Logan's Roadhouse, Longhorn Stea Los Amigos, Los Garcia's, McAlister's Deli, Olive Garden, Pa ra Bread, Pizza Hut, Qdoba, Red Lobster, Sonic, Starbuc Steak'n Shake, Taco Bell, Taco John's, Tokyo Hibachi, TX Ro house, Wendy's, Zaxby's Country Inn&Suites, Drury Suit EconoLodge, PearTree Inn, Quality Suites, Super 8 $Ge eral, $Tree, AAA, Advance Parts, Aldi Foods, AT&T, Best B Books-A-Million, Dick's, Dillard's, Goodyear/auto, Hob Lobby, Home Depot, JC Penney, Kohl's, Lowe's, Menar Michael's, Office Depot, Old Navy, Petsmart, Plaza Tire, Sar Club/gas, TJ Maxx, Tuesday Morning, Verizon, Walmart
3	KY 305, to Paducah, N Shell/dsl, Superway/dsl B Value Inn, Comfort Inn/rest., Red Roof Inn, S Maratho Charley's/Noble Romans/dsl/e85, Pilot/Subway/d scales/24hr El Torito, Waffle Hut Baymont Inn Fe Lake Camping
0mm	Kentucky/Illinois state line, Ohio River

INTERSTATE 64

GRAYSON

Exit #	Services
192mm	Kentucky/West Virginia state line, Big Sandy River
191	US 23, to Ashland, **1-2 mi** N Exxon, Marathon/Subway/d Speedway/dsl Arby's, Little Caesar's, McDonald's, Wa House, Wendy's Ramada Ltd H, IGA Foods, Rite A USPO
185	KY 180, Cannonsburg, **0-3 mi** N Exxon/dsl, Maratho dsl, Shell/McDonald's/USPO, Superquik Arby's, Bob E ans, Burger King, DQ, Gatti's Pizza, Hermanos Nunez Mexica KFC, Subway, Taco Bell, Waffle House, Wendy's Days In Fairfield Inn, Hampton Inn, Holiday Inn Express $Tree, Walmart/Subway, S FLYING J/Denny's/dsl/LP/scales/24
181	181 US 60, to Princess, N BP/dsl, S Marathon/dsl
179	rd 67, Industrial Pkwyttttfds, N KOA/@
174mm	**eb, full facilities, litter barrels, petwalk, , , vendi**
173mm	**wb, full facilities, litter barrels, petwalk, , , vendi**
172	rd 1, rd 7, Grayson, N Marathon/dsl, Superquik/dsl/24 A&W/LJ Silver, Huddle House, KFC, Pizza Hut, Shoney's, Su way Days Inn, Econolodge, Quality Inn $General, $Tr Chrysler/Dodge/Jeep, Ford, Save-A-Lot Foods, URGENT CAF S BP, Exxon/Hardees, Love's/Wendy's/scales/dsl/24 Marathon, Shell/dsl, Speedway/dsl Arby's, Biscuit Wor China House, DQ, Little Caesar's, McDonald's, Papa John's, Ta Bell, Toro Loco Super 8 $General, Advance Parts, AT&T, A toZone, Family$, Food Fair, O'Reilly Parts, Rite Aid, USPO, Veriz
161	US 60, to Olive Hill, N BP Spanish Manor Motel Carter Caves SP
156	rd 2, to KY 59, to Olive Hill, S BP
148mm	**weigh sta wb**
141mm	**both lanes, full facilities, litter barrels, petwalk, , vending**

KY

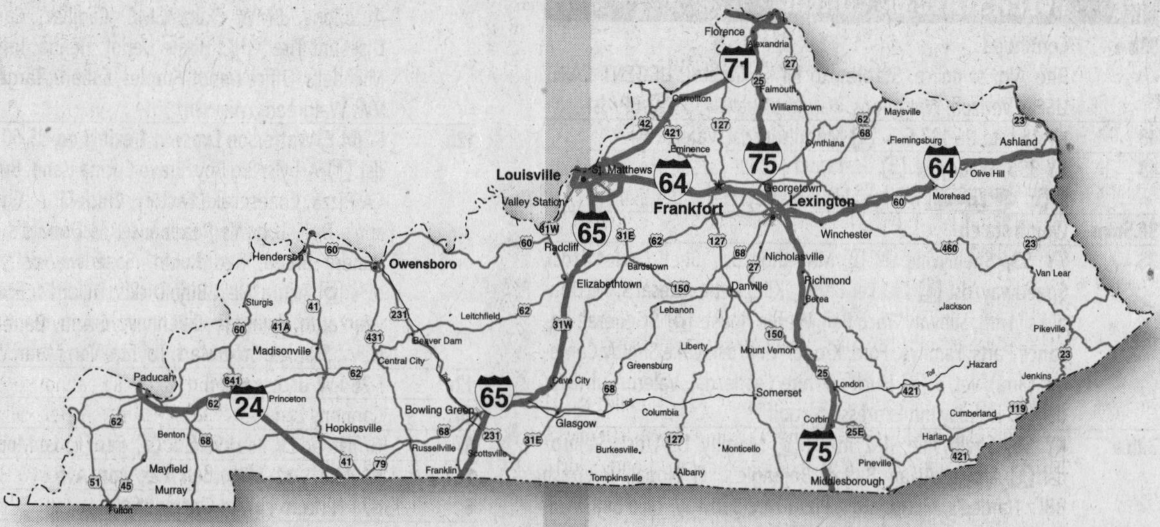

INTERSTATE 64 Cont'd

Exit #	Services
137	KY 32, to Morehead, N BP/dsl, Speedway/dsl DQ, Huddle House AT&T, Big Lots, Kroger/dsl, Lowe's, Walmart/Subway, S BP/McDonald's/dsl/24hr, Marathon/dsl China Star, Cracker Barrel, Domino's, Don Señor, Hardee's, Lee's Chicken, Reno's Roadhouse Best Western, Days Inn, Hampton Inn, Motel 6, Red Roof Inn H, $General, Ace Hardware, auto repair, AutoZone, st police
133	rd 801, to Sharkey, Farmers, N Shell/dsl Chrysler/Dodge/Jeep/Ford, S BP/Subway/dsl Comfort Inn Outpost RV Park (4mi)
123	US 60, to Salt Lick, Owingsville
121	KY 36, to Owingsville, N BP/dsl, Exxon/dsl, Valero/dsl DQ, McDonald's, Subway $General, Family$, S Save-a-Lot Foods
113	US 60, to Mt Sterling, N Shell/dsl, S Pilot/McDonald's/Subway/dsl/scales/24hr
110	US 460, KY 11, Mt Sterling, N Shell/Krystal/Subway/dsl, Valero/dsl Cattleman's Roadhouse, Cracker Barrel Comfort Inn, Ramada Ltd, S BP/dsl, Exxon, Marathon, Marathon/dsl, Murphy Express/dsl, Speedway/dsl Applebee's, Arby's, Asian Buffet, Bojangle's, Burger King, Capt D's, City King Buffet, Don Señor, El Camino Real, Hardee's, KFC, Lee's Chicken, Little Caesar's, LJ Silver, Los Rodeos, McDonald's, Pizza Hut, Subway, Taco Bell, Waffle House, Wendy's Budget Inn, Days Inn H, $Tree, Advance Parts, Advance Parts, AT&T, AutoZone, Chevrolet, Chrysler/Dodge/Jeep, CVS Drug, Family$, Ford, JC Penney, Kroger, Lowe's, O'Reilly Parts, Verizon, Walmart/Subway
101	US 60
98.5mm	**eb, full facilities, litter barrels, petwalk, vending**
98	KY 402 (from eb), S Natural Bridge Resort SP
96b a	KY 627, to Winchester, Paris, N 96 Truck Plaza/dsl/rest./scales, BP/dsl, S Baymont Inn, Hampton Inn, Red Roof Inn Buick/Chevrolet/GMC
94	KY 1958, Van Meter Rd, Winchester, N Marathon/dsl/24hr, Shell/scales/dsl Comfort Inn, Value Stay Inn, S BP/dsl, Marathon/dsl, Murphy Express/dsl, Shell/dsl, Speedway/dsl Applebee's, Arby's, Big Boy, Bojangle's, Burger King,
94	Continued Capt D's, Dickey's BBQ, Domino's, Don Senor, DQ, El Camino Real, Fazoli's, Golden Corral, Great Wall Chinese, Hardee's, Jade Garden Chinese, Jimmy John's, KFC, Little Caesar's, McDonald's, Papa John's, Pizza Hut, Puerta Grande, Rally's, Sakura Express, Sir Pizza, Sonic, Starbucks, Subway, Taco Bell, Taste Of China, Waffle House, Wendy's Holiday Inn Express H, $Tree, Advance Parts, AT&T, auto repair, AutoZone, Chrysler/Dodge/Jeep, Kroger/dsl, Lowe's, Office Depot, O'Reilly Parts, Rite Aid, Tire Discounters, to Ft Boonesborough Camping, Verizon, Walgreens, Walmart/Subway
87	KY 859, Blue Grass Sta
81	I-75 S, to Knoxville
I-64 and I-75 run together 7 mi. See I-75, exits 113-115.	
75	I-75 N, to Cincinnati, access to KY Horse Park
69	US 62 E, to Georgetown, N antiques (6mi), to Georgetown Coll., S Equus Run Vineyards (2mi)
65	US 421, Midway, S BP/dsl, Shell/dsl McDonald's, Subway
60mm	**both lanes, full facilities, litter barrels, petwalk, vending**
58	US 60, Frankfort, N BP/dsl, Five Star/dsl, Shell/dsl, Speedway/dsl Arby's, Buffalo Wild Wings, Capt. D's, Cattleman's Roadhouse, DQ, KFC, McDonald's, Miguel's Mexican, Starbucks, Subway, Taco Bell, Waffle House, Wendy's, White Castle, Zaxby's Best Western, Bluegrass Inn, Fairfield Inn $General, $Tree, Buick/Chevrolet/GMC, Chrysler/Dodge/Jeep, Dick's, ElkHorn Camping (5mi), Ford/Lincoln, GNC, Honda, Kohl's, Kroger/gas, KYSU, Michael's, Nissan, TireDiscounters, TJ-Maxx, to KY St Capitol, to Viet Vets Mem, Toyota, Walgreens, S Cracker Barrel, Logan's Roadhouse
55mm	Kentucky River
53b a	US 127, Frankfort, N Marathon, Speedway/dsl, Speedway/dsl Applebee's, Arby's, Baskin-Robbins, Beef O'Brady's, Big Boy, Burger King, Capt D's, Carino's Italian, Chili's, China Buffet, CookOut, DQ, Fazoli's, Ginza Japanese, Hardee's, KFC, Longhorn Steaks, McDonald's, My Guadalajara, O'Charley's, Panera Bread, Penn Sta Subs, Qdoba Mexican, Sonic, Starbucks, Staxx BBQ, Steak'n Shake, Subway, Taco Bell, Tacos n More, Wendy's Best Value Inn, Days Inn, Hampton Inn, Holiday Inn Express H, $General, Advance Parts, Ancient Age Tour, AT&T, AutoZone, BigLots, Big-O Tire, Family$, GNC, Goodyear/auto, JC Penney, Kroger/gas, Lowe's, Midas, Office Depot, Petco,

FRANKFORT

KY

INTERSTATE 64 Cont'd

53b a Continued
Rite Aid, st police, Staples, to KY St Capitol, URGENT CARE, USPO, Verizon, Walgreens, Walmart/Subway, **S** BP/dsl

48 KY 151, to US 127 S, **S** Marathon/dsl, Valero/dsl

43 KY 395, Waddy, **N** FLYING J/Denny's/dsl/LP/scales/24hr, **S** Loves/McDonald's/Subway/dsl/scales/24hr

38.5mm **weigh sta eb**

35 KY 53, Shelbyville, **N** Marathon/dsl, Shell/Circle K/dsl, Speedway/dsl Cracker Barrel, KFC, Little Caesar's, McDonald's (1mi), Subway, Taco Bell, Waffle House $General, Advance Parts, Family$, Ford, Kroger/deli/dsl, Lake Shelby Camping (3mi), vet, **S** Huck's/White Castle/dsl, Valero/Subway/dsl Holiday Inn Express golf

32b a KY 55, Shelbyville, **1-2 mi N** Murphy USA/dsl, Valero/dsl Arby's, Asian Buffet, Bojangle's, El Nopal, Firefresh BBQ, Hardee's, McDonald's, Pizza Hut, Subway, Taco Bell, Waffle House, Wendy's, Zaxby's Best Western, Econolodge, Red Roof Inn H, $Tree, AutoZone, Big O Tire, Buick/Chevrolet/GMC, Chrysler/Dodge/Jeep, CVS Drug, Lowe's, Rolling Hills Camping (16mi), Verizon, Walgreens, Walmart, **S** Cattleman's Roadhouse Ramada Taylorsville Lake SP

28mm **eb, full facilities, info, litter barrels, petwalk, , , vending**

28 KY 1848, Veechdale Rd, Simpsonville, **N** Pilot/Wendy's/dsl/scales/24hr DQ, Subway, Zaxby's Hampton Inn golf, **S** Bob Evans, Culver's, McDonald's Blue Grass Outlets/famous brands

19b a I-265, Gene Snyder Fwy, **N** to Tom Sawyer SP

17 S Blankenbaker, **N** Shell/Circle K/dsl Mellow Mushroom Pizza, Zaxby's Staybridge Suites Harley-Davidson, **S** Marathon, Speedway/Subway/dsl, Thornton's/dsl Arby's, BackYard Burger, Burger King, Cracker Barrel, El Caporal Mexican, HomeTown Buffet, KFC, Kingfish Rest., LJ Silver/Taco Bell, Logan's Roadhouse, McDonald's, Penn Sta Subs, Qdoba, Ruby Tuesday, Starbucks, Waffle House, Wendy's Comfort Suites, Country Inn&Suites, Extended Stay America, Fairfield Inn, Hampton Inn, Hawthorn Suites, Hilton Garden, Holiday Inn Express, La Quinta, Microtel, Quality Inn, Sleep Inn, Wingate Inn, Woodspring Suites Lexus, Sam's Club/gas

15 Hurstbourne Pkwy, Louisville, **0-2 mi N** Shell/Circle K/dsl, Speedway, Thorton's/dsl Arby's, Bob Evans, Bonefish Grill, Carrabba's, Chili's, Fazoli's, Firehouse Subs, IHOP, Jimmy John's, Macaroni Grill, McDonald's, Mimi's Cafe, Momma's BBQ, Noodles&Co, Olive Garden, Panda Express, Panera Bread, Papa John's, PF Changs, Pita Pit, Qdoba, Sichuan Garden, Skyline Chili, Smashburger, Starbucks, Subway, Waffle House Baymont Inn, Courtyard, Days Inn, Drury Inn, Holiday Inn, Hyatt Place, Red Roof Inn, Residence Inn Barnes&Noble, Kroger/gas, Lowe's, Towery's Auto, Tuesday Morning, Walgreens, **S** Applebee's, BoomBozz Pizza, Buca Italian, Buffalo Wild Wing, Burger King, Cattleman's Roadhouse, Chick-fil-A, ChuckeCheese, Coldstone, DQ, El Marlin Seafood, El Torazo Mexican, Famous Daves, Happy China, Home Run Burgers, J Gumbo's Cajun, Jason's Deli, Jumbo Buffet, Kansai Japanese, Longhorn Steaks, McAlister's Deli, McDonald's, Melting Pot, Moe's SW Grill, O'Charley's, Old Chicago, Panera Bread, Penn Sta. Subs, Pizza Hut, Qdoba, Shogun Japanese, Smokey Bones BBQ, Starbucks, Steak'n Shake, Taco Bell, Tumbleweed SW Grill, Wendy's, White Castle, Yen Ching Best Western, Extended Stay America, Marriott, Ramada, Red Carpet Inn $Tree,

15 Continued
AutoZone, BMW, Buick/GMC, Cadillac, Carmax, Chevro Discount Tire, GNC, Home Depot, Honda, Infiniti, Kroger/g Michael's, Office Depot, Staples, Subaru, Target, Verizon, Vol VW, Walgreens, Walmart

12b I-264 E, Watterson Expswy, **1 exit N on US 60** Thornto dsl Arby's, Big Boy, Bravo Cucina Italin, Buffalo Wild Wir CA Pizza, Cheesecake Factory, Chick-Fil-A, Chuy's Mexican, son's Deli, Logan's Roadhouse, McDonald's, Outback Stea Panera Bread, Red Robin, Speedway/dsl, Taco Bell, W dy's Acura, Best Buy, Dick's, Dillard's, Ford/Lincoln, Go year/auto, Hyundai, JC Penney, Jo-Ann, Kia, Kohl's, Macy's, Navy, Staples, SteinMart, Toyota, Von Maur, Whole Foods M

12a I-264 W, access to H

10 Cannons Lane

8 Grinstead Dr, Louisville, **S** gas Le Moo

7 US 42, US 62, Mellwood Ave, Story Ave

6 I-71 N (from eb), to Cincinnati

5a I-65, S to Nashville, N to Indianapolis

5b 3rd St, Louisville, **N** Joe's CrabShack, **S** Galt House tel, Marriott H

4 9th St, Roy Wilkins Ave, **S** KY Art Ctr, science muse downtown

3 US 150 E, to 22nd St, **S** Marathon/dsl, Shell/Circle K McDonald's Family$

1 I-264 E, to Shively, **S** , zoo

0mm Kentucky/Indiana state line, Ohio River

INTERSTATE 65

Exit # Services

138mm Kentucky/Indiana state line, Ohio River

137 I-64 W, I-71 N, I-64 E, **W** to Galt House, downtown

136c Jefferson St, Louisville, **E** H, Walgreens, **W** S McDonald's, Papa John's, Subway, White Castle Co yard, EconoLodge, Fairfield Inn, Hampton Inn, Hyatt, Marri SpringHill Suites Tires+

136b Broadway St, Chestnut St (from nb), **E** H, NAPA, W greens, **W** Shell, Thornton's McDonald's, Subw White Castle Courtyard, Fairfield Inn, Hampton Inn, Hy Marriott, Springhill Suites same as 136c, Tires+

135 W St Catherine, **E** Shell

134b a KY 61, Jackson St, Woodbine St, **W** Shell/Circle K D Inn, Quality Inn Harley-Davidson

133b US 60A, Eastern Pkwy, Taylor Blvd, **E** Denny's, Subw **W** Speedway/dsl Cracker Barrel, McDonald's, P John's Churchill Downs, museum, U of Louisville

133a Crittenden Dr (132from sb), **E** Denny's, same as 1 **W** BP Arby's, Burger King, Cracker Barrel, Hall of Fa Cafe Country Inn&Suites, Hilton Garden, Holiday Inn, mada Inn, Sheraton, Super 8

131b a I-264, Watterson Expswy, **W** , Cardinal Stadium, E Center

130 KY 61, Preston Hwy, **E on Ky 61** Shell/Circle K, Speedw dsl, Thornton's Bob Evans, Domino's, Fazoli's, Little C sar's, McDonald's, Papa John's, Popeye's, Rally's, Slabho BBQ, Subway, Waffle House, Wendy's EconoLodge, Roof Inn, Super 8 $General, $Tree, Aamco, AutoZone, O Tire, BigLots, Chevrolet/Kia, Dodge, Ford, GNC, O'Reilly P Sav-A-Lot Foods, Tires+, U-Haul

128 KY 1631, Fern Valley Rd, **E** BP, Mapco/dsl/e85, Marath Circle K, Thornton's/dsl Big Boy, Dunkin', El Nopal Mexi Hardee's, Indi's Rest., McDonald's, Outback Steaks, Shon

SHELBYVILLE LOUISVILLE LOUISVILLE KY

INTERSTATE 65 Cont'd

128 Continued
Subway, Taco Bell, Waffle House, Wendy's, White Castle, Zaxby's Baymont Inn, Comfort Suites, Days Inn, Holiday Inn, InTown Suites Sam's Club/gas, Walgreens, **W** UPS Depot

127 KY 1065, outer loop, **E** Cheddar's, TX Roadhouse, **W** McDonald's/RV Parking

125b a I-265 E, KY 841, Gene Snyder Fwy

121 KY 1526, Brooks Rd, **E** BP, Marathon Burger King, Cracker Barrel, McDonald's, Subway, Tumbleweed Grill Comfort Inn, Fairfield Inn, Holiday Inn Express H, **W** BP/dsl, Pilot/Subway/dsl/scales/24hr Taco Bell, Waffle House Baymont Inn, EconoLodge, Hampton Inn, Quality Inn

117 KY 44, Shepherdsville, **E** BP/dsl, Valero Denny's Best Western/rest., Garden Inn KOA (2mi), vet, **W** Marathon, Speedway/dsl Arby's, Big Boy, Cattlemans Roadhouse, China Buffet, Domino's, DQ, El Nopal, El Tarasco, Fazoli's, KFC, Little Caesar's, LJ Silver, McDonald's/playplace, Mr Gatti's, Papa John's, Penn Sta Subs, Quiznos, Sonic, Starbucks, Subway, Taco Bell, Waffle House, Wendy's, White Castle Country Inn&Suites, Motel 6, Sleep Inn, Super 8 $General, Advance Parts, AT&T, AutoZone, BigLots, Family$, Kroger/dsl, Lowe's, NAPA, O'Reilly Parts, Rite Aid, SaveALot, Towery Tire/auto, Walgreens, Walmart/dsl

116.5mm Salt River

116 KY 480, to KY 61, **E** Loves/Chester's/Subway/dsl/scales/24hr, Valero/dsl House of Quilts, **W** Marathon/dsl Grandma's RV Park/flea mkt

114mm **sb, full facilities, litter barrels, petwalk, , , vending**

112 KY 245, Clermont, **E** Valero/dsl Bernheim Forest, Jim Beam Outpost, to My Old Kentucky Home SP (15mi)

105 KY 61, Lebanon Jct, **W** Pilot/McDonald's/Subway/dsl/scales/24hr/@, Speedway/dsl

102 KY 313, to KY 434, Radcliff, **W** to Patton Museum

94 US 62, Elizabethtown, **E** BP/dsl, Marathon/dsl Denny's, Waffle House, White Castle Days Inn, Quality Inn, Super 8 $General, **W** BP/dsl, Speedway/dsl Arby's, Burger King, Chalupa's Mexican, Cracker Barrel, Gatti's Pizza, HoneyBaked Ham, KFC/Taco Bell, McDonald's, Papa John's, Pizza Hut, Ruby Tuesday, Ryan's, Shoney's, Subway, TX Outlaw Steaks, TX Roadhouse, Wendy's Baymont Inn, Comfort Suites, Fairfield Inn, Hampton Inn, Holiday Inn Express, La Quinta, Motel 6, Ramada Inn, Wingfield Inn H, $General, Advance Parts, AutoZone, Crossroads Camping, Kroger/gas, Skagg's RV Ctr, st police, USPO, visitors ctr, Walgreens

93 to Bardstown, to BG Pky, **E** Maker's Mark Distillery (27mi), to My Old KY Home SP (25mi)

91 US 31 W, KY 61, WK Pkwy, Elizabethtown, **E** Marathon/dsl LJ Silver, Subway Best Value Inn, Royal Inn $General, to Lincoln B'Place, **W** Doug's/dsl, Marathon H

90mm weigh sta sb only

86 KY 222, Glendale, **E** Pilot/McDonalds/dsl/scales/24hr Glendale Camping, trk repair, **W** Petro/Dunkin'/dsl/scales/24hr/@ Glendale Economy Inn Blue Beacon

83mm Nolin River

81 KY 84, Sonora, **E** Pilot/Subway/dsl/scales/24hr to Lincoln B'Place, **W** Five Star/dsl

76 KY 224, Upton, **E** Marathon/dsl, **W** to Nolin Lake

75mm eastern/central time zone

71 KY 728, Bonnieville

BOWLING GREEN

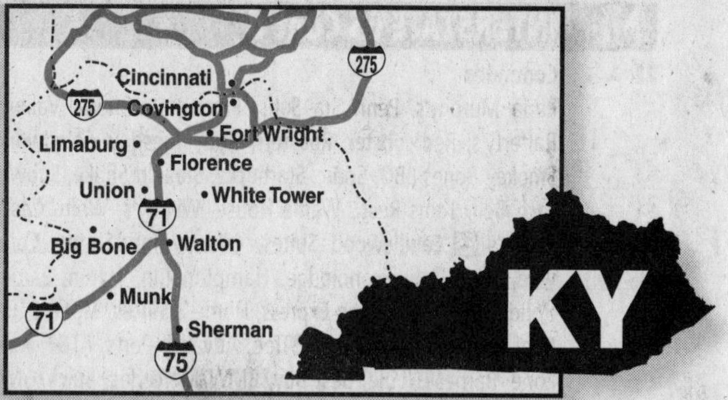

65 US 31 W, Munfordville, **E** BP/Subway/dsl, FiveStar/dsl DQ, El Mazatlan, King Buffet, McDonald's, Pizza Hut, Sonic Super 8 $General, Advance Parts, Fred's Store, IGA Foods, Save-A-Lot, **W** Marathon/dsl, Shell Bucky Bee's BBQ, to Nolin Lake

61mm **both lanes, full facilities, Green River, info, litter barrels, petwalk, , , vending**

58 KY 218, Horse Cave, **E** Loves/McDonald's/dsl/scales/24hr/@ H, **W** Hampton Inn, Quality Inn KOA, to Mammoth Cave NP

53 KY 70, KY 90, Cave City, **E** BP/dsl, Gulf/dsl/repair, Shell/Subway/Sonic/dsl A&W/LJ Silver, Cracker Barrel, El Mazatlan, KFC, McDonald's, Pizza Hut, Wendy's Baymont Inn, Comfort Inn, Days Inn/rest., Motel 6, Red Roof Inn, Sleep Inn, Super 8 H, $General, Barren River Lake SP (24mi), Olde General Store, **W** Watermill Rest. Jellystone Camping, Mammoth Cave NP, Onyx Cave

48 KY 255, Park City, **E** Shell/Subway/dsl $General, Park Mammoth Resort, **W** Diamond Caverns Resort, to Mammoth Cave NP

43 Nun/Cumberland Pky, **E** to Barren River Lake SP

38 KY 101, Smiths Grove, **W** Exxon/dsl/scales, Marathon/Subway/dsl, Shell/Schlotsky's/dsl Bestway Pizza, McDonald's, Miss Betty's Diner, Wendy's Bryce Inn $General, auto repair, city park, IGA Foods

36 US 68, KY 80, Oakland, (no nb return)

31 to Bristol Rd

28 rd 446, to US 31 W, Bowling Green, **W** Huck's/dsl, Shell/dsl Hardee's, Jerry's Rest., McDonald's, Wendy's Best Value Inn, Country Hearth Inn, Super 8, Value Lodge H, Corvette Museum/cafe, to WKYU

26 KY 234, Bowling Green, **W** Shell/dsl Subway H, IGA Foods

22 US 231, Bowling Green, **E** Exxon/dsl, Marathon/Godfather's, Shell, Shell/dsl Cracker Barrel, Culver's, Domino's, El Maguey, El Mazatlan, Hardee's, Motor City Grill, Ryan's, Sonic, Waffle House, Zaxby's Baymont Inn, Best Western, Days Inn, Greenwood Hotel, HomeTowne Suites, Jameson Inn, La Quinta, Microtel, Quality Inn, Ramada Inn, Sleep Inn, Super 8 $General, Camping World, Harley-Davidson, URGENT CARE, USPO, **W** Marathon/dsl, Speedway/dsl Applebee's, Arby's, Beijing Chinese, Bob Evans, Bojangles, Bruster's, Buffalo Wild Wings, Burger King, Capt D's, Chick-fil-A, Chipotle, ChuckeCheese, Chuy's Mexican, Corner Bakery Cafe, Double-Dog's Chowhouse, Fazoli's, Firehouse Subs, Five Guys, Freddy's, Gondolier Italian, Honeybaked Ham, IHOP, Jersey Mike's, Jimmy John's, KFC, Krystal, Kyoto Steaks, Logan's Roadhouse, Longhorn Steaks, McDonald's, Moe's SW Grill, MT Grille, O'Charley's, Olive Garden, Outback Steaks, Panera Bread,

INTERSTATE 65 Cont'd

22 Continued
Papa Murphy's, Penn Sta Subs, Pizza Hut, Puerto Vallarta, Rafferty's, Red Lobster, Roosters, Ruby Tuesday, Saladworks, Smokey Bones BBQ, Sonic, Starbucks, Steak'n Shake, Subway, Taco Bell, Toots Rest., Waffle House, Wendy's, White Castle, Zaxby's Candlewood Suites, Country Inn&Suites, Courtyard, Drury Inn, Econolodge, Hampton Inn, Hilton Garden, Holiday Inn, Holiday Inn Express, Home 2 Suites, Motel 6, Red Roof Inn H, $General, $Tree, Advance Parts, AT&T, AutoZone, Barnes&Noble, Best Buy, BMW/Mercedes, Buick/GMC/Cadillac, Cabela's, Chevrolet, Chrysler/Dodge/Jeep, CVS Drug, Dick's, Dillard's, Ford/Lincoln, Goodyear/auto, Hobby Lobby, Home Depot, Honda, Hyundai, JC Penney, Kia, KOA, Kohl's, Kroger/gas, Lowe's, Meijer, Michael's, Nissan, Old Navy, PetCo, Petsmart, Sam's Club/gas, Staples, Target, TJ Maxx, Toyota, Tuesday Morning, U-Haul, URGENT CARE, Walgreens, Walmart/McDonald's

20 WH Natcher Toll Rd, to Bowling Green, access to W KY U, W st police

6 KY 100, Franklin, E Shell/dsl/24hr truckwash, W Pilot/Subway/dsl/scales/24hr, Pilot/Wendy's/dsl/scales/24hr El Potrero Comfort Inn, Days Inn, Knights Inn H, Bluegrass RV Park, SpeedCo, TA Truck Service, truck&tires/repair, truckwash, Volvo Trucks

FRANKLIN

4mm weigh sta nb

2 US 31 W, to Franklin, E FLYING J/Denny's/dsl/LP/scales/24hr, Keystop/Marathon/Burger King/dsl/24hr, W BP/dsl Cracker Barrel, Franklin Steakhouse, McDonald's, Oasis SW Grill, Solazteca, Waffle House Baymont Inn, EconoLodge, Hampton Inn, Holiday Inn Express, Quality Inn, Super 8 H, antiques

1mm Welcome Ctr nb, full facilities, litter barrels, petwalk, vending

0mm Kentucky/Tennessee state line

INTERSTATE 71

Exit #	Services
100	Kentucky/Ohio state line, Ohio River

I-71 and I-75 run together 19 miles, See I-75, exits 175-192.

77[173] I-75 S, to Lexington

75mm weigh sta sb

72 KY 14, to Verona, E BP/dsl, Marathon/dsl Oak Creek Camping (5mi)

62 US 127, to Glencoe, E 62 TrkPlaza/rest./dsl, W Valero/dsl/rest. 127 Motel

57 KY 35, to Sparta, E Marathon/dsl Eagle Valley Camping (10mi), Sparta RV Park (3mi), W BP/dsl Ramada KY Speedway

55 KY 1039, W Loves/McDonald's/Subway/dsl/scales/24hr casino, KY Speedway

44 KY 227, to Indian Hills, W Marathon/dsl, Marathon/dsl, Murphy USA/dsl, Valero/dsl Arby's, Burger King, El Nopal, Hometown Pizza, KFC, McDonald's, Mi Viejo Mexican, New China, Subway, Taco Bell, Waffle House Hampton Inn, Holiday Inn Express, Quality Inn, Red Roof Inn, Super 8 H, $General, $Tree, AutoZone, Chevrolet, Ford, Gen. Butler SP, Kroger/dsl, Save-a-Lot Foods, URGENT CARE, Verizon, Walmart

43.5mm Kentucky River

43 KY 389, to KY 55, English

34 US 421, New Castle, Campbellsburg, W Marathon/Valero/Subway/dsl st police

28 KY 153, KY 146, to US 42, Pendleton, E Pilot/Subway/dsl/scales/24hr/@, Valero/dsl, W Pilot/McDonald's/scales/dsl/24hr truck repair

22 KY 53, La Grange, E Murphy USA/dsl, Speedway/ly's/dsl, Valero/dsl Applebee's, Beef O'Brady's, Burger King, Jumbo Buffet, Papa John's, Papa Murphy's, Subway, Waffle House, Wendy's Best Western-Ashbury, Comfort Inn H, $General, AT&T, Big-O Tire, GNC, Kroger/gas, Towery's Tire/auto, Verizon, Walgreens, Walmart/Subway, W Marathon/dsl Arby's, Cracker Barrel, Domino's, El Nopal, Hometown Pizza, KFC, LJ Silver, McDonald's, Taco Bell Quality Suites, Super 8 $Tree, Advance Parts, Buick/Chevrolet/GMC, Lee Tires, NAPA, Rite Aid, USPO, vet

18 KY 393, Buckner, W Marathon/dsl Subway For

17 KY 146, Buckner, W Thornton's/dsl/24hr USPO

LOUISVILLE

14 KY 329, Crestwood, Pewee Valley, Brownsboro, E dsl DQ, Hometown Pizza, McDonald's, Sonic, Starbucks, Subway

13mm both lanes, full facilities, litter barrels, petwalk, vending

9b a I-265, KY 841, Gene Snyder Fwy, E Drury Inn, Hilton Garden Cabela's, Costco/gas, H, to Sawyer SP

5 I-264, Watterson Expswy (exits left from sb), E to Sawyer

2 Zorn Ave, E VA H, W Shell/dsl, Valero El Nopal Mexican, KingFish Rest. Ramada Inn WaterTower Museum

1b I-65, S to Nashville, N to Indianapolis

INTERSTATE 75

Exit #	Services
193mm	Kentucky/Ohio state line, Ohio River

COVINGTON

192 5th St (from nb), Covington, E BP/dsl, Shell/Circle K, Speedway/dsl Big Boy, Burger King, GoldStar Chili, McDonald's, Popeyes, Riverfront Pizza, Skyline Chili, Subway, Taco Bell, Waffle House, Wendy's, White Castle Courtyard, Extended America, Holiday Inn, Radisson Lexus, Riverboat Cas W Hampton Inn

191 12th St, Covington, E H, museum, same as 192

189 KY 1072, Kyles Lane, W BP/dsl, Shell/dsl Big Skyline Chili, Substation II Subs Rodeway Inn same 188, Walgreens

188 US 25, US 42, Dixe Hwy, E Marathon Starbucks, Subway GNC, Kroger/dsl, Tuesday Morning, W Rodeway Inn Mercedes, same as 189

186 KY 371, Buttermilk Pike, Covington, E BP/dsl, Marathon/DQ/dsl Graeter's Ice Cream, Oriental Wok, Papa John's Montgomery Inn, Super 8, W BP, Speedway/Sunoco/dsl Arby's, Baskin-Robbins/Dunkin', Bonefish Grill, Burger King, Cancun Mexican, Chipotle Mexican, Domino's, Empire Buffet, Firehouse Subs, GoldStar Chili, Jimmy John's, Rosa's Pizza, Marco's Pizza, McDonald's, Miyako Steaks, Outback Steaks, Skyline Chili, Subway, Sweet Basil Thai $Tree, Field & Stream, Home Depot, Petco, Remke Foods, Staples, Verizon, Walgreens

185 I-275 E and W, W to

184 KY 236, Donaldson Rd, to Erlanger, E BP, Erlan Dunkin' Double Dragon Oriental, W Racers/Subway/dsl, Speedway/dsl Peecox Grill, Waffle House Country Hearth Inn, EconoLodge, Red Roof Inn, Wingate Inn Goodyear/auto

INTERSTATE 75 Cont'd

Exit # Services

182 KY 1017, Turfway Rd, E [gas] BP/dsl, Shell/dsl [food] Bamboo Garden, Big Boy, China City, Lee's Chicken, McDonald's, Papa John's, Subway, Taco Bell [lodging] Baymont Inn, Courtyard, Days Inn, Woodspring Suites [other] BigLots, CVS Drug, Family$, Office Depot, Remke Foods, USPO, W [food] Applebee's, Chick-fil-A, Chili's, CiCi's Pizza, Cracker Barrel, Famous Dave's BBQ, Firebowl Grill, Longhorn Steaks, Noodles&Co., O'Charley's, Potbelly, Rafferty's, Skyline Chili, Steak'n Shake, Subway, Wendy's [lodging] Comfort Inn, Extended Stay America, Hampton Inn, Hilton, Hyatt Place, La Quinta, SpringHill Suites [other] [H], Best Buy, Dick's, Home Depot, Jo-Ann, Kohl's, Lowe's, Meijer, Michael's, Petsmart, Sam's Club, Target, Turfway Park Racing

181 KY 18, Florence, E [gas] Speedway/dsl, TA/Valero/Pizza Hut/Popeye's/Subway/dsl/24hr/@ [food] Kiwha Korean, Waffle House [lodging] Best Value Inn, Best Western, Heritage Inn [other] Chevrolet, W [gas] BP/dsl, Marathon/dsl, Speedway/dsl [food] Buffalo Wild Wings, Cheddar's, Chipotle Mexican, Chuy's Mexican, City BBQ, Currito Burrito, El Rio Grande, Fazoli's, Firehouse Subs, Fuji Steaks, Hooters, IHOP, Jersey Mike's, La Rosa's, Laughing Noodle, Logan's Roadhouse, Miyoshi Japanese, Panda Express, Panera Bread, Red Robin [lodging] Homewood Suites, Stay Lodge [other] AT&T, Buick/GMC, Chrysler/Jeep/Dodge, Ford, Honda, Hyundai, Mazda, Nissan, Tire Discounters, Toyota, URGENT CARE, Verizon, VW, Walmart/Subway

180a Mall Rd (from sb), W [food] Asian Buffet, BJ's Rest., Buca Italian, ChuckeCheese, GoldStar Chili, HoneyBaked Ham, Jimmy John's, Olive Garden, Pizza Hut, Qdoba, Skyline Chili, Smokey Bones BBQ, Starbucks, Subway, Taco Bell, Which Wich? [other] $General, $Tree, AT&T, Barnes&Noble, Harley Davidson, Hobby Lobby, JC Penney, Kroger/dsl, Macy's, Old Navy, same as 180, Staples, TJ Maxx, Tuesday Morning

180 US 42, US 127, Florence, Union, E [gas] BP/dsl, Speedway/dsl [food] Big Boy, Bob Evans, Capt D's, Chipotle Mexican, El Nopal Mexican, Mai Thai, McDonald's, Penn Sta Subs, Rally's, Red Lobster, Subway, Wendy's [lodging] Holiday Inn, Howard Johnson, Knights Inn, Motel 6, Quality Inn, Super 8 [other] Cadillac, funpark, Subaru, W [gas] Marathon/dsl, Murphy USA/dsl, Speedway/dsl [food] Arby's, Chick-fil-a, Dave&Buster's, KFC, Little Caesar's, LJ Silver, outback, Ponderosa, Waffle House, White Castle [lodging] Magnuson Hotel, Travelodge [other] CarX, Costco/dsl, Midas, O'Reilly Parts, PepBoys, Tire Discounters, Tires+, Walgreens

178 KY 536, Mt Zion Rd, E [gas] Marathon/Rally's/dsl, Speedway/dsl, Sunoco/Subway/dsl [food] Buffalo Bob's, Chopsticks, GoldStar Chili, Hot Head Burritos, Jersey Mike's Subs, La Fuentes Mexican, La Rosa's Pizza, Mad Mike's Burgers, Sonic, Steak'n Shake, Taco Bell [other] AutoZone, Goodyear/auto, Kroger

177mm **Welcome Ctr sb/[RS] nb, full [handicapped] facilities, litter barrels, [phone], [picnic], RV dump, vending**

175 KY 338, Richwood, E [gas] Pilot/Subway/dsl/24hr, TA/BP/Country Pride/Taco Bell/dsl/24hr/@ [food] Arby's, Burger King, White Castle [lodging] Richwood Inn, W [gas] BP/dsl, Pilot/Subway/dsl/scales/24hr, Shell/dsl [food] GoldStar Chili, Gourmet Cafe, Hong Kong Cafe, McDonald's, Papa Dino's Pizza, Penn Sta Subs, Skyline Chili, Snappy Tomato Pizza, Waffle House, Wendy's [lodging] EconoLodge, Holiday Inn Express [other] to Big Bone Lick SP

173 I-71 S, to Louisville

171 KY 14, KY 16, to Verona, Walton, E [gas] BP/dsl, Marathon/DQ/dsl [food] China Moon, El Toro Mexican, McDonald's, Pizza Hut, Starbucks, Subway, Waffle House [other] AT&T, AutoZone, Kohl's, Kroger/dsl, Tire Discounters, URGENT CARE, Walton Drug,

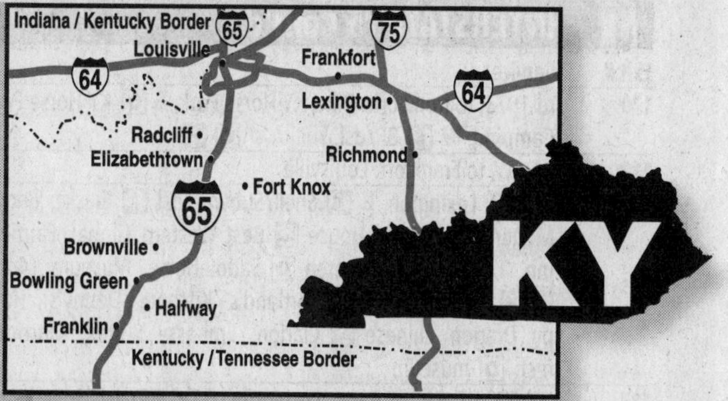

171 Continued
W [gas] FLYING J/Denny's/dsl/scales/24hr [other] Blue Beacon, Delightful Days RV Ctr, Oak Creek Camping (1mi), to Big Bone Lick SP, vet

168mm **weigh sta/rest haven sb**

DRY RIDGE

166 KY 491, Crittenden, E [gas] BP/dsl, Sunoco/dsl [food] McDonald's [other] Chrysler/Dodge/Jeep, Cincinnati S Camping (2mi), W [gas] Marathon/dsl, Shell/Gold Star Chili [food] China Castle, Subway, Wendy's [other] $General, Grant Co Drugs

159 KY 22, to Owenton, Dry Ridge, E [gas] BP, Shell/dsl, Speedway/dsl [food] Arby's, Burger King, Happy Dragon Chinese, KFC/Taco Bell, La Rosa's, LJ Silver, McDonald's, Pizza Hut, Skyline Chili, Subway, Waffle House, Wendy's [lodging] Microtel, Red Roof Inn [other] [H], $General, Buick/Chevrolet, O'Reilly Parts, Verizon, Walmart, W [gas] Marathon/dsl, Speedway/dsl [food] Beavis Cafe/Bakery, Big Boy, Cracker Barrel [lodging] Hampton Inn, Quality Inn [other] Camper Village, Dry Ridge TowneCtr, Sav-A-Lot, Tire Discounters, Toyota

156 Barnes Rd, E [other] [H]

154 KY 36, Williamstown, E [gas] Marathon/dsl, Shell/dsl [other] [H], to Kincaid Lake SP, W [gas] Sunoco/dsl [food] El Jalisco Mexican [lodging] Best Value Inn, Sunrise Inn

144 KY 330, to Owenton, Corinth, E [gas] Noble's Trk Plaza/rest./dsl, Sunoco/dsl, W [gas] BP [food] North Star Cafe [lodging] North Star Inn

136 KY 32, to Sadieville, E [gas] Loves/Hardee's/dsl/scales/24hr

130.5mm **weigh sta nb**

129 rd 620, Cherry Blossom Wy, E [gas] Pilot/Wendy's/dsl/scales/24hr/@ [food] Waffle House [lodging] Days Inn, Motel 6, W [gas] Pilot/McDonald's/dsl/scales/24hr, Shell [other] Whispering Hills RV Park (3mi)

127mm **[RS] both lanes, full [handicapped] facilities, litter barrels, petwalk, [phone], [picnic], vending**

GEORGETOWN

126 US 62, to US 460, Georgetown, E [gas] Marathon/dsl, Murphy USA/dsl [food] Applebee's, Asian Royal Buffet, Big Boy, Buffalo Wild Wings, Gold Star Chili, Jimmy John's, McDonald's, O'Charley's, Papa John's, Penn Sta Subs, Pepe's Mexican, Qdoba, Starbucks, Steak'n Shake, Subway [lodging] Holiday Inn Express [other] AT&T, Kohl's, Lowe's, Tire Discounters, URGENT CARE, Verizon, Walmart/Subway, W [gas] Marathon, Shell/Subway, Speedway/dsl [food] Cane's, Chick-fil-A, Cracker Barrel, Culver's, Fazoli's, KFC, Panera Bread, Ruby Tuesday, Waffle House [lodging] Baymont Inn, Best Western, Comfort Suites, Country Inn&Suites, Fairfield Inn, Hampton Inn, Hilton Garden, Microtel, Super 8 [other] [H], Buick/Chevrolet, Chrysler/Dodge/Jeep, same as 125, to Georgetown Coll

125 US 460 (from nb), Georgetown, E [gas] BP, Shell [food] FatKats Pizza [lodging] Knights Inn, W [gas] Swifty/dsl, Valero/dsl [food] Arby's, DQ, Little Caesar's, LJ Silver, Taco Bell, Wendy's [lodging] Winner's Circle Motel [other] $Tree, Advance Parts, BigLots, Camping World, Midas, Outlets/Famous Brands, same as 126

INTERSTATE 75 Cont'd

Exit #	Services
120	rd 1973, to Ironworks Pike, KY Horse Park, E [other] KY Horse Park Camping, W [gas] BP/dsl, Shell/dsl [other] [H]
118	I-64 W, to Frankfort, Louisville
115	rd 922, Lexington, E [gas] Shell/Subway/dsl [food] Cracker Barrel, McDonald's, Waffle House [lodging] Best Western Global, Fairfield Inn, La Quinta, Sheraton [other] SaddleHorse Museum (4mi), W [gas] Marathon/dsl [food] Cortland's Kitchen, Denny's, Happy Dragon Chinese [lodging] Clarion, Embassy Suites, Marriott/rest. [other] museum
113	US 27, US 68, to Paris, Lexington, E [gas] BP/dsl, Speedway/dsl [food] Waffle House [lodging] Ramada Inn, W [gas] Marathon/dsl, Shell, Shell/dsl [food] Arby's, Burger King, Capt D's, Donato's Pizza, DQ, Fazoli's, Golden Corral, Hardee's, Horseshoes Grill, Little Caesar's, McDonald's, Penn Sta Subs, Rally's, Subway, Taco Bell, Wendy's, Zaxby's [lodging] Catalina Motel, Days Inn, Red Roof Inn [other] Advance Parts, AutoZone, Bluegrass RV Ctr, Chevrolet, CVS Drug, Northside RV Ctr, O'Reilly Parts, Rupp Arena, to UK, Walmart
111	I-64 E, to Huntington, WV
110	US 60, Lexington, W [gas] Murphy USA/dsl, Shell/dsl, Speedway/dsl, Thorntons/dsl [food] A&W Cafe, Arby's, Bob Evans, Calistoga Cafe, Cane's Chicken, Cracker Barrel, FirstWatch Cafe, McDonald's, Smashing Tomato, Starbucks, Tom+Chee Rest., Waffle House, Wendy's [lodging] Baymont Inn, Comfort Inn, Country Inn&Suites, Guesthouse Inn, Hampton Inn, Holiday Inn Express, Howard Johnson, Microtel, Motel 6, Quality Inn, Super 8 [other] [H], Hobby Lobby, Lowe's, Rite Aid, Walmart/Subway
108	Man O War Blvd, E [gas] Shell [food] Freddy's [other] Cabela's, Costco/gas, Rite Aid, W [gas] Marathon/dsl, Meijer/dsl, Shell/KFC/Pizza Hut/Wendy's/dsl [food] Applebee's, Arby's, Asuka Grill, Backyard Burger, BD Mongolian Grill, Big Boy, Blaze Pizza, BoneFish Grill, Carino's, Carrabba's, Cheddar's, Chick-fil-A, Chipotle Mexican, Coldstone, Culver's, Fazoli's, GoldStar Chili, IChing Asian, Logan's Roadhouse, Malone's, McDonald's, Old Chicago, Outback Steaks, Qdoba, Rafferty's, Red Lobster, Saul Good Rest., Starbucks, Steak'n Shake, Subway, Taco Bell, Ted's MT Grill, TGIFriday's, Waffle House [lodging] Courtyard, Hilton Garden, Homewood Suites, Hyatt Place, Residence Inn, Sleep Inn, TownePlace Suites [other] [H], AT&T, Audi, Barnes&Noble, Best Buy, BigLots, Dick's, GNC, Gordmans, Harley-Davidson, Kohl's, Marshall's, Michael's, Old Navy, Petsmart, Ross, Staples, Target, Tire Discounters, Verizon, Walgreens
104	KY 418, Lexington, E [gas] BP/dsl, Shell/McDonald's [lodging] Clarion, Comfort Inn, Days Inn, EconoLodge, La Quinta, W [gas] BP/dsl, Speedway/dsl [food] Wendy's [other] [H]
99	US 25 N, US 421 N, Clays Ferry
98mm	Kentucky River
97	US 25 S, US 421 S, Clay's Ferry
95	rd 627, to Boonesborough, Winchester, E [gas] BP/dsl, Loves/Arby's/dsl/scales/24hr [other] camping, Ft Boonesborough SP, W [gas] Shell/Subway/dsl
90	US 25, US 421, Richmond, E [gas] Shell [food] Cracker Barrel [lodging] La Quinta, Red Roof Inn, Relax Inn, Super 7, W [gas] BP, Gulf/dsl, Marathon, Shell, Valero [food] Big Boy, DQ, Hanger's Rest., Hardee's, McDonald's, Pizza Hut, Subway, Taco Bell, Waffle House, Wendy's [lodging] Days Inn, Super 8 [other] $General, vet
87	rd 876, Richmond, E [gas] BP/dsl, Marathon/dsl, Shell/dsl, Speedway/dsl [food] A&W/LJ Silver, Arby's, Casa Fiesta Mexican, CookOut, Domino's, Fazoli's, Fong's Chinese, Hardee's, Hooters, King Buffet, Lee's Chicken, Little Caesar's, McAlister's Deli,
87	Continued McDonald's, Papa John's, Qdoba, Rally's, Subway, Taco Bell, W fle House, Wendy's [lodging] Best Western, Country Hearth Inn, Q ity Quarters Inn [other] [H], $General, Aamco, Ace Hardware, A BigLots, Goodyear/auto, Rite Aid, to EKU, vet, W [gas] Marath Circle K, Shell/dsl [food] Bob Evans, Buffalo Wild Wings, Bu King, Cane's, Chick-fil-A, Culver's, Firehouse Subs, Golden Co IHOP, Koto Japanese, Logan's Roadhouse, Olive Garden, Pa Bread, Ryan's, Starbucks, Steak'n Shake, Subway [lodging] Com Suites, Hampton Inn, Holiday Inn Express, Quality Inn, Tov Place Suites [other] Belk, Dick's, GNC, JC Penney, Meijer/dsl, chaels, Petsmart, Tire Discounters, TJ Maxx, Verizon
83	to US 25, rd 2872, Duncannon Ln, Richmond, E [other] Blueg Army Depot
77	rd 595, Berea, E [other] [H], KY Artisan Ctr/Cafe/Travelers Ct Berea Coll, W [gas] Shell/dsl, Valero/Subway/dsl [food] Sm house Grill [lodging] Motel 6, Quality Inn, Red Roof Inn [other] $Gen
76	KY 21, Berea, E [gas] BP, Marathon/Circle K, Shell/Burger K Speedway/dsl [food] A&W/LJ Silver, Arby's, Cracker Barrel, Di Bell Rest., Gold Star Chili, Hong Kong Buffet, Mario's Pizza, Donald's, Old Town Amish Rest., Papa John's, Pizza Hut, way, Taco Bell, Wendy's, Wings Etc, Yamato Japanese [lodging] Value Inn, Holiday Motel, Knights Inn [other] [H], $General, $T URGENT CARE, Walmart, W [gas] 76 Fuel/dsl, BP/dsl, Marath dsl [food] Lee's Chicken [lodging] EconoLodge, Fairfield Inn, Hol Inn Express [other] Oh! Kentucky Camping, tires, Walnut Mea RV Park
62	US 25, to KY 461, Renfro Valley, E [gas] Derby City/rest. Shell [food] Hardee's, Little Caesar's [lodging] Baymont Inn [other] (2mi), Renfro Valley RV Park/rest, W [gas] BP, Marathon, Marathon/Wendy's/dsl, Shell [food] Arby's, El Dorado Mexi Godfather's/Subway, KFC, Limestone Grill, McDonald's, Bell [lodging] Days Inn, EconoLodge [other] [H], Lake Cumberland, Aid, to Big South Fork NRA
59	US 25, to Livingston, Mt Vernon, E [gas] Shell, TravelCtr/dsl [food] Cazador Mexican, Pizza Hut [lodging] Kastle Inn, W [gas] BP [lodging] View Inn
51mm	Rockcastle River
49	KY 909, to US 25, Livingston, E [other] Camp Wildcat W [gas] 49er/dsl/24hr [other] RV Park, truck/tire repair
41	rd 80, to Somerset, London, E [gas] Speedway/dsl [food] Ar Azteca Mexican, Burger King, Gondolier Italian, KFC, McD ald's, Subway, White Castle [lodging] Days Inn, EconoLodge, Qu Inn, Red Roof Inn, Super 8 [other] [H], $General, Advance P AutoZone, CVS Drug, Kroger/deli, Parsley's Tire/repair, st lice, W [gas] BP/Home Cooker/dsl/24hr, Marathon/McDona Shell/pizza, Sunoco/dsl, Valero/dsl [food] Buffalo Wings&Ri Cheddar's, Cracker Barrel, LJ Silver, Old Town Grill, Shiloh R house, Smokin' Barrel BBQ, Subway, Taco Bell, Waffle Ho Wendy's [lodging] Budget Host, Fairfield Inn, Hampton Inn [other] Patch Ctr
38	rd 192, to Rogers Pkwy, London, E [gas] BP/dsl, Marathon, M phy USA/dsl, Shell/Mama's Subs/dsl, Speedway/dsl [food] Boy, Burger King, Capt D's, Dino's Italian, Domino's, Dunkin'/Baskin Robins, El Dorado Mexican, Fazoli's, Go Corral, Great Wall Chinese, Hardee's, Huddle House, Krystal, Donald's, Penn Sta Subs, Pizza Hut, Starbucks, Steak'n Sh Subway, Sun Buffet, Taco Bell [lodging] Baymont Inn, Comfort Su Country Inn&Suites, Holiday Inn Express, Microtel [other] $ Advance Parts, [RV dump], AT&T, camping, E Kentucky RV Ctr, Ford, coln, Kroger/dsl, Lowe's, NAPA, Nissan, Office Depot, Pete Rogers Pkwy to Manchester/Hazard, to Levi Jackson SP, U

LEXINGTON

RICHMOND

BEREA

LONDON

KY

INTERSTATE 75 Cont'd

38	Continued Verizon, Walgreens, Walmart/Subway, **W** (H), to Laurel River Lake RA
34mm	**truck haven, weigh sta both lanes**
30.5mm	Laurel River
29	US 25, US 25E, Corbin, **E** Marathon, Murphy USA, Pilot/McDonald's/Subway/dsl/scales/24hr, Spur Oil David's Steaks, DQ, Huddle House, Mi Jalisco Mexican, Taco Bell Super 8 Aldi Foods, AutoZone, Blue Beacon, Lowe's, to Cumberland Gap NP, Walmart/Subway, **W** BP/Krystal/dsl, Loves/Hardee's/dsl/scales/24hr/@, Marathon, Shell/dsl Cracker Barrel, Sonny's BBQ Baymont Inn, Fairfield Inn, Hampton Inn, Knights Inn, Quality Suites KOA, tires/repair, to Laurel River Lake RA
25	US 25W, Corbin, **E** Speedway/dsl Applebee's, Arby's, Bojangle's, Burger King, Cayenne SW Grill, CB's Grill, Dino's Italian, McDonald's, Taco Bell, Wendy's EconoLodge, Holiday Inn Express, Landmark Inn, Red Roof Inn (H), auto repair/tires, **W** Shell El Dorado Mexican, Subway, Waffle House Best Western to Cumberland Falls SP
15	US 25W, to Williamsburg, Goldbug, **W** Shell, Xpress/dsl Cumberland Falls SP
14.5mm	Cumberland River
11	KY 92, Williamsburg, **E** BP/dsl, Shell Arby's, El Dorado Mexican, Hardee's, KFC, Little Caesar's, McDonald's, Pizza Hut, Subway, Taco Bell Budget Inn, Cumberland Inn, Super 8 $General, Advance Parts, AutoZone, Family$, museum, Sav-A-Lot, Windham Drug, **W** Pilot/Wendy's/dsl/scales/24hr, Shell Burger King, DQ, Huddle House, Krystal, LJ Silver Hampton Inn $Tree, to Big South Fork NRA, Walmart
1.5mm	**Welcome Ctr nb, full facilities, litter barrels, petwalk, vending**
0mm	Kentucky/Tennessee state line

INTERSTATE 275 (Cincinnati)

Exit #	Services
84	I-71, I-75, N to Cincinnati, S to Lexington, Louisville
83	US 25, US 42, US 127, **S** Shell/Circle K/dsl, Thornton's/dsl Abuelo's Mexican, Buffalo Wings&Rings, Carrabba's, Chipotle, Coldstone, Dewey's Pizza, Donato's Pizza, First Watch Cafe, Five Guys, Gold Star Chili, Jimmy John's, KFC, Max&Erma's, McAlister's Deli, McDonald's, Moe's SW Grill, Panera Bread, Starbucks, Subway, Taco Bell, The Pub, Wendy's $Tree, CarX, Dillard's, GNC, Verizon, Walgreens
82	rd 1303, Turkeyfoot Rd, **S** TGIFriday's (H)
80	KY 17, Independence, **N** Speedway/dsl, United/dsl Arby's, Big Boy, Bob Evans, Buffalo Wild Wings, Burger King, El Ranchero Mexican, Golden Corral, Hot Head Burrito, Penn Sta Subs, Snappy Tomato Pizza, Subway, Taco Bell, TX Roadhouse, Wendy's, White Castle AT&T, Petco, TireDiscounters, Verizon, Walmart/Subway, **S** Thornton's/dsl McDonald's, Waffle House
79	KY 16, Taylor Mill Rd, **N** BP, Marathon, Speedway/dsl Domino's, Goldstar Chili, McDonald's, Peking Chinese, Subway, Wendy's $General, $Tree, Big Lots, Burlington Coats, CVS Drug, Kroger/gas, URGENT CARE, Walgreens, **S** BP/dsl El Jinete Mexican, Graeter's Rest., KFC/Taco Bell, La Rosa's Pizza, Marco's Pizza, McDonald's, Original Wok, Skyline Chili, Subway Remke's Mkt, Verizon, vet

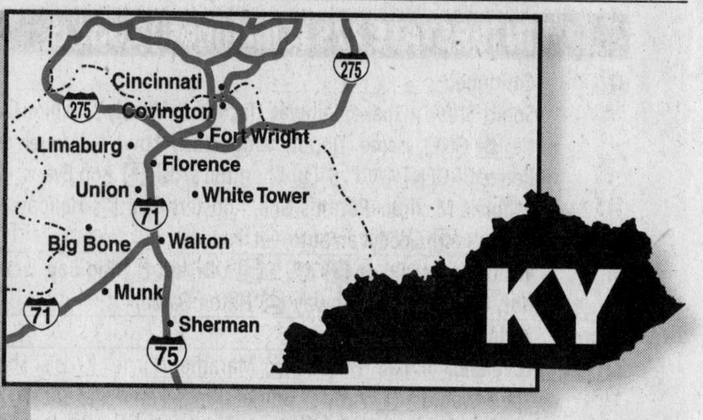

77	KY 9, Maysville, Wilder, **N** Hampton Inn, **S** Speedway/dsl, Thorntons/dsl, UDF/dsl DQ, Goldstar Chili, McDonald's, Mellow Mushroom Pizza, Subway, Waffle House Country Inn Suites
76	Three Mile Rd
74a	Alexandria, (exits left from sb), to US 27
74b	I-471 N, Newport, Cincinnati, **N** (H)
73mm	OH/KY state line, OH River
72	US 52 W, Kellogg Ave, **S** Marathon (2mi) Coney Island Funpark
71	US 52 E, New Richmonds
69	5 Mile Rd, **W** BP/dsl Big Boy, Carrabba's, Firehouse Subs, IHOP, La Rosa's Mexican, McDonald's, Moe's SW Grill, Outback, TGIFriday's (H), CVS, Kroger/gas, TireDiscounters
65	OH 125, Beechmont Ave, Amelia, **E** Shell, Speedway, UDF/dsl Hibachi Grill, Los Cazadores, Red Lobster, Ron's Chinese, Tender Towne, Wendy's Beechmont Motel CarX, Family$, Ford, Lowe's, Tires+, Walgreens, **W** BP, Marathon, Speedway/dsl Big Boy, Bob Evans, Burger King, Butterbee's Grille, Chick-fil-A, Chipotle Mexican, McDonald's, Olive Garden, Peking Chinese, Skyline Chili, Smashburger, Starbucks, Waffle House, White Castle Best Western, Days Inn, Red Roof Inn $Tree, Aldi Foods, AT&T, Audi, AutoZone, BigLots, Goodyear/auto, Home Depot, Honda, Kroger, O'Reilly Parts, Staples, Sumerel Tire/repair, Target, TireDiscounters, TJ Maxx, Toyota, Tuesday Morning, Verizon
63b a	OH 32, Batavia, Newtown, **E** UDF Applebee's, Big Boy, Bob Evans, Burger King, Chick-fil-A, China Buffet, Chipotle, ChuckECheese, City BBQ, Firehouse Subs, Five Guys, Fuji Steaks, Golden Corral, Hwy 55 Cafe, Jimmy John's, KFC, LaRosa's Pizza, LJ Silver, Logan's Roadhouse, Longhorn Steaks, McDonalds, O'Charley's, Panera Bread, Penn Sta Subs, Pizza Hut, Popeye's, Skyline Chili, Skyline Chili, Sonic, Starbucks, Steak'n Shake, Taco Bell, Wendy's, White Castle Comfort Inn, Fairfield Inn, Hampton Inn, Holiday Inn $Tree, Advance Parts, Aldi Foods, AT&T, Best Buy, Dick's, Dillard's, Firestone/auto, Hobby Lobby, JC Penney, Jo-Ann Fabrics, Jungle Jim's Mkt, Kohl's, Kroger/dsl, Marshall's, Meijer/dsl, PepBoys, Petsmart, Sam's Club/gas, URGENT CARE, Walmart/Subway, **W** Marathon, Speedway/dsl, Sunoco Gold Star Chili, Gramma's Pizza Kroger, Midas
59	OH 452, US 50, Milford Pkwy, Hillsboro, **S** UDF/dsl Buffalo Wild Wings, Cracker Barrel, Dos Amigos, Goldstar Chili, Mint Bistro, Quaker Steak&Lube, Red Robin, Roney's Rest., Ruby Tuesday, Subway, TX Roadhouse, Wendy's Homewood Suites Office Depot, Petsmart, Target, Verizon, Walmart
57	OH 28, Blanchester, Milford, **0-1 mi N** Arby's, Burger King, Chipotle Mexican, Donato's Pizza, DQ, Dunkin', Goldstar Chili, IHOP, KFC, Panera Bread, Papa John's, Penn Sta Subs, Skyline Chili,

INTERSTATE 275 (Cincinnati) Cont'd

57 Continued
Sonic, Steak'n Shake, Subway, Taco Bell, Wendy's, White Castle GNC, Home Depot, Kroger/dsl, Lowe's, Meijer/dsl, Petco, URGENT CARE, S Thornton's/dsl Bob Evans, Cazadore's Mexican, Putter's Grill, Roosters Grill Holiday Inn Express Goodyear/auto, vet

54 Wards Corner Rd, N BP, S UDF/dsl Big Boy, Dominos, Goldstar Chili, Subway Hilton Garden

53mm Little Miami River

52 Loveland, Indian Hill, N Marathon/Circle K/dsl, Shell, Speedway/dsl Arby's, Burger King, Penn Sta Subs, Pizza Hut, Skyline Chili, Starbucks, Subway, Taco Bell, Wendy's CVS Drug, Indian Motorcycles, URGENT CARE, Verizon, vet, Walgreens

50 US 22, OH 3, Montgomery, N Shell Buffalo Wild Wings, Chili's, deSha's Tavern, Dewey's Pizza, Donato's Puzza, DQ, Johnny Chan's, Melting Pot, Panera Bread, Starbucks, Subway, Taco Casa, Which Wich? Acura, AT&T, Fresh Thyme Mkt, GNC, Hyundai, Kroger/dsl, TJ Maxx, S BP/dsl, Shell/Subway/Dunkin' El Jinete, Goldstar Chili, McDonald's, Merlot's Rest., Skyline Chili, Wendy's H

49 I-71 N to Columbus, S to Cincinnatis

47 Reed Hartman Hwy, Blue Ash, S Chipotle, Jersey Mike's, Jimmy John's, Kanpai Japanese, Ruby Tuesday, Smashburger, Starbucks, Tropical Cafe DoubleTree, Hyatt Place, Quality Inn, Residence Inn

46 US 42, Mason, N BP Chipotle, KFC, Marie's Scrambler, Max&Erma's, McDonald's, Skyline Chili, Taco Bell, Wendy's, White Castle Holiday Inn, Motel 6, Woodspring Suites Advance Parts, CVS Drug, Goodyear/auto, Kroger/dsl, Walgreens, S Marathon/dsl, Shell, Speedway/dsl, UDF/dsl Arby's, El Rancho Grande, Waffle House Days Inn Midas, Mr Transmission, Tire Discounters

44 Mosteller Rd, N Subway, S Homewood Suites

43b a I-75, N to Dayton, S to Cincinnatis

42 OH 747, Springdale, Glendale, N Sunoco, Thorntons $General, Staples, S Shell/dsl BJ's Brewhouse, Blue Agave Mexican, Chick-fil-A, Chipotle, Firehouse Subs, La Rosa's Pizza, McDonald's, Noodles&Co, Panera Bread, Steak'n Shake, TGIFriday's BigLots, Chevrolet, Chrysler/Dodge/Jeep, Dillard's, Hancock Fabrics, Hobby Lobby, Lowe's, Macy's, Michael's, Office Depot, Petsmart, TJ Maxx, Verizon

41 OH 4, Springdale Pkwy, N Shell, Speedway/dsl, Sunoco/dsl Burger King, Hooters, Olive Garden, Pappadeaux, Rib City, Skyline Chili, SmoQ Rest., Wendy's La Quinta, S BP, UDF/dsl Beef'O'Brady's, DJ's Tavern, DQ, Goldstar Chili, Outback Steaks, Penn Sta Subs, Subway, White Castle Extended Stay America, Howard Johnson, Super 8 CVS Drug, Family$, O'Reilly Parts

39 Winton Rd, Winton Woods, N BP Asian Buffet, Chipotle, Golden Corral, IHOP, McDonald's, Old Spaghetti Factory, Panera Bread, Red Lobster, Steak'n Shake Comfort Suites, Hampton Inn Bass Pro Shops, CarMax, Home Depot, Kohl's, Meijer/dsl, Tire Discounters, S Marathon/dsl, Shell/dsl, UDF/dsl Big Boy, Cancun Mexican, China Garden, Cracker Barrel, Izzy's Cafe, Jade House Chinese, Jax Tavern, KFC, La Fiesta Mexican, Papa John's, Penn Sta Subs, Popeye's, Skyline Chili, Starbucks, Subway, Taco Bell, Wendy's Quality Inn, SpringHill Suites $Tree, AAA, Aldi Foods, AutoZone, Kroger/gas, Tires+, vet, Walmart

36 US127, Hamilton, MtHealthy, N Marathon/CircleK/dsl, Speedway Wendy's CVS Drug, S Shell/dsl, Sunoco, UDF

36 Continued
Big Boy, China Island, La Rosa's Pizza, Little Caesars, Donald's, Rally's, Subway, Taco Bell Advance Parts, Fa ly$, O'Reilly Parts

33 US 27, US 126, Colerain Ave, N Speedway/dsl Bu er King, Skyline Chili, Steak'n Shake, Wendy's Dic Jo-Ann, Lowe's, Petsmart, TireDiscounters, Walmart/Subw S Shell Applebee's, Arby's, Big Boy, Bob Evans, Buf Wild Wings, Burger King, Cheddar's, Chipotle, Five Guys, H eybaked Ham, IHOP, KFC, La Piñata Mexican, La Rosa's Pizza Silver, Logan's Roadhouse, Longhorn Steaks, McDonald's, O Garden, Outback Steaks, Panera Bread, Pizza Hut, Popey Potbelly, Qdoba, Red Lobster, Starbucks, Taco Bell, TGIFrida White Castle Aldi Foods, AT&T, Best Buy, GNC, Hobby L by, JC Penney, Kroger, Macy's, Marshalls, Meijer/dsl, Micha Old Navy, Sumerel Tire/auto, Tires+, Tuesday Morning, GENT CARE, Verizon, Walgreens

31 Ronald Reagan Hwy, Blue Rock Rds

28 I-74, US 52, E to Cincinnati, W to Indianapolis

25 I-74, E to Cincinnati, W to Indianapolis

21 Kilby Rd, Indian Springs Camping (3mi)

18mm Ohio/Indiana State Line

16 US 50, Greendale, Lawrenceburg, W Ameristop/dsl, Sh Circle K/Subway, Sinclair/dsl Buffalo Wings&Rings, Bur King, KFC, La Rosa's Pizza, Maverick's Grill, McDonald's, T Bell, Waffle House, White Castle Baymont Inn, Holiday Express, Quality Inn, Riverside Inn casino, Chevrolet, Ch ler/Dodge/Jeep, Ford, TireDiscounters, Walgreens

14mm Kentucky/Indiana state line, Ohio River

11 Petersburg

8b a KY 237, Hebron, N Marathon/DQ/dsl, UDF/dsl Ag Mexican, Arby's, China Wok, Hebron Grille, Jets Pizza, J my John's, Longnecks Grill, Papa John's, Penn Sta Subs, Pi Hut, Strong's Pizza, Wendy's Remke's Mkt, URGENT CA S Speedway/Subway/dsl Burger King, Goldstar C Skyline Chili, Sonic, Waffle House

4a b KY 212, KY 20, N Shell/dsl Comfort Suites, Co try Inn&Suites, Hampton Inn, Marriott, S DoubleT (2mi) H,

2 Mineola Pike, N Mobil/Rally's/Subway/dsl Holi Inn, Quality Inn, S Shell/dsl Hot Head Burrito, S way Courtyard Inn, Residence Inn

NOTES

KY

LOUISIANA

INTERSTATE 10

Exit #	Services
274mm	Louisiana/Mississippi state line, Pearl River
272mm	West Pearl River
270mm	**Welcome Ctr wb, full facilities, info, litter barrels, petwalk, , , RV dump**
267b	I-12 W, to Baton Rouge
267a	I-59 N, to Meridian
266	US 190, Slidell, N RaceTrac/dsl, Shell/dsl, TA/Country Pride/dsl/scales/24hr/@ Baskin-Robbins, Cane's, Chick-fil-A, Copeland's Rest., Firehouse Subs, Golden Dragon Chinese, Los Tres Amigos, McDonald's, NO Rest., NOLA Southern Grill, Panda Express, Rotolo's Pizza, Sonic, Subway, Taco Bell Best Value Inn, Best Western+, Country Inn Suites, Motel 6, Red Roof Inn H, CVS Drug, Firestone/auto, GNC, Harley-Davidson, Hobby Lobby, Office Depot, O'Reilly Parts, PepBoys, Petco, Rouse's Mkt, U-Haul, Walgreens, S Chevron/dsl, Murphy USA/dsl, RaceTrac/dsl Applebee's, Big Easy Diner, Cracker Barrel, Fuji Yama Hibachi, Hooters, McAlister's Deli, Outback Steaks, Popeye's, Sonic, Starbucks, TX Roadhouse, Waffle House Days Inn, La Quinta, Wingate Inn H, $General, $Tree, AT&T, CVS, Home Depot, Lowe's, repair/transmissions, vet, Walgreens, Walmart/Subway
265	US 190, Fremaux Ave, N RaceTrac/dsl BJ's Rest., Cheddar's, Chipotle, Five Guys, Longhorn Steaks, Lost Cajun, Panera Bread, Red Robin, Saltgrass Steaks, Starbucks, Which Wich? TownePlace Suites BAM, Best Buy, Dick's, Dillard's, GNC, Goodyear/auto, Kohl's, Michael's, Petsmart, TJ Maxx, Verizon

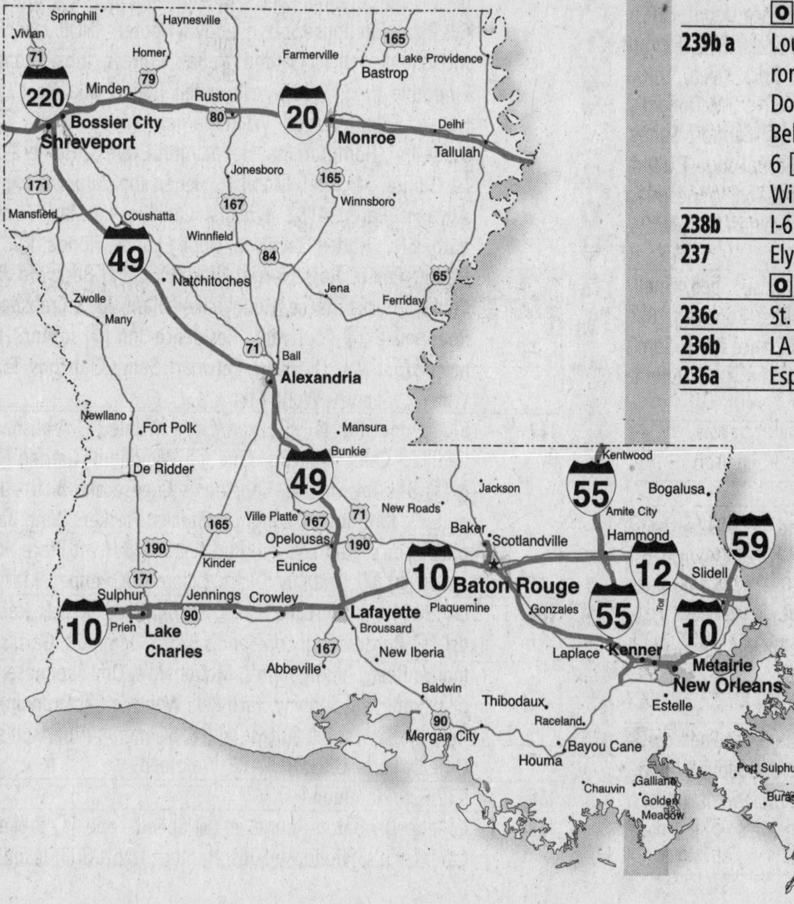

Exit #	Services
263	LA 433, Slidell, N Exxon/Circle K/dsl, Shell/dsl, Valero Oishii Buffet, Waffle House Hampton Inn, Super 8 repair, S Circle K/Subway/scales/dsl, Exxon/Circle K/dsl McDonald's, Taco Bell, Wendy's Holiday Inn Buick/GMC, Chevrolet/Cadillac, Chrysler/Dodge/Jeep, Ford, Honda, Hyundai, Kia, Nissan, NO East RV Park (1mi), Pinecrest RV Park, Toyota
261	Oak Harbor Blvd, Eden Isles, N Exxon/Circle K/dsl Waffle House Sleep Inn, S Shell/Subway/dsl Bayou Country Store
255mm	Lake Pontchartrain
254	US 11, to Northshore, Irish Bayou
251	Bayou Sauvage NWR, S swamp tours
248	Michoud Blvd
246b a	I-510 S, LA 47 N, S to Chalmette, N to Little Woods
245	Bullard Ave, N Chevron/dsl, Shell/dsl Bullard Diner, Waffle House Comfort Suites, Holiday Inn Express Family$, Honda, S Chevron/dsl, Shell Burger King, IHOP, KFC/Taco Bell, McDonald's, NO Rest., Papa John's, Subway, Super Cajun Seafood, Wendy's Motel 6, Quality Inn Chrysler/Dodge/Jeep, Home Depot, Nissan, NTB, PepBoys, Toyota, Walgreens, Walmart
244	Read Blvd, N Shell/dsl McDonald's Walgreens, S EZ Stop/dsl Popeye's, Subway, Waffle House, Wendy's Days Inn, Knights Inn, Wyndham Garden H, CVS, SaveALot Foods
242	Crowder Blvd, N Chevron, S Crowder Ctr, Exxon/dsl Subway Rodeway Inn Family$, Walgreens, $General
241	Morrison Rd, N Big E-Z/dsl, FuelXpress/dsl
240b a	US 90 E, Chef Hwy, Downman Rd, N Shell/dsl Super 8 Chevrolet, U-Haul, USPO, S DZ/dsl, DZ/dsl Delta Tires
239b a	Louisa St, Almonaster Blvd, N Big Easy TP/rest./dsl, Chevron/dsl, FuelZone/dsl Burger King, Cane's, Church's, McDonald's, Min Moon Chinese, Popeye's, Rally's, Subway, Taco Bell, Waffle House, Wendy's Days Inn, EconoLodge, Motel 6 $General, Family$, Goodyear/auto, Walgreens, Walmart, Winn-Dixie, S Day&Night/dsl
238b	I-610 W (from wb)
237	Elysian Fields Ave, N Mardi Gras Trkstp/Subway/dsl Lowe's
236c	St. Bernard Ave
236b	LA 39, N Claiborne Ave
236a	Esplanade Ave, downtown
235a	Orleans Ave, to Vieux Carre, French Qtr, S Chevron/dsl Clarion, Marriott, Sheraton
235b	Poydras St, N H, S to Superdome, downtown
234a	US 90A, Claiborne Ave, to Westbank, S Superdome
232	US 61, Airline Hwy, Tulane Ave, N Burger King, S Exxon, Shell McDonald's, Popeye's, Rallys, Subway, Wendy's Costco/gas, CVS, Family$, Firestone/auto, Pepboys, to Xavier U, USPO, vet
231b	Florida Blvd, WestEnd
231a	Metairie Rd
230	I-610 E (from eb), to Slidell
229	Bonnabel Blvd

INTERSTATE 10 Cont'd

NEW ORLEANS AREA

Exit #	Services
228	Causeway Blvd, N Exxon/dsl, Shell/dsl Buffalo Wild Wings, Cheesecake Factory, Cucina Italiana, Outback Steaks, PF Chang's, Red Lobster, Ruth's Chris Steaks, TGIFriday's Best Western, Hampton Inn, Ramada Dick's, Dillard's, JC Penney, Macy's, Whole Foods Mkt, S DZ, Exxon/Circle K IHOP, Little Tokyo Courtyard, Extended Stay America, Holiday Inn, La Quinta, Ramada Inn, Residence Inn, Sheraton
226	Clearview Pkwy, Huey Long Br, N Chevron/dsl, Exxon/Circle K/dsl Cafe Dumonde, Cane's, Chili's, Copeland's Cheesecake Bistro, Corky's BBQ, Don's Seafood Hut, Hooters, Houston's Rest., Izzo's Burrito, Jimmy John's, Popeye's, Romano Italian, Starbucks, Taco Bell, Taco Tico, Zea Rotisserie Sleep Inn NTB, Target, Walgreens, S Chevron, Danny&-Clyde Beijing Chinese, Burger King, Piccadilly, Smoothie King, Subway In Town Suites, Super 8 H, AT&T, Buick/GMC, Firestone/auto
225	Veterans Blvd, N Chevron, DZ/dsl, Shell Bonefish, Burger King, Coyote Blues, Denny's, Hooters, McDonald's, Panera Bread, Pei Wei La Quinta CVS Drug, Honda, Hyundai, Rite Aid, Rouses Mkt, URGENT CARE, S Shell/dsl Burger King, Casa Garcia, ChuckeCheese, Little Caesar's, Louisiana Purchase Kitchen, New Orleans Burgers, O'Henry's, Popeye's, Starbucks, Subway, Tiffin Pancakes, Wendy's Evergreen Inn, Wyndham Garden $General, Acura, Best Buy, BigLots, BMW, Chevrolet, GNC, Home Depot, Jo-Ann Fabrics, Kia, Lexus, Michael's, Nissan, Office Depot, PepBoys, Petsmart, TJ Maxx, Verizon, vet, VW, Walgreens, Walmart
224	Power Blvd (from wb)
223b a	LA 49, Williams Blvd, N DZ/dsl, Exxon/dsl, Shell/dsl Cafe Dumonde, Cane's Chicken, Fisherman's Cove, IHOP, Popeye's, Rally's, Subway, Taco Bell, Wendy's Fairfield Inn $Tree, AutoZone, Carmax, Dillards, Family$, Ford, Office Depot, PetCo, Save-a-Lot Foods, Target, TrueValue, Walmart Mkt, S Exxon/Circle K/dsl, Shell American Pie Diner, Brick Oven, Chick-fil-A, Don Jose's Grill, Dot's Diner, KFC/LJ Silver, McDonald's, Pollo Campero, Sonic, Subway, Taco Tico Comfort Suites, Contempra Inn, Crowne Plaza, DoubleTree, EconoLodge, Extended Stay America, Holiday Inn, La Quinta, Radisson, Woodspring Suites $General, CVS Drug, Family$, Goodyear/auto, NAPA, NTB, Toyota, U-Haul, USPO, Winn-Dixie
221	Loyola Dr, N Circle K, Exxon/Circle K/dsl, Shell, Shell/dsl Church's, Little Caesar's, McDonald's, Popeye's, Rally's, Subway, Taco Bell, VooDoo BBQ Advance Parts, Sam's Club/gas, S Citgo/dsl, DZ Red Roof Inn $General, Family$
220	I-310 S, to Houma
214mm	Lake Pontchartrain
210	I-55N (from wb)
209	I-55 N, US 51, to Jackson, LaPlace, Hammond, N Shell/Huddle House/casino/dsl Suburban Lodge, S Chevron/dsl, Circle K/dsl, Pilot/Subway/dsl/24hr/scales Burger King, McDonald's, Waffle House, Wendy's Best Western, Days Inn, Hampton Inn, Holiday Inn Express, Quality Inn, TownePlace Suites
207mm	**weigh sta both lanes**
206	LA 3188 S, La Place, S Circle K/dsl, Marathon/dsl, Shell/dsl Fairfield Inn H, Chrysler/Dodge/Jeep, Ford, Goodyear/auto
194	LA 641 S, to Gramercy, 4-6 mi S Marathon, Shell, Taylors/dsl Golden Grove Rest., McDonald's, Popeye's H, plantations

GONZALES

Exit #	Services
187	US 61, N to Sorrento, S to Gramercy
182	LA 22, Sorrento, N Shell/Popeye's/dsl, Texaco S Marathon/Subway/dsl/scales/24hr, SJ/dsl McDonald's, Waffle House tourist info
179	LA 44, Gonzales, 1 mi N Exxon/Popingo's Cafe/dsl, Murphy USA/dsl Alabasha Cafe, Subway $General, Buick/GMC, Chabill's Automotive, Fred's Store, Walgreens
177	LA 30, Gonzales, N Circle K/dsl, Shell/dsl Buffalo Wild Wings, Burger King, Chick-fil-A, El Paso Mexican, Jack-in-Box, McDonald's, Outback Steaks, Taco Bell, Waffle House, Zaxby's Best Value Inn, Budget Inn, Clarion, Days Inn, Highland Inn, Western Inn H, Home Depot, O'Reilly P... S Marathon/dsl, RaceTrac/dsl, Shell/dsl Berger..., Chili's, Cracker Barrel, Don's Seafood Hut, Firehouse Subs, Logan's Roadhouse, Mooyah Burger, Popeye's, Sonic, Starbucks, Tang Buffet, Tilted Kilt, Wendy's, Which Wich? Best Western+, Candlewood Suites, Comfort Suites, Hampton Inn, Holiday Inn Express, Home 2 Suites, La Quinta, Quality Inn, SpringHill Suites, TownePlace Suites Cabela's, Tanger famous brands, Vesta RV Park
173	LA 73, to Geismar, Prairieville, N Circle K/dsl, Shell vet, S Exxon/dsl, Marathon/dsl, Mobil/McDonald's, RaceTrac/dsl, Sunoco/dsl Burger King, DQ, Griffin Grill, ... Wok, Las Palmas Mexican, Pizza Hut, Popeye's, Smoothie K..., Sonic, Subway Mainstay Suites, Sleep Inn O'Reilly P... repair, Twin Lakes RV Park (1mi), Walgreens
166	LA 42, LA 427, Highland Rd, Perkins Rd, N Circle ... Church's/dsl, Exxon/Circle K/dsl Las Palmas Mex..., Popeye's, Ruffino's Italian, Sonic, Starbucks, Waffle H..., Zoe's Kitchen Alexander's Mkt, funpark, Goodyear/a..., Home Depot, Tire Engineers/auto, S Shell/dsl, Texaco, Subway

BATON ROUGE

Exit #	Services
163	Siegen Lane, N Marathon/dsl, RaceTrac/dsl, Shell/Circ... dsl Burger King, Cane's, CC's Coffee, Chick-fil-A, China ... Ci's Pizza, Firehouse Subs, Freddy's, Hooters, IHOP, Jason's ..., McDonald's, Olive Garden, PoBoy Express, Ribs Chopho..., Smoothie King, Subway, Taco Bell, Twin Peaks Rest., W... House, Whataburger, Whataburger, Which Wich? ... Value Inn, Hampton Inn, Holiday Inn Express, Home 2 Su..., La Quinta, Microtel, Motel 6, Siegen Inn, Super 8 $... Advance Parts, AT&T, BigLots, Cadillac, CarMax, Firest... auto, GNC, Harley-Davidson, Hobby Lobby, Honda, Kia, C... Depot, PetCo, Ross, Target, Verizon, S Backyard Bu..., Chili's, ChuckeCheese, Honeybaked Ham, Joe's Crabshack, Roadhouse Courtyard, Residence Inn Jo-Ann, K... Lowe's/Subway, Old Navy, Petsmart, Sam's Club/gas, TJ M... Walmart/Subway, World Mkt
162	Bluebonnet Rd, N Exxon/Circle K/dale Albasha ... Cadillac Cafe, Francois Cafe Wyndham Garden ... S BJ's Brewhouse, Copeland's Cheesecake Bistro, J... ander's, King Buffet, Longhorn Steaks, Pluckers Wing Bar, ...ph&Kacoo's, Red Lobster, Red Robin Hyatt Place, Renaissance H, Best Buy, Dick's, Dillard's, JC Penney, Macy's
160	LA 3064, Essen Lane, S Exxon/Circle K/dsl, Race... dsl Burger King, Copeland's Bistro, Domino's, Gatti's P... India's Rest., Jimmy John's, McDonald's, Omi Japanese, P... dilly, Popeye's, Subway, Taco Bell, Wendy's Drury Inn, ... field Inn, Springhill Suites H, $General, Albertson's, O'Reilly Parts, URGENT CARE, Walgreens
159	I-12 E, to Hammond
158	College Dr, Baton Rouge, N Speed Zone Broken ... Cafe, Cane's, Firehouse Subs, Hooters, Izzo's Grill, Jason's

LA

INTERSTATE 10 Cont'd

158 Continued

Mansurs Rest., Marble Slab Creamery, Subway, Sullivan's Rest., Waffle House, Wendy's Candlewood Suites, Cloverleaf Suites, Extended Stay America, Homewood Suites, Marriott, Richmond Inn, Tru Hilton H, Barnes&Noble, Meineke, Midas, **S** Exxon/Circle K/dsl, Shell/Circle K Chick-fil-A, Chili's, Don Jose's, Gino's Rest., IHOP, McDonald's, Panda Express, Ruth's Chris Steaks, Starbucks, Subway, Taco Bell, Tio Javi's Mexican Best Value, Comfort Inn, Comfort Suites, Crowne Plaza, DoubleTree, Embassy Suites, Hampton Inn, Holiday Inn $Tree, Albertson's, AutoZone, Hobby Lobby, Office Depot, USPO, Verizon, Walgreens, Walmart/Subway

157b Acadian Thwy, **N** Chevron/dsl Mestizo Grill, Rib's Rest. La Quinta, Radisson H, **S** Shell/Circle K/dsl Acme Oyster House, Juban's Rest., Outback Steaks, Provisions, Saltgrass Steaks Courtyard AT&T, PetCo, Trader Joe's, Tuesday Morning

157a Perkins Rd (from eb), same as 157b

156b Dalrymple Dr, **S** to LSU

156a Washington St

155c Louise St (from wb)

155b I-110 N, to Baton Rouge bus dist, **N**

155a LA 30, Nicholson Dr, Baton Rouge, **N** Belle Hotel, **S** Shell/Circle K/dsl to LSU

154mm Mississippi River

153 LA 1, Port Allen, **N** Chevron, Shell/Circle K/dsl Church's, Pizza Hut AutoZone, Family$, Kenworth, NAPA, O'Reilly Parts, repair, Walgreens, **S** LA 1S TP/Exxon/Casino/dsl/scales/24hr, RaceTrac/dsl, Sunoco Domino's, Hardee's, Waffle House Red Roof Inn $Tree, Verizon, Walmart/Subway

151 LA 415, to US 190, **N** Cash's Trk Plaza/dsl/scales/casino, Chevron/dsl, Emerald Plaza Trkstp/Champs Chicken/dsl, Exxon/dsl, Nino's/dsl/casino, Shell/Circle K/dsl Burger King, KFC/Taco Bell, McDonald's, Popeye's, Subway, Waffle House Best Western, Comfort Suites, Hampton Inn, Holiday Inn Express, La Quinta, Quality Inn, TownePlace Suites, West Inn $General, **S** Loves/Arby's/dsl/scales/24hr, Mobil/dsl/24hr Audubon Inn, Motel 6, Super 8, Super 8 truck repair

139 LA 77, Grosse Tete, **N** Shell/Subway/dsl Big Heads BBQ Chevrolet, **S** Tiger/Country Store/dsl/rest./@

135 LA 3000, to Ramah

127 LA 975, to Whiskey Bay

126.5mm Pilot Channel of Whiskey Bay

122mm Atchafalaya River

121 Butte La Rose, **N** **Visitors ctr/ both lanes, full facilities, litter barrels, petwalk, tourist info, vending,** **S** Lazy Cajun Grill (2mi) Frenchman's Wilderness Camground (.5mi)

115 LA 347, to Cecilia, Henderson, **N** Exxon/dsl/24hr, Shamrock/dsl, Texaco/dsl Chicken on the Bayou, Landry's Seafood Holiday Inn Express casinos, **S** Chevron/dsl, Exxon/Subway/dsl, Shell/McDonald's/dsl, Texaco/dsl, Valero/dsl Popeye's, Waffle House $General

109 LA 328, to Breaux Bridge, **N** Shell/dsl, Texaco/Hardee's/dsl/casino Microtel, **S** Exxon/Domino's/dsl, Murphy USA/dsl, Pilot/Arby's/dsl/scales/24hr, Valero/Popeye's/dsl Burger King, City Buffet, Crazy Bout Cajun, Hacienda Real, McDonald's, Pizza Hut, Sonic, Taco Bell, Waffle House, Wendy's, Zapote Mexican Best Value Inn, Super 8 $General, $Tree, AT&T, AutoZone, Chevrolet, Chrysler/Dodge/Jeep, city park, Dixie RV Ctr, Family$, Ford/Lincoln, O'Reilly Parts, Pioneer RV Park, Super 1 Foods, USPO, Walgreens, Walmart/Subway

LAFAYETTE

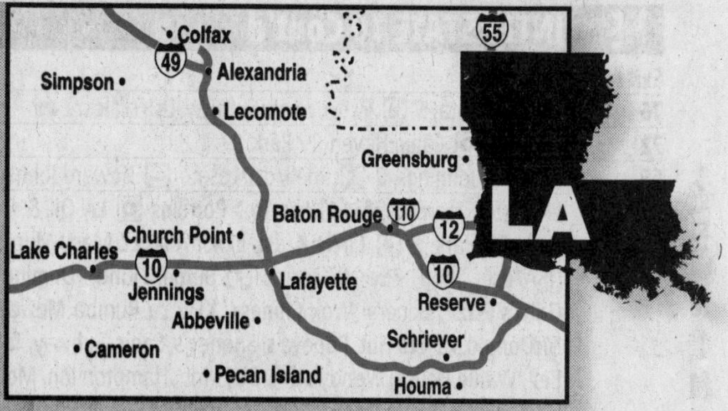

108mm **weigh sta both lanes**

104 Louisiana Ave, **S** RaceTrac/dsl Chick-fil-A, McDonald's, Subway, Taco Bell AT&T, GNC, JC Penney, Office Depot, PetCo, Ross, Target, Verizon

103b I-49 N, to Opelousas

103a US 167 S, to Lafayette, **S** Circle K, Murphy USA/dsl, RaceTrac/dsl, Shell/dsl Checkers, McDonald's, Popeye's, Sonic, Subway, Taco Bell, Waffle House, Wendy's Baymont Inn, Best Western, Fairfield Inn, Holiday Inn, Howard Johnson, La Quinta, Motel 6, Quality Inn, Super 7, Super 8 H, $Tree, Home Depot, Super 1 Foods/gas, transmissions

101 LA 182, to Lafayette, **N** McDonald's, Shell/Circle K/Subway/dsl, TA/Country Pride/dsl/scales/24hr/@ Burger King, Waffle House, Whataburger Red Roof Inn, **S** Chevron/dsl, Citgo, Exxon Church's, Cracker Barrel, KFC Days Inn, Drury Inn, Hilton Garden (2mi), King Motel, Peartree Inn H, $General, Advance Parts, Family$, O'Reilly Parts, Valero/dsl

100 Ambassador Caffery Pkwy, **N** Exxon/dsl Gauthier's RV Ctr, Peterbilt, Ryder Trucks, **S** Chevron/dsl, RaceTrac/dsl, Shell/Circle K/dsl Burger King, McDonald's, Sonic, Taco Bell, Waffle House, Wendy's Ambassador Inn, Hampton Inn, Microtel, Sleep Inn H, Southern Tire Mart

97 LA 93, to Scott, **N** La Rumba Mexican Super 1 Foods/dsl, **S** Chevron/McDonald's, Shell/Church's/dsl Billy's Cracklings, Fezzo's Seafood, Huddle House, Popeye's, Rochetto's Pizza Comfort Inn, Holiday Inn Express, Howard Johnson Harley-Davidson, KOA

92 LA 95, to Duson, **N** Exxon/dsl/casino/RV dump/scales/24hr, Loves/Chester's/Wendy's/dsl/scales/24hr, **S** Chevron/dsl, Marathon/Subway/dsl/casino, Roady's/cafe/dsl/casino Super 8 Frog City RV Park

87 LA 35, to Rayne, **N** Chevron/dsl, Shell/Subway/casino/dsl Burger King, Chef Roy's Rest., McDonald's, Taco Bell Days Inn $General, **S** Circle K/dsl, Citgo/dsl, Frog City/Exxon/Cajun Rest./dsl, Shop Rite, Texaco/dsl Candyland Ice Cream, Domino's, DQ, Gabe's Café, Great Wall Chinese, Pizza Hut, Popeye's, Sonic Best Western Advance Parts, Family$, O'Reilly Parts, Super 1 Foods, Walgreens

82 LA 1111, to E Crowley, **S** Chevron/dsl, Murphy USA Chili's, Wendy's H, AT&T, GNC, Lowe's, Walgreens, Walmart/Subway

CROWLEY

80 LA 13, to Crowley, **N** Conoco/Exit 80/dsl/rest./24hr DQ, Fezzo's Seafood/steaks, Waffle House Crowley Inn, Days Inn, Motel 6 Buick/Chevrolet, vet, **S** Chevron/dsl, Exxon, Raceway/dsl, Tobacco+/gas, Valero/dsl Asian Buffet, Burger King, Cajun Way, China Dragon, El Dorado Mexican, Gatti's Pizza, KFC, Little Caesar's, McDonald's, Pizza Hut, PJ's Grill, Popeye's, Sonic, Subway, Taco Bell $General, $Tree, AutoZone, Ford, O'Reilly Parts, Super 1, Verizon

INTERSTATE 10 Cont'd

JENNINGS

Exit #	Services
76	LA 91, to Iota, S Petro/Shell/Subway/dsl/scales/24hr
72	Egan, N Cajun Haven RV Park
65	LA 97, to Jennings, S Shell/dsl/casino Howard Johnson
64	LA 26, to Jennings, N Los Tres Potrillos LA Oil & Gas Park, RV Park, S Circle K/dsl, Exxon/dsl, EZ Mart, Murphy USA/dsl, Shop Rite/dsl/casino Burger King, Domino's, Gatti's Pizza, General Wok Chinese, KFC, La Rumba Mexican, McDonald's, Pizza Hut, Popeye's, Shoney's, Sonic, Subway, Taco Bell, Waffle House, Wendy's Days Inn, Hampton Inn, Motel 6 H, $General, $Tree, AT&T, AutoZone, O'Reilly Parts, Verizon, Walgreens, Walmart/Subway
59	LA 395, to Roanoke, N Peto's TrvlCtr/Chevron/dsl/scales/24hr
54	LA 99, Welsh, S Citgo, Exxon/dsl/24hr, Valero DQ, Subway
48	LA 101, Lacassine, S Exxon
44	US 165, to Alexandria, N Quiet Oaks RV Park (10mi), S Rabideaux's Cajun
43	LA 383, to Iowa, N Loves/Hardee's/dsl/scales/24hr, Pilot/Arby's/PJ Fresh/dsl/scales/24hr Burger King Howard Johnson Express, La Quinta, S Citgo/dsl, Shell/McDonald's/dsl, Texaco Boudreaux's Cajun, Sonic, Subway $General, I-10 Outlet/famous brands
36	LA 397, to Creole, Cameron, N Jean Lafitte RV Park (2mi), S Cash Magic/grill/dsl/RV Dump, Chevron/dsl Los Ponchos Red Roof Inn casino, Country Oaks RV Park
34	I-210 W, to Lake Charles
33	US 171 N, N Chevron/dsl, Conoco/dsl, RaceWay/dsl/E85, Shell/dsl, Time/dsl Burger King, Church's, KFC, Subway, Taco Bell Best Western, Comfort Suites, Motel 6, Richmond Suites $General, AutoZone, Family$, O'Reilly Parts, to Sam Houston Jones SP, S EconoLodge, Holiday Inn Express, Super 10
32	Opelousas St, N Exxon, S EconoLodge, Holiday Inn Express, Super 10
31b	US 90 E, Shattuck St, to LA 14, N Chevron/dsl/casino, S Valero/dsl
31a	US 90 bus, Enterprise Blvd, S Valero/dsl Popeye's
30b	downtown
30a	LA 385, N Lakeshore Dr, Ryan St, N Citgo Steamboat Bill's Rest., Waffle House Days Inn, Oasis Inn, S Wendy's Quality Suites
29	LA 385 (from eb), same as 30a
28mm	Calcasieu Bayou, Lake Charles
27	LA 378, to Westlake, N Chevron/dsl, Conoco/dsl, Texaco/dsl, Valero Burger King, El Tapatia Mexican, McDonald's, Popeye's, RoundTop Burger, Sonic, Subway La Quinta $General, Bumper Parts, Family$, Fred's, MarketBasket, O'Reilly Parts, to Sam Houston Jones SP (6mi), S Inn at the Isle Riverboat Casinos
26	US 90 W, Southern Rd, Columbia, N Exxon/dsl
25	I-210 E, to Lake Charles
23	LA 108, to Sulphur, N Chevron, Circle K, Exxon/dsl, Murphy USA, Shell Bergeron's Cajun Diner, Burger King, Cane's, Chili's, China Wok, Kyoto, McDonald's, Popeye's, Subway, Taco Bell, Wendy's Quality Inn $General, $Tree, AT&T, Bumper Parts, Lowe's, Verizon, Walgreens, Walmart/Subway, S Chevron/Jack-in-the-Box/dsl, Citgo/Cash Magic/dsl, Sulphur Trkstp/Shell/Subway/dsl/casino Cracker Barrel, Waffle House Best Western+, Comfort Suites, Days Inn, Holiday Inn Express, HomeTowne Studios, Studio 6, Super 8 Southern Tire Mart
21	LA 3077, Arizona St, N Conoco/dsl, Shell Boiling P Cajun, China Taste, Papa John's, Starbucks H, $Ge al, AT&T, Chevrolet, CVS Drug, Ford, GNC, Kroger/gas, N Walgreens, S Chevron/dsl, Shell/dsl, Valero/dsl/ca Hidden Ponds RV Park
20	LA 27, to Sulphur, N Chevron/dsl, Circle K, Conoco Gulf, Valero/dsl Burger King, Casa Ole Mexican, Chec Gatti's Pizza, Hollier's Cajun, Hong Kong Chinese, Joe's Pi pasta, La Rumba Mexican, LeBleu's Landing Cajun, Little sar's, McDonald's, Pitt Grill Cajun, Popeye's, Ruiz's Steaks, way, Taco Bell, Wendy's Best Value, Hampton Inn, M 6 H, Brookshire Bros/gas, Family$, Firestone/auto, G year/auto, Jiffy Lube, S Chevron/dsl, Shell/dsl rosky's Burgers, Pizza Hut, Sonic, Waffle House Bayn Inn, Candlewood Suites, Days Inn, Fairfield Inn, Holiday Red Roof Inn, Wingate Inn Stine, to Creole Nature Trai
8	LA 108, Vinton, N Chevron/dsl, Exxon/dsl Cajun C boy's Rest. V RV Park
7	LA 3063, Vinton, N FuelStop/dsl Burger King, ic, Subway Cobblestone Inn $General, casino, Loves/Arby's/dsl/scales/24hr
4	US 90, LA 109, Toomey, N Cash Magic/dsl/grill/ca Chevron/dsl/casino, Shell/dsl truck repair, S Con dsl, Exxon/dsl, Valero/dsl/rest. Subway Best W ern casinos, RV Park
2.5mm	**weigh sta wb lanes**
1.5mm	**Welcome Ctr eb, full facilities, litter barrels, petwalk,**
1	(from wb), Sabine River Turnaround
0mm	Louisiana/Texas state line, Sabine River

LAKE CHARLES

SULPHUR

INTERSTATE 12

Exit #	Services
85c	I-10 E, to Biloxi. **I-12 begins/ends on I-10, exit 267.**
85b	I-59 N, to Hattiesburg
85a	I-10 W, to New Orleans
83	US 11, to Slidell, N Circle K/dsl, Exxon/dsl Burger McDonald's, Sonic, Waffle House, S RaceTrac/dsl, S Subway/dsl H
80	Airport Dr, North Shore Blvd, N Circle K/Kry dsl Dickey's BBQ, IHOP, PJ's Coffee, Sonic Com Inn AT&T, Petsmart, Ross, Target, S Chevron, S dsl Burger King, Chili's, ChuckECheese's, Domino's, Donald's, Olive Garden, Starbucks, Subway, Taco Bell, W House, Wendy's, Zea Grill Candlewood Suites, Holida Express, Homewood Suites, La Quinta $Tree, Burlin Dillard's, Goodyear/auto, Home Depot, Jo-Ann, Mars Sam's Club/gas, Walgreens, Walmart
74	LA 434, to Lacombe, N Chevron/Subway/dsl Steve's RV Ctr, S Big Branch Marsh NWR
68	LA 1088, to Mandeville
65	LA 59, to Mandeville, N Chevron/dsl, Exxon/Dan Clyde's/cafe/dsl, Shell/dsl Fat Spoon Cafe, Pope Smoothie King, Sonic, Subway, Waffle House Co Suites, S Circle K/Arby's/dsl, Valero/Domino's/dsl Rancho Mexican, Liu's Wok, McDonald's, PJ's C Quiznos camping, to Fontainebleau SP, vet, Winn-Dix
63b a	US 190, Covington, Mandeville, N Chevron/dsl, E RaceTrac, Shell/Circle K Acme Oyster House, Apple Burger King, Cane's, Chick-fil-A, Copeland's Grill, Dakota Don's Seafood, Dunkin', Four Seasons Chinese, HoneyB Ham, IHOP, Jimmy John's, Johnny's Pizza, La Carreta, Lee's burgers, McAlister's Deli, Mellow Mushroom Cafe, North S

LA

E INTERSTATE 12 Cont'd

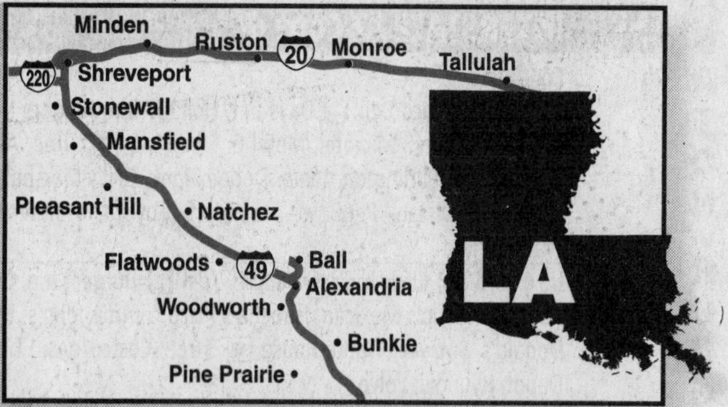

63b a Continued
Empress Asian, Osaka Japanese, Outback Steaks, Papi's Fajita Factory, Piccadilly, Sonic, Starbucks, Subway, Thai Chili, Waffle House, Wendy's, Zea Rotisserie [lodging] Best Western, Clarion, Comfort Inn, Country Inn&Suites, Courtyard, Hampton Inn, Hilton Garden, Holiday Inn, Homewood Suites, Residence Inn, Staybridge Suites, Super 8 [other] Ace Hardware, AT&T, AutoZone, Chevrolet, Chrysler/Dodge/Jeep, CVS Drug, Firestone/auto, GNC, Home Depot, Honda, Hyundai, Lowe's, Nissan, Office Depot, Petsmart, Rouse's Mkt, Subaru, Toyota, Verizon, Walmart/McDonald's, **S** [other] [H], st police, to New Orleans via **toll** causeway

60 Pinnacle Pkwy, to Covington, same as 59

59 LA 21, to Covington, Madisonville, **N** [gas] Chevron/dsl, Kangaroo, Shell/dsl [food] Buffalo Wild Wings, Cafe Du Monde, Carreta's Grill, Chili's, Cracker Barrel, Firehouse Subs, Five Guys, Golden Wok, Isabella's Pizza, Italian Pie, Izzo's Burrito, Jimmy John's, McDonald's, Olive Garden, Panda Buffet, Panera Bread, PJ's Coffee, Safa Mediterranean, Sake Steaks, Seafood Grill, Smoothie King, Steak'n Shake, Subway, TX Roadhouse [lodging] La Quinta [other] [H], $Tree, AT&T, AutoZone, CVS Drug, Hobby Lobby, Kohl's, Petco, URGENT CARE, Walgreens, Winn-Dixie, **S** [gas] Valero/Domino's [food] Chick-fil-A, ChuckECheese's, Dickey's BBQ, Habaneros Mexican, Longhorn Steaks, Pardo's Grill, Taco Bell, Wendy's, Which Wich?, Zoe's Kitchen [lodging] Holiday Inn Express [other] Belk, Best Buy, Fairview Riverside SP, GNC, JC Penney, Marshall's, Michael's, Ross, Sam's Club/dsl, Target, Verizon, World Mkt

57 LA 1077, to Goodbee, Madisonville, **S** [gas] QuickWay/PoBoys/dsl [food] Best Wok, Pizza Hut, PJ's Coffee, Subway [other] to Fairview Riverside SP, vet

47 LA 445, to Robert, **1-3 mi N** [other] Jellystone Camping, to Global Wildlife Ctr, **S** [gas] Chevron/dsl

42 LA 3158, to Airport, **N** [gas] Chevron/Quiznos/dsl/24hr, Texaco/dsl [food] McDonald's, Popeye's [lodging] Friendly Inn, **S** [gas] Shell/Subway/dsl [other] [H], Berryland RV Ctr

40 US 51, to Hammond, **N** [gas] RaceTrac/dsl, Shell/Circle K [food] Burger King, Cane's, Chick-fil-A, China Garden, Church's, Coldstone, Don's Seafood, East of Italy, IHOP, Jimmy John's, McDonald's, Nagoya Rest., Olive Garden, Ryan's, Santa Fe Steaks, Shane's Rib Shack, Smoothie King, Sonic, Subway, Taco Bell, Wendy's, Which Wich? [lodging] Best Western, Courtyard, Holiday Inn, Quality Inn [other] AT&T, Best Buy, Books-A-Million, Dillard's, GNC, Harley-Davidson, JC Penney, Rite Aid, Target, TJ Maxx, U-Haul, Verizon, Walgreens, **S** [gas] Petro/Mobil/Subway/dsl/scales/24hr/@, Pilot/Arby's/dsl/scales/24hr, Shell/dsl [food] Waffle House [lodging] Colonial Inn, Days Inn, La Quinta [other] [H], $General, Blue Beacon, SpeedCo

38b a I-55, N to Jackson, S to New Orleans

37mm **weigh sta both lanes**

35 Pumpkin Ctr, Baptist, **N** [gas] Texaco/dsl [other] $General, Dixie Camping World RV Service/Supplies, Punkin RV Park (2mi), **S** [gas] Chevron/Bayou Boyz/Subway/dsl

32 LA 43, to Albany, **N** [gas] Chevron/Subway/dsl, Exxon/dsl, Shell/Big River/dsl [food] McDonald's, **S** [other] to Tickfaw SP (11mi), tourist info

29 LA 441, to Holden, **N** [gas] Sunoco/dsl [other] Berryland Campers

22 LA 63, to Frost, Livingston, **N** [gas] Chevron/dsl, Marathon/dsl [food] Pizza Hut, Subway, Wayne's BBQ [other] Carters Foods, Family$, Thrift Town Drug, USPO, **S** [other] Lakeside RV Park (1mi)

19 to Satsuma, Colyell, **N** [gas] Exxon/dsl [food] Subway

15 LA 447, to Walker, **N** [gas] Murphy Express/dsl, Shell/Subway/dsl, Texaco/dsl [food] Burger King, China Wok, Domino's, Foochow Buffet, Jack-in-the-Box, McDonald's, Papa John's, Papa Murphy's, Pizza Hut, Popeye's, Quiznos, Sherwood PoBoy's, Sombrero Mexican, Sonic, Taco Bell, Waffle House, Wendy's [lodging] La Quinta [other] $General, $Tree, AT&T, AutoZone, NAPA, O'Reilly Parts, Verizon, Walgreens, Walmart/Subway, Winn-Dixie, **S** [gas] Chevron/dsl [other] [H]

12 LA 1036, Juban Rd, **N** [food] Marble Slab, Moe's SW [other] Belk, Kohl's, Michael's, Old Navy, Petsmart, Ross, Rouse's Mkt, TJ Maxx, Verizon, **S** [gas] Shell/dsl

10 LA 3002, to Denham Springs, **N** [gas] Chevron, Exxon, RaceTrac/dsl, Shell/Circle K/dsl [food] Arby's, Baskin-Robbins, Burger King, Cactus Café, Cane's, Chili's, Church's, Domino's, Don's Seafood, Gatti's Pizza, IHOP, McDonald's, Papa John's, Papi's Fajita, Pizza Hut, Popeye's, Ron's Seafood, Ryan's, Sonic, Starbucks, Subway, Taco Bell, Waffle House, Wendy's [lodging] Best Value Inn, Candlewood Suites, Carom Inn, Comfort Suites, Hampton Inn, Motel 6 [other] $General, $Tree, Advance Parts, Albertsons, AT&T, AutoZone, CVS Drug, Home Depot, Meineke, NTB, Office Depot, O'Reilly Parts, PetCo, Rite Aid, Tire Pros, Walgreens, Walmart/Subway, **S** [gas] Pilot/Subway/dsl/scales/24hr, Shell [food] Cafe Phoenicia, El Rancho Mexican, Hardee's, Hooters, Islamorada Fish Co, Longhorn Steaks, Piccadilly, Rotolo's Pizza, VooDoo BBQ [lodging] Days Inn, Highland Inn [other] Bass Pro Shops, Cavender's, Chrysler/Dodge/Jeep, Ford, KOA, Sam's Club/dsl, Walgreens

8.5mm Amite River

7 O'Neal Lane, **N** [gas] Mobil, RaceTrac/dsl [lodging] La Quinta, Quality Inn [other] Hobby Lobby, Toyota, **S** [gas] Murphy USA/dsl, RaceTrac/dsl, Shell, Texaco/Subway/dsl [food] China King, Hardee's, Las Palmas Mexican, Little Caesar's, LoneStar Steaks, McDonald's, Popeye's, Rice Bowl, Sonic, Taco Bell, Waffle House, Wendy's [other] [H], $Tree, AutoZone, O'Reilly Parts, Walgreens, Walmart/Subway

6 Millerville Rd, **N** [gas] Chevron/dsl [food] Chick-fil-A, Chili's, Golden Corral [other] Best Buy, Honda, Lowe's, Office Depot, Petsmart, Super Target, **S** [gas] Texaco/dsl [food] Rotolo's Pizza, Subway [other] Ace Hardware

4 Sherwood Forest Blvd, **N** [gas] Exxon, Shell/Circle K/dsl [food] Burger King, ChuckECheese, Egg Roll King, Jack-in-the-Box, McDonald's, Pizza Hut, Popeye's, Sonic, Subway, Taco Bell, Waffle House [lodging] Crossland Suites, Red Roof Inn, Super 8, Woodspring Suites [other] Fred's, Goodyear/auto, Rite Aid, **S** [gas] RaceTrac/dsl, Shell/dsl [food] Cane's, DQ, Dunkin', Hardee's, Nagoya, Piccadilly, Podnuh's BBQ, Sherwood PoBoys [lodging] Calloway Inn [other] AT&T, auto care

2b US 61 N, **N** [gas] Chevron/dsl, Mobil/dsl, Rende's/dsl, Shell/Circle K [food] Applebee's, Chinese Inn, Cracker Barrel, Little Caesar's,

BATON ROUGE

INTERSTATE 12 Cont'd

2b Continued
McDonald's, Taco Bell [lodging] Days Inn, Holiday Inn, Knights Inn, Magnuson Hotel, Microtel, Motel 6, Sleep Inn [other] $Tree, Albertsons/gas, Burlington Coats, Dodge/Ram, GNC, Marshall's, Michael's, Nissan, PepBoys, SteinMart, Toyota, Walgreens, Walmart Mkt

2a US 61 S, **S** [gas] Circle K, Exxon/Circle K/dsl [food] Burger King, China 1, Fernando's Mexican, Isabella's Pizza, Jimmy John's, McDonald's, Subway, Waffle House [other] $Tree, Costco/gas, Home Depot, Hyundai, Volvo

1b LA 1068, to LA 73, Essen Lane, **N** [gas] Shell/Circle K/dsl [food] Cane's, China Wok, McDonald's, VooDoo BBQ [other] Family$, Le Blanc's Mkt, **S** [other] [H]

1a I-10 (from wb). **I-12 begins/ends on I-10, exit 159 in Baton Rouge.**

INTERSTATE 20

Exit # Services

189mm Louisiana/Mississippi state line, Mississippi River

187mm **weigh sta both lanes**

186 US 80, Delta, **S** [gas] Chevron/Subway/dsl/24hr

184mm **[rest stop] wb, full [handicapped] facilities, litter barrels, petwalk, [phone], [picnic], RV dump**

182 LA 602, Mound

173 LA 602, Richmond

171 US 65, Tallulah, **N** [gas] Chevron/Subway/dsl, Shell/dsl [food] Chopsticks Buffet, McDonald's, Wendy's [lodging] Days Inn, Super 8 [other] [H], **S** [gas] Exxon/dsl/scales, Loves/Arby's/dsl/scales/24hr, TA/Country Pride/dsl/scales/24hr/@, Texaco [food] Red Top Grill

164mm Tensas River

157 LA 577, Waverly, **N** [gas] Waverly Trkstp/rest./dsl/24hr, **S** [gas] Chevron/Hunt Bros Pizza/dsl/24hr, Shell/rest./dsl/24hr [other] Casino, to Tensas River NWR

RAYVILLE

155mm Bayou Macon

153 LA 17, Delhi, **N** [gas] Chevron/Subway, Texaco/dsl [food] Boomers, Burger King, Pizza Hut, Sonic [other] [H], $General, AT&T, Brookshire's Foods, Family$, Fred's, USPO, **S** [gas] Valero/dsl [lodging] Best Western, Executive Inn

148 LA 609, Dunn

145 LA 183, rd 202, Holly Ridge

141 LA 583, Bee Bayou Rd

138 US 425, Rayville, **N** [gas] Bud's, Pilot/Wendy's/dsl/scales/24hr [food] Fox's Pizza, McDonald's, Sonic [lodging] Days Inn [other] [H], $General, $Tree, AutoZone, Brookshire's Foods, Buick/Chevrolet, Family$, repair, Verizon, Walmart, **S** [gas] Chevron/Subway/dsl/24hr, Exxon/Circle K/Quiznos/dsl, RaceWay/dsl [food] Big John's Rest., Popeye's, Waffle House [lodging] Super 8

135mm Boeuf River

132 LA 133, Start, **N** [gas] Exxon/dsl

128mm Lafourche Bayou

124 LA 594, Millhaven, **N** [gas] Shell/dsl [other] st police, to Sage Wildlife Area

120 Garrett Rd, Pecanland Mall Dr, **N** [gas] Chevron/dsl [food] Applebee's, ChuckECheese, Copeland's Rest., Fiesta Linda, IHOP, Longhorn Steaks, McAlister's, O'Charleys, Olive Garden, Red Lobster, Ronin Habachi, Sonic [lodging] Courtyard, Residence Inn, TownePlace Suites [other] $Tree, AT&T, Belk, Best Buy, Dick's, Dillard's, Firestone/auto, Home Depot, JC Penney, Kohl's, Michael's, Old Navy, PetCo, Petsmart, Ross, Stein Mart, Target, TJ Maxx, **S** [gas] Shell/dsl [lodging] Best Western, Days Inn, Hampton Inn [other] Harley-Davidson, Hope's Campers, Lowe's, Ouachita RV Park, Pecanland RV Park, Sam's Club/gas

MONROE

118b a US 165, **N** [gas] Valero/dsl [lodging] Clarion, Motel 6, Stratford Ho Inn [other] Hyundai, Kia, Nissan, to NE LA U, **S** [gas] Chevron, C oco/dsl, Exxon, Now Save/dsl, Shell/Circle K [food] Burger K Capt D's, Church's, KFC, McDonald's, Popeye's, Sonic, Subw Taco Bell, Wendy's [lodging] Comfort Suites, Hampton Inn, Mote Super 8

117b LA 594, Texas Ave, **N** [gas] Now Save/deli/dsl

117a Hall St, Monroe, **N** [other] [H], Civic Ctr

116b US 165 bus, LA 15, Jackson St, **N** [other] [H]

116a 5th St, Monroe

115 LA 34, Mill St, **N** [gas] Chevron

114 LA 617, Thomas Rd, **N** [gas] Murphy USA, RaceWay/dsl [food] B er King, Cane's, Capt D's, Cheddar's, Chick-fil-A, El Chico, El C Verde, Five Guys, Grandy's, Hibachi Grill, IHOP, KFC, McAlist Deli, McDonald's, Podnuh's BBQ, Popeye's, Subway, Taco Waffle House, Wendy's [lodging] Best Value Inn, Super 8, Wing Inn [other] [H], AT&T, BigLots, Hobby Lobby, Office Depot, Rite Walgreens, Walmart/McDonald's, **S** [gas] Chevron, Exxon/Ci K/Subway/dsl [food] Buffalo Wild Wings, Chili's, Cracker Ba El Sombrero, Four Bros Rest., Genghis Grill, Hooters, Log Roadhouse, Outback Steaks, Peking Chinese, Pizza Hut, Rc Hibachi, Sonic, TX Roadhouse, Waffle House [lodging] Best West Comfort Inn, La Quinta, Motel 6, Quality Inn, Red Roof Inn

113 Downing Pines Rd, **S** [lodging] Fairfield Inn, Hampton Inn, Hi Garden, Holiday Inn Express, Home 2 Suites [other] Chrys Dodge/Jeep, Hyundai

112 Well Rd, **N** [gas] Conoco, Now Save/dsl, Shell/Circle K/dsl, aco/dsl [food] Burger King, DQ, McDonald's, Sam's Eatery, Francisco TexMex, Sonic, Subway, Taco Bell, Waffle House, by's [other] Advance Parts, CVS Drug, Mac's Fresh Mkt, vet, greens, Walmart Mkt/dsl, **S** [gas] Pilot/Subway/Wend dsl/scales/24hr [other] Pavilion RV Park

108 LA 546, to US 80, Cheniere, **N** [gas] Shell/dsl, Smart/dsl

107 Camp Rd, rd 25, Cheniere

103 US 80, Calhoun, **N** [gas] Chevron, USA/dsl/24hr [food] Johnny's za (1mi) [lodging] Avant Motel

101 LA 151, to Calhoun, **S** [gas] Chevron/Huddle House/Subway/ Exxon [food] Sonic [other] 101 RV Park

97mm **[rest stop] wb, full [handicapped] facilities, litter barrels, petwalk, [phone], [picnic], dump**

95mm **[rest stop] eb, full [handicapped] facilities, litter barrels, petwalk, [phone], [picnic], RV du**

93 LA 145, Choudrant, **S** [gas] Choudrant [other] camping, Jimmie vis SP (28mi)

86 LA 33, Ruston, **N** [gas] Murphy USA, RaceWay/dsl, Shell/Ci K/Quiznos/dsl, Texaco/dsl [food] Arby's, Cane's Chicken, Ch burger Cheeburger, Chili's, El Jarrito Mexican, Hot Rod B Huddle House, Log Cabin Grill, Logan's Roadhouse, Po Grill, Ronin Hibachi, Ryan's, Sonic, Taco Bell, Whataburge Buffet [lodging] Comfort Inn, Days Inn, Home 2 Suites [other] $T AT&T, Buick/GMC, Cadillac/Chevrolet, Chrysler/Dodge/Je Ford/Lincoln, Fred's, GNC, Lowe's, Toyota, vet, Walmart/S way, **S** [gas] Spirit/dsl [lodging] Best Western, Fairfield Inn, Holi Inn Express

RUSTON

85 US 167, Ruston, **N** [gas] Chevron/Subway, Exxon, Shell/Ci K [food] Applebee's, Burger King, Capt D's, Little Caesar's, McD ald's, Peking Chinese, Wendy's [lodging] Courtyard, Hampton Relax Inn [other] $General, Office Depot, Super 1 Foods, True ue, Walgreens, **S** [gas] Texaco, Valero/dsl [food] Pizza Hut [lodging] E Value Inn, Sleep Inn [other] [H], Advance Parts, Verizon

84 LA 544, Ruston, **S** [gas] Chevron/dsl, Exxon [food] Domino's, Jo ny's Pizza, Pizza Inn, Smoothie King, Starbucks, Subway, Wa House [lodging] Super 8

LA

INTERSTATE 20 Cont'd

Exit #	Services
81	LA 149, Grambling, S Chevron/Church's/dsl, Exxon to Grambling St U
78	LA 563, Industry, S Texaco/dsl
77	LA 507, Simsboro
69	LA 151, Arcadia, N Chevron/dsl, Mobil/Burger King/dsl La Fogata Mexican, S Exxon/dsl, Gulf/dsl, Shell/Church's/dsl El Jarrito Mexican, McDonald's, Sonic, Subway Days Inn H, $General, Brookshire Foods, Bumper Parts, Factory Stores/famous brands, Fred's, tires/repair
67	LA 9, Arcadia, N to Lake Claiborne SP, S Shell/dsl/repair
61	LA 154, Gibsland, N to Lake Claibourne SP
55	US 80, Ada, Taylor
52	LA 532, to US 80, Dubberly, N Exxon/dsl, Texaco/CJ's Diner/dsl
49	LA 531, Minden, N Loves/Arby's/dsl/scales/24hr, Murphy USA (3mi), Quick Draw TrkStp/Shell/dsl/rest./24hr, QuickDraw/Subway/dsl KFC (3mi), Pizza Hut (3mi), Taco Bell (3mi) Walmart (3mi), S truck/tire repair
47	US 371 S, LA 159 N, Minden, N Chevron/dsl, Exxon/dsl, Valero/dsl Beanie&Bubba's Grill Best Western, Exacta Inn/rest., Holiday Inn Express, Southern Inn H, Ford, S camping, to Lake Bistineau SP
44	US 371 N, Cotton Valley, N Exxon/Huddle House/dsl Crawfish Hole #2, Nicky's Cantina, Sonic Minden Motel (2mi) Cinnamon Creek RV/camping, Family$, Lakeside RV Camping
38	Goodwill Rd, S Gulf/Rainbow Diner/dsl/24hr Ammo Plant, truck/trailer repair
33	LA 157, Fillmore, S Exxon, Pilot/Arby's/dsl/scales/24hr Pizza Hut, Waffle House $General, Family$, Fred's, Lake Bistineau SP, USPO
26	I-220, Shreveport, 1 mi N RaceWay/dsl Comfort Suites, Holiday Inn, Springhill Suites Casino
23	Industrial Dr, N Exxon/dsl, Shell/Circle K, Valero/dsl McDonald's, Popeye's, Sue's Country Kitchen, Taco Bell, Wendy's Ramada Inn O'Reilly Parts, RV Repair, st police, S Mobil/dsl EconoLodge Peterbilt, Southern RV Ctr
22	Airline Dr, N Citgo/dsl, Mobil/McDonald's/dsl, Shell/Circle K, Valero/dsl Applebee's, Arby's, Burger King, Chili's, China Flag, DQ, Five Guys, Gatti's Pizza, IHOP, Johnny's Pizza, Logan's Roadhouse, Notini's Italian, Popeye's, Red Lobster, Shogun Steaks, Sonic, Starbucks, Subway, Taco Bell, TX Street Steaks, Waffle House Country Hearth Inn, Crossland Suites, Rodeway Inn, Super 8 H, Albertsons, BigLots, Books-A-Million, CVS Drug, Dillard's, Firestone/auto, JC Penney, Meineke, Michael's, Office Depot, PepBoys, Tuesday Morning, Verizon, Walgreens, S Exxon/dsl, Gulf/dsl Beard's Catfish/seafood, Capt John's, Church's, Griff's Burgers, Outback Steaks Microtel, Quality Inn, Red Carpet Inn AutoZone, Fred's, Super1 Foods, to Barksdale AFB
21	LA 72, to US 71 S, Old Minden Rd, N Shell/Circle K/dsl, Valero DAQ's Grill, Denny's, Johnny's Pizza, McDonald's, Pancho's Mexican, Podnah's BBQ, Posado's Mexican, Ralph&Kacoo's, Subway, TX Roadhouse, Whataburger Best Value Inn, Hampton Inn, Hilton Garden, Homewood Suites, La Quinta, MainStay Suites, TownePlace Suites $General, Bayou RV Ctr, O'Reilly Parts, USPO, VW, S RaceWay Waffle House, Wendy's Days Inn, Motel 6, Woodspring Suites

SHREVEPORT

GREENWOOD

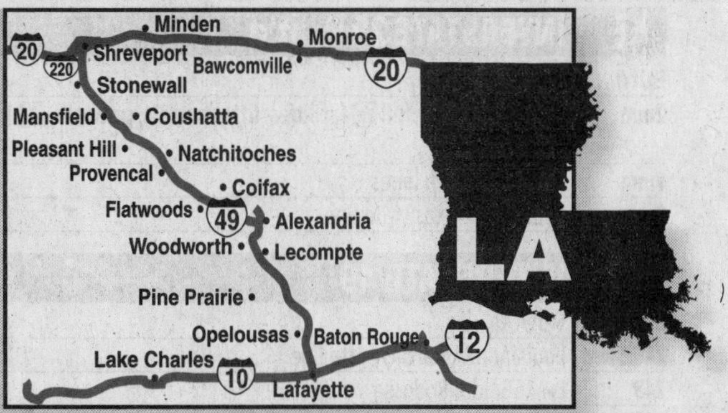

Exit #	Services
20c	to US 71 S, to Barksdale Blvd
20b	LA 3, Benton Rd, same as 21
20a	Hamilton Rd, Isle of Capri Blvd, N Circle K Quality Inn, Wingate Inn, S Exxon Bossier Inn, Travelodge casino
19b	Traffic St, Shreveport, N Courtyard Bass Pro Shop, casino, Chevrolet, S casino, downtown
19a	US 71 N, LA 1 N, Spring St, Shreveport, N Chateau Suites, Hilton, Shreveport Hotel
18b-d	Fairfield Ave (from wb), S H, downtown Shreveport
18a	Line Ave, Common St (from eb), S H, downtown
17b	I-49 S, to Alexandria
17a	Lakeshore Dr, Linwood Ave
16b	US 79/80, Greenwood Rd, N H, S Citgo/dsl El Chico Travelodge
16a	US 171, Hearne Ave, N Shell/dsl Subway H, vet, S Raceway/dsl KFC, Wendy's Cajun Inn
14	Jewella Ave, Shreveport, N Clark/dsl, Phillips 66/dsl, Valero Burger King, Church's, McDonald's, Popeye's, Sonic, Subway, Whataburger AutoZone, County Mkt Foods, Family$, O'Reilly Parts, Rite Aid, Super 1 Foods, Walgreens
13	Monkhouse Dr, Shreveport, N Bro's Cafe Best Western, Days Inn, Residence Inn, Super 8, Value Inn, S Citgo/dsl, Exxon/Subway/dsl, Valero/dsl Waffle House Baymont Inn, Hampton Inn, Holiday Inn Express, Merryton Inn, Moonrider Inn, Motel 6, Quality Inn, Regency Inn to
11	I-220 E, LA 3132 E, to I-49 S
10	Pines Rd, N Chevron/dsl DQ, Johnny's Pizza, Pizza Hut, Popeye's, Sam's Eatery, Subway Meineke, S Circle K, Exxon/dsl, Murphy USA/dsl, Shell/Circle K/Quiznos/dsl Burger King, CiCi's Pizza, Cracker Barrel, Domino's, Dragon Chinese, Great Wall Chinese, IHOP, KFC, McDonald's, Nicky's Mexican, Papa John's, Sonic, Taco Bell, Waffle House, Wendy's, Whataburger Comfort Suites, Courtyard, Fairfield Inn, Hilton Garden, Holiday Inn, Homewood Suites, La Quinta, Sleep Inn, Woodspring Suites $Tree, CVS Drug, Family$, GNC, Home Depot, O'Reilly Parts, Rite Aid, USPO, Verizon, Walgreens, Walmart/Subway
8	US 80, LA 526 E, N Red Roof Inn Freightliner, repair, tires, S Chevron/dsl, Citgo/dsl, Petro/Shell/Iron Skillet/dsl/scales/@ Wendy's Blue Beacon, Blue Beacon, Camper's RV Ctr/park, Tall Pines RV Park (1mi)
5	US 79 N, US 80, to Greenwood, N Outpost Travel Ctr/dsl, TA/Valero/Country Pride/Subway/dsl/scales/24hr/@ Country Inn, Mid Continent Motel RV park, S Pizza Hut $General, Southern Living RV Park
3	US 79 S, LA 169, Mooringsport, N Gator's RV Park (4mi), S FLYING J/Denny's/dsl/LP/scales/24hr, Loves/Arby's/dsl/scales/24hr Sonic SpeedCo

INTERSTATE 20 Cont'd

Exit #	Services
2mm	**Welcome Ctr eb, full facilities, litter barrels, petwalk, , , RV dump**
1mm	**weigh sta both lanes**
0mm	Louisiana/Texas state line

INTERSTATE 49

SHREVEPORT

Exit #	Services
246.5mm	Louisiana/Arkansas state line
245	LA 168, Ida, Rodessa
241	Rd 16, Mira Myrtis Rd, to Mira, **E** Exxon/pizza/dsl
237	LA 2, Plain Dealing, Hosston
234	US 71, Gilliam, Hosston
231	LA 170, Gilliam, Vivian, **W**
228	LA 530, Belcher, Oil City
223	LA 169, Mooringsport
221	LA 173, Dixie, Blanchard
215	LA 1, N Market St, **E** Family$, vet, **W** Exxon/dsl, Walmart/dsl China Wok, Johnny's Pizza, McDonald's, Popeye's, Sonic, Subway, Taco Bell, Trejo's Mexican, Wendy's, Zaxby's Verizon, Walmart
211	LA 3194, MLK JR Dr, **E** Chevron/dsl Checkers, Domino's, Pizza Hut, Sonic, Subway, Waffle House, Whataburger Brookshire's/gas, Walgreens
210b a	**I-220, I-49 begins/ends in Shreveport on I-20, exit 17.**
206	I-20, E to Monroe, W to Dallas.
205	King's Hwy, **E** Tesla EVC Cane's, McDonald's, Piccadilly, Taco Bell Dillard's, **W** Circle K/dsl Burger King, LJ Silver, Subway Sleep Inn
203	Hollywood Ave, Pierremont Rd, **W** Chevron/dsl
202	LA 511, E 70th St, **E** RaceWay/dsl, **W** Circle K SC Chicken $General, Family$
201	LA 3132, to Dallas, Texarkana
199	LA 526, Bert Kouns Loop, **E** Chevron/Arby's/dsl/24hr, Shell/Circle K Burger King, KFC, Taco Bell, Wendy's Comfort Inn Home Depot, **W** RaceWay/dsl McDonald's, Sonic, Starbucks, Subway, Waffle House Audi/Porsche, Brookshire Foods, Verizon, Walmart Mkt
196	Southern Loop
196mm	Bayou Pierre
191	LA 16, LA 3276, to Stonewall, **W** Chevrolet/Buick
186	LA 175, to Frierson, Kingston, **E** Trailerhood RV Park (3mi), **W** Relay Sta./rest./casino/dsl/scales Heart of Haynesville RV Park (7mi)
177	LA 509, to Carmel, **E** Texaco/Eagles Trkstp/casino/dsl/rest., **W** Hwy 509 RV Park (4mi)

NATCHITOCHES

Exit #	Services
172	US 84, to Grand Bayou, Mansfield, **W** Civil War Site, New Rockdale RV Park (4mi)
169	Aseff Rd
162	US 371, LA 177, to Evelyn, Pleasant Hill
155	LA 174, to Ajax, Lake End, **W** Country Livin' RV Pk, Cowboys/dsl
148	LA 485, Powhatan, Allen
142	LA 547, Posey Rd
138	LA 6, to Natchitoches, **E** French Mkt/cafe/dsl, RaceWay/dsl Cane's (5mi), IHOP, Popeye's, Wendy's Best Western, Comfort Suites, Days Inn, Fairfield Inn, Holiday Inn Express , Walmart (5mi), **W** Chevron/dsl, Exxon, Texaco/dsl Burger King, El Patio, Huddle House, McDonald's, Ribfin's, Subway EconoLodge, Hampton Inn, Quality Inn Nakatosh RV Park, to Kisatchie NF

ALEXANDRIA

Exit #	Services
132	LA 478, rd 620
127	LA 120, to Cypress, Flora, **E** Exxon/dsl to Cane Ri Plantations
119	LA 119, to Derry, Cloutierville, **E** to Cane River Plantations
113	LA 490, to Chopin, **E** Express Mart TrkStp/dsl
107	to Lena, **E** USPO
103	LA 8 W, to Flatwoods, **E** Chevron/dsl, **W** RV campi to Cotile Lake
99	LA 8, LA 1200, to Boyce, Colfaxm **6 mi W** Cotile Lake Camping
98	LA 1 (from nb), to Boyce
94	rd 23, to Rapides Sta Rd, **E** Rapides/dsl, **W** Love Arby's/dsl/scales/24hr Alexandria RV Park (2mi), I-49 RV
90	LA 498, Air Base Rd, **W** Chevron/dsl/CNG/24hr, Exxon/S way/dsl, Shell/dsl, Texaco/Eddie's BBQ/dsl Burger Ki Cracker Barrel, McDonald's Comfort Suites, Hampton La Quinta, Rodeway Inn, Super 8 Cabana RV Park
86	US 71, US 165, MacArthur Dr, **0-2 mi W** Conoco/dsl, Exx dsl, Mobil/dsl, Shell/Circle K/dsl, Texaco/dsl, Valero, Vale dsl Applebee's, Burger King, Cane's, Chick-fil-A, Churc CiCi's Pizza, Dominos, DQ, Eddie's BBQ, El Paso Mexican Reparo Mexican, Firehouse Subs, Golden Corral, Little C sar's, McDonald's, Outlaw's BBQ, Piccadilly, Popeye's, Sch zsky's, Sonic, Steamboat Bill's, Subway, Taco Bell, TX Ro house Alexandria Inn, Baymont Inn, Best Value Inn, B Western, Candlewood Suites, Comfort Inn, Guesthouse Inn, H iday Inn Express, Motel 6, Quality Inn, Red Roof Inn $G eral, $Tree, Advance Parts, AutoZone, Buick/GMC, Kia, Krog gas, NAPA, Office Depot, O'Reilly Parts, Petco, Super 1 Foo Tuesday Morning, Verizon
85b	Monroe St, Medical Ctr Dr (from nb), **E**
85a	LA 1, 10th St, MLK Dr, downtown
84	US 167 N, LA 28, LA 1, Pineville Expswy (no EZ nb return)
83	Broadway Ave, **E** Fuel+ $General, **1 mi W** M phy USA/dsl Checker's, Little Caesar's, Sonic, W dy's $Tree, AutoZone, Harley-Davidson, Walmart
81	US 71 N, LA 3250, Sugarhouse Rd, MacArthur Dr (from sb) same as 80 and 83
80	US 71 S, US 167, MacArthur Dr, Alexandria, **0-3 mi W** Ch ron/dsl, Exxon/dsl, Shell Buffalo Wild Wings, Burger Ki Capt D's, Carino's Italian, Chili's, IHOP, KFC, Logan's Ro house, McDonald's, Outback Steaks, Panda Express, Pizza H Popeye's, Sonic, Taco Bell Courtyard, Fairfield Inn, Ho 2 Suites, TownePlace Suites $General, Albertson's, B Buy, Dillard's, Family$, Ford/Lincoln, Hyundai, JC Penney, M shall's, Mazda, Michael's, Old Navy, Petsmart, Sam's Club/g U-Haul
73	LA 3265, rd 22, to Woodworth, **W** Chevron/dsl LA C Ctr, RV camping, to Indian Creek RA
66	LA 112, to Lecompte, **E** Chevron/dsl Burger Ki **W** Exxon/dsl museum (10mi)
61	US 167, to Meeker, Turkey Creek, **E** to Loyd Hall Plantat (3mi)
56	LA 181, Cheneyville
53	LA 115, to Bunkie, **E** Sammy's/Chevron/dsl/casino/2 Knights Inn
46	LA 106, to St Landry, **W** to Chicot SP
40	LA 29, to Ville Platte, **E** Pilot/PJ Fresh/Subway/d scales/24hr
35mm	**E /rec area both lanes, full facilities, litter barrels, p walk, , RV dump, vending**
27	LA 10, to Lebeau

LA

INTERSTATE 49 Cont'd

Exit #	Services
25	LA 103, to Washington, Port Barre, **W** [gas] Citgo [other] Family$
23	US 167 N, LA 744, to Ville Platte, **E** [gas] Chevron/Subway/Stuckey's/dsl/scales/casino, Valero/dsl/casino, **W** [gas] Texaco/dsl/casino [other] visitors ctr
19b a	US 190, to Opelousas, **E** [other] Evangeline Downs Racetrack, **W** [gas] Chevron/dsl, Exxon/dsl, RaceTrac/dsl, Valero [other] [H], CVS Drug, Lowe's, USPO
18	LA 31, to Cresswell Lane, **E** [gas] Murphy USA/dsl [food] Waffle House [lodging] Comfort Inn, Hampton Inn, Holiday Inn [other] $Tree, Chrysler/Dodge/Jeep, Ford/Lincoln, URGENT CARE, Verizon, Walmart/Subway, **W** [gas] Chevron/dsl, Circle K/dsl, Shell/dsl [food] Burger King, Cane's, Cresswell Lane, Domino's, Gatti's Pizza, Jimmy John's, McDonald's, Pedro's Mexican, Peking Buffet, Pizza Hut, Subway, Taco Bell, Wendy's [lodging] Days Inn, Super 8 [other] AT&T, Buick/GMC, Cashsaver, Danny's Tires, Family$, Walgreens
17	Judson Walsh Dr, **E** [gas] Valero/dsl
15	LA 3233, Harry Guilbeau Rd, **W** [lodging] Motel 6 [other] [H], Courvelle RV Ctr, Nissan, Toyota
11	LA 93, to Grand Coteau, Sunset, **E** [gas] Chevron, Exxon/Popeye's/dsl, Texaco/Huddle House/dsl/24hr [food] McDonald's [other] Primeaux RV Ctr, vet, **W** [food] Subway [other] $General, Family$, Janise's Foods
7	LA 182, **W** [other] Primeaux RV Ctr
4	LA 726, Carencro, **E** [food] Dickey's BBQ, Don's, Hardee's, La Pizzaria, Pizza Hut, Popeye's, Rotolo's Pizza, Taco Bell, Tropical Cafe [other] $Tree, AT&T, GNC, Super 1 Foods/gas, URGENT CARE, Walmart, **W** [gas] Chevron/dsl, Texaco/dsl [food] Burger King, King Wok, McDonald's [lodging] Economy Inn [other] $General, Champagne's Mkt, Family$, Fred's, USPO
2	LA 98, Gloria Switch Rd, **E** [gas] Chevron/deli/dsl [food] Chili's, IHOP, Prejean's Rest., Wendy's [other] Lowe's, **W** [gas] Shell/Circle K/Church's/dsl [food] Domino's, El Paso Mexican, Great Wall Buffet, Subway
1c	Pont Des Mouton Rd, **E** [gas] Circle K/dsl, Shell/dsl, Texaco/dsl [food] Buffalo Wild Wings, Burger King [lodging] Plantation Inn, Rodeway Inn [other] CVS, Walgreens, **W** [gas] Exxon/dsl [other] Firestone/auto, Ford
0b a	I-10, W to Lake Charles, E to Baton Rouge, **US 167 S** [gas] Circle K, Murphy USA/dsl, RaceTrac/dsl, Shell/Circle K/dsl [food] Checker's, McDonald's, Popeye's, Sonic, Subway, Taco Bell, Waffle House, Wendy's [lodging] Baymont Inn, Best Western, Express Inn, Fairfield Inn, Garden Plaza Hotel, Holiday Inn, Howard Johnson, La Quinta, Motel 6, Quality Inn, Super 8 [other] [H], $Tree, Home Depot, Super 1 Foods/gas, transmissions

I-49 begins/ends on I-10, exit 103.

INTERSTATE 55

Exit #	Services
66mm	**Louisiana/Mississippi state line**
65mm	**Welcome Ctr sb, full [handicapped] facilities, litter barrels, petwalk, [phone], [picnic], tourist info**
64mm	**weigh sta nb**
61	LA 38, Kentwood, **E** [gas] Chevron/dsl, Texaco [food] Jam Chicken, Popeye's, Sonic [other] $General, AutoZone, Family$, Fred's, IGA Foods, Super$, **W** [gas] Kangaroo/dsl, Kangaroo/dsl (2)
58.5mm	**weigh sta sb**
57	LA 440, Tangipahoa, **E** [other] to Camp Moore Confederate Site
53	LA 10, to Greensburg, Fluker, **W** [other] [H]

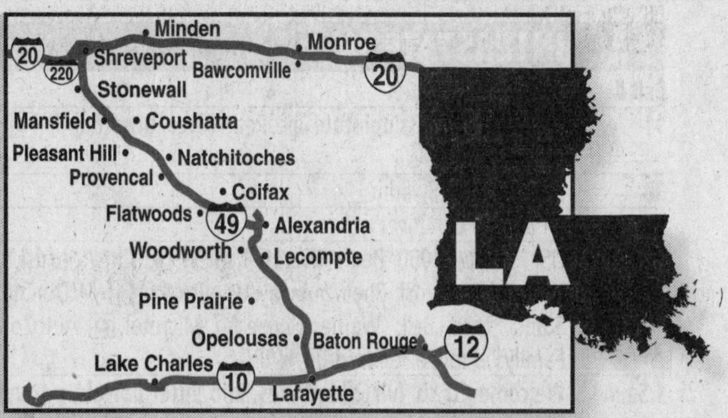

AMITE

Exit #	Services
50	LA 1048, Roseland, **E** [gas] Chevron/dsl [food] Subway (1mi)
46	LA 16, Amite, **E** [gas] Exxon/dsl, Murphy USA/dsl, RaceTrac/dsl [food] Burger King, Master Chef, McDonald's, Mike's Catfish, Panda Garden, Popeye's, Smoothie King, Sonic, Subway, Taco Bell, Waffle House, Wendy's, Yamato Japanese [lodging] Comfort Inn [other] [H], $Tree, AutoZone, Fred's, O'Reilly Parts, to Bogue Chitto SP, Verizon, Walgreens, Walmart/Subway, Winn-Dixie, **W** [lodging] Colonial Inn, Holiday Inn Express [other] Buick/Chevrolet/GMC
40	LA 40, Independence, **E** [gas] Best Stop [other] [H], **W** [other] Indian Cr Camping (2mi)
36	LA 442, Tickfaw, **E** [gas] Chevron/dsl [other] to Global Wildlife Ctr (15mi), **W** [gas] Exxon/dsl
32	LA 3234, Wardline Rd, **E** [gas] Chevron, Kangaroo/dsl, Texaco [food] Burger King, McDonald's, Popeye's, Sarita Grill, Sonic, Subway, Taco Bell, Wendy's [lodging] Lexington Inn [other] Tony's Tire
31	US 190, Hammond, **E** [gas] Chevron/dsl/scales/24hr, Exxon/dsl, Murphy USA/dsl, RaceTrac/dsl [food] Applebee's, Baskin-Robbins, Buffalo Wild Wings, Burger King, Cane's, Chili's, CiCi's Pizza, Cracker Barrel, Firehouse Subs, Hi-Ho 1 BBQ, McDonald's, Pizza Hut, Sonic, Starbucks, Taco Bell, Voodoo BBQ, Waffle House, Wendy's [lodging] Comfort Inn, Hampton Inn, Super 8, Western Inn, Woodspring Suites [other] [H], $General, $Tree, Advance Parts, AT&T, AutoZone, Chrysler/Dodge/Jeep, CVS Drug, Family$, Hobby Lobby, LeBlanc's Foods Lowe's, Lowe's, Office Depot, Ross, Sav-A-Lot Foods, Tuesday Morning, URGENT CARE, Walgreens, Walmart/Subway, Winn-Dixie
29b a	I-12, W to Baton Rouge, E to Slidell
28	US 51 N, Hammond, **E** [gas] Exxon, RaceTrac/dsl, Valero/dsl [food] Don's Seafood/Steaks, Great Wall Chinese [lodging] Best Value Inn, Red Roof Inn [other] [H], Buick/GMC, dsl repair, Mitchell RV Ctr, Toyota
26	LA 22, to Springfield, Ponchatoula, **E** [gas] Chevron/dsl, Exxon/dsl, Murphy Express/dsl, RaceTrac/dsl/e85, Shell/dsl [food] Burger King, China King, Hi-Ho BBQ, McDonald's/playplace, Papa John's, Pizza Hut, Popeye's, Smoothie King, Sonic, Subway, Taco Bell, Waffle House, Wendy's [lodging] Microtel [other] AutoZone, Bohning's Foods, CVS Drug, Family$, Ford, O'Reilly Parts, Rouse's Mkt, Walgreens, Walmart/Subway, **W** [gas] Kangaroo/Domino's/dsl [other] $General, Tickfaw SP (13mi)
23	US 51, Ponchatoula
22	frontage rd (from sb)
15	Manchac, **E** [food] Middendorf Café [other] [phone], swamp tours, USPO
7	Ruddock
1	US 51, to I-10, Baton Rouge, La Place, **S** [gas] Chevron/dsl, Circle K/dsl, Pilot/Subway/dsl/24hr/scales, Shell/Huddle House/casino/dsl [food] Burger King, McDonald's, Waffle House, Wendy's [lodging] Best Western, Days Inn, Hampton Inn, Holiday Inn Express, Quality Inn, Suburban Lodge, TownePlace Suites

HAMMOND

I-55 begins/ends on I-10, exit 209.

= gas = food = lodging = other = rest stop

INTERSTATE 59

Exit #	Services
11	Louisiana/Mississippi state line, Pearl River Turnaround, to Bogue Chitto NWR
5b	Honey Island Swamp
5a	LA 3081, Pearl River
3	US 11 S, LA 1090, Pearl River, 0-1 mi W Chevron/dsl, Interstate Fuels/dsl, Shell/Subway/dsl, Texaco McDonald's, Sonic, Taco Bell, Waffle House Microtel AutoZone, Family$, Jubilee Foods/drug, NAPA
1.5mm	**Welcome Ctr sb, full facilities, info, litter barrels, petwalk, , , RV dump**
1c b	I-10, E to Bay St Louis, W to New Orleans
1a	I-12 W, to Hammond. I-59 begins/ends on I-10/I-12.

INTERSTATE 210 (Lake Charles)

LAKE CHARLES

Exit #	Services
12	**I-210 begins/ends on I-10, exit 34.**
11	US 90, Broad St, Fruge St, E Exxon/dsl, Shell/dsl, W Best Value Inn
10	Legion St, E Shell/dsl , Luke's RV Ctr, W Kia, Nissan
8	LA 14, Gerstner Mem Dr, N Citgo/dsl Chili's, IHOP Hobby Lobby, S Murphy USA/dsl, Valero ChuckECheese, Kyoto, Logan's Roadhouse, Outback, Panda Buffet, Sonic, Taco Bell, Wendy's Quality Inn, Woodspring Suites $Tree, AT&T, Chrysler/Jeep/Dodge, GMC, Home Depot, Lowe's, Old Navy, Toyota, VW, Walmart
7b	Enterprise Blvd, LA Blvd, N Conoco/dsl, Exxon/dsl Sonic, Subway Best Western, Super 8 $General, AutoZone, O'Reilly Parts, S Shell/dsl Chevrolet/Cadillac, Ford, Honda, Hyundai
6a	LA 385, Ryan St, N Burger King, McDonald's, Popeye's, Tony's Pizza Comfort Inn Aamco, S Church's, CiCi's, Gatti's Pizza, Jason's Deli $General, Firestone/auto, Goodyear/auto, Tuesday Morning
5	Lake St, N McAlister's Deli, Wendy's Best Value Inn H, AT&T, Best Buy, Dick's, Dillard's, Kohl's, Petco, Verizon
4	LA 1138, Nelson Rd, N Buffalo Wild Wings, Jo Jo's Chinese, Mongolian Grill, O'Charley's, Olive Garden, Sonic, Subway Candlewood Suites, Courtyard, Hampton Inn, La Quinta, Residence Inn, Springhill Suites, Wingate Inn Marshall's, Ross, Sam's Club/gas, Target, S Murphy USA/dsl, Tobacco+ Chick-fil-A, Panera Bread, Starbucks, TX Roadhouse Walmart/Subway
3	Golden Nugget Blvd, Prien Lake Rd, N casino/hotel
1b a	**I-210 begins/ends on I-10, exit 25.**

INTERSTATE 220 (Shreveport)

SHREVEPORT

Exit #	Services
I-220 begins/ends on I-20, exit 26.	
17b	I-20, W to Shreveport, E to Monroe
17a	US 79, US 80, N RaceWay/dsl, Shell/Circle K Taco Bell, Waffle House Comfort Suites, Holiday Inn, SpringHill Suites Racetrack/casino, S Chevron/Huddle House/dsl Silver Star Smokehouse
15	Shed Rd
13	Swan Lake Rd
12	LA 3105, Airline Dr, N Baskin-Robbins, Chick-fil-A, Dickey's BBQ, Firehouse Subs, Izzo's Burrito, McAlister's Deli, Newk's Eatery, Olive Garden, Papa Murphy's, Santa Fe Steaks,
12	Continued Starbucks, Subway, TaMolly's H, AT&T, Belk, Best B GNC, Old Navy, Petsmart, Ross, Sam's Club/gas, Target, V izon, Walgreens, S Exxon/dsl, Murphy USA/dsl, Vale dsl Applebee's, Burger King, Cane's, Capt D's, China F McDonald's, Nicky's Rest., Panda Express, Ruby Tuesday, an's, Smashburger, Sonic, Taco Bell, Trejo's Mexican, Wen Hampton Inn $Tree, Gateway Tire, Hobby Lobby, Ho Depot, Kroger/dsl, Lowe's, vet, Walmart
11	LA 3, Bossier City, N RaceWay/dsl H, Buick/G Ford, Harley-Davidson, Lexus, RV Park, Subaru, Suzuki, Toyo S Valero/dsl Chrysler/Dodge/Jeep, Nissan
7b a	US 71, LA 1, Shreveport, N Chevron/dsl, Exxon/dsl Che ers, Domino's, Johnny's Pizza, Papa John's, Pizza Hut, Sonic, S way, Waffle House, Whataburger/24hr Brookshire Foo gas, Family$, Walgreens, S RaceWay/dsl, Shell Bur King, Carl's Jr, Church's, KFC, McDonald's, Podnah's BBQ, P eye's, Taco Bell, Wendy's Royal Inn Advance Parts, toZone, CVS Drug, Family$, O'Reilly Parts, repair/transmissic Shoppers Foods, U-Haul
6	I-49 N
5	LA 173, Blanchard Rd, N Citgo/dsl
2	Lakeshore Dr
1a	Jefferson Paige Rd, S Days Inn, Hampton Inn, Merryton I Ramada Inn, Residence Inn, Super 8, Value Inn
1b c	I-20, E to Shreveport, W to Dallas. **I-220 begins/ends on I- exit 11.**

INTERSTATE 610 (New Orleans)

Exit #	Services
I-610 begins/ends on I-10.	
4	Franklin Ave (from eb)
3	Elysian fields, S B Express, Shell Burger King, McDonald's, Waffle House H, Lowe's
2b	US 90, N Broad St, New Orleans St (from wb)
2c	Paris Ave (from wb, no return), S Jimmy's, Shell/2 Popeye's
2a	St Bernard Ave (from eb), to LSU School of Dentistry, S a racetrack
1a	Canal Blvd
1b	I-10, to New Orleans
I-610 begins/ends on I-10.	

NOTES

MAINE

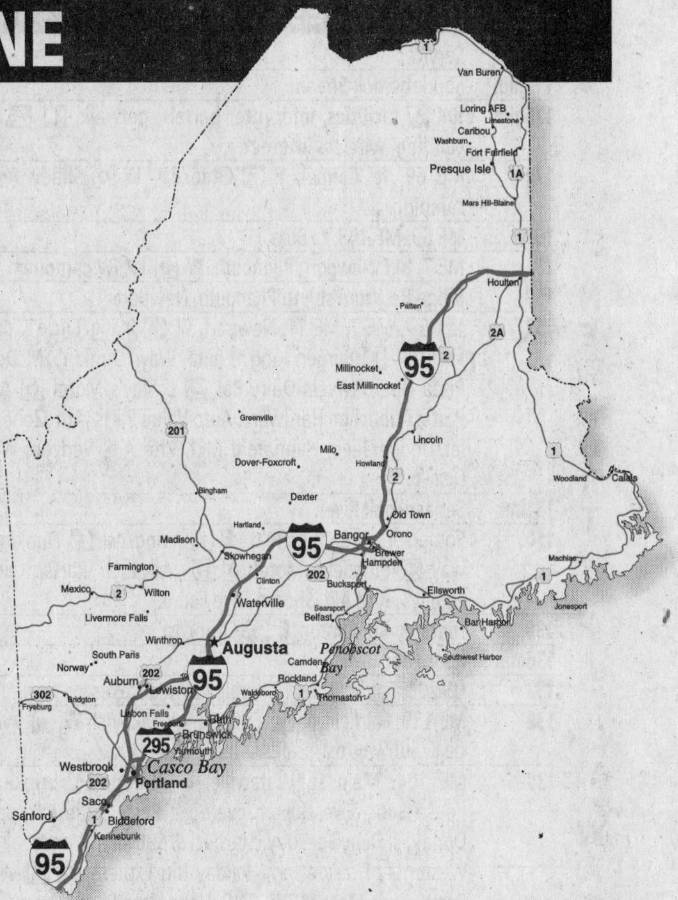

INTERSTATE 95

Exit #	Services
305mm	US/Canada border, Maine state line, US Customs. **I-95 begins/ends.**
305	US 2, to Houlton, **E** [other] DFA Duty Free Shop, Houlton Airport
303mm	Meduxnekeag River
302	US 1, Houlton, **E** [gas] Irving/Circle K/dsl/24hr [food] Burger King, Domino's, McDonald's, Pizza Hut, Tang's Chinese [other] [H], IGA Foods, Mardens, O'Reilly Parts/VIP Service, Rite Aid, **W** [RS] **both lanes, full [handicap] facilities, litter barrels, petwalk, [phone], [picnic]** [gas] Citgo/Subway/dsl, Irving/Circle K/dsl/scales/@, Shell/Dunkin'/dsl [food] Tim Hortons/Coldstone [lodging] Ivey's Motel, Shiretown Motel [other] Arrowstook SP, Family$, Ford, Hannaford Mkt, Toyota, Walmart
301mm	B Stream
291	US 2, to Smyrna, **E** [lodging] Brookside Motel/rest.
286	Oakfield Rd, to ME 11, Eagle Lake, Ashland, **W** [gas] Irving/Circle K/dsl, Sunoco/dsl [food] A Place To Eat [other] USPO
277mm	Mattawamkeag River, W Branch
276	ME 159, Island Falls, **E** [gas] Islands Falls Onestop, Porter's/rest. [other] Bishop's Mkt, USPO, **W** [other] to Baxter SP (N entrance)
264	to ME 11, Sherman, **E** [gas] Shell/dsl/LP/rest., **W** [gas] Irving/Circle K/dsl [lodging] Katahdin Valley Motel [other] to Baxter SP (N entrance)
259	Benedicta (from nb, no re-entry)
252mm	scenic view Mt Katahdin, nb
247mm	Salmon Stream
244	ME 157, to Medway, E Millinocket, **W** [gas] Irving/Circle K/dsl [lodging] Gateway Inn [other] [H], city park, Katahdin Shadows Camping, to Baxter SP (S entrance), USPO
244mm	Penobscot River
243mm	**full [handicap] facilities, litter barrels, petwalk, [phone], [picnic], [RS] both lanes**
227	to US 2, ME 6, Lincoln, **4 mi E** [other] [H], RV camping, food, gas, lodging
219mm	Piscataquis River
217	ME 6, Howland, **E** [gas] Irving/95 Diner/dsl [other] camping, Citgo/95er Towing/repair, LP
201mm	Birch Stream
199	ME 16 (no nb re-entry), to LaGrange
197	ME 43, to Old Town, **E** gas/dsl
196mm	Pushaw Stream, Pushaw Stream
193	Stillwater Ave, to Old Town, **E** [gas] Citgo/dsl, Gulf/dsl, Irving/Circle K/dsl [food] Burger King, China Garden, Dunkin', Governor's Rest., McDonald's, Wendy's [lodging] Black Bear Inn [other] $Tree, IGA Foods, O'Reilly Parts/VIP Service
191	Kelly Rd, to Orono, **2-3 mi E** camping, food, gas, lodging
187	Hogan Rd, Bangor Mall Blvd, to Bangor, **E** [gas] Citgo [food] Denny's [lodging] Courtyard, Hampton Inn, Hilton Garden, TownePlace Suites [other] Audi/VW, Buick/GMC, Cadillac/Chevrolet, Chrysler/Dodge/Jeep, Firestone/auto, Ford, Honda, Hyundai, Mazda, Mercedes, Nissan, Sam's Club/gas, Subaru, Volvo, **W** [gas] Citgo/dsl, Irving/Circle K/dsl [food] Applebee's, Buffalo Wild Wings, Burger King, Chicago Grill, Chick-fil-A, Chili's, Chipotle, Dunkin', Elevation Burger, Five Guys, Green Tea Japanese, Happy China, KFC, Kobe Japanese, Las Palapas, Longhorn Steaks, McDonald's, Miguel's Mexican, Olive Garden, Papa Johns, Pizza Hut, Starbucks, Subway, TX Roadhouse, Wendy's [lodging] Bangor Motel, Comfort Inn, Country Inn, Quality Inn [other] $Tree, AT&T, AutoZone,
187	Continued Best Buy, BJ's/gas, BooksAMillion, Dick's, Hannaford Foods, Hobby Lobby, Home Depot, JC Penney, Jo-Ann Fabrics, Kia, Kohl's, LL Bean, Lowe's, Old Navy, O'Reilly Parts/VIP Service, PetCo, Petsmart, Staples, Sullivan Tire/auto, Target, Town Fair Tire, URGENT CARE, Verizon, Walmart
186	Stillwater Ave, same as 187
185	ME 15, to Broadway, Bangor, **E** [gas] Irving/Circle K/dsl [food] Tri-City Pizza [other] [H], **W** [gas] Citgo [food] Amato's, China Light, Coldstone/Tim Hortons, Governor's Rest., KFC, McDonald's, Moe's BBQ, Pizza Hut, Subway, Taco Bell [other] Advance Parts, Hannaford Foods, TJ Maxx, Walgreens
184	ME 222, Union St, to Ohio St, Bangor, **E** [gas] Citgo, Irving [other] Walgreens, **W** [gas] Citgo, Shell/dsl [food] Burger King, Dunkin', McDonald's, Nicky's Rest., Wendy's [lodging] Sheraton [other] $Tree, auto repair, Hannaford Foods, Marshall's, Midas, to [airport]
183	US 2, ME 2, Hammond St, Bangor, **E** [gas] Citgo, Shell [food] Angelo's Pizza, Papa Gambino's Pizza [other] Corner Store, Fairmont Hardware, Fairmont Mkt, NAPA, **W** [other] [airport]
182b	US 2, ME 100 W, **W** [gas] Irving/Circle/Subway/dsl, Shell/dsl [food] Dunkin', Ground Round, Tim Hortons [lodging] Fairfield Inn, Holiday Inn, Howard Johnson, Motel 6, Quality Inn, Ramada Inn, Rodeway Inn, Super 8, Travelodge [other] O'Reilly Parts/VIP Service, Pumpkin Patch RV Resort, Tire Whse
182a	I-395, to US 2, US 1A, Bangor, downtown
180	Cold Brook Rd, to Hampden, **E** [gas] Citgo [food] Angler's Rest. (1mi), **W** [gas] Citgo/dsl/24hr/@, Dysarts Fleet Fuel/dsl [lodging] Best Western [other] dsl repair, Mack, Volvo
178mm	[RS] **sb, full [handicap] facilities, info, litter barrels, petwalk, [phone], [picnic], vending, wireless internet**

INTERSTATE 95 Cont'd

NEWPORT

Exit #	Services
177mm	Soudabscook Stream
176mm	**full facilities, info, litter barrels, petwalk, nb, vending, wireless internet**
174	ME 69, to Carmel, **E** Citgo/dsl, **W** Shady Acres RV camping
167	ME 69, ME 143, to Etna
161	ME 7, to E Newport, Plymouth, **W** LP, RV camping
159	Ridge Rd (from sb), to Plymouth, Newport
157	to US 2, ME 7, ME 11, Newport, **W** Irving/Circle K/dsl/24hr, Shell/dsl Burger King, China Way, Dunkin', McDonald's, Pizza Hut, Sawyers Dairy Bar Lovley's Motel Advance Parts, Aubuchon Hardware, Auto Value Parts, AutoZone, Chrysler/Dodge/Jeep, Hannaford Mkt, Rite Aid, Verizon, Walmart/Deli
151mm	Sebasticook River
150	Somerset Ave, Pittsfield, **E** Irving/dsl Dunkin', Subway Pittsfield Motel H, Advance Parts, Chevrolet, Family$, Rite Aid, Shop'n Save Foods
138	Hinckley Rd, Clinton, **E** Citgo/dsl
134mm	Kennebec River
133	US 201, Fairfield, **E** Purple Cow Pancakes
132	ME 139, Fairfield, **E** EVC, Gene's Mkt/dsl, **W** Irving/Circle K/Subway/dsl/scales/24hr

WATERVILLE

Exit #	Services
130	ME 104, Main St, Waterville, **E** Citgo Dunkin', Firehouse Subs, Five Guys, Governor's Rest., Little Caesar's, McDonald's, Ruby Tuesday, Starbucks, Subway, Wendy's Best Western+, Fireside Inn, Holiday Inn Express H, Advance Parts, Audi/Mazda/VW, GNC, Hannaford Foods, Home Depot, JC Penney, O'Reilly Parts/VIP Service, Staples, Verizon, Walmart
129mm	Messalonskee Stream
127	ME 11, ME 137, Waterville, Oakland, **E** EVC, Irving/dsl/24hr, Xpress/dsl Applebee's, Burger King, DQ, Dunkin', KFC/Taco Bell, McDonald's, Pad Thai, Pizza Hut, Subway, Supreme Buffet Budget Host, Hampton Inn H, AutoZone, Buick/Chevrolet, Chrysler/Dodge/Jeep/Fiat, CVS Drug, Hannaford Foods, Jo-Ann Fabrics, Marden's, Shaw's Foods/Osco Drug, Tire Whse, TJ Maxx, Toyota, Verizon, **W** Shell/dsl Aubuchon Hardware, Ford/Lincoln, NAPA
120	Lyons Rd, Sidney
117mm	**weigh sta both lanes**

AUGUSTA

Exit #	Services
113	ME 3, Augusta, Belfast, **W** H
112	ME 27, ME 8, ME 11, Augusta, **E** Citgo, Tesla EVC Chipotle, Denny's, DQ, Dunkin', Elevation Burger, IHOP, Longhorn Steaks, Olive Garden, Panera Bread, Red Robin, Ruby Tuesday, Sam's Italian, Subway Best Western+ Barnes&Noble, Dick's, GNC, Home Depot, Kohl's, Michaels, Old Navy, Sam's Club, TJ Maxx, TownFair Tire, Verizon, Walmart, **W** Irving/Circle K/dsl/24hr 99 Rest., Great Wall Chinese, KFC/Taco Bell, Wendy's Comfort Inn, Fairfield Inn Advance Parts
109	US 202, ME 11, ME 17, ME 100, Augusta, **E** Citgo/dsl, Irving/Circle K/dsl Amato's Rest., Amazing Garden, Applebee's, Arby's, Burger King, Damon's Italian, Domino's, Five Guys, Little Caesar's, McDonald's, Pizza Hut, Starbucks, Subway, Wendy's Senator Inn $Tree, Best Buy, BigLots, Lowe's, O'Reilly Parts/VIP Service, Petsmart, Shaw's Foods/Osco Drug, Staples, Target, U-Haul, USPO, vet, Walgreens, **W** Kenoco Margarita's Mexican, TX Roadhouse Days Inn, Hampton Inn, Homewood Suites, Quality Inn, Super 8 CarQuest, Chrysler/Dodge, Hannaford Foods, Honda, Hyundai, Jeep, Kia, Nissan, PetCo, Subaru, Toyota
103	to I-295 S (from sb), ME 9, ME 126, to Gardiner, service za, Citgo Burger King, Popeye's, Starbucks Z
102	to I-295 S (from nb), rd 9, rd 106, **service plaza E** go Burger King, Popeye's, Starbucks ZMkt
100mm	**toll plaza**
99mm	Cobbosseecontee Stream

LEWISTON

Exit #	Services
86	to ME 9, Sabattus
84mm	Sabattus Creek
80	ME 196, Lewiston, **W on ME 196** Coast Fuels, Gendr dsl, Shell/dsl, XPress/dsl Burger King, Canton Wok, D gelo, Domino's, Dunkin', Governor's Rest., KFC/Taco Bell, Donald's, Papa John's, Sam's Italian, Subway Adv Parts, Motel 6, Ramada Inn, Super 8 H, $Tree, NAPA, ples, USPO
78mm	Androscoggin River
75	US 202, rd 4, rd 100, to Auburn, **E** Irving/Circle K/dsl, bil/Subway/dsl Dunkin', Peking Chinese Fireside **W** H
71mm	Royal River
66mm	**toll plaza**
63	US 202, rd 115, rd 4, to ME 26, Gray, **E** Citgo, Cumbe Farms/dsl, Mobil, Sunoco China Gray, Dunkin', Goody' za, McDonald's, Subway $General, $Tree, Ace Hardw NAPA, Shop'n Save Mkt
59mm	**service plaza both lanes,** Citgo/dsl Burger King
55mm	Piscataqua River

PORTLAND

Exit #	Services
53	to ME 26, ME100 W, N Portland, **E** Irving/Circle K/Sub dsl Dunkin', Maddens Grill H, Hannaford Foods
52	to I-295, US 1, Freeport
48	ME 25, to Portland, **E** Applebee's, Asian Bistro, P Garden, Subway Portland Inn $Tree, BigLots, Whse/gas, Chevrolet, CVS Drug, Fiat, Jo-Ann Fabrics, Lo Sullivan Tire, vet, **W** Irving/Circle K/dsl, Mobil Am Rest., Burger King, Chipotle, Dunkin', Egg&I Cafe, KFC/ Bell, McDonald's, Panera Bread, Pizza Hut, Ruby Tuesday, dy's Fireside Inn, Motel 6, Ramada, Super 8 Adv Parts, AT&T, Chrysler/Dodge/Jeep, Ford, Harley-Davic Home Depot, Hyundai, Kohl's, Lexus/Toyota, Lincoln, M NAPA, O'Reilly Parts/VIP Service, Shaw's Foods/Osco Drug, livan Tire, Tire Whse, vet
47	to ME 25, Rand Rd
47mm	Stroudwater River
46	to ME 22, Congress St, same as 45
45	to US 1, Maine Mall Rd, S Portland, **E** Citgo/dsl, Sun dsl, Tesla EVC Burger King, Chili's, Chipotle Mexican, C er Barrel, Dunkin', Five Guys, Food Court, Friendly's, Great Chinese, Heidi's Brooklyn Deli, HomeTown Buffet, IHOP, I rial China, Kobe Steakhouse, Longhorn Steaks, Macaroni McDonald's, Olive Garden, On the Border, Panda Express, P ra Bread, Popeye's, Qdoba, Sebago Brewing Rest., Starb Tuscan Table, UNO Pizzaria, Villa Italian, Wendy's Cor Inn, Courtyard, Days Inn, DoubleTree, EconoLodge, Fair Inn, Hampton Inn, Home 2 Suites, Homewood Suites, Tru ton $Tree, Best Buy, BooksAMillion, Carmax, Dick's, naford Foods, Honda, JC Penney, Macy's, Michael's, Nis Old Navy, PetCo, Staples, TJ Maxx, TownFair Tire, Veri **W** Applebee's, Starbucks Holiday Inn Express, S aton Target
44	I-295 N (from nb), to S Portland, Scarborough, **1 mi E on** 114 Cumberland Chia Sen Chinese, KFC/Taco Bell, Le Kitchen, Little Caesar's, Red Robin, Subway, TX Roadhous Candlewood Suites, Extended Stay America, Homev

ME

INTERSTATE 95 Cont'd

44	Continued Suites, Residence Inn AT&T, Lowe's, Marshall's, NAPA, O'Reilly/VIP Parts/service, Sam's Club/gas, Shaw's Foods/Osco Drug, Walmart/Dunkin'
42mm	Nonesuch River
42	to US 1, **E** Famous Dave's, Portland Pie Cabela's, Scarborough Downs Racetrack (seasonal)
36	I-195 E, to Saco, Old Orchard Beach, **E** Hampton Inn KOA, Paradise Park Resort RV
35mm	**E** Ramada Inn/Saco Hotel Conference Ctr
33mm	Saco River
32	ME 111, to Biddeford, **E** Irving/Circle K/Subway/dsl Amato's Sandwiches, Dunkin', Wendy's Best Value Inn, Holiday Inn Express AAA, AutoZone, O'Reilly/VIP Parts/Service, Walmart, **W** Cumberland/dsl Applebee's, Casa Fiesta Mexican, Kobe Japanese, Longhorn Steaks, Panera Bread GNC, Home Depot, Kohl's, MarketBasket Foods, Michael's, Petsmart, Staples, Target, TJ Maxx, TownFair Tire, Verizon
25mm	Kennebunk River
25	ME 35, Kennebunk Beach, **service plaza both lanes E** car repair, vet, **W** Shell Hampton Inn, Kennebunk Lodge, Citgo/dsl, Tesla EVC (nb&sb) Burger King (sb), Popeye's (nb), Starbucks (nb&sb) Zmkt
24mm	Mousam River
19.5mm	Merriland River
19	ME 9, ME 109, to Wells, Sanford, **W** to Sanford RA
7mm	Maine Tpk begins/ends, **toll booth**
7	ME 91, to US 1, The Yorks, **(last exit before toll rd nb)**, **E** Irving/Circle K/dsl, Mobil/dsl, Shell Bamboo Garden, Norma's Rest., Ruby's Grill, Wild Willy's Burgers, York 54 Pizza Best Western, Microtel Ford, Hannaford Foods, Rite Aid, vet
5.5mm	**weigh sta nb**
5mm	York River
4mm	**weigh sta sb**
3mm	**Welcome Ctr nb, full facilities, info, litter barrels, petwalk, vending, wireless**
2	(2 & 3 from nb), US 1, to Kittery, **E on US 1** 7-11/dsl, Irving/Circle K/dsl/scales Burger King, DQ, McDonald's, Robert's Maine Grill, Starbucks, Subway, Sunrise Grill, Tasty Thai, Weathervane Seafood Rest. Days Inn, Hampton Inn, Kittery Inn, Northeaster Hotel, Ramada Inn Outlets/Famous Brands, vet
1	ME 103 (from nb, no re-entry), to Kittery
0mm	Maine/New Hampshire state line, Piscataqua River

INTERSTATE 295

Exit #	Services
52mm	**I-295 begins/ends on I-95 exit 103.**
51	ME 9, ME 126, to Gardiner, Litchfield, **toll plaza, W service plaza,** Citgo Burger King, Popeye's, Starbucks ZMkt
49	US 201, to Gardiner
43	ME 197, to Richmond, **E** Irving/dsl Dunkin', Subway, **W** KOA (5mi)
37	ME 125, Bowdoinham, **W** USPO
31b a	ME 196, to Lisbon, Topsham, **E** EVC, Gibbs/dsl, Irving/Circle K/Dunkin'/Subway 99 Rest., Arby's, Fairground Cafe, Firehouse Subs, Little Caesars, McDonald's, Panera Bread, Romeo's Pizza, Ruby Tuesday, Starbucks, Wendy's $Tree,
31b a	Continued AT&T, Best Buy, Dick's, Hannaford Foods, Home Depot, Jo-Ann Fabrics, Meineke, Nissan, O'Reilly Parts/VIP Service, PetCo, Rite Aid, Target, Tire Whse, Town Fair Tire, Toyota, Verizon, **W** ΔXpress Stop/dslΔ
30mm	Androscoggin River
28	US 1, Bath, **1 mi E on US 1** Cumberland/dsl, Irving/dsl, Shell Amato's, Dunkin', McDonald's, Pancho Villa, Subway Best Value Inn, Comfort Inn, Fairfield Inn, Relax Inn, Travelers Inn Chevrolet/Mazda, Chrysler/Dodge/Jeep
24	to Freeport (from nb), **services 1 mi E on US 1**
22	ME 125, to Pownal, **1 mi E on US 1** Irving/Circle K Azure Cafe, Jameson Rest., Linda Bean's ME Kitchen, McDonald's, Mediterranean Rest., Sam's Italian, Starbucks, Subway, Tuscan Bistro Harraseeket Inn, Hilton Garden CVS Drug, LL Bean, outlets/famous brands, USPO, **W** to Bradbury Mtn SP
20	Desert Rd, Freeport, **E** Irving/Circle K Antonia's Pizza, Buck's BBQ, Dunkin', Thai Garden Rest. Econolodge, Hampton Inn, Holiday Inn Express, Quality Suites, Super 8 Shaw's Foods
17	US 1, Yarmouth, **E both lanes, full facilities, info** Day's Takeout, Muddy Rudder Rest. Best Western Delorme Mapping, Ford, **W** Citgo/Dunkin'/dsl, Cumberland/dsl Pat's Pizza Ace Hardware, Hannaford Foods, O'Reilly Parts/VIP Service, Tire Whse
15	US 1, to Cumberland, Yarmouth, **W** Mobil, Sunoco/dsl 233 Grill, Chopstick Asian, Romeo's Pizza, Subway AT&T, Rite Aid
11	to I-95, ME Tpk (from sb)
10	US 1, to Falmouth, **E** Citgo/dsl, Irving/dsl Dunkin', Foreside Rest., Leavitt & Sons Deli, McDonald's, Orchid Thai, Ricetta's Pizza, Starbucks, Subway Falmouth Inn Ace Hardware, Audi/VW, Mazda, Rite Aid, Shaw's Foods, Staples, Sullivan Tire/auto, vet, Walmart
9mm	Presumpscot River
9	US 1 S, ME 26, to Baxter Blvd
8	ME 26 S, Washington Ave, **E** U-Haul
7	US 1A, Franklin St, **E** Miss Portland Diner AT&T, Tire Whse, Trader Joe's, Verizon, Walgreens, Whole Foods Mkt
6b a	US 1, Forest Ave, **E** Citgo Chipotle, Leavitt & Son Deli USPO, **W** Mobil/dsl Burger King, Leonardo's Pizza, Stavros Pizza CVS Drug, Hannaford Foods, U of SME, Walgreens
5b a	ME 22, Congress St, **E** Amato's Rest., D'Angelos, Denny's, Dunkin', McDonald's, Subway La Quinta Sullivan Tire, **W** Gulf, Mobil/dsl Anania's Italian Clarion
3mm	Fore River, Fore River
4	US 1 S, to Main St, to S Portland, **E** services on US 1
3	ME 9, to Westbrook St, no sb return, **W** Citgo/dsl, Irving/Circle K/dsl Buffalo Wild Wings, El Rodeo Mexican, Guerrero Maya, Olive Garden, Seadog Brew Co., Subway Chevrolet, Home Depot
2	to US 1 S, S Portland, **E** Irving/Circle K/dsl, Mobil Dunkin' Best Western, Budget Inn, Howard Johnson, Quality Inn, **services E on US 1**
1	to I-95, to US 1, **multiple services E on US 1**
	I-295 begins/ends on I-95, exit 44.

FREEPORT

PORTLAND

ME

MARYLAND

INTERSTATE 68

HANCOCK

Exit #	Services
82c	I-70 W, to Breezewood. **I-68 begins/ends on I-70, exit 1.**
82b	I-70 E, US 40 E, to Hagerstown
82a	US 522, Hancock, **S** Mobil/dsl, Sheetz/dsl Hardee's, Park'n Dine, Pizza Hut, Subway Hancock Motel, Super 8 $General, Chevrolet, Happy Hills Camping, NAPA, Save-A-Lot Foods
77	US 40, MD 144, Woodmont Rd, **S** RV camping
75mm	**runaway truck ramp eb**
74mm	**Sideling Hill /exhibit both lanes, full facilities, vending,** 1269 ft (seasonal)
74	US 40, Mountain Rd (no return from eb)
73mm	Sideling Hill Creek
72	US 40, High Germany Rd, Swain Rd, **S** Citgo/dsl Oak Barrel Cafe
68	Orleans Rd, **N** Exxon/dsl
67mm	Town Hill, elevation 940 ft, Town Hill
64	MV Smith Rd, **S** scenic overlook, elevation 1040 ft, to Green Ridge SF HQ
62	US 40, 15 Mile Creek Rd, **N** Billmeyer Wildlife Mgt Area
58.7mm	Polish Mtn, elevation 1246 ft
57mm	Town Creek
56mm	Flintstone Creek
56	MD 144, National Pike, Flintstone, **S** Billie's Gas&Grub Seven C's Lodge USPO
52	MD 144, Pleasant Valley Rd (from eb), National Pike
50	Pleasant Valley Rd, **N** Tesla EVC Lakeside Grill, Signature's Grill Rocky Gap Lodge/golf/rest. to Rocky Gap SP
47	US 220 N, MD 144, Dehaven Rd (from wb), Old National Pike, Bedford, **S** Loves/Arby's/dsl/scales/24hr Sleep Inn
46	US 220 N, Dehaven Rd, Baltimore Pike, Naves Crossroads, **N** Sheetz/dsl Cumberland Motel $General, Advance Parts, **S** Loves/Arby's/dsl/scales/24hr Puccini's Rest. Sleep Inn
45	Hillcrest Dr, **S** Sunoco/dsl
44	US 40A, Baltimore Ave, Willow Brook Rd, to Allegany Comm Coll, **N** Hampton Inn, **S** H, to Allegany Comm Coll
43d	Maryland Ave, **N** Ramada USPO, **S** Gulf/7-11/Subway Chick-fil-A, Papa John's H, AT&T, AutoZone, Martin's Foods/gas
43c	downtown, same as 43b
43mm	Youghiogheny River
43b	MD 51, Industrial Blvd, **N** McDonald's, Subway Ramada Family$, SaveALot Foods, **S** Sunoco/dsl Roy Rogers, Taco Bell, Wendy's Fairfield Inn
43a	to WV 28A, Beall St, Industrial Blvd, to Cumberland, Johnson St, **N** Sheetz
42	US 220 S, Greene St, Ridgedale
41	Seton Dr (from wb, no directory turn)
41mm	Haystack Mtn, elev 1240 ft
40	US 220 S, to US 40A, Vocke Rd, La Vale, **N** BP/dsl, Sheetz/dsl, Tesla EVC Arby's, Asian Garden, Bob Evans, Burger King, Cracker Barrel, D'Atri Rest., Denny's, DQ, KFC, LJ Silver, McDonald's, New Orient, Pizza Hut, Rio Grande Mexican, Rita's Custard, Ruby Tuesday, Subway, TX Grill, Wendy's Best Western, Comfort Inn, Holiday Inn Express, Super 8 $General, Advance Parts, AT&T, AutoZone, CVS Drug, Harley-Davidson,

FROSTBURG

Exit #	Services
40	Continued Jo-Ann Fabrics, Lowe's, Mr Tire, NAPA, st police, Staples, URG CARE, **S** Applebee's, Buffalo Wild Wings, Chick-fil-A, Wa Japanese Motel 6 $Tree, Aldi Foods, JC Penney, Ko Martin's Foods/gas, Petsmart, Walmart/McDonald's
39	US 40A (from wb), same as 40
34	MD 36, to Westernport, Frostburg, **N** Sheetz/dsl, Val dsl Burger King, Fox's Pizza, Mario's Italian, McDona Pizza Hut, Subway Hampton Inn, Quality Inn H, $G eral, Rite Aid, Save-A-Lot, Weis Mkt, **S** to Dans Mtn SP
33	Midlothian Rd, to Frostburg, **N** H, **S** to Dans Mt S
31mm	**weigh sta eb**
30mm	Big Savage Mtn, elevation 2800 ft
29	MD 546, Finzel, **N** Hen House Rest. (2mi) Mason-D Camping (4mi/seasonal), **S** Savage River Lodge/rest. (
25.8mm	eastern continental divide, elevation 2610 ft
24	Lower New Germany Rd, to US 40A, **S** to New German to Savage River SF
23mm	Meadow Mtn, elevation 2780 ft
22	US 219 N, to Meyersdale, **N** Pilot/Arby's/dsl/scales/2 Sunoco/dsl Burger King, IHOP, Little Caesar's, Penn Rest., Subway $General, Ford, Hilltop Fruit Mkt, N Rite Aid, Shop'n Save, TrueValue, **S** Valero/dsl Com Inn New Germany SP, Savage River SF
20mm	Casselman River
19	MD 495, to US 40A, Grantsville, **N** Exxon/Subway/dsl, noco/dsl Casselman Motel/rest. Medicine Shoppe, U
15mm	Mt Negro, elevation 2740 ft
14mm	Keyser's Ridge, elevation 2880 ft
14b a	US 219, US 40 W, Oakland, **N** 7-11/dsl, Liberty/Ridge/re dsl McDonald's, repair
6mm	**Welcome Ctr eb, full facilities, info, litter barrels, petw , vending**
4.5mm	Bear Creek
4	MD 42, Friendsville, **N** Exxon/dsl, Liberty/dsl Yo Valley Motel S&S Mkt, USPO, **S** Sunset Inn to D Creek Lake SP
0mm	Maryland/West Virginia state line

INTERSTATE 70

BALTIMORE

Exit #	Services
I-70 begins/ends in Baltimore at Cooks Lane.	
94	Security Blvd N, **S** Shell
91b a	I-695
87b a	US 29 (exits left from wb)to MD 99, Columbia, **2 mi S on 40** BP/dsl, Exxon/dsl, Gulf, Shell/dsl, Sunoco Ar Baskin-Robbins/Dunkin', Boston Mkt, Burger King, Check Domino's, Jimmy John's, McDonald's, Papa John's, Pizza Qdoba, Starbucks, Subway 7-11, Acura, Advance Pa Cadillac/Chevrolet, Carmax, CVS Drug, Giant Foods, Goodye auto, H Mart Foods, Home Depot, Honda, Infiniti, Kia, N Foods, Midas, Mr Tire, Nissan, Rite Aid, Safeway Foods, V zon, Walgreens, Walmart
83	US 40, Marriottsville (no EZ wb return), **2 mi S** Turf Va Hotel/Country Club/rest.
82	US 40 E (from eb), same as 83
80	MD 32, Sykesville, **N** golf, **S** High's/dsl Subv Tony's Pizzeria
79mm	**weigh/insp sta wb,**

MD

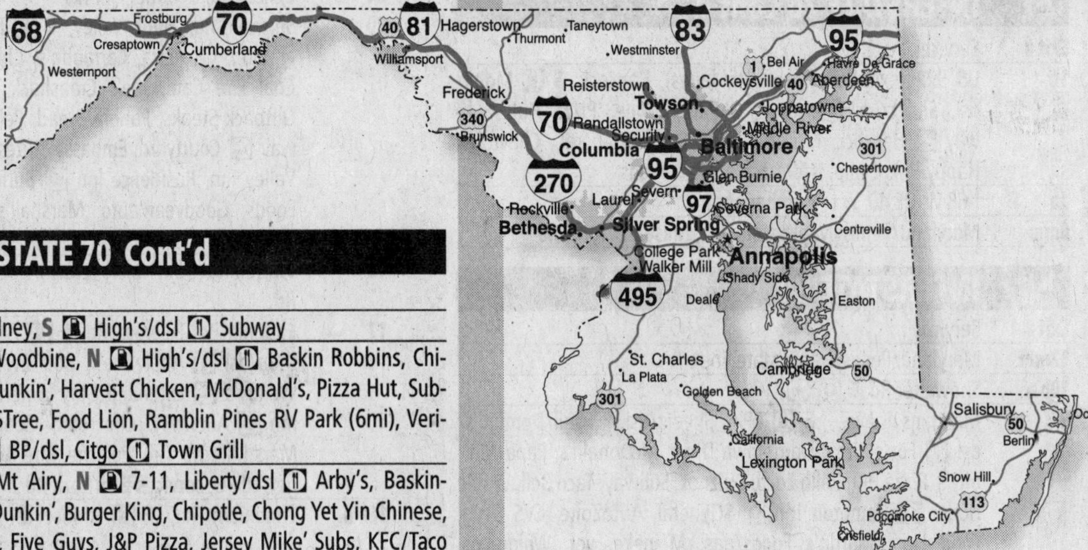

INTERSTATE 70 Cont'd

Exit #	Services
76	MD 97, Olney, S High's/dsl Subway
73	MD 94, Woodbine, N High's/dsl Baskin Robbins, China Yee, Dunkin', Harvest Chicken, McDonald's, Pizza Hut, Subway $Tree, Food Lion, Ramblin Pines RV Park (6mi), Verizon, S BP/dsl, Citgo Town Grill
68	MD 27, Mt Airy, N 7-11, Liberty/dsl Arby's, Baskin-Robbns/Dunkin', Burger King, Chipotle, Chong Yet Yin Chinese, Domino's, Five Guys, J&P Pizza, Jersey Mike' Subs, KFC/Taco Bell, Ledo's Pizza, McDonald's, Papa John's, Pizza Hut, Rita's Custard, Starbucks, Subway Ace Hardware, Advance Parts, AT&T, Food Lion, GNC, Goodyear, Mr Tire, Rite Aid, Safeway, Verizon, Walmart, S Exxon/dsl, Shell/dsl Budget Inn
66mm	**truckers parking area eb**
64mm	**weigh/insp sta eb**
62	MD 75, Libertytown, N Falcon Fuels, High's/dsl Asian Bistro, Baskin Robbins, Burger King, Domino's, Dunkin', McDonald's, Morgan's Grill CVS Drug, Food Lion, New Market Hist Dist
59	MD 144
57mm	Monocacy River
56	MD 144, N BP, Sheetz Beijing, Burger King, JR's Pizza, McDonald's, Roy Rogers, Taco Bell, Wendy's to Hist Dist, S Chesaco RV Ctr
55	South St, **1 mi N** BP, Sheetz/dsl same as 56
54	Market St, to I-270, N Costco/gas Super 8, S 7-11, Sheetz/dsl, Shell/dsl, SouStates/dsl, Valero/dsl, Wawa/dsl Applebee's, Arby's, BJ's Rest., Burger King, Checker's, Chick-fil-A, ChuckeCheese, Cracker Barrel, Golden Corral, KFC/Taco Bell, Longhorn Steaks, McDonald's, Olive Garden, Panera Bread, Papa John's, Peking Gourmet, Popeye's, Red Robin, Ruby Tuesday, Sonic, Subway, Waffle House Clarion, Country Inn Suites, Courtyard, Days Inn, EconoLodge, Extended Stay America, Fairfield Inn, Hampton Inn, Hilton Garden, Residence Inn, Sleep Inn $Tree, AAA, Aamco, Audi, Barnes&Noble, Best Buy, Buick/GMC, Chrysler/Dodge/Jeep, Dick's, Home Depot, Honda, Hyundai, JC Penney, Kia, Kohl's, Lincoln, Lowe's, Macy's, Michael's, Mr Tire, Nissan, Petsmart, Ross, Sam's Club/dsl, Staples, Target, Tires+, TJMaxx, Toyota, Volvo, Walmart
53b a	I-270 S, US 15 N, US 40 W, to Frederick
52b a	US 15 S, US 340 W, Leesburg
49	US 40A, Braddock Heights, **N on US 40** Carroll/dsl, Citgo/dsl, Exxon/dsl, GetGo, Shell/dsl, Sunoco, WaWa/dsl Arby's, Bob Evans, Boston Mkt, Burger King, Casa Rico Mexican, Chipotle, Denny's, Domino's, Dunkin', Famous Dave's BBQ, Flaming Grill, HoneyBaked Ham, KFC, Los Trios, McDonald's, Mtn View Diner, Outback Steaks, Pizza Hut, Popeye's, Red Horse Rest., Red Lobster, Roy Rogers, Starbucks, Subway, Taco Bell, Wendy's Comfort Inn, Motel 6 H, $General, $Tree, 7-11, Aldi Foods, AT&T, AutoZone, Boscov's, CVS Drug, Giant Eagle Foods, Home Depot, Meineke, Mr Tire, NTB, PepBoys, PetCo, Subaru, Verizon, Weis Foods, S camping, to Washington Mon SP,
48	US 40 E, US 340 (from eb, no return), **1 mi N** same as 49
42	MD 17, Myersville, N Exxon, Sunoco/dsl Burger King, McDonald's, Old Town Diner Greenbrier SP (4mi), to Gambrill SP (6mi), S Crown/dsl Subway
39mm	**both lanes, full facilities, litter barrels, petwalk, vending**
35	MD 66, to Boonsboro, S Sheetz/dsl (1mi) camping, to Greenbrier SP
32b a	US 40, Hagerstown, **0-3 mi N** 7-11/dsl, BP, Exxon/dsl, Sheetz/dsl, Sunoco Baskin-Robbins/Dunkin', Bob Evans, Burger King, Cancun Cantina, Checkers, Coldstone, Denny's, DQ, El Ranchero Mexican, Family Diner, Five Guys, Jimmy John's, KFC, Ledo's Pizza, Little Caesar's, McDonald's, Papa John's, Pizza Hut, Popeye's, Sonic, Subway, Supreme Buffet, Taco Bell, TX Roadhouse, Wendy's Baymont Inn, Comfort Suites, Days Inn, Garden Plaza Hotel, Hampton Inn, Quality Inn, Super 8 H, $General, $Tree, Advance Parts, Aldi Foods, AT&T, AutoZone, Cadillac/Chevrolet, Chrysler/Dodge/Jeep, CVS Drug, Family$, Martin's Foods, Mercedes, Midas, Mr Tire, Nissan, Tires+, Toyota, URGENT CARE, Walgreens, Weis Foods, S Buick/GMC, Honda, Kia, Subaru/Mazda/VW
29b a	MD 65, to Sharpsburg, N EVgo EVC, Exxon/Subway/dsl, Sheetz/dsl, Tesla EVC FoodCourt, Longhorn Steaks H, Prime Outlets/famous brands, S EVC, Liberty/7-11/dsl Burger King, Cracker Barrel, McDonald's, Waffle House, Wendy's Sleep Inn Jellystone Camping, st police, to Antietam Bfd, Walmart
28	MD 632, Hagerstown
26	I-81, N to Harrisburg, S to Martinsburg
24	MD 63, Huyett, N Pilot/Subway/dsl/24hr, Sheetz/dsl (2mi), S Red Roof Inn C&O Canal, KOA (2mi)
18	MD 68 E, Clear Spring, N BP/dsl, Liberty Al's Grill, McDonald's Holiday Inn Express, Sleep Inn, S Exxon/dsl Wendy Hill Café
12	MD 56, Indian Springs, S Exxon/dsl Ft Frederick SP
9	US 40 E (from eb, exits left), Indian Springs
5	MD 615 (no immediate wb return), N Log Cabin Rest. (2mi)
3	MD 144, Hancock (exits left from wb), S ACT/Exxon/dsl, Liberty/rest./dsl/24hr Hardee's, Park'n Dine Hilltop Inn Blue Goose Mkt

HAGERSTOWN

INTERSTATE 70 Cont'd

Exit #	Services
1b	US 522 (exits left from both lanes), Hancock, S [gas] Mobil/dsl, Sheetz/dsl [food] Hardee's, Park'n Dine, Pizza Hut, Subway [lodging] Hancock Motel, Super 8 [other] $General, Chevrolet, Happy Hills Camp, NAPA, Save-A-Lot Foods
1a	I-68 W, US 40, W to Cumberland
0mm	Maryland/Pennsylvania state line, Mason-Dixon Line

INTERSTATE 81

HAGERSTOWN

Exit #	Services
12mm	Maryland/Pennsylvania state line
10b a	Showalter Rd, E [other] [airport]
9	Maugans Ave, E [gas] BP, Sheetz/dsl, Shell/Domino's/dsl [food] Fox's Pizza, Hometown Diner, McDonald's, Papa Murphy's, Pizza Hut, Pollo Loco, Quiznos, Subway, Taco Bell, Waffle House [lodging] Hampton Inn [other] $General, AutoZone, CVS Drug, Food Lion, Martin's Foods/gas, Meineke, vet, Walgreens, W [food] Burger King, Dunkin' [lodging] Microtel [other] Kenworth, Volvo
7b a	MD 58, Hagerstown, same as 6
6b a	US 40, Hagerstown, E [gas] Shell [other] [H], W [food] Arby's, Chipotle Mexican, Five Guys, IHOP, Jersey Mike's Subs, KFC, McDonald's, Number One Chinese, Panera Bread, Ryan's, Starbucks, Subway, TGIFriday's, Uno Pizza, Wendy's [other] $Tree, AT&T, Best Buy, Dick's, GNC, Home Depot, Marshall's, Petsmart, Walmart
5b a	Halfway Blvd, E [gas] AC&T/dsl [food] Bob Evans, Boston Mkt, Boston Mkt, Buffalo Wild Wings, Burger King, Chick-fil-A, ChuckECheese's, CiCi's Pizza, Cinco de Mayo, Coldstone, El Ranchero Mexican, Fireside Rest., Golden Corral, Hard Times Cafe, Jimmy John's, McDonald's, Nikko Japanese, Noodles&Co, Olive Garden, Outback Steaks, Papa John's, Pizza Hut, Popeye's, Red Lobster, Red Robin, Roy Rogers, Ruby Tuesday, Sakura Steaks, Starbucks, Taco Bell, Tilted Kilt, Wendy's [lodging] Country Inn&Suites, Courtyard, Holiday Inn Express, Homewood Suites, Motel 6, Ramada, SpringHill Suites [other] $Tree, BigLots, BonTon, CVS Drug, Firestone/auto, Ford, Hobby Lobby, Hyundai, JC Penney, Kohl's, Lowe's, Martin's Foods/gas, Michael's, PetCo, Ross, Sam's Club/gas, Staples, Target, W [gas] Exxon/dsl/scales/24hr, Pilot/McDonald's/Subway/dsl/scales/24hr [lodging] Super 8 [other] Freightliner
4	I-70, E to Frederick, W to Hancock, to I-68
2	US 11, Williamsport, E [gas] AC&T/dsl, W [gas] Exxon/dsl, Sunoco/dsl [food] China 88, McDonald's, Subway, Waffle House [lodging] Red Roof Inn [other] auto repair, KOA (4mi)
1	MD 63, MD 68, Williamsport, E [gas] Bowman/dsl [other] Jellystone, to Antietam Bfd, W [gas] Citgo [other] $General, KOA, NAPA
0mm	Maryland/West Virginia state line, Potomac River

INTERSTATE 83

BALTIMORE

Exit #	Services
38mm	Maryland/Pennsylvania state line, Mason-Dixon Line
37	to Freeland (from sb)
36	MD 439, Bel Air, W [gas] Filler-Up [food] Maryland Line Inn Grill [other] Holiday Travel Park (5mi), Merry Meadows Camping (5mi)
35mm	**weigh/insp sta sb**
33	MD 45, Parkton, E [other] USPO
31	Middletown Rd, to Parkton, E [other] golf
27	MD 137, Mt Carmel, Hereford, E [gas] Exxon/dsl [food] Michael's Pizza, Monkton Grill, Subway [other] 7-11, Graul's Foods, Hereford Drug, Mt Carmel Drug, USPO, vet
24	Belfast Rd, to Butler, Sparks
20	Shawan Rd, Hunt Valley, E [gas] Exxon/dsl, Mobil [food] B... er King, CA Pizza, Carrabba's, Chick-fil-A, Chipotle Mexi... Coal Fire Cafe, Joe's Crabshack, McDonald's, Noodles&... Outback Steaks, Panera Bread, Pei Wei, Sakura Hibachi, S... way [lodging] Courtyard, Embassy Suites, Holiday Inn Express, H... Valley Inn, Residence Inn [other] Burlington Coats, Dick's, G... Foods, Goodyear/auto, Marshall's, Verizon, vet, Wegm... Foods
18	Warren Rd (from nb, no return), Cockeysville, **services E on Y... Rd**
17	Padonia Rd, Deereco Rd, E [gas] 7-11, BP/dsl, Gulf/dsl, M... thon/dsl [food] Applebee's, Bob Evans, Chili's, Macaroni G... Wendy's [lodging] Extended Stay America, Hampton Inn, Holi... Inn [other] Audi/VW, Chevrolet, Goodyear/auto, Lowe's W... Mars Mkt, Mr Tire, Porsche, Rite Aid, Sam's Club, Subaru, ... get, USPO, **services E on York Rd**
16b a	Timonium Rd, E [gas] Sunoco/dsl [food] Baja Fresh, Fireho... Subs, Little Caesar's, McDonald's [lodging] N Baltimore Plaza ... tel, Red Roof Inn [other] Infiniti/Nissan, Petsmart, REI, Rite ... ShopRite Foods, **services E on York Rd**
14	I-695 N
13	I-695 S, Falls Rd, E [other] [H], W [other] st police
12	Ruxton Rd (from nb, no return)
10b a	Northern Parkway, E [gas] Exxon, Shell, W [other] [H]
9b a	Cold Spring Lane
8	MD 25 N (from nb), Falls Rd
7b a	28th St, E [other] [H], W [other] Baltimore Zoo
6	US 1, US 40T, North Ave, downtown
5	MD Ave (from sb), downtown
3	Chase St, Gilford St, downtown
2	Pleasant St (from sb), downtown
1	Fayette St, downtown Baltimore, **I-83 begins/ends.**

INTERSTATE 95

Exit #	Services
110mm	Maryland/Delaware state line
109b a	MD 279, to Elkton, Newark, E [gas] CF/dsl, Flying J/G... en Corral/dsl/scales/24hr/@ [food] Cracker Barrel, KFC/Taco B... McDonald's, Waffle House [lodging] Days Inn, Elkton Lodge, Ha... ton Inn, Knights Inn, La Quinta, Motel 6 [other] [H], Blue Beac... W [gas] 7-11, TA/Country Pride/dsl/24hr/@, WaWa/dsl [lodging] H... day Inn Express [other] to U of DE
100	MD 272, to North East, Rising Sun, E [gas] Flying J/Denn... dsl/LP/24hr, Sunoco/dsl [food] Burger King, Dunkin', Frank's Pi... Little Caesar's, McDonald's, Waffle House, Wendy's [lodging] Com... Inn, Holiday Inn Express [other] $General, $Tree, Advance Pa... AT&T, auto repair, Food Lion, Lowe's, PetCo, st police, to ... Neck SP, Verizon, Walgreens, Walmart/Subway, W [gas] Hig... dsl [food] Hunan Wok, Pizza Hut [lodging] Best Western [other] zoo
96mm	**Chesapeake House service area (exits left from both lan...** [gas] Sunoco/dsl [food] Burger King, Peets Coffee, Pizza Hut, P... eye's, Wendy's
93	MD 275, to Rising Sun, US 222, to Perryville, E [gas] Exx... dsl, Pilot/Subway/dsl/scales/24hr [food] Denny's [lodging] Days ... [other] [H]
92mm	**weigh sta/toll booth**
91.5mm	Susquehanna River
89	MD 155, to Havre de Grace **(last nb exit before toll), 1-3...** E [food] Burger King, Chesapeake Grill, Dunkin', MacGreg... Rest., McDonald's, Waffle House [lodging] Super 8, Van Div... B&B [other] [H], W [other] to Susquehanna SP

MD

INTERSTATE 95 Cont'd

Exit #	Services
85	MD 22, to Aberdeen, **E** [gas] 7-11, Crown/dsl, Royal Farms/dsl, Shell/dsl [food] Applebee's, Baskin-Robbins/Dunkin', Bob Evans, Burger King, Chap's Pit Beef, Chick-fil-A, IHOP, KFC, La Tolteca Mexican, Little Caesar's, McDonald's, Olive Tree Italian, Panera Bread, Papa John's, Rita's Custard, Subway, Taco Bell, Wendy's [lodging] Comfort Inn, Days Inn, Hampton Inn, Hilton Garden, Holiday Inn Express, La Quinta, Red Roof Inn, Super 8, Travelodge [other] $General, $Tree, Firestone/auto, GNC, Home Depot, Rite Aid, ShopRite Foods, Target, Verizon, Walgreens, **W** [lodging] Courtyard, Residence Inn
81mm	**MD House service area (exits left from both lanes)** [gas] Sunoco/dsl [food] Dunkin', Jerry's, Phillips Seafood, Starbucks, Wendy's
80	MD 543, to Riverside, Churchville, **E** [gas] 7-11, BP/Burger King, Shell/dsl, Sunoco [food] Arby's, China Moon, Cracker Barrel, Lee's Asian Bistro, McDonald's, Pizza Hut, Riverside Grille, Riverside Pizzeria, Ruby Tuesday, Subway, Waffle House [lodging] Candlewood Suites, Country Inn&Suites, Extended Stay America, Homewood Suites, SpringHill Suites, Wingate Inn [other] Bar Harbor RV Park (4mi), Rite Aid, ShopRite Foods
77b a	MD 24, to Edgewood, Bel Air, **E** [gas] Exxon/dsl, Royal Farms/dsl, Sunoco/dsl [food] Denny's, My 3 Sons Rest., Subway, Waffle House [lodging] Comfort Inn, Hampton Inn, Holiday Inn Express, La Quinta, Motel 6, Ramada, Red Roof Inn, Sleep Inn [other] Old Navy, **W** [gas] Exxon/dsl, WaWa/dsl [food] Boston's, Chick-fil-A, Dickey's BBQ, KFC/Taco Bell, McDonald's, Panda Express, Panera Bread, Starbucks [other] H, $Tree, BJ's Whse, GNC, JC Penney, Lowe's, Petsmart, Target, Walmart/Subway, Wegman's Foods
74	MD 152, Fallston, Joppatowne, **E** [gas] CF/dsl, Exxon/dsl, WaWa/dsl [food] Friendly's, Subway [lodging] Super 8 [other] Toyota (1mi), **W** [gas] Royal Farms/dsl
70mm	[other] Big Gunpowder Falls
67b a	MD 43, US 1, US 40, **E** [gas] BP/dsl [food] Applebee's, Chick-fil-A, Chipotle, Five Guys, Jimmy John's, Ledo Pizza, McDonald's, Noodles&Co, Panda Express, Panera Bread, Pie Five, Qdoba, Starbucks, Subway, Zoe's Kitchen [lodging] Home 2 Suites [other] Best Buy, Carmax, Chevrolet, Dick's, Lowe's, Michael's, on White Marsh Blvd, Petco, Target, TJ Maxx, **W** [gas] 7-11, Exxon/dsl [food] All About Burger, Bertucci's, Buffalo Wild Wings, Burger King, Chili's, China Wok, Coldstone, Don Pablo, Kobe Japanese, McDonald's, Olive Garden, PF Chang's, Red Brick Sta., Red Lobster, Red Robin, Starbucks, Taco Bell, TGIFriday's, Tilted Kilt, TX Roadhouse, Wendy's [lodging] Fairfield Inn, Hampton Inn, Hilton Garden, Residence Inn, Woodspring Suites [other] AT&T, Barnes&Noble, Giant Foods, IKEA, JC Penney, Macy's, Mr Tire, Old Navy, Staples, to Gunpowder SP, USPO, Verizon
64b a	I-695 (exits left), E to Essex, W to Towson
62	to I-895 (from sb)
61	US 40, Pulaski Hwy, **E** [gas] BP, Shell/dsl [food] McDonald's
60	Moravia Rd
59	Eastern Ave, **W** [gas] BP/dsl, Exxon, Royal Farms/dsl, WaWa [food] Broadway Diner, McDonald's, Subway, Wendy's [other] H, Home Depot, Shoppers Foods
58	Dundalk Ave, (from nb), **E** [gas] Citgo
57	O'Donnell St, Boston St, **E** [gas] TA/Buckhorn/Country Pride/Subway/dsl/scales/motel/@ [food] McDonald's [lodging] Best Western
56	Keith Ave
56mm	McHenry Tunnel, **toll plaza** (north side of tunnel)
55	Key Hwy, to Ft McHenry NM, last nb exit before **toll**
54	MD 2 S, to Hanover St, **W** [other] H, Harris Teeter, downtown

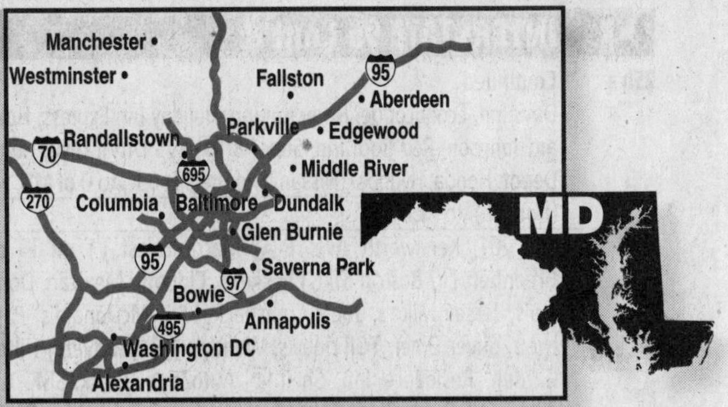

COLUMBIA

Exit #	Services
53	I-395 N, to MLK, **W** [other] Oriole Park, downtown
52	Russell St N, **W** [other] H
51	Washington Blvd
50.5mm	**inspection sta nb**
50	Caton Ave, **E** [gas] Marathon/dsl, Shell/dsl, US/dsl [food] Caton House, Loafers Grill, McDonald's [lodging] Motel 6 [other] 7-11, Aldi Foods, auto repair, Midas, Toyota, **W** [other] H
49b a	I-695, E to Key Bridge, Glen Burnie, W to Towson, to I-70, to I-83
47b a	I-195, to MD 166, to BWI Airport, to Baltimore
46	I-895, to Harbor Tunnel Thruway
43b a	MD 100, to Glen Burnie, **1 mi E on US 1** [gas] Exxon/Wendy's/dsl, Xtra [lodging] Best Western
41b a	MD 175, to Columbia, **E** [gas] BP/dsl, Exxon/dsl, Shell/dsl, TA/Country Pride/Subway/dsl/scales/24hr/@ [food] Arby's, Burger King, Frank's Diner, IHOP, McDonald's, Panda Express, Starbucks [lodging] Comfort Suites, Holiday Inn, La Quinta, Red Roof Inn, Sleep Inn, Super 8 [other] $Tree, Advance Parts, Mom's Organic Mkt, **W** [gas] Exxon [food] Bob Evans, Fat Burger, Houlihan's, Jersey Mike's, McDonald's, Mimi's Cafe, Olive Garden, On the Border, TGIFriday's [lodging] Extended Stay America, Homewood Suites [other] H, Best Buy, Costco/gas, CVS Drug, Lowe's, Loyola U, Office Depot, Royal Farms, to Johns Hopkins U, Trader Joe's
38b a	MD 32, to Ft Meade, **2 mi E on US 1** [gas] BP/dsl, Exxon/Wendy's/dsl, Royal Farms, Shell/dsl [food] Burger King, Dunkin', McDonald's, Subway, Taco Bell [lodging] Comfort Inn, Extended Stay America [other] H, to BWI Airport
37mm	**Welcome Ctr both lanes, full [handicapped] facilities, info, litter barrels, petwalk, [phone], [picnic], RV Dump, vending**
35b a	MD 216, to Laurel, **E** [gas] Exxon, Shell/dsl [food] McDonald's, Subway [other] Weis Food/drug
34mm	Patuxent River
33b a	MD 198, to Laurel, **E** [gas] Exxon [other] H, **W** [gas] Exxon/Blimpie/dsl, Shell [food] Outback Steaks [lodging] Holiday Inn
31	MD 200 (toll), to I-270
29	MD 212, to Beltsville, **E** [other] Cherry Hill RV Resort, **W** [gas] Exxon/Blimpie/dsl [food] Baskin-Robbins, Danny's Subs, KFC, McDonald's, Taco Bell, The Villa Rest., TJ's Rest., Wendy's [lodging] Comfort Inn, Sheraton [other] CVS Drug, Giant Foods
27	I-495 S around Washington
25b a	US 1, Baltimore Ave, to Laurel, College Park, **E** [gas] 7-11, BP/dsl, Exxon/dsl, Shell, Sunoco, Wawa/dsl [food] Arby's, Buffalo Wild Wings, Burger King, Chipotle, Domino's, Dunkin', McDonald's, Moose Creek Steaks, Panera Bread, Papa John's, Pizza Hut/Taco Bell, Potbelly's, Starbucks, Subway, Wendy's [lodging] Holiday Inn [other] Advance Parts, Aldi Foods, AutoZone, Cherry Hill RV Resort, Costco/gas, CVS Drug, IKEA, PetCo, Rite Aid, URGENT CARE, US Agri Library, Verizon, **W** [gas] BP/24hr, Exxon, Shell, Xtra [food] Azteca, Burger King, College Park Diner, Denny's, Dunkin', Hard Times Cafe, IHOP, Mamma Lucia, McDonald's, Pizza Hut, Sakura Seafood Buffet, Starbucks, Taco Bell [lodging] Clarion,

= gas = food = lodging = other = rest stop

INTERSTATE 95 Cont'd

WASHINGTON DC AREA

25b a Continued
Days Inn, EconoLodge, Hampton Inn, Holiday Inn Express, Howard Johnson, Red Roof Inn, Super 8 CVS Drug, GNC, Home Depot, Honda, Hyundai, Nissan, Shoppers Foods, to U of MD, vet

24 (from sb), to metro

23 MD 201, Kenilworth Ave, **E** Marriott/rest., **1 mi W on Greenbelt** Boston Mkt, Checker's, Chipotle Mexican, Domino's, Jersey Mike's, Joe's Crabshack, KFC, McDonald's, Popeye's, Silver Diner, TGIFriday's, Wendy's Courtyard, Hilton Garden, Residence Inn, Shell AutoZone, Buick/GMC/Cadillac, CVS Drug, Giant Food/drug, Jo-Ann Fabrics, Marshall's, Staples, Target, URGENT CARE

22 Baltimore-Washington Pkwy, **E** to NASA

20b a MD 450, Annapolis Rd, Lanham, **E** Burger King, McDonald's, Red Lobster Best Western, Days Inn/rest., Red Roof Inn Ford/KIA, NTB, **W** 7-11/dsl, BP, Citgo, Shell Bojangles, Chipotle, Dunkin', El Gran Chaparral, Jersey Mike's, KFC, King Pollo, Papa John's, Popeye's, Starbucks, Subway, Wendy's Metro Points Hotel H, Advance Parts, Chrysler/Dodge/Jeep, CVS Drug, Family$, Foodway Foods, JustTires, Lowe's, Meineke, SaveALot, Shoppers Foods, Staples

19b a US 50, to Annapolis, Washington

17 MD 202, Landover Rd, to Upper Marlboro, **E** Chipotle, Copper Canyon, Jasper's Rest., Kobe Japanese, Outback Steaks, Ruby Tuesday Doubletree, Hampton Inn, Holiday Inn Express Best Buy, Costco/gas, Old Navy, Petco, Wegman's, **W** FedEx Center

16 Arena Dr, **E** Carolina Kitchen, Chick-fil-A, ChuckeCheese, Famous Dave's, Five Guys, Golden Corral, Kobe Japanese, Longhorn Steaks, Panda Express, TGIFriday's Courtyard, Residence Inn, **W** to FedEx Field

15 MD 214, Central Ave, **E** Extended Stay America, Hotel Largo to Six Flags, **W** BP, Exxon/dsl, Shell Checker's, Dunkin', IHOP, KFC, McDonald's, Panda Express, Taco Bell, Wendy's Fairbridge Inn&Suites, La Quinta Family$, Goodyear/auto, Home Depot, NTB, U-Haul, URGENT CARE

13 Ritchie-Marlboro Rd, Capitol Hgts, **W** WaWa/dsl Chick-fil-A, Chipotle, Dave&Buster's, Five Guys, Ledo Pizza, McDonald's, Popeye's, Sonic, Tropical Cafe $Tree, Advance Parts, Big Lots, BJ Whse/gas, Honda, Hyundai, Tires+, TJ Maxx

11 MD 4, Pennsylvania Ave, to Upper Marlboro, **W** Exxon, Shell, Sunoco Applebee's, Arby's, Domino's, IHOP, LJ Silver, Starbucks, Subway, Taco Bell, Wendy's $Tree, CVS Drug, JC Penney, Marshall's, PetCo, Shoppers Foods, Target

9 MD 337, to Allentown Rd, **E** Exxon, Shell/repair Checker's, Dunkin', McDonald's, Popeye's Days Inn, Quality Inn, Rodeway Inn, Super 8 to Andrews AFB, U-Haul, **W** Sunoco

7 MD 5, Branch Ave, to Silver Hill, **E** Citgo, Exxon, Sunoco Dunkin', Wendy's, **W** Shell/Subway/dsl Red Lobster Country Inn Suites, Hampton Inn, Holiday Inn Express H, BMW, Chrysler/Dodge/Jeep, Ford, Infiniti, KIA, Mazda, Nissan, Toyota

4b a MD 414, St Barnabas Rd, Marlow Hgts, **E** Citgo/dsl, Zip-in Bojangle's, Burger King, Checker's, IHOP, KFC, McDonald's, Outback Steaks, Wendy's Red Roof Inn $Tree, CVS Drug, GNC, Home Depot, Petsmart, Ross, Safeway Foods, Staples, **W** Exxon/7-11/dsl, Shell/autocare China Best, McDonald's, Subway Family$

3b a MD 210, Indian Head Hwy, to Forest Hgts, **E** Gulf, Sunoco Popeye's, Subway, Taco Bell Comfort Inn, Ramada

3b a Continued
Advance Parts, Aldi Foods, MGM Casino, Sav-A-Lot Fo Shoppers Foods, Tanger Outlets/famous brands, U **W** BP/dsl, Citgo, Shell 7-11, Burger King, CVS D Family$, Giant Foods, Goodyear/auto, McDonald's, John's, Popeye's, Rite Aid, Subway, **S** Exxon/dsl P Hut, Rita's Marshall's, Safeway

2b a I-295, N to Washington

0mm Maryland/Virginia state line, Potomac River, Woodrow W Bridge

INTERSTATE 97

GLEN BURNIE

Exit #	Services
17	I-695. **I-97 begins/ends on I-695.**
16	MD 648, Ferndale, Glen Burnie, **E** BP, Crown Dun Hong Kong Cafe, McDonald's, Rita's Custard, Wendy's $G eral, Giant Foods, Roses, **W** Carroll UHaul
15b a	MD 176 W, Dorsey Rd, Aviation Blvd, **E** BP, Cr Dunkin', McDonald's, Wendy's, **W** st police, to BWI
14b a	MD 100, Ellicott City, Gibson Island
13b a	MD 174, Quarterfield Rd, **E** 7-11, Gulf, Liberty Squisito Pizza, Subway, The Grill, **W** Shell/dsl, Wa dsl Chick-fil-A, Ichiban, Pizza Hut AT&T, Kohl's, Lov Rite Aid, Sam's Club/dsl, Shoppers Foods, Walmart/Subway
12	MD 3, New Cut Rd, Glen Burnie, **E on Veterans Hwy** Exxon, Gulf, Royal Farms, Sunoco, WaWa/dsl Burger K Domino's, Dunkin', Fortune Cooky, Hardee's, KFC, McDona Popeye's, Steak'n Shake, Subway, Taco Bell, Wendy's CVS Drug, Giant Foods, Goodyear/auto, Shoppers, Target, V zon, vet, Walgreens
10b a	Benfield Blvd, Severna Park, **E** BP/dsl, Exxon/dsl, Tra dsl/scales Baskin-Robbins/Dunkin', Hella's Rest., Le Pizza $General, 7-11, access to same as 12
7	MD 3, MD 32, Bowie, Odenton, **E** White Gables Mc **W** KOA
5	MD 178 (from sb, no EZ return), Crownsville

I-97 begins/ends on US 50/301.

INTERSTATE 270 (Rockville)

FREDERICK

Exit #	Services
32	**I-270 begins/ends on I-70, exit 53.**
31b a	MD 85, **N** 7-11, Sheetz/24hr, Shell/dsl, SouStates/c Valero/dsl, Wawa/dsl Applebee's, Arby's, BJ's Rest., Evans, Burger King, Checker's, Chick-fil-A, ChuckeChe Golden Corral, Jersey Mike's, KFC/Taco Bell, Longhorn Ste McDonald's, Olive Garden, Panera Bread, Papa John's, Pek Gourmet, Pizza Hut, Popeye's, Red Robin, Roy Rogers, R Tuesday, Smashburger, Sonic, Subway, Tilted Kilt, UNO G Waffle House Country Inn Suites, Days Inn, EconoLod Holiday Inn, Sleep Inn, Super 8 $Tree, AAA, Aamco, A Barnes&Noble, Best Buy, Buick/GMC, CarMax, Chrys Dodge/Jeep, Costco/gas, Dick's, Harley-Davidson, Home pot, Hyundai, JC Penney, Kohl's, Lincoln, Lowe's, Macy's, chael's, Mr Tire, Nissan, Office Depot, Petsmart, Ross, Sa Club/dsl, Staples, Target, Tires+, TJ Maxx, Verizon, Vo Walmart, **S** BP Cafe Rio, Chipotle Mexican, Ci Cracker Barrel, Firehouse Subs, Five Guys, IHOP, Jimmy Joh Macaroni Grill, McDonald's, Noodles&Co, Panda Express, S bucks, TGIFriday's, TX Roadhouse Comfort Inn, Courty Extended Stay America, Fairfield Inn, Hampton Inn, Hi Garden, Homewood Suites, MainStay Suites, Residence TownePlace Suites Honda, Toyota

MD

INTERSTATE 270 (Rockville) Cont'd

Exit #	Services
30mm	Monocacy River
28mm	scenic view wb, no rest rooms
26	MD 80, Urbana, **N** [gas] 7-11, Exxon, Royal Farms/dsl, Shell/dsl [food] Black Hog BBQ, Buffalo Wild Wings, Burger King, China Taste, Dunkin', Jimmy John's, Ledo's Pizza, McDonald's, Waffle House [other] Advance Parts, CVS Drug
22	MD 109, to Barnesville, Hyattstown, **N** [gas] Carroll/dsl [food] Denise Deli, Dunkin', Laurienzo Cafe [other] Food+
21mm	**weigh/insp sta both lanes**
18	MD 121, to Clarksburg, Boyds, **N** Little Bennett Pk, **S** [other] Clarksburg Outlets/famous brands, Blackhill Pk
16	MD 27, Father Hurley Blvd, to Damascus, **N** [gas] Exxon, Free State/dsl, Sunoco, Washington Express [food] Applebee's, Bob Evans, Jersey Mike's Subs, McDonald's, Starbucks [lodging] Extended Stay America [other] AT&T, Best Buy, Giant Foods, GNC, Home Depot, Kohl's, Michael's, PepBoys, Petsmart, Target, TJ Maxx, Verizon, Walmart
15b a	MD 118, to MD 355, **N** [lodging] Holiday Inn Express, **S** [gas] 7-11, BP/dsl, Exxon/Circle K, Sunoco/dsl [food] Baja Fresh, Burger King, Carrabba's, Chick-fil-A, Chipotle, Domino's, Firehouse Subs, Five Guys, Greene Turtle, IHOP, Longhorn Steaks, McDonald's, Panda Express, Panera Bread, Pizza Hut, Red Robin, Ruby Tuesday, Senor Tequilas, Starbucks, Taco Bell, Wendy's, Zoe's Kitchen [lodging] Extended Stay America, Fairfield Inn [other] Giant Foods, Honda, Mercedes/Smart Car, Nissan, Petco, Rite Aid, Safeway Foods
13b a	Middlebrook Rd (from wb)
11	MD 124, Quince Orchard Rd, **N** [gas] Exxon, Exxon [food] Boston Mkt, ChuckeCheese, Ichiban Rest., KFC, McDonald's, Panera Bread, Popeye's, Subway [lodging] Hampton Inn, Hilton, Holiday Inn, Homewood Suites, TownePlace Suites [other] Aamco, Acura, AT&T, Costco, CVS Drugs, Ford, Hyundai/Subaru, JC Penney, Lincoln, Lord&Taylor, Macy's, Mazda, Mini, Ross, Sam's Club, Toyota, Verizon, VW/Kia, **S** [gas] Shell/dsl [food] Buffalo Wild Wings, Dunkin', Jerry's Subs, Jimmy John's, McDonald's, Starbucks [lodging] Motel 6 [other] Advance Parts, Aldi Foods, Chevrolet, Chrysler/Dodge/Jeep, Fiat, Giant Foods, JoAnn Fabrics, Rite Aid, Seneca Creek SP, Staples
10	MD 117, Clopper Rd (from wb), same as 11
9b a	I-370, to Gaithersburg, Sam Eig Hwy, **S on Washington Blvd,** [food] Copper Canyon Grill, Corner Cafe Bakery, Joe's Crabshack, Pizza Hut, Uncle Julio's [lodging] Courtyard [other] Barnes&Noble, Dick's, Kohl's, Target
8	Shady Grove Rd, **N** [gas] Shell/dsl [food] Burger King, Five Guys, Red Lobster, Subway [lodging] Red Roof Inn, Sheraton [other] 7-11, Best Buy, Home Depot, Office Depot, vet, **S** [food] Thatsamore [lodging] Courtyard, Marriott, Radisson, Residence Inn, Sleep Inn, SpringHill Suites [other] [H]
6b a	MD 28, W Montgomery Ave, **S** [gas] Shell [lodging] Best Western
5b a	MD 189, Falls Rd
4b a	Montrose Rd, **S** [food] Elevation Burger, Starbucks, Zoe's Kitchen [other] Harris Teeter, Walgreens
2	I-270/I-270 spur diverges eb, converges wb
1b a	MD 187, Old Georgetown Rd, **S** [gas] Exxon [food] Chipotle, Not Your Joe's, Subway [other] [H], Balducci's Foods, Giant Foods, Verizon
1	(I-270 spur)Democracy Blvd, **E** [lodging] Marriott, **W** [gas] Exxon/dsl, Shell/dsl [other] Macy's, Nordstrom

I-270 begins/ends on I-495, exit 35.

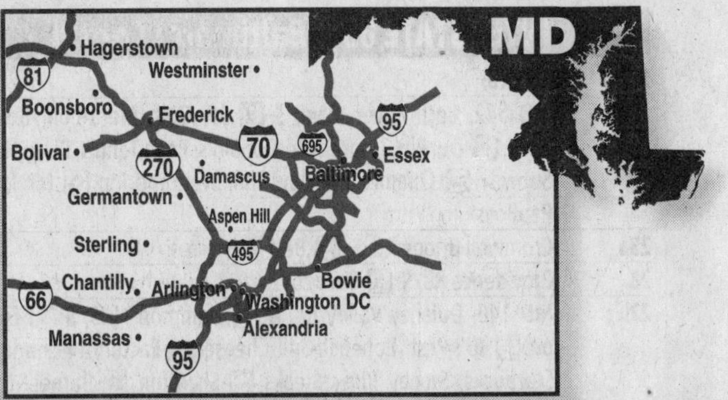

INTERSTATE 495 (DC)

See Virginia Interstate 495 (DC)

INTERSTATE 695 (Baltimore)

Exit #	Services
48mm	Patapsco River, Francis Scott Key Br
44	Broening Ave (from nb)
43	MD 157, **toll plaza**
42	MD 151 S, Sparrows Point (last exit before **toll** sb), **E** [gas] Citgo/dsl [other] North Point SP
41	MD 20, Cove Rd, **W** [gas] Royal Farms/dsl, WaWa [food] Burger King, McDonald's
40	MD 150, MD 151, North Point Blvd, (nb only)
39	Merritt Blvd, **W** [gas] BP [food] Burger King, Dunkin', McDonald's, Rita's [other] $Tree, Aldi Foods, Ford, Giant Foods, Honda, Hyundai, JC Penney, Mazda, Mr Tire, Walmart
38b a	MD 150, Eastern Blvd, to Baltimore, **E** [gas] Royal Farms, **W** [food] Applebee's, Arby's, Checker's, Chick-fil-A, Dunkin', Hibachi Buffet, Hip Hop Fish&Chicken [other] $Tree, AT&T, JC Penney, Kia/Nissan, Staples
36	MD 702 S (exits left from sb), Essex
35	US 40, **N** [gas] Sunoco, WaWa/dsl [food] Arby's, Chipotle Mexican, DQ, Dunkin', IHOP, Longhorn Steaks, Panda Express, Panera Bread, Sonic [other] Aldi Foods, Best Buy, Harley-Davidson, Home Depot, Mr Tire, NTB, Office Depot, PetCo, same as 34, Sam's Club/gas, U-Haul, Walmart
34	MD 7, Philadelphia Rd, **N** [food] McDonald's, Panda Express, Popeye's [lodging] La Quinta [other] [H], $General, $Tree, Giant Foods, Goodyear/auto, Marshall's, **S** [gas] Exxon/dsl [other] same as 35, Walgreens
33b a	I-95, N to Philadelphia, S to Baltimore
32b a	US 1, Bel Air, **N** [gas] Exxon [food] Bob Evans, Burger King, Dunkin', Golden Corral, IHOP, McDonald's, Peking House, Taco Bell [other] $Tree, 7-11, BJ's Whse, Giant Foods, Merchants Tire/auto, Mr Tire/auto, Nissan, Toyota, Verizon, vet, Walmart, **S** [gas] Shell [food] Baskin-Robbins/Dunkin', Carrabba's, Papa John's, Rita's Custard, Subway, Szechuan Taste [other] 7-11, Goodyear/auto, Verizon
31c	MD 43 E (from eb, exits left)
31b a	MD 147, Harford Rd, **N** [gas] 7-11/dsl, BP, CF/dsl, CF/dsl (2), Sunoco [food] Dunkin', Wendy's [other] Chrysler/Dodge/Jeep, CVS Drug, Honda, VW, Walgreens, Weis Foods
30b a	MD 41, Perring Pkwy, **N** [gas] Shell [food] Bateman's Bistro, Burger King, Checker's, Chick-fil-A, Denny's, Dunkin', Five Guys, Hibachi Buffet, KFC, McDonald's, Popeye's, Rita's Custard, Starbucks, Subway, Taco Bell [other] $Tree, Advance Parts, Chevrolet, Ford/Lincoln, Goodyear/auto, Home Depot, Jo-Ann Fabrics, NTB, Office Depot, Ross, Safeway Foods, Shoppers Foods, Tuesday Morning, Verizon

[gas] = gas [food] = food [lodging] = lodging [other] = other [rest stop] = rest stop

INTERSTATE 695 (Baltimore) Cont'd

Exit #	Services
29b	MD 542, Loch Raven Blvd, S [gas] BP, Gulf, Marathon, Royal Frms [food] Dunkin', Hooters, McDonald's, Papa John's, Pizza Hut, Subway [lodging] Comfort Inn, Days Inn, Welcome Inn [other] Mr Tire, PepBoys
29a	Cromwell Bridge Rd, S [lodging] Best Western
28	Providence Rd, S [gas] Sunoco
27b a	MD 146, Dulaney Valley Rd, N [other] Hampton NHS, S [gas] Exxon [food] BJ's Rest., Bonefish Grill, Cheesecake Factory, PF Chang's, Starbucks, Stoney River Steaks [lodging] Sheraton [other] Barnes&Noble, Fresh Mkt, Macy's, Trader Joe's
26b a	MD 45, York Rd, Towson, N [gas] BP, Citgo, Exxon/dsl, Oceanic, Sunoco/dsl [food] Dunkin', Ocean Pride Rest., Pizza Hut, Subway [other] Best Buy, Firestone/auto, Kia, Mazda, Mr Tire, NTB, Petco, Rite Aid, S [gas] Exxon, Shell [food] Burger King, Five Guys, McDonald's, Towson Diner [other] CVS Drug, Goodyear/auto, Honda, Hyundai, Lexus, Safeway Foods, Verizon, vet, Walgreens
25	MD 139, Charles St, S [other] H
24	I-83 N, to York
23b	MD 25, Falls Rd, Baltimore, N [gas] Exxon/Circle K/dsl
23a	I-83 S, MD 25 N, Baltimore
22	Greenspring Ave
21	MD 129, to Stevenson Rd, Park Hghts Rd
20	MD 140, Reisterstown Rd, Pikesville, N [gas] Exxon/7-11/dsl [food] Chipotle Mexican, Starbucks [other] AT&T, Barnes&Noble, Trader Joe's, S [gas] BP/dsl, Shell/dsl, Sunoco/Subway [food] McDonald's, Olive Branch Italian [lodging] Doubletree, Ramada Inn [other] Target, vet
19	I-795, NW Expswy
18b a	MD 26, Randallstown, Lochearn, E [gas] Shell/dsl, Sunoco/dsl [food] Baskin-Robbins/Dunkin', KFC, Popeye's, Subway [other] $General, Family$, W [gas] BP, Exxon/dsl, Shell/dsl [food] Burger King, Dunkin', McDonald's, Sonic, Subway, Taco Bell [other] H, 7-11, Firestone/auto, Giant Foods, Shoppers Foods, vet, Walgreens
17	MD 122, Security Blvd, E [gas] BP/repair, Shell [food] City View Grill, Dunkin', Little Caesar's, McDonald's, Subway, Taco Bell [lodging] Days Inn, Knights Inn, Motel 6 [other] Chevrolet, Family$, Nissan, PriceRite Foods, Rite Aid, W [gas] Carroll/dsl, Exxon/dsl [food] Burger King, Chipotle, Five Guys, McDonald's, Panera Bread, Popeye's, Rita's Custard [lodging] Hampton Inn, Quality Inn [other] Ford, Macy's, Old Navy, Rite Aid, Weis Foods
16b a	I-70, E to Baltimore, W to Frederick
15b a	US 40, Ellicott City, Baltimore, E [gas] BP [food] Burger King, Checker's, Chick-fil-A, ChuckECheese's, KFC, McDonald's, Panda Express, Quiznos, Shirley's Diner, Subway [lodging] Holiday Inn Express,
15b a	Continued Quality Inn [other] $Tree, BigLots, CVS Drug, Dodge, Firest auto, Lowe's, Marshall's, Mr Tire, Rite Aid, Ross, Safe Foods/gas, Sam's Club/gas, Shoppers Foods, U-Haul, greens, W [gas] BP/dsl, Exxon/dsl, Shell, Shell [food] Appleb Bob Evans, McDonald's, Popeye's, Starbucks, Starbucks, way, Taco Bell, TT Diner [lodging] Ramada [other] $Tree, Aamco, Foods, Chrysler/Jeep, Firestone/auto, Giant Foods, Goody auto, Home Depot, Hyundai, NTB, Office Depot, Office pot, PepBoys, Petsmart, Staples, Toyota, Verizon, Walgre Walmart/McDonald's
14	Edmondson Ave, E [food] Grilled Cheese&Co [other] Royal Fa W [gas] Carroll [food] Papa John's
13	MD 144, Frederick Rd, Catonsville, W [gas] BP, Gas+, [food] Baskin-Robbins/Dunkin', McDonald's, Subway [other] 7-1
12c b	MD 372 E, Wilkens, E [other] H
11b a	I-95, N to Baltimore, S to Washington
10	US 1, Washington Blvd (from wb only), E [gas] Royal Farms. WaWa [food] 3 Bros Pizza, Chick-fil-A, Dunkin', IHOP, Quiz Wendy's [lodging] Beltway Motel/rest. [other] Home Depot, Office pot, PetCo, Walmart, W [food] Burger King
9	Hollins Ferry Rd, Lansdowne, E [gas] Carroll/Circle K/Subw Sunoco/7-11/dsl [food] Victor's Deli [other] Royal Farms
8	MD 168, Nursery Rd, N [gas] Exxon, Shell [food] Hardee's, McDonald's, Taco Bell, Wendy's [lodging] Motel 6, S [gas] BP, Car dsl [food] Dunkin', G&M Rest., Happy Garden Chinese, Rita's tard, Seasons Pizza
7b a	MD 295, N to Baltimore, S [other] BWI Airport
6b a	Camp Mead Rd (from eb)
5	MD 648, Ferndale, N [gas] Exxon/7-11/dsl, Shell/dsl [food] Ch er's, Dunkin' [lodging] Best Western, Comfort Inn [other] NAPA, [food] Wok
4b a	I-97 S, to Annapolis
3b a	MD 2, Brooklyn Park, S [gas] Exxon, Royal Farms/dsl, Sh dsl [food] Bob Evans, BoneFish Grill, Checker's, Chick-fi ChuckECheese's, Coldstone, Denny's, Five Guys, Golden ral, Hibachi Buffet, HipHop Fish&Chicken, Ledo Pizza, McD ald's, Moe's SW, Noodles&Co, Panera Bread, Pappas Rest., Five, Pizza Hut, Qdoba, Starbucks, Subway, Taco Bell, W dy's [lodging] Days Inn, Extended Stay America, Hampton Inn, Quinta [other] $Tree, Advance Parts, Aldi Foods, AT&T, AutoZ Best Buy, BigLots, Buick/GMC, Dick's, Hyundai, Just Ti Lowe's, Office Depot, PetCo, Salvo Parts, ShopRite Foods, Su ru, Target, Tuesday Morning, Verizon, Walgreens, Walmart
2	MD 10, Glen Burnie, S [food] McDonald's [other] Costco/gas, Ho Depot, Petsmart
1	MD 174, Hawkins Point Rd, S [gas] Citgo/deli/dsl

NOTES

MD

MASSACHUSETTS

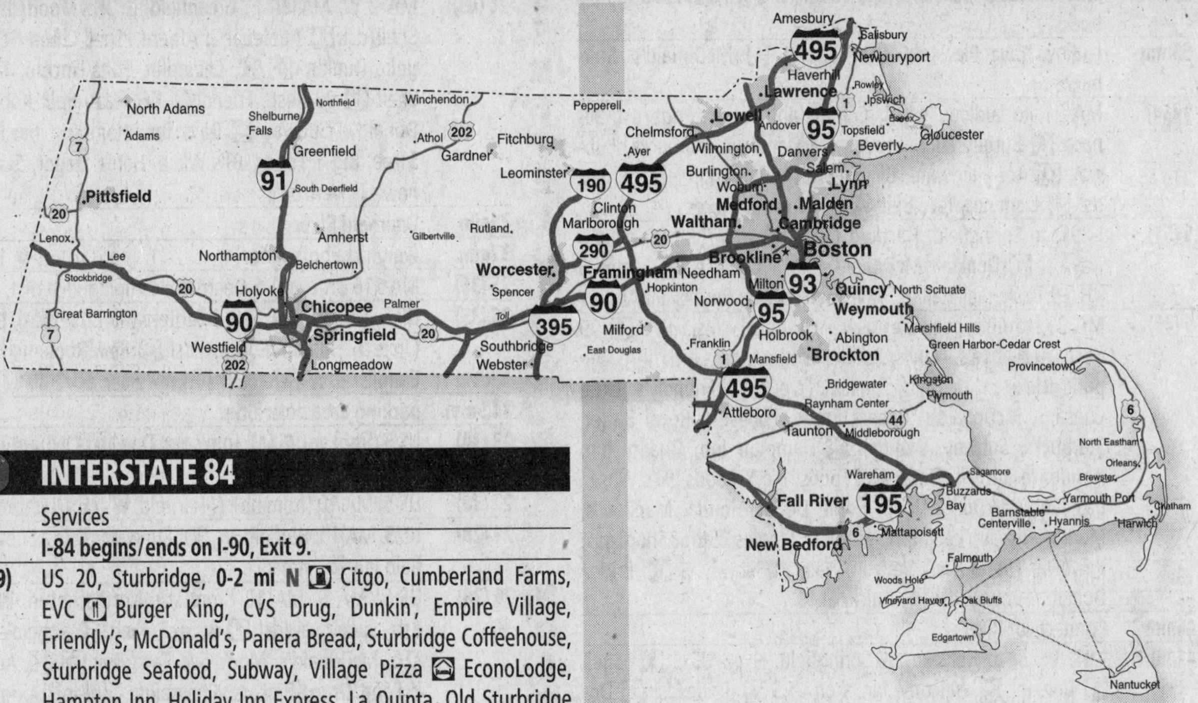

INTERSTATE 84

Exit #	Services
4 (11)	**I-84 begins/ends on I-90, Exit 9.**
3b a (9)	US 20, Sturbridge, **0-2 mi N** Citgo, Cumberland Farms, EVC Burger King, CVS Drug, Dunkin', Empire Village, Friendly's, McDonald's, Panera Bread, Sturbridge Coffeehouse, Sturbridge Seafood, Subway, Village Pizza EconoLodge, Hampton Inn, Holiday Inn Express, La Quinta, Old Sturbridge Lodges, Super 8 USPO, **0-2 mi S** S&S, Shell/Dunkin'/Subway Applebee's, Cracker Barrel, Uno Pizzaria, Wendy's Comfort Inn Marshall's, Michael's, Petco, Staples, Stop&Shop, Verizon, vet, Walmart/Subway
2 (5)	MA 131, to Old Sturbridge Village, Sturbridge, **2 mi S** Publick House, RV camping
4mm	**picnic area wb, litter barrels**
1 (3)	Mashapaug Rd, to Southbridge, **S** Mobil/dsl, Pilot/deli/dsl/scales/24hr/@ Days Inn H
2mm	**weigh sta both lanes**
0.5mm	**picnic area eb**
0mm	Massachusetts/Connecticut state line

INTERSTATE 90

Exit #	Services
140mm	**I-90 begins/ends near Logan Airport**
25	to I-93, to downtown Boston
24	to I-93, to downtown Boston
22 (134)	Presidential Ctr, downtown
20 (132)	MA 28, Alston, Brighton, Cambridge, **N** Courtyard, Doubletree Inn H, **S** Mobil
131mm	**toll plaza**
18 (130)	MA Ave (from eb), **N** IHOP, Starbucks
17 (128)	Centre St, Newton, **N** Bertucci's, Starbucks Crowne Plaza Honda, Walgreens
16 (125)	MA 16, W Newton, **N** Shell/repair Blue Ribbon BBQ CVS Drug
15 (124)	I-95, **N** Speedway Marriott
123mm	**toll plaza**
14 (122)	MA 30, Weston
117mm	**Natick Travel Plaza eb,** EVC, Gulf/dsl Dunkin', McDonald's, Papagino's/d'Angelo's
13 (116)	MA 30, Natick, **S** Cumberland, EVC, Mobil, Shell, Tesla EVC Boston Mkt, Burger King, Chick-fil-A, Dunkin', Five Guys, Lotus Flower Chinese, McDonald's, Panera Bread,
13 (116)	Continued Stop&Shop Courtyard, Monticello Inn, Red Roof+ Best Buy, BJ's Whse, Home Depot, Kia, Kohl's, Lowe's, Marshall's, REI, Target, TJ Maxx, USPO, Walmart
114mm	**Framingham Travel Plaza wb, S** EVC, Gulf/dsl Boston Mkt, McDonald's, Starbucks
12 (111)	MA 9, Framington, **N** BP, Speedway Dunkin', Godavari Framingham, Wendy's Motel 6, Sheraton, **S** China Gourmet Toyota
11a (106)	I-495, N to NH, S to Cape Cod
105mm	**Westborough Travel Plaza wb,** Gulf/dsl Boston Mkt, D'angelo, Dunkin', Papagino's
11 (96)	MA 122, to Millbury, **N** UMA Med Ctr
10a (95)	MA 146
94mm	Blackstone River
10 (90)	I-395 S, to Auburn, I-290 N, Worcester, **N** Outback, Papa Gino's Comfort Inn, La Quinta, **S** Shell, Shell/repair/24hr Applebee's, D'angelo, Dunkin', Friendly's, Wendy's Fairfield Inn, Hampton Inn, Holiday Inn Express CVS Drug, Hyundai, Park'n Shop, TJ Maxx
84mm	**Charlton Travel Plaza wb,** Gulf/dsl McDonald's, Papa Gino's/d'Angelo's
80mm	**Charlton Travel Plaza eb,** Gulf/dsl McDonald's, Papa Gino's st police
79mm	**toll plaza**
9 (78)	I-84, to Hartford, NYC, Sturbridge, access to same services as I-84, exit 3., **S** access to H
67mm	Quaboag River
8 (62)	MA 32, to US 20, Palmer, **S on MA 32** Pride, Shell/dsl Domino's, Dunkin', McDonald's, Subway, Wendy's H, Big Y Foods, Chevrolet, CVS Drug, repair/transmissions, Rite Aid, vet
58mm	Chicopee River

MA

INTERSTATE 90 Cont'd

Exit #	Services
56mm	**Ludlow Travel Plaza wb,** [gas] Gulf/dsl [food] Papa Gino's, Starbucks
55mm	**Ludlow Travel Plaza eb,** [gas] Gulf/dsl [food] McDonald's , Starbucks
7 (54)	MA 21, to Ludlow, **N** [gas] Cumberland Farms, Pride/dsl, Sunoco [food] Burger King, Dunkin', McDonald's, Starbucks, Subway [O] Ace Hardware, Big Y Foods, CVS Drug, **S** [gas] Shell/dsl [food] Dominos, Taco Bell [lodging] Holiday Inn Express
6 (51)	I-291, to Springfield, Hartford CT, **N** [gas] Pride/50's Diner/Subway/dsl [food] Dunkin', McDonald's, Po's Chinese [lodging] Motel 6 [O] H, Basketball Hall of Fame, Mercedes, to Bradley Int Airport
5 (49)	MA 33, to Chicopee, Westover AFB, **N** [gas] Tesla EVC [food] 99 Rest., Applebee's, Arby's, Buffalo Wild Wings, Chick-fil-A, Chipotle Mexican, Denny's, Dunkin', Five Guys, Friendly's, Little Caesar's, McDonald's, Panera Bread, Popeye's, Royal Buffet, Starbucks, Subway, Wendy's [lodging] Hampton Inn, Quality Inn, Residence Inn [O] $Tree, Aldi Foods, Big Y Foods, BJ's Whse/gas, Chrysler/Dodge/Jeep, Home Depot, Honda, Marshall's, Monro, Nissan, Petsmart, Staples, Staples, Stop&Shop/gas, TownFair Tire, U-Haul, Verizon, Walmart/Subway, **S** [gas] Pride/Dunkin'/Subway/dsl [O] Buick/GMC
46mm	Connecticut River
4 (46)	I-91, US 5, to Holyoke, W Springfield, **N on US 5** [gas] Shell [food] Dunkin' [lodging] Welcome Inn, **S on US 5** [gas] Pride/dsl [food] Donut Dip, Five Guys, Hooters, On the Border, Outback Steaks, Subway [lodging] Hampton Inn, Red Roof+, Residence Inn, Springfield Inn, Super 8 [O] BMW, Honda/Lexus/Toyota
41mm	st police wb
3 (40)	US 202, to Westfield, **N** [gas] Mobil [food] Alessio's Pizza, **S** [gas] Citgo/Subway/dsl, Shell/dsl [food] Dunkin', Friendly's, McDonald's, Wendy's [lodging] Hampton Inn, Quality Inn [O] H, repair, vet
36mm	Westfield River
35.5mm	**runaway truck ramp eb**
29mm	Blandford/Ludlow TP both lanes, [gas] Gulf/dsl [food] McDonald's [O] info
20mm	highest point on MA Tpk, 1724 ft
14.5mm	Appalachian Trail
2 (11)	US 20, to Lee, Pittsfield, **N** [gas] Citgo, Shell/dsl, Sunoco [food] Athena's Rest., Dunkin', Friendly's, McDonald's, Rose's Rest., Subway [lodging] Morgan House/rest., Pilgrim Inn, Sunset Motel, Super 8 [O] Rite Aid, True Value, **S** [gas] Big Y/dsl [food] Orient Taste, Subway, Villa Pizza [O] Big Y Foods, Lee Outlets/famous brands
10.5mm	Hoosatonic River
8mm	**Lee Travel Plaza both lanes,** [gas] EVC, Gulf/dsl [food] McDonald's, Papa Gino's [O] info
4mm	**toll booth,** [phone]
1 (2)	MA 41 (from wb, no return), to MA 102, W Stockbridge, the Berkshires, **N** [lodging] Pleasant Valley Motel [O] to Bousquet Ski Area
0mm	Massachusetts/New York state line

PITTSFIELD

INTERSTATE 91

Exit #	Services
55mm	Massachusetts/Vermont state line
54mm	**parking area both lanes,** [RS]
28 (51)	US 5, MA 10, Bernardston, **E** [lodging] Fox Inn, **W** [gas] Sunoco [food] Antonio's II Ristorante, Four-leaf Clover Rest., Hillside Organic Pizza [O] Country Corner Store, USPO
27 (45)	MA 2 E (exits left from sb), Greenfield, **US 5 E** [gas] Cumberland Farms, Speedway, Stop&Shop, Sunoco/dsl [food] Denny's Pantry, Domino's, Dunkin', McDonald's, Subway [O] H,
27 (45)	Continued $General, AT&T, Aubuchon Hardware, AutoZone, Chry Dodge/Jeep, Honda, O'Reilly Parts, Walgreens
26 (43)	MA 2 W, MA 2A E, Greenfield, **E** [gas] Mobil/dsl, Planet Shell/dsl [food] Applebee's, Athens Pizza, China Gourmet, D gelo, Dunkin' [O] H, Chevrolet, Ford/Lincoln, Toyota, **W** Shell [food] 99 Rest., Friendly's, KFC/Taco Bell, Kobe Asian, Donald's, Subway [lodging] Days Inn, Hampton Inn [O] $Gen $Tree, Big Y Foods, BJ's Whse, Home Depot, Staples, to hawk Tr, Verizon
39mm	Deerfield River
37mm	**weigh sta both lanes**
25 (36)	MA 116 (from sb), S Deerfield, camping, hist dist, same as
24 (35)	US 5, MA 10, MA 116, Deerfield (no EZ return), **E** [gas] Irv Circle K/Dunkin'/Subway/dsl [lodging] Red Roof+ [O] vet, Yar Candle Co, **W** [gas] Roady's Trkstp/diner/dsl/24hr [food] 24hr D
34.5mm	**parking area both lanes**
23 (34)	US 5 (from sb), **E** [food] Tom's Hot Dog [O] Orchard Trailers, R bow Motel/camping
22 (30)	US 5, MA 10 (from nb), N Hatfield, **W** [O] Diamond RV Ctr
21 (28)	US 5, MA 10, Hatfield, **W** [gas] Sunoco/dsl [food] Subway [lodging] field Inn [O] st police
20 (26)	US 5, MA 9, MA 10 (from sb), Northampton, **W** [gas] Pr dsl, Speedway/dsl [food] Burger King, D'angelo's, Domir KFC, McDonald's, Moe's SW, Taco Bell [O] H, AutoZone, Y Food/Drug, BigLots, Chevrolet, Chrysler/Dodge/Jeep, Drug, Firestone/auto, Ford, Goodyear/auto, Honda, Hyun Stop&Shop/gas, TownFair Tire, Toyota, U-Haul, Verizon, Walgreens, Walmart/Subway
19 (25)	MA 9, to Amherst, Northampton, **0-2 mi E** [gas] Big Y Cumberland Farms, Phillips 66, Pride/Subway/dsl [food] Pr Pizza [lodging] Hampton Inn [O] Nissan, to Elwell SP, vet
18 (22)	US 5, Northampton, **W** [gas] Shell/Dunkin' [lodging] Fairfield Quality Inn [O] to Smith Coll
18mm	scenic area both lanes
17b a (16)	MA 141, S Hadley, **E** [gas] Mobil/dsl, Shell/dsl [food] Dunkin', R China, Subway [lodging] Motel 6 [O] Meineke, Walgreens
16 (14)	US 202, Holyoke, **W** Soldier's.Home
15 (12)	to US 5, Ingleside, **E** [gas] Shell/Dunkin' [food] Applebee's, Chi go Grill, Chipotle, Cracker Barrel, JP's Rest., McDonald's, Robin [lodging] Fairfield Inn [O] H, Barnes&Noble, Best Buy, Drug, Hobby Lobby, JC Penney, Macy's, Old Navy, PetCo, Tar TJ Maxx, **W** [lodging] Homewood Suites
14 (11)	to US 5, to I-90 (Mass Tpk), E to Boston, W to Albany, **E** [O]
13b a (9)	US 5 N, W Springfield, **E** [gas] Pride/dsl [food] Donut Dip, F Guys, Hooters, On-the-Border, Outback Steaks, Shallot T Subway, Tap House Grill [lodging] Express Inn, Red Roof+, Reside Inn, Springfield Inn, Super 8 [O] BMW, Lexus/Toyota, **W** Pride/dsl, Shell/dsl, Tesla EVC [food] 99 Rest., Burger King, C Grill, Carrabba's, Chili's, D'angelo's, Dunkin', Friendly's, IH KFC, Longhorn Steaks, McDonald's, Nippon Grill, Olive G den, Panera Bread, Pizza Hut, Tokyo Cuisine, Wendy's [lodging] Air Inn, Best Western, Candlewood Suites, Clarion, Courtya EconoLodge, Hampton Inn, Quality Inn, Red Carpet Inn, Tra Inn [O] $Tree, Aldi Foods, AT&T, Chrysler/Dodge/Jeep, Cost CVS Drug, Dick's, Fiat, GNC, Home Depot, Honda, Kohl's, M da, Michael's, Nissan, Staples, Stop&Shop, Subaru, TownF Tire, Verizon
12 (8.5)	I-391 N, to Chicopee
11 (8)	Birnie Ave (from sb), **E** [gas] Mobil [O] H
10 (7.5)	Main St (from nb), Springfield, **E** [gas] Mobil

GREENFIELD

NORTHAMPTON

SPRINGFIELD

INTERSTATE 91 Cont'd

Exit #	Services
9 (7)	US 20 W, MA 20A E (from nb), E McDonald's, W Pride/Subway/dsl
8 (6.5)	I-291, US 20 E, to I-90, E downtown
7 (6)	Columbus Ave (from sb), E Pride/Subway/dsl Sheraton, Tower Square, W to Basketball Hall of Fame
6 (5.5)	Springfield Ctr, E Pride/Dunkin'/Subway/dsl Starbucks, W Coldstone, Plan B Burger Basketball Hall of Fame
5 (5)	Broad St, same as 4, E Shell/dsl Hampton Inn Hyundai, W Sunoco/dsl Chicago Grill, Subway Hilton Garden Buick/GMC
4 (4.5)	MA 83, Broad St, Main St, same as 5, E Shell/dsl Antonio's Grinders Hyundai, W Sunoco/dsl Chicago Grill, Subway Hilton Garden Buick/GMC, Chevrolet
3 (4)	US 5 N, to MA 57, Columbus Ave, W Springfield, E Sunoco Antonio's Pizza, W Chevrolet
2 (3.5)	MA 83 S (from nb), to E Longmeadow
1 (3)	US 5 S (from sb)
0mm	Massachusetts/Connecticut state line, callboxes begin/end

INTERSTATE 93

Exit #	Services
47mm	Massachusetts/New Hampshire state line, callboxes begin/end
48 (46)	MA 213 E, to Methuen, E H
47 (45)	Pelham St, Methuen, E Sunoco Dunkin', Heavenly Donuts, McDonald's, Outback Steaks, W BP, Irving/Circle K/Subway/dsl Fireside Rest. Day's Hotel/rest. Chrysler/Dodge/Jeep
46 (44)	MA 110, MA 113, to Lawrence, E BP/repair, Mobil, Shell Burger King, Dunkin', KFC/Taco Bell, McDonald's, Pizza Hut H, $Tree, MktBasket Foods, Rite Aid, W Super Anthony's Roast Beef, Dunkin', Irish Cottage, Royal Roast Beef Passport Inn
45 (43)	Andover St, River Rd, to Lawrence, E Courtyard, Doubletree, Homewood Suites, W Mobil/Dunkin' Chateu Italian, Chili's La Quinta, Residence Inn, Sonesta Suites, SpringHill Suites vet
44b a (40)	I-495, to Lowell, Lawrence, E H
43 (39)	MA 133, N Tewksbury, E Mobil/Dunkin', W 99 Rest.
42 (38)	Dascomb Rd, East St, Tewksbury, W Citgo/dsl Dunkin', Luna Rossa Italian, Subway 7-11
41 (35)	MA 125, Andover, E EVC Dunkin' Hampton Inn Target
40 (34)	MA 62, Wilmington
39 (33)	Concord St, E Dunkin', Mona's Kitchen Shriners Auditorium, URGENT CARE
38 (31)	MA 129, Reading, W Mobil/Dunkin'/Subway/dsl Burger King, Pacific Grove Chinese, Red Heat Tavern
37c (30)	Commerce Way, Atlantic Ave, W Chipotle Mexican, Firehouse Subs, Starbucks Red Roof+, Residence Inn PetCo, Petsmart, Target, Verizon
37b a (29)	I-95, S to Waltham, N to Peabody
36 (28)	Montvale Ave, E Mobil/Circle K Deli Works, Dunkin' Courtyard, W BP, Gulf, Speedway/dsl Bickford's Grille, Dunkin', McDonald's, Polcari's Italian, Wendy's Best Western+, Comfort Inn H
35 (27)	Winchester Highlands, Melrose, E H (no EZ return to sb)
34 (26)	MA 28 N (from nb, no EZ return), Stoneham, E Mobil/Circle K/dsl Friendly's, W H

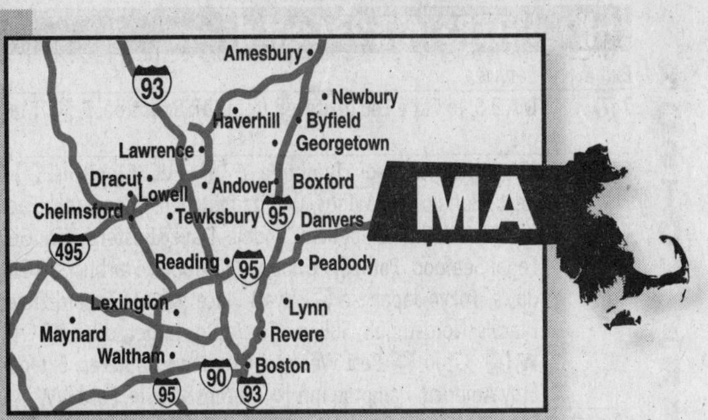

BOSTON AREA

Exit #	Services
33 (25)	MA 28, Fellsway West, Winchester, W H
32 (23)	MA 60, Salem Ave, Medford Square, W Hyatt Place H, to Tufts U
31 (22)	MA 16 E, to Revere (no EZ return sb), W Fred's Gas, Mobil/dsl, Mr. C's/dsl Avellino's Italian, Burger King, Dunkin' AutoZone, Chrysler/Dodge/Jeep, Infiniti, Nissan
30 (21)	MA 28, MA 38, Mystic Ave, Somerville, W Mr. C's/dsl Burger King AutoZone, VW
29 (20)	MA 28 (from nb), same as 30, Somerville, E 99 Rest., Dunkin', Starbucks La Quinta Home Depot, Staples, TJ Maxx, Trader Joe's, W Gulf, Speedway Dunkin' Stop&Shop
28 (19)	Sullivans Square, Charles Town, downtown
27	US 1 N (from nb)
26 (18.5)	MA 28 N, Storrow Dr, North Sta, downtown
25	Haymarket Sq, Gov't Center
24 (18)	Callahan Tunnel, E
23 (17.5)	High St, Congress St, W Harborside Inn
22 (17)	Atlantic Ave, Northern Ave, South Sta, Boston World Trade Ctr
21 (16.5)	Kneeland St, ChinaTown
20 (16)	I-90 W, to Mass Tpk
19 (15.5)	Albany St (from sb), W H
18 (15)	Mass Ave, to Roxbury, W H
17 (14.5)	E Berkeley (from nb)
16 (14)	S Hampton St, Andrew Square, W Applebee's, Chipotle, Olive Garden, Panera Bread, Wahlburgers Courtyard, Holiday Inn Express Best Buy, Home Depot, Marshall's, Old Navy, Stop&Shop/gas, Target, TJ Maxx
15 (13)	Columbia Rd, Everett Square, E DoubleTree JFK Library, to UMA, W Gulf, Speedway
14 (12.5)	Morissey Blvd (from nb no return), E JFK Library, W Shell
13 (12)	Freeport St, to Dorchester, (from nb), W 7-11, Citgo Deadwood Cafe, Dunkin', Ruritan Pizza, Subway Comfort Inn, Ramada CVS Drug, Honda, Lambert's Mkt, Stop&Shop, Toyota
12 (11.5)	MA 3A S (from sb, no EZ return), Quincy, E Express, tires Best Western, W Gulf/Dunkin', Speedway/dsl PapaGino's AutoZone, CVS Drug, Staples, Verizon, Walgreens
11b a (11)	to MA 203, Granite Ave, Ashmont
10 (10)	Squantum Ave (from sb), Milton, W H
9 (9)	Adams St, Bryant Ave, to N Quincy, E Dunkin', House of Pizza, W Shell/repair USPO
8 (8)	Brook Pkwy, to Quincy, Furnace, E Gulf/dsl, Mobil/dsl

= gas = food = lodging = other = rest stop

BOSTON AREA

INTERSTATE 93 Cont'd

Exit #	Services
7 (7)	MA 3 S, to Cape Cod (exits left from sb), Braintree, E Marriott
6 (6)	MA 37, to Holbrook, Braintree, E EVC, Mobil/dsl 99 Rest., Buffalo Wild Wings, CA Pizza Kitchen, Cheesecake Factory, Chicago Grill, Chipotle, D'angelo, Dave&Buster's, Five Guys, Legal Seafood, Potbelly, Qdoba, Red Robin, Starbucks, TGIFriday's, Tokyo Japanese Hyatt Place AT&T, Lord&Taylor, Macy's, Nordstrom's, Sullivan Tire/auto, Target, URGENT CARE, W Citgo Best Western, Candlewood Suites, Extended Stay America, Hampton Inn Barnes&Noble, Ford, VW
5b a (4)	MA 28 S, to Randolph, Milton, E Mobil/dsl, Shell/dsl Domino's, Dunkin', La Scala, Lombardo's, Randolph Cafe, Wong's Chinese Comfort Inn AT&T
4 (3)	MA 24 S (exits left from sb), to Brockton
3 (2)	MA 138 N, to Ponkapoag Trail, Houghtons Pond
2b a (1)	MA 138 S, to Stoughton, Milton, E golf, W BlueHill/dsl, Mobil/dsl, Shell/dsl Blue Hills Grill, Dunkin' Homewood Suites
1 (0)	I-95 N, S to Providence. **I-93 begins/ends on I-95, exit 12.**

INTERSTATE 95

AMESBURY

PEABODY

Exit #	Services
89.5mm	**Welcome Ctr/ sb, full facilities, litter barrels,** , Massachusetts/New Hampshire state line
60 (89)	MA 286, to Salisbury, beaches, E Mobil/dsl Cosmos Rest., Dunkin', Lena's Seafood Rest. Black Bear Camping (seasonal)
59 (88)	I-495 S (from sb)
58b a (87)	rd 110, to I-495 S, to Amesbury, Salisbury, E Sunoco/Dunkin'/Subway/dsl China Buffet, Niko's Place, Sylvan St Grille, Winner's Circle Rest. $Tree, Ford, U-Haul, vet, W EVC, Irving Gas/Circle K, Mobil, Sunoco/dsl, Tesla EVC Acapulco's Mexican, Burger King, Dunkin', Friendly's, McDonald's, Subway Fairfield Inn, Hampton Inn AT&T, Chevrolet, Stop&Shop, Verizon
57 (85)	MA 113, to W Newbury, E Mobil/dsl, Shell/dsl/repair, Sunoco China Wok, Dunkin', Giuseppe's Italian, Hana Japan, McDonald's, Moe's SW, Panera Bread, Wendy's H, 7-11, CVS Drug, GNC, Marshall's, Midas, MktBasket Foods, Shaw's Foods, Verizon, Walgreens
56 (83)	Scotland Rd, to Newbury, E st police
55 (82)	Central St, to Byfield, E Rusty Can, W Prime/dsl/repair
54b a (78)	MA 133, E to Rowley, W to Groveland, E vet
77mm	**weigh sta both lanes**
53b a (76)	MA 97, S to Topsfield, N to Georgetown
52 (74)	Topsfield Rd, to Topsfield, Boxford
51 (72)	Endicott Rd, to Topsfield, Middleton
50 (71)	US 1, to MA 62, Topsfield, E Gulf/dsl, Mobil/dsl Honda, W S&S Break Away Rest., Supino's Rest., TX Roadhouse DoubleTree, Knights Inn CVS Drug, st police, Staples, Stop&Shop, USPO
49 (70)	MA 62 (from nb), same as 50, Danvers, Middleton
48 (69)	Hobart St (from sb), W Calitri's Italian Best Western+, Comfort a Inn, Motel 6 Home Depot
47b a (68)	MA 114, to Middleton, Peabody, E Gulf/Dunkin', Sunoco Dunkin', Honey Dew Donuts, McDonald's, Olive Garden, Outback Steaks, Pizza Hut Audi, CarMax, Chevrolet, Chrysler/Dodge/Jeep, Infiniti, Lexus, Lowe's, NTB, Petsmart, Subaru, TJ Maxx, Toyota, Trader Joe's, Verizon, vet, VW, Walmart/Subway, **W on US 1** Cumberland Farms, Speedway/dsl
47b a (68)	Continued Chili's, Hardcover Rest., TGIFriday's Motel 6, Reside Inn, TownePlace Suites Costco/gas, Home Depot, La Rover, Mazda, Meineke, NAPA
46 (67)	to US 1, W Best, Gulf/dsl, Mobil, Sunoco/dsl Dunk Dunkin' (2), Honey Dew Donuts auto repair
45 (66)	MA 128 N, to Peabody
44b a (65)	US 1 N, MA 129, E H, W 7-11, Gulf, Shell Bert ci's, Bros Kouzina Rest., Dunkin', Marco's Italian, Santarpi Pizza, Sonic, Wendy's Hampton Inn, Holiday Inn, Hom wood Suites, Plaza Inn, SpringHill Suites
43 (61)	Walnut St, Lynnfield, E 99 Rest. golf, to Saugus I Works NHS (3mi), W Panera Bread, Starbucks, Ya house Sheraton EVC, Whole Foods
42 (62)	Salem St, Montrose, E Irving/Circle K/Subway, Su co Dunkin', W Sheraton
41 (60)	Main St, Lynnfield Ctr, E Shell, W vet
40 (59)	MA 129, Wakefield Ctr, N Reading, E Bellino's Itali Honey Dew Donuts city park, vet, W Cumberla Farms Dunkin', Mandarin Chinese Chevrolet, Mazda,
39 (58)	North Ave, Reading, E Lakeside Inn city park, Su aru, W Shell/dsl Anthony's Pizza, Bertucci's, Chil Chipotle, Fuddrucker's, Longhorn Steaks, Oye's Rest., St bucks Home Depot, Honda, Mkt Basket Foods, Stapl Stop&Shop Foods, URGENT CARE, Verizon
38b a (57)	MA 28, to Reading, E Gulf/repair, Mobil, Speedwa dsl 99 Rest., Burger King, D'Angelo's/PapaGino's, Dunki Dunkin', Five Guys, Loui Loui Advance Parts, AutoZor Ford, GNC, Marshall's, Michael's, Stop&Shop/gas, Target, Ve izon, Walgreens, W Citgo, Mobil/dsl, Shell Anthony Roast Beef, Burger King, Calareso's Farm Stand, China Moo Domino's, Dunkin', Harrow's Chicken Pies, McDonald's, Sta bucks Meineke
37b a (56)	I-93, N to Manchester, S to Boston
36 (55)	Washington St, to Winchester, E B Good, Chick-fil- Dunkin', Red Robin, Sal's Pizza, Starbucks, Subway H ton BJ's Whse/gas, Hogan Tire/auto, Nissan, Staple Toyota, W Sunoco 99 Rest., Bertucci's, China Pea Dave&Buster's, Dunkin', Joe's Grill, On the Border, Qd ba Courtyard, Fairfield Inn, Holiday Inn Express, Re Roof+ $Tree, AT&T, CVS Drug, Kohl's, Lowe's, Mkt Bask Foods, NTB, TJ Maxx, Town Fair Tire, USPO
35 (54)	MA 38, to Woburn, E Scoreboard Grill Crowne Pl za H, W Mobil/dsl Applebee's, Dunkin', Sichua Garden Extended Stay America city park, CVS Dru Stop&Shop Foods
34 (53)	Winn St, Woburn
33b a (52)	US 3 S, MA 3A N, to Winchester, E Bickford's Grille, Caf Escadrille, Capital Grille, Coldstone, Dunkin', NYA Joe's Gri Panera Bread, Potbelly, Seasons 52 Grill, Starbucks, Su way Hyatt House CVS Drug, Honda, LL Bean, Ma shall's, Michael's, W EVC, Prime, Speedway Chopp Grill Marriott H, Audi/Porsche, Kia, Mercedes, repai
32b a (51)	US 3 N, MA 2A S, to Lowell, E Mobil/dsl, Shell Burge King, Burton's Grill, Chateau Italian, Dunkin', Five Guys, Mc Donald's Hilton Garden, Sonesta Suites Best Buy, Jo Ann, Midas, Mkt Basket Foods, Nordstrom, Old Navy, PetCo Trader Joe's, W Border Cafe, Buffalo Wild Wings, Cheese cake Factory, Chipotle, Del Frisco's Grill, Legal Seafoods, Mac aroni Grill, Wendy's Candlewood Suites, Extended Sta America AT&T, Barnes&Noble, Kohl's, Lord&Taylor, Macy's Nordstrom, Staples, URGENT CARE, Verizon

READING

MA

INTERSTATE 95 Cont'd

Exit #	Services
31b a (48)	MA 4, MA 225, Lexington, E Gulf, Mobil/dsl/repair Alexander's Pizza, Qdoba, Starbucks Stop&Shop, Walgreens, W Gulf, Shell Chipotle, Dunkin', Great Wall, Margarita's, McDonald's, Minuteman Diner Bedford Plaza Hotel, Quality Inn Stop&Shop, TJ Maxx, vet
30b a (47)	MA 2A, Lexington, E Sunoco/Dunkin'/dsl H, W ALoft, Element Hotel Hanscom AFB, to MinuteMan NP
46.5mm	**travel plaza nb,** Gulf/dsl/CNG Honey Dew Donuts, McDonald's, Original Boston Pizza
29b a (46)	MA 2 W, Cambridge
28b a (45)	Trapelo Rd, Belmont, E Gulf/dsl, Mobil/dsl Boston Mkt, Burger King, Dunkin', Panera Bread, Papa Gino's, Starbucks, Subway city park, Star Mkt/Osco Drugs, Verizon
27b a (44)	Totten Pond Rd, Waltham, E Shell Copper House, D'Angelo, Dunkin', Osteria Posto, Ruth's Chris Best Western+, Courtyard, Extended Stay America, Extended Stay America (2), Hilton Garden, Holiday Inn Express, Home Suites, Hyatt, Westin Hotel, W Bertucci's Rest., Green Papaya Thai Embassy Suites/The Grille, Hampton Inn AT&T, Costco, Home Depot
26 (43)	US 20, to MA 117, to Waltham, E Sunoco/dsl, W Mobil/dsl Dunkin' NTB, vet
25 (42)	I-90, MA Tpk
24 (41)	MA 30, Newton, Wayland, E Speedway Marriott/rest.
23 (40)	Recreation Rd (from nb), to MA Tpk
22b a (39)	Grove St, E Hotel Indigo golf
38.5mm	**travel plaza sb,** Gulf/dsl McDonald's
21b a (38)	MA 16, Newton, Wellesley, E H, W Sunoco Dunkin', North End Pizza, Papa Razzi, Starbucks CVS Drug
20b a (36)	MA 9, Brookline, Framingham
19 (35)	Highland Ave, Newton, Needham, E EVC, Speedway Anthony's Pizza, Chef Mike's, Chipotle Mexican, Five Guys, Mandarin Cuisine, Mighty Subs, Panera Bread, Petsmart, Starbucks Residence Inn, Sheraton/rest. AAA, Advance Parts, CVS Drug, Marshall's, Michael's, PetCo, Staples, TJ Maxx, W Three Squares Rest. Chevrolet, Ford
18 (34)	Great Plain Ave, W Roxbury
33.5mm	**parking area sb**
17 (33)	MA 135, Needham, Wellesley
32mm	**truck turnout sb**
16b a (31)	MA 109, High St, Dedham, W Mobil/dsl
15b a (29)	US 1, MA 128, **0-2 mi** E Gulf Dunkin', Harrow's Chicken Pies, Hooters, Joe's Grill, Panera Bread, PapaGino's, PF Chang's, Qdoba, Starbucks, Subway, TGI Friday's, Victory Grille, Yard House Rest. Fairfield Inn, Holiday Inn, Residence Inn AT&T, AutoZone, Best Buy, BJ's Whse, Costco/gas, CVS Drug, LL Bean, NTB, PepBoys, PetCo, Staples, Star Mkt, Tesla, Verizon, vet, Whole Foods Mkt, **0-2 mi** W Irving/dsl, Shell/dsl Burger King, Dunkin', Jade Chinese, McDonald's Budget Inn AAA, Acura, AT&T, Audi, Buick/GMC, Chevrolet, Chrysler/Dodge/Jeep, Fiat, Honda, Hyundai, Kia, Mercedes, Porsche, Toyota
14 (28)	East St, Canton St, E Hilton
27mm	**sb, full facilities, litter barrels,**
13 (26.5)	University Ave, W EVC Anthony's Pizza, Chipotle, Del Frisco's, Joe's Grill, Panda Express, Panera Bread, Smashburger, Starbucks, Which Wich? GNC, Michael's, Petsmart, Target, Verizon, Wegman's Mkt
12 (26)	I-93 N, to Braintree, Boston, motorist callboxes end nb
11b a (23)	Neponset St, to Canton, E Citgo/repair, Sunoco/dsl Dunkin', **2 mi W on US 1** Gulf/dsl, Sunoco Jake&Joe's,

NEWTON
DEDHAM

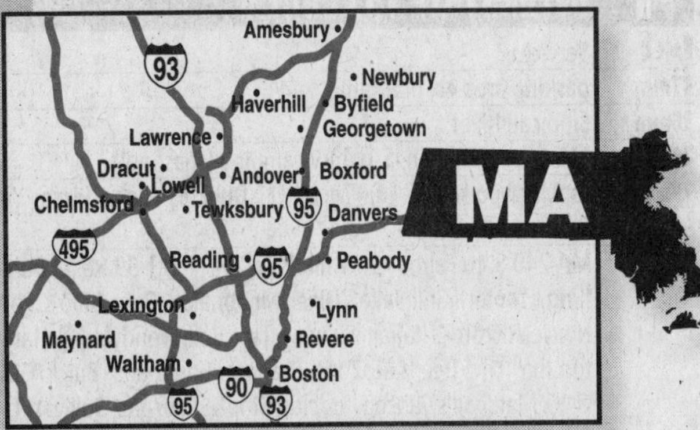

ATTLEBORO

Exit #	Services
11b a (23)	Continued The Chateau Hampton Inn H, Chevrolet, Ferrari, Ford, Honda, Hyundai, Maserati, Nissan, Toyota, Volvo
22.5mm	Neponset River
10 (20)	Coney St (from sb, no EZ return), to US 1, Sharon, Walpole, **1 mi W on US 1** BJ's Gas, Mobil 99 Rest., Bertucci's, Chili's, Chipotle Mexican, Dunkin', Five Guys, Friendly's, IHOP, McDonald's, Panda Express, Panera Bread, Starbucks, Subway, Taco Bell, TX Roadhouse, Wendy's Courtyard, Holiday Inn Express, Residence Inn, Sheraton Advance Parts, Barnes&Noble, CarMax, Home Depot, Jo-Ann, Kohl's, Old Navy, O'Reilly Parts, PetCo, Petsmart, Staples, Stop&Shop, TownFair Tire, VW, Walgreens
9 (19)	US 1, to MA 27, same as 10, Walpole, W Gulf, Mobil/dsl Applebee's, Dunkin', Starbucks Best Western+, EconoLodge BigY Foods/drug, Lexus, Walmart
8 (16)	S Main St, Sharon, E Dunkin', Starbucks Shaw's Foods
7b a (13)	MA 140, to Mansfield, E 99 Rest., Jake'nJoe's Grille Comfort Inn, Courtyard, Holiday Inn, Red Roof+, Residence Inn Stop&Shop/gas, W Shell/HoneyDew Donuts/dsl Dunkin', PapaGino's $Tree
6b a (12)	I-495, S to Cape Cod, N to NH
10mm	**Welcome Ctr/ nb, full facilities, info, litter barrels, petwalk,**
9mm	**truck parking area sb**
5 (7)	MA 152, Attleboro, E H, W Gulf/dsl Barett's Alehouse, Wendy's Shaw's Foods/Osco Drug
4 (6)	I-295 S, to Woonsocket
3 (4)	MA 123, to Attleboro, E Shell/dsl Dunkin' H, zoo
2.5mm	**parking area/weigh sta both lanes, litter barrels, no restrooms**
2b a (1)	US 1A, Newport Ave, Attleboro, E Mobil/dsl McDonald's, Olive Garden Hobby Lobby, Home Depot, Market Basket Foods, TJ Maxx, Verizon, W Grampy's/dsl Kia
1 (.5)	US 1 (from sb), E Attleboro Inn Rite Aid, Volvo, W Speedway/dsl
0mm	Massachusetts/Rhode Island state line

INTERSTATE 195

Exit #	Services
22 (41)	I-495 N, MA 25 S, to Cape Cod. **I-195 begins/ends on I-495, exit 1.**
21 (39)	MA 28, to Wareham, N BB's Rest., Casa Cancun, Cosi, Gourmet Garden, Longhorn Steaks, Qdoba Mexican, Red Robin Aldi, AutoZone, GNC, JC Penney, LL Bean, Lowe's, Michael's, Old Navy, PetCo, Staples, Target, TJ Maxx, Verizon, Walmart/Subway, S Gateway Star/dsl, Mobil/Dunkin/Subway/dsl 99 Rest., Five Guys, Saga Fusion TownPlace Suites H

= gas = food = lodging = other = rest stop

INTERSTATE 195 Cont'd

Exit #	Services
37mm	parking area eb, boatramp, info
36mm	Sippican River
20 (35)	MA 105, to Marion, S RV camping (seasonal)
19b a (31)	to Mattapoisett, S Mobil Dunkin', Nick's Pizza, Ying Dynasty USPO
18 (26)	MA 240 S, to Fairhaven, 1 mi S 7-11 99 Rest., Burger King, Frontera Grill, Jake's Diner, McDonald's, PapaGino's, Pasta House, Riccardi's Italian, Subway, Taco Bell, Wendy's Hampton Inn $Tree, AutoZone, Brahmin Handbags, Buick/GMC, GNC, Marshall's, Mazda, Staples, Stop&Shop/gas, Sullivan Tire, TownFair Tire, Walgreens, Walmart/Subway
25.5mm	Acushnet River
17 (24)	Coggeshall St, (from wb only), same as 16, New Bedford, N 7-11/gas, Petro/dsl, Sunoco HoneyDew Donuts, Little Caesar's, McDonald's, Popeye's, Subway, Taco Bell GNC, Market Basket Foods, URGENT CARE
16 (23)	Washburn St (from eb), N Sunoco McDonald's
15 (22)	MA 18 S, New Bedford, S Mutual hist dist, to downtown, Whaling Museum
14 (21)	Penniman St (from eb), New Bedford, downtown
13b a (20)	MA 140, N , S Sunoco H, Buttonwood Park/zoo, CVS Drug, Shaw's Foods, Walgreens
12b a (19)	N Dartmouth, S Mobil/dsl, Mobil/Subway/dsl, Speedway 99 Rest., Applebee's, Azuma Asian, Buffalo Wild Wings, Burger King, Chipotle, ChuckeCheese, Coldstone, Dunkin', Five Guys, Friendly's, IHOP, Jimmy's Pizza, McDonald's, Olive Garden, Panera Bread, Peking Garden, Starbucks, Subway, Taco Bell, TGIFriday's, Tropical Smoothie, TX Roadhouse, Wendy's Residence Inn $Tree, AT&T, Barnes&Noble, Best Buy, BJ's Whse/gas, Chevrolet, Dick's, Firestone/auto, Home Depot, JC Penney, Jo-Ann, Kia, Kohl's, Lowe's, Macy's, Michael's, Nissan, Old Navy, PetCo, Stop&Shop/gas, Target, TJ Maxx, TownFair Tire, Toyota, USPO, Walgreens, Walmart
11b a (17)	Reed Rd, to Dartmouth, 2 mi S Shell Dunkin'
10 (16)	MA 88 S, to US 6, same as 9, Westport, S Cumberland CVS Drug
9 (15.5)	MA 24 N (from nb), Stanford Rd, Westport, S Rte 6 Gas, Supreme, Valero Dunkin', Galley Grill Hampton Inn White's Hospitality
8b	MA 24 N, (exits left from eb)
8a (15)	MA 24 S, Fall River, Westport
7 (14)	MA 81 S, Plymouth Ave, Fall River, N Speedway 99 Rest., Boston Mkt, Burger King, Dunkin', HoneyDew Donuts, KFC, Subway, Wendy's H, CVS Drug, Hyundai, S Gulf, Shell Applebee's, McDonald's Stop&Shop, Sullivan Tire, Walgreens
6 (13.5)	Pleasant St, Fall River, downtown
5 (13)	MA 79, MA 138, to Taunton, S 7-11, Speedway/dsl Dunkin'
12mm	Assonet Bay
4b a (10)	MA 103, to Swansea, Somerset, N Wilbur's Rogers Rest. repair, vet, S Shell Jillian's Grill Riverview Inn
3 (8)	US 6, to MA 118, Swansea, Rehoboth, N Mobil/Dunkin', Speedway Five Guys, Friendly's, McDonald's, Subway, Thai Taste, Wendy's $Tree, AT&T, BigLots, Firestone/auto, JoAnn Fabrics, Marshall's, Petsmart, Price Rite Foods, Target, Verizon, Walmart/Subway, S Cumberland Farms/dsl Umi Japanese Holiday Inn Express, Rodeway Inn Kia, NAPA, USPO
5.5mm	parking area wb
2 (5)	MA 136, to Newport, S Mobil/24hr, Shell/24hr Dunk McDonald's, Subway CVS Drug, Toyota
3mm	weigh sta eb
1 (1)	MA 114A, to Seekonk, N Exxon, Global/Subway/c Shell/dsl 99 Rest., Dunkin', Newport Creamery Mo 6 vet, S Mobil/24hr, Speedway/dsl, Stop&Shop Ga repair, Sunoco Applebee's, Buffalo Wild Wings, Burg King, Chick-fil-A, Chili's, Chipotle, Dunkin', Five Guys, Ichi Ichie Japanese, IHOP, Joe's Kitchen, Longhorn Steaks, McDo ald's, Moe's SW, Outback Steaks, Panera Bread, Papa Johr PapaGino's, Rebeco Mexican, Starbucks, Subway, Taco B TGIFriday's, Wendy's Best Western, Clarion, Extended St America, Hampton Inn, Knights Inn, Mary's Motel, Qual Inn $Tree, Acura, Advance Parts, AT&T, Best Buy, BigLo BJ's/gas, Bob's Stores, Dick's, Firestone/auto, GNC, Hobby Lo by, Home Depot, Kohl's, Lowe's, Michael's, PepBoys, Petco, St ples, Stop&Shop Foods, Target, TJMaxx, TownFair Tire, Verizo Walmart
0mm	Massachusetts/Rhode Island state line. **Exits 8-1 are in RI.**
8 (5)	US 1A N, Pawtucket, S Mobil/dsl Dunkin', Su way CVS Drug, Walgreens
7 (4)	US 6 E, CT 114 S, to Barrington, Seekonk
6 (3)	Broadway Ave, N Monro
5 (2.5)	RI 103 E, Warren Ave
4 (2)	US 44 E, RI 103 E, Taunton Ave, Warren Ave
3 (1.5)	Gano St, S EVC Hilton Garden
2 (1)	US 44 W, Wickenden St, India Pt, downtown , N Shell/d S EVC Hilton Garden
1 (.5)	Providence, downtown

I-195 begins/ends on I-95, exit 20 in Providence, RI. Exits 1-8 are in RI.

FALL RIVER

SEEKONK

PROVIDENCE

INTERSTATE 290

Exit #	Services
26b a (20)	I-495. **I-290 begins/ends on I-495, exit 25.**
25b a (17)	Solomon Pond Mall Rd, to Berlin, N EVC Bertucci's, O ive Garden, TGIFriday's Quality Inn, Residence Inn Be Buy, JC Penney, Macy's, Old Navy, Target, S Cafe Norma
24 (15)	Church St, Northborough
23b a (13)	MA 140, Boylston, N Gulf/Dunkin'/dsl, Shell/dsl
22 (11)	Main St, Worchester, N Dunkin'
21 (10)	Plantation St (from eb), N Dunkin', same as 20
20 (8)	MA 70, Lincoln St, Burncoat St, N Gulf/Subway/dsl, Shel dsl Crown Chicken, Denny's, Dunkin', Five Guys, KFC, Ky to, McDonald's, PapaGino's/D'Angelo, Ruby Tuesday, Subwa Taco Bell, TX Roadhouse, Wendy's Quality Inn, Suburba Inn $Tree, Aldi Foods, AT&T, AutoZone, Barnes&Nobl CVS Drug, Dick's, Kohl's, Lowe's, Staples, Stop&Shop, Targe URGENT CARE, USPO, Walgreens
19 (7)	I-190 N, MA 12
18	MA 9, Framington, Ware, N Worcester Airport, S H
16	Central St, Worcester, N 99 Rest., Starbucks Hilton Gar den, Holiday Inn Express USPO
14	MA 122, Barre, Worcester, downtown
13	MA 122A, Vernon St, Worcester, downtown
12	MA 146 S, to Millbury
11	Southbridge St, College Square, N Shell/dsl Culpep per's Cafe, Wendy's Family$
10	MA 12 N (from wb), Hope Ave
9	Auburn St, to Auburn, E Shell Arby's, Auburn Town Piz za, Dunkin', McDonald's, Outback, PapaGino's, Starbucks, Sub way, Yong Shing Comfort Inn, Holiday Inn Express (1mi)

WORCESTER

INTERSTATE 290 Cont'd

9	Continued La Quinta [other] Acura, AutoZone, Big Lots, Firestone/auto, Macy's, Midas, Monro, Petco, Shaw's Foods, Staples, TownFair Tire, USPO, Verizon
8	MA 12 S (from sb), Webster, **W** [gas] Shell [lodging] Holiday Inn Express
7	I-90, E to Boston, W to Springfield. **I-290 begins/ends on I-90.**

INTERSTATE 395

Exit #	Services
12.5	**I-395 begins/ends on I-290, exit 10.**
7 (12)	to I-90 (MA Tpk), MA 12, same as 6b, **E** [lodging] Holiday Inn Express, **W** [gas] Shell [food] Bentley Cafe
6b a (11)	US 20, **E** [gas] Cumberland [food] Major League Roast Beef, Tiny Tim's [other] NAPA, truck tires/repair, VW, **W** [gas] Shell [food] Applebee's, Chuck's Steakhouse, D'angelo, Dunkin', Friendly's, Wendy's [lodging] Fairfield Inn, Hampton Inn [other] BJ's Whse/dsl, Buick/Cadillac/GMC, Chevrolet, CVS, Ford, Home Depot, Hyundai, Nissan, TJ Maxx
5 (8)	Depot Rd, N Oxford
4b a (6)	Sutton Ave, to Oxford, **E** [gas] Shell/Dunkin'/dsl [other] $Tree, Home Depot, MktBasket Foods, URGENT CARE, **W** [gas] Mobil/dsl [food] Dunkin', McDonald's, NE Pizza, Subway [other] Cumberland Farms, CVS Drug
3 (4)	Cudworth Rd, to N Webster, S Oxford
2 (3)	MA 16, to Webster, **E** [other] RV Camping, Subaru, **W** [gas] BP/repair, Gulf, Sunoco [food] Burger King, D'angelo, Dunkin', Empire Wok, Friendly's, HoneyDew Donuts, KFC/Taco Bell, Little Caesar's, McDonald's, Mexicali Grill, Panera Bread, PapaGino's, Wendy's [other] [H], $Tree, Advance Parts, AutoZone, Big Lots, CVS Drug, Ford, GNC, O'Reilly Parts, PriceChopper Foods, Rite Aid, Verizon, Walgreens
1 (1)	MA 193, to Webster, **E** [other] [H], **W** [gas] Mobil/dsl [food] Golden Greek Rest., Wind Tiki Chinese [other] Goodyear/auto
0mm	**Massachusetts/Connecticut state line**

INTERSTATE 495

Exit #	Services
119	**I-495 begins/ends on I-95, exit 59.**
55 (119)	MA 110 (from nb, no return), to I-95 S, **E** [gas] EVC, Irving/Circle K, Mobil, Sunoco/dsl [food] Acapulco Mexican, Burger King, Dunkin', Friendly's, McDonald's, Subway [lodging] Fairfield Inn, Hampton Inn [other] AT&T, Chevrolet, Stop&Shop, Verizon, **W** [gas] Cumberland Farms/dsl [other] CVS, NAPA
54 (118)	MA 150, to Amesbury, **W** [other] RV camping
53 (115)	Broad St, Merrimac, **W** [food] Dunkin', Osaka
114mm	**parking area sb, litter barrels (6AM-8PM), [rest stop], restrooms**
52 (111)	MA 110, to Haverhill, **E** [other] [H], **W** [gas] Mobil, Racing Mart [food] Biggart Ice Cream, Dunkin'
110mm	**parking area nb, litter barrels, [rest stop]**
51 (109)	MA 125, to Haverhill, **E** [gas] Gulf, Mobil [food] Bros Pizza, China King, Dunkin' [other] [H], **W** [gas] Mobil/dsl [food] Applebee's, Burger King, Dunkin', Five Guys, Friendly's, Li's Asian, Longhorn Steaks, Lucky Corner Chinese, McDonald's, Mr Mikes Grill, Starbucks, Taco Bell, Wendy's [other] Monro Service
50 (107)	MA 97, to Haverhill, **W** [food] Starbucks [other] Ford, Target
49 (106)	MA 110, to Haverhill, **E** [gas] Cumberland Farms, Sunoco [food] 99 Rest., Athens Pizza, Dunkin', McDonald's, Oriental Garden, PapaGino's [lodging] Best Western, Hampton Inn [other] Buick/Chevrolet/GMC, Chrysler/Dodge/Jeep, CVS Drug, Marshall's, MktBasket Foods, Tire Whse, Walgreens
105.8mm	Merrimac River

HAVERHILL

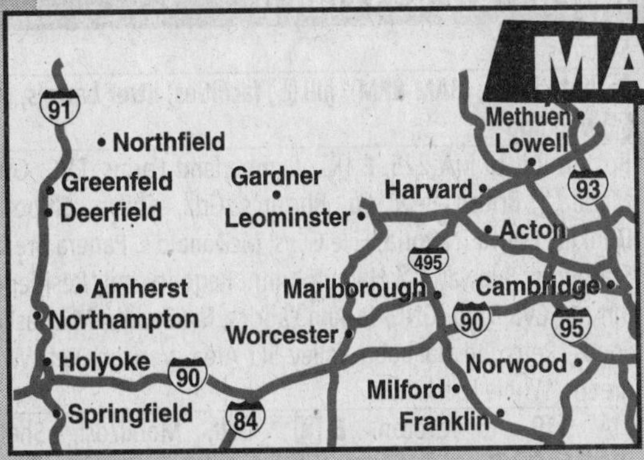

48 (105.5)	MA 125, to Bradford, **E** [gas] BJ's Whse/Subway/gas
47 (105)	MA 213, to Methuen, **1-2 mi W** [gas] EVC, Haffner's, Shell [food] Burger King, Chick-fil-A, Chipotle, ChuckeCheese, Joe's Grill, Margaritas Mexican, McDonald's, Olive Garden, Starbucks, TGIFriday's, Wendy's [other] [H], Home Depot, Marshall's, MktBasket Foods, Old Navy, Stop&Shop, Target, The Mann Orchards/Bakery, Walmart/Subway
46 (104)	MA 110, **E** [gas] Giovanni's Deli, Sunoco [food] Tekila's Mexican, **W** [other] [H]
45 (103)	Marston St, to Lawrence, **W** [other] Chevrolet, Honda, Kia, Nissan, VW
44 (102)	Merrimac St, to Lawrence
43 (101)	Mass Ave, **W** [gas] Mobil
42 (100)	MA 114, **E** [gas] Gulf, Mobil, Wave [food] Bollywood Grill, Boston Mkt, Burger King, Burtons Grill, Chipotle Mexican, Dunkin', Friendly's, Lee Chin Chinese, Panera Bread [lodging] Holiday Inn Express [other] Ace Hardware, AT&T, CVS Drug, Kohl's, MktBasket Foods, PetCo, Staples, TJ Maxx, Walgreens, **W** [gas] Gas'n Go [food] Dunkin's, KFC, Little Caesar's, Starbucks, Subway, Taco Bell, Wendy's [other] [H], Advance Parts, America's Food Basket, Family$, Marshall's, Monro Service, O'Reilly Parts/VIP Service, vet
41 (99)	MA 28, to Andover, **E** [food] Dunkin' [other] Cadillac/Chevrolet
40b a (98)	I-93, N to Methuen, S to Boston
39 (94)	MA 133, to Dracut, **E** [gas] Speedway [food] Longhorn Steaks, McDonald's [lodging] Extended Stay America, **W** [gas] Mobil/Circle K/dsl [food] Cracker Barrel, Wendy's [lodging] Fairfield Inn, Holiday Inn/rest., Residence Inn, TownePlace Suites
38 (93)	MA 38, to Lowell, **E** [gas] Cumberland Farms/dsl, EVC, Petroil/dsl [food] 99 Rest., Applebee's, Burger King, Dunkin', Harrow's Chicken Pie, IHOP, Jade East, Vic's Waffle House [lodging] Motel 6 [other] AT&T, Home Depot, Honda, TownFair Tire, Toyota, URGENT CARE, Verizon, Walmart, **W** [gas] Citgo, Mobil, NTB, Sunoco [food] Dunkin', Jillie's Rest., McDonald's, Milan Pizza, Wendy's [other] Buick/GMC, Chevrolet, Chrysler/Dodge/Jeep, CVS Drug, Hannaford Foods, Hogan Tire/auto, Marshall's, Mazda, MktBasket Foods
37 (91)	Woburn St, to S Lowell, **W** [gas] Gulf/Dunkin'/Subway
35c (90)	to Lowell SP, Lowell ConX, **0-2 mi W on US 3** [food] Chili's, Outback Steaks [lodging] Courtyard [other] Kia/VW, Lincoln, Shop&Save, Target, Walgreens
35b a (89)	US 3, S to Burlington, N to Nashua, NH
34 (88)	MA 4, Chelmsford, **E** [gas] Ampet, EVC, Mobil, Sunoco [food] 110 Grill, Domino's, Dunkin', Jimmy's Pizza, PapaGino's [lodging] Radisson [other] CVS Drug, USPO, Walgreens, **W** [gas] Shell [food] Moonstone's Rest. [lodging] Best Western+
33	MA 4, N Chelmsford (from nb)

LOWELL

= gas = food = lodging = other = rest stop

INTERSTATE 495 Cont'd

Exit #	Services
87mm	both lanes, (8AM-8PM), full facilities, litter barrels, vending
32 (83)	Boston Rd, to MA 225, E Cumberland Farms, EVC, Gulf, Mobil British Beer Co, Burton's Grill, Chili's, Chipotle, Dunkin', Evviva Trattoria, Five Guys, McDonald's, Panera Bread, Starbucks, Subway Hampton Inn, Regency Inn, Residence Inn CVS Drug, GNC, Jo-Ann Fabrics, Marshall's, MktBasket Foods, Petco, to Nashoba Valley Ski Area, Verizon, vet, Walgreens, Whole Foods Mkt
31 (80)	MA 119, to Groton, E Gulf, Mobil/dsl, Shell/Dunkin' Dunkin', Littleton Subs, Subway, Yangtze River Chinese Aubuchon Hardware, CVS Drug, Donelan's Foods, Toyota, Verizon, vet, W Anthony's Pizza, Moe's SW, Starbucks Courtyard AT&T, Market Basket, Town Fair Tire
30 (78)	MA 110, to Littleton, E EVC Littleton Cafe, W Mobil/Dunkin' vet
29b a (77)	MA 2, to Leominster, E to Walden Pond St Reserve
28 (75)	MA 111, to Boxborough, Harvard, E Gulf/Dunkin' Bravo Pizza Boxboro Regency, W vet
27 (70)	MA 117, to Bolton, E Mobil/dsl Dunkin', Subway, W vet
26 (68)	MA 62, to Berlin, E Gulf/Dunkin', Tesla EVC 110 Grill, Panera Bread, Qdoba, Subway Holiday Inn Express BJ's Whse/gas, Cabela's, GNC, Lowe's, Market Basket, Michael's, Petsmart, TJ Maxx, URGENT CARE, Verizon, W Mobil/dsl
66mm	Assabet River
25b (64)	I-290, to Worchester
25a	to MA 85, Marlborough, 1 mi E Cumberland Farms, Mobil/dsl, Stop&Shop Gas 99 Rest., Applebee's, Burger King, Checkerboards Rest., Dunkin', HoneyDew Donuts, KFC/Taco Bell, McDonald's, PapaGino's $Tree, AutoZone, Chevrolet, CVS Drug, GMC Trucks, Hogan Tire/auto, PetCo, Shaw's Foods, Stop&Shop, Verizon, Walgreens, Walmart/Subway, W Residence Inn
24b a (63)	US 20, to Northboro, Marlborough, E Mobil/dsl D'angelo, Dunkin', Lake Williams Pizza Holiday Inn, W EVC, EVC, Gulf/Dunkin', Shell 99 Rest., Boston Mkt, Chick-fil-A, China Taste, Chipotle Mexican, Five Guys, Friendly's, Japan 1, Jersey Mike's, Longhorn Steaks, McDonald's, Panera Bread, Qdoba, Starbucks, Subway, Wendy's Best Western, Courtyard, Embassy Suites, Extended Stay America, Fairfield Inn, Hampton Inn, Hyatt Place $Tree, AT&T, Hannaford Foods, Sullivan Tire/auto, URGENT CARE
23c (60)	Simrano Dr, Marlborough
23b a (59)	MA 9, to Shrewsbury, Framingham, E Cumberland/Dunkin', Gulf Wendy's Red Roof Inn Cadillac, Volvo, 0-2 mi W Mobil/dsl, Shell Bertucci's, Chateau Rest., Chipotle Mexican, Dunkin', Harry's Rest., Mandarin, McDonald's, Starbucks, Subway Courtyard, Doubletree Inn, Extended Stay America, Extended Stay America (2), Extended Stay America (3), Hampton Inn, Residence Inn H, Buick/GMC, CarMax, Chrysler/Dodge/Jeep, Marshall's, Staples, Stop&Shop, VW
22 (58)	I-90, MA TPK, E to Boston, W to Albany
21b a (54)	MA 135, to Hopkinton, Upton, E Cumberland, Mobil/Dunkin' 110 Grill, Dynasty Chinese, Hiller's Pizza, Starbucks Verizon
20 (50)	MA 85, to Milford, E Dunkin', W Gulf/dsl/LP, Mobil/dsl 99 Rest., Pizza 85/deli, TGIFriday's, Wendy's Best Western, Courtyard, Fairfield Inn, Holiday Inn Express H, Best Buy, Lowe's, PetCo, Staples, Target, Toyota
19 (48)	MA 109, to Milford, W Mobil/Circle K/dsl, Shell A plebee's, Burger King, Chipotle, Dunkin', Five Guys, IH KFC, McDonald's, Panera Bread, PapaGino's, Red Heat Tave Starbucks, Subway Doubletree, La Quinta $Gene $Tree, AutoZone, Big Y Foods, CVS Drug, Jo-Ann Fabrics, Koh Stop&Shop, TJ Maxx, TownFair Tire
18 (46)	MA 126, to Bellingham, E Chili's, McDonald's, Mo SW Barnes&Noble, Michael's, MktBasket Foods, Old Na Staples, Verizon, Walmart/Subway, Whole Foods Mkt, W Mobil, Speedway/dsl, Sunoco/dsl Chicago Grill, Dunki Outback Steaks Home Depot, Petsmart
17 (44)	MA 140, to Franklin, Bellingham, E BP/7-11, Mobil/d Shell/dsl 3 Rest., British Beer Co, Burger King, Chipot Dunkin', Firehouse Subs, Five Guys, HoneyDew Donuts, Lon horn Steaks, Panera Bread, PapaGino's, Pepper Terrace Th Starbucks, Subway, Taco Bell, Wendy's AT&T, AutoZo Buick/GMC, CVS Drug, GNC, Marshall's, Midas, Stop&Sho URGENT CARE, Verizon, W Stop&Shop Gas 99 Res Ichigo Ichie Hibachi Residence Inn BJ's Whse/Subwa gas
16 (42)	King St, to Franklin, E BP/7-11 Dunkin', King St Ca Spruce Pond Creamery Hampton Inn, W Hawthc Suites
15 (39)	MA 1A, to Plainville, Wrentham, E Assisi Pizza repa W Mobil/dsl Chicago Grill, Cracker Barrel, Dunki Ruby Tuesday Premium Outlets/famous brands
14b a (37)	US 1, to N Attleboro, E Shell/dsl Luciano's Rest. A bor Motel Bass Pro Shops (4mi), W Mobil Chili Dunkin', Panera Bread Holiday Inn Express casin Lowe's, NTB, Pete's RV Ctr, Stop&Shop, Target, TJ Maxx, vet
13 (32)	I-95, N to Boston, S to Providence, W H
12 (30)	MA 140, to Mansfield, E Tesla EVC Bertucci's Italia Buffalo Wild Wings, Chipotle Mexican, Coldstone, Dunki Longhorn Steaks, Papa Gino's, Qdoba Mexican, Sake Japanes TGIFriday's AT&T, Best Buy, Firestone/auto, GNC, Hon Depot, Kohl's, LL Bean, Michael's, PetCo, Shaw's Foods, Staple Verizon
11 (29)	MA 140 S (from sb), 1 mi W Cumberland, Mobil Be Sandwich, Dunkin', Fiesta Mexican, Mandarin Chinese, McDo ald's $Tree, Roche Bros Mkt
10 (26)	MA 123, to Norton, E Dunkin' QuickStop, W H
9 (24)	Bay St, to Taunton, E Chateau Rest., W Dunkin', Ja bo Cafe, Ruby Tuesday, Subway, Wendy's Extended Sta America, Holiday Inn $Tree, BJ's Whse, Tadeschi Food Watson Pond SP
8 (22)	MA 138, to Raynham, E Mobil/dsl, Speedway/dsl Ho eyDew Donuts, W AARC/dsl/repair, Gulf/Dunkin', Stop Go/dsl Brothers Pizza, Cape Cod Cafe, D'angelo, Hone Dew Donuts, Lucky Corner Chinese, McDonald's, PieZoni Pizza H, Ace Hardware, Mkt Basket Foods, O'Reilly Part USPO, Walmart
7b a (19)	MA 24, to Fall River, Boston, 1/2 mi E Mobil/dsl Bur er King
18mm	weigh sta both lanes
17mm	Taunton River
6 (15)	US 44, to Middleboro, E Super/dsl Burger Kin Dunkin', Friendly's, PapaGino's, Subway, W Irving/Circ K/Dunkin'/dsl Fairfield Inn, Holiday Inn Express
5 (14)	MA 18, to Lakeville, E Shell, Super/dsl D'Angel Dave's Diner, Harry's Grille, Lorenzo's Rest, PapaGino's, Persy Place Cafe CVS Drug, Kelly's Tire, Trucchi's Mkt, W Mas sasoit SP, RV camping (seasonal)

MILFORD

MARLBORO

MILFORD

MA

INTERSTATE 495 Cont'd

Exit #	Services
4 (12)	MA 105, to Middleboro, E Cumberland/dsl, Petro-Max Best Pizza, China Sails, DQ, Dunkin', McDonald's AutoZone, Family$, Hannaford Mkt, Rite Aid
11mm	parking area eb
10mm	parking area both lanes
3 (8)	MA 28, to Rock Village, S Middleboro, E GeKo/dsl repair, W Mobil/Dunkin'/Subway/dsl
2 (3)	MA 58, W Wareham, E Mobil/dsl (2mi) Dunkin' (2mi) RV camping, to Myles Standish SF, W Shell/dsl
2mm	Weweantic River
I-495 begins/ends on I-195, MA 25 S	

NOTES

MICHIGAN

INTERSTATE 69

Exit #	Services
273mm	Welcome Ctr/ eb, full facilities, litter barrels, petwalk
199	Lp 69 (from eb, no return), to Port Huron, 0-2 mi S on Lp 69 Mobil/dsl, Speedway Arby's, Burger King, Jimmy John's, KFC, Little Caesar's, McDonald's, Subway, Taco Bell, Tim Horton's, Wendy's $General, Advance Parts, AutoZone, Kroger/gas, repair, Sam's Club/gas, to Port Huron, USPO
I-69 E and I-94 E run together into Port Huron. See I-94, exits 274-275mm.	
198	I-94, to Detroit and Canada
196	Wadhams Rd, N BP/Wendy's, Marathon, Speedy Q/dsl Hungry Howie's, McDonald's, Peking Kitchen, Subway, Taco Bell KOA (1mi), Vinckier Foods, Wadham's Drugs, S Pilot/Subway/dsl/scales/24hr golf
194	Taylor Rd, N Goodells CP, RV camping
189	Wales Center Rd, to Goodells, S golf
184	MI 19, to Emmett, N Sunoco/dsl/scales/24hr repair, USPO, S Marathon/dsl/24hr
180	Riley Center Rd, N KOA
176	Capac Rd, N BP/dsl/scales, Loves/Chester's/McDonald's/dsl/scales/24hr
174mm	wb, full facilities, litter barrels, petwalk, vending
168	MI 53, Imlay City, N BP/dsl, Speedway/dsl Big Boy, Burger King, DQ, Hungry Howie's, Jet's Pizza, John's Country Kitchen, Little Caesar's, Lucky's Steaks, McDonald's, New China, Taco Bell, Wah Wong Chinese, Wendy's/Tim Horton Days Inn, M53 Motel, Super 8 AutoZone, Chevrolet, Chrysler/Dodge/Jeep, CVS Drug, Ford, GNC, Kroger/dsl, NAPA, O'Reilly Parts, Verizon
163	Lake Pleasant Rd, to Attica
160mm	eb, full facilities, litter barrels, petwalk, vending
159	Wilder Rd
158mm	Flint River
155	MI 24, Lapeer, 1 mi N Speedy Q/dsl, Sunoco/dsl Apple Tree Rest., Applebee's, Arby's, Blind Fish Rest., Brian's Rest., Buffalo Wild Wings, Burger King, Checkers, DQ, Jet's Pizza, Jimmy John's, KFC, Leo's Coney Island, Little Caesar's, Mancino's, McDonald's, Nick's Grill, Sonic, Starbucks, Subway, Taco Bell, Tim Horton, Wah Wong Chinese, Wendy's Best Western, Holiday Inn Express H, $Tree, Aldi Foods, AT&T, AutoZone, Belle Tire, Home Depot, Honda, Kohl's, Kroger/gas, Marshall's, Meijer/dsl, Michael's, Office Depot, O'Reilly Parts, Rite Aid, st police, URGENT CARE, Verizon, vet, Walgreens, S Mobil/dsl Chrysler/Dodge/Jeep, Harley Davidson

LAPEER

153	Lake Nepessing Rd, S camping, golf, to Thumb Correctional
149	Elba Rd, N Torzewski CP, S Country Mkt, RV/truck repair
145	MI 15, Davison, N Marathon, Speedway/dsl, Sunoco/dsl Apollo Rest., Applebee's, Arby's, Big Boy, Burger King, Chee Kong Chinese, Flag City Diner, Hungry Howie's, Italia Gardens, Jimmy John's, KFC, Little Caesar's, Lucky's Steaks, McDonald's, Pizza Hut, Senor Lucky, Subway, Taco Bell, Tim Horton, Tropical Smoothie Best Western AutoValue Parts, Buick/GMC, Davison Automotive, GNC, Monro Tire, Rite Aid, Verizon, Walgreens, YaYa Chicken, S Mobil/dsl Sicilian Pizza vet
143	Irish Rd, N Speedway/dsl Menard's, S Sunoco/McDonald's/24hr Meijer/dsl/e85
141	Belsay Rd, Flint, N Marathon/Wendy's/dsl/24hr, Mobil Halo Burger, KFC, McDonald's, Subway, Taco Bell $Tree, Walmart/Subway, S Sunoco/Tubby's/dsl Little Caesar's
139	Center Rd, Flint, N Speedway/dsl Applebee's, Domino's, El Cozumel Mexican, Empire Wok, Halo Burger, Leo's Coney Island, Quiznos, Starbucks, Subway, Tim Horton Aldi Foods, Big Lots, Discount Tire, GNC, Home Depot, JC Penney, Jo-Ann Fabrics, Staples, 0-2 mi S China 1, Coney Island, DQ, Hungry Howie's, McDonald's, Red Baron Rest., Subway Burton Inn $Tree, AT&T, Belle Tire, Meijer/dsl, TJ Maxx, Verizon
138	MI 54, Dort Hwy, N BP/dsl, Speedway/dsl, Sunoco/dsl Big John's Rest., Little Caesar's, Rally's, Tom's Coney Island, YaYa's Chicken H, $General, KanRock Tires, Rite Aid, Save-a-Lot, Walgreens, 0-2 mi S Marathon, Marathon, Sunoco American Diner Coney Island, Arby's, Big John Steak, Burger King, Church's, Empress of China, KFC, McDonald's, Taco Bell, The Coney Grill Travel Inn $General, Advance Parts, AutoZone, Burton Tire/auto, Family$, O'Reilly Parts, Tuffy Auto, U-Haul, Walgreens
137	I-475, UAW Fwy, to Detroit, Saginaw
136	Saginaw St, Flint, N Sunoco/dsl H, U MI at Flint
135	Hammerberg Rd, industrial area
133b a	I-75, S to Detroit, N to Saginaw, US 23 S to Ann Arbor
131	MI 121, to Bristol Rd, 1/2 mi N on Miller Rd Bar Louie, BD Mongolian BBQ, Buffalo Wild Wing, Casa Real, Chili's, Chipotle, ChuckeCheese, Famous Dave's BBQ, Golden Corral, Golden Moon Chinese, Halo Burger, Hooters, Jimmy John's, Leo's Coney Island, LJ Silver, Logan's Roadhouse, Olive Garden,

FLINT

MI

INTERSTATE 69 Cont'd

131	Continued Osaka Buffet, Outback Steaks, Panda Express, Panera Bread, Red Robin, Subway, Taco Bell, Telly's Coney Island, TX Roadhouse $Tree, AT&T, Barnes&Noble, Belle Tire, Best Buy, BigLots, Hobby Lobby, JC Penney, Jo-Ann Fabrics, Kohl's, Macy's, Michael's, Old Navy, PetCo, Petsmart, Target, TJ Maxx, USPO, Valley Tire, Verizon
129	Miller Rd, **S** Arby's, Burger King, McDonald's, Subway, Taco Bell, Wendy's Kroger/gas, O'Reilly Parts
128	Morrish Rd, **N** Meijer/dsl/e85, **S** Admiral, Mobil/dsl Hungry Howie's
126mm	**eb, full facilities, info, litter barrels, petwalk,**
123	MI 13, to Saginaw, Lennon, **N** Speedway/dsl USPO
118	MI 71, to Corunna, Durand, **N** Durand Automotive, **S** Shell/dsl, Valero China House, Hungry Howie's, McDonald's, Subway, Wendy's Quality Inn Ace Hardware, CarQuest, Chevrolet, Family$, golf, Rite Aid
115mm	Shiawassee River
113	Bancroft, **S** BP/dsl (1.5mi) RV camping
105	MI 52, to Owosso, Perry, **S** Citgo/Subway/dsl, Exxon/7-11, Mobil/dsl, Sunoco/dsl/scales/24hr Burger King, Cafe Sports, China Garden, Hungry Howie's, McDonald's, Taco Bell Heb's Inn $General, Carl's Mkt, Family$, Rite Aid, truck repair (1mi), USPO
101mm	**wb, full facilities, litter barrels, petwalk,**
98.5mm	Vermilion River
98	Woodbury Rd, to Laingsburg, Shaftsburg
94	Lp 69, Marsh Rd, to E Lansing, Okemos, **S** Speedway/dsl McDonald's Gillette RV Ctr, Meijer/Subway/dsl/e85, Monticello's Mkt
92	Webster Rd, Bath
89	US 127 S, to E Lansing
87	Old US 27, to Clare, Lansing, **N** Marathon, Speedway/Speedy's Café/dsl Arby's, Bob Evans, Burger King, China Gourmet, FlapJack Rest., Little Ceasar's, Mancino's, McDonald's, Subway, Tim Horton Sleep Inn Chevrolet, Meijer/dsl, Price Rite RV Ctr, Verizon, vet, **S** Speedway/dsl American Inn
85	DeWitt Rd, to DeWitt
84	Airport Rd
91	I-96 (from sb), W to Grand Rapids, Grand River Ave, Frances Rd, **W** FLYING J/Denny's/dsl/24hr
93b a	MI 43, Lp 69, Saginaw Hwy, to Grand Ledge, **0-2 mi N** EVC, Shell, Speedway/dsl Applebee's, Buffalo Wild Wings, Burger King, Carrabba's, Cheddar's, Chick-fil-A, Chipotle, Denny's, Finley's Grill, Frank's Grill, Hibachi Grill, Honeybaked Ham, Houlihan's, Jets Pizza, Logan's Roadhouse, Longhorn Steaks, Marco's Pizza, McDonald's, Outback Steaks, Panera Bread, Qdoba, Red Robin, Subway Comfort Inn, Fairfield Inn, Hampton Inn, Hilton Garden, Motel 6, Quality Inn, Ramada Inn, Red Roof Inn, Residence Inn H, $Tree, Aldi, AT&T, Barnes&Noble, Best Buy, BigLots, Chrysler/Dodge/Jeep, Hobby Lobby, JC Penney, Kohl's, Kroger/dsl, Meijer/dsl/24hr, Target, TJ Maxx, vet, Walgreens, **S** QD, Shell/Dunkin', Sunoco/McDonald's Arby's, Biggby Coffee, Bob Evans, Cancun Mexican, Cracker Barrel, Culver's, Steak'n Shake SpringHill Suites Belle Tire, Buick/GMC, Discount Tire, Lowe's, Mazda/Volvo, Menards, Michael's, PetsMart, Staples, Walmart/Subway
95	I-496, to Lansing
72	I-96, E to Detroit, W to Grand Rapids
70	Lansing Rd

LANSING

MARSHALL

COLDWATER

68mm	**nb, full facilities, litter barrels, petwalk, , vend**
66	MI 100, to Grand Ledge, Potterville, **W** BP/dsl, Shell/Subway/dsl Charlie's Grill, McDonald's, to Fox Co Park
61	Lansing Rd, **E** Murphy USA/dsl Applebee's Comfort Inn $Tree, AT&T, AutoZone, Buick/Chevrolet/GMC, Verizon, Walmart/Subway, **W** QD, Speedway/dsl Arby's, Big Boy, Biggby Coffee, Burger King, Jersey Subs, J... Pizza, KFC, Little Caesar's, McDonald's, Pizza Hut, Rally's, Taco Bell, Tasty Twist, Top Chinese, Wendy's H, Ace Hardw... Advance Parts, Family$, Ford, NAPA, O'Reilly Parts, Tire City,
60	MI 50, Charlotte, **E** Holiday Inn Express Meijer/dsl, ...GENT CARE, **W** Admiral Best Value Inn H
57	Lp 69, Cochran Rd, to Charlotte
51	Ainger Rd, **1 mi E** gas food RV camping
48	MI 78, to Bellevue, Olivet, **1 mi E** Cenex/Subway/dsl Olivet Coll
42	N Drive N, Turkeyville Rd, **W** Osprey Grille
41mm	**sb, full facilities, litter barrels, petwalk,**
38	I-94, E to Detroit, W to Chicago
36	Michigan Ave, to Marshall, **E** Admiral, Citgo/dsl/e..., Shell/Subway/dsl Applebee's, Arby's, Biggby Coffee, Little Caesar's, McDonald's, Pizza Hut, Speedy Chick, Starbucks, Taco Bell, Wendy's, Yin Hai Chinese Quality Inn $General, $Tree, Ace Hardware, AT&T, AutoZone, Chevrolet, Family F... Mkt/gas, NAPA, O'Reilly Parts, Rite Aid, Save-A-Lot, Tuffy Au... Verizon, **W** Arbor Inn H, Chrysler/Dodge/Jeep
32	F Drive S, **E** Shell/dsl RV Camping
25	MI 60, to Three Rivers, Jackson, **E** BP/dsl, Sunoco/dsl, Shell/Country Pride/dsl/scales/24hr/@ McDonald's, Subway $General, Auto Value Parts, RV camping
23	Tekonsha, **W** access to RV camping
16	Jonesville Rd, **W** Waffle Farm Camping (2mi)
13	US 12, to Quincy, Coldwater, **E** Speedway/dsl Applebee's, Biggby Coffee, Bob Evans, Buffalo Wild Wings, Gra... Buffet Hampton Inn, Holiday Inn Express, Red Roof Inn $Tree, Aldi Foods, AT&T, AutoZone, Belle Tire, BigLo... Buick/Chevrolet/GMC, GNC, Haylett RV Ctr, Home Depot, Meijer/dsl, Verizon, Walmart/Subway, **W** Citgo/dsl, Speedwa... dsl Arby's, Burger King, Coldwater Garden Rest., Cotta... Inn Pizza, Culver's, Dickey's BBQ, Jimmy John's, KFC, Little Caesar's, McDonald's, Pizza Hut, Subway, Taco Bell Best Western+, Quality Inn H, auto repair, Ford/Lincoln, O'Rei... Parts, Rite Aid, st police, Walgreens
10	Lp 69, Fenn Rd, to Coldwater, **W** Harbor Cove RV Park (4m...
8mm	**weigh sta nb**
6mm	**Welcome Ctr nb, full facilities, litter barrels, petwalk, , vending**
3	Copeland Rd, Kinderhook, **W** BP/dsl
0mm	**Michigan/Indiana state line**

INTERSTATE 75

Exit #	Services
395mm	US/Canada Border, Michigan state line, **I-75 begins/ends** ... **toll bridge to Canada.**
394	Easterday Ave, **E** Citgo/Krist/dsl Holiday Inn Express Ramada Inn (2mi) H, to Lake Superior St U, **W Welcome Ctr/ , info** Admiral/dsl, Holiday/dsl/currency exchange
392	3 Mile Rd, Sault Ste Marie, **E** Admiral/dsl, Holiday/dsl, Marathon/dsl, Shell/dsl, Sunoco/dsl Applebee's, Arby's, Asia... Buffet, Buffalo Wild Wings, Burger King, Domino's, DQ, Fu... Steaks, Great Wall Chinese, Indo China Garden, Jimmy John's, Little Caesar's, McDonald's, Pizza Hut, Subway, Taco Be...

INTERSTATE 75 Cont'd

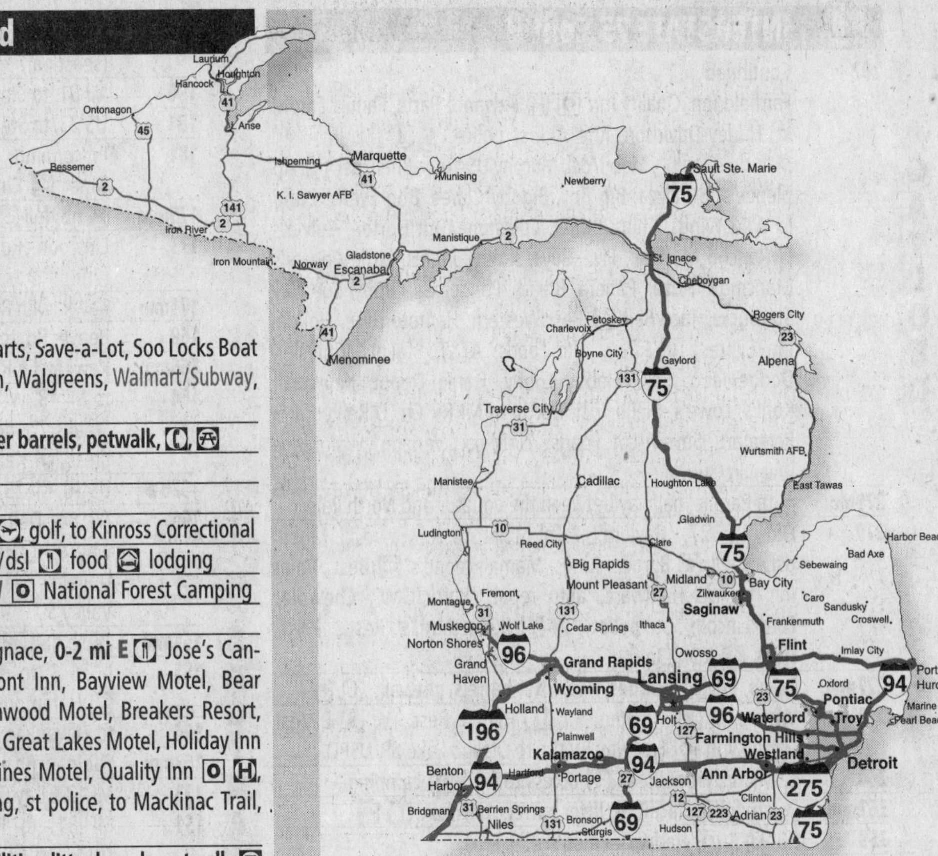

392 Continued
Wendy's Best Value Inn, Best Western, Comfort Inn, Days Inn, Hampton Inn, Plaza Motel, Skyline Motel, Super 8 H, $Tree, Advance Parts, AT&T, AutoZone, BigLots, Buick/Chevrolet/GMC, Family$, Goodyear/auto, Jo-Ann Fabrics, Kohl's, NAPA, O'Reilly Parts, Save-a-Lot, Soo Locks Boat Tours, st police, TJ Maxx, Verizon, Walgreens, Walmart/Subway, **W** Meijer/dsl

389mm **nb, full facilities, info, litter barrels, petwalk,**

386 MI 28, **W** to Brimley SP

379 Gaines Hwy, **E** to Barbeau Area

378 MI 80, Kinross, **E** BP/dsl , golf, to Kinross Correctional

373 MI 48, Rudyard, **2 mi W** gas/dsl food lodging

359 MI 134, to Drummond Island, **W** National Forest Camping

352 MI 123, to Moran, Newberry

348 H63, to Sault Reservation, St Ignace, **0-2 mi E** José's Cantina Bavarian Haus, Baymont Inn, Bayview Motel, Bear Cove Inn, Best Value Inn, Birchwood Motel, Breakers Resort, Cedars Motel, Evergreen Motel, Great Lakes Motel, Holiday Inn Express, NorthernAire Motel, Pines Motel, Quality Inn H, casino, Castle Rock Camping, st police, to Mackinac Trail, **W** Castle Rock Gifts

346mm **/scenic turnout sb, full facilities, litter barrels, petwalk,**

345 Portage St (from sb), St Ignace

344b US 2 W, **W** BP/dsl, Holiday/dsl, Shell/dsl Big Boy, Burger King, Clyde's Drive-In, McDonald's, Subway, Suzy's Pasties Quality Inn, Sunset Motel, Super 8 Ford, golf, KOA, Lakeshore RV Park

344a Lp 75, St Ignace, **0-2 mi E** Shell BC Pizza, Bentley's Cafe, Galley Rest., Mackinac Grille, MI Patio Grill Aurora Borealis Motel, Boardwalk Inn, Cedar Hill Lodge, Colonial House, Moran Bay Motel, Normandy Motel, Thunderbird Motel, Village Inn/rest., Voyager Motel H, $General, Ace Hardware, Bay Drug, Family Fare Mkt, Family$, NAPA, public marina, st police, Straits SP, to Island Ferrys, TrueValue, USPO

343mm **E Welcome Ctr nb, full facilities, litter barrels, , W museum, toll booth to toll bridge**

341mm **toll bridge**, Lake Huron, Lake Michigan

339 US 23, Jamet St, **E** Audie's Rest. Days Inn, Knights Inn, LightHouse View Motel, Parkside Motel, Riviera Motel, Super 8, **W** Shell Bridgeview Diner, Darrow's Rest., Mackinaw Cookie Co Holiday Inn Express, Vindel Motel Wilderness SP

338 US 23 (from sb), same as 337, **E** Marathon/dsl BC Pizza, Burger King, DQ, KFC, Mama Mia's Pizza, Pancake Chef, Subway, Wienerlicious Baymont Inn, Court Plaza Hotel Mackinaw Mkt, Mackinaw Outfitters, USPO, **W** Holiday Inn Express

337 MI 108 (from nb, no EZ return), Nicolet St, Mackinaw City, **E Welcome Ctr/**, Citgo/dsl/LP, Tesla EVC Blue Water Grill, Lighthouse Rest., Mackinaw Pastie&Cookie Co., Starbucks Bayside Inn, Beach House Cottages, BeachComber Motel, Bell's Melody Motel, Best Value Inn, Best Western, Bridge Vista Beach Motel, Bridgeview Motel, Budget Inn, Capri Motel, Clarion, Clearwater Lakeshore Motel, Comfort Inn, Crown Choice Inn, Days Inn, EconoLodge, Fairview Inn, Great Lakes Inn, Hamilton Inn, Mackinaw Inn, North Winds Motel,

MACKINAW CITY

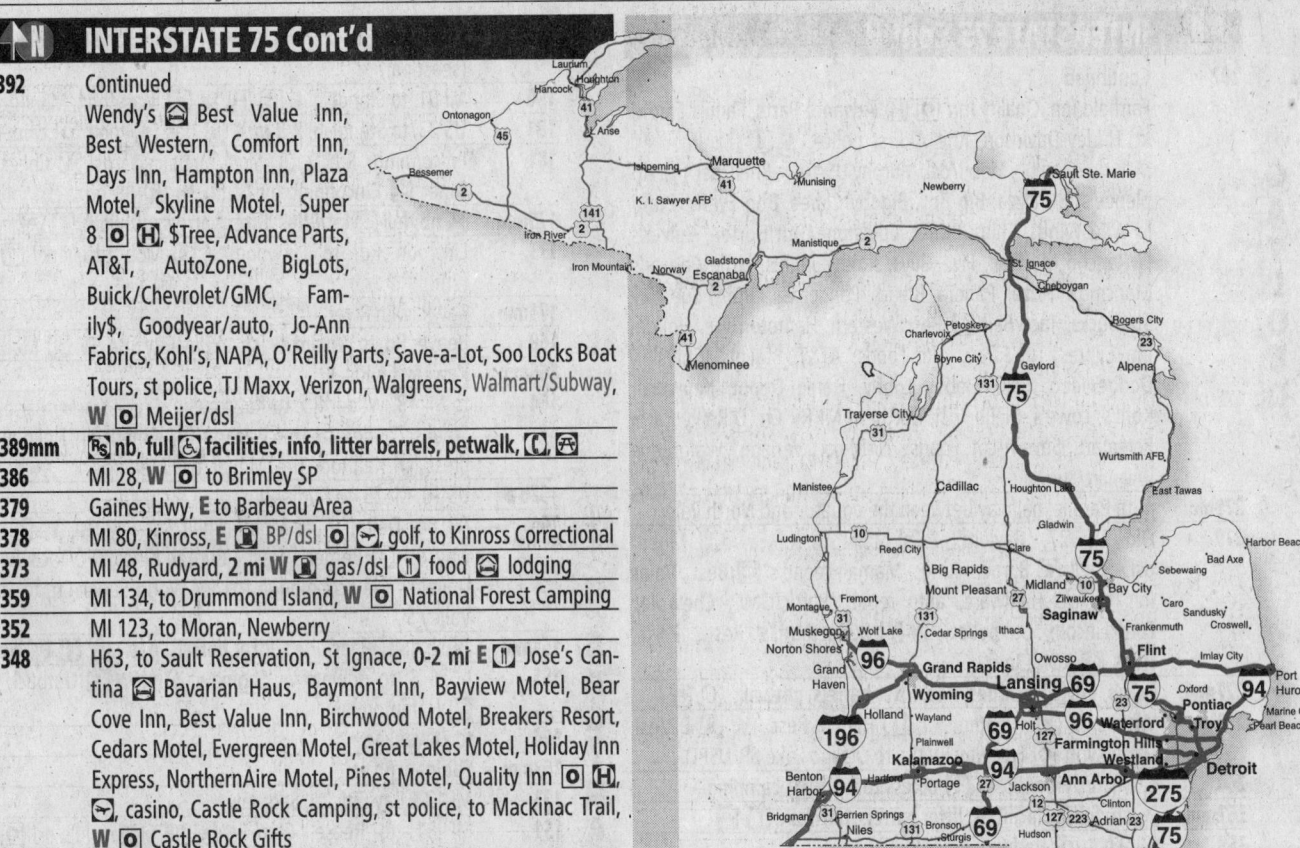

337 Continued
Quality Inn, Rainbow Motel, Ramada Ltd, Sundown Motel, Sunrise Beach Motel, Super 8, Thunderbird Inn, Waterfront Inn Harley-Davidson, Old Mill Creek SP, Tee Pee Camping, to Island Ferrys **W** KOA, Wilderness SP

336 US 31 S (from sb), to Petoskey

328mm **sb, full facilities, info, litter barrels, petwalk,**

326 C66, to Cheboygan, **E** Andy's/dsl H, Sea Shell City/gifts

322 C64, to Cheboygan, **E** H, , LP, st police

317mm **/scenic turnout nb, full facilities, info, litter barrels, petwalk,**

313 MI 27 N, Topinabee, **E** Indian River RV Resort/Camping, Topinabee Motel

311mm Indian River

310 MI 33, MI 68, **E** Hometown Inn Michigan Oaks Camping (3mi), **W** Marathon, Shell/McDonald's Burger King, Subway, Wilson's Rivers Edge Rest. Coach House Motel, Indian River Motel auto repair, Family$, Ken's Mkt/gas, to Burt Lake SP, to Indian River Trading Post/RV Resort

301 C58, Wolverine, **E** Marathon/dsl Whistle Stop Rest. Elkwood Campground (5mi), **W** Sturgeon Valley Campground (3mi)

297mm Sturgeon River

290 Vanderbilt, **E** Marathon/dsl/LP/RV dump, Spirit/dsl Elk Horn Grill USPO, Village Mkt Foods, **W** Mobil/dsl Black Bear Golf Resort (2mi)

287mm **sb, full facilities, info, litter barrels,**

282 MI 32, Gaylord, **E** Family Fare/dsl, Holiday, Speedway/dsl Arby's, Arlene's Diner, Big Buck Steaks, Burger King, DQ, Jet's Pizza, KFC, La Senorita Mexican, McDonald's, Qdoba Mexican, Subway, Wendy's Alpine Lodge, Baymont Inn,

MI

INTERSTATE 75 Cont'd

GAYLORD

282 Continued
Fairfield Inn, Quality Inn H, Advance Parts, Family FareMkt, Harley-Davidson, Rite Aid, st police, W Marathon/dsl, Marathon/dsl (2), Mobil/dsl, Murphy USA/dsl, Shell/dsl Applebee's, BC Pizza, Big Boy, Biggby Coffee, Bob Evans, Buffalo Wild Wings, China Buffet, Coldstone/Tim Horton, Culver's, El Rancho Mexican, Five Guys, Jimmy John's, Little Caesar's, Mancino's Pizza, Panera Bread, Ponderosa, Ruby Tuesday, Starbucks, Taco Bell Best Western, Hampton Inn, Holiday Inn Express $Tree, Aldi Foods, AT&T, BigLots, Chrysler/Dodge/Jeep, GNC, Hobby Lobby, Home Depot, Kenworth, Kohl's, Lowe's, Meijer/dsl, Northern MI RV Ctr, O'Reilly Parts, Petsmart, Save-A-Lot Foods, TJ Maxx, Verizon, Walgreens, Walmart/Subway

279mm 45th Parallel halfway between the equator and North Pole

279 Old US 27, Gaylord, E Marathon/Subway/dsl, Mobil/dsl, Shell Burger King, Mama Leone's Best Value Inn Ace Hardware, auto repair, Buick/GMC, Chevrolet, Ford/Lincoln, st police, W Bennethum's Rest., Porter Haus KOA (3mi)

277mm nb, full facilities, info, litter barrels, petwalk

270 Waters, E Marathon/dsl Hilltop Rest., W BP/dsl, Waters Inn Freeway RV Ctr, to Otsego Lake SP, USPO

264 Lewiston, Frederic, W access to food camping

262mm sb, full facilities, litter barrels, petwalk

259 MI 93, E Hartwick Pines SP

GRAYLING

256 (from sb), to MI 72, Grayling, access to same as 254

254 MI 72 (exits left from nb, no return), Grayling, 1 mi W Admiral/dsl, Marathon/dsl, Shell, Speedway/dsl Burger King, DQ, Keg'O'Nails, Little Caesar's, McDonald's, Pizza Hut, Subway, Taco Bell, Wendy's Days Inn, Ramada H, $General, 7-11, Ace Hardware, AT&T, Auto Value Parts, Family Fare Mkt, Family$, Ford, NAPA, O'Reilly Parts, Save-A-Lot Foods, Verizon, Walgreens

251mm nb, full facilities, info, litter barrels, petwalk, vending

251 4 Mile Rd, E Jellystone RV Park (5mi), W Marathon/Arby's/dsl/scales/RV Dump/24hr Super 8

249 US 127 S (from sb), to Clare

244 MI 18, Roscommon, 3 mi E Shell/dsl McDonald's, W Valero/dsl Higgins Lake SP, KOA (1mi)

239 MI 18, Roscommon, S Higgins Lake SP, 3 mi E Shell/McDonald's/dsl camping, W camping, Higgins Lake SP

235mm sb, full facilities, info, litter barrels, petwalk, vending

227 MI 55 W, rd F97, to Houghton Lake, 5 mi W food

222 Old 76, to St Helen, 2-4 mi E food lodging camping

215 MI 55 E, West Branch, E Shell/dsl H

212 MI 55, West Branch, E Mobil/dsl, Murphy USA/dsl, Shell/Subway/dsl Applebee's, Arby's, Big Boy, Burger King, KFC, Lumberjack Rest., McDonald's, Ponderosa, Rally's, Taco Bell, Tim Hortons, Wendy's Quality Inn, Super 8 H, Home Depot, st police, Walmart/Subway, West Branch Outlets/famous brands, W Marathon/dsl

210mm nb, full facilities, info, litter barrels, petwalk, vending

202 MI 33, to Rose City, Alger, E Marathon/Narski's Mkt/jerky, Mobil/jerky outlet/dsl, Shell/Subway/dsl Greenwood Camping

201mm sb, full facilities, litter barrels, petwalk, vending

195 Sterling Rd, to Sterling, 6 mi E gas Riverview Cam (seasonal)

190 MI 61, to Standish, E H, W Marathon, Mobil/jerky

188 US 23, to Standish, 2-3 mi E gas food camping

181 Pinconning Rd, E Shell/McDonald's/dsl Cheeseho Diner Pinconning Inn (2mi), W BP/pizza/dsl/24hr

175mm nb, full facilities, litter barrels, petwalk, vend

173 Linwood Rd, to Linwood, E Mobil/dsl/jerky Ar (2mi)

171mm Kawkawlin River

168 Beaver Rd, to Willard, E to Bay City SRA, W Mobil/je

166mm Kawkawlin River

164 to MI 13, Wilder Rd, to Kawkawlin, E Cracker Barrel, Lu Steaks, Ponderosa, Uno Pizzaria AmericInn, Holiday Inn Express KanRock Tire, Meijer/dsl, Menards

162b a US 10, MI 25, to Midland

160 MI 84, Delta, E Mobil, Shell/Subway/dsl, W Spe way/dsl Berger's Rest., Burger King, KFC/Taco Bell, Donald's Econolodge RV World Super Ctr, to Sagin Valley SU

SAGINAW

158mm sb, full facilities, litter barrels, petwalk, vendi

155 I-675 S, to downtown Saginaw, 4 mi W Outback Ste Hampton Inn

154 to Zilwaukee

153mm Saginaw River

153 MI 13 E Bay City Rd, Saginaw

151 MI 81, to Reese, Caro, E BP/McDonald's/dsl Vo Trucks, W FLYING J/Wendy's/dsl/LP/24hr

150 I-675 N, to downtown Saginaw, 6 mi W Outback Ste Hampton Inn

149b a MI 46, Holland Ave, to Saginaw, W BP, Speedwa dsl Arby's, Big John's Steaks, Burger King, McDonal Popeye's, Subway, Taco Bell Red Roof Inn, Welco Inn H, Advance Parts, USPO

144b a Bridgeport, E Loves/Hardee's/dsl/scales/24 Speedway/dsl Jellystone Camping (9mi), W Mob dsl/e85, TA/Country Pride/dsl/scales/24hr/ @ Arby's, Boy, Cracker Barrel, Hungry Howie's, McDonald's, Subway, Ta Bell, Wendy's Baymont Inn, Knights Inn $Gener Family$, Kroger/gas, Rite Aid, st police, USPO

143mm Cass River

138mm pull off both lanes

136 MI 54, MI 83, Birch Run, E Mobil/dsl/24hr Halo Burg KFC, Subway Best Value Inn, Best Western, Comfort Ir Hampton Inn, Holiday Inn Express Advance Parts, Gen al RV Ctr, Mejier/dsl/e85, Totten Tires, W BP, Citgo/7-1 Marathon A&W, Applebee's, Arby's, Bagger Dave's Bur ers, Beijing Express, Bob Evans, Buffalo Wild Wings, Culver DQ, Dunkin', Jimmy John's, Leo's Coney Island, Little Ca sar's, McDonald's, Sonic, Starbucks, Taco Bell, Tony's Res Uno Grill, Victor&Merek's Pizza, Wendy's Country Inn Suites Birch Run Outlet/famous brands, Buick/Chevrole Family$, GNC, Old Navy, USPO

131 MI 57, to Montrose, E Arby's, Big John's Steaks, Bur er King, DQ, KFC, McDonald's, Oriental Express, Subway, Ta Bell, Tim Hortons, Twins Pizza, Wendy's AutoZone, Che rolet, Chrysler/Dodge/Jeep, KanRock Tire, Tradewinds RV C vet, W Mobil/Rally's/dsl, Murphy USA/dsl Applebee Big Boy, Lucky Steaks, Tropical Smoothie Cafe $Tree, au repair, Menards, Verizon, Walmart/Subway

129mm both lanes, full facilities, litter barrels, petwalk, vending

INTERSTATE 75 Cont'd

Exit #	Services
126	to Mt Morris, **E** [gas] B&B/A&W/dsl/scales/24hr, **W** [gas] BP/dsl
125	I-475 S, UAW Fwy, to Flint
122	Pierson Rd, to Flint, **E** [gas] BP/dsl, Marathon/dsl [food] McDonald's, Papa's Coney's, Subway [other] Family$, O'Reilly Parts, Tuffy Auto, **W** [gas] Citgo/dsl, ClicMart/dsl [food] Arby's, Big John's, Cracker Barrel, Domino's, Halo Burger, Red Lobster, Taco Bell, Tim Hortons, YaYa Chicken [lodging] Baymont Inn [other] $General, $Tree, Aldi Foods, AT&T, Belle Tire, Discount Tire, Home Depot
118	MI 21, Corunna Rd, **E** [gas] [food] Badawest Lebanese, Big John's Steaks, Burger King, Church's, Hungry Howie's, Little Caesar's, Taco Bell, Wing Fong Chinese, YaYa Chicken [other] [H], Advance Parts, Family$, Kroger/gas, Rite Aid, **W** [gas] BP/dsl, Marathon/Wendy's, Mobil, Speedway/dsl, Valero [food] Burger King, KFC, Mega Diner, Rally's, Tim Horton, White Castle [lodging] Economy Motel [other] $General, Aldi Foods, AutoZone, Buick, Chevrolet, GMC, Home Depot, KanRock Tire, Kroger/gas, O'Reilly Parts, Rite Aid, Sam's Club/gas, st police, Verizon, Walgreens, Walmart
117b	Miller Rd, to Flint, **E** [gas] Speedway/dsl [food] Applebee's, Arby's, Cottage Inn Pizza, Domino's, Fuddrucker's, McDonald's, Popeye's, Qdoba, Sonic, Subway, Vehicle City Diner, West Side Diner [lodging] Knights Inn, Quality Inn, Rodeway Inn [other] Harley Davidson, Tuffy Auto, **W** [gas] Mobil [food] Bar Louie, BD's Mongolian BBQ, Bob Evans, Buffalo Wild Wings, Casa Real, Chili's, Chipotle, ChuckeCheese, Famous Dave's BBQ, Five Guys, Golden Corral, Golden Moon, Halo Burger, HoneyBaked Ham, Hooters, IHOP, Italia Garden, Jimmy John's, Logan's Roadhouse, Olive Garden, Outback Steaks, Panda Express, Panera Bread, Pizza Hut, Red Robin, Starbucks, Subway, Taco Bell, Telly's Coney Island, Tim Horton, TX Roadhouse [lodging] Red Roof Inn, Super 8 [other] AT&T, Barnes&Noble, Belle Tire, Best Buy, Big Lots, Hobby Lobby, JC Penney, Jo-Ann Fabrics, Macy's, Michael's, Midas, Office Depot, Old Navy, Petsmart, Target, U-Haul, Valley Tire, Verizon, vet
117a	I-69, E to Lansing, W to Port Huron
116	MI 121, Bristol Rd, **E** [gas] Mobil, Speedway/dsl [food] Capitol Coney Island, KFC, McDonald's, Subway [other] Advance Parts, AutoZone, **W** [gas] Marathon/dsl [other] [airport]
115	US 23 (from sb) on Hill Rd, **W** [gas] Citgo, Mobil [food] Arby's, Hill Rd Grille, Jimmy John's, McDonald's, Redwood Steaks, Subway, Taco Bell, Tim Hortons [lodging] Best Western+, Courtyard, Hampton Inn, Holiday Inn, Residence Inn [other] $Tree, Meijer/dsl
111	I-475 N (from nb), UAW Fwy, to Flint
109	MI 54, Dort Hwy (no EZ return to sb)
108	Holly Rd, to Grand Blanc, **E** [gas] Sunoco/dsl [food] Bagger Dave's Burgers, Big Apple Bagels, Buffalo Wild Wings, Culver's, Freakin' Burger, Qdoba, Taco Bell [lodging] Fairfield Inn, Holiday Inn Express, Quality Inn [other] BMW/Mercedes/Toyota, Nissan, URGENT CARE, **W** [gas] BP/McDonald's/dsl [food] Arby's [other] [H]
106	Dixie Hwy (exits left from sb, no nb return), Saginaw Rd, to Grand Blanc
101	Grange Hall Rd, Ortonville, **E** [gas] Shell/dsl [other] Groveland Oaks Camping, Holly RA, KOA, **W** [gas] Shell/dsl [other] to Seven Lakes SP
98	E Holly Rd, **E** [gas] Mobil/Tubby's/dsl [other] Ford, golf
96mm	**[RS] nb, full [handicapped] facilities, info, litter barrels, petwalk, [phone], [picnic], vending**
95mm	**[RS] sb, full [handicapped] facilities, info, litter barrels, petwalk, [phone], [picnic], vending**

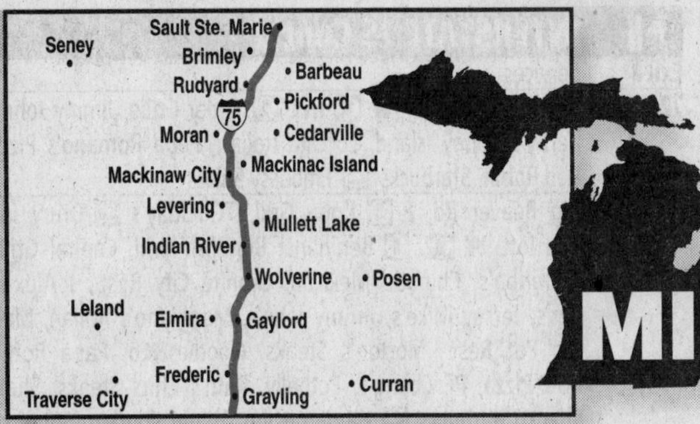

Exit #	Services
93	US 24, Dixie Hwy, Waterford, **E** [gas] BP/dsl [food] McDonald's [other] Chrysler/Dodge/Jeep, General RV Ctr, Kroger/gas (2mi), **W** [food] Kruse's Deer Lake Inn, Wendy's [other] CVS Drug, Office Depot, to Pontiac Lake RA, Walgreens
91	MI 15, Davison, Clarkston, **E** [gas] Sunoco/dsl, **W** [gas] BP/dsl [food] Andiamo Italian [other] URGENT CARE
89	Sashabaw Rd, **E** [gas] Mobil/dsl [food] Arby's, Culver's, Ruby Tuesday, Taco Bell, Tropical Smoothie Cafe [other] county park, **W** [gas] BP, Citgo [food] Chicken Shack, Dunkin', E Ocean Chinese, Guido's Pizza, Hong Kong Chinese, Hungry Howie's, Jimmy John's, Leo's Coney Island, Little Caesar's, McDonald's, Sagano Japanese, Starbucks, Subway, Tim Horton, Wendy's [other] $Tree, AT&T, CVS Drug, Kroger/dsl, vet
86mm	**weigh sta sb**
84b a	Baldwin Ave, **E** [gas] BP/dsl [food] Arby's, Big Boy, Chipotle, Joe's Crabshack, Longhorn Steaks, Panera Bread, Patty Burger, Potbelly, Starbucks, Taco Bell, Wendy's [other] $Tree, Best Buy, Costco/gas, Discount Tire, Kohl's, Michael's, Nordstrom Rack, Old Navy, PetCo, Staples, **W** [gas] Mobil [food] Bar Louie, Chili's, Five Guys, Jimmy John's, Kerby's Coney Island, McDonald's, On-the-Border, Oriental Forest Buffet, Qdoba Mexican, Rainforest Cafe, Starbucks, Steak'n Shake, Subway [lodging] TownePlace Suites [other] AT&T, Bass Pro Shops, Batteries+Bulbs, Great Lakes Crossing Outlet/famous brands, Hampton Inn, Holiday Inn Express, Marshall's, TJ Maxx, USPO, Verizon, Vitamin Shoppe
83b a	Joslyn Rd, **E** [gas] Tesla EVC [food] Biggby Coffee, Checkers, Logan's Roadhouse, Olive Garden, Panda Express, Subway [other] Belle Tire, Home Depot, Jo-Ann Fabrics, Meijer/dsl, Sam's Club/gas, Target, **W** [gas] BP
81	MI 24, Pontiac (no EZ return), **E** [other] The Palace Arena, to Bald Mtn RA
79	University Dr, **E** [gas] [food] BD Mongolian, Blaze Pizza, Dibella's Subs, Domino's, Dunkin', Jersey Mike's, Jimmy John's, Spargo Coney Island, Starbucks, Subway, Taste of Thailand, Ziggy's Cheesesteak [lodging] Extended Stay America [other] AT&T, **W** [gas] Mobil, Speedway/dsl [food] Burger King, KFC, Lelli's Steaks, McDonald's, Taco Bell, Wendy's/Tim Horton [lodging] Baymont Inn, Comfort Suites, Courtyard, Crowne Plaza, Extended Stay America, Extended Stay America (2), Hampton Inn, Hawthorn Suites, Hilton, Holiday Inn Express, Hyatt Place, Quality Inn, Rodeway Inn, Sonesta Suites, Staybridge Suites [other] [H]
78	Chrysler Dr, **E** [other] Chrysler, Chrysler Museum, Oakland Tech Ctr
77b a	MI 59, to Pontiac, **2 mi E on Adams** [food] 112 Pizza, Five Guys, Grand Tavern, Kerby's Coney Island, Panera Bread [lodging] Holiday Inn Express, Woodspring Suites [other] GNC, Meijer/dsl, Petsmart, Walmart/Subway
75	Square Lake Rd (exits left from nb), to Pontiac, **W** [other] [H], St Mary's Coll
74	Adams Rd

AUBURN HILLS

MI

INTERSTATE 75 Cont'd

TROY

Exit #	Services
72	Crooks Rd, to Troy, W [gas] EVC [food] Cedar Grille, Jimmy John's, Kerby's Coney Island, Loccino Italian, Papa Romano's Pizza, Red Robin, Starbucks [lodging] Embassy Suites
69	Big Beaver Rd, E [food] Kona Grill, TGIFriday's [lodging] Drury Inn, Marriott, W [gas] [food] Benihana, Bonefish Grill, Capital Grille, Carrabba's, Chipotle Mexican, Granite City Rest., J Alexander's, Jersey Mike's, Jimmy John's, Maggiano's Italian, Melting Pot Rest., Morton's Steaks, Noodles&Co, Papa Romano's Pizza, PF Chang's, Potbelly, Ruth's Chris Steaks, Shake Shack, Starbucks [lodging] Hampton Inn, Hilton Garden, Somerset Inn [other] AT&T, Macy's, Neiman Marcus, Nordstrom, Verizon
67	Rochester Rd, to Stevenson Hwy, E [gas] BP, Shell/dsl, Sunoco [food] Bahama Breeze, Burger King, Detroit Burger Bar, Domino's, El Charro, First Watch, Gran Castor Mexican, Hills City Grille, Hungry Howies, Jimmy John's, McDonald's, Mission BBQ, MOD Pizza, Orchid Cafe, Panera Bread, PeiWei, Picano's Italian, Qdoba, Sakura Japanese, Subway, Taco Bell, Tim Hortons, Troy Deli, Wendy's [other] Discount Tire, Fresh Thyme Mkt, Nordstrom Rack, Petsmart, REI, Tuesday Morning, vet, W [gas] [lodging] Courtyard, Quality Inn, Red Roof Inn [other] Pepboys
65b a	14 Mile Rd, Madison Heights, E [gas] Mobil/dsl, Shell/dsl [food] Bob Evans, Burger King, Chili's, Chipotle, ChuckeCheese, Coldstone, Grand Azteca, Jersey Mike's, Jimmy John's, Krispy Kreme, Logan's Roadhouse, McDonald's, Panda Express, Panera Bread, Pizza Hut, Pizza Papalis, Red Robin, Sonic, Starbucks, Steak'n Shake, Taco Bell, Wendy's [lodging] Motel 6, Red Roof Inn [other] $Tree, AT&T, Barnes&Noble, Belle Tire, Best Buy, BigLots, CVS Drug, Dick's, Field & Stream, Firestone/auto, Ford, JC Penney, Jo-Ann Fabrics, Kohl's, Macy's, Michael's, Target, TJ Maxx, Verizon, W [gas] Mobil [food] Applebee's, McDonald's, NY Coney Island, Outback Steaks, Twin Peaks [lodging] Baymont Inn, Courtyard, Days Inn, Extended Stay America, Fairfield Inn, Hampton Inn, Holiday Inn Express, Residence Inn, Rodeway Inn, TownPlace Suites [other] Costco/gas, Value Ctr Foods
63	12 Mile Rd, E [gas] Marathon/dsl [food] Culver's, Green Lantern Rest., McDonald's, Penn Sta Subs, Red Lobster, Sero's Rest., Starbucks, Tim Hortons, TX Roadhouse [other] Home Depot, Lowe's, Midas, Sam's Club/gas, Uncle Ed's Oil, USPO, vet, W [gas] Marathon, Mobil/dsl, Speedway [other] Chevrolet, Costco/gas, Family$
62	11 Mile Rd, E [gas] Exxon/dsl, Mobil [food] Biggby Coffee, Boodles Rest., Happy's Pizza, Jets Pizza, Telway Burgers [other] 7-11, Advance Parts, CVS Drug, repair/tires, Save-a-Lot, Tirezfactory, Walgreens, W [gas] BP, Marathon/dsl [food] Taco Bell, Tim Hortons, Tubby's Subs [other] Belle Tire, vet
61	I-696 E, to Port Huron, W to Lansing, to Hazel Park Raceway
60	9 Mile Rd, John R St, E [food] Checkers, China 1 Buffet, Hardee's, McDonald's, Subway, Tim Hortons [other] $General, CVS Drug, Kroger/gas, O'Reilly Parts, USPO, W [gas] Exxon, Marathon, Mobil [food] Tubby's Subs, Wendy's [other] Hasting's Parts, repair
59	MI 102, 8 Mile Rd
58	7 Mile Rd, W [gas] BP/dsl
57	McNichols Rd, E [gas] Mobil/dsl [food] LA Coney Island
56b a	Davison Fwy
55	Holbrook Ave, Caniff St, E [gas] Mobil/dsl, W [food] Grandy's Coney Island
54	E Grand Blvd, Clay Ave, W [gas] Mobil/dsl
53b	I-94, Ford Fwy, to Port Huron, Chicago
53a	Warren Ave, E [gas] Mobil, W [gas] BP
52	Mack Ave, E [gas] Exxon/dsl [food] McDonald's

DETROIT AREA

Exit #	Services
51c	I-375 to civic center, tunnel to Canada, downtown
51b	MI 3 (exits left from nb), Gratiot Ave, downtown
50	Grand River Ave, downtown
49b	MI 10, Lodge Fwy, downtown
49a	Rosa Parks Blvd, E [other] Firestone, Tiger Stadium, W [gas] Mobil,
48	**I-96 begins/ends**
47b	Porter St, E **MI Welcome Ctr**, bridge to Canada, DutyFree/24
47a	MI 3, Clark Ave, E [gas] BP/Subway/dsl, W [gas] Marathon
46	Livernois Ave, to Hist Ft Wayne
45	Fort St, Springwells Ave, W [gas] Mobil [food] McDonald's
44	Deerborn St (from nb)
43b a	MI 85, Fort St, to Schaefer Hwy, E [gas] Exxon/dsl, W [gas] Marathon Refinery [other] to River Rouge Ford Plant
42	Outer Dr, E [gas] Marathon/dsl [food] Happy's Pizza, W [gas] Qu Fuel/dsl [other] Family$, truck tires
41	MI 39, Southfield Rd, to Lincoln Park, E [food] A&W, Tim H tons, White Castle [other] Aldi Foods, Family$, O'Reilly Pa Walgreens, W [gas] Citgo/Tim Hortons, Mobil [food] Burger Ki Checkers, Hungry Howie, McDonald's, Pizza Hut, Starbuc Taco Bell, Wendy's [lodging] Royal Choice Inn [other] $Tree, AT&T, B Tire, Kroger/gas, Verizon
40	Dix Hwy, E [gas] AAA/A&W/dsl, Marathon/dsl, Sunoco, W come [food] Baskin-Robbins/Dunkin', China Bowl, Sonic, Tom Coney Island [other] 7-11, CVS Drug, Dix Parts, Meijer, W [gas] go, Marathon [food] Big Boy, Burger King, Checkers, DQ, M Donald's, Papa John's, Pizza Hut, Starbucks, Taco Bell, W dy's [other] $Tree, AT&T, Belle Tire, Family$, Kroger/gas, Tire Tra Auto/repair, Verizon
37	Allen Rd, North Line Rd, to Wyandotte, E [gas] BP/dsl, Shell/T Hortons [lodging] Hampton Inn, Holiday Inn [other] [H], Sam's Club/g W [gas] Citgo/dsl, Sunoco [food] Arby's, Burger King, Mallie's G McDonald's, Wendy's [lodging] Comfort Suites, La Quinta, Motel
36	Eureka Rd, E [gas] Speedway, Sunoco [food] Bob Evans, Burrito press, Denny's, Golden Corral, Tim Hortons [lodging] Super 8 [other] W [food] Culver's, Famous Dave's, HoneyBaked Ham, Hooters, Ji my John's, Leo's Coney Island, Little Daddy's Grill, McDonal Olga's Kitchen, Panera Bread, Penn Sta Subs, Pizza Papalis, manti Bros, Qdoba, Starbucks, Subway, Tropical Smoothie, Roadhouse, Wahlburgers, Wendy's [lodging] Red Roof Inn [other] $Tr AT&T, Belle Tire, Best Buy, Big Lots, Dick's, Discount Tire, Hob Lobby, Home Depot, JC Penney, Jo-Ann, Kohl's, Macy's, Meij dsl, Petsmart, Target, Verizon, Walgreens
35	US 24, Telegraph Rd, (from nb, exits left)
34b	Sibley Rd, Riverview, W [gas] Sunoco/Baskin-Robbins/Dunki Subway [other] General RV Ctr
34a	to US 24 (from sb), Telegraph Rd
32	West Rd, to Trenton, Woodhaven, E [gas] EVC, EVC, FLYING Detroiter/IHOP/dsl/LP/scales/24hr/@, Speedway/dsl [food] A plebee's, Baskin-Robbins/Dunkin', Blue Margarita, Bob Eva Buffalo Wild Wings, Chipotle, Christoff's Rest., Coldstone, Fi house Subs, Five Guys, Jersey Subs, MOD Pizza, Olga's Kit en, Panda Express, Panera Bread, Qdoba, Starbucks, Steak Shake, Subway, Taco Bell, Tim Hortons, Wendy's, White C tle [other] Aldi Foods, Belle Tire, Chevrolet, Chrysler/Dodge/Je Discount Tire, Firestone/auto, Ford, GNC, Home Depot, Kohl Lowe's, Marshall's, Meijer/dsl, Michael's, Office Depot, O'Re Parts, Petsmart, Target, URGENT CARE, Verizon, Walmart/Su way, W [gas] BP, BP/Tim Hortons, Circle K/Hardee's/dsl [food] A dy's Pizza, DQ, Jimmy John's, Little Caesar's, McDonald's, Sp ta Coney Island, Subway [lodging] Best Western/rest., Holiday I Express, Westwood Inn [other] [H], $Tree, AT&T, CVS Drug, Kroge dsl, Walgreens

INTERSTATE 75 Cont'd

Exit #	Services
29	Gilbralter Rd, to Flat Rock, Lake Erie Metropark, E [gas] Citgo/dsl [food] McDonald's, Peking Chinese, Sammy's Pizza, Subway, Tim Horton, Wendy's [other] [H], GNC, Kroger/gas, W [gas] Marathon/Burger King/dsl [lodging] Baymont Inn [other] Ford
28	rd 85 (from nb), Fort St, E [other] [H]
27	N Huron River Dr, to Rockwood, E [gas] Marathon/7-11/dsl [food] Benito's Pizza, Marco's Pizza, Subway [other] $General, Rite Aid, SaveALot, USPO, W [gas] Speedway/dsl [food] River Village Rest.
26	S Huron River Dr, to S Rockwood, E [gas] Sunoco/dsl [food] Dixie Cafe [other] USPO
21	Newport Rd, to Newport, E [gas] BP/Subway/dsl, W [gas] Marathon/Burger King/dsl/24hr
20	I-275 N, to Flint
18	Nadeau Rd, E [gas] Loves/Hardee's/dsl/scales/24hr, W [gas] Pilot/Taco Bell/dsl/scales/24hr [other] [H]
15	MI 50, Dixie Hwy, to Monroe, E [gas] Citgo [food] Burger King, Red Lobster, Subway [lodging] Best Value Inn, Days Inn, Hampton Inn, Holiday Inn Express [other] to Sterling SP, W [gas] Pilot/Subway/dsl/scales/24hr, TA/BP/Fazoli's/Popeye's/Tim Hortons/dsl/scales/24hr/@ [food] Cracker Barrel, Denny's, El Maguey, IHOP, McDonald's, Taco Bell, Wendy's [lodging] Quality Inn [other] [H], to Viet Vet Mem
14	Elm Ave, to Monroe
13	Front St, Monroe
11	La Plaisance Rd, to Bolles Harbor, W [gas] Marathon/Taco Bell/dsl, Speedway/dsl [food] McDonald's, Monroe's Hotdogs [lodging] Econolodge, Harbor Town RV Resort
10mm	**Welcome Ctr nb, full [handicap] services, info, litter barrels, petwalk, [phone], [picnic], vending**
9	S Otter Creek Rd, to La Salle, W [other] antiques
7mm	**weigh sta both lanes**
6	Luna Pier, E [gas] Sunoco/Subway/dsl/scales [food] Beef Jerky Un-Ltd., Ganders Rest. [lodging] Pier Inn [other] USPO
5	to Erie, Temperance
2	Summit St (no nb re-entry)
0mm	Michigan/Ohio state line

INTERSTATE 94

Exit #	Services
275mm	**I-69/I-94 begin/end on MI 25, N Pinegrove Ave in Port Huron,** [gas] BP, Shell/dsl, Speedway/dsl [food] Arby's, McDonald's, Tim Horton, Wendy's [lodging] Comfort Inn, Days Inn [other] Family$, Honda, Rite Aid, **tollbridge to Canada**
274.5mm	Black River
274	Water St, Port Huron, N [gas] Tesla EVC [food] Cracker Barrel [lodging] Best Western [other] Lake Port SP, Port Huron RV Park, S [gas] SpeedyQ/dsl [food] Bob Evans [lodging] Fairfield Inn, Hampton Inn, Holiday Inn Express, Quality Inn [other] Menard's, O'Reilly Parts
273mm	**Welcome Ctr/[RS] wb, full [handicap] facilities, [picnic], litter barrels, petwalk**
271	**I-69 E and I-94 E run together eb,** Lp I-69, 0-2 mi S on Lp 69 [gas] Mobil/dsl, Speedway [food] Arby's, Burger King, Jimmy John's, KFC, Little Caesar's, McDonald's, Subway, Taco Bell, Tim Horton's, Wendy's [other] $General, Advance Parts, AutoZone, Kroger/gas, repair, Sam's Club/gas, to Port Huron, USPO
269	Dove St, Range Rd, N [gas] Speedway/dsl [food] Theo's Rest. [lodging] Baymont Inn
266	Gratiot Rd, Marysville, 0-2 mi S [gas] BP, Marathon/dsl/scales/24hr, Speedway/dsl [food] Arby's, Big Boy, Burger King,

Exit #	Services
266	Continued China Lite, Dairy Boy, Daliono's, Four Star Grille, Hungry Howie's, Jets Pizza, Jimmy John's, KFC, Little Caesar's, McDonald's, Mr Pita, Pelican Café, Subway, Taco Bell, Tim Horton [lodging] Super 8 [other] [H], $General, $Tree, Advance Parts, AutoZone, CVS Drug, Meijer/dsl, O'Reilly Parts, Rite Aid, Verizon, vet, Wally's Mkt
262	Wadhams Rd, N [gas] Loves/Subway/dsl/scales/24hr, S [gas] Mobil/dsl
257	St Clair, Richmond, N [gas] Sunoco/dsl, S [gas] BP/dsl
255mm	**[RS] eb, full [handicap] facilities, info, litter barrels, petwalk, [phone], [picnic]**
251mm	**[RS] wb, full [handicap] facilities, info, litter barrels, petwalk, [phone], [picnic]**
248	26 Mile Rd, to Marine City, N [food] McDonald's (2mi), S [gas] Mobil/7-11, Shell [food] Subway, Taco Bell, Tim Horton [other] Mejier/dsl
247mm	Salt River
247	MI 19 (no eb return), New Haven
243	MI 29, MI 3, Utica, New Baltimore, N [gas] BP/Dunkin', EVC, Marathon/dsl, Sunoco/dsl [food] Applebee's, Arby's, Buffalo Wild Wings, Burger King, Chapo's Tacos, Chipotle, Chophouse, Coldstone, Coney Island, Dave's Pizza, Del Taco, Detroit Wings, Dimitri's Rest., Eagles Grill, Happy's Pizza, Jersey Mike's, Little Caesar's, McDonald's, MOD Pizza, Noodles&Co, Olga's Kitchen, Panda Express, Panera Bread, Potbelly, Qdoba, Ruby Tuesday, Starbucks, Tim Horton, TX Roadhouse, Wendy's, White Castle [other] $Tree, AutoZone, Belle Tire, Best Buy, Big Jim's Automotive, Big Lots, Dick's, Discount Tire, GNC, Hobby Lobby, Home Depot, JC Penney, Jo-Ann Fabrics, Kohl's, Lowe's, Meijer/Subway/dsl, Michael's, NAPA, Old Navy, O'Reilly Parts, PetCo, PetsMart, Rite Aid, Staples, Target, TJ Maxx, URGENT CARE, Verizon, Walgreens, S [gas] Marathon/dsl/24hr, Speedway/dsl/24hr [food] Big Boy, Buscemi's Pizza, Checkers, Taco Bell [lodging] LodgeKeeper [other] Chevrolet
241	21 Mile Rd, same as 240, Selfridge, N [gas] Exxon/dsl/e85, Speedway/dsl [food] China King, Hungry Howie's, Jets Pizza, Jimmy John's [other] Advance Parts, AT&T, CVS Drug, Verizon, vet
240	to MI 59, N [gas] 7-11/gas, BP, Mobil [food] Arby's, Bob Evans, Burger King, Coney Island, Culver's, KFC, McDonald's, Taco Bell, Twisted Rooster [lodging] Fairfield Inn, Hampton Inn, Holiday Inn Express [other] $Tree, Ford, Harley-Davidson, Kia, Menard's, Subaru, Toyota, Walmart
237	N River Rd, Mt Clemens, N [gas] BP/dsl, Mobil/Subway/dsl [food] Clinton River Cruise Co, McDonald's [other] [H], General RV Ctr
236.5mm	Clinton River
236	Metro Parkway, S [food] Big Apple Bagels, Empire Chinese, Little Caesar's, McDonald's, Subway [other] [H], CVS Drug, Kroger, URGENT CARE, Verizon
235	Shook Rd (from wb)
234b a	Harper Rd, 15 Mile Rd, N [gas] BP/McDonald's, Marathon/dsl, SpeedyQ, Sunoco/dsl [food] Domino's, Gina's Cafe, Tim Horton's [other] Family$, vet, S [gas] Shell [food] China Moon, Subway, Travis Rest., Winners Grill

INTERSTATE 94 Cont'd

DETROIT AREA

Exit #	Services
232	Little Mack Ave (from wb only), same as 231, N Marathon, Mobil, Shell, Sunoco Chipotle, Coldstone, Denny's, Hooters, McDonald's, Pizza Hut, Potbelly, Red Robin Hampton Inn, Holiday Inn Express, Red Roof Inn, Relax Inn, Super 8, Victory Inn Advance Parts, Aldi Foods, AT&T, Belle Tire, Discount Tire, Firestone/auto, O'Reilly Parts, Sam's Club/gas, Target, Tuesday Morning, S Kroger/dsl, Speedway/dsl Cracker Barrel, Culver's, IHOP Baymont Inn Home Depot, Jo-Ann Fabrics, Kroger, Meijer/dsl/24hr, PetsMart, URGENT CARE
231	(from eb), MI 3, Gratiot Ave, N Exxon/dsl, Marathon Applebee's, Arby's, Bob Evans, Burger King, Chili's, Chipotle, ChuckeCheese, Del Taco, Denny's, Famous Dave's BBQ, Huddle Grill, Jersey Mike's, Logan's Roadhouse, McDonald's, National Coney Island, Panera Bread, PetCo, Pizza Hut, Potbelly, Qdoba, Ruby Tuesday, Starbucks, Subway, Tim Horton, TX Roadhouse Days Inn, Extended Stay America, Hampton Inn, Microtel Belle Tire, Best Buy, Dick's, Discount Tire, Firestone/auto, Honda/Acura, Kia, Kohl's, Kroger, Michael's, Nissan, Sam's Club/gas
230	12 Mile Rd, N Mobil/dsl, Sunoco/dsl Jimmy John's, Outback Steaks, Starbucks, Taco Bell $Tree, AT&T, CVS Drug, Marshall's, Verizon, Walmart/Subway, S Marathon
229	I-696 W, Reuther Fwy, to 11 Mile Rd, S Shell/dsl, Speedway/dsl $General, 7-11
228	10 Mile Rd, N 7-11, BP Baskin-Robbins, Donna's Rest., Eastwind Chinese, Jet's Pizza, Little Italy Pizza, Sugarbush Rest. $General, Save Mor Drugs, URGENT CARE
227	9 Mile Rd, N BP, Metro, Mobil/dsl, Speedway/dsl DQ, McDonald's, Milestone Grill, Popeye's, Subway, Taco Bell, Tim Horton's, Wendy's $Tree, Aldi Foods, CVS Drug, Family$, Fresh Choice Mkt, Office Depot, TrueValue, vet, S Mobil/dsl Shore Pointe Motel Cadillac, Mercedes
225	MI 102, Vernier Rd, 8 Mile Rd, S BP/Subway, Mobil, Sunoco/dsl Coney Island, KFC, Taco Bell, Wendy's Kroger, Walgreens
224b	Allard Ave, Eastwood Ave
224a	Moross Rd, S Citgo H, Family Foods Mkt
223	Cadieux Rd, S BP/Subway, Marathon/dsl, Mobil, Sunoco Checkers, Papa's Pizza, Popeye's, Tubby's Subs, Wendy's, White Castle Family$, Rite Aid
222b	Harper Ave (from eb), S Hastings Auto Parts
222a	Chalmers Ave, Outer Dr, N 76, BP/Subway/dsl Coney Island, KFC, Little Caesar's Family$
220b	Conner Ave, N BP, Sunoco
220a	French Rd, S Mobil
219	MI 3, Gratiot Ave, N 76, Marathon/Subway Coney Island, McDonald's $General, Farmer John's Foods, USPO, S Citgo Burger King
218	MI 53, Van Dyke Ave, N BP, Mobil/dsl
217b	Mt Elliott Ave, S Citgo, Mobil/dsl Royal BBQ
217a	E Grand Blvd, Chene St, S Marathon
216b	Russell St (from eb), to downtown
216a	I-75, Chrysler Fwy, to tunnel to Canada
215c	MI 1, Woodward Ave, John R St
215b	MI 10 N, Lodge Fwy
215a	MI 10 S, tunnel to Canada, downtown
214b	Trumbull Ave, N to Ford Hospital
214a	(from wb)Grand River Ave
213b	I-96 W to Lansing, E to Canada, bridge to Canada, to Tiger Stadium
213a	W Grand (exits left from eb)
212b	Warren Ave (from eb)
212a	Livernois Ave, S BP/dsl, Marathon/Subway/dsl
211b	Cecil Ave (from wb), Central Ave
211a	Lonyo Rd, S Sunoco Ford
210	US 12, Michigan Ave, Wyoming Ave, N Mobil/d S BP/dsl, Sunoco/dsl Checkers
209	Rotunda Dr (from wb)
208	Greenfield Rd, Schaefer Rd, N Mobil/dsl Senate Con Island, Wendy's/Tim Horton 7-11, S River Rouge Fo Plant
207mm	Rouge River
206	Oakwood Blvd, Melvindale, N EVC, Marathon, Shell A plebee's, Biggby Coffee, Chili's, Chipotle, Coldstone, Con Island, Five Guys, Jimmy John's, Little Caesar's, Longho Steaks, Olga's Kitchen, On-the-Border, Panda Express, Pane Bread, Potbelly, Qdoba, Starbucks, Subway, Taco Bell AA Barnes&Noble, Best Buy, GNC, Greenfield Village Museu Home Depot, Jo-Ann Fabrics, Lowe's, Meijer, Michael's, C Navy, PetCo, Staples, Target, TJ Maxx, USPO, Verizon, S B dsl Burger King, McDonald's, Ming Sun Chinese, Mr Steve Pizza, Sabina's, Tim Horton's Best Western, Comfo Inn $General, $Tree, 7-11, CVS Drug, O'Reilly Parts, Ri Aid
205mm	Largest Uniroyal Tire in the World
204b a	MI 39, Southfield Fwy, Pelham Rd, N Mobil, Valer dsl 7-11, to Greenfield Village, S Exxon/dsl, Mar thon/dsl, Marathon/dsl Walgreens
202b a	US 24, Telegraph Rd, N Citgo, Mobil, Sunoco Burg King, Checkers, Dunkin', Jets Pizza, KFC, McDonald's, Pa John's, Pizza Hut, Ram's Horn Rest., Subway, Taco Bell, We dy's Advance Parts, Aldi Foods, Walgreens, **0-2 mi** S B Citgo/dsl, Marathon/dsl, Valero/dsl Arby's, Big Boy, Bur er King, Dunkin', Hungry Howie's, Jersey Mike's, Jimmy John KFC, Leon's Rest., Leo's Coney Island, Little Caesar's, Lucky St Buffet, Marina's Pizza, McDonald's, New Hong Kong, Pancho Mexican, Pizza Hut, Popeye's, Subway, Taco Bell, Teppany ki, Tim Horton's/Coldstone, Tubby's, Wendy's Comfo Inn $Tree, AT&T, AutoZone, Family$, Firestone/auto, Hom Depot, H, Rite Aid, st police, U-Haul, Verizon, vet, Walgreen Walmart/Burger King
200	Ecorse Rd, (no ez eb return), to Taylor, N Marathon/Subwa dsl/scales Tim Horton's, S Citgo/dsl, Rich
199	Middle Belt Rd, S BP/dsl Checkers, McDonald's, Wer dy's Days Inn, Knights Inn, Quality Inn
198	Merriman Rd, N Citgo/dsl, Marathon, Speedway/Speec Cafe/dsl Big Boy, Bob Evans, Capitol Bistro, Fortune Ch nese, Leonardo's Italian, McDonald's, Merriman St Grill, Su way, Urban Steak Baymont Inn, Best Value Inn, Clario Comfort Inn, Courtyard, Delta Hotel, Embassy Suites, Extende Stay America, Fairfield Inn, Hampton Inn, Hilton Garden, Ho day Inn, Holiday Inn Express, Howard Johnson, La Quinta, Mag nuson Hotel, Marriott, Rodeway Inn, Sheraton, Sheraton Fo Points, SpringHill Suites, Travelodge, Wyndham Garden Hote S Wayne Co Airport
197	Vining Rd
196	Wayne Rd, Romulus, N Shell/dsl Little Caesar's, M Donald's, Taco Bell $General, S Mobil/dsl Burg King, Jimmy John's, Subway
194b a	I-275, N to Flint, S to Toledo
192	Haggerty Rd, N BP/Tubby's/dsl, Mobil/dsl, S Low Huron Metro Park

DETROIT AREA

MI

INTERSTATE 94 Cont'd

Exit #	Services
190	Belleville Rd, to Belleville, N EVC, Marathon, Mobil/dsl Applebee's, Arby's, Asian Garden, Coney Island, Cracker Barrel, Culver's, Dunkin', Happy's Pizza, Hungry Howie's, McDonald's, Qdoba, Starbucks, Taco Bell, Tim Horton, Twisted Rooster, Wendy's Hampton Inn, Holiday Inn Express, Red Roof Inn $Tree, Aldi Foods, AT&T, AutoZone, Belle Tire, Camping World RV Ctr, CVS Drug, Firestone/auto, Ford, Meijer/dsl, Menards, National RV Ctr, O'Reilly Parts, Verizon, Walgreens, Walmart, S Shell Burger King, China City, China King, Dos Pesos Mexican, Subway Baymont Inn, Super 8 URGENT CARE, USPO
189mm	**wb, full facilities, info, litter barrels, petwalk, , , vending**
187	Rawsonville Rd, N Freightliner, S Mobil/dsl, Speedway/dsl Burger King, Denny's, KFC, Little Caesar's, McDonald's, Pearl River Chinese, Pizza Hut, Taco Bell, Tim Horton, Wendy's $General, $Tree, Detroit Greenfield RV Park
185	US 12, Michigan Ave (from eb, exits left, no return), to frontage rds, N
184mm	S Ford Lake
183	US 12, Huron St, Ypsilanti, N Citgo/dsl H, to E MI U, S Shell Buffalo Wild Wings, Coney Island, Jet's Pizza, McDonald's, Tim Horton's Fairfield Inn, Marriott Kroger/dsl, USPO
181b a	US 12 W, Michigan Ave, Ypsilanti, N Speedway/dsl Dunkin', Hong Kong Chinese, Koney Island, Popeye's, Taco Bell, Tim Horton/Wendy's H, Aamco, BigLots, GNC, Walmart/Subway, **0-2 mi** S Mobil/Circle K, Shell/Subway/dsl, Sunoco/dsl Harvest Moon Cafe, McDonald's Sam's Club/gas
180b a	US 23, to Toledo, Flint
177	State St, N BP, Mobil, Shell/dsl Bravo Italiana, Buffalo Wild Wings, Burger King, CA Pizza, Chipotle, Los Amigos, Macaroni Grill, Mediterrano Rest, Olive Garden, Panda Express, PF Chang's, Red Robin, Relish Rest., Wendy's Comfort Inn, Courtyard, Extended Stay America, Extended Stay America, Fairfield Inn, Hampton Inn, Hilton Garden, Holiday Inn, Holiday Inn Express, Kensington Court Inn, Red Roof Inn, Sheraton, Sonesta Suites, TownePlace Suites Firestone/auto, Honda, JC Penney, Macy's, Porsche, to UMI, URGENT CARE, Von Maur, VW, World Mkt, S Citgo/Subway/dsl, Speedway/dsl Black Rock Grill, Coney Island, Jimmy John's, McDonald's, Taco Bell, Tim Horton's Motel 6, Staybridge Suites Belle Tire, Costco/gas, U-Haul
175	Ann Arbor-Saline Rd, N Shell/Tim Horton's Applebee's, Blaze Pizza, Dibella Subs, Moe's SW Grill, Panera Bread, Potbelly, Tropical Smoothie, Zamaan Cafe Candlewood Suites REI, to UMI Stadium, vet, Whole Foods Mkt, S Tesla EVC Bob Evans, Buddy's Pizza, ChuckECheese's, Five Guys, Jets Pizza, McDonald's, Nick's Pancakes, Outback Steaks, Panchero's, Starbucks, Subway, TGIFriday's, TX Roadhouse AT&T, Best Buy, BigLots, Dick's, Jo-Ann Fabrics, Kohl's, Meijer/dsl/e85, Petsmart, Target
172	Jackson Ave, to Ann Arbor, S Marathon Weber's Rest. Hampton Inn, Wyndham Garden Belle Tire, Chevrolet/Cadillac, Ford, Hyundai, Mini, Nissan, Subaru, Toyota, N on Stadium Ave Marathon, Shell/dsl Cottage Inn Pizza, DQ, Jersey Mike's, McDonald's, Noodles&Co, Quarter Rest., Subway, Taco Bell, Zingerman's Roadhouse H, CVS, Goodyear/auto, Kroger, Midas, O'Reilly Parts, Plum Mkt, Rite Aid, Staples, TJ Maxx, Verizon, Walgreens

ANN ARBOR

Exit #	Services
171	MI 14 (from eb, exits left), Ann Arbor, to Flint by U.S. 23
169	Zeeb Rd, N BP/dsl Grand Traverse Pies Co, Kathy's Pancakes, McDonald's, Metzger's Rest. Holiday Inn Express, S Citgo/dsl Arby's, Burger King, Culver's, Domino's, Panera Bread, Standard Grill, Subway, Taco Bell, Wendy's AutoZone, CVS Drug, Discount Tire, Lowe's, Meijer/dsl, Menard's, vet
167	Baker Rd, Dexter, N Pilot/Subway/scales/dsl/24hr, S Pilot/Arby's/dsl/scales/24hr, TA/BP/Popeye's/dsl/scales/24hr/@ McDonald's Blue Beacon
162	Jackson Rd, Fletcher Rd, S Marathon/Krispy Chicken/dsl/24hr Stiver's Rest.
161mm	**eb, full facilities, litter barrels, petwalk, , , vending**
159	MI 52, Chelsea, N Shell/dsl, Speedway/dsl, Sunoco/dsl Big Boy, Biggby Coffee, China Garden, Chinese Tonite, Jimmy John's, KFC/Taco Bell, McDonald's, Subway, Uptown Coney Island, Wendy's Baymont Inn, Comfort Inn H, $Tree, Ace Hardware, AutoZone, Chrysler/Dodge/Jeep, Country Mkt Foods/drug, CVS Drug, Travel Land RV Ctr, USPO, Verizon, S Buick/Chevrolet
157	Jackson Rd, Pierce Rd, N Gerald Eddy Geology Ctr
156	Kalmbach Rd, N to Waterloo RA
153	Clear Lake Rd, N Marathon/dsl
151.5mm	**weigh sta both lanes**
150	to Grass Lake, S Mobil/Dunkin'/Subway/dsl
150mm	**wb, full facilities, litter barrels, petwalk, , , vending**
147	Race Rd, N Hideaway RV Park, to Waterloo RA, S Joy Motel Holiday RV Camp
145	Sargent Rd, S BP, Marathon/145 Auto Trk Plaza McDonald's, Wendy's Colonial Inn $General
144	Lp 94 (from wb), to Jackson
142	US 127 S, to Hudson, **1 mi** S Meijer/dsl, Speedway/dsl Arby's, Bob Evans, KFC, McDonald's, Taco Bell, Wendy's $General, $Tree, Advance Parts, AT&T, Rite Aid, to MI Speedway, Verizon, Walgreens
141	Elm Rd, N Travelodge Chevrolet, Chrysler/Dodge/Jeep, Ford/Lincoln, Honda, Nissan, S H
139	MI 106, Cooper St, to Jackson, N st police/prison, S Citgo/Subway H, Meekhof Tire
138	US 127 N, MI 50, to Lansing, Jackson, N Red Lobster, Yen King Chinese Baymont Inn, Comfort Inn, Fairfield Inn, Hampton Inn, Super 8 vet, S Admiral, BP/dsl, Shell/dsl Arby's, Bob Evans, Buffalo Wild Wings, Burger King, Dunkin', Fazoli's, IHOP, KFC, LJ Silver, Los Tres Amigos, McDonald's, Outback Steaks, Panda Express, Panera Bread, Papa John's, Potbelly, Qdoba, Rally's, Starbucks, Subway, TX Roadhouse, Wendy's Best Value Inn $Tree, Advance Parts, Aldi Foods, AT&T, AutoZone, Belle Tire, Best Buy, BigLots, Discount Tire, Home Depot, JoAnn Fabrics, Kohl's, Kroger/gas,

JACKSON

MI

INTERSTATE 94 Cont'd

Exit	Services
138	Continued Lowe's, Michael's, Midas, O'Reilly Parts, Petsmart, Target, TJ Maxx, Verizon, Walgreens
137	Airport Rd, N Marathon/dsl, Shell/Taco Bell Burger King, Denny's, McDonald's, Steak'n Shake, Subway, Wendy's Holiday Inn 7-11, Meijer/dsl, S BP/dsl Cracker Barrel, Culver's, Olive Garden Holiday Inn Express Sam's Club/gas, Save-A-Lot Foods
136	Lp 94, MI 60, to Jackson
135mm	**eb, full facilities, litter barrels, petwalk, vending**
133	Dearing Rd, Spring Arbor, S to Spring Arbor U
130	Parma, S $General
128	Michigan Ave, N BP/Burger King/scales/dsl/24hr, Marathon/deli/dsl Zephyr Hill Farms
127	Concord Rd
124	MI 99, to Eaton Rapids
121	28 Mile Rd, to Albion, N Mobil/Subway/dsl Arby's Days Inn, S Marathon/dsl, Speedway/dsl, Sunoco/dsl Frosty Dan's, KFC, La Casa Mexican, McDonald's, Pizza Hut, Taco Bell Super 9 Inn H, $General, AutoZone, Buick/Chevrolet, Family Fare Foods, Family$, Ford, O'Reilly Parts, Tire City/auto
119	MI 199, 26 Mile Rd
115	22.5 Mile Rd, N Citgo/115 Rest./dsl/24hr
113mm	**wb, full facilities, litter barrels, petwalk, vending**
112	Partello Rd, S Loves/Hardee's/scales/dsl/24hr Schuler's Rest. (2mi)
110	Old US 27, Marshall, N Shell/Country Kitchen/Subway/dsl/24hr, S Citgo/dsl, Tesla EVC Denny's, Schuler's Rest. (2mi) Hampton Inn, Holiday Inn Express H, sheriff
108	I-69, US 27, N to Lansing, S to Ft Wayne
104	11 Mile Rd, Michigan Ave, N Pilot/McDonald's/dsl/scales/24hr, TA/Country Pride/dsl/scales/24hr/@, S Citgo/Subway/dsl/e85 Quality Inn/rest. casino
102mm	Kalamazoo River
100	rd 294, Beadle Lake Rd, N Moonraker Rest., S Citgo/dsl/repair Binder Park Zoo
98b	I-194 N, to Battle Creek
98a	MI 66, to Sturgis, same as 97, S Citgo/Tim Horton/dsl Chili's, Los Aztecas, McDonald's, Ruby Tuesday, Schlotzsky's, Starbucks, Steak'n Shake Courtyard, Holiday Inn, TownePlace Suites AT&T, Best Buy, Discount Tire, Kohl's, Lowe's, Meijer/dsl, Menards, Michael's, PetCo, Sam's Club/gas, Staples, TJ Maxx, Verizon, Walgreens, Walmart/Subway
97	Capital Ave, to Battle Creek, N BP, Marathon Arby's, Domino's, Lux Cafe, McDonald's, Old China, Red Lobster Knights Inn, Quality Inn, S BP/Subway, Shell/dsl Applebee's, Bob Evans, Buffalo Wild Wings, Burger King, Cracker Barrel, Culver's, Denny's, Fazoli's, Hibachi Steaks, Jimmy John's, La Cocina, Panera Bread, Pizza Hut, Qdoba, Taco Bell Baymont Inn, Best Value Inn, Best Western, Fairfield Inn, Hampton Inn, Red Roof Inn, Rodeway Inn, Travelodge $Tree, AAA, Barnes&Noble, Belle Tire, BigLots, Firestone/auto, Harley Davidson, Hobby Lobby, Jo-Ann Fabrics, Target, Uncle Ed's Oil Shoppe, URGENT CARE, vet
96mm	**eb, full facilities, litter barrels, petwalk, vending**
95	Helmer Rd, 2 mi N Citgo/dsl Arby's, Big Boy Meijer/dsl/e85
92	Lp 94, rd 37, to Battle Creek, Springfield, N BP/Arlene's Trkstp/dsl/rest./24hr, Shell to Ft Custer RA
88	Climax, N Galesburg Speedway

MARSHALL

Exit	Services
85	35th St, Galesburg, N Shell/dsl McDonald's, Subway Galesburg Speedway, River Oaks CP, to Ft Custer S Colebrook CP, Scott's Mill CP
85mm	**wb, full facilities, litter barrels, petwalk, vendi**
81	Lp 94 (from wb), to Kalamazoo
80	Cork St, Sprinkle Rd, to Kalamazoo, N Marathon/Speedway/dsl, Sunoco/dsl Arby's, Burger King, Cr Rest., Denny's, Godfather's, Taco Bell Baymont Inn, Cl ion, Holiday Inn Express, Red Roof Inn, Sheraton Mon vet, S BP/dsl, Speedway/dsl McDonald's, Michel Rest., Nob Hill Grill, Subway, Wendy's Candlewood Suit EconoLodge, Fairfield Inn, Motel 6, Quality Inn
78	Portage Rd, Kilgore Rd, N Mobil/Circle K China Hut, Su mer Thyme Cafe Comfort Inn, Residence Inn H, repai Marathon/dsl, Shell, Speedway Angelo's Italian, Bigg Coffee, Bravo Rest., Brewster's Jct., Café Meli, McDonald's, Piz King, Subway, Taco Bell, Travelers Cafe Country Inn&Suit Days Inn, Hampton Inn AutoValue Parts, Fields Fabrics
76	Westnedge Ave, N Meijer/dsl, Speedway/dsl Gra Traverse Pie Co, Hibachi Buffet, IHOP, Jersey Giant Subs, Le Chicken, McDonald's, Old Chicago Grill, Outback Steaks, Pa Murphy's, Pizza Hut, Qdoba, Riviera Mayo, Root Beer Sta Steak'n Shake, Subway, Taco Bell, Theo&Stacy's Rest. Cou yard, Homewood Suites $Tree, Advance Parts, Discount Ti Earth Fare, Firestone/auto, Goodyear/auto, Lowe's, Midas, W greens, S Shell Antique Kitchen Rest., Applebee's, Big by Coffee, Blaze Pizza, Bob Evans, Brann's Steaks, Burger Kir Carrabba's, Chick-fil-A, Chili's, ChuckECheese's, Coldstone, Co Life Eatery, Culver's, Five Guys, HoneyBaked Ham, Jimmy John KFC, Little Caesar's, Logan's Roadhouse, Los Amigos Mexica McDonald's, Moe's SW Grill, Noodles&Co, Olive Garden, Pane Bread, Penn Sta Subs, Qdoba Mexican, Red Lobster, Red Ro in, Schlotzsky's, Starbucks, Subway, Taco Bell, Tim Horton, Roadhouse, Wendy's, Zoup! Holiday Motel $Tree, Al Foods, AT&T, AutoZone, Barnes&Noble, Belle Tire, Best Bu BigLots, Buick/Cadillac/GMC, Dick's, Fannie May Candies, Fi stone/auto, Harding's Mkt, Hobby Lobby, Home Depot, JC Pe ney, JoAnn Fabrics, Kohl's, Macy's, Michael's, Monro, Old Nav O'Reilly Parts, PepBoys, Petco, Sam's Club/gas, Target, TJMax Tuesday Morning, Tuffy Auto, Verizon, Walgreens, World Mkt
75	Oakland Dr
74b a	US 131, to Kalamazoo, N Kalamazoo Coll, to W MI U
72	9th St, Oshtemo, N Citgo/dsl, Speedway/dsl Arby Culver's, McDonald's, Starbucks, Taco Bell, Wendy's Ham ton Inn, S Fairfield Inn, Microtel, Towne Place Suites
66	Mattawan, N Citgo/dsl, Speedway/Subway/dsl/scale 24hr Chinn Chinn, Mancino's Italian $General, Family Freightliner, R&S RV Service, vet, S Shell/dsl Pizza Hu Subway USPO, Wagoner's Foods
60	MI 40, Paw Paw, N Citgo, Speedway/dsl Arby Biggby Coffee, Burger King, Chicken Coop, Copper Gril McDonald's, Pizza Hut, Red's Root Beer, Subway, Taco Be Wendy's Comfort Inn, EconoLodge, Travelodge Advance Parts, AT&T, Buick/Chevrolet/GMC, Chrysler/Dodge Jeep, Family Fare Mkt, Ford, O'Reilly Parts, St Julian Winer Walgreens, S Walmart/Subway
56	MI 51, to Decatur, N st police, S Citgo/dsl, Marathon/d
52	Lawrence
46	Hartford, N Shell/dsl McDonald's, Panel Room Rest Subway
42mm	**wb, full facilities, litter barrels, petwalk, vendin**

KALAMAZOO

INTERSTATE 94 Cont'd

Exit #	Services
41	MI 140, to Niles, Watervliet, N Casey's/dsl, Citgo, Marathon/dsl, Shell/dsl Burger King, Chicken Coop, Frosty Boy, Mill Creek Charlie's Rest., Subway, Taco Bell Fairfield Inn H, KOA (Apr-Oct) (7mi)
39	Millburg, Coloma, Deer Forest, 0-1 mi N BP/dsl, Shell/dsl, Speedway/dsl, Wesco/dsl DQ, El Asadero Mexican, Friendly Grill, McDonald's, Subway Family$, Krenek RV Ctr, S fruit mkt, wine tasting
34	I-196 N, US 31 N, to Holland, Grand Rapids
33	Lp I-94, to Benton Harbor, 2-4 mi N
30	Napier Ave, Benton Harbor, N Pilot/Wendy's/dsl/LP/24hr/@, Shell/dsl American Inn H, Blue Beacon
29	Pipestone Rd, Benton Harbor, N Applebee's, Asian Grille, Burger King, El Rodeo Mexican, IHOP, McDonald's, Popeye's, Sophia's Pancake House, Steak'n Shake, Super Buffet, TX Corral Best Western, Days Inn, Hilton Garden, Red Roof Inn, Travelodge Aldi Foods, Best Buy, Big Lots, Chrysler/Dodge/Jeep, Home Depot, JC Penney, Jo-Ann Fabrics, Lowe's, Meijer/dsl, Staples, USPO, Walmart/Subway, S BP/dsl Bob Evans Comfort Suites, Holiday Inn Express
28	US 31 S, MI 139 N, Scottdale Rd, to Niles, N Citgo/dsl, Marathon/dsl Burger King, Chicken Coop, Country Kitchen, Henry's Burgers, Jimmy John's, Joey C Pizza, KFC, Little Caesar's, Pizza Hut, Sonic, Subway, Taco Bell, Wendy's Best Value Inn, Loyalty Inn H, $General, $Tree, AutoZone, Belle Tire, Chevrolet/Buick/GMC, Family$, Kohl's, M&W Tire, Michael's, Midas, NAPA, O'Reilly Parts, Petsmart, radiators/repair/transmissions, Save-A-Lot, TJ Maxx, U-Haul, vet, Walgreens
27mm	St Joseph River
27	MI 63, Niles Ave, to St Joseph, N Citgo Nye's Apple Barn, S Tesla EVC Five Guys, Moe's SW Grill, Panera Bread Goodyear
23	Red Arrow Hwy, Stevensville, N Admiral, BP/Taco John's, Marathon/dsl, Mobil/Dunkin', Shell/dsl Big Boy, Burger King, Coach's Grill, Cracker Barrel, Crimson Cafe, Culver's, DQ, LJ Silver, McDonald's, Papa John's Baymont Inn, Candlewood Suites, Comfort Suites, Fairfield Inn, Super 8 Honda, Walgreens, S Hampton Inn Meijer/dsl
22	John Beers Rd, Stevensville, N Chalet on the Lake to Grand Mere SP, S Marathon/dsl
16	Bridgman, N BP/Quiznos/dsl camping, to Warren Dunes SP, S Citgo Early Bird Eatery, Lydia's Rest., McDonald's, Pizza Hut, Roma Pizza, Subway Bridgman Inn auto repair, Chevrolet, Chrysler/Dodge/Jeep, Ford/Mazda, vet
12	Sawyer, N Marathon/deli/dsl/scales/24hr truck wash, S TA/Burger King/Popeye's/Taco Bell/scales/dsl/24hr/@ Greenbush Brewing Super 8 Family$, USPO
6	Lakeside, Union Pier, N Round Barn Winery, St Julian Winery, S RV camping
4b a	US 12, to Three Oaks, New Buffalo, N Pizza Hut, Redamak's Hamburgers, Roma Pizza
2.5mm	weigh sta both lanes
1	MI 239, to Grand Beach, New Buffalo, 0-2 mi N Shell/Subway/dsl Brewster's Italian, Casey's Grille, McDonald's, Nancy's, Rosie's Rest., Stray Dog Grill, Subway Baymont Inn, Fairfield Inn, Holiday Inn Express, Quality Inn, Super Inn $General, S Days Inn casino
0.5mm	**Welcome Ctr eb, full facilities, info, litter barrels, petwalk, vending**
0mm	Michigan/Indiana state line

DETROIT AREA

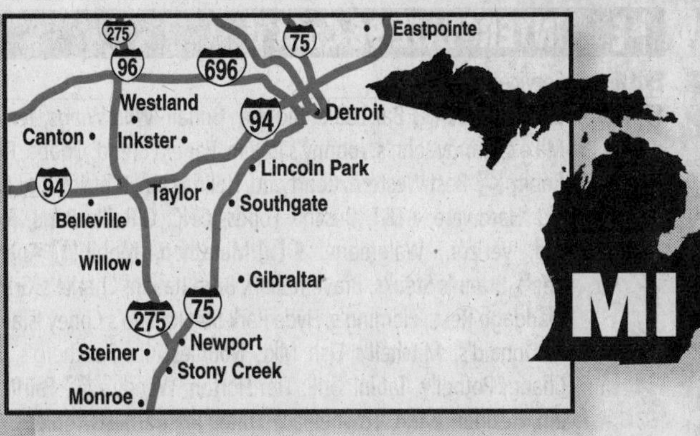

INTERSTATE 96

Exit #	Services
	I-96 begins/ends on I-75, exit 48 in Detroit.
191	I-75, N to Flint, S to Toledo, US 12, to MLK Blvd, to Michigan Ave
190b	Warren Ave, N BP/dsl
190a	I-94 E to Port Huron
189	W Grand Blvd, Tireman Rd, N Citgo/dsl, Mobil
188b	Joy Rd, N Church's
188a	Livernois, N Exxon/Subway, Mobil Burger King, KFC, McDonald's, Wendy's
187	Grand River Ave (from eb)
186b	Davison Ave, I-96 local and I-96 express divide, no exits from express
186a	Wyoming Ave
185	Schaefer Hwy, to Grand River Ave, N Citgo, Mobil Coney Island, McDonald's CVS Drug, S Sunoco/dsl
184	Greenfield Rd
183	MI 39, Southfield Fwy, exit from expswy and local
182	Evergreen Rd
180	Outer Dr, N BP/dsl/lube
180mm	I-96 local/express unite/divide
179	US 24, Telegraph Rd, N BP, Marathon/dsl Arby's, Baskin-Robbins/Dunkin', China King, Little Caesar's, McDonald's, Tim Horton's, White Castle AutoZone, Chevrolet, Family$, Family$, O'Reilly Parts, URGENT CARE, S Marathon/dsl, Shell/dsl
178	Beech Daly Rd, N Sunoco
177	Inkster Rd, N BP/Tim Horton Best Value Inn $General, 7-11, URGENT CARE
176	Middlebelt Rd, N Bob Evans, IHOP, Olive Garden Comfort Inn Aldi Foods, H, 0-1 mi S Applebee's, Chili's, Culver's, Del Taco, Five Guys, Jimmy John's, Leo's Coney Island, Logan's Roadhouse, McDonald's, MOD Pizza, Noodles&Co, Outback, Panda Express, Panera Bread, Pizza Hut, Popeye's, Potbelly, Qdoba, Red Lobster, Starbucks Hampton Inn, Holiday Inn Express, Hometowne Suites $Tree, AT&T, AutoZone, BigLots, Costco/gas, Dick's, Firestone/auto, GNC, Goodyear/auto, Home Depot, Jo-Ann Fabrics, Marshall's, Meijer, Menard's, Michael's, Office Depot, Petsmart, Target, URGENT CARE, Verizon, Walgreens, Walmart
175	Merriman Rd, N Mobil/dsl, Speedway/dsl, S Exxon/dsl Prime Grill
174	Farmington Rd, N Mobil/dsl, Sunoco Looney Baker, S KFC vet
173b	Levan Rd, N H, to Madonna U
173a	Newburgh Rd
	I-275 and I-96 run together 9 miles

MI

INTERSTATE 96 Cont'd

DETROIT AREA

Exit #	Services
170	6 Mile Rd, N Bar Louie, Big Boy, Buffalo Wild Wings, Jersey Mike's, Jimmy John's, Johnny's Italian, Panera Bread, Qdoba, Red Robin Best Western, Courtyard, Holiday Inn, Marriott H, Ace Hardware, AT&T, Busch's Foods, GNC, O'Reilly Parts, Rite Aid, Verizon, Walgreens, S Marathon, Mobil Applebee's, Brann's Steaks, Bravo Italian, Buca Italian, Charlie's Grille, Claddagh Rest., Fleming's, Hyde Park Steaks, Leo's Coney Island, McDonald's, Mitchell's Fish Mkt, Noodles&Co, Panchero's, PF Chang, Potbelly, Tahini Grill, Tim Horton, Wendy's Fairfield Inn, Residence Inn, TownePlace Suites Barnes&Noble, CVS, Kroger, Office Depot, Petsmart, REI
169b a	7 Mile Rd, N Dave&Buster's, Los Amigos Embassy Suites, S EVC Andiamo's Cafe, Bahama Breeze Rest., BJ's Rest., Burger Fi, Chipotle, Gaucho Brazilian, Granite City Grill, J Alexander's Rest., Jimmy John's, Macaroni Grill, MOD Pizza, Rusty Bucket Rest. Hyatt Place AT&T, Home Depot, Trader Joe
167	8 Mile Rd, to Northville, S BP/dsl, Speedway/dsl Benihana, Big Boy, Chili's, Five Guys, Kerby's Koney Island, McDonald's, Mission BBQ, On-the-Border, Panera Bread, Qdoba, Starbucks, Taco Bell, Twin Peaks, Zoup! Country Inn Suites, Extended Stay America, Hampton Inn, Holiday Inn Express, Sheraton Best Buy, Costco/gas, Dick's, Firestone/auto, Kohl's, Meijer/dsl, Target, to Maybury SP, Verizon
165	I-696, I-275, MI 5, Grand River Ave.
I-275 and I-96 run together 9 miles.	
163	I-696 (from eb)
162	Novi Rd, to Walled Lake, Novi, N Bar Louie, Black Rock Rest., Buddy's Pizzaria, Buffalo Wild Wings, CA Pizza, Carrabba's, Cheesecake Factory, ChuckECheese's, Coldstone, McDonald's, Novi Chophouse, Red Lobster, Starbucks, Subway, Taco Bell Hilton Garden, Renaissance, Residence Inn BigLots, Dick's, JC Penney, JoAnn Fabrics, Kohl's, Lord&Taylor, Macy's, Marshalls, Michael's, Midas, Nordstrom, Old Navy, S Mobil/dsl, Sunoco/dsl Athenian Coney Island, Bagger Dave's Burgers, BD Mongolian BBQ, Blaze Pizza, Bonefish Grill, Boston Mkt, Chipotle, Famous Dave's, Genji Japanese, Honeybaked Express, IHOP, Jersey Mike's, Maisano's Italian, Noodles&Co, Olive Garden, Panda Express, Panera Bread, Pei Wei, Pizza Hut, Potbelly, Primanti Bros, Qdoba, Red Robin, Steve&Rocky's, TGIFriday's, Tony Sacco Pizza, Wasabi, Wendy's Courtyard, DoubleTree, Homewood Suites, Towne Place Suites H, Advance Parts, AT&T, Belle Tire, Better Health Mkt, Chevrolet, Discount Tire, Hobby Lobby, Kia, Monro/auto, NAPA, O'Reilly Parts, TJ Maxx, URGENT CARE, Verizon, Walmart
160	Beck Rd, 12 Mile Rd, S EVC, Shell/Tim Horton Applebee's, China King, Guido's Pizza, La Herraduro Mexican, Leo's Coney Island, Olga's Kitchen, Outback Steaks, Starbucks, Subway, Zoup! Hyatt Place, Staybridge Suites H, GNC, Home Depot, Kroger, Staples, to Maybury SP
159	Wixom Rd, Walled Lake, N Marathon/dsl, Sunoco/dsl Culver's, Denise's Grill, Quiznos, Wendy's Holiday Inn Express, My Place, Springhill Suites Aldi Foods, General RV Ctr, Meineke, Menard's, to Proud Lake RA, S Exxon, Mobil/dsl, Valero/dsl A&W/KFC, Arby's, Baskin-Robbins/Dunkin', Burger King, Dickey's BBQ, Grand Diner, Jimmy John's, McDonald's, Red Olive Rest., Shakers Grill, Stinger's Grill, Taco Bell, Tropical Cafe Comfort Suites AutoZone, Lincoln, Meijer/dsl, Sam's Club/gas, Target

HOWELL

Exit #	Services
155b a	to Milford, New Hudson, N Camp Dearborn (5mi), Fo to Lyon Oaks CP, S Sunoco Applebee's, Arby's, Bigg Coffee, Jet's Pizza, Jimmy John's, Kensington Grill, Leo's Cor Island, McDonald's, Starbucks, Subway, Tim Horton's AA AT&T, Belle Tire, Chevrolet, Discount Tire, Hyundai, Lowe's, U GENT CARE, Verizon, Walmart
153	Kent Lake Rd, N Kensington Metropark, S E dsl Country Meadows Inn (3mi)
151	Kensington Rd, N Kensington Metropark, S Isla Lake RA
150	Pleasant Valley Rd (no return wb)
148b a	US 23, N to Flint, S to Ann Arbor
147	Spencer Rd, N Mobil/dsl Cheryl's Cafe st poli S to Brighton St RA
145	Grand River Ave, to Brighton, N BP, Shell/dsl Arby Baskin-Robbins/Dunkin', Cracker Barrel, Outback Steaks, Piz Hut Courtyard H, $General, Buick/GMC, Ford, Hon Mazda, URGENT CARE, vet, S Marathon/Subway Boy, Burger King, Chili's, Chipotle, Firehouse Subs, Five Gu Gourmet Garden, IHOP, Jimmy John's, Leo's Coney Island, Chef, McDonald's, MOD Pizza, Olga's Kitchen, Panda Expre Panera Bread, Pi's Asian, Potbelly, Red Robin, Starbucks, Ta Bell, Tim Horton, Wendy's Homewood Suites, Winga Inn $Tree, AAA, Advance Parts, Aldi Foods, AT&T, Belle Ti Best Buy, Bob's Tire, CVS Drug, Home Depot, JoAnn Fabri Marshalls, Meijer/dsl, Michael's, O'Reilly Parts, Petsmart, S ples, Target, to Brighton Ski Area, USPO, Verizon, Walgreens
141	Lp 96 (from wb, return at 140), to Howell, **0-2 mi** N BP/c Shell/Tim Horton/dsl, Speedway, Sunoco/dsl Applebee Arby's, Asian Fusian Buffet, Aubree's Pizzaria, Biggby Coff Bluefin Steaks, Bob Evans, Buffalo Wild Wings, Jimmy John KFC, Leo's Coney Island, Little Caesar's, Los Tres Amigos, M Donald's, Panera Bread, Qdoba, Subway, Taco Bell, White C tle $Tree, AT&T, Belle Tire, Big Lots, Chevrolet, Disco Tire, GNC, Home Depot, Kohl's, Lowe's, Meijer, O'Reilly Pa Petsmart, URGENT CARE, Walmart
140	S Latson Rd, same as 141
137	D19, to Pinckney, Howell, N Marathon, Mobil/dsl, Spee way/dsl, Sunoco/Baskin-Robbins/Dunkin'/dsl All S Coney Island, Block Brewing Co, Joanna's 2 Go, Taco B Wendy's Kensington Inn H, Parts+, Spartan Tire, Tr Value, USPO, S Wooly Bully's Rest. Magnuson Hotel
135mm	**eb, full facilities, litter barrels, petwalk, , , vendi**
133	MI 59, Highland Rd, N Marathon/McDonald's/dsl by's, Jersey Giant Subs, Leo's Coney Island Baymont, H iday Inn Express Tanger Outlets/famous brands
129	Fowlerville Rd, Fowlerville, N BP/dsl, Marathon/dsl, Sur co/dsl Great Lakes Rest., McDonald's, Pizza Hut/Taco B Wendy's Magnuson Hotel Chevrolet, O'Reilly Par Walmart, S Mobil/dsl Subway Chysler/Dodg Jeep, Ford
126mm	**weigh sta both lanes**
122	MI 43, MI 52, Webberville, N Mobil/dsl/24hr McDo ald's
117	to Dansville, Williamston, N Marathon/Jersey's Giant Sub dsl, S Sunoco/dsl
111mm	**wb, full facilities, litter barrels, petwalk, , , vendi**
110	Okemos, Mason, N Marathon/dsl, Sunoco/Dunkin' A plebee's, Arby's, Backyard BBQ, Big John's Steaks, Biggby C fee, Coldstone/Tim Horton, Cracker Barrel, Culver's, Grand T verse Pie Co., Hibachi Grille, Jimmy John's, Leaf Salad Bar, Lit Caesar's, Lucky's Steaks, McDonald's, Ozzy Mediterranea

INTERSTATE 96 Cont'd

110 Continued
Panchero's Mexican, Starbucks, Stillwater Grill, Subway, Taco Bell Comfort Inn, Fairfield Inn, Hampton Inn, Holiday Inn Express, Staybridge Suites 7-11, BMW/Porsche, Mercedes, to stadium, Verizon

106b a I-496, US 127, to Jackson, Lansing, N St Police

104 Lp 96, Cedar St, to Holt, Lansing, N Admiral, Speedway/dsl Applebee's, Arby's, Asia's Finest, Big John's, Biggby Coffee, Blimpie, Bob Evans, Boston Mkt, Burger King, China King, Domino's, Fazoli's, Happy's Pizza, Hooters, Jet's Pizza, KFC, Los Tres Amigos, Mikado Grill, Panda Gourmet, Pizza Hut, Steak'n Shake, Taco Bell, TX Roadhouse, Wendy's, Zeus Coney Island Best Value Inn H, $Tree, Aldi Foods, AT&T, auto repair, Belle Tire, Cadillac, Chevrolet, Chrysler/Dodge/Jeep, Discount Tire, Family$, GNC, Kia, Lexus, Meijer/dsl, Menards, Target, Toyota, Tuffy Auto, Verizon, vet, S Speedway/dsl Aldaco's Taco Bar, Burger King, Champion's Grill, China East Buffet, Dairy Dan, Hungry Howie's, McDonald's, Starbucks, Subway, Taco Bell Causeway Bay Hotel Advance Parts, AutoZone, Budget Tire, CVS Drug, Family$, Kroger/gas, Lowe's, NAPA, O'Reilly Parts, Rite Aid, URGENT CARE, Verizon

101 MI 99, MLK Blvd, to Eaton Rapids, **0-3 mi N** QD, S Mobil/Tim Horton, Speedway/Subway/dsl Coach's Grill, McDonald's, Wendy's

98b a Lansing Rd, to Lansing, N Arby's, Wendy's Comfort Inn, Holiday Inn Express Harley-Davidson, S st police

97 I-69, US 27 S, S to Ft Wayne, N to Lansing

95 I-496, to Lansing

93b a MI 43, Lp 69, Saginaw Hwy, to Grand Ledge, **0-2 mi N** Shell, Speedway/dsl Applebee's, Buffalo Wild Wings, Burger King, Carrabba's, Cheddar's, Chick-fil-A, Chipotle, Denny's, Finley's Grill, Frank's Grill, Hibachi Grill, Honeybaked Ham, Houlihan's, Logan's Roadhouse, Longhorn Steaks, McDonald's, Outback Steaks, Panera Bread, Qdoba, Red Robin, Subway Comfort Inn, Fairfield Inn, Hampton Inn, Motel 6, Quality Inn, Ramada Inn, Red Roof Inn, Residence Inn H, $Tree, Aldi, AT&T, Barnes&Noble, Best Buy, BigLots, Chrysler/Dodge/Jeep, Hobby Lobby, JC Penney, Kohl's, Kroger/dsl, Macy's, Meijer/dsl/24hr, Target, TJ Maxx, vet, Walgreens, S QD, Shell/Dunkin', Sunoco/McDonald's Arby's, Biggby Coffee, Bob Evans, Cancun Mexican, Cracker Barrel, Culver's, Steak'n Shake SpringHill Suites Belle Tire, Buick/GMC, Discount Tire, Lowe's, Mazda/Volvo, Menards, Michael's, Petsmart, Staples, Walmart/Subway

92mm Grand River

91 I-69 N (from wb), US 27 N, to Flint

90 Grand River Ave, to (from wb), S FLYING J/Denny's/dsl/24hr

89 I-69 N, US 27 N (from eb), to Flint

87mm **eb, full facilities, litter barrels, petwalk, , , vending**

86 MI 100, Wright Rd, to Grand Ledge, S Mobil/McDonald's/dsl, Speedway/Subway/24hr

84 to Eagle, Westphalia

79mm **wb, full facilities, info, litter barrels, petwalk, , , vending**

77 Lp 96, Grand River Ave, Portland, N Citgo/dsl, Shell/Subway, Speedway/dsl Arby's, Biggby Coffee, Burger King, Little Caesar's, McDonald's, New China Buffet, Red Tomato Pizza American Heritage Inn CarQuest, Family$, Rite Aid, Tom's Foods, Verizon, S Tom's/dsl Wendy's

76 Kent St, Portland

76mm Grand River

73 to Lyons-Muir, Grand River Ave

69mm **weigh sta both lanes**

67 MI 66, to Ionia, Battle Creek, N Pilot/Subway/dsl/scales/24hr Corner Landing Grill Midway Motel, Super 8 H, Alice Springs RV Park (3mi), Lakeside Camping, Meijer/dsl (4mi), Walmart (4mi)

64 to Lake Odessa, Saranac, N Ionia St RA, S I-96 Speedway

63mm **eb, full facilities, litter barrels, petwalk, , , vending**

59 Clarksville

52 MI 50, to Lowell, N Mobil/Subway/dsl, S Marathon/dsl (2mi)

46mm Thornapple River

46 rd 6, to rd 37

44 36 St, S

CASCADE

43b a MI 11, 28th St, Cascade, N Bagger Dave's, Biggby Coffee, Brann's Steaks, Culver's, Dan's Diner, Dunkin'/Baskin Robbins, Firehouse Subs, Freddy's, Gipper's Grill, Jet's Pizza, Jimmy John's, Korean BBQ, Leo's Coney Island, New Beginnings Rest., Panera Bread, Pit Stop BBQ, Pizza Hut, Qdoba, Starbucks, Subway, Sundance Grill, Taco Bell Baymont Inn, Best Western, Country Inn&Suites, Crowne Plaza, EconoLodge, Holiday Inn Express Ace Hardware, AT&T, Audi/Porsche/Subaru, Fresh, Mkt, GNC, Meijer/dsl, Mercedes/Volvo/VW, Verizon, Walmart, **0-3 mi S** Citgo, Shell, Speedway/dsl Applebee's, Arby's, Arby's, Arnie's Rest., Bob Evans, Buddy's Pizza, Burger King, Cantina Mexican, Chick-fil-A, Chipotle Mexican, ChuckeCheese, Dave&Buster's, Denny's, Five Guys, Grand Coney, Grand Traverse Pie Co, Honey Baked Ham, IHOP, Jersey Mike's, Jimmy John's, Krispy Kreme, Longhorn Steaks, McDonald's, Moe's SW Grill, Noodles&Co, Old Chicago, Olive Garden, Osaka Japanese, Outback Steaks, Panera Bread, Pizza Hut, Pizza Ranch, Potbelly, Red Lobster, Smokey Bones, Starbucks, Steak'n Shake, Subway, Taco Bell, Tropical Cafe, TX Roadhouse, Wendy's Clarion, Comfort Inn, Courtyard, Delta Marriott, DoubleTree, Drury Inn, Extended Stay America, Fairfield Inn, Hampton Inn, Hawthorn Suites, Homewood Suites, Motel 6, Red Roof Inn, Residence Inn, Sleep Inn, SpringHill Suites, Tru Hilton, Wyndham Garden $General, $Tree, Advance Parts, Aldi Foods, Belle Tire, Best Buy, Big Lots, Costco/gas, Dick's, Ford/Mazda, Hobby Lobby, Home Depot, Honda, Hyundai/Kia, Jo-Ann Fabrics, Lowe's, Michael's, Monro Auto, Nissan, Old Navy, Petsmart, Sam's Club/gas, Staples, Target, TJ Maxx, Trader Joe's, Tuesday Morning, U-Haul, World Mkt

40b a Cascade Rd, N BP/dsl, Forest Hills Fuel Biggby Coffee, Great Harvest, Jets Pizza, Little Bangkok, Little Caesar's, Manna Cafe, Noco Provisions, Subway Forest Hills Mkt, vet, Walgreens, S Shell/dsl, Speedway/dsl Bonefish Grill, Jimmy John's, Zoup! H

MI

INTERSTATE 96 Cont'd

Exit #	Services
39	MI 21 (from eb), to Flint
38	E Beltline Ave, to MI 21, MI 37, MI 44, **N** Applebee's, Fuji Yama Japanese, Red Hot Inn Rest., Wendy's Meijer/dsl, URGENT CARE, Verizon, **S** Gravity Grille Country Inn&Suites
37	I-196 (from wb, exits left), Gerald Ford Fwy, to Grand Rapids
36	Leonard St, **2 mi S** Arby's, Jimmy John's, McDonald's
33	Plainfield Ave, MI 44 Connector, **N** Citgo/dsl, Speedway/dsl Anna's House, Arby's, Biggby Coffee, Charlie's Grille, Cheers Grill, Freddy's, Fred's Italian, Jimmy John's, KFC, Little Caesar's, Loco Taco, McDonald's, Pizza Hut, Rice Wok, Russ' Rest., Subway, Taco Bell, Tim Horton's, Wendy's Lazy T Motel, Motel 6 $Tree, AAA, AutoZone, Belle Tire, BigLots, Chevrolet, Chrysler/Jeep/Dodge, CVS, Discount Tire, Firestone/auto, Ford, Kia, Lowe's, Meijer/dsl, Midas, NAPA, Nissan/VW, O'Reilly Parts, Quality/auto, Toyota, U-Haul, vet, Walgreens, **S** Denny's
31mm	Grand River
31b a	US 131, N to Cadillac, S to Kalamazoo, **1 mi N** Speedway/Subway/dsl McDonald's
30b a	Alpine Ave, Grand Rapids, **N** BP/dsl, Marathon/dsl, Mobil Applebee's, Buffalo Wild Wings, Checkers, ChuckeCheese, Culver's, El Burrito Mexican, Empire Buffet, Firehouse Subs, First Wok, Five Guys, Freddy's, Golden Corral, Hibachi Grill, IHOP, Jersey Mike's, Jimmy John's, Little Caesar's, Logan's Roadhouse, McDonald's, MOD Pizza, Olive Garden, Outback Steaks, Panda Express, Panera Bread, Qdoba, Russ' Rest., Sonic, Starbucks, Steak'n Shake, Subway, Taco Bell, TGIFriday's, Three Happiness Chinese Hampton Inn, Holiday Inn Express, SpringHill Suites $Tree, Aldi Foods, AT&T, AutoZone, Belle Tire, Best Buy, Discount Tire, Ford, GNC, Hobby Lobby, Jo-Ann, Kohl's, Marshall's, Menards, Michael's, NAPA, PepBoys, PetCo, Sam's Club/gas, Target, TJ Maxx, Verizon, Walgreens, Walmart, **S** Admiral/dsl, Speedway/dsl Arby's, Burger King, Fazoli's, Jimmy John's, KFC, LJ Silver, McDonald's, Papa John's, Wendy's Best Value Inn Goodyear/auto, Home Depot, Meijer/dsl, Midas, O'Reilly Parts, U-Haul, URGENT CARE
28	Walker Ave, **S** Meijer/dsl/24hr Bob Evans, McDonald's Baymont Inn, Quality Inn
26	Fruit Ridge Ave, **N** Citgo/dsl, **S** Marathon/deli/dsl
25mm	**eb, full facilities, litter barrels, petwalk,**
25	8th Ave, 4Mile Rd (from wb), **S** Marathon/dsl Wayside Motel
24	8th Ave, 4Mile Rd (from eb), **S** Marathon/dsl Wayside Motel
23	Marne, **N** tires, **S** Depot Café, Rinaldi's Café Ernie's Mkt, fairgrounds/raceway, USPO
19	Lamont, Coopersville, **S** LP
16	B-35, Eastmanville, **N** Citgo/Subway/dsl, Shell/Burger King/dsl, Speedway/dsl/24hr #1 Chinese, Arby's, Biggby Coffee, Hungry Howie's, Little Caesar's, McDonald's, New Beginnings Rest., Taco Bell Rodeway Inn Buick/Chevrolet, Chrysler/Dodge/Jeep, Family Fare Foods, Family$, Ford, Fun 'N Sun RV Ctr, Rite Aid, vet, **S** Pacific Pride/dsl RV camping
10	B-31 (exits left from eb), Nunica, **N** Turk's Rest., **S** Conestoga RV camping, golf course/rest.
9	MI 104 (from wb, exits left), to Grand Haven, Spring Lake, **S** Marathon/dsl to Grand Haven SP, vet
8mm	**wb, full facilities, litter barrels, petwalk, , vend**
5	Fruitport (from wb, no return)
4	Airline Rd, **S** Speedway/dsl, Wesco/dsl Bur Crest Diner, McDonald's, Norm's Ice Cream, Subway, Villa Inn $General, Grover Drug, Orchard Mkt Foods, to PJ H master SP, USPO
1c	Hile Rd (from eb), **S** Tesla EVC Arby's, Asian Buffet, E Evans, Brann's Grille, Buffalo Wild Wings, Burger King, Chuc Cheese, Five Guys, Golden Corral, Grand Traverse Pie Co, zumi Steaks, KFC/Taco Bell, Logan's Roadhouse, McDonal Olive Garden, Qdoba, Red Lobster, Red Robin, Starbucks, S way, TX Roadhouse Baymont Inn, Fairfield Inn, Hamp Inn $Tree, Aldi Foods, AT&T, Barnes&Noble, Belle Tire, B Buy, Dick's, Hobby Lobby, JC Penney, Jo-Ann Fabrics, Koh Meijer/dsl, Menards, Old Navy, PetCo, Target, TJ Maxx, Veriz VW/Audi/Nissan/Subaru/Toyota
1b a	US 31, to Ludington, same as 1c, Grand Haven, **2 mi N Sherman Blvd** Applebee's, Arby's, Fazoli's, Los Amigos, Donald's, Panera Bread, Pizza Ranch, Red Wok, Subway, T Bell, Tim Horton, Wendy's Airline Motel, Alpine Mo Bel-aire Motel, Quality Inn/rest. , $Tree, All Seasons Ctr, Big Lots, GNC, Lowe's, Marathon/dsl, Norton Automot Petsmart, Sam's Club/gas, Staples, Walmart

I-96 begins/ends on US 31 at Muskegon.

GRAND RAPIDS

INTERSTATE 196 (Grand Rapids)

Exit #	Services
81mm	**I-196 begins/ends on I-96, 37mm in E Grand Rapids.**
79	Fuller Ave, **N** sheriff, **S** Shell/dsl, Speedw dsl Biggby Coffee, Bill's Rest., Checkers, Elbow Room, K Subway, Taco Bell, Wendy's , Ace Hardware, Fami Verizon, Walgreens
78	College Ave, **S** Mobil/Circle K McDonald's, Omele Shop , Ford Museum
77c	Ottawa Ave, **S** Gerald R Ford Museum, downtown
77b a	US 131, S to Kalamazoo, N to Cadillac
76	MI 45 E, Lane Ave, **S** Gerald R Ford Museum, John Park&Zoo
75	MI 45 W, Lake Michigan Dr, **S** to Grand Valley St U
74mm	Grand River
73	Market Ave, **N** to Vanandel Arena
72	Lp 196, Chicago Dr E (from eb)
70	MI 11 (exits left from wb), Grandville, Walker, **S** Citgo/ Shell New Beginnings Best Western+ USPO, ve
69c	Baldwin St (from wb)
69b a	Chicago Dr, **N** Speedway Biggby Coffee, Culver's, D ey's BBQ, Domino's, Fazoli's, Jimmy John's, KFC, McDonal Peppino's Pizza, Subway, Taco Bell $Tree, Advance Pa Aldi Foods, AutoZone, Meijer/dsl, O'Reilly Parts, USPO, V greens, **S** Admiral, Speedway/dsl Adobe Mexic Arby's, Brann's Steaks, Little Caesar's, Rainbow Grill, R Rest., Wings&More Grand Village Inn, Holiday Inn press NAPA
67	44th St, **N** Mobil/dsl Burger King, Cracker Ba Panera Bread, Steak'n Shake Comfort Suites H da, Walmart/Subway, **0-2 mi S** Anna's House, Applebe Big Boy, Carrabba's, China One, Famous Dave's, IHOP, Jim John's, Logan's Roadhouse, Noodles&Co, Olive Garden, On Border, Qdoba, Red Lobster, Red Robin, Sakura Japanese, S bucks, Subway, TGIFriday's, Tropical Smoothie, TX Roadho

GRAND RAPIDS

INTERSTATE 196 (Grand Rapids) Cont'd

67	Continued Uccello's Ristorante, Wendy's Residence Inn $Tree, Barnes&Noble, Best Buy, Chrysler/Dodge/Jeep, Costco/gas, Dick's, Discount Tire, Family Fare Foods, Fiat, Gordman's, Hobby Lobby, Home Depot, JC Penney, Kohl's, Lowe's, Macy's, Marshall's, Meijer/zeal, Michael's, Old Navy, Petsmart, Verizon, World Mkt
64	MI 6 E, to Lansing (exits left from wb)
62	32nd Ave, to Hudsonville, **N** BP/dsl, Citgo/dsl Arby's, Biggby Coffee, Burger King, Hudsonville Grille, Little Caesar's, McDonald's Quality Inn Chevrolet, **S** Mobil/Subway/dsl/24hr, Tesla EVC Rainbow Grill, Wendy's Travelodge Harley-Davidson, Harvest Foods, Meijer/dsl
58mm	**eb, full facilities, litter barrels, petwalk, , vending**
55	Byron Rd, Zeeland, **N** Citgo/7-11 Blimpie, McDonald's , to Holland SP
52	16th St, Adams St, **2 mi N** Speedway/dsl Burger King, Jimmy John's, Papa Murphy's, Pizza Ranch, Wendy's , Meijer/dsl/e85, **S** Loves/Hardee's/dsl/scales/24hr, Mobil/Subway/dsl
49	MI 40, to Allegan, **N** BP/McDonald's/dsl Residence Inn, **S** Pilot/Arby's/dsl/scales/24hr, Tulip City/Marathon/Subway/dsl/scales/24hr truck repair, truck wash
44	US 31 N (from eb), to Holland, **3-5 mi N** , food, gas
43mm	**wb, full facilities, info, litter barrels, petwalk, , , vending**
41	rd A-2, Douglas, Saugatuck, **N** Marathon/dsl, Marathon/dsl, Shell/Subway/dsl Burger King, Dairy Dayz, Spectators Grill Best Western (1mi) $General, NAPA, to Saugatuck SP, **S** Belvedere Inn/Rest.
38mm	Kalamazoo River
36	rd A-2, Ganges, **N** Shell Christo's Rest., Pizza Mambo, Saugatuck Brewing Co AmericInn, Blue Star Motel
34	MI 89, to Fennville, **N** to West Side CP, **S** Shell Cranes Pie Pantry (4mi), Lyons Farm Mkt
30	rd A-2, Glenn, Ganges, **N** to Westside CP (4mi)
28mm	**eb, full facilities, litter barrels, petwalk, , , vending**
26	109th Ave, to Pullman, **N** Dutch Farm Mkt
22	N Shore Dr, **N** Cousin's RV Camping/rest., to Kal Haven Trail SP
20	rd A-2, Phoenix Rd, **N** BP/dsl, Marathon/dsl Arby's, China Buffet, Taco Bell , $Tree, AutoZone, Meijer/dsl, Walgreens, **S** Murphy USA/dsl, Shell/dsl Big Boy, McDonald's, Sherman's Dairybar, Wendy's Baymont Inn, Comfort Suites, Hampton Inn, Holiday Inn Express $General, Aldi Foods, Menards, Walmart
18	MI 140, MI 43, to Watervliet, **0-2 mi N** Shell/dsl Burger King, Little Caesar's, McDonald's, Pizza Hut Great Lakes Inn, LakeBluff Motel , auto repair, AutoValue Parts, Buick/Cadillac/GMC, Chevrolet, Chrysler/Dodge/Jeep, Ford/Lincoln, Village Mkt Foods, **7 mi S** KOA (Apr-Oct)
13	to Covert, **N** RV camping, to Van Buren SP
7	MI 63, to Benton Harbor, **N** DiMaggio's Pizza
4	to Coloma, Riverside, **S** Shell/dsl KOA (Apr-Oct)
2mm	Paw Paw River
1	Red Arrow Hwy, **N** SW Michigan Airport
0mm	I-94, E to Detroit, W to Chicago

I-196 begins/ends on I-94, exit 34 at Benton Harbor.

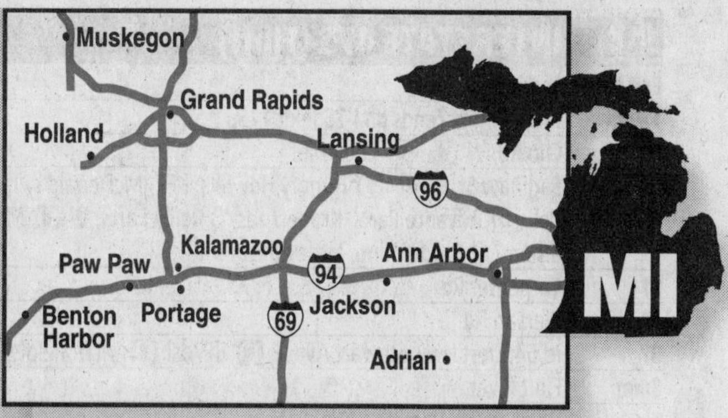

LIVONIA

INTERSTATE 275 (Livonia)

Exit #	Services
I-275 and I-96 run together 9 miles. See I-96, exits 165-170.	
29	I-96 E, to Detroit, MI 14 W, to Ann Arbor
28	Ann Arbor Rd, Plymouth, **E** BP/Dunkin', Mobil, Shell/dsl Little Caesar's, Los Tres Amigos, McDonald's Red Roof Inn $Tree, Verizon, **W** Burger King, Firehouse Subs, Grand Traverse Pie Co., Lee's Coney Island, Tropical Smoothie Comfort Inn Cadillac, CVS Drug, Lincoln, vet
25	MI 153, Ford Rd, Garden City, **E** Logan's Roadhouse, Parthenon Coney Island, Starbucks, Subway Home Depot, Sam's Club, Walmart, **W** BP, Speedway, Sunoco/dsl Applebee's, Arby's, Basement Burger Bar, BD Mongolian BBQ, Black Rock Grill, Bob Evans, Boston Mkt, Bowery Grill, Buffalo Wild Wings, Burger King, Carrabba's, Carvel Ice Cream, Chili's, Chipotle, Chopstick House, ChuckeCheese, Coldstone, Dunkin'/Baskin-Robbins, Five Guys, Jersey Mike's, Jimmy John's, KFC, Little Caesar's, McDonald's, Mexican Fiesta, MOD Pizza, Olga's Kitchen, Outback Steaks, Panera Bread, Potbelly, Qdoba, Starbucks, Subway, Taco Bell, TGIFriday's, Tim Hortons, Wendy's, White Castle Baymont Inn, Comfort Suites, Extended Stay America, Fairfield Inn, Hampton Inn, La Quinta, TownePlace Suites Advance Parts, Aldi Foods, CVS Drug, Discount Tire, Firestone/auto, GNC, Hobby Lobby, IKEA, JC Penney, Jo-Ann, Kohl's, Lowe's, Marshall's, Meijer/dsl, Michael's, Midas, PetCo, Target, Tuesday Morning, URGENT CARE, Verizon, vet, Walgreens
23	**nb, full (facilities), info, litter barrels, ,**
22	US 12, Michigan Ave, to Wayne, **E** BP/dsl, Mobil/dsl, Shell, Valero/dsl Arby's, Jonathan's Rest., McDonald's, Quiznos, Subway, Wendy's EconoLodge, Fellows Cr Motel, Holiday Inn Express, Super 8, Willo Acres Motel, **W** Marathon/dsl Jimmy John's Kia, Nissan, vet
20	Ecorse Rd, to Romulus, **E** Mobil/7-11, Shell/Tubby's/dsl, **W** BP/Burger King/scales/dsl/24hr
17	I-94 E to Detroit, W to Ann Arbor, **E**
15	Eureka Rd, **E** Shell/Subway/dsl
13	Sibley Rd, New Boston, **W** Mobil/Subway/dsl to Lower Huron Metro Park
11	S Huron Rd, **W** Sunoco/Burger King/dsl Iron Mike's Rest.
8	Will Carleton Rd, to Flat Rock
5	Carleton, South Rockwood, **W** Speedway/dsl, Sunoco/Subway/dsl $General, USPO
4mm	**sb, full facilities, litter barrels, ,**
2	US 24, to Telegraph Rd, **W** BP/dsl, Marathon/Subway/dsl $General
0mm	**I-275 begins/ends on I-75, exit 20.**

MI

FLINT

INTERSTATE 475 (Flint)

Exit #	Services
17mm	I-475 begins/ends on I-75, exit 125.
15	Clio Rd, W Chevrolet
13	Saginaw St, E Hungry Howie's, KFC, McDonald's, Taco Bell Advance Parts, Kroger/gas, O'Reilly Parts, W Marathon Burger King, Little Caesar's
11	Carpenter Rd
10	Pierson Rd
9	rd 54, Dort Hwy, Stewart Ave, E BP/dsl McDonald's
8mm	Flint River
8b	Davison Rd, Hamilton Ave
8a	Longway Blvd, W Holiday Inn Express H, USPO
7	rd 21, Court St, downtown Flint
6	I-69, W to Lansing, E to Port Huron
5	Atherton Rd (from sb), E Marathon/dsl
4	Hemphill Rd, Bristol Rd, E Speedway/dsl Rally's, Subway Rite Aid, W Speedway/dsl Little Caesar's, Tim Horton/Wendy's $General, Kroger/dsl, vet
2	Hill Rd, E Speedway Applebee's, Bob Evans Wingate Inn vet, W Mobil, Speedway/dsl Arby's, Burger King, Burger St Grill, Little Caesar's, McDonald's, Starbucks, Taco Bell, Wendy's Rite Aid
	I-475 begins/ends on I-75, exit 111.

DETROIT

INTERSTATE 696 (Detroit)

Exit #	Services
	I-696 begins/ends on I-94.
28	I-94 E to Port Huron, W to Detroit, 11 Mile Rd, E 7-11, Shell/dsl, Speedway/dsl $General
27	MI 3, Gratiot Ave, N BP, Marathon, Valero Checkers, Firehouse Subs, McDonald's, National Coney Island, Tubby's Subs Costco/gas, S Marathon, Mobil/McDonald's/dsl, Shell Biggby Coffee, Burger King, JW Ice Cream, KFC, Subway, Taco Bell, Tim Horton's, White Castle Belle Tire, Chrysler/Dodge/Jeep, Family$, Firestone/auto, GNC, Kroger/gas, Rite Aid, Sav-A-Lot Foods, TJ Maxx
26	MI 97, Groesbeck Ave, Roseville, N BP/dsl, S Tim Horton
24	Hoover Rd, Schoenherr Rd, N Burger King, KFC, S BP/dsl, Mobil/7-11 Boston Mkt, Del Taco, DQ, Grubhouse, Little Caesar's, Popeye's, Red Lobster, Subway, Taco Bell, Tim Horton, Wendy's Holiday Inn Express $Tree, Advance Parts, CVS Drug, GNC, Home Depot, Kroger
23	MI 53, Van Dyke Ave, N BP, Marathon, Mobil/dsl Applebee's, Arby's, Baskin-Robbins/Dunkin', McDonald's, Simple Palate Rest., Subway $General, Cadillac, Dodge/Ram, Toyota, Walmart, S Luca's Coney Island Chevrolet/Buick/GMC, Discount Tire, Ford, Rite Aid, USPO, vet
22	Mound Rd, N BP/Burger King, Mobil/dsl
20	Ryan Rd, Dequindre Rd, N Citgo, Mobil/7-11, Su co Knights Inn, Red Roof Inn auto repair, BigLots, v S Church's, LA Coney Island, McDonald's Best Inn, V tory Suites transmissions
19	Couzens St, 10 Mile Rd, S Hazel Park Racetrack
18	I-75 N to Flint, S to Detroit
17	Campbell Ave, Hilton Ave, Bermuda, Mohawk, S Ma thon/dsl
16	MI 1, Woodward Ave, Main St, N zoo, S Sunoco
14	Coolidge Rd, 10 Mile Rd, S Speedway Hungry Hc ie's, Jade Palace Chinese, Little Caesar's, Sahara Grill, S way CVS Drug, Family$, URGENT CARE
13	Greenfield Rd, N Marathon, Mobil L George Coney land, McDonald's, Popeye's, Subway, White Castle $Tr Aldi Foods, Family$, Save a Lot Foods, Sol's Automotive, U GENT CARE, S Shell, Sunoco Baskin-Robbins/Dunk Front Page Deli, Pita Cafe, Starbucks Rite Aid
12	MI 39, Southfield Rd, 11 Mile Rd, N Panera Bread D count Tire, S Shell Happy's Pizza AT&T
11	Evergreen Rd, S Mobil, Speedway/dsl Benito's P za, China Gourmet, Chipotle, Coldstone/Tim Horton's, F drucker's, Jimmy John's, Potbelly, Qdoba, Subway, TGI day's Hawthorn Suites, Holiday Inn Express
10	US 24, Telegraph Rd, N Marathon, Mobil, Sunoco C potle, DiBella Subs, Five Guys, Jimmy John's, Mezzanine Me terranian, Noodles&Co, Panera Bread, Popeye's, Potbelly, Q ba, Starbucks, Wendy's Extended Stay America, Red R Inn, Springhill Suites AT&T, Belle Tire, Best Buy, Bui GMC, Chevrolet, Chrysler/Dodge/Jeep, Ford, Honda, Hy dai, Kia, Lexus, Lincoln, Lowe's, Meijer/dsl, Michael's, M Nissan, Office Depot, Petsmart, Subaru, Verizon, S M bil/7-11, Sunoco Kerby's Koney Island, Starbucks, Tim H ton's Best Western, Candlewood Suites, Courtyard, Holi Inn Express, Marriott, Quality Inn AutoZone, Family$
8	MI 10, Lodge Fwy
7	American Dr (from eb), S Extended Stay America, Hil Garden
5	Orchard Lake Rd, Farmington Hills, N BP/dsl, Marath Mobil/dsl, Sunoco Arby's, Burger King, Camelia's Mexic Hong Hua Chinese, Jet's Pizza, Jimmy John's, Kabuki Japane Marie's Scrambler, Roberto's, Ruby Tuesday, Starbucks, S way, Wendy's Comfort Inn, Extended Stay America, F field Inn, Radisson CVS, Discount Tire, Holocaust Muse Petco, to St Mary's Coll, Verizon
1	(from wb), I-96 W, I-275 S, to MI 5, Grand River Ave

NOTES

MINNESOTA

MN

INTERSTATE 35

Exit #	Services
260mm	**I-35 begins/ends on MN 61 in Duluth.**
259	MN 61, London Rd, to Two Harbors, North Shore, **W** BP/dsl, Holiday/dsl, Holiday/dsl (2), ICO/dsl Blackwoods Grill, Dunn Bros Coffee, KFC, McDonald's, Perkins, Subway, Taco John's, Wendy's Days Inn, Esdgewater Inn
258	21st Ave E (from nb), to U of MN at Duluth, same as 259
256b	Mesaba Ave, Superior St, **E** ICO/DQ Bellisio's, Caribou Coffee, Famous Dave's BBQ, Grandma's Grill, Greenmill Rest., Grizzly's, Little Angie's Cantina, Old Chicago, Red Lobster, Smokehouse Rest., Subway, Timberlodge Steaks Canal Park Lodge, Comfort Suites, Hampton Inn, Inn at Lake Superior, Suites Hotel, **W** Holiday Inn, Radisson, Sheraton
256a	Michigan St, **E** waterfront, **W** H, downtown
255a	US 53 N (exits left from nb), **W** Mobil Kia, downtown
255b	I-535 spur, to Wisconsin
254	27th Ave W, **W** Holiday/Burger King/dsl, KwikTrip/dsl Duluth Grill, Little Caesar's, Subway Motel 6 USPO
253b	40th Ave W, **W** Holiday/dsl/CNG Perkins Comfort Inn, Super 8
253a	US 2 E, US 53, to Wisconsin
252	Central Ave, W Duluth, **W** Holiday/dsl, Mobil/Charley's/dsl China King Buffet, Domino's, Jimmy John's, KFC, McDonald's, Pizza Hut, Subway, Taco John's $Tree, Advance Parts, CVS Drug, Menards, O'Reilly Parts, Super 1 Foods, USPO, Walgreens
251b	MN 23 S, Grand Ave
251a	Cody St, **E** Allyndale Motel zoo
250	US 2 W (from sb), to Grand Rapids, **1/2 mi W** Holiday/dsl, Mobil/dsl/LP Blackwoods Grill AmericInn
249	Boundary Ave, Skyline Pkwy, **E** Holiday/dsl McDonald's Best Western to ski area, to Spirit Mtn RA, **W** Rs **both lanes, full facilities, info, litter barrels, vending** Exxon/Subway/dsl Blackwoods Grill AmericInn, Best Value Inn Mack/Volvo
246	rd 13, Midway Rd, Nopeming, **W** Armor/dsl Dry Dock Rest.
245	rd 61, **E** Buffalo House Rest./camping
242	rd 1, Esko, Thomson, **E** Mobil
239.5mm	St Louis River
239	MN 45, to Cloquet, Scanlon, **E** Jay Cooke SP, KOA (May-Oct) (3mi), **W** Holiday, KwikTrip/dsl/e85 Trapper Pete's Steaks Golden Gate Motel H, Coates RV Ctr, dsl repair
237	MN 33, Cloquet, **1 mi W** Lemon Tree/dsl, Mobil, Murphy USA/dsl Applebee's, Arby's, DQ, Erbert&Gerberts, Little Caesar's, McDonald's, Papa Murphy's, Perkins, Pizza Hut, South Gate Pizza, Subway, Taco John's/Steak Escape, Wendy's AmericInn, Super 8 H, $Tree, AT&T, AutoZone,

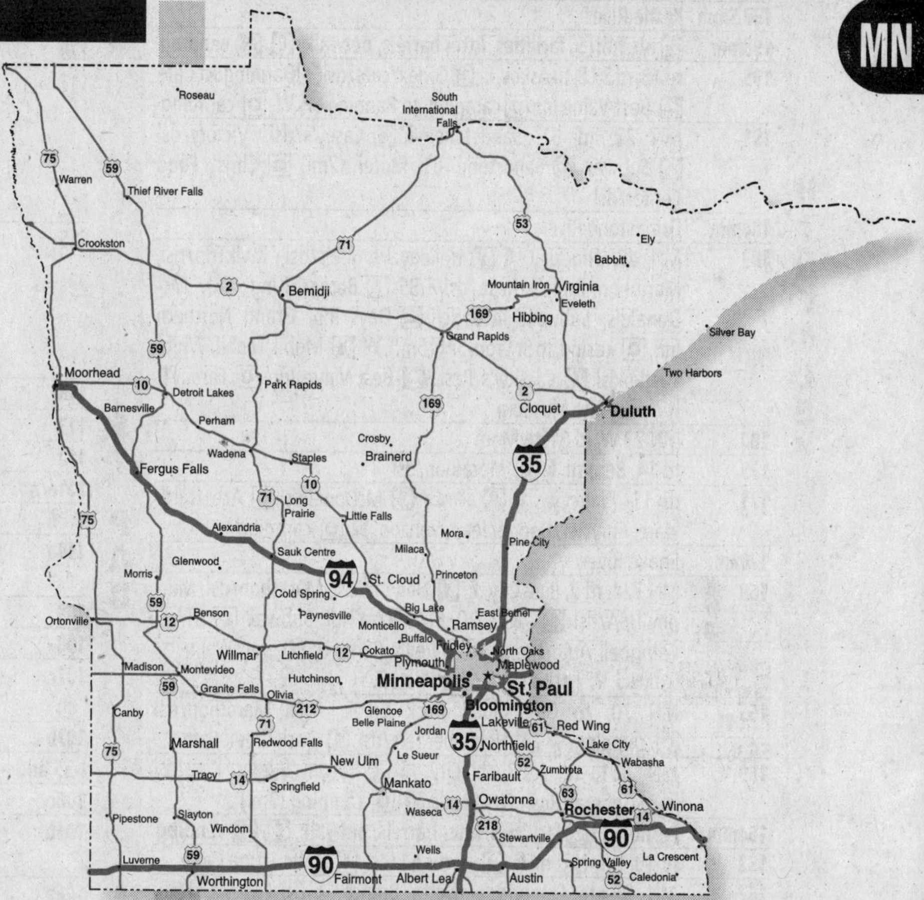

Exit #	Services
237	Continued Chrysler/Dodge/Jeep, Family$, Ford, NAPA, O'Reilly Parts, Super 1 Foods, Verizon, Walgreens, Walmart/Subway
236mm	**weigh sta both lanes**
235	MN 210, to Cromwell, Carlton, **E** BP/rest./dsl, ICO/dsl/24hr Spirits Rest. AmericInn, Royal Pines Motel to Jay Cooke SP, **W** Black Bear Casino/Hotel/rest.
235mm	Big Otter Creek
233mm	Little Otter Creek
227	rd 4, Mahtowa, **E** camping, **W** TJ's Country Store/gas (2 mi)
226mm	Rs **nb, full facilities, litter barrels, petwalk, vending**
220	rd 6, Barnum, **E** Bear Lake Camping, **W** Mobil/café/dsl/24hr Lazy Bear Rest. Northwoods Motel Munger Tr
219mm	Moose Horn River
218mm	Moose Horn River
216	MN 27 (from sb, no EZ return), Moose Lake, **1-2 mi W** Cenex/dsl, Holiday/dsl Art's Café, DQ, Lazy Moose Grille Days Inn. (4mi), Moose Lake Motel H, 1918 Museum, Ace Hardware, AutoValue Parts, Mkt Place Foods, O'Reilly Parts, to Munger Trail
214	rd 73, **E** camping, Moose Lake SP (2mi), **W** KwikTrip/dsl/e85/scales, Mobil/dsl McDonald's, Subway Days Inn, Moose Lake Motel H, Munger Trail, Red Fox Camping
209	rd 46, Sturgeon Lake, **E** Mobil/dsl Doc's Cafe Sturgeon Lake, **W** Ernie's Rest. (seasonal) Sturgeon Lake Motel camping (3mi)
209mm	Rs **sb, full facilities, litter barrels, petwalk, vending**
206.5mm	Willow River

MN

INTERSTATE 35 Cont'd

HINCKLEY

Exit #	Services
205	rd 43, Willow River, W BP/cafe/dsl camping (2mi)
198.5mm	Kettle River
198mm	**nb, full facilities, litter barrels, petwalk, , vending**
195	rd 18, rd 23 E, to Askov, E Cenex/cafe/dsl Banning Jct Cafe Best Value Inn camping, to Banning SP, W camping
191	MN 23, rd 61, Sandstone, E Casey's/dsl, Victory/dsl Subway Sandstone 61 Motel (2mi) Chris' Food Center/dsl
184mm	Grindstone River
183	MN 48, Hinckley, E Holiday/Hardee's/dsl, KwikTrip/dsl, Marathon/Tobie's Rest./dsl/E-85 Burger King, DQ, McDonald's, Subway, Taco Bell Days Inn, Grand Northern Inn casino, to St Croix SP (15mi), W Mobil, Mobil/White Castle/dsl Cassidy's Rest. Best Value Inn Family$, Hinckley Fire Museum
180	MN 23 W, rd 61, to Mora
175	rd 14, Beroun, E Marathon/dsl
171	rd 11, Pine City, E SA/dsl McDonald's Ace Hardware, Chrysler/Dodge/Jeep, Verizon, W camping
170mm	Snake River
169	MN 324, rd 7, Pine City, E Holiday/dsl, Marathon/dsl, Murphy USA/dsl A&W, DQ, KFC, Pizza Hut, Subway $Tree, Campbell Auto/tire, Ford, O'Reilly Parts, USPO, vet, Walmart/Subway, W to NW Co Fur Post HS
165	MN 70, to Grantsburg, Rock Creek, E Marathon/dsl camping, W Heidelbergers/dsl Rock Creek Cafe
159	MN 361, rd 1, Rush City, E Holiday/Burger King/dsl $General, Rush City Foods, W camping (2mi)
154mm	**nb, full facilities, litter barrels, petwalk, , vending**
152	rd 10, Harris, **1 mi E** Harris 61/dsl Kaffe Stuga Caffe
147	MN 95, to Cambridge, North Branch, E Casey's, Holiday/dsl China Taste, Domino's, DQ, McDonald's, Oak Inn Rest., Perkins, Subway, Taco Bell AmericInn, Budget Host Family$, Fisk Tire, NAPA, O'Reilly Parts, to Wild River SP (14mi), vet, W Holiday/dsl/e85 Burger King, Denny's, Dickey's BBQ, Don Lulu Mexican, Papa Murphy's Chevrolet, County Mkt Foods, Ford, North Branch Outlets/famous brands, USPO, Verizon
143	rd 17, W Tesoro/dsl
139	rd 19, Stacy, E Gas+ Rustic Inn Rest., Stacy Grill, Subway city park, W KwikTrip/dsl/e85 A-1 Tires
135	US 61 S, rd 22, Wyoming, E Casey's, Sinclair/dsl DQ, Linwood Pizza, Subway, Tasty Asia H, CarQuest, IGA Foods, WY Drug, W Shell/dsl McDonald's, Village Inn Rest. camping (10mi), golf, vet
132	US 8 (from nb), to Taylors Falls
131	rd 2, Forest Lake, E BP, Holiday/dsl, SA/dsl Applebee's, Arby's, Burger King, Culver's, Joy Garden, KFC, McDonald's, Papa John's, Perkins, Quack's Cafe, Subway, Taco Bell, White Castle AmericInn Aldi Foods, AutoZone, O'Reilly Parts, RV/Auto repair, Target, Tires+, Verizon, Walgreens, Walmart/Subway, W Holiday/dsl Famous Dave's BBQ, Jimmy John's, Papa Murphy's, Starbucks, Taco John's, Wendy's Country Inn&Suites AT&T, Buick/GMC, Cadillac/Chevrolet, Chrysler/Dodge/Jeep, Cub Foods, GNC, Home Depot, Jiffy Lube, Menards
131mm	**sb, full facilities, litter barrels, petwalk, , vending**
129	MN 97, rd 23, E Kwik Trip/dsl/e85 camping (6mi), W Holiday/dsl camping (1mi), Coates RV Ctr,
128mm	**weigh sta both lanes**

FOREST LAKE

ST PAUL

Exit #	Services
127	I-35W, S to Minneapolis. See I-35W.
123	rd 14, Centerville, E Kwik Trip Blue Heron Grill, Du Bros Coffee, McDonald's, Papa Murphy's Festival Foo vet, White Bear RV Ctr, W Mobil, Shell/Circle K DQ, esta Cancun, WiseGuys Pizza auto repair
120	rd J (from nb, no return)
117	rd 96, E SA/dsl Burger King, Carbone's Pizza A ericInn Goodyear/auto, NAPA, W Holiday $5 za, Applebee's, Arby's, Caribou Coffee, Culver's, McDonal Noodles&Co, Punch Pizza, Subway, Zen Asia AutoZo Cub Foods, Tires+, USPO, Walgreens
115	rd E, E BP/repair, SA/dsl Jimmy John's, Jimmy's Re Perkins, Savoy Pizza Country Inn&Suites, Fairfield Inn, H iday Inn Express URGENT CARE, W Chipotle Mexic KFC, Mad Jack's Cafe, Panera Bread, Papa Murphy's, W dy's $Tree, AT&T, Fresh Thyme Mkt, GNC, Target, Walma
114	I-694 E (exits left from sb)
113	I-694 W
112	Little Canada Rd, E BP, W Porterhouse Rest.
111a/b	MN 36 E, to Stillwater/MN 36 W, to Minneapolis
110b	Roselawn Ave
110a	Wheelock Pkwy, E BP, Gulf May's Deli, Roadside Piz Subway
109	Maryland Ave, E SA/dsl, W Wendy's K-Mart
108	Pennsylvania Ave, downtown
107c	University Ave, E SA/dsl, W H, to st capitol, dow town
107b a	I-94, W to Minneapolis, E to St Paul.
I-35 and I-94 run together.	
106c	11th St (from nb), Marion St, downtown
106b	Kellogg Blvd (from nb), E Eagle St Grill Holi Inn H; downtown
106a	Grand Ave, E H
105	St Clair Ave
104c	Victoria St, Jefferson Ave
104b	Ayd Mill Rd (from nb)
104a	Randolph Ave
103b	MN 5, W 7th St, E Burger King, W SA/dsl Mic USPO
103a	Shepard Rd (from nb)
102mm	Mississippi River
102	MN 13, Sibley Hwy, W BP, Holiday/Subway
101b a	MN 110 W, E BP/dsl Caribou Coffee, McDonald's, S way, Teresa's Mexican, Tommy Chicago's Pizza Veriz Walgreens, W SA/dsl/e85
99b a	I-494 W/I-494 E
98	Lone Oak Rd, E Extended Stay America, Microtel Sa Club/gas, URGENT CARE, USPO, W Shell Far Grandson's Eatery Hampton Inn, Sonesta Suites
97b	Yankee Doodle Rd, E Applebee's, Arby's, Buffalo W Wings, Burger King, Chipotle, Coldstone, Culver's, Domin DQ, Genghis Grill, Houlihan's, Jake's Grille, Jersey Mik Jimmy John's, KFC, Noodles&Co, Old Chicago Pizza, Pa Express, Panera Bread, Papa John's, Papa Murphy's, Perk Pizza Man, Potbelly, Qdoba, Smashburger, Taco Bell $T AT&T, Barnes&Noble, Best Buy, BigLots, GNC, Home De Kohl's, Lunds&Byerly's Mkt, Michael's, Old Navy, O'Re Parts, Petsmart, TJ Maxx, Verizon, Walgreens, Walmart/S way, W BP/dsl, SA/dsl El Loro Mexican, Granite C Starbucks, Subway Best Western, Extended Stay Am ca Hobby Lobby, HyVee Foods, Marshall's, NAPA

MN

INTERSTATE 35 Cont'd

Exit #	Services
97a	Pilot Knob Rd, E Holiday, SA Chili's, McDonald's, Wendy's SpringHill Suites, TownePlace Suites Discount Tire, Excel Repair, Firestone/auto, Kohl's, Tires+, Walmart/Subway, W BP/dsl, SA/dsl Starbucks Best Western, Holiday Inn Express, same as 97b
94	rd 30, Diffley Rd, to Eagan, E Holiday/dsl Andiamo Italian CVS Drug, Kowalski's Mkt/Starbucks, URGENT CARE, W Sinclair/dsl Goodyear/auto
93	rd 32, Cliff Rd, E Holiday/dsl Bonfire Grill, Sarpino's Pizza, Subway Ace Hardware, W Holiday/dsl Burger King, Caribou Coffee, Casper's Rest., Chipotle Mexican, Dolittle's Grill, DQ, Green Mill Rest., Hong Wong Chinese, Jimmy John's, Leeann Chin's, Noodles&Co, Papa John's, Papa Murphy's, Pizza Hut, Starbucks, Taco Bell, Wendy's, Which Wich? Hilton Garden, Quality Inn, Staybridge Suites $Tree, Cub Foods, O'Reilly Parts, Target, USPO, Walgreens
92	MN 77, Cedar Ave, E Zoo, 1 mi W access to Cliff Rd services
90	rd 11, E KwikTrip Pizza Man, Subway Valley Natural Foods, vet, W SA/dsl
88b	rd 42, Crystal Lake Rd, E Chianti Grill Lund's&Byerly's Mkt, Petsmart, W BP, Holiday/dsl, SA/dsl, Shell Applebee's, Arby's, Buca Italian, Burger Jones, Burger Jones, Burger King, Cam Ranh Bay, Chick-fil-A, Chili's, Chipotle Mexican, ChuckECheese, HoneyBaked Ham, IHOP, Jimmy John's, KFC, LeeAnn Chin, Little Caesar's, McDonald's, Noodles&Co, Old Country Buffet, Olive Garden, Outback Steaks, Panera Bread, Papa John's, Papa Murphy's, Pizza Hut, Porter Creek Grill, Red Lobster, Roasted Pear, Royal Buffet, Shogun Japanese, Smashburger, Starbucks, Taco Bell, TGIFriday's, Wendy's AmericInn, Best Western, Fairfield Inn, Hampton Inn, InTown Suites H, $Tree, Ace Hardware, Advance Parts, AT&T, Barnes&Noble, Best Buy, Costco/gas, Cub Foods, Dick's, Discount Tire, Home Depot, JC Penney, Kohl's, Macy's, Michael's, Old Navy, PetCo, Target, Tires+, Tuesday Morning, Verizon, VW, Walgreens
88a	I-35W (from nb), N to Minneapolis. **See I-35W.**
87	Crystal Lake Rd (from nb), W Kwik Trip/dsl Honda/Nissan, Hyundai, Mazda, Toyota
86	rd 46, E KwikTrip/dsl, SA/dsl KFC, Starbucks Harley-Davidson, W McDonald's auto repair, O'Reilly Parts
85	MN 50, E F&F/dsl, SA/dsl Caribou Coffee, Culver's, Domino's, DQ, Eddie Cheng, Gerbert's Sandwiches, Green Mill Rest., Jimmy John's, Lakeville Chinese, Little Caesar's, Starbucks, Subway, Taco Bell, Wendy's Quality Inn $Tree, Advance Parts, Cub Foods, CVS Drug, GNC, Goodyear/auto, NTB, O'Reilly Parts, Verizon, Walgreens, W Holiday/dsl Cracker Barrel, Perkins, Pizza Ranch Baymont Inn,
84	185th St W, Orchard Trail, E SA/dsl Applebee's, Buffalo Wild Wings, Caribou Coffee, Quiznos, SawaJapan Marshall's, Target
81	rd 70, Lakeville, E Holiday/dsl Baldy's BBQ, McDonald's, Min Garden, Subway Holiday Inn/rest., Motel 6, W SA/dsl Harry's Cafe Candlewood Suites Walmart/Subway
76	rd 2, Elko, W Endzone Grill Elko Speedway
76mm	**Rs sb, full facilities, litter barrels, petwalk, , , vending**
69	MN 19, to Northfield, New Prague, 7 mi E KwikTrip Applebee's, Big Steer Rest., Caribou Coffee, McDonald's, Quarterback Rest., Subway, Taco Bell AmericInn, College City Motel, Country Inn&Suites, Super 8 H, Carleton Coll, St Olaf Coll, W FLYING J/Subway/dsl/scales/24hr

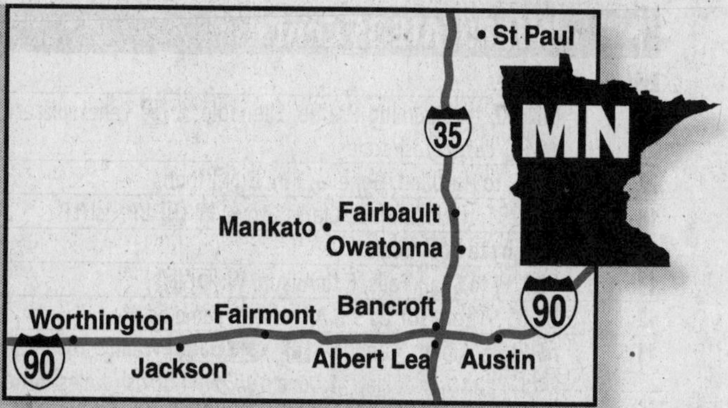

FARIBAULT

Exit #	Services
68mm	**Rs nb, full facilities, litter barrels, petwalk, , , vending**
66	rd 1, to Dundas, 1 mi W Boonie's Grill
59	MN 21, Faribault, 0-2 mi E KwikTrip, SA/Family Diner/dsl/scales/24hr A&W, Arby's, Burger King, DQ, Hardee's, Joe's Cafe, KFC, Pizza Hut, Taco Bell, Taco John's Best Value Inn, Days Inn, Grandstay Aldi Foods, Buick/Chevrolet/GMC, Chrysler/Dodge/Jeep, O'Reilly Parts, repair, Satakah St Trail, vet, W Harley-Davidson, 0-2 mi S Ford/Lincoln
56	MN 60, Faribault, E KwikTrip A&W, Arby's, Asian Buffet, Burger King, Jimmy John's, KFC, Little Caesar's, McDonald's, Perkins, Subway, Taco John's H, $Tree, Aldi Foods, AutoValue Parts, AutoZone, Buick/Chevrolet/GMC, Chrysler/Dodge/Jeep, Family$, Goodyear/auto, Hy-Vee Foods/dsl, Jo-Ann, O'Reilly Parts, Petsmart, TrueValue, Verizon, Walmart/Subway, W Country Kitchen, DQ Regency Inn Sakatah Lake SP, same as 59
55	rd 48, (from nb, no return), 1 mi E KwikTrip, Mobil/dsl, SA/dsl A&W, Arby's, Broaster Rest., Burger King, DQ, El Tequila Mexican, KFC, Southern China Cafe, Subway, Taco John's
48	rd 12, rd 23, Medford, E Casey's/dsl, W McDonald's Outlet Mall/famous brands
45	rd 9, Clinton Falls, W KwikTrip/dsl/scales Caribou Coffee, Famous Dave's BBQ, Sportsman's Grille, Subway, TimberLodge Steaks, Wendy's Comfort Inn, Holiday Inn Buick/Chevrolet/Cadillac, Cabela's Sporting Goods, Russell-Stover Candies

OWATONNA

Exit #	Services
43	rd 34, 26th St, Owatonna, E Noble RV Ctr, W H
42b a	US 14 W, rd 45, to Waseca, Owatonna, E Hardee's, Kernel Rest. Valu Stay Inn AutoZone, CashWise Foods, Chrysler/Dodge/Jeep, Ford/Lincoln, O'Reilly Parts, repair, vet, W KwikTrip/dsl Buffalo Wild Wings, Culver's, Don Juan Cantina, East Wind Buffet, McDonald's, Olivia's Rest., Panda Express, Perkins Best Budget Inn, Super 8 $Tree, Aldi, GNC, Kohl's, Lowe's, Verizon, Walmart/Subway
41	Bridge St, Owatonna, E Holiday/dsl Applebee's, Arby's, Asian Kitchen, Burger King, DQ, Jimmy John's, KFC, Papa Murphy's, Red&Green Burrito, Starbucks, Subway, Taco Bell Baymont Inn, Country Inn&Suites Verizon, W F&F/dsl Microtel Target
40	US 14 E, US 218, Owatonna, 1 mi E on rd 45 Godfather's, Little Caesar's, Taco John's Oakdale Motel Hy-Vee Foods/dsl, vet, Walgreens, WholesaleTire
38mm	Turtle Creek
35mm	**Rs both lanes, full facilities, litter barrels, petwalk, , , vending**
34.5mm	Straight River
32	rd 4, Hope, 1/2 mi E Hope Oak Knoll Camping, 1 mi W gas food

INTERSTATE 35 Cont'd

ALBERT LEA

Exit #	Services
26	MN 30, to Blooming Prairie, Ellendale, E Cenex/pizza/dsl, W Casey's/dsl/scales
22	rd 35, to Hartland, Geneva, 1 mi E food
18	MN 251, to Hollandale, Clarks Grove, W BP/dsl/LP
17mm	**weigh sta both lanes**
13b a	I-90, W to Sioux Falls, E to Austin, W H
12	US 65 S (from sb), Lp 35, Albert Lea, same as 11
11	rd 46, Albert Lea, E Loves/Wendy's/dsl/scales/24hr, Petro/Iron Skillet/McDonald's/Pizza Hut/dsl/scales/24hr/@ Comfort Inn, Holiday Inn Express dsl repair, KOA (may-oct/6mi), to Myre-Big Island SP, W Casey's, KwikTrip Burger King, Casa Zamora Mexican, GreenMill Rest., KFC, Perkins, Subway, Taco John's, Taco King, Trumble's Rest., Wok'n Roll Best Value Inn, Country Inn&Suites, Countryside Inn, Heritage Hotel, Motel 6 H, $Tree, Advance Parts, AutoValue Parts, AutoZone, Buick/GMC, CarQuest, Chrysler/Dodge/Jeep, Ford, Home Depot, Honda, Lincoln, NAPA, Nissan/VW, O'Reilly Parts, Volvo Trucks, Walmart/Subway
9mm	Albert Lea Lake
8	US 65, Lp 35, Albert Lea, 2 mi W Freeborn City Co-op/dsl DQ, Hardee's
5	rd 13, to Glenville, Twin Lakes, 3 mi W camping
2	rd 5
1mm	**Welcome Ctr nb, full facilities, litter barrels, petwalk, , vending**
0mm	Minnesota/Iowa state line

INTERSTATE 35 West

MINNEAPOLIS

Exit #	Services
41mm	**I-35W begins/ends on I-35, exit 127.**
36	rd 23, E Holiday/dsl, W Minnoco/dsl Caribou Coffee, Don Julio, DQ, McDonald's, Subway, Tasty Asia Hampton Inn AT&T, Discount Tire, Kohl's, Super Target, Verizon
33	rd 17, Lexington Ave, E F&F/dsl, Holiday/dsl Burger King, Walmart/Subway Aldi Foods, W Applebee's, Arby's, Bonfire Rest., Caribou Coffee, Green Mill Rest., Taco Bell, Wendy's, Zantigo's Mexican Cub Foods, GNC, Home Depot, Michael's, Walgreens
32	95th Ave NE, to Lexington, Circle Pines, W Nat Sports Ctr
31b a	Lake Dr, E Shell/Circle K/dsl Quizno's, Red Ginger Asian Country Inn&Suites
30	US 10 W, MN 118, to MN 65
29	rd I, W Cenex/dsl
28c b	rd 10, rd H, W BP McDonald's, Mermaid Café, Taco Bell AmericInn, Days Inn
28a	MN 96, E Holiday/dsl, W Homewood Suites
27b a	I-694 E and W
26	rd E2, W Exxon/Circle K/dsl Jimmy John's, Limu Coffee USPO
25b	MN 88, to Roseville (no EZ return to sb), same as 25a
25a	rd D (from nb), E BP/dsl Courtyard, Fairfield Inn, Residence Inn, W Marathon/dsl, SA/dsl, Shell Barley John's, Caribou Coffee, Jake's Café, McDonald's, New Hong Kong, Perkins/24hr, Sarpino's Italian, Subway
24	rd C, E Burger King, India Palace Rest., Joe Senser's Rest. Hampton Inn, Home 2 Suites, Key Inn, Motel 6, Radisson USPO, Walmart, W Holiday Inn Express Buick/GMC, Chevrolet, Chrysler/Dodge/Jeep, Norm's Tires
23b	Cleveland Ave, MN 36
23a	MN 280, Industrial Blvd (from sb)
22	MN 280, Industrial Blvd (from nb), E Ramada Plaza
21b a	Broadway St, Stinson Blvd, E Ford/Isuzu Trucks, W Sol, Burger King, Caribou Coffee, Leeann Chin, McDona Taco Bell Cub Foods, GNC, Home Depot, Target
19	E Hennepin (from nb)
18	US 52, 4th St SE, University Ave, to U of MN
17c	11th St, Washington Ave, E Courtyard, W Mobil US Bank Stadium
17b	I-94 W (from sb)
17a	MN 55, Hiawatha
16b a	I-94 (from nb), E to St Paul, W to St Cloud, to MN 65
15	31st St (from nb), Lake St, E McDonald's, Taco Bell AutoZone
14	35th St, 36th St
13	46th St
13mm	Minnehaha Creek
12b	Diamond Lake Rd
12a	60th St (from sb), W Mobil Cub Foods
11b	MN 62 E, to , to
11a	Lyndale Ave (from sb)
10b	MN 62 W, 58th St
10a	rd 53, 66th St, E SA
9c	76th St (from sb)
9b a	I-494, MN 5, to , to
8	82nd St, E BMW, W Applebee's, Caribou Coffee, Ji John's, Panda Express, Red Lobster, Sonic, Starbucks, Sub Timberlodge Steaks, Wendy's Embassy Suites Ch let, Chrysler/Dodge/Jeep, GNC, Infiniti, Kia, Kohl's, TJ M Verizon, Walgreens
7b	90th St
7a	94th St, E Goodyear/auto, W Holiday Inn
6	rd 1, 98th St, E Applebee's, Bakers Square, Domino's, my John's, Leeann Chin, McDonald's, Starbucks, Subway, dy's, White Castle Bloomington Drug, Festival Foods, URGENT CARE, Walgreens, W SA/dsl
5	106th St
5mm	Minnesota River
4b	113th St, Black Dog Rd
4a	Cliff Rd, E Dodge, Subaru, Walmart
3b a	MN 13, Shakopee, Canterbury Downs, W Perkins
2	Burnsville Pkwy, E BP Carbone's Pizza, W day Clive's Roadhouse, Denny's, Gourmet Chinese, kins Best Value Inn, LivInn, Norwood Inn, Prime Rate tel auto repair, vet
1	rd 42 (from sb), Crystal Lake Rd, E Shell Arby's, B King, Chianti Grill, HoneyBaked Ham, McDonald's, Old Co Buffet, Roasted Pear, Taco Bell AmericInn, Best Wes Fairfield Inn, Hampton Inn H, Home Depot, Lunds& ly's Mkt, PetsMart, W Holiday/dsl, SA/dsl Appleb Buca Italian, Burger Jones, Burger King, Cam Ranh Bay, C fil-A, Chili's, Chipotle, ChuckECheese, IHOP, Jimmy John's, LeAnn Chin, Little Caesar's, Noodles&Co, Olive Garden, back Steaks, Panera Bread, Papa John's, Papa Murphy's, Hut, Porter Creek Grill, Red Lobster, Royal Buffet, Shogun anese, Smashburger, Starbucks, TGIFriday's, Wendy's Town Suites $Tree, Ace Hardware, Advance Parts, Barnes&Noble, Best Buy, Costco/gas, Cub Foods, Dick's, count Tire, JC Penney, Kohl's, Macy's, Michael's, Old Navy Co, Target, Tires+, Tuesday Morning, Verizon, VW, Walgre

I-35W begins/ends on I-35, exit 88a.

MN

E INTERSTATE 90

Exit #	Services
278mm	Minnesota/Wisconsin state line, Mississippi River
276	US 14, US 61, to MN 16, La Crescent, N **Welcome Ctr wb, full [handicapped] facilities, info, litter barrels, petwalk, [phone], [picnic], vending,** S [gas] Kwik Trip (1mi)
273b a	Dresbach
271	Dakota
270	US 14, US 61, to Winona (from wb), N to OL Kipp SP/camping
267	rd 12, Nodine, N [other] Great River Bluffs SP, S [gas] Kwik Trip/Hearty Platter Rest./dsl/e-85/scales/24hr/@
261mm	**weigh sta both lanes**
258	MN 76, to Houston, Ridgeway, Witoka, N [gas] gas, S [other] camping
252	MN 43 N, to Winona, **7 mi** N [food] Taco Bell [lodging] Express Inn, Holiday Inn Express, Plaza Hotel, Quality Inn [other] [H], S [other] vet
249	MN 43 S, to Rushford, N [other] Peterbilt Trucks/repair
244mm	**[RS] eb, full [handicapped] facilities, litter barrels, petwalk, [phone], [picnic], vending**
242	rd 29, Lewiston
233	MN 74, to Chatfield, St Charles, N [gas] Kwik Trip/LP/24hr (2mi) [food] A&W (2mi), Subway (2mi) [other] Whitewater SP, S [gas] BP/Amish Ovens Rest./dsl/RV dump/LP
229	rd 10, Dover
224	MN 42, rd 7, Eyota, N [gas] KwikTrip/dsl/e85 (3mi) [food] Country Cafe (3mi)
222mm	**[RS] wb, full [handicapped] facilities, litter barrels, petwalk, [phone], [picnic], vending**
218	US 52, to Rochester, S [gas] BP/dsl [other] KOA (Mar-Oct) (1mi)
209b a	US 63, MN 30, to Rochester, Stewartville, **8-10 mi** N [lodging] Clarion, EconoLodge, Hampton Inn, Super 8, **1 mi** S [gas] KwikTrip/dsl [food] DQ, Pizza Ranch, Subway [lodging] Best Inn [other] Family$, Verizon
205	rd 6
202mm	**[RS] eb, full [handicapped] facilities, litter barrels, petwalk, [phone], [picnic], vending**
193	MN 16, Dexter, N [gas] BP/Oasis Rest./dsl, S [lodging] Windmill Motel
189	rd 13, to Elkton
187	rd 20, S [other] Jellystone Camping
183	MN 56, to Rose Creek, Brownsdale, S [gas] Freeborn County Co-op/dsl/LP
181	28th St NE
180b a	US 218, 21st St NE, to Austin, Oakland Place, S [gas] Shell [lodging] Rodeway Inn
179	11th Dr NE, to Austin, N [gas] KwikTrip/dsl/24hr
178b	6th St NE, to Austin, S [other] Spam Museum
178a	4th St NW, N [food] Culver's, Jimmy John's, Perkins, Torge's Grille [lodging] AmericInn, Days Inn, Holiday Inn [other] Buick/Chevrolet/GMC, vet, S [gas] KwikTrip/dsl [food] Burger King, Hardee's, Subway [other] [H]
177	US 218 N, to Owatonna, Austin, Mapleview, N [food] Applebee's, Arby's, China Star, El Patron Mexican, KFC, King Buffet, Pizza Hut, Pizza Ranch, Wendy's [other] $Tree, Aldi Foods, AT&T, AutoZone, Hy-Vee Foods/gas, JoAnn Fabrics, O'Reilly Parts, Verizon, Walmart/Subway, S [gas] Sinclair/McDonald's/dsl [lodging] Super 8
175	MN 105, rd 46, to Oakland Rd, N [lodging] Econolodge, S [gas] BP/dsl, Shell/dsl [other] Chrysler/Dodge/Jeep, Ford/Lincoln, vet
171mm	**[RS] wb, full [handicapped] facilities, litter barrels, petwalk, [phone], [picnic],**
166	rd 46, Oakland Rd, N [other] KOA/LP
163	rd 26, Hayward, S [gas] Freeborn County Co-op/dsl [food] McDonald's (4mi), Pizza Hut (4mi), Trails Rest. (4mi) [lodging] Holiday Inn Express (4mi) [other] KOA, Myre-Big Island SP
161.5mm	**[RS] eb, full [handicapped] facilities, petwalk, [phone], [picnic] litter barrels**

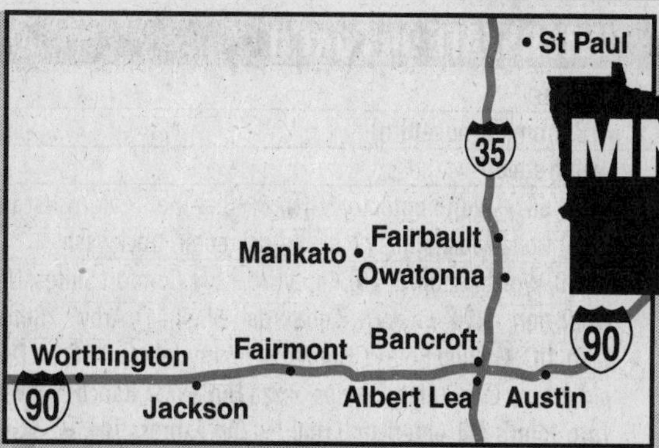

ALBERT LEA

Exit #	Services
159b a	I-35, N to Twin Cities, S to Des Moines
157	rd 22, Albert Lea, N [other] Kenworth, S [gas] HyVee/dsl [food] Applebee's, Arby's, Caribou Coffee, DQ, KwikTrip/dsl, McDonald's, Pizza Ranch, Plaza Morina Mexican [lodging] AmericInn, Best Western+ [other] [H], Ace Hardware, Chevrolet, Harley-Davidson, Herberger's, Hy-Vee Foods, Verizon
154	MN 13, to US 69, to Manchester, Albert Lea, N [gas] SA/dsl, **3 mi** S [lodging] Best Value Inn
146	MN 109, to Wells, Alden, S [gas] Cenex/dsl/rest., Freeborn Co-Op Gas/dsl/E-85 [other] truck/dsl repair
138	MN 22, to Wells, Keister, N [gas] Casey's (6mi)
134	MN 253, rd 21, to Bricelyn, MN Lake
128	MN 254, rd 17, Frost, Easton
119	US 169, to Winnebago, Blue Earth, S [gas] Blue Earth/dsl, Shell/dsl [food] Country Kitchen, DQ, McDonald's, Pizza Hut, Subway [lodging] AmericInn, Super 8 [other] [H], $General, Jolly Green Giant, Bomgaars
119mm	**[RS] both lanes, full [handicapped] facilities, litter barrels, petwalk, [phone], [picnic], playground**
113	rd 1, Guckeen

FAIRMONT

Exit #	Services
107	MN 262, rd 53, to East Chain, Granada, S [other] camping (May-Oct) (1mi), gas/dsl
102	MN 15, to Madelia, Fairmont, N [gas] Verizon, Walmart/Subway, **0-2 mi** S [gas] BP, Cenex/dsl, SA/dsl/24hr [food] Arby's, Bean Town a Grill, Burger King, China Buffet, DQ, Green Mill Rest., Hardee's, McDonald's, Perkins, Pizza Ranch, Ranch Family Rest., Subway [lodging] Budget Inn, Hampton Inn, Holiday Inn, Quality Inn, Super 8 [other] [H], $Tree, Ace Hardware, Advance Parts, auto repair, Chevrolet, Chrysler/Dodge/Jeep, Fareway Foods, Ford, Freightliner, Goodyear/auto, Hy-Vee Foods, NAPA, O'Reilly Parts, USPO, Walgreens
99	rd 39, Fairmont
93	MN 263, rd 27, Welcome, **1/2 mi** S [gas] Casey's/dsl [other] camping
87	MN 4, Sherburn, N [other] Fox Lake Camping (3mi), S [gas] Casey's/dsl, Kum&Go/Subway/dsl/E-85
80	rd 29, Alpha
73	US 71, Jackson, N [gas] SA/dsl [food] Burger King [lodging] EconoLodge, Super 8 [other] KOA, to Kilen Woods SP, S [gas] BP/DQ, Casey's/dsl [food] Embers Rest., Pizza Ranch, Subway [lodging] AmericInn, Earth Inn, Prairie Winds Motel [other] [H], Ace Hardware, Buick/Chevrolet, Chrysler/Dodge/Jeep, city park, Family$, Sunshine Foods, to Spirit Lake
72.5mm	W Fork Des Moines River
72mm	**[RS] wb, full [handicapped] facilities, litter barrels, petwalk, [phone], [picnic], vending**
69mm	**[RS] eb, full [handicapped] facilities, litter barrels, petwalk, [phone], [picnic], vending**
64	MN 86, Lakefield, N [gas] gas/dsl [food] food [other] camping, to Kilen SP (12mi)
57	rd 9, to Heron Lake, Spafford
50	MN 264, rd 1, to Brewster, Round Lake

MN

INTERSTATE 90 Cont'd

WORTHINGTON

Exit #	Services
47	rd 3 (from eb, no return)
46mm	**weigh sta eb**
45	MN 60, Worthington, **N** BP/Blueline Cafe/dsl/scales, **S** Holiday/dsl/scales/24hr dsl repair, truckwash
43	US 59, Worthington, **N** Casey's/dsl Comfort Suites, Norwood Inn, **S** Casey's, Cenex/dsl, Shell Arby's, Burger King, DQ, Ground Round, Hardee's, Jimmy John's, KFC, McDonald's, New City Buffet, Perkins, Pizza Hut, Pizza Ranch, Subway, Taco John's AmericInn, Holiday Inn Express H, $General, Ace Hardware, CarQuest, Chevrolet, Fareway Foods, Ford, Hy-Vee Foods/dsl, NAPA, O'Reilly Parts, Verizon, Walgreens, Walmart/Subway
42	MN 266, rd 25, to Reading, **S** Days Inn, Super 8
33	rd 13, to Wilmont, Rushmore
26	MN 91, Adrian, **S** Cenex/dsl, Kum&Go/Subway/dsl/E-85/24hr Countryside Steaks $General, Adrian Camping, city park
25mm	**wb full facilities, litter barrels, petwalk,**
24mm	**eb full facilities, litter barrels, petwalk,**
18	rd 3, Kanaranzi, Magnolia, **N** camping
12	US 75, Luverne, **N** BP/dsl/E-85, Casey's/dsl, Holiday/Subway/dsl McDonald's, Papa's Place Rest., Taco John's, Tasty Drive-In Cozy Rest Motel (1mi), GrandStay Hotel, Quality Inn H, $General, Buick/Cadillac/Chevrolet/GMC, Chrysler/Dodge/Jeep, Ford, Lewis Drugs, Pipestone NM, Sturdevant's Parts, to Blue Mounds SP, **S** Blue Stem Rest. Super 8
5	rd 6, Beaver Creek, **N** Local/dsl
3	rd 4 (from eb), Beaver Creek
1	MN 23, rd 17, to Jasper, **N** access to gas/dsl, to Pipestone NM
0mm	Minnesota/South Dakota state line, **Welcome Ctr eb, full facilities, info, litter barrels,**

INTERSTATE 94

ST PAUL

Exit #	Services
259mm	Minnesota/Wisconsin state line, St Croix River
258	MN 95 N, to Stillwater, Hastings, Lakeland, **N** Bungalow Rest.
257mm	**Welcome Ctr wb, full facilities, litter barrels, petwalk, , vending, weigh sta wb**
253	MN 95 S, rd 15, Manning Ave, **N** StoneRidge Golf, **S** ski area, to Afton Alps SP
251	rd 19, Keats Ave, Woodbury Dr, **S** KwikTrip, SA/dsl Applebee's, Arby's, Burger King, Caribou Coffee, Chili's, Chipotle Mexican, ChuckECheese, Culver's, Dino's Rest., Dunn Bros Coffee, Fiesta Brava, Jersey Mike's, Lakes Grill, LeeAnn Chin, Little Chopstix, McDonald's, Noodles&Co, Papa Murphy's, Quiznos, Ray J's Grill, SmashBurger, Starbucks, Subway, Which Wich? Extended Stay America, Holiday Inn Express $Tree, AT&T, Discount Tire, Hobby Lobby, Michael's, Sam's Club/gas, Staples, Target, Trader Joe's, Verizon, Walmart/Subway, Woodbury Lakes Outlets/famous brands
250	rd 13, Radio Dr, Inwood Ave, **N** Buffalo Wild Wings, Caribou Coffee, Five Guys, Machine Shed Rest., Milio's Rest., Olive Garden, Red Lobster Hilton Garden, Holiday Inn Best Buy, **S** Holiday/e85 Domino's, DUC Vietnamese, Firehouse Subs, Jamba Juice, Little Caesar's, Pei Wei, Piada Italian, Pie Five, Potbelly, Qdoba, Starbucks, Taco Bell, Tamarack Rest.,
250	Continued Wendy's, Wild Bill's Grill, Zupas Residence Inn Foods, BigLots, Cabela's, Cub Foods, CVS Drug, Dick's, Fa May, GNC, Gordman's, Heppner's Auto Ctr, Home Depo Penney, Jo-Ann, LandsEnd Inlet, Old Navy, Petsmart, Ti Verizon, vet
249	I-694 N & I-494 S
247	MN 120, Century Ave, **N** Denny's LivInn ley-Davidson, **S** SA/dsl GreenMill Rest. Cou Inn/rest. CarQuest, Chevrolet
246c b	McKnight Ave, **N** 3M, **S** Holiday Inn
246a	Ruth St (from eb, no return), **N** BP Culver's, Domi Hoho Chinese, Jimmy John's, Leeann Chin $Tree, Foods, Firestone/auto, GNC, TJ Maxx
245	White Bear Ave, **N** SA/dsl Subway Mote Walgreens, **S** BP Arby's, Davanni's Pizza/subs, Ocampo, McDonald's, Papa John's, Popeye's, Sonic, Taco Wendy's Aldi Foods, Family$, NAPA, O'Reilly Parts, Tar
244	US 10 E, US 61 S, **S** Mounds/Kellogg
243	US 61, Mounds Blvd, **S** River Centre
242d	US 52 S, MN 3, 6th St, (exits left from wb), **N** Holi dsl Subway
242c	7th St, **S** SA
242b a	I-35E N, US 10 W, I-35E S (from eb)
241c	I-35E S (from wb)
241b	10th St, 5th St, to downtown
241a	12th St, Marion St, Kellogg Blvd, **N** Best Western+, **S** Paul's Cathedral
240	Dale Ave
239b a	Lexington Pkwy, Hamline Ave, **N** BP, SA DQ, Hard Leeann Chin, Noodles&Co, Popeye's, White Castle $ Aldi, AutoZone, Cub Foods, Discount Tire, Herberger's, O'R Parts, Target, TJ Maxx, Verizon, **S** H
238	MN 51, Snelling Ave, **N** Culver's, Little Caesar's, Mc ald's, Peking Garden, Perkins CVS Drug, Family$, Rainbow Foods, same as 239, Walgreens, Walmart/Sub **S** Tires+
237	Cretin Ave, Vandalia Ave, to downtown
236	MN 280, University Ave, to downtown
235b	Huron Blvd
235mm	Mississippi River
235a	Riverside Ave, 25th Ave, **N** Fina Starbucks, **S** kins, Taco Bell
234c	Cedar Ave, downtown
234b a	MN 55, Hiawatha Ave, 5th St, **N** Courtyard to down
233b	I-35W N, I-35W S (exits left from wb)
233a	11th St (from wb), **N** downtown
231b	Hennepin Ave, Lyndale Ave, to downtown
231a	I-394, US 12 W, to downtown
230	US 52, MN 55, 4th St, 7th St, Olson Hwy, **N** US Bank S um, **S** H, Int Mkt Square
229	W Broadway, Washington Ave, **N** EZ Stop/dsl, Holi dsl Broadway Pizza, **S** Winner Burger King, Caesar's, McDonald's, Subway, Taco Bell, Wendy's $ AutoZone, Cub Foods, Family$, Walgreens
228	Dowling Ave N
226	53rd Ave N, 49th Ave N
225	I-694 E, MN 252 N, to Minneapolis

I-94 and I-494 run together. See I-494/694, exits 28-34.

MINNEAPOLIS

Exit #	Services
216	I-94 W and I-494s
215	rd 109, Weaver Lake Rd, **N** SA/dsl, Shell Angeno by's, Broadway Pizza, Burger King, Caribou Coffee, Chin

INTERSTATE 94 Cont'd

215	Continued ChuckECheese's, Domino's, DQ, El Rodeo Mexican, Famous Dave's BBQ, Frankie's Pizza, Golden Corral, Great Harvest Bread Co., Jimmy John's, McDonald's, Papa John's, Papa Murphy's, Rita's, Starbucks, Subway, Taco Bell, Wendy's AT&T, Barnes&Noble, Cub Foods, GNC, Goodyear/auto, JC Penney, Kohl's, Lund&Byerly's Foods, Michael's, Midas, Old Navy, PetCo, same as 28, Tires+, USPO, Verizon, Walgreens, **S** Applebee's
214mm	**eb, full facilities, litter barrels**
213	rd 30, 95th Ave N, Maple Grove, **N** SA/dsl Chipotle Mexican, Subway Cambria Suites Aldi Foods, GNC, Home Depot, Target, **S** Holiday/dsl Caribou Coffee, Culver's, Jersey Mike's, Jets Pizza, Leeann Chin, McDonald's, Starbucks, Teresa's Mexican, Which Wich?, White Castle $Tree, AT&T, BigLots, Discount Tire, Firestone/auto, Goodyear/auto, Hobby Lobby, KOA (2mi) (Apr-Oct), Menards, Sam's Club/gas, Verizon, Walgreens, Walmart/Subway
212	101st Ave (from eb)
207	MN 101, to Elk River, Rogers, **N** Holiday/dsl, SA/dsl, TA/Country Pride/dsl/scales/24hr/@ Applebee's, Arby's, Burger King, China Kitchen, Chipotle, Culver's, Davanni's Pizza, Denny's, Dickey's BBQ, Domino's, DQ, Hardee's, Jimmy John's, Maynard's, McDonald's, Noodles&Co, Papa Murphy's, Starbucks, Subway, Taco Bell, Wendy's Hampton Inn, Holiday Inn Express, Super 8 $Tree, AT&T, Cabela's, Camping World, Cub Foods, Discount Tire, GNC, Kohl's, NAPA, NTB, O'Reilly Parts, Target, Tires+, Verizon, vet, Walgreens, **S** BP/Circle K/dsl, Holiday BoBo Asian, Guadalajara Mexican, Minne's Diner AmeriInn Chevrolet, CVS Drug, TrueValue, URGENT CARE, USPO
205.5mm	Crow River
205	MN 241, rd 36, St Michael, **S** KwikTrip/dsl, SA/dsl
202	rd 37, Albertville, **N** Shell/dsl Emma Krumbee's Rest., **S** BP/dsl, SA/dsl, same as 201
201	rd 19 (from eb), Albertville, St Michael, **N** Andy's Pizza, Burger King, Five Guys, Hana Steaks, Michael B's Grill, Subway Country Inn&Suites Albertville Outlets/famous brands, Old Navy, **S** Casey's, Mobil/Circle K Caribou Coffee, China Dragon, Culver's, Little Caesar's, Papa Murphy's, Space Aliens Grill, Subway, Taco Bell Ace Hardware, auto repair, Coburn's/dsl, Goodyear/auto, Verizon
194	rd 18, rd 39, Monticello, **N** KwikTrip/dsl Caribou Coffee, Little Caesar's AT&T, GNC, Home Depot, Marshall's, Petsmart, Target, Verizon
193	MN 25, to Buffalo, Monticello, Big Lake, **N** Holiday/dsl Burger King, Caribou Coffee, KFC, Papa Murphy's, Perkins, Quiznos, Rancho Grande Mexican, Taco Bell AmericInn AutoValue Parts, Cub Foods, USPO, Walgreens, **S** Holiday/dsl, SA/dsl Applebee's, Arby's, Buffalo Wild Wings, China Buffet, Culver's, DQ, Jimmy John's, McDonald's, Pizza Ranch, Subway, Taco John's Best Western, Days Inn, Super 8 $Tree, Aldi Foods, AutoZone, Buick/GMC, Chevrolet, Goodyear/auto, Lake Maria SP, NAPA, O'Reilly Parts, Verizon, Walmart/Subway
187mm	**eb, full facilities, litter barrels, petwalk, vending**
183	rd 8, to Silver Creek, Hasty, Maple Lake, **S** SA/rest./dsl/scales/24hr/@ camping, to Lake Maria SP
178	MN 24, to Annandale, Clearwater, **N** Holiday/Petro/dsl/scales/24hr/@ Burger King, DQ, Kettle, Subway, Taco Gringo Best Value Inn Clearwater Hardware, Coburn's Foods/gas, Parts City, repair, USPO, **S** A-J Acres RV Camping (Apr-Oct), Recreation Outdoor RV Ctr

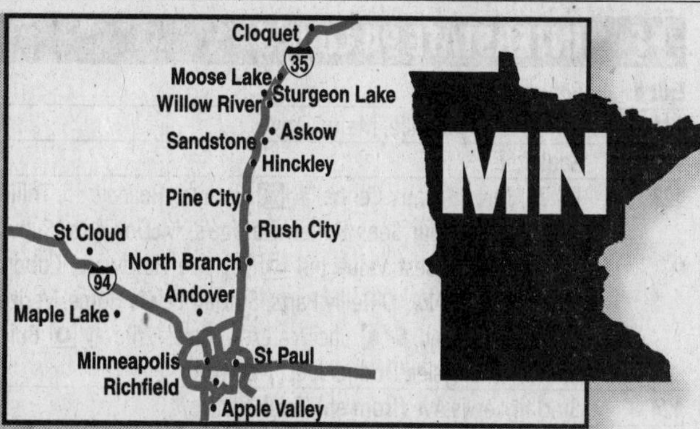

ST CLOUD

178mm	**wb, full facilities, litter barrels, petwalk, vending**
173	Opportunity Dr
171	rd 7, rd 75, St Augusta, **N** Pilot/dsl/scales/24hr, Shell/Burger King/dsl McDonald's, RJ's Grill, Subway AmericInn, Holiday Inn Express, Travelodge Goodyear/auto, **S** BP Freightliner, Pleasureland RV Ctr
167b a	MN 15, to St Cloud, Kimball, 4 mi **N** Holiday, SA/dsl Applebee's, Arby's, Bonanza, Boulder Taphouse, Buffalo Wild Wings, Burger King, Caribou Coffee, Chick-fil-A, Chipotle, ChuckECheese's, Coldstone, Famous Dave's BBQ, Five Guys, Granite City Grill, Grizzly's Grill, IHOP, La Casita Mexican, Leeann Chin, McDonald's, Noodles&Co, Old Chicago Pizza, Olive Garden, Panda Express, Perkins, Pizza Ranch, Red Lobster, Red Robin, Sammy's Pizza, Starbucks, Subway, Taco Bell, Taco John's, TX Roadhouse, Wendy's, White Castle Country Inn&Suites, Days Inn, Fairfield Inn, Hampton Inn, Holiday Inn, Homewood Suites, Quality Inn, Super 8 AT&T, Barnes&Noble, Best Buy, CashWise Foods, Dick's, Fresh Thyme Mkt, Hobby Lobby, Home Depot, JC Penney, Jo-Ann Fabrics, Kohl's, Macy's, Michael's, Office Depot, Old Navy, Petsmart, Sam's Club, Save-A-Lot, Scheel's Sports, Subaru, Target, Walgreens, Walmart
164	MN 23, to St Cloud, Rockville, 4-6 mi **N** KwikTrip/dsl, SA/dsl Culver's, IHOP, KFC, Subway, Wendy's Astaria Inn $Tree, Discount Tire, Grande Depot Gourmet Foods, Honda, Hyundai, Kia, Menards, Petsmart, same as 167, Toyota
162.5mm	Sauk River
160	rd 2, to Cold Spring, St Joseph, **N** BP Coll of St Benedict
158	rd 75 (from eb exits left), to St Cloud, 3 mi **N** same as 160
156	rd 159, St Joseph, **S** St Johns U
153	rd 9, Avon, **N** Casey's/dsl, Tesoro/McDonald's/dsl Subway Budget Host city park, USPO, **S** El Rancho Manana Camping (10mi)
152mm	**both lanes, full facilities, litter barrels, petwalk, vending**
147	MN 238, rd 10, Albany, **N** Holiday/dsl, Shell/Godfather's/dsl A&W/Subway, DQ, Hillcrest Rest. Baymont Inn CVS Drug, golf, **S** Chrysler/Dodge/Jeep, NAPA, vet
140	rd 11, Freeport, **N** Cenex/dsl, Sinclair/dsl Ackie's Pioneer Rest., Charlie's Café auto repair, vet
137	MN 237, rd 65, New Munich
137mm	Sauk River
135	rd 13, Melrose, **N** Sinclair/dsl/repair, Victory/Subway/dsl Burger King, Cornerstone Buffet $General, **S** Casey's/dsl DQ, El Portal Mexican Super 8 TrueValue, vet
132.5mm	Sauk River

MN

INTERSTATE 94 Cont'd

Exit #	Services
131	MN 4, to Paynesville, Meire Grove
128mm	Sauk River
127	US 71, MN 28, Sauk Centre, N Casey's, Holiday/dsl, Trillium CNG DQ, Four Seas Buffet, Hardee's, McDonald's, Subway AmericInn, Best Value Inn H, Ace Hardware, Coborn's Foods, Ford, NAPA, O'Reilly Parts, Sinclair Lewis Home, Verizon, Walmart/Subway, S Shell/café/dsl/scales/24hr/@ Buick/ Chevrolet/Chrysler/Dodge/Jeep, Kenworth
124	Sinclair Lewis Ave (from eb), Sauk Centre
119	rd 46, West Union
114	MN 27, rd 3, to Westport, Osakis, 3 mi N gas A&W, Subway lodging
105mm	wb, full facilities, litter barrels, petwalk, vending

ALEXANDRIA

Exit #	Services
103	MN 29, to Glenwood, Alexandria, N F&F/dsl, Holiday/dsl, Simonson/dsl Arby's, Burger King, Caribou Coffee, China Buffet, Culver's, Dolittle's Grill, Great Hunan, Hardee's, Jimmy John's, KFC, McDonald's, Perkins, Qdoba, Subway, Taco Bell, TN Roadhouse, Wendy's AmericInn, Best Western, Days Inn, Hampton Inn, Super 8 H, $Tree, Aldi Foods, AT&T, AutoZone, Cadillac/Chevrolet/Mazda, Cub Foods, Goodyear/ auto, Harley-Davidson, Herberger's, Jo-Ann Fabrics, Mazda, Menards, Target, Verizon, Walmart/Subway, S Holiday/ dsl Country Inn&Suites, Holiday Inn Alexandria RV Ctr, Buick/GMC
100	MN 27, N Pilot/Subway/dsl/scales/24hr/@ Best Inn/ Alexandria RV Park (2mi) H, S camping
100mm	Lake Latoka
99mm	eb, full facilities, litter barrels, petwalk, vending
97	MN 114, rd 40, to Lowry, Garfield
90	rd 7, Brandon, S camping, ski area
82	MN 79, rd 41, to Erdahl, Evansville, 2 mi N BP/dsl H, S camping
77	MN 78, rd 10, to Barrett, Ashby, N gas/dsl camping, S camping
69mm	wb, full facilities, litter barrels, petwalk, vending
67	rd 35, Dalton, N camping, S camping

FERGUS FALLS

Exit #	Services
61	US 59 S, rd 82, to Elbow Lake, N Tesoro/café/dsl/LP/24hr H, camping (4mi), S camping
57	MN 210 E, rd 25, Fergus Falls, N H
55	rd 1, to Wendell, Fergus Falls, N antiques
54	MN 210 W, Lincoln Ave, Fergus Falls, N Cenex/dsl, F&F/dsl, Tesoro/dsl Applebee's, Arby's, Burger King, Family Diner, Hardee's, Hunan Spring Buffet, McDonald's, Papa Murphy's, Perkins, Pizza Hut, Pizza Ranch, Subway, Thrifty White Drug AmericInn, Best Value Inn, Best Western, Comfort Inn, Motel 7, Super 8 H, $Tree, Aldi Foods, AT&T, Chrysler/Dodge/ Jeep, Ford/Lincoln, GMC, Herberger's, Home Depot, Kenworth, museum, NAPA, O'Reilly Parts, SunMart Foods/dsl, Target, Tires+, Toyota, USPO, S Mabel Murphy's Rest. Walmart
50	rd 88, rd 52, to US 59, to Fergus Falls, Elizabeth, camping
38	rd 88, Rothsay, S Tesoro/cafe/dsl/24hr Powerhouse Grill Comfort Zone Inn tires
32	MN 108, rd 30,to Pelican Rapids, Lawndale, 19 mi N Maplewood SP
24	MN 34, Barnesville, N Renee's Drive-in, 1 mi S Cenex/ dsl, Tesoro/dsl DQ, Subway $General, city park, Wagner Park Camping (May-Oct)
22	MN 9, Barnesville, 1 mi S Cenex/dsl, Tesoro/dsl DQ, Subway $General
15	rd 10, Downer
8mm	Buffalo River
6	MN 336, rd 11, to US 10, Dilworth, N to Buffalo River S
5mm	Red River weigh sta eb

MOORHEAD

Exit #	Services
2b	34th St, Moorhead, 2 mi N Casey's/dsl, Holiday/dsl/e Tesoro Arby's, Fry'n Pan, Hardee's, McDonald's, Perk Pizza Ranch, Subway Travelodge H, $Tree, CVS D Menards, Target, Tires+, Walmart/Subway
2a	no service
1mm	Welcome Ctr eb, full facilities, info, litter barrels, vending
1b	20th St, Moorhead (from eb, no return)
1a	US 75, Moorhead, N Cenex/dsl Burger King, Crave B er Co., Jimmy John's, Little Caesar's, Noodles&Co, Papa phy's, Qdoba, Starbucks, Village Inn Courtyard Fa Fare Foods, Verizon, S Casey's, Holiday/dsl Panch Mexican, Sarpino's Pizza, Snapdragon Asian, Speak Easy R Subway Days Inn, Grand Inn, Microtel, Super 8 CVS D Hornbacher's Mkt, Subaru, vet, Walgreens
0mm	Minnesota/North Dakota state line, Red River

INTERSTATE 494/694

Exit #	Services
	I-494/I-694 loops around Minneapolis/St Paul.
71	rd 31, Pilot Knob Rd, N Courtyard, Fairfield Inn, S day Inn
70	I-35E, N to St Paul, S to Albert Lea
69	MN 149, MN 55, Dodd Rd, S Caribou Coffee, Jimmy Jo McDonald's, Subway Country Inn&Suites
67	MN 3, Roberts St, 1 mi N BP, Holiday Applebee's by's, Baker's Square, Burger King, Chick-fil-A, Chipotle Mex Culver's, Jimmy John's, KFC, Noodles&Co, Panda Express, P ra Bread, Papa Murphy's, Taco Bell, White Castle $ Aamco, Aldi Foods, AT&T, Best Buy, Buick/GMC, Chevrolet, Foods, Discount Tire, Ford, Home Depot, Honda, Hyundai, Lincoln, Lowe's, Mazda, NAPA, Nissan, NTB, O'Reilly Parts, Boys, Petco, Target, Toyota, VW, Wagreens, Walmart
66	US 52, S SA Applebee's, B-52 Burger, Out Steaks AmericInn, Holiday Inn Express, Microtel
65	7th Ave, 5th Ave
64b a	MN 56, Concord St, N KwikTrip/dsl/scales Burger Subway Clarion Goodyear, Peterbilt, Stockmens S Holiday/dsl Chrysler/Jeep/Dodge, Parts+
63mm	Mississippi River
63c	Maxwell Ave
63b a	US 10, US 61, to St Paul, Hastings, S BP, SA B King, Subway Boyd's Motel NAPA
60	Lake Rd, E SA/dsl Carbone's Pizza, Milio's Sandwi W H
59	Valley Creek Rd, E BP/repair, SA/dsl/LP Appleb Chipotle Mexican, Coldstone, DQ, Jersey Mike's, Jimmy Jo Noodles&Co, Panda Express, Papa Murphy's, Perkins, belly, Red's Savoy Pizza, Starbucks, Yang's Chinese Inn $Tree, Barnes&Noble, GNC, Kohl's, Lunds&Byerly's Marshall's, PetCo, Target, URGENT CARE, USPO, Walgr W Shell Bonfire Rest., Burger King, Keys Cafe, Mc ald's, Sole Mio Italian, Subway Hampton Inn H Hardware, Goodyear
58c	Tamarack Rd, E Tavern Grill, Woodbury Cafe La Qu Sheraton
58b a	I-94, E to Madison, W to St Paul. **I-494 S begins/ends, I-6 begins/ends.**

INTERSTATE 494/694 Cont'd

Exit #	Services
57	rd 10, 10th St N, E SA/dsl IHOP, Pizza Man, Sgt Peppers Grill, Wild Boar Grill Best Western, W Holiday/dsl Burger King, Caribou Coffee, Hardee's, Hunan Buffet, KFC, Papa Murphy's, Starbucks $Tree, Cub Foods, HyVee/dsl
55	MN 5, E SA/dsl McDonald's Target, W Holiday/dsl, KwikTrip/dsl Subway Menards, st patrol
52b a	MN 36, N St Paul, to Stillwater, W F&F/dsl Burger King, Caribou Coffee, DQ
51	MN 120, E BP, SA/dsl Dulano's Pizza, Jethro's, Tacos Fresh, W The Corner/gas vet
50	White Bear Ave, N SA/dsl Cub Foods, Sam's Club/gas, S Acapulco, Arby's, Bakers Square, Buffalo Wild Wings, Caribou Coffee, Chili's, Chipotle, Denny's, Great Moon Buffet, IHOP, Jake's Grill, Jimmy John's, McDonald's, Noodles&Co, Olive Garden, Osaka, Outback Steaks, Perkins/24hr, Pizza Hut, Pizza Ranch, Popeye's, Red Lobster, Taco Bell, TGI Friday, Wendy's Emerald Inn Aamco, Barnes&Noble, Best Buy, Firestone/auto, Hobby Lobby, JC Penney, Jo-Ann Fabrics, Kohl's, Macy's, Marshall's, Michael's, Tires+, Verizon, Walgreens
48	US 61, N KwikTrip/dsl Acura, Chrysler/Dodge/Jeep, Ford, Honda, Hyundai, Kia, Lincoln, Subaru, S Chili's, Jake's Grill, McDonald's, Olive Garden, Subway H, Audi/Porsche, CarMax, Costco/gas, Lexus, Mercedes, Nissan, Toyota, Venburg Tire, Volvo
47	I-35E, N to Duluth
46	I-35E, US 10, S to St Paul
45	rd 49, Rice St, N Gas+, Mobil/dsl Subway, Taco Bell, S Burger King, Caribou Coffee
43b	Victoria St
43a	Lexington Ave, N Greenmill Rest., Red Robin Best Western+, Hilton Garden, S Exxon/Circle K/dsl Arby's, Cane's, Caribou Coffee, Chipotle, Davanni's Pizza, Five Guys, Jimmy John's, Leeann Chin, Noodles&Co, Papa John's, Papa Murphy's, Perkins, Potbelly, Starbucks, Subway, Wendy's Quality Inn AT&T, Cub Foods, GNC, Target, Trader Joe's
42b	US 10 W (from wb), to Anoka
42a	MN 51, Snelling Ave, 1 mi S Shell/dsl Flaherty's Grill, Lindey's Steaks, McDonald's Country Inn&Suites vet
41b a	I-35W, S to Minneapolis, N to Duluth
40	Long Lake Rd, 10th St NW
39	Silver Lake Rd, N BP Acapulco Mexican, McDonald's, Subway Ford, U-Haul
38b a	MN 65, Central Ave, N Holiday/dsl Subway, S SA A&W/KFC, Applebee's, Asia Rest., Big Marina Deli, Chipotle, Domino's, Embers Rest., Flameburger Rest., Jimmy John's, La Casita Mexican, Leeann Chin, Little Caesar's, McDonald's, Papa John's, Pizza Hut, Sonic, Starbucks, Subway, Taco Bell, Wendy's LivInn Hotel $General, Advance Parts, Aldi Foods, AT&T, AutoZone, Discount Tire, Menards, Noodles&Co, PetCo, Target, Tires+, vet, Walgreens
37	rd 47, University Ave, N Holiday, SA/dsl Burger King, McDonald's, Panchero's, Papa Murphy's Pizza, Zantigo's Rest. Cub Foods, CVS Drug, Duluth Trading, Home Depot, NTB, S Bona Bros/repair, Shell
36	E River Rd
35mm	**I-494 W begins/ends, I-694 E begins/ends.**
35c	MN 252, N Holiday, SA
35b a	I-94 E to Minneapolis
34	to MN 100, Shingle Creek Pkwy, N Denny's Best Western, Country Inn&Suites, Doubletree, Extended Stay America,

MINNEAPOLIS

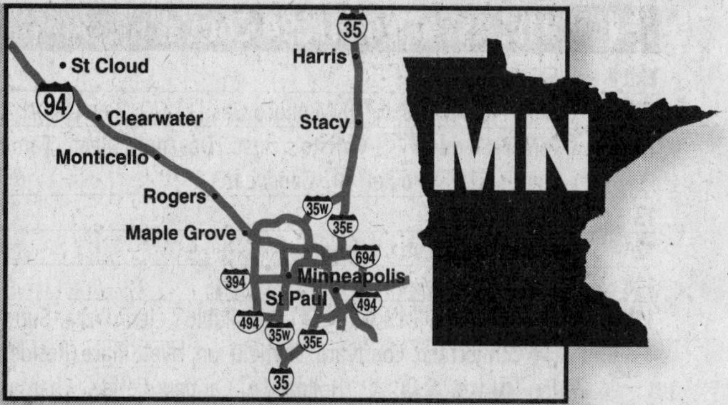

Exit #	Services
34	Continued Motel 6, Norwood Inn, Quality Inn, Super 8, S Ocean Buffet, Panera Bread, Rose Garden Embassy Suites AT&T, Target, Tires+, Walmart
33	rd 152, Brooklyn Blvd, N SA/dsl Culver's, Slim's Café, Subway Buick/GMC, Chevrolet, Honda, Toyota, USPO, VW, S BP AutoZone, Family$, Sun Foods, Walgreens
31	rd 81, Lakeland Ave, N SA/dsl Chipotle Mexican, Wagner's Drive-In, Wendy's CarMax, Target, U-Haul, S Northstar Inn
30	Boone Ave, N La Quinta, Marriott, S Home Depot
29b a	US 169, to Hopkins, Osseo
28	rd 61, Hemlock Lane, **N on Elm Creek** Arby's, Benihana, Biaggi's Italian, Buca Italian, Chick-fil-A, Chipotle Mexican, Coldstone, Dave&Buster's, Dickey's BBQ, Firehouse Subs, Five Guys, Freddy's, Granite City Rest., Leeann Chin, Malone's Grill, Mongo's Grill, Noodles&Co, Olive Garden, Panda Express, Panera Bread, Patrick's Cafe, PF Chang's, Pittsburgh Blue, Potbelly's, Red Lobster, Redstone Grill, Starbucks, Subway, TGIFriday's, Wild Bill's Café, Zupas Courtyard, Hampton Inn, Holiday Inn, Staybridge Suites $Tree, Best Buy, Costco/gas, Dick's, Jo-Ann Fabrics, Lowe's, Marshalls, Petsmart, REI, Trader Joe's, Verizon, Whole Foods Mkt, World Mkt, S BP Perkins Asteria Suites
27	I-94 W to St Cloud, I-94/694 E to Minneapolis
26	rd 10, Bass Lake Rd, E Freedom Caribou Coffee, Culver's, McDonald's, Subway Extended Stay America vet, W BP, Holiday/dsl Jimmy John's, Pancake House, Pizza Hut, Rusty Taco, Solos Pizza Hilton Garden auto repair, CVS Drug
23	rd 9, Rockford Rd, E Holiday Chili's, Domino's, Five Guys, Sunshine Factory Grill AT&T, GNC, Kohl's, O'Reilly Parts, PetsMart, Target, TJ Maxx, Walgreens, W BP, Freedom/dsl DQ, LeAnn Chin, Subway, Toppers Pizza, Caribou Coffee
22	MN 55, E Holiday/dsl Broadway Pizza, Caribou Coffee, Green Mill Rest., Jimmy John's, McDonald's, Red Robin, Solos Pizza, Starbucks, Subway Crowne Plaza, Ramada, Red Roof Inn, Residence Inn, W Holiday/dsl Arby's, Burger King, Davanni's Rest., Firehouse Subs, Jake's Rest., Perkins, Wendy's Comfort Inn, Days Inn Goodyear/auto, Tires+
21	rd 6, E KwikTrip Discount Tire, Home Depot
20	Carlson Pkwy, E Holiday/dsl Pizza Hut, Subway, W Grizzy's Grill Country Inn&Suites
19b a	I-394 E, US 12 W, to Minneapolis, **1/2 mi W** BP, Holiday Chipotle, KFC, McDonald's BMW, Chevrolet, Goodyear/auto, Lexus, Nissan, **1 mi E off of I-394** Wendy's Barnes&Noble, Best Buy, Ford, JC Penney, Jo-Ann Fabrics, Lunds&Byerly's Foods, Mazda, Mercedes, Office Depot, Petco, Subaru, Target, Tires+, Whole Foods

[gas] = gas [food] = food [lodging] = lodging [O] = other [RS] = rest stop

INTERSTATE 494/694 Cont'd

Exit #	Services
17b a	Minnetonka Blvd, E Minnoco Gas DQ, Royal Subs
16b a	MN 7, 1 mi W Christo's Rest., Davanni's Rest., Famous Dave's BBQ, Taco Bell Goodyear
13	MN 62, rd 62
12	Valleyview Rd, rd 39 (from sb)
11c	MN 5 W, same as 11 a b
11b a	US 169 S, US 212 W, N Don Pablo's, Jets Pizza, Subway Comfort Inn, Courtyard, Fairfield Inn, Hyatt Place, Residence Inn vet, S BP, Holiday Caribou Coffee, Champp's, Davanni's Rest., Jake's Grill, Leeann Chin, McDonald's, Old Chicago, Osaka Japanese, Panera Bread, Papa John's, Popeye's, Qdoba, Redstone Rest., Starbucks, Wildfire Steaks Extended Stay America, SpringHill Suites, TownePlace Suites $Tree, Barnes&Noble, Best Buy, Costco/gas, Cub Foods, Discount Tire, JC Penney, Office Depot, Petco, Target, Walgreens, Walmart
10	US 169 N, to rd 18
8	rd 28 (from wb, no return), E Bush Lake Rd, same as 7 a b
7b a	MN 100, rd 34, Normandale Blvd, N Shell/dsl Burger King, Chili's, DQ, Jimmy John's, Starbucks, Subway, TGIFridays Days Inn, Doubletree, Sheraton, S Holiday/dsl El Loro Country Inn&Suites, Crowne Plaza, Hampton Inn, Hilton Garden, La Quinta, Staybridge Inn
6b	rd 17, France Ave, N Mobil Fuddrucker's, Perkins Holiday Inn Express, Park Plaza Hotel, Residence Inn H, Marshall's, Michael's, Staples, Trader Joe's, World Mkt, S Denny's, Joe Senser's Grill, Olive Garden AmeriInn, Hilton Buick/GMC, Hyundai, Mercedes, Toyota
6a	Penn Ave (no EZ eb return), S Applebee's, Caribou Co[ffee], Jimmy John's, McDonald's, Red Robin, Starbucks, Sub[way], Which Wich? Embassy Suites, Home 2 Suites A[...] Chevrolet, Chrysler/Jeep/Dodge, Fresh Thyme Mkt, Herb[erg]er's, Hobby Lobby, Kohl's, Target, TJ Maxx, Walgreens
5b a	I-35W, S to Albert Lea, N to Minneapolis
4b	Lyndale Ave, N BP, SA Boston Mkt, Chipotle Mexi[can], DQ, Eddie Cheng's, Noodles&Co, Papa John's, Potbelly, Sa[...]no's Pizza, Starbucks, Subway Candlewood Suites, S[her]aton Best Buy, Honda, Lands End, PetsMart, S Exte[nd]ed Stay America Acura/Subaru, Lincoln, REI
4a	MN 52, Nicollet Ave, N SA/dsl Taco Bell Mena[rds], S Holiday/dsl Culver's, McDonald's La Quinta, [Su]per 8 Home Depot, Sam's Club
3	Portland Ave, 12th Ave (from eb), N Arby's, Kh[...] BBQ AmericInn, S BP $Tree, Denny's, Jim[my] John's, Outback Steaks, Pizza Hut, Subway Comfort [Inn], Microtel, Quality Inn, Residence Inn Walgreens, Walm[art], Subway
2c b	MN 77, N SA Motel 6, S Outback Steaks C[om]fort Inn, Courtyard, Fairfield Inn, Hampton Inn, Hilton Gar[den], JW Marriott, Marriott, Northwood Inn, Radisson, Residence [Inn], SpringHill Suites, TownePlace Suites IKEA, Macy's, Ma[ll of] America, Nordstrom's
2a	24th Ave, same as 2c b
1b	34th Ave, Nat Cemetary, N Holiday/dsl, S Crowne [Pla]za, Embassy Suites, Hilton, Hyatt Place, Hyatt Regency
1a	MN 5 E, N [O] [airport]
0mm	Minnesota River. **I-494/I-694 loops around Minneapolis/St P[aul]**

NOTES

MISSISSIPPI

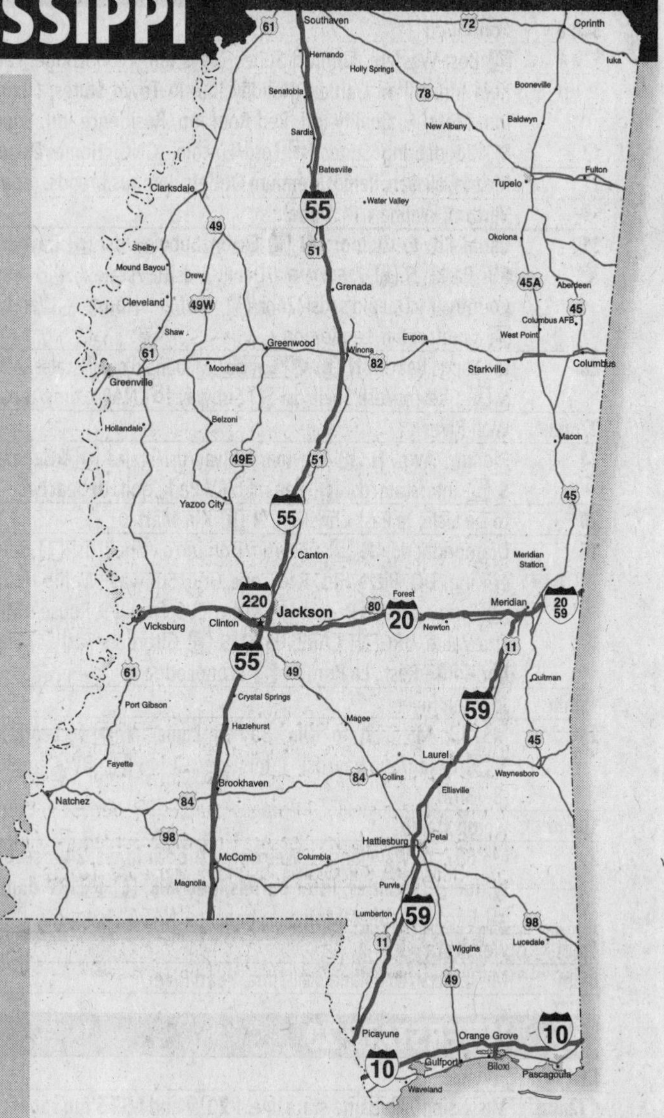

MS

INTERSTATE 10

Exit #	Services
77mm	Mississippi/Alabama state line, **weigh sta wb**
75	Franklin Creek Rd
75mm	**Welcome Ctr wb, full facilities, litter barrels, petwalk, , RV dump, weigh sta eb**
74mm	Escatawpa River
69	MS 63, to E Moss Point, **N** Raceway/dsl, Shell/Circle K/Domino's/dsl/24hr Waffle House Best Value, La Quinta, Motel 6, **S** Chevron/dsl, Exxon/Subway/dsl, Pilot/Moe's SW/dsl/scales/24hr, Shell Burger King, Cracker Barrel, Hardee's, KFC, McDonald's, Pizza Hut, Ruby Tuesday, San Miguel Mexican, Taco Bell, Waffle House, Wendy's Best Western, Comfort Inn, Days Inn, EconoLodge, Hampton Inn, Holiday Inn Express, Quality Inn H, Toyota
68	MS 613, to Moss Point, Pascagoula, **N** Chevron/dsl, Texaco/dsl Coco Loco Mexican, Tugus' Rest. Super 8, **S** Marathon/dsl H, Pelican Landing Conf Ctr
64mm	Pascagoula River
63.5mm	**both lanes, 24hr security, full facilities, litter barrels, petwalk, , , RV dump**
61	to Gautier, **N** MS Nat Golf Course, **1-3 mi S** Marathon/dsl Hardee's, KFC, McDonald's, Pizza Hut, Sonic, Wendy's Best Western, Suburban Lodge Sandhill Crane WR, Shephard Camping
57	MS 57, to Vancleave, **N** Chevron/dsl Shed BBQ Journey's End Camping, tires/repair, **S** Exxon
50	MS 609 S, Ocean Springs, **N** Shell/Circle K/Domino's/dsl Waffle House Best Western+, Country Inn&Suites, Motel 6, Quality Inn, Ramada Ltd, Red Roof Inn, Super 8 Martin Lake Camping (1mi), tires/repair, **S** Chevron/McDonald's, Circle K/Subway/dsl, Marathon/dsl, RaceTrac/dsl Denny's, El Rancho Mexican, Waffle House, Wendy's Comfort Suites, Days Inn, Hampton Inn, Holiday Inn Express, Magnuson $General, $Tree, Nat Seashore
46b a	I-110, MS 15 N, to Biloxi, **N** Chevron/dsl, Murphy USA/dsl Beef O'Brady's, Beijing Chinese, Buffalo Wild Wings, Chick-fil-A, Chili's, Cici's, Dickey's BBQ, Five Guys, IHOP, Logan's Roadhouse, Moe's SW Grill, Newk's Cafe, Olive Garden, Osaka Japanese, Outback Steaks, Panda Palace, Papa John's, Red Lobster, Ruby Tuesday, Salsarita 's, Samurai, Sonic, Starbucks, Subway, Twin Peaks, Waffle House, Wendy's, Whataburger, Which Wich? Comfort Inn, Courtyard, Home2 Suites, Regency Inn AT&T, Best Buy, CVS, Dick's, GNC, Kohl's, Lowe's, Marshall's, Mercedes, Michaels, NTB, Office Depot, Petsmart, Ross, Target, URGENT CARE, Verizon, vet, VW, Walgreens, Walmart, **S** H, BMW, Buick/GMC, to beaches
44	Cedar Lake Rd, to Biloxi, **N** Loves/Subway/dsl/scales/24hr Chevrolet, **S** Exxon/Circle K/dsl, Shell/dsl Applebee's, El Saltillo, KFC/LJ Silver, McDonald's, Pop's Pizza, Sonic, Subway, Taco Bell, Waffle House La Quinta H, $General, Biloxi Nat Cem, Cedar Lake Drug, Harley-Davidson, Home Depot, O'Reilly Parts, to Jeff Davis Shrine (Beauvoir), vet
41	MS 67 N, to Woolmarket, **N** Chevron/dsl, Texaco/dsl golf (6mi), **S** Camping World, Freightliner, Mazalea RV Prk, Parkers Landing RV Prk, Southern Tire Mart
39.5mm	Biloxi River
38	Lorraine-Cowan Rd, **N** Chevron/dsl, Exxon/Subway, Shell/Circle K/dsl Domino's, McDonald's, Sonic Toyota, **S** RaceTrac/dsl Baywood RV Park (3mi), Foxes RV Park (8mi), to beaches
34b a	US 49, to Gulfport, **N** Circle K/dsl, Exxon, Shell/Circle K/dsl Buffalo Wild Wings, Burger King, Cane's, Chick-fil-A, Chili's, ChuckeCheese, Cracker Barrel, Dickey's BBQ, Domino's, Firehouse Subs, Five Guys, Golden Corral, Hardee's, KFC, Krystal, Little Caesar's, Logan's Roadhouse, Longhorn Steaks, Marble Slab, McDonald's, Newk's Cafe, O'Charley's, O'Neal's PoBoy, Panda Palace, Papa John's, Pepper's Deli, Pizza Hut, Popeye's, Sicily's Italian Buffet, Sonic, Starbucks, Subway, Taco Bell, Taco Sombrero, TGIFriday's, TX Roadhouse, Waffle House, Wendy's, Whataburger Hampton Inn, Home 2 Suites, Sleep Inn H, $Tree, Advance Parts, AT&T, Barnes&Noble, Belk, Best Buy, Buick/Cadillac/Chevrolet, CVS Drug, Foley's RV Ctr, Food Giant/gas, Fred's Store, Goodyear/auto, Hobby Lobby, Honda, Michael's, NTB, Office Depot, Old Navy, Petsmart, Rite Aid, Ross, Sam's Club/dsl, TJ Maxx, URGENT CARE, USPO, Walgreens, Winn-Dixie, **S** Circle K/dsl, Murphy USA, RaceWay/dsl, Shell/dsl, Shell/Subway Applebee's, Arby's, Aztecas Mexican, Burger King, Food Court, Hibachi Express, Hooters, IHOP, Jimmy John's, Krispy Kreme, McAlister's Deli, McDonald's, Shrimp Basket, Sonic, Taco Bell, Waffle House, Wendy's

GULFPORT

MS

INTERSTATE 10 Cont'd

GULFPORT

34b a	Continued Best Western, Comfort Suites, Days Inn, EconoLodge, Fairfield Inn, Hilton Garden, Holiday Inn, In Town Suites, Luxury Inn, Motel 6, Quality Inn, Red Roof Inn, Residence Inn, Super 8, Woodspring Suites Ford/Lincoln, GNC, Home Depot, Mazda, Nissan, Petco, Premium Outlets/famous brands, repair, Verizon, Walmart/McDonald's
31	Canal Rd, to Gulfport, N Exxon/Subway/dsl Bayberry RV Park, S FLYING J/Denny's/dsl/LP/scales/24hr, Pure Country/McDonald's/dsl/24hr Waffle House, Wendy's Comfort Inn, Legacy Inn
28	to Long Beach, N Loves/McDonald's/dsl/scales/24hr, S Chevron/dsl, Shell/dsl Subway NAPA, tires/repair
27mm	Wolf River
24	Menge Ave, N Chevron/Subway/dsl/scales $General, S Interstate/dsl flea mkt/RV Park, golf, to beaches
20	to De Lisle, to Pass Christian, N Kin-Mart
16	Diamondhead, N Chevron/Domino's, Shell/dsl Burger King, DQ, Pizza Hut, Red Zone Grill, Subway, Waffle House Diamondhead Resort $Tree, CVS, Family$, Rouse's Mkt, TrueValue, URGENT CARE, USPO, S Giterdone/dsl Harbor House Rest., La Rumba EconoLodge
15mm	Jourdan River
13	MS 43, MS 603, to Kiln, Bay St Louis, N McLeod SP, S Exxon/Subway/dsl, Interstate/dsl H, RV Camping (8-13mi)
10mm	**weigh sta eb**
2	MS 607, to Waveland, S **Welcome Ctr both lanes, 24hr security, full facilities, litter barrels, petwalk, , RV dump,** Buccaneer SP, camping, to beaches, NASA Visitor Ctr
1mm	**weigh sta wb**
0mm	Mississippi/Louisiana state line, Pearl River

INTERSTATE 20

MERIDIAN

Exit #	Services
172mm	Mississippi/Alabama state line. **I-20 W and I-59 S run together to Meridian.**
170mm	**weigh sta both lanes**
169	US 11, US 80, Kewanee, S Kewanee Trkstp/BBQ/dsl Simmons-Wright Gen Store
165	to US 11, Toomsuba, N Dee's/dsl, Sunoco/Subway, S Loves/Arby's/dsl/scales/24hr KOA (2mi)
164mm	**Welcome Ctr wb, 24hr security, full facilities, litter barrels, petwalk, , , RV dump, vending, wi-fi**
160	to Russell, N TA/Country Pride/dsl/scales/24hr/@ Nanabe RV Camping (1mi), S Chevron/dsl KOA (4mi)
157b a	US 45, to Macon, Quitman
156	Jimmie Rodgers Pkwy
154b a	MS 19 S, MS 39 N, Meridian, N MapleLeaf/dsl, Shell, Texaco/dsl Applebee's, Buffalo Wild Wings, Cracker Barrel, IHOP, Logan's Roadhouse, Penn's Rest, Waffle House, Western Sizzlin Days Inn, Drury Inn, Fairfield Inn, Hampton Inn, Hilton Garden, Holiday Inn, Home 2 Suites, Relax Inn, Rodeway Inn, Sleep Inn, Super 8, Super Inn, Western Motel auto repair, Back Country RV Ctr, Chrysler/Dodge/Jeep/Kia, U-Haul, S Chevron/dsl, Texaco/dsl Chick-fil-A, Chili's, CiCi's, Dickey's BBQ, Honey Baked Ham, McAlister's Deli, McDonald's, O'Charley's, Olive Garden, Outback Steaks, Popeye's, Red Lobster, Ryan's, Taco Bell Baymont Inn, Comfort Inn, Country Inn&Suites, Microtel $Tree, AT&T, Belk, Best Buy, Books-A-
154b a	Continued Million, Dillard's, Harley-Davidson, Jo-Ann Fabrics, PetCo, P Sam's Club/gas, TJ Maxx, Tuesday Morning
153	MS 145 S, 22nd Ave, Meridian, N Shell, Xp Lane Arby's, Bumper's Drive-In, Burger King, Capt China Buffet, Hardee's, KFC, McDonald's, Pizza Hut, Sub Wendy's H, $General, CarQuest, Cash Saver Foods, F Nissan, Fred's, Goodyear/auto, S Exxon/dsl, Murphy U dsl, Texaco/dsl, Valero/dsl A&W/LJ Silver, Checkerb Kitchen, El Norte Mexican, Waffle House Astro Motel, get 8 Motel, EconoLodge, Extended Suites, Hamilton Inn, iday Inn Express, La Quinta, Motel 6, Sleep Inn Chevr Lowe's, Office Depot, Verizon, Walmart/McDonald's
152	29th Ave, 31st Ave, Meridian, N Chevron/dsl Ram Ltd, S Royal Inn
151	James Chaney Dr, N tires, S Pilot/Subway/ scales/24hr stockyards
150	US 11 S, MS 19 N, Meridian, N Exxon/dsl, Queen City stp/dsl/rest./@ McDonald's, Waffle House Okatib Lake, RV camping, S Chevron/Stuckey's/Subway/dsl, S dsl , Peterbilt
130[149]	I-59 S, to Hattiesburg. **I-20 E and I-59 N run together.**
129	US 80 W, Lost Gap, S Spaceway/Grill King/dsl/RV Dump/
121	Chunky
119mm	Chunky River
115	MS 503, Hickory
109	MS 15, Newton, N Shell/Jct Deli/dsl/24hr Los Pa leros Thrifty Inn H, lube/repair, S Chevron Newton Jct/dsl, Texaco/dsl Cooks BBQ, Hardee's, K Taco Bell, McDonald's, Panda Buffet, Pizza Hut, Sonic, Subw Zack's Steaks Days Inn $General, Advance Parts, A AutoZone, Fred's, Piggly Wiggly, Walmart/Subway
100	US 80, Lake, Lawrence, N Marathon/rest/dsl
96	Lake, S Loves/Chester's/Subway/dsl/scales/24hr
95mm	Bienville NF, eastern boundary, Bienville Nat Forest, Bien Nat Forest
90mm	**eb, 24hr security, full facilities, litter barrels, petw , , RV dump**
88	MS 35, Forest, N Murphy USA/dsl, Shell, Texaco/C ter's/dsl, Valero/dsl KFC, Las Parrillas Mexican, McD ald's, Popeye's, Taco Bell, Waffle House, Wendy's, Zh Garden Best Value Inn, Days Inn, EconoLodge, Hol Inn Express H, $Tree, AT&T, O'Reilly Parts, Walgre Walmart/Subway, S Chevron/dsl Penn's Rest.
80	MS 481, Morton, S RV Camping
77	MS 13, Morton, N Exxon/McDonald's/dsl, Tex dsl H, Green Tree RV Park (4mi), to Roosevelt S Shell/Subway/dsl
76mm	Bienville NF, western boundary
75mm	**wb, 24hr security, full facilities, litter barrels, petw , , RV dump**
68	MS 43, Pelahatchie, N Chevron/Subway/dsl, Texaco/r dsl/24hr Jellystone Camping, S Marathon/dsl
59	US 80, E Brandon, **2 mi** S Shell/dsl
56	US 80, Brandon, N Shell/dsl El Potrillo Mexican, K tal, Sonny's BBQ, Taco Bell Microtel AT&T, AutoZ O'Reilly Parts, USPO, Verizon, S BP, Chevron, Exxon, M Gas, Texaco/dsl DQ, Penn's Rest., Sonic, Waffle Ho Wendy's Best Value Inn, Red Roof Inn Auto+, to Barnett Reservoir, vet
54	Crossgates Blvd, W Brandon, N Circle K/dsl, Exxon, Mu USA Abner's Chicken, Applebee's, Burger King, Chick-f

MERIDIAN NEWTON FOREST BRANDON

INTERSTATE 20 Cont'd

54 Continued
China Buffet, Fernando's Fajita Factory, KFC, Little Caesar's, Mazzio's, McAlister's Deli, McDonald's, Newk's Rest, Papa John's, Pizza Hut, Popeye's, Subway, Waffle House H, $Tree, BigLots, Buick/GMC, Chevrolet, CVS Drug, Ford/Lincoln, Fred's, GNC, Kroger/dsl, Nissan, Office Depot, Piggly Wiggly, Scotty's Tire/repair, Toyota, Tuesday Morning, Walgreens, Walmart/Subway, S Circle K/dsl, Exxon/dsl, Mobil/Domino's/dsl Steak Escape, Wendy's La Quinta Home Depot, Honda, Tire Pros

52 MS 475, N Exxon/Subway/dsl, RaceWay/dsl, Texaco/dsl Waffle House Quality Inn, Ramada, Sleep Inn, Super 8 Peterbilt, to Jackson Airport

48 MS 468, Pearl, N Exxon/dsl, Shell/dsl, Texaco Arby's, Baskin Robbins, Bumpers Drive-In, Cracker Barrel, Domino's, DQ, Dunkin', Jose's Rest., KFC, Kobe Japanese, Logan's Roadhouse, LoneStar Steaks, Los Parrilleros, McAlister's Deli, McDonald's, Mikado, Mikado Japanese, Moss Creek Fishouse, O'Charley's, Popeye's, Ruby Tuesday, Ryan's, Ryan's, Sonic, Subway, Waffle House, Wendy's Baymont Inn, Best Western, Comfort Inn, Courtyard, Days Inn, Fairfield Inn, Hampton Inn, Hilton Garden, Holiday Inn Express, Motel 6 AT&T, CarCare, S Exxon/dsl, Mobil/dsl Candlewood Suites, Country Inn&Suites, La Quinta $General, Family$

47b a US 49 S, Flowood, N FLYING J/Denny's/dsl/LP/RV dump/24hr, Loves/Subway/dsl/scales/24hr Western Sizzlin Airport Inn, Holiday Inn Bass Pro Shop, MS Outlets/famous brands, Sam's Club/dsl, SpeedCo, **2-3 mi** S Race-Way/dsl Waffle House Freightliner, Kenworth, tires

46 I-55 N, to Memphis

45b US 51, State St, to downtown

45a Gallatin St, to downtown, N BP/dsl, Petro/Iron Skillet/dsl/scales/24hr/@, Shell Blue Beacon, tires/truck repair, vet, S Pilot/McDonald's/dsl/scales/24hr Hilltop Inn Nissan

44 I-55 S (exits left from wb), to New Orleans

43b a Terry Rd, N Exxon/dsl, Jasco Apache RV Ctr

42b a Ellis Ave, Belvidere, N BP, Citgo/dsl, Shell Capt D's, Church's, McDonald's, Pizza Hut, Popeye's, Sonny's BBQ, Wendy's Best Inn, Metro Inn, Scottish Inn, Super 8 $Tree, Advance Parts, AutoZone, CarQuest, Family$, Firestone/auto, O'Reilly Parts, Sav-a-Lot Foods, transmissions, U-Haul, zoo, S Citgo/dsl, Exxon/dsl DQ

41 I-220 N, US 49 N, to Jackson

40b a MS 18 W, Robinson Rd, N Exxon/dsl, Jasco/dsl, Shell/dsl Arby's, Krystal, Mazzio's, Piccadilly, Popeye's $General, AT&T, Office Depot, USPO, S Chevron, Citgo/dsl, Murphy USA, RaceWay/dsl, Shell/Church's/dsl Chan's Garden, IHOP, McDonald's, Subway, Waffle House, Wendy's Quality Inn H, $Tree, GNC, Lowe's, Walmart/Subway

36 Springridge Rd, Clinton, N Chevron/Burger King, Citgo/dsl, Murphy USA/dsl, Shell Capt D's, Chick-fil-A, China Buffet, Chopstick Buffet, DQ, El Sombrero, Hungry Howie's, KFC, Kroger/dsl, Little Ceasar's, Mazzio's, McAlister's, McDonald's, Newk's Cafe, Smoothie King, Sonic, Starbucks, Subway, Taco Bell, Waffle House, Wendy's, Zaxby's Comfort Inn, Days Inn, Fairfield Inn $Tree, Advance Parts, AT&T, BigLots, CVS Drug, Family$, Fred's, Home Depot, Kroger/gas, O'Reilly Parts, Verizon, Walgreens, Walmart (2mi), S Exxon/Baskin-Robbins/Quiznos/dsl, Valero/dsl Applebee's, Bonsai, Froghead Grill, Pizza Hut, Popeye's, Salsa's Mexican, Shoney's Best Western,

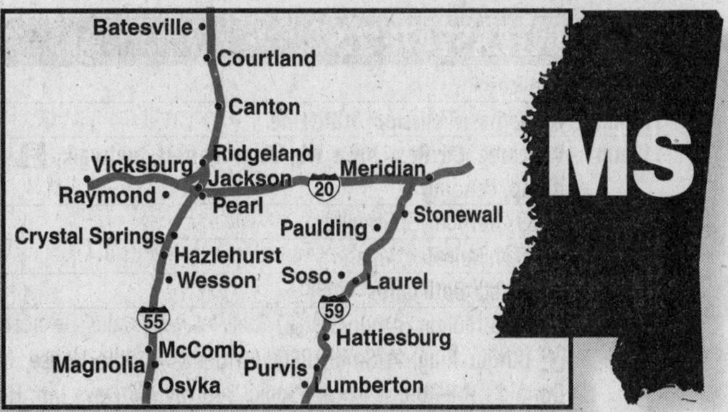

36 Continued
Econolodge, Hampton Inn, Holiday Inn Express, Quality Inn, Super 8 $General, Davis Tire, Springridge RV Park, vet

35 US 80 E, Clinton, N Chevron, Circle K/dsl, Shell/dsl vet

34 Natchez Trace Pkwy

31 Norrell Rd

27 Bolton, S Chevron/dsl

19 MS 22, Edwards, Flora, N Askew's Landing Camping (2mi), S Exxon/dsl, Shell/dsl Relax Inn

17mm Big Black River

15 Flowers

11 Bovina, N Exxon/Subway/dsl/24hr RV camping

10mm **weigh sta wb**

8mm **weigh sta eb**

6.5mm **parking area eb**

5b a US 61, MS 27 S, N Exxon/dsl, Shell/dsl Sonic, S same as 4a

4b a Clay St, N Shell Hampton Inn, Motel 6, Super 8, Vicksburg Inn H, RV Park, to Vicksburg NP, S Shell/dsl, Texaco Baskin Robbins, Bumper's Drive-In, China Buffet, Cracker Barrel, Little Caesar's, McAlister's deli, Pizza Inn, Rowdy's Rest., Subway, Waffle House, Wendy's Beechwood Inn/rest., Comfort Suites, Courtyard, Econolodge, Holiday Inn Express, La Quinta, Quality Inn, Scottish Inn $General, Outlet Mall/famous brands/deli, same as 5

VICKSBURG

3 Indiana Ave, N Shell/Subway/dsl China King, McDonald's, Papa John's, Waffle House Best Western, Deluxe Inn Chevrolet, Chrysler/Dodge/Jeep, Corner Mkt Foods, Ford/Lincoln, Honda, Mazda, Nissan, Rite Aid, Toyota, S Shell/dsl Goldie's BBQ, Heavenly Ham, KFC Best Inn Buick/Cadillac/GMC, Family$

1c Halls Ferry Rd, N Exxon/dsl Burger King, Sonic Travel Inn H, CVS Drug, Durst Drugs, S Shell/dsl Asian Kitchen, Capt D's, Chick-fil-A, DQ, El Sombrero Mexican, Garfield's Rest., Goldie's Express, Little Caesar's, Newk's Eatery, Pizza Hut, Popeye's, Shoney's, Subway, Taco Bell, Taco Casa, Wendy's, Whataburger Candlewood Suites, Holiday Inn, Howard Johnson, Ramada Inn, Rodeway Inn $General, Advance Parts, AT&T, Belk, BigLots, Dillard's, Fred's, Hobby Lobby, Home Depot, Kroger/dsl, TJ Maxx, USPO, Walgreens

1b US 61 S, S Murphy Express/dsl, Shell/Domino's/dsl McDonald's, Panda Buffet, Waffle House $Tree, same as 1c, Verizon, Walmart/Subway

1a Washington St, Vicksburg, N **Welcome Ctr both lanes, full facilities,** Shell/dsl AmeriStar Hotel/Casino/RV Park, S Waffle House Best Value Inn, Days Inn

0mm Mississippi/Louisiana state line, Mississippi River

MS

INTERSTATE 22

Exit #	Services
118mm	Alabama/Mississippi State Line
115mm	**Welcome Ctr/Rest Area wb, litter barrels, petwalk, , RV dump, vending**
113	rd 23, Tremont, Smithville
108	rd 25 N, Belmont, Iuka
106mm	**weigh sta both lanes**
104	rd 25 S, Fulton, Amory, N Shell/cafe/dsl/scales, Texaco/dsl Burger King, Ft Smith BBQ, Hardee's, Huddle House, McDonald's, Mi Toro Mexican, Sonic, Subway Days Inn, Holiday Inn Express $General, AutoZone, Brown's Auto Repair, Food Giant/dsl, Fred's, O'Reilly Parts, RV camping, Whitten HS, S Murphy USA/dsl Peking Palace AT&T, KFC, Los Compadres Mexican, Pizza Hut, URGENT CARE, Walmart, Wendy's
104mm	Tombigbee River/Tenn-Tom Waterway
101	rd 178, rd 363, Peppertown, Mantachie, N Marathon, S Dorsey Fuel/dsl (2mi)
97	Fawn Grove Rd
94	rd 371, Mantachie, Mooreville, N Woodchuck's/pizza/dsl
90	Auburn Rd, N Chevron/dsl
87	Veterans Blvd, N Shell/Chix Rest/dsl Huddle House Wingate Inn E. Presley Campground/Park, S Tombigbee SP
86	US 45 N, Tupelo, to Corinth, **1 exit** N Shell/dsl, Texaco, Valero Abner's Rest., Applebee's, Baskin Robbins, Buffalo Wild Wings, Burger King, Capt D's, Chick-fil-A, Chili's, ChuckeCheese, Cracker Barrel, Crossroads Rib Shack, D'Casa Grill, Dickey's BBQ, Five Guys, IHOP, Kyoto Japanese, Lenny's Subs, Logan's Roadhouse, Longhorn Steaks, Margaritas Mexican, McDonald's, Mt Fuji Japanese, New China Buffet, Newk's Eatery, O'Charley's, Olive Garden, Pizza Hut, Pizza Pro, Red Lobster, Ryan's, Sake Japanese, Sonic, Subway, Taco Bell, Thai Garden, Waffle House, Wendy's Best Inn, Best Western, Econolodge, Fairfield Inn, Hampton Inn $Tree, AT&T, AutoZone, Barnes&Noble, Belk, Best Buy, CarMax, Dick's, Ford/Lincoln, Hobby Lobby, Home Depot, Hyundai, JC Penney, Jo-Ann, Kohl's, Kroger/gas, Lowe's, Mazda, Midas, NAPA, Nissan, Old Navy, Petsmart, Ross, Sam's Club/gas, Staples, TJ Maxx, Toyota, Tuesday Morning, URGENT CARE, Verizon, Walgreens, Walmart
85	Natchez Trace Pkwy
82	Barnes Crossing Rd, Coley Rd
81	rd 178, McCullough Blvd, N Loves/McDonald's/dsl/scales/24hr Best Value Inn, S Exxon/dsl, Shell/dsl Old Venice Pizza, Sonic Super 8 $General, USPO
76	rd 9 S, Sherman, Pontotoc, N Wild Bill's/dsl Sherman RV Ctr
73	rd 9 N, to Magnolia Way, Blue Springs
64	rd 15, rd 30 E, Pontotoc, Ripley, N Eagle/dsl, S Circle K/dsl, Pilot/Arby's/scales/dsl/24hr
63	New Albany, N Dee's Oil/dsl Buick/Chevrolet/GMC, Ford
62mm	Tallahatchie River
61	rd 30 W, W New Albany, N Dee's China Buffet, Cracker Barrel, McAlister's Deli, McDonald's, Pizza Hut, Subway, Waffle House, Wendy's Hampton Inn H, Rite Aid, Walgreens, S Exxon, Murphy USA/dsl, Shell Burger King, Capt D's, Domino's, El Agave Mexican, Huddle House, KFC, Mi Pueblo Mexican, Taco Bell, Zaxby's Comfort Inn, Economy Inn, Hallmarc Inn, Holiday Inn Express $Tree, AT&T, Lowe's, to U of MS, Verizon, Walmart
60	Glenfield, to Oxford, N Pure Budget Inn Tire Pros, S to U of MS
55	Myrtle
48	rd 178, Hickory Flat, S Exxon/Trkstp/rest/dsl/24hr
41	rd 346, Potts Camp, S Flicks/dsl $General, NAPA
41mm	Tippah River
37	Lake Center, N Chewalla Lake/RV camping
30	rd 7, rd 4, Holly Springs, Oxford, N Exxon, Shell/C ter's/BBQ Burger King, Domino's, El Nopalito, Hu House, KFC, Little Caesar's, McDonalds, Panda Buffet, F Hut, Popeye's, Sonic, Subway, Taco Bell, Wendy's Ma lia Inn $General, AT&T, AutoZone, Liddy's Drug, O'R Parts, Save-a-Lot, Wall Doxey SP/RV camping, S Sl dsl Days Inn, Quality Inn Walmart
26	W Holly Springs
21	Red Banks, N Dee's Oil/dsl, Texaco/dsl
18	Victoria, E Byhalia, N Marathon/dsl, S Victoria/dsl
14	rd 309, Byhalia, N BP/dsl, Shell/dsl Best V Inn Autozone, Fred's
12	I-269, MS 304
10	W Byhalia, N Marathon/dsl
6	Bethel Rd, Hacks Crossroad, N FLYING J/Subw dsl/scales/LP/RV dump/24hr, BP, Exxon/Baskin Robb dsl JR's Grill, Rancho Grande, Tops BBQ Best W ern+, Super 8 truck repair, S H
4	rd 305, Olive Branch, Independence, N BP/dsl, Sh Circle K, Valero/Huddle House DQ, Old Style BBQ, P Hut Holiday Inn Express $General, Piggly Wi USPO, S Exxon/dsl CVS Drug
3.5mm	**weigh sta both lanes**
2	rd 302, Olive Branch, N Murphy Express/dsl Abb Rest., Baskin-Robbins, Buffalo Wild Wings, Chick-fil-A, Ch Colton's Steaks, IHOP, Krystal, Lenny's Subs, McAlisters Mis Pueblos Mexican, O'Charley's, Starbucks, Wendy's dlewood Suites, Comfort Suites, Hilton Garden $Tree, F Home Depot, Lowe's, Verizon, Walmart/Subway, S Cl ron/dsl, Shell/Circle K Applebees, Backyard Burger, Bu King, Casa Mexicana, Honeybaked Ham, Hunan Chinese, Donald's, Panera Bread, Papa John's, Steak Escape, Subv Taco Bell, Waffle House, Zaxby's Comfort Inn, Hampton Home 2 Suites AutoZone, CVS Drug, GNC, Goodyear/a Kroger/dsl, Petco
1	Craft Rd, N Candlewood Suites Camping World RV Chevrolet, Hyundai
0mm	Mississippi/Tennessee state line, **I-22 begins/ends. US 78 tinues wb.**

CORINTH

OLIVE BRANCH

SOUTHAVEN

INTERSTATE 55

Exit #	Services
291.5mm	Mississippi/Tennessee state line
291	State Line Rd, Southaven, E Exxon, RaceWay/dsl, Sh dsl Interstate BBQ, Little Caesar's, Subway, Tops E Waffle House Days Inn, Quality Inn, Southern Inn, Su 8 Family$, Firestone/auto, Goodyear/auto, Kroger/ Southaven RV Park, Walgreens, W Exxon, Valero C D's, Checker's, Dale's Rest., El Patron Mexican, Lucky Ch Sonic, Taco Bell, Wendy's BigLots, Fred's, Mainstreet A motive, Rite Aid, tires, USPO, Walgreens
289	MS 302, to US 51, Horn Lake, E BP/Circle K, Shell/C K Abbays Rest., Backyard Burger, Baskin-Robbins, falo Wild Wings, Burger King, Chick-fil-A, Chili's, Dun Fazoli's, Firehouse Subs, Five Guys, Fox&Hound, Hu Rest., IHOP, Jimmy John's, Krystal, Kublai Khan, Len Subs, Logan's Roadhouse, Longhorn Steaks, McDona

INTERSTATE 55 Cont'd

289 Continued
Mi Pueblo, Nagoya Japanese, Naru Japanese, Newk's Eatery, O'Charley's, Olive Garden, On-the-Border, Outback Steaks, Red Lobster, Sonic, Starbucks, Steak'n Shake, Subway, Swanky's Tacos, Swanky's Tacos, TGIFriday's, Wendy's, Wing Stop, Wing Stop [lodging] Candlewood Suites, Comfort Suites, Courtyard, Fairfield Inn, Hampton Inn, Hilton Garden, Holiday Inn, Holiday Inn Express, Home2Suites, Homewood Suites, Residence Inn [other] [H], $Tree, Advance Parts, Aldi Foods, AT&T, Best Buy, Books-A-Million, Buick/GMC, Chevrolet, Chrysler/Dodge/Jeep, CVS Drug, Dillard's, Discount Tire, Ford, GNC, Gordman's, JC Penney, Jo-Ann Fabrics, Lowe's, Marshall's, Nissan, Office Depot, Old Navy, PetCo, Sam's Club/gas, Tuesday Morning, URGENT CARE, Verizon, Walmart/Subway, **W** [gas] BP/Circle K, Phillips 66/dsl, Shell/Circle K/dsl [food] Applebee's, Arby's, ChuckECheese's, Country Home Buffet, Cracker Barrel, Grand Buffet, Hardee's, Hooters, KFC, McDonald's, Memphis BBQ, Papa John's, Pizza Hut, Popeye's, Starbucks, Taco Bell, TX Roadhouse, Waffle House, Wendy's, Zaxby's [lodging] Best Value Inn, Best Western, Comfort Inn, Drury Inn, EconoLodge, La Quinta, Motel 6, Sleep Inn [other] CVS Drug, Family$, Gateway Tires/repair, Home Depot, Kroger, Meineke, Save-a-Lot Foods, Target, Walgreens

287 Church Rd, **E** [gas] Citgo/dsl [food] Area 50 Grill, Domino's [other] AutoZone, Tanger Outlets/famous brands, **W** [gas] Citgo/dsl, Mapco/dsl/deli, Shell/Circle K/dsl [food] Boiling Point Seafood, Casa Mexicana, Dixie Queen, McDonald's, Sonic, Subway, Taco Bell, Three Guys Pizza, Waffle House [lodging] Homegate Inn, Magnolia Inn [other] El Daze RV Camping (1mi), Family$, Fred's, Harley-Davidson, Jellystone Camping, Southaven RV Ctr, Walgreens

285mm **weigh sta both lanes**

284 to US 51, Nesbit Rd, **W** [gas] Shell [food] Happy Daze Dairybar [other] USPO

283 I-69, MS 304, Tunica

280 MS 304, US 51, Hernando, **E** [gas] Exxon, Murphy USA/dsl [food] Arby's, Buon Cibo, Capt D's, Domino's, Fins Grill, Guadalajara Mexican, KFC, Royal Buffet, Sonic, Steak Escape, Taco Bell, Zaxby's [lodging] Days Inn, Hampton Inn [other] $Tree, AT&T, GNC, Ultimate Tires/repair, URGENT CARE, Walgreens, Walmart/Subway, **W** [gas] Mobil, Shell/Circle K/dsl [food] Brick Oven Rest., Coleman's BBQ, Lenny's Subs, Little Caesar's, McDonald's, Mi Pueblo, Mr Chen's, Papa John's, Pizza Hut, Subway, Taco Felix, Waffle House, Wendy's [lodging] Super 8 [other] AutoZone, Bryant Repair, Desoto Museum, Fred's, Kroger/gas, NAPA, to Arkabutla Lake, USPO, vet

279mm **Welcome Ctr sb, 24hr security, full [handicapped] facilities, litter barrels, petwalk, [phone], [picnic], RV dump**

276mm **[rest stop] nb, 24hr security, full [handicapped] facilities, litter barrels, petwalk, [phone], [picnic], RV dump**

273mm Coldwater River

271 MS 306, Coldwater, **W** [gas] Shell [food] Subway [other] Lake Arkabutla, Memphis S RV Park

265 MS 4, Senatobia, **W** [gas] Marathon/dsl, Pilot/Huddle House/dsl/scales/24hr, Shell/dsl [food] Applebee's, Coleman's BBQ, Domino's, Hardee's, KFC, McDonald's, New China Buffet, Pizza Hut, Popeye's, Rio Lindo Mexican, Sonic, Subway, Taco Bell, Waffle House, Wendy's, Zaxby's [lodging] Best Value Inn, Magnolia Inn [other] [H], CarQuest, Fred's, Kaye Mkt, USPO

263 rd 740, S Senatobia

257 MS 310, Como, **E** [other] N Sardis Lake, **W** [gas] Citgo/dsl [food] Windy City Grille (1mi) [other] $General

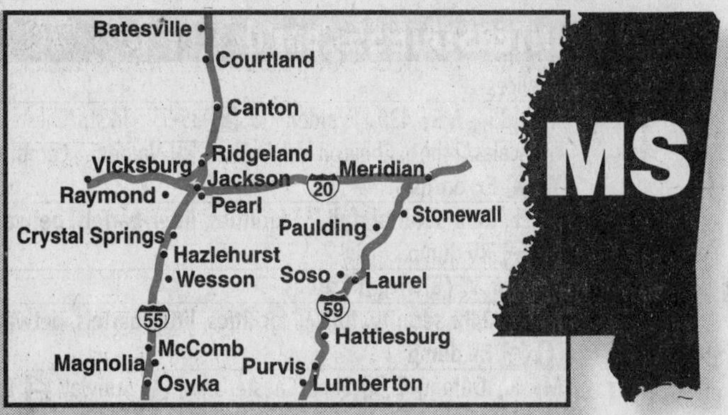

MS

BATESVILLE

252 MS 315, Sardis, **E** [gas] Chevron/dsl, Local/dsl [food] McDonald's [lodging] Lake Inn, Rodeway Inn [other] NAPA, repair, RV camping, Sardis Dam, to Kyle SP, **W** [gas] BP/Subway/dsl, Shell/dsl [food] Sonic [other] $General, Fred's

246 MS 35, N Batesville, **E** [other] to Sardis Lake, **W** [gas] Loves/McDonald's/Subway/dsl/scales/24hr, Shell/dsl

243b a MS 6, to Batesville, **E** [gas] Marathon/dsl, Mobil/dsl, Murphy USA/dsl, RaceWay/dsl [food] Backyard Burger, Chili's, Mi Pueblo Mexican, Zaxby's [lodging] Comfort Suites, Home 2 Suites [other] [H], $Tree, Lowe's, to Sardis Lake, to U of MS, Walmart/Subway, **W** [gas] BP, Exxon/dsl, Phillips 66/dsl, Shell/dsl [food] Burger King, Burn's BBQ, Cafe Ole, Capt D's, Cracker Barrel, Domino's, Hardee's, Huddle House, KFC, Little Caesar's, McDonald's, New China, Pizza Hut, Popeye's, Sonic, Subway, Taco Bell, Waffle House, Wendy's, Yamato Hibachi [lodging] Best Value Inn, Days Inn, EconoLodge, Hampton Inn, Holiday Inn [other] $General, AT&T, AutoZone, Factory Stores/famous brands, Family$, Fred's, Kroger/dsl, O'Reilly Parts, Piggly Wiggly, Save-a-Lot, URGENT CARE, USPO, Walgreens

240mm **[rest stop] both lanes, 24hr security, full [handicapped] facilities, litter barrels, petwalk, [phone], [picnic], RV dump**

237 to US 51, Courtland, **E** [gas] Pure/dsl, **W** [other] $General

233 to Enid Dam, **E** [other] RV camping, to Enid Lake

227 MS 32, Oakland, **E** [other] to Cossar SP, **W** [gas] Sayle/Baskin Robbins/dsl, Shell/dsl [food] Country Catfish [other] $General

220 MS 330, Tillatoba, **E** [gas] Conoco/rest./dsl/@

211 MS 7 N, to Coffeeville, **E** [other] Frog Hollow RV Park, **W** [gas] Exxon/Aunt M's/dsl, Marathon/dsl

GRENADA

208 Papermill Rd, **E** [gas] Monroe's/Chester's/dsl/scales [other] Grenada Airport

206 MS 8, MS 7 S, to Grenada, **E** [gas] Exxon/dsl, Shell/dsl, Sprint [food] Applebee's, China Buffet, Church's, Great Wall Chinese, Jake&Rip's Catfish, La Cabana Mexican, Little Caesar's, McAlister's Deli, McDonald's, No Way Jose, Pizza Hut, Pizza Inn, Shoney's, Simply Southern Cafe, Subway, Taco Bell, Wendy's [lodging] Baymont Inn, Best Value Inn, EconoLodge, Grenada Inn, Hampton Inn, Holiday Inn Express, Knights Inn, Relax Inn, Rodeway Inn [other] [H], $General, $Tree, Advance Parts, AT&T, AutoZone, Chevrolet, CVS Drug, GNC, O'Reilly Parts, SaveALot, to Grenada Lake/RV camping, Walmart/McDonald's, **W** [gas] Exxon/Huddle House, Sayle/Baskin Robbins/dsl [food] Waffle House [lodging] Comfort Inn, Hilltop Inn [other] Ford/Lincoln, Nissan, Toyota

199 Troutt Rd, S Grenada, **E** [other] to camp McCain

195 MS 404, Duck Hill, **E** [other] to Camp McCain, **W** [gas] Conoco/dsl

185 US 82, Winona, **E** [gas] Exxon, Shell/Kangaroo/Little Caesar's/dsl [food] Huddle House, KFC, McDonald's, Sonic, Subway, Waffle House [lodging] Best Value Inn, Holiday Inn Express, Magnolia Lodge, Relax Inn [other] [H], **W** [gas] Pilot/Taco Bell/dsl/scales/24hr/@

MS

INTERSTATE 55 Cont'd

Exit #	Services
174	MS 35, MS 430, Vaiden, E 35-55 Trkstp/Chester's/dsl/scales/24hr, Chevron/dsl, Shell Vaiden Camping, W Exxon/dsl
173mm	sb, 24hr security, full facilities, litter barrels, petwalk, RV dump
164	to West, W West Trkstp/dsl
163mm	nb, 24hr security, full facilities, litter barrels, petwalk, RV dump
156	MS 12, Durant, E Shell/Chester's/dsl Subway Durant Motel/rest. (3mi), Oak Tree Inn, W H (7mi)
150	E Holmes Co SP, RV camping
146	MS 14, Goodman, W to Little Red Schoolhouse
144	MS 17, to Pickens, W Marathon/Baskin-Robbins/dsl/24hr to Little Red Schoolhouse
139	MS 432, to Pickens
133	Vaughan
128mm	Big Black River
124	MS 16, to N Canton
119	MS 22, to MS 16 E, Canton, E Exxon, Kangaroo/Subway/dsl, Marathon/dsl, Shell/Domino's, Valero/dsl El Sombrero Mexican, McDonald's, Pizza Hut, Popeye's, Sonic, Waffle House, Wendy's Best Value Inn, Best Western, Econolodge, Hampton Inn, Holiday Inn Express, La Quinta, Relax Inn, Super 8 H, $General Mkt, Family$, Nissan, O'Reilly Parts, to Ross Barnett Reservoir, W Chevron/KFC/dsl, Citgo, Loves /Arby's/dsl/scales/24hr/@, Texaco/Penn's/dsl Bumpers Drive-In, Two Rivers Steaks Walmart
118a b	Nissan Parkway, E to Nissan
114a b	Sowell Rd
112	US 51, Gluckstadt, E Exxon/Krystal/dsl Sonic Super 8 Goodyear/auto, W Shelk/Pizza Hut/dsl Camper Corral RV Ctr, vet
108	MS 463, Madison, E Kangaroo/Mobil/dsl, Shell/dsl Applebee's, Backyard Burger, Burger King, Chick-Fil-A, Chili's, Corner Bakery Café, Dickey's BBQ, El Potrillo, Jimmy John's, La Guadalupe Mexican, Little Caesar's, Longhorn Steaks, Subway $Tree, AT&T, Best Buy, Dick's, GNC, Lowe's, Michael's, Office Depot, PetCo, SteinMart, Walmart, W Exxon/KFC/dsl BoneFish Grill, KFC, Nagoya Japanese, Papito's Grill, Pizza Inn, Schlotsky's, Subway, Tay's BBQ, Wendy's Hilton Garden CVS Drug, Home Depot, Kroger, Walgreens
107	Colony Park Blvd, Madison Ave, E Sam's Club/dsl
105c b	Old Agency Rd, E Chevron/dsl Home2Suites Honda, Hyundai, W Biaggi's Ristorante, Five Guys, Panera Bread, PF Changs, Ruth's Chris Steaks, Smoothie King, Starbucks Hyatt Place Barnes&Noble, Fresh Mkt Foods, GNC
105a	Natchez Trace Pkwy
104	I-220, to W Jackson
103	County Line Rd, E Chevron, Exxon/dsl, Murphy Express/dsl Bop's Custard, Bulldog Grill, Burgers&Blues Cafe, Cane's, Chick-fil-A, ChuckECheese's, Drago's Rest., Fortune Chinese, Grand China, HoneyBaked Ham, Jason's Deli, KFC, King Buffet, Krispy Kreme, Papito's Grill, Pizza Hut, Popeye's, Taco Bell, Wendy's, Whataburger, Zaxby's Cabot Lodge, Courtyard, Days Inn, EconoLodge, Extended Stay America, Hilton, Quality Inn, Red Roof Inn, Staybridge Suites $Tree, Acura, Belk, BigLots, Cadillac, Dillard's, JC Penney, Lowe's, Marshall's, Old Navy, Ross, TJ Maxx, to Barnett Reservoir, Tuesday Morning, Verizon, Walmart, W Logan's Roadhouse, Nagoya Japanese, Olive Garden, Red Lobster, Subway Drury Inn,

CANTON

MADISON

Exit #	Services
103	Continued Holiday Inn Express, Motel 6 Home Depot, Jo-Ann Fab Petsmart, Target, Upton Tire
102b	Beasley Rd, Adkins Blvd, E Sunoco Cracker Barrel, C back Steaks, Twin Peaks Rest. Super 8 Chevrolet, F Nissan, Toyota, W Shell/dsl, Texaco/dsl Baskin-R bins, Burger King, Chili's, Fuddrucker's, IHOP, Luby's, McD ald's, Waffle House Baymont Inn, Comfort Inn, Extend Stay America, Fairfield Inn, Howard Johnson, InTown Suites, Quinta CarMax, Chrysler/Dodge/Jeep, frontage rds acc 102a, Mercedes, Save-A-Lot Foods
102a	Briarwood, E Rodeway Inn Buick/GMC, W C D's, Popeye's Clarion Chrysler/Dodge/Jeep, Porsche
100	North Side Dr W, E Chevron, Marathon/dsl, Sprint Bu er King, Char Rest., McAlister's Deli, Papa John's, Piccadill Pizza Hut, Starbucks, Subway, Wendy's Extended S America $Tree, Audi, Books-A-Million, CVS Drug, Fir tone/auto, Goodyear/auto, Jaguar/LandRover, Kroger/ Office Depot, SteinMart, Verizon, vet, VW, Walgreens, Wh Foods Mkt, W Exxon/dsl, FastLane, Shell Domin Hooters, Waffle House Select Motel, USA Inn
99	Meadowbrook Rd, Northside Dr E (from nb), E Newk's Eat
98c b	MS 25 N, Lakeland Dr, E Shell/dsl Parkside Inn Fleur's Bluff SP, museum, W H,
98a	Woodrow Wilson Dr (exits left from nb), downtown
96c	Fortification St, E Studio 6 Suites, W H, Bellhaven Colle
96b	High St, Jackson, E BMW, Chevrolet, Infiniti, Lex W Exxon/Subway/dsl, Valero/Kangaroo/dsl Arb Chimneyville Cafe, Domino's, Popeye's, Taco Bell, Waffle Hou Wendy's, Whataburger Best Value Inn, Best Western, Co fort Inn, Hampton Inn, Holiday Inn Express, Red Roof Inn, gency Hotel H, fairgrounds, Honda, museum, st capi Subaru/Volvo
96a	Pearl St (from nb), Jackson, W access to same as 96b, downto
94	(46 from nb), I-20 E, to Meridian, US 49 S
45b[I-20]	US 51, State St, N Marathon, Petro/Iron Skillet/c scales/24hr, Shell, S Pilot/McDonald's/dsl/scales/24 to downtown
45a	Gallatin St (from sb), W Blue Beacon, N Marath Petro/Iron Skillet/dsl/scales/24hr, Shell, S Pilot/McD ald's/dsl Nissan
92c	(44 from sb), I-20 W, to Vicksburg, US 49 N
92b	US 51 N, State St, Gallatin St
92a	McDowell Rd, 1 mi E Petro/Iron Skillet/dsl/scales/24 Pilot/McDonald's/dsl, W Citgo/dsl, Exxon, Maratho dsl, Shell McDonald's, Waffle House Family$, Food pot, Fred's, Rite Aid, Roses
90b	Daniel Lake Blvd (from sb), W Shell Harley-Davidsor
90a	Savanna St, E transmissions, W Gas Caney Cre RV Ctr
88	Elton Rd, W Exxon/dsl, Shell/Subway/dsl Campi World RV Ctr
85	Byram, E Blue Sky/dsl, Hungry Jack's/dsl Daddi BBQ, Krystal, Mexican Grill Comfort Inn, Woodspring Sui Swinging Bridge RV Park, W Byram/dsl, Chevron/ Exxon/dsl, Mobil/Kangaroo/dsl Backyard Burger, Burg King, Capt D's, Domino's, KFC, Mazzio's, McAlister's Deli, M Donald's, New China, Newk's Eatery, Papa John's, Pizza Hut, Po eye's, Sonic, Subway, Taco Bell, Waffle House, Wendy's B Value Inn, Holiday Inn Express $General, AutoZone, Famil Mkt Place Foods, NAPA, O'Reilly Parts, Tire Depot, Walgree Walmart/Subway

JACKSON

INTERSTATE 55 Cont'd

Exit #	Services
81	Wynndale Rd, E repair, W Chevron/dsl
78	Terry, E Citgo/dsl, Texaco/Subway/dsl Buick/Chevrolet/GMC (1mi), Fred's, USPO, W Quick Trip $General
72	MS 27, Crystal Springs, E Exxon/Subway/dsl, Phillips 66/dsl Louise's Pit BBQ, McDonald's, Popeye's Ford
68	to US 51, S Crystal Springs, E gas/dsl Red Barn Produce, vet
65	to US 51, Gallman, E Stuckey's/dsl
61	MS 28, Hazlehurst, E Exxon/Circle K/Subway/dsl, Murphy Express/dsl, Phillips 66/dsl Burger King, KFC/Taco Bell, Los Parrilleros, McDonald's, Pizza Hut, Sonic, Waffle House, Wendy's Best Value Inn, Rodeway Inn, Western Inn H, $General, $Tree, Advance Parts, AT&T, Family$, Fred's, Piggly Wiggly, SaveALot, Verizon, Walgreens, Walmart
59	to S Hazlehurst
56	to Martinsville
54mm	**both lanes, 24hr security, full facilities, litter barrels, petwalk, RV dump, vending**
51	to Wesson, E Lake Lincoln SP, W Texaco/Country Jct Trkstp/dsl/rest.
48	Mt Zion Rd, to Wesson
42	to US 51, N Brookhaven, E Exxon/Subway, Shell/Gridiron Grill/dsl/scales/24hr H, W Super 8
40	to MS 550, Brookhaven, E Blue Sky, Exxon/Subway, Marathon/Domino's/dsl, Murphy USA/dsl, Shell/dsl Bowie BBQ, Burger King, China Buffet, Cracker Barrel, DQ, El Dorado Mexican, Hudgey's Rest., KFC, Krystal, Little Caesar's, Little Tokyo, Los Parrilleros, McDonald's, Mitchell's Steaks, Pizza Hut, Popeye's, Sonic, Taco Bell, Waffle House, Wards Burgers, Wendy's Best Value Inn, Comfort Inn, Hampton Inn, Holiday Inn Express, Lincoln Inn, Rodeway Inn, Spanish Inn H, $General, $Tree, AT&T, AutoZone, Buick/Cadillac/Chevrolet/GMC, CarQuest, Family$, Ford/Lincoln, Fred's, Gene's Tires, GNC, Honda, Nissan, O'Reilly Parts, Rite Aid, Save-A-Lot Foods, Toyota, Walgreens, Walmart/Subway, W IHOP Home Depot
38	US 84, S Brookhaven, W Chevron/dsl
30	Bogue Chitto, Norfield, E Shell/BogueChitto/dsl
24	Johnston Station, E to Lake Dixie Springs
20b a	US 98 W, to Natchez, Summit, E Marathon/dsl, Shell/dsl, Stop'n Shop/dsl, W Exxon/Subway/dsl, ShawnMart/dsl
18	MS 570, Smithdale Rd, N McComb, E Marathon, Murphy USA/dsl Burger King, McDonald's, Piccadilly's, Ruby Tuesday Holiday Inn Express H, AT&T, Belk, Hobby Lobby, JC Penney, Kia, Lowe's, Walgreens, Walmart/Subway, W Chevron/Mr Whiskers/dsl Applebee's, Arby's, El Dorado Mexican, Santa Fe Steaks Comfort Inn, Deerfield Inn, Hampton Inn Ford/Lincoln
17	Delaware Ave, McComb, E Blue Sky, Chevron/dsl, Exxon/Penn's Rest., Marathon/Subway/dsl, Pump&Savor Burger King, Domino's, Golden Corral, Kyoto Steaks, Little Caesar's, Pizza Hut, Popeye's, Smoothie King, Sonic, Taco Bell, Tortillo Soup, Waffle House, Wendy's Best Western, Quality Inn H, $General, AutoZone, Chrysler/Dodge/Jeep, CVS Drug, Family$, Fred's, Kroger, McComb Mkt, Office Depot, O'Reilly Parts, Rite Aid, Verizon, W Days Inn
15b a	US 98 E, MS 48 W, McComb, **1 mi** E Citgo/dsl, Exxon/Subway, Presley QuikStop/dsl, Pump&Savor, Shell Church's, KFC Camellian Motel $General, $Tree, Advance Parts, Family$, tires, vet, $Tree, W Marathon/dsl
13	Fernwood Rd, E truck repair, W Loves/Chester's/McDonald's/dsl/scales/24hr/@ golf, to Percy Quin SP

LAUREL

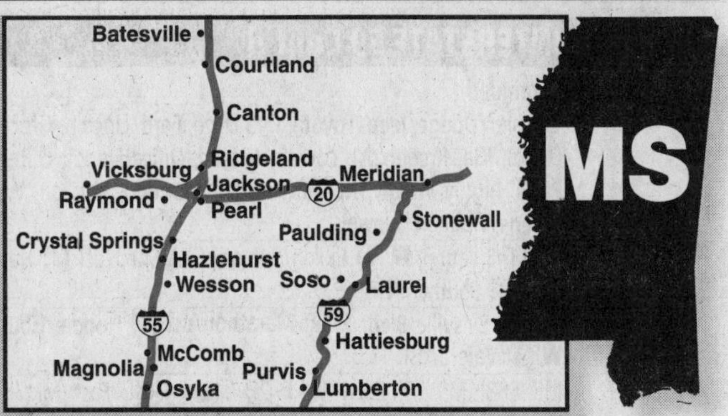

Exit #	Services
10	MS 48, Magnolia, **1 mi** E Exxon/Subway/dsl, Marathon, Shell/dsl RV camping, Marathon
8	MS 568, Magnolia
4	Chatawa
3mm	**Welcome Ctr nb, 24hr security, full facilities, litter barrels, petwalk, RV dump**
2mm	**weigh sta nb**
1	MS 584, Osyka, Gillsburg
0mm	Mississippi/Louisiana state line

INTERSTATE 59

Exit #	Services
172mm	Mississippi/Alabama state line
I-59 S and I-20 W run together to Meridian. See I-20, exits 170mm-150.	
142	to US 11, Dunns Falls, Savoy
137	to N Enterprise, to Stonewall
134	MS 513, S Enterprise, E FastStop
126	MS 18, to Rose Hill, Pachuta, E Alliance/dsl, Pachuta TP/dsl
118	to Vossburg, Paulding
113	MS 528, to Heidelberg, E Chevron/dsl, Exxon/Subway/dsl, Valero/dsl Ward's Burgers
109mm	**parking area sb, litter barrels, no rest rooms**
106mm	**parking area nb, litter barrels, no restrooms**
104	Sandersville
99	US 11, E Sleepy Hollow RV Park (1mi)
97	US 84 E, E Circle K/Subway/dsl, Exxon/Huddle House/dsl/scales Hardee's, Ward's Burgers, W Shell KFC, Vic's Rest.
96b	MS 15 S, Cook Ave
96a	Masonite Rd, 4th Ave
95d	(from nb)
95c	Beacon St, Laurel, W Burger King, Church's, McDonald's, Popeye's TownHouse Motel $General, Family$, Firestone/auto, Grocery Depot, H, JC Penney, museum of art, NAPA, USPO
95b a	US 84 W, MS 15 N, 16th Ave, Laurel, **0-2 mi** W Alliance/dsl, Exxon/dsl, Fast Stop, Murphy Express/dsl, Shell Applebee's, Arby's, Buffalo Wild Wings, Buffet Palace, Burger King, Cane's, Capt D's, Checkers, Chick-fil-A, China Town, Dickey's BBQ, Domino's, DQ, Hardee's, KFC, Laredo Grill, Little Caesar's, McDonald's, Mi Casita, Panda Express, Papa John's, Popeye's, Shipley's Donuts, Shoney's, Sonic, Subway, Taco Bell, Tokyo Grill, Waffle House, Ward's Burgers, Wendy's Baymont Suites, Best Western, EconoLodge, Hampton Inn, Holiday Inn Express, Rodeway Inn, Super 8 H, $General, $Tree, Advance Parts, AT&T, auto tech, AutoZone, BigLots, Chevrolet,

MS

= gas = food = lodging = other = rest stop

MS

INTERSTATE 59 Cont'd

LAUREL

95b a	Continued Chrysler/Dodge/Jeep/Toyota, CVS Drug, Ford/Lincoln, Grocery Depot, Kia, Kroger/dsl, Lowe's, Nissan, Office Depot, O'Reilly Parts, Piggly Wiggly, Roses, Tuesday Morning, Verizon, Walgreens, Walmart/Subway
93	US 11, S Laurel, W Exxon/Subway/dsl, Shell/dsl Hardee's Southern Tires
90	US 11, Ellisville Blvd, E Marathon/dsl Huddle House, W Valero/dsl
88	MS 588, MS 29, Ellisville, E Chevron/dsl, Fast Mkt/dsl, Keith's/dsl Domino's, KFC, Little Caesar's, McDonald's, Pizza Hut, Sonic, Subway, Ward's Burgers $General, AutoZone, CashSaver, Ellisville Drug, Family$, NAPA, O'Reilly Parts, W Shell/dsl Millennium Inn
85	MS 590, to Ellisville, W Texaco/dsl
80	to US 11, Moselle, E Chevron/dsl
78	Sanford Rd
76	W to Hattiesburg-Laurel Reg Airport
73	Monroe Rd, to Monroe
69	MS 42 E, Gandy Pkwy, to Petal, Eatonville
67b a	US 49, Hattiesburg, E Clark's/dsl, Exxon, Exxon/dsl/scales, Shell, Texaco Arby's, Burger King, Cracker Barrel, DQ, Krystal, McDonald's, Popeye's, Waffle House Budget Inn, EconoLodge, Executive Inn, Holiday Inn, Howard Johnson, Magnuson, Quality Inn, Red Roof Inn, Sleep Inn, Sunset Inn, Super 8, University Inn $General, Hattiesburg Cycles, W Chevron, MapleLeaf/dsl, Pure/dsl, Shell/Subway, Stuckey's Express/dsl, Texaco, Valero Sonic, Waffle House, Ward's Burgers, Wendy's Candlewood Suites, DoubleTree Inn, Northgate Inn
65b a	US 98 W, Hardy St, Hattiesburg, E Shell/dsl, Valero Applebee's, Baskin Robbins, Buffalo Wild Wings, Cane's, Checkers, CiCi's Pizza, Cookout, Crab House, Crescent City Grill, Domino's, Ed's Burger Joint, Firehouse Subs, IHOP, Jimmy John's, Lenny's Subs, Little Caesar's, McDonald's, Papa John's, Pizza Hut, Qdoba, Smoothie King, Starbucks, Subway, Tabella Italian, Taco Bell, Topher's, Ward's Burgers Courtyard, Days Inn, Fairfield Inn, Hotel Indigo, La Quinta, Residence Inn, Super 8, TownePlace Suites, Western Motel Corner Mkt Foods, CVS Drug, Goodyear/auto, Home Depot, H, to USM, URGENT CARE, Verizon, vet, Walgreens, W Chevron, Circle K, Exxon/Domino's, Shell/Jimmy John's/dsl Arby's, Burger King, Chesterfield's Rest., Chick-fil-A, Chili's, China Buffet, ChuckECheese's, City Buffet, Dickey's BBQ, FireHouse Subs, Five Guys, Gatti Town Pizza, Georgia Blue Rest., Golden Corral, Hardee's, HoneyBaked Ham, Hooters, Krispy Kreme, Logan's Roadhouse, Longhorn Steaks, Marble Slab, McAlister's Deli, McDonald's, Newk's Eatery, O'Charley's, Olive Garden, Outback Steaks, Panda Express, Pepper's Deli, Pizza Hut, Plaid Rhino Burger, Popeye's, Red Lobster, Super King Asian, Taco Bell, TGIFriday's, Waffle House, Ward's Burgers, Wendy's, Which Wich?, Yamato Japan, Zaxby's Baymont Inn, Best Western, Comfort Suites, Hampton Inn, Hilton Garden, Home 2 Suites, InTown Suites, Microtel, Red Lion Inn H, $Tree, Aamco, Advance Parts, AT&T, AutoZone, Belk, Best Buy, BigLots, Books-A-Million, Dick's, Dillard's, Firestone/auto, Goodyear/auto, Hobby Lobby, JC Penney, Jo Ann, Kohl's, Lowe's, Michael's, Nissan, Office Depot, Old Navy, PetCo, Petsmart, Ross, Sam's Club/gas, SteinMart, Target, TJ Maxx, Tuesday Morning, Verizon, Walgreens, Walmart, Winn-Dixie
60	US 11, S Hattiesburg, E Shell/TX BBQ/dsl, W Circle K/Subway/dsl/24hr, Texaco, Valero/dsl Freightliner, Peterbilt

HATTIESBURG

59	US 98 E, to US 49, Lucedale, MS Gulf Coast
56mm	**parking area both lanes, litter barrels, no restrooms**
51	rd 589, to Purvis, W Chevron/dsl, Pinebelt Oil/dsl, Shell/ (2mi) Little Caesar's, McDonald's (2mi), Pizza Hut (2mi) Little Black Cr Water Park
48mm	Little Black Creek
41	MS 13, to Lumberton, W Marathon/dsl $General, Little Black Cr Water Park
35	Hillsdale Rd, E to Kings Arrow Ranch
32mm	Wolf River
29	rd 26, to Poplarville, W Loves/Arby's/dsl/scales/24 Pure/dsl NAPA, tires/repair
27	MS 53, to Poplarville, Necaise, W Chevron/dsl McDonald's
19	to US 11, Millard
15	to McNeill, W McNeill Trkstop/rest./dsl
10	to US 11, Carriere, E Texaco/cafe/dsl Clearwater Camp (5mi)
6	MS 43 N, N Picayune, E Mi Sol Azteca, Paul's Pastri W Chevron/dsl DQ, McDonald's, Sonic, Subway, W fle House Super 8 H, Claiborne Hill Mkt, CVS Dr Family$, Walgreens
4	MS 43 S, to Picayune, E Murphy USA/dsl, RaceTr dsl McDonald's, Rio Grande Mexican, Ryan's $Tr AT&T, Buick/Cadillac/Chevrolet/GMC, Chrysler/Dodge/Je GNC, Home Depot, Nissan, Verizon, Walgreens, Walma W Exxon/dsl, Keith's/dsl, Shell/dsl Applebee's, Bur King, Domino's, Don's Seafood, Hardee's, IHOP, Little Caesa New Buffet City, Papa John's, Pizza Hut, Popeye's, Subw Taco Bell, Tokyo Grill, Waffle House, Wendy's Days I EconoLodge, Heritage Inn, Holiday Inn Express H, $G eral, Advance Parts, AutoZone, Family$, Ford/Lincoln, Gen Tire/auto, O'Reilly Parts, Paw Paw's RV Ctr, Shoppers Val URGENT CARE
3mm	**Welcome Ctr nb, full facilities, litter barrels, petwalk, RV dump, vending**
1.5mm	**weigh sta both lanes**
1	US 11, MS 607, E NASA, W Shell/dsl $General
0mm	Mississippi/Louisiana state line, Pearl River

PICAYUNE

INTERSTATE 220 (Jackson)

Exit #	Services
11mm	**I-220 begins/ends on I-55, exit 104.**
9	Hanging Moss Rd, County Line Rd, E Marathon/dsl
8	Watkins Dr, E Exxon/Subway, Shell/Chester's/dsl
5b a	US 49 N, Evers Blvd, to Yazoo City, E Citgo KFC, Sc ic Star Motel $General, Family$, Food Depot/g W Exxon/Burger King, Forty Nine TS/Subway/dsl, She Baskin Robbin/dsl $General
3	Industrial Dr
2b a	Clinton Blvd, Capitol St, E to Jackson Zoo, W RaceW Shell McDonald's, Popeye's, Sonic Family$
1b a	US 80, E Citgo/dsl, Shell Capt D's, Country Fisherma DQ, KFC, McDonald's, Pizza Hut, Popeye's, Taco Bell, We dy's Best Inn, Scottish Inn AutoZone, Firestone/au Mr Transmission, UHaul, W Citgo/dsl, Exxon/dsl A by's, Krystal $General
0mm	**I-220 begins/ends on I-20, exit 41.**

MISSOURI

INTERSTATE 29

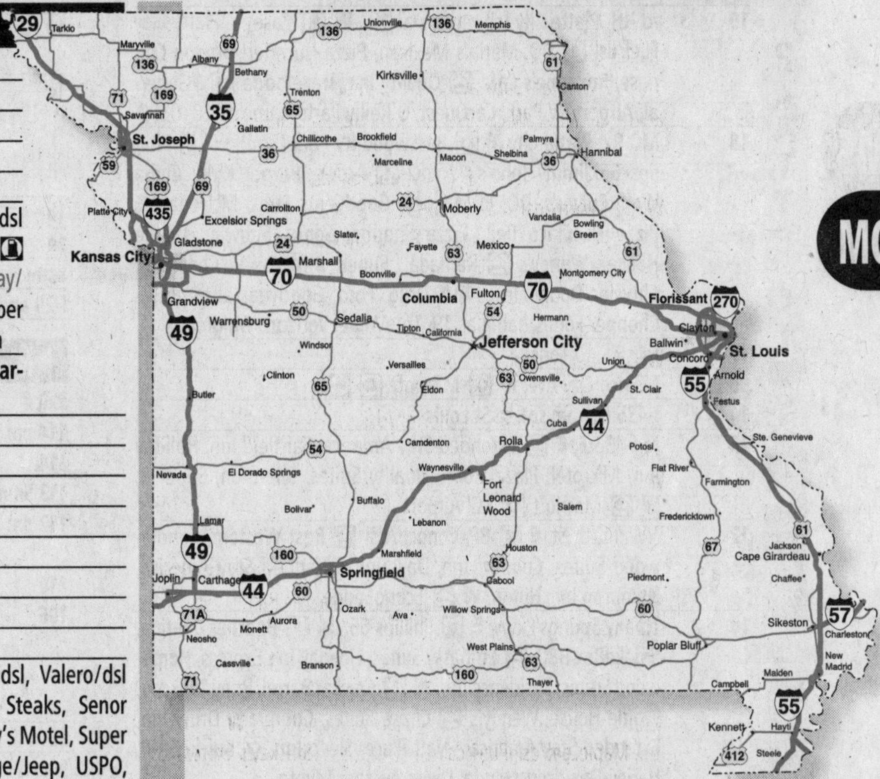

Exit #	Services
124mm	Missouri/Iowa state line
123mm	Nishnabotna River
121.5mm	**weigh sta both lanes**
116	rd A, rd B, to Watson, **W** fireworks
110	US 136, Rock Port, Phelps City, **E** Sinclair/dsl fireworks, Rockport Inn, to NW MO St U, **W** Cenex/Godfather's/dsl/24hr, Phillips 66/Subway/dsl/24hr McDonald's, Trails End Rest. Super 8 fireworks, Rivers Edge RV Park, truck wash
109.5mm	**Welcome Ctr sb, full facilities, info, litter barrels, petwalk,**
107	MO 111, to Rock Port
106.5mm	Rock Creek
102mm	Mill Creek
99	rd W, Corning
97mm	Tarkio River
92	US 59, to Fairfax, Craig, **W** Sinclair/dsl
90.5mm	Little Tarkio Creek
86.5mm	Squaw Creek
84	MO 118, Mound City, **E** Sinclair/Subway/dsl, Valero/dsl Breadeaux Pizza, McDonald's, Quacker's Steaks, Senor Barrigas Mexican, Shakers Icecream Audrey's Motel, Super 8 $General, Bumper Parts, Chrysler/Dodge/Jeep, USPO, **W** BP/dsl Big Lake SP (12mi)
82mm	**truck parking both lanes, limited facilities**
79	US 159, Rulo, **E** Phillips 66 Trkstp/dsl/rest/RV dump/@, **W** to Big Lake SP (12mi), to Squaw Creek NWR (3mi)
78mm	Kimsey Creek
75	US 59, to Oregon
67	US 59 N, to Oregon
66.5mm	Nodaway River
65	US 59, rd RA, to Fillmore, Savannah, **E** Trex/dsl antiques, fireworks
60	rd K, rd CC, Amazonia, **W** Hunt's Fruit Barn
58.5mm	Hopkins Creek
56b a	I-229 S, US 71 N, US 59 N, to St Joseph, Maryville
55mm	Dillon Creek
53	US 59, US 71 bus, to St Joseph, Savannah, **E** AOK Camping, **W** Phillips 66/dsl antiques, fireworks
50	US 169, St Joseph, King City, **1-3 mi W on Belt Hwy** Cenex/dsl, Conoco, Shell, Sinclair/Subway/dsl 54th St Grill, Bob Evans, Buffalo Wild Wings, Cheddar's, Chick-fil-A, Chili's, Chipotle Mexican, Coldstone, Culver's, Famous Dave's, Hardee's, IHOP, KFC, McDonald's, Olive Garden, Panda Express, Ryan's, Sonic, Starbucks, Subway, Taco Bell Candlewood Suites, Fairfield Inn, Holiday Inn Express Advance Parts, Aldi Foods, AT&T, Autozone, Best Buy, Dick's, Home Depot, Kohl's, Lowe's, Michael's, Old Navy, Petco, Petsmart, Sam's Club/gas, Target, Tires+, TJ Maxx, URGENT CARE, Walgreens, Walmart/Subway
47	MO 6, Frederick Blvd, to Clarksdale, St Joseph, **E** Conoco Bandanas BBQ Days Inn, Drury Inn H, **W** Sinclair/dsl Applebee's, Arby's, Burger King, Cracker Barrel, Denny's, Dunkin', El Maguey Mexican, Fazoli's, Five Guys, Golden Corral, LJ Silver, McAlister's Deli, McDonald's, New China Super Buffet, Pancheros, Panera Bread, Papa John's,

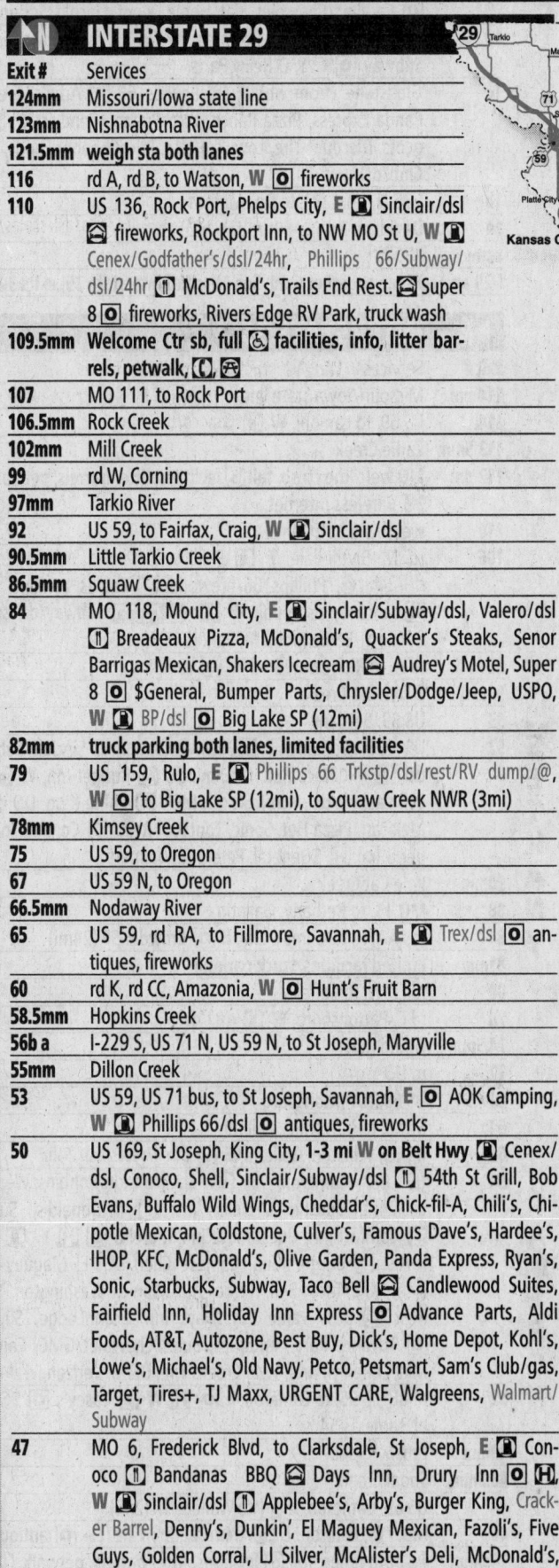

ST JOSEPH

Exit #	Services
47	Continued Papa Murphy's, Perkins, Pizza Hut, Red Lobster, Rib Crib BBQ, Sonic, Starbucks, Subway, Taco Bell, TX Roadhouse, Wendy's, Whiskey Creek Steaks Best Value Inn, Hampton Inn, Motel 6, Quality Suites, Ramada, Stoney Creek Inn $General, Apple Mkt Foods, BigLots, Buick/GMC, Chevrolet, CVS Drug, Dillard's, Firestone/auto, Ford/Lincoln, Hobby Lobby, Honda, HyVee Foods/dsl, JC Penney, Jo-Ann Fabrics, Nissan, Office Depot, Taco John's, Toyota, U-Haul, Verizon, vet, Walgreens
46b a	US 36, to Cameron, St Joseph, **E** to MWSU, **1 mi W on US 169** BP/dsl, FP/dsl, Murphy USA/dsl, Roadstar/dsl, Sinclair/dsl Burger King, Jimmy John's, Pizza Hut, Taco John's, Wendy's $General, Ace Hardware, AT&T, CVS, KIA, Klein RV Ctr, O'Reilly Parts, Walgreens, Walmart/Subway
44	US 169, to Gower, St Joseph, **E** Loves/Arby's/dsl/scales/24hr, Phillips 66 Nelly's Mexican, Subway Guesthouse Inn dsl repair, **W** Murphy USA/dsl, Shell/dsl/24hr DQ, El Maguey, Goodcents Subs, McDonald's, San Jose Steaks, Sonic, Taco Bell, Waffle House $Tree, Apple Mkt Foods, Chrysler/Dodge/Jeep, Harley-Davidson, Hyundai, Menards, Walmart/Subway
43	I-229 N, to St Joseph
39.5mm	Pigeon Creek
35	rd DD, Faucett, **W** Farris Trkstp/dsl/motel/rest/24hr/@
33.5mm	Bee Creek
30	rd Z, rd H, Dearborn, New Market, **E** Trex/Subway/dsl/24hr
29.5mm	Bee Creek
27mm	**both lanes, full facilities, litter barrels, petwalk, vending**
25	rd E, rd U, to Camden Point, **E** Trex/dsl
24mm	**weigh sta nb/truck parking sb**
20	MO 92, MO 273, to Atchison, Leavenworth, **W** antiques, to Weston Bend SP

MO

= gas = food = lodging = other = rest stop

INTERSTATE 29 Cont'd

PLATTE CITY

KANSAS CITY

Exit #	Services
19.5mm	Platte River
19	rd HH, Platte City (sb returns at 18), W Casey's, Platte-Clay Fuel/dsl DQ, Maria's Mexican, Pizza Hut, Red Dragon Chinese, Roxanne's Cafe Quality Inn, Travelodge $General, Airport RV Park, CarQuest, O'Reilly Parts, same as 18, USPO
18	MO 92, Platte City, E Basswood RV Park (5mi), W Phillips 66/Jimmy John's, QT/dsl Arby's, Burger King, China Wok, Culver's, DQ, El Maguey, GoodCents Subs, McDonald's, Pizza Hut/Taco Bell, Pizza Shoppe, Sonic, Subway, Waffle House, Wendy's Ramada, Super 8 Buick/Chevrolet, Chrysler/Dodge/Jeep, CVS Drug, Ford, Goodyear/auto, PriceChopper Foods, same as 19, TrueValue, Verizon, Walgreens
17	I-435 S, to Topeka
15	Mexico City Ave, W Marriott
14	I-435 E (from sb), to St Louis
13	to I-435 E, E Extended Stay America, Fairfield Inn, Holiday Inn, Microtel, Plaza Hotel, Quality Suites, Sheraton, Super 8, W Marriott KCI Airport
12	NW 112th St, E BP, Conoco/dsl Best Western, Candlewood Suites, Comfort Inn, Days Inn, Extended Stay America, Hampton Inn, Hilton, W EconoLodge
10	Tiffany Springs Pkwy, E Phillips 66/dsl Beaches Cantina, SmokeBox BBQ Embassy Suites, Holiday Inn Express, Homewood Suites, Residence Inn, W Cracker Barrel, Ruby Tuesday, Waffle House, Wendy's Chase Suites, Courtyard, Drury Inn, Extended Stay America, Hyatt Place, Sleep Inn Buick/GMC, Harley-Davidson, Honda, Lexus, Nissan, Toyota
9b a	MO 152, to Liberty, Topeka
8	MO 9, rd T, NW Barry Rd, E Phillips 66/dsl Applebee's, Big Biscuit, Burger King, Chick-fil-A, Chili's, China Wok, Chipotle Mexican, ChuckeCheese, Dickey's BBQ, Five Guys, Golden Corral, Honeybaked Cafe, Hong's Buffet, Hooters, Houlihan's, Jason's Deli, Kato Japanese, On the Border, Panchero's, Panda Express, Panera Bread, Papa Murphy's, Rally House, Sheridan's Custard, Starbucks, Subway, Taco Bell, Wendy's, Winstead's Rest. H, $Tree, AutoZone, Best Buy, Ford, Hobby Lobby, Home Depot, HyVee/dsl, JC Penney, Lowe's, NTB, Petsmart, Ross, Target, Verizon, vet, Walmart, W Phillips 66/dsl, QT/dsl 54th St Grill, A&W/LJSilver, Abuelo's, Arby's, Bar Louie, BoLings Chinese, Bravo Italian, Buffalo Wild Wings, Granite City, Hardee's, Hereford House, Jimmy John's, McDonald's, Minsky's Pizza, Noodles&Co, Outback Steaks, Rainbow Oriental, Smokehouse BBQ, Sonic, Stone Canyon Pizza, Taco Bueno La Quinta, Motel 6, Super 8 AT&T, Barnes&Noble, CVS Drug, Dick's, Dillard's, Marshall's, Michael's, Old Navy, Staples, Tires+, Verizon
6	NW 72nd St, Platte Woods, E Sinclair/dsl vet, W Phillips 66 Iron Wok, Papa John's, Tasty Thai K-Mart
5	MO 45 N, NW 64th St, W Shell/dsl Bonefish Grill, Caribou Coffee, Chamas Brazilian Grill, Culver's, Goodcents Subs, IHOP, Luna Azteca, McDonald's, Papa Murphy's, Quiznos, Saki Asian, Starbucks, Subway, Taco Bell $General, CVS Drug, GNC, Hen House Mkt, HyVee, Sprouts Mkt, Tuesday Morning, vet
4	NW 56th St (from nb), W Phillips 66
3c	rd A (from sb), Riverside, W QT/dsl Corner Café, Sonic Rverside Automotive, USPO
3b	I-635 S
3a	Waukomis Dr, rd AA (from nb)
2b	US 169 S (from sb), to KC
2a	US 169 N (from nb), to Smithville
1e	US 69, Vivion Rd, E Phillips66/dsl Steak'n Sh Cadillac/Chevrolet, Fiat, Home Depot, Lincoln, Subaru
1d	MO 283 S, Oak Tfwy (from sb), W BP/dsl McDona Subway CVS, O'Reilly Parts
1c	Gladstone (from nb), E Phillips 66 Arby's, Fredd Panda Express, Pizza Ranch, Taco Bueno, Wendy's H gLots, Discount Tire, Lowe's, Petco, PriceChopper Foods, Sa Club/dsl
1b	I-35 N (from sb), to Des Moines
1a	Davidson Rd
8mm	I-35 N.

I-29 and I-35 run together 6 mi. See Missouri Interstate 35, exits 3-8a

INTERSTATE 35

BETHANY

CAMERON

Exit #	Services
114mm	Missouri/Iowa state line
114	US 69, to Lamoni, W Conoco/dsl/24hr
113.5mm	Zadie Creek
112mm	**MO welcome ctr sb, full facilities, litter barrels, petwalk, , wireless internet**
110	**weigh sta both lanes**
106	rd N, Blythedale, E Phillips 66/Dinner Bell Cafe/mo dsl/24hr/@, Phillips 66/fireworks Eagles Landing M camping, dsl repair, W Loves/Subway/dsl/sca 24hr Eagle Ridge RV Park (2mi), fireworks
99	rd A, to Ridgeway, 5 mi W camping
94mm	E Fork Big Creek
93	US 69, Bethany
92	US 136, Bethany, E Casey's/dsl/scales, Sinclair/Subw dsl KFC/Taco Bell, McDonald's Budget Inn, W dsl, Casey's/dsl, Kum&Go/dsl, MFA China King, DQ, Nc Mexican, Pizza Hut, Sonic, TootToot Rest. Comfort Inn, per 8 H, $General, Peterbilt, Walmart
90mm	Pole Cat Creek
88	MO 13, to Bethany, Gallatin
84	rds AA, H, to Gilman City, E Crowder SP (24mi)
81mm	**limited facilities, truck parking**
80	rds B, N, to Coffey
78	rd C, Pattonsburg, W gas/dsl
74.5mm	Grand River
72	rd DD
68	US 69, to Pattonsburg
64	MO 6, to Maysville, Gallatin
61	US 69, Winston, Gallatin, E Shell/rest./dsl/24hr
54	US 36, Cameron, E Shell/Baskin-Robbins/Wendy dsl/24hr, Sinclair/dsl/scales/24hr McDonald's, Subw Comfort Inn, Guesthouse Inn, Motel 6 H, W Va ro/dsl Burger King, Chinese Chef, DQ, El Maguey M ican, KFC/Taco Bell, Pizza Hut, Sonic, Washington St Rest. Best Value Inn, Days Inn, EconoLodge, Supe Advance Parts, antiques, Buick/Chevrolet/GMC, Came Mkt, O'Reilly Parts, Twin Creeks Tire, USPO, Verizon, Walma
52	rd BB, Lp 35, to Cameron, E H, W Casey's $Gen al, same as 54
49mm	Brushy Creek
48.5mm	Shoal Creek
48	US 69, Cameron, E to Wallace SP (2mi)
40	MO 116, Lathrop, E Trex/Country Cafe/dsl antiques
34.5mm	**both lanes, full facilities, litter barrels, petwalk, , vending**

INTERSTATE 35 Cont'd

Exit #	Services
33	rd PP, Holt, E [other] auto repair, W [gas] BP/dsl, Conoco/dsl [lodging] American Eagle Inn [other] $General
30mm	Holt Creek
26	MO 92, Kearney, E [gas] Casey's/dsl, Phillips 66/dsl, QT/dsl [food] China Wok, Jimmy John's, McDonald's, Papa Murphy's, Pizza Hut, Sonic [lodging] Comfort Inn, Super 8 [other] CVS Drug, Price Chopper, to Watkins Mill SP, True Value, Verizon, W [gas] Pilot/Taco Bell/dsl/scales/24hr [food] Arby's, Burger King, Hunan Garden Chinese, JJ's Homestead Rest., Pizza Shoppe, Stables Grill, Subway [lodging] EconoLodge, Quality Inn [other] Goodyear/auto, O'Reilly Parts, to Smithville Lake
22mm	**parking area sb, weigh sta nb**
20	US 69, MO 33, to Excelsior Springs, E [other] H
17	MO 291, rd A, **1 mi** E [gas] BP, QT/dsl [food] A&W, CiCi's, Dickey's BBQ, Firehouse Subs, Hardee's, LJ Silver, McDonald's, Minsky's Pizza, Papa John's, Papa Murphy's, Perkins, Sonic, Subway, Taco Bell [other] $General, Chevrolet, Days Inn, Firestone/auto, KC Auto, Liberty RV Ctr, O'Reilly Parts, same as 16, Walgreens, W [gas] Phillips 66/dsl, QT [food] DQ, Masabi Japanese, McDonald's, Nicky's Pizza, Sonic, Subway, Zaxby's [lodging] Sleep Inn, Woodspring Suites Inn [other] Price Chopper Foods, to KCI Airport, URGENT CARE, Walgreens
16	MO 152, Liberty, E [gas] EVC, Phillips 66 [food] Baskin-Robbins, Chick-fil-A, CiCi's Pizza, Culver's, Domino's, Five Guys, IHOP, Jimmy John's, Margarita's, MOD Pizza, Olive Garden, Perkins, Pizza Hut, Pizza Ranch, Planet Sub, Red Robin, Starbucks, TX Roadhouse, Wendy's [lodging] Days Inn, Super 8 [other] H, Advance Parts, AutoZone, Chevrolet, CVS Drug, Dick's, Discount Tire, Firestone/auto, Gordman's, Hy-Vee/gas, Lowe's, Ross, URGENT CARE, Walgreens, W [gas] Murphy USA/dsl, Phillips 66/dsl [food] 54th St Grill, Applebee's, Arby's, Buffalo Wild Wings, Burger King, Cheddar's, Chili's, Chipotle Mexican, Corner Cafe, Cracker Barrel, Fanner's Grill, Freddy's Burgers, Jose Peppers, Joy Wok, KFC, LongHorn Steaks, McDonald's, Noodles&Co, Old Chicago Pizza, Panda Express, Panera Bread, PepperJax Grill, Qdoba, Steak'n Shake, Subway, Taco Bell, Ted's Cafe Escondido, Waffle House [lodging] Comfort Suites, Fairfield Inn, Hampton Inn, Holiday Inn Express [other] Aldi Foods, AT&T, Best Buy, Christian Bros Auto, Ford, Home Depot, JC Penney, Jiffy Lube, Kohl's, Michael's, NAPA, NTB, Office Depot, Petsmart, Sam's Club/dsl, Sprouts Mkt, Target, TJ Maxx, Tuesday Morning, URGENT CARE, Verizon, Walmart/Subway
14	US 69 (exits left from sb), Liberty Dr, to Glenaire, Pleasant Valley, E [gas] Phillips 66, Sinclair/dsl, W [gas] QT/dsl/scales/24hr
13	US 69 (from nb), to Pleasant Valley, E [gas] Phillips 66, Sinclair/dsl, W [gas] QT/dsl/scales/24hr
12b a	I-435, to St Louis
11	US 69 N, Vivion Rd, E [gas] BP/dsl, Phillips 66/dsl [food] Church's, McDonald's, W [gas] QT/dsl [food] Sonic, Stroud's Rest., Subway [other] CVS Drug, O'Reilly Parts, USPO, vet
10	N Brighton Ave (from nb), W [gas] QT/dsl [food] Church's, Sonic [other] CVS Drug
9	MO 269 S, Chouteau Trfwy, E [gas] Phillips 66 [food] IHOP, McDonald's, Ming Garden, Papa Murphy's, Subway, Wing Stop [other] Festival Foods, GNC, Harrah's Casino/rest., Target, W [food] Wendy's (1mi)
8c	MO 1, Antioch Rd, E [gas] 7-11 [food] Domino's [lodging] Best Western [other] auto repair, W [gas] Phillips 66, QT [food] Dickey's BBQ, Waffle House [other] AT&T, Walgreens
8b	I-29 N, US 71 N, KCI [airport]

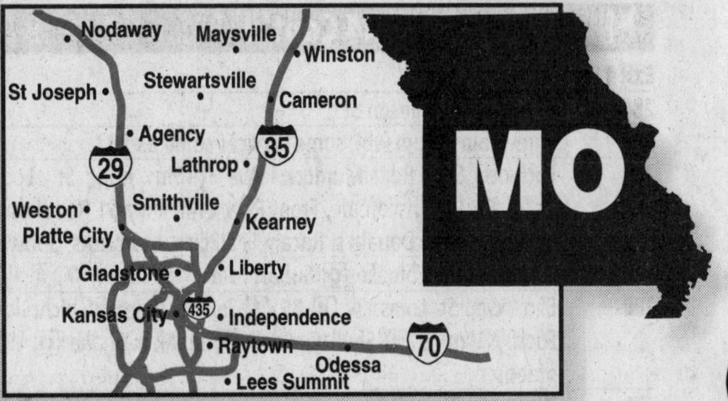

KANSAS CITY

Exit #	Services
	I-35 S and I-29 S run together 6 mi.
8a	Parvin Rd, E [gas] BP/dsl, Shell/dsl [food] Subway [other] O'Reilly Parts
6b a	Armour Rd, E [gas] Phillips 66/dsl [food] Arby's, Burger King, Denny's, McDonald's, Quiznos, Subway [lodging] EconoLodge, La Quinta [other] H, repair, to Riverboat Casino, W [gas] Flash/dsl, Phillips 66, QT [food] DQ, Jimmy John's, Lucky Dragon Chinese, Pizza Hut, Subway, Taco Bell, Wendy's [lodging] American Inn, Holiday Inn Express [other] URGENT CARE, USPO
5b	16th Ave, industrial district
5a	Levee Rd, Bedford St, industrial district
4.5mm	Missouri River
4b	Front St, E [other] Isle of Capri Riverboat Casino/rest.
4a	US 24 E, Independence Ave
3	I-70 E, US 71 S, to St Louis
2g	**I-35 N and I-29 N run together 6 mi.**
2e	Oak St, Grand-Walnut St, E [gas] Phillips 66 [lodging] Marriott
2d	Main-Delaware, Wyandotte St, downtown
2a	I-70 W, to Topeka
2y	US 169, Broadway, to downtown
2w	12th St, Kemper Arena, to downtown
2v	14th St, to downtown
2u	I-70 E, to Broadway, E [food] Denny's
1e	US 69, Vivion Rd, E [gas] Phillips66/dsl
1d	20th St (from sb), E [gas] Phillips 66
1c	27th St, SW Blvd, W Pennway (from nb), E [gas] Phillips 66 [other] H
1a	SW Trafficway (from sb)
0mm	Missouri/Kansas state line

INTERSTATE 44

ST LOUIS

Exit #	Services
293mm	**I-44 begins/ends on I-70, exit 249 in St Louis.**
290a	I-55 S, to Memphis
290c	Gravois Ave (from wb), 12th St, S [food] Jack-in-the-Box
290b	18th St (from eb), downtown
289	Jefferson Ave, St Louis, N [gas] Phillips 66 [food] Subway [lodging] Hotel Avyan, Residence Inn [other] Family$, SaveALot, S [gas] Conoco [food] Lee's Chicken, McDonald's [other] $General
288	Grand Blvd, St Louis, N [gas] BP [lodging] Water Tower Inn [other] H, vet, S [food] Domino's, Jack-in-the-Box, Jimmy John's, Starbucks, Subway [other] Family$
287b a	Kingshighway, Vandeventer Ave, St Louis, N [gas] BP, QT/dsl [other] H, Jiffy Lube, U-Haul, S [other] Chevrolet, to MO Botanical Garden
286	Hampton Ave, St Louis, N [gas] BP, Circle K, Mobil, Phillips 66 [food] Courtesy Diner, Denny's, Jack-in-the-Box, McDonald's, Steak'n Shake, Subway, Taco Bell [other] zoo, S [gas] Circle K/dsl [food] Bartolino's Rest., Hardee's, Wendy's [lodging] Drury Inn, Holiday Inn, Red Roof Inn
285	SW Ave (from wb, no EZ return)

gas = gas, food = food, lodging = lodging, other = other, rest stop = rest stop

MO

INTERSTATE 44 Cont'd

Exit #	Services
284b a	Arsenal St, Jamieson St
283	Shrewsbury (from wb), some services same as 282
282	Laclede Sta Rd, Murdock Ave (from eb), St Louis, N BP Frisco Cafe, Front Row Grill, Hwy 61 Roadhouse, Imo's Pizza, McDonald's, Racanelli's Pizza, Starbucks, Subway, Webster Wok Chinese Subaru, vet
280	Elm Ave, St Louis, N BP Jamba Juice Schnuck's Foods, 1 mi S Shell/Circle K Steak'n Shake Walgreens
279	(from wb), Berry Rd
278	Big Bend Rd, St Louis, N Culver's, Hardee's H, Sam's Club/gas, URGENT CARE, S Mobil/dsl, QT
277b	US 67, US 61, US 50, Lindbergh Blvd, N Arby's, Blaze Pizza, Buffalo Wild Wings, Cane's, Chili's, Chipotle Mexican, Dunkin', Jason's Deli, Sonic, TX Roadhouse, White Castle Best Western H, $Tree, Aldi Foods, AT&T, AutoZone, Harley-Davidson, Hobby Lobby, Lowe's Whse, Office Depot, Target, TJ Maxx, Walmart, S Circle K/dsl, Phillips 66/dsl Burger King, Chick-fil-A, Denny's, Five Guys, Fuddrucker's, Helen Fitzgerald's Grill, IHOP, Lion's Choice, Longhorn Steaks, Panda Express, St Louis Bread, Steak'n Shake, Subway, Walnut Grill Days Inn/rest., Hilltop Hotel, Holiday Inn Dobb's Auto/Tire, Home Depot, Marshall's, Old Navy, Petsmart, Ross, Stein Mart
277a	MO 366 E, Watson Rd, access to same as 277b S
276b a	I-270, N to Chicago, S Memphis
275	N Highway Dr (from wb), Soccer Pk Rd, N Road Ranger/Subway/dsl
274a b	Bowles Ave, N Road Ranger/Subway/dsl, S Phillips 66/dsl, QT/dsl Bandana's BBQ, Cracker Barrel, Jack-in-the-Box, Krispy Kreme, McDonald's, White Castle Drury Inn, Fairfield Inn, Holiday Inn Express, Motel 6, PearTree Inn, Stratford Inn, Super 8, TownePlace Suites
272	MO 141, Fenton, Valley Park, N Motomart, S Phillips 66/dsl, ZX Bob Evans, Hardee's, Jimmy John's, Psghetti's, Ruby Tuesday, Starbucks, Steak'n Shake, Subway, Sugarfire BBQ, Taco Bell Drury Inn, Hampton Inn Save-A-Lot Foods
269	Antire Rd, Beaumont
266	Lewis Rd, N golf, Rte 66 SP
266mm	Meramec River
265	Williams Rd (from eb)
264	MO 109, rd W, Eureka, N Phillips 66/dsl Arby's, Burger King, Culver's, Domino's, Jimmy John's, McDonald's, Pizza Hut, Poor Richard's, Smokers BBQ, St Louis Bread, Taco Bell, White Castle AT&T, Byerly RV Ctr, O'Reilly Parts, Schnuck's Foods, to Babler SP, Valvoline, Verizon, S QT/dsl Walgreens
261	Lp 44, to Allenton, N Motomart/McDonald's/dsl China King, Denny's, Imo's Pizza, Lion's Choice, Steak'n Shake, Subway Best Inn, Holiday Inn, Super 8 $Tree, AutoZone, Jellystone RV Camping, same as 264, to Six Flags, Walmart, S Circle K/dsl, Circle K/dsl (2) KOA
257	(256 from eb) Lp 44, Pacific, N Phillips 66/dsl, Pilot/Subway/dsl/scales/24hr Comfort Inn fireworks, S BP/dsl, Mobil/dsl, Motomart Domino's, El Agave Mexican, Hardee's, KFC, McDonald's, New China, Pizza Hut, Taco Bell Quality Inn $General, B&H Foods, Chrysler/Dodge/Jeep, CVS Drug, O'Reilly Parts, SaveALot, st police
253	MO 100 E, to Gray Summit, S Mobil/dsl fireworks, Shaw Nature Preserve
251	MO 100 W, to Washington, N BP/dsl, Mr Fuel/dsl/scales, Phillips 66/Burger King/dsl $General, H (11mi)

SULLIVAN

CUBA

ROLLA

Exit #	Services
247	US 50 W, rd AT, rd O, to Union, N Pin Oak Creek RV P S to Robertsville SP
247mm	Bourbeuse River
242	rd AH, to Hist Rte 66
240	MO 47, St Clair, N Phillips 66/Taco Bell/dsl Bu King tire/auto, S Mobil/dsl Domino's, McD ald's, Subway Budget Lodge, Super 8 $General, Co try Mart Foods, NAPA, O'Reilly Parts, Save-A-Lot Foods, USF
239	MO 30, rds AB, WW, St Clair, N repair, S Phillips 66.
238mm	**weigh sta both lanes**
235mm	**both lanes (both lanes exit left), full facilities, litter b rels, petwalk, , , vending**
230	rds W, Stanton, S Amstar/fireworks KOA, Mera Caverns Camping (3mi), USPO
226	MO 185 S, Sullivan, N FLYING J/Denny's/dsl/ scales/24hr vet, S Circle K/dsl Applebee's, Arb China Buffet, DQ, Imo's Pizza, KFC, Little Caesar's, McD ald's, Starbucks, Subway, Taco Bell $General, $Tree, Foods, AT&T, AutoZone, Lowe's, O'Reilly Parts, same as 225 Meramec SP, Walmart
225	MO 185 N, rd D, Sullivan, N Mobil, Phillips 66/dsl Do ino's, Du Kum Inn Rest., Jimmy John's Baymont Inn, B Value Inn, Motel 6, Super 8 Chevrolet/Buick/GMC, Chrys Dodge/Jeep, Ford, S BP/Fas-Trip/dsl/café, ZX Crac Barrel, El Nopal Mexican, Jack-in-the-Box, Lion's Choice, Pi Hut Comfort Inn H, city park, same as 226
218	rds N, C, J, Bourbon, N ZX/dsl Budget Inn, S Mo dsl Planet Sub, Subway $General, Blue Sprgs Camp (6mi), Bourbon RV Ctr, Riverview Ranch Camping (8mi), Si Drug, Town&Country Mkt
214	rd H, Leasburg, N Mobil/dsl, S Skippy's Rte Rest. to Onandaga Cave SP (7mi)
210	rd UU, N Meremac Valley Resort, S MO Hick B (3mi) winery
208	MO 19, Cuba, N Midwest/Phillips 66/Dotty's Rest./c scales/24hr/@ Huddle House, Pizza Hut Cuba I Super 8 antiques, Blue Beacon, S Casey's, Mobil/ East Sun Chinese, Hardee's, Jack-in-the-Box, McDonal Sonic, Subway, Taco Bell Days Inn $General, $Tr Mace Foods, O'Reilly Parts, to Ozark Nat Scenic Riverw (74mi), Walmart
203	rds F, ZZ, S Rosatti Winery (2mi)
195	MO 8, MO 68, St James, Maramec Sprg Park, N BP/Ci K/dsl, Mobil/dsl China King, McDonald's, Pizza Hut, S ic, Subway Economy Inn, Greenstay Inn $Gene Ford, O'Reilly Parts, Ray's Tires, to Maremac Winery, tours S Casey's/dsl, Phillips 66/dsl Burger King Fin Motel CountryMart Foods
189	rd V, Industrial Park Dr, Hypoint, N Loves/McDo ald's/Subway/dsl/scales/24hr, S Mule Trading Post
186	US 63, MO 72, Rolla, N Sinclair/dsl Steak'n Sha Drury Inn, Hampton Inn, Motel 6 Big O Tire, Kia, Koh Lowe's, Nissan, Plaza Tire, S BreakTime/dsl, Mobil/c Phillips 66/dsl Buffalo Wild Wings, Colton's Steaks, Do King, IHOP, Koi Chinese, Lee's Chicken, Panera Bread, St bucks Budget Motel H
185	rd E, to Rolla, N hwy patrol, S ZX Arby's, DQ, Ha ee's, Huddle House, Jimmy John's, Kyoto Japanese, LJ Silv Papa John's, Subway, Taco Bell, Wendy's H, CVS Dr Ford, Kroger, UMO at Rolla
184	US 63 S, to Rolla, N Comfort Suites, Holiday Inn press Menards, Petsmart, Ross, TJMaxx, S MotoMart,

INTERSTATE 44 Cont'd

184	Continued Arby's, Bandana's BBQ, Denny's, Dickey's BBQ, Little Caesar's, LJ Silver, Lucky House Chinese, Maid-Rite, McDonald's, Penelope's Rest., Pizza Hut, Sirloin Stockade, Subway, Waffle House, Wendy's Baymont Inn, Best Western, EconoLodge, Quality Inn, Sunset Inn, Super 8 H, Buick/Cadillac/GMC, Chevrolet, city park, CVS Drug, Kroger
179	rds T, C, to Doolittle, Newburg, S Phillips 66/dsl Cookin' From Scratch Rest. $General
178mm	**truck parking both lanes, restrooms**
176	Sugar Tree Rd
172	rd D, Jerome
169	rd J
166	to Big Piney
164mm	Big Piney River
163	MO 28, to Dixon, N Road Ranger/Chesters/Subway/dsl/scales/24hr, S Phillips 66/dsl Best Western, Days Inn, Motel 6 RV Park, Uranus Fudge Factory
161b a	rd Y, to Ft Leonard Wood, N Mobil/dsl, Murphy USA/dsl, One Stop/dsl Cracker Barrel, Domino's, Ocean Buffet, Papa Murphy's, Pizza Hut, Rte 66 Diner, Ruby Tuesday, Wendy's Baymont Inn, Best Value Inn, Candlewood Suites, Comfort Inn, Fairfield Inn, Hampton Inn, Hawthorn Suites, Mainstay Suites, Red Roof Inn Lowe's, Toyota, visitors ctr, Walmart/Subway, S Casey's/dsl, Kum&Go/dsl Arby's, Buffalo Wild Wings, Cantina Bravo, Colton's Steaks, Culver's, Freddy's, Hardee's, Little Caesar's, McDonald's, Panera Bread, Papa John's, Starbucks, Subway, Taco Bell, Waffle House Budget Inn, EconoLodge, Holiday Inn Express, Liberty Lodge, Quality Inn, ZLoft Hotel $General, $Tree, AT&T, AutoZone, Chrysler/Dodge/Jeep, Family$, Ford/Lincoln, Mazda, NAPA, O'Reilly Parts, Verizon
159	Lp 44, to Waynesville, St Robert, N DQ, Sonic All Star Motel, Super 8 auto repair, O'Reilly Parts, S Cenex/dsl El Cabrito Alliance Inn Big O Tire, Cadillac/GMC
158mm	Roubidoux Creek
156	rd H, Waynesville, N Express Stop/Burger King/dsl/e85, Gulf/dsl, Kum&Go/dsl McDonald's, Subway $General, Chevrolet, Price Cutter+
153	MO 17, to Buckhorn, N Ft Wood Inn, S Gulf/dsl Glen Oaks RV Park
150	MO 7, rd P to Richland
145	MO 133, rd AB, to Richland, N Sinclair/Oasis/cafe/dsl/24hr
143mm	Gasconade River
140	rd N, to Stoutland, S Cenex/pizza/dsl
139mm	Bear Creek
135	rd F, Sleeper
130	rd MM, N Cenex/dsl, Express Stop/Taco John's/dsl Andy's Rest. EconoLodge, Munger Moss Inn, S Kum&Go/dsl H
129	MO 5, MO 32, MO 64, to Hartville, Lebanon, N Applebee's, Arby's, Bamboo Garden, Bandana's BBQ, Burger King, DQ, Elm St Eatery, Jimmy John's, KFC, Little Caesar's, LJ Silver, McDonald's, Papa Murphy's, Sonic, Steak'n Shake, Subway, Taco Bell, Wendy's Aldi Foods, AT&T, AutoZone, Chevrolet, Ford, King Cashsaver, O'Reilly Parts, repair, Rte 66 Museum, to Bennett Sprgs SP, to Lake of the Ozarks, Verizon, Walgreens, Walnut Bowl Factory, S Cenex/dsl, Phillips 66/dsl Capt D's, Denny's, Domino's, Hardee's, La Tolteca, Pizza Hut H, $Tree, Lowe's, O'Reilly Parts, Sawyer Tire/auto, Walmart/Subway

LEBANON

MO

LEBANON

127	Lp 44, Lebanon, N Cenex/dsl, Gulf/B&D/J Diner/dsl/scales/24hr Dowd's Catfish&BBQ, El Sombrero Mexican, Slim Chickens, Subway, Tequila Mexican, Waffle House Best Value Inn, Days Inn, Hampton Inn, Holiday Inn Express, Midwest Inn, Rte 66 Motel, Super 8 $General, Chrysler/Dodge/Jeep, Cutlery/Walnut Bowl Outlet, Firestone/auto, S Conoco/McDonald's/dsl Dickey's BBQ Buick/Cadillac/GMC, Harley-Davidson, Russell Stover
123	County Rd, S antiques, Happy Trails RV Ctr, Happy Trails RV Park
118	rds C, A, Phillipsburg, S Phillips 66 Redmon's Gifts, tourist info
113	rds J, Y, Conway, N Conoco/dsl Rockin Chair Café Budget Inn to Den of Metal Arts, S Sinclair/dsl $General, SummerFresh Foods, USPO
111mm	**both lanes, full facilities, litter barrels, petwalk, playground, vending**
108mm	Bowen Creek
107	Sparkle Brooke Rd, Sampson Rd
106mm	Niangua River
100	MO 38, rd W, Marshfield, N Murphy USA/dsl, Phillips 66 $Tree, auto repair, Chevrolet, Chrysler/Dodge/Jeep, Ford, Walmart/Subway, S Casey's/dsl, Cenex/dsl, Shell/dsl Burger King, DQ, El Charro, Golden China, Grillos Cafe, KFC/Rib Crib, McDonald's, Pizza Hut, Sonic, Subway, Taco Bell Holiday Inn Express $General, AutoZone, O'Reilly Parts, RV Express RV Park, Verizon, Walgreens
96	rd B, Northview, N Rustic Meadows RV Park (2mi)
89mm	**weigh sta both lanes**
88	MO 125, to Fair Grove, Strafford, N Loves/Hardee's/dsl/scales/rv dump/24hr, TA/Subway/Taco Bell/dsl/scales/24hr/@ McDonald's Camping World RV Ctr, truckwash, vet, S Breaktime/dsl, Kum&Go Pizza Hut Super 8 $General, Strafford RV Park
84	MO 744, S Peterbilt
82b a	US 65, to Branson, Fedalia, S Kum&Go/dsl, Phillips 66/dsl Waffle House Bull Shoals Lake, Kenworth, st patrol, to Table Rock Lake
80b a	rd H to Pleasant Hope, Springfield, N Conoco/rest./dsl/scales/24hr, Kum&Go/dsl, Shell/dsl, Sinclair, Tesla EVC Tropical Cafe, Waffle House Days Inn, Holiday Inn Express, Red Roof Inn, Super 8 $General, S Casey's, Kum&Go/dsl, Phillips 66/dsl, Shell Andy's Custard, Applebee's, Braum's, Burger King, Carriage House, Cracker Barrel, Culver's, El Maguey Mexican, Fazoli's, Freddy's, Hardee's, Hong Kong Inn, Houlihan's, Ichiban Buffet, Jose Locos, King's Asian Chef, Little Tokyo, LJ Silver, McDonald's, Panda Express, Pizza Hut, Rib Crib, Royal Buffet, Ruby Tuesday, Schlotzsky's, Shanghai Inn,

MARSHFIELD

MO

SPRINGFIELD

INTERSTATE 44 Cont'd

80b a Continued
Sonic, Steak'n Shake, Subway, Taco Bell, Whole Hog Cafe, Ziggies Cafe Baymont Inn, Best Western, Campus Inn, Candlewood Suites, Comfort Inn, Dogwood Park Inn, Doubletree Hotel, Drury Inn, EconoLodge, Economy Inn, Fairfield Inn, Flagship Motel, Hampton Inn, Holiday Inn, Home 2 Suites, Lamplighter Hotel, Motel 6, Plaza Inn, Quality Inn, Springfield Inn, Springhill Suites H, Aldi Foods, AutoZone, Big O Tire, O'Reilly Parts, Tire Express, U-Haul, Walmart/Subway

77 MO 13, KS Expswy, N Kum&Go/dsl/e85 Lowe's, S Casey's/dsl, Phillips 66/dsl Arby's, Braum's, Buffalo Wild Wings, Chuckwagon BBQ, El Charro, Five Guys, Golden Corral, Goodcents, IHOP, Jimmy John's, McAlister's Deli, McDonald's, New China, Panera Bread, Papa John's, Papa Murphy's, Subway, Taco Bell, Waffle House $Tree, AT&T, BigLots, Drug Mart, GNC, Goodyear/auto, Hobby Lobby, PriceCutter Foods, Verizon, Walgreens, Walmart

75 US 160 W byp, to Willard, Stockton Lake, S Kum&Go/dsl Wendy's Courtyard, La Quinta

72 MO 266, to Chesnut Expwy, S Casey's, Cenex, FLYING J/Wendy's/PJ Fresh/dsl/scales/24hr, Kum&Go/dsl/e85 Alli's Rest., Arby's, China Wok, Hardee's, KFC, LJ Silver, McDonald's, Pizza Hut, Plaza Mexico, Sonic, Subway, Taco Bell, Waffle House Best Budget Inn, Best Western+, Redwood Motel $General, AutoZone, city park, PriceCutter Foods

70 rds MM, B, N fireworks, S KOA (1mi), Wilson's Creek Nat Bfd (5mi)

69 to US 60, Springfield

67 rds N, T, Bois D' Arc, to Republic, S Conoco/dsl AmericInn (5mi) art glass

66mm Pond Creek

64.6mm Dry Branch

64.5mm Pickerel Creek

61 rds K, PP, N Cenex/Hoods/dsl/scales/LP/24hr, Phillips 66 Hood I-44 Motel

58 MO 96, rds O, Z, to Carthage, Halltown, S Shell/dsl truck repair

57 to rd PP (from wb)

56.5mm Turnback Creek

56mm Goose Creek

52.5mm **truck parking both lanes**

49 MO 174E, rd CCW, Chesapeake

46 MO 39, MO 265, Mt Vernon, Aurora, N Casey's/dsl, Gulf/dsl, Kum&Go/dsl, TA/Conoco/Subway/dsl/scales/24hr/@ Bamboo Garden Chinese, El Azteca Mexican, KFC/LJ Silver, Mazzio's, McDonald's, Pizza Hut, Sonic, Subway, Taco Bell Best Western, USA Inn $General, O'Reilly Parts, True Value, S Cenex/dsl Quality Inn to Table Rock Lake

44 rd H, to Monett, Mt Vernon, N Subway (1mi) Mid-America Dental/Hearing, Walmart

43.5mm Spring River

38 MO 97, to Stotts City, Pierce City, N gas/dsl/repair/tires, S U of MO SW Ctr (4mi)

33 MO 97 S, to Pierce City

29 rd U, to La Russell, Sarcoxie, N antiques, Beagle Bay RV Camping, OzarkLand Gifts, S Casey's (1mi), Kum&Go/Subway/dsl antiques

29mm Center Creek

26 MO 37, to Reeds, Sarcoxie, N Bill's Truck/trailer repair

22 rd 100 N, N Colaw RV Ctr, S Consignment RV Sales

21mm Jones Creek

JOPLIN

18b a I-49 N, US 71 N, MO 59 S, to Carthage, Neosho, N Coa light RV Ctr/Camping

15 MO 66 W, Lp 44 (from wb), Joplin, N Tara Motel

15mm Grove Creek

14mm Turkey Creek

13 Prigmore Ave, S Skyline Travel Plaza/dsl/scales/24hr

11b a I-49 S, US 71 S, MO 249 N, to Neosho, Ft Smith, S FLYING Denny's/dsl/LP/scales/24hr/@, Speedco Blue Beacon, Go year Tires/repair, Kenworth

8b a US 71, to Neosho, Joplin, N Cenex/dsl, Conoco/ Kum&Go/dsl, Phillips 66/dsl Andy's Custard, Applebe Arby's, Billy Sims BBQ, Braum's, Buffalo Wild Wings, Bu er King, Carino's Italian, Casa Montez Mexican, Chedda Chick-fil-A, Chipotle, ChuckeCheese, CiCi's, Denny's, Domin El Vallarta Mexican, Firehouse Subs, First Watch, Five Gu Freddy's, Golden Corral, Golden Dragon, Hardee's, Hu IHOP, Jimmy John's, Jimmy's Egg, Little Caesar's, Logan's Ro house, Longhorn Steaks, McAlister's, McDonald's, Old Chica Olive Garden, On the Border, Outback Steaks, Panda Expre Pizza Hut, Popeye's, Qdoba, Red Hot&Blue Grill, Red Lobs Rib Crib, Schlotzsky's, Sonic, Starbucks, Steak'n Shake, S way, Taco Bell, TX Roadhouse, Waffle House, Wasab Stea Wendy's Best Western, Candlewood Suites, Comfort I Days Inn, Drury Inn, EconoLodge, Fairfield Inn, Hampton I Hilton Garden, Holiday Inn, Homewood Suites, La Quin Motel 6, Quality Inn, Residence Inn, Sunrise Inn, Super 8, T Hilton $Tree, Aldi Foods, AT&T, AutoZone, Best Buy, Boo A-Million, Chrysler/Dodge/Jeep, Discount Tire, Firestone/au Food4Less, Ford/Lincoln, Freightliner, Goodyear/auto, Hob Lobby, Home Depot, Honda, Hyundai, JC Penney, Jo-Ann Fa rics, Kia, Kohl's, Lowe's, Macy's, Mercedes, Michael's, Nissa Office Depot, O'Reilly Parts, Petsmart, Ross, Sam's Club/g Subaru, Target, TJ Maxx, Toyota, Verizon, Walgreens, Walma Subway, S Casey's Cracker Barrel, Fazoli's Micro TownePlace Suites vet, Wheelen RV Ctr

6 MO 86, MO 43 N, to Racine, Joplin, N Phillips 66 Jim John's, Moe's SW Grill, Schlotzsky's CVS Drug, Walgree S Kum&Go/dsl/e15 H, Harley-Davidson

5.5mm Shoal Creek

4 MO 43 to Seneca, N Loves/Hardee's/dsl/scales/24 S Conoco/Subway/dsl, Petro/Iron Skillet/Pizza Hut/Taco Be dsl/scales/24hr/@, Pilot/Wendy's/dsl/scales/24hr M Donald's Sleep Inn $General, fireworks, IA 80 Truc omat, KOA

3mm **weigh sta both lanes**

2mm **Welcome Ctr eb, full facilities, litter barrels, , , strooms, vending; truck parking wb**

1 US 400, US 166W, to Baxter Springs, KS, N Downstrea dsl Downstream Casino/RV Park, Downstream RV Pa S Sandstone Gardens

0mm Missouri/Oklahoma state line

INTERSTATE 49

Exit # Services

184 I-435, I-470.

I-49 begins/ends, continues N as US 71.

182 Red Bridge Rd, Longview Rd, E Sinclair/dsl McDo ald's, Taco Bell auto repair, W Phillips 66/dsl Woo spring Suites

181 Blue Ridge Blvd, E Shell/dsl Church's Best Val Inn NAPA, U-Haul, W BP/dsl, Conoco/dsl 54th Grill, Arby's, Chipotle, Hardee's, IHOP, KFC, McAlister's De

INTERSTATE 49 Cont'd

181	Continued Papa John's, Pizza Hut, Starbucks, Wendy's [other] $Tree, Advance Parts, AT&T, AutoZone, Burlington Coats, CVS, GNC, Petco, Price Chopper, Tires+, TJ Maxx
180	(from sb), same as 181 w, W [other] Jerry's Auto Repair
179	Main St, E [gas] Conoco [food] Burger King, Capestre Mexican, Capt D's, Popeye's, Providence Pizzeria [other] $General, Firestone/auto, Holiday Inn Express, to Longview Lake CP, W [gas] Phillips 66/dsl [food] Taco Bell, Waffle House [other] transmissions, USPO, Walgreens
178	140th St, W [gas] Phillips 66/dsl [food] Pizza Hut [other] $General
177	MO 150, E [gas] Phillips 66/dsl, QT/dsl [food] Sonic, Subway [other] Harley Davidson
176	155th St, to Belton, W [gas] Cenex/dsl [other] $General
175	rd Y, 163rd St, Belton, E [food] Cracker Barrel [lodging] Hampton Inn [other] [H], W [gas] Phillips 66/dsl, QT/dsl [food] Fazoli's, Knead-er's, Pizza Hut, Taco Bueno [other] AutoZone, CVS, Hobby Lobby, Marshall's, Menards, O'Reilly Parts, Petco, Price Chopper, Ross
174	MO 58, Belton, E [gas] QT/dsl, Shell/dsl [food] Burger King, China Star, Church's, Firehouse Subs, Golden Corral, KFC, MOD Pizza, Panda Express, Papa John's, Pizza Hut, Qdoba, Steak'n Shake, Taco Bell, Waffle House, Wendy's [lodging] Quality Inn [other] Advance Parts, AT&T, Big O Tire, Chrysler/Dodge/Jeep, Firestone/auto, [H], Lowe's, Sam's Club/dsl, Transwest RV Ctr, Walmart/Subway, W [food] Applebee's, Arby's, Buffalo Wild Wings, Chipotle, Freddy's, Hawaiian Bros, IHOP, Jimmy John's, Jose Pepper's, Longhorn Steaks, McDonald's, Panera Bread, Papa Murphy's, Pepper Jax Cafe, Starbucks, Subway, TX Roadhouse [lodging] EconoLodge, Fairfield Inn [other] $Tree, Aldi Foods, Discount Tire, Express Auto Service, GNC, Home Depot, HyVee/dsl, Jo-Ann, Kohl's, Petsmart, Target, Verizon, Walgreens
172	N Cass Pkwy
168	Peculiar Way
167	MO C, J, Peculiar, E [gas] Casey's, FLYING J/Denny's/dsl/Lp/scales/24hr [food] Subway [lodging] Highland Inn [other] Peculiar RV Park, W [food] Sonic [other] CountryMart/dsl, USPO
160	MO 291 N, Harrisonville, E [gas] Casey's/dsl, Murphy USA, QT/dsl [food] Applebee's, Arby's, Branding Iron BBQ, Capt D's, El Maguey Mexican, Hardee's, Jimmy John's, KFC, McDonald's, Subway, Sunrise Chinese, Taco Bell, Wendy's [lodging] Best Value Inn, Budget Motel, Harrisonville Inn [other] $Tree, AT&T, GNC, [H], vet, Walmart, W [other] Ford
159	MO 2 W, 7 N, Mechanic St, Harrisonville, E [gas] BP, Casey's/dsl, Phillips 66/dsl [food] Burger King, China Wok, DQ, Papa Murphy's, Pizza Hut, Starbucks [other] CVS, DLS Tire/auto, Price Chopper, Verizon, vet, Walgreens
158	MO 2 E, Commercial Blvd, Harrisonville, E [gas] Conoco/dsl, Phillips 66 [food] Best Burrito [lodging] Comfort Inn [other] Russell Stover, Sutherland's, W [gas] Love's/McDonald's/Subway/dsl/scales/24hr
157mm	**weigh sta both lanes**
157	MO 7 S, to Clinton, E [other] [airport], W [gas] BP/dsl, Sapp Bros/dsl/scales/24hr [lodging] Slumber Inn
153	307th St
148mm	S Grand River
147	MO A, B, Archie, Drexel, W [gas] Phillips 66, Phillips 66/dsl [food] Mama's Kitchen, S [other] $General
144	MO E, AA, Crescent Hill
141	MO 18, Adrian, to Clinton, W [gas] Casey's/dsl [food] Gray's Cafe [other] $General
136	rds D, F, Passaic, to Butler, W [other] McBee's Bratwurst/BBQ

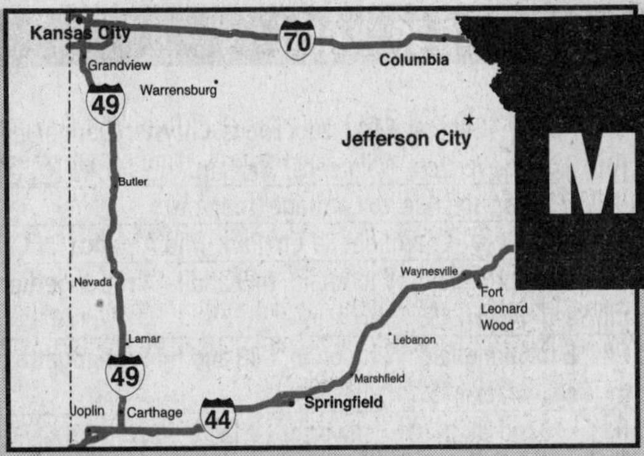

MO

131	MO 52 W, Butler, Amoret, E [gas] Conoco [food] McDonald's, Pizza Hut, Sonic, Subway, Taco Bell [lodging] Days Inn, Super 8 [other] $General, Chrysler/Dodge/Jeep/Ford, [H], O'Reilly Parts, Walmart, W [food] El Charro
130	US 71 Bus (from nb), to Butler
129	MO 52 E, Appleton City
120	rds B, A, Rich Hill, to Osceola, W [gas] Phillips 66/dsl [food] Swope's Drive In [other] $General, Food Fair Mkt/drug
116	Rd TT, to Panama
112	Horton, W [other] Farm Mkt
110	Rd D, Stotesbury
107	Rd M, Compton Jct
103	Highland Ave, to Nevada, W [other] $General, Buick/Chevrolet/GMC, Osage Prairie RV Park
102b	49 Bus, W [other] same as 103
102a	US 54, Nevada, to El Dorado Springs, W [gas] MFA/dsl/e85 [food] 54 Cafe [other] Centennial Park, Highly Tires
101	Rd K, Nevada, to Camp Clark, E [gas] Conoco/dsl, W [gas] Hot Spot/dsl, Murphy USA/dsl, Pilot/dsl/scales/24hr [food] Burger King, Buzz's BBQ, Pizza Hut, Sonic, Subway [lodging] Best Value Inn, Country Inn&Suites, Holiday Inn Express, Nevada Inn, Super 8 [other] AutoZone, Chrysler/Dodge/Jeep/Ford, Verizon, Walmart/Subway, Wilson Tire
95	Rd E, Milo
91	Rds DD, BB, to Bellamy
88	Rds B, N, Sheldon, Bronaugh, E [other] to Stockton Lake (33 mi)
83	Rds C, V, Irwin
80	Rds EE, DD
77	US 160, Lamar, Mindenmines, E [gas] Phillips 66, Sinclair/dsl/scales/24hr [food] Bamboo House, McDonald's, Pizza Hut, Sonic, Subway, Taco Bell, Taco Palace [lodging] Blue Top Inn, Super 8 [other] $Tree, Blue Top Quiltshop, O'Reilly Parts, truckwash, W [gas] Murphy USA/dsl, Phillips 66/Roady's/dsl [food] DQ [other] [H], Lamar Truck/tire, Walmart
74	30th Rd
70	MO 126, Golden City, Pittsburg
66	Rds K, H, Jasper, W [gas] Judy's Trkstp/Cafe/dsl, Phillips 66/dsl [other] $General
63	Rds N, M
56	Garrison Ave (from sb), to Carthage, E [lodging] Best Inn (2mi)
55	Civil War Rd, to Carthage
53	MO 571 S, MO 96, MO 171 N, Central Ave, Carthage, E [gas] Casey's/dsl, Phillips 66/dsl [food] Arby's, Boomer's BBQ, Burger King, LJ Silver, McDonald's, Sirloin Stockade, Sonic, Subway [lodging] Days Inn [other] $General, King Cashsaver
51	Fairview Ave, to Carthage
50	Rd HH, Fir Rd, E [gas] Murphy USA, Phillips 66/McDonald's/dsl [food] Big Ben's BBQ, Hardee's, Iggy's Diner, KFC, Little Caesar's, Peck&Jen's Custard, Taco Bell, Wendy's [lodging] Quality Inn,

BELTON HARRISONVILLE NEVADA CARTHAGE

MO

INTERSTATE 49 Cont'd

50	Continued Super 8 $General, $Tree, Aldi Foods, Chrysler/Dodge/Jeep, Ford, Lowe's, Verizon, Walgreens, Walmart/Subway, W
49	MO 571, Garrison Ave, to Carthage (from nb)
47	Cedar Rd, W Coachlight RV Ctr/Park, Mid America RV Ctr
46mm	I-44, E to Springfield, W to Joplin. **I-49 and I-44 run together 7 mi. See I-44, exit 15.**
39b	I-44, E to Springfield, W to Joplin. **I-49 and I-44 run together 7 mi. See I-44, exit 15.**
39a	Rd FF, 32nd St, E Kenworth, W FLYING J/Denny's/dsl/LP/scales/24hr/ Blue Beacon, Goodyear Tires/repair, Speedco
35	Rd V, Diamond, E G Washington Carver NM
33	MO 175, Gateway Dr, W Phillips 66/dsl/deli Shoal Creek RV Park
30	Iris Rd
27	MO 86, to Neosho, Racine, E Loves/McDonald's/Subway/dsl/scales/24hr, Phillips 66/dsl, W Freightliner
24	US 60, to Neosho, Seneca, E Kum&Go/dsl/e85, Murphy USA Burger King, Burger King, Denny's, El Charro, KFC, LJ Silver, Taco Bell Best Western, Super 8 $Tree, Aldi, Lowe's, Verizon, Walmart, W Whispering Woods RV Park (12 mi)
20	Rd AA
17	Rds C, B, to Goodman, E truck repair
16	MO 59 (from sb), Kelley Springs
10	MO 76, to Anderson, W Cenex/Subway/dsl Mazzio's EconoLodge Harps/dsl
7	Rd EE, to Pineville, Lanagan, E Sugar Island Camping
5	Rd H, to Pineville.

I-49 begins/ends, US 71 continues S, W Lazy Days Camping

INTERSTATE 55

ST LOUIS

Exit #	Services
209mm	Missouri/Illinois state line at St. Louis, Mississippi River
209b	to I-70 W to Kansas Citys
209a	W Busch Stadium, to Arch
208	Park Ave, 7th St, W BP Rally's, Taco Bell, White Castle Hilton
207c b	I-44W, Truman Pkwy, to Tulsa
207a	Gravois St (from nb), E Midwest Petroleum, W A-1 Chinese Wok, Jack-in-the-Box
206c	Arsenal St, E Anheuser-Busch Tour Ctr, W Shell/dsl
206b	Broadway (from nb), Broadway (from nb)
206a	Potomac St (from nb)
205	Gasconade, W
204	Broadway, E Phillips 66, W Conoco/dsl Hardee's, McDonald's, Subway Family$, O'Reilly Parts, Walgreens
203	Bates St, Virginia Ave, W BP 7-11
202c	Loughborough Ave, W Burger King, China King, Little Caesar's, Qdoba, St Louis Bread Co, Starbucks AutoZone, Firestone/auto, Lowe's Whse, Schnuck's Foods
202b	Germania (from sb)
202a	Carondelet (from nb)
201b	Weber Rds
201a	Bayless Ave, E BP McDonald's, W 7-11/gas, Mobil/dsl DQ, Jack-in-the-Box, Subway, Taco Bell auto repair
200	Union Rd (from sb)
199	Reavis Barracks Rd, E Shell/Circle K STL BBQ
197	US 50, US 61, US 67, Lindbergh Blvd, E Phillips 66 Applebee's, Arby's, Buffalo Wild Wings, ChuckeCheese, CiCi's, Dillar... Hometown Buffet, HoneyBaked Ham, Hooters, IHOP, Imo's P... za, KFC, Krispy Kreme, McAlister's, Noodles&Co, Penn Sta Su... Qdoba, Starbucks, Steak'n Shake, Subway, Taco Bell, Tuck... Place, Wendy's Holiday Inn AT&T, Best Buy, Chrysl... Dodge/Jeep, CVS Drug, Dick's, Dobbs Tire, Ford/Lincoln, Ho... Depot, JC Penney, Jo-Ann Fabrics, Macy's, Marshall's, NTB, Ve... zon, vet, W QT/dsl Bob Evans, Culvers, Denny's, Gold... Corral, O'Charley's, Panda Express, Pasta House Best Val... Inn Aldi Foods, AT&T, CarMax, Chevrolet, Costco/gas, Ho... da, Hyundai, Kia, Mazda, Nissan, Target, VW
196b	I-270 W, to Kansas City
196a	I-255 E, to Chicago
195	Butler Hill Rd, E Phillips 66 Hampton Inn Advan... Parts, Walgreens, Holiday Inn Express, Popeye's, W Phi... lips 66 Burger King, Hardee's, Subway, Taco Bell, Waf... House Schnuck's Foods, tires/repair
193	Meramec Bottom Rd, E QT/dsl Cracker Barrel Be... Western Midwest RV Ctr
191	MO 141, Arnold, E QT 54th St Grill, Applebee's, A... by's, Bandana's BBQ, Capt D's, Chick-fil-A, China King, De... ny's, Dunkin'/Baskin Robbins, Fazoli's, Five Guys, Jack-in-th... Box, Jimmy John's, Las Fuentes, Lee's Chicken, Lion's Choi... LJ Silver, McDonald's, Panda Express, Papa John's, Rally... Starbucks, Steak'n Shake, Super China Buffet, Taco Bell, Te... razza Grill, Wendy's Drury Inn, Pear Tree Inn A... Foods, AT&T, CVS Drug, Dobbs Tire, Gordman's, Hobby Lo... by, Kohl's, NAPA, O'Reilly Parts, PetCo, Shop'n Save Foo... vet, Walgreens, Walmart/Subway, W Phillips 66/Circle... dsl Chili's, First Wok, Pasta House, Penn Sta Subs, Qdob... St Louis Bread, Sunny St Cafe, TX Roadhouse Woodspri... Suites $Tree, Dierberg's Foods, GNC, Lowe's, Office Dep... Petsmart, Ross, Verizon
190	Richardson Rd, E BP/McDonald's, Hucks, Phillips 66/d... Shell/Circle K/dsl Culver's, Domino's, DQ, Pizza Hut, Po... derosa, Taco Bell, White Castle $Tree, Advance Parts, Au... Tire, Firestone, Save-A-Lot Foods, URGENT CARE, W Phi... lips 66/dsl, Shell/Circle K/dsl Burger King, Front Row Gri... Happy Wok, Imo's Pizza, McDonald's/playplace, Mr. Goodcen... Subs, Ruby Tuesday, Waffle House Quality Inn 7-1... Aamco, AutoZone, GNC, Home Depot, Plaza Tire, Schnuck... Foods, Target, Walgreens
186	Imperial, Kimmswick, E Mobil, Shell/Circle K Big Car... BBQ, Blue Owl (1mi) auto repair, W Phillips 66/Jac... in-the-Box/dsl China Wok, Domino's, Ginono's Grill, Pap... John's, Scottie's Grill, Subway to Mastodon SP, USPO
185	rd M, Barnhart, Antonia, W Phillips 66, Phillips 66... dsl Karsch's Mkt, USPO, Walgreens
180	rd Z, to Hillsboro, Pevely, E Mobil/dsl Burger Kin... Domino's, Main St BBQ, Pizza Hut, Subway, Taco Bell $Gen... eral, Queens Foods, W Mr Fuel/dsl, Phillips 66/McDonald'... dsl/scales Super 8 auto repair, rv camping
178	Herculaneum, E QT/Wendy's/dsl/scales, Shell/Circle... Cracker Barrel, DQ, Jack-in-the-Box, La Pachanga Mexica... Subway Toyota, Little Caesar's, W Buick/GMC, Cadi... lac/Chevrolet, Ford, vet
175	rd A, Festus, E Mobil, Murphy USA/dsl, Phillips 66/d... Arby's, Bob Evans, Burger King, Capt D's, China 1, Fazoli'... Hibachi Grill, Imo's Pizza, Jack-in-the-Box, McDonald's/play... place, Oriental Buffet, Panda Express, Papa John's, Sonic, S... Louis Bread Co, Steak'n Shake, Subway, Taco Bell, White Cast...

INTERSTATE 55 Cont'd

175 Continued
La Quinta, Quality Inn $Tree, Advance Parts, Aldi Foods, AT&T, AutoZone, CVS Drug, Dobbs Tire, GNC, Home Depot, Plaza Tire, Schnuck's Foods/gas, URGENT CARE, Walgreens, Walmart, Verizon, W Phillips 66/7-11/dsl, Phillips 66/Domino's/dsl Hardee's, Jimmy John's, Ruby Tuesday, Waffle House, Whittaker's Pizza Comfort Inn, Holiday Inn Express Chrysler/Dodge/Jeep, Lowe's

174b a US 67, Lp 55, Festus, Crystal City, E Phillips 66/dsl H

170 US 61, W BP/dsl/LP Gators Grill

165 rd TT (from sb)

162 rds DD, OO

160mm **nb/weigh sta sb, full facilities, litter barrels, petwalk, , vending**

157 rd Y, Bloomsdale, E Phillips 66/Subway, W Love's/Chester's/McDonald's/dsl/scales/24hr

154 rd O, to St Genevieve

150 MO 32, rds B, A, to St Genevieve, E BP DQ H, Hist Site (6mi), W Phillips 66/dsl Hawn SP (11mi)

143 rds J, M, N, Ozora, W Exxon/Subway/dsl/scales/24hr Econolodge truckwash

141 rd Z, St Mary

135 rd M, Brewer

129 MO 51, to Perryville, E MotoMart/McDonald's/dsl Burger King, KFC, Ponderosa, Taco Bell H, Ford, W Rhodes/IMO's/dsl China Buffet, Five Star Chinese, Subway Comfort Inn, Days Inn, Super 8 AT&T, Buick/Chevrolet, Chrysler/Dodge/Jeep, Walmart, Holiday Inn

123 rd B, Biehle, W Rhodes/dsl

119mm Apple Creek

117 rd KK, to Appleton

111 rd E, Oak Ridge

110mm **sb/full facilities, truck parking nb**

105 US 61, Fruitland, E Casey's, Phillips 66/dsl, Rhodes/dsl $General, Purcell Tires/repair, Trail of Tears SP (11mi), W D-Mart/dsl Bavarian Halle, DQ, Pizza Inn Drury Inn

102 LaSalle Ave, E Main St

99 US 61, MO 34, to Jackson, E RV camping, W Delmonico's Steaks Comfort Suites Hill Top RV, McDowell South RV Ctr

96 rd K, to Cape Girardeau, E Phillips 66/dsl Applebee's, Buffalo Wild Wings, Burger King, Chick-fil-A, China Town, CiCi's Pizza, Cracker Barrel, Daddy's Cheesecake, Denny's, Dexter BBQ, DQ, El Acapulco, Firehouse Subs, Golden Corral, Great Wall Chinese, Honey Baked Ham, IHOP, Logan's Roadhouse, O'Charley's, Olive Garden, Panera Bread, Papa Murphy's, Popeye's, Qdoba, Red Lobster, Ruby Tuesday, Starbucks, Steak'n Shake, Subway, Taco Bell, TX Roadhouse, Wendy's Auburn Place, Drury Lodge/rest., Hampton Inn, Holiday Inn Express, PearTree Inn H, AT&T, Barnes&Noble, Best Buy, BigLots, CVS Drug, Hobby Lobby, JC Penney, Macy's, Old Navy, Schnuck's Foods, to SEMSU, Verizon, W Shell McDonald's/playplace, Outback Steaks, Penn Sta Subs, White Castle Drury Suites, Quality Inn $Tree, Chrysler/Dodge/Jeep, Honda, Hyundai, Kohl's, Lowe's, Mazda, Nissan, PetCo, Plaza Tire, Sam's Club, Sears Grand, Staples, Target, TJ Maxx, Toyota, Walmart/Subway

95 MO 74 E, E Mercato/dsl Candlewood Suites URGENT CARE, W Menard's

93a b MO 74 W, Cape Girardeau

MINER

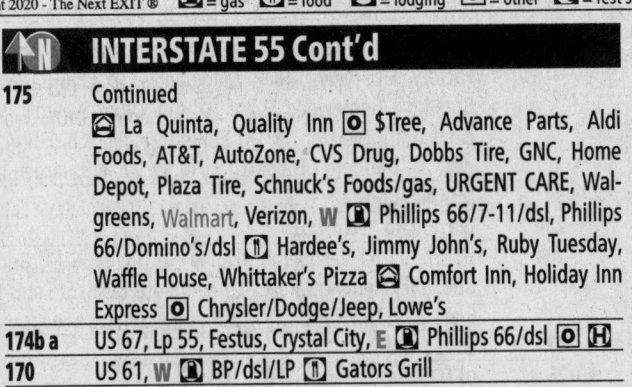

91 rd AB, to Cape Girardeau, E Rhodes/IMO's/dsl Staxx Diner Harley-Davidson, tire repair, vet, W Capetown RV Ctr

89 US 61, rds K, M, Scott City, E Rhodes Burger King, Ice Cream Corner, Las Brisas Mexican, Pizza Hut, Pizza Pro, Subway $General, Bob's Foods, Medicap Drug, NAPA, Plaza Tire/auto

87 MO PP

80 MO 77, Benton, E Express/dsl, W Exxon/McDonald's/dsl/fireworks Subway antiques, winery (8mi)

69 rd HH, to Sikeston, Miner, E Peterbilt, W H, golf

67 US 60, US 62, Miner, E Breaktime/dsl Best Value Inn, Best Western+, Motel 6 Hinton RV Park, 0-2 mi W Conoco, Hucks, Jasper's Gas, Mobil, QuickCheck Bo's BBQ, Buffalo Wild Wings, Burger King, Dexter BBQ, El Tapatio Mexican, Lambert's Rest., Little Caesar's, McDonald's, Papa Murphy's, Pizza Hut, Pizza Inn, Ruby Tuesday, Sergio's Mexican, Sonic, Subway, Taco John's, Wendy's Comfort Inn, Country Hearth Inn, Drury Inn, PearTree Inn, Super 8 H, $General, AutoZone, Buick/Chevrolet, Cadillac/GMC, CVS Drug, Family$, Food Giant, Food Giant, Raben Tires, Sikeston Outlets/famous brands, Walgreens

66b US 60 W, to Poplar Bluff, 3 mi W on US 61/62 Breaktime/E-85 A&W/LJ Silver, Applebee's, Arby's, China Buffet, Colton's Steaks, DQ, El Bracero Mexican, Hardee's, La Ruleta Mexican, McDonald's, Sonic, Taco Bell Days Inn, Holiday Inn Express $Tree, Aldi Foods, AT&T, Chrysler/Dodge/Jeep, Ford/Lincoln, GNC, JC Penney, Lowe's, O'Reilly Parts, Walmart/Subway, Hampton Inn, Love's/Dunkin'/dsl/scales/24hr, Watami, Zaxby's

66a I-57 E, to Chicago, US 60 W

59mm St Johns Bayou

58 MO 80, Matthews, E TA/Taco Bell/dsl/scales/24hr/@ to Big Oak Tree SP (24mi), truck repair, W FLYING J/Denny's/dsl/LP/RV dump/scales/24hr, LNG, Love's/Chester's/Subway/dsl/scales/24hr repair

52 rd P, Kewanee, E Mobil/BJ Trvl Ctr/BBQ/dsl

49 US 61, US 62, New Madrid, E Hunter-Dawson HS (3mi)

44 US 61, US 62, Lp 55, New Madrid, E Higgerson School Hust Site

42mm **sb/full facilities, truck parking nb**

40 rd EE, St Jude Rd, Marston, E Pilot/Subway/dsl/scales/24hr Hunter Lodge, W MFA Travelodge

32 US 61, MO 162, Portageville, W Casey's, Phillips 66/dsl China King, McDonald's, Sonic, Subway $General

27 rds K, A, BB, to Wardell, E RV camping (2mi), W Delta Research Ctr

20mm **nb, full facilities, litter barrels, petwalk, , picnic table, vending**

HAYTI

19 MO 84, Hayti, E Double Nickel/dsl, Pilot/Arby's/dsl/scales/24hr, Shell KFC/Taco Bell, McDonald's, Pizza Hut Quality Inn, Regency Motel Lady Luck Casino/camping, Burger King, W Exxon/Hayti Trvl Ctr/Subway/dsl,

MO

INTERSTATE 55 Cont'd

19	Continued Phillips/dsl, R&P/dsl Apple Barrel, Chubby's BBQ, Los Portales, Patty Ann's BBQ Drury Inn H, $General, CarQuest, Fred's Store, Hay's Foods, repair, USPO
17b a	I-155 E, US 412, to TN
14	rds J, H, U, to Caruthersville, Braggadocio
10mm	**weigh sta nb**
8	US 61, MO 164, Steele, E truck repair, W Shell/Subway/dsl/scales Deerfield Inn
4	rd E, to Holland, Cooter
3mm	**truck parking both lanes**
1	US 61, rd O, Holland, W Shell/dsl/24hr
0mm	Missouri/Arkansas state line

INTERSTATE 57

Exit #	Services
22mm	Missouri/Illinois state line, Mississippi River
18.5mm	**weigh sta both lanes**
12	US 62, MO 77, Charleston, E FLYING J/Huddle House/dsl/scales/24hr Eagle Inn JSH Towing/repair, W Casey's/dsl Las Brisas Mexican Super 8 vet, Waffle&Pancake House
10	MO 105, Charleston, E Exxon/Boomland/dsl McDonald's, Wally's Eatery Boomland RV Park, W Casey's China Buffet, Pizza Hut, Subway Quality Inn city park, CountryMart Foods, Plaza Tire
4	rd B, Bertrand
1b a	I-55, N to St Louis, S to Memphis.

I-57 begins/ends on I-55, exit 66.

INTERSTATE 64

ST LOUIS

Exit #	Services
41mm	Missouri/Illinois state line, Mississippi River
40b a	Broadway St, to Stadium, to the Arch, N Hilton, Sheraton, stadium, S Dobb's Tire
40c	(from wb), I-44 W, I-55 Ss
39c	11th St (exits left), downtown
39b	14th St, N Sheraton, S BP, downtown
39a	21st St, Market St (from wb), N Drury Inn, Hampton Inn
38d	Chestnut at 20th St, N Drury Inn, Hampton Inn
38c	Jefferson Ave, St Louis Union Sta, N Joplin House, S Residence Inn
38a	Forest Park Blvd (from wb), N Shell
37b a	Market St, Bernard St, Grand Blvd, N Shell Del Taco Adam's Mark Hotel, Courtyard, Drury Inn, Hampton Inn, Hyatt, Marriott
36d	Vandeventer Ave, Chouteau Aves
36b a	Kingshighway, N H, S BP
34d c	Hampton Ave, Forest Park, N museums, zoo, S BP, Mobil, Phillips 66 Courtesy Diner, Hardee's, Imo's Pizza, Jack-in-the-Box, Smokin' Al's BBQ, Steak'n Shake, Subway, Taco Bell Hampton Inn
34a	Oakland Ave, N BP Del Taco, Subway H
33d	McCausland Ave, N BP Del Taco
33c	Bellevue Ave, N H
33b	Big Bend Blvd
32b a	Eager Rd, Hanley Rd, S Shell Chick-fil-A, Chipotle, Lion's Choice, McDonald's, Panda Express, Subway Best Buy, Dierberg's Foods, Home Depot, Petco, Petsmart, REI, Target, Trader Joe's, Whole Foods Mkt

CHESTERFIELD

31b a	I-170 N, N Burger King, CA Pizza Kitchen, Cheese Factory, Five Guys, IHOP, Maggiano's, PF Chang's, St Bread Homewood Suites CVS Drug, Dillard's, Ma Nordstrom, Verizon, S Bonefish Grill, Chick-fil-A, way Dierberg's Foods, Drury Inn, Michael's, Target
30	McKnight Rd
28b	Clayton Rd (from wb)
28a	US 67, US 61, Lindbergh Blvd, N Honda, S Brick Brio Grill, Fleming's Rest., Schneithouse Rest., St Louis Br Starbucks, Tim Hortons Hilton Shnuck's Foods
27	Spoede Rd
26	rd JJ, Ballas Rd, N H, S H
25	I-270, N to Chicago, S to Memphis
24	Mason Rd, N Courtyard, Marriott hwy patrol, LDS Ter
23	Maryville Centre Dr (from wb), N Courtyard, Marriott
22	MO 141, N H, S Five Guys, Hot Wok
21	Timberlake Manor Pkwy
20	Chesterfield Pkwy (from wb), same as 19b a
19b a	MO 340, Chesterfield Pkwy, Olive Blvd, N BP, Shell C lie Gitto's, Sheridan's Custard, Taco Bell DoubleTree H Hampton Inn, Homewood Suites, Residence Inn, Spring Suites Dobb's Tire, Schnucks Foods, USPO, Walgre S Mobil California Pizza Kitchen, Cheesecake Fact Chili's, Edgewild Rest., PF Chang's, Twin Peaks Drury Pl Hotel, Hyatt Place Dillard's, mall
17	Boones Crossing, Long Rd, Chesterfield Airport Rd, N P tige Outlets/famous brands, S Mobil 54th St Grill, Louie, Brickhouse Tavern, Buffalo Wild Wings, Cane's, Ch fil-A, Culver's, East Coast Pizza, Fox&Hound, Hardee's, IH Jason's Deli, Kaldi's Coffee, Lion's Choice, Longhorn Ste McDonald's, Mimi's Cafe, Old Spaghetti Factory, Olive Garc Original Pancakes, Panda Express, Pie Five, Qdoba Mexic Red Lobster, Red Robin, SmokeHouse Rest., Sonic, St Lo Bread, St Louis Bread, Steak'n Shake, Subway, Syberg's C Taco Bell, Wendy's Courtyard, Hampton Inn, Hilton G den $Tree, Aldi Foods, AutoTire Care, AutoZone, Best B Dick's, Dobb's Tire, Firestone/auto, Ford, GNC, Gordma Home Depot, Lowe's, Michael's, Old Navy, Petsmart, Ro Sam's Club, Target, Verizon, Walgreens, Walmart, WorldMkt
16	Long Rd (from wb)
14	Chesterfield Airport Rd (from eb), S BP/dsl, Phillips dsl Comfort Inn Premium Outlets/famous brands
13mm	Missouri River
11	Research Park Ctr Dr, S Wingate Inn
10	MO 94 (from wb), N Mercedes
9	rd k, O'Fallon, N Mobil, QT/dsl Arby's, Cracker Bar Culver's, Denny's, Las Margaritas, McDonald's, Starbucks, S way, Walnut Grill, Wendy's Holiday Inn Express, Reside Inn, Sleep Inn, Staybridge Suites Chevrolet, Honda, H, W greens
6	rd DD, Wing Haven Blvd, N Phillips 66 Bristol Seafo Hunan King, Massa's Italian, Outback Steaks, Subway H ton Garden vet
4	rd N, N Phillips 66 Qdoba Mexican, Red Robin Penney, Petco, Shop'n Save, Target, S Murphy USA/c Phillips 66 Arby's, El Maguay, Jack-in-the-Box, McDonalc Sonic, St. Louis Bread Co., Starbucks, Steak'n Shake, Subw Taco Bell, Wendy's, White Castle $Tree, Aldi Foods, Au Zone, Dobb's Tire, Firestone/auto, GNC, Lowe's, Walmart
2	Lake St. Louis Blvd, N Hucks/dsl BC's Rest., Max& ma's Old Navy, Schnuck's Foods, Von Maur, Walgreens
1	Prospect Rd
0mm	I-70 E to St Louis, W to Kansas City

INTERSTATE 70

Exit #	Services
251.5mm	Missouri/Illinois state line, Mississippi River
251a	I-55 S, to Memphis, to I-44, to downtown/no return
249b	Tucker Blvd, downtown St Louis, S Mobil/dsl
249a	I-44 W, I-55 S
248b	St Louis Ave, Branch St
248a	Salisbury St, McKinley Br, S BP, Phillips 66
247	Grand Ave, N BP, Phillips 66/Subway/dsl Western Inn
246b	Adelaide Ave
246a	N Broadway, O'Fallon Park, N Loves/McDonald's/Subway/dsl/scales/24hr, Mobil/dsl Freightliner, truck tires
245b	W Florissant
245a	Shreve Ave, S BP
244b	Kingshighway, S BP Burger King, McDonald's, Subway Walgreens
244a	Bircher Blvd, Union Blvd, N BP/dsl, Mobil/dsl
243b	(243c from eb)Bircher Blvd
243a	Riverview Blvd
243	Goodfellow Blvd, N BP, Conoco/dsl
242b a	Jennings Sta Rd, S Western Inn
241b	Lucas-Hunt Rd, N Shell/Circle K, 3/4 mi S Church's, Lee's Chicken, McDonald's Walgreens
241a	Bermuda Rd, S H
240b a	Florissant Rd, N BP/McDonald's Family$, Schnuck's Foods
239	N Hanley Rd, N Hilton Garden, S BP
238c b	I-170 N, I-170 S, no return
238a	N Lambert-St Louis Airport, S Renaissance Hotel
237	Natural Bridge Rd (from eb), S Phillips 66, Shell Church's, Jack-in-the-Box, Rally's, Steak'n Shake, Waffle House Ramada Inn, Renaissance, Travelodge
236	Lambert-St Louis Airport, S BP/dsl Bandana's BBQ, Golden Pancake, Lombardo's Café Rafferty's Rest., Subway Best Value Inn, Drury Inn, Econolodge, Hampton Inn, Hilton, Holiday Inn, Holiday Inn Express, Marriott, Peartree Inn, Quality Inn
235c	Cypress Rd, rd B W, N to
235b a	US 67, Lindbergh Blvd, N Airport Plaza Hotel, S Lion's Choice Rest., TGIFriday's Crowne Plaza, Embassy Suites, Extended Stay America Menard's
234	MO 180, St Charles Rock Rd, N BP, Phillips 66/dsl A&W/LJ Silver, Applebee's, Arby's, Chimi's Mexican, Chipotle, Fazoli's, HomeTown Buffet, Imo's Pizza, Jack-in-the-Box, Jimmy John's, LoneStar Steaks, McDonald's, New China Buffet, Pizza Hut, Ponderosa, Red Lobster, St Louis Bread, Subway, Taco Bell, Wendy's, White Castle, Ya Hala Mediterranean H, $Tree, Aldi Foods, AT&T, AutoZone, Best Buy, CVS Drug, Hobby Lobby, Kohl's, Meineke, NTB, Office Depot, Petsmart, Save-A-Lot Foods, Target, Verizon, Walgreens, Walmart/Burger King, S QT IHOP, Lion's Choice Chrysler/Dodge/Jeep, Home Depot, Schnuck's, Shamel Tires/repair, Walgreens
232	I-270, N to Chicago, S to Memphis
231b a	Earth City Expwy, N Motomart, Phillips 66/Jack-in-the-Box/dsl Malone's Grill, McDonald's Candlewood Suites, Courtyard, Extended Stay America, Holiday Inn, Residence Inn, SpringHill Suites, S Mobil Burger King, Dave&Buster's, Subway Holiday Inn Express, Homewood Suites, La Quinta Hollywood Casino/Hotel, Riverport Ampitheatre
230mm	Missouri River

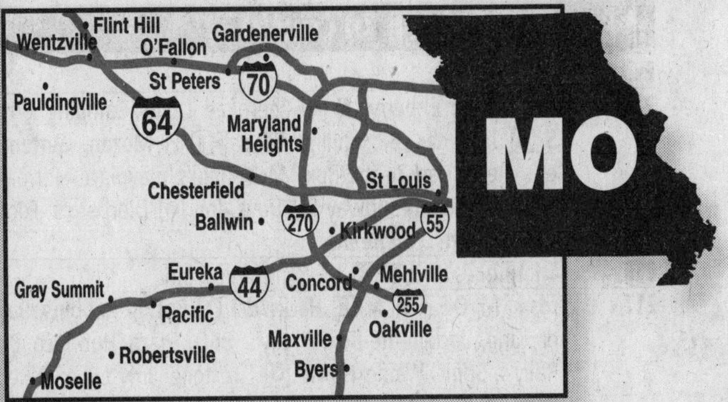

ST CHARLES

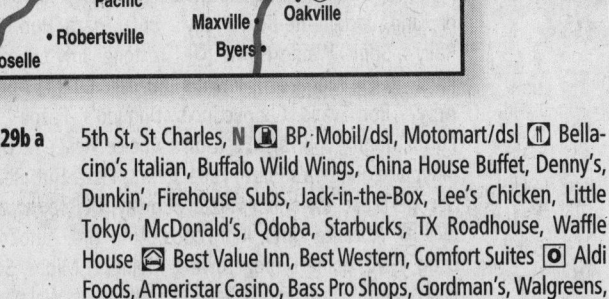

Exit #	Services
229b a	5th St, St Charles, N BP, Mobil/dsl, Motomart/dsl Bellacino's Italian, Buffalo Wild Wings, China House Buffet, Denny's, Dunkin', Firehouse Subs, Jack-in-the-Box, Lee's Chicken, Little Tokyo, McDonald's, Qdoba, Starbucks, TX Roadhouse, Waffle House Best Value Inn, Best Western, Comfort Suites Aldi Foods, Ameristar Casino, Bass Pro Shops, Gordman's, Walgreens, S QT/dsl Bar Louie, Cracker Barrel, Five Guys, Tuscanos Brazilian Drury Suites, Embassy Suites, Fairfield Inn
228	MO 94, to Weldon Springs, access to 227, St Charles, N Mobil/dsl, QT/dsl Arby's, DQ, Imo's Pizza, Papa John's, Steak'n Shake Advance Parts, AutoZone, CVS Drug, GNC, NAPA, Schnuck's, Valvoline, S Mobil/dsl, QT Chinese Express, ChuckECheese, Fazoli's, Gingham's Rest., Grappa Grill, Jimmy John's, McAlister's Deli, Outback Steaks, Pizza Hut, Tilted Kilt Intown Suites $General, Dobb's Tire
227	Zumbehl Rd, access to 228, N Phillips 66/dsl, ZX Culpepper's Grill Super 8 Ford, Lowe's, Sav-A-Lot Foods, S BP, Hucks/dsl Applebee's, Big Woody's BBQ, Bob Evans, Capt D's, El Mariachi Mexican, Fratelli's Ristorante, Golden Corral, Hardee's, Hoho Chinese, Jack-in-the-Box, McDonald's, Papa Murphy's, Penn Sta Subs, Shogun, Smashburger, St Louis Bread, Subway, Taco Bell Red Roof Inn, TownePlace Suites $Tree, Dierberg's Foods, GNC, Jiffy Lube, Michael's, NTB, Petco, Petsmart, Sam's Club/gas, Schnuck's Foods, URGENT CARE, vet, Walgreens, Walmart
225	Truman Rd, to Cave Springs, N Phillips 66/dsl Hampton Inn, Rodeway Inn Buick/GMC, Cadillac, Harley Davidson, Indian Motorcycles, Mazda, Subaru, U-Haul, VW, S Conoco, QT Bandanas BBQ, Burger King, Chimi's Mexican, Culver's, Denny's, Hibachi Grill, Hooters, IHOP, Jack-in-the-Box, KFC, Lion's Choice Rest., LJ Silver, Longhorn Steaks, Los Chavez Mexican, McDonald's, O'Charley's, Pasta House, Red Lobster, Steak'n Shake, Subway, Taco Bell, Thai Kitchen, Wendy's, White Castle Country Inn&Suites, Courtyard H, Advance Parts, AT&T, Batteries+Bulbs, Chrysler/Dodge/Jeep, Firestone, Hobby Lobby, Home Depot, Kia, Office Depot, Shop'n Save, Target, TJ Maxx, URGENT CARE, Verizon
224	MO 370 E
222	Mid-Rivers Mall Dr, rd C, St Peters, N QT/dsl/24hr Burger King CarMax, Chevrolet, Honda, Lincoln, Toyota, S Mobil/dsl Arby's, Bob Evans, Buffalo Wild Wings, Chili's, China Wok, Domino's, Fazoli's, HoneyBaked Ham, Joe's Crabshack, Max & Erma's, McDonald's/playplace, Olive Garden, Planet Sub, Qdoba, Red Robin, Ruby Tuesday, St Louis Bread, Steak'n Shake, Subway, Taco Bell, Wendy's Drury Inn, Extended Stay America Aldi Foods, Barnes&Noble, Best Buy, BigLots, Costco/gas, Dick's, Dillard's, Hyundai/Nissan/VW, JC Penney, Jo-Ann Fabrics, Kia, Macy's, Marshall's, NTB, Verizon

ST PETERS

= gas = food = lodging = other = rest stop Copyright 2020 - The Next E

MO

INTERSTATE 70 Cont'd

O'FALLON

WENTZVILLE

WARRENTON

Exit #	Services
220	MO 79, to Elsberry, N Cherokee Lakes Camping (7mi), S 7-11/gas, BP, Phillips 66/dsl El Mezon, Gettemeier's Rest., Jack-in-the-Box, McDonald's/playplace, Pirrone's Pizzaria, Sonic, Subway Days Inn Dierberg's Foods, O'Reilly Parts, Walgreens
219	T R Hughes Blvd, S QT Comfort Inn
217	rds K, M, O'Fallon, N Hucks/dsl Baskin-Robbins, Burger King, Jack-in-the-Box, Piggy's BBQ, Pizza Hut/Taco Bell, Rally's, Sonic, Waffle House Firestone, Jiffy Lube, O'Reilly Parts, S Mobil/dsl, Phillips 66/dsl, QT Applebee's, Arby's, Bob Evans, Cappuccino's, Domino's, Fazoli's, Golden Corral, Jimmy John's, KFC, Lion's Choice Rest., McDonald's/playplace, Pantera's Pizza, Papa John's, Pizza Hut, Red Robin, St Louis Bread, Stefanina's Pizza, Subway, TX Roadhouse, Wendy's Advance Parts, Aldi Foods, Auto Tire, AutoZone, CVS Drug, GNC, Home Depot, Lowe's, Meineke, Midas, Schnuck's Foods, Shop'n Save Foods, Verizon, Walgreens, Walmart
216	Bryan Rd, N Super 8 Ford, Peterbilt, St Louis RV Ctr, S Conoco, Phillips 66/Jack-in-the-Box/dsl, QT DQ, Little Caesar's, Mr. Goodcents, Wendy's
214	Lake St Louis, N Phillips 66/McDonald's/dsl, S Phillips 66/dsl, Shell/Circle K Denny's, Hardee's Best Value Inn H
212	rd A, N Economy Inn Camping World, S Mobil Pizzamenti's Cafe Regency Plaza Hotel Chrysler/Dodge/Jeep
210b a	I-64, US 40 E, US 61 N, S H
209	rd Z, Church St, New Melle, N DQ Holiday Inn Express, S Phillips 66/dsl Stone Summit Steaks Hampton Inn
208	Pearce Blvd, Wentzville Pkwy, Wentzville, N Mobil/dsl, QT/dsl 54th St Grill, 88 China, Applebee's, Arby's, Bob Evans, Buffalo Wild Wings, Chick-fil-A, China Buffet, Culver's, Domino's, El Maguey, Fritz's Custard, Hardee's, Jack-in-the-Box, Jimmy John's, KFC, Lion's Choice, Little Caesar's, McDonald's, Olive Garden, Panda Express, Papa John's, Penn Sta., Pizza Hut, Pizza Pro, Ruby Tuesday, St Louis Bread, Starbucks, Steak'n Shake, Subway, Sunny St Cafe, Taco Bell, Waffle House, Wendy's, White Castle Fairfield Inn H, $General, AT&T, AutoZone, Chevrolet, Dick's, Dierberg's Foods, Dobb's Tire, GNC, Home Depot, Kohl's, Lowe's, Michael's, NAPA, O'Reilly Parts, Petsmart, Ross, Sam's Club/dsl, Save-A-Lot, Schnuck's Food, Target, URGENT CARE, Verizon, Walgreens, Walmart, S BP/dsl Bandana's BBQ, Chimi's FreshMex, IHOP, TX Roadhouse Super 8 Hyundai, Thomas RV Ctr
204mm	**weigh sta both lanes**
203	rds W, T, Foristell, N Mr Fuel/dsl/scales, TA/BP/Pizza Hut/Popeye's/Taco Bell/dsl/scales/24hr/@ Quality Inn, S Phillips 66/McDonald's/dsl dsl repair
200	rds J, H, F (from wb), Wright City, N Phillips 66/dsl Ruiz Castillo's Mexican (1mi) $General, S BP Subway Super 7 Inn
199	rd J, H, F, Wright City, N Shell/McDonald's/dsl $General, S Super 7 Inn Volvo Trucks
198mm	**both lanes, full facilities, litter barrels, petwalk,**
193	MO 47, Warrenton, N Fast Lane/DQ/dsl, Mobil/dsl 1st Wok, Applebee's, Burger King, China House, Dominos, DQ, El Jimador Mexican, Jack-in-the-Box, Little Caesar's, McDonald's, Pizza Hut, Subway, Waffle House, Wendy's Best Value Inn, Holiday Inn Express, Super 8 Aldi Foods, AT&T, Mosers Foods, Walmart, S BP/dsl, Conoco/dsl, Phillips 66/dsl

COLUMBIA

Exit #	Services
193	Continued Denny's, Imo's Pizza, Papa John's, Taco Bell Bayn Inn AutoZone, CarQuest, Chevrolet, NAPA, O'Reilly P Walgreens
188	rds A, B, to Truxton, S FLYING J/Denny's/dsl/LP/RV Du scales/24hr Motel 6
183	rds E, NN, Y, Jonesburg, **1 mi** N Jonesburg Gardens Ca ing, S Phillips 66/Chester's/dsl USPO
179	rd F, High Hill, S Colonial Inn, Motel 70
175	MO 19, New Florence, N BP/dsl, Shell/dsl/24hr D Jct Cafe, McDonald's Best Inn, Best Value Inn, I Inn auto repair, Stone Hill Winery/gifts (15mi)
170	MO 161, rd J, Danville, N Red's/dsl Kan-Do RV Par Graham Cave SP, S Lazy Day RV Park
169.5mm	**truck parking**
168mm	Loutre River
167mm	**truck parking eb**
161	rds D, YY, Williamsburg, N Cranes/mkt Marle Rest. USPO
155	rds A, Z, to Calwood, N antiques
148	US 54, Kingdom City, N BP/dsl, Phillips 66/Burger Ki dsl Taco Bell MO Tourism Ctr, to Mark Twain Lak Fast Lane/DQ/dsl, Gulf/Gasper's/Arby's/dsl/scales/@, Pe Mobil/Iron Skillet/dsl/scales/24hr/@, Phillips 66/Subway/ scales/24hr Denny's, McDonald's Days Inn, Holi Inn Express, Motel 6, Quality Inn, Super 8 Ozarkland G Wheeler's Truckwash
144	rds M, HH, to Hatton, S fireworks
137	rds DD, J, to Millersburg, Stephens, S Ranch Ho BBQ antiques, Freightliner, to Little Dixie WA (4mi)
133	rd Z, to Centralia, N Gander RV Ctr
131	Lake of the Woods Rd, N BP, Phillips 66/Subway Buckingham BBQ, George's Rest, Sonic Super 8 H ley-Davidson, S Conoco/dsl Jimmy John's Holiday
128a	US 63, to Jefferson City, Columbia, N CNG, Mobil/ QT Bandanas BBQ, Bob Evans, Burger King, China Gard Cracker Barrel, Golden Corral, Hooters, KFC, McDonald's, Pi Hut, Ruby Tuesday, Steak'n Shake, Taco Bell, Wendy's, Wh Castle Best Western+, Fairfield Inn, Hampton Inn, Hil Garden, Red Roof Inn, Residence Inn, SpringHill Suites, Su 8 Bass Pro Shop, Home Depot, Menard's, Pine Grove Park, S BreakTime/dsl Applebee's, Baskin-Robbi Chili's, Chipotle Mexican, CiCi's, Culver's, El Maguey, Fi house Subs, Five Guys, Freddy's, Good Cents Subs, Houliha IHOP, Kobe Japanese, Little Caesar's, Longhorn Steaks, P da Express, Panera Bread, Sonic, Starbucks, Subway, TGI day's Country Inn&Suites, Drury Plaza, Motel 6, Quality I Ramada, Staybridge Suites, Suburban Inn, Wingate Inn $Tree, HyVee Foods, Lowe's/Subway, Patricia's Foods, Sa Club, Staples, Verizon, Walmart/McDonald's
128	Lp 70 (from wb), same as 128a, Columbia, N Shell Ha ee's Honda, S Eastwood Motel H, Big O Ti NAPA
127	MO 763, to Moberly, Columbia, N Waffle House Bu get Host Chrysler/Dodge/Jeep, Fiat, Hyundai, Mazda, To ota, transmissions, VW, S Phillips 66/dsl Super 7 Mo
126	MO 163, Providence Rd, same as 127, Columbia, N Ph lips 66/dsl Country Kitchen Quality Inn, R Roof Inn CarQuest, McKnight Tire, S BreakTim dsl Burger King, Carlito's Mexican, Church's, DQ, LJ Silv McDonald's, Pizza Hut, Subway, Taco Bell H, AutoZor Buick/Cadillac/Chevrolet/GMC, Nissan, O'Reilly Parts

INTERSTATE 70 Cont'd

Exit #	Services
125	Lp 70, West Blvd, same as 124, Columbia, N Comfort Suites, S Phillips 66/dsl Agave Mexican, Cheddar's, Domino's, Fazoli's, Imo's Pizza, JJ's Cafe, Olive Garden, Teppanyaki Grill Days Inn Aldi Foods, BMW, Firestone/auto, Kia, Mercedes, Mosers Foods, Subaru, U-Haul, vet
124	MO 740, rd E, Stadium Blvd, same as 125, Columbia, N Extended Stay America, S BreakTime, Phillips 66/dsl Applebee's, ChuckECheese, Denny's, Five Guys, Hardee's, Jazz Kitchen, KFC, Lee's Chicken, McDonald's, Pancheros, Panera Bread, Pizza Hut, Red Lobster, Ruby Tuesday, Smokehouse BBQ, Sports Zone Grill, Steak'n Shake, Subway, Taco Bell, TX Roadhouse, Wendy's Best Value Inn, Drury Inn, Holiday Inn, La Quinta, Royal Inn $Tree, AT&T, Barnes&Noble, Best Buy, Dick's, Dillard's, Ford, Hobby Lobby, JC Penney, Marshalls, Michael's, Natural Grocers, Old Navy, O'Reilly Parts, PetCo, Petsmart, Target, to U of MO, URGENT CARE, Verizon
122mm	Perche Creek
121	US 40, rd UU, Midway, N Midway/dsl/rest., Phillips 66 Budget Inn tires/repair, S golf
117	rds J, O, to Huntsdale, Harrisburg
115	rd BB N, Rocheport, N to Katy Tr SP, winery
114.5mm	Missouri River
111	MO 98, MO 179, to Wooldridge, Overton, S Cenex/dsl/repair RV Park
106	MO 87, Bingham Rd, to Boonville, S Cenex/dsl
104mm	both lanes, full facilities, litter barrels, petwalk, vending
103	rd B, Main St, Boonville, N Breaktime, Casey's/dsl, Murphy USA/dsl China One Buffet, La Hacienda Mexican, McDonald's, Pizza Hut, Sonic, Subway, Taco Bell Days Inn, Super 8 H, NAPA, RV Express Camping, to Katy Tr SP, Walmart/Subway, S Cenex/dsl Rte B Cafe QT Inn Buick/Chevrolet/GMC
101	US 40, MO 5, to Boonville, N Pilot/Wendy's/dsl/24hr Arby's Comfort Inn, Holiday Inn Express, Isle of Capri Hotel (3mi) Buick/Cadillac/Chevrolet/GMC, Ford, Russell Stover Candies, S Love's/Hardee's/scales/dsl/24hr to Lake of the Ozarks
98	MO 41, MO 135, Lamine, N tires, to Arrow Rock HS (13mi), S Conoco/Ma's Kettle/dsl, Settlers/dsl repair
93mm	Lamine River
89	rd K, to Arrow Rock, N to Arrow Rock HS
84	rd J, N truck repair, Valero/DQ/Stuckey's
78b a	US 65, to Marshall, N Conoco/dsl fireworks, RV Park
77mm	Blackwater River
74	rd YY, N Cenex/Betty's/cafe/dsl/repair/24hr Welcome Motel
71	rds EE, K, to Houstonia
66	MO 127, Sweet Springs, N H, S BreakTime/dsl, Casey's/dsl Brownsville Sta Rest. Night Inn, Super 8 $General, Bumper Parts
65.5mm	Davis Creek
62	rds VV, Y, Emma
58	MO 23, Concordia, N TA/Country Pride/Subway/dsl/scales/24hr/@ El Patron, McDonald's $General, Bratchers Mkt, truck/RV wash, S Breaktime/dsl, Casey's/dsl, Cenex/dsl Dempsey's BBQ, Pizza Hut Best Value Inn, Budget Inn, Days Inn Bumper Parts
57.5mm	both lanes, full facilities, litter barrels, petwalk, vending

MO

Exit #	Services
52	rd T, Aullville
49	MO 13, to Higginsville, N Casey's/dsl, Pilot/McDonald's/Subway/dsl/scales/24hr Sure Stay Inn to Confederate Mem, S Super 8 Great Escape RV Park
45	rd H, to Mayview
43mm	weigh sta both lanes
41	rds O, M, to Lexington, Mayview
38	MO 131 (from wb), same as 37, Odessa, S BP/dsl, Phillips 66/dsl, Shell McDonald's, Pizza Hut, Sonic, Subway, Taco John's, Thompson's Country Kitchen $General Mkt, $Tree, O'Reilly Parts
37	MO 131, same as 38, Odessa, N Country Gardens RV Park/dump, S BP/dsl, Phillips 66/dsl, Shell El Camino Real, McDonald's, Pizza Hut, Sonic, Subway, Taco John's, Thompson's Country Kitchen Parkside Inn $General Mkt, $Tree, fireworks, NAPA, O'Reilly Parts, Sunrise Mkt
35mm	truck parking both lanes
31	rds D, Z, to Bates City, Napoleon, N Bates City RV Camping, S Valero/dsl Bates City BBQ fireworks
29.5mm	Horse Shoe Creek
28	rd H, rd F, Oak Grove, N TA/Country Pride/Popeye's/dsl/scales/24hr/@ Oak Grove Inn Blue Beacon, KOA, S Casey's, Petro/BP/Iron Skillet/DQ/Wendy's/scales/dsl/@, QT/dsl China Buffet, Hardee's, KFC/Taco Bell, McDonald's, Pizza Hut, PJ's Rest., Subway, Waffle House EconoLodge Cash Saver Foods, Lake Paradise RV/Camping (9mi), O'Reilly Parts, SpeedCo Lube, Walgreens, Walmart
24	US 40, rds AA, BB, to Buckner, N Casey's/dsl Papa Murphy's Best Value Inn, Comfort Inn LifeStyle RV Ctr, Price Chopper, vet, S Conoco/Subway/dsl/scales/24hr McDonald's, Sonic Advance Parts, Trailside RV Park/Ctr
21	Adams Dairy Pkwy, N Camping World RV Ctr (1mi), S Murphy USA/dsl, Phillips 66/Burger King/dsl Arby's, Cane's, Chick-fil-A, Chipotle Mexican, Five Guys, Jersey Mike's, Olive Garden, Panda Express, Panera Bread, Pepper Jax Grill, Planet Sub, Sonic, Subway, Taco Bell, TX Roadhouse Courtyard AT&T, GNC, Gordman's, Home Depot, Kohl's, Michael's, NTB, PetCo, Ross, Target, TJ Maxx, Verizon, Walmart
20	MO 7, Blue Springs, N Phillips 66/dsl, QT/dsl Backyard Burger, Bob Evans, China 1, Custard's, Dunkin', Goodcents Subs, Minsky's Pizza, Papa Murphy's, Rancho Grande, Sonic, Subway Best Value Inn, Days Inn, Econolodge, Rodeway Inn $General, Ace Hardware, CVS Drug, NAPA, O'Reilly Parts, PriceChopper Foods, Walgreens, Walmart Mkt, S BP/dsl, QT, Valero/dsl Applebee's, Big Biscuit, Denny's, Firehouse Subs, Jack-in-the-Box, Jimmy John's, KFC, LJ Silver, McDonald's, Original Pizza, Starbucks, Subway, Taco Bell, Taco Bueno, Wendy's, Winsteads Cafe, Zarda's BBQ Hampton Inn, Quality Inn H, Advance Parts, Aldi Foods, AutoZone,

ODESSA

BLUE SPGS

CONCORDIA

MO

INTERSTATE 70 Cont'd

20	Continued BigLots, Chevrolet, Firestone/auto, Goodyear/auto, Hobby Lobby, Hy-Vee Foods/gas, Office Depot, Russell Stover, transmissions, URGENT CARE
18	Woods Chapel Rd, same as 20, N La Quinta, Motel 6, Super 8, Welcome Inn Harley-Davidson, S Conoco/dsl, Phillips 66/dsl, QT, QT (2) China Kitchen, KFC/Taco Bell, Las Playas Mexican, McDonald's, Pizza Hut, Sonic, Subway, Taco John's, Waffle House CVS Drug, Ford, Hyundai
17	Little Blue Pkwy, 39th St, N QT/dsl Buffalo Wild Wings, Coldstone, DQ, Hereford House, Jimmy John's, Joe's Crabshack, Lion's Choice, On the Border, Saints Grill, Sonic, Twin Peaks Hilton Garden H, Menard's, World Mkt, S QT Arby's, BD Mongolian, Carrabba's, Chipotle Mexican, Corner Cafe, Culver's, Golden Corral, Hooters, IHOP, Kobe Steaks, McDonald's, Outback Steaks, Panera Bread, Pie Five, Qdoba, Red Robin, Subway Comfort Suites, Drury Inn, Holiday Inn Express, My Place Candlewood Suites, Carmax, Costco/gas, Lowe's
16mm	Little Blue River, Little Blue River
15b	MO 291 N, Independence, **1 exit N on 39th St** Phillips 66, QT 54th St Grill, Applebee's, Burger King, Chick-fil-A, Chili's, ChuckECheese, Famous Dave's, Fazoli's, Logan's Roadhouse, Longhorn Steaks, McDonald's, Noodles&Co, Perkins, Smokehouse BBQ, Starbucks, Taco Bell, Zio's Italian Fairfield Inn, Residence Inn, Staybridge Suites H, AT&T, AutoZone, Barnes&Noble, Best Buy, Dick's, Dillard's, JC Penney, Jo-Ann, Kohl's, Macy's, Marshalls, NTB, Petsmart, Ross, Sam's Club/gas, Target, Walmart
15a	I-470 S, MO 291 S, to Lee's Summit, same as 14
14	Lee's Summit Rd, **1 mi N** Longhorn Steaks, S Tesla EVC Cheddar's, Cracker Barrel, Los Cabos, Old Chicago, Pizza Ranch, Slim Chickens Stoney Creek Hotel Bass Pro Shops, Duluth Trading, Hobby Lobby, Home Depot
12	Noland Rd, Independence, N Conoco/dsl, QT, Shell China Town, Denny's, Domino's, Hardee's, Mr Goodcents, Pizza St, Sheridan's Custard, Sonic, Subway Best Western, Super 8 $General, Advance Parts, Buick/GMC/Cadillac, Chevrolet, Chrysler/Jeep, CVS Drug, Firestone/auto, Ford, Office Depot, to Truman Library, TrueValue, Walgreens, Walmart Mkt, S Phillips 66/Kicks Arby's, Bandana's BBQ, Baskin Robbins, Burger King, HoneyBaked Ham, KFC/Taco Bell, Krispy Kreme, Ma Ma Garden, McDonald's, Olive Garden, Pizza Hut, Quiznos, Red Lobster, Ruby Tuesday, Steak'n Shake, Wendy's American Inn, Best Value Inn, Days Inn, Quality Inn, Red Roof Inn $Tree, BigLots, GNC, Gordman's, HyVee Foods/gas, Old Time Pottery, Petco, PriceChopper Mkt, Tires+, U-Haul
11	US 40, Blue Ridge Blvd, Independence, N QT A&W/LJ Silver, La Fuentes, Rosie's Cafe, Sonic, Subway, V's Italian, S 7-11, BP, Murphy USA/dsl, Sinclair Applebee's, Big Boy Burgers, Chipotle Mexican, Church's, East Buffet, Firehouse Subs, IHOP, McDonald's, Papa John's, Samurai Chef, Starbucks Family$, GNC, Lowe's, O'Reilly Parts, Verizon, vet, Walmart/Subway
10	Sterling Ave (from eb), same as 11
9	Blue Ridge Cutoff (from wb), N Denny's Adams Mark, Drury Inn, Woodspring Suites, S BP, Phillips 66/Subway Taco Bell Sheraton Sports Complex
8b a	I-435, N to Des Moines, S to Wichita
7b	Manchester Trafficway

INDEPENDENCE

KANSAS CITY

7mm	Blue River
7a	US 40 E, 31st St
6	Van Brunt Blvd, N Conoco/7-11, Phillips 66/dsl, S McDonald's VA H
5c	Jackson Ave (from wb)
5b	31st St (from eb)
5a	27th St (from eb)
4c	23rd Ave
4b	18th St
4a	Benton Blvd (from eb), Truman Rd, N Super Stop/Wendy's/dsl Subway Advance Parts, Save-A-Lot Foods
3c	Prospect Ave, N BP Church's, S McDonald's
3b	Brooklyn Ave (from eb), N BP Church's, S Shell/ McDonald's
3a	Paseo St, S BP/dsl tires
2m	US 71 S, downtown
2l	I-670, to I-35 S
2j	11th St, downtown
2g	I-29/35 N, US 71 N, to Des Moines
2h	US 24 E, downtown
2e	MO 9 N, Oak St, S Phillips 66 Marriott
2d	Main St, downtown
2c	US 169 N, Broadway, S Phillips 66 Marriott
2b	Beardsley Rd
2a	I-35 S, to Wichita
0mm	Missouri/Kansas state line, Kansas River

INTERSTATE 270 (St Louis)

Exit #	Services
15b a	I-55 N to Chicago, S to St Louis. **I-270 begins/ends in Illinois I-55/I-70, exit 20.**
12	IL 159, to Collinsville, **1 mi N** QT/dsl, ZX/dsl App bee's, Denny's, DQ, Hardee's, IHOP, Jack-in-the-Box, Jimm John's, KFC, Little Caesar's, Papa John's, Subway A Foods, AT&T, Chrysler/Dodge/Jeep, Home Depot, Lowe PetsMart, Sam's Club/dsl, Walgreens, Walmart, S H
9	IL 157, to Collinsville, N Comfort Inn, S BP/ Hampton Inn
7	I-255, to I-55 S to Memphis
6b a	IL 111, N FLYING J/Denny's/dsl/scales/24hr Hen Hou Rest. Motel 6 Blue Beacon/scales, Speedco, truck/tra er repair, S Mobil/dsl Denny's, McDonald's/playpla Taco Bell Best Western+, Days Inn, Fairfield Inn, La Quint Super 8 to Pontoon Beach
4	IL 203, Old Alton Rd, to Granite City
3b a	IL 3, N Riverboat Casino, S Phillips 66 Hardee Waffle House Budget Motel, EconoLodge, Economy In Sun Motel KOA, MGM Camping
2mm	Chain of Rocks Canal
0mm	Illinois/Missouri state line, Mississippi River
34	Riverview Dr, to St Louis, N **Welcome Ctr/ both lanes, full facilities, info, litter barrels,** Moto Mart/Subway
33	Lilac Ave, N USPO, S Phillips 66/Jack-in-the-Box/dsl, Q dsl/scales/24hr Hardee's
32	Bellefontaine Rd, N Shell/Circle K China King, M Donald's, Pizza Hut, Steak'n Shake Budget Inn A vance Parts, Family$, Firestone/auto, Schnuck's Food S BP White Castle Aldi Foods
31b a	MO 367, N BP, QT/dsl Jack-in-the-Box, Little Caesar McDonalds, Subway, Taco Bell H, $General, CVS Dru Family$, Shop'n Save Foods, U-Haul, Walgreens

INTERSTATE 270 (St Louis) Cont'd

Exit #	Services
30b a	Hall's Ferry Rd, rd AC, N [gas] Conoco/dsl, QT/dsl, Shell/dsl [food] Applebee's, Capt. D's, White Castle [lodging] Knights Inn [other] Ford/Lincoln, Kia, S [gas] BP/dsl, Conoco, Phillips 66 [food] China Wok, Church's, Cracker Barrel, IHOP, Steak'n Shake, Subway [other] AutoZone, Home Depot, Meineke, O'Reilly Parts, Shop'n Save Foods
29	W Florissant Rd, N [food] China Moon, Jack-in-the-Box, Lion's Choice, Pasta House [other] $General, Aldi Foods, Dobb's Tire/auto, Family$, Firestone, GNC, Ross, S [gas] Phillips 66/dsl, QT/dsl [food] Arby's, Burger King, Domino's, Hibachi Grill, Krispy Kreme, Little Caesar's, McDonald's, Starbucks [other] $General, $Tree, AT&T, NTB, Sam's Club/gas, Walmart
28	Elizabeth Ave, Washington St, N [gas] Phillips 66/dsl [food] Jack-in-the-Box, Subway, Taco Bell [other] Chevrolet, Schnuck's Foods, Walgreens
27	New Florissant Rd, rd N, N [gas] Shell/Circle K [other] CVS Drug
26b	Graham Rd, N Hanley, N [gas] Phillips 66/7-11/dsl [food] Arby's, LJ Silver, Starbucks [lodging] Quality Inn, Red Roof Inn [other] H, $Tree, S [food] McDonald's [lodging] Days Inn [other] $General
26a	I-170 S
25b a	US 67, Lindbergh Blvd, N [gas] BP, Phillips 66, QT/dsl [food] Bandana's BBQ, Burger King, Church's, Domino's, Five Guys, IHOP, Imo's Pizza, Jack-in-the-Box, Jimmy John's, McDonald's, Papa John's, Pizza Hut, Pueblo Nuevo Mexican, Starbucks, Subway, Taco Bell, Waffle House, Wendy's [lodging] Comfort Inn, Holiday Inn Express, InTown Suites, La Quinta [other] $General, AutoZone, Dierberg's Deli, Family$, Firestone/auto, Ford, GNC, Hyundai, NAPA, Nissan, O'Reilly Parts, Sav-a-Lot Foods, Schnuck's Foods, Toyota, Walgreens, S [food] Jimmy John's [lodging] Budget Inn, Crossland Suites [other] Honda, USPO, VW
23	McDonnell Blvd, E [food] Denny's, Quiznos [lodging] Motel 6, W [gas] Mobil/dsl, QT/dsl [food] Arby's, Jack-in-the-Box, Lion's Choice, McDonald's, Steak'n Shake, Subway, Taco Bell [other] Buick/GMC
22b a	MO 370 W, to MO Bottom Rd
20c	MO 180, St Charles Rock Rd, E [gas] BP, Phillips 66/dsl [food] A&W/LJ Silver, Applebees, Arby's, Chick-fil-A, Chimi's Mexican, Chipotle, Fazoli's, Hometown Buffet, Imo's Pizza, Jack-in-the-Box, Jimmy John's, Lonestar Steaks, McDonald's, New China Buffet, Pizza Hut, Qdoba, Red Lobster, St. Louis Bread, Subway, Taco Bell, Wendy's, White Castle, Ya Hala Mediterranean [other] H, $Tree, Aldi Foods, AT&T, AutoZone, Best Buy, CVS Drug, Hobby Lobby, Kohl's, Meineke, NTB, Office Depot, Petsmart, Save-a-Lot, Target, Verizon, Walgreens, Walmart/Burger, W [gas] QT [food] Bob Evans, Olive Garden, Waffle House [lodging] Best Value Inn, Motel 6, Super 8
20b a	I-70, E to St Louis, W to Kansas City
17	Dorsett Rd, E [food] Bandana's BBQ, Papa John's, Syberg's Grill, Waffle House [lodging] Drury Inn, Hampton Inn, Homewood Suites, W [gas] Mobil, Phillips 66/dsl, Shell [food] Arby's, Denny's, Firehouse Subs, McDonald's, MOD Pizza, Steak'n Shake, Subway [lodging] Motel 6 [other] GNC, Schnuck's Mkt, Walgreens
16b a	Page Ave, rd D, MO 364 W, E [gas] BP, QT, Shell/Circle K/dsl [food] Hardee's, Hooters, McDonald's, Spazio Café, Starbucks [lodging] Comfort Inn, Courtyard, Days Inn, DoubleTree, Extended Stay America, Extended Stay America (2), Extended Stay America (3), Fairfield Inn, Hawthorn Suites, La Quinta, Red Roof Inn, Residence Inn, Sheraton, Sonesta Suites
14	MO 340, Olive Blvd, E [gas] Phillips 66/dsl [food] Applebee's, Bristol Cafe, Five Guys, Granite City, Lion's Choice Rest., McDonald's, Pasta House, Pei Wei, Pieology, Potbelly, Qdoba, Starbucks,

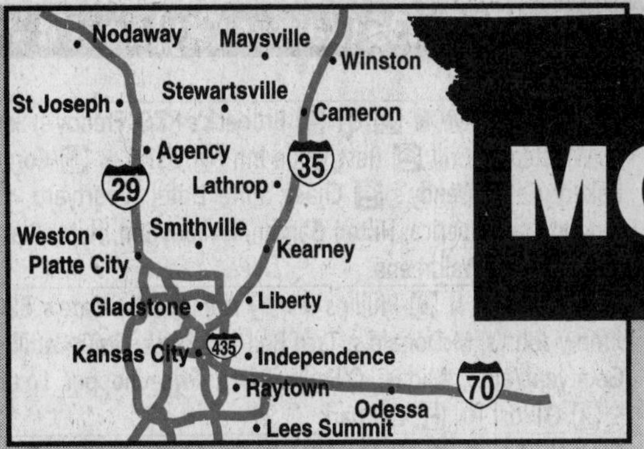

Exit #	Services
14	Continued Subway [lodging] Courtyard, Drury Inn [other] Aldi Foods, AT&T, BMW/Audi/Infiniti, Chevrolet, CVS Drug, Dierberg's Mkt, Land Rover/Jaguar, Lexus, Mercedes, Verizon, W [food] Coldstone, IMO's Pizza, Jet's Pizza, La Salsa, Subway, TGIFriday's [other] H, Dierberg's Foods, Kohl's, Schnuck's Mkt, vet, Walgreens
13	rd AB, Ladue Rd
12b a	I-64, US 40, US 61, E to St Louis, W to Wentzville, E [other] H
9	MO 100, Manchester Rd, E [food] Bravo, Cane's, Chick-fil-A, Elephant Bar, Five Guys, Imo's Pizza, J Gilbert's Rest., Jimmy John's, McAlister's Deli, McDonald's, Qdoba, Subway [other] Barnes&Noble, Dick's, Macy's, Nordstrom, Schnuck's, W [gas] Shell [food] Red Robin
8	Dougherty Ferry Rd, 2 mi S [gas] Citgo/7-11, Mobil [food] McDonald's [other] H
7	Big Ben Rd, N [other] H
5b a	I-44, US 50, MO 366, E to St Louis, W to Tulsa
3	MO 30, Gravois Rd, N [gas] BP, Phillips 66 [food] Bandana BBQ, Olive Garden, Outback Steaks [other] Ford
2	MO 21, Tesson Ferry Rd, N [gas] BP, Mobil [food] 54th St Grill, Baskin Robbins, Burger King, Church's, Jack-in-the-Box, Jimmy John's, Joey B's, Olive Garden, Outback Steaks, Panda Chinese, Pizza Hut, Quizno's, Red Lobster, Shogun Japanese, Subway, Taco Bell, TGIFriday's, Waffle House, White Castle [other] Acura, AutoZone, Buick/GMC, Dobb's Auto, Honda, O'Reilly Parts, Schnuck's Foods, Shop'n Save, Toyota, Walgreens, S [gas] Shell/Circle K/dsl [food] Chevy's Mexican, Little Caesar's [other] Dierberg's Foods
1b a	I-55 N to St Louis, S to Memphis

INTERSTATE 435 (Kansas City)

Exit #	Services
83	I-35, N to KS City, S to Wichita
82	Quivira Rd, Overland Park, N [food] Burger King, Cheddar's, Chick-fil-A, KFC, Mimi's Cafe, Outback Steaks, Sonic, Taco Bell [other] H, AT&T, Dillard's, JC Penney, Macy's, Nordstrom's, Target, S [food] Boston Mkt, Domino's, McDonald's, Subway, Taco Bell, Wendy's [lodging] Extended Stay America [other] CVS Drug, Hen House Mkt
81	US 69 S, to Ft Scott
80	Antioch Rd
79	Metcalf Ave, N [gas] Conoco/7-11, Phillips 66/dsl/repair [food] Buffalo Wild Wings, Carrabba's, Chartroose Caboose, ChuckECheese, D'Bronx Pizza, Denny's, Fox&Hound, Hardee's, Hooters, Jack-in-the-Box, Jose Pepper's, Krispy Kreme, Subway [lodging] Comfort Inn, Days Inn, Embassy Suites, Extended Stay America, Hampton Inn, Homewood Suites, La Quinta, Motel 6, Overland Park Place Hotel, Super 8 [other] H, AAA, Office Depot, vet, Walmart Mkt, S [food] Applebee's, McDonald's, Panera Bread [lodging] Drury Inn, Marriott, PearTree Inn

= gas = food = lodging = other = rest stop

MO

INTERSTATE 435 (Kansas City) Cont'd

Exit #	Services
77b a	Nall Ave, Roe Ave, N QT Brobeck's BBQ, Freddy's, Sonic, Winstead's Grill Best Value Inn USPO, S Corner Bakery Cafe, Wendy's Chase Suite Hotel, Courtyard, Extended Stay America, Hilton Garden, Holiday Inn, Hyatt Place, Sheraton Walgreens
75b	State Line Rd, N Phillips 66 Applebee's, Gate's BBQ, Jimmy John's, McDonald's, Taco Bell Buick/GMC/Cadillac, Goodyear/auto, Midas, O'Reilly Parts, PriceChopper Foods, S QT/dsl H, city park
75a	Wornall Rd, N QT Applebee's, China King, Coach's Grill, Dunkin', Fuzzy's Taco Shop, McDonald's, Panera Bread, Pizza Hut, Subway Acura, Audi, Chevrolet, Honda, Nissan, Price Chopper, Toyota, VW
74	Holmes Rd, N Phillips 66/dsl Subway, Thai House, S Courtyard, Extended Stay America
73	103rd St (from wb)
71b a	I-470/US 50 E, I-49/US 71S
70	Bannister Rd, E Phillips 66 Wendy's Walgreens, W Taco Bell Firestone/auto, Home Depot
69	87th St., E Conoco/dsl, QT McDonald's Capital Inn Advance Parts, W Days Inn
67	Gregory Blvd (same as 66a b), W Nature Ctr, zoo
66	MO 350 E, 63rd st
65	Eastwood Tfwy, W Conoco Church's, McDonald's, Peachtree Rest.
63c	Raytown Rd, Stadium Dr (nb only), E to Sports Complex
63b a	I-70, W to KC, E to St Louis
61	MO 78, 2 mi E Church's
60	MO 12 E, Truman Rd, 12th St, E Phillips 66/dsl, W QT
59	US 24, Independence Ave, E QT to Truman Library, W Hardee's CarQuest
57	Front St, E FLYING J/Conoco/rest/dsl/scales/24hr Blue Beacon, Kenworth, W Phillips 66/dsl, QT, Sinclair/dsl Denny's, McDonald's, Smugglers Rest., Subway, Waffle House Howard Johnson Plaza, Quality Inn URGENT CARE
56mm	Missouri River
55b a	MO 210, E Phillips 66/dsl, Pilot/PJ Fresh/dsl/scales/24hr Subway Ameristar Hotel/Casino, Motel 6 Ford/Volvo/GMC/Mercedes Trucks, Riverboat Casino
54	48th St, Parvin Rd, E Funpark, W QT All Star Grill, Taco Bell, Waffle House, Wendy's Best Inn, Candlewood Suites, Comfort Inn, Days Inn, Hampton Inn, Holiday Inn, Hometowne Suites, Springhill Suites, Super 8, SureStay Inn
52a	US 69, E Phillips 66/dsl, W McDonald's, Pizza Hut, Subway $General, Walgreens
52b	I-35, S to KC
51	Shoal Creek Dr, W LDS Temple
49b a	MO 152 E, to I-35 N, Liberty, 2 mi E 54th St Grill, Applebee's, Bob Evans, Buffalo Wild Wings, Cracker Barrel, Longhorn Steaks, Steak'n Shake Best Western, Comfort Inn, Fairfield Inn, Hampton Inn, Holiday Inn Express, Super 8
47	NE 96th St
46	NE 108th St
45	MO 291, NE Cookingham Ave, to I-35 N
42	N Woodland Ave
41b a	US 169, Smithville, 4 mi N Kum&Go Burger King, McDonald's, Sonic Super 8
40	NW Cookingham
37	NW Skyview Ave, rd C, N Cenex (1mi), S golf (3mi)
36	to I-29 S, to KCI Airport, N Cenex, S Extended S America, Fairfield Inn, Holiday Inn, Marriott, Microtel, P Hotel, Quality Suites, Sheraton, Super 8
31	I-29 N, to St Joseph, S to KC, Prairie Creek
29	rd D, NW 120th St
24	MO 152, rd N, NW Berry Rd
22	MO 45, Weston, Parkville, E The Station/DiBella's Pizza/
20mm	Missouri/Kansas state line, Missouri River
18	KS 5 N, Wolcott Dr, E to Wyandotte Co Lake Park
16	Donohoo Rd
15b a	Leavenworth Rd, E Conoco/Subway/dsl Comfort Sui Woodlands Racetrack
14b a	Parallel Pkwy, E Honda, Toyota, W Phillips 66/7- Subway/dsl Applebee's, Arby's, Bob Evans, Bryant's B Carino's Italian, Chick-fil-A, Chili's, Chipotle Mexican, Chuisar Brick Oven, Culver's, Danny's Grill, Dave&Buster's, Five Gu Fuddrucker's, Granite City Rest, Hooters, IHOP, Jack-in-the-B Jose Pepper's Grill, Longhorn Sreaks, McDonald's, Olive Gard Panda Express, Panera Bread, Pizza Hut, Red Lobster, Sherida Custard, Sonic, Starbucks, Stix Asian, Taco Bell, Taco Bueno, We dy's Candlewood Suites, Country Inn&Suites, Holiday Inn press, Residence Inn AT&T, JC Penney, Kohl's, NTB, Old Na Sam's Club/dsl, Target, TJ Maxx, Verizon, Walmart
13b a	US 24, US 40, State Ave, E Frontier Steaks wa park, W Casa Agave, Famous Dave's BBQ, Lones Steaks Best Western, Chateau Avalon, Great Wolf Lod Hampton Inn Cabela's, KS Race Track, Russell Stovers
12b a	I-70, KS Tpk, to Topeka, St Louis
11	Kansas Ave
9	KS 32, KS City, Bonner Springs, W Phillips 66/dsl
8b	Woodend Rd, E Peterbilt, W Shell/Subway/dsl/scales
8.8mm	Kansas River
8a	Holliday Dr, to Lake Quivira
6c	Johnson Dr
6b a	Shawnee Mission Pkwy, E Chili's, Grand Wok, IHOP, M Donald's, Pizza Hut, Subway Aldi Foods, GNC, Home Dep Kohl's, Lowe's, Michael's, NTB, Petsmart, Target, Walmart/Subw
5	Midland Dr, Shawnee Mission Park, E Conoco, Phillips 66/ 11/Subway/dsl Barley's Brewhaus, Chen's Kitchen, Egg Jose Pepper's Grill, Minsky's Pizza, Paula&Bill's Ristoran Wendy's Hampton Inn, W Hereford House Cou yard, Holiday Inn Express
3	87th Ave, E BP, Phillips 66/dsl Freddy's, McDo ald's, Panera Bread, Papa John's, Papa Murphy's, Sonic, Ta Bell Ace Hardware, Aldi Foods, Sprouts Mkt, Walgreer W Gambino's Pizza, Grand St Cafe, Hen House Mkt, Su way Hyatt Place
2	95th St
1b	KS 10, to Lawrence
1a	Lackman Rd, N Phillips 66/dsl Suburban Lodge
0mm	**I-435 begins/ends on I-35.**

KANSAS CITY

NOTES

MONTANA

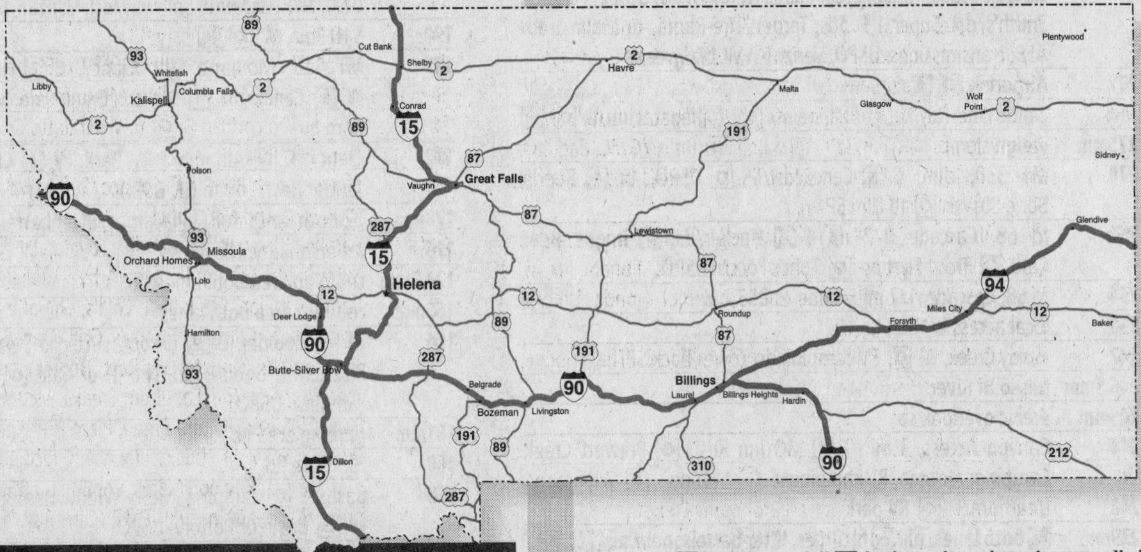

INTERSTATE 15

Exit #	Services
398mm	Montana/US/Canada Border, Sweetgrass
397	Sweetgrass, W both lanes, full facilities, litter barrels, petwalk, , , Gastrak Glocca Morra Motel/cafe Duty Free
394	ranch access
389	MT 552, Sunburst, W CFN/dsl Sunburst Mercantile, Sunburst RV Park, USPO
385	Swayze Rd
379	MT 215, MT 343, to Kevin, Oilmont, W Four Corners Café
373	Potter Rd
369	Bronken Rd
366.5mm	**weigh sta sb**
364	Shelby, E Lewis&Clark RV Park, W
363	US 2, Shelby, to Cut Bank, Shelby, 0-1 mi E Cenex, Pilot/Exxon/Country Skillet/dsl/scales/24hr, Sinclair/dsl Dash Drive-In, Dixie Inn Steaks, Kowloon Chinese, Pizza Hut, Subway, The Griddle Comfort Inn, Crossroads Inn, Glacier Motel/RV Park, O'Haire Motel , Albertsons, CarQuest, city park, Mark's Tire, Parts+, Shelby RV Park, TrueValue, USPO, visitor info, W Best Western to Glacier NP
361mm	**parking area nb**
358	Marias Valley Rd, to Golf Course Rd, E camping
357mm	Marias River
352	Bullhead Rd
348	rd 44, to Valier, W Lake Frances RA (15mi)
345	MT 366, Ledger Rd, E to Tiber Dam (42mi)
339	Conrad, E /weigh sta both lanes, full facilities, , litter barrels, petwalk, W Calumet/dsl, Cenex/dsl, Conoco/dsl, Exxon/Subway/dsl A&W/Chester's, Home Cafe, Main Drive-In Northgate Motel, Super 8 , Buick/Chevrolet/GMC, CarQuest, Conrad Tire/repair, Ford, IGA Foods, museum, Olson's Drug, Pondera RV Park, TrueValue, USPO, vet, Village Drug, Westco RV Ctr
335	Midway Rd, Conrad, 4 mi W gas food lodging , RV camping
328	MT 365, Brady, W Mtn View Co-op/dsl city park, USPO
321	Collins Rd
319mm	**both lanes, full facilities, litter barrels, petwalk, , , Teton River**
313	MT 221, MT 379, Dutton, W Cenex/dsl The Drive-In city park, USPO
302	MT 431, Power
297	Gordon
290	US 89 N, rd 200 W, to Choteau, W Conoco/dsl, Sinclair/dsl/LP/RV dump USPO
288mm	**parking area both lanes**
286	Manchester, W livestock auction, same as 290 (2mi)
282	US 87 N (from sb), NW bypass, **2-3 mi** E Conoco/dsl, Holiday/dsl Arby's, Buffalo Wild Wings, Burger King, Little Caesar's, McDonald's, New Peking, Subway, Taco Bell, Taco John's Days Inn $Tree, Ace Hardware, Albertsons/Osco, O'Reilly Parts, Sam's Club/gas, Staples, Tire-Rama, TJ Maxx, Walgreens, Walmart
280	US 87 N, Central Ave W, Great Falls, E Loaf 'N Jug/dsl A&W/KFC, Ford's Drive-In, Lippi's Kitchen, Papa John's Alberta Inn, Central Motel, Days Inn (3mi), Staybridge Suites city park, to Giant Sprgs SP, U-Haul/LP, vet, Whalen Tire
280mm	Sun River
278	US 89 S, rd 200 E, 10th Ave, Great Falls, E Calumet/dsl, Cenex/dsl, Conoco/dsl, Exxon/dsl, Holiday/Subway/dsl, Sinclair/dsl, Town Pump/dsl 4B's Rest., Applebee's, Arby's, Baskin-Robbins, Beef'O'Brady's, Best Wok, Boston's Pizza, Burger King, Café Rio, Chili's, Classic 50s Diner/casino, Coldstone, DQ, Fuddrucker's, Golden Corral, Hardee's, Jaker's Rest., JB's Rest., Jimmy John's, Little Caesar's, MacKenzie River Pizza, McDonald's, Ming's Chinese, Noodle Express, Papa John's, Papa Murphy's, Pita Pit, Pizza Hut, Sonic, Starbucks, Subway, Taco Bell, Taco Del Mar, Taco John's, Taco Treat, Wendy's, Wheat MT, ZPizza Best Western, Comfort Inn, Comfort Inn (2), Extended Stay America, Fairfield Inn, Hampton Inn, Hilton Garden, Holiday Inn, Holiday Inn Express, La Quinta, Motel 6, Super 8, Western Motel , $Tree, Ace Hardware, Albertsons/Osco, AT&T, AT&T, AutoZone, Barnes&Noble, Big O Tire, BigLots, Cadillac/Chevrolet/Toyota, CarQuest, Chrysler/Dodge/Jeep, CVS Drug, Dick's RV Park, Firestone/auto, Ford, Gardner's RV Ctr, Harley-Davidson, Herberger's, Home Depot, Honda, JC Penney,

SHELBY

CONRAD

GREAT FALLS

= gas = food = lodging = other = rest stop

MT

INTERSTATE 15 Cont'd

278 Continued
Jo-Ann Fabrics, KOA, Michael's, Midas, NAPA, Nissan, Old Navy, O'Reilly Parts, PetCo, Pierce RV Ctr, Ross, Scheels Sports, Smith's/dsl, Super 1 Foods, Target, Tire-Rama, to Malmstrom AFB, transmissions, USPO, Verizon, VW, Walgreens

277 Airport Rd, E FLYING J/Denny's/dsl/scales/24hr, Pilot/Conoco/Subway/casino/dsl/scales/24hr Crystal Inn, W

275mm **weigh sta nb**

270 MT 330, Ulm, E Cenex/dsl/LP USPO, W Beef'n Bone Steaks to Ulm SP

256 rd 68, Cascade, **1/2 mi** E Sinclair/dsl Angus Bear Cafe Trout Flyshop Tom's Foods, USPO

254 rd 68, Cascade, **1/2 mi** E same as 256

250 local access

247 Hardy Creek, W RV camping, to Tower Rock SP

246.5mm Missouri River

245mm scenic overlook sb

244 Canyon Access, **2 mi** W MO Inn Rest. Prewett Creek Camping, rec area, RV camping

240 Dearborn, E RV park

239mm **both lanes, full facilities, litter barrels, petwalk,**

238mm Stickney Creek

236mm Missouri River

234 Craig, E Izaak's Cafe, Trout Shop Café/lodge Flyshop boating, camping, rec area

228 US 287 N, to Augusta, Choteau

226 MT 434, Wolf Creek, E Exxon/dsl Oasis Café Wolf Creek Angler camping, to Holter Lake, W Frenchman&Me Café USPO

222mm **parking area both lanes**

219 Spring Creek, Recreation Rd (from nb), Spring Creek, boating, camping

218mm Little Prickly Pear Creek

216 Sieben

209 E to Gates of the Mtns RA

202mm **weigh sta sb**

200 MT 279, MT 453, Lincoln Rd, W Sinclair/Bob's Mkt/dsl GrubStake Rest. Lincoln Rd RV Park, to ski area

194 Custer Ave, E Conoco/dsl Chili's, Hardee's, IHOP, Nagoya Japanese, Qdoba Comfort Suites, Residence Inn Costco/gas, GNC, Hobby Lobby, Home Depot, Staples, Super 1 Foods, TJ Maxx, W Cenex/dsl, Conoco/dsl, Exxon/dsl Applebee's, Arby's, Buffalo Wild Wings, Burger King, DQ, Jade Garden, Mackenzie River Pizza, McDonald's, Panda Express, Papa Murphy's, Pizza Hut, Quiznos, Steve's Cafe, Subway, Taco Bell, Taco Del Mar Holiday Inn Express $Tree, Albertson's, AT&T, AutoZone, CVS Drug, Helena RV Park (5mi), Jo-Ann, Lowe's, Macy's, Murdoch's, Natural Grocers, PetCo, Petsmart, Ross, Target, Verizon

193 Cedar St, Helena, E W Conoco/dsl, Conoco/dsl, Exxon/dsl Godfather's, Little Caesar's, Perkins, Steffano's Pizza, Subway, Taco John's Quality Inn, Wingate Inn Ace Hardware, Chevrolet/Buick/GMC, O'Reilly Parts, Tire Rama, USPO, vet

192b a US 12, US 287, Helena, Townsend, E Cenex, Conoco/dsl Burger King, Pizza Hut Hampton Inn Big Lots, Chrysler/Dodge/Jeep, D&D RV Ctr, Ford/Lincoln, Honda, Nissan, Schwab Tire, st patrol, Toyota, Walmart/Subway, W Exxon/dsl, Holiday, Sinclair/dsl DQ, Jimmy John's, L&D Chinese, McDonald's, Overland Express Rest., Papa John's, Papa Murphy's, Rte 12 Diner, Starbucks, Steve's Cafe, Taco John's, Taco Treat,

HELENA

192b a Continued
Village Inn Pizza, Wendy's Baymont Inn, Days Inn, Fairfield Inn, Howard Johnson, Jorgenson's Inn, La Quinta, Motel 6, Radisson, Shilo Inn, Super 8 H, Albertson's, CVS Drug, GNC, J&J Tire/auto, Safeway/dsl, Verizon, Walgreens

190 S Helena, W H

187 MT 518, Montana City, Clancy, E Hugo's Pizza/casino, W Cenex/dsl Jackson Creek Cafe, MT City Grill Elkhorn Inn

182 Clancy, E Alhambra RV Park, W Chubby's Grill, Legal Tender Rest. to NF, USPO

178mm **both lanes, full facilities, litter barrels, petwalk,**

176 Jefferson City, NF access

174.5mm chain up area both lanes

168mm **chainup area both lanes**

164 rd 69, Boulder, E Exxon/dsl/casino Elkhorn Cafe, Jo... Pizza, Mtn Good Rest., The River Café auto repair, RV camping, USPO

161mm **parking area nb**

160 High Ore Rd

156 Basin, E camping, Merry Widow Health Mine/RV camping, W Basin Cr Pottery, USPO

154mm Boulder River

151 to Boulder River Rd, Bernice, W camping, picnic area

148mm **chainup area both lanes**

143.5mm **chainup area both lanes**

138 Elk Park, W Sheepshead Picnic Area, wildlife viewing

134 Woodville

133mm continental divide, elev 6368, continental divide

130.5mm scenic overlook sb

129 I-90 E, to Billings

I-15 S and I-90 W run together 8 mi.

127 Harrison Ave, Butte, E Cenex/dsl, ConocoPhillips/dsl, Exxon/dsl, Exxon/dsl (2), Sinclair/dsl A&W/KFC, Arby's, Asia Buffet, Buffalo Wild Wings, Burger King, MacKenzie River Pizza, McDonald's, MT Club Rest., Perkins, Pizza Hut, Pizza Ranch, Silver Bow Pizza, Starbucks, Subway, Taco Bell, Three Amigos, Wendy's Best Western, Comfort Inn, Hampton Inn, Super 8 $Tree, American Car Care, Buick/Chevrolet/GMC, CarQuest, casinos, Chrysler/Dodge/Jeep, Ford, Hart's RV Ctr, Herberger's, Honda, Jo-Ann Fabrics, Kia, Murdoch's, NAPA, Petco, Rocky Mtn RV Ctr, Staples, Subaru, Toyota, Verizon, vet, Walmart/Subway, W Cenex/dsl, Conoco/dsl Derby Steaks, Domino's, DQ, El Taco Mexican, Hanging 5 Rest., Hardee's, John's Rest., Papa John's, Papa Murphy's, Quiznos, Royse's Burgers, Taco John's Days Inn, Fairfield Inn, Holiday Inn Express, La Quinta, Quality Inn Ace Hardware, AutoZone, Lisac's Tires, O'Reilly Parts, Safeway, Walgreens

BUTTE

126 Montana St, Butte, E Conoco/dsl, Exxon/dsl, W Chef Garden Italian Eddy's Motel H, Safeway, Schwab Tire

124 I-115 (from eb), to Butte City Ctr

123mm **weigh sta sb**

122 Rocker, E Pilot/Conoco/McDonald's/Subway/dsl/scales/24hr Econolodge casino, weight sta nb, W FLYING J Exxon/rest./dsl/LP/24hr Best Value Inn 2 Bar Lazy-H RV Camping

I-15 N and I-90 E run together 8 mi.

121 I-90 W, to Missoula

119 Silver Bow, W Port of MT Transportation Hub

116 Buxton

112mm Continental Divide, elevation 5879

111 Feely

INTERSTATE 15 Cont'd

Exit #	Services
109mm	/weigh sta both lanes, full facilities, litter barrels, petwalk,
102	rd 43, to Wisdom, Divide, W rv camping (2mi), to Big Hole Nat Bfd (62mi)
99	Moose Creek Rd
93	Melrose, W Hitchin Post Rest., Melrose Café/grill/dsl Great Waters Inn (5mi), Pioneer Mtn Cabins Sportsman Motel/RV Park, Sunrise Flyshop, USPO
85.5mm	Big Hole River
85	Glen, E Willis Sta RV camping (3mi)
74	Apex, Birch Creek
64mm	Beaverhead River
63	Lp 15, rd 41, Dillon, Twin Bridges, E Cenex/dsl/LP/RV Dump, Exxon/dsl, Phillips 66/dsl 4B's Rest., Lions Den, McDonald's, Pizza Hut, Subway Best Western/rest., Fairbridge Inn, Motel 6, Quality Inn, Sundowner Motel, Super 8 H, auto repair/tires, Buick/Chevrolet, CarQuest, city park, Family$, KOA, Les Schwab Tire, Murdoch's, museum, NAPA, O'Reilly Parts, Safeway/dsl, W MT U
62	Lp 15, Dillon, E DQ, Sparky's Rest., Taco John's Flyshop Inn H, KOA, Southside RV Park, to W MT U, Van's/IGA Foods
60mm	Beaverhead River
59	MT 278, to Jackson, W Bannack SP, Countryside RV Park/LP
56	Barretts, E RV camping, W Sinclair/RV Park/dsl
55mm	**parking area sb, litter barrels**
52	Grasshopper Creek
51	Dalys (from sb, no return)
50mm	Beaverhead River
46mm	Beaverhead River
45mm	Beaverhead River
44	MT 324, E Buffalo Lodge Armstead RV Park, W Clark Cyn Reservoir/RA, RV camping
38.5mm	Red Rock River
37	Red Rock
34mm	**parking area both lanes, litter barrels, restrooms**
29	Kidd
23	Dell, E Cenex/dsl Yesterdays Calf-a USPO
16.5mm	**weigh sta both lanes**
15	Lima, E both lanes, facilities, litter barrels, petwalk, Exxon/dsl, Tesla EVC Jan's Café Mtn View Motel/RV Park ambulance, Big Sky Tire/auto, Ralph's Tire, USPO
9	Snowline
0	Monida, E to Red Rock Lakes
0mm	Montana/Idaho state line, Monida Pass, elevation 6870

INTERSTATE 90

Exit #	Services
554.5mm	Montana/Wyoming state line
549	Aberdeen
544	Wyola
530	MT 463, Lodge Grass, 1 mi S gas/dsl food lodging
517.5mm	Little Bighorn River
514	Garryowen, N Conoco/Subway Custer Bfd Museum, S 7th Ranch RV camp (3mi)
511.5mm	Little Bighorn River
510	US 212 E, N Conoco/café/dsl/gifts casino, casino, H, to Little Bighorn Bfd
509.5mm	**weigh sta both lanes exit left**
509.3mm	Little Bighorn River

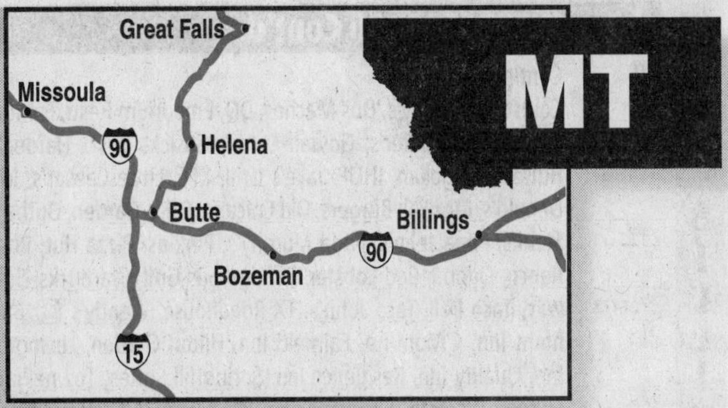

MT

HARDIN

Exit #	Services
509	Crow Agency, N Conoco, S to Bighorn Canyon NRA
503	Dunmore
498mm	Bighorn River
497	MT 384, 3rd St, Hardin, N fireworks, S Western Motel H, Bighorn Cty Museum
495	MT 47, City Ctr, Hardin, N Cenex/dsl, Loves/Hardee's/dsl/scales/24hr Golden Bridge Chinese KOA, S Cenex/dsl, Exxon/dsl, FLYING J/Conoco/Subway/dsl/LP/24hr DQ, McDonald's, Pizza Hut, Taco John's Rodeway Inn, Super 8, Western Motel H, Chevrolet, Grand View Camping/RV Park, Sunset Village RV Park
484	Toluca
478	Fly Creek Rd
477mm	**both lanes, full facilities, litter barrels, petwalk,**
469	Arrow Creek Rd
462	Pryor Creek Rd
456	I-94 E, to Bismarck, ND
455	Johnson Lane, N Pilot/Conoco/McDonald's/dsl/scales/24hr, S FLYING J/dsl/LP/scales/24hr, Exxon/A&W/dsl Burger King, Domino's, DQ, Jin's Chinese, Subway Holiday Inn Express Bretz RV Ctr, Verizon, Whalen Tire
452	US 87 N, City Ctr, Billings, **2-4 mi N on US 87** Conoco/Arby's/dsl/LP Applebee's, Arby's, Burger King, Domino's, DQ, Fuddrucker's, Godfather's, Golden Phoenix, Jimmy John's, MacKenzie River Pizza, McDonald's, Panda Express, Papa John's, Papa Murphy's, Pizza Hut, Sonic, Starbucks, Subway, Taco Bell, Taco John's, Wendy's Boothill Inn, Country Inn&Suites, Heights Motel Ace Hardware, Albertsons/Osco, American Spirit RV Ctr, AT&T, AutoZone, BigLots, CarQuest, Cenex/dsl, CVS Drug, GNC, Holiday/dsl, Metra Rv Ctr, O'Reilly Parts, Petsmart, Target, Tire Rama, U-Haul, Verizon, vet, Walgreens, Walmart, S Cenex/dsl RV Camping
451.5mm	Yellowstone River
450	MT 3, 27th St, Billings, N Conoco/dsl Blondy's Cafe, Pizza Hut Doubletree, Vegas Motel H, CarQuest, city park, USPO, visitor ctr, S KOA, Yellowstone River Camping
447	S Billings Blvd, N Conoco/Subway/dsl, Holiday/dsl 4B's Rest., Burger King, DQ, Fiddlers Green Grill, McDonald's, Popeye's, Taco Bell Best Western/Kelly, Comfort Suites, Days Inn, Extended Stay America, Hampton Inn, Ledgestone Hotel, My Place, Sleep Inn, Super 8 Cabela's Sporting Goods, NAPA, Sam's Club/dsl, S Freightliner, Kenworth, KOA (2mi), Yellowstone River Campground
446	King Ave, Billings, N Conoco/dsl, Conoco/dsl, Holiday/dsl, Phillips 66/dsl Applebee's, Arby's, Asian Sea Grill, Bruno's Italian, Buffalo Wild Wings, Burger King, Cactus Creek Steaks, Café Rio, Carino's Italian, ChuckECheese's, City Brew Coffee,

BILLINGS

INTERSTATE 90 Cont'd

BILLINGS

446 Continued
Coldstone, Denny's, Dos Machos, DQ, Emporium Rest., Famous Dave's, Fuddrucker's, Golden Corral, Gusicks Rest., Hardee's, HuHot Mongolian, IHOP, Jake's Grill, KFC, Little Caesar's, McDonald's, MooYah Burgers, Old Chicago, Olive Garden, Outback Steaks, Papa John's, Papa Murphy's, Perkins, Pizza Hut, Pizza Ranch, Qdoba, Red Lobster, Rendezvous Grill, Starbucks, Subway, Taco Bell, Taco John's, TX Roadhouse, Wendy's 🛏 Baymont Inn, C'Mon Inn, Fairfield Inn, Hilton Garden, Lexington Inn, Quality Inn, Residence Inn, SpringHill Suites, TownePlace Suites, Western Executive Inn ⓞ $Tree, Albertsons/Osco, AT&T, AutoZone, Barnes&Noble, Best Buy, Chevrolet, Chrysler/Dodge/Jeep, Costco/gas, Dillards, Ford, Hobby Lobby, Home Depot, JC Penney, JoAnn Fabrics, Kia, Lisac's Tire, Lowe's, Mercedes, Michael's, Natural Grocers, Nissan, Office Depot, Old Navy, O'Reilly Parts, Petsmart, Ross, Subaru, USPO, Verizon, vet, Walmart/Subway, World Mkt, **S** ⛽ Conoco/dsl 🍴 Cracker Barrel, Emporium Rest. 🛏 EconoLodge, Howard Johnson, Kelly Inn, La Quinta, Motel 6, Motel 6 (2), Radisson, Red Lion Inn ⓞ Volvo/Mack Trucks

443 Zoo Dr, to Shiloh Rd, **N** ⛽ Holiday/dsl 🍴 Five Guys, MT Rib/Chophouse 🛏 Bighorn Resort/waterpark, Hampton Inn, Holiday Inn Express, Homewood Suites ⓞ Honda, Hyundai/Volvo/Buick, Pierce RV Ctr, zoo, **S** ⓞ Harley-Davidson, vet

439mm **weigh sta both lanes**

437 E Laurel, **S** ⛽ TA/Sinclair/cafe/dsl/scales/casino/motel/RV Park/24hr

434 US 212, US 310, to Red Lodge, Laurel, **N** ⛽ Cenex/dsl, Conoco/dsl, Exxon/dsl 🍴 Beartooth Grill, City Brew Coffee, Gauica's Mexican, Hardee's, McDonald's, Pizza Hut, Subway, Taco Bell, Taco John's 🛏 Best Western, Locomotive Inn ⓞ Ace Hardware, AutoZone, Chevrolet, CVS Drug, Ford, IGA Foods, O'Reilly Parts, Rapid Tire, Verizon, Walmart/Subway, **S** ⓞ Riverside Park/RV Camping, to Yellowstone NP

433 Lp 90 (from eb), same as 434

426 Park City, **S** ⛽ Cenex/café/dsl/24hr, KwikStop 🍴 The Other Cafe ⓞ USPO

419mm **Rs both lanes, full ♿ facilities, litter barrels, petwalk, ☎, 🧺**

408 rd 78, Columbus, **N** ⓞ Mtn Range RV Park, **S** ⛽ Conoco, Pilot/Exxon/dsl/24hr 🍴 Bearstone Cafe, McDonald's, Subway 🛏 Big Sky Motel, Super 8 ⓞ casino, city park, Family$, H, IGA Foods, tires/repair, to Yellowstone

400 Springtime Rd

398mm Yellowstone River

396 ranch access

392 Reed Point, **N** ⛽ Sure Stop/dsl ⓞ Old West RV Park, USPO

384 Bridger Creek Rd

381mm **Rs both lanes, full ♿ facilities, litter barrels, petwalk, ☎, 🧺**

377 Greycliff, **S** ⓞ KOA, Prairie Dog Town SP

370 US 191, Big Timber, **1 mi N** ⛽ Sinclair/dsl 🛏 Grand Hotel, Lazy J Motel ⓞ H, Spring Creek RV Ranch (4mi), USPO, vet

369mm Boulder River

367 US 191 N, Big Timber, **N** ⛽ Conoco/dsl, Exxon/dsl 🍴 Country Skillet 🛏 River Valley Inn, Super 8 ⓞ CarQuest, Family$, historic site/visitor info, Spring Creek Camping (3mi)

362 De Hart

354 MT 563, Springdale

352 ranch access

350 East End access

343 Mission Creek Rd, **N** ⓞ Ft Parker HS

340 US 89 N, to White Sulphur Sprgs, **S** ⓞ ✈

LIVINGSTON

337 Lp 90, to Livingston, **2 mi N** ⓞ services in Livingston

333mm Yellowstone River

333 US 89 S, Livingston, **N** 🍴 Clark's Rest., DQ, Mark's In&Ou[t], Pizza Hut, Taco John's 🛏 Budget Host, Livingston Inn, Qua[l]ity Inn, Rodeway Inn, Yellowstone Pioneer Lodge ⓞ H, A[ce] Hardware, Chrysler/Dodge/Jeep, Town&Country Foods, Tr[ue] Value Hardware, Verizon, Western Drug, **S** ⛽ Cenex/d[sl], Conoco/dsl, Exxon/dsl 🍴 Arby's, McDonald's, Rosa's Pizz[a], Subway 🛏 Comfort Inn, Super 8 ⓞ Albertsons/Osco, KO[A] (10mi), Osen's RV Park/Lp, to Yellowstone, URGENT CARE, ve[t]

330 Lp 90, Livingston, **1 mi N** ⛽ Cenex/Yellowstone Trkstp/ds[l]/rest./24hr

326.5mm **chainup/chain removal area both lanes**

324 ranch accesss

323mm **chainup/chain removal area wb**

322mm Bridger Mountain Range

321mm turnouts/hist marker both lanes

319 Jackson Creek Rd

319mm **chainup area both lanes**

316 Trail Creek Rd

313 Bear Canyon Rd, **S** ⓞ Bear Canyon Camping

BOZEMAN

309 US 191 S, Main St, Bozeman, **N** ⓞ Subaru, Sunrise R[V] Park, **S** ⛽ Cenex/dsl, Conoco/dsl, Exxon/dsl 🍴 MT Al[e] Works 🛏 Ranch House Motel, Western Heritage Inn ⓞ H, East Main Foods, repair, Tire Rama, to Yellowstone

306 MT 205, N 7th, to US 191, Bozeman, **N** ⛽ Cenex 🍴 McDon[ald's], Panda Buffet 🛏 Fairfield Inn, La Quinta, Microtel, M[o]tel 6, Ramada, Rodeway Inn, Super 8 ⓞ Murdoch's, ski are[a], Whalen Tire, **S** ⛽ Conoco/Arby's/dsl, Exxon 🍴 Applebee'[s], Bar-3 BBQ, Dominos, DQ, Famous Dave's BBQ, Papa John'[s], Santa Fe Red's Cafe, Taco John's, Village Inn Pizza 🛏 Be[st] Western, Bozeman Inn, Comfort Inn, Days Inn, Hampton In[n], Holiday Inn, Homewood Suites, Royal 7 Inn ⓞ Big O Tire, Fir[e]stone/auto, Museum of the Rockies, U-Haul, Verizon, Walmar[t]/McDonald's

305 MT412, N 19th Ave, **N** 🍴 Exxon 🛏 Mountainview Inn, 0-[1] mi **S** Rs, **full ♿ facilities, petwalk, 🧺/litter barrels,** ⛽ Co[n]oco/dsl 🍴 A&W/KFC, Buffalo Wild Wings, Carino's Italia[n], City Brew Coffee, Clarks Fork Rest., Corner Bakery Cafe, Fiv[e] Guys, IHOP, Jimmy John's, Mongolian BBQ, Noodles&Co, O[ld] Chicago Pizza, Olive Garden, Outback Steaks, Papa Murphy'[s], Starbucks, Subway, Wasabi Grill, Wendy's 🛏 C'mon In[n], Comfort Suites, Country Inn Suites, Hilton Garden, Holida[y] Inn Express, My Place Extended Stay, Residence Inn, Spring[Hill] Suites ⓞ AT&T, Costco/gas, Ford/Lincoln/RV Ctr, Hom[e] Depot, Lowe's, Michael's, Office Depot, Petsmart, REI, Ros[s], Smith's Foods/dsl, Staples, Target, TJMaxx, USPO, Verizon, ve[t], World MKT

BELGRADE

299 Airway Blvd, **N** ⓞ ✈

298 MT 291, rd 85, Belgrade, **N** ⛽ Cenex/dsl, Exxon/Subway/dsl 🍴 Burger King, DQ, McDonald's, Papa Murphy's, Pizz[a] Hut, Rosa's Pizza, Starbucks, Taco Bell, Taco Time 🛏 Hol[i]day Inn Express ⓞ Albertson's/Osco, NAPA, Town&Countr[y] Foods, Verizon, Whalen Tire, **S** ⛽ FLYING J/Conoco/ds[l]/scales/LP, Pilot/Conoco/dsl/scales/24hr 🍴 Fiesta Mex[i]cana 🛏 La Quinta, Quality Inn, Super 8 ⓞ Freightliner, Ha[r]ley-Davidson, repair, Tire Factory, to Yellowstone NP, TrueValu[e]

292.5mm Gallatin River

288 MT 288, MT 346, Manhattan, **N** ⛽ Conoco/Subway/d[sl] ⓞ RV camping

283 Logan, **S** ⓞ Madison Buffalo Jump SP (7mi)

INTERSTATE 90 Cont'd

Exit #	Services
279mm	Madison River
278	MT 205, rd 2, Three Forks, Trident, N Missouri Headwaters SP, **1 mi S** Conoco/dsl Iron Horse Cafe Broken Spur Motel, Lewis&Clark Motel, Sacajawea Hotel CarQuest, golf
277.5mm	Jefferson River
274	US 287, to Helena, Ennis, N Conoco/dsl Wheat MT Bakery/deli Ft 3 Forks Motel/RV Park dsl repair, to Canyon Ferry SP, S Pilot/Exxon/Subway/dsl/scales/24hr Camp 3 Forks, Lewis&Clark Caverns SP, to Yellowstone NP
267	Milligan Canyon Rd
261.5mm	**chain-up area**
257mm	Boulder River
256	MT 359, Cardwell, S Cenex/dsl/RV Park Lewis&Clark Caverns SP, RV camping, to Yellowstone NP
249	rd 55, to rd 69, Whitehall, S Exxon/dsl A&W/KFC, Subway Rodeway Inn casino, Cliff's Tire/auto, to Virginia City NHS
241	Pipestone
240.5mm	**chainup/chain removal area both lanes**
238.5mm	**runaway ramp eb**
237.5mm	**pulloff eb**
235mm	**truck parking both lanes, litter barrels, restrooms**
233	Continental Divide, elev 6393, Homestake
230mm	**chain-up area both lanes**
228	MT 375, Continental Dr, S Conoco/dsl Harley-Davidson, Three Bears Foods
227	I-15 N, to Helena, Great Falls
I-90 and I-15 run together 8 mi. See Montana I-15, exits 122-127.	
123mm	**weight sta wb**
219	I-15 S, to Dillon, Idaho Falls
216	Ramsay
211	MT 441, Gregson, **3-5 mi S** Fairmont RV Park (Apr-Oct), food, lodging
210.5mm	**parking area wb**, Pintlar Scenic route info
208	rd 1, Pintler Scenic Loop, Georgetown Lake RA, Opportunity, Anaconda, **S RS both lanes, full facilities, petwalk, , litter barrels, RV camp/dump,** H, food, gas, lodging, ski area
201	Warm Springs, S MT ST H
197	MT 273, Galen, S to MT ST H
195	Racetrack
187	Lp 90, Deer Lodge (no wb return), **2 mi S** Travelodge H, KOA (seasonal), Old MT Prison/auto museum, same as 184, Valley Foods
184	Deer Lodge, **0-1 mi S** Conoco/dsl/casino, Exxon/dsl/casino, Sinclair/Subway/dsl 4B's Rest., A&W, McDonald's, Pizza Hut Travelodge, Western Big Sky Inn H, city park, Family$, Grant-Kohrs Ranch NHS, Indian Creek Camping, KOA, Safeway/deli, Schwab Tire, USPO
179	Beck Hill Rd
175	US 12 E, Garrison, N hist site, RiverFront RV Park
175mm	Little Blackfoot River
174	US 12 E (from eb), S same as 175
170	Phosphate
166	Gold Creek, S Camp Mak-A-Dream, USPO
162	Jens
154	to MT 1 (from wb), Drummond, S Cenex/dsl, Conoco/dsl Parker's Rest., Wagon Wheel Café Drummond Motel, Sky Motel, Wagon Wheel Motel city park, Front St Mkt, Georgetown Lake RA, Pintler Scenic Lp
153	MT 1 (from eb), **S** same as 154

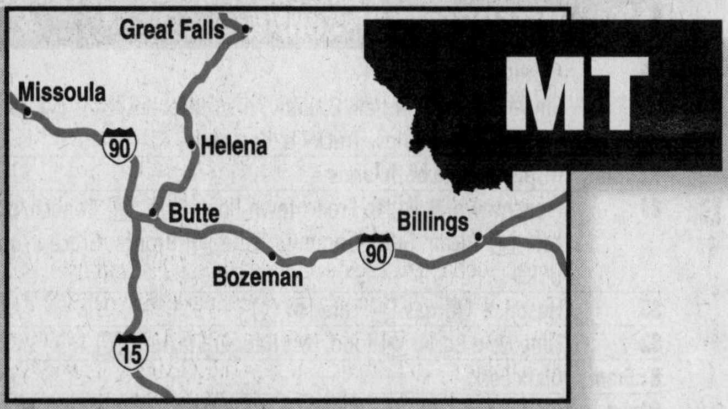

MISSOULA

Exit #	Services
150.5mm	**weigh sta both lanes**
143mm	**RS both lanes, full facilities, litter barrels, petwalk,**
138	Bearmouth Area, N Chalet Bearmouth Camp/rest.
130	Beavertail Rd, S to Beavertail Hill SP
128mm	**parking area both lanes, litter barrels/restrooms**
126	Rock Creek Rd, S rec area
120	Clinton, N Conoco/dsl Poor Henry's Café (1mi W on frtg rd) Clinton Market, S USPO
113	Turah, S Turah RV Park/gas
109.5mm	Clark Fork
109mm	Blackfoot River
109	MT 200 E, Bonner, N Pilot/Exxon/Arby's/Subway/dsl/scales/casino/LP/24hr River City Grill hist site, USPO
108.5mm	Clark Fork
107	E Missoula, N Ole's/Conoco/dsl, Sinclair Reno Cafe Aspen Motel dsl repair
105	US 12 W, Missoula, S Cenex/dsl, Conoco/dsl, Sinclair/dsl Burger King, Five Guys, McDonald's, Pizza Hut, Qdoba, Subway, Taco Bell Campus Inn, Comfort Inn, DoubleTree, Motel 6, Thunderbird Motel Ace Hardware, Albertson's, Kingfisher Flyshop, O'Reilly Parts, U of MT, Verizon
104	Orange St, Missoula, S Conoco/dsl Pagoda Chinese, Taco John's Mtn Valley Inn, Red Lion Inn H, TireRama, to City Ctr
101	US 93 S, Reserve St, N Conoco/dsl Cracker Barrel, MacKenzie River Pizza, Starbucks Best Western+, C'Mon Inn, Motel 6, My Place ski area, **0-2 mi S** Cenex/dsl/LP, Conoco/dsl, Exxon/Subway/dsl Arby's, Buffalo Wild Wings, Burger King, Cafe Rio, Chipotle, Coldstone, Domino's, DQ, Famous Dave's BBQ, Freddy's, Fuddrucker's, HoagiVille, IHOP, Jimmy John's, Little Caesar's, McDonald's, MOD Pizza, MT Club Rest./casino, Old Chicago, Outback Steaks, Panda Express, Perkins, Pizza Hut, Popeye's, Quiznos, Rowdy's Cabin Rest., Stone Of Accord, Taco Bell, Taco Time/TCBY, Wendy's Courtyard, EconoLodge, Hampton Inn, Hilton Garden, Holiday Inn Express, La Quinta, Quality Inn, Ruby's Inn/rest., Staybridge Suites, Super 8, TownePlace Suites, Travelers Inn Albertson's, AT&T, Barnes&Noble, Best Buy, Bretz RV/Marine, Chevrolet/Cadillac, Costco/gas, dsl repair, Firestone/auto, GNC, Home Depot, Lowe's, Michael's, Old Navy, Petsmart, REI, Ross, Staples, Target, TJ Maxx, Verizon, VW, Walgreens, Walmart/Subway
99	Airway Blvd, S Mobil/dsl/24hr, Sinclair/dsl Stone Creek Lodge, Wingate Inn , Chrysler/Dodge/Jeep, Harley-Davidson, Kia
96	US 93 N, MT 200W, Kalispell, N Conoco/rest./dsl/scales/24hr/@, FLYING J/Exxon/McDonald's/dsl/scales/24hr WheatMT/deli Days Inn/rest. Jellystone RV Park (1mi), Jim&Mary's RV Park (1mi), Peterbilt, to Flathead Lake&Glacier NP, S Love's/Hardee's/dsl/scales/24hr,

MT

MT

INTERSTATE 90 Cont'd

96	Continued Sinclair/dsl, TA/Sinclair/Country Pride/dsl/scales/24hr Tamarack Inn Harlow Truck Ctr, Kenworth
92.5mm	**inspection sta both lanes**
89	Frenchtown, N to Frenchtown Pond SP, S Conoco/dsl/café Alcan Grill, Gammy's Cafe Broncs Grocery/gas, USPO
85	Huson, S gas cafe
82	Nine Mile Rd, N food, Hist Ranger Sta/info,
81.5mm	Clark Fork
80mm	Clark Fork
77	MT 507, Petty Creek Rd, Alberton, S access to gas food lodging
75	Alberton, N Cenex/dsl USPO, S River Edge Rest. casino, motel, RV camp
73mm	**parking area wb, litter barrels**
72mm	**parking area eb, litter barrels**
70	Cyr
70mm	Clark Fork
66	Fish Creek Rd
66mm	Clark Fork
61	Tarkio
59mm	Clark Fork
58mm	**both lanes, full facilities, litter barrels, NF camping (seasonal), petwalk, ,**
55	Lozeau, Quartz
53.5mm	Clark Fork
49mm	Clark Fork
47	MT 257, Superior, N Conoco/dsl, Energy Partners/LP Durango's Rest./gas Big Sky Motel, Hilltop Motel , Family Foods, Mineral Drug, NAPA, USPO, S Pilot/Exxon/dsl/casino/24hr
45mm	Clark Fork
43	Dry Creek Rd, N NP camping (seasonal)
37	Sloway Area
34mm	Clark Fork
33	MT 135, St Regis, N Conoco/rest/dsl/gifts, Exxon, Sinclair Frosty Drive-In, Huck's Grill, Jasper's Rest., OK Café/casino Little River Motel, St Regis Motel, Super 8 antiques, city park, Nugget Camground, St Regis Campground (seasonal), to Glacier NP, USPO
30	Two Mile Rd, S fishing access
29mm	fishing access wb
26	Ward Creek Rd (from eb)
25	Drexel
22	Camels Hump Rd, Henderson, N antiques (1mi), camping (seasonal)
18	DeBorgia, N O'aces Rest. Black Diamond Guest Ranch, USPO
16	Haugan, N Exxon/dsl/24hr 50000 Silver $/motel/rest./casino/RV park
15mm	**weigh sta both lanes, exits left from both lanes**
10	Saltese, N Mangold's Motel
10mm	St Regis River
5	Taft Area, access to Hiawatha Trail
4.5mm	**both lanes, chainup/removal, full facilities, , litter barrels, petwalk**
0	Lookout Pass, access to Lookout Pass ski area/lodge, info
0mm	Montana/Idaho state line, Central/Pacific time zone, Lookout Pass elev 4680

GLENDIVE

MILES CITY

INTERSTATE 94

Exit #	Services
250mm	Montana/North Dakota state line
248	Carlyle Rd
242	MT 7 (from wb), Wibaux, S **both lanes, full facilities, lit barrels, , ,** Amsler's/dsl, Cenex/dsl/service Tas Hut Beaver Creek Inn
241	MT 261 (from eb), to MT 7, Wibaux, S same as 242
240mm	**weigh sta both lanes**
236	ranch access
231	Hodges Rd
224	Griffith Creek, frontage road
222.5mm	Griffith Creek
215	MT 335, Glendive, City Ctr, N Cenex/dsl C's Fam Café, Penny's Diner Astoria Suites, Comfort Inn, Days I Holiday Inn Express, Oak Tree Inn, Super 8 Glendive Cam ing (apr-oct), museum, Running's Hardware, S Exxon/ Holiday/dsl Subway El Centro Motel, Glendive Inn, Quinta , to Makoshika SP, Verizon
215mm	Yellowstone River
213	MT 16, to Sidney, Glendive, N Town Pump/dsl/scales patrol, S Cenex/dsl, Sinclair/dsl Pizza Hut Riv side Inn Albertson's/Osco, Ford, NAPA, Reynolds Mkt
211	MT 200S (from wb, no EZ return), to Circle
210	Lp 94, to rd 200 S, W Glendive, S Cenex/dsl, Exx dsl Buick/Chevrolet, I-94 RV Park, Makoshika SP, Tire Ra
206	Pleasant View Rd
204	Whoopup Creek Rd
198	Cracker Box Rd
192	Bad Route Rd, S **/weigh sta both lanes, camping, full cilities, litter barrels, petwalk, , , weather info**
187mm	Yellowstone River
185	MT 340, Fallon, S café
184mm	O'Fallon Creek
176	MT 253, Terry, N Cenex/dsl, Four Corners/dsl Di Diner Kempton Hotel , museum, Terry RV Oasis
170mm	Powder River
169	Powder River Rd
159	Diamond Ring
148	Valley Access
141	US 12 E, Miles City, N RV Camping
138	rd 59, Miles City, N Cenex/dsl, Conoco/dsl, Pilot/E on/dsl/24hr 4B's Rest., Arby's, Black Iron Grill, Boardw Rest., City Brew Coffee, DQ, Gallagher's Rest., Little Caesa McDonald's, Mexico Lindo, MT Rib&Chophouse, Pizza Hut, S way, Taco John's, Wendy's Best Western, EconoLodge, M tel 6, Sleep Inn , $Tree, Ace Hardware, Albertsons/Os Buick/Chevrolet, casinos, Murdoch's, O'Reilly Parts, Veriz Walmart, S Cenex/dsl New Hunan Chinese Co fort Inn, Guesthouse Inn, MC Hotel, Super 8
137mm	Tongue River
135	Lp 94, Miles City, N KOA (Apr-Oct)
128	local access
126	Moon Creek Rd
117	Hathaway
114mm	**eb, full facilities, litter barrels, petwalk, ,**
113mm	**wb, full facilities, litter barrels, overlook, petwalk, ,**
106	Butte Creek Rd, to Rosebud, N food
103	MT 446, MT 447, Rosebud Creek Rd, N food
98.5mm	**weigh sta both lanes**
95	Forsyth, N Exxon/dsl, Forsyth Watering Hole Sundowner Inn , Ford, NAPA, to Rosebud RA, Van IGA, vet, S Wagon Wheel Camping

INTERSTATE 94 Cont'd

Exit #	Services
93	US 12 W, Forsyth, N [gas] Exxon/dsl, Forsyth Watering Hole [food] Fitzgerald's Rest., Top That Eatery [lodging] Rails Inn, Restwel Inn, WestWind Motel [other] [H]
87	rd 39, to Colstrip
82	Reservation Creek Rd
72	MT 384, Sarpy Creek Rd
67	Hysham, 1-2 mi N [gas] gas [food] food [other] [phone]
65mm	**[RS] both lanes, full [handicap] facilities, litter barrels, petwalk, [phone], [picnic]**
63	ranch access
53	Bighorn, access to [phone]
52mm	Bighorn River
49	MT 47, to Hardin, Custer, S [food] Ft Custer Café [other] camping, to Little Bighorn Bfd
47	Custer, S [gas] Cenex/Custer Sta/dsl [food] Jct City Saloon/café [other] USPO
41.5mm	**[RS] wb, full [handicap] facilities, litter barrels, petwalk, [phone], [picnic]**
38mm	**[RS] eb, full [handicap] facilities, litter barrels, petwalk, [phone], [picnic]**

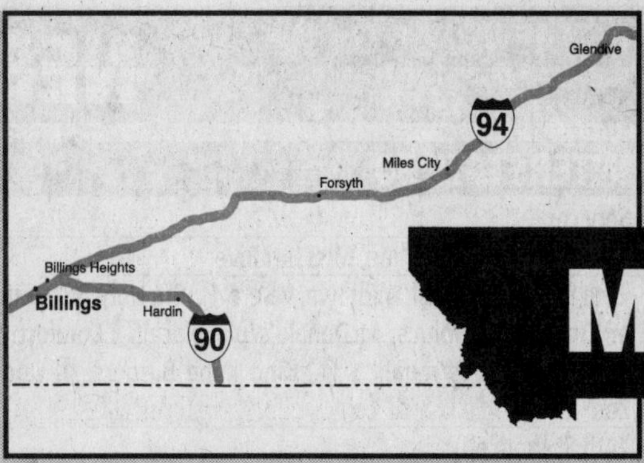

Exit #	Services
36	frontage rd, Waco
23	Pompeys Pillar, N [other] Pompeys Pillar Nat Landmark
14	Ballentine, Worden, S [food] Long Branch Café/casino
6	MT 522, Huntley, N [food] Pryor Creek Café/casino, S [food] golf
0mm	I-90, E to Sheridan, W to Billings, **I-94 begins/ends on I-90, exit 456.**

MT

NOTES

NE

NEBRASKA

INTERSTATE 80

OMAHA

Exit #	Services
455mm	Nebraska/Iowa state line, Missouri River
454	13th St, N BP/dsl, Midtown, Valero Big Horn BBQ, Burger King, Jimmy John's, McDonald's/playplace Comfort Inn Family$, tires/repair, S King Kong Burgers Doorly Zoo
453	24th St (from eb)
452b	I-480 N, US 75 N, N Eppley Airfield
452a	US 75 S
451	42nd St, N BP/dsl H, S Phillips 66 Burger King, McDonald's, Taco Bell Pitstop Lube
450	60th St, N Phillips 66 NAPA, to U of NE Omaha, S Casey'/dsl transmissions
449	72nd St, to Ralston, N BP, QT Burger King, Spezia Italian Baymont Inn, Best Value Inn, Comfort Inn, DoubleTree, Quality Inn, Ramada, Super 8 H, Walmart, S Cenex/dsl Anthony's Steaks
448	84th St, N BP/dsl Arby's, Crane Coffee, Denny's, Farmhouse Café, Great Wall Chinese, Husker Hounds, La Casa, Little Caesar's, McDonald's, Pizza Ranch, Subway, Taco Bell Motel 6 Ace Hardware, Advance Parts, CVS Drug, Jensen's Tire/auto, Mangelson's Crafts, USPO, S Kum&Go/dsl/e85, QT, Shell/dsl Wendy's Chevrolet, Kia
446	I-680 N, to Boystown
445	US 275, NE 92, I thru L St, N Casey's/dsl Buffalo Wings&Rings, Cheddar's, Famous Dave's BBQ, Hardee's, Jason's Deli, Noodles&Co, Pita Pit, Qdoba, SmashBurger, Starbucks, Wendy's Carol Hotel Book-A-Million, Buick/GMC, Home Depot, Michael's, Nelsen's RV Ctr, PetCo, Sam's Club/gas, Super Target, Verizon, Walmart, S BP, QT/dsl Arby's, Brew Burgers, Burger King, Dunkin', Godfather's Pizza, Hog Wild BBQ, Hunan Garden, Jimmy' Egg Cafe, Jimmy John's, LJ Silver, McDonald's, Runza, Subway, Taco Bell, Valentino's, Village Inn Best Western, La Quinta, Motel 6, Super 8, Victorian Inn, Victorian Inn, Westmont Inn Bag'n Save Foods, Family$, Jensen Automotive, O'Reilly Parts, URGENT CARE
444	Q St, N Casey's/dsl
442	126th St, Harrison St, N Chrysler/Dodge/Jeep, Toyota, VW, S Phillips 66/dsl Amigo's Mexican, Burger King, Coldstone, Dunkin', Houston's, Jimmy John's, Pizza West, Runza, Sonic, Summer Kitchen Comfort Suites, Courtyard, Embassy Suites, Hampton Inn, My Place, Woodspring Suites Cabela's, Costco/gas
440	NE 50, to Springfield, N BP/dsl/e85, Phillips 66/dsl, Sapp Bros/Subway/dsl/24hr/@ Azteca Mexican, Cracker Barrel, Hardee's, McDonald's Countryside Suites, EconoLodge, Hometown Lodge, Motel 6, Quality Inn, Red Carpet Inn Ford, tires, S BP, to Platte River SP H
439	439 NE 370, to Gretna, N Kum&Go/dsl Arby's, Taco John's Holiday Inn Express Walmart/Subway, S H, museum, Volvo Trucks
432	US 6, NE 31, to Gretna, N Pump&Pantry/dsl/24hr McDonald's, Subway Super 8 KOA, Nebraska X-ing/famous brands, S FLYING J/Denny's/dsl/LP/24hr to Schramm SP
431mm	**wb, full facilities, info, litter barrels, petwalk,**

LINCOLN

YORK

Exit #	Services
427mm	Platte River
426	NE 66, to Southbend, N museum, rv camping, to Mahoney
425.5	**eb, full facilities, litter barrels, petwalk, , vend**
420	NE 63, Greenwood, N Cenex/cafe/dsl/scales/24hr P Grove RV Park, S Shell/dsl antiques, to Platte River WWII Museum
416mm	**weigh sta both lanes**
409	US 6, to E Lincoln, Waverly, N Casey's (2mi) McD ald's (2mi), Subway (2mi), S H
405	US 77 N, 56th St, Lincoln, S Phillips 66 H, antiq Freightliner, Peterbilt, truck service/wash/tires
403	27th St, Lincoln, **0-3 mi** S Mobil, Phillips 66/Subway/ Phillips 66/Wendy's/dsl, Shell Amigos Mexican, Applebe Arby's, Asian Buffet, Burger King, Cane's, Carlos O'Kelly's, Ch Inn, CiCi's Pizza, Cracker Barrel, Culver's, daVinci's Italian, Dick BBQ, DQ, Fazoli's, Golden Corral, IHOP, Jimmy John's, King K Burger, Mazatlan Mexican, McDonald's, Papa John's, Papa M phy's, Pizza Hut, Popeye's/Taco Inn, Ruby Tuesday, Runza, Sch zsky's, Sonic, Taco Bell, Taco John's, Village Inn Americ Best Western+, Country Inn&Suites, Countryside Suites, Fairf Inn, Hampton Inn, Holiday Inn Express, La Quinta, Microtel, M tel 6, Quality Inn, Red Roof Inn, Sleep Inn, Staybridge Sui Super 8, TownePlace Suites, Woodspring Suites $Tree, A Zone, BMW, Buick/Chevrolet/GMC, Chrysler/Dodge/Jeep, Fo Lincoln, GNC, Gordman's, Haas Tire, Home Depot, HyVee Fo Lexus, Menards, Mercedes, Petsmart, Sam's Club/dsl, Su Saver Foods, to U NE, Toyota, URGENT CARE, Verizon, Walma McDonald's
401b	US 34 W, S RV camping
401a	I-180, US 34 E, to 9th St, Lincoln
399	NW 12th St, Lincoln, N Gulf/FatDogs/dsl, Phillips dsl Baskin-Robbins, Big Ten Subs, McDonald's B Value Inn, Comfort Inn, Country Inn Suites, Fairfield Inn, Har ton Inn, Holiday Inn Express, Horizon Inn, Luxury Inn, Qua Inn, Rodeway Inn, Sunset Inn, Travelodge to, S sey's/dsl Subway EconoLodge
397	US 77 S, to Beatrice
396	US 6, West O St (from eb), S Rodeway Inn, Super 8
395	US 6, NW 48th St, S Phillips 66/dsl, Shoemaker's/Shell/ scales/@ Cobbler Inn Harley-Davidson, truck repair
388	NE 103, to Crete, Pleasant Dale
382	US 6, Milford, S Phillips 66/dsl
381mm	**eb, full facilities, litter barrels, petwalk, , vendi**
379	NE 15, to Seward, N Buick/Chevrolet/GMC, Ford, H (3r S Shell/dsl
375mm	**truck parking (wb)**
373	80G, Goehner, N gas
369	80E, Beaver Crossing, **3 mi** S H, food, RV camping
366	80F, to Utica
360	93B, to Waco, N Phillips 66/Waco Rest/dsl/24hr, S D ble Nickel Camping
355mm	**wb, full facilities, info, litter barrels, petwalk,** **vending**
353	US 81, to York, N Conoco/dsl, Pump-N-Pantry/e85, S pBros/Sinclair/Subway/scales/dsl, Shell/dsl Arby's, Bur King, China Buffet, Dickey's BBQ, DQ, Golden Gate Chine KFC/Taco Bell, La Carreta Mexican, McDonald's, Runza, St bucks, Taco John's, The Kitchen, Wendy's Best Value I Comfort Inn, Days Inn, Hampton Inn, Holiday Inn Expre

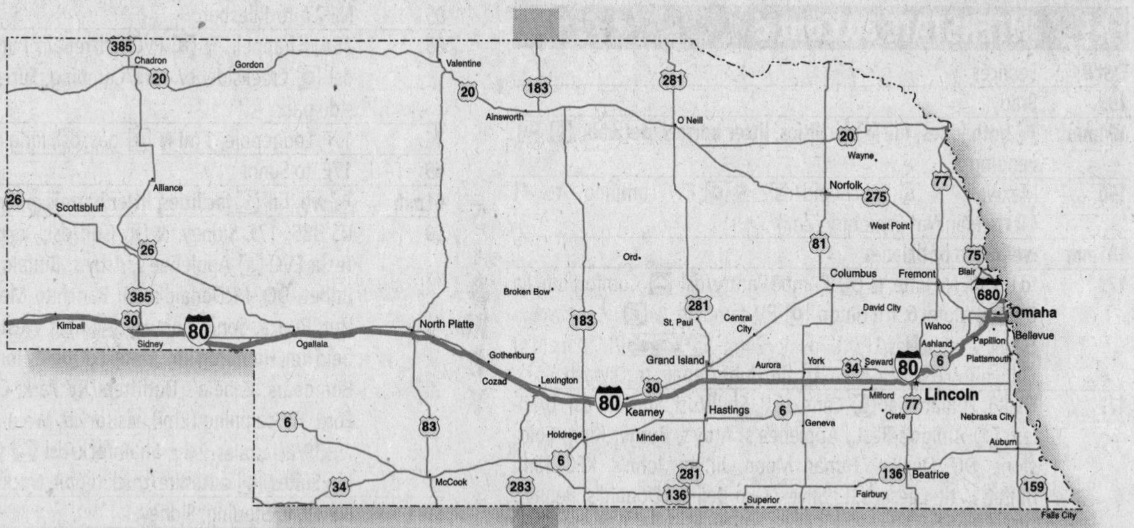

NE

INTERSTATE 80 Cont'd

Exit	Services
353	Continued New Victorian Inn, Super 8, Yorkshire Motel H, Buick/GMC, Chevrolet, Elms RV Park, Ford, RV Camp, Walmart/Subway, S Petro/Phillips 66/Iron Skillet/Pizza Hut/dsl/24hr/@, Shell/Huddle House/dsl Applebee's Best Western+, Motel 6 Blue Beacon, Freightliner, tires/wash/lube
351mm	**eb, full facilities, info, litter barrels, petwalk, vending**
348	93E, to Bradshaw
342	93A, Henderson, N Prairie Oasis Camping, S Henderson Trkstp/dsl Subway Sun Motel H
338	41D, to Hampton
332	NE 14, Aurora, 2-3 mi N Casey's McDonald's, Pizza Hut, Subway Budget Host H, Ford, to Plainsman Museum, S Loves/Arby's/dsl/scales/24hr
324	41B, to Giltner
318	NE 2, to Grand Island, S KOA (seasonal)
317mm	**wb, full facilities, info, litter barrels, petwalk, vending**
315mm	**eb, full facilities, info, litter barrels, petwalk, vending**
314mm	Platte River
314	Locust Street, to Grand Island, 4-6 N food, gas, lodging
312	US 34/281, to Grand Island, N Bosselman/Pilot/Little Caesar's/Subway/scales/dsl/24hr, Fat Dogs Thunder Road Grill Motel 6, USA Inn H, Mormon Island RA, to Stuhr Pioneer Museum, S Phillips 66/Arby's/dsl Days Inn, Quality Inn/Riverfront Grille Hastings Museum (15mi), Peterbilt
305	40C, to Alda, N Sinclair/dsl, TA/Country Pride/dsl/scales/24hr/@, S **Crane Meadows Nature Ctr/**
300	NE 11, Wood River, N to Cheyenne SRA, S Pilot/Subway/dsl/scales/24hr motel/RV park
291	10D, Shelton, N War Axe SRA
285	10C, Gibbon, N Petro Oasis/dsl RV camping, Windmill SP, S Country Inn
279	NE 10, to Minden, N Conoco/dsl, S Pioneer Village Camping (13mi)
275	NE 10, Kearney, N Archway Mon
275mm	The Great Platte River Road Archway Monument
272	NE 44, Kearney, N Casey's, Casey's/dsl, Cenex/dsl, Phillips 66/Subway/dsl, Pump&Pantry/dsl Amigo's, Angus Burger,
272	Continued Arby's, Burger King, Coppermill Steaks, DQ, Egg&I, El Limon, El Maguey, Firehouse Subs, Freddy's, Gourmet House Japanese, Hunan's Rest., King's Buffet, LJ Silver, McDonald's, Moe's SW, Old Chicago, Perkins, Pizza Hut, Red Lobster, Ruby Tuesday, Runza, Taco Bell, Taco John's, USA Steaks, Wendy's, Whiskey Creek AmericInn, Candlewood Suites, Comfort Inn, Country Inn&Suites, Days Inn, EconoLodge, Fairfield Inn, Hampton Inn, Holiday Inn, Howard Johnson, La Quinta, Microtel, Midtown Western Inn, Motel 6, New Victorian Inn, Quality Inn, Ramada Inn, Rodeway Inn, Super 8, Western Inn South, Wingate Inn H, $General, Apache Camper Ctr, Boogaart's, Buick/Cadillac, Chevrolet, Chrysler/Dodge/Jeep, Kearney RV Park/camping, Museum of NE Art, to Archway Mon, U NE Kearney, Verizon, Walmart (3mi), S Conoco/dsl Skeeter's BBQ Best Western+, Holiday Inn Express
271mm	**wb, full facilities, info, litter barrels, petwalk,**
269mm	**eb, full facilities, info, litter barrels, petwalk,**
263	Rd 10 b, Odessa, N Sapp Bros./Apple Barrel Rest./dsl UP Wayside
257	US 183, Elm Creek, N Pilot/Subway/dsl/scales/24hr Rodeway Inn Antique Car Museum, Sunny Meadows Camping, S Nebraska Prairie Museum (9mi)
248	Overton, N Jay Bros/dsl
237	US 283, Lexington, N Casey's, Cenex/dsl, Gulf/dsl, Phillips 66/dsl Arby's, Baskin-Robbins, Burger King, Delight Donuts, DQ, Hong Kong Buffet, Little Caesar's, McDonald's, Pizza Hut, San Pedro Mexican, Sonic, Wendy's Comfort Inn, Days Inn, Econolodge, Holiday Inn Express, Minute Man Motel H, $General, $Tree, Advance Parts, Buick/Chevrolet, Military Vehicle Museum, O'Reilly Parts, Plum Creek Foods, Verizon, Walmart/Subway, S Sinclair/dsl/@ Kirk's Café Super 8 to Johnson Lake RA (6mi)
231	Darr Rd
227mm	**both lanes, full facilities, info, litter barrels, petwalk, vending**
222	NE 21, Cozad, N Casey's/dsl, Cenex/dsl Burger King, DQ, Panda Buffet, Pizza Hut, Runza, Subway Knights Inn, Rodeway Inn H, $General, Firestone/auto, museum
211	NE 47, Gothenburg, N Cenex/dsl, Cenex/dsl/24hr Lasso Espresso, McDonald's, Mi Ranchito Mexican, NE Grill, Pizza Hut, Runza Comfort Suites, Howard Johnson, Travel Inn H, Buick/Chevrolet, Carquest, Pony Express Sta Museum (1mi), S Blue Heron Camping/Gas

AURORA

KEARNEY

LEXINGTON

= gas = food = lodging = other = rest stop

NE

INTERSTATE 80 Cont'd

	Exit #	Services
	199	Brady
	194mm	**both lanes, full facilities, litter barrels, petwalk, , , vending**
	190	Maxwell, N Ranchland/dsl, S RV camping, to Ft McPherson Nat Cemetary (2mi)
	181mm	**weigh sta both lanes**
N PLATTE	179	to US 30, N Platte, N Pump&Pantry/dsl Comfort Inn, La Quinta, Motel 6, Tru Hilton RV camping, S FLYING J/Denny's/dsl/scales/LP/RV dump/24hr, Loves/McDonald's/Subway/dsl/scales/24hr tire/lube/repair, truckwash
	177	US 83, N Platte, N Cenex/dsl, Shell/dsl, Sinclair/dsl, U-Fillem Amigo's Rest., Applebee's, Arby's, Burger King, Coldstone, DQ, Dunkin', Hunan Moon, Jimmy John's, KFC, King Buffet, Little Caesar's, LJ Silver/Taco Bell, McDonald's, Penny's Diner, Perkins, Pizza Hut, Qdoba, Quiznos, Ruby Tuesday, Runza, San Pedro Mexican, Sonic, Starbucks, Subway, Wendy's, Whiskey Creek Steaks Baymont Inn, Blue Spruce Motel, Fairfield Inn, Hampton Inn, Howard Johnson, Knights Inn, Motel 6, Quality Inn H, $General, $Tree, Advance Parts, Goodyear/auto, Harley-Davidson, Herberger's, Holiday RV Park, museum, Staples, SunMart Foods, Tire Pros, to Buffalo Bill's Ranch, Verizon, visitor ctr, Walgreens, Walmart/Subway, S Cenex, Gulf/Taco Bell/dsl/24hr, U-Fillem/Subway/dsl/RV dump Taco John's Best Western+, Comfort Inn, Days Inn, Holiday Inn Express, Super 8 Chevrolet/Cadillac, Chrysler/Dodge/Jeep, dsl repair, Ford/Lincoln, Hobby Lobby, Honda, Menards, Nissan, Seevers Tire/auto, to Lake Maloney RA, Toyota, vet, veterans memorial/info
	164	56C, Hershey, N Shell/Western Cafe/dsl/24hr/@ KJ's Ranch Store
	160mm	**both lanes, full facilities, info, litter barrels, petwalk, ,**
	158	NE 25, Sutherland, N Park Motel (1mi) RV camping, S Sinclair/Godfather's Pizza/dsl RV camping
	149mm	Central/Mountain time zone
	145	51C, Paxton, N Shell/dsl/24hr Days Inn RV camping
	133	51B, Roscoe
	132mm	**wb, full facilities, info, litter barrels, petwalk, ,**
OGALLALA	126	US 26, NE 61, Ogallala, N Casey's/dsl, Cenex/dsl, Kwik Stop, Sapp Bros/Shell/dsl/24hr, Watering Hole/dsl, Western/dsl Arby's, Front Street Cafe, Golden Village Chinese, Margarita's, McDonald's, Peking Chinese, Pizza Hut, Runza, Spur Steaks, Valentino's Days Inn, Lonesome Dove Lodge, Quality Inn, Travelodge H, $General, Bomgaars, Buick/Chevrolet/GMC, Chrysler/Dodge/Jeep, Firestone/auto, Ford/Lincoln, NAPA, O'Reilly Parts, SunMart Foods, to Lake McConaughy, U-Save Drug, Verizon, S EVC, Gulf/Subway/dsl, TA/Country Pride/dsl/scales/24hr/@ DQ, Mi Ranchito Mexican, Royal Buffet, Wendy's Hampton Inn, Holiday Inn Express, Rodeway Inn, Super 8 Ace Hardware, Countryview Camping, Sleepy Sunflower RV Park, truck repair, Walmart/dsl
	124mm	**eb, full facilities, info, litter barrels, petwalk, s,**
	117	51A, Brule, N Happy Jack's/dsl Riverside RV camping
	107	25B, Big Springs, N Big Springs/dsl, FLYING J/Grandma Max's/Subway/dsl/scales/24hr/@ Sam Bass' Steaks Motel 6 truckwash, S McGreer's Camping
	102	I-76 S, to Denver
	102mm	S Platte River
	101	US 138, to Julesburg, S truck parking
	99mm	scenic turnout eb
	95	NE 27, to Julesburg
	85	25A, Chappell, N FVC/dsl/repair, Pump&Pantrydsl, She dsl Creekside RV Park/Camping, Super Foods, USPO, w side park
	76	17F, Lodgepole, 1 mi N gas/dsl, lodging
	69	17E, to Sunol
	61mm	**wb, full facilities, litter barrels, petwalk, , , vendi**
SIDNEY	59	US 385, 17J, Sidney, N Gulf/dsl, Sapp Bros/Shell/dsl/24 Tesla EVC Applebee's, Arby's, Buffalo Point Rest., China Buffet, DQ, McDonald's, Mi Ranchito Mexican, Perkins, Piz Hut, Runza, Sonic, Subway Best Western+, Days Inn, Fa field Inn, Hampton Inn, Motel 6, Quality Inn auto/dsl repa Bomgaars, Cabela's Outfitters/RV Park, Chrysler/Dodge/Jee Ford, RV camping (2mi), visitor ctr, Walmart, S Lov /IHOP/dsl/scales/24hr, Shamrock/dsl Comfort Inn, Coun Inn Suites auto tire/truck repair, truckwash
	55	NE 19, to Sterling, Sidney
	51.5mm	**/hist marker eb, full facilities, litter barrels, petwalk, , vending**
	48	to Brownson
	38	rd 17 b, Potter, N FVC/dsl/LP repair
	29	53A, Dix, 1/2 mi N food, gas
KIMBALL	22	53E, Kimball, 1-2 mi N Kwik Stop, Vince's/dsl Piz Hut, Subway Days Inn, Motel Kimball, Sleep4Less Mo city park, Kimball RV Park (seasonal), Main St Mkt, NAPA
	20	NE 71, Kimball, 0-2 mi N Conoco/dsl, FVC/dsl, Kwik Sto Vince's/dsl O'Henry's Diner, Pizza Hut, Subway 1st terstate Inn, Days Inn, Motel Kimball, Sleep4Less Motel, Sup 8 city park, Kimball RV Park (seasonal), Main St Mkt, NA
	8	53C, to Bushnell
	1	53B, Pine Bluffs, 1 mi N RV camping
	0mm	Nebraska/Wyoming state line

INTERSTATE 680 (Omaha)

Exit #	Services
I-680 begins/ends on I-80, exit 27.	
29b a	I-80, W to Omaha, E to Des Moines.
28	IA 191, to Neola, Persia
21	L34, Beebeetown
19mm	**wb, full facilities, info, litter barrels, petwalk, ,**
16mm	**eb, full facilities, info, litter barrels, petwalk, ,**
15mm	scenic overlook
71	I-29 N, to Sioux City
66	Honey Creek
3b a	(61 b a from wb) I-29, S to Council Bluffs, IA 988, to Crescen E Casey's/dsl to ski area
1	County Rd
14mm	Nebraska/Iowa state line, Missouri River, Mormon Bridge
13	US 75 S, 30th St, Florence, E Shell/dsl Enzo's, Zesto Di er HyVee Drug, LDS Temple, Mormon Trail Ctr, W Fl ence/dsl
12	US 75 N, 48th St, E Cenex/dsl Burger King (2mi), Ta Bell (2mi)
9	72nd St, 1-2 mi E Kwikshop Burger King, Gold Corral, Jimmy John's, KFC, Panda Express, Taco Bell, Villa Inn H, Big Lots, Marshall's, Petsmart, Target, Walgree W Cunningham Lake RA
6	NE 133, Irvington, E BP, MurphyUSA/dsl Burger Kin Jimmy John's $Tree, Verizon, Walmart/Subway/drugs/24 W Legend's Grill, Villagio Pizzeria, Zesto Cafe Fairfie Inn, Holiday Inn Express

INTERSTATE 680 (Omaha)

Exit #	Services
5	Fort St, W KwikShop, QT Dunkin' CVS Drug, HyVee Foods, Walgreens
4	NE 64, Maple St, E BP, W Kum&Go/dsl, Megasaver Burger King, China 1, Godfather's Pizza, Jimmy John's, La Mesa Mexican, McDonald's, Pizza Hut, Runza, Subway, Taco Bell, Taco John's Comfort Suites, La Quinta $General, Family Fare, O'Reilly Parts, vet
3	US 6, Dodge St, E Cheesecake Factory, Granite City Rest., JC Mandarin Chinese, Panera Bread, PF Chang's AmericInn, Marriott AAA, Audi/VW, BMW, Dick's, Hyundai, Jaguar/Land Rover, JC Penney, Mazda, Mini, Subaru, Von Maur, Whole Foods Mkt, W Phillips 66 Burger King, Chick-fil-A, China Buffet, Cilantro's, DQ, Jimmy John's, McDonald's, Starbucks, Subway, Which Wich? Best Western, Hampton Inn, Sheraton, Super 8, TownPlace Suites Cadillac, Chevrolet, Costco/gas, Discount Tire, Menard's
2	Pacific St, E Conoco Subway, W BP

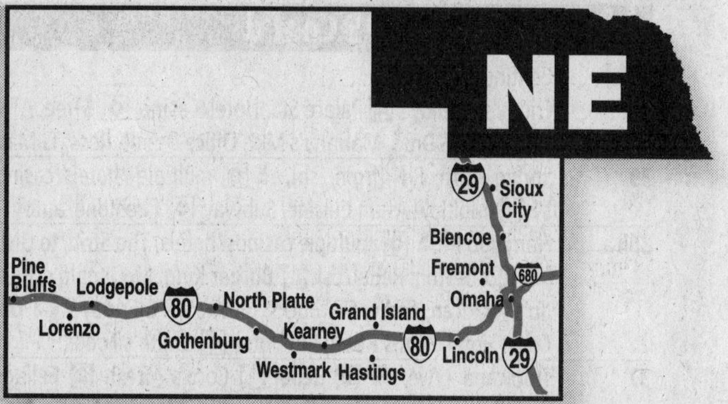

1	NE 38, W Center Rd, E Cenex/dsl Don Carmelo's, Don&Millie's Rest., Subway, W Phillips 66 Arby's, Burger King, Dickey's BBQ, IHOP, Krispy Kreme, McAlister's Deli, Ozark BBQ, Starbucks, Subway, Taco Bell, Wendy's $Tree, Baker's Foods/dsl, Office Depot, TJ Maxx, Tuesday Morning
0mm	**I-680 begins/ends on I-80, exit 446.**

NE NV

NEVADA

INTERSTATE 15

Exit #	Services
123mm	Nevada/Arizona state line, Pacific/Mountain time zone
122	Lp 15, Mesquite, E **NV Welcome Ctr both lanes, full facilities, petwalk,** Arco, Maverik/dsl, Shell/DQ/dsl Alberto's Mexican, Cafe Rio, Canton Chinese, Cucina Italiano, Dominos, Golden West Rest./casino, Jack-in-the-Box, KFC, Los Lupes, Panda Garden, Peggy Sue's Cafe, Taco Bell Best Western, Rising Star $General, Ace Hardware, AutoZone, Big O Tire, CarQuest, city park, Smith's/Subway/dsl, Sun Resort RV Park, USPO, Walgreens, W 76/dsl/LP/RV park McDonald's, Starbucks Eureka Motel/casino, Virgin River Hotel/casino
120	Lp 15, Mesquite, Bunkerville, E Shell/dsl, Sinclair/dsl, Terrible's McDonald's Casablanca Resort/casino/RV Park, Oasis Resort RV Park USPO, W Chevron/dsl Del Taco, Popeye's, Roberto's Tacos Holiday Inn Express H, $Tree, Ford/RV Ctr, Verizon, Walmart/Subway
118	Lower Flat Top Dr, W FLYING J/dsl/scales24hr
112	NV 170, Riverside, Bunkerville
110mm	**truck parking both lanes, litter barrels**
100	to Carp, Elgin
96mm	**truck parking both lanes, litter barrels**
93	NV 169, to Logandale, Overton, E Chevron (3mi) Lake Mead NRA, Lost City Museum
91	NV 168, Glendale, W Arco/dsl Muddy River Rest. USPO
90.5mm	Muddy River
90	NV 168 (from nb), Glendale, Moapa, W gas Moapa Indian Reservation, USPO
88	Hidden Valley
88mm	**parking area both lanes, litter barrels**
84	Byron
80	Ute
75	Valley of Fire SP, Lake Mead NRA, E Chevron/dsl casino, fireworks
64	US 93 N, Great Basin Hwy, to Ely, Great Basin NP, W Loves/Subway/Godfather's/dsl/scales/24hr

LAS VEGAS

60mm	**livestock check sta sb**
58	NV 604, Las Vegas Blvd, to Apex, Nellis AFB
54	Speedway Blvd, Hollywood Blvd, E Petro/Sinclair/dsl/scales/24hr/@ Race Day Cafe Las Vegas Speedway, W Speedee Mart/dsl
52	rd 215 W
50	Lamb Ave, **1-2 mi** E Comfort Inn Hitchin Post RV Park
48	Craig Rd, E Arco, Pilot/KFC/Pizza Hut/dsl/scales/24hr, Shell, Sinclair/Subway/dsl Burger King, Jack-in-the-Box, Taco Bell, Zapata's Cantina Comfort Inn 7-11, Firestone/auto, Freightliner, to Nellis AFB, W 7-11 Cane's, Cannery Grill, Carl's Jr, Chipotle Mexican, Del Taco, Famous Dave's BBQ, Five Guys, In-N-Out, Jamba Juice, Marble Slab, Mulligan's, Panda Express, Sonic, Starbucks, Subway Best Western, Hampton Inn, Springhill Suites Batteries&Bulbs, Lowe's, Sam's Club/gas
46	Cheyenne Ave, E CiCi's Pizza, Marianna's Mkt, Panda Express, Subway, Taco Bell $Tree, 7-11, NAPA, vet, W 7-11, Valero/Mortons/Subway/dsl/LP24hr Denny's, McDonald's, Tacos El Gordo Sunrise Inn Aamco, Blue Beacon, dsl repair, Kenworth, SpeedCo, tires
45	Lake Mead Blvd, E Chevron, Rebel/dsl Arby's, Burger King, Jack-in-the-Box, McDonald's 7-11, PepBoys, W Arco/dsl
44	Washington Ave (from sb), E casinos
43	D St (from nb), same as 44
42b a	I-515 to LV, US 95 N to Reno, US 93 S to Phoenix
41b a	NV 159, Charleston Blvd, E 7-11, Arco/dsl Cheesecake Factory, Chipotle Premium Outlets/famous brands, Walgreens, W Chevron, Rebel/dsl Carl's Jr, Del Taco, Jimmy John's, McDonald's, Starbucks, Wendy's H, CVS Drug, Smith's Foods
40	Sahara Ave, E Artisan Hotel multiple casinos/hotels, The Strip, W 7-11, Arco/dsl, Chevron, Rebel/dsl, Shel Carl's Jr, Chipotle Mexican, DQ, El Pollo Loco, In-N-Out, KFC, Landry's Seafood, Los Tacos, Macaroni Grill, McDonald's, Panda Express, PDQ Cafe, Pizza Hut, Shilla BBQ, Starbucks, Subway, TGI

NV

INTERSTATE 15 Cont'd

LAS VEGAS

40	Continued Friday's, Wendy's Palace Sta. Hotel/Casino $Tree, AT&T, casinos, CVS Drug, Mariana's Mkt, Office Depot, Ross, TJ Maxx
39	Spring Mtn Rd (from sb), E multiple hotels/casinos, W Multiple Asian Cuisine, Subway Firestone/auto
38b a	Flamingo Rd, E multiple casinos/hotels, The Strip, to UNLV, W Chevron, Rebel/dsl Burger King, McDonald's, Ricardo's Mexican, Sonic, Starbucks, Subway, TGIFriday's Gold Coast Hotel, Palms Hotel, Rio Hotel Smith's Foods
37	Tropicana Ave, E Rebel Coco's Rest. Bellagio, Excaliber Hotel, Hooters Hotel/casino, Mandalay Bay, MGM Grand, Monte Carlo, Motel 6, Tropicana Hotel multiple hotels/casinos, W Rebel/dsl, Shell/Subway, Standard, Texaco Burger King, Cane's, Dennys, In-N-Out, Jack-in-the-Box, McDonald's, Wendy's Budget Suites, Days Inn, Hampton Inn, La Quinta, Motel 6, Orleans Hotel, Siegel Suites
36	Russell Rd, E multiple hotels/casinos, to , W Chevron/Herbst/dsl Courtyard, Fairfield Inn, Holiday Inn Express, Residence Inn, Staybridge Suites
34	to I-215 E, Las Vegas Blvd, to The Strip, E McCarran Airport
33	NV 160, to Blue Diamond, Death Valley, E 7-11, Chevron/dsl, Rebel/dsl Bootlegger Bistro, Buffalo Wild Wings, Burger King, Cane's, Chili's, Chipotle Mexican, Denny's, Dickey's BBQ, Dunkin', Five Guys, Hawaiian BBQ, IHOP, Jersey Mikes, McDonald's, NY Pizza, Outback Steaks, Panda Express, Popeyes, Smashburger, Starbucks, Subway, Wienerschnitzel Baymont Inn, Budget Suites, Caribe Resort, Hilton Garden CVS Drug, factory outlet/famous brands, Oasis RV Resort, Smith's Foods, W Chevron/dsl, Shell, TA/Burger King/Subway/TacoTime/dsl/LP/scales/24hr/@ Cafe Rio, Carl's Jr, Chipotle, Del Taco, Domino's, Famous Dave's BBQ, In-N-Out, Jack-in-the-Box, McDonald's, Panda Express, Papa Murphy's, Subway Silverton Lodge/Casino AT&T, $Tree, 99c Store, Albertson's, Bass Pro-Shops, BigLots, Discount Tire, GNC, Kohl's, Meineke, Office Depot, PetCo, Ross, Target, Verizon, Walgreens, WorldMkt
31	Silverado Ranch Blvd, E Steak'n Shake South Point Hotel/Casino
30	W Cactus Ave, W Chevron/dsl
27	NV 146, to Henderson, Lake Mead, Hoover Dam, **0-2 mi** E Arco, Chevron/dsl, Shell Burger King, Jack-in-the-Box, Starbucks, Subway Best Western, Hampton Inn Camping World, casino, W vet
25	NV 161, Sloan, **1 mi** E Camping World
24mm	**bus/truck check sta nb**

JEAN

12	NV 161, to Goodsprings, Jean, E Shell/dsl Denny's Gold Strike Casino/hotel, NV Correctional, NV HP, skydiving, USPO, W Chevron/dsl
1	Primm, E Chevron/Subway/dsl, Texaco/dsl Carl's Jr, Dennys, KFC, Mad Greek Cafe, McDonald's, Panda Express, Starbucks, Taco Bell Buffalo Bill's Resort/casino, factory outlets, Primm Valley Resort/casino, W FLYING J/Subway/Qdoba/DQ/dsl/scales Whiskey Pete's Hotel/casino
0mm	Nevada/California state line

INTERSTATE 80

WENDOVER

Exit #	Services
411mm	Nevada/Utah state line
410	US 93A, to Ely, W Wendover, **S NV Welcome Ctr/info, full facilities** Chevron/dsl, Pilot/Arby's/dsl/scales/24hr, Shell/Taco Time/dsl Burger King, McDonald's, Pizza Hut, Subway
410	Continued Knights Inn, Motel 6, Nugget Hotel/casino, Peppermill Hotel/casino/RV parking, Rainbow Hotel/casino, Red Garter Hotel/casino Best Hardware, city park, KOA, Smith's Foods/dsl
407	Ola, W Wendover
405mm	Pacific/Mountain time zone
398	to Pilot Peak
390mm	Silverzone Pass, elevation 5940
387	to Shafter
378	NV 233, to Montello, Oasis
376	to Pequop
373mm	Pequop Summit, elev 6967, **both lanes, litter barrels, rest rooms**
365	to Independence Valley, N prison camp
360	to Moor
354mm	**parking area eb**

WELLS

352b a	US 93, Great Basin Hwy, E Wells, N Chevron/dsl/LP, Conoco/dsl, Petro/Dunkin'/dsl/café/casino Bella's Diner, Burger King/Subway Motel 6, Rest Inn Motel, Sharon Motel, Super 8 Crossroads RV Park, repair, Tire Factory, S FLYING J/dsl/scales/LP/casino/RV Dump/24hr, LNG, Loves/McDonalds/dsl/scales/24hr Hampton Inn Great Basin NP
351	W Wells, N Wells/dsl/LP Family$, Mtn Shadows RV Park, Roy's Foods, USPO, Well's Hardware, S Angel Lake RV Park, to Angel Lake RA
348	to Beverly Hills, N RV camping
343	to Welcome, Starr Valley, N food , Welcome RV P
333	Deeth, Starr Valley
328	to River Ranch
321	NV 229, Halleck, Ruby Valley
318mm	N Fork Humboldt River
317	to Elburz
314	to Ryndon, Devils Gate, N Sinclair/cafe/dsl, S camping
312mm	**check sta both lanes**
310	to Osino, **4 mi S** Valley View RV Park

ELKO

303	E Elko, N Flyers/CFN/dsl, Sinclair/Arctic Circle/dsl/2 Wingers Holiday Inn Express, Home 2 Suites, Ledstone Hotel, TownePlace Suites, S Chevron/dsl, Conoco/dsl, Maverik/dsl, Sinclair/dsl Blue Moon Rest., Burger King, Chef Cheng's Chinese, Domino's, DQ, Garibaldi's Mexican, McDonald's/playplace, Monkey Sun Chinese, Pizza B, Pizza Hut, Quiznos, Subway, Taco Time, Toki Ona Diner, Wendy's Best Value Inn, Best Western, Budget Inn, Comfort, Days Inn, High Desert Inn, Hilton Garden, Holiday Motel, Motel 6, Quality Inn, Red Lion Inn/casino, Sheraton Four Points, Super 8, Travelodge H, Albertson's, AT&T, Big O Tires, Buick/Cadillac/Chevrolet/GMC, Cal Ranch Store, city park, Double Dice RV Park, Ford, Gold Country RV Park, Goodyear/auto, Iron Horse RV Park, JC Penney, Kenworth, NE NV Museum, Valley View RV Park
301	NV 225, Elko, N Maverik/dsl 9 Beans/Burrito, Arby's, Burger King, Denny's, Greatwall Chinese, Jack-in-the-Box, Jimmy John's, Mattie's Grill, McDonald's/playplace, Papa Murphy's, Port of Subs, RoundTable Pizza Baymont, Shilo Inn Suites AT&T, GNC, Home Depot, JoAnn Fabrics, Marshall's, Petco, Raley's Foods, Ross, Verizon, Walmart/Subway, S Shell, Shell/dsl Costa Vida, Dos Amigos, Little Caesar's, Sergio's Mexican, Starbucks, Subway, Taco Bell American Inn, Centre Motel, Economy Inn, Elko Inn, Esquire Inn, Hampton Inn, Manor Inn, Midtown Motel, Rodeway Inn, Scottish Inn, Stampede Motel, Stockmen's Hotel/casino

INTERSTATE 80 Cont'd

301 Continued
Thunderbird Motel [other] [H], Advance Parts, [RV], AutoZone, Cimarron West RV Park, CVS Drug, Family$, O'Reilly Parts, Smith's Foods/dsl, transmission, Verizon

298 W Elko, **S** [gas] Sinclair/Port of Subs/dsl

292 to Hunter, **N** [other] CA Trail Interpretive Ctr

285mm Humboldt River, tunnel

282 NV 221, E Carlin, **N** [other] prison area

280 NV 766, Carlin, **N** [food] Pizza Factory [other] Desert Gold RV Park, dsl repair, **S** [gas] Chevron/dsl, Pilot/Subway/dsl/scales/24hr [food] Chin's Cafe, Rigobertos Mexican, State Café/casino [lodging] Carlin Inn, Cavalier Motel [other] Ace Hardware, Family$, tires, USPO

279 NV 278 (from eb), to W Carlin, **1 mi S** [gas] Flyers/dsl

271 to Palisade

270mm Emigrant Summit, elevation 6114, **truck parking both lanes, litter barrels**

268 to Emigrant

261 NV 306, to Beowawe, Crescent Valley

259mm **[RS] both lanes, full [handicap] facilities, litter barrels, petwalk, [picnic]**

257mm Humboldt River

254 to Dunphy

244 to Argenta

233 NV 304, to Battle Mountain, **N** [gas] Conoco/dsl [food] Mama's Pizza/deli [lodging] Royal Inn [other] [H], Ace Hardware, FoodTown

231 NV 305, Battle Mountain, **1 mi N** [gas] FLYING J/76/Blimpie/dsl/casino/24hr, Chevron/dsl, Maverik/dsl [food] El Aguila Real, Hide-a-way Steaks, McDonald's, Ming Dynasty, Owl Rest., Pizza Factory, Port of Subs [lodging] Big Chief Motel, Nevada Hotel, Owl Motel, Super 8 [other] [H], city park, Family$, Mills Drug, NAPA, NAPA Care, Tire Factory, USPO

229 NV 304, W Battle Mountain, **N** [gas] FLYING J/76/dsl/casino/scales/24hr, Shell/dsl [food] Colt Rest./casino [lodging] Big Chief Motel, Rodeway Inn [other] Colt RV camping, NAPA Care, Tire Factory

222 to Mote

216 Valmy, **N** [gas] Chevron/USPO/dsl, **S** **[RS] both lanes, full [handicap] facilities, litter barrels, petwalk, [phone], [picnic], RV dump**

212 to Stonehouse

205 to Pumpernickel Valley

203 to Iron Point

200 Golconda Summit, elevation 5159, [other] **truck parking both lanes, litter barrels**

194 Golconda, **N** [other] USPO

187 to Button Point, **N** **[RS] both lanes, full [handicap] facilities, litter barrels, petwalk, [phone], [picnic], RV dump**

180 NV 794, E Winnemucca Blvd

178 NV 289, Winnemucca Blvd, Winnemucca, **S** [gas] Chevron/dsl, Maverik/dsl [food] Rte 66 Grill, Sonoma Grill [lodging] Budget Inn, Candlewood Suites, Cozy Motel, Frontier Motel, Valu Motel [other] [H], Advance Parts, carwash

176 US 95 N, Winnemucca, **N** [gas] Pacific Pride/dsl, **S** [gas] FLYING J/dsl/LP/RV dump/24hr, Chevron/dsl/24hr, Conoco/dsl, G Gas, Kwik Serv/dsl [food] Burger King, China Garden, Dos Amigos Mexican, Dotty's, Griddle Rest., Jack-in-the-Box, KFC/LJ Silver, Little Caesar's, McDonald's/playplace, Pig BBQ, Pizza Hut, Port of Subs, RoundTable Pizza, Sid's Rest., Subway, Taco Bell, Taco Time [lodging] Best Western, Country Hearth Inn, Economy Inn, Holiday Inn Express, Holiday Motel, Model T Motel/casino/RVPark, Motel 6, Park Hotel, Pyrenees Motel, Quality Inn, Regency Inn, Santa Fe Inn, Scott Motel, Scottish Inn, Super 8, Winnemucca Inn/casino, Winner Hotel/casino [other] [H], auto/truck repair,

LOVELOCK

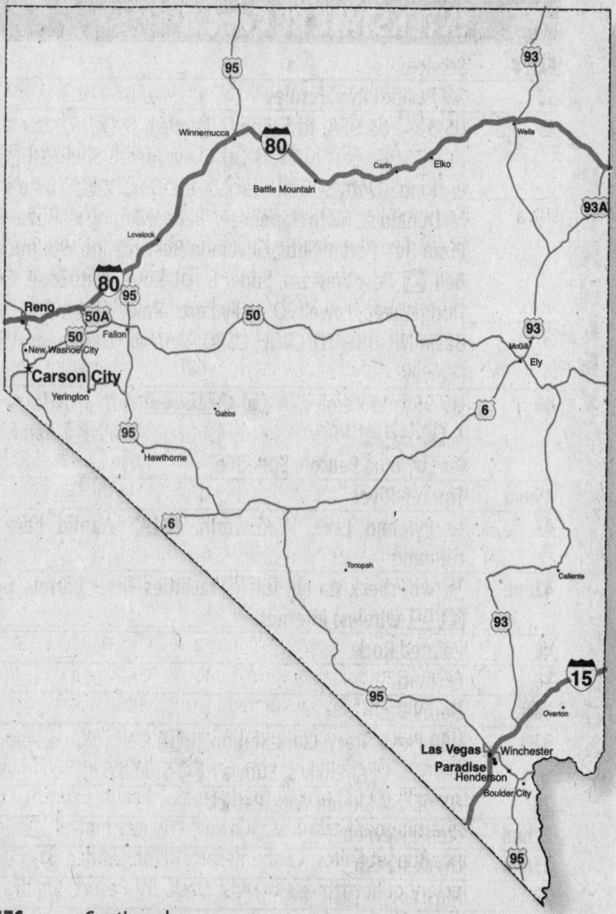

176 Continued
AutoZone, Ford, O'Reilly Parts, Ridley's Foods, RV camping, Schwab Tire, Verizon, Walmart/Subway

173 W Winnemucca, **N** [gas] Pilot/Subway/dsl/scales/24hr, **S** [other] [RV]

168 to Rose Creek, **S** [other] prison area

158 to Cosgrave, **S** **[RS] both lanes, full [handicap] facilities, litter barrels, petwalk, [phone], [picnic]**

151 Mill City, **N** [gas] TA/Subway/Taco Bell/Fork/dsl/casino/24hr/@

149 NV 400, Mill City, **1 mi N** [gas] TA/Subway/Taco Bell/Fork/dsl/24hr/@, **S** [other] Star Point Gen. Store/RV camping

145 Imlay, **S** [other] Star Peak RV Park

138 Humboldt

129 Rye Patch Dam, **N** [other] to Rye Patch SRA, **S** [gas] Chevron/Rye Patch Trkstp/dsl

119 to Rochester, Oreana

112 to Coal Canyon, **S** [other] to correctional ctr

107 E Lovelock (from wb), same as 106

106 Main St, Lovelock, **N** [gas] Chevron/dsl/LP, PJ's Gas/subs/dsl [food] Black Rock Grill, Cowpoke Cafe, McDonald's, Pizza Factory [lodging] Cadillac Inn, Covered Wagon Motel, Punch Inn/casino, Royal Inn, Super 10 Motel [other] [H], auto care, city park/playground/restrooms, Family$, Lazy K Camping, Safeway Foods, USPO, **S** [gas] Conoco/Port of Subs/dsl24hr

105 W Lovelock (from eb), **N** [gas] Shop'n Go/dsl, Valero/dsl [food] La Casita Mexican [lodging] Lovelock Inn [other] [H], Brookwood RV Park, museum, NAPA, same as 106

93 to Toulon, **S** [other] [RV]

83 US 95 S, to Fallon, **S** **[RS] both lanes, full [handicap] facilities, litter barrels, [phone], [picnic]**

78 to Jessup

65 to Hot Springs, Nightingale

NV

INTERSTATE 80 Cont'd

FERNLEY

Exit #	Services
50	NV Pacific Pkwy, Fernley
48	US 50A, US 95A, to Fallon, E Fernley, N FLYING J/Denny's/dsl/scales/Lp/24hr, S Chevron/dsl, Shell/dsl Burger King, Dotty's Grill, Jack-in-the-Box, KFC, Louie's China, McDonald's, Moto Japanese, Papa Murphy's, Pizza Factory, Pizza Hut, Port of Subs, Silverado Rest./casino, Starbucks, Taco Bell Best Western, Super 8 $Tree, AutoZone, Chrysler/Dodge/Jeep, Lowe's, O'Reilly Parts, Raley's Mkt, tires, to Great Basin NP, URGENT CARE, USPO, Verizon, Walgreens, Walmart/Subway
46	US 95A, W Fernley, N Loves/Arby's/dsl/scales/24hr, S Pilot/DQ/Wendy's/dsl/scales/24hr Comfort Suites Blue Beacon, SpeedCo
45mm	Truckee River
43	to Pyramid Lake, Wadsworth, N Pyramid Lake/dsl/RV camping
42mm	**wb, check sta eb, full facilities, litter barrels, petwalk, , wireless internet**
40	Painted Rock
38	Orchard
36	Derby Dam
32	USA Pkwy, Tracy, Clark Station, S Golden Gate/Port of Subs/dsl/scales Philly's, Subway Studio 6
28	NV 655, Waltham Way, Patrick
27mm	scenic view eb
25mm	**check sta wb**
23	Mustang, S Chevron/dsl
22	Lockwood
21	Vista Blvd, Greg St, Sparks, N Chevron/McDonald's, Qwik-Stop Del Taco Fairfield Inn, Woodspring Suites H, S Petro/Iron Skillet/dsl/24hr/@ Super 8 Peterbilt, truckwash
20	Sparks Blvd, Sparks, N 7-11, Shell/dsl BJ's Rest., Buffalo Wild Wings, Burrito Bandito, Carl's Jr, Chick-fil-A, Chipotle, Fuddruckers, Jersey Mike's, Jimmy John's, Olive Garden, Outback Steaks, Panda Express, Papa John's, Popeye's, Starbucks, Subway, Taco Bell Hampton Inn, Residence Inn AT&T, Best Buy, Discount Tire, GNC, Lowe's, Old Navy, Petco, Scheel's Sports, Schwab Tire, Target, Tires+, TJ Maxx, Verizon, water funpark, S Petro/Iron Skillet/dsl/scales/24hr/@ Super 8 Freightliner
19	E McCarran Blvd, Sparks, N Arco, Chevron/dsl, Sinclair/dsl, TA/Fuddrucker's/dsl/scales/@ Applebee's, Baskin-Robbins, BJ's BBQ, Black Bear Diner, Burger King, Cane's, China King, Domino's, El Pollo Loco, Jack-in-the-Box, KFC, Little Caesar's, McDonald's, Pizza Hut, Pizza+, Port Of Subs, Sizzler, Taco Bell, Wendy's, Wienerschnitzel Aloha Inn, Sunrise Motel, Windsor Inn $Tree, 99c Store, AutoZone, BigLots, CVS Drug, Family$, Foodmaxx Foods, O'Reilly Parts, Ross, Victorian RV Park, S Denny's, Super Burrito Best Western+ NAPA

SPARKS

NV

RENO

Exit #	Services
18	NV 445, Pyramid Way, Sparks, N 7-11 In-N-Out Bourbon Square Casino, Nugget Courtyard, S Nugget Hotel/casino
17	Rock Blvd, Nugget Ave, Sparks, N Arco, Chevron, dsl Safari Motel, Victorian Inn, Wagon Train Motel casinos, O'Reilly Parts, S Nugget Hotel/casino
16	B St, E 4th St, Victorian Ave, N Arco Jack's Cafe Motel 6 Rail City Casino, S Chevron/repair
15	I-580 S, US 395, to Carson City, Susanville, **0-1 mi** S Best Western, Holiday Inn Express, Hyatt Place, La Quinta Costco/gas, Grand Sierra Resort, USPO, Walmart/McDonald's
14	Wells Ave, Reno, N Motel 6, S Chevron/dsl Denny's America's Best Inn, Days Inn, Ramada Inn auto repair, Goodyear, Tire Pros
13	US 395, Virginia St, Reno, N Shell/dsl Taco Shop, S H, Circus Circus, to downtown hotels/casinos, to UNR, Walgreens
12	Keystone Ave, Reno, N Arco Pizza Hut, Starbucks Gateway Inn, Motel 6 7-11, CVS Drug, Raley's Foods, S Chevron/dsl Burger King, Jack-in-the-Box, KFC, Little Caesar's, McDonald's, Port of Subs, Round Table Pizza, Taco Bell, Wendy's casinos, Keystone RV Park, Meineke, NAPA, O'Reilly Parts, SaveMart/drug
10	McCarran Blvd, Reno, N 7-11/dsl, Arco Applebee's, Asian Wok, Baskin-Robbins, Bully's Grill, Burger King, Carl's Jr, Chili's, Chipotle, Del Taco, El Pollo Loco, Hawaiian BBQ, IHOP, Jack-in-the-Box, KFC, Little Caesar's, McDonald's, Papa Murphy's, Pizza+, Popeyes, Qdoba Mexican, RoundTable Pizza, Silver Chop Chinese, Starbucks, Subway, Taco Bell, Taco el Rey $Tree, AT&T, AutoZone, Big O Tires, Discount Tire, Kohl's, O'Reilly Parts, Petsmart, Ross, Safeway/dsl, SaveMart Foods, Staples, Tires+, Walgreens, Walmart/McDonald's, S 7-11 Home Depot, URGENT CARE, vet
9	Robb Dr, N Chevron/dsl, Maverik/dsl Bully's Grill, Burger Me, Casa Grande, China Kitchen, Dickey's BBQ, Domino's, Jimmy John's, Moxie's Cafe, Port Of Subs, Starbucks, Subway Hampton Inn CVS Drug, Raley's Foods, URGENT CARE
8	W 4th St (from eb), Robb Dr, Reno, S RV camping
7	Mogul
6.5mm	**truck parking**/hist marker/scenic view both lanes
5	to E Verdi (from wb no return), N Maria's Mexican
4.5mm	scenic view eb
4	Garson Rd, Boomtown, N Chevron/Boomtown Hotel/dsl/casino Mel's Rest. Cabela's, KOA/RV dump
3.5mm	**check sta eb**
3	Verdi (from wb)
2.5mm	Truckee River
2	Lp 80, to Verdi, N Sinclair/dsl/24hr Jack-in-the-Box Gold Ranch RV Resort/casino
0mm	Nevada/California state line

NOTES

NEW HAMPSHIRE

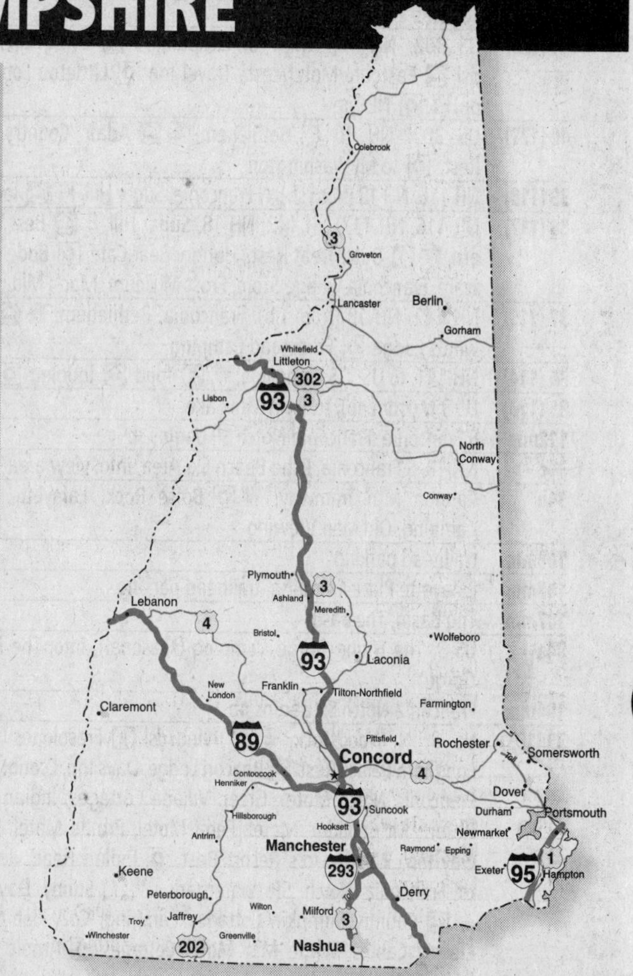

INTERSTATE 89

Exit #	Services
61mm	New Hampshire/Vermont state line, Connecticut River
20 (60)	NH 12A, W Lebanon, **E** Sunoco 99 Rest., Chili's, Dunkin', KFC/Taco Bell, Lui Lui Pizza, Subway GNC, Hannaford Foods, Jo-Ann Fabrics, LL Bean, Rite Aid, Shaw's Foods, TJ Maxx, Town Fair Tire, USPO, **W** Tesla EVC 110 Grill, Applebee's, D'angelo's, Denny's, Five Guys, Koto Japanese, McDonald's, Moe's SW Grill, Panera Bread, Starbucks, Weathervane Seafood, Wendy's Baymont Inn, Fireside Inn $Tree, AT&T, Best Buy, BJ's Whse/dsl, CVS Drug, Home Depot, JC Penney, Kohl's, Michael's, Midas, Old Navy, Petsmart, PriceChopper Foods, Staples, Verizon, Walgreens, Walmart
19 (58)	US 4, NH 10, W Lebanon, **E** Gulf/dsl, Mobil China Station AutoZone, Family$, Ford, Harley-Davidson, Honda, Pricechopper Foods, **W** Sunoco/Maplewoods/dsl O'Reilly Parts
57mm	**Welcome Ctr/ /weigh sta sb, full facilities, litter barrels, petwalk, , , vending, weigh sta nb**
18 (56)	NH 120, Lebanon, **E** Irving/dsl/scales Courtyard (3mi), Hilton Garden, Quality Inn, Residence Inn (2mi) H, Chrysler/Dodge/Jeep, Freightliner, Nissan, to Dartmouth Coll, Volvo/VW, Wilson Tire/repair, **W** Mobil/Subway/dsl, Shell/dsl U-Haul
17 (54)	US 4, to NH 4A, Enfield, **E** vet
16 (52)	Eastman Hill Rd, **E** Gulf/Subway/dsl, **W** Mobil/Dunkin'/dsl Whaleback Ski Area
15 (50)	Montcalm
14 (47)	NH 10 (from sb), N Grantham
13 (43)	NH 10, Grantham, **E** Irving/Gen Store/dsl, **W** Irving/Circle K Dunkin', Pizza Chef vet
40mm	**nb, full facilities, info, litter barrels, petwalk, , picnic table, vending**
12A (37)	Georges Mills, **W** food, lodging, , RV camping, to Sunapee SP
12 (34)	NH 11 W, New London, **2 mi E** Irving/dsl McKenna Rest. Maple Hill Country Inn, New London Inn H
11 (31)	NH 11 E, King Hill Rd, New London, 2-3 mi **E** Fairway Motel, New London Inn
10 (27)	to NH 114, Sutton, **E** to Winslow SP, **1 mi W** to Wadleigh SP
26mm	**sb, full facilities, info, litter barrels, petwalk, , , vending**
9 (19)	NH 103, Warner, **E** Irving/Circle K/Dunkin'/dsl, Shell/Subway/pizza McDonald's Aubuchon Hardware, MktBasket Foods, Rollins SP, **W** to Sunapee SP
8 (17)	NH 103 (from nb, no EZ return), Warner, **1 mi W** gas food museum, to Rollins SP
15mm	Warner River
7 (14)	NH 103, Davisville, **W** Pleasant Lake Camping
12mm	Contoocook River
6 (10)	NH 127, Contoocook, **E** Sunoco Everyday Cafe vet, **W** Elm Brook Park, Sandy Beach Camping (3mi)
5 (8)	US 202 W, NH 9 (exits left from nb), Hopkinton, **W** food RV camping (seasonal)
4 (7)	NH 103, Hopkinton (from nb, no EZ return), **E** gas
3 (4)	Stickney Hill Rd (from nb)
2 (2)	NH 13, Clinton St, Concord, **E** H, **W** NH Audubon Ctr
1 (1)	Logging Hill Rd, Bow, **E** Mobil Chen Yang Li Chinese Hampton Inn
0mm	I-93 N to Concord, S to Manchester, **I-89 begins/ends on I-93, 36mm.**

LITTLETON

INTERSTATE 93

Exit #	Services
2 (11)	I-91, N to St Johnsbury, S to White River Jct. **I-93 begins/ends on I-91, exit 19.**
1 (8)	VT 18, to US 2, to St Johnsbury, 2 mi **E** gas food camping, lodging
1mm	**Welcome Ctr nb, full facilities, info, litter barrels, petwalk, , , vending, WiFi**
131mm	Vermont/New Hampshire state line, Connecticut River, exits 1-2 are in VT.
44 (130)	NH 18, NH 135, **W Welcome Ctr (8am-8pm) /scenic vista both lanes, full facilities, info, litter barrels, petwalk, ,**
43 (125)	NH 135 (from sb), to NH 18, Littleton, 1-2 mi **W** H, same as 42
42 (124)	US 302 E, NH 10 N, Littleton, **E** Citgo/Quiznos, Cumberland Farms, Sunoco/dsl Burger King, Deluxe Pizza, Dunkin', Littleton Diner, Pizza Hut, Subway Littleton Motel Family$, Rite Aid, USPO, Walgreens, **W** Cumberland Farms/dsl, Mobil 99 Rest., Applebee's, Domino's, McDonald's Hampton Inn $Tree, Buick/Chevrolet, Chrysler/Dodge/Jeep/Fiat, Home Depot, KOA (5mi), Lowe's, O'Reilly Parts/VIP Service, Shaw's Foods/Osco Drug, Staples, Tire Whse, TJ Maxx, Town Fair Tire, Verizon, Walmart/Dunkin'

NH

INTERSTATE 93 Cont'd

Exit #	Services
41 (122)	US 302, NH 18, NH 116, Littleton, E Irving/Circle K/dsl Eastgate Motel/rest., Travel Inn Littleton Food Co-op, W NE Tire
40 (121)	US 302, NH 10 E, Bethlehem, E Adair Country Inn/Rest. to Mt Washington
39 (119)	NH 116, NH 18 (from sb), N Franconia, Sugar Hill, W lodging
38 (117)	NH 116, NH 117, NH 142, NH 18, Sugar Hill, E Best Western, W DutchTreat Rest., Hungry Bear Café Bode Hardware, Franconia Village Store, Frost Museum, Mac's Mkt, USPO
37 (115)	NH 142, NH 18 (from nb), Franconia, Bethlehem, W Hillwinds Lodge Franstead Camping
36 (114)	NH 141, to US 3, S Franconia, W food lodging golf
35 (113)	US 3 N (from nb), to Twin Mtn Lake
112mm	S Franconia, Franconia Notch SP begins sb
34c	NH 18, S Franconia, Echo Beach Ski Area, info, view area
34b	Cannon Mtn Tramway, W Boise Rock, Lafayette Place Camping, Old Man Viewing
109mm	trailhead parking
108mm	Lafayette Place Camping, trailhead parking
107mm	The Basin, The Basin
34a	US 3, The Flume Gorge, camping (seasonal), info, The Flume Gorge
104mm	Franconia Notch SP begins nb
33 (103)	US 3, N Woodstock, E Irving/dsl Fresolones Pizza, Longhorn Palace Rest. Beacon Lodge, Days Inn, EconoLodge, Franconia Notch Motel, Green Village Cottages, Indian Head Resort, Mt Coolidge Motel, Pemi Motel, Profile Motel, Rodeway Inn, Woodward's Resort/Rest. Indian Head viewing, to Franconia Notch SP, waterpark, W Sunny Day Diner Country Bumpkin Cottages/Camping, Cozy Cabins, Mt Liberty Cabins, White Mtn Motel/Cottages Arnold's NAPACare, Clark's Trading Post, Tim's Repair, vet
32 (101)	NH 112, Loon Mtn Rd, N Woodstock, E BP/7-11/dsl, Citgo, Mobil/dsl Black Mtn Burger, Cafe Nacho's, Cheng Garden Chinese, Common Man Rest., Dunkin', El Charro, Enzo's Pizza, Flapjack's Pancakes, GH Pizza, Gordi's Fish&Steaks, Gypsy Cafe, McDonald's, Subway, White Mtn Bagel Deli Holiday Inn Express, Kancamagu's Lodge, Lincoln Sta. Lodge, Nordic Inn, South Mtn Resort Aubuchon Hardware, Family$, NAPA, PriceChopper Foods, Rite Aid, USPO, W Citgo Imperial Chinese, Lafayette Dinner Train, Landmark II Rest., Peg's Café, Truant's Rest., Woodstock Inn Rest. Alpine Lodge, Cascade Lodge USPO
31 (97)	to NH 175, Tripoli Rd, W KOA (2mi)
30 (95)	US 3, Woodstock, E Lanterns End Grill Jack-O-Lantern Inn/rest. golf
29 (89)	US 3, Thornton, E Pemi River RV Park/LP, W Gilcrest Motel
28 (87)	NH 49, Campton, E Gulf, Mobil Dunkin', Exit 28 Pizza Handy Man Hardware, USPO, W Irving/dsl Sunset Grill Branch Brook Camping, Chelsey's Pizza, Mtn Vista RV Park, repair
27 (84)	Blair Rd, Beebe River, E Covered Bridge Farm Table Days Inn, Red Sleigh Condos
26 (83)	US 3, NH 25, NH 3A, Tenney Mtn Hwy, W Common Man Inn, EconoLodge, Pilgrim Inn H
25 (81)	NH 175 (from nb), Plymouth, W Citgo/dsl, Irving/Circle K/dsl Downtown Pizza, Fracher's Diner, HongKong Garden, Lucky Dog Grill, Thai Smile H, Chase St Mkt, Plymouth State U, USPO

WOODSTOCK

Exit #	Services
24 (76)	US 3, NH 25, Ashland, E Irving/Circle K/dsl, Mobil, ing Mart Ashland Pizza, Burger King, Common Diner, Dunkin', La Catrina, Lucky Dragon Chinese, Vil Grill Comfort Inn $General, Bob's Mkt, Jellystone Camp (4mi), repair, USPO
23 (71)	NH 104, NH 132, to Mt Washington Valley, New Hamp E Irving/Circle K/dsl, Mobil/dsl Dunkin', Rossi Ita Subway Jellystone, USPO
22 (62)	NH 127, Sanbornton, **1-5 mi W** H, food, gas/dsl,
61mm	**sb, full facilities, info, litter barrels, petwalk, vending**
20 (57)	US 3, NH 11, NH 132, NH 140, Tilton, E Irving/Circle dsl/24hr, Shell/Subway/dsl 99 Rest., Applebee's, Bu King, Dunkin', Five Guys, Green Ginger Chinese, KFC, McD ald's, Starbucks, Taco Bell, Thai Cuisine, Tilt'n Diner, UNO, perCrust Pizza, Wendy's Hampton Inn, Holiday Inn Exp Super 8 BJ's Whse/gas, Hobby Lobby, Home Depot, Old Navy, O'Reilly Parts/VIP Service, Staples, Subaru, Ta Outlet/famous brands, Verizon, Walgreens, W Chili's, P Hut Chrysler/Dodge/Jeep, Ford, Kohl's, Lowe's, MktBa Foods, Nissan, USPO, VW, Walmart/Subway
56mm	Winnipesaukee River
19 (55)	NH 132 (from nb no ez return), Franklin, W Gulf Italian H, NH Vet Home
51mm	**nb, full facilities, info, litter barrels, petwalk, vending**
18 (49)	to NH 132, Canterbury, E to Shaker Village HS
17 (46)	US 4 W, to US 3, NH 132, Boscawen, W Mobil/Dunkin'
16 (41)	NH 132, E Concord, E Mobil/dsl Quality Cash Mkt
15W (40)	US 202 W, to US 3, N Main St, Concord, W Citgo, Cum land/Dunkin', Speedway Domino's, Friendly's C yard/café
15E	I-393 E, US 4 E, to Portsmouth
14 (39)	NH 9, Loudon Rd, Concord, E Mobil, Shell/dsl DQ Rest., Applebee's, Arnie's Place, B Good, Buffalo Wild Wi Burger King, Chicago Grill, Chipotle, D'angelo's, Dunkin Rodeo Mexican, Five Guys, Friendly's, LJ Silver/Taco Longhorn Steaks, McDonald's, Moritomo Japanese, New Lobster House, Olive Garden, Panera Bread, PapaGino's, P Hut, Red Apple Buffet, Red Arrow Diner, Starbucks, Suns Oriental, TGIFriday's, Wendy's, Windmill Rest. $Tree, 7 AAA, Ace Hardware, Advance Parts, Aldi Foods, AutoZone, Buy, BonTon, BooksAMillion, city park, CVS, Dick's, GNC, naford Foods, Home Depot, Irving/Circle K/Subway/dsl, JC ney, LLBean, Lowe's, Meineke, Michael's, Midas, Mkt Ba Foods, PetCo, Petsmart, Rite Aid, Sam's Club/gas, Shaws Fo Shaw's Foods (2), Shell/dsl, Staples, Target, TJ Maxx, T Fair Tire, URGENT CARE, USPO, Verizon, Walgreens, Waln W Citgo, Cumberland, Speedway Domino's, Tea den Rest. Holiday Inn hist sites, Jo-Ann, Marsh MktBasket, museum, to state offices
13 (38)	to US 3, Manchester St, Concord, E Cumberland, Sun dsl/deli Beefside Rest., Brookside Pizza, Dunkin', Ich Japanese, Red Blazer Rest., Veano's Italian Buick/C Cadillac/Chevrolet, Chrysler/Dodge/Jeep, Harley-Davic Kia, Nissan, O'Reilly Parts/VIP Service, Outdoor RV Ctr S ru, Stratham's Tire, Subaru, Tire Whse, Volvo, W Mobil Speedway/dsl Burger King, Common Man Diner, D'a lo's, Dunkin', KFC, McDonald's Best Western, Comfort Fairfield Inn, Residence Inn H, Aubuchon Hardware, Drug, Firestone, Goodyear/auto

CONCORD

NH

INTERSTATE 93 Cont'd

Exit #	Services
12N (37)	NH 3A N, S Main, E gas 7-11, Irving/Subway/dsl/24hr food Dunkin' lodging Tru Hilton other Ford, Honda, Hyundai, Mazda, Toyota, W other H
12S	NH 3A S, Bow Junction, E gas 7-11, Irving/Circle K/Subway/dsl food Dunkin' lodging Tru Hilton other Ford/Mazda, Honda, Hyundai, Toyota
36mm	I-89 N to Lebanon, **toll road begins/ends**
31mm	**Welcome Ctr both lanes, full facilities,** gas Irving/dsl food Hi-Way Diner other General Store
11 (28)	NH 3A, to Hooksett, **4 mi** E gas Pilot/dsl/rest., **toll plaza**
28mm	I-293, Everett Tpk
10 (27)	NH 3A, Hooksett, E gas Irving/Circle K/dsl food Dunkin', Subway, Wendy's other Home Depot, Kohl's, Petco, Target, Verizon, W gas Irving/Circle K/Dunkin'/dsl, Mr Gas other Bass Pro Shop, MktBasket Foods, Walmart/Subway
26mm	Merrimac River
9N S (24)	US 3, NH 28, Manchester, E gas Irving/Dunkin'/Circle K/dsl lodging Fairfield Inn, W gas Sunoco/dsl food Burger King, Cheng Du Chinese, Happy Garden Chinese, La Carreta Mexican, Lusia's Italian, Mr Mac's Cafe, PapaGino's, Puritan Rest., Shorty's Mexican, Subway, Villaggio Ristorante other Chrysler/Dodge/Jeep, city park, Hannaford Foods, Lincoln, O'Reilly Parts/VIP Service, U-Haul
8 (23)	to NH 28a, Wellington Rd, W other H, Currier Gallery
7 (22)	NH 101 E, to Portsmouth, Seacoast
6 (21)	Hanover St, Candia Rd, Manchester, E food Dunkin', Wendy's other vet, W gas Citgo, Mobil/dsl, Shell food Dunkin', McDonald's other H, GNC, Granite State Tire/auto, Hannaford Foods
19mm	I-293 W, to Manchester (from nb), other to airport
5 (15)	NH 28, to N Londonderry, E gas Irving/Dunkin'/dsl, Sunoco/dsl food Poor Boy's Diner, W gas Shell/dsl food Subway lodging Sleep Inn
4 (12)	NH 102, Derry, E gas Mobil/dsl, Mutual, Rte 102, Shell/Dunkin'/dsl, Sunoco/dsl food Burger King, Cracker Barrel, Derry Rest., Juliano's Pizza, Subway other H, Advance Parts, R. Frost Farm, W gas 7-11, Global, Speedway food 99 Rest., Dunkin', KFC/Taco Bell, La Carreta Mexican, McDonald's, PapaGino's, Starbucks, Wendy's other AT&T, Ford, GNC, Hannaford Foods, Home Depot, Mkt Basket Foods, O'Reilly Parts/VIP Service, Shaw's Foods, Staples, TJ Maxx, Town Fair Tire, USPO, Verizon
7mm	**weigh sta both lanes**
3 (6)	NH 111, Windham, E gas Mobil/McDonald's food House of Pizza, Windham Rest. other URGENT CARE, vet, W gas B&H food 33 Hilltop, Dunkin', Klemm's Bakery other Castleton Conference Ctr, CVS Drug, Osco Drug, Shaw's Foods, USPO
2 (3)	to NH 38, NH 97, Salem, E food Tuscan Kitchen lodging Red Roof Inn, W food Blackwater Grill, Dunkin', Margarita's Cafe, Michael's Flatbread lodging Holiday Inn, La Quinta other URGENT CARE
1 (2)	NH 28, Salem, E gas Citgo/dsl, Gulf food 99 Rest., Chili's, LJ Silver, Mary Ann's Diner, McDonald's, Panera Bread, PapaGino's, Taco Bell, T-Bones lodging Park View Inn other AT&T, Best Buy, Dick's, Home Depot, JC Penney, Kohl's, Lord&Taylor, Macy's, Marshall's, Meineke, Michael's, MktBasket Foods, NTB, PetCo, Petsmart, Staples, Target, TJ Maxx, TownFair Tire, Verizon, vet, Walgreens
1mm	**Welcome Ctr nb, full (handicapped) facilities, info, litter barrels, petwalk,** (phone), (picnic), **vending**
0mm	New Hampshire/Massachusetts state line

PORTSMOUTH

SEABROOK

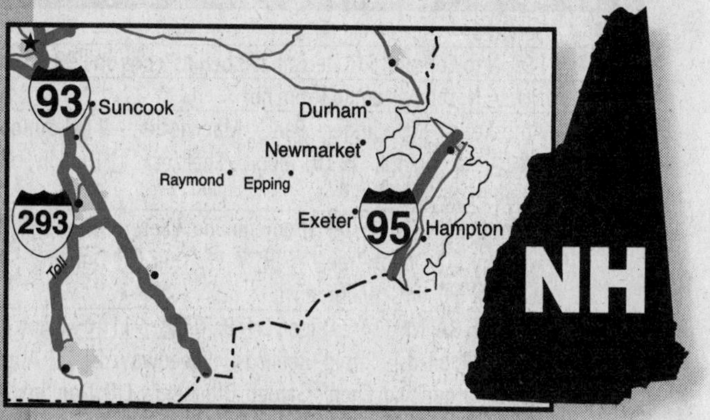

INTERSTATE 95

Exit #	Services
17mm	New Hampshire/Maine state line, Piscataqua River
7 (16)	Market St, Portsmouth, Port Authority, E lodging Hampton Inn, Hilton Garden, Residence Inn, Sheraton, **0-2 mi** W gas BP, Mobil food Applebee's, D'Angelo, Dunkin', Panera Bread, Qdoba, Starbucks, Wendy's lodging Courtyard, Homewood Suites other $Tree, AutoZone, BJ's Whse/gas, Marshall's, MktBasket Foods, PepBoys, PetCo, Rite Aid, TJ Maxx, Verizon, vet, other waterfront hist sites
6 (15)	Woodbury Ave (from nb), Portsmouth, E lodging Howard Johnson, W same as 7
5 (14)	US 1, US 4, NH 16, The Circle, Portsmouth, E gas Bypass Gas, Shell/dsl food Roudabout Diner lodging Anchorage Inn, Best Western+, Fairfield Inn, Holiday Inn, Howard Johnson, Port Inn other H, Buick/Cadillac/GMC, Chevrolet, U-Haul, W food Chipotle, Longhorn Steaks, McDonald's lodging Hampton Inn, Motel 6, Residence Inn other Barnes&Noble, Best Buy, Dick's, Ford/Lincoln, Home Depot, Kohl's, Mazda, Michael's, Nissan, Old Navy, Staples, Trader Joe's
4 (13.5)	US 4 (exits left from nb), to White Mtns, Spaulding TPK, E other H, W other to Pease Int Trade Port
3a (13)	NH 33, Greenland
3b (12)	NH 33, to Portsmouth, E other H, **0-2 mi** W gas Sunoco/dsl, TA/Country Pride/dsl/scales/24hr/@ food Dunkin', McDonald's, Starbucks other Lowe's, Mercedes, Target, VW
6.5mm	**toll plaza**
2 (6)	NH 101, to Hampton, W other H
4mm	Taylor River
1 (1)	NH 107, to Seabrook, **toll rd begins/ends,** E gas BP, Irving/Circle K/dsl, Mobil/dsl, Prime, Richdale, Shell, Sunoco/Subway/dsl food 99 Rest., Applebee's, Burger King, Chili's, Dunkin', Five Guys, IHOP, KFC/Taco Bell, McDonald's, Outback Steaks, Panera Bread, Pizza Hut, Starbucks, Wendy's lodging Best Western Hampshire Inn, Holiday Inn Express other $Tree, Advance Parts, AutoZone, CVS Drug, Dick's, GNC, Hobby Lobby, Home Depot, Jo-Ann Fabrics, Kohl's, Lowe's, Meineke, MktBasket Foods, NTB, Petsmart, Staples, Sullivan Tire, TJ Maxx, Town-Fair Tire, Verizon, Walmart, W gas Citgo food McGrath's Dining lodging Seabrook Inn other NAPA
.5mm	**Welcome Ctr nb, full (handicapped) facilities, litter barrels, petwalk,** (phone), (picnic), **vending**
0mm	New Hampshire/Massachusetts state line

NH

MANCHESTER

INTERSTATE 293 (Manchester)

Exit #	Services
8 (9)	I-93, N to Concord, S to Derry. **I-293 begins/ends on I-93, 28mm.**
7 (6.5)	NH 3A N, Dunbarton Rd (from nb)
6 (6)	Amoskeag Rd, Singer Park, Manchester, **E** Sunoco/dsl La Quinta, **W** Mobil, Shell/dsl Dunkin', Hot Stone Pizza H
5 (5)	Granite St, Manchester (from nb, no EZ return), **E** The Foundry DoubleTree, **W** 7-11, Gulf Dunkin', Subway H, tires, Walgreens
4 (4)	US 3, NH 3A, NH 114A, Queen City Br, **E** 7-11 Elliott H, **W** Mobil/dsl, Rapid Refill/dsl, Speedway/dsl Applebee's, Burger King, Chen's Garden, D'angelo's, DQ, Dunkin', KC's Rib Shack, KFC, KFC, Little Caesar's, McDonald's, Panera Bread, Taco Bell, Wendy's Comfort Inn, EconoLodge $Tree, Family$, Subaru, Walmart
3 (3)	NH 101, **0-2 mi W on US 3** Carrabba's, Chipotle, Dunkin', IHOP, Outback Steaks, Panera Bread, Starbucks, T-Bones, Whole Foods Mkt Country Inn& Suites, Hampton Inn CVS Drug, Hannaford's, Kohl's, Lexus, Lowe's, Marshall's, Mini, O'Reilly Parts/VIP Service, Rite Aid, Staples, Target, Trader Joe's, URGENT CARE, vet
2.5mm	Merrimac River
2 (2)	NH 3A, Brown Ave, **S** Mobil/dsl, Shell/Subway/dsl A port Diner, Dunkin', McDonald's Holiday Inn, Homewo Suites, Springhill Suites, Super 8 Manchester Airport
1 (1)	NH 28, S Willow Rd, **N** Mobil/dsl, Sunoco/dsl B ton Mkt, Burger King, Chipotle Mexican, CJ's Grill, Coldsto Dunkin', Firehouse Subs, Five Guys, Friendly's, McDonal Panera Bread, Papa John's, Pizza Hut, Sal's Pizza, Starbuc Subway, Taco Bell, Wendy's, Yee Dynasty Chinese Fairfi Inn, Holiday Inn Express, Quality Inn H, $Tree, Aldi Foo AT&T, AutoZone, Batteries+Bulbs, BJ's Whse, Buick/GM Chevrolet, CVS Drug, Hannaford Foods, Harley-Davidson, Ho Depot, Kia, Mazda, Mercedes, Michael's, PepBoys, Pet Petsmart, Sullivan Tire/repair, TJ Maxx, TownFair Tire, U-Ha URGENT CARE, Verizon, vet, VW, Walmart, **S** Shell Rest., Bertucci's, Buffalo Wild Wings, ChuckeCheese, D'an lo's, FoodCourt, Great Buffet, La Carreta, Longhorn Steaks, M Japanese Steaks, Olive Garden, Red Robin, TGIFriday's, Roadhouse Courtyard, TownePlace Suites Barnes& ble, Best Buy, BMW, CarMax, Ford, Hobby Lobby, Honda, Hy dai, JC Penney, Macy's, Nissan, NTB, Old Navy, Staples, Toy
0mm	I-93, N to Concord, S to Derry. **I-293 begins/ends on I-93.**

NH

NJ

NEW JERSEY

NEWARK

CLINTON

INTERSTATE 78

Exit #	Services
58b a	US 1N, US 9N, NJ Tpk
57	US 1S, US 9S, **N** Doubletree, Howard Johnson, Ramada Inn, **S** Courtyard, Fairfield Inn, SpringHill Suites to Newark Airport
56	Clinton Ave (exits left from eb)
55	Irvington (from wb), **N** Speedway/dsl Burger King, Dunkin', Wendy's, White Castle H, AutoZone
54	Hillside, Irvington (from eb), **N** Speedway/dsl Burger King, Dunkin', Wendy's, White Castle H, AutoZone
52	Garden State Pkwy
50b a	Millburn (from wb), **N** BP, Exxon, Lukoil Manny's Wieners Best Buy, Firestone/auto, Ford/Lincoln, Home Depot Superstore, Target, USPO, Whole Foods Mkt
49b a	NJ 124 (from eb), to Maplewood, same as 50b a
48	to NJ 24, to I-287 N, (exits left from eb), Springfield
48mm	I-78 eb divides into express & local
45	NJ 527 (from eb), Glenside Ave, Summit
44	(from eb), to Berkeley Heights, New Providence
43	to New Providence, Berkeley Heights
41	to Berkeley Heights, Scotch Plains
40	NJ 531, The Plainfields, **S** H
36	NJ 651, to Warrenville, Basking Ridge, **N** Exxon, Tesla EVC Dunkin', **S** Exxon
33	NJ 525, to Martinsville, Bernardsville, **N** 3West Rest., LingLing Chinese, Starbucks Courtyard USGA Golf Museum, **S** Exxon/7-11 Chipotle, Panera Bread Mavis Tire, Verizon
32mm	scenic overlook wb
29	I-287, to US 202, US 206, I-80, to Morristown, Somerville, **S** H
26	NJ 523 spur, to North Branch, Lamington
24	NJ 523, to NJ 517, to Oldwick, Whitehouse, **2-3 mi S** Exx dsl, Gulf/dsl Readington Diner, Starbucks, Subway Ki Mkt, Rite Aid, Walgreens
20b a	NJ 639 (from wb), to Cokesbury, Lebanon, **S** Exxon, noco Dunkin', Janina Bistro, Kirsten's Italian Co yard to Round Valley RA, vet
18	US 22 E, Annandale, Lebanon, **N** same as 17, **S** H, Hon
17	NJ 31 S, Clinton, **N** Exxon, Speedway, Valero Baskin-Robbins/Dunkin', Finnigel's, McDonald's Ma Tire/auto, to Voorhees SP
16	NJ 31 N (from eb), Clinton, **N** same as 17
15	NJ 173 E, to Pittstown, Clinton, **N** Express/repair, Sh dsl Subway Holiday Inn, **S** Cracker Barrel, Fra Italian, Hunan Wok Hampton Inn H, GNC, Shop Foods, TJ Maxx, Verizon, Walmart/Dunkin'
13	NJ 173 W (from wb), same as 12, **N** Clinton Sta Diner
12	NJ 173, to Jutland, Norton, **N** Clinton/dsl, Exxon/Dunk dsl, Pilot/Subway/dsl/scales/24hr to Spruce Run vet, **S** Shell Bagelsmith Deli
11	NJ 173, West Portal, Pattenburg, **N** Mobil, Shell/piz dsl American Spirits Rest., Chalet Rest. Jugtown Ca ing, st police
8mm	**both lanes, litter barrels, no restrooms,**
7	NJ 173, to Bloomsbury, West Portal, **N** RV camp **S** Citgo/deli, Pilot/Subway/dsl/scales/24hr, TA/Bu King/Country Pride/dsl/scales/24hr/@
6mm	**weigh sta both lanes**
6	Warren Glen, Asbury (from eb)
4	Warren Glen, Stewartsville (from wb)
3	US 22, NJ 173, to Phillipsburg, **0-2 mi N** BP/dsl, Penn Je Trkstp/dsl/scales/24hr, Speedway/dsl, US/dsl, Wawa plebee's, Chick-fil-A, Dunkin', Frank's Trattoria, IHOP, Key Diner, McDonald's, Panera Bread, Pizza Hut, Quaker St Ruby Tuesday, Starbucks, Taco Bell, Teppanyaki, White Ca

INTERSTATE 78 Cont'd

3 Continiued
Best Value H, $Tree, Advance Parts, Aldi, AutoZone, Best Buy, Hobby Lobby, Home Depot, Honda, Kohl's, Lowe's, Marshall's, Meineke, Michael's, Old Navy, PetCo, ShopRite Foods, Stop&Shop, Target, Verizon, Walmart/Subway

0mm New Jersey/Pennsylvania state line, Delaware River

INTERSTATE 80

Exit # Services

I-80 begins/ends on I-95, exit 69.

68 Leonia, Teaneck, N Starbucks Hampton Inn, Marriott H

68b a I-95, N to New York, S to Philadelphia, to US 46

67 to Bogota (from eb)

66 Hudson St, to Hackensack

65 Green St, S Hackensack

64b a NJ 17 S, to US 46 E, Newark, Paramus, S BP/dsl Crow's Nest Rest. Hilton Stop&Shop

63 NJ 17 N, N Amoco/7-11/dsl, BP, EVC, Exxon/dsl, Shell/dsl, Sunoco, Wawa/dsl Boston Mkt, Chipotle, Longhorn Steaks, Outback Steaks, Starbucks H, Acura, BMW, Harley-Davidson, Home Depot

62b a GS Pkwy, to Saddle Brook, N Dunkin' Garden Plaza, Marriott, S Crowne Plaza

61 NJ 507, to Garfield, Elmwood Park, N Marcal Paper Co

60 NJ 20, N to Hawthorne, N H, Lowe's, Pepboys, Stern Tire/auto

59 Market St (from wb), to Paterson

58b a Madison Ave, to Paterson, Clifton, S H

57c Main St (from wb), to Paterson

57b a NJ 19 S, to Clifton, downtown Paterson

56b a Squirrelwood Rd, to Paterson, S Lukoil/Dunkin'

55b a Union Blvd (from wb, no EZ return), Totowa, N Shell/dsl, S Holiday Inn Cadillac

54 Minnisink Rd, to Paterson, S Dunkin' Home Depot

53 US 46 E, to NJ 3 (no eb return), to Wayne, Cliffton, **0-2 mi S** Exxon Applebee's, Bahama Breeze, Blaze Pizza, Brio Tuscan Grill, CA Pizza, Chipotle, IHOP, Olive Garden, Qdoba, Sonic, Starbucks, TGIFriday's Bloomingdale's, Costco/gas, Hobby Lobby, JC Penney, Lord&Taylor, Macy's, Nissan, Office Depot, Old Navy

52 US 46, the Caldwells

48 to Montville (from wb), Pine Brook

47b US 46 W, to Montclair, N Sunoco Five Guys, IHOP, Longhorn Steaks, Moe's SW, Wendy's Holiday Inn, Travelodge Home Depot, ShopRite Foods

47a I-280 E, to The Oranges, Newark

45 to US 46, Lake Hiawatha, Whippany, **0-2 mi N on US 46** BP/dsl, Gulf/dsl, Sunoco/dsl Applebee's, Buffalo Wild Wings, Cuba Mia, Dunkin', Eccola Rest., Empire Diner, Five Guys, IHOP, Jasper Chinese, Longhorn Steaks, McDonald's, Moe's SW Grill, Outback Steaks, Panera Bread, Quin Dynasty, Sakura Japanese, Smashburger, Starbucks, Subway, Taco Bell, Wendy's Budget Inn, Holiday Inn/rest., Ramada Ltd, Red Roof Inn, Travelodge $Tree, Advance Parts, Firestone, Home Depot, Michael's, PepBoys, PetCo, ShopRite Foods, Staples, Verizon, Walgreens

43b a I-287, to US 46, Boonton, Morristown

42b a US 202, US 46, to Morris Plains, same as 39, Parsippany, **0-1 mi N on US 46** 76/Dunkin'/dsl, Exxon Fuddrucker's, McDonald's, TGIFriday's, Wendy's Courtyard, Days Inn, Fairfield Inn, Hampton Inn Marshall's, Subaru

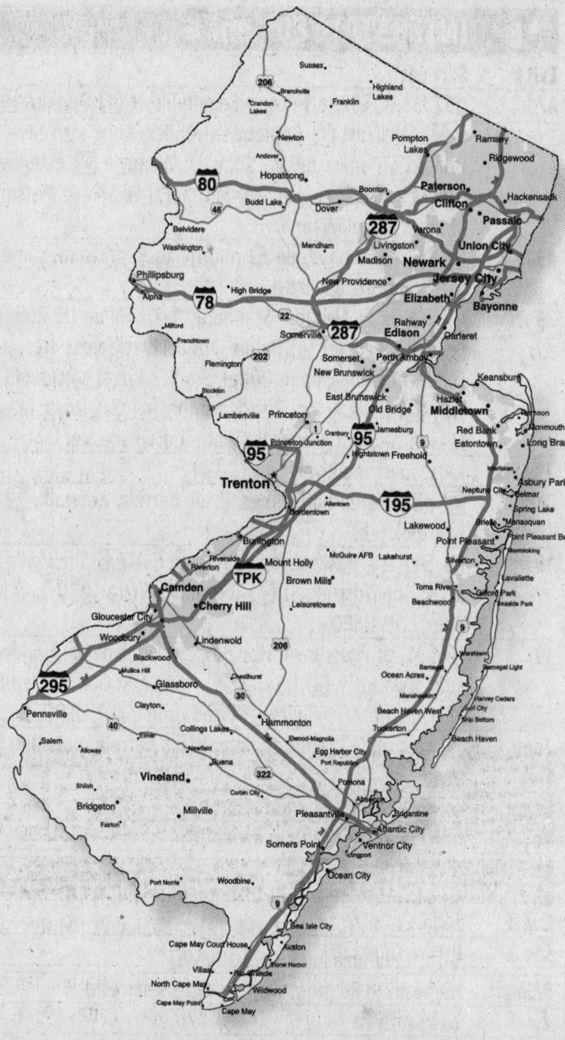

39 (38 from eb), US 46 E, to NJ 53, Denville, **0-2 mi N on US 46** Citgo/dsl, Enrite Gas, Exxon, Speedway/Dunkin', Sunoco Burger King, Casa Bella Italian, Charlie Brown's Steaks, Dunkin', Moe's SW Grill, Paul's Diner, Summit West Diner H, Chevrolet, Verizon, Walgreens, S Delta Verizon

37 NJ 513, to Hibernia, Rockaway, N Exxon/dsl, Shell Dunkin', Hibernia Diner, River Barn Rest. Hampton Inn, S BP H

35b a to Dover, Mount Hope, S Exxon Buffalo Wild Wings, Chipotle, Coldstone, Dunkin', Olive Garden, Red Robin, Riviera Mexican Hilton Garden, Homewood Suites, TownePlace Suites H, Best Buy, JC Penney, Lord&Taylor, Macy's, Michael's, Verizon

34b a NJ 15, to Sparta, Wharton, N Exxon/dsl Fortune Buffet Rite Aid, USPO, S Dunkin', Five Guys, Frank's Pizza, Panera Bread, Qdoba, Starbucks, Townsquare Diner H, $Tree, Big Lots, Costco/gas, Dick's, Home Depot, Petsmart, ShopRite Foods, Target, Walmart/Subway

32mm truck wb

30 Howard Blvd, to Mt Arlington, N Exxon/dsl, Quickchek Gas Blossom Asian, Cracker Barrel, Davy's Hotdogs, Dunkin', Frank's Pizza Courtyard, Holiday Inn Express $Tree

28 US 46, to NJ 10, to Ledgewood, Lake Hopatcong, **1-2 mi S on US 46, NJ 10** Speedway/dsl, Sunoco/dsl Boston Mkt, Domino's, Dunkin', Fuddruckers, KFC, McDonald's, Muldoons Diner, Outback Steaks, Panera Bread, Red Lobster, Taco Bell, TGIFriday's, Wendy's, White Castle AutoZone, Barnes&Noble, BJ's Whse, CVS Drug, Home Depot, Jo-Ann, Kohl's, Petco, ShopRite Foods, Toyota, Walgreens, Walmart

= gas = food = lodging = other = rest stop

STANHOPE

INTERSTATE 80 Cont'd

Exit #	Services
27	US206S, NJ182, to Netcong, Somerville, N Dunkin' Ford, S Shell/dsl Applebee's, Chili's, Longhorn Steaks, McDonald's, Panera Bread, Subway, Wendy's Extended Stay America $Tree, Lowe's, Michael's, Old Navy, Petsmart, TJ-Maxx, Verizon, Walmart
26	US 46 W (from wb, no EZ return), to Budd Lake, same as 27, S Conoco, Shell/dsl
25	US 206 N, to Newton, Stanhope, **1-2mi N on US 206** Exxon/dsl, Shell/dsl Bellas Pizza, Blackforest Rest., Byram Diner, Dunkin', Empire Buffet, Frank's Pizza, McDonald's, Subway Holiday Inn, Residence Inn CVS Drug, Mavis Tire, Nissan, ShopRite Foods, to Waterloo Village, vet
23.5mm	Musconetcong River
21mm	**picnic area both lanes, litter barrels, petwalk, , scenic overlook (eb)**
19	NJ 517, to Hackettstown, Andover, N Shell/dsl, 1-2 mi S Shell/dsl/repair Terranova Pizza H, 7-11, Stephen's SP, USPO
12	NJ 521, to Blairstown, Hope, N Dunkin' Harley-Davidson, st police, S US Gas Hope Mkt Deli Jenny Jump SF, Land of Make Believe, RV camping (5mi), USPO
7mm	**eb, full facilities, info, litter barrels, petwalk, , , vending**
6mm	scenic overlook wb, no trailers
4c	to NJ 94 N (from eb), to Blairstown
4b	to US 46 E, to Buttzville
4a	NJ 94, to US 46 E, to Portland, Columbia, N TA/Pizza Hut/Taco Bell/dsl/scales/24hr/@ McDonald's RV camping, S Columbia Inn Rest. USPO
3.5mm	Hainesburg Rd (from wb), accesses services at 4
2	**weigh sta eb**
1mm	N Worthington SF
1	to Millbrook (from wb), N Worthington SF
0mm	New Jersey/Pennsylvania state line, Delaware River

INTERSTATE 95

Exit #	Services
124mm	New Jersey/New York state line, Hudson River, Geo Washington Br
123mm	Palisades Pkwy (from sb)
73	NJ 67, Lemoine Ave, W Sunoco Five Guys, McDonald's A&P Mkt, GNC, Verizon, Walgreens
72(122)	US 1, US 9, US 46, Ft Lee, E Doubletree, W Sunoco McDonald's
71(121)	Broad Ave, Leonia, Englewood, E Lukoil, W Speedway Holiday Inn
70(120)	to NJ 93, Leonia, Teaneck, W Hampton Inn, Marriott
69(119)	I-80 W (from sb), to Paterson
68(118)	US 46, Challenger Blvd, Ridgefield Park, E Exxon Lan Garden Chinese Day's Inn, Hampton Inn, Hilton Garden
117mm	**I-95 and NJ Turnpike run together sb.**

NEW JERSEY TURNPIKE

NEW JERSEY TURNPIKE

Exit #	Services
	I-95 and NJ Turnpike run together sb.
18(117)	US 46 E, Ft Lee, Hackensack, **last exit before toll sb.**
17(116)	Lincoln Tunnel
115mm	**Vince Lombardi Service Plaza nb, W** Sunoco/dsl Burger King, Nathan's, Popeye's
114mm	toll plaza,
16W(113)	NJ 3, Secaucus, Rutherford, E Shell, Speedway Hilt W Extended Stay America Meadowlands
112mm	**Alexander Hamilton Service Area sb,** Sunoco/dsl R Rogers gifts
16E(112)	NJ 3, Secaucus, E Lincoln Tunnel
15W(109)	I-280, Newark, The Oranges
15E(107)	US 1, US 9, Newark, Jersey City, E Lincoln Tunnel
14c	Holland Tunnel
14b	Jersey City
14a	Bayonne
14(105)	I-78 W, US 1, US 9, **2 mi W** Courtyard, Fairfield Inn, Spri Hill Suites
102mm	**Halsey Service Area,** Sunoco/dsl Roy Rogers, other s vices in Elizabeth
13a(102)	Elizabeth, E Country Inn Suites, Courtyard, Embassy Sui Extended Stay America, Residence Inn, W McDona Crowne Plaza, Days Inn, Hampton Inn, Hilton, Rennaisar services on US1/US9
13(100)	I-278, to Verrazano Narrows Bridge
12(96)	Carteret, Rahway, E McDonald's Holiday Inn C Drug, Walgreens, W Executive Suites
93mm	**Cleveland Service Area nb, T Edison Service Area sb,** Bur King, Dunkin', Popeye's, Roy Rogers, Sbarro's, Starbucks, Starbu
11(91)	US 9, Garden State Pkwy, to Woodbridge, E McD ald's Hampton Inn $Tree, Home Depot, Walm W Speedway/dsl Residence Inn, The Forge Inn
10(88)	I-287, NJ 514, to Perth Amboy, E Speedway/dsl Co yard, Edison Hotel
9(83)	US 1, NJ 18, to New Brunswick, E Brunswick, E Gulf, M bil/dsl, Speedway/dsl Bone Fish Grill, Boston Mkt, Bur King, Carrabba's, Dunkin', Grand Buffet, Hooters, Jersey Mik KFC, McDonald's, Perkins, Popeye's, Starbucks Days tel, Motel 6 $Tree, AT&T, Best Buy, Dick's, Kohl's, Low Petsmart, ShopRite Foods, TJ Maxx, Walmart/Subway, W Exxon Famous Dave's, Houlihan's, On the Border ton, Holiday Inn Express
79mm	**Kilmer Service Area nb, Kilmer Service Area,** Burger K Cookies and Creamery, Sbarro, Starbucks Sunoco/dsl
8a(74)	to Jamesburg, Cranbury, W Courtyard, Crowne Plaza
72mm	**Pitcher Service Area,** Sunoco/dsl Cinnabon, Dick Cla AB Grill, Nathan's, Roy Rogers, Starbucks
8(67)	NJ 33, NJ 571, Highstown, E Petro/dsl, Shell/Dunkin'/ Speedway/dsl Prestige Diner Days Inn, Hampton Holiday Inn CVS Drug, vet, W Quality Inn, Townhouse M
7a(60)	I-195 W to Trenton, E to Neptune
59mm	**Richard Stockton Service Area sb** Sunoco/dsl Bur King, Nathan's, Pizza Hut, Quiznos, Roy Rogers, Starbu TCBY, **Woodrow Wilson Service Area nb** Sunoco
7(54)	US 206, to Bordentown, to Ft Dix, McGuire AFB, to I-295, Tren W AmeriGas, Delta/dsl, Exxon, Gulf, Loves/Wenc dsl/scales/24hr, Petro/Iron Skillet/dsl/scales/24hr/@, Sun Valero/dsl Denny's, Dunkin', McDonald's Best West Comfort Inn, Days Inn, Hampton Inn, Ramada Inn WaWa
6(51)	I-276, to PA Tpk
5(44)	to Mount Holly, Willingboro, E AJ's Gas/dsl Ap bee's, Charlie Brown's Steaks, Cracker Barrel, McDonald's, covery Grill Best Western, Hampton Inn, Hilton Gar Quality Inn vet, W BP, Exxon/dsl, Valero/dsl B er King, China House, Dunkin', IHOP, TGIFriday's Courty Holiday Inn Express $Tree, AT&T, Dick's, Home De Kohl's, Motel 6, Target

NJ

NEW JERSEY TURNPIKE Cont'd

Exit #	Services
39mm	**James Fenimore Cooper Service Area nb,** Sunoco/dsl Burger King, Cinnabon, Popeye's, Roy Rogers, TCBY gifts
4(34)	NJ 73, to Philadelphia, Camden, E US Gas, WaWa/dsl Applebee's, Chili's, Cracker Barrel, Dunkin', Kazumi, McDonald's, On-the-Border, Sage Rest., TGIFriday's, Wendy's Candlewood Suites, Comfort Inn, Extended Stay America, Hampton Inn, Hilton Garden, Holiday Inn Express, Hyatt House, Hyatt Place, Knights Inn, La Quinta, Rodeway Inn, Staybridge Suites, Wyndham Hotel BMW, Cadillac, Lexus, Mini, Toyota, Verizon, Whole Foods Mkt, W Lukoil Bob Evans, Miller's Alehouse, Starbucks aLoft, Courtyard, Fairfield Inn, Hotel ML, Red Roof Inn, Super 8, Westin
30mm	**Walt Whitman Service Area sb, Walt Whitman Service Area,** Sunoco Cinnabon, Nathan's, Roy Rogers, TCBY gifts
3(26)	NJ 168, Atlantic City Expwy, Walt Whitman Br, Camden, Woodbury, E Pioneer, WaWa/dsl Antonietta's, Luigi's Pizza, Pat's Pizza, Phily Diner, Rita's Custard Days Inn, La Quinta Advance Parts, CVS Drug, Toyota, Walgreens, W Riggins, Shell/dsl, Valero/dsl Burger King, Club Diner, Dunkin', Vero Pizzaria, Wendy's Bellmawr Motel, EconoLodge, Howard Johnson, Red Roof Inn, Super 8
2(13)	US 322, to Swedesboro, W Shell/Dunkin'/dsl
5mm	**Barton Service Area sb, Fenwick Service Area nb,** Sunoco/dsl Burger King, Nathan's, Pizza Hut, Starbucks, TCBY
1(1.2)	Deepwater, W Gulf, Pilot/Subway/dsl/scales/24hr Comfort Inn, Friendship Motor Inn, Holiday Inn Express, Red Carpet Inn
1mm	**toll road begins/ends**
2(I-295)	**I-295 N divides from toll road, I-295 S converges with toll road.**
1(I-295)	NJ 49, to Pennsville, E WaWa/dsl Applebee's, Burger King, Cracker Barrel, Dunkin', KFC/Taco Bell, McDonald's Hampton Inn, Super 8 Peterbilt, W Coastal Seaview Motel
0mm	New Jersey/Delaware state line, Delaware River, Delaware Memorial Bridge

INTERSTATE 195

Exit #	Services
36	Garden State Parkway N. **I-195 begins/ends on GS Pkwy, exit 98.**
35b a	NJ 34, to Brielle, GS Pkwy S., Pt Pleasant, 0-2 mi S Exxon/dsl, Getty/dsl, Lukoil/dsl Legends Japanese
31b a	NJ 547, NJ 524, to Farmingdale, N to Allaire SP
28b a	US 9, to Freehold, Lakewood, N LukOil/7-11/dsl, WaWa/dsl Ivy League Grill, Lino's Pizza, Stewart's Drive-In At 9 Motel, S Exxon, Gulf, LukOil, QuickChek/dsl, WaWa Applebee's, Arby's, Baskin-Robbins/Dunkin', Boston Mkt, Chick-fil-A, China Moon, Chipotle, Dunkin', Five Guys, IHOP, Jersey Mike's Subs, Longhorn Steaks, Luigi's Pizza, McDonald's, Panera Bread, Pizza Hut, Ruby Tuesday, Sonic, Starbucks, Subway, Taco Bell $Tree, Advance Parts, AT&T, Barnes&Noble, Best Buy, BJ's/dsl, CVS Drug, GNC, Hobby Lobby, Kohl's, Lowe's, Michael's, PepBoys, PetCo, Petsmart, repair, ShopRite Foods, Staples, Stop&Shop, Target, TJ Maxx, USPO, Verizon, vet, Walgreens, Walmart/McDonald's
22	to Jackson Mills, Georgia, N to Turkey Swamp Park, 2 mi S McDonald's ShopRite Foods
21	NJ 526, NJ 527, to Jackson, Siloam
16	NJ 537, to Freehold, N Citgo/dsl, Sunoco FoodCourt, GianMarco's Pizza H, Jackson Outlets/famous brands, S WaWa/dsl Burger King, Chicken Holiday, Dunkin', KFC/LJ Silver, McDonald's, McGinns Pizzaria, Rio Grande Mexican, Tommy's Rest. Six Flags

MAHWAH

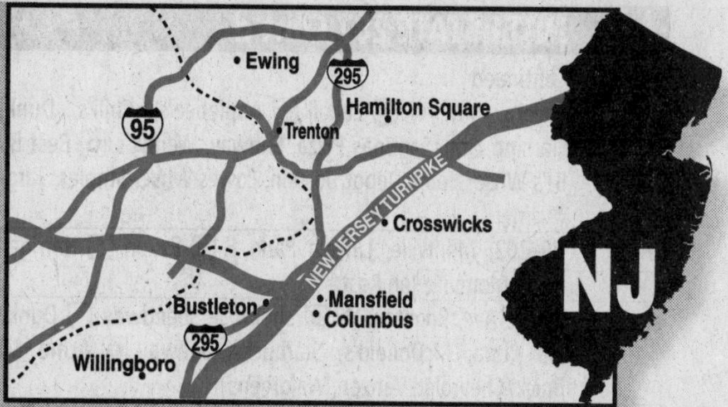

Exit #	Services
11	NJ 524, Imlaystown, N to Horse Park of NJ
8	NJ 539, Hightstown, Allentown, S Shell (1mi), Valero/repair Sam's Deli vet
7	NJ 526, Robbinsville, Allentown, N Hampton Inn, 1 mi S La Piazza Ristorante
6	NJ Tpk, N to NY, S to DE Memorial Br
5b a	US 130, N Delta/dsl/repair, Valero/dsl Domino's, Dunkin', Rusert's Deli, ShrimpKing Rest., Taco Bell Homewood Suites AAA, vet, S GS Fuel/dsl, WaWa/dsl Chick-fil-A, Chili's, China Grill, Cracker Barrel, DQ, Jersey Mike's Subs, Longhorn Steaks, McDonald's, Outback Steaks, Panchero's, Panera Bread, Red Robin, Ruby Tuesday, Subway, TGIFriday's, Wendy's Hilton Garden, Residence Inn $Tree, AT&T, Barnes&Noble, BJ's Whse, GNC, Harry's Army Navy, Home Depot, Honda, Kohl's, Lowe's, Michael's, Old Navy, Petsmart, Ross, ShopRite Foods, Staples, to state aquarium, USPO, Verizon, Walmart
3b a	Hamilton Square, Yardville, N H
2	US 206 S, S Broad St, Yardville, S BP, Shell/dsl Subway $Tree, 7-11, CVS Drug, Rite Aid
1b a	US 206 (eb only), N Circle Deli, Taco Bell Advance Parts, Midas, S Papa John's ShopRite Foods
0mm	**I-295, I-195 begins/ends.**

INTERSTATE 287

Exit #	Services
68mm	New Jersey/New York state line
66	NJ 17 S, Mahwah, 1-3 mi E Amoco/dsl, BP, Liberty/dsl, Pilot/dsl, Sunoco/dsl, Valero/Subway/dsl Boston Mkt, Burger King, Dunkin', McDonald's Comfort Suites, Courtyard, Doubletree, Hampton Inn, Homewood Suites, Sheraton, Super 8 Buick/GMC, Cadillac, Chrysler/Dodge/Jeep, Home Depot, Honda, Hyundai
59	NJ 208 S, Franklin Lakes
58	US 202, Oakland, E Lukoil/dsl Jr's Pizza, Luca Pizza, Mike's Doghouse, Pizza Hut, Starbucks, Subway $Tree, Staples, USPO, Walgreens, W Exxon
57	Skyline Dr, Ringwood
55	NJ 511, Pompton Lakes, E Frank's Pizza, Starbucks, Thatcher McGhee Eatery, Wendy's, W Gulf/dsl Baskin-Robbins, Burger King, Dunkin' Holiday Inn Express CVS Drug, Stop'n Shop
53	NJ 511A, rd 694, Bloomingdale, Pompton Lakes, E Sunoco, Valero Dunkin', Karen's Country Kitchen USPO
52b a	NJ 23, Riverdale, Wayne, Butler, 0-3 mi E Amoco/dsl, BP, BP/dsl, Delta, Sunoco 23 Buffet, Dunkin', Jersey Mike's, Moe's SW Grill, Pompton Queen Diner, Stefano's Pizza H, 7-11, GNC, Honda, Kia, Pepboys, Stop&Shop, Subaru, TJ Maxx,

= gas = food = lodging = other = rest stop

INTERSTATE 287 Cont'd

52b a	Continued Toyota, VW, W Lukoil Applebee's, Chili's, Dunkin, Flaming Grill, Santinas Pizza, Subway, Wendy's Best Buy, BJ's Whse, Home Depot, Jo-Ann, Lowes Whse, Staples, Target, Walmart
47	US 202, Montville, Lincoln Park, E Exxon Harrigan's Rest., Montville Inn Rest.
45	Myrtle Ave, Boonton, W Shell/dsl, Speedway Dunkin', Jr's Pizza, McDonald's, Starbucks, Subway Acme Mkt, Buick/Chevrolet, Verizon, Walgreens
43	Intervale Rd, to Mountain Lakes, E Valero/dsl
42	US 46, US 202 (from sb only), W Conoco/Dunkin'/dsl, Exxon Fuddrucker's, McDonald's, TGIFriday's, Wendy's Courtyard, Day's Inn, Embassy Suites, Fairfield Inn, Hampton Inn CVS Drug, Marshall's, Subaru, USPO
41b a	I-80, E to New York, W to Delaware Water Gap
40	NJ 511, Parsippany Rd, to Whippany, W Petro Hub, Shell/dsl, Woroco Gas Carrot Chinese, Frank&Son Pizza, Subway Embassy Suites (1mi) vet
39b a	NJ 10, Dover, Whippany, E Exxon, Quickchek/dsl Brookside Diner, Dunkin', Jersey Mike's, Palermo's Pizza, Pancake House, Whippany Diner CVS Drug, W Liberty/dsl, Lukoil, Raceway Chick-fil-A, Chipotle, Dunkin', Smashburger, Subway, Wendy's, Zin Burger Best Value Inn, Hilton, Hyatt House, Marriott Barnes&Noble, Buick/GMC, GNC, Harley Davidson, Kohl's, Stop'n Shop, Verizon
37	NJ 24 E, Springfield
36b a	rd 510, Morris Ave, Lafayette
35	NJ 124, South St, Madison Ave, Morristown, E Friendly's Richie's Country Store, vet, W Best Western+ H, Rite Aid, Walgreens
33	Harter Rd
33mm	**E truck nb, full facilities, litter barrels, petwalk, vending**
30b a	to US 202, N Maple Ave, Basking Ridge, E The Ridge, W EVC, Gulf, Lukoil GrainHouse Rest., Vine Rest. Olde Mill Inn/rest.
26b a	rd 525 S, Mt Airy Rd, Liberty Corner, **3 mi** E Exxon Chipotle, Panera Bread Courtyard, Somerset Hotel
22b a	US 202, US 206, Pluckemin, Bedminster, E Exxon, Exxon/dsl Coldstone, Dunkin', Golden Palace, Panchero's, Rocco's Pizza, Starbucks, Subway CVS Drug, Fresh Mkt, King's Foods, URGENT CARE, Verizon
21b a	I-78, E to NY, W to PA
17	US 206 (from sb), Bridgewater, W Exxon Buffalo Wild Wings, CA Pizza, Cheesecake Factory, Chipotle Mexican, Dunkin', KFC, Maggiano's Italian, McDonald's, Redstone, Seasons 52 Grill, Taco Bell, TGIFriday, Wendy's Marriott Best Buy, Bloomingdale's, Lord&Taylor, Macy's
14b a	US 22, to US 202/206, E Speedway/dsl Chevrolet/Lexus, W BP, Sunoco/dsl, Valero/dsl Houlihan's, Red Lobster Hampton Inn Acura, Chrysler/Dodge/Jeep, Fiat, Ford, Infiniti, Kia, Mercedes, Nissan, Volvo
13b a	NJ 28, Bound Brook, E 76/dsl, BP/dsl 30 Burgers, Burger King, Dunkin', Frank's Pizza, Girasole Rest., Little Caesar's 7-11, AT&T, AutoZone, QuickChek Mkt, ShopRite Foods, Walgreens, W WaWa/dsl Applebee's, Chuckecheese, McDonald's, Panchero's Hilton Garden H, 7-11, Costco, Home Depot, Marshall's, Michael's, Old Navy, PepBoys, PetsMart, Target
12	Weston Canal Rd, Manville, E USPO, W Hooters Clar
10	NJ 527, Easton Ave, New Brunswick, E Hotel Somers W Exxon Dunkin', Ichiban, Ruby Tuesday, Subw Wild Ginger Asian Candlewood Suites, Comfort Inn, Cou yard, Doubletree, Extended Stay America, Fairbridge Inn, F field Inn, Homewood Suites, Residence Inn, Sonesta Suit Springhill Suites H, Garden State Conv Ctr
9	NJ 514, River Rd, W Delta Dunkin' Embassy Suit Radisson
8.5mm	**weigh sta nb**
8	Possumtown Rd, Highland Park
7	S Randolphville Rd, Piscataway, E Lukoil/dsl
6	Washington Ave, Piscataway, E Shell/7-11/dsl P eye's AutoZone, W Applebee's, Chand Palace, Gour Pizza, Healthy Garden, Longhorn Steaks, Olive Garden, Pan Bread, Piscataway Pizza, Smashburger, Starbucks, Subway, T Friday's, Thai Basil 99c Depot, Aldi Foods, GNC, Lowes W PetCo, same as 5, ShopRite Foods, Walmart/McDonald's
5	NJ 529, Stelton Rd, Dunellen, E BP/dsl, Gulf/dsl, Luk dsl Enzo's Pizza, KFC Red Carpet Inn Adva Parts, Goodyear/auto, Home Depot, Meineke, Stop'n Sh W Exxon, WaWa/dsl Brickhouse Rest., Burger K Chipotle, Dunkin', El Toro Loco, Five Guys, Fontainbleu Di Gabrieles Grill, Gianni Pizza, IHOP, Joe's Crabshack, Panda press, Pizza Hut, Red Lobster, Red Robin, Taco Bell, Villa Pi Wendy's, White Castle Garden Executive Hotel, Hamp Inn, Holiday Inn, Motel 6, Woodspring Suites $Tree, B ington Coats, Dick's, Kohl's, Marshall's, Mavis Tire, NAPA, Boys, Staples, Target, Tuesday Morning, Verizon
4	Durham Ave (from nb, no EZ return), S Plainfield, E lOne/dsl McDonald's, Subway H, Firestone/auto
3	New Durham Rd (from sb), E Shell, W Dunkin', Onion Chinese Fairfield Inn, Home 2 Suites, Red Inn Walgreens
2b a	NJ 27, Metuchen, New Brunswick, E Brownstone W BP, Lukoil Dunkin' Costco/gas, Petsmart, U Walmart/Subway
1b a	US 1, N Exxon/dsl, Raceway/dsl, Shell, Tesla EVC B hana, Cheesecake Factory, Dunkin', Famous Dave's BBQ, lihan's, IHOP, Little Italy, Macaroni Grill, McDonald's, M Park Diner, Panera Bread, Seasons 52 Grill, Sonic, White tle Barnes&Noble, Firestone/auto, Goodyear/auto, Ma Midas, Nordstrom's, Target, S Shell/7-11/dsl Ap bee's, Boston Mkt, ChuckeCheese, Jersey Mike's, McDona Starbucks, Zinburger Comfort Inn, Quality Inn $T AT&T, BJ's Whse, Home Depot, Infiniti, Land Rover/Jag Porche, Mercedes, Office Depot, PepBoys, PetCo, Sam's C gas, Stop&Shop Foods, Volvo
0mm	**I-287 begins/ends on NJ 440. I-95/NJ Tpk**

PISCATAWAY

BRIDGEWATER

NJ

INTERSTATE 295

Exit #	Services
77mm	New Jersey/Delaware state line, Delaware River, Delaware morial Bridge
76	1 NJ 29, to Trenton, **2 mi** W st police museum
75	NJ 579, to Harbourton, E LukOil (1mi) Dunkin', Star Pizza 7-11, W BP
73b a	Scotch Rd, E Courtyard, W H
72b a	NJ 31, to Ewing, Pennington, E Citgo/repair, Exxo pair, LukOil/Dunkin'/dsl SpringHill Suites Robbins W Exxon, LukOil/Blimpie/dsl Mizuki Asian, Starb ShopRite Foods, Stop&Shop Foods

INTERSTATE 295 Cont'd

Exit #	Services
71b a	Federal City Rd (sb only)
69b a	US 206, W [gas] LukOil/dsl [food] Fox's Pizza, Starbucks
68b a	NJ 583, NJ 546, to Princeton Pike
67b a	US 1, to Trenton, New Brunswick, E [gas] Shell, WaWa/McDonald's/dsl [food] Michael's Diner [lodging] Howard Johnson, Sleepy Hollow Motel [other] Acura, 0-3 mi W [gas] LukOil/dsl [food] Applebee's, Bahama Breeze, Big Fish Bistro, Bonefish Grill, Brick House Tavern, Brio Grille, Buffalo Wild Wings, Cheesecake Factory, Chipotle, ChuckECheese's, Corner Bakery Cafe, Dunkin', Firehouse Subs, Hooters, Houlihan's, Jersey Mike's, Joe's Crabshack, Olive Garden, On-the-Border, Outback Steaks, Panera Bread, Pei Wei, PF Chang's, Red Lobster, Seasons 32, Smashburger, Starbucks, Subway, TGIFriday's, Wendy's [lodging] Clarion, Comfort Inn, Extended Stay America, Hyatt Place, Hyatt Regency, Red Roof Inn, Residence Inn [other] $Tree, AT&T, Barnes&Noble, Best Buy, Buick/Cadillac/GMC, Chevrolet, Dick's, Firestone/auto, Hobby Lobby, Home Depot, JC Penney, Jo-Ann Fabrics, Kohl's, Lord&Taylor, Lowe's, Macy's, malls, Marshall's, Michael's, Mini, NTB, Old Navy, PepBoys, PetCo, Petsmart, REI, Ross, ShopRite Foods, Staples, Target, TJ Maxx, Trader Joe's, Verizon, Walmart, Wegman's Foods, Whole Foods Mkt
65b a	Sloan Ave, E [gas] Exxon [food] Burger King, DeLorenzo's Pizza, Dunkin', Five Guys, New China Buffet, Subway, Taco Bell, Uno Grill [other] Goodyear/auto, Risoldi's Mkt
64	NJ 535 N (from sb), to NJ 33 E, same as 63
63b a	NJ 33 W, rd 535, Mercerville, Trenton, E on rd 33 [gas] Lukoil, Speedway/dsl, Valero [food] Applebee's, Lucky Star Buffet, McDonald's, Pizza Hut, Popeye's, Stewart's Rootbeer, Subway, Vincent's Pizza [other] Ace Hardware, auto repair, CVS Drug, Ford/Subaru, Rite Aid, USPO, W [gas] Exxon [food] Dunkin', White Horse Diner [other] Advance Parts, Family$, transmissions, Walgreens, Walmart, WaWa
62	Olden Ave N (from sb, no return), W [gas] Delta, Exxon
61b a	Arena Dr, White Horse Ave, W [other] 7-11
60b a	I-195, to I-95, W to Trenton, E to Neptune
58mm	scenic overlook both lanes
57b a	US 130, to US 206, E [gas] Amera, Valero [food] Denny's, Dunkin', McDonald's, Rosario's Pizza [lodging] Best Western, Days Inn, Ramada Inn [other] Aldi, W [food] Starbucks [lodging] Candlewood Suites [other] Acme Foods, st police, Verizon
56	to US 206 S (from nb, no return), to NJ Tpk, Ft Dix, McGuire AFB, E [gas] Loves/Wendy's/dsl/scales/24hr, Petro/Iron Skillet/dsl/scales/24hr/@ [lodging] Days Inn, Hampton Inn [other] Blue Beacon, same as 57, W [lodging] Candlewood Suites [other] st police
52b a	rd 656, to Columbus, Florence, 3 mi E [gas] Loves/Wendy's/dsl/scales/24hr, Petro/Iron Skillet/dsl/scales/24hr/@
47b a	NJ 541, to Mount Holly, NJ Tpk, Burlington, E [gas] BP, Exxon/dsl, Valero/dsl [food] Applebee's, Burger King, China House, Cracker Barrel, Dunkin', IHOP, Recovery Grill, TGIFriday's [lodging] Best Western, Courtyard, Hampton Inn, Hilton Garden, Holiday Inn Express, Motel 6, Quality Inn [other] $Tree, AT&T, Dick's, Home Depot, Kohl's, Target, W [gas] BP, Citgo/dsl, Gulf/dsl, WaWa/dsl [food] Checker's, Chick-fil-A, Dunkin', Kum Fong, Subway, Villa Pizza, Wendy's [other] [H], AutoZone, Marshall's, ShopRite, Walmart/Subway
45b a	to Mt Holly, Willingboro, W [gas] LukOil/dsl [other] [H], auto repair
43b a	rd 636, to Rancocas Woods, Delran, W [gas] Exxon [food] Carlucci's Rest.
40b a	NJ 38, to Mount Holly, Moorestown, E [food] Ruby Tuesday [lodging] Residence Inn, W [gas] Amera/dsl, WaWa/dsl [food] Anthony's

CHERRY HILL

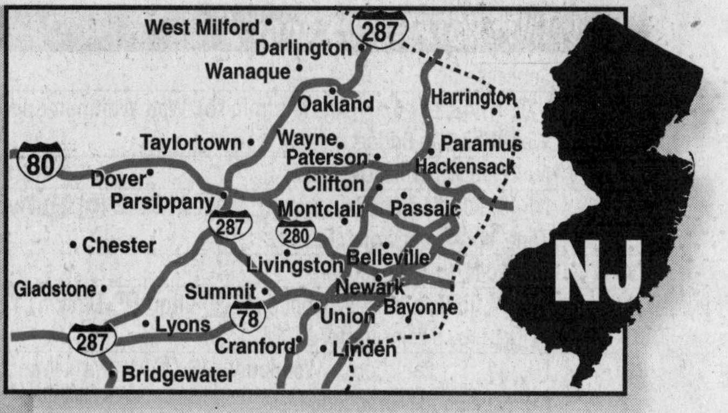

Exit #	Services
40b a	Continued Pizza, Arby's, Chick-fil-A, Chipotle, Dunkin', Jimmy John's, Naf Naf Grill, Panera Bread, Qdoba, Starbucks, Subway, TGIFriday's, Wendy's [lodging] SpringHill Suites [other] [H], Costco/gas, GNC, Jo-Ann Fabrics, Petsmart, Target, TJ Maxx, UHaul, Wegman's Foods
36b a	NJ 73, to NJ Tpk, Tacony Br, Berlin, E [gas] LukOil/dsl [food] Bob Evans, Miller's Alehouse, Starbucks [lodging] aLoft, Courtyard, EconoLodge, Fairfield Inn, Hotel ML, Red Roof Inn, Super 8, TownePlace Suites, Westin, W [gas] Citgo, Shell, WaWa/dsl [food] Bertucci's, Boscov's, Boston Mkt, Buffalo Wild Wings, Burger King, Chick-fil-A, Chipotle Mexican, Corner Cafe, Don Pablo, Dunkin', Five Guys, Friendly's, Jersey Mike's, Old Town Buffet, Panera Bread, Pei Wei, Perkins, PJ Whelahin's, Popeye's, The Melting Pot, Uno Grill, Wendy's [lodging] Crossland Suites, Homewood Suites, Motel 6, Quality Inn [other] $Tree, Acura, Advance Parts, AT&T, AutoZone, Barnes&Noble, Best Buy, Dick's, Fiat, Ford/Lincoln, Home Depot, Infiniti, Lord&Taylor, Lowe's, Marshall's, Michael's, Mr Tire, Old Navy, PepBoys, PepBoys, Petsmart, Ross, ShopRite Foods, Staples
34b a	NJ 70, to Camden, Cherry Hill, E [gas] BP, Exxon, WaWa [food] Burger King, Dunkin', PJ Whelihans, Rock Hill Rest., Stacy's Korean BBQ [lodging] Extended Stay America, Residence Inn [other] Mavis Tire, Tires+, W [gas] Jersey Gas, LukOil, US Gas [food] Dunkin', Famous Dave's BBQ, Han Dynasty, McDonald's, Norma's Rest., Ponzio's Rest, Qdoba, Rita's, Salad Works, Seasons Pizza, Starbucks [lodging] Woodspring Suites [other] [H], $Tree, AT&T, CVS Drug, Goodyear/auto, Mom's Mkt, Rite Aid, vet, WaWa, Whole Foods Mkt
32	NJ 561, to Haddonfield, Voorhees, E [gas] LukOil/dsl [food] Herman's Deli, Hunan Wok, Tucchi's Pizza, Vito's Pizza [other] [H], $Tree, Trio Tire, USPO, W [gas] Pioneer/dsl [food] Burger King, Dunkin', Subway, Tutti Toscani [other] 7-11, Ford
31	Woodcrest Station
30	Warwick Rd (from sb)
29b a	US 30, to Berlin, Collingswood, E [gas] Astro/dsl, Citgo/dsl, Valero/dsl, WaWa/dsl [food] Arby's, Church's, Dunkin', McDonald's, Popeye's, Wendy's, Wild Wing Cafe [other] AutoZone, Home Depot, Lowe's, Petsmart, ShopRite
28	NJ 168, to NJ Tpk, Belmawr, Mt Ephraim, E [gas] Riggins, Shell/dsl, Valero/dsl [food] Burger King, Club Diner, Dunkin', Vero Pizzaria, Wendy's [lodging] Bellmawr Motel, EconoLodge, Howard Johnson, Red Roof Inn, Super 8, W [gas] BP, Conoco, Speedway/dsl, WaWa/dsl [food] Applebee's, Arby's, Black Horse Diner, Chick-fil-A, Da Vinci'sRest., Domino's, Dunkin', Little Caesar's, McDonald's, Pizza Hut/Taco Bell, Sonic [other] Acme Foods, AutoZone, Chrysler/Dodge, CVS Drug, Firestone/auto, Harley-Davidson, Meinke, Midas, Mr Tire, PepBoys, URGENT CARE, USPO, Walgreens, Walmart/Subway

INTERSTATE 295 Cont'd

Exit #	Services
26	I-76, NJ 42, to I-676 (exits left from sb), Walt Whitman Bridge, Walt Whitman Bridge
25b a	NJ 47, to Westville, Deptford
24b a	NJ 45, NJ 551 (no EZ sb return), to Westville, E [O] [H], AutoZone, W [O] Chevrolet, Family$
23	US 130 N, to National Park
22	NJ 644, to Red Bank, Woodbury, E [gas] Citgo [food] Dunkin', 1 mi W [gas] Crown Point Trkstp/dsl/@
21	NJ 44 S, Paulsboro, Woodbury, W [food] WaWa, Wendy's [lodging] Westwood Motor Lodge
20	NJ 44, rd 643, to National Park, Thorofare, E [lodging] Best Western, W [lodging] Red Bank Inn
19	to NJ 44, rd 656, Mantua
18b a	rd 667, to rd 678, Clarksboro, Mt Royal, E [gas] Exxon/dsl, TA/Shell/Country Pride/dsl/scales/@ [food] Dragon Nest Chinese, Dunkin', McDonald's [O] RV camping, W [gas] Valero, WaWa/dsl
17	rd 680, to Mickleton, Gibbstown, W [food] Burger King, Domino's, Dunkin', Mr Bee's Deli [O] $General, Advance Parts, Family$, GNC, Rite Aid, ShopRite Foods
16b	rd 551, to Gibbstown, Mickleton
16a	rd 653, to Paulsboro, Swedesboro
15	rd 607, to Gibbstown
14	rd 684, to Repaupo
13	US 130 S, US 322 W, to Bridgeport (from sb, no return)
11	US 322 E, to Mullica Hill
10	Ctr Square Rd, to Swedesboro, E [gas] Citgo/dsl, Wa dsl [food] Applebee's, Ciconte's Pizza, Dunkin', McDonald's, W dy's [lodging] Hampton Inn, Holiday Inn, TownePlace Suites [O] A Foods/Sav-On, Firestone/auto, Rite Aid, URGENT CARE, Veri W [O] Camping World RV Supplies/service
7	to Auburn, Pedricktown
4	NJ 48, Woodstown, Penns Grove
3mm	**weigh sta nb**
2mm	**[RS] nb, full [handicapped] facilities, info, litter barrels, [phone], picnic tabl dump, vending**
2c	to US 130 (from sb), Deepwater, E same as 2b, W [gas] FLYIN Denny's/dsl/scales/LP/24hr, Sunoco/Dunkin'/dsl/scales/24hr
2b	US 40 E, to NJ Tpk, E [gas] Gulf, Pilot/Subway/ scales/24hr [lodging] Comfort Inn, Friendship Motor Inn, Holiday Express, Red Carpet Inn, W same as 2c
2a	to Delaware Bridge, US 40 W (from nb)
1c	NJ 551 S, Hook Rd, to Salem, E [lodging] White Oaks Motel
1b	US 130 N (from nb), Penns Grove
1a	NJ 49 E, to Pennsville, Salem, E [gas] WaWa/dsl [food] Appleb Burger King, Cracker Barrel, Dunkin', KFC/Taco Bell, McD ald's [lodging] Hampton Inn, Super 8 [O] Peterbilt, W [gas] Coas dsl [lodging] Seaview Motel
0mm	New Jersey/Pennsylvania state line, Delaware River

NJ

NM

NEW MEXICO

INTERSTATE 10

LAS CRUCES

Exit #	Services
164.5mm	New Mexico/Texas state line
164mm	**Welcome Ctr wb, full [handicapped] facilities, litter barrels, petwalk, [phone], [picnic]**
162	NM 404, Anthony, S [gas] Alon/dsl [O] El Paso West RV Park, Family$
160mm	**weigh sta wb**
155	NM 227 W, to Vado, N [O] Western Sky's RV Park, S [gas] Chevron/El Viajero/dsl/scales/24hr, NTS/dsl/scales/24hr/@ [O] $General, El Camino Real HS
151	Mesquite
144	I-25 N, to Las Cruces
142	Rd 188, Rd 101, Valley Dr, Las Cruces, N [gas] Chevron/dsl [food] Chilito's Mexican, Dick's Cafe, IHOP, Jimmy John's, Whataburger [lodging] Best Western, EconoLodge, Holiday Inn Express, Motel 6, Quality Inn, Ramada Inn, Super 8, Teakwood Inn [O] [H], auto/RV repair/tires, Cadillac/Chevrolet, Dalmont's RV Camping, Ford/Lincoln, Honda, Hyundai, Mazda, Nissan, NMSU, vet, S [gas] Alon/dsl [O] USPO
140	NM 28, to Mesilla, Las Cruces, N [gas] Alon/dsl [food] Applebee's, Blake's Lotaburger, BurgerTime, Cracker Barrel, Domino's, Golden Corral, K-Bob's, McDonald's, Murry Express, Starbucks, Subway [lodging] Best Value Inn, Days Inn, Drury Inn, Hampton Inn, La Quinta, SpringHill Suites [O] Buick/GMC, Kia, Toyota, VW, Walmart/McDonald's, S [food] LunaRossa Pizza [lodging] Comfort Inn [O] Harley-Davidson, Holiday World RV Ctr, Siesta RV Park, United RV Ctr
139	NM 292, Amador Ave, Motel Blvd, Las Cruces, N [gas] Pilot/Subway/dsl/scales/24hr, TA/Burger King/Pizza Hut/Taco Bell/dsl/24hr/scales/@, S [food] PitStop Café [lodging] Coachlight Inn/RV Park [O] NAPACare

DEMING

Exit #	Services
138mm	Rio Grande River
135.5mm	**[RS] eb, full [handicapped] facilities, litter barrels, petwalk, [picnic], scenic vi**
135	US 70 E, to W Las Cruces, Alamogordo, 1 mi N [O] KOA
132	N [O] fairgrounds, to [airport], S [gas] Loves/Subway/dsl/sca 24hr
127	Corralitos Rd, N [gas] Exxon [O] Bowlin's Trading Post, to fairgrou
120.5mm	**insp sta wb**
116	NM 549
111mm	**parking area wb, litter barrels**
102	Akela, N [gas] Exxon/dsl/gifts
85	East Motel Dr, Deming, S [gas] Chevron/dsl, Con dsl [lodging] Hampton Inn, Holiday Inn Express, La Quinta, M 6, Quality Inn [O] Buick/Cadillac/Chevrolet/GMC, Chrys Dodge/Jeep, Dreamcatcher RV Park
82b	Railroad Blvd, Deming, N [gas] Chevron/dsl, S [gas] Con dsl [food] DQ, Golden Star Chinese, IHOP, KFC, Little Caes Ranchers Grill, Wendy's [lodging] Days Inn, Grand Motel [O] $G eral, $Tree, AutoZone, Big O Tire, Deming Visitors Ctr, L Vinyard RV Park, NAPA, O'Reilly Parts, Roadrunner RV P st police, Sunrise RV Park, to Rock Hound SP, Verizon, Wa Wheel RV Park, Walmart/Subway
82a	US 180, NM 26, NM 11, Deming, N [gas] Chevron/dsl [food] Bla Lotaburger, S [gas] Exxon, Phillips 66 [food] Burger King, na Rest., Denny's, Domino's, KFC, Palma's Italian, Pizza Rancher's Grill, Si Senor [lodging] Butterfield Stage Motel [O] Budget Tire, CarQuest, museum, Rockhound SP, to Pancho SP, Walgreens
81	NM 11, W Motel Dr, Deming, S [gas] Circle K/dsl, CNG [food] ji's Rest, El Camino Real, McDonald's, Sonic, Subway, Bell [lodging] Best Western, Comfort Inn, Deming Motel, Execu Motel, Super 8, Western Motel [O] [H], 81 Palms RV Park, park, Hitchin Post RV Park, Rock Hound SP, to Pancho Villa

INTERSTATE 10 Cont'd

Exit #	Services
68	NM 418, S [gas] Petro/Iron Skillet/Starbucks/dsl/scales/24hr [other] tires/repair
62	Gage, S [gas] Butterfield Station/Exxon/DQ/dsl
61mm	**[rest stop] wb, full [handicapped] facilities, litter barrels, petwalk, [picnic], vending**
55	Quincy
53mm	**[rest stop] eb, full [handicapped] facilities, litter barrels, petwalk, [picnic], vending**
51.5mm	ContinentalDivide, elev 4585
49	NM 146 S, to Hachita, Antelope Wells
42	Separ, S [other] Bowlin's Continental Divide Trading Post/Gifts
34	NM 113 S, Muir, Playas
29	no service
24	US 70, E Motel Dr, Lordsburg, N [gas] FLYING J/Denny's/dsl/LP/scales/RV Dump/24hr, Pilot/Arby's/dsl/scales/24hr [lodging] American Motel [other] Horseman RV Park
23.5mm	**weigh sta both lanes**
22	NM 494, Main St, Lordsburg, N [food] McDonald's [lodging] Comfort Inn, Hampton Inn [other] $General, Family$, NAPA, Saucedo's Foods, USPO, S [gas] Circle K/dsl [food] Kranberry's Rest. [lodging] EconoLodge, Motel 10, Motel 6, Plaza Inn [other] KOA
20b a	W Motel Dr, Lordsburg, N [gas] Loves/Godfather's Pizza/Subway/scales/dsl [lodging] Days Inn, S [gas] Chevron/dsl, **Visitors Ctr/full [handicapped] facilities** [other] info
15	to Gary
11	NM 338 S, to Animas
5	NM 80 S, to Road Forks, S [other] dsl/tire repair, fireworks
3	Steins
0mm	New Mexico/Arizona state line

INTERSTATE 25

Exit #	Services
460.5mm	New Mexico/Colorado state line
460	Raton Pass Summit, elev 7834, **weigh sta sb**, E [other] Cedar Rail Campground
454	2nd St, Lp 25, Raton, 2 mi W [gas] Crossroads [lodging] Budget Host [other] [H], CarQuest, Ford
452	NM 72 E, Raton, E [other] to Sugarite Canyon SP, W [gas] Conoco
451	US 64 E, US 87 E, Raton, E [gas] 87 Express/dsl, Chevron/dsl, CR/dsl/24hr [food] Subway [other] Summerlan RV Park, to Capulin Volcano NM, W [gas] Conoco/dsl, CR/dsl, Loaf'n Jug/dsl, Phillips 66 [food] Arby's, Denny's, Domino's, DQ, K-Bob's, McDonald's, Sand's Rest., Sonic [lodging] Best Value Inn, Best Western, Microtel, Oasis Motel/rest, Quality Inn, Robin Hood Motel, Rodeway Inn, Super 8, Texan Motel, Travelodge, Village Inn Motel [other] [H], $General, Ace Hardware, AutoZone, Family$, KOA, O'Reilly Parts, Super Save Foods, Visitor's Ctr/info
450	Lp 25, Raton, W [lodging] Holiday Inn Express, Oasis Motel/rest. [other] [H], AutoZone, KOA, vet
446	US 64 W, to Cimarron, Taos, 4 mi W [other] camping, NRA Whittington Ctr
440mm	Canadian River
435	Tinaja
434.5mm	**[rest stop] both lanes, full [handicapped] facilities, litter barrels, petwalk, [picnic], weather info**
426	NM 505, Maxwell, W [gas] Maxwell Station/dsl [other] to Maxwell Lakes, USPO
419	NM 58, to Cimarron, E [gas] Chevron/Russell's/Subway/dsl/scales/24hr/@
414	US 56, Springer, 1 mi E [gas] Conoco/dsl, Crossroads/dsl [food] Minnie's Dairy Delite [lodging] Broken Arrow Motel, Oasis Motel [other] Old Santa Fe Trail RV Park

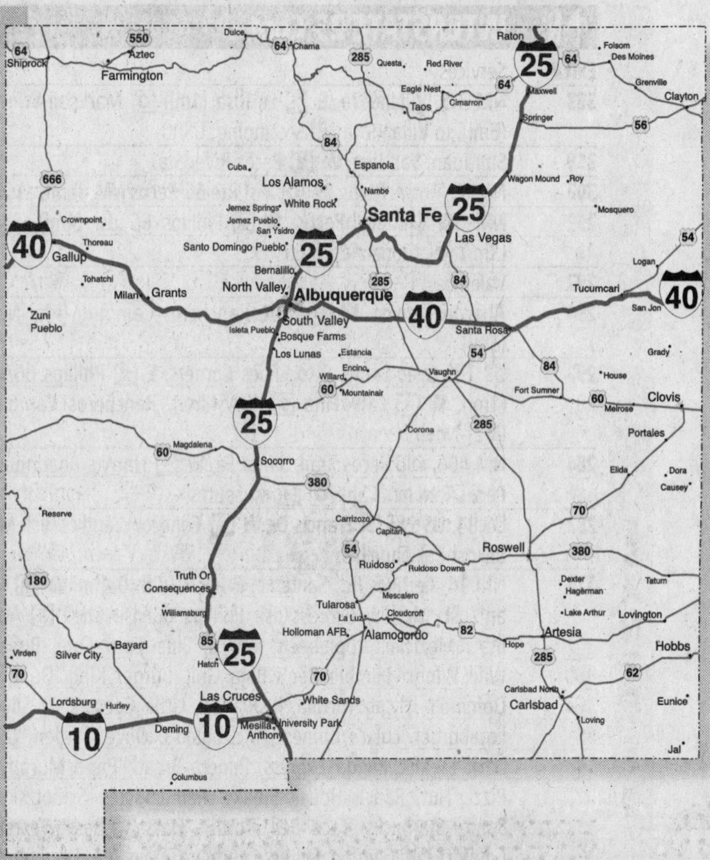

Exit #	Services
412	US 56 E, US 412 E, NM 21, NM 468, Springer, **1 mi E** [gas] Alon [lodging] Brown Hotel/cafe [other] CarQuest, Family$, Springer Foods, USPO
404	NM 569, Colmor, Charette Lakes
393	Levy
387	NM 120, to Roy, Wagon Mound, E [gas] Conoco/dsl, Phillips 66/dsl
376mm	**[rest stop] sb, full [handicapped] facilities, litter barrels, petwalk, [phone], [picnic], RV camp**
374mm	**[rest stop] nb, full [handicapped] facilities, litter barrels, petwalk, [phone], [picnic], RV camp**
366	NM 97, NM 161, Watrous, Valmora, W [other] Ft Union NM, Santa Fe Trail
364	NM 97, NM 161, Watrous, Valmora
361	no service
360mm	**parking area both lanes**
356	Onava, Onava
352	E [other] [airport], RV camping
347	to NM 518, Las Vegas, **0-2 mi W** [gas] Loves/Chester's/dsl/scales/24hr, Phillips 66/Burger King, Pino/dsl/rest. [food] Arby's, Hillcrest Rest., KFC, Little Moon Chinese, McDonald's, Sonic, Taco Bell, Wendy's [lodging] Best Western, Budget Inn, Comfort Inn, Days Inn, Palamino Inn, Regal Motel, Super 8 [other] [H], Storrie Lake SP
345	NM 65, NM 104, University Ave, Las Vegas, E [other] to Conchas Lake SP, W [gas] Allsups, Crossroads/dsl [food] DQ, Hillcrest Rest., Johnny's Kitchen, KFC [lodging] El Fidel, Knights Inn [other] [H], Hist. Old Town Plaza
343	to NM 518 N, Las Vegas, E [other] Garcia Tires, **0-2 mi W** [gas] Alon, Phillips 66/dsl [lodging] Holiday Inn Express, Thunderbird Motel [other] auto repair
339	US 84 S, to Santa Rosa, Romeroville, E [other] KOA, W [gas] Phillips 66/Subway/dsl
335	Tecolote
330	Bernal
325mm	**parking area both lanes, no rest rooms**

LAS VEGAS

NM

INTERSTATE 25 Cont'd

SANTA FE

Exit #	Services
323	NM 3 S, Villanueva, E La Risa (1mi) Madison Winery (6mi), to Villanueva SP/rv camping, USPO
319	San Juan, San Jose, W Pecos River Sta.
307	NM 63, Rowe, Pecos, W Hist Rte 66, Pecos NM, same as 299
299	NM 50, Glorieta, Pecos, W Phillips 66 dsl (4mi), Shell (3mi) Glorieta Conf Ctr
297	Valencia
294	Apache Canyon, W KOA, Rancheros Camping (Mar-Nov) (3mi)
290	US 285 S, to Lamy, S to Clines Corners, E Phillips 66/dsl (1mi), W Cafe Fina KOA (3mi), Rancheros Camping (Mar-Nov)
284	NM 466, Old Pecos Trail, Santa Fe, W Harry's Roadhouse, Pecos Trail Inn/Cafe H, museums
282	US 84, US 285, St Francis Dr, W Conoco/Wendy's/dsl, Mobil/dsl Church's
278	NM 14, Cerrillos Rd, Santa Fe, E RV Ctr, 0-4 mi W Giant/dsl, Murphy Express/dsl, Phillips 66/dsl, Shell Adelita's Mexican, Applebee's, Arby's, Blue Corn Cafe, Buffalo Wild Wings, Bumble Bee's Baja Grill, Burger King, Denny's, Domino's, Flying Tortilla, IHOP, KFC, Little Caesars, LJ Silver, Lotaburger, LuLu's Chinese, McDonald's, Olive Garden, Outback Steaks, Panda Express, Panera Bread, Papa Murphy's, Pizza Hut, Ranch House Steaks, Red Lobster, Schlotzsky's, Sonic, Starbucks, Taco Bell, Tortilla Flats Best Western, Comfort Inn, Comfort Suites, Courtyard, Days Inn, Doubletree, EconoLodge, Fairfield Inn, Hampton Inn, Holiday Inn Express, Hyatt Place, La Quinta, Motel 6, Quality Inn, Santa Fe Inn, Super 8, Tranquilla Inn AAA, Albertson's, AT&T, Best Buy, BigLots, BMW, Buick/GMC, Cadillac/Chevrolet, Chrysler/Dodge/Jeep, CVS Drug, Dillard's, Discount Tire, Firestone/auto, Ford/Lincoln, Harley-Davidson, Home Depot, Honda, JC Penney, Jo-Ann Fabrics, Kohl's, Land Rover, Lexus, Los Campos RV Park, Lowe's, Mazda, Mecedes/Smart, Meineke, Michaels, Natural Grocers, Peerless Tire, Penske, PepBoys, Petsmart, Ross, Sam's Club/gas, Santa Fe Outlets/famous brands, Sprouts Mkt, Staples, Subaru/VW, Target, TJ Maxx, Tuesday Morning, Verizon, Volvo, Walgreens, Walmart
276b a	NM 599, to NM 14, to Madrid, E Phillips 66/Allsup's Santa Fe Skies RV Park, 4 mi W Shell Sunrise Springs
271	CR 50F, La Cienega
269mm	**nb, full facilities, litter barrels, petwalk,**
267	Waldo Canyon Rd, **insp sta., access to nb**
264	NM 16, Pueblo, W to Cochiti Lake RA
263mm	Galisteo River
259	NM 22, to Santo Domingo Pueblo, W Phillips 66/cafe/dsl to Cochiti Lake RA (11mi)
257	Budaghers, W Mormon Battalion Mon
252	San Felipe Pueblo, E San Felipe TC/dsl San Felipe Casino/rest.
248	Rte 66, Algodones
242	US 550, NM 44 W, NM 165 E, to Farmington, Aztec, **0-2 mi** W Chevron/dsl, Conoco/dsl, M&M/Burger King/dsl, Phillips 66/dsl, Valero/dsl Denny's, Guang Dong Chinese, IHOP, KFC, Lotaburger, McDonald's, Pizza Hut, Sonic, Starbucks, Subway, Taco Bell, Twisters, Wendy's Days Inn, Holiday Inn Express, Motel 6, Super 8 $General, AutoZone, Casino, Home Depot, KOA, O'Reilly Parts, to Coronado SP, Walgreens, Walmart

NM

ALBUQUERQUE

Exit #	Services
240	NM 473, to Bernalillo, W Conoco/dsl Abuelita's M can, Range Café KOA, to Coronado SP, USPO, vet
234	NM 556, Tramway Rd, E Valero/Subway/dsl ca W Phillips 66/dsl
233	Alameda Blvd, E Chevron Burger King Com Suites, Motel 6, Staybridge Suites Audi/Porsche, Lin Meineke, Mercedes, Toyota, Volvo, W Phillips 66/Circ dsl Carl's Jr Best Value, Holiday Inn Express loon Fiesta Park, CarMax
232	Paseo del Norte, Paseo del Norte, E Chick-fil-A, China L Chipotle Mexican, Five Guys, Freddy's Steakburgers, Jas Deli, Jimmy John's, McDonald's, Panda Express, Panera Br Starbucks, Subway, Tomato Cafe, Wendy's Howard J son Aloha RV Ctr, AutoZone, Discount Tire, Kohl's, Low Office Depot, Target, Verizon, Walgreens, W Shell/C K Arby's Courtyard, Marriott
231	San Antonio Ave, E Alon/7-11 Cracker Barrel, Den Lotaburger Comfort Suites, Hilton Garden, Homew Suites, La Quinta, Quality Inn H, USPO, W Bayn Inn, Crossland Suites, LaQuinta Mazda, VW
230	San Mateo Blvd, Osuna Rd, Albuquerque, E Chevron, C K, Giant/dsl, Phillips 66/Circle K, Shell Applebee's, Ar Azuma Grill, Bob's Burgers, Burger King, Chick-fil-A, Chili's ci's Pizza, Firehouse Subs, Furrs Buffet, Golden Corral, Hay Hooters, Jack-in-the-Box, KFC, LJ Silver, McDonald's, Olive den, Papa John's, Pizza Hut/Taco Bell, Popeyes, Schlozts Sonic, Souper Salad, Starbucks, Subway, SweetTomatoes, Bueno, Taco Cabana, Teriyaki Chicken, TX Roadhouse, Vil Inn, Wendy's, Wienerschnitzel Nativo Lodge $Tree bertson's, AT&T, AutoZone, Brake Masters, Cadillac, CVS D Fiat, Firestone, Firestone/auto, GNC, Just Brakes, Midas, N O'Reilly Parts, Peerless Tire, PepBoys, PetCo, Ross, Sprouts Subaru, Tuesday Morning, U-Haul, Walgreens, W Circl dsl, Valero/dsl McDonald's, Quiznos, Weck's Break lunch, Whataburger Studio 6 BMW/Mini
229	Jefferson St, E ClaimJumper, Outback Steaks Hol Inn same as 230, W Boston's Pizza, Chama River R Cheddar's, Chile Rio, Coldstone, Dickey's BBQ, Fox&Hound, drucker's, Genghis Grill, Mimi's Café, Nick&Jimmy's Grill, padeaux, Pars Cuisine, PF Chang's, Plum Cafe Asian, Red in, Subway, Twin Peaks Rest., TX Land&Cattle Steaks D Inn, Hampton Inn, Hampton Inn, Residence Inn, TowneP Suites Lexus
228	Montgomery Blvd, E Alon/7-11/dsl, Chevron/dsl, Con dsl Fiestas Cantina, Lotaburger Best Western Discount Tire, W Shell/Circle K Arby's, Carl's Jr, I McDonald's, Panda Express, Starbucks, Wendy's InTo Suite Acura, Costco/gas, Ford, Home Depot, Infiniti, O Depot, Petsmart, REI, Sam's Club/gas, Sportsman's Whse
227b	Comanche Rd, Griegos Rd, E UPS Depot
227a	Candelaria Rd, Albuquerque, E Circle K/dsl, Pump'n'Sa dsl, Shell, TA/Valero/Country Pride/dsl/scales/24hr/@ plebee's, Little Anita's, Mesa Grill, Range Cafe, Subway, lage Inn Candlewood Suites, Crowne Plaza, Days Elegante Hotel, Fairfield Inn, Holiday Inn Express, La Qui Motel 1, Motel 76, Quality Inn, Rodeway Inn, Super 8, T elodge Kenworth, W Chevron/dsl Ambassa Inn, Rodeway Inn Penske
226b a	I-40, E to Amarillo, W to Flagstaff
225	Lomas Blvd, E Phillips 66 Plaza Inn/rest. Che let, W FillUp, Shell/Circle K/McDonald's Burger K Carl's Jr, Starbucks Embassy Suites H

INTERSTATE 25 Cont'd

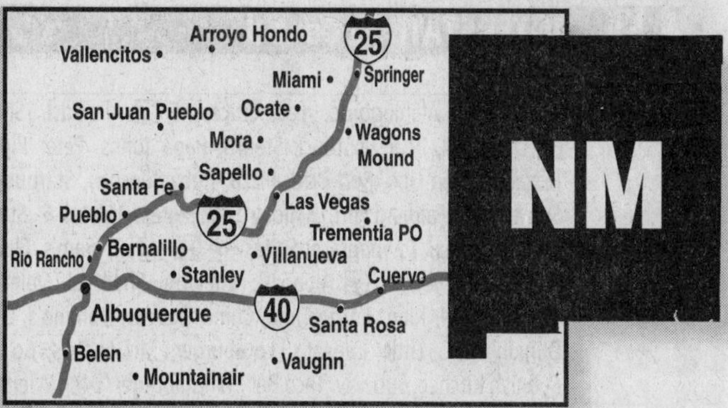

Exit #	Services
224	Lead Ave, Coal Ave, Grand Ave, Central Ave, E Alon/7-11 66 Diner Crossroads Motel H, W M&M Best Value Inn, EconoLodge, Hotel Parq Central, Knights Inn
223	Chavez Ave, E Motel 6 sports arena
222b a	Gibson Blvd, E Phillips 66/dsl Applebee's, Buffalo Wild Wings, Burger King, Dion's Pizza, Fuddrucker's, IHOP, Subway, Village Inn, Waffle House AmericInn, Best Western, Comfort Inn, Country Inn&Suites, Courtyard, Days Inn, Extended Stay America, Fairfield Inn, Hawthorn Suites, Hilton Garden, Holiday Inn Express, La Quinta, Quality Suites, Ramada Inn, Residence Inn, Sleep Inn, TownePlace Suites H, Kirtland AFB, museum, vet, W Alon/7-11/dsl Church's, Lotaburger
221	Sunport, E Holiday Inn, Homewood Suites, Hyatt Place, Staybridge Suites , USPO
220	Rio Bravo Blvd, Mountain View, E golf, **1-2 mi** W Shell/dsl, Valero/dsl Bob's Burgers, Burger King, Church's, KFC/Taco Bell, McDonald's, Pizza Hut, Subway Albertsons/Sav-On, Family$, O'Reilly Parts, vet, Walgreens
215	NM 47, E Isleta One Stop/dsl, Phillips 66/Subway/dsl casino, golf, st police, to Isleta Lakes RA/RV Camping
214mm	Rio Grande
213	NM 314, Isleta Blvd, W Chevron/Subway/dsl $General, vet
209	NM 45, to Isleta Pueblo
203	NM 6, to Los Lunas, E Chevron/dsl, Murphy USA/dsl, Shell/Circle K/Wendy's/dsl/24hr, Valero/dsl Applebee's, Benny's Burger, Del Taco, Denny's, Sonic, Starbucks Days Inn, Los Lunas Inn AutoZone, Big O Tire, Chevrolet, Chrysler/Dodge/Jeep, Ford, Home Depot, Lowe's, URGENT CARE, Walgreens, W Phillips 66/Subway/dsl Carl's Jr, Chili's, Coldstone, KFC, Mariscos Altamar, Panda Express Western Skies Inn Buick/GMC, Discount Tire, Verizon, Walmart/McDonald's
195	Lp 25, Los Chavez, **1 mi** E Roadrunner/grill/dsl Pizza Hut/Taco Bell Walmart/Subway
191	NM 548, Belen, E Conoco/dsl, Loves/Arby's/dsl/scales/24hr McDonald's, Pizza Hut Super 8 $General, USPO, Walgreens, W Rio Grande Diner Holiday Inn Express, RV park
190	Lp 25, Belen, **1-2 mi** E Conoco/dsl, Phillips 66 A&W/LJ Silver, McDonald's, Pizza Hut Super 8 $General, Affordable Tire/repair, AutoZone, USPO, Walgreens
175	US 60, Bernardo, E Salinas NM, W Kiva RV Park
174mm	Rio Puerco
169	E La Joya St Game Refuge Sevilleta NWR
167mm	**both lanes, full facilities, litter barrels, petwalk, , vending**
166mm	Rio Salado
165mm	**weigh sta/parking area both lanes**
163	San Acacia
156	Lemitar, W Phillips 66/dsl/24hr
152	Escondida, W to st police
150	US 60 W, Socorro, W Chevron/dsl, Exxon/dsl, Phillips 66/dsl, Valero/dsl Bodega Burger Co, Burger King, China Best, Denny's, Domino's, K-Bob's, Little Caesar's, Lotaburger, McDonald's, Pizza Hut, Socorro Springs Rest., Sofia's Kitchen, Sonic, Subway Best Value, Best Western, Comfort Inn, Days Inn, EconoLodge, Economy Inn, Holiday Inn Express, Sands Motel, Super 8 $General, Ace Hardware, AutoZone, Brooks Foods, CarQuest, Family$, Ford, NAPA, Smith's Foods, to NM Tech, Verizon, vet, Walmart
147	US 60 W, Socorro, W Chevron/dsl, Conoco/dsl/LP, Pump-N-Save/dsl, Shell/Circle K/dsl Arby's Rodeway Inn H, repair/transmissions, Socorro RV Park, to
139	US 380 E, to San Antonio, E to Bosque Del Apache NWR
124	to San Marcial, E Ft Craig, to Bosque del Apache NWR
115	NM 107, E Truck Plaza/dsl/rest./24hr to Camino Real Heritage Ctr
114mm	**both lanes, full facilities, litter barrels, petwalk, , RV parking, vending**
107mm	Nogal Canyon
100	Red Rock
92	Mitchell Point
90mm	La Canada Alamosa, La Canada Alamosa
89	NM 181, to Cuchillo, to Monticello, RV Park (4mi)
83	NM 52, NM 181, to Cuchillo, **3 mi** E Ivory Tusk Inn& Tavern Elephant Butte Inn/rest. Elephant Lake Butte SP, RV Park
82mm	**insp sta nb**
79	Lp 25, to Truth or Consequences, E Chevron/dsl, Circle K, Shell/dsl Blakes's Lotaburger, Denny's, K-Bob's, La Cocina Mexican, Los Arcos Steaks, McDonald's, Pizza Hut, Sonic, Subway Ace Lodge, Comfort Inn, Desert View Motel, Holiday Inn Express, Hot Springs Inn, Motel 6, Oasis Motel H, $General, AutoZone, O'Reilly Parts, to Elephant Butte SP, USPO, Verizon, Walmart
76	(75 from nb)Lp 25, to Williamsburg, E Conoco/dsl, FillUp/dsl, Phillips 66/dsl, Shell/dsl Maria's Mexican Rio Grande Motel Alco, auto/tire repair, Buick/Chevrolet/GMC, Cielo Vista RV Park, city park, Rio Grande RV Park, RJ RV Park, Shady Corner RV Park
71	Las Palomas
63	NM 152, to Hillsboro, Caballo, E Lakeview RV Park/dsl/LP
59	rd 187, Arrey, Derry, E to Caballo-Percha SPs
58mm	Rio Grande
51	rd 546, to Arrey, Garfield, Derry
41	NM 26 W, Hatch, **1 mi** W Alon/Subway/dsl Burgers&More, Sparky's Cafe Kings Pillow Inn Chile Pepper Outlets, Franciscan RV Ctr, USPO
35	NM 140 W, Rincon
32	Upham
27mm	litter barrels, , scenic view nb
26mm	**insp sta nb**
23mm	**both lanes, full facilities, litter barrels, petwalk, , vending**
19	Radium Springs, W Family$, Fort Selden St Mon, Leasburg SP, RV camping, USPO
9	Dona Ana, W Chucky's/dsl, Circle K/dsl Chachi's Mexican, Jake's Cafe $General, Family$, RV camping, USPO

T O R C

NM

= gas = food = lodging = other = rest stop

NM

INTERSTATE 25 Cont'd

LAS CRUCES

Exit #	Services
6	US 70, to Alamogordo, Las Cruces, E Alon/dsl, Shell Domino's, IHOP, Outback Steaks, Papa Johns, Peter Piper Pizza, Pizzaria Uno, Red Brick Pizza, Ruby Tuesday, Starbucks, Subway Fairfield Inn, Holiday Inn Express, Motel 6, Staybridge Suites, Towneplace Suites H, AT&T, Sam's Club/gas, USPO, vet, W Alon/dsl, Chevron, Shell/dsl, Valero/dsl Burger King, BurgerTime, China Express, Domino's, DQ, Dunkin', KFC, Little Caesar's, Lotaburger, McDonald's, Sonic, Spanish Kitchen, Subway, Taco Bell, Whataburger/24hr, Wienerschnitzel $General, $Tree, Albertson's, AutoZone, CVS Drug, Family$, Kohl's, Lowe's, O'Reilly Parts, Verizon, vet, Walgreens
3	Lohman Ave, Las Cruces, E Alon/dsl, Shell Applebee's, Buffalo Wild Wings, Burger King, Cattle Baron Steaks, Chili's, ChuckeCheese, Dumkin Donuts, Empire Buffet, Farley's Grill, Fidencio's Mexican, Five Guys, Genghis Grill, Golden Corral, Hooters, Jack-in-the-Box, Jason's Deli, KFC, McAlister's Deli, Olive Garden, Pecan Grill, Red Lobster, Sonic, Starbucks, Village Inn, Whataburger Hotel Encanto Albertsons, AutoZone, Barnes&Noble, Dick's, Dillard's, Discount Tire, Home Depot, JC Penney, Marshalls, PetCo, Ross, Target, W Giant/dsl, Valero/dsl Arby's, Carl's Jr, Corner Bakery Cafe, McDonald's, Papa Murphy's, Quiznos, Subway, Taco Bell, TX Roadhouse, Wendy's Hampton Inn AT&T, Best Buy, Big Lots, Brake Masters, Hobby Lobby, NAPA, Old Navy, PepBoys, Petsmart, Staples, URGENT CARE, Verizon, vet, Walgreens, Walmart
1	University Ave, Las Cruces, E AlonSubway/dsl Hilton Garden H, golf, museum, st police, W Giant/dsl Dublin's Cafe, Lorenzo's Italian, McDonald's, Schlotsky's Comfort Suites, Sleep Inn, Woodspring Suites $Tree, Jo-Ann Fabrics, NMSU, Tuesday Morning
0mm	**I-25 begins/ends on I-10, exit 144 at Las Cruces.**

INTERSTATE 40

TUCUMCARI · SANTA ROSA · MORIARTY

Exit #	Services
373.5mm	New Mexico/Texas state line, Mountain/Central time zone
373mm	**Welcome Ctr wb, full facilities, litter barrels, petwalk,**
369	NM 93 S, NM 392 N, Endee, N Chevron/Russell's Truck&Travel/Subway/dsl/scales/24hr
361	Bard
358mm	**weigh sta both lanes**
356	NM 469, San Jon, N Phillips 66/Dhillon//cafe/dsl repair, to Ute Lake SP, S Valero/dsl San Jon Motel city park, USPO
343	no service
339	NM 278, N
335	Lp 40, E Tucumcari Blvd, Tucumcari, N Conoco/dsl Best Value, EconoLodge, Motel 6, Quality Inn, Rodeway Inn, Super 8 to Conchas Lake SP, S KOA
333	US 54 E, Tucumcari, **0-1 mi** N FLYING J/Phillips 66/dsl/LP/scales/24hr, Loves/Arbys/Chester's/Godfather's/dsl/scales Fairfield Inn city park, Mtn Rd RV Park, truck repair, truckwash
332	NM 209, NM 104, 1st St, Tucumcari, **0-2 mi** N Shell/Circle K/Subway/dsl, Valero/Allsups/dsl Blake's Lotaburger, K-Bob's, McDonald's, Pizza Hut, Sonic, Taco Bell Best Western, Days Inn, Desert Inn, Holiday Inn Express, La Quinta H, $General, Ace Hardware, Dinosaur Museum, Family$, Lowe's Foods, st police, to Conchas Lake SP
331	Camino del Coronado, Tucumcari
329	US 54, US 66 E, W Tucumcari Ave
321	Palomas
311	Montoya
302mm	**both lanes, full facilities, litter barrels, petwalk, RV dump**
300	NM 129, Newkirk, N Rte 66/dsl to Conchas Lake USPO
291	to Rte 66, Cuervo, N Cuervo Gas/repair
284	no service
277	US 84 S, to Ft Sumner, N Phillips 66/dsl, Pilot/Subw dsl/scales/24hr Annie's Rest., DQ, Silver Moon Café Western, Budget Inn, Comfort Inn, Hampton Inn, Holiday Express, Motel 6, Quality Inn NAPACare, S Lov Carl's Jr/dsl/24hr, TA/Shell/Subway/dsl/24hr/@ truck/tire re
275	US 54 W, Santa Rosa, N Chevron/dsl, Valero sup's McDonald's, Rte 66 Rest., Santa Fe Grill Days Econolodge, La Quinta, Rodeway Inn Santa Rosa Camp st police, S Shell/Circle K/dsl Joseph's Grill La Motel/RV Park, Rodeway Inn, Sun'n Sand Motel/rest., Sup Tower Motel H, $General, CarQuest, city park, Fam NAPA, USPO
273.5mm	Pecos River
273	US 54 S, Santa Rosa, N Santa Rosa Lake SP, S Phi 66/dsl Best Value Inn NAPACare, to Carlsbad Cav NP
267	Colonias, N Sinclair/dsl
263	San Ignacio
256	US 84 N, NM 219, to Las Vegas
252	no service
251.5mm	**both lanes, full facilities, litter barrels, petwalk, RV dump**
243	Milagro, N Phillips 66/dsl
239	no service
234	N Exxon/Flying C/DQ/dsl/gifts
230	NM 3, to Encino, N to Villanueva SP
226	no service
220mm	**parking area both lanes, litter barrels**
218b a	US 285, Clines Corners, N Conoco/dsl/24hr, Phillips dsl Clines Corners Rest., Subway, S to Carlsbad erns NP
208	Wagon Wheel
207mm	**both lanes, full facilities, litter barrels, petwalk,**
203	no service
197	to Rte 66, Moriarty, S Lisa's TC/dsl/rest./@ auto/RV pair, Glider Museum, same as 194
196	NM 41, Howard Cavasos Blvd, N Pilot/Subw dsl/scales/24hr, S Lisa's TC/dsl, Phillips 66/Circle K Blakes Lotaburger Quality Inn, Sunset Motel a repair, city park, Family$, to Salinas NM (35mi), USPO
194	NM 41, Moriarty, S Alon/7-11/dsl, Conoco/dsl, TA/Sh Burger King/Country Pride/Pizza Hut/dsl/24hr/scales/@ by's, Chili Hills Mexican, El Comedor Mexican, KFC/Taco Subway Best Value Inn, Best Western, Motel 6, Ponde Motel, Super 8 $General, Chevrolet/GMC, Moriarty Fo RV Ctr, URGENT CARE
187	NM 344, Edgewood, N Conoco/DQ/dsl D ny's Walmart/McDonald's, S Phillips 66/dsl Hills Mexican, China Chef, Domino's, McDonald's, Pizza B Sonic, Subway Comfort Inn $Tree, auto/rv repair, A Zone, Ford, O'Reilly Parts, Rte 66 RV Park, RV Camping, Smi Foods/dsl, USPO, Walgreens

E INTERSTATE 40 Cont'd

Exit #	Services
181	NM 217, Sedillo, S Route 66/dsl
178	Zuzax, S Zuzax/dsl/repair Hidden Valley RV Park, Leisure Mtn RV Park
175	NM 337, NM 14, Tijeras, N to Cibola NF, Turquoise Trail RV Park, S Subway USPO
170	Carnuel
167	Central Ave, to Tramway Blvd, S Alon/7-11, Alon/7-11/dsl, Phillips 66/Circle K/dsl Blakes Lotaburger, Happy Garden, KFC, McDonald's, Starbucks, Subway, Taco Bell, Waffle House Budget Host, Deluxe Inn, EconoLodge, Motel 6, Quality Inn, Rodeway Inn, Suburban Lodge, Woodspring Suites $Tree, Rocky Mtn RV/marine, Smith's/gas, Sprouts Mkt, to Kirtland AFB, Valvoline
166	Juan Tabo Blvd, N Phillips 66/Circle K, Texaco/dsl AA Buffet, Dominos, McDonald's, Olive Garden, Peter Piper Pizza, Pizza Hut, Starbucks, Subway, Taco Bell, Twisters Diner, Village Inn Rest., Weck's Rest., Wendy's Guest Gate Inn, Super 8 $General, Albertson's, Discount Tire, Family$, Hobby Lobby, Midas, Sav-On Drug, Tuesday Morning, vet, S Sonic, Wienerschnitzel $General, Chisholm Trail RV Ctr, Holiday RV Ctr, KOA/LP, Myer's RV Ctr, repair
165	Eubank Blvd, N Chevron, Phillips 66/Circle K Applebee's, Owl Cafe, Panda Express, Sadie's Rest., Sonic Days Inn, Econolodge, Holiday Inn Express, Ramada $Tree, Best Buy, CarQuest, city park, PetCo, Target, S Circle K/dsl, Conoco/dsl Bob's Burgers, Boston Mkt, Burger King, Chick-fil-A, Chili's, Church's, Del Taco, Freddy's, IHOP, Jack-in-the-Box, Starbucks, Subway, Taco Bell, Taco Cabana, Twister's Burritos, Wendy's AutoZone, Costco/gas, Home Depot, O'Reilly Parts, Peerless Tires, Petsmart, repair, Ross, Sam's Club/gas, Toyota, Walgreens, Walmart/McDonald's
164	Lomas Blvd, Wyoming Blvd, N Circle K/dsl, Phillips 66/dsl Black Angus, Chick-fil-A, Dickey's BBQ, Dominos, Furr's Buffet, Krispy Kreme, Subway, Wendy's H, $Tree, NAPA, vet, Walgreens, Walmart, S Chrysler/Dodge/Jeep, Ford, Harley-Davidson, Honda, Hyundai, Kirtland AFB, Mazda, Subaru, transmissions, VW
162b a	Louisiana Blvd, N BJ's Rest., Blaze Pizza, Bravo Italian, Buca Italian, CA Pizza Kitchen, Cheesecake Factory, Chili's, Chipotle, Dave & Buster's, Elephant Bar Rest., Firehouse Subs, Five Guys, Fuddrucker's, Garduno's Mexican, Genghis Grill, Jasons Deli, La Madeleine, LePeep, Longhorn Steaks, Macaroni Grill, McAlister's Deli, Melting Pot, Ojos Locos, Panera Bread, Red Robin, Ruth's Chris, Seasons Grill 52, Starbucks, Subway Hilton Garden, Homewood Suites, Hyatt Place, Marriott, Sheraton AT&T, Barnes&Noble, Big O Tire, Dick's, Dillard's, Firestone/auto, JC Penney, Kohl's, Macy's, Petsmart, Target, TJ Maxx, Trader Joe's, Verizon, S Shell Burger King atomic museum
161b a	San Mateo Blvd, Albuquerque, N Giant/dsl, Shell Bob's Burgers, Denny's, Domino's, KFC, Pizza Hut, Starbucks, Subway, Taco Bell San Mateo Inn $Tree, Office Depot, Old Navy, Walmart Mkt, S Chevron/dsl Starbucks
160	Carlisle Blvd, Albuquerque, N Circle K/gas, Murphy Express/dsl, Shell, USA Applebee's, Blakes Lotaburger, China Wok, Jack-in-the-Box, Little Anita's, McDonald's, Papa Murphy's, Range Cafe, Rudy's BBQ, Sonic, Subway, Twisters Grill, Village Inn Rest., Whataburger Best Value Inn, Candlewood Suites, Crowne Plaza, Days Inn, EconoLodge, Elegante Hotel, Fairfield Inn, Hampton Inn, Holiday Inn Express,

ALBUQUERQUE

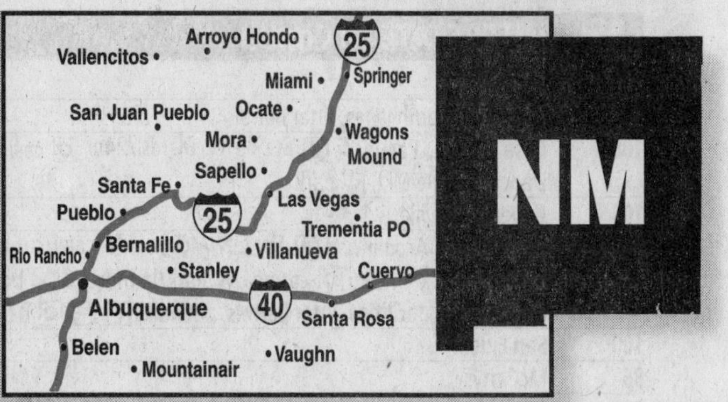

Exit #	Services
160	Continued La Quinta, Motel 6, Quality Inn, Residence Inn, Suburban Motel, Super 8, Wyndham AutoZone, Firestone/auto, Walgreens, Walmart, S Chevron/dsl, Circle K Burger King Home 2 Suites H, Whole Foods Mkt
159b c	I-25, S to Las Cruces, N to Santa Fe
158	6th St, 8th St, 12th St, Albuquerque, N Loves/Subway/dsl $ General, U-Haul, S Chevron/dsl Comfort Inn
157b	12th St (from eb), N Four Winds/Burrito Co/dsl Laguna Burgers, McDonald's, Starbucks Holiday Inn Express Lowe's, Walgreens
157a	Rio Grande Blvd, Albuquerque, N Chevron Range Cafe, S Shell Ben Michaels, Blakes Lotaburger, Burger King, Little Anita's, Starbucks Best Western+/grill, Hotel Albuquerque repair
156mm	Rio Grande River
155	Coors Rd, Albuquerque, N Circle K, Mobil, Valero/dsl Applebee's, Arby's, Baskin-Robbins, Burger King, Chili's, Chipotle, Cracker Barrel, Golden Corral, IHOP, Krispy Kreme, McDonald's, Mimmo's Pizza, Panda Express, Panera Bread, Papa Murphy's, Sonic, Starbucks, Subway, Taco Cabana, Twisters Burritos, Wendy's, Wienerschnitzel, Wing Stop $Tree, AutoZone, Brake Masters, Family$, Firestone, GNC, Home Depot, Jiffy Lube, Verizon, Walgreens, Walmart/Subway, S Chevron/dsl, Phillips 66/Circle K/dsl, Shell, Valero Altamar Mexican, Blakes Lotaburger, Buffalo Wild Wings, China Buffet, Del Taco, Denny's, Dion's, Freddy's, McDonald's, Papa John's, Pizza Hut/Taco Bell, Subway, Twisters Burritos Days Inn, EconoLodge, Hampton Inn, La Quinta, Motel 6, Motel 76, Quality Inn, Rodeway Inn, Super 8 BigLots, Discount Tire, O'Reilly Parts
154	Unser Blvd, N Valero, Walmart/dsl McDonald's, Starbucks, Taco Bell GNC, to Petroglyph NM, Verizon, Walmart Mkt
153	98th St, S FLYING J/Denny's/dsl/LP/24hr, LNG, Valero-dsl Burger King, Church's, Godfather's, Jack-in-the-Box, Little Caesars, McDonald's, Starbucks, Subway, Wing Stop Microtel $Tree, AutoZone, truckwash/tire/lube
149	Central Ave, Paseo del Volcan, N Camping World, Enchanted Trails RV Camping, Freightliner, LaMesa RV Ctr, to Shooting Range SP, S Loves/Carl's Jr/dsl/scales 24hr American RV Park, High Desert RV Park
140.5mm	Rio Puerco River, N 66 Pit Stop
140	Rio Puerco, N 66 Pit Stop/dsl, S Rte 66 TC/DQ/Road Runner Cafe/hotel/casino/dsl/@
131	Canoncito
126	NM 6, to Los Lunas
120mm	Rio San Jose, Rio San Jose
117	Mesita
114	NM 124, Laguna, 1/2 mi N 66 Pit Stop/dsl

NM

= gas = food = lodging = other = rest stop

INTERSTATE 40 Cont'd

GRANTS

Exit #	Services
113.5mm	scenic view both lanes, litter barrels
108	Casa Blanca, Paraje, S Rte 66 TC/DQ/dsl/24hr casino, Dancing Eagle Mkt, RV park
104	Cubero, Budville
102	Sky City Rd, Acomita, N Sky City/McDonald's/hotel/casino/dsl Huwak'a Rest. casino, RV Park/laundry, S **both lanes, full facilities, litter barrels, petwalk,**
100	San Fidel
96	McCartys
89	NM 117, to Quemado, N Sky City/Subway/dsl/gifts, S El Malpais NM
85	NM 122, NM 547, Grants, N Alon/dsl, Phillips 66/dsl, Shell/dsl Asian Buffet, Blakes Lotaburger, Canton Cafe, Denny's, Pizza Hut, Subway, Taco Bell Best Western, Days Inn, Holiday Inn Express, Motel 6, Quality Inn, Sands Motel, Super 8, SureStay $Tree, AutoZone, Delta Tire, O'Reilly Parts, repair/transmissions/towing, Walgreens, Walmart, S Lavaland RV Park
81b a	NM 53 S, Grants, N Phillips 66/dsl Domino's, KFC, McDonald's, Sonic Ford, NAPA, USPO, S Blue Spruce RV Park, El Malpais NM, KOA/Cibola Sands RV Park
79	NM 122, NM 605, Milan, N Chevron/dsl, Loves/Chester's/Subway/dsl/scales/24hr DQ Crossroads Motel $ General, Bar-S RV Park, S Petro/Iron Skillet/dsl/scales/24hr/@ dsl repair, Speedco Lube
72	Bluewater Village, N Exxon/DQ/dsl
63	NM 412, Prewitt, S to Bluewater Lake SP (7mi)
53	NM 371, NM 612, Thoreau, N Giant/Blimpie/dsl Family$, NAPA, USPO
47	Continental Divide, elevation 7275, N Phillips 66 Continental Divide Trdg Post, towing/repair, S USPO
44	Coolidge
39	Refinery, N FLYING J/Subway/Dennys/dsl/scales/24hr/@
36	Iyanbito
33	NM 400, McGaffey, Ft Wingate, N museum, RV camping, to Red Rock SP
26	E 66th Ave, E Gallup, N Shell/Subway/dsl Denny's Comfort Suites, Holiday Inn Express, La Quinta, Sleep Inn,

GALLUP

Exit #	Services
26	Continued TownePlace Suites museum, Red Rock Camping, st poli to Red Rock SP, on Rte 66, S Conoco/dsl, Giant/dsl, Pr to Express, Shell/Ortega Gifts Blakes Lotaburger, Bur King, KFC, McDonald's, Sonic, Wendy's Days Inn, Fairfi Inn, Hacienda Motel, Roadrunner Motel $Gene Family $, Verizon
22	Montoya Blvd, Gallup, N **both lanes, full facilities, ir** on Rte 66, S Duke City/dsl, Gas Up, Giant/dsl, Phill 66 Big Cheese Pizza, Church's, Domino's, DQ, Earl's Re Hong Kong Buffet, LJ Silver, Papa John's, Pizza Hut, Subway, T Bell Blue Spruce Motel, El Capitan Motel, El Rancho Mot rest. Albertson's, O'Reilly Parts, Shop'n Save, Walgreens
20	US 491, to Shiprock, Gallup, N Alon/dsl, Giant/dsl A plebee's, Arby's, Big Cheese Pizza, Blakes Lotaburger, Bur King, CA Chinese, Carl's Jr., Church's, Cracker Barrel, Del Ta Denny's, DQ, Freddy's, Golden Corral, KFC, King Dragon C nese, Little Caesars, McDonald's, Panda Express, Pizza Hut, S zler, Sonic, Subway, Super Buffet, Taco Bell, Wendy's Co fort Inn, Hampton Inn, Hilton Garden, Quality Inn, Spring Suites $Tree, AT&T, AutoZone, Beall's, Big Lots, CarQue Chrysler/Dodge/Jeep, Family$, Hobby Lobby, Home Dep JC Penney, Nissan, O'Reilly Parts, PepBoys, Safeway, Veriz Walmart/McDonald's, on Rte 66, S Phillips 66/dsl B lands Grill, Blakes Lotaburger, Don Diego's, El Charrito, El So brero Mexican, Garcia's Rest., McDonald's, Rte 66 Diner, S ic Best Value Inn, Days Inn, Golden Desert Motel, Knig Inn, Rodeway Inn, Royal Holiday Motel, Super 8 Fo Lincoln, Tire Factory
16	NM 118, W Gallup, Mentmore, N Loves/Cheste Subway/dsl/24hr, Navajo/dsl/24hr, TA/Country Pride/c scales/ 24hr/@, USave Trkstp/dsl Ace Truck/dsl Servi Blue Beacon, NKS Truck Repair, S Conoco/dsl, Shell/c Valero/Allsup's Taco Bell, Virgie's Mexican Budget I EconoLodge, Hampton Inn, Knights Inn, Microtel, Motel 6, R Roof Inn, Travelodge Family $, USA RV Park
12mm	**inspection/weigh sta eb**
8	to Manuelito
3mm	**Welcome Ctr eb, full facilities, litter barrels, petwalk,**
0mm	New Mexico/Arizona state line

NM

NOTES

NEW YORK

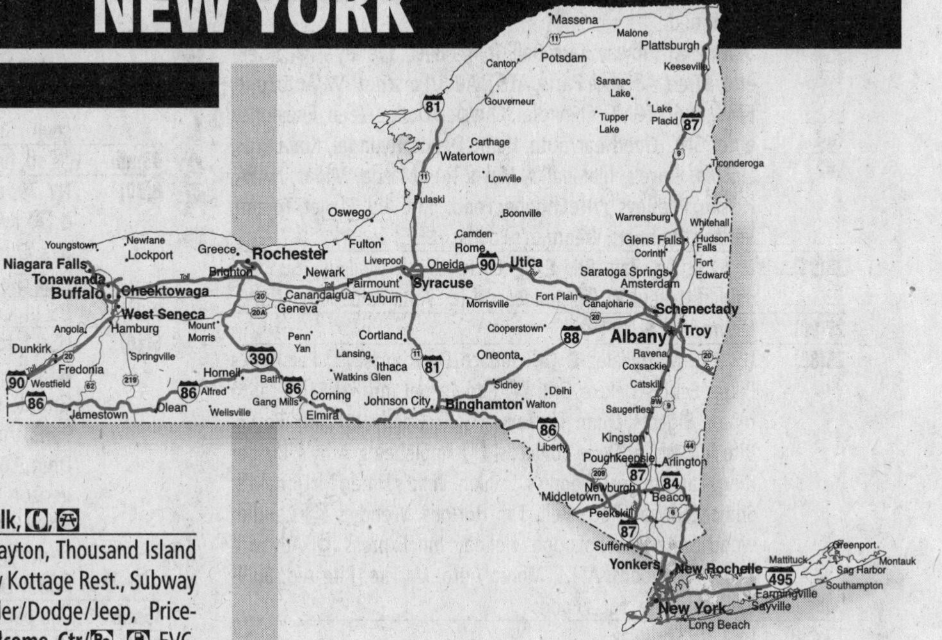

INTERSTATE 81

Exit #	Services
184mm	US/Canada border, New York state line. **I-81 begins/ends.**
183.5mm	US Customs (sb)
52(183)	Island Rd, to De Wolf Point, last US exit nb, last US exit nb
51(180)	Island Rd, to Fineview, Islands Parks, **E** Torchlite Lodge USPO, **W** Sunoco Thousand Islands Park
179mm	St Lawrence River
178.5mm	Thousand Islands Toll Bridge Booth, **NY Welcome Ctr/ sb, full facilities, litter barrels, petwalk, ,**
50NS(178)	NY 12, E to Alexandria Bay, W to Clayton, Thousand Island Region, **E** Sunoco/dsl Kountry Kottage Rest., Subway PineHurst Motel , Chrysler/Dodge/Jeep, Price-Chopper Mkt, st police, **W NY Welcome Ctr/**, EVC, Mobil Bridgeview Motel vet
174mm	**nb, full facilities, litter barrels, petwalk, , , vending**
49(171)	NY 411, to Theresa, Indian River Lake
168mm	**parking area sb, picnic table**
161mm	**parking area nb**
48a	I-781, CR 16, to Ft Drum
48(158)	US 11, NY 37, **E** Circle K/dsl, Mobil/Dunkin'/dsl Longway's Diner Allen's Budget Motel, Royal Inn Long-Park Tire
156.5mm	**parking area both lanes**
47(155)	NY 12, Bradley St, Watertown, **E** Sunoco/Subway/dsl, Valero Frosty Dairy Bar , Honda, **W** Rainbow Motel
154.5mm	Black River
46(154)	NY 12F, Coffeen St, Watertown, **E** Mobil/Dunkin/dsl Cracker Barrel, Shorty's Diner Home Depot, URGENT CARE, **W** Sunoco/Tim Horton/dsl
45(152)	NY 3, to Arsenal St, Watertown, **E** Mobil/Tim Horton/dsl, Sunoco, Tesla EVC Apollo Rest., Applebee's, Arby's, Buffalo Wild Wings, Burger King, Camino Real, Chipotle Mexican, Daily Buffet, Denny's, Dunkin', Five Guys, Ichiban, Jreck Subs, KFC, Lotus Rest., McDonald's, Moe's SW Grill, Mustard Seed Cafe, Ruby Tuesday, Sonic, Starbucks, Taco Bell Comfort Inn, EconoLodge, Fairfield Inn, Hampton Inn, Hilton Garden, Holiday Inn Express, Travelodge $General, $Tree, Advance Parts, Aldi Foods, AT&T, AutoZone, BigLots, Jo-Ann Fabrics, Mavis Discount Tire, Midas, Monro, Mr Tire, PriceChopper Foods/24hr, Staples, TJ Maxx, USPO, Walgreens, **W** Fastrac Bob Evans, Olive Garden, Panera Bread, Pizza Hut, Red Lobster, Super Wok, TGIFriday's, TX Roadhouse Ramada Inn Best Buy, Burlington Coats, Dick's, GNC, Hannaford Foods, JC Penney, Kohl's, Lowe's, Michael's, Old Navy, PetCo, Sam's Club, Target, to Sackets Harbor, Verizon, Walmart/Dunkin'
149mm	**parking area nb**
44(148)	NY 232, to Watertown Ctr, **3 mi E**
147mm	**sb, full facilities, litter barrels, petwalk, , , vending**
43(146)	US 11, to Kellogg Hill
42(144)	NY 177, Adams Center, **E** Sunoco/Mama Mia's Pizza/dsl Harley Davidson, Tugger's Camping (12mi)
41(140)	NY 178, Adams, **E** Sunoco/dsl Dunkin', McDonald's Willows on the Lake RV Park, **W** KOA, st police
138mm	South Sandy Creek
40(135)	NY 193, to Ellisburg, Pierrepont Manor
134mm	**parking area/ both lanes**
39(133)	Mannsville
38(131)	US 11
37(128)	Lacona, Sandy Creek, **E** Two Bros Pizza Harris Lodge USPO, **W** Mobil/dsl New China One Pink House Inn B&B $General, CarQuest, Colonial Court Camping (3mi), Sandy Island Beach SP, Tops/dsl, USPO
36(121)	NY 13, Pulaski, **E** Byrne Dairy/dsl, Valero Ponderosa Red Carpet Inn Buick/Chevrolet, Ford, **W** Fas-Trac/dsl, KwikFill/dsl Arby's, Burger King, Dunkin', McDonald's, Paulanjo's Pizza, River House Rest., Stefano's Rest. 1880 House B&B, Super 8 Advance Parts, Aldi Foods, Family$, Kinney Drug, Mavis Tire, NAPA, Rite Aid, to Selkirk Shores SP, Top's Foods, URGENT CARE, Verizon
35(118)	to US 11, Tinker Tavern Rd, **E** Streamside RV Park
34(115)	NY 104, to Mexico, **E** Mobil/Maple View Rest./dsl/scales, **W** Feeder Creek Lodge (5mi) Jellystone Camping (9mi)
33(111)	NY 69, Parish, **E** Sunoco/dsl/24hr Grist Mill Rest. $General, Up Country RV Park (8mi), **W** Gulf, Mirabito/Dunkin'/dsl Passarella Pizza USPO
32(103)	NY 49, to Central Square, **E** Mirabito/dsl Good Golly's Rest. Murphy's Automotive, **W** Fastrac/gas Burger King, Dunkin', McDonald's, Taco Bell $Tree, Advance Parts, Ford, NAPA, Rite Aid, URGENT CARE, Verizon, Walmart/Subway
31(99)	to US 11, Brewerton, **E** Oneida Shores Camping, **W** Circle K/dsl, Mirabito/Tim Hortons/dsl Dunkin', Lin Li's Chinese, Little Caesar's, McDonald's, Subway Days Inn $General, AT&T, Kinney Drugs, USPO, vet
30(96)	NY 31, to Cicero, **E** Fastrac/dsl, Speedway/dsl Arby's, Cracker Barrel, Dunkin', McDonald's, Sapori Pizza Comfort Suites, Holiday Inn Express $Tree, Aldi, **W** Kwikfill Cicero Diner, Cicero Pizza Burdick's RV Ctr
29(93)	I-481 S, NY 481, to Oswego, Syracuse, **1 mi W on US 11** EVC, Speedway Burger King, Chick-fil-A, Copper Top Tavern, Denny's, DQ, Dunkin', Jimmy John's, KFC, Little Caesar's, McDonald's, Moe's SW Grill, Panera Bread, Pizza Hut,

WATERTOWN

PULASKI

NY

INTERSTATE 81 Cont'd

SYRACUSE

29(93) Continued
Starbucks, Subway, Taco Bell, Tully's Rest., Wendy's $General, $Tree, Advance Parts, AT&T, Audi/Porsche/VW, AutoZone, BMW, Buick/GMC, Chevrolet, Chrysler/Dodge/Jeep, Firestone/auto, GNC, Goodyear/auto, Home Depot, Hyundai, Kia, Lexus, Lincoln, Lowe's, Marshall's, Mavis Tire, Mazda, Midas, NAPA, Nissan, PepBoys, PriceChopper Foods, Rite Aid, Target, Toyota, Verizon, Walmart, Wegman's Foods

28(91) N Syracuse, Taft Rd, **E** Circle K/dsl, KwikFill, Sunoco/dsl U-Haul, **W** Sunoco/dsl Auto Value Parts, USPO

27(90) N Syracuse, **E**

26(89) US 11, Mattydale, **E** Sunoco/Dunkin/dsl Paladino's Pizza, Zebb's Deluxe Grill Red Carpet Inn $Tree, auto repair, BigLots, Dunn Tire/auto, GNC, Goodyear/auto, PetCo, Rite Aid, **W** Delta Sonic/dsl Applebee's, Arby's, Burger King, Camino Real, Denny's, Dunkin', Julie's Diner, McDonald's, Sonic, Subway, Taco Bell, Tim Hortons, Wendy's Candlewood Suites, EconoLodge, Holiday Inn Express Advance Parts, Aldi Foods, AT&T, Monro Auto, Mr Tire, Rite Aid, Sullivan's Car Care, Top's Foods

25a(88) I-90, NY Thruway

25(87.5) 7th North St, **E** Pilot/McDonald's/dsl/scales/24hr NAPA Autocare, **W** EVC, Sunoco/dsl Burger King, Denny's, Dunkin', Little Caesar's, Subway, Tully's Rest. Comfort Inn, Country Inn Suites, Hampton Inn, Maplewood Inn/cafe, Super 8, Tru Hilton

24(86) NY 370 W, to Liverpool, same as 23

23(86) NY 370 E, Hiawatha Blvd, **E** Stella's Diner, Wendy's Family$, **W** EVC, Speedway/Dunkin' Cheesecake Factory, Dave&Busters, Panera Bread, PF Chang's Best Buy, Dick's, JC Penney, Lord&Taylor, Macy's, TJ Maxx

22(85) NY 298, Court St

21(84.5) Spencer St, Catawba St (from sb), industrial area

20(84) I-690 W (from sb), Franklin St, West St

19(84) I-690 E, Clinton St, Salina St, to E Syracuse

18(84) Harrison St, Adams St, **E** Crowne Plaza H, to Syracuse U, **W** Civic Ctr

17(82) Brighton Ave, S Salina St, **W** Conoco/Chicken Basket

16a(81) I-481 N, to DeWitt

16(78) US 11, to Nedrow, Onondaga Nation, 1-2 mi **W** Valero McDonald's, Pizza Hut $General, Aldi, Mr Tire

15(73) US 20, La Fayette, **E** Cirvle K/dsl New LaFayette Inn, Old Tymes Rest. $General, NAPA, st police, USPO, vet, **W** McDonald's

71mm **truck insp sta both lanes**

14(67) NY 80, Tully, **E** Circle K/deli/dsl A Pizza More, Tasty China Quality Inn $General, Chevrolet, Kinney Drug, USPO, **W** Burger King

13(63) NY 281, Preble, **E** Mirabito/Dunkin'/Subway/dsl to Song Mtn Ski Resort

60mm **/truck insp nb, full facilities, litter barrels, petwalk, , vending**

12(53) US 11, NY 281, to Homer, **W** KwikFill, Sunoco, Sunoco/Dunkin'/dsl Little Italy H, $General, st police, to Fillmore Glen SP

11(52) NY 13, Cortland, **E** Perkins Clarion Inn, Holiday Inn Express, Quality Inn, **W** Mobil/Dunkin'/dsl Arby's, Denny's, Friendly's, McDonald's, Starbucks, Subway, Taco Bell, Wendy's Hampton Inn, Ramada Inn, Red Roof Inn Advance Parts, Family$, Jo-Ann Fabrics, Mr Tire, P&C Foods

CORTLAND

10(50) US 11, NY 41, to Cortland, McGraw, **W** Pitstop/Dunkin'/Speedway/dsl/24hr, Sunoco Cortland Motel, Motel 6

9(38) US 11, NY 221, **W** Sunoco/XtraMart/dsl/24hr, Varo NY Pizzaria, Reilly's Cafe Greek Peak Lodge, The Bear Inn/rest. city park, Country Hills Camping, Maple Museum, Robinson's Repair, st police, USPO

33mm **sb, full facilities, litter barrels, petwalk, , vendi**

8(30) NY 79, to US 11, NY 26, NY 206 (no EZ return), Whitney **E** Kwikfill, Speedway, Sunoco Aiello's Ristorante, by's, Dunkin', McDonald's, Subway Hotel Griffin $Geral, Gregg's Mkt, NAPA, Parts+, to Dorchester Park, USPO

7(21) US 11, Castle Creek, **W** Mirabito/Subway/Tim Hortons/

6(16) US 11, to NY 12, I-88E, Chenango Bridge, **E on US 11** Mbito/dsl, Sunoco/dsl Arby's, Burger King, Denny's, Dunk Grande Pizza, Moe's SW Grill, Subway, Wendy's Adva Parts, AutoZone, Big E Tire/auto, Chrysler/Dodge/Jeep, Drug, Lowe's, Mavis Tire, Monro, Mr Tire, Rite Aid, Valvoli Verizon, Weis Foods, on US 11, **W** KwikFill, Tesla E Wave/dsl China Star, Nirchi's Pizza, Sonic, Spot Diner, St bucks Comfort Inn, Motel 6, Quality Inn Aldi Foo Harley Davidson

BINGHAMTON

15mm I-88 begins eb

5(14) US 11, Front St, 1 mi **W** Mirabito/Subway/dsl, Suno McDonald's/dsl, Tesla EVC Applebee's, Cracker Bar Starbucks, Thai Front EconoLodge, Fairfield Inn, Red R Inn Cutler Botanical Garden

4(13) NY 17, Binghamton

3(12) Broad Ave, Binghamton, **W** Mirabito KFC C Drug, Weis Mkt

3(10) Industrial Park, same as 2

2(8) US 11, NY 17, 1-2 mi **W** Love's/Wendy's/dsl/scales/24 Mirabito/Dunkin'/dsl, TA/Country Pride/dsl/scales/24hr Burger King, McDonald's, Subway, Taco Bell Del Mo

1(4) US 11, NY 7, Kirkwood, 1-2 mi **W** Mirabito/dsl K wood Motel

2mm **Welcome ctr nb, full facilities, litter barrels, petwalk, , vending**

1mm **truck insp sta nb**

0mm New York/Pennsylvania state line

INTERSTATE 84

Exit #	Services
71.5mm	New York/Connecticut state line
69	US 6, US 202, NY 121 (from wb), N Salem, same as 20
68N	NY 22, Palling, **N** Mobil, Shell/dsl, Valero Dunkin', Ptofinos Ford, Honda, Subaru
68S	I-684, to NYC
65	NY 312, Carmel, **S** Applebee's, Dunkin', Eveready Dir Gaetano's Deli H, DeCicco's Mkt, Home Depot, Koh Marshall's, Michael's, Verizon
61	NY 311, Lake Carmel, **S** La Famiglia
58	Ludingtonville Rd, **S** Speedway/dsl, Sunoco/dsl Cu lo's Rest., Dunkin', Gappy's Pizza, Lou's Rest.
56mm	elevation 965 ft
55mm	**both lanes, full facilities, litter barrels, petwalk, , vending**
52	Taconic Parkway, N to Albany, S to New York
50	CR 27, Lime Kiln NY, 3 mi **N** Shell Dunkin' Ar Ridge Inn
46	US 9, to Poughkeepsie, **N** Mobil/deli, Mobil/dsl, Phill 66/Dunkin'/dsl A&W/KFC, Boston Mkt, Charlie Brow Chipotle, Coldstone, Cracker Barrel, Fishkill Grill, Five Gu

NY

INTERSTATE 84 Cont'd

46 Continued
Hudson Buffet, Panera Bread, Red Line Diner, Starbucks, Subway, Taco Bell, Wendy's [lodging] Courtyard, Extended Stay America, Extended Stay America, Hampton Inn, Hawthorn Inn, Hilton Garden, Holiday Inn Express, Hyatt House, Magnuson Hotel, Ramada Inn, Springhill Suites [other] AT&T, Sam's Club, Verizon, Walmart, **S** [gas] Speedway/dsl [food] Maya Cafe, McDonald's [other] Home Depot

44 NY 52 E, Fishkill, **N** [gas] Valero/dsl [food] Golden Buddha, Green Garden [other] CVS Drug, USPO, **S** [gas] Mobil, Sunoco/dsl [food] 84 Diner, Hometown Deli [lodging] Quality Inn

41 NY 9D, to Wappingers Falls, **1 mi N** [gas] Gulf/dsl, Mobil/dsl

41mm toll booth

40mm Hudson River

39 US 9W, NY 32, to Newburgh, **N** [gas] Citgo/dsl, Sunoco [food] Alexis Diner, Burger King, Domino's, Dunkin', Green Garden Chinese, KFC, McDonald's, New China, Papa John's, Pizza Hut, Planet Pizza, Subway [other] $Tree, Advance Parts, BigLots, Family$, Firestone/auto, Monro, PriceChopper Foods, Shop Rite Foods, Verizon, Walgreens, **S** [gas] Citgo/dsl, Shell/dsl, Sunoco [food] Dunkin' [other] [H]

37 NY 52, to Walden, **N** [gas] Conoco/dsl

36b NY 300, Newburgh, **N** [gas] Mobil [food] DQ, Dunkin', Flaming Grill Buffet, Leo's Pizzaria, McDonald's, Newburgh Buffet, Perkins, Taco Bell, Wendy's [other] $Tree, AT&T, AutoZone, GNC, Marshall's, Mavis Tire, Midas, Office Depot, Stop&Shop Foods, Verizon, **S** [gas] Mobil, Speedway/dsl, Sunoco/dsl [food] Applebee's, Burger King, Chili's, China City, Cosimos Ristorante, Denny's, Five Guys, IHOP, Ikaros Diner, Longhorn Steaks, Orange Hill Bistro, Panera Bread, Pizza Mia, Sonic, Starbucks, Subway, TGIFriday's, Union Sq Rest., Yobo Asian [lodging] Days Inn, Hampton Inn, Howard Johnson, Hudson Valley Hotel, Ramada Inn, Super 8 [other] $General, Adam's Farm Mkt, Aldi Foods, Barnes&Noble, Buick/GMC, Cadillac/Chevrolet, Chrysler/Dodge/Jeep, Ford/Lincoln, Home Depot, Honda, Kohl's, Lowe's, Meineke, Michael's, Nissan, PetsMart, Target, Tesla EVC, Verizon, Walmart

36a I-87, NY Thruway, Albany, to NYC

34 NY 17K, to Newburgh, **N** [gas] Mobil/dsl, Pilot/Arby's/dsl/scales/24hr [food] Airport Diner [lodging] Sheraton, **S** [gas] Shell/Dunkin'/dsl [lodging] Courtyard, Hampton Inn, Howard Johnson [other] Toyota

32 NY 747, International Blvd, **S** [lodging] Homewood Suites [other] to Stewart Airport

28 NY 208, Maybrook, **N** [gas] Mobil/dsl, Sunoco/dsl [food] Burger King, Dunkin', McDonald's [lodging] Holiday Inn Express [other] AutoPro Parts, Rite Aid, ShopRite Foods, Verizon, Walgreens, Winding Hills Camping, **S** [gas] Speedway/dsl, TA/Shell/Country Pride/Pizza Hut/dsl/scales/24hr/@ [food] Renee's Deli, Subway [lodging] Super 8 [other] Advance Parts, auto/truck repair, Blue Beacon, st police

24mm [rest stop] wb, full [handicapped] facilities, litter barrels, petwalk, [phone], [picnic], vending

19 NY 17, Middletown, **N** [gas] Mobil/24hr, Tesla EVC [food] Americana Diner, Applebee's, Boston Mkt, Buffalo Wild Wings, Burger King, Chipotle, Cosimo's Italian, Denny's, Dunkin'/Baskin-Robbins, Five Guys, Fuji Japanese, Golden Corral, KFC, McDonald's, Olive Garden, Panera Bread, Pizza Hut, Popeye's, Red Lobster, Ruby Tuesday, Sonic, Starbucks, Subway, Taco Bell, TX Roadhouse, Wendy's, Youyou Asian [lodging] Home 2 Suites, Middletown Motel, Super 8 [other] $Tree, Aldi Foods, AT&T, AutoZone, Best Buy, Big Lots, CVS Drug, Dick's, Firestone/auto, GNC, Hannaford Foods, Hobby Lobby, Home Depot, Honda, JC Penney,

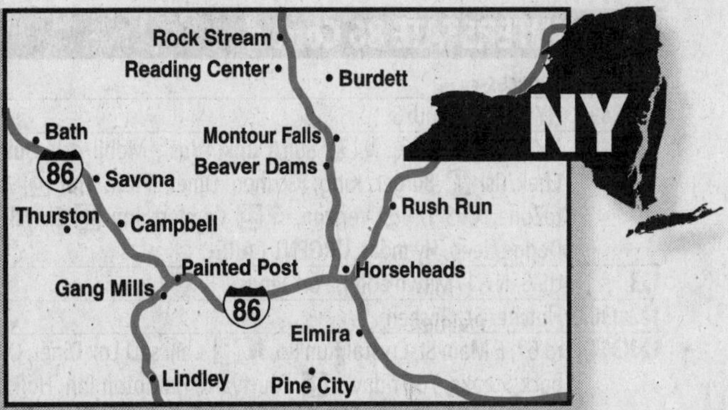

MIDDLETOWN

19 Continued
Jo-Ann Fabrics, Kohl's, Lowe's, Macy's, Marshall's, Mavis Tire/auto, Michael's, Midas, Old Navy, PetCo, PetsMart, PriceChopper Foods, Rite Aid, Sam's Club/dsl, ShopRite/gas, Staples, Target, Tire Discount, TJ Maxx, U-Haul, Verizon, Walmart/Subway, **S** [food] Chili's, D lux Diner, Dunkin', El Bandido Mexican, Outback Steaks, TGIFriday [lodging] Courtyard, Hampton Inn, Holiday Inn, Microtel [other] [H], st police

17mm [rest stop] eb, full [handicapped] facilities, litter barrels, petwalk, [phone], [picnic], vending

15 US 6, to Middletown, **N** [gas] Citgo/dsl, Mobil, QuickChek/dsl, Shell, Sunoco [food] DQ, Dunkin', IHOP, McDonald's, Peking Chinese, Rita's Custard, Subway, Taco Bell, Wendy's [lodging] Sleep Inn [other] $General, Acura, AutoZone, Buick/Chevrolet, Family$, Lexus, Mavis Discount Tire, Mazda, Meineke, Monro Automotive, NAPA, ShopRite Foods, Subaru, Verizon, VW, Walgreens, **S** [gas] Geo/Dunkin'/dsl, Sunoco/dsl [lodging] Days Inn [other] Kia, Nissan, Toyota, USPO

4 Mountain Rd, **S** [food] Firehouse Deli

4mm elevation 1254 ft wb, 1272 ft eb

3mm parking area both lanes

1 US 6, NY 23, Port Jervis, **N** [food] Arlene'n Tom's Diner, Dunkin'/Baskin-Robbins [other] [H], Ford, **S** [gas] BP/dsl/LP, Citgo/dsl, Gulf/dsl, Pilot/Subway/dsl, Shell/dsl, Valero/dsl [food] DQ, McDonald's, Village Pizza [other] $Tree, GNC, ShopRite Foods, TJ Maxx

0mm New York/Pennsylvania state line, Delaware River

INTERSTATE 86

Exit # Services

I-86 begins/ends on I-87, exit 16, toll booth

131(379) NY 17, **N** [food] Chipotle, Food Court, Starbucks [other] Outlets/famous brands, **S** [gas] EVC, Gulf/dsl [food] Chili's, Dunkin', El Castillo Mexican, IHOP, KFC/Taco Bell, Outback Steaks, Panera Bread, TGIFriday's, Uno Grill, Wendy's [lodging] Hampton Inn [other] $Tree, Best Buy, BJ's Whse, BMW, GNC, Home Depot, Kohl's, Mercedes, Michael's, Old Navy, Petsmart, Staples, Target, TJMaxx, Verizon, Walmart/Subway

130a(378) US 6, Bear Mtn, to West Point (from eb, no return)

130(377) NY 208, Monroe, Washingtonville, **N** [food] 208 Grill, **S** [gas] Exxon, Mobil/dsl, Sunoco/dsl [food] Burger King, Domino's, Dunkin', Empire Diner, Wayback Burger [other] $Tree, Rite Aid, ShopRite Foods, USPO, Verizon

129(375) Museum Village Rd

128(374) rd 51 (only from wb), Oxford Depot

127(373) Greycourt Rd (from wb only), Sugar Loaf, Warwick

126(372) NY 94 (no EZ wb return), Chester, Florida, **N** [gas] Mobil, Shell, Sunoco/dsl [food] Bro Bruno Pizza, Burger King, Chester Diner, Dunkin', McDonald's, Subway, Taco Bell, Wendy's [lodging] Holiday Inn Express [other] CVS Drug, GNC, Goodyear/auto, Rite Aid, ShopRite Foods, USPO, Verizon, **S** [other] Lowe's

NY

INTERSTATE 86 Cont'd

MIDDLETOWN

Exit #	Services
125(369)	NY 17M E, South St
124(368)	NY 17A, NY 207, N Gulf/Dunkin'/dsl, Mobil/dsl, Quick-Chek/dsl Burger King, Goshen Diner, Pizza Hut AutoZone, CVS Drug, Verizon, S Comfort Inn Chrysler/Dodge/Jeep, Hyundai, URGENT CARE
123	US 6, NY 17M (wb only), Port Jervis
122a(367)	Fletcher St, Goshen
122(364)	rd 67, E Main St, Crystal Run Rd, N Chili's, D Lux Diner, Outback Steaks, TGIFriday's Courtyard, Hampton Inn, Holiday Inn, Microtel URGENT CARE, S El Bandido Rest. H
121(363)	I-84, E to Newburgh, W to Port Jervis
120(363)	NY 211, N Mobil, Tesla EVC Buffalo Wild Wings, Cosimo's Ristorante, Fuji Japanese, Olive Garden Home 2 Suites, Middletown Motel, Super 8 Best Buy, Dick's, Hannaford's Foods, Honda, JC Penney, Lowe's, Macy's, Mavis Discount Tire, PetCo, Sam's Club/dsl, Target, S Americana Diner, Applebee's, Boston Mkt, Burger King, Chipotle, Denny's, Dunkin', Five Guys, Franco Di Roma Italian, Golden Corral, KFC, McDonald's, Panera Bread, Papa John's, Pizza Hut, Popeye's, Red Lobster, Ruby Tuesday, Sonic, Starbucks, Subway, Taco Bell, TX Roadhouse, Wendy's, Yu Yu Chinese $General, $Tree, Aldi Foods, AT&T, AutoZone, BigLots, CVS Drug, Firestone/auto, GNC, Hobby Lobby, Home Depot, Jo-Ann, Kohl's, Marshall's, Michael's, Midas, Old Navy, Petsmart, PriceChopper, ShopRite/gas, Staples, Tire Discount Ctr, TJMaxx, U-Haul, Verizon, Walmart/Subway
119(360)	NY 302, Circleville, to Pine Bush, Pine Bush, S Citgo/dsl, Exxon/Dunkin'/dsl Subway
118a(358)	NY 17M, Fair Oaks
118(358)	Fair Oaks, Circleville, N Economy Inn, S Citgo/dsl, Mobil/dsl
116(355)	NY 17K, Bloomingburg, N Mtn View Rest., S Citgo/dsl Quickway Diner
115	Burlingame Rd
114	Wurtsboro, Highview (from wb)
113(350)	US 209, Wurtsboro, Ellenville, N Mobil/dsl, Stewarts/gas Danny's Steaks Days Inn G-Mart Foods, S Giovanni's Café (2mi)
112(347)	Masten Lake, Yankee Lake, N Days Inn, S Yankee Lake
111(344)	(eb only), Wolf Lake, S Global/dsl
110(343)	Lake Louise Marie
109(342)	Rock Hill, Woodridge, N Citgo/dsl, EVC Bernie's Holiday Rest., Dunkin', Dutch's Cafe, Pizza Rock Sullivan Ramada Ace Hardware, auto repair, Hilltop Farms Camping (6mi), Super Mkt Trading Post, USPO, S Mobil/dsl Windsong B&B
108(341)	Bridgeville, same as 109
107(340)	Thompsonville, S Chevrolet, Chrysler/Dodge/Jeep, Toyota
106(339)	East Broadway, E. Broadway, N Ford/Lincoln, S Mobil/dsl Super 8 (2 mi) GMC Trucks, Hyundai, Toyota
105(337)	NY 42, Monticello, N Mobil/dsl Bro Bruno's Pizza, Burger King, China City, Dunkin', Giovanni's Rest, KFC, McDonald's, Subway, Taco Bell AutoZone, Home Depot, museum, ShopRite Foods, Walmart/McDonald's, S Citgo/dsl, Sunoco/dsl Monticello Diner, Pizza Hut, Stewart's, Wendy's EconoLodge, Heritage Inn, Super 8 Advance Parts, Family$, NAPA, Verizon, Walgreens
104(336)	NY 17B, Raceway, Monticello, S Citgo/dsl, Mobil/Subway/dsl Albella Rest., Colosseo Rest., Dunkin', Tilly's Diner Best Western, Raceway Motel AT&T, Swinging Bridge Camp

NY

WINDSOR

Exit #	Services
103	Rapp Rd (wb only)
102(332)	Harris, N H
101(327)	Ferndale, Swan Lake, S Mobil/dsl
100(327)	NY 52 E, Liberty, N Citgo/dsl, Sam's, Sunoco Bur King, Dunkin', Joseph's Italian, Last Licks Cafe, Liberty Diner, Donald's, Piccolo Italian, Pizza Hut, Subway, Taco Bell D Inn, Knights Inn $Tree, Ace Hardware, Advance Parts, toZone, Rite Aid, ShopRite Foods, USPO, Verizon, S Linc Motel Buick/Cadillac, Chrysler/Dodge/Jeep, Ford/Linc NAPA
100a	NY 52 W (no wb return), Liberty, S st police
99(325)	NY 52 W, to NY 55, Liberty, S Sunoco Catskill Motel
98(321)	Cooley, Parksville, N Mobil/dsl
97(319)	Morsston
96(316)	Livingston Manor, S Citgo, EVC, Sunoco Robin H Diner Covered Bridge Camping, Mongaup Pond Campi Peck's Mkt, to Covered Bridge, USPO
313mm	**eb, truck insp. sta, full facilities, litter barrels, petw, vending**
94(311)	NY 206, Roscoe, Lew Beach, N Mobil/dsl, Sunoco/Tesla EVC Raimondo's Diner, Roscoe Diner Creeks B&B, Reynolds House Motel, Rockland House Motel, Ros Motel Beaverkill St Camping (8mi), Roscoe Mkt, st pol USPO, S Mobil/dsl Tennanah Lake Motel
93(305)	to Cooks Falls (from wb)
92(303)	Horton, Cooks Falls, Colchester, S Sunoco/dsl Rivers Café/lodge Russell Brook Camping
90(297)	NY 30, East Branch, Downsville, N Sunoco Beaver-Camping, Oxbow Camping, Peaceful Valley Camping, S Branch Motel
295mm	**wb, full facilities, litter barrels, petwalk, , vend**
89(293)	Fishs Eddy
87a(288)	NY 268 (from wb, no ez-return), same as 87
87(284)	NY 97, to NY 268, to NY 191, Hancock, Cadosia, S Mi bito/Subway/dsl, Sunoco, Valero McDonald's, New C na Hancock House Hotel, Upper Delaware Inn Famil NAPA, Rite Aid, Tops Foods
276mm	**parking area wb**
84(274)	Deposit, N Mirabito/dsl BC Pizza, Honey's Cafe, W dy's Deposit Motel, Laurel Bank Motel Family$, st lice
83(272)	Deposit, Oquaga Lake
82(270)	NY 41, McClure, Sanford, N Cornerstone Cafe a repair, Kellystone Park, Oquaga Creek SP, S Scott's Fan Resort Guestward Camping (3mi)
265mm	**parking area eb, litter barrels,**
81(263)	E Bosket Rd
80(261)	Damascus, N Mirabito/dsl auto repair, Forest Hill La Park Camping (3mi)
79(259)	NY 79, Windsor, N Sunoco/dsl China Star, Pizza Win Subway Big M Mkt, USPO, S Marian's Pizza/Su Windsor Diner $General, Lakeside Camping (8mi)
78(256)	Dunbar Rd, Occanum
77(254)	W Windsor, N Sunoco/dsl McDonald's $Genera
76(251)	Haskins Rd, to Foley Rd
75(250)	I-81 S, to PA (exits left from wb)
3	Colesville Rd (from eb), S Loves/Wendy's/dsl/scal 24hr, Mirabito/Dunkin'/dsl, TA/Country Pride/dsl/scales/24hr Subway
I-86/I-81 run together 4 miles.	
3	Broad Ave (from wb, no return)
4s	NY 7, **I-86/I-81 run together 4 miles.**

INTERSTATE 86 Cont'd

Exit #	Services
72(244)	I-81 N, US 11, Front St, Clinton St, (no wb re-entry)
71(242)	Airport Rd, Johnson City, S Mirabito Microtel Walmart
70(241)	NY 201, Johnson City, N Mirabito, Speedway/dsl Arby's, Dunkin', Food&Fire BBQ, Friendly's, Great China, McDonald's, Papa John's, Pizza Hut, Ruby Tuesday, Taco Bell Baymont Inn, Hampton Inn, La Quinta, Red Roof Inn $Tree, JC Penney, Mavis Tire, Mr Tire, PetCo, Wegman's Foods, S Home Depot
69(239)	NY 17C
238mm	Susquehanna River
68(237)	NY 17C, Old Vestal Rd, (from eb, no re-entry)
67(236)	NY 26, NY 434, Vestal, Endicott, S on NY 434 Mirabito/dsl, Mirabito/Dunkin', Speedway/dsl, Stop'N Gas A&W/LJ Silver, Applebee's, Arby's, Blaze Pizza, Burger King, CA Grill, Chili's, ChuckECheese, Denny's, Dunkin', IHOP, Jimmy John's, KFC, McDonald's, Moe's SW Grill, Olive Garden, Outback Steaks, Panera Bread, Pudgie's Pizza, Red Lobster, Red Robin, Starbucks, Subway, Taco Bell, TGIFriday's, Wendy's Candlewood Suites, Comfort Suites, Courtyard, Hampton Inn, Holiday Inn Express, Homewood Suites, Parkway Motel $Tree, Aldi Foods, AT&T, Barnes&Noble, Best Buy, Big E Tire/auto, BigLots, Chrysler/Dodge/Jeep, CVS Drug, Dick's, Ford/Lincoln, Jo-Ann Fabrics, Kohl's, Lowe's, Mavis Tire, Michael's, Mr Tire, Nissan, Old Navy, Petsmart, Price Rite Foods, Rite Aid, Sam's Club, Staples, Target, TJ Maxx, U-Haul, USPO, Verizon, vet, Volvo, VW, Walmart/Dunkin', Wies Foods
66(231)	NY 434, Apalachin, S KwikFill Big Dipper Drive-In, Blue Dolphin Diner, Dunkin', McDonald's, Perkins, Subway Apalachin Inn, Comfort Inn
65(225)	NY 17C, NY 434, Owego, N Speedway A&W/KFC, Arby's, McDonald's, Panda Wok, Subway, Wendy's Hampton Inn, Holiday Inn Express, Treadaway Inn/rest. $General, Buick/GMC, Hickories Park Camping, Mr Tire, Top's Foods, Verizon, S st police
64(223)	NY 96, Owego, N Dunkin' AutoZone, CVS Drug, Rite Aid, USPO, S Mobil/dsl
222mm	**wb, full facilities, litter barrels, petwalk, picnic Tables, vending**
63(218)	Lounsberry, S Valero/rest./dsl/24hr
62(214)	NY 282, Nichols, S Citgo/pizza/dsl Jim's RV Ctr, Tioga Downs Race Track (2mi)
212mm	**eb, full facilities, litter barrels, petwalk, , vending**
208mm	Susquehanna River
61(206)	NY 34, PA 199, Waverly, Sayre, N $General, Goodyear/gas, S Gulf Best Western/rest. Chrysler/Dodge/Jeep, Joe's RV Ctr, Nissan, Subaru
60(204)	US 220, to Sayre, Waverly, N O'brien's Inn, S Citgo/dsl, Mirabito/Dunkin'/dsl, Tesla EVC Wendy's (3mi) Candlewood Suites, Comfort Inn, Hampton Inn Advance Parts, Aldi Foods, Rite Aid, Top's Foods, Toyota
59a(202)	Wilawana, S Sunoco/Subway/dsl
59(200)	NY 427, Chemung, N Dandy/dsl
58a(197)	to CR 60, Lowman
57(195)	rd 2, Lowman, Wellsburg, N Gardner Hill Campsites (4mi), USPO
56(190)	Jerusalem Hill, N Hilltop Rest., S Citgo/dsl, Sunoco/Dandy Pizza/Subway/dsl Dunkin', McDonald's Holiday Inn, Mark Twain Motel (3mi) H
54(186)	NY 13, to Ithaca

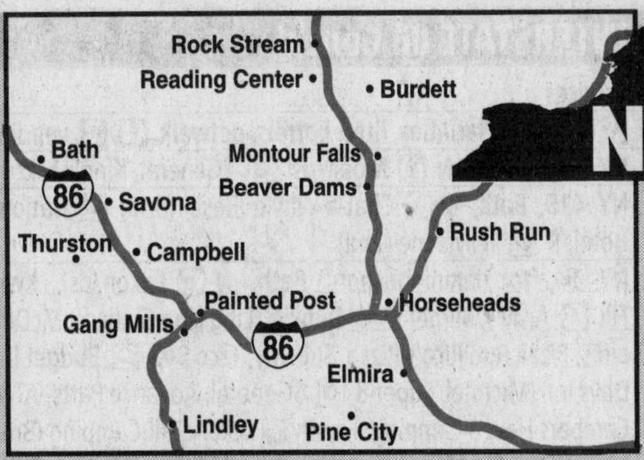

ELMIRA

Exit #	Services
53(185)	Horseheads, S Speedway/dsl Burger King, Domino's, Dunkin', Guiseppe's Pizza, Lin Buffet, McDonald's, Rico's Pizza, Subway, Wendy's Red Carpet Inn, Travelodge Advance Parts, Family$, Rite Aid
52b(184)	NY 14, to Watkins Glen, N Friendly's Knights Inn, Quality Inn, S Denny's, Rita's Custard
52a(183)	Commerce Ctr, S Buffalo Wild Wings, Cracker Barrel, Red Robin, TX Roadhouse Fairfield Inn Aldi Foods, AT&T, Dick's, Jo-Ann Fabrics, Kohl's, Mavis Discount Tire, Petsmart, Walmart/McDonald's
51a(182)	Chambers Rd, N Sunoco/Subway/dsl Chili's, Dunkin', McDonald's, Olive Garden, Outback Steaks, Red Lobster, Ruby Tuesday Candlewood Suites, Country Inn&Suites, Courtyard, Hampton Inn, Hilton Garden JC Penney, Nissan, S Applebee's, Charley's Subs, Five Guys, Moe's SW, Mt Fuji Japanese, Old Country Buffet, Panera Bread, Popeye's, Taco Bell, TGIFriday's, Wendy's EconoLodge $Tree, Barnes&Noble, Best Buy, Buick/GMC/Cadillac, Field&Stream, Hobby Lobby, Honda, Hyundai, Lowe's, Michael's, Mr Tire, Old Navy, PetCo, Sam's Club, Staples, Subaru, Target, TJ Maxx, Top's Foods, Toyota, URGENT CARE, Verizon
50(180)	Kahler Rd, N to Airport
49(178)	Olcott Rd, Canal St, Big Flats, N antiques, S Sunoco Picnic Pizza Comfort Suites USPO
48(171)	NY 352, E Corning, N Citgo Budget Inn, Gate House Motel H
47(174)	NY 352, Gibson, E Corning, N Budget Inn, Gate House Motel
46(171)	NY 414, to Watkins Glen, Corning, N Ferenbaugh Camping (5mi), KOA (14mi), Watkins Glen Camping, S Sunoco Pizza Hut Comfort Inn, Radisson, Staybridge Suites Corning Glass Museum
45(170)	NY 352, Corning, S Fastrac Bob Evans, Subway, Wendy's Fairfield Inn Advance Parts, AutoZone, Rite Aid, Tops/gas
44a	I-99 S, US 15 S, NY 417 W, Gang Mills, N Mobil McDonald's, S Gulf, Sunoco Applebee's, Arby's, Taco Bell Best Value Inn, Corning Inn, EconoLodge, Hampton Inn, Ramada Inn $Tree, Aldi Foods, Buick/GMC, Chevrolet, Home Depot, Verizon, Walmart
43(167)	NY 415, Painted Post, N Citgo Burger King $General, AutoValue Parts, Big Lots, Firestone/auto, S 7-11 Denny's, Dunkin' Hampton Inn, Holiday Inn Express
167mm	**parking area wb, litter barrels**
42(165)	Coopers Plains, N st police
41(161)	rd 333, Campbell, N Sunoco/Subway/dsl Camp Bell Camping (1mi), S Sunoco antiques, Cardinal Campsites (6mi)

CORNING

NY

INTERSTATE 86 Cont'd

Exit #	Services
160mm	**eb, full facilities, litter barrels, petwalk, , , vending**
40(156)	NY 226, Savona, N Mobil/dsl $General, King's Mkt
BATH	
39(153)	NY 415, Bath, N Chat-a-Whyle Rest. (3mi) National Hotel, S Jellystone (2mi)
38(150)	NY 54, to Hammondsport, Bath, N Exxon/dsl, Kwik-Fill Arby's, Burger King, Dunkin', Ling Ling Chinese, McDonald's, Pizza Hut, Rico's Pizza, Subway, Taco Bell Budget Inn, Days Inn, Microtel, Super 8 $General, Advance Parts, AT&T, Campers Haven Camping, Family$, Hickory Hill Camping (3mi), Meyer's RV Ctr, Monro, museum, Rite Aid, SaveALot, st police, to Keuka Lake, Top's Foods/gas, Verizon, Walgreens
147mm	**wb, full facilities, litter barrels, petwalk, , , vending**
37(146)	NY 53, to Prattsburg, Kanona, S Pilot/Subway/dsl/scales/24hr/@, Sunoco/Smokey's/dsl/scales st police, USPO, Wilkin's RV Ctr (1mi)
36(145)	I-390 N, NY 15, to Rochester
HORNELL	
35(138)	Howard, S to Lake Demmon RA
34(130)	NY 36, Hornell, Arkport, **0-2 mi** S KwikFill, Mobil/dsl Applebee's, Country Kitchen, Dunkin', McDonald's, Pizza Hut, Subway Days Inn, EconoLodge, Sunshine Motel $General, $Tree, Advance Parts, Aldi Foods, AutoZone, Chrysler/Dodge/Jeep, Ford/Nissan, GNC, Lowe's, NAPA, Verizon, Walmart/Subway, Wegman's Foods
125mm	scenic overlook eb
33(124)	NY 21, to Alfred, Almond, Andover, S 7-11/dsl Kanakadea Camping, Lake Lodge Camping (8mi), USPO
117mm	highest elevation on I-86, elev 2110 ft eb, 2080 ft wb
32(116)	W Almond
31(108)	Angelica, N Valero/dsl American House Inn
30(104)	NY 19, Belmont, Wellsville, N Letchworth SP (27mi), S , st police
101mm	**eb, full facilities, litter barrels, petwalk, , , vending**
29(99)	NY 275, to Bolivar, Friendship, S Miller&Brandes Gas, Mobil/Subway/dsl
28(92)	NY 305, Cuba, N Moonwink's Rest. EconoLodge $General, Maple Lane RV Park, S Sunoco/dsl, Valero/dsl Charlie's Chicken Pizza, McDonald's, Subway , Cuba Cheese Shop, Cuba Drug, Family$, Giant Foods
27(84)	NY 16, NY 446, Hinsdale, N food, S gas lodging
OLEAN	
26(79)	NY 16, Olean, S 7-11 Burger King, Pizza Hut, Subway, Wendy's Holiday Inn Express
25(77)	Buffalo St, Olean, S Citgo/dsl , **2 mi** S **on** NY 417 Tesla EVC Applebee's, Burger King, Coldstone/Tim Hortons, Domino's, Dunkin', Friendly's, Lakeview Chinese, Little Caesar's, McDonald's, Perkins, Subway Best Western+, Fairfield Inn, Microtel $Tree, Advance Parts, Aldi Foods, AT&T, BJ's Whse/gas, GNC, Home Depot, Jo-Ann Fabrics, KwikFill, Old Navy, St Bonaventure U, Staples, Tops Foods/gas, Verizon, Walmart/Subway
SALAMANCA	
24(74)	NY 417, Allegany, S Mobil/7-11/dsl $General, to St Bonaventure U
73mm	**wb, full facilities, litter barrels, petwalk,**
23(68)	US 219 S, N M&M Jct./Subway/dsl, Sassy's Trkstp/dsl
66mm	Allegheny River
21(61)	US 219 N, Salamanca
20(58)	NY 417, NY 353, Salamanca, N Allegany Gas, Antone's Gas, Grand Ctr Sta, Nafco Quickstop/Burger King/24hr, Seneca OneStop/dsl/24hr Burger King, Little Caesar's, McDonald's Holiday Inn Express, Hotel Westgate AutoZone, Rail Museum, Seneca-Iroquis Museum, S casino
19(54)	N Red House Area, S Allegany SP
18(51)	NY 280, S Allegany SP, Quaker Run Area
17(48)	NY 394, Steamburg, S Steamburg, WW/dsl
16(41)	W Main St, Randolph, N Mobil/7-11/dsl R Rest. RV camping
40mm	**parking area,**
15(39)	School House Rd
39mm	**parking area,**
JAMESTOWN	
14(36)	US 62, Kennedy, **1 mi** N Keystone Gas Office Pi Subs, S RV camping
32mm	Cassadaga Creek
13(31)	NY 394, Falconer, S Keystone, Mobil/dsl Burger K Budget Inn, Quality Inn CVS Drug, Harley-Davidson
12(28)	NY 60, Jamestown, N KwikFill/dsl st police, S bil/McDonald's/dsl Bob Evans, Tim Horton Com Inn, Hampton Inn, Holiday Inn Express
11(25)	to NY 430, Jamestown, S gas/dsl food lodging
22mm	**Welcome ctr/ eb, full facilities, litter barrels, petwalk, vending**
10(21)	NY 430 W, Bemus Point
9(20)	NY 430 E (no EZ eb return), N Mobil/dsl Bemus P Rest.
19mm	Chautauqua Lake
8(18)	NY 394, Mayville, N USPO, vet
7(15)	Panama
6(9)	NY 76, Sherman, N Keystone Gas $General, city p NAPA, Sherman Drug, USPO
4(1)	NY 430, Findley Lake, N Holiday Inn Express, S B Heron Inn, Peek'n Peak Conference Ctr to Peek'n Peak Area
0mm	New York/Pennsylvania state line. **Exits 3-1 are in PA.**
3	PA 89, North East, Wattsburg, N gas food
1ba	I-90, W to Erie, E to Buffalo.

I-86 begins/ends on I-90, exit 37.

INTERSTATE 87

Exit #	Services
176mm	US/Canada Border, NY state line, **I-87 begins/ends.**
43(175)	US 9, Champlain, E Duty Free America, W Peterbilt stp/deli/dsl/scales/24hr/@ repair
42(174)	US 11 S, to Rouse's Point, Champlain, E Irving/dsl, Suno Subway Empire Buffet, Pizza+ $General, $Tree, Hardware, Chevrolet (3mi), Kinney Drug, PriceChopper, R Aid, USPO, W Mobil/dsl, Valero/dsl Dunkin', McD ald's, Nathan's
41(167)	NY 191, Chazy, E st police, W Miner Museum
162mm	**both lanes, full facilities, info, litter barrels, petwalk,**
PLATTSBURGH	
40(160)	NY 456, Beekmantown, E Mobil/dsl Conroy's Org ics Pt Auroche Lodge, Stonehelm Motel/café, W Tw Ells Camping
39(158)	NY 314, Moffitt Rd, Plattsburgh Bay, E Mobil/dsl, Ste arts Dunkin', Gus' Rest Rip van Winkle Motel, Su 8 $General, Plattsburgh RV Park, to VT Ferry, W Sha Oaks Camping, to Adirondacks
38(154)	NY 22, NY 374, to Plattsburgh, E Mobil/dsl S way Kinney Drug, W RV Store
37(153)	NY 3, Plattsburgh, E Stewarts #1 Chinese, Buffalo W Wings, Burger King, Chick-fil-A, China Buffet, Chipotle, Do no's, Dunkin', Five Guys, Golden Palace, Guiseppe's Pizza, Ja Buffet, KFC, Koto Japanese, McDonald's, Michigans+ Re Panera Bread, Perkins, Pizza Hut, Starbucks, Subway, Taco B

INTERSTATE 87 Cont'd

37(153) Continued
TX Roadhouse, Wendy's Comfort Inn, Holiday Inn H, Aldi Foods, BigLots, Buick/GMC, Family$, Ford, GNC, Kinney Drug, Michael's, Petsmart, Sam's Club/dsl, Staples, TJ Maxx, TrueValue, Verizon, vet, Walgreens, Walmart, **W** Mobil/dsl, Shell, Sunoco/Lambo's Subs, Tesla EVC 99 Rest., Anthony's Rest., Applebee's, Butcher Block Rest., Dickey's BBQ, Dunkin', Friendly's, Ground Round, PriceChopper Mkt, Subway, Uno Best Value Inn, Best Western+, Days Inn, Hampton Inn, La Quinta, Microtel, Quality Inn $Tree, Advance Parts, AT&T, AutoZone, Best Buy, Dick's, Hannaford Foods, Harley-Davidson, Hobby Lobby, Honda, JC Penney, Kinney Drug, Lowe's, Midas, Prays Mkt, Target, vet

151mm Saranac River

36(150) NY 22, Plattsburgh AFB, **E** Mobil/dsl st police, U-Haul, **W** Shell/Dunkin'/dsl

146mm **nb, litter barrels, petwalk, , full facilities, truck insp sta both lanes**

35(144) NY 442, to Port Kent, Peru, **2-8 mi E** Iroquois/Ausable Pines Camping, to VT Ferry, **W** Mobil/Dunkin'/Subway/dsl, Mobil/repair Dunkin', Livingood's Rest., McDonald's, Pasquale's Rest. Aubuchon Hardware, Tops Foods, USPO

143mm emergency at 2 mi intervals begin sb/end nb

34(137) NY 9 N, Ausable Forks, **E** Sunoco/dsl Big Daddy's BBQ, Pleasant Corner Rest., **W** Ausable River RV Camping, auto repair, Prays Mkt

136mm Ausable River

33(135) US 9, NY 22, to Willsboro, **E** gas/dsl food lodging RV camping, to Essex Ferry

125mm N Boquet River

32(124) Lewis, **E** RV Camping, **W** Beavers Trkstp Diner RV Camping, st police

120mm Boquet River

31(117) NY 9 N, to Elizabethtown, Westport, **E** Mobil/dsl Hill-Top Motel RV camp/dump, **W** H, st police, vet

30(104) US 9, NY 73, Keene Valley

99mm **both lanes, full facilities, litter barrels, petwalk, , , trk insp sta**

29(94) N Hudson, **E** Jellystone Camping, USPO, **W** Blue Ridge Falls Camping

28(88) NY 74 E, to Ticonderoga, Schroon Lake, **E** Mt Severance Country Store, Sunoco/dsl Maple Leaf Motel, Schroon Lake B&B RV camp/dump, services on US 9, st police

83mm **parking area nb**

27(81) US 9 (from nb, no EZ return), Schroon Lake, **E** to gas/dsl food lodging

26(78) US 9 (from sb, no EZ return), Pottersville, Schroon Lake, **E** Lee's Corner Motel Wakonda Camping, **W** Mobil/dsl Black Bear Diner USPO

25(73) NY 8, Chestertown, **E** Crossroads Country Store Country Haven Camping, **W** Stewart's/dsl

24(67) Bolton Landing, **E** RV camping

67mm Schroon River

66mm **parking area sb,**

64mm **parking area nb,**

23(58) to US 9, Diamond Point, Warrensburg, **W** Citgo/dsl, Cumberland, Gulf, Stewarts, Sunoco/Dunkin'/dsl Dragon Lee Chinese, George Henry's Rest., McDonald's, Subway Super 8 Central Adirondack Tr, Family$, Ford, PriceChopper Foods, Riverview Camping, Schroon River Camping (3mi), ski area, Tops Foods

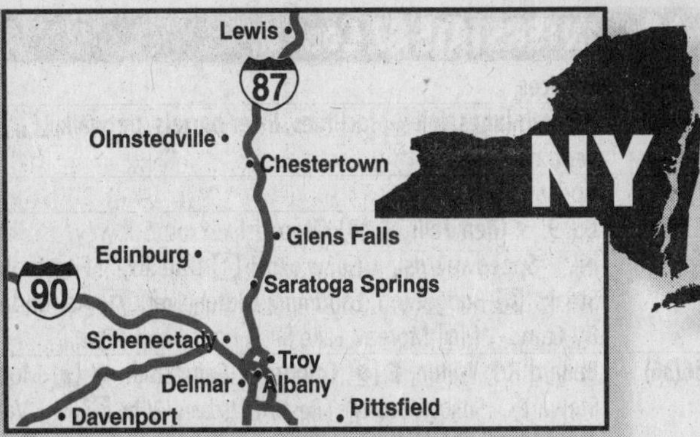

LAKE GEORGE

22(54) US 9, NY 9 N, to Diamond Pt, Lake George, **E on US 9** Gino&Tony's, Guiseppe's Pizza, Mario's Italian, Monte Cristo's, Moose Tooth Grill, Number 1 7 Dwarfs Motel, Admiral Motel, Balsam Motel, Barberry Ct, Best Value Inn, Blue Moon Motel, Brookside Motel, Courtyard, EconoLodge, Georgian Lakeside Resort, Heritage Motel, Lake Crest Inn, Lake George Inn, Lake Haven Motel, Lake Motel, Marine Village Resort, Motel Montreal, Nordick's Motel, Oasis Motel, O'Sullivan's Motel, Park Lane Motel, Sundowner Motel, Surfside Motel multiple services, PriceChopper Foods, same as 21, **W parking area both lanes**

21(53) NY 9 N, Lake Geo, Ft Wm Henry, **E on US 9** Stewarts, Sunoco/dsl, Valero A&W, Adirondack Brewery, Barnsider BBQ, Blacksmith Rest., Dining Room, DJ's Cafe, Gaslight Grill, Jasper's Steaks, Lobster Pot, Mama Riso's Italian, McDonald's, Mezzaluna's, Pizza Hut Best Western, Ft William Henry Inn, Hampton Inn, Holiday Inn Resort, Lake View Inn, Lincoln Log Motel, Motel 6, Quality Inn, Rodeway Inn, Super 8, Tiki Hotel, Travelodge, Villager Motel, Windsor Hotel, Wingate Inn city park, Harley-Davidson, King Phillip Camping, Lake George Camping, multiple services, Rite Aid, same as 22, USPO, waterpark, **W** Mobil/dsl/LP Kathy's Cottages

51mm Adirondack Park

20(49) NY 149, to Ft Ann E, **E on US 9** Mobil/Dunkin'/dsl, Sunoco/dsl Blue Moose Rest., Frank's Pizza, Johnny Rocket's, Logjam Rest., Olde Post Grille, Subway Clarion, Comfort Suites, French Mtn Inn, Great Escape Lodge, Mohican Motel Factory Outlets/famous brands, Ledgeview RV Park (3mi), Six Flags Funpark, waterpark

GLENS FALLS

19(47) NY 254, Glens Falls, **E** Mobil/dsl, Speedway, Sunoco, Tesla EVC 99 Rest., Ambrosia Diner, Burger King, Chicago Grill, Dickey's BBQ, Dunkin', Five Guys, Friendly's, Giavano's Pizza, Golden Corral, KFC, Liberty Pizza, McDonald's, Moe's SW Grill, Mr B's Rest., Old China Buffet, Olive Garden, Outback Steaks, Panera Bread, Papa John's, Pizza Hut, Red Lobster, Silo Rest., Starbucks, Subway, Taco Bell/LJ Silver, Wendy's Alpen Haus Motel, Budget Inn, EconoLodge, Home 2 Suites, Quality Inn, Red Roof Inn, Sleep Inn $Tree, Ace Hardware, Advance Parts, AT&T, AutoZone, Dick's, Goodyear, Hobby Lobby, Home Depot, JC Penney, Jo-Ann Fabrics, Meineke, Petco, Price Rite Foods, PriceChopper Foods, Rite Aid, Staples, Target, TJ Maxx, Tuesday Morning, USPO, Verizon, Walmart, **W** Mobil/Dunkin'/Subway/dsl Baymont Inn st police

18(45) Glens Falls, **E** Cumberland Farms/Subway/e-85/dsl, Speedway/dsl, Sunoco/dsl Dunkin', Pizza Hut, Steve's Place Rest., Subway Days Inn, Fairfield Inn H, $General, CVS Drug, Hannaford Foods, Toyota, U-Haul, Walgreens, **W** Fastrac/dsl, Stewarts McDonald's, Taco Bell Holiday Inn Express Super 8

NY

INTERSTATE 87 Cont'd

SARATOGA SPRINGS

Exit #	Services
43mm	**both lanes, full facilities, litter barrels, petwalk, , , vending**
42mm	Hudson River
17(40)	US 9, S Glen Falls, **E** Citgo/dsl, Exxon/Subway/dsl, Mobil, Speedway/dsl, Sunoco/dsl Dunkin', Fitzgerald's Steaks Budget Inn, Landmark Motel (1mi) Adirondack RV Camp, **W** Moreau Lake SP
16(36)	Ballard Rd, Wilton, **E** Coldbrook Campsites, **W** Mobil, Stewart's, Sunoco/Scotty's Rest./dsl/scales/24hr Mt View Acres Motel Alpin Haus RV Ctr, golf
15(30)	NY 50, NY 29, Saratoga Springs, **E** Speedway/dsl, Sunoco 99 Rest., Applebee's, Burger King, Chipotle Mexican, Denny's, Dunkin', Five Guys, Friendly's, Golden Corral, Jersey Mike's, KFC/Taco Bell, McDonald's, Moe's SW Grill, Osaka, Panera Bread, Red Robin, Subway, Sunny Wok, TGIFriday's Comfort Inn AT&T, Barnes&Noble, Best Buy, BJ's Whse, Dick's, Ford, GNC, Hannaford Foods, Healthy Living Mkt, Home Depot, JC Penney, Kohl's, Lowe's, Old Navy, Petsmart, PriceChopper Mkt, Rite Aid, Staples, Subaru, Target, TJ Maxx, Toyota, Walgreens, Walmart, **W** Residence Inn H
14(28)	NY 9P, Schuylerville, **2 mi W** Hampton Inn, Holiday Inn H, museum, racetrack
13(25)	US 9, Saratoga Springs, **E** Andy's Grille, DeLucia's Deli Budget Inn, Locust Grove Motel Ballston Spa SP, Nissan, **W** Mobil/dsl, Stewarts 13 North Rest., PJ's BBQ Best Western+, Design Motel, Roosevelt Inn/rest., Top Hill Hotel Saratoga SP
12(21)	NY 67, Malta, **E** Citgo/dsl, Cumberland Farms/dsl, Sunoco/dsl Bentley's Rest., Dunkin', KFC/Taco Bell, Malta Diner, McDonald's, Panera Bread, Starbucks, Subway Fairfield Inn, Home 2 Suites CVS Drug, GNC, PriceChopper Foods, Saratoga NHP, st police, Stewart's, Verizon, **W** Hyatt Place URGENT CARE
11(18)	Round Lake Rd, Round Lake, **W** Gulf/dsl, Stewarts/dsl Governor's Rest. Hannaford Foods, Walgreens
10(16)	Ushers Rd, **E** Speedway/Dunkin'/dsl, Xtra/dsl auto repair, **W** Stewarts
14mm	**nb, full facilities, info, litter barrels, petwalk, , , vending**
9(13)	NY 146, Clifton Park, **E** Speedway/Dunkin'/dsl, USA Burger King, Caputo's Pizza, Chili's, Cracker Barrel, Delmonico's Steaks, Harborhouse Fish Fry, Mr Subb, Peddler's Grill, Pizza Hut, Red Robin, Snyder's Rest., Subway, Wheatfields Bistro Holiday Inn Express, Park Manor Inn, Residence Inn Advance Parts, Aldi Foods, AutoZone, BigLots, Goodyear/auto, Home Depot, Kohl's, Lowe's, Michael's, Midas, Petco, Red Roof Inn, Rite Aid, Target, **W** Mobil, Sunoco/dsl 99 Rest., Bellini's Italian, Blaze Pizza, Brick House Pizza, Buffalo Wild Wings, Chipotle Mexican, Dunkin', East Wok, Five Guys, Friendly's, IHOP, La Fiesta, McDonald's, Moe's SW Grill, Olive Garden, Outback Steaks, Panera Bread, Pasta Pane, Salad Creations, Starbucks, Subway, Taco Bell, TGIFriday's, Wendy's Best Western, Hampton Inn, Hilton Garden, Homewood Suites $Tree, AT&T, Chevrolet, CVS Drug, Firestone/auto, GNC, Hannaford Foods, JC Penney, Jo-Ann Fabrics, Marshall's, Petsmart, PriceChopper Mkt, st police, Staples, Verizon, Walgreens
8a(12)	Grooms Rd, to Waterford
8(10)	Crescent, Vischer Ferry, **E** Speedway/dsl McDonald's USPO, **W** Stewart's/dsl, Sunoco Dunkin', Mangia Pizza, Pancho's Mexican CVS Drug

ALBANY

Exit #	Services
8mm	Mohawk River
7(7)	NY 7, Troy, **E on US 9 N** Speedway/dsl Century Ho Mr Subb Comfort Inn, Holiday Inn Express, Sycamore tel $General, Acura, Chrysler/Dodge/Jeep, Ford, Infi Lexus, Nissan, Walgreens, **E on US 9 S** Sunoco Burg Fi, Dunkin', McDonald's, Red Robin, Subway AT&T, Au Zone, Hobby Lobby, Marshall's
6(6)	NY 2, to US 9, same as 7, Schenectady, **E** Mobil, Spe way Applebee's, Boston Mkt, ChuckeCheese, Circle Di Jersey Mike's, Mr Subb, Panera Bread, Red Robin, Starbu Wendy's Golden Circle Inn, La Quinta $Tree, CVS D Dick's, Field&Stream, GNC, Hannaford Foods, Home De Lowe's, Mavis Discount Tire, Mkt Bistro, Petsmart, Sam's C Staples, Toyota, VW, Walmart/Subway, **W** Mobil/dsl, St art's Carrabba's, Chipotle Mexican, Denny's, DiBella's Su Dunkin', Ruby Tuesday, Sake Japanese, Sonic, Subway crotel, Quality Inn, Super 8, TownePlace Suites Goodye auto, Michael's, Target, TJ Maxx, Verizon
5(5)	NY 155 E, Latham, **E** DeeDee's Rest., Philly's Grill US
4(4)	NY 155 W, Wolf Rd, **E on Wolf Rd** Mobil/Subway, Spe way/dsl, Sunoco 99 Rest., Arby's, Capital Buffet, Chipc Mexican, CiCi's Pizza, Denny's, Dunkin', Honeybaked Ha Longhorn Steaks, Macaroni Grill, Maxie's Grill, McDonal Moe's SW Grill, Olive Garden, Outback Steaks, Pizza Hut, R Lobster, Reel Seafood Co, Samurai, Smashburger, Starbuc Subway, Ted's Fishfry, TX Roadhouse, Whse Grill BBQ, Wo 1-11 Courtyard, Fairfield Inn, Hampton Inn, Holiday I Home 2 Suites, Homewood Suites, Marriott, Red Lion Inn, R Roof Inn, Residence Inn, Staybridge Suites, SureStay+ Che rolet, CVS Drug, Firestone/auto, Hannaford Foods, Trader Jo **W** Blu Stone Bistro, Koto Japanese Desmond Ho Hotel Indigo to Heritage Park
2(2)	NY 5, Central Ave, **E** Mobil/dsl, Sunoco, Tesla EVC E Rest., Buca Italian, Cheesecake Factory, Chili's, Five Guys, Ho eybaked Ham, Hooters, IHOP, Panera Bread, PF Chang's, St bucks, Taco Bell, Wendy's Cocca's Inn, Holiday Inn Expre Scottish Inn, SpringHill Suites, Staybridge Suites, Travelodge Barnes&Noble, BJ's Whse/gas, Goodyear/auto, Jo-Ann Fabrics, Bean, Lowe's, Macy's, Marshall's, Mr Tire, PetCo, Staples, Targ Whole Foods Mkt, **W** Cumberland Farms/dsl, Gulf/dsl, Mo USA/dsl Brazilian Steaks, Delmonico's Steaks, DQ, Dunkin', Fiesta Mexican, McDonald's, Moe's SW Grill, Mr Subb, Smok Bones BBQ, Subway, Wendy's Days Inn, EconoLodge, Howa Johnson, Motel 6, Quality Inn, Red Carpet Inn Advance Pa AT&T, AutoZone, Buick/GMC, Cadillac, Krause's Candy, Mid PepBoys, ShopRite/gas, Subaru, Verizon, Walgreens
1W(1)	NY State Thruway (from sb), I-87 S to NYC, I-90 W to Buffalo
1E(1)	I-90 E (from sb), to Albany, Boston
1S(1)	to US 20, Western Ave, **E on US 20** Mobil B Good, Bla Pizza, Burger King, Chipotle Mexican, Coldstone, Dunkin', Fi Guys, J&A Italian, Starbucks, TGIFriday's Days Inn, Ham ton Inn AT&T, CVS Drug, USPO, Verizon, **W on US 20** M bil, USA Capital City Diner, Dunkin', El Charro, Hana Gr McDonald's Homewood Suites, Tru Hilton Adironda Tires, PriceChopper Foods
1N(1)	I-87 N (from nb), to Plattsburgh
149	NY State Thruway goes west to Buffalo (I-90), S to NYC (I-8 I-87 N to Montreal
24(148)	I-90 and I-87 N
23(142)	I-787, to Albany, US 9 W, **E on US 9 W** Cumberland Farm Dunkin'/dsl, Sunoco/dsl Comfort Inn transmission **W** Stewarts Johnny B's Diner Quality Inn

NY

INTERSTATE 87 Cont'd

Exit #	Services
139mm	**parking area sb, litter barrel,**
22(135)	NY 396, to Selkirk
21a(134)	I-90 E, to MA Tpk, Boston
127mm	**New Baltimore Travel Plaza both lanes,** Mobil/dsl Famous Famiglia, Quiznos, Roy Rogers, Starbucks, TCBY atm, info, wi-fi
21b(124)	US 9 W, NY 81, to Coxsackie, **W** 21B Travel Plaza/rest./dsl/scales/24hr, Sunoco/dsl Dunkin', McDonald's Best Western, Holiday Inn Express Boat'n RV Whse, repair, vet
21(114)	NY 23, Catskill, **E** Stewart's, Sunoco/dsl Pelokes Motel (2mi) Home Depot, to Rip van Winkle Br, visitors ctr, **W** Anthony's Banquet Hall Astoria Motel, Rip Van Winkle Motel to Hunter Mtn/Windham Ski Areas
103mm	**Malden Service Area nb,** Mobil/dsl Carvel Ice Cream, Hotdogs, McDonald's atm, **parking area sb,**
20(102)	NY 32, to Saugerties, **E** Mobil/dsl, Stewart's, Sunoco Dunkin', Frederico's Pizza, McDonald's, Pizza Star, Starway Café, Subway Advance Parts, Big Lots, Chrysler/Dodge/Jeep, CVS Drug, Family$, PriceChopper Foods, Verizon, **W** Speedway/dsl, Sunoco/dsl Michelle's Diner Comfort Inn, Holiday Inn Express, Howard Johnson/rest. Blue Mtn Campground (5mi), Brookside Campground (10mi), KOA (2mi), Rip Van Winkle Campground (3mi), to Catskills
99mm	**parking area nb, litter barrels,**
96mm	**Ulster Travel Plaza sb,** Sunoco/dsl Burger King, Nathan's, Pizza Hut, Starbucks, TCBY atm, , wi-fi
19(91)	NY 28, Rhinecliff Br, Kingston, **E** QuickChek/dsl Olympic Diner, Picnic Pizza, Stadium Diner Best Western+, Super 8 access to I-587 E, Advance Parts, Advance Parts, CVS Drug, Hannaford Foods, Kia, Walgreens, **W** Roudigan's Steaks Motel 19, Quality Inn, Rodeway Inn access to US 209, Camping World RV Ctr, Chrysler/Dodge/Jeep/Fiat, Ford, Nissan
18(76)	NY 299, to Poughkeepsie, New Paltz, **E** Mobil, Shell/dsl 87 Motel, EconoLodge, Rodeway Inn Lowe's, to Mid-Hudson Br, **W** EVC, Sunoco Burger King, Dunkin', Gadaletos Seafood, McDonald's, Pasquale's Pizza, Plaza Diner, Rino's Pizza, Rococo's Pizza, Subway Best Value Inn, Hampton Inn Advance Parts, AT&T, KOA (10mi), Midas, Rite Aid, ShopRite Foods, Tops Mkt, Verizon
66mm	**Modena service area sb,** Sunoco/dsl Carvel's Ice Cream, Chicago Grill, McDonald's, Moe's SW Grill atm, UPS, wi-fi
65mm	**Plattekill Travel Plaza nb,** Sunoco/dsl Nathan's, Roy Rogers, Starbucks atm, info, wi-fi
17(60)	I-84, NY 17K, to Newburgh, **E on NY 300 N** Mobil Buffalo Wild Wings, DQ, Dunkin', Flaming Grill, Joe's Deli, McDonald's, Newburgh Buffet, Perkins, Pizza Union, Taco Bell, Wendy's $Tree, AT&T, AutoZone, BonTon, Marshall's, Mavis Tire, Midas, Office Depot, Stop&Shop, **E on NY 300 S** Speedway/dsl, Sunoco/dsl, Tesla EVC Applebee's, Burger King, Chili's, China City, Cosimos Ristorante, Denny's, Five Guys, IHOP, Ikaros Diner, Longhorn Steaks, Neptune Diner, Panera Bread, Pizza Mia, Sonic, Starbucks, Subway, TGIFriday's, Union Sq Rest., Yobo Asian Days Inn, Hampton Inn, Howard Johnson, Hudson Valley Hotel, Ramada Inn, Super 8 $General, Adam's Food Mkt, Aldi Foods, Barnes&Noble, Buick/GMC, Cadillac/Chevrolet, Chrysler/Dodge/Jeep, Ford/Lincoln, Home Depot, Honda, Kohl's, Lowe's, Meineke, Michael's, Nissan, Petsmart, Target, Verizon, Walmart/McDonald's

NEWBURGH

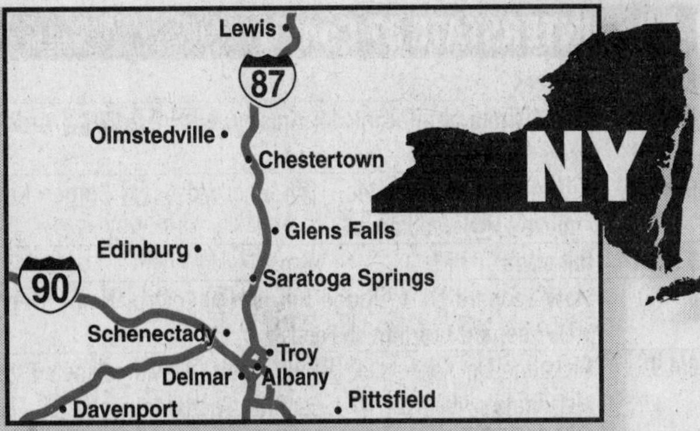

Exit #	Services
16(45)	US 6, NY 17, to West Point, Harriman, **W** Gulf/dsl Applebee's, Chicago Grill, Chili's, Dunkin', KFC, Outback Steaks, Panera Bread, TGIFriday's, Wendy's Days Inn, Hampton Inn $Tree, Best Buy, BJ's Whse, BMW, GNC, Home Depot, Kohl's, Michaels, Old Navy, Petsmart, st police, Staples, Target, TJ Maxx, Verizon, Walmart/Subway, Woodbury Outlet/famous brands
34mm	**Ramapo Service Area sb,** Sunoco/dsl Carvel, McDonald's, Uno Pizza atm, wi-fi
33mm	**Sloatsburg Travel Plaza nb,** Sunoco/dsl Burger King, Dunkin', Quiznos, Sbarro's atm, gifts, info
15a(31)	NY 17 N, NY 59, Sloatsburg
15(30)	I-287 S, NY 17 S, to NJ. **I-87 S & I-287 E run together.**
14b(27)	Airmont Rd, Montebello, **E** Crowne Plaza, **W on NY9** Gulf/Dunkin'/dsl Airmont Diner, AJ's, Bagel Boys Cafe, Le Brick, Starbucks, Sutter's Mill Rest. Howard Johnson H, ShopRite Foods, Tallman Tires, Walgreens, Walmart
14a(23)	Garden State Pkwy, to NJ, Chestnut Ridge
14(22)	NY 59, Spring Valley, Nanuet, **E** 76/dsl, Citgo/dsl, Shell/dsl Burger King, Deliziosa Pizza, Domino's, IHOP, McDonald's, Planet Wings, Subway Candlewood Suites, Quality Inn BMW, Costco/gas, Lowe's, Maserati/Ferrari, Michael's, Target, **W** 76, Citgo, Gulf Baskin-Robbins/Dunkin', ChuckeCheese, Dunkin', Franco's Pizza, KFC/Taco Bell, Nanuet Diner, Panera Bread, Red Lobster, Smashburger, Starbucks, White Castle, Zinburger Days Inn, Hampton Inn, Hilton Garden $Tree, AT&T, Barnes&Noble, Fairway Mkt, Home Depot, Macy's, Marshall's, Mavis Tires, Midas, PetCo, Staples, Stop&Shop Foods, Verizon
13(20)	Palisades Pkwy, N to Bear Mtn, S to NJ
12(19)	NY 303, Palisades Ctr Dr, W Nyack, **W** Mobil Buffalo Wild Wings, Cheesecake Factory, Outback Steaks, Panera Bread Tappan Zee Hotel Barnes&Noble, Best Buy, BJ's Whse, Dave&Buster's, Dick's, Home Depot, Lord&Taylor, Macy's, Mavis Tire/repair, Old Navy, Staples, Target, Verizon
11(18)	US 9W, to Nyack, **E** Mobil, Shell/dsl West Gate Inn H, Walgreens, **W** Shell/dsl Dunkin', McDonald's Super 8 J&L Repair/tire, Midas, Old World Food Mkt
10(17)	Nyack (from nb), same as 11
14mm	Hudson River, Tappan Zee Br
13mm	**toll plaza**
9(12)	to US 9, to Tarrytown, **E** Shell, Speedway/dsl CVS Drug, **W** BP, EVC DoubleTree Hotel Honda, Mavis Tire
8(11)	I-287 E, to Saw Mill Pkwy, White Plains, **E** Extended Stay America, Hampton Inn, Marriott, Sheraton
7a(10)	Saw Mill River Pkwy S, to Saw Mill River SP

NYACK

INTERSTATE 87 Cont'd

NYC AREA

Exit #	Services
7(8)	NY 9A (from nb), Taconic SP, Ardsley, E H, W Ardsley Acres Motel
6mm	Ardsley Travel Plaza nb, Sunoco/dsl Burger King, Popeye's vending
5.5mm	toll plaza
6ba(5)	Stew Leonard Dr, to Ridge Hill, W Costco, Home Depot, Stew Leonard's Farmfresh Foods
6(4.5)	Tuckahoe Dr, Yonkers, E BP/repair Marcellino's Pizza, McDonald's, Subway ShopRite Foods/drug, W Gulf, Mobil/dsl Domino's, Dunkin', Kim Wei Chinese Ramada Inn, Royal Regency Hotel
5(4.3)	NY 100 N (from nb), Central Park Ave, White Plains
4(4)	Cross Country Pkwy, Mile Sq Rd, E Applebee's, Boston Mkt, Chipotle, Panda Express, Panera Bread, Red Lobster, Starbucks Hyatt Place Ford/Lincoln/Subaru, Macy's, Marshall's, TJ Maxx, W BP, Shell/dsl, Shell/Dunkin'/dsl Burger King Chevrolet, Mavis Tire
3(3)	Mile Square Rd, E Stop&Shop, W Citgo
2(2)	Yonkers Ave (from nb), Westchester Fair, E Mobil Yonkers Speedway
1(1)	Hall Place, McLean Ave, E Dunkin' Acme Mkt/Subway
0mm	New York St Thruway and I-87 N run together to Albany
14(11)	McLean Ave, E Acme/dsl Dunkin', Subway
13(10)	E 233rd, NE Tollway, service plaza both lanes, Gulf/Dunkin'
12(9.5)	Hudson Pkwy (from nb), Sawmill Pkwy
11(9)	Van Cortlandt Pk S
10(8.5)	W 230th St (from sb), W 240th (from nb), E Citgo, W Dunkin' H, Marshall's, Target
9(8)	W Fordham Rd, E BP/dsl Dallas BBQ H
8(7)	W 179th (from nb), W Roberto Clemente SP
7(6)	I-95, US 1, S to Trenton, NJ, N to New Haven, CT
6(5)	E 153rd t, River Ave, Stadium Rd, E Yankee Stadium
5(5)	E 161st, Macombs Dam Br, (exit 4 from nb), E AT&T, Best Buy, Michael's, Target, Yankee Stadium
3(3)	E 138th St, Madison Ave Br, E BP/dsl
2(2)	Willis Ave, 3rd Ave Br, E Mobil/dsl, W McDonald's
1(1)	Brook Ave, Hunts Point, E BP, W Speedway
0mm	**I-87 begins/ends on I-278.**

INTERSTATE 88

COBLESKILL

Exit #	Services
25a	I-90/NY Thruway. **I-88 begins/ends on I-90, exit 25a.**
117mm	**toll booth** (to enter or exit NY Thruway)
25(116)	NY 7, to Rotterdam, Schenectady, **3 mi S** Pilot/Dunkin'/Subway/dsl/scales/24hr Peppino's Pizza Frosty Acres Camping
24(112)	US 20, NY 7, to Duanesburg, N Stewart's, Valero/dsl Duanesburg Diner, Dunkin' st police, S USPO
23(101)	NY 30, to Schoharie, Central Bridge, N Apple Food/dsl Hideaway Camping (2mi), Locust Park Camping, S Mobil/Subway/dsl Apple Barrel Cafe, Dunkin' Quality Inn, Wedgewood B&B (2mi)
22(95)	NY 7, NY 145, to Cobleskill, Middleburgh, **2-5 mi N** Speedway/dsl, Stewart's/dsl, Sunoco Dunkin', Pizza Hut, Subway Colonial CT Motel, Super 8 H, $General, $Tree, Advance Parts, AT&T, Buick/Chevrolet/GMC, Chrysler/Dodge/Jeep, Howe Caverns Camping, PriceChopper Foods, to Howe Caverns, Walmart/McDonald's, S Twin Oaks Camping (5mi)
21(90)	NY 7, NY 10, to Cobleskill, Warnerville, **2-3 mi N** Mobil/ Speedway/Dunkn'/dsl, Stewart's/dsl Arby's, Burger Ki KFC/Taco Bell, McDonald's, Pizza Hut, Subway H, $G eral, Ace Hardware, CVS Drug, Mavis Tire, NAPA, PriceChop Foods, SavaLot, Walmart/McDonald's
20(87)	NY 7, NY 10, to Richmondville, S Mobil/dsl, Su co/dsl Reinhardt's Deli, Sub Express Countrys Inn USPO
79mm	**wb, full facilities, litter barrels, petwalk, , , vendi**
19(76)	to NY 7, Worcester, N Stewart's, Sunoco/dsl
73mm	**eb, full facilities, , litter barrels**
18(71)	to Schenevus, N Mirabito/dsl Schenevus Rest.
17(61)	NY 7, to NY 28 N, Colliersville, Cooperstown, N Su co Best Western (14mi), Redwood Inn to Baseball H of Fame

ONEONTA

Exit #	Services
16(59)	NY 7, to Emmons, N Arby's, Brooks BBQ, Farmhou Rest., Morey's Rest., Pizza Hut Amber Life Motel, Rainb Inn PriceChopper Foods, Rite Aid
15	NY 28, NY 23, Oneonta, N Speedway Dunk KFC Townhouse Inn H, Advance Parts, to Soccer H of Fame, USPO, S Mirabito/dsl, Speedway/dsl App bee's, Buffalo Wild Wings, Burger King, Denny's, Five Gu McDonald's, Moe's SW, Mt Fuji Japanese, Panera Bread, Su way, Taco Bell, Tim Horton, Wendy's Budget Inn, Courtya Holiday Inn Express, Quality Inn, Super 8 $Tree, Aldi Foo AT&T, BJ's Whse/gas, Dick's, Ford, Hannaford Foods, Ho Depot, JC Penney, Lowe's, Mr Tire, Petco, TJ Maxx, Veriz Walmart
14(55)	Main St (from eb), Oneonta, N Stewart's, Sunoco fresco's Italian Advance Parts
13(53)	NY 205, **1-2 mi N** Mirabito, Speedway, Valero/dsl D Dunkin', McDonald's Celtic Motel, Hampton Inn, Mo 88 Buick/Cadillac/Chevrolet/GMC, Gilbert Lake SP (11m Honda, NAPA, Nissan, repair, Rite Aid, st police, Subaru, Ve zon
12(47)	NY 7, to Otego, S Mirabito/Subway/Tim Hortons/dsl/24 Sunoco/dsl
42	**wb, facilities, tables, litter barrels**
11(40)	NY 357, to Unadilla, Delhi, S KOA
39mm	**eb, full facilities, litter barrels, petwalk, , , vendin**
10(38)	NY 7, to Unadilla, **2 mi N** KwikFill, Mirabito Count Motel (4mi) Family$, st police, USPO
9(33)	NY 8, to Sidney, N Citgo/dsl, Sunoco China Buffet, L tle Caesar's, McDonald's, Pizza Hut, Subway Algonkin M tel, Country Motel, Super 8 H, $General, Advance Par PriceChopper Foods, Tall Pines Camping, USPO
8(29)	NY 206, to Bainbridge, N Citgo/dsl, Sunoco Bob's Far ily Diner, China Star, Dunkin' Algonkin Motel, Susqueha na Motel Auto Parts+, Chevrolet/GMC, Family$, Riversi RV Park, USPO, S to Ouage Creek Park
7(22)	NY 41, to Afton, **1-2 mi N** Mirabito, Sunoco/dsl Ma St Grill, RiverClub Rest. Afton Golf/rest., Kellystone Par Smith-Hale HS
6(16)	NY 79, to NY 7, Harpursville, Ninevah, S Mirabito/Subwa dsl Pantheon Rest. Family$, to Nathanial Cole Park
5(12)	Martin Hill Rd, to Belden, N Belden Hill Camping
4(8)	NY 7, to Sanitaria Springs, S Speedway/dsl
3(4)	NY 369, Port Crane, N to Chenango Valley SP, S Fa trac/dsl, KwikFill Subway
2(2)	NY 12a W, to Chenango Bridge, N Mirabito USPO
1(1)	NY 7 W (no wb return), to Binghamton
0mm	I-81, N to Syracuse, S to Binghamton. **I-88 begins/ends on I-8**

INTERSTATE 90

Exit #	Services
0mm	New York/Massachusetts state line
0(B23)	NY 22, to Austerlitz, New Lebanon, W Stockbridge, N Citgo/dsl/scales/24hr, Loves/Dunkin'/Subway/dsl/scales/24hr, S Sunoco/dsl Berkshire Travel Lodge Woodland Hills Camp (3mi)
0(B17)	toll plaza,
0(B15)	NY 295, Taconic Pkwy, 1-2 mi S gas
0(B7)	US 9, NY Thruway W, to I-87, , toll booth
12(20)	US 9, to Hudson, N Pilot/Subway/dsl/scales/24hr, 0-3 mi S to Van Buren NHS
18.5mm	/weigh sta wb, full facilities, litter barrels, petwalk, , vending
11(15)	US 9, US 20, E Greenbush, Nassau, N Speedway/dsl, Sunoco/dsl Dunkin' st police, S Stewart's Mercato's Pizza, My Place Host Field Inn, Knights Inn Rite Aid, USPO, vet
10(10)	Miller Rd, to E Greenbush, S Mobil/dsl Dunkin' Comfort Inn
9(9)	US 4, to Rensselaer, Troy, N Mobil/dsl Applebee's, Domino's, Dunkin', Five Guys, McDonald's, Moe's SW, OffShore Pier Rest., Panera Bread, Starbucks, Subway, Taco Bell, The Sports Grill Holiday Inn Express, Residence Inn $Tree, AT&T, CVS Drug, Home Depot, Mavis Tire/auto, PetsMart, Staples, Target, Walmart, S Mobil/dsl, Stewart's Cracker Barrel, Denny's, Dunkin' Hampton Inn Fairfield Inn
8(8)	NY 43, Defreestville
7(7)	Washington Ave (from eb), Rensselaer
6.5mm	Hudson River
6a	I-787, to Albany
6(4.5)	US 9, Northern Blvd, to Loudonville, N Stewart's Mr Subb, NY Pizza Red Carpet Inn H
5a(4)	Corporate Woods Blvd
5(3.5)	Everett Rd, to NY 5, Central Ave, S on NY 5 ShopRite, Speedway/dsl Dunkin', Gateway Diner, Hokkaido Asian, Little Caesar's, McDonald's, Popeye's, Subway, Taco Bell Motel 6, Ramada H, $Tree, Aamco, Advance Parts, AutoZone, Chevrolet, Chrysler/Dodge/Jeep, CVS Drug, Fiat, Ford, Hannaford's Foods, Home Depot, Hyundai, Kia, Mavis Tire, Mazda, Monro, Nissan, PepBoys, PriceChopper Foods, Rite Aid, ShopRite Foods, Verizon
4(3)	NY 85 S, to Slingerlands
3(2.5)	S State Offices
2(2)	Fuller Rd, Washington Ave, same as 1, S on Washington Sunoco/Subway Dunkin' Courtyard, CrestHill Suites, Extended Stay America, Fairfield Inn, Hilton Garden, Red Carpet Inn, TownePlace Suites same as 1S
1N(1)	I-87 N, to Montreal, to Albany Airport
1S(1)	US 20, Western Ave, S Mobil Black&Blue Rest., Blaze Pizza, Burger King, Capital City Diner, Chipotle Mexican, Coldstone, Creo Rest., Dave&Buster's, Dunkin', Five Guys, Hana Grill, Ichiban Japanese, McDonald's, Moe's SW Grill, Panera Bread, Peaches Cafe, Provence Rest., Starbucks, TGIFriday's, Uno Grill Hampton Inn, Residence Inn AT&T, Best Buy, CVS Drug, Dick's, Home Depot, JC Penney, Macy's, Michael's, Old Navy, PetsMart, PriceChopper Foods, USPO, Verizon, Walmart
24(149)	I-87 N to Albany, Montreal, S to NYC
153mm	Guilderland Service Area eb, Mobil/dsl McDonald's
25(154)	I-890, NY 7, NY 146, to Schenectady

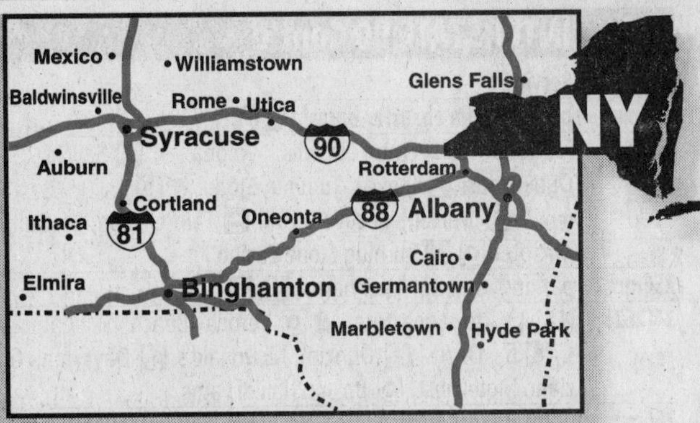

Exit #	Services
25a(159)	I-88 S, NY 7, to Binghamton, S Pilot/Dunkin'/Subway/dsl/scales/24hr
26(162)	I-890, NY 5 S, Schenectady
168mm	Pattersonville Service Area wb, Mobil/dsl Hershey's, Roy Rogers, Starbucks atm, NY Mkt, wi-fi
172mm	Mohawk Service Area eb, Mobil/dsl McDonald's
27(174)	NY 30, Amsterdam, N Mobil/dsl, Valero/Dunkin'/dsl Knight Inn, Super 8 Alpin Haus RV Ctr (3mi)
28(182)	NY 30A, Fonda, N Citgo/rest/dsl/motel/24hr, Sunoco/dsl, TA/Country Pride/dsl/motel/scales/24hr/@ Dunkin', McDonald's Riverside Motel H, st police, truck repair
184mm	parking area/truck insp area both lanes, litter barrels,
187mm	wb, full facilities, living history site
29(194)	NY 10, Canajoharie, N Cumberland, Stewart's/dsl McDonald's, Subway $General, BigLots, Rite Aid, Riverfront Park, USPO, S Beavers/dsl, Citgo/dsl, Sunoco Mercato Pizza, Village Rest. USPO
210mm	Indian Castle Service area eb, Iroquois Service Area wb, Mobil/dsl Burger King, Hershey's Ice Cream, Roy Rogers, Starbucks atm, Dunkin', wi-fi
29a(211)	NY 169, to Little Falls, N Travelodge (3mi) H, to Herkimer Home
30(220)	NY 28, to Mohawk, Herkimer, N FasTrac/dsl, Stewart's, Sunoco/Subway/dsl Applebee's, Burger King, Denny's, Dunkin', KFC/Taco Bell, McDonald's, Pizza Hut, Tony's Pizzaria, Vinny's Pizza Budget Motel, Inn Towne Motel, Red Roof Inn $General, $Tree, Advance Parts, AutoZone, Mavis Tire/auto, Rite Aid, Verizon, vet, Walmart, S FasTrac Little Caesar's, Red Apple Chinese Family$, to Cooperstown (Baseball Hall of Fame)
227mm	Schuyler Service Area wb, Mobil/dsl Breyer's, McDonald's atm, st police
31(233)	I-790, NY 8, NY 12, to Utica, N Citgo/dsl, Fastrac, Sunoco Applebee's, Burger King, Charlie's Pizza, Franco's Pizza, Good Friend Chinese $Tree, Aldi Foods, Bass Pro Shop, BigLots, BJ's Whse/gas, Lowe's, PriceChopper Foods, Rite Aid, Walmart/McDonald's, S Speedway/dsl Babe's Grill, Delmonico's Steaks, Denny's, Dunkin', McDonald's, Moe's SW, Subway, Taco Bell, Wendy's Best Western, Days Inn, EconoLodge, Fairfield Inn, Hampton Inn, Happy Journey Motel, Holiday Inn Epress, Red Roof Inn, Rest Inn AT&T
236mm	I-790 (from eb), to Utica
237.5mm	Erie Canal
238mm	Mohawk River
32(243)	NY 232, Westmoreland, N Travel Inn, S Stewart's USPO
244mm	Oneida Service Area eb, Sunoco/dsl Burger King, Sbarro's, Starbucks atm, gifts

NY

INTERSTATE 90 Cont'd

SYRACUSE

Exit #	Services
250mm	**parking area eb, litter barrel,**
33(253)	NY 365, to Vernon Downs, Verona, **N** SavOn Gas/Dunkin'/dsl Inn at Turning Stone, **S** SavOn Gas/LP/repair Dunkin', Recovery Grill Fairfield Inn, La Quinta, Microtel H, Turning Stone Casino
256mm	**parking area wb, litter barrel,**
34(262)	NY 13, to Canastota, **N** Verona Beach SP Camping, **S** SavOn/dsl Dunkin', McDonald's Days Inn, Graziano Motel/rest. Boxing Hall of Fame
266mm	**Chittenango Service Area wb,** Sunoco/dsl Sbarro's, Starbucks atm
34a(277)	I-481, to Syracuse, Chittenango
35(279)	NY 298, The Circle, Syracuse, **S** Xpress Mart Burger King, Denny's, Dunkin', East Wok, Grimaldi's, Jimmy John's, Joey's Italian, Jreck Subs, McDonald's, Ruby Tuesday Best Western+, Magnuson Inn, Best Value Inn, Candlewood Suites, Comfort Inn, Courtyard, Cresthill Suites, Days Inn, Doubletree Inn, Embassy Suites, Extended Stay America, Fairfield Inn, Hampton Inn, Hilton Garden, Homewood Suites, Motel 6, Quality Inn, Ramada, Red Roof Inn, Residence Inn, Rodeway Inn, SpringHill Suites Stevenson's Tire/auto, Verizon
280mm	**Dewitt Service Area eb,** Sunoco/dsl McDonald's
36(283)	I-81, N to Watertown, S to Binghamton
37(284)	7th St, Electronics Pkwy, to Liverpool, **N** Best Western+, **S** Speedway/Dunkin' KFC/Taco Bell Holiday Inn, Homewood Suites, Knights Inn, Staybridge Suites Kinney Drug
38(286)	NY 57, to Liverpool, Syracuse, **N** Fastrac/dsl, KwikFill, Speedway Bangkok Thai, Dunkin', Pizza Hut Super 8 $Tree, Aldi Foods, Midas, NAPA, Rite Aid
39(290)	I-690, NY 690, Syracuse, **N** Comfort Inn/rest. Camping World RV Ctr, **S** Holiday Inn Express
292mm	**Warners Service Area wb,** Mobil/dsl Boston Pizza, McDonald's
40(304)	NY 34, to Owasco Lake, Weedsport, **N** Riverforest RV Park, **S** Fastrac, KwikFill, Sunoco/dsl Arby's, Arnold's Rest., Cj's Rest., DB's Drive-In, Dunkin', NY Pizzaria Days Inn, Rodeway Inn $General, Ace Hardware, Bass Pro Shops (12mi), Kinney Drug, NAPA, USPO, Weedsport Foods
310mm	**Port Byron Service Area eb,** Mobil/dsl Boston Pizza, Edy's Ice Cream
318mm	**parking area wb, litter barrels**
41(320)	NY 414, to Cayuga Lake, Waterloo, **S** Byrne Dairy/dsl, Circle K/dsl, Petro/Iron Skillet/dsl/scales/24hr/@ MaGee Country Diner Hampton Inn (4mi), Microtel (4mi), Quality Inn (4mi) Cayuga Lake SP/camping, Waterloo Outlets/famous brands (3mi)
324mm	**Junius Ponds Service Area wb,** Sunoco/dsl Dunkin', Roy Rogers atm, wi-fi
42(327)	NY 14, to Geneva, Lyons, **S** Mobil/7-11/dsl/scales Belhurst (6mi), Best Value Inn (6mi), Days Inn (6mi), Hampton Inn (6mi), Ramada Inn (6mi) Junius Ponds RV Camping, Waterloo Outlets/famous brands (3mi)
337mm	**Clifton Springs Service Area eb,** Sunoco/dsl Burger King, Sbarro's, Starbucks atm
43(340)	NY 21, to Palmyra, Manchester, **N** Hill Cumorah LDS HS (2mi), **S** Sunoco/dsl Dunkin', McDonald's Manchester Inn KOA (6mi)
44(347)	NY 332, Victor, **S** 7-11/dsl, Mobil/Subway, Speedway, Sunoco/dsl Burger King, Dunkin', KFC, McDonald's, Park Place Rest.

ROCHESTER

BATAVIA

DEPEW

Exit #	Services
44(347)	Continued Budget Inn, Comfort Inn, Travelodge $General, $T Aldi Foods, AutoZone, casino, CVS Drug, KOA (4mi), st po Top's Foods
350mm	**Seneca Service Area wb,** Mobil/dsl Checker's, Pizza atm, wi-fi
45(351)	I-490, NY 96, to Rochester, **N** Mobil/dsl Bone Grill, Champp's Grill, Chipotle, City Tavern, Distillery R Five Guys, Longhorn Steaks, McDonald's, Moe's SW Grill, ive Garden, Panera Bread, PF Chang's, Pi Craft Pizza, Starbu Subway Hampton Inn, Springdale Farm B&B $T AT&T, Best Buy, BJ's Whse/gas, Dick's, GNC, Home De JC Penney, Kohl's, Lord&Taylor, Macy's, Michael's, Old N Petsmart, Staples, Target, Verizon, Von Maur, Walm **S** KwikFill/dsl Burger King, Chili's, Denny's, Taco Wendy's Best Western+, Holiday Inn Express, Homew Suites, Microtel, Royal Inn Wilkins RV Ctr
353mm	**parking area eb, litter barrels**
46(362)	I-390, to Rochester **N on NY 253 W** Gulf/dsl, Mobil/ Speedway/Dunkin'/dsl McDonald's, Peppermint's R Tim Hortons, Wendy's Days Inn, Fairfield Inn, Microtel, Roof Inn, Super 8 Buick/GMC
366mm	**Scottsville Service Area eb,** Mobil/dsl by's atm, info
376mm	**Ontario Service Area wb,** Sunoco/dsl Boston Piz Edy's Ice Cream, McDonald's atm, wi-fi
47(379)	I-490, NY 19, to Rochester, **N** 490 Truckstop/dsl Ed House B&B Timberline Camping
48(390)	NY 98, to Batavia, **N** Fairbridge Inn, Hampton Inn, Holic Inn Express, **S** Citgo Applebee's, Bob Evans, Five Gu Subway, Taco Bell, Tim Horton's, Yume Asian Bistro B Western, Budget Inn, Days Inn, La Quinta, Quality Inn, Red R Inn, Relax Inn, Super 8 AT&T, AutoZone, BJ's Whse, Dic Home Depot, Kohl's, Marshall's, Michael's, PetCo, Rite Aid, T get, Tops Foods, Verizon, Walmart/Subway
397mm	**Pembroke Service Area eb,** Sunoco/dsl Tim Horto atm, gifts
48a(402)	NY 77, Pembroke, **S** FLYING J/Denny's/Subway/dsl/ scales/24hr, TA/Mobil/Country Pride/dsl/scales/24hr/@ S way Darien Lake Lodge/camping, EconoLodge Slee Hollow Camping (8mi)
412mm	**Clarence Service Area wb,** Sunoco/dsl Arby's, T Hortons atm, full facilities, info, wi-fi
49(417)	NY 78, Depew, **0-3 mi N** Delta Sonic, Mobil/dsl, Suno Sunoco, Tesla EVC Applebee's, Arby's, Burger King, Chil Chipotle, Cracker Barrel, Deep South Taco, Dibella's Subs, D Duff's Wings, Dunkin', Firehouse Subs, Five Guys, Fuji Gr Jimmy John's, KFC, La Divina Dos, La Tolteca, McDonalc Mighty Taco, Moe's SW Grill, Old Country Buffet, Olive Gard Panera Bread, Picasso's Pizza, Pita Gourmet, Pizza Plant, P tocol Rest., Red Lobster, Russel's Steaks, Salsarita's, Santor Pizza, Starbucks, Starbucks, Subway, Taco Bell, Ted's HotDo Tim Horton, Tully's Rest., Wendy's Clarion, Home 2 Suit Motel 6, Salvatore's Hotel, Springhill Suites, Staybridge Suit Super 8, Tru Hilton $Tree, Acura, Advance Parts, Aldi Foo AT&T, AutoZone, Barnes&Noble, Best Buy, BigLots, BJ's Whs gas, Buick/GMC, Chevrolet, Chrysler/Dodge/Jeep, Dick's, Du Tire, Firestone/auto, Ford, Goodyear/auto, Hobby Lobby, Hor Depot, Honda, Hyundai, JC Penney, Jo-Ann Fabrics, Kohl Lowe's, Marshall's, Mavis Tire, Michael's, Office Depot, PetC PetsMart, Rite Aid, SteinMart, Target, TJ Maxx, Top's Food/de Tuesday Morning, Verizon, vet, Walgreens, Walmart/Subwa

INTERSTATE 90 Cont'd

49(417)	Continued Wegman's Foods, S [gas] Kwikfill, Mobil/dsl [food] China 1, Italian Village, John&Mary's Cafe, McDonald's, Salvatore's Italian, Subway, Tim Horton [lodging] Garden Place Hotel, Hospitality Inn, La Quinta, Red Roof Inn [other] $Tree, 7-11, Advance Parts, Mavis Tire, Top's Foods/gas
419mm	toll booth
50(420)	I-290 to Niagara Falls
50a(421)	Cleveland Dr (from eb)
51(422)	NY 33 E, Buffalo, S [other] [airport], st police
52(423)	Walden Ave, to Buffalo, N [food] Applebee's, Burger King, Chipotle, Famous Dave's BBQ, IHOP, McDonald's, Ruby Tuesday, Starbucks, Subway, TGIFriday's, Tim Horton [lodging] Hampton Inn, Holiday Inn Express, Residence Inn [other] $Tree, Aldi Foods, AT&T, AutoZone, Firestone/auto, Ford, Home Depot, Michael's, Office Depot, PetsMart, PriceRite Mkt, Target, Top's Foods, S [gas] Delta Sonic, Jim's Trk Plaza/Sunoco/dsl/rest./scales/24hr, KwikFill [food] Alton's Rest., Bar Louie's, Bravo Italiano, Cheesecake Factory, Dick's, Dunkin', Five Guys, Gordon Biersch arrest., Longhorn Steaks, McDonald's, Melting Pot, Mighty Taco, Milton's Rest., Moe's SW, Olive Garden, Panera Bread, PF Chang's, Pizza Hut, Popeye's, Smokey Bones BBQ, Sonic, Taco Bell, Texas de Brazil Steaks, Tim Horton, Zahng's Buffet [lodging] Baymont Inn, Home 2 Suites, Millenium Hotel [other] Best Buy, Burlington Coats, Cabela's, Dave&Buster's, Dunn Tire, JC Penney, Lord&Taylor, Macy's, Marshall's, Mavis Tire, Sam's Club, Verizon
52a(424)	William St
53(425)	I-190, to Buffalo, Niagara Falls, N [lodging] Best Western+
54(428)	NY 400, NY 16, to W Seneca, E Aurora
55(430)	US 219, Ridge Rd, Orchard Park, S [gas] Delta Sonic, Sunoco [food] Denny's, Ferro's NY Pizza, Mighty Taco, Subway, Tim Horton, Wendy's [lodging] Country Inn&Suites, Hampton Inn, Staybridge Suites [other] $General, Aldi Foods, BigLots, Goodyear/auto, Home Depot, Mr Tire, Pepboys, Petco, Tops Foods/gas, Verizon, Wegman's Foods
431mm	toll booth
56(432)	NY 179, Mile Strip Rd, N [gas] Gulf/dsl, Mobil, Sunoco [food] Blasdell Pizza, China King, DiPaolo's Rest., Odyssey Rest., Whse Rest. [lodging] EconoLodge [other] $General, Advance Parts, CVS Drug, repair, SaveALot Foods, USPO, S [food] Applebee's, Chipotle, ChuckeCheese, El Canelo Mexican, Firehouse Subs, Five Guys, McDonald's, Mongolian Buffet, Olive Garden, Outback Steaks, Panera Bread, Pizza Hut, Popeye's, Red Lobster, Starbucks, Subway, TGIFriday's, Wendy's [other] $Tree, Aldi Foods, Barnes&Noble, Best Buy, BJ's Whse, Firestone/auto, Hobby Lobby, Home Depot, JC Penney, Jo-Ann Etc, Old Navy, PepBoys, TJ Maxx, Wegman's Foods
57(436)	NY 75, to Hamburg, N [gas] Mobil/Dunkin'/dsl [food] Arby's, Blasdell Pizza, Denny's, Hat Trix, McDonald's, Tim Horton, Uncle Joe's Diner, Waterstone Grill, Wendy's [lodging] Comfort Inn, Holiday Inn Express, Motel 6, Red Roof Inn [other] Chevrolet, Chrysler/Dodge/Jeep, Ford, Honda, Lowe's, Pepboys, transmissions, Walmart/Subway, S [gas] Go Gas, Kwikfill/dsl, Mad J's [food] Burger King, Mexico City, Pizza Hut, Savory Cafe, Subway, Tim Horton [lodging] Hampton Inn, Quality Inn, Super 8 [other] $General, Advance Parts, AutoZone, Gander RV Ctr, Goodyear/auto, Monro Automotive, NAPA, USPO, vet
442mm	parking area both lanes, litter barrels
57a(445)	to Eden, Angola, N [gas] Mobil/dsl
447mm	Angola Service Area both lanes, [gas] Sunoco/dsl [food] McDonald's, Moe's SW Grill, Subway [other] atm, gifts, wi-fi

HAMBURG

FREDONIA

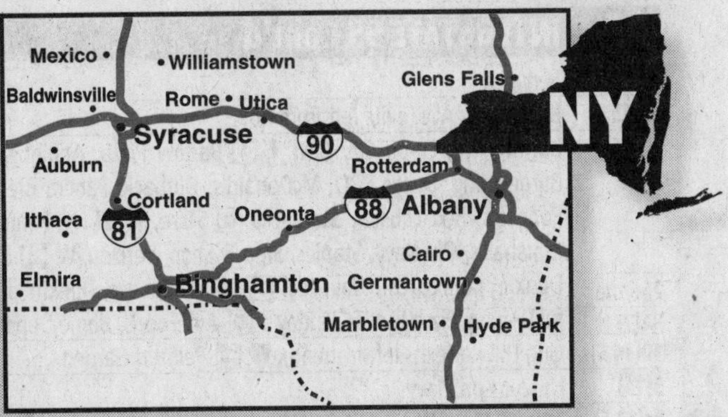

58(456)	US 20, NY 5, to Silver Creek, Irving, N [gas] Kwikfill, Seneca Hawk Trkstp/dsl [food] Burger King, Colony Rest., McDonald's, Millie's Rest., Sunset Bay, Sunset Grill, Tim Hortons, Tom's Rest. [lodging] Lighthouse Inn [other] [H], auto repair, to Evangola SP, USPO
59(468)	NY 60, Fredonia, Dunkirk, N [lodging] Clarion (2mi), Dunkirk Motel (4mi) [other] Lake Erie SP/camping (7mi), S [gas] Country Fair/dsl, Kwikfill/dsl [food] Applebee's, Arby's, Azteca Cantina, Bob Evans, Burger King, Denny's, Dunkin', KFC/Taco Bell, Little Caesar's, McDonald's, Pizza Hut, Subway, Tim Horton, Tim Hortons, Wendy's, Wing City Grille [lodging] Best Western, Econolodge/Suburban Lodge, Quality Inn [other] $General, $Tree, Advance Parts, Aldi Foods, AT&T, AutoZone, BigLots, Chrysler/Dodge/Jeep, Ford/Lincoln, GMC, GNC, Home Depot, Midas, Monro, Petsmart, Rite Aid, TJ Maxx, Tops Foods/gas, Verizon, Walmart/Subway
60(485)	NY 394, Westfield, N [other] Brookside Beach Camping, KOA, to Lake Erie SP/camping, S [lodging] Holiday Motel, Webb's Resort [other] [H]
494mm	toll booth
61(495)	Shortman Rd, to Ripley, N [other] Lakeside RV Park
496mm	New York/Pennsylvania state line

INTERSTATE 95

Exit #	Services
32mm	New York/Connecticut state line
22(30)	Midland Ave (from nb), Port Chester, Rye, W [food] Dunkin' [lodging] Courtyard [other] [H], Home Depot, Staples, Whole Foods Mkt
21(29)	I-287 W, US 1 N, to White Plains, Port Chester, Tappan Zee
20(28)	US 1 S (from nb), Port Chester, E [gas] Shell [other] CVS Drug, Ford, Subaru, USPO
19(27)	Playland Pkwy, Rye, Harrison
18b(25)	Mamaroneck Ave, to White Plains, E [gas] Shell, Speedway [food] Domino's, Jimmy's Pizza [other] Mavis Tire
18a(24)	Fenimore Rd (from nb), Mamaroneck, E [gas] Conoco, Gulf
17(20)	Chatsworth Ave (from nb, no return), Larchmont
19.5mm	toll plaza
16(19)	North Ave, Cedar St, New Rochelle, E [food] Applebee's, Buffalo Wild Wings, Subway, TX Roadhouse [lodging] Radisson, Residence Inn [other] ShopRite, Toyota, USPO, W [other] [H]
15(16)	US 1, New Rochelle, The Pelhams, E [gas] SuperGas, Wave/dsl [food] Dunkin', New China, New Rochelle Diner [other] AutoZone, Costco/gas, CVS Drug, Harley-Davidson, Home Depot, Walgreens, W [other] repair
14(15)	Hutchinson Pkwy (from sb), to Whitestone Br
13(16)	Conner St, to Mt Vernon, E [gas] Gulf/dsl [food] Taco Bell [lodging] Ramada Inn, W [gas] [food] McDonald's [lodging] Holiday Motel [other] [H], Co-Op City Tire/auto, Pepboys

NY

= gas = food = lodging = other = rest stop

NYC AREA

INTERSTATE 95 Cont'd

Exit #	Services
12(15.5)	Baychester Ave (exits left from nb)
11(15)	Bartow Ave, Co-op City Blvd, E Bartow Pizza, Applebee's, Burger King, Dallas BBQ, McDonald's, Outback, Panera Bread, Popeye's, Red Lobster, Starbucks $Tree, AT&T, JC Penney, Marshall's, Old Navy, Staples, Stop & Shop, Verizon, W BP/Dunkin', Sunoco/dsl, Wave/dsl ChuckeCheese, Dunkin', Joyful Dragon, Pizza Hut, TGIFriday's Aldi Foods, Home Depot
10(14.5)	Gun Hill Rd (exits left from nb), W Pelham Garden
9(14)	Hutchinson Pkwy
8c(13.5)	Pelham Pkwy W
8b(13)	Orchard Beach, City Island
8a(12.5)	Westchester Ave (from sb)
7c(12)	Pelham Bay Park (from nb), Country Club Rd
7b(11.5)	E Tremont (from sb), W Super FoodTown
7a(11)	I-695 (from sb), to I-295 S, Throgs Neck Br
6b(10.5)	I-278 W (from sb), I-295 S (from nb)
6a(10)	I-678 S, Whitestone Bridge
5b(9)	Castle Hill Ave, W Sunoco McDonald's, Subway $Tree
5a(8.5)	Westchester Ave, White Plains Rd
4b(8)	Bronx River Pkwy, Rosedale Ave, E BP/Dunkin'
4a(7)	I-895 S, Sheridan Expsy
3(6)	3rd Ave, W H
2b(5)	Webster Ave, W H
2a(4)	Jerome Ave, to I-87
1c(3)	I-87, Deegan Expswy, to Upstate
1b(2)	Harlem River Dr
1a(1)	US 9, NY 9A, H Hudson Pkwy, 178th St, downtown
0mm	New York/New Jersey state line, Hudson River, Geo Washington Br

NIAGARA FALLS

INTERSTATE 190 (Buffalo)

Exit #	Services
25.5mm	US/Canada Border, US Customs
25b a	R Moses Pkwy, NY 104, NY 265, Lewiston, E H
24	NY 31, Witmer Rd, E H, st police
23	NY 182, Porter Rd, Packard Rd, E EVC, Sunoco/dsl Applebee's, Burger King, Chili's, Chipotle, DQ, Five Guys, Longhorn Steaks, Mighty Taco, Olive Garden, Panera Bread, Subway, Tim Horton $Tree, Advance Parts, Big Lots, Chrysler/Dodge/Jeep, Fashion Outlets/famous brands, Firestone/auto, Goodyear/Auto, Hobby Lobby, Jo-Ann Fabrics, Marshall's, Mavis Tire, Mr Tire, NAPA, Petco, Sam's Club/gas, U-Haul, Verizon, Walmart/Subway, Wegman's, W Wendy's Aldi Foods
22	US 62, Niagara Falls Blvd, E Sunoco Arby's, Bob Evans, Burger King, Denny's, Dunkin', KFC, Mandalay Rest., McDonald's, Pizza Hut, Popeye's, Starbucks, Subway, Taco Bell, Wendy's Beat Value Inn, Budget Host, Caravan Motel, Hampton Inn, Pelican Motel, Quality Inn, Red Carpet Inn, Super 8, Swiss Cottage Inn $Tree, Advance Parts, AT&T, Dunn Tire, Ford, Rite Aid, Target, TJ Maxx, Top's Foods/gas, Walgreens, W Comfort Inn, Econolodge, La Quinta Home Depot
21a	La Salle Expswy
21	NY 384, Buffalo Ave, R Moses Pkwy, E Aashram Hotel, Sheraton, W Gulf American Falls, casino, to NF SP
20.5mm	Niagara River East, toll booth sb
20b a	Long Rd, E Budget Motel Kelly's Country Store
19	Whitehaven Rd, E Noco Express/dsl McDonald's Chateau Motel (2mi) $Tree, funpark, KOA (1mi), Top's Foods/gas, W Chevrolet, Hyundai, Toyota, vet
18b a	NY 324 W, Grand Island Blvd, E NOCO/dsl, Sp way/dsl Burger King, McDonald's, Tim Horton, W dy's Chateau Motel, Grand Suites $Tree, Adva Parts, Tops/gas, W Beaver Island SP
17.5mm	Niagara River East, **toll booth**
17	NY 266, last free exit nb

BUFFALO

Exit #	Services
16	I-290 E, to I-90, Albany
15	NY 324, Kenmore Ave, E 7-11 city park, W U-H
14	Ontario St, E KwikFill McDonald's, Tim Horton vance Parts, Family$
13	(from nb), same as 14
12	Amherst St, (from nb), downtown
11	NY 198, Buffalo, E First Line
9	Porter Ave, to Peace Bridge, Ft Erie
8	NY 266, Niagara St, E Buffalo Grand Hotel, W Co yard, downtown
7	NY 5 W, Church St, Buffalo, downtown
6	Elm St, E H, downtown, W Arena
5	Louisiana St, Buffalo, downtown
4	Smith St, Fillmore Ave, Buffalo, downtown
3	NY 16, Seneca St, from sb, W Tim Horton
2	US 62, NY 354, Bailey Ave, Clinton St
1	Ogden St, E Sunoco Wendy's Best Western+, Co fort Inn Big Lots, CVS Drug, Family$
.5mm	**toll plaza nb**
0mm	**I-90. I-190 begins/ends on I-90, exit 53.**

NYC AREA

INTERSTATE 287 (New York City)

Exit #	Services
12	I-95, N to New Haven, S to NYC. **I-287 begins/ends on I-95, exit**
11	US 1, Port Chester, Rye, N BP, Mobil, Sunoco Bur King, Domino's, Dunkin', McDonald's, Popeye's, Port Ches Diner, Subway, Taco Bell Courtyard H, Goodye auto, Home Depot, Kohl's, Mavis Discount Tire, Nissan, Stap Verizon, Whole Foods Mkt
10	Bowman Ave, Webb Ave
9N S	Hutchinson Pkwy, Merritt Pkwy, to Whitestone Br
9a	I-684, Brewster
8	Westchester Ave, to White Plains, S BP, Mobil Buff Wild Wings, Cheesecake Factory, Chipotle, Five Guys, M ton's Steaks, Panera Bread, PF Chang's, Westchester Bur Co Crowne Plaza Chrysler/Dodge/Jeep, H, Neim Marcus, Nordstrom, Stop&Shop Foods, Walmart, Westches Mall Place, Whole Foods Mkt
7	Taconic Pkwy (from wb), to N White Plains
6	NY 22, White Plains
5	NY 100, Hillside Ave, S Gulf, Lukoil Applebee's, Chip tle, Dunkin', Planet Pizza, Smashburger, Subway Aam AutoZone, GNC, Lexus, Mazda, vet
4	NY 100A, Hartsdale, N Shell H, S Mobil Ba boo Garden Chinese, Burger King BMW/Mini, Jaguar, Ma da/Subaru, Staples
3	Sprain Pkwy, to Taconic Pkwy, NYC
2	NY 9A, Elmsford, N BP, Citgo, Gulf, Mobil, Sun co Dunkin', Subway, Taco Bell Mavis Discount Ti NAPA, Sam's Club, S Shell Wendy's
1	NY 119, Tarrytown, N Shell/dsl, Tesla EVC Coope Mill, Qdoba, Ruth's Chris Steaks Marriott, Sherato S BP/dsl El Dorado Diner Extended Stay Ameri Hampton Inn
0	**I-287 runs with I-87 N.**

NY

INTERSTATE 290 (Buffalo)

Exit #	Services
8	I-90, NY Thruway, **I-290 begins/ends on I-90, exit 50.**
7b a	NY 5, Main St, **N** [gas] Mobil/dsl, Sunoco [food] La Nova Pizza/Wings, McDonald's, Panera Bread, Starbucks, Tim Horton, Wendy's [lodging] Hampton Inn, Wyndham Garden [other] Tops Foods, Walgreens, **S** [gas] Valero [lodging] Hyatt Place
6	NY 324, NY 240, **N** [gas] Marathon/dsl [lodging] Courtyard [other] Cadillac, **S** [food] China Star, ChuckeCheese, McDonald's, Sheridan Rest., Subway [other] 7-11, Aamco, CVS Drug, Hyundai, Kia/Mazda, Lexus, Nissan, Subaru, URGENT CARE, Walgreens
5b a	NY 263, to Millersport, **N** [gas] Gulf [food] Santora's Pizza, Zetti's Pizza [lodging] Candlewood Suites, Comfort Inn, DoubleTree, Marriott, Red Roof+, Residence Inn, **S** [gas] Mobil [lodging] Homewood Suites [other] Mr Tire, Toyota, VW, Walgreens
4	I-990, to St U
3b a	US 62, to Niagara Falls Blvd, **N** [gas] Mobil/7-11, Valero [food] Anderson's Rest., Bob Evans, Checkers, Dunkin', Just Pizza, Pancake House, Roadhouse Grill, Ted's Hot Dogs [lodging] Econolodge, Extended Stay America, Knight's Inn, La Quinta, Red Carpet Inn, Rodeway Inn, Sleep Inn [other] CarMax, Chrysler/Dodge/Jeep, Home Depot, Honda, NAPA, Rite Aid, URGENT CARE, vet, **S** [gas] Delta Sonic, Sunoco/dsl [food] Applebee's, Blaze Pizza, BoneFish Grill, Buffalo Wild Wings, Burger King, Carrabba's, Cheeburger, Chili's, Chipotle, Denny's, Dibella's Subs, Domino's, Five Guys, John's Pizza, McDonald's, Moe's SW Grill, Olive Garden, Outback Steaks, Panera Bread, Papa John's, Pl Pizza, Starbucks, TGIFriday, Tim Horton, Tulley's [lodging] Days Inn, Royal Inn [other] $Tree, AT&T, Barnes&Noble, Best Buy, BJ's/gas, Christmas Tree Shop, Dick's, Firestone/auto, GNC, Goodyear/auto, JC Penney, Jo-Ann Fabrics, Lowes Whse, Macy's, Michael's, Old Navy, Pepboys, PetCo, PetsMart, Target, TJ Maxx, Trader Joe's
2	NY 425, Colvin Blvd, **N** [food] Athena's Rest., KFC, McDonald's, Subway, Texas Roadhouse, Tim Horton, Wendy's [other] [H], Big Lots, Family$, Top's Foods/gas, **S** [gas] KwikFill [food] Just Pizza [other] Pepboys
1b a	Elmwood Ave, NY 384, NY 265, **N** [gas] KwikFill [food] Franco's Pizza, John's Pizza/Subs, Subway, Touch of Italy [lodging] Center Way Motel [other] [H], $Tree, auto repair, Rite Aid, **S** [gas] Sunoco/dsl [food] Arby's
0mm	I-190. **I-290 begins/ends on I-190 in Buffalo.**

INTERSTATE 390 (Rochester)

Exit #	Services
20b a	I-490. **I-390 begins/ends on I-490 in Rochester.**
19(75)	NY 33a, Chili Ave, **N** [other] AutoZone, URGENT CARE, **S** [gas] Sunoco [food] Burger King, KFC, Little Caesar's, Pizza Hut, Subway [lodging] Motel 6, Quality Inn [other] $General
18b a	NY 204, Brooks Ave, **N** [lodging] Ramada Inn, **S** [lodging] Fairfield Inn [other] [airport]
17(73)	NY 383, Scottsville Rd, **S** [gas] 7-11/dsl, Fastrac/dsl
16(71)	NY 15a, to E Henryetta, **N** [other] [H], Costco/gas, **S** [food] Delmonico's Rest., TGI Friday's [lodging] Country Inn&Suites, Courtyard, Hampton Inn, Holiday Inn Express [other] Rite Aid
15(70)	I-590, Rochester
14(68)	NY 15a, NY 252, **E** [food] Dunkin', Gray's Cafe, Jeremiah's, Outback Steaks, Tully's Rest. [lodging] Extended Stay America, Residence Inn [other] $Tree, Top's Foods/gas, **W** [gas] Mobil/dsl [food] Bar Louie, Boston Mkt, Buffalo Wild Wings, Burger King, Dunkin', Five Guys, Jimmy John's, Moe's SW, Sonic, Starbucks, Subway, Taco Bell [lodging] Best Western, DoubleTree Inn, Hampton Inn, Holiday Inn, Home 2 Suites [other] Big Lots, Staples, Verizon

R
O
C
H
E
S
T
E
R

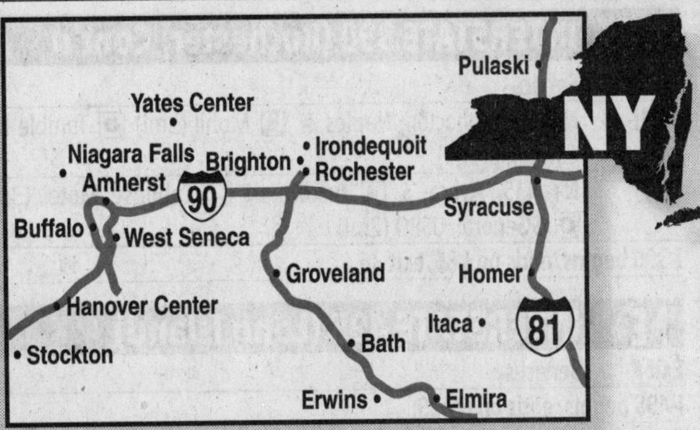

Exit #	Services
13(67)	Hylan Dr, **E** [gas] Fastrac/dsl [food] Cracker Barrel [lodging] Comfort Suites, Homewood Suites, **W** [gas] Mobil/dsl [food] Chili's, Chipotle, ChuckECheese, IHOP, Joe's Crabshack, Longhorn Steaks, McDonald's, Olive Garden, Panera Bread, Qdoba, Red Robin, Smashburger, Starbucks, Subway, Tim Hortons, TX Roadhouse, Uno Grill, Wendy's [other] Aldi Foods, Best Buy, BJ's Whse, Dick's, JC Penney, Lowe's, Marshall's, Michael's, Old Navy, PepBoys, PetCo, Target, Walmart, Wegman's Foods
12(66)	I-90. NY Thruway, NY 253, **W** [gas] Gulf/dsl/scales, Mobil/dsl, Speedway [food] Lehigh Rest., McDonald's, Peppermint's Rest., Tim Hortons, Wendy's [lodging] Country Inn&Suites, Days Inn, Fairfield Inn, Microtel, Red Carpet Inn, Red Roof Inn, Super 8 [other] Buick/GMC
11(62)	NY 15, NY 251, Rush, Scottsville, **2 mi N** [food] McDonald's, Tim Hortons, Wendy's [lodging] Fairfield Inn, Red Roof Inn
10(55)	US 20, NY 5, Avon, Lima, **N** [gas] Exxon [food] Countryside Diner [lodging] CrestHill Inn, Stratford Inn, **S** [gas] Quicklee's/dsl [food] Avon Cafe (3mi), Dutch Hollow Cafe (3mi), McDonald's (3mi), Subway (3mi), Tom Wahls Cafe (3mi) [lodging] Avon Cedar Lodge (3mi) [other] Chrysler/Dodge/Jeep, Ford, Sugar Creek Camping (3mi)
9mm	scenic area wb
9(52)	NY 15, **N** [gas] Mobil/Dunkin'/dsl [food] Fratelli's Rest., Lakeville Rest., McDonald's, Tee&Gee Cafe [lodging] Rodeway Inn [other] Chevrolet
8(48)	US 20a, Geneseo, **N** [other] Conesus Lake Camping, **2 mi S** [gas] Mobil/Dunkin' [food] Applebee's, Denny's, KFC/Taco Bell, McDonald's, Subway, Tim Hortons, Wendy's [lodging] Hampton Inn, Quality Inn [other] $Tree, Aldi Foods, AT&T, AutoZone, GNC, Petsmart, Verizon, Walmart, Wegman's
7(39)	NY 63, NY 408, Geneseo, **N** [other] st police, **S** [gas] Doughboys/dsl, KwikFill, Valero/dsl [food] Dunkin', McDonald's [lodging] Alligence B&B, Country Inn&Suites, Geneseo River Hotel/Rest., Greenway Motel [other] Bonadonna Auto, Family$, Letchworth SP, Ridge Camping, Rite Aid, Save-A-Lot Foods
38mm	[rest stop] **both lanes, full [handicapped] facilities, litter barrels, petwalk, [picnic], vending**
6(33)	NY 36, Mt Morris, Sonyea
5(26)	NY 36, Dansville, **N** [gas] KwikFill/dsl, Mobil/7-11/dsl [food] Arby's, Burger King, Dunkin', McDonald's, Pizza Hut, Subway, Taco Bell [other] $Tree, Advance Parts, BigLots, Chevrolet, Chrysler/Dodge/Jeep, CVS Drug, Rite Aid, Save-A-Lot Foods, Top's Foods/gas, Verizon, **S** [gas] TA/Valero/Country Pride/dsl/scales/24hr/@
4(23)	NY 36, Dansville, **N** [gas] Sunoco/dsl [lodging] Logan's Inn [other] [H], **S** [other] Skybrook Camping, Stonybrook Park Camping, Sugar Creek Camping, Sunvalley Camping
3(17)	NY 15, NY 21, Wayland, **N** [other] CarQuest (1mi), Holiday Hill Campground (7mi), st patrol

NY

INTERSTATE 390 (Rochester) Cont'd

Exit #	Services
2(11)	NY 415, Cohocton, Naples, N Mobil (2mi) Tumble Hill Camping (3mi)
1(2)	NY 415, Avoca, S Arrowmart Caboose Motel (3mi) $General, USPO (2mi)

I-390 begins/ends on I-86, exit 36.

INTERSTATE 495 (Long Island)

RIVERHEAD

Exit #	Services
I-495 begins/ends on NY 25.	
73	rd 58, Old Country Road, to Greenport, Orient, **0-2 mi E** Petsmart, **0-2 mi S** BP, Citgo, EVC, Mobil/dsl, Speedway/dsl Applebee's, Buffalo Wild Wings, Chipotle, IHOP, Panera Bread, Starbucks, Taco Bell, TGIFriday's, Wendy's Hilton Garden, Holiday Inn Express Aldi Foods, AT&T, Best Buy, Buick/GMC, Chevrolet, Costco/gas, CVS Drug, Dick's, Ford/Lincoln, Harley-Davidson, Home Depot, Honda, Kia/Mazda, Lowe's, Michael's, Nissan/Hyundai, PetCo, Stop&Shop, Subaru/VW, Tanger/famous brands, Target, Toyota, Volvo, Walgreens, Walmart/Subway
72	NY 25, (no ez eb return), Riverhead, Calverton (no EZ eb return), N funpark, S Speedway Hotel Indigo Tanger/famous brands/foodcourt
71	NY 24, to Hampton Bays (no ez eb return), Calverton, N Exxon/dsl
70	NY 111, to Eastport, Manorville, S 7-11, Cumberland Farms/dsl, EVC McDonald's, Starbucks, Wendy's CVS Drug, King Kullen Food/drug
69	Wading River Rd, Center Moriches, S golf
68	NY 46, to Shirley, Wading River, S Mobil Carlo's Pizzaria 7-11
67	Yaphank Ave, N USPO
66	NY 101, Sills Rd, Yaphank, N Shell/dsl
65.5mm	**parking area both lanes**
65	Horse Block Rd, N Baskin-Robbins/Dunkin' $Tree
64	NY 112, to Coram, Medford, N Speedway DQ, Subway 7-11, Family$, Lowe's, Michael's, Sam's Club, Target, TJ Maxx, Verizon, Walgreens, S BP (2), BP/Dunkin', Sunoco/dsl J&R Steaks, Starbucks Comfort Inn, Fairfield Inn 7-11, AutoZone
63	NY 83, N Ocean Ave, N Speedway/dsl, Stop'n Shop/gas Applebee's, Burger King, McDonald's, Starbucks, Taco Bell, TGIFriday's 7-11, CVS Drug, Hampton Inn, S BP/dsl, Gulf/dsl Sonoma Grill Ramada Plaza
62	Nicolls Rd, rd 97, to Blue Point, Stony Brook, N BP, S Chili's, On the Border, Subway, Wendy's Residence Inn
61	rd 19, to Patchogue, Holbrook, N Mobil, S BP/dsl, Speedway/dsl China 4, Greek Islands Rest., Joe's Pizza/Pasta, Outback Steaks, Subway 7-11, Advance Parts, CVS Drug
60	Ronkonkoma Ave, N USPO, S Mobil Red Lobster, Smokey Bones BBQ Courtyard, Homewood Suites
59	Ocean Ave, to Oakdale, Ronkonkoma, S BP/Dunkin', Sunoco Hilton Garden (2mi) 7-11
58	Old Nichols Rd, Nesconset, N Gulf/Dunkin' Starbucks Jake's 58 Hotel BJ's Whse
57	NY 454, Vets Hwy, to Hauppauge, N BP/dsl TGIFriday's, S BP, Mobil, Shell, Sunoco Dave&Buster's, Islandia Buffet Hampton Inn 7-11, AT&T, Mavis Tire, Stop&Shop Foods, TJ Maxx, Verizon, Walgreens, Walmart/McDonald's

MEDFORD

NY

HICKSVILLE

Exit #	Services
56	NY 111, Smithtown, Islip, N BP/Dunkin' Trop Smoothie, S Sunoco/dsl Steve's Italian Holiday Express
55	rd 67, Motor Pkwy, Central Islip, N Mobil Chip Dunkin', IHOP, Madison Steaks, Subway, S Shell/dsl
54	Wicks Rd
53	Sagkitos Pkwy, Bay Shore, Kings Park, Bayshore, N B 11 Applebee's Radisson, S Mobil
52	rd 4, Commack Rd, N Babylon, Commack, N Citgo/dsl, C berland Farms, Shell/dsl Ara Greek Kitchen, Chick-fi Premier Diner, Red Robin, Starbucks, Starbucks (2) Ha ton Inn Costco, Home Depot, Jo-Ann, Kohl's, Lowe's, M shall's, ShopRite Mkt, Verizon, Walmart
51.5mm	**LI Welcome Ctr eb, full facilities/parking area wb, litter bar**
51	NY 231, to Northport, Babylon
50	Bagatelle Rd, to Wyandanch
49N	NY 110 N, to Huntington, N Marriott, S Jewel Rest.
49S	NY 110 S, to Amityville
48	Round Swamp Rd, Old Bethpage, S Cumberland Far dsl Hilton Garden, Homewood Suites, Sheraton USP
46	Sunnyside Blvd, Plainview, N Holiday Inn, S 7-11
45	Manetto Hill Rd, Plainview, Woodbury
44	NY 135, to Seaford, Syosset
43	S Oyster Bay Rd, to Syosset, Bethpage, N BP
42	Northern Pkwy, rd N, Hauppauge
41	NY 106, NY 107, Hicksville, Oyster Bay, N Starbucks, Wh Foods Mkt CVS Drug, Marshall's, USPO, S BP, Mobil, noco Arby's, Boston Mkt, Broadway Diner, Chick-fil-A, Chi tle, Dunkin', Five Guys, McDonald's, On the Border, Red Lobs Starbucks $Tree, AT&T, Goodyear/auto, Petco, Verizon
40	NY 25, Mineola, Syosset, S BP, Speedway/dsl Bu er King, Dunkin', KFC, Kobe Hibachi, McDonald's, W dy's Hampton Inn, Jericho Inn 7-11, Chrysler/Dodg Jeep, Home Depot, Kohl's
39	Glen Cove Rd, N Mobil
38	(from eb) Northern Pkwy E, Meadowbrook Pkwy, to Jones Bea
37	Willis Ave, to Roslyn, Mineola, N BP, Shell Dunk Green Cactus Mexican, Skinny Pizza, S Mobil/dsl L Joe Rest.
36	Searingtown Rd, to Port Washington, N H
35	Shelter Rock Rd, Manhasset, S H
34	New Hyde Park Rd
33	Lakeville Rd, to Great Neck, N H
32	Little Neck Pkwy, N Shell/Burger King Centre Piz Chipotle, Five Guys, Panera Bread, Starbucks Petco, Veriz
31	Douglaston Pkwy, S BP/service Grimaldi's Pizza, Ja Asian Fairway Mkt, USPO, vet
30	E Hampton Blvd, Cross Island Pkwy
29	Springfield Blvd, S BP/Dunkin' Starbucks GNC
27	I-295, Clearview Expswy, Throgs Neck, N Barney's Bl Bay Diner 7-11, EVC
26	Francis Lewis Blvd
25	Utopia Pkwy, 188th St, N Citgo, Mobil Courtyar Fairfield Inn, S Gas Sale/dsl, Gulf, Mobil Applebee Arby's, Dunkin', Five Guys, Hooters, Qdoba, Subway Wyn ham Garden Michael's, USPO
24	Kissena Blvd, N BP/dsl Dunkin', Subway, S Mobi
23	Main St, N Lake Pavilion
22	Grand Central Pkwy, to I-678, College Pt Blvd, N Holid Inn Express
21	108th St, N BP/7-11, Mobil Holiday Inn Express

INTERSTATE 495 (Long Island) Cont'd

Exit #	Services
19	NY 25, Queens Blvd, Woodhaven Blvd, to Rockaways, N Applebee's, Cheesecake Factory, Chick-fil-A, Longhorn Steaks, McDonald's, Olive Garden, Popeye's JC Penney, Macy's, S Mobil Burger King, Chipotle, Dallas BBQ, Starbucks, Subway Wyndham Garden Aldi Foods, Costco, CVS, Kohl's, Marshall's, Old Navy, TJ Maxx, USPO
18.5	69th Ave, Grand Ave (from wb)
18	Maurice St, N Exxon/Dunkin'/dsl Comfort Inn dsl repair, S Maspeth Deli, McDonald's Holiday Inn Express
17	48th St, to I-278, N Mobil City View Inn
16	**I-495 begins/ends in NYC.**

NOTES

NORTH CAROLINA

INTERSTATE 26

Exit#	Services
71mm	North Carolina/South Carolina state line
69mm	N Pacolet River
67.5mm	**Welcome Ctr wb, full facilities, litter barrels,**
67	US 74 E, to NC 108, Columbus, Tryon, N Shell//dsl, Vgo/dsl Cocula Mexican, Joy Wok, Larkin's Carolina Grill, McDonald's, Subway, Waffle House, Wendy's Advance Parts, CVS Drug, Family$, Food Lion, S Exxon/dsl KFC/Taco Bell, Mtn View Deli Days Inn H, $General, Bi-Lo
59	Saluda, N Saluda Mtn Lodge, S BP/dsl, Marathon/Subway/dsl Crust&Kettle Cafe, Saluda Rest. Orchard Inn B&B (2mi) $General, AppleMill Outlet, Atkins Fruit, camping, repair, vet
56mm	Green River
54	US 25 (from eb), to Greenville, E Flat Rock, to Carl Sandburg Home
53.5mm	2130 ft, Eastern Continental Divide
53	Upward Rd, Hendersonville, N Marathon/Dunkin'/dsl Waffle House, Zaxby's Fairfield Inn, Mtn Inn&Suites Bloomfields Giftshop, Lakewood RV Park, Wildflower RV Park, S Exxon/McDonald's, Shell/pizza Cracker Barrel, Poplar Leaf Cafe, Subway Holiday Inn Express, Quality Inn repair, to Carl Sandburg Home
49b a	US 64, Hendersonville, N Marathon/dsl, Shell/dsl, Sunoco/dsl Chick-fil-A, Golden Corral, Jack-in-the-Box, Moose Cafe, O'Charley's, Sonic, Starbucks, Waffle House, Zaxby's Best Western, Hampton Inn, Quality Inn, Ramada Inn $Tree, Advance Parts, Ingles/gas, PetCo, Sam's Club/gas, Staples, Walmart, World of Clothing, S Exxon/dsl/LP, Shell/dsl Applebee's, Arby's, Binion's Roadhouse, Bojangles, Burger King, China Buffet, Denny's, Fatz Café, Hardee's, Harry's Rest., HoneyBaked Ham, KFC, Krispy Kreme, LJ Silver, Lon Sen Chinese, McDonald's, Outback Steaks, Pizza Hut, Subway, Taco Bell, Tequila's Grill, Wendy's Days Inn, EconoLodge, Red Roof Inn H, Aldi Foods, Belk, BigLots, Bi-Lo Foods, Chrysler/Dodge/Jeep, Clark Tire/auto, CVS Drug, Family$, Home Depot, Jo-Ann, Lowe's, NAPA, TJ Maxx, Tuesday Morning, Verizon
46mm	**weigh sta both lanes,**
44	US 25, Fletcher, N Exxon/dsl Hardee's, Subway flea mkt/campground, vet, S Citgo/dsl, Shell/DQ/dsl/scales/24hr, Sonny's/dsl Bojangles, Burger King, McDonald's, Valentina's Mexican Mountain Inn&Suites H, Camping World RV Ctr, USPO
41mm	**both lanes, full facilities, litter barrels, , vending**
40	NC 280, Arden, N Fastop/dsl, Shell/Arby's Bojangles, Carrabba's, Casa Torres, Chili's, Cracker Barrel, Firehouse Subs, IHOP, Jersey Mike's, Little Caesar's, Lonestar Steaks, McDonald's, Moe's SW Grill, Olive Garden, Ruby Tuesday, Sonic, Tamarind Thai, Tokyo Express Budget Motel, Clarion, Comfort Inn, Courtyard, EconoLodge, Hampton Inn, Knight's Inn Acura/Honda, Aldi Foods, Best Buy, BigLots, Dick's, Lowe's, Marshalls, Michael's, Old Navy, Petsmart, Ross, Rutledge Lake RV Park, Target, World Mkt, S Citgo/dsl Circle B Ranch BBQ, J&S Cafeteria Fairfield Inn Asheville Airport, BMW
37	NC 146, Skyland, N BP Arby's, Brixx Pizza, Broken Egg Cafe, Coldstone, Hickory Tavern, McDonald's, Neo Burrito, PF Chang's, Starbucks, Waffle House, Which Wich? Hilton, Quality Inn Barnes&Noble, CVS Drug, Ingles/gas, REI, S Chevrolet
34mm	French Broad River
33	NC 191, Brevard Rd, 2 mi N Asheville Farmers Mkt, Bear Creek RV Camp, Toyota, S Citgo, HotSpot/dsl Apollo Flame, Harbor Inn Seafood, LJ Silver, McDonald's, Papa's Mexican, Ryan's, Shogun Buffet, Stoneridge Grill, Subway, Taco Bell, Waffle House Comfort Suites, Country Inn&Suites, Fairfield Inn, Hampton Inn, Hilton Garden, Holiday Inn Express, Rodeway Inn $Tree, Asheville Outlets, Belk, Dillards, Field&Stream, Ingles Foods/dsl, Kia, PetCo, to Blue Ridge Pkwy, Verizon
31b a	I-40, E to Statesville, W to Knoxvilles
27mm	I-240 E, Patton Ave
	I-26 and I-240 run together 3 mi. See NC I-240 exits 1-4.
25	rd 251, N to UNCA
24	Elk Mtn Rd, Woodfins
23	Merrimon Ave, N Asheville, N Gulf/dsl, HotSpot Bellagio Bistro, Frank's Pizza, Moe's BBQ Days Inn camping, vet
21	New Stock Rd, N Citgo/dsl, Shell Domino's, Granny's Kitchen, Pizza Hut $General, Campfire Lodge RV Park, CVS, Ingles/gas
19b a	N US 25, W US 70, Marshall, N Shell/dsl Arby's, Bojangles, Burger King, Chapala Mexican, IHOP, KFC, La Carreta Mexican, Little Caesars, McDonald's, Peking East, Subway, TCBY, Waffle House, Zaxby's Ace Hardware, Advance Parts, Aldi Foods, AutoZone, BigLots, Ingles/dsl, Roses, URGENT CARE, Verizon, S Shell/DQ/dsl Steak'n Shake $Tree, CVS, Lowe's, Walmart/Subway
18	Weaverville (no EZ return from eb)s

HENDERSONVILLE

ARDEN

ASHEVILLE

INTERSTATE 26 Cont'd

Exit #	Services
17	to Flat Creeks
15	rd 197, to Jupiter, Barnardsvilles
13	Forks of Ivy, N [gas] Mkt Ctr/dsl, S [gas] Exxon/dsl
11	rd 213, to Mars Hill, Marshall, N [other] tires, S [gas] Exxon//Hardee's/dsl, TriCo [food] Bojangles, Osaka Japanese, Subway, Waffle House, Wagon Wheel Rest. [lodging] Comfort Inn [other] $General, CVS, Ingles/dsl, NAPA
9	Burnsville, Spruce Pine, N [other] to Mt Mitchell SP
7mm	**runaway truck ramp eb**, scenic overlook wb
6mm	**Welcome Ctr/[rest stop] eb, full [handicap] facilities**
5.5mm	**runaway truck ramp eb**
5mm	Buckner Gap, elev. 3370
3	to US 23 A, Wolf Laurel, N [gas] Exxon/dsl [food] Little Creek Cafe [other] to ski areas
2.5mm	**eb runaway truck ramp**
.5mm	**eb brake insp sta**
0mm	North Carolina/Tennessee state line

INTERSTATE 40

WILMINGTON

Exit #	Services
420mm	**I-40 begins/ends at Wilmington, Services N on US 17** [food] Buffalo Wild Wings, Hiro Japanese Steaks [lodging] Hampton Inn, TX Roadhouse [other] CarQuest, Home Depot, Hyundai, Kia, Kohl's, Land Rover, Mazda, Nissan, Subaru, Toyota, Volvo, **Services S on US 17** [gas] Exxon, Murphy USA/dsl [food] Arby's, Bojangles, Bonefish Grill, Carrabba's, Chick-fil-A, ChopStix, Church's, Cracker Barrel, Dunkin', Elizabeth's Pizza, Hieronymus Seafood Co, Hooters, IHOP, Jason's Deli, McDonald's, Olive Garden, Sonic, Subway, Taco Bell, Waffle House [lodging] AmeriStay, Best Western+, Budgetel, Comfort Suites, Country Inn Suites, Days Inn, Extended Stay America, Holiday Inn, Jameson Inn, MainStay Suites, Quality Inn, Red Roof Inn, Rodeway Inn, Sleep Inn, Staybridge Suites, Travel Inn, Wingate Inn [other] Advance Parts, AutoZone, Batteries+, Black's Tires/auto, Cadillac, Costco/gas, Petsmart, Target, URGENT CARE, VW, Walgreens, Walmart, **Services 2-4 mi S on US 117/NC 132** [gas] BP/dsl, Exxon/dsl [food] Applebee's, Bojangles, Carolina Ale House, Chili's, CiCi's Pizza, College Diner, Cookout, Golden Corral, HoneyBaked Ham, Jersey Mike's, Jimmy John's, Kickback Jack's, Little Caesar's, McAlister's Deli, McDonald's, Mission BBQ, Okami Japanese, Outback Steaks, Starbucks, Wendy's [lodging] Baymont Inn, Comfort Inn, Courtyard, Holiday Inn Express [other] $Tree, AT&T, Best Buy, Buick/GMC, Chevrolet, Chrysler/Dodge/Jeep, Dick's, Harris-Teeter, Honda, Jo-Ann, Lowe's Foods, Lowe's Whse, Mercedes, Old Navy, PetCo, Ross, Sam's Club/gas, Staples, TJ Maxx, to UNCW, Verizon
420b a	Gordon Rd, NC 132 N, 2 mi N [gas] Shell/dsl [other] KOA (4mi), S [gas] BP/dsl, Circle K/dsl, Go Gas/dsl [food] China Wok, Dunkin', McDonald's, Subway, Taco Bell [other] $General, Family$, Lowe's Foods, Rite Aid
416b a	I-140, US 17, to Topsail Island, New Bern, Myrtle Beach
414	Holly Shelter Rd, to Brunswick Co beaches, Castle Hayne, S [gas] BP, Circle K/dsl, GoGas/dsl [food] Carolina Cafe, Domino's, Hardee's, Hwy 55 Cafe, Subway [other] $General, CVS Drug, Fresh Foods IGA, USPO
413mm	NE Cape Fear River
408	NC 210, N [other] Mack/Volvo/Isuzu, S [gas] Phoenix TC/Exxon/Subway/dsl/scales, Shell/Freshway Cafe/dsl, Speedway/Wendy's/dsl [food] Hardee's, McDonald's [other] Advance Parts, Family$, Food Lion, to Moore's Creek Nat Bfd/camping, USPO
398	NC 53, Burgaw, 2 mi S [gas] Shell/dsl, Walmart/dsl [food] Bojangles, Domino's, Hardee's, KFC, McDonald's, Subway, Taco Bell [lodging] Burgaw Motel [other] [H], $Tree, Advance Parts, Food Lion, Walmart
390	to US 117, Wallace
385	NC 41, Wallace, N [gas] Exxon/Village Subs, Tesla EVC [food] Bojangles, Mad Boar Rest. [lodging] Holiday Inn Express [other] Lake Leamon Camping, 1.5 mi S [gas] Murphy USA/dsl, Speedway/dsl [food] Burger King, Domino's, McDonald's, Sensation Farmhouse Rest., Subway, Taco Bell, Zaxby's [other] $General, $Tree, Food Lion, O'Reilly Parts, Verizon, Walgreens, Walmart/Subway
384	NC 11, Wallace
380	Rose Hill, S [gas] BP/Subway/dsl (1mi), Comco, Kwikstop (1mi) [other] Duplin Winery, Family$
373	NC 24 E, NC 903, Magnolia, N [gas] BP/dsl, Exxon/dsl/e85 [other] [H], Cowan Museum
369	US 117, Warsaw
364	NC 24, to NC 50, Clinton, N [gas] Pilot/Arby's/Dunkin/dsl/24hr, S [rest stop] **both lanes, full [handicap] facilities, litter barrels, petwalk, [phone], [picnic], vending** [gas] BP/dsl, Citgo [food] Bojangles, Cookout, KFC, McDonald's, Smithfield's BBQ, Subway, Taco Bell, Waffle House, Wendy's [lodging] Best Value Inn, Quality Inn
355	NC 403, to US 117, Goldsboro, Faison, 3 mi N [gas] Exxon
348	Suttontown Rd
343	US 701, Newton Grove, 1 mi N [gas] Exxon/dsl, to Bentonville B...
341	NC 50, NC 55, to US 13, Newton Grove, 1.5 mi N [gas] Exxon/dsl [food] Hardee's [other] Food Lion, S [gas] BP/McDonald's, Shell/Subway/dsl [food] Smithfield BBQ [other] Family Auto/tire
334	NC 96, Meadow, S [gas] Short Stop/dsl [other] $General
328b a	I-95, N to Smithfield, S to Benson
325	NC 242, to US 301, to Benson, S [gas] Marathon/dsl
324mm	[rest stop] **both lanes, full [handicap] facilities, litter barrels, no overnight parking, petwalk, [phone], [picnic], vending**
319	NC 210, McGee's Crossroads, N [gas] BP/BBQ/dsl, Shell/Dunkin/dsl [food] McDonald's [other] [H], vet, S [gas] Mobil/dsl, Sheetz/dsl [food] Bojangle's, China Star, Domino's, Italian Pizza/Pasta, KFC/Taco Bell, Subway, Wendy's [other] $General, AutoZone, CVS Drug, Food Lion
312	NC 42, to Clayton, Fuquay-Varina, N [gas] Murphy Express/dsl, Speedway/Dunkin'/dsl/24hr, Speedway/Wendy's/dsl [food] Applebee's, China King, Cookout, Cracker Barrel, Divano's Pizza, Fiesta Mexicana, Hibachi&Co, Hwy 55 Burger, Jersey Mike's Subs, King Chinese, Pizza Inn, Ruby Tuesday, Smithfield BBQ, Wendy's [lodging] Comfort Inn, Holiday Inn Express, Super 8, Woodspring Suites [other] $Tree, JustTires, Lowe's, URGENT CARE, Verizon, Walmart/McDonald's, S [gas] BP/Subway/dsl, Exxon/Burger King, Marathon/dsl, Shell/dsl [food] Bojangle's, Domino's, DQ, Jumbo China, KFC/Taco Bell, Little Caesar's, McDonald's, Snoopy Hotdogs, Waffle House, Yummi Japan [lodging] Hampton Inn, Sleep Inn [other] AutoZone, CVS Drug, Food Lion, vet, Walgreens
309	US 70 E, Goldsboro, Smithfield
306b a	US 70 E bus, to Smithfield, Garner, Goldsboro, 1 mi N [gas] Citgo/dsl, Kangaroo/Subway/dsl [other] Chrysler/Dodge/Jeep, S [gas] Sheetz/dsl [food] Blaze Pizza, Buffalo Bros Pizza, Buffalo Wild Wings, Carolina Alehouse, Char-Grill, Chick-fil-A, Chili's, Chipotle, City BBQ, Coldstone, Five Guys, Kaze Japanese, La Cocina Mexican, Logan's Roadhouse, Longhorn Steaks, McDonald's, Moe's SW Grill, New Japan Express, Panera Bread, Prima Vera Pizza, Red Robin, Starbucks, Subway, TGIFriday's, Wendy's, Zaxby's [other] $Tree, AT&T, Best Buy, BJ's Whse/gas, Burlington, Cabela's, Dick's, GNC, Kohl's, Michael's, Petsmart, Ross, Staples, Target, TJ Maxx

NC

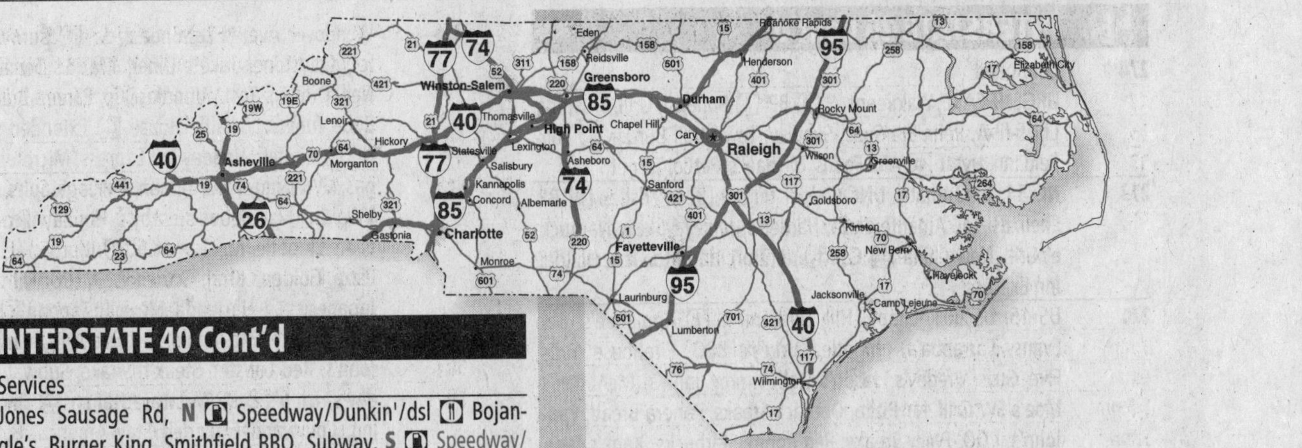

INTERSTATE 40 Cont'd

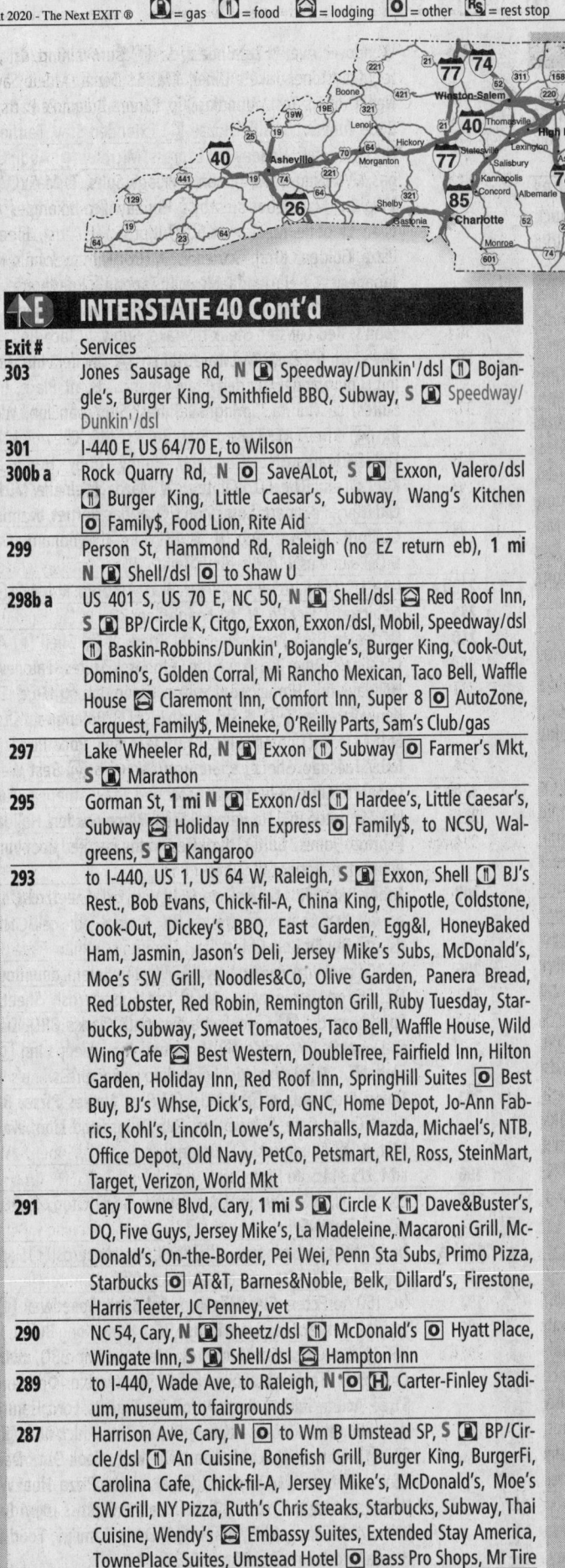

Exit #	Services
303	Jones Sausage Rd, N Speedway/Dunkin'/dsl Bojangle's, Burger King, Smithfield BBQ, Subway, S Speedway/Dunkin'/dsl
301	I-440 E, US 64/70 E, to Wilson
300b a	Rock Quarry Rd, N SaveALot, S Exxon, Valero/dsl Burger King, Little Caesar's, Subway, Wang's Kitchen Family$, Food Lion, Rite Aid
299	Person St, Hammond Rd, Raleigh (no EZ return eb), 1 mi N Shell/dsl to Shaw U
298b a	US 401 S, US 70 E, NC 50, N Shell/dsl Red Roof Inn, S BP/Circle K, Citgo, Exxon, Exxon/dsl, Mobil, Speedway/dsl Baskin-Robbins/Dunkin', Bojangle's, Burger King, Cook-Out, Domino's, Golden Corral, Mi Rancho Mexican, Taco Bell, Waffle House Claremont Inn, Comfort Inn, Super 8 AutoZone, Carquest, Family$, Meineke, O'Reilly Parts, Sam's Club/gas
297	Lake Wheeler Rd, N Exxon Subway Farmer's Mkt, S Marathon
295	Gorman St, 1 mi N Exxon/dsl Hardee's, Little Caesar's, Subway Holiday Inn Express Family$, to NCSU, Walgreens, S Kangaroo
293	to I-440, US 1, US 64 W, Raleigh, S Exxon, Shell BJ's Rest., Bob Evans, Chick-fil-A, China King, Chipotle, Coldstone, Cook-Out, Dickey's BBQ, East Garden, Egg&I, HoneyBaked Ham, Jasmin, Jason's Deli, Jersey Mike's Subs, McDonald's, Moe's SW Grill, Noodles&Co, Olive Garden, Panera Bread, Red Lobster, Red Robin, Remington Grill, Ruby Tuesday, Starbucks, Subway, Sweet Tomatoes, Taco Bell, Waffle House, Wild Wing Cafe Best Western, DoubleTree, Fairfield Inn, Hilton Garden, Holiday Inn, Red Roof Inn, SpringHill Suites Best Buy, BJ's Whse, Dick's, Ford, GNC, Home Depot, Jo-Ann Fabrics, Kohl's, Lincoln, Lowe's, Marshalls, Mazda, Michael's, NTB, Office Depot, Old Navy, PetCo, Petsmart, REI, Ross, SteinMart, Target, Verizon, World Mkt
291	Cary Towne Blvd, Cary, 1 mi S Circle K Dave&Buster's, DQ, Five Guys, Jersey Mike's, La Madeleine, Macaroni Grill, McDonald's, On-the-Border, Pei Wei, Penn Sta Subs, Primo Pizza, Starbucks AT&T, Barnes&Noble, Belk, Dillard's, Firestone, Harris Teeter, JC Penney, vet
290	NC 54, Cary, N Sheetz/dsl McDonald's Hyatt Place, Wingate Inn, S Shell/dsl Hampton Inn
289	to I-440, Wade Ave, to Raleigh, N H, Carter-Finley Stadium, museum, to fairgrounds
287	Harrison Ave, Cary, N to Wm B Umstead SP, S BP/Circle/dsl An Cuisine, Bonefish Grill, Burger King, BurgerFi, Carolina Cafe, Chick-fil-A, Jersey Mike's, McDonald's, Moe's SW Grill, NY Pizza, Ruth's Chris Steaks, Starbucks, Subway, Thai Cuisine, Wendy's Embassy Suites, Extended Stay America, TownePlace Suites, Umstead Hotel Bass Pro Shops, Mr Tire
285	Aviation Pkwy, to Morrisville, N Sheetz/dsl Hilton Garden Raleigh/Durham Airport
284	Airport Blvd, N Capital City Chophouse Cambria Suites, Country Inn&Suites, Hyatt Place to RDU Airport, S BP/Circle/dsl, Mobil Bojangles, Carmen's, Cracker Barrel, Hooters, KFC/Taco Bell, Los Tres Magueyes, Peng's Asian, TX Steaks, Waffle House, Wendy's Courtyard, Days Inn, Extended Stay America, Fairfield Inn, Hampton Inn, Holiday Inn, Holiday Inn Express, La Quinta, Microtel, Residence Inn, Sheraton, Staybridge Suites Morrisville Outlets/famous brands/food court
283	I-540 E, toll I-540 W, to US 70, Aviation Pkwy
282	Page Rd, S Arby's, Bojangles, Jimmy John's, McDonald's, Mez Cafe, Page Road Grill, Starbucks Comfort Suites, DoubleTree, Sheraton, Sleep Inn, Wingate Inn Office Depot
281	Miami Blvd, N Extended Stay America, Hilton Garden, Marriott, S BP, Shell/dsl Arby's, Bojangles, Burger King, McDonald's, Quiznos, Randy's Pizza, Serena, Subway, Tropical Smoothie, Wendy's, Wok'n Grill, Zaxby's Extended Stay America, Holiday Inn Express, Homewood Suites, Hotel Indigo Office Depot
280	Davis Dr, N to Research Triangle
279b a	NC 147 N, Triangle Expwy, to Durham, N H
278	NC 55, to NC 54, Apex, Foreign Trade Zone 93, N Marathon Jimmy's Hotdogs, Sansui Grill, Waffle House Comfort Inn, DoubleTree, EconoLodge, La Quinta, Red Roof Inn, S BP, Exxon/dsl, Mobil/dsl Arby's, BBQ Pit, Bojangles, Brigs Rest., Capt D's, Chick-fil-A, Cinco de Mayo, CookOut, El Dorado Mexican, Golden Corral, Hardee's, Little Caesar's, McDonald's, Papa John's, Pizza Hut, Starbucks, Subway, Taco Bell, Thai 55, Wendy's, William's Kitchen Candlewood Suites, Courtyard, Crossland Suites, Extended Stay America, Residence Inn $Tree, Aamco, Advance Parts, AutoZone, BigLots, Colonial Tire, CVS Drug, Firestone/auto, Food Lion, Jiffy Lube, Just Tires, Meineke, NAPA, O'Reilly Parts, Precision Tune, Walgreens
276	Fayetteville Rd, N Circle K/dsl, Exxon/Circle K/dsl China Cafe, City BBQ, McDonald's, Melting Pot, Orient Garden, Ruby Tuesday, Waffle House, Wendy's GNC, Kroger/dsl, Roses, to NC Central U, Walgreens, S Bufflo Wild Wings, CA Pizza Kitchen, Champp's Rest, Cheesecake Factory, Chili's, Chipotle, Firebird's, Fork-in-the-Road Cafe, Jersey Mike's, Los Tres Mexican, Maggiano's, McAlister's Deli, Melting Pot, Moe's SW Grill, Panera Bread, PF Chang's, Ruth's Chris Steaks, Starbucks, Ted's MT Grill Hilton Garden AT&T, Barnes&Noble, Belk, Best Buy, Buick/Cadillac/GMC, Chevrolet, JC Penney, Macy's, Mercedes, Nordstrom, Old Navy, Porsche, REI, World Mkt
274	NC 751, to Jordan Lake, N BP, Marathon Asian Kitchen, Burger King, Char Grill, Denny's, Dunkin', Jimmy John's, KFC, Marco's Pizza, Taco Bell, Which Wich?, Wing Stop Advance Parts, CVS Drug, Harris Teeter, Honda, Lexus, Rite Aid, Sheetz/dsl,

RALEIGH

CARY

NC

 = gas = food = lodging = other = rest stop

INTERSTATE 40 Cont'd

CHAPEL HILL

274 Continued
URGENT CARE, Walgreens, S BP Bonefish Grill, Bruster's, Chick-fil-A, Penn Sta Subs, Subway, Town Hall Burger Fairfield Inn, Hyatt Aldi Foods, Michael's, PetCo, Target

273 NC 54, to Durham, UNC-Chapel Hill, N BP/dsl, S BP, Shell/dsl Amante Pizza, Hardee's, Jersey Mike's, Nantucket Grill, New China Courtyard (2mi), Hampton Inn, Holiday Inn Express

270 US 15, US 501, Chapel Hill, Durham, N Applebee's, Bob Evans, Carrabba's, Chipotle, Dickey's BBQ, Firehouse Subs, Five Guys, Freddy's, Jason's Deli, Jimmy John's, McAlister's, Moe's SW Grill, NY Pizza, Outback Steaks, Panera Bread, Papa John's, PDQ, Philly Steaks, Red Robin, Starbucks, Xank's Japanese Comfort Inn, Home 2 Suites, Homewood Suites, SpringHill Suites, Staybridge Suites $Tree, AT&T, Barnes&Noble, Best Buy, Dick's, Home Depot, H S, Kohl's, Kroger/dsl, Marshalls, Michael's, Old Navy, Petsmart, to Duke U, Verizon, Walmart/Subway, S Petco Hardee's, La Hacienda, McDonald's, Starbucks, Subway, Wendy's Quality Inn, Red Roof Inn, Residence Inn, Sheraton, University Inn Acura, Advance Parts, AutoZone, BMW, CVS Drug, Food Lion, Lowe's, Mr Tire, Subaru, Trader Joe's

266 NC 86, to Chapel Hill, **2 mi** S BP, Exxon, Speedway/dsl Jersey Mike's, Subway

263 New Hope Church Rd

261 Hillsborough, **1.5 mi** N BP/Circle K, Citgo/dsl McDonald's, Pizza Hut Holiday Inn Express

259 I-85 N, to Durham

I-40 and I-85 run together 30 mi. See I-85, exits 131-161.

GREENSBORO

226 McConnell Rd, S Exxon

224 E Lee St, to US 29 N, to US 220 N, N BP/dsl, Shell/dsl Holiday Inn Express, Rodeway Inn

223 to N US 29, E US 70, N US 20, Reidsville

222 MLK Jr (from eb), Sanford, S Arby's, Biscuitville, Burger King, McDonald's, Subway, Taco Bell Domino's, Ocean Blue Seafood Rest., Wendy's Advance Parts, CVS Drug, Food Lion, Hall Tire Co, Walmart Mkt

221 S Elm-Eugene St, N Citgo/dsl, Valero AutoZone, Family$, Food Lion, O'Reilly Parts, S BP, Shell/dsl EconoLodge, Super 8 Home Depot

220 Randleman Rd, US 220 S, to Greensboro, Ashboro, N Marathon/dsl, Valero Biscuitville, Church's, KFC, McDonald's, Pizza Hut, Sub Sta 2, Subway Greensboro Tire, Harley-Davidson, Rite Aid, Save-A-Lot, S BP, Kangaroo Cook-Out, Mayflower Seafood, Waffle House, Wendy's

219 US 29 S, W US 70, Highpoint (exits left from wb), Charlotte

218 US 220, Freeman Mill Rd, Ashboro

217 Highpoint Rd, Koury Blvd (from wb), N Exxon, Shell/dsl Biscuitville, Burger King, Chili's, Ham's Rest, Hooters, Ichiban Grill, J Butler's Grille, Little Caesar's, Olive Garden, Sakura Japanese, Santa Fe Mexican, Subway, Taco Bell DoubleTree Hotel, Hampton Inn, Holiday Inn, Quality Inn, Red Roof Inn, Super 8 $General, $Tree, Office Depot, S Shell Bonefish Grill, Carrabba's, Darryl's Grill, Jimmy John's, Krispy Kreme, McDonald's, Popeye's, Smokey Bones BBQ, Waffle House, Wendy's, Zaxby's Baymont Inn, Best Western, Comfort Suites, Drury Inn, Howard Johnson, Ramada Inn, Sheraton, Studio 6 Dillard's, Discount Tire, JC Penney, O'Reilly Parts, Walmart Mkt

216 (from eb), Greensboro, N coliseum

NC

WINSTON•SALEM

214 Wendover Ave, N Sheetz/dsl Burger King, China B fet, Coldstone, Jake's Diner, Mario's Pizza, Moe's SW G New Orleans Rest., Noodles&Co, Panera Bread, Penn Sta Su Ruby Tuesday, Waffle House Extended Stay, Fairfield Hilton Garden, Holiday Inn Express, Microtel Audi, Cost gas, CVS Drug, Ford, Nissan, PetCo, Staples, TJ Maxx, Veriz VW, S Applebee's, Arby's, Biscuitville, Bojangles, Chi fil-A, Chipotle Mexican, CookOut, Cracker Barrel, Elizabet Pizza, Golden Corral, Golden Wok, IHOP, Jimmy John's, Kab Japanese, La Hacienda Mexican, Logan's Roadhouse, Lo horn Steaks, McDonald's, O'Charley's, Panda Express, Pa John's, Red Lobster, Steak'n Shake, Subway, Taco Bell, TGI day's, Tripp's Rest., Villarosa Italian Comfort Inn, Comf Inn, Courtyard, Extended Stay America, Hyatt Place, InTo Suites, La Quinta, SpringHill Suites, Suburban Inn, Winga Inn $Tree, AT&T, Best Buy, Buick/GMC, Chevrolet, Dick Field&Stream, GNC, Goodyear, Hobby Lobby, Home Dep Kohl's, Land River/Jaguar, Lowe's, Mazda, Meineke, Michae Old Navy, Petsmart, Ross, Sam's Club/gas, Target, Walmart

213 Guilford College Rd, N BP/dsl Wyndham Gard S same as 214, Sheetz vet

212b a I-73, US 241 S, to I-85, to Bryan Blvd, Ashboro, N to

211 Gallimore Dairy Rd, N Freightliner

210 NC 68, to High Point, Piedmont Triad, N Shell Arby Carolina's Diner Days Inn, Embassy Suites, Fairview In Holiday Inn, Homewood Suites, Sleep Inn Ford Truc Kenworth, to , S Exxon/dsl Bojangles, Dunki Fatz Cafe, McDonald's, Pizza Hut/Taco Bell, Pollo Pizza/Pas Ruby Tuesday, Shoney's, Subway, Wendy's Best Weste Comfort Suites, Courtyard, Extended Stay America, Fairfie Inn, Hampton Inn, Hawthorn Suites, Hilton Garden, Holiday I Express, Home 2 Suites, Motel 6, Quality Inn, Red Roof Inn, Re idence Inn, SpringHill Suites

208 Sandy Ridge Rd, N Exxon/Subway/dsl, Sheetz/dsl, Spee way/dsl Camping World RV Ctr, S Shell/Circle dsl Out Of Doors Mart

206 Lp 40 (from wb), to Kernersville, Winston-Salem, downtown

203 NC 66, to Kernersville, N QM/Subway/dsl, Sheetz/d Speedway/dsl Capt Tom's Seafood, Clark's BBQ, Dairi- McDonald's, Wendy's Hampton Inn, Sleep Inn Ford, NTB, S Shell/dsl Holiday Inn Express

201 Union Cross Rd, N BP/dsl Blue Naples Pizza, Burg King, China Café, Subway CVS Drug, Food Lion, Walma Mkt, S Sheetz/dsl Bojangle's

196 I-74, US 311 S, to High Point

195 US 311 N, NC 109, to Thomasville, S Citgo, Speedwa dsl Family$

193b a US 52, NC 8, to Lexington, S Shell, Speedway/dsl Hardee

193c Silas Creek Pkwy (from eb), same as 192

192 NC 150, to Peters Creek Pkwy, N Shell, Speedway Bo jangles, Burger King, Hero House Rest, Hong Kong Buffet, IHO KFC, Little Caesar's, Monterrey Mexican, Mr BBQ, Subwa Taco Bell, Tokyo Japanese University Inn $Genera $Tree, Acura/Subaru, Audi, AutoZone, BigLots, Ford, Hamrick' Hyundai, Infiniti, Mazda, Office Depot, Rite Aid, VW, S B QM Arby's, Baskin-Robbins/Dunkin', Cook-Out, Dairi-C K&W Cafeteria, McDonald's, Papa John's, Pizza Hut, Waff House, Wendy's, Zaxby's Holiday Inn Express Advanc Parts, Aldi Foods, BMW/Mini, CVS Drug, Family$, Food Lio Honda, Mock Tire, Toyota

190 Hanes Mall Blvd (from wb, no re-entry), N Carolina Alehous Chipotle Mexican, Coldstone, Elizabeth's Pizza, Genghis Gril

INTERSTATE 40 Cont'd

E

190 Continued
Jimmy John's, McDonald's, Ruby Tuesday, TGIFriday's, Tripp's Rest. Best Western Belk, Dick's, Dillard's, Firestone/auto, JC Penney, Macy's, Marshalls, same as 189, S Bad Daddy's Burger, Burger King, ChuckECheese, Outback Steaks, Pan Asian, Starbucks, Subway Comfort Suites, Microtel

189 US 158, Stratford Rd, Hanes Mall Blvd, N BJ's Rest., Bojangles, Chili's, Golden Corral, Honeybaked Ham, Olive Garden, Red Lobster, Red Robin, Taco Bell, TX Roadhouse Courtyard, Fairfield Inn H, Belk, Buick/GMC, Cadillac, Chevrolet, Dillard's, JC Penney, Macy's, Walgreens, S Shell Applebee's, Bleu Rest., Brixx Pizza, Buffalo Wild Wings, Cheddar's, Chick-fil-A, Firebirds Grill, Five Guys, Hooters, Jason's Deli, Jersey Mike's, KFC/LJ Silver, Longhorn Steaks, Mario's Pizza, Moe's SW Grill, Panera Bread, Qdoba, Subway, Tin Tin Asian, Twin Peaks, Village Tavern, Which Wich?, Zaxby's Extended Stay America, Hampton Inn, Hilton Garden, La Quinta, Residence Inn, Sleep Inn, SpringHill Suites $Tree, AT&T, Barnes&Noble, Best Buy, Costco/gas, CVS Drug, Discount Tire, Hobby Lobby, Home Depot, Kohl's, Lowe's, Michael's, NTB, Petsmart, Ross, Sam's Club/gas, Target, Verizon

188 US 421, to Yadkinville, to WFU (no EZ wb return), Winston-Salem1/2mi off US 421, N BP, Exxon, Kangaroo, Shell Arby's, Burger King, Cook-Out, Dickey's BBQ, McDonald's, Starbucks, Waffle House, Wendy's CarMax, Lexus, Mercedes, Verizon, vet, Walmart/Subway

184 to US 421, Clemmons, N Mobil/7-11, Shell Applebee's, Dairi-O, Dunkin', IHOP, K&W Cafe, KFC, Milner Bros Rest., Panera Bread, Steak Escape Quality Inn, S BP/dsl, Circle K, Speedway/dsl Arby's, Biscuitville, Brick Oven Pizza, Burger King, Cracker Barrel, Domino's, Kimono Japanese, Krispy Kreme, Little Richard's BBQ, McDonald's, Mi Pueblo Mexican, Mtn Fried Chicken, Pizza Hut, Ruby Tuesday, Sonic, Starbucks, Subway, Taco Bell, Time to Eat Cafe, Waffle House, Wendy's Super 8, Village Inn $Tree, Advance Parts, AutoZone, BigLots, CVS Drug, GNC, Lowe's Foods, Meineke, NTB, O'Reilly Parts, Staples, USPO, Verizon, vet, Walgreens, Walmart Mkt

182 Bermuda Run, Tanglewood, S Chang Thai, Jersey Mike's, Lee's Chinese, Monte De Rey Mexican, Papa John's, Subway Harris-Teeter, Tanglewood Camping

182mm Yadkin River

180 NC 801, Tanglewood, N Sheetz/dsl Capt's Galley Seafood, Domino's, La Carreta Mexican, Subway Hampton Inn H, Lowe's Foods/dsl, Rite Aid, S BP/McDonald's/dsl, Speedway/dsl Asian View, Bojangles, Jade Garden, Miyabi Japanese, Venezia Italian, Wendy's, Zaxby's $General, Ace Hardware, CVS Drug, Food Lion, Walgreens

177mm both lanes, full facilities, litter barrels, petwalk, vending

174 Farmington Rd, N Shell/dsl, S vineyards

170 US 601, Mocksville, N Citgo/dsl, Murphy USA/dsl, TA/Shell/Country Pride/Popeye's/dsl/scales/24hr JinJin Chinese, La Carreta Mexican $Tree, Campers Inn RV Ctr, GNC, Verizon, Walmart/Subway, S BP, Sheetz/dsl, Speedway/Taco Bell Arby's, Bojangles, Burger King, China Grill, Domingo's Mexican, Dunkin', Dynasty Chinese, East Coast Grill, KFC, Marco's Pizza, McDonald's, Papa John's, Pizza Hut, Sagebrush Steaks, Shiki Japanese, Subway, Waffle House, Wendy's Comfort Inn, Days Inn, HighWay Inn, Scottish Inn H, $General, Advance Parts, Lowe's, O'Reilly Parts, USPO, vet, Walgreens

MOCKSVILLE

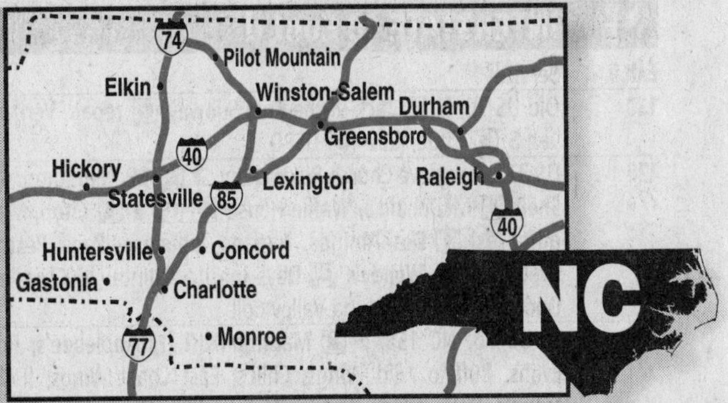

MOCKSVILLE

168 US 64, to Mocksville, N Exxon/dsl Lake Myers RV Resort (3mi), S BP/dsl H

162 US 64, Cool Springs, N Lake Myers RV Resort (5mi), S Shell/dsl Midway Camping

161mm S Yadkin River

154 to US 64, Old Mocksville Rd, N H, S Citgo/dsl, Loves/McDonald's/dsl/scales/24hr Jaybee's Hotdogs repair/tires

153 US 64 (from eb), 1/2 mi S Citgo/dsl Jaybee's Hotdogs repair/tires

152b a I-77, S to Charlotte, N to Elkin

STATESVILLE

151 US 21, E Statesville, N Marathon/DQ/dsl, Speedway/dsl Applebee's, Baskin-Robbins/Dunkin', Bojangles, Chick-fil-A, Chili's, Cook-Out, Cracker Barrel, K&W Cafeteria, KFC, Logan's Roadhouse, McDonald's, Mi Pueblo Café, Red Lobster, Ruby Tuesday, Shiki Japanese, Sorrento's Italian, Taco Bell, Wendy's, Zaxby's Days Inn, Sleep Inn $Tree, Advance Parts, Aldi Foods, AutoZone, BigLots, Chevrolet, CVS Drug, GNC, Hobby Lobby, Home Depot, Lowe's, Meineke, Michael's, NTB, Petsmart, Staples, TJ Maxx, URGENT CARE, Verizon, Verizon, Walmart/Subway, S Exxon BJ Hibachi, Greg's BBQ, Lonestar Steaks, Olde 1847 Pizza&Wing, Sonic, Waffle House Holiday Inn Express, Masters Inn, Quality Inn H, $General, URGENT CARE

150 NC 115, Statesville, N BP/dsl, Citgo, Sheetz/dsl, Shell/Subway Amalfi's Italian, Little Caesar's, Ol'Bob's BBQ, Waffle Shop $General, CVS Drug, Food Lion, Fred's, museum

148 US 64, NC 90, W Statesville, N Citgo/dsl, Shell Arby's, BoxCar Grille, Burger King, McDonald's, Shiki Japanese, Subway, Village Inn Pizza Economy Inn $General, CVS Drug, Ingles Foods

146 Stamey Farm Rd, N truck repair

144 Old Mountain Rd, N Backyard's Troy's Rest., S BP/dsl, Shell/dsl

143mm weigh sta both lanes

141 Sharon School Rd, N Citgo/dsl

140mm Catawba River

138 NC 10 W, Oxford School Rd, to Catawba, N Valero/dsl

136mm both lanes, full facilities, litter barrels, petwalk, vending

135 Claremont, S Shell/7-11 BoxCar Grille, Burger King, Hannah's BBQ, Hardee's, New Panda, Subway Rodeway Inn $General, Carolina Coach RV Ctr, Lowe's Foods

133 Rock Barn Rd, N Shell/dsl, S Pilot/Subway/dsl/scales/24hr

132 to NC 16, Taylorsville, W Hwy 55 Cafe, N Marathon/Kangaroo, Murphy USA/dsl, Shell/dsl Burger King, Jin's Buffet, Subway, Zaxby's Holiday Inn Express $Tree, AT&T, AutoZone, Walmart

NC

= gas = food = lodging = other = rest stop

INTERSTATE 40 Cont'd

Exit #	Services
130	Old US 70, N Jack-in-the-Box, Subway repair, Verizon, vet, S Citgo, Pure USPO
128	US 321, Fairgrove Church Rd, Hickory, N BP, Marathon/dsl, Shell McDonald's, Waffle House H, S Citgo, Marathon/dsl Dos Amigos, Nagano Japanese, Papa Pesto's Greek/Italian, Wendy's Days Inn, La Quinta Chrysler/Dodge/Jeep, to Catawba Valley Coll
126	to US 70, NC 155, S Marathon/dsl Applebee's, Bob Evans, Buffalo Wild Wings, Chili's, East Coast Wings, IHOP, Jason's Deli, Krispy Kreme, McDonald's, O'Charley's, Olive Garden, Panera Bread, Popeye's, Taco Bell Holiday Inn Express Barnes&Noble, Discount Tire, Hickory Furniture Mart, Lowe's, Michael's, PetCo, Ross, Sam's Club/gas, URGENT CARE, Walmart/McDonald's
125	Hickory, N RaceWay/dsl Bojangles, Dickey's BBQ, Golden Corral, Hardee's, Kickback Jack's Grill, Mellow Mushroom, Rancho Viejo, Starbucks, TX Roadhouse Red Roof Inn $General, Aamco, Advance Parts, Firestone/auto, S Shell/dsl, Speedway/dsl Arby's, Atlanta Bread, Burger Fi, Carrabba's, Chick-fil-A, Chipotle, ChuckECheese, CiCi's Pizza, Coldstone, Cracker Barrel, Five Guys, Hooters, J&S Cafeteria, Jack-in-the-Box, KFC, Kobe Japanese, Longhorn Steaks, NY Hibachi Buffet, Outback Steaks, PDQ Rest., Red Lobster, Ruby Tuesday, Tony's Pizza, Waffle House, Wendy's, Which Wich?, Wild Wok, Zaxby's Baymont Inn, Best Western, Courtyard, Crowne Plaza, Fairfield Inn, Hampton Inn, Hilton Garden, Quality Inn, Sleep Inn $Tree, Aldi Foods, AT&T, Belk, Best Buy, Carmax, Dick's, Dillard's, Food Lion, Ford, Hamrick's, Harley-Davidson, Home Depot, Honda, JC Penney, Kohl's, Mazda, NAPA, Nissan, NTB, Office Depot, Old Navy, O'Reilly Parts, Petsmart, Sunrise Camping Ctr, Suzuki, Target, TJ Maxx, Toyota, Verizon
123	US 70/321, to NC 127, Hickory
121	Long View, N Kenworth
119b a	Hildebran, N Shell/Subway Bojangles, Hardee's $General
118	Old NC 10, N Pure, Shell/dsl
116	Icard, S Marathon/McDonald's/dsl Burger King, Granny's Kitchen Icard Inn USPO
113	Connelly Springs, N Citgo/dsl Patsy Ann's Rest, Subway H, CVS Drug, Ford/Hyundai, Walgreens
112	Mineral Springs Mtn Rd, Valdese
111	Valdese
107	NC 114, to Drexel
106	Bethel Rd, S Exxon/dsl Economy Inn/rest.
105	NC 18, Morganton, N BP/Dunkin'/dsl Abele's Rest., Arby's, Capt D's, Cracker Barrel, Fatz Café, Harbor Inn Seafood, Las Salsas, McDonald's, Sonic, Wendy's, Zaxby's, Zeko's Italian Hampton Inn H, Chevrolet/Buick/GMC, S Shell/dsl El Paso Mexican, Sagebrush Steaks, Waffle House Quality Inn, Sleep Inn to South Mtns SP
104	Enola Rd, S Chen's Garden $Tree, BigLots, Food Lion
103	US 64, Morganton, N Citgo/dsl, Exxon/dsl Allison's Rest., Chick-fil-A, Cook-Out, Village Inn Pizza Days Inn, S Marathon, RaceWay/dsl Bojangles, Butch's BBQ, Denny's, Hardee's, KFC, Subway, Taco Bell, Tokyo Diner Comfort Inn $General, Clark Tire/auto, Food Lion, Honda, Ingles Foods, Lowe's
100	Jamestown Rd, N BP/dsl Waffle Shop Chrysler/Dodge/Jeep, Ford/Lincoln
98	Causby Rd, to Glen Alpine, S B&B/food
96	Kathy Rd
94	Dysartsville Rd, Lake James, N Lake James SP
90	Lake James, Nebo, N Nebo/dsl to Lake James S Marathon/dsl Springs Creek RV Ctr
86	NC 226, to Spruce Pine, Marion, N Exxon, Subway/Godfather's/dsl/scales/24hr Hardee's, KFC, Wa House Jellystone RV Park (2mi)
85	US 221, Marion, N Hampton Inn to Mt Mitchell S Marathon/dsl Best Value Inn, Super 8 $Gene
83	Ashworth Rd
82mm	both lanes, full facilities, litter barrels, petwalk, vending
81	Sugar Hill Rd, to Marion, N BP/dsl, Murphy Expre dsl Arby's, Bojangle's, Hwy 55 Cafe, Japanese Expre New China, Nopale's Mexican, Waffle House H, $Tr Chrysler/Dodge/Jeep, GNC, Walmart/Subway, S Subway/dsl
76mm	Catawba River
75	Parker Padgett Rd, S Exxon/Stuckey's/DQ/dsl
73	Old Fort, N BP/dsl Hardee's Auto+, S Sunoc dsl McDonald's
72	US 70 (from eb), Old Fort, N B&B
71mm	Pisgah NF, eastern boundary
67.5mm	truck eb
66	Ridgecrest, N B&B
65	(from wb), to Black Mountain, Black Mtn Ctr
64	NC 9, Black Mountain, N Shell/Subway Pizza Hut, Starbucks Hampton Inn, S BP/dsl Denny's, McDonald's, Phil's BBQ, Starbucks, Taco Bell, Wendy's Quality I Ingles Foods/gas, Walgreens
63mm	Swannanoa River
59	Swannanoa, N BP/Subway, Shell/dsl Athens Pizz Burger King, Don Chon Chinese, Papa John's Ace Hardware, CVS Drug, Family$, Harley-Davidson, Ingles Foods/ga KOA (2mi), Miles RV Ctr/Park, to Warren Wilson Coll, USPO, v S Mama Gertie's Camping
55	US 70, E Asheville, N BP, Citgo/Subway, Mobil Arby Bojangles, Cocula Mexican, Domino's, Gondolier Italian, Waffle House, Zaxby's Days Inn, Holiday Inn, Motel 6, Quali Inn Family$, Folk Art Ctr, Go Groceries, Tap's RV park, to Mitchell SP, VA H, vet
53b a	I-240 W, US 74 a, to Asheville, Bat Cave, S Shell/dsl So ic, Subway CVS Drug, Ingles, to Blue Ridge Pkwy, N on Fa view Rd Ay Carumba Mexican, China Buffet, J&S Cafeteri KFC, Little Caesars, McDonald's, Papa John's, Pizza Hut, Subway Ramada Inn $General, Advance Parts, Citgo/d CVS Drug, Hamrick's, Home Depot, Meineke
51	US 25A, Sweeten Creek Rd, S Subway Brookstone Lod
50	US 25, Asheville, N Market Ctr, Shell, Shell/dsl Arby' Asaka Japanese, Chapala Mexican, Hardee's, Jimmy John's, Silver, McDonald's, Moe's SW Grill, Ruth's Chris Steaks, Starbucks, Subway, TGIFriday's, TX Roadhouse, Wendy's, Zoe Kitchen Baymont Inn, Biltmore Village Lodge, Doubletree Inn, Grand Bohemian Hotel, Guesthouse Inn, Residen Inn H, to Biltmore House, URGENT CARE, S Speedway/dsl Apollo Flame Rest., Atl Bread Co, Bojangles, Hu dle House, Juicy Lucy's Advance Parts, Ingles/deli
47mm	French Broad River
47	NC 191, W Asheville, N Bear Creek RV Camping, S BP Subway Moose Cafe Comfort Suites, Country Inn& Suites, Fairfield Inn, Hampton Inn, Holiday Inn Express, Rodeway Inn Audi/Porsche/VW, Farmer's Mkt, Ford, Nissan

HICKORY

MORGANTON

ASHEVILLE

NC

INTERSTATE 40 Cont'd

Exit #	Services
46b a	I-26 & I-240 Em, **2 mi N** multiple services from I-240
44	US 19, US 23, W Asheville, **N** BP, Shell/DQ/dsl, Speedway/dsl Applebee's, Arby's, Bojangle's, Burger King, Cracker Barrel, Dunkin', El Chapala Mexican, Fatz Cafe, Hardee's, IHOP, Subway, Waffle House, Wendy's, Yao Grill Comfort Inn, Country Inn&Suites, Ramada Inn, Red Roof Inn, Rodeway Inn, Sleep Inn, Whispering Pines Motel Chevrolet, Chrysler/Dodge/Jeep, Lowe's, Mazda/Mercedes, **S** McDonald's, Zaxby's Asheville Inn, Holiday Inn, Woodspring Suites Bi-Lo Foods, CVS Drug, Home Depot
41mm	**weigh sta both lanes**
37	Candler, **N** Sunoco, TA/Country Pride/dsl/scales/24hr/@ Goodyear/truck tires, **S** Exxon/dsl Days Inn, Plantation Motel $General, KOA
33	Newfound Rd, to US 74, **S** Exxon
31	Rd 215, Canton, **N** Sagebrush Steaks Best Value Inn URGENT CARE, **S** BP/dsl, Marathon/DQ, Shell/dsl Arby's, Bojangles, Burger King, McDonald's, Starbucks, Subway, Taco Bell, Waffle House Quality Inn Ford, Ingles Foods/dsl, RV/truck repair
27	US 19/23, to Waynesville, Great Smokey Mtn Expswy, **3 mi S** Burger King, Coffee Cup Cafe, Subway Super 8 H, $Tree, Food Lion, GNC, Lowe's, to WCU (25mi)
24	NC 209, to Lake Junaluska, **N** Pilot/Subway/dsl/scales/24hr/@ Midway Motel, **S** Shell/cafe/dsl/24hr H
20	US 276, to Maggie Valley, Lake Junaluska, **S** BP/dsl, Exxon/dsl, Marathon (2mi) Creekwood RV Park, Pride RV Resort, Winngray RV Park
16mm	Pigeon River
15	Fines Creek
13mm	Pisgah NF eastern boundary
10mm	**both lanes, full facilities, litter barrels, petwalk, ,** **vending**
7	Harmon Den
4mm	tunnel both lanes
0mm	North Carolina/Tennessee state line

INTERSTATE 74

Exit #	Services
23	US 220 S, **I-74/73 begins/ends.**
25	US 220 N, Ellerbe
28	to NC 73 W, Millstone Rd
30	Haywood Parker Rd
33	NC 73
35	Norman
39	Tabernacle Church Rd
41	US 220 S, US 220 A N, Candor
44	NC 211, Candor, Pinehurst, **N** Exxon/dsl, Pilot/Dunkin'/Wendy's/dsl/scales/24hr, **S** Citgo/dsl $General
49	NC 24, 27, Troy, Carthage, **S** Citgo Bojangle's, Hardee's, Waffle House Day Inn $General
52	Star, Robbins
56	US 220 A, Ether, Steeds
58	Black Ankle Rd
60	**/visitor ctr both lanes, full facilities**
61	NC 705, Seagrove, Robbins, **N** Citgo/Hardee's/dsl
66	New Hope Church Rd
68	US 220, NC 134, Ulah, Troy

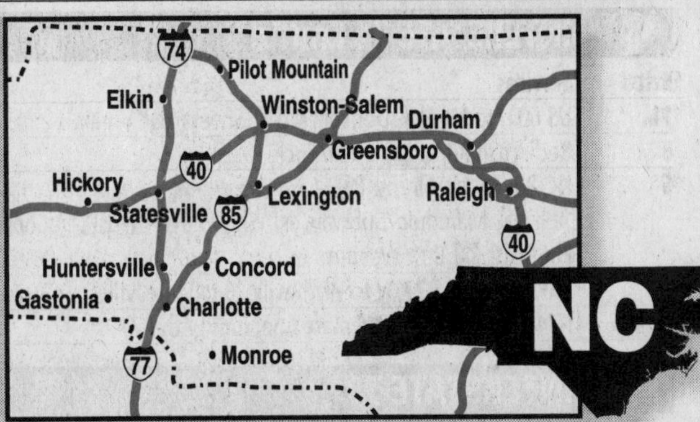

ASHEBORO

Exit #	Services
71	McDowell Rd, **N** Tank$Tommy, **S** K&W Cafeteria
72b a	US 64, NC 49, To Lexington, **N** BP, Speedway/dsl Arby's, Bamboo Garden, Biscuitville, Bojangle's, Burger King, Dunkin', Huddle House, McDonald's, Taco Bell, Wendy's Comfort Inn Lowe's Foods, **S** Citgo/dsl Subway Randolph Inn Food Lion
74	(exits left) Salisbury St, Sunset Ave
75	W Presnell St
76	Vision Dr
77	Spero Rd
79	Pineview St
86	(80 from wb) I-73 N (exits left from eb, runs with I-74)
84	US 311 S, Randleman, **S** Citgo USPO
79	Cedar Square Rd, Archdale
75	I-85, N to Greensboro, S to Charlotte
71b	I-85BR, US 29
71a	E Green St
70	MLK Dr, **S** H
69	Greensboro Rd, Jamestown, **N** Exxon Bojangle's Holiday Tire/auto, vet, **S** Citgo McDonald's Family$, SaveALot
67	NC 68, Eastchester Dr, to I-40, **S** Marathon/dsl Barbarito's, Honeybaked Ham URGENT CARE
66	Johnson St
65	US 311, N Main St, High Point, **S** Sheetz/dsl McDonald's Aldi Foods
63	NC 66, Kernersville
60	High Point Rd
59	Union Cross Rd
56	Ridgewood Rd
I-74 begins/ends on I-40, exit 196.	
Future I-74 connects via US 52 to US 311 around Winston Salem.	
122	Moore-RJR Dr, **N** Hanging Rock SP
123	King, Tobaccoville, **N** Exxon/7-11 Bojangle's, Burger King, KFC, Little Caesar's, Little Italy, McDonald's, Papa John's, Pizza Hut, Stratford BBQ, Subway, Taco Bell, Waffle House, Wendy's Bestway Inn $General, $Tree, Advance Parts, CVS Drug, Family$, Food Lion, Lowe's Foods, O'Reilly Parts, Rite Aid, USPO, vet, Walmart
127mm	scenic overlook wb
129	Pinnacle, **N** BP/dsl, **S** Marathon
131	Pilot Mtn SP
134	NC 268, Pilot Mtn, Elkin, **N** Exxon/dsl McDonald's, Mtn View Rest. Econolodge Advance Parts, **S** Shell/Circle K/dsl, Speedway/Dunkin'/dsl Wendy's
135	Pilot Mtn
136	Cook School Rd, **N** Blue Mtn/dsl, Gas&Go Ford
17	US 52 N, to Mt Airy
13	Park Dr

KING

PILOT MTN

NC

INTERSTATE 74 Cont'd

Exit #	Services
11	US 601, to Mt Airy, Dobson, N Sheetz/dsl
8	Red Brush Rd, N Shell/Circle K/dsl
6	NC 89, to Mt Airy, S FLYING J/Brintle's Rest./dsl/scales/24hr/@, Marathon/Subway/dsl, Shell/Circle K/dsl Copper Pot Rest. Best Western
5	(101 from eb) I-77, N to Wytheville, S to Statesville
0mm	**I-74 begins/ends at NC state line, runs with I-77.**

INTERSTATE 77

Exit #	Services
105mm	North Carolina/Virginia state line
105mm	**Welcome Ctr sb, full facilities, info, litter barrels, petwalk, , , vending**
103mm	**weigh sta both lanes**
101	I-74 E, to Mt Airy, Winston-Salem, Greensboro, E (12mi)
100	NC 89, to Mt Airy, E FLYING J/Brintle's Rest./dsl/scales/24hr/@, Marathon/Subway/dsl, Shell/Circle K/dsl Copper Pot Rest. Best Western dsl repair, (12mi)
93	to Dobson, Surry, E BP/DQ/dsl, Exxon/Circle K/dsl Diner, Harvest Grill (2mi), Putters Grill Hampton Inn, Surry Inn
85	NC 118, CC Camp Rd, to Elkin, 1-3 mi W Exxon/7-11/dsl, Murphy Express/dsl, Sheetz/dsl, Speedway/dsl Burger King, KFC, Mazzini's Italian, McDonald's, Sonic, Taco Bell, Zaxby's Fairfield Inn , $Tree, AT&T, BigLots, Food Lion, Lowe's, Rite Aid, Walmart/Subway
83	US 21 byp, to Sparta (from nb)
82.5mm	Yadkin River
82	NC 67, Elkin, E BP/Subway/dsl, Citgo/Case Outlet/dsl, Exxon/dsl Arby's, Cracker Barrel, Sixty Seven Pizza Best Western Holly Ridge Camping (8mi), W Speedway/Dunkin'/dsl Bojangles, Breakfastime, McDonald's, Valentino's Pizza, Waffle House, Wendy's Days Inn, Hampton Inn, Quality Inn $General, D-Rex Drug, Food Lion, URGENT CARE, vet
79	US 21 S, to Arlington, E Citgo/Subway/dsl Royal Inn, W BP/dsl Glenn's BBQ Best Value Inn
73b a	US 421, to Winston-Salem, 1 mi E Exxon/Subway/7-11/dsl
72mm	**nb, full facilities, litter barrels, petwalk, , , vending**
65	NC 901, to Union Grove, Harmony, E Van Hoy Farms Camping, W BP/dsl, Exxon/Subway/7-11/dsl Burger Barn $General, Ace Hardware, Fiddler's Grove Camping (2mi)
63mm	**sb, full facilities, litter barrels, petwalk, , , vending**
59	Tomlin Mill Rd, W Valero/dsl
58	**both lanes, full facilities**
56.5mm	S Yadkin River
54	US 21, to Turnersburg, E Citgo, W Exxon/7-11/dsl Arby's, Baskin-Robbins/Dunkin', Chick-fil-A, CookOut, Golden Corral, Zaxby's
51b a	I-40, E to Winston-Salem, W to Hickory
50	E Broad St, Statesville, E Citgo, Exxon/Kangaroo/dsl, Shell Arby's, Bojangles, Burger King, Domino's, Dunkin'/Hungry Howie's, East Coast Grill, IHOP, Little Caesar's, Los Compadres Mexican, McDonald's, Papa John's, Papa Murphy's, Pizza Hut, Shanghai Buffet, Starbucks, Subway, Taco Bell, Wendy's Brookwood Inn, Red Roof Inn $General, $Tree, AT&T, Belk, Bi-Lo, Food Lion, Rite Aid, URGENT CARE
49b a	US 70, G Bagnal Blvd, to Statesville, E BP, Citgo/dsl, Citgo/dsl, Marathon/dsl, Shell, Solo KFC, Outback Steaks, Rice Fun Chinese, Subway, Village Inn Pizza, Waffle House Best
49b a	Continued Value Inn, Best Western, Comfort Inn, Courtyard, Hamp Inn, Motel 6, Ramada Inn auto repair, Camping W RV Ctr, Ford/Lincoln, Harley-Davidson, Honda, Nissan, To ta, W Citgo/dsl, Exxon/dsl Hilton Garden, Micr Buick/GMC, Carquest, Chrysler/Dodge/Jeep
45	to Troutman, Barium Springs, E KOA, RV Repair
42	US 21, NC 115, to Troutman, Oswalt, E Pilot/Subw Dunkin'/dsl/scales/24hr, Sheetz/dsl Bojangles, McD ald's, Taco Bell, Wendy's AutoZone, Lowe's, W Cl Exxon/dsl Arby's to Lake Norman SP
39mm	**both lanes, full facilities, litter barrels, petwalk, , vending**
36	NC 150, Mooresville, E Circle K/dsl, Exxon, QT/dsl, Sh dsl Applebee's, CookOut, Denny's, Domino's, Fat Boys Re Hong Mei Buffet, Pizza Hut, Pomodoro's, Popeyes, Sonny's B Taco Bell, Waffle House, Wendy's, Zaxby's Days Inn, Fairfi Inn, Holiday Inn Express, Quality Inn $Tree, Belk, Big L Cadillac/Chevrolet, GNC, Jo-Ann Fabrics, Kia, Kohl's, Suba Tuesday Morning, URGENT CARE, Walmart/Subway, W cle K/dsl, Qt/dsl, Shell/dsl, Speedway/dsl Baskin-Robbi Dunkin', Bojangles, Buffalo Wild Wings, Charanda Mexic Chick-fil-A, Chili's, Chipotle, Chopstix, Cracker Barrel, Duckwort Grill, Firehouse Subs, Five Guys, Golden Corral, Hardee's, Hick Tavern Grill, Hooters, IHOP, Iron Thunder Grill, LoneStar Stea McAlister's Deli, McDonald's, Moe's SW Cafe, Noodles& O'Charley's, Panera Bread, Papa Murphy's, Red Robin, Rita's C tard, Sagebrush Steaks, Showmar's, Smoothie King, Sonic, St bucks, Steak'n Shake, Subway Carolina Inn, Hampton I Sleep Inn, Wingate Inn Advance Parts, AT&T, AutoZone, B Buy, BJ's Whse/gas, CVS Drug, Dick's, Discount Tire, Food Li Hobby Lobby, Lowe's, Michael's, NTB, Old Navy, PetCo, Petsm Ross, Sam's Club/dsl, Staples, Target, TJ Maxx, Tuffy Auto, V zon, vet, Walgreens, World Mkt
35	Brawley School Rd
33	US 21 N, E Shell Brusco's Pizza, China Express, I Iron Grill Japanese, Jeffrey's Rest, Jets Pizza, McDonal Starbucks, Subway Candlewood Suites, Hilton Gard SpringHill Suites, TownePlace Suites , W Citgo/ Marathon/dsl Arby's, Baskin-Robbins/Dunkin', Sauz Mexican Food Lion, vet
31	Langtree Rd, W Shell/dsl
30	Davidson, E BP, Exxon/dsl Char-Grill, Ming's Chine Subway Homewood Suites Harris-Teeter, to Davids College, Woodie's Auto Service, W North Harbor Rest
28	US 21 S, NC 73, Cornelius, Lake Norman, E Cashion/dsl, C go Acropolis Cafe Days Inn, Hampton Inn NAF vet, W Marathon/Circle K Asiana, Bojangles, Chica Dog, Choplin's Rest., Domino's, Dragon Buffet, Fresh Chef Ca Honeybaked Ham, Jersey Mike's, Jimmy John's, KFC, Little Ca sar's, Mac's BBQ, McAlister's Deli, McDonald's, Pizza Hut, St bucks, Subway, Taco Bell, Waffle House, Wendy's Clari Comfort Inn, EconoLodge, Microtel $Tree, Chrysler/Dodg Jeep, Fresh Mkt, Goodyear/auto, Hyundai, Infiniti, SteinMa USPO, Walgreens
25	NC 73, Concord, Lake Norman, E Exxon/7-11/dsl Bu er King, Chick-fil-A, Chili's, Duckworth's Grill, IHOP, Longho Steaks, McDonald's, Melting Pot, Moe's SW Grill, Panda E press, Panera Bread, Papa John's, Showmar's Rest., St bucks, Subway, Zaxby's Country Inn&Suites, Holiday I Express, Quality Inn , AAA, Advance Parts, AT&T, GN Harris-Teeter, Home Depot, Kohl's, Lowe's, Marshall's, PetC

ELKIN

STATESVILLE

MOORESVILLE

CONCORD

NC

INTERSTATE 77 Cont'd

25	Continued Staples, Target, Tuffy Auto, Verizon, vet, W Shell/Circle K/dsl Bob Evans, Bojangles, Bonefish Grill, Carrabba's, Chipotle, Hickory Tavern Grill, House of Taipei, Jason's Deli, Jimmy John's, Kabuto Japanese, Outback Steaks, Qdoba, Red Rock's Cafe, Starbucks, Subway, Taco Mac, Viva Chicken, Which Wich?, Zoe's Kitchen Candlewood Suites, Courtyard, Sleep Inn Barnes&Noble, Dick's, Office Depot, to Energy Explorium, Walgreens, Whole Foods Mkt
23	Gilead Rd, to US 21, Huntersville, E BP, Pittstop, Shell Baskin-Robbins/Dunkin Dounuts, Bojangles, Chico's Mexican, CookOut, Hardee's, Huntersville Rest., Jersey Mike's, Little Caesar's, Rocky's Pizza, Romanello's Subs, Subway, Taco Bell, Waffle House, Wendy's Best Western, Comfort Suites, Hampton Inn, Super 8 AutoZone, Buick/GMC, Food Lion, Ford, Goodyear/auto, Honda, Mazda, O'Reilly Parts, Rite Aid, Toyota, Tuesday Morning, USPO, vet, VW, W Shell/7-11/dsl Domino's, Firehouse Subs, Five Guys, Fusion Asian, Groucho's Deli, Hawthorne's Pizza, Killington's Rest., McDonald's, Papa Murphy's, Pizza Hut, Starbucks H, Batteries+, CVS Drug, Earth Fare, GNC, Harris-Teeter, Publix, URGENT CARE, Walgreens
19b a	S I-485 Outer, Rd 115, to Spartanburg
18	Harris Blvd, Reames Rd, E BP/Arby's, Shell/7-11/dsl Azteca Mexican, Bob Evans, Hickory Tavern, Jack-in-the-Box, Jimmy John's, Subway, Waffle House Comfort Suites, Courtyard, Fairfield Inn, Hilton Garden, Holiday Inn Express, Suburban Lodge H, Advance Parts, Staples, to UNCC, Univ Research Park, URGENT CARE, W Bravo Italian, Buffalo Wild Wings, Chick-fil-A, Chili's, East Coast Grill, Edomae Grill, Firebirds Grill, Firehouse Subs, Five Guys, Fox&Hound, Jersey Mike's, Mimi's Cafe, Moe's SW Grill, Olive Garden, On-the-Border, Panera bread, PF Chang's, Red Robin, Shane's Rib Shack, TGI Friday's, Wendy's Drury Inn $Tree, AT&T, Belk, Best Buy, Dick's, Dillard's, Discount Tire, Lowe's, Macy's, Old Navy, Petsmart, REI, Target, Verizon
16b a	US 21, Sunset Rd, E Circle K, QT/dsl, Shell/7-11/dsl Capt D's, Hardee's, KFC, McDonald's, Papa John's, Subway, Taco Bell, Wendy's Days Inn, Super 8 $General, AutoZone, Just$ave Foods, NAPA, O'Reilly Parts, W Circle K/dsl, Citgo/dsl, Shell/dsl/scales/24hr Baskin-Robbins/Dunkin', Bojangles, Bubba's BBQ, CookOut, Denny's, Domino's, Jack-in-the-Box, Little Caesar's, Subway, Waffle House Microtel, Sleep Inn Advance Parts, Aldi Foods, CVS Drug, Family$, Food Lion, Meineke, Walgreens
13b a	I-85, S to Spartanburg, N to Greensboro
12	La Salle St, W Marathon/dsl, Shell/dsl
11b a	I-277, Brookshire Fwy, NC 16
10b	Trade St, 5th St, E to Discovery Place, W Circle K Bojangles, Church's Family$
10a	US 21 (from sb), Moorhead St, downtown
9	I-277, US 74, to US 29, John Belk Fwy, downtown, E H, stadium
8	Remount Rd (from nb, no re-entry)
7	Clanton Rd, E QT/dsl, Shell/dsl Quality Inn, Super 8 Family$, W 7-11/dsl, BP
6b a	US 521, Billy Graham Pkwy, E Citgo, Exxon/dsl, Exxon/dsl (2), QT/dsl Arby's, Azteca Mexican, Bojangles, Burger King, Capt D's, Carolina Prime Steaks, Domino's, Dragon House, Firehouse Subs, HoneyBaked Ham, IHOP, KFC, Papa John's, Tres Pesos Grill, Waffle House Baymont Inn, Best Western, Clarion, Days Inn, Ramada, Sheraton CVS Drug, Family$,

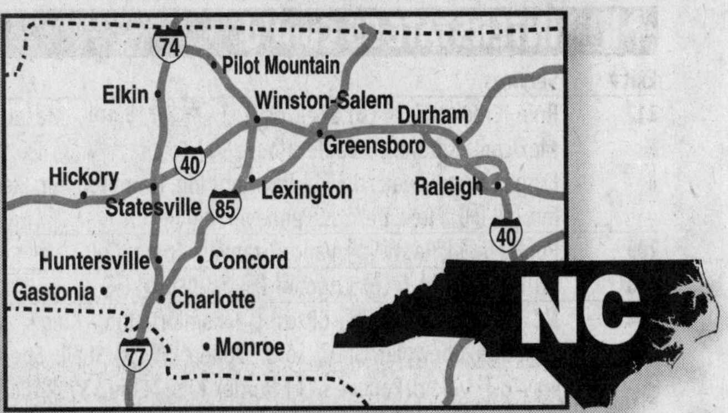

6b a	Continued Home Depot, TJ Maxx, to Queens Coll, Walgreens, W Circle K Courtyard, Embassy Suites, Extended Stay America, Hyatt House, InTowne Suites, La Quinta, Sleep Inn
5	Tyvola Rd, E Circle K, Exxon/7-11/dsl, Shell Chili's, Kabuto, McDonald's, Sonny's BBQ, Subway Cloverleaf Suites, Comfort Inn, Crowne Plaza, Extended Stay America, Hawthorn Suites, Hilton, Wyndham Garden Aldi Foods, Costco/gas, Maserati, Meineke, Verizon, W Extended Stay America, Home 2 Suites, Wingate Inn
4	Nations Ford Rd, E Citgo, Shell/Circle K Best Value Inn, Knights Inn, W Mobil/Burger King
3	Arrowood Rd, E Cafe South, Jack-in-the-Box, Sonic, Starbucks, Wendy's Courtyard, Fairfield Inn, Holiday Inn Express, Hyatt Place, Mainstay Suites, Sonesta Suites, TownePlace Suites, W Ruby Tuesday Drury Inn, Hampton Inn
2	I-485
1.5mm	**Welcome Ctr nb, full facilities, info, litter barrels, petwalk, vending**
1	Westinghouse Blvd, to I-485 (from nb), E BP/dsl Jack-in-the-Box, Subway, Waffle House Super 8, W Mobil/7-11/dsl
0mm	North Carolina/South Carolina state line

INTERSTATE 85

Exit #	Services
234mm	North Carolina/Virginia state line
233	US 1, to Wise
231mm	**Welcome Ctr sb, full facilities, litter barrels, petwalk,**
229	Oine Rd, to Norlina, E BP, W SRA
226	Ridgeway Rd, W to Kerr Lake, to SRA
223	Manson Rd, E USPO, W to Kerr Dam
220	US 1, US 158, Flemingtown Rd, to Middleburg, E Mobil/dsl, W Exxon/dsl/scales/truck wash Chex Trkstp/motel/rest.
218	US 1 S (from sb exits left), to Raleigh
217	Nutbush Bridge, E auto repair, W Kerr Lake RA
215	US 158 BYP E, Henderson (no EZ return from nb), E Citgo, Shell, Speedway/dsl Burger King, Forsyth's BBQ, Golden China, Subway Budget Host, EconoLodge, Scottish Inn $General, Food Lion, repair/tires, Roses, services on US 158
214	NC 39, Henderson, E BP, W Mobil/dsl, Shell to Kerr Lake RA
213	US 158, Dabney Dr, to Henderson, E Marathon, Valero Bamboo Garden, Big Cheese Pizza, Bojangles, Denny's, Domino's, Ichibar Chinese, KFC, McDonald's, Papa John's, Pino's Italian, Subway, Wendy's Family$, Food Lion, Roses, vet, W Shell Chick-fil-A, Golden Corral, Mayflower Seafood, Pizza Hut, Ruby Tuesday, Smithfields BBQ, Taco Bell Red Roof Inn Advance Parts, Buick/Chevrolet/GMC, Chrysler/Dodge/Jeep, Ford/Lincoln, Lowe's, Rite Aid, Staples, Verizon

= gas = food = lodging = other = rest stop

INTERSTATE 85 Cont'd

Exit #	Services
OXFORD	
212	Ruin Creek Rd, E Shell/dsl Cracker Barrel, Mazatlan Mexican, Ribeye's, Waffle House Toyota, W Exxon/Burger King, Sheetz/dsl Baymont Inn, Hampton Inn, Sleep Inn H, $Tree, Belk, JC Penney, Walmart
209	Poplar Creek Rd, W Vance-Granville Comm Coll
206	US 158, Oxford, E Citgo, W BP/dsl
204	NC 96, Oxford, E BP/dsl Comfort Inn, King's Inn Buick/Chevrolet/GMC, Ford, Honda, W Shell, Speedway/dsl, Valero/Popeye's Burger King, China Wok, Cook-Out, Domino's, KFC/Taco Bell, McDonald's, Pizza Hut, Subway, Wendy's Clarion H, GNC
202	US 15, Oxford, W Murphy Express/dsl Bojangles, Hwy 55 Cafe Crown Motel (2mi) $Tree, Verizon, Walmart
199mm	**both lanes, full facilities, litter barrels, petwalk,**
198mm	Tar River
BUTNER	
191	NC 56, Butner, E BP/dsl, Speedway/dsl Arby's, Bob's BBQ, Bojangles, Diner 56, Domino's, El Rio Mexican, KFC/Taco Bell, McDonald's, Pizza Hut, Pizza Mia, Sonic, Subway, Taste of China, Wendy's Inn at Creedmoor $General, $Tree, Advance Parts, AutoZone, Food Lion, M&H Tires, O'Reilly Parts, Rite Aid, to Falls Lake RA, Verizon, vet, W Exxon, Shell/dsl Hardee's, Old South Rest. Best Western, EconoLodge, Quality Inn auto repair
189	Butner, 1 mi W BP/dsl, Exxon/dsl, Valero BBQ Barn, Subway repair, 1 mi N $General
186b a	US 15, to Creedmoor, E Variety Mart/dsl
185mm	Falls Lake
183	Redwood Rd
182	Red Mill Rd, E Exxon/dsl Kenworth/Isuzu Trucks
180	Glenn School Rd, E Citgo/dsl Hwy 55 Cafe $Tree, AT&T, Verizon, Walmart/Subway
179	E Club Blvd, E Exxon
178	US 70 E, to Raleigh, Falls Lake RA, Research Triangle, E RDU Airport
DURHAM	
177	Avondale Dr, NC 55, W BP, Shell American Hero, Arby's, Guanajuato, McDonald's, Subway, Waffle House Advance Parts, AutoZone, Family$
176b a	Gregson St, US 501 N, E Mobil Burger King, Kickback Jack's, PanPan Diner, Randy's Pizza, Ruby Tuesday Hampton Inn W H, Museum of Life&Science
175	Guess Rd, E Citgo Hog Heaven BBQ, Pad Thai Holiday Inn Express, Super 8 Rite Aid, W BP/dsl, Exxon/dsl, Pure/dsl Bojangles, IHOP, Jimmy's Hotdogs, McDonald's, Popeye's, TX Roadhouse Red Roof Inn $Tree, Costco/gas, Family$, GNC, Home Depot, PetsMart, Ross, Verizon, vet
174a	Hillandale Rd, W BP Bleu Olive, China King, El Corral, Pomodoro Italian Comfort Inn, Courtyard URGENT CARE, Walgreens
174b	US 15 S, US 501 S
173	US 15, US 501, US 70, Colemill Rd, W Durham, E BP, Exxon/dsl, Mobil, Sheetz/dsl Arby's, Biscuitville, Bojangles, Chick-fil-A, Cookout, Cracker Barrel, DogHouse Rest., Domino's, Japan Express, KFC/Taco Bell, Krispy Kreme, McDonald's, Shanghai Chinese, Subway, Waffle House, Wendy's, Zaxby's Days Inn, Hilton, Motel 6, Quality Inn H, $General, Advance Parts, AutoZone, CVS Drug, Mr Tire, O'Reilly Parts, Rite Aid
172	NC 147 S, to US 15 S, US 501 S (from nb), Durham
170	to NC 751, to Duke U (no EZ return from nb), E Durham Skyland Inn, Scottish Inn, W to Eno River SP

165	NC 86, to Chapel Hill, E Eagles/Burger King/dsl, She dsl China Fuji, Hwy 55, Papa John's, Subway $Tree, vance Parts, Home Depot, vet, Walmart, W BP/dsl repair
164	Hillsborough, E BP, Citgo/dsl McDonald's Holiday Express, W Shell Bojangles, Colorado Burrito, Domi Hardee's, Jimmy's Hotdogs, KFC/Taco Bell, Pueblo Viejo M can, Subway, Waffle House, Wendy's Microtel $Gen $Tree, AutoZone, Food Lion, Ford, Goodyear/auto
163	I-40 E, to Raleigh.
I-85 S and I-40 W run together 38 mi.	
161	to US 70 E, NC 86 N
160	to NC 86 N, Efland, W Exxon/dsl Missy's Grill drew's Repair
158mm	**weigh sta both lanes**
MEBANE	
157	Buckhorn Rd, E BP/dsl, Petro/Marathon/Dunkin'/Iron let/dsl/scales/24hr/@, W Citgo
154	Mebane-Oaks Rd, E Murphy USA/dsl, Sheetz/dsl na Garden, Ciao Pizza, Hwy 55 Cafe, Starbucks, Subway, Bell, Wendy's, Zaxby's $Tree, AT&T, GNC, Walmart/Subw W BP, Shell/dsl, Speedway/dsl Biscuitville, Blue bon Diner, Bojangles, La Fiesta Mexican, McDonald's, Rc Pizza, Sake Japanese, Waffle House Budget Inn vance Parts, AutoZone, CVS Drug, Lowe's Foods, Tanger C lets/famous brands, URGENT CARE, Verizon, vet, Walgreens
153	NC 119, Mebane, E BP/KFC/Pizza Hut/Taco Bell A Maria's Pizza, Cracker Barrel, Hibachi, Hursey's BBQ, Jer Mike's, La Cocina Mexican, Moe's SW Grill, Ruby Tues Sakura Japanese, Smithfield's BBQ Fairfield Inn, Hamp Inn, Holiday Inn Express $General, Lowe's, O'Reilly Pa vet, W Exxon/Burger King Asian Harbor, Catrin Domino's, Papa John's, Subway Food Lion
152	Trollingwood Rd, E Pilot/McDonald's/dsl/scales/2 W Love's/Hardee's/dsl/scales/24hr
150	to Roxboro, Haw River, W Flying J/Denny's/dsl/ scales/24hr, Pilot/DQ/Wendy's/dsl/scales/24hr, Spee Days Inn Blue Beacon
BURLINGTON	
148	NC 54, Graham, E BP/dsl, Exxon/Circle K, Shell/dsl W fle House Quality Inn, W AmMex 2 Cafe
147	NC 87, to Pittsboro, Graham, E Sheetz/dsl AnnaMar Pizzeria, Arby's, Bojangles, Great Wall Chinese, Guerrero M can, Pizza Hut, Popeye's, Subway, Wendy's Advance Pa AutoZone, Champion Tire/Repair, Family$, Food Lion, Fc Just Save, O'Reilly Parts, Rite Aid, W Citgo/dsl, Exxon/ Shell/dsl Biscuitville, Cook-Out, Golden China, La Fie Mexican, McDonald's, Taco Bell, Zaxby's $General, C Drug, Verizon, Walgreens
145	NC 49, Burlington, E BP/dsl, Sheetz/dsl, Shell/dsl C D's EconoLodge, Microtel, Motel 6 Harley-Davids W BP/dsl Biscuitville, Bojangles, Burger King, Ch Inn, Hardee's, KFC, Subway Red Carpet Inn, Red Roof I Royal Inn $General, Chrysler/Dodge/Jeep, Family$, Fc Lion, Rite Aid
143	NC 62, Burlington, E Sav-Way Hardee's, Waffle Hou Wendy's JR Outlet, to Alamance Bfd, W Marath Sheetz/dsl Biscuitville, Cutting Board Rest., K&W Cafete Ramada Inn $General, auto repair, Cadillac, Chevro Food Lion, Ford, Home Depot, Mazda, vet
141	Huffman Mill Rd, Burlington, E BP, Circle K IHOP, M flower Seafood, Outback Steaks Hampton Inn, Holiday Express H, Nissan, W Applebee's, Arby's, Biscuitvi Bojangles, Cancun Mexican, Chick-fil-A, China Gate, Cook-O

NC

INTERSTATE 85 Cont'd

Exit	Services
141	Continued Cracker Barrel, East Coast Cafe, Fire Pit, Golden Corral, Grill 584, Hibachi Buffet, HoneyBaked Ham, Hooters, KFC, Krispy Kreme, La Cocina Mexican, Longhorn Steaks, McDonald's, Mellow Mushroom, O'Charley's, Panera Bread, Sal's Italian, Starbucks, Steak'n Shake, Subway, Taco Bell, Village Grill Best Western+, Country Inn&Suites, Courtyard, Super 8 $Tree, Harris Teeter/dsl, Hyundai, Lowe's, Subaru/Volvo/VW, to Elon Coll, URGENT CARE, Verizon, Walgreens, Walmart/McDonald's
140	University Ave, E Toyota, W Brixx Pizza, Buffalo Wing Wings, Burger King, Chick-fil-A, Chili's, Coldstone, Freddy's, Jimmy John's, Little Italy, McDonald's, Moe's SW Grill, Olive Garden, Peking House, Red Bowl Asian, Red Lobster, Red Robin, San Marcos Mexican, Smithfield's BBQ, Starbucks, TX Roadhouse Drury Inn AT&T, Barnes&Noble, Belk, Best Buy, BJ's Whse/gas, Dick's, Dillard's, Discount Tire, GNC, Hobby Lobby, JC Penney, Kohl's, Michael's, Petsmart, Ross, Target, TJ Maxx, Verizon
139mm	**both lanes, full facilities, litter barrels, , , vending**
138	NC 61, Gibsonville, W TA/BP/Burger King/Popeye's/dsl/scales/24hr/@ truckwash
135	Rock Creek Dairy Rd, W Circle K, Citgo Bojangles, China 1, Ciao Italian, Domino's, Guacamole Mexican, Jersey Mike's Subs, McDonald's, Osaka Japanese, Pizza Hut/Taco Bell, Subway, Zaxby's Comfort Suites $General, CVS Drug, Food Lion, Verizon
132	Mt Hope Church Rd, E Shell/Subway/dsl McDonald's, Pascali's Pizza, W Liberty/dsl, Pilot/Wendy's/dsl/24hr Hampton Inn
131	to I-85 S, to I-73 N, to US 421, Highpoint, Charlotte
129	Youngsmill Rd, W KOA (4mi)
128	Alamance Church Rd, E Citgo/Subway/dsl
126b a	US 421, to Sanford, E Hagan Stone Park Camping, W Circle K/dsl, Exxon/Circle K/dsl
124	S Elm, Eugene St, E Murphy Express/dsl Waffle House, W Bamboo Grill, Bojangles, Cracker Barrel, Hwy 55 Cafe, McDonald's, Pizza Hut, Smithfield's BBQ, Starbucks, Subway, Taco Bell, Wendy's, Zaxby's AT&T, Lowe's, Verizon, Walmart/McDonald's
122c b a	US 220, to Greensboro, Asheboro (from sb)
121	I-40 W, I-73 N, to Winston-Salem
120	N US 29, E US 70, to I-40 W
119	Groometown Rd, from nb, W Citgo/dsl
118	US 29 S, US 70 W, to High Point, Jamestown, W Grandover Resort
115mm	Deep River
113c	I-74, US 311, Ashboro, to Winston-Salem
113a	NC 62, Archdale, E Citgo/dsl, W BP/dsl Quality Inn
111	US 311, to High Point, Archdale, E Sheetz/dsl Bamboo Garden, Bojangles, Carolina's Diner, Hardee's, Pizza Hut, Subway, Taco Bell, Wendy's, Zaxby's Days Inn $General, CVS Drug, Food Lion, Lowe's Foods, Walmart Mkt, W Citgo, McDonald's, Mobil/dsl, Shell/Circle K/dsl, Valero/dsl Biscuitville, Cabo Grill, Rancho Rest., Waffle House Comfort Inn, Country Inn&Suites, Fairfield Inn, Hampton Inn, Holiday Inn Express , O'Reilly Parts, tires, USPO, vet
108	Hopewell Church Rd, Trinity
106	Finch Farm Rd, E BP/dsl, W Sheetz/dsl BBQ Joe's, Subway (1mi)
103	NC 109, to Thomasville, E Exxon/dsl, Mobil/7-11/dsl, Murphy USA/dsl, Sheetz/dsl Arby's, Chen's Kitchen, Cookout

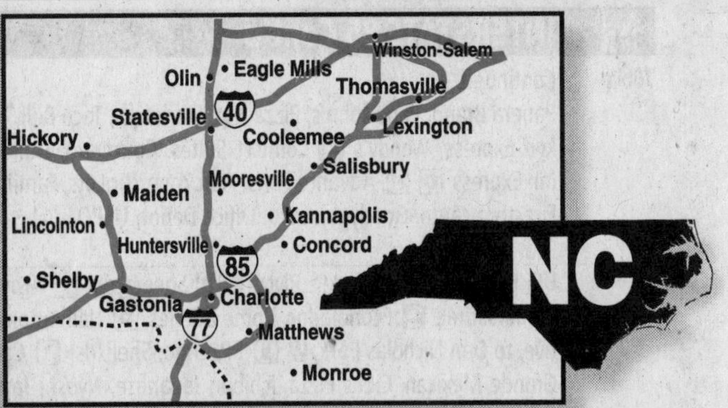

THOMASVILLE

Exit	Services
103	Continued Burgers, Elizabeth's Pizza, Subway, Taco Bell, Zaxby's Staylodge $Tree, CVS Drug, Ingles Foods, Lidl Mkt, Walmart/McDonald's, W Exxon/dsl, Fast Fuels/dsl, Shell, Speedway/dsl BBQ Shack, Biscuitville, Bojangles, Burger King, China Garden, Denny's, E Coast Grill, Hardee's, Hunan Chinese, KFC, La Carreta Mexican, Little Caesar's, Mandarin Express, Mazatlan Mexican, McDonald's, Papa John's, Pizza Hut, Ruby Tuesday, Sonic, Sunrise Diner, Waffle House, Wendy's Davidson Lodge, Quality Inn $General, Advance Parts, Aldi Foods, AutoZone, Family$, Food Lion, Mighty$, NAPA, NTB, O'Reilly Parts, Peebles, Rite Aid, UHaul, Verizon, Walgreens
102	Lake Rd, W Marathon/dsl, Sunoco/dsl Comfort Inn, Microtel
100mm	**both lanes, full facilities, litter barrels, petwalk, , , vending**
96	US 64, to Asheboro, Lexington, E Citgo/dsl Modern Tire, NC Zoo, W Exxon/dsl, Gulf/dsl Randy's Rest. to Davidson Co Coll
94	Old US 64, E Shell, W Timberlake Gallery
91	NC 8, to Southmont, E BP/dsl, Citgo/dsl, Mobil/7-11 Biscuit King, Bojangle's, Christo Rest., Hunan Express, Kabuki Japanese, KFC, McDonald's, Ocean View Seafood, Subway, Waffle House, Wendy's Days Inn, Red Roof Inn Food Lion, High Rock Lake Camping (7mi), Mock Tire, W Exxon/dsl, Shell/dsl Applebee's, Arby's, Burger King, Cagney's Kitchen, Chick-fil-A, Cracker Barrel, Golden Corral, La Carreta Mexican, Little Caesar's, Mi Pueblo, Pizza Hut (1mi), Subway, Taco Bell, Zaxby's Country Hearth Inn, Quality Inn , $Tree, Belk, GNC, Lidl Mkt, Lowe's (1mi), Walgreens, Walmart
88	Linwood, W Affordable Suites
87	US 29, US 70, US 52 (from nb), High Point, W ,
86	Belmont Rd, W Bill's Trkstp/dsl/scales/24hr/@
84	US 29 S, US 70 W, NC 150 (from nb), to Spencer
82	US 29, US 70 (from sb), to Spencer
81.5mm	Yadkin River
81	Long Ferry Rd, Spencer, E BP/dsl
79	Spencer Shops SHS, Spencer, E Spencer, **1 mi** W Citgo Bojangles, Subway $General, Food Lion
76b a	US 52, to Albemarle, Salisbury, E BP, Citgo Applebee's, Buffalo Wild Wings, Capriano's, Chipotle, ColdStone, E Coast Grill, IHOP, Pancho Villa, Top China, Which Wich?, Zaxby's Days Inn, Economy Inn, Happy Traveler Inn $Tree, Aldi Foods, AT&T, CVS Drug, Food Lion, GNC, Harley-Davidson, Lowe's, Marshall's, NTB, Old Navy, Petsmart, Rite Aid, Staples, Verizon, vet, Walgreens, W Murphy Express/dsl, Shell/Circle K/dsl, Speedway/dsl Blue Bay Seafood, Bojangles, Burger King, Capt D's, Chick-fil-A, China Buffet, Christo's Rest., Cookout, Cracker Barrel, Hardee's, HoneyBaked Ham, Jersey Mike's, KFC, Marco's Pizza, McDonald's, O'Charley's, Outback Steaks,

SALISBURY

NC

INTERSTATE 85 Cont'd

76b a Continued
Panera Bread, Papa John's, Pizza Hut, Starbucks, Taco Bell, Tokyo Express, Wendy's Comfort Suites, Courtyard, Holiday Inn Express H, Advance Parts, AutoZone, BigLots, Family$, Firestone/auto, Goodyear/auto, Office Depot, USPO, Walmart/Subway

75 US 601, Jake Alexander Blvd, E Sheetz/dsl Arby's, Breakfastime Econolodge, Home 2 Suites Hall Automotive, to Dan Nicholas Park, W BP, Citgo, Shell/dsl Casa Grande Mexican, CiCi's Pizza, Ichiban Japanese, Nyoshi Japanese, Waffle House, Wendy's Hampton Inn, Holiday Inn, Quality Inn Buick, Cadillac/Chevrolet, Chrysler/Dodge/Jeep, Ford, GMC, Honda, Kia, Nissan, Toyota

74 Julian Rd, E Honeybaked Ham, Salsarita's Dick's, Hobby Lobby, W Longhorn Steaks, Los Arcos, Olive Garden, Starbucks, Subway $Tree, Belk, Kohl's, Michael's

72 Peach Orchard Rd

71 Peeler Rd, E Loves/Chester's/McDonald's/dsl/scales/24hr, W Pilot/Dunkin'/Subway/dsl/scales/24hr Bojangle's dsl repair

70 Webb Rd, E flea mkt, W Shell/dsl st patrol

68 US 29, US 601, to Rockwell, China Grove, W BP Bojangle's, Domino's, Gary's BBQ, Hardee's, Jimmie's Rest., Papa John's, Pizza Hut, Subway $General, AutoZone, Family$, Food Lion, Rite Aid

63 Kannapolis, E Pilot/Subway/dsl/scales Waffle House Motel 6, W QT/dsl URGENT CARE

60 Earnhardt Rd, Copperfield Blvd, E Exxon/dsl, Shell/Circle K/dsl Bojangles, Breakfast Time Rest., Copper Grill, Cracker Barrel, Waffle House Country Inn&Suites, Hampton Inn, Sleep Inn H, Discount Tire, URGENT CARE, W Shell/Kangaroo/dsl Casa Grande Mexican, Dragon Wok, Dunkin', East Coast Wings, Firehouse Subs, Little Caesar's, Logan's Roadhouse, McDonald's, Ruby Tuesday, Steak'n Shake, Subway, Taco Bell, Wendy's Holiday Inn Express AT&T, Hobby Lobby, Kohl's, Lowe's, Petco, Sam's Club/gas, Walmart

59mm **both lanes, full facilities, litter barrels, petwalk, vending**

58 US 29, US 601, Concord, E BP, Marathon/Circle K/dsl, Marathon/dsl, Shell/dsl Applebee's, Capt D's, Chick-fil-A, Chili's, Chipotle, Freddy's, Golden Corral, Jimmy John's, McDonald's, Moe's SW Grill, Mr C's Rest., O'Charley's, Panera Bread, Popeye's, Starbucks, Subway, Wendy's Best Value Inn, Quality Inn, Rodeway Inn H, Belk, Family$, Harris Teeter, JC Penney, Staples, Verizon, Walgreens, W BP, QT/dsl, Speedway/dsl CiCi's, IHOP Comfort Inn, Econolodge, Microtel $General, Ford, Home Depot, st patrol, vet

55 NC 73, to Davidson, Concord, E Shell McDonald's, W Shell/Circle K/dsl Days Inn

54 Kannapolis Pkwy, George W Lyles Pkwy, E QT/dsl, SM/Subway/dsl Bojangles, China Garden, Marco's Pizza, Off-the-Grill Advance Parts, AutoZone, CVS Drug, Firestone/auto, Food Lion, Harris Teeter, URGENT CARE, vet, Walgreens, W Circle K/dsl Arby's, Asian Cafe, Buffalo Wild Wings, Chick-fil-A, Dunkin', Jersey Mike's, McDonald's, Mi Pueblo, Showmar's Rest., Starbucks, Zaxby's $Tree, Best Buy, Dick's, Goodyear/auto, Marshall's, Petsmart, Steinmart, Super Target, Verizon

52 Poplar Tent Rd, E Mobil/7-11/dsl R&R BBQ to Lowe's Speedway, W Exxon/7-11/dsl

NC

CONCORD

49 Bruton Smith Blvd, Concord Mills Blvd, E BP/McDonal Mobil/7-11/dsl Bojangles, Carrabba's, ChuckECheese, C co de Mayo Mexican, Cookout, Cracker Barrel, Firehouse Su Five Guys, Hooters, Hot Shots Grill, Jack-in-the-Box, KFC/Ta Bell, Ruby Tuesday, Sonic, Sonny's BBQ, Starbucks, Subw Taco Bell, TX Land&Cattle Steaks, TX Roadhouse, Waffle Hou Wendy's, Zaxby's Comfort Suites, Courtyard, Emba Suites, Great Wolf Lodge, Hampton Inn, Hilton Garden, Holid Inn Express, Home Towne Suites, Homewood Suites, Resider Inn, Sleep Inn, SpringHill Suites, Wingate Inn BJ's Whs gas, Camping World, Camping World Resort (1.5mi), Chrysl Dodge/Jeep, Harley-Davidson, Honda, Kia, to Lowe's Mo Speedway, Toyota, VW, W Circle K/dsl Bonefish G Burger King, Carolina Alehouse, Charanda Mexican, Chick-fil Chipotle, Dave&Buster's, Denny's, Dunkin', Foster's Grille, Fre dy's, Jason's Deli, Jim'n Nick's BBQ, Jimmy John's, Mayflow Seafood, McAlisters Deli, Olive Garden, On-the-Border, O back Steaks, Panera Bread, PDQ Cafe, Queen City Q, Razzo Cafe, Red Lobster, Steak'n Shake, Sticky Fingers, TGI Friday Tijuana Flats, Twin Peaks $Tree, AT&T, BassPro Shops, B Buy, BooksAMillion, Concord Mills Mall, Discount Tire, Fir tone/auto, Goodyear/auto, Lowe's, Old Navy, PetCo, Ross, Maxx, URGENT CARE, Verizon, Walmart/Subway

48 I-485, to US 29, to Rock Hill

46 Mallard Creek Church Rd, E Exxon/7-11, Kangaroo, Spee way/dsl China Cafe, Giacomos Pizza, Jack-in-the-B Wild Wing Cafe Research Park, vet, W Shell/Cir K Farley's Pizzaria, Hickory Tavern, Rita's, Starbucks, Th Taste, Toyama Express, Zoe's Kitchen PetCo, Trader Joe's

45b a Harris Blvd, E Applebee's, Bar Louie, Blaze Pizza, Bojangl Buffalo Wild Wings, Burger King, Cheddar's, Chick-fil-A, Chil China Buffet, China Palace, Chipotle, City BBQ, Dunkin', Five Gu IHOP, Jersey Mike's Subs, Jimmy John's, Los Arcos, McDonal Nakato Steaks, Noodles&Co, Panera Bread, Papa John's, Pei W Picasso's Pizza, Qdoba, Shane's Rib Shack, Shoney's, Showma Rest., Starbucks, Taco Bell, Taco Mac Grill, TGIFriday's, Tijua Flats, Tropical Cafe Country Inn&Suites, Courtyard, Dr Inn, Extended Stay America, Hampton Inn, Hilton, Holiday I Homewood Suites, Microtel, Residence Inn, Sleep Inn Food Lion, Kohl's, Michael's, Office Depot, Ross, Sam's Club, Miz Scarlett's, to UNCC, U Research Park, Verizon, Walgree Walmart/McDonald's, **0-2 mi** W Longhorn Steaks, Macar Grill, Red Robin, Tony's Pizza SpringHill Suites, TownePla Suites Harris Teeter, Rite Aid

43 University City Blvd, E Circle K/dsl, Circle K/Subway/ Chipotle, Culver's, Golden Corral, Honeybaked Ham, Outba Steaks, Pablo's, Starbucks, Taco Bell, Zaxby's Extended St America, Holiday Inn Express, InTowne Suites AT&T, Chev let, Discount Tire, Firestone/auto, GNC, Hobby Lobby, IKEA, M shall's, Old Navy, Petsmart, TJ Maxx, Walmart, World Mkt

42 US 29 (nb only)

41 Sugar Creek Rd, E Shell/dsl, Exxon/7-11/gas B jangles, McDonald's, Taco Bell, Wendy's Best Val Inn, Brookwood Inn, Continental Inn, Motel 6 Family W Shell/Circle K/dsl Chicken Box Rest., Cookout, Ranch Steaks Days Inn, Quality Inn, Red Roof Inn, Rodew Inn, Super 8

40 Graham St, E Exxon/7-11/dsl Budget Inn repa UPS, Volvo, Western Star, W Marathon/dsl Freightlin

39 Statesville Ave, E Pilot/Subway/dsl/scales/24hr A vance Parts, repair, W Citgo/dsl, Shell/dsl Bojangl Family$

CHARLOTTE

INTERSTATE 85 Cont'd

Exit #	Services
38	I-77, US 21, N to Statesville, S to Columbia
37	Beatties Ford Rd, E 7-11/dsl Burger King, McDonald's, Tops China CVS Drug, Family$, Food Lion, USPO, W Citgo
36	NC 16, Brookshire Blvd, E Rodeway Inn repair, W Exxon/7-11/dsl, Mobil/dsl, QT/dsl, RaceWay/dsl Burger King, Jack-in-the-Box, Subway Family$, Griffin Tire
35	Glenwood Dr, E Exxon Knights Inn, W Shell/dsl
34	NC 27, Freedom Dr, E Citgo/dsl, Shell/Circle K Beauregard's Rest., Bojangles, Capt D's, Cookout, Domino's, KFC, McDonald's, Pizza Hut, Showmar's, Subway, Taco Bell, Wendy's $Tree, Advance Parts, Aldi Foods, AutoZone, Family$, Goodyear/auto, URGENT CARE, Walgreens, W Charlotte Express
33	US 521, Billy Graham Pkwy, E Shell/dsl Bojangles, KFC/Taco Bell, McDonald's, Wendy's Baymont Inn, Comfort Suites, Royal Inn, Sheraton, SpringHill Suites , W Exxon/dsl Cracker Barrel, Ichiban, Waffle House EconoLodge, Holiday Inn Express, La Quinta, Microtel, Motel 6, Quality Inn, Suburban Lodge, Super 8
32	Little Rock Rd, E Mobil/7-11/dsl Airport Inn, Courtyard, Hampton Inn, Holiday Inn, W 76/dsl, BP/dsl, Mobil/7-11 Arby's, Showmar's Rest., Subway Country Inn&Suites, Day's Inn, Wingate Inn Family$, Food Lion, Griffin Tire, Walgreens
30b a	I-485, to 1-77, Pineville
29	Sam Wilson Rd, W Loves/Chester's/dsl/scales/24hr, Shell/dsl, S camping
28mm	**weigh sta both lanes**
27.5mm	Catawba River
27	NC 273, Mt Holly, E BP/Dunkin'/dsl, Murphy USA/dsl Arby's, Captain's Cap Seafood, Chick-fil-A, KFC, Pizza Hut, Sake Japanese, Starbucks, Subway, Taco Bell, Waffle House, Wendy's Big Lots, CVS Drug, Family$, Firestone/auto, Lowe's, NAPA, Walgreens, Walmart/Subway, W Citgo/dsl Holiday Inn Express
26	NC 7, E BP/dsl, Shell/Circle K/dsl Bojangles, Estia's Rest., Hardee's, McDonald's, New China, Papa John's Hampton Inn $Tree, Advance Parts, Aldi Foods, AT&T, AutoZone, Ford, Verizon, W Belmont Abbey Coll
24mm	South Fork River
23	NC 7, McAdenville, W Exxon/dsl, Shell/Subway/dsl Hardee's, Hillbilly's BBQ/Steaks
22	Cramerton, Lowell, E Shell/Circle K/dsl, Speedway/dsl Chick-fil-A, CiCi's, Denny's, Jack-in-the-Box, Jersey Mike's Subs, Moe's SW, Popeye's, Popeye's, Portofino's, Sakura Japanese, Schlotzsky's, Shane's Ribshack, Showmar's, Wild Wing Cafe, Zaxby's Books-A-Million, Buick/Cadillac/Chevrolet/GMC, Honda, Kia, Kohl's, Lowe's, Old Navy, Petsmart, Sam's Club/gas, U-Haul
21	Cox Rd, E Shell Akropolis Cafe, Buffalo Wild Wings, Cheddar's, Chili's, Chipotle, ChuckeCheese, Cookout, Dynasty Buffet, Firehouse Subs, Five Guys, Golden Corral, Jimmy John's, Krispy Kreme, La Fuente, Logan's Roadhouse, Longhorn Steaks, McAlister's Deli, McDonald's, Noodles&Co, Olive Garden, On the Border, Panera Bread, Peking Garden, Qdoba, Ruby Tuesday, Starbucks, Steak'n Shake Hilton Garden $Tree, AT&T, Best Buy, Chrysler/Dodge/Jeep, Dick's, Discount Tire, Ford/Subaru, GNC, Hobby Lobby, Home Depot, Michael's, Nissan, NTB, Office Depot, O'Reilly Parts, PepBoys, Petco, Ross, Target, TJ Maxx, Verizon, vet, Walgreens, Walmart/Subway, W Shell/dsl Arby's, Brixx Pizza, IHOP Super 8 H, $General, Medical Ctr Drug

GASTONIA

ROANOKE RAPIDS

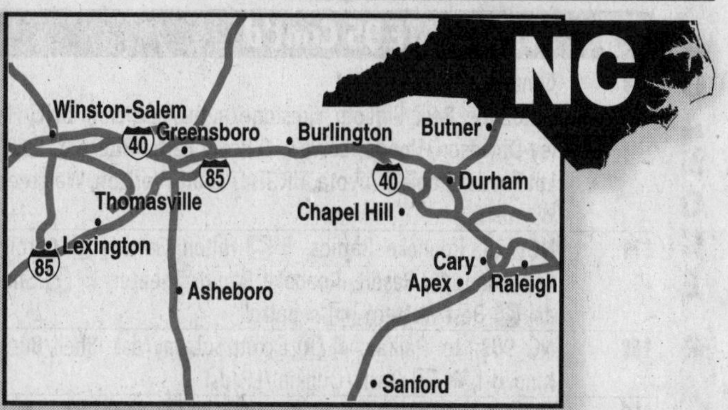

Exit #	Services
20	NC 279, New Hope Rd, E World Capt D's, Dunkin', Jackson's Cafeteria, Los Arcos Mexican, McDonald's, O'Charley's, Red Lobster, Sake Japanese, Taco Bell, Tres Pesos, Wendy's Advance Parts, AutoZone, Belk, Family$, Firestone/auto, Tuesday Morning, W Bojangles, Cracker Barrel, Honeybaked Ham, KFC, Outback Steaks, TX Roadhouse, Waffle House Best Western, Comfort Suites, Courtyard, Fairfield Inn, Hampton Inn H, CarMax
19	NC 7, E Gastonia, E Shell
17	US 321, Gastonia, E Citgo/dsl/LP Los Arcos Mexican Days Inn, Woodspring Suites Family$, W QT/dsl, Shell/Circle K/dsl Dunkin', Hardee's, Papa John's Holiday Inn Express, Lakeside Lodge, Motel 6
14	NC 274, E Bessemer, E Citgo/dsl, Murphy USA/dsl Walmart, W Citgo/dsl, Shell/Subway Bojangles, Waffle House Express Inn
13	Edgewood Rd, Bessemer City, E to Crowders Mtn SP, W Exxon/dsl
10b a	US 74 W, US 29, Kings Mtn
8	NC 161, to Kings Mtn, E Holiday Inn Express camping, W BP/dsl Los Tarascos, McDonald's, Subway, Taco Bell, Waffle House, Wendy's Comfort Inn, Quality Inn H, $General, Campers Inn RV Ctr
5	Dixon School Rd, E Trkstp/dsl/24hr truck/tire repair
4	US 29 S (from sb)
2.5mm	**Welcome Ctr nb, full facilities, info, litter barrels, petwalk, , , vending**
2	NC 216, Kings Mtn, E to Kings Mtn Nat Military Park
0mm	North Carolina/South Carolina state line

INTERSTATE 95

Exit #	Services
181mm	North Carolina/Virginia state line, **Welcome Ctr sb, full facilities, litter barrels, petwalk, , , vending**
180	NC 48, to Gaston, to Lake Gaston, Pleasant Hill, W Pilot/Subway/dsl/scales/24hr
176	NC 46, to Garysburg, W Shell/dsl Burger King Super 8
174mm	Roanoke River
173	US 158, Roanoke Rapids, Weldon, E BP/dsl, Shell/dsl Frazier's Rest., Ralph's BBQ, Waffle House Days Inn, Econolodge, W BP/dsl, Exxon/DQ/Stuckey's, Murphy USA/dsl, Sheetz/dsl, Shell/dsl Applebee's, Arby's, Bojangles, Burger King, Carolina BBQ, Chick-fil-A, China Lin, Cookout, Cracker Barrel, Hardee's, Ichiban, KFC, Little Caesar's, Logan's Roadhouse, Mayflower Seafood, McDonald's, New China, Papa John's, Pizza Hut, Popeyes, Ruby Tuesday, San Jose Mexican, Starbucks, Subway, Subway, Taco Bell, TX Steaks, Waffle House, Wendy's, Zaxby's BaymontInn, Hampton Inn, Holiday Inn Express, Motel 6, Sleep Inn H, $General, $Tree, Advance Parts,

NC

INTERSTATE 95 Cont'd

ROANOKE RAPIDS

173	Continued AutoZone, Belk, BigLots, Firestone/auto, Food Lion, GNC, Harley-Davidson, Honda, Lowe's, O'Reilly Parts, Rite Aid, Save a Lot Foods, Staples, Toyota, URGENT CARE, Verizon, Walgreens, Walmart
171	NC 125, Roanoke Rapids, E Hilton Garden Carolina Crossroads RV Resort, Roanoke Rapids Theater, W Shell/dsl Best Western st patrol
168	NC 903, to Halifax, E Exxon/Subway/dsl, Shell/Burger King/dsl, W Oasis/Dunkin'/LP/dsl
160	NC 561, to Brinkleyville, E Exxon, W Shell/dsl
154	NC 481, to Enfield, 1 mi W KOA
151mm	**weigh sta both lanes**
150	NC 33, to Whitakers, E golf, W BP/Subway/DQ/Stuckey's/dsl
145	NC 4, to US 301, Battleboro, E BP/dsl, Exxon/dsl, Marathon/dsl, Shell Carolina BBQ, Denny's, Hardee's, Waffle House Ashburn Inn, Best Western, Deluxe Inn, EconoLodge, Economy Inn, Quality Inn, Red Carpet Inn, Travelers Inn
142mm	**both lanes, full facilities, litter barrels, petwalk, vending**
141	NC 43, Red Oak, E BP/dsl, Exxon/dsl/LP $General, Smith's Foods
138	US 64, **1 mi E on Winstead** BP/dsl, Speedway/dsl Bojangles, Cracker Barrel, Gardner's BBQ, Hardee's, Highway Diner, Outback Steaks, TX Steaks, Waffle House Candlewood Suites, Comfort Inn, Country Inn&Suites, Courtyard, Doubletree, Hampton Inn, Holiday Inn, Residence Inn H, Buick/GMC, Harley-Davidson, Honda, Rite Aid, to Cape Hatteras Nat Seashore, URGENT CARE
132	to NC 58, E Pitstop/dsl, **1 mi W** BP/dsl
128mm	Tar River
127	NC 97, to Stanhope, E
121	US 264a, Wilson, **0-4 mi E** BP, Kangaroo/dsl/LP, Marathon, Murphy USA/dsl, Shell, Speedway/dsl Applebee's, Arby's, Buffalo Wild Wings, Burger King, Chick-fil-A, Chili's, Chopstix, Cookout, Denny's, El Tapatio, Golden Corral, Hardee's, Hibachi Buffet, Jersey Mike's, KFC/LJ Silver, Kobe Express, Mama Mia's Pizzaria, McDonald's, Moe's SW Grill, Olive Garden, Quizno's, Red Chileez Grill, Ruby Tuesday, San Jose Mexican, Sonic, Starbucks, Subway, Teppanyaki, TX Steaks, Waffle House, Wendy's, Zaxby's's Candlewood Suites, Hampton Inn, Quality Inn H, $General, $Tree, Aldi Foods, AT&T, AutoZone, Belk, Best Buy, Big Lots, Chevrolet, Chrysler/Dodge/Jeep, Ford/Lincoln, GNC, Harris-Teeter, Hobby Lobby, Honda, Lowe's, Marshall's, Mr Tire, Nissan, O'Reilly Parts, Petsmart, Ross, Staples, Target, Toyota, URGENT CARE, Verizon, vet, Walmart, White's Tires, W BP Best-N-Burgers, Bojangles, Burger King, Cracker Barrel, McDonald's, Pino's Pizza Comfort Suites, Country Inn&Suites, Fairfield Inn, Hampton Inn, Holiday Inn Express, Jameson Inn, Microtel, Sleep Inn to Country Dr Museum
119b a	I-795 S, US 264, US 117
116	NC 42, to Clayton, Wilson, E Shell/dsl H, W Exxon/dsl Rock Ridge Camping (2mi)
107	US 301, Kenly, E BP/dsl, Citgo, Exxon/McDonald's/dsl, Fuel Doc, PitStop Andy's Cafe, Golden China, Nik's Pizza, Norman's BBQ, Subway Budget Inn, Deluxe Inn, Quality Inn $General, CarQuest, Family$, Food Lion, Ford, O'Reilly Parts, Piggly Wiggly, Tobacco Museum
106	Truck Stop Rd, Kenly, E FLYING J/Denny's/dsl/LP/scales/24hr, W Kenly 95/Petro/DQ/Subway/Wendy's/dsl/scales/24hr/@,

WILSON

KENLY

106	Continued Pilot/Arby's/dsl/scales/24hr Waffle House Days Motel 6 Blue Beacon, Speedco Lube, Truck-o-Mat
105.5mm	Little River
105	Bagley Rd, Kenly, E Big Boys/Shell/105 Pizza/dsl/scal 24hr Lowell Mill Rest.
102	Micro, W Shop'N-Go Backdoor Cafe $General, park, USPO
101	Pittman Rd
99mm	**both lanes, full facilities, hist marker, litter barrels, p walk, vending**
98	to Selma, E RVacation
97	US 70 A, to Pine Level, Selma, E Mobil/dsl Denn Robbins Nest Rest. Days Inn J&R Outlet, W dsl, Exxon/dsl, Shell/dsl Bojangles, Cookout, Don to's Tacos, KFC, McDonald's, Shoney's, Waffle House, W dy's EconoLodge, Hampton Inn, Masters Inn, Qua Inn H
95	US 70, Smithfield, E Best Value Inn, Village Mo W Sheetz/dsl, Speedway/dsl, Sunoco/dsl Bob Eva Burger King, Checker's, CiCi's Pizza, Coldstone, Cracker Barrel Sombrero Mexican, Golden Corral, Outback Steaks, Ruby Tu day, San Marcos Mexican, Subway, TX Steaks, Waffle Hou Zaxby's Baymont Inn, Best Western, Comfort Inn, Fairfi Inn, Sleep Inn, Super 8 H, Ava Gardner Museum, Carol Premium Outlets/famous brands, Harley-Davidson
93	Brogden Rd, Smithfield, W BP/dsl, Citgo $General
91.5mm	Neuse River
90	US 301, US 701, to Newton Grove, E BP/dsl, Vale dsl Travelers Inn Happy Trails RV Park, Raleigh O RV Resort, Ronnie's Tires, to Bentonville Bfd (14mi), W E on/dsl Holt Lake BBQ Four Oaks Motel/RV Park
87	NC 96, Four Oaks, W BP/dsl, Speedway/dsl, Walmart press/dsl McDonald's, Subway $General
81b a	I-40, E to Wilmington, W to Raleigh
79	NC 50, to NC 27, to NC 242, Benson, Newton Grove, E go/dsl, Short Stop/dsl Char-Grill, Waffle House Har ton Inn auto repair, W Exxon/Burger King/dsl C na 8, Domino's, McDonald's, Pizza Hut, Subway, Taco B White Swan BBQ Days Inn Advance Parts, auto rep Family$, Food Lion, Walgreens
78mm	Neuse River
77	Hodges Chapel Rd, E Loves/Subway/dsl/scales/ dump/24hr
75	Jonesboro Rd, W Exxon/Milestone Diner, Pilot/Sh DQ/Quiznos/dsl/scales/24hr/@
73	US 421, NC 55, to Dunn, Clinton, E Cracker Barrel, H 55 Cafe, McDonald's, Mi Casita Mexican, Panda House C nese Chevrolet, Chrysler/Dodge/Jeep, Family$, Food Li W Exxon/dsl, Shell, Speedway/dsl Bojangles, Bur King, El Charro Mexican, Fishing Chicken, Hot Dog&Hambur Heavan, Sagebrush Steaks, Subway, Taco Bell, Triangle W fle Baymont Inn, Days Inn, Hampton Inn, Quality Inn, Su 8 Charlie C's IGA, museum, to Campbell U.
72	Pope Rd, E Comfort Inn, Royal Inn, W BP, Pure/ Brass Lantern Steaks Fairfield Inn Cadillac/GMC
71	Longbranch Rd, E Pilot/Circle K/Hardee's/dsl/scal 24hr, W to Averasboro Bfd
70	SR 1811, E Relax Inn
65	NC 82, Godwin, E Falcon Children's Home, W Godw Mart/dsl

SMITHFIELD

DUNN

NC

INTERSTATE 95 Cont'd

Exit #	Services
61	to Wade, E Lucky 7 Trkstp/dsl Fayetteville RV Resort Cottages, W Exxon/dsl
58	US 13, to Newton Grove, I-295 to Fayetteville, E Shell/dsl/scales Subway, Waffle House Econolodge
56	Lp 95, to US 301 (from sb), Fayetteville, W Circle K/dsl, Epco/dsl H, Pope AFB, to Ft Bragg
55	NC 1832, Murphy Rd, W Circle K/dsl, Epco/dsl
52	NC 24, Fayetteville, W botanical gardens, museum, Pope AFB, to Ft Bragg
49	NC 53, NC 210, Fayetteville, E BP/dsl, BP/dsl, Exxon/dsl, Marathon Burger King, McDonald's, Pizza Hut, Taco Bell, Waffle House Days Inn, Deluxe Inn, Hampton Inn, Motel 6, Tru Hilton $General, W BP/Subway/dsl, Exxon/dsl, Sunoco/dsl Bojangle's, Cracker Barrel, Ruby Tuesday Baymont Inn, Comfort Inn, Doubletree, EconoLodge, Fairfield Inn, Holiday Inn, Holiday Inn Express, Quality Inn, Red Roof Inn, Sleep Inn, Super 8, Sure Stay Inn
48mm	**both lanes, full facilities, litter barrels, petwalk, vending**
47mm	Cape Fear River
46b a	NC 87, to Fayetteville, Elizabethtown, W H
44	Claude Lee Rd, W Lazy Acres Camping, to
41	NC 59, to Hope Mills, Parkton, E Circle K/Subway/dsl Bojangles, W BP/dsl Grandsons Buffet Camping World RV Ctr, Lake Waldo's Camping, Spring Valley RV Park
40	Lp 95, to US 301 (from nb), to Fayetteville, services on US 301 (5-7mi)
33	US 301, St Pauls, E BP/dsl
31	NC 20, to St Pauls, Raeford, E BP, Marathon/Huddle House/dsl, Mobil/McDonald's, Valero Burger King, Hardee's Days Inn Volvo Trucks, Walgreens, Walmart Mkt, W BP/dsl, Sunoco Taco Bell Food Lion
25	US 301, E Sun-Do/dsl
24mm	**weigh sta both lanes**
22	US 301, E BP, Marathon, Shell/DQ Burger King, Chick-fil-A, China Wok, Denny's, Firehouse Subs, Golden Corral, Hardee's, IHOP, Outback Steaks, Panera Bread, Papa John's, Pizza Hut, Ruby Tuesday, San Jose Mexican, Shogun, Smithfield BBQ, Starbucks, TX Steaks, Waffle House, Wendy's, Zaxby's Best Western, Comfort Suites, Hampton Inn, Holiday Inn, Super 8 $Tree, AT&T, Chrysler/Dodge/Jeep, Goodyear/auto, Honda, Lowe's, Lowe's Foods, McDonald's, Toyota, URGENT CARE, Verizon, Walmart/Subway, W Gulf, Sun-Do/dsl, Sunoco/dsl Bojangles Springhill Suites Ford/Lincoln, Kia
20	NC 211, to NC 41, Lumberton, E BP/dsl, Citgo/dsl, Liberty/dsl Arby's, Arnold's Rest., Bojangles, Burger King, Capt D's, Christopher's, CiCi's Pizza, Cook Out, Dunkin', Hardee's, Hong Kong Chinese, Hwy 55 Cafe, Kami Japanese, KFC, McDonald's, Shoney's, Sonic, Subway, Taco Bell, Tokyo Express, Village Sta. Rest., Waffle House Deluxe Inn, Red Roof Inn H, Advance Parts, AutoZone, Belk, city park, CVS Drug, Food Lion/deli, JC Penney, Nissan, O'Reilly Parts, Verizon, Walgreens, W Marathon/dsl, Sun-do/dsl Cracker Barrel, San Jose Mexican Comfort Inn, Country Inn&Suites, Days Inn/rest., Fairfield Inn, Knights Inn
19	Carthage Rd, Lumberton, E BP Rodeway Inn, W Sunoco Motel 6, Royal Inn
18mm	Lumber River
17	NC 72, Lumberton, Pembroke, E Atkinson's/dsl, BP/dsl, Go-Gas/dsl, Mobil/dsl, Sunoco Burger King, China Garden,

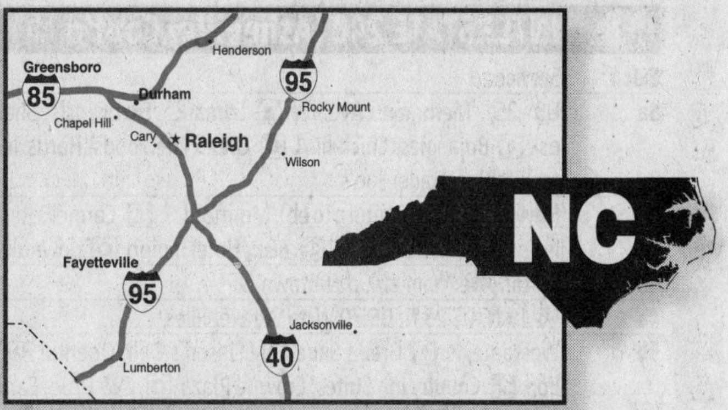

Exit #	Services
17	Continued Hardee's, Huddle House, McDonald's, Papa Bill's Ribs, Pizza Hut, Ruby Tuesday, Subway, Waffle House Atkinson Inn, Budget Inn, Southern Inn $General, $Tree, Advance Parts, AutoZone, CVS Drug, Food Lion, Walmart Mkt/dsl, W KOA (3mi)
13	I-74, US 74, Rockingham, Wilmington, E SE NC Beaches, U.S.S Wilmington
10	US 301, to Fairmont
7	to McDonald, Raynham
5mm	**Welcome Ctr nb, full facilities, litter barrels, petwalk, vending**
2	NC 130, to NC 904, Rowland
1b a	US 301, US 501, Dillon, E Sunoco, Sunoco (2) Hot Tamale Rest., Peddler Steaks, Pedro's Trkstp Budget Motel, South-of-the-Border Motel Pedro's Campground, W Shell/dsl Waffle House
0mm	North Carolina/South Carolina state line

INTERSTATE 240 (Asheville)

Exit #	Services
9mm	**I-240 begins/ends on I-40, exit 53b a.**
8	Fairview Rd, N Shell/dsl Ay Carumba, Cheddar's, China Buffet, Coldstone, J&S Cafeteria, KFC, Little Caesar's, McDonald's, Papa John's, Subway Ramada Inn $General, Advance Parts, Aldi Foods, Bi-Lo Foods, CVS Drug, Discount Tire, Hamrick's, Kohl's, Petsmart, U-Haul, Walmart/McDonald's, S Citgo Pizza Hut Home Depot
7.5mm	Swannanoa River
7	US 70, N Enmark Best Western Hyundai, Kia, Subaru, S Shell/dsl Applebee's, Bonefish Grill, Buffalo Wild Wings, Burger King, Carrabba's, Chick-fil-A, Chili's, Chuckecheese, Cici's Pizza, Cook Out, Cornerstone Rest., Cracker Barrel, DQ, Firehouse Subs, IHOP, Jersey Mike's Subs, Longhorn Steaks, McAlister's Deli, McDonald's, McDonald's, Mikado Japanese, O'Charley's, Olive Garden, Outback Steaks, Papa's Mexican, Red Lobster, Starbucks, Subway, Taco Bell, Waffle House, Wild Wok Country Inn&Suites, Courtyard, Days Inn, EconoLodge, Extended Stay America, Hampton Inn, Holiday Inn, Homewood Suites, InTown Motor Inn, Mountaineer Inn, SpringHill Suites, Super 8 $Tree, AT&T, Barnes&Noble, Belk, Best Buy, BigLots, Clark Tire/auto, Dick's, Dillards, Firestone/auto, Ingles Foods/gas, JC Penney, Jo-Ann, Lowe's, Michael's, Midas, Office Depot, Old Navy, Ross, Target, TJ Maxx, Walgreens, Whole Foods Mkt
6	Tunnel Rd (from eb), same as 7
5b	US 70 E, US 74A, Charlotte St, N Exxon, Shell Charlotte St. Grill, Fuddruckers, Starbucks, Two Guys Hogi B&B vet, S Chop House Rest. Renaissance Hotel, Sheraton Civic Ctr

INTERSTATE 240 (Asheville) Cont'd

Exit #	Services
5a	US 25, Merrimon Ave, N Enmark, Exxon/dsl, Shell/dsl Bojangles, Chick-fil-A Green Life Foods, Harris Teeter, Staples, Trader Joe's
4c	Haywood St (no EZ return to eb), Montford, S Carmel's Rest., Isa's Bistro, Roman's Deli B&B, Hotel Indigo downtown
4b	Patton Ave (from eb), downtown
4a	US 19 N, US 23 N, US 70 W, to Weavervilles
3b	Westgate, N Green Sage Cafe, Jason's Deli, Oriental Pavillion Country Inn Suites, Crowne Plaza CVS Drug, EarthFare Foods, Mr Transmission, Sam's Club/gas, Tuesday Morning
3a	US 19 S, US 23 S, W Asheville, N Shell/dsl A&W/LJ Silver, Bojangles, Burger King, CookOut, Denny's, Dragon China, El Que Pasa Mexican, Firehouse Subs, Green Tea Japanese, Jersey Mike's, KFC, Krispy Kreme, Little Caesar's, McDonald's, Neo Burrito, New 1 China, Papa John's, Pizza Hut, Sonic, Subway, Taco Bell, Wendy's, Yoshida Japanese, Zingers Cafe $General, Advance Parts, Aldi Foods, AT&T, AutoZone, Clark Tire/auto, Ingles Foods, Sav-Mor Foods, URGENT CARE, vet, Walgreens
2	US 19, US 23, W Asheville, N Haywood Quickstop/dsl Zia Mexican, S B&B Drug
1c	Amboy Rd (from eb)s
1b	NC 191, to I-40 E, Brevard Rd, S camping, farmers mkt
1a	I-40 W, to Knoxvilles
0mm	**I-240 begins/ends on I-40, exit 46b a.**

INTERSTATE 440 (Raleigh)

Exit #	Services
16	I-40. **I-440 begins/ends on I-40.**
15	Poole Rd, E BP, Exxon, W Circle K, Citgo/dsl, Valero/dsl Burger King, Family$, Food Lion, KFC/Taco Bell, McDonald's, Subway, Wang's Kitchen
14	I-495, US 64/264, to Wilson, to Rocky Mount
13b a	US 64 bus, New Bern Ave, to Wilson, 0-2 mi E BP/Circle K, Circle K, Exxon, Exxon/dsl, Murphy USA/dsl, Shell/dsl Bojangles, Burger King, Domino's, McDonald's, Papa John's, Pizza Hut, Popeye's, Ruby Tuesday, Starbucks, Subway, Waffle House, Wendy's Comfort Suites, Holiday Inn Express, Knights Inn, Microtel, Quality Inn Advance Parts, AutoZone, CVS Drug, Firestone/auto, Food Lion, O'Reilly Parts, Plemmons RV Ctr, U-Haul, vet, Walgreens, Walmart, W H
12	Yonkers Rd, Brentwood Rd
11b a	US 1, US 401, Capital Blvd N, N BP, BP, Exxon, Mobil, Sunoco, Valero/dsl Baskin-Robbins/Dunkin', Buffalo Bros Pizza, Burger King, ChuckeCheese, Cici's, Cookout, Golden Corral, IHOP, Mayflower Seafood, McDonald's, Outback Steaks, Popeye's, Starbucks, Taco Bell, Vallerta Mexican, Waffle House Best Value Inn, Best Western, Extended Stay America, Holiday Inn, La Quinta, Motel 6, Quality Inn $Tree, Advance Parts, AT&T, AutoZone, Food Lion, U-Haul
10	Wake Forest Rd, N Bahama Breeze, Denny's Days Inn, Extended Stay America, Hilton, Hyatt Place, Residence Inn H, CVS Drug, S BP Applebee's, Arby's, Biscuitville, BurgerFi, El Rodeo Mexican, Jersey Mike's, Jimmy John's, Jumbo China, McDonald's, Melting Pot Rest., Papa John's, Pizza Hut, Qdoba, Subway, Tropical Smoothie Comfort Inn, Courtyard, Extended Stay America Advance Parts, AutoZone, Buick/GMC, Costco/gas, Discount Tire, Hyundai, Mazda, Ross, Staples, Subaru, Trader Joe's
8b a	6 Forks Rd, North Hills, N Exxon/repair, Tesla EVC Bo fish Grill, Capital Grille, Chick-fil-A, Chuy's, Firebirds Grill, Guys, Fox&Hound Grille, Moe's SW Grill, Panera Bread, P la Pizza, Pieology, Ruths Chris Steaks, Starbucks, Zoe's Ki en AC Hotel Marriott, Hyatt House, Renaissance AT GNC, Harris Teeter, JC Penney, REI, Target
7b a	US 70, NC 50, Glenwood Ave, Crabtree Valley, N BP (2), dsl Brio Grill, Cheesecake Factory, Fleming's, Kanki Ja nese, McDonald's, Panera Bread, PF Chang's Candlew Suites, Courtyard, Embassy Suites, Fairfield Inn, Hampton Hilton Garden, Holiday Inn, La Quinta, Marriott, Reside Inn Barnes&Noble, Belk, Best Buy, Macy's, McCormick& micks, Old Navy
6	Ridge Rd (from nb), same as 7
5	Lake Boone Tr, W Shell/Circle K Chick-fil-A, McD ald's, Starbucks, Village Deli H, Food Lion, Rite Aid
4b a	to I-40 W, Wade Ave, to RDU
3	NC 54, Hillsboro St, E BP, Exxon Arby's, Bean Sp Chinese, IHOP, Snoopy's Hotdogs, Waffle House to M dith Coll, to St Mary's, W to Carter-Finley Stadium
2b a	Western Blvd, E Domino's, Exxon, Shell/Circle K, Spe way/dsl Amedeo's Italian, Bojangles, Cookout, Dun McDonalds, Popeye's, Subway, Taco Bell, Wendy's Adva Parts, Food Lion, Roses, Shaw U, to NCSU, vet
1d	Melbourne Rd (from sb)
1c	Jones-Franklin Rd
1b a	I-40. **I-440 begins on I-40.**

INTERSTATE 485 (Charlotte)

Exit #	Services
67	I-77, US 21, to Charlotte, Columbia, **I-485 begins/ends**
65	South Blvd, N Kangaroo Chick-fil-A, Golden ral, Hooters, McDonald's, Popeyes, Steak'n Shake, Wen $Tree, Advance Parts, Big Lots, Chevrolet, Discount T Honda, Jo-Ann, Kohl's, Nissan, Old Navy, Petsmart, Ross, Su ru, Target, Toyota, Verizon, VW, World Mkt, S Arby's dillac, CarMax, Mercedes, NAPA, TreadQtrs Auto/tire, vet
64b a	rd 51, N Exxon/dsl, Shell/Circle K/dsl Bojang Chili's, CiCi's, CookOut, Firehouse Subs, Jimmy John's, K Cafeteria, KFC, McDonald's, Outback Steaks, Pizza Hut, S bucks, Wendy's Extended Stay America H, Aldi Fo AutoZone, Bi-Lo, Family$, Firestone/auto, S Kanga Shell/7-11 Applebee's, Buca Italian, Burger King, Capt China Buffet, Harper's Rest., IHOP, Jason's Deli, Longhorn Ste McAlister's Deli, Olive Garden, Red Lobster, Sky Asian, Subw Taco Bell Comfort Suites, Hampton Inn, Hilton Garden, H day Inn Express, Quality Inn $General, Barnes&Noble, B Best Buy, Dick's, Dillard's, Food Lion, Home Depot, JC Pen Macy's, Meineke, Midas, Office Depot, REI, Rite Aid, Sam's C gas, SteinMart, Tire Kingdom, TJ Maxx
61b a	US 521 S, Johnston Rd, N Global Rest., Hickory Tavern, Robin, Ruby Tuesday, Sticky Fingers, Viva Chicken Ho wood Suites, SpringHill Suites Earth Fare Foods, S K garoo/dsl 5 Guys Burgers, Duckworth's Grill, Me Mushroom Rest., Pei Wei, Starbucks, Stone Mtn Grill, Subw Tony's Pizza, Vine American Kitchen Ballantyne Ho Courtyard, Staybridge Suites CVS Drug
59	Rea Rd, E Exxon/7-11 1511 Cantina, Applebe Boneheads Grill, Chick-fil-A, City Tavern, Firebirds Grill, Ma Slab, Noodles Rest., Qdoba, Smashburger, Starbucks, True za, Wendy's Residence Inn GNC, Goodyear/auto, H ris-Teeter, Michaels, Target, vet

INTERSTATE 485 (Charlotte) Cont'd

Exit #	Services
57	Providence Rd, rd 16, E Kangaroo/Wendy's Hickory Tavern, Ilios Noche, Papa John's, Penn Sta, The Wok Harris-Teeter, USPO, W Exxon/7-11, Shell BBQ Shack, BT Burgers, Macaroni Grill, On the Border, Red Bowl Rest., Showmars Rest., Starbucks, Subway, Wolfman Pizza CVS Drug, Harris-Teeter, Home Depot, Lowes Whse, Rite Aid, Staples, SteinMart, vet
52	E John St, to Matthews
51b a	US 74, to Charlotte, Monroe, E Circle K/dsl Country Inn&Suites, InTown Suites, Quality Inn Toyota, W Citgo/dsl, Exxon/7-11, Shell Bojangles, Golden Corral, Pizza Hut, TX Roadhouse, Wendy's Courtyard, EconoLodge, Microtel H, Aamco, AutoZone, Best Buy, Black's Auto/tire, Costco/gas, Firestone/auto, Lowe's Whse, Sam's Club/gas, Target, Tuesday Morning
49	Idlewild Rd, E Exxon/7-11/dsl Cactus Rose Mexican, China Cafe, Mama's Pizza $Tree, GNC, Harris-Teeter, Meineke, Rite Aid
47	Lawyers Rd, E Gate/dsl Bellacino's Pizza, Best China, Carnita's Mexican, Domino's, McDonald's, Subway CVS Drug, Firestone/auto, Harris-Teeter, vet
44	rd 218, to Mint Hill, W BP/dsl, Shell/7-11 $General, city park, CVS
43	rd 51, to Mint Hill
41	rd 24, rd 27, to Albemarle, E Speedway/dsl Bojangles
39	Harrisburg Rd, W BP/EVC China Garden, Papa John's, Wendy's Food Lion
36	Rocky River Rd, E BP/dsl, Gate/dsl Best China, Bojangles, Capriccio Pizza, Subway CVS Drug, Discount Tire, EMERGENCY, GNC, Harris-Teeter, Tuffy Auto
33	rd 49, to Harrisburg, E Speedway/dsl Cici's Pizza Food Lion, USPO, W BP, Circle K/dsl, Exxon/7-11, Shell/7-11/dsl Arby's, Chopsticks, Domino's, Little Caesar's, Wendy's Family$
32	US 29, N QT/dsl CVS Drug, Walmart Mkt, S Exxon/7-11/dsl, Kangaroo, Speedway/dsl Jack-in-the-Box H, Tire Kingdom
30b a	I-85, N to High Point, S to Charlotte
28	Mallard Creek Rd
26	Benfield Rd, Prosperity Church Rd, Prosperity Ridge Rd, N BP/dsl Bojangle's, IHOP, Jersey Mike's, Papa Murphy's, Starbucks, Subway Aldi Foods, Giffen Bros Automotive, Harris Teeter, Publix, Rite Aid, S Shell/Circle K/dsl
23c	rd 115, to Huntersville, N Shell/7-11/dsl Audi, BMW, Lexus, Mercedes, Walmart
23b a	I-77, to Charlotte, Statesville

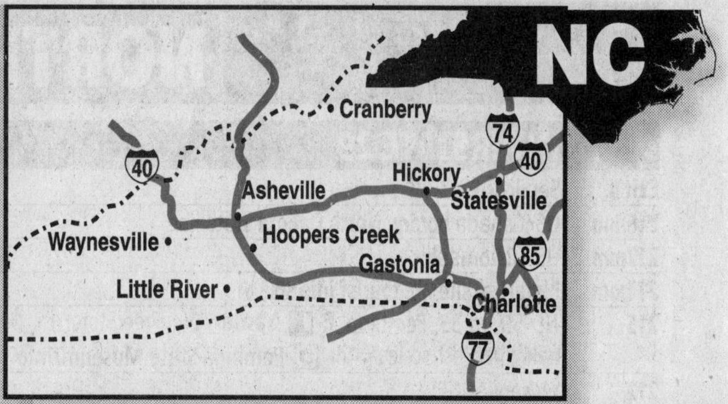

Exit #	Services
21	rd 24, Harris Blvd, S Bravo Italian, Buffalo Wild Wings, Chick-fil-A, Chili's, East Coast Grill, Edomae Grill, Firebirds Grill, Firehouse Subs, Five Guys, Fox&Hound, Jersey Mike's, McDonald's, Mimi's Cafe, Moe's SW Grill, Olive Garden, On-the-Border, Panera bread, PF Chang's, Red Robin, Shane's Rib Shack, TGI Friday's, Wendy's Drury Inn $Tree, AT&T, Belk, Best Buy, Dick's, Dillard's, Discount Tire, Lowe's Whse, Macy's, Old Navy, Petsmart, REI, Target, Verizon
16	rd 16, to Newton, Brookshire Blvd, E city park, W Bojangles, Bull&Barrister Grille, Chick-fil-A, Domino's, Los Arcos, McDonald's, Papa John's, Pizza Hut, Red Bowl Asian, Subway, Wendy's AT&T, AutoZone, Harris-Teeter, Rite Aid, URGENT CARE, vet, Walmart/Subway
14	rd 27, to Mt Holly Rd, W BP (2mi) Sonic (2mi) Food Lion (2mi), Meineke (2mi)
12	Moores Chapel Rd, E Jin Jin Chinese, Subway Advance Parts, CVS Drug, Family$, Food Lion
10b a	I-85, to Spartanburg, Greensboros
9	US 29, US 74, Wilkinson Blvd, S BP camping
6	West Blvd
4	rd 160, to Fort Mill, N Exxon/7-11/dsl CVS Drug, S BP/dsl Bojangles Charlotte Premium Outlets/famous brands
3	Arrowood Rd, S Quizno's, Siam Garden
1	S Tryon St, NC 49, N Citgo, Exxon/7-11 Arby's, Bojangles, Chick-fil-A, Chili's, Dragon Buffet, IHOP, Lenny's Subs, Luigi's Pizza, McDonald's, O'Charley's, Panera Bread, Qdoba, Showmars Rest., Waffle House, Zaxby's Family$, GNC, Lowe's Whse, Rite Aid, Walmart, S Kangaroo/dsl, QT/dsl Mac's BBQ, Applebee's, Baskin-Robbins/Dunkin', Burger King, Domino's, Don Pedro Mexican, Firehouse Subs, Fortune Cookie, Hungry Howie's, Joe Momma's Pizza, KFC, McAlister's Deli, Pan China, Portofino's, Starbucks, Subway, Taco Bell, Wild Wing Cafe Hilton Garden, Homewood Suites $Tree, AT&T, AutoZone, Discount Tire, Food Lion, NAPA, Office Depot, Tire Kingdom, Tuffy Auto, URGENT CARE

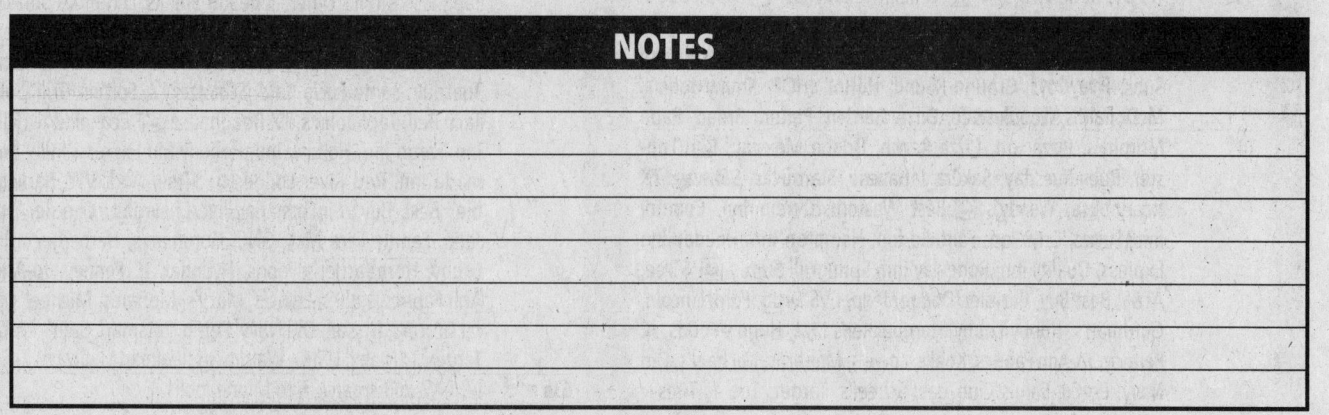

NC

NOTES

NORTH DAKOTA

INTERSTATE 29

Exit #	Services
218mm	US/Canada border, North Dakota state line
217mm	US Customs sb
216mm	historical site nb, tourist info sb
215	ND 59, rd 55, Pembina, E Gastrak/DutyFree Store/dsl, Gastrak/pizza/dsl/scales/24hr Pembina State Museum/info
212	no service
208	rd 1, to Bathgate
203	US 81, ND 5, to Hamilton, Cavalier, W to Icelandic SP (25 mi), **weigh sta both lanes**
200	no service
196	rd 3, Bowesmont
193	no service
191	rd 11, to St Thomas
187	ND 66, to Drayton, E Cenex/pizza/dsl/E-85, Tesoro/dsl Motel 66 city park, USPO
184	to Drayton, **2 mi** E gas/dsl USPO
180	rd 9
179mm	**both lanes (both lanes exit left), full facilities, litter barrels, petwalk, , , vending**
176	ND 17, to Grafton, **10 mi** W gas food lodging
172	65th St NE
168	rd 15, to Minto, Warsaw
164	57th St NE
161	ND 54, rd 19, to Ardoch, Oslo
157	32nd Ave
152	US 81, to Gilby, Manvel, W Manvel/dsl/food
145	US 81 bus, N Washington St, to Grand Forks
141	US 2, Gateway Dr, Grand Forks, E Cenex, Loaf'N Jug/dsl, University Sta/dsl Burger King, Far East Buffet, Little Caesar's, McDonald's, Northside Cafe, Papa Murphy's, Subway, Taco John's Best Value Inn, Budget Inn, EconoLodge, Grand Forks Inn, Ramada Inn, Select Inn, Super 8 , AT&T, Freightliner, Hugo's Foods, Kia, O'Reilly Parts, Subaru, to U of ND, transmissions, U-Haul, visitors ctr, W Simonson/café/dsl/24hr, StaMart/dsl/RV dump/scales/24hr/@ Hardee's Knights Inn , Budget RV Ctr, dsl repair, Mack/Volvo, NW Tire, to AFB, vet, Walmart/Subway
140	DeMers Ave, E Cenex/dsl, Loaf'N Jug/dsl, Valley Dairy Red Pepper Cafe, Tim Hortons Baymont Inn, Canada Inn, Expressway Suites, Hilton Garden, La Quinta, My Place Suites, Sleep Inn, Staybridge Suites , Alerus Ctr, to U of ND
138	US 81, 32nd Ave S, E Cenex, Holiday/dsl Applebee's, Arby's, Buffalo Wild Wings, Burger King, Cherry Berry Yogurt, Coldstone, Culver's, Denny's, DQ, Erbert&Gerbert's, Firehouse Subs, Five Guys, Ground Round, HuHot, IHOP, Jimmy John's, McDonald's, Noodles&Co, Olive Garden, Panera Bread, Papa Murphy's, Pizza Hut, Pizza Ranch, Qdoba Mexican, Red Lobster, Ruby Tuesday, Sakura Japanese, Starbucks, Subway, TX Roadhouse, Wendy's Best Western, C'mon Inn, Country Inn&Suites, Days Inn, Fairfield Inn, Hampton Inn, Holiday Inn Express, Quality Inn, Rodeway Inn, SpringHill Suites $Tree, AT&T, Best Buy, Chrysler/Dodge/Jeep, CVS Drug, Ford/Lincoln, Gordman's, Hobby Lobby, Hornbacher's Mkt, Hugo's Foods, JC Penney, Jo-Ann Fabrics, Kohl's, Lowe's, Menards, Michael's, Old Navy, PetCo, Sam's Club/gas, Scheel's, Target, Tire 1, Tires+,

ND

GRAND FORKS

Exit #	Services
138	Continued TJ Maxx, Toyota, Verizon, vet, Walmart/Subway, White D Natural Grocers, W FLYING J/Subway/dsl/LP/scales dump/24hr Grand Forks Camping
130	ND 15, rd 81, Thompson, **1 mi** W gas food
123	to Reynolds, E to Central Valley School
120	**truck insp sb**
118	to Buxton
111	ND 200 W, to Cummings, Mayville, W Big Top Firework Mayville St U
104	Hillsboro, E Casey's, Cenex/Burger King/dsl/LP/24hr S way Hillsboro Inn , Hillsboro Camping, USPO
100	ND 200 E, ND 200A, to Blanchard, Halstad
99mm	**both lanes, full facilities, litter barrels, petwalk, , vending**
92	rd 11, Grandin, W Stop&Shop/dsl
86	Gardner
78	Argusville
74.5mm	Sheyenne River
72	rd 17, rd 22, Harwood, E Cenex/pizza/dsl/LP/café/24hr
69	rd 20
67	US 81 bus, 19th Ave N, **1 mi** E Applebee's, Bu Wild Wings, Burger King, McDonald's, Pizza Hut, Subv Taco Bell Candlewood Suites, Days Inn, Homew Suites CVS Drug, Hector Int Airport, VA
66	12th Ave N, E StaMart/dsl/scales/24hr Marlin's F Woodspring Suites , to ND St U, tuck re W Cenex/dsl Arby's Super 8
65	US 10, Main Ave, W Fargo, E Tesoro/dsl CarQu NAPA, OK Tire, vet, W Cenex/Subway/dsl, Simonson Hardee's, O'Kelly's Rest., Season Buffet Chinese more on Main Inn CarQuest, Honda, Kia, Lincoln, M Hardware, Mazda, Mercedes, O'Reilly Parts, Recreation RV Toyota, VW
64	13th Ave, Fargo, E Don's, Exxon, Kum&Go/dsl, Pet erve/dsl Acapulco Mexican, Applebee's, Arby's, Bu Rest, Burger King, ChuckeCheese, DQ, Erbert&Gerbert's S GreenMill Rest., Ground Round, Little Caesar's, Perkins, S ie's Garage, Subway, Taco John's, Wendy's Americ Baymont Inn, Country Inn&Suites, Days Inn, EconoLo EconoLodge, Grand Inn, Motel 6, Quality Inn, Quality Suites, per 8 AT&T, CashWise Foods/drug/gas, CVS Drug, Fami Goodyear/auto, Meineke, O'Reilly Parts, Tires+/transmissi Tuesday Morning, Verizon, White Drug, W All-Stop/dsl, sey's, Cenex Applebee's, Arby's, Buffalo Wild Wings, Ch Culver's, Denny's, Domino's, DQ, Happy Joe's Pizza, KFC, K Japanese, Kroll's Diner, LoneStar Steaks, Longhorn Steaks, Donald's, Olive Garden, Osaka Japanese, Panchero's Mexi Panera Bread, Paradiso Mexican, Pizza Hut, Red Lobster, R Tuesday, Santa Lucia Cafe, Schlotzsky's, Spitfire Grill, Subv Taco Bell, Taco John's, TX Roadhouse Econolodge, Fair Inn, Fargo Inn, Holiday Inn, Holiday Inn Express, Kelly Inn, mada Inn, Red River Lodge $Tree, Audi/VW, Barnes& ble, Best Buy, BigLots, Cadillac/Chevrolet, Chrysler/Do Jeep, Family Fare Mkt, GNC, Gordman's, Herberger's, Ho Lobby, Hornbacher's Foods, Hyundai, JC Penney, Jo-Ann, Ann Fabrics, Kohl's, Lowe's, Macy's, Menards, Michael's, N ral Grocers, Nissan, Old Navy, PetCo, Petsmart, Sam's Club/ Target, TJ Maxx, USPO, Walgreens, Walmart/Subway
63b a	I-94, W to Bismarck, E to Minneapolis

FARGO

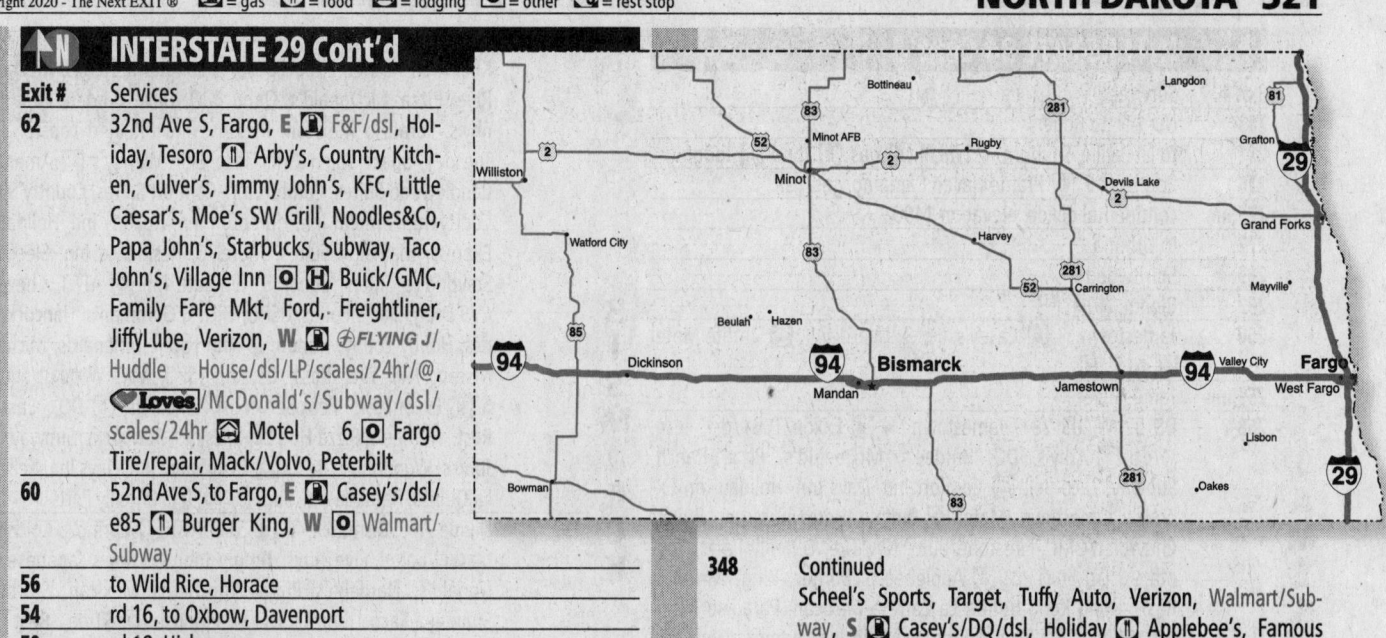

INTERSTATE 29 Cont'd

Exit #	Services
62	32nd Ave S, Fargo, E F&F/dsl, Holiday, Tesoro Arby's, Country Kitchen, Culver's, Jimmy John's, KFC, Little Caesar's, Moe's SW Grill, Noodles&Co, Papa John's, Starbucks, Subway, Taco John's, Village Inn Buick/GMC, Family Fare Mkt, Ford, Freightliner, JiffyLube, Verizon, W FLYING J/Huddle House/dsl/LP/scales/24hr/@, Loves/McDonald's/Subway/dsl/scales/24hr Motel 6 Fargo Tire/repair, Mack/Volvo, Peterbilt
60	52nd Ave S, to Fargo, E Casey's/dsl/e85 Burger King, W Walmart/Subway
56	to Wild Rice, Horace
54	rd 16, to Oxbow, Davenport
50	rd 18, Hickson
48	ND 46, to Kindred
44	to Christine
42	rd 2, to Walcott
37	rd 4, to Abercrombie, Colfax, E to Ft Abercrombie HS, 3 mi W gas
31	rd 8, Galchutt
26	to Dwight
24mm	**weigh sta both lanes exit left**
23b a	ND 13, to Wahpeton, Mooreton, 10 mi E H, ND St Coll of Science
15	rd 16, to Mantador, Great Bend
8	ND 11, to Hankinson, Fairmount, E Tesoro/dsl, 3 mi W camping
3mm	**Welcome Ctr nb, full facilities, litter barrels, petwalk,**
2	rd 22
1	rd 1E, E Dakota Magic Casino/Hotel/rest./gas/dsl
0mm	North Dakota/South Dakota state line

INTERSTATE 94

Exit #	Services
352mm	North Dakota/Minnesota state line, Red River
351	US 81, Fargo, N Casey's, Loaf'n Jug Duane's Pizza, Great Harvest Breads, Great Wall Chinese, Taco Shop H, Hornbacher's Foods, Medicine Shoppe, vet, S Tesoro/dsl Burger King, Happy Joe's Pizza, McDonald's, Pepper's Café, Randy's Diner, Subway, Taco Bell Rodeway Inn, Vista Inn Hornbacher's/gas, O'Reilly Parts, Verizon
350	25th St, Fargo, N Casey's, S Loaf'n Jug/dsl, Phillips/dsl Dolittle's Grill, Ruby Tuesday
349b a	I-29, N to Grand Forks, S to Sioux Falls, **services 1 mi N exit 64**
348	45th St, N **Visitor Ctr/full facilities, litter barrels,** Holiday/dsl, Petro/dsl/Lp/24hrs/@ Carino's, Chipotle, Coldstone, Culver's, Denny's, Dunn Bros Coffee, Granite City, HuHot Mongolian, IHOP, Kroll's Diner, Little Caesar's, Longhorn Steaks, Maddio's Pizza, McDonald's, Noodles&Co, Panda Express, Papa Murphy's, Pizza Hut, Potbelly, Qdoba, Smashburger, Space Aliens Grill, Subway, Wendy's, Wild Bill's Best Western, C'Mon Inn, Expressway Suites, Hilton Garden, Holiday Inn Express, Home 2 Suites, MainStay Suites, Ramada Inn, Red Roof Inn, Staybridge Suites, Wingate Inn Blue Beacon, Hobby Lobby, Home Depot, Kohl's, NAPA, Old Navy, Sam's Club,

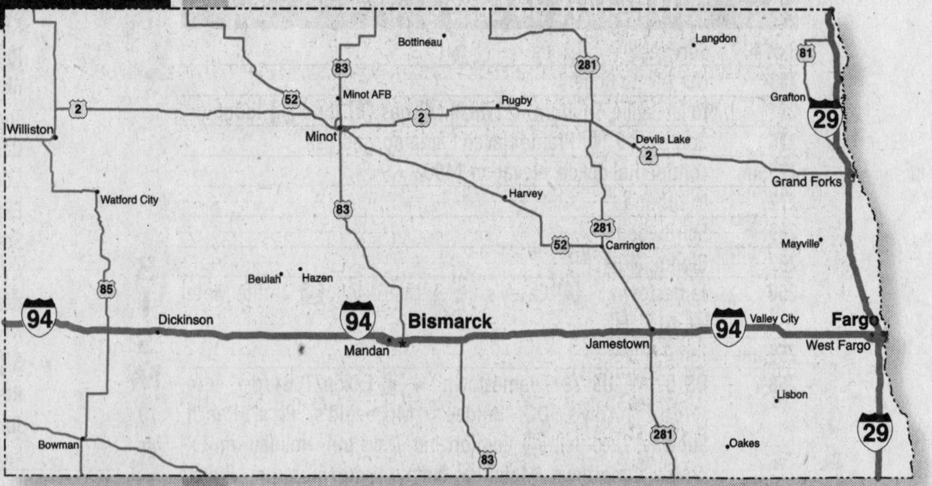

Exit #	Services
348	Continued Scheel's Sports, Target, Tuffy Auto, Verizon, Walmart/Subway, S Casey's/DQ/dsl, Holiday Applebee's, Famous Dave's BBQ, Five Guys, Hardee's, Korean BBQ, Mexican Village, Old Chicago Pizza, Pizza Ranch, Sonic, Taco John's, Taco Shop AmericInn, Comfort Suites, Hampton Inn, La Quinta, Residence Inn, Sheraton, Sleep Inn AT&T, Red River Zoo
347	9th St E, Veterans Blvd, N Blarney Stone Cambria Inn, Element Hotel, S Casey's/dsl Firehouse Subs, McDonald's, Papa John's, Subway, Taco Bell Microtel, My Place Hotel Cash Wise Foods/dsl, Costco/gas, H
346b a	to Horace, W Fargo, S repair, Tesoro/dsl Harley Davidson
343	US 10, Lp 94, W Fargo, N Cenex/dsl Adventure RV Ctr, Pioneer Village, Red River Valley RV Park
342	38th St NE
342mm	**weigh sta wb**
340	to Kindred
338	Mapleton, N Tesoro/dsl
337mm	truck parking wb, litter barrels
331	ND 18, to Leonard, Casselton, N Tesoro/Subway/dsl Country Kitchen Days Inn/RV park
328	to Lynchburg
327mm	**truck parking eb, litter barrels**
324	Wheatland, to Chaffee
322	Absaraka
320	to Embden
317	to Ayr
314	ND 38 N, to Alice, Buffalo, 3 mi N gas food
310	36th St SE
307	to Tower City, N Cenex/café/dsl/RV Park/24hr, motel
304mm	**both lanes (both lanes exit left), full facilities, info, litter barrels, petwalk, vending**
302	ND 32, to Fingal, Oriska, 1 mi N city park
298	123rd Ave SE
296	121st Av SE
294	Lp 94, to Kathryn, Valley City, N H, camping
292	Valley City, N PetroServe/Tesoro/café/dsl Sabir's Rest. AmericInn, Grand Stay Hotel, Super 8, Wagon Wheel Inn/rest. H, Ford, to Bald Hill Dam, S Ft Ransom SP (35mi)
291	Sheyenne River
290	Lp 94, Valley City, N Casey's/dsl Burger King, Kenny's Rest., Kirin House Chinese, Pizza Ranch, Subway H, Buick/Chevrolet/GMC, Chrysler/Dodge/Jeep, Family$, Firestone/auto, NAPA, O'Reilly Parts
288	ND 1 S, to Oakes, S Fort Ransom SP (36 mi)

ND

INTERSTATE 94 Cont'd

Exit #	Services
283	ND 1 N, to Rogers
281	to Litchville, Sanborn, **1-2 mi N** gas food lodging
276	Eckelson, **S** Prairie Haven Camping/gas/dsl
275mm	continental divide, elevation 1490
272	to Urbana
269	Spiritwood
262	Bloom, **N**
260	Jamestown, **N** Casey's, Cenex/café/dsl/@ Starlite Motel to St H
259mm	James River
258	US 52 W, US 281, Jamestown, **N** Exxon/TCBY/dsl, Tesoro/dsl Arby's, DQ, Hardee's, McDonald's, Pizza Ranch, Subway, Taco Bell Comfort Inn, Days Inn, Holiday Inn Express, Jamestown Motel Buffalo Herd/museum, Buick/Chevrolet/GMC, Firestone/auto, NW Tire, O'Reilly Parts, Toyota, **S** Shell/dsl Applebee's, Burger King, Grizzly's Rest., Hong Kong Buffet, La Carreta Mexican, Paradiso Mexican, Perkins EconoLodge, Fairfield Inn, Hampton Inn, My Place, Quality Inn, Super 8 $Tree, AT&T, Chrysler/Dodge/Jeep, Ford/Lincoln, GNC, Harley-Davidson, Mac's Hardware, Menards, Verizon, Walmart
257	Lp 94 (from eb, exits left), to Jamestown, **N** dsl repair
256	US 52 W, US 281 N, **S** H, Jamestown Campground/RV dump (1mi)
254mm	**both lanes, full facilities, litter barrels, petwalk, , , vending**
251	Eldridge
248	74th Ave SE
245	70th Ave SE
242	Windsor
238	to Gackle, Cleveland
233	58th Ave SE
230	Medina, **1 mi N** Famer's Union/dsl/LP DairyTreat city park, Medina RV Park, USPO
228	ND 30 S, to Streeter
224mm	**wb, full facilities, litter barrels, petwalk, , , vending**
221	Crystal Springs
221mm	**eb, full facilities, litter barrels, petwalk, , , vending**
217	Pettibone
214	Tappen, **S** gas/dsl/food
208	ND 3 S, Dawson, **N** RV camping, **1/2 mi S** gas food RV camping, to Camp Grassick
205	Robinson
200	ND 3 N, to Tuttle, Steele, **S** Shell/Subway/Pizza Hut/dsl Cobblestone Inn truckwash
195	20th Ave SE
190	Driscoll, **S** food
182	US 83 S, ND 14, to Wing, Sterling, **S** Cenex/dsl Top's Motel (1mi)
176	McKenzie
170	Menoken, **S** RV Park, to McDowell Dam
168mm	**both lanes, full facilities, litter barrels, petwalk, , , vending, wifi**
161	Lp 94, Bismarck Expswy, Bismarck, **N** Cenex/dsl/LP/24hr, Exxon/dsl My Place Peterbilt, Toyota, **S** Holiday/dsl, Tesoro/Marlin's Rest./dsl/scales/24hr McDonald's Ramada Ltd Capital RV Ctr, Dakota Zoo, dsl repair, Freightliner, Kenworth, OK Tires
159	US 83, Bismarck, **N** Holiday/dsl, Simonson/dsl Applebee's, Arby's, Buffalo Wings&Rings, China Star, Hong Kong Chinese,

JAMESTOWN

BISMARCK

Exit #	Services
159	Continued KFC, Kroll's Diner, Little Caesar's, Longhorn Steaks, MacKe River Pizza, McDonald's, Oahu BBQ, Olive Garden, Papa M phy's, Paradiso Mexican, Perkins, Pita Pit, Red Lobster, R Tuesday, Space Alien Grill, Taco Bell, Wendy's Americ Candlewood Suites, Comfort Inn, Comfort Suites, Country Su Courtyard, Fairfield Inn, Hampton Inn, Holiday Inn, Holiday Express, Mainstay Suites, Motel 6, Residence Inn, Sleep Staybridge Suites, Super 8, Wingate Inn AT&T, Chevr CVS Drug, Dan's Foods/USPO, Dick's, Gordman's, Hancock rics, Hobby Lobby, Honda, Jo-Ann Fabrics, Menards, Micha Nissan, NW Tire, Ross, UHaul, USPO, VW, Walmart/Subw **S** Exxon/dsl, PetroServe/dsl, Shell/dsl DQ, East Rest., Hardee's, Pizza Hut, Schlotzsky's, Starbucks, Subway, John's, Woodhouse Rest. Best Value Inn, Days Inn, Kelly La Quinta, Ramada Inn, Super 8 H, O'Reilly Parts
157	Divide Ave, Bismarck, **N** Shell/dsl Carino's, Coldst Cracker Barrel, Five Guys, Jimmy John's, Kobe's Japanese, Donald's, Nardello's Pizza, Pancheros Mexican, Starbu Subway, Taco John's, TX Roadhouse $Tree, Best GNC, Kohl's, Lowe's, Old Navy, Petsmart, TJ Maxx, Veri visitor ctr, **S** Cenex/dsl/E85/LP/RV Dump Stad Café Hampton Inn Dan's Mkt/USPO
156mm	Missouri River
156	I-194, Bismarck Expswy, Bismarck City Ctr, **1/2 mi S** Dakota
155	to Lp 94 (exits left from wb), Mandan, City Ctr, same as 153
153	ND 1806, Mandan Dr, Mandan, **1/2 mi S** Cenex/dsl, M dsl, PetroServe/dsl, Tesoro Bonanza, Burger King, Da ta Farms Rest., Domino's, DQ, Hardee's, Papa Murphy's, za Hut, Pizza Ranch, Subway, Taco John's North Cou Inn Chevrolet, Dacotah Centennial Park, Family$, Ft Lin SP (5mi), Goodyear/auto, NAPA, NW Tire, O'Reilly Parts, Su ru, Verizon
152	Sunset Dr, Mandan, **N** Tesoro/dsl Baymont Inn, C fort Inn Thrifty White Drug, Walmart/Subway, **S** Tes RV dump Fried's Rest. H
152mm	scenic view eb
147	ND 25, to ND 6, Mandan, **S** FLYING J/Shell/Subway/ scales/24hr
140	to Crown Butte
135mm	scenic view wb, litter barrel
134	to Judson, Sweet Briar Lake
127	ND 31 N, to New Salem, **N** Knife River Indian Vill (35mi), **S** Cenex/dsl, Tesoro/dsl Sunset Cafe Arr head Inn/café DFC/dsl, vet, World's Largest Cow
123	to Almont
120	no service
119mm	**both lanes, full facilities, litter barrels, petwalk,**
117	no service
113	no service
110	ND 49, to Glen Ullin
108	to Glen Ullin, Lake Tschida, **3 mi S** gas food lo ing camping
102	Hebron, to Glen Ullin, to Lake Tschida, **3 mi S** food lodging camping
97	Hebron, **2 mi N** gas food lodging
96.5mm	central/mountain time zone
90	no service
84	ND 8, Richardton, **N** Cenex/dsl H, Schnell RA, Spr field Mkt, to Assumption Abbey
78	to Taylor
72	to Enchanted Hwy, Gladstone

BISMARCK

MANDAN

HEBRON

ND

INTERSTATE 94 Cont'd

Exit #	Services
64	Dickinson, S Cenex/Tiger Truckstop/rest./dsl/24hr, Dakota Diner dsl repair, Ford/Lincoln, Honda, NW Tire, Toyota
61	ND 22, Dickinson, N Cenex/dsl/LP, Mobil/Schlotsky's/dsl/scales/24hr, Simonson/dsl Applebee's, Arby's, Burger King, City Brew Coffee, DQ, El Sombrero Mexican, Jimmy John's, Papa Murphy's, Pizza Ranch, Qdoba, Sakura Japanese, Sanford's Rest., Taco Bell, Taco John's, Wendy's AmericInn, Astoria Suites, Best Western, Candlewood Suites, Comfort Inn, Hampton Inn, Holiday Inn Express, Microtel, My Place, Ramada, Red Roof Inn, TownePlace Suites AT&T, Cashwise Foods, Chevrolet/Cadillac, Family Fare Mkt, Goodyear/auto, Herberger's, Midas, O'Reilly Parts, Runnings Hardware, USPO, Verizon, Walmart/Subway, White Drug, S Cenex/dsl, Conoco/repair, Holiday/dsl, Tesoro/Domino's/dsl A&W/KFC, Country Kitchen, Don Pedro's Mexican, King Buffet, McDonald's, Perkins, Subway La Quinta, Motel 6, Quality Inn, Relax Inn, Rodeway Inn, Travel Inn H, Ace Hardware, museum, visitor info
59	Lp 94, to Dickinson, N Buffalo Wild Wings Hawthorn Suites, Woodspring Suites Family Fare/dsl, Menard's, Verizon, S camping, H, to Patterson Lake RA, services in Dickinson
56	116th Ave
51	South Heart
42	US 85, to Grassy Butte, Belfield,Williston, N MVP/dsl T Roosevelt NP (52mi), S Cenex/dsl/24hr, Conoco/dsl Trapper's Kettle Rest. Trapper's Inn NAPA
36	Fryburg
32	T Roosevelt NP, N **both lanes, full facilities, scenic overlook**
27	Lp 94, S Historic Medora (from wb), T Roosevelt NP
24.5mm	Little Missouri Scenic River
24	Medora, Historic Medora, S Chateau de Mores HS, T Roosevelt NP, visitors ctr
23	West River Rd (from wb)
22mm	scenic view eb
18	Buffalo Gap, N Buffalo Gap Camping (seasonal)
10	Sentinel Butte, Camel Hump Lake, S gas
7	Home on the Range
1	ND 16, S **Welcome/Visitor Ctr, full facilities, litter barrels, petwalk,** FLYING J/Subway/dsl/scales/LP/24hr, Cenex/dsl/LP/24hr Buckboard Inn Beach RV Park
1mm	**weigh sta eb, litter barrel**
0mm	North Dakota/Montana state line

OHIO

INTERSTATE 70

Exit #	Services
225.5mm	Ohio/West Virginia state line, Ohio River
225	US 250 W, OH 7, Bridgeport, N Marathon, StarFire, Sunoco/dsl DQ, Papa John's, Pizza Hut Advance Parts, AutoZone, Family$, Meineke, NAPA, S Clark, Exxon/dsl Domino's
220	US 40, rd 214, N Marathon, Sunoco/dsl Comfort Inn, S Exxon/dsl Days Inn vet
219	I-470 E, to Bel-Aire, Washington PA, (from eb)
218	Mall Rd, to US 40, to Blaine, N BP, Exxon/Subway/dsl, Sheetz/dsl Applebee's, Arby's, Burger King, DeFelice Pizza, Denny's, Eat'n Park, HoneyBaked Ham, King Buffet, Little Caesar's, Outback Steaks, Pizza Hut, Red Lobster, Starbucks, Steak'n Shake, Taco Bell, Tlaquepaque Mexican, Undo's Rest., W Texas Steaks, Wendy's Best Value Inn, Hawthorn Suites, Holiday Inn Express, Knights Inn, Microtel, Red Roof Inn, Super 8, Wingate Inn $General, $Tree, AAA, Advance Parts, Aldi Foods, AT&T, AutoZone, Buick/Cadillac/Chevrolet, CVS Drug, Kroger, Lowe's, Sam's Club, Staples, Stewarts RV Ctr, URGENT CARE, Verizon, Walmart/McDonald's, S Bob Evans, Buffalo Wild Wings, Chipotle, Cracker Barrel, Garfield's Rest., KFC/LJ Silver, Longhorn Steaks, McDonald's, Osaka Steaks, Panera Bread, Starbucks, Zhuzi Chinese Candlewood Suites, Fairfield Inn, Residence Inn Boscov's, Chrysler/Dodge/Jeep, Jo-Ann Fabrics, Macy's, Marshall's, NTB
216	OH 9, St Clairsville, N BP
215	National Rd, N Burger King, Domino's, WenWu Chinese Riesbeck's Foods, USPO
213	OH 331, Flushing, S BP, Marathon/Subway/dsl, Sunoco/dsl
211mm	**both lanes, full facilities, litter barrels, petwalk, , vending**
208	OH 149, Morristown, N Exxon/McDonald's/dsl Schlepp's Rest. Arrowhead Motel (1mi), Days Inn $General, Cannonball Speedway, Ford/Lincoln, S Marathon/Quiznos/dsl,
208	Continued Pilot/Subway/dsl/scales/24hr Sleep Inn Barkcamp SP, Harley-Davidson
204	US 40 E (from eb, no return), National Rd
202	OH 800, to Barnesville, S Sunoco/dsl H
198	rd 114, Fairview
193	OH 513, Middlebourne, N BP, FuelMart/dsl fireworks
189mm	**eb, full facilities, litter barrels, petwalk, , vending**
186	US 40, OH 285, to Old Washington, N Marathon/dsl $General, S GoMart/dsl, Speedway/dsl/scales/24hr
180b a	I-77 N, to Cleveland, to Salt Fork SP, I-77 S, to Charleston
178	OH 209, Cambridge, **0-1 mi** N BP/dsl, Sheetz/dsl Bob Evans, Coldstone/Tim Hortons, Cracker Barrel, Denny's, DQ, Forum Rest., KFC, McDonald's, Papa John's, Pizza Hut, Ruby Tuesday, Subway, Wendy's Comfort Inn, Days Inn, Hampton Inn, Holiday Inn Express, Microtel, Quality Inn, Sleep Inn, Southgate Hotel H, $General, Advance Parts, AutoZone, BigLots, Cash Saver Foods, Family$, Ford, O'Reilly Parts, Verizon, S Murphy USA/dsl, Pilot/Subway/dsl/scales/24hr Arby's, Buffalo Wild Wings, Burger King, Great Chinese, Little Caesar's, Taco Bell, Tlaquepaque Mexican Baymont Inn $Tree, Aldi Foods, AT&T, Chevrolet, Chrysler/Dodge/Jeep, Spring Valley RV Park (1mi), Verizon, Walmart/Subway
176	US 22, US 40, to Cambridge, N Sunoco/dsl Budget Inn RV camping, st patrol, vet
173mm	**weigh sta both lanes**
169	OH 83, to Cumberland, New Concord, N Marathon/dsl Garland Hotel John&Annie Glen Historic Site, RV camping, to Muskingum U
164	US 22, US 40, Norwich, N Baker's Motel, Zane Gray Museum, S antiques, pottery
163mm	**wb, full facilities, litter barrels, petwalk, , vending**
160	OH 797, Airport Rd, N Loves/Arby's/dsl/scales/24hr, S BP, Marathon/Subway/dsl Denny's, McDonald's, Wendy's Best Western, Economy Inn, Kautilya Zanesville Hotel , st patrol

CAMBRIDGE

ND OH

INTERSTATE 70 Cont'd

ZANESVILLE

Exit #	Services
157	OH 93, Zanesville, N BP, S Marathon, Shell/dsl st patrol
155	OH 60, OH 146, Underwood St, Zanesville, N Bob Evans, Olive Garden, Oriental Buffet, Red Lobster, Steak'n Shake, Tumbleweed Grill Hampton Inn, Holiday Inn Express, Quality Inn, Wingate Inn H, Riesbeck's Mkt, USPO, S Marathon/dsl Cracker Barrel, Subway, Wendy's Baymont Inn, Travel Inn Rite Aid
154	5th St (from eb)
153b	Maple Ave (no EZ return from wb), N DQ, Italian Eatery, Papa John's, Tee Jaye's Rest. H, CVS Drug, Family$
153a	State St, N Speedway/dsl to Dillon SP (8mi), USPO
153mm	Licking River
152	US 40, National Rd, N BP/A&W/Subway/dsl, Shell/dsl McDonald's Super 8
142	US 40 (from wb, no EZ return), Gratiot, N RV camping
141	OH 668, US 40 (from eb, no return), to Gratiot, same as 142
132	OH 13, to Thornville, Newark, N Dawes Arboretum (3mi), S BP, Shell Subway (2mi)
131mm	**both lanes, full facilities, litter barrels, petwalk, , , vending**
129b a	OH 79, to Buckeye Lake, Hebron, N Subway Best Western Advance Parts, Kroger/gas, S Donato's Pizza, McDonald's, Subway, Taco Bell, Wendy's Motel 6 CarQuest, KOA (2mi)
126	OH 37, to Granville, Lancaster, N Marathon/dsl, Pilot/Chester's/Subway/dsl/scales/24hr, S IA 80 Truckomat/truckwash, TA/BP/Bob Evans/Popeye's/Sbarro's/dsl/scales/24hr/@ Deluxe Inn, Red Roof Inn KOA
122	OH 158, to Baltimore, Kirkersville, N Regal Inn, S FLYING J/Denny's/dsl/LP/scales/24hr fireworks
118	OH 310, to Pataskala, N BP/McDonald's, Shell/dsl, Speedway/dsl DQ, S BP/Duke's/Subway/dsl RCD RV Ctr
112c	OH 204, to Blecklick Rd (from eb)
112	OH 256, to Pickerington, Reynoldsburg, N BP, Shell/McDonald's Buffalo Wild Wings, Chipotle Mexican, Culver's, Five Guys, IHOP, Logan's Roadhouse, Noodles&Co, O'Charley's, Olive Garden, Panera Bread, Penn Sta, Smokey Bones BBQ, Subway, TGIFriday's Fairfield Inn, Holiday Inn Express AT&T, Best Buy, Jo-Ann Fabrics, Marshall's, NTB, Old Navy, Petco, Petsmart, Sam's Club/gas, Staples, Target, Tire Discounters, Verizon, Walgreens, Walmart/Subway, S Speedway/dsl Arby's, Bob Evans, Cane's, Cold Stone, Cracker Barrel, Donato's Pizza, Firehouse Subs, Iron Chef, Jimmy John's, KFC, La Fogata Mexican, LJ Silver, Longhorn Steaks, Max&Erma's, Omezzo Italian, Red Robin, Skyline Chili, Starbucks, Steak'n Shake, Wendy's Best Western, Comfort Inn, Hampton Inn Advance Parts, Barnes&Noble, Kohl's, Kroger/E85, URGENT CARE, Verizon
110	Brice Rd, to Reynoldsburg, N Speedway/dsl, Sunoco Burger King, Donato's, Genji Japanese, Golden China, Popeye's, Subway, TeeJaye's Rest., Tim Horton's, Waffle House Days Inn, Extended Stay America, La Quinta, Red Roof Inn BigLots, Family$, Goodyear/auto, Home Depot, O'Reilly Parts, S BP, Speedway/dsl Applebee's, Arby's, Asian Star, Boston Mkt, Chipotle Mexican, KFC, McDonald's, Starbucks, Subway, Taco Bell, Waffle House Comfort Suites, Motel 6, Rodeway Inn $Tree, Acura, Advance Parts, Aldi Foods, Family$, Fiat, Firestone/auto, Honda, Lowe's, Michael's, Toyota, Walgreens
108b a	I-270 N to Cleveland, access to H, I-270 S to Cincinnati

COLUMBUS AREA

Exit #	Services
107a	OH 317, Hamilton Rd, to Whitehall, S Shell/dsl Arby Burger King, Capt D's, ChuckeCheese, Ichiban Japanese, M Donald's, Papa John's, Pizza Hut, Popeye's, Red Lobster, Steal Shake, Taco Bell Hampton Inn, InTown Suites $Gen al, AT&T, PepBoys
105a	US 33, to Lancaster, **2 mi** N Tat Italian
105b	US 33, James Rd, Bexley, N Tat Italian
103b a	Livingston Ave, to Capital University, N Exxon, Spe way/dsl Mr Hero Subs, Peking Dynasty, Popeye's, Subw Taco Bell, Tim Horton's, Wendy's auto repair, Katz Ti S Marathon, Shell McDonald's, Rally's, White Cas Family$
102	Kelton Ave, Miller Ave
101a	I-71 N, to Cleveland
100b	US 23, to 4th St, downtown
99c	Rich St, Town St (exits left from wb)
99b	OH 315 N, downtown
99a	I-71 S, to Cincinnati
98b	Mound St (from wb, no EZ return), S Speedway Li Caesar's, McDonald's, Rally's Aldi Foods, Family$
98a	US 62, OH 3, Central Ave, to Sullivant, same as 98b
97	US 40, W Broad St, N Arby's, Burger King, McDonald's, S way, Taco Bell, Tim Horton's Knights Inn, Motel 6 Aa co, CVS Drug, U-Haul, USPO
96	I-670 (exits left from eb), to
95	Hague Ave (from wb), S Exxon
94	Wilson Rd, N Marathon/Circle K/Subway/dsl, UDF, S Pilot/Wendy's/dsl/scales/24hr, Shell/dsl, Speedway Donald's, Waffle House EconoLodge vet
93b a	I-270, N to Cleveland, S to Cincinnati
91b a	to Hilliard, New Rome, N GetGo, Shell, Speedway/ Applebee's, Arby's, Buffalo Wild Wings, Burger Ki Chick-fil-A, Chipotle, Cracker Barrel, Culver's, Daruma Japane Donato's Pizza, El Vaquero Mexican, Fazoli's, Firehouse Su Five Guys, Golden Chopsticks, Hot Head Burrito, IHOP, K McDonald's, Olive Garden, Outback Steaks, Panda Expre Panera Bread, Perkins, Red Robin, Rooster's Rest., Skyline C Subway, Supreme Buffet, Taco Bell, Tim Horton's/Coldstone, Roadhouse, Wendy's, White Castle, Wild Ginger Asian B Value Inn, Comfort Suites, Fairfield Inn, Hampton Inn, Hawth Inn, Holiday Inn, La Quinta, Motel 6, Red Roof Inn $T Advance Parts, AT&T, Dick's, Discount Tire, Firestone/a Ford, GNC, Kohl's, Marshall's, Meijer/dsl, Michael's, Mi Old Navy, Petsmart, Sam's Club/gas, Target, URGENT CA Verizon, Walmart/Subway, S BP/dsl, Marathon/dsl Evans, Handel's Ice Cream, Steak'n Shake Best Weste Country Inn&Suites, Super 8
85	OH 142, to Plain City, W Jefferson, N Prairie Oaks S Battelle Darby SP
80	OH 29, to Mechanicsburg, S hwy patrol
79	US 42, to London, Plain City, N Pilot/Arby's/ scales/24hr Waffle House Camping World RV truck/auto repair, S Speedway/Subway/dsl, TA/BP/P Hut/Popeye's/dsl/scales/24hr/@ McDonald's, Taco E Wendy's Holiday Inn Express, Motel 6 H
72	OH 56, to London, Summerford, N Marathon/Subway/ 4 mi S H
71mm	**both lanes, full facilities, litter barrels, petwalk, , vending**
66	OH 54, to Catawba, South Vienna, N Fuelmart/dsl/sca S Speedway/dsl

OH

INTERSTATE 70 Cont'd

Exit #	Services
62	US 40, Springfield, N Harmony Motel antiques, auto repair, Harmony Farm Mkt, to Buck Creek SP, S Beaver Valley Camping
59	OH 41, to S Charleston, N Harley-Davidson, st patrol, S BP/dsl, Loves/Subway/Wendy's/dsl/scales/24hr antiques
54	OH 72, to Cedarville, Springfield, N BP/dsl, Shell, Speedway/dsl, Sunoco/dsl A&W/LJ Silver, Arby's, Bob Evans, Burger King, Cassano's Pizza/subs, Cracker Barrel, Domino's, Dunkin', El Toro Mexican, Hardee's, Lee's Chicken, Little Caesar's, McDonald's, Panda Chinese, Popeye's, Rally's, Rudy's Smokehouse, Subway, Taco Bell Baymont Inn, Comfort Suites, Hampton Inn, Holiday Inn Express, Motel 6, Quality Inn, Red Roof Inn, USA Suites Advance Parts, BigLots, Family$, Kroger/deli, Rite Aid, Walgreens, S Marathon/dsl
52b a	US 68, to Urbana, Xenia, S to John Bryan SP
48	OH 4 (from wb), to Enon, Donnelsville, N camping, S Speedway
47	OH 4 (from eb), to Springfield, N Enon Beach Camping, S Speedway
44	I-675 S, Spangler Rd, to Cincinnati
43mm	Mad River
41b a	OH 4, OH 235, to Dayton, New Carlisle, N Shell/dsl McDonald's, Taco Bell, Wendy's Freightliner, Kenworth
38	OH 201, Brandt Pike, N Marathon/dsl Meijer/Subway/dsl/E85, S Shell, UDF/dsl Bob Evans, Hardee's, Sonic, Tim Horton's, Waffle House, Wendy's Comfort Inn, Red Roof Inn vet, Walmart
36	OH 202, Huber Heights, N Speedway/dsl Applebee's, Big Boy, Dragon City, El Toro Grill, Fazoli's, Firehouse Subs, Osaka Japanese, Steak'n Shake, Taco Bell, Waffle House Baymont Inn $Tree, AT&T, Big Lots, Dick's, GNC, Hobby Lobby, Kia, Kohl's, Lowe's, Marshall's, Petsmart, Staples, Target, Verizon, vet, S BP/dsl, Marathon/dsl Arby's, Buffalo Wild Wings, Burger King, Chipotle Mexican, CiCi's Pizza, IHOP, McDonald's, Panera Bread, Rooster's Rest., Skyline Chili, Subway, TGIFriday's, TX Roadhouse Days Inn, Hampton Inn, Holiday Inn Express Kroger/gas
33b a	I-75, N to Toledo, S to Dayton
32	to US 40, Vandalia, N to Dayton Intn'l Airport
29	OH 48, to Dayton, Englewood, N BP, Speedway/dsl, Sunoco/dsl, Valero Arby's, Big Boy, Bob Evans, Buffalo Wild Wings, Company BBQ, Domino's, Firehouse Subs, Hot Head Burrito, Lee's Chicken, Perkins, Pizza Hut, Popeye's, Skyline Chili, Taco Bell, Tim Horton's, Tony's Italian, Wendy's, Yen Ching Chinese Best Western+, Clarion, Hampton Inn $Tree, Advance Parts, Aldi Foods, AutoZone, Family$, Grismer/auto, Midas, O'Reilly Parts, Petco, Verizon, vet, S Chipotle, El Toro, McDonald's, MOD Pizza, Panera Bread, Starbucks, Steak'n Shake, Waffle House Comfort Inn, Motel 6 AT&T, Meijer/dsl/E85
26	OH 49 S, N Murphy USA/dsl Bob Evans, La Rosa's Pizza, Sonic, Subway URGENT CARE, Verizon, Walmart/Subway, S Shell/dsl Burger King, Wendy's
24	OH 49 N, to Greenville, Clayton, N KOA (seasonal)
21	Arlington Rd, Brookville, N Speedway/Subway/dsl, S Speedway/dsl Arby's, Brookville Grille, Great Wall Chinese, KFC/Taco Bell, K's Rest., Lee's Chicken, McDonald's, Pizza Hut, Rob's Rest., Subway, Waffle House, Wendy's Brookville Inn, Holiday Inn Express $General, Advance Parts, Brookville Parts, Chevrolet, Family$, IGA Foods, Rite Aid

CLEVELAND

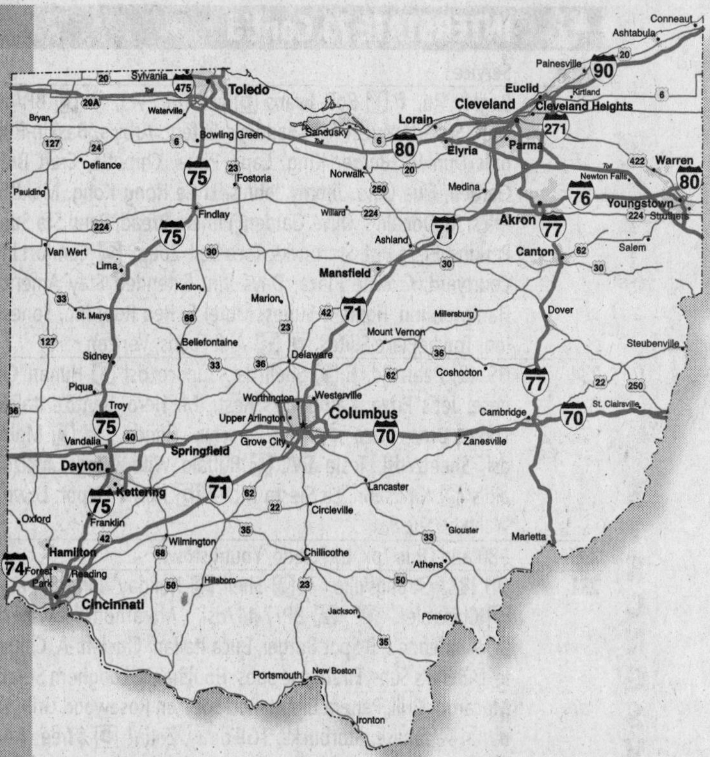

Exit #	Services
14	OH 503, to West Alexandria, Lewisburg, N Marathon/Subway/dsl Dari Twist Super Inn $General, S Sunoco/dsl
10	US 127, to Eaton, Greenville, N TA/BP/Burger King/Subway/dsl/scales/24hr/@, S Pilot/Subway/dsl/scales/24hr Budget Inn
3mm	**Welcome Ctr eb/ both lanes, full facilities, litter barrels, petwalk, , vending**
1	US 35 E (from eb), to Eaton, New Hope
0mm	Ohio/Indiana state line, Welcome Arch, **weigh sta eb**

INTERSTATE 71

Exit #	Services
I-71 begins/ends on I-90, exit 170 in Cleveland.	
247b	I-90 W, I-490 E.
247a	W 14th, Clark Ave, E Applebee's, Chipotle, Five Guys, IHOP, Panda Express, Taco Bell Walmart
246	Denison Ave, Jennings Rd (from sb)
245	US 42, Pearl Rd, E BP/7-11, Gas&Go zoo, W
244	W 65th, Denison Ave (exits left from nb)
242b a	W 130th, to Bellaire Rd, W Sunoco
240	W 150th, E Marathon, Speedway/dsl, Sunoco Burger King, Denny's, Happy's Pizza Marriott AutoZone, Goodyear/auto, Marc's Foods, W BP/Subway/7-11/dsl Hub Grill La Quinta, Sheraton
239	OH 237 S (from sb), W to
238	I-480, Toledo, Youngstown, W
237	Snow Rd, Brook Park, E GetGo, Marathon/Circle K, Shell Arby's, Bob Evans, Burger King, Dunkin', Garden Rest., Goody's Rest., KFC, Little Caesar's, McDonald's, Rally's, Reddi's Pizza, Subway, Taco Bell Best Western, Holiday Inn Express, Howard Johnson $General, $Tree, Advance Parts, AutoZone, Conrad Tire/repair, CVS Drug, Giant Eagle, O'Reilly Parts, Rite Aid, W to

OH

INTERSTATE 71 Cont'd

STRONGSVILLE

Exit #	Services
235	Bagley Rd, E Bob Evans Mr Tire, vet, W BP/dsl, Gulf, Speedway/dsl Aladdin's Eatery, Arby's, Baskin-Robbins/Dunkin', Burger King, Capri Pizza, Chipotle, Craft Brew Garden, Five Guys, Jimmy John's, Little Hong Kong, Max&Erma's, McDonald's, Olive Garden, Panera Bread, Penn Sta Subs, Perkins, Pizza Hut, Starbucks, Taco Bell, Zoup! Comfort Inn, Courtyard, Crowne Plaza, Days Inn, Extended Stay America, Hampton Inn, Home 2 Suites, Motel 6, Red Roof Inn, Sonesta Inn, TownePlace Suites H, Aldi Foods, Verizon
234	US 42, Pearl Rd, E Shell/dsl, Sunoco/dsl Hunan Chinese, Jet's Pizza, Katherine's Rest., Mr Hero, Santo's Italian, Three Bros Pizza Audi/Porsche, Honda, W Mobil/dsl, Sheetz/dsl, Tesla EVC Buffalo Wild Wings, McDonald's Kings Inn, La Siesta Motel Home Depot, Lowe's, Walmart/Subway
233	I-80 and Ohio Tpk, to Toledo, Youngstown
231	OH 82, Strongsville, E Shell Holiday Inn, Super 8 Chevrolet, W BP/7-11/dsl, Marathon/Subway/dsl Applebee's, B Spot Burger, Buca Italian, Chick-fil-A, Chipotle, DiBella's Subs, Firehouse Subs, Houlihan's, Longhorn Steaks, Macaroni Grill, Panera Bread, Red Lobster, Rosewood Grill, Samurai Japanese, Starbucks, TGIFriday, Zoup! $Tree, AAA, AT&T, Best Buy, Costco/gas, Dick's, Dillard's, Heinen's Mkt, JC Penney, Kohl's, Macy's, Michael's, Midas, NTB, Old Navy, PetCo, Target, TJ Maxx, Verizon
226	OH 303, Brunswick, E Shell/dsl Antonio's Pizza Chrysler/Dodge/Jeep, Hyundai, Subaru, Toyota, vet, VW, W Speedway/dsl, Sunoco/dsl Applebee's, Arby's, Bob Evans, Burger King, Chipotle, Georgio's Pizza, House of Pearl, KFC, McDonald's, Muchos Buenos Mexican, Panera Bread, Panini's Grill, Pizza Hut, Starbucks, Steak'n Shake, Subway, Taco Bell, Wendy's Quality Inn $General, Ford, Giant Eagle Mkt, GNC, Home Depot, Marc's Mkt, Verizon, Comfort Suites, Jersey Mike's
225mm	**nb, full facilities, litter barrels, petwalk,**
224mm	**sb, full facilities, litter barrels, petwalk,**
222	OH 3, Medina, Hinckley, W st patrol
220	I-271 N, (from nb) to Erie, Pa
218	OH 18, to Akron, Medina, E BP/dsl, Marathon/dsl, Sunoco/dsl Baskin-Robbins/Dunkin', Burger King, DQ, Fresh Food Deli, Master Pizza, Pizza Hut Holiday Inn Express, Quality Inn, Super 8 Kia, Nissan, Verizon, W GetGo, Speedway/dsl Arby's, Bob Evans, Brown Derby, Buffalo Wild Wings, Chipotle, Denny's, McDonald's, Rocknes Rest., Starbucks, Taco Bell, Waffle House, Wendy's Fairfield Inn, Hampton Inn, Motel 6, Red Roof Inn H, Aldi Foods, Buehler's Foods, Buick/Cadillac/GMC, Chrysler/Dodge/Jeep, Firestone/auto, Harley-Davidson, Honda, Verizon
209	I-76 E, to Akron, US 224, W Pilot/Subway/dsl/scales/24hr, TA/Country Pride/Burger King/Popeye's/dsl/scales/24hr/@ Arby's, McDonald's, Starbucks Super 8 Blue Beacon, Chippewa Valley Camping (1mi), SpeedCo
204	OH 83, Burbank, E BP/dsl, Duke/dsl, Loves/Hardee's/dsl/scales/24hr Plaza Motel, W Pilot/Wendy's/dsl/scales/24hr Arby's, Bob Evans, Burger King, McDonald's H, OH Sta Outlets/famous brands
198	OH 539, W Salem
196mm	**both lanes, full facilities, litter barrels, petwalk, vending**
196	OH 301 (from nb, no re-entry), W Salem

AKRON

OH

MANSFIELD

Exit #	Services
186	US 250, Ashland, E Marathon Grandpa's Villa cheese/gifts, Perkins Hickory Lakes Camping (7mi), Goasis/BP/Pizza Hut/Popeye's/Starbucks/Taco Bell/dsl/2 Marathon/Subway/dsl Buffalo Wild Wings, Chipotle, D ny's, Dunkin', Jake's Rest., McDonald's, Wendy's Hamp Inn, Holiday Inn Express, Motel 6, Quality Inn, Super 8 $Tree, Aldi Foods, AT&T, Buehler's Foods, GNC, Home Depo patrol, to Ashland U, URGENT CARE, Verizon, Walmart/Subw
176	US 30, to Mansfield, E Heritage Inn fireworks
173	OH 39, to Mansfield
169	OH 13, Mansfield, E Marathon/7-11/dsl, Murphy U dsl Applebee's, Chipotle, Cracker Barrel, Steak'n Sha Wendy's Best Western, La Quinta Mohican Walmart/Subway, W BP/7-11 Arby's, Bob Eva Burger King, El Charrito Mexican, McDonald's, Subway, T Bell Hampton Inn, Super 8, Travelodge H, st patro
165	OH 97, to Bellville, E BP, Shell/Dunkin'/dsl, Speedw dsl Buckeye Express Diner, Burger King, Der Dutchm KC's Rib House, McDonald's Comfort Inn, Economy Mid Ohio Inn, Quality Inn to Mohican SP, W Lov /Subway/Taco John's/dsl/scales/24hr Wendy's
151	OH 95, to Mt Gilead, E Duke/BP/deli, Marathon, T EVC Eight Sisters Cafe, McDonald's, Wendy's Western st patrol, W Shell/dsl, Sunoco/ e85 Subway Knights Inn H, Mt Gilead SP (6mi
149mm	**truck parking both lanes**
140	OH 61, Mt Gilead, E Pilot/Arby's/dsl/scales/24hr, W BP/Taco Bell, Marathon/Subway Legacy Rest. Card Ctr Camping
131	US 36, OH 37, to Delaware, E FLYING J/Denny's/dsl/ scales/24hr/@, Pilot/Subway/dsl/scales/24hr Bu King Harley-Davidson, W BP/dsl, Shell/Tim Hor Arby's, Bob Evans, Cracker Barrel, KFC/LJ Silver, McDona Panera Bread, Starbucks, Taco Bell, Waffle House, Wen White Castle Hampton Inn, Holiday Inn Express, T elodge H, Alum Cr SP, Cross Creek Camping (6mi)
128mm	**both lanes, full facilities, litter barrels, petwalk, vending**
121	Polaris Pkwy, to Gemini Pl, E BP, Shell/dsl, UDF Bo fish Grill, Buffalo Wild Wings, Canes, Carfagna's Kitchen, E capulco, Firehouse Subs, First Watch, Five Guys, McDona Mellow Mushroom Pizza, Polaris Grill, Skyline Chili, Starbu Steak'n Shake, Subway, Tim Horton's Fairfield Inn, F Points Sheraton, Hampton Inn, Holiday Inn Express, Homew Suites Firestone/auto, Mr Tire, W BP, Sunoco plebee's, Arby's, Bar Louie, Benihana, Bibibop Asian, BJ's R Brio Grille, Burger King, CA Pizza, Cantina Laredo, Carrab Charley Subs, CheeseCake Factory, Chick-fil-A, Chipotle M can, Coldstone, Corner Bakery Cafe, Dave&Buster's, Domir El Vaquero Mexican, Firebird's Grill, Honey Baked Ham, Jas Deli, Jersey Mike's, Jimmy John's, Krispy Kreme, Marcella's ian, Matt the Miller's Tavern, McDonald's, McKenzie River Pi Merlot's Rest., Mimi's Cafe, Mitchell Steaks, MOD Pizza, M Woo's, Noodles&Co, O'Charley's, Olive Garden, Panda Expr Panera Bread, Papa John's, Penn Sta Subs, Potbelly's, Qd Quaker Steak, Red Lobster, Red Robin, Rooster's Grill, Sc Starbucks, Subway, Taco Bell, TX Roadhouse, Waffle Ho Wendy's Cambria Suites, Candlewood Suites, Comfort Extended Stay America, Hilton, Hilton Garden, Residence Staybridge Suites AT&T, AutoZone, Barnes&Noble, Buy, BigLots, Cabela's, Costco/gas, Dick's, Field&Stream, park, GNC, Hobby Lobby, JC Penney, Jo-Ann Etc, Kroger/

INTERSTATE 71 Cont'd

121 Continued
Lowe's, Macy's, NTB, Old Navy, Petsmart, Target, TireDiscounters, TJ Maxx, Verizon, Von Maur, Walgreens, World Mkt

119b a I-270, to Indianapolis, Wheeling

117 OH 161, to Worthington, E BP/dsl, Shell, Speedway/dsl, Sunoco/dsl Burger King, Carfagna's Italian, Casa Hacienda, China Dynasty, Chipotle, Dunkin'/Baskin Robbins, KFC, Massey's Pizza, McDonald's, Penn Sta Subs, Popeye's, Rally's, Red Lobster, Subway, Super Seafood Buffet, Taco Bell, Wendy's, White Castle Best Value Inn, Haven Inn, Norwood Inn, Red Roof Inn $General, auto repair, CVS Drug, Family$, Walgreens, W Shell, Speedway/dsl Asian Kitchen, China Jade, Domino's, McDonald's, Pizza Hut, Subway, Tim Hortons, Waffle House, Wendy's Baymont Inn, Continent Inn, Crowne Plaza, Extended Stay America, Hawthorn Suites, Hometowne Studios, Super 8 Advance Parts, AutoZone, Chevrolet, Family$, Premier Tire

116 Morse Rd, Sinclair Rd, E BP, Marathon/dsl, Shell/dsl, Speedway/dsl, Turkey Hill/dsl Chipotle, Dunkin'/Robbins Robins, Jimmy John's, Little Caesar's, McDonald's, Papa John's, Subway, Taco Bell, Tim Horton's Extend Suites $General, $Tree, Buick/GMC, Chrysler/Dodge/Jeep, CVS Drug, Firestone/auto, Ford, Menard's, Mr Tire, PepBoys, Save-A-Lot Foods, URGENT CARE, W Sunoco Best Value Inn, Motel 6 NTB

115 Cooke Rd

114 N Broadway, W Sunoco/dsl Subway, Tim Horton

113 Weber Rd, W Speedway/dsl Advance Parts

112 Hudson St, E Marathon, Shell/dsl Wendy's Holiday Inn Express Family$, W Aldi Foods, Lowe's, NTB

111 17th Ave, W McDonald's Comfort Suites, Days Inn

110b 11th Ave

110a 5th Ave, E Sunoco Royal Fish&Chicken, White Castle, W Exxon Burger King, Church's, KFC, Wendy's AutoZone

109a I-670

109b OH 3, Cleveland Ave

109c Spring St (exits left from sb)

108b US 40, Broad St, downtown, downtown

108a Main St

101a[70] I-70 E, US 23 N, to Wheeling

100b a[70] US 23 S, Front St, High St, downtown

106a I-70 W, to Indianapolis

106b OH 315 N, Dublin St, Town St

105 Greenlawn, E BP Jimmy John's, White Castle Berliner Park, W Marathon

104 OH 104, Frank Rd, W Marathon/Subway/dsl/scales

101b a I-270, Wheeling, Indianapolis

100 Stringtown Rd, E BP, Tesla EVC Bibibop Asian, Bob Evans, Buffalo Wings & Rings, Charley's Grilled Subs, Chick-fil-A, Chipotle, Coldstone, DQ, El Vaquero Mexican, Five Guys, Fusion Steaks, Honey Baked Ham, Jersey Mike's, Longhorn Steaks, O'Charley's, Olive Garden, Panda Express, Panera Bread, Red Robin, Roosters Grill, Smokey Bones BBQ, Sonic, Starbucks, Steak'n Shake, TX Roadhouse, White Castle Best Western, Candlewood Suites, Courtyard, Drury Inn, Fairfield Inn, Hampton Inn, Hilton Garden, Holiday Inn Express, La Quinta, Quality Inn, Red Roof Inn, Springhill Suites AT&T, Best Buy, Dick's, Discount Tire, Firestone/auto, GNC, Hobby Lobby, Home Depot, Kohl's, Michael's, Petsmart, Staples, Target, TJMaxx, Verizon, vet, Walmart/Subway, W BP, GetGo, Speedway/dsl, Sunoco/dsl,

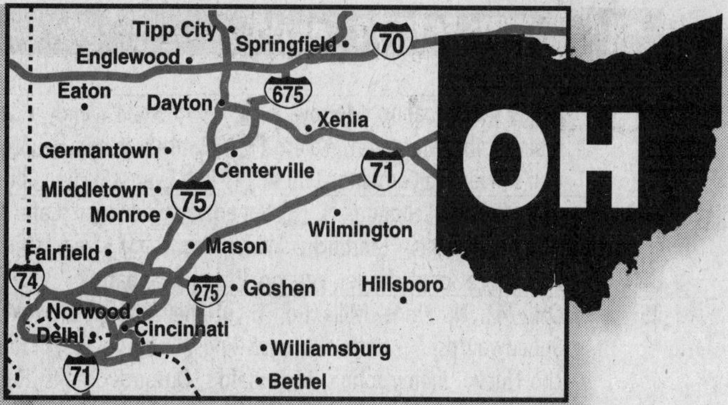

100 Continued
Turkey Hill/dsl Applebee's, Arby's, Cane's Chicken Fingers, China Bell, City BBQ, Cracker Barrel, Donato's Pizza, Fazoli's, Golden Corral, IHOP, KFC, Mariachi Mexican, Massey's Pizza, McDonald's, Papa John's, Pizza Hut, Rally's, Ruby Tuesday, Starbucks, Subway, Taco Bell, TeeJaye's Rest., Tim Horton, Waffle House, Wendy's Comfort Inn, Comfort Suites, Days Inn, Motel 6, Travelodge Advance Parts, Aldi Foods, AutoZone, BigLots, CVS Drug, Giant Eagle Foods, GNC, Goodyear/auto, Kroger/dsl, Tuffy Auto, USPO, Walgreens

97 OH 665, London-Groveport Rd, E Marathon/Circle K Arby's, Jimmy John's, McDonald's, Subway, Sunny St Cafe, Taco Bell, Tim Horton/Wendy's $Tree, Chevrolet, CVS Drug, Kroger/gas/e85, Meijer/e85, Tire Discounters, to Scioto Downs, URGENT CARE, Verizon, vet, KFC, Starbucks, Waffle House

94 US 62, OH 3, Orient, E $General, W Sunoco/Subway/dsl Eddie's Repair

84 OH 56, Mt Sterling, E BP/Subway/dsl to Deer Creek SP (9mi)

75 OH 38, Bloomingburg, E fireworks, W Sunoco/dsl

69 OH 41, OH 734, Jeffersonville, E FLYING J/Denny's/dsl/scales/LP/24hr H, Walnut Lake Camping, W BP, Shell/Subway/dsl Arby's, Wendy's Quality Inn Family$, Buckeye RV Ctr, Buckeye RV Ctr

68mm both lanes, full facilities, litter barrels, petwalk, vending

65 US 35, Washington CH, E Shell/dsl, Speedway/Speedy Cafe/dsl, TA/BP/Pizza Hut/Popeye's/dsl/scales/24hr/@ A&W/KFC, Bob Evans, Chipotle Mexican, LJ Silver/Taco Bell, McDonald's, Subway, Waffle House, Wendy's, Werner's BBQ Baymont Inn, Fairfield Inn, Hampton Inn H, Tanger Outlets/famous brands, EVC, EVC, Starbucks, Starbucks, W Love's /Hardee's/dsl/scales/24hr EconoLodge

58 OH 72, to Sabina

50 US 68, to Wilmington, E H, W BP/DQ/dsl, Pilot/Subway/dsl/scales/24hr, Shell/dsl Max&Erma's, McDonald's, Wendy's Holiday Inn, repair/tires Robert's Centre

49mm weigh sta nb

45 OH 73, to Waynesville, E BP, Shell/dsl 73 Grill H, W Caesar Creek Camping (3mi), Caesar Creek SP (5mi), flea mkt

36 Wilmington Rd, E Olive Branch Camping, to Ft Ancient St Mem

35mm Little Miami River

34mm both lanes, full facilities, litter barrels, petwalk, scenic view, vending

INTERSTATE 71 Cont'd

Exit #	Services
32	OH 123, to Lebanon, Morrow, E FLYING J/Wendy's/dsl/scales/24hr, Marathon, Valero Country Kitchen Morgan's Riverside Camping, 3 mi W Bob Evans, Skyline Chili
28	OH 48, S Lebanon, E Speedway/Speedy's Cafe/dsl Dickey's BBQ, Starbucks, White Castle $Tree, Kohl's, Lowe's, Petsmart, Target, Verizon, W hwy patrol
25	OH 741 N, Kings Mills Rd, E Shell/Popeye's/Dunkin', Speedway/dsl Buffalo Wings&Rings, Chipotle, DQ, El Rancho Nuevo, Jimmy John's, McDonald's, Outback Steaks, Ruby Tuesday, Taco Bell, Wendy's Comfort Suites, Great Wolf Lodge, Kings Island Resort, Residence Inn Harley-Davidson, USPO, Verizon, W Ameristop/Subway, BP Arby's, Big Boy, Burger King, Panera Bread, Perkins, Pizza Hut, Skyline Chili, Starbucks, Waffle House, Woodhouse Kitchen Baymont Inn, Hampton Inn, Microtel, Super 8, Tru Hilton CarX, CVS Drug, GNC, Kroger/dsl, vet
24	Western Row, King's Island Dr (from nb), E Sunoco Eli's Grill, Fantastic Wok King's Island Resort
19	US 22, Mason-Montgomery Rd, E Speedway/dsl Arby's, Big Boy, Boston Mkt, Burger King, Cane's, Cracker Barrel, Dunkin', Flipdaddy's Burgers, Fricker's, Golden Corral, Honey-Baked Ham, Hot Head Burrito, Iron Chef Grill, KFC, Longhorn Steaks, McDonald's, Olive Garden, Potbelly, Slim Chickens, Taco Bell, Wendy's, White Castle Comfort Inn, Red Roof Inn, SpringHill Suites, TownePlace Suites Aldi Foods, AT&T, AutoZone, Barnes&Noble, Best Buy, Buick/GMC, Chevrolet, Chrysler/Dodge/Jeep, Costco/gas, Firestone/auto, Ford, GNC, Honda, Infiniti, JC Penney, Kia, Kohl's, Kroger, Lexus, Mazda, Meijer/dsl, Michael's, Nissan, Old Navy, Petco, Porsche, Subaru, Target, Tire Discounters, Tires+, Toyota, Tuffy Auto, USPO, Verizon, VW, Walgreens, W BP/dsl, Shell/Dunkin' Blaze Pizza, Bravo Italian, Carrabba's, Chick-fil-A, Chipotle Mexican, DiBella Subs, Dickey's BBQ, Firebirds Grill, Five Guys, Fox-&Hound Grill, Graeter's Cafe, Hooters, IHOP, Jimmy John's, Kirkwood's Kitchen, Maplewood Kitchen, McAlister's Deli, Mission BBQ, Noodles&Co, O'Charley's, Panda Express, Panera Bread, Piada Italian, Popeye's, Qdoba, Red Robin, Rusty Bucket, Skyline Chili, Steak'n Shake, Taziki's Cafe, Waffle House, Wendy's, Zoup! Best Western, Drury Inn, Hilton Garden, Holiday Inn Express, Homewood Suites, Hyatt Place, La Quinta, Marriott, Mason Inn Dick's, Hobby Lobby, Home Depot, Lowe's, Marshall's, NAPA, Staples, vet, Walmart/Subway, Whole Foods Mkt
17b a	I-275, to I-75, OH 32
15	Pfeiffer Rd, E H, W BP, Shell/dsl, Sunoco/dsl Bob Evans, Buffalo Wild Wings, City BBQ, Firehouse Grill, Subway Comfort Inn, Courtyard, Embassy Suites, Holiday Inn Express, Quality Hotel, Red Roof Inn, Wingate Inn, Springhill Suites
14	OH 126, Reagan Hwy, Blue Ash
12	US 22, OH 3, Montgomery Rd, E BP/dsl, Shell/Dunkin'/Subway, Sunoco Arby's, Bob Evans, Chipotle Mexican, Chuy's, Coopers Hawk, Currito, Delicious Coal Fired Pizza, Ember's, First Watch, Fusian, Jimmy John's, Outback Steaks, Panera Bread, Penn Sta Subs, Red Lobster Hampton Inn Tuesday Morning, W BP, Marathon Cheesecake Factory, Chick-fil-A, Chipotle, Honeybaked Ham, IHOP, Jersey Mike's, Maggiano's, McDonald's, Potbelly, Ruby Tuesday, Starbucks, Taziki's Grill, TX Roadhouse, Wendy's Best Western+ H, AT&T, Dick's, Dillard's, Firestone/auto, Fresh Mkt Foods, Macy's, Marshall's, Old Navy, PepBoys, Staples, Tire Discounters, TJ Maxx, Trader Joe's, Verizon
11	Kenwood Rd, (from nb), W H, same as 12
10	Stewart Rd (from nb), to Silverton, E BMW/N W Marathon/dsl
9	Redbank Rd, to Fairfax, (no ez sb return), E UDF Ra
8	Kennedy Ave, Ridge Ave W, E Meijer/dsl IHOP tel 6 Kroger/dsl, Petsmart, Target, W Marathon, Shell/Subway/Dunkin'/dsl Gold Star Chili, Hooliga Jack-in-the-Box, LJ Silver, McDonald's, Wendy's, White tle Quality Inn $Tree, Aldi Foods, Buick/GMC, Burl ton Coats, Home Depot, Lowes Whse, Sumeral Tire
7	(from sb) OH 562, Ridge Ave E, Norwood
6	Edwards Rd, E BP, Shell/Popeye's/Dunkin', Speedw dsl BJ's Rest., Boston Mkt, Bravo Italiana, Buca Ital Buffalo Wild Wings, Capital Grille, Donato's, First Watch, Guys, J Alexander's Rest., Jason's Deli, Longhorn Steaks, M co's Pizza, PF Chang's, Potbelly, Qdoba, Rusty Bucket, Seas 52 Grill, Starbucks, The Pub Courtyard AT&T, GNC, Navy, REI, SteinMart, TJ Maxx, URGENT CARE, Whole Fo Mkt, W Shell
5	Dana Ave, Montgomery Rd, W Xavier Univ, Zoo
3	Taft Rd (from sb), W U of Cincinnati
2	US 42, Reading Rd, Gilbert ave (from sb), E art muse W H, ballpark stadium arena, downtown
1k j	I-471 S
1d	Main St, downtown
1c b	Pete Rose Way, Fine St, downtown, stadium
1a	I-75 N, US 50, to Dayton
1	**I-71 S and I-75 S run together.**
0mm	Ohio/Kentucky state line, Ohio River

INTERSTATE 74

Exit #	Services
20	I-75 (from eb), N to Dayton, S to Cincinnati, **I-74 begins/e on I-75.**
19	Gilmore St, Spring Grove Ave
18	US 27 N, Colerain Ave
17	Montana Ave (from wb), N BP
14	North Bend Rd, Cheviot, N Shell, Speedway/dsl Boy, Dunkin', Jersey Mike's, McDonald's, Papa John's, line Chili, Subway, Taco Bell, Wendy's Family$, Kro Petco, Sam's Club/gas, Tire Discounters, Verizon, Walgre S Shell Bob Evans vet
11	Rybolt Rd, Harrison Pike, S Chipotle, Longhorn Ste Marco's Pizza, McDonald's, Penn Sta Subs, Sakura Steaks, line Chili, Starbucks, Wendy's, White Castle Holiday Inn press AT&T, Kohl's, Meijer/gas, Verizon
9	I-275 N, to I-75, N to Dayton, (exits left from eb)
8mm	Great Miami River
7	OH 128, to Hamilton, Cleves, N BP/dsl, Sunoco Wendy's
5	I-275 S, to Kentucky
3	Dry Fork Rd, N BP/dsl, S Marathon/dsl, Shell/Dun dsl Monk's Kitchen vet
2mm	**weigh sta eb**
1	New Haven Rd, to Harrison, N BP/dsl Bob Evans, Bu lo Wild Wings, China Garden, Chipotle Mexican, Cracker Ba Dunkin', Little Caesar's, O'Charley's, Subway Best W ern+ Ford, Home Depot, Kia, Remke Mkt, Staples, Tire URGENT CARE, Verizon, S Circle K, Speedway/dsl, Sun White Castle, UDF A&W/KFC, Arby's, Big Boy, Burger K

CINCINNATI AREA

CINCINNATI

HARRISON

INTERSTATE 74 Cont'd

1	Continued Domino's, DQ, El Mariachi Cantina, Firehouse Subs, Freddy's, Happy Garden, Marco's Pizza, McDonald's, Penn Sta Subs, Pizza Hut, Skyline Chili, Taco Bell, Valle Escondidos, Waffle House, Wendy's Holiday Inn Express, Super 8 $General, $Tree, Advance Parts, AT&T, AutoZone, BigLots, CVS Drug, Family$, Firestone/auto, GNC, Kroger/dsl, Meineke, NAPA, O'Reilly Parts, Sumerel Tire/auto, Tire Discounters, Walgreens
0mm	Ohio/Indiana state line

INTERSTATE 75

Exit #	Services
211mm	Ohio/Michigan state line
210	OH 184, Alexis Rd, to Raceway Park, W BP/Circle K/dsl, Pilot/Subway/dsl/scales/24hr Arby's, Bob Evans, Burger King, McDonald's, Taco Bell, Wendy's Courtyard, Fairfield Inn, Hampton Inn, Holiday Inn Express Aldi Foods, AutoZone, Meijer/dsl, Menards, URGENT CARE
210mm	Ottawa River
209	Ottawa River Rd (from nb), E BP, Sunoco China King, Little Caesar's, Marco's Pizza, River Diner Kroger/e85, Rite Aid, Verizon, vet
208	I-280 S, to I-80/90, to Cleveland
207	Stickney Ave, Lagrange St, E BP, Stop&Go Arby's, KFC, Marco's Pizza, McDonald's, Wendy's Family$, Rite Aid
206	to US 24, Phillips Ave, W auto repair, transmissions
205b	Berdan Ave, E H, W Burger King, Subway $General
205a	to Willys Pkwy, to Jeep Pkwy
204	I-475 W, to US 23 (exits left fom nb), to Maumee, Ann Arbor
203b	US 24, to Detroit Ave, W Gas Express/dsl, Sunoco KFC, McDonald's, Rally's, Wendy's Family$, Rite Aid, U-Haul
203a	Bancroft St, downtown
202	Washington St, Collingwood Ave (from sb, no EZ return), E H, $Tree, Art Museum, W China Star, McDonald's $General
201b a	OH 25, Collingwood Ave, W Toledo Zoo
200	South Ave, Kuhlman Dr
200mm	Maumee River
199	OH 65, Miami St, to Rossford, E Days Inn
198	Wales Rd, Oregon Rd, to Northwood, E Mobil/Subway/dsl, S&G/dsl Arby's, Arturo's Kitchen, Coney Island, Fried Rice, Jimmy John's Best Value Inn, BridgePointe Inn
197	Buck Rd, to Rossford, E Shell/dsl Tim Horton's, Wendy's, W BP, Sunoco/dsl Denny's, McDonald's, Subway Knights Inn, Motel 6
195	to I-80/90, OH 795, OH Tpk (**toll**), Perrysburg, E BP/Subway/dsl Country Inn&Suites, Courtyard, Hampton Inn, Staybridge Suites Bass Pro Shops, Camping World RV Ctr
193	US 20, US 23 S, Perrysburg, E BP/dsl Arby's, Big Boy, Bob Evans, Burger King, Chick-fil-A, Chili's, China City, Chipotle, Cocina de Carlos, Cracker Barrel, Dickey's BBQ, First Wok, Five Guys, Fricker's, IHOP, Jimmy John's, KFC, McDonald's, Panda Express, Panera Bread, Penn Sta Subs, Sonic, Starbucks, Subway, Taco Bell, Tim Horton's, Wendy's Baymont Inn, Candlewood Suites, Comfort Suites, EconoLodge, Holiday Inn, Quality Inn $Tree, Aldi Foods, Belle Tire, Best Buy, Discount Tire, GNC, Hobby Lobby, Home Depot, KOA (7mi), Kohl's, Kroger/gas/e85, Lowe's, Meijer/dsl, Michael's, Petsmart, Target, TJ Maxx, Tuffy, Walgreens, Walmart/Subway, W Speedway/dsl La Quinta AutoZone, Harley-Davidson

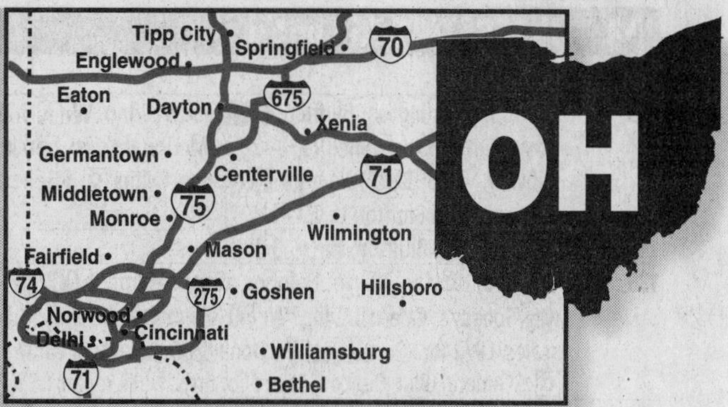

FINDLAY

192	I-475, US 23 N (exits left from nb), to Maumee, Ann Arbor
187	OH 582, to Luckey, Haskins
181	OH 64, OH 105, to Pemberville, Bowling Green, E Holiday Inn Express Meijer/dsl/e85, W BP/dsl, Circle K/Subway/dsl, Speedway/dsl Bob Evans, Buffalo Wild Wings, Burger King, Chipotle Mexican, Coldstone/Tim Horton's, El Zarape Mexican, Fricker's Rest., Jimmy John's, McDonald's, Panera Bread, Penn Sta Subs, Starbucks, Waffle House, Wendy's Best Western, Days Inn, Fairfield Inn, Hampton Inn, Home 2 Suites H, to Bowling Green State U, USPO, Verizon
179	US 6, to Fremont, Napoleon, E museum
179mm	**both lanes, full facilities, litter barrels, petwalk, vending**
175mm	**weigh sta nb**
171	OH 25, Cygnet
168	Eagleville Rd, Quarry Rd, E FuelMart/dsl
167	OH 18, to Fostoria, North Baltimore, E Petro/BP/Iron Skillet/dsl/scales/24hr/@ McDonald's, W Loves/Arby's/dsl/scales/24hr, Sunoco $General, Great Scot Mkt
165mm	Rocky Ford River
164	OH 613, to McComb, Fostoria, E RV camping, Van Buren SP, W Pilot/Subway/Taco Bell/dsl/scales/24hr
162mm	**weigh sta sb**
161	rd 99, E Shell/Subway/dsl, Speedway/Speedy's Cafe/dsl Comfort Suites Ford/Lincoln, hwy patrol, Kia, URGENT CARE, VW, W antiques
159	US 224, OH 15, Findlay, E Exxon/dsl, Marathon/dsl, Speedway/Speedy's Cafe/dsl Burger King, Culver's, Dakota Grill, Fin's Seafood Grill, Jimmy John's, KFC/LJ Silver, McDonald's, Ming's Great Wall, Pizza Hut, Ralphie's, Steak'n Shake, Subway, Taco Bell, Wendy's Drury Inn, Findley Value Inn, Rodeway Inn, Super 8 H, Advance Parts, W Murphy USA/dsl, Shell/dsl Bob Evans, Coldstone/Tim Horton's, Cracker Barrel, Denny's, Hokkaido Steaks, Jac&Do's Pizza, Outback Steaks, Penn Sta Subs, Tony's Rest., TX Roadhouse, Waffle House Country Inn&Suites, Hampton Inn, Hilton Garden, Holiday Inn Express, Quality Inn AT&T, AutoZone, Best 1 Tires/repair, Chrysler/Dodge/Jeep, Peterbilt, Verizon, Walmart/Subway
158mm	Blanchard River
157	OH 12, Findlay, E Marathon/dsl, W Fricker's Rest. EconoLodge vet
156	US 68, OH 15, to Carey, E H
Exit #	Services
153mm	**both lanes, full facilities, litter barrels, petwalk, vending**
145	OH 235, to Ada, Mount Cory, E Twin Lakes Camping

OH

INTERSTATE 75 Cont'd

Exit #	Services
142	OH 103, to Arlington, Bluffton, E Fairway Inn, W Marathon/Circle K/dsl, Shell Arby's, McDonald's/rv parking, Subway, Taco Bell, Wendy's Comfort Inn $General, auto repair, to Bluffton U, vet
140	Bentley Rd, to Bluffton, W
135	OH 696, to US 30, to Delphos, Beaverdam, E Speedway/Speedy's Cafe/dsl/24hr, W FLYING J/Denny's/dsl/scales/LP/24hr/@, Pilot/McDonald's/Subway/dsl/24hr/ @ $General, Blue Beacon, SpeedCo, tires, truck repair
134	Napolean Rd (no nb re-entry), to Beaverdam
130	Bluelick Rd, E Clark
127b a	OH 81, to Ada, Lima, W Fuelstop/dsl Subway, Waffle House Comfort Inn, Red Carpet Inn
126mm	Ottawa River
125	OH 309, OH 117, Lima, E Murphy USA/dsl, Speedway/Speedy's Cafe/dsl Applebee's, Bob Evans, Buffalo Wings & Rings, Burger King, Capt D's, China Buffet, China Buffet, Cracker Barrel, El Cazadore, Hunan Garden, McDonald's, Olive Garden, Panera Bread, Red Lobster, Skyline Chili, Subway, Taco Bell, TX Roadhouse, Wendy's Courtyard, Hampton Inn, Howard Johnson, Motel 6 $Tree, Aldi Foods, AT&T, BigLots, Ford/Lincoln, Sam's Club/gas, Verizon, Walgreens, Walmart/Burger King, W Arby's, Kewpee Hamburger's, Yamato Steaks Country Inn&Suites, Holiday Inn, Travelodge, $General, Advance Parts, Best 1 Tires/repair, O'Reilly Parts, Rite Aid, Save-A-Lot Foods, Verizon
124	4th St, E Ford/Lincoln, hwy patrol
122	OH 65, Lima, E Speedway/Speedy Cafe/dsl, W Marathon/Subway/dsl Family$, Freightliner, truck repair, Volvo
120	Breese Rd, Ft Shawnee, W Shawnee Fuelstop/dsl Harley-Davidson
118	to Cridersville, W Casey's/dsl, Fuelmart/Subway/dsl, Speedway/dsl $General, Community Mkt, vet
114mm	**both lanes, hadicapped facilities, litter barrels, pet walk, , vending**
113	OH 67, to Uniopolis, Wapakeneta
111	Bellefontaine St, Wahpakeneta, E TA/Hub Room Rest./dsl/scales/@ Red Roof Inn KOA, truck tires, W Clark/dsl, Murphy USA/dsl, Shell Arby's, Bob Evans, Burger King, Capt D's, DQ, El Azteca, Lucky Steer Rest., McDonald's, Pizza Hut, Subway, Taco Bell, Waffle House, Wendy's Best Western, Holiday Inn Express, Super 8 Advance Parts, Aldi Foods, CVS Drug, Lowe's, Neil Armstrong Museum, O'Reilly Parts, st patrol, URGENT CARE, Verizon, Walmart
110	US 33, to St Marys, Bellefontaine, E hwy patrol, KOA
104	OH 219, W Circle K/Subway/dsl, Gulf/dsl, Marathon Budget Host $General
102	OH 274, to Jackson Ctr, New Breman, E air stream tours, W bicycle museum
99	OH 119, to Minster, Anna, E 99/dsl, Marathon/dsl, W Shell, Speedway/Taco Bell/dsl Subway, Wendy's Family$, lube/wash/repair
94	rd 25A, Sidney, E Marathon/deli
93	OH 29, to St Marys, Sidney, W Camp Qtokee, Lake Loramie SP
92	OH 47, to Versailles, Sidney, E Speedway/dsl Arby's, China Garden, Coldstone, Fuji Steakhouse, Little Caesar's, Subway, Time Horton's, Wendy's , Advance Parts, AutoZone, CVS Drug, NAPA, URGENT CARE, Walgreens, W Murphy USA/dsl, Sunoco/dsl, VP Applebee's, Big Boy, Bob Evans,
92	Continued Buffalo Wild Wings, Burger King, Cazadores Mexican, Chipotle, Culver's, Fricker's, Hong Kong Buffet, KFC, McDonald's, Perkins, Pizza Hut, Smokin Jo's BBQ, Taco Bell, Wa House Days Inn, Holiday Inn Express, Motel 6, Quality Super 8 $Tree, Aldi Foods, AT&T, Buick/Cadillac/Chevro GMC, Chrysler/Dodge/Jeep, Ford/Lincoln, Kroger/dsl, Low Menards, Verizon, Walmart/Subway
90	Fair Rd, to Sidney, E Sunoco/dsl, W Loves/Cter's/Godfather's/Hardee's/dsl/scales/24hr, Marathon/dsl Hampton Inn
88mm	Great Miami River
83	rd 25A, Piqua, W Sunoco/MaidRite Cafe/dsl Chrys Dodge/Jeep, Sherry RV Ctr, to Piqua Hist Area
82	US 36, to Urbana, Piqua, E Marathon, Murphy U dsl A&W/LJ Silver, Arby's, China East, China Garden, KFC, Subway, Taco Bell, Waffle House, Wendy's $Tree, Foods, AT&T, BigLots, Harley-Davidson, Home Depot, Jo Fabrics, st patrol, Verizon, vet, Walmart/Subway, W Spe way Bob Evans, Buffalo Wings&Rings, Cracker Ba McDonald's, Red Lobster Budgetel, Comfort Inn, La Q ta Elder Beerman, JC Penney
81mm	**both lanes, full facilities, litter barrels, , , vendir**
78	rd 25A, E
74	OH 41, to Covington, Troy, E BP/dsl Al's Pizza, G en Bowl, Little Caesar's, McDonald's, Pizza Hut, Subway, T Bell to Hobart Arena, URGENT CARE, vet, W Circle dsl, Shell, Speedway/dsl Applebee's, Big Boy, Bob Ev Buffalo Wild Wings, Burger King, Cassano's Pizza, Chick-fi Chipotle Mexican, Culver's, Fazoli's, Fricker's, J's Cuisine, J my John's, KFC, Logan's Roadhouse, Los Pitayos Mexic Marion's Pizza, Outback Steaks, Panera Bread, Penn Sta S Ruby Tuesday, Sakai Japanese, Skyline Chili, Starbucks, Stea Shake, Tim Horton Comfort Suites, Fairfield Inn, Hamp Inn, Holiday Inn Express, Residence Inn, Super 9 $Ger al, $Tree, AT&T, AutoZone, GNC, Grismer Auto Service, Ko Lowe's, Meijer/dsl, Petco, Staples, Tire Discounters, Veriz Walmart/Subway
73	OH 55, to Ludlow Falls, Troy, E BP, Shell Asian Cotta Boston Stoker Coffee House, Honeybaked Ham, Hot Head B rito, Lincoln Sq Rest., Papa John's, Starbucks, Subway, Wa House, Wendy's Budget Inn, Motel 6, Royal Inn $G eral, Kroger/e85, Verizon
69	rd 25A, E Casey's/dsl, Circle K/dsl, Shell/dsl Arbog RV Ctr, Buick/GMC, Chrysler/Dodge/Jeep, Ford
68	OH 571, to West Milton, Tipp City, E BP/dsl, Shell, Spe way/dsl Burger King, Cassano's Pizza, Domino's, Gre fire Bistro, Hickory River BBQ, Hong Kong Kitchen, Hot H Burritos, McDonald's, Subway AT&T, CVS Drug, Fami FoodTown, Goodyear/auto, Honda, O'Reilly Parts, W M athon, Speedway/dsl Arby's, Big Boy, Bob Evans, Taco B Wendy's Holiday Inn Express, La Quinta Lee's Gara Menards, vet
64	Northwoods Blvd, E El Toro Mexican, Fu Ying $T Kroger/dsl, W FLYING J/Subway/dsl/scales/RV dump/2
63	US 40, to Donnelsville, Vandalia, E Speedway/dsl B ker's Grill, Dragon China, Fricker's AutoZone, O'Reilly Pa repair, W BP/dsl, Shell, Speedway/dsl Arby's, Bu King, Domino's, Hot Head Burrito, KFC/LJ Silver, McDona Pizza Hut, Subway, Taco Bell, Waffle House, Wendy's Su 8 Goodyear/auto, Rite Aid
61b a	I-70, E to Columbus, W to Indianapolis, to Dayton Int Airpor

LIMA

SIDNEY

TROY

OH

INTERSTATE 75 Cont'd

Exit #	Services
59	Wyse Rd, Benchwood Rd, E [food] Little York Pizza, Shen's [lodging] Hawthorn Suites, Knights Inn [other] BMW/Volvo/VW, Discount Tire, W [gas] Speedway/dsl, Valero/dsl [food] Arby's, Asian Buffet, Big Boy, Bob Evans, Burger King, Cassano's Pizza, Chick-fil-A, Chipotle Mexican, Coldstone, Cousin Vinny's Puzza, Cracker Barrel, El Toro Mexican, Fazoli's, Fricker's, Golden Corral, Hooters, Longhorn Steaks, McAlister's Deli, McDonald's, O'Charley's, Olive Garden, Outback Steaks, Panera Bread, Red Lobster, Red Robin, Ruby Tuesday, Sake Japanese, Skyline Chili, SmashBurger, SmokeyBones BBQ, Subway, Taco Bell, Tesla EVC, Tim Horton's [lodging] Comfort Inn, Courtyard, Days Inn, Drury Inn, Extended Stay America, Hampton Inn, Home 2 Suites, Motel 6, Quality Inn, Red Lion Inn, Red Roof Inn, Residence Inn, Springhill Suites, TownePlace Suites [other] Office Depot, Sam's Club/gas, Verizon, Walmart/Subway
58	Needmore Rd, to Dayton, E [gas] BP/dsl, Shell/McDonald's [food] Hardee's [other] Goodyear/auto, to AF Museum, W [gas] Marathon/dsl, Speedway/Speedy's Cafe, Sunoco/dsl [food] A&W/LJ Silver, Church's, Domino's, Subway, Tim Horton's, Waffle House, Wendy's [other] $General, $Tree, Advance Parts, auto repair, AutoZone, Family$, Kroger/gas, Midas, O'Reilly Parts, USPO, vet
57b	Wagner Ford Rd, Siebenthaler Rd, Dayton
57a	Neva Rd
56	Stanley Ave, Dayton, E [gas] Shell, W [food] Dragon City Chinese, Great Steak, McDonald's, Pancake House, Taco Bell [lodging] Dayton Motel
55b a	Keowee St, Dayton, downtown
54c	OH 4 N, Webster St, to Springfield, downtown
54mm	Great Miami River
54b	OH 48, Main St, Dayton, E [gas] Chevrolet, Honda, W [other] [H], Family$
54a	Grand Ave, Dayton, downtown
53b	OH 49, 1st St, Salem Ave, Dayton, downtown
53a	OH 49, 3rd St, downtown
52b a	US 35, E to Dayton, W to Eaton
51	Edwin C Moses Blvd, Nicholas Rd, E [lodging] Courtyard, Marriott [other] [H], to U of Dayton, W [gas] BP/dsl, Loves/Hardee's/dsl/scales/24hr [food] McDonald's, Wendy's [lodging] Holiday Inn Express [other] SunWatch Indian Village
50b a	OH 741, Kettering St, Dryden Rd, E [other] [H], vet, W [gas] Marathon/dsl [lodging] Red Roof Inn
47	Dixie Dr, W Carrollton, Moraine, E [gas] Sunoco/dsl [food] Big Boy, Domino's, Waffle House [other] $General, auto repair, W [gas] Shell/dsl, Speedway/dsl [food] El Meson, KFC, McDonald's, Pizza Hut, Sonic, Taco Bell, Wendy's [other] $General, USPO
44	OH 725, to Centerville, Miamisburg, E [gas] BP/dsl, Shell, Speedway/dsl [food] Applebee's, Big Boy, Bonefish Grill, Bravo Italiana, Chick-fil-A, ChuckeCheese, Dunkin'/Baskin-Robbins, El Toro Mexican, Fazoli's, FirstWatch Cafe, Fricker's, Godfather's, Golden Corral, Hardee's, Jimmy John's, KFC, Logan's Roadhouse, Marion's Pizza, McDonald's, O'Charley's, Olive Garden, Outback Steaks, Panera Bread, Penn Sta Subs, PF Chang's, Red Lobster, Rusty Bucket Grill, Sake Japanese, Skyline Chili, SmashBurger, Starbucks, Steak'n Shake, Subway, Taco Bell, Waffle House, Wendy's [lodging] Comfort Suites, Courtyard, DoubleTree Suites, Extended Stay America, Hampton Inn, Hawthorn Suites, Homewood Suites, InTowne Suites, Motel 6, SpringHill Suites, Studio 6, Woodspring Suites [other] [H], $Tree, Advance Parts, Aldi Foods, AT&T, Audi/VW/Porsche/Jaguar, Barnes&Noble, Best Buy, Burlington Coats, Dick's, Discount Tire, Grismer Auto Service,

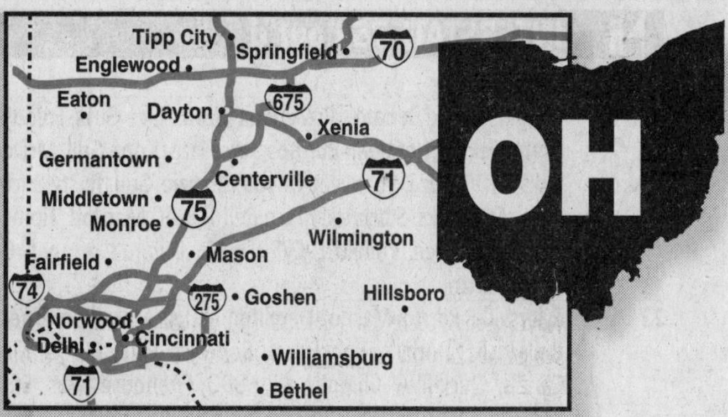

Exit #	Services
44	Continued Hobby Lobby, Home Depot, Honda/Nissan/Mazda, JC Penney, Jo-Ann Fabrics, Kia, Lowe's, Macy's, Menard's, Michael's, Midas, Monro, Office Depot, PepBoys, Petsmart, Target, Tire Discounters, Toyota, Verizon, vet, Walmart, W [gas] BP, Marathon, Shell/dsl [food] Bob Evans, LJ Silver, Perkins, Tim Horton's [lodging] Knights Inn, Quality Inn, Red Roof Inn, Super 8 [other] [H], $General, CarMax, Chevrolet, Ford, NAPA, transmissions
43	I-675 N, to Columbus
41	Austin Blvd, E [food] BJ's Rest., Broken Egg Cafe, Chipotle, Chuy's, Coldstone, Dewey's Pizza, Firebirds, Five Guys, Noodles&-Co, Panera Bread, Spicy Olive [lodging] Hilton Garden [other] AT&T, Field&Stream, GNC, Kohl's, Kroger/dsl, TJ Maxx
38	OH 73, Springboro, Franklin, E [gas] Shell, Speedway/dsl, Thornton's/dsl [food] Applebee's, Arby's, Bob Evans, Burger King, China Garden, Chipotle Mexican, KFC, LJ Silver, McDonald's, Papa John's, Pizza Hut, Popeye's, Skyline Chili, Starbucks, Subway, Taco Bell, Tim Horton's, Waffle House, Wendy's [lodging] Hampton Inn, Quality Inn [other] Kroger, O'Reilly Parts, Tire Discounters, USPO, vet, W [gas] Murphy USA/dsl, Speedway/dsl, Sunoco [food] A&G Pizza, Big Boy, Domino's, El Vaquero Mexican, GoldStar Chili, Lee's Chicken, McDonald's [lodging] EconoLodge, Holiday Inn Express [other] $General, $Tree, Auto Doc, AutoZone, NAPA, URGENT CARE, USPO, Walgreens, Walmart
36	OH 123, to Lebanon, Franklin, E [gas] Marathon/Mom's Rest./dsl, Pilot/Subway/Pizza Hut/dsl/scales/24hr/@, Shell/Wendy's/dsl [food] McDonald's, Waffle House [lodging] Motel 6, W [gas] Marathon/White Castle/dsl, Sunoco
32	OH 122, Middletown, E [food] McDonald's [lodging] Days Inn, Red Roof Inn, Super 8 [other] [H], CVS Drug, W [food] Applebee's, Arby's, Big Boy, Bob Evans, Cracker Barrel, El Rancho Grande, Fricker's, Golden Corral, GoldStar Chili, Hot Head Burritos, KFC, La Rosa's Pizza, O'Charley's, Olive Garden, Sonic, Wendy's, White Castle [lodging] Drury Inn, Fairfield Inn, Hampton Inn, Holiday Inn Express, Quality Inn [other] $General, Aldi Foods, AT&T, AutoZone, BigLots, Kohl's, Kroger/dsl, Lowe's, Meijer/dsl, Petco, Staples, Tire Discounters, URGENT CARE, Verizon, Walmart/Subway
29	OH 63, to Hamilton, Monroe, E [gas] Shell/Popeye's/dsl [food] Burger King, Chipotle, Culver's, DQ, Dunkin', GoldStar Chili, Skyline Chili, Tim Horton/Wendy's, Waffle House [lodging] Comfort Inn [other] Premium Outlets/Famous Brands, Tire Discounters, Trader's World, W [gas] Speedway/dsl [food] Froggy's, McDonald's, Richard's Pizza, Subway [lodging] Best Western, Motel 75 [other] Honda
27.5mm	**[rest stop] both lanes, full [handicapped] facilities, info, litter barrels, petwalk, [phone], [picnic], vending**
24	OH 129 W, to Hamilton, E [lodging] Holiday Inn Express, Hyatt, W [gas] Kroger/dsl, Tesla EVC, UDF [food] Buffalo Wings & Rings, BibibopAsian, BigBoy, BrioTuscanGrille, BurgerKing, Chick-fil-A,

MIDDLETOWN

OH

= gas = food = lodging = other = rest stop

INTERSTATE 75 Cont'd

24	Continued Coopers Hawk, Donato's Pizza, First Watch, Five Guys, Freddy's, Grand Peking, Hot Head Burritos, Jets Pizza, Kona Grill, McDonald's, MOD Pizza, Popeye's, Qdoba, Rodizio Grill, Rusty Bucket Rest., Starbucks, Starbucks, Taco Bell AC Marriott, Home 2 Suites $Tree, Cabela's, CVS, Dick's, Dillard's, Kroger, Old Navy, Verizon
22	Tylersville Rd, to Mason, Hamilton, E Marathon, Thornton's/dsl Arby's, Bob Evans, BoneFish Grill, Burger King, Cane's, Chick-fil-A, Chipotle, City BBQ, Firehouse Subs, Fricker's, Graeter's Grill, IHOP, Jack-in-the-Box, Jimmy John's, KFC, LJ Silver, Longhorn Steaks, McAlister's Deli, McDonald's, Miyako Grill, Noodles&Co, Panda Express, Panera Bread, Perkins, Pizza Hut, Skyline Chili, SmashBurger, Soho Japanese, Starbucks, Taco Bell, Taziki Grill, TGIFriday's, Twin Dragon, Waffle House, Wayback Burger, Wendy's H, AT&T, Big Lots, Discount Tire, Firestone/auto, Fresh Mkt, GNC, Home Depot, Kohl's, Kroger, Michael's, Office Depot, Petsmart, Target, TJ Maxx, URGENT CARE, Walgreens, W Speedway/dsl Sheraton Aldi Foods, CarX, Lowe's, Meijer/dsl, Tire Discounters
21	Cin-Day Rd, E Big Boy Quality Inn, W EVC, Shell/dsl, Speedway/dsl, UDF/Subway/dsl Arby's, Domino's, Dunkin', El Rancho Nuevo, La Rosa's Pizza, Little Caesar's, Papa John's, Sonic, Tikka Grill, Waffle House, Wendy's, White Castle AutoZone, Christian Bros Automotive, USPO, Walgreens, Walmart/Subway
19	Union Centre Blvd, to Fairfield, E Bravo Italiana, Chuy's, Mitchell's Fish Mkt, Original Pancakes, Panera Bread, PF Chang's, Red Robin, Smokey Bones BBQ AT&T, Barnes&Noble, Verizon, W BP/dsl, Marathon/Circle K, Shell Aladdin's Eatery, Applebee's, Bob Evans, Buffalo Wild Wings, Burger King, Chipotle Mexican, Dingle House, First Watch, Jag's Steaks, Jimmy John's, McDonald's, Mellow Mushroom, Palermo Italian, Rancho Nuevo, Skyline Chili, Starbucks, Subway, Tom+Chee, Uno, Wendy's, Yummy Bowl Aloft, Comfort Inn, Courtyard, Hampton Inn, Hilton Garden, Holiday Inn, Homewood Suites, Marriott, Residence Inn, Staybridge Suites IKEA, Mercedes, Monro, Volvo
16	I-275 to I-71, to I-74
15	Sharon Rd, to Sharonville, Glendale, E Sunoco, Thornton's/dsl Big Boy, Bob Evans, Cracker Barrel, Ruby Tuesday, Skyline Chili, Subway, Waffle House Baymont Inn, Drury Inn, Hawthorn Suites, Hilton Garden, Holiday Inn Express, La Quinta, Quality Inn, Red Roof Inn, Travel Inn, ÷on Kemper, W÷ Sunoco Burger King, Cane's, Chick-fil-A, Chili's, ChuckeCheese, Cindy Crab Seafood, Five Guys, Habaneros, LJ Silver, McDonald's, Panera Bread, Penn Sta Subs, Pizza Hut, Taco Bell, Tokyo Japanese, Vincenzo's Italian Fairfield Inn, Home Towne Studios, LivInn Suites, Motel 6, Sharonville Hotel, Sonesta Suites AT&T, Best Buy, Costco/gas, Hyatt Place Conv Ctr, Lowe's, Nissan, Sam's Club, Target
14	OH 126, to Woodlawn, Evendale, E GE Plant, W Sunoco/dsl
13	Shepherd Lane, to Lincoln Heights, E GE Plant, W Wendy's
12	Wyoming Ave, Cooper Ave, to Lockland, W Marathon/dsl
10a	OH 126, Ronald Reagan Hwy
10b	Galbraith Rd (exits left from nb), Arlington Heights
9	OH 4, OH 561, Paddock Rd, Seymour Ave, E to Cincinnati Gardens, W fairgrounds
8	Towne St, Elmwood Pl (from nb)
7	OH 562, to I-71, Norwood, Cincinnati Gardens
6	Mitchell Ave, St Bernard, E Mobil, Shell, Sunoco P eye's, White Castle Quality Inn to Cincinnati Zoo Xavier U, Walgreens, W BP/dsl Gold Star Chili, McD ald's, Rally's Advance Parts, Family$, Ford, Honda, Hyu ai, Kia, Kroger, Tires+, S AutoZone
4	I-74 W, US 52, US 27 N, to Indianapolis
3	to US 27 S, US 127 S, Hopple St, E Big Boy, Wh Castle Budget Host H, U of Cincinn W Shell Wendy's
2b	Harrison Ave, W Family$, industrial district
2a	Western Ave, Liberty St (from sb)
1g	Ezzard Charles Dr ((from sb), W Quality Inn
1f	US 50W, Freeman Ave (from sb), W Marathon/ Shell/Subway Big Boy, Taco Bell, Wendy's, White C tle Quality Inn Ford, NAPA, USPO
1e	7th St (from sb), downtown
1c	5th St, E Hilton, Hyatt, Millennium Hotel, Westin Duke Energy Center, downtown
1a	I-71 N, to Cincinnati, downtown, to stadium
0mm	Ohio/Kentucky state line, Ohio River

INTERSTATE 76

Exit #	Services
65	Ohio/Pennsylvania state line. **See OH TPK, exits 232-234.**
60mm	I-76 eb joins Ohio TPK **(toll)**
57	to OH 45, Bailey Rd, to Warren
54	OH 534, to Newton Falls, Lake Milton, N RV campi S Sunoco/dsl to Berlin Lake
52mm	Lake Milton
48	OH 225, to Alliance, N to W Branch SP, S to Berlin La to Lake Milton SP
45mm	**both lanes, full facilities, litter barrels, petwalk,**
43	OH 14, to Alliance, Ravenna, N to W Branch SP, S Ma thon/Subway/dsl fireworks
38b a	OH 5, OH 44, to Ravenna, N BP/dsl, Speedway/dsl by's, McDonald's/rv parking, Wendy's, S Marathon/Circ Cracker Barrel H, $General, auto parts, Giant Ea Foods, RV camping
33	OH 43, to Hartville, Kent, N BP/dsl Los Girasoles Mexi Comfort Inn, Days Inn, EconoLodge, Hampton Inn, Holi Inn Express, Super 8 to Kent St U, S Circle K, Spe way/dsl Gionino's Pizza, McDonald's, Pizza Hut, Subw Wendy's $General, Goodyear Tire/brakes, vet
31	rd 18, Tallmadge, N Murphy USA/dsl #1 Chine Applebee's, Arby's, Beef'O'Brady's, Chipotle, DQ, La Terr Mexican, Panera Bread $Tree, AT&T, GNC, Kohl's, Low Marshall's, Petco, Verizon, Walmart/Subway
29	OH 532, Tallmadge, Mogadore
27	OH 91, Canton Rd, Gilchrist Rd, N Bob Evans, S Ma thon/Subway/dsl Hardee's EconoLodge
26	OH 18, E Market St, Mogadore Rd, N Marathon/dsl mad Tire/repair, S Arby's, Dunkin', McDonald's, Subw Wendy's $General
25b a	Martha Ave, General St, Brittain, N Circle K/dsl Hil Garden Mercedes, Toyota, S Goodyear HQ
24	Arlington St, Kelly Ave, S Goodyear HQ
23b	OH 8, Buchtell Ave, to Cuyahoga (exits left from eb), to U of Ak
23a	I-77 S, to Canton
22a	Main St, Broadway, N Aldi Foods, downtown
21c	OH 59 E, Dart Ave, N H
21b	Lakeshore St, Bowery St (from eb)

CINCINNATI AREA

AKRON

OH

INTERSTATE 76 Cont'd

Exit #	Services
21a	East Ave (from wb)
20	I-77 N (from eb), to Cleveland
19	Battles Ave, Kenmore Blvd
18	I-277, US 224 E, to Canton, Barberton
17b	OH 619, Wooster Rd, S Sunoco/dsl, tires/repair
17a	(from eb, no return) State St, to Barberton, S Papa John's, Papa Roni's Pizza Walgreens
16	Barber Rd, S Rocky's/dsl/e85 DQ, Tomaso's Italian Chrysler/Dodge/Jeep
14	Cleve-Mass Rd, to Norton, S BP/dsl, Circle K/dsl Arby's, Casa Del Mar Mexican, Marco's Pizza, McDonald's, Ming Garden, Pizza Hut, Subway, Wendy's $General, Ace Hardware, Acme Fresh Mkt, Advance Parts, CVS Drug, Ritzman Drug, USPO, Verizon
13b a	OH 21, N to Cleveland, S to Massillon
11	OH 261, Wadsworth, N Speedway/dsl, S GetGo/e85, Giant Eagle Antonio's Pizza, Beef'O'Brady's, Wayback Burger AAA, GNC, Kohl's, Lowe's, PetCo, Target, Verizon
9	OH 94, to N Royalton, Wadsworth, N GetGo, Marathon/Circle K Applebee's, Arby's, Bob Evans, Burger King, China Express, Chipotle Mexican, El Rincon Mexican, Galaxy Rest., Little Caesar's, Marie's Cafe, McDonald's, Panera Bread, Pizza Hut, Romeo's Pizza, Starbucks, Taco Bell, Wendy's Comfort Inn, Holiday Inn Express $Tree, Aldi Foods, BigLots, Buehler's Foods, DrugMart, Goodyear/auto, Home Depot, NTB, Verizon, Walmart/Subway, S Marathon/DQ/dsl, Sunoco Casa Del Rio, Dunkin', KFC, Papa John's Legacy Inn Advance Parts, auto repair, AutoZone, CVS Drug, Rite Aid, vet
7	OH 57, to Rittman, Medina, N Marathon/dsl, S
6mm	**weigh sta eb**
2	OH 3, to Medina, Seville, N Marathon/Circle K/dsl Digsby Pizza, DQ, Hardee's, Huddle House, Subway Hawthorn Suites, Quality Inn Maple Lakes Camping (seasonal), S Clark, Shell/dsl #1 Chinese, E of Chicago Pizza, El Patron Mexican $General
1	I-76 E, to Akron, US 224on US 224, W Pilot/Subway/dsl/scales/24hr, TA/BP/Burger King/Popeye's/dsl/scales/24hr/@ Arby's, McDonald's, Starbucks Super 8 Blue Beacon, Chippewa Valley Camping (1mi), SpeedCo
0mm	**I-76 begins/ends on I-71, exit 209.**

INTERSTATE 77

Exit #	Services
	I-77 begins/ends on I-90, exit 172 in Cleveland.
163c	I-90, E to Erie, W to Toledo
163b	E 9th St, Tower City
162b	E 22nd St, E 14th St (from nb)
162a	E 30th St, Woodland Ave, Broadway St (from nb), W USPO
161b	I-490 W, to I-71, E 55th, E
161a	OH 14 (from nb), Broadway St
160	Pershing Ave (from nb), W
159b	Fleet Ave, E BP/7-11/dsl
159a	Harvard Ave, Newburgh Heights, W BP/Subway/dsl
158	Grant Ave, Cuyahoga Heights
157	OH 21, OH 17 (from sb), Brecksville Rd
156	I-480, to Youngstown, Toledo
155	Rockside Rd, to Independence, E Shell, Sunoco/dsl Aladdin's, Bob Evans, Bonefish Grill, Chipotle, Delmonico's Steaks, Denny's, DiBella's Subs, Jimmy John's, McDonald's,

CLEVELAND

Exit #	Services
155	Continued Melt Grill, Outback Steaks, Panera Bread, Potbelly, Red Robin, Shula's Steaks, Starbucks, Wendy's, Winking Lizard Grill, Zoup! Comfort Inn, DoubleTree, Embassy Suites, Holiday Inn, La Quinta, Red Roof Inn, Springhill Suites AT&T, Drugmart, to Cuyahoga Valley NP, Verizon, Walgreens, W Applebee's, Longhorn Steaks, Wasabi Steaks Courtyard, Crowne Plaza, Hampton Inn, Home 2 Suites, Hyatt Place, Residence Inn
153	Pleasant Valley Rd, to Independence, 7 Hills
151	Wallings Rd
149	OH 82, to Broadview Heights, Brecksville, 1 mi E Shell/dsl Austin's Grille, Courtyard Cafe, Panera Bread, Sakura Japanese, Simon's Rest., Starbucks, Subway CVS Drug, Marc's Foods, vet, Walgreens, W BP, GetGo/dsl Bob Evans, Chipotle, McDonald's, Starbucks, Wild Eagle Steaks Giant Eagle Foods
147	to OH 21, Miller Rd (from sb)
146	I-80/Ohio Tpk, to Youngstown, Toledo
145	OH 21 (from nb), E Pilot/Wendy's/dsl/scales Cozumel Mexican, Subway Days Inn, Hampton Inn, Holiday Inn Express, Motel 6, Super 8
144	I-271 N, to Erie
143	OH 176, to I-271 S, W Shell McDonald's, Panda Chinese, Richfield Cafe, Subway, Teresa's Pizza
141mm	**both lanes, full facilities, litter barrels, petwalk, vending**
138	Ghent Rd, W Circle K/dsl Gasoline Alley, Lanning's Rest.
137b a	OH 18, to Fairlawn, Medina, E Circle K, GetGo, Shell, Speedway Applebee's, A-Wok, Bob Evans, Boston Mkt, Bravo Italiana, Burntwood Tavern, Chick-fil-A, Chili's, Chipotle Mexican, Coldstone, Cracker Barrel, Donato's Pizza, First Watch, Five Guys, Fleming's Steaks, Gionino's Pizza, HoneyBaked Ham, Hyde Park Grille, Jimmy John's, Macaroni Grill, McDonald's, Menchie's, Olive Garden, Pad Thai, Panera Bread, Penn Sta Subs, PF Chang's, Red Lobster, Robeck's FruitJuice, Starbucks, Steak'n Shake, Subway, Taco Bell, Wendy's, Winking Lizard Grill, Zoup! Courtyard, DoubleTree, EconoLodge, Fairfield Inn, Hampton Inn, Hilton, Holiday Inn, Homewood Suites, Motel 6, Quality Inn $Tree, Acme Fresh Mkt, Aldi Foods, AT&T, Barnes&Noble, Best Buy, Dick's, Dillard's, Earth Fare Foods, Ford, Giant Eagle Foods, Goodyear/auto, Hobby Lobby, Home Depot, JC Penney, Jo-Ann Fabrics, Lowe's, Macy's, Michael's, NTB, Old Navy, Petsmart, Sam's Club, Staples, TJ Maxx, Verizon, Walmart, World Mkt, W Sunoco DQ, Hooley House Rest., Kingfish Rest., Longhorn Steaks, Outback Steaks, Tres Potrillos, Wasabi Grill Baymont Inn, Best Western+, Extended Stay America, Extended Stay America 2, Fairbridge Suites, Radisson, Residence Inn, Super 8
136	(exits left from nb) OH 21S, to Massillon

FAIRLAWN

OH

INTERSTATE 77 Cont'd

Exit #	Services
135	Cleveland-Massillon Rd (from nb, no return)
133	Ridgewood Rd, Miller Rd, E Circle K/dsl, W Old Carolina BBQ, Teresa's Pizza, Tiffany's Bakery Conrad's Automotive
132	White Pond Dr, Mull Ave
131	OH 162, Copley Rd, E Circle K China Star, Little Caesar's Save-A-Lot Foods, Walgreens, W BP/dsl McDonald's, Pizza Hut vet
130	OH 261, Wooster Ave, E Circle K, Sunoco/dsl Ann's Place, Burger King, Church's, McDonald's, New Ming Chinese, Rally's, Subway Advance Parts, AutoZone, O'Reilly Parts, W Chevrolet, Toyota, U-Haul
129	I-76 W, to I-277, to Kenmore Blvd, Barberton
I-77 S and I-76 E run together. See I-76, exits 21a-22b.	
125b	I-76 E, to Youngstown, I-77 and I-76 run together
125a	OH 8 N, to Cuyahoga Falls, U of Akron
124b	Lover's Lane, Cole Ave
124a	Archwood Ave, Firestone Blvd (from sb)
123b	OH 764, Wilbeth Rd, E DQ to
123a	Waterloo Rd (from sb), W BP, GetGo Burger King, House of Hunan, Hungry Howies, Mi Casa, Papa John's, Rally's, Subway, Waterloo Rest. $General, $Tree, Big Lots, Giant Eagle Foods, GNC, Marc's Mkt, Rite Aid, Walgreens
122b a	I-277, US 224 E, to Barberton, Mogadore
120	Arlington Rd, to Green, E Speedway/dsl Applebee's, Denny's, Golden Corral, IHOP, Jimmy John's, Mr Hero, Shogun, Starbucks, Waffle House EconoLodge, Red Roof Inn AT&T, AutoZone, Home Depot, Kohl's, O'Reilly Parts, Staples, Walmart/Subway, W Bob Evans, Burger King, Chipotle Mexican, CiCi's Pizza, McDonald's, Panera Bread, Subway, Taco Bell, TGIFriday's, Wendy's Fairfield Inn, Hampton Inn, Holiday Inn Express, Residence Inn, Woodspring Suites $Tree, Acura, Buick/GMC, Camping World RV Ctr, Chevrolet, Circle K, GNC, Goodyear/auto, Honda, Hyundai, Infiniti, Lexus, Lowe's, Nissan, Subaru, Target, Verizon
118	OH 241, to OH 619, Massillon, E Sheetz/dsl, Speedway/dsl Gionino's Pizza, Handel's Ice Cream, Hunan Dragon, Subway, W Circle K/dsl, GetGo, Tesla EVC Arby's, DQ, Dunkin', Hungry Howie's, Jimmy John's, Kasai Japanese, Lucky Star Chinese, McDonald's, Menches Rest., Starbucks, Subway, Tom Chee Cafe Cambria Suites, Super 8 H, $General, Acme Fresh Mkt, Advance Parts, Aldi Foods, Conrad Automotive, CVS Drug, Giant Eagle Foods
113	W Hilton Garden Akron-Canton Airport, General RV Ctr (2mi)
112	Shuffel St, E Embassy Suites
111	Portage St, N Canton, E Circle K, Sunoco/dsl, TA/Country Pride/dsl/scales/24hr/@ Burger King, KFC, Palombo's Italian, Quaker Steak, Subway, Sylvester's Italian Mr Tire, TrueValue, W BP/dsl, Speedway/dsl Aladdin's Eatery, BJ's Rest., Bonefish Grill, Carrabba's, ChuckeCheese, Coldstone, Cracker Barrel, Dunkin'/Baskin-Robbins, Five Guys, IHOP, Longhorn Steaks, McDonald's, Menchie's, Outback Steaks, Panera Bread, Red Robin, Rockne's Cafe, Romeo's Pizza, Samantha's Rest., Starbucks, Taco Bell, Wasabi Japanese, Wendy's, Zoup! Best Western+, Microtel, Rodeway Inn AAA, AT&T, Best Buy, BJ's Whse, Book A Million, Chevrolet, DrugMart, Giant Eagle Foods, Goodyear/auto, Harley-Davidson, Home Depot, Lowe's, Marshall's, Michael's, Old Navy, Sam's Club/gas, Walgreens, Walmart/Subway

Exit #	Services
109b a	Everhard Rd, Whipple Ave, E Marathon/Subway/ Speedway/dsl Denny's, Fat Head's Brewery, Fazoli's, Je Mike's, Moe's SW, Waffle House Baymont Inn, Comfort Fairfield Inn, Hampton Inn, Home 2 Suites, Hyatt Place, R dence Inn, Staybridge Suites Buick/GMC, Ford, W M athon A1 Japanese Steaks, Applebee's, Arby's, Bob Ev Bravo Italiana, Brown Derby, Buffalo Wild Wings, Buffet nasty, Burnt Wood Tavern, Cane's, Chick-fil-A, Chili's, Chip Mexican, CiCi's Pizza, DiBella Subs, Dunkin', Firehouse S Golden Corral, HoneyBaked Ham, Jerzees Grille, Jimmy Joh Katana Buffet, KFC, McDonald's, Mission BBQ, Mr Hero, M gan's, Olive Garden, Original Steaks & Hoagies, Panda Expr Panera Bread, Papa Bear's, Papa Gyros, Penn Sta Subs, P Hut, Red Lobster, Robek's, Ruby Tuesday, Sahara Grill, Sak Japanese, Starbucks, Steak'n Shake, Subway, Taco Bell, TG day's, TX Roadhouse Courtyard, Holiday Inn, Knights Quality Inn, Ramada, Red Roof Inn, Springhill Suites $T Aldi Foods, AT&T, Burlington Coats, Dick's, Dillard's, Firesto auto, Goodyear/auto, Jo-Ann Fabrics, Kohl's, Macy's, Mag son, Marc's Foods, NTB, Petsmart, Target, TJ Maxx, Tues Morning, Verizon, World Mkt
107b a	US 62, OH 687, Fulton Rd, to Alliance, E Marathon/Ci K/Subway Jerzee's Grille city park, W Circle Dunkin' Pro Football Hall of Fame
106	13th St NW, E H
105b	OH 172, Tuscarawas St, E Lindsey's, McDona W KFC, Subway AutoZone, CVS
105a	6th St SW (no EZ return from sb), E Sunoco McD ald's Ford, W Subway H, AutoZone
104b a	US 30, US 62, to E Liverpool, Massillon
103	OH 800 S, E Marathon/Subway/dsl, Speedway Arb DQ, Italo's Pizza, McDonald's, Peking Chinese, Taco Bell, Wa House $Tree, Advance Parts, auto repair, Family$, Go year/auto, O'Reilly Parts, Save-A-Lot Foods, W Fireston
101	OH 627, to Faircrest St, E Pilot/Subway/dsl/scales/2 Speedway/McDonald's Wendy's Fairfield Inn
99	Fohl Rd, to Navarre, E KOA (4mi), W Sunoco
93	OH 212, to Zoar, Bolivar, E Speedway/dsl McDonal Pizza Hut, Wendy's Sleep Inn $General, Giant Ea Foods, NAPA, to Lake Atwood Region, vet, Zoar Tavern (3mi), W Marathon/DQ/Subway/dsl
87	US 250W, to Strasburg, W BP/Taco Bell/dsl, Marath dsl Hardee's, Manor Rest., McDonald's, Subway mada Ltd Family$, Verizon
85	Schneiders Crossing Rd, to Dover, E Marathon F dy's, Subway Buehler's Mkt/gas
83	OH 39, OH 211, to Sugarcreek, Dover, E BP/dsl, Speedw Speedy's Cafe/dsl Bob Evans, KFC, McDonald's, Shone Wendy's 77 Inn/Grill H, Chrysler/Dodge/Jeep, Flyr Tires, Ford, Honda, Lincoln, Nissan, W Comfort Inn, Cour Inn&Suites vet
81	US 250, to Uhrichsville, OH 39, New Philadelphia, E Shee dsl, Speedway Buffalo Wild Wings, Burger King, Denny's San Jose Mexican, Hog Heaven BBQ, LJ Silver, Pizza Hut, St bucks, Taco Bell, TX Roadhouse Best Western, Hampton Holiday Inn Express, Schoenbrunn Inn, Travelodge $Ger al, $Tree, Advance Parts, Aldi Foods, BigLots, O'Reilly Pa Walmart/Subway, W Eagle TP/rest./dsl/scales/24hr H ley-Davidson
73	OH 751, to rd 53, Stone Creek, W Marathon/dsl
65	US 36, Port Washington, Newcomerstown, W BP, D TP/rest./dsl Speedway/Wendy's McDonald's, Taco Hampton Inn, Super 8

INTERSTATE 77 Cont'd

Exit #	Services
64mm	Tuscarawas River
54	OH 541, rd 831, to Plainfield, Kimbolton, W BP
47	US 22, to Cadiz, Cambridge, E to Salt Fork SP (6mi), W BP/repair , to Glass Museum
46b a	US 40, to Old Washington, Cambridge, W Marathon/Wendy's/dsl, Speedway/dsl Burger King, Hunan Chinese, Lee's Rest., LJ Silver, McDonald's Family$, Riesbeck's Food
44b a	I-70, E to Wheeling, W to Columbus
41	OH 209, OH 821, Byesville, W BP, Circle K, Clark McDonald's, Subway $General, Family$, museum
39mm	**nb, full facilities, litter barrels, petwalk, , vending**
37	OH 313, Buffalo, E Dough Boys Pizza, Subway to Senecaville Lake, USPO
36mm	**sb, full facilities, litter barrels, petwalk, , vending**
28	OH 821, Belle Valley, E Sunoco/dsl RV camping, to Wolf Run SP, USPO
25	OH 78, Caldwel, E Pilot/Arby's/dsl/scales/24hr, Sunoco/Subway/dsl DQ, Lori's Rest., McDonald's Best Western, Days Inn, Microtel, W Comfort Inn
16	OH 821, Macksburg
6	OH 821, to Devola, E BP/Subway/dsl, W Marathon/dsl/LP
3mm	**nb, full facilities, info, litter barrels, petwalk, , , vending**
1	OH 7, to OH 26, Marietta, E GoMart/dsl/24hr DQ, IHOP, Subway Baymont Inn, Comfort Suites, Fairfield Inn, Holiday Inn Express, Quality Inn, Red Roof Inn $Tree, Aldi Foods, Buick/GMC, Cadillac/Chevrolet, Chrysler/Dodge/Jeep, Ford/Lincoln, GNC, Lowe's, Toyota, Walmart/McDonald's, W BP/dsl, GetGo/dsl, Marathon/dsl, Speedway/dsl Applebee's, Arby's, Biscuit World, Bob Evans, Burger King, Capt D's, China Fun, E Chicago Pizza, Empire Buffet, KFC, Las Trancas Mexican, Little Caesar's, LJ Silver, McDonald's, Napoli's Pizza, Papa John's, Pizza Hut, Qdoba, Shogun Hibachi, Shoney's, Subway, Taco Bell, Wendy's Hampton Inn, Microtel, Super 8 Advance Parts, AT&T, AutoZone, Big Lots, Family$, JoAnn Fabrics, Kroger, Rite Aid, TrueValue, Verizon, Walgreens
0mm	Ohio/West Virginia state line, Ohio River

INTERSTATE 80

Exit #	Services
237mm	Ohio/Pennsylvania state line
237mm	**Welcome Ctr wb, full facilities, info, litter barrels, petwalk, , , vending**
234b a	US 62, OH 7, Hubbard, to Sharon, PA, Hubbard, N FLYING J/Denny's/dsl/LP/scales/24hr, Shell/rest./dsl/scales/motel/24hr/@ Arby's, Burger King, Dunkin', McDonald's, Waffle House Best Western, Travelodge Blue Beacon, Homestead RV Ctr., tire/dsl repair, S Love's/Chester's/Subway/dsl/scales/24hr Chevrolet
232mm	**weigh sta wb**
229	OH 193, Belmont Ave, to Youngstown, N GetGo, Speedway/dsl Chad Anthony's Italian, Fortune Garden, Handel's Ice Cream, Sta Square Italian, Subway Comfort Suites, Hampton Inn, Motel 6, Rodeway Inn Giant Eagle Foods, S BP/dsl, Shell Arby's, Bob Evans, Denny's, El Tapatio, Golden Hunan Chinese, Happy Buffet, Jimmy's Italian, KFC,

YOUNGSTOWN

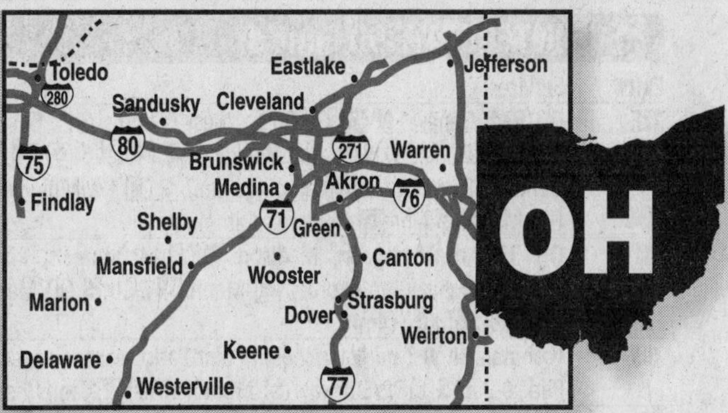

Exit #	Services
229	Continued Little Caesar's, LJ Silver, McDonald's, Nonni's Ristorante, Pizza Hut, Señor Jalapeño Mexican, Subway, Taco Bell, Tim Horton, Uptown Pizza, Wendy's Days Inn, Quality Inn $General, $Tree, Advance Parts, Aldi Foods, AutoZone, Firestone/auto, Goodyear/auto, O'Reilly Parts, Rite Aid, SaveALot Foods, USPO, vet, Walgreens, Walmart/Subway
228	OH 11, to Warren (exits left from eb), Ashtabula
227	US 422, Girard, Youngstown, N Shell/dsl, Sunoco Burger King, DQ, El Torero, JibJab Hotdogs, Subway
226	Salt Springs Rd, to I-680 (from wb), N BP/Dunkin'/dsl, Sheetz/dsl McDonald's, Waffle House vet, S Mr Fuel/Road Rocket Diner/dsl/24hr, Petro/Shell/Iron Skillet/dsl/scales/24hr/@, Pilot/Subway/dsl/scales/24hr Blue Beacon, Quality Truckwash, SpeedCo
224b	I-680 (from eb), to Youngstown
224a	OH 11 S, to Canfield
223	OH 46, to Niles, N Country Fair/dsl, Pilot/McDonald's/dsl/scales/24hr Bob Evans, Dunkin', IceHouse Rest., Los Girasoles California Palms, Candlewood Suites, Comfort Inn, Holiday Inn Express, S BP/Subway/dsl, Sunoco, TA/Counry Pride/dsl/scales/24hr/@ Arby's, Cracker Barrel, LJ Silver/Taco Bell, Perkins, Quaker Steak&Lube, Starbucks, Wendy's Country Inn&Suites, Fairfield Inn, Hampton Inn, Quality Inn, Sleep Inn, Super 8 Freightliner, Harley-Davidson
221mm	Meander Reservoir
219mm	**I-80 wb joins Ohio Tpk (toll)**

For I-80 exits 2-218, see Ohio Turnpike.

INTERSTATE 90

Exit #	Services
244mm	Ohio/Pennsylvania state line
242mm	**/weigh sta wb, full facilities, info, litter barrels, petwalk, ,**
241	OH 7, to Andover, Conneaut, N Burger King, McDonald's (2mi) Days Inn , AutoZone, Evergreen RV Park, S Love's/McDonald's/Subway/dsl/scales/24hr
235	OH 84, OH 193, to Youngstown, N Kingsville, N Grab&Go/gas, Marathon/Circle K Dav-Ed Motel Village Green Camping (2mi), S Circle K/Subway/dsl, TA/BP/Burger King/dsl/scales/24hr/@ Kay's Place Diner Kingsville Motel towing/repair
228	OH 11, to Ashtabula, Youngstown, N (4mi)
223	OH 45, to Ashtabula, N FLYING J/Denny's/Shell/dsl/LP/scales/24hr Austinburg Inn, Best Value Inn, Holiday Inn Express, Sleep Inn, S Pilot/Subway/dsl/scales/24hr, SpeedCo Burger King, Clay St Grill, McDonald's, Taco Bell, Waffle House Hampton Inn auto repair

INTERSTATE 90 Cont'd

Exit #	Services
218	OH 534, Geneva, N GetGo Best Friend's Grill, Chop's Grille, McDonald's, Pizza Hut, Wendy's Motel 6 H, to Geneva SP, Willow Lake Camping (4mi), S KwikFill, Kwik-Fill/dsl/scales/24hr Kenisse's Camping
212	OH 528, to Thompson, Madison, N McDonald's, Pizza Roto Holiday Inn Express Mentor RV Ctr, S Marathon/dsl KOA (4mi)
205	Vrooman Rd, 0-2 mi N Indian Point Park, Masons Landing Park, 0-2 mi S BP/Subway/dsl, Marathon/dsl Capps Pizza
200	OH 44, to Painesville, Chardon, S BP/7-11/dsl, Shell/dsl B2B Burgers, Chipotle, McDonald's, Paninis Grill, Pizza Roto, Red Hawk Grille, Starbucks, Sunny St Cafe, Waffle House Comfort Inn, Holiday Inn Express, Quail Hollow Resort H, URGENT CARE, Verizon
198mm	**both lanes, full facilities, litter barrels, petwalk, , , vending**
195	OH 615, Center St, Kirtland Hills, Mentor, 1-2 mi N Best Western+
193	OH 306, to Mentor, Kirtland, 0-2 mi N BP/7-11/dsl, Shell McDonald's Mentor Home Inn H, S Speedway/dsl Burger King Days Inn, Red Roof Inn Kirtland Temple LDS Historic Site
190	Express Lane to I-271 (from wb)
189	OH 91, to Willoughby, Willoughby Hills, N BP/7-11/dsl, Shell/dsl Applebee's, Big Cheese Pizza, Bob Evans, Café Europa, Cracker Barrel, Peking Chef, Subway, TX Roadhouse, Wendy's Courtyard, Motel 6, Travelodge H, CVS Drug, Walgreens, S BMW/Mini, Lexus
188	I-271 S, to Akron
187	OH 84, Bishop Rd, to Wickliffe, Willoughby, S BP/7-11/dsl, Shell Dunkin', Golden Mtn Chinese, McDonald's, Subway, Tony's Pizza Fairbridge Inn H, $Tree, Chevrolet, CVS Drug, Giant Eagle Foods, Marc's Foods, Mazda/VW, NTB, O'Reilly Parts
186	US 20, Euclid Ave, N Sunoco EconoLodge, Quality Inn Ford, radiators/transmissions, Subaru, S Shell Arby's, Asian Express, KFC, Popeye's, R-Ribs, Sidewalk Cafe, Taco Bell $General, Advance Parts, Family$, Firestone/auto, Save-a-Lot Foods
185	OH 2 E (exits left from eb), to Painesville
184b	OH 175, E 260th St, N Shell USPO, S auto/tire repair
184a	Babbitt Rd, N Buick/GMC
183	E 222nd St, N repair, S BP, Sunoco/dsl vet
182b a	185 St, 200 St, N BP/7-11/dsl Subway Home Depot, Honda, Hyundai, S Marathon/dsl, Shell/dsl, Speedway/dsl
181b a	E 156th St, S BP/Mr Hero
180b a	E 140th St, E 152nd St
179	OH 283 E, to Lake Shore Blvd
178	Eddy Rd, to Bratenahl
177	University Circle, MLK Dr, N Cleveland Lake SP, S H, Rockefeller Park
176	E 72nd St
175	E 55th St, Marginal Rds
174b	OH 2 W, to Lakewood, downtown, N Browns Stadium, Rock&Roll Hall of Fame
174a	Lakeside Ave
173c	Superior Ave, St Clair Ave, N BP, downtown
173b	Chester Ave, S BP
173a	Prospect Ave (from wb), downtown
172d	Carnegie Ave, S Shell/dsl Burger King, KFC, McDonald's Cadillac, downtown
172c b	E 9th St, S H, to Cleveland St U
172a	I-77 S, to Akron
171b a	US 422, OH 14, Broadway St, Ontario St, N Hilton Garc
171	Abbey Ave, downtown
170c b	I-71 S, to I-490
170a	US 42, W 25th St, S Royal
169	W 44th St, W 41st St, N H
167b a	OH 10, West Blvd, 98th St, to Lorain Ave, N H, S E dsl CVS Drug
166	W 117th St, N BP/dsl, GetGo/dsl, Shell Penn Sta St Advance Parts, AutoZone, Giant Eagle Foods, Home Dep Staples, Target, S Gas USA Monro
165	W 140th St, Bunts Rd, Warren Rd, S H
164	McKinley Ave, to Lakewood
162	Hilliard Blvd (from wb), to Westway Blvd, Rocky River, S Shell Ferris Steaks, Joe's Rest. USPO, vet
161	OH 2, OH 254 (from eb, no EZ return), Detroit Rd, Rocky Rive
160	Clague Rd (from wb), same as 159, S H
159	OH 252, Columbia Rd, N EVC Carrabba'a, Dave&Buste Hooley House Grille, Outback Steaks, Si Senor Courtya Super 8, TownePlace Suites BMW, S BP/7-11 by's, Domino's, Houlihan's, Jets Pizza, KFC, McDonald's, Pan Bread, Taco Bell, Urban Grill H, Chevrolet, NTB
156	Crocker Rd, Bassett Rd, Westlake, Bay Village, N Shell DoubleTree, Extended Stay America, Holiday Express, Red Roof Inn, Sonesta Suites, S BP/7-11, Spee way Aladdin's Eatery, Bar Louie, Bob Evans, Bonefish G Brio, Cheesecake Factory, Don Ramon Mexican, First Wat Five Guys, Jersey Mike's, Jimmy John's, McDonald's, Pizza Robert, Robeks, Starbucks, Subway, TGIFriday's, Wendy's, Ya House, Zoup! Hampton Inn, Hyatt Place H, Aldi Foo Barnes & Noble, CVS Drug, Dick's, Fresh Thyme Mkt, Giant gle, GNC, Marc's Foods, Monro, Trader Joe's, Verizon
155	Nagel Rd, Avon Lake, N GetGo/dsl Residence In S Dunkin' Drugmart, Meijer/dsl
153	OH 83, Avon Lake, N Circle K/Dunkin'/dsl, GetG dsl Arby's, Buffalo Wild Wings (2mi), Culver's, Fujiyan King Yuan, Panda Express, Perkins, Rush Inn Grille, We dy's Ali Foods, AutoZone, Best Buy, Cabela's, Discount Ti Duluth Trading, Firestone/auto, JC Penney, Lowe's, Menard PetCo, Walmart, S Antonio's Pizza, Applebee's, Bob Eva Burger King, Chipotle, Five Guys, IHOP, Jimmy John's, Manda House, Moe's SW Grill, Panera Bread, Penn Sta Subs, R Robin, Starbucks, Subway, Taco Bell, Winking Lizard Tave Zoup! Cambria Hotel AT&T, Costco/gas, CVS Dru GNC, Heinen's Mkt, Home Depot, Kohl's, Marc's Foods, M shall's, Michael's, Old Navy, Target, USPO, Verizon, World M
151	OH 611, Avon, N BP/7-11/dsl, Pilot/Subway/dsl/24 McDonald's Fairfield Inn, Woodspring Suites Buic GMC, Chevrolet, Harley-Davidson, NAPA, S BJ's Whse/g Dunkin', Mulligan's Grille
148	OH 254, Sheffield, Avon, N Quaker Steak&Lube Hom wood Suites Ford, Kia, Mazda, Nissan, S BP, GetGo, Shee dsl, Speedway/dsl Arby's, China Star, Cracker Barrel, KFC, Ma co's Pizza, McDonald's, Panera Bread, Pizza Hut, Ruby Tuesda Sorrento Pizzaria, Starbucks, Steak'n Shake, Subway, Sugarcre Rest., Taco Bell, Wendy's $General, $Tree, Aldi Foods, Aut Zone, Drug Mart, Giant Eagle Mkt, Sam's Club/gas, Verizon
147mm	Black River

EUCLID

CLEVELAND

AVON

OH

INTERSTATE 90 Cont'd

Exit #	Services
145	OH 57, to Lorain, I-80/Ohio Tpk E, Elyria, N Burger King, George's Rest. $General, Save-a-Lot, U-Haul, S Speedway/dsl Applebee's, Bob Evans, Buffalo Wild Wings, Burger King, Chipotle Mexican, Denny's, Golden Corral, Harry Buffalo, Honeybaked Ham, IHOP, McDonald's, Olive Garden, Red Lobster, Subway, TX Roadhouse, Wasabi Grill, Wendy's Best Western, Country Inn&Suites, Days Inn, Hampton Inn, Quality Inn, Red Roof Inn $General, $Tree, AT&T, Best Buy, Conrad's Automotive, Dick's, Firestone/auto, Giant Eagle Mkt, Home Depot, Honda, Hyundai, JC Penney, Jo-Ann Fabrics, Lowe's, Marc's Foods, Petsmart, Staples, Target, Tuffy Repair, Verizon
144	OH 2 W (from wb, no return), to Sandusky

I-90 wb joins Ohio Tpk. WB exits to Ohio/Indiana state line are on Ohio Turnpike, exits 142-0.

INTERSTATE 270 (Columbus)

Exit #	Services
55	I-71, to Columbus, Cincinnati
52b a	US 23, High St, Circleville, N Marathon/Circle K, Speedway/dsl, Turkey Hill/dsl Arby's, Bob Evans, Burger King, China City, KFC, Little Caesar's, LJ Silver, Los Mariachis, McDonald's, Pizza Hut, Ponderosa, Skyline Chili, Subway, Taco Bell, Tim Horton's, Waffle House, Wendy's, White Castle Kozy Inn $General, $Tree, Advance Parts, Aldi Foods, AutoZone, CVS Drug, Family$, Firestone/auto, Kroger/gas, Lowe's, NAPA, O'Reilly Parts, Walgreens, Walmart, S BP/dsl Kioto Downs
49	Alum Creek Dr, N BP/dsl, Shell/dsl, Thornton's/dsl Donato's Pizza, KFC/LJ Silver, Subway $General, Family$, S BP/dsl Arby's, McDonald's, Taco Bell, Wendy's Comfort Inn, Quality Inn
46b a	US 33, Bexley, Lancaster
43b a	I-70, E to Cambridge, W to Columbus
41b a	US 40, E Shell, Speedway Bob Evans, City BBQ, Honeybaked Ham, McDonald's, Outback Steaks, Rally's, Steak'n Shake, Taco Bell, Texas Roadhouse auto repair, AutoZone, Family$, NAPA, TJ Maxx, Verizon, Walgreens, W Shell/dsl, Speedway, UDF Golden Corral, Hunan Chinese, McDonald's, Mi Mexico, Poblanos Mexican, Subway $General, Family$
39	OH 16, Broad St, E GetGo, Speedway/dsl Arby's, Cane's, Chick-fil-A, Chipotle, Donato's Pizza, Dunkin', Five Guys,
39	Continued Hot Head Burrito, Jets Pizza, Jimmy John's, McDonald's, Noodles&Co, Panera Bread, Penn Sta Subs, Potbelly's, Sonic, Starbucks, Subway, Sunny St Cafe, Taco Bell, Tim Horton's, Waffle House, Wendy's, White Castle Comfort Suites H, Giant Eagle Mkt, Goodyear/auto, Grismer Auto Service, Kroger, Menard's, URGENT CARE, Verizon, Walgreens, W Shell, Speedway/dsl Chevrolet
37	OH 317, Hamilton Rd, E BP/dsl, Speedway/dsl Arby's, Big Boy, Bob Evans, Burger King, Chinese Express, Chipotle, Dunkin', Firehouse Subs, Jersey Mike's, McDonald's, Panera Bread, Penn Sta Subs, Rusty Bucket, Starbucks, Taco Bell, Tim Horton's Holiday Inn Express Firestone/auto, GNC, Kroger/dsl, W Fairfield Inn, Hampton Inn, Hilton Garden Buick/GMC, Subaru/Jaguar/Porsche, Volvo, VW/Audi
35b a	I-670W, US 62, E Speedway/dsl City BBQ, Little Caesar's, McDonald's, Tim Horton's Advance Parts, AutoZone, CVS Drug, Family$, W I-670
33	Easton Way

COLUMBUS

Exit #	Services
32	Morse Rd, E Marathon/DM, Speedway/dsl, UDF CVS Drug, Mazda, Nissan, Toyota, W BP, Shell/Subway, UDF/dsl Abuelo's, Applebee's, BJ's Rest., Champp's Grill, Donato's Pizza, HomeTown Buffet, J Akexander's, Kobe Japanese, Logan's Roadhouse, McDonald's, On-the-Border, Papa John's, Pei Wei, Red Robin, Sakura Steaks, Smokey Bones, Steak'n Shake, Taco Bell, Wendy's Courtyard, Extended Stay America, Hampton Inn, Holiday Inn Express, Residence Inn, Woodspring Suites AT&T, Best Buy, Cadillac, Carmax, Costco/gas, Dick's, Discount Tire, Field&Stream, Infiniti, Jo-Ann Fabrics, Lexus, Lowe's Whse, Macy's, Mercedes, Michael's, Nordstrom's, NTB, Old Navy, Petsmart, REI, Sam's Club, Staples, Target, TJ Maxx, Trader Joe's, Verizon, Walmart/McDonald's, Whole Foods Mkt, World Mkt
30	OH 161 E to New Albany, W to Worthington
29	OH 3, Westerville, N BP/dsl, Shell Arby's, Bob Evans, Chipotle Mexican, City BBQ, Fazoli's, McDonald's, Pizza Hut, Tim Horton's, Wendy's Red Roof Inn Advance Parts, AT&T, Big Lots, CarQuest, Firestone/auto, Kohl's, Kroger, Marc's Mkt, vet, Walmart, S Clark/dsl, Speedway/dsl Carsoni's Italian, China House, Domino's, Subway Aldi Foods, Family$, Grismer Tire/auto, Midas, Monro, USPO
27	OH 710, Cleveland Ave, N Speedway/dsl Subway, Wendy's Ramada Inn $General, CVS Drug, NAPA Autocare, Tuffy, S Turkey Hill/dsl El Rancho Allegre, McDonald's, O'Charley's Embassy Suites Home Depot
26	I-71, S to Columbus, N to Cleveland
23	US 23, Worthington, N Bob Evans, Chipotle Mexican, Columbus Fish Mkt, Cucina Italiana, El Acapulco, Hyde Park Steaks, J Alexander's, J Gilbert's Steaks, Lotus Grill, Ruth's Chris Steaks, Starbucks, Subway, Sushiko Japanese, Winking Lizard Courtyard, DoubleTree, Extended Stay America, Homewood Suites, Hyatt Place, Motel 6, Quality Inn, Red Roof Inn, Residence Inn, Sheraton, TownePlace Suites, Woodspring Suites, S Aladdin's Eatery, Buca Italian, Cosi Grill, Jimmy John's, McDonald's, Panera Bread, Piada Italian, Starbucks Econolodge, Holiday Inn Kroger
22	OH 315, N BP/dsl, Marathon/dsl Subway
20	Sawmill Rd, N BP, Marathon/dsl Burger King, IHOP, Logan's Roadhouse, Max&Erma's, McDonald's, Olive Garden, Papa John's, Subway, Taco Bell, Wendy's Fairfield Inn Buick/GMC, CVS Drug, Ford, Hyundai, Kroger/gas, Lincoln, Mazda, NTB, Subaru, vet, S Shell, Speedway Applebee's, Arby's, bd Mogolian, Blue Ginger Asian, Bob Evans, Bonchon, Burger King, Cane's, Charlie's Subs, Chick-fil-A, Chili's, Chipotle Mexican, ChuckeCheese, El Vaquero Mexican, Firehouse Subs, Genji Japanese, Golden Corral, HoneyBaked Cafe, Jimmy John's, Joe's Crabshack, KFC, Krispy Kreme, McDonald's,

INTERSTATE 270 (Columbus) Cont'd

COLUMBUS

Exit #	Services
20	Continued Mellow Mushroom, Panera Bread, Pizza Hut, Red Lobster, Ruby Tuesday, Starbucks, Steak'n Shake, Subway, Ted's MT Grill, Vicenzos Italian Cloverleaf Suites, Hampton Inn, Quality Inn $Tree, Advance Parts, AT&T, AutoZone, Barnes&Noble, Big Lots, Cadillac/Honda, CarMax, Dick's, Discount Tire, Firestone/auto, GNC, Hobby Lobby, Home Depot, Infiniti, Jo-Ann Fabrics, Kohl's, Lexus, Lowe's Whse, Meijer, Meineke, Michael's, Mr Tire, Old Navy, PetCo, Petsmart, Sam's Club/gas, Staples, SteinMart, Target, Toyota, Trader Joe's, Verizon, vet, Whole Foods Mkt
17b a	US 33, Dublin-Granville Rd, E Marathon, Sunoco Bob Evans, Hyde Park Steaks, Jason's Deli, Max&Erma's, McDonald's, Pizza Hut, Subway Courtyard, Crowne Plaza, Embassy Suites, Extended Stay America, Hilton Garden, Red Roof Inn, Residence Inn CVS Drug, Fiat, Kroger, Mr Tire, USPO
15	Tuttle Crossing Blvd, E BP, UDF BJ's Rest., Bob Evans, Boston Mkt, Chipotle Mexican, DiBella's Subs, House of Japan, Longhorn Steaks, Macaroni Grill, McDonald's, Noodles&Co, Panera Bread, PF Chang's, River City Grill, Taco Bell, Wendy's Drury Inn, Homewood Suites, Hyatt Place, La Quinta, Marriott JC Penney, W Shell, Turkey Hill/Subway/dsl Steak'n Shake, Uno Pizzaria Staybridge Suites Best Buy, NTB, vet, Walmart/Subway, World Mkt
13	Cemetery Rd, Fishinger Rd, E Exxon/Subway, Shell, Speedway Burger King, Carrabba's, Chipotle Mexican, Damon's, Dave&Buster's, Donato's Pizza, KFC, Lunada Mexican, Panera Bread, Skyline Chili, Spageddie's, Starbucks, Steak&Shake, Tim Horton's Comfort Suites, Homewood Suites $Tree, CVS Drug, Discount Tire, GNC, Home Depot, Lowe's Whse, NTB, Staples, Tire Dicounters, Tuesday Morning, W GetGo/dsl, Speedway Bob Evans, Marie's Scrambler, Max&Erma's, McDonald's, Rusty Bucket Rest., Tim Horton's, Wendy's Hampton Inn, Knights Inn Giant Eagle Mkt, Nissan
10	Roberts Rd, E Marathon, Thornton's/dsl Subway, Tim Horton's, Wendy's Woodspring Suites, W Speedway/dsl Tim Horton's, Waffle House Courtyard, Quality Inn, Royal Inn CVS Drug, Family$, O'Reilly Parts
8	I-70, E to Columbus, W to Indianapolis
7	US 40, Broad St, E BP, Speedway/dsl Bob Evans, Boston Mkt, BurgerKing, ChuckeCheese, McDonald's, PeacockWest, Popeye's, TeeJay's, White Castle Advance Parts, Big Lots, Buick/GMC, Chevrolet, GNC, Target, W GetGo, Speedway/dsl, Thornton's A&W/LJ Silver, Arby's, Canes, KFC, McDonald's, Papa John's, Tim Horton's, Waffle House Red Roof Inn H, CVS Drug, Family$, Giant Eagle Foods, Goodyear/auto, Home Depot, Jo-Ann Fabrics, O'Reilly Parts, Walgreens
5	Georgesville, E Shell/dsl, Sunoco/dsl, UDF/dsl Jimmy John's, Starbucks Verizon, Walmart, W Applebee's, Arby's, Bob Evans, Buffalo Wild Wings, Chipotle Mexican, DQ, Fiesta Mariachi, KFC/LJ Silver, McDonald's, O'Charley's, Red Lobster, Steak'n Shake, Subway, Taco Bell, Wendy's, White Castle Advance Parts, AT&T, Chrysler/Dodge/Jeep, GNC, Honda, Hyundai/Subaru, Kia, Kroger/gas, Lowe's Whse, NTB, TireDiscounters, Toyota, VW
2	US 62, OH 3, Grove City, N Turkey Hill/dsl Woodspring Suites, S Marathon, Shell, Speedway/dsl Big Boy, Burger King, Domino's, Donato's Pizza, Little Caesar's, McDonald's, Subway, Tim Horton/Wendy's, Waffle House, Wedgewood Pizza CVS Drug, Verizon
0mm	I-71

INTERSTATE 271 (Cleveland)

CLEVELAND

MACEDONIA

Exit #	Services
39mm	**I-271 begins/ends on I-90, exit 188.**
36	Wilson Mills Rd, Highland Hts, Mayfield, E Shell A din's Eatery, Austin's Steaks, Jersey Mike's, Yours T Rest. Hilton Garden, Holiday Inn Chrysler/Dodge/J CVS Drug, Heinen's Mkt, vet, W Marathon/dsl Bur 2 Beer, Chipotle, Denny's, Hibachi Steaks, Panera Bread Lots, DrugMart, Home Depot, Kohl's, Tuesday Morning, Ver
34	US 322, Mayfield Rd, E BP/7-11, Circle K Chipotle, Bella's Subs, First Watch, Five Guys, Fox&Hound Grille, Georg Pizza, Jimmy John's, Piccolo Italian, Scramblers, Starbucks, S way, Wendy's H, Aldi Foods, CVS Drug, Marc's Foods, chael's, Mr Tire, Old Navy, Rite Aid, Target, Tire Pros, Walm W Marathon, Shell, Speedway Arby's, Bob Evans, Bu King, Chick-fil-A, ChuckECheese, Dunkin', Firehouse Subs, Ga no's Italian, McDonald's, Otani Japanese, Panera Bread, Penr Subs, Pizza Hut, Sonic, Subway, Taco Bell, TGI Friday's $T AT&T, AutoZone, Best Buy, Conrad's Tire/auto, Costco/gas, Drug, Ford/Lincoln, Fresh Thyme Mkt, Giant Eagle Mkt, C JoAnn Fabrics, Marshall's, Midas, Nissan, NTB, O'Reilly P Petsmart, Staples, Verizon, World Mkt
32	Brainerd Rd, E Burntwood Tavern, J Alexander's USPO
29	US 422 W, OH 87, Chagrin Blvd, Harvard Rd, E Shell, Spe way, Sunoco Bahama Breeze, Bob Evans, Bravo Ital Chipotle, Corky&Lenny's Rest., McDonald's, Mitchell's Mkt, Paladar Latin Kitchen, Pancake House, Red Lobster, S bucks, Stone Oven, Tenas de Brazil, Wasabi Japanese, W dy's Courtyard, Extended Stay America, Extended America, Fairfield Inn, Hampton Inn AT&T, Barnes&No CVS Drug, Rite Aid, TJ Maxx, Trader Joe's, W BP/Subw Shell/dsl Giovanni's Ristorante, Hyde Park Steaks, Chang's, Tres Potrillos, Winking Lizard Tavern Clarion, D bleTree, Embassy Suites, Home 2 Suites, Homewood Suites, tel Indigo, Residence Inn H, Buick/GMC, Cadillac, Infi NTB, Porsche, Verizon
28b	Harvard Rd, E Coopers Hawk, Firebirds, Syman's ern Drury Inn REI, Verizon, Whole Foods Mkt, W falo Wild Wings, Chick-fil-A, Chipotle, DiBella's Subs, Five G Olive Garden, Panera Bread, Piada Italian, River City Gr Robeks Cafe, Zoup! Aloft, Marriott H, Marshall's
28a	OH 175, Richmond Rd, Emery Rd, E BP, GetGo/dsl, Marath Circle K/Subway/dsl Baskin-Robbins/Dunkin', Don Rar Mexican, Jimmy John's, McDonald's vet, W BJ's Whse
27b	I-480 W
27a	US 422 E, E CarMax, Chevrolet, Lowe's
26	Rockside Rd, E Speedway/dsl, Sunoco/dsl Bu King, Subway Family$
23	OH 14 W, Forbes Rd, Broadway Ave, E Sunoco B BBQ, McDonald's, Subway, Wendy's Hampton Inn, Qua Inn Sam's Club/dsl, W Gasway, Marathon/Circle K
21	I-480 E, OH 14 E (from sb), to Youngstown
19	OH 82, Macedonia, E Speedway/dsl/e85 Dunkin', P Sta Subs, Pizza Hut, W Tesla EVC Antonio's Pizza, Ap bee's, Arby's, Chick-fil-A, Chili's, Chipotle, Culver's, First Wa Fuji Japanese, Golden Corral, Jersey Mike's, McDonald's, C back Steaks, Panera Bread, Popeye's, Starbucks, Steak'n Sh Taco Bell, Wendy's Aldi Foods, AT&T, Best Buy, Chevro Discount Tire, Giant Eagle Foods, GNC, Hobby Lobby, Home pot, Kohl's, Lowe's, NTB, O'Reilly Parts, PetCo, Petsmart, Tar Verizon, Verizon, Walgreens, Walmart/Subway

OH

INTERSTATE 271 (Cleveland) Cont'd

Exit #	Services
18b a	OH 8, Boston Hts, to Akron, (exits left from sb), E GetGo, Speedway/dsl Bob Evans, KFC Country Inn&Suites, Key Inn, Knights Inn, La Quinta, W same as 19
12	OH 303, Richfield, Peninsula
10	I-77, to I-80, OH Tpk (from nb), to Akron, Cleveland
9	I-77 S, OH 176 (from nb), to Richfield
8mm	both lanes, full facilities, litter barrels, petwalk
3	OH 94, to I-71 N, Wadsworth, N Royalton, W PetroUSA/dsl
0mm	I-271 begins/ends on I-71, exit 220.

INTERSTATE 275 (Cincinnati)

See Kentucky Interstate 275

INTERSTATE 280 (Toledo)

Exit #	Services
13	I-280 begins/ends on I-75, exit 208.
12	Manhattan Blvd, E Sunoco, W Sunoco/dsl
11	OH 25 S, Eerie St, W Huntington Ctr
10mm	Maumee River
9	OH 65, Front St, E Sunoco Subway, Tony Packo's Cafe, W Sunoco/dsl
8	Starr Ave, (from sb only)
7	OH 2, Oregon, E Circle K/dsl, Sunoco Arby's, Bob Evans, Briskets, Burger King, Coldstone/Tim Horton's, Empire, McDonald's, Sonic, Taco Bell, Wendy's Comfort Inn, Hampton Inn, TownePlace Suites H, Ford, to Maumee Bay SP, Walgreens
6	OH 51, Woodville Rd, Curtice Rd, E BP/dsl, Marathon Bob Evans, Burger King Menards, W Speedway/dsl Applebee's, Arby's, Big Boy, Gino's Pizza, KFC, LJ Silver, McDonald's, Subway, Taco Bell Sleep Inn H, $Tree, Advance Parts, Meijer/dsl, Midas, O'Reilly Parts
4	Walbridge
2	OH 795, Perrysburg, W Sunoco/dsl
1b	Bahnsen Rd, E FLYING J/Denny's/dsl/LP/scales/24hr Best Value Inn, Regency Inn, W Loves/Arby's/dsl/scales/24hr, Petro/BP/Iron Skillet/dsl/scales/24hr/@ Budget Inn Blue Beacon, SpeedCo, Super 8
1a	I-280 begins/ends on I 80/90, OH Tpk, exit 71., S FuelMart/Subway/dsl/scales, Pilot/McDonald's/dsl/scales/24hr, TA/BP/Taco Bell/dsl/scales/24hr/@ KOA

INTERSTATE 475 (Toledo)

Exit #	Services
20	I-75. I-475 begins/ends on I-75, exit 204.
19	ProMedica Pky, Central Ave, S Burger King, Gino's Pizza, Subway H
18b	Douglas Rd (from wb)
18a	OH 51 W, Monroe St
17	Secor Rd, N Marathon, Shell/dsl, Stop'n Shop, Sunoco Applebee's, Bambino's Pizza, Bob Evans, Boston Mkt, Burger King, Famous Dave's BBQ, Hooters, KFC, Monroe St Diner, Netty's, Penn Sta Subs, Red Robin, Rudy's Hot Dogs, Tim Horton's H, $Tree, Advance Parts, AT&T, Barnes&Noble, Best Buy, Jo -AnnFabrics, Kohl's, Kroger/dsl, O'Reilly Parts, Rite Aid, Walgreens, S Bubba's 33, Big Boy, Chick-fil-A, Chipotle Mexican, El Vaquero, First Watch, Five Guys, Fusion, Jamba Juice, Jersey Mike's, McDonald's, Original Pancakes, Packo's, Piada Italian, Pizza Fire, Pizza Hut, Popeye's, Scrambler's, Sonic, Starbucks, Subway, Taco Bell, TX Roadhouse, Uncle John's Pancakes

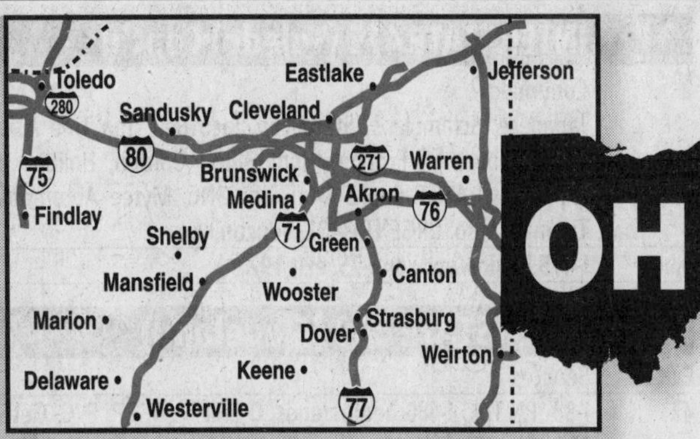

Exit #	Services
17	Continued Courtyard, Hampton Inn, Holiday Inn Express, Quality Inn, Ramada Inn, Red Roof Inn Batteries+Bulbs, Costco/gas, Fresh Mkt, Home Depot, Rite Aid, Steinmart, U of Toledo
16	Talmadge Rd (from wb, no return), N BP/dsl, Speedway/dsl Arby's, Bar Louie, bd Mongolian BBQ, Bravo Italiana, Chick-fil-A, Chipotle, Coldstone, IHOP, J Alexander's, Jimmy John's, Longhorn Steaks, McDonald's, Panera Bread Dick's, JC Penney, Kohl's, Macy's, Old Navy
15	Corey Rd (from eb, no return)
14	US 23 N, to Ann Arbor
13	US 20, OH 120, Central Ave, E Speedway/dsl Bob Evans, Magic Wok, McDonald's, Rally's, Subway, Wendy's Buick/GMC, Cadillac, Chrysler/Dodge/Jeep, Fiat, Ford, Honda, Hyundai, Kia, Mazda, Nissan, Subaru, Toyota, Walmart, W BP, Speedway Buffalo Wild Wings, Chick-fil-A, Jimmy John's, KFC, Tim Horton's, Waffle House Lowe's, Verizon
8b a	OH 2, E BP/dsl Fire Station Grill, Penn Sta Subs, TGIFriday's, TX Roadhouse Extended Stay America, Hawthorn Suites, Knights Inn, Red Roof Inn H, Home Depot, Kohl's, Old Navy, to OH Med Coll, W Speedway/dsl Arby's, Bob Evans, Boston Mkt, Burger King, Chick-fil-A, Chili's, Chipotle Mexican, Cinco de Mayo, Hot Head Burritos, IHOP, Jimmy John's, Little Caesar's, Magic Wok, Mancino's Pizza, Marco's Pizza, McDonald's, New Empire, Panda Express, Panera Bread, Starbucks, Subway, Taco Bell, Tim Horton's, Waffle House, Wendy's Courtyard, EconoLodge, Quality Inn $Tree, Aldi Foods, Best Buy, BigLots, Dick's, Firestone/auto, GNC, Kroger/dsl, Menard's, Michael's, Petsmart, Sam's Club/gas, Target, TJ Maxx, Verizon, Walmart/Subway
6	Dussel Dr, Salisbury Rd, to I-80-90/tpk, E Applebee's, Arby's, Bangkok Kitchen, Bluewater Grille, Buffalo Wild Wings, Coldstone, Cracker Barrel, Don Juan's, Gino's Pizza, Jimmy John's, Longhorn Steaks, Max&Erma's, McDonald's, Outback Steaks, Panera Bread, Rayoka Japanese, Rusty Taco, Sam's Diner, Scrambler's, Smokey Bones BBQ, Subway, Wendy's Country Inn&Suites, Courtyard, Extended Stay America, Fairfield Inn, Homewood Suites, Residence Inn, Super 8 Ford/Lincoln, W Bob Evans, Briarfield Café, Carrabba's, JoJo's Pizza Best Western Churchill's Mkt, vet
4	US 24, to Maumee, Napolean, N H, Toledo Zoo
3mm	Maumee River
2	OH 25, to Bowling Green, Perrysburg, N BP/dsl, Circle K/dsl, Shell American Table Rest., Arby's, Biggby Coffee, Dunkin', El Vaquero, Gino's Pizza, Jersey's Grill, Marco's Pizza, McDonald's, Subway, Wendy's Auto Value, Churchill's Mkt, Costco/dsl, GMC, Goodyear/auto, Hyundai, URGENT CARE, Volvo, VW, S Marathon, Speedway/dsl Bar Louie's, Biaggi's, Blue Pacific Grill, Bob Evans, Max&Erma's, Nagoya

OH

INTERSTATE 475 (Toledo) Cont'd

2	Continued Japanese, Scrambler's, Starbucks, Taco Bell, Tea Tree Asian, Waffle House Economy Inn, Hilton Garden, Holiday Inn Express AT&T, Books-A-Million, GNC, Mytee Automotive, Tireman/auto, URGENT CARE, Verizon, vet
0mm	**I-475 begins/ends on I-75, exit 192.**

INTERSTATE 480 (Cleveland)

Exit #	Services
42	I-80, PA Tpk, **I-480 begins/ends, 0-2mi** S BP, EVC, GetGo, Marathon/Circle K, Marathon/Circle K, Sheetz/24hr, Shell, Tesla EVC Applebee's, Arby's, Baskin Robbins/Dunkin', Bob Evans, Brown Derby Roadhouse, Buffalo Wild Wings, Burger King, China Chef, Chipotle, Denny's, DQ, El Campesino, Fun Buffet, Happy Moose Grill, Honeybaked Ham, Jimmy John's, KFC, Little Caesar's, McDonald's, Mr Hero, New Peking Chinese, Panda Express, Rockne's Grill, Ruby Tuesday, Sonic, Starbucks, Steak'n Shake, Taco Bell, Wendy's Comfort Inn, Econolodge, Fairfield Inn, Hampton Inn, Holiday Inn Express, Motel 6, Quality Inn, TownePlace Suites, Wingate Inn H, $General, $Tree, Aldi Foods, All Seasons RV Ctr, AT&T, AutoZone, Giant Eagle Mkt, GNC, Home Depot, Honda, Hyundai, Kia, Lowes Whse, Midas, Nissan, NTB, Save-a-Lot Foods, Staples, Target, Tire Source/auto, to Kent St U, U-Haul, USPO, Van's Tires, Verizon, vet, VW, Walgreens, Walmart
41	Frost Rd, Hudson-Aurora
37	OH 91, Solon, Twinsburg, N Arby's, Brewster's, Chipotle, DQ, Mandarin Buffet, Panera Bread, Panini's Grill, Pizza Hut, Taco Bell Comfort Suites, Giant Eagle Mkt, GNC, S BP/7-11
36	OH 82, Aurora, Twinsburg, N BP, McDonald's, Sheetz/dsl Burger King Super 8, S Cracker Barrel, Get'n Go, Wendy's Blue Canyon Rest. Hilton Garden
26	I-271, to Erie, PA
25a b c	OH 8, OH 43, Northfield Rd, Bedford, S Marathon, Shell, Sunoco Giant Eagle Mkt
24	Lee Rd (from wb)
23	OH 14, Broadway Ave, N Marathon H, S Freightliner
22	OH 17, Garanger, Maple Hts, Garfield Hts
21	Transportation Blvd, to E 98th St, N H, S GetGo Applebee's, Chipotle, Penn Sta Subs, Starbucks AT&T, Giant Eagle Foods, Verizon
20b a	I-77, Cleveland
17	OH 176, OH 17, Cleveland
16	OH 94, to OH 17 S, State Rd, N auto repair, Convenient Mart, transmissions, S BP/7-11, Sunoco/dsl Kia
15	US 42, Ridge Rd, N Applebee's, Baskin-Robbins/Dunkin', Boston Mkt, CiCi's Pizza, Coldstone Creamery, Kintaro Hot Pot, McDonald's, Mr Hero, Penn Sta Subs, Pizza Hut, Plaza Nuevo, Rockne's Rest., Starbucks, TX Roadhouse $General, Giant Eagle Mkt, GNC, Lowe's, Marc's Foods, Michael's, TJMaxx, URGENT CARE, USPO, Verizon, S GetGo, Speedway/Speedy's Cafe/dsl Arby's, Denny's, DQ, Taco Bell, Wendy's $Tree, Advance Parts, AT&T, Best Buy, Buick/GMC, Hyundai, Meineke, Staples, Verizon, Walgreens
13	Teideman Rd, Brooklyn, S BP/dsl, Sheetz/dsl, Speedway/dsl Buffalo Wild Wings, Burger King, Carrabba's, Chipotle Mexican, Cracker Barrel, Golden Corral, Hooley House Grill, Hungry Howie's, Ice House Grill, IHOP, La Casa Mexican, LJ Silver, McDonald's, Panera Bread, Subway, TGIFriday's Extended Stay America, Hampton Inn Aldi Foods, Home Depot, Jaguar, LandRover, Mazda, Sam's Club/gas, Volvo, Walmart
12b	W 150th, W130th, Brookpark, N Marathon Fam S Marathon/dsl, Shell/dsl Big Boy, Bob Evans, way Best Value Inn Acura, Chevrolet, Chrysler/Doc Jeep, Infiniti, Lexus, Mini, Toyota
11	I-71, Cleveland, Columbus
10	S Rd 237, Airport Blvd (wb only)
9	OH 17, Brookpark Rd, N Graytown Rd Tavern, way Hilton Garden, Woodspring Suites H, S 1 Bomb Group Rest. Sheraton
7	(wb only)Clague Rd, to WestLake
6	OH 252, Great Northern Blvd, to N Olmsted, N BP, S Speedway/dsl Applebee's, Arby's, Bamboo Garden, Rest., Bob Evans, Boston Mkt, Brown Bag Burgers, Burger K Chick-fil-A, Chili's, ChuckeCheese, Denny's, Famous Dave's, Guys, Frankie's Italian, Great Wall Buffet, Harry Buffalo, Je Mike's, Jimmy John's, Little Caesar's, Macaroni Grill, McAlis Deli, Moe's SW Grill, Olive Garden, Panera Bread, Penn Sta S Popeye's, Rail Burger Bar, Red Lobster, Red Robin, Ruby T day, Scrambler's, Subway, Wendy's, Wild Mango Rest. dlewood Suites, Courtyard, Extended Stay America, Exten Stay America, Hampton Inn, La Quinta, Radisson $T Aldi Foods, AT&T, Best Buy, Big Lots, Buick/GMC/Cadillac, potle Mexican, Conrad's Tire/auto, Dick's, Dillard's, Firestc auto, Home Depot, Honda, Hyundai/VW, JC Penney, Jo-Ann Macy's, Marc's Foods, Monro, NTB, Petsmart, Subaru, Targe Maxx, Toyota, Verizon, Walmart, World Mkt
3	Stearns Rd, N H, S Razzle's Cafe (2 mi) CVS Drug (2
2	OH 10, Lorain Rd, to OH Tpk, S BP, Sheetz/dsl, Speedv dsl Burger King, Chipotle, Dunkin', Gourme Rest., Lone Tavern, McDonald's, Panera Bread, Taco Bell Motel 6, Sup
1	OH 10 W, to US 20 (from wb), Oberlin
0mm	OH 10, to Cleveland, **I-480 begins/ends on exit 151, OH Tpk**

INTERSTATE 680 (Youngstown)

Exit #	Services
14	OH 164, to Western Reserve Rd, **I-680 begins/ends on OH T exit 234,** S Shell/Subway/dsl Cafe 422, Carme Cafe, Dunkin', Ely's, McDonald's, Pizza Hut, Taco Bell, W dy's H
11b a	US 224, S BP, GetGo, Shell/dsl Aladdin's Eatery, plebee's, Burger King, Chick-fil-A, Chipotle, Domino's, Dun Honeybaked Ham, IHOP, Jersey Mike's, KFC, Longhorn Ste McDonald's, O'Charley's, Olive Garden, Outback Steaks, P da Express, Panera Bread, Papa John's, Perkins, Primanti B Red Lobster, Springfield Grill, Starbucks, Subway, Taco E TX Roadhouse Best Western+, Days Inn, Fairfield Inn, Ha ton Inn, Holiday Inn, Red Roof Inn, Residence Inn H, $T Aldi Foods, AT&T, Best Buy, Big Lots, Giant Eagle, GNC, Ho Lobby, Lowe's, Marc's Foods, Marshall's, NTB, Petsmart, Sa Club/gas, Tuesday Morning, URGENT CARE, Walmart/Subway
9b a	OH 170, Midlothian Blvd, Struthers, S Shell/dsl, Spe way/dsl McDonald's, Subway $General, Rite Aid, W greens
8	Shirley Rd, downtown
7	US 62, OH 7, South Ave, downtown
6b a	US 62, OH 7, Mkt St, downtown
5	Glenwood Ave, Mahoning Ave, downtown
4b a	OH 193, to US 422, Salt Springs Rd, N H, museum
3c b	Belle Vista Ave, Connecticut Ave
3a	OH 711 E, to I-80 E
2	Meridian Rd, S Ford/Peterbilt Trucks
1	OH 11

OH

OHIO TURNPIKE

Exit #	Services
241mm	Ohio/Pennsylvania state line
239mm	toll plaza,
237mm	**Mahoning Valley Travel Plaza eb, Glacier Hills Travel Plaza wb, Sunoco/dsl/24hr DQ (sb), Panera Bread (wb)**
234	I-680 (from wb), to Youngstown
232	OH 7, to Boardman, Youngstown, **N** Marathon/dsl, Sheetz DQ, Los Gallos Mexican, Rita's Custard, Steamer's Stonewall Tavern Budget Inn, Holiday Inn Express, Quality Inn, Skylight Inn $General, antiques, **S** Pilot/McDonald's/dsl/scales/24hr Davis Motel, Liberty Inn
218	I-80 E, to Youngstown. OH Tpk runs with I-76 eb, I-80 wb, Niles
216	Lordstown (from wb), **N** GM Plant
215	Lordstown (from eb), **N** GM Plant
210mm	Mahoning River
209	OH 5, to Warren, **N** Budget Lodge, **S** Marathon/dsl EconoLodge, Holiday Inn Express
197mm	**Portage Service Plaza wb, Bradys Leap Service Plaza eb,** Sunoco/dsl/24hr McDonald's, Starbucks
193	OH 44, to Ravenna
192mm	Cuyahoga River
187	OH 14 S, I-480, to Streetsboro, **0-2 mi S** EVC, GetGo, Marathon/Circle K, Marathon/Circle K, Sheetz, Tesla EVC Applebee's, Arby's, Baskin Robbins/Dunkin', Bob Evans, Brown Derby Roadhouse, Buffalo Wild Wings, Burger King, China Chef, Chipotle, Denny's, El Campesino, Fun Buffet, Happy Moose Grill, Honeybaked Ham, Jimmy John's, KFC, Little Caesar's, McDonald's, Mr Hero, New Peking Chinese, Panda Express, Rockne's Grill, Ruby Tuesday, Sonic, Starbucks, Steak'n Shake, Taco Bell, Wendy's Comfort Inn, EconoLodge, Fairfield Inn, Hampton Inn, Holiday Inn Express, Motel 6, Quality Inn, TownePlace Suites, Wingate Inn H, $General, $Tree, Aldi Foods, All Seasons RV Ctr, AT&T, AutoZone, Giant Eagle Mkt, GNC, Home Depot, Honda, Hyundai, Kia, Lowe's, Midas, NAPA, Nissan, NTB, Save-a-Lot Foods, Staples, Target, Tire Source/auto, to Kent St U, U-Haul, USPO, Van's Tires, Verizon, vet, VW, Walgreens, Walmart
180	OH 8, to I-90 E, **N** Valley Jct Rest. Baymont Inn Costco/dsl, **S** BP/dsl to Cuyahoga Valley NRA
177mm	Cuyahoga River
173	OH 21, to I-77, **N** Pilot/Wendy's/dsl/scales Holiday Inn Express, Motel 6, **S** Cozumel Mexican, Subway Days Inn, Hampton Inn, Super 8
170mm	**Towpath Service Plaza eb, Great Lakes Service Plaza wb,** Sunoco/dsl/24hr Burger King, FoodCourt, Panera Bread, Pizza Hut, Starbucks
161	US 42, to I-71, Strongsville, **N on US 42** Mobil/dsl, Sheetz/dsl Buffalo Wild Wings, McDonald's, O'Charlie's Kings Inn, La Siesta Motel Home Depot, Lowe's, vet, Walmart/Subway, on US 42, **S** Elmhaven Motel DQ, Fiat, J-Bella Rest., KFC, Marco's Pizza, Mr Hero, Olympia's Cafe, Staples, vet
152	OH 10, to Oberlin, I-480, Cleveland, **N** BP, Sheetz/dsl, Speedway/dsl Burger King, Chipotle, Dunkin', Gourme Rest., Lone Tree Tavern, McDonald's, Panera Bread, Taco Bell Motel 6, Super 8
151	I-480 E (from eb), to Cleveland, **N**
146mm	Black River
145	OH 57, to Lorain, to I-90, Elyria, **N** Speedway/dsl Applebee's, Bob Evans, Buffalo Wild Wings, Burger King, Chipotle Mexican, Denny's, Giant Eagle Mkt, Golden Corral, Harry Buffalo, Honeybaked Ham, IHOP, Jimmy John's, McDonald's, Olive Garden, Red Lobster, Subway, TX Roadhouse, Wasabi Grill, Wendy's Courtyard, Best Western, Country Inn&Suites,

STREETSBORO

LORAIN

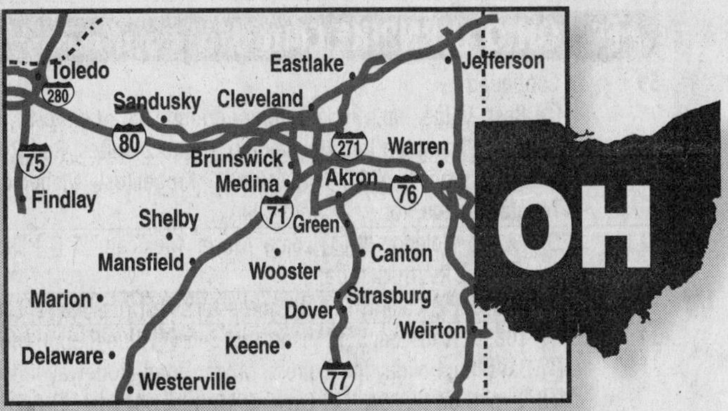

Exit #	Services
145	Continued Days Inn, Hampton Inn, Quality Inn, Red Roof Inn $General, $Tree, AT&T, Best Buy, Conrad's Automotive, Dick's, Firestone/auto, Home Depot, Honda, Hyundai, JC Penney, Jo-Ann Fabrics, Lowe's, Marc's Foods, Petsmart, Staples, Target, Tuffy, Verizon, **S** Shell, Speedway/dsl Super 8
142	I-90 (from eb, exits left), OH 2, to W Cleveland
140	OH 58, Amherst, **N** Sunoco/Subway DQ, Moosehead Grill $General, Chrysler/Dodge/Jeep, **S** Ford
139mm	**Service Plaza both lanes,** Sunoco/dsl/24hr Burger King, Panera Bread, Popeye's, Starbucks
135	rd 51, Baumhart Rd, to Vermilion
132mm	Vermilion River
118	US 250, to Norwalk, Sandusky, **N** Circle K/dsl, Marathon/dsl McDonald's, Subway Country Inn Suites, Days Inn, Hampton Inn, Motel 6, Quality Inn, Red Roof Inn, Super 8 Milan RV Park, **S** Colonial Inn to Edison's Birthplace
110	OH 4, to Bellevue
100mm	**Service Plaza both lanes,** Sunoco/dsl/24hr Burger King, Sbarro's, Starbucks
93mm	Sandusky River
91	OH 53, to Fremont, Port Clinton, **N** Days Inn, **0-2 mi S** Murphy USA/dsl, Shell/Subway/dsl/24hr Applebee's, Bob Evans, Buffalo Wild Wings, Burger King, Fricker's, Jimmy John's, McDonald's, Subway, Taco Bell Comfort Inn, Delux Inn, Hampton Inn, Holiday Inn Express, Quality Inn H, $Tree, Aldi Foods, AT&T, AutoZone, Ford/Lincoln, GNC, Lowe's, Rutherford B. Hayes Library, Staples, URGENT CARE, USPO, Verizon, vet, Walmart
81	OH 51, Elmore, Woodville, Gibsonburg
80.5mm	Portage River
77mm	**Service Plaza both lanes,** Sunoco/dsl/24hr Hardee's (eb), Red Burrito
71	I-280, OH 420, to Stony Ridge, Toledo, **N** FLYING J/Denny's/dsl/scales/LP/24hr, Loves/Arby's/dsl/scales/24hr, Petro/BP/Iron Skillet/dsl/scales/24hr/@ Best Value Inn, Budget Inn, Regency Inn, Super 8 Blue Beacon, SpeedCo, **S** FuelMart/Subway/dsl/scales, Pilot/McDonald's/dsl/scales/24hr, TA/BP/Taco Bell/dsl/scales/24hr/@ KOA
64	I-75 N, to Toledo, Perrysburg, **S** BP/Subway/dsl Country Inn&Suites, Courtyard, Hampton Inn, Staybridge Suites Bass Pro Shops, Camping World RV Ctr
63mm	Maumee River
59	US 20, to I-475, Maumee, Toledo, **N** Shell/dsl, Speedway/dsl Bob Evans, Golden Lily, Marco's Pizza, McDonald's, Nick's Cafe, Olive Garden, Steak'n Shake, Subway, Waffle House Motel 6 $Tree, Goodyear/auto, Jo-Ann Fabrics, NAPA, O'Reilly Parts, Rite Aid, to Toledo Stadium, Walgreens, **S** Shell/dsl, Speedway/dsl Big Boy, Chipotle Mexican, Deet's BBQ, Five Guys, Fricker's, La Fiesta Mexican, Packo's, Pizza Hut, Red Lobster, Schlotzsky's, Steak Escape, Taco Bell, Tim Horton's

TOLEDO

OH

OHIO TURNPIKE Cont'd

WAUSEON

59	Continued Best Value Inn, Budget Inn, Comfort Inn, Comfort Inn, Days Inn, Hampton Inn, Holiday Inn, Home 2 Suites, Red Roof Inn antiques, AT&T, Ford, Honda, Kroger/dsl, Meijer/dsl, Toyota, Verizon, vet
52	OH 2, to Toledo, N Loma Linda Mexican, S Days Inn , RV/truck repair
39	OH 109, S Country Corral/Winchester's Rest./dsl/scales/24hr
34	OH 108, to Wauseon, S Sunoco/dsl/24hr Blue Ribbon Diner Days Inn, Holiday Inn Express, M Star Hotel, Rodeway Inn H, **2 mi S on US 20A** Circle K, Murphy USA/dsl Burger King, DQ, Kamwa Chinese, McDonald's, Pizza Hut, Subway, Taco Bell, Wendy's Ace Hardware, AutoZone, Rite Aid, Walmart
25	OH 66, Burlington, N Harrison Lake SP (3mi), S Sauder Village Museum/Inn
24.5mm	Tiffen River
20	**Indian Meadow wb/Tiffen River eb Service Plaza,** Sunoco/dsl Burger King (eb), Sbarro's, Starbucks
13	OH 15, to Bryan, Montpelier, S Marathon/dsl, Sunoco Four Seasons Rest., JJ Winn's Rest. EconoLodge, Holiday Inn Express, Quality Inn, Rainbow Motel Hutch's Dsl Repair
11.5mm	St Joseph River
3mm	**toll plaza,**
2	OH 49, to US 20, N Subway truck repair, truck wash
0mm	Ohio/Indiana state line

NOTES

OKLAHOMA

INTERSTATE 35

Exit #	Services
236mm	Oklahoma/Kansas state line
235	**weigh sta sb**
231	US 177, Braman, E Conoco/deli/dsl casino
230	Braman Rd
229mm	Chikaskia River
225mm	**Welcome Ctr sb, full facilities, litter barrels, petwalk, s, , vending**
222	OK 11, to Blackwell, Medford, Alva, Newkirk, E Conoco/dsl, Shell/dsl Braum's, Cobb's Rest., KFC/Taco Bell, Los Potros Mexican, McDonald's, Subway Best Way Inn, Best Western, Econolodge, Holiday Inn Express, Sleep Inn H
218	Hubbard Rd
217mm	**weigh sta both lanes**
214	US 60, to Tonkawa, Lamont, Ponka City, N OK Coll, E RV Park, W Casey's/dsl, Pilot/Taco Bell/dsl/scales/24hr, Shell/dsl New Western Inn casino
213mm	Salt Fork of Arkansas River
211	Fountain Rd, E Loves/Chester's/Subway/dsl/scales/24hr/RV Dump
209mm	**parking area, litter barrels**
203	OK 15, to Marland, Billings, E Phillips 66/DQ/Subway/dsl/CNG/scales/24hr
199mm	Red Rock Creek
195mm	**parking area both lanes, litter barrels**
194b a	US 412, US 64 W, Cimarron Tpk, to Cimarron, Enid, W Phillips U
193	Rd (from nb, no return)
191mm	Black Bear Creek
186	US 64 E, to Fir St, Perry, E Mobil/Subway/dsl Braum's, McDonald's Super 8 H, museum, W Exxon/dsl

GUTHRIE

186	Continued Comfort Suites, Holiday Inn Express, Microtel, Regency I Chevrolet/Buick/GMC
185	US 77, to Covington, Perry, E American Inn, W Philli 66/rest/motel/dsl/24hr
180	Orlando Rd
174	OK 51, to Stillwater, Hennessee, E Phillips 66/dsl Smok Pokey Cafe Fairfield Inn (12mi), Hampton Inn (12mi), Quinta (12mi), Residence Inn (12mi) Lake Carl Blackw RV Park, to OSU
173mm	**parking area sb, parking only, litter barrels**
171mm	**parking area nb, parking only, litter barrels**
170	Mulhall Rd
166mm	Cimarron River
157	OK 33, to Cushing, Guthrie, E Loves/Carl's Jr/ds scales/24hr, Valero/Golden Chick/dsl Langston U, W Loves/Subway/dsl, Road Star, Shell/dsl, Valero A by's, Braum's, El Rodeo Mexican, Pizza Hut, Sonic, The Ri shack Best Value Inn, Hampton Inn, Holiday Inn Expres Interstate Motel, La Quinta, Sleep Inn H, OK Terr Museu RV camping
153	US 77 N (exits left from nb), Guthrie, W McDonald's (3mi Taco Bell (3mi) Buick/Cadillac/GMC, Chevrolet, Chrysle Dodge/Jeep, Ford
151	Seward Rd, E Shell/cafe/dsl Lazy E Arena (4mi), Pi neer RV park
146	Waterloo Rd, E Phillips 66/dsl, Shell/Subway/dsl
143	Covell Rd, E Phillips 66/dsl Subway, W Hilton Garde
142	Danforth Rd (from nb)
141	US 77 S, OK 66E, to 2nd St, Edmond, Tulsa, W Conoco/ds Phillips 66/dsl Best Western, Fairfield Inn, Hampton In Holiday Inn Express, Home 2 Suites, La Quinta H, vet

OH

OK

INTERSTATE 35 Cont'd

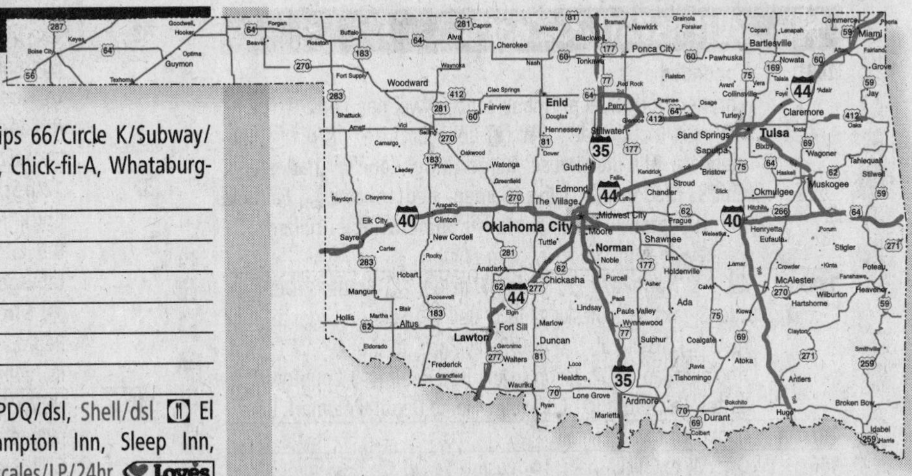

Exit #	Services
140	SE 15th St, Spring Creek, Arcadia Lake, Edmond Park, W Phillips 66/Circle K/Subway/dsl Braum's, Buffalo Wild Wings, Chick-fil-A, Whataburger Sam's Club/dsl, Walmart
139	SE 33rd St
138d	Memorial Rd
138c	Sooner Rd (from sb)
138b	Kilpatrick Tpk
138a	I-44 Tpk E to Tulsa

I-35 S and I-44 W run together 8 mi.

Exit #	Services
137	NE 122nd St, to OK City, E PDQ/dsl, Shell/dsl El Patio, IHOP Budget Lodge, Hampton Inn, Sleep Inn, W FLYING J/Huddle House/dsl/scales/LP/24hr, Love's/Godfathers/Subway/dsl/24hr, Valero/dsl/scales Cracker Barrel, McDonald's, Sonic, Waffle House Baymont Inn, Best Value Inn, Days Inn, Economy Inn, Holiday Inn Express, Motel 6, Super 8 Abe's RV Park, Frontier City Funpark, Oklahoma Visitors Ctr/info/restrooms
136	Hefner Rd, W Conoco/dsl same as 137
135	Britton Rd
134	Wilshire Blvd, W Executive Inn Blue Beacon

I-35 N and I-44 E run together 8 mi.

Exit #	Services
133	I-44 W, to Amarillo, W Cowboy Hall of Fame, st capitol
132b	NE 63rd St (from nb), 1/2 mi E Conoco/dsl Braum's Remington Inn
132a	NE 50th St, Remington Pk, W funpark, museum, zoo
131	NE 36th St, W Phillips 66/Circle K/dsl 45th Inf Division Museum
130	US 62 E, NE 23rd St, E Shell/dsl, W to st capitol
129	NE 10th St, E Valero/McDonald's/dsl Family$
128	I-40 E, to Ft Smith
127	Eastern Ave, OK City, W Checkers/Subway/dsl/scales/24hr/@, Petro/Iron Skillet/dsl/24hr/@ Waffle House Comfort Inn, EconoLodge, Motel 6, Ramada Lewis RV Ctr
126a	I-40, W to Amarillo, I-235 N, to st capitol
126b	I-35 S to Dallas
125d	SE 15th St, E Conoco/dsl Holiday Inn Express
125b	SE 22nd St (from nb)
125a	SE 25th, same as 124b
124b	SE 29th St, E China Queen, Denny's, El Sombrero, McDonald's, Sonic, Taco Bell Best Value Inn, Days Inn, Plaza Inn, Royal Inn, W Phillips 66/Circle K Mama Lou's Rest. Executive Inn same as 125a
124a	Grand Blvd, E Studio 6, Super 8, W Drover's Inn
123b	SE 44th St, E Shell Domino's, Sonic Best Value Inn, Courtesy Inn, Motel 6 $General, W Phillips 66 Subway, Taco Mayo $General, Family$, USPO
123a	SE 51st St, E Conoco/dsl Best Value Inn
122b	SE 59th St, E Phillips 66/dsl, W Shell/dsl, Valero/dsl U-Haul
122a	SE 66th St, E Burger King, Subway, TX Roadhouse Fairfield Inn, Magnuson Hotel, Residence Inn, W 7-11 Arby's
121b	US 62 W, I-240 E
121a	SE 82nd St, (from sb), W Days Inn, Rodeway Inn
120	SE 89th St, E Valero/dsl/scales Ford, W Love's Subway/dsl/24hr Classic Parts
119b	N 27th St, E Shell/Circle K/dsl Starbucks, W Pickles Rest.
119a	Shields Blvd (exits left from nb)
118	N 12th St, E Mazzio's, Peking Buffet Super 8, W 7-11, Shell, Valero/dsl A&W/LJ Silver, Arby's, Braum's, Grandy's, KFC, Mamma Lou's, McDonald's, Papa John's, Subway, Taco Bell, Wendy's, Western Sizzlin Best Western, Candlewood Suites, Econolodge, Hampton Inn, SpringHill Suites $General, AutoZone, vet
117	OK 37, S 4th St, W 7-11, On Cue/dsl/CNG/e10 H, USPO
116	S 19th St, E Sam's Club/dsl, Shell Braum's, Garage Burgers, Genghis Grill, Jimmy John's, McDonald's, Ricky's Cafe, Slim Chickens, Taco Bell, Taco Bueno, Waffle House, Whataburger, Zaxby's American Automotive, AT&T, Best Buy, Firestone/auto, GNC, Hobby Lobby, JC Penney, Office Depot, Petsmart, Ross, URGENT CARE, W Murphy USA Alfredo's Mexican, Applebee's, Arby's, Buffalo Wild Wings, Burger King, Cane's, Carl's Jr, Chicken Express, Chick-fil-A, Chili's, China House, Del Taco, DQ, Earl's Ribs, Firehouse Subs, Five Guys, Freddy's Custard, Furr's Buffet, Hollies Steaks, IHOP, Jack-in-the-Box, Jersey's Mike's Subs, Jimmy's Egg, Luigi's Bistro, Mazzio's, McAlister's Deli, Oliveto's Italian, Panda Express, Pei Wei, Qdoba Mexican, Schlotzsky's, Smashburger, Sonic, Starbucks, Subway, Taco Mayo, Tropical Cafe La Quinta $Tree, Aldi Foods, AT&T, AutoZone, Dick's, Discount Tire, Gordman's, Harley-Davidson, Home Depot, Kohl's, Lowe's, Target, Tires+, Verizon, Walmart
114	Indian Hill Rd, E Woodspring Suites, W Double Dave's Pizza Cadillac, funpark
113	US 77 S (from sb, exits left), Norman
112	Tecumseh Rd, W McDonald's, Sonic H, CVS Drug, Nissan, Toyota, URGENT CARE
110b a	Robinson St, E Carl's Jr, Cheddar's, Chipotle, ChuckECheese, Five Guys, Logan's Roadhouse, Panda Express, Pei Wei, Qdoba Mexican, Sonic, Starbucks, Subway, Taco Bell, Wing Stop, Zio's Italian, Zoe's Kitchen Embassy Suites, Holiday Inn Express, Motel 6 H, $Tree, AT&T, Buick/GMC, Crest Mkt, Discount Tire, Ford, GNC, Homeland Foods/gas, Honda, Hyundai, Kohl's, Mazda, Michael's, Office Depot, PetCo, Target, Tires+, TJ Maxx, Verizon, VW, W Conoco/Subway Arby's, Braum's, Cafe Escondido, Chuy's Mexican, Cracker Barrel, Domino's, Jersey Mike's, Outback Steaks, Papa John's, Papa Murphy's, Rib Crib, Saltgrass Steaks, Waffle House, Yamato Steaks Comfort Inn, Courtyard, Hilton Garden, Norman Hotel Kia
109	Main St, E Murphy USA/dsl, Phillips 66/dsl, Shell/Circle K, Sinclair Arby's, Chick-fil-A, DQ, Golden Corral, Jimmy's Egg, Little Caesar's, Panera Bread, Subway, Waffle House, Wendy's, Whataburger, Zaxby's Days Inn, EconoLodge, Super 8, Travelodge Aldi Foods, AT&T, AutoZone, Best Buy, BigLots,

OKLAHOMA CITY

NORMAN

INTERSTATE 35 Cont'd

NORMAN

109	Continued Chrysler/Dodge/Jeep, Hobby Lobby, Kwik Kar, Lowe's, Tires+, Walmart/McDonald's, W Conoco/Circle K/dsl Applebee's, BJ's Brewhouse, Burger King, Cane's, Charleston's, Chili's, McDonald's, Olive Garden, Red Lobster Fairfield Inn, Hampton Inn, La Quinta Barnes&Noble, Dillard's, JC Penney, Jo-Ann, Old Navy, Sam's Club
108b a	OK 9 E, Norman, E Conoco/Circle K Braum's, Del Rancho Steaks, Schlotzsky's, Taco Bell Sooner Legends Inn/rest. $General, NAPA, O'Reilly Parts, to U of OK, W Carino's Italian, IHOP, Jason's Deli, Red Robin Country Inn&Suites, La Quinta Chevrolet, Home Depot, Petsmart, Ross
107mm	Canadian River
106	OK 9 W, to Chickasha, E Casino, W Loves/Subway/dsl/24hr, Shell McDonald's, Sonic Sleep Inn casino, URGENT CARE, vet
104	OK 74 S, Goldsby, E Floyd's RV Ctr, W CNG, Valero/dsl Libby's Cafe
101	Ladd Rd
98	Johnson Rd, E Funtown RV Ctr
95	US 77 (exits left from sb), Purcell, E Conoco/dsl KFC, Mazzio's, Van's BBQ H, $General, AutoZone, Ford
91	OK 74, to OK 39, Maysville, E Conoco/dsl, Murphy USA/dsl, Phillips 66/dsl Braum's, McDonald's, New China, Subway, Taco Mayo EconoLodge, Executive Inn, Ruby's Inn/rest. AT&T, Walmart/Subway, W Shell/dsl A&W/LJ Silver, Taco Bell

PAULS VALLEY

86	OK 59, Wayne, Payne, E American RV Park
79	OK 145 E, Paoli, E Phillips 66/dsl
76mm	Washita River
74	Kimberlin Rd, to OK 19
72	OK 19, Paul's Valley, E Conoco/dsl, Murphy USA/dsl, Sunoco/dsl/rest/24hr Arby's, Braum's, Chicken Express, Green Tea Chinese, Happy Days Diner, KFC/Taco Bell, McDonald's, Riviera Maya, Snider's Buffet, Sonic, Subway, Tio's Mexican American Inn, Best Value Inn, Comfort Inn, Days Inn, Hampton Inn, Holiday Inn Express, Relax Inn AT&T, Buick/Cadillac/GMC, Chrysler/Dodge/Jeep, URGENT CARE, Walmart, W Phillips 66/dsl/24hr, Shell/dsl Ford/Lincoln, truckwash
70	Airport Rd, E Loves/Burger King/dsl/LP/scales/24hr/@ H, W T&R RV Resort
66	OK 29, Wynnewood, E Kent's Motel, W Shell/dsl
64	OK 17A E, to Wynnewood, E GW Exotic Animal Park
60	Ruppe Rd
59mm	**both lanes, full facilities, litter barrels, petwalk, , picnic table, RV dump**
55	OK 7, Davis, E Conoco/dsl, Phillips 66/A&W/dsl/24hr The Inn to Chickasaw NRA, Treasure Valley Casino/Inn, W **Chickasaw Nation Welcome Ctr,** Phillips 66/dsl to Arbuckle Ski Area
54.5mm	Honey Creek Pass
53mm	**weigh sta both lanes**
51	US 77, Turner Falls, E Arbuckle Mtn Motel, Mtnview Inn (3mi) RV camping, to Arbuckle Wilderness, W Sinclair/rv park
49mm	scenic turnout both lanes
47	US 77, Turner Falls Area
46mm	scenic turnout both lanes
42	OK 53 W, Springer, Comanche, W Exxon/Subway/dsl
40	OK 53 E, Gene Autry, E Valero/dsl/café/24hr Gene Autry Museum (8mi)

ARDMORE

33	OK 142, Ardmore, E Shell, Valero/dsl IHOP, Jim Egg Cafe Best Value Inn, Courtyard, Holiday Inn, La Q ta, Nissan, Red Roof Inn, SpringHill Suites, Super 8 Ho regional park, tires, W FLYING J/Huddle House/dsl scales/24hr
32	12th St, Ardmore, E Phillips 66/dsl, Shell Arby's, Brau Chick-fil-A, Chili's, Cotton Patch Cafe, Freddy's, Quiz Rib Crib, Sakura Hibachi, Santa Fe Steaks, Starbucks, W taburger Baymont Inn, Candlewood Suites, La Qu $Tree, AT&T, Chevrolet, Hilton Garden, Hyundai, Low PetCo, Ross, Toyota, W Loves/Godfather's/Subw dsl/24hr/@ McDonald's Microtel
31b a	US 70 W, OK 199 E, Ardmore, E Shell/dsl, Valero/dsl plebee's, Burger King, Denny's, El Chico, El Tapatio, Interu Grill, Jack-in-the-Box, KFC, McDonald's, Papa John's, Pizza Prairie Kitchen, Two Frogs Grill Best Western+, Com Inn, Days Inn, Hampton Inn, Lexington Inn, Motel 6, Quality AutoZone, Econolodge, Kia, O'Reilly Parts, W Conoco Ardmore RV Park, Chrysler/Dodge/Jeep, Ford/Lincoln, ve
29	US 70 E, Ardmore, E to Lake Murray SP/lodge (8 W Hidden Lake RV Park
24	OK 77 S, E By the Lake RV Park, Red River Livestock Mk Lake Murray SP
22.5mm	Hickory Creek
21	Oswalt Rd, W Valero/dsl Ardmore Marietta RV Par
15	OK 32, Marietta, E Valero/dsl/24hr Carl's Jr, La R Mexican, McDonald's, Robertson's Sandwiches, Sonic, S way H, $General, Homeland Foods, to Lake Texoma W Gulf/dsl, Shell/dsl
5	OK 153, Thackerville, W Red River Ranch RV Park, Shor Foods/gas
3.5mm	**Welcome Ctr nb, full facilities, litter barrels, petwalk, , vending**
3	Winstar Blvd, E casino, same as 1
1	US 77 N, E Phillips 66/dsl/CNG Sonic Best We ern, Red River Suites, The Inn RV park, Winstar Casi W Red River RV Resort (3mi)
0mm	Oklahoma/Texas state line, Red River

INTERSTATE 40

Exit #	Services
331mm	Oklahoma/Arkansas state line
330	OK 64D S (from eb), Ft Smith
329mm	**weigh sta wb**
325	US 64, Roland, Ft Smith, N Cherokee Trkstp/Valero/Subwa dsl/scales/24hr Four Star Diner Best Value Inn, Che kee Inn casino, S Pilot/Wendy's/dsl/scales/24 QS/dsl, Shell/dsl/scales Arby's, El Celaya Mexican, Mazzic McDonald's, Sonic, Subway, Taco Bell Interstate $General, Marvin's Foods, O'Reilly Parts
321	OK 64b N, Muldrow, S Arena/dsl Executive Inn au dsl repair
316mm	**eb, full facilities, info, litter barrels, petwalk, , vending**
313mm	**wb, full facilities, info, litter barrels, petwalk, , dump, vending**
311	US 64, Sallisaw, N Ed's Truckstop/Phillips 66/diner/d Mr Jiff, Sunoco/dsl El Toro Mexican, Hardee's, KFC/Ta Bell, Pizza Hut, Simple Simon's Pizza Motel 6, Sallisa Inn H, $General, AutoZone, Brushy Lake SP (10mi), O'Re ly Parts, Sequoya's Home (12mi)

ROLAND

OK

INTERSTATE 40 Cont'd

Exit #	Services
308	US 59, Sallisaw, N Murphy USA/dsl, Sunoco/dsl A&W/LJ Silver, Arby's, Asian Star, Braum's, Cazadore Mexican, China Harbor, Mazzio's, McDonald's, Roma's Italian, Sonic, Subway, Taco Bueno Days Inn, Economy Inn, Golden Spur Motel, Super 8 H, $General, $Tree, AT&T, casino, Verizon, Walmart/Subway, S Valero/dsl Chen's Garden Buick/Chevrolet/GMC, Chrysler/Dodge/Jeep, Ford, KOA, to Kerr Lake, truck/tire repair
303	Dwight Mission Rd
297	OK 82 N, Vian, N FL/dsl Simple Simon, Subway Cherokee Landing SP (24 mi), IGA Foods, to Tenkiller Lake RA (12 mi), USPO, S Sequoia NWR
291	OK 10 N, to Gore, N Greenleaf SP (10mi), Tenkiller SP (21mi)
290mm	Arkansas River
287	OK 100 N, to Webbers Falls, N Loves/Burger King/Subway/dsl/24hr Cox's Buffet Greenleaf SP, parts/tires/repair, Tenkiller SP
286	Muskogee Tpk, to Muskogee
284	Ross Rd
283mm	**parking area both lanes, litter barrels**
278	US 266, OK 2, Warner, N Conoco, Sinclair/dsl (2), Sinclair/McDonald's/dsl El Jaracho Mexican, Sonic, Subway Ambassadors Inn & RV $General
270	Texanna Rd, to Porum Landing, S Campbell's/BBQ
265	US 69 bus, Checotah, N Kwik'n Easy Pizza Hut, Sonic, S Phillips 66/dsl Budget Inn Chevrolet/Chrysler/Dodge/Jeep
264b a	US 69, to Eufaula, 1 mi N FLYING J/Denny's/dsl/LP/scales/24hr, Casey's/dsl, Phillips 66/dsl/24hr Charlie's Chicken, McDonald's, Simple Simon's Pizza, Taco Bell Best Value Inn $General, AT&T, O'Reilly Parts, repair, TrueValue, Walmart/Subway
262	to US 266, Lotawatah Rd, N Sunshine
261mm	Lake Eufaula
259	OK 150, to Fountainhead Rd, S Shell/dsl Lake Eufaula Inn to Lake Eufaula SP
255	Pierce Rd, N KOA
251mm	**both lanes**
247	Tiger Mtn Rd, S Quilt Barn/antiques
240b a	US 62 E, US 75 N, Henryetta, N Conoco/dsl, Loves/dsl, Phillips 66, Shell Arby's, Braum's, Classic Diner, El Charro Mexican, KFC, Mazzio's, McDonald's, Shoney's, Sonic, Subway, Taco Bell, Taco Bueno Days Inn, Economy Inn, Relax Inn Chevrolet, Chrysler/Dodge/Jeep, Ford, O'Reilly Parts, tires/repair, Walmart, S Indian Nation Tpk
237	US 62, US 75, Henryetta, N Shell/dsl Cowboy Corner Rest. Green Country Inn H, Henryetta RV Park (2mi), S Super 8
231	US 75 S, to Weleetka, N Sinclair/dsl Cowpoke's Cafe
227	Clearview Rd, S casino
221	US 62, OK 27, Okemah, N $General/dsl, Express/Subway/dsl/24hr, Phillips 66/McDonald's Mazzio's, Pepino's Mexican, Simple Simon's, Sonic Days Inn $General, Chevrolet, Homeland Foods, NAPA, TrueValue, S Loves/Chester Fried/dsl/24hr casino, H, truck repair
217	OK 48, to Bristow, Bearden, S gas/dsl
216mm	N Canadian River
212	OK 56, to Cromwell, Wewoka, N auto/tire repair, S Valero/Chester's/Subway/dsl to Seminole Nation Museum (16mi)

HENRYETTA

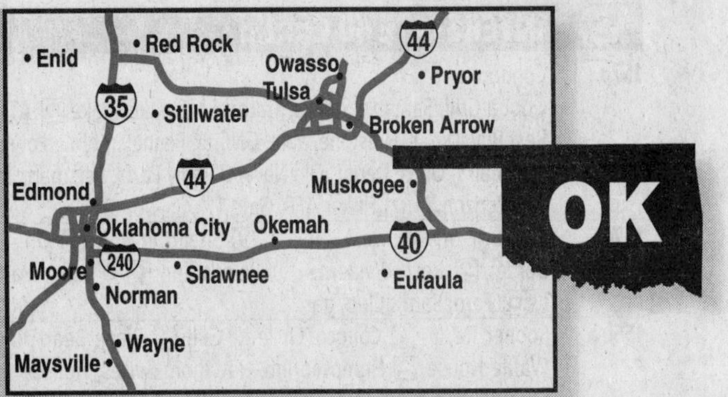

SHAWNEE

Exit #	Services
208mm	Gar Creek
202mm	Turkey Creek
200	US 377, OK 99, to Little, Prague, N Bar H Bar TC/Shell/dsl/RV park RoadHouse Diner, S Conoco/dsl, Loves/Subway/dsl/24hr, Sinclair/dsl Robertson's Ham Sandwiches, Roundup Rest/RV Park H
197mm	**both lanes, full facilities, litter barrels, petwalk,**
192	OK 9A, Earlsboro, S Valero/Godfather's/Cafe/dsl
189mm	N Canadian River
186	OK 18, to Shawnee, N Phillips 66, Sinclair Denny's American Inn, Comfort Inn, Days Inn, La Quinta, Quality Inn, Super 8, S Shell/Domino's/dsl, Sinclair/dsl Carl's Jr, Cazadorez, Golden Corral, Sonic, Subway, Van's BBQ Colonial Inn Chrysler/Dodge/Jeep, Homeland Foods
185	OK 3E, Shawnee Mall Dr, to Shawnee, N Murphy USA/dsl Buffalo Wild Wings, Chili's, Garage Burgers, KFC, Panda Express, Red Lobster, Santa Fe Steaks, Taco Bueno, Wendy's Holiday Inn Express $Tree, AT&T, Chevrolet, Dillard's, Ford, JC Penney, Jo-Ann, Kohl's, Ross, Walgreens, Walmart/McDonald's, S Phillips 66/Circle K/Quiznos/dsl Braum's, Burger King, Chick-fil-A, Cracker Barrel, Delta Cafe, Freddy's, IHOP, Mazzio's, McAlister's Deli, McDonald's, Popeye's, Qdoba, Rib Crib BBQ, Schlotzky's, Sonic, Starbucks, Subway, Taco Bell, Whataburger Hampton Inn Aldi Foods, CVS Drug, Discount Tire, Hobby Lobby, Kwik Kar, Lowe's, O'Reilly Parts, Petsmart, Staples, TJ Maxx, Verizon
181	US 177, US 270, to Tecumseh, S Shell/dsl Rosa's Mexican dsl repair, Prestige RV Ctr
180mm	N Canadian River
178	OK 102 S, Dale, N Grand TC/Subway/hotel/casino/dsl
176	OK 102 N, McLoud Rd, S Loves/Subway/dsl/24hr, Sinclair/dsl Curtis Watson Rest.
172	Newalla Rd, to Harrah
169	Peebly Rd
166	Choctaw Rd, to Woods, N Loves/McDonald's/Subway/dsl/scales/24hr KOA, S Pilot/Wendy's/dsl/scales/24hr Sonic to Lake Thunderbird SP (11mi)
165	I-240 W (from wb), to Dallas
162	Anderson Rd, N Leisure Time RV Ctr, LP
159b	Douglas Blvd, N OnCue/dsl, Shell/Circle K/dsl A&W/LJ Silver, Denny's, Freddy's, Jimmy John's, KFC, McDonald's, Pizza Hut, Sonic, Subway, Taco Bell, Whataburger Eastland Hills RV Park, S H, Tinker AFB
159a	Hruskocy Gate, N Chrysler/Dodge/Jeep, same as 157, U-Haul, S Tinker AFB, Gate 7
157c	Eaker Gate, Tinker AFB, same as 159
157b	Air Depot Blvd, N Shell/Circle K Bricktown Brewery, Cane's, Cheddar's, Chick-fil-A, Chili's, Jack-in-the-Box, Logans Roadhouse, McAlister's Deli, Panda Express, Panera Bread, Pei Wei,

OK

INTERSTATE 40 Cont'd

OKLAHOMA CITY

157b Continued
Qdoba Grill, Santa Fe Steaks, Starbucks, Steak&Shake AT&T, Best Buy, Dick's, Firestone/auto, GNC, JC Penney, Kohl's, Lowe's, Marshall's, Office Depot, Old Navy, O'Reilly Parts, Petsmart, Target, Verizon, S Tinker AFB, Gate 1

157a SE 29th St, Midwest City, N Shell/Circle K On the Border Best Western+, Traveler's Inn O'Reilly Parts, S Ford, Sam's Club/gas

156b a Sooner Rd, N Conoco/Circle K, Gulf Black Bear Diner, Waffle House Hampton Inn, Hawthorn Suites, Holiday Inn Express, Home 2 Suites, La Quinta, Motel 6, Sheraton, Studio 6 Hobby Lobby, Home Depot, Walmart/Subway, S Best China, Buffalo Wild Wings, Carl's Jr, Garage Grill, Hungry Howie's, Ted's Mexican Candlewood Suites, SpringHill Suites, Super 8 AT&T, Chevrolet/GMC, Discount Tire, Tires+, Toyota, Verizon

155b SE 15th St, Del City, N Valero/dsl Peter Piper Pizza Family$, Nissan

155a Sunny Lane Rd, Del City, N Conoco/Subway/dsl Hyundai, U-Haul, S Braum's, Church's, Dunkin', Sonic $ Tree, $General, Save ALot Foods

154 Reno Ave, Scott St, N Woodspring Suites vet, S 7-11

152 (153 from wb)I-35 N, to Wichita

127 Eastern Ave (from eb), Okla City, N Checkers/Subway/dsl/scales/24hr, Petro/Iron Skillet/dsl/scales/@ Waffle House Comfort Inn, Econolodge, Motel 6 Lewis RV Ctr

151b c I-35, S to Dallas, I-235 N, to downtown, st capitol

151a Lincoln Blvd, N Conoco/Subway/Circle K/dsl Earl's Rib Palace, McDonald's, Sonic Hampton Inn, Homewood Suites, Residence Inn Bass Pro Shop, Bricktown Stadium

150c Robinson Ave (from wb), OK City, N Spaghetti Whse, Zio's Italian Courtyard, Hilton Garden, Residence Inn U-Haul, SpringHill, Staybridge Suites

150b Harvey Ave (from eb), N Courtyard, Hilton Garden, Renaissance Hotel, Sheraton, downtown

150a Shields Blvd (from eb), N to downtown

149b Classen Blvd (from wb), same as 149a, to downtown

149a Western Ave, Reno Ave, N Conoco/dsl, Shell/dsl, VP/Subway/dsl McDonald's, Sonic, Sweis Gyros, Taco Bell

148c Virginia Ave (from wb), to downtown

148b Penn Ave (from eb), N Valero/dsl

148a Agnew Ave, Villa Ave, N VP/dsl

147c May Ave

147b a I-44, E to Tulsa, W to Lawton

146 Portland Ave (from eb, no return), N Phillips 66/Subway/dsl

145 Meridian Ave, OK City, N Conoco/Circle K/dsl, Shell/Circle K/dsl Denny's, Earl's Ribs, Louie's Grill, McDonald's, On the Border, Portofinos Italian, Trapper's Rest. Best Western, Biltmore Hotel, Days Inn, Extended Stay America, Howard Johnson, Red Roof Inn, Sonesta Suites, Studio 6, Super 8, S Phillips 66/Circle K/dsl Arby's, Billy Sims BBQ, Burger King, Charleston Rest., Chili's, Cracker Barrel, Five Star Grill, Frosted Mug Grill, Golden Palace Chinese, IHOP, Mackie's Steaks, San Marcos Mexican, Shorty Smalls Ribs, Sonic, Subway, Taco Bell, Taco Bueno, Waffle House, Whataburger, Zapata's, Zio's Italian AmericInn, Baymont Inn, Best Value Inn, Cambria Suites, Candlewood Suites, Clarion, Comfort Suites, Comfort Suites (2), Country Inn&Suites, Courtyard, Embassy Suites, Fairfield Inn, Governors Suites, Hampton Inn, Hilton Garden, Holiday Inn, Holiday Inn Express, Home 2 Suites, Hyatt Place, La Quinta, Meridian Inn, Motel 6,

145 Continued
Oak Tree Inn, Quality Inn, Ramada, Residence Inn, Sherat Sleep Inn, Staybridge Suites, TownePlace Suites, Tru, Wing Inn, Woodspring Suites, Wyndham Garden Boot Barn

144 MacArthur Blvd, N Phillips 66/dsl, Shell/Circle K/dsl A plebee's, Arby's, Chick-fil-A, China One, Coldstone, Del Ta Firehouse Subs, Five Guys, Golden Corral, Jack-in-the-Box, Jim John's, KFC, McDonald's, Olive Garden, Panda Express, Pan Bread, Qdoba, Sonic, Starbucks, Steak'n Shake, Taco Bueno, Tw Peaks, TX Roadhouse, Zaxby's SpringHill Suites $Tr AT&T, GNC, Hobby Lobby, Office Depot, Petsmart, Ross, Targ Verizon, Walmart/McDonald's, S Comfort Inn, Green Car Inn, Microtel, Travelers Inn Sam's Club/gas

143 Rockwell Ave, N 7-11/dsl, Shell/dsl Buffalo Wild Win Burger Joint, Jersey Mike's, Pizza Inn, Taco Bell Homewo Suites, Rodeway Inn Best Buy, Dick's, Discount Tire, Har Davidson, Home Depot, McClain's RV Ctr, Tires+, S Sar Motel/RV Park/LP Rockwell RV Park

142 Council Rd, N On Cue/dsl/CNG, Tesla EVC BJ's Re Braum's, Garage Burgers, Jimmy's Egg, McDonald's, Subw Taco Mayo, Ted's Mexican, Whataburger Super 40 Inn repair, S TA/Country Pride/dsl/scales/24hr/@ Eco Inn Council Rd RV Park, Ford/Peterbilt, truckwash

140 Morgan Rd, N Pilot/McDonald's/dsl/24hr/@, TA/Popeye's/Fazoli's/dsl/24hr/@ Blue Beacon, S FLYING Huddle House/dsl /LP/scales/24hr, LNG, Loves/Subwa dsl/scales/24hr Ricky's Cafe, Sonic Speedco

139 Kilpatrick Tpk

YUKON

138 OK 4, to Yukon, Mustang, N Catfish Cove Best Val Inn, Comfort Suites, Motel 6 Chrysler/Dodge/Jeep, v S Conoco/Circle K/dsl Braum's, Burger King, Gold Chick, IHOP, Interurban Grill, Mama Mo's Pizza, McDonald Sonic, Subway, Taco Bell Best Western+, Home 2 Suite Hyatt Place, La Quinta Aamco, CVS Drug, Homeland Foo drug, Mustang Run RV Park, URGENT CARE

137 Cornwell Dr, Czech Hall Rd, N On Cue/dsl Homela Food/drug, URGENT CARE

136 OK 92, Garth Brooks Blvd, Yukon, N Murphy USA/dsl, She Circle K A&W/LJ Silver, Billy Sims BBQ, Braum's, Cane Chelino's Mexican, CiCi's Pizza, KFC, McDonald's, Popeye Primo's Italian, Subway, Taco Mayo, Waffle House, Wendy Wendy's, Yukon Buffet Hampton Inn $Tree, AutoZon Big O Tire, GNC, NAPA, repair, Sprouts Mkt, Tuesday Mornin USPO, Verizon, Walgreens, Walmart, S Shell/dsl Alfredo's Mexican, Arby's, Buffalo Wild Wings, Buffalo Wild Wing Carino's Italian, Cheddar's, Chicken Express, Chick-fil-A, Chili Del Taco, DQ, Freddy's, Hideaway Pizza, Hooters, Jersey Mike Jimmy's Egg Café, Johnnie's Broiler, Logan's Roadhouse, Louie Grill, McAlister's Deli, Panda Express, Pizza Hut, Rib Crib, Soni Starbucks, Taco Bueno, Tokyo Moon, Zaxby's Fairfield In Holiday Inn Express, Sleep Inn H, Aldi, AT&T, Big Lots, Discount Tire, Ford, GNC, Hobby Lobby, Kohl's, Kwik Kar, Lowe' Marshall's, Petco, PetsMart, Ross, Staples, Target, Tires+

132 Cimarron Rd, S

130 Banner Rd, N Shell/dsl/rest.

129mm **weigh st both lanes**

127 S Radio Rd, S Loves Carl's Jr/dsl/scales/24hr

125 US 81, to El Reno, N Loves/Subway/dsl, Phillips 66 dsl, Shell/dsl Chelino's Mexican, China King, Swadley' BBQ, Taco Mayo Best Value Inn, Economy Express, Range Motel $General, Buick/GMC, Chevrolet, Chrysler/Dodge Jeep, Ford/Lincoln

INTERSTATE 40 Cont'd

Exit #	Services
123	Country Club Rd, to El Reno, N Murphy USA/dsl, Phillips 66, Shell/dsl, Valero/dsl Arby's, Braum's, Burger King, Greatwall Chinese, KFC, Little Caesar's, McDonald's, Pizza Express, Pizza Hut, Subway, Taco Bell, Taco Bueno Fairfield Inn, Hampton Inn, Home 2 Suites, Motel 6 H, AT&T, AutoZone, Walgreens, Walmart, S Denny's, MT Mikes Steaks Baymont Inn, Best Western/RV Park, Days Inn, Holiday Inn Express, Regency Motel
119	Lp 40, to El Reno
115	US 270, to Calumet
111mm	**picnic area eb, litter barrels**
108	US 281, to Geary, N Shell/Subway/dsl/24hr KOA/Indian Trading Post, to Roman Nose SP, S Phillips 66/Pizza Inn/dsl
105mm	S Canadian River
104	Methodist Rd
101	US 281, OK 8, Hinton, N Territory Rte 66 RV Park, to Roman Nose SP, S Loves/Chester's/Godfather's/Sonic/dsl/scales Subway Hinton Country Inn, Sugar Creek Inn casino, Chevrolet, to Red Rock Canyon SP
95	Bethel Rd
88	OK 58, to Hydro, Carnegie
84	Airport Rd, N Phillips 66/dsl/CNG/scales/24hr Lucille's Roadhouse Holiday Inn Express, Travel Inn H, Buick/Cadillac/Chevrolet/GMC, Stafford Aerospace Museum, S La Quinta Chrysler/Dodge/Jeep, Ford/Lincoln
82	E Main St, Weatherford, N Conoco/dsl, Phillips 66/dsl, Shell/dsl Arby's, BBQ Shed, Braum's, Carl's Jr, Chicken Express, Hibachi Buffet, Jerry's Rest., KFC, Little Caesar's, McDonald's, Pizza Hut, Qdoba, Sonic, Subway, Taco Mayo Best Western+, Comfort Inn, Fairfield Inn, Scottish Inn H, $General, Ace Hardware, AT&T, GNC, NAPA, O'Reilly Parts, Savealot Foods, to SW OSU, United Mkt, Walgreens, S Walmart/Subway
80a	(from eb), N Phillips/dsl Casa Soto Mexican
81	E Main St (from eb), same as 82
80	W Main St, Mountainview, Thomas, N Best Value Inn NAPAcare
71	Custer City Rd, N Loves/Subway/dsl/24hr Cherokee Trading Post/rest.
69	Lp 40 (from wb, no return), to Clinton
67.5mm	Washita River
66	US 183, Clinton, S Shell/dsl Ford
65a	10th St, Neptune Dr, Clinton, N Branding Iron Rest., China King, Picante Grille Days Inn, Relax Inn, Super 8 United Foods, S Phillips 66/dsl EconoLodge, Holiday Inn Express Hargus RV Park
65	Gary Blvd, Clinton, N Hutch/dsl Braum's, Italian Villa, KFC/Taco Bell, LJ Silver, Mazzio's, McDonald's, MT Mike's, Palacios Mexican, Pizza Hut, Subway, Taco Mayo Hampton Inn, Motel 6, Ramada Inn, Tradewinds Inn H, $General, $Tree, Rte 66 Museum, Rte 66 Museum, S Holiday Inn Express, La Quinta
62	Parkersburg Rd, S Hargus RV Ctr
61	Haggard Rd
57	Stafford Rd
53	OK 44, Foss, N to Foss SP, S Cenex/dsl
50	Clinton Lake Rd, N KOA/LP/dsl
47	Canute, S Shell/dsl
41	OK 34 (exits left from eb), Elk City, N Hutch's/dsl, Loves/Subway/dsl Home Cooking Rest. Elk City Motel, HomeTowne Inn, La Quinta, Motel 6, Sleep Inn, Super 8, Travel Inn H, Elk Run RV Park

WEATHERFORD

CLINTON

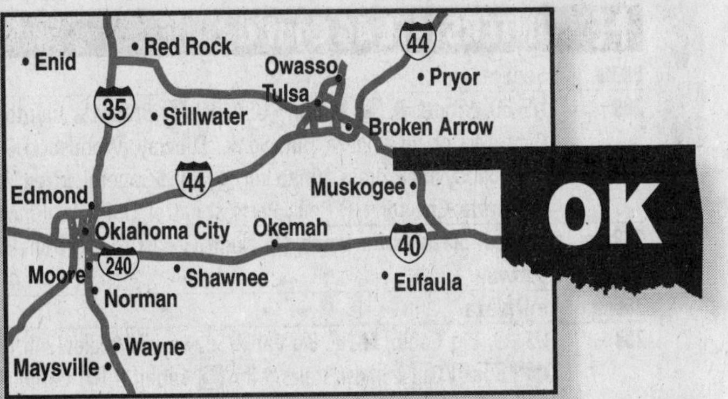

ELK CITY

SAYRE

Exit #	Services
40	E 7th St, Elk City, N Holiday Inn Express Chrysler/Dodge/Jeep, S Hutch's/dsl/CNG Huddle House, Rib Crib Hampton Inn Hobby Lobby, same as 41, Walmart/McDonald's, Wendy's
38	OK 6, Elk City, N Conoco/dsl, Phillips 66/dsl Arby's, Billy Sims BBQ, Boomtown Grill, China Super Buffet, LJ Silver, McDonald's, Western Sizzlin Bedford Inn, Days Inn Ace Hardware, Elk Creek RV Park, tires, S Phillips 66/dsl Best Western+, Clarion Inn, Comfort Inn Elk City RV Ctr, to Quartz Mtn SP
34	Merritt Rd
32	OK 34 S (exits left from eb), Elk City
26	Cemetery Rd, N Shell/dsl dsl repair, S TA/Taco Bell/Subway/dsl/scales/24hr/@
25	Lp 40, Sayre, 1 mi N Hutch's/dsl/CNG Western Motel, Windgate Hotel H, Bobcat Creek RV Park, Chevrolet/GMC, Ford
23	OK 152, Sayre, S Cenex/dsl
22.5mm	N Fork Red River
20	US 283, Sayre, N FLYING J/Denny's/dsl/LP/RV dump/scales/24hr McDonald's AmericInn to Washita Bfd Site (25mi), Truck lube, truckwash
14	Hext Rd
13.5mm	**check sta both lanes, litter barrels**
11	Lp 40, to Erick, Hext
10mm	**Welcome Ctr/ both lanes, full facilities, litter barrels, petwalk, , , RV dump**
7	OK 30, Erick, N Motel 6, S Loves/Subway/dsl/scales Simple Simon's Pizza Days Inn
5	Lp 40, Honeyfarm Rd
1	**weigh Sta eb**
1	Texola, S RV camping
0mm	Oklahoma/Texas state line

INTERSTATE 44

Exit #	Services
329mm	Oklahoma/Missouri state line
321mm	Spring River
314mm	**Oklahoma Welcome Ctr wb, full facilities**
313	OK 10, Miami, N Loves/dsl, Phillips 66, Phillips 66/dsl Donut Palace, Subway Days Inn, Deluxe Inn, EconoLodge, Hampton Inn, Holiday Inn Express, Microtel, Motel 6 H, auto repair, Miami RV Park, to NE OK A&M Coll, S Chrysler/Dodge/Jeep
312mm	Neosho River
302	US 59, US 69, Afton, S Buffalo Ranch/Subway/dsl Rte 66 Motel $General

OK

= gas = food = lodging = other = rest stop

E INTERSTATE 44 Cont'd

VINITA

Exit #	Services
289	US 60, Vinita, N Murphy USA/dsl Braum's, Clanton's Cafe, McDonald's, Pizza Hut, Sonic, Subway, Woodshed Deli Holiday Inn Express, Vinita Inn H, $General, $Tree, Ace Hardware, Chevrolet, O'Reilly Parts, st patrol, USPO, Walmart
288mm	**service plaza both lanes,** Kum&Go/dsl McDonald's, Subway
286mm	**toll plaza**
283	US 69, Big Cabin, N Big Cabin/Subway/dsl/scales/24hr/@, Loves/Carl's Jr/dsl/scales/24hr Super 8 Cabin RV Park, trk repair
269	OK 28 (from eb, no re-entry), to Adair, Chelsea
255	OK 20, to Pryor, Claremore, **0-2 mi N** Kum&Go/dsl/e85, Murphy USA/dsl, QT/dsl Carl's Jr Hampton Inn, Holiday Inn Express, Super 8, Travel Inn, Will Rogers Inn H, $General, museum, to Rogers U, Walgreens, Walmart, Will Rogers Memorial
248	to OK 266, Port of Catoosa, N QT/dsl Hampton Inn (4mi), Microtel (2mi), Quality Inn (4mi), Will Rogers Inn (4mi) Dave's RV Ctr
244mm	Kerr-McClellan Navigation System
241mm	**Will Rogers Tpk begins eb, ends wb,**
241b	US 412 E (34 from wb), Choteau
241	(35 from wb)OK 66 E, to Catoosa
240a	OK 167 N, 193rd E Ave, N Freddy's, IHOP, McDonald's, OK Joe's BBQ, Panda Express, Taco Bell, Taco Bueno, Waffle House, Wendy's Cherokee Inn/Casino, Fairfield Inn, Hampton Inn, Hardrock Hotel/Casino, Homewood Suites, La Quinta AT&T, GNC, Petco, Ross, Tate Boys Automotive, Walgreens, Walmart, S QT Mazzio's, Port City Diner, Sonic, Subway Comfort Suites, Holiday Inn Express, Motel 6 $General, O'Reilly Parts, tires/repair
238	161st E Ave, N **Cherokee Nation Welcome Ctr,** QT/dsl/scales/24hr truckwash, S Arby's, Burger King Microtel truckwash
236b	I-244 W, to downtown Tulsa, N
236a	129th E Ave, N FLYING J/Denny's/dsl/LP/24hr Southern Tire Mart, S McDonald's
235	E 11th St, Tulsa, N QT/dsl Mazzio's, Sonic, Subway Economy Inn, Executive Inn, Garnett Inn, Knights Inn, Travelodge $General, O'Reilly Parts, Walgreens, S Braum's Whse Mkt
234b	same as 235
234a	US 169, N to Owasso, S to Broken Arrow, to
233	E 21st St, N Golden Corral Camping World RV Ctr, Family$, S El Chico
231	US 64, OK 51, to Muskogee, E 31st St, Memorial Dr, N QT/dsl Sonic, Speedy Gonzales Mexican, Subway Delux Inn, Homestay Inn, Ramada Inn, Tulsa Inn Walgreens, S Shell/Taco Silvia Cracker Barrel, IHOP, McDonald's, Pizza Hut, Ruby Tuesday, Village Inn Best Value Inn, Best Western+, Clarion, Comfort Suites, Courtyard, EconoLodge, Embassy Suites, Extended Stay America, Fairfield Inn, Hampton Inn, Quality Suites, Sleep Inn, Super 8 Cavender's Boots, Chevrolet, Harley-Davidson, Nissan
230	E 41st St, Sheridan Rd, N Shell Carl's Jr, Chick-fil-A, Chipotle, Desi Wok, Jimmy John's, On-the-Border, Panera Bread, Schlotzsky's, Starbucks, Subway, Top That! Pizza AT&T, Barnes&Noble, Cartec Automotive, JC Penney, Jo-Ann Fabrics, Michael's, Old Navy, Petco, Petsmart, Reasor's Foods, Ross,

TULSA

OK

Exit #	Services
230	Continued Verizon, S Buffalo Wild Wings, Carino's Italian La Quinta Batteries+Bulbs, Best Buy, Home Depot
229	Yale Ave, Tulsa, N Shell El Chico, McDonald's, Subway Firestone/auto, JC Penney, PetCo, S Kum&Go/dsl/e85, QT Andy's Custard, Applebee's, Arby's, Braum's, Cane's, Jack-in-the-Box, Outback Steaks, Qdoba, Red Lobster, Saltgrass Steaks, Sonic, Taco Bell, Village Inn Comfort I[nn], Hilton Garden, Holiday Inn Express, Motel 6, Red Roof Inn, Residence Inn H, Kia, vet
228	Harvard Ave, Tulsa, N QT/dsl Casa Tequila Mexic[an], McDonald's, NYC Pizza Tradewinds Motel, S A&W, Silver, Chili's, Freckle's Frozen Custard, Jamil's Rest, Mario's Pizza, Papa John's, Starbucks, Subway Wingate Inn $Tr[ee], Hobby Lobby, SteinMart
227	Lewis Ave, Tulsa, S Goldie's Grill Walgreens
226b	Peoria Ave, Tulsa, N Kum&Go/dsl, QT/dsl Arby['s], Brookside Diner, Burger St., Charleston's Rest., China W[ok], CiCi's, Egg Roll Express, Jimmy's Egg, KFC, Little Caesa[rs], Mazzio's, Pizza Hut, Sonic, Subway, Super Wok, Taco Bell, Ta[co] Bueno Peoria Inn $Tree, Harley-Davidson, O'Rei[lly] Parts, Reasor's Mkt, Robertson Tire, Verizon, Walmart M[kt], Whole Foods Mkt, S Braum's, Golden Palace $Gener[al], AutoZone, Family$, Walgreens
226a	Riverside Dr
225mm	Arkansas River
225	Elwood Ave, N Chevrolet, Ford, S Budget Inn
224b a	US 75, to Okmulgee, Bartlesville, N QT/dsl KF[C], Mazzio's, Sonic $General, vet, Whse Mkt, S Roy[al] Inn Hurley RV Ctr
223c	33rd W Ave, Tulsa, N Braum's, Domino's, S Cono[co] Rib Crib BBQ
223b	51st St (from wb)
223a	I-244 E, to Tulsa, downtown
222c	from wb), S Value Inn
222b	55th Place, N Capri Motel, Crystal Motel, S Best Val[ue] Inn, Winston's Inn
222a	49th W Ave, Tulsa, N Carl's Jr, Monterey Mexican, Subway Gateway Motel, Interstate Inn, Motel 6 $Genera[l], BigLots, Mack Trucks, S QT/Kitchens/dsl/scales/24hr Arby's, McDonald's, Taco Bueno, Waffle House Comfort In[n], Super 8 Buick/GMC, Freightliner, Kenworth
221a	57th W Ave, (from wb), S Buick/GMC
221mm	**Turner Tkp begins wb, ends eb.**
218	Creek Tpk E (from eb)
215	OK 97, to Sand Sprgs, Sapulpa, S Kum&Go/dsl/e8[5], Freddie's Rest., Subway Super 8 H, Hunter RV Ct[r], Route 66 RV Park
211	OK 33, to Kellyville, Drumright, S Heyburn Lake SP
207	no service
196	OK 48, Bristow, S Kenny's/dsl, Phillips 66/dsl Mazzio's, McDonald's, Pizza Hut, Sonic, Steak'nEgg Rest, Taco Mayo Carolyn Inn $General, $Tree, Ford, O'Reilly Parts, Walmart
182mm	**toll plaza**
179	OK 99, to Drumright, Stroud, N Ranch House Rest. Cattle Country Lodge, S Kids/dsl, Phillips 66/Subway/dsl 5Star BBQ, Cozumel Mexican, Mazzio's, McDonald's, Pepe's Mexican, Sonic Hampton Inn, Skyliner Motel, Sooner Motel H, auto/tire repair, USPO

INTERSTATE 44 Cont'd

Exit #	Services
178mm	**Hoback Plaza both lanes (exits left),** Phillips 66/dsl McDonald's
167mm	**service plaza (from eb),** Phillips 66/dsl
166	OK 18, to Cushing, Chandler, **S** Phillips 66/dsl Sonic Lincoln Motel Chandler Tire, Chevrolet/GMC, Ford
158	OK 66, to Wellston, **N** Phillips 66/Subway/dsl/24hr Butcher BBQ $General
147	N Luther Rd
146	Luther-Jones
138d	to Memorial Rd, to Enterprise Square
138a	I-35, I-44 E to Tulsa, Turner Tpk
I-44 and I-35 run together 8 mi. See I-35, exits 137-134.	
135mm	**Turner Tpk begins eb, ends wb.**
130	I-35 S, to Dallas, access to services on I-35 S
129	MLK Ave, Remington Park, **N** Park Hill Inn Cowboy Museum, **S** McDonald's, Sonic, Subway Family$
128b	Kelley Ave, OK City, **N** Conoco, VP/Subway/dsl Gabriella's Italian
128a	Lincoln Blvd, **S** Lincoln Mart/dsl Lincoln Inn Express, Oxford Inn st capitol
127	I-235 S, US 77, City Ctr, Broadway St, **N on 63rd St** Conoco/Circle K, Shell/Circle K Holiday Inn, Surestay URGENT CARE
126	Western Ave, **S** Sleep Inn
125c	NW Expressway (exits left from sb)
125	Classen Blvd, (exits left from wb), OK City, **N** Cheesecake Factory, Chili's, Freebirds Burrito, Jamba Juice, Olive Garden, Pei Wei, Smashburger, Subway, Whiskey Cake Kitchen AT&T, Dillard's, JC Penney, Macy's, Old Navy, Ross, Verizon, Walmart/McDonald's, **S** IHOP, McDonald's, Milagro Mexican Courtyard, Hyatt Place
125a	OK 3A, Penn Ave, to NW Expswy, **N** VP Express, **S** Shell/Circle K, Valero Braum's auto/tire repair, Family$
124	N May, **N** Shell/Circle K/Subway Azteca Mexican Days Inn, Motel 6, Super 8 O'Reilly Parts, Sam's Club/dsl, **S** Valero Dunkin', Jersey Mike's, Starbucks, Wendy's Aamco, Advance Parts, Family$, Ford, Lowe's
123b	OK 66 W, NW 39th, to Warr Acres, **N** 7-11, Shell, Valero/McDonald's/dsl Braum's, Carl's Jr, Jimmy's Egg, Sonic Hospitality Inn Family$, U-Haul
123a	NW 36th St, **S** Woodspring Suites
122	NW 23rd St, **N** 7-11, Conoco/dsl Church's, EggRoll King Tires+, **S** Conoco Arby's, Sonic Family$
121b a	NW 10th St, **N** On Cue/dsl, **S** 7-11, Shamrock $General, fairgrounds, Family$, Whittaker's Foods
120b a	I-40, W to Amarillo, E to Ft Smith
119	SW 15th St
118	OK 152 W, SW 29th St, OK City, **E** 7-11, Shamrock A&W/LJ Silver, Burger King, CiCi's Pizza, KFC, McDonald's, Pizza Hut, Sonic, Subway, Taco Bueno $General, $Tree, Advance Parts, AT&T, AutoZone, Buy-4-Less Foods, city park, O'Reilly Parts, Walgreens, **W** Alon/dsl city park, transmissions, U-Haul/LP, **S** Jimmy's Egg
117	SW 44th St, **W** auto repair
116b	Airport Rd (exits left from nb), **W**
116a	SW 59th St, **E** Conoco/Circle K Subway Family$, **W** Will Rogers Airport, **S** Waffle House
115	I-240 E, US 62 E, to Ft Smith
114	SW 74th St, OK City, **E** Valero/dsl Braum's, Burger King, Perry's Rest. Motel 6 $General
113	SW 89th St, **E** 7-11, Loves/Subway/dsl, Valero/dsl Sonic H, CVS Drug

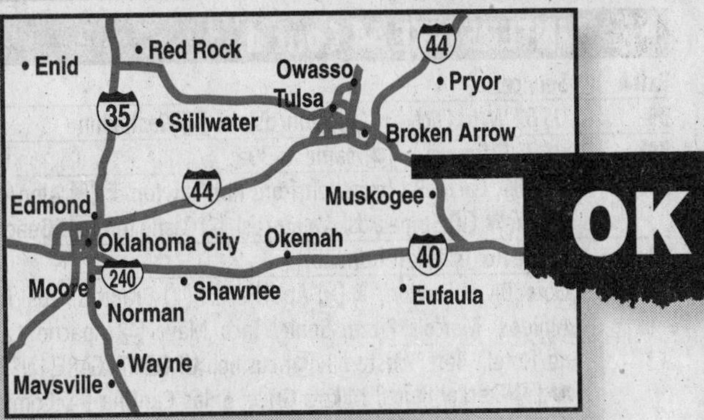

Exit #	Services
112	SW 104th St, **E** Valero, Walmart/dsl Arby's, McDonald's, Starbucks, Subway, Taco Bell $General, Crest Mkt, Firestone/auto, Verizon, Walmart
111	SW 119th St, **E** 7-11, On Cue/dsl Little Caesar's, Sonic
110	OK 37 E, to Moore, **E** H
109	SW 149th St, **E** JR's Grill
108mm	S Canadian River
108	OK 37 W, to Tuttle, **W** Conoco/dsl, Phillips 66/dsl Arby's, Braum's, Carlito's Mexican, Jimmy's Egg, KFC/Taco Bell, Little Caesar's, McDonald's, New China, Sonic, The Pizza Shop, Tri City Diner $General, AT&T, AutoZone, O'Reilly Parts, Walgreens, Walmart/Subway
107	US 62 S (no wb return), to Newcastle, **E** Comfort Inn, Newcastle Motel casino, Newcastle RV, **S** Loves/Subway/Dunkin'/dsl/scales/24hr
99	H E Bailey Spur, rd 4, to Blanchard, Tuttle, Norman
97mm	**toll booth**
85.5mm	**service plaza, both lanes exit left,** Phillips 66/dsl McDonald's
83	US 62, Chickasha, **W** Jay's/dsl, Valero/dsl Best Western+ Southern Plains Indian Museum (18mi)
80	US 81, Chickasha, **E** Circle K/dsl, Shell/dsl La Fiesta Mexican, Western Sizzlin Best Value Inn, Fairfield Inn, Hampton Inn, Holiday Inn Express, Super 8 Buick/GMC, Cadillac/Chevrolet, Chrysler/Dodge/Jeep, vet, **W** Loves/dsl, Murphy USA/dsl, Valero Arby's, Braum's, Chicken Express, China Dream, China Moon, Cotton Patch Cafe, Domino's, KFC, Little Caesar's, Mazzio's Pizza, McDonald's, New China, Pizza Hut, Sims BBQ, Sonic, Subway, Taco Bell, Taco Mayo, Tropical Cafe Quality Inn, Ranch House Motel H, $General, $Tree, Ace Hardware, Aldi Foods, AT&T, AutoZone, Chickasha RV Park, CVS Drug, Ford, Griffith's Repair, O'Reilly Parts, Ralph&Son's Tires/repair, Save-A-Lot Foods, URGENT CARE, Verizon, Walgreens, Walmart/Subway
78	no service
66mm	**toll plaza both lanes**
62	to Cyril (from wb)
53	US 277, Elgin, Lake Ellsworth, **E** Shamrock, Valero/McDonald's/dsl Billy Sim's BBQ, China Garden, Sonic, Subway $General, Family$, tires
46	US 62 E, US 277, US 281, to Elgin, Apache, Comanche Tribe, **last free exit eb**
45	OK 49, to Medicine Park, **W** Loves/Subway/dsl/24hr Burger King, Sonic $General, Wichita NWR
41	to Ft Sill, Key Gate, **W** Ft Sill Museum
40c	Gate 2, to Ft Sill
40a	to Cache

CHICKASHA

OK

= gas = food = lodging = other = rest stop

INTERSTATE 44 Cont'd

LAWTON

Exit #	Services
39	US 62 W, to Cache, E Alon/dsl, W Castle Inn
39b	US 281 (from sb), same as 39a
39a	US 281, Cache Rd (exits left from nb), Lawton, E Alon/dsl, 1-3 mi W Stripes/dsl, Valero/dsl Castle Inn $General
38	Cache Rd (exits left from nb)
37	Gore Blvd, Lawton, E Apache/dsl Braum's, Los Tres Amigos, Marco's Pizza, Sonic, Taco Mayo Apache Casino/Hotel, Best Western+ casino, URGENT CARE, USPO, W Cracker Barrel, Mike's Grille, Salas Cantina Comfort Suites, Fairfield Inn, Hilton Garden, Holiday Inn Express, Homewood Suites, Sleep Inn, SpringHill Suites $Tree, AT&T, Chrysler/Dodge/Jeep, Dick's, Harley-Davidson, Jo-Ann, Kohl's, Nissan, Petco
36a	OK 7, Lee Blvd, Lawton, E Phillips 66/dsl, W Alon/dsl/repair, Barefoot/dsl, Shamrock/dsl Braum's, Burger King, KFC/Taco Bell, Leo&Ken's Rest., McDonald's Motel 6 H, $General, Advance Parts, CVS Drug, vet
33	US 281, 11th St, Lawton, W
30	OK 36 (last free exit sb), Geronimo
20.5mm	**Elmer Graham Plaza (both lanes exit left),** Phillips 66/dsl Back 40 BBQ info
20	OK 5, to Walters
19.5mm	**toll plaza**
5	US 277 N, US 281, Randlett, last free exit nb, E Loves/Subway/dsl/scales/24hr
1	OK 36, to Grandfield, E Comanche Nation TP/dsl, W Kiowa Hotel/casino
0mm	Oklahoma/Texas state line, Red River

INTERSTATE 240 (Oklahoma City)

OKLAHOMA CITY

Exit #	Services
16mm	**I-240 begins/ends on I-40.**
14	Anderson Rd, S Conoco/dsl
11b a	Douglas Blvd, N Tinker AFB
9	Air Depot Blvds
8	OK 77, Sooner Rd, N Phillips 66/dsl/CNG/e85 S URGENT CARE, S Phillips 66/Popeye's/dsl, Valero, Donald's/dsl H
7	Sunnylane Ave, S Valero/Subway/dsl Woodspring S
6	Bryant Aves
5	S Eastern Aves
4c	Pole Rd, N Burger King, Subway, TX Roadhouse field Inn, Magnuson Hotel, Residence Inn
4b a	I-35, N to OK City, S to Dallas, US 77 S, US 62/77 Ns
3b	S Shields, N Valero/dsl Braum's Chrysler/Doc Jeep, Home Depot, S Discount Tire, Nissan, Subaru
3a	S Santa Fe, N Kia, S Murphy USA/dsl Chili's, I Jersey Mike's, Panda Express Lowe's, Staples, Walm McDonald's
2b	S Walker Ave, N 7-11, Shell/Circle K Johnnie's B er, Rib Crib, S Burger Joint, Carino's, ChuckeCheese, Bites, Jimmy's Egg Grill, On-the-Border Holiday Inn press PepBoys
2a	S Western Ave, N 7-11, Conoco Braum's, Burger K CiCi's Pizza, House of Szechwan, Taste of China $Ge al, Advance Parts, Hyundai, Tires+, vet, S 7-11, Vale dsl A&W/LJ Silver, Chick-fil-A, Garage Burgers, Granc Hibachi Buffet, Jimmy John's, KFC, McDonald's, Popeye's, Lobster Best Western, Comfort Inn, Hampton Inn, Hom Suites, Quality Inn Chevrolet, Honda, Office Depot
1c	S Penn Ave, N Conoco/dsl Cane's, Carl's Jr, Char ton's Rest., Denny's, Golden Corral, Hooters, Old Chicago Piz Olive Garden, Outback Steaks, Pioneer Pies, SaltGrass Stea Schlotsky's AT&T, Best Buy, BigLots, GNC, Green Acres M Hobby Lobby, Marshall's, Michaels, Old Navy, Petsmart, R Verizon, S Shell/Circle K Hunan Buffet, Joe's Cr shack, Mazzio's, Papa John's, Starbucks, Subway, Taco Bue Western Sizzlin $Tree, URGENT CARE
1b	S May Ave, N 7-11/gas Abel's Mexican, Jack-in-t Box, New Mandarin, Taco Bell, Waffle House O'Re Parts, S Nova, Valero/dsl Braum's, Burger King, Per Rest. Cambridge Inn, Knights Inn $General
1a	I-44, US 62, **I-240 begins ends on I-44.**

OREGON

INTERSTATE 5

PORTLAND

Exit #	Services
308.5mm	Oregon/Washington state line, Columbia River
308	Jansen Beach Dr, E Chevron/dsl Burger King, Hooters, Starbucks, Taco Bell Oxford Suites, Red Lion Safeway, W BJ's Rest., Bradley's Grill, CJ's Deli, Denny's, Jersey Mike's, Jimmy John's, McDonald's, Panera Bread, Stanford's Rest., Starbucks, Subway Best Buy, Burlington Coats, GNC, Home Depot, Jansen Beach RV Park, Michael's, Old Navy, PetCo, Ross, Staples, Target, TJ Maxx, Verizon
307	OR 99E S, MLK Blvd, Union Ave, Marine Dr (sb only), E 76/dsl, Jubitz Trvl Ctr/rest/dsl/@ Pizza Mia, Portland Cascade Grill, Subway Courtyard, Fairfield Inn, Portlander Inn, Residence Inn Blue Beacon, truck repair, W Expo Ctr
306b	Interstate Ave, Delta Park, E Arco Burger King, Burrito House, Elmer's, Mars Meadows Chinese, Shari's Best Western, Days Inn, Motel 6 $Tree, Baxter Parts, Dick's, Lowe's, Portland Meadows, vet, Walmart
306a	Columbia (from nb), same as 306b
305b a	US 30, Lombard St (from nb, no return), E Little Ca sar's Knecht's Parts, W Astro/dsl, Shell/dsl Pan Express, Subway, Wendy's Fred Meyer
304	Rosa Parks Way, W 76/dsl, Arco Nite Hawk Cafe king Motel U of Portland
303	Alberta St, Swan Island, E H, W Subway, Ta Bell Monticello Motel, Westerner Motel CarQuest
302b	I-405, US 30 W, W to ocean beaches
302a	Rose Qtr, City Ctr, E 76/Circle K/dsl, Shell/dsl B lagio's Pizza, Burger King, Chipotle Mexican, Jersey Mike McDonald's, Muchas Gracias, Qdoba Mexican, Starbucks, We dy's Courtyard, Crowne Plaza, Shiloh Inn H, 7-11, K Schwab Tire, Toyota, Verizon, Walgreens, W coliseum
301	I-84 E, US 30 E, **services E off I-84 exits**
300	US 26 E (from sb), Milwaukie Ave, W Hilton, Marriott
299b	I-405, US 26 W, to city ctr
299a	US 26 E, OR 43 (from nb), City Ctr, to Lake Oswegos
298	Corbett Aves

OK OR

INTERSTATE 5 Cont'd

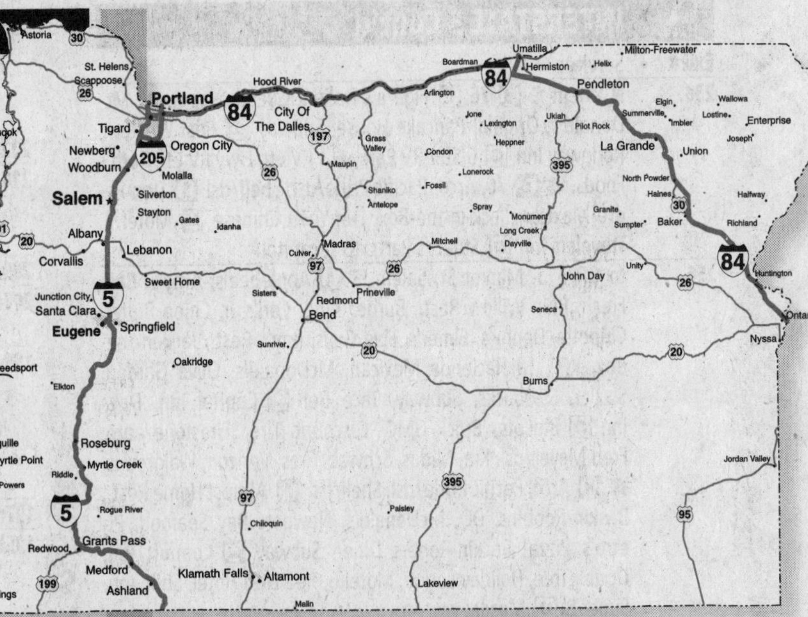

Exit #	Services
297	Terwilliger Blvd, W Baja Fresh, KFC, La Costita, Starbucks Fred Meyer, to Lewis and Clark Coll.
296b	Multnomah Blvd (from sb), W Safeway, same as 296a
296a	(from sb), Barbur, W 76/dsl, Chevron/dsl Bellagio's Pizza, Frack Burger, Subway Aladdin Inn, Budget Lodge, Capitol Hill Motel 7-11, AT&T, Schwab Tire
295	Capitol Hwy (from sb), Taylors Ferry Rd (from nb), E Shell/dsl McDonald's, Sho Japanese, Starbucks, Thai Orchid Hospitality Inn, W Taco Time, Wendy's Walgreens
294	Barbur Blvd, OR 99W, to Tigard, E Comfort Suites, W 76, Chevron, Shell Arby's, Baja Fresh, Banning's Rest., Baskin-Robbins, Burger King, Buster's BBQ, Carl's Jr, Chang's Mongolian Grill, Gators Eatery, Jimmy John's, Mazatlan Mexican, McDonald's, Starbucks, Subway, Taco Bell Quality Inn, Regency Inn $Tree, Americas Tire, auto repair, Baxter Parts, Costco, Fred Meyer, JoAnn Fabrics, NAPA, PetCo, Petsmart, Schwab Tire, transmissions, U-Haul, vet, Walmart/Subway, Winco Foods
293	Haines St, W Ford/Lincoln
292	OR 217, Kruse Way, Lake Oswego, E Shell/dsl Applebee's, Chevy's Mexican, Chipotle, Olive Garden, Oswego Grill, Potbelly, Stanford's Rest., Starbucks Crowne Plaza, Fairfield Inn, Hilton Garden, Phoenix Inn, Residence Inn LDS Temple, W Extended Stay America Lowe's
291	Carman Dr, W 76/dsl, Chevron Burgerville, Domino's, El Sol De Mexico, Starbucks, Subway, Sweet Tomatoes Courtyard, Holiday Inn Express Home Depot, Office Depot
290	Lower Boonsferry Rd, Lake Oswego, E Chevron/dsl, Space Age/dsl/LP Arby's, Baja Fresh, Baskin-Robbins, Burger King, Cafe Yumm, Carl's Jr., Fuddruckers, Miller's Rest., Nicoli's Grill, Panda Express, Starbucks, Subway, Taco Bell Motel 6 Dick's, Safeway Foods, See's Kitchen, Walgreens, W CA Pizza Kitchen, Claim Jumper, Jamba Juice, Jimmy John's, McCormick&Schmick's, Pastini Pastaria, PF Chang's, Qdoba Mexican, Royal Panda, Starbucks, Twigs Bistro, Village Inn Grand Hotel Barnes&Noble, Verizon, Whole Foods Mkt
289	Tualatin, E 76, Shell/dsl Chipotle Mexican, Famous Dave's BBQ, Jamba Juice, McDonald's, Panera Bread, Starbucks, Subway 7-11, Best Buy, Old Navy, Petsmart, vet, W Applebee's, Buffalo Wild Wings, Carl's Jr, Coldstone, Dickie Jo's Burgers, Hayden's Grill, Jack-in-the-Box, McDonald's, Outback Steaks, Pieology Pizzaria, Pizza Hut, Shari's, Starbucks, Subway, Taco Bell, Thai Rest., Wendy's Century Hotel, Comfort Inn Cabela's, Fred Meyer, Haggen's Foods, Michael's, New Seasons Mkt, O'Reilly Parts, PetCo, Staples, TJ Maxx
288	I-205, to Oregon City
286	Elligsen Rd, Boonsferry Rd, Stafford, E 76/dsl Burger King, Cafe Yumm!, Moe's SW Grill, Panda Express, Pizza Schmizza, Starbucks, Subway, Zoup! La Quinta, Motel 6 Chrysler/Dodge/Jeep, Costco/gas, Discount Tire, Ferrari/Maserati, Mercedes, Office Depot, Petsmart, Pheasant Ridge RV Resort, Target, W Chevron/dsl Boone Town Bistro, Carl's Jr Holiday Inn/rest. Audi, Camping World RV Ctr, Chevrolet, Nissan, Toyota

WILSONVILLE

Exit #	Services
283	Wilsonville, E 76 Abella Italian, Arby's, Chipotle, Denny's, Jamba Juice, Jimmy John's, Juan Colorado, McDonald's, Noodles&Co, Papa Murphy's, Red Robin, Shari's, Starbucks, Subway, Taco Bell, Thai Rest., Wanker's Café, Wendy's, Wong's Chinese GuestHouse Inn, Quality Inn, SnoozInn $Tree, Ace Hardware, AT&T, Fry's Electronics, funpark, GNC, Honda, NAPA, Rite Aid, Safeway, Schwab Tire, URGENT CARE, USPO, vet, W Fred Meyer/dsl Baskin-Robbins, Biscuits Cafe, Boone's Jct Pizza, Burger King, Domino's, Hunan Kitchen, Little Caesar's, McMenamin's Rest., Oswego Grill, Perfect Pizza, Qdoba, RAM Rest., Sonic, Starbucks, Subway, Wow Burger Best Western Wilsonville 7-11, auto repair, Fred Meyer/dsl, O'Reilly Parts, Verizon, Walgreens
282.5mm	Willamette River
282	Charbonneau District, E Langdon Farms Rest. Langdon Farms Golf
281.5mm	both lanes, coffee, full facilities, info, litter barrels, petwalk, vending
278	Donald, E 76/dsl/LP Aurora Acres RV Park, W FLYING J/Subway/dsl/scales/24hr, TA/Country Pride/Popeye's/dsl/scales/24hr/@ NAPA Truck Parts, SpeedCo Lube, to Champoeg SP, truckwash
274mm	weigh sta both lanes
271	OR 214, Woodburn, E Arco/dsl, Chevron Burger King, Denny's, DQ, KFC, McDonald's, Subway, Taco Bell Best Western, Super 8 76/repair, Al's RV Ctr, vet, Walgreens, Walmart/McDonald's, W Shell/dsl Arby's, Elmer's, Jack-in-the-Box, Jamba Juice, Panera Bread, Starbucks La Quinta Ford, Woodburn Outlets/famous brands, Woodburn RV Park
263	Brooks, Gervais, E Brooks Mkt/deli, W Pilot/Subway/Taco Bell/dsl/LP/scales/24hr Carl's Jr., Chalet Rest. Antique Powerland Museum, Freightliner, Willamette Mission SP (4mi)
260b a	OR 99E, Chemawa Rd, Keizer, W Burger King, Firehouse Subs, Jamba Juice, McDonald's, Outback Steaks, Panda Express, Panera Bread, RoundTable Pizza, Starbucks, Subway, Taco Bell, Taco del Mar Holiday Inn Express AT&T, GNC, Lowe's, Marshall's, Michael's, Old Navy, PetCo, REI, Ross, Staples, Target, Verizon, World Mkt
259mm	45th parallel, halfway between the equator and N Pole

= gas = food = lodging = other = rest stop

INTERSTATE 5 Cont'd

SALEM

Exit #	Services
258	N Salem, E 76 Figaro's Italian, Guesthouse Rest., McDonald's, Original Pancake House, Subway Best Western, Rodeway Inn 5 Star RV Park, Al's RV Ctr, Hwy RV Ctr, Roth's Foods, W 76, Arco, Pacific Pride/dsl, Shell/dsl Don Pedro Mexican, Jack-in-the-Box, LumYuen Chinese Motel 6, Travelers Inn Stuart's Parts, to st capitol
256	to OR 213, Market St, Salem, E Applebee's, Arby's, Baja Fresh, Blue Willow Rest., Burger King, Carl's Jr, China Buffet, Chipotle, Denny's, Elmer's, Five Guys, Izzy's Rest., Jack-in-the-Box, KFC, La Hacienda Mexican, McDonald's, Olive Garden, Sizzler, Starbucks, Subway, Taco Bell Capital Inn, Days Inn BigLots, Buick/GMC, Discount Tire, Firestone/auto, Fred Meyer/dsl, Kia, Midas, Schwab Tires, Verizon, Walgreens, W Arco, Pacific Pride/dsl, Shell/dsl Almost Home Rest., Baskin-Robbins, DQ, McDonald's, Newport Bay Seafood, Pietro's Pizza, Rockin-Rogers Diner, Subway Comfort Inn, DoubleTree, Holiday Lodge, Motel 6, Red Lion Hotel, Shilo Inn, Super 8 Mazda, vet
253	OR 22, Salem, Stayton, E Chevron, Shell/dsl, Space Age/dsl Burger King, Carls Jr, Las Polomas Mexican, McDonalds/playplace, Shari's, Subway $Tree, Home Depot, Salem Camping/RV Park, to Detroit RA, WinCo Foods, W Shell/dsl Carl's Jr, Denny's, DQ, Jack-in-the-Box, Panda Express, Popeyes, Taco Del Mar Best Western+, Comfort Suites, Hampton Inn, La Quinta, Residence Inn H, AAA, Chrysler/Jeep, Costco/gas, Lowe's, Nissan, Schwab Tire, st police, Walmart
252	Kuebler Blvd
249	to Salem, 2 mi W 76, Arco Arby's, Burger King, Carl's Jr Phoenix Inn Safeway/gas
248	Sunnyside, E Enchanted Forest Themepark, Willamette Valley Vineyards, W Pacific Pride/dsl
244	to N Jefferson, E Emerald Valley RV Park
243	Ankeny Hill
242	Talbot Rd
241mm	**both lanes, full facilities, info, litter barrels, petwalk,**
240.5mm	Santiam River
239	Dever-Conner
238	S Jefferson, Scio, W Loves/Arby's/dsl/scales/24hr
237	Viewcrest (from sb)
235	Millersburg
234	OR 99E, Albany, E Cascade Grill Comfort Suites, Holiday Inn Express Knox Butte Camping/RV dump, W Chevron Burger King, Carl's Jr, DQ, Golden Town Buffet, McDonald's, Muchas Gracias, Subway, Taco Bell Budget Inn, Motel 6, Quality Inn, Super 8 H, Costco/gas, Kohl's, NAPA, to Albany Hist Dist
233	US 20, Albany, E 76/dsl, Chevron/dsl/LP Denny's, LumYuen Chinese Best Western+, Phoenix Inn, Rodeway Inn Blue Ox RV Park, Chevrolet, Home Depot, Honda, Lassen RV Ctr, st police, Toyota, Walmart, W Shell/dsl, Space Age/dsl Abby's Pizza, Arby's, Baskin-Robbins, Burgerville, Carl's Jr, El Trio Loco, Elmer's, Fox Den Pizza, Golden Wok, Jack-in-the-Box, Los Dos Amigos, Los Tequilos Mexican, Original Breakfast Cafe, Pizza Hut, Sizzler, Skipper's, Starbucks, Sweetwaters Rest., Taco Time, Wendy's Valu Inn H, $Tree, Bi-Mart, CarQuest, Chrysler/Dodge/Hyundai/Jeep/Subaru, Fred Meyer/dsl, Hyundai, JoAnn Fabrics, Knechts's Parts, Old Navy, O'Reilly Parts, Rite Aid, Ross, Schwab Tires, Staples, Target, Walgreens

ALBANY

OR

SPRINGFIELD / EUGENE

Exit #	Services
228	OR 34, to Lebanon, Corvallis, E 76/dsl, Leather's/dsl Pine Cone Cafe Mallard Creek Golf/RV Resort, W Arc dsl, Chevron/CFN/A&W/dsl, Shell/dsl Subway K (5mi), to OSU
222mm	Butte Creek
216	OR 228, Halsey, Brownsville, E 76/Pioneer Villa TrkStp/de dsl/24hr/@ Travelodge, W Mobil/dsl parts/repa towing
209	to Jct City, Harrisburg, W Diamond Hill RV Park
206mm	**both lanes, full facilities, info, litter barrels, petwalk,**
199	Coburg, E Fuel'n Go/dsl Premier RV Resort, W She McDonald's/dsl, TA/Country Pride/Truck'n'Travel Motel/d scales/24hr/@ Coburg Crossing Cafe Camping Wor dsl repair, Eugene Kamping RV Park, Evert RV Ctr, Freightlin hist dist, RV Corral, Volvo
197mm	McKenzie River
195b a	N Springfield, E Arco, Chevron/dsl Applebee's, Bu falo Wild Wings, Cafe Yummi, Carl's Jr, China Sun, Ciao Pizz Denny's, Elmer's Rest., FarMan Chinese, Five Guys, Hacien Amigo Mio, HomeTown Buffet, Hop Valley Rest., IHOP, Jac in-the-Box, Jimmy John's, KFC, McDonald's, Outback Steak Panda Express, Roadhouse Grill, Shari's, Sizzler, Starbucks, Su way, Taco Bell, Taco Grande Best Western, Comfort Suite Courtyard, Hilton Garden, Holiday Inn, Holiday Inn Expres Motel 6, Quality Inn, Super 8 H, Best Buy, Cabela's, Kohl Michael's, Ross, st police, Staples, Target, USPO, Walmart Mk W Taco Bell Costco/gas, Office Depot, Petsmart, to
194b a	OR 126 E, I-105 W, Springfield, Eugene, 1 mi W 76, Chevro Mobil Carl's Jr, MOD Pizza, PF Chang's, Starbucks L Quinta, Residence Inn Albertson's, Natural Grocers, Ni san, Old Navy, Subaru, U Of O
193mm	Willamette River
192	OR 99 (from nb), to Eugene, E Candlewood Suites, Fairfie Inn, W 76 House Of Chen, Starbucks, Subway Bes Western, Days Inn, Holiday Inn Express, University Inn M Of Choice, to U of O
191	Glenwood, W 76/dsl, Shell/dsl/LP Denny's Com fort Suites, Motel 6
189	30th Ave S, Eugene, E Shell/dsl/LP Harley-Davidsor NW RV Supply, Shamrock RV Park, W Chevron/dsl, SeQun tial/dsl
188b	OR 99 S (nb only), Goshen
188a	OR 58, OR 99 S to Oakridge, E Deerwood RV Park W Pacific Pride/dsl tires
186	Dillard Rd, to Goshen (from nb)
182	Creswell, E DQ, Subway Comfort Inn $General, Bi Mart, golf, OR RV Ctr, W 76/dsl, Arco/dsl China Wok Creswell Cafe, Figaro's Pizza, Joe's Diner, TJ's Rest. Supe 8 $Tree, Creswell Automotive, Dari Mart, Meadowlark RV Park, NAPA
180mm	Coast Fork of Willamette River
178mm	**both lanes, coffee, full facilities, litter barrels, petwalk**
176	Saginaw
175mm	Row River
174	Cottage Grove, E Chevron/dsl/repair, Pacific Pride/dsl Arby's, Chalerm Thai, Subway, Taco Bell Village Resort/RV park H, AutoZone, Chevrolet/GMC, Chrysler/Dodge/Jeep, Walmart, W Chevron/dsl/LP, Mobil/dsl, Shell/dsl Burger King, Carl's Jr, Jack-in-the-Box, KFC, McDonald's/RV parking, Papa Murphy's, Pinocchio's Pizza,

INTERSTATE 5 Cont'd

174	Continued Taco Time, Torero's Mexican, Vintage Rest. Best Western, Quality Inn, Relax Inn $Tree, Bi-Mart Foods, Grocery Outlet, O'Reilly Parts, Safeway/dsl, Walgreens
172	6th St (from sb), Cottage Grove Lake (from sb), 2 mi W Cottage Grove RV Village
170	to OR 99, London Rd (nb only), Cottage Grove Lake, 6 mi W Cottage Grove RV Village
163	Curtin, E Stardust Motel antiques, W Pass Creek Park/camping
162	OR 38, OR 99, to Drain, Elkton
161	Anlauf (from nb)
160	Salt Springs Rd
159	Elk Creek, Cox Rd
154	Yoncalla, Elkhead
150	OR 99, to OR 38, Yoncalla, Red Hill, W Eagle Valley RV Park
148	Rice Hill, E Arco/LP, FLYING J/Denny's/Subway/dsl/scales/24hr, Pacific Pride/dsl Ranch Rest. Ranch Motel, Rodeway Inn Rice Hill RV Park, towing/dsl repair, W K-R Drive-In
146	Rice Valley
144mm	**sb, full facilities, litter barrels, petwalk,**
143mm	**nb, full facilities, litter barrels, petwalk,**
142	Metz Hill
140	OR 99 (from sb), Oakland, E Tolly's Rest. Oakland Hist Dist
138	OR 99 (from nb), Oakland, E Tolly's Rest. Oakland Hist Dist
136	OR 138W, Sutherlin, E Chevron/dsl, Mobil/dsl Abby's Pizza, Apple Peddler Rest., Burger King, Domino's, McDonald's, Papa Murphy's, Pedotti's Italian, Sol de Sutherlin, Yummy House Best Western+, Motel 6, Relax Inn $Tree, Autocare, AutoZone, I-5 RV Ctr, NAPA, W Shell/dsl Dakota St Pizza, DQ, Si Casa Flores, Starbucks, Subway, Taco Bell Hi-Way Haven RV Camp, Umpqua RV Park
135	Wilbur, Sutherlin, E CFN/dsl, Shell/dsl/LP vet
129	OR 99, Winchester, E Del Ray Cafe Kamper Korner RV Ctr (1mi), Rivers Edge RV Park, st police
129mm	N Umpqua River, N Umpqua River
127	Stewart Pkwy, Edenbower Rd, N Roseburg, E Shell/dsl Shari's Rest., Subway Motel 6, Super 8 Costco/gas, Home Depot, Honda, Lowe's, Mt Nebo RV Park, Verizon, W Mobil, Valero/dsl Applebee's, Del Taco, McDonald's/playplace, Red Robin, Subway, Yummy Chinese Sleep Inn H, Albertson's, Big O Tire, Macy's, Sherm's Foods, vet, Walmart
125	Garden Valley Blvd, Roseburg, E Abby's Pizza, China Buffet, Elmer's, Gilberto's Mexican, Jack-in-the-Box, KFC, Los Dos Amigo's Mexican, McDonald's, Smokin' Friday BBQ, Sonic, Subway, Taco Bell Comfort Inn, Hampton Inn, Quality Inn AT&T, AutoZone, BigLots, Buick/Chevrolet/GMC, Ford/Lincoln, Honda, NAPA, Safeway/dsl, Toyota, U-Haul, Verizon, vet, Walgreens, W Shell/LP/repair Burger King, Carl's Jr, Fox Den Pizza, Panda Express, Pita Pit, Rodeo Steaks, RoundTable Pizza, Si Casa Flores Mexican, Sizzler, Starbucks, Wendy's Best Western, Days Inn H, $Tree, Bi-Mart Foods, Fred Meyer/dsl, JC Penney, JoAnn Fabrics, Marshall's, Michael's, O'Reilly Parts, PetCo, Rite Aid, Ross, Staples, Walgreens
124	OR 138, Roseburg, City Ctr, E Chevron/dsl, Texaco/dsl Denny's Baymont Inn, Holiday Inn Express, Rodeway Inn, Travelodge Rite Aid, W 76/dsl, Mobil/dsl Charley's BBQ, Domino's, KFC/LJ Silver, Pete's Drive-In, Subway, Taco Time Grocery Outlet, Harvard Ave Drug

SUTHERLIN

ROSEBURG

123	Roseburg, E camping, museum, to Umpqua Park
121	McLain Ave
120.5mm	S Umpqua River
120	OR 99 N (no EZ nb return), Green District, Roseburg, E Rodeway Inn, Shady Oaks Motel, W auto repair
119	OR 99 S, OR 42 W, Winston, E Ingram Dist., W Chevron/A&W/dsl, Loves/Arby's/dsl/scales/LP/24hr, Shell/dsl McDonald's, Papa Murphy's, Subway, Taco Bell $General, Ray's Foods, Rising River RV Park, Western Star RV Park
113	Clarks Branch Rd, Round Prairie, W Quikstop Motel On the River RV Park (2mi)
112.5mm	S Umpqua River, S Umpqua River
112	OR 99, OR 42, Dillard, E Rivers West RV Park
111mm	**weigh sta both directions**
110	Boomer Hill Rd
108	Myrtle Creek, E Chevron Armando's Mexican, Golf Course Cafe, Subway, Tommy's Cafe city park, Myrtle Creek RV Park, Ray's Foods
106	Weaver Rd
103	Tri City, Myrtle Creek, E Tri-City RV Park, W Chevron/A&W/dsl, Pacific Pride McDonald's
102	Gazley Rd, E Surprise Valley RV Park (1mi)
101.5mm	S Umpqua River
101	Riddle, Stanton Park, W camping
99	Canyonville, E Penny Pincher Burger King, El Paraiso 7 Feathers Hotel/casino, Riverside Motel Canyon Mkt, city park, W 7 Feathers Trkstp/café/dsl/scales/24hr/@ Creekside Rest. Holiday Inn Express 7 Feathers RV Resort
98	OR 99, Canyonville, Days Creek, E Arco/dsl, Mobil/dsl Ken's Cafe, Papa Morgan's Rest., Subway Leisure Inn $General, auto repair, Canyonville Hardware, NAPA, Ray's Foods, USPO, vet, W museum
95	Canyon Creek
90mm	Canyon Creek Pass, elevation 2020
88	Azalea
86	Barton Rd, Quine's Creek, E Quines Creek/dsl Heaven on Earth Rest./rest., Meadow Wood RV Park (3mi)
83	Barton Rd (from nb), E Meadow Wood RV Park/camping
80	Glendale, W Cow Creek/Lp/Rest.
79.5mm	Stage Road Pass, elevation 1830
78	Speaker Rd (from sb)
76	Wolf Creek, W 76/deli/dsl, Pacific Pride/dsl, Shell/dsl Wolf Creek Inn Rest. Creekside RV park, USPO
74mm	Smith Hill Summit, elevation 1730
71	Sunny Valley, E Covered Bridge Store/gas, W Sunny Valley RV Park/motel
69mm	Sexton Mtn Pass, elevation 1960

= gas = food = lodging = other = rest stop

INTERSTATE 5 Cont'd

Exit #	Services
66	Hugo, E KOA, W Pottsville Museum (3mi)
63mm	**both lanes, full facilities, info, litter barrels, petwalk, , vending**
61	Merlin, W Valero/dsl $General, Almeda RV Park, Beaver Creek RV Resort (2mi), OR RV Ctr, Ray's Foods, repair
58	OR 99, to US 199, Grants Pass, W 76/Circle K/dsl, CFN/dsl, Chevron, Mobil/dsl, Shell/dsl/repair, TownePump Gas Black Bear Diner, Burger King, Carl's Jr, China Hut, Denny's, DQ, In-N-Out, Jack-in-the-Box, McDonald's, Muchas Gracias Mexican, Nano's Mexican, Papa Murphy's, Sizzler, Subway, Taco Bell, Uptown Grill, Wendy's Best Way Inn, Buona Sera Inn, Hampton Inn, Hawks Inn, La Quinta, Motel 6, Quality Inn, Red Lion Inn, Redwood Motel, Sunset Inn, Super 8, SweetBreeze Inn, Travelodge H, $Tree, AutoZone, Chevrolet/Honda, Chrysler/Dodge/Jeep, Jack's RV Resort, Nissan, repair, Rouge Valley RV Park, Schwab Tire, st police, towing
55	US 199, Redwood Hwy, E Grants Pass, W Arco/dsl, Mobil/dsl Abby's Pizza, Applebee's, Arby's, Carl's Jr, Elmer's, Jersey Mike's, KFC, Kobe Buffet, La Burrita, McDonald's, MOD Pizza, Panda Express, Pizza Hut, Shari's, Si Casa Flores Mexican, Starbucks, Subway, Taco Bell Best Western, Holiday Inn Express H, $Tree, Albertson's, AT&T, BigLots, Fred Meyer/dsl, Grocery Outlet, Home Depot, Jo-Ann, Moon Mtn RV Park (2mi), O'Reilly Parts, Petco, Rite Aid, RiverPark RV Park (4mi), Ross, Siskiyou RV Ctr, Staples, Verizon, Walmart, Winco Foods
48	Rogue River, E 76/dsl, Chevron/Circle K/dsl Abby's Pizza, Cottage Cafe, Homestead Rest., Subway $General, Ace Hardware, auto repair, Rogue River RA, vet, W La Guayacama, Mkt Basket Deli Bella Rosa Inn, Best Western Bridgeview RV Park, Chinook Winds RV Park, visitors ctr/info, Whispering Pines RV Park
45b	**W Valley of the Rogue SP/ both lanes, camping, full facilities, litter barrels, petwalk,**
45mm	Rogue River
45a	OR 99, Savage Rapids Dam, E Cypress Grove RV Park
43	OR 99, OR 234, to Crater Lake, Gold Hill, E RoadRiver B&B, Rock Point RV Park
40	OR 99, OR 234, Gold Hill, E Figaro's Pizza $General, KOA, Lazy Acres Motel/RV Park, Running Salmon RV Park, W Dardanelle's/gas Dardanelle's Trailer Park
35	OR 99, Blackwell Rd, Central Point, 2-4 mi W gas food lodging Jacksonville Nat Hist Landmark, st police
33	Central Point, E Chevron, LNG, Pilot/Subway/Taco Bell/dsl/scales/24hr Burger King, KFC, Shari's Rest., Sonic Candlewood Suites (2mi), Courtyard (2mi), Holiday Inn Express, La Quinta, Super 8 Costco/dsl, funpark, W 76/Circle K/dsl, Shell/dsl Abby's Pizza, Little Caesar's, Mazatlan Mexican, McDonald's Albertson's, AT&T, USPO
30	OR 62, to Crater Lake, Medford, E Arco, Chevron/dsl, Witham Trkstp/rest./dsl/24hr/@ Abby's Pizza, Applebee's, Asian Grill, Baskin Robbins, Buffalo Wild Wings, Burger King, Carl's Jr, Del Taco, Denny's, DQ, Elmer's, McDonald's, Olive Garden, Outback Steaks, Panda Express, Papa John's, Papa Murphy's, Pita Pit, Pizza Hut, Red Robin, RoundTable Pizza, Sizzler, Sonic, Starbucks, Subway, Taco Bell, Taco Delite, Thai Bistro, TX Roadhouse, Wayback Burger, Wendy's Comfort Inn, Hampton Inn, Motel 6, Quality Inn, Ramada, Rogue Regency Hotel, Shilo Inn H, $Tree, AT&T, AutoZone, Barnes&Noble, Best Buy, BigLots, Bi-Mart, Chevrolet/Buick/GMC, Discount Tire, Food4Less, Ford/Lincoln, Fred Meyer/dsl, Hobby Lobby, JoAnn,
30	Continued Lowe's, Mazda, Mercedes, Michael's, NAPA, Office Depot, O Navy, O'Reilly Parts, Petsmart, Ross, Safeway, Schwab Tire, police, Subaru, TJ Maxx, USPO, Verizon, vet, Walmart/Subw W 76/dsl, Spirit/dsl Chipotle, In-n-Out, Jack-in-th Box, Kaleidoscope Pizza, KFC, MOD Pizza, Red Lobster, Subw Wendy's CarQuest, JC Penney, Kohl's, Macy's, Natural G cers, Petco, REI, Target, Toyota, Trader Joe's, Verizon
27	Barnett Rd, Medford, E Black Bear Diner, DQ B Western, Days Inn/rest., Hilton Garden, Homewood Suit Motel 6, Travelers Inn H, W 76/Circle K/dsl, Che ron/dsl Abby's Pizza, Arby's, Burger King, Carl's Jr, Do ino's, El Arriero Mexican, HomeTown Buffet, Jack-in-the-Bo KFC, McDonald's, McGrath's FishHouse, Panda Express, Piz Hut, Rooster's Rest., Shari's, Starbucks, Subway, Taco Be Wendy's Comfort Inn, Holiday Inn Express, Medford In Royal Crest Motel, Sovana Inn, SpringHill Suites, TownePla Suites $Tree, AT&T, Fred Meyer/dsl, GNC, Grocery Outl Harry&David's, O'Reilly Parts, Staples, Verizon, Walgreen Walmart/McDonald's, WinCo Foods
24	Phoenix, E Petro/Iron Skillet/dsl/scales/RV dump/24hr/ Shell/dsl Best Value/PearTree RV park Home Depo Peterbilt, W Chevron/Circle K/dsl Amigos Mexica Angelo's Pizza, Jack-in-the-Box, McDonald's auto repa Harley Davidson, Holiday RV Park, Ray's Foods, Rite Aid
22mm	**sb, full facilities, litter barrels, petwalk, , vendin**
21	Talent, W 76/dsl, Chevron/dsl Subway GoodNig Inn $General, Ashland Talent RV Resort, vet
19	Valley View Rd, Ashland, W 76/dsl, Pacific Pride/dsl, Shel dsl/LP Burger King, El Tapatio Mexican Comfort In EconoLodge/RV Park Acura, Chevrolet, Ford
18mm	**weigh sta both lanes**
14	OR 66, to Klamath Falls, Ashland, E Chevron/dsl, Mobil/ds LP, Valero/dsl El Paraiso Mexican, OakTree Rest. As land Hills Inn & Suites, Best Western, Holiday Inn Express, Rela Inn Emigrant Lake Camping (3mi), Glenyan RV Park (3m W Arco, Shell Señor Sam's Mexican, Subway, Taco Be Wendy's, Wild Goose Cafe Rodeway Inn, Super 8 H $Tree, Albertson's, AT&T, Bi-Mart, CarQuest, Rite Aid, Schwa Tire, Shop'n Kart, U-Haul, vet
12	**nb, full facilities**
11	OR 99, Siskiyou Blvd (nb only, no return)
6	to Mt Ashland, E Callahan's Siskiyou Lodge/rest. s area
4mm	Siskiyou Summit, elevation 4310, brake check both lanes
1	to Siskiyou Summit (from nb, no return)
0mm	Oregon/California state line

INTERSTATE 84

Exit #	Services
378mm	Oregon/Idaho state line, Snake River
377.5mm	**Welcome Ctr wb, full facilities, info, litter barrels, petwal , vending**
376b a	US 30, to US 20/26, Ontario, Payette, N Chevron/ds A&W/KFC, Burger King, Carl's Jr, China Buffet, Countr Kitchen, Denny's, Domino's, DQ, Dutch Bros Coffee, Little Cae sar's, McDonald's, Panda Express, Papa Murphy's, Starbucks Subway, Taco Time, Wingers Best Western, Clarion, Mo tel 6, Quality Inn, Red Lion Inn, Sleep Inn $Tree, AT&T GNC, Home Depot, st police, Staples, Toyota, Verizon, Wal greens, Walmart/Subway, Waremart, S Pilot/Arby's/dsl scales/24hr, Sinclair/dsl East Side Cafe, Gandolfo's Deli

GRANTS PASS
MEDFORD
ASHLAND
ONTARIO
OR

INTERSTATE 84 Cont'd

376b a	Continued Ogawa's Japanese, Sweet Caroline's, Taco Bell Holiday Inn Express, OR Trail Motel, Stockman's Motel, Super 8 H, Commercial Tire, Les Schwab Tire, NAPA
374	US 30, OR 201, to Ontario, N to Ontario SP, S Loves /Chester's/Subway/dsl/scales/24hr/@ , Pacific Pride Budget Inn H
373.5mm	Malheur River
371	Stanton Blvd, 2 mi S to correctional institution
362	Moores Hollow Rd
356	OR 201, to Weiser, ID, 3 mi N Catfish Junction RV Park, Oasis RV Park
354.5mm	**weigh sta eb**
353	US 30, to Huntington, N info, RV camping, to Farewell Bend SP, **weigh sta wb**
351mm	Pacific/Mountain time zone
345	US 30, Lime, Huntington, 1 mi N gas food lodging to Snake River Area, Van Ornum BFD
342	Lime (from eb)
340	Rye Valley
338	Lookout Mountain
337mm	Burnt River
335	to Weatherby, N **both lanes, full facilities, litter barrels, Oregon Trail Info, petwalk, , vending**
330	Plano Rd, to Cement Plant Rd, S cement plant
329mm	**pulloff eb**
327	Durkee, N Co-op/dsl/LP/café
325mm	Pritchard Creek
321mm	Alder Creek
317	to Pleasant Valley (from wb)
315	to Pleasant Valley (from wb)
313	to Pleasant Valley (from eb)
306	US 30, Baker, 2-3 mi S Chevron/dsl Baker City Motel, Bridge Street Hotel, OR Trail Motel/rest. H, Les Schwab Tire, same as 304, to st police
304	OR 7, Baker, N Chevron/dsl Super 8, Welcome Inn Grocery Outlet, S Maverik/dsl, Shell/dsl, Sinclair/dsl/rest./scales/24hr, USA/dsl Big Chief's BBQ, Golden Crown, McDonald's, Papa Murphy's, Pizza Hut, Rising Sun Chinese, Starbucks, Subway, Sumpter Jct Rest., Taco Time Eldorado Inn, Geiser Grand Motel, Rodeway Inn, Sunridge Inn H, $Tree, Albertson's, Bi-Mart, Carquest, CarQuest, city park, Mtn View RV Park/LP (3mi), museum, O'Reilly Parts, Paul's Transmissions/repair, Rite Aid, Safeway Foods, to hist dist, Verizon
302	OR 86 E to Richland, S H, A Frame RV Park/LP, st police
298	OR 203, to Medical Springs
297mm	Baldock Slough
295mm	**both lanes, full facilities, info, litter barrels, petwalk, , , vending**
289mm	Powder River
287.5mm	45th parallel, halfway between the equator and north pole
286mm	N Powder River
285	US 30, OR 237, North Powder, N North Powder Motel/cafe, S ski area, to Anthony Lakes
284mm	Wolf Creek
283	Wolf Creek Lane
278	Clover Creek
273	Frontage Rd
270	Ladd Creek Rd (from eb, no return)
269mm	**both lanes, full facilities, info, litter barrels, petwalk, , , vending**

BAKER

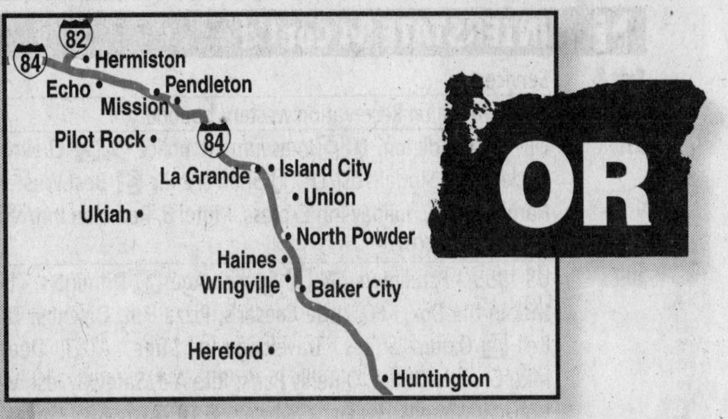

LA GRANDE

268	Foothill Rd
265	OR 203, LaGrande, N , Eagles Hot Lake RV Park, S FLYING J/rest./dsl/scales/24hr SmokeHouse Rest. (2mi) Freightliner
261	OR 82, LaGrande, N Chevron/dsl, Shell/dsl Denny's, Little Caesar's, Pizza Hut, Primo's Pizza, Starbucks, Taco Bell LaGrande Inn AT&T, Chrysler/Dodge/Jeep, Ford, Grocery Outlet, Thunder RV Ctr, Verizon, vet, Walmart/Subway, S 76/Baskin-Robbins/Subway/dsl, Chevron/dsl, Texaco/dsl Chen's Chinese, Domino's, DQ, Dutch Bro's Coffee, KFC, La Fiesta Mexican, Local Harvest Eatery, McDonald's, Moy's Dynasty, Nell's Steakburger, Papa Murphy's, Taco Time, Wendy's Best Western+, Royal Motel, Sandman Inn/Best Value, Super 8 H, $General, $Tree, Ace Hardware, E OR U, O'Reilly Parts, Rite Aid, Safeway/dsl, Schwab Tire, Wallowa Lake
260mm	Grande Ronde River
259	US 30 E (from eb), to La Grande, 1-2 mi S Chevron/dsl, Mobil/dsl Burger King Greenwell Motel/rest., Rodeway Inn, Royal Motel, same as 261
257	Perry (from wb)
256.5mm	**weigh sta eb**
256	Perry (from eb)
255mm	Grande Ronde River
254mm	scenic wayside
252	OR 244, to Starkey, Lehman Springs, S camping, chainup area, Hilgard SP
251mm	Wallowa-Whitman NF, eastern boundary
248	Spring Creek Rd, to Kamela, 3 mi N Oregon Trail Visitors Park
246mm	Wallowa-Whitman NF, western boundary
243	Summit Rd, Mt Emily Rd, to Kamela, 2 mi N Emily Summit SP, Oregon Trail info
241mm	Summit of the Blue Mtns, elevation 4193
238	Meacham
234	Meacham, S Emigrant Sprs SP
231.5mm	Umatilla Indian Reservation, eastern boundary
228mm	Deadman Pass, **both lanes, full facilities, litter barrel, Oregon Trail info, petwalk, (wb), picnic table, RV Dump (wb), vending**
227mm	**weigh sta wb, brake check area**
224	Poverty Flats Rd, Old Emigrant Hill Rd, to Emigrant Springs SP
223mm	wb viewpoint, no restrooms
221.5mm	eb viewpoint, no restrooms
220mm	**runaway truck ramp wb**
216	Mission, McKay Creek, N Arrowhead Trkstp/Pacific Pride/McDonald's/dsl/24hr DQ, Subway Wildhorse Casino/RV Park
213	US 30 (from wb), Pendleton, 3-5 mi N Chevron/dsl Travelers Inn Pendleton NHD

= gas = food = lodging = other = rest stop

INTERSTATE 84 Cont'd

PENDLETON

Exit #	Services
212mm	Umatilla Indian Reservation western boundary
210	OR 11, Pendleton, N museum, st police, S Chevron/Circle K/dsl, Sinclair/dsl/LP Shari's/24hr Best Western, Hampton Inn, Holiday Inn Express, Motel 6, Red Lion Inn/rest., Super 8 KOA
209	US 395, Pendleton, N Space Age Domino's, DQ, Jack-in-the-Box, KFC, Little Caesar's, Pizza Hut, Quiznos, Taco Bell Oxford Suites, Travelodge $Tree, AT&T, Dean's Mkt, Grocery Outlet, O'Reilly Parts, Rite Aid, Safeway/dsl, Verizon, Walgreens, Walmart/Subway, S Astro/dsl, Sinclair/dsl Abby's Pizza, Burger King, Denny's, Dickey's BBQ, McDonald's, Rooster's Rest, Starbucks, Subway, Wendy's Motel 6 H, Les Schwab, Thompson RV Ctr
208mm	Umatilla River
207	US 30, W Pendleton, N Sinclair/dsl/LP Lookout RV Park, truck repair
202	Barnhart Rd, to Stage Gulch, N Woodpecker Truck Repair
199	Stage Coach Rd, Yoakum Rd
198	Lorenzen Rd, McClintock Rd, N trailer/reefer repair
193	Echo Rd, to Echo, Oregon Trail Site
188	US 395 N, Hermiston, N Chevron/dsl (5mi), Pilot/Subway/McDonald's/dsl/24hr/RV park Denny's/24hr (5mi), Jack-in-the-Box (5mi), McDonald's (5mi), Shari's/24hr (5mi) Best Western (5mi), Holiday Inn Express, Motel 6, Oxford Suites (5mi) H (5mi), S Echo HS, Henrietta RV Park (1mi)
187mm	**both lanes, full facilities, info, litter barrels, petwalk,**
182	OR 207, to Hermiston, N Space Age/A&W/dsl/LP/24hr Comfort Inn
180	Westland Rd, to Hermiston, McNary Dam, N trailer repair, S Western Express/dsl Freightliner
179	I-82 W, to Umatilla, Kennewick, WA
177	Umatilla Army Depot
171	Paterson Ferry Rd, to Paterson
168	US 730, to Irrigon, 8 mi N Green Acres RV Park, Oasis RV Park, Oregon Trail info
165	Port of Morrow, S Pacific Pride/dsl
164	Boardman, N Chevron/Circle K/dsl, Sinclair/dsl C&D Drive-In, Smiley's Cafe, Sunrise Cafe, Village Rest. Knights Inn, Riverview Motel Boardman RV/Marina Park, city park, USPO, S Shell/dsl Subway Boardman Tire, NAPA, Oregon Trail Library, Rodeway Inn Harvest Town Mkt
161mm	**both lanes, full facilities, litter barrels, petwalk, , , vending**
159	Tower Rd, S Loves/Carl's Jr/dsl/scales/24hr
151	Threemile Canyon
147	OR 74, to Ione, Blue Mtn Scenic Byway, Heppner, Oregon Trail Site
137	OR 19, Arlington, S Shell/Circle K/dsl Happy Canyon Cafe, Pheasant Grill, Rivers Edge Deli Rodeway Inn Arlington Hardware, Arlington RV Park/dump, city park, Thrifty Foods
136.5mm	viewpoint wb, , litter barrels
131	Woelpern Rd (from eb, no return)
129	Blalock Canyon, Lewis&Clark Trail
123	Philippi Canyon, Lewis&Clark Trail
114.5mm	John Day River
114	S LePage Park
112	**parking area both lanes, litter barrels, N** John Day Dam

BOARDMAN

THE DALLES

Exit #	Services
109	Pendleton, N John Day Visitor Ctr, S Sincla dsl Bob's T-Bone, Bull Dog Diner Hillview Motel, Ty Motel Ed's RV Park, Family Mkt/deli, Rufus RV Park
104	US 97, Biggs, N Des Chutes Park Bridge, Maryhill M seum, S 76/Circle K/Noble Roman's/dsl/24hr, Pilo McDonald's/dsl/scales/24hr, Shell/Subway/dsl Linda's Re Dinty's Motel, Three Rivers Inn Dinty's Mkt, dsl/tire rep
100mm	Columbia River Gorge Scenic Area, Deschutes River
97	OR 206, Celilo, N Celilo SP, restrooms, S Deschutes Indian Village
92mm	**pull off eb**
88	N to The Dalles Dam
87	US 30, US 197, to Dufur, N 76/dsl/24hr, Chevro dsl McDonald's, Portage Grill Comfort Inn, Sh Inn Columbia Hills RV Park, Lone Pine RV Park, st poli S Big Jim's Drive-In Celilo Inn
85	The Dalles, N **Riverfront Park, litter barrels, , , pla ground, restrooms,** marina, S 76/dsl, Chevron, Si clair Burgerville, Canton Wok, Clock Tower Rest., Domino River Tap Rest. Dalles Inn, Oregon Motel H, AJ's Ra ators, Dalles Parts, to Nat Hist Dist, TrueValue, USPO
83	(84 from wb)W The Dalles, N Casa El Mirador Le ends Hotel/Casino S-Point Automotive, S Astro/d Chevron/dsl, Fred Meyer/dsl Burger King, Denny's, D Dutch Bro's Coffee, Ixtapa Mexican, Jack-in-the-Box, KFC, M Donald's, Papa Murphy's, Pizza Hut, Shari's Rest., Starbuck Subway, Taco Bell, Taco Time, The BBQ Cousin's Inn/res Fairfield Inn, Motel 6, Super 8 H, $Tree, AT&T, AutoZon Buick/Chevrolet/GMC, Chrysler/Dodge/Jeep, Ford, Fred Mey Grocery Outlet, Honda, Jo-Ann Fabrics, Nissan, O'Reilly Par PetCo, Rite Aid, Safeway/dsl, Staples, Subaru, Toyota, Verizo Walgreens
82	Chenowith Area, S 76/dsl Spooky's Café Bi-Mart Food Columbia Discovery Ctr, Home Depot, museum, same as 83
76	Rowena, N Lewis & Clark info, Mayer SP, Memaloose S windsurfing
73mm	**both lanes, full facilities, litter barrels, petwalk, , RV dump** camping, Memaloose SP
69	US 30, Mosier, S USPO
66mm	**N wb, full facilities, litter barrels, ,** Koberg Beach S
64	US 30, OR 35, to White Salmon, Hood River, N Chevro dsl, Shell McDonald's, Riverside Grill, Starbucks Be Western marina, museum, st police, visitors info
63	Hood River, City Ctr, N Valero/dsl Hampton In S Astro 3 River's Grill, Andrew's Pizza, Big Horse Rest Hood River Rest., Pietro's Pizza Hood River Hotel, Oakstre Hotel H, USPO
62	US 30, Westcliff Dr, W Hood River, N Charburger, Whit Buffalo Rest. Columbia Gorge Hotel, Vagabond Lodg S 76/dsl, Chevron/dsl/LP Domino's, DQ, Egg Rive Cafe, HoHo Chinese, McDonald's, Pelinti Cafe, Red Carpet Caf Starbucks, Subway, Taco Bell Holiday Inn Express, Prater Motel, Riverview Lodge H, AT&T, Les Schwab Tire, Rit Aid, Safeway, Verizon, Walmart
61mm	**pulloff wb**
60	service rd wb (no return)
58	Mitchell Point Overlook (from eb)
56	N RV camping, Viento SP
55	Starvation Peak Tr Head (from eb), restrooms
54mm	**weigh sta wb**
51	Wyeth, S camping
49mm	**pulloff eb**

HOOD RIVER

OR

INTERSTATE 84 Cont'd

Exit #	Services
47	Forest Lane, Hermon Creek (from wb), [other] camping
45mm	**weigh sta eb**
44	US 30, to Cascade Locks, **N** [gas] Chevron/dsl, Shell/dsl [food] Bridgeside Rest., Cascade Inn Rest., Eastwind Drive-In, Waterfront Cafe [lodging] Best Western+, Bridge of the Gods Motel, Cascade Motel, Columbia Gorge Inn [other] Columbia Mkt, KOA, Stern Wheeler RV Park, to Bridge of the Gods, USPO
41	[other] Eagle Creek RA (from eb), to fish hatchery
40	**N** [other] Bonneville Dam NHS, info, to fish hatchery
37	Warrendale (from wb)
35	Historic Hwy, Multnomah (exits left from both lanes), **S** [other] Ainsworth SP, Fishery RV Park, scenic loop highway, waterfall area
31	Multnomah Falls (exits left from both lanes), **S** [food] Multnomah Falls Lodge/Rest. (hist site) [other] camping
30	**S** [other] Benson SRA (from eb)
29	Dalton Point (from wb)
28	to Bridal Veil (7 mi return from eb), **S** [other] USPO
25	**N** [other] Rooster Rock SP
23mm	[other] hist marker, viewpoint wb
22	Corbett, **2 mi S** [gas] Corbett Mkt [food] View Point Rest. [other] Crown Point RV Camping
19mm	[other] Columbia River Gorge scenic area
18	Lewis&Clark SP, to Oxbow SP
17.5mm	Sandy River
17	Marine Dr, Troutdale, **N** [food] DQ [lodging] Comfort Inn, **S** [gas] Chevron/dsl, Loves/Chester's/dsl/LP/scales/24hr, TA/Shell/Country Pride/Popeye's/Subway/dsl/scales/24hr/@ [food] Arby's, McDonald's, Shari's/24hr, Subway, Taco Bell [lodging] Holiday Inn Express, Motel 6 [other] Premium Outlets/famous brands, Sandy Riverfront RV Resort
16	238th Dr, Fairview, **N** [gas] Arco/dsl/24hr [food] Bronx Eatery, Burger King, Jack-in-the-Box [lodging] Travelodge [other] Camping World, Walmart/Subway, **S** [gas] 76 [other] [H]
14	207th Ave, Fairview, **N** [gas] Shell/dsl [food] Parkway Grill [other] auto repair, Portland RV Park, Rolling Hills RV Park
13	181st Ave, Gresham, **N** [gas] Chevron/dsl [lodging] Hampton Inn, **S** [gas] 76, Arco, Shell [food] Burger King, Canton Pearl, Carl's Jr, Elmer's, McDonald's, Pizza Hut, Shari's, Subway, Wendy's [lodging] Bridgeway Inn, Days Inn, Extended Stay America, Portland Suites, Sheraton [other] $Tree, 7-11, U-Haul, vet
10	122nd Ave (from eb)
9	I-205, S to Salem, N to Seattle, to [airport], (to 102nd Ave from eb)
8	I-205 N (from eb), **N** [other] to [airport]
7	Halsey St (from eb), Gateway Dist
6	I-205 S (from eb)s
5	OR 213, to 82nd Ave (eb only), **N** [lodging] Days Inn, **S** [food] Eastern Cathay [lodging] Comfort Inn
4	68th Ave (from eb), to Halsey Aves
3	58th Ave (from eb), **S** [gas] 76, Shell/dsl [other] [H], Fred Meyer
2	43rd Ave, 39th Ave, Halsey St, **N** [gas] 76 [food] Burger King, Panera Bread, Starbucks [lodging] Banfield Motel [other] Rite Aid, Trader Joe's, **S** [other] [H], same as 1
1	33rd Ave, Lloyd Blvd (eb only), downtown, **N** [gas] Shell/dsl [food] Burger King, Starbucks [other] AT&T, **S** [food] Wendy's [other] Schwab Tire, same as 2
1	to downtown (wb only), **N** [food] Applebee's [lodging] Doubletree, Residence Inn [other] $Tree, Macy's, Marshall's, Nordstrom, Safeway, **S** [other] Cadillac
0mm	**I-84 begins/ends on I-5, exit 301.**

TROUTDALE

PORTLAND

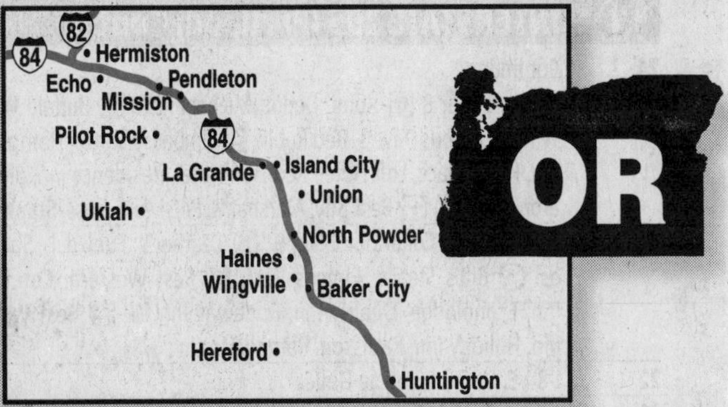

PORTLAND AREA

INTERSTATE 205 (Portland)

Exit #	Services
37mm	**I-205 begins/ends on I-5. Exits 36-27 are in Washington.**
36	NE 134th St (from nb), **E** [gas] Chevron/dsl [lodging] Holiday Inn Express [other] [H], **W** [gas] 7-11, Arco, Mobil, Shell [food] Applebee's, Baskin-Robbins, Billygan's Roadhouse, Burger King, Burgerville, El Tapatio, Jack-in-the-Box, McDonald's, Muchas Gracias, Panda Express, Papa Murphy's, PizzaSchmitzza, Round Table Pizza, Starbucks, Subway, Taco Bell [lodging] La Quinta, Shilo Inn, Vancouver Inn [other] 99 RV Park, Albertson's, Fred Meyer, Safeway/dsl, Verizon, Walgreens
32	NE 83rd St, Andreson Rd, Battle Ground, **W** [gas] Shell/dsl/24hr [food] Burger King, Emporor Chinese, Krispy Kreme, Panda Express, Starbucks, Subway, Taco Bell, Taste of China, Weinerschnitzel, Wendy's [other] Costco/gas, Home Depot, vet
30c b a	WA 500, Orchards, Vancouver, **E** [gas] 76, Shell, Shell, USA [food] ABC Buffet, Applebee's, Burger King, Burgerville, DQ, Imperial Palace, KFC, McDonald's, Papa Murphy's, Subway, Wendy's [other] 7-11, GNC, Jo-Ann Crafts, Midas, Office Depot, PetCo, repair, Sportsman's Whse, Toyota, Walgreens, **W** [gas] 7-11/dsl, Chevron/dsl, Shell/dsl [food] Burgerville, ChuckeCheese, Golden Tent BBQ, Great Taste Chinese, Hometown Buffet, IHOP, Jack-in-the-Box, Jamba Juice, LaCosta Mexican, Muchas Gracias, Olive Garden, Outback Steaks, Popeyes, Red Lobster, Red Robin, RoundTable Pizza, Shari's, Starbucks, Subway, Taco Bell [lodging] Best Western, Comfort Suites, Day's Inn, Heathman Lodge, Holiday Inn Express, Howard Johnson's, Residence Inn, Staybridge Inn [other] $Tree, Americas Tire, auto repair, Barnes&Noble, GNC, JC Penney, Macy's, Old Navy, Petsmart, Ross, Target, TJ Maxx, URGENT CARE, Verizon
28	Mill Plain Rd, **E** [gas] 76, Chevron [food] Applebee's, Baskin-Robbins, Breakfast At Valerie's, Burger King, Burgerville, DQ, Elmer's Rest., Irishtown Grill, Jimmy John's, Kings Buffet, McDonald's, McGrath's Fish House, Muchas Gracias Mexican, Pizza Hut, Shari's, Starbucks, Starbucks, Sweet Tomatoes, Taco Bell, Yummy Mongolian [lodging] Best Western, DoubleTree Hotel, Extended Stay America, The Guesthouse Motel [other] $Tree, 7-11, Fred Meyer/dsl, O'Reilly Parts, PetCo, Schwab Tire, Trader Joe's, **W** [gas] 7-11, 76 [food] Arby's, Jack-in-the-Box, Little Caesar's, Subway [other] [H], auto/tire repair, Walgreens, Walmart/McDonald's
27	WA 14, Vancouver, Camas, Columbia River Gorge
25mm	Oregon/Washington state line. Columbia River. **Exits 27-36 are in Washington.**
24	122nd Ave, Airport Way, **E** [gas] 7-11/dsl [food] Burger King, China Wok, Dutch Bros Coffee, Jack-in-the-Box, McDonald's, Panera Bread, Shari's, Subway [lodging] Candlewood Suites, Clarion, Comfort Suites, Courtyard, Fairfield Inn, Hilton Garden, Holiday Inn Express, La Quinta, Shilo Inn/rest., SpringHill Suites, Staybridge

OR

= gas = food = lodging = other = rest stop

INTERSTATE 205 (Portland) Cont'd

PORTLAND AREA

24 Continued
Suites, Super 8 Home Depot, Michael's, **W** Buffalo Wild Wings, Famous Dave's, Red Robin Embassy Suites, Hampton Inn, Hyatt Place, Loft Hotel, Red Lion Hotel, Residence Inn, Sheraton/rest. Best Buy, Marshall's, PetsMart, Ross, Staples

23b a US 30 byp, Columbia Blvd, **E** Leather's Fuel/dsl, Shell/dsl Bill's Steaks, Elmer's Rest. Best Western, Comfort Inn, Econolodge, Quality Inn, Rodeway Inn, **W** Best Value Inn, Holiday Inn, Radisson, Ramada Inn

22 I-84 E, US 30 E, to The Dalles

21b I-84 W, US 30 W, to Portland

21a Glisan St, **E on NE 102nd St** 76, Arco Applebee's, Carl's Jr, Izzy's Pizza, Jamba Juice, Starbucks, Subway Fred Meyer, Kohl's, Office Depot, Ross, WinCo Foods

20 Stark St, Washington St, **E** 76/7-11, Chevron/dsl Arby's, Baja Fresh, Burger King, Denny's, Elmer's Rest., Hometown Buffet, Jack-in-the-Box, McMenamin's Rest., Old Chicago Pizza, Olive Garden, Panda Express, Portland Seafood Co, Red Robin, Saylor's, Starbucks, Subway, Village Inn Chestnut Tree Inn, Ramada $Tree, Big Lots, Home Depot, Target, Tuesday Morning, Verizon, **W** Stark St Pizza, Taco Bell Motel 6 7-11

19 US 26, Division St, **E** Space Age/dsl H, **W** Shell Burgerville, ChuckeCheese, McDonald's

17 Foster Rd

16 Johnson Creek Blvd, **W** 76, Arco Applebee's, Bajio, Burger King, Carl's Jr, Five Guys, Hog Wild BBQ, Jack-in-the-Box, Jimmy John's, Krispy Kreme, McDonald's, McDonald's, Outback Steaks, Panda Express, RoundTable Pizza, Starbucks, Taco Bell 7-11, Best Buy, Dick's, Firestone/auto, Fred Meyer/dsl, Home Depot, Knecht's Parts, O'Reilly Parts, PetsMart, RV Ctrs, Trader Joe's, Walgreens, Walmart/Subway

14 Sunnyside Rd, **E** 76/dsl A&W/KFC, Baja Fresh, Domino's, Gustav's Grill, Jersey Mike's, McMenamin's, Papa John's, Starbucks Clarion, Sunnyside Inn H, Office Depot,

14 Continued
W Chevron/dsl Burger King, CA Pizza Kitch Cheesecake Factory, Chick-fil-A, Chipotle, Claim Jumper, D e&Buster's, Denny's, DQ, Jimmy John's, McDonald's, Much Gracias, Noodles&Co, Old Spaghetti Factory, Olive Gard Panera Bread, Pieology Pizzaria, Pizza Hut, RAM Rest., R Robin, Stanford's Rest., Wendy's Courtyard, Monarch H tel/rest. Barnes&Noble, Discount Tire, Hobby Lobby, Penney, Kohl's, Macy's, Nordstroms, Old Navy, PetCo, REI, T get, U-Haul, Verizon, World Mkt

13 OR 224, to Milwaukie, **W** CarMax, Lowe's

12 OR 213, to Milwaukie, **E** Chevron/dsl, Pacific Pri Shell Denny's, Elmer's, KFC, McDonald's, New Cath Chinese, Pronto Pizza, Subway, Taco Bell, Wendy's Cla amas Inn, Hampton Inn $Tree, 7-11, Fred Meyer, USP **W** Comfort Suites

11 82nd Dr, Gladstone, **W** Arco, Chevron High Roc Rest., McDonald's, Starbucks, Subway Holiday Inn E press Harley-Davidson, Safeway

10 OR 213, Park Place, **E** Chevron/dsl H, Home Depot, Oregon Trail Ctr

9 OR 99E, Oregon City, **E** 76, Chevron/dsl KFC H, pair, Subaru, **W** La Hacienda Mexican, McDonald's, Shari Starbucks, Subway, Thai Rest. Best Western+ $Tre AT&T, Firestone/auto, Michael's, Rite Aid, Ross, URGENT CAR

8.5mm Willamette River

8 OR 43, W Linn, Lake Oswego, **E** 76 museu **W** Chevron/dsl, Shell/dsl Starbucks Mkt of Choic USPO, Verizon, vet

7mm viewpoint nb, hist marker

6 10th St, W Linn St, **E** Chevron/LP Five Guys, Ixta Mexican, McDonald's, McMenamin's Rest., Papa Murphy Willamette Coffee House Ace Hardware, Les Schwa **W** Biscuit's Cafe, Subway

4mm Tualatin River

3 Stafford Rd, Lake Oswego, **W** Wanker's Country Sto H

0mm **I-205 begins/ends on I-5, exit 288.**

NOTES

OR

PENNSYLVANIA

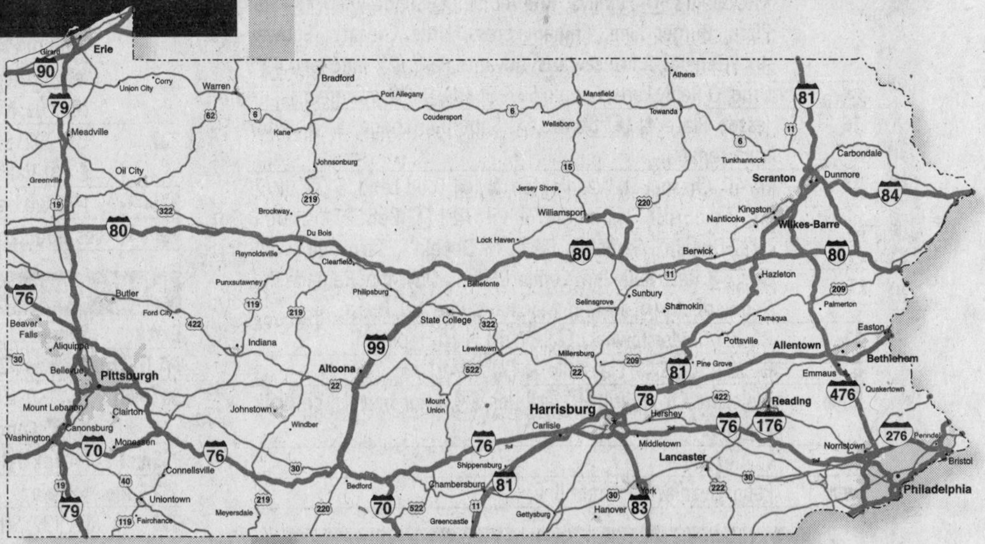

INTERSTATE 70

Exit #	Services
171mm	Pennsylvania/Maryland state line, **Welcome Ctr wb, full** facilities, info, litter barrels, petwalk, vending
168	US 522 N, Warfordsburg, **N** Fuel/dsl, **S** fireworks
163	PA 731 S, Amaranth
156	PA 643, Town Hill
153mm	eb, full facilities, litter barrels, petwalk, vending
151	PA 915, Crystal Spring, **N** auto repair, **S** Country Store/USPO
149	US 30 W, to Everett, S Breezewood (no immediate wb return), **3 mi S** McDonald's Wildwood Motel
147	US 30, Breezewood, **services on US 30** Exxon/dsl, FLYING J/Perkins/dsl/scales/24hr, Sheetz/dsl, Shell, Shell/Dunkin'/Subway/dsl, Sunoco/dsl, TA/Valero/Gateway Rest./Subway/dsl/scales/24hr/@ Bob Evans, Classic American Diner, Hardee's, McDonald's, Pizza Hut, Starbucks, Subplicity, Taco Bell Best Western, EconoLodge, Holiday Inn Express, Quality Inn, Wiltshire Motel Blue Beacon
I-70 and I-76/PA Tpk run together 71 mi. See I-76/PA Tpk exits 148mm-75.	
77	I-70 E runs with I-76/PA Turnpike eb
58	PA Tpk. I-70 E and I-76/PA Turnpike E run together.
57b a	I-70 W, US 119, PA 66 (**toll**), New Stanton, **N** Exxon, Sheetz/dsl BBG Grill, Bob Evans, Eat'n Park, McDonald's, Pagano's Rest., Pizza Hut, Subway, Szechuan Wok, Wendy's Budget Inn, Comfort Inn, Days Inn, EconoLodge, Fairfield Inn, Garden Inn, Hampton Inn, Motel 6, Super 8, **S** Marathon/dsl, Sunoco/dsl Cracker Barrel, La Tavola Ristorante $General, USPO
54	Madison, **N** KOA, **S** truck repair
53	Yukon
51b a	PA 31, West Newton, **S** Volvo/Mack
49	Smithton, **N** Citgo/rest./dsl/scales/@, FLYING J/Denny's/dsl/LP/scales/24hr/@
46b a	PA 51, Pittsburgh, **N** Sunoco/dsl Burger King Comfort Inn Buick/Cadillac/Chevrolet, Ford/Kia, Honda, **S** GetGo/dsl, PP/dsl Clubhouse Grille Budget Inn, Clarion golf
44	Arnold City
43b a	(43 from eb)PA 201, to PA 837, Fayette City, **S** Exxon/dsl A&W/LJ Silver, Burger King, Denny's, Domino's, Eat'n Park, Hibachi Buffet, Hoss' Rest., KFC, Little Bamboo, McDonald's, Old Mexico, Pizza Hut, Rita's Custard, Sonny's Grille, Starbucks, Subway, Taco Bell, Wendy's Candlewood Suites, Fairfield Inn, Hampton Inn, Holiday Inn Express $General, $Tree, Advance Parts, Aldi Foods, AT&T, BigLots, CVS Drug, Giant Eagle Foods, GNC, Jo-Ann Fabrics, Lowe's, NAPA, Staples, URGENT CARE, Verizon, Walmart
42a	Monessen
42	N Belle Vernon, **S** BP/McDonald's/7-11, Sunoco/dsl DQ
41	PA 906, Belle Vernon
40mm	Monongahela River
40	PA 88, Charleroi, **N** Gulf, Sunoco McDonald's, My Girl's Rest., Subway/TCBY Rite Aid, Valley Tire
39	Speers, **S** Exxon/dsl
37b a	PA 43 (**toll**), N to Pittsburgh, S to CA
36	Lover (from wb, no re-entry)
35	PA 481, Centerville
32b a	PA 917, Bentleyville, **S** BP/dsl, Pilot/DQ/Subway/dsl/scales/24hr Burger King, King's Rest., McDonald's, Pizza Hut Best Western, Holiday Inn Express $General, Advance Parts, AutoZone, Blue Beacon, Giant Eagle Foods, Rite Aid
31	to PA 136, Kammerer, **N** Carlton Motel
27	Dunningsville, **S** Avalon Motel
25	PA 519, to Eighty Four, **S** BP/7-11 Diner/dsl/24hr, Sunoco/dsl
21	I-79 S, to Waynesburg.
I-70 W and I-79 N run together 3.5 mi.	
20	PA 136, Beau St, **S** to Washington&Jefferson Coll
19b a	US 19, Murtland Ave, **N** BP/dsl, GetGo Applebee's, Arby's, Asahi Buffet, Buffalo Wild Wings, Chick-fil-A, Cracker Barrel, Five Guys, Fusion Steaks, Ichiban Steaks, Jimmy John's, Krispy Kreme, Longhorn Steaks, Max&Erma's, McDonald's, Moe's SW Grill, Noodles&Co, Olive Garden, Outback Steaks, Panera Bread, Penn Sta Subs, Plaza Azteca, Red Lobster, Red Robin, Rita's Custard, Starbucks, Subway, Taco Bell, TGIFriday's, TX Roadhouse, Wong's Wok, Zoup! SpringHill Suites $Tree, Aldi Foods, AT&T, Dick's, Field&Stream, Ford, Giant Eagle Foods, GNC, Hobby Lobby, Honda, Hyundai, Kohl's, Lowe's, Mercedes, Michael's, Nissan, PetCo, Petsmart, Sam's Club/gas, Save-A-Lot Foods, Target, Toyota, URGENT CARE, Verizon, Walmart/McDonald's, **S** BP/dsl, Exxon/dsl, Sunoco, Sunoco/dsl A&W/LJ Silver, Bob Evans, Donut Connection, Dunkin', Eat'n Park, Grand China, KFC, Old Mexico, Papa John's, Pizza Hut, Waffle House Hampton Inn, Motel 6, BigLots, Buick/GMC, Chevrolet, Firestone/auto, Home Depot, Jo-Ann Fabrics, Mazda, Pepboys, Staples, Subaru
18	I-79 N, to Pittsburgh.
I-70 E and I-79 S run together 3.5 mi.	

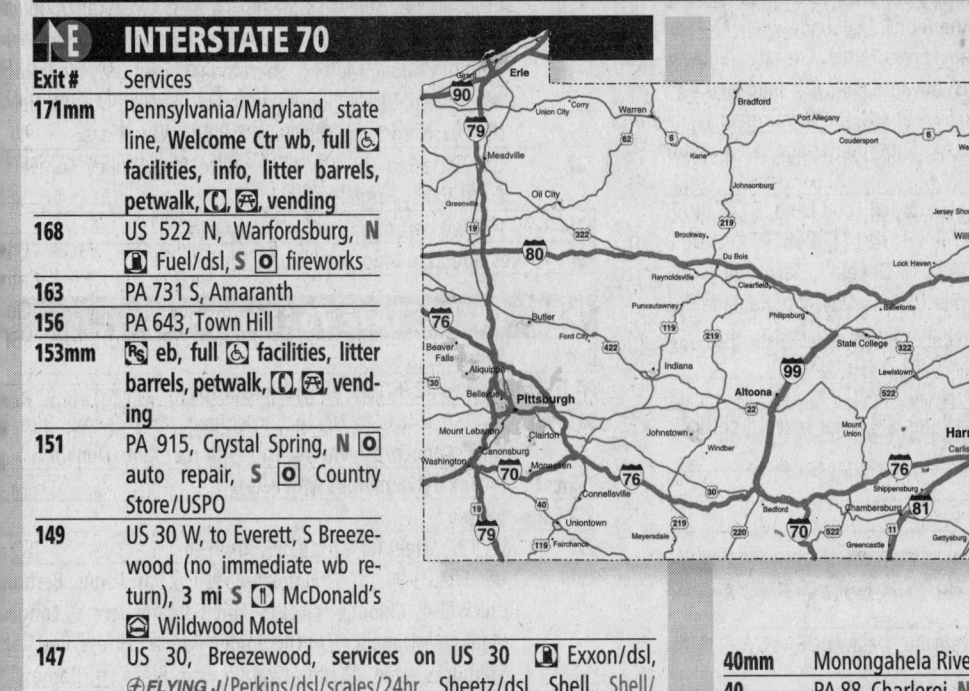

WASHINGTON

INTERSTATE 70 Cont'd

Exit #	Services
17	PA 18, Jefferson Ave, Washington, N GetGo/dsl DQ, McDonald's Family$, Rite Aid, S Sunoco/dsl 4Star Pizza, Burger King, China Express, Little Caesar's, Subway $General, Advance Parts, Advance Parts (2), AutoZone, CVS Drug, O'Reilly Parts, Shop'n Save Foods, USPO, Walgreens
16	Jessop Place, N Dean's Suburban Lodge, S auto/truck repair
15	US 40, Chesnut St, Washington, N Food Land, S BP/7-11, Exxon/dsl, Marathon, Sunoco/dsl Bob Evans, Denny's, Dunkin', Garfield's Rest., McDonald's, Taco Bell, Wendy's Best Value Inn, Comfort Suites, Days Inn, Ramada Inn, Red Roof Inn Jo-Ann, Marshalls, Rite Aid, Ross
11	PA 221, Taylorstown, N BP/dsl, S repair
6	PA 231, to US 40, Claysville, N BP/dsl
5mm	**Welcome Ctr eb, full facilities, litter barrels, petwalk, vending**
1	W Alexander
0mm	Pennsylvania/Ohio state line

PHILADELPHIA

INTERSTATE 76

Exit #	Services
354mm	Pennsylvania/New Jersey state line, Delaware River, Walt Whitman Br
351	Front St, I-95 (from wb), N to Trenton, S to Chester
350	Packer Ave, 7th St, to I-95 (from eb), S Holiday Inn to sports complex
349	to I-95, PA 611, Broad St, N Citgo Talk of the Town
348	PA 291, W to Chester (exits left from wb)
347a	to I-95 S (exits left from wb)
347b	Passyunk Ave, Oregon Ave, N Burger King, KFC, Little Caesar's, McDonald's, Pizza Hut BJ's Whse, Home Depot, Ross, ShopRite, S FDR Park
346c	28th St, Vare Ave, Mifflin St (from wb)
346b	Grays Ferry Ave, University Ave, N Fresh Grocer, Little Caesar's, McDonald's H, USPO, S 76, Speedway/dsl Dunkin'
346a	South St (exits left from wb)
345	30th St, Market St, downtown
344	I-676 E, US 30 E, to Philadelphia (no return from eb), N LDS Temple
343	Spring Garden St, Haverford
342	US 13, US 30 W, Girard Ave, N E Fairmount Park, S Philadelphia Zoo
341	Montgomery Dr, W River Dr, W Fairmount Park, S W Fairmount Park
340b	US 1 N, Roosevelt Blvd, to Philadelphia
339	US 1 S, S CA Pizza Kitchen, Chili's, Chipotle Mexican, Houlihans, PeiWei Asian, Starbucks, TGIFriday's Dave's Hotel Target, Verizon
340a	Lincoln Dr, Kelly Dr, to Germantown
338	Belmont Ave, Green Lane, S 76, Sunoco UHaul, WaWa
337	Hollow Rd (from wb), Gladwyne
332	PA 23 (from wb), Conshohocken, N Marriott
331b a	I-476, PA 28 (from eb), to Chester, Conshohocken
330	PA 320, Gulph Mills, S to Villanova U
329	Weadley Rd (from wb), N Exxon
328b a	US 202 N, to King of Prussia, N Exxon/dsl, Lukoil, Shell, Sunoco, WaWa Bahama Breeze, Baja Fresh, Burger King, CA Pizza Kitchen, Capital Grille, Champp's, Cheesecake Factory,
328b a	Continued Chili's, Fox&Hound, Hooters, Joe's Crabshack, Maggiano's, M ton's Steaks, Panera Bread, Red Lobster, Ruby's Diner, Rut Chris Steaks, Sullivan's Steaks Best Western, Doubletr Fairfield Inn, Hampton Inn, Holiday Inn Express, Hyatt, Inn King of Prussia, Motel 6, Sheraton Best Buy, Blooming le's, Costco, Dick's, Home Depot, Lord&Taylor, Macy's, Neim Marcus, Nordstrom, Old Navy, S Crowne Plaza
327	US 202 S, to US 420 W, Goddard Blvd, Valley Forge Pa E Valley Forge Park
326	I-76 wb becomes I-76/PA Tpk to Ohio

For I-76 westbound to Ohio, see I-76/PA Turnpike.

INTERSTATE 76 (Turnpike)

Exit #	Services
	PA Tpk runs wb as I-276/I-95, eb ends on NJ Tpk.
6a (I-95)	US 130 exit is in NJ, to Bordentown, N $Tree, Rite A S Conoco/dsl, WaWa/dsl Burger King, Dunkin'
355mm	**PA Tpk/I-276 merges with I-95 N**
352.5mm	**toll plaza**
352	PA 132, Street Rd, EZ tag only, from eb
351	US 1, to I-95, to Philadelphia, N Bar Louie, Bertucc Chick-fil-A, Chipotle, Cracker Barrel, Jimmy John's, Longh Steaks, McDonald's, On The Border, Panda Express, Red Rob Starbucks, Uno, Wendy's Crowne Plaza Barnes&N ble, Buick/GMC, CVS Drug, Home Depot, Lowes Wh Target, Walmart, S 7-11/dsl, Classic/wash, Sunoc dsl Dunkin' Best Western, Comfort Inn, Courtya Hampton Inn, Knights Inn, Neshaminy Inn, Quality Inn, Rad son, Red Roof Inn Indian Motorcycles, Toyota
343	PA 611, Willow Grove, N BP/dsl, Shell/dsl, Speedway/c Sunoco Carrabba's, Dunkin', Sonic Courtyard, Fa field Inn, SpringHill Suites 7-11, Home Depot, Lexus, N S Bonefish Grill, China Garden, Domino's, Dunkin', Oo Japanese, Tony Roni's Pizza Hampton Inn 7-11, Au Infiniti, Best Buy, PepBoys, repair, Staples, transmissions
340	to VA Dr, EZ tag only, from wb, no trucks, WaWa/dsl, tagholder only
339	PA 309, Ft Washington, N LukOil/dsl Friendly's, Su way Best Western, Hilton Garden, Holiday Inn Expre BMW, Mercedes, Volvo, WaWa
334	PA Tpk NE Extension, I-476, S to Philadelphia, N to Allentow
333	Germantown Pike, to Norristown, N Lukoil, Sunoco A teca, Bertucci's, California Pizza Kitchen, Chipotle, Da e&Buster's, Dunkin', Elevation Burger, PF Chang's, Red Sto Grill, Starbucks, Zoup! Courtyard, DoubleTree, Extend Stay America, SpringHill Suites H, Boscov's, Verizo Whole Foods, S LukOil
328mm	**King of Prussia Service Plaza wb,** Sunoco/dsl/24 Burger King, Starbucks
	PA Tpk runs eb as I-276, wb as I-76.
326	I-76 E, to US 202, I-476, Valley Forge, N Shell Rad son, S Exxon, LukOil, Shell, Sunoco, WaWa CA Piz Kitchen, Cheesecake Factory, Chili's, Hooters, Maggiano's, R Lobster, Ruth's Chris Steaks, Sullivan Steaks Best Wester Hampton Inn, Holiday Inn Express, Hyatt, Inn of King of Pruss Motel 6, Sheraton Best Buy, Costco, Dick's, Home Dep Macy's, Neiman Marcus, Nordstrom, Walmart, Wegman's
325mm	**Valley Forge Service Plaza eb,** Sunoco/dsl/24hr La son Grill, Starbucks

PA

E INTERSTATE 76 (Turnpike) Cont'd

Exit #	Services
312	PA 100, to Downingtown, Pottstown, N WaWa/dsl CarSense, Harley-Davidson, S Sunoco/dsl, WaWa Applebee's, Chick-fil-A, Isaac's Deli, Red Robin, Starbucks, Uno Grill, Wendy's Clarion, Comfort Suites, Extended Stay America, Fairfield Inn, Hampton Inn, Hilton Garden, Residence Inn Giant Foods, Target, Walgreens
305mm	**Camiel Service Paza wb,** Sunoco/dsl/24hr Roy Rogers, Starbucks
298	I-176, PA 10, to Reading, Morgantown, N Arby's, DQ, Dunkin', Sonic, Subway USA Inn $Tree, AutoZone, Lowe's, Mavis Tire, Verizon, Walmart, S Exxon, Sheetz/dsl McDonald's, Rita's Custard Holiday Inn Chevrolet, Rite Aid, USPO
290mm	**Bowmansville Service Plaza eb,** Sunoco/dsl/24hr Burger King, Hershey's, Starbucks
286	US 322, PA 272, to Reading, Ephrata, N Citgo/dsl Baskin-Robbins/Dunkin', Park Place Diner, Subway, Zia Maria's Eatery Black Horse Inn/rest., S Turkey Hill Comfort Inn, Econolodge, Hampton Inn (11mi), Red Carpet Inn, Red Roof Inn
266	PA 72, to Lebanon, Lancaster, N Speedway/dsl, Sunoco/Chester's Comfort Inn Holiday Inn Express (17 mi) H, auto repair, Harley-Davidson, NAPA, S Hampton Inn Mt Hope Winery, Pinch Pond Camping
259mm	**Lawn Service Plaza wb,** Sunoco/dsl/24hr Burger King, Starbucks RV dump
250mm	**Highspire Service Plaza eb,** Sunoco/dsl/24hr Starbucks, Steak'n Shake
247	I-283, PA 283, to Harrisburg, Harrisburg East, Hershey, N Exxon/dsl, Sheetz/dsl, Sunoco Bob Evans, Capitol Diner, Chick-fil-A, Chili's, Five Guys, Friendly's, Gilligan's Steaks, McDonald's, Moe's SW, Subway, Taco Bell, Wendy's Best Western, Courtyard, Harrisburg Hotel, Holiday Inn, La Quinta, Red Lion, Red Roof Inn, Sheraton, Sleep Inn, Super 8 GNC, Harrisburg East Camping, JC Penney, Kia, Petco, Target, Verizon
246mm	Susquehannah River
242	I-83, Harrisburg West, N Shell/dsl, Speedway, Sunoco Bob Evans, John's Diner, McDonald's, Pizza Hut Best Western, Budget Inn, Clarion Inn, Fairfield Inn, Holiday Inn Express, La Quinta, Motel 6, Quality Inn, Scottish Inn vet, S Rutter's/dsl Days Inn, Red Carpet Inn
236	US 15, to Gettysburg, Gettysburg Pike, Harrisburg, N Exxon, Gulf/dsl Isaac's Rest, Marzoni's, McDonald's, Papa John's, Peppermill Rest, Subway, Subway (2) Comfort Inn, Country Inn&Suites, Courtyard, EconoLodge, Hampton Inn, Homewood Suites, TownePlace Suites H, U-Haul, vet, S Sheetz Arby's, Bros Pizza, Burger King, Cracker Barrel, Subway, Wendy's Motel 6, Wingate Inn $Tree, Giant Food/gas, GNC, Rite Aid
226	US 11, to I-81, to Harrisburg, Carlisle, N FLYING J/Denny's/dsl/LP/scales/24hr/@, Gulf/dsl, Loves/Wendy's/dsl/scales/24hr, Petro/Iron Skillet/dsl/scales/24hr/@, Pioneer/dsl, Sunoco/Subway/dsl Arby's, Bob Evans, Carelli's Subs, Dunkin', Embers Steaks, McDonald's, Middlesex Diner, Rte 11 Diner, Waffle House Best Value Inn, Days Inn, EconoLodge, Hampton Inn, Hotel Carlisle, Knights Inn, Quality Inn, Red Roof Inn, Residence Inn, Rodeway Inn, Super 8, Travelodge Blue Beacon, S Rutter's/dsl Hoss' Rest. Best Western, Holiday Inn Express, Motel 6 H, U-Haul, vet

HARRISBURG

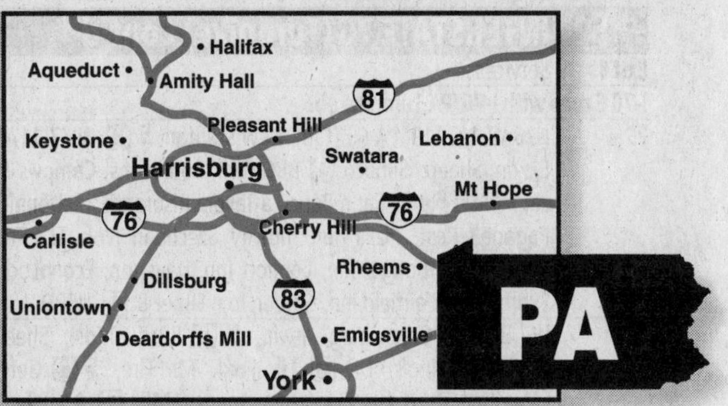

Exit #	Services
219mm	**Plainfield Service Plaza eb,** Sunoco/dsl/24hr Hershey's Ice Cream, Roy Rogers, Starbucks
203mm	**Blue Mtn Service Plaza wb,** Sunoco/dsl/24hr Hershy's Ice Cream, Pizza Hut, Roy Rogers, Starbucks
201	PA 997, to Shippensburg, Blue Mountain, S Kenmar Motel auto/truck repair
199mm	Blue Mountain Tunnel
197mm	Kittatinny Tunnel
189	PA 75, Willow Hill, S Double Dip Drive-In, Pizza Star Willow Hill Motel/rest.
187mm	Tuscarora Tunnel
180	US 522, Mt Union, Ft Littleton, N Cutchall's/dsl, Noname/dsl The Family Rest. Downes Motel
172mm	**Sideling Service Plaza both lanes,** Sunoco/dsl/24hr Burger King, Famiglia Pizza, Hershey's, Popeye's, Starbucks
161	US 30, Breezewood, **Services N on US 30** Exxon/dsl, FLYING J/Perkins/dsl/scales/24hr, Sheetz/dsl, Shell, Shell/Dunkin'/Subway/dsl, Sunoco/dsl, TA/Valero/Gateway Rest./Subway/dsl/scales/24hr/@ Bob Evans, Classic American Diner, Hardee's, McDonald's, Pizza Hut, Starbucks, Subplicity, Taco Bell Best Western, EconoLodge, Holiday Inn Express, Quality Inn, Wiltshire Motel Blue Beacon
161mm	**I-70 W and I-76/PA Turnpike W run together.**
148mm	**Midway Service Plaza both lanes,** Sunoco/dsl/24hr Sbarro's, Starbucks, Steak'n Shake
146	I-99, US 220, Bedford, N GetGo/McDonald's/dsl, PP/dsl, Sheetz/dsl/24hr, Shell/Subway/dsl Bedford Diner, Clara's Place, Denny's, Ed's Steaks, Hoss' Rest., LJ Silver, Pizza Hut, Salsa's Mexican, Wendy's Best Value Inn, Budget Host, Fairfield Inn, Quality Inn, Rodeway Inn, Travelodge Blue Knob SP (15mi), to Shawnee SP (10mi), S Hampton Inn
123mm	Allegheny Tunnel
112mm	**Somerset Service Plaza both lanes,** Sunoco/dsl/24hr Burger King, Pizza Hut, Popeye's, Starbucks
110	PA 601, to US 219, Somerset, N KwikFill/dsl, Sheetz Hoss' Rest., King's Rest., Pizza Hut $Inn, Economy Inn Advance Parts, Ford, tires, S Somerset TravelCtr/dsl/@, Tesla EVC, Turkey Hill Arby's, Bruster's Ice Cream, DQ, Eat'n Park, KFC, LJ Silver, McDonald's, Pine Grill, Ruby Tuesday, Starbucks, Subway, Summit Diner, Wendy's Budget Host, Budget Inn, Comfort Inn, Days Inn, Econolodge, Hampton Inn, Holiday Inn Express, Quality Inn, Super 8 Harley-Davidson
91	PA 711, PA 31, to Ligonier, Donegal, N Tall Cedars Rest., S BP/McDonald's, Sunoco/dsl DQ, Subway Days Inn, Holiday Inn Express camping, golf
78mm	**New Stanton Service Plaza wb,** Sunoco/dsl/24hr Burger King, Hershey's Ice Cream, Quiznos, Starbucks

BREEZEWOOD

INTERSTATE 76 (Turnpike) Cont'd

Exit #	Services
	I-70 E runs with I-76/PA Turnpike eb.
75	I-70 W, US 119, PA 66 (toll), New Stanton, S BP/7-11/dsl, Exxon, Sheetz, Sunoco BBG Grill, Bob Evans, Campy's Pizza, Cracker Barrel, Eat'n Park, La Tavola Risorante, McDonald's, Pagano's Rest., Pizza Hut, Subway, Szechuan Wok, TJ's Rest., Wendy's Budget Inn, Comfort Inn, Days Inn, EconoLodge, Express Inn, Fairfield Inn, Garden Inn, Super 8 USPO
67	US 30, to Greensburg, Irwin, N BP/7-11/dsl, Sheetz/dsl Domino's, DQ Ford, Mr Tire, S GetGo, Marathon/7-11/dsl, Sheetz/dsl, Sunoco/24hr Applebee's, Arby's, Atria's, Bob Evans, Burger King, Denny's, Double Wide Grill, Dunkin', Eat'n Park, Fire Pit Grill, Five Guys, KFC, Little Caesar's, McDonald's, Panera Bread, Pizza Hut, Starbucks, Subway, Taco Bell, Wendy's Hampton Inn, Holiday Inn Express $Tree, Advance Parts, Aldi Foods, AT&T, Giant Eagle Foods/24hr, GNC, Kohl's, Rite Aid, Target, Verizon, Walgreens, Walmart
61mm	parking area eb
57	I-376, US 22, to Pittsburgh, Monroeville, S Marathon, Sheetz, Sunoco Arby's, Blaze Pizza, Chick-fil-A, China Palace, Chipotle, Denny's, El Campesino, Five Guys, Golden Corral, Max&Erma's, McDonald's, Outback Steaks, Panda Express, Panera Bread, Penn Sta Subs, Primanti Bros, Red Lobster, Starbucks, Subway, Taco Bell, Wendy's Comfort Suites, Courtyard, Day's Inn, Extended Stay America, Hampton Inn, Holiday Inn Express, Red Roof Inn AT&T, Big Lots, CVS Drug, GNC, Honda, Lowes Whse, Marshall's, NTB, Old Navy, Pet Land, PetCo, Rite Aid, to Heinz Field, URGENT CARE
49mm	Oakmont Service Plaza eb, Sunoco/dsl/e85/24hr Burger King, Starbucks litter barrels
48.5mm	Allegheny River
48	PA 28, to Pittsburgh, Allegheny Valley, New Kensington, N Exxon, Sunoco Rite Aid, S GetGo, Marathon/dsl, Sheetz/dsl Bob Evans, Burger King, Denny's, Dunkin', Gino Bro's Pizza, KFC, McDonald's, Pizza Hut, Primanti Bros, Subway, Wendy's Day's Inn, Hampton Inn, Holiday Inn Express, Quality Inn, TownePlace Suites, Valley Motel Advance Parts, AutoZone, Ford, Target
41mm	parking area/call box eb
39	PA 8, to Pittsburgh, Butler Valley, 0-1 mi N Exxon, GetGo, Sheetz/dsl, Sunoco Applebee's, Atria's Rest., Bruno's Pizza, Buffalo Wild Wings, Eat'n Park, King's Rest., McDonald's, Starbucks, Taco Bell, Wendy's Quality Inn $Tree, Advance Parts, Chrysler/Dodge/Jeep, Dunkin', Giant Eagle Foods, GNC, Kohl's, Lowes Whse, Petco, Shop'n Save Foods, Target, TJ Maxx, USPO, Walmart/Subway, S BP, Sunoco/dsl Arby's, Bruster's, Burger King, China Bistro, Domino's, KFC, Little Caesar's, McDonald's, Panera Bread, Pasquales Pizza, Pizza Hut, Primanti Bros, Starbucks, Subway, Vocelli Pizza AT&T, AutoZone, CVS Drug, Firestone/auto, Home Depot, Mr. Tire, NTB, O'Reilly Parts, Pepboys, Rite Aid, USPO
31mm	Toll Plaza wb
28	to I-79, to Cranberry, Pittsburgh, N BP/7-11/dsl, GetGo, Marathon/dsl, Sheetz/dsl, Sunoco/dsl Aladdin's Eatery, Arby's, Bob Evans, Boston Mkt, Bravo Italian, Buffalo Wild Wings, Burger King, Chipotle Mexican, Denny's, Domino's, Dunkin', Dynasty, Eat'n Park, Emiliano's, Firehouse Subs, Five Guys, HotDog Shoppe, Houlihan's, Ichiban Steakhouse, Jason's Deli, Jersey Mike's, Jimmy John's, Mad Mex, Max-&Erma's, McDonald's, Monte Cello's Grill, Panda Express,
28	Continued Panera Bread, Perkins, Pizza Hut, Pizza Roma, Primanti Bro Saga Steaks, Subway, Vocelli Pizza, Wendy's Candlewoo Suites, Clarion, Comfort Inn, Doubletree, Hampton Inn, Hya Place, Motel 6, Quality Inn, Red Roof Inn, Residence Inn, Sup 8, Woodspring Suites $Tree, Aldi Foods, AT&T, AutoZon Barnes&Noble, Best Buy, Costco/gas, Field&Stream, Fireston auto, Giant Eagle Foods, GNC, Home Depot, Jo-Ann Fabric Marshall's, Michael's, NAPA, PepBoys, Petco, Rite Aid, Toyot Tuesday Morning, USPO, Verizon, Walgreens, Walmart
23.5mm	pulloff eb
17mm	parking area eb
13.4mm	parking area eb
13mm	Beaver River
13	PA 8, to Ellwood City, Beaver Valley, N Al's Corner Subway Beaver Falls Motel, Lark Motel, Park Inn S Super 8
10	PA 60 (toll), to New Castle, Pittsburgh, S to
6mm	pulloff eb
2mm	pulloff eb
1mm	toll plaza eb, toll plaza eb
0mm	Pennsylvania/Ohio state line

PITTSBURGH

CRANBERRY

INTERSTATE 78

Exit #	Services
77mm	Pennsylvania/New Jersey state line, Delaware River
76mm	Welcome Ctr wb, toll booth wb, full facilities, litter barrel petwalk, vending
75	to PA 611, Easton, N TurkeyHill/dsl Dunkin', McDonald's (1mi), Subway Crayola Factory, CVS Drug, S Exxon/dsl
71	PA 33, to Stroudsburg, 1 mi N on Freemansburg Ave Chipotle, CJT Asian, Frank's Pizza, MOD Pizza, Panera Bread, Ruby Tuesday, Starbucks, TGIFriday's, TX Roadhouse, Wayback Burgers Courtyard Barnes&Noble, Best Buy, Dick's, Lowe's, Michael's, Pet Supplies+, ShopRite Mkt, Staples, Verizon
67	PA 412, Hellertown, N TurkeyHill/gas Wendy's Comfort Suites (3mi) Chevrolet, S Citgo/dsl, Exxon/dsl, Sunoco Bella's Ristorante, Dunkin', Papa John's, Rocco Pizza, Roma Pizza, Vassi's Drive-In, Waffle House Holiday Inn Express 7-11, CVS Drug, repair
60b a	PA 145 N, PA 309 S, South Fort St, Quakertown
59	to PA 145 (from eb), Summit Lawn
58	Emaus St (from wb), S Gulf $General
57	Lehigh St, N Sunoco/dsl, WaWa/dsl Arby's, China House, Dunkin', IHOP, Palumbo Pizza, Queen City Diner, Subway, Willy Joe's Rest. Red Roof Inn $Tree, AAA, BigLots, CVS Drug, Family$, Ford/Lincoln, Home Depot, Infiniti, Kia, Mavis Tires/repair, Redner's Whse, Toyota, VW, S Sunoco, TurkeyHill, Valero A1 Japanese, Bangkok, Brass Rail Rest., Domino's, Dunkin', McDonald's, Papa John's, Perkins, Pizza Hut/Taco Bell, Rodizio Grill, Rossi's Pizza, Starbucks, Subway, Tilted Kilt Eatery, Wendy's Acura, AT&T, Audi/Mercedes/Porsche, BonTon, Bottom$ Mkt, Buick/GMC, Cadillac, Chevrolet, Chrysler/Dodge/Jeep, Honda, Hyundai, Kost Tire, Mazda, Midas, Ross, Staples, SteinMart, Verizon, Volvo, Williams Tire/auto
55	PA 29, Cedar Crest Blvd, N Shell, S
54b a	US222, Hamilton Blvd, N Speedway, WaWa/dsl Bamboo Asian, Baskin-Robbins/Dunkin', Boston Mkt, Carrabba's, Gourmet Buffet, Ice Cream World, McDonald's, Menchie's, Perkin

ALLENTOWN

PA

INTERSTATE 78 Cont'd

54b a	Continued Pizza Hut, Subway, TGIFriday's, Wendy's Holiday Inn Express, Howard Johnson Dorney Funpark, Office Depot, Rite Aid, USPO, Weis Foods, **S** WaWa Dunkin', Hunan Springs Holiday Inn Audi, Costco/gas, Subaru, Target
53	PA 309 (wb only)
51	to I-476, US 22 E, PA 33 N (eb only), Whitehall
49b a	PA 100, Fogelsville, **N** Arby's, Cracker Barrel, LJ Silver, Panda&Fish Chinese, Pizza Hut, Steak'n Shake, Windsor Deli Comfort Inn, Hawthorn Inn KOA (7mi), Mavis Tire/repair, Rite Aid, **S** Shell/Dunkin', Sunoco, WaWa/dsl Arooga's Grill, Burger King, Florence Italian, Starlite Diner, Taco Bell, Yocco's Hotdogs Allentown Park Hotel, Hilton Garden, Holiday Inn, Sleep Inn, Staybridge Suites Clover Hill Winery, st police, Toyota
45	PA 863, to Lynnport, **N** Exxon/dsl, Sunoco/New Smithville Diner/dsl truck service, **S** Demarco's Italian Super 8
40	PA 737, Krumsville, **N** Pine Hill Campground, Robin Hill RV Park (4mi)
35	PA 143, Lenhartsville, **3 mi S** Robin Hill Park
30	Hamburg, **S** Hamburg Mkt
29b a	PA 61, to Reading, Pottsville, **N** Shell/dsl, WaWa/dsl Baskin-Robbins/Dunkin', Burger King, Cracker Barrel, Five Guys, JA Buffet, LJ Silver/Taco Bell, Logan's Roadhouse, McDonald's, Pizza Hut, Red Robin, Starbucks, Wendy's Microtel $Tree, Advance Parts, Aldi, AT&T, Boat'n RV Ctr RV, Cabela's Outdoor, GNC, Harley-Davidson (8mi), Hyundai, Lowe's, Pet Supplies+, Russell Stover, Toyota, Verizon, Walmart/Subway
23	Shartlesville, **N** Chromeshop/dsl, Loves/McDonald's/Subway/dsl/scales/24hr Dunkin' Dutch Motel Appalachian Campsites, **S** Blue Mtn Family Rest. Motel 6 antiques, camping, Dutch Haus/gifts, USPO
19	PA 183, Strausstown, **N** Sheepskin Mkt, **S** Power/dsl
17	PA 419, Rehrersburg, **N** US Gas truck/tire repair
16	Midway, **N** Exxon/dsl, Sunoco/dsl J&S Pizza, Midway Diner Quality Inn
15	Grimes
13	PA 501, Bethel, **N** Valero/dsl, **S** Bethel/dsl, Sheetz/dsl dsl repair, USPO
10	PA 645, Frystown, **S** FLYING J/Huddle House/Subway/dsl/scales/24hr/@ Travel Inn
6	(8 from wb, US 22)PA 343, Fredricksburg, **1 mi S** PP/dsl, Redner's Whse/mkt Esther's Rest. KOA (5mi)

I-81. I-78 begins/ends on I-81, exit 89.

INTERSTATE 79

Exit #	Services
183b a	PA 5, 12th St, Erie, **E** H, Valley Tire, **W** Country Fair/dsl, Gulf/dsl Applebee's, Arby's, Bob Evans, Bruster's, Chipotle, Domino's, Dunkin', El Canelo Mexican, Five Guys, Hibachi Japanese, IHOP, Jimmy John's, KFC, McDonald's, Moe's SW Grill, Panera Bread, Pizza Hut, Popeye's, Serafini's, Starbucks, Taco Bell, Tim Hortons, Wendy's Comfort Inn (2mi) $General, $Tree, Advance Parts, Aldi Foods, BigLots, CVS Drug, Dunn Tire, Family$, Giant Eagle Foods, GNC, Save-a-Lot Foods, Tires-4-Less, to Presque Isle SP, Tuesday Morning, U-Haul, Verizon, vet
182	US 20, 26th St, **E** Country Fair/dsl, KwikFill Subway H, CVS Drug, Family$, Tops Foods/gas/24hr, **W** Country Fair/dsl Arby's, Burger King, DQ, Hong Kong Chinese,

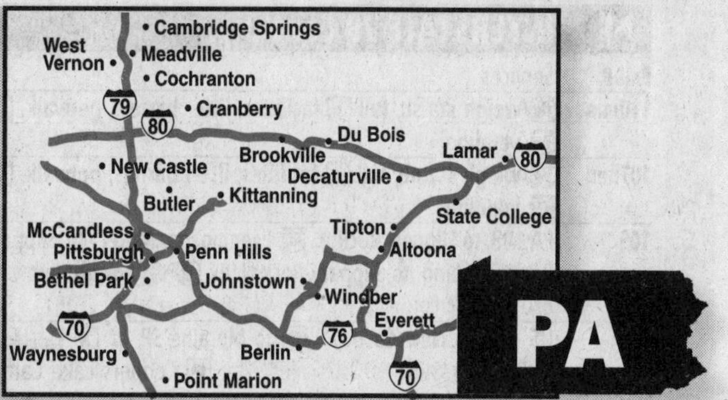

182	Continued Hoss's Steaks, Hungry Howie's, Little Caesar's, LJ Silver, McDonald's, Pizza Pete's, Subway, Tim Hortons Glass House Inn $General, AT&T, AutoZone, Ford, Giant Eagle Foods, Monro, O'Reilly Parts, TrueValue, URGENT CARE, USPO, vet, Volvo
180	US 19, to Kearsarge, **E** Aoyama Japanese, Arby's, Buffalo Wild Wings, Cheddar's, Coldstone, Firebirds Grill, Fox&Hound, KFC, Mad Mex, Max&Erma's, McDonald's, Moe's SW Grill, O'Charley's, Olive Garden, Outback Steaks, Primanti Bros, Red Lobster, Smokey Bones BBQ, Sonic, Starbucks, Wendy's Candlewood Suites, Fairfield Inn, Homewood Suites, SpringHill Suites, TownePlace Suites H, Audi/Cadillac, Barnes&Noble, Chrysler/Dodge/Jeep, Dick's, Field & Stream, Firestone/auto, JC Penney, Macy's, Michael's, Petco, Rite Aid, Ross, TJ Maxx, Toyota, Verizon, **W** Country Fair/dsl
178b a	I-90, E to Buffalo, W to Cleveland
174	to McKean, **E** access to gas/dsl, **W** KOA
166	US 6N, to Edinboro, **E** Country Fair/dsl, Sheetz McDonald's (3mi), TacoBell (2mi), Wendy's Comfort Suites Advance Parts, vet, Walmart/Subway
163mm	**both lanes, full facilities, litter barrels, petwalk, , , vending**
154	PA 198, to Saegertown, Conneautville, **E** Erie NWR (17mi)
147b a	US 6, US 19, US 322, to Meadville, **E** Country Fair/dsl, GetGo, Sheetz/dsl Applebee's, Arby's, Chovy's Italian, Cracker Barrel, DQ, Five Guys, Hoss's Rest., KFC, Perkins, Pizza Hut, Subway, Super China, Taco Bell EconoLodge, Holiday Inn Express H, Advance Parts, AT&T, Family$, Giant Eagle Foods, Home Depot, Jo-Ann Fabrics, Save-a-Lot Foods, **W** Sheetz/dsl Burger King, Compadres Mexican, King's Rest., McDonald's, Red Lobster, Subway, Tim Hortons, Yuen's Garden Hampton Inn, Quality Inn $Tree, Aldi Foods, AutoZone, Buick/GMC, Chevrolet, GNC, to Pymatuning SP, Toyota, URGENT CARE, Verizon, Walmart/Subway
141	PA 285, to Geneva, **E** to Erie NWR (20mi), **W** Aunt Bee's Rest./dsl, Citgo/dsl
135mm	**/weigh sta both lanes, full facilities, litter barrels, petwalk, , , vending**
130	PA 358, to Sandy Lake, **W** H (13mi), to Goddard SP
121	US 62, to Mercer, **E** Valley Tire, **W** Sunoco/dsl st police
116b a	I-80, E to Clarion, W to Sharon
113	PA 208, PA 258, to Grove City, **E** Country Fair/dsl, Marathon/dsl Compadres Mexican H, **W** KwikFill/Subway, Sheetz/dsl, Tesla EVC Eat'n Park, Hoss' Rest., McDonald's, My Bro's Place, Palato's Italian, Primanti Bros, Taco Bell, Timber Creek Rest., Wendy's Best Western, Candlewood Suites, Comfort Inn, Hampton Inn, Holiday Inn Express, Microtel, Super 8, TownePlace Suites KOA (3mi), Premium Outlets/famous brands

MEADVILLE

PA

INTERSTATE 79 Cont'd

Exit #	Services
110mm	/weigh sta sb, full facilities, litter barrels, petwalk, , , vending
107mm	/weigh sta nb, full facilities, litter barrels, petwalk, , , vending
105	PA 108, to Slippery Rock, E Evening Star Motel Slippery Rock Camping, to Slippery Rock U, W Loves/Subway/dsl/scales24hr
99	US 422, to New Castle, E to Moraine SP, W Pilot/McDonald's/Subway/dsl/scales/24hr Coopers Lake Camping, to Rose Point Camping
96	PA 488, Portersville, E Bear Run Camping, Moraine SP, W Marathon/dsl Brown's Country Kitchen McConnell's Mill SP (3mi), USPO
88	(87 from nb) US 19, PA 68, Zelienople, W Exxon/dsl Burger King, Fox's Pizza, Log Cabin Inn Rest., Pizza Hut
85	(83 from nb), PA 528 (no quick return), to Evans City, W Buick/GMC
83	PA 528, Evans City
80mm	weigh sta both lanes
78	(76 from nb, exits left from nb), US 19, PA 228, to Mars, access to I-76, PA TPK, E GetGo/dsl, Gulf/7-11/dsl Anthony's Pizza, Applebee's, Chick-fil-A, Cracker Barrel, DiBella's Subs, Firebirds, Jimmy Wan's Chinese, Juniper Grill, Longhorn Steaks, McDonald's, Moe's SW Grill, Noodles&Co, Olive Garden, Patron Mexican, Red Robin, River City Grille, Smokey Bones BBQ, Starbucks, Subway Best Western+, Courtyard, Hilton Garden, Home 2 Suites, Marriott, TownePlace Suites Dick's, GNC, Kohl's, Lowe's, Petsmart, Staples, Target, TJ Maxx, Verizon, on US 19, W Aladdin's Eatery, Arby's, Bob Evans, Boston Mkt, Bravo Italian, Buffalo Wild Wings, Burger King, Chipotle Mexican, Denny's, Domino's, Dunkin', Dynasty, Eat'n Park, Emiliano's Mexican, Firehouse Subs, Five Guys, HotDog Shoppe, Houlihan's, Ichiban Steakhouse, Jason's Deli, Jersey Mike's, Jimmy John's, Mad Mex, Max&Erma's, McDonald's, Monte Cello's Grill, Panda Express, Panera Bread, Perkins, Pizza Hut, Pizza Roma, Primanti Bros, Saga Steaks, Subway, Vocelli Pizza, Wendy's Candlewood Suites, Clarion, Comfort Inn, Doubletree, Hampton Inn, Hyatt Place, Motel 6, Quality Inn, Red Roof Inn, Residence Inn, Super 8, Woodspring Suites H, $Tree, Aldi Foods, AT&T, AutoZone, Barnes&Noble, Best Buy, BP/7-11/dsl, Costco/gas, Field&Stream, Firestone/auto, GetGo, Giant Eagle Foods, GNC, Home Depot, Jo-Ann Fabrics, Marathon/dsl, Marshall's, Michael's, NAPA, PepBoys, PetCo, Rite Aid, Sheetz/dsl, Sunoco/dsl, Toyota, Tuesday Morning, USPO, Verizon, Walgreens, Walmart
77	I-76/Tpk, to Youngstown
75	US 19 S (from nb), to Warrendale, services on US 19
73	PA 910, to Wexford, E Eat'n Park, Starbucks EconoLodge Rite Aid, W Exxon/dsl, Sheetz/dsl, Tesla EVC Hampton Inn
72	I-279 S (from sb, exits left), to Pittsburgh
68	Mt Nebo Rd, E Sheetz/dsl
66	to PA 65, Emsworth
65	to PA 51, Coraopolis, Neville Island, E Speedway/Speedway Cafe Kings Grille Fairfield Inn Penske Trucks, W Subway
64.5mm	Ohio River
64	PA 51 (from nb), to Coraopolis, McKee's Rocks
60	PA 60, Crafton, E GetGo/dsl Primanti Bros Comfort Inn, EconoLodge, Hilltop Motel, Motel 6 H, W Juliano's Rest. Meineke
59b	I-376 W, US 22 W, US 30 (from nb), W
59a	I-376 E, to Pittsburgh
57	to Carnegie
55	PA 50, to Heidelberg, E on PA 50 Advance Parts, Marathon dsl, Sunoco Arby's, Bob Evans, ChuckeCheese, Eat'n Park, Jersey Mike's, LJ Silver, McDonald's, Moe's SW, Panera Bread, Pizza Hut, Sonic, Starbucks, Subway, Taco Bell, TX Roadhouse, Walnut Grill, Wendy's $Tree, BigLots, Firestone/auto, Ford, Giant Eagle Foods, GNC, Home Depot, Jo-Ann Fabrics, Lowe's, Mr Tire, Pepboys, Rite Aid, Shop'n Save, TJ Maxx, Tuesday Morning, Walgreens, Walmart
54	PA 50, to Bridgeville, E BP/dsl, GetGo Chipotle, Jimmy John's, McDonald's, Starbucks Holiday Inn Express Aldi Foods, Chevrolet, Midas, Monro, NAPA, Rite Aid, USPO, W Sunoco/dsl Five Guys Hampton Inn
50mm	/weigh sta both lanes, full facilities, litter barrels, petwalk, , , vending
48	South Pointe, W Jackson's Rest., Subway Holiday Inn Express, Hilton Garden, Homewood Suites
45	to PA 980, Canonsburg, E Sheetz Toyota, W Chicago Dunkin', Hogfathers BBQ, KFC/Taco Bell, Little Caesar's, McDonald's, Papa John's, Pizza Hut, Starbucks, Subway, WaiWai Grill, Wendy's Super 8 $General, Advance Parts, auto/transmission repair, AutoZone, Walgreens
43	PA 519, Houston, E BP/dsl, W Sunoco Freightliner
41	Race Track Rd, E Marathon/dsl Burger King, Dunkin', McDonald's, Waffle House, Wendy's Cambria Suites, Candlewood Suites, Comfort Inn, Country Inn&Suites, Courtyard, Doubletree, Hampton Inn, Holiday Inn Express, Hyatt Place Audi, Old Navy, racetrack, Tanger Outlets/famous brands, W BP/dsl Microtel Trolley Museum
40	Meadow Lands, W golf, racetrack, Trolley Museum (3mi)
38	I-70 W, to Wheeling
I-79 and I-70 run together 3.5 mi. See I-70, exits 19b-20.	
34	I-70 E, to Greensburg
33	US 40, to Laboratory, W KOA
31mm	weigh sta sb
30	US 19, to Amity, W Exxon/Subway/dsl
23	to Marianna, Prosperity
19	US 19, to PA 221, Ruff Creek, W BP/dsl
14	PA 21, to Waynesburg, E Bob Evans Comfort Inn, Microtel Walmart/Subway, W BP/7-11/dsl, Exxon/dsl, GetGo, Marathon, Sheetz, Sunoco Burger King, DQ, Golden Wok, Hardee's, KFC, Little Caesar's, McDonald's, Pizza Hut, Subway, Taco Bell, Wendy's EconoLodge, Hampton Inn, Super 8 H, $General, $Tree, Advance Parts, Aldi Foods, AT&T, AutoZone, BigLots, Cadillac/Chevrolet/Subaru, Chrysler/Dodge/Jeep, CVS Drug, Giant Eagle Foods, Rite Aid, st police, Subaru, Verizon
7	to Kirby
6mm	Welcome Ctr/weigh sta nb, full facilities, litter barrels, petwalk, , , vending
1	Mount Morris, E Sunoco/Huddle House/dsl/scales/24hr Honda/Mazda, W Marathon/dsl
0mm	Pennsylvania/West Virginia state line

CRANBERRY · PITTSBURGH · WAYNESBURG

INTERSTATE 80

Exit #	Services
311mm	Pennsylvania/New Jersey state line, Delaware River
310.5	toll booth wb
310	PA 611, Delaware Water Gap, Welcome Ctr/, S Fuel One, Gulf Apple Pie Bakery, Doughboys Pizza, Sango Kura

PA

INTERSTATE 80 Cont'd

Exit #	Services
309	US 209 N, PA 447, to Marshalls Creek, N Gulf DQ, Dunkin', Huddle House, Landmark Cafe Days Inn, Staybridge Suites H
308	East Stroudsburg, N Exxon/Subs Now H, WaWa, S Roasted Tomato Grill Quality Inn, Super 8
307	PA 191, Broad St, N Hampton Inn H, S Sunoco Compton's Rest. Bridgeview Inn
306	Dreher Ave (from wb, no EZ return), N WaWa
305	US 209, Main St, N Gulf/dsl, Sunoco Perkins Pocono Plaza Inn, S Exxon/dsl
304	US 209, to PA 33, 9th St (from wb)
303	9th St, (from eb), N Burger King, Dunkin', Five Guys, McDonald's, Olive Garden, Panera Bread, Popeye's, Ruby Tuesday, TX Roadhouse, Wendy's $Tree, Best Buy, BJ's/Subway/gas, Buick/GMC, Chevrolet, CVS Drug, Home Depot, Hyundai, JC Penney, Kia, Michael's, Midas, Old Navy, Petsmart, Staples, Target, Target, TJ Maxx, URGENT CARE, Walgreens, Weis Foods/gas
302	PA 611, to Bartonsville, N Exxon/dsl Chili's, Dunkin', East Gourmet Buffet, Frank's Pizza, Ichiban Steaks, Longhorn Steaks, Moe's SW Grill, Red Lobster, Red Robin, Sonic Baymont Inn, Fairfield Inn, Hampton Inn, Howard Johnson, Springhill Suites $Tree, Advance Parts, AT&T, Dick's, Giant Foods/gas, Kohl's, Lowe's, Mavis Tire, URGENT CARE, Verizon
299	PA 715, Tannersville, N Citgo/dsl, Mobil/Burger King/dsl, Tesla EVC, Turkey Hill DQ, Dunkin', FoodCourt, Friendly's, Pocono Diner Best Western+, Scotrun Motel $General, CVS Drug, The Crossing Factory Outlet/famous brands, Weis Foods, S Sunoco/dsl Days Inn to Big Pocono SP, to Camelback Ski Area
298	PA 611 (from wb), to Scotrun, N Fill&Fly/dsl Brick Oven Pizza Great Wolf Lodge, Scotrun Diner/motel to Mt Pocono
295mm	**eb, full facilities, litter barrels, petwalk, vending**
293	I-380 N, to Scranton, (exits left from eb)
284	PA 115, to Wilkes-Barre, Blakeslee, N Citgo, WaWa/dsl Dunkin' Best Western st police, S Gulf/dsl Fern Ridge Camping, to Pocono Raceway
277	PA 940, to PA Tpk (I-476), to Pocono, Lake Harmony, Allentown, N WaWa Arby's, Burger King, McDonald's Comfort Inn, EconoLodge, Holiday Inn Express, Mtn Laurel Resort, Pocono Inn/Resort, Quality Inn, Split Rock Resort
274	PA 534, N Hickory Run/Exxon/rest./dsl/scales/24hr, Sunoco/Subs Now/dsl/24hr towing/repair, S to Hickory Run SP (6mi)
273mm	Lehigh River
273	PA 940, PA 437, to Freeland, White Haven, N Exxon, Fuel One, S Powerhouse Eatery
270mm	**eb, full facilities, info, litter barrels, petwalk, vending**
262	PA 309, to Hazleton, Mountain Top, N Citgo/Dunkin' Mary's Rest., Wendy's EconoLodge auto/truck repair, Nescopeck SP (5mi), S Valero/dsl Holiday Inn Express
260b a	I-81, N to Wilkes-Barre, S to Harrisburg
256	PA 93, to Nescopeck, Conyngham, N Citgo/repair, Pilot/Subway/dsl/scales/24hr, S Hampton Inn (4mi), Motel 6 H, towing/truck repair
251mm	Nescopeck River
246mm	**/weigh sta both lanes, full facilities, litter barrels, petwalk, vending, weather info**
242	PA 339, to Mainville, Mifflinville, N Loves/Arby's/dsl/scales/24hr, Sunoco/Burger King/Subway/dsl McDonald's Super 8, S Delta/dsl Comfort Inn

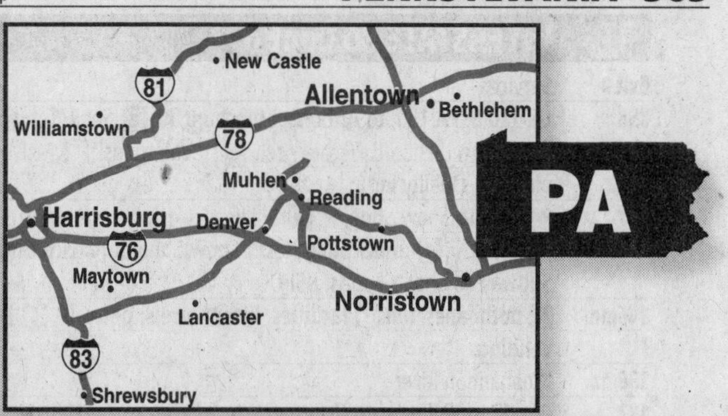

Exit #	Services
241mm	Susquehanna River
241b a	US 11, to Berwick, Lime Ridge, Bloomsburg, N Red Maple Inn (2mi) H, 2-5 mi S Sheetz/dsl, Sunoco/Subs Now/dsl Applebee's, Arby's, Burger King, China Queen, Domino's, Dunkin', Kemler's Rest., Little Caesar's, Marley's Grill, McDonald's, Morris Rest., Oliran Japanese, Pizza Hut, Rita's Custard, Subway, Taco Bell, Taste of Italy, Wendy's Motel 6, Relax Inn AAA, Ace Hardware, Advance Parts, BigLots, Buick/GMC, Cadillac/Chevrolet, CVS Drug, Ford/Honda, Giant Foods/gas, Kost Tire, Rite Aid, Staples, U-Haul, Verizon, Weis Foods/gas
236	PA 487, to Bloomsburg, Lightstreet, N Tesla EVC Fairfield Inn, S Sunoco Denny's Hampton Inn, Turkey Hill Inn H, to Bloomsburg U
232	PA 42, Buckhorn, N Exxon/Subs Now, TA/Country Pride/Subway/dsl/scales/24hr/@, Tesla EVC Burger King, Cracker Barrel, KFC, Perkins, Quaker Steak&Lube, Ruby Tuesday, Starbucks, Wendy's Holiday Inn Express, Quality Inn AT&T, Home Depot, S Gourmet Buffet, Olive Garden, Panera Bread Comfort Suites $Tree, Indian Head Camping (3mi), Lowe's, Marshall's, PetCo, Verizon, Walmart/McDonald's
224	PA 54, to Danville, N Exxon/Subway/dsl Quality Inn, S Mobil/dsl Friendly's, McDonald's Best Western, Hampton Inn, Red Roof Inn, Super 8 H
219mm	**both lanes, full facilities, info, litter barrels, petwalk, vending**
215	PA 254, Limestonevill, S FLYING J/Penn 80 Rest./Subway/dsl/scales/24hr/@ Eagle Truckwash
212b a	I-180 W, PA 147 S, to Muncy, Williamsport, S Sunoco (1mi)
210.5mm	Susquehanna River
210b a	US 15, to Williamsport, Lewisburg, S Sunoco/dsl Bonanza Holiday Inn Express, Quality Inn H, KOA (5mi)
199	Mile Run
194mm	**/weigh sta both lanes, full facilities, litter barrels, petwalk, vending**
192	PA 880, to Jersey Shore, N Sunoco/dsl H, S Valero/dsl towing/truck repair
185	PA 477, Loganton, N Valero, S Twilight Diner RB Winter SP (12mi)
178	US 220, Lock Haven, 5 mi N KwikFill/dsl, Sheetz/dsl Little Caesar's, Original Italian Pizza, Ruby Tuesday H, $General, $Tree, Advance Parts, Lowe's, Walmart/Subway, Weis Foods
173	PA 64, Lamar, N Pilot/Subway/dsl/scales/24hr Cottage Rest., McDonald's Hampton Inn, Quality Inn/rest. repair, S FLYING J/Denny's/Dunkin'/dsl/LP/scales/24hr/, TA/Country Pride/dsl/scales/24hr/@, Valero
161	I-99, US 220 S, PA 26, to Bellafonte, N Bellefonte Camping, KOA (2mi), S to PSU

LAMAR

PA

INTERSTATE 80 Cont'd

Exit #	Services
158	US 220 S, PA 150, to Altoona, Milesburg, N Shell/Subway, TA/Country Pride/dsl/scales/24hr/@, Valero/dsl McDonald's Quality Inn
147	PA 144, to Snow Shoe, N Phillips 66/dsl/repair/24hr, Sunoco/dsl/24hr Snow Shoe Rest., Snow Shoe Sandwich Shop, Subway Hall's Foods, USPO
146mm	**both lanes, full facilities, litter barrels, petwalk, vending**
138mm	Moshannon River
133	PA 53, to Philipsburg, Kylertown, N Exxon, KwikFill/motel/dsl/scales Roadhouse Rest. $General, Mtn View Mkt, USPO, S H, Black Moshannon SP (9mi)
123	PA 970, to Shawville, Woodland, N Woodland Camping, S Gio's BBQ/dsl (2mi), PP/dsl st police, USPO
120mm	Susquehanna River, W Branch
120	PA 879, Shawville, Clearfield, N Sapp Bros/rest./dsl/scales/24hr/@ Peterbilt, S BP/dsl, Sheetz, Snappy's Arby's, Burger King, Dunkin', Dutch Pantry, KFC, McDonald's Best Western+, Comfort Inn, Hampton Inn, Holiday Inn Express, Red Roof Inn, Super 8 H, Lowe's, Walmart/Subway
111mm	highest point on I-80 east of Mississippi River, 2250 ft
111	PA 153, to Penfield, N to Parker Dam, to SB Elliot SP, S H
101	PA 255, Du Bois, N Snappy's/Grille /dsl camping, 1-2 mi S Sheetz/dsl A&W/LJ Silver, Burger King, Dunkin', Eat'n Park, Fusion Buffet, Italian Oven, Japan One, McDonald's, Napoli Pizzeria, Perkins, Pizza Hut, Red Lobster, Ruby Tuesday, Station 101 Grill, Subway, Taco Bell, Wendy's Fairfield Inn, Hampton Inn, Homewood Suites H, $General, $Tree, Aldi Foods, BigLots, CVS Drug, JC Penney, Jo-Ann Fabrics, Lowe's, Old Navy, PetCo, Rite Aid, Ross, st police, Staples, TJ Maxx, Verizon, Walmart/Subway
97	US 219, to Brockway, Du Bois, S Pilot/Arby's/dsl/scales/24hr, Sheetz/dsl/24hr Dutch Pantry Rest., Hoss' Rest. (2mi) Best Western (2mi), Clarion, Holiday Inn Express H, Advance Parts (2mi), AutoZone (2mi), Freightliner
90	PA 830 E, N Du Bois Regional Airport
87.5mm	**both lanes, full facilities, litter barrels, petwalk, vending**
86	PA 830, to Reynoldsville
81	PA 28, to Brookville, Hazen, S hist dist (2mi)
78	PA 36, to Sigel, Brookville, N FLYING J/Denny's/dsl/LP/scales/24hr, TA/BP/Taco Bell/dsl/scales/24hr/@ McDonald's, Pizza Hut Super 8 NAPA, to Cook Forest SP, S GetGo/dsl, O Ring CNG, Sheetz/dsl Arby's, Burger King, China Wok, Plyler's Buffet, Subway Gold Eagle Inn, Rodeway Inn $General, Chrysler/Dodge/Jeep, Family$, truckwash
73	PA 949, Corsica, N to Clear Creek SP, S USPO
70	US 322, to Strattanville
64	PA 66 S, to New Bethlehem, Clarion, N to Clarion U
62	PA 68, to Clarion, N BP, KwikFill/dsl Applebee's, Arby's, Burger King, Cozumel, Eat'n Park, Hunan King, McDonald's, Perkins, Pizza Hut, RRR Roadhouse, Sakura Buffet, Subway, Taco Bell Clarion, Hampton Inn, Holiday Inn Express, Motel 6, Quality Inn, Ramada H, $Tree, Advance Parts, Aldi Foods, AT&T, AutoZone, JC Penney, Verizon, Walmart/Subway, S Microtel
61mm	Clarion River
60	PA 66 N, to Shippenville, N Jiffy/dsl camping, to C Forest SP
56mm	**weigh sta both lanes**
53	to PA 338, to Knox, N Satterlee Gas/dsl (cardlock) Country Rest. Countryside Crafts/Quilts, Wolf's Cam Resort, S Good Tire Service
45	PA 478, to St Petersburg, Emlenton
44.5mm	Clarion River, Allegheny River
42	PA 38, to Emlenton, N Exxon/Subway/dsl, Pilot/r dsl/scales/24hr Emlenton Motel Gaslight RV P truck/RV repair
35	PA 308, to Clintonville, N Family$
30.5mm	**both lanes, full facilities, litter barrels, petwalk, vending**
29	PA 8, to Franklin, Barkeyville, N Speedway/Speedway Cafe Arby's, Burger King, King's Rest. Motel 6, Quality Inn Freightliner, S Heath/dsl, KwikFill/dsl/scales/motel/24hr, BP/Subway/dsl/scales/24hr/@ to Slippery Rock U, truckw
24	PA 173, to Grove City, Sandy Lake, S H, Grove City Col
19b a	I-79, N to Erie, S to Pittsburgh
15	US 19, to Mercer, N PP/dsl, Shell Burger King, M garita King Mexican Comfort Inn, 2 mi S Iron Bri Rest. KOA (4mi)
4b a	I-376, PA 60, to PA 18, to Sharon-Hermitage, New Ca N Sheetz/dsl, Sunoco/Subway/dsl EconoLodge, Ha ton Inn, Holiday Inn Express, Park Inn, Quality Inn, Red Roof Super 8, S DQ, MiddleSex Diner $General
2.5mm	Shenango River
1mm	**Welcome Ctr eb, full facilities, litter barrels, petwalk, vending**
0mm	Pennsylvania/Ohio state line

INTERSTATE 81

Exit #	Services
233mm	Pennsylvania/New York state line
232mm	**Welcome Ctr/weigh sta sb, full facilities, litter barrels, walk,**
230	PA 171, Great Bend, E Valero Lakeside Camping (5 W Exxon/Tim Hortons/dsl, Sunoco/dsl Bluestone za, Burger King, Dobb's Country Kitchen, Dunkin', McDona Subway Colonial Brick Motel Family$, Reddon's Dr Rob's Foods
223	PA 492, New Milford, E East Lake Camping/RV Park (3 W Citgo/dsl, Gulf/dsl Green Gables Rest. Ridge Motel, Lynn Lee B&B (1.5mi)
219	PA 848, to Gibson, E Sunoco/Burger King/ W FLYING J/Denny's/dsl/scales/24hr, Exxon/McD ald's/dsl/24hr Holiday Inn Express, st police
217	PA 547, Harford, E Exxon/Subway/dsl/24hr, Mobil/dsl/2
211	PA 92, Lenox, E Elk Mtn Ski Area, Shady Rest Camp (3mi), W Gulf/dsl, Pump-N-Pantry/dsl Bingha Rest., Lenox Rest. Lenox Drug
209mm	**sb, full facilities, litter barrel, petwalk, vendi**
206	PA 374, to Glenwood, Lenoxville, E Sunoco/dsl to Mountain Ski Resort
203mm	**nb, full facilities, litter barrels, petwalk, vend**
202	PA 107, to Fleetville, Tompkinsville
201	PA 438, East Benton, W Duchniks/dsl/repair B&B R
199	PA 524, Scott, E Gulf/dsl, W Exxon/Subway M 81 to Lackawanna SP
197	PA 632, Waverly, E Rite Aid, Weis Foods, W Sun Doc's Deli Camelot Inn/rest

INTERSTATE 81 Cont'd

Exit #	Services
194	US 6, US 11, to I-476/PA Tpk, Clarks Summit, W [gas] Exxon/dsl, Sheetz/dsl, Sunoco/dsl, Valero [food] Burger King, Dino&Francesco's, Domino's, DQ, Dunkin', Krispy Kreme, Kyoto Japanese, McDonald's, Moe's SW Grill, Starbucks, Starbucks, Subway, Sunny Chinese, Taco Bell, Waffle House, Wendy's [lodging] Comfort Inn, EconoLodge, Hampton Inn, Nichols Village Inn, Ramada Inn [other] Ace Hardware, Advance Parts, Kost Tire, Monro, Rite Aid, Verizon, Weis Mkt
191b a	US 6, US 11, to Carbondale, E [gas] Sheetz/dsl, Sunoco [food] A&W/LJ Silver, Applebee's, Buffalo Wild Wings, Burger King, China Palace, Chipotle, ChuckECheese, Colarusso's Pizza, Denny's, DQ, Dunkin', Five Guys, HoneyBaked Ham, Jersey Mike's, La Tonalateca, McDonald's, Olive Garden, Panera Bread, Perkins, Perkins, Primanti Bros, Quaker Steak&Lube, Red Lobster, Red Robin, Rita's Custard, Roma Pizza, Royal Buffet, Ruby Tuesday, Starbucks, Subway, Taco Bell, TGIFriday's, TX Roadhouse, Uno Grill, Viewmont Diner [lodging] Days Inn, Holiday Inn Express, Home 2 Suites [other] $Tree, Aldi Foods, AT&T, Books-A-Million, Dick's, Field&Stream, Firestone/auto, Harley-Davidson, Hobby Lobby, Home Depot, Hyundai, JC Penney, Jo-Ann Crafts, Kohl's, Macy's, Marshall's, Michael's, Old Navy, PepBoys, Petsmart, Target, TJ Maxx, Verizon, Walmart, Wegman's Mkt, William's Tires, W [other] to Anthracite Museum
190	Main Ave, Dickson City, E [food] Wendy's [lodging] Fairfield Inn, Microtel, Residence Inn [other] auto repair, Best Buy, Ford, Lowe's, Sam's Club/gas, Staples, vet, W [other] Schiff's Mkt, Toyota
188	PA 347, Throop, E [gas] Sheetz/dsl, Sunoco/dsl [food] McDonald's, Wendy's [lodging] Dunmore Inn, Quality Inn, Rodeway Inn, Sleep Inn [other] Advance Parts, BigLots, Kost Tire, Monro, Nissan, PriceChopper Foods, st police, URGENT CARE, W [gas] Exxon/Subway/dsl [food] Burger King, Dunkin', Friendly's
187	to I-84, I-380, US 6 (no return from nb)
186	PA 435, Drinker St (from nb), E [gas] Valero/dsl, W [gas] Exxon/dsl
185	Central Scranton Expwy (exits left from nb), W [other] [H]
184	to PA 307, River St, W [gas] Exxon/Subway/dsl, Valero, Vamco [food] Asian Taste, Dunkin' [lodging] Sheraton [other] [H], $Tree, CVS Drug, Gerrity Foods
182	Davis St, Montage Mtn Rd, E [gas] EVC, Exxon/Coldstone/Subway/dsl, Tesla EVC [food] Burger King, Food&Fire BBQ, Gourmet Slice Pizza, Harvest Seasonal Grill, Longhorn Steaks, Marzoni's Brick Oven, Nonno's Pizza, Panchero's Mexican, Panera Bread, Ruby Tuesday, Starbucks [lodging] Comfort Suites, Courtyard, Hampton Inn, Springhill Suites, TownePlace Suites [other] AT&T, GNC, Verizon, W [gas] Sunoco [food] Dunkin', Waffle House, Wendy's [lodging] EconoLodge [other] CVS Drug, USPO
180	to US 11, PA 502, to Moosic, (exits left from nb)on US 11, W [gas] Citgo/dsl, Sunoco [food] Subway
178b a	to US 11, Avoca, E [lodging] Best Western+, W [gas] Petro/Shell/Iron Skillet/dsl/scales/24hr/@
175b a	PA 315 S, to I-476, Dupont, E [gas] Exxon/Subway/dsl, Sunoco/dsl [food] Arby's, McDonald's, Perkins [lodging] Knights Inn [other] Volvo, W [gas] Pilot/Wendy's/dsl/scales/24hr [food] Burger King, Denny's, Star Asia Buffet, Taco Bell, Uncle Joe's Pizza [lodging] Holiday Inn Express [other] truck repair, Verizon, Walmart/Subway
170b a	PA 115, PA 309, Wilkes-Barre, E [gas] Exxon/Subway/dsl, Sunoco/dsl, Tesla EVC [lodging] Holiday Inn, W [gas] Citgo, Sunoco/dsl [food] Buffalo Wild Wings, Burger King, Denny's, Domino's, Dunkin', Friendly's, Grotto Pizza, Hardee's, Harvest Buffet, IHOP, Jersey Mike's, Longhorn Steaks, McDonald's, Moe's SW Grill, Red Lobster, Sonic, Taco Bell, TGIFriday's, Wendy's [lodging] Days Inn,

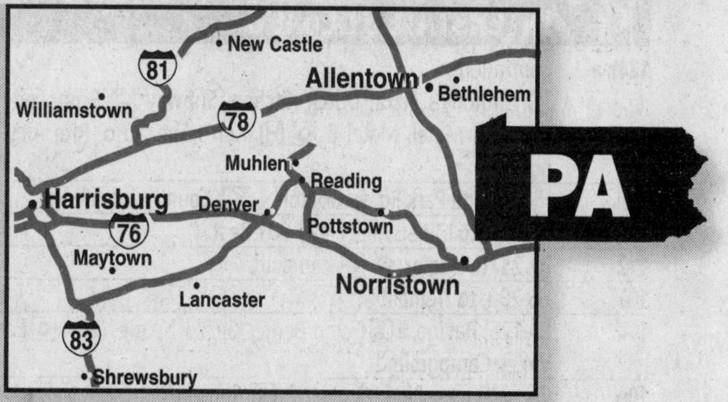

WILKES BARRE

Exit #	Services
170b a	Continued Extended Stay America, Fairfield Inn, Holiday Inn Express, Host Inn, Quality Inn, Red Roof Inn, Woodspring Suites [other] [H], $General, AutoZone, Chevrolet, JC Penney, Macy's, to Pocono Downs, Williams Tire/auto
168	Highland Park Blvd, Wilkes-Barre, W [gas] Sheetz/dsl, Sunoco/Subway/dsl, Tesla EVC [food] Applebee's, Bob Evans, Chili's, Chipotle, ChuckeCheese, Cracker Barrel, Five Guys, King's Buffet, La Tolteca Mexican, Miller's Alehouse, Mizu Steaks, Nello's Pizza, Olive Garden, Outback Steaks, Popeye's, Red Robin, Smokey Bones BBQ, Starbucks, TX Roadhouse, Wendy's [lodging] Courtyard, Hampton Inn, Hilton Garden, Motel 6 [other] AT&T, Barnes&Noble, Best Buy, Dick's, Firestone/auto, Home Depot, Kohl's, Kost Tire/auto, Lowe's, Marshall's, Michael's, Nissan, Old Navy, PepBoys, PetCo, Petsmart, PriceChopper, Ross, Sam's Club/gas, Staples, Target, TJ Maxx, Tuesday Morning, U-Haul, URGENT CARE, Verizon, Walgreens, Walmart/Subway, Wegman's Foods
165b a	PA 309 S, (exits left from nb), Wilkes-Barre, W [gas] Citgo/dsl, Gulf [food] Dunkin', McDonald's, Perkins, Taco Bell [lodging] Comfort Inn, EconoLodge [other] $Tree, Advance Parts, Rite Aid
164	PA 29, to Nanticoke, Ashley
159	Nuangola, W [gas] Valero/Subs Now/dsl [other] camping (10mi)
157mm	**[RS]/weigh sta sb, full [handicapped] facilities, litter barrels, petwalk, [phone], [picnic], vending**
156mm	**[RS]/weigh sta nb, full [handicapped] facilities, litter barrels, petwalk, [phone], [picnic], vending**
155	to Dorrance, E [gas] Sunoco/dsl, W [gas] Blue Ridge Plaza/dsl
151b a	I-80, E to Mountaintop, W to Bloomsburg
145	PA 93, W Hazleton, E [gas] Sunoco/Dunkin'/dsl, TurkeyHill/dsl [food] Applebee's, Arby's, Bonanza, Damon's, Denny's, Five Stars Chinese, LJ Silver, McDonald's, Panera Bread, Perkins, Pizza Hut, Popeye's, Subway, Taco Bell, Wendy's [lodging] Comfort Inn, Fairfield Inn, Forest Hill Inn, Ramada Inn (2mi) [other] [H], $Tree, Advance Parts, Aldi Foods, AT&T, Big Lots, Boscov's, Buick/Cadillac/GMC, Chrysler/Dodge/Jeep, Lowe's, Mazda, Michael's, Old Navy, Petsmart, st police, Verizon, Walmart/McDonald's, Weis Foods, W [gas] JN Delimart [food] Damenti's, Top of the 80's [lodging] Candlewood Suites, Hampton Inn
143	PA 924, to Hazleton, W [gas] Fuelon/Subs Now/dsl/scales, Sunoco/Subway, TurkeyHill/dsl [food] Burger King, Sonic [lodging] Residence Inn
141	PA 424, S Hazleton Beltway, E [lodging] Mt Laurel Motel
138	PA 309, to McAdoo, 2 mi E [lodging] Pines Motel
134	to Delano
132mm	**parking area/weigh sta both lanes**
131b a	PA 54, Mahanoy City, E [other] to Tuscarora/Locust Lake SP, W [gas] Gulf/dsl, Sunoco/dsl [lodging] Comfort Inn & Suites
124b a	PA 61, to Frackville, E [food] Cracker Barrel, McDonald's [lodging] Holiday Inn Express [other] BigLots, W [gas] Exxon, Gulf/dsl, Speedway

HAZLETON

PA

INTERSTATE 81 Cont'd

LEBANON

124b a Continued
Anthony's Pizza, Dutch Kitchen, Subway EconoLodge, Granny's Motel, Motel 6 H, Ken's Tire/auto, Rite Aid, st police

119 High Ridge Park Rd, to Gordon, E Country Inn&Suites

116 PA 901, to Minersville, E 901 Rest.

112 PA 25, to Hegins, W camping

107 US 209, to Tremont

104 PA 125, Ravine, E Exxon/Burger King/dsl/scales/24hr Echo Valley Campground

100 PA 443, to Pine Grove, E Sunoco/dsl Arby's, McDonald's Comfort Inn, Seasons Inn $General, W Pilot/DQ/Subway/dsl/scales/24hr, Pilot/dsl Diner Hampton Inn truckwash, vet

90 PA 72, to Lebanon, E Exxon/Subway, Loves/McDonald's/dsl/scales/24hr, Speedway/Dunkin'/dsl Burger King, Wendy's Days Inn, Fairfield Inn KOA, st police, W Comfort Inn

89 I-78 E, to Allentown

85b a PA 934, to Annville, 2 mi W Funck's Rest. to Indian-Town Gap Nat Cem

80 PA 743, Grantville, E Shell/dsl Days Inn, Hampton Inn, W Exxon/dsl Italian Delight Comfort Suites, Holiday Inn racetrack

79mm **/weigh sta both lanes, full facilities, litter barrels, petwalk, , vending**

77 PA 39, to Hershey, E Pilot/Pizza Hut/dsl/scales/24hr, Sheetz/dsl Hershey Rd Rest. Country Inn&Suites, EconoLodge, La Quinta, Motel 6, Super 8 st police, to Hershey Attractions, W FLYING J/Perkins/dsl/24hr/@, TA/Country Pride/dsl/scales/24hr/@ McDonald's Holiday Inn Express Goodyear, SpeedCo, truck repair

HARRISBURG

72 to US 22, Linglestown, E Sheetz/dsl, Speedway/Dunkin'/dsl, Sunoco/dsl Burger King, Chipotle Mexican, Five Guys, McDonald's, Red Robin, Starbucks, Subway, Tonino's Pizza Baymont Inn, Quality Inn Advance Parts, Chrysler/Dodge/Jeep, Costco/gas, CVS Drug, Harley-Davidson, Hobby Lobby, Karn's Foods, Target, Toyota, U-Haul, W Turkey Hill Mikado Japanese Candlewood Suites, Ramada Inn $General

70 I-83 S, to York,

69 Progress Ave, E Cracker Barrel, Dunkin', Harvest Grill, Macaroni Grill, Starbucks, Tonino's Grill Home 2 Suites AT&T, CVS Drug, st police, Susquehanna Shoppes, W Turkey Hill/dsl Arby's, YP Rest. Best Western, Hampton Inn, Red Roof Inn, SpringHill Suites

67b a US 22, US 322 W, PA 230, Cameron St, to Lewistown

66 Front St, E H, W Exxon, Sunoco Front St Diner, McDonald's, Pizza Hut, Simply Turkey, Two Guys Pizza, Wendy's Best Value, Days Inn

65 US 11/15, to Enola, 1 mi E Sunoco/dsl, Tom's Al's Pizza, China Taste, Domino's, DQ, Dunkin', McDonald's, Squeaky Rail Diner, Subway, Wendy's Quality Inn $Tree, Advance Parts, Fischer Parts, Rite Aid

61 PA 944, to Wertzville, E Burger King, Taco Bell Holiday Inn Express H, AT&T, Giant/dsl, Weiss Mkt, W Turkey Hill/dsl Best Western+

59 PA 581, to US 11, to I-83, Harrisburg, **3 mi E on Carlisle Pk** Sheetz/dsl, Sunoco Applebee's, Burger King, Carrabba's, Denny's, Dunkin', McDonald's, Outback Steaks, TGIFriday's, Wayback Burger, Wendy's Park Inn AutoZone,

PA

CARLISLE

59 Continued
Buick/GMC, Home Depot, Hyundai, Lowe's, Nissan, NTB, Pe boys, Petsmart, TJ Maxx

57 PA 114, to Mechanicsburg, **2 mi E** Sheetz/dsl Alfred Pizza, Arby's, Dickey's BBQ, Great Wall Chinese, Isaac's Re KFC/LJ Silver, McDonald's, Olive Garden, Pizza Hut, Red Ro in, Silver Spring Diner, Subway, Taco Bell Home 2 Suit La Quinta CarMax, Giant Foods/gas, Sam's Club/g Walmart

52b a US 11, to I-76/PA Tpk, Middlesex, E FLYING J/Denny dsl/scales/24hr/@, I-81/dsl, Sheetz/dsl, Tesla EVC Dunk Hickory Ridge, Middlesex Diner Best Value Inn, Quality I Red Roof Inn, Super 8 H, W Gulf, Loves/Wendy dsl/24hr, Petro/Iron Skillet/dsl/24hr/@, Rutters/dsl, Sunoc Subway/dsl Arby's, Carelli's Subs, McDonald's, Mira Mile Diner, Waffle House Best Western, Comfort Inn, Da Inn, Diamond Carlisle Inn, EconoLodge, Hampton Inn, Ho day Inn Express, Motel 6, Residence Inn, Rodeway Inn, Tr elodge H, Blue Beacon

49 PA 74 (no EZ sb return), same as 48, E Sheetz/dsl Ha ee's, W Trindle Grill AAA

48 PA 74, York Rd (no EZ nb return), E Red Robin, Starbuc Subway Microtel $Tree, Aldi Foods, Kohl's, Michae Petsmart, Rite Aid, Target, Verizon, W Gulf/dsl, Spee way Burger King, Farmers Mkt Diner, Little Caesar's, M Donald's, Neato Burrito, Pizza Hut, Scalles Whse Rest., Ta Bell CVS Drug, Dunkin', Ford, Jo-Ann, Lowe's, Midas, W Mkt

47 PA 34, Hanover St, E Chili's, Cracker Barrel Sle Inn Home Depot, W Applebee's, Bruster's/Natha Chick-fil-A, China Palace, Chipotle, DQ, Five Guys, Pan Bread, Papa John's, Rita's Custard, Subway, Super Buffet, V ny's Rest., Wendy's AT&T, CVS Drug, Rite Aid, Staples, Maxx, Walmart/McDonald's

45 College St, E Gulf/dsl Alfredo Pizza, Arby's, Hos Rest., McDonald's, Subway, Walnut Bottom Diner Ho Ava, Super 8 H, Giant Food Mkt, Monro, Tire Pros, Veriz

44 PA 465, Allen Rd, to Plainfield, E Country Inn&Suites, Fa field Inn H, st police, W Sheetz/dsl Burger Ki Subway

38.5mm **both lanes, full facilities, litter barrels, petwalk, ,**

37 PA 233, to Newville, E Pine Grove Furnace SP, W Denning SP

29 PA 174, King St, E Sunoco/dsl Rodeway I W Gulf, Rutter's/dsl Bros Pizza, Burger King, C na House, Domino's, KFC, Little Caesar's, Subway, Taco B Wendy's Best Western, Holiday Inn Express, Theo's M tel $General, Advance Parts, Aldi Foods, AT&T, Cadill Chevrolet, CVS Drug, Ford, Verizon, vet, Walmart

24 PA 696, Fayette St, E Sheetz/dsl, W Pacific Pride/ds

20 PA 997, Scotland, E Citgo/dsl McDonald's Comf Inn, Super 8, W Sunoco Quality Inn

17 Walker Rd, W Sheetz/dsl Aki Japanese, Bruster's/N than's, Buffalo Wild Wings, Cafe del Sol, Chick-fil-A, Chipo Mexican, Five Guys, Fuddrucker's, Jersey Mike's, Jimmy John Longhorn Steaks, MOD Pizza, Olive Garden, Panera Bre Red Robin, Sonic, Starbucks, Subway, TGIFriday's, TX Ro house Candlewood Suites, Country Inn&Suites, Spring Suites Aldi Foods, AT&T, BJ's/dsl, Buick/Chevrolet/GM Ford, Giant Foods/gas, Kohl's, Michael's, Mr Tire, Petsma Staples, Target, URGENT CARE, Verizon

INTERSTATE 81 Cont'd

Exit #	Services
16	US 30, to Chambersburg, E Sheetz/dsl Arby's, Bonanza, Bro's Pizza, Burger King, Chris's Kitchen, Domino's, DQ, Dunkin', Hoss's Rest., KFC, Little Caesar's, Perkins, Popeye's, Supreme Buffet, Waffle House, Wendy's Days Inn $Tree, AAA, Dick's, Harley-Davidson, Hobby Lobby, Jo-Ann Fabrics, Lowe's, NAPA, Nissan/Toyota, Petco, TJ Maxx, U-Haul, vet, Walmart/Subway, W Big Oak Cafe, Burger King, Chambersburg Diner, Copper Kettle, LJ Silver, McDonald's, Pizza Hut, Ruby Tuesday, Taco Bell Best Western, Clarion, La Quinta H, Advance Parts, AutoZone, Lincoln, Walgreens
14	PA 316, Wayne Ave, E Sheetz/dsl Bob Evans, Cracker Barrel Baymont Inn, Hampton Inn, Red Carpet Inn, W KwikFill Applebee's, Arby's, China Wok, Denny's, Mario's Italian, Montezuma Mexican, Papa John's, Red Lobster, Stoner's Rest., Subway, Twin Dragon Chinese, Volcano Japanese, Wendy's Holiday Inn Express, Motel 6, Red Roof Inn $Tree, CVS Drug, Giant Foods/gas, GNC, Mr Tire, Save-a-Lot Foods, Verizon, Weis Mkt
12mm	**weigh sta sb**
10	PA 914, Marion
7mm	**weigh sta nb**
5	PA 16, Greencastle, E Shell/dsl, Sunoco/grill/dsl, TA/Country Pride/dsl/scales/24hr/@ Burger King, McDonald's, Taco Bell Super 8 truckwash, Whitetail Ski Resort, W Exxon/Dunkin'/dsl Green Motel AutoZone
3	US 11, E Sunoco/dsl Bro's Pizza Comfort Inn Bowers Tire/auto, W Sheetz/dsl Chevrolet
2mm	**Welcome Ctr nb, full facilities, litter barrels, petwalk, vending**
1	PA 163, Mason-Dixon Rd, W Hoffman's Grill Stateline Inn Keystone RV Ctr
0mm	Pennsylvania/Maryland state line, Mason-Dixon Line

INTERSTATE 83

Exit #	Services
51b a	**I-83 begins/ends on I-81, exit 70.**
50b a	US 22, Jonestown Rd, Harrisburg, E Speedway/dsl, Sunoco/dsl, USA Applebee's, Arby's, Buffalo Wild Wings, Chipotle Mexican, Cold Stone, Colonial Park Diner, Domino's, El Rodeo Mexican, Five Guys, Gilligan's Grill, Hibachi Grill, LJ Silver, Longhorn Steaks, McDonald's, Mission BBQ, Noodles&Co, Old Country Buffet, Olive Garden, Panera Bread, Pizza Hut, Red Lobster, Red Robin, Shogun Asian, Starbucks, Subway, Taco Bell, Wendy's Advance Parts, Aldi Foods, AT&T, AutoZone, Best Buy, BooksAMillion, Boscov's, Costco/gas, Dick's, Ford, Goodyear/auto, Hobby Lobby, Home Depot, Jo-Ann, Kohl's, Marshall's, Meineke, Michael's, NTB, Old Navy, PepBoys, PetCo, Rite Aid, Ross, Shannon Tire/auto, Target, Tires+, U-Haul, Verizon, vet, Weis Foods, William's Tires/repair, W Sunoco/dsl Crave Diner, DQ, Dunkin', Gabriella's Italian, KFC, Roberto's Pizza Rite Aid
48	Union Deposit Rd, E Sunoco Arby's, Burger King, Dunkin', Infinito's Buffet, Panera Bread Best Western, Hampton Inn H, $Tree, Giant Foods/gas, Rite Aid, Staples, URGENT CARE, W Gulf/dsl, Sheetz/dsl, Tesla EVC Chipotle, ChuckeCheese, Empire Asian Bistro, Great Wall Chinese, HFC Pizza, IHOP, Jimmy John's, McDonald's, Naples Pizza, New China, Outback Steaks, Rita's Ice Cream, Starbucks, Subway, TX Roadhouse, Waffle House, Wendy's Country Inn&Suites,

LEWISBERRY

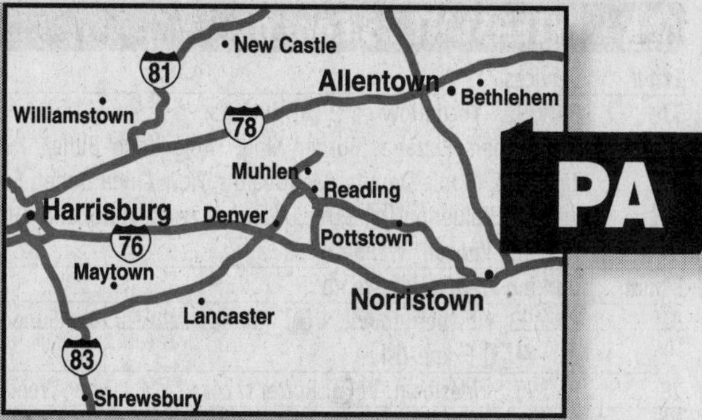

Exit #	Services
48	Continued EconoLodge, Fairfield Inn, Holiday Inn Express $General, $Tree, BigLots, Lowe's, PriceRite Foods, Weis Foods
47	(46b from nb), US 322 E, to Hershey, Derry St, E Speedway/Dunkin' Papa John's, Pizza Hut Home Depot, Petsmart
46b a	I-283 S, to I-76/PA Tpk, **services E off I-283** Sunoco/dsl Bob Evans, Capitol Diner, Chick-fil-A, Chili's, Five Guys, Friendly's, Lancaster Brewing Rest., Leeds Rest., McDonald's, Moe's SW Grill, Subway Courtyard, EconoLodge, Howard Johnson, La Quinta, Red Lion Inn, Red Roof Inn, Sheraton, Sleep Inn, Super 8 $General, GNC, JC Penney, Kia, Petco, Target, Verizon
45	Paxton St, E Sheetz/dsl Applebee's, Burger King, Cafe Fresco, Capt Don's Rest., Dunkin', Fiesta Mexico, Hibachi Buffet, McDonald's, Melting Pot, Papa Joe's Pizza, Pizza Hut, Qdoba, Ruby Tuesday, Starbucks, Tomato Pie Cafe Hilton Garden, Homewood Suites, Towneplace Suites $Tree, Advance Parts, AutoZone, Bass Pro Shops, Macy's, Meineke, Nissan, Subaru, Toyota
44b	17th St, 19th St, E Sunoco, Turkey Hill Dunkin', Hardee's, Kajimachi Japanese Advance Parts, AutoZone, Buick/GMC, Firestone/auto, Honda, Hyundai, Midas
44a	PA 230, 13th St, Harrisburg, E Family$, W Chevrolet, VW, downtown
43	2nd St, Harrisburg, W Crowne Plaza, Hilton H, st capitol, downtown
42.5mm	Susquehanna River
42	Lemoyne
41b	Highland Park, E Turkey Hill Burger King, KFC, W Sunoco Vito's Italian Ace Hardware, Weis Foods
41a	US 15, PA 581 W, to Gettysburg
40b	New Cumberland, W Gulf/dsl Cedar Cliff Pizza, McDonald's, New China, Starbucks, Subway $General, CVS Drug
40a	Limekiln Rd, to Lewisberry, E Shell/dsl, Sunoco John's Diner, McDonald's, Pizza Hut Budget Inn, Capital Inn, Clarion, Fairfield Inn, Holiday Inn Express, La Quinta, W Speedway/Dunkin' Best Western+, Motel 6, Scottish Inn vet
39b	I-76/PA Tpk
39a	PA 114, Lewisberry Rd, E EVC, Rutter's/dsl Days Inn, Highland Inn, Red Carpet Inn
38	Reesers Summit
36	PA 262, Fishing Creek, E Speedway/Dunkin' Bruster's, Culhane's Steaks, Mamma's Pizza CVS Drug
35	PA 177, Lewisberry, E Patriot Pizza/subs, W Exxon Francesco's Pizza, Summit Rest.
34mm	**parking area/weigh sta sb**
34	Valley Green (from nb), same as 33

YORK

INTERSTATE 83 Cont'd

Exit #	Services
33	PA 392, Yocumtown, E Rutter's, Speedway/Dunkin'/dsl Brothers Pizzaria, Burger King, Hong Kong Buffet, KFC/Taco Bell, Maple Donuts, McDonald's, New China Buffet, Subway Value Inn $Tree, Advance Parts, AutoZone, GNC, Rite Aid, Verizon, Walmart/Subway
33mm	**parking area/weigh sta nb**
32	PA 382, Newberrytown, E Rutter's/deli/dsl/24hr, Sunoco/dsl, W Exxon/dsl
28	PA 295, Strinestown, W Rutter's/24hr 83 Diner, Wendy's
24	PA 238, Emigsville, W Sunoco/dsl Four Bros Rest.
22	PA 181, N George St, same as 21b, E Rutter's Comfort Inn, Homewood Suites
21b a	US 30, Arsenal Rd, to York, E Sheetz/dsl Cheddar's, Clock Diner, Qdoba, Starbucks Days Inn, EconoLodge, Motel 6, Sheraton, Tru Hilton AT&T, Buick/GMC, W Dickey's BBQ, Royal Farms/dsl, Rutter's/dsl, Sheetz/dsl Arby's, Bob Evans, Buffalo Wild Wings, Burger King, Chick-fil-A, Chili's, China Buffet, Chipotle, Denny's, Domino's, DQ, Dunkin', El Rodeo Mexican, Friendly's, Fujihana Japanese, Great Wall, Hardee's, Hoss's, Infinito's, Jersey Mike's, Jimmy John's, KFC, Little Caesar's, LJ Silver, Logan's Roadhouse, Lyndon Diner, Maple Donuts, McDonald's, Mission BBQ, MOD Pizza, Old Country Buffet, Olive Garden, Outback Steaks, Panera Bread, Pizza Hut, Quaker Steak, Rita's Custard, Smokey Bones BBQ, Subway, Taco Bell, Wendy's Best Western, La Quinta, Motel 6, Super 8, Wingate Inn $General, $Tree, Advance Parts, Aldi Foods, AutoZone, BJ's Whse/gas, BMW, Cadillac/Chevrolet, Chrysler/Dodge/Jeep, CVS Drug, Giant Foods/gas, Harley-Davidson, Honda, Kia, Kohl's, Lowe's, NTB, Old Navy, PepBoys, PetCo, Petsmart, Ross, Staples, Subaru, Target, TJ Maxx, URGENT CARE, Verizon, Walmart/McDonald's, Weis Foods/gas
19	PA 462, Market St, E Rutter's/dsl Applebee's, Arby's, Aroma Buffet, Buffalo Wild Wings, Chick-fil-A, ChuckECheese's, DQ, Dunkin', Fiesta Mexico, Firehouse Subs, Fuddruckers, Guadalajara Mexican, Jimmy John's, KFC, MOD Pizza, Moe's SW, Panera Bread, Papa John's, Red Lobster, Rita's Custard, Starbucks, Taco Bell, Tokyo Diner, Wendy's Quality Inn $General, $Tree, Advance Parts, Aldi Foods, Burlington Coats, Firestone/auto, Giant Foods/gas, Goodyear/auto, Home Depot, Lowe's, Meineke, Nissan, NTB, Petco, Sam's Club/gas, Verizon, Volvo, Walgreens, Walmart, Weis Mkt, W H
18	PA 124, Mt Rose Ave, Prospect St, E Rutters Arooga's Grille, Burger King, Five Guys, Nino's Pizza, Parma Pizza Grill, Pizza Hut $Tree, Grocery Outlet, Nello Tire
16b a	PA 74, Queen St, E Sunoco Baskin-Robbins/Dunkin', Cracker Barrel, IHOP, Imperial Gourmet, Isaac's Rest., JJ Panda, John's Pizza Shop, Maple Donuts, MOD Pizza, Primanti Bros, Starbucks, Stone Grille Country Inn&Suites, Hampton Inn, Home 2 Suites Giant Foods/gas, W Sheetz/dsl Chipotle, Infinito's Pizza, Jersey Mike's, Jimmy John's, Little Caesar's, McDonald's, Noodles&Co, Panera Bread, Pizza Hut/Taco Bell, Starbucks, Subway, Wendy's $General, $Tree, AT&T, CVS Drug, Jo-Ann Fabrics, Monro, Price Rite Foods, Tuesday Morning, vet, Walgreens, Weis Mkt
15	S George St, I-83 spur into York, W H
14	PA 182, Leader Heights, E Sheetz/dsl, Tesla EVC Arby's, Domino's, First Wok, Subway vet, W Rutter's McDonald's Holiday Inn Express Rite Aid
10	PA 214, Loganville, W Rutter's/dsl Mamma's Pizza Midway Motel st police, TrueValue

SHREWSBURY

Exit #	Services
8	PA 216, Glen Rock, W Shrewsbury Mkt (2mi)
4	PA 851, Shrewsbury, E Tom's/dsl/24hr Bill Batema Grill, Burger King, Cracker Barrel, Papa John's, Ruby Tu day Hampton Inn Home Depot, TrueValue, W E on/dsl Arby's, Chick-fil-A, Chipotle, Coachlight Rest., E erald Garden Chinese, Five Guys, KFC/Taco Bell, McDonal Panera Bread, Rita's Custard, Sons of Italy Pizzaria, Starbuc Subway, Wendy's $Tree, AAA, Advance Parts, Giant Foo GNC, Mr Tire, Saubel's Foods, Verizon, Walmart
2mm	**Welcome Ctr nb, full facilities, litter barrels, petwalk, vending**
0mm	Pennsylvania/Maryland state line

INTERSTATE 84

Exit #	Services
54mm	Pennsylvania/New York state line, Delaware River
53	US 6, PA 209, Matamoras, N **Welcome Ctr/both lanes, full facilities, litter barrels, petwalk, vending,** Go Shell, TurkeyHill/dsl The Grill, Two Rivers Grille Ap Inn AutoZone, fireworks, PriceChopper, S Suno dsl Dunkin', Goodfella's Italian, McDonald's, Peking G den, Perkins, Roy Rogers, Subway, Taco Bell, Village Di Wayback Burger, Wendy's Best Western, Hampton Scottish Inn $Tree, Advance Parts, Home Depot, Low Mavis Tire/auto, Staples, Tristate RV Park, Verizon, Walm Subway
46	US 6, to Milford, N Sunoco/dsl, 0-2 mi S Exxon/ Gulf, TurkeyHill Apple Valley Rest., Chang Mao Chine China Buffet, Dimmick Inn Steaks Rodeway Inn Food Mkt, NAPA, Rite Aid, USPO
34	PA 739, to Lords Valley, Dingmans Ferry, S Mirabito/ Sunoco/Dunkin'/dsl Bruno Pizza, McDonald's, Panda C nese, Portobello's Family$, Rite Aid, Weis Foods
30	PA 402, to Blooming Grove, N st police, to Lake Wall paupack
26	PA 390, to Tafton, N Exxon/dsl Tanglewood Ski A (4mi), to Lake Wallenpaupack, S to Promised Land SP
26mm	**/weigh sta both lanes, full facilities, litter barrels, p walk, vending**
20	PA 507, Greentown, N Exxon/dsl, Sunoco/Subv John's Italian Animal Park (5mi)
17	PA 191, to Newfoundland, Hamlin, N Howe's/Exxon/ scales/24hr Twin Rocks Diner Comfort Inn dsl rep
8	PA 247, PA 348, Mt Cobb, N Gulf/dsl, Sunoco/Burger K Tim Hortons/dsl $General
4	I-380 S, to Mount Pocono
2	PA 435 S, to Elmhurst
1	Tigue St, N Holiday Inn, S Valero/dsl
0mm	**I-84 begins/ends on I-81, exit 54.**

INTERSTATE 90

Exit #	Services
46mm	Pennsylvania/New York state line, **Welcome Ctr/weigh sta full facilities, litter barrels, petwalk, vending**
45	US 20, to State Line, N KwikFill/dsl/scales McDonal S Shell/Subway/dsl Red Carpet Inn fireworks, agara Falls Info
41	PA 89, North East, N Shell/repair New Har Rest. Holiday Inn Express, S Creekside Camping (4r
37	I-86 E, to Jamestown
35	PA 531, to Harborcreek, N TA/Country Pride/Pizza Hut/ way/dsl/scales/24hr/@ Blue Beacon, dsl repair

INTERSTATE 90 Cont'd

Exit #	Services
32	PA 430, PA 290, to Wesleyville, **N** [gas] Country Fair, GetGo/dsl
29	PA 8, to Hammett, **N** [gas] Country Fair [food] Wendy's [other] [H], **S** [lodging] Best Value [other] dsl repair
27	PA 97, State St, Waterford, **N** [gas] Country Fair/dsl [food] Arby's, Barbato's Italian, Doc Holiday's Grill, McDonald's [lodging] Days Inn, La Quinta, Motel 6, Red Roof Inn [other] [H], **S** [gas] Pilot/Subway/dsl/scales/24hr, Sheetz/dsl, Shell/Tim Hortons/dsl [food] Taco Bell [lodging] Baymont Inn, Quality Inn, Super 8 [other] $General, casino
24	US 19, Peach St, to Waterford, **N** [gas] Country Fair/dsl, Delta Sonic/Subway, GetGo/dsl, KwikFill, Tesla EVC [food] Applebee's, Burger King, Chick-fil-A, Chipotle Mexican, ChuckeCheese, Cracker Barrel, Dunkin', Eat'n Park, Five Guys, Golden Corral, KFC, Krispy Kreme, Longhorn Steaks, McDonald's, Olive Garden, Panera Bread, Quaker Steak&Lube, S&S Buffet, Starbucks, Steak'n Shake, Taco Bell, TGIFriday's, Tim Hortons, Torero's Mexican, TX Roadhouse [lodging] Courtyard, Hilton Garden [other] [H], $Tree, Advance Parts, Aldi Foods, AT&T, Best Buy, Hobby Lobby, Home Depot, Jo-Ann Fabrics, Kohl's, Lowe's, Marshall's, Old Navy, Petsmart, Sam's Club/gas, Staples, Target, URGENT CARE, Verizon, Walmart/Subway, Wegman's Foods, **S** [gas] Country Fair, Shell/Subway [food] Blotto's Grill, Bob Evans, IHOP [lodging] Best Western+, Comfort Inn, Country Inn&Suites, Hampton Inn, Holiday Inn Express, Home 2 Suites, Microtel, Residence Inn, Solstice Inn, Wingate Inn [other] waterpark
22b a	I-79, N to Erie, S to Pittsburgh, **3-5 mi N** services in Erie
18	PA 832, Sterrettania, **N** [gas] Marathon/dsl [other] Presque Passage RV Park, to Presque Isle SP, Waldameer Park (8mi), **S** [food] Beechwood Rest. [lodging] Quality Inn [other] golf, KOA, West Haven RV Park/camping
16	PA 98, to Franklin Center, Fairview, **S** [other] Follys Camping (2mi), Mar-Da-Jo-Dy Camping (5mi)
9	PA 18, to Girard, Platea, **N** [other] Fiesler's Service/repair/tires, st police, **S** [lodging] Green Roof Inn (2mi)
6	PA 215, to Albion, East Springfield, **N** [lodging] lodging
3	US 6N, to Cherry Hill, West Springfield, **N** [lodging] lodging on US 20
2.5mm	**[RS]/weigh sta eb, full [handicapped] facilities, info, litter barrels, petwalk, [phone], [picnic], vending**
0mm	Pennsylvania/Ohio state line

INTERSTATE 95

Exit #	Services
	Pennsylvania/New Jersey state line, Delaware River. **I-276 runs eb to NJ TPK.**
42 (I-95)	US 13, Delaware Valley, **N** [gas] [food] Dallas Diner, McDonald's [lodging] Motel 6 [other] 7-11, auto repair, U-Haul, **S** [gas] G Fuel, LukOil/dsl, Sunoco/dsl, Valero/dsl, WaWa/dsl [food] Burger King, Dunkin', Golden Eagle Diner, Italian Family Pizza, Porfirio's Pizza [lodging] Rodeway Inn, Villager Lodge [other] $General, Meineke
40	(from nb) I-295 N, to NJ. **I-95 N merges with PA Tpk/276 to NJ Tpk**
39	PA 413, I-276, to Bristol Bridge, Burlington
37	PA 132, to Street Rd, **W** [gas] BP/dsl, Liberty, Sunoco/dsl [food] Burger King, Chick-fil-A, China Sun Buffet, Dunkin', Golden Corral, Krispy Kreme, Little Caesar's, McDonald's, Popeye's, TX Roadhouse, Wendy's [other] $General, Advance Parts, Aldi Foods, GNC, Goodyear/auto, PepBoys, U-Haul, Walgreens, WaWa
35	PA 63, to US 13, Woodhaven Rd, Bristol Park, **W** [gas] BP/Dunkin', Sunoco/dsl [food] Arby's, Bob Evans, Boston Mkt, Burger King, Dunkin', Grand China Buffet, KFC, McDonald's, Old Haven Pizza,

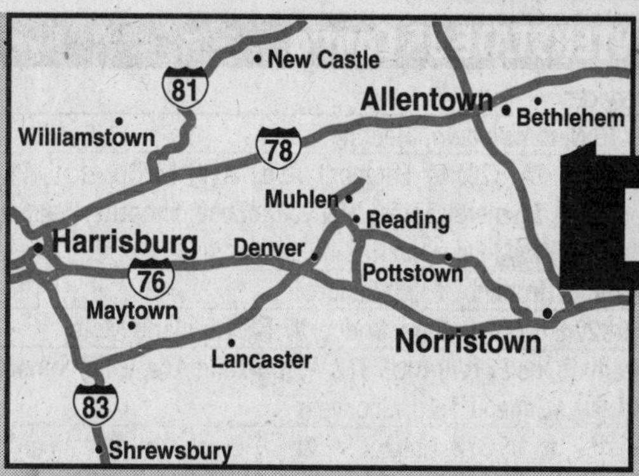

PA

PHILADELPHIA AREA

Exit #	Services
35	Continued Pizza Hut, Rita's Custard, Taco Bell, Wendy's [lodging] Holiday Inn Express [other] [H], $Tree, Acme Foods, Dick's, Home Depot, Marshall's, NTB, TJ Maxx, Verizon, Walmart, WaWa
32	Academy Rd, **W** [gas] Lukoil [food] Dunkin', KFC, McDonald's [other] [H], AutoZone
30	PA 73, Cottman Ave, **W** [gas] Sunoco
27	Bridge St, **W** [gas] 7-11, Citgo/dsl, Exxon, Lukoil [food] Dunkin' [other] [H], Rite Aid
26	to NJ 90, Betsy Ross Br, **W** [gas] BP/Dunkin', Speedway, Sunoco/dsl, WaWa/dsl [food] Applebee's, Boston Mkt, Burger King, Chick-fil-A, KFC, McDonald's, Sonic, Taco Bell, Wendy's [other] $Tree, Advance Parts, Home Depot, Lowe's, Rite Aid, ShopRite Foods, Target, Walmart
25	Allegheny Ave, **W** [gas] Sunoco/dsl [other] [H], WaWa
23	Lehigh Ave, Girard Ave, **E** [other] casino, **W** [gas] Exxon [food] Applebee's, Arby's, Coldstone, Dunkin', Rita's Custard [other] [H], $Tree, AutoZone, CVS Drug, GNC, PepBoys, Rite Aid, WaWa/dsl
22	I-676, US 30, to Central Philadelphia, Independence Hall
20	Columbus Blvd, Penns Landing, **1-2 mi E on Columbus** [gas] BP, Liberty/WaWa/dsl [food] Burger King, Chick-fil-A, ChuckECheese, Dunkin', Famous Dave's BBQ, IHOP, Longhorn Steaks, McDonald's, Ruby Buffet, Wendy's [lodging] Holiday Inn Express [other] $Tree, Acme Mkt, AT&T, Best Buy, GNC, Home Depot, IKEA, Lowe's, Marshall's, Old Navy, PepBoys, Staples, Target, Verizon, Walmart, **1-2 mi W on Columbus** [lodging] Marriott
19	I-76 E, to Walt Whitman Bridge, **W** [gas] BP, Liberty, Sunoco/dsl [food] Dunkin', KFC, Little Caesar's, McDonald's, Popeye's [other] $General, Aldi Foods, to stadiums
17	PA 611, to Broad St, Pattison Ave, **W** [other] [H], to Naval Shipyard, to stadium
15mm	Schuykill River
15	Enterprise Ave, Island Ave (from sb)
14	Bartram Ave, Essington Ave (from sb)
13	PA 291, to I-76 W (from nb), to Central Philadelphia, **E** [lodging] Aloft, Doubletree, Hawthorn Suites, Marriott, Renaissance Inn, Sheraton Four Points, Sheraton Suites, **W** [lodging] Residence Inn
12	Philadelphia Intl Airport, **E** services same as 10
10	PA 291, Bartrom Ave, (from nb), Cargo City, **E** [lodging] Marriott, Renaissance Hotel, **W** [gas] WaWa/dsl [food] Ruby Tuesday [lodging] Courtyard, Embassy Suites, Extended Stay America, Extended Stay America, Fairfield Inn, Hampton Inn, Microtel [other] Heinz NWR
9b a	PA 420, to Essington, Prospect Park, **E** [gas] Sunoco/dsl, Valero/dsl [food] Denny's, Lehmans Rest., Mel's Diner, Philly Diner [lodging] Clarion, La Quinta, Motel 6, Red Roof+, SpringHill Suites, Wyndham Garden [other] USPO, WaWa
8	to Chester Waterfront, Ridley Park, **E** [gas] Royal Farms [food] Cracker Barrel, Wendy's [lodging] Microtel, SpringHill Suites, **W on US 13** [food] Stargate Diner

INTERSTATE 95 Cont'd

Exit #	Services
7	I-476 N, to Plymouth, Meeting
6	PA 352, PA 320, to Edgmont Ave, E McDonald's, Popeye's $General, $Tree, AT&T, AutoZone, Shoprite, Walmart/Subway, W Days Inn
5	Kerlin St (from nb), E Sunoco
4	US 322 E, to NJ, to Barry Bridge, W Highland Motel
3	(from nb, no EZ return)US 322 W, Highland Ave, E Sunoco/dsl $General, Ford, Goodyear
2	PA 452, to US 322, Market St, W Exxon/dsl, Royal Farms/dsl Dunkin', McDonald's, Subway
1	Chichester Ave, E Sunoco fireworks, W Dunkin' transmissions, WaWa
0mm	Pennsylvania/Delaware state line, **Welcome Ctr/weigh sta nb, full facilities, litter barrels, petwalk,**

INTERSTATE 99

Exit #	Services
85	**I-99 begins/ends on I-80, exit 161.**
83	PA 350, Bellefonte, E Tesla EVC, Weis Foods/gas Wendy's, W Lyken's Mkt Burger King, Pizza Hut, Sammi's Rest. Rite Aid, TrueValue
81	PA 26 S, to PA 64, to Pleasant Gap
80	Harrison Rd (from nb, no re-entry)
78b a	PA 150, to Bellafonte, W Sheetz/dsl Dunkin' EconoLodge auto repair, Ford
76	Shiloh Rd, E Sheetz/dsl McDonald's, Perkins, Quaker Steak, Rey Azteca Best Western+, Ramada $Tree, AAA, Advance Parts, Barnes&Noble, BigLots, Chevrolet, Jo-Ann Fabrics, Ross, Sam's Club, Subaru, Walmart/Subway
74	Innovation Park, Beaver Stadium, Penn State U
73	US 322 E, Lewiston, State College
71	Woodycrest, Tofftrees, E Sheetz/dsl Applebee's, Chick-fil-A, Cracker Barrel, McDonald's, Olive Garden, Outback Steaks, Panda Express, Qdoba, Red Lobster, Starbucks, TX Roadhouse Hampton Inn, Holiday Inn Express, SpringHill Suites $Tree, Best Buy, Dick's, Kohl's, Michael's, PetCo, Target, Verizon, Walmart, Wegman's Foods, W Down Under Cafe Carnegie Inn, Toftrees Golf Resort
69	US 322 E, Valley Vista Dr, E Sheetz/dsl Home Depot, Lowe's
68	Skytop Mtn Rd, Grays Woods, Waddle
62	US 322 W, to Phillipsburg (from sb)
61	to US 322 W, Port Matilda, E Lykens Mkt/Sub Express/dsl Brother's Pizza Port Matilda Hotel USPO
52	PA 350, W Snappy's/Subway/dsl
48	PA 453, Tyrone, W Sheetz/dsl Burger King, Nino's Pizza, Subway H, Advance Parts, USPO
45	Tipton, Grazierville, W Rossi's H, DelGrosso's Funpark, Ford
41	PA 865 N, Bellwood, E Ft Roberdeau HS (6mi), W Martin Gen Store/dsl, Sheetz/dsl DelGrosso's Funpark (3 mi)
39	PA 764 S, Pinecroft, W Comfort Inn, Days Inn, Elizabeth Rest B&B Martin's Foods, Oak Spring Winery
33	17th St, same as 32, Altoona, W Sheetz/dsl Aldi Foods, Lowe's, Railroader Museum, U-Haul
32	PA 36, Frankstown Rd, Altoona, E GetGo, Sheetz/dsl Chili's, Chipotle, DQ, Panera Bread, Subway, TX Roadhouse Barnes&Noble, Best Buy, Boscov's, Canoe Cr SP, Dick's, Giant Eagle Foods, GNC, Home Depot, Kohl's, Michael's,
32	Continued PetCo, Ross, Staples, Verizon, W Sheetz/dsl Chuc Cheese, Dunkin', El Campesino Mexican, Five Guys, Honeyba Ham, McDonald's, Olive Garden, Papa John's, Perkins, Pi Hut, Popeye's, Red Lobster, Subway, Wendy's EconoLod Quality Inn, Super 8 H, $Tree, AT&T, AutoZone, Chrys Dodge/Jeep, CVS Drug, Jo-Ann Fabrics, Nissan, O'Reilly Pa Rite Aid, Save-A-Lot, URGENT CARE, USPO, Walgreens
31	Plank Rd, Altoona, E Chick-fil-A, Dunkin', Jethro's Re King's Rest., Outback Steaks Altoona Grand Hotel, Co yard, Holiday Inn Express Field&Stream, Firestone/a Petco, Sam's Club/gas, st police, Target, TJ Maxx, Walmart/ Donald's, W Applebee's, Arby's, Bob Evans, Burger Ki Casa Valadez, Champs Grill, Chinese Gourmet, Cracker Ba Denny's, Eat'n Park, KFC, Little Caesar's, LJ Silver, Longh Steaks, Panda Express, Red Robin, Taco Bell Hampton Motel 6 Advance Parts, BigLots, Buick/GMC, Hobby Lo JC Penney, Macy's, Martin's/gas, Monro, Verizon, Weis Foo
28	US 22, to Ebensburg, Holidaysburg
23	PA 36, PA 164, Roaring Spring, Portage, E GetGo/ Sheetz/24hr, Turkey Hill H, truck repair, Walmart/Subw
15	Claysburg, King, Claysburg, King, W Sheetz/dsl $Gen
10	to Imler, W Slick's Ivy Stone Rest. (2mi) Blue Knob SP (8
7	PA 869, Osterburg, St Clairsville, W Slick's Ivy Stone R (2mi) Blue Knob SP
3	PA 56, Johnstown, Cessna, E st police, truck parts
1	I-70/76, E GetGo/McDonald's/dsl, Pacific Pride/dsl, She dsl, Shell/Subway/dsl Arby's, Bedford Diner, Denny's, Steaks, Hoss' Rest, Pizza Hut, Taco Bell, Wendy's Budget H Fairfield Inn, Hampton Inn, Quality Inn, Rodeway Inn, Super
0	I-99 begins/ends on US 220.

ST COLLEGE

ALTOONA

INTERSTATE 295

Exit #	Services
10mm	Pennsylvania/New Jersey state line, Delaware River
10	PA 32, to New Hope, W Washington Crossing Hist Park
9mm	**Welcome Ctr sb, full facilities, litter barrels, petwalk, vending**
8	PA 332, to Yardley, Newtown, W Dunkin' Hampton H, to Tyler SP
5b a	US 1, W to I-276/PA TPK, Langhorne, Oxford Valley, W
3	US 1 bus, to PA 413, Penndel, Levittown, E Shell/7- dsl Arrano Hibachi Steaks, ChuckECheese's, Dun Friendly's, Hong Kong Pearl, Olive Garden, Panera Bread, Lobster, Ruby Tuesday, Subway, Uncle Bill's Homestyle, W dy's $Tree, Acura, Chevrolet, Chrysler/Dodge/Jeep, F stone/auto, Ford, Goodyear/auto, Harley-Davidson, Ho Hyundai, Kia, Lowe's, Marshall's, Redner's Whse Mkt, Sa Club, Subaru, Subaru, Target, VW/Volvo, W Denny's, Donald's H, Toyota, U-Haul

I-295 begins/ends on I-276/I-95/PA Tpk.

INTERSTATE 476

Exit #	Services
131	US 11, US 6. **I-476 begins/ends on I-81. Services same as exit 194.**
122	Keyser Ave, Old Forge, Taylor
121mm	**toll plaza**
115	I-81, PA 315, Wyoming Valley, Pittston, W Exxon/Subv dsl, Pilot/Wendy's/dsl/scales/24hr, Sunoco/dsl Ar Burger King, Denny's, McDonald's, Perkins Holiday Inn press, Knight's Inn Volvo, Walmart/Subway

INTERSTATE 476 Cont'd

Exit #	Services
112mm	**toll plaza**
105	PA 115, Wilkes-Barre, Bear Creek, E Exxon, Mobil Dunkin'
95	I-80, PA 940, Pocono, Hazleton, W WaWa Arby's, Burger King, McDonald's Comfort Inn, EconoLodge, Holiday Inn Express, Mtn Laurel Resort, Pocono Inn/Resort, Quality Inn, Split Rock Resort
87	PA 903, Jim Thorpe (tag holder only)
86mm	**Hickory Run Service Plaza both lanes, Sunoco/dsl Burger King, Jamba Juice, Quizno's, Starbucks**
74	US 209, Mahoning Valley, Lehighton, Stroudsburg, W Citgo, Shell/Subway/dsl Country Inn&Suites, Hampton Inn
71mm	Lehigh Tunnel
56	I-78, US 22, PA 309, Lehigh Valley, E Tesla EVC China House, Dunkin', Jamba Juice, Moe's SW, Red Robin, Subway, Trivet Diner, Wendy's, Zio's Pizza Parkview Inn BMW/Mini, Lexus, Maserati, Staples, Tuesday Morning, on US 22, W Exxon, Trexler Plaza Chris Rest., Potsy Pizza Holiday Inn Express, Motel 6 CVS Drug, Dan's Auto Repair, Jaguar, Land Rover, S Dunkin'
56mm	**Allentown Service Plaza both lanes, Sunoco/dsl Famiglia Pizza, Hershey's Ice Cream, Roy Rogers, Starbucks**
44	PA 663, Quakertown, Pottstown, E BP, Exxon/Subway/dsl, Wawa/dsl Caitlyn&Cody's Diner, Dunkin', Faraco's Pizza Hampton Inn, Holiday Inn Express, Quality Inn, SpringHill Suites
31	PA 63, Lansdale, E Lukoil, Royal Farms Margaritas Mexican, Osaka Japanese, The Mill Rest. Courtyard, Holiday Inn USPO, Walgreens, WaWa
20	Germantown Pike W, to I-276 W, PA Tpk W
19	Germantown Pike E
18b a	(18 from sb), Conshoshocken, Norristown, E Lukoil, Sunoco Andy's Diner, Burger King, Cracker Barrel, Domino's, Dunkin', Five Guys, Illiano's Pizza, McDonald's, Outback Steaks, Panera Bread, Qdoba, Rita's Ice Cream, Ruby Tuesday, Salad Works, Starbucks, Tony Roni Pizza Hampton Inn AT&T, Barnes&Noble, Best Buy, Dick's, Giant Foods, Lowe's, Marshall's, Old Navy, Petsmart, REI, Rite Aid, Ross, Target, Toyota, Verizon, Weis Mkt, W Papa John's, Uno, Wendy's Audi, BJ's Whse, Ford, Home Depot, Honda, Hyundai, IKEA, Kia, Mazda, Michael's, Nissan, Porsche
16b a	(16 from sb), I-76, PA 23, to Philadelpia, Valley Forge
13	US 30, E Liberty Campus Pizza, First Watch Cafe, Nova Grill, Snap Kitchen, Starbucks, Winger's to Villanova U, USPO
9	PA 3, BrooUpper Darby, E Barnaby's Rest. URGENT CARE
5	US 1, Lima, Springfield, E Chipotle, Hibachi Japanese, Smashburger, Subway AT&T, Giant Foods, Jo-Ann Fabrics, Marshall's, Old Navy, Staples, Verizon, Walmart
3	Baltimore Pike, Media, Swarthmore, E Mobil/dsl Carrabba's, Dunkin', Olive Garden, Outback Steaks, Panera Bread, Qdoba, Ruby Tuesday, Starbucks Macy's, Swarthmore Coll, Target
1	McDade Blvd, E Exxon Dunkin', McDonald's, Panda Chinese $Tree, CVS Drug
0mm	**I-476 begins/ends on I-95, exit 7.**

RHODE ISLAND

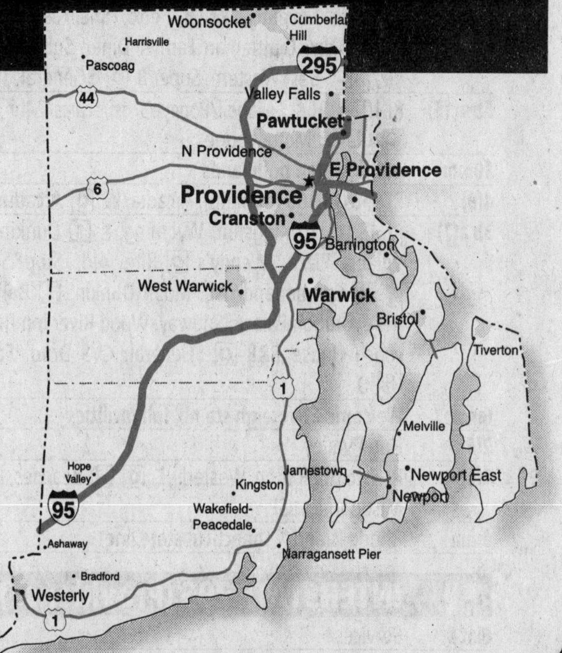

INTERSTATE 95

Exit #	Services
43mm	Rhode Island/Massachusetts state line
30(42)	East St, to Central Falls, E Dunkin', Subway
29(41)	US 1, Cottage St, W d'Angelo
28(40)	RI 114, School St, E Sunoco to hist dist, Yarn Outlet
27(39)	US 1, RI 15, Pawtucket, W EVC, Shell/repair/dsl, Sunoco/dsl/24hr Burger King, Dunkin', Murphy's Law Hampton Inn
26(38)	RI 122, Lonsdale Ave (from nb), E U-Haul
25(37)	US 1, RI 126, N Main St, Providence, E Shell/dsl, Speedway/dsl Chili's, Dunkin', Gregg's Rest. $Tree, Firestone/auto, PepBoys, Walgreens, W Speedway Burger King, Chelo's Rest. Aamco
24(36.5)	Branch Ave, Providence, W Stop&Shop/gas Wendy's Home Depot, Stop&Shop, URGENT CARE, Walmart/Subway, downtown
23(36)	RI 146, RI 7, Providence, E Mobil/dsl Marriott, W USPO
22(35.5)	US 6, RI 10, Providence, E Cheesecake Factory, Dave&Buster's, Fleming's Steaks, Panera Bread, PF Chang's CVS Drug, Macy's
21(35)	Broadway St, Providence, E Starbucks Hilton
20(34.5)	I-195, to E Providence, Cape Cod
19(34)	Eddy St, Allens Ave, to US 1, W Dunkin', Wendy's
18(33.5)	US 1A, Thurbers Ave, W Shell/dsl Burger King
17(33)	US 1 (from sb), Elmwood Ave, W Dunkin' Tires Whse, USPO
16(32.5)	RI 10, Cranston, E Williams Zoo/park
15(32)	Jefferson Blvd, E Mobil Dunkin', Shogun Steaks Courtyard, La Quinta, Motel 6, W Ryder Trucks
14(31)	RI 37, Post Rd, to US 1, W Shell/dsl Burger King Aldi, CVS Drug, Ford/Lincoln, Mazda, Volvo
13(30)	TF Green Airport Connector Rd, E Shell, Sunoco/Dunkin' Bertucci's, Chelo's Grill, Chipotle, HoneyDew Donuts, IHOP, Subway, Tuscan Grille, Wendy's Best Western, Extended

PA
RI

INTERSTATE 95 Cont'd

E GREENWICH

13(30) Continued
Stay America, Fairfield Inn, Hampton Inn, Hilton Garden, Holiday Inn Express, Homewood Suites, Radisson, Sheraton, Sonesta Suites TF Green Airport

12b(29) RI 2, I-295 N (from sb)

12a RI 113 E, to Warwick, E Shell/Dunkin'/dsl Crowne Plaza Hotel Lowe's, Stop&Shop, W Sunoco BJ's Rest., ChuckeCheese, On the Border, Wendy's Kohl's, Walmart/Subway

11(29) I-295 N (exits left from nb), to Woonsocket

10b a(28) RI 117, to Warwick, W H

9(25) RI 4 S, E Greenwich

8b a(24) RI 2, E Greenwich, E Shell/dsl, Tesla EVC Dunkin', McDonald's, Outback Steaks, Panera Bread, PieZone Pizza, TX Roadhouse Extended Stay America AT&T, CVS Drug, Dave's Mkt, **0-2 mi** W Sunoco/dsl Applebee's, Carrabba's, Chick-fil-A, Chili's, Denny's, Dunkin', Five Guys, KFC, Moe's SW, Olive Garden, PapaGino's Pizza, Smokey Bones BBQ, Starbucks, TGIFriday's, Wendy's SpringHill Suites Acura, Aldi Foods, Arlington RV Ctr, Audi/Bentley/BMW/Inifinti/Lexus/Mini/Porsche, Barnes&Noble, Best Buy, Cadillac, Home Depot, Honda, Jaguar, Jo-Ann Fabrics, Land Rover, Lowe's, Mercedes, Michael's, Nissan, PepBoys, Petco, Petsmart, Staples, Stop&Shop/gas, Subaru, Target, vet, VW

7(21) to Coventry, E Mobil/dsl, W Cumberland/dsl Applebee's, Cracker Barrel, Denny's, Dunkin', McDonald's, Wendy's Hampton Inn, Holiday Inn Express, Residence Inn BJ's Whse/gas, CVS Drug, Firestone/auto, GNC, Home Depot, URGENT CARE, Verizon, Walmart/Subway

6a(20) Hopkins Hill Rd, W Dunkin' park&ride

6(18) RI 3, to Coventry, W Petro, Shell/dsl/24hr, Sunoco/dsl Dunkin', Gentleman Farmer Diner, Subway, Wicked Good Pizza Best Western, Super 8 $General, TrueValue, vet

5b a(15) RI 102, W TA/Shell/Popeye's/dsl/scales/24hr Dan's Rest. Classic Motor Lodge

10mm **parking area both lanes**

4(9) RI 3, to RI 165 (from nb), Arcadia, W Arcadia SP, camping

3b a(7) RI 138 E, to Kingston, Wyoming, E Dunkin', McDonald's, Village Pizza, Wendy's Rite Aid, Stop&Shop/gas, vet, W Cumberland/dsl, Mobil/Dunkin' Bali Village Chinese, Dragon Palace, Subway, Wood River Inn Rest. Stagecoach House B&B $General, CVS Drug, Family$, NAPA, USPO

6mm **Welcome Ctr/weigh sta nb, full facilities**

2(4) Hope Valley

1(1) RI 3, to Hopkinton, Westerly, E H, beaches, RV camping, to Misquamicut SP

0mm Rhode Island/Connecticut state line

INTERSTATE 295 (Providence)

PROVIDENCE

Exit # Services

4b a(4) I-95, N to Boston, S to Providence. **I-295 begins/ends on I-95, exit 4 in MA. Exits 2-1 are in MA.**

2b a(2) US 1, E Mobil/Dunkin'/dsl 99 Rest., Chicago Grill, Chick-fil-A, Chipotle, ChuckeCheese, d'Angelo, Five Guys, Friendly's, Longhorn Steaks, Moe's SW, Panera Bread, PapaGino's Italian, Ruby Tuesday, Smashburger, TGIFriday's $Tree, AT&T, Best Buy, BJ's Whse, Buick/Chevrolet/GMC, CVS Drug, Dick's, Firestone/auto, JC Penney, Jo-Ann Fabrics, Lowe's, Macy's, Marshall's, Michael's, Old Navy, Petco, Petsmart, Staples,

2b a(2) Continued
Stop&Shop/gas, Target, Verizon, Walmart/Dunkin', W G
Shell/dsl Applebee's, Dunkin' Holiday Inn Expre
Knights Inn, Pineapple Inn CarMax, CVS Drug, Nissan, S
aru, Toyota

0mm Rhode Island/Massachusetts state line. **Exits 1-2 are in MA.**

22(24) RI 114, to Cumberland, E Shell/dsl, Sunoco Dunk
HoneyDew Donuts CVS Drug, Dave's Foods, US
W J's Deli, Saki's Pizza/subs Diamond Hill SP

20(21) RI 122, E Gulf Bollywood Grill, Burger King, Dunk
McDonald's Verizon, W Fortune House Chinese, H
eyDew Donuts, Paradise Pointe, Subway AAA, Ace Ha
ware, CVS Drug, Rite Aid, Seabra Foods, URGENT CARE

20mm Blackstone River

19.5mm **(full facilities) nb, weigh sta**

18b a(19) RI 146, Woonsocket, Lincoln, E EVC, Sunoco/dsl As
Grill, Chili's, Dunkin', Five Guys, McDonald's, Panera Bre
Starbucks Courtyard $Tree, AT&T, GNC, Marsha
Stop&Shop/gas, Target

15b a(16) RI 7, N Smithfield, E Terrazza Ristorante Home
Suites, W 7-11/dsl Biagio's Pizza, Dunkin', Paren
Rest. Hampton Inn, Holiday Inn Express Smith-App
by House

12b a(13) US 44, Centerdale, E Speedway Cancun Mexican, Dunk
Parma Ristorante H, NAPA, repair, W Exxon/dsl, Mo
Shell/dsl Applebee's, Burger King, Chelo's Grill, Chicago G
Chili's, Chipotle, D'angelo, Domino's, Dunkin', KFC/Taco Bell, M
Donald's, Panera Bread, PapaGino's, Sonic, Starbucks, Subw
TinTsin Chinese, Yamato Steaks $Tree, AT&T, Barnes&No
CVS Drug, Dave's Foods, Dick's, Home Depot, Kohl's, Michae
Old Navy, Rite Aid, Staples, Stop&Shop, Target, TJ Maxx, to Po
der Mill Ledges WR, URGENT CARE, Verizon

10 RI 5, Greenville Ave

9c(10) US 6, to Providence, E Shell/Dunkin' Atwood Grill, Bu
er King, Denny's, Dunkin', Five Guys, Hei Place, Jersey Mik
KFC, Popeye's, Smashburger, Starbucks, Subway AT
AutoZone, BJ's Gas, Buick/GMC, Chevrolet, Chrysler/Dod
Jeep, CVS Drug, Honda, Hyundai, Kia, Stop&Shop/gas, To
Fair Tire, USPO

9a(9) US 6 E Expswy, E Chipotle, McDonald's, Taco Bell $Tr
BJ's Whse, Home Depot, Petsmart

7(8) RI Resource Recovery Industrial Park

6(7) RI 14, Plainfield Pk, E Speedway/dsl McDona
$Tree, Walmart/Subway, W Gulf, Mobil/dsl/2
Dunkin', Palmieri Pizza, Subway CVS Drug, repair

3b a(4) rd 37, Phenix Ave, E TF Green Airport

1b(2) RI 2 S, to Warwick, E EVC Buffalo Wild Wings, Chic
Grill, Longhorn Steaks, Red Robin Extended Stay Ame
$Tree, JC Penney, Macy's, Marshalls, Old Navy, Target, V
zon, W Mobil, Sunoco/Subway BJ's Rest., Burger K
Chili's, Chipotle Mexican, ChuckeCheese, Dunkin', McDona
Olive Garden, On-the-Border, Panera Bread, Smashbur
Smokey Bones, Sonic, Starbucks, Subway, Taco Bell, W
dy's AT&T, AutoZone, Barnes&Noble, Best Buy, Chrys
Dodge/Keep/Kia, Dick's, Hobby Lobby, Home Depot, Jag
Kia, Kohl's, Petco, PetsMart, Price Rite Foods, Rite Aid, Stap
Target, TJMaxx, TownFair Tire, Trader Joe's, Verizon, Walm
Subway

1a(1) RI 113 W, to W Warwick, same as 2

0mm **I-295 begins/ends on I-95, exit 11.**

SOUTH CAROLINA

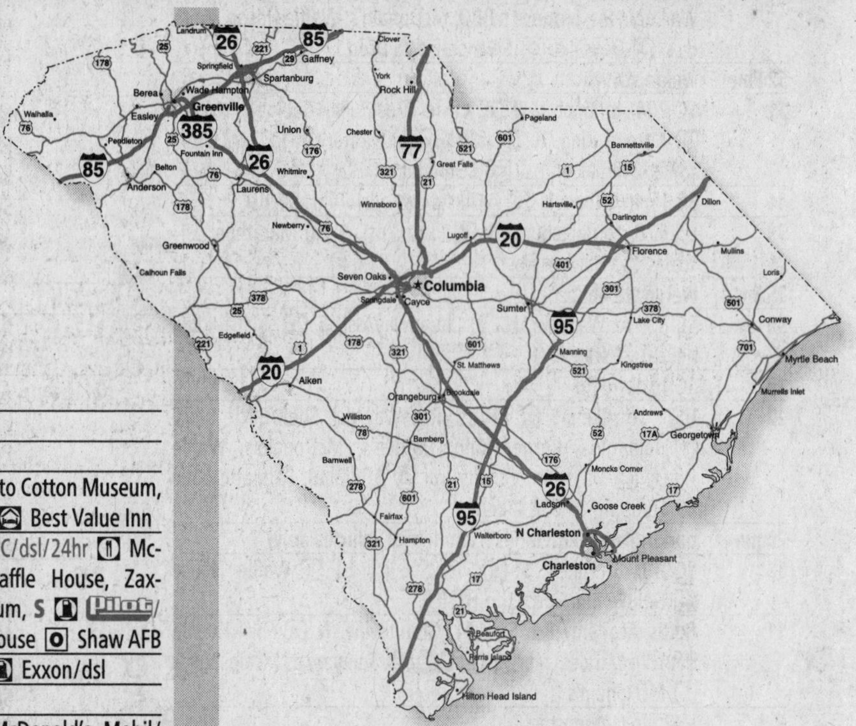

INTERSTATE 20

Exit #	Services
141b a	I-95, N to Fayetteville, S to Savannah. **I-20 begins/ends on I-95, exit 160. See Interstate 95, exit 160a for services.**
137	SC 340, to Timmonsville, Darlington, N BP/dsl (1mi) $General (1mi), S Marathon
131	US 401, SC 403, to Hartsville, Lamar, N Exxon/dsl to Darlington Raceway, S Shell/Markette/dsl
129mm	parking area both lanes (commercial vehicles only)
123	SC 22, N camping, Lee SP
121mm	Lynches River
120	SC 341, Bishopville, Elliot, N BP/dsl to Cotton Museum, S Exxon/dsl Taste of Country Rest. Best Value Inn
116	US 15, to Sumter, Bishopville, N Shell/KFC/dsl/24hr McDonald's, Pizza Hut, Subway (1mi), Waffle House, Zaxby's Red Roof Inn to Cotton Museum, S Pilot/DQ/Wendy's/dsl/scales/24hr Huddle House Shaw AFB
108	SC 34, to SC 31, Manville, N BP/dsl, S Exxon/dsl
101	rd 329, Dr Humphries Rd
98	US 521, to Camden, N BP/dsl, Exxon/McDonald's, Mobil/Circle K/dsl, Shell/dsl Fatz Cafe, Waffle House Comfort Suites, Hampton Inn, Holiday Inn Express H, to Revolutionary War Park
96mm	Wateree River
93mm	both lanes, full facilities, litter barrels, petwalk, vending
92	US 601, to Lugoff, N Mobil, Pilot/DQ/Subway/dsl/scales/24hr, Shell/Bojangles/dsl Hardee's, Waffle House Days Inn, EconoLodge
87	SC 47, to Elgin, N BP/dsl, Shell/dsl, S Loves/Hardee's/dsl/scales24hr
82	SC 53, to Pontiac, N Mobil, Shell Blimpie, Burger King, Egg Roll Express Woodspring Suites $General, Harley-Davidson, vet, S BP/dsl Clothing World Outlet
80	Clemson Rd, N Circle K, Exxon/dsl, Shell/Bojangles/dsl China Garden, D's, Dunkin', Groucho's Deli, Henry's, J Peters Grill, Krispy Kreme, Maurice's BBQ, McDonald's, San Jose Mexican, Subway, Sumo Japanese, Travinia Italian, Waffle House, Zaxby's Hampton Inn, Holiday Inn Express CVS Drug, Firestone/auto, S Wendy's Chevrolet, Ft Jackson Nat Cem, Hyundai
76b	Alpine Rd, to Ft Jackson, N Sesquicentennial SP
76a	(76 from eb), I-77, N to Charlotte, S to Charleston
74	US 1, Two Notch Rd, to Ft Jackson, N Mobil/dsl Chili's, Fazoli's, Hooters, IHOP, Lizard's Thicket, Outback Steaks, Waffle House Best Western+, Comfort Suites, EconoLodge, Fairfield Inn, Hampton Inn, La Quinta, Microtel, Motel 6, Red Roof Inn Home Depot, to Sesquicentennial SP, USPO, S BP, Exxon, Shell Applebee's, Bojangles, Brickhouse, China Garden, Church's, Harbor Inn Seafood, Hardee's, Honeybaked Ham, Jasmine Buffet, Maurice's BBQ, McDonald's, Monterrey Mexican, Substation II Days Inn Advance Parts, AT&T, AutoZone, Best Buy, Firestone/auto, Lowe's, Marshall's, Verizon
73b	SC 277 N, to I-77 N
73a	SC 277 S, to Columbia, S H
72	SC 555, Farrow Rd
71	US 21, N Main, to Blythewood, Columbia, N BP/dsl, Save-a-Ton/dsl, TA/Subway/Taco Bell/dsl/scales/24hr/@ McDonald's Days Inn tires/repair, truckwash, S Shell
70	US 321, Fairfield Rd, S FLYING J/Denny's/dsl/LP/24hr, Exxon Hardee's Super 8 Blue Beacon, truck repair
68	SC 215, Monticello Rd, to Jenkinsville, N Exxon/dsl, Shell/dsl, S Shell/dsl
66mm	Broad River
65	US 176, Broad River Rd, to Columbia, N CK Mart, BP, Exxon, Shell/Circle K Bojangles, Rush's BBQ, Sonic, Subway, Waffle House Economy Inn $Tree, Aamco, CVS Drug, Family$, U-Haul, Walgreens, S Speedway/dsl Arby's, Baskin-Robbins/Dunkin', Chick-fil-A, Church's, KFC, Lizard's Thicket, McDonald's, Nick's, Ocean View Seafood, Ruby Tuesday, Sandy's HotDogs, Scholtzsky's, Taco Bell, Wendy's, Zaxby's American Inn, InTown Suites, Ramada Ltd, Regency Inn, Royal Inn $General, Advance Parts, Office Depot, PepBoys
64b a	I-26, US 76, E to Columbia, W to Greenville, Spartanburg
63	Bush River Rd, N Shell/Circle K Burger King, Cracker Barrel, Real Mexican, Subway Quality Inn CVS Drug, S Marathon, Murphy USA/dsl, Sunoco/dsl Fuddrucker's Best Western, DoubleTree, Knights Inn, Sleep Inn AutoZone, Hamrick's, Walmart
61	US 378, W Cola, N Exxon, Murphy Express/dsl Chick-Fil-A, Chili's, Jewell's BBQ, McDonald's, Starbucks, Substation II, Taco Bell Wingate Inn Honda, S BP/dsl, Shell/Burger King/dsl Waffle House $General
58	US 1, W Columbia, N Shell/Subway/dsl, Sunoco Waffle House, S Murphy Express/dsl Bojangles, San Jose Mexican Woodspring Suites auto repair, County Tire
55	SC 6, to Lexington, N BP/Circle K/dsl, Shell/dsl Blue Pig Hampton Inn (2mi) John's RV Ctr, S BP/dsl,

COLUMBIA

INTERSTATE 20 Cont'd

55	Continued Pops, Shell/Circle K/DQ/dsl Bojangles, Dunkin', Great Wall Chinese, Maurice's BBQ, McDonald's, Waffle House, Wendy's Days Inn $General, CVS Drug
52.5mm	weigh sta wb
51	SC 204, to Gilbert, N Circle K/dsl, Shell/Subway/dsl/24hr Burger King, S Loves/Chester's/McDonald's/dsl/scales/24hr, Mobil/dsl $General
44	SC 34, to Gilbert, N 44Trkstp/rest./dsl/24hr, BP/dsl
39	US 178, to Batesburg, N Exxon/dsl, S Marathon/dsl/scales Hillview Rest.
35.5mm	weigh sta eb
33	SC 39, to Wagener, N Cheapway/dsl, S Shell/Huddle House/dsl/scales
29	SC 49, Wire Rd
22	US 1, to Aiken, S BP/dsl, RaceWay/dsl, Shell/Circle K/dsl Bojangle's, Burger King, Hardee's, McDonald's, Waffle House Days Inn, Quality Inn $General, Palmetto Lake RV Camping, to USC Aiken
20mm	parking area both lanes (commercial vehicles only)
18	SC 19, to Aiken, S Shell/Subway/dsl Waffle House Deluxe Inn, Guest Inn H
11	Bettis Academy Rd, SC 144, Graniteville, N Shell/Huddle House/dsl/scales/24hr, S Pilot/Subway/dsl/scales/24hr McDonald's
6	I-520 to N Augusta
5	US 25, SC 121, N BP/repair/dsl, Circle K/dsl, Shell/Circle K/dsl/scales Bojangles, Burger King, Checkers, Crazy Buffet, DQ, Jersey Mike's, Little Caesar's, McDonald's, Pablo's Mexican, Sonic, Subway, Wendy's, Zaxby's Holiday Inn Express $General, Advance Parts, Food Lion, GNC, Verizon, Walmart, S Marathon Waffle House Sleep Inn
1	SC 230, Martintown Rd, N Augusta, N Gas+/dsl, S Shell/Circle K/Subway/dsl Waffle House to Garn's Place
.5mm	Welcome Ctr eb, full facilities, litter barrels, petwalk, vending
0mm	South Carolina/Georgia state line, Savannah River

INTERSTATE 26

Exit #	Services
221	Meeting St, Charleston, E Church's Courtyard, Embassy Suites, Hampton Inn, Hyatt Place Family$
221b	US 17 N, to Georgetown
I-26 begins/ends on US 17 in Charleston, SC.	
221a	US 17 S, to Kings St, to Savannah
220	Romney St (from wb)
219b	Morrison Dr, East Bay St (from eb), N Exxon
219a	Rutledge Ave (from eb, no EZ return), to The Citadel
218	Spruill Ave (from wb), N Charleston
217	N Meeting St (from eb)
216b a	SC 7, Cosgrove Ave, to US 17 S
215	SC 642, Dorchester Rd, N Charleston, N Cheapway/dsl Charleston Grand, S BP/Circle K/dsl Charleston Inn Best Value Inn
213b a	Montague Ave, Mall Dr, N Cowboys Brazilian, Hello Deli, Red Lobster Courtyard, Marriott, Woodspring Suites Charles Towne Square, S BP/Circle K/dsl, Mobil, Spinx/dsl Arby's, Big Billy's Burgers, Bonefish Grill, Bufflo Wild Wings, Burger King, Chick-fil-A, Chipotle, CiCi's Pizza, Community Pizza, Domino's, Dunkin', Firehouse Subs, Five Guys,
213b a	Continued Golden Corral, Grand Buffet, IHOP, Jersey Mike's, Jimmy Joh Jim'N Nick's BBQ, La Hacienda, McAlister's Deli, McDona Mellow Mushroom, Panda Express, Panera Bread, Sake Ja nese, Starbucks, Steak'n Shake, Taste of Tokyo, Waffle Ho Zaxby's ALoft, Comfort Inn, Crowne Plaza, EconoLod Embassy Suites, Extended Stay America, Extended Stay Am ica (2), Fairfield Inn, Hampton Inn, Hilton Garden, Holiday Express, Home 2 Suites, Homewood Suites, Hyatt Place, InTo Suites, Quality Inn, Residence Inn, Rodeway Inn, TowneP Suites, Wingate Inn $Tree, AT&T, Field&Stream, Old N Sam's Club/gas, Staples, Tanger Outlet/Famous Brands, V zon, vet, Walmart/Subway
212c b	I-526, E to Mt Pleasant, W to Savannah, S
212a	Remount Rd, Hanahan, N on US 52/78 Sunoco/dsl K Taco Bell Advance Parts, AutoZone, Ford
211b a	Aviation Pkwy, N on US 52/78 Citgo, Exxon Arb Burger King, Capt D's, Church's, KFC, McDonald's, Nick's Gyr Papa John's, Popeye's, Schlotzky's, Smokey Bones, Sonic, S way, Super Buffet, Taco Bell Masters Inn O'Reilly Pa PepBoys, U-Haul, USPO, S Circle K/dsl Waffle Ho Budget Inn
209	Ashley Phosphate Rd, to US 52, N Exxon, Kangaroo plebee's, Cane's, Carrabba's, Chick-fil-A, China Buffet, Chip Mexican, ChuckECheese, Coldstone, Denny's, Dickey's B Firehouse Subs, Five Guys, Hardee's, Hooters, Jersey Mi Subs, Jimmy John's, King Street Grill, Longhorn Steaks, Reyes, Moe's SW Grill, Noisy Oyster, O'Charley's, Olive Gard Outback Steaks, Panda Express, Smokey Bones BBQ, S bucks, Subway, Taco Bell, Waffle House, Wendy's, Wild W Cafe Candlewood Suites, Country Inn&Suites, DoubleT Extended Stay America, Hawthorn Inn, Holiday Inn Express, Town Suites, Red Roof Inn, Rodeway Inn, Suburban Inn $General, $Tree, AT&T, Barnes&Noble, Belk, Best Buy, BigL Books-A-Million, Dillard's, Firestone/auto, GNC, Hobby Lob Home Depot, JC Penney, Lowe's, Michael's, Nissan, NTB, O Depot, Old Navy, Petco, Petsmart, Ross, Target, Toyota, Tu day Morning, URGENT CARE, Verizon, Walgreens, Walma McDonald's, S BP, RaceWay/dsl, Speedway/dsl, Suno dsl Bojangles, Cracker Barrel, IHOP, McDonald's, Os Asian, Ruby Tuesday, Waffle House Best Western, Fairf Inn, Hampton Inn, Hyatt Place, InTown Suites, La Quinta, M 6, Quality Inn, Relax Inn, Residence Inn, Sleep Inn, Staybri Suites, Woodspring Suites
209a	to US 52 (from wb), to Goose Creek, Moncks Corner
205b a	US 78, to Summerville, N BP/Dunkin', Speedway/dsl, noco/dsl Arby's, Bruster's, Cook-Out, East Bay Deli, F house Subs, Fortune Garden, Jersey Mike's, Sonic, Starbu Subway, Waffle House, Wendy's, Willie Jewell's BBQ, Z by's Fairfield Inn, Hampton Inn, Holiday Inn Express, W gate Inn H, Charleston Southern U, CVS Drug, Fami S Citgo, Speedway/dsl, Sunoco/dsl Burger King, C na Chef, KFC, Subway, Taco Bell Advance Parts, CVS Dr KOA, Piggly Wiggly
204mm	eb, full facilities, litter barrels, petwalk, vendi
203	College Park Rd, Ladson, N BP, Sunoco/dsl McD ald's, Waffle House Best Western, Days Inn, S Spi dsl KOA (2mi)
202mm	wb, full facilities, litter barrels, petwalk, vend
199b a	US 17 A, to Moncks Corner, Summerville, N BP, Kangar dsl, Marathon, Pilot/McDonald's/dsl/scales/24hr, Speedw Dunkin'/dsl Carolina Alehouse, China Chef, China W

CHARLESTON

NORTH CHARLESTON

E INTERSTATE 26 Cont'd

199b a	Continued KFC, Pizza Hut, Subway Courtyard $General, Advance Parts, AutoZone, BiLo, Buick/GMC, CVS Drug, Family$, O'Reilly Parts, vet, **S** Shell/Circle K Applebee's, Atlanta Bread, Bojangles, Box Car Betty's, Burger King, Chick-fil-A, China Token, Cracker Barrel, Domino's, Dunkin', Five Guys, Hardee's, IHOP, Jersey Mike's Subs, La Hacienda, Logan's Roadhouse, Marble Slab, McAlisters Deli, Mellow Mushroom, Moe's SW Grill, Newk's Eatery, O'Charleys, Panera Bread, Papa John's, Ruby Tuesday, Ryan's, Shoney's, Smashburger, Starbucks, Sticky Fingers, Waffle House, Which Wich?, Zaxby's Comfort Inn, Comfort Suites, Country Inn&Suites, EconoLodge, Economy Inn, Hampton Inn, Holiday Inn Express, Quality Inn, Sleep Inn AT&T, Belk, Best Buy, Chrysler/Dodge/Jeep, Dick's, Earthfare Mkt, GNC, Home Depot, Jo-Ann, Kohl's, Lowe's, NTB, Petco, Petsmart, Ross, Staples, Target, TJ Maxx, Verizon, Walgreens, Walmart/McDonald's, World Mkt
194	SC 16, to Jedburg, **E** access to Foreign Trade Zone 21, **W** FLYING J/PJ Fresh/Wendy's/dsl/scales/24hr
187	SC 27, to Ridgeville, St George, **N** Shell, **S** BP/dsl Francis Beidler Forest (10mi)
177	SC 453, to Holly Hill, Harleyville, **S** Shell/dsl Ashley Lodge/RV park
174mm	**weigh sta both lanes**
172b a	US 15, to Santee, St George, **S** Horizon/Domino's/Subway/dsl/e-85/scales/24hr
169b a	I-95, N to Florence, S to Savannah
165	SC 210, to Bowman, **N** Exxon/dsl, **S** BP/dsl
159	SC 36, to Bowman, **N** Pilot/McDonald's/dsl/scales/24hr/@, **S** Exxon
154b a	US 301, to Santee, Orangeburg, **N** Days Inn, **S** Exxon, Loves/Chesters/Subway/dsl/scales/24hr, Shell/dsl Waffle House
152mm	**wb, full facilities, litter barrels, petwalk, , , vending**
150mm	**eb, full facilities, litter barrels, petwalk, , , vending**
149	SC 33, to Cameron, to SC State Coll, Orangeburg, Claflin Coll
145b a	US 601, to Orangeburg, St Matthews, **S** BP/dsl, Exxon, Shell, Sunoco/dsl, United/dsl Burger King, Chick-fil-A, Cracker Barrel, Fatz Café, Hardee's, McDonald's, Ruby Tuesday, Seafood Academy, Subway, Waffle House, Wendy's, Zaxby's Carolina Lodge, Comfort Inn, Country Inn&Suites, Days Inn, Fairfield Inn, Hampton Inn, Holiday Inn Express, Howard Johnson, Quality Inn, Sleep Inn, Southern Lodge H, $General, Cadillac/Chevrolet, Chrysler/Dodge/Jeep, Ford, Nissan, Toyota
139	SC 22, to St Matthews, **S** Horizon/e85, Mobil, Pilot/Dunkin'/Arby's/dsl/scales/24hr Sweetwater Lake Camping (2.5mi)
136	SC 6, to North, Swansea, **N** Exxon/dsl
129	US 21, **N** Shell/dsl
125	SC 31, to Gaston, **N** Wolfe's Truck/trailer repair
123mm	**both lanes, full facilities, litter barrels, petwalk, , , vending**
119	US 176, US 21, to Dixiana, **S** BP/Subway/dsl, Exxon/dsl
116	I-77 N, to Charlotte, US 76, US 378, to Ft Jackson
115	US 176, US 21, US 321, to Cayce, **N** BP, Gulf, RaceWay, Shell/dsl Pizza Hut, Waffle House $General, $Tree, Advance Parts, Bi-Lo, CVS Drug, Family$, Reid's Foods, **S** Pilot/DQ/Wendy's/dsl/scales/24hr, Shell/dsl Bojangles, Carolina Wings, Great China, Hardee's, McDonald's, Sonic, Subway Country Hearth Inn Firestone, Piggly Wiggly

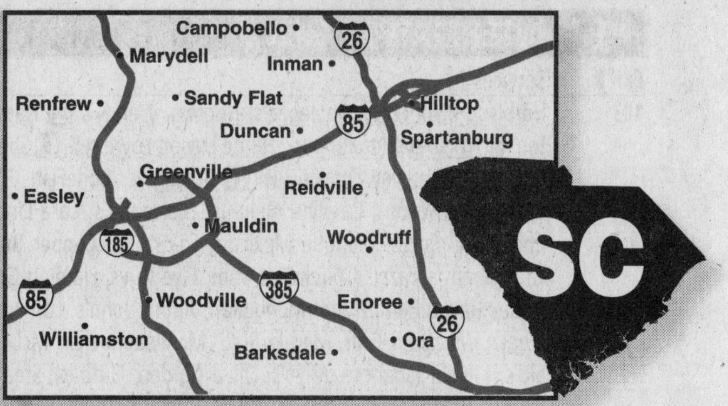

CAYCE

113	SC 302, Cayce, **N** Marathon, Mobil/Burger King, Sunoco/dsl Waffle House Airport Inn, Knights Inn, Masters Inn $General, AutoZone, O'Reilly Parts, Rite Aid, Save-A-Lot, Toyota, Walgreens, **S** BP/dsl, RaceWay, Shell/Circle K Lizard's Thicket, Shoney's, Subway, Waffle House Carolina Lodge, Country Inn&Suites, Days Inn, Sleep Inn, Travelers Inn , NAPA
111b a	US 1, to W Columbia, **N** Murphy USA/dsl, RaceWay, Shell/Circle K/dsl Chick-fil-A, Domino's, Dragon City Chinese, Hardee's, Little Caesar's, Maurice's BBQ, Moe's SW Grill, Ruby Tuesday, San Jose, Sonic, Subway, Tokyo Grill, Waffle House, Zaxby's Clarion, Delta Motel, Quality Inn $General, $Tree, AT&T, Bi-Lo, GNC, Hobby Lobby, Pet Supplies+, to USC, Walgreens, Walmart, **S** Speedway/dsl Applebee's, China Chef, Fat Boy Greek, Popeye's, Wendy's Aldi Foods, BigLots, Family$, Lowe's, U-Haul

COLUMBIA

110	US 378, to W Columbia, Lexington, **N** Grecian Gardens, Happy China, Lizard's Thicket, McDonald's, Rush's Rest., Subway, Waffle House America's Inn, Hampton Inn, Holiday Inn CVS Drug, Family$, Food Lion, Toyota, **S** Mobil/dsl, Shell/Circle K Atlanta Bread, Bojangles, China Dragon, Firehouse Subs, La Fogata, Pizza Hut Executive Inn H, URGENT CARE
108b a	I-126 to Columbia, Bush River Rd, **N** BP, Exxon/dsl, Shell/dsl Capt D's, Chick-fil-A, Hardee's, Ruby Tuesday, Schlotzsky's, Waffle House, Wendy's, Zaxby's Comfort Inn, Embassy Suites, Extended Stay America, Homewood Suites $General, Advance Parts, Chrysler/Jeep/Dodge, Dodge/Ram, Firestone/auto, Ford/Lincoln, Hyundai, Kia, Mazda, Midas, Office Depot, Riverbanks Zoo, Verizon, **S** City Gas, Murphy USA/dsl, Sunoco/dsl Bamboo House, Fuddrucker's, Pizza Hut, Tokyo Grill Baymont Inn, Best Western, DoubleTree, Hawthorn Suites, Knights Inn, Sleep Inn AutoZone, GNC, Hamrick's, Walmart
107b a	I-20, E to Florence, W to Augusta
106b a	St Andrews Rd, **N** Exxon/dsl ChuckECheese, IHOP, Papa John's, Sonic, Top China Buffet Motel 6 $Tree, Bi-Lo, Camping World RV Ctr, CVS Drug, Infiniti, Jaguar, Nissan, Walgreens, **S** BP/dsl, Shell, Speedway/Dunkin'/dsl Domino's, King Buffet, Maurice's BBQ, McDonald's, Nick's Grill, Pizza Hut, Sandy's Hot Dogs, Substation II, Waffle House, WG's Wings, Zaxby's EconoLodge, Red Roof Inn $General, KJ's IGA, Tire Kingdom, vet
104	Piney Grove Rd, **N** Sunoco/dsl Hardee's, San Jose Mexican, Waffle House Quality Inn Costco/gas, Sportsmans Whse, vet, **S** Exxon, Shell/dsl Country Inn&Suites, Microtel Carmax, Land Rover

INTERSTATE 26 Cont'd

IRMO

Exit #	Services
103	Harbison Blvd, N Applebee's, Hooters, Wendy's Hampton Inn Chevrolet, funpark, Home Depot, Lowe's, S Shell/Circle K, Speedway/Dunkin'/dsl Bojangles, BoneFish Grill, Buffalo Wild Wings, Carolina Alehouse, Carrabba's, Casa Linda, Chick-fil-A, Chili's, Chipotle Mexican, Coldstone, Copper River Grill, Denny's, Fazoli's, Firehouse Subs, Five Guys, Flaming Grill, Honey Baked Ham, Huhot Mongolian, Jimmy John's, Longhorn Steaks, Macaroni Grill, Marble Slab, McAlister's Deli, McDonald's, Miyabi Japanese, Miyo's, Olive Garden, Outback Steaks, Panera Bread, Rioz Brazilian, Rita's Custard, Ruby Tuesday, Rush's BBQ, Ryan's, Sonic, Starbucks, Subway, Tokyo Grill, Tsunami Steaks, TX Roadhouse, Which Wich?, Wild Wing Cafe, Yamato Japanese Comfort Suites, Fairfield Inn, Hilton Garden, Holiday Inn Express, Home Towne Suites, InTown Suites, Wingate Inn $Tree, AT&T, Belk, Best Buy, Buick/GMC, Dick's, Dillard's, Firestone/auto, Goodyear/auto, JC Penney, Kohl's, Marshalls, Michael's, Midas, NTB, Old Navy, Petsmart, Publix, Ross, Sam's Club/dsl, Staples, SteinMart, Target, TJ Maxx, Verizon, Walmart
102	SC 60, Ballentine, Irmo, N Cracker Barrel Extended Stay Deluxe, Hyatt Place H, S JP/dsl, Shell Arby's, Bellacino's Pizza, Dunkin', Groucho's Deli, Marco's Pizza, Maurice's BBQ, Moe's SW Grill, Papa John's, Smashburger, Taco Bell, Zaxby's, Zoe's Kitchen Residence Inn AAA, CVS Drug, Jiffy Lube, same as 103
101b a	US 76, US 176, to N Columbia, 1/2 mi N Exxon/Subway/dsl Bojangles, China House, Fatz Café, Fuji Cafe, HotDog Heaven, Jersey Mike's Subs, Zorba's $General, AutoZone, Food Lion, Harley-Davidson, Publix, Rite Aid, Walgreens, S BP, Hickory Point/dsl, Mobil, Shell/dsl Burger King, Lucky's BurgerShack, Waffle House $General, Toyota
97	US 176, to Ballentine, Peak, N China 1, Subway Food Lion, S Exxon/dsl
94mm	**weigh sta wb**
91	SC 48, to Chapin, S BP/dsl, Exxon/Taco Bell/dsl, Shell/dsl Bojangles, Farm Boys BBQ, McDonald's, Waffle House to Dreher Island SP, URGENT CARE
85	SC 202, Little Mountain, Pomaria, S to Dreher Island SP
82	SC 773, to Prosperity, Pomaria, N Exxon/Circle K/Subway/dsl/24hr, Pilot/Wendy's/dsl/scales/24hr Waffle House
81mm	**weigh sta eb**
76	SC 219, to Pomaria, Newberry, N Love's/McDonald's/Chester's/dsl/scales/24hr, 0-2 mi S BP, Murphy USA Burger King, Wendy's Hampton Inn (4mi), Holiday Inn Express to Newberry Opera House, Walmart
74	SC 34, to Newberry, N BP/dsl, Shell/dsl Bill&Fran's Café, 2-4 mi S Citgo/dsl Arby's, Capt D's, Hardee's, McDonald's, Waffle House Days Inn, Days Inn, Economy Inn H, to NinetySix HS
72	SC 121, to Newberry, S Citgo/dsl H, to Newberry Coll
66	SC 32, to Jalapa
63.5mm	**both lanes, full facilities, litter barrels, petwalk, vending**
60	SC 66, to Joanna, S BP/dsl Magnolia RV Park
54	SC 72, to Clinton, N BP/dsl, S Citgo/dsl Fatz Cafe, Zaxby's Hampton Inn H, to Presbyterian Coll
52	SC 56, to Clinton, N Pilot/Subway/dsl/scales/24hr Blue Ocean Rest., McDonald's Comfort Suites, Quality Inn, S Citgo/dsl Hardee's, Waffle House, Wendy's Days Inn H
51	I-385, to Greenville (from wb)
45.5mm	Enoree River

SPARTANBURG

Exit #	Services
44	SC 49, to Cross Anchor, Union
41	SC 92, to Enoree, N Valero
38	SC 146, to Woodruff, N HotSpot/Shell/Hardee's/dsl/scales/
35	SC 50, Walnut Grove Rd, to Woodruff, S BP/dsl
33mm	S Tyger River
32mm	N Tyger River
28	US 221, to Spartanburg, N Circle K/dsl/24hr, Shell/Subway/dsl Bojangles, Burger King, Italian Pizza, W... House H, Pine Ridge Camping (3mi), to Walnut G... Plantation
22	SC 296, Reidville Rd, to Spartanburg, N Exxon/dsl, M...athon/Kangaroo/dsl, Spinx/dsl Arby's, Blue Bay R... Bruster's, Chief's Rest., Fatz Cafe, Fuddrucker's (1mi), L... Caesars, McDonald's, Outback Steaks, Substation II, W... House, Wasabi Japanese, Wayback Burger, Zaxby's $G...eral, Advance Parts, to Croft SP, USPO, vet, S 7-11/dsl, ... dsl, Sunoco/dsl Clock Rest., Denny's, Domino's, Dunki... Limon Mexican, Hardee's, Hong Kong Express, Hunan K, Pa... Garden, Papa John's, Subway Sleep Inn, Southern Su... Super 8 $General, Abbott Farms, Bi-Lo, CVS Drug, Hyu... Midas, Rite Aid, Toyota, vet, VW, Walgreens
21b a	US 29, to Spartanburg, N Marathon/Circle K, Sp... dsl A&W/LJ Silver, Bojangles, Brasilia Steaks, Buffalo W... Wings, Burger King, Chick-fil-A, Chipotle Mexican, Chu... Cheese, CiCi's, City Range Steaks, Corona Mexican, DQ, ... house Subs, FoodCourt, Golden Corral, Jack-in-the-Box, Jas... Deli, Jin Jin Buffet, Kanpai Tokyo, KFC, La Taverna Italian, Lo...horn Steaks, McAlister's Deli, Moe's SW Grill, O'Charley's, C... Garden, Panera Bread, Pizza Hut, Red Bowl Asian, Red Lob... Ruby Tuesday, Ryan's, Starbucks, Subway, Wendy's C...fort Suites, Hampton Inn, Hilton Garden, Holiday Inn Expr... Residence Inn AT&T, Barnes&Noble, Belk, Best Buy, Cos...gas, Dick's, Dillard's, Discount Tire, Firestone/auto, Hamri... Home Depot, JC Penney, Jo-Ann Fabrics, Lowe's, Meineke, ...chael's, Office Depot, Old Navy, Petsmart, Rite Aid, Ross... Maxx, Tuesday Morning, USPO, Verizon, Walmart/McDona... S Marathon/dsl, Shell/dsl Apollo's Pizza, Applebe... Compadre's TexMex, IHOP, McDonald's, Shogun Japan... Starbucks, Taco Bell, Waffle House $Tree, Advance P... CarQuest, Hobby Lobby, Ingles Foods/gas, Kohl's, Sam's Cl... gas, Target, TrueValue
19b a	Lp I-85, Spartanburg, N BP/dsl, Valero Cracker Ba... Subway Residence Inn, S Valero Brookwood In...
18b a	I-85, N to Charlotte, S to Greenville
17	New Cut Rd, S BP/dsl, Exxon/dsl Burger King, ... Café, McDonald's, Waffle House Days Inn, Howard Jo...son, Red Roof Inn, Rodeway Inn
16	John Dodd Rd, to Wellford, N Exxon/Circle K/Aunt M... dsl Camping World RV Ctr
15	US 176, to Inman, N Breakers, Shell/Circle K/dsl/sc... Waffle House H, S QT/dsl Simply RV Ctr
10	SC 292, to Inman, N Shell/Hot Spot/Subway/dsl/scales/2...
7.5mm	Lake William C. Bowman
5	SC 11, Foothills Scenic Dr, Chesnee, Campobello, N K...garoo/Pilot/Subway/dsl/scales/24hr, S Marathon... Cricket/dsl
3mm	**Welcome Ctr eb, full facilities, info, litter barrels, petw... vending, wi-fi**
1	SC 14, to Landrum, S Shell/Burger King/dsl Bo...gles, China Cafe, Papa John's, Pizza Hut (1mi), Starbucks, S...way $General, Bi-Lo Foods, Ingles/café/gas, Verizon, v...
0mm	South Carolina/North Carolina state line

INTERSTATE 77

Exit #	Services
91mm	South Carolina/North Carolina state line
90	US 21, Carowinds Blvd, E Mobil/Circle K/dsl, QT/dsl Bojangles, Burger King, McDonald's, Zaxby's H, fireworks, W Circle K/Subway, Exxon/7-11, QT/dsl, Shell/Circle K/Wendy's/dsl Cracker Barrel, Culver's, Famous Dave's, KFC, Moe's SW, Panchito's Mexican Best Western, Clarion, Comfort Inn, Country Inn Suites, Motel 6, Quality Inn Cabela's, Carowinds Camping, Carowinds Funpark
89.5mm	**Welcome Ctr sb, full facilities, info, litter barrels, petwalk/ weigh sta nb, , vending**
88	Gold Hill Rd, to Pineville, E URGENT CARE, W QT/dsl, Shell/dsl, Valero/dsl Dunkin', Hardee's, Marco's Pizza WingBonz Cantina Chrysler/Dodge/Jeep, Fiat, Ford, Hyundai, KOA, Publix, vet
85	SC 160, Ft Mill, Tega Cay, E Exxon Brixx Pizza, Carolina Alehouse, Panera Bread, Smashburger, Starbucks Courtyard Ft Mill Drug, W BP/dsl, QT/dsl, Shell/Circle K/dsl Akahana Asian, Big Wok, Burger King, Charanda Mexican, Chick-fil-A, Empire Pizza, Fratelli's Italian, Jimmy John's, Killington's Rest., McAlister's Deli, Moe's SW Grill, Papa John's, Pizza Hut, Starbucks, Wendy's, Zaxby's Hampton Inn, Holiday Inn Express CVS Drug, Firestone/auto, Goodyear/auto, Harris-Teeter, Lowe's, Meineke, vet, Walgreens
84.5mm	**weigh sta sb**
83	SC 49, Sutton Rd, W Loves/Chester/Subway/dsl/scales/24hr
82.5mm	Catawba River
82c	US 21, SC 161, Rock Hill, Ft Mill, E Exxon Freddy's, IHOP, Sonny's BBQ, Steak'n Shake, Zaxby's Comfort Inn Home Depot, Lidl, Petsmart, W Mobil/dsl, QT/dsl, Shell/Circle K, Shell/dsl, Valero Big Wok, Chinese Bistro Deli, Empire Pizza, Hooters, Krispy Kreme, McDonald's, Outback Steaks, Sonic, Starbucks Courtyard H, $General, Food Lion, TreadQtrs Auto, Walgreens
82b a	E Exxon Comfort Inn, Ramada Inn, W Shell/Circle K/dsl Arby's, Bojangles, Burger King, Chick-fil-A, China Kitchen, CiCi's Pizza, Cookout, Fuji Japan, Golden Corral, HoneyBaked Ham, HongKong Chinese, Little Caesar's, Luigi& Sons Italian, Mario's Pizza, McDonald's, Nick's Gyros, Penn Sta. Subs, Pizza Hut, Popeye's, Rock Hill Diner, Sakura Japanese, Subway, Taco Bell, Waffle House, Wendy's Baymont Inn, Best Way, Best Western, Country Inn&Suites, Days Inn, EconoLodge, Economy Express Inn, Howard Johnson, Microtel, Motel 6, Quality Inn, Red Roof Inn $General, $Tree, Advance Parts, Aldi Foods, AutoZone, BigLots, Cadillac/Chevrolet, city park, Family$, Firestone/auto, Midas, NAPA, Office Depot, O'Reilly Parts, PepBoys, Publix, Verizon, York Co Museum
79	SC 122, Dave Lyle Blvd, to Rock Hill, E BP/dsl, Murphy USA/dsl Amber Buffet, Applebee's, Buffalo Wild Wings, Charanda Mexican, Chick-fil-A, Cracker Barrel, Five Guys, Hardee's, Jersey Mike's, Longhorn Steaks, Newk's Eatery, O'Charley's, Ruby Tuesday, TX Roadhouse Comfort Suites, Fairfield Inn, Hampton Inn, Holiday Inn, Home 2 Suites, La Quinta, Staybridge Suites, TownePlace Suites, Tru, Wingate Inn $Tree, AT&T, Belk, Buick/GMC, Discount Tire, Food Lion, Harley Davidson, Hobby Lobby, Honda, JC Penney, Kohl's, Lowe's, Meineke, Nissan, NTB, Sam's Club/dsl, Staples, Toyota, Verizon, Walmart, W Circle K/dsl Baskin Robins/Dunkin', Bob Evans, Chili's, DQ, Firehouse Subs, Jack-in-the-Box, McAlister's Deli,

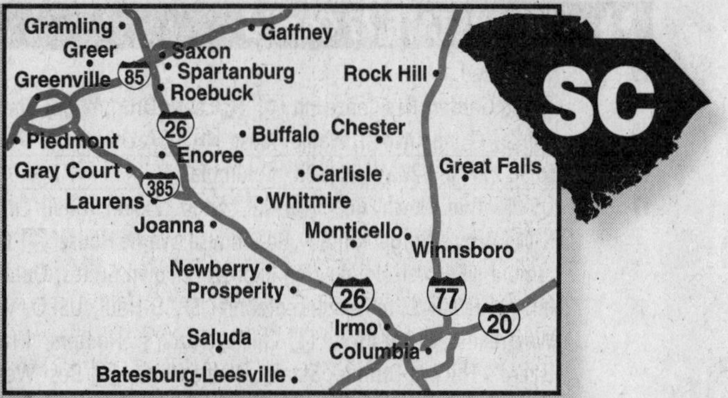

Exit #	Services
79	Continued McDonald's, Mellow Mushroom Pizza, Moe's SW Grill, Olive Garden, Panera Bread, Subway, Taco Bell, Wendy's Extended Stay America, Hilton Garden Best Buy, Books-A-Million, Dick's, Ford, Michael's, Ross, Target, TJ Maxx, URGENT CARE
77	US 21, SC 5, to Rock Hill, E BP/Subway/dsl, Pilot/dsl, QT/dsl to Andrew Jackson SP (12mi), W Valero/dsl Waffle House to Winthrop Coll
75	Porter Rd, E Crown fireworks
73	SC 901, to Rock Hill, York, E FLYING J/Denny's/dsl/scales/LP/24hr, Exxon/dsl W H
66mm	**both lanes, full facilities, litter barrels, petwalk, , , vending**
65	SC 9, to Chester, Lancaster, E BP/dsl, Citgo/dsl, QT/dsl, Shell/Subway/dsl Bojangles, China Wok, Waffle House Days Inn, EconoLodge $General, IGA Foods/gas, W Exxon/dsl Burger King, Country Omelet, Front Porch Rest., KFC/Taco Bell, McDonald's, Zaxby's Motel 6, Quality Inn, Super 8 H, vet
62	SC 56, to Fort Lawn, Richburg
55	SC 97, to Chester, Great Falls, E Exxon/dsl, W H, to Chester SP
48	SC 200, to Great Falls, E Shell/Grand Central Rest./dsl/@, W Pilot/Wendy's/DQ/dsl/scales/24hr/
46	SC 20, to White Oak
41	SC 41, to Winnsboro, E to Lake Wateree SP
34	SC 34, to Winnsboro, Ridgeway, E Am Pm/dsl Ridgeway Motel (1mi) Bryan's Auto/tire, Ridgeway Camping (1mi), W Exxon/dsl Waffle House Ramada Ltd
32	Peach Rd, Ridgeway, Little Cedar Creek Camping (2mi)
27	Blythewood Rd, E BP/Dunkin', Exxon/Bojangles/dsl/24hr Carolina Wings, China King, Hardee's, KFC/Pizza Hut, McDonald's, San Jose Mexican, Subway, Valentina's Greek, Waffle House, Wendy's Comfort Inn, Days Inn, Holiday Inn Express $General, IGA Foods, repair/tires, USPO, vet, W Lizard's Thicket Food Lion, Groucho's Deli
24	US 21, to Wilson Blvd., E BP/dsl, Shell/Subway/dsl auto repair, W Exxon/dsl
22	Killian Rd, E Mobil/Burger King/dsl, Murphy Express/dsl Applebee's, Bojangles, Chick-fil-A, Firehouse Subs, Freddy's, Hardee's, McDonald's, Panda Express, Popeye's, Salsarita's, Steak'n Shake, Subway, Taco Bell, Tropical Cafe, Zaxby's Hampton Inn Acura, Aldi Foods, AutoZone, BMW, CVS Drug, Discount Tire, Firestone, Honda, Kia, Kroger/dsl, Lowe's, Mazda, Rite Aid, Subaru, Toyota, VW, Walgreens, W China Dragon, Monterrey's Mexican Lexus/Buick/GMC/Cadillac, Verizon, Walmart/McDonald's
19	SC 555, Farrow Rd, E BP/dsl, Exxon, Shell/dsl Bojangles, Cracker Barrel, Sonic, Subway, Wendy's Courtyard,

INTERSTATE 77 Cont'd

COLUMBIA

19	Continued Hilton Garden, Residence Inn H, Longs Drug, W Shell/dsl China Kitchen, Waffle House SC Archives
18	to SC 277, to I-20 W (from sb), Columbia
17	US 1, Two Notch Rd, E BP, Citgo, Exxon, Shell/Circle K Arby's, Burger King, TX Roadhouse, Waffle House Columbia NE Hotel, Holiday Inn Express, InTown Suites, Quality Inn Family$, to Sesquicentennial SP, U-Haul, USPO, vet, Walgreens, W Mobil Chili's, Fazoli's, Hooters, IHOP, Lizard's Thicket, Outback Steaks, Waffle House Best Western+, Comfort Suites, EconoLodge, Fairfield Inn, Hampton Inn, La Quinta, Microtel, Red Roof Inn Home Depot
16b a	I-20, W to Augusta, E to Florence, Alpine Rd
15b a	SC 12, to Percival Rd, W Shell
13	Decker Blvd (from nb), W El Cheapo, Spinx/dsl
12	Forest Blvd, Thurmond Blvd, E to Ft Jackson, W BP/dsl, Shell/dsl/24hr Chick-fil-A, Cookout, Domino's, Eastern Buffet, Fatz Café, Golden Corral, McDonald's, Pancho's, Sonic, Subway, Wendy's Extended Stay America, Super 8 H, $Tree, AT&T, Hobby Lobby, museum, Sam's Club/gas, Tuesday Morning, Verizon, vet, Walmart
10	SC 760, Jackson Blvd, E to Ft Jackson, 2 mi W Shell Applebee's, Bojangles, Buffalo Wild Wings, Maurices BBQ, Moe's SW, Ruby Tuesday, Smashburger, Subway EconoLodge Bilo, Staples, Walgreens, Whole Foods Mkt
9b a	US 76, US 378, to Sumter, Columbia, 0-2 mi E BP, Citgo, Murphy USA/dsl, Shell, Shell/Burger King, Sunoco/dsl Arby's, Bojangles, Capt D's, Chick-fil-A, Domino's, Ichiban, KFC, McDonald's, Pizza Hut, Popeye's, Ruby Tuesday, Rush's Rest., Shoney's, Subway, Taco Bell, Waffle House, Waffle House, Wendy's, Zaxby's Baymont Inn, Candlewood Suites, Comfort Inn, Country Inn&Suites, Days Inn, Hampton Inn, Hampton Inn, Holiday Inn Express, La Quinta, Microtel, Quality Inn, Sleep Inn, TownePlace Suites $Tree, Advance Parts, Aldi Foods, AutoZone, CVS Drug, Family$, Firestone/auto, Ford, Interstate Batteries, Lowe's, NTB, O'Reilly Parts, URGENT CARE, USPO, Verizon, Walgreens, Walmart, W Circle K, Shell CiCi's Pizza, Eric's Mexican, Hardee's, Jimmy John's, Krispy Kreme, Panera Bread, Sonic, Starbucks, Sub Station, Wendy's Best Value Inn H, $General, BigLots, GNC, Goodyear/auto, Rite Aid, Sav-A-Lot Foods, Target
6b a	Shop Rd, W fairgrounds, to USC Coliseum
5	SC 48, Bluff Rd, W Loves/McDonald's/Subway/dsl/scales/24hr, Shell/Burger King/dsl Bojangles (2mi) $General, Petro/Starbucks/dsl/scales/24hr
3mm	Congaree River
2	SC 35, to Cayce, W Columbia
1	US 21, US 176, US 321 (from sb), Cayce, W accesses same as SC I-26, exit 115.

I-77 begins/ends on I-26, exit 116.

INTERSTATE 85

GAFFNEY

SPARTANBURG

Exit #	Services
106.5mm	South Carolina/North Carolina state line
106	US 29, to Grover, W Exxon/dsl, Hickory Point/gas, Mobil/dsl/fireworks, Pilot/Wendy's/DQ/dsl/scales/24hr
104	SC 99, Tribal Rd, E Loves/McDonald's/Subway/dsl/scales/24hr, W fireworks
103mm	Welcome Ctr sb, full facilities, info, litter barrels, petwalk, vending
102	SC 198, to Earl, E BP/dsl, Exxon Hardee's, W FLYING J/Denny's/dsl/scales/LP/24hr, Citgo/dsl McDonald's, Waffle House
100mm	Buffalo Creek
100	SC 5, to Blacksburg, Shelby, W Citgo, Exxon/dsl/scales/
98	Frontage Rd (from nb)
97mm	Broad River
96	SC 18, E Circle K/Krystal/dsl
95	SC 18, to Gaffney, E Exxon/Circle K/dsl, PetroMax Mr Waffle Gaffney Inn, Shamrock Inn H, to Limestone Coll
92	SC 11, to Gaffney, E Circle K/Subway/dsl, Fast Point Murphy USA/dsl Aegean Pizza, Applebee's, Bojang Burger King, Chick-fil-A, China Express, CookOut, Daddy J BBQ, Domino's, Firehouse Subs, KFC, Little Caesar's, McDonald's, Olive Garden, Papa John's, Pete's, Pizza Hut, Popeye Sonic, Taco Bell, Waffle House, Wendy's, Wings Etc., by's Baymont Inn, Super 8 $General, $Tree, Adva Parts, Aldi Foods, AT&T, Belk, BigLots, BiLo, Ingles Fo Lowe's, O'Reilly Parts, to Limestone Coll, USPO, Verizon, W greens, Walmart, W Fatz Cafe EconoLodge, Qua Inn Chevrolet, Foothills Scenic Hwy, to The Peach
90	SC 105, SC 42, to Gaffney, E Pilot/Arby's/dsl/scales/2 QT/dsl Bojangles, Clock Rest., Starbucks, Subway, Wa House Red Roof Inn, Sleep Inn, W Citgo/dsl, Exx Burger King Cracker Barrel, El Michoacan, Food Court, O back Steaks Hampton Inn fruit stand, Gaffney Outl famous brands, Hamrick's
87	SC 39, E KOA
83	SC 110, E fruit stand, W Westar/dsl/scales/24h fruitstand, to Cowpens Bfd
82	Frontage Rd (from nb)
80.5mm	Pacolet River
80	SC 57, to Gossett, E Hot Spot/Shell/dsl
78	US 221, Chesnee, E Citgo/dsl Hardee's Red R Inn, W QT/dsl, RaceWay/dsl Arby's, Bojangles, Bu er King, McDonald's, Southern BBQ, Subway, Waffle Ho Wendy's Hampton Inn, Holiday Inn Express $Gene Advance Parts, Harley-Davidson, Ingles Foods/cafe/dsl
77	Lp 85, Spartanburg, services along Lp 85 exits E
75	SC 9, Spartanburg, E Spinx/dsl Denny's Best Western+ $General, W QT/dsl, RaceWay/dsl Bruste Capri's Italian, CookOut, Copper River Grill, Fatz Café, Gra vine Rest, La Paz Mexican, McDonald's, Pizza Hut, Wa House, Zaxby's Comfort Inn, Days Inn CVS Drug, gles/cafe/gas, Parr 3 Automotive, USPO
72	US 176, to I-585, E to USCS, Wofford/Converse C W Kangaroo/dsl, RaceWay/dsl China Fun, El Lin Mexican, Subway, Waffle House $General, Ingles Foo cafe/gas
70b a	I-26, E to Columbia, W to Asheville
69	Lp 85, SC 41 (from nb), to Fairforest
68	SC 129, to Greer
67mm	N Tyger River
66	US 29, to Lyman, Wellford, E Exxon/Subway/dsl Wa House
63	SC 290, to Duncan, E Exxon/Circle K/dsl, QT/dsl, Spi Dunkin'/dsl Bojangles, Chick-Fil-A, Clock Rest., Cracker rel, El Primo Mexican, Firehouse Subs, Fudd's Burger, KFC, Pai nos Italian, Pizza Inn, Sake Japanese, Starbucks, Taco Bell, T Garden, Waffle House, Zaxby's Baymont Inn, Fairfield Hampton Inn, Home 2 Suites, Microtel, W BP, Marathon/

INTERSTATE 85 Cont'd

63 Continued [Pilot]/Wendy's/dsl/scales/24hr, TA/BP/DQ/rest./dsl/scales/24hr/@ [food] Demetre's Grill, El Molcajete Mexican, Hardee's, McDonald's [lodging] Day's Inn, Holiday Inn Express, Quality Inn, Woodspring Suites [other] Blue Beacon, Sonny's RV Ctr, Speedco

62.5mm S Tyger River

60 SC 101, to Greer, E [gas] Marathon, QT/dsl [food] Landmark Diner, Subway, Theo's Rest, W [gas] Spinx/Burger King/dsl [food] Bojangles, Waffle House [lodging] Super 8 [other] BMW Visitor Ctr

58 Brockman-McClimon Rd

57 W [other] Greenville-Spartanburg Airport

56 SC 14, to Greer, E [gas] Citgo/dsl [other] [H], W [gas] QT/dsl, Spinx/dsl [other] Goodyear Truck Tires, Ledford's Adventure RV Ctr

55mm Enoree River

54 Pelham Rd, E [gas] Exxon/Circle K, Stop-A-Minute/dsl [food] Burger King, Corona Mexican, Skin's Hotdogs, Waffle House [lodging] Best Western, Subrban Lodge, W [gas] BP/dsl [food] Asian Kitchen, Bertolos Pizza, Bojangles, California Dreaming Rest., Chick-fil-A, Chophouse 47, Dunkin', Eggs Up Grill, Firehouse Subs, Five Guys, Frankie's Pizza, Hardee's, Jimmy John's, Joe's Crabshack, Joy of Tokyo, Logan's Roadhouse, Macaroni Grill, McDonald's, Moe's SW Grill, On the Border, Palmetto Alehouse, Panera Bread, PDQ Rest., Red Bowl Asian, Schlotzsky's, Starbucks, Taco Bell, Taziki's Cafe, Tropical Cafe, Wendy's [lodging] Courtyard, EconoLodge, Extended Stay America, Fairfield Inn, Hampton Inn, Holiday Inn Express, Home2 Suites, MainStay Suites, Marriott, Residence Inn, Wingate Inn, Wyndham Garden [other] Advance Parts, Bi-Lo, CVS Drug, EarthFare Foods, GNC, Goodyear/auto, Verizon, Walgreens, Walmart

51 I-385, SC 146, Woodruff Rd, E [food] Brixx Pizza, Buffalo Wild Wings, Chipotle Mexican, Coldstone, Cracker Barrel, Fuddrucker's, Genghis Grill, IHOP, La Parrilla, Lieu's Bistro, Longhorn Steaks, Oriental House, Panera Bread, PF Chang's, Red Robin, Sticky Fingers [lodging] Drury Inn, Hampton Inn, Hilton Garden, Homewood Suites, Residence Inn, Staybridge Suites, Tru Hilton [other] Barnes&Noble, Best Buy, Dick's, Goodyear/auto, Hamrick's Outlet, Lowe's, Marshalls, PetCo, Petsmart, REI, Ross, Verizon, vet, Whole Foods Mkt, W [gas] QT/dsl, RaceWay/dsl [food] Bad Daddy's Burger, Carolina Alehouse, Carrabba's, Cheddars, Chuy's Mexican, Dave&Busters's, Firebirds, Grimaldi's, HuHot Mongolian, McDonald's, MidTown Deli, Panda Express, Ruby Tuesday, Ruth's Chris Steaks, Starbucks, Strossner's Cafe, Subway, TGIFriday's, Tin Lizzy's, Tropical Cafe, Tucanos Brazilian Grill, Twin Peaks Rest., Waffle House, Wild Wing Cafe, Yardhouse Rest., Zoe's Kitchen [lodging] Baymont Inn, Candlewood Suites, Comfort Inn, Crowne Plaza, Days Inn, Embassy Suites, Holiday Inn Express, La Quinta, Microtel, My Place [other] AT&T, Cabela's, Costco/gas, Firestone/auto, Home Depot, Old Navy, Target, Trader Joe's, Hyundai

48b a US 276, Greenville, E [gas] BP/dsl, QT/dsl [food] Waffle House [lodging] Red Roof Inn [other] BMW/Mini, CarMax, to ICAR, W [gas] Exxon/dsl [food] Arby's, Burger King, Happy China, Hooters, McDonald's, Olive Garden, Starbucks, Subway, Taco Bell [lodging] Country Inn&Suites, Embassy Suites [other] $Tree, Acura, Audi/Porsche/VW, Bi-Lo, Buick/GMC, Chevrolet/Cadillac, Chrysler/Dodge/Jeep, CVS Drug, Ford/Lincoln, GNC, Honda, Infiniti, Jaguar, Kia, Lexus, Mazda, Meineke, Mercedes, Michael's, Nissan, Office Depot, Old Time Pottery, PepBoys, Petsmart, SteinMart, Subaru, Toyota, Volvo

46c rd 291, Pleasantburg Rd, Mauldin Rd, W [gas] BP, Citgo/dsl, QT/dsl [food] Jack-in-the-Box, Papa John's, Subway [lodging] Greenville Inn, InTown Suites, Super Lodge, Woodspring Suites [other] Aamco, Advance Parts, Aldi, Home Depot, NTB, same as 46ba

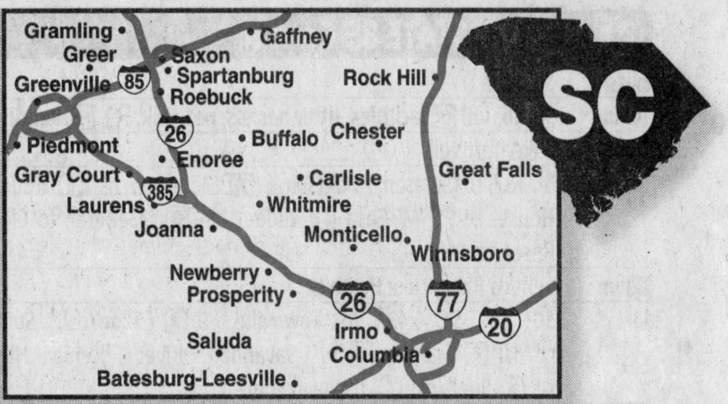

46b a US 25 bus, Augusta Rd, E [gas] Mike&Jack/dsl, QT/dsl, Spinx/dsl, Vgo [food] Burger King, Waffle House [lodging] Country Hearth Inn, Southern Suites, W [lodging] Economy Inn, Traveler's Inn [other] Home Depot, same as 46c

44 US 25, White Horse Rd, E [gas] Spinx/Subway/dsl, W [gas] Citgo/McDonald's, Fastfuels/dsl [food] Waffle House [other] [H], Freightliner

44a SC 20 (from sb), to Piedmont

42 I-185, to Greenville, I-185 S (toll), Columbia, W [other] [H]

40 SC 153, to Easley, E [gas] BP/dsl [food] Waffle House, W [gas] 7-11/dsl, Citgo/dsl, QT/dsl, RaceWay/dsl, Spinx/dsl [food] Arby's, Big Clock, Bojangles, Burger King, Chick-Fil-A, Cracker Barrel, Dunkin', El Sureno Mexican, Firehouse Subs, Huddle House, KFC, Little Caesar's, Los Amigos, McDonald's, Papa John's, Pizza House, Pizza Hut, Subway, Taco Bell, Zaxby's [lodging] Best Western+, Comfort Suites, Executive Inn, Hampton Inn (4mi), Holiday Inn Express, Super 8 [other] $General, Advance Parts, AutoZone, Bi-Lo, CVS Drug, O'Reilly Parts, Verizon, Walgreens, Walmart

39 SC 143, to Piedmont, E [gas] Vgo/dsl, W [gas] Shell/dsl

35 SC 86, to Easley, Piedmont, E [gas] BP/Subway (1.5mi), [Pilot]/McDonald's/dsl/scales/24hr [food] Cancun Mexican, Hardee's (1.5mi), Sweet P's, Tony' Pizza [other] O'Reilly Parts, repair/tires, Walgreens, W [gas] QT/dsl, Spinx/dsl [food] Bojangles

34 US 29 (from sb), to Williamston

32 SC 8, to Pelzer, Easley, E [gas] 7-11/dsl, Shell/dsl

27 SC 81, to Anderson, E [gas] BP/dsl, Exxon/dsl, Stop A Minit/dsl [food] Arby's, McDonald's, Papa's Mexican, Waffle House [lodging] Hampton Inn, Holiday Inn Express [other] [H]

23mm **[Rs] sb, full [handicapped] facilities, litter barrels, petwalk, [phone], [picnic], vending**

21 US 178, to Anderson, E [gas] BP/dsl, QT/dsl [food] Burger King, Waffle House

ANDERSON

19b a US 76, SC 28, to Anderson, E [gas] Exxon/dsl, QT/dsl, Shell/dsl, Stop A Minit/dsl [food] Applebee's, Barbarito's, Bojangles, Carson Steaks, Chick-fil-A, Chili's, Chipotle, CookOut, Denny's, Five Guys, Fuddruckers, Golden Corral, Golden Corral, Grand China, Hardee's, Hardee's, Hibachi Grill, Jack-in-the-Box, Logan's Roadhouse, Longhorn Steaks, O'Charley's, Olive Garden, Panera Bread, Red Lobster, Starbucks, Tucker's Rest., TX Roadhouse, Zaxby's [lodging] Best Value Inn, Days Inn, Hilton Garden, Holiday Inn, Rodeway Inn, Super 8 [other] $General, $Tree, Advance Parts, Aldi Foods, AT&T, Best Buy, Chrysler/Dodge/Jeep, Dick's, Ford/Mazda, GNC, Goodyear, Harley-Davidson, Hobby Lobby, Home Depot, Honda, Kohl's, Lowe's, Meineke, Michael's, Nissan, Office Depot, Old Navy, O'Reilly Parts, Petsmart, Publix/deli, Ross, Russell Stover, Sam's Club, Staples, Target, TJ Maxx, Toyota, Verizon, vet, Walmart/Subway, W [gas] RaceWay/dsl, Shell/McDonald's [food] Arby's, Cracker Barrel, Fatz Cafe, Hooters, J Peters Grill, Outback Steaks, Starbucks, Subway, Waffle House, Wendy's, Wild Wing Cafe [lodging] Baymont Inn, Comfort Suites, Country Inn&Suites, Fairfield Inn, Hampton Inn, Holiday Inn Express, Microtel, Residence Inn [other] to Clemson U (11mi)

INTERSTATE 85 Cont'd

Exit #	Services
18mm	**nb, full facilities, litter barrels, petwalk, , , vending**
15mm	Lake Hartwell
14	SC 187, to Clemson, Anderson, E Marathon/dsl Huddle House, W Mi Casa Budget Inn $General, to Clem Research Pk
12mm	Seneca River, Lake Hartwell
11	SC 24, SC 243, to Townville, E Exxon/dsl, Sunoco/dsl Subway to Savannah River Scenic Hwy, W Shell/dsl Townville Cafe
9mm	**weigh sta nb**
4	SC 243, to SC 24, Fair Play, E Loves/Arby's/dsl/scales/24hr, Mobil/dsl
2	SC 59, to Fair Play, W fireworks
1	SC 11, to Walhalla, W Gazebo Rest. fireworks, to Lake Hartwell SP
.5mm	**Welcome Ctr nb, full facilities, info, litter barrels, petwalk, , , vending**
0mm	South Carolina/Georgia state line, Lake Hartwell, Tugaloo River

INTERSTATE 95

DILLON

Exit #	Services
198mm	South Carolina/North Carolina state line
196mm	**Welcome Ctr sb, full facilities, info, litter barrels, petwalk, , , vending**
195mm	Little Pee Dee River
193	SC 9, SC 57, to N Myrtle Beach, Dillon, E Exxon/dsl, Mobil/dsl, Murphy Express/dsl, Sunoco/dsl B&C Steak/BBQ, Burger King, CookOut, Huddle House, Little Caesar's, Pizza Hut, Popeye's, Subway, Tokyo Cafe, Waffle House, Wendy's, Zaxby's Best Value Inn, Days Inn, Quality Inn, Red Roof Inn, Taco Bell H, $General, $Tree, Advance Parts, AutoZone, CVS Drug, fireworks, Food Lion, O'Reilly Parts, SaveALot Foods, Walgreens, Walmart, W Eastern Cafe Chines Economy Inn Bass Lake RV Camp/LP
190	SC 34, to Dillon, W Loves/Arby's/dsl/scales/24hr
181	SC 38, Oak Grove, E FLYING J/dsl/LP/scales/24hr, BP/Subway/dsl/24hr, Shell/McDonald's/dsl/24hr Shuler's BBQ (5mi) fireworks, W Pilot/DQ/Wendy's/dsl/scales/24hr Best Western
175mm	Pee Dee River
170	SC 327, E BP, Pilot/Wendy's/dsl/scales/24hr McDonald's, Subway, Waffle House, Zaxby's Holiday Inn Express Harley Davidson, Missile Museum, to Myrtle Beach
169	TV Rd, to Florence, E dsl repair, Florence RV Park, W BP, Petro/Shell/Iron Skillet/dsl/scales/24hr/@ Best Value Inn Blue Beacon, dsl repair, Peterbilt
164	US 52, to Darlington, Florence, E Exxon/dsl, RaceWay, Shell/dsl Cracker Barrel, McDonald's, Quincy's, Ruby Tuesday, Waffle House, Wendy's Baymont Inn, Best Western, EconoLodge, Rodeway Inn, Suburban Lodge, Super 8 H, Chrysler/Dodge/Jeep, W Mobil, Pilot/Subway/Taco Bell/dsl, TA/BP/Popeye's/dsl/scales/@ Arby's, Dickey's BBQ, Dunkin', Fatz Café, Hardee's, Krispy Kreme, Shoney's, Young's Pecans, Zaxby's Comfort Suites, Country Inn&Suites, Days Inn, Hampton Inn, La Quinta, Microtel, Motel 6, Sleep Inn, Travel House Inn, Tru Hilton to Darlington Raceway, transmissions
160b	I-20 W, to Columbia

FLORENCE

Exit #	Services
160a	Lp 20, to Florence, E Exxon/dsl, Murphy USA/dsl, T EVC Arby's, Bruster's Ice Cream, Buffalo Wild Wings, B er King, Chick-fil-A, Chili's, Chipotle, ChuckeCheese, Fireho Subs, Golden Corral, Hibachi Grill, Hwy 55 Cafe, IHOP, La Ba Mexican, Longhorn Steaks, Mellow Mushroom, Olive Gar Outback Steaks, Panera Bread, Percy&Willie's, Red Bowl As Red Lobster, Ruby Tuesday, San Jose's, Subway, Taco Bell, W fle House, Western Sizzlin, Which Wich? Courtyard, D Inn, Fairfield Inn, Hampton Inn, Hilton Garden, Holiday Express, Home 2 Hilton, Homewood Suites, Quality Inn, Roof Inn, Residence Inn, SpringHill Suites, Staybridge Su TownePlace Suites $Tree, Aldi Foods, AT&T, Barnes&No Belk, Best Buy, Big Lots, Dick's, Discount Tire, Hamrick's, Ho Lobby, Home Depot, JC Penney, Kohl's, Lowes Whse, Petsm Sam's Club/dsl, Target, Verizon, Walmart
157	US 76, Timmonsville, Florence, E Citgo/dsl, Kangaroo/ Marathon/dsl, Shell/McDonald's Peking Asian, Wa House Florence Inn, Travelodge Abbott Farms Peac W Mobil/dsl Palmetto Inn, Swamp Fox Camping (1 Tree Top Inn auto repair
153	Honda Way, W Exxon/dsl Honda Plant
150	SC 403, to Sardis, E Mobil/dsl/scales Hotp Cafe Budget Inn, W Marathon/dsl
147mm	Lynches River
146	SC 341, to Lynchburg, Olanta, E Relax Inn
141	SC 53, SC 58, to Shiloh, E DonMar RV Ctr, to Woods Bay W Shell
139mm	**both lanes, full facilities, litter barrels, petwalk, , vending**
135	US 378, to Sumter, Turbeville, E BP/dsl, Citgo/dsl/2 Day's Inn, W Exxon/Subway/dsl
132	SC 527, to Sardinia, Kingstree
130mm	Black River
122	US 521, to Alcolu, Manning, W Exxon/dsl
119	SC 261, to Paxville, Manning, **0-1 mi** E Murphy USA/ Shell/dsl, TA/BP/Pizza Hut/Popeye's/dsl/scales/24hr/@ jangles, Burger King, CookOut, Golden Chick, Huddle Ho Mariachi's Mexican, McDonald's, Shoney's, Sonic, Subw Taco Bell, Waffle House, Wendy's, Yucatan Mexican, Z by's Baymont Inn, Days Inn, Hampton Inn, Quality SureStay H, $General, AutoZone, Chrysler/Dodge/Je CVS Drug, Ford, O'Reilly Parts, truckwash, Verizon, Walm W Enmarket/dsl/e85, Marathon Super 8
115	US 301, to Summerton, Manning, W Shell/dsl Ge gio's Rest Ashburn Inn
108	rd 102, Summerton, E BP/DQ, Travel Depot/dsl Ta Caw Camping (6mi), W Days Inn
102	US 15, US 301 N, to N Santee, E Marathon/dsl San Resort/Motel KOA, Palmetto Shores Resort, W H zon/dsl/e85 to Santee NWR
100mm	Lake Marion
99mm	**both lanes, full facilities, info, litter barrels, petwalk, , vending**
98	SC 6, to Eutawville, Santee, E BP/Bojangles, Citgo, Ex Mobil Huddle House, Pizza Hut, Subway, Taco Bell B Western+, Clarion, Econolodge, Fairfield Inn, Hamp Inn, Red Roof Inn, Super 8, Travelodge $General, Foods, W Horizon/dsl/e85, Marathon/dsl, Shell, Su co Burger King, Cracker Barrel, McDonald's, Waffle Hou Wendy's Clark Inn/rest., Comfort Inn, Holiday Inn, Knig Inn, Lake Marion Inn, Quality Inn CarQuest, CVS Drug, Fa ily$, Food Lion, Rivers Country Store, to Santee SP (3mi), US

MANNING

SANTEE

INTERSTATE 95 Cont'd

Exit #	Services
97	US 301 S (from sb, no return), to Orangeburg
93	US 15, to Santee, Holly Hill
90	US 176, to Cameron, Holly Hill, W Exxon/dsl
86b a	I-26, W to Columbia, E to Charleston
82	US 178, to Bowman, Harleyville, E Enmarket/Subway, Pilot/Wendy's/DQ/Dunkin'/dsl/scales/24hr Peachtree Inn, W Shell/dsl tires/truck repair
77	US 78, to Bamberg, St George, E Enmarket/Subway/dsl/e85, FLYING J/Denny's/dsl/scales/24hr, Monoco, Sunoco Empire Chinese, Georgio's Rest., Hardee's, KFC, McDonald's, Pizza Hut, Skynyrd's Grill, Waffle House Best Value Inn, Days Inn/RV Park, EconoLodge, Quality Inn $General, Ace Hardware, BiLo, Chevrolet/GMC, CVS Drug, Family$, USPO, W BP, Shell/Taco Bell/dsl Country Hearth Inn, Knights Inn
74mm	**parking area c(ommercial vehicles only sb), weigh sta nb**
68	SC 61, Canadys, E BP, Crosco Express, Shell/Subway/dsl to Colleton SP (3mi)
62	McLeod Rd
57	SC 64, Lodge, Walterboro, E Citgo/dsl, Horizon/e85, Shell/DQ, Sunoco/dsl Arby's, Bojangles, Burger King, Capt D's, China Wok, Dimitrio's Rest., Domino's, Dunkin', EVC, Hardee's, Huddle House, McDonald's, Olde House Café, Starbucks, Subway, Taco Bell, Waffle House, Wendy's Carolina Lodge, Sleep Inn, Southern Inn H, $General, Ace Hardware, Advance Parts, AutoZone, Belk, Family$, Ford, GNC, O'Reilly Parts, W Murphy USA/dsl China Buffet, Fat Jack's, IHOP, KFC, Zaxby's Super 8 $Tree, AT&T, PetCo, Verizon, Walmart
53	SC 63, to Varnville, Walterboro, Hampton, E BP/McDonald's, Circle K/dsl, El Cheapo, Exxon, Shell/DQ Ruby Tuesday, Shoney's, Waffle House Baymont Inn, Best Western, Comfort Inn, EconoLodge, Palms Inn, Ramada Inn, Red Roof Inn, Rodeway Inn fireworks, W Enmarket/dsl Cracker Barrel Days Inn, Hampton Inn, Holiday Inn Express, Microtel, Motel 6, Quality Inn New Green Acres Camping
47mm	**both lanes, full facilities, litter barrels, petwalk, vending**
42	US 21, to Yemassee, Beaufort
40mm	Combahee River
38	SC 68, to Hampton, Yemassee, E Enmarket/dsl/e85 Family$, W BP/Subway/TCBY, Exxon/dsl, Love's/Hardee's/dsl/scales/24hr, Shell/dsl
33	US 17 N, to Beaufort, E BP/dsl, Exxon/McDonald's, Marathon/Subway/TCBY, Shell 17 W Kitchen, Waffle House, Wendy's Best Western, Hampton Inn, Motel 6, Red Roof Inn Confederate Railroad Museum, KOA, The Oaks RV Camping
30.5mm	Tullifinny River
29mm	Coosawhatchie River
28	SC 462, to Coosawhatchie, Hilton Head, Bluffton, W Exxon/dsl, Gen Store
22	US 17, Ridgeland, W Sunoco H
21	SC 336, to Hilton Head, Ridgeland, E Citgo/dsl, Marathon/dsl McDonald's, Wendy's Boat'n RV Whse, W BP/DQ/dsl, Enmarket/dsl, Shell Burger King, Chef Donald's, Hong Kong Chinese, KFC, Subway, Waffle House Carolina Lodge, Days Inn, Oyo Motel, Quality Inn H, $General, Harvey's Foods, Rite Aid
18	SC 13, to US 17, US 278, to Switzerland, Granville, Ridgeland
17mm	**parking area both lanes (commercial vehicles only)**

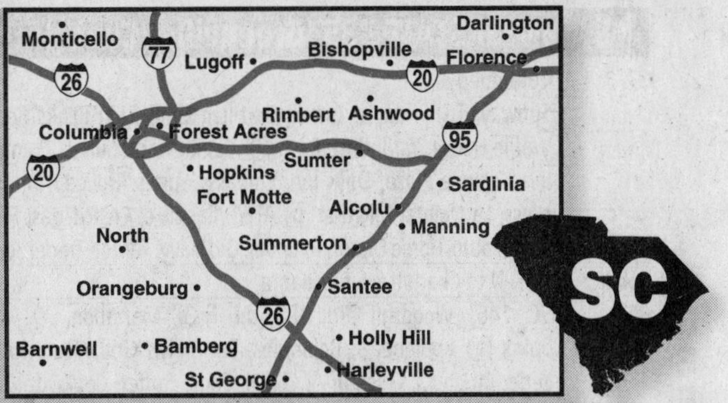

HARDEEVILLE

Exit #	Services
8	US 278, to Bluffton, Hardeeville, E BP/Burrito/dsl/scales, Circle K/McDonald's, Exxon Dunkin', Waffle House H, W Horizon/Subway/dsl, Shell/dsl Holiday Inn Express, Motel 6
5	US 17, US 321, to Savannah, Hardeeville, E BP/dsl, Parker's/dsl, Pilot/Subway/dsl/scales/24hr Chicken Lickin, Mi Tierrita Mexican, Waffle House Days Inn, Economy Inn, Sleep Inn fireworks, to Savannah NWR, W Butlers/dsl/repair, Octane/dsl, Speedway/dsl, Sunoco/dsl Burger King, Wendy's Best Western+, Deluxe Inn, Hardeeville Inn, Knights Inn, Magnolia Motel, Quality Suites, Red Roof Inn, Super 8, Travelodge $General, Advance Parts, Family$, fireworks, NAPA
4.5mm	**Welcome Ctr nb, full facilities, info, litter barrels, petwalk, vending, wi-fi**
4mm	**weigh sta both lanes**
0mm	South Carolina/Georgia state line, Savannah River

INTERSTATE 385 (Greenville)

GREENVILLE

Exit #	Services
42	US 276, Stone Ave, to Travelers Rest, **I-385 begins/ends on US 276**, E CarQuest, vet, **1-2 mi** W Spinx/dsl multiple services on US 276, to Greenville Zoo
40b a	SC 291, Pleasantburg Dr, E Sunoco Jack-in-the-Box, Little Caesar's, Olive Tree, S&S Cafeteria, Sonic, Starbucks, Subway, Taco Casa, Wendy's $Tree, CVS Drug, Family$, Furman U, to BJU, Walgreens, W Citgo/dsl, QT/dsl Domino's, Krispy Kreme Phoenix Inn/Rest., Sleep Inn Cottman Transmissions, Midas
39	Haywood Rd, E Spinx Noodleville, Outback Steaks, Portofino's, Tony's Pizzeria Clarion, Courtyard, Hawthorn Inn, Hilton, Hyatt Place, La Quinta Firestone/auto, USPO, W Spinx/dsl Applebee's, Backyard Burger, Burger King, Chick-fil-A, Chili's, Chipotle, ChuckeCheese, CiCi's Pizza, CityRange Steaks, Clock Rest., Copper River Grill, Don Pablo, Firehouse Subs, Five Guys, Fried Green Tomatoes, Grille 33, Habiba Mediterranean, Halton Country Buffet, Harbor Inn Seafood, Jason's Deli, Jimmy John's, Kanpai Tokyo, McAlister's Deli, Miyabi Japanese, Moe's SW Grill, Monterrey Mexican, Panera Bread, Papa's&Beer, Rafferdi's, Saskatoon Rest, Starbucks, Stax Grill, Steak'n Shake, Waffle House Baymont Inn, Extended Stay America, Hampton Inn AT&T, Barnes&Noble, Belk, Dillard's, Discount Tire, JC Penney, Jo-Ann, Macy's, TJ Maxx, Verizon, vet
37	Roper Mtn Rd, W Marathon/Kangaroo/dsl, QT/dsl, RaceWay/dsl Carrabba's, Cheddar's, Chuy's Mexican, Dave&Busters, HuHot Mongolian, Krystal, McDonald's, MidTown Deli, RubyTuesday, RuthsChrisSteaks, Starbucks, Strossner's Cafe,

INTERSTATE 385 (Greenville) Cont'd

GREENVILLE

37	Continued Subway, TGI Friday's, Tucnos Brazilian Grill, Twin Peaks Rest., Waffle House, Yardhouse Rest. Candlewood Suites, Comfort Inn, Crowne Plaza, Days Inn, Embassy Suites, Holiday Inn Express, La Quinta, Microtel AT&T, Cabela's, Costco/gas, Firestone/auto, Home Depot, Hyundai, Old Navy, Target, Trader Joe's
36b a	I-85, N to Charlotte, S to Atlanta
35	SC 146, Woodruff Rd, **0-2 mi E** Marathon, QT/dsl, Spinx Applebee's, Bojangles, Bone Fish Grill, Boston Pizzeria, Bruster's, Chick-fil-A, Chili's, China Buffet, CookOut, Culver's, Dunkin', Epic Curean Rest., Firehouse Subs, Great Harvest Bread, Green Tomato Buffet, Hardee's, Hibachi Grill, Jersey Mike's, JP's 4 Corners SW Rest., KFC, Krispy Kreme, Little Caesar's, McAlister's Deli, McDonald's, Mimi's Japanese Steaks, Moe's SW Grill, Pizza Inn, Sonic, Starbucks, Stevi B's, Subway, Taco Bell, Topper's Rest., Travinia Italian, Waffle House, Wendy's, Your Pizza Pie, Zaxby's $Tree, AAAAZ, Ace Hardware, Aldi Foods, BigLots, Bi-Lo Foods, Discount Tire, GNC, Hobby Lobby, Kohl's, O'Reilly Parts, Publix, Rite Aid, Sam's Club/gas, Save-a-Lot Foods, Staples, Tire Kingdom, URGENT CARE, USPO, Walmart, **W** Red Robin Brixx Pizza, Buffalo Wild Wings, Chipotle Mexican, Coldstone, Cracker Barrel, Fuddrucker's, Genghis Grill, IHOP, La Parrilla Mexican, Lieu's Bistro, Longhorn Steaks, Oriental House, Panera Bread, PF Chang's, Red Robin, Sticky Fingers, Which Wich? Drury Inn, Hampton Inn, Hilton Garden, Homewood Suites, Residence Inn, Staybridge Suites, Tru Hilton Barnes&Noble, Best Buy, Dick's, Goodyear/auto, Hamrick's Outlet, Lowe's, Marshall's, Petco, Petsmart, REI, Ross, Verizon, vet, Whole Foods Mkt, World Mkt
34	Butler Rd, Mauldin, **E** Spinx/dsl Arby's, **W** Bojangles, Dino's Rest., Moretti's Pizzeria, Sub Sta. 2 $General
33	Bridges Rd, Mauldin
31	**I-185 toll**, SC 417, to Laurens Rd, **E** Marathon, Shell/dsl Hardee's, McDonald's, Subway BiLo, SaveALot Foods, **W** Spinx/dsl
30	I-185 **toll**, US 276, Standing Springs Rd
29	Georgia Rd, to Simpsonville, **W** Woodspring Suites
27	Fairview Rd, to Simpsonville, **E** Shell Carolina Rest., CoachHouse Rest., JB's BBQ, Little Caesar's, McDonald's, Milano Pizzeria, Subway Palmetto Inn H, $General, Advance Parts, AutoZone, Big Lots, CVS Drug, O'Reilly Parts, **W** Exxon, Murphy USA, Spinx/dsl Anthony's Pizza, Applebee's, Arby's, AZ Steaks, Baskin-Robbins, Bellacino's, Bruster's, Burger King, Chick-fil-A, Cracker Barrel, Epic Buffet, Firehouse Subs, Five Guys, Hibachi House, Hungry Howie's, IHOP, Jack-in-the-Box, Jersey Mike's, KFC, La Fogata Mexican, Mad Cuban, McDonald's, Mei Mei House, Moe's SW Grill, O'Charley's, Panera Bread, Pizza Hut, Ruby Tuesday, Sonic, Starbucks, Subway, Taco Bell, Tequila's Mexican, Waffle House, Wendy's, Zaxby's Comfort Suites, Days Inn, Hampton Inn, Holiday Inn Express, Motel 6, Quality Inn $Tree, AT&T, Belk, Bi-Lo, CVS Drug, GNC, Goodyear/auto, Home Depot, Ingles Foods, Kohl's, Lowe's, Publix, Ross, Target, Tire Kingdom, TJ Maxx, URGENT CARE, USPO, Verizon, Walgreens, Walmart
26	Harrison Bridge Rd, **W** 7-11/dsl, QT/dsl, same as 27
24	Fairview St, **E** Marathon Hardee's, Waffle House
23	SC 418, to Fountain Inn, Fork Shoals, **E** Exxon/pizza/subs/dsl Bojangles, Zaxby's $General, O'Reilly Parts, USPO, **W** Sunoco/dsl
22	SC 14 W, Old Laurens Rd, to Fountain Inn

SIMPSONVILLE

19	SC 14 E, to Gray Court, Owings
16	SC 101, to Woodruff, Gray Court
10	rd 23, Barksdale, Ora
9	US 221, to Laurens, Enoree, **E** S&H Trkstp/dsl W House Budget Lodge, **W** Walmart Dist Ctr
6mm	**both lanes (both exit left), full facilities, litter rels, petwalk, , vending**
5	SC 49, to Laurens, Union
2	SC 308, to Clinton, Ora, **W** H, to Presbyterian Coll in Cli
0mm	I-26 S to Columbia, **I-385 begins/ends on I-26 at 52mm.**

INTERSTATE 526 (Charleston)

Exit #	Services
33mm	**I-526 begins/ends.**
32	US 17, **0-1 mi N** Shell, Speedway/dsl Atl Bread, Bo gles, Burger King, Burton's Grill, Cane's, Five Guys, Grima Brick Oven, IHOP, PF Chang's, Qdoba, Sonic, Taco Bell, TG day, Zoe's Kitchen Courtyard, Hampton Inn Adva Parts, AT&T, Barnes&Noble, Belk, BiLo, Chevrolet, CVS D GNC, Lowes Whse, Midas, Old Navy, Rite Aid, Tire Kingo TrueValue, Verizon, Walgreens, **0-1 mi S** Shell/Circle K, noco/dsl Applebees, Arby's, Chick-fil-A, Cici's, Fireh Subs, Hardee's, Huddle House, Jimmy John's, La Hacienda M icana, Liberty Rest., McDonald's, Melvin's Ribs& Cue, Moe's Grill, Momma Goldberg's Deli, Outback Steaks, Sticky Fing Subway, Wendy's, Zeus Grill Best Western, Clarion, D Inn, Extended Stay America, Hampton Inn, Hilton Garden, H day Inn, Holiday Inn Express, Mainstay Suites, Quality Inn, Roof Inn, Sleep Inn $Tree, Bi-Lo, CVS Drug, Firestone/a Harris Teeter, Jiffy Lube, Marshall's, Michaels, NAPA, Office pot, O'Reilly Parts, Petco, Publix, Staples, TJ Maxx, Trader Jo USPO, Verizon, vet, VW, Walmart, Whole Foods Mkt
28	Long Point Rd, **N** Exxon, Shell Another Broken Bamboo Garden, Chick-fil-A, McAlister's, Moe's SW Grill, S bucks, Subway, Waffle House, Wendy's Charles Pinck NHS, CVS Drug, Harris Teeter Foods, PetsMart, Steinmart
26mm	Wando River
24	Daniel Island, **S** Exxon Domino's, Dragon Palace, S way, Wasabi Hampton Inn, Home 2 Suites Publix
23b a	Clements Ferry Rd
21mm	Cooper River
20	Virginia Ave (from eb), **S** Speedway Depot
19	N Rhett Ave, **N** Exxon, Kangaroo/Subway/dsl, Pilot by's/dsl/scales/24hr Bojangles, Waffle House Fami Food Lion, **S** Kwikstop
18b a	US 52, US 78, Rivers Ave, **N** BP/dsl, Circle K/dsl auto pair, Family$, H&L Foods, **S** 76/dsl Woodspring Sui
17b a	I-26, E to Charleston, W to Columbia
16	Montague Ave, Airport Rd, **S** Bonefish Grill, Chili's, D ny's, Jersey Mike's, La Hacienda, Panera Bread, Starbu Wendy's Embassy Suites, Hilton Garden, Holiday I Homewood Suites, Residence Inn Sam's Club/gas, Stap Tanger Outlet/famous brands, Walmart/Subway
15	SC 642, Dorchester Rd, Paramount Dr, **N** Shell/Ci K auto service, Family$, **S** Citgo/dsl, Sunoco B er King, Checker's, Domino's, East Bay Deli, Huddle Ho Little Caesar's, Pizza Hut, Subway Airport Inn Adva Parts, Bi-Lo Foods, CVS Drug, Family$, Food Lion, Harley-vidson, U-Haul
14	Leeds Ave, **S** Woodspring Suites boat marina
13mm	Ashley River

CHARLESTON

SC

INTERSTATE 526 (Charleston) Cont'd

Exit #	Services
11b a	SC 61, Ashley River Rd, N Baron's Pizza, Chick-fil-A, McDonald's, O'Charley's Food Lion, Home Depot, Jo-Ann, Kohl's, Lowes Whse, Marshall's
10	US 17, SC 7, **services from US 17 E** BP Bessinger's BBQ, Capt D's, Chick-fil-A, CookOut, Dunkin', Five Guys, Hopsing's Asian, IHOP, King St Grille, Krispy Kreme, La Fontana Italian, McDonald's, Panera Bread, Red Lobster, Ruby Tuesday, Taco Bell Best Western, Evergreen Motel, Holiday Inn Express, Motel 6, Sleep Inn, Town & Country Suites AutoZone, Belk,
10	Continued BiLo, BMW/Mini, Buick/GMC/Cadillac, Chevrolet, Chrysler/Dodge/Jeep, Dick's, Dillard's, Ford/Lincoln, Honda, Hyundai, Infiniti, Jaguar/Range Rover/Porsche, JC Penney, Maserati, Mercedes, Nissan, Pepboys, Petsmart, Ross, Smart, Target, Tire Kingdom, vet, Volvo, **services from US 17 W** AMFlag, Shell/Circle K, Speedway/dsl China Fun, Hardees, Inyabi Japanese, Subway, Waffle House Comfort Suites, Econolodge, Hampton Inn, Hawthorn Suites, InTown Suites Acura, Advance Parts, Audi, Carmax, Costco/gas, CVS Drug, DriveTime, Family$, Food Lion, Kia, Lexus, Toyota
9	**I-526 begins/ends on US 17.**

SOUTH DAKOTA

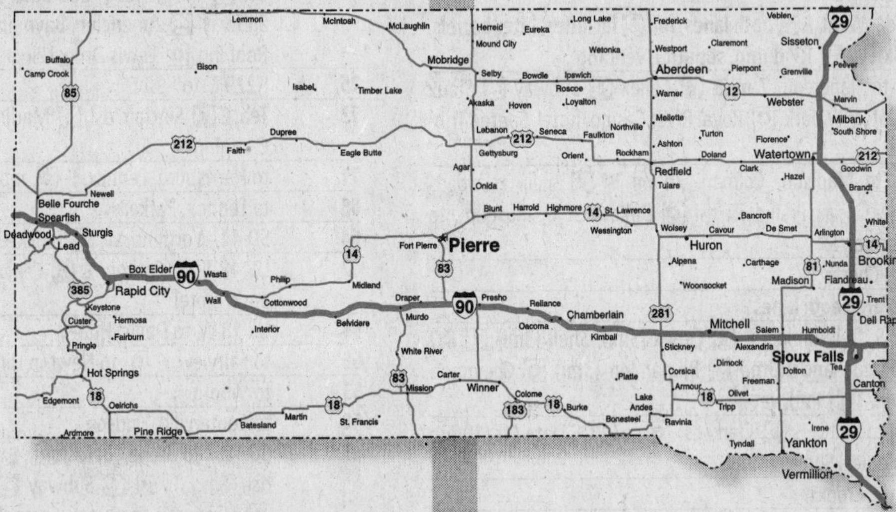

INTERSTATE 29

WATERTOWN

Exit #	Services
253mm	South Dakota/North Dakota state line
251mm	**Welcome Ctr sb, full facilities, info, litter barrels, petwalk, , RV dump**
246	SD 127, to Rosholt, New Effington, **3 mi W** gas food RV camping, Sica Hollow SP (24mi)
242	110th St
235mm	**weigh sta sb**
232	SD 10, Sisseton, **E** Dakota Connection/dsl/casino/24hr Crossroads Cafe, **1-3 mi W** Amstar/dsl, FuelMax/dsl, Sinclair/dsl/e85, Tesoro Cottage Rest, DQ, Pizza Hut, Subway, Taco John's Holiday Motel, I-29 Motel, Super 8 Camp Dakotah, Family$, Ft Sisseton SP (35mi), NAPA, Teals Mkt, to Roy Lake SP (25mi)
224	Peever, Sioux Tribal Hqtrs, **E** I-29 Food'n Fill/dsl, **W** Pickerel Lake (16mi)
213	SD 15, to Wilmot, **E both lanes, full facilities, litter barrels, petwalk, , st patrol, RV dump,** to Hartford Beach SP (17mi)
207	US 12, Summit, **E** Cenex/Pizza Hut/Subway/dsl/24hr County Line Camping (1mi), **W** Blue Dog Fish Hatchery (15mi), Waubay NWR (19mi)
201	to Twin Brooks
193	SD 20, to South Shore, Stockholm
185	to Waverly, **W** Dakota Sioux Casino/Cenex/rest. (4mi)
180	US 81 S, to Watertown, **5 mi W** Sinclair , Bramble Park Zoo
177	US 212, Watertown, **E** Tesoro/Grainery Cafe/dsl/24hr Holiday Inn Express fireworks, truck repair, truck wash, WW Tires, **0-2 mi W** Cenex/Subway/dsl, Cenex/Subway/dsl (2), Freedom/dsl, Sinclair/dsl, Tesoro/dsl Applebee's, Arby's, Buffalo Wild Wings, Burger King, China Buffet, Culver's, Domino's, DQ, Firehouse Subs, Four Seasons Buffet, Godfather's, Guadalajara Mexican, Hardee's, IHOP, Jimmy John's, KFC, Little Caesar's, Marco's Pizza, McDonald's, Papa Murphy's, Perkins, Pizza Hut, Qdoba, Senor Max's Mexican, Starbucks, Subway, Taco Bell, Taco John's Country Inn Suites, Days Inn, Econolodge, Hampton Inn, Quality Inn $Tree, Advance Parts, AT&T, Chrysler/Dodge/Jeep, Ford/Lincoln, Goodyear/auto, Harley-Davidson, Herberger's, Hobby Lobby, , Hy-Vee Foods, Menards, NAPA, O'Reilly Parts, Target, Tires+, to Sandy Shore RA (10mi), Verizon, Walgreens, Walmart/Subway
164	SD 22, to Castlewood, Clear Lake, **9 mi E** Cenex/dsl
161mm	**both lanes, full facilities, litter barrels, petwalk, , vending**
157	to Brandt
150	SD 28, SD 15 N, to Toronto, **7 mi W** gas food lodging Lake Poinsett RA (24 mi), SD Amateur Baseball Hall of Fame (24 mi)

SD

INTERSTATE 29 Cont'd

BROOKINGS

Exit #	Services
140	SD 30, to White, Bruce, W Oakwood Lakes SP (12mi)
133	US 14 byp, Brookings, E WW Tires, W Laura Ingalls Wilder Home (43 mi), museums, to SD St U
132	US 14, Lp 29, Brookings, E Cenex/dsl Applebee's, Whiskey Creek Grill Fairfield Inn, Hampton Inn, Holiday Inn Express, My Place Hotel, Super 8, W BP Arby's, Backyard BBQ, Buffalo Wild Wings, Burger King, Culver's, DQ, Ground Round, Guadalajara Mexican, Hardee's, Jimmy John's, KFC, King's Wok, McDonald's, Papa John's, Papa Murphy's, Perkins, Pizza Ranch, Qdoba Mexican, Subway, Taco Bell Comfort Suites, Days Inn, Econolodge, Quality Inn H, Advance Parts, AT&T, Buick/Chevrolet/GMC, CarQuest, city park, Lowe's, Verizon, Walmart/Subway
127	SD 324, to Elkton, Sinai
124mm	Big Sioux River
121	to Nunda, Ward, E **both lanes, full facilities, litter barrels, petwalk, , , RV dump, st patrol, vending**
114	SD 32, to Flandreau, **7 mi** E Cenex Subway Sioux River Motel/RV park Royal River Casino/hotel, Santee Tribal Hqtrs
109	SD 34, to Madison, Colman, **20 mi** W Shell/Crossroads Rest./dsl, Sinclair/Prairie Jct/dsl Dakota St U, museum, to Lake Herman SP
104	to Trent, Chester
103mm	**parking area both lanes**
98	SD 115 S, Dell Rapids, E Cenex (3mi), Shell (3mi) DQ (3mi), Pizza Ranch (3mi) Bilmar Inn (3mi) Chevrolet, dsl service, H (3mi), vet
94	SD 114, to Baltic, E Clark/dsl to EROS Data Ctr (10mi), US Geological Survey (10mi)
86	to Renner, Crooks
84b a	I-90, W to Rapid City, E to Albert Lea
83	SD 38 W, 60th St, E FLYING J/Denny's/dsl/LP/scales/24hr/@ Burger King Quality Suites Freightliner, Harley-Davidson, Indian Motorcycles, Truckwash, W fireworks, hwy patrol, Walmart/Subway
82	Benson Rd, E BeefOBrady's Fairfield Inn
81	SD 38 E, Russell St, Sioux Falls, E BP, Food'n Fuel/Quiznos Roll'n Pin Rest. Arena Motel, Best Western+, Dakotah Lodge, Guesthouse Inn, Motel 6, Ramada Inn, Sheraton, Sioux Falls Inn, Sleep Inn, Super 8 golf, Schaap's RV Ctr, W Subway
80	Madison St, E Sinclair/dsl to fairgrounds
79	SD 42, 12th St, E BP, Freedom Burger King, Burger Time, Fry'n Pan, Golden Harvest Chinese, KFC, McDonald's, Pizza Hut, Sneaky's Chicken, Subway, Taco Bell, Taco John's, Tomacelli's Pizza, Wendy's Ramada, Woodspring Suites H, $General, Ace Hardware, BMW/Cadillac/Mercedes, Chevrolet, city park, Lewis Drug, NAPA, Nissan, to Great Plains Zoo/museum, Toyota, USPO, Walgreens, W BP/dsl, Cenex/Chester's/dsl, Food'n Fuel Hardee's Meineke, Tower RV Park
78	26th St, Empire St, E BP/dsl/e85 Buffalo Wild Wings, Carino's Italian, Carnaval Brazillian Grill, Chevy's Mexican, ChuckeCheese, Coldstone, Cracker Barrel, Culver's, Domino's, Granite City Rest, Outback Steaks, Puerto Vallarta, Ruby Tuesday, Sonic ClubHouse Suites, Hampton Inn, Holiday Inn Express, StayBridge Suites BigLots, Home Depot, Michael's, Petsmart, Sam's Club/gas, USPO, World Mkt, W DQ, Papa

SIOUX FALLS

Exit #	Services
78	Continued John's, Starbucks TownePlace Suites Hy-Vee Foo gas, Lowe's, Tuffy Auto, Verizon
77	41st St, Sioux Falls, E BP, SA/dsl, Shell, Sinclair/dsl plebee's, Arby's, Burger King, Chili's, Firehouse Subs, F Pan Rest., Fuddrucker's, HuHot Mongolian, KFC, Lones Steaks, McDonald's, Old Chicago Pizza, Olive Garden, P cake House, Panda Express, Papa Murphy's, Perkins, Pi Hut, Pizza Ranch, Qdoba Mexican, Red Lobster, Starbu Subway, Szechwan Chinese, Taco Bell, Taco John's, TX Ro house, Valentino's, Wendy's Best Western, Comfort Sui Courtyard, Fairfield Inn, Microtel, MyPlace Hotel, Red Rock Residence Inn, SpringHill Suites, Super 8 Advance Pa Barnes&Noble, Best Buy, Dick's, Ford/Lincoln, Goodyear/a Gordman's, Hyundai, Hy-Vee Foods/dsl, JC Penney, Koh Macy's, Mazda, Menards, Old Navy, PetCo, Target, Tires+ Maxx, Verizon, Walgreens, Walmart/Subway, W Holid dsl Burger King, Godfather's, IHOP, Little Caesar's, Perk Subway AmericInn, Baymont Inn, Days Inn, La Quinta, Roof Inn Lewis Drug, USPO
75	I-229 E, to I-90 E
73	Tea, E Sinclair/dsl Marlin's Rest, **1.5 mi** W Red B Camping
71	to Harrisburg, Lennox, E repair, W RV camping
68	to Lennox, Parker
64	SD 44, Worthing, W Buick/Chevrolet, New Prairie RV Ct
62	US 18 E, to Canton, E Cenex/pizza/dsl Countryside park/motel
59	US 18 W, to Davis, Hurley
56	to Fairview, E to Newton Hills SP (12mi)
53	to Viborg
50	to Centerville, Hudson
47	SD 46, to Irene, Beresford, E BP/Burger King, Casey dsl, Sinclair/dsl Subway Crossroads Motel, Super $General, CarQuest, Chevrolet, Fiesta Foods, Jet Auto pair, Lewis Drug, W Conoco/Dutch Rest./dsl/scales/24hr
42	to Alcester, Wakonda
41mm	**truck check (from sb)**
38	to Volin, E to Union Co SP (3mi)
31	SD 48, to Akron, Spink
26	SD 50, to Vermillion, E **Welcome Ctr/ both lanes, full cilities, info, litter barrels, petwalk, , ,** W BP/Subw Pizza Hut/dsl Burger King (6mi), Godfather's Pizza (6 Jimmy John's (6mi), Red Steakhouse (6mi), Subway (6mi), T John's (6mi) Best Western (6mi), Comfort Inn (6mi), H day Inn Express (6mi), Prairie Inn (6mi), Super 8 (6mi) (6mi), Hy-Vee Foods (6mi), to Lewis & Clark RA (6mi), to U of (6mi), Walmart (6mi)
18	Lp 29, to Burbank, Elk Point, E A-1/dsl, Casey's Hon Towne Inn
15	to Elk Point, E Kum&Go/Subway/dsl, W fireworks
13mm	**weigh sta nb, parking area sb**
9	SD 105, Jefferson, E Conoco/Choice Cut Rest.
4	North Shore Dr, McCook, **1 mi** W Adams Homestead/ ture preserve, KOA (seasonal)
2	SD 105, N Sioux City, E Goode/casino/dsl/E10/20/ McDonald's, Subway, Taco John's fireworks, US W Casey's, Clark Days Inn, Hampton Inn, Red Car Inn, Super 8 KOA
1	Dakota Dunes Blvd, W Cenex/dsl Graham's G Country Inn&Suites Dakota Dunes Golf Resort
0mm	South Dakota/Iowa state line, Big Sioux River

INTERSTATE 90

Exit #	Services
412.5mm	South Dakota/Minnesota state line
412mm	**Welcome Ctr wb/ eb, full facilities, info, litter barrels, petwalk, , , RV dump (wb), weigh sta (wb)**
410	Valley Springs, N Palisades SP (7mi), S gas food Beaver Creek Nature Area
406	SD 11, Brandon, Corson, N Palisades SP (10mi), S BP/dsl, Holiday/McDonald's/dsl, Local Brandon Steaks, DQ, Great Wall, Papa Murphy's, Pizza Hut, Pizza Ranch, Subway, Taco John's, Tailgator's Grill Holiday Inn Express, Quality Inn Ace Hardware, Lewis Drug, Sturdevant's Parts, Sunshine Foods, to Big Sioux RA (4mi), Verizon
402	EROS Data Ctr, N Jellystone RV Park, tires
400	I-229 S
399	SD 115, Cliff Ave, Sioux Falls, N KOA, Spader RV Ctr, S BP/Get'n Go/dsl, Conoco, Holiday/dsl/e85, Love's/Grandma Max's/Subway/dsl/scales/24hr/@, Sinclair/dsl Arby's, Burger King, McDonald's/truck parking, Perkins, Taco Bell, Taco John's Cloud Nine Motel, Days Inn, EconoLodge, Super 8 H, Graham Tire, Kenworth, Peterbilt, Volvo
398mm	Big Sioux River
396b a	I-29, N to Brookings, S to Sioux City
395	Marion Rd, Marion, S Walmart/Subway
390	SD 38, Hartford, N Pizza Ranch (3mi) Goos RV Ctr, S Cowboy Town/dsl
387	rd 17, Hartford, N BP/dsl Midway Grill, Pizza Ranch (1.6mi) AmericInn
379	SD 19, Humboldt, N Clark/dsl USPO
375mm	E Vermillion River
374	to SD 38, Montrose, 5 mi S Battle Creek Res., Lake Vermillion RA, RV camping
368	Canistota, 5 mi S Best Western, Canistota Depot Inn, Ortman Hotel
364	US 81, to Yankton, Salem, 1 mi N Cenex Home Motel Camp America
363.5mm	W Vermillion River
363mm	**both lanes, full facilities, litter barrels, petwalk, , , RV dump, st patrol, vending**
357	to Bridgewater, Canova
353	Spencer, Emery, S FuelMart/Subway/dsl/casino/24hr
352mm	Wolf Creek
350	SD 25, Emery, Farmer, N to DeSmet, Home of Laura Ingalls Wilder
344	SD 262, to Fulton, Alexandria, S Sinclair/dsl
337mm	**parking area both lanes**
335	Riverside Rd, N KOA (1mi)
334.5mm	James River
332	SD 37 S, to Parkston, Mitchell, N Cenex/Chester's/dsl, Clark, I-90/Holiday/Marlin's Rest./Subway/dsl/scales/24hr, Mobil/Jimmy John's, Sinclair Arby's, Cattleman's Club Steaks, Chef Louie Steaks, Corona Village Mexican, McDonald's, Perkins, Pizza Hut, Pizza Ranch, Twin Dragon Chinese AmericInn, Corn Palace Inn, Days Inn, Quality Inn, Super 8/truck parking, Thunderbird Motel H, Advance Parts, AutoZone, Chrysler/Dodge/Jeep, Museum of Pioneer Life, O'Reilly Parts, Rondee's Campground, to Corn Palace, transmissions, URGENT CARE, Verizon, Walgreens, S Shell/Godfather's/Taco Bell/dsl/24hr Culver's, Hardee's, Quiznos, Ruby Tuesday, Whiskey Creek Grill Comfort Inn, Hampton Inn, Holiday Inn Express, Kelly Inn $Tree, AT&T, Cabela's, Menards, Verizon, Walmart/Subway

MITCHELL

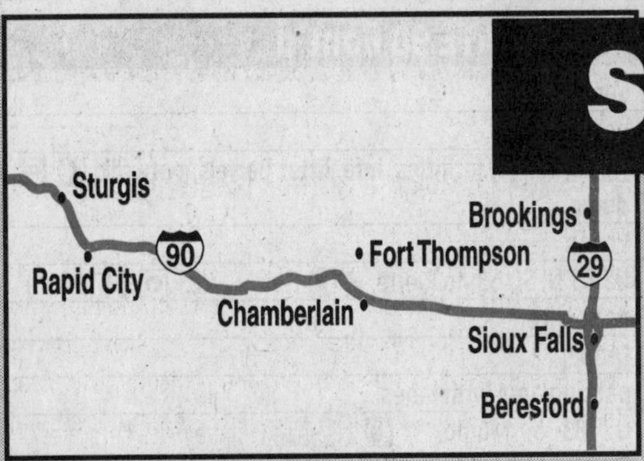

Exit #	Services
330	SD 37 N, Mitchell, N Cenex/Chester's/dsl, Shell/dsl, Sinclair/dsl DQ Budget Inn, Motel 6, Ramada Inn, Siesta Motel, Travelodge H, County Fair Foods, Jack's Campers/RV Ctr, Lewis Drug, Mr. Tire, museum, to Corn Palace, weigh sta, S Dakota RV Park
325	Betts Rd, S Famil-e-Fun Camping
319	Mt Vernon, 1 mi N Sinclair/dsl, Westey's One Stop/dsl
310	US 281, to Stickney, S Sinclair/Deli Depot/dsl/24hr to Ft Randall Dam
308	Lp 90, to Plankinton, N Sinclair/Al's Cafe/dsl Cabin Fever Motel/RV Park, Smart Choice Inn Gordy's Camping, Hills RV Park, repair, USPO
301.5mm	**both lanes, full facilities, litter barrels, , , RV dump**
296	White Lake, 1 mi N Hillman's/dsl A-Z Motel USPO, S Siding 36 Motel/RV Park
294mm	Platte Creek
289	SD 45 S, to Platte, S to Snake Cr/Platte Cr RA (25mi)
284	SD 45 N, Kimball, N Clark, Conoco/Ditty's/Diner/dsl. Frosty King Dakota Winds Motel, Westwood Inn Parkway Campground, repair/tires, S tractor museum
272	SD 50, Pukwana, 2 mi N gas food lodging, S Snake/Platte Creek Rec Areas (25mi)
265	SD 50, Chamberlain, N Cenex/DQ/dsl AmericInn H, St Joseph Akta Lakota Museum (4mi), vet, S SA/dsl Happy Camper Campground
264mm	**both lanes, full facilities, info, litter barrels, , , scenic view**
263	Chamberlain, N Sinclair/dsl McDonald's, Pizza Hut, Subway (1mi), Taco John's Bel Aire Motel (1mi), Best Western (1mi), Super 8 Crow Creek Sioux Tribal Hqtrs, SD Hall of Fame
262mm	Missouri River
260	SD 50, Oacoma, N Clark/dsl, Phillips 66/Arby's/dsl, Shell/dsl Al's Oasis/Motel/Camping/cafe/mkt, Baymont Inn, Cedar Shore Motel/Camping (3mi), Econolodge, Howard Johnson, Quality Inn antiques, Buick/Chevrolet, Dakota Camping, Oasis Camping, Old West Trading Post
251	SD 47, to Winner, Gregory
248	SD 47, Reliance, N Cenex (1mi), Farmer's Union/dsl (1mi) Sioux Tribal Hqtrs, to Big Bend RA
241	to Lyman
235	SD 273, Kennebec, N Clark/dsl Hot Rods Steaks Budget Host, Kings Inn auto repair, KOA, USPO
226	US 183 S, Presho, N Cenex/dsl, Sinclair/dsl Hutch's Motel/café New Frontier RV Park, pioneer museum, repair, vet
225	lp 90, Presho, same as 226
221mm	**wb, full facilities, info, litter barrels, petwalk, , , RV dump**

CHAMBERLAIN

[gas] = gas [food] = food [lodging] = lodging [other] = other [RS] = rest stop

SD

INTERSTATE 90 Cont'd

	Exit #	Services
	220	no service
	218mm	**[RS] eb, full [handicapped] facilities, info, litter barrels, petwalk, [phone], [picnic], RV dump**
	214	Vivian
	212	US 83 N, SD 53, to Pierre, N [gas] Sinclair/dsl [other] [H] (34mi)
	208	no service
	201	Draper
	194mm	**parking area both lanes**
MURDO	192	US 83 S, Murdo, N [gas] Pilot/Subway/dsl/Lp/scales/24hr, Pioneer/dsl [food] Buffalo Rest., Covered Wagon Cafe, Murdo Drive-In, Prairie Pizza, Rusty Spur Steaks, Star Rest. [lodging] American Inn, Best Western, Iversen Inn, Range Country Lodge, Sioux Motel, Super 8 [other] American RV Park/camping, auto museum, city park, Ford, Murdo Foods, USPO, S [lodging] Country Inn [other] to Rosebud
	191	Murdo, N same as 192
	188mm	**parking area both lanes**
	183	Okaton, S [other] Ghost Town
	177	no service
	175mm	central/mountain timezone
	172	to Cedar Butte
	170	SD 63 N, to Midland, N [gas] Conoco/dsl [other] 1880's Town, KOA
	167mm	**[RS] wb, full [handicapped] facilities, litter barrels, petwalk, [phone], [picnic], RV dump**
	165mm	**[RS] eb, full [handicapped] facilities, litter barrels, petwalk, [phone], [picnic], RV dump**
	163	SD 63, Belvidere, S [gas] Belvidere Store/dsl [food] JR's Grill
KADOKA	152	Lp 90, Kadoka, N [gas] Conoco/rest./dsl/24hr, S [other] Badlands Petrified Gardens
	150	SD 73 S, Kadoka, N [lodging] Dakota Inn/rest., S [gas] Conoco/dsl, Sinclair/pizza/dsl [food] Subway, Sunset Grill [lodging] Best Value Inn, Budget Host, El Centro Motel/rest., Ponderosa Motel/RV Park, Wagon Wheel Motel, West Motel [other] Kadoka Kampground, repair, to Buffalo Nat Grasslands
	143	SD 73 N, to Philip, **15 mi** N [other] [H]
	138mm	scenic overlook wb
	131	SD 240, N [other] Minuteman Missle NHS, S [gas] Conoco [lodging] Badlands Inn (9mi), Cedar Pass Lodge/rest. (9mi) [other] Circle 10 Camping, KOA (11mi), Prairie Home NHS, to Badlands NP
	129.5mm	scenic overlook eb
	127	no service
	121	Bigfoot Rd
	116	239th St
	112	US 14 E, to Philip
WALL	110	SD 240, Wall, N [gas] Conoco/dsl, Exxon, Phillips 66/Subway [food] Cactus Cafe, DQ, Red Rock Rest., Roadtrip Cafe, Wall Drug Rest. [lodging] Ann's Motel, Best Value Inn, Best Western, Days Inn, EconoLodge, Fountain Hotel, Sunshine Inn, Super 8, The Wall Motel, Travelodge, Welsh Motel [other] Ace Hardware, Arrow Campground, Harley Davidson, National Grasslands Visitor Ctr, Pronto Parts, Sleepy Hollow RV Park/Camping, Wall Drug, Wall Foods, Wounded Knee Museum, S [lodging] Frontier Cabins Motel [other] RV camping, to Badlands NP
	109	W 4th Ave, Wall, **1-2 mi** N access to same as 110
	107	Cedar Butte Rd
	101	Jensen Rd, to Schell Ranch
	100mm	**[RS] both lanes, full [handicapped] facilities, info, litter barrels, petwalk, [phone], [picnic], RV dump, vending**
	99.5mm	Cheyenne River
	98	Wasta, N [gas] Mobil/dsl [other] 24 Express RV Camping, USPO
	90	173rd Ave, to Owanka
	88	171st Ave(from eb, no re-entry)

	84	167th Ave, N [other] Olde Glory Fireworks
	78	161st Ave, New Underwood, S [gas] Sinclair/dsl, Steve's Gen Store/dsl/motel/rest. [food] Harry's Hideaway Rest, [lodging] BJ's tel [other] Boondocks Camping
	69mm	**parking area both lanes**
	67	to Box Elder, N [gas] Love's/Hardee'sdsl/scales/24hr [other] Air&Sp Museum, Ellsworth AFB
	63	(eb only) to Box Elder, S [gas] Phillips 66/dsl, [other] Ellsworth
	61	Elk Vale Rd, N [gas] FLYING J/Conoco/CountryMkt/dsl/e-LP/RV dump/scales/24hr/@ [food] Quaker Steak [lodging] Cam an Suites, MainStay Suites, My Place [other] Black Hills Vis Ctr, Cabela's, Dakota RV Ctr, S [gas] Conoco/dsl, Sinclair/ e85 [food] Arby's, Dakotah Steakhouse, Marco's Pizza, McD ald's, Perkins, Taco Bell [lodging] Baymont Inn, Comfort Su Fairfield Inn, Home 2 Suites, La Quinta, Residence Inn, Sl Inn [other] KOA (2mi seasonal)
	60	Lp 90, to Mt Rushmore, Rapid City, N [other] Buick/GMC, Che let, Ford/Lincoln, Great Western Tire, Kenworth/Volvo, Niss Toyota, S [gas] Holiday/dsl [food] Blaze Pizza, Culver's, Fam Dave's, Five Guys, Fuji Japanese Steaks, HuHot Mongoli Longhorn Steaks, MacKenzie River, Native Grill, Noodle Co, On the Border, Panera Bread, Pizza Ranch, Popeyes, Q ba Mexican, Smiling Moose Deli, Starbucks [lodging] Staybri Suites [other] [H], $Tree, Aamco, AT&T, Gordman's, Menards, chael's, Nat Coll of Mines/Geology, PetCo, Ross, Sam's Cl dsl, Scheel's Sports, Target, TJ Maxx, Verizon
RAPID CITY	59	La Crosse St, Rapid City, N [gas] Mobil/dsl, Phillips 66 [food] B ton's Rest., Burger King, Denny's, Fuddrucker's, Minerva's Re Outback Steaks, Starbucks, TGIFriday's, TX Roadhouse [lodging] B Western, Country Inn&Suites, EconoLodge, Hilton Garden, H iday Inn Express, Super 8 [other] Herberger's, Hobby Lobby, st trol, S [gas] Exxon/24hr, Sinclair [food] Arnold's Diner, China W Golden Corral, Little Caesar's, MillStone Rest., Mongolian G Pacific Rim Cafe, Perkins, Philly Ted's, Subway [lodging] Americl Days Inn, Fair Value Inn, Foothills Inn, Grand Gateway Ho Hampton Inn, Microtel, Motel 6, Quality Inn, Ramada, Rodew Inn [other] AT&T, URGENT CARE, Walgreens, Walmart/McDonal
	58	Haines Ave, Rapid City, N [gas] Fresh Start/dsl [food] Applebe Chili's, Hardee's, IHOP, Olive Garden, Red Lobster [lodging] Best V ue Inn, Grand Stay Motel [other] BAM!, Best Buy, Herbergers, Penney, Jo-Ann, Kohl's, Lowe's, Petsmart, Tires+, to Rushm Mall, S [gas] Loaf'n Jug, Maverik/dsl [food] ChuckECheese, Di ey's BBQ, Jimmy John's, Papa John's, Pizza Hut, Taco Joh Wendy's [other] [H], Family$, URGENT CARE
	57	I-190, US 16, to Rapid City, Mt Rushmore, **1 mi** S **on No St** [gas] Exxon [food] Panchero's Mexican [lodging] Holiday Inn, Howa Johnson, The Rushmore Hotel [other] Family Thrift Foods, Kne Home Ctr, Office Depot
	55	Deadwood Ave, N [other] Dakota RV Ctr, Harley-Davidson/ca S [gas] Pilot/Subway/dsl/scales/24hr/@ [food] Marlin's Rest. dsl repair
	52	Peaceful Pines Rd, Black Hawk, N [other] Lazy JD RV Park (4m Three Flags Camping (1mi), S [food] BJ's/dsl, Godfather's Piz Longhorn Rest. [other] Family$, USPO
	48	Stagebarn Canyon Rd, S [gas] Conoco/Haggar's Mkt/food, P Stop/dsl [food] Pizza Hut [lodging] Ramada [other] $General, Campi World RV Ctr
	46	Piedmont Rd, Elk Creek Rd, N [food] Elk Creek Steakhouse [other] Creek RV Park, to Petrified Forest, S [gas] Mobil/Country Corn Cafe/Papa John's/dsl [food] Sacora Sta Rest. [other] Sacora Sta Campi
	44	Bethlehem Rd, S [other] Jack's RV Ctr (2mi)
	42mm	**parking area both lanes**

SD

INTERSTATE 90 Cont'd

Exit #	Services
40	Tilford, S RV Park
39mm	weigh sta eb
37	Pleasant Valley Rd, N Kickstands Camp, S Bulldog Camping, Rush-No-More Camping
34	S Black Hills Nat Cemetary, No Name City RV Park
32	SD 79, Jct Ave, Sturgis, N Conoco/dsl, Exxon/dsl Sturgis Grill, Taco John's Best Western H, Ford, Grocery Mart, NAPA, to Bear Butte SP, vet, S Mobil/Arby's/Papa John's/dsl Ford
30	US 14A W, SD 34E, to Deadwood, Sturgis, N Cenex/dsl, Phillips 66/dsl McDonald's, Pizza Hut, Shanghai Chinese, Sturgis Coffee Co $General, CarQuest, Day's End Camping, Family$, Indian Motorcycles, Mr Tire, O'Reilly Parts, USPO, S Conoco/dsl, RanchMart Burger King, DQ, Kang San Asian, Pizza Ranch, Subway Days Inn, Holiday Inn Express, Super 8 BMW Motorcycles, Chevrolet, Verizon
23	SD 34 W, to Belle Fourche, Whitewood, N Northern Hills RV Ctr, S Howdy's/dsl, Mobil/Sonset Sta/dsl Hideaway Diner Tony's Motel USPO
17	US 85 S, to Deadwood, S Cenex/Dickey's BBQ/dsl Deadwood NLH (17mi), Elkhorn Ridge RV Resort, KOA (9mi)
14	US 14A, Spearfish Canyon, N FreshStart/dsl Applebee's, Culver's, Subway Fairfield Inn, Hampton Inn, Holiday Inn/rest., Quality Inn $Tree, AutoZone, Verizon, Walmart, S Phillips 66/dsl KFC/LJ Silver, Perkins, Pizza Ranch, Roma's Rest. Baymont Inn, Super 8, Travelodge Ace Hardware, Bomgaars, Ford/Lincoln, transmissions
12	Jackson Blvd, Spearfish, S Conoco/dsl, Exxon, Loaf'n Jug, Phillips 66/dsl Arby's, Barbacoa's, Domino's, Jade Palace Chinese, McDonald's, Millstone Rest., Papa Murphy's, Pizza Hut, Taco John's Best Western H, Black Hills St U, CarQuest, Chrysler/Dodge/Jeep, historic fish hatchery, same as 10
10	US 85 N, to Belle Fourche, S Burger King, Cedar House Rest., City Brew, Golden Dragon Chinese, Little Caesar's, McDonald's, Philly Ted's, Qdoba, Subway, Taco Bell Days Inn H, Buick/Chevrolet, Cadillac/GMC, KOA, Safeway/dsl, same as 12, USPO, Walgreens
8	McGuigan Rd, W Spearfish, S Phillips 66/dsl KOA (1mi)
2	1 mi N McNenny St Fish Hatchery
1mm	Welcome Ctr eb, full facilities, info, litter barrels, petwalk, RV dump
0mm	South Dakota/Wyoming state line

INTERSTATE 229 (Sioux Falls)

Exit #	Services
10b a	I-90 E and W. **I-229 begins/ends on I-90, exit 400.**
9	Benson Rd, W Sinclair/pizza/dsl DQ, Jimmy John's, Marlin's Rest. Ford Trucks, Western Star
7.5mm	Big Sioux River
7	Rice St, E winter sports, W to stockyards
6	SD 38, 10th St, E Sinclair A&W, Applebee's, Arby's, Denny's, Domino's, DQ, Fryn' Pan Rest., Jimmy John's, KFC, Pizza Hut, Pizza Ranch, Taco Bell, Tokyo Hibachi, Tomacelli's Italian Super 8 AT&T, AutoZone, Family$, Hy-Vee Foods, O'Reilly Parts, Sturdevant's Parts, USPO, Valvoline, vet, W BP/dsl, Casey's/dsl, Shell Burger King, BurgerTime, Hardee's, Little Caesar's, McDonald's, Pita Pit, Pizza Inn, Pizza Man, Puerto Vallarta, Qdoba Mexican, Subway, Taco John's Rushmore Motel Lewis Drug, vet

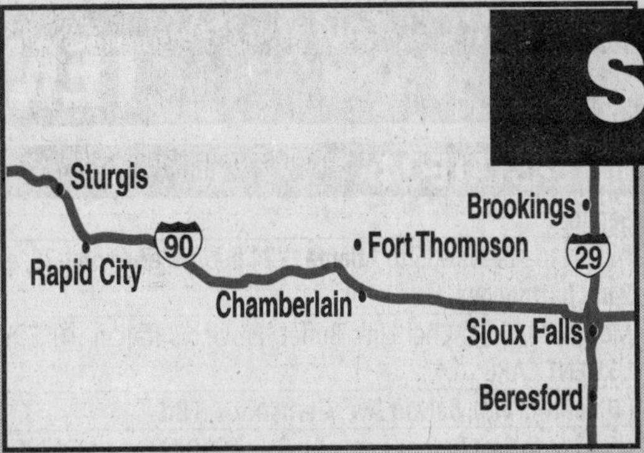

SIOUX FALLS

Exit #	Services
5.5mm	Big Sioux River
5	26th St, E Holiday/dsl Burger King, Cherry Creek Grill, Dario's Pizza, McDonald's, Saigon Panda city park, W H
4	Cliff Ave, E BP
3	SD 115, Lp 229, Minnesota Ave, E city park, W BP/dsl, Sinclair Arby's, Burger King, Camilles Cafe, Culver's, DQ, Famous Dave's BBQ, Golden Bowl Chinese, Hardee's, Little Caesar's/TCBY, McDonald's, Subway $Tree, Ace Hardware, Acura, Buick/GMC, Costco/gas, Hy-Vee Foods/dsl, Kia, Lewis Drug, Staples, tires, USPO, vet
2	Western Ave, E Holiday/dsl Bracco Cafe, DQ, Scooters Coffee, Starbucks, W Cenex/dsl, Holiday Buck's Roadhouse, Burger King, China Buffet, Huhot Mongolian, Lone Star Steaks, Papa Murphy's, PepperJax Grill, Perkins, Qdoba Mexican, Redrossa Pizza, Scheel's, Valentino's H, Advance Parts, AutoZone, Best Buy, Goodyear/auto, Hancock Fabrics, Tuesday Morning
1.5mm	Big Sioux River
1c	Louise Ave, E Holiday/dsl Comfort Suites, Hampton Inn, Holiday Inn Express, Homewood Suites H, Chrysler/Dodge/Jeep, Fiat, Lewis Drug, W BP Burger King, Five Guys, Jimmy John's, Marco's Pizza, McDonald's, Noodles&Co, Panera Bread, Qdoba Mexican, Royal Palace, Spezia's Rest, Taco John's, Wendy's Hilton Garden Inn Barnes&Noble, Dick's, Honda, Hy-Vee Foods/dsl, JC Penney, Jo-Ann Fabrics, Kohl's, Target, Verizon, Walgreens
1b a	**I-29 N and S. I-229 begins/ends on I-29, exit 75.**

NOTES

= gas = food = lodging = other = rest stop Copyright 2020 - The Next EX

TENNESSEE

TN

INTERSTATE 24

CHATTANOOGA

Exit #	Services
185b a	I-75, N to Knoxville, S to Atlanta. **I-24 begins/ends on I-75, exit 2 in Chattanooga.**
184	Moore Rd, **S** Chef Lin's Buffet, Provino's Italian $Tree, URGENT CARE
183	(183a from wb), Belvoir Ave, Germantown Rd
181a	US 41 S, to East Ridge (from eb), **S** 2503 Station Grill, Sugar's Ribs
181	Fourth Ave, to TN Temple U, Chattanooga, **N** Citgo/dsl, Exxon/dsl, Hi-Tech Fuel, Stop'n Save Bojangles, Burger King, Capt D's, Hunan Wok, Krystal, Subway, Waffle House Chatt Inn $General, Family$, Food City, Mack/Volvo Trucks, NAPA, O'Reilly Parts, repair, vet, **S** Mystik
180b a	US 27 S, TN 8, Rossville Blvd, **N** Best One Tires/service, to UT Chatt, **S** Mapco/dsl, Mobil/dsl Hamilton Inn Family$, to Chickamauga Battlefield
178	US 27 N, Market St, to Lookout Mtn, Chattanooga, **N** BP/dsl, Citgo District 3 Hotel, Marriott, Staybridge Suites Chevrolet, Ford/Lincoln, Midas, Nissan, to aquarium, to Chattanooga ChooChoo, U-Haul, **S** RaceWay/dsl KFC Comfort Inn, Motel 6, Red Roof+
175	Browns Ferry Rd, to Lookout Mtn, **N** BP, Spirit/dsl China Gourmet Best Value Inn, La Quinta CVS Drug, vet, **S** Mapco/dsl Hardee's, McDonald's Comfort Inn, EconoLodge, Travelodge $General
174	US 11, US 41, US 64, Lookout Valley, **N** Waffle House Days Inn Racoon Mtn Camping (1mi), st patrol, **S** BP/dsl, Exxon/Circle K/dsl, Murphy USA/dsl Cracker Barrel, Jack's Rest., Logan's Roadhouse, Los 3 Amigos, New China, Sonic, Taco Bell, Waffle House, Wendy's Best Western, Budget Motel, Clarion, Country Inn&Suites, Fairfield Inn, Hampton Inn, Holiday Inn Express, Quality Inn, Red Roof Inn, Super 8 $Tree, Ace Hardware, URGENT CARE, Verizon, Walmart/Subway
172mm	**eb, full facilities, litter barrels, petwalk, , , vending**
171mm	Tennessee/Georgia state line
169	GA 299, to US 11, **N** Mapco/dsl, **S** BP/Krispy Chicken/dsl/24hr, Citgo, Pilot/Subway/dsl/scales/24hr $General
167	I-59 S, to Birmingham
167mm	Tennessee/Georgia state line, Central/Eastern time zone
161	TN 156, to Haletown, New Hope, **N** Anchor Inn/dsl (1mi) Hales Bar RV Park (2.5mi), **S** Chevron/fireworks
160mm	Tennessee River/Nickajack Lake
159mm	**Welcome Ctr wb/ eb, full facilities, litter barrels, petwalk, , , vending**
158	US 41, TN 27, Nickajack Dam, **N** Love's/McDonald's/Subway/dsl/scales/24hr, **S** Shellmound Camping (2.5mi), Speedway/Speedy's Cafe/24hr
155	TN 28, Jasper, **N** Hi-Tech/dsl Hardee's, Western Sizzlin Quality Inn, **S** BP/Mapco/dsl H
152	US 41, US 64, US 72, Kimball, S Pittsburg, **N** Phillips 66/fireworks, RaceWay/dsl, Shell/dsl A&W/LJ Silver, Arby's, China Buffet, Cracker Barrel, Domino's, El Toril, KFC, Krystal, Little Caesar's, McDonald's, Pizza Hut, Shoney's, Subway, Taco Bell, Waffle House, Wendy's Best Value Inn, Comfort Inn, Hampton Inn, Holiday Inn Express, Super 8 $Tree, Buick/Chevrolet/GMC, GNC, Lowe's, Walmart, **3 mi S** Lodge Cast Iron, to Russell Cave NM

MONTEAGLE

MANCHESTER

Exit #	Services
143	Martin Springs Rd, **N** Citgo/dsl
135	US 41 N, Monteagle, **N** Marathon/dsl, Pilot/Wendy's/scales/24hr High Point Rest., Rocky Top Rest., Shan Chi Family$, Monteagle Parts, USPO, **S** Red Roof Inn
134	US 64, US 41A, to Sewanee, Monteagle, **N** BP/Map McDonald's/dsl Sonic American Eagle Inn Drug, to S Cumberland SP, **S** Exxon/dsl, Marathon/Kangaroo Hardee's, Pizza Hut, Smokehouse BBQ, Subway, Wa House Best Western, Mountain Inn, Super 8 $Gene Auto/tire repair, Fred's, Piggly Wiggly, to U of The South
133mm	**both lanes, full facilities, litter barrels, petwalk, , vending**
128mm	Elk River
127	US 64, TN 50, to Winchester, Pelham, **N** Citgo, Marath dsl, **S** Gulf/dsl to Tims Ford SP/RV camping
119mm	**trucks only parking area both lanes**
117	to Tullahoma, USAF Arnold Ctr, UT Space Institute
116mm	**weigh sta both lanes**
114	US 41, Manchester, **N** Exxon/24 Truckers/scales/dsl, Marathon/dsl, Murphy USA/dsl, Shell/dsl Great Wall Chine Logan's Roadhouse, O'Charley's, Potrillos Mexican, St bucks Comfort Suites, Holiday Inn Express, Motel 6, Quality Inn, Scottish Inn, Sleep Inn, Truckers Inn $Tree, AT Home Depot, KOA, Nissan, tire/truck repair, Toyota, Veriz Walmart/Subway, **S** Mobil/Circle K, RaceWay/dsl by's, Baskin-Robbins, Bojangles, Burger King, Capt D's, Hong Kong Buffet, KFC, Krystal, McDonald's/playplace, Papa Joh Pizza Hut, Rafael's Italian, Subway, Taco Bell, Waffle Hou Wendy's Days Inn, Microtel, Red Roof Inn, Regency I Royal Inn Advance Parts, AutoZone, Family$, Ford/Linc O'Reilly Parts, Russell Stover, USPO, vet
111	TN 55, Manchester, **N** BP/dsl, Co-op/dsl, Mobil/Circle K H, to Rock Island SP, vet, **S** Hardee's, J&G Pizza Steaks, Sonic $General, Gateway Auto, Old Stone Fort Rite Aid, to Jack Daniels Dist HS, Walgreens
110	TN 53, Manchester, **N** Exxon, Mobil/Circle K/dsl, Pet dsl Cracker Barrel, Emma's Rest., Las Fajitas Mexican, C Rest. Ambassador Inn, Econolodge, Economy Inn, Hampton Inn H, **S** Shell/dsl Los 3 Amigos, Prater's BB Waffle House repair
110mm	Duck River
105	US 41, **N** Exxon/dsl, Marathon/dsl, **S** Dickel HS, tire repair, to Normandy Dam, Whispering Oaks Camping (1.5mi
97	TN 64, to Shelbyville, Beechgrove, **S** Marathon/dsl
89	Buchanan Rd, **N** Love's/McDonald's/dsl/scales/24 Subway, **S** Shell/dsl $General, A&L RV Ctr
84	Joe B. Jackson Pkwy, **N** Subway
81	US 231, Murfreesboro, **N** Exxon, Gulf/dsl, Mapco, Sh Cathay Asian, Cracker Barrel, Krystal, Parthenon Gril Shoney's, Sports Seasons Grill, Wendy's Best Value In Knights Inn, Quality Inn, Ramada Ltd, Regal Inn H, Chrysler/Dodge/Jeep, Honda, **S** Kangaroo, Mapco/dsl, Mob Pilot/Arby's/scales/dsl/24hr Bojangles, Burger King, Siesta Mexican, McDonald's/playplace, Pizza Hut, Rick's BB Sonic, Starbucks, Subway, Taco Bell, Waffle House, Whitt's BB Zaxby's Select Inn, Vista Suites $General, Advan Parts, AutoZone, Discount Tire, Gateway Auto, Kroger/d O'Reilly Parts, Rite Aid, Toyota, vet

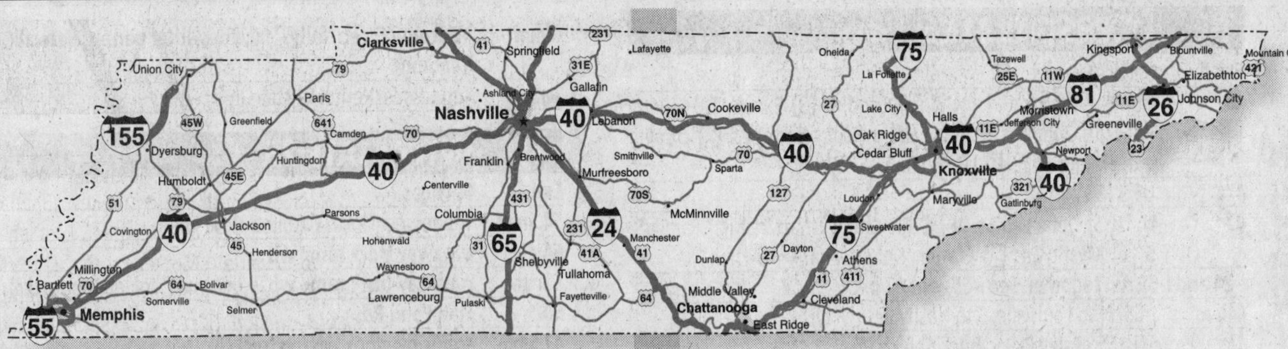

TN

INTERSTATE 24 Cont'd

NASHVILLE

MURFREESBORO

Exit #	Services
80	New Salem Hwy, rd 99, S Speedway/Speedy's Cafe/dsl Domino's, Marco's Pizza, Subway
78	TN 96, to Franklin, Murfreesboro, N Marathon, Murphy USA/dsl, Phillips 66/Church's/White Castle/dsl, Shell/Jack-in-the-Box Arby's, Baskin-Robbins, Bonefish Grill, Buffalo Wild Wings, Carrabba's, Cheddar's, Chick-fil-A, Chipotle, Chophouse, ChuckECheese, Coconut Bay Cafe, Cracker Barrel, Egg&I Cafe, Fazoli's, Firehouse Subs, Five Guys, IHOP, Jason's Deli, Jimmy John's, Jim'n Nick's BBQ, KFC, McDonald's, Mi Patria, Moe's SW Grill, Old Chicago, Olive Garden, Outback Steaks, Panda Express, Panera Bread, Red Lobster, Red Robin, Sam's Grill, Samurai's Cuisine, Sandwich Factory, SmashBurger, Starbucks, Steak'n Shake, Subway, TGIFriday's, Waffle House, Wendy's, Zaxby's Baymont Inn, Best Western, Candlewood Suites, Clarion, Comfort Suites, Country Inn&Suites, Days Inn, DoubleTree, EconoLodge, Fairfield Inn, Hampton Inn, Holiday Inn Express, Microtel, Motel 6, Red Roof Inn, Sleep Inn, Super 8 $Tree, Aldi Foods, AT&T, Books-A-Million, Dillard's, Discount Tire, Firestone, Hobby Lobby, Home Depot, JC Penney, Jo-Ann Fabrics, Lowe's, Marshalls, NTB, Petsmart, Ross, Staples, SteinMart, Target, TJ Maxx, to Stones River Bfd, Verizon, vet, Walgreens, Walmart, S Kangaroo/dsl, Mapco, Marathon/dsl, Shell/dsl Camino Real Mexican, Capt D's, China Garden, Dos Rancheros, DQ, Hardee's, Jersey Mike's Subs, McDonald's, O'Charley's, Papa Murphy's, Pizza Garden, Pizza Hut, Sonic, Subway, Taco Bell, Waffle House, Wasabi Japanese Woodspring Suites $General, auto repair, AutoZone, Kohl's, Kroger/dsl, Old Time Pottery, O'Reilly Parts, Rite Aid, Sam's Club/gas, vet, Walgreens
76	Fortress Blvd, Manson Pike, Medical Center Pkwy, N Thornton's/dsl Bar Louie, Chili's, Culver's, Genghis Grill, Longhorn Steaks, Macaroni Grill, Mimi's Cafe, Newk's Eatery, Peter D's, Starbucks, Subway, Which Wich? Embassy Suites, Hilton Garden, Holiday Inn, Residence Inn H, Barnes&Noble, Belk, Best Buy, Dick's, GNC, Michael's, Old Navy, Petco, Tire Discounters, to Stones River Nat. Bfd, World Mkt, S Exxon/dsl Sonic Chevrolet/Cadillac/GMC/Buick, Toyota
74b a	TN 840, to Lebanon, Franklin
70	TN 102, Lee Victory Pkwy, Almaville Rd, to Smyrna, N Speedway/Speedy Cafe/dsl/scales Asian Cafe, Bojangles, Mi Tierro Mexican, Naked Fish Publix, S Kangaroo/Little Caesar's/dsl, Mapco, Shell/dsl Legends Steaks, McDonald's, Sonic, Subway Deerfield Inn $General
66	TN 266, Sam Ridley Pkwy, to Smyrna, N Shell/dsl A&W/LJ Silver, Arby's, Asuka Hibachi, Blue Coast Burrito, Buffalo Wild Wings, Cheddar's, Chick-fil-A, Chili's, Chipotle, CiCi's Pizza, DQ, Famous Dave's BBQ, Firehouse Subs, Five Guys, Hickory Falls Cafe,
66	Continued IHOP, Jersey Mike's Subs, Jim'n Nick's BBQ, Krispy Kreme, La Siesta Mexican, Logan's Roadhouse, Longhorn Steaks, Panda Express, Panera Bread, Papa Murphy's, Pollo Tropical, Razz Grill, Smoothie King, Sonic, Starbucks, Subway, Waffle House, Wendy's, Zaxby's H, $General, $Tree, AT&T, CVS Drug, Discount Tire, Firestone/auto, GNC, Home Depot/gas, Kohl's, Kroger/dsl, Lowe's, Nashville I-24 Camping (3mi), Petsmart, Publix, Ross, Staples, Target, Tire Discounters, URGENT CARE, Verizon, Walgreens, S Cracker Barrel, O'Charley's, Ruby Tuesday Candlewood Suites, Comfort Suites, Fairfield Inn, Hampton Inn, Hilton Garden, Holiday Inn Express, Home 2 Suites, La Quinta, Sleep Inn, TownePlace Suites
64	Waldron Rd, to La Vergne, N Kangaroo, Kwik Sak, Pilot/Subway/dsl/scales/24hr Arby's, Hardee's, Krystal, McDonald's, Waffle House Comfort Inn, Quality Inn, Ramada Inn, S Mapco/dsl $General
62	TN 171, Old Hickory Blvd, N Citgo/Subway/dsl, Shell/dsl, TA/BP/Burger King/Popeye's/dsl/scales/24hr/@ Acapulco Burrito Rodeway Inn
60	Hickory Hollow Pkwy, N Exxon/dsl, Mapco, Thornton's/dsl 360 Burger, Burger King, ChuckECheese, KFC/LJ Silver, Logan's Roadhouse, McDonald's/Playplace, New Century Buffet, O'Charley's, Red Lobster, Starbucks, Subway, Taco Bell, Wendy's, Zaxby's Country Inn&Suites, Hampton Inn, Holiday Inn Express Chevrolet, Chrysler/Dodge/Jeep, Family$, Firestone/auto, Kroger/gas, Mazda, Office Depot, S BP/Quiznos/dsl, Shell/Dunkin' Camino Real Mexican, Casa Fiesta Mexican, IHOP, Olive Garden, Shoney's, Steak'n Shake Antioch Qtrs, Knights Inn, Super 8 Home Depot, Kia, vet
59	TN 254, Bell Rd, same as 60
57	Haywood Lane, N Kwik Sak/dsl Hardee's, Whitt's BBQ $General, Walgreens, S Kangaroo, Shell
56	TN 255, Harding Place, N Delta/dsl, Exxon, Shell/dsl Applebee's, Bar-B-Cutie, Chicago Gyros, Dunkin', KFC, McDonald's, Mikado Japanese, Pizza Hut/Taco Bell, Subway, Waffle House, Wendy's Executive Inn, M Motel, Stay Lodge, Thrifty Inn $Tree, Sam's Club/gas, S Delta/dsl, Shell/dsl Burger King, Hooters, Jack-in-the-Box, La Fiesta Best Value Inn, Travelodge H
54b a	TN 155, Briley Pkwy, to Opryland
53	I-440 W, to Memphis
52	US 41, Murfreesboro Rd, N Phillips 66/dsl, Shell Waffle House Best Western, Days Inn, Holiday Inn Express, Rodeway Inn, Super 8, S Mapco/dsl, SpeedCo/dsl/e85 BP/dsl NAPA
52b a	I-40, E to Knoxville, W to Memphis
I-24 and I-40 run together 2 mi. See I-40, exits 212-213.	
50b	I-40 W
49	Shelby Ave, (from wb only), S Exxon to LP Field

= gas = food = lodging = other = rest stop

TN

NASHVILLE / CLARKSVILLE

INTERSTATE 24 Cont'd

Exit #	Services
48	James Robertson Pkwy, N Citgo, S Exxon, TA/Country Pride/dsl/24hr/@ Gerst Haus Rest., Shoney's Quality Inn, Stadium Inn LP Stadium, st capitol
47a	US 31E
47	N 1st St, Jefferson St, N BP, Citgo, Zmart/dsl Family$, S Mystic Gas Clarion, Knights Inn U-Haul
I-24 and I-65 run together. See I-65, exit 87 b a.	
44b a	I-65, N to Louisville, S to Nashville
43	TN 155, Briley Pkwy, Brick Church Pike
40	TN 45, Old Hickory Blvd, N Marathon/Subway/dsl, Phillips 66/dsl, Shell/dsl El Rey Azteca Super 8
35	US 431, to Joelton, Springfield, N H, S BP/Heritage TC/DQ/Subway/dsl, Shell/dsl, Tfuel/dsl Family Rest., Mazatlan Mexican, McDonald's, Taco Bell Days Inn $General, auto repair, OK Camping
31	TN 249, New Hope Rd, S Marathon/dsl, Shell/dsl Jardin Mexican
24	TN 49, to Springfield, Ashland City, N Mapco/dsl, Marathon/Pizza Hut/dsl Quality Inn H, S Shell/dsl, SS/Dunkin'/Wendy's/dsl Burger King, Hardee's, KFC/Taco Bell, Sidelines Grill, Sonic, Subway Hampton Inn $General Mkt, city park, Hill Foods, O'Reilly Parts, USPO, vet
19	TN 256, Maxey Rd, to Adams, N Phillips 66/dsl, S Shell/dsl $General
11	TN 76, to Adams, Clarksville, N Shell/dsl, S Citgo, Exxon/dsl Domino's, El Rancho Grande, McDonald's, Pancho Villa Grille, Subway, Waffle House Baymont Inn, Comfort Inn, Days Inn, Super 8 H, $General, Publix, vet
9mm	Red River
8	TN 237, Rossview Rd, N Burger King, Popeye's, S Dunbar Cave SP
4	US 79, to Clarksville, Ft Campbell, N Exxon/dsl, Shell/dsl Cracker Barrel Best Western+, Hilton Garden, Sleep Inn Sam's Club/gas, Spring Creek Camping (2mi), S BP/dsl, Murphy USA/dsl, Shell/Subway/dsl Applebee's, Arby's, Baskin-Robbins, Buffalo Wild Wings, Burger King, Canela Mexican, Capt D's, Cheddar's, Chick-Fil-A, Chili's, China King, Chipotle, ChuckeCheese, Church's/White Castle, DQ, Fazoli's, Firehouse Subs, Golden Corral, Harbor Cafe, IHOP, Jersey Mike's, KFC, Krispy Kreme, Krystal, LJ Silver, Logan's Roadhouse, Longhorn Steaks, McDonald's, Moe's SW Grill, Noodles&Co, O'Charley's, Old Chicago Pizza, Olive Garden, Outback Steaks, Panera Bread, Rafferty's, Red Lobster, Shogun Japanese, Shoney's, Starbucks, Steak'n Shake, Subway, Taco Bell, Tilted Kilt, TX Roadhouse, Waffle House, Wendy's, Zaxby's Baymont Inn, Best Inn, Best Value Inn, Candlewood Suites, Country Inn&Suites, Courtyard, Days Inn, EconoLodge, Fairfield Inn, Gateway Inn, Guesthouse Inn, Hampton Inn, Hometowne Suites, La Quinta, Mainstay Suites, Microtel, Quality Inn, Ramada Ltd, Red Roof Inn, Rodeway Inn, Super 8, Woodspring Suites H, $Tree, AT&T, Belk, Best Buy, Books-A-Million, Buick/GMC, Dick's, Firestone/auto, Goodyear/auto, Hobby Lobby, Home Depot, Hyundai, JC Penney, Kohl's, Kroger/dsl, Lowe's, Mazda, Office Depot, Petco, Petsmart, Ross, Subaru, Target, TJ Maxx, to Austin Peay St U, to Land Between the Lakes, Toyota, U-Haul, Verizon, Walmart/McDonald's
1	TN 48, to Clarksville, Trenton, N Exxon/dsl, Shell/dsl Clarksville RV Camping, S Exxon/dsl, Shell/dsl Bojangles, Burger King, Coldstone, Dunkin Donuts, El Bracero Mexican, Little Caesar's, Marco's Pizza, McDonald's, Sonic, Starbucks, Subway, Wendy's, Zaxby's $General, AT&T, AutoZone, Walgreens
.5mm	**Welcome Ctr eb, full facilities, litter barrels, petwalk, vending**
0mm	Tennessee/Kentucky state line

ERWIN / JOHNSON CITY

INTERSTATE 26

Exit #	Services
54.5mm	Tennessee/North Carolina state line
54mm	**runaway truck ramp wb**
52mm	**runaway truck ramp wb, scenic overlook eb (no trucks)**
50	Flag Pond Rds
47.5mm	scenic overlook wb (no trucks)
46mm	**N Welcome Ctr/ both lanes, full facilities, litter barr petwalk,**
44mm	Higgins Creek
43	US 19 W, rd 352, Temple Hill Rds
42mm	S Indian Creek
40	Jackson-Love Hwy, Erwin, Jonesborough, N Valero/ Mtn Inn H, Nolichucky Gorge Camping (2mi)
37	TN 81, rd 107, Erwin, Jonesborough, N Shell Bojangl Huddle House, McDonald's, Pal's Drive-Thru, Taco Bell USPO, Walgreens, S Super 8 A. Johnson NHS (31m River Park Camping (5mi)
36	Main St, Erwin, N BP/dsl, Exxon/dsl/e-85 Azteca Mexican, Hardee's, KFC, Little Caesars, Pizza Hut, Subway, Wendy's $General, Advance Parts, AutoZone, Firestone, Rite A
34	Tinker Rd, N Murphy USA/dsl Los Jalapenos, Prim Pizza Walmart
32	rd 173, Unicoi Rd, to Cherokee NF, N Jerry's Mkt Clarence's Drive-In, Whistle Stop Deli $General, Grandvie Ranch Camping (7mi), USPO, S Woodsmoke Camping
27	rd 359 N, Okolona Rd, N BP Budget Inn (3mi) tru repair
24	US 321, TN 67, Elizabethton, N Shell/Dunkin'/dsl Ro Mtn SP, S BP/dsl Arby's, Burger King, Fox's Pizza, Litt Caesar's, LJ Silver, Subway Comfort Inn H, Advan Parts, CVS, Food City/gas, Price Less Foods, to ETSU, Walgree
23	rd 91, Market St, N DQ, McDonald's, S museum
22	rd 400, Unaka Ave, Watauga Ave
20b a	US 11 E, US 19 N, to Roan St, N Shell/dsl, Sunoco/dsl Arby's, Cootie Brown's Rest., Harbor House Seafood, Hardee Little Caesar's, LJ Silver, Mellow Mushroom Pizza, Moto Japanese, Peerless Rest., Perkins, Popeye's, Sonic Best Wester Holiday Inn, Ramada Ltd, Super 8 Acura, Advance Part AT&T, AutoZone, BigLots, Ford, Fred's, Honda, Hyundai, Mazd NAPA Repair, O'Reilly Parts, Subaru, Tuesday Morning, UHa VW, S Applebees, Babylon Grill, Bojangles, Bonefish Gri Brusco's Pizza, Fazoli's, Five Guys, Greg's Pizza, Hana Steak Hibachi Grill, Hooters, Jack's City Grill, KFC, Longhorn Steak McAlister's Deli, McDonald's, O'Charley's, Olive Garden, Pap Murphy's, Red Lobster, Shoney's, Smokey Bones BBQ, Starbucks, Subway, Taco Bell, TX Roadhouse, Zaxby's Doubletree, Motel 6, Red Roof Inn $General, $Tree, Belk, Books-A Million, CVS, Dick's, FreeService Tire/auto, JC Penney, Kroge Office Depot, Target, TJ Maxx, Verizon, Walgreens
19	TN 381, to St of Franklin Rd, to Bristol, N Murphy USA dsl, Valero/McDonald's Golden Corral, Honeybaked Han Logan's Roadhouse, Outback Steaks, Subway Comfo Suites Walmart, **0-2 mi** S Amigo Mexican, Barberito Grille, Buffalo Wild Wings, Carrabba's, Cheddar's, Chick-fil-A Chili's, ChuckECheese's, East Coast Wings, Fuddruckers, IHO Jason's Deli, Mad Greek, Ming's Asian, Panera Bread, Rita Custard, Wendy's, Which Wich? Courtyard, Hampton In

TN

INTERSTATE 26 Cont'd

19	Continued Sleep Inn H, AT&T, Barnes&Noble, Best Buy, Home Depot, Kohl's, Lowe's, Michael's, Natural Foods Mkt, Old Navy, PetsMart, Ross, Sam's Club/gas, Steinmart, USPO, Verizon, vet
17	Boone St, N BP, QP/dsl Beef'o Brady's, Bob Evans, Giovanni's Italian, Hardee's, McDonald's, Pal's Drive-in, Pizza+ $General, Ingles Foods/dsl, S Exxon/e-85, Shell/Subway/dsl Cracker Barrel, Domino's, Poblano's Mexican, Waffle House, Wendy's Holiday Inn Express, Quality Inn, Woodspring Suites
13	rd 75, Bobby Hicks Hwy, N BP, Shell Burger King, China Luck, DQ, La Carreta, McDonald's, Pal's Drive-Thru, Papa John's, Pizza Hut, Sicily Italian, Subway, Taco Bell, Yong Asian $General, Advance Parts, Food City/gas, O'Reilly Parts, USPO, Walgreens, S Exxon/dsl
10	Eastern Star Rd, N Phil's Dream Pit BBQ
8b a	I-81, to Bristol, Knoxville
6	rd 347, Rock Springs Rd, S Rite Quik/dsl
5mm	**Welcome Ctr/, full facilities both lanes, , litter barrels, petwalk**
4	TN 93, Wilcox Dr, N BP/Subway, Mobil/McDonald's/dsl Burger King, Hardee's, La Carreta Mexican, Pizza Hut, Wendy's Comfort Suites, Hampton Inn, Holiday Inn Express, Quality Inn $General, Cave's Drug, Price Less Foods, S Exxon, Mobil/Arby's/dsl/e-85 Pizza+
3	Meadowview Pkwy, N Marriott
1	US 11 W, West Stone Dr, N Shell Little Caesar's, Molcajete's Mexican Super 8 H, Walgreens, S Exxon, Murphy USA/dsl Bojangles, China Star, Fatz Cafe, Sonic, Subway $Tree, Lowe's, Walmart

I-26 begins/ends on US 23.

INTERSTATE 40

Exit #	Services
451mm	Tennessee/North Carolina state line
451	Waterville Rd
447	Hartford Rd, N Citgo/dsl, S BP/dsl Bean Tree Cafe, Pigeon River Smokehouse Foxfire Camping, Shauan's Riverside RV Park, USPO, whitewater rafting
446mm	**Welcome Ctr wb, full facilities, litter barrels, NO TRUCKS, petwalk, , , vending**
443	Foothills Pkwy, to Gatlinburg, Great Smoky Mtns NP
443mm	Pigeon River
440	US 321, to Wilton Spgs Rd, Gatlinburg, N 76/440 Trkstp/cafe/dsl, S Marathon Broasted Chicken Arrow Creek Camping (14mi), CrazyHorse Camping (14mi)
439mm	Pigeon River
435	US 321, to Gatlinburg, Newport, N Exxon/Biodsl/e-85, JSK Express, Marathon, Rite Quik/dsl, Weigel/dsl Arby's, Burger King, Hardee's, KFC, Lois' Country Kitchen, McDonald's, Pizza Hut, SageBrush Steaks, Subway, Taco Bell Motel 6 H, CVS Drug, O'Reilly Parts, Town&Country Drug, USPO, Walgreens, S Mobil/dsl, Murphy USA/dsl Bojangle's, Brooklyn Pizza, Cracker Barrel, Monterrey Mexican, New China, Papa John's, Papa Murphy's, Portabella's, Ruby Tuesday, Waffle House, Wendy's Best Western, Family Inn, Hampton Inn, Holiday Inn Express, Knights Inn, Quality Inn $General, $Tree, AT&T, Lowe's, Save-A-Lot Foods, Verizon, Walmart/Subway
432b a	US 70, US 411, US 25W, to Newport, N Exxon/dsl, Marathon/dsl, TimeOut TC/BP/Huddle House/dsl/scales/ Comfort Inn, Relax Inn Buick/Chevrolet, Chrysler/Dodge/Jeep, KOA (2mi),

NEWPORT

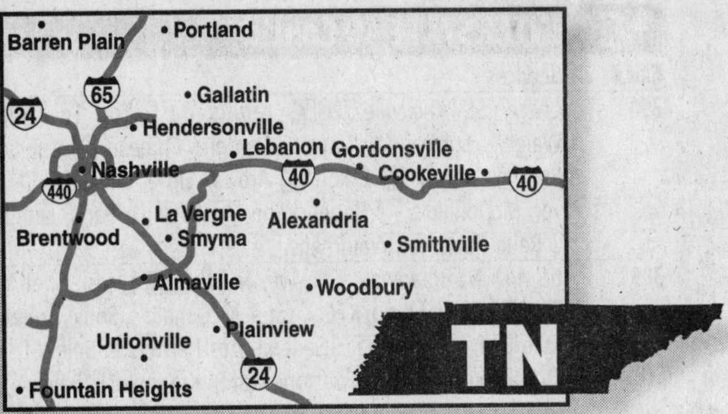

DANDRIDGE

432b a	Continued Tana-See RV Park, truck service, Westgate Tire, S Citgo/dsl, Marathon/dsl, Shell/dsl Family Inn/rest. $General
426mm	**wb, full facilities, litter barrels, petwalk, , , vending**
425mm	French Broad River
424	TN 113, Dandridge, N Marathon/dsl
421	I-81 N, to Bristol
420mm	**eb, full facilities, litter barrels, petwalk, , , vending**
417	TN 92, Dandridge, N Marathon/dsl, Pilot/Subway/dsl/scales/24hr/@ Capt's Galley, Hardee's, McDonald's, Perkins, Ruby Tuesday, Taste of Dandridge Rodeway Inn, S Exxon/Wendy's/dsl, Marathon/dsl, Weigel's/dsl Arby's, Bojangles, LJ Silver/Taco Bell, Shoney's, Waffle House Hampton Inn, Holiday Inn Express, Jefferson Inn, Quality Inn, Super 8 Advance Parts
415	US 25W, US 70, to Dandridge, S Marathon/dsl Sonic (3mi)
412	Deep Sprgs Rd, to Douglas Dam, N Loves/Chester's/Subway/dsl/scales/24hr, Speedway/Speedy's Cafe/dsl
407	TN 66, to Sevierville, Pigeon Forge, Gatlinburg, N Shell/Subway/dsl Chophouse, Cracker Barrel, McDonald's, Uncle Buck's Grill Best Value Inn, Fairfield Inn, Hampton Inn, Holiday Inn Express Bass Pro Shops, Harley Davidson, RV Camping, Smoky Mtn Visitor's Ctr, S BP/Subway/dsl, Exxon/dsl, Mobil/Dunkin'/dsl, Shell/Krystal/dsl Burger King, FlapJack's, Wendy's Best Western, Comfort Suites, Days Inn, Quality Inn Chrysler/Dodge/Jeep, flea mkt, Russell Stover, RV Camping, TN Tourist Info, USPO, multiple services/outlets
402	Midway Rd
398	Strawberry Plains Pk, Strawberry Plains Pk, N BP/dsl, Citgo/dsl, Exxon/dsl, Shell/dsl Aubrey's Rest., McDonald's, Outback Steaks, Waffle House, Wendy's EconoLodge, Hampton Inn, Holiday Inn Express, Knight's Inn, Quality Inn, Red Roof Inn, Rodeway Inn, Super 8 TN RV Ctr, S Pilot/Subway/dsl/scales/24hr, Weigel's Arby's, Burger King, Cracker Barrel, Golden Wok Chinese, KFC, Krystal, Puleo's Grille, Taco Bell Best Western, Comfort Suites, Fairfield Inn, La Quinta, Motel 6
395mm	Holston River
394	US 70, US 11E, US 25W, Asheville Hwy, N BP, Pilot/dsl, Shell/dsl Papa John's, Subway, Wendy's Gateway Inn Advance Parts, AutoZone, city park, S Exxon, Mapco/dsl Habaneros Mexican, Pizza Hut, Scott's Place, Waffle House Days Inn $General, CVS Drug, Family$, Kroger/gas, NAPA, vet, Walgreens
393	I-640 W, to I-75 N
392	US 11W, Rutledge Pike, N Citgo/dsl $General, truck repair, U-Haul, S Shell Buddy's BBQ, Hardee's, Shoney's NAPA, Sav-A-Lot Foods, to Knoxville Zoo, transmissions

= gas = food = lodging = other = rest stop

TN

INTERSTATE 40 Cont'd

KNOXVILLE

Exit #	Services
390	Cherry St, Knoxville, N Marathon/dsl, Top Fuel Mart, Weigel's/Subway Happy Garden Chinese Knoxville Inn tires, S Exxon Arby's, Little Caesar's, LJ Silver, McDonald's Regency Inn Advance Parts, Family$, O'Reilly Parts, vet, Walgreens
389	US 441 N, Broadway, 5th Ave, N Pilot/dsl, Shell/dsl, Star Burger King, KFC, Krystal, McDonald's, Sonic, Subway, Taco Bell, Wendy's $General, Ace Hardware, Belew Drug, CVS Drug, Family$, Firestone/auto, Kroger/dsl, Save-A-Lot Foods, USPO, Walgreens/24hr
388	US 441 S (exits left from wb), S Crowne Plaza, Hilton, Holiday Inn downtown, to Smokey Mtns, to U of TN
387a	I-275 N, to Lexington
387	TN 62, 17th St, N Gas'N Go, Pilot/dsl Hamilton Inn, Royal Inn $General, Food City, vet
386b a	US 129, University Ave, to UTs
385	I-75 N, I-640 E
I-40 W and I-75 S run together 17 mi.	
383	Papermill Rd, N Red Roof Inn, S Exxon/dsl, Pilot/dsl Barberitos, Buddy's BBQ, Burger King, Five Guys, Krispy Kreme, Sonic, Twin Peaks, Waffle House Courtyard, Hampton Inn, Holiday Inn Express, Travelodge Food City, same as 380, Walgreens
380	US 11, US 70, West Hills, S Delta Express, Mapco/dsl Arby's, Brazeiro's Brazilian Steaks, Brixx Pizza, Burro Flojo Mexican, Cheesecake Factory, Chick-fil-A, Chili's, Cookout, Doc's Grille, Dunkin', Firehouse Subs, Hardee's, Honeybaked Ham, Hooters, IHOP, Jets Pizza, Jimmy John's, Longhorn Steaks, McAlister's Deli, McDonald's, Mooyah Burger, Mr Gatti's, O'Charley's, Olive Garden, Papa John's, Penn Sta Subs, Petro's Chili, PF Chang's, Pizza Hut, PlumTree Chinese, Qdoba Mexican, Red Lobster, Salsarita's Cantina, Starbucks, Subway, Taco Bell, Tropical Smoothie Cafe, TX Roadhouse, Zaxby's Extended Stay America, Ramada Inn $Tree, AT&T, Barnes&Noble, Belk, Dillards, Food City, JC Penney, Kohl's, Office Depot, Old Navy, O'Reilly Parts, Petsmart, REI, Ross, Steinmart, Target, TJ Maxx, Trader Joe's, U-Haul, Walgreens, Whole Foods Mkt
379	Bridgewater Rd, N Exxon/Subway/dsl, Pilot/McDonald's/dsl Taco Bell Sam's Club/gas, Walmart/Subway, S Conoco/dsl, Marathon/dsl Asia Kitchen, Buddy's BBQ, Burger King, Cheddar's, ChuckeCheese, CiCi's Pizza, Makino Japanese, Misaki Japanese, Shoney's, Sonic, Wendy's InTown Suites Aamco, Advance Parts, AutoZone, Books-A-Million, Buick/GMC, Chrysler/Dodge/Jeep, Firestone/auto, Ford/Lincoln, Hyundai/Subaru, Mazda, Nissan, NTB, Tire Barn, Transmission World
378	Cedar Bluff Rd, N Pilot/Taco Bell/dsl, Shell, Weigel's/dsl Arby's, Burger King, Cracker Barrel, Dunkin', KFC, Little Caesar's, McDonald's, Old Mill Bread Co., Papa John's, Starbucks, Subway, Waffle House, Wendy's Country Inn&Suites, Days Inn, Hampton Inn, Holiday Inn, Quality Inn H, $General, S Exxon Applebee's, Blaze Pizza, Cancun Mexican, Capt D's, Carrabba's, Chipotle, Chuy's Mexican, Famous Dave's BBQ, Firehouse Subs, Fuddrucker's, Hardee's, Jason's Deli, Koko Japanese, Krystal, La Rosa's, Lenny's Subs, Newk's Cafe, Outback Steaks, Panera Bread, Parkside Grill, Peerless Grill, Penn Sta. Subs, Pizza Hut, Puleo's Grill, Rafferty's, Salsarita's, Starbucks, Which Wich?, Zaxby's Baymont Inn, Best Western, Comfort Inn, Courtyard, Embassy Suites, Extended Stay America, Hilton Garden, Home 2 Suites, Microtel, Motel 6,
378	Continued Red Roof Inn, Residence Inn, Towne Place Suites $T Aldi Foods, AT&T, Best Buy, Cadillac, Chevrolet, CVS D Dick's, Fiat, Ford/Lincoln, GNC, Home Depot, Jo-Ann Fab Kia, Kroger/dsl, Lowe's, Pepboys, Staples, Tuesday Morni Volvo, Walgreens
376	I-140 E, TN 162 N, to Maryville, N to Oak Ridge Museum
374	TN 131, Lovell Rd, N Shell/dsl, Speedway/Speedy Cafe/ scales/24hr, TA/Country Pride/dsl/scales/24hr/@ Bojang Subway, Waffle House Econolodge Harley-Davids S Pilot/Wendy's/dsl/24hr Abuelo's Mexican, Arb Baskin-Robbins, Bonefish Grill, Brixx Pizza, Buffalo Wild Wi Calhoun's Rest., Chick-fil-A, Chipotle, Connor's Rest., Eg Cafe, Flemings, Hurricane Grill, IHOP, Jimmy John's, Kab Japanese, Krystal, Lenny's Subs, McAlister's Deli, McDonal Mimi's Cafe, Moe's SW Grill, Noodles&Co, O'Charley's, O Garden, Panera Bread, Pei Wei, Red Robin, Salsarita's Canti Smokey Mtn Brewery, Sonic, Starbucks, Steak'n Shake, T Bell, TX Roadhouse, Wasabi Japanese, Zoe's Kitchen B get Inn, Candlewood Suites, Homewood Suites, Spring Suites H, $Tree, Advance Parts, AutoZone, Belk, Best B BMW/Mini, CarMax, Costco/gas, EarthFare Foods, GNC, Hob Lobby, Honda, Land Rover, Lexus, Marshall's, Mercedes, Navy, Petsmart, Ross, Target, Toyota, Walgreens, Walmart/S way, World Mkt
373	Campbell Sta Rd, N Marathon/dsl, Shell/dsl Comf Suites, Country Inn&Suites, Fairfield Inn, Holiday Inn Expre Super 8 Buddy Gregg RV Ctr, S Exxon/dsl, Pilo dsl, Weigel's Bad Daddy's Burger, Cracker Barrel, Dunk Hardee's, La Parrilla, Longhorn Steaks, Mellow Mushroo Newk's Grill, Panda Express, Potbelly, Seasons Grille, Taco B Wild Wing Cafe, Zaxby's Clarion, Hampton Inn, Staybrid Suites AT&T, JC Penney, Publix, Verizon, Walgreens
372mm	**weigh sta both lanes**
369	Watt Rd, N FLYING J/Denny's/dsl/LP/scales/RV dum 24hr, Speedco Blue Beacon, S Petro/Iron Skillet/d scales/24hr/@, TA/Marathon/Burger King/Pizza Hut/Popeye Subway/dsl/24hr/@ Knoxville Coach & RV
I-40 E and I-75 N run together 17 mi.	
368	I-75 and I-40
364	US 321, TN 95, Lenoir City, Oak Ridge, N Crosseyed Cric Camping (2mi), **4-5 mi** S Loves/McDonald's/Subwa dsl/24hr Ruby Tuesday Days Inn, EconoLodge, Ham ton Inn, Holiday Inn Express
362	Industrial Park Rd
360	Buttermilk Rd, N Soaring Eagle RV Park
356	TN 58 N, Gallaher Rd, to Oak Ridge, N Marathon/dsl, W gels/dsl Motel 6 $General, 4 Seasons Camping
355	Lawnville Rd, N Pilot/Subway/dsl
352	TN 58 S, Kingston, N Lakeview Inn, S Exxon/dsl, M bil/dsl, RaceWay Buddy's BBQ, Hardee's, Little Caesar McDonald's, Sonic, Subway, Taco Bell Super 8 $Gen al, Cash Saver Foods, Family$, Marina RV Park, to Watts B Lake, USPO
351mm	Clinch River
350	US 70, Midtown, S Weigel's/dsl Bojangles, Gondol Italian, Subway, Zaxby's H, AT&T, Caney Creek Campi (3mi), Kroger, Lowe's, Walgreens
347	US 27, Harriman, N Phillips 66/dsl Hardee's, KFC, Silver, Los Primos Mexican, McDonald's, Pizza Hut, Ruby Tue day, Subway, Taco Bell, Wendy's Days Inn Big S Fo NRA, to Frozen Head SP, Verizon, **2-3 mi** S Murphy USA/d

HARRIMAN

INTERSTATE 40 Cont'd

347 Continued
Shell/Krystal/dsl/24hr, Sunoco/dsl Cancun Mexican, Capt D's, China King, Cracker Barrel, Domino's, McDonald's, Shoney's, Sonic Comfort Inn, Holiday Inn Express, Quality Inn, Rodeway Inn H, Ace Hardware, BigLots, vet, Walmart

340 TN 299 N, Airport Rd

339.5mm eastern/central time zone line

338 TN 299 S, Westel Rd, **S** Exxon/dsl, Sunoco/dsl Boat-N-RV Ctr/Park

336mm **parking area/weigh sta eb, litter barrel**

329 US 70, Crab Orchard, **N** Citgo/dsl, Marathon/dsl KOA (4mi), **S** Cumberland Trails SP, Wilson SP

327mm **wb, full facilities, litter barrels, petwalk, , vending**

324mm **eb, full facilities, litter barrels, petwalk, , vending**

322 TN 101, Peavine Rd, Crossville, **N** Exxon/Subway/dsl, Volunteer/dsl Hardee's, McDonald's Holiday Inn Express Deer Run RV Resort, KOA Camping, Roam-Roost RV Campground, to Fairfield Glade Resort, **S** Shell/dsl Cancun Mexican, Taco Bell Comfort Suites, Hampton Inn, Super 8 H, Chestnut Hill Winery, Cumberland Mtn SP

320 TN 298, Crossville, **N** Pilot/Wendy's/dsl/scales/24hr Butcher's Block Rest., Lefty's BBQ antiques, winery, **S** Shell/DQ/dsl, Speedway/dsl Log Cabin Rest. H, auto repair/tires, Crossville Outlet/famous brands, Save-A-Lot Foods

318mm Obed River

317 US 127, Crossville, **N** Exxon/dsl, Shell/Circle K/dsl Shoney's, Subway Baymont Inn, Motel 6, Quality Inn repair, to Big South Fork RA, to York SP, **0-2 mi S** Jiffy, Marathon/dsl, Murphy USA/dsl, Shell Arby's, Bojangles, Burger King, Cancun Mexican, Cracker Barrel, La Costa Mexican, McDonalds, Papa John's, Romo's Mexican, Ruby Tuesday, Ryan's, Sonic, Subway, Taco Bell, Tokyo Steaks, Vegas Steaks, Waffle House, Zaxby's Economy Inn, Red Roof Inn H, $General, $Tree, Buick/Cadillac/Chevrolet/GMC, Chrysler/Dodge/Jeep, Ford, GNC, Lowe's, Rite Aid, Shadden Tires, Staples, to Cumberland Mtn SP, Verizon, Walgreens, Walmart

311 Plateau Rd, **S** BP/dsl, Exxon/Hunt Bros Pizza

307mm **parking area/weigh sta wb, litter barrels**

301 US 70 N, TN 84, Monterey, **N** Shell Burger King, DQ, Rocky Pops BBQ/Catfish, Subway Bethel Inn

300 US 70, Monterey, **N** Citgo/dsl DQ, Hardee's

291mm Falling Water River

290 US 70, Cookeville, **S** Super/dsl Fiesta Cancun Alpine Suites

288 TN 111, to Livingston, Cookeville, Sparta, **N** Hull SP, **S** Sunoco/dsl, Super Truck&TravelCtr/dsl/24hr Subway Fall Creek Inn

COOKEVILLE

287 TN 136, Cookeville, **N** Marathon/dsl, Murphy USA/dsl, Shell/dsl Applebee's, Arby's, Baskin-Robbins, Blue Coast Burrito, Buffalo Wild Wings, Bully's Rest., Burger King, Capt D's, Cheddars, Chick-fil-A, Chili's, Cookout, Cracker Barrel, Dunkin', Fazoli's, Firehouse Subs, Fuji Japanese, Golden Corral, Hibachi Buffet, IHOP, Krystal, LJ Silver, Logan's Roadhouse, Longhorn Steaks, Marco's Pizza, McDonald's, Nick's Rest., O'Charley's, Olive Garden, Outback Steaks, Papa Murphy's, Pizza Hut, Red Lobster, Ruby Tuesday, Shoney's, Sonic, Starbucks, Steak'n Shake, Subway, Taco Bell, Wendy's Best Value Inn, Best Western, Clarion, Comfort Inn, Comfort Suites, Days Inn, Hampton Inn, Red Roof Inn Aldi Foods, BigLots, Firestone/auto, Harley-Davidson, JC Penney, Kroger/gas, Lowe's,

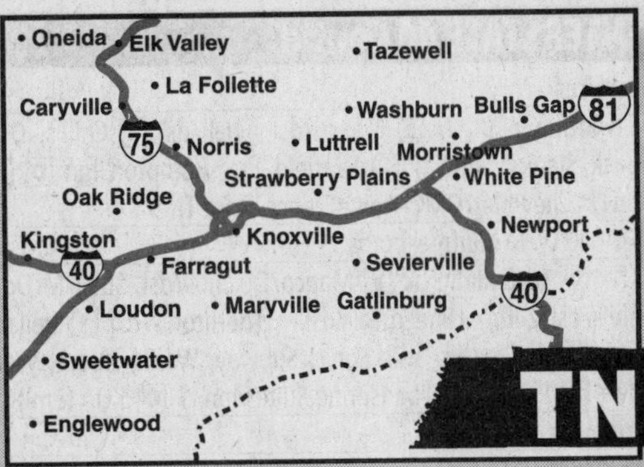

287 Continued
Nissan, st patrol, transmissions, Verizon, Walmart, **S** Marathon/Godfather's/dsl, Pilot/dsl Gondola, KFC, Waffle House Country Inn&Suites, Fairfield Inn, Holiday Inn Express, La Quinta, Motel 6, TownePlace Suites Sam's Club/gas, URGENT CARE

286 TN 135, Burgess Falls Rd, **N** Exxon, Gulf, RaceWay/dsl, Shell/dsl Arby's, Hardee's, Waffle House H, Chrysler/Dodge/Jeep, Ford/Lincoln, Goodyear/auto, Hyundai, Kia, to TTU, Toyota, USPO, **S** Sunoco/dsl Star Motor Inn Burgess Falls SP (8mi)

280 TN 56 N, Baxter, **N** Loves/McDonalds/Subway/dsl/scales/24hr, Speedway/dsl/24hr Huddle House Camp Discovery (2mi), Twin Lakes RV Park (2mi)

276 Old Baxter Rd

273 TN 56 S, to Smithville, **S** Shell Rose Garden Rest. USPO

268 TN 96, Buffalo Valley Rd, **N** Grandville Marina Camping (11mi), **S** to Edgar Evins SP/RV camping

267mm Caney Fork River

267mm **both lanes, full facilities, info, litter barrels, petwalk, , vending**

266mm Caney Fork River

263mm Caney Fork River

258 TN 53, Gordonsville, **N** Exxon/KFC/Taco Bell, Shell/dsl McDonald's, Subway, Timberloft Café, Waffle House Comfort Inn to Cordell Hull Dam, **S** Mobil/dsl, Pilot/Wendy's/dsl/scales/24hr Arby's, Cornerstone Cafe, El Corral Mexican, KFC/Taco Bell $General

254 TN 141, to Alexandria

252mm **parking area/truck sta both lanes, litter barrels,**

245 Linwood Rd

LEBANON

239 US 70, Lebanon, **N** RaceWay/dsl, Shell $General, **S** Phillips 66/Uncle Pete's/dsl/scales Jalisco Mexican

238 US 231, Lebanon, **N** Exxon, Mapco/dsl, Murphy Express/dsl, Shell/dsl Applebee's, Arby's, Chick-fil-A, Cici's Pizza, Cracker Barrel, Demo's Steaks, El Molino Mexican, Hardee's, Jack-in-the-Box, KFC, Logan's Roadhouse, Los Compadres, McDonald's, Panda Express, Pizza Hut, Ryan's, Shoney's, Starbucks, Subway, Sunset Rest., Taco Bell, Waffle House, Wendy's, White Castle, Whitt's BBQ, Zaxby's Days Inn, EconoLodge, Executive Inn, Holiday Inn Express, Quality Inn, Ramada H, $Tree, Aldi Foods, AT&T, Discount Tire, Lowe's, to Bledsoe SP (23mi), Verizon, Walgreens, Walmart/Subway, **S** Citgo/Pizza Inn/Quiznos/dsl, LNG, Pilot/Subway/DQ/dsl/scales/24hr, Shell/dsl, Speedway/dsl/e85 O'Charley's, Sonic Comfort Suites, Knights Inn, La Quinta, Travel Inn Family RV Ctr, Lebanon Outlets/famous brands, Shady Acres Camping, Timberline Campground, to Cedars of Lebanon SP

= gas = food = lodging = other = rest stop

TN

INTERSTATE 40 Cont'd

Exit #	Services
236	S Hartmann Dr, N Mapco/dsl, Shell/dsl Chili's, Outback Steaks, Subway Fairfield Inn, Hampton Inn H, Buick/Chevrolet/GMC, Home Depot, Rose Tire
235	TN 840 W, to Murfreesboros
232	TN 109, to Gallatin, N Mapco/Quiznos/dsl, Shell/McDonald's/dsl/24hr, Speedway/dsl, Thornton's/dsl Bellacino's Pizza, Coach's Grill, Sonic, Subway, Waffle House, Wendy's Sleep Inn, Woodspring Suites Inn, S KOA (3mi)
228mm	**truck sta, wb only**
226mm	**truck sta**
229b a	Beckwith Rds
226	TN 171, Mt Juliet Rd, N BP/McDonald's/dsl, Exxon/dsl, Murphy Express/dsl, Shell/dsl Arby's, Capt D's, Cheddars, Don Pancho Mexican, Far East Buffet, Five Guys, Longhorn Steaks, Subway Comfort Suites $Tree, Aldi Foods, Firestone/auto, Lowe's, NTB, URGENT CARE, Walmart, S Mapco/Quiznos/dsl Blue Coast Burrito, Bonfire Japanese Steaks, Buffalo Wild Wings, Chick-fil-A, ChuckECheese, Cori's Dog House, Cracker Barrel, Firehouse Subs, Fulin's Asian, Jonathan's, Logan's Roadhouse, Marble Slab, Martin's BBQ, McDonald's, Mi Casa Mexican, NY Pizza, O'Charley's, Olive Garden, Panera Bread, Penn Sta Subs, Pizza Hut, Red Lobster, Red Robin, Salsarita's Cantina, Sonic, Steak'n Shake, Taco Bell, Taziki's Cafe, Waffle House, Wasabi Steaks, Wendy's, Which Wich?, Zaxby's Hampton Inn, Holiday Inn Express, Quality Inn AT&T, Belk, Best Buy, Books-A-Million, Dick's, Discount Tire, Ford, GNC, JC Penney, JoAnn Fabrics, Kroger/dsl, Old Navy, Petsmart, Publix, Ross, Staples, Target, Tire Discounters, TJ Maxx, to Long Hunter SP, Verizon, vet, Walgreens
221	TN 45 N, Old Hickory Blvd, to The Hermitage, **0-2 mi N** BP, Delta/dsl, Exxon, RaceWay/dsl Applebee's, Baskin-Robbins/Dunkin', Buffalo Wild Wings, Burger King, Chick-fil-A, Chili's, Cinco de Mayo, Domino's, DQ, Famous Dave's, Fazoli's, Firehouse Subs, Golden Corral, Hardee's, IHOP, Jack-in-the-Box, Jets Pizza, Las Palmas Mexican, O'Charley's, Outback Steaks, Panera Bread, Penn Sta Subs, Pizza Hut, Qdoba Mexican, Starbucks, Steak'n Shake, Subway, Taziki's Cafe, Waffle House Best Value Inn, Suburban Lodge, Super 8, Vista Inn H, Home Depot, Kroger, Lowe's, PetCo, Staples, Verizon, Walgreens, S Kwik Sak/dsl, Marathon/dsl, Phillips 66/White Castle, Shell/McDonald's
219	Stewart's Ferry Pike, N Mapco/dsl, S Mapco/Subway/dsl, Shell/dsl, Thornton's/dsl China King, Cracker Barrel, La Hacienda Mexican, Sal's Pizza, Subway, Waffle House Comfort Suites, Country Inn&Suites, Days Inn, EconoLodge, Family Inn, Motel 6, Sleep Inn $General, Food Lion, Fred's, vet
216	(216 c from eb)TN 255, Donaldson Pk, N BP/dsl, Mapco, RaceWay/dsl, Shell/dsl Arby's, Backyard Burger, Bar-B-Cutie, Darfon's, Jalisco Mexican, KFC, McDonald's, Panera Bread, Ruby Tuesday, Shoney's, Sonic, Subway, Taco Bell, Waffle House, Wendy's BNA Inn, Country Inn&Suites, Drury Inn, Hampton Inn, Holiday Inn Express, Hyatt Place, La Quinta, Radisson, Red Roof Inn, Sheraton, SpringHill Suites, Super 8 Advance Parts, USPO, Walgreens, S
216b a	(from eb), S Nashville Intn'l Airport
215b a	TN 155, Briley Pkwy, to Opryland, **N on Elm Hill** Citgo, Mapco Jack-in-the-Box, Waffle House Alexis Inn, Baymont Inn, Club Hotel, Comfort Suites, Courtyard, Doubletree, Extended Stay, Hilton Garden, Holiday Inn, Homewood Suites, La Quinta, Marriott, Nashville Inn, Quality Inn, Residence Inn,
215b a	Continued TownePlace Suites URGENT CARE, S Phillips 6 dsl Dunkin', Mazatlan Mexican, Panda House, Subw Hamilton Inn, Hotel Preston
213	US 41 (from wb no return), to Spence Lane, N CNG K worth, S Phillips 66/dsl, Shell Waffle House B Western, Days Inn, Holiday Inn Express, Rodeway Inn, Su 8 same as 212
213b	I-24 W
213a	I-24 E/I-440, E to Chattanooga
212	Fessler's Lane (from eb, no return), N Freightliner, H ley-Davidson, S BP/dsl, Mapco/dsl, Shell/Dunk SpeedCo/dsl/e85 Burger King, McDonald's, Sonic, We dy's Scottish Inn Chevrolet, NAPA, same as 213
211mm	Cumberland River
211b	I-24 W
211a	I-24E, I-40 W
210c	US 31 S, US 41A, 2nd Ave, 4th Ave, N Hilton, Renaissan Hotel, Sheraton, S museum
210b a	I-65 S, to Birmingham
209b a	US 70 S, Charlotte Ave, Nashville, N Exxon McDo ald's Sheraton Conv Ctr, Country Music Hall of Fam Firestone, Mazda, S Exxon Burger King, Jack Ca thon's BBQ, Krystal, Sonic, Subway, White Castle Comfo Inn, Hilton Garden Buick/GMC, Hyundai, Toyota, URGE CARE, Walgreens
208b a	I-65, N to Louisville
207	28th Ave, Jefferson St, Nashville, N BP Subway, We dy's Family$, to TN St U, S H
206	I-440 E, to Knoxville
205	46th Ave, W Nashville, S Shell/dsl M L Rose Burge McDonald's USPO
204	TN 155, Briley Pkwy, S BP/dsl Burger King, China Bu fet, Church's/White Castle, Cinco De Mayo, Domino's, Hat B's Chicken, Jack-in-the-Box, KFC, Las Palmas, Papa John Shoney's, Subway, Waffle House, Wendell Smith's Rest., Whi Castle, Whitt's BBQ Best Western, Comfort Inn, Days In Holiday Inn Express CVS Drug, Family$, Firestone/auto, Kr ger/gas, O'Reilly Parts, PepBoys, Sav-a-lot Foods, Walgreens
201b a	US 70, Charlotte Pike, N Exxon, Shell/dsl, Thornton's/d Bojangles, Cracker Barrel, El Sombrero, Jim 'N Nick's BB Krystal, Little Caesar's, Waffle House, Wayback Burger, We dy's Super 8 GNC, Kwik Kar, Lowe's Whse, vet, Walmar Subway, S BP, Delta Express/dsl Arby's, Blue Coa Burrito, Buffalo Wild Wings, Chick-fil-A, Firehouse Subs, IHO Logan's Roadhouse, McDonald's, Pizza Hut, Red Robin, Tac Bell $Tree, AT&T, Best Buy, Big Lots, Books-A-Million, Costc gas, Dick's, Firestone/auto, GNC, Marshall's, Old Navy, PetsMa Publix, Ross, Target, Uhaul, URGENT CARE, Verizon, World Mkt
199	rd 251, Old Hickory Blvd, N Shell/dsl $Genera S BP, Mapco/dsl Sonic, Subway
196	US 70, to Bellevue, Newsom Sta, N Mapco/dsl Shoney' S BP, Mapco/dsl, Shell/dsl Arby's, Asihi Asian, Bask Robbins, El Agavero, Jonathan's Grill, O'Charley's, Pizza Hu Sir Pizza, Sonic, Subway, Taco Bell, Waffle House, Wendy Hampton Inn, Microtel $Tree, AutoZone, Firestone auto, Home Depot, Michael's, PetCo, Publix, Staples, USP Verizon, Walgreens
195mm	Harpeth River
192	McCrory Lane, to Pegram, N Eddie's Mkt (1mi), 4 m S Loveless Cafe Natchez Trace Pkwy
190mm	Harpeth River

NASHVILLE

INTERSTATE 40 Cont'd

Exit #	Services
188mm	Harpeth River
188	rd 249, Kingston Springs, N BP, Mapco/Quiznos/dsl, Shell/Arby's/dsl El Jardin Mexican, McDonald's/playplace, Sonic, Subway Best Western, Mid-Town Inn, Relax Inn USPO, S Petro/BP/Quick Skillet/dsl/scales/showers/24hr/@ vet
182	TN 96, to Dickson, Fairview, N BP/dsl Fairview Inn M Bell SP (16mi), S FLYING J/Denny's/dsl/LP/scales/24hr, Citgo/Backyard Burger/Dunkin'/dsl Deerfield Inn
176	I-840
172	TN 46, to Dickson, N Marathon/dsl, Pilot/Wendy's/dsl/scales/24hr, Shell/Dunkin'/Taco Bell/dsl Arby's, Bojangle's, Camino Real, Cracker Barrel, Hardee's, Logan's Roadhouse, McDonald's, Ruby Tuesday, Waffle House Best Western, Comfort Inn, EconoLodge, Fairfield Inn, Hampton Inn, Motel 6, Rodeway Inn, South-Aire Inn, Super 8 H, $General, auto repair, Chappell's Foods, Chevrolet/Buick/GMC, Dickson RV Park, Ford, Nissan, to M Bell SP, truck repair, S Marathon/dsl, Shell/dsl Colton's Steaks, O'Charley's, Sonic Days Inn, Holiday Inn Express, Quality Inn
170	both lanes, full facilities, litter barrels, petwalk, vending
166mm	Piney River
163	rd 48, to Dickson, N Loves/McDonald's/Subway/dsl/scales/24hr, Phillips 66/dsl tire repair, S Shell Pinewood Camping (7mi), Tanbark Camping
152	rd 230, Bucksnort, N Sunoco/dsl Rodeway Inn
149mm	Duck River
148	rd 50, Barren Hollow Rd, to Turney Center
143	TN 13, to Linden, Waverly, N Pilot/Arby's/dsl/scales/24hr, Shell Jen's Rest, Log Cabin Rest., Loretta Lynn's Kitchen, McDonald's, Rochelle's BBQ Days Inn, Holiday Inn Express, Knights Inn, Quality Inn KOA/LP, S Speedway/dsl Scottish Inn
141mm	Buffalo River
137	Cuba Landing, N TN River RV Park, S Cuba Landing Rest./gas
133mm	Tennessee River
133	rd 191, Birdsong Rd, 9 mi N Good Sam RV Park, Songbird RV Resort/marina
131mm	both lanes, full facilities, litter barrels, petwalk, vending
126	US 641, TN 69, to Camden, N Marathon/Subway/dsl, Shell/North 40/dsl Burger Barn $ General, Paris Landing SP, tire/truck repair, to NB Forrest SP, truck wash, S Marathon/dsl, Shell/dsl Days Inn H, Mouse-tail Landing SP (24mi)
116	rd 114, S RV camping, to Natchez Trace SP
110mm	Big Sandy River
108	TN 22, to Lexington, Parkers Crossroads, N Marathon/dsl/24hr, Phillips 66/dsl, Shell/McDonald's/dsl DQ, Smarter's Rest, Subway Knights Inn city park, USPO, S Exxon Becky's Kitchen, Patty's Rest. Best Value Inn H, $ General, Parkers Crossroads Bfd Visitors Ctr, to Shiloh NMP (51mi)
103mm	parking area/truck sta eb, litter barrels
102mm	parking area/truck sta wb, litter barrels
101	rd 104, N 101 TP/Real Food/dsl/tires/24hr golf (3mi)
93	rd 152, Law Rd, N Phillips 66/deli/dsl/24hr, S Shell/dsl
87	US 70, US 412, Jackson, N Gulf/dsl, Mapco/Deli/dsl/e85, S Loves/Hardee's/dsl/scales/24hr, Skyline Express/dsl, Speedway/dsl/e85

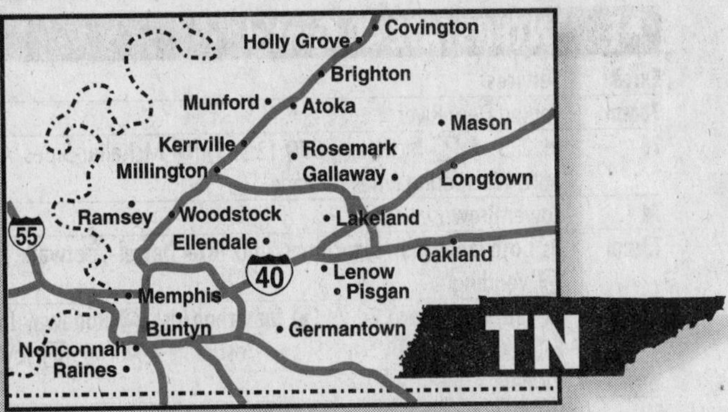

JACKSON

Exit #	Services
85	Christmasville Rd, to Jackson, N Exxon/dsl, Pilot/Denny's/dsl/scales/24hr, Speedway/dsl Comfort Inn $General, S Shell/Pizza Pro/dsl Burger King, Jack's, Jet's Pizza, Jiang Jun Chinese, Lenny's Subs, Los Portales, McDonald's, Reggi's BBQ, Sonic, Sparky's, Subway, Taco Bell, Waffle House Holiday Inn Express $Tree, Food Giant
83	Campbell st, N Shell/Old Madina Mkt/dsl Residence Inn, S Courtyard, Hampton Inn
82b a	US 45, Jackson, N Dodge's/dsl, Marathon/dsl Cracker Barrel Best Value Inn, Knights Inn Batteries+Bulbs, Smallwoods RV Ctr (4mi), S Exxon, Hucks/dsl Baskin-Robbins, Burger King, Catfish Galley, Chucke-Cheese, DQ, KFC, Krystal, Little Caesar's, LJ Silver, Los Portales Mexican, McDonald's/playplace, Papa John's, Pizza Hut, Popeye's, Sakura Japanese, Sonic, Starbucks, Subway, Taco Bell, Tulum Mexican, Waffle House, Wendy's Executive Inn, La Quinta, Ramada Ltd, Scottish Inn, Travellers Motel $General, $Tree, Advance Parts, AT&T, AutoZone, Belk, BigLots, Firestone/auto, Fred's, Goodyear/auto, JC Penney, Kroger/dsl, Macy's, O'Reilly Parts, Office Depot, vet
80b a	US 45 Byp, Jackson, 0-2 mi N Exxon, Shell/dsl Arby's, Asahi Japanese, Backyard Burger, Baskin-Robbins, Buffalo Wild Wings, Casa Adobe, Cheddar's, Chick-fil-A, Chili's, CookOut, Don Pancho, DQ, Dunkin', Fazoli's, Firehouse Subs, Five Guys, Flat Iron Grill, Fujiyama Japanese, Genghis Grill, HoneyBaked Ham, IHOP, Jason's Deli, Jersey Mike's, Jimmy John's, Lenny's Subs, Longhorn Steaks, Maggie Moo's, Marco's Pizza, McAlisters Deli, Moe's SW Grill, Olive Garden, Outback Steaks, Panda Express, Panera Bread, Perkins, Popeye's, Red Lobster, Red Robin, Snappy Tomato, Sonic, Starbucks, Steak'n Shake, Subway, TGIFriday's, Wendy's, Zaxby's Baymont Inn, Fairfield Inn, Hilton Garden, Howard Johnson $Tree, Aldi Foods, AT&T, AutoZone, Best Buy, Books-A-Million, Buick/Cadillac/Chevrolet/GMC, CarMax, Dick's, Firestone/auto, Gateway Tires/repair, Hobby Lobby, Home Depot, JoAnn Fabrics, Kia, Kohl's, Lowe's, Marshall's, Nissan, Old Navy, Petsmart, Ross, Sam's Club/gas, SteinMart, Target, TJ Maxx, Toyota, Verizon, Walmart/gas, S BP, G/dsl, Mobil/dsl, Shell/dsl Arby's, Asia Garden, Baudo's Rest., Burger King, Checkers, Heavenly Ham, Logan's Roadhouse, McDonald's, O'Charley's, Old Hickory Steakhouse, Old Town Spaghetti, Pizza Hut, Red Bones Grill, Subway, Taco Bell, Waffle House Best Western, Casey Jones Motel, Clarion, Comfort Suites, Days Inn, DoubleTree, EconoLodge, Jackson Hotel, Motel 6, Old Hickory Inn, Quality Inn, Super 8 H, $General, Chickasaw SP, Chrysler/Dodge/Jeep, Ford/Lincoln, Harley-Davidson, Honda, Hyundai, to Pinson Mounds SP, Tuesday Morning
79	US 412, Jackson, S Citgo/Subway/dsl, Exxon, Valero Rodeway Inn Jackson RV Park

TN

INTERSTATE 40 Cont'd

Exit #	Services
78mm	Forked Deer River
76	rd 223, S McKenzie BBQ (2.5mi) McKellar-Sipes Airport, Whispering Pines RV Park
74	Lower Brownsville Rd
73mm	**both lanes, full facilities, info, litter barrels, petwalk, , vending**
68	rd 138, Providence Rd, N Marathon/dsl Rodeway Inn, S Citgo/dsl, TA/Shell/Subway/dsl/scales/24hr/@ Joy-O RV Park
66	US 70, to Brownsville, N Ft Pillow SHP (51mi), S Exxon/dsl Motel 6
60	rd 19, Mercer Rd
56	TN 76, to Brownsville, N Delta/dsl, Marathon DQ, KFC, McDonald's/playplace, Pizza Hut, Taco Bell Comfort Inn, Days Inn, Econolodge, Rodeway Inn, S Exxon/Breakfast Cove/dsl, Valero
55mm	Hatchie River
52	TN 76, rd 179, Koko Rd, to Whiteville, S Koko Mkt
50mm	**weigh sta both lanes**
47	TN 179, to Stanton, Dancyville
42	TN 222, to Stanton, S Exxon/dsl, Pilot/Chester's/Subway/dsl/scales/24hr Deerfield Inn
35	TN 59, to Somerville, S Shelldsl/scales Longtown Rest.
29.5mm	Loosahatchie River
29	TN 196, Hickory Withe Rd
25	TN 205, Airline Rd, to Arlington, N Shell/dsl, S Exxon/Taco bell/dsl vistor ctr
24	I-269, TN 385, rd 204, to Arlington, Millington, Collierville
20	Canada Rd, Lakeland, N Mobil/dsl, Shell/dsl Cracker Barrel, Waffle House Motel 6, Relax Inn, Super 8, S Exxon/Subway/dsl fireworks, Memphis East Camping
18	US 64, to Bartlett, N Shell/Burger King Abuelo's, Buffalo Wild Wings, El Porton Mexican, Firebird's Grill, Hooters, Longhorn Steaks, McAlister's Deli, O'Charley's, Olive Garden, Panera Bread, Steak'n Shake, TGI Friday's, TX Roadhouse Best Western, Fairfield Inn, Holiday Inn, Home 2 Suites, La Quinta, SpringHill Suites Buick/GMC, Firestone/auto, Lowe's, Pepboys, same as 16, Sam's Club/gas, Verizon, Walmart, S Circle K/dsl, Citgo, Marathon Backyard Burger, Dunkin', KFC, Lenny's Subs, Papa John's, Papa Murphy's, Pizza Hut, Subway AT&T, Family$, Kroger/dsl, Sprouts Mkt, Walgreens, Zaxby's
16b a	TN 177, to Germantown, N BP/Circle K, Shell/Circle K Abuelo's, Arby's, Bahama Breeze, Baskin Robbins, Buffalo Wild Wings, Burger King, Casa Mexicana, Cheesecake Factory, Chick-fil-A, Chili's, Colton's Steaks, Cook Out, Dave & Buster's, IHOP, J. Alexander's, Joe's Crabshack, Logan's Roadhouse, McDonald's/playplace, On-the-Border, Red Lobster, Red Sun Buffet, Redlands Grill, Starbucks, Subway, Taco Bell, TCBY, Tellini's Italian, Waffle House, Wendy's Extended Stay America, Hampton Inn, Hyatt Place H, $Tree, Barnes&Noble, Best Buy, BigLots, CarMax, Chevrolet, Chrysler/Dodge/Jeep, Dillard's, Ford, Hobby Lobby, Home Depot, Honda, Hyundai, JC Penney, Macy's, Michael's, Nissan, Office Depot, Old Navy, Petsmart, Target, TJ Maxx, Walgreens, **0-2 mi** S BP/Circle K, Shell/Circle K Abbay's Rest., Arby's, Backyard Burger, Burger King, Cheddar's, ChuckeCheese, Corky's BBQ, Genghis Grill, Honeybaked Ham, Howard's Donuts, Jason's Deli, Jimmy John's, Jim'n Nick's BBQ, La Hacienda, Lenny's Subs, Little Caesar's, Margarita's Mexican, McDonald's, Newk's Cafe, Osaka, Pei Wei Chinese, Pyros Pizza, Shogun Japanese, Subway,

MEMPHIS

Exit #	Services
16b a	Continued Waffle House, Wendy's Comfort Suites, Country Inn Suites, Hilton Garden, Microtel, Quality Suites Aldi Foo AT&T, AutoZone, Costco/gas, Dick's, GNC, Gordman's, Koh Kroger/gas, Marshall's, Rite Aid, Ross, Steinmart, Toyota, Tuesday Morning, URGENT CARE, Verizon, vet
15b a	Appling Rd, N BP/Circle K/dsl, Shell/dsl H, S Marathon/dsl Subway Family $
14	Whitten Rd, N Mapco, Shell/Burger King, Valero/ Walmart/dsl Hardee's, McDonald's, Sidecar Café, Taco B Firestone/auto, Harley-Davidson, Walmart, S BP/Circle K, Shell/Backyard Burger/dsl Dunkin', Subway, Supreme H Wings Candlewood Suites Family$, Walgreens
12	Sycamore View Rd, N Citgo/dsl, Murphy Express/d Shell/dsl Capt D's, Church's, Cracker Barrel, IHOP, Kryst McDonald's, Ruby Tuesday, Shoney's, Sonic, Starbucks, Ta Bell, Waffle House Baymont Inn, Best Value Inn, Co fort Inn, Extended Stay America, GardenTree Hotel, Motel Red Roof Inn $General, AutoZone, Family$, Walgree S BP/Circle K/dsl, Exxon, Mapco Beijing Chinese, Bu er King, Dos Amigos, Pizza Hut, Popeye's, Subway, Tops BB Wendy's Knights Inn, Budgetel, Days Inn, Econolodg Fairfield Inn, La Quinta, Memphis Inn, Quality Inn, Rodew Inn Bass Pro Shops
10.5mm	Wolf River
10b a	(from wb) I-240 W around Memphis, I-40 E to Nashville
12c	(from eb) I-240 W, to Jackson, I-40 E to Nashville
12b	Sam Cooper Blvd (from eb)
12a	US 64/70/79, Summer Ave, N Mapco/dsl, Marathon/ Asian Palace, Waffle House Welcome Inn U-Ha S Exxon McDonald's, Subway $Tree, Fireston auto, Fred's
10	TN 204, Covington Pike, N BP/Circle K McDonald Wendy's Audi/VW, Buick/GMC, Chevrolet, Chrysle Dodge/Jeep/Fiat, Honda, Hyundai, Kia, Mazda, Nissan, Sam Club, Subaru, SuperLo Food
8b a	TN 14, Jackson Ave, N Citgo/dsl Motel 6, Sleep In Raleigh Tire, S Citgo/dsl, Valero AutoZone, Family$, O'Reilly Parts, repair
6	Warford Rd
5	Hollywood St, N Marathon, Valero/dsl Burger Kin Popeye's Family$, S Memphis Zoo
3	Watkins St, N Highway/dsl, Jubilee/dsl, Marathon Family$, U-Haul
2a	rd 300, to US 51 N, Millington, N Meeman-Shelby SP
2	Smith Ave, Chelsea Ave, S Valero
1e	I-240 E
1d c b	US 51, Danny Thomas Blvd, N Ronald McDonald House, Jude Research Ctr
1a	2nd St (from wb), downtown, S Crowne Plaza, Holiday In Sheraton Conv Ctr
1	Riverside Dr, Front St (from eb), Memphis, S Comfort In Courtyard, Sleep Inn Conv Ctr, Riverfront, Visitors Ctr
0mm	Tennessee/Arkansas state line, Mississippi River

INTERSTATE 55

Exit #	Services
13mm	Tennessee/Arkansas state line, Mississippi River
12c	Delaware St, Memphis, W Super 8
12b	Riverside Dr, E **TN Welcome Ctr**, downtown Memphis
12a	E Crump Blvd (from nb), E Exxon Capt D's, KFC, LJ Silver, Taco Bell Family$

INTERSTATE 55 Cont'd

Exit #	Services
11	McLemore Ave, Presidents Island, industrial area
10	S Parkway, 1/2 mi E Marathon/dsl
9	Mallory Ave, industrial area
8	Horn Lake Rd (from sb)
7	US 61, 3rd St, E Exxon, Shell Church's, Interstate BBQ, McDonald's $Tree, AutoZone, Family$, Kroger, NAPA, Roses, Save-A-Lot Foods, Walgreens, W MapCo, Marathon/Chester's/dsl KFC, McDonald's, Subway Rest Inn Fuller SP, Indian Museum
6b a	I-240
5b	US 51 S, Elvis Presley Blvd, to Graceland, **0-2 mi W on US 51** Citgo/dsl, Dodge's/dsl, Exxon, Marathon, Shell/dsl Baskin-Robbins, BJ's Wings, Burger King, Checker's, Exline Pizza, KFC, Krispy Kreme, Little Caesar's, McDonald's, Piccadilly's, Subway, Taco Bell American Inn, Days Inn, Guesthouse at Graceland, Heartbreak Hotel/RV Park, Memory Lane Inn H, $General, $Tree, Advance Parts, Aldi Foods, CVS, D&N RV Ctr, Family$, Memphis Visitors Ctr, Presley RV Park, to Graceland, Walgreens, Walgreens
5a	Brooks Rd, E BP, Exxon, Mapco/dsl Burger King, Papa John's, Popeye's Airport Inn, Best Value Inn, Kings Hotel, Motel 6 Freightliner, Peterbilt
2b a	TN 175, Shelby Dr, Whitehaven, E Citgo/Subway/dsl, Exxon, Phillips 66/dsl, Qmart/dsl Colonial Inn, W Exxon/dsl, Shell/dsl, Valero/dsl Burger King, Dixie Queen Burgers, IHOP, McDonald's, Popeye's $General, Family$, Kroger/gas, Save-a-Lot Foods, Toyota, U-Haul, Walgreens
0mm	Tennessee/Mississippi state line

MEMPHIS

INTERSTATE 65

Exit #	Services
121.5mm	Tennessee/Kentucky state line
121mm	**Welcome Ctr sb, full facilities, litter barrels, petwalk, vending**
120	Highland Rd
119mm	**weigh/insp sta both lanes**
117	TN 52, Portland, E Exxon/Godfather's/Quiznos/dsl, Shell/dsl/fireworks Comfort Suites H, Bledsoe Cr SP (20mi), W Shell/dsl Budget Host fireworks
116mm	Red River
113mm	Red River
112	TN 25, Cross Plains, E Shell/dsl/fireworks $General, antiques, Bledsoe Cr SP (20mi), W Mapco/Subway/dsl
108	TN 76, White House, E Murphy USA/dsl, Nervous Charlie's/dsl, Shell, Speedway/dsl A&W/KFC, Arby's, Bojangles, China Spring, Cracker Barrel, DQ, Dunkin', Hardee's, Little Caesar's, Los Agaves, McDonald's, Mr Wok, Papa Murphy's, Sonic, Subway, Taco Bell, Waffle House, Wendy's, Zaxby's Hampton Inn, Holiday Inn Express, Motel 6, Quality Inn Ace Hardware, AT&T, city park/playground, Kroger/gas, O'Reilly Parts, Rite Aid, USPO, Walgreens, Walmart/Subway, W Loves/IHOP/dsl/scales/24hr, Shell/dsl Days Inn
104	rd 257, Bethel Rd, W Shell/dsl Owl's Roost Camping
98	US 31 W, Millersville, E Shell/dsl Subway, Waffle House $General, auto repair, Grand Ol' RV Resort, W Marathon Economy Inn fireworks
97	rd 174, Long Hollow Pike, E BP/dsl, Exxon, Mapco Arby's, Capt D's, Cracker Barrel, Domino's, Happy Asian, Kabuto Japanese, KFC, McDonald's, Papa Murphy's, Quiznos, Shoney's, Subway, Taco Bell, Waffle House, Wendy's Baymont Inn,

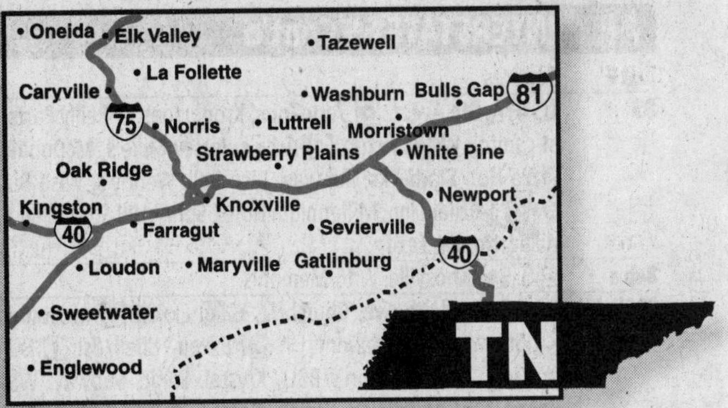

NASHVILLE

Exit #	Services
97	Continued Courtyard, Days Inn, Hampton Inn, Quality Inn, Red Roof Inn, Somotel, TownePlace Suites Kroger/dsl, USPO, Walgreens, W Shell/dsl Buck's BBQ, DQ, Hardee's, Krystal, Poncho Villa Grill, Sonic La Quinta, Motel 6 Rite Aid, Walgreens
96	Rivergate Pky, E Phillips 66/dsl, Shell/dsl Checkers, Chicago Gyros, El Chico, Fuji Steaks, HoneyBaked Ham, Hooters, Las Palmas Mexican, McDonald's, O'Charley's, Pizza Hut, Subway, Wendy's Best Value Inn, Comfort Suites, Country Inn Suites, Magnuson Hotel, Rodeway Inn H, Dillard's, JC Penney, Macy's, W Marathon, Volunteer, E on Gallatin Arby's, Bar-B-Cutie, Burger King, Chick-fil-A, Chili's, ChuckeCheese, CiCi's, Cookout, Domino's, Fazoli's, IHOP, Jersey Mike's, Jets Pizza, Jimmy John's, Krispy Kreme, Las Fiestas, Logan's Roadhouse, Longhorn Steaks, Olive Garden, Outback Steaks, Panda Express, Panera Bread, Pollo Tropical, Popeye's, Rafferty's, Red Lobster, Ryan's, Sonic, Starbucks, Steak'n Shake, Taco Bell, TGI Friday's, Zaxby's $General, $Tree, $Tree, AT&T, Best Buy, Big Lots, Books-A-Million, Buick/GMC, CarMax, Chevrolet, Chrysler/Dodge/Jeep, CVS Drug, Dick's, Discount Tire, Firestone/auto, Goodyear/auto, Harley-Davidson, Hobby Lobby, Home Depot, Honda, Jo-Ann's Etc, Kia, Lowe's, Nissan, Office Depot, Old Navy, O'Reilly Parts, PepBoys, Petsmart, Target, TJ Maxx, Toyota, URGENT CARE, Verizon, VW, Walgreens, Walmart/Subway/gas
95	TN 386, Vietnam Veterans Blvd (from nb)
92	rd 45, Old Hickory Blvd, E to Old Hickory Dam, W H
90b	TN 155 E, Briley Pkwy, E to Opryland
90a	US 31W, US 41, Dickerson Pike, E Citgo/dsl, Delta/dsl, Exxon/dsl Arby's, Capt D's, Chicago Gyros, China King, Church's, Domino's, Jay's Rest., KFC, Little Caesar's, McDonald's, Pizza Hut, Subway, Taco Bell, Waffle House, Wendy's Days Inn, EconoLodge, Sleep Inn, Super 8 $General, Advance Parts, AutoZone, Family$, O'Reilly Parts, Walgreens, W Murphy USA/dsl $Tree, Lowe's, Walmart
88b a	I-24, W to Clarksville, E to Nashville
87b a	US 431, Trinity Lane, E BP, Loves/Subway/dsl/scales/24hr Church's/White Castle, Krystal, Sonic Cumberland Inn, Delux Inn Piggly Wiggly, W BP, Exxon, Shell/dsl, Victory/dsl Fat Mo's, Jack-in-the-Box, Jack's BBQ, McDonald's, Subway, Taco Bell, Waffle House Best Value Inn, Days Inn, EconoLodge, Halmark Inn, Howard Johnson, King's Inn, Magnuson Hotel, Ravin Hotel, Red Roof Inn, Regency Inn, Rodeway Inn $General, Family$
86	I-24 E, to I-40 E, to Memphis
86mm	Cumberland River

TN

INTERSTATE 65 Cont'd

BRENTWOOD

FRANKLIN

Exit #	Services
85	US 41A, 8th Ave, E AutoZone, Kroger/gas, O'Reilly Parts, to st capitol, W Exxon Arby's, Jersey Mike's, McDonald's, Pizza Hut, Starbucks, Subway, Taco Bell, Wendy's, Wise Burger Fairfield Inn, Millennium Hotel, SpringHill Suites Cadillac, Honda, Lexus
84b a	I-40, E to Knoxville, W to Memphis
209[I-40]	US 70, Charlotte Ave, Church St, E Exxon McDonald's Sheraton Firestone, W Exxon, Shell/dsl Burger King, Jack Cawthon's BBQ, Krystal, Sonic, Subway, White Castle Comfort Inn, Hilton Garden Hyundai, URGENT CARE, Walgreens
82b a	I-40, W to Memphis, E to Nashville
81	Wedgewood Ave, W BP, Exxon, Shell/dsl Burger King, Subway $General, U-Haul
80	I-440, to Memphis, Knoxville
79	Armory Dr, E on Powell Shell Applebee's, Firehouse Subs, Jersey Mike's, Logan's Roadhouse, Panda Express, Panera Bread, Pizza Hut, Rafferty's, Subway, Taco Bell, Wendy's BMW, CarMax, Home Depot, Michael's, Petsmart, Ross, Staples, TJ Maxx, Walmart
78b a	rd 255, Harding Place, E Mapco, Pure, Shell Beijing Chinese, Cracker Barrel, Sub House, Waffle House La Quinta, Red Roof Inn CVS Drug, URGENT CARE
74	TN 254, Old Hickory Blvd, to Brentwood, E Coldstone, Fulin's Asian, Longhorn Steaks, Panera Bread, Qdoba Mexican, Waffle House Best Western, Holiday Inn Express, Hyatt Place, Sheraton GNC, Target, W BP, Gulf, Shell/dsl, Twice Daily/dsl Backyard Burger, Blaze Pizza, BurgerFi, Chick-fil-A, Chili's, Chipotle Mexican, Corky's BBQ, Dunkin' Donuts, FirstWatch, Five Guys, Jimmy John's, McAlister's Deli, McDonald's, Moe's SW Grill, Newk's Eatery, O'Charley's, Papa John's, Papa Murphy's, Pei Wei, Pizza Hut, Ruby Tuesday, Starbucks, Subway, Taco Bell, Taziki 's Cafe, Wendy's, Which Wich?, Zoe's Baymont, Courtyard, Extended Stay (2), Extended Stay America, Hampton Inn, Hilton Garden, Hilton Suites, Mainstay Suites Cadillac, CVS Drug, Firestone/auto, Fresh Mkt Foods, Kroger, Land Rover, Office Depot, PetCo, Publix, REI, TJ Maxx, Walgreens
71	TN 253, Concord Rd, to Brentwood
69	rd 441, Moores Lane, Galleria Blvd, E MapCo/dsl, Shell, Tesla EVC Amerigo's Grill, Baskin-Robbins, Cheddar's, Dicky's BBQ, Dunkin', Fuji Japanese, Hungry Howie's, Mexicali Grill, Outback Steaks, Papa Murphy's, Shogun Japanese, Sonic, Sportsman's Grille, Starbucks Hilton Garden, Holiday Inn, Holiday Inn Express, Hyatt Place Acura/Lexus, Advance Parts, Christian Bros. Auto, CVS Drug, Home Depot/dsl, Michael's, Petsmart, Publix, vet, Walgreens, W BP, Shell/dsl Backyard Burger, Buca Italian, Burger King, Capt D's, Cheesecake Factory, Chili's, Cracker Barrel, Famous Dave's, HoneyBaked Ham, Honeysuckle Grill, J Alexander's Rest., Krispy Kreme, Logan's Roadhouse, Macaroni Grill, McDonald's, Peking Palace, Pizza Hut/Taco Bell, Red Lobster, Schlotzsky's, Stoney River Steaks, Subway, Twin Peaks Sleep Inn $Tree, Barnes&Noble, Belk, Best Buy, Costco/gas, Dillard's, Discount Tire, Firestone/auto, JC Penney, Macy's, NTB, Old Navy, Ross, Target, UHaul
68b a	Cool Springs Blvd, E Jersey Mike's, Noodles&Co, Swankys Tacos, Tupelo Honey Cafe Courtyard, Embassy Suites, Marriott, Residence Inn, W Exxon, Shell BoneFish Grill, Burger Up, Canton Buffet, Carrabba's, Chick-fil-A, Chipotle,
68b a	Continued ChuckeCheese, Chuy's Mexican, Five Guys, Genghis Grill, G Cafe, J Christopher's, Jack-in-the-Box, Jason's Deli, Je Mike's, Jim 'N Nicks BBQ, Jimmy John's, Jonathan's Grille, Palmas, McAlister's Deli, McDonald's, Moe's SW Grill, Nev Eatery, Old Chicago, Panda Express, Panera Bread, Papa Joh PF Chang's, Pie Five Pizza, Pizza Hut, Pollo Tropical, Saladwo Sperry's, Starbucks, Subway, TGIFriday's, Wendy's, Which W Wild Wing Cafe, Zoe's Kitchen ALoft, Country Inn&Sui Hampton Inn, TownePlace Suites Acura, AT&T, Dick's, G Harley-Davidson, Jo-Ann Fabrics, Kroger, Lowe's, Marsha Mazda, Office Depot, Sam's Club/gas, Staples, TJ Maxx, to C leria Mall, Verizon, vet, Walgreens
67	McEwen Dr, E Homewood Suites, W Blue Coast B rito, Brick Top's, Buffalo Wild Wings, Culver's, Firehouse Su Granite City, Jamba Juice, Little Caesar's, Marco's Pizza, Wei, Sonic, Subway, Tazikis Mediterranean Cafe Dr Inn CarMax, CVS, Kohl's, Petco, Toyota, Walmart, Wh Food Mkt
65	TN 96, to Murfreesboro, Franklin, E Mapco, Shell/K tal Cracker Barrel, Sonic, Steak'n Shake Best Value I Comfort Inn, Days Inn, La Quinta, Ramada Inn auto rep Baymont Inn, Buick/GMC, Chevrolet, Honda, Kia, O'Reilly Pa Subaru, URGENT CARE, Volvo, Walgreens, W BP/dsl, Sh Shell/dsl Arby's, Backyard Burger, Bar-B-Cutie, Bleach Sports Grill, El Agave Mexican, Franklin Chophouse, Fra lin Chophouse, Guacamole Mexican, Hardee's, IHOP, Jers Mike's, KFC, La Terraza Mexican, McDonald's, Nashville Piz O'Charley's, Pancho's Mexican, Papa John's, Shoney's, St bucks, Subway, Taco Bell, Waffle House, Wendy's, Whitts BB Zaxby's Best Western, Best Western, Quality Inn $Ge eral, $Tree, Aldi Foods, AT&T, BigLots, Chrysler/Dodge/Jee Discount Tire, Fiat, Ford/Lincoln, Hobby Lobby, Home Dep Kroger/dsl, Publix/gas, Rite Aid, Sprouts Mkt, SteinMart, Confederate Cem at Franklin, Tuesday Morning, Verizon, v Walgreens
64mm	Harpeth River
61	TN 248, Peytonsville Rd, to Spring Hill, E TA/BP/Coun Pride/dsl/scales/24hr/@, W Mapco, Shell/dsl Goo Creek Inn
59b a	I-840, Memphis, Knoxville
58mm	W Harpeth River
53	TN 396, Saturn Pkwy, Spring Hill, to TN Scenic Pkwy, Columbi
48mm	**truck insp/weigh sta nb**
46	US 412, TN 99, to Columbia, Chapel Hill, E Loves Arbys/dsl/scales/24hr, Marathon/dsl Sleep Inn Ha ley-Davidson, Henry Horton SP, W Citgo/Subway/dsl, Ex on, Shell, Stan's/Country Store Burger King, Cracker Barr McDonald's, Waffle House Best Value Inn, Comfort In Comfort Suites, Fairfield Inn, Hampton Inn, Holiday Inn Expres Super 8 H
40.5mm	Duck River
37	TN 50, to Columbia, Lewisburg, E H, TN Walking Hors HQ, W BP/dsl to Polk Home
32	rd 373, to Lewisburg, Mooresville, E BP/dsl
27	rd 129, to Lynnville, Cornersville, E Texas T Camping
25mm	**parking area sb**
24mm	**parking area nb**
22	US 31A, to Pulaski, E Tennesseean Trkstp/Exxon/Pop's BBQ dsl/scales/24hr/@ McDonald's, Subway EconoLodge W Pilot/dsl/scales/24hr, Shell/dsl

TN

INTERSTATE 65 Cont'd

Exit #	Services
14	US 64, to Pulaski, E Exxon/dsl, Shell/dsl Sarge's Shack Rest. Motel 6 to Jack Daniels Distillery (30mi)
6	rd 273, Bryson, E Shell/rest./dsl/repair Best Value Inn dsl repair, W Marathon/dsl (2mi)
5mm	**weigh sta nb**
4mm	Elk River
3mm	**Welcome Ctr nb, full facilities, info, litter barrels, petwalk,**
1	US 31, rd 7, Ardmore, E Chevron/dsl, Shell, Victory/Huddle House/dsl $General, Burger King, El Olmeca Mexican, Hardee's, KFC/Taco Bell, McDonald's, Sonic, Subway, Whitts BBQ $General Mkt, $Tree, Daly Tire, O'Reilly Parts
0mm	Tennessee/Alabama state line

INTERSTATE 75

Exit #	Services
161.5mm	Tennessee/Kentucky state line
161mm	**Welcome Ctr sb, full facilities, litter barrels, petwalk, vending**
160	US 25W, Jellico, E Sunoco/dsl, VP/dsl, W Exxon/Wendy's/dsl, Shell/Arby's/dsl Hardee's, Heritage Pizza, McDonald's, Subway Days Inn, Parkway Inn H, fireworks, to Indian Mtn SP
156	Rarity Mtn Rd
144	Stinking Creek Rd, 4 mi E Ride Royal Blue Camping
141	TN 63, to Royal Blue, Huntsville, E Shell/dsl El Rey Azteca, W Pilot/Subway/dsl/scales/24hr, TA/Shell/Popeye's/dsl Hardee's Comfort Inn fireworks, repair/truckwash, to Big South Fork NRA
134	US 25W, TN 63, Caryville, E Shell Takumi Japanese, Waffle House Hampton Inn, Holiday Inn Express, Red Roof Inn, Super 8 H, $General, Cumberland Gap NHP, to Cove Lake SP, W Exxon/dsl Scotty's Hamburgers, Shoney's Budget Host USPO
129	US 25W S, Lake City, W BP/dsl, Marathon/Sonic/dsl, Pilot/dsl, Shell/dsl Cracker Barrel, Domino's, Glenn's Pizza, KFC/Taco Bell, La Fiesta Mexican, McDonald's, Subway Blue Haven Motel, Econolodge, Lamb's Inn/rest., Scottish Inn $General, Family$, fireworks, same as 128
128	US 441, to Lake City, E Sunoco Mtn Lake Marina Camping (4mi), W BP/dsl, Marathon, Weigel's/dsl Blue Haven Motel $General, Advance Parts, antique cars, Family$, same as 129, to Norris Dam SP
126mm	Clinch River
122	TN 61, Bethel, Norris, E Mobil/dsl, Wiegel's/dsl Shoney's antiques, KOA, Museum of Appalachia, Toyota, W BP/dsl, Exxon/Burger King/Subway/dsl, Git'n Go/dsl, Phillips 66/dsl, Shell/Baskin-Robbins Arby's, Bojangles, Firehouse Subs, Golden Girls Rest., Gondolier Italian, Hardee's, Harrison's Grill, Krystal, LJ Silver, McDonald's, Petro's Chili, Waffle House, Wendy's, Zaxby's Baymont Inn, Hampton Inn, Holiday Inn Express, Quality Inn, Red Roof Inn, Super 8 AT&T, Big Pine Ridge SP, Ford, Verizon, Walgreens, Walmart/McDonald's
117	rd 170, Racoon Valley Rd, E BP/dsl/scales/24hr, W Valley Inn Racoon Valley RV Park, Volunteer RV Park
112	rd 131, Emory Rd, to Powell, E Pilot/DQ/Taco Bell/dsl, Shell/Buddy's BBQ/dsl Arby's, Bruster's, Chick-fil-A, Cook-Out, Firehouse Subs, Five Guys, Jets Pizza, Krystal, McDonald's/playplace, Petro's Cafe, Ruby Tuesday, Starbucks, Steak'n

BETHEL

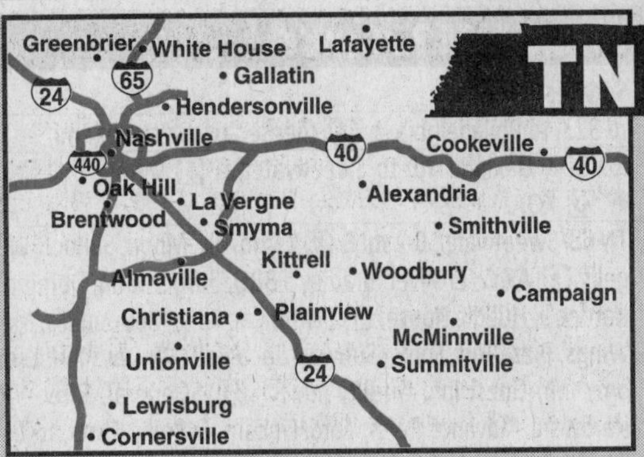

KNOXVILLE

Exit #	Services
112	Continued Shake, Subway, Taco Bell, Wendy's, Zaxby's Comfort Inn, Holiday Inn Express, La Quinta H, CVS Drug, Ingles/gas, O'Reilly Parts, Rigg's Drug, Verizon, W Exxon/dsl, Shell/dsl, Weigel's/dsl Aubrey's Rest., Hardee's, Shoney's, Waffle House Super 8 Kroger/dsl
110	Callahan Dr, E Weigel's/dsl Archer's BBQ, Asian Cafe Baymont Inn, Express Inn Honda, W Scottish Inn Kia, Mack/Volvo
108	Merchants Dr, E Delta/dsl, Marathon/dsl, Mobil/dsl, Pilot/dsl Applebee's, Cracker Barrel, El Chico, Hooters, Monterrey Mexican, O'Charley's, Pizza Hut, Puelo's Grill, Starbucks, Waffle House Best Western, Clarion, Comfort Suites, Hampton Inn, Mainstay Suites, Quality Inn, Red Roof Inn, Sleep Inn Ingles, Valvoline, W Exxon/dsl, Pilot/Domino's/dsl Austin's Steaks, Burger King, Capt D's, Dunkin', IHOP, Mandarin House, McDonald's, Nixon's Deli, Outback Steaks, Red Lobster, Subway, Taco Bell Best Value Inn, EconoLodge, Motel 6, Select Inn, Super 8 CVS Drug, Walgreens
107	I-640 & I-75
3b[I-640]	US 25W, (from nb), W Chevrolet, Ford, Nissan
1[I-640]	rd 62, Western Ave, E Hardee's, Krystal Advance Parts, Family$, O'Reilly Parts, W Exxon/dsl, Marathon/dsl, RaceWay/dsl Central Park, Firehouse Subs, KFC, Little Caesars, LJ Silver, McDonald's, Panda Chinese, Shoney's, Subway, Taco Bell, Wendy's CVS Drug, Kroger/dsl, Walgreens
I-75 and I-40 run together 17 mi. See I-40, exits 369 through 385.	
84[368]	I-40, W to Nashville, E to Knoxville
81	US 321, TN 95, to Lenoir City, E Exxon/Subway/dsl, Mobil, Murphy USA/dsl, Shell/Buddy's BBQ/TCBY/dsl, Shell/dsl, Weigel's/dsl Arby's, Aubrey's Rest., Bella Hibachi, Bojangles, Burger King, Capt D's, Chick-fil-A, Chili's, China Buffet, Cinco Amigos Mexican, Cracker Barrel, Domino's, Dunkin', Firehouse Subs, Gondolier Italian, Hardee's, KFC, McDonald's, Panda Express, Papa John's, Papa Murphy's, Pizza Hut, Shoney's, Starbucks, Subway, Taco Bell, Waffle House, Wendy's, Zaxby's Fairfield Inn, Hampton Inn, Holiday Inn Express, King's Inn/rest. H, $General Mkt, $Tree, Advance Parts, Aldi Foods, AT&T, AutoZone, Big Lots, CVS Drug, Food City/gas, Ford, Ft Loudon Dam, GNC, Great Smokies NP, Home Depot, Ingles, Lazy Acers RV Park (7mi), O'Reilly Parts, Verizon, Walgreens, Walmart/Subway, W Citgo/dsl Krystal, Ruby Tuesday Comfort Inn, EconoLodge Crosseyed Cricket Camping (6mi), Matlock Tires/Repair
76	rd 324, Sugar Limb Rd, W to TN Valley Winery
74mm	Tennessee River
72	TN 72, to Loudon, E Exxon/Wendy's/dsl, Shell/McDonald's, Weigel's/dsl Bojangles, KFC, Romeo's Pizza, Taco Bell Inn of Loudon, La Quinta to Ft Loudon SP, W Marathon Best Value Inn Express RV Park

TN

INTERSTATE 75 Cont'd

SWEETWATER

Exit #	Services
68	rd 323, to Philadelphia, E cheese factory/store (2mi)
62	RD 322, Oakland Rd, to Sweetwater, E Dinner Bell Rest., W KOA
60	TN 68, Sweetwater, **0-2 mi** E Citgo/dsl, Mobil, Sunoco, Weigel's A&W/LJ Silver, Bradley's BBQ, Burger King, Domino's, Hardee's, Huddle House, KFC, Little Caesar's, McDonald's, Mexi Wings, Pizza Hut, Sonic, Subway, Taco Bell Days Inn, Economy Inn, Guest Inn, Quality Inn H, $General, $Tree, Ace Hardware, Advance Parts, Ford/Lincoln, O'Reilly Parts, to Lost Sea Underground Lake, Verizon, Walgreens, W Kangaroo/dsl, Marathon Holiday Inn Express, Motel 6 flea mkt, to Watts Bar Dam, vet
56	rd 309, Niota, E Pilot/Wendy's/dsl/scales/24hr TN Country Camping, W repair
52	rd 305, Mt Verd Rd, to Athens, E Marathon/dsl (2mi), Sunoco/dsl Subway (2mi) Overniter RV Park, W BP Athens Lodge

ATHENS

Exit #	Services
49	TN 30, to Athens, E Exxon, Kangaroo, Mobil/dsl, Murphy USA/dsl Applebee's, Arby's, Betty's BBQ, Buddy's BBQ, Burger King, Capt D's, China Wok, Cookout, Dunkin', Firehouse Subs, Hardee's, KFC, Krystal, Little Caesar's, McDonald's, Mexi Wing, Ming Dynasty, Papa John's, Pizza Hut, Ruby Tuesday, Shoney's, Sonic, Subway, Subway, Taco Bell, Waffle House, Wendy's, Western Sizzlin, Zaxby's Days Inn, EconoLodge, Hampton Inn, Holiday Inn Express, Motel 6, Scottish Inn, Super 8 H, $General, $Tree, Advance Parts, AT&T, Athens I-75 Camping, Belk, BigLots, GNC, Russell Stover, Staples, to TN Wesleyan Coll, URGENT CARE, Verizon, Walgreens, Walmart/Subway, W Mobil/dsl, Speedway/Speedy's Cafe/dsl Cracker Barrel Best Value Inn, Comfort Inn, Fairfield Inn
45mm	**both lanes, full facilities, litter barrels, petwalk, vending**
42	rd 39, Riceville Rd, E Citgo/dsl Relax Inn, Rice Inn (2mi) $General (2mi)
36	rd 163, to Calhoun, E Hardee's (3mi) Hiwassee/Ocoee River SP
35mm	Hiwassee River
33	rd 308, to Charleston, E Marathon/dsl Hardee's, W Loves/McDonald's/Subway/dsl/scales/24hr

CLEVELAND

Exit #	Services
27	Paul Huff Pkwy, **1 mi** E Murphy USA, Shell/dsl Applebee's, Buffalo Wild Wings, Capt D's, Chili's, CiCi's, DQ, Fazoli's, Firehouse Subs, Five Guys, Golden Corral, IHOP, Little Caesar's, Longhorn Steaks, Marco's Pizza, McDonald's, O'Charley's, Olive Garden, Outback Steaks, Panera Bread, Papa Murphy's, Pita Pit, Pizza Hut, Royal Buffet, Six Happiness, Sonic, Starbucks, Steak'n Shake, Subway, Taco Bell Baymont Inn, Holiday Inn Express $Tree, Aldi Foods, auto repair/tires, AutoZone, Belk, Buick/Cadillac/GMC, CVS Drug, Discount Tire, Food Lion, Hobby Lobby, Home Depot, JC Penney, Lowe's, NTB, PetCo, Petsmart, Publix, Staples, TJ Maxx, Verizon, Walgreens, Walmart, W EVC, Exxon/dsl, Orbit/dsl, Shell/Subway Burger King, Denny's, Fulin's Asian, Hardee's, Honeybaked Ham, Shane's Ribshack, Waffle House, Wendy's Clarion, Classic Suites, Hampton Inn, Quality Inn, Red Roof Inn, Royal Inn, Super 8 AT&T, Books-A-Million, Kohl's, Ross, Target
25	TN 60, Cleveland, E Chevron/dsl, RaceWay/dsl, Shell/dsl, Sunoco/dsl Bojangles, Burger King, Checkers, Cracker Barrel, Dunkin', Hardee's, Las Margaritas, McDonald's, Old Fort Rest., Sonic, Subway, Waffle House, Zaxby's Days Inn, Douglas Inn, EconoLodge, Economy Inn, Fairfield Inn, Howard Johnson,
25	Continued Knights Inn, Motel 6 H, $General, Ace Hardware, BigLc Cherokee Drug, NAPA, to Lee Coll, Tuesday Morning, v W BP Cleveland Hotel, Comfort Inn, La Quinta, Mtn Vi Inn
23mm	**truck/weigh sta nb**
20	US 64 byp, to Cleveland, **1-4 mi** E FuelMart Ford, Honda, Kia, W Exxon/dsl, Pilot/McDonald's/Subway/d scales/24hr fireworks, KOA (1mi), Toyota
16mm	scenic view sb
13mm	**truck/weigh sta, litter barrels sb**

CHATTANOOGA

Exit #	Services
11	US 11 N, US 64 E, Ooltewah, E BP/Circle K, EVC, Map Murphy USA/dsl, RaceWay/dsl Arby's, Bojangles, Burg King, Chick-fil-A, China Rose, Cracker Barrel, El Cortes Mexica Hardee's, Jersey Mike's, Little Caesar's, McDonald's, Pan Express, Pizza Hut, Puleo's Grille, Sonic, Starbucks, Subwa Taco Bell, Wendy's, Zaxby's Hampton Inn, Holiday I Express, Springhill Suites $General, Ace Hardware, Al Foods, AutoZone, Food City, GNC, O'Reilly Parts, Verizon, v Walgreens, Walmart/Subway, W BP/Circle K/Dunkin', Exxon/dsl Beef'o Brady's, Krystal, Waffle House Sup 8 Publix, Tire Discounters, to Harrison Bay SP
9	TN 317, Apison Pk, Volkswagen Dr, E Shell
7b a	US 11, US 64, Lee Hwy, E Exxon/dsl, W BP, EV EVC, Speedway/Speedy's Cafe/dsl City Cafe, Waf House Airport Inn, Best Inn, Best Value Inn, Best Weste EconoLodge, Motel 6, Woodspring Suites Denton's Repa Harley-Davidson, Jaguar/Land Rover/Porsche/Infiniti
5	Shallowford Rd, same as 4a, E Acropolis Grill, Arby Chuy's, CiCi's, Forbidden City Chinese, Imperial Garden, J. A exanders, James Co Grill, Jersey Mike's, Krystal, McAliste Deli, McDonald's, Mellow Mushroom Pizza, Miller's Alehous Newk's Eatery, Outback Steaks, Panda Express, Pier 88, Ruth Chris Steaks, Smokey Bones BBQ, Starbucks, Steak'n Shak Taco Bell, Zaxby's Courtyard, Embassy Suites, Studio Wingate Inn Best Buy, Firestone/auto, Fresh Mkt, Hob Lobby, Home Depot, Lowe's, Office Depot, Old Navy, Petc Petsmart, Publix, REI, SteinMart, Target, Walgreens, Walmar Subway, World Mkt, W BP, Citgo/dsl, Exxon/dsl, She Speedway/Speedy's Cafe/dsl Cracker Barrel, Fazoli's, Fire box Grill, Fuji Steaks, O'Charley's, Papa John's, Shoney's, Soni Subway, TX Roadhouse, Waffle House, Wendy's Athen Inn, Baymont Inn, Comfort Inn, Days Inn, Fairfield Inn, Hilto Garden, Holiday Inn, Home 2 Suites, Homewood Suites, L Quinta, La Quinta, MainStay Suites, Microtel, Quality Inn, Re Roof Inn, Residence Inn, Sleep Inn, Staybridge Suites, Super 8 SureStay+, TownePlace Suites, Travelodge, Tru Hilton H CarMax, CVS Drug, Family$, Food City, Goodyear/auto, SaveAl ot, U of TN/Chatt
4a	(from nb) Hamilton Place Blvd, same as 5, E Shell Abuelo's, Acropolis, Big River Grille, BoneFish Grill, Capt D's, Carrab ba's, Cheddar's, Cheesecake Factory, Chick-fil-A, Chili's, Cho House, DQ, El Meson Mexican, Firebirds, Firehouse Subs, Fiv Guys, Golden Corral, Hana Steak, Honeybaked Ham, Jason's Del Jim'n Nick's BBQ, McDonald's, Moe's SW Grill, Olive Garden, Outback Steaks, Panera Bread, PF Chang's, Red Lobster, Red Robir Salsarita's Mexican, Shogun Japanese, Starbucks, Sticky Finger BBQ, Taziki's Cafe Hampton Inn, InTown Suites $Tree AT&T, Barnes&Noble, Belk, Big Lots, Dick's, Dillard's, Earthfare Firestone/auto, JC Penney, Jo-Ann, Kohl's, Marshall's, Michael's Pepboys, Ross, Staples, Target, TJ Maxx, Verizon, World Mkt
4	TN 153, Chickamauga Dam Rd,

TN

INTERSTATE 75 Cont'd

Exit #	Services
3b a	TN 320, Brainerd Rd, E BP/Circle K Baskin-Robbins, Subway, W BMW
2	I-24 W, to I-59, to Chattanooga, Lookout Mtn
1.5mm	**Welcome Ctr nb, full facilities, litter barrels, petwalk, , , vending**
1b a	US 41, Ringgold Rd, to Chattanooga, E BP/Circle K, Shell/dsl Buddy's BBQ, Chick-fil-A, Starbucks, Wendy's Best Western+, EconoLodge, Hampton Inn, La Quinta, Motel 6, Quality Inn Bass Pro Shops, Camping World RV Ctr/park, Family$, W Citgo/dsl, Mapco/dsl, Valero/dsl Arby's, Baskin-Robbins, Burger King, Cracker Barrel, Dunkin', Firehouse Subs, Hardee's, Krystal, Marco's Pizza, McDonald's, Pizza Hut, Popeye's, PortoFino Italian, Sonic, Subway, Taco Bell, Teriyaki House, Waffle House, Wally's Rest. Budgetel, Fairfield Inn, Four A's Inn, Holiday Inn Express, Super 8, Waverly Motel $General, Advance Parts, AutoZone, Family$, Food Lion, O'Reilly Parts, U-Haul, Walgreens
0mm	Tennessee/Georgia state line

INTERSTATE 81

Exit #	Services
75mm	Tennessee/Virginia state line, **Welcome Ctr sb, full facilities, info, litter barrels, petwalk, , , vending**
74b a	US 11W, to Bristol, Kingsport, E Fairfield Inn, Hampton Inn H, W Tesla EVC, Valero/dsl Aubrey's Rest., Bojangle's, Brusco's Pizza, Chick-fil-A, Drake's Rest., Jersey Mike's, La Carreta, McDonald's, Moe's SW, Outback Steaks, Pal's Drive-Thru, Panda Express, Starbucks, Steak'n Shake, Zaxby's Bass Pro Shops, Belk, CarMax, Dick's, GNC, Marshall's, Michael's, Old Navy, Verizon
69	TN 394, to Blountville, E BP/Subway/dsl Arby's, Domino's Advance Parts, Bristol Int Speedway, Lakeview RV Park (8mi), Shadrack Camping
66	rd 126, to Kingsport, Blountville, W Shell/dsl McDonald's
63	rd 357, E BP/Krystal/dsl, Shell/Subway/dsl Cracker Barrel, Wendy's La Quinta, Sleep Inn Hamricks, Tri-Cities Airport, W Citgo/dsl Econolodge dsl repair, KOA, Rocky Top Camping
60mm	Holston River
59	rd 36, to Johnson City, Kingsport, E Marathon/dsl Super 8, W Exxon/dsl, Marathon, Shell/dsl, Sunoco Arby's, Fisherman's Dock Rest., Hardee's, HotDog Hut, Jersey Mike's Subs, La Carreta Mexican, Little Caesar's, Little Caesar's, McDonald's, Moto Japanese, Pal's Drive-Thru, Perkins, Pizza Hut, Plum Tree Rest., Raffaele's Pizza, Sonic, Subway, Taco Bell, The Shack BBQ, Zachary's Steaks Comfort Inn, Motel 6 $General, Advance Parts, CVS Drug, Ingles/deli, Murphy's Automotive, O'Reilly Parts, to Warrior's Path SP, URGENT CARE, USPO, Verizon, Walgreens
57b a	I-26
56	Tri-Cities Crossing
50	TN 93, Fall Branch, W auto auction, st patrol
44	Jearoldstown Rd, E Marathon
41mm	**sb, full facilities, litter barrels, petwalk, , , vending**
38mm	**nb, full facilities, litter barrels, petwalk, , , vending**
36	rd 172, to Baileyton, E Pilot/Subway/dsl/scales/24hr, W Marathon/dsl, Shell/Subway/dsl/24hr, TA/Country Pride/dsl/scales/24hr/@ Pizza+ 36 Motel $General, Around Pond RV Park, Family$, KOA (2mi)

KINGSPORT

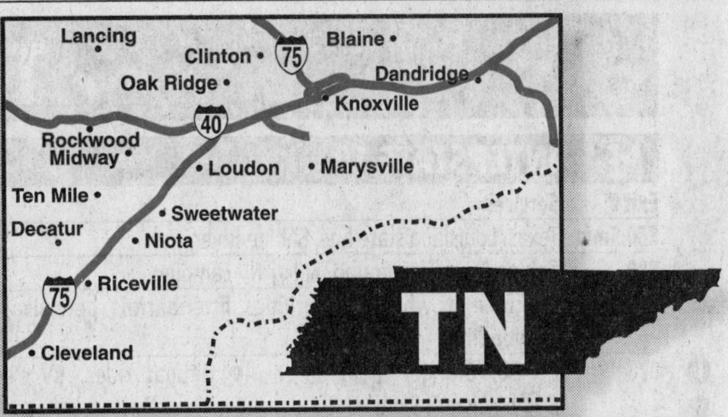

Exit #	Services
30	TN 70, to Greeneville, E Marathon/DQ/Stuckey's/dsl
23	US 11E, to Greeneville, E Marathon/Wendy's, Mobil/Subway/dsl Crockett SP, to Andrew Johnson HS, Tri-Am RV Ctr, W Exxon/DQ/dsl, Phillips 66/dsl/rest./scales McDonald's, Pizza+, Taco Bell Quality Inn, Super 8 Tony's Repair
21mm	**weigh sta sb**
15	rd 340, Fish Hatchery Rd
12	TN 160, to Morristown, E Phillips 66/dsl, W Gulf/dsl Days Inn (6mi), Hampton Inn (12mi), Holiday Inn Express (5mi), Super 8 (5mi) to Crockett Tavern HS
8	US 25E, to Morristown, E Sonic (2mi), W Weigel's/dsl Bojangle's, Cracker Barrel, Fastop/Subway/dsl, Hardee's, McDonald's Best Western+, Hampton Inn, Parkway Inn, Super 8 to Cumberland Gap NHP
4	rd 341, White Pine, E Pilot/McDonald's/dsl/scales/24hr Subway, W Pilot/Dunkin'/Wendy's/dsl/scales/24hr Taco Bell Econolodge to Panther Cr SP
2.5mm	**sb, full facilities, litter barrels, petwalk, , , vending**
1b a	I-40, E to Asheville, W to Knoxville. **I-81 begins/ends on I-40, exit 421.**

INTERSTATE 640 (Knoxville)

Exit #	Services
9mm	**I-640 begins/ends on I-40, exit 393.**
8	Millertown Pike, Mall Rd N, N Exxon/DQ, Shell Applebee's, Burger King, China Wok, Honeybaked Ham, KFC, Krystal, Mandarin Palace, McDonald's, Pizza Hut, Taco Bell, TX Roadhouse, Wendy's $Tree, AT&T, Belk, Food City/dsl, Jo-Ann, Kohl's, Marshall's, Old Navy, Ross, Sam's Club/dsl, Target, Walmart, S Shell/dsl Amigo's, Cracker Barrel, Little Caesar's, O'Charley's, Sonic Home Depot, Lowe's Whse, PepBoys
6	US 441, to Broadway, N Citgo/dsl, Pilot/dsl Arby's, Cancun Mexican, Chick-fil-A, Chop House, CiCi's, Firehouse Subs, Hardee's, Krispy Kreme, Lenny's Subs, LJ Silver, McDonald's, Panera Bread, Papa John's, Papa Murphy's, Penn Sta Subs, Ruby Tuesday, Sonic, Subway, Taco Bell $General, Advance Parts, AutoZone, BigLots, CVS Drug, Firestone, Food City/gas, Kroger, O'Reilly Parts, repair/tires, Verizon, Walgreens, S Bojangle's, Buddy's BBQ, Little Caesar's, Shoney's $General, $Tree, Food City, Office Depot
3a	I-75 N to Lexington, I-275 S to Knoxville
3b	US 25W, Clinton Hwy, N Chevrolet, Ford, Nissan, services on frontage rds
1	TN 62, Western Ave, N Exxon/dsl, Marathon/dsl, Raceway/dsl Central Park, Firehouse Subs, KFC, Little Caesars, LJ Silver, McDonald's, Panda Chinese, Shoney's, Subway, Taco Bell, Wendy's CVS Drug, Kroger/dsl, Walgreens, S Hardee's, Krystal Advance Parts, Family$, O'Reilly Parts
	I-640 begins/ends on I-40, exit 385.

KNOXVILLE

TX

TEXAS

INTERSTATE 10

ORANGE

Exit #	Services
880.5mm	Texas/Louisiana state line, Sabine River
880	Sabine River Turnaround, N [other] RV camping
879mm	**Welcome Ctr wb, full [handicapped] facilities, litter barrels, petwalk, [phone], [picnic], vending**
878	US 90, Orange, N [gas] Gulf/dsl [other] airboat rides, RV Park, S [other] Western Store
877	TX 87, 16th St, Orange, N [gas] Exxon/dsl, Shamrock/dsl [food] Little Caesar's, Pizza Hut, Subway [lodging] Hampton Inn [other] Ace Hardware, Market Basket/deli, S [gas] Get'n Go/dsl, Kwik Stop/dsl, Shell/dsl, Valero/dsl [food] 2 Amigo's Mexican, Casa Ole, Church's, DQ, General Wok, Jack-in-the-Box, McDonald's, Popeye's, Sonic, Taco Bell [other] $General, CVS Drug, Family$, Goodyear/auto, HEB Foods, Kroger/dsl, Modica Tires, O'Reilly Parts, Verizon, Walgreens
876	Adams Bayou, frontage rd, N [food] Gary's Café, Señor Toro's Mexican, Taste of Orange Rest., Waffle House [lodging] Best Price Motel, Best Texan Inn, Days Inn, EconoLodge, Executive Inn, Knights Inn, Motel 6 [other] Toyota, S [gas] Chevron/dsl [lodging] Holiday Inn Express [other] same as 877
875	FM 3247, MLK Dr, N [gas] Exxon/dsl, S [other] [H], Chrysler/Dodge/Jeep
874	US 90, Womack Rd, to Orange, S [other] [H]
873	TX 62, TX 73, to Bridge City, N [gas] FLYING J/Denny's/dsl/LP/scales/24hr, Fuel Tec/dsl/24hr [lodging] Studio 6 [other] Blue Beacon, Oak Leaf RV Park, S [gas] Pilot/Subway/Wendy's/dsl/scales/24hr, Shell/Church's/dsl, Valero/dsl [food] McDonald's, Sonic, Waffle House, Whataburger [lodging] Best Western, Comfort Inn, La Quinta
872	N Mimosa Ln, Jackson Dr, from wb
870	FM 1136
869	FM 1442, to Bridge City, S [gas] Exxon/dsl
867	frontage rd (from eb)
865	Doty Rd (from wb), frontage rd
864	FM 1132, FM 1135, N [lodging] Budget Inn [other] TX Star RV Park
862	Lakeside St, Timberlane Dr, N [gas] Conoco

VIDOR

Exit #	Services
861	FM 105, Vidor, N [gas] Chevron/dsl, Citgo/dsl, Conoco/dsl, Valero/dsl [food] Casa Ole, Domino's, DQ, Jack-in-the-Box, Little Caesars, McDonald's/playplace, Ming's Buffet, Novrosky's Burgers, Popeye's, Waffle House [other] AutoZone, CVS, Mktbasket Foods, Modica Bros Tires, O'Reilly Parts, Verizon, Walgreens, Walmart, S [gas] Citgo/dsl, Exxon/dsl [food] Burger King, Pizza Hut, Sonic, Subway, Taco Bell, Whataburger [lodging] Best Western+, Holiday Inn Express [other] auto repair, Family$
860	Dewitt Rd, frontage rd, W Vidor, S [gas] Citgo, Exxon, Mobil/dsl [food] Burger King, Pizza Hut, Sonic, Subway, Taco Bell, Whataburger [lodging] Best Western, Holiday Inn Express [other] Family$, repair
859	Bonner Turnaround (from eb), Asher Turnaround (from wb), N [other] Boomtown RV Park, S [gas] Chevron/Gateway/dsl/24hr
858	Rose City
856	Old Hwy 90 (from eb), Rose City
855b	Magnolia St (from wb)
855a	US 90 bus, to downtown, Port of Beaumont
854	ML King Pkwy, Beaumont, N [gas] Chevron/dsl, Valero/dsl [food] Jack-in-the-Box, S [gas] Jet/dsl, Shamrock/dsl [food] McDonald's
853b	11th St, N [gas] Valero/dsl [food] Cafe Del Rio, Red Lobster, Waffle House [lodging] Beaumont Lodge, Days Inn, EconoLodge, Holiday Inn, Merit Inn, Sleep Inn, Studio 6 [other] MktBasket, S [gas] Chevron/dsl, Shamrock [food] Checker's, Chula Vista Mexican, Dunkin',

BEAUMONT

Exit #	Services
853b	Continued Jack-in-the-Box, Luby's [lodging] HomeBridge Suites, Rodeway [other] [H]
853a	US 69 N, to Lufkin
852	Harrison Ave, Calder Ave, Beaumont, N [gas] Shell/dsl, Va ro/dsl [food] Casa Ole Mexican, Casa Tapatia Mexican, Chi Frankie's Italian, Olive Garden, Saltgrass Steaks, Tony's B S [food] Church's, McDonald's [lodging] La Quinta, Scottish Inn [other]
851	US 90, College St, N [gas] Chevron/dsl, Exxon/dsl, Racewa dsl [food] Carrabba's, Chicken Express, Floyd's Cajun Cafe, Golc Corral, Hooters, Lupe Tortilla, Outback Steaks, Sartin's Seafo Tokyo Japanese, Waffle House [lodging] Howard Johnson, Quality I Ramada, Red Roof Inn [other] Advance Parts, AutoZone, Harley-D vidson, Indian Motorcycles, O'Reilly Parts, URGENT CARE, Ve zon, Volvo Trucks, S [gas] Exxon/dsl, Mobil, Shell/dsl [food] Cane Chick-fil-A, China Hut, DQ, IHOP, Pizza Hut, Sonic, Taco B Wendy's, Whataburger [lodging] Best Value, Courtyard, Elegante M tel, Fairfield Inn, Regency Inn, Woodspring Suites [other] [H], $Tr BMW, Chrysler/Dodge/Jeep, CVS Drug, Discount Tire, Firestor auto, HEB Foods, Honda, Mercedes, Nissan, NTB, Office Dep Sam's Club/gas, U-Haul, VW, Walgreens
850	wb only, same as 851
849	US 69 S, Washington Blvd, to Port Arthur, N [other] [airport]
848	Walden Rd, N [gas] Shell/dsl [food] Pappadeaux Seafood, Sor Subway, Taco Bell [lodging] Comfort Suites, Holiday Inn/rest., Quinta [other] USPO, S [gas] Chevron/dsl, Petro/Iron Skillet/d scales/24hr/@, Shell/dsl [food] Cheddar's, Cracker Barrel, Jack-i the-Box, Joe's Crabshack, Twin Peaks, Waffle House [lodging] Ca dlewood Suites, Executive Inn, Hampton Inn, Hilton Garde Home 2 Suites, Homewood Suites, Residence Inn, Super 8
847	Brooks Rd (from wb), (845 from eb), S [other] Gulf Coast RV R sort, Hidden Lake RV Park
845	TX 364
843	Smith Rd, N [gas] Love's/Arby's/Chester's/Godfather's/d scales/24hr
838	FM 365, Fannett, N [food] Alligator Park/Rest., Shell/Bar-H BB gas [other] T&T RV Park
837.5mm	no service
833	Hamshire Rd, N [gas] Valero/Sonic/dsl

WINNIE

Exit #	Services
829	FM 1663, Winnie, N [gas] Exxon/dsl, Mobil/Burger King/d Shell/dsl/24hr [food] McDonald's, Taco Bell, Whataburger/24 [lodging] Days Inn [other] RV Park, S [gas] Chevron/Chester's/dsl, Gu Subway/Pizza Hut/dsl/scales/24hr, Texaco/dsl [food] Al-T's Se food, Exxon/dsl, Hart's Chicken, Jack-in-the-Box, Joe's Italia Waffle House [lodging] Best Value Inn, Comfort Inn, Hampton In Holiday Inn Express, La Quinta, Motel 6, Winnie Inn/RV Pa [other] [H], Chrysler/Jeep/Dodge
828	TX 73, TX 124 (from eb), to Winnie, S [other] [H], same as 829
827	FM 1406
822	FM 1410
821	**insp sta wb**
819	Jenkins Rd, N [gas] Chevron/Dunkin'/dsl, S [gas] Exxon/Stuc ey's/Chester's/dsl
817	FM 1724
814	frontage rd, from eb, **[Rs] both lanes, full [handicapped] facilities, [picnic], litte barrels**
813	TX 61 (from wb), Hankamer, N [gas] Shell/dsl [lodging] Palace In S [gas] Exxon/DJ's Diner/dsl [food] McDonald's [other] same as 812
812	TX 61, Hankamer

TX

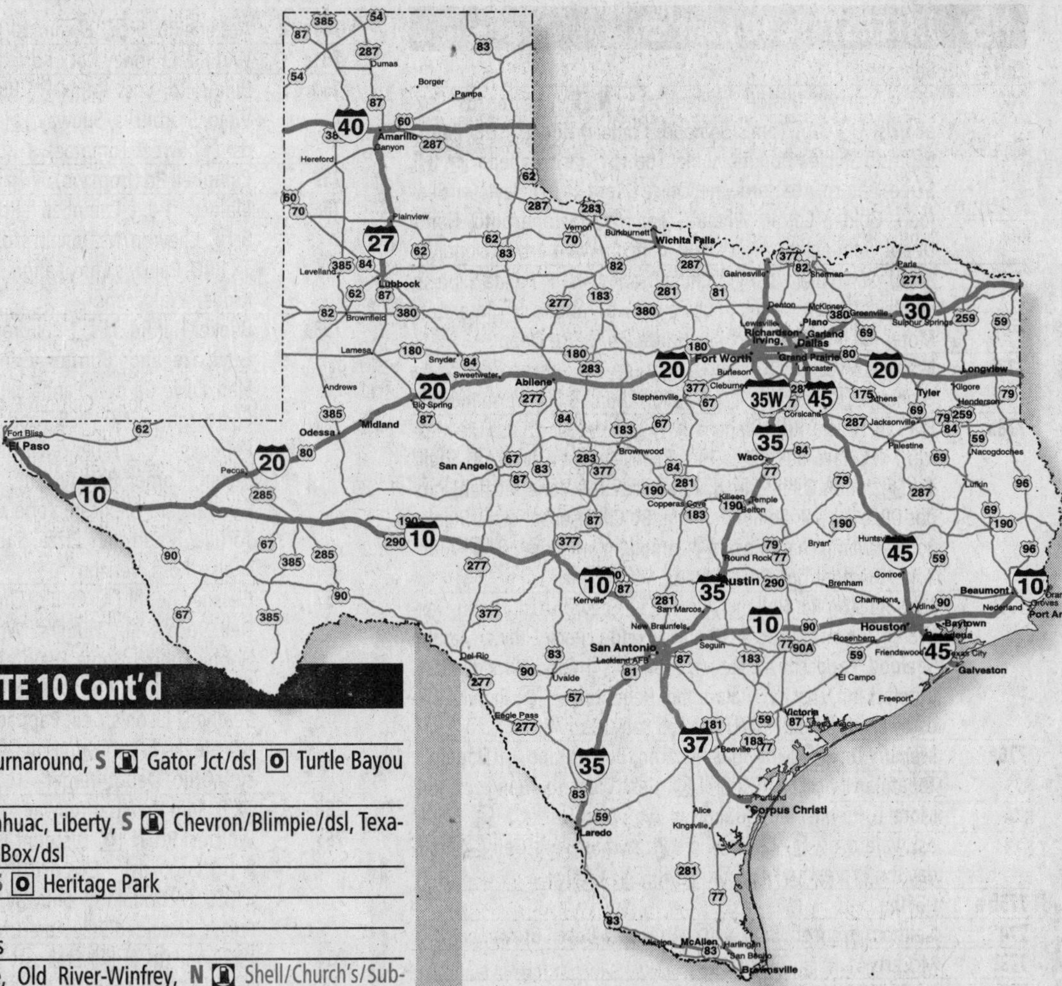

INTERSTATE 10 Cont'd

Exit #	Services
811	Turtle Bayou Turnaround, S Gator Jct/dsl Turtle Bayou RV Park
810	FM 563, to Anahuac, Liberty, S Chevron/Blimpie/dsl, Texaco/Jack-in-the-Box/dsl
807	to Wallisville, S Heritage Park
805.5mm	Trinity River
804mm	Lost, Old Rivers
803	FM 565, Cove, Old River-Winfrey, N Shell/Church's/Subway/dsl/scales/24hr Lost River RV Park, S Chevron/Checkers/dsl, Valero/dsl
800	FM 3180, N Exxon/dsl Burger King, Popeye's, Taco Bell HEB/gas, vet
799	TX 99, Grand Pkwy
797	(798 from wb) TX 146, **99 toll**, Baytown, N Chevron/Subway/dsl/scales, Conoco/dsl/scales, Shell/dsl DQ, El Hacendado, Iguana Joe's Mexican, McDonald's, Waffle House Crystal Inn, Motel 6, Super 8 L&R RV Park, Value RV Park, S Exxon, RaceWay/dsl, Stripes/Taco Co/dsl, Texaco/Popeye's/dsl Baytown Seafood, Chick-fil-A, Freddy's, Jack-in-the-Box, KFC/Taco Bell, Sonic, Wendy's, Whataburger Magnuson Hotel Houston East RV Park, vet, Walmart
796	frontage rd, N Chevron/Phillips/Chemical Refinery
795	Sjolander Rd, S Chevron/dsl
793	N Main St, S Valero/Dickey's BBQ/dsl/24hr
792	Garth Rd, N Chevron/dsl Chicken Express, Cracker Barrel, Denny's, Jack-in-the-Box, Red Lobster, Richard's Cajun, Sonic, Starbucks, Subway, Tuscany Italian, Waffle House, Whataburger Baymont Inn, Comfort Suites, Days Inn, EconoLodge, Hampton Inn, Holiday Inn, La Quinta, Motel 6, SpringHill Suites Buick/GMC, Chrysler/Jeep/Dodge, Honda, Hyundai, Kia, Nissan, O'Reilly Parts, Toyota, Walgreens, S RaceWay/dsl, Shell/dsl Buffalo Wild Wings, Carino's Italian, Carl's Jr, Chili's, Firehouse Subs, Lee Palace, McDonald's, Olive Garden, Outback Steaks, Panda Express, Panera Bread, Pizza Hut/Taco Bell, Popeye's, Subway, Tortuga Mexican, TX Rodehouse, Wendy's Palace Inn, Quality Inn, Scottish Inn H, $General, AT&T, JC Penney, Kohl's, Macy's, Marshall's, Michael's, Tuesday Morning, Verizon
791	John Martin Rd, S Buc-ee's/dsl Cheddar's, Saltgrass Steaks Best Western+, Woodspring Suites Cadillac/Chevrolet, Ford
790	Ellis School Rd, N Super 8
789	Thompson Rd, N Loves/McDonald's/dsl/scales/24hr/@ Super 8, S FLYING J/Denny's/dsl/scales/24hr/@, TA/Country Pride/dsl/scales/24hr/@ Blue Beacon, Truck Lube
788.5mm	**eb, full facilities, litter barrels, petwalk,**
788	sp 330 (from eb), to Baytown
787	sp 330, Crosby-Lynchburg Rd, to Highlands, N Exxon/Domino's/dsl RV Camping (1mi), S Phillips 66/dsl Four Corners BBQ to San Jacinto SP
786.5mm	San Jacinto River
786	Monmouth Dr
785	Magnolia Ave, to Channelview, N Shell/dsl/scales, S Exxon/dsl truckwash
784	Cedar Lane, Bayou Dr, N Valero/dsl Rodeway Inn, TX Inn
783	Sheldon Rd, N Chevron/dsl, Shell/dsl, Valero/dsl Burger King, Church's, Jack-in-the-Box, Pizza Hut, Pizza Inn, Popeye's, Subway, Taco Bell, Whataburger Days Inn, Grand Inn, Holiday Inn, Leisure Inn, Palace Inn, Parkway Inn, Travelers Inn AutoZone, Discount Tire, Family$, FoodFair, USPO, S Chevron/dsl, Texaco/dsl McDonald's, Wendy's Deluxe Inn, Fairfield Inn, Scottish Inn auto repair
782	Dell-Dale Ave, N Exxon/dsl Dell-Dale Motel, Luxury Inn H, S Channelview RV Ctr
781b	Market St, N Clarion H
781a	TX 8, Sam Houston Pkwy, S Gulf/dsl

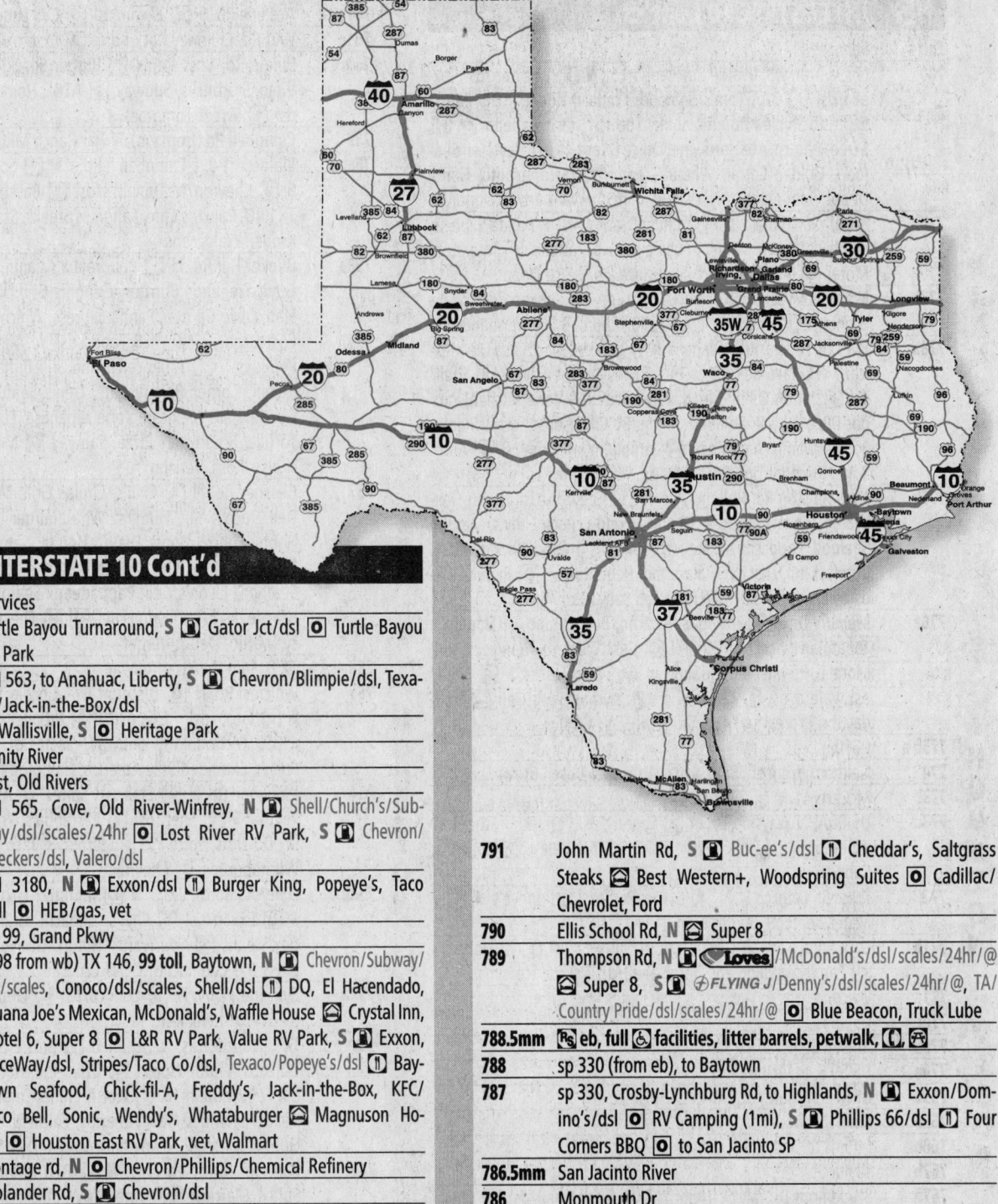

= gas = food = lodging = other = rest stop

TX

INTERSTATE 10 Cont'd

HOUSTON

Exit #	Services
780	(779a from wb) Uvalde Rd, Freeport St, N Chevron/dsl, Texaco/dsl Capt Tom's Seafood, China Dragon, IHOP, Panda Express, Shipley Donuts, Sonic, Subway, Taco Cabana H, $Tree, Aamco, Ace Hardware, Office Depot, S Baytown Seafood, Golden Corral, Whataburger Firestone/auto, Home Depot, Sam's Club/gas, U-Haul, Verizon, Walmart/McDonald's
779b	N Gulf, Valero/dsl China Dragon, IHOP, Panda Express, Shipley's Donuts, Sonic, Subway, Taco Cabana Interstate Motel $Tree, Aamco, Ace Hardware, Office Depot
778b	Normandy St, N Shell/Jack-in-the-Box, Texaco/dsl La Quinta, S Citgo/dsl Cafe Ko, Church's Normandy Inn
778a	FM 526, Federal Rd, Pasadena, N Burger King, Casa Ole Mexican, KFC/Taco Bell, Pizza Hut, Popeye's, Subway, S Shell/dsl James Coney Island, Pappadeaux Seafood Kitchen, Pappas BBQ, Pappa's Seafood, Peking Bo Chinese, Saltgrass Steaks, Sonic, Swamp Shack Rest. Lamplight Inn, Super 8 AutoZone, Discount Tire, O'Reilly Parts, Scottish Inn
776b	John Ralston Rd, Holland Ave, N Chevron/dsl, Exxon, Texaco Chulas Mexican, Denny's, Fuddruckers, Luby's, Mambo Seafood, Pappasito's Cantina, Subway Candlewood Suites, Comfort Inn, Day Inn, Palace Inn, Regency Inn Family$, Fiesta Foods, NTB, URGENT CARE, S same as 778
776a	Mercury Dr, N Arandas Mexican, Burger King, McDonald's, Tepatillan Mexican, TX Grill Best Western, Hampton Inn, Motel 6, Premier Inn, Quality Inn Volvo Trucks, S Shell/dsl, Valero/dsl Chili's, Cici's Pizza, Murphy's Deli Holiday Inn Express CVS Drug, URGENT CARE
775b a	I-610
774	Gellhorn (from eb) Blvd, S Anheuser-Busch Brewery
773b	McCarty St, N Chevron/dsl, Shell
773a	US 90A, N Wayside Dr, N Speedy/dsl Jack-in-the-Box, Whataburger, S Chevron/dsl, Shell/dsl, Valero Church's, Subway
772	Kress St, Lathrop St, N Exxon, Pemex Popeye's, S 7 Mares Seafood, Burger King
771b	Lockwood Dr, N Chevron/Subway/dsl McDonald's Family$, Walgreens, S Shell/dsl Palace Inn
771a	Waco St
770c	US 59 N
770b	Jenson St, Meadow St, Gregg St
770a	US 59 S, to Victoria
769c	McKee St, Hardy St, Nance St, downtown
769a	Smith St (from wb), to downtown
768b a	I-45, N to Dallas, S to Galveston
767b	Taylor St
767a	Studemont Dr, Yale St, Heights Blvd, S Shell/dsl Chick-fil-A, Chili's, Dickey's BBQ, KFC/Taco Bell, Panda Express, Subway AT&T, Petsmart, Staples, Target
766	(from wb), Heights Blvd, Yale St
765b	N Durham Dr, N Shepherd Dr, N Shell/dsl Wendy's Howard Johnson vet, S Valero/dsl Saltgrass Steaks
765a	TC Jester Blvd, S Exxon/dsl, Texaco/dsl Golden Hunan, Starbucks vet
764	Westcott St, Washington Ave, Katy Rd, N Denny's Hampton Inn, S Chevron IHOP, McDonald's Scottish Inn
763	I-610
762	Silber Rd, Post Oak Rd, N Chick-fil-A, Dave&Buster's, Jimmy John's, Panda Express, Red Robin, SteaKountry Chrysler/Dodge/Jeep, Fiat, Firestone/auto, IKEA, Walmart, S Jack-in-the-Box, Shipley Donuts Crowne Plaza, Holiday Inn Express

HOUSTON

Exit #	Services
761b	Antoine Rd, S Exxon/dsl CVS Drug
761a	Wirt Rd, Chimney Rock Rd, S Exxon/dsl CVS Drug
760	Bingle Rd, Voss Rd, N Burger Shack, Hunan Chef, Pue Viejo, Starbucks, Subway AT&T, Home Depot, S She dsl Sweet Tomatoes
759	Campbell Rd (from wb), N Ranch Mkt, same as 758b
758b	Blalock Rd, Campbell Rd, N Sonic H, Lowe S Chevron/McDonald's/dsl Baskin-Robbins, Goode TX BBQ, Pappy's Cafe, Saltgrass Steaks, Starbucks cleane Kroger, Walgreens
758a	Bunker Hill Rd, N Boudreaux's Cajun, Dennys, Egg&I, F Guys, Freebirds Burritos, Genghis Grill, Jimmy John's, Mar Slab, Olive Garden, Panda Express, Which Wich? Best B Costco/gas, GNC, HEB Foods/dsl, Jo-Ann, Lowe's, Michae PepBoys, S American Island Grill, Buffalo Wild Wings, Cir Italian, Corner Bakery Cafe, Denis Seafood, Firehouse Su Guadalajara Mexican, Kobe Japanese, Longhorn Steaks, Lu Tortilla, Russo's NY Pizza, Subway Memorial Inn M shall's, Ross, Verizon
757	Gessner Rd, N Chili's, Chulas Grill, McDonald's, Murph Deli, Taco Bell, Wendy's, Whataburger AT&T, CVS Dr Hobby Lobby, Home Depot, Honda, Sam's Club/gas, U-Ha S 59 Diner, Cheesecake Factory, Fuddrucker's, Goode Seafood, Jason's Deli, Pappadeaux Seafood, Pappasito's, P ry's Steaks Westin Hotel H, Firestone/auto, Ford, M cy's, Office Depot, Target
756	TX 8, Sam Houston Tollway
755	Willcrest Rd, N Discount Tire, Lincoln, Mazda, NTB, U-Ha S Citgo/dsl, Exxon/dsl Brenner's Steaks, Denny IHOP, McDonald's, Subway, Taste of TX Candlewo Suites, Extended Stay America, Hampton Inn, Sheraton
754	Kirkwood Rd, N Embassy Suites Audi/Porsche, Linco Toyota, S Shell/dsl Carrabba's, Prince's Burgers, Shi ley Do-Nuts, Spicy Pickle, Starbucks, Taco Cabana, Twin Pea Whataburger Chevrolet
753b	Dairy-Ashford Rd, N Infiniti, Lexus, Nissan, Vol S Exxon/dsl Chili's, Hibachi Grill, Subway, TX C tle Steaks Courtyard, Hilton Garden, Holiday Inn E press Cadillac, URGENT CARE
753a	Eldridge Pkwy, N Conoco/dsl Omni Hotel, S Va ro/dsl Kwik Kar
751	TX 6, to Addicks, N Shell Bros Pizza, Cattlegard Res Quiznos, Waffle House Drury Inn, Homewood Suites, S dio 6, Wyndham, S North China, Salata, Subway Be Value, Extended Stay America, Fairfield Inn, Hyatt House, Quinta, Motel 6, TownePlace Suites USPO
750	Park Ten Blvd, eb only, N Red Roof Inn, S Embas Suites, Marriott Acura, BMW, Buick/GMC, Hoover RV Ctr
748	Barker-Cypress Rd, N Exxon/Subway BurgerTex Gr Coaches Grill, El Rancho Mexican, Firehouse Subs, Popey Smoothie Factory, Tony's Mexican Residence Inn S Cracker Barrel Hyundai, Subaru, vet, VW
747b a	Fry Rd, N Gulf/dsl, Shell/dsl Applebee's, Arby Buffalo Wild Wings, Burger King, Chipotle, Denny's, D Five Guys, Jimmy John's, McDonald's, Panda Express, Pan ra Bread, Pizza Hut, Smoothie King, Sonic, Souper Sala Starbucks, Subway, Taco Bell, Waffle House, Whatabu er Candlewood Suites AAA, Best Buy, HEB Foo gas, Hobby Lobby, Home Depot, Jo-Ann, Kohl's, Kroge dsl, Ross, Sam's Club/gas, URGENT CARE, Verizon, v Walgreens, Walmart, S Shell/dsl Captain To Seafood, Fazoli's, IHOP, McDonald's, Outback Steaks, P belly, Quiznos, Smashburger, Star Chinese, Starbuc

E INTERSTATE 10 Cont'd

Exit	Services
747b a	Continued TX Mesquite Grill, Wendy's, Willie's Woodspring Suites Hotel H, A&T, Katy Drug, Lowe's, NTB, Office Depot, Petsmart, Randall's Mkt, Target, TJ Maxx, U-Haul
746	W Green Blvd, N RaceWay/dsl BJ's Rest., Chang's Chinese, Cheddar's, Chuy's Mexican, Firehouse Subs, Kublai Khan Stirfry, Longhorn Steaks, Nagoya Japanese, Olive Garden, Orleans Seafood Kitchen, Springcreek BBQ, Stadia Grill, Steak'n Shake, TX Roadhouse, Wild Wings Cafe Holiday Inn Express, Palace Inn, S Carl's Jr, Jimmy Changas TexMex Home2 Christian Bros Automotive, CVS Drug, Ford, Honda
745	Mason Rd, N CarMax, S Shell/dsl, Valero/dsl Babin's Seafood, Blackeyed Pea, Burger King, Carino's Italian, Chick-fil-A, Chili's, CiCi's, Dickey's BBQ, DQ, El Patron Mexican, Freebirds Burrito, Hooters, Jack-in-the-Box, Jason's Deli, KFC, Landry's Seafood, Luby's, McDonald's, Panda Express, Papa John's, Pizza Hut, Popeye's, Rudy's BBQ/gas, SaltGrass Steaks, Schlotzsky's, Subway, Taco Bell, Taco Cabana, Whataburger, Which Wich? Comfort Inn&Suites, Hampton Inn, La Quinta, Motel 6, Super 8 $Tree, 99c Store, AutoZone, Chevrolet, Chrysler/Dodge/Jeep, Discount Tire, Fiesta Foods, Firestone/auto, Goodyear/auto, HEB Food/gas, Kia, Toyota, transmissions, Walgreens
743	TX 99, Grand Pkwy, Peek Rd, N La Madeleine, Red Robin H, JC Penney, S Freddy's Steakburgers, Subway Costco/gas, URGENT CARE
741	(742 from wb)Katy-Fort Bend County Rd, Pin Oak Rd, S Murphy USA/dsl, Shell/dsl, Texaco/dsl Alegra Brazilian, Alicia's Mexican, Antonia's Rest, Chick-fil-A, ChuckECheese, CiCi's Pizza, Denny's, Fuddruckers, Jack-in-the-Box, Jimmy John's, JoJo's Mongolian Grill, KFC, LJ Silver/Taco Bell, Los Cucos, Pizza Hut, Popeyes, Rainforest Cafe, Red Lobster, Smashburger, Starbucks, Subway, Subway, TGIFriday's, Whataburger Best Western, Comfort Suites, Country Inn & Suites, Courtyard, Hilton Garden, Holiday Inn, Homewood Suites, Residence Inn, SpringHill Suites H, $Tree, AT&T, BassPro Shops, BooksAMillion, Discount Tire, HEB/dsl, Katy Mills Outlet/famous brands, Marshall's, Nissan, Ross, URGENT CARE, Verizon, Walgreens, Walmart/McDonald's
740	FM 1463, N Exxon/dsl, S Shell/McDonald's/dsl Starbucks
739	Cane Island Pkwy, N Buc-ee's/dsl, S Camping World
737	Pederson Rd, N Buc-ee's/dsl, Loves/Arby's/dsl/scales/24hr, S Camping World RV Super Ctr, Holiday World RV Ctr
735	Igloo Rd
734	Woods Rd
732	FM 359, to Brookshire, N FLYING J/Denny's/dsl/LP/scales/24hr/@, Exxon/Chester's/dsl, Shell Church's, Orlando's Pizza, Subway Executive Inn, S Chevron/dsl, Shell/McDonald's/dsl Burger King, Jack-in-the-Box, Popeye's, Taco Bell Holiday Inn Express, Super 8 truck lube, truckwash
731	FM 1489, to Koomey Rd, N Exxon/dsl Ernesto's Mexican Brooke Hotel Houston W RV Park, S Texaco/Dickey's BBQ/dsl La Quinta
729	Peach Ridge Rd, Donigan Rd (730 from wb), S Kathy's/dsl/rest./24hr
726	Chew Rd (from eb), S golf
725	Mlcak Rd (from wb), S Kathy's Korner/dsl
723	FM 1458, to San Felipe, N Exxon/Subway/dsl/scales/ 24hr Peterbilt, to Stephen F Austin SP (3mi), S Riverside Tire

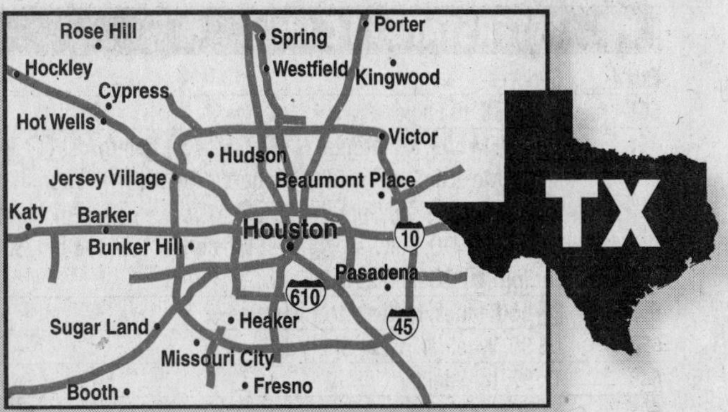

SEALY • COLUMBUS

Exit	Services
721	(from wb) US 90, N Shell/Chester's/dsl Chrysler/Dodge/Jeep, Ford
720a	Outlet Ctr Dr, N Shell/Chester's/dsl
720	TX 36, to Sealy, N Shell/dsl DQ, Hartz Chicken Buffet, McDonald's, Sonic, Tony's Rest. $General, Jones RV Ctr, O'Reilly Parts, Walgreens, S Chevron/Burger King/dsl, Murphy USA/dsl, Shell/dsl, Texaco/dsl Cazadore's Mexican, Chicken Express, Domino's, Ernesto's Cantina, Hinze's BBQ, Jack-in-the-Box, Jin's Asian, Pizza Hut, Subway, Whataburger Best Value Inn, Countryside Inn, Holiday Inn Express, Super 8 $Tree, Verizon, Walmart/Subway
718	US 90 (from eb), to Sealy, N Valero/Huddle House/Subway/dsl, S Exxon/Prasek's Smokehouse/dsl
716	Pyka Rd, N Sunoco/dsl/rest./showers/24hr/@
713	Beckendorff Rd
709	FM 2761, Bernardo Rd, N TA/Carl's Jr/Subway/Dunkin'/dsl/scales/24hr
704	FM 949, N Happy Oaks RV Park (3mi)
699	FM 102, to Eagle Lake, N Happy Oaks RV Park, S Eagle Lake SP (14mi)
698	Alleyton Rd, N Mikeska's BBQ, S Shell/Taco Bell/BBQ/dsl, Valero/Subway/dsl Chrysler/Dodge/Jeep, Ford
697mm	Little Colorado River
696	TX 71, Columbus, N Exxon/Burger King/dsl, Shell/dsl #1 Buffet, Blake St. Grill, Jack-in-the-Box, Pizza Hut, Schobel's Rest., Whataburger, Zapata Mexican Columbus Inn, Holiday Inn Express H, AT&T, AutoZone, HEB Foods, Walmart, S Chevron/dsl, Conoco/Church's/Subway/dsl, Phillips 66/dsl Los Cabos Mexican, McDonald's, Nancy's Steaks, Sonic Baymont Inn, Best Value, LaQuinta Columbus RV Park
695	TX 71 (from wb), to La Grange
693	FM 2434, to Glidden
692mm	**both lanes, full facilities, litter barrels, petwalk, RV dump, vending**
689	US 90, to Hattermann Lane, N Whispering Oaks RV Park
682	FM 155, to Wiemar, N Shell/dsl, Valero/dsl DQ, McDonald's, Subway/Texas Burger Motel 6 H, $General, Lowe's Mkt, Tire Pros, S 76/Church's/dsl/24hr, Loves/Chester's/Wendy's/dsl/scales/24hr Buick/Chevrolet/GMC
678mm	E Navidad River
677	US 90
674	US 77, Schulenburg, N Pilot/Taco Bell/PJ Fresh/dsl/scales/24hr, Sunoco/Stripes/Taco Co Oak Ridge Smokehouse Best Value Inn, Executive Inn Ford, Potter Country Store, S Exxon/dsl, Valero/Subway DQ, Los Agaves, Lucy's Grill, Taco Rodeo, Whataburger Best Western+, Holiday Inn Express $General, Family$, O'Reilly Parts, Schulenberg RV Park
672mm	W Navidad River

= gas = food = lodging = other = rest stop

TX

INTERSTATE 10 Cont'd

Exit #	Services
668	FM 2238, to Engle
661	TX 95, FM 609, to Flatonia, N Citgo/dsl, Valero/dsl Jessito's Mexican, Joel's BBQ, Robert's Steaks Flatonia RV Ranch (1mi), S Shell/McDonald's/Grumpy's Rest./motel/dsl, Valero DQ, Subway Best Western+, Carefree Inn, Sunset Inn $General, NAPA
658mm	both lanes, tables, litter barrels
653	US 90, Waelder, N Shell/dsl
649	TX 97, to Waelder
642	TX 304, to Gonzales
637	FM 794, to Harwood
632	US 90/183, to Gonzales, N Love's/Subway/dsl/scales/24hr Best Western+, Coachway Inn (2mi), La Quinta, S Buc-ee's/dsl camping, to Palmetto SP (5mi)
630mm	San Marcos River
628	TX 80, to Luling, N Citgo (2mi), Valero/pizza/dsl/24hr H, Riverbend RV Park
625	Darst Field Rd
624.5mm	Smith Creek
621mm	weigh sta both lanes
620	FM 1104
618mm	both lanes, full facitlities, petwalk,
617	FM 2438, to Kingsbury
614	toll 130 N, to Austin, Waco
612	US 90
611mm	Geronimo Creek
610	TX 123, to San Marcos, N Exxon/Circle K/dsl, Shell/Subway/dsl Chili's, Giuseppe Pizza, IHOP, Los Cucos Mexican, Starbucks Comfort Inn, Days Inn, Hampton Inn, Holiday Inn Express, TownePlace Suites Carters Tires, S Valero/dsl Taco Cabana H
609	TX 123, Austin St, S Phillips 66/dsl, Sunoco/dsl Chevrolet, Home Depot
607	TX 46, FM 78, to New Braunfels, N Valero/Jack-in-the-Box/dsl Motel 6 Ford, S Exxon/dsl, Shell/Circle K/dsl Bill Miller BBQ, Dixie Grille, Garcia's Mexican, McDonald's, Subway, Whataburger Best Value, La Quinta Chrysler/Dodge/Jeep
605	FM 464, N Twin Palms RV Park
605mm	Guadalupe River
604	FM 725, to Lake McQueeney, N Love's/Arby's/dsl/scales/24hr Twin Palms RV Park
603	US 90 E, US 90A, to Seguin, N D&A RV Park, Seguin RV Ctr, S Explore USA RV Ctr
601	FM 775, to New Berlin, N Chevron/Subway/dsl/scales/24hr
600	Schwab Rd
599	FM 465, to Marion
599mm	Santa Clara Creek
597	Santa Clara Rd, N auto racetrack
595	Zuehl Rd
594mm	Cibolo Creek
593	FM 2538, Trainer Hale Rd, N Texaco/dsl tires, S Exxon/Lucille's Rest./dsl/24hr
593mm	Woman Hollering Creek
591	FM 1518, to Schertz, N Alamo Trvl Ctr/Shell/dsl repair, S Valero/Circle K/dsl/e85
589	Pfeil Rd, Graytown Rd
589mm	Salatrillo Creek
587	LP 1604, Randolph AFB, to Universal City, N EVC/CNG, S Shell/McDonald's/dsl Whataburger

KIRBY

SAN ANTONIO

585.5mm	Escondido Creek
585	FM 1516, to Converse, N Chevron/Church's/dsl/scales/2 Best Western+, S Kenworth, Peterbilt/GMC/Freightlin
585mm	Martinez Creek
583	Foster Rd, N FLYING J/Denny's/dsl/LP/scales/24hr/ Valero/Subway/dsl/24hr Jack-in-the-Box Comfort I La Quinta Blue Beacon, Speedco Lube, Tire Mart, S T Chevron/Burger King/Pizza Hut/Popeye's/dsl/24hr/@
582.5mm	Rosillo Creek
582	Ackerman Rd, Kirby, N Pilot/Subway/dsl/scales/24 S Petro/Iron Skillet/dsl/scales/24hr/@ El Rodeo Me ican Knights Inn Blue Beacon, Petrolube
581	I-410
580	LP 13, WW White Rd, N Chevron/dsl, Valero/dsl Playa Seafood, Wendy's Red Roof Inn, Rodeway Inn, S per 7 tires, S Exxon/7-11, Valero Bill Miller BB El Rodeo Mexican, Lazaritas Mexican, McDonald's, Pizza H Popeye's, Subway Best Value, Motel 6, Super 8 Far ly$, Ford/Volvo Trucks, tires/repair
579	Houston St, N Valero/dsl Starbucks Quality I Penske, S Chevron, Stripes/Valero/dsl Days I Knights Inn, Upland Inn
578	Pecan Valley Dr, ML King Dr, S Shell/Subway/dsl
577	US 87 S, to Roland Ave, S Whataburger Best Western+, Super 8
576	New Braunfels Ave, Gevers St, S Valero McDonald's
575	Pine St, Hackberry St, S Little Red Barn Steaks
574	I-37, US 281
573	Probandt St, N Jack-in-the-Box, Miller's BBQ, S Va ro tires/repair, to SA Missions HS
I-10 and I-35 run together 3 miles. See I-35, exits 156-154a.	
569c	Santa Rosa St, to Our Lady of the Lake U, downtown
568	spur 421, Culebra Ave, Bandera Ave, S to St Marys U
567	Lp 345, Fredericksburg Rd (from eb upper level accesses I-35 I-10 E, US 87 S, lower level accesses I-35 N)
566b	Fresno Dr, S Exxon/dsl Galaxy Inn
566a	West Ave, N Exxon/7-11 DQ, Subway, Whatabur er CarCare
565c	(from wb), access to same as 565 a b, S Shell Jimad Mexican, Starbucks La Quinta
565b	Vance Jackson Rd, N Murphy USA/dsl Bill Miller BB IHOP Comfort Inn, Days Inn, EconoLodge Walma S Shell/dsl Holiday Inn Express
565a	Crossroads Blvd, Balcone's Heights, N Shell/dsl Hov ard Johnson vet, S Valero/dsl Crossroads BB Dave&Buster's, Denny's, El Pollo Loco, McDonald's, Wh taburger SpringHill Suites Firestone/auto, Hobby Lo by, Mazda, Office Depot, Target
564b a	I-410, services off of I-410 W, Fredericksburg Rd
563	Callaghan Rd, N Valero Las Palapas Mexican, Subw Embassy Suites, Marriott $General, Ford, Sprouts Mk Toyota, S Exxon/7-11 Mamacita's Rest. Lowe's
561	Wurzbach Rd, N Texaco/dsl Bolo's Grille, Broadw 5050 Grill, County Line BBQ, Egg&I, Firehouse Subs, Fuddruc er's, Honeybaked Ham, Jason's Deli, Pappasito's Cantin Popeye's, Sea Island Shrimphouse, Taste Of China, TX Land Cattle, Wasabi Grill Extended Stay America, Homewoo Suites, Hyatt Place, Motel 6, Staybridge Suites AutoZon BigLots, HEB Food/gas, Office Depot, Porsche, Tuesday Mor ing, S Shell/dsl 210 Ceviche Seafood, Alamo Café, A by's, Chester's Burgers, China Sea, Church's, Denny's, El Ta Tote, Jack-in-the-Box, Mamma Margie's Mexican, McDonald'

INTERSTATE 10 Cont'd

561	Continued Pizza Hut, Ruby Tuesday, Sumo Japanese, Taco Bell, Wendy's [lodging] Baymont Inn, Best Western, Candlewood Suites, Drury Inn, Hawthorn Suites, La Quinta, Motel 6, Sleep Inn [other] [H], CarMax
560b	frontage rd (from eb), same as 561
560a	Huebner Rd, N [food] CA Pizza Kitchen, Chipotle, Fare Wok, Genghis Grill, La Madeleine, Macaroni Grill, Panera Bread, Pericos Mexican, Salata, SaltGrass Steaks [other] Cadillac, Chrysler/Jeep/Dodge, Fiat, Nissan, Old Navy, Ross, S [gas] Chevron, Exxon, Shell/Jack-in-the-Box/dsl [food] Cracker Barrel, Jim's Rest., Miller's BBQ [lodging] Days Inn, Quality Inn, TownePlace Suites
559	Lp 335, US 87, Fredericksburg Rd, N [food] Pearl Inn [lodging] Holiday Inn Express [other] Acura, S [food] Krispy Kreme, Shell/Jack-in-the-Box/dsl [lodging] Comfort Suites, Days Inn, HomeGate Studios, Rodeway Inn, SpringHill Suites [other] Infiniti
558	De Zavala Rd, N [gas] Chevron, Shell/Subway [food] Bill Miller BBQ, Burger King, Carrabba's, Chick-fil-A, Chili's, Five Guys, Fox&Hound, KFC/Taco Bell, Logan's Roadhouse, McDonald's, Outback Steaks, Sonic, Starbucks, Taco Cabana, The Earl of Sandwich, Wendy's [other] HEB Foods, Home Depot, Marshall's, PetCo, Petsmart, Steinmart, Target, S [food] IHOP, Popeye's, Schlotzsky's [lodging] Days Inn, SpringHill Suites, Studio 6 [other] Discount Tire, Sam's Club/gas, Verizon, Walmart
557	Spur 53, N [gas] Exxon/7-11/dsl [food] Cheddar's, Chuy's Mexican [lodging] Best Western, EconoLodge, Embassy Suites, Howard Johnson, Super 8 [other] Audi, Chevrolet, Hyundai, Jaguar/Mazerati/Ferrari, S [gas] Valero/Subway/dsl [food] A&W/LJ Silver, Cici's Pizza, Huhot Chinese, IHOP, Matamoro's Cantina, Quiznos, Twin Peaks, Whataburger, Zio's Italian [lodging] Holiday Inn [other] Costco/gas, Land Rover, Sams Club/gas, Univ of TX at San Antonio, Walmart
556b	frontage rd
556a	to Anderson Lp, S [other] to Seaworld, Six Flags
555	La Cantera Pkwy, N [food] 54th St Rest., BJ's Rest., Bob's Chophouse, Chick-fil-A, Coldstone, Freddy's Steakburger, Islamorada Rest., Maggiano's Little Italy, McDonald's/playplace, Mimi's Cafe, Panera Bread, Popeye's, Potbelly, Red Robin, Sonic, Starbucks, Tiago's, Whataburger, Which Wich? [lodging] Courtyard, Hilton Garden, Residence Inn [other] $Tree, AT&T, Bass Pro Shops, Best Buy, Dick's, GNC, Hobby Lobby, JC Penney, Lowe's, Michaels, Old Navy, Petsmart, Ross, Staples, Target, TJ Maxx, World Mkt, S [food] Applebee's, Longhorn Steaks, Olive Garden, Red Lobster [lodging] Drury Inn, La Quinta, Motel 6 [other] Honda, to La Cantera Pkwy
554	Camp Bullis Rd, N [gas] Texaco/dsl [other] Russell CP, S [gas] Shell/dsl [lodging] Rodeway Inn
552	Dominion Dr, Stonewall Pkwy, S [food] Aldo's Rest., Bourbon St. Kitchen, La Gloria [other] Audi, CVS Drug, Lexus, Subaru, VW
551	Boerne Stage Rd (from wb), to Leon Springs, N [gas] Shamrock/dsl [food] Rudy's BBQ, Sonic, S [food] Las Palapas Mexican, Longhorns Rest., Papa Nacho's, Starbucks, Subway [other] CarX, GNC, HEB Foods/dsl, Tesla
550	FM 3351, Ralph Fair Rd, N [gas] Exxon/McDonald's/dsl, Valero/dsl [food] Rudy's BBQ/gas, Willie's Cafe [lodging] La Quinta, S [gas] Shell/Domino's/dsl [food] Bill Miller's BBQ, Laguna Madre, Schlotsky's, Taco Cabana, Whataburger [other] Walgreens, Walmart
546	Fair Oaks Pkwy, Tarpon Dr, N [gas] Shell/dsl [food] Papa John's [other] American Dream RV Ctr, CVS Drug, ExploreUSA RV Ctr, Harley-Davidson, vet, S [gas] Chevron/dsl/café, Exxon/dsl/café [other] Belden's Automotive, Fair Oaks Automotive, Hoover RV Ctr

SAN ANTONIO

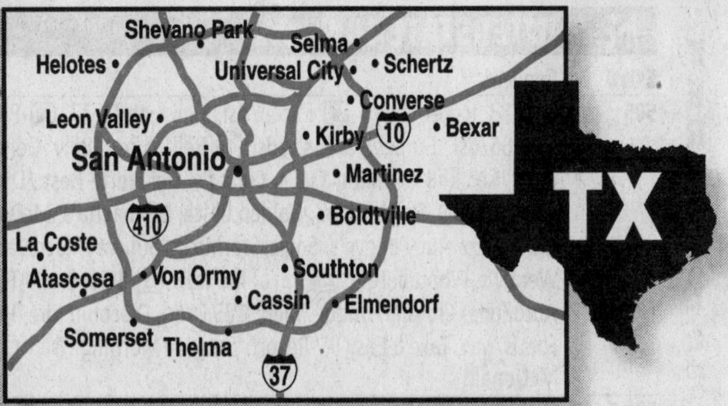

TX

543	Boerne Stage Rd, to Scenic LP Rd, N [gas] Valero/Circle K/Subway/dsl [lodging] Fairfield Inn [other] Ancira RV Ctr, Buick/GMC, Chevrolet, Chrysler/Dodge/Jeep, Ford, NAPA, tires/repair, to Cascade Caverns/camping (3mi), S [other] Explore USA RV Ctr, Infiniti, Mercedes, Nissan, Toyota
542	(from wb), N [gas] Shamrock [food] Domino's, Pizza Hut, Subway, Wendy's [other] $Tree, Alamo Fiesta RV Park, O'Reilly Parts, same as 540, Verizon
540	TX 46, to New Braunfels, N [gas] Exxon/Taco Bell/dsl, Murphy USA/dsl, Shell/dsl [food] Burger King, Centinela Mexican, Church's, Denny's, DQ, Guadalajara Mexican, Little Caesar's, Papa Murphy's, Pizza Hut, Shanghai Chinese, Sonic, Subway, Taco Cabana, Wendy's [lodging] Comfort Inn, Days Inn, Motel 6 [other] AutoZone, Discount Tire, HEB Food/dsl, Verizon, vet, Walgreens, Walmart, S [food] Chili's, Starbucks, Whataburger [lodging] Hampton Inn [other] [H], Home Depot
539	Johns Rd, N [lodging] Best Western, S [gas] Valero/dsl/LP
538mm	Cibolo Creek
538	Ranger Creek Rd
537	US 87, to Boerne
533	FM 289, Welfare, N [food] PoPo Family Rest. [other] Top of the Hill RV Park (1mi)
532mm	Little Joshua Creek
531mm	**[picnic] wb, tables, litter barrels**
530mm	Big Joshua Creek
529.5mm	**[picnic] eb, tables, litter barrels**
527	FM 1621 (from wb), to Waring
526.5mm	Holiday Creek
524	TX 27, FM 1621, to Waring, N [other] vet, **1 mi** S [gas] Chevron, Shell/dsl
523.5mm	Guadalupe River
523	US 87 N, to Comfort, N [gas] Chevron/Chicken Express/dsl, Loves/McDonald's/Subway/dsl/scales/24hr, S [gas] Exxon/dsl [food] DQ [lodging] Executive Inn [other] $General, RV Park/LP
521.5mm	Comfort Creek
520	FM 1341, to Cypress Creek Rd
515mm	Cypress Creek
514mm	**[rest stop] both lanes, full [handicapped] facilities, litter barrels, petwalk, [phone], [picnic], playground, RV dump, vending, wireless internet**
508	TX 16, Kerrville, N [gas] Exxon/dsl [other] Buick/Cadillac/Chevrolet, **0-2 mi** S [gas] Exxon, Shell/McDonald's/dsl/24hr, Stripes/Taco Co, Valero/dsl/e-85 [food] Margarita's Mexican, Bella Sera Italian, Burger King, Chicken Express, Cracker Barrel, Good Taste Asian, IHOP, Jack-in-the-Box, Little Caesar's, McDonald's, Schlotzsky's, Sonic, Taco Bell, Taco Casa [lodging] Best Western, Days Inn, Hampton Inn, Holiday Inn Express, La Quinta, Motel 6, Quality Inn, Super 8, Yo Ranch Hotel [other] [H], $Tree, Advance Parts, BigLots, Home Depot, Kerrville RV Ctr, Lowe's, O'Reilly Parts, Walgreens

KERRVILLE

TX

INTERSTATE 10 Cont'd

KERRVILLE

Exit #	Services
505	FM 783, to Kerrville, S Exxon/dsl, 3 mi S on TX 27 Phillips 66/dsl, Stripes/Taco Co/dsl Belle Vita, Billy Gene's Rest., Chick-fil-A, Chili's, CiCi's, Culver's, Del Norte Rest., Dickey's BBQ, DQ, Fuddruckers, Golden Chick, Mamacita's, McDonald's, Pizza Hut, Popeye's, Sonic, Starbucks, Subway, Taco Casa, Wendy's, Whataburger Inn of the Hills $General, AT&T, AutoZone, Chrysler/Dodge/Jeep, CVS Drug, Discount Tire, HEB Foods/gas, Take It Easy RV Resort, Tuesday Morning, Walmart/McDonald's
503.5mm	scenic views both lanes, litter barrels
501	FM 1338, N Buckhorn RV Resort, S KOA (2mi)
497mm	scenic views both lanes, litter barrels
492	FM 479
490	TX 41
488	TX 27, to Ingram, Mountain Home
484	Midway Rd
477	US 290, to Fredericksburg
476.5mm	service rd eb
472	Old Segovia Rd
465	FM 2169, to Segovia, S Phillips 66/rest./dsl River Valley Inn/RV park
464.5mm	Johnson Fork Creek
462	US 83 S, to Uvalde
461mm	eb, tables, litter barrels
460	(from wb), to Junction
459mm	wb, tables, litter barrels
457	FM 2169, to Junction, N Shell/dsl, S Econolodge RV camping, S. Llano River SP

JUNCTION

Exit #	Services
456.5mm	Llano River
456	US 83/377; Junction, N Alon/dsl, Chevron/dsl, Shell/McDonald's/dsl/24hr Cooper's BBQ, Tia Nena's Mexican Motel 6, S Conoco/dsl, Exxon/dsl, Phillips 66/dsl, Pilot/Subway/PJ Fresh/dsl/scales/24hr DQ, Isaack Rest., La Familia Mexican, Lum's BBQ, Sonic Best Western, Holiday Inn Express, Lazy T Motel, Legends Inn, Rodeway Inn, Sun Valley Motel, The Hills Motel H, $General, Best Hardware, Family$, Lowe's Mkt, Plumley's Store, S Llano RV Park, to S Llano River SP
452.5mm	Bear Creek
451	RM 2291, to Cleo Rd
448mm	North Creek
445	RM 1674, S camping
444.5mm	Stark Creek
442mm	Copperas Creek
442	RM 1674, to Ft McKavett, N to Ft McKavett SHS
439mm	N Llano River
438	Lp 291 (from wb), to Roosevelt, same as 437
437	Lp 291 (from eb, no EZ return), to Roosevelt, 1 mi N Simon Bros Mercantile/dsl USPO
429	RM 3130, to Harrell
423mm	parking area both lanes, litter barrels
420	RM 3130, to Baker Rd
412	Allison Rd, RM 3130

SONORA

Exit #	Services
404	RM 3130, RM 864, N to Ft McKavett St HS, 3 mi S Love's/Chester's/dsl/scales/24hr, Stripes/Taco Co H
400	US 277, Sonora, N Road Ranger/Church's/desk Sutton Co Steaks Motel 6, S Alon/7-11/dsl, Sunoco/dsl, Sunoco/Stripes/dsl DQ, La Mexicana Rest., Pizza Hut, Sonic, Taco Grill Quality Inn, Super 8, Surestay Family$, USPO
399	(from eb)LP 467, Sonora, N Motel 6, S Sunoco/dsl, Sunoco/Stripes/Taco Co DQ H, RV camping

Exit #	Services
394mm	both lanes, full facilities, litter barrel, petwalk, RV dump
392	RM 1989, Caverns of Sonora Rd, 8 mi S Caverns of Sonc Camping
388	RM 1312 (from wb)
381	RM 1312 (from eb)
372	Taylor Box Rd, N Exxon/rest./dsl/scales/24hr Super auto museum, Circle Bar RV Park
368	LP 466, N same as 365 & 363

OZONA

Exit #	Services
365	TX 163, Ozona, N Stripes/Godfather's/Taco Co/dsl, S noco/dsl, Valero/dsl Cafe Next Door, DQ, Sonic, Su way Best Value Inn, Economy Inn/RV Park, Hampton I Hillcrest Inn, Holiday Inn Express, Quality Inn H, $Gener dsl/auto repair, NAPA, to David Crockett Mon, S Pilot dsl, Sunoco/Stripes El Chato's city park
363	Lp 466, to Ozona
361	RM 2083, Pandale Rd
357mm	Eureka Draw
351mm	Howard Draw
350	FM 2398, to Howard Draw
349mm	parking area wb, litter barrels
346mm	parking area eb, litter barrels
343	TX 290 W, S Ft. Lancaster Historic Site
337	Live Oak Rd
336.5mm	Live Oak Creek
328	River Rd, Sheffield
327.5mm	Pecos River
325	TX 290, TX 349, to Iraan, Sheffield, N H
320	frontage rd
314	frontage rd
309mm	both lanes, full facilities, litter barrels, petwalk, wireless internet
307	US 190, FM 305, to Iraan, N H
298	RM 2886
294	FM 11, Bakersfield, N Exxon, S Chevron/café/
288	Ligon Rd, N many windmills
285	McKenzie Rd, S Domaine Cordier Ste Genevieve Winery
279mm	eb, tables, litter barrels
277	FM 2023
273	US 67/385, to McCamey, wb, tables, litter barrels
272	University Rd
264	Warnock Rd, N Fort Stockton RV Park/Roadrunner Cafe
261	US 290 W, US 385 S, N Exxon/dsl, S Love's/Ca Jr/dsl/scales/24hr, Shell/dsl, Stripes/dsl DQ, Pizza H Sonic, Subway All Inn, Budget Inn, Deluxe Inn, Executi Inn H, RV camping, to Big Bend NP

FT STOCKTON

Exit #	Services
259b a	(259 from eb)TX 18, FM 1053, Ft Stockton, N Shell/Bur er King/dsl I-10 RV Park, S FLYING J/Subway/ds scales/24hr H
257	US 285, to Pecos, Ft Stockton, N Stripes/Sunoco/Taco C dsl/scales24hr Camp Stockton RV Park, golf, S Chevro dsl, Exxon/dsl, Shell/dsl, Valero/dsl Bush's Chicken, Dic ey's BBQ, DQ, KFC/Taco Bell, Little Caesar's, McDonald's, P cos Roadhouse, Pizza Hut, Pizza Pro, Sonic, Steak House, Su way Atrium West Inn, Best Western+, Candlewood Suite Days Inn, Fairfield Inn, Hampton Inn, La Quinta, Quality In Texan Inn $General, $Tree, Ace Hardware, Advance a Par AutoZone, Buick/Chevrolet, Comanche Land RV Park, Family Firestone/auto, Lowe's Foods, O'Reilly Parts, Williams Tires
256	to US 385 S, Ft Stockton, N HillTop RV, S Shell/d Walmart/dsl Domino's, Howard's Drive-In, K-Bob's Steal

INTERSTATE 10 Cont'd

256 Continued
Subway [lodging] Comfort Suites, Holiday Inn Express, Motel 6, Sleep Inn, Super 8 [other] auto/RV repair, Big Bend NP, Chrysler/Jeep/Dodge, Ford, to Ft Stockton Hist Dist, vet, Walmart

253 FM 2037, to Belding

248 US 67, FM 1776, to Alpine, S [other] to Big Bend NP

246 Firestone

241 Kennedy Rd

235 Mendel Rd

233mm **[Rs] both lanes, full [handicapped] facilities, litter barrels, petwalk, [phone], [picnic]**

229 Hovey Rd

222 Hoefs Rd

214 (from wb), FM 2448

212 TX 17, FM 2448, to Pecos, N [other] [picnic], litter barrels, S [gas] Saddleback RV Camping, Valero/I-10 Fuel/café/dsl

209 TX 17, S [other] Ft Davis NHS, to Balmorhea SP, to Davis Mtn SP

206 FM 2903, to Balmorhea, Toyah, 2 mi S [gas] GasCard [food] Uncles Rest. [other] to Balmorhea SP, USPO

192 FM 3078, to Toyahvale, S [other] to Balmorhea SP

188 Giffin Rd

187 I-20, to Ft Worth, Dallas

186 I-10, E to San Antonio (from wb)

185mm **[picnic] both lanes, tables, litter barrels**

184 Springhills

181 Cherry Creek Rd, S [gas] Chevron/dsl

176 TX 118, FM 2424, to Kent, S [other] Davis Mtn SP, Ft Davis, to McDonald Observatory

173 Hurd's Draw Rd

166 Boracho Sta

159 Plateau, N [gas] Exxon/rest./dsl/24hr

153 Michigan Flat

146 Wild Horse Rd, Wild Horse Rd

146mm **weigh sta wb**

145mm **[Rs] both lanes, full [handicapped] facilities, litter barrels, petwalk, [picnic], wireless internet**

140b Ross Dr, Van Horn, N [gas] Love's/Subway/dsl/scales/24hr, Valero/dsl [lodging] Days Inn, Desert Inn, Sands Motel/rest. [other] Desert Willow RV Park, repair, S [other] Mountain View RV Park/dump

140a US 90, TX 54, Van Horn Dr, N [gas] Alon/dsl [lodging] Hotel El Capitan [other] [H], NAPA, S [gas] Pilot/Wendy's/dsl/scales/24hr, Valero/dsl [food] Papa's Pantry [other] dsl/tire repair, RV Dump, Van Horn RV Park

138 Lp 10, to Van Horn, N [food] Chuy's Rest. [lodging] Budget Inn, EconoLodge, Economy Inn, Knights Inn, Motel 6, Red Roof Inn, Value Inn [other] $General, auto/dsl repair, city park, Oasis RV Park, Porter Foods, Southern Star RV Park, UPSO, visitor info, S [gas] Chevron/dsl/24hr, Tesla EVC [food] McDonald's [lodging] Hampton Inn, Holiday Inn Express, Quality Inn, Super 8 [other] tires/repair

137mm **weigh sta eb**

136mm **scenic overlook wb, [picnic], litter barrels**

135mm Mountain/Central time zone

133 (from wb) frontage rd

129 to Hot Wells, Allamore

108 to Sierra Blanca (from wb), same as 107

107 FM 1111, Sierra Blanca Ave, N [gas] Exxon/Subway/dsl/24hr [food] Delfina's Mexican [other] to Hueco Tanks SP, truck/tire repair, USPO, S [gas] Chevron/dsl [lodging] Americana Inn [other] Stagecoach Trading Post

105 (106 from wb) Lp 10, Sierra Blanca, same as 107

102.5mm **insp sta eb**

99 Lasca Rd, N [other] **[picnic] both lanes, litter barrels, no restrooms**

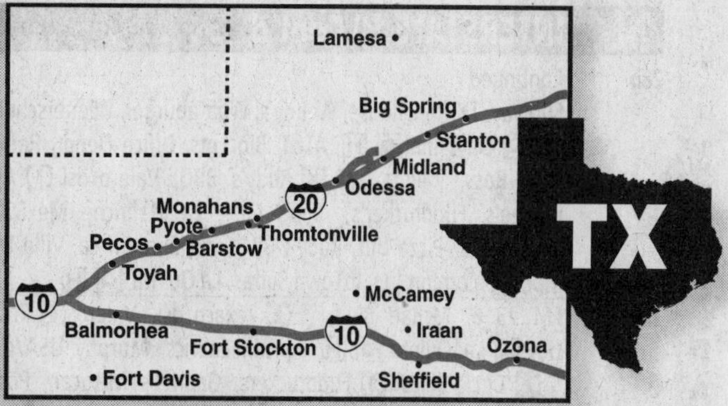

98mm **[picnic] eb, litter barrels, no restrooms**

95 frontage rd (from eb)

87 FM 34, S [gas] DriversMart/dsl

85 Esperanza Rd

81 FM 2217

78 TX 20 W, to McNary

77mm **truck parking area wb**

72 spur 148, to Ft Hancock, S [gas] Shell/dsl [food] Angie's Rest. [lodging] Ft Hancock Motel [other] Family$, USPO

68 Acala Rd

55 Tornillo

51mm **[Rs] both lanes, full [handicapped] facilities, litter tables, petwalk, [picnic]**

49 FM 793, Fabens, S [gas] Shell/dsl [food] Church's, Little Caesar's, McDonald's, Subway [lodging] Fabens Inn/Cafe [other] Family$, San Eli Foods

42 FM 1110, to Clint, S [gas] Express/dsl [food] Cotton Eyed Joe's, Mamacita's Rest. [lodging] Adobe Inn, Best Western, Cotton Valley Motel/RV Park/rest./dump

37 FM 1281, Horizon Blvd, N [gas] Flying J/Denny's/dsl/scales/24hr/@, Love's/Chester's/Subway/dsl/scales/24hr/@ [lodging] Americana Inn [other] Freightliner, RV Camping, Speedco Lube, S [gas] Petro/Valero/Iron Skillet/Subway/dsl/scales/24hr/@ [food] McDonald's [lodging] Deluxe Inn [other] Blue Beacon

35 Eastlake Blvd.

34 TX 375, Americas Ave, N [gas] Chevron/dsl, Valero/Subway/dsl [lodging] Motel 6, Woodspring Suites [other] Mission RV Camping, Peterbilt, U-Haul, S [other] El Paso Museum of Hist

32 FM 659, Zaragosa Rd, N [gas] Alon/7-11 [food] Applebee's, Barrigos Mexican, BJ's Rest., Cheddar's, Chico's Tacos, Chipotle Mexican, Corner Bakery Cafe, Famous Dave's, Five Guys, Furr's Buffet, Genghis Grill, Great American Steaks, IHOP, Jack-in-the-Box, Jason's Deli, Krispy Kreme, La Malinche Mexican, Logan's Roadhouse, Macaroni Grill, Mama Fu's Asian, McDonald's, Outback Steaks, Pei Wei, Peter Piper Pizza, Potbelly, Sonic, Starbucks, Taco Bell, Village Inn, Whataburger [lodging] Courtyard, Hampton Inn, Holiday Inn Express [other] AT&T, Chevrolet, Discount Tire, GNC, Kohl's, Lowe's, Michaels, Nissan, Office Depot, Ross, Walgreens, Which Wich, World Mkt, S [gas] Valero/dsl [food] Gallego's Mexican [other] city park, vet, Volvo/Mack

30 Lee Trevino Dr, N [gas] Exxon [food] Denny's, Los Canarios Mexican, Whataburger [lodging] La Quinta, Motel 6, Red Roof Inn, Studio 6 [other] Discount Tire, Firestone/auto, Ford, Home Depot, Kenworth/Ford Trucks, Lexus, Mazda, Toyota, S [other] Chrysler/Dodge/Jeep

29 Lomaland Dr, S [gas] Alon/7-11 [lodging] Ramada [other] Harley-Davidson

28b Yarbrough Dr, El Paso, N [gas] Murphy USA, Shell/Coldstone/dsl, Texaco [food] Buffalo Wild Wings, Burger King, ChuckECheese, Corner Bakery, Dunkin', Grandy's, Hayashi Japanese, Hong Kong Buffet, LJ Silver, McDonald's, Peter Piper Pizza, Sonic,

TX

INTERSTATE 10 Cont'd

EL PASO

28b Continued
Subway, TX Roadhouse, Wendy's, Whataburger, Wienerschnitzel Days Inn H, AT&T, Big Lots, Office Depot, Ranch Mkt, Ross, Walmart, S Rudy's BBQ, Valero/dsl Applebee's, Fuddrucker's, Julio's Cafe, La Malinche Mexican, Lin's Buffet, Pizza Hut, Rudy's BBQ/gas, Shangri-La, Villa Del Mar Comfort Inn, InTown Suites, La Quinta H

28a FM 2316, McRae Blvd, N Texaco/dsl, Valero Pizza Hut La Quinta H, Jo-Ann Fabrics, Murphy USA/dsl, S Circle K/dsl Fuddruckers, Gabriel's Mexican, Pizza Hut La Quinta, Quality Inn NAPA, vet

27 Hunter Dr, Viscount Blvd, N Alon/7-11, Valero/dsl Grand China Buffet, Taco Bell La Quinta $General, $Tree, Jo-Ann, S Alon/7-11, Exxon/dsl Whataburger Family$, Food City

26 Hawkins Blvd, El Paso, N Shamrock, Shell Arby's, Chipotle Mexican, Firehouse Subs, Five Guys, Landry's Seafood, Luby's, Olive Garden, Starbucks, Twin Peaks AT&T, Barnes&Noble, Best Buy, Dick's, Dillard's, JC Penney, Macy's, Old Navy, Petsmart, Sam's Club/gas, Steinmart, TJ Maxx, Verizon, Walgreens, Walmart, S Circle K/dsl McDonald's, Village Inn Super 8 Tony Lama Boots

25 Airway Blvd, N Shell/dsl Carino's, Famous Dave's, Starbucks, Whataburger Comfort Inn, Courtyard, Hampton Inn, Holiday Inn, Residence Inn El Paso Airport, VW/Volvo/Mercedes, S Chevron/Subway/dsl/24hr Holiday Inn Express, Staybridge Suites

24b Geronimo Dr, N El Taco Tote, Taco Cabana Wingate Inn $Tree, Costco/gas, Kohl's, Marshall's, Office Depot, Ross, Target, Walgreens, S Alon/7-11/dsl, Circle K Denny's, IHOP Embassy Suites, Hilton Garden, Homewood Suites, Hyatt Place, La Quinta URGENT CARE

24a Trowbridge Dr, N Luby's, McDonald's, Whataburger Ford, Nissan, Walgreens

23b US 62/180, to Paisano Dr, N Jack-in-the-Box, McDonald's, Whataburger Budget Inn, Soluna Inn Ford, to Carlsbad, U-Haul

EL PASO

23a Raynolds St, S Arby's Best Value Inn, Motel 6 H

22b US 54, Patriot Fwy

22a Copia St, El Paso, N Alon/7-11, Shamrock KFC

21 Piedras St, El Paso, N Burger King, McDonald's Family$

20 Dallas St, Cotton St, N Valero Church's, Subway

19 TX 20, El Paso, downtown, N Chevron, S Camino Real Hotel, DoubleTree Inn, Holiday Inn Express

18b Franklin Ave, Porfirio Diaz St

18a Schuster Ave, N Sun Bowl, S to UTEP

16 Executive Ctr Blvd, N Valero Best Value Inn

13b a US 85, Paisano Dr, to Sunland Park Dr, N Valero Barrigo's Café, Buffalo Wild Wings, Carino's Italian, ChuckECheese, Corner Bakery Cafe, Five Guys, Grand China, IHOP, Olive Garden, PF Chang's, Red Lobster, Sonic, Whataburger $Tree, AT&T, Barnes&Noble, Best Buy, Dillard's, JC Penney, Marshall's, Michael's, Office Depot, Old Navy, Petsmart, Ross, Sprouts Mkt, Target, URGENT CARE, Verizon, vet, S Shamrock/dsl, Shell State Line BBQ, Bob-O's Funpark, La Malinche Mexican, Little Caesar's, McDonald's, Sonic, Subway Best Western, Country Inn Suites, Extended Stay America, Quality Inn, Sleep Inn Buick/GMC, Chrysler/Dodge/Jeep, Family$, Vista Mkt

12 Resler Dr (from wb)

11 TX 20, to Mesa St, Sunland Park, N Chevron/dsl, Circle Mobil/dsl, Valero/dsl AJ's Diner, Chick-fil-A, Chili's, CiC Coldstone, Cracker Barrel, El Taco Tote, Famous Dave's BB Golden Corral, Krispy Kreme, Leo's Mexican, PacoWong's C nese, Panda Express, Pei Wei, Popeye's, Schlotsky's, Souper S ad, Subway, Taco Bell, TX Roadhouse, Wendy's, Wienerschn zel Comfort Suites, EconoLodge, Fairfield Inn, La Quir (2), LaQuinta, Red Roof Inn, SpringHill Suites $Gener Albertson's, BigLots, Family$, Firestone/auto, GNC, Home D pot, PepBoys, SteinMart, TirePros, USPO, Verizon, Walmart/M Donald's, S Chevron/dsl, Valero/dsl Ay Caramba M ican, Burger King, Church's, Golden Buddha, Jack-in-the-B KFC, McDonald's, Pizza Hut, Starbucks, Subway, Taco Caba Village Inn Days Inn, Motel 6, Travelodge $Gener $Tree, AutoZone, Big 8 Foods, Hobby Lobby, Martin Tires, Sar Club/gas, Walgreens

9 Redd Rd, N Circle K Applebee's, Burger King, Dou Dave's Pizza, Peter Piper Pizza, Starbucks, Subway A ertson's, Ford, Kohl's, Lowe's, O'Reilly Parts, S Circle dsl, Valero Chevrolet, Honda, Mazda, URGENT CARE, V Walmart Mkt

8 Artcraft Rd, N Walmart Gas/dsl Cane's, Chipo McDonald's, Panda Express, Pieology, Starbucks, Taco B AT&T, Cabela's, Petsmart, Ross, TJ Maxx, Tuesday Morni Verizon, Walmart, S Shell/dsl Carl's Jr, Church's, Ruc BBQ/dsl, Subway Hampton Inn, Holiday Inn Express, Qu ity Inn $Tree, Nissan

6 Lp 375, to Canutillo, N Shell/DQ/dsl Franklin Mtns to Trans Mountain Rd, S Shell/McDonald's IHOP, Pi Hut, Sonic, Starbucks, Whataburger Discount Tire, El P Shops/Famous Brands, GNC, Martin Tire

5mm truck check sta eb

ANTHONY

2 Westway, Vinton, N Petro/Valero/Subway/c scales/24hr/@ American RV Park, Camping World (1r PetroLube/tires, S truck repair/tires

1 **S Welcome Ctr eb, full facilities, info, litter barrels, petw**, **weigh sta wb,** Great American Steaks Anth RV Ctr, funpark

0 FM 1905, Anthony, N FLYING J/Denny's/dsl/LP dump/24hr, Loves/Chester's/McDonald's/dsl/scales/2 Carl's Jr Best Value Inn, S Alon/7-11/dsl, Pilo Subway/Wendy's/dsl/24hr/@ Burger King, KFC/Taco Best Western $General, $Tree, Anthony RV Ctr, Bi Foods, funpark, tires, truckwash, Walgreens

0mm Texas/New Mexico state line

INTERSTATE 20

Exit #	Services
636mm	Texas/Louisiana state line
635.5mm	**Welcome Ctr/ wb, full facilities, litter barrels, petw**
635	TX 9, TX 156, to Waskom, N Chevron/Burger King/dsl, E on/McDonald's/dsl DQ, Jim's BBQ Family$, USPO
633	US 80, FM 9, FM 134, to Waskom, N Shell Catfish lage Rest., S Miss Ellie's RV Park
628	to US 80, to frontage rd
624	FM 2199, to Scottsville
620	FM 31, to Elysian Fields, N Timberline RV Park (3mi)
617	US 59, Marshall, 0-2 mi N Exxon/dsl, Shell Applebe Burger King, Cafe Italia, Catfish Express, Golden Chick, Gol Corral, IHOP, In Japan Steaks, Jalapeño Tree, KFC, Little C sars, LJ Silver, McDonald's, Pizza Hut, Porky's Smokeho

INTERSTATE 20 Cont'd

617	Continued Sonic, Subway, Taco Bell, Waffle House, Wendy's, Whataburger Baymont Inn, Best Western, Best Western, Comfort Suites, Days Inn, Fairfield Inn, Hampton Inn, Quality Inn $General, Chevrolet, Chrysler/Dodge/Jeep, Ford/Lincoln, NAPA, Save-A-Lot Foods, Toyota, S Chevron/dsl, Conoco/Pony Express/dsl/scales/@, Rudy's/dsl, Valero/dsl JW's Diner Best Value Inn, EconoLodge, Holiday Inn Express, La Quinta, Motel 6, Super 8 Holiday Springs RV Park (2mi)
614	TX 43, to Marshall, S to Martin Creek Lake SP
610	FM 3251
604	FM 450, Hallsville, N Valero/dsl 450 Hitchin' Post RV Park, to Lake O' the Pines
600mm	Mason Creek
599	FM 968, Longview, N Kenworth, S Exxon/Sonic/dsl, Valero Travel Plaza/@ Cowboy RV Park (5mi), Goodyear Truck Tire, truck repair, truck/rv wash
596	US 259 N, TX 149, to Lake O' Pines, N Exxon/Grandy's/dsl, Shell/Sonic/TX Smokehouse/dsl Burger King, Denny's, Whataburger Centerstone Suites, Microtel, Super 8 H, S Valero/dsl Cracker Barrel Holiday Inn Express to Martin Lake SP
595b a	TX 322, Estes Pkwy, N Exxon/dsl, EZ Mart Hajalmer's Rest., Jack-in-the-Box, McDonald's, Waffle House Best Value Inn, Best Western, Express Inn, Guest Inn, Knight's Inn, La Quinta Family$, S Alon/dsl, Murphy USA/dsl KFC/Taco Bell Baymont Inn, Days Inn, Motel 6 auto repair, Walmart/Subway
593mm	Sabine River
591	FM 2087, FM 2011, S Fernbrook RV Park (2mi)
589b a	US 259, TX 31, Kilgore (exits left from wb), 1-3 mi S Chevron/dsl, Exxon/dsl Chili's, Kilgore Café, Mazzio's, McDonald's, Taco Bueno Best Value Inn, Comfort Suites, Hampton Inn, Holiday Inn Express AutoZone, Chevrolet, E Texas Oil Museum, Ford, O'Reilly Parts
587	TX 42, Kilgore, N Exxon/dsl Bodacious BBQ, S Shell/Wendy's/dsl Denny's Days Inn Big Rig Lube, E TX Oil Museum, Walmart (3mi)
583	TX 135, to Kilgore, Overton, N EZmart/dsl Liberty City RV Park, Shallow Creek RV Resort
582	FM 3053, Liberty City, N Mobil/Subway/dsl, Shell/Whataburger/dsl Bob's BBQ, DQ, Los Enchiladas, Pizza Boy, Sonic
579	Joy-Wright Mtn Rd
575	Barber Rd
574mm	**both lanes, accessible, litter barrels**
571b	FM 757, Omen Rd, to Starrville
571a	US 271, to Gladewater, Tyler, S Shell/Sonic/Texas Smokehouse/dsl/scales/24hr
567	TX 155, Winona, N Valero/dsl/24hr, S DQ (2mi) Best Value Inn H, Freightliner
565	FM 2015, to Driskill-Lake Rd
562	FM 14, N Bodacious BBQ to Tyler SP, S Pilot/McDonald's/dsl/scales/24hr Northgate RV Park (4mi)
560	Lavender Rd, S 5 Star RV Park (2 mi)
557	Jim Hogg Rd, N Shell/dsl TX Rose RV Park
556	US 69, to Tyler, N Gulf/dsl, Murphy USA/dsl, RaceWay/dsl Burger King, Chicken Express, Chili's, Cole's Grill, Domino's, Eastern Buffet, IHOP, KFC\LJ Silver, McDonald's, Pizza Hut, Pizza Inn, Posado's Cafe, Sonic, Subway, Taco Bell Best Western, Comfort Suites, Hampton Inn, La Quinta, Motel 6 $General,

CANTON

TERRELL

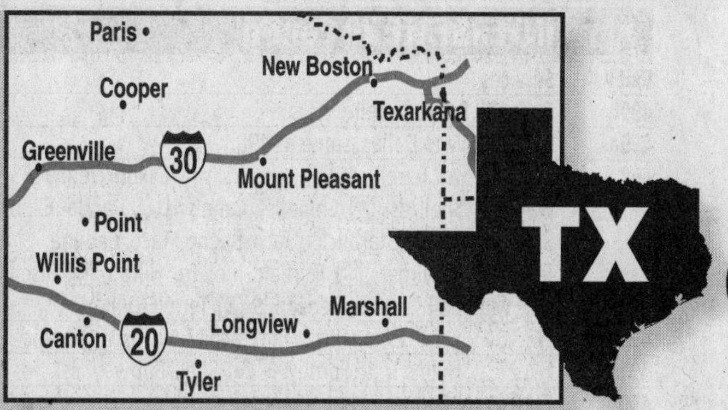

556	Continued Family$, Fred's, Kwik Kar, Lowe's, Verizon, Walmart/Subway, S Chevron/DQ, Exxon/dsl Cracker Barrel, Wendy's Best Value Inn
554	Harvey Rd
553	TX 49 S (**toll**), CR 411
552	FM 849, N Valero/dsl Collin St Bakery, Subway vet
548	TX 110, to Grand Saline, N Exxon/dsl, S Valero/dsl
546mm	**cmv insp sta both lanes**
544	Willow Branch Rd, N Willow Branch RV Park
540	FM 314, to Van, N Loves/Carl's Jr/dsl/scales/24hr Bush's Chicken, DQ, Farmhouse Rest, Sonic, Soul Mans BBQ, Subway Fairfield Inn, Van Inn
538mm	**both lanes, full facilities, litter barrels, petwalk, , , vending**
537	FM 773, FM 16
536	Tank Farm Rd
533	Oakland Rd, to Colfax, N Shell/Pilot/A&W/LJ Silver/dsl
530	FM 1255, Canton
528	FM 17, to Grand Saline, N Chrysler/Dodge/Jeep
527	TX 19, N Exxon/dsl Bunker Rest., Chicken Express, Denny's, Jalapeño Tree, Whataburger Motel 6, Quality Inn, Super 8, S Circle K/dsl/24hr, Mobil/dsl, Shell/dsl Dairy Palace, DJ's BBQ, DQ, King's Fish House, McDonald's, Subway, Taco Bell Best Western, Days Inn Ford, Mill Creek Ranch RV Resort, to First Monday SP
526	FM 859, to Edgewood, N water park
523	TX 64, Wills Point, N Shell/dsl/24hr Duke's Rest., Taco Casa Bluebird RV Park, repair
521	Myrtle Springs Rd, S Explore USA RV Ctr, repair, RV camp/dump
519	Turner-Hayden Rd, S Canton RV Park
516	FM 47, to Wills Point, N Fourwinds Steaks, to Lake Tawakoni, S Texaco/dsl Robertson's Café/gas Interstate Motel
512	FM 2965, Hiram-Wills Point Rd
512mm	**cmv inspection sta both lanes**
509	Hiram Rd, S Shell/dsl/cafe/24hr
506	FM 429, FM 2728, College Mound Rd, N Blue Bonnet Ridge RV Park
503	Wilson Rd, S TA/Shell/Country Pride/Pizza Hut/Subway/dsl/LP/24hr/@
501	TX 34, to Terrell, N Exxon/dsl, QT/dsl/scales/24hr, Shell/Subway/dsl Church's, Italrican Cafe, Schlotzsky's, Sonic, Starbucks, Steak&Grill, Waffle House Baymont Inn, Days Inn, Gateway Inn, La Quinta, Motel 6, Quality Inn H, Home Depot, S Circle K/dsl, Valero/dsl/24hr Applebee's, Carmona's Cantina, IHOP, McDonald's, Wendy's Holiday Inn Express, Super 8 Old Navy, Tanger Outlet/famous brands

TX

TX

DALLAS

INTERSTATE 20 Cont'd

Exit #	Services
499b	Rose Hill Rd, to Terrell
499a	to US 80, W to Dallas, same as 498
498	FM 148, to Terrell, N Buc-ee's/dsl, Exxon/Denny's/Subway/dsl, Shell/dsl Chipotle, Cane's, DQ, Panda Express, Soulman's BBQ, Starbucks, Taco Bueno, Taco Cabana, Chick-fil-A, Whataburger Fairfield Inn, Tru Hilton, Discount Tire, Marshall's, Petco, Verizon, S Terrell RV Park
493	FM 1641, S Exxon/Pizza Inn/Taco Mayo/dsl Sonic
491	FM 2932, Helms Tr, to Forney, N Shell/Subway/dsl
490	FM 741, to Forney, N $General
487	FM 740, to Forney, S Forney RV park
483	Lawson Rd, Lasater Rd
482	Belt Line Rd, to Lasater, N Exxon/dsl Smokehouse BBQ, Sonic, S Shell/KFC/Pizza Hut/Subway RV park
481	Seagoville Rd, N Shell/Church's/Dickey's BBQ, Valero/dsl Motel 6, S Lindy's Rest.
480	I-635, N to Mesquite
479b a	US 175, S Marlow/dsl
477	St Augustine Rd, N Family$, S Shell/dsl Sonic
476	Dowdy Ferry Rd
474	TX 310 N, Central Expsy
473b a	JJ Lemmon Rd, I-45 N to Dallas, S to Houston
472	Bonnie View Rd, N FLYING J/Denny's/dsl/LP/24hr, Shell Jack-in-the-Box EconoLodge Blue Beacon, Kenworth, Speedco Lube, S TA/Exxon/Burger King/Taco Bell/dsl/scales/24hr/@
470	TX 342, Lancaster Rd, N Chevron/dsl, Exxon/Popeye's/Subway/dsl/scales/24hr Soulman's BBQ, S Pilot/Wendy's/dsl/scales/24hr LJ Silver/Taco Bell, McDonald's, Sonic, Whataburger, William's Chicken Days Inn
468	Houston School Rd, S Exxon/dsl, QT/dsl Whataburger
467b a	I-35E, N to Dallas, S to Waco, **1 mi N off of I-35E** Chevron, Shell McDonald's
466	S Polk St, N Exxon/dsl, Texaco/dsl DQ, Sonic, Subway Family$, S Loves/Carl's Jr/dsl/scales/24hr
465	Wheatland/S Hampton Rds, N Shell/Subway Chick-fil-A, Chili's, Furr's Cafeteria $Tree, Aldi Foods, CVS Drug, GNC, Office Depot, Petsmart, Ross, Target, S Chevron/McDonald's, Murphy USA/dsl, QT/dsl, RaceWay/dsl Arby's, Burger King, Cheddar's, Jack-in-the-Box, Panda Express, Popeye's, Sonic, Spring Creek BBQ, Taco Bell, Wendy's Super 8 H, Home Depot, Honda, Hyundai, Kia, Lowe's, Nissan, Sam's Club/gas, Toyota, Walmart
464b a	US 67, Love Fwy
463	Camp Wisdom Rd, N Chevron/7-11, Exxon Catfish King Rest., Denny's, Taco Bell/LJ Silver, Taco Cabana Best Value Inn, Quality Inn, Royal Inn, Super 7 $Tree, Chrysler/Dodge/Jeep, S Shamrock Burger King, Chubby's Rest., Dave's BBQ, Olive Garden, Red Lobster, Subway, Tortilla Factory
462b a	Duncanville Rd (no EZ wb return), S QT, Shell/dsl Church's, Jack-in-the-Box, Los Lupes Mexican, Popeye's, Whataburger Hilton Garden, Motel 6 Firestone/auto, Kroger
461	Cedar Ridge Rd, S RaceWay/dsl
460	TX 408
458	Mt Creek Pkwy
457	FM 1382, to Grand Prairie, N Shell/7-11/dsl, Valero/dsl Waffle House, S RaceTrac/dsl Jack-in-the-Box to Joe Pool Lake
456	Carrier Pkwy, to Corn Valley Rd, N QT Chick-fil-A, Dickey's BBQ, Domino's, Don Pablo, Popeyes, Sonic, Starbucks, Taco Cabana, Whataburger AutoZone, Home Depot, Kohl's, Target,
456	Continued S Shell Baskin-Robbins, Boston Mkt, Chapp's Ca Cheddar's, Chili's, Chipotle, Denny's, IHOP, Little Caesa McDonald's, Spring Creek BBQ, Subway Holiday Inn press Albertsons/gas, CVS Drug, GNC, Tom Thumb Foo gas, Verizon, Walgreens
455	TX 151, S QT/dsl
454	Great Southwest Pkwy, N Exxon/dsl, Mobil/7-1 dsl Beto's, Carino's Italian, China Dragon, ChuckeChee DQ, Golden Corral, KFC, McDonald's, Taco Bell, Taco B no, TX Roadhouse, Waffle House, Wendy's, Wienerschi zel Comfort Suites, Heritage Inn, Quality Inn Firestone/auto, Harley-Davidson, U-Haul, S 7-11, QT/ Shell/Subway/dsl, Valero/dsl Applebee's, Arby's, Buff Wild Wings, Burger King, Schlotzsky's, Sonic La Quin Super 8 $Tree, AT&T, Discount Tire, Kroger, Office Dep Petsmart, RaceTrac/dsl, Sam's Club, to Joe Pool Lake, W greens, Walmart/McDonald's
453b a	TX 360
452	Frontage Rd
451	Collins St, New York Ave, N Exxon/dsl, RaceTrac/dsl, dy's Store/BBQ/dsl Cotton Patch Cafe, Golden Corral, Ja in-the-Box, Whataburger Chrysler/Dodge/Jeep, Kia/M da/VW, URGENT CARE, S QT, Shell, Valero/dsl Chic Express, KFC/Taco Bell, McDonald's, Sonic, Subway, Taco B no Hampton Inn Buick/GMC, Nissan
450	Matlock Rd, N Abuelo's Mexican, Bar Louie, BJ's Re Black-eyed Pea, Bone Daddy's, Boomer Jack's Grill, Chu Mexican, Coldstone, Dave&Buster's, Genghis Grill, Houliha India Grill, Jason's Deli, Kincaide's Burgers, McAlister's D Melting Pot, Mercado Juarez, Mimi's Cafe, PF Changs, Plu ers's Wings, Potbelly, Red Robin, Starbucks, Sweet Tomato The Keg Steaks, Wendy's, Which Wich Courtyard, Qua Inn, Residence Inn H, AT&T, Costco/gas, Jo-Ann Fab Lowe's, Old Navy, Petsmart, Staples, World Mkt, S 7- RaceWay/dsl, Shell/7-11 Joe's Pizza, Pizza Patron, S bucks Fry's Electronics, O'Reilly Parts
449	FM 157, Cooper St, N Shell/dsl Cane's, Cheesec Factory, Chili's, Corner Bakery, Grandy's, Honeybaked Ha IHOP, In-N-Out, McDonald's, Nagoya Japanese, On-the-Bor Outback Steaks, Pei Wei, Razzoo's Cajun Café, Red Lobs Rockfish Seafood, Salt Grass Steaks, Souper Salad, Spagh ti Whse, Spring Creek BBQ, Whataburger Best Weste Days Inn, Holiday Inn Express, La Quinta, Studio 6, Su 8 Barnes&Noble, Best Buy, Dick's, Dillard's, Discount T JC Penney, Macy's, Michael's, Office Depot, Target, TJ Ma Verizon, S Shell Applebee's, Arby's, Boston Mkt, Bu er St, Carl's Jr, Chick-fil-A, Chipotle, Denny's, El Arroyo, El Fe Mexican, Lin's Buffet, LJ Silver, Macaroni Grill, McDonald's, ive Garden, Panda Express, Peter Piper Pizza, Schlotsky's, S bucks, Subway, Taco Bueno, Taco Cabana, TGIFriday Town Suites, Microtel $Tree, AAA, Acura, Chevrolet, Fo Hobby Lobby, Home Depot, Honda, Hyundai, NTB, Ross, Suz Toyota, Walmart/McDonald's
448	Bowen Rd, N QT, RaceTrac/dsl Cracker Barrel, So S Shell
447	Kelly-Elliott Rd, Park Springs Blvd, N 7-11, Val S Exxon/Subway city park
445	Green Oaks Blvd, N Conoco/dsl, Shell/7-11/dsl Arb Boston Mkt, Braum's, Burger St, Cafe Acapulco, Chapp's C Chick-fil-A, Church's, CiCi's, Colter's BBQ, Fuzzy's Tacos, Hoot Jack-in-the-Box, Jay Jay Rest., Joe's Pizza, Mijo's Cafe, Quizn

INTERSTATE 20 Cont'd

445 Continued
Schlotzsky's, Starbucks, Taco Bell, Taco Cabana, Taco Casa, Tai-Pan, Wendy's, Whataburger [other] $Tree, Ace Hardware, Albertsons, AT&T, CVS Drug, Firestone, Kroger/dsl, Meineke, Office Depot, Verizon, Walgreens, **S** [gas] 7-11, Murphy Express/dsl, QT/dsl, Valero/dsl [food] Cheddar's, Corky's Pizza, Golden Buffet, IHOP, McDonald's, Pancho's Mexican, Panda Express, Sonic, Subway, Taco Bueno, Waffle House [other] $General, AutoZone, BigLots, Discount Tire, O'Reilly Parts, Tuesday Morning, vet, Walmart/Subway

444 US 287 S, to Waxahatchie, from eb, same as 445

443 Bowman Springs Rd (from wb)

442b a I-820 to Ft Worth, US 287 bus, **N** [gas] Valero [lodging] Great Western Inn, Knights Inn, **S** [gas] QT/dsl

441 Anglin Dr, Hartman Lane, **N** [lodging] Woodspring Suites, **S** [gas] Conoco/dsl

440b Forest Hill Dr, **S** [gas] Shell/7-11/dsl [food] Braum's, Capt D's, CiCi's Pizza, Jack-in-the-Box, Luby's, Sonic, Starbucks, Subway, Taco Bell [lodging] La Quinta [other] $General, $Tree, AutoZone, CVS Drug, Discount Tire, O'Reilly Parts, Super 1 Foods, Walgreens

440a Wichita St, **N** [gas] Chevron/dsl, QT/dsl [food] #1 Chinese, Starbucks, Taco Casa, Wendy's, **S** [gas] Texaco/dsl, Valero [food] Chicken Express, Denny's, Domino's, McDonald's, Pizza Hut, Schlotzsky's, Taco Bueno, Whataburger [lodging] Best Western, Comfort Inn, Hampton Inn

439 Campus Dr, **N** [other] Chrysler/Dodge/Jeep, Ford, **S** [other] Sam's Club/gas

438 Oak Grove Rd, **S** [gas] Valero

437 I-35W, N to Ft Worth, S to Waco

436b Hemphill St, **N** [gas] Shell/dsl, **S** [other] Chevrolet

436a FM 731 (from eb), to Crowley Ave, **N** [gas] Conoco/dsl, Valero/dsl [food] China Express [other] $General, Sav-a-Lot Foods, **S** [food] BurgerBox, Pizza Hut/Taco Bell, Subway [other] transmissions

435 McCart St, **N** [gas] Shamrock, Shell/dsl, **S** [gas] Mobil/dsl

434b Trail Lakes Dr, **S** [gas] Shell [food] Sonic, Starbucks, Subway, Wendy's [other] CVS Drug, Family$

434a Granbury Rd

433 Hulen St, **N** [gas] Shell/dsl [food] Chef Chen, ChuckECheese, Honeybaked Ham, Hooters, Olive Garden, Papa Murphy's, Souper Salad, Subway, TX Roadhouse [lodging] TownePlace Suites [other] Albertsons, Home Depot, NTB, Petsmart, Sprouts Mkt, TJ Maxx, **S** [food] Abuelo's Mexican, BJ's Rest., Denny's, Five Guys, In-N-Out, Jack-in-the-Box, Kincaide's Burgers, McDonald's, Panera Bread, Pizza Inn, Potbelly, Red Lobster, Red Robin [lodging] Hampton Inn [other] Barnes&Noble, Dillard's, Hobby Lobby, Macy's, Michael's, Office Depot, Old Navy, Ross

431 (432 from wb), TX 183, Bryant-Irvin Rd, **N** [gas] Chevron [food] Chipotle Mexican, Genghis Grill, Keg Steaks, Mimi's Café, On-the-Border, Taste of Asia [other] Best Buy, Cavender's Boots, Kohl's, Lowe's, Petsmart, Sam's Club/gas, **S** [gas] Chevron, Shell/dsl [food] Blackeyed Pea, Chicken Express, Chick-fil-A, Cousin's BBQ, Fox & Hound, Fuddruckers, IHOP, Jimmy John's, Lonestar Oysters, Outback Steaks, Pei Wei, Pizza Hut, Razzoo's Cajun, Rio Mambo, SaltGrass Steaks, Schlotzsky's, Sonic, Starbucks, Subway, Szechuan [lodging] Courtyard, Extended Stay America, Holiday Inn Express, Homewood Suites, Hyatt Place, La Quinta [other] H, AT&T, Costco/gas, Firestone/auto, Ford, Goodyear/auto, Infiniti, Kwik Kar, Lexus, Mazda, PetCo, Staples, Target, Verizon, Walgreens

430mm Clear Fork Trinity River

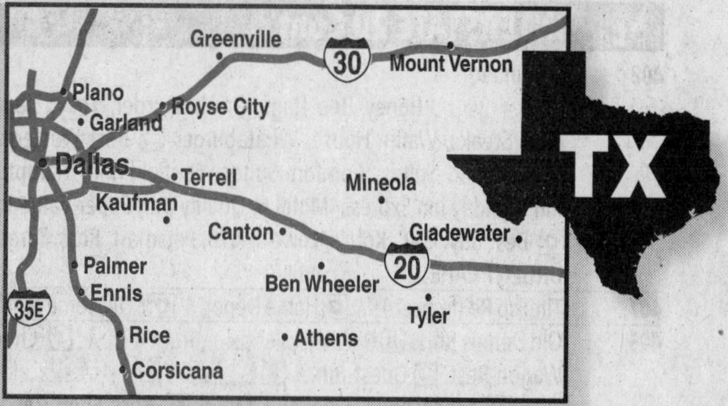

TX

429b Winscott Rd, **N** [gas] Circle K/dsl [food] Cracker Barrel [lodging] Best Western, Comfort Suites

429a US 377, to Granbury, **S** [gas] QT/dsl, RaceTrac/dsl, Shell/dsl, Valero [food] 7-11/dsl, Arby's, Braum's, Burger King, Chicken Express, Chick-fil-A, Domino's, Golden Chick, Jack-in-the-Box, KFC/Taco Bell, McDonald's, NY Pizza, Panda Express, Pizza Hut, Ricky's BBQ, Sonic, Starbucks, Subway, Taco Casa, Taco Villa, Waffle House, Waffle House, Whataburger [lodging] Motel 6 [other] $General, AutoZone, CVS Drug, O'Reilly Parts, USPO, Walgreens, Walmart

428 I-820, N around Ft Worth

426 RM 2871, Chapin School Rd

425 Markum Ranch Rd

421 I-30 E (from eb), to Ft Worth

420 FM 1187, Aledo, Farmer, parking & ride

419mm weigh sta eb

418 Ranch House Rd, Willow Park, **N** [gas] Exxon/Taco Casa, Shell/dsl [food] Pizza Hut, Sonic, Subway, Whataburger, **S** [gas] Chevron/dsl [food] Alex's Pizza, Chicken Express, Domino's, Domino's, McDonald's, Railhead BBQ [lodging] Quality Inn [other] $General, Brookshire Foods/gas, Cowtown RV Park, Texas RV Outlet

417mm **N** [food] Cafe 23:5, Sunny Street Cafe [other] H

415 FM 5, Mikus Rd, Annetta, **N** [other] vet, **S** [gas] Shell/dsl [other] 415 RV Ctr

413 (414 from wb), US 180 W, Lake Shore Dr, **N** [gas] Murphy USA/dsl, RaceTrac/dsl, Shell/dsl [food] Chick-fil-A, DQ, Golden Chick, McDonald's, Paleo's Pizza, Sonic, Subway, Taco Bell, Waffle House [other] Buick/Cadillac/Chevrolet/GMC, Ford, HEB Mkt, Hyundai, Lincoln, Nissan, Toyota, Verizon, Walgreens, Walmart/Subway, **S** [gas] Valero/dsl

411 Service Rd (from wb), same as 413

410 Bankhead Hwy, **S** [gas] Love's/Subway/dsl/24hr

409 FM 2552 N, Clear Lake Rd, **N** [gas] Petro/Valero/Iron Skillet/dsl/24hr/@ [food] Antonio's Mexican, Granny's Kitchen, Jack-in-the-Box, Little Panda Chinese, Popeyes [lodging] Heritage Inn, SleepGo Motel [other] H, Blue Beacon, **S** [gas] Shell/dsl

WEATHERFORD

408 TX 171, FM 1884, FM 51, Tin Top Rd, Weatherford, **N** [gas] Exxon, Mobil, Murphy USA/dsl [food] Applebee's, Baker's Ribs, Braum's, Buffalo Wild Wings, Cane's, Chicken Express, China Harbor, CiCi's Pizza, Cotton Patch Cafe, IHOP, Kincade's Burgers, LJ Silver, Logan's Roadhouse, McAlister's Deli, McDonald's, MT Rest., Olive Garden, Panda Express, Rosa's Cafe, Schlotzsky's, Starbucks, Subway, Taco Bell, Taco Bueno, Taco Cabana, Whataburger, Wild Mushroom Steaks [lodging] La Quinta, Sleep Inn, Super 8 [other] $Tree, AT&T, AutoZone, Belk, Christian Bros Auto, Discount Tire, Firestone/auto, JC Penney, Just Brakes, Michael's, TJ Maxx, Verizon, Walgreens, Walmart/Subway, **S** [gas] Exxon/Subway/dsl, Shell/Burger King/dsl [food] Chick-fil-A, Chili's, Chipotle,

= gas = food = lodging = other = rest stop Copyright 2020 - The Next EXI

TX

INTERSTATE 20 Cont'd

408 Continued
Cracker Barrel, Honey Bee Ham, On-the-Border, Tokyo Japanese Steaks, Waffle House, Whataburger Best Western+, Candlewood Suites, Comfort Suites, Fairfield Inn, Hampton Inn, Holiday Inn Express, Motel 6, Quality Inn, Super Value Inn Best Buy, GNC, Kohl's, Lowe's, NTB, Petsmart, Ross, Target, URGENT CARE

407 Tin Top Rd (from eb), N Home Depot, S KOA, same as 408

406 Old Dennis Rd, N QT/dsl/scales/24hr, Truck'n Travel Chuck Wagon Rest. Quest Inn, S Pilot/Wendy's/dsl/scales/24hr EconoLodge, Quality 1 Motel Boss Shop Repair, Honda

404 Williams Memorial Dr

402 (403 from wb), TX 312, to Weatherford

397 FM 1189, to Brock, N Valero/dsl Oak Creek RV Park

394 FM 113, to Millsap

393mm Brazos River

391 Gilbert Pit Rd

386 US 281, to Mineral Wells, Stephenville, N Shell/Subway/dsl Gilbert Pecans, S Chevron/Maverick TC/Taco Casa/dsl, Sunoco/Stripes/Taco Co/dsl DQ

380 FM 4, Santo, S RV Park

376 Blue Flat Rd, Panama Rd

373 TX 193, Gordon

370 TX 108 S, FM 919, Gordon, N Texaco/Bar-B/dsl, S Exxon/dsl Cactus Rose RV Park, Longhorn Inn/Country Store

367 TX 108 N, Mingus, N Smoke Stack Café Thurber Sta, S NY Hill Rest.

364mm Palo Pinto Creek

363 Tudor Rd, **litter barrels**

362mm Bear Creek, **both lanes, litter barrels**

361 TX 16, to Strawn

359mm **wb, full facilities, , litter barrels, petwalk**

358 (from wb), frontage rd

356mm Russell Creek

354 Lp 254, Ranger

353 **eb, full facilities, , litter barrels, vending**

351 (352 from wb), College Blvd

349 FM 2461, Ranger, N Loves/Godfather's/Subway/dsl/scales/24hr DQ Rodeway Inn RL RV Park, S Phillips 66/dsl repair

347 FM 3363 (from wb), Olden, S TX Steakhouse

345 FM 3363 (from eb), Olden, S TX Steakhouse

343 TX 112, FM 570, Eastland, Lake Leon, N Alon/7-11/Subway, Murphy USA/dsl, Shell/Taco Casa/dsl Chicken Express, Domino's, DQ, Heff's Burgers, McDonald's, Pizza Heaven, Pizza Hut, Sonic, Taco Bell Holiday Inn Express, La Quinta, Super 8/RV park $General, AT&T, AutoZone, Buick/Cadillac/Chevrolet/GMC, Chrysler/Dodge/Jeep, Ford, O'Reilly Parts, TrueValue, Walmart, S Exxon/dsl Pulido's Mexican Budget Host, Days Inn

340 TX 6, Eastland, N Valero/dsl H, S Shell/dsl

337 spur 490, N The Wild Country RV Park

332 US 183, Cisco, N Alon/Allsups/dsl Chicken Express, DQ, Pizza Heaven, Sonic, Subway Cisco Inn, Executive Inn/RV Park $General, Family$, Hilton Mon (1mi), NAPA

330 TX 206, Cisco, N Sunoco/Stripes/Tacos/dsl/scales/24hr Best Value Inn H, S FLYING J/Denny's/dsl/scales/ 24hr

329mm **wb, litter barrels, accessible**

327mm **eb, litter barrels, accessible**

324 Scranton Rd

322 Cooper Creek Rd

320 FM 880 N, FM 2945 N, to Moran

319 FM 880 S, Putnam, N Fillin Sta/café USPO

316 Brushy Creek Rd

313 FM 2228

310 Finley Rd

308 Lp 20, Baird

307 US 283, Clyde, N Loves/Chester's/Subway/dsl/scal 24hr DQ Baird Motel/RV park/dump, S Alon/ sups/7-11, Conoco/dsl Robertson's Café

306 FM 2047, Baird, N Chevrolet/GMC, Hanner RV Ctr

303 Union Hill Rd

301 FM 604, Cherry Lane, N Exxon/dsl McDonald's, S ic, Whataburger NAPA, S Alon/7-11, Alon/7-11/ Chicken Express, Pizza House, Subway Family$, Uni Mkt, USPO

300 FM 604 N, Clyde, N Chrysler/Dodge/Jeep, S Cono dsl White's RV Park/dump

299 FM 1707, Hays Rd

297 FM 603, Eula Rd

296.5mm **both lanes, full facilities, litter barrels, petwalk, , wireless internet**

294 Buck Creek Rd, N Big Counry RV Ctr/park, Buck Creek Park/dump, S Abilene RV Park

292b Elmdale Rd

292a Lp 20 (exits left from wb)

290 TX 36, Lp 322, S , zoo

ABILENE

288 TX 351, N Alon/7-11/dsl, Murphy USA/dsl Buf Wild Wings, Chick-fil-A, Chili's, Cracker Barrel, DQ, Golden Ch Jason's Deli, Oscar's Mexican, Panda Express, Subway, T Casa, Wendy's Comfort Suites, Courtyard, Days Inn, Ex utive Inn, Holiday Inn Express, Knights Inn, Quality Inn, F idence Inn, TownePlace Suites, Whitten Inn $Tree, AT Lowe's, Walmart/Subway, S Super 8 H

286c FM 600, Abilene, N Alon/7-11/dsl, Alon/Allsups/dsl Denny's Best Western, Hampton Inn, Holiday Inn, La Q ta, S Alon/7-11/dsl Sleep Inn

286 US 83, Pine St, Abilene, S Alon/Allsups Frontier H

285 Old Anson Rd, S Alon/Allsups/dsl Best Value Inn

283b N US 277, U83, Anson

283a US 277 S, US 83 (exits left from wb)

282 FM 3438, Shirley Rd, S Motel 6 KOA

281 Fulwiler Rd, to Dyess AFB, S to Dyess AFB

279 US 84 E, to Abilene, **1-3 mi S** access to facilities

278 Lp 20, N Conoco/dsl/24hr dsl repair, S Westgo Phillips 66/Huddle House/dsl/scales/24hr/@ Mack Tru Volvo

277 FM 707, Tye, N FLYING J/Denny's/dsl/LP/24hr Pe bilt, truck lube, Tye RV Park, S Alon/7-11/dsl South Tire Mart, USPO

274 Wells Lane

272 Wimberly Rd

270 FM 1235, Merkel, N Alon/dsl/24hr, Conoco/dsl

269 FM 126, N Sonic, Subway Scottish Inn, S Alon/7- dsl, Phillips 66/dsl DQ, Skeet's BBQ CarQuest, Famil

267 Lp 20, Merkel, **1 mi S** access to gas, food, lodging

266 Derstine Rd

264 Noodle Dome Rd

263 Lp 20, Trent, N RV Park

262 FM 1085, S Alon/7-11/dsl

261 Lp 20, Trent

E INTERSTATE 20 Cont'd

Exit #	Services
259	Sylvester Rd
258	White Flat Rd, oil wells
257mm	**both lanes, full facilities, litter barrels, petwalk, vending**
256	Stink Creek Rd
255	Adrian Rd
251	Eskota Rd
249	FM 1856, N Lonestar RV Park
247	TX 70 N, Sweetwater
246	Alabama Ave, Sweetwater
245	Arizona Ave (from wb), same as 244
244	TX 70 S, Sweetwater, N Alon/7-11/dsl/24hr, Chevron/Subway/dsl, Murphy USA/dsl Dickey's BBQ, Domino's, DQ, Golden Chick, McDonald's, Subway, Wendy's Best Western, Budget Inn, La Quinta, Motel 6 H, AT&T, AutoZone, Medicine Place Drug, Verizon, Walmart, S Shell/dsl Big Boy's BBQ, Buck's BBQ, Great Wall Buffet, Schlotzsky's, Skeet's Grill, Taco Bell Country Hearth Inn, Hampton Inn, Holiday Inn Express, Ranch House Motel/rest., Stay Express Inn Chaparral RV Park, Ford, Rainbolt RV Park
243	Hillsdale Rd, Robert Lee St, N Family RV Ctr
242	Hopkins Rd, N Loves/Arby's/dsl/scales/24hr Microtel, S TA/Alon/Pizza Hut/Popeye's/dsl/scales/24hr/@ Rolling Plains RV Park, truck wash, truck/tire repair
241	Lp 20, Sweetwater, N gas food lodging, S RV camping
240	Lp 170, N , camping
239	May Rd
238b a	US 84 W, Blackland Rd
237	Cemetery Rd
236	FM 608, Roscoe, N Alon/dsl, Sunoco/Stripes/Taco Co/dsl NAPA, S Retta Mae's Rest
235	to US 84, Roscoe
230	FM 1230, many wind turbines
229mm	**wb, litter barrels, accessible**
228mm	**eb, litter barrels, accessible**
227	Narrell Rd
226b	Lp 20 (from wb), Loraine
226a	FM 644 N, Wimberly Rd
225	FM 644 S, 1 mi S access to gas food
224	Lp 20, to Loraine, 1 mi S gas food
223	Lucas Rd, S 223 RV Park
221	Lasky Rd
220	FM 1899
219	Lp 20, Country Club Rd, Colorado City
217	TX 208 S, N Sunoco/Stripes/Taco Co/dsl/scales/24hr La Quinta, S Santiago's Lone Wolf RV Park
216	TX 208 N, N Chevron/Subway/dsl DQ Sleep Inn, S Sunoco/Stripes/Taco Co/dsl Golden Chick, Pizza Hut, Sonic American Inn, Hotel Texas, Motel 6, Super 8 H, $General, City RV Park, Parts+
215	FM 3525, Rogers Rd, N Motel 6 Extended, 2 mi S access to gas food H
214.5mm	Colorado River
213	Lp 20, Enderly Rd, Colorado City
212	FM 1229
211mm	Morgan Creek
210	FM 2836, S Country Store camping, , to Lake Colorado City SP
209	Dorn Rd

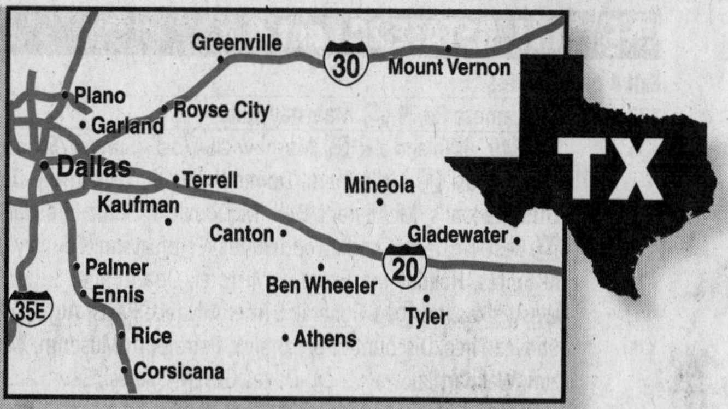

BIG SPRING

Exit #	Services
207	Lp 20, Westbrook
206	FM 670, to Westbrook
204mm	**N wb, full facilities, litter barrels, petwalk**
200	Conaway Rd
199	Iatan Rd
195	frontage rd (from eb)
194a	E Howard Field Rd
192	FM 821, many oil wells
191mm	**eb, full facilities, litter barrels, petwalk**
190	Snyder Field Rd
189	McGregor Rd
188	FM 820, Coahoma, N Sunoco/Stripes/Taco Co/dsl DQ Coahoma Inn Coahoma RV Park, USPO
186	Salem Rd, Sand Springs
184	Moss Lake Rd, Sand Springs, N Alon/dsl $General, S RV camping
182	Midway Rd
181b	Refinery Rd, N Alon Refinery
181a	FM 700, N , RV camping, 2 mi S H
179	US 80, Big Spring, S Alon/7-11 Denny's Camlot Inn, Quality Inn, Super 8 $General, Buick/Cadillac/Chevrolet
178	TX 350, Big Spring, N Shell/dsl tire/truck service, S Pilot/McDonald's/dsl/scales/24hr
177	US 87, Big Spring, N Exxon/dsl, TA/Subway/Popeye's/dsl/scales/24hr/@ Texas Cajan Cafe Advantage Inn, La Quinta, Plaza Inn, W Texas Inn, S Alon/dsl, Sunoco/Stripes/dsl Casa Blanca Mexican, DQ, McAlister's Deli, Starbucks Baymont Inn, Best Western, Hampton Inn, Sleep Inn MainStay Suites, Spring City Inn, TownePlace Suites Chrysler/Dodge/Jeep
176	TX 176, Andrews
174	Lp 20 E, Big Springs, S Shell/dsl H, , Big Spring SP
172	Cauble Rd
171	Moore Field Rd
169	FM 2599
168mm	**both lanes, litter barrels**
165	FM 818
158	Lp 20 W, to Stanton, N RV camping
156	TX 137, Lamesa, S Phillips 66/Stripes/Subway/dsl/24hr Sonic Cobblestone Inn, Comfort Inn, Super 8
154	US 80, Stanton, 2 mi S access to gas food lodging
151	FM 829 (from wb)
144	Loop 250, 2-3 mi N services in Midland
143mm	frontage rd (from eb)
142mm	**both lanes, litter barrels, hits marker**
140	FM 307 (from eb)
138	TX 158, FM 715, Greenwood, N Pilot/dsl, Valero/dsl KD's BBQ, Whataburger, S FLYING J/Moe's/dsl/scales/24hr, Sunoco/Stripes/Subway/dsl, Sunoco/Stripes/Taco Co/dsl Baymont Inn

TX

INTERSTATE 20 Cont'd

MIDLAND / ODESSA / MONAHANS / PECOS

Exit #	Services
137	Old Lamesa Rd, N Mainstay Suites
136	TX 349, Midland, N Murphy USA/dsl, Sunoco/Stripes/Taco Co/dsl Cici's Pizza, Domino's, IHOP, Jack-in-the-Box, Little Caesar's, McAlister's Deli, McDonald's, Sonic, Starbucks Best Western, Candlewood Suites, Comfort Inn, Country Inn&Suites, Holiday Inn Express, Microtel, Quality Inn, Super 8, West Texas Inn $General, $Tree, Advance Parts, AutoZone, Chavez Tires, Discount Tire, Family$, Petroleum Museum, Verizon, Walmart/Subway, S Daves Gas/NAPA/dsl, Exxon/Burger King/dsl, Pilot/dsl, Stripes/Taco Co/dsl
135	Cotton Flat Rd, S H
134	Midkiff Rd, **0-1 mi (Wall St)** N Alon/7-11, Exxon/dsl, Shell, Sunoco/Stripes/Subway/dsl Denny's, DQ Best Value Inn, Bradford Inn, Days Inn, Executive Inn, La Quinta, Studio 6, Super 8 H, Chevrolet, Chrysler/Dodge/Jeep, Ford/ Lincoln, Honda, Midland RV Park, Subaru
131	TX 158, Midland, N Motel 6 Midland RV Park, S Love's/Chester's/Subway/dsl/scales/24hr Suburban Inn
126	FM 1788, N Pilot/McDonald's/dsl/scales/24hr, Sunoco/Stripes/Taco Co/dsl Steak'n Shake, Subway Carquest, Main Street Mkt/Subway/dsl, museum, Western Auto
121	Lp 338, Odessa, **0-3 mi (TX 191)** N Alon/7-11, Stripes/Taco Co/dsl Carino's, Casa Ole, Cheddar's, Chili's, Dickey's BBQ, Domino's, Fazoli's, Five Guys, Fuddruckers, Genghis Grill, Golden Corral, Harigan's Grill, Hooters, IHOP, KFC, Logan's Roadhouse, McDonald's, Panda Express, Pizza Hut, Red Lobster, Rosa's Cafe, Schlotzsky's, Sonic, Subway, Twin Peaks Rest, Wendy's, Whataburger Comfort Suites, Days Inn, Elegante Hotel, Fairfield Inn, Hampton Inn Express, Hilton Garden, Holiday Inn, Holiday Inn Express, La Quinta, Parkway Inn, Quality Inn, Sleep Inn, Studio 6, Super Inn $General, $Tree, AT&T, Buick/GMC, Chevrolet, Dillard's, Hobby Lobby, Home Depot, Honda, Hyundai, JC Penney, Lowe's, Mazda, Mkt Street, Nissan, Sam's Club/gas, Staples, Target, Toyota, U of TX Permian Basin, USPO, Walmart/Subway, S Flying J/McDonald's/dsl/scales/24hr
120	JBS Pkwy, N Candlewood Suites, Comfort Inn, Staybridge Suites, Super 8 Mack/Volvo
118	FM 3503, Grandview Ave, N Alon/dsl Freightliner/Peterbilt
116	US 385, Odessa, N Chevron/dsl, Stripes/Taco Co/dsl DQ, La Margarita Delux Inn, Ramada, Villa West Inn H, $General, city park, Family$, S Alon/dsl, Valero/dsl MainStay Suites, Motel 6
115	FM 1882, N Sunoco/Stripes/Taco Co/dsl, S Love's/McDonald's/Subway/dsl/scales/24hr Blue Beacon
113	TX 302, Odessa
112	FM 1936, Odessa, N Red X Trkstp/dsl
108	Moss Ave, Meteor Crater, Meteor Crater, N Road Ranger/Church's/Subway/dsl/scales/24hr
104	FM 866, Meteor Crater Rd, Goldsmith, N RV park
103.5mm	**weigh sta both directions**
101	FM 1601, to Fenwell, Penwell
93	FM 1053, to Ft Stockton
86	TX 41, N camping, Monahans Sandhills SP
83	US 80, Monahans, **2 mi** N H, RV camping
80	TX 18, Monahans, N Chevron/dsl Bar-H Steaks, DQ, Great Wall Buffet, McDonald's, Pappy's BBQ, Pizza Hut, Sonic Candlewood Suites, Holiday Inn Express H, $General, Alco, Family$, Lowe's Foods, O'Reilly Parts, repair/tires,
80	Continued Verizon, S Alon/dsl, Sunoco/Stripes/Subway/dsl, Texa Huddle House/dsl/24hr Huddle House Best Value Best Western, Comfort Inn, Texan Inn Buick/Chevro GMC, Chrysler/Dodge/Jeep, RV Park, vet
79	Lp 464, Monahans, S La Quinta
76	US 80, Monahans, **2 mi** N RV camping, to Million Ba Museum
73	FM 1219, Wickett, N Alon/Allsup's/dsl, S Main St/S way/dsl
70	TX 65
69.5mm	**both lanes, full facilities, litter barrels, petwalk, , wi-fi**
66	TX 115, FM 1927, to Pyote, N Alon/dsl
58	frontage rd, multiple oil wells
52	Lp 20 W, to Barstow
49	FM 516, to Barstow
48mm	Pecos River
44	Collie Rd
42	US 285, Pecos, N Flying J/Denny's/dsl/scales/24hr, A Sunoco/Stripes/dsl/e85 Alfredo's Mexican, DQ, El Ro Mexican, Golden Palace Chinese, Pizza Hut Holiday Express, Motel 6, OakTree Inn, Quality Inn AutoZone, seum, tire repair, Walmart, S Love's/McDonald's/S way/Chester's/dsl/scales/24hr/@ Microtel
40	Country Club Dr, N Cobblestone Inn, Comfort Suites, F field Inn st patrol, S Stripes/Subway Alpine Lo Rest. Best Western/rest., La Quinta municipal p Pecos Park/Zoo, RV camping
39	TX 17, Pecos, N Pilot/Dunkin'/PJ Fresh/dsl/scales/2 H, S Sunoco/Stripes/Subway/dsl/24hr Hampton La Bonita Inn Buick/Chevrolet/GMC, Pecos Tire, Trapark Park
37	Lp 20 E
33	FM 869
29	Shaw Rd, S to TX AM Ag Sta
25mm	**both lanes, accessible, litter barrels, tables**
22	FM 2903, to Toyah, N Valero/dsl
13	McAlpine Rd
7	Johnson Rd
3	Stocks Rd

I-20 begins/ends on I-10, 187mm.

INTERSTATE 27

AMARILLO

Exit #	Services
	I-27 begins/ends on I-40, exit 70 in Amarillo.
123b	I-40, W to Albuquerque, E to OK City
123a	26th Ave, E DJ Gas
122c	from sb only
122a	34th Ave, Tyler St, E Toot'n Totem Sonic $Gen
122b	FM 1541, Washington St, Parker St, Moss Lane, W T Bell, Thai Express
121a	Hawthorne Dr, Austin St, E Amarillo Motel, W Scot Transmissions
121b	Georgia St, E Murphy USA/dsl Buick/GMC, Ho Mazda, Subaru, Walmart/McDonald's
120b	45th Ave, E Waffle House O'Reilly Parts, W To Totum, Valero Abuelo's Mexican, Donut Stop, Gatti's Pi Grandma's Cocina, McDonald's, Sonic, Whataburger $G eral, Advance Parts, BMW, Chrysler/Dodge/Jeep, Drug Emp um, vet, Walgreens
120a	Republic Ave

INTERSTATE 27 Cont'd

Exit #	Services
119b a	(from sb) Western St, 58th Ave, E Phillips 66/dsl Sonic, Subway $General, Fiesta Foods, W Valero/dsl Arby's, Braum's, Thai Palace, Wendy's Aamco, U-Haul, USPO, Walgreens
119a	(from nb) W Hillside
117	Bell St, Arden Rd, W Valero/dsl Popeye's, Sonic $General
116	Lp 335, Hollywood Rd, E Loves/Subway/dsl/scales/24hr, Phillips 66/dsl McDonald's, Waffle House, Whataburger Comfort Suites, Motel 6, W Holiday Inn Express H (8mi)
115	Sundown Lane
113	McCormick Rd, E $General, Ford, W Family Camping Ctr
112	FM 2219, E Stater's RV Ctr
111	Rockwell Rd, W Buick/GMC
110	US 87 S, US 60 W, Canyon
109	Buffalo Stadium Rd, W stadium
108	FM 3331, Hunsley Rd
106	TX 217, to Palo Duro Cyn SP, Canyon, E Palo Duro Canyon SP (10mi), Palo Duro RV Park, 3 mi W McDonald's Best Western, Buffalo Inn, Holiday Inn Express Plains Museum, to W TX A&M
103	FM 1541 N, Cemetery Rd
99	Hungate Rd
98mm	**parking area both lanes, litter barrels**
96	Dowlen Rd
94	FM 285, to Wayside
92	Haley Rd
90	FM 1075, Happy, W gas/dsl
88b a	US 87 N, FM 1881, Happy, same as 90
83	FM 2698
82	FM 214
77	US 87, Tulia
75	NW 6th St, Tulia, 1 mi E Phillips 66/dsl Pizza Hut, Sonic Lasso Motel, W same as 74
74	TX 86, Tulia, E Lasso Motel H, W Pilot/Valero/Subway/dsl/scales/24hr Executive Inn
70mm	**parking area both lanes, litter barrels**
68	FM 928
63	FM 145, Kress, 1 mi E gas/dsl food
61	US 87, County Rd
56	FM 788
54	FM 3183, to Plainview
53	Lp 27, Plainview, E H, access to gas, camping, food, lodging
51	Quincy St
50	TX 194, Plainview, E Valero/dsl H, to Wayland Bapt U
49	US 70, Plainview, E AllStar/dsl, Allsup's, Cefco/dsl, Phillips 66/Stripes/dsl, Valero/dsl 910 Smokehouse BBQ, A&W/LJ Silver, Carlito's Mexican, China Dragon, Cotton Patch Café, Domino's, Leal's Mexican, Pizza Hut, Tokyo Japanese Comfort Suites, Days Inn, Quality Inn $Tree, AutoZone, Beall's, GNC, NAPA, O'Reilly Parts, United Foods, W Allsup's/dsl, Murphy USA/dsl, Valero/dsl Burger King, Chicken Express, Chili's, Dos Jefes, Empire Buffet, IHOP, McDonald's, Mia's Italian, Sonic, Subway, Taco Bell, Wendy's Holiday Inn Express, Plainview Inn, Super 8 AT&T, GNC, Verizon, Walmart/McDonald's
48	FM 3466, Plainview (from nb), E Chevrolet/Buick/GMC, Chrysler/Dodge/Jeep
45	Lp 27, to Plainview

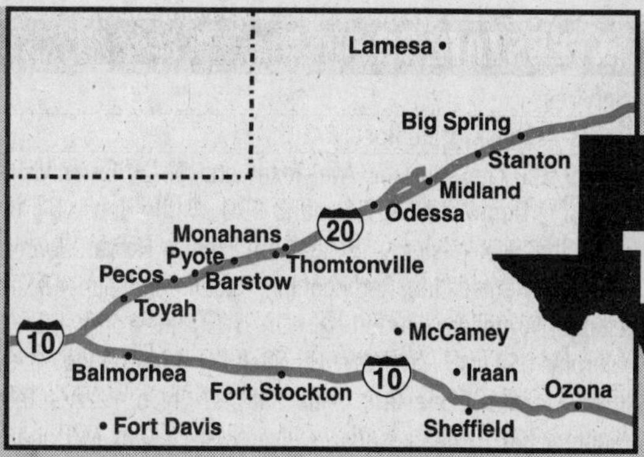

Exit #	Services
43	FM 2337
41	County Rd
38	Main St
37	FM 1914, Cleveland St, W Allsups/dsl city park, Family$, Lowe's Foods
36	FM 1424, Hale Center
32	FM 37 W
31	FM 37 E
29mm	**both lanes, full facilities, litter barrels, petwalk, tornado shelter, vending**
27	County Rd
24	FM 54, W RV park/dump
22	Lp 369, Abernathy
21	FM 597, Main St, Abernathy, W HH Farms/dsl DQ $General, USPO
20	FM 597, Abernathy (from nb)
17	CR 53
15	Lp 461, to New Deal, same as 14
14	FM 1729, E Alon/rest./dsl/scales/24hr
13	Lp 461, to New Deal
12	access rd (from nb)
11	FM 1294, Shallowater
10	Keuka St, E Fed Ex
9	Airport Rd, E, W Lubbock RV Park/LP/dump
8	FM 2641, Regis St, E, W Loves/Subway/Chester's/dsl/scales/24hr
7	Yucca Lane, E Pharr RV Ctr
6b a	Lp 289, Ave Q, Lubbock, E Pharr RV
5	B. Holly Ave, Municipal Dr, E Mackenzie SP, W Civic Ctr
4	US 82, US 87, 4th St, to Crosbyton, E funpark, W FLYING J/Subway/dsl/LP/scales/24hr to TTU
3	US 62, TX 114, 19th St, Floydada, E Phillips 66 NAPA
2	34th St, E Phillips 66/dsl Pete's Drive Inn, W Valero Josie's #5, Phillips 66, Subway AutoZone, Raff&Hall Drug, U-Haul
1c	50th St, E Buddy's El Charro Family$, W Alon/7-11, Valero/dsl A&W/LJ Silver, Bryan's Steaks, Burger King, China Star, Church's, Domino's, KFC, La Bella Pizza, McDonald's, Pizza Hut/Taco Bell, Subway, Wienerschnitzel Howard Johnson, Microtel $General, O'Reilly Parts, United Food/gas, USPO, Walgreens
1b	US 84, E Best Value Inn, Days Inn, W Best Western+, Country Inn Suites, EconoLodge, Holiday Inn Express, La Quinta, Motel 6, Quality Inn, Red Roof Inn, Super 8, Woodspring Suites Chevrolet
1a	Lp 289
1	82nd St, W Phillips 66/dsl, **I-27 begins/ends on US 87 at 82nd St in S Lubbock.**

LUBBOCK

TX

INTERSTATE 30

TEXARKANA

Exit #	Services
223mm	Texas/Arkansas state line
223b a	US 59, US 71, State Line Ave, Texarkana, N Exxon/dsl, EZ Mart Denny's, IHOP, Naaman's BBQ, Waffle House Baymont Inn, Best Western+, Holiday Inn Express, Howard Johnson, Ramada, Ramada Inn, Red Roof Inn, Regency Inn, Super 8, Travelodge, Wyndham Garden KOA, S Chevron/dsl, Exxon, Murphy USA/dsl, RaceWay/dsl, Shell Burger King, Cattleman's Steaks, China Inn, China King, El Chico, Fuzzy's Tacos, Hooters, KFC, Little Caesar's, LJ Silver, Marble Slab, McDonald's, Papa John's, Popeye's, Schlotzsky's, Slim Chickens, Sonic, Starbucks, Subway, Taco Bell, Wendy's, Whataburger Ambassador Inn, Best Value Inn, Days Inn, EconoLodge, Executive Inn, Magnuson Hotel, Motel 6, Rodeway Inn $General, $Tree, Albertson's/Sav-On, AutoZone, CVS Drug, O'Reilly Parts, VW, Walgreens, Walmart/Subway
223mm	**Welcome Ctr wb, full facilities, info, litter barrels, petwalk, vending**
222	TX 93, FM 1397, Summerhill Rd, N Shell, Valero/Subway/dsl Applebee's, McDonald's, The One Buffet, Waffle House Motel 6 AT&T, Goodyear Truck Tire, Hyundai, URGENT CARE, S Exxon/dsl Catfish King, Sonic Ford, Gateway Tires, Nissan, Walmart Mkt/dsl
220b	FM 559, Richmond Rd, N Shell Buffalo Wild Wings, Burger King, Cane's, Chick-fil-A, Chipotle, CiCi's Pizza, Coldstone Creamery, Cracker Barrel, Domino's, DQ, Fuji Grill, Genghis Grill, Gusano's Pizza, Jason's Deli, Jimmy John's, Larry's Pizza, Little Caesar's, Longhorn Steaks, McAlister's Deli, Mooyah Burgers, On-the-Border, Osaka Japanese, Papa Murphy's, Pizza Hut, Red Lobster, Reggie's Cafe, Ruby Tuesday, Schlotzky's, Silver Star Smokehouse, Smashburger, Sonic, Starbucks, Steak'n Shake, Taco Bell, TaMolly's Mexican, TX Roadhouse, Wendy's, Wing Stop Comfort Suites, Courtyard, Residence Inn, TownePlace Suites $General, $Tree, AT&T, Best Buy, Chevrolet, Discount Tire, Home Depot, Honda, Kohl's, Kwik Kar, Office Depot, Old Navy, Petsmart, Sam's Club/gas, Super 1 Food/gas, Target, TJ Maxx, Verizon, Walmart Mkt/dsl, S Valero/dsl Arby's, Chili's, ChuckeCheese, Firehouse Subs, Golden Chick, Golden Corral, Grandy's, Lee's China, McDonald's, Newk's, Olive Garden, Outback Steaks, Subway, Taco Bueno, Tacos 4Life Candlewood Suites, Hampton Inn, Hilton Garden/Conv Ctr, Holiday Inn Express Albertson's/Sav-On, AT&T, Books-A-Million, Cavender's Boots, CVS Drug, Dillard's, Hobby Lobby, JC Penney, Michael's, Ross, Tuesday Morning, Walgreens
220a	I-369 S, US 59 S, Texarkana
219	Pecan St, University Ave, S Exxon, Murphy USA Subway, Wendy's Country Inn&Suites, Fairfield Inn Buick/GMC, Cadillac, Chrysler/Dodge/Jeep, Harley-Davidson, Kia, Lowe's, Mazda, Mercedes, vet, Walmart
218	FM 989, Nash, N Road Runner/dsl Dixie Diner, S 76/TX Best BBQ/Steak'n Shake/Golden Chick/Dunkin/dsl, Exxon/Burger King/dsl Sonic GMC/Peterbilt, to Lake Patman, Toyota, USPO
213	FM 2253, Leary, S Love's/McDonald's/Subway/dsl/scales/24hr
212	spur 74, S Lone Star Army Ammo Plant
208	FM 560, Hooks, N Valero/dsl, S Truckstp/dsl/scales/24hr DQ, Sonic $General, Family$, Hooks Tire
207	rd 594, Red River Army Depot
206	TX 86, S Red River Army Depot

NEW BOSTON

Exit #	Services
201	TX 8, New Boston, N Exxon/Burger King/dsl, Valero, Pitt Grill Tex Inn Chevrolet, Chrysler/Dodge/Je S Murphy USA/dsl, Shell/dsl Catfish King, Churc Domino's, DQ, KFC/Taco Bell, McDonald's, Pizza Hut, Ran BBQ, Sonic Best Value Inn, Bostonian Inn, Holiday Inn press $Tree, Brookshire's Foods/gas, Ford, O'Reilly Pa Verizon, Walmart/Subway
199	US 82, New Boston, **1/2 mi N** VP/dsl, S Exxon/Denny's
198	TX 98, **1/2 mi N** VP/dsl
193mm	Anderson Creek
192	FM 990
186	FM 561
181mm	Sulphur River
178	US 259, to DeKalb, Omaha
174mm	White Oak Creek
170	FM 1993
165	FM 1001

MT PLEASANT

Exit #	Services
162b a	US 271, FM 1402, FM 2152, Mt Pleasant, N Exxon Applebee's, Blalock BBQ Holiday Inn Express, Su 8 $General, KOA, S Shell/dsl, Sunoco/Subway Burger King, McDonald's, Popeye's, Sonic Best West H, $General, Cadillac/Chevrolet, Chrysler/Dodge/J Family$, Ford, vet
160	US 271, FM 1734, Mt Pleasant, N Texaco/dsl Se rita's Mexican La Quinta Buick/GMC (1mi), Low Ramblin Fever RV Park (2mi), Toyota, S Exxon/dsl, Sh dsl IHOP, Jalapeño Tree Executive Inn, Hampton Motel 6, Quality Inn Sandlin SP
158mm	**weigh sta both lanes**
156	frontage rd
153	spur 185, to Winfield, Miller's Cove, N Hana/Exxon/Win Cafe/dsl, Winfield/dsl
150	Ripley Rd, N Lowe's Distribution
147	spur 423, N Love's/Chester's/Subway/dsl/scales/2 American Inn tires/repair, S Duke's/Shell/Taco C BBQ/dsl
146	TX 37, Mt Vernon, N Sonic $General, auto repair, Br shire Foods/gas, O'Reilly Parts, S Cefco/Huddle Ho dsl/24hr, Exxon/dsl Burger King, DQ, El Manna, McDon Super 8 auto/dsl repair, to Lake Bob Sandlin SP
142	County Line Rd (from eb)
141	FM 900, Saltillo Rd
136	FM 269, Weaver Rd
135	US 67 N
131	FM 69

SULPHUR SPGS

Exit #	Services
127	US 67, Lp 301, N Days Inn, Econolodge, Ferrari Inn, M 6 H, S Shell Best Western
126	FM 1870, College St, S Shell Best Western F tone/auto, same as 127
125	Bill Bradford Rd, same as 124
124	TX 11, TX 154, Sulphur Springs, N Exxon/dsl Bodac BBQ, Broadway Buffet, Chicken Express, Don Ialo's Mexi IHOP, Juan Pablo's Mexican, Metro Diner, Pizza Hut, Schlotzs Soulman's BBQ, Subway, Wendy's Hampton Inn, Hol Inn Express, Royal Inn H, $General, AutoZone, Brooksh Foods/gas, CVS Drug, Family$, Ford/Lincoln, FSA Outlet/fan brands, O'Reilly Parts, USPO, VF Outlet/famous brands, greens, S Exxon/dsl, Murphy USA/dsl, Shell/dsl, Brau Burger King, Chili's, Domino's, DQ, Furr's Rest., Jack-in-the- McDonald's, Panda Express, Pizza Inn, Roma Italian, Sonic, bucks, Taco Bell/LJ Silver, Whataburger AT&T, Cody D Discount Wheel&Tire, Lowe's, Verizon, Walmart/Subway

E INTERSTATE 30 Cont'd

Exit #	Services
123	FM 2297, League St, N Shamrock/dsl, Shell
122	TX 19, to Emory, N Shamrock/dsl H, Chrysler/Dodge/Jeep, to Cooper Lake SP, Travel Time RV Ctr, S CNG, Loves/Carl's Jr/dsl/scales/24hr, Pilot/Arby's/dsl/scales/24hr, Valero/dsl dsl repair
120	US 67 bus
116	FM 2653, Brashear Rd, S USPO
112	FM 499 (from wb)
111mm	both lanes, full facilities
110	FM 275, Cumby, N Phillips 66/dsl, S Valero/dsl
104	FM 513, FM 2649, Campbell, S to Lake Tawakoni
101	TX 24, TX 50, FM 1737, to Commerce, N Exxon/dsl to TX A&M-Commerce
97	Lamar St, N Exxon/dsl Budget Inn, S vet
96	Lp 302
95	Division St, S H
94b	US 69, US 380, Greenville, N Valero/dsl Collin St Bakery, Golden Chick, Senorita's Mexican Knights Inn, Royal Inn H, S Exxon, QT/dsl Arby's, McDonald's, Racho Viejo Economy Inn, Express Inn, Guest Inn, Motel 6, Super 8
94a	US 69, US 380, Greenville, S QT/dsl, Valero/Subway/dsl Chrysler/Dodge/Jeep
93b a	US 67, TX 34 N, N Chevron/Taco Casa/dsl, Exxon/dsl, RaceTrac/dsl, Shell/dsl, Texaco Applebee's, Braum's, Buffet Palace, Chicken Express, Chick-fil-A, Chipotle, CiCi's, Cotton Patch Cafe, DQ, El Fenix, Firehouse Subs, Grandy's, IHOP, Jack-in-the-Box, Jimmy John's, KFC, Little Caesar's, Panera Bread, Pizza Hut, Schlotzsky's, Sonic, Starbucks, Subway, Taco Bell, Taco Bueno, Tony's Italian, Wendy's, Whataburger Hampton Inn H, Aldi Foods, AT&T, Beall's, Belk, BigLots, Brookshire's Foods, Cavender's Outfitter, Discount Tire, Hobby Lobby, Kwik Kar, Lowe's, Marshall's, O'Reilly Parts, Petco, Ross, Staples, URGENT CARE, USPO, Verizon, Walgreens, S Exxon/dsl, Murphy USA/dsl, Shell/dsl Burger King, Chili's, Cracker Barrel, Molina's Mexican, Panda Express, Papa John's, Popeye's, Red Lobster, Rib Crib BBQ, Shogun Hibachi, Soulman's BBQ, Subway, TaMolly's Mexican Best Western+, Comfort Suites, Holiday Inn Express $Tree, Buick/GMC, Ford/Lincoln, Home Depot, Hyundai, Nissan, NTB, Walmart
92	Stratton Pkwy, S Chevrolet/Cadillac
90mm	Farber Creek
89	FM 1570, S Luxury Inn
89mm	E Caddo Creek
87	FM 1903, N Shell/dsl fireworks, S Pilot/McDonald's/dsl/scales/24hr, Texaco/Huddle House/dsl Baker's Ribs tire repair
87mm	Elm Creek
85	FM 36, Caddo Mills, N Dallas NE RV Park
85mm	W Caddo Creek
83	FM 1565 N, N Exxon/Pizza Inn/dsl
79	FM 2642, N Budget RV Ctr, S Buc-ee's/dsl vet
77b	FM 35, Royse City, N Texaco/Subway/dsl/scales/24hr Soulman's BBQ Family$
77a	TX 548, Royse City, N Shell/dsl Jack-in-the-Box, McDonald's American Inn AutoZone, tires, S Exxon Denny's, Pizza Hut, Rice Express, Sonic, Taco Bell Holiday Inn Express
76	Campbell Blvd, N Murphy Express/dsl Arby's, Burger King, DQ, Palio's Pizza Cafe, Panda Express, Papa John's, Popeye's, Whataburger AT&T, CVS Drug, Kwik Kar, O'Reilly Parts, URGENT CARE, Walmart/Subway

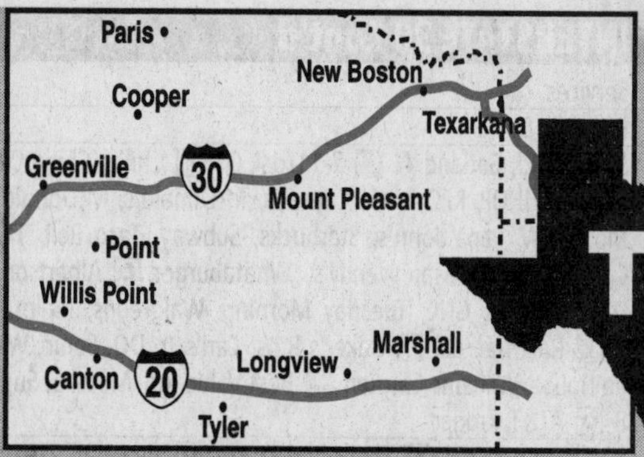

ROCKWALL

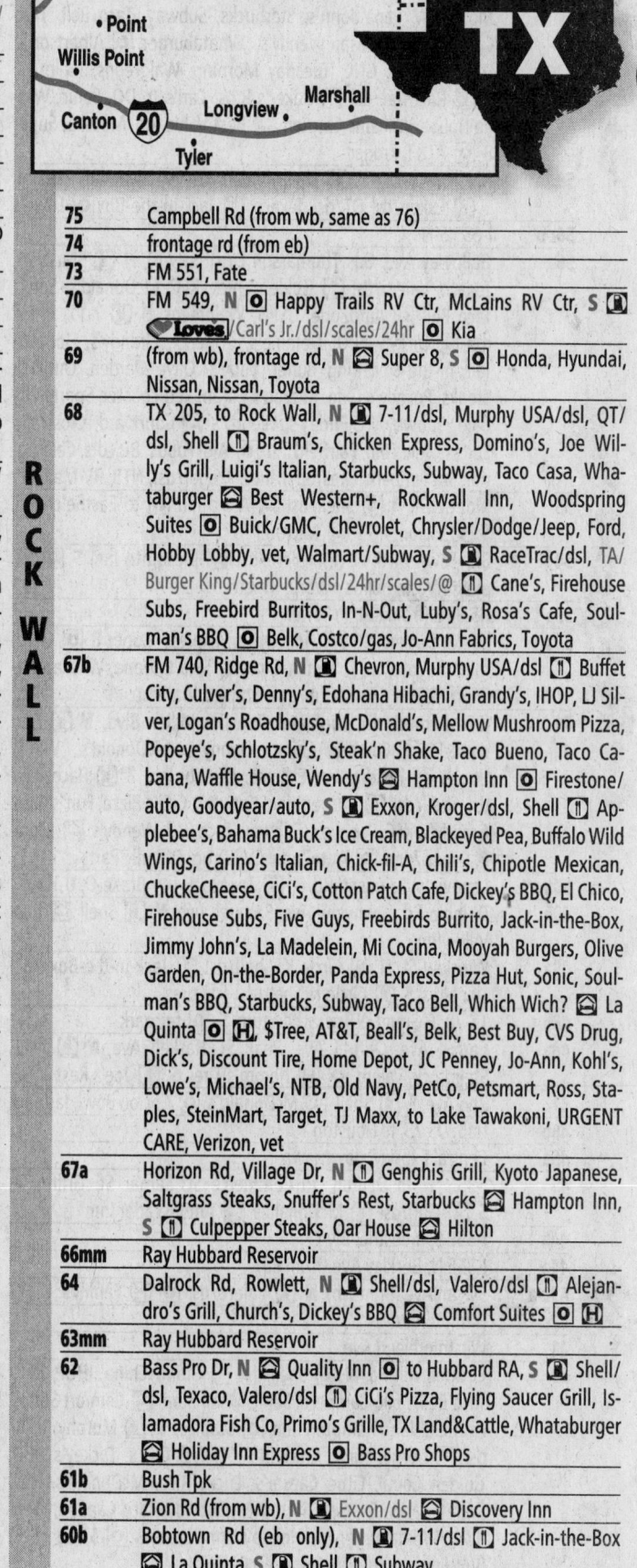

Exit #	Services
75	Campbell Rd (from wb, same as 76)
74	frontage rd (from eb)
73	FM 551, Fate
70	FM 549, N Happy Trails RV Ctr, McLains RV Ctr, S Loves/Carl's Jr./dsl/scales/24hr Kia
69	(from wb), frontage rd, N Super 8, S Honda, Hyundai, Nissan, Nissan, Toyota
68	TX 205, to Rock Wall, N 7-11/dsl, Murphy USA/dsl, QT/dsl, Shell Braum's, Chicken Express, Domino's, Joe Willy's Grill, Luigi's Italian, Starbucks, Subway, Taco Casa, Whataburger Best Western+, Rockwall Inn, Woodspring Suites Buick/GMC, Chevrolet, Chrysler/Dodge/Jeep, Ford, Hobby Lobby, vet, Walmart/Subway, S RaceTrac/dsl, TA/Burger King/Starbucks/dsl/24hr/scales/@ Cane's, Firehouse Subs, Freebird Burritos, In-N-Out, Luby's, Rosa's Cafe, Soulman's BBQ Belk, Costco/gas, Jo-Ann Fabrics, Toyota
67b	FM 740, Ridge Rd, N Chevron, Murphy USA/dsl Buffet City, Culver's, Denny's, Edohana Hibachi, Grandy's, IHOP, LJ Silver, Logan's Roadhouse, McDonald's, Mellow Mushroom Pizza, Popeye's, Schlotzsky's, Steak'n Shake, Taco Bueno, Taco Cabana, Waffle House, Wendy's Hampton Inn Firestone/auto, Goodyear/auto, S Exxon, Kroger/dsl, Shell Applebee's, Bahama Buck's Ice Cream, Blackeyed Pea, Buffalo Wild Wings, Carino's Italian, Chick-fil-A, Chili's, Chipotle Mexican, ChuckeCheese, CiCi's, Cotton Patch Cafe, Dickey's BBQ, El Chico, Firehouse Subs, Five Guys, Freebirds Burrito, Jack-in-the-Box, Jimmy John's, La Madelein, Mi Cocina, Mooyah Burgers, Olive Garden, On-the-Border, Panda Express, Pizza Hut, Sonic, Soulman's BBQ, Starbucks, Subway, Taco Bell, Which Wich? La Quinta H, $Tree, AT&T, Beall's, Belk, Best Buy, CVS Drug, Dick's, Discount Tire, Home Depot, JC Penney, Jo-Ann, Kohl's, Lowe's, Michael's, NTB, Old Navy, PetCo, Petsmart, Ross, Staples, SteinMart, Target, TJ Maxx, to Lake Tawakoni, URGENT CARE, Verizon, vet
67a	Horizon Rd, Village Dr, N Genghis Grill, Kyoto Japanese, Saltgrass Steaks, Snuffer's Rest, Starbucks Hampton Inn, S Culpepper Steaks, Oar House Hilton
66mm	Ray Hubbard Reservoir
64	Dalrock Rd, Rowlett, N Shell/dsl, Valero/dsl Alejandro's Grill, Church's, Dickey's BBQ Comfort Suites H
63mm	Ray Hubbard Reservoir
62	Bass Pro Dr, N Quality Inn to Hubbard RA, S Shell/dsl, Texaco, Valero/dsl CiCi's Pizza, Flying Saucer Grill, Islamadora Fish Co, Primo's Grille, TX Land&Cattle, Whataburger Holiday Inn Express Bass Pro Shops
61b	Bush Tpk
61a	Zion Rd (from wb), N Exxon/dsl Discovery Inn
60b	Bobtown Rd (eb only), N 7-11/dsl Jack-in-the-Box La Quinta, S Shell Subway

TX

TX

INTERSTATE 30 Cont'd

Exit #	Services
	GARLAND
60a	Rose Hill Dr
59	Beltline Rd, Garland, N 7-11/dsl, QT Chili's, China City, Denny's, IHOP, KFC, Little Caesar's, McDonald's, McDonald's, Moe's SW, Papa John's, Starbucks, Subway, Taco Bell, Taco Cabana, Taco Casa, Wendy's, Whataburger Albertson's, Discount Tire, GNC, Tuesday Morning, Walgreens, Walmart, S RaceTrac/dsl Baker's Ribs, Carl's Jr, DQ, Sonic, Waffle House, Williams Chicken Best Value Inn, Motel 6, Super 8 AT&T, Kroger
58	Northwest Dr, N Shell, Valero/dsl Hyundai, Nissan, S Exxon/dsl, QT/dsl, Texaco Jack-in-the-Box Lowe's
56c b	I-635 S-N
56a	Galloway Ave, Gus Thomasson Dr (from eb), N Star USA, Texaco, Valero/dsl Golden Chick, KFC, McDonald's, Sonic, Taco Bell AutoZone, USPO, Walgreens, S 7-11, Chevron Dicky's BBQ, Domino's, El Fenix, Grandy's, Hooters, Jack-in-the-Box, King Buffet, Luby's, Olive Garden, Outback Steaks, Posado's Cafe, Razzoo's Cajun, Red Lobster, Sports City Cafe, Subway, TGIFriday's, Wendy's Courtyard, Crossland Suites, Delux Inn, Fairfield Inn Aldi Foods, BigLots, Celebration Sta Funpark, Firestone/auto, Kroger/dsl, NTB, RV Max
	DALLAS
55	Motley Dr, N Shell/dsl Astro Inn to Eastfield Coll, S Exxon/7-11 Microtel
54	Big Town Blvd, N Valero/dsl Mesquite Inn, S Explore RV Ctr, Holiday World RV Ctr
53b	US 80 E (from eb), to Terrell
53a	Lp 12, Buckner, N Holiday Inn Express, Super 8 Chevrolet, Toyota, S Panda Express, Taco Cabana, Whataburger $Tree, Sam's Club/gas, Staples, Walmart
51	(52 a from wb), Highland Rd, Jim Miller Blvd, N Exxon/7-11 Country China, Denny's, McDonald's, Waffle House Holiday Inn Express, Quality Inn, S RaceWay/dsl, Shell/dsl Burger King, Capt D's, CiCi's Pizza, Furr's Cafe, Grandy's, KFC, Popeye's, Subway, Taco Bell, Wendy's Motel 6, Super 7 Inn AutoZone, CVS Drug, O'Reilly Parts
50b a	Longview, Ferguson Rd, N Texaco, S Brake-O, U-Haul
49b	Dolphin Rd, Lawnview Ave, Samuell Ave, N Shell Best Value Inn
49a	Winslow St, N Circle K, Shell/dsl Jack-in-the-Box, McDonald's, S Circle K, Shell/dsl tires
48b	TX 78, E Grand, N arboretum, S fairpark
48a	Carroll Ave, Central Ave, Peak St, Haskell Ave, N 7-11, Shamrock, Valero H, Hamm's Tires, S Joe's Rest
47	2nd Ave, S Shell McDonald's Cotton Bowl, fairpark
46b	I-45, US 75, to Houston
46a	Central Expswy, downtown
45	I-35E, N to Denton, to Commerce St, Lamar St, Griffin St, S Gulf/dsl McDonald's Ambassador Inn
44b	I-35E S, Industrial Blvd
44a	I-35E N, Beckley Ave (from eb)
43b a	Sylvan Ave (from wb), N Valero/dsl H, Family$, USPO
42	Hampton Rd
41	Westmoreland Ave
39	Cockrell Hill Rd, N Shell/dsl Grand China, IHOP, KFC/Taco Bell, Pollo Campero, Sonic, Wing Stop Comfort Suites, Fairfield Inn, Hampton Inn Staples, S Murphy USA/dsl Burger King, Chick-fil-A, Chili's, CiCi's, Dickey's BBQ, Golden Corral, Little Caesar's, Lucky Rice, McDonald's, New Buffet, Panda Express, Starbucks, Subway, Taco Cabana, Wendy's, Whataburger Holiday Inn Express $Tree, Best Buy, Lowe's, Ross, Walmart/McDonald's
	ARLINGTON
38	Lp 12, 1 mi N Exxon/7-11, Texaco/dsl, VP/dsl Bur King
36	MacArthur Blvd, S U-Haul
34	Belt Line Rd, N QT/dsl, RaceTrac/dsl Studio 6, Su 8 Ford, Ripley's Museum, S RaceTrac/dsl, Shell/S way/dsl, Valero/dsl Burger King, Popeye's, Schlotzsk Starbucks city park, vet
32b a	George Bush Tpk, toll, N Valero/dsl
30	TX 360, Six Flags Dr, Arlington Stadium, N Shell, Vale dsl Boston's, Cracker Barrel, Grand Buffet, Saltgrass Ste Steak'n Shake, The Rock Grill, Wendy's Best Inn, Bud Suites, Candlewood Suites, Crowne Plaza, Extended Stay Am ica, Extended Stay America, Fairfield Inn, Hawthorn Sui Hilton, Hilton Garden, Hyatt Place, Motel 6, Residence Studio 6, Wingate Inn, S Shell/7-11/dsl, Valero D ny's, Humperdink's Rest., Jack-in-the-Box, Mariano's Mexi McDonald's, Red Neck Heaven Rest, Subway Baymont Holiday Inn Express, Homewood Suites, Hyatt Place, Knig Inn, La Quinta, Quality Inn, Ranger Inn, Sleep Inn Ford/ coln, Six Flags Funpark
29	Ball Park Way, N Chevron/7-11, QT, Valero/dsl Dic BBQ, Rio Mambo, Sonic Hampton Inn, Springhill Sui Towneplace Suites Auto Nation/Toyota, USPO, S the-Border, Vila Brazil Howard Johnson, Sheraton Flags Funpark
28b a	FM 157, Collins St, N Chevron/dsl Chipotle, IH Mooyah Burgers, Pei Wei, Potbelly, Starbucks, Waffle H EconoLodge, Holiday Inn BMW, Cadillac, Chrys Dodge/Jeep, Mini, Walmart, Whole Foods Mkt, S Ar Asian Buffet, Blackeyed Pea, Blue Mesa Grill, Buffalo Wings, Cane's, Chili's, El Chico, Gino's East Pizzaria, Hoo Jason's Deli, Joe's Crab Shack, Lupe's Grill, Olive Garden, da Express, Panera Bread, Pappadeaux, Pappasito's Can Popeye's, Sherlock's Grill, Subway, Taco Bell, Taco Bueno, Friday's, TX Land&Cattle, Wendy's, Which Wich? Co Suites, Courtyard, Days Inn $Tree, GNC, Home Depot, chael's, Office Depot, PepBoys, Petsmart, Ross, SteinMar Stadium, Walgreens
27	Lamar Blvd, Cooper St, N Gulf Jack-in-the-Box, way BigLots, Family$, Kroger/dsl, vet, S 7-11, QT Shell/dsl Burger King, Pappasito's Cantina, Tom's B ers Comfort Suites
26	Fielder Rd, S to Six Flags (from eb)
25mm	Village Creek
24	Eastchase Pkwy, N Jack-in-the-Box, Panda Express Quinta CarMax, Lowe's, Sam's Club/gas, Ver Walmart/McDonald's, S Chevron/7-11/dsl, RaceTrac Shell/7-11/dsl Burger King, Chicken Express, CiCi's P IHOP, McDonald's, No Frills Grill, Pizza Hut, Schlotzsky's, way, Taco Bell, Wendy's, Whataburger $Tree, Aldi Fo AT&T, GNC, Marshall's, Office Depot, Ross, Target
23	Cooks Lane, S Shell/dsl
21c b	I-820
21a	Bridgewood Dr, N Chevron/dsl Braum's, Dickey's Jack-in-the-Box, KFC, Luby's, Subway, Taco Casa, We $General, Albertson's, Discount Tire, Firestone/auto, H Depot, U-Haul, S Conoco, Phillips 66/dsl, QT Taco no, Whataburger/24hr
19	Brentwood Stair Rd (from eb), N Shell, S Sham Texaco Family$
18	Oakland Blvd, N Circle K, Shell/dsl Taco Bell, W House Motel 6

TX

INTERSTATE 30 Cont'd

Exit #	Services
16c	Beach St, S 7-11 Motel 6, Stay Express Hotel
16b a	Riverside Dr (from wb), S Great Western Inn
15b a	I-35W N to Denton, S to Waco
14b	Jones St, Commerce St, Ft Worth, downtown
14a	TX 199, Henderson St, Ft Worth, downtown
13b	TX 199, Henderson St, N Holiday Inn Express, Omni, Sheraton
13a	8th Ave, N Holiday Inn Express
12b	Forest Park Blvd, N Pappadeaux Café, Pappa's Burgers, Pappasito's, S H, URGENT CARE
12a	University Dr, City Parks, S SpringHill Suites
11	Montgomery St, S Shell/7-11/dsl Railhead BBQ, Taco Bell, Whataburger
10	Hulen St, Ft Worth, S Buttons Rest., Chick-fil-A, McDonald's, Mi Cocina, Potbelly, Smoothie King, Starbucks Central Mkt, WorldMkt
9b	US 377, Camp Bowie Blvd, Horne St, N Uncle Julio's Mexican, S 7-11, Exxon/7-11, Texaco/dsl Campisi's Italian, Chipotle, Jack-in-the-Box, Jason's Deli, Jersey Mike's, Jimmy John's, McDonald's, Mexican Inn Cafe, Schlotzsky's, Smashburger, Sonic, Starbucks, Subway, Taco Bueno, Wendy's AT&T, Batteries+Bulbs, URGENT CARE, Walgreens
9a	Bryant-Irvin Rd, S Shell same as 9b
8b	Ridgmar, Ridglea
8a	TX 183, Green Oaks Rd, N Applebee's, Arby's, Asia Bowl, Cane's, Chick-fil-A, Chipotle, Cowtown BBQ, Del Taco, Don Pablo's, Firehouse Subs, Grand Buffet, Jack-in-the-Box, McDonald's, Olive Garden, Panda Express, Papa Murphy's, Sonic, Subway, Taco Bueno, Whataburger, Woody Creek BBQ Courtyard $Tree, Albertson's, Aldi Foods, AT&T, Best Buy, BigLots, Dillard's, Firestone/auto, JC Penney, Jo-Ann Fabrics, Lowe's, Neiman Marcus, NTB, Office Depot, Old Navy, PetCo, Petsmart, Ross, Sam's Club/gas, Target, U-Haul, Verizon, Walmart/Subway, S Fairfield Inn, Hampton Inn
7b a	Cherry Lane, TX 183, spur 341, to Green Oaks Rd, N Shell/7-11, Texaco/dsl, Valero/dsl ChuckECheese, IHOP, Popeye's, Subway, Wendy's Comfort Inn, Motel 6, Scottish Inn O'Reilly Parts, same as 8a, U-Haul, S QT/dsl Holiday Inn, Holiday Inn Express, La Quinta, Quality Inn, Super 8
6	Las Vegas Trail, N Chevron/McDonald's/dsl, Conoco/dsl Jack-in-the-Box, Waffle House Days Inn Hyundai, Lincoln, S Shell/7-11/dsl, Texaco, Valero/dsl Best Value Inn, Knights Inn, Relax Inn AutoZone, Kia, vet
5b c	I-820 N and S
5a	Alemeda St (from eb, no EZ return)
3	RM 2871, Chapel Creek Blvd, S Exxon/Church's/Subway/dsl Sonic
2	spur 580 E
1b	Linkcrest Dr, S Gulf/dsl
0mm	I-20 W. **I-30 begins/ends on I-20, exit 421.**

INTERSTATE 35

Exit #	Services
504mm	Texas/Oklahoma state line, Red River
504	frontage rd, access to **Texas Welcome Ctr**
503mm	**parking area both lanes**
502mm	**Welcome Ctr sb, full facilities, litter barrels, , TX Tourist Bureau/info, wireless internet**
501	FM 1202, Prime Outlets Blvd, E Chrysler/Dodge/Jeep, Ford, W Conoco/café/dsl Applebee's, Cracker Barrel Hampton Inn, La Quinta Prime Outlets/famous brands, RV camping, Western Outfitter

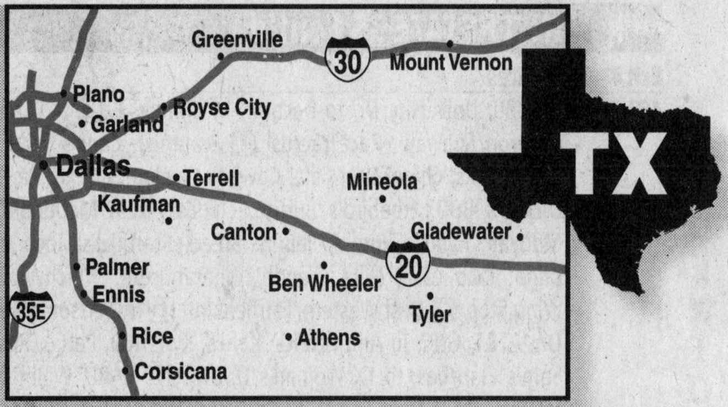

GAINESVILLE

Exit #	Services
501	Continued Hampton Inn, La Quinta Prime Outlets/famous brands, RV camping, Western Outfitter
500	FM 372, Gainesville, W Hitchin' Post/Shell/dsl
498b a	US 82, to Wichita Falls, Gainesville, Sherman, E Chevron/dsl, Shell/dsl, Valero/dsl Luigi's Italian Budget Host, Super 8 H, AT&T, URGENT CARE, W Exxon/dsl Comfort Suites, Days Inn, Rodeway Inn
497	frontage rd, W Valero/dsl
496b	TX 51, FM 51, California St, Gainesville, E Chevron Arby's, Braum's, Fera's Mexican, IHOP, McDonald's, Sonic, Starbucks, Starbucks, Taco Bell, Taco Casa, Wendy's Holiday Inn Express, Quality Inn Kwik Kar/auto, Lowe's Mkt, W Valero Chili's N Central TX Coll
496a	to Weaver St
496mm	Elm Fork of the Trinity River
495	frontage rd
494	FM 1306
492mm	**sb, litter barrels, tables**
491	Spring Creek Rd
490mm	**nb, litter barrels**
489	FM 1307, to Hockley Creek Rd
487	FM 922, Valley View, W Shell/Subway/Taco Tico/dsl, Valero/dsl DQ USPO
486	Fm 1307, W Texaco/dsl Texas Inn $General
485	frontage rd (from sb)
483	FM 3002, Lone Oak Rd, E Shell/Church's/Subway/dsl Roberts Lake SP, RV Guys
482	Chisam Rd
481	View Rd, W McClain's RV Ctr
480	Lois Rd, E Walmart Dist Ctr
479	Belz Rd, Sanger, same as 478
478	FM 455, to Pilot Pt, Bolivar, E QuickTrack, Shell/dsl DQ, Fuzzy's Tacos, Miguelito's, Pizza Hut, Sonic, Subway, Taco Bell Sanger Inn RV park, USPO, W Chevron/dsl, Conoco/Chicken Express/dsl Domino's, Jack-in-the-Box, McDonald's Chevrolet, Family$, Kwik Kar Lube, O'Reilly Parts, Ray Roberts Lake and SP, Super Save Foods, Verizon
477	Keaton Rd, E Exxon/dsl
475b	Rector Rd
475a	FM 156, to Krum (from sb)
474	Cowling rd (from nb)
473	FM 3163, Milam Rd, E Love's/Subway/dsl/scales/24hr
472	Ganzer Rd, W Crandell RV Ctr
471	US 77, FM 1173, Lp 282, to Denton, Krum, E TA/Pizza Hut/Taco Bell/dsl/scales/24hr/@ H, W Love's/Godfather's/Subway/Wendy's/dsl/scales/24hr Foster's Western Shop, to Camping World RV Supply
470	Lp 288, same services as 469 from sb

TX

DENTON

INTERSTATE 35 Cont'd

Exit #	Services
469	US 380, University Dr, to Decatur, McKinney, E [gas] 7-11/dsl, Chevron/Subway, RaceTrac/dsl [food] Braum's, Cane's, Chick-fil-A, Chili's, ChinaTown Café, Cowboy Chicken, Cracker Barrel, Dickey's BBQ, Freebird's Burrito, Luigi's Pizza, McDonald's, Mooyah, Panda Express, Panera Bread, Starbucks, Taco Cabana, Taco Casa, Villa Grande, Whataburger, WhichWich?, Wing Stop [lodging] Best Western, Fairfield Inn [other] Albertson's/Sav-On, AT&T, GNC, Jo-Ann Fabrics, Kohl's, Kwik Kar, PetCo, Ross, Sam's Club/gas, to TX Woman's U, URGENT CARE, Walmart/McDonald's, Winco Foods, W [gas] Exxon/dsl, QT/dsl [food] Brisket Burger, Denny's, DQ, Shell/dsl, Waffle House [lodging] Comfort Inn, Days Inn, Holiday Inn Express, Howard Johnson, La Quinta, Motel 6, Woodspring Suites Inn [other] [H], Camping World RV Supply, I-35 RV Ctr
468	FM 1515, Airport Rd, W Oak St, E [other] [H]
467	I-35W, S to Ft Worth
I-35 divides into E and W sb, converges into I-35 nb. See Texas I-35 W.	
466b	Ave D, E [food] Central Grill, Chicken Express, IHOP, Pancho's Mexican [other] $General, to NTSU
466a	McCormick St, E [gas] EKon, Shell/7-11/dsl [food] Pancho's Mexican [other] $General
465b	US 377, Ft Worth Dr, E [gas] RaceTrac/dsl, Valero [food] Layalina Mediterranean, Taco Bell, Whataburger [lodging] Motel 6, W [gas] 7-11/dsl [food] Outback Steaks, Sonic [lodging] Knights Inn
465a	FM 2181, Teasley Ln, E [gas] 7-11 [food] Applebee's, Braum's, Carino's, ChuckeCheese, Domino's, Hooters, KFC, Little Caesar's, Pizza Hut, Subway [lodging] Hampton Inn, Quality Inn [other] Brookshires Foods, U-Haul, W [gas] Exxon, Shell/dsl [food] La Milpa Mexican, Rudy's BBQ/gas [lodging] Best Value Inn, Super 8 [other] vet
464	US 77, Pennsylvania Dr, Denton, same as 463
463	Lp 288, to McKinney, E [gas] Murphy USA, RaceTrac/dsl [food] Arby's, Buffalo Wild Wings, Buffet King, Burger King, Carl's Jr, Chick-fil-A, Chipotle, CiCi's Pizza, Corner Bakery Cafe, Egg&I Cafe, El Fenix, Five Guys, Fuddrucker's, Golden Corral, Gulf Coast Kitchen, Jason's Deli, Jersey Mike's, Jimmy John's, LJ Silver, McAlister's Deli, McDonald's, Mooyah, Olive Garden, On-the-Border, Palio's Pizza, Panda Express, Pei Wei, Pollo Tropical, Red Lobster, Sonic, Starbucks, Taco Bell, TX Roadhouse, Wendy's, Whataburger [lodging] Best Western, Courtyard, Hilton Garden [other] $General, $Tree, AT&T, Barnes&Noble, Best Buy, BigLots, Burlington Coats, Dillard's, Discount Tire, Firestone/auto, Goodyear/auto, Hobby Lobby, Home Depot, JC Penney, Kroger/dsl, Kwik Kar, Lowe's, Macy's, Michael's, NTB, Office Depot, Old Navy, PetCo, Petsmart, Ross, Staples, Target, TJ Maxx, Verizon, Walgreens, Walmart, W [gas] Chevron/dsl [food] BJ's Rest., Bone Daddy's, Chili's, Chuy's Mexican, Fuzzy's Tacos, Jack-in-the-Box, Papa John's, Schlotzsky's, Wing Stop [lodging] Homewood Suites [other] EMERGENCY CARE, same as 464, vet
462	State School Rd, Mayhill Rd, E [gas] QT [food] Dickey's BBQ, Subway [lodging] Residence Inn [other] [H], URGENT CARE, W [gas] Exxon [food] Shogun Japanese, Sonic [other] Buick/GMC, Cadillac, Chevrolet, Chrysler/Dodge/Jeep, Honda, Toyota
461	Sandy Shores Rd, Post Oak Dr, E [other] Explore USA RV Ctr, Ford, Hyundai, vet, W [other] Christian Bros Auto, Chrysler/Dodge/Jeep, Kia, Mazda, Nissan, Subaru
460	Corinth Pkwy, E [other] McClains RV Ctr, W [other] Harley-Davidson
459	frontage rd, W [other] Destiny RV Resort
458	FM 2181, Swisher Rd, E [gas] Circle K, QT/dsl [lodging] Best Western, Comfort Inn [other] O'Reilly Parts, W [gas] Chevron/McDonald's, Exxon/7-11, Murphy USA/dsl [food] Chicken Express, Chick-fil-A, Denny's,

LEWISVILLE

Exit #	Services
458	Continued IHOP, Jack-in-the-Box, KFC/Taco Bell, Los Cabos, Pizza Hut, S Starbucks, Subway, Wendy's, Whataburger [other] Albertson's, Foods, AT&T, AutoZone, Discount Tire, Firestone/auto, GNC, Kar, URGENT CARE, Verizon, Walgreens, Walmart
457b	Denton Rd, Hundley Dr, Lake Dallas
457a	Hundley Dr (from nb), Lake Dallas
456	Highland Village
456mm	Lewisville Lake
454b	Garden Ridge Blvd
454a	FM 407, Justin, E [gas] Valero [food] Old House BBQ, W [gas] dsl [food] McDonald's, Subway
453	Valley Ridge Blvd, E [other] Ford, May's RV, W [gas] Chev dsl [food] Burger King, Fat Cow BBQ, Subway [other] Home De Kohl's, Lowe's, Staples
452	FM 1171, to Flower Mound, E [food] IHOP, Taco Bueno [lodging] Se Inn [other] [H], W [gas] Shell [food] Buffet Palace, Burger King, Ca Chick-fil-A, Chipotle Mexican, CiCi's Pizza, Grandy's, Korner C McDonald's, Panda Express, Pizza Hut, Regal Buffet, Smashb er, Sonic, Taco Bell, Taco Cabana, Whataburger [other] $Tree, ertson's, CVS, DQ, Midas, PetCo, same as 451, Sam's Club/ transmissions, U-Haul, URGENT CARE, Walmart
451	Fox Ave, E [gas] Shell/dsl [food] Braum's, W [gas] Chevron [food] Cracker Barrel, Starbucks [lodging] Baymont Inn, EconoLo [other] VW
450	TX 121, Grapevine, E [gas] 7-11, Exxon/dsl [lodging] Texan [other] Chrysler/Dodge/Jeep, W [gas] Chevron, Conoco/dsl [food] B er King, Church's, Subway, Taco Bell, Waffle House [other] Fi tone/auto, Kwik Kar, Nissan, Toyota
449	Corporate Drive, E [gas] Valero/dsl [food] Hooters, Kyoto, On- Border, Razzoo's Cajun [lodging] Extended Stay America, M 6, Suburban Lodge [other] Cavender's Boots, Chevrolet, Ho W [gas] Valero [food] Cantina Loredo, Chili's, Denny's, El Fe Outback Steaks [lodging] Best Western [other] $Tree, Hobby Lobby, Ann Fabrics, Marshall's, NTB, Petsmart, Tuesday Morning
448b a	Round Grove Rd, TX 121, Rayburn Fwy, E [gas] 7-11 [food] A KFC, Cane's, ChuckeCheese, Dickey's BBQ, Jack-in-the- Joe's Crabshack, LJ Silver/Taco Bell, Olive Garden, Pei W Souper Salad, Starbucks, Subway, Taco Casa [lodging] Homew Suites [other] Honda, Ross, Target, W [gas] Exxon/7-11, RaceT dsl [food] Applebee's, Arby's, BJ's Grill, Buffalo Wild Wings, Ch fil-A, Chipotle Mexican, Christina's Mexican, Cotton Patch R Firehouse Subs, Five Guys, Freebirds Burrito, Honeybaked H Jason's Deli, Jimmy John's, La Madeline Bakery, Logan's Ro house, Macaroni Grill, McDonald's, Panda Express, Par Bread, Penn Sta Subs, Popeye's, Red Lobster, Redneck Hea BBQ, Saltgrass Steaks, Schlotzsky's, Sonic, Spring Creek B Starbucks, Steak'n Shake, Subway, Taco Bueno, Taco Caba TGIFriday's, Twin Peaks, Wendy's, Which Wich? [lodging] Com Suites, Country Inn&Suites, Courtyard, Fairfield Inn, Hamp Inn, Hilton Garden, Holiday Inn Express, Residence Inn, Sp ghill Suites, TownePlace Suites [other] AT&T, Barnes&Noble, Buy, Costco/gas, Dillard's, Discount Tire, JC Penney, Ma Michael's, Old Navy, URGENT CARE, Verizon
447a	TX 121, Rayburn Fwy
446	Frankford Rd, E [gas] RaceTrac [food] La Hacienda Ranch Grill
445b a	Pres Geo Bush Tpk
444	Whitlock Lane, Sandy Lake Rd, E [gas] Shell [food] La Hac da [lodging] Rodeway Inn [other] Buick/GMC, Kia, W [food] McDona Starbucks [lodging] Delux Inn [other] Harley-Davidson
443	Belt Line Rd, Crosby Rd, E [gas] RaceTrac [food] Subway [other] F Hyundai, W [gas] Shell [other] Chevrolet, U-Haul

INTERSTATE 35 Cont'd

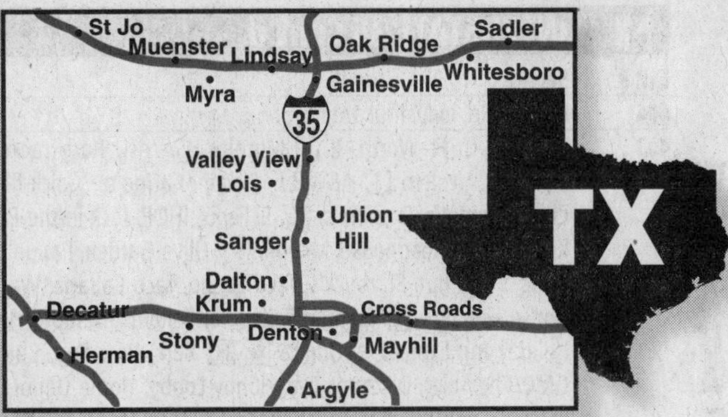

Exit #	Services
442	Valwood Pkwy, E Chevron/Subway/dsl, Conoco/dsl DQ, Grandy's, Jack-in-the-Box, Taco Bueno, Waffle House Guest Inn, LoneStar Inn, Super 8, W Gas/dsl transmissions
441	Valley View Lane, W Chevron, Shell/dsl Best Value Inn, Days Inn, Motel 6
440b	I-635 E
440c	I-635 W, to DFW Airport
439	Royal Lane, E Shell/dsl, Valero/7-11/dsl McDonald's, Wendy's, W Chevron/7-11, Exxon/dsl Jack-in-the-Box
438	Walnut Hill Lane, E Chevron/dsl, Shell, Valero/dsl Burger King, Denny's, Trail Dust Steaks, Wild Turkey Grill Hampton Inn, La Quinta, Quality Inn, W Gulf/dsl, Shell/dsl
437	Manana Rd (from nb), same as 438
436	TX 348, to DFW, Irving, E Shell/dsl Finish Line Grill, IHOP, Starbucks, Waffle House Baymont Inn, Best Western, Country Inn Suites, Days Inn, Elegante Hotel, Holiday Inn Express, SpringHill Suites, Studio 6, W Exxon/dsl, Valero/dsl Chili's, Gino's Pizzaria, Humperdinks, Jack-in-the-Box, Jason's Deli, Joe's Crabshack, Mambo Seafood, McDonald's, Ojos Locos Cantina, Olive Garden, Papadeaux Seafood, Pappa's BBQ, Pappas Bros Steaks, Pappasito's Mexican, Red Lobster, Taco Bell, TX L&C, Wendy's Budget Suites, Century Inn
435	Harry Hines Blvd (from nb)
434b	Regal Row, E Chevron/Grandy's/dsl Sam's Grill, Whataburger Motel 6, W Ramada Inn
434a	Empire, Central, E Shell/McDonald's Kay's Rest, Sonic Budget Suites, Candlewood Suites, InTown Suites, Wingate Inn Office Depot, W Exxon/dsl Bombshells Rest., Burger King, Schlotzsky's, Taco Bell
433b	Mockingbird Lane, E Shell/dsl Jack-in-the-Box Budget Suites, Comfort Inn, Crowne Plaza, Hawthorn Suites, Love Field Hotel, Residence Inn Love Field Airport, W Starbucks
433a	(432b from sb) TX 356, Commonwealth Dr
432a	Inwood Rd, E Exxon/7-11 H, Chevrolet, URGENT CARE, W Shell, Texaco/Subway/dsl Taco Cabana, Whataburger Embassy Suites, Extended Stay America, Hampton Inn, Holiday Inn Express, Homewood Suites
431	Motor St, E Chevron Denny's H, W Shell/7-11 Alamo Rest Marriott Suites
430c	Wycliff Ave, E Holiday Inn, Renaissance Hotel, W Hilton Anatole, Hilton Garden
430b	Mkt Ctr Blvd, E World Trade Ctr, W Shell Denny's Best Western, Courtyard, Days Inn, DoubleTree, Fairfield Inn, Sheraton Suites
430a	Oak Lawn Ave, E Holiday Inn, W Shell/dsl Denny's, Medieval Times Rest. to Merchandise Mart
429c	HiLine Ave (from nb)
429b	Continental Ave, Commerce St W, E Hooters, W Exxon, Shell McDonald's, Popeye's, downtown
429a	to I-45, US 75, to Houston
428e	Commerce St E, Reunion Blvd, Dallas, downtown
428d	I-30 W, to Ft Worth
428a	I-30 E, to I-45 S
428b	Industrial Blvd, E Exxon, W Fuel City/dsl, Shamrock
427b	I-30 E
427a	Colorado Blvd, E H
426c	Jefferson Ave, E Shell/dsl
426b	TX 180 W, 8th St, E Shell/dsl
426a	Ewing Ave, E McDonald's, Popeye's
425c	Marsalis Ave, W Chevron, GME Mart Jack-in-the-Box
425b	Beckley Ave, 12th St, sb only, W QT, Shell Wendy's
425a	Zang Blvd, same as 425b
424	Illinois Ave, E Chevron William's Chicken, W Exxon/7-11 Burger King, Church's, Jack-in-the-Box, Little Caesar's, Pancake House, Popeye's, Sonic, Subway, Taco Bell Oak Tree Inn Kroger, Ross, Walgreens
423b	Saner Ave
423a	(422b from nb) US 67 S, Kiest Blvd, W Shell/repair Golden Chick, McDonald's, Subway
421b	Ann Arbor St, W Exxon/dsl
421a	Lp 12E W, E RaceWay/dsl Motel 6, W QT/dsl IHOP, Subway $Tree, Walmart
420	Laureland, E 7-11/dsl Plaza Inn, W Exxon/dsl, Texaco Linfield Inn
419	Camp Wisdom Rd, E Exxon Jack-in-the-Box Oak Cliff Inn, W Chevron, Shell McDonald's Grand Inn U-Haul
418c	Danieldale Rd (from sb)
418b	I-635/I-20 E, to Shreveport
418a	I-20 W, to Ft Worth
417	Wheatland Rd (from nb)
416	Wintergreen Rd, W 7-11 Cracker Barrel, Waffle House Clarion, Days Inn, Hampton Inn, Holiday Inn Express
415	Pleasant Run Rd, E Shell/dsl, Valero/Church's/dsl Bienvenidos Mexican, Chicken Express, Chili's, CiCi's Pizza, Grandy's, IHOP, In-N-Out, Logan's Roadhouse, Sonic, Subway, Taco Cabana, Waffle House Great Western Inn, Hwy Express Inn, Motel 6, Spanish Trails Motel Family$, Home Depot, NAPA, W Burger King, Dicky's BBQ, El Chico, KFC, LJ Silver, Luby's, McDonald's, On the Border, Outback Steaks, Pollo Tropical, Starbucks, Taco Bueno, Wendy's Best Value Inn, La Quinta AT&T, Chevrolet, Discount Tire, Firestone/auto, Ford, Kroger, Office Depot, Ross
414	FM 1382, Desoto Rd, Belt Line Rd, E Murphy USA/dsl Taco Bell, Whataburger Verizon, Walmart/McDonald's, W QT/dsl $Tree
413	Parkerville Rd, W Exxon/Subway/dsl U-Haul
412	Bear Creek Rd, W Shell/dsl Jack-in-the-Box transmissions
411	FM 664, Ovilla Rd, E Exxon/dsl, Murphy USA/dsl, RaceTrac Burger King, Denny's, Dickey's BBQ, DQ, LJ Silver/Taco Bell, McDonald's, Panda Express, Whataburger Comfort Inn Brookshire's Foods, CVS Drug, USPO, Walgreens, Walmart, W Exxon/Subway, Valero
410	Red Oak Rd, E Shell/Pizza Inn/Subway/dsl, Valero/dsl Motel 6, W Hilltop Travel Trailers
408	US 77, TX 342, to Red Oak, E golf
406	Sterrett Rd, E fireworks
405	FM 387, E Phillips 66/dsl, QT/dsl

TX

INTERSTATE 35 Cont'd

WAXAHATCHIE

Exit #	Services
404	Lofland Rd, industrial area
403	US 287, to Ft Worth, E Murphy USA/dsl, RaceTrac/dsl, Shell/dsl, Valero A&W/LJ Silver, Carino's, Chick-fil-A, Chili's, Chipotle, Domino's, DQ, El Fenix, IHOP, Jack-in-the-Box, KFC, Logan's Roadhouse, McDonald's, Olive Garden, Panda Express, Pizza Hut, Starbuck's, Taco Bueno, Taco Cabana, Waffle House, Wendy's Comfort Suites, Fairfield Inn, Hampton Inn, Holiday Inn Express, LaQuinta H, Belk, Best Buy, Buick/GMC/Chevrolet, Discount Tire, Hobby Lobby, Home Depot, JC Penney, Lowe's, Office Depot, Petsmart, Ross, Target, Walmart, W Chrysler/Dodge/Jeep, Ford
401b	US 287 bus, Waxahatchie, E Motel 6, Super 8
401a	Brookside Rd, E Dallas Suites, Executive Inn
399b	FM 1446
399a	FM 66, FM 876, Maypearl, E Texas Inn, W Exxon/dsl, Shell/Sonic/dsl
397	to US 77, to Waxahachie
391	FM 329, Forreston Rd
386	TX 34, Italy, E Loves/Carl's Jr/dsl/scales/24hr, Shell/Smokehouse BBQ/dsl Sonic $General, W Exxon/Grandy's/McDonald's/dsl/scales Pizza Inn, Subway, Taco Bell Italy Inn truckwash
384	Derrs Chapel Rd
381	FM 566, Milford Rd
377	FM 934
374	FM 2959, Carl's Corner, W Petro/Exxon/Dunkin'/Iron Skillet/dsl/scales/24hr/@
373	I-35E
371	I-35 W. **I-35 divides into E and W nb, converges sb. See Texas I-35 W.**
370	US 77 N, FM 579, Hillsboro, E TA/Shell/Country Pride/Burger King/dsl/scales/24hr/@ Rangers Cafe
368b	FM 286 (from sb), E LoneStar Café, Taco Bell, Wendy's Hampton Inn, W Exxon, Valero/dsl Braum's, El Conquistador Mexican, El Taco Jalisco, Pizza Hut, Up In Smoke BBQ Best Value Inn, EconoLodge, La Quinta H
368a	TX 22, TX 171, to Whitney, E 7-11, Loves/Chester's/Subway/dsl/scales/24hr Dickey's BBQ, DQ, Golden Buffet, IHOP, McDonald's, Starbucks Comfort Suites, Days Inn, Motel 6, Quality Inn, Super 8 Hillsboro Outlets/Famous Brands, W 7-11, Chevron/dsl, Mobil, Murphy USA/dsl $Tree, Chicken Express, Jack-in-the-Box, Schlotzsky's, Sonic, Whataburger Thunderbird Motel/rest. AT&T, Chrysler/Dodge/Jeep, Ford, Walmart/Subway
367	Old Bynum Rd (from nb), same as 368
364b	TX 81 N, to Hillsboro (from nb, exits left)
364a	FM 310 (from sb)
363	CR 3111s
362mm	**both directions, full facilities, litter barrels, petwalk,**
359	FM 1304, W Gulf/dsl/24hr truckwash
358	FM 1242 E, Abbott, E Still Smokin' BBQ
356	Co Rd 3102
355	County Line Rd, E Waco North RV Park
354	Marable St, E Waco North RV Park
353	FM 2114, West, E Chevron/dsl, Shell/Czech Bakery Bush's Chicken, Sonic, Subway Ford, W Exxon/Slovacek's/dsl Best Western Czech Inn Chevrolet, Vintage Automotive
351	FM 1858, E tires/repair
349	Wiggins Rd

HILLSBORO

WACO

Exit #	Services
347	FM 3149, Tours Rd
346	Ross Rd, W Exxon/Church's/dsl/24hr antiques, I-35 Park/LP
345	Old Dallas Rd, W I-35 RV Park/LP
345a	frontage rd, same as 345
343	FM 308, Elm Mott, E Exxon/DQ, Shell/Jct Cafe/ scales/24hr, W $General
342b	US 77 bus, W North Crest RV Park
342a	FM 2417, Crest Dr, W Valero/dsl Bush's Chicken, Motel 6 auto repair, Family$
341	Craven Ave, Lacy Lakeview, E Freightliner, W Chev Shell
340	Myers Lane (from nb)
339	to TX 6 S, FM 3051, Lake Waco, E Murphy USA, Vale dsl Casa Ole, Cici's Pizza, Domino's, El Conquistador, Ja in-the-Box, Luby's, Pizza Hut, Popeye's, Sonic, Subway, W dy's, Whataburger, WingStop Holiday Inn $Gene $Tree, Advance Parts, Discount Tire, Home Depot, NAPA, to Walmart, W 7-11/dsl, Chevron, Shell, Valero/dsl Bu er King, Cracker Barrel, Heitmiller Steaks, KFC, McDonal Starbucks, Taco Bell Fairfield Inn, Hampton Inn AT URGENT CARE
338b	Behrens Circle (from nb), same as 339, E Jack-in-the-E Little Caesar's, Sonic GNC, W Shell/dsl/LP Crac Barrel Best Western, Comfort Suites, Days Inn, Delta Hampton Inn, Knights Inn, Motel 6, Quality Inn
338a	US 84, to TX 31, Waco Dr, E Chopstix, Collin St Bak Denny's, Subway Woodspring Suites AutoZone, Fa ly$, HEB Food/gas, O'Reilly Parts, Sam's Club/gas, Tesla E W Comfort Suites H
337	US 77 business
335c	Lake Brazos Dr, MLK Blvd, E Baylor Stadium, W B zard Billy's Red Roof Inn, Scottish Inn H
335mm	Brazos River
335b	FM 434, University Parks Dr, E Starbucks Baylor U, Ranger Museum, W 7-11/dsl In-N-Out, Jack-in-t Box Residence Inn
335a	4th St, 5th St, E Exxon/Subway/dsl IHOP La Qu ta Baylor U, W Valero/dsl Cane's, Chick-fil-A, Fa li's, Freddy's, LJ Silver, McAlister's Deli, McDonald's, Pan Bread, Papa John's, Sonic, Taco Bell, Taco Cabana, Wend Whataburger CVS Drug
334b	US 77 S, 17th St, 18th St, E Shell/dsl, Valero/dsl Bur King, Fuego Grill, Jimmy John's, Pizza Hut, Popeye's, Sch zsky's, Vitek's BBQ Budget Inn, Deluxe Inn, La Quinta, per 8, W Shell Taquerias Mexican H
333a	Lp 396, Valley Mills Dr, E 7-11/dsl El Chico, Elite Ca Rudy's BBQ/gas, Trujillo's Mexican, TX Roadhouse Com Suites, Motel 6 Kia, Mazda, W RaceWay/dsl, Vale dsl Bubba's Rest., Bush's Chicken, Catfish King, Chi Church's, George's Rest., Jack-in-the-Box, Little Caesar's, za Patron, Potbelly, Sonic, Starbucks, Subway, Zoe's Kit en Home 2 Suites Aamco, Advance Parts, AutoZo CVS Drug, Family$, HEB Foods/dsl, Lincoln, Walgreens
331	New Rd, E Phillips 66/dsl Candlewood Suites, N Road Inn, Relax Inn, Rodeway Inn, W FLYING J/D ny's/dsl/scales/24hr Burger King, Carl's Jr, Hoot IHOP Quality Inn Harley Davidson
330	Lp 340, TX 6, W Chevron/dsl Buffalo Wild Win Bush's Chicken, Chuy's Mexican, Don Carlo's Mexican, Heitm er Steaks, Logan's Roadhouse, Newk's Eatery, Panda Expre Panera Bread, Saltgrass Steaks, Sonic, Starbucks, Subw

INTERSTATE 35 Cont'd

330 Continued
Hampton Inn, Holiday Inn Express, Homewood Suites, TownePlace Suites H, $Tree, AT&T, Belk, Best Buy, Cabela's, Cavender's Boots, Fiat/Alpha Romeo, Ford, Honda, Hyundai, Jo-Ann, Kohl's, Marshall's, Nissan, Office Depot, Old Navy, Petco, Ross, Toyota, URGENT CARE, World Mkt

328 FM 2063, FM 2113, Moody, E Pilot/Subway/Wendy's/dsl/scales/24hr/@ McDonald's Robinson Inn Kenworth, W Shell/dsl, Valero/dsl DQ Ramada Inn, Sleep Inn

325 FM 3148, Moonlight Dr, W Valero/dsl FunTown RV Ctr

323 FM 2837 (from sb), Lorena, W Brookshire Bros/Conoco/dsl Pizza House, Sonic

322 Lorena, E Phillips 66/dsl, W Bush's Chicken, Pizza House $General

321 Callan Ranch Rd

319 Woodlawn Rd

318b a Bruceville

315 TX 7, FM 107, Eddy, E Bruceville-Eddy RV Park, W Family$, to Mother Neff SP

314 Old Blevins Rd

311 Big Elm Rd, E fireworks

308 FM 935, Troy, E Loves/Subway/McDonald's/s/dsl/scales/24hr, Shell/dsl, Valero/dsl, W $General, dsl repair

306 FM 1237, Pendleton, W Goodyear Truck Tires

305 Berger Rd, W Lucky's RV Park, repair

304 Lp 363, Dodgen Loop, E Buc-ee's/dsl, W Shell/Wendy's/dsl Freightliner

303 spur 290, N 3rd St, Temple, E S-2 Gas Texas Inn

302 Nugent Ave, E Exxon/dsl Baymont Inn, Best Value Inn, EconoLodge, Motel 6, W TX Roadhouse Best Western, Days Inn, Knights Inn, Motel 6

301 TX 53, FM 2305, Adams Ave, E Exxon/dsl, Valero Arby's, Chick-fil-A, KFC, Little Caesar's, LJ Silver, McDonald's, Pizza Hut, Starbucks, Subway, Taco Bell, Whataburger La Quinta H, Advance Parts, HEB Foods/dsl, O'Reilly Parts, URGENT CARE, W TX Roadhouse Best Western

300 Ave H, 49th –57th Sts, E Clem Mikeskas BBQ

299 US 190 E, TX 36, E Shell/dsl Cracker Barrel, Jack-in-the-Box, Luby's, Olive Garden, Sol de Jalisco Budget Inn, Residence Inn, Travelodge H, AT&T, Chrysler/Dodge/Jeep, Natural Grocers, Tires To You, URGENT CARE, Verizon, W BJ's Rest., Chili's, Chipotle Mexican, Five Guys, IHOP, McDonald's, Subway, Taco Cabana Hampton Inn Best Buy, Firestone/auto, GNC, Home Depot, Michael's, Petsmart, Target

298 nb only, to frontage rd, E Longhorn Steaks Residence Inn

297 FM 817, Midway Dr, E Phillips 66/dsl Golden Corral Holiday Inn, Super 8/rest. Buick/GMC/Cadillac, Nissan, W Valero/dsl Goodyear/auto, VW

294b FM 93, 6th Ave, E Shell/dsl McDonald's Chevrolet, Ford/Lincoln, Toyota, W Subway River Forest Inn Harley-Davidson, U of Mary Hardin Baylor

294a Central Ave, E Taco Bell, W Shell/dsl Burger King, El Mexicano Grill, Jimmy John's, Pizza Hut, Schlotzsky's, Schoepf's BBQ, Sonic, Starbucks, Whataburger Knights Inn AutoZone, city park, O'Reilly Parts, Parts+, USPO

293b TX 317, FM 436, Main St

293a US 190 W, to Killeen, Ft Hood

292 Lp 121 (same as 293a), E Valero/dsl/24hr Budget Host, W 7-11/dsl, Exxon/dsl Oxbow Steaks La Quinta Belton RV Park, Sunbelt RV Ctr

290 Shanklin Rd

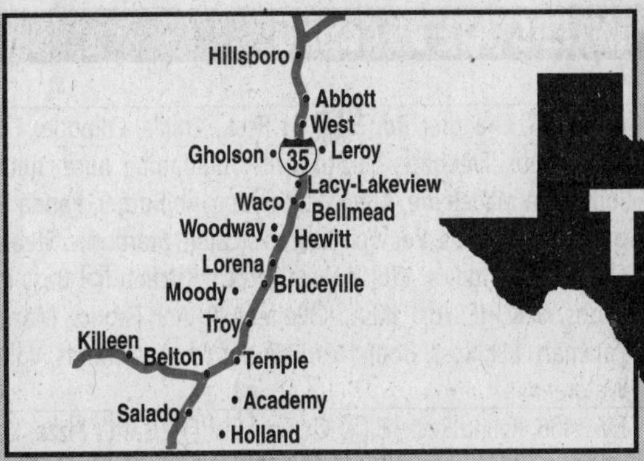

GEORGETOWN

289 Tahuaya Rd

287 Amity Rd

286 FM 2484, E Days Inn, Holiday Inn Express, W to Stillhouse Hollow Lake, Tranquil RV Park (2mi)

285 FM 2268, Salado, E Conoco/dsl Subway Holiday Inn Express Brookshire Foods/gas, W Cefco/dsl, Gulf Bush's Chicken, Robertson's Rest., Sonic

284 Stagecoach Rd, E Stagecoach Inn, W Johnny's Steaks

283 FM 2268, FM 2843, to Holland, Salado, E Stagecoach Inn

282 FM 2115, E Valero/dsl

281mm **both lanes, full facilities, litter barrels, petwalk, table, RV dump, vending**

280 Grainger Rd, Hackberry Rd, Prairie Dell

279 Hill Rd

277 Rd 305

275 FM 487, to Florence, Jarrell, E Exxon/dsl $General, W Shell/dsl (2), Shell/Krispy Kreme/Pizza Inn/dsl USPO

274 Rd 312, E Exxon/Subway/dsl, FLYING J/Burger King/Denny's/dsl/scales McDonald's

271 Ronald Reagan Blvd, W Shell/Subway/dsl/24hr

268 fm 972, Walburg, E Crestview RV Ctr

266 TX 195, E Phillips 66/dsl, Shell TC/dsl/scales/24hr, W Shell/dsl

265 TX 130 Toll S, to Austin

264 Lp 35, Georgetown

262 RM 2338, Lake Georgetown, E Valero Chipotle Mexican, KFC, McDonald's, Papa John's, Pizza Hut, Sonic, Starbucks, Subway, Verts Grill $Tree, CVS Drug, Parts+, URGENT CARE, W DQ, Frankie's Pizza, Plaka Greek, Whataburger Candlewood Suites, Georgetown Inn, Holiday Inn Express, La Quinta

261 TX 29, Georgetown, E Shell/dsl Applebee's, Burger King, Chili's, Domino's, Jack-in-the-Box, Jimmy John's, KFC, La Playa, McDonald's, Schlotzsky's, Taco Bell Best Western, Comfort Suites, Hampton Inn HEB Foods, Hobby Lobby, Midas, O'Reilly Parts, same as 262, Tuesday Morning, W Murphy USA/dsl Cane's, Carl's Jr, Casa Ole, Chick-fil-A, CiCi's, Cotton Patch Cafe, Five Guys, George's Rest., IHOP, Longhorn Steaks, Mama Fu's, McAlister's Deli, Panda Express, Panera Bread, Pie Five, Popeye's, Salsa's Mexican, Souper Salad, Starbucks, Taco Cabana, Wendy's AT&T, Beall's, Best Buy, Discount Tire, Home Depot, Kohl's, Michael's, Natural Grocers, Office Depot, Old Navy, Petsmart, Ross, Target, TJ Maxx, Verizon, Walgreens, Walmart/McDonald's

260 RM 2243, Leander, E H, USPO, W Chevron/dsl, Exxon/dsl, Texaco Jack-in-the-Box Econolodge

259 Lp 35, W RV Outlet Ctr, to Interspace Caverns

257 Westinghouse Rd, E Buick/Chevrolet, Chrysler/Dodge/Jeep, Ford/Lincoln, Mazda, Mercedes, Subaru/Volvo, VW

= gas = food = lodging = other = rest stop

TX

INTERSTATE 35 Cont'd

ROUND ROCK

Exit #	Services
256	RM 1431, Chandler Rd, E BJ Rest., Chili's, Chipotle, Firehouse Subs, Freebirds Burrito, In-N-Out, Jamba Juice, Jimmy John's, La Madeleine, Mimi's Cafe, Mooyah Burger, Panda Express, Papa John's, Pei Wei, Razzoo's Cajun, Starbucks, Steak'n Shake, TGI Friday's, Which Wich?, Zoe's Kitchen Bass Pro Shops, GNC, HEB/dsl, IKEA, JC Penney, Jo-Ann Fabrics, Mazda, Petsmart, REI, Ross, Round Rock Outlet/famous brands, Volvo, Walgreens
254	FM 3406, Round Rock, E Chevron/dsl Gatti's Pizza, Kerby Lane Cafe, La Tapatia, McDonald's, Saucy Rooster Best Western $General, Firestone/auto, Harley-Davidson, Honda, Hyundai, Kia, Toyota, W EVC, Shell/dsl Chuy's Mexican, Cover 3 Rest., Cracker Barrel, Denny's, Double Dave's Pizza, Jack Allen's Kitchen, Mellow Mushroom, Rudy's BBQ/gas, Salt Traders Rest., SaltGrass Steaks Courtyard, Hilton Garden, Holiday Inn, Holiday Inn Express, La Quinta, Red Roof Inn, SpringHill Suites, Woodspring Suites CVS Drug, GMC, Nissan
253b	US 79, to Taylor, E Chevron/dsl, Texaco/dsl Baskin-Robbins, Casa Garcia's, DQ, Fuddrucker's, KFC, La Tapatia, LJ Silver, Pizza Hut, Short Stop Dogs, Sirloin Stockade Best Western, Wingate Inn $General, Advance Parts, AutoZone, Beall's, Cottman Transmissions, Just Brakes, W Shell/dsl Gatti's Pizza, Hunan Lion, IHOP, La Margarita, Poke Joe's BBQ, Popeye's, Starbucks, Thundercloud Subs Country Inn&Suites, La Quinta, Motel 6, Red Roof Inn, Woodspring Suites $Tree, USPO
253a	Frontage Rd, same as 253 b
252b a	RM 620, E Shell/dsl Candlewood Suites, Extended Stay America NAPA, W Mobil/dsl Corner Cafe Bakery, Freddy's Steakburgers, Jimmy John's, Little Caesar's, McDonald's, Starbucks, Wendy's Comfort Suites, Staybridge Suites Office Depot, Sprouts Mkt, Tuesday Morning
251	Lp 35, Round Rock, E CiCi's Pizza, Outback Steaks, Papa John's, Pluckers Wings, Smokey Mo's BBQ, Whataburger Residence Inn Aamco, BigLots, Brake Check, W Shell Burger King, Jack-in-the-Box, Luby's, Taco Cabana Days Inn, Marriott, Sleep Inn Austin's Automotive, GNC, NTB, transmissions, Walgreens
250	TX 45, Lp 1, E Chick-fil-A, Chili's, El Taquito, Firehouse Subs, Five Guys, Green Mesquite BBQ, Jason's Deli, Joe's Crabshack, Macaroni Grill, McDonald's, Panda Express, Subway, Twin Peaks Rest. Hampton Inn, Homewood Suites, Residence Inn $Tree, AT&T, Best Buy, Discount Tire, Home Depot, Michael's, Petsmart, Ross, Steinmart, Target, URGENT CARE, Walmart/Subway, W Applebee's, Chipotle, Egg&I Cafe, Hooters, Jimmy John's, Logan's Roadhouse, Longhorn Steaks, Olive Garden, Red Lobster, Schlotzsky's, Tokyo Steaks Extended Stay America, La Quinta Barnes&Noble, Hobby Lobby, Kohl's, Lowe's, Marshall's, Old Navy, PetCo, Sam's Club, World Mkt
248	Grand Ave Pkwy, E 7-11/Subway/dsl, Citgo, Shell/dsl Chucho's Mexican, Gatti's Pizza, Thundercloud Subs, TX Roadhouse Comfort Suites URGENT CARE, W Exxon/McDonald's/dsl
247	FM 1825, Pflugerville, E Exxon/7-11/dsl Bombshells Rest., Burger King, Cheddar's, Domino's, FD's Grillhouse, Jack-in-the-Box, Subway, Taco Cabana, Wendy's Comfort Suites Firestone/auto, GNC, HEB Foods/gas, W Exxon/7-11, Shell/Church's KFC, Miller's BBQ, Sonic Country Inn Suites Goodyear, McSpadden Automotive, Tires4Less
246	Howard Lane, E Citgo, Exxon/7-11/dsl Arby's, Acapulco, McDonald's, Subway, Wings'n More Home Depot, Kohl's, NTB, W Valero/dsl IHOP, Whatabu Sleep Inn CarMax
245	FM 734, Parmer Lane, to Yager Lane (244 from nb), E Cari Chick-fil-A, Chili's, Freebirds Burrito, In-N-Out, Jersey Mike's, my John's, Kublai Khan, Little Caesar's, Masala Wok, MOD P My Fit Grill, Panda Express, Pei Wei, Schlotzsky's, Souper S Subway, Verts Grill, Zed's Rest Homewood Suites $ HEB Food/E-85, Hobby Lobby, JC Penney, Kohl's, PetCo, Petsm Ross, Sears Grand, Verizon, W Conoco/dsl, Exxon/7-11 Murphy USA/dsl Buffalo Wild Wings, Golden Corral, Chinese, Red Robin Courtyard, Fairfield Inn, Hilton Ga Residence Inn, SpringHill Suites, Staybridge Suites A CarMax, Discount Tire, Lowe's, Walmart/McDonald's
244	Tech Ridge Blvd, Yager Lane, (from nb), same as 245
243	Braker Lane, E Valero/dsl Whataburger U-Hau Citgo, Shell/dsl Austin Motel, Woodspring Su $General
241	Rundberg Lane, E Exxon/7-11 Grand China Bu Jack-in-the-Box Extended Stay America, Orangewood $General, Chevrolet, U-Haul, W Chevron, Shell tin Suites, Budget Inn, Budget Lodge, Economy Inn, Holiday Express, Motel 6, Motel 6 (2), Red Roof Inn, Super 8
240a	US 183, Lockhart, E Exxon Jack-in-the-Box Inn, Orangewood Inn, W Chevron/dsl Motel 6, Roof Inn, Super 8
239	St John's Ave, E Shell Burger King, Chili's, Japon anese, Pappadeaux, Pappasito's Mexican Crowne Pl Days Inn, DoubleTree, Drury Inn, Econolodge, Hampton Studio 6 USPO, W Exxon/7-11, Mobil/dsl, Val dsl Applebee's, Buffalo Wild Wings, Carrabba's, Den IHOP, Ojos Locos, Panda Express, Wendy's Best Value Comfort Inn, Country Inn&Suites, Courtyard, Holiday Inn, H Place, La Quinta, Motel 6, Ramada Inn Ford, Office Dep
238b	US 290 E, RM 222, frontage rds connect several exits, sam 238a
238a	51st St, E Buffet King, Chipotle, Church's, CiCi's, J ba Juice, La Madeleine, McDonald's, Papa John's, Pie gy, SmashBurger, Subway, Tino's Greek, TX Steaks, W Wich? DoubleTree Hotel, Drury Inn, EconoLodge, Emb Suites $Tree, Advance Parts, AutoZone, Best Buy, H Depot, Marshall's, Old Navy, Petsmart, Ross, Staples, Tar Walgreens, W Shell Baby Acapulco, Capt Benny's food Capital Inn, Courtyard, Fairfield Inn, Motel 6, Supe
237b	51st St, same as 238a
237a	Airport Blvd, W In-N-Out, Jack-in-the-Box, Wen GNC, Goodyear, HEB Foods, PetCo
236.7	lower level accesses downtown, upper level is I-35 thru
236b	39th St, E Chevron/dsl Short Stop Burgers, Sub Fiesta Foods, O'Reilly Parts, U-Haul, W Shell/dsl U of TX
236a	26th-32nd Sts, E Los Altos Mexican, Subway Days W Rodeway Inn H
235b	Manor Rd, E Denny's DoubleTree, W Rodeway st capitol, U of TX, same as 236a
235a	MLK, 15th St, W H
234.9	lower level accesses downtown, upper level is I-35 thru
234c	11th St, 12th St, E Chevron/dsl, Shell/dsl D ny's, Wendy's DoubleTree Hotel, Super 8 CVS D W Gulf/dsl, Shell Hilton, Hilton Garden, La Qui Marriott, Omni Motel, Radisson, Sheraton H, museum capitol, downtown

AUSTIN

INTERSTATE 35 Cont'd

Exit #	Services
234b	8th-3rd St, W IHOP
234a	Cesar Chavez St, Holly St, E Shell/dsl, W Chevron/dsl Holiday Inn, downtown
233mm	Little Colorado River
233	Riverside Dr, Town Lake, E Gulf, Shell/dsl Chipotle, Church's, MOD Pizza, Starbucks AT&T, Walgreens
232b	Woodland Ave
232a	Oltorf St, E Chevron/dsl, Gulf, Shell/dsl Donn's BBQ, Luby's, Sonic Best Value, Howard Johnson, La Quinta, Motel 6, Parkwest Inn, W Conoco/dsl, Exxon/7-11 Denny's, Starbucks Best Western, Simco Plaza
231	Woodward St, E same as 232, Wyndham Garden, W Home Depot, Walmart
230b a	US 290 W, TX 71, Ben White Blvd, St Elmo Rd, E Shell/Circle K/dsl Baymont Inn, Courtyard, Fairfield Inn, Hampton Inn, Homewood Suites, Marriott, Omni Hotel, Quality Inn, Red Roof Inn, Residence Inn, SpringHill Suites Acura, W Burger King Candlewood Suites, Days Inn, La Quinta H, Audi, CarMax, Chrysler/Dodge/Jeep, Ford, Hyundai, Kia, Mazda, Nissan, NTB, Toyota
229	Stassney Lane, W Buffalo Wild Wings, Chili's, Chipotle, Jimmy John's, Krispy Kreme, Logan's Roadhouse, Macaroni Grill, Pizza Hut, Trudy's Grill, Twin Peaks Rest., TX Cattle Co Steaks Holiday Inn Express, Staybridge Suites Fiesta Foods/gas, Lowe's
228	Wm Cannon Drive, E Exxon, Valero Applebee's, McDonald's, Subway, Taco Bell Brake Check, Discount Tire, HEB Foods, Nissan, W Shell/dsl Burger King, China Harbor, Gatti's Pizza, Golden Corral, KFC, LJ Silver, Taco Cabana, Wendy's, Whataburger Advance Parts, AT&T, BigLots, Chevrolet, Firestone
227	Slaughter Lane, Lp 275, S Congress, E Shell/dsl ChuckE-Cheese, Don Dario's, IHOP Home Depot, Lone Star RV Resort, U-Haul, W Murphy USA/dsl, Valero, Valero/dsl Carino's, Chick-fil-A, Chili's, Chipotle Mexican, Fuddrucker's, Gatti Town, Jack-in-the-Box, Jason's Deli, Longhorn Steaks, Luby's, Mama Fu's, Miller BBQ, Panda Express, Serrano's TexMex, Smashburger, Sonic, Starbucks, Steak'n Shake, Subway, Taco Bell, TGIFriday's, TX Roadhouse, Wendy's, Whataburger $Tree, AT&T, Best Buy, Firestone/auto, GNC, Hobby Lobby, JC Penney, Jo-Ann, Marshall's, Petsmart, Ross, Sam's Club/dsl, Target, URGENT CARE, Verizon, VW, Walgreens, Walmart
226	Slaughter Creek Overpass
225	FM 1626, Onion Creek Pkwy, E Texaco, Valero Subway Harley-Davidson
224	frontage rd (from nb)
223	FM 1327, rd 45 **toll**
221	Lp 4, Buda, E Chevron/McDonald's Starbucks Best Value Inn, Candlewood Suites, Comfort Suites, Holiday Inn Express Ford, Kenworth, W Murphy USA/dsl, Shell/dsl Arby's, Chili's, Cracker Barrel, Dan's Burgers, Domino's, Jack-in-the-Box, KFC/LJ Silver, Little Caesar's, Logan's Roadhouse, Miller BBQ, Papa John's, Pizza Hut, Sonic, Subway, Taco Bell, Whataburger, Zaxby's Hampton Inn, Microtel AT&T, AutoZone, Cabela's, HEB Food/dsl/E-85, O'Reilly Parts, USPO, Verizon, Walgreens, Walmart
220	FM 2001, Niederwald, E Shell Burger King Camper Clinic RV Ctr, Marshall's RV Park, W Crestview RV Ctr/Park, Peterbilt

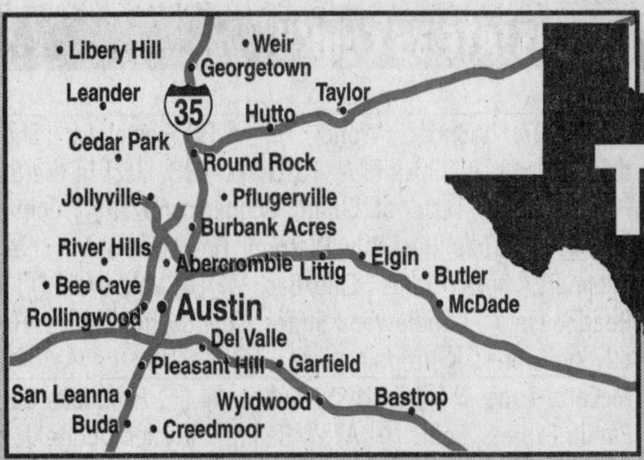

SAN MARCOS

Exit #	Services
217	Lp 4, Buda, E Exxon/dsl La Quinta Mack/Volvo, W Valero/dsl Burger King Quality Inn Christian Bros Auto, Home Depot
215	Bunton Overpass, E Exxon/KFC/LJ Silver, Walmart/dsl Carl's Jr, Dickey's BBQ, Dunkin'/Baskin Robbins, Firehouse Subs, Pollo Tropical, Popeye's, Taco Bell, Taco Cabana, Wendy's Hampton Inn H, AT&T, Discount Tire, Firestone/auto, Lowe's, Walgreens, Walmart, W Conoco/dsl, Sunoco/Schlotzky's/dsl Applebee's, Casa Garcia's, Chicken Express, Chick-fil-A, Five Guys, IHOP, Jack-in-the-Box, Jersey Mike's, Little Caesar's, Mama Fu's, McDonald's, MOD Pizza, Panda Express, Papa Murphy's, Starbucks, Subway, Whataburger Comfort Suites $Tree, Explore USA RV Ctr, GNC, HEB Foods/dsl/e85, Kohl's, PetCo, Ross, Target, URGENT CARE, Verizon
213	FM 150, Kyle, E 7-11/dsl, Valero/dsl DQ AutoZone, O'Reilly Parts, W Conoco/dsl Casa Maria Mexican Advance Parts, CVS Drug, repair
210	Yarrington Rd, E Hyundai, W Buick/Chevrolet/GMC, Ford, Plum Creek RV Park
209	**weight sta (sb only)**
208mm	Blanco River
208	Frontage Rd, Blanco River Rd, W Hilton Garden Buick/Chevrolet/GMC
206	Lp 82, Aquarena Springs Rd, E Conoco, Valero/dsl San Marcos RV Park, W Exxon/dsl, Shell, Shell/dsl Inn-N-Out, Pancake House, Pollo Tropical, Popeye's, Sonic Best Value Inn, Howard Johnson, La Quinta, Motel 6, Quality Inn, Ramada Ltd, Rodeway Inn, Summit Inn, Super 8 to SW TX U
205	TX 80, TX 142, Bastrop, E 7-11/dsl, Exxon, RaceWay/dsl, Shell/dsl, Valero/dsl Cane's, China Palace, Fazoli's, Freebirds Burrito, Jason's Deli, Little Caesar's, Pizza Hut, Subway, Wing Stop Executive Inn, Fairfield Inn $General, AutoZone, CVS Drug, Hobby Lobby, Verizon, Walmart, W Valero A&W/LJ Silver, Burger King, Church's, Chuy's, Five Guys, IHOP, Kobe Japanese, Logan's Roadhouse, McDonald's, Taco Cabana, Wendy's Best Western, Budget Inn, Days Inn, Gateway Inn, Knights Inn, Red Roof Inn, Rodeway Inn Brake Check, city park, HEB/gas, Office Depot, Walgreens
204mm	San Marcos River
204b	CM Allen Pkwy, W Shell/dsl, Spirit/dsl Casa Maria, DQ, Krispy Kreme, La Fonda Rest., Mazatlan, Plucker's Grill, Sonic Best Western, EconoLodge AutoZone, O'Reilly Parts, transmissions
204a	Lp 82, TX 123, to Seguin, E Conoco, Exxon/dsl 54th St Grill, Burger King, Bush's Chicken, Carino's, Chicken Express, Chili's, Freddy's, Luby's, McDonald's, Newk's Eatery, Red Lobster, Starbucks, Whataburger Comfort Suites, Hampton Inn, Wingate Inn H, Aamco

TX

INTERSTATE 35 Cont'd

NEW BRAUNFELS

Exit #	Services
202	FM 3407, Wonder World Dr, E Exxon/dsl, Shell/dsl Carl's Jr, Chick-fil-A, Fuschaks BBQ, Jack-in-the-Box, Panera Bread, Taste of China, Wienerschnitzel Comfort Inn H, $Tree, Best Buy, Discount Tire, Lowe's, Marshall's, Petsmart, Ross, Sams Club/gas, W Valero/dsl TX Roadhouse Candlewood Suites, Country Inn&Suites, Holiday Inn Express repair
201	McCarty Lane, E Embassy Suites, W Firehouse Subs, Panda Express, Sonic AT&T, Beall's, Chrysler/Dodge/Jeep, Firestone/auto, JC Penney, Nissan, Target, URGENT CARE
200	Centerpoint Rd, E Chipotle, Cracker Barrel, Outback Steaks, Subway, Taco Bell, Wendy's GNC, Old Navy, San Marcos Outlets/famous brands, Tanger Outlet/famous brands, W Sunoco/dsl McDonald's, Starbucks, Subway, Whataburger, Zaxby's Baymont Inn, Courtyard Honda
199	Posey Rd, E same as 200, Tanger Outlets/famous brands, Toyota
196	FM 1106, York Creek Rd, W Canyon Trail RV Park
195	Watson Lane, Old Bastrop Rd
193	Conrads Rd, Kohlenberg Rd, W TA/Shell/Country Fare/Popeye's/Subway/dsl/scales/24hr/@ Camping World RV Ctr
191	FM 306, FM 483, Canyon Lake, E Buc-ee's BJ's Rest, Las Palapas, Longhorn Steaks, Newk's Eatery, Panda Express, Panera Bread, Sea Island Shrimphouse, Shogun Japanese, Subway, Whataburger, Which Wich?, Willie's Grill AT&T, Belk, Best Buy, Dick's, GNC, Hobby Lobby, JC Penney, Petsmart, Ross, Target, TJ Maxx, URGENT CARE, Verizon, Walmart Dist Ctr, W Exxon/dsl Burger King, HEB/e85 Wingate Inn Nissan, transmissions
190c	Post Rd
190b	frontage rd, New Braunfels, E Evergreen RV Ctr
190a	frontage rd, same as 189
189	TX 46, Seguin, E Shell/dsl Chili's, Denny's, Golden Corral, Logan's Roadhouse, Olive Garden, Peter Piper Pizza, Sonic, Taco Palenque Best Value Inn, Courtyard, EconoLodge, Hampton Inn, La Quinta, Super 8, Travelodge Discount Tire, Home Depot, Kohl's, Office Depot, vet, W Texaco, Valero Applebee's, Bush's Chicken, Chipotle Mexican, IHOP, Mama Fu's, McDonald's, Miller's BBQ, Pizza Hut, Subway, Taco Bell, Taco Cabana, TJ's Burgers, Wendy's Baymont, Best Western, Candlewood Suites, Comfort Suites, Country Inn Suites, Days Inn, Edelweiss Inn, Fairfield Inn, Hilton Garden, Holiday Inn Express, Howard Johnson, Microtel, Motel 6, Quality Inn, Ramada Inn, Rodeway Inn, Sleep Inn H, Walgreens
188	Frontage Rd, W Garden Buffet, Mamacita's Rest. River Ranch Resort Hyundai, Tuesday Morning
188mm	Guadalupe River
187	FM 725, Lake McQueeny Rd, E A&W/LJ Silver, Arby's, Burger King, CiCi's, River Hofbrau, Whataburger $Tree, Aamco, BigLots, Chevrolet, Ford/Lincoln, Jeep, Meineke, vet, W Adobe Café, DQ, Jack-in-the-Box, Jason's Deli Budget Inn H, CVS Drug, River Ranch RV Resort
186	Walnut Ave, E Exxon/Subway, Murphy USA/dsl, Valero/dsl Carl's Jr, Chick-fil-A, Firehouse Subs, McDonald's, Popeye's, Schlotzsky's, Taco Bell Red Roof Inn Jo-Ann, Lowe's, Verizon, Walmart, W Shell/dsl Baskin-Robbins, Bonzai Japanese, Chicken Express, Panda Express, Papa John's, Papa Murphy's, Pollo Tropical, Starbucks $Tree, AutoZone, GNC, HEB Foods/gas, U-Haul, Walgreens
185	FM 1044

SAN ANTONIO

Exit #	Services
184	FM 482, Lp 337, Rueckle Rd, E Shell/dsl Hill Cou RV Park, Kia, Mazda, W Pilot/McDonald's/Subway/ scales Jack-in-the-Box
183	Solms Rd, W Exxon/Circle K/dsl
182	Engel Rd
180	Schwab Rd
178	FM 1103, Cibolo Rd, Hubertus Rd, E Exxon/7-11 McDonald's Walgreens, W Valero/Subway/dsl
177	FM 482, FM 2252, W Stone Creek RV Park
176	Weiderstein Rd, same as 175
175	FM 3009, Natural Bridge, E Valero/dsl Chili's, IH Mama Margie's Mexican, McDonald's, Miller's BBQ, Sch zsky's, Sonic, Taco Cabana Fairfield Inn, Hampton HEB Food/dsl/E-85, Lowe's, Verizon, vet, W Mur USA/dsl, Shell/dsl, Valero/Subway/dsl Abel's Diner, Arb Cane's, Chick-fil-A, Denny's, Domino's, Jack-in-the-Box, Jim John's, KFC/Pizza Hut/Taco Bell, Panda Express, Pollo Tropi Starbucks, Wendy's, Whataburger, Wing Stop Best W ern, La Quinta $Tree, URGENT CARE, Walmart/McDona
174b	Schertz Pkwy, E Shell Chevrolet, W Crestview RV
174a	FM 1518, Selma, E Phillips 66/dsl Rudy's BBQ A Buick/GMC, Honda, Subaru, W Comfort Inn Crestv RV Ctr
173	Old Austin Rd, Olympia Pkwy, E Baskin Robbins, Charl Subs, Cheddar's, Chick-fil-A, Chili's, Chipotle Mexican, Ci Firehouse Subs, Five Guys, Freddy's, Genghis Grill, Hoot IHOP, Las Palapas, Macaroni Grill, Outback Steaks, Panda press, Panera Bread, Papouli's Greek, Peter Piper Pizza, Robin, Sea Island Srimp, Starbucks, Subway, Wendy's H day Inn Express AT&T, Beall's, Best Buy, Costco/gas, count Tire, GNC, Hobby Lobby, Home Depot, Kohl's, Michae NTB, Old Navy, Petsmart, Ross, Target, TJ Maxx, URGENT CA Verizon, WorldMkt, W ChuckeCheese, Chuy's Mexic Freebirds Burritos, Houlihan's Hampton Inn
172	TX 218, Anderson Lp, P Booker Rd, E Buffalo Wild Wir Coldstone, Gino's East Pizza, IHOP, Jimmy John's, TX Ro house, Zio's Hilton Garden, Woodspring Suites Niss to Randolph AFB, W Comfort Inn, to SeaWorld
171	Topperwein Rd, same as 170
170	Judson Rd, to Converse, E Carl's Jr, Denny's, Whatabur Great Value Inn, La Quinta H, Ford, Hyundai, Niss Toyota, W Exxon/7-11 Best Western Kia, Maz Sam's Club/gas
169	O'Conner Rd, Wurzbach Pkwy, E Exxon/7-11/dsl Donald's, Quiznos, Subway, Taco Cabana Comfort Su CarMax, Chrysler/Dodge/Jeep, Lowe's, Walgreens, W Shell/dsl, Valero/dsl Jack-in-the-Box, Jim's Rest., So Mi Casa Inn Kia, Mazda
168	Weidner Rd, E Citgo/dsl Comfort Suites, Days W Chevron Econolodge, Super 8 Harley-Davids Volvo Trucks
167b	Thousand Oaks Dr, Starlight Terrace, E Valero/dsl
167a	Randolph Blvd, E Valero/dsl, W Days Inn, Delta Midtowne Suites, Motel 6
166	I-410 W, Lp 368 S, W to Sea World
165	FM 1976, Walzem Rd, E Shell, Valero/dsl Applebe Baskin Robbins/Dunkin', Benny's, Buffalo Wild Wings, Bur King, Bush's Chicken, China Harbor, Church's, Domino's, IH In-n-Out, Jack-in-the-Box, KFC/Taco Bell, Las Palapas Mexic Little Caesar's, LJ Silver, Luby's, McDonald's, Miller's BBQ, O Garden, Pizza Hut, Red Lobster, Shoney's, Starbucks, Subw Taco Cabana, Whataburger Drury Inn $Tree, 99c St

INTERSTATE 35 Cont'd

165 Continued
AutoZone, Cavender's Boots, CVS Drug, Discount Tire, Firestone/auto, HEB/dsl, Home Depot, Office Depot, PepBoys, Petsmart, Ross, Walgreens, Walmart/Subway/dsl, W Sonic NTB

164b Eisenhauer Rd, E Exxon/7-11 Hampton Inn, La Quinta, Mainstay Suites, Super 8, Woodspring Suites Inn $General

164a Rittiman Rd, E Exxon/7-11, Shell/dsl, Valero/dsl Burger King, Church's, Cracker Barrel, Denny's, Hacienda Tapatia, Jack-in-the-Box, McDonald's, Taco Bell, Taco Cabana, Whataburger Best Western, Comfort Suites, Hallmark Inn, Hampton Inn, La Quinta, Mainstay Suites, Motel 6, Motel 6 (2), Rittiman Inn, Super 8, Travel Inn, Woodspring Suites Inn, W Valero Bill Miller BBQ, Popeye's, Sonic, Subway

163 I-410 S (162 from nb, exits left from sb)

161 Binz-Engleman Rd (from nb), same as 160

160 Splashtown Dr, E Valero/Subway/dsl/24hr Motel 6, W Grady's BBQ Best Value Inn, Budget Lodge, Days Inn, Howard Johnson, Microtel, Motel 6, Travelodge

159b Walters St, E McDonald's, W EconoLodge to Ft Sam Houston

159a New Braunfels Ave, E Shell/dsl, Texaco/Burger King auto/dsl repair, W Chevron/dsl, Valero/dsl Miller BBQ, Sonic Antonian Suites to Ft Sam Houston

158c N Alamo St, Broadway

158b I-37 S, US 281 S, to Corpus Christi, to Alamo

158a US 281 N (from sb), to Johnson City

157b a Brooklyn Ave, Lexington Ave, N Flores, E Super 8, W Luby's H, downtown

156 I-10 W, US 87, to El Paso

155b Durango Blvd, E Best Western, Courtyard, Fairfield Inn, Holiday Inn, La Quinta, Residence Inn H, W McDonald's Candlewood Suites, Doubletree, Motel 6, downtown

155a South Alamo St, E Exxon, Shell/dsl Church's, Huevos Nuevos, McDonald's, Wendy's Best Western, Days Inn, Holiday Inn, La Quinta, Residence Inn, Travelodge Advance Parts, USPO, W Knights Inn

154b S Laredo St, Ceballos St, same as 155b

154a Nogalitos St

153 I-10 E, US 90 W, US 87, Lackland AFB, to Kelly AFB

152b Malone Ave, Theo Ave, E Taco Cabana, W Shell

152a Division Ave, E Chevron Bill Miller BBQ, Las Cazuelas Mexican, Whataburger/24hr Econolodge, W Sonic transmissions

151 Southcross Blvd, E Exxon/7-11/dsl, Shell, W Shell/dsl Mazatlan Mexican

150b Lp 13, Military Dr, E Valero Applebee's, Carl's Jr, Denny's, Don Pedro Mexican, Papa John's, Starbucks, Subway, Taco Cabana La Quinta AutoZone, Discount Tire, Meineke, U-Haul, W Exxon Buffalo Wild Wings, Burger King, Chick-fil-A, Chili's, CiCi's, Freddy's Custard, Hungry Farmer Rest, IHOP, Jack-in-the-Box, KFC, Lin's Buffet, Little Caesar's, LJ Silver, Longhorn Steaks, Mama Margie's Mexican, McDonald's, Olive Garden, Panda Express, Popeye's, Red Lobster, Sea Island Shrimp House, Wendy's, Whataburger $Tree, AT&T, Dick's, Firestone/auto, HEB Foods, Home Depot, JC Penney, Lowe's, Macy's, Office Depot, Old Navy, Ross, Target, Verizon, Walgreens

150a Zarzamora St (149 fom sb), same as 150b

149 Hutchins Blvd (from sb), E Valero/dsl Motel 6, Woodspring Suites, W H, Chevrolet, Ford, Honda, Hyundai, Kia

148b Palo Alto Rd

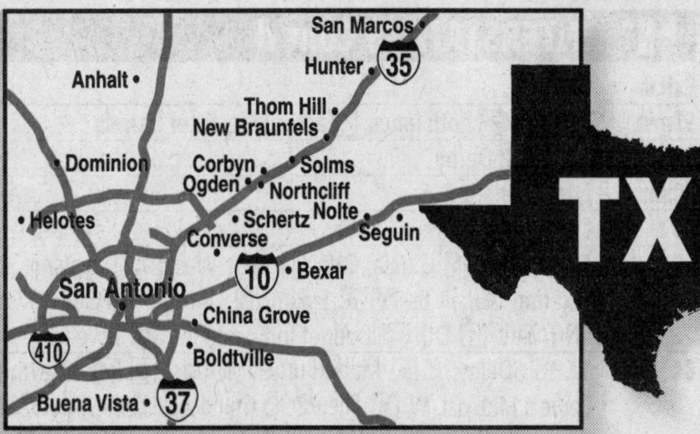

148a TX 16 S, spur 422 (from nb), Poteet, E Chevron/dsl, Murphy USA/dsl Golden Chick Days Inn CVS Drug, Walmart/Subway, W $General

147 Somerset Rd, E Shell/dsl Ford, W Chrysler/Dodge/Jeep

146 Cassin Rd (from nb)

145b Lp 353 N

145a I-410, TX 16

144 Fischer Rd, E Valero/7-11/Subway/dsl/scales/24hr D&D Motel, W Loves/Carl's Jr/dsl/scales/24hr/@ Toyota

142 Medina River Turnaround (from nb)

141 Benton City Rd, Von Ormy, E USPO, W Shell/Parador Café/dsl

140 Anderson Lp, 1604, E Exxon/dsl/24hr Burger King, W Pilot/Subway/dsl/scales/24hr Alamo River RV Resort, to Sea World

139 Kinney Rd

137 Shepherd Rd, E truck repair, W Exxon/Choke Canyon BBQ/dsl/24hr dsl repair

135 Luckey Rd

133 TX 132 S (from sb), Lytle, same as 131

131 FM 3175, FM 2790, Benton City Rd, E Best Western, W HEB/dsl/24hr Bill Miller BBQ, Little Caesar's, McDonald's, Sonic, Subway, Whataburger Days Inn/cafe $General, AutoZone, CVS Drug, Family$, HEB Food/dsl, USPO

129mm **both lanes, full facilities, litter barrels, petwalk, vending**

127 FM 471, Natalia, W Loves/Subway/Wendy's/dsl/scales/24hr/@

125 FM 770

124 FM 463, Bigfoot Rd, E Ford

122 TX 173, Divine, E Exxon/dsl Chevrolet, Chrysler/Dodge/Jeep, W Chevron/McDonald's/Subway/dsl, Exxon, Shell/dsl CCC Steaks, Church's, Pizza Hut, Sonic, Viva Zapatas Mexican Country Corner Inn O'Reilly Parts, Walmart/Subway

121 TX 132 N, Devine

118.5mm **weigh sta both lanes**

114 FM 462, Yancey, Bigfoot, E Lucky/dsl, W Shell/dsl USPO

PEARSALL

111 US 57, to Eagle Pass, W Road Ranger/Valero/Subway/Chester's/dsl/scales/24hr

104 Lp 35

101 FM 140, Pearsall, E Chevron/dsl Cowpokes BBQ, Jalisco's Mexican Baymont Inn, Garden Inn, Hampton Inn, Pearsall Inn, Royal Inn HEB Foods/dsl, W Exxon/Subway/Church's/dsl/24hr, Petro/Valero/Iron Skillet/dsl/scales/24hr Hungry Hunter Grill Days Inn, Holiday Inn Express, La Quinta, Rio Frio Motel, Southern Inn H

99 FM 1581, to Divot, Pearsall

= gas = food = lodging = other = rest stop

TX

INTERSTATE 35 Cont'd

Exit #	Services
93mm	**parking/ both lanes, accessible, litter barrels**
91	FM 1583, Derby
90mm	Frio River
86	Lp 35, Dilley
85	FM 117, E Garcia Café Best Western, Days Inn, Relax Inn, Super 8, W Exxon/dsl, Phillips 66/Church's/dsl/CNG/24hr DQ Budget Inn, Sona Inn RV park
84	TX 85, Dilley, E Mobil/Burger King/dsl H, Chevrolet, Lowe's Mkt/dsl, W Shell/Pollo Grande/dsl/24hr, Valero/Subway/dsl/24hr Best Value Inn, Executive Inn NAPA
82	County Line Rd, to Dilley, Dilley
77	FM 469, Millett
74	Gardendale
69	(68 from nb), Lp 35, Cotulla, E Phillips 66/dsl Family$, Lowe's Mkt, W FLYING J/Subway/PJ Fresh/dsl/scales/24hr, Stripes/Taco Co/dsl/scales/24hr McDonald's, Sonic Days Inn, Fairfield Inn, Mainstay Suites, Microtel
65	Lp 35, Cotulla
67	FM 468, to Big Wells, E Exxon/Wendy's/dsl/24hr, JJ's/dsl, Valero/deli/dsl/24hr DQ, El Charro Mexican, Golden Chick, Pizza Hut, Subway, Taco Palenque Baymont Inn, Candlewood Suites, Comfort Suites, Executive Inn, Hampton Inn, Holiday Inn Express, La Quinta, Quality Inn, Super 8, Village Inn truck repair, W Chevron/dsl/scales/24hr LaSalle Steakhouse Best Western, Hotel Cotulla, Residency Suites Mack/Volvo
63	Elm Creek Interchange
59mm	**both lanes, full facilities, litter barrels, petwalk, , , vending**
56	FM 133, Artesia Wells
48	Caiman Creek Interchange
39	TX 44, Encinal, E Loves/Chester Fried/Subway/dsl/scales/24hr, Road Ranger/Church's/dsl/scales/24hr, W Chevron/dsl
38	TX 44 (from nb), Encinal
32	San Roman Interchange
29mm	**inspection sta nb**
27	Callaghan Interchange
24	**255 toll, Camino Colombia toll rd**, to Monterrey
22	Webb Interchange
18	US 83 N, to Carrizo Springs, E **TX Travel Info Ctr (8am-5pm) / , full facilities, litter barrels, petwalk, , wireless internet,** W RV Camping
14mm	**parking area sb**
12b	(13 from sb) Uniroyal Interchange, E Pilot/McDonald's/Subway/dsl/scales/24hr Blue Beacon, Southern Tire Mart, W FLYING J/Denny's/dsl/scales/24hr, TA/Burger King/Subway/Taco Bell/dsl/scales/24hr/@
12a	Port Loredo
10	Port Laredo Carriers Dr (from nb)
9	Industrial Blvd, to Bob Bullock Lp (from sb only)
8b	Lp 20 W, to Solidarity Bridge
8a	Lp 20 W, to to World Trade Bridge, Milo
5	San Isidro Pkwy
4b	Las Cruces Dr, E Valero/dsl El Pescador
4a	FM 1472
4	FM 1472, Del Mar Blvd, E Exxon/Burger King/dsl Applebee's, Carino's Italian, CiCi's, IHOP, Jack-in-the-Box, McDonald's, Quiznos, Whataburger Extended Stay America, Hampton Inn Best Buy, BigLots, HEB Foods/gas, Marshall's, Old Navy, Target, W La Noria/dsl Days Inn Harley-Davidson

LAREDO

Exit #	Services
3b	Mann Rd, E Buffalo Wild Wings, Krispy Kreme, Lin's nese Residence Inn Ford/Lincoln, Honda, Kia, Low Mazda, URGENT CARE, W Chili's, Golden Corral, Ke Pancake House, Subway, Taco Palenque, TX Roadhouse, W taburger Best Value, Family Garden Inn, Gateway Inn Hacienda Motel, Monterey Inn, Motel 6, Red Roof Inn, Sp gHill Suites $Tree, AT&T, Home Depot, Kohl's, Micha Office Depot, PetCo, Ross, Verizon, Walmart/McDonald's
3a	San Bernardo Ave, E Chick-fil-A, ChuckeCheese, El T Tote, Emperor Garden, Fuddrucker's, LJ Silver, Logan's Ro house, Luby's, Luby's, Olive Garden, Peter Piper Pizza, Red I ster, Sirloin Stockade, Tony Roma's Fairfield Inn $G eral, Advance Parts, HEB Foods/gas, Macy's, NAPA, PepB SteinMart, W Valero Burger King, Danny's Rest., McDonald's, Pizza Hut, Popeye's, Taco Bell, Taco Palenc Wendy's Family$, O'Reilly Parts, Sam's Club/gas
2	US 59, Saunders Rd, E Conoco, Shell Jack-in-the- H, W Exxon/Burger King/dsl, Shell/dsl Churc Denny's, Subway Best Western, Courtyard, La Quinta, mada Plaza, Super8 Advance Parts, AutoZone, AutoZo Mexico Insurance
1b	Park St, to Sanchez St, W Conoco/dsl La Mexic Rest., Pizza Hut, Popeye's
1a	Victoria St, Scott St, Washington St (from sb), E Val W Chevron, Valero/dsl Dos Marias, McDonald's, W dy's Firestone/auto
I-35 begins/ends in Laredo at Victoria St, access to multiple services.	

INTERSTATE 35 (West)

Exit #	Services
I-35W begins/ends on I-35, exit 467.	
85b	W Oak St, E H
85a	I-35E S
84	FM 1515, Bonnie Brae St, E H
82	FM 2449, to Ponder
79	Crawford Rd
76	FM 407, to Justin, Argyle, W Exxon/dsl Paradise Mk
76mm	**both lanes, tables, litter barrels**
74	FM 1171, to Lewisville
72	Dale Earnhardt Way, W Marriott TX Motor Speedw
70	TX 114, to Dallas, Bridgeport, E QT/dsl, Shell/Subway/ Valero/dsl/e85 BurgerIM, IHOP, Rose's Cafe, Popey Sonic Holiday Inn Express, Home 2 Suites, La Quin Quality Inn, Motel 6, North Lake RV Park, to DFW Airp W Buc-ee's, EVC Buffalo Wild Wings, Cane's, Ch fil-A, In-N-Out, Panda Express, Olive Garden, Smoothie Ki Starbucks, Whataburger Marriott Tanger Outlets/ mous brands, TX Motor Speedway
68	Eagle Pkwy, W
67	Alliance Blvd, W FedEx, to Alliance Airport
66	to Westport Pkwy, Keller-Haslet Rd, E Hampton Inn, Hil Garden, Residence Inn, W 7-11/Wendy's/dsl Brya BBQ, Schlotzsky's, Snooty Pig, Subway, Taco Bueno USP
65	TX 170 E, E Pilot/McDonald's/dsl/scales/24hr IH Cabela's/cafe
64	Golden Triangle Blvd, to Keller-Hicks Blvd, E QT/dsl, Ra Trac/dsl/e85 Chrysler/Dodge/Jeep, Kia
63	Heritage Trace, Park Glen, E 7-11 BJ's Rest., Chedda Chick-fil-A, Chipotle, Chuy's, Coldstone, Costa Vida, Cous BBQ, Free Birds Burritos, Houlihan's, Jason's Deli, McAliste Deli, McDonald's, Mi Cocina, Panera Bread, Pei Wei, Pie Fi Razzoo's Cajun, Smoothie King, Starbucks, Subway, The Ro

INTERSTATE 35 (West) Cont'd

63 Continued
Kitchen, Which Wich?, Zoe's Kitchen [lodging] Courtyard [other] Belk, Best Buy, Dick's, GNC, JC Penney, Kroger/dsl, Petsmart, Verizon, W [gas] 7-11/dsl

62 North Tarrant Pkwy, E [food] 54th St Grill, Chili's, Firehouse Subs, Five Guys, Fuzzy's Tacos, HaNaBi Hibachi, Olive Garden, Pizza Inn, Pluckers, Thai Fusion [other] [H], W [food] Cane's, Chick-fil-A, ChuckECheese, El Pollo Loco, In-N-Out, Jimmy John's, La Madeleine, Old Chicago, Pollo Tropical, Potbelly, Starbucks, Taco Cabana, Tom+Chee, Uncle Julio's, Wendy's [other] $Tree, AT&T, Costco/gas, Hobby Lobby, Old Navy, Petco, Ross, Target, TJ Maxx, Tuesday Morning, URGENT CARE, Winco

60 US 287 N, US 81 N, to Decatur

59 Basswood (sb only), E [gas] Chevron/Jack-in-the-Box/dsl [food] Chicken Express, DQ, Sonic, Subway, Taco Bell [other] Home Depot, NTB

58 Western Ctr Blvd, E [gas] 7-11/dsl, Shell/Church's [food] BoomerJack's, Braum's, Brick House, Chili's, Denny's, Dublin Square Rest., Flips Grill, Genghis Grill, Jake's Burgers, Jimmy John's, On-the-Border, Posados Cafe, Rudy's BBQ, SaltGrass Steaks, Shady Oak Grill, Twin Peaks, Wendy's, Which Wich?, Wing Stop [lodging] Magnuson Hotel, Residence Inn [other] AT&T, W [food] Boston's, Firehouse Subs, Joe's Crabshack, McDonald's, Popeye's, Rosa's Cafe, Smoothie King, Starbucks, Subway, Waffle House, Whataburger [lodging] Comfort Inn, Holiday Inn Express, Staybridge Suites [other] repair, URGENT CARE

57b a I-820 E&W

56b Melody Hills Dr

56a Meacham Blvd, E [gas] Shell/7-11 [lodging] Hilton Garden, Knights Inn, La Quinta, W [gas] Texaco/dsl [food] Cracker Barrel, McDonald's, Subway [lodging] Holiday Inn, Quality Inn, Radisson, Super 8 [other] USPO

55 Pleasantdale Ave (from nb)

54c 33rd St, Long Ave (from nb), W [gas] Drivers TC/Subway/dsl/scales [lodging] Motel 6

54b a TX 183, NE 28th St, E [food] Lisa's Chicken/dsl, W [gas] QT/dsl [lodging] Stockyards Motel 6 Inn

53 North Side Dr, Yucca Dr, E [gas] Shell/7-11/dsl, W [food] Mercado Juarez Café [lodging] Country Inn&Suites

53mm Trinity River

52e Carver St (from nb)

52d Pharr St (exits left from nb)

52b US 377N, Belknap

52a US 377 N, TX 121, to DFW

51a I-30 E, to Avalene (from nb), downtown Ft Worth

50c a I-30 W, E to Dallas

50b TX 180 E (from nb)

49b Rosedale St, E [gas] 7-11/dsl [food] Jack-in-the-Box, W [other] [H]

49a Allen Ave, E [gas] Valero/dsl, W [other] [H]

48b Morningside Ave (from sb), same as 48a

48a Berry St, E [gas] Chevron/McDonald's [other] AutoZone, El Rio Grande Foods, Family$, W [gas] RaceTrac/dsl [other] U-Haul, zoo

47 Ripy St, E [other] transmissions

46b Seminary Dr, E [gas] RaceWay [food] Grandy's, Jack-in-the-Box, Taco Cabana, Whataburger [lodging] Days Inn, Delux Inn, Motel 6, Super 7 Inn [other] NAPA, W [gas] Shell, Valero [food] Chalio Mexican, ChuckECheese, Denny's, Sonic, Wendy's [other] Firestone/auto, Pepboys, Ross

46a Felix St, E [gas] Valero [lodging] Dalworth Inn, W [food] Cesar's Tacos, McDonald's [other] Family$

45b a I-20, E to Dallas, W to Abilene

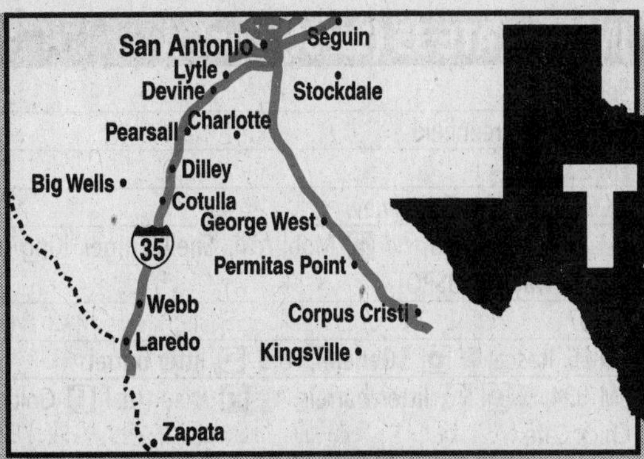

44 Altamesa, E [lodging] Radisson, W [gas] Conoco/dsl [food] Rig Steaks, Waffle House [lodging] Baymont Inn, Comfort Suites, Motel 6, South Lp Inn, Super 8

43 Sycamore School Rd, W [gas] Exxon/7-11/dsl [food] Chicken Express, Jack-in-the-Box, Jimmy John's, Sonic, Subway, Whataburger [lodging] Scottish Inn [other] $General, Home Depot

42 Everman Pkwy, E [food] McDonald's, Starbucks, W [gas] QT/dsl/scales, Shell/dsl

41 Risinger Rd, E [other] Chrysler/Dodge/Jeep, W [other] Camping World RV Service/Supplies, McClain's RV Ctr

40 Garden Acres Dr, E [gas] Loves/Subway/dsl/scales/24hr [lodging] Motel 6 [other] [H], W [gas] 7-11/dsl [food] Chicken Express, Taco Bell

39 FM 1187, McAlister Rd, E [gas] QT/dsl [other] [H], W [gas] Shell/dsl, Valero/dsl [food] Buffalo Wild Wings, Charley's Subs, Firehouse Subs, Logan's Roadhouse, McAlister's Deli, Mooyah Burger, Olive Garden, Panda Express, Red Lobster, Subway, TGIFriday's, Waffle House [lodging] Magnuson [other] AT&T, Best Buy, Kohl's, Michael's, Old Navy, Petsmart, Ross, Staples, TJ Maxx, URGENT CARE, Verizon

38 Alsbury Blvd, E [gas] Mobil/dsl [food] Chili's, Cracker Barrel, Hibachi Japanese, IHOP, McDonald's, Mexican Inn Cafe, On-the-Border, Our Place Grill, Outback Steaks, Spring Creek BBQ [lodging] Fairfield Inn, Hampton Inn, Holiday Inn Express, La Quinta, Super 8 [other] Discount Tire, Ford, Lowe's Whse, W [gas] 7-11/dsl, RaceTrac/dsl [food] Applebee's, Arby's, Burger King, Chick-fil-A, Cotton Patch Cafe, Denny's, El Fenix, Sonic, Taco Cabana, Wendy's [other] Albertson's, Chevrolet, GNC, JC Penney, Michael's, PetsMart, Ross, URGENT CARE, vet

37 TX 174, Wilshire Blvd, to Cleburne, (from sb)

36 FM 3391, TX 174S, Burleson, E [gas] 7-11/dsl, Mobil [food] Miranda's Cantina, Sonic, Waffle House [lodging] Best Western, Days Inn, Quality Inn [other] Harley Davidson, Honda, Hyundai, Nissan, Sam's Club/dsl, W [other] $General, transmissions

35 Briaroaks Rd (from sb), E [other] same as 36, W [other] Mockingbird Hill RV Park (2mi)

32 Bethesda Rd, E [gas] Valero [lodging] Five Star Inn [other] RV Ranch Park, W [other] Mockingbird Hill RV Park

30 FM 917, Mansfield, E [gas] Shell/Sonic/dsl [other] $General, W [gas] Shell/dsl

27 Rd 604, Rd 707

26b a US 67, Cleburne, E [gas] Chevron/dsl, Exxon/dsl, Texaco/dsl [food] Chicken Express, Domino's, DQ, Lin's Chinese, Little Caesar's, McDonald's, Pizza Hut, Sonic, Subway, Taco Bell, Waffle House, Whataburger [lodging] Comfort Inn, Holiday Inn Express, La Quinta, Motel 6, Super 8 [other] $General, AutoZone, Brookshire Foods, Family$, Motor Home Specialists, Parts+, RV Tech Ctr, W [gas] QT/dsl [food] Burger King [other] CVS Drug

24 FM 3136, FM 1706, Alvarado, E [gas] Shell/LJ Silver/dsl/scales/24hr

TX

INTERSTATE 35 (West) Cont'd

Exit #	Services
21	Rd 107, to Greenfield
17	FM 2258
16	TX 81 S, Rd 201, Grandview
15	FM 916, Maypearl, W Mobil/dsl, Shell/Burger King/dsl Subway USPO
12	FM 67
8	FM 66, Itasca, W $General, Ford, litter barrels
7	FM 934, E litter barrels, W Exxon/dsl Golden Chick Cafe
3	FM 2959, E to Hillsboro Airport

I-35W begins/ends on I-35, 371mm.

INTERSTATE 37

SAN ANTONIO

Exit #	Services
142b a	I-35 S to Laredo, N to Austin. **I-37 begins/ends on I-35 in San Antonio.**
141c	Brooklyn Ave, Nolan St (from sb), downtown
141b	Houston St, E Comfort Suites, Red Roof Inn Theo's Tires, W Denny's Crockett Hotel, Days Inn, Fairfield Inn, Hampton Inn, Hyatt Hotel, La Quinta, Marriott, Residence Inn, SpringHill Suites Macy's, to The Alamo
141a	Commerce St, E Best Western, Staybridge Suites, W Denny's Hyatt, La Quinta, Marriott Macy's
140b	Durango Blvd, E Bill Miller BBQ to Alamo Dome, downtown
140a	Carolina St, Florida St, E Shell/dsl
139	I-10 W, US 87, US 90, to Houston, W to Sea World
138c	Fair Ave, Hackberry St, E DQ, Jack-in-the-Box, La Tapatia Mexian, Popeye's Brake Check, Family$, Home Depot, W Exxon/7-11, Shell
138b	E New Braunfels Ave (from sb), E Burger King, Chick-fil-A, IHOP, McDonald's, Taco Cabana, Wendy's Beall's, HEB/dsl, Marshall's, W Exxon Sonic
138a	Southcross Blvd, W New Braunfels Ave, E McDonald's, Taco Cabana, Wendy's Golden Chick, Panda Express, W Exxon Burger King, Sonic
137	Hot Wells Blvd, E Chevron/dsl, W IHOP Motel 6, Super 8
136	Pecan Valley Dr, E Citgo/dsl Church's, KFC/Taco Bell, Pizza Hut Pecan Valley Inn AutoZone, O'Reilly Parts, W H
135	Military Dr, Lp 13, E Shell/dsl, Valero Jack-in-the-Box, Rancho Grande Quality Inn CVS Drug, Mission Trail RV park, W Valero/Subway/dsl A&W/LJ Silver, Buffalo Wild Wings, Buffet Seafood, Burger King, Carino's Italian, Chaba Thai, Chick-fil-A, Chili's, Cracker Barrel, IHOP, Little Caesar's, Longhorn Cafe, Panda Express, Papa John's, Peter Piper Pizza, Sonic, Starbucks, Subway, Whataburger Hampton Inn, Holiday Inn Express, La Quinta H, $Tree, Advance Parts, AT&T, AutoZone, Best Buy, BigLots, Discount Tire, HEB Food/gas, Home Depot, Lowe's, Office Depot, PetCo, Ross, Sam's Club/dsl, Target, to Brooks AFB, Walgreens, Walmart/McDonald's
133	I-410, US 281 S
132	US 181 S, to Floresville, E Shell/7-11/dsl $General
130	Donop Rd, Southton Rd, E Valero/7-11/dsl Tom's Burgers Days Inn Braunig Lake RV Resort, W Shell/dsl car/truckwash
127	San Antonio River Turnaround (from nb), Braunig Lake
127mm	San Antonio River
125	FM 1604, Anderson Lp, E Mobil/dsl/24hr Burger King fireworks, W Exxon/dsl, Pilot/Subway/dsl/scales/2 Shell/dsl Miller's BBQ, Sonic, Whataburger fireworks, t
122	Priest Rd, Mathis Rd, E Valero/dsl $General
120	Hardy Rd
117	FM 536
113	FM 3006
112mm	**both lanes, litter barrels**
109	TX 97, to Floresville, E Chevron/dsl, Exxon/dsl Por lo's Mexican Chrysler/Dodge/Jeep
106	Coughran Rd
104	spur 199, Leal Rd, to Pleasanton (no immediate sb retu same as 103
103	US 281 N, Leal Rd, to Pleasanton, E Valero/dsl K&K Cafe Kuntry Inn
98	TX 541, McCoy
92	US 281A, Campbellton
88	FM 1099, to FM 791, Campbellton
83	FM 99, Whitsett, Peggy, E Shell/cafe/dsl, W C Fue dsl, Exxon/dsl Choke Canyon BBQ
82mm	**sb, full facilities, litter barrels,**
78mm	**nb, full facilities, litter barrels,**
76	US 281A, FM 2049, Whitsett
75mm	**truck weigh sta sb**
74mm	**truck weigh sta nb**
72	US 281 S, Three Rivers, W Loves/McDonald's/Subw dsl/scales/24hr/@ Sonic, Van's BBQ Motel 6 to Grande Valley
69	TX 72, Three Rivers, W Valero/Subway/dsl/24hr Reb Rose RV Park, to Choke Cyn SP
65	FM 1358, Oakville, E Van's BBQ
59	FM 799
56	US 59, George West, E FLYING J/McDonald's/dsl/scal 24hr, Stripes/Taco Co/dsl/24hr, W Shell/BBQ/dsl/24hr, Va ro/Burger King/dsl/24hr
51	Hailey Ranch Rd
47	FM 3024, FM 534, Swinney Switch Rd, W Swinney Swi Cafe Mike's Mkt/gas, Mustang Hollow Camping (4mi)
44mm	**parking area sb**
42mm	**parking area nb**
40	FM 888
36	TX 359, to Skidmore, Mathis, W Road Ranger/Subway/d scales, Shell/McDonald's/dsl, Valero/dsl (1mi) Pizza H Smolik's Smokehouse La Quinta Lake Corpus Christi S
34	TX 359 W, E Adventure TX RV Ctr/LP, W Shell, Vale dsl Church's, Sonic DQ, Pizza Hut $General, O'R ly Parts, to Lake Corpus Christi SP
31	TX 188, to Sinton, Rockport
22	TX 234, FM 796, to Odem, Edroy
20b	Cooper Rd
19.5mm	**both lanes, accessible, litter barrels**
17	US 77 N, to Victoria
16	LaBonte Park, W info, litter barrels,
15	Sharpsburg Rd (from sb), Redbird Ln
14	I-69, US 77 S, Redbird Ln, to Kingsville, Robstown, **1 mi W** FM 624 RaceWay/dsl, Shell/dsl, Valero/Burger King/ Chili's, CiCi's, Denny's, El Tapatio Mexican, Good'n Crisp Chi en, Miller's BBQ, Papa John's, Pizza Hut, Popeye's, Sonic, Subw Whataburger, Wienerschnitzel Comfort Inn, Holiday Inn press H, $General, $Tree, AT&T, AutoZone, Beall's, CVS Dr Discount Tire, Firestone/auto, GNC, Hobby Lobby, Home Dep O'Reilly Parts, Petco, Ross, Verizon, Walmart/McDonald's

INTERSTATE 37 Cont'd

Exit #	Services
13b	Sharpsburg Rd (from nb)
13a	FM 1694, Callicoatte Rd, Leopard St
11b	FM 24, Violet Rd, Hart Rd, E [gas] Shell/Subway/dsl [food] Chicken Shack, W [gas] Exxon/dsl, Valero/dsl [food] Domino's, DQ, Fliz Amancer Mexican, KFC/LJ Silver, Little Caesar's, McDonald's, Pizza Hut, Schlotzsky's, Sonic, Subway, Taco Bell, Whataburger [lodging] Hampton Inn, Super 8 [other] Advance Parts, AutoZone, Family$, HEB Food/gas, O'Reilly Parts, Walgreens
11a	McKinzie Rd, E [gas] Shell [food] Jack-in-the-Box [lodging] La Quinta, W [gas] Valero/dsl
10	Carbon Plant Rd
9	FM 2292, Up River Rd, Rand Morgan Rd, W [gas] Valero/dsl [food] Whataburger
7	Suntide Rd, Tuloso Rd, Clarkwood Rd, W [other] CC RV Ctr, Freightliner
6	Southern Minerals Rd, E [gas] refinery
5	Corn Products Rd, Valero Way, E [other] Kenworth/Mack, W [gas] Gascard/dsl [food] Jalisco II Rest. [lodging] Best Value, Howard Johnson, ValStay
4b	Lantana St, McBride Lane (from sb), W [lodging] Airport Inn, Motel 6
4a	TX 358, to Padre Island, W [lodging] Holiday Inn, Plaza Inn [other] Walmart (4mi)
3b	McBride Lane (from nb), W [other] Gulf Coast Racing
3a	Navigation Blvd, E [gas] Valero/dsl [lodging] Rodeway Inn, W [gas] Exxon/7-11/dsl [food] Denny's, La Milpas, Miller BBQ [lodging] Hampton Inn, Holiday Inn Express, Knights Inn, La Quinta, Super 8 [other] CarQuest
2	Up River Rd, E [other] refinery, W [food] Mr G's BBQ
1e	Lawrence Dr, Nueces Bay Blvd, E [other] refinery, W [gas] Valero [food] Church's [lodging] Red Roof Inn [other] Aamco, AutoZone, Firestone, HEB Foods, USPO
1d	Port Ave (from sb), W [gas] Coastal, Shell [food] Vick's Burgers [lodging] EconoLodge [other] Port of Corpus Christi
1c	US 181, TX 286, Shoreline Blvd, Corpus Christi, W [other] H
1b	Brownlee St (from nb)
1a	Buffalo St (from sb), 0-1 mi W on Shoreline [gas] Sunoco/dsl [food] Burger King, Joe's Crabshack, Landry's Seafood, Subway, Waterstreet Seafood, Whataburger [lodging] Bayfront Inn, Best Western, Holiday Inn, Omni Hotel, Super 8 [other] U-Haul, USPO, **I-37 begins/ends on US 181 in Corpus Christi.**

CORPUS CHRISTI

INTERSTATE 40

Exit #	Services
177mm	Texas/Oklahoma state line
176	spur 30 (from eb), to Texola
169	FM 1802, Carbon Black Rd
167	FM 2168, Daberry Rd
165mm	check sta wb
164	Lp 40 (from wb), to Shamrock, 1 mi S [lodging] EconoLodge [other] H, check sta eb, museum
163	US 83, to Wheeler, Shamrock, N [gas] Chevron/Taco Bell/dsl [lodging] Best Western+, Motel 6 [other] Ace Hardware, S [gas] Conoco/dsl, Tesla EVC, Valero/Subway/dsl [food] McDonald's [lodging] EconoLodge, Holiday Inn Express, Sleep Inn, Western Motel [other] Family$
161	Lp 40, Rte 66 (from eb), to Shamrock
157	FM 1547, Lela, 1 mi S [other] West 40 RV Camping
152	FM 453, Pakan Rd
148	FM 1443, Kellerville Rd
146	County Line Rd

SHAMROCK

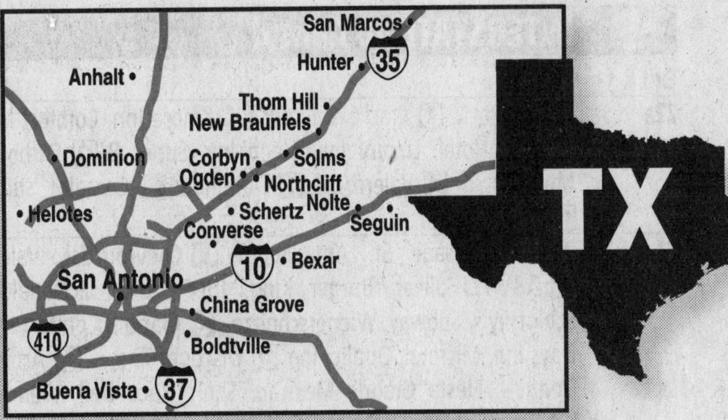

Exit #	Services
143	Lp 40 (from wb), to McLean, N [other] to Rte 66/dsl
142	TX 273, FM 3143, to McLean, N [gas] Conoco/dsl [food] Red River Steaks [lodging] Cactus Inn [other] RV Camping/dump, USPO
141	Rte 66 (from eb), McLean, same as 142
135	FM 291, Rte 66, Alanreed, S [gas] Conoco/motel/café/RV park/dump [other] USPO
132	Johnson Ranch Rd, ranch access
131mm	**[rest stop] wb, full [handicapped] facilities, litter barrels, petwalk, [phone], [picnic]**
129mm	**[rest stop] eb, full [handicapped] facilities, littler barrels, petwalk, [phone], [picnic], playground**
128	FM 2477, to Lake McClellan, N [other] Lake McClellan RA/RV Dump
124	TX 70 S, to Clarendon, S [other] RV camping/dump (11mi)
121	TX 70 N, to Pampa
114	Lp 40, Groom, N [other] dsl repair
113	FM 2300, Groom, S [gas] Phillips 66/dsl [food] DQ [lodging] Chalet Inn
112	FM 295, Groom, S [gas] gas [other] Biggest Cross
110	Lp 40, Rte 66
109	FM 294
105	FM 2880, grain silo
98	TX 207 S (from wb), to Claude
96	TX 207 N, to Panhandle, N [gas] Love's/Subway/dsl/24hr, S [lodging] Conway Inn/cafe, Executive Inn
89	FM 2161, to Rte 66
87	FM 2373
87mm	**[picnic] both lanes, litter barrels**
85	Amarillo Blvd, Durrett Rd, access to camping
81	FM 1912, N [gas] Valero/dsl
80	FM 228, N [other] AOK RV Park
78	US 287 S (from eb), FM 1258, Pullman Rd, same as 77
77	FM 1258, Pullman Rd
76	spur 468, N [gas] FLYING J/Denny's/dsl/LP/RV dump/scales/24hr, Phillips/dsl [food] Buffalo Wild Wings [lodging] Fairfield Inn, Holiday Inn Express, La Quinta [other] Mack/Volvo Trucks, S [gas] Speedco [other] Custom RV Ctr, TX info
75	Lp 335, Lakeside Rd, N [gas] Pilot/Subway/McDonald's/dsl/scales/24hr/ [lodging] Hampton Inn, Holiday Inn, Knights Inn, Super 8 [other] KOA (2mi), Overnite RV Park, S [gas] Petro/dsl/rest./scales/@, Valero/dsl [other] Blue Beacon
74	Whitaker Rd, N [food] Big Texan Inn [other] RV camping, S [gas] Love's/Subway/dsl/scales/@, TA/Exxon/FoodCourt/dsl/scales/24hr/@ [other] Blue Beacon, Eagle Truckwash, Peterbilt
73	Eastern St, Bolton Ave, Amarillo, N [gas] TT/dsl [lodging] Express Inn, Motel 6, Wood Spring Suites, S [gas] Valero/dsl [lodging] Best Western
72b	Grand St, Amarillo, N [gas] Valero/dsl [food] Henk's BBQ [lodging] Value Inn [other] O'Reilly Parts, S [gas] Murphy USA/dsl, Phillips 66, Valero [food] Braum's, Chicken Express, McDonald's, Pizza Hut, Sonic, Starbucks, Subway, Taco Villa, Whataburger [lodging] Best Value Inn [other] $Tree, Advance Parts, Amigo's Foods, AutoZone, BigLots, GNC a, Meineke, same as 73, URGENT CARE, Walmart

AMARILLO

TX

INTERSTATE 40 Cont'd

AMARILLO

Exit #	Services
72a	Nelson St, N [food] Cracker Barrel [lodging] Ashmore Inn, Comfort Inn, La Kiva Hotel, Luxury Inn, Sleep Inn, Super 8 [other] Qtrhorse Museum, S [gas] Valero/dsl [food] Domino's [lodging] Camelot Suites [other] transmissions
71	Ross St, Osage St, Amarillo, N [gas] Chevron/dsl, Valero [food] A&W/LJ Silver, Burger King, IHOP, KFC, McDonald's, Schlotsky's, Subway, Wienerschnitzel [lodging] Clarion, Comfort Inn, Days Inn, Microtel, Quality Inn [other] Discount Tire, S [food] Arby's, Denny's, Fiesta Grande Mexican, Sonic, Taco Bell, Wendy's [lodging] Baymont Inn, La Quinta, Red Roof Inn [other] Chevrolet, Ford, Hyundai, Sam's Club/gas, USPO
70	I-27 S, US 60 W, US 87, US 287, to Canyon, Lubbock, to downtown Amarillo
69b	Washington St, Amarillo, S [gas] TT/dsl [food] DQ [other] CVS Drug, Subway
69a	Crockett St, access to same as 68b
68b	Georgia St, N [gas] TT/dsl [food] Dyer's BBQ, Schlotzky's, Sharky's Burrito Co, S [gas] Valero [food] Burger King, Church's Chicken, Coldstone, Denny's, Firehouse Subs, Jersey Mike's, Pizza Hut, Sonic, Starbucks, TX Roadhouse, Whataburger [lodging] Holiday Inn Express [other] Home Depot, Office Depot, Walgreens
68a	Julian Blvd, Paramount Blvd, N [food] Chili's, Rosa's Cafe [lodging] same as 67, S [gas] Valero [food] Burger King, Chick-Fil-A, Chipotle, Panda Express, Popeyes, Red Lobster, Ruby Tequila's Mexican, TX Roadhouse [lodging] Holiday Inn Express, Motel 6, Super 8, Travelodge [other] Home Depot, Office Depot, Bubba's BBQ, El Patron, Five Guys
67	Western St, Amarillo, N [gas] Phillips 66 [food] Braum's, Burger King, McAlister's Deli, McDonald's, Papa Murphy's, Sonic, Subway, Taco Bell, Wendy's, Aspen Creek Grill, S [gas] Murphy Express/dsl, Rudy's/BBQ/dsl, Valero [food] Blue Sky Rest., Cheddar's, IHOP, Jimmy John's, Olive Garden, Waffle House, Wienerschnitzel [lodging] Baymont Inn, Candlewood Suites, Comfort Suites, Staybridge Suites [other] Discount Tire, Firestone/auto, Michael's, O'Reilly Parts, Petco, same 68
66	Bell St, Amarillo, N [gas] Cefco/dsl [lodging] Fairfield Inn, Red Roof Inn, Relax Inn, Residence Inn [other] Harley-Davidson, S [food] Donut Stop, Taco Bueno [other] CashSaver
65	Coulter Dr, Amarillo, N [gas] Phillips 66/dsl [food] Arby's, Golden Corral, Subway, Taco Bell, Waffle House [lodging] Days Inn, Executive Inn, Holiday Inn, Holiday Inn Express, La Quinta [other] [H] Cadillac/Chevrolet, Chrysler/Dodge/Jeep, Firestone/auto, S [gas] Chevron/Chicken Express/dsl [food] ChinaStar, CiCi's, Hoffbrau Steaks, Outback Steaks, Pizza Hut, Whataburger [lodging] 5th Season Inn, Hampton Inn, Sleep Inn [other] AT&T, Goodyear/auto, Verizon
64	Soncy Rd, to Pal Duro Cyn, N [food] Fuddrucker's, Furr's Buffet, Jimmy John's, Lin's Chinese, Plaza Rest., Red Robin [lodging] Comfort Inn, Country Inn&Suites, Drury Inn, Hilton Garden, Holiday Inn, Homewood Suites [other] USPO, Cavender's Boots, Courtyard, Discount Tire, Extended Stay America, Kabuki, Logan's Roadhouse, Longhorn Steaks, My Place, Saltgrass Steaks, SpringHill Suites, Tru, S [gas] Valero/dsl/24hr [food] Applebee's, ChuckeCheese, DQ, Fazoli's, Hooters, Marble Slab Creamery, McAlisters Deli, McDonald's, On-the-Border, Pei Wei, Starbucks, Subway [other] $Tree, Barnes&Noble, Best Buy, Dillard's, Ford, Home Depot, JC Penney, Jo-Ann Fabrics, Kohl's, Lincoln, Old Navy, PetsMart, Ross, Sam's Club/dsl, Target, Verizon, World Mkt
62b	Lp 40, Amarillo Blvd, N [other] Gander Outdoors, S [other] Sundown RV Resort
62a	Hope Rd, Helium Rd, S [other] Cadillac RV camping

VEGA

Exit #	Services
60	Arnot Rd, S [gas] Loves/Subway/dsl [other] Oasis RV Reso dump
57	RM 2381, Bushland, N [gas] Falcon Stop/dsl [other] grain silos [gas] Phillips 66/dsl [food] Bushland Burger, Joe's Pizza [other] US vet
55mm	**parking area wb, litter barrels, litter barrels, parking area w**
54	Adkisson Rd
53.5mm	**parking area eb, litter barrels**
49	FM 809, Wildorado, S [gas] Crist Fuel/dsl/LP
42	Everett Rd
37	Lp 40 W, to Vega, 1 mi N [lodging] Bonanza Motel [other] same as Walnut RV Park
36	US 385, Vega, N [gas] Alon/dsl, Shamrock, Valero/Allsup's/c scales/24hr [food] DQ, Subway [lodging] Days Inn [other] RV Park, $ Ger al, S [gas] Pilot/PJ Fresh/dsl/scales/24hr, Vega Trk Stop/cafe/
35	to Rte 66, to Vega, N [lodging] Best Value Inn, Bonanza Motel (1 [other] same as 36, Walnut RV Park (1mi)
32mm	**[RS] both lanes, litter barrels**
28	to Rte 66, Landergin
23	to Adrian, Vega, same as 22
22	TX 214, Adrian, N [food] Midpoint Cafe [other] auto repair, US S [gas] Valero/dsl
18	FM 2858, Gruhlkey Rd
15	Ivy Rd
13mm	**[RS] both lanes, litter barrels**
0	Lp 40, to Glenrio
0mm	Texas/New Mexico state line, Central/Mountain time zone

INTERSTATE 44

WICHITA FALLS

Exit #	Services
15mm	Texas/Oklahoma state line, Red River
14	Lp 267, E 3rd St, W [other] historical marker, KOA
13	Glendale St, W [food] Subway
12	Burkburnett, E [gas] Valero/dsl [lodging] Best Western, W [gas] Alon/ 11/dsl [food] Braum's, Chicken Express, Feedlot Rest., Lite P Asian, McDonald's, Whataburger [other] Chevrolet, Ford, NAPA
11	FM 3429, Daniels Rd
9mm	**[RS] both lanes, litter barrels, petwalk**
7	East Rd
6	Bacon Switch Rd
5a	FM 3492, Missile Rd, E [food] El Mejicano Rest., Marco's Piz [other] st patrol, W [gas] Exxon/dsl
5	Access Rd
4	City Loop St
3c	FM 890, W [gas] Murphy USA/dsl [food] Cracker Barrel, Gold Chick, Jack-in-the-Box, KFC/Taco Bell, Parkway Grill, Subw [other] Walmart/Subway
3b	sp 325, Sheppard AFB
3a	US 287 N, to Amarillo, W [gas] Shell/dsl [food] Carl's Jr [lodging] How ard Johnson
2	Maurine St, E [gas] Alon/7-11/dsl [lodging] Best Value Inn, Exe utive Inn, Motel 6, Quality Inn [other] Chevrolet, Mazda/V W [gas] Alon/7-11 [food] Denny's, LJ Silver, Whataburger [lodging] Ca dlewood Suites, Comfort Inn, La Quinta, Red Roof Inn, Super
1d	US 287 bus, Lp 370, W [gas] Valero/dsl [lodging] Travelodge
1c	Texas Travel Info Ctr, E [gas] $Saver
1b	Scotland Park (from nb)
1a	US 277 S, to Abilene, W [food] Arby's [lodging] EconoLodge
1	Holliday St, W [gas] Valero/dsl [food] Arby's, Burger King, Carl's IHOP, McDonald's, Subway [lodging] Delux Inn, EconoLodge [other] Family$, Walgreens
0mm	Witchita Falls. I-44 begins/ends on US 287.

INTERSTATE 45

Exit #	Services
286	to I-35 E, to Denton. **I-45 begins/ends in Dallas.**
285	Bryan St E, US 75 N
284b a	I-30, W to Ft Worth, E to Texarkana, **E** [other] access to [H]
283b	Pennsylvania Ave, to MLK Blvd, **E** [gas] Kwikstop
283a	Lamar St
281	Overton St (from sb), **W** [gas] Chevron
280	Illinois Ave, Linfield St, **E** [lodging] Star Motel, **W** [gas] Exxon, Shell/dsl
279b a	Lp 12
277	Simpson Stuart Rd, **W** [other] to Paul Quinn Coll
276b a	I-20, W to Ft Worth, E to Shreveport
275	TX 310 N (from nb, no re-entry)
274	Dowdy Ferry Rd, Hutchins, **E** [gas] Exxon/Subway/dsl, Shell/McDonald's/dsl [lodging] Gold Inn, La Quinta, Motel 6 [other] auto repair, **W** [gas] Top Fuel/dsl [food] DQ, Jack-in-the-Box, Whataburger
273	Wintergreen Rd, **W** [gas] QT/dsl/scales/24hr
272	Fulghum Rd, **E** [gas] Love's/Carl's Jr/dsl/scales/24hr, **W** [other] **weigh sta both lanes**
271	Pleasant Run Rd
270	Belt Line Rd, to Wilmer, **E** [gas] Chevron/Pizza Inn/dsl, **W** [gas] Exxon/Sonic/dsl, Shell/Church's/Subway/dsl [food] Denny's [other] $General, Family$, USPO
269	Mars Rd
268	Malloy Bridge Rd
267	Frontage Rd
266	FM 660, **E** [food] Jack-in-the-Box, **W** [gas] Valero/dsl [food] DQ, Pizza Hut
265	Lp 45, Ferris, nb only
263a b	Lp 561
262	frontage rd
260	Lp 45, **E** [food] Traylor RV Park, **W** [gas] Shell/Sonic/dsl
259	FM 813, FM 878, Jefferson St
258	Lp 45, Palmer, **E** [gas] Chevron/Subway/dsl/scales/24hr [other] golf
255	FM 879, Garrett, **E** [gas] Exxon/dsl, **W** [gas] Chevron/dsl
253	Lp 45, **W** [gas] Shell/Subway/dsl
251b	TX 34, Ennis, **E** [gas] Alon/dsl, QT/dsl [food] Bubba's BBQ, Cotton Patch Cafe, McDonald's [lodging] Baymont Inn, Comfort Suites, Days Inn, Holiday Inn Express, La Quinta [other] Ford, URGENT CARE, **W** [gas] Chevron/dsl, Exxon/dsl/24hr, Murphy USA/dsl, Valero [food] Braum's, Burger King, Chili's, Chipotle, Denny's, Domino's, DQ, Golden Chick, Grand Buffet, Hilda's Kitchen, IHOP, Jack-in-the-Box, Little Caesar's, Papa John's, Sonic, Starbucks, Subway, Taco Bell, Taco Cabana, Tokyo Grill, Waffle House, Wall Chinese, Wendy's, Whataburger [lodging] Quality Inn [other] [H], $Tree, AT&T, AutoZone, Beall's, Chevrolet, Chrysler/Dodge/Jeep, RV camping, Walmart/McDonald's
251a	Creechville Rd, FM 1181, Ennis, **W** [other] [H]
249	FM 85, Ennis, **E** [lodging] Budget Inn, **W** [gas] Exxon/Subway/dsl [other] Blue Beacon, repair
247	US 287 N, to Waxahatchie
246	FM 1183, Alma, **E** [gas] Love's/Subway/dsl/scales/24hr, **W** [gas] Chevron/dsl
244	FM 1182
243	Frontage Rd
242	Calhoun St, Rice, **W** [gas] Shell/Sonic/dsl [other] Family$
239	FM 1126, **W** [gas] Conoco/dsl [other] Rendell RV Ctr
238	FM 1603, **E** [gas] Exxon/rest./dsl/24hr [other] Casita RV Trailers
237	Frontage Rd
235b	Lp I-45 (from sb), to Corsicana

ENNIS

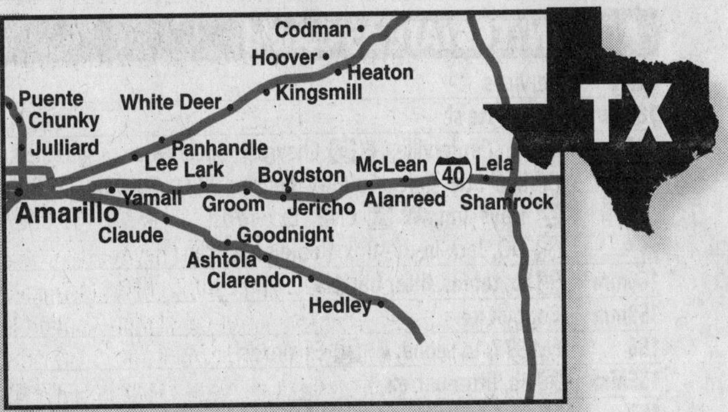

CORSICANA

FAIRFIELD

Exit #	Services
235a	Frontage Rd
232	Roane Rd, E 5th Ave
231	TX 31, Corsicana, **E** [gas] Mobil/Taco Casa/dsl, Valero/dsl [food] Jack-in-the-Box [lodging] Best Western, La Quinta, Super 8 [other] Buick/Cadillac/Chevrolet/GMC, **W** [gas] Exxon/dsl, Shell/Subway/dsl [food] Bill's Fried Chicken, McDonald's [lodging] Comfort Inn [other] [H], Chrysler/Dodge/Jeep, Ford/Lincoln, to Navarro Coll
229	US 287, Palestine, **E** [gas] Exxon/Wendy's/dsl, Shell/dsl [food] Applebee's, Chili's, Collin St Bakery, Denny's, DQ, Panda Express, Schlotsky's, Sonic, Subway, Taco Bell, Whataburger [lodging] Hampton Inn, Holiday Inn Express [other] Corsicana Outlets, Home Depot, Office Depot, Russell Stover Candies, **W** [food] Waffle House [lodging] Days Inn, Motel 6, Traveler's Inn
228b	Lp 45 (exits left from nb), Corsicana, **2 mi W** services in Corsicana
228a	15th St, Corsicana, **W** [other] Toyota
225	FM 739, Angus, **E** [gas] Conoco/dsl [other] RV park, to Chambers Reservoir
221	Frontage Rd
220	Frontage Rd
219b	Frontage Rd
219a	TX 14 (from sb), to Mexia, Richland, **W** [gas] Shell
218	FM 1394 (from nb), Richland, **W** [gas] Shell
217mm	[RS] **both lanes, full [handicapped] facilities, litter barrels, petwalk, [phone], [picnic], vending**
213	TX 75 S, FM 246, to Wortham, **W** [gas] Exxon/dsl, Valero/dsl
211	FM 80, to Streetman, Kirvin
206	FM 833, **W** [other] I-45 RV Park (3mi)
198	FM 27, to Wortham, **E** [gas] Shell/Cole's BBQ [food] Gilberto's Mexican [lodging] La Quinta [other] [H], **W** [gas] Cooper Farms/dsl, Love's/Burger King/dsl/scales/24hr [lodging] Budget Inn [other] I-45 RV Park (4mi)
197	US 84, Fairfield, **E** [gas] Chevron/dsl, Exxon/dsl, Shell/dsl [food] Bush's Chicken, DQ, Jack-in-the-Box, McDonald's, Sam's Rest., Something Different Rest, Sonic, Subway/TX Burger [lodging] Days Inn, Holiday Inn Express, Super 8 [other] Brookshire Foods/gas, Chevrolet, Chrysler/Dodge/Jeep, Fred's Store, **W** [gas] Exxon/dsl, Shell/dsl [food] I-45 Rest., KFC/Taco Bell, Mesquite Grill, Pizza Hut, Ponte's Diner [lodging] Budgetel, Regency Inn [other] Ace Hardware, Ford
189	TX 179, to Teague, **E** [gas] Exxon/Dinner Bell Rest/dsl, **W** [gas] Valero/Chester's/Huddle House/dsl
180	TX 164, to Groesbeck
178	US 79, Buffalo, **E** [gas] Chevron/dsl, Conoco/dsl, Mobil/dsl, Shell/dsl [food] Pizza Hut, Subway/TX Burger [other] $General, Brookshire Foods/gas, Family$, **W** [gas] Exxon/Church's/Subway/Pizza Inn/dsl/scales, Pilot/PJ Fresh/Taco Bell/dsl/scales/24hr, Texaco/dsl [food] Anthony's Rest., Dickey's BBQ, DQ, McDonald's, Rancho Viejo, Sonic [lodging] Best Value Inn, Hampton Inn, Quality Inn, Super 8
175mm	Bliss Creek

TX

INTERSTATE 45 Cont'd

Exit #	Services
166mm	**weigh sta sb**
164	TX 7, Centerville, E Chevron, Shell/Woody's BBQ/dsl Broken Star Cafe, Country Cousins BBQ, Subway/TX Burger Days Inn, W CNG, Exxon/dsl, Shell/Woody's BBQ/dsl DQ, Jack-in-the-Box, Roble's Mexican
160mm	**sb, tables, litter barrels**
159mm	Boggy Creek
156	FM 977, to Leona, W Exxon/dsl
155mm	**nb, litter barrels**
152	TX OSR, to Normangee, W Shell/Arby's/dsl Yellow Rose RV Park
146	TX 75
142	US 190, TX 21, Madisonville, E Buc-ees/dsl, Exxon/dsl Dickey's BBQ, Shipley's Donuts, Subway Best Western, Madisonville Inn URGENT CARE, W Exxon, Mobil/Church's/dsl, Shell/Subway Jack-in-the-Box, Lakeside Rest, McDonald's, Pizza Hut, Sonic, Taco Bell, TX Burger Budget Motel, Days Inn, Motel 6 H, Ford, Toyota
136	spur 67, E Home on the Range RV camping/LP (3mi)
132	FM 2989
124mm	**both lanes, full facilities, litter barrels, petwalk, , , vending**
123	FM 1696
118	TX 75, E Shell/Hitchin Post/dsl/24hr/@ Texas Prison Museum, truckwash, W Pilot/Wendy's/dsl/scales/24hr, Shell/Dickey's BBQ/Subway/dsl Chicken Express
116	US 190, TX 30, E Conoco/dsl, Phillips 66/dsl, Valero/dsl Arby's, Bandera Grill, Church's, Golden Corral, Los Panchitos, Mama Juanita's, McDonald's, Popeye's, Schlotzsky's, Sonic, Whataburger Days Inn, EconoLodge, Holiday Inn Express, La Quinta, Motel 6 AutoZone, Brookshire Foods/gas, Buick/Cadillac/Chevrolet/GMC, Cavander's Boots, Chrysler/Dodge/Jeep, CVS Drug, Family$, Firestone/auto, O'Reilly Parts, vet, Walgreens, W Chevron/dsl, Exxon/dsl, Murphy USA/dsl, Shell Bob Luby's Seafood, Buffalo Wild Wings, Burger King, Cane's, Chili's, Chipotle, Denny's, Five Guys, Grand Buffet, Hartz Chicken, IHOP, Jack-in-the-Box, Little Caesar's, Moe's SW, Olive Garden, Panda Express, Pizza Hut, Rodeo Mexican, Starbucks, Subway, Taco Bell, Wing Stop, Yummy Mongolian Best Western, Hampton Inn H, $Tree, AT&T, Discount Tire, GNC, Hobby Lobby, Home Depot, JC Penney, Kroger/dsl, Marshall's, Office Depot, Petco, Ross, Target, USPO, Verizon, Walmart
114	FM 1374, E Exxon/dsl, Shell DQ, Margaritas Rest. Red Roof Inn, Super 8, W Texaco/dsl, Valero/dsl Country Inn Steaks Best Value Inn, Quality Suites H, Ford, Hyundai
113	TX 19 (from sb), Huntsville, W Ford, Hyundai
112	TX 75, E Big E's Houston Statue, museum, to Sam Houston St U
109	Park 40, W to Huntsville SP
103	FM 1374/1375 (from sb), to New Waverly, W Chevron/Burger King/dsl
102	FM 1374/1375, TX 150 (from nb), to New Waverly, E Valero/dsl (1mi) Waverly Rest., W Chevron/Burger King/dsl (1mi)
101mm	**weigh sta nb**
98	TX 75, Danville Rd, Shepard Hill Rd, E Convenience RV Ctr/repair
97	Calvary Rd

HUNTSVILLE

Exit #	Services
95	Longstreet Rd, Calvary Rd, Willis, E Holiday World, W Loves/Subway/Wendy's/dsl/scales/24hr
94	FM 1097, Longstreet Rd, to Willis, E Kwik Stop Jack-in-the-Box, Sonic, Taco Bell $General, AutoZ W Chevron/Popeye's, Shell/dsl Burger King, Ch fil-A, Cilantros Mexican, Little Caesar's, McDonald's, P John's, Pizza Hut, Scholtzsky's, Shipley's Donuts, Subw Whataburger, WingStop, Yummy Mongolian Best W ern GNC, Kroger/dsl, Verizon, Walgreens
92	FM 830, Seven Coves Dr, W Omega Farms RV Park (2 RV Park on the Lake (3mi), Thousand Trails Resort (2mi)
90	League Line Rd, E Mobil/McDonald's, Shell/dsl Ma Juanita's Mexican, Waffle House, Wendy's Com Inn, Days Inn, La Quinta Conroe Outlets/famous bra W Chevron/Jack-in-the-Box Cracker Barrel
89	FM 3083, Teas Nursery Rd, Montgomery Co Park, E E on/dsl Applebee's, Buffalo Wild Wings, Popeye's, Lobster, Smokey Mo's BBQ Fairfield Inn, Homew Suites AT&T, Kohl's, Old Navy, Petsmart, Ross, TJ Ma W Firehouse Subs, Olive Garden, Wengs Wok, Wild Gin Japanese Woodspring Suites Inn Cavender's Boots, Penney, Verizon
88	Lp 336, to Cleveland, Navasota, E Valero/dsl Arb Burger King, Carl's Jr, Chili's, China Delight, Denny's, Do ino's, Dunkin'/Baskin Robbins, Los Cucos Mexican, Ma Slab Creamery, Margarita's Mexican, McDonald's, Papa Joh Pizza Hut, Potbelly, Sonic, Subway, Supreme Buffet, TX Ro house, Whataburger, Wing Stop Hampton Inn, Holi Inn Express $Tree, Advance Parts, CVS Drug, Discount T Discount Tire, GNC, HEB Foods/gas, Hobby Lobby, Kroger/g Michael's, vet, Walgreens, W Chevron/24hr Casa Mexican, Culver's, Dickey's BBQ, Hunan Village, Jack-in-t Box, KFC, Ryan's, Starbucks 99c Store, Big Lots, Low PetCo, Sam's Club/gas, Tuesday Morning, Walmart
87	TX 105, Conroe, E Burger King, CiCi's, El Charrito, Freebi Burrito, Golden Corral, La Mariposa, McDonald's, Outba Steaks, Popeye's, Saltgrass Steaks Super 8 $Gen al, CVS Drug, Firestone/auto, NTB, W Exxon Cane Chick-fil-A, Chipotle, El Bosque Mexican, Five Guys, Luby's, Pa da Express, Panera Bread, Papa Murphy's, Schlotzsky's, Shog Japanese, Smoothie King, Starbucks, Subway, Vero Itali Whataburger H, Best Buy, Buick/GMC, GNC, Home Dep Hyundai, Office Depot, Target, Verizon
85	FM 2854, Gladstell St, E Shell/dsl Ford, Honda, K Nissan, UHaul, W Valero Best Value Inn, Motel H, Chevrolet, Chrysler/Dodge/Jeep, DeMontrond RV C Mazda, Toyota
84	TX 75 N, Frazier St, E Chevron/dsl Corporate In Econolodge, W Shell/dsl China Buffet, IHOP, Incredib Pizza, Pizza Hut, Subway, Taco Cabana, Waffle House Ba mont Inn H, Discount Tire, Kroger/dsl, Verizon
83	Crighton Rd, Camp Strake Rd
82	River Plantation Dr
82mm	San Jacinto River
81	FM 1488, to Hempstead, Magnolia, E Citgo/dsl, Valero/Subway/dsl CamperLand RV Ctr
80	Needham Rd (from sb)
79	TX 242, Needham, E Shell/McDonald's Mama Juan ta's Mexican Best Western Costco/dsl, Mercedes, Mi VW, W Exxon, Murphy USA/dsl Arby's, Burger Kin ChuckeCheese, Domino's, Dunkin', LJ Silver/Taco Bell, Outba Steaks, Panera Bread, Popeye's, Sonic, Starbucks, Subwa

CONROE

INTERSTATE 45 Cont'd

79 Continued
Taco Cabana, Twin Peaks, Wendy's, Whataburger, Willie's Grill, Wings'N More Fairfield Inn, Springhill Suites, TownPlace Suites BMW/Mini, Firestone/auto, Kohl's, Lowe's Whse, Walgreens, Walmart

78 Needham Rd (from sb), Tamina Rd, access to same as 77

77 Woodlands Pkwy, Robinson, Chateau Woods, E Chevron Babin's Seafood, BJ's Rest., Buca Italian, Buffalo Wild Wings, Chuy's, El Bosque Mexican, Hooters, Lupe Tortilla, Mi Rancho Mexican, Pappadeaux, PeiWei, Red Robin, Saltgrass Steaks, Spring Creek BBQ, Subway Best Value Inn, Courtyard, Holiday Inn Discount Tire, GNC, Home Depot, Michael's, NTB, Old Navy, Petsmart, Sam's Club/gas, SteinMart, vet, Walgreens, W Shell/dsl, Texaco, Valero/dsl, Valero/dsl Blackeyed Pea, Brazilian Steaks, Cane's, Chick-fil-A, Chili's, Chipotle Mexican, Culver's, Denny's, Freebirds Burrito, Guadalajara Mexican, Jack-in-the-Box, Jason's Deli, Jimmy John's, Kirby's Steaks, Luby's, Olive Garden, Red Lobster, Sweet Tomatoes, TGIFriday's, Zoe's Kitchen Clarion, Days Inn, Drury Inn, Hampton Inn, Homewood Suites, La Quinta, Marriott Best Buy, Dillard's, HEB Foods, Macy's, Marshall's, Ross, Target, World Mkt

76 Research Forest Dr, Tamina Rd, E Pappas BBQ Firestone/auto, Office Depot, PepBoys, URGENT CARE, W Shell/dsl Bonefish Grill, Carrabba's, Firehouse Subs, Fukuda Japanese, IHOP, Landry's Seafood, Longhorn Steaks, Macaroni Grill, Noodles&Co, Olive Garden, Starbucks, Sweet Tomatoes, TGIFriday's Courtyard, Residence Inn JC Penney, Woodlands Mall

73 Rayford Rd, Sawdust Rd, E Shell/dsl, Valero Cane's, Hartz Chicken, Jack-in-the-Box, McDonald's, Popeye's, Sonic, Starbucks, Thomas BBQ Holiday Inn Express, La Quinta Aamco, AutoZone, O'Reilly Parts, Walgreens, W Shell/dsl Carrabba's, Gino's Pizza, IHOP, Pizza Hut Extended Stay America, Super 8 Brake Check, Discount Tire, GNC, Harley-Davidson, HEB Foods, Jo-Ann

72a Spring Crossing Dr, W Texaco/dsl Fairfield Inn

72b to Hardy Toll Rd from sb

70b Spring-Stuebner Rd, E Hampton Inn Vaughn RV Ctr

70a FM 2920, to Tomball, E Exxon/dsl, Rudy's BBQ/dsl, Shell/dsl Arby's, Chick-fil-A, El Palenque Mexican, Golden Jade Chinese, Hartz Chicken, McDonald's, Subway, Taco Cabana, Wendy's, Whataburger, Zaxby's Best Western, Comfort Suites $Tree, Hyundai, Kohl's, Michael's, O'Reilly Parts, Ross, Toyota, Vaughn's RV Ctr, Verizon, Walmart, W RaceWay Palace Inn U-Haul, vet

68 Holzwarth Rd, Cypress Wood Dr, E Golden Corral, Burger King, Freddy's, Gringo's TexMex, McAlister's Deli, Pizza Hut/Taco Bell, Sonic, Starbucks AT&T, Pepboys, W Exxon/dsl, Murphy Express/dsl, Smashburger Bombshells Rest., Cheddar's, Chipotle, Denny's, Dickey's BBQ, Firehouse Subs, Jack-in-the-Box, Lenny's Subs, Panera Bread, Pizza Hut, Popeye's, Razzoo's Cajun, Schlotsky's, Starbucks EconoLodge, Motel 6, Scottish Inn Advance Parts, Best Buy, Chrysler/Dodge/Jeep, Firestone/auto, Ford/Lincoln, Home Depot, Lowe's Whse, Office Depot, PetCo, Staples, Target, Walgreens

66 FM 1960, to Addicks, E Chevron/dsl Subway, TX Roadhouse Acura, AT&T, BMW, Chevrolet, Honda, Mercedes, Petsmart, Subaru, W Exxon, Valero Chick-fil-A, Cilantros Mexican, Hooters, James Coney Island, McDonald's, Outback Steaks, Panda Express, Pollo Campero, Red Lobster

HOUSTON

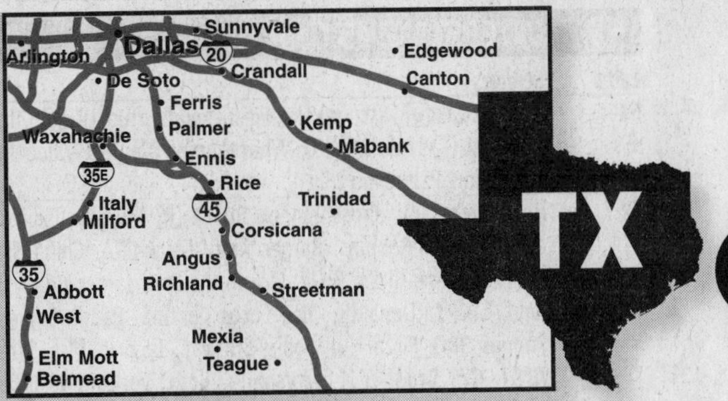

66 Continued
Baymont Inn, Fairfield Inn, Hampton Inn, Hilton Garden, Palace Inn, Quality Inn, Studio 6 $Tree, Audi, Infiniti, Jaguar/LandRover, Kroger/dsl, Lexus, NTB, Porsche, U-Haul

64 Richey Rd, E Buffalo Wild Wings, Olive Garden, Taco Bell Best Value Inn, Downtowner Inn, Super 8 CarMax, Discount Tire, Sam's Club/dsl, W FLYING J/Denny's/dsl/scales/24hr Chula's Cantina, El Toro Loco, Joe's Crabshack, Lupe Tortilla, Mamacita's Mexican, Michoacan Rest, SaltGrass Steaks, Subway, Wings'n More SpringHill Suites

63 Airtex Dr, E Exxon/dsl, Sunoco/dsl, Valero/Church's China Bear, Pappasito's Cantina Comfort Suites, Woodspring Suites Inn Cadillac, LoneStar RV Ctr, Nissan, W Exxon/dsl Cracker Barrel, Jack-in-the-Box, Popeye's, Whataburger Best Western, Holiday Inn Express, Sleep Inn

62 Rankin Rd, Kuykendahl, E Best Classic Inn, Scottish Inn, W Chevron/McDonald's, RaceWay/dsl, Shell Shiply Donuts, Sonic Extended Stay Amerca, Palace Inn, SunSuites Buick/GMC, DeMontrond RV Ctr, Kia, Lamborghini, Volvo, VW, Walgreens

61 Greens Rd, E Exxon Brown Sugar's BBQ, IHOP, Luna's Mexican Knights Inn Dillard's, W Luby's, Panda Chinese, Subway Comfort Inn 99c Store, Burlington Coats

60c Beltway E

60 (b a from nb) TX 525, W Pappas Seafood U-Haul

59 FM 525, West Rd, E Shell/dsl, Shell/dsl/repair A&W/LJ Silver, Burger King, China Border, CiCi's, Denny's, Domino's, Hanz Diner, Mambo Seafood, McDonald's, Michoacan Rest., Pizza Hut Holiday Inn Express AutoZone, Chrysler/Dodge/Jeep, Family$, Firestone/auto, W Exxon/dsl, Shell/dsl Chili's, Jalisco's Mexican, Panda Express, Papa John's Pizza, Starbucks, Subway, Taco Bell, Taco Cabana, Wendy's, Whataburger, Wing Stop Best Value Inn $Tree, AT&T, Best Buy, Discount Tire, Fry's Electronics, Home Depot, Office Depot, PepBoys, Ross, Verizon, Walmart

57 (b a from nb) TX 249, Gulf Bank Rd, Tomball, E Chevron, Gulf/dsl, Texaco/Church's Subway, W Shell Sonic, Tampico Seafood Days Inn, Quality Inn CVS Drug, Family$, Giant$

56 Canino Rd, E Taj Inn Suites, W Texaco Denny's, Luby's Deluxe Inn, Gulfwind Motel Ford, Isuzu, Walgreens

55 (b a from nb) Little York Rd, Parker Rd, E Chevron/dsl, Exxon/dsl, Texaco Burger King, China One, McDonald's, Ranchero King Buffet, Subway, Whataburger Advance Parts, Family$, FoodTown, W KFC, La Chicken, Popeye's Walgreens

54 Tidwell Rd, E Exxon/dsl Aunt Bea's Rest, Burger King, Chacho's Mexican, China Border, Pancho's Mexican, Thomas BBQ 99c Store, CVS Drug, W Chevron, Shell Hartz Chicken, McDonald's Guest Motel, Southwind Motel, Symphony Inn, Town Inn Family$, U-Haul

= gas = food = lodging = other = rest stop

TX

INTERSTATE 45 Cont'd

HOUSTON

Exit #	Services
53	Airline Dr, E Discount Tire, Fiesta Foods/drug, W Citgo, Shell/dsl Little Mexico, Whataburger Best Value Inn, Luxury Inn, Palace Inn
52	(b a from nb) Crosstimbers Rd, E Murphy Express/dsl Baskin-Robbins, Burger King, Chick-fil-A, China Star, ChuckeCheese, Cici's, IHOP, Jack-in-the-Box, James Coney Island, KFC, McDonald's, Ojos Locos Cantina, Panda Express, Pappas BBQ, Pizza Hut, Sonic, Subway, Taco Bell $Tree, AT&T, CVS Drug, GNC, Marshall's, Ross, Verizon, Walmart, W Texan Inn
51	I-610
50	(b a from nb) Patton St, Calvacade St, Link Rd, E Citgo, Exxon, Loves/Wendy's/dsl/scales/24hr, Shell Best Value Inn, Luxury Inn, W Astro Inn AutoZone, Family$, NAPA, USPO
49b	N Main St, Houston Ave, E Citgo, Loves/Wendy's/dsl/scales/24hr Best Value Inn, Luxury Inn, W Exxon/dsl Domino's, McDonald's, Subway, Whataburger/24hr Sleep Inn O'Reilly Parts
48b a	I-10, E to Beaumont, W to San Antonio
47d	Dallas St, Pierce St (from sb), E H
47c	McKinney St (from sb, exits left)
47b	Houston Ave, Memorial Dr, W DoubleTree, downtown
47a	Allen Pkwy (exits left from sb)
46b a	US 59, N to Cleveland, S to Victoria, W Chevron, Texaco McDonald's BMW
45b a	South St, Scott St, Houston, E Phillips 66/Church's/dsl, Shell Scott Inn, W to TSU
44	Cullen Blvd, Houston, W to U of Houston
43b	Telephone Rd, Houston, E Valero/dsl
43a	Tellepsen St, E Luby's, W U of Houston
41b	US 90A, Broad St, S Wayside Dr, E Houston Inn, Palace Inn Walmart/McDonald's, W Chevron/dsl, Exxon Burger King, Chick-fil-A, Jack-in-the-Box, Little Caesar's, McDonald's, Taco Cabana AT&T
41a	Woodridge Dr, E Shell Chinese Buffet, Church's, Denny's, James Coney Island, McDonald's, Pappa's Seafood House, Pizza Hut, Schlotsky's King$, W Bonebrake BBQ, Boudreaux Cajun, China Star, ChuckeCheese, CiCi's, Doneraki Mexican, IHOP, KFC/Taco Bell, Panda Express, Pappas BBQ, Sonic, Starbucks, Subway, Taco Palenque, Wendy's, Whataburger Best Buy, HEB Food/gas, Home Depot, Lowe's, Marshall's, Office Depot, Old Navy, Ross, Verizon
40c	I-610 W
40b	I-610 E, to Pasadena
40a	Frontage Rd (from nb)
39	Park Place Blvd, Broadway Blvd, E Shell/dsl, W Pemex/dsl, Shell/dsl Kelley's Rest., Papa John's, Subway Chrysler/Dodge/Jeep, Family$
38b	Howard Dr, Bellfort Dr (from sb), E Shell Jack-in-the-Box, Wendy's, W Shell/dsl, Texaco/dsl Chilo's Seafood, VStar Seafood Buffet Camelot Inn, Moonlight Inn, Mustang Inn, Palace Inn
38	TX 3, Monroe Rd, E Shell/dsl, Sunoco/Stripes/dsl, Valero/dsl DQ, Jack-in-the-Box, Ninfa's Mexican, Starbucks, Wendy's Palace Inn AutoZone, Family$, URGENT CARE, W Chevron/dsl, Texaco/dsl Mannie's Seafood, Pappa's BBQ, Subway Holiday Inn Express, Sheraton Firestone/auto, U-Haul
36	College Ave, Airport Blvd, E Valero Aranda's Ba Burger House, Church's, DQ, Jack-in-the-Box, Shipley Do Subway, Waffle House Holiday Inn Express O'R Parts, W Gulf/dsl, Shell/dsl, Valero/dsl Denny's, ny's, Taco Cabana Best Western, Comfort Suites, Court Days Inn, Drury Inn, Hampton Inn, Holiday Inn, La Quinta, riott, Motel 6, SpringHill Suites Discount Tire
35	Edgebrook Dr, E Chevron, RaceWay/dsl, Shell/dsl A da's Mexican, Burger King, Chilo's Rest., Jack-in-the-Box, Popeye's, Subway, Taco Bell Family$, Fiesta Foods, F tone/auto, Office Depot, vet, W Citgo/dsl James C Island, Mambo Seafood, McDonald's, Pizza Hut, Whatab er $General, Cavender's Boots, O'Reilly Parts, Verizon
34	S Shaver Rd, E Conoco McDonald's Island Su Ford, Kia, Nissan, Toyota, W MurphyUSA/dsl by's, China Star Buffet, Chopstix, Ojos Locos, Pancho's Mexi Pizza Patron, Starbucks, Subway, Wendy's $Tree, 99c St AT&T, Discount Tire, Firestone/auto, GNC, Honda, Macy's, M shall's, NTB, PetsMart, Ross, Staples, Walmart/McDonald's
33	Fuqua St, E Chili's, Denny's, Fuddrucker's, Las Hacien Luby's, Olive Garden, Schlotzky's, TGIFriday's Studio 6, Suites Lincoln, Volvo, W Bayou City Wings, Blacke Pea, Bombshells Grill, Boudreaux's, Casa Ole, Cici's Pizza, F &Hound, Golden Corral, Gringo's Mexican, IHOP, Joe's Cr shack, McDonald's, Outback Steaks, Subway, Taco Bell, T Cabana, TX Land&Cattle Steaks, Whataburger Buick/G CarMax, Chevrolet, Home Depot, Sam's Club/gas
32	Sam Houston Tollway
31	FM 2553, Scarsdale Blvd, W Chevrolet
30	FM 1959, Dixie Farm Rd, Ellington Field, E Shell/dsl Nopalito, Subway Motel 6 H, Chrysler/Dodge/Je Fiat, Infiniti, Subaru, W Exxon/dsl, RaceWay, Shell/ McDonald's, Popeye's Palace Inn Lonestar RV, V
29	FM 2351, Clear Lake City Blvd, to Clear Lake RA, Friendswo W Hyundai
27	El Dorado Blvd, E Exxon/dsl Carl's Jr, Chick-fil-A, Pa ra Bread, Starbucks, Taco Bell Firestone/auto, Home Dep W Bar Louie, Kona Grill, Maggiano's, Perry's Steakhou Sonic, Subway, TX Roadhouse, Whataburger, Yardhouse G Cadillac, Kohl's, Lexus, Sam's Club/gas, Walmart/McDonal
26	Bay Area Blvd, E Chevron Bonefish Grill, Buffalo W Wings, Chick-fil-A, La Madeleine, Longhorn Steaks, Lupe T tilla, Noodles&Co, Pei Wei, Potbelly, Red Lobster, Taco C bana, TGIFriday's, Zio's Kitchen Best Western, Hampt Inn, Hilton Garden, La Quinta H, Barnes&Noble, B Buy, Lowe's, Michael's, Staples, to Houston Space Ctr, Wo Mkt, W Valero/dsl Burger King, Cheesecake Fac ry, Chick-fil-A, ChuckeCheese, Dave&Buster's, Denny's, Fi Guys, Los Cucos, McDonald's, Olive Garden, Panda Expre PF Chang's, Starbucks, Subway, Zoe's Kitchen Holiday I Express AT&T, Dillard's, Fresh Mkt, JC Penney, Jo-Ann Fa rics, Macy's, Marshall's, Office Depot, Old Navy, Petsmart, Ro Target, Verizon, vet
25	FM 528, NASA rd 1, E Chevron/dsl, Valero/dsl Bo Daddy's, Cheddar's, Chili's, Chuy's Mexican, Fuddrucker's, L Hacienda Mexican, Luby's, Marble Slab, McAlister's Deli, Mic ru Asian, Pappa's Seafood, Pappasito's Cantina, Rudy's BB dsl, Saltgrass Steaks, Steak'n Shake, Twin Peaks Rest., Waf House Motel 6, Springhill Suites H, BigLots, Cave dar's Boots, Fry's Electronics, Hobby Lobby, Honda, Mazd W Floyd's Cajun, Hooters, James Coney Island, Pappa Cafe, Subway Tuesday Morning

TX

INTERSTATE 45 Cont'd

Exit #	Services
23	FM 518, League City, E RaceWay/dsl, Shell/dsl Center Buffet, La Brisa, Sonic, Subway $Tree, Kroger, W Chevron/dsl, Valero Cracker Barrel, McDonald's, Taco Bell, Waffle House, Wendy's Super 8 Discount Tire, Space Ctr RV Park, U-Haul
22	Calder Dr, Brittany Bay Blvd, E BMW/Mini, Mercedes, Nissan, Toyota, W Acura, Holiday World RV Ctr
20	FM 646, Santa Fe, Bacliff, E MurphyUSA/dsl Chick-fil-A, Cici's Pizza, Denny's, Five Guys, Freebirds Burrito, Jack-in-the-Box, Jimmy Changas, Logan's Roadhouse, Marble Slab, McDonald's, NY Pizzaria, Panda Express, Panera Bread, Pollo Tropical, Quaker Steak, Schlotzky's, Spring Creek BBQ, Subway, Whataburger, Which Wich? Candlewood Suites, Hampton Inn $Tree, AT&T, Best Buy, Firestone/auto, GNC, Hobby Lobby, Home Depot, JC Penney, Lowe's, Michael's, NTB, PetsMart, Ross, Staples, Target, TJ Maxx, URGENT CARE, Walmart/McDonald's, W Chevron/dsl 888 Chinese Rest., Chili's, Subway, Taco Cabana Cabela's, HEB Foods/gas, Kohl's, PetCo, Verizon, Walgreens
19	FM 517, Dickinson Rd, Hughes Rd, E Jack-in-the-Box, Little Mexico Buick/GMC, CVS Drug, Family$, Kia, W Conoco/dsl, Shell/dsl KFC, McDonald's, Pizza Hut, Sonic, Starbucks, Subway, Taco Bell, Wendy's, Whataburger/24hr Days Inn Chrysler/Dodge/Jeep, Ford, Kroger
17	Holland Rd, W Buc-ee's/dsl Tanger Outlets/Famous Brands, to Gulf Greyhound Park
16	FM 1764 E (from sb), Texas City, same as 15
15	FM 2004, FM 1764, Hitchcock, E Beyond Burger, Gringo's Cafe, Jack-in-the-Box, Olive Garden, Ryan's Best Western, Fairfield Inn, Holiday Inn Express, Woodspring Suites H, Chevrolet/Toyota, DeMontrond RV Ctr, W Gulf/Subway, MurphyUSA/dsl, Shell Best Wok, IHOP, Little Caesar's, Pizza Hut, Rose Garden Chinese, Sonic, Waffle House, Wendy's, Whataburger, WingStop AT&T, Gulf Greyhound Park, Sam's Club/gas, URGENT CARE, Verizon, Walmart/McDonald's
13	Century Blvd, Delany Rd, W Barcema's Mexican Best Value Inn, Super 8 Lazy Days RV Park, VF Factory Outlet/famous brands
12	FM 1765, La Marque, E Chevron/dsl Domino's, Jack-in-the-Box, Kelley's Rest., Sonic $General, CVS Drug, Family$, W Texaco/dsl Little Thicket RV Park, UHaul
11	Vauthier Rd
10	E Exxon, Valero KFC, McDonald's, PitStop BBQ, Subway, W Shell/dsl Hoover RV Ctr, Oasis RV Park
9	Frontage Rd (from sb, no return/turnaround)
8	Frontage Rd (from nb)
7c	Frontage Rd
7b	TX 146, TX 6 (exits left from nb), Texas City
7a	TX 146, TX 3
6	Frontage Rd (from sb)
5	Frontage Rd
4	Frontage Rd, Village of Tiki Island, W **Welcome Ctr** Valero/dsl public boat ramp
4mm	West Galveston Bay
1c	TX 275, FM 188 (from nb), Port Ind Blvd, Teichman Rd, Port of Galveston, E Citgo, Exxon/dsl, Valero/dsl Howard Johnson, Motel 6 Buick/Chevrolet/GMC, Ford, Toyota
1b	71st St (from sb), E Best Value Inn same as 1c
1a	TX 342, 61st St, to W Beach, E RaceWay Subway, WingStop Candlewood Suites Big Lots, Family$, GNC,

GALVESTON

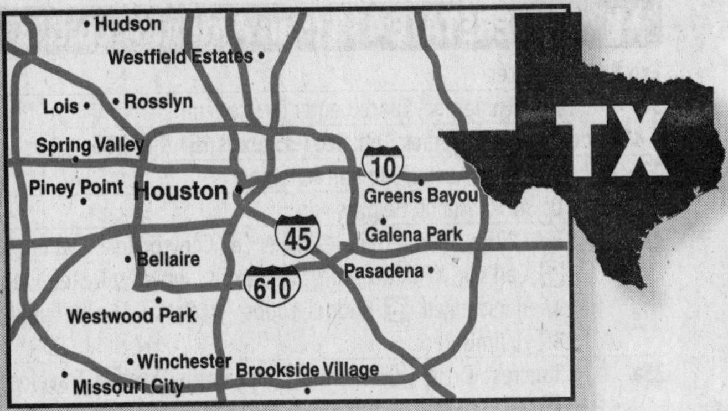

Exit #	Services
1a	Continued Home Depot, NTB, PetsMart, Target, **0-2 mi** W Chevron/dsl, Citgo, Exxon, Murphy USA/dsl, Shell/Burger King/dsl, Texaco/dsl, Valero Cici's Pizza, Domino's, Golden Corral, Happy Buddah, Healthy Chinese, Jack-in-the-Box, Jimmy John's, KFC, Little Caesar's, Marble Slab, Mario's, McAlister's Deli, McDonald's, Papa John's, Popeye's, Schlotsky's, Sonic, Starbucks, Subway, Taco Bell, Taco Cabana, Waffle House, Whataburger, Yamato Japanese Baymont Inn, Comfort Inn, Hilton, Quality Inn, Red Roof Inn, Rodeway Inn, Springhill Suites, Super 8 $Tree, AT&T, AutoZone, CVS Drug, Family$, Firestone/auto, Kroger/dsl, KwikCar, Marshall's, Office Depot, O'Reilly Parts, Randall's Food/gas, Ross, Tuesday Morning, URGENT CARE, USPO, Verizon, Walgreens, Walmart

I-45 begins/ends on TX 87 in Galveston.

INTERSTATE 410 (San Antonio)

Exit #	Services
53	I-35, S to Laredo, N to San Antonio
51	FM 2790, Somerset Rd
49	TX 16 S, spur 422, N Chevron, Texaco/dsl Church's, Domino's, Sonic, Subway, Whataburger Days Inn H, to Palo Alto Coll, S Valero/dsl Jack-in-the-Box Best Western
48	Zarzamora St, S Valero/dsl
47	Turnaround (from eb)
46	Moursund Blvd
44	US 281 S, spur 536, Roosevelt Ave, N Shell/McDonald's/dsl, Valero/dsl Subway, S Jack-in-the-Box Holiday Inn Express
43	Espada Rd (from eb)
42	spur 122, S Presa Rd, N to San Antonio Missions Hist Park, S Valero/dsl
41	I-37, US 281 N
39	spur 117, WW White Rd
37	Southcross Blvd, Sinclair Rd, Sulphur Sprs Rd, N Shell/dsl, Valero H, Family$
35	US 87, Rigsby Ave, E Exxon/7-11, Murphy USA/dsl, Valero/dsl Denny's, El Rodeo Mexican, Jack-in-the-Box, KFC/Taco Bell, McDonald's $Tree, AT&T, Walmart/McDonald's, W Chevron/dsl Bill Miller BBQ, Burger King, Domino's, El Tapico Mexican, Habachi Buffet, Laguna Madre, Sonic, Taco Cabana, Whataburger Days Inn, Holiday Inn Express Aamco, Advance Parts, Gascard/dsl, U-Haul, vet, Walgreens
34	FM 1346, E Houston St, W Valero/dsl USPO
33	I-10 E, US 90 E, to Houston, I-10 W, US 90 W, to San Antonio
32	Dietrich Rd (from sb), FM 78 (from nb), to Kirby
31b	Lp 13, WW White Rd
31a	FM 78, Kirby

SAN ANTONIO

= gas = food = lodging = other = rest stop

TX

INTERSTATE 410 (San Antonio) Cont'd

Exit #	Services
30	Binz-Engleman, Space Center Dr (from nb)
I-410 and I-35 run together 7 mi. See I-35, exits 161 thru 165.	
27	I-35, N to Austin, S to San Antonio
26	Lp 368 S, Alamo Heights
25b	FM 2252, Perrin-Beitel Rd, N Chevron/dsl, Valero/dsl Carl's Jr, KFC/Taco Bell, Schlotsky's, Subway, Tastee-Freez/ Wienerschnitzel Budget Lodge Brake Check, Family$, S Jim's Rest.
25a	Starcrest Dr, N Valero Jack-in-the-Box Travelodge H
24	Harry Wurzbach Hwy, N Taco Cabana, S BBQ Sta. VW
23	Nacogdoches Rd, N Shell/dsl Bill Miller BBQ, Church's, Formosa Chinese, IHOP, Jimmy John's, Luby's, Pizza Hut, Sonic Crowne Plaza, S Chevron/7-11 Volvo
22	Broadway St, N Shell/dsl Chili's, Fuddrucker's, McDonald's Cambria Suites, Courtyard, Home2 Suites, S Citgo, Valero/dsl Cane's, Chesters Hamburgers, Jim's Rest., Little Caesar's, Martha's Mexican, Taco Palenque, Whataburger Residence Inn, Springhill Suites, TownHouse Motel
21	US 281 S, Airport Rd, Jones Maltsberger Rd, N Applebee's Drury Suites, Hampton Inn, Holiday Inn, Holiday Inn Express, PearTree Inn, Sheraton, S Murphy USA/dsl Cracker Barrel, Logan's Roadhouse, Pappadeaux, Texas Land&Cattle, Whataburger Best Western, Courtyard, Days Inn, Fairfield Inn, Home2 Suites, La Quinta, Staybridge Suites, TownePlace Suites Nissan, TJ Maxx, Walmart/McDonald's/24hr
20	TX 537, N Valero Arby's, Chick-fil-A, Jack-in-the-Box, Jason's Deli, Rosario's Mexican, Subway, TGIFriday's, Wendy's DoubleTree Hotel, Hilton Barnes&Noble, Best Buy, Brake Check, Cavender's Boots, Chevrolet, Honda, Jo-Ann Fabrics, Lexus, Lincoln, Mazda, Mercedes, Office Depot, PetCo, Ross, Subaru, S Cheesecake Factory, Chipotle, Dickey's BBQ, Earth Burger, Egg&I, El Pollo Loco, Freddy's, Jimmy John's, La Madeleine, Longhorn Steaks, Luby's, Panda Express, Starbucks, Taco Cabana, Twin Peaks Aloft AT&T, Chrysler/ Dodge/Jeep, CVS Drug, Dillard's, JC Penney, Macy's, Saks 5th, Target, Verizon
19b	FM 1535, FM 2696, Military Hwy, N Guajillos Mexican, Souper Salad, S Denny's, Jim's Rest.
19a	Honeysuckle Lane, Castle Hills
17b	(18 from wb), S Shell Bill Miller BBQ, Burger King, Pollo Tropical, Subway HEB Foods/gas, NAPA, vet
17	Vance Jackson Rd, N Valero/dsl Jack-in-the-Box, McDonald's, Sonic, Starbucks, Taco Cabana, Whataburger Embassy Suites, Marriott Aamco, AT&T, Discount Tire, S Petronic, Shell Church's, Subway U-Haul
16b a	I-10 E, US 87 S, to San Antonio, I-10 W, to El Paso, US 87 N
15	Lp 345, Fredericksburg Rd, E Citgo, EVC Church's, Dave&Buster's, Denny's, El Pollo Loco, El Rodeo, Jack-in-the-Box, Jim's Rest., Luby's, McDonald's, Peter Piper Pizza, Taco Cabana, Wendy's, Whataburger Best Value Inn, SpringHill Suites Family$, Firestone/auto, Hobby Lobby, SteinMart, Target, W Chevron/7-11/dsl CVS Drug
14	(c b a from sb) Callaghan Rd, Babcock Ln, E Chevron/dsl, Valero/dsl Marie Callender's, Popeye's, Red Lobster, Whataburger BestWestern, QualityInn Hyundai, W Exxon, Shell, Valero Burger King, Chili's, ChopSticks Chinese, DingHow Chinese, Golden Corral, Henry's Tacos, IHOP, Jack-in-the-Box, Jim's Rest, Joe's Crabshack, Las Palapas Mexican,

SAN ANTONIO

Exit #	Services
14	Continued (Louie Italian, McDonald's, Nicha's Mexican, Pizza Hut, C no's, Subway, Taco Cabana, Wendy's H, Cavan Boots, Chevrolet, Home Depot, NTB, Petsmart, Sam's Club/ Walmart/Subway/24hr
13	(b a from sb) TX 16 N, Bandera Rd, Evers Rd, Leon Va E Outback Steaks, Panda Express Audi, HEB Foods/ Office Depot, Toyota, UHaul, W Bill Miller BBQ, Henry's cos, Jim's Rest., Schlotzsky's, Sonic, Taco Cabana Chevr
12	(from sb), W Fortune Cookie Chinese, Jason's D Ojos Locos, Olive Garden, Sea Island Shrimp House, S bucks $Tree, AT&T, Barnes&Noble, Best Buy, Marsha Michael's, Old Navy, Petco, Ross
11	Ingram Rd, E Shell/dsl KFC/Taco Bell, Los Robert Saltgrass Steaks, TX Roadhouse, Vallarta Mexican Com Suites, Courtyard, Days Inn, Holiday Inn Express, Red Roof Residence Inn Aamco, Chrysler/Dodge/Jeep, Mazda, san, W Chick-fil-A, ChuckeCheese, Denny's, Fuddrucke Jack-in-the-Box, Whataburger Best Western Dillar Firestone/auto, JC Penney, Macy's
10	FM 3487, Culebra Rd, E Denny's, J Anthony's Seafood, Donald's, Wendy's La Quinta, Ramada Ltd Harley-vidson, to St Mary's U, W Phillips 66 Ford
9	(b a from sb) TX 151, E Subway, W Murphy U dsl 54th St Grill, Buffalo Wild Wings, Carino's Itali Cheddar's, Chili's, Chipotle Mexican, Cracker Barrel, Dicke BBQ, Firehouse Subs, IHOP, McAlister's Deli, Panda Expre Schlotsky's, Starbucks, TGIFriday's, Twin Peaks, Whatabu er Homewood Suites, Quality Inn, Sleep Inn, Spring Suites $Tree, AT&T, GNC, Home Depot, Lowe's Whse, Of Depot, Petsmart, Ross, Target, to Sea World, URGENT CA Verizon, Walmart/McDonald's
7	(8 from sb) Marbach Dr, E Exxon/7-11 Churc Golden Wok, IHOP PepBoys, W Chevron/dsl, Shell/ Burger King, Chick-fil-A, Jack-in-the-Box, Jimmy Joh Jim's Rest., KFC, LJ Silver, McDonald's, Peter Piper Pizza, Pi Hut, Popeye's, Red Lobster, Sonic, Subway, Taco Bell, Taco C bana, Whataburger/24hr Knights Inn, Motel 6 $Tr Advance Parts, BigLots, BrakeCheck, Discount Tire, Fireston auto, HEB Foods/gas
6	US 90, E Country Inn Motel to Lackland AFB, W Shell/dsl, Valero/dsl Best Western Explore USA RV C
4	Valley Hi Dr, to Del Rio, San Antonio, E Valero/dsl Bu er King, Church's, Little Caesar's, McDonald's, Panda Expre Pizza Hut, Sonic, Subway AutoZone, Family$, HEB Foo gas, O'Reilly Parts, W Valero Jack-in-the-Box Lackland AFB, Walgreens
3	(b a from sb) Ray Ellison Dr, Medina Base, E Chevron/d W Exxon/dsl, Valero/Subway/dsl Walmart/Subway
2	FM 2536, Old Pearsall Rd, E Shell/dsl, Valero/dsl B Miller BBQ, Church's, Domino's, Little Caesar's, McDonald Mexico Taqueria, Sonic, Subway AutoZone, CVS Dru O'Reilly Parts
1	Frontage Rd, W Toyota

INTERSTATE 610 (Houston)

Exit #	Services
38c a	TX 288 N, access to zoo, downtown
37	Scott St, N Citgo, Exxon Family$
36	FM 865, Cullen Blvd, N Crystal Inn, S Chevron/McDonald's, Shell Cullen Inn
35	Calais Rd, Crestmont St, MLK Blvd, S Shell Subway

INTERSTATE 610 (Houston) Cont'd

Exit #	Services
34	S Wayside Dr, Long Dr, N Citgo, Shell/dsl, Sunoco/Stripes/dsl Church's, S Shell, Valero/dsl Jack-in-the-Box NAPA
33	Woodridge Dr, Telephone Rd, N Shell/dsl ChuckeCheese, Cici's Pizza, Doneraki Mexican, IHOP, KFC/Taco Bell, McDonald's, Panda Express, Pappas BBQ, Starbucks, Taco Palenque, Wendy's Advance Parts, Best Buy, Brake Check, Harley Davidson, HEB Foods/gas, Lowe's, Marshall's, Old Navy, Ross, Verizon, S Citgo/dsl Spanky's Pizza
32b a	I-45, S to Galveston, N to Houston, to
31	Broadway Blvd, S Phillips 66/dsl, Valero/dsl
30c b	TX 225, to Pasadena, San Jacinto Mon
29	Port of Houston Main Entrance
28	Clinton Dr, W Shell/Burger King/dsl, to Galina Park
27	Turning Basin Dr, industrial area
26b	Market St
26a	I-10 E, to Beaumont, I-10 W, to downtown
24	(b a from sb) US 90 E, Wallisville Rd, E Citgo/dsl, Gulf/dsl, Loves/Arby's/dsl/scales/24hr, Pilot/McDonald's/dsl/scales, Valero/dsl, Valero/Hartz Chicken/dsl/scales/24hr Chevron/dsl Blue Beacon, W Citgo/dsl
23b	N Wayside, N Valero
23a	Kirkpatrick Blvd
22	Homestead Rd, Kelley St, N Shell/dsl Whataburger Super 8, S Chevron/Subway/dsl/scales
21	Lockwood Dr, W Texaco/Subway/dsl, N Chevron/McDonald's, Shell/dsl Church's, Timmy Chan Chinese H, Family$, Fiesta Foods
20a b	US 59, to downtown
19b	Hardy Toll Rd
19a	Hardy St, Jensen Dr (from eb)
18	Irvington Blvd, Fulton St, N Chevron, S Shell/dsl
17b c	I-45, N to Dallas, S to Houston
17a	(eb only) Airline Dr, S Shell/dsl Jack-in-the-Box Western Inn
16	(b a from eb) Yale St, N Main St, Shamrock, N Exxon/dsl Harley-Davidson, S Texaco Burger King, KFC/Taco Bell, Starbucks
15	TX 261, N Shepherd Dr, N Five Guys, Gabby's BBQ, Sonic, Starbucks, Taco Cabana, S Chevron/dsl, Shell Chick-fil-A, Wendy's, Whataburger Home Depot, PepBoys
14	Ella Blvd, N Exxon Cane's, Carl's Jr, El Pollo Loco, KFC, McDonald's, Popeye's, Taco Bell, S Murphy USA/dsl, Shell Chipotle, Thomas BBQ H, BrakeCheck, CVS Drug, Lowe's Whse, Office Depot
13c	TC Jester Blvd, N Shell Antone's Po' Boys, Denny's, Juanita's Mexican Courtyard, SpringHill Suites, S Phillips 66/dsl
13b a	US 290 (exits left from nb)
12	W 18th St, E Applebee's, Whataburger, W Shell Burger King Sheraton
11	I-10, W to San Antonio, E to downtown Houston
10	Woodway Dr, Memorial Dr, W Chevron/Pizza Inn/dsl, Shell/dsl Goodyear
9b	Post Oak Blvd, E Drury Inn, Hampton Inn, La Quinta, W McCormick&Schmick's Café, Starbucks
9a	San Felipe Rd, Westheimer Rd, FM 1093, E Chevron/dsl, Shell Grotto Rest., Jack-in-the-Box, Le Peep Cafe, Starbucks, Sullivan Steaks Extended Stay America, Hampton Inn, La Quinta CVS Drug, NTB, Target, W Shell CA Pizza Kitchen, Five Guys, Jamba Juice, Panera Bread, Yia Yia Mary's Courtyard, Extended Stay America, Marriott, Sheraton AT&T, Best Buy, Dillard's, Nieman-Marcus, Whole Foods Mkt
8a	US 59, Richmond Ave, E Extended Stay America CVS Drug, W Shell Holiday Inn Dillards
7	Bissonet St, West Park Dr, Fournace Place, E Beudreax's Kitchen Candlewood Suites Home Depot, Petsmart, W Shell/dsl/repair
6	Bellaire Blvd
5b	Evergreen St
5a	Beechnut St, E Chevron Boston Mkt, IHOP, Lowe's, McDonald's, Outback Steaks, Panda Express, Subway Hobby Lobby, Verizon, W Phillips 66, Shell Becks Prime, Chick-fil-A, Escalante Mexican Grill, Fadi's Grill, James Coney Island, La Madeleine, Los Tios Mexican, Saltgrass Steaks, Smoothie King, Starbucks AT&T, Best Buy, GNC, JC Penney, Marshall's, Old Navy, Ross, SteinMart, Target
4a	S Post Oak Rd, Brasswood, E Outback Steaks, W Target, Walmart
3	Stella Link Rd, N Mobil Domino's 99c Store, Discount Tire, O'Reilly Parts, S Valero/dsl Brake Check, vet
2	US 90A, N Exxon/dsl, Mobil, Texaco, Valero Burger King, Chacho's Cantina, Denny's/24hr, KFC, McDonald's, Popeye's, Starbucks, Subway, Wendy's Holiday Inn Express CVS Drug, Discount Tire, Family$, Ford, Honda, Mazda, Walgreens, S Chevron/dsl Golden Corral, Taco Bell, Whataburger/24hr Candlewood Suites, CareFree Inn, Motel 6, Motel 6 (2), RainTree Inn Nissan, to Buffalo Speedway
1c	Kirby Dr (from eb), N Crowne Plaza, Quality Inn, Sterling Inn, S Joe's Crabshack, Pappadeaux Seafood, Pappasito's Cantina Cavender's Boots, Chevrolet, Hyundai, NTB, Toyota
1b a	FM 521, Almeda St, Fannin St, N Chevron/dsl, Shell Burger King NRG Arena, S Shell/dsl McDonald's Aamco, Chrysler/Dodge/Jeep, to Six Flags

HOUSTON

TX

NOTES

= gas = food = lodging = other = rest stop

UT

UTAH

INTERSTATE 15

Exit #	Services
400.5mm	Utah/Idaho state line
398	Portage
392	UT 13 S, Plymouth, E United/A&W/dsl
385	UT 30 E, to Riverside, Fielding, 1 mi E Sinclair/Riverside Grill/dsl
381	Tremonton, Garland, 2 mi E H, food, gas, lodging
379	I-84 W, to Boise
376	UT 13, to Tremonton, 2-3 mi E Texaco/Arby's/dsl/scales/24hr JC'S Diner, Subway, Taco Time Marble Motel, N Sandman Motel (3mi)
372	UT 240, to UT 13, to rec area, Honeyville, E Crystal Hot Springs Camping
370mm	sb, full facilities, info, litter barrels, petwalk, vending
BRIGHAM CITY	
365	UT 13, Brigham City, W to Golden Spike NHS
363	Forest St, Brigham City, E Loves/Carl's Jr/Subway/dsl/scales/24hr Holiday Inn Express, W Bear River Bird Refuge
362	US 91, to US 89, Brigham City, Logan, E 7-11/dsl, Chevron/dsl, Exxon, Phillips 66/dsl, USA Burger King, Costa Vida, Domino's, Floriberto's Mexican, Hunan Chinese, J&D's Rest., KFC/Taco Bell, McDonald's, Old Grist Mill Bread, Pizza Hut, Sonic, Subway, Taco Time, Wendy's, Wingers Crystal Inn, Howard Johnson Express H, Verizon, $Tree, AT&T, AutoZone, Buick/Cadillac/Chevrolet, Golden Spike RV Park, John Watson, Chiropractor (5mi), KOA (4mi), O'Reilly Parts, Schwab Tires, to Yellowstone NP via US 89, Walmart/Subway, W Maverick/DQ/dsl/scales/24hr Days Inn
361mm	nb, full facilities, litter barrels, petwalk, vending
359	Port of Entry both lanes
357	UT 315, to Willard, Perry, E FLYING J/Subway/dsl/LP/scales/24hr KOA (2mi), Willard Peak Camping
351	UT 126, to US 89, to Utah's Fruit Way, Willard Bay, W Smith & Edwards Hardware
349	UT 134, N Ogden, Farr West, E 7-11, EVC, Exxon/Wendy's/dsl, Maverik/dsl Arby's, Bella's Mexican, Burger King, Del Taco, Domino's, Jumbo Burger, McDonald's, Subway, Taco Bell Comfort Inn Jiffylube, Wasatch View RV park, W Chevron/dsl
346	to Harrisville, W Chevron/Subway/dsl, dsl repair, Maverik/dsl GriDeli's, Taco Time, Zhang's Chinese Cal Ranch, vet
OGDEN	
344	UT 39, 12th St, Ogden, E 7-11/dsl, Chevron/dsl, Old Frontier Best Western+ to Ogden Canyon RA, W Pilot/Subway/Taco Bell/dsl/24hr Sleep Inn Sierra RV Ctr
343	UT 104, 21st St, Ogden, E FLYING J/Denny's/dsl/LP/24hr, Phillips 66/dsl Cactus Red's SW Grill, McDonalds Comfort Suites, Holiday Inn Express, Motel 6, Woodspring Suites RV Repair, W Shell/Blimpie/dsl Super 8 Bideaux RV Ctr, Century RV Park
342	(from nb, no return) UT 53, 24th St, Ogden
341b a	UT 79 W, 31st St, Ogden, W , 1-2 mi E on Wall St Longhorn Steaks H, Big O Tires, Chevrolet, Costco/gas, Dillard's, Ford, Hyundai, to Weber St U
340	I-84 E (from sb), to Cheyenne, Wyo
339	UT 26 (from nb), to I-84 E, Riverdale Rd, E Exxon/dsl, S clair/dsl Applebee's, Arby's, Buffalo Wild Wings, Carl's Chili's, Chipotle, Honeybaked Ham, IHOP, Jamba Juice, Jers Mike's, Lucky Buffet, McDonald's, MOD Pizza, Starbucks, S way, Sweet Burrito, Wendy's Motel 6 $Tree, Best B Buick/GMC, Cadillac, Chrysler/Dodge/Jeep, Good Earth Na ral Foods, Gordman's, Harley-Davidson, Home Depot, Hon Jo-Ann Fabrics, Kia, Maverik/dsl, Nissan, Petsmart, Sam's Clu gas, Schwab Tire, Target, Toyota, Verizon, Walmart
ROY	
338	UT 97, Roy, Sunset, E Air Force Museum, W 7-11, EV Exxon/dsl, Maverik/dsl, Sinclair/dsl A&W/KFC, Arby's, Be Cafe, Burger King, Five Star Thai, Greek Olive Rest., Japane Wasabi, McDonald's, Papa Murphy's, Rancherito's Mexican, Ta Bell, Village Inn Rest., Wendy's AutoZone, Citte RV Ctr, C Drug, Harmon's Mkt, Midas, O'Reilly Parts, Sacco's Fresh M Schwab Tires, Smith's/dsl, transmissions, vet, vet, Walgreens
335	UT 103, Clearfield, E Jimmy John's, Popeye's, Starbuc Hill AFB, W Phillips 66/dsl, Shell/dsl, Sinclair Bu er King, Carl's Jr, KFC, McDonald's, Subway, Taco Bell, Winge Days Inn, EconoLodge C&M Tires
334	UT 193, Clearfield, E Chevron/dsl, Maverik to Hill AF W 7-11, Maverik/dsl AutoZone
332	UT 108, Syracuse, E Applebee's, Boston's Rest., Cafe R Carl's Jr, Chick-fil-A, Chili's, Chipotle, Cracker Barrel, Famo Dave's, Five Guys, Golden Corral, Hook&Reel Seafood, Jimn John's, Lucky Slice Pizza, MacCool's Grill, MOD Pizza, Moe's S Noodles&Co, Outback Steaks, Panda Express, Papa Murphy Popeye's, Red Robin, Rumbi Island Grill, Sonic, Tepanya Zupas Cafe Courtyard, Fairfield Inn, Hampton Inn, Hilt Garden, Holiday Inn Express, Home 2 Suites, La Quinta, Town Place Suites Barnes&Noble, Lowe's Whse, Michael's, Pe co, Ross, Target, Tire Pros, URGENT CARE, Verizon, Walgreen W Exxon/Subway/dsl Arby's, Burger King, Crow Burger, McDonald's H, 7-11, Ford, to Antelope Island
LAYTON	
331	UT 232, UT 126, to I-84, Layton, E Buffalo Wild Wing Costa Vida, Denny's, Garcia's, La Puente, McDonald's, Oliv Garden, Red Lobster, Sizzler, TX Roadhouse, Wendy's Be Western+, Comfort Inn $Tree, Dick's, JC Penney, to Hill AF S Gate, W Exxon/dsl Asian Buffet, Burger King, Cant na SW Grill, ChuckeCheese, Coldstone, Del Taco, HuHot Mong lian, IHOP, KFC, Krispy Kreme, Pace's Rest., Rancheritos Mex can, Taco Bell AT&T, Batteries+Bulbs, Big Lots, Buick/GM Chevrolet, Chrysler/Dodge/Jeep, Discount Tire, Hobby Lobb Home Depot, Kia, Petsmart, Sam's Club/gas, Staples, Walmart McDonald's
330	Layton Pkwy, to UT 126, Layton, E Little Orient Chines Tire Pros, W Cafe Sabor Camping World RV Ctr
KAYSVILLE	
328	UT 273, Kaysville, E 7-11/dsl, Chevron/McDonald's, EV Big Daddy's Pizza, Domino's, Dylan's Drive-In, Granny Ar nie's Rest., Pizza Hut, Subway, Taco Time, Wendy's, Winger AutoZone, Big O Tire, O'Reilly Parts, Schwab Tire, USPO Walgreens, W Maverick/dsl Camping World
325mm	parking area both lanes
325	UT 225, Lagoon Dr, Farmington, E Chevron Subwa Hampton Inn camping, funpark, Mercedes, W Blaze Pizza, Cafe Rio, Chick-fil-A, Costa Vida, Habit Burge McDonald's, Panda Express, R&R BBQ, Starbucks, Subway Zupas Hyatt Place AT&T, Cabela's, Gordman's, Har mon's Mkt, Marshall's, Old Navy, Petco, Ross

INTERSTATE 15 Cont'd

Exit #	Services
324	US 89 N, UT 225, Legacy Pkwy (from sb), E Maverik/dsl, Smith's Foods/dsl Burger King, Chevron/dsl, Chopstix Chinese, Javier's Mexican, Papa John's, Subway Hampton Inn Aunt Pam's, Burt Bros/Goodyear/auto, Mercedes, RV Park
322	UT 227 (from nb), Lagoon Dr, to Farmington, E Subway Lagoon Funpark/RV Park
319	UT 105, Parrish Lane, Centerville, E 7-11/dsl, Chevron/Jimmy John's/dsl, Phillips 66/dsl Arby's, Carl's Jr, Chick-fil-A, Chili's, Costa Vida, Domino's, DQ, IHOP, In-N-Out, Little Caesar's, McDonald's, Papa Murphy's, Rancheritos, Sonic, Starbucks, Subway, Taco Bell, Wendy's $Tree, Dave's Auto Repair, Dick's Mkt, Home Depot, Jo-Ann, Kohl's, Land Rover, O'Reilly Parts, Petsmart, Schwab Tire, Target, Tire Factory, Walmart
317	US 89 S (exits left from sb), UT 131, 500W, S Bountiful, E Chevron/dsl, Exxon/dsl, Sinclair/7-11/dsl Chipotle, Culver's, Five Guys, Jimmy John's, Texas Roadhouse Country Inn Suites Chrysler/Dodge/Jeep, Costco/gas, Office Depot, PetCo, Verizon
316	UT 68, 500 S, W Bountiful, Woods Cross, E Shell Applebee's, Barbacoa Mexican, Cafe Rio, Carl's Jr, Chipotle, Chuck-aRama, Coldstone, Del Taco, Five Guys, Jimmy John's, KFC, McDonald's, Mikado Japanese, Panda Express, Pizza Hut, Sizzler, Starbucks, Subway, Taco Bell, TX Roadhouse, Wendy's H, $Tree, AT&T, AutoZone, Barnes&Noble, Costco/gas, GNC, Lowe's, Michael's, Office Depot, O'Reilly Parts, Petco, Ross, Tire Pros, TJ Maxx, Walgreens, W Phillips 66/A&W/dsl In-Town Suites vet
315	26th S, N Salt Lake, E Chevron/dsl, Sinclair Apollo Burger, Arby's, Black Bear Diner, Cafe Zupas, Jersey Mike's, Kneaders Bakery Cafe, McDonald's, MOD Pizza, Nielsen's Frozen Custard, Pappa's Steaks, R&R BBQ, Starbucks, Subway, Taco Time, Village Inn, Wendy's Best Western+, Comfort Inn AT&T, Buick/GMC, Burt Bros Tires, Chevrolet, Discount Tire, Ford/Lincoln, Honda, Mazda, Nissan, Schwab Tire, Smith's Foods, Southfork Hardware, Toyota, Tunex, U-Haul, Verizon, Walgreens, W IHOP, Lorena's Mexican Hampton Inn, Motel 6
314	Center St, Cudahy Lane (from sb), N Salt Lake, E Chevron
313	I-215 W (from sb), W to
312	US 89 S, to Beck St, N Salt Lake
311	2300 N
310	900 W (from sb), W Salt City Inn
309	600 N, E H, downtown, LDS Temple, W to UT State FairPark
308	I-80 W, to Reno, W
307	400 S, downtown
306	600 S, SLC City Ctr, 1 mi E Chevron, Fastbreak/dsl, Maverik, Sinclair, Tesla EVC Alberto's Mexican, Denny's, McDonald's, R&R BBQ, Starbucks, Street Tacos, Subway Comfort Inn, Crystal Inn, DoubleTree, Grand America, Hampton Inn, Hilton Garden, Hotel RL, Little America, Motel 6, Quality Inn, Sheraton, SpringHill Suites Hyundai, LDS Church Offices, to Temple Square, Toyota
305c-a	1300 S, 2100 S UT 201 W, SLC, downtown, E Chevron/dsl Carl's Jr, ChuckECheese, Dickey's BBQ, IHOP, Jimmy John's, McDonald's, Starbucks $Tree, Best Buy, Costco/gas, Home Depot, Office Depot, PetsMart, Sams Club/dsl, U-Haul, Walmart, W FLYING J/Denny's/dsl/LP/24hr Blue Beacon
304	I-80 E, to Denver, Cheyenne
303	UT 171, 3300 S, S Salt Lake, E 7-11, Maverik/dsl Apollo Burgers, Carl's Jr, Crown Burger, Jimmy John's, McDonald's, Starbucks, Taco Bell InTowne Suites, Motel 6, W Maverik Buick/GMC
301	UT 266, 4500 S, Murray, Kearns, E Maverik McDonald's, Subway Discount Tire, W Chevron/Burger King/dsl, Exxon/dsl, Texaco/dsl Denny's, Wendy's Baymont Inn, Fairfield Inn, Hampton Inn Lowe's Whse
300	UT 173, 5300 S, Murray, Kearns, E H, W Chevron/dsl, Exxon/dsl, Sinclair/dsl Papa Murphy's, Subway, Taco Time Quality Inn Smith's Foods
298	I-215 E and W
297	UT 48, 7200 S, Midvale, E Chevron, Phillips 66/dsl Arctic Circle, Betos Mexican, Denny's, Korean BBQ, McDonald's, Mekong Café, Mi Rico Burrito, Midvale Mining Cafe, Sweet Ginger Chinese Day's Inn, Discovery Inn, InTowne Suites, La Quinta, Motel 6, Park Inn Family$, Schwab Tire, Solitude Ski Areas, to Brighton, vet, Walgreens, W Chevron/dsl Arby's, Culver's, Dunkin', Freddy's, Jimmy John's, Popeye's, Subway, WinCo Foods, Zaxby's Staybridge Suites
295	UT 209, 9000 S, Sandy, E Chevron/dsl, Sinclair/dsl Arby's, Korean BBQ, Schlotzky's, Sconecutter's Rest., Sizzler, Starbucks, Subway EconoLodge Alta Ski Areas, Discount Tire, NAPA, Rio Rinto Stadium, to Snowbird, W Maverik/dsl, Maverik/dsl (2) H, Aamco, BMW Motorcycles, Harley-Davidson, URGENT CARE
293	106th S, Sandy, S Jordan, E Exxon, Shell//dsl Burger King, Carl's Jr, Carver's Steak&Seafood, Chick-fil-A, Chili's, Chipotle Mexican, Costa Vida, Dog Haus, El Pollo Loco, Firehouse Subs, Five Guys, HuHot, IHOP, Jamba Juice, Jim's Rest., Krispy Kreme, La Puente, Legends Grill, Los Cucos Mexican, Mazza, Mimi's Cafe, Noodles&Co, Olive Garden, Pei Wei, Potbelly, Rumbi Island Grill, Sonic, Starbucks, Subway, Sweet Tomatoes, Taco Bell, TX Roadhouse, Village Inn, Wendy's Best Western+, Courtyard, Extended Stay America, Hampton Inn, Hilton Garden, Holiday Inn Express, Hyatt House, Residence Inn Barnes&Noble, Chrysler/Dodge/Jeep, Goodyear/auto, Honda, JC

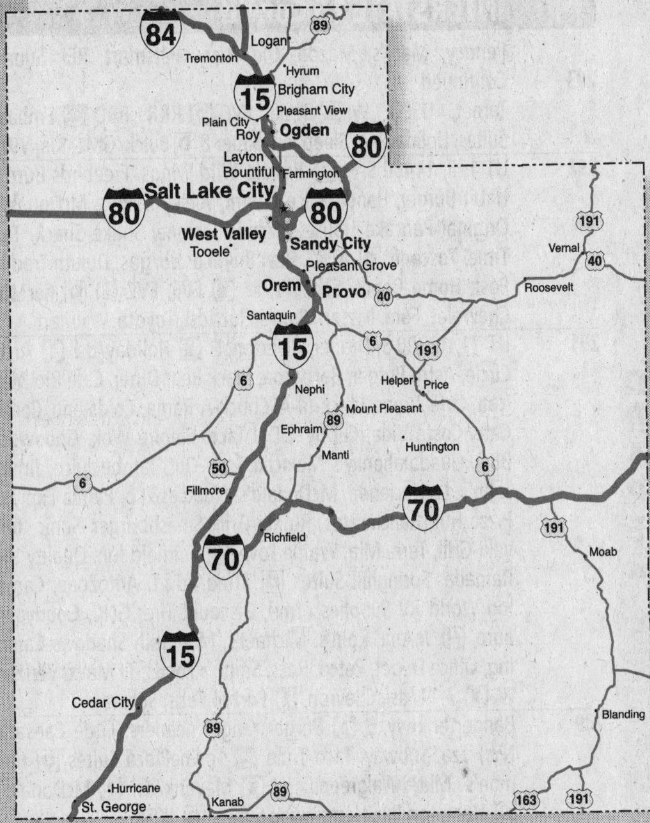

SALT LAKE

SALT LAKE

SANDY

UT

UT

INTERSTATE 15 Cont'd

DRAPER

293 Penney, Macy's, Mazda, Old Navy, Petsmart, REI, Subaru, Continued
Target, USPO, W Tesla EVC R&R BBQ Embassy Suites, Holiday Inn, Sleep Inn, Super 8 Buick/GMC, Kia, VW

292 UT 175, 11400 S, E Buffalo Wild Wings, Freebirds Burrito, Habit Burger, Handel's Ice Cream, Jersey Mike's, McDonald's, Original Pancake House, Pizzeria Limone, Shake Shack, Taco Time, Toscano AT&T, Best Buy, Costco/gas, Duluth Trading Post, Home Depot, Scheel's, W EVC, EVC (2) CarMax, Chevrolet, Ford, Nissan, Sam's Club/dsl, Toyota, Walmart

291 UT 71, 12300 S, Draper, Riverton, E Holiday/dsl Arctic Circle, Astro Burger, Barbacoa, Black Bear Diner, Café Rio Mexican, Cafe Zupas, Chick-fil-A, Chuck-A-Rama, Coldstone, Corner Cafe, Costa Vida, Cubby's, Del Taco, Empire Wok, Goodwood BBQ, Guadalahonky's Mexican, In-N-Out, Jamba Juice, Jimmy John's, La Hacienda, McDonald's, Noodles&Co, Panda Express, Pizza Hut, Rancheritos, Rumbi Grill, Smashburger, Sonic, Teriyaki Grill, Terra Mia, Waffle Love Fairfield Inn, Quality Inn, Ramada, Springhill Suites $Tree, AT&T, AutoZone, Camping World RV Supplies (1mi), Discount Tire, GNC, Goodyear/auto, H, JoAnn, Kohl's, Michael's, Mountain Shadows Camping, Office Depot, Petco, Ross, Smith's Foods, TJ Maxx, Verizon, W 7-11/dsl, Chevron Port of Subs, Subway

289 Bangerter Hwy, E Burger King, Kneaders, Little Caesar's, NY Pizza, Subway, Taco Time TownePlace Suites Harmon's Mkt, Walgreens, W Maverik/dsl McDonald's Hampton Inn, Homewood Suites IKEA

288 UT 140, Bluffdale, E 7-11/dsl, Chevron/dsl, Maverik/dsl General RV Ctr

284 UT 92, Timpanogas Hwy, to Alpine, Highland, E EVC Blaze Pizza, Braza Grill, Cafe Rio, Chick-fil-A, Chipotle, Five Guys, Jamba Juice, McDonald's, Panda Express, PDQ, Pieology, Rumbi, Slapfish, Taco Bell, Village Baker, Wendy's Hilton Garden, Hyatt Place, Staybridge Suites AT&T, Audi/Porsche, Cabela's, Harmon's Mkt, to Timpanogas Cave, Traverse Mtn Outlets/famous brands, W 7-11/Subway/dsl, Maverik/dsl Arby's, Carl's Jr, Costa Vida, Cubby's Cafe, Del Taco, Dickey's BBQ, Firehouse Subs, JCW Burgers, Popeye's, Smashburger, Starbucks, Zaxby's, Zupas Kitcken Courtyard, Hampton Inn, Home 2 Suites, SpringHill Suites Lone Peak RV Ctr, Thanksgiving Point/café

282 US 89 S, 12th W, to UT 73, Lehi, W Exxon/dsl

LEHI

279 UT 73, to Lehi, E Texaco/dsl Buffalo Wild Wings, Cafe Rio, Chili's, ChuckARama, Culver's, Del Taco, Denny's, El Pollo Loco, Hibachi House, Jimmy John's, One Man Band Diner, Panda Express, Popeye's, TX Roadhouse, Which Wich? Motel 6 Costco/gas, Home Depot, Lowe's Whse, Petsmart, Schwab Tire, Verizon, Walgreens, Walmart/Burger King, W Chevron/dsl, CNG, Phillips 66/7-11/Wendy's Arctic Circle, KFC/Pizza Hut, McDonald's, Moochie's, Papa Murphy's, Subway, Tepanyki Japanese Best Western, Comfort Inn, Day's Inn Big O Tire, Dave's Chiropractic, Macey's, O'Reilly Parts, USPO, vet

278 Main St, American Fork, E Chevron Cafe Zupas, Chili's, Del Taco, In-N-Out, Olive Garden, Pier 49, Rodizio Grill, Sonic, Zaxby's H, $Tree, Chrysler/Dodge/Jeep, Home Depot, Kia, Kohl's, Office Depot, Old Navy, Subaru, Target, Walmart, W Phillips 66/dsl Woodspring Suites

276 5th E, Pleasant Grove, E Exxon, Phillips 66 Arby's, Beto's, Carl's Jr, KFC, McDonald's, Starbucks, Subway, Taco Bell, Wendy's Holiday Inn Express H, CVS Drug, Stewart's RV Ctr, W Buick/GMC, Chevrolet, Ford, Land Rover

275 Pleasant Grove, E Holiday/dsl Costa Vida, Jersey Mike's, Panda Express, R&R BBQ, Starbucks Hyatt House BMW, Macey's Foods

OREM

273 Orem, Lindon, E Chevron, Maverik/dsl Costa Vida Mexican, Del Taco Discount Tire, Home Depot, Hyundai, Lex Schwab Tire, W Harley-Davidson

272 UT 52, to US 189, 8th N, Orem, E Maverik/dsl by's, Culver's, McDonald's, Milagros, Sonic, Starbucks, Su way Fairfield Inn, La Quinta, TownePlace Suites Honda, to Sundance RA, Winco Foods

271 Center St, Orem, E 7-11, Chevron Burger King, Chuck Cheese, McDonald's, Panda Express, Taco Bell, Wendy's, Za by's H, Target, USPO, W Maverik/dsl DQ

269 UT 265, 12th St S, University Pkwy, E Chevron, EVC, Te aco/Wendy's/dsl Applebee's, Arby's, Carrabba's, Chil Chipotle, El Pollo Loco, Golden Corral, HoneyBaked Ham, IHC In-n-Out, J Dawgs, Krispy Kreme, McDonald's, Noodles & C Outback Steaks, Pizza Hut, Sizzler, Starbucks, Thai Evergree Village Inn Comfort Inn, Hampton Inn, La Quinta $Tre Barnes&Noble, Best Buy, Dick's, Hobby Lobby, Honda, Jo-A Fabrics, Lowe's Whse, Mazda, Michael's, Nissan, Office Dep Old Navy, Petsmart, Ross, Staples, TJ Maxx, to BYU, Toyo Tuesday Morning, Verizon, VW, Walmart, W Chevron/d CNG Domino's, Subway Holiday Inn Express

PROVO

265b a UT 114, Center St, Provo, E Maverik/dsl Joe Vera Mexican, Salt Marriott H, auto repair, Fresh M W Chevron, Phillips 66/7-11/Wendy's, Shell/dsl Gre Steak Rest., Subway Best Value Inn Lakeside RV Cam ing, to Utah Lake SP

263 US 189 N, University Ave, Provo, E Exxon/dsl, Maverik/d Phillips 66/dsl, Shell/dsl A&W/KFC, Arby's, Burger Kin Cafe Rio, ChuckaRama, Kyoto, McDonald's, Papa Murphy Rancheritos, Ruby River Steaks, Sizzler, Subway, Taco Bell, V lage Inn Rest., Wendy's Fairfield Inn, Hampton Inn, Litt Suites, Ramada, Residence Inn, Sleep Inn $Tree, Dillard Discount Tire, Home Depot, JC Penney, Les Schwab, Ross, Sam Club/gas, Staples, to BYU, transmissions

SPRINGVILLE

261 UT 75, Springville, E FLYING J/Denny's/dsl/scales/24h Maverik McDonald's (1mi) Best Western, Holiday In Express KOA, RestStop

260 UT 77, Springville, Mapleton, E Phillips 66/7-11/dsl A by's, Del Taco, IHOP, Mongolian Grill, Papa John's, Pizza Hu Taco Bell, Wendy's Big O Tire, JiffyLube, Walmart/Subway, W Chevron/Subway/dsl, Love's/Chester's/McDonald's/ds scales/24hr Cracker Barrel Days Inn, Microtel Qua ty RV Ctr

257b a US 6 E, UT 156, Spanish Fork, E Chevron/dsl, Sinclair, Te soro/dsl, Texaco/dsl/LP Amber Rest., Arby's, Burger King Cafe Rio, Carl's Jr, China Wok, Costa Vida, Cubby's Cafe, Cu ver's, Five Guys, Italian Place, Jimmy John's, KFC, Kneaders, Li tle Caesar's, McDonald's, One Man Band Diner, Papa Murphy's Pizza Factory, Rita's, Sonic, Starbucks, Subway, Taco Bell, Tac Time, Wendy's, Zupas Kitchen $Tree, AT&T, AutoZone, Bi O Tire, Cal Store, Costco/gas, Fresh Mkt/gas, GNC, Good Eart Mkt, Jo-Ann Fabrics, Macey's Foods, O'Reilly Parts, Verizon Walmart/Subway, W Chevrolet

253 UT 164, to Spanish Fork

250 UT 115, Payson, E Chevron/dsl McDonald's, Subwa Quality Inn H, Mt Nebo Loop, O'Reilly Parts, Payso Foods, RiteAid

248 Payson, Salem, E Chevron/dsl, Exxon/Arby's/Subway/ds Costa Vida, Hunan City, Papa John's, Papa Murphy's, Pizza Hut, Taco Bell, Tsing Tao Asian $Tree, AT&T, AutoZone Big O Tire, Verizon, Walmart/Subway, W Phillips 66/Wendy's/7-11/dsl

INTERSTATE 15 Cont'd

Exit #	Services
244	US 6 W, Santaquin, E Maverik/dsl Cubby's Diner, DQ Tire Trax Auto, TrueValue, W Chevron/dsl, Sinclair/dsl Brumby's Cafe, Family Tree Rest., Hot Rod Diner, Main St Pizza, Subway, Taco Time auto/tire care, Family$, Ford, Main St Mkt, Nat Hist Area, USPO
242	to S Santaquin, W Chevron/dsl
233	UT 54, Mona, W Shell/Subway/dsl
228	UT 28, to Nephi, 2-4 mi W services
225	UT 132, Nephi, E Exxon/dsl/LP Main St Pizza, One Man Band Diner, Taco Time, W Chevron/Arby's/dsl, Phillips 66/7-11/Wendy's/dsl Economy Inn H, Big O Tire
222	UT 28, to I-70, Nephi, E Chevron/dsl, Exxon/scales/dsl/24hr, Texaco/dsl Burger King, Mickelson's Rest., Subway Motel 6, National 9 Inn, Super 8 dsl repair, W FLYING J/Denny's/dsl/LP/scales/24hr Lisa's Country Kitchen Best Western, Safari Motel H, dsl repair, High Country RV Park
207	to US 89, Mills
202	Yuba Lake, access to boating, camping, rec services
188	US 50 E, to I-70, Scipio, E Chevron/Subway/dsl, Texaco/dsl Scipio Hotel, W FLYING J/DQ/dsl/rest stop/24hr
184	ranch exit
178	US 50, to Delta, W to Great Basin NP
174	to US 50, Holden, W to Great Basin NP
167	Lp 15, Fillmore, E Chevron/dsl, Sinclair/dsl 5 Buck Pizza Best Western/rest. H, CarQuest, city park, golf, Goodyear, KOA (3mi), WagonsWest RV Park, W Chevron/Subway/rest stop/dsl, Texaco/dsl Carl's Jr tires/repair
163	Lp 15, to UT 100, Fillmore, E Conoco/Burger King/Costa Vida/dsl, Maverik/dsl Hong Kong Chinese, Larry's Drive-In Comfort Inn H, KOA, W Chevron/dsl Travel & Rest Inn
158	UT 133, Meadow, E Conoco/dsl, Shell/dsl
153mm	view area sb
151mm	view area nb
146	Kanosh, 2 mi E gas chainup area
138	ranch exit
135	Cove Fort Hist Site, E Chevron/Subway/rest stop/dsl repair/tires
132	I-70 E, to Denver, E Capitol Reef NP, Fremont Indian SP
129	Sulphurdale, chainup area
125	ranch exit
120	Manderfield, chainup area nb
112	to UT 21, Beaver, Manderfield, E Chevron/dsl, Conoco/dsl, Sinclair/dsl Arshel's Café, Carl's Jr, Crazy Cow Cafe, Hunan Chinese, McDonald's, Subway Beaver Lodge, Best Western, Country Inn, De Lano Motel/RV Park, Motel 6 H, auto/RV/dsl repair, Family$, Hometown Mkt, KOA (1mi), W FLYING J/cafe/dsl/scales/24hr Denny's, Wendy's Days Inn, Super 8 to Great Basin NP
109	to UT 21, Beaver, E Phillips 66/dsl, Shell/Burger King/dsl/RV dump, Spirit/dsl Best Western, Comfort Inn H, auto repair, Cache Valley Cheese, Mike's Foodtown, NAPA, United Camping, W Blu LNG, Chevron/DQ/dsl KanKun Mexican, Timberline Rest. Quality Inn to Great Basin NP, truck wash
100	ranch exit
95	UT 20, to US 89, to Panguitch, E Bryce Canyon NP
88mm	**both lanes, full facilities, hist site, litter barrel, petwalk, picnic table**
82	UT 271, Paragonah
78	UT 141, 1 mi E Chevron/dsl, Maverik Days Inn NAPA, ski areas, W TA/Subway/Taco Bell/LP/dsl/scales/24hr/@

FILLMORE

BEAVER

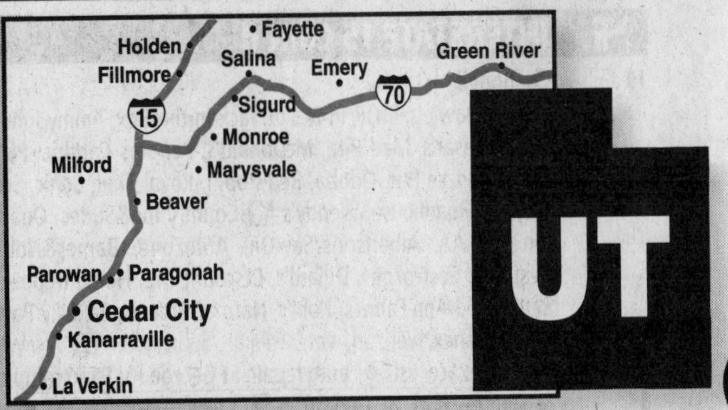

CEDAR CITY

Exit #	Services
75	UT 143, 2 mi E Chevron, Maverik, Phillips 66/dsl Days Inn Parowan Mkt, to Brian Head/Cedar Breaks Ski Resorts
71	Summit
62	UT 130, Cedar City, E Loves/Carl's Jr/Subway/dsl/scales/24hr, Phillips 66/dsl Allberto's Mexican H, Country Aire RV Park, KOA (2mi), st patrol, W Maverik/dsl, Shell/dsl/24hr/dsl repair/@ Travelodge
59	UT 56, Cedar City, 0-2 mi E Chevron/DQ/dsl, Conoco/dsl, Maverik, Phillips 66/dsl/LP, She'll/dsl A&W/KFC, Arby's, Burger King, China Kitchen, Denny's, Depot Grill, Firehouse Subs, Great Harvest Bread Co., Hermie's Drive-In, Hong Kong Buffet, IHOP, Jimmy John's, Little Caesar's, McDonald's/playplace, Papa Murphy's, Pizza Factory, Sizzler, Sonny Boy's BBQ, Subway, Taco Bell, Valerie's Tacos, Wendy's, Zaxby's Abbey Inn, Best Value Inn, Best Western, Quality Inn, Stratford Hotel Buick/Chevrolet, Goodyear/auto, Lin's Mkt, Mr Tire, NAPA, Tire Pros, USPO, Verizon, W Maverik/dsl, Sinclair/dsl Subway Motel 6, Ramada, Super 8
57	Lp 15, to UT 14, Cedar City, 0-2 mi E Chevron/repair/24hr, Phillips 66/dsl, Shell, Sinclair/dsl DQ, Golden Corral, Subway, Taco Time Clarion, Comfort Inn, Courtyard, Holiday Inn Express, La Quinta, SpringHill Suites H, $Tree, AutoZone, Big O Tire, Bryce Cyn, CAL Ranch, Duck Crk, Jo-Ann Fabrics, NAPACare, Navajo Lake, O'Reilly Parts, Smith's Food/dsl, Staples, TJ Maxx, to Cedar Breaks, Verizon, W Chevron/dsl, USA Applebee's, Cafe Rio, Chili's, Costa Vida, Del Taco, Dickey's BBQ, Five Buck Pizza, Jack-in-the-Box, Lupita's Mexican, Ninja Japanese, Panda Express, Papa John's, Starbucks, Subway, Winger's Hampton Inn GNC, Home Depot, Tunex, Verizon, Walgreens, Walmart/McDonald's
51	Kanarraville, Hamilton Ft
44mm	**both lanes, full facilities, hist site, litter barrels, petwalk,**
42	New Harmony, Kanarraville, W Shell/dsl
40	to Kolob Canyon, E scenic drive, tourist info/ , Zion's NP
36	Black Ridge
33	Snowfield
31	Pintura
30	Browse
27	UT 17, Toquerville, E Grand Canyon, Lake Powell, to Zion NP
23	Leeds, Silver Reef (from sb), 3 mi E hist site, Leed's RV Park/gas, museum
22	Leeds, Silver Reef (from nb), same as 23

Exit #	Services
16	UT 9, to Hurricane, E Texaco/dsl Holiday Inn Express Harley-Davidson, Walmart Dist Ctr
13	Washington Pkwy, E Maverik/dsl Black Bear Diner
10	Middleton Dr, Washington, E Phillips 66/dsl, Sinclair/dsl, USA Alvero's Mexican, Arby's, Arctic Circle, Benja's Thai, Bishop's Cafe, Buca Italian, Burger King, Costa Vida, Del Taco, Dickey's BBQ, Don Pedro's Mexican, El Pollo Loco, Freddy's,

INTERSTATE 15 Cont'd

ST GEORGE

10 Continued
Hungry Howie's, IHOP, In-N-Out, Jack-in-the-Box, Jimmy John's, Little Caesar's, Mad Pita, McDonald's, Peppers Cantina, Pizza Factory, Pizza Hut, Qdoba, Red Robin, Royal Thai, Sonic, Subway, TX Roadhouse, Wendy's Country Inn&Suites, Quality Inn AAA, Albertsons/Sav-On, AutoZone, Barnes&Noble, Best Buy, Costco/gas, Dillard's, Discount Tire, Home Depot, JC Penney, Jo-Ann Fabrics, Kohl's, Natural Grocers, O'Reilly Parts, PetCo, Tunex, Verizon, vet, Walmart/Subway, **W** Chevron/dsl/LP, Texaco/dsl auto repair, St George RV Park/camping

8 St George Blvd, St George, **E** Chevron/Subway/dsl, Texaco/dsl Apollo Burger, Applebee's, Brick Oven, Buffalo Wild Wings, Carl's Jr, Chick-fil-A, Chick-fil-A, Chili's, Chipotle, Chuck-aRama, Coldstone, Firehouse Subs, Five Guys, Golden Corral, Habit Burger, Iggy's Grill, Jimmy John's, Mongolian BBQ, Olive Garden, Outback Steaks, Panda Express, Paradise Bakery & cafe, Red Lobster, Smashburger, Starbucks, Subway, Village Inn Rest., Winger's Best Inn, Courtyard, Hampton Inn, Ramada Inn, TownePlace Suites $Tree, AT&T, Dick's, Harmon's Foods, Lowe's, Old Navy, Petsmart, Ross, Staples, Sunrise Tire, Target, TJ Maxx, Tuesday Morning, Verizon, Zion Outlets/famous brands, **W** Conoco/dsl, Maverik, Shell/dsl, Sinclair/dsl, Texaco/dsl A&W/KFC, Burger King, Cafe Rio, Denny's, Iceberg Drive-In, Larsen's Drive-In, McDonald's, Ocean Buffet, Panda Garden, Papa John's, Port of Subs, Red Ginger Asian, Sakura Japanese, Taco Bell, Taco Time, Tropical Smoothie, Wendy's Best Western, Chalet Motel, Coronada Inn, Days Inn, EconoLodge, Econo-my Inn, Knights Inn, Motel 6, Rodeway Inn, Sands Motel, Sun-Time Inn, Super 8 Auto Tech/tires, Big O Tire, Desert Coach RV Ctr, NAPA, O'Reilly Parts, Rite Aid, to LDS Temple, vet

6 UT 18, Bluff St, St George, **E** Chevron/dsl, Sinclair/dsl, Texaco/dsl Cracker Barrel, Culver's, Jack-in-the-Box, Player's Grill, Rib Chop House, Subway Ambassador Inn, Comfort Inn, Fairfield Inn, Hilton Garden Buick/GMC, Hyundai, Kia, museum, Subaru, VW, **W** Shell, Texaco Arby's, Beijing Buffet, Black Bear Diner, Burger King, Denny's, Domino's, DQ, Jimmy John's, McDonald's, Pizza Hut, Ricardo's Rest., SF Pizza Best Value Inn, Best Western, Claridge Inn, Clarion Suites, Crystal Inn, Howard Johnson, Lexington Hotel, Quality Inn, St George Inn auto/truck repair, AutoZone, Big O Tire, Cadillac/Chevrolet, Camping World RV Ctr, Chrysler/Dodge/Jeep, Ford/Lincoln, funpark, Goodyear/auto, Honda, Mazda, Nissan, TempleView RV Park, Toyota, U-Haul

5 Dixie Dr

4 Brigham Rd, Bloomington, **E** Pilot/Burger King/dsl/scales/24hr La Quinta, **W** Chevron/Subway/Taco Time/dsl, USA/dsl Dickey's BBQ, Hungry Howie's, Peppers Cantina, Wendy's Wingate Inn Walmart/Subway

2 UT 7 E, Southern Pkwy, **E** , **W** Terrible Herbst/dsl Hampton Inn

1 Port of Entry/**weigh sta both lanes**

0mm Utah/Arizona state line

INTERSTATE 70

Exit #	Services
232mm	Utah/Colorado state line
227	Westwater
221	ranch exit
214	to Cisco
204	UT 128, to Cisco
193	Yellowcat Ranch Exit
190mm	**Welcome Ctr wb, full facilities, info, litter barrels, , vending**
187	Thompson, **N** Exxon/7-11/dsl Ballard RV Park
185mm	**parking area eb**
182	US 191 S, Crescent Jct, to Moab, **N** Papa Joe's, **S** Arches/Canyonlands NP
181mm	**eb, full facilities, litter barrels, , scenic view**
175	ranch exit
164	UT 19, Green River, **1-3 mi N** Phillips 66/Burger King/d Pilot/Westwinds/rest/dsl/scales/24hr, Silver Eagle/Blimpi dsl, Tesla EVC Tamarisk Rest. Best Value Inn, Comfort I Holiday Inn Express, Knights Inn, Motel 6, River Terrace Inn, S per 8 KOA, Powell River Museum, same as 160, tires/repai
160	UT 19, Green River, **0-2 mi N** Chevron/Subway/dsl, Cor co/Arby's/dsl Cathy's Pizza, Chowhound, La Veracruzar Ray's Rest. Budget Inn, Robbers Roost, Sleepy Hollow M tel Ace Hardware, city park, Green River SP, NAPA/repa same as 164, Shady Acres RV Park, USPO
157	US 6 W, US 191 N, to Price, Salt Lake
149	UT 24 W, to Hanksville, to Capitol Reef, Lake Powell, Go lin Valley SP
146	**restrooms wb, view area**
144mm	**runaway truck ramp eb**
143mm	**restrooms, view area both lanes**
142mm	**runaway truck ramp eb**
138mm	**brake test area, restrooms eb**
131	Temple Mt Rd
122mm	**Ghost Rock View Area both lanes, restrooms**
116	to Moore, **N** view area both lanes
115	**N** view area eb
108	ranch exit
105mm	Salt Wash View Area both lanes
99	ranch exit
91	UT 10 N, UT 72, to Emery, Price, **12 mi N** gas, **S** to Ca itol Reef NP
86mm	**S both lanes, full facilities, litter barrels, petwalk**
73	ranch exit
63	Gooseberry Rd
56	US 89 N, to Salina, US 50 W, to Delta, NEXT SERVICES 109 M EB, **0-1 mi N** Conoco/dsl, Maverik/dsl, Phillips 66/Carl's J dsl, Sinclair/Burger King/dsl Denny's, El Mexicano Mex can, Losta Motsa Pizza, Mom's Cafe, Subway EconoLodg Rodeway Inn, Super 8 Barretts Foods, Butch Cassidy R Camp, Family$, NAPA, Peterbilt, truck/RV/auto repair, **S** Loves/Arby's/dsl/scales/24hr, Xpress/Little Caesar's/dsl
48	UT 24, to US 50, Sigurd, Aurora, **1-2 mi S** gas foo Capitol Reef NP, to Fishlake NF
40	Lp 70, Richfield, **0-2 mi S** FLYING J/Pepperoni's/ds LP/rest./24hr, Chevron/dsl, Maverik/dsl, Texaco/dsl A by's, Frontier Village Rest., Papa Murphy's, Subway, Tac Time Best Western, Budget Host, Days Inn/rest., Holida Inn Express, Super 8 Big O Tire, Buick/Cadillac/Chevro let/GMC, Chrysler/Dodge/Jeep, city park, Fresh Mkt, IFA Stor NAPA, RV/truck repair, USPO
37	Lp 70, Richfield, **1-2 mi S** Phillips 66/Wendy's/dsl, Si ver Eagle/Burger King/dsl Dickey's BBQ, KFC/Tac Bell, Little Caesar's, Lotsa Motsa Pizza, McDonald's, Pi za Hut, Steve's Steaks, Wingers Comfort Inn, Fairfie Inn, Hampton Inn, Motel 6, New West Motel, Quality Inn Royal Inn $Tree, Ace Hardware, AutoZone, Ford, gol Home Depot, KOA, O'Reilly Parts, Pearson Tire, st patro to Fish Lake/Capitol Reef Parks, Verizon, Walmart/Subwa
31	Elsinore, Monroe, **S** Silver Eagle/DQ/dsl
25	UT 118, Joseph, Monroe, **S** Flying U Country Store/dsl/RV park
23	US 89 S, to Panguitch, Bryce Canyon
17	**N** camping, chain-up area (WB), Fremont Indian SP, info museum,

GREEN RIVER

SALINA

RICHFIELD

INTERSTATE 70 Cont'd

Exit #	Services
13mm	brake test area eb
7	Ranch Exit
3mm	Western Boundary Fishlake NF
1	N Chevron/Subway/rest stop (2mi) Historic Cove Fort
0mm	I-15, N to SLC, S to St George.

I-70 begins/ends on I-15, exit 132.

INTERSTATE 80

Exit #	Services
197mm	Utah/Wyoming state line, Utah/Wyoming state line
191	Wahsatch
187	ranch exit
185	Castle Rock
182mm	Port of Entry/**weigh sta wb**
178	Emery (from wb)
170	**Welcome Ctr wb/ eb, full facilities, litter barrels, petwalk, , , RV dump, vending**
169	Echo
168	I-84 W, to Ogden, I-80 E, to Cheyenne
166	view area both lanes, litter barrels
162	Coalville, N Phillips 66/dsl/mart Best Western CamperWorld RV Park, Holiday Hills RV Camp/LP, S Chevron/dsl, Sinclair/dsl Polar King, Subway Griffith's Foods, NAPA, to Echo Res RA, USPO
155	UT 32 S, Wanship, S Sinclair/dsl to Rockport SP
150	toll gate promontory
146b a	US 40 E, to Heber, Provo, N Sinclair/Blimpie/Pizza Hut/dsl, S Phillips 66/7-11/dsl Burt Bros Tires, Home Depot
146	view area/**chain up wb**
145	UT 224, Kimball Jct, to Park City, N Chevrolet, Ford, Park City RV Park, vet, S Chevron/dsl Arby's, Cafe Rio, Coldstone, Del Taco, Five Guys, Freebirds Burrito, Ghidottis Italian, Great Harvest Bread Co, Jimmy John's, Loco Lizard Cantina, McDonald's, Panda Express, Papa John's, Pizza Hut, Red Rock Cafe, Ruby Tuesday, Starbucks, Subway, Szechwan Chinese, Taco Bell, Wendy's, Whole Foods Mkt Best Western, Hampton Inn, Holiday Inn Express Best Buy, Best Buy, GNC, Michaels, Outlet Mall/famous brands, Petco, RV camping, Smith's Foods/dsl, Staples, TJ Maxx, to ski areas, USPO, visitors info, Walmart
144mm	view area eb
141	ranch exit, N Phillips 66/Subway/dsl Burt Bros Tires, to Jeremy Ranch, S Billy Blanco Mexican camping, Fresh Mkt, ski area
140	Parley's Summit, Parley's Summit, S Sinclair/dsl No Worries Café
137	Lamb's Canyon
134	UT 65, Emigration Canyon, East Canyon, Mountaindale RA
133	utility exit (from eb)
132	ranch exit
131	(from eb) Quarry
130	I-215 S (from wb)
129	UT 186 W, Foothill Dr, Parley's Way, N H
128	I-215 S (from eb)
127	UT 195, 23rd E St, to Holladay
126	UT 181, 13th E St, to Sugar House, N Chevron A&W/KFC, Carl's Jr, Chick-fil-A, Olive Garden, Red Lobster, Sizzler, Taco Bell, Training Table, Wendy's Extended Stay America Verizon
125	UT 71, 7th E St, N Dee's Rest., Jimmy John's, Little Caesar's, Olympian Rest., Starbucks AT&T, Firestone, Pepboys

KIMBALL JCT

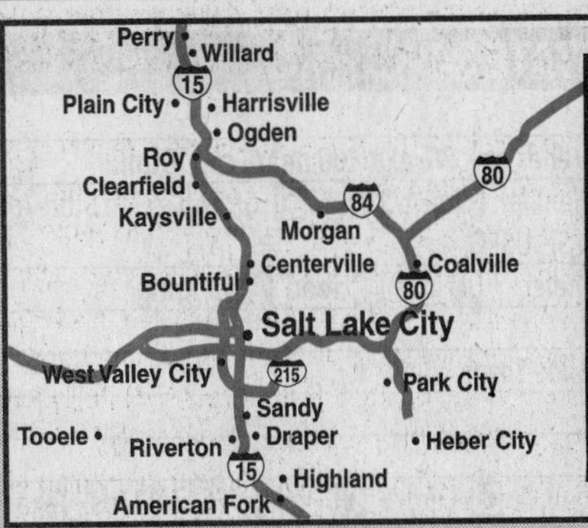

SALT LAKE CITY

Exit #	Services
124	US 89, S State St, N 7-11 Astro Burgers, Burger King, Strarbucks, Subway, Taco Bell Access RV Ctr, Chrysler/Dodge/Jeep, Discount Tire, vet, S A&W/KFC Ramada Inn
123mm	I-15, N to Ogden, S to Provo

I-80 and I-15 run together approx 4 mi. See I-15, exits 305-307.

Exit #	Services
121	600 S, to City Ctr
120	I-15 N, to Ogden
118	UT 68, Redwood Rd, to N Temple, N Chevron/Subway/dsl, Loves/Arby's/dsl/scales/24hr A&W/KFC, Apollo Burger, Burger King, Carl's Jr, Denny's, Taco Bell, Wendy's Airport Inn, Candlewood Suites, Comfort Suites, Holiday Inn Express, Motel 6, Radisson, Ramada 7-11, S Maverik/dsl H
117	I-215, N to Ogden, S to Provo
115b a	Bangerter Hwy, N to Salt Lake Airport
114	Wright Bros Dr (from wb), N same as 113
113	5600 W (from eb), N EVC, Phillips 66/dsl Perkins, Port of Subs, Subway Best Western+, Comfort Suites, Courtyard, DoubleTree, Fairfield Inn, Hampton Inn, Hilton Garden, Holiday Inn, Homewood Suites, Hyatt Place, La Quinta, Microtel, Quality Inn, Ramada Inn, Residence Inn, Sheraton, SpringHill Suites, Super 8, Tru Hilton
111	7200 W
104	UT 202, Saltair Dr, to Magna, N beaches, Great Salt Lake SP
102	UT 201 (from eb), to Magna
101mm	view area wb
99	UT 36, to Tooele, S FLYING J/Denny's/dsl/scales/LP/24hr, Chevron/Subway/dsl, TA/Burger King/Taco Bell/dsl/scales/24hr/@, Texaco/dsl Del Taco, McDonald's Comfort Inn/Suites, Oquirrh Motel/RV Park H, SpeedCo
88	to Grantsville
84	UT 138, to Grantsville, Tooele
77	UT 196, to Rowley, Dugway
70	to Delle, S Delle/Tesoro/café/dsl
62	to Lakeside, Eagle Range, military area
56	to Aragonite
55mm	**both lanes, full facilities, litter barrels, petwalk, , , vending**
49	to Clive
41	Knolls
26mm	architectural point of interest
10mm	**both lanes, full facilities, litter barrels, observation area, petwalk, , , vending**
4	Bonneville Speedway, N Sinclair/dsl/café/24hr
3mm	Port of Entry, **weigh sta both lanes**
2	UT 58 (no EZ wb return), Wendover, S Shell/dsl, Sinclair/dsl Subway Best Western+, Bonneville Inn, Knights Inn, Motel 6, Nugget Hotel/casino, Quality Inn, Super 8, Western Ridge Motel auto repair, Carquest, Family$, KOA, Montego Bay Hotel/Casino, USPO
0mm	Utah/Nevada state line, Mountain/Pacific time zone

UT

INTERSTATE 84

Exit #	Services
120	**I-84 begins/ends on I-80, exit 168 near Echo, Utah.**
115	Ut 65 S, to Henefer, Echo, 1/2 mi S Grump's Gen Store/gas, to E Canyon SP, USPO
112	UT 86 E, Henefer, S gas food lodging
111	Croydon
111mm	Devil's Slide Scenic View
108	Taggart
106	ranch exit
103	UT 66, Morgan, N Ford, S Phillips 66/7-11/dsl, Texaco/dsl J's Drive-in, Spring Chicken Café, Subway Ace Hardware, city park, E Canyon SP, Family$, Ridley's Mkt, URGENT CARE, USPO
96	Peterson, N Sinclair/dsl (3mi) Nordic Valley Ski Areas, Powder Mtn, to Snow Basin, S Phillips 66/dsl
94mm	**wb, full facilities, litter barrels, petwalk,**
92	UT 167 (from eb), to Huntsville, N Sinclair/dsl (2mi) city park (2mi), to ski areas
91mm	**S eb, full facilities, litter barrels, petwalk,**
87b a	US 89, to Ogden, Layton, Ogden, N McDonald's (2mi), Wendy's (2mi) Best Western Cheese Outlet, Goodyear/auto, S to Hill AFB
85	S Weber, Uintah
81	to I-15 S, UT 26, Riverdale Rd, N Exxon/dsl, Maverik/dsl, Sinclair/dsl Applebee's, Arby's, Buffalo Wild Wings, Carl's Jr, Chili's, Chipotle, El Pollo Loco, Habit Burger, Honeybaked Ham, IHOP, Jamba Juice, Jersey Mike's, Lucky Buffet, McDonald's, MOD Pizza, Starbucks, Subway, Sweet Burrito, Wendy's $Tree, AT&T, Best Buy, Buick/GMC, Good Earth Foods, Gordman's, Harley-Davidson, Hobby Lobby, Home Depot, Honda, Jo-Ann, Kia, Lowe's Whse, Nissan, PepBoys, Petsmart, Sam's Club/gas, Schwab Tire, Target, Toyota, Verizon, Walmart/McDonald's, S Motel 6 Chrysler/Dodge/Jeep

RIVERDALE

I-84 and I-15 run together. See I-15, exits 344 through 379.

Exit #	Services
41	I-15 N to Pocatello
40	UT 102, Tremonton, Bothwell, N Chevron/Poblano's/dsl/wash/24hr, Maverik/dsl, Sinclair/Burger King/dsl/scales/@, Tesla EVC Denny's, McDonald's, Wendy's Hampton Inn, Western Inn C&R Rv Ctr, H (4mi), O'Reilly Parts, RV/truck/tire repair, S to Golden Spike NHS
39	to Garland, Bothwell, N H
32	ranch exit
26	UT 83 S, to Howell, S to Golden Spike NHS
24	to Valley
20	to Blue Creek
17	ranch exit
16	to Hansel Valley (from wb)
12	ranch exit
7	Snowville, N FLYING J/Pepperoni's/dsl/LP/24hr, Sinclair/A&W/dsl Mollie's Café, Ranch House Diner Outsiders Inn city park, Lotti-Dell RV camping, USPO
5	UT 30, to Park Valley
0mm	Utah/Idaho state line

INTERSTATE 215

Exit #	Services
29	**I-215 begins/ends on I-15.**
28	UT 68, Redwood Rd, E Pony Express RV Park, W FLYING J/Pepperoni's/dsl/LP/24hr/@, Maverik/dsl Lotus Chinese
26	Legacy Pkwy
25	22nd N
23	7th N, E Exxon/dsl, Loves/Arbys/dsl/scales/2 (1.5 mi), Maverik Denny's, KFC, Little Caesar's, McDonald's, Papa Murphy's, Subway, Taco Bell, Wendy's Mo 6 $Tree, Family$, Super Saver Mkt, W Airport Inn, Candlewood Suites, Comfort Suites, Holiday Inn Express, Radiss
22b a	I-80, W to Wendover, E to Cheyenne
21	California Ave, E Sapp Bros/Sinclair/Burger King/dsl/@, soro/7-11/dsl RV/Truckwash, W Chevron/dsl P of Subs
20b a	UT 201, W to Magna, 21st S, W Maverik/dsl Taco Goodyear, Kenworth
18	UT 171, 3500 S, W Valley, E 7-11 Applebee's, Chi Costa Vida Mexican, Cracker Barrel, Greek Souvlaki, IHOP, Ko loon Cafe Baymont Inn, Country Inn Suites, Crystal I Extended Stay America, Holiday Inn Express, La Quinta, Sle Inn, Staybridge Suites H, PepBoys, W Cafe Rio, In-Out, Jimmy John's, Olive Garden, Pizza Hut, Red Robin, Sma burger, TGIFriday's, Wendy's, Winger's, Zupas Emba Suites AT&T, Big O Tire, Costco/gas, CVS Drug, JC Penn Office Depot, Petco, Ross, Staples, Verizon
15	UT 266, 47th S, E 7-11, Conoco/dsl Dee's Rest., K Mad Greek, Pizza Hut, Taco Time, Village Inn, Wendy's Fre Mkt, Goodyear/auto, Rite Aid, Walgreens, W Chevro dsl Arby's, Arctic Circle, Tammie's Diner vet, Sinclair/dsl
13	UT 68, Redwood Rd, E Chevron, Shell/dsl Apollo Bur er, Applebee's, Arby's, Burger King, Carl's Jr, City Buffet, Dic ey's BBQ, Domino's, Francesco's Rest., Freebirds Burrito, Hon Baked Ham, McDonald's/playplace, Panda Express, Starbuc Subway, TX Roadhouse Extended Stay America $Tre AT&T, Harmon's Mkt, Jo-Ann Fabrics, PetsMart, Ross, Verizo Walmart/McDonald's
12	I-15, N to SLC, S to Provo
11	same as 10 (from eb)
10	UT 280 E, E Tesoro Papa John's AutoZone, Sam Club/gas, W A&W/KFC, Applebee's, Arby's, Braza Gr Brio Grill, CA Pizza, Cheesecake Factory, ChuckARama, Corn Bakery Cafe, Jason's Deli, Macaroni Grill, McDonald's, Oliv Garden, Panda Express, Red Lobster, Red Robin, RedRock Caf Starbucks, Subway, Taco Bell, Village Inn H, Dillard's, Fir stone/auto, Honda, Marshalls, Midas, Nordstrom, Pepboy Sprouts Mkt, Verizon
9	Union Park Ave, E Applebee's, Bucca Italian, Buffalo Wi Wings, Cafe Rio, Carl's Jr, Chick-fil-A, Chili's, Chipotle, Den ny's, Dickey's BBQ, Famous Dave's BBQ, Firehouse Subs, Fiv Guys, Longhorn Steaks, Noodles&Co, Panda Express, Pei We Smashburger, Subway, Wendy's Hawthorn Suites, Sup 8 $Tree, Barnes&Noble, Dick's, GNC, Gordman's, Home De pot, Michaels, Old Navy, Petco, Ross, Smith's Foods, Target, Maxx, Verizon, Walmart/Subway, W Shell Crystal Inn Motel 6 Extended Firestone/auto, Office Depot
8	UT 152, 2000 E, E Chevron KFC, McDonald's, Soni Taco Bell Whole Foods Mkt, W Phillips 66/dsl Sub way, Wendy's Discount Tire
6	6200 S, E Jimmy John's, Luna Blanca, Pie Five, Starbuck Trio Cafe, Zupas Hyatt Place, Residence Inn Alta, Brigh ton, Snowbird, Solitude/ski areas
5	UT 266, 45th S (from sb), Holladay, W Sinclair
4	39th S, E Chevron/dsl, Sinclair/dsl Barbacoa Grill, Rock Mtn Pizza, Subway Ace Hardware, Dan's Mkt, W H
3	33rd S, Wasatch, W Smith's/dsl Cafe Rio, Fiv Guys, KFC/Taco Bell, McDonald's, Shivers Burgers, Wen dy's Petsmart, REI, Smith's Mkt
2	I-80 W
0	**I-215 begins/ends on I-80, exit 130.**

SALT LAKE CITY

VERMONT

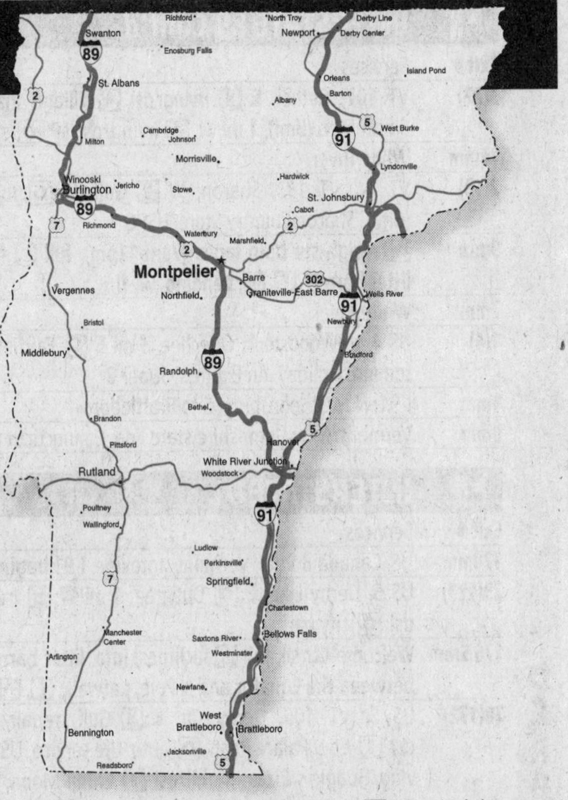

VT

INTERSTATE 89

Exit #	Services
130mm	US/Canada Border, Vermont state line, **I-89 begins/ends.**
22(129)	US 7 S, Highgate Springs, **E** Irving/dsl DutyFree
129mm	Latitude 45 N, midway between N Pole and Equator
128mm	Rock River
21(123)	US 7, VT 78, Swanton, **E** Shell/dsl, **W** Mobil/Subway/dsl, Shell, Sunoco/dsl Dunkin', McDonald's, Pam's Pizza, Shaggy's Snack Bar $General, Aubuchon Hardware, Hannaford Foods, NAPA
20(118)	US 7, VT 207, St Albans, **E** Chevrolet, Toyota, **W** Mobil/Subway/dsl, Sunoco Burger King, Dunkin', KFC/Taco Bell, McDonald's, Oriental Kitchen, Pizza Hut H, Advance Parts, AT&T, Aubuchon Hardware, Buick/GMC/Cadillac, Ford, Hannaford Foods, Jo-Ann Fabrics, Kinney Drug, PriceChopper Foods, TJ Maxx, URGENT CARE, Verizon, Walmart/Subway
19(114)	US 7, VT 36, VT 104, St Albans, **W** Mobil/dsl, Shell/dsl Dunkin', Subway La Quinta H, st police, vet
111mm	**both lanes, full facilities, info, litter barrels, petwalk, , , vending, wifi**
18(107)	US 7, VT 104A, Georgia Ctr, **E** Mobil/dsl, Shell/dsl GA Farmhouse Rest. $General, GA Auto Parts, repair, USPO
17(98)	US 2, US 7, **E** Mobil, Shell/dsl camping (4mi), **W** camping (6mi)
96mm	**weigh sta both lanes**
16(92)	US 7, US 2, Winooski, **E** Mobil Lighthouse Rest. Hampton Inn Costco/gas, CVS Drug, Osco Drug, Shaw's Foods, **W** Citgo, Shell/dsl Athens Diner, Burger King, McDonald's, Subway Motel 6, Quality Inn
15(91)	VT 15 (from nb no return), Winooski, **E** Days Inn, Handys Extended Stay Suites to St Michael's Coll, **W** Mobil/dsl, Shell
90mm	Winooski River
14(89)	US 2, Burlington, **E** Gulf, Mobil, Shell/dsl, Sunoco/dsl, Sunoco/repair, Valero Al's Cafe, Applebee's, Chicken Charlie's, Dukes Public House, Dunkin', Hana Japanese, IHOP, Leonardo's Pizza, McDonald's, Moe's SW Grill, Outback Steaks, Pulcinella's, Rotisserie, Starbucks, Subway, Wind Jammer Rest., Zachary's Pizza Anchorage Inn, Best Western+, Comfort Inn, Delta Hotel, Holiday Inn, Homewood Suites, La Quinta Aubuchon Hardware, Barnes&Noble, CVS, Hannaford Foods, Healthy Living Mkt, JC Penney, Jo-Ann Fabrics, Kohl's, Midas, PriceChopper, Rite Aid, Target, Trader Joe's, USPO, **W** Mobil/dsl, Shell DoubleTree H, Advance Parts, Michael's, PetCo, Staples, to UVT, Verizon
13(87)	I-189, to US 7, Burlington, **2 mi W on US 7 N** Citgo/dsl, Sunoco/dsl Buffalo Wild Wings, China Express, Chipotle, Five Guys, Starbucks, Subway $Tree, GNC, Hyundai/Subaru, Kinney Drug, PriceChopper Mkt, Shaw's Foods, TJ Maxx, USPO, Walgreens, **2 mi W on US 7 S** Gulf, Irving, Mobil/dsl, Shell/dsl, Sunoco Burger King, Chicago Grill, Denny's, Koto Japanese, Lakeview House Rest., McDonald's, Olive Garden, Panera Bread, Pauline's Cafe, Zen Garden Comfort Suites, Holiday Inn Express, North Star Motel, Travelodge Acura/Audi, Advance Parts, Buick/Cadillac/GMC, Chevrolet, Chrysler/Dodge, Ford, Hannaford Foods, Jeep, Lowe's, Nissan, O'Reilly Parts, Tire Whse, Toyota, URGENT CARE, Verizon, VW
12(84)	VT 2A, to US 2, to Essex Jct, Williston, **E** EVC, Mobil, Sunoco/Dunkin'/dsl 99 Rest., Chili's, Friendly's, Longhorn Steaks, Moe's SW Grill, Panera Bread, Starbucks, TX Roadhouse, VT Taphouse Fairfield, TownePlace Suites Best Buy, CVS Drug, Dick's, Hannaford Foods, Home Depot, Marshall's, Natural Provisions Mkt, Old Navy, Petsmart, Shaws Foods/Osco, st police, Staples, Town Fair Tire, Verizon, Walmart, **W** Courtyard, Sonesta Suites
82mm	**both lanes (7am-11pm), full facilities, litter barrels, petwalk, , , vending, WiFi**
11(79)	US 2, to VT 117, Richmond, **W** Mobil/dsl
67mm	**parking area/weigh sta sb**
66mm	**weigh sta nb**
10(64)	VT 100, to US 2, Waterbury, **E** Mobil/dsl, Shell/dsl Hong Kong Chinese, Thai Smile Best Western+, Fairfield Inn Shaws Foods/Osco Drug, TrueValue, **W** Citgo/dsl Maxi's Rest., Zachary's Pizza USPO
9(59)	US 2, to VT 100B, Middlesex, **W** EVC Red Hen Baking Co museum, st police
8(53)	US 2, Montpelier, **1 mi E** Citgo, Cumberland Farms /dsl, Mobil/dsl, Shell/dsl China Star, Domino's, Dunkin', Julio's, Sarducci's Rest. Capitol Plaza Hotel Aubuchon Hardware, camping (6mi), O'Reilly Parts, Rite Aid, Shaw's Foods, Sunoco/repair, to VT Coll
7(50)	VT 62, to US 302, Barre, **E** Tesla EVC, Irving/dsl Applebee's Comfort Suites, Hilltop Inn H, camping (7mi), Honda, JC Penney, Shaw's Foods, Subaru, Toyota, Walmart
6(47)	VT 63, to VT 14, S Barre, **4 mi E** camping, food, gas, info, lodging
5(43)	VT 64, to VT 12, VT 14, Williamstown, **6 mi E** camping, food, gas/dsl, lodging, **W** to Norwich U
41mm	1752 ft, highest elevation on I-89
34.5mm	**weigh sta both lanes**
4(31)	VT 66, Randolph, **E** RV camping (seasonal 1mi), **W** Mobil/Subway/dsl lodging (3mi), McDonald's H, RV camping (5mi)
30mm	**parking area sb**

BURLINGTON

MONTPELIER

= gas = food = lodging = other = rest stop Copyright 2020 - The Next EX

VT

INTERSTATE 89 Cont'd

Exit #	Services
3(22)	VT 107, Bethel, E Irving/dsl Village Pizza to Jos Smith Mon (8mi), 1 mi W Irving/dsl/LP st police, vet
14mm	White River
2(13)	VT 14, VT 132, Sharon, W Gulf/dsl Jos Smith Mon (6mi), Sharon Country Store, USPO
9mm	/weigh sta both lanes (7am-11pm), full facilities, info, litter barrels, , , vending, wi-fi
7mm	White River
1(4)	US 4, to Woodstock, Quechee, 3 mi E Fairfield Inn, Hampton Inn, Holiday Inn Express, Super 8
1mm	I-91, N to St Johnsbury, S to Brattleboro
0mm	Vermont/New Hampshire state line, Connecticut River

INTERSTATE 91

Exit #	Services
178mm	US/Canada Border, Vermont state line, I-91 begins/ends.
29(177)	US 5, Derby Line, E Dutyfree, 1 mi W Irving/Circle K/dsl city park
176.5mm	Welcome Ctr sb, full facilities, info, litter barrels, Midpoint between the Equator and N Pole, petwalk, , , wi-fi
28(172)	US 5, VT 105, Derby Ctr, E Gulf, repair, Sunoco/dsl/dsl Cow Palace Rest. auto/tire service, USPO, W Irving/Hoagie's Pizza, Mobil/dsl China Moon, Dunkin', McDonald's, Roasters Cafe, VT Pie&Pasta 4 Seasons , $General, $Tree, Advance Parts, Chrysler/Dodge/Jeep, Kinney Drug, O'Reilly Parts, PriceChopper Foods, Rite Aid, Shaw's Foods, st police, Verizon
27(170)	VT 191, to US 5, VT 105, Newport, 3 mi W , Border Patrol, camping, info
167mm	parking area/weigh sta both directions
26(161)	US 5, VT 58, Orleans, E Pit Stop, Sunoco/dsl Subway Family$, Thibaults Mkt, TrueValue, USPO
156.5mm	Barton River
25(156)	VT 16, Barton, 1 mi E Irving/Circle K/dsl Parson's Corner Rest. C&C Foods, Kinney Drug, O'Reilly Parts, USPO
154mm	parking area nb
150.5mm	highest elevation on I-91, 1856 ft
143mm	scenic overlook nb
141mm	sb, full facilities, info, litter barrels, ,
24(140)	VT 122, Wheelock, 2 mi E food, gas, lodging
23(137)	US 5, to VT 114, Lyndonville, E Irving/dsl, Mobil/Dunkin' Hoagie's Pizza, Lyndon Buffet, McDonald's, Miss Lyndonville Diner, Pizza Man Colonnade Inn $General, CarQuest, Kinney Drug, Rite Aid, TrueValue, White Mkt Foods, W Lyndon Motel
22(132)	to US 5, St Johnsbury, 1-2 mi E Sunoco/dsl KFC/Taco Bell, Kham's Cuisine, Pizza Hut , Buick/GMC, Chrysler/Dodge/Jeep, Kinney Drug, O'Reilly Parts, PriceChopper Foods, repair, Subaru
21(131)	US 2, to VT 15, St Johnsbury, 1-2 mi E services
20(129)	US 5, to US 2, St Johnsbury, E Mobil, Sunoco/dsl, Valero/dsl Anthony's Diner, Domino's, Dunkin', East Garden Chinese, Subway, Winegate Rest. welcome ctr, Family$, Kevin's Repair, NAPA, Rite Aid, W Comfort Inn st police
19(128)	I-93 S to Littleton NH
122mm	scenic view nb
18(121)	to US 5, Barnet, E camping (5mi), W camping (5mi)
115mm	parking area sb
113mm	parking area nb
17(110)	US 302, to US 5, Wells River, NH, E (5mi), W Mobil/P&H Trkstp/rest./dsl/scales/24hr camping (9mi)
100mm	nb, full facilities, info, litter barrels, petwalk, , sb parking area
16(98)	VT 25, to US 5, Bradford, E Mobil/dsl/LP/café Hun Bear Grill Bradford Motel Family$, Hannaford Foo Kinney Drug, NAPA, O'Reilly Parts, Pierson Farm Mkt, W st po
15(92)	Fairlee, E Irving/dsl, Mobil/7-11, Sunoco/dsl Fair Diner, Lunchbox Deli $General, USPO, Wings Mkt/d W golf
14(84)	VT 113, to US 5, Thetford, 1 mi E food, Rest-n-Nest Camping, W camping
13(75)	US 5, VT 10a, Hanover, NH, E , to Dartmouth, W go Norwich Inn Rest. auto service, USPO
12(72)	US 5, White River Jct, Wilder, E Cumberland Farms/dsl, Mo
11(71)	US 5, White River Jct, E Mobil/dsl, Shell/Subway/dsl China Moon, Crossroads Country Café, McDonald's Comf Inn Chevrolet, Hyundai, Subaru, Toyota, USPO, W Sunoco/dsl Dunkin' Fairfield Inn, Hampton Inn, Holic Inn Express, Super 8, White River Inn
10N(70)	I-89 N, to Montpelier
10S	I-89 S, to NH,
68mm	Welcome Ctr sb, full facilities, weigh sta nb
9(60)	US 5, VT 12, Hartland, E , W Mobil (1mi) Hartland Diner
8(51)	US 5, VT 12, VT 131, Ascutney, E Irving/Subway, Sunoco/dsl Ascutney House Rest. , Getaway Camping (2m USPO
7(42)	US 5, VT 106, VT 11, Springfield, W Irving/Circle K/Subway/dsl/scales/24hr Holiday Inn Express (5mi)
39mm	weigh sta both lanes, weigh sta sb
6(34)	US 5, VT 103, to Bellows Falls, Rockingham, E Shell/c Leslie's Rest. Rodeway Inn, W Sunoco/dsl
5(29)	VT 121, to US 5, to Bellows Falls, Westminster, 3 mi E food, ga lodging,
24mm	parking area both lanes
22mm	weigh sta sb
20mm	weigh sta nb
4(18)	US 5, Putney, E Putney Inn/rest., W Rod's/repair, Sunoco/dsl/24hr Putney Diner, Putney Food Coop/deli Putney Gen Store/deli, USPO
3(11)	US 5, VT 9 E, Brattleboro, E Agway/dsl, Citgo/dsl, Mobil/dsl, Sunoco 99 Rest., China Buffet, Dunkin', Fast Eddy Caf KFC, McDonald's, Panda North, Ramunto's Brick Oven, Taco Bell, Village Pizza, Wendy's Black Mtn Inn, Colonial Mote Comfort Inn, Covered Bridge Inn, Hampton Inn, Holiday Ir Express, Motel 6, Quality Inn Advance Parts, Aldi Food AT&T, Buick/Chevrolet/GMC, Chrysler/Dodge/Jeep, Family Ford, GNC, Hannaford Foods, O'Reilly Parts, Staples, Subaru TrueValue, URGENT CARE, USPO, Verizon
2(9)	VT 9 W, to rd 30, Brattleboro, W VT Country Deli Marlboro Coll
1(7)	US 5, Brattleboro, E Gulf/dsl, Irving/Circle K/dsl, Mobil Dunkin', Shell/Subway/dsl Domino's, FC Chinese, VT In Pizza EconoLodge , $Tree, PriceChopper Mkt, Rite Aid, to Ft Dummer SP, vet, Walgreens
6mm	Welcome Ctr nb, full facilities, info, litter barrels, petwalk , , playground, vending, wi-fi
0mm	Vermont/Massachusetts state line

DERBY CTR

ST JOHNSBURY

BRATTLEBORO

INTERSTATE 93

See New Hampshire Interstate 93

VIRGINIA

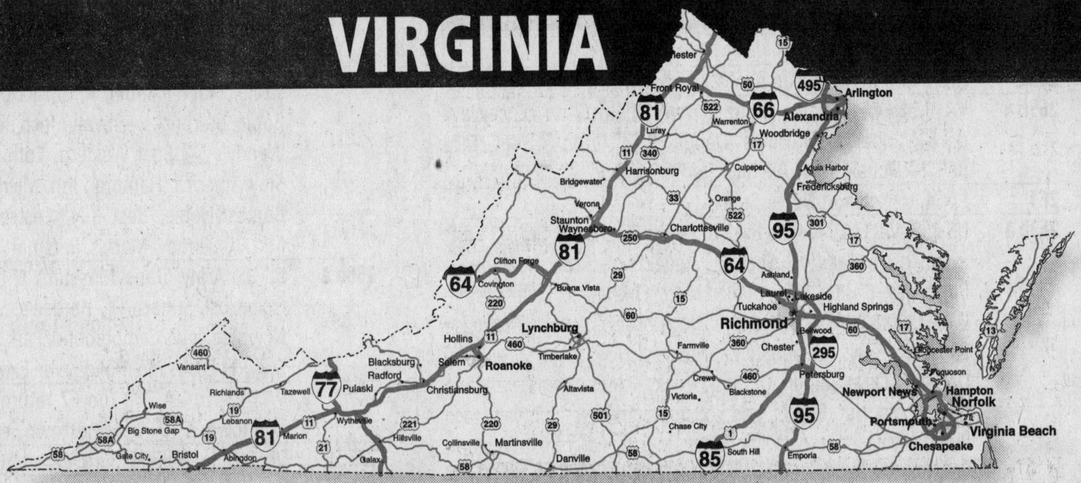

INTERSTATE 64

Exit #	Services
299b a	I-264 E, to Portsmouth. **I-64 begins/ends on I-264.**
297	US 13, US 460, Military Hwy, N 7-11, Exxon McDonald's, Papa John's
296b a	US 17, to Portsmouth, N 7-11 Hardee's, McDonald's, Papa John's, Pizza Hut, Subway, Zino's Cafe Comfort Inn $General, Food Lion, USPO, vet
294mm	S Br Elizabeth River
292	VA 190, to VA 104 (from eb, no EZ return), Dominion Blvd, S 7-11 #1 China, Burger King, Royal China, Subway Family$, Food Lion
291b a	I-464 N, VA 104 S, to Elizabeth City, Outer Banks, same services as 292
290b a	VA 168, Battlefield Blvd, to Nag's Head, Manteo, N Burger King Woodspring Suites $General, BigLots, Kroger, Merchant's Auto Ctr, NAPA, S 7-11, BP/DQ, Shell Applebee's, Baskin-Robbins, Burger King, Carrabba's, Chick-fil-A, ChuckECheese's, CookOut, Denny's, Dunkin', Five Guys, Golden Corral, Grand China Buffet, Hardee's, Hunan Wok, Jade Garden, Little Caesar's, Panda Express, Sonic, Starbucks, Taco Bell, TGIFriday's, Tropical Smoothie Café, TX Roadhouse, Waffle House, Wendy's, Wildwing Café Hampton Inn, InTown Suites, Quality Inn, Studios For Less H, $Tree, AT&T, Goodyear/auto, Home Depot, Kohl's, Lowe's, Nissan, Rite Aid, Sam's Club/gas, USPO, vet, Walgreens, Walmart
289b a	Greenbrier Pkwy, N 7-11, Citgo/dsl, WaWa/dsl Burger King, McDonald's, Subway, Taco Bell, Wendy's Extended Stay America, Hampton Inn, Holiday Inn Express, Marriott, Red Roof Inn, Staybridge Suites, Wingate Inn Acura, auto repair, Chevrolet, Chrysler/Jeep, Dodge, Ford, GMC, Hyundai, JoAnn Fabrics, Kia, Lincoln, Mazda, Toyota, U-Haul, vet, VW, S 7-11 Abuelo's Mexican, Baker's Crust, Boston Mkt, Buffalo Wild Wings, Chipotle, Coldstone, Cracker Barrel, Fazoli's, Firehouse Subs, Hooters, Jason's Deli, Jersey Mike's Subs, Jimmy John's, Joe's Crabshack, Kyoto Japanese, Los Burritos, McDonald's, Moe's SW, Olive Garden, Panera Bread, Pizza Hut, Pop's Diner, Qdoba, Red Robin, Ruby Tuesday, Smokey Bones BBQ, Starbucks, Subway, Tropical Smoothie, Zero's Subs, Zoe's Kitchen Aloft Hotel, Comfort Suites, Courtyard, Extended Stay, Fairfield Inn, Hilton Garden, Homewood Suites, Residence Inn, SpringHill Suites, Sun Suites AT&T, Barnes&Noble, Best Buy, Dillard's, Food Lion, Harris Teeter, Macy's, Marshall's, Michael's, Office Depot, Old Navy, Petsmart, Ross, Steinmart, Target, TJ Maxx, Verizon, Walgreens
286b a	Indian River Rd, N BP/dsl, Gulf, SkyMart/dsl, Speedway/dsl Dunkin', Golden China, Hardee's CVS, S Exxon/dsl CookOut, Ellen's BBQ, Oriental Cuisine, Oriental Cuisine, Waffle House 7-11
285mm	E Branch Elizabeth River
284a	I-264, to Norfolk, to VA Beach (exits left from eb)
284b	Newtown Rd
282	US 13, Northampton Blvd, N Citgo/dsl Krispy Kreme, McDonald's, Starbucks, Taco Bell, Wendy's Quality Inn, Sleep Inn to Chesapeake Bay Br Tunnel
281	VA 165, Military Hwy (no EZ eb return), N Shell/dsl EconoLodge Aamco, Chysler/Dodge/Jeep, Fiat, S 7-11, Citgo Burger King, Chick-fil-A, CookOut, Firehouse Subs, Hooters, IHOP, Jersey Mike's Subs, Jimmy John's, KFC, Little Caesar's, Logan's Roadhouse, Max&Erma's, Panera Bread, Qdoba, Ruby Tuesday, Sonic, Starbucks, Taco Bell, Wendy's Candlewood Suites, Days Inn, Doubletree, Hampton Inn, Holiday Inn, Holiday Inn Express, InTown Suites, La Quinta, Residence Inn BJ's Whse/dsl, FarmFresh Foods, Food Lion, GNC, Home Depot, Lowe's, Nissan, Pep Boys, Petco, Petsmart, Target, TJ Maxx, Verizon, Walgreens, Walmart/Subway
279	Norview Ave, N WaWa/dsl China House, Franco's Italian, Golden Corral, Pizza Hut, Wendy's $General, $Tree, 7-11/dsl, Food Lion, Tire City, to & botanical garden
278	VA 194 S (no EZ return)
277b a	VA 168, to Tidewater Dr, N 7-11, Shell Bojangles, Domino's, Fuddrucker's, Hardee's, Ruby Tuesday Advance Parts, Food Lion, Walmart/Subway, S Honda
276c	to US 460 W, VA 165, Little Creek Rd, (from wb only), N Race Coast/dsl, S BP, Shell Firehouse Subs, KFC, McDonald's, Moe's SW, Papa John's, Starbucks, Taco Bell, Wendy's AutoZone, FarmFresh Foods, GNC, Harris Teeter, Kroger, Rite Aid, USPO, Walgreens
276b a	I-564 to Naval Base (exits left from wb)
274	Bay Ave (from wb), S to Naval Air Sta
273	US 60, 4th View St, Oceanview, N 7-11/dsl Economy Inn, Motel 6 Oceanview Pier
272	W Ocean View Ave, N Willoughby Seafood, S Sunset Grill
270mm	Chesapeake Bay Tunnel
269mm	**weigh sta eb**
268	VA 169 E, to Buckroe Beach, Ft Monroe, N Citgo Hardee's, McDonald's, S to VA Air&Space Ctr
267	US 60, to VA 143, Settlers Ldg Rd, S Golden City Chinese, Subway, Tropical Smoothie H, to Hampton U

= gas = food = lodging = other = rest stop

VA

HAMPTON

WILLIAMSBURG

INTERSTATE 64 Cont'd

Exit #	Services
265c	(from eb), to Armistead Ave, N to Langley AFB
265b a	VA 134, VA 167, to La Salle Ave, N Citgo, RaceWay/dsl Super 8 Home Depot, S Citgo KFC/Taco Bell, McDonald's Advance Parts, Family$
264	I-664, to Newport News, Suffolk
263b a	US 258, VA 134, Mercury Blvd, to James River Br, N 7-11, BP, Exxon/dsl, Miller's/dsl, Shell Abuelo's Mexican, Applebee's, Bojangles, Boston Mkt, Burger King, Chick-fil-A, Chili's, China Wok, Chipotle Mexican, Denny's, Dog House, El Azteca, Firehouse Subs, Five Guys, Golden Corral, Hooters, IHOP, Jason's Deli, McDonald's, Olive Garden, Outback Steaks, Panera Bread, Parklane Rest., Pizza Hut, Rally's, Red Lobster, Starbucks, Subway, Taco Bell, Tokyo Japanese, Waffle House, Wendy's Best Western, Courtyard, Days Inn, Embassy Suites, Holiday Inn Express, Quality Inn, Red Roof Inn $Tree, AT&T, Barnes&Noble, Chevrolet/Mazda, FarmFresh Foods, Food Lion, Ford, GNC, Goodyear/auto, JC Penney, Jo-Ann Fabrics, Marshall's, Michael's, NAPA, Nissan, Office Depot, PetCo, Ross, Target, U-Haul, USPO, Verizon, Volvo, Walgreens, Walmart, S Citgo/dsl, Miller's/dsl, WaWa/dsl Burritos Mexican, Chick-fil-A, CiCi's Pizza, Coldstone, Cracker Barrel, Domino's, Dunkin', Joe's Crabshack, La Parrilla, Little Caesar's, Longhorn Steaks, Pizza Hut, Rita's, Sonic, Steak'n Shake, Waffle House, Zaxby's Ambassador Inn Suites, Hilton Garden, InTown Suites, Relax Inn, SpringHill Suites $General, 7-11, Aamco, Advance Parts, BassPro Shop, BigLots, BJ's Whse/Subway/gas, CVS Drug, Firestone/auto, Lowe's, Office Depot, PepBoys, Toyota, Walmart Mkt
262	VA 134, Magruder Blvd (from wb, no EZ return), N 7-11, Exxon Country Inn&Suites, Suburban Lodge Audi, Hyundai, Mercedes
261b a	Center Pkwy, to Hampton Roads, N Candlewood Suites, Hampton Inn (2mi), S 7-11, Shell Anna's Italian, ChuckECheese's, Fortune Garden Chinese, Gus's NY Pizza, McDonald's, Peking Chinese, Pizza Hut/Taco Bell, Plaza Azteca, Ruby Tuesday, Subway $Tree, FarmFresh Foods, Food Lion, GNC, Rite Aid, TJMaxx
258b a	US 17, J Clyde Morris Blvd, N BP, Shell/dsl Domino's, New China, Waffle House BudgetLodge, Country Inn&Suites, Holiday Inn Express, Host Inn, PointPlaza Hotel, Quality Inn 7-11, Advance Parts, Family$, Food Lion, S Kangaroo, WaWa/dsl Angelo's Steaks, Burger King, DQ, KFC/Taco Bell, McDonald's, Papa John's, Starbucks, Subway, Vinny's Pizza, Wendy's Motel 6 H, museum, Rite Aid, Subaru, VW
256b a	Victory Blvd, Oyster Point Rd, N Kangaroo/dsl, Murphy USA/dsl Arby's, Burger King, Chick-fil-A, China Ocean, Hardee's, McDonald's, Panda Express, Pizza Hut, Ruby Tuesday, Saisaki Asian, Sonic, Starbucks, Subway, Three Amigos Mexican, TX Roadhouse, Uno Grill CandleWood Suites, Courtyard, Hampton Inn, Hilton Garden, Staybridge Suites, TownePlace Suites $Tree, FarmFresh Foods, GNC, Goodyear/auto, Kroger, Walgreens, Walmart, S Crestwood Suites, Jameson Inn
255b a	VA 143, to Jefferson Ave, N Exxon/dsl, Shell/dsl Chili's, CookOut, Donato's Pizza, Firehouse Subs, Five Guys, Golden Corral, HoneyBaked Ham, Hooters, Jason's Deli, Longhorn Steaks, McDonald's, Moe's SW Grill, Olive Garden, Panera Bread, Papa John's, Red City Buffet, Red Lobster, Smokey Bones BBQ, Sonic, Starbucks Comfort Suites H, Acura, Buick/Cadillac/GMC, Chrysler/Dodge/Jeep, FarmFresh Foods/deli, Fiat, GNC, Home Depot, Kohl's, Lowe's, Michael's, PetCo, Ross, Sam's Club/gas, TJ Maxx, Trader Joe's, Tuesday Morning,
255b a	Continued Walgreens, Walmart, S Applebee's, Buffalo Wild Win Carrabba's, Cheddar's, Chick-fil-A, Chipotle Mexican, Co stone, Cracker Barrel, KFC, McDonald's, Outback Steaks, R Robin, Starbucks, Subway, Taco Bell, TGIFriday's, Waffle Hou Wendy's Best Western, Comfort Inn, Courtyard, Extend Stay America, Hampton Inn, Microtel, Residence Inn 7-1 Barnes&Noble, Best Buy, Costco/dsl, Dick's, Dillard's, Fre Mkt, JC Penney, Macy's, Petsmart, Target, Verizon, World Mk
250b a	to US Army Trans Museum, N 7-11/gas, Dodge's Sto Exxon/dsl, Sunoco Hardee's, Subway B&L Auto Rep Newport News Campground/Park (1mi), to Yorktown Victory C S Ft Eustis Inn, Holiday Inn Express, Mulberry Inn 7-11
247	VA 143, to VA 238 (no EZ return wb), N 7-11/gas Yorktown, S to Jamestown Settlement
243	VA 143, to Williamsburg, exits left from wb, S same as 242a
242b a	VA 199, to US 60, to Williamsburg, N Wyndham G den Best Buy, Dick's, Kohl's, Target, to Yorktown NHS, w ter funpark, **1 mi** S 7-11/gas, Sunoco, WaWa/dsl C na's Cuisine, Doraldo's Italian, KFC, McDonald's, Sportsma Grille, Starbucks, Subway, Taco Bell, Wendy's, Whaling Rest. Country Inn&Suites, Courtyard, Quality Inn Bus Gardens, to Jamestown NHS, to William&Mary Coll
238	VA 143, to Colonial Williamsburg, Camp Peary, **2-3 mi** S **US 60** Exxon/7-11, Shell Aberdeen Barn Rest., A plebee's, Arby's, Chili's, Chipotle Mexican, Cracker Barrel, D Firehouse Subs, Five Guys, Golden Corral, Hooters, IHOP, Je ferson Steaks, KFC, Kyoto, McDonald's, Outback Steaks, Pa cake House, Pizza Hut, Plaza Azteca, Red Hot&Blue, Sal's Res Seafare Rest., Smokehouse Grill, Subway, Taco Bell, Uno Gril Wendy's Best Inn, Best Western, Comfort Inn, Country I n&Suites, Days Inn, EconoLodge, Embassy Suites, Fairfield In Hampton Inn, Hampton Inn, Hilton Garden, Holiday Inn Expres Holiday Inn/rest., Homewood Suites, La Quinta, Quality In Residence Inn, Sleep Inn, SpringHill Suites, Travelodge Anvil Camping (4mi), CVS Drug, Goodyear/auto
234	VA 646, to Lightfoot, **1-2 mi** N KOA, **2-3 mi** S Exxo dsl, Shell/dsl Burger King, Chick-fil-A, China Wok, Har ee's, IHOP, McDonald's, Sonic, Starbucks, Subway Gre Wolf Lodge, Holiday Inn Express, Super 8 H, $Tree, Fo Home Depot, Lowe's, PetCo, Ross, Toyota, USPO, Walmart, W liamsburg Campark
231b a	VA 607, to Norge, Croaker, N 7-11/gas to York Riv SP, **1-3 mi** S **on US 60** Shell/dsl Candle Light Kitc en, China Star, Daddy-O's Pizza, Jimmy's Grill, Pizza H EconoLodge American Heritage RV Park, CVS Dru FarmFresh Deli/gas, Food Lion, Honda, Hyundai, USPO
227	VA 30, to US 60, to West Point, Toano, S Shell/dsl, Sta Subway/dsl McDonald's
220	VA 33 E, to West Point, N Mobil/dsl
214	VA 155, to New Kent, Providence Forge, S Exxon/DC dsl Antonio's Pizza, Tops China
213mm	**both lanes, full facilities, litter barrels, petwalk, vending**
211	VA 106, to Talleysville, to James River Plantations, S Loves/Arby's/dsl/scales/24hr, Pilot/Subway/dsl/scales 24hr Burger King
205	VA 33, VA 249, to US 60, Bottoms Bridge, Quinton, N Exx on/dsl, Star Express, Valero Julio's Mexican, Maria's Ita ian, Panda Garden, Pizza Hut, Subway, Wendy's Food Lio Verizon, S FasMart, Shell/dsl Bojangle's, McDonald Food Lion, Rite Aid

INTERSTATE 64 Cont'd

Exit #	Services
204mm	Chickahominy River
203mm	**weigh sta both lanes**
200	I-295, N to Washington, S to Rocky Mount, to US 60
197b a	VA 156, Airport Dr, to Highland Springs, **N** Shell/dsl, Valero Antonio's Pizza, Domino's, Hardee's, Subway, Tops China $General, 7-11, Advance Parts, CVS Drug, Farmers Foods, **S** BP, Chubby's/dsl, Shell/7-11, WaWa Arby's, Burger King, Mexico Rest., Pizza Hut, Roberto's Italian, The Patron, Waffle House All Day Inn, Best Value Inn, Courtyard, EconoLodge, Hampton Inn, Hilton Garden, Holiday Inn, Holiday Inn Express, Homewood Suites, Microtel, Motel 6, Quality Inn, Red Roof Inn, Super 8 to
195	Laburnum Ave, **N** auto repair, **S** 7-11, Exxon, WaWa/dsl Applebee's, Capt D's, Chick-fil-A, China King, CiCi's Pizza, CookOut, Cracker Barrel, Firehouse Subs, Five Guys, Hardee's, IHOP, KFC, Little Caesar's, Longhorn Steaks, McDonald's, Olive Garden, Panera Bread, Papa John's, Popeye's, Qdoba Mexican, Red Lobster, Steak'n Shake, Subway, Taco Bell, TGIFriday's, Wendy's Hyatt Place, Sheraton $General, $Tree, AT&T, CarQuest, CVS Drug, GNC, JC Penney, Kroger, Lowe's, Michael's, Petsmart, Publix, Target, Walgreens
193b a	VA 33, Nine Mile Rd, **N** Exxon/Subway/dsl, Sunoco/dsl PepBoys, **S** H
192	US 360, to Mechanicsville, **N** Exxon/dsl, Shell McDonald's Tuffy Repair, **S** Shell, Valero
190	I-95 S, to Petersburg, 5th St. **S** Hilton, Marriott coliseum, st capitol
I-64/I-95 run together, see VA I-95 exits 76-78.	
187	I-95 N (exits left from eb), to Washington.
186	I-195, to Powhite Pkwy, from wb, Richmond
185b a	US 33, Staples Mill Rd, Dickens Rd
183c	from wb, US 250 W, Broad St, Glenside Dr N, same as exit 183
183b a	US 250, Broad St E, Glenside Dr S., **N** Sheetz/dsl McDonald's, Mission BBQ, Nanking, Olive Garden, Subway, Taco Bell, TGIFriday's, Waffle House Best Western, Econolodge/Rodeway, Embassy Suites, Hampton Inn, Knights Inn, Residence Inn, Super 8, Woodspring Suites AutoZone, Honda, vet, Volvo, **S** Chipotle, Denny's, Jersey Mike's, O'Charley's, Plaza Azteca, Starbucks Candlewood Suites, Courtyard, Westin H, Aldi Foods, Home Depot, Target, to U of Richmond, vet, Walmart
181b a	Parham Rd, **N** Citgo, Exxon Chrysler/Dodge/Jeep
180	Gaskins Rd, **N** BP, Shell/dsl Applebee's, Coldstone, Cracker Barrel, Dickey's BBQ, Golden Corral, IHOP, Kickback Jack's Rest., McDonald's, O'Charley's, Pizza Hut, Starbucks, Subway, Taco Bell 7-11, Exxon, Fairfield Inn, Holiday Inn Express, Mapco, SpringHill Suites $Tree, Advance Parts, AutoZone, Costco/gas, Goodyear/auto, Kroger/gas, Lowe's, Martin's Foods, Mazda, Michael's, Sam's Club/gas, Tesla
178b a	US 250, Broad St, Short Pump, **N** 7-11, Exxon, Wawa/dsl Blaze Pizza, BurgerWorks, Capital Alehouse, Chipotle Mexican, Corner Bakery Cafe, DQ, Dunkin', Firehouse Subs, Five Guys, Hondo's Rest., Joey's Hotdogs, Leonardo's Pizza, Moe's SW Grill, Noodles, Panera Bread, Potbelly, Silver Diner, Starbucks, Taziki's Comfort Suites, Courtyard, Extended Stay America, Hampton Inn, Hilton Garden, Homestead Suites, Hyatt Place, Residence Inn CarMax, CVS Drug, Firestone/auto, Ford, Marshall's, Ross, Verizon, **S** 7-11, Shell Arby's, Bertucci's, BJ's Rest., Bonefish Grill, Buffalo Wild Wings, Burger King, Capt D's, Carolina Alehouse, Carrabba's, Cheesecake Factory,

RICHMOND

CHARLOTTESVILLE

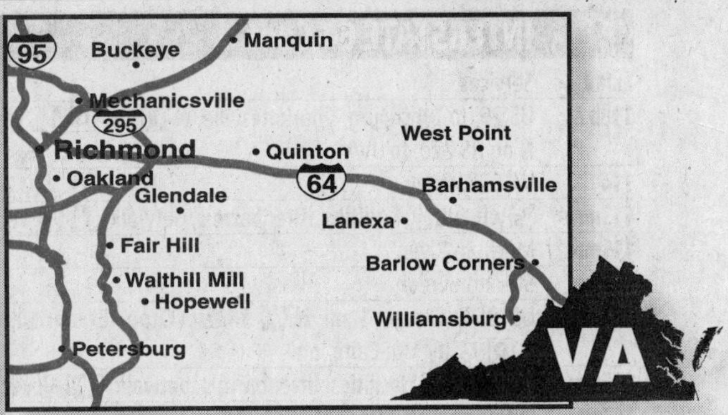

Exit #	Services
178b a	Continued Chick-fil-A, Chili's, Chipotle Mexican, Chuy's Mexican, Dave&Buster's, Domino's, Genghis Grill, HoneyBaked Ham, Jason's Deli, Jersey Mike's Subs, Jimmy John's, Kanpai, KFC, Kona Grill, LJSilver, Longhorn Steaks, Maggiano's Italian, McDonald's, Olive Garden, Panda Express, Panera Bread, Plaza Azteca, Qdoba, Shula's Steaks, Sonic, Starbucks, Taco Bell, TGIFriday's, Wendy's Candlewood Suites, Hilton, Hyatt House, Wingate Inn $Tree, AT&T, Barnes&Noble, Best Buy, Buick/Chevrolet/GMC, CarQuest, Dick's, Dillard's, GNC, Hobby Lobby, Home Depot, Kohl's, Kroger, Lowe's, Macy's, Martin's Foods, Nissan, Nordstrom, NTB, Petco, Petsmart, REI, Staples, Steinmart, Target, Tom Leonard's Mkt, Trader Joe's, Verizon, Walmart, Whole Foods Mkt, World Mkt
177	I-295, to I-95 N to Washington, to Norfolk, VA Beach, Williamsburg
175	VA 288, Chesterfield
173	VA 623, to Rockville, Manakin, **0-2 mi S** Exxon/dsl, Shell/dsl, Valero/Subway/dsl McDonald's, Sunset Grill, Taco Bell $General, Food Lion, vet
169mm	**both lanes, full facilities, litter barrels, petwalk, , , vending**
167	VA 617, to Goochland, Oilville, **N** Exxon/dsl, **S** BP/dsl
159	US 522, to Goochland, Gum Spring, **N** Exxon/dsl, **S** BP/DQ/dsl, Citgo
152	VA 629, Hadensville, **1 mi S** BP, Liberty
148	VA 605, Shannon Hill
143	VA 208, to Louisa, Ferncliff, **N** Small Country Camping (7mi), **S** Citgo/dsl, Exxon/dsl
136	US 15, to Gordonsville, Zion Crossroads, **N** Sheetz/dsl Arby's, Dunkin', IHOP, Lelo's Pizza, Popeye's, Subway, Taco Bell, Wendy's Best Western+ Advance Parts, Lowe's, Verizon, Walmart, **S** BP/McDonald's/dsl/24hr, Exxon/Burger King/dsl, Shell/dsl/scales Crescent Rest.
129	VA 616, Keswick, Boyd Tavern
124	US 250, to Shadwell, **2 mi N** BP, Exxon, Mobil/dsl, Shell, Speedway Applebee's, Bojangle's, Burger King, Chick-fil-A, Chipotle, Dunkin', Guadalajara Mexican, Hardee's, Jersey Mike's, Jimmy John's, McDonald's, Shadwell's Rest., Starbucks, Taco Bell, TipTop Rest., Wendy's Hilton Garden H, Audi/VW, BMW, CarMax, Ford, Giant Foods, Kia, Mercedes, Porsche, Rite Aid, Toyota, **S** Comfort Inn
123mm	Rivanna River
121	VA 20, to Charlottesville, Scottsville, **N** BP/dsl, **S** KOA (10mi), to Monticello
120	VA 631, 5th St, to Charlottesville, **N** Exxon/dsl, Sunoco/dsl Burger King, Domino's, Hardee's, Subway, Taco Bell, Waffle House Holiday Inn, Sleep Inn CVS Drug, Family$, Food Lion

VA

= gas = food = lodging = other = rest stop

VA

INTERSTATE 64 Cont'd

WAYNESBORO

Exit #	Services
118b a	US 29, to Lynchburg, Charlottesville, N BP, services N on US 220, to UVA
114	VA 637, to Ivy
113mm	wb, full facilities, litter barrels, petwalk, , vending
111mm	Mechum River
108mm	Stockton Creek
107	US 250, Crozet, 1 mi N BP/dsl, Citgo, Exxon/dsl, 1 mi S Misty Mtn Camping
105mm	eb, full facilities, litter barrels, petwalk, , vending
104mm	scenic area eb, litter barrels, no truck or buses
100mm	scenic area eb, hist marker, litter barrels, no truck or buses
99	US 250, to Waynesboro, Afton, N Colony Motel Skyline Drive, to Blue Ridge Pkwy, to Shenandoah NP, S Afton Inn
96	VA 622, to Lyndhurst, Waynesboro, 3 mi N Shell, Speedway Quality Inn Waynesboro Camping
95mm	South River
94	US 340, to Stuarts Draft, Waynesboro, N 7-11/dsl, Exxon/dsl Applebee's, Buffalo Wild Wings, Cracker Barrel, Five Guys, Golden Corral, KFC, Outback Steaks, Panera Bread, Pizza Hut, Plaza Azteca, Ruby Tuesday, Silk Road Rest., Sonic, Starbucks, Waffle House, Wendy's Best Western+, Comfort Inn, Days Inn, Holiday Inn Express, Residence Inn, Super 8 , Home Depot, Lowe's, Martin's Food/gas, Verizon, vet, Walmart, Waynesboro N 340 Camping (9mi), S Mobil/dsl Chick-fil-A, McAlister's Deli, McDonald's Aldi Foods, AT&T, Books-A-Million, GNC, Kohl's, Michael's, Petsmart, Ross, Target
91	Va 608, to Stuarts Draft, Fishersville, N Citgo/Subway (1mi), Shell/dsl Hampton Inn , Eaver's Tires, S Sheetz/dsl McDonald's, Wendy's Shenadoah Acres Camping (8mi), Walnut Hills Camping (9mi)
89mm	Christians Creek
87	I-81, N to Harrisonburg, S to Roanoke

LEXINGTON

I-64 and I-81 run together 20 miles. See I-81, exits 195-220.

Exit #	Services
55	US 11, to VA 39, N Exxon Burger King, Crystal Chinese, Naples Pizza, Ruby Tuesday, Waffle House Best Western+, Sleep Inn, Super 8, Wingate Inn $Tree, Ford, Lowe's, Stonewall Jackson Museum, Verizon, Walmart, S Marathon/7-11/Subway, Mobil/DQ/dsl Applebee's, Country Cookin Best Western, Comfort Inn, Country Inn&Suites, Holiday Inn Express, Motel 6
50	US 60, rd 623, to Kerrs Creek, Lexington
43	rd 780, to Goshen
35	VA 269, rd 850, Longdale Furnace
33mm	truck eb
29	VA 269, VA 42 E, S Sunoco/dsl
27	US 60 W, US 220 S, VA 629, Clifton Forge, N to Douthat SP, S BP/dsl, Exxon Bella Pizza, Pizza Hut (2mi) CVS Drug, Family$, Kroger
24	US 60, US 220, Clifton Forge, 1 mi S Shell/dsl DQ, Hardee's auto repair
21	to rd 696, Low Moor, N Love's/McDonald's/Subway/dsl/scales/24hr, S Exxon Penny's Diner Travelodge
16	US 60 W, US 220 N, to Hot Springs, Covington, N BP/Subway/dsl, Exxon/dsl, Shell Burger King, Cucci's, San Juan Mexican, Western Sizzlin Best Value Inn, Hampton Inn, Magnuson Hotel, Pinehurst Hotel to ski area, S McDonald's Compare Inn, Taco Bell
14	VA 154, to Hot Springs, Covington, N Citgo, Exxon/Arby's KFC, LJ Silver, Subway, Wendy's $General, Advance Parts,

COVINGTON

Exit #	Services
14	Continued AutoZone, CVS Drug, Family$, Food Lion, URGENT CARE, V izon, S Applebee's, China House, Trani's Grille $Tr Chevrolet, Walmart
10	US 60 E, VA 159 S, Callaghan, S Marathon/dsl/LP
7	rd 661
2.5mm	**Welcome Ctr eb, full facilities, litter barrels, no trucks, p walk, ,**
1	Jerry's Run Trail, N to Allegheny Trail
0mm	Virginia/West Virginia state line

INTERSTATE 66

DC AREA

Exit #	Services
77mm	Constitution Ave, to Lincoln Mem. **I-66 begins/ends in Was ington, DC.**
76mm	Potomac River, T Roosevelt Memorial Bridge
75	US 50 W (from eb), to Arlington Blvd, G Wash Pkwy, I-395, US S Iwo Jima Mon
73	US 29, Lee Hwy, Key Bridge, to Rosslyn, N Marric S Holiday Inn
72	to US 29, Lee Hwy, Spout Run Pkwy (from eb, no EZ retur N Shell Virginia Inn, S Starbucks, Tarbouch G CVS Drug, Giant Foods, Walgreens
71	VA 120, Glebe Rd (no EZ return from wb), N S Sunoco Booeymonger Grill, IHOP, Melting Pot, Chang's Comfort Inn, Holiday Inn
69	US 29, Sycamore St, Falls Church, N Exxon/7- S EconoLodge vet
68	Westmoreland St (from eb), same as 69
67	to I-495 N (from wb), to Baltimore, Dulles Airport
66b a	VA 7, Leesburg Pike, to Tysons Corner, Falls Church, N E on, Sunoco China King, Jason's Deli, Ledo Pizza, Noodles Co, Starbucks, Subway, Tara Thai 7-11, Trader Joe's, Ve zon, Whole Foods Mkt, S Citgo Baja Fresh, Domino Jimmy John's, McDonald's, Starbucks, Subway CVS Dru Giant Foods, GNC, Kia, Staples, vet, Volvo
64b a	I-495 S, to Richmond
62	VA 243, Nutley St, to Vienna, S Citgo Baja Fresh, Do ino's, McDonald's, Starbucks, Subway CVS Drug, Michae Safeway Foods/gas, Walgreens
60	VA 123, to Fairfax, S Exxon, Shell, Sunoco 29 Din Denny's, Freddy's Steakburgers, Fuddruckers, Hooters, McDo ald's, Outback Steaks, Panera Bread, Papa John's, Red Lobst Smashburger, Subway Best Western, Hampton Inn, Ho day Inn Express, Residence Inn Chevrolet, CVS Drug, K Mazda, Rite Aid, Subaru, to George Mason U, Toyota
57b a	US 50, to Dulles Airport, N Brio Tuscan, Cheesecake Fac ry Extended Stay America, Marriott access to same 55, JC Penney, Lord&Taylor, Macy's, S BP, Shell/dsl C potle, Chuy's, Jimmy John's, McDonald's, Wendy's Comf Inn/rest., Courtyard, SpringHill Suites AT&T, Ford, Gia Foods, Honda, Nissan, NRA Museum, VW/Volvo, Walmart
55	Fairfax Co Pkwy, to US 29, N Exxon, Sunoco Applebe Blue Iguana Café, Burger King, Cantina Italiana, Chick-fil-A, C potle, Dunkin', Guapo's, Jason's Deli, Jersey Mike's, Joe's Cra shack, Logan's Roadhouse, McDonald's, Noodles&Co, Olive Ga den, Pizza Hut, Red Robin, Starbucks, Subway, Taco Bell, Wend Hyatt Regency, Residence Inn , Best Buy, BJ's Whs gas, Dick's, Fair Oaks Mall, GNC, Kohl's, Michael's, Petsmart, Ta get, Verizon, Walmart, Whole Foods Mkt, World Mkt
53b a	VA 28, to Centreville, S same as 52, Dulles Airport, Manass Museum

INTERSTATE 66 Cont'd

Exit #	Services
52	US 29, to Bull Run Park, Centreville, N Sunoco/dsl Bull Run Park/RV Dump, Goodyear/auto, S Exxon, Sunoco/dsl Charlie Chang's, Dickey's BBQ, Five Guys, IHOP, My Thai, Pancho Villa, Panda Express, Pizza Hut, Starbucks, Subway $Tree, Advance Parts, AT&T, Giant Foods, SpringHill Suites, Trader Joe's, USPO, vet, Walgreens
49mm	**both lanes, full facilities, litter barrels, petwalk,**
47b a	VA 234, to Manassas, N Shell/dsl Cracker Barrel, Golden Corral, Jerry's Subs, Uno, Wendy's Courtyard, Holiday Inn Express, La Quinta, Wyndham Garden Duluth Trading Co, Kohl's, Manassas Nat Bfd, Old Navy, S 7-11, BP, Exxon, RaceWay/dsl, Shell/repair, Sunoco Arby's, Baja Fresh, Bob Evans, Burger King, Cafe Rio, Checker's, Chick-fil-A, Chili's, China Palace, Chipotle Mexican, ChuckECheese's, CiCi's, City Grille, Coldstone, Denny's, Domino's, DQ, Dunkin', Firehouse Subs, Food Lion, Great American Buffet, Hibachi Buffet, Hooters, IHOP, Jersey Mike's, Jimmy John's, KFC, Logan's Roadhouse, McDonald's, Olive Garden, Panda Express, Panera Bread, Papa John's, Pizza Hut, Pollo Campero, Popeye's, Potbelly's, Red Hot&Blue BBQ, Red Lobster, Starbucks, Subway, Subway, Taco Bell, TGIFriday's, Wendy's Best Western, Comfort Suites, Days Inn, Hampton Inn, Holiday Inn, Quality Inn, Red Roof Inn, Residence Inn, Woodspring Suites $Tree, Advance Parts, Aldi Foods, AT&T, AutoZone, Barnes&Noble, Best Buy, Buick/GMC, Burlington Coats, Chevrolet, Costco/gas, CVS Drug, Dick's, Family$, Giant Foods, GNC, Home Depot, Honda, Lowe's, Macy's, Marshall's, Merchant Auto Ctr, Michael's, Mr Tire, NTB, Office Depot, PepBoys, Petsmart, Reines RV Ctr, Ross, Shopper's Foods, Staples, Toyota, Tuesday Morning, URGENT CARE, Verizon, vet, Walgreens, Walmart
44	VA 234 S, Manassas, S to Bristoe Sta Bfd SP
43b a	US 29, to Warrenton, Gainesville, S 7-11, BJ's/gas, Sunoco/dsl, WaWa BJ's Rest, Burger King, Chick-fil-A, Chili's, Chipotle, Coldstone, Domino's, Famous Dave's, Firebirds Grill, Five Guys, Grafton St Rest., IHOP, Joe's Pizza/Subs, KFC, McDonald's, MOD Pizza, Out of the Blue Seafood, Panera Bread, PeiWei, Potbelly, Qdoba, Smashburger, Starbucks, Subway, Taco Bell, Uncle Julio's Hampton Inn, SpringHill Suites, Woodspring Suites Advance Parts, Best Buy, Cabela's, CVS Drug, Giant Food/drug, GNC, Lowe's, Petsmart, Piedmont Tire/auto, Target, Verizon, Walgreens
40	US 15, Haymarket, N Greenville Farms Camping (5mi), H, S Sheetz/dsl Burapa Cafe, Chick-fil-A, Foster's Grill, Giuseppe's Italian, Little Caesar's, McDonald's, Papa John's, Penn Sta Subs, Starbucks, Subway, Young Chow Cafe CVS Drug, Food Lion, Kohl's, Verizon, Walmart
31	VA 245, to Old Tavern, 1 mi N Sunoco/dsl USPO
28	US 17 S, Marshall, N BP/McDonald's/dsl Anthony's Pizza, Foster's Grille, Great Wall Chinese, Old Salem Cafe, Subway Food Lion, vet
27	VA 55 E, Rd 647, Marshall, 1 mi N Citgo/dsl, Exxon/dsl/LP Marshall Diner
23	US 17 N, VA 55, Delaplane (no re-entry from eb)
20mm	Goose Creek
18	VA 688, Markham
13	VA 79, to VA 55, Linden, Front Royal, S 7-11/dsl, Exxon/dsl Applehouse Rest./BBQ/gifts Skyline Drive, to Shenandoah NP
11mm	Manassas Run
7mm	Shenandoah River

WYTHEVILLE

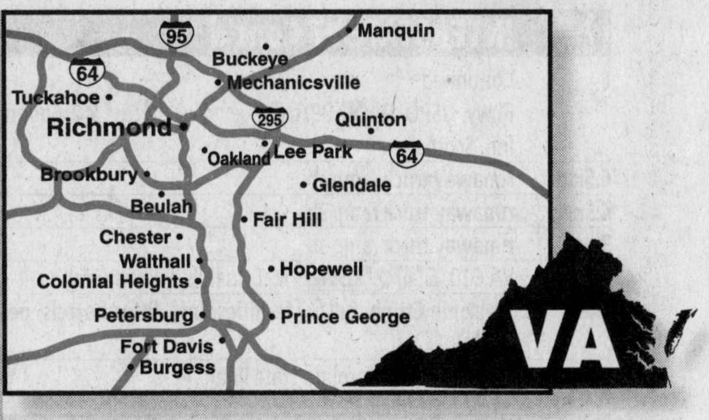

Exit #	Services
6	US 340, US 522, to Winchester, Front Royal, N 7-11, Mobil/7-11/dsl Applebee's, Checkers, China City Buffet, Cracker Barrel, IHOP, Ledo Pizza, Los Potrillos, McAlister's Deli, Mikado, Panda Express, Roy Rogers, Starbucks, TGIFriday's, Tropical Cafe TownePlace Suites $Tree, Aldi Foods, AT&T, Buick/GMC, Ford, GNC, Lowe's, PetCo, Staples, Target, URGENT CARE, Walmart, S 7-11, Exxon/Dunkin'/Subway, Shell McDonald's Hampton Inn Poe's Southfork Camping (2mi)
1b a	I-81, N to Winchester, S to Roanoke
0mm	**I-66 begins/ends on I-81, exit 300.**

VA

INTERSTATE 77

Exit #	Services
67mm	Virginia/West Virginia state line, East River Mtn
66	VA 598, to East River Mtn
64	US 52, VA 61, to Rocky Gap
62	VA 606, to South Gap
62mm	**Welcome Ctr sb, full facilities, info, litter barrels, petwalk, , vending**
59mm	**nb, full facilities, litter barrels, petwalk, , , vending**
58	US 52, to Bastian, E BP/Front Porch Cafe/dsl, W Exxon/Circle K, Loves/Arby's/dsl/scales/24hr
56mm	**runaway ramp nb**
52	US 52, VA 42, Bland, E Sunoco Subway $General, W Circle K/DQ/dsl Big Walker Motel
51.5mm	**weigh sta both lanes**
48mm	Big Walker Mtn
47	VA 717, 6 mi W to Deer Trail Park/NF Camping
41	VA 610, Peppers Ferry, Wytheville, E Sagebrush Steaks Best Western, Sleep Inn, Super 8, W Exxon/dsl/scales/24hr, TA/BP/Country Pride/Popeye's/Subway/Taco Bell/dsl/scales/24hr/@ Southern Diner Comfort Suites, Country Inn&Suites, Fairfield Inn, Hampton Inn, Ramada Inn, Tru Hilton
40	I-81 S, to Bristol, US 52 N
I-77 and I-81 run together 9 mi. See I-81, exits 73-80.	
32	I-81 N, to Roanoke
26mm	New River
24	VA 69, to Poplar Camp, E New River Trail Info Ctr, to Shot Tower HP, W Circle K/Subway/dsl
19	VA 620, W
14	US 58, US 221, to Hillsville, Galax, E Mobil/Subway Peking Palace Red Carpet Inn H, LakeRidge RV Resort (14mi), W BP, Exxon/dsl, Gulf/dsl/24hr McDonald's, Pizza Inn, Shoney's, TCBY, Wendy's Comfort Inn, Hampton Inn, Holiday Inn Express, Motel 6, Quality Inn, Super 8 Carrollwood Camping, Chevrolet
8	VA 148, VA 775, to Fancy Gap, E Gulf Fancy Gap Cafe (2mi) Lakeview Motel/rest., Mountain Top Motel $General, Chance's Creek RV Ctr, KOA (2mi), to Blue Ridge

VA

INTERSTATE 77 Cont'd

8	Continued Pkwy, USPO, W BP/dsl, Exxon/Circle K/dsl Countryview Inn, Scottish Inn
6.5mm	runaway truck ramp sb
4.5mm	runaway truck ramp sb
3mm	runaway truck ramp sb
1	VA 620, E Loves/McDonald's/Subway/dsl/scales/24hr
.5mm	**Welcome Ctr nb, full facilities, info, litter barrels, petwalk,**
0mm	Virginia/North Carolina state line

INTERSTATE 81

Exit #	Services
324mm	Virginia/West Virginia state line
323	rd 669, to US 11, Whitehall, E Exxon, W FLYING J/Denny's/Subway/dsl/LP/scales/24hr
321	rd 672, Clearbrook, E Citgo/Old Stone Cafe/dsl Woolen Mills Grill
320mm	**Welcome Ctr sb, full facilities, litter barrels, petwalk, , vending**
317	US 11, Stephenson, E Chick-fil-A, Guan's Garden, Las Trancas, McDonald's, Subway, Tropical Smoothie Café, TX Roadhouse AT&T, Lowe's, Petsmart, Target, Verizon, W Exxon/Dunkin'/dsl, Sheetz, Shell/7-11/Burger King, Sunoco/dsl Denny's, Pizza Hut/Taco Bell Comfort Inn, EconoLodge, Holiday Inn Express (3mi) H, Candy Hill Camping
315	VA 7, Winchester, E Exxon, Sheetz/dsl Bamboo Garden, Ledo's Pizza, Little Caesars, Sonic, Starbucks, Waffle House TownePlace Suites $Tree, Chrysler/Dodge/Jeep, GNC, Goodyear/auto, Martin's Foods/gas, PetCo, URGENT CARE, Walgreens, W Exxon/Dunkin'/Subway, Liberty/dsl, Shell/dsl 5 Guys Burgers, Apple Blossom Diner, Arby's, Camino Real Mexican, KFC, McDonald's, NIK Italian, Pizza Hut, Wendy's Hampton Inn, Winchester Inn AutoZone, CVS Drug, Family$, Food Lion, Food Maxx, Sharp Shopper Mkt, TrueValue
314mm	Abrams Creek
313	US 17/50/522, Winchester, E Exxon/Baskin-Robbins/Dunkin'/Subway, Liberty/dsl, Mobil/7-11/dsl, Shell/dsl Apple Valley Diner, Chinatown, Cracker Barrel, Golden Corral, Hibachi Grill, IHOP, Los Tolteco's Mexican, TX Steaks, Umberto's Pizza Aloft Hotel, Candlewood Suites, Fairfield Inn, Holiday Inn, Red Roof Inn, Sleep Inn, Super 8, Travelodge BigLots, Costco/gas, Food Lion, Jo-Ann Fabrics, Nissan, vet, W Sheetz/dsl Bob Evans, Buca Italian, Chili's, China Jade, China Wok, Chipotle Mexican, ChuckECheese's, CiCi's, Coldstone, Dickey's BBQ, Five Guys, Glory Days Grill, Ichiban Japanese, Jimmy John's, KFC, Longhorn Steaks, McDonald's, Okinawa Steaks, Olive Garden, Panera Bread, Perkins, Rancho Mexican, Red Lobster, Roy Rogers, Ruby Tuesday, Subway, Taco Bell, TGIFriday's, Waffle House, Wendy's Best Western, Hampton Inn, Hilton Garden, Wingate Inn $Tree, AT&T, Belk, Best Buy, Books-A-Million, Dick's, Hobby Lobby, Home Depot, JC Penney, Kohl's, Lowe's, Martin's Foods, Merchants Tire, Michael's, Old Navy, PepBoys, Petsmart, Ross, Staples, Target, TJ Maxx, to Shenandoah U, URGENT CARE, Verizon, Walgreens, Walmart
310	VA 37, to US 50W, W Citgo/dsl, Shell/7-11/dsl Carrabba's, McDonald's, Outback Steaks, Subway Country Inn&Suites H, Aldi Foods, Camping World, Candy Hill Camping (6mi), CarQuest, Honda, Volvo, VW

WINCHESTER

WOODSTOCK

HARRISONBURG

307	VA 277, Stephens City, E Liberty/dsl, Shell/Burger King/dsl, Shell/Subway/dsl Arby's, China House, Del Rio Mexican, Domino's, Ginger Asian, KFC/Taco Bell, McDonald's, Pizza Hut, Roma Italian, Waffle House, Wendy's Comfort Inn, Holiday Inn Express $General, 7-11, Advance Parts, AutoZone, Food Lion, Martin's Foods/gas, Rite Aid, Verizon, W Exxon/Dunkin', Sheetz/dsl
304mm	**weigh sta both lanes**
302	rd 627, Middletown, E Exxon/dsl, W 7-11, Liberty/dsl McDonald's Econolodge $General, to Wayside Theatre
300	I-66 E, to Washington, Shenandoah NP, Skyline Dr
298	US 11, Strausburg, E Exxon/McDonald's/dsl/LP, Shell/7-11/dsl Anthony's Pizza, Arby's, Burger King, Castiglia Italian, Ciro's Pizza, Denny's, Golden China, Great Wall Buffet Fairfield Inn, Ramada Inn Advance Parts, Family$, Food Lion, Verizon, W Battle of Cedar Grove Camping, to Belle Grove Plantation
296	US 48, VA 55, Strausburg, E museums
291	rd 651, Toms Brook, E Budget Inn (3mi), W Loves/Arby's/dsl/scales/24hr, Pilot/DQ/Subway/dsl/scales/24hr truckwash/repair
283	VA 42, Woodstock, E Liberty/7-11, Sheetz, Shell/Dunkin' Arby's, Burger King, China Wok, KFC, Las Trancas, McDonald's, Pizza Hut, Taco Bell, Tony's Pizza, Wendy's Comfort Inn, Hampton Inn, Holiday Inn Express H, CVS Drug, Family$, Food Lion, Rite Aid, to Massanutten Military Academy, W Exxon/dsl, Sunoco China Wok, Cracker Barrel, Domino's, Paisano's Pizza, Subway $Tree, Ford, Lowe's, NAPA Care, Walmart
279	VA 185, rd 675, Edinburg, E Exxon/dsl, Shell/dsl S... Italian Bistro auto repair, Creekside Camping (2mi), USPO
277	rd 614, Bowmans Crossing
273	VA 292, RD 703, Mt Jackson, E 7-11, Exxon/dsl, Liberty/dsl/scales/24hr, Sheetz/dsl/scales/24hr Burger King, China King, Denny's, Italian Touch, Subway Motel 6 $General, Food Lion, to Mt Jackson Hist Dist, USPO
269	rd 730, to US 11, Shenandoah Caverns, E Shell/..., W Shenandoah Valley Camping
269mm	N Fork Shenandoah River
264	US 211, New Market, E Exxon/Subway/dsl, Liberty/dsl, Mobil/dsl, Shell/dsl Appleseed's Rest., Burger King, Italian Job, McDonald's Quality Inn Endless Caverns Camping, Skyline Dr, to Shenandoah NP, W 7-11 Days Inn New Market Bfd SHP
262mm	**both lanes, full facilities, litter barrels, petwalk, , vending**
257	US 11, VA 259, to Broadway, **3-5 mi** E Liberty/7-11/Burger King/dsl Endless Caverns Camping, KOA
251	US 11, Harrisonburg, W Exxon/dsl, Pilot/Subway/dsl/scales/24hr Economy Inn
247b a	US 33, Harrisonburg, E Citgo/dsl, Exxon/dsl, Royal/dsl, Sheetz/dsl, Shell/dsl, Walmart Applebee's, Aroma Buffet, Bob Evans, Bravo Italian, Bruster's, Buffalo Wild Wings, Burger King, Chick-fil-A, Chili's, Chipotle, CiCi's Pizza, Cook Out, Domino's, Dunkin', El Charro Mexican, Firehouse Subs, Five Guys, Franco's Pizza, Golden Corral, Great Wok, IHOP, Jess' Lunch, Jimmy John's, McAlister's Deli, McDonald's, O'Charley's, O'Neill's Grill, Outback Steaks, Panera Bread, Qdoba, Quaker Steak&Lube, Red Lobster, Ruby Tuesday, South Fork BBQ, Subway, Taco Bell, Tilted Kilt, TX Roadhouse, Waffle House, Wendy's, Which Wich?, Wok Grill Buffet Best Western, Candlewood Suites, Comfort Inn

INTERSTATE 81 Cont'd

247b a Continued
Courtyard, Doubletree, EconoLodge, Fairfield Inn, Hampton Inn, Motel 6, Quality Inn, Residence Inn, Sleep Inn $Tree, AT&T, Barnes&Noble, Belk, Best Buy, Books-A-Million, Cadillac/Chevrolet, Costco/gas, Dick's, Firestone/auto, Home Depot, JC Penney, Kohl's, Kroger, Lowe's, Martin's Foods/gas, Michael's, Nissan, Old Navy, PetCo, Petsmart, Ross, Staples, Target, TJ Maxx, to Shenandoah NP, to Skyline Dr, Tuesday Morning, URGENT CARE, Verizon, Walmart/McDonald's, **W** Exxon/dsl, Liberty/dsl, Royal/dsl, Sheetz/dsl Arby's, Ciro's Pizza, DQ, Dragon Palace, Golden China, Hardee's, KFC, Kyoto, L'Italia, Little Caesars, McDonald's, Papa John's, Sam's Hotdogs, Subway Advance Parts, BigLots, CVS Drug, Family$, Food Lion, URGENT CARE

245 VA 659, Port Republic Rd, **E** Campus Corner, Exxon/dsl, Liberty/dsl, Royal/dsl China Express, Corgan's Publick House, El Charro, McDonald's, Subway, Tropical Smoothie, Vito's Italian Days Inn H, CVS Drug, Food Lion, **W** Asian City, Jimmy John's, Starbucks to James Madison U

243 US 11, to Harrisonburg, **0-2 mi W** Exxon/dsl, Harrisonburg Travel Ctr/diner/dsl/scales, Liberty, Sheetz/dsl, Shell/7-11/dsl Burger King, Cracker Barrel, Griddle&Grill, McDonald's, Pano's Rest., Pizza Hut, Subway, Taco Bell Country Inn Suites, Hampton Inn, Holiday Inn Express, Microtel, Motel 6, Ramada Inn, Super 8 $General, Advance Parts, AutoZone, CarMax, Family$, Ford, Honda, Hyundai, Kia, Lincoln, Subaru, Toyota, USPO

240 VA 257, rd 682, Mount Crawford, **E** Shell/7-11/dsl McDonald's, **W** Exxon/Burger King/dsl (1mi)

235 VA 256, Weyers Cave, **E** Shell/dsl, **W** BP/Subway/dsl, Exxon/dsl Freightliner, to Grand Caverns

232mm **both lanes, full facilities, litter barrels, petwalk, vending**

227 rd 612, Verona, **E** BP/Subway/dsl Waffle Inn, **W** 7-11/Wendy's, Exxon, Shell/dsl Burger King, Ciro's Pizza, Hardee's, McDonald's Knights Inn $General, antiques, Food Lion, Good Sam RV Park (3mi), Rite Aid

225 VA 262, Woodrow Wilson Pkwy, **E** Motel 6, **W** Days Inn, Holiday Inn/rest.

222 US 250, Staunton, **E** BP, Royal/dsl Cracker Barrel, Hometown Grill, McDonald's, Mrs Rowe's Rest., TX Steaks Best Western, Red Roof Inn, Sleep Inn, **W** Sheetz, Speedway/dsl Baskin-Robbins/Dunkin', Burger King, Chili's, Country Cookin, Firehouse Subs, KFC, Massaki Japanese, Pizza Hut, Starbucks, Waffle House Comfort Inn, EconoLodge American Frontier Culture Museum, AT&T, auto repair, AutoZone, Lowe's, Martin's Foods/gas, Toyota, URGENT CARE, Walmart/Subway

221 I-64 E, to Charlottesville, Skyline Dr, Shenandoah NP

220 VA 262, to US 11, Staunton, **1 mi W** Citgo, Exxon, Shell A&W/LJ Silver, Applebee's, Arby's, Burger King, CiCi's Pizza, El Puerto, Jimmy John's, Kathy's Rest., Kline's Dairy Bar, Maria's Italian, McDonald's, Papa John's, Red Lobster, Sam's HotDogs, Sauced Grill, Subway, Taco Bell, Wendy's Budget Inn, Hampton Inn $General, $Tree, Advance Parts, Belk, Buick/GMC, Cadillac/Chevrolet, Chrysler/Dodge/Jeep, CVS Drug, Food Lion, Ford/Lincoln, Harley-Davidson, Honda, Hyundai, JC Penney, Kia/Mazda, Kroger/dsl, Nissan, NTB, Obaugh RV Ctr, Petco, Staples, Subaru, TJ Maxx, Verizon, vet, VW

217 Rd 654, to Mint Spring, Stuarts Draft, **E** GB/dsl Days Inn, **W** Exxon/Circle K/dsl/24hr, Liberty/LP Relax Inn KOA

LEXINGTON

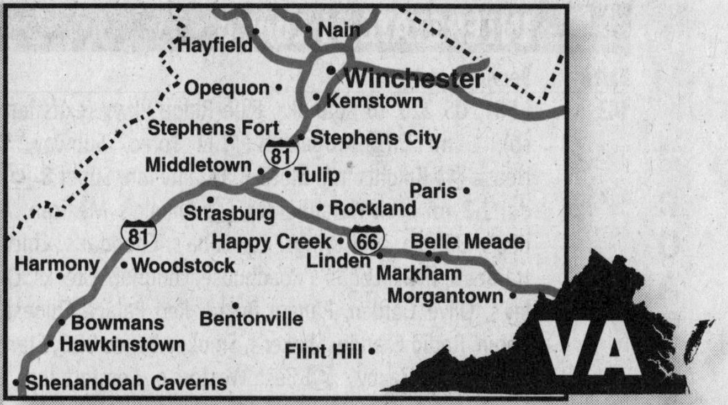

213b a US 11, US 340, Greenville, **E** BP/Subway, Loves/McDonalds/dsl/scales/24hr, Pilot/Arby's/scales/dsl/24hr, Shell Edelweiss Rest. Hometowne Inn KOA (3mi)

205 Rd 606, Raphine, **E** BP/dsl, Exxon/Burger King/dsl, Fuel City/Smiley's BBQ/dsl/24hr, Petro/Iron Skillet/Papa John's/Popeye's/Subway/dsl/scales/24hr/@ Blue Beacon, **W** Pilot/Wendy's/dsl/scales/24hr Comfort Inn/rest. Peterbilt

200 RD 710, Fairfield, **E** BP/McDonald's/dsl, Pure Frank's Pizza, **W** Exxon/Subway/dsl, Shell/dsl

199mm **sb, full facilities, litter barrels, petwalk, vending**

195 US 11, Lee Hwy, **E** Maple Hall Country Inn, **W** Exxon/dsl, TA/Shell/IHOP/dsl/scales/24hr/@ Days Inn, Howard Johnson, Quality Inn Lee-Hi Camping, repair

191 I-64 W (exits left from nb), US 60, to Charleston

188b a US 60, to Lexington, Buena Vista, **3-5 mi E** BP, Exxon Burger King, Hardee's Buena Vista Inn $General, Family$, Food Lion, to Blue Ridge Pkwy, to Glen Maury Park, to Stonewall Jackson Home, **W** Exxon/dsl, Exxon/McDonald's/dsl Hardee's, Pizza Hut, Taco Bell Hampton Inn H, Food Lion, Marshall Museum, to Washington&Lee U, VMI

180 US 11, Natural Bridge, (180a exits left from sb), **E** Relax Inn Cave Mtn NF, Jellystone Camping, **W** Shell/dsl Pink Cadillac Diner Budget Inn KOA

175 US 11 N, to Glasgow, Natural Bridge, **E** Exxon Natural Bridge Hotel/rest. (2mi) Jellystone Camping (6.5mi), to James River RA

168 VA 614, US 11, Blue Ridge Pkwy, Arcadia, **E** Shell/dsl Mtn View Rest. Wattstull Inn Middle Creek Camping (6mi), **2 mi W** Exxon Burger King

167 US 11 (from sb), Buchanan

162 US 11, Buchanan, **E** Exxon/dsl to BR Pkwy, **W** Citgo/Subway

158mm **sb, full facilities, litter barrels, petwalk, vending**

156 RD 640, to US 11, **E** Exxon/Brugh's Mill/dsl

150 US 11/220, to Fincastle, **E** Circle K/dsl/24hr, Dodge's/dsl, Pilot/Subway/dsl/24hr Angelle's Diner, Bella Pizza, Country Cookin, Cracker Barrel, Hardee's, McDonald's, Shoney's, Taco Bell Comfort Inn, Holiday Inn Express, Motel 6, Quality Inn, Red Roof Inn $General Mkt, Berglund RV Ctr, truckwash, **W** BP/dsl, Exxon/dsl, GB Bojangle's, Little Caesar's, Pancho's Mexican, Pizza Hut, Three Lil' Pigs BBQ, Wendy's Howard Johnson, Super 8 Kroger/dsl, Verizon, vet

149mm **weigh sta both lanes**

146 VA 115, Cloverdale, **E** BP/dsl, Exxon, Shell/dsl El Rodeo Mexican, Hardee's, McDonald's, Subway Country Inn&Suites, Days Inn/rest., Fairfield Inn, Hampton Inn, Tru Hilton Camping World, CVS, to Hollins U

VA

VA

INTERSTATE 81 Cont'd

ROANOKE

SALEM

CHRISTIANSBURG

Exit #	Services
143	I-581, US 220, to Roanoke, Blue Ridge Pkwy (exits left from sb), **1 mi** E Kroger/dsl El Toreo, Subway, Waffle House Knights Inn, Motel 6, Quality Inn, Super 8 Honda, **2-3 mi** E **on Hershberger** Abuelo's Mexican, Applebee's, Buffalo Wild Wings, Carrabba's, Cheddar's, Chick-fil-A, Hardee's, IHOP, Logan's Roadhouse, Longhorn Steaks, O'Charley's, Olive Garden, Panera Bread, Red Palace Chinese, Red Robin, Rodio Grande, Shaker's, Smokey Bones BBQ, Starbucks, TGIFriday's, Zaxby's Best Western+, Comfort Inn, Courtyard, Extended Stay America, Hampton Inn, Holiday Inn, Home 2 Suites, Hyatt Place, MainStay Suites, Residence Inn, Sheraton $Tree, AT&T, Barnes&Noble, Belk, Best Buy, BigLots, Dick's, Exxon, Home Depot, Macy's, Michael's, Murphy USA/dsl, NTB, Old Navy, Petsmart, Shell, Staples, Target, U-Haul, Verizon, Walmart
141	VA 419, Salem, E Liberty/7-11/dsl, Marathon/Burger King Hardee's, IHOP, McDonald's, Starbucks Baymont Inn, Days Inn, Fairfield Inn, Holiday Inn Express, La Quinta H, Chevrolet, GNC, Kroger/gas, **1 mi** W BP/Subway/dsl, Citgo Billy's Barn Rest.
140	VA 311, Salem, **1 mi** E Mac&Bob's Cafe, **1 mi** W BP/Subway/dsl, Citgo Billy's Barn Rest., Hanging Rock Grill/golf
137	VA 112, VA 619, Salem, E BP, Exxon/dsl, Go-Mart, Marathon, Sheetz/dsl Angelle's Diner, Anthony's Cafe, Applebee's, Arby's, Bojangle's, Burger King, Chick-fil-A, Denny's, DQ, Dunkin', Dynasty Buffet, El Rodeo Mexican, Firehouse Subs, Hardee's, Jimmy John's, K&W Cafeteria, KFC, Mamma Maria Italian, McDonald's, Omelette Shoppe, Pizza Hut, Starbucks, Subway, Taco Bell, Tokyo Express, Waffle House, Wendy's, Zaxby's Comfort Suites, Motel 6, Quality Inn, Super 8 $General, $Tree, Aamco, Advance Parts, AutoZone, BigLots, Food Lion, Goodyear, Kroger/dsl, Lowe's, NTB, O'Reilly Parts, Verizon, Walgreens, Walmart/Subway, W Hampton Inn, Howard Johnson
132	VA 647, to Dixie Caverns, E Citgo/dsl Blue Jay Motel Dixie Caverns Camping
129mm	**nb, full facilities, litter barrels, petwalk, , vending**
128	US 11, VA 603, Ironto, E Shell, W Exxon/Dixie's/Subway/dsl/24hr
118c b a	US 11/460, Christiansburg, E Shell/dsl Cracker Barrel, Denny's Days Inn, Fairfield Inn, Holiday Inn Express, Homewood Suites, Quality Inn, Super 8, Wyndham, W Exxon/Subway/dsl, Liberty/7-11/dsl, Shell Country Cookin, Hardee's, LJ Silver, McDonald's, Pizza Hut, Ruby Tuesday, Wendy's EconoLodge, Shayona Inn H, $General, Advance Parts, Chevrolet, Chrysler/Dodge/Jeep, Food Lion, Ford, Honda, Hyundai, Kia, Subaru, to VA Tech, Toyota
114	VA 8, Christiansburg, E to Blue Ridge Pkwy, **0-1 mi** W Citgo/dsl Burger King, Pizza Inn, Subway Budget Inn $General Mkt, USPO
109	VA 177, VA 600, E H, **0-2 mi** W Exxon/dsl, Marathon Best Western, Comfort Inn, La Quinta, Super 8 (2mi) Buick/Cadillac/Chevrolet
107mm	**both lanes, full facilities, litter barrels, petwalk, , , vending**
105	VA 232, RD 605, to Radford, **2-4 mi** W Citgo, Exxon/dsl Sal's Italian Executive Motel museum
101	RD 660, to Claytor Lake SP, E Claytor Lake Inn, Sleep Inn repair, W Exxon/DQ/dsl, Shell/Omelette Shoppe/Taco Bell/dsl/scales/@

WYTHEVILLE

Exit #	Services
98	VA 100 N, to Dublin, E Exxon/Subway/dsl, Marathon Bojangles, Shoney's Hampton Inn, Holiday Express, Quality Inn to Wilderness Rd Museum, W erty/dsl, Marathon/dsl, Shell/Papa John's/dsl Arby's, Burger King, Domino's, El Ranchero Mexican, Fatz Cafe, McDonald's, Waffle House, Wendy's Super 8 $General, NA O'Reilly Parts, Verizon, Walmart/Subway
94b a	VA 99 N, to Pulaski, **0-3 mi** W BP, Exxon/dsl, Speedw dsl China Wall, Compadre's Mexican, Domino's, Harde KFC, Kimono Japanese, Little Caesar's, McDonald's, Sonic, S way, Taco Bell, Wendy's H, $General, Advance Parts, C Family$, Food Lion, O'Reilly Parts
92	Rd 658, to Draper, E BP to New River Trail SP
89b a	US 11 N, VA 100, to Pulaski, E auto/truck repair
86	Rd 618, Service Rd, W Sunoco/Appletree Rest./dsl rep
84	Rd 619, to Grahams Forge, W Exxon/Circle K/DQ/dsl/2 Loves/Chester's/Subway/dsl/scales/24hr Fox Mtn Trail Motel
	I-81 S and I-77 N run together 9 mi.
81	I-77 S, to Charlotte, Galax, to Blue Ridge Pkwy
80	US 52 S, VA 121 N, to Ft Chiswell, E FLYING J/Denny's/ scales/24hr/@, Exxon/Burger King/dsl Wendy's Hamp Inn, Super 8 Blue Beacon, Ft Chiswell RV Park, NAPA, W Circle K/dsl, Citgo McDonald's Comfort Inn Speed
77	Service Rd, E FLYING J/Denny's/dsl/scales/LP/RVDump/2 Circle K/Subway/dsl/24hr, Speedway/Dunkin'/dsl Burger K KOA, W Exxon/dsl, Pilot/Arby's/DQ/dsl/scales/2 st police
73	US 11 S, Wytheville, E Exxon/dsl, Go-Mart Applebe Bob Evans, Cracker Barrel, Dawghouse, El Puerto Mexic Hardee's, Papa John's, Peking Chinese, Shoney's, Sonic, Wa House, Wendy's Budget Host, Days Inn, EconoLodge, H day Inn Express, La Quinta, Motel 6, Quality Inn, Red Roof Rodeway Inn, Travelodge H, $General, AutoZone, Bui Chevrolet/GMC, CVS Drug, Food Lion, Ford, Goodyear/a Harley-Davidson, Nissan, Rite Aid, Rural King
	I-81 N and I-77 S run together 9 mi.
72	I-77 N, to Bluefield, **1 mi** N **on I-77 exit 41** E Sagebr Steaks, Best Western, Sleep Inn, Super 8, **1 mi** N **on exit 41** W Exxon/Circle K/dsl/24hr, TA/Country Pride/P eye's/Subway/Taco Bell/dsl/scales/24hr/@ Southern D er Comfort Suites, Country Inn&Suites, Fairfield Inn, Har ton Inn, Ramada/rest., Tru Hilton
70	US 21/52, Wytheville, E BP/dsl, Sheetz/dsl Bojang China Wok, El Patio Mexican, KFC/Taco Bell, Little Caesar's, Donald's, Ruby Tuesday, Starbucks, Subway, Tokyo Japan Wendy's H, $Tree, Food Lion, GNC, Lowe's, O'Reilly Parts, Co, Verizon, Walmart/Subway, W Kangaroo Comfort Inn
67	US 11 (from nb, no re-entry), to Wytheville
61mm	**nb, full facilities, litter barrels, NO TRUCKS, petwalk, , vending**
60	VA 90, Rural Retreat, E Shell/dsl Dutch Pantry, McD ald's $General, camping, to Rural Retreat Lake
54	rd 683, to Groseclose, E Exxon, Sunoco/dsl The B Rest. Relax Inn Settler's Museum
53.5mm	**sb, full facilities, litter barrels, petwalk, , , vendi**
50	US 11, Atkins, W Circle K/Subway/dsl/24hr, Exxon C fort Inn NAPA Care
47	US 11, to Marion, W Citgo/Subway, Gas'N Go, Sh dsl Arby's, Bojangle's, Burger King, Charley's Philly Ste China House, KFC/Taco Bell, Little Caesar's, McDonald's, Puerto Mexican, Pizza Hut, Sonic, Wendy's Best Value

INTERSTATE 81 Cont'd

47	Continued EconoLodge, Travel Inn H, $General, $Tree, Advance Parts, AutoZone, Buick/Chevrolet/GMC, CVS Drug, Food City, Food Lion, Ford, Ingles, Marion Drug, O'Reilly Parts, to Hungry Mother SP (4mi), Verizon, Walgreens, Walmart
45	VA 16, Marion, E Valero/dsl Mt Rogers NRA, to Grayson Highlands SP, W Sunoco Hardee's NAPA, USPO
44	US 11, Marion, W $General, Vet
39	US 11, rd 645, Seven Mile Ford, W Interstate Camping
35	VA 107, Chilhowie, E Chilhowie Pizza, Hardee's Knights Inn, W Exxon/dsl, Gas'N Go, Mobil/Main St Mkt, Shell/dsl McDonald's, Riverfront Rest., Subway, Taco Bell $General, Food City, Greever's Drugs, USPO
32	US 11, to Chilhowie
29	VA 91, to Damascus, Glade Spring, E Marathon/Subway/dsl, Petro/Iron Skillet/dsl/24hr/@, Valero/Wendy's Giardino's Italian, Pizza+ EconoLodge, Knights Inn $General, Peterbilt, W Exxon, Shell/dsl, Spirit El Burrito Loco vet
26	rd 737, Emory, W Macado's (1mi) to Emory&Henry Coll, USPO (1mi)
24	VA 80, Meadowview Rd, E Loves/McDonald's/Subway/dsl/scales/24hr, W Harvest Table
22	rd 704, Enterprise Rd, E Marathon/dsl H
19	US 11/58, to Abingdon, E Shell/Subway/Dunkin'/dsl, Walmart/dsl Bojangle's, DQ, McDonald's, Pizza+ $Tree, Lowe's, to Mt Rogers NRA, URGENT CARE, vet, Walmart, W BP/dsl, Exxon/dsl, Marathon/Huddle House Bella's Pizza, Burger King, Cracker Barrel, Harbor House Seafood, Papa Tom's Cantina, Pita's Country Inn Suites, Fairfield Inn, Quality Inn, Red Roof Inn $General
17	US 58A, VA 75, Abingdon, E Mobil/dsl Domino's, LJ Silver Hampton Inn, W Exxon, Gas'n Go Arby's, Capt D's, Charley's Philly Steaks, China Wok, Fuji Express, Hardee's, Little Caesar's, Los Arcos, McDonald's, Papa John's, Shoney's, Subway, Taco Bell, Wendy's Super 8 Advance Parts, Food City, GNC, Kroger/dsl
14	US 19, VA 140, Abingdon, W BP/dsl, Exxon, Shell/dsl McDonald's, Milano's Italian, Moon Dog Cafe, Subway Comfort Inn, Comfort Suites Chevrolet, Ford/Lincoln, Riverside Camping (10mi)
13.5mm	**nb, full facilities, litter barrels, TRUCKERS ONLY vending**
13	VA 611, to Lee Hwy, W Shell/dsl Kenworth, Mack, Volvo
10	US 11/19, Lee Hwy, W Exxon, Marathon/dsl, Shell/dsl Deluxe Inn, Economy Inn, Evergreen Inn, Red Carpet Inn
7	Old Airport Rd, E Shell/dsl Bojangles, Cheddar's, Cracker Barrel, Sonic Days Inn, Hilton Garden, W Marathon, Sunoco/Wendy's, Valero/dsl Chick-fil-A, Chili's, Cook-Out, Domino's, El Patio Mexican, Five Guys, Golden Corral, IHOP, Jersey Mike's Subs, Kobe Japanese, Logan's Roadhouse, Los Arcos, Mellow Mushroom, O'Charley's, Olive Garden, Pal's Drive-In, Perkins, Red Lobster, Starbucks, Subway, Taco Bell Courtyard, Holiday Inn, Motel 6, Quality Inn $General, $Tree, Advance Parts, AT&T, AutoZone, Best Buy, Books-A-Million, Food City/gas, Home Depot, Office Depot, Petsmart, Ross, Sam's Club/gas, Sugar Hollow Camping, Target, TJ Maxx, Verizon, Walmart
5	US 11/19, Lee Hwy, E Shell Arby's, Burger King, Hardee's, KFC, LJ Silver, McDonald's, Shoney's Budget Inn, Red Roof Inn Harley-Davidson, O'Reilly Parts, Price Less Foods, USPO, W Exxon/dsl, Sheetz/dsl Buffalo Wild Wings, Zaxby's Comfort Inn Aldi Foods, Buick/GMC, Cabela's, Hobby Lobby, Kings Tire, Lowe's
3	I-381 S, to Bristol, **1 mi** E Gas'n Go/dsl, Mobil/dsl, Shell/dsl Krystal, Subway EconoLodge Food City, vet
1b a	US 58/421, Bristol, 1 mi E 5 Mart/dsl, Exxon/dsl, Shell Burger King, Capt D's, KFC, McDonald's, Sonic, Subway, Taco Bell, Wendy's Rodeway Inn H, $Tree, Chrysler/Dodge/Jeep, CVS Drug, Kroger/dsl, Toyota, UHaul, Verizon, vet, Walgreens
0mm	Virginia/Tennessee state line, **Welcome Ctr nb, full facilities, info, litter barrels, NO TRUCKS, petwalk, vending**

BRISTOL

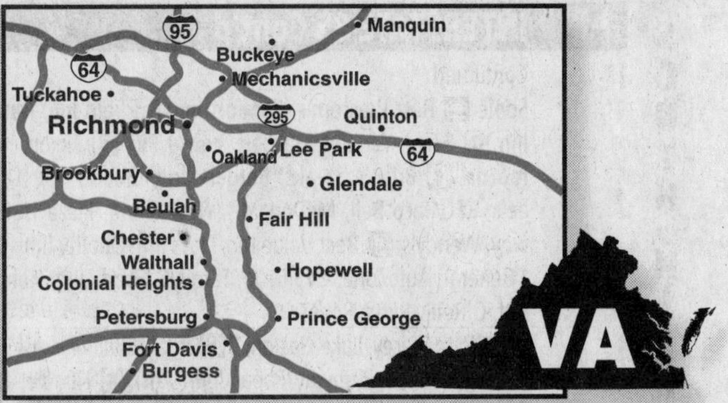

VA

INTERSTATE 85

Exit #	Services
I-85 begins/ends on I-95.	
69	US 301, I-95 N, Wythe St, Washington St, Petersburg
68	I-95 S, US 460 E, to Norfolk, Crater Rd
65	Squirrel Level Rd, E to Richard Bland Coll, W BP
63b a	US 1, to Petersburg, E Chubby's/dsl, Exxon/KFC/dsl, Shell/Burger King/dsl Hardee's, Taco Bell, Waffle House Holiday Inn Express $General, W BP McDonald's
61	US 460, to Blackstone, E Mapco/Subway/dsl Joe's Rest., W auto repair
55mm	**both lanes, full facilities, litter barrels, petwalk, vending**
53	VA 703, Dinwiddie, W Exxon/dsl to 5 Forks Nat Bfd
52mm	Stony Creek
48	VA 650, DeWitt
42	VA 40, McKenney, W BP, Citgo, Exxon
40mm	Nottoway River
39	VA 712, to Rawlings, W Davis TC/Exxon/Dunkin'/Subway/dsl/scales/24hr, Race-In/Nottoway Rest.
34	VA 630, Warfield, W Exxon/dsl
32mm	**both lanes, full facilities, litter barrels, petwalk, vending**
28	US 1, Alberta, W Exxon Family Dollar
27	VA 46, to Lawrenceville, E to St Paul's Coll
24	VA 644, to Meredithville
22mm	**weigh sta both lanes**
20mm	Meherrin River
15	US 1, to South Hill, E Hines, W Hot Food/dsl, Loves/Subway/McDonald's/dsl/scales/24hr El Saucito, Kahill's Rest. Holiday Inn Express
12	US 58, VA 47, to South Hill, E Exxon/dsl, Pilot/Shell/dsl, RaceWay, Sunoco/dsl Applebee's, Arby's, Bojangles, Domino's, Five Guys, Glass House Grill, Luca's Italian, Papa John's,

PETERSBURG

SOUTH HILL

SOUTH HILL

INTERSTATE 85 Cont'd

12 Continued
Sonic Best Western+, Comfort Inn, Fairfield Inn, Hampton Inn $Tree, Verizon, Walmart/Subway, **W** Exxon, Kangaroo/dsl Brian's Steaks, Burger King, Cracker Barrel, Hardee's, KFC/Taco Bell, McDonald's, New China, Pizza Hut, Subway, Wendy's Best Value Inn, Days Inn, Quality Inn H, $General, AutoZone, CVS Drug, Family$, Food Lion, Home Depot, O'Reilly Parts, Roses

4 VA 903, to Bracey, Lake Gaston, **E** Exxon/Simmon's/dsl/scales/24hr/@, Sunoco/Subway/Papa John's/dsl Huddle House, Top This Pizza $General, Americamps Camping (5mi), **W** Shell/Pizza Hut/Quizno's Lake Gaston Inn

3mm Lake Gaston

1mm **Welcome Ctr nb, full facilities, litter barrels, petwalk, vending**

0mm Virginia/North Carolina state line

VA

INTERSTATE 95

Exit # Services

178mm Virginia/Maryland state line, Potomac River, W Wilson Br

DC AREA

177c b a US 1, to Alexandria, Ft Belvoir, **E** Great American Steaks Budget Host, Hampton Inn, Red Roof Inn, Relax Inn Chevrolet, Chrysler/Dodge/Jeep, **W** Liberty/repair, Speedway

176b a VA 241, Telegraph Rd, **E** BP, Speedway/dsl, **W** Ted's MT Grill Courtyard, Extended Stay America, Holiday Inn, SpringHill Suites

174 Eisenhower Ave Connector, to Alexandria

173 rd 613, Van Dorn St, to Franconia, **E** Comfort Inn, **1 mi W** Exxon, Shell Dunkin', Jerry's Subs, McDonald's, Red Lobster Aamco, Giant Foods, NTB

170a I-495 N, **I-495 & I-95 N run together to MD, to Rockville.**

170b I-395 N, to Washington

169b a rd 644, Springfield, Franconia, **E** Bertucci's, Dunkin', Houlihan's, Silver Diner, Starbucks, Subway, TGIFriday's Best Western, Comfort Inn, Courtyard, Extended Stay America, Hampton Inn, Hilton H, AT&T, Barnes&Noble, Best Buy, Dick's, Firestone/auto, Ford, Home Depot, JC Penney, Macy's, Michael's, Nissan, Old Navy, Petsmart, Staples, Subaru, Target, **W** BP, Shell, Sunoco Blue Pearl Buffet, Chick-fil-A, Chipotle Mexican, Deliah's Grill, Domino's, Dunkin', Five Guys, Hard Times Cafe, KFC, McDonald's, Noodles&Co, Outback Steaks, Panda Express, Popeye's, Starbucks, Subway Holiday Inn Express, Homewood Suites, Motel 6, Residence Inn, TownePlace Suites 7-11, Advance Parts, CarQuest, Chrysler/Dodge/Jeep, CVS Drug, Giant Foods, GNC, Goodyear/auto, Mr Tire, Toyota, Trader Joe's, USPO, Verizon, vet, VW

167 VA 617, Backlick Rd (from sb), **W** InterFuel/dsl

166b a VA 7100, Newington, to Ft Belvoir, **E** Pkwy Express Wendy's Embassy Suites NTB, Toyota, U-Haul, **W** Exxon/7-11/dsl McDonald's Costco

163 VA 642, Lorton, **E** Shell/repair, Sunoco/dsl auto repair, **W** Shell/dsl Antoneli's Pizza, Burger King, Gunston Wok, Kabob Factory Rest.

161 US 1 S (exits left from sb, no reentry nb), to Ft Belvoir, Mt Vernon, Woodlawn Plantation, Gunston Hall

160.5mm Occoquan River

160b a VA 123 N, Woodbridge, Occoquan, **E** Sunoco Taco Bell Hampton Inn, Quality Inn Aldi Foods, Food Lion, Mr Transmissions, **W** Exxon/repair/dsl, Fast Fuels, Shell/dsl

160b a Continued
KFC, Madigan's Waterfront Rest., McDonald's, VA C Wendy's 7-11, same as 161

158b a VA 294, Prince William Pkwy, Woodbridge, **W** 7-11, Ex Shell, Sunoco/dsl Bonefish Grill, Boston Mkt, Bungalow house, Chick-fil-A, Chipotle Mexican, ChuckeCheese, Coldst Famous Dave's BBQ, Firehouse Subs, Hooters, IHOP, Maca Grill, McDonald's, Noodles&Co, Old Country Buffet, On-Border, Panda Express, Panera Bread, Qdoba, Red Lobster, Robin, Smokey Bones BBQ, Starbucks, Taco Bell, TGIFrid Wendy's Country Inn&Suites, Courtyard, Fairfield Inn, day Inn Express, Residence Inn, SpringHill Suites $Tree, vance Parts, Best Buy, CarMax, Dick's, GNC, JC Penney, Lov Michael's, Office Depot, Petsmart, Sam's Club/gas, Shopp Foods, Target, Verizon, Walmart/Subway

156 VA 784, Potomac Mills, **E** Brixx Woodfired Grill, Fireb Grill, PF Chang's, Potbelly, Starbucks, Travinia Italian, U Julio's Grill, Zoe's Kitchen Hilton Garden, Homew Suites H, AT&T, Old Navy, REI, to Leesylvania SP, W man's Mkt, **W** Mobil/dsl, Shell/dsl, Sunoco/dsl Ba ma Breeze, Bob Evans, Bobby's Burger, Buffalo Wild Wi Burger King, Char Broil Grill, Cheesecake Factory, Chili's, na King Buffet, Denny's, Domino's, DQ, Guapo's, Hard Ti Cafe, Los Amigos, McDonald's, Olive Garden, Outback Ste Paisano's, Popeye's, Sakura Japanese, Silver Diner, Subv Wendy's Best Western, Wytestone Suites Costco/ Family$, Firestone/auto, IKEA, Jo-Ann Fabrics, Marshalls, N strom Rack, NTB, Potomac Mills Outlets/Famous Brands, ples, Tuesday Morning, U-Haul, vet

154mm **/weigh sta both lanes**

DUMFRIES

152 VA 234, Dumfries, to Manassas, **E** BP/dsl, Express, on/dsl, Shell/dsl, Valero/Subway Applebee's, China C KFC, McDonald's, Ruby Tuesday, Taco Bell Sleep Inn, per 8 7-11, Food Lion, Meineke, NAPA Autocare, Walm Weems-Botts Museum, **W** 7-11, Exxon Asian Chick-fil-A, Cracker Barrel, Five Guys, IHOP, Jerry's Subs, M Clair Rest., Panera Bread, Starbucks, Subway, Tiziano Ital Waffle House Comfort Inn, Days Inn, EconoLodge, Ha ton Inn, Holiday Inn AT&T, Prince William Camping, Aid, Shoppers Foods, Target, URGENT CARE

150 VA 619, Quantico, to Triangle, **E** Dunkin', McD ald's Ramada Inn 7-11, to Marine Corps Base, **W** Pri William Forest Park

148 to Quantico (2mi), **E** Gulf/dsl Subway Co yard to Marine Corps Base

143b a to US 1, VA 610, Aquia, **E** 7-11, Exxon/Circle K/dsl, V ro Carlos O'Kelly's, El Gran Charro, KFC, McDonald's, Mi Rest., Papa John's, Pizza Hut, Ruby Tuesday, Subway Western, Fairfield Inn, Hampton Inn, Staybridge Suites, S urban Extended Stay, Towne Place Suites Aquia Pi Camping, Nissan, Rite Aid, Tires+, **W** 7-11, Exxon/ Kangaroo, WaWa 5 Guys Burgers, Applebee's, Baskin-R bins/Dunkin', Bob Evans, Buffalo Wild Wings, Burger K Chick-fil-A, Chili's, China Wok, CiCi's, Firehouse Subs, Harde Hibachi Buffet, IHOP, Jersey Mike's, Jimmy the Greek, K Japanese, Little Caesar's, McDonald's, Moe's SW Grill, Outb Steaks, Pancho Villa, Panera Bread, Popeye's, Starbucks, T Bell, Umi Japanese, Wendy's Comfort Inn, Country In Suites, Quality Inn, Super 8, Wingate Inn $General, $T Aldi Foods, AutoZone, Best Buy, CVS Drug, Giant Foods, G Home Depot, Kohl's, Lowe's, Merchant's Tire, Michael's, Pe Petsmart, Ross, Shopper's Foods, Staples, Target, TJ Maxx, T ota, URGENT CARE, Verizon, Walmart/McDonald's

INTERSTATE 95 Cont'd

Exit #	Services
140	VA 630, Stafford, E 7-11, Sunoco/dsl, Valero McDonald's O H, W Exxon/dsl, Shell/dsl
137mm	Potomac Creek
136	rd 8900, Centreport, 2 mi E Valero/dsl, W
133b a	US 17 N, to Warrenton, E Exxon/dsl Arby's Knights Inn, Motel 6 O 7-11, auto/truck repair, CarQuest, W EastCoast/Subway/dsl, Shell/dsl, WaWa/dsl Aladin Grill, Burger King, Dunkin', Hardee's, McDonald's, Pancho Villa Mexican, Panera Bread, Perkins, Ponderosa, Popeye's, Sam's Pizza&Subs, Subway, Taco Bell, Waffle House, Wendy's Best Value Inn, Clarion, Comfort Suites, Country Inn&Suites, Days Inn, Holiday Inn Express, Quality Inn, Sleep Inn, Super 8, Super Value Inn, Wingate Inn O Advance Parts, AutoZone, Blue Beacon, Food Lion, Honda, Petsmart, Target, Verizon
132.5mm	Rappahannock River
132mm	sb, full facilities, litter barrels, petwalk, , , vending
130b a	VA 3, to Fredericksburg, E BP/dsl, Gulf/dsl, Shell/dsl, Wawa Aladin Cafe, Arby's, Bob Evans, Dixie Bones BBQ, Dunkin', Friendly's, Honeybaked Ham, KFC, Lonestar Steaks, McDonald's, Pizza King, Popeye's, Shoney's, Starbucks, Subway, Teppanyaki Buffet, Wendy's Best Western, Quality Inn O H, AutoZone, Batteries+Bulbs, BigLots, Home Depot, PepBoys, Staples, Tuesday Morning, U-Haul, Verizon, W Exxon/dsl, Murphy USA, Sheetz/dsl, Valero, WaWa 5 Guys Burgers, A&W/LJ Silver, Applebee's, BoneFish Grill, Bravo!, Buffalo Wild Wings, Burger King, Cancun Mexican, Carrabba's, Checker's, Cheeburger Cheeburger, Chick-fil-A, Chili's, Chipotle Mexican, ChuckeCheese, CiCi's Pizza, Cracker Barrel, Dunkin', Firebirds Grill, Firehouse Subs, Hibachi Buffet, IHOP, Jimmy John's, Joe's Crabshack, Krispy Kreme, Logan's Roadhouse, McDonald's, Melting Pot, Noodles&Co, O'Charley's, Olive Garden, Outback Steaks, Pancho Villa, Panda Express, Panera Bread, Park Lane Grill, Peter Chang, Potbelly, Qdoba, Quaker Steak, Red Lobster, Ruby Tuesday, Ryan's, Sam's Pizza, Santa Fe Grill, Shane's Ribshack, Smokey Bones BBQ, Starbucks, Subway, Taco Bell, TGIFriday's, Tito's Diner, TX Roadhouse Best Western, Hampton Inn, Hilton Garden, Homewood Suites, Hospitality House, Residence Inn, Super 8, WoodSpring Inn O $General, $Tree, AAA, Aldi Foods, AT&T, AutoZone, Barnes&Noble, Belk, Best Buy, BJ's Whse, Books A Million, Costco/gas, CVS Drug, Dick's, Food Lion, GNC, Hobby Lobby, JC Penney, Kohl's, Lowe's, Macy's, Meineke, Mercedes, Merchants Tire, Michael's, NTB, Office Depot, Old Navy, Petsmart, Target, Verizon, vet, Volvo, Walmart, Wegman's Foods, Yankee Candle
126	US 1, US 17 S, to Fredericksburg, E 7-11/dsl, BP/dsl, Exxon/Circle K, Gulf/dsl, Shell/dsl, Wawa Arby's, Denny's, DQ, Friendly's, Golden Corral, Hardee's, Hooters, McDonald's, Pizza Hut, Poncho Villa Mexican, Ruby Tuesday, Subway, Taco Bell, Vita Felice Italian, Waffle House Best Value Inn, Country Inn&Suites, Days Inn/rest., EconoLodge, Fairfield Inn, Hampton Inn, Howard Johnson, Knights Inn, Motel 6, Royal Inn, TownePlace Suites O H, $General, $Tree, Advance Parts, Aldi Foods, AutoZone, BMW Cycles, Buick/GMC, Chrysler/Dodge/Jeep, CVS Drug, Family$, Fiat, Food Lion, Hyundai, Kia, Little Tires, Mazda, Midas, Nissan, Rite Aid, Subaru, Tires+, VW, W 7-11, 95 Fuel Stop/dsl, Exxon/Circle K, WaWa/dsl 5 Guys Burgers, Applebee's, Arby's, Asian Diner, Bob Evans, Buffalo Wild Wings, Burger King, Chick-fil-A, Chili's, China King, Chipotle Mexican, Coldstone Creamery, Cracker Barrel, Dickey's BBQ, El Charro Mexican, Famous Dave's BBQ, Firehouse Subs, Golden China,

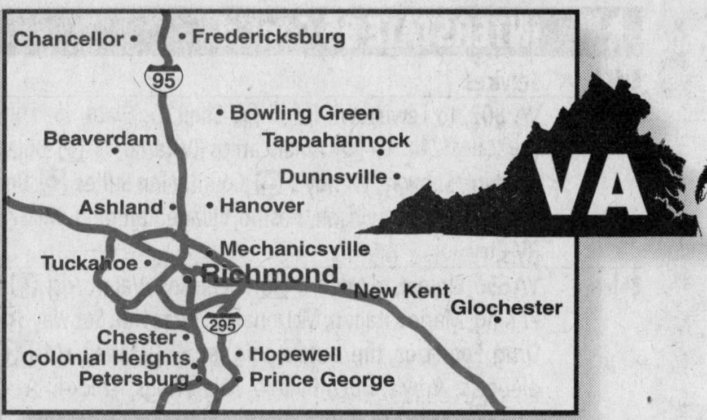

FREDERICKSBURG

Exit #	Services
126	Continued KFC, Kobe Japanese, Legends Grill, Longhorn Steaks, Mad Crab Grill, McDonald's, Mexico Rest., Mimi's Cafe, Panera Bread, Papa John's, Red Robin, Salsarita's Cantina, Sonic, Starbucks, Steak'n Shake, Subway, Taco Bell, Wendy's Candlewood Suites, Holiday Inn Express, Sleep Inn, WyteStone Suites O AT&T, Carmax, CVS Drug, Dick's, Firestone/auto, GNC, Jo-Ann Fabrics, Kohl's, Lowe's, Marshalls, Merchant Tire/auto, Petsmart, Rite Aid, Ross, Staples, Target, URGENT CARE, USPO, Verizon, vet, Walmart/Subway, World Mkt
118	VA 606, to Thornburg, E Shell/dsl O Camping World, to Stonewall Jackson Shrine, W 7-11, Citgo/dsl, Exxon, Shell/DQ/dsl, Valero Angela's Italian, Domino's, McDonald's, Subway, Taco Bell Best Western+, Holiday Inn Express, Quality Inn O $General, Family$, Food Lion, KOA (7mi), to Lake Anna SP, USPO
110	VA 639, to Ladysmith, E Shell/dsl, W Citgo/dsl, Exxon/dsl Domino's, Guiseppe's Rest., Lin's Gourmet, McDonald's, Subway, Timbers Rest. O $General, Family$, Food Lion, Lady Smith Drug, Lady Smith Tire/repair, Verizon
108mm	both lanes, full facilities, litter barrels, pet walk, s, , vending
104	VA 207, to US 301, Bowling Green, E Exxon/dsl, FLYING J/Golden Corral/dsl/Lp/scales/24hr/@, Gulf/7-11/dsl, Loves/DQ/Subway/dsl/scales/24hr, Mr Fuel/dsl, Valero/dsl Arby's, McDonald's, Wendy's Knights Inn, Super 8 O Blue Beacon, SpeedCo, to Ft AP Hill, W FLYING J/Denny's/dsl/scales/RV dump/24hr, Exxon/dsl Waffle House City Studio, Comfort Inn, Days Inn/rest., EconoLodge O CarQuest, USPO
98	VA 30, Doswell, E 7-11, Doswell TP/motel/dsl/scales/24hr/@, Exxon Burger King, Denny's Best Western, Country Inn&Suites, Days Inn, La Quinta O Camp Wilderness, King's Dominion Camping, to King's Dominion Funpark, truckwash/service
92	VA 54, Ashland, E Sunoco, W 7-11/dsl, EC/Krispy Kreme/dsl, Exxon/Subway, Kangeroo/dsl, Shell/dsl, Sunoco/Circle K/dsl, TA/Valero/Country Pride/dsl/scales/24hr/@ Anthony's Pizza, Applebee's, Arby's, Brickoven Rest., Burger King, Capt D's, Chick-fil-A, China Wok, Cracker Barrel, DQ, El Azteca, GNC, Hardee's, Jersey Mike's Subs, KFC/LJ Silver, McDonald's, New China Buffet, Pizza Hut, Ponderosa, Ruby Tuesday, Starbucks, Taco Bell, Tops China, Waffle House, Wendy's Apple Garden Inn, Ashland Inn, Days Inn, EconoLodge, Hampton Inn, Holiday Inn Express, Howard Johnson, Motel 6, Sleep Inn, Super 8 O $General, $Tree, Ace Hardware, Advance Parts, AutoZone, Buick/GMC, CarQuest, CVS Drug, Family$, Food Lion, Martin's Foods/dsl, O'Reilly Parts, Rite Aid, Tuesday Morning, Verizon, Walmart/Subway

= gas = food = lodging = other = rest stop

VA

INTERSTATE 95 Cont'd

Exit #	Services
89	VA 802, to Lewistown Rd, E Shell, TA/Pizza Hut/Popeye's/dsl/scales/24hr/@ Americamps RV Camp, W Bojangles, Dunkin', Subway, Wendy's Country Inn Suites Bass Pro Shops, Harley Davidson, Kosmo Village Camping, McGeorge's RV Ctr
86b a	VA 656, Elmont, to Atlee, E Sheetz/dsl, Valero/dsl Burger King, Mario's Italian, McDonald's, Pizza Hut, Subway CVS Drug, Food Lion, tire/auto repair, vet, W Wawa/dsl Applebee's, Arby's, BBQ, Buffalo Wild Wings, Chick-fil-A, Chili's, Chipotle Mexican, CiCi's Pizza, Coldstone Creamery, Famous Dave's BBQ, Firehouse Subs, Halligan BBQ, Jade Chinese, Jersey Mike's Subs, McDonald's, O'Charley's, O'Dragon Buffet, Panera Bread, Papa John's, Pizzaro, Plaza Azteca Mexican, Red Robin, Roda Japanese, Shoney's, Sonic, Starbucks, Subway, TX Roadhouse, Wendy's Candlewood Suites, Comfort Suites, Courtyard, Hampton Inn, SpringHill Suites $Tree, 7-11, AT&T, Barnes&Noble, Best Buy, Burlington, Dick's, Firestone/auto, GNC, Goodyear/auto, Home Depot, JC Penney, Martin's Foods, Merchant's Tire, Michael's, Petsmart, Ross, Shell/dsl, Target, Tire America, Walgreens
84b a	I-295 W, to I-64, to Norfolk
83b a	VA 73, Parham Rd, W 7-11, Exxon/DQ, Shell/dsl, Wawa Aunt Sarah's, Burger King, Firehouse Subs, Frida's Cafe, Hardee's, Hawks BBQ, KFC/Taco Bell, McDonald's, Popeyes, River City Diner, Starbucks, Subway, Waffle House, Wendy's Best Value Inn, Best Western, Cavalier Motel, Days Inn, EconoLodge, Knights Inn, Quality Inn, Sleep Inn $Tree, BigLots, Food Lion, Lowe's, Verizon, Walmart
82	US 301, Chamberlayne Ave, E BP/dsl, Sunoco/dsl, Valero/dsl, Wawa KFC, McDonald's, Pizza Hut/Taco Bell, Subway Super 8 $Tree, Family$, Food Lion, USPO, W Exxon/Circle K
81	US 1, Chamberlayne Ave (from nb), same as 82
80	Hermitage Rd, Lakeside Ave (from nb, no return), W Citgo/Subway Ginter Botanical Gardens, Goodyear/auto
79	I-64 W, to Charlottesville, I-195 S, to U of Richmond
78	Boulevard (no EZ nb return), E BP Clarion, W H, stadium, to VA HS
76	Chamberlayne Ave, Belvidere, E H, VA Union U
75	I-64 E, VA Beach, to Norfolk,
74c	US 33, US 250 W, to Broad St, W H, Museum of the Confederacy, st capitol
74b	Franklin St, E Richmond Nat Bfd Park
74a	I-195 N, to Powhite Expswy, downtown
73.5mm	James River
73	Maury St, to US 60, US 360, industrial area
69	VA 161, Bells Rd, E Port of Richmond, W Exxon/dsl, Shell/dsl McDonald's, Subway Candlewood Suites, Hampton Inn, Holiday Inn, Red Roof Inn
67b a	VA 895 (toll E), VA 150, to Chippenham Pkwy, Falling Creek, W BP/dsl, RaceWay/dsl, Shell/dsl Burger King, Hardee's Food Lion, U-Haul
64	VA 613, to Willis Rd, E BP, Exxon/Circle K/dsl Waffle House Best Value Inn, Knights Inn, W 7-11, Citgo/dsl, Shell/dsl, Sunoco Burger King, Maury's BBQ, McDonald's, Subway Country Inn&Suites, La Quinta, Sleep Inn,. VIP Inn Drewry's Bluff Bfd, flea mkt
62	VA 288 N, to Chesterfield, Powhite Pkwy, W to
61b a	VA 10, Chester, E RaceWay/dsl Don Pepe Mexican, Hardee's Comfort Inn, Courtyard, Hampton Inn, Holiday Inn

ELMONT

RICHMOND

CHESTER

PETERSBURG

Exit #	Services
61b a	Continued Express, Homewood Suites, Quality Inn H, City Point N Petersburg NBF, to James River Plantations, W Exx Circle K/dsl, Gulf/dsl, Mobil/Circle K/dsl, Shell/dsl, Sunc dsl Applebee's, Bojangles, Brass Monkey Grill, Bu lo Wild Wings, Burger King, Capt D's, Chili's, Chipotle, C Pizza, Cracker Barrel, Denny's, Don Papa Mexican, Friend Hardee's, Hooters, IHOP, KFC, Logan's Roadhouse, McDona O'Charley's, Panera Bread, Peking Chinese, Pizza Hut, Shone Sonic, Starbucks, Subway, Taco Bell, The Patron Cantina, W dy's Country Inn&Suites, Days Inn, Fairfield Inn, InTov Suites, Suburban Lodge, Super 8 $General, $Tree, Aar AT&T, Big Lots, Chevrolet, CVS Drug, Food Lion, GNC, Home pot, Kohl's, Kroger/gas, Lowe's, Martin's Foods, NAPA, Pe Rite Aid, Target, to Pocahontas SP, Verizon
58	VA 746, to Ruffinmill Rd, E Pilot/Wendy's/dsl/scales/2 Honda, Hyundai, Kia, Nissan, Subaru, Toyota, VW, W 7-11, Exxon/Subway/dsl, Wawa/dsl McDonald's C dlewood Suites, Comfort Inn, EconoLodge Family$
54	VA 144, Temple Ave, Hopewell, to Ft Lee, E Exxon/Bur King, Sheetz/dsl, Shell, Sunoco/Circle K/dsl, Wawa/dsl plebee's, Arby's, Buffalo Wild Wings, Chick-fil-A, China Bu Chipotle, CiCi's Pizza, Denny's, Firehouse Subs, Five Guys, G en Corral, Great China, IHOP, Jimmy John's, Longhorn Ste McDonald's, Olive Garden, Outback Steaks, Panera Bread, P Hut, Red Lobster, Ruby Tuesday, Sonic, Starbucks, Subway, T Bell, TX Roadhouse, Wendy's Comfort Suites, Hampton Hilton Garden, Holiday Inn, Woodspring Suites $Tree, A AT&T, Best Buy, BooksAMillion, Dick's, Discount Tire, Home pot, JC Penney, Jo-Ann Fabrics, Macy's, Marshall's, Micha NTB, Old Navy, Petsmart, Sam's Club/gas, Staples, Target, izon, Walmart/Subway, W Circle K/dsl DQ, Harde Waffle House to VSU, U-Haul
53	S Park Blvd, E same as 54
52.5mm	Appomattox River
52	Washington St, Wythe St, E Marathon/dsl, Valero Jade Garden Knights Inn, Royal Inn Petersburg Bfd, W Liberty H
51	I-85 S, to South Hill, US 460 W
50d	Wythe St, (from nb), same as 52
50b c	E 7-11 Flagship Inn
50a	US 301, US 460 E, to Crater Rd, County Dr, E BP, RaceW dsl, Star Express Hardee's American Inn, Budget California Inn, EconoLodge H
48b a	Wagner Rdon Crater Rd, W Gulf/dsl, Wawa Arb Bojangles, Burger King, Capt D's, KFC, King's BBQ, Little C sar's, Pizza Hut, Plaza Mexico, Subway, Taco Bell, Taste of Ch Country Inn&Suites, Super 8 $General, $Tree, Adva Parts, H, Martin's Foods, O'Reilly Parts, PepBoys, USPO, V zon, Walgreens, Walmart
47	VA 629, to Rives Rd, W Citgo, Shell/dsl Bojangles, K Outlaw's Rest. Heritage Motel Ace Hardware, sam 48 on US 301, Softball Hall of Fame Museum, Walmart
46	I-295 N (exits left from sb), to Washington
45	US 301, E Shell/dsl, W Exxon/Circle K Lightho Rest., Nanny's Rest., Steven Kent Rest. Comfort Inn, D Inn, Hampton Inn, Holiday Inn Express, Howard Johnson, Q ity Inn
41	US 301, VA 35, VA 156, E Exxon/dsl/scales/24hr Nir N Italian Rest. EconoLodge South 40 camp res W Travelers Inn
40mm	weigh sta both lanes

INTERSTATE 95 Cont'd

Exit #	Services
37	US 301, Carson, W [gas] BP/dsl, Shell/dsl
36mm	**[rest stop] nb, full [handicapped] facilities, litter barrel, petwalk, [phone], [picnic], vending**
33	VA 602, W [gas] Davis/Exxon/Subway/Starbucks/dsl/scales/24hr, Moble/Wendys/dsl [food] Denny's, Little Italy, Popeye's [lodging] Hampton Inn, Sleep Inn
31	VA 40, Stony Creek, to Waverly, W [gas] Citgo/dsl, Shell/dsl [food] Tastee Hut [other] Family$
24	VA 645
20	VA 631, Jarratt, W [gas] Exxon/Blimpie/Pizza Hut/dsl/24hr, Sunoco/dsl [other] $General, Ford
17	US 301, 1 mi E [lodging] Knights Inn, Reste Motel [other] Jellystone Park Camping
13	VA 614, to Emporia, E [gas] Exxon/Chester's/dsl, Shell/dsl
12	US 301 (from nb)
11b a	US 58, Emporia, to South Hill, E [gas] Citgo/Burger King, Exxon/Blimpie/LJ Silver, Shell/dsl [food] Applebee's, Arby's, Carolina BBQ, Cracker Barrel, Domino's, Hardee's, KFC, McDonald's, Pizza Hut, Taco Bell, Wendy's, Wong's Garden [lodging] Country Inn&Suites, Fairfield Inn, Rodeway Inn [other] [H], Advance Parts, Buick/Chevrolet/GMC, CVS Drug, Family$, Food Lion, NAPA, O'Reilly Parts, Rite Aid, Verizon, Walmart, W [gas] Exxon, Pilot/Sadler/5 Guys Burgers/dsl/scales/24hr/@, Race-In/Quiznos/dsl [food] Bojangles, Pino's Pizza, Shoney's [lodging] Best Western, Days Inn, Hampton Inn, Holiday Inn Express, Quality Inn, Sleep Inn
8	US 301, E [gas] Citgo, Simmons/Exxon/Huddle House/dsl/scales/24hr [lodging] Motel 6, Red Carpet Inn [other] truck repair
4	VA 629, to Skippers, E [gas] Loves/McDonald's/dsl/scales/24hr, Pilot/Dunkin'/Subway/dsl/scales/24hr, Shell/IHOP, W [lodging] AmericanInn
3.5mm	Fountain's Creek
.5mm	**Welcome Ctr nb, full [handicapped] facilities, litter barrels, petwalk, [phone], [picnic], vending**
0mm	Virginia/North Carolina state line

INTERSTATE 264 (Norfolk)

Exit #	Services
23mm	**I-264 begins/ends.** [gas] BP, Shell [other] convention ctr
22	Birdneck Rd, N [food] Pizza Hut [other] museum, vet, S [gas] Shell/dsl [food] Dunkin', Max&Erma's, McDonald's/playplace, Subway [lodging] DoubleTree [other] Family$, Food Lion, O'Reilly Parts
21	VA Beach Blvd, First Colonial Rd, N [gas] BP, Shell [food] Applebee's, Arby's, Burger King, Chick-fil-A, China Wok, Chipotle, DQ, Five Guys, IHOP, KFC, McDonald's, Moe's SW Grill, Otani Japanese, Outback Steaks, Panera Bread, Pizza Hut, Plaza Azteca, Schlotzsky's, Shogun Japanese, Sonic, Starbucks, Subway, Taco Bell, Virginian Steaks, Wendy's, Zero's Subs [other] Advance Parts, CVS, GNC, JoAnn Fabrics, Kroger/dsl, Michael's, Office Depot, Petsmart, Rite Aid, SteinMart, Target, Toyota, Trader Joe's, USPO, Verizon, vet, Walgreens, Whole Foods Mkt, S [gas] Shell, Wawa/dsl [other] 7-11, CarQuest, Firestone/auto, NAPA
20	US 58 E, to VA Beach Blvd (eb only), N [gas] Kangaroo, Wawa/dsl [food] Bojangle's, Capt. George's Seafood, China Moon, Hardee's, Ruby Tuesday, Starbucks, Subway [other] 7-11, Family$, Food Lion, Kia/Lincoln, Lowe's, PepBoys, TJ Maxx, Tuesday Morning, vet
19	Lynnhaven Pkwy, N [gas] 7-11, Wawa [food] Ensenada Mexican, Iggle's, Lucky Express, Subway [other] Audi, Chevrolet, Ford, Hobby Lobby, Hyundai, Jaguar, Porsche, Subaru, VW, S [food] Five Guys, McDonald's, Olive Garden, Starbucks, Taco Bell [other] Walmart

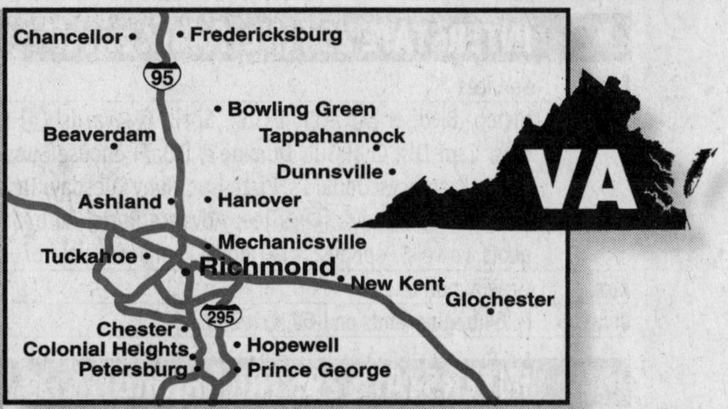

Exit #	Services
18	Rosemont, N [gas] Exxon [food] Bonefish Grill, Burger King, Denny's, Hardee's, Jade Garden, KFC, LJ Silver, McDonald's, Mi Casita Mexican, Papa John's, Pizza Hut, Starbucks, Taco Bell, Wendy's, Zero's Subs [lodging] EconoLodge [other] $Tree, Acura, AutoZone, BJ's Whse/gas, CarMax, Chrysler/Dodge/Jeep, Food Lion, Home Depot, Honda, Kroger, Merchant's Tire/Auto, Nissan, Petsmart, Rite Aid, Sam's Club/gas, Walgreens, S [gas] Speedway/dsl, Wawa/dsl [food] Four Seasons Chinese [other] $General, CVS
17.5mm	**inspection sta wb only**
17a b	Independance Blvd, N [gas] Exxon [food] Bahama Breeze, Cheesecake Factory, Chipotle, IHOP, Jason's Deli, Macaroni Grill, Max-&Erma's, McDonald's, Mission BBQ, Panera Bread, PF Chang's, Ruby Tuesday, Smokey Bones BBQ, Starbucks, Taco Bell, Village Inn, Wendy's [lodging] Candlewood Suites, Crowne Plaza, Days Inn, Extended Stay, Hilton Garden, Motel 6, Westin [other] Barnes&Noble, Best Buy, Dick's, Kohl's, Michael's, Old Navy, Steinmart, Target, Walgreens, S [gas] 7-11, Exxon/dsl, Wawa/dsl [food] Arby's, Azteca Mexican, Domino's, Firehouse Subs, Golden Corral, Hardee's, KFC, Panda China, Quiznos, Starbucks, Subway, Taco Bell, TX Roadhouse, Zero Subs [lodging] InTown Suites [other] $General, auto repair, Food Lion, Mazda, Rite Aid, vet
16	Witchduck Rd
15a b	Newtown Rd, N [food] Capt D's, Domino's, McDonald's, Taco Bell, Wendy's [lodging] Homewood Suites, TownePlace Suites [other] 7-11, AutoZone, S [gas] BP, Shell [food] Denny's [lodging] Courtyard, Hampton Inn, Holiday Inn, La Quinta, Red Roof Inn, SpringHill Suites [other] 7-11, Rite Aid
14b a	I-64, US 13, to Military Hwy
13	US 13, Military Hwy, N [gas] Shell [food] Arby's, Boston Mkt, Lonestar Steaks, Mongolian BBQ, Norfolk Garden Korean, Piccadilly, Schlotzsky's [lodging] Days Inn, EconoLodge, Motel 6, Ramada Ltd [other] Costco/gas, CVS, Firestone/auto, Ross
12	Ballentine Blvd, N [other] [H], Norfolk SU
11b a	US 460, VA 166/168, Brambleton Ave, Campostello Rd, N [gas] 7-11 [food] Chick-fil-A
10	Tidewater Dr, City Hall Ave, exits left from eb, N [gas] Shell [food] McDonald's, Popeye's
9	St Paul's Blvd, Waterside Dr, S [other] to Harbor Park Stadium
8	I-464 S, to Chesapeake
7.5mm	tunnel
7b a	VA 141, Effingham St, Crawford St, N [gas] Shell [other] Naval [H], S [gas] Citgo [other] Shipyard
6	Des Moines Ave (from eb)
5	US 17, Frederick Blvd, N [gas] WaWa/dsl [food] Chick-fil-A, Dunkin', IHOP, Little Caesar's, Rally's, Taco Bell, Wendy's [other] [H], Advance Parts, CVS Drug, Kroger, to Midtown Tunnel, Walgreens, Walmart, S [gas] BP [other] Harley-Davidson
4	VA 337, Portsmouth Blvd

VA

VA

INTERSTATE 264 (Norfolk) Cont'd

Exit #	Services
3	Victory Blvd, N 7-11, Exxon, Shell, WaWa/dsl Bojangles, Capt D's, CookOut, Domino's, DQ, Firehouse Subs, KFC, Krispy Kreme, McDonald's, Pizza Hut, Ruby Tuesday, Taco Bell, Tops China, Wendy's $Tree, Advance Parts, AutoZone, BigLots, Lowe's, PepBoys, S Royal Farms/dsl, Valero/dsl
2b a	Greenwood Dr
0mm	**I-264 begins/ends on I-64, exit 299.**

INTERSTATE 295 (Richmond)

MECHANICSVILLE

Exit #	Services
53b a	I-64, W to Charlottesville, E to Richmond, to US 250, **I-295 begins/ends.**
51b a	Nuckols Rd, **1 mi** N Miller's/dsl, Valero Cheeburger, Chen's Chinese, Home Team Grill, McDonald's, Nonna's Pizzaria, Pizza Hut, Rico's Mexican, Samurai Japanese, Starbucks, Subway, Tropical Smoothie Cafe CVS Drug, Food Lion, Walgreens, S Exxon/Mkt Cafe USPO
49b a	US 33, Richmond, S JJ's Grille, Little Angela's, Little Caesar's, Little Szechuan, Nuevo Mexico $ General, 7-11, CVS
45b a	Woodman Rd, **1-2 mi** S 7-11 Little Caesar's $General, CVS Drug, Meadow Farm Museum
43	I-95, US 1, N to Washington, S to Richmond (exits left from nb) on US 1, N Shell/dsl Applebee's, Arby's, BBQ, Buffalo Wild Wings, Chick-fil-A, Chili's, Chipotle Mexican, Coldstone, Famous Dave's BBQ, Firehouse Subs, McDonald's, O'Charley's, O'Dragon buffet, Panera Bread, Papa John's, Pizzaro, Plaza Azteca Mexican, Red Robin, Roda Japanese, Shoney's, Starbucks, Subway, TX Roadhouse, Wendy's Candlewood Suites, Comfort Suites, Courtyard, Hampton Inn, SpringHill Suites $Tree, AT&T, Barnes&Noble, Best Buy, Burlington, Dick's, Firestone/auto, GNC, Goodyear/auto, Home Depot, JC Penney, Macy's, Martin's Foods, Merchant's Tire, Michael's, Petsmart, Ross, Target, Tire America, Walgreens, **1-2 mi** S 7-11, Shell, WaWa Aunt Sarah's, Burger King, Frida's Mexican, Hardee's, KFC/Taco Bell, McDonald's, Ming's Dynasty, Starbucks, Subway, Waffle House, Wendy's Best Value Inn, Cavalier Motel, Days Inn, EconoLodge, Knights Inn, Sleep Inn $Tree, Food Lion, Lowe's, Walmart
41b a	US 301, VA 2, E BP/dsl, Valero/dsl, WaWa/dsl Bojangles, Burger King, China Kitchen, Dunkin', Marty's Grill, McDonald's, Popeye's, Stevi B's, Subway, Tropical Smoothie Cafe, Wendy's, Zheng Chinese $General, AT&T, AutoZone, Kroger/gas, URGENT CARE, Verizon, vet, Walgreens, **0-4 mi** W Exxon/dsl Friendly's Holiday Inn, Super 8, Travelodge
38b a	VA 627, Pole Green Rd, **0-1 mi** E 7-11, Exxon/dsl, Sunoco/dsl Antonio's Pizza, Bell Cafe, Bruster's, Chen's Rest., Mimmo's Rest., Patron Mexican, Subway Food Lion, vet, W 7-11, Valero Pasta House CVS, H
37b a	US 360, E BP, Shell/dsl, Valero Applebee's, Arby's, Buffalo Wild Wings, Burger King, Chick-fil-A, Cookout, Cracker Barrel, DQ, Franco's, Gus' Italian, IHOP, Jersey Mike's, KFC, McDonald's, Mexico Rest., Moe's SW Grill, Noodles&Co, Outback Steaks, Panera Bread, Papa John's, Peking Chinese, Pizza Hut, Roma Italian, Ruby Tuesday, Shoney's, Starbucks, Subway, Taco Bell, Waffle House, Wendy's Hampton Inn, Holiday Inn Express $Tree, Advance Parts, Aldi Foods, AT&T, Best Buy, BJ's Whse/gas, CVS, Food Lion, GNC, Home Depot, Kohl's, Marshall's, Old Navy, Petsmart, Target, Verizon, Walgreens, Walmart/Burger King, W 7-11, Sunoco/dsl, Valero/dsl $General, to Mechanicsville

HOPEWELL

Exit #	Services
34b a	VA 615, Creighton Rd, E 7-11, Valero
31b a	VA 156, E Exxon/dsl to Cold Harbor Bfd, W S (4mi), Valero Hardee's (4mi) Courtyard (4mi), EconoLo (4mi), Holiday Inn Express (4mi), Motel 6 (4mi)
28	I-64, to US 60, W museum
25	Rd 895 W (**toll**), to Richmond
22b a	VA 5, Charles City, E Exxon/dsl DQ Shirley Plantation, W Valero/Subway/dsl China Taste, Portabe Cafe Food Lion, Richmond Nat Bfd, Rite Aid
18mm	James River
16	Rivers Bend Blvd
15b a	VA 10, Hopewell, E BP/dsl Burger King H, Ja River Plantations, W EC/Subway/dsl, Exxon/McDonal dsl, Sheetz, WaWa/dsl Cesare's Ristorante, Chen's Re Jalapeno's, Rivers Bend Grill, Taco Bell, Wendy's, Wing's za Hyatt Place, Residence Inn CVS Drug, Food Lion
13mm	Appomattox River
9b a	VA 36, Hopewell, E Citgo, Gulf, WaWa/dsl Bojang El Nopal, Hardee's, KFC, Little Caesar's, McDonald's, Ro Italian Best Western, EconoLodge, Fairfield Inn, StayC Suites $General, Advance Parts, AutoZone, Family$, O'R ly Parts, Verizon, vet, Walgreens, W BP/dsl, Exxon, Sh dsl, Sunoco/dsl Burger King, Denny's, DQ, Dragon Expr Dunkin', Kanpai Japanese, McDonald's, Papa John's, Pizza Ruby Tuesday, Shoney's, Starbucks, Subway, Taco Bell, T China, Waffle House, Wendy's Baymont Inn, Candlew Suites, Hampton Inn, Quality Inn $Tree, Chevrolet, Fami Food Lion, Rite Aid, to Petersburg Nat Bfd, U-Haul, US A Museum
5.5mm	Blackwater Swamp
3b a	US 460, Petersburg, to Norfolk, E EC/Subway/dsl, Pilo Wendy's/dsl/scales/24hr Prince George BBQ, **1-2 mi** W BP/dsl McDonald's
1	I-95, N to Petersburg, S to Emporium, **I-295 begins/ends.**

INTERSTATE 495 (DC)

WASHINGTON AREA

Exit #	Services
57	I-95 S, I-395 N, I-95 N. **I-495 & I-95 N run together. See MD I- exits 25b a-2b a.**
54b a	VA 620, Braddock Rd, S Shell/dsl Hong Kong Exp 7-11, Ctr for the Arts, Geo Mason U, NTB, Rite Aid, Safe Foods, USPO
52b a	VA 236, Little River Tpk, Fairfax, E Liberty/dsl, Suno repair Chicken Loco, KFC/Taco Bell, Little Caesar's, Donald's, Wendy's $Tree, 7-11, Advance Parts, GNC, Pe Safeway Foods
51	VA 657, Gallows Rd, W Exxon H, 7-11
50b a	US 50, Arlington Blvd, Fairfax, Arlington, E Marri W Shell, Sunoco/dsl Chevy's Mexican, Five G Grevey's Rest, Jasmine Garden, McDonald's, Panda Expr Panera Bread, Papa John's, Starbucks, Sweetwater Tavern, U Grill, Wendy's Residence Inn H, CVS Drug, Midas, ples, Target, URGENT CARE, vet
49c b a	I-66 (exits left from both lanes), to Manassas, Front Royal
47b a	VA 7, Leesburg Pike, Tysons Corner, Falls Church, E Wes W BP/dsl, Exxon, Shell/dsl BJ's Rest., Chili's, Jim John's, McDonald's, Olive Garden, On-the-Border, Pan Bread, Silver Diner, Starbucks, Subway, Wendy's Emb sy Suites, Hilton Garden AT&T, Best Buy, Bloomingdal Buick/Chevrolet/GMC, Chrysler/Dodge/Jeep, CVS Drug, M shall's, Mr Tire, PetCo, Petsmart, Staples, Subaru/VW, TJ Ma

INTERSTATE 495 (DC) Cont'd

Exit #	Services
46b a	VA 123, Chain Bridge Rd, W Gulf/dsl, Sunoco/dsl Cheesecake Factory, Maggiano's, PF Chang's Courtyard, Crowne Plaza Macy's
45b a	VA 267 W (toll), to I-66 E, to Dulles Airport
44	VA 193, Langley
43	G Washington Mem Pkwy, no trucks
42mm	Virginia/Maryland state line, Potomac River. **Exits 41-27 are in Maryland.**
41	Clara Barton Pkwy, Carderock, Great Falls, no trucks
40	Cabin John Pkwy, Glen Echo (from sb), no trucks
39	MD 190, River Rd, Washington, Potomac
38	I-270, to Frederick
36	MD 187, Old Georgetown Rd, S H
35	(from wb), I-270
34	MD 355, Wisconsin Ave, Bethesda
33	MD 185, Connecticut Ave, N LDS Temple, S Citgo/repair, Giant/dsl, Liberty Chevy Chase Mkt, Starbucks
31b a	MD 97, Georgia Ave, Silver Spring, N H, S BP/dsl, Exxon/dsl, Shell, W Express/dsl Armand's Pizza, Domino's, Mayflower Chinese CVS Drug, Snider's Foods, Staples, vet
30b a	US 29, Colesville, N BP/dsl, Citgo, Shell Chipotle, McDonald's, Papa John's, Red Maple Asian, Starbucks, Subway 7-11/Jerry's Subs, CVS Drug, Safeway Foods
29b a	MD 193, University Blvd
28b a	MD 650, New Hampshire Ave, N BP, Exxon/dsl, Shell/repair Domino's, Quizno's, Starbucks, Urban BBQ 7-11, CVS Drug, Safeway Foods
27	I-95, N to Baltimore, S to Richmond.

I-495 & I-95 S run together. See MD I-95, exits 25b a-2b a.

INTERSTATE 664 (Norfolk)

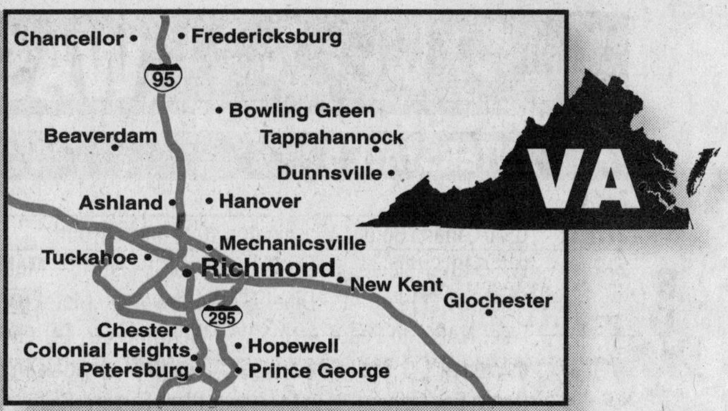

PORTSMOUTH

Exit #	Services
15b a	I-64 to Chesapeake, I-264 E to Portsmouth & Norfolk. **I-664 begins/ends on I-64, exit 299.**
13b a	US 13, US 58, US 460, Military Hwy, E Shell/Frank's/dsl Bowers Hill Inn
12	VA 663, Dock Landing Rd
11b a	VA 337, Portsmouth Blvd, E 7-11, Citgo, Shell/dsl, Speedway Applebee's, Arby's, Buffet City, Burger King, Chick-fil-A, Chili's, ChuckECheese, DQ, Dunkin', Five Guys, Golden Corral, IHOP, McDonald's, Olive Garden, Outback Steaks, Piccadilly, Pizza Hut, Pizza Hut, Red Lobster, Red Robin, Starbucks, Subway, Taco Bell, Wendy's Extended Stay 4 Less, Hampton Inn, Holiday Inn Express $Tree, AutoZone, Best Buy, Big Lots, BJ's Whse/gas, Buick, Firestone/auto, Food Lion, Ford, Home Depot, Merchant's Auto Ctr, Michael's, Old Navy,
11b a	Continued Petsmart, Ross, Sam's Club/gas, Target, Tuesday Morning, Walmart, W 7-11 Burger King, Cracker Barrel, Old Bay Seafood, Subway, Waffle House Candlewood Suites, Fairfield Inn Lowe's
10	VA 659, Pughsville Rd, E 7-11, Citgo, Shell La Tolteca Food Lion, Rite Aid, vet
9b a	US 17, US 164, E 7-11, Speedway/dsl, Wawa Burger King, Capt D's, Domino's, DQ, Dunkin', Great Wall Chinese, KFC, McDonald's, Papa John's, Pizza Hut, Sonic, Taco Bell, Waffle House, Wendy's Budget Lodge, Extended Stay America, Sleep Inn, Studios & Suites for Less, Super 8 $Tree, Advance Parts, Chevrolet, Honda, Hyundai, Kia, NAPA, Nissan, O'Reilly Parts, tires, Toyota, W Buffalo Wild Wings, Subway Comfort Suites, Hilton Garden H, Harris Teeter, to James River Br
8b a	VA 135, College Dr, E 7-11, Murphy USA/dsl Applebee's, Arby's, Chick-fil-A, Chipotle, Firehouse Subs, IHOP, McDonald's, Panda Express, Panera Bread, Ruby Tuesday, Subway, Taco Bell, TX Roadhouse, Wendy's, Zaxby's Dick's, Discount Tire, Food Lion, GNC, Kohl's, Petsmart, Rite Aid, TJ Maxx, Walmart, W Riverstone Chophouse Courtyard, TownePlace Suites
11.5mm	insp sta nb
9mm	James River
8mm	tunnel
7	Terminal Ave
6	25th St, 26th St, E 7-11 McDonald's, W Subway
5	US 60 W, 35th St, Jefferson Ave, E Fast&Easy #1 Chinese, Church's, King's Pizza Hornsby Tire
4	Chesnut Ave, Roanoke Ave
3	Aberdeen Rd, W 7-11 Hardee's, McDonald's, Wendy's
2	Powhatan Pkwy, E 7-11, **1-2 mi** W Coldstone, Joe's Crabshack, Longhorn Steaks Hilton Garden, SpringHill Suites Bass Pro Shop, BJ's Whse/gas, Lowe's
1b a	I-64, W to Richmond, E to Norfolk. **I-664 begins/ends on I-64.**

VA

NOTES

= gas = food = lodging = other = rest stop

WASHINGTON

INTERSTATE 5

BLAINE

Exit #	Services
277mm	USA/Canada Border, Washington state line, customs
276	WA 548 S, Blaine, E Chevron/dsl, Exxon/dsl, Mobil/dsl, Shell/dsl Big Al's Diner Northwoods Motel Duty Free, NAPA, to Peace Arch SP, W **Welcome Ctr**, Chevron/dsl/repair Back Forest Steaks, Chada Thai, Edaleen Dairy, Ocean Bay Chinese, Pasa Del Norte, Pizza Factory, Railway Cafe, Starbucks, Tony's Cafe Anchor Inn, Bay Side Motel, Cottage by the Bay B&B, International Motel, Sunset Inn Blaine Marine Park, USPO
275	WA 543 N (from nb, no return), E Chevron/dsl, Mkt/dsl, Shell/dsl Burger King, Subway $Tree, Border Tire, Cost-Cutter Foods, Rite Aid, truck customs
274	Peace Portal Drive (from nb, no return), Blaine W Shell/dsl Lizzie's Cafe Semi-ah-moo Resort
270	Birch Bay, Lynden W Shell/Domino's/Subway/dsl Bob's Burgers, Jack-in-the-Box, Subway Semi-ah-moo Resort Birch Bay Mkt, Thousand Trails Camping, vet
269mm	**Welcome Ctr sb, full facilities, info, litter barrels, petwalk, vending**
267mm	**nb, full facilities, info, litter barrels, petwalk, vending**
266	WA 548 N, Grandview Rd, Custer W Arco Birch Bay SP
263	Portal Way, E Pacific Pride/dsl, Shell/dsl El Nopal Mexican AA RV Park, Cedars RV Park
263mm	Nooksack River
262	Main St, Ferndale, E Chevron/dsl, Pilot/Subway/dsl/scales/24hr McDonald's Super 8 GCR Tires, vet, W Gull/dsl, Shell/dsl Bob's Burgers, Domino's, DQ, Jack-in-the-Box, Papa Murphy's, Sonic, Starbucks, Taco Time Motel 6 $Tree, Grocery Outlet, Haggen's Foods, NAPA, O'Reilly Parts, Schwab Tire, Verizon, vet, Walgreens
260	Slater Rd, Lummi Island, E Arco/dsl antiques, El Monte RV Ctr, 4 mi W Silver Reef Hotel/Casino Lummi Ind Res
258	Bakerview Rd, E Asian Fusion, Five Guys, IHOP, Jack-in-the-Box, Papa Murphy's, Port of Subs, Starbucks, Subway, Taco Time La Quinta Costco/dsl, Fred Meyer/dsl, Verizon, W 76/7-11, Arco, Mkt/dsl Mykono's Greek Rest. Holiday Inn Express, Hotel Bellingham, Shamrock Motel , Bellingham RV Park, st patrol
257	Northwest Ave, E Jack-in-the-Box, Starbucks Home 2 Hilton, La Quinta, SpringHill Suites, TownePlace Suites Cadillac/Chevrolet
256b	Bellis Fair Mall Pkwy (from nb), E JC Penney, Target
256a	WA 539 N, Meridian St, E Shell/dsl, Super Gas/dsl Arby's, Asian 1, Boston's Rest., Buffalo Wild Wings, Burger King, China Palace, Chipotle, Denny's, Domino's, DQ, Jimmy John's, Lilia's Mexican, McDonald's, Mi Mexico, Olive Garden, Red Robin, Shari's, Starbucks, Subway, Taco Bell, Taco Time, Thai House Rest., Wendy's, Wonderful Buffet Baymont Inn, Best Western, Comfort Inn, Holiday Inn Express, Oxford Suites, Quality Inn $Tree, AT&T, Barnes&Noble, Best Buy, Dick's, Hobby Lobby, Home Depot, JC Penney, Kohl's, Macy's, Marshall's, Michael's, Midas, O'Reilly Parts, Office Depot, O'Reilly Parts, PetCo, Petsmart, Rite Aid, Ross, Schwab Tire, Sierra Trading Post, Target, TJ Maxx, U-Haul, Verizon, Walgreens, Walmart/McDonald's, WinCo Foods, W Slo Pitch Grill EconoLodge, Rodeway Inn

WA

BELLINGHAM

255	WA 542 E, Sunset Dr, Bellingham, E 76, Chevron/dsl, Sh dsl A&W/KFC, Applebee's, El Gitano Mexican, Hawaii B Jack-in-the-Box, Panda Express, Panda Palace, RoundTable za, Starbucks, Taco Bell Jo-Ann Fabrics, Lowe's, Rite Safeway/dsl, to Mt Baker, Tuesday Morning, USPO, Veriz Walgreens, W
254	Iowa St, State St, Bellingham, E 76, Mobil/dsl Au VW, Chrysler/Dodge/Jeep, Honda, Hyundai, Kia, Mercedes, san, Subaru, Toyota, Volvo, W Chevron/dsl, Shell McDonald's, Starbucks, Subway AutoZone, Ford, Mi NAPA, O'Reilly Parts
253	Lakeway Dr, Bellingham, E Little Caesar's, Papa Joh Papa Murphy's, Port of Subs, Rhodes Cafe, Sol de Mex Subway, Woods Coffee Guesthouse Inn, Sheraton F Points 7-11, Discount Tire, Fred Meyer/dsl, URGENT CA Whole Foods Mkt, W same as 252
252	Samish Way, Bellingham, E same as 253, W 76, Chevr dsl, SuperGas/dsl Boomers Drive-In, Busara Thai Cuis Domino's, El Agave, El Albanil Mexican, Five Columns Gr Kyoto Steaks, McDonald's, Pizza Hut, Sehome Diner, Starbu Subway, Taco Time, Wendy's Bay City Motel, Belling Lodge, Cascade Inn, Coachman Inn, Days Inn, Motel 6, Inn $Tree, Ace Hardware, AT&T, Haggen Foods, REI, Aid, URGENT CARE, vet, Walgreens
250	WA 11 S, Chuckanut Dr, Bellingham, Fairhaven Hist Dist W Arco, Shell/repair Starbucks, Subway to Alaska Ferry Larrabee SP
246	N Lake Samish, E Lake Padden RA, W Shell/dsl
242	Nulle Rd, S Lake Samish
240	Alger, E Shell/dsl/LP/RV dump Alger Grille W pering Firs Motel/RV Parking
238mm	**both lanes, full facilities, litter barrels, petwalk, vending**
236	Bow Hill Rd, E Skagit Hotel Casino/rest./dsl/LP
235mm	**weigh sta sb**
234mm	Samish River
232	Cook Rd, Sedro-Woolley, E Chevron/dsl, Shell/dsl, Tesla Bob's Burgers, Jack-in-the-Box, Starbucks, Subway F field Inn , KOA (3mi)
231	WA 11 N, Chuckanut Dr, E Camping World RV Ctr, Ha man's RV Ctr, Kia, vet, W st patrol, to Larrabee SP (14m
230	WA 20, Burlington, E Chevron, Shell/dsl Applebe Carino's Italian, Jack-in-the-Box, Mi Mexico, MOD Pizza, back Steaks, Papa Murphy's, Pizza Factory, Pizza Hut/Taco Popeye's, Red Robin, Starbucks Cocusa Motel, Ster Motel , $Tree, 7-11, AutoZone, Fred Meyer/dsl, Hag Foods, JC Penney, Macy's, Schwab Tire, Skagit Transmissi Target, to N Cascades NP, Walgreens, W Pacific Pr dsl McDonald's Holiday Inn Express Harley-Da son, Hyundai, to San Juan Ferry
229	George Hopper Rd, E Arco, Mobil/dsl Carl's Jr, Chip Mexican, Five Guys, Jamba Juice, Jimmy John's, McDona Olive Garden, Panera Bread, Sakura Japanese, Shari's, bucks, Subway, Taco Del Mar, Wendy's Candlewood Su Hampton Inn AT&T, Best Buy, Costco/gas, Dick's, Disc Tire, Home Depot, Kohl's, Michael's, Old Navy, Outlet Sho famous brands, Petsmart, Ross, See's Candies, Verizon, W Chrysler/Jeep/Dodge, Ford/Lincoln, Honda, Mazda, san, Subaru, Toyota, VW

BURLINGTON

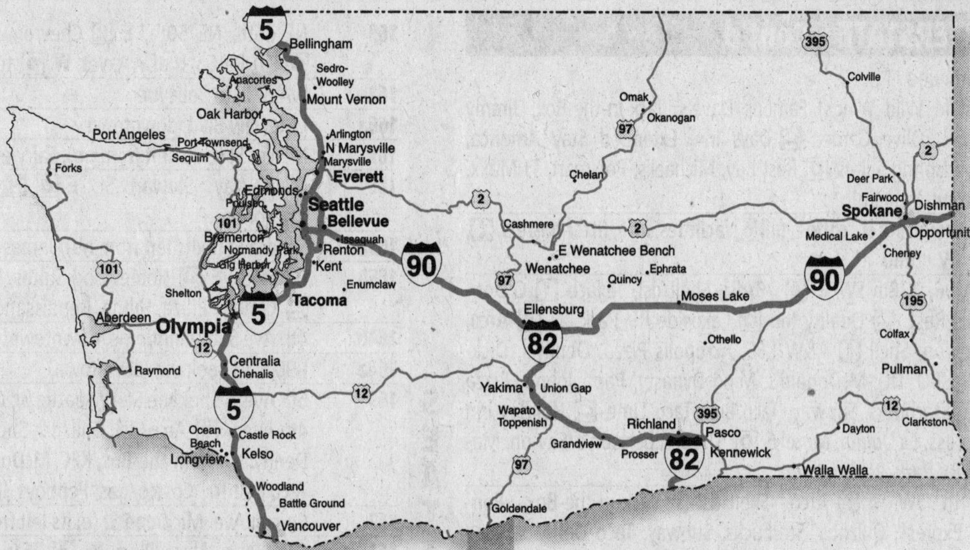

WA

INTERSTATE 5 Cont'd

Exit #	Services
228mm	Skagit River
227	WA 538 E, College Way, Mt Vernon, E A&W, Big Scoop Rest., Denny's, Dragon Inn, El Gitano, Firehouse Subs, Hong Kong Rest., Jack-in-the Box, Jersey Mike's, KFC, Max Dale's Steak Chops, Moreno's Mexican, Papa Murphy's, Pizza Hut, Riverside Cafe, RoundTable Pizza, Starbucks, Subway, Taco Bell, Taco Time Days Inn, West Winds Motel $Tree, Ace Hardware, AutoZone, Grocery Outlet, Hobby Lobby, Jo-Ann Fabrics, Motorworks, Office Depot, O'Reilly Parts, PepBoys, PetCo, Rite Aid, Safeway/dsl, Tire Factory, Verizon, W APP/dsl, Shell/dsl Arby's, Burger King, Burgermaster, DQ, Fortune Chinese, IHOP, Los Compadres, Panda Express, Royal Star Buffet Best Western, Quality Inn, Tulip Inn Blade RV Ctr, Chevrolet, Lowe's, Riverbend RV Park, URGENT CARE, Walmart/Subway
226	WA 536 W, Kincaid St, E H, W Old Towne Grainery Rest., Skagit River Brewing Co City Ctr, NAPA, Red Apple Mkt, visitor info
225	Anderson Rd, E 76/dsl CarQuest, Country Motorhomes, W Chevron Evert's RV Ctr, Freightliner, Poulsbo RV Ctr
224	WA 99 S (from nb, no return), S Mt Vernon, E food, gas/dsl
221	WA 534 E, Conway, Lake McMurray, E 76/dsl farmers mkt, W 76/dsl, Chevron/dsl/LP Conway Deli Channel Lodge/Rest. (11mi) Blake's RV Park/marina (6mi), USPO
218	Starbird Rd
215	300th NW W Interstate/dsl
214mm	weigh sta nb
212	WA 532 W, Stanwood, Bryant W 76/dsl, Shell/Burger Stop/dsl Camano Island SP (19mi)
210	236th NE, E Angel Winds Casino, River Rock/dsl
209mm	Stillaguamish River
208	WA 530, Silvana, Arlington, E 76, A1/dsl, Arco/dsl, Chevron/dsl, Pilot/PJ Fresh/dsl/scales/24hr Denny's, Subway Arlington Motel Chevrolet, to N Cascades Hwy, W Mobil/dsl
207mm	both lanes, coffee, full facilities, litter barrels, petwalk, RV dump, vending
206	WA 531, Lakewood, E 7-11, 76/dsl, Arco, Shell Alfy's Pizza, Buzz Inn Steaks, Domino's, Jack-in-the-Box, Jersey Mike's, Jimmy John's, KFC, Little Caesar's, McDonald's, Moose Creek BBQ, Olympia Pizza, Panda Express, Papa Murphy's, Peking Palace, Starbucks, Subway, Taco Time, Wendy's Best Western+,
206	Continued Quality Inn, Wyndham Garden $Tree, AT&T, Chrysler/Dodge/Jeep, Ford, Harley-Davidson, Honda, Jo-Ann Fabrics, Lowe's, O'Reilly Parts, Rite Aid, Safeway/dsl, Schwab Tire, vet, Walmart/Subway, W Bonefish Grill, Boston's, Buffalo Wild Wings, Burger King, Chipotle, Coldstone, Firehouse Subs, Five Guys, Hop Jack's, IHOP, Jamba Juice, MOD Pizza, Outback Steaks, Pizza Hut, Popeye's, Qdoba, Red Robin, Starbucks, Taco Bell, Taco Bell AT&T, Best Buy, Costco/gas, Dick's, Discount Tire, Firestone/auto, Hobby Lobby, Marshall's, Michael's, Office Depot, PetCo, Target, to Wenburg SP, Tuesday Morning, Verizon
202	116th NE, E Shell/dsl Arby's, Blazing Onion Burger, Carl's Jr, DQ, Papa John's, Popeye's, Sonic, Starbucks, Subway, Taco Bell Home 2 Suites $Tree, Kohl's, Petsmart, Rite Aid, Ross, URGENT CARE, Verizon, WinCo Foods, W Chevron/dsl, Donna's Trkstp/Gull/dsl/scales/24hr/@ McDonald's, Olive Garden, RAM Rest. Seattle Outlets/famous brands, st patrol, Tulalip Resort/Casino
200	88th St NE, Quil Ceda Way, E 7-11, Shell/dsl/LP Applebee's, Jersey Mike's, Mkt St Cafe, Starbucks Holiday Inn Express Haggen's Foods, W USA Bob's Burgers, Panera Bread, Port of Subs Cabela's, casino, Home Depot, Walmart/McDonald's
199	WA 528 E, Marysville, Tulalip, E 76, Arco, Chevron/dsl, Shell/dsl Burger King, Don's Rest./24hr, DQ, Jack-in-the-Box, Jimmy John's, Las Margaritas Mexican, MOD Pizza, Subway Village Motel/Rest. Albertson's, AT&T, Big Lots, JC Penney, Petco, Rite Aid, Staples, Verizon, Walgreens, W 76, Chevron/dsl McDonald's, Taco Time, Wendy's Quality Inn casino, Chevrolet, Robinson RV Ctr, Subaru, to Tulalip Indian Res
198	Port of Everett (from sb), Steamboat Slough, st patrol
195mm	Snohomish River
195	Port of Everett (from nb), Marine View Dr
194	US 2 E, Everett Ave W Shell/dsl City Ctr, Schwab Tire
193	WA 529, Pacific Ave (from nb) W 76 Denny's, Hunan Palace Best Western, Delta Hotel, Travelodge H, Lowe's
192	Broadway, to 41st St W 76/dsl, Chevron, Shell Buzz Inn Steaks, IHOP, Little Caesar's, Quiznos, Starbucks, Subway Travelodge City Ctr, Verizon
189	WA 526 W, WA 527, Everett Mall Way, Everett, E Arco, Chevron, Shell/dsl Alfy's Pizza, Burger King, Buzz Inn Steaks, Subway, Wendy's EconoLodge, Extended Stay America Costco/gas, vet, WinCo Foods, W Shell/dsl Bob's Burgers,

WA

INTERSTATE 5 Cont'd

SEATTLE

Exit	Services
189	Continued Buffalo Wild Wings, Famous Dave's, Jack-in-the-Box, Jimmy John's, Olive Garden Days Inn, Extended Stay America, Woodspring Suites Best Buy, Michael's, Petsmart, TJ Maxx, Verizon, Walmart
188mm	**/weigh sta sb, coffee, full facilities, info, litter barrels, , RV dump**
186	WA 96, 128th SW, **E** 76/dsl, Shell/dsl, Texaco O'Donnells Rest. Quality Inn Lakeside RV Park, **W** Arco, Chevron, Shell A&W/KFC, Acropolis Pizza, Denny's, Dickey's BBQ, DQ, McDonald's, Ming Dynasty, Papa John's, Pizza Hut, Starbucks, Subway, Taco Bell, Taco Time Holiday Inn Express, La Quinta, Motel 6 $Tree, Albertson's/Sav-on, Maple RV Park, PepBoys, vet
183	164th SW, **E** Arco, Shell/dsl Jack-in-the-Box, Panda Express, Quiznos, Starbucks, Subway, Taco Del Mar, Taco Time Walgreens, Walmart, **W** Chevron/dsl Five Guys, MOD Pizza, Subway Fred Meyer/dsl, vet
182	WA 525, Alderwood Mall Blvd, to Alderwood Mall, **E** I-405 S, to Bellevue, **W** Arco Anthony's SeafoodGrill, Azteca Mexican, Buffalo Wild Wings, Cafe Rio, Claim Jumper, Fatburger, Jersey Mike's, Keg Steaks, Macaroni Grill, Panera Bread, PF Chang's, Qdoba Mexican, Red Robin, TCBY Homewood Suites, Residence Inn JC Penney, Kohl's, Macy's, Nordstrom, REI, Rite Aid, Ross, See's Candies, Target, vet, World Mkt
181	44th Ave W, to WA 524, Lynnwood, **E** 76/dsl, Arco, Shell Chick-fil-A, Jimmy John's, Little Caesar's, McDonald's/playplace, Old Spaghetti Factory, Starbucks Embassy Suites, Extended Stay America, Hampton Inn, Holiday Inn Express Albertson's, Barnes&Noble, Best Buy, Jaguar, Land Rover, Lowe's, Old Navy, O'Reilly Parts, PetCo, Staples, Verizon, vet, Whole Foods Mkt, **W** 76/dsl, Arco, Shell/repair Applebee's, Arby's, Buca Italian, Chipotle Mexican, ChuckeCheese, Denny's, Ezell's Chicken, Harbour Buffet, IHOP, Jack-in-the-Box, KFC, McDonald's, Olive Garden, Panda Express, Red Lobster, Rock Woodfire Pizza, Starbucks, Subway, Taco Bell, Taco del Mar, Taco Time, Todo Mexico, Wendy's, Zeeks Pizza Best Value Inn, Best Western, Courtyard, La Quinta 7-11, Fred Meyer/dsl, Goodyear/auto, Grocery Outlet, Schwab Tire, URGENT CARE, USPO, vet
179	220th SW, Mountlake Terrace, Mountlake Terrace **W** Shell/dsl Azteca Mexican, Port of Subs, Subway H, vet
178	236th St SW (from nb), Mountlake Terrace
177	WA 104, Edmonds, **E** Chevron/dsl, Shell/dsl Domino's, Gabriel's Fire BBQ, Mazatlan Mexican, McDonald's/playplace, Pagliacchi Pizza, Starbucks, Subway, Time Out Burger, Todo Mexico Motel 6 O'Reilly Parts, RiteAid, Thriftway Foods, URGENT CARE
176	NE 175th St, Aurora Ave N, to Shoreline, **E** Safeway/dsl
175	WA 523, NE 145th, 5th Ave NE
174	NE 130th, Roosevelt Way
173	1st Ave NE, Northgate Way, **E** EVgo EVC Azteca Mexican, BlueFin Grill, CA Pizza Kitchen, Chipotle Mexican, Domino's, Five Guys, Gate Buffet, Jimmy John's, Mama Stortini's, Ram Rest., Red Robin, Stanford's Rest. Barnes&Noble, Best Buy, Dick's, Discount Tire, JC Penney, Macy's, Nordstrom, Old Navy, Petco, Ross, Target, Verizon, **W** 76, Chevron, Shell/dsl McDonald's, Saffron Grill, Starbucks Hotel Nexus 7-11
172	N 85th, Aurora Ave
171	WA 522, Lake City Way, Bothell
170	Ravenna Blvd, **E** Shell/dsl

SEATTLE

Exit	Services
169	NE 45th, NE 50th, **E** Chevron, Shell Qdoba, Sub H, PetCo, U of WA, vet, **W** to Seattle Pacific U, zoo
168b	WA 520, to Bellevue
168a	Lakeview Blvd, downtown
167	Mercer St (exits left from nb), Fairview Ave, Seattle Ctr
166	Olive Way, Stewart St, **E** H, **W** SpringHill Su Honda
165a	Seneca St (exits left from nb), James St, **E** H
165b	Union St, **E** Homewood Suites, **W** Ruth's Chris St Crowne Plaza, Hilton, Renaissance Inn, Sheraton
164b	4th Ave S, to Kingdome, downtown
164a	I-90 E, to Spokane, downtown
163	6th Ave, S Spokane St, W Seattle Br, Columbian Way, **1 mi W 4th Ave S** Arco/dsl, Gull/dsl, Shell Arby's, Burger K Denny's, Jack-in-the-Box, KFC, McDonald's, Starbucks, Sub Taco Bell Costco/gas, Pepboys, USPO
162	Corson Ave, Michigan St (exits left from nb), same as 161
161	Swift Ave, Albro Place **W** 76/dsl, Shell/dsl Starb Georgetown Inn Verizon
158	Pacific Hwy S, E Marginal Way **W** Chevron/dsl NAP
157	ML King Way
156	WA 539 N, Interurban Ave (no EZ return to sb), Tukw **E** Pacific Pride/dsl Billy Baroos Rest., **W** 76 Shell/dsl Jack-in-the-Box, Quiznos, Starbucks, Sunny yaki Days Inn
154b	WA 518, Burien **W** Extended Stay America
154a	I-405, N to Bellevues
153	S Center Pkwy, (from nb), **E** Chevron/dsl Appleb Azteca Mexican, Bahama Breeze, BJ's Rest., Buffalo Wild Wi Burger King, CA Pizza Kitchen, Cheesecake Factory, Chip Mexican, ClaimJumper, Coldstone, Duke's ChowderHouse, mous Dave's, Five Guys, Grazie Ristorante, IHOP, Jamba J Mayflower of China, McDonald's, Mizuki Buffet, Mizuki Japa Steaks, Mongolian Grill, Old Spaghetti Factory, Olive Gar Outback Steaks, Panda Express, Panera Bread, Qdoba Mexi Red Robin, Simply Thai, Sizzler, Stanford's Rest., Starbucks, way, Thai Cuisine, Zoopa DoubleTree Inn, Holiday Inn press, Hotel Interurban $Tree, Acura, AT&T, Barnes&No Best Buy, Big Lots, Firestone/auto, JC Penney, Jo-Ann Fab Kohl's, Lowe's, Macy's, Michael's, Nordstrom, Nordstrom R Office Depot, Old Navy, PetCo, Petsmart, REI, Ross, See's Can Target, Tuesday Morning, Verizon, World Mkt
152	S 188th, Orillia Rd **W** 76/dsl Dave's Diner, Den Jack-in-the-Box, Taco Bell DoubleTree Hotel, Hampton La Quinta, Motel 6 city park, to
151	S 200th, Military Rd, **E** 76/Subway/dsl Motel **W** 7-11, 76, Chevron IHOP Best Value Inn, Western, Comfort Inn, Country Inn Suites, Days Inn, Fair Inn, Hampton Inn, Holiday Inn Express, Residence Inn, S Inn AutoZone, city park, O'Reilly Parts, U-Haul
149	WA 516, to Kent, Des Moines, **E** Century Motel P bo RV Ctr, **W** Arco, Chevron/dsl, Shell/dsl Chur Los Cabos Mexican, McDonald's, Pizza Hut, Starbucks, way Garden Suites, Kings Arms Motel $Tree, Lov Meineke, to Saltwater SP, Walgreens
147	S 272nd, **E** Chevron/dsl, **W on Pacific Hwy** Arco, S dsl Jack-in-the-Box, Little Caesar's, McDonald's, F Murphy's, Starbucks, Subway, Taco Bell AutoZone, Ba Drug, Safeway
143	S 320th, Federal Way **W** 76/dsl, Arco Applebee's, teca Mexican, Black Angus, Black Bear Diner, Buffalo Wild Wi Cafe Rio, Chick-fil-A, Chipotle Mexican, Church's, Colds

INTERSTATE 5 Cont'd

143 Continued
Denny's, Domino's, Grand Peking, Ivar's Seafood, Jasmine Mongolian, Jimmy John's, McDonald's, Mika Japanese Buffet, Old Country Buffet, Panda Express, Panera Bread, Papa Murphy's, Qdoba Mexican, Ram Rest., Red Lobster, Red Robin, Starbucks, Subway, Taco Time, Tokyo Japanese Steaks, Village Inn, Wendy's Best Western+, Clarion, Comfort Inn, Courtyard, Extended Stay America, Hampton Inn AT&T, Barnes&Noble, Best Buy, Campeon Mkt, Dick's, Jo-Ann Fabrics, Kohl's, Macy's, Marlene's Natural Mkt, Michael's, O'Reilly Parts, PetCo, Petsmart, Rite Aid, Ross, Safeway/dsl, Target, TJ Maxx, to Dash Point SP, Trader Joe's, Tuesday Morning, Verizon, Walmart/McDonald's

142b a WA 18 E, S 348th, Enchanted Pkwy, E funpark, W Chevron, Shell/dsl Arby's, Biscuits Cafe, Burger King, Del Taco, Denny's, Jack-in-the-Box, Jamba Juice, Jimmy Mac's Roadhouse, KFC, McDonald's, Olive Garden, Panda Express, Popeye's, Puerta Vallarta, Quiznos, RoundTable Pizza, Shari's, Starbucks, Subway, Taco Bell, Taco Del Mar, Taco Time, Thai Bistro, The Rock Pizza, Time Out Grill Day's Inn, Quality Inn, Red Lion Inn H, AT&T, Chevrolet, Costco/gas, Discount Tire, Hobby Lobby, Home Depot, Lowe's, Office Depot, O'Reilly Parts, Pepboys, Schwab Tire, UHaul, Verizon, Walmart/Subway

140mm **both lanes, full facilities, litter barrels, petwalk, RV dump, weigh sta nb**

137 WA 99, Fife, Milton, E 76/dsl, Chevron/dsl, Shell DQ, Johnny's Rest., Warthog BBQ Motel 6 Acura, Cadillac, RV Country, visitor info, W 76/dsl, 76/dsl Arby's, Denny's, Fife Thai Rest., Jersey Mike's, KFC, McDonald's, Pick Quick Burgers, Pizza Hut, Poodle Dog, Sapporo Japanese, Starbucks, Subway, Taco Bell, Taco Time, Wendy's Days Inn, EQC Motel/casino, Quality Inn 7-11, Audi/Porsche, Mercedes, O'Reilly Parts, Schwab Tire, Tacoma RV Ctr, Verizon

136b a Port of Tacoma, E CFN/dsl Baydos RV Ctr, BMW, Costco, Honda, I-5 Motors, Mini, Peterbilt, W 76/dsl, Gull/dsl, Love's/Chester's/Subway/dsl/scales/LP/RV dump/24hr, Shell/dsl Jack-in-the-Box Extended Stay America, Guesthouse Inn, Port of Tacoma Inn, Rodeway Inn, Sunshine Motel, Travelodge Fife RV Ctr, Goodyear/biodsl, Harley-Davidson, Johnson RV Ctr, Land Rover/Jaguar/Lexus, Meineke, NAPA, Poulsbo RV Ctr, truck repair, Volvo

135 Bay St, Puyallup, E 76/Tahoma Express Majestic RV Park (4mi), W Subway La Quinta to Tacoma Dome

134 Portland Ave (from nb), same as 135

133 WA 7, I-705 W Best Western, Courtyard, Holiday Inn Express City Ctr, museum, Tacoma Dome

132 WA 16 W, S 38th, Gig Harbor, to Bremerton W Adriatic Grill, BJ's Rest., Buffalo Wild Wings, Chipotle, Five Guys, Jamba Juice, Jimmy John's, Krispy Kreme, Panera Bread, Red Robin, Wendy's $Tree, Best Buy, Costco/gas, Firestone/auto, Ford/Toyota, Goodyear/auto, JC Penney, JoAnn Fabrics, Macy's, Nordstrom, Old Navy, PetCo, REI, to Pt Defiance Pk/Zoo, Verizon, World Mkt

130 S 56th, Tacoma Mall Blvd W Shell/dsl Axteca Mexican, ChuckeCheese, Jack-in-the-Box Extended Stay America

129 S 72nd, S 84th, E Chevron, Valero Applebee's, Burger King, DQ, Elmer's, Famous Dave's, IHOP, Jack-in-the-Box, Jimmy John's, Mongolian Grill, Olive Garden, Popeye's, Red Lobster, RoundTable Pizza, Shari's, Starbucks, Subway Hampton Inn, Motel 6, Shilo Inn Bass Pro Shops, WinCo Foods, W Hooters Clarion Home Depot, to Steilacoom Lake

128 S 84th St (from nb)same as 129, E 76, Shell/dsl Denny's, Ginger Palace, Greatwall Chinese, Subway American Lodge, Comfort Inn, Crossland Suites, Econolodge, Hampton Inn, Holiday Inn Express, Howard Johnson, Red Lion Hotel, Rothem Inn, Travelodge, W Shell/dsl $Tree, Discount Tire

127 WA 512, S Tacoma Way, Puyallup, Mt Ranier W 7-11, 76/7-11, Arco/dsl AAA Buffet, DQ, Ivar's Seafood, Mazatlan Mexican, McDonald's, Sizzler, Starbucks, Taco Time, Wendy's Candlewood Suites, Western Inn Advance Parts, Grocery Outlet, O'Reilly Parts

125 to McChord AFB, Lakewood W 76/Circle K/dsl, Chevron, Mobil, Shell/dsl A&W/KFC, Carr's Rest., Church's, Denny's, Greek Cafe, Jack-in-the-Box, Pizza Hut, Subway, Wendy's Holiday Inn Express, Home Motel, TownePlace Suites H, 7-11, Aamco, Ford, NAPA, O'Reilly Parts, tires/repair, U-Haul

124 Gravelly Lake Dr W 76/Circle K, Arco/repair El Toro Mexican, Pizza Casa, same as 125

123 Thorne Lane, Tillicum Lane

122 Berkeley St, Camp Murray W Chevron/repair Gertie's Grill, Jack-in-the-Box, KFC, McDonald's, Papa John's, Popeye's, Starbucks, Subway, Taco Bell 7-11, AutoZone

120 Ft Lewis, E Ft Lewis Military Museum

119 Du Pont Rd, Steilacoom, E to Ft Lewis, W 76 Happy Teriyaki, Starbucks, Subway Hampton Inn, Home 2 Suites

118 Center Dr W Chevron/dsl Farrelli's Pizza, Fortune Cookie Chinese, Jack-in-the-Box, Koko's Wok, McDonald's, McNamara's Eatery, Pizza Hut, Quiznos, Starbucks, Subway, Super Buffet, Viva Mexico Best Western, Fairbridge Inn, Fairfield Inn

117mm **weigh sta nb**

116 Mounts Rd, Old Nisqually, E golf, W Eagles Pride Grill

115mm Nisqually River

114 Nisqually, E Arco/dsl, Chevron/repair/Lp Medicine Creek Cafe, Nisqually Grill Nisqually Auto Repair, Nisqually RV Park, River Bend RV Park (3mi), WLYH RV Park (2mi)

111 WA 510 E, Marvin Rd, to Yelm, E 76/Circle K, Chevron/dsl, Shell/dsl Burger King, Chipotle, Coldstone, Domino's, Firehouse Subs, Hawk's Prairie Rest./casino, Jack-in-the-Box, Jamba Juice, Jersey Mike's, KFC/LJ Silver, Lemon Grass Rest., McDonald's, Panda Express, Panera Bread, Papa Murphy's, Popeye's, Puerto Vallarta, RAM Rest., Red Robin, Starbucks, Subway, Super Buffet, Taco Del Mar, Taco Time, Vinny's NY Pizza Best Western+, Day's Inn $Tree, AT&T, Best Buy, BigLots, Costco/gas, Grocery Outlet, Harley Davidson, Home Depot, O'Reilly Parts, Petco, Rite Aid, Safeway/gas, Schwab Tire, Verizon, Walgreens, Walmart/Subway, WLYH RV Park (2mi), W 7-11/dsl Mayan Mexican, Meconi's Subs Cabela's, Tolmie SP (5mi)

WA

INTERSTATE 5 Cont'd

OLYMPIA

Exit #	Services
109	Martin Way, Sleator-Kenny Rd, E (food) Main Chinese Buffet, Taco Bell, The Rock Pizza (other) Discount Tire, W (gas) 76/dsl, Shell/dsl (food) Brewery City Pizza, Burger King, Casa Mia, Denny's, Domino's, El Serape Mexican, Jimmy John's, Red Lobster, Shari's, Subway (lodging) Comfort Inn, La Quinta, Quality Inn, Ramada Inn, Super 8 (other) H, Point S Tire
108	Sleater-Kinney Rd, E (gas) Shell/dsl (food) Applebee's, Arby's, Carl's Jr, McDonald's/playplace, Pizza Hut/Taco Bell, Starbucks, Wendy's (lodging) Candlewood Suites, Holiday Inn Express (other) $Tree, Firestone/auto, Fred Meyer/dsl, GNC, Kohl's, Marshall's, Michael's, Office Depot, Petsmart, Rite Aid, Target, Tuesday Morning, Verizon, W (gas) Arco/dsl, Shell (food) Casa Mia, Dirty Dave's, El Sarape Mexican, Jack-in-the-Box, Panda Express, Starbucks, Subway (lodging) Hampton Inn, Ramada Inn (other) H, AT&T, Lowe's, Point S Tires, Safeway/gas, same as 109
107	Pacific Ave, E (gas) Shell/dsl/E-85 (food) DQ, Fajita Grill, Izzy's Pizza, Shari's, Subway, Taco Time (other) Albertson's, Home Depot, Ross, vet, W (other) H, Coumbs RV Ctr
105	St Capitol W (gas) 76/Subway/dsl, Chevron/dsl (lodging) Quality Inn (other) to St Capitol
104	US 101 N, W Olympia, to Aberdeen W (gas) 7-11, Arco, Chevron/dsl, Shell/Oly Burger/dsl (food) Jack-in-the-Box (lodging) Extended Stay America, Red Lion Hotel (other) Buick/GMC, Chevrolet/Cadillac, Ford, Honda, Hyundai, Kia, Lincoln/Mazda, Nissan, Subaru, VW
103	2nd Ave, Deschutes Ave, to hist dist
102	Trosper Rd, Black Lake, E (gas) Shell (food) Brewery City Pizza, Burger King, DQ, El Sarape Mexican, Jack-in-the-Box, KFC, McDonald's, Starbucks, Subway, Taco Bell, Taco Time (lodging) Best Western, Motel 6, Tumwater Inn (other) O'Reilly Parts, Schwab Tire, Tumwater Auto Repair, Verizon, W (gas) Chevron, Mobil (food) Best Buffet, Little Caesar's, Panda Express, Papa Murphy's, Pizza Hut, Starbucks, Subway, Taco Del Mar, The Brick Rest. (other) Albertson's, Alderbrook RV Park, AutoZone, Costco/gas, Fred Meyer/dsl, GNC, Home Depot, URGENT CARE, Walgreens, Walmart
101	Tumwater Blvd, E (gas) Chevron, Shell/dsl (food) DQ (1mi), Inferno's Pizza, Meconi's Pizza, Red Wagon Burgers (lodging) Comfort Inn, GuestHouse Inn, Olympia Camping (other) 7-11, USPO
99	WA 121 S, 93rd Ave, Scott Lake, E (gas) Pilot/McDonald's/Subway/dsl/scales/24hr (other) Ace Hardware, American Heritage Camping, Olympia Camping
95	WA 121, Littlerock, 3 mi E (other) Millersylvania SP, RV camping, W (gas) Chevron/dsl (3mi) (food) Farmboy Drive-In (other) Freightliner
93.5mm	**RS sb, coffee, full ♿ facilities, info, litter barrels, petwalk, ☎, picnic, vending**
91mm	**RS nb, coffee, full ♿ facilities, info, litter barrels, petwalk, ☎, picnic, vending**
88	US 12, Rochester, E (other) Blair's I-5 RV Ctr, I-5 Truckwash, W (gas) Arco, CFN/dsl, Chehalis/Burger King/dsl, Chevron/dsl, Shell (food) DQ, Figaro's Pizza, Jack-in-the-Box, Jack-in-the-Box, Mariachi Mexican, McDonald's, Quiznos, Starbucks (lodging) Fairfield Inn, Great Wolf Lodge (other) auto repair, Outback RV Park (2mi)
82	Harrison Ave, Factory Outlet Way, Centralia, E (gas) Arco (food) Burger King, Burgerville, Casa Ramos Mexican, DQ, Jimmy John's, Panda Chinese, Papa Pete's Pizza, Peking House Chinese, Pizza Hut, Quiznos, Thai Dish, Wendy's (lodging) Centralia Inn, King Oscar Motel, Motel 6, Quality Inn (other) AutoZone, VF/famous brands, W (gas) Chevron/dsl, Mobil/dsl, Texaco (food) Arby's, Bill&Bea's, Country Cousin Rest., Denny's, Domino's, Jack-in-the-Box, McDonald's, Papa Murphy's, Starbucks, Subway,

CENTRALIA

KELSO

Exit #	Services
82	Continued Taco Bell (lodging) Motel 6 (other) AT&T, Centralia Outlets/fam brands, city park, Midway RV Park, O'Reilly Parts, Rite Safeway/dsl, Schwab Tire, Verizon
82mm	Skookumchuck River
81	WA 507, Mellen St, E (gas) Chevron/dsl, Shell/dsl (food) Sub (lodging) Empress Inn, Lakeview Inn, Pepper Tree Motel/RV P dump, W (other) H
79	Chamber Way, E (gas) Mobil/dsl (food) Jalisco Mexican (other) Ch ler/Dodge/Jeep/Fiat, museum, Tires, Inc., vet, visitor W (gas) Chevron/dsl/LP/e85 (food) Applebee's, Burger King, Donald's, Sonic, Starbucks, Subway, Taco Bell, Taco Del Wendy's (other) $Tree, GNC, Grocery Outlet, Home Depot, chael's, O'Reilly Parts, st patrol, Toyota, Verizon, Walgre Walmart/McDonald's
77	WA 6 W, Chehalis, E (gas) 76/dsl, Cenex/dsl/LP (food) Dairy Jeremy's Cafe (lodging) Holiday Inn Express (other) NAPA, Schwab USPO, W (other) Rainbow Falls SP (16mi), truck parts, vete museum
76	13th St, E (gas) Arco, Chevron/dsl (food) Denny's, Jack-in-the- Kit Carson Rest., Subway (lodging) Best Western+, Econolodge, lax Inn (other) Awesome I-5 RV Ctr/RV dump, Baydo's RV Ctr, F W (other) RV park/dump
74	Labree Rd
72	Rush Rd, Napavine, E (gas) Shell/dsl/scales (food) Burger K McDonald's, RibEye Rest., Subway (other) Country Canopy Ctr/repair, W (gas) Loves/Carl's Jr/dsl/scales/24hr, Sh dsl (food) Arby's, Starbucks, Taco Bell
72mm	Newaukum River
71	WA 508 E, Onalaska, Napavine, E (gas) 76/dsl (other) KC Truck Pa
68	US 12 E, Morton, E (gas) Arco/dsl, Texaco/dsl (food) Spiffy's R (other) Mt Ranier NP, to Lewis&Clark SP, W (gas) 76/rest./dsl
63	WA 505, Winlock W (gas) Shell/Chesters/dsl/LP
60	Toledo Vader Rd, Toledo
59	WA 506 W, Vader, E (gas) Shell/dsl (food) Beesley's Cafe (other) Park, W (gas) Chevron/Subway/dsl (food) Country House Rest.
59mm	Cowlitz River
57	Jackson Hwy, Barnes Dr, E (other) R&R Tires, W (gas) Texaco/G Cee's/café/dsl/scales/24hr/@ (other) repair, RV camping
55mm	**RS both lanes, full ♿ facilities, litter barrels, petwalk, ☎, vending**
52	Barnes Dr, Toutle Park Rd, E (other) Paradise Cove RV Park/ger al store, W (other) Toutle River RV Resort
50mm	Toutle River
49	WA 504 E, Castle Rock, E (gas) Chevron/dsl/LP, Shell/dsl (food) 4 Diner, Burger King, C&L Burgers, El Compadre Mexican, Pa Pete's Pizza, Subway (lodging) 7 West Motel, Mt St Helens Mo Timberland Inn (other) Seaquest SP (5mi), W (food) McDona (other) visitor info
48	Castle Rock, E (other) Cedars RV Park/dump, W (other) city park
46	Pleasant Hill Rd, Headquarters Rd, E (other) Cedars RV Park/dum
44mm	**weigh sta sb, weigh sta sb**
42	Bridge Dr, Lexington W (gas) Chevron/dsl (food) Subway (other) a repair
40	to WA 4, Kelso-Longview W (gas) Texaco (lodging) Econolodge
39	WA 4, Kelso, to Longview, E (gas) Arco, Shell (food) Denn Jack-in-the-Box, McDonald's, Shari's, Starbucks, Subway, Ta Time (lodging) Motel 6, Red Lion Hotel, Super 8 (other) $Tree, Br Hollow RV Park, city park, Rite Aid, Verizon, W (food) Burger Ki DQ, Fiesta Bonita Mexican, Izzy's Pizza, Panera Bread, Red L ster, Taco Bell (lodging) Comfort Inn, GuestHouse Inn (other) JC Penn museum, Safeway/dsl, Target

WA

INTERSTATE 5 Cont'd

Exit #	Services
36	WA 432 W, to WA 4, to US 30, Kelso, **E** [other] U-Neek RV Ctr, **W** [other] RV Camping, Toyota
32	Kalama River Rd, **E** [food] Fireside Café [other] Camp Kalama RV Park/camping/gifts
31mm	Kalama River
30	Kalama, **E** [gas] Chevron/dsl [food] Burger Bar, Columbia Rest., Lucky Dragon Chinese, Playa Azul Mexican, Poker Pete's Pizza, Subway [lodging] Motel 6 [other] antiques, Godfrey's Drug, USPO, **W** [gas] Spirit/dsl [lodging] McMenamin's Kalamazoo Inn [other] RV camping
27	Todd Rd, Port of Kalama, **E** [gas] Rebel/Shell/café/dsl/24hr
22	Dike Access Rd **W** [food] Taco Bell [other] Columbia Riverfront RV Park, O'Reilly Parts, Schwab Tire, Verizon, Walmart/Subway
21	WA 503 E, Woodland, **E** [gas] Arco/dsl, Chevron, Pacific Pride/dsl, Shell/LP/dsl [food] America's Diner, Burgerville, Casa Tapatia, DQ, Fat Moose Grill, Grocery Outlet, Guilliano's Pizza, Mali Thai, OakTree Rest., Rosie's Rest. [lodging] Best Western, Lewis River Inn, Rodeway Inn [other] Ace Hardware, Hi-School Drug, Woodland Shores RV Park, **W** [gas] Astro [food] Antony's Pizzaria, Carl's Jr, Guadalajara Mexican, Los Pepes Mexican, McDonald's, Papa Murphy's, Starbucks, Subway [other] $Tree, NAPA, repair/tires, Safeway/dsl
20mm	N Fork Lewis River
18mm	E Fork Lewis River
16	NW La Center Rd, La Center, **E** [gas] Shell/dsl [food] Twin Dragons Rest. (2mi) [other] Paradise Point SP, Tri-Mountain Golf/rest., **W** [lodging] Ilani Casino/Hotel
15mm	**weigh sta nb**
14	WA 501 S, Pioneer St, Ridgefield, **E** [gas] Arco [food] Country Café, Papa Pete's Pizza, Subway, Teriyaki Thai [other] Big Fir RV Park (4mi), Ridgefield WR, to Battleground Lake SP (14mi), Tri-Mountain RV Park, vet, **W** [gas] Chevron/dsl
13mm	**[rest stop] sb, full [handicapped] facilities, info, litter barrels, petwalk, [phone], [picnic], RV dump, vending**
11	WA 502, Battleground, **[rest stop] nb, full [handicapped] facilities, info, litter barrels, petwalk, [picnic], RV dump, vending**
9	NE 179th St **W** [gas] Chevron/dsl [other] RV Park
7	I-205 S (from sb), to I-84, WA 14, NE 134th St, **E** [gas] 7-11, Arco, Mobil [food] Applebee's, Billygan's Roadhouse, Burger King, Burgerville, Jack-in-the-Box, McDonald's, Muchas Gracias, Panda Express, Round Table Pizza, Starbucks, Subway, Taco Bell [lodging] Holiday Inn Express, Quality Inn, Shilo Inn [other] [H], 99 RV Park, Albertson's, Safeway/dsl, Verizon, Walgreens, **W** [gas] Shell [food] Baskin-Robbins, Bruchi's, El Tapatio, Garlic Jim's Pizza, Papa Murphy's, PizzaSchmitzza, Planet Thai, Starbucks, Subway [lodging] La Quinta [other] AT&T, Fred Meyer, URGENT CARE
5	NE 99th St, **E** [food] Burgerville, Carl's Jr, Del Taco, Domino's, Fat Dave's Rest., Popeyes, Quiznos [other] 7-11, AutoZone, Harley-Davidson, Walgreens, Walmart/Subway, Winco Foods/gas, **W** [gas] Arco/dsl, Chevron/dsl [food] Applebee's, Bortolami's Pizza, McDonald's, Subway, Taco Del Mar [other] $Tree, Grocery Outlet, Kohl's, Office Depot, PetCo, Target, Verizon
4	NE 78th St, Hazel Dell, **E** [gas] 7-11, 76 [food] Baja Fresh, Baskin Robbins, Burger King, Canton Chinese, Don Pedro Mexican, Dragon Buffet, Izzy's Grill, KFC, McDonald's, Muchas Gracias Mexican, PeachTree Rest., Pizza Hut, Skipper's, Starbucks, Subway, Taco Bell [lodging] Quality Inn [other] Aamco, AT&T, CarQuest, CostLess Parts, Firestone, Fred Meyer, Jo-Ann, O'Reilly Parts, Tire Factory, U-Haul, **W** [gas] Shell/dsl/LP [food] Buffalo Wild Wings, Chipotle Mexican, Five Guys, Jack-in-the-Box, Jazzy John's BBQ,

VANCOUVER

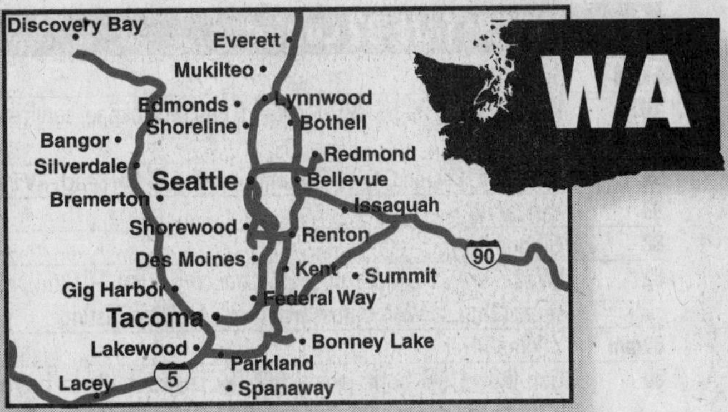

Exit #	Services
4	Continued Jimmy John's, Little Caesar's, Panda Express, Pita Pit, RoundTable Pizza, Starbucks, Wendy's [other] GNC, Hancock Fabrics, Natural Grocers, Petsmart, Ross, Safeway, Tuesday Morning
3	NE Hwy 99, Main St, Hazel Dell, **E** [gas] 7-11 [food] Muchas Gracias Mexican, Pizza Hut, Skippers, **W** [gas] Arco/dsl, Chevron/dsl [food] Papa Murphy's [other] Safeway, transmissions
2	WA 500 E, 39th St, to Orchardss
1d	E 4th, Plain Blvd W, to WA 501, Port of Vancouvers
1c	Mill Plain Blvd, City Ctr, **E** [other] Clark Coll, **W** [gas] Chevron [food] Black Angus [lodging] Comfort Inn [other] st patrol
1b	6th St, **E** [food] Joe's Crabshack, Who Song & Larry's Mexican, **W** [lodging] EconoLodge, Hilton, Red Lion Hotel
1a	WA 14 E, to Camus, **E** [other] [H], **W** [lodging] EconoLodge, Hilton
0mm	Washington/Oregon state line, Columbia River

WA

INTERSTATE 82

Exit #	Services
11mm	**I-82 Oregon begins/ends on I-84, exit 179.**
10	Westland Rd, **E** [other] to Umatilla Army Depot
5	Power Line Rd
1.5mm	Umatilla River
1	US 395/730, Umatilla, **E** [food] Jack-in-the-Box (5mi) [lodging] Best Western (8mi), Motel 6 (8mi), Oxford Inn (5mi), Quality Inn/rest. (2mi) [other] Hatrock Camping (8mi), to McNary Dam, **W Welcome Ctr, weigh sta,** [gas] Chevron/dsl, Mobil/Subway/dsl, Shell/Crossroads Trkstp/dsl/rest./24hr [lodging] Tillicum Motel, Umatilla Inn [other] Harvest Foods, st police, Umatilla Marina/RV Park, USPO
132mm	Washington/Oregon state line, Columbia River
131	WA 14 W, to McNary Dam, Plymouth, **N** [other] RV camping
130mm	**weigh sta wb**
122	Coffin Rd
114	Locust Grove Rd
113	US 395 N, to I-182, Kennewick, Pasco, st patrol, **2-4 mi N** [gas] Exxon/Circle K/dsl, Metro/dsl, USA/dsl [food] A&W/KFC, Azteca Mexican, Bob's Burgers, Burger King, Carl's Jr, Costa Vida, Denny's, Dickey's BBQ, DQ, Jack-in-the-Box, Little Caesar's, McDonald's, Original Pancake House, Osaka Asian, Panda Express, Papa John's, Starbucks, Subway, Taco Bell, Taco Bell [lodging] Baymont Inn, Best Western+, Comfort Suites, Hampton Inn, La Quinta, Motel 6 [other] [H], AT&T, Blue Dog RV Ctr, Fred Meyer/dsl, GNC, Harley-Davidson, Home Depot, PetCo, Rite Aid, Safeway/dsl, st patrol, Traveland RV Ctr, Verizon, vet, Walgreens, Walmart/Subway
109	Badger Rd, W Kennewick, **N** [gas] Exxon/Subway/dsl, Sunmart/dsl [food] Silo Grill [lodging] Quality Inn (3mi), Red Lion Hotel (3mi), Super 8 (3mi), **S** [other] Columbia Sun RV Park
104	Dallas Rd, **3 mi N** [gas] Conoco/dsl

KENNEWICK

= gas = food = lodging = other = rest stop Copyright 2020 - The Next E

INTERSTATE 82 Cont'd

Exit #	Services
102	I-182, US 12 E, to US 395, Richland, Pasco, Spokane, services in Richland
96	WA 224 E, Benton City, N Conoco/cafe/dsl Beach RV Park
93	Yakitat Rd
88	Gibbon Rd
82	WA 22, WA 221, Mabton, S Conoco/dsl H (2mi), museum (2mi), to WAS U Research (2mi), to Wine Tasting
82mm	Yakima River
80	Gap Rd, S **both lanes, full facilities, litter barrels,** **rv dump,** Chevron/dsl, Loves/Carl's Jr/dsl/scales/24hr, Pacific Pride/dsl, Shell/dsl/scales Barn Rest., Burger King, Domino's, Dutch Bros Coffee, El Rancho Alegre, Golden Horse Chinese, KFC/Taco Bell, McDonald's, Starbucks, Subway Best Western+, Holiday Inn Express, Vintners Inn H, Ford, Schwab Tire, URGENT CARE, Verizon, Wine Country RV Park
76mm	**weigh sta eb**
75	County Line Rd, Grandview, S Cenex/Deli/dsl, Safeway/dsl Papa Murphy's O'Reilly Parts, same as 73
73	Stover Rd, Wine Country Rd, Grandview, S Chevron/Subway/dsl, Conoco/dsl 10-4 Café, DQ, Eli&Kathy's Rest., Garcia's Mexican, New Hong Kong Apple Valley Motel, Grandview Motel Chrysler/Dodge/Jeep, IGA Mercado, RV park/dump, Safeway/dsl, Schwab Tire
69	WA 241, to Sunnyside, N Arco/dsl, Shell/dsl/scales/24hr A&W, Burger King, Carl's Jr, China Buffet, El Charrito Mexican, Green Olive Cafe, KFC, Little Caesar's, McDonald's, Mongolian BBQ, Panda Garden, Papa Murphy's, Pizza Hut, Popeye's, Subway, Taco Bell Best Western+, Quality Inn $Tree, AT&T, auto repair, AutoZone, Buick/Chevrolet, Fiesta Foods, GNC, Grocery Outlet, JC Penney, Nissan, O'Reilly Parts, Rite Aid, Ross, Walmart/Subway
67	Sunnyside, Port of Sunnyside, N Chevron/CFN/dsl, Conoco/dsl/e85 Jack-in-the-Box H, BiMart Foods, S Dari-Gold Cheese
63	Outlook, Sunnyside, **3 mi** N Snipe's Rest. Rodeway Inn, Sunnyside Inn Sunnyside RV Park
58	WA 223 S, to Granger, S Arco/dsl/tacos, Conoco/dsl
54	Division Rd, Yakima Valley Hwy, to Zillah, S Teapot Dome NHS
52	Zillah, Toppenish, N 76/dsl, Chevron/Circle K/dsl, Shell/Circle K/dsl El Porton Mexican, McDonald's, Pizza Hut, Subway Best Western+
50	WA 22 E, to US 97 S, Toppenish, **3-4 mi** S Legends Buffet/casino, McDonald's Quality Inn H, Murals Museum, RV Park, to Yakima Nation Cultural Ctr
44	Wapato, N Donald Store/dsl
40	Thorp Rd, Parker Rd, Yakima Valley Hwy
39mm	Yakima River
38	Union Gap (from wb), **1 mi** S gas, lodging, museum
37	US 97 (from eb), S Conoco/dsl
36	Valley Mall Blvd, Yakima, S Arco/dsl, Cenex/dsl, Chevron/Gearjammer/Subway/dsl/scales/24hr/@ A&W/KFC, Applebee's, Buffalo Wild Wings, Burger King, Carl's Jr, Denny's, El Porton Mexican, Famous Dave's, Jack-in-the-Box, Krispy Kreme, McDonald's, Miner's Drive-In, Old Country Buffet, Old Town Sta Rest., Outback Steaks, Panda Express, Panera Bread, SeaGalley Rest., Shari's, Starbucks, Subway, Taco Bell Best Western+, Quality Inn, Super 8 AT&T, Best Buy, Cabela's, Canopy RV Ctr, Costco/gas, Dick's, Frank's Tire, Gap Autoparts, Hobby Lobby, Home Depot, JC Penney, Kohl's, Lowe's, Macy's, Marshall's,
36	Continued Michael's, Office Depot, Old Navy, PetCo, Petsmart, Rite Ross, st patrol, TJ Maxx, Toyota, URGENT CARE, Verizon, W Foods
34	WA 24 E, Nob Hill Blvd, Yakima, N dsl/repair, Sports SP, S 76/dsl, Arco/dsl, CFN/dsl, Nob Hill/dsl H, Hole RV Park, Circle K, Fiesta Foods, Freightliner, Kenw O'Reilly Parts, Peterbilt, Volvo
33	Yakima Ave, Yakima, E Baymont Inn, My Place, N C ron/dsl, Shell/dsl Burger King, El Mirador Mexican ford Inn&Suites Chevrolet, Honda, Walmart/McDona S 7-11, Arco Bob's Burgers, Domino's, DQ, Pizza Taco Bell Fairfield Inn, Hilton Garden, Holiday Inn, Hov Johnson, Ledgestone Hotel, Motel 6, Red Lion Hotel, Red Inn $Tree, BigLots, Schwab Tire, Target
31b a	US 12 W, N 1st St, to Naches, S Arco/dsl, Conoco/dsl, S Golden Moon Chinese, Jack-in-the-Box, Mel's Diner, Teryaki, Red Lobster, Subway, Tammy's Mexican, Waffle's Best Western+, Budget Inn, Days Inn, Econolodge, Econ Inn, Fairbridge Inn, Red Apple Motel, Sun Country Inn, Suns Motel, Yakima Inn Harley-Davidson, Trailer Inns RV Par
30	WA 823 N, Rest Haven Rd, to Selah
29	E Selah Rd, N fruits/antiques
26	WA 821 N, to WA 823, Canyon Rd, N Chevron/Noble mans/Subway/dsl
24mm	**eb, full facilities, litter barrels, RV dump**
23mm	Selah Creek
22mm	**wb, full facilities, litter barrels, RV dump**
21mm	S Umptanum Ridge, elevation 2265
19mm	Burbank Creek
17mm	N Umptanum Ridge, elevation 2315
15mm	Lmuma Creek
11	Military Area, Military Area
8mm	Manastash Ridge, elevation 2672, view point both lanes
3	WA 821 S, Thrall Rd
0mm	I-90, E to Spokane, W to Seattle. **I-82 begins/ends on I-90, exit 1**

SUNNYSIDE

YAKIMA

WA

INTERSTATE 90

Exit #	Services
300mm	Washington/Idaho state line, Spokane River
299	State Line, Port of Entry, N Panda Express Cabel Walmart/Subway
297	**weigh sta wb**
296	Otis Orchards, Liberty Lakes, N 76/dsl Legend's G Best Western+ Buick/GMC, Kia, Mercedes, Porsc S Cenex/dsl, Chevron/LP Barlow's Rest., Carl's Jr, D How Asian, Domino's, Field House Pizza, Jimmy John's, McD ald's, Papa Murphy's, Pizza Hut, Starbucks, Subway, Taco B Taco Time Quality Inn Safeway, Home Depot, O'Re Parts, Peterbilt, RnR RV Ctr, TireRama, URGENT CARE, vet, W greens, Yoke's Mkt
294	Country Vista Dr, Appleway Ave
293	Barker Rd, Greenacres, N Chevron/Trkstp/dsl/scales, Co oco/dsl Wendy's Camping World RV Ctr, Freedo RV Ctr, Harley-Davidson, S Exxon/Subway/dsl, Mobil/ NW RV Ctr, repair, USPO
291b	Sullivan Rd, Veradale, N Arby's, Hong Kong Buffet, Kris Kreme, Outback Steaks, Panera Bread Hampton Inn, N Place, Oxford Suites, Residence Inn AT&T, Barnes&Nob Best Buy, Jo-Ann Fabrics, Verizon, S Chevron/dsl, Conoco/ DQ, Five Guys, Jack-in-the Box, Jimmy John's, KFC, Little Ca sar's, Max Rest., McDonald's, Mongolian BBQ, Noodle Expres

INTERSTATE 90 Cont'd

291b Continued
Panda Express, Pizza Hut, Pizza Pipeline, RoundTable Pizza, Schlotzsky's, Shari's, Starbucks, Subway, Taco Bell, Wendy's, Zelia's Cafe [lodging] Mirabeau Park Hotel, Ramada Inn [other] $Tree, Ace Hardware, Fred Meyer/dsl, GNC, Hancock Fabrics, Kohl's, Lowe's, Michael's, NAPA, PetCo, Petsmart, Ross, Schwab Tire, USPO, Walgreens, Walmart/McDonald's

291a Evergreen Rd, **N** [food] Azteca Mexican, Black Angus, Boston's Rest, Buffalo Wild Wings, Cafe Rio, Honeybaked Ham, IHOP, Red Robin, Twigs Bistro [other] Dick's, Hobby Lobby, JC Penney, Macy's, Old Navy, Staples, TJ Maxx, **S** [gas] Exxon/dsl, Maverik/dsl

289 WA 27 S, Pines Rd, Opportunity, **N** [gas] Sam's/dsl [food] Black Pearl Rest., Subway [other] 7-11, **S** [gas] Cenex, Conoco/dsl, Holiday/dsl [food] Applebee's, DQ, Jack-in-the-Box, Jimmy John's, Qdoba Mexican [lodging] Comfort Inn [other] [H], NW Auto, repair, Walgreens

287 Argonne Rd, Millwood, **N** [gas] Holiday/dsl [food] Burger King, Caruso's Sandwiches, Denny's, Domino's, DQ, Jack-in-the-Box, Longhorn BBQ, McDonald's, Panda Express, Papa Murphy's, Pizza Hut, Starbucks, Subway, Taco Time, Timber Creek Grill, Wendy's [lodging] Baymont Inn, Motel 6, Super 8 [other] $Tree, Albertson's, O'Reilly Parts, Savon, URGENT CARE, Verizon, vet, Walgreens, Yoke's Foods, **S** [gas] Cenex/dsl, Conoco [food] Casa de Oro Mexican, Jimmy John's, Little Caesar's, Starbucks [lodging] Fairfield Inn, Holiday Inn Express [other] Ace Hardware, Rite Aid, Safeway

286 Broadway Ave, **N** [gas] FLYING J/Conoco/rest./dsl/LP/scales/24hr/@, Chevron/dsl [food] Goodyear, Smacky's Cafe, Zip's Burgers [lodging] Rodeway Inn [other] International Trucks, Kenworth, Schwab Tire, **S** [other] 7-11

SPOKANE

285 Sprague Ave, **N** [food] Dragon Garden Chinese, IHOP, Jack-in-the-Box, McDonald's, Panda Express, Starbucks, Subway, Wendy's [lodging] ParkLane Motel/RV Park [other] $Tree, Advance Parts, AutoZone, Costco/gas, Home Depot, Lowe's, O'Reilly Parts, Verizon, Volvo Trucks, Walmart, **S** [gas] Conoco [food] Burger Express, Cottage Cafe, Puerta Vallarta Mexican, Starbucks, Taco Time [other] Acura, CarMax, Chevrolet, Chrysler/Dodge, Ford, Honda, Hyundai, Mazda, Nissan, Toyota, transmissions, vet

284 Havana St (from eb, no EZ return), **N** [gas] Mobil/dsl, **S** [gas] Conoco/dsl [other] Fred Meyer/dsl

283b Freya St, Thor St, **N** [gas] Chevron/dsl, Mobil/dsl, **S** [gas] Conoco/dsl [other] Fred Meyer/dsl

283a Altamont St

282b 2nd Ave, **N** [gas] Conoco/dsl [lodging] Ramada Inn [other] Office Depot

282a WA 290 E, Trent Ave, Hamilton St, **N** [gas] Conoco/dsl [lodging] Comfort Inn [other] Office Depot

281 US 2, US 395, to Colville, **N** [gas] 7-11, Conoco, Exxon, Mobil/dsl [food] Arby's, Dick's Hamburgers, Frankie Doodles Rest., Starbucks, Taco Time [lodging] Days Inn, FairBridge Inn [other] Firestone/auto, Schwab Tire, U-Haul, **S** [lodging] Quality Inn [other] [H], URGENT CARE

280b Lincoln St, **N** [gas] 76/dsl, Chevron [food] Atilano's Mexican, Carl's Jr, Domino's, Jack-in-the-Box, McDonald's, Molly's Rest., Taco Bell, Thai Cuisine, Zip's Burgers [other] Honda, Lexus, Subaru, Toyota, Troy's Tire, **S** [other] [H]

280a Spokane, downtown, **N** [gas] 76/dsl, Chevron/McDonald's/dsl, Conoco [food] Frank's Diner, Jenny's Diner, Pizza Hut, Subway [other] Grocery Outlet

279 US 195 S, Pullman, to Colfax

277b a US 2 W (no ez wb return), to Grand Coulee Dam, **N** [lodging] Blvd Motel, EconoLodge, Hampton Inn, Motel 6, Quality Inn [other] Fairchild AFB

276 Geiger Blvd, **N** [gas] FLYING J/dsl/LP/24hr [food] Denny's, Subway [lodging] Airway Express Inn, Best Western+ [other] st patrol, USPO, **S** [gas] Conoco/dsl

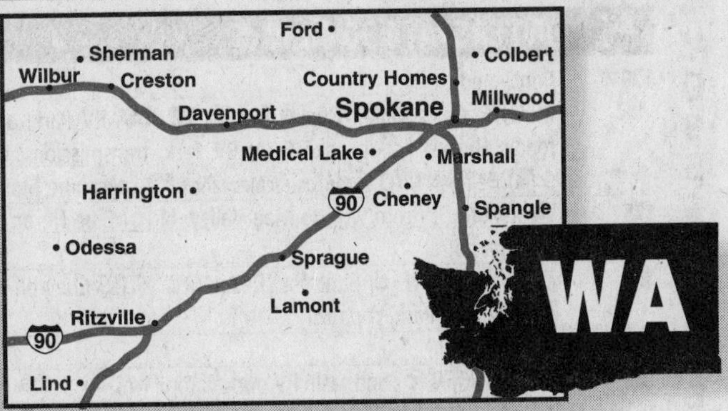

CHENEY

272 WA 902, Medical Lake, **N** [gas] Mobil/dsl [other] Overland Sta/RV Park, **S** [gas] Exxon/Subway/dsl, Petro/Iron Skillet/Subway/dsl/scales/24hr/@ [food] McDonald's [lodging] Super 8 [other] Freightliner, Ponderosa Falls RV Resort, Speedco, truck repair

270 WA 904, Cheney, Four Lakes, **S** [gas] 76 [lodging] Holiday Inn Express (4mi), Willow Springs Motel (6mi) [other] E WA U, Peaceful Pines RV Park (7mi)

264 WA 902, Salnave Rd, to Cheney, Medical Lake, **2 mi N** camping

257 WA 904, Tyler, to Cheney, **S** [other] Peaceful Pines RV Park (10mi), to Columbia Plateau Trail SP, Tyler RV Park

254 Fishtrap, **S** [other] Fishtrap RV camping/tents

245 WA 23, Sprague, **S** [gas] Chevron/dsl [food] Viking Drive-In [lodging] Sprague Motel/RV park [other] 4 Seasons RV Park (6mi), Sprague Lake Resort/RV Park

242mm **[RS] both lanes, full [handicapped] facilities, litter barrels, petwalk, [phone], [picnic], RV dump (eb), tourist/weather info**

231 Tokio, **N** [other] **weigh sta both lanes, S** [gas] Templin's Café/CFN/dsl [other] RV Park

226 Schoessler Rd

221 WA 261 S, Ritzville, City Ctr, **N** [gas] Chevron/McDonald's, Conoco/dsl, Exxon/Circle K/Subway/dsl [food] Cow Creek Cafe/gifts, Ritz Roadhouse, Starbucks, Taco Del Mar, Zip's Rest. [lodging] Best Western, Days Inn/RV park, Empire Motel, Top Hat Motel [other] [H], hist dist, **S** [gas] Love's/Carl's Jr/dsl/scales/24hr

220 to US 395 S, Ritzville, **N** [gas] Bronco/dsl, Texaco/dsl [food] Jake's Cafe [lodging] Top Hat Motel [other] Days Inn/RV Park, Harvest Foods, NAPA, Schwab Tire, st patrol

215 Paha, Packard

206 WA 21, Odessa, to Lind

199mm **[RS] both lanes, full [handicapped] facilities, litter barrels, petwalk, [phone], [picnic], RV dump, vending**

196 Deal Rd, to Schrag

188 U Rd, to Warden, Ruff

184 Q Rd

182 O Rd, to Wheeler

179 WA 17, Moses Lake, **N** [gas] Chevron/dsl, Conoco/Subway/dsl, Ernie's Trkstp/76/café/dsl/24hr, Sunval/dsl, Texaco/dsl [food] Arby's, Bob's Cafe, Burger King, Carl's Jr., Denny's, DQ, Dragon Express, McDonald's, Shari's, Starbucks, Subway, Taco Bell, Wendy's [lodging] Comfort Suites, El Rancho Motel, Fairfield Inn, Holiday Inn Express, Moses Lake Inn, Ramada Inn, Sure Stay Inn+, Wingate Inn [other] [H], $Tree, Chevrolet, Chrysler/Dodge/Jeep, Ford, Honda, Lowe's, Toyota, vet, **S** [other] I-90 RV, Mardon RV Park (15mi), Potholes SP (22mi), Willows RV Park (2mi)

177mm Moses Lake

176 WA 171, Moses Lake, **N** [gas] 76/dsl, Cenex/dsl, Chevron/dsl, Shell, SP/dsl, Sunval/dsl [food] El Rodeo Mexican, Michael's Rest., Subway, Taco Del Mar [lodging] Best Western+, Interstate Inn,

WA

INTERSTATE 90 Cont'd (E)

MOSES LAKE

176 Continued
Motel 6, Oasis Motel, Quality Inn, AAA RV Park, auto repair, Harvest Foods, Lake Front RV Park, transmissions, vet, **S** Half-Sun TP/Chevron/dsl/scales/24hr, Lakeshore Motel

175 Westshore Dr (from wb), to Mae Valley, **N** Blue Heron SP, **S** st patrol

174 Mae Valley, **N** Suncrest Resort/RV, **S** Chevron/dsl, Pier 4 RV Park, st patrol

169 Hiawatha Rd

164 Dodson Rd, **N** Sunbasin RV park/camp (1mi)

162mm **wb, full facilities, litter barrels, petwalk, RV dump**

161mm **eb, full facilities, litter barrels, petwalk, RV dump**

154 Adams Rd

151 WA 281 N, to Quincy, **N** Shell/pizza/subs/dsl (12mi), Shady Grove RV park, to Grand Coulee Dam

149 WA 281 S, George, **N** (12mi), **S** BW&M/Chester's/dsl, Shree's Trkstp/Subway/dsl/scales/24hr

143 Silica Rd, **N** to The Gorge Ampitheatre

139mm **N** Wild Horses Mon, scenic view both lanes

137 WA 26 E, to WA 243, Othello, Richland

137mm Columbia River

136 Huntzinger Rd, Vantage, **N** Chevron/dsl, Blustery's Burger Drive-in, Golden Harvest Rest., Riverstone Vantage Resort/RV Park, to Ginkgo SP, Vantage Gen. Store, **S** to Wanapum SP (3mi)

126mm Ryegrass, elevation 2535, **both lanes, full facilities, litter barrels, petwalk**

115 Kittitas, **N** Shell/dsl/LP, Main Stop Rest., Olmstead Place SP, UHaul

ELLENSBURG

110 I-82 E, US 97 S, to Yakima

109 Canyon Rd, Ellensburg, **N** 76, Astro/dsl, Chevron, Exxon/Circle K, Arby's, Burger King, Carl's Jr, Fiesta Mexican, Jimmy John's, Los Cabos Mexican, McDonald's, Oyama Japanese, Papa Murphy's, RanchHouse Rest., Roadhouse Grill, Rodeo City BBQ, Starbucks, Subway, Taco Bell, Taco Del Mar, Teriyaki Wok, Wendy's, Westside Pizza, Best Western+, Comfort Inn, Holiday Inn Express, Red Lion Inn, Super 8, Advance Parts, AutoZone, Chevrolet, NAPA, O'Reilly Parts, Rite Aid, Schwab Tire, Super 1 Foods, TrueValue, **S** Conoco/Sak's/dsl/scales/LP/24hr, Buzz Inn Steaks, Days Inn/RV park

106 US 97 N, to Wenatchie, **N** 76/dsl, Chevron/dsl, Conoco/dsl, Loves/Subway/dsl/scales/24hr, DQ, IHOP, Perkins, Econolodge, Hampton Inn, Buick/Cadillac/GMC, Canopy Country RV Ctr, Chrysler/Dodge/Jeep, truck repair, Truck/RV Wash, **S** KOA, st patrol

101 Thorp Hwy, **N** Arco/dsl, antiques/fruits/vegetables

93 Elk Heights Rd, Taneum Creek

92.5mm Elk Heights, elev 2359

89mm Indian John Hill, elevation 2141, **both lanes, full facilities, litter barrels, petwalk, RV dump, vending**

CLE ELUM

85 WA 970, WA 903, to Wenatchie, **N** 76/dsl, Gas Save/dsl, Shell/dsl, Cottage Café, Giant Burger, Homestead BBQ, Aster Inn, Chalet Motel, Cle Elum Traveler's Inn, EconoLodge, Trailer Corral RV Park, vet

84 Cle Elum (from eb, return at 85), **N** Chevron/dsl, Short Stop/Subway/dsl, Warrior's/dsl, Best Thai, Burger King, Caboose Grill, DQ, El Caporal Mexican, Los Cabos Mexican, MaMa Vallones, McDonald's, Sunset Café, Taco Bell, Best Western Snowcap, Stewart Lodge, Timber Lodge Inn, $Tree, Cle Elum Hardware, museum, Safeway/dsl, URGENT CARE, USPO

81mm Cle Elum River

80 Roslyn, Salmon la Sac, **N** Suncadia Resort/rest. (4mi)

80mm **weigh sta both lanes**

78 Golf Course Rd, **S** Sun Country Golf/RV Park

74 W Nelson Siding Rd

71 Easton, **S** Easton Store/dsl/LP, Easton Motel, Horse SP, John Wayne Tr, USPO

71mm Yakima River

70 Sparks Rd, Easton, Lake Easton SP, **N** Shell/RV Town/café, Backwoods Cafe, Mtn High Burger, repair, Si Ridge Ranch RV Park, **S** Lake Easton RV Camping, L Easton SP

63 Cabin Creek Rd

62 Stampede Pass, elev 3750, to Lake Kachess, **N** Lake Kach Lodge

54 Hyak, Gold Creek, **S** Ski Area

53 Snoqualmie Pass, elev 3022, **S** Chevron, Summit P cake House, Summit Lodge, info, Lee's Summit Mkt, rec areas

52 W Summit (from eb), same as 53

47 Tinkham Rd, Denny Creek, Asahel Curtis, **N** chain ar **S** RV camping/dump

45 USFS Rd 9030, **N** to Lookout Point Rd

42 Tinkham Rd

38 **N** fire training ctr

35mm S Fork Snoqualmie River

34 468th Ave SE, Edgewick Rd, **N** Gull/dsl/deli, Shell/dsl, T Country Pride/Popeyes/dsl only/24hr/@, Warriors/dsl, Edgwick Inn, Norwest RV Park

32 436th Ave SE, **1 mi N** Snoqualmie Ranger Sta, gas, lodgi **S** Riverbend Cafe, Iron Horse SP (3mi)

31 WA 202 W, North Bend, Snoqualmie, **N** Chevron/dsl, She dsl, Arby's, Blimpie, Burger King, Los Cabos, McDonalc Mongolian Grill, Papa Murphy's, Starbucks, Subway, Ta Time, North Bend Motel, Sallish Lodge, Sunset Motel NorthBend Outlets/famous brands, O'Reilly Parts, Safeway/ds

27 North Bend, Snoqualmie (from eb), **N** Woodman's Stea

25 WA 18 W, Snoqualmie Pkwy, Tacoma, to Auburn, **N** She dsl/e85 (1.5mi), weigh sta

22 Preston, **N** Shell/dsl, Rhodes BBQ, Subway, LP, USP **S** Blue Sky RV Park

20 High Point Way

ISSAQUAH

18 E Sunset Way, Issaquah, **S** Shell (1mi), Flying Pie Pi za, Las Margaritas, Mandarin Garden, Stan's BBQ, Sunset A house, $Tree

17 E Sammamish Rd, Front St, Issaquah, **N** 76, Coho Ca Coldstone, Fatburger, Ivan's Rest., Jamba Juice, Krispy Krem McDonald's, Panda Express, Papa John's, Qdoba Mexican, Sta bucks, Subway, AT&T, Bartell Drug, Best Buy, Fred Meye Home Depot, URGENT CARE, Walgreens, **S** Arco/dsl, Ce ex/dsl, Chevron/dsl, Shell/dsl, Boehms Chocolates, Dom no's, Stan's BBQ, Subway, XXX Rootbeer, Big O Tire

15 WA 900, Issaquah, Renton, **N** Arco/dsl, Chevron, IHO O'Char Thai, Red Robin, Taco Time, Tully's Coffee, Holid Inn, Motel 6, Barnes&Noble, Big Lots, Costco/gas, Lowe' Michael's, Office Depot, PCC Natural Mkt, Petsmart, to Lk Sam mamish SP, **S** Shell/dsl, 12th Ave Cafe, Baskin-Robbin Burger King, Cafe Rio, Chipotle Mexican, Corner Cafe Baker Dickey's BBQ, Five Guys, Frankie's Pizza, Issaquah Cafe, Jac in-the-Box, Jamba Juice, Jersey Mike's, KFC/Taco Bell, La V nadita, McDonald's, Panera Bread, Papa Murphy's, Potbell

INTERSTATE 90 Cont'd

15	Continued Starbucks, Starbucks(2), Subway, Taco Time, The Egg&Us Rest., Tuttabella Pizza, WildFin Grill [lodging] Hilton Garden, Homewood Suites [other] Chevrolet, Firestone/auto, Ford, GNC, Hobby Lobby, O'Reilly Parts, PetCo, QFC Foods, REI, Rite Aid, Ross, Safeway, See's Candies, Target, Trader Joe's, USPO, Verizon
13	SE Newport Way, W Lake Sammamish, S [gas] 76/dsl [food] Starbucks, Subway [other] Matthew's Thriftway Mkt, vet
11	SE 150th, 156th, 161st, Bellevue, N [gas] Shell [food] Cypress Coffee, DQ, Jack-in-the-Box, Lil' Jon Rest., McDonald's, Shibuya Grill, Starbucks, Subway [lodging] Embassy Suites, Hyatt House, Quality Inn, Silver Cloud Inn [other] 7-11, LDS Temple, Nissan, Subaru/VW, Toyota, vet, S [gas] 76, Chevron, Shell/dsl, Standard/dsl [food] Domino's, Outback Steaks, Pizza Hut, Starbucks [lodging] Larkspur Landing Suites [other] Honda, O'Reilly Parts, Rite Aid, Safeway, Trailer Inn RV Park
10	I-405, N to Bellevue, S to Renton, services located off I-405 S, exit 10
9	Bellevue Way
8	E Mercer Way, Mercer Island
7c	80th Ave SE (exits left from wb)
7b a	SE 76th Ave, 77th Ave, Island Crest Way, Mercer Island, S [gas] Chevron/dsl, Shell/dsl [food] McDonald's, Qdoba, Starbucks, Subway, Thai Rest. [other] New Seasons Mkt, QFC Mkt, Walgreens
6	W Mercer Way (from eb), same as 7
5mm	Lake Washington
3b a	Ranier Ave, Seattle, downtown, N [gas] Shell/dsl
2c b	I-5, N to Vancouver, S to Tacoma
2a	4th Ave S, to stadiums
0	**I-90 begins/ends on I-5, exit 164.**

S
T
T
L
E

INTERSTATE 182 (Richland)

Exit #	Services
I-182 begins/ends on US 395 N.	
14b a	US 395 N, WA 397 S, OR Ave, N [gas] FLYING J/dsl/scales/24hr, King City/Shell/rest/dsl/@ [food] Burger King, Subway [other] Arrowhead RV Park, Freightliner, Peterbilt, S [lodging] Knights Inn
13	N 4th Ave, Cty Ctr, N [gas] CFN/dsl [lodging] Airport Motel, Starlite Motel, S [gas] 76/dsl, Chevron/dsl [other] [H], Green Tree RV park, Tire Pros, vet
12b	N 20th Ave, N [lodging] Best Western+, Red Lion Hotel
12a	US 395 S, Court St, **S on Court St** [gas] Chevron, Circle K/dsl, Conoco, Exxon/Jack-in-the-Box, Petro, Shell/dsl, USA [food] A&W/KFC, Andy's Rest., Baskin-Robbins, Burger King, Domino's, El Mirador Mexican, Little Caesar's, McDonald's, Oriental Express, Papa Murphy's, Pizza Hut, RoundTable Pizza, Subway, Taco Bell, Wendy's [other] $Tree, Albertson's, AutoZone, Blue Dog RV Ctr, Cadillac/Chevrolet, Dean RV Ctr, Ford, Hyundai, Mazda, Nissan, Rite Aid, U-Haul, USPO, Walgreens
9	rd 68, Trac, N [gas] Exxon/Circle K/dsl, Maverik/dsl, Porter's/dsl [food] Antonio's Pizza, Applebee's, Arby's, Bruchi's, Cousin's Rest., Dickey's BBQ, Domino's, DQ, Fiesta Mexican, Hacienda del Sol, IHOP, Jack-in-the-Box, Little Caesar's, McDonald's, Panda Express, Pier 39 Seafood, Pita Pit, Pizza Hut, Shakey's Pizza, Sonic, Starbucks, Subway, Taco Bell [lodging] Hampton Inn, Holiday Inn Express, MyPlace [other] $Tree, AT&T, Discount Tire, Firestone/auto, Franklin County RV Park, Grocery Outlet, Lowe's, O'Reilly Parts, Schwab Tire, URGENT CARE, Verizon, Walgreens, Walmart/Subway, Yokes Foods, S [gas] Maverik/dsl

RICHLAND

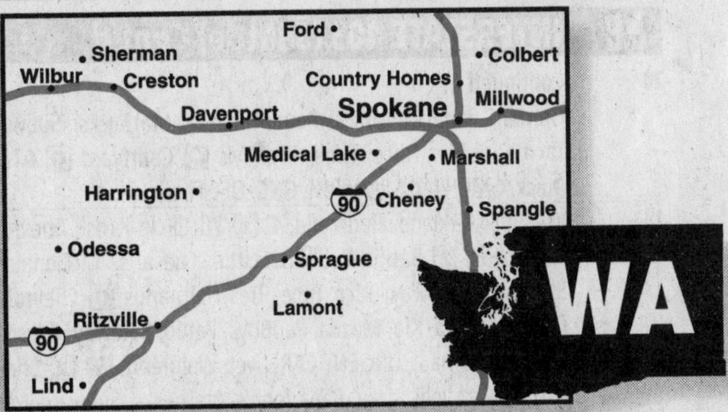

7	Broadmoor Blvd, N [lodging] Sleep Inn [other] Camping World, GNC, Subaru, vet, S [gas] Exxon/Circle K/dsl [other] Broadmoor RV Ctr, KOA
6.5mm	Columbia River
5b a	WA 240 E, Geo Washington Way, to Kennewick, N [gas] Conoco/dsl [food] Anthony's Rest., Applebee's, Jack-in-the-Box, Starbucks [lodging] Courtyard, Economy Inn, Hampton Inn, Red Lion Hotel, Shilo Inn, TownePlace Suites [other] $Tree, AT&T, Winco Foods
4	WA 240 W, N [gas] Shell/dsl [food] El Porton Mexican, McDonald's, Starbucks [other] BMW, Fred Meyer/dsl
3.5mm	Yakima River
3	Keene Rd, Queensgate, N [gas] Exxon/Circle K, Maverik/dsl, USA/dsl [food] A&W/KFC, Bob's Burgers, Burger King, Costa Vida, Dickey's BBQ, Fiesta Mexican, Five Guys, Krispy Kreme, LJ Silver, McDonald's, Panda Express, Panera Bread, Qdoba, Starbucks, Sterling's Rest., Stick+Stone Pizza, Subway, Taco Bell [other] AT&T, GNC, Home Depot, Marshall's, PetCo, Ross, Schwab Tire, Target, Tire Factory, Verizon, Walmart/Subway, S [gas] Chevron/dsl [food] MOD Pizza [other] tires/repair
0mm	**I-182 begins/ends on I-82, exit 102.**

WA

INTERSTATE 405 (Seattle)

Exit #	Services
30	I-5, N to Canada, S to Seattle, **I-405 begins/ends on I-5, exit 182.**
26	WA 527, Bothell, Mill Creek, E [food] McDonald's, Rama House Thai, Starbucks [lodging] Extended Stay America, W [gas] Shell/dsl [food] Applebee's, Arby's, Bamboo House, Bangkok Cafe, Baskin-Robbins, Bonefish Grill, Chick-fil-A, Crystal Creek Cafe, Five Guys, Grazie Ristorante, Imperial Wok, Jack-in-the-Box, Jimmy John's, Little Caesar's, MOD Pizza, Outback Steaks, Papa Murphy's, Qdoba Mexican, Starbucks, Subway, Taco Bell, Taco Time, Wendy's, Zeek's Pizza [lodging] Comfort Inn, Extended Stay America, Hilton Garden, Holiday Inn Express [other] 7-11, Bartell Drug, Goodyear/auto, Lake Pleasant RV Park, QFC Foods, Rite Aid, URGENT CARE, vet
24	NE 195th St, Beardslee Blvd, E [gas] Chevron/dsl [food] Subway, Teryaki Etc. [lodging] Country Inn&Suites, Red Lion Inn, Residence Inn [other] Exotic vet
23b	WA 522 W, Bothell
23a	WA 522 E, to WA 202, Woodinville, Monroe
22	NE 160th St, E [gas] Chevron, Shell/dsl [food] Top Mkt/deli
20	NE 124th St, E [gas] Arco, Shell/dsl [food] Brown Bag Cafe, Cafe Veloce, Jack-in-the-Box, KFC, Santa Fe Mexican, Shari's, Subway, Taco Bell [lodging] Baymont Inn, Comfort Inn, Motel 6 [other] [H], 7-11, AutoZone, Chrysler/Dodge/Jeep, Discount Tire, Fiat, Firestone/auto, Ford, Hyundai, NAPA, O'Reilly Parts, Rite Aid, Ross, Schwab Tire, Toyota, Verizon, VW, Whole Foods Mkt, W [gas] 76/dsl [food] Azteca Mexican, Burger King, Five Guys, Izumi Japanese, Jimmy John's, McDonald's, Mediterranean Kitchen, Olive

SEATTLE

INTERSTATE 405 (Seattle) Cont'd

20 Continued
Garden, Papa Murphy's, Romio's Pizza, Starbucks, Subway, Taco Del Mar, Taco Time, Wendy's [lodging] Courtyard [O] AT&T, Buick/GMC, Fred Meyer/dsl, GNC, QFC Foods

18 WA 908, Kirkland, Redmond, **E** [gas] 76/Circle K/dsl, Chevron, Texaco/dsl [food] Baskin-Robbins, Little Caesar's, McDonald's, Starbucks, Subway, Taco Time, Tres Hermanos [O] Chevrolet, Costco, Honda, Kia, Mazda, PepBoys, PetCo, Safeway, Tuesday Morning, U-Haul, URGENT CARE, vet, Walgreens, **W** [gas] Shell/dsl [food] Acropolis Pizza, Papa John's, Starbucks, Subway, Wendy's [O] QFC Foods, Tire Pros

17 NE 70th Pl

14b a WA 520, Seattle, Redmond

13b NE 8th St, **E** [gas] Arco, Chevron/dsl, Shell/dsl [food] Burger King, Chick-fil-A, Taco del Mar [lodging] Hotel 116 [O] [H], Bartell Drugs, Best Buy, Cadillac, Chevrolet, Ford, Home Depot, Infiniti, Mercedes, Porsche, Volvo, Whole Foods Mkt, **W** [food] Starbucks, Subway [lodging] Courtyard, Hyatt

13a NE 4th St, **E** [lodging] Extended Stay America, Hampton Inn [O] Chrysler/Dodge/Jeep, Lexus, **W** [food] Azteca Mexican, Subway [lodging] Hilton, Hotel Bellevue, Marriott, Red Lion/Bellevue Inn, Residence Inn, Sheraton

12 SE 8th St **W** [lodging] Residence Inn

11 I-90, E to Spokane, W to Seattle

10 Cold Creek Pkwy, Factoria, **E on Factoria Blvd** [gas] 76, Chevron [food] Applebee's, Burger King, Chipotle, Coldstone, Domino's, El Tapatio Mexican, Goldberg's Rest., Great Harvest Bread, Jamba Juice, Jimmy John's, KFC, McDonald's, MOD Pizza, Novilhos Brazilian Steaks, Panda Express, Panera Bread, Ricardo's Mexican, Romio's Pizza, Shanghai Cafe, Starbucks, Subway, Taco Bell, Taco Time, Thai Ginger, Tokyo Japanese [O] 7-11,

10 Continued
AT&T, Bartell Drug, Midas, Old Navy, O'Reilly Parts, PetCo, Q Foods, Rite Aid, Safeway, Target, TJ Maxx, Verizon, Walmart

9 112th Ave SE, Newcastle, [C]

7 NE 44th St, **E** [food] Denny's, McDonald's, Starbucks, Subw Taco Del Mar, Teriyaki Wok [lodging] EconoLodge

6 NE 30th St, **E** [gas] Arco, **W** [gas] Chevron/dsl, Shell/dsl [O] 7-

5 WA 900 E, Park Ave N, Sunset Blvd NE **W** [food] Five Guys, Ji my John's, Panda Express, Panera Bread, Potbelly, Red Rob Torero's Mexican [lodging] Hampton Inn, Hyatt House, Resider Inn [O] AT&T, Dick's, Fry's Electronics, GNC, Lowe's, Marsha Petsmart, Ross, Staples, Target, Verizon, World Mkt

4 WA 169 S, Wa 900 W, Renton, **E** [food] Shari's [lodging] Quality [O] Aqua Barn Ranch Camping, **W** [food] Burger King, Piz Dudes, Subway [lodging] Renton Inn [O] $Tree, 7-11

2 WA 167, Rainier Ave, to Auburn, **E** [lodging] Hilton Garden, La spur Landing, SpringHill Suites, TownePlace Suites [O] **W** [gas] Arco/dsl, Chevron, Chevron, Mobil/dsl [food] A&W/K Applebee's, Baskin-Robbins, Chipotle, Domino's, IHOP, Jack-the-Box, Jimmy John's, Jimmy Mac's Roadhouse, King Buff Little Caesar's, Mazatlan Mexican, McDonald's, Papa Murphy Pizza Hut, Popeye's, Sonic, Starbucks, Subway, Taco Bell, Ta Time, Wendy's, Yankee Grill [lodging] Red Lion Hotel [O] AutoZor Buick/Cadillac/GMC, Chevrolet, Chrysler/Dodge/Jeep, D count Tire, Firestone/auto, Ford, Fred Meyer/dsl, Hyundai, K Mazda, Midas, O'Reilly Parts, Safeway/gas, Schwab Tire, Sub ru, Toyota, vet, Walgreens, Walmart

1 WA 181 S, Tukwila, **E** [gas] Chevron/dsl [food] Jack-in-the-Bo Taco Bell, Wendy's [lodging] Courtyard, Embassy Suites, Exten ed Stay America, Hampton Inn, Ramada, Residence In Woodspring Suites [O] 7-11, **W** [gas] 76 [food] Subway, Taco D Mar [lodging] Comfort Suites, Homewood Suites [O] fun center

0mm I-5, N to Seattle, S to Tacoma, WA 518 W. **I-405 begins/ends o I-5, exit 154.**

NOTES

WA

WEST VIRGINIA

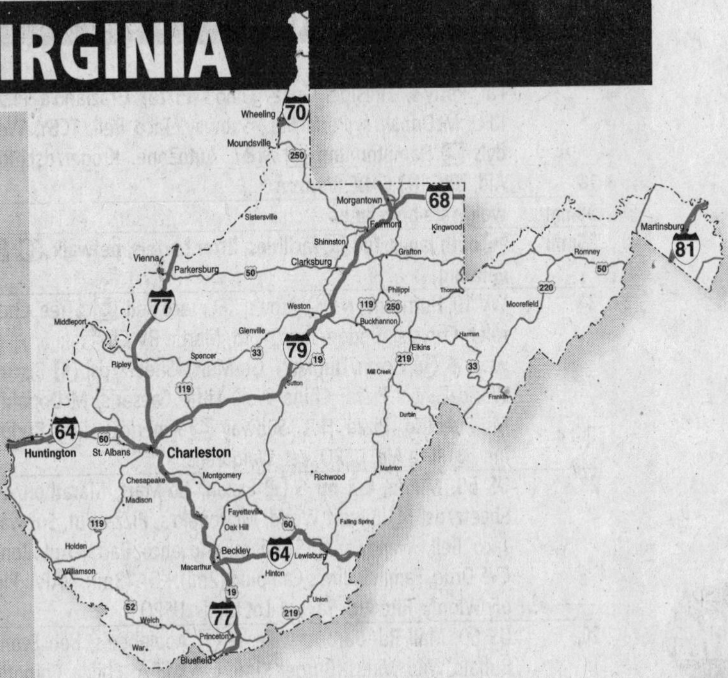

INTERSTATE 64

Exit #	Services
184mm	West Virginia/Virginia state line
183	VA 311, (from eb, no reentry), Crows (from eb)
181	US 60, WV 92 (no ez wb return), White Sulphur Springs, **0-2 mi N** GoMart/dsl, Marathon/Godfather's, Shell April's Pizzaria, Hardee's Budget Inn, Greenbrier Resort, Old White Motel autocare, Family$, Food Lion, Rite Aid, ski area, to Midland Trail, USPO
179mm	**Welcome Ctr wb, full facilities, info, litter barrels, petwalk,**
175	US 60, WV 92, Caldwell, **N** Exxon, Shell/Subway/dsl, Sunoco/Mountaineer Mart/dsl Cook's Country Kitchen, McDonald's, Wendy's $General, **S** Greenbrier SF
173mm	Greenbrier River
169	US 219, Lewisburg, Hist Dist, **N** Shell Biscuit World Relax Inn Federated Parts, **S** Exxon/dsl, Gomart, Shell, Walmart/dsl Applebee's, Arby's, Bellacino's, Bob Evans, China Palace, Dickey's BBQ, Hardee's, Papa John's, Ruby Tuesday, Shoney's, Subway, Taco Bell Fairfield Inn, Hampton Inn, Holiday Inn Express, Quality Inn, Super 8 H, $Tree, AT&T, AutoZone, Buick/Chevrolet, Ford, Lowe's, URGENT CARE, Verizon, Walmart
161	WV 12, Alta, **S** Citgo/dsl Alta Sta/cafe Greenbrier River Camping (14mi)
156	US 60, Midland Trail, Sam Black Church, **N** Exxon/Arby's/dsl, Shell/dsl
150	rd 29, rd 4, Dawson, **S** Exxon Cheddar's Cafe Dawson Inn RV camping
147mm	**runaway truck ramp wb**
143	WV 20, Green Sulphur Springs, **N** Liberty/dsl
139	WV 20, Sandstone, Hinton, **S** Citgo/dsl Blue Stone SP (16mi), Richmonds Store/USPO, to Pipestem Resort Park (25 mi)
138mm	New River
136mm	**runaway truck ramp eb**
133.1mm	Sandstone Mtn, elev 2765
133	WV 27, Pluto Rd, Bragg, **S** RV camping, mandatory truck stop eb
129	WV 9, Shady Spring, **N** to Grandview SP, **S** Exxon/dsl, Shell/dsl Subway Little Beaver SP
125b a	WV 307, Airport Rd, Beaver, **N** Shell/dsl Biscuit World Sleep Inn, **1 mi S** GoMart/gas, Marathon/dsl, Sheetz/dsl Arby's, Dickey's BBQ, DQ, El Mariachi, Hardee's, KFC, Little Caesar's, LJ Silver, McDonald's, Subway, Wendy's Advance Parts, CVS Drug, Family$, Kroger, USPO, Walgreens
124	US 19, Eisenhower Dr, E Beckley, **1-2 mi N** GoMart/gas Capt D's, Raleigh Diner Green Bank Motel, Microtel H, $General, last exit before **toll** rd wb
121	I-77 S, to Bluefield

I-64 and I-77 run together 61 mi. See I-77, exits 42 through 100.

Exit #	Services
59	I-77 N (from eb), to I-79
58c	US 60, Washington St, **N** BP, Exxon, GoMart/dsl Family$, **S** 5th Quarter Steaks, Capt D's, Panera Bread, Shoney's, Wendy's Courtyard, Embassy Suites, Hampton Inn, Holiday Inn Express, Marriott H, civic ctr, Goodyear/auto, Macy's, mall
58b	US 119 N (from eb), Charleston, downtown, same as 58c
58a	US 119 S, WV 61, MacCorkle Ave
56	Montrose Dr, **N** Exxon/dsl, Marathon/dsl, Speedway/dsl Hardee's, Los Agaves Mexican Holiday Inn, Microtel,

CHARLESTON

Exit #	Services
56	Continued Wingate Inn $General, Acura, Advance Parts, Chevrolet, Dodge, Hyundai, Kia, NAPA, Rite Aid, VW
55	Kanawha Tpk (from wb)
54	US 60, MacCorkle Ave, **N** Burger King, Casa Garcia, Graziano's Pizza, Krispy Kreme, Subway $Tree, AT&T, Kroger/dsl, TJ Maxx, **S** Bob Evans, Husson's Pizza, KFC, LJ Silver, McDonald's, Pizza Hut, Schlotzsky's, Taco Bell, Wendy's H, Aamco, Family$, Harley-Davidson, Honda, Mazda, URGENT CARE
53	Roxalana Rd, to Dunbar, **S** GoMart/dsl BiscuitWorld, Capt D's, Gino's Pizza, Graziano's Pizza, Los Agaves, McDonald's, Subway, Wendy's Dunbar Plaza Motel, Super 8 $General, Advance Parts, Aldi Foods, CVS Drug, Family$, Jo-Ann Fabrics, Kroger/dsl, NTB, Rite Aid
50	VW 25, Institute, **S** GoMart/dsl
47b a	WV 622, Goff Mtn Rd, **N** Exxon/dsl, GoMart, Speedway/dsl BiscuitWorld, Bob Evans, Capt D's, Domino's, Gino's Pizza, Little Caesar's, McDonald's, Papa John's, Pizza Hut, Subway, Taco Bell, Wendy's Motel 6 Advance Parts, AT&T, Autozone, Family$, Kroger/gas, Rite Aid, Save-a-Lot, URGENT CARE, Walgreens, **S** Arby's, Asian Buffet, Barnyard BBQ, Buffalo Wild Wings, Burger King, Cracker Barrel, Golden Corral, HoneyBaked Ham, La Roca Mexican, Sakura Japanese, TGIFriday's Comfort Inn, Holiday Inn Express, Sleep Inn $Tree, Lowe's, Staples, Walmart
45	WV 25, Nitro, **N** Pilot/Arby's/dsl/scales/24hr Chevrolet, **S** Exxon/dsl, GoMart, Speedway/dsl BiscuitWorld, Checker's, DQ, Gino's Pizza, McDonald's, Subway, Wendy's $General
44.3mm	Kanawha River
44	US 35, St Albans, **S** Shell/7-11/dsl
40	US 35 N, Winfield, Pt Pleasant, **S** Sheetz/dsl, Speedway/dsl DQ
39	WV 34, Winfield, **N** BP/Arby's, GoMart/dsl Applebee's, Bob Evans, Rio Grande Mexican, Taste of Asia Holiday Inn Express, Red Roof Inn $General, $Tree, Advance Parts, Aldi Foods, BigLots, Elder-Beerman, GNC, Home Depot, USPO, **S** GoMart, TA/Country Pride/dsl/scales/24hr/@ Biscuit World, Burger King, Capt D's, China Chef, El Rancho Grande,

= gas = food = lodging = other = rest stop

INTERSTATE 64 Cont'd

39	Continued Fat Patty's, Fireside Grille, Gino's Pizza, Graziano's Pizza, KFC, McDonald's, Penn Sta., Subway, Taco Bell, TCBY, Wendy's Hampton Inn AT&T, AutoZone, Kroger/dsl, Rite Aid, URGENT CARE, Verizon
38mm	**weigh sta both lanes**
35mm	**both lanes, full facilities, litter barrels, petwalk, , , vending**
34	WV 19, Hurricane, N Arby's, KFC, Taco Bell $Tree, Chevrolet, Chrysler/Dodge/Jeep, Ford, Martin RV Ctr, Walmart/Subway, S Exxon/Dunkin', Go-Mart, Sheetz/dsl Biscuit-World/Gino's Pizza, China Wok, Little Caesar's, McDonald's, Mi Pueblito, Pizza Hut, Subway American Inn, Budget Inn Rite Aid, USPO, vet, Walgreens
28	US 60, Milton, **0-2 mi** S Exxon, Go-Mart, Marathon/dsl, Sheetz/dsl Biscuit World, McDonald's, Pizza Hut, Subway, Taco Bell, Wendy's $General, Advance Parts, AutoZone, CVS Drug, Family$, Jim's Camping (2mi), KOA (3mi), NAPA, Piggly Wiggly, Rite Aid, Save-A-Lot foods, USPO
20	US 60, Mall Rd, Barboursville, N Applebee's, Bob Evans, Buffalo Wild Wings, Burger King, Chick-fil-A, Chili's, Chipotle, IHOP, Logan's Roadhouse, McDonald's, Olive Garden, Panera Bread, Qdoba Mexican, Ruby Tuesday, Super China, Wendy's Comfort Inn BAM!, Best Buy, Dick's, Drug Emporium, Elder-Beerman, Firestone/auto, Hobby Lobby, JC Penney, Jo-Ann Fabrics, Kohl's, Lowe's, Macy's, Michael's, NTB, Old Navy, Walmart/Subway, S BP/dsl, Sheetz/dsl Cracker Barrel, Fat Patty's, Outback Steaks, Shogun Japanese, Sonic, Steak&Shake, Subway, Taco Bell Best Western, Hampton Inn, Holiday Inn Toyota
18	US 60, to WV 2, Barboursville, N Bellacino's, O'Charley's, Starbucks $Tree, Home Depot, Marshall's, Office Depot, Petco, Target, S Shell/7-11 Biscuit World, Gino's, Giovanni's Pizza, Hardee's, Papa John's Food Fair, Kia, Kroger/gas, NAPA, Rite Aid, Walgreens
15	US 60, 29th St E, N GoMart/dsl, Shell/dsl, Speedway/dsl #1 Kitchen, Arby's, Biscuit World, Burger King, Honeybaked Ham, Subway, Waffle House, Wendy's Huntington Motel, Quality Inn H, $General, AT&T, BigLots, NAPA, Save-a-Lot Foods, st police, Verizon, Walmart/McDonald's, S Exxon Fazoli's, Golden Corral, KFC, Little Caesar's, Marco's Pizza, McDonald's, Penn Sta., Taco Bell Days Inn, Red Roof Inn Buick/Cadillac/GMC, CVS Drug, Honda, Nissan, Subaru, VW
11	WV 10, Hal Greer Blvd, **0-2 mi** N Marathon/Subway Arby's, Baskin-Robbins, Biscuit World, Bob Evans, El Ranchito Mexican, Frostop Drive-In, McDonald's, Papa John's, Ritzy's Cafe, Wendy's Fairfield Inn, Hampton Inn, Ramada Ltd, Super 8, TownePlace Suites H, AutoZone, Chrysler/Dodge/Jeep, Rite Aid, S Beech Fork SP (8mi)
10mm	**Welcome Ctr eb, full facilities, litter barrels, petwalk, , , vending**
8	WV 152 S, WV 527 N, N URGENT CARE, vet, S GoMart/dsl, Speedway/dsl
6	US 52 N, W Huntington, Chesapeake, N Sheetz/dsl, Speedway/dsl Pizza Hut, Shoney's, Wendys H, $General, AutoZone, BigLots, Family$, Save-A-Lot Foods
1	US 52 S, Kenova, **0-1 mi** N Exxon, Shell/dsl Burger King, Evaroni's Pizza, Gino's Pizza, Hermanos Nunez Mexican, McDonald's, Stewart's Hotdogs, Taco Bell Hollywood Motel $General, Advance Parts, CVS Drug, NAPA, Save-A-Lot, USPO
0mm	West Virginia/Kentucky state line, Big Sandy River

HUNTINGTON

MORGANTOWN

WV

INTERSTATE 68

Exit #	Services
32mm	West Virginia/Maryland state line
31mm	**Welcome Ctr wb, full facilities, litter barrels, petwalk, , vending**
29	rd 5, Hazelton Rd, N Sunoco/dsl Microtel (1 S Big Bear Camping (3mi), Pine Hill RV Camp (4mi)
23	WV 26, Bruceton Mills, N BFS/Subway/dsl/24hr, Sunoco/Little Sandy's Rest./dsl/24hr Mill Stone Rest. Maple L Motel antiques, Auto+ Parts, Family$, USPO
18mm	Laurel Run
17mm	**runaway truck ramp eb**
16mm	**weigh sta wb**
15	WV 73, WV 12, Coopers Rock, N Chestnut Ridge SF, S Springs Camping (2mi)
12mm	**runaway truck ramp wb**
10	WV 43 N, to rd 857, Fairchance Rd, Cheat Lake, N B DQ/Little Caesar's/dsl, Exxon/dsl Angelo's Pizza, Drag Cafe USPO, vet, S Burger King Lakeview Resort
9mm	Cheat Lake
7	rd 705, Pierpont Rd, N BFS/Little Caesar's/Subway/TC Exxon/Taco Bell/dsl Fox's Pizza Den, Fujiyama Stea Honeybaked Ham, IHOP, McDonald's, Outback Steaks, Ru Tuesday, Wendy's Holiday Inn Express, Super 8 Books-A-Million, Family$, GNC, Lowe's, Michael's, Shop'n Sa Foods, to WVU Stadium, S Sunoco/dsl Apple Annie Don Patron Mexican, Rita's Custard Chrysler/Dodge
4	rd 7, to Sabraton, N BFS/Subway/dsl, Sheetz/dsl A by's, Burger King, Dunkin', Hardee's, KFC, LJ Silver, McDonalc Popeye's, Shoney's, Wendy's SpringHill Suites, Suburb Lodge $General, $Tree, Advance Parts, AutoZone, C Drug, Family$, Kroger/dsl, NAPA, Save-A-Lot Foods, USP S Marathon/Circle K, Sunoco/dsl China City
3mm	Decker's Creek
1	US 119, Morgantown, N Go-Mart/dsl Morgantown In rest., Quality Inn tires, S Sheetz/dsl, Tesla EVC De ny's, Mariachi Loco $Tree, to Tygart L SP, Walmart/Subway
0mm	I-79, N to Pittsburgh, S to Clarksburg. **I-68 begins/ends on I-7 exit 148.**

INTERSTATE 70

Exit #	Services
14mm	West Virginia/Pennsylvania state line
13.5mm	**Welcome Ctr wb, full facilities, litter barrels, petwalk, , vending**
11	WV 41, Dallas Pike, N TA/Country Pride/dsl/scales/24hr/ Comfort Inn, S Exxon, Marathon/DQ/dsl EconoLodg RV camping
10	rd 65, to Cabela Dr, N Sheetz/dsl Applebee's, Bob E ans, Cheddar's, Coldstone, Eat'n Park, El Paso Mexican, Fiv Guys, Fusion Steaks, Jimmy John's, Logan's Roadhouse, M Donald's, Olive Garden, Panera Bread, Primanti Bros, Quake Steak, TX Roadhouse, Wendy's Fairfield Inn, Hampto Inn, Hawthorn Suites, Microtel AT&T, Best Buy, Books A-Million, Cabela's, GNC, JC Penney, Kohl's, Old Navy, PetC Russell Stover Candies, Target, TJ Maxx, Verizon, Walmart Subway, S Sheetz/dsl Holiday Inn Express, Suburba Lodge Buick/GMC, Chevrolet, Ford/Lincoln, Honda, Hyun dai, Nissan, Toyota
5	US 40, WV 88 S, Tridelphia, N Marathon/dsl Pizz Hut, Subway, Wendy's Super 8 Chrysler/Dodge/Jeep

INTERSTATE 70 Cont'd

WHEELING

5	Continued Family$, Riesbeck's Foods, Subaru/VW, URGENT CARE, vet, **S** Marathon/dsl Arby's, DQ, McDonald's, Undo's Rest. Advance Parts, AT&T, AutoZone, museum, Rite Aid
5a	I-470 W, to Columbus
4	WV 88 N (from eb), Elm Grove, same as 5
3.5mm	**weigh sta eb**
2b	Washington Ave, **N** $General, **S** Figaretti's Italian
2a	rd 88 N, to Oglebay Park, **N** Marathon/dsl, Sheetz AC Buffet, Bob Evans, DeFelice Bros Pizza, Hardee's, Little Caesar's, Papa John's, Perkins, Subway, Tim Hortons Hampton Inn, SpringHill Suites Advance Parts, CVS Drug, Kroger/gas, NTB, URGENT CARE, Verizon
1b	US 250 S, WV 2 S, S Wheeling
1mm	**tunnel**
1a	US 40 E, WV 2 N, Main St, downtown, **S** Knights Inn
0	(from wb) US 40 W, Zane St, Wheeling Island, **N** Exxon/dsl Burger King, KFC
0mm	West Virginia/Ohio state line, Ohio River

INTERSTATE 77

PARKERSBURG

Exit #	Services
186mm	West Virginia/Ohio state line, Ohio River
185	WV 14, WV 31, Williamstown, **W WV Welcome Ctr/, full facilities, info, litter barrels,** Clark, GoMart/dsl, Shell (1mi) Dutch Pantry Econolodge/Rodeway Inn Glass Factory Tours
179	WV 2 N, WV 68 S, to Waverly, **E** Exxon/dsl, **W** BP/dsl Burger King, Hardee's (3mi) Red Carpet Inn, Sleep Inn
176	US 50, 7th St, Parkersburg, **E** to North Bend SP, **W** BP/7-11, GoMart Domino's, DQ, Hardee's, Little Caesar's, McDonald's, Mountaineer Rest./24hr, Omelette Shoppe, Wendy's Economy Inn, Travelodge Advance Parts, AutoZone, Chrysler/Dodge/Jeep, CVS Drug, Family$, Ford/Lincoln, Honda, Hyundai, Kroger/dsl, Mercedes, NAPA, Rite Aid, to Blennerhassett Hist Park, Toyota
174	WV 47, Staunton Ave, **1 mi E** GoMart/Sub Express/dsl $General
174mm	Little Kanawha River
173	WV 95, Camden Ave, **E** Marathon/dsl, **1-4 mi W** BP Hardee's Blennerhassett Hotel
170	WV 14, Mineral Wells, **E** BP/dsl/repair, GoMart/Taco Bell/dsl, Liberty Trkstp/dsl/24hr McDonald's, Wendy's Comfort Suites, Hampton Inn, **W** Cracker Barrel, Napoli's Pizza Holiday Inn Express, Microtel, Mineral Wells Inn
169mm	**weigh sta both lanes,**
166mm	**both lanes, full facilities, litter barrels, petwalk, , , RV dump, vending**
161	WV 21, Rockport, **W** Marathon/dsl
154	WV 1, Medina Rds
146	WV 2 S, Silverton, Ravenswood, **E** Ruby Lake Camping (4mi), **W** Exxon/DQ, Marathon/dsl McDonald's (3mi), Subway (4mi), Wendy's (3mi) Scottish Inn
138	US 33, Ripley, **E** BP/dsl, Marathon/dsl, Murphy USA/dsl, Sheetz/dsl Arby's, KFC, Las Trancas Mexican, LJ Silver, McDonald's, Pizza Hut, Taco Bell, Wendy's Holiday Inn Express, Super 8 $Tree, AutoZone, Family$, Kroger/dsl, NAPA, Rite Aid, Save-A-Lot Foods, Verizon, Walmart/Subway, **W** Exxon/dsl Bob Evans, Ponderosa, Shoney's, Subway Quality Inn

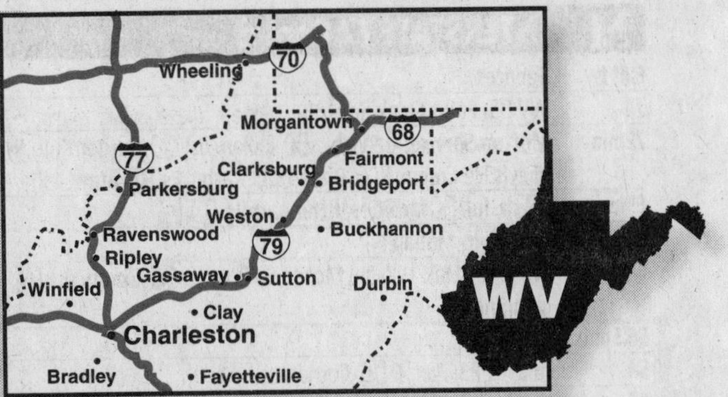

CHARLESTON

132	WV 21, Fairplain, **E** BP/7-11/dsl, GoMart/dsl, Speedway/dsl/24hr Burger King, Fratello's Italian $General, Ford, Statts Mills RV Park (6mi), **W** Loves/Chester's/McDonald's/dsl/scales/24hr
124	WV 34, Kenna, **E** Exxon Your Family Rest.
119	WV 21, Goldtown, same as 116
116	WV 21, Haines Branch Rd, Sissonville, **4 mi E** Rippling Waters Camping
114	WV 622, Pocatalico Rd, **E** BP/dsl $General
111	WV 29, Tuppers Creek Rd, **W** BP/Subway/dsl Gino's (2mi), McDonald's (2mi), Tudor's Biscuit World, Wendy's (2mi)
106	WV 27, Edens Fork Rd, **W** Marathon/dsl/country store Sunset Motel (3mi)
104	I-79 N, to Clarksburg
102	US 119 N, Westmoreland Rd, **E** BP/7-11, GoMart Hardee's Foodland/gas
101	I-64, E to Beckley, W to Huntington
100	Broad St, Capitol St, **W** Subway Best Western, Charleston Capitol Hotel, Marriott Cadillac/GMC, Firestone, Rite Aid, USPO
99	WV 114, Capitol St, **E** , **W** BP/7-11, Exxon/Noble Roman's Domino's, McDonald's, Wendy's st capitol, to museum
98	35th St Bridge (from sb), **W** Shell/7-11/dsl Husson's Pizza, KFC, McDonald's, Steak Escape, Subway, Taco Bell, Wendy's , Rite Aid, to U of Charleston
97	US 60 W (from nb), Kanawha Blvd
96	US 60 E, Midland Trail, Belle, **W** Anchor Pizza, Biscuit World, Gino's Budget Host
96mm	**W Va Turnpike begins/ends.**
95.5mm	Kanawha River
95	WV 61, to MacCorkle Ave, **E** GoMart/dsl/24hr, Marathon/Subway/dsl Bob Evans, IHOP, McDonald's, TX Steaks Country Inn&Suites, Days Inn, Holiday Inn Express, Knights Inn, Motel 6, Red Roof Inn Advance Parts, AutoZone, **W** Exxon/dsl, GoMart, Shell/7-11/dsl Applebee's, Arby's, Bojangle's, Burger King, Capt D's, China Buffet, Cracker Barrel, Firehouse Subs, Fujiyama Japanese, Hooters, La Carreta, Little Caesar's, Pizza Hut, Taco Bell $Tree, AT&T, Drug Emporium, GNC, GNC, Kings Tire, Kroger/dsl, Lowe's, Piggly Wiggly, URGENT CARE, Verizon, vet
89	WV 61, WV 94, to Marmet, **E** Exxon/Subway/dsl/24hr, GoMart/dsl, Sunoco/dsl BiscuitWorld, Gino's Pizza, Hardee's, LJ Silver, Wendy's $General, Family$, Family$, Ford, Kroger/dsl, NAPA, Rite Aid, USPO
85	US 60, WV 61, East Bank, **E** Marathon/dsl, Shell/Arby's/dsl Gino's Pizza, McDonald's, Shoney's $General, Chevrolet, Rite Aid
82.5mm	**toll booth**
79	Cabin Creek Rd, Sharon

WV

= gas = food = lodging = other = rest stop

INTERSTATE 77 Cont'd

BECKLEY

Exit #	Services
74	WV 83, Paint Creek Rd
72mm	**Morton Service Area nb,** Exxon/dsl Burger King, Hershey's Ice Cream, KFC, Pizza Hut, Starbucks atm
69mm	**sb, full facilities, litter barrels,**
66	WV 15, to Mahan
60	WV 612, Oak Hill, to Mossy, **1/2 mi E** Exxon/dsl RV camping
56.5mm	**toll plaza**
54	rd 2, rd 23, Pax, **E** Corner/dsl
48	US 19, N Beckley, **1-4 mi E on US 19/WV 16** Exxon/Subway, Sheetz/dsl Bob Evans, Buffalo Wild Wings, Burger King, Cheddar's, Chick-fil-A, Chili's, Dickey's BBQ, Five Guys, Honeybaked Ham, LJ Silver, Logan's Roadhouse, McDonald's, Olive Garden, Panera Bread, Peking Buffet, Qdoba, Rally's, Ryan's, Starbucks, Subway, Taco Bell, Wendy's Days Inn $General, $Tree, Advance Parts, AT&T, AutoZone, Belk, BigLots, Buick/GMC, Chevrolet, Chrysler/Dodge/Jeep, CVS Drug, Dick's, Food Lion, Goodyear/auto, Hobby Lobby, Honda, Hyundai, JC Penney, Jo-Ann Fabrics, Kia/Subaru, Kohl's, Kroger/gas, Lowe's, NAPA, Nissan, Petsmart, Rite Aid, RV Ctr, Sam's Club/gas, Staples, TJ Maxx, Toyota, U-Haul, Walgreens, Walmart
45mm	**Tamarack Service Area both lanes, W** Exxon/dsl Burger King, Hershey's Ice Cream, Quiznos, Sbarro's, Starbucks gifts
44	WV 3, Beckley, **E** Exxon/dsl, Marathon/dsl, Shell/Dickey's BBQ Applebee's, Bojangle's, Burger King, Campestre Mexican, DQ, Fujiyama Japanese, Hooters, IHOP, McDonald's, Omelet Shoppe, Outback Steaks, Pizza Hut Courtyard, EconoLodge, Fairfield Inn, Howard Johnson, Quality Inn/rest., Super 8, Travelodge H, Advance Parts, CVS Drug, Kroger/gas, Rite Aid, Tires, URGENT CARE, **W** BP/Subway/dsl, Go-Mart/dsl Bob Evans, Cracker Barrel, Pasquale Italian, Ruby Tuesday, Sam's Hotdogs, TX Steaks, Wendy's Baymont Inn, Comfort Inn, Country Inn&Suites, Hampton Inn, Holiday Inn, Microtel
42	WV 16, WV 97, to Mabscott, **2 mi E** H, **W** BP/dsl, Go-Mart Arby's, Gino's Pizza/Biscuit World, Subway AutoValue Repair, O'Reilly Parts, USPO, Walmart/Subway
40	I-64 E, to Lewisburg
30mm	**toll booth**
28	WV 48, to Ghent, **E** Exxon/dsl, Marathon/dsl Subway Appalachian Resort Inn (12mi), Glade Springs Resort (1mi) to ski area, **W** Knight's Inn
26.5mm	elevation 3252, Flat Top Mtn
20	US 19, to Camp Creek, **E** Exxon/dsl, **W** Camp Creek SP/RV camping
18.5mm	Bluestone River, scenic overlook/parking area/**weigh sta sb**
17mm	**Bluestone Service Area/weigh sta nb, full facilities, picnic area, scenic view** Exxon/dsl Blimpie, Hershey's Ice Cream, Starbucks, Uno Pizza atm/fax, 14 WV 20, Athens Rd, Pipestem Resort SP, to Concord U
9mm	**WV Turnpike begins/ends.**
9	US 460, Princeton, **E Welcome Ctr/Rest Area both lanes, full facilities, litter barrels, petwalk** Walmart/dsl Campestre Mexican, Kimono Japanese, Outback Steaks, Ryan's Country Inn&Suites, Fairfield Inn $Tree, AT&T, URGENT CARE, Verizon, Walmart/Subway, **W** BP/dsl, Exxon, Sheetz/dsl, Shell/Subway Applebee's, Arby's, Bob Evans, Bojangles, Capt D's, Chick-fil-A, Chili's, Cracker Barrel, Dolly's Diner, DQ, Hardee's, McDonald's, Shoney's, Starbucks, Taco Bell, TX Steaks, Wendy's Days Inn, Eden Rock Motel, Hampton Inn, Holiday Inn Express, Microtel, Quality Inn, Sleep Inn, Turnpike Motel H, Hyundai, Lowe's

PRINCETON

Exit #	Services
7	WV 27, Twelve Mile Rd
5	WV 112 (from sb, no re-entry), to Ingleside
3mm	East River
1	US 52 N, to Bluefield, **4 mi W** KFC/LJ Silver, Wend EconoLodge, Quality Inn H, to Bluefield St Coll
0mm	West Virginia/Virginia state line, East River Mtn

MORGANTOWN

INTERSTATE 79

Exit #	Services
160mm	West Virginia/Pennsylvania state line
159	**Welcome Ctr sb, full facilities, info, litter barrels, petwa , vending**
155	US 19, WV 7, **0-3 mi E** GetGo, Sheetz/dsl Cheddar Chili's, Chipotle, CiCi's Pizza, Cracker Barrel, Evergreen Buff Golden Corral, Longhorn Steaks, McDonald's, Olive Garde Red Lobster, Starbucks, TX Roadhouse Best Wester EconoLodge, Fairfield Inn H, $Tree, Barnes&Noble, Be Buy, Buick/Chevrolet/GMC, CVS Drug, Dick's, Giant Eag Foods, GNC, Old Navy, PetCo, Sam's Club/dsl, Target, TJ Max to WVU, Walmart/Subway, **W** BFS/dsl Burger King, D Firehouse Subs, Little Caesar's, Tim Hortons Candlewo Suites, La Quinta Harley-Davidson, Hobby Lobby
153	University Towne Ctr, **E** Buffalo Wild Wings, Fusion Japanese, Wendy's Courtyard, Hampton Inn Kia
152	US 19, to Morgantown, **E** BFS/dsl, Exxon Arby's, Chir Wok, McDonald's, Pizza Hut, Subway, Taco Bell EconoLodg Advance Parts, BigLots, URGENT CARE, **W** Bob Evan Burger King, Garfield's Rest. Microtel Belk, Elder-Bee man, JC Penney, Lowe's
150mm	Monongahela River
148	I-68 E, to Cumberland, MD, **1 mi E** Go-Mart/dsl, Sheetz dsl, Tesla EVC Denny's, Mariachi Loco, Subway Mo gantown Motel, Quality Inn, Ramada Inn $Tree, tires, t Tygart Lake SP, Walmart
146	WV 77, to Goshen Rd, **W** Pilot/deli/dsl/scales/24hr (R accessible dsl only)
141mm	**weigh sta both lanes**
139	WV 33, E Fairmont, **E** Sunoco, **W** Exxon, K&T/dsl/scale repair, RV camping, to Prickett's Ft SP
137	WV 310, to Fairmont, **E** Exxon/dsl, Sunoco Clari on to Valley Falls SP, vet, **W** Shell/dsl Domino's KFC, McDonald's, Subway, Wendy's H, $General, Advanc Parts, Family$, Shop'n Save Foods
136	rd 273, Fairmont
135	WV 64, Pleasant Valley Rd
133	Kingmont Rd, **E** Exxon/Fazoli's/dsl, Marathon/Subway/dsl Cracker Barrel Hampton Inn, Holiday Inn Express, Super 8, **W** Shell/Quiznos/dsl DJ's Diner Quality Inn
132	US 250, S Fairmont, **E** BFS/DQ/dsl, Walmart/dsl Applebee's, Arby's, Bob Evans, Colasessano's Italian, Dutchman's Daughter, El Rey Mexican, Firehouse Subs, Granc China, Hardee's, Little Caesar's, McDonald's, Mi Pueblo, Subway, Taco Bell Days Inn, Fairfield Inn, Microtel, Red Roo Inn $General, Ace Hardware, Advance Parts, Chrysler/Dodge/Jeep, GNC, NAPA, Sav-A-Lot Foods, Shop'n Save, to Tygart Lake SP, Walmart/Subway, **W** Exxon/dsl, GoMart/dsl, Sunoco/dsl Burger King, Steak Escape H, AT&T, Buick/GMC, Ford/Lincoln, Toyota, Trailer City RV Ctr
125	WV 131, Saltwell Rd, to Shinnston, **E** Oliverio's Rest. (4mi) Kia, **W** BFS/Burger King/dsl, Exxon/dsl
124	rd 279, Jerry Dove Dr, **E** BFS, Exxon/Dunkin'/dsl Buffalo Wild Wings, DQ, Firehouse Subs, Little Caesar's, Mi

WV

INTERSTATE 79 Cont'd

124 Continued
Margherita Microtel, Wingate Inn, **W** Sheetz/dsl IHOP, Subway, TGIFriday Comfort Suites, Courtyard, Hawthorn Suites, Holiday Inn Express

123mm **both lanes, full facilities, info, litter barrels, petwalk, RV dump, vending**

121 WV 24, Meadowbrook Rd, **E** GoMart, Sheetz/dsl Biscuit World, Bob Evans, Gino's Pizza Hampton Inn Hyundai/Subaru, **W** Exxon/dsl Burger King, Garfield's Rest., Outback Steaks Super 8 Dick's, Honda, JC Penney, Jo-Ann Fabrics, Marshall's, NTB, Old Navy, Target

119 US 50, to Clarksburg, **E** A&W/LJ Silver, Brickside Grille, Chick-fil-A, Denny's, Eat'n Park, Grand China, KFC, Las Trancas, Little Caesar's, McDonald's, McDonald's (2), Panera Bread, Pizza Hut, Primanti Bros, Starbucks, Taco Bell, TX Roadhouse, Wendy's Best Western+, Days Inn, Sleep Inn, SpringHill Suites, Sutton Inn, Townplace Suites $Tree, Advance Parts, Autozone, BigLots, Family$, GNC, Home Depot, Kohl's, Kroger/dsl, Lowe's, Monro, Sam's Club/gas, URGENT CARE, USPO, Verizon, Walgreens

117 WV 58, to Anmoore, **E** BFS/dsl Applebee's, Arby's, Burger King, Honeybaked Ham, Ruby Tuesday, Ryan's, Subway Hilton Garden Aldi Foods, AT&T, El Rey Mexican, Staples, Walmart/Subway

115 WV 20, Nutter Fort, to Stonewood, **E** BP/7-11/dsl, Exxon/dsl $General, Stonewood Bulk Foods, **W** Greenbrier Motel (5mi)

110 Lost Creek, **E** General Store/dsl USPO

105 WV 7, to Jane Lew, **E** Jane Lew Trkstp/dsl/rest., Valero/dsl/rest. Days Inn, **W** GoMart $General, Kenworth/Mack/Volvo

99 US 33, US 119, to Weston, **E** GoMart/dsl, Marathon/DQ/Little Caesars/dsl, Sheetz/dsl Burger King, Gino's Pizza, McDonald's, Patron Mexican, Peking Buffet, Steer Steakhouse, Subway Hampton Inn (9mi), Holiday Inn Express, Quality Inn/rest., Super 8 $Tree, Advance Parts, Blackwater Falls, GNC, to Canaan Valley Resort, Walmart/dsl, **0-2 mi W** Exxon/Arby's, Go-Mart Domino's, Giovanni's, Hardee's, KFC, LJ Silver, Pizza Hut, Subway, Wendy's H, $General, Chrysler/Dodge/Fiat, CVS Drug, Ford, NAPA, NAPACare, Rite Aid, Save-a-Lot

96 WV 30, to S Weston, **E** Broken Wheel Camping, to S Jackson Lake SP

91 US 19, to Roanoke, **E** Marathon/dsl Stillwaters Rest. camping, to S Jackson Lake SP

85mm **both lanes, full facilities, info, litter barrels, petwalk, RV dump, vending**

79.5mm Little Kanawha River

79 WV 5, Burnsville, **E** Exxon 79er Motel/rest. Burnsville Dam RA, **W** GoMart Cedar Cr SP

76mm Saltlick Creek

67 WV 4, to Flatwoods, **E** BP/Arby's/dsl, Go-Mart/dsl, Shell/dsl Custard Stand, KFC/Taco Bell, McDonald's, Subway Day's Hotel antiques, Buick/Chevrolet, KOA, to Sutton Lake RA, **W** Exxon/dsl, Pilot/Moe's SW Grill/dsl/scales/24hr China Buffet, Shoney's, Starbucks, Wendy's Bulk Foods, Flatwood Factory Stores, Walmart

62 WV 4, Gassaway, to Sutton, **E** Elk Motel Sutton Lake Camping, **W** GoMart LJ Silver, Pizza Hut Microtel H, AutoZone, CVS Drug, Ford, Kroger/deli

57 US 19 S, to Beckley

52mm Elk River

51 WV 4, to Frametown, **E** antiques, food

CLARKSBURG

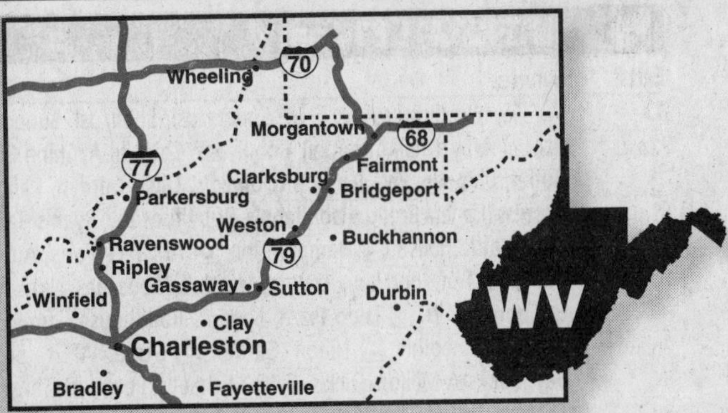

CHARLESTON

49mm **both lanes, full facilities, litter barrels, petwalk, RV dump, vending**

46 WV 11, Servia Rd

40 WV 16, to Big Otter, **E** GoMart/dsl, **W** Exxon/dsl

34 WV 36, to Wallback, **10 mi E** BiscuitWorld, Gino's Diner, Subway

25 WV 29, to Amma, **E** Exxon/dsl

19 US 119, VW 53, to Clendenin, **E** BP/7-11/dsl Rite Aid (3mi), Speedway/dsl (3mi)

9 WV 43, to Elkview, **E** GoMart/dsl Burger King, Penn Sta Subs AutoZone, **W** Exxon/Arby's/dsl, Speedway/dsl La Carreta, Little Caesar's, McDonald's, Picanha Steaks, Subway La Quinta $Tree, Advance Parts, AT&T, CVS Drug, Kroger/dsl

5 WV 114, to Big Chimney, **1 mi E** Exxon Hardee's Rite Aid, Smith's Foods

1 US 119, Mink Shoals, **E** Harding's Family Rest. Sleep Inn

0 I-77, S to Charleston, N to Parkersburg. **I-79 begins/ends on I-77, exit 104.**

INTERSTATE 81

Exit # Services

26mm West Virginia/Maryland state line, Potomac River

25mm **Welcome Ctr sb, full facilities, info, litter barrels, petwalk,**

23 US 11, Marlowe, Falling Waters, **E** Exxon/AC&T/Subway/dsl Kings Rest., Red Lantern Chinese $General, Falling Waters Camping (1mi), Food Lion, **W** BP/dsl 7-11, Outdoor Express RV Ctr

20 WV 901, Spring Mills Rd, **E** Sheetz/dsl China Spring, Cinco de Mayo, Little Caesar's, McDonald's, Pizza Montese, Popeye's, Tokyo Cafe Motel 6 $Tree, Advance Parts, Walmart/Subway, **W** Shell/dsl Burger King, Domino's Quality Inn

16 WV 9, N Queen St, Berkeley Springs, **E** Crown/dsl, Exxon/Subway/dsl, Sheetz Arby's, China King, Domino's, Dunkin', Hoss's, KFC, La Trattoria, LJ Silver, McDonald's, Meridian Cafe, Mrs McCracken's Diner, Pizza Hut, Popeye's, Rita's Custard, Subway, Taco Bell, Waffle House Care Free Inn, Comfort Inn, Knights Inn, Super 8 Advance Parts, Aldi Foods, AutoZone, BigLots, Carquest, CVS Drug, Family$, Food Lion, URGENT CARE, USPO, Walgreens, **W** Shell/Subway/dsl

14 rd 13, Dry Run Rd, **E** H, **W** Butler's Farm Mkt (1mi)

13 rd 15, Kings St, Martinsburg, **E** BP/Subway/dsl, Sheetz/dsl Applebee's, Buffalo Wild Wings, Burger King, Cracker Barrel, Daily Grind, Fiesta Tapatia, Golden Corral, Jerry's Subs, Kobe Japanese, Las Trancas, Outback Steaks, Pizza Hut, Wendy's Days Inn, Fairfield Inn, Holiday Inn/rest. H, Chevrolet/Toyota, Office Depot, Walmart

MARTINSBURG

WV

= gas = food = lodging = other = rest stop

INTERSTATE 81 Cont'd

Exit #	Services
12	WV 45, Winchester Ave, E Sheetz/dsl, Shell/dsl, Sunoco/dsl Arby's, Asian Garden, Bob Evans, Chick-fil-A, China City Buffet, Chipotle, Five Guys, McDonald's, Olive Garden, Panda Express, Panera Bread, Papa John's, Ruby Tuesday, Ryan's, Taco Bell, Waffle House Hampton Inn Advance Parts, AutoZone, BonTon, Food Lion, Lowe's, Martin's Foods/gas, Nahkeeta Camping, W Ledo Pizza, Logan's Roadhouse, Subway, Tropical Smoothie Hilton Garden $Tree, AT&T, Best Buy, Books-A-Million, Dick's, GNC, Michael's, Petsmart, Target, TJ Maxx, URGENT CARE
8	rd 32, Tablers Sta Rd, E Sheetz/dsl
5	WV 51, Inwood, to Charles Town, E 7-11, BP, Liberty, Sheetz/dsl, Shell/dsl Arby's, Burger King, Domino's, DQ, McDonald's, Pizza Hut, Pizza Oven, Subway, Waffle House Hampton Inn Advance Parts, CVS Drug, Family$, Food Lion, NAPA, Rite Aid, URGENT CARE, USPO, W Lazy-A Camping (9mi)
2mm	**Welcome Ctr/weigh sta nb, full facilities, info, litter barrels, petwalk, , , vending**
0mm	West Virginia/Virginia state line

NOTES

WV

WI

WISCONSIN

INTERSTATE 39

WASSAU

Exit #	Services
211	US 51, rd K, Merrill, 2 mi W Cenex Chip's Burgers, Hardee's, Pine Ridge Rest., Pizza Hut
208	WI 64, WI 17, Merrill, E KFC, Taco Bell, W KwikTrip/dsl, Mobil/Arby's/dsl China Inn, Culver's, Los Mezcales, Mama De Luca's Pizza, McDonald's, Subway Americinn, Cobblestone Inn, EconoLodge H, $Tree, Chrysler/Dodge/Jeep, O'Reilly Parts, to Council Grounds SP, Verizon, Walmart
206mm	Wisconsin River
205	US 51, rd Q, Merrill, E BP/Hwy 51/rest./dsl/24hr fireworks
197	rd WW, to Brokaw, W Mobil/dsl
194	US 51, rd U, rd K, Wausau, E F&F/dsl, KwikTrip/dsl McDonald's, Subway, Taco Bell, W BP/Arby's/dsl Ford, Kia, Nissan, Subaru, Toyota
193	Bridge St, E CVS Drug, W H
192	WI 29 W, WI 52 E, Wausau, to Chippewa Falls, same as 191 b
191b	Sherman St, E BP, Holiday/dsl, Shell Applebee's, Buffalo Wild Wings, Great Dane Rest., Jimmy John's, King Buffet, Little Caesar's, McDonald's, Milwaukee Burger Co, Noodles&Co, Panera Bread, Papa Murphy's, Pizza Hut, Qdoba, Starbucks, Subway, Toppers Pizza Courtyard, Hampton Inn, La Quinta, Motel 6, Plaza Hotel, Super 8 County Mkt/USPO, Trig's Foods, Walgreens, W KwikTrip/dsl 2510 Deli, Hardee's H, Cadillac, Home Depot, Honda, Menards
191a	WI 29, Chippewa Falls
190mm	Rib River
190	rd NN, E BP/Burger King El Tequila Salsa, IHOP Hilton Garden, W The Store/Subway/dsl Quality Inn Granite Mtn Ski Area, Rib Mtn Ski Area, st patrol
188	rd N, E KwikTrip/dsl Dunkin', Fazoli's, HuHot, McDonald's, Olive Garden, Panda Express, Red Robin, Rococo Pizza, Ropa Pizza, Starbucks, TX Roadhouse Days Inn $Tree, Aldi Foods, AT&T, Audi/VW, Barnes&Noble, Best Buy, Chevrolet, Dick's, GNC,

STEVENS PT

Exit #	Services
188	Continued Gordman's, Hobby Lobby, Hyundai, JoAnn Fabrics, King's RV C Kohl's, Michael's, Old Navy, PetCo, Petsmart, Sam's Club/gas/d Tires+, TJ Maxx, Walmart/Subway, W Rib Mtn SP
187mm	**I-39 begins/ends. Freeway continues N as US 51.**
187	WI 29 E, to Green Bay
186mm	Wisconsin River
185	US 51, Rothschild, Kronenwetter, E BP/dsl Arby's, Culver's, Denny's, Green Mill Rest., Subway, Wausau Grill Be Western+, EconoLodge, Grand Lodge, Holiday Inn, Motel Stoney Creek Inn Harley-Davidson, Pick'n Save Foods
181	Maple Ridge Rd, Kronenwetter, Mosinee, E Peterbilt, ve Volvo, W Kenworth
179	WI 153, Mosinee, W BP/Subway/dsl, KwikTrip/dsl, Shel dsl McDonald's, StageStop Rest. Quality Inn vet
175	WI 34, Knowlton, to WI Rapids, 1 mi W Mullins Cheese Facto
171	rd DB, Knowlton, W gas food lodging Rive Edge Camping
165	US 10 W, to Marshfield (no nb re-entry)
163	Casimir Rd
161	US 51, Stevens Point, W BP, Kwik Trip/dsl, Th Store Burger King, China Wok, Coldstone, Cousins Subs Culver's, Hardee's, Jimmy John's, KFC, McDonald's, Michele' Rest., Noodles&Co, Perkins, Pizza Hut, Rococo's Pizza, Star bucks, Subway, Taco Bell, Topper's Pizza Baymont Inn Country Inn&Suites, Days Inn $Tree, Trig's Foods, Verizon
159	WI 66, Stevens Point, W KwikTrip/dsl H, Ford, Honda Hyundai, Nissan, VW
158	US 10, Stevens Point, E F&F/dsl, KwikTrip/dsl/e85, Mobil dsl, The Store/Subway/dsl Amber Grill, Arby's, Asian Buffet, Buffalo Wild Wings, Burger King, Culver's, DQ, El Mezca Mexican, Fazoli's, Grazie's Grill, McDonald's, Qdoba, Tac Bell Fairfield Inn, Holiday Inn, Holiday Inn Express Ald Foods, Chrysler/Dodge/Jeep, Target, Verizon, W BP dsl Hilltop Grill EconoLodge, La Quinta

INTERSTATE 39 Cont'd

Exit #	Services
156	rd HH, Whiting, E The Store/Subway/dsl Charcoal Grill, Chili's, McDonald's, Monk's Grill, Panda Express, Panera Bread, Pizza Ranch, Starbucks $Tree, AT&T, Best Buy, GNC, JoAnn Fabrics, Kohl's, Lowe's, Michael's, PetCo, Staples, TJ Maxx, Walmart/Subway
153	rd B, Plover, W BP, Kwik Trip/dsl, Mobil/Dunkin'/dsl Arby's, Bamboo House, Burger King, Culver's, Happy Wok, IHOP, Jimmy John's, KFC, McDonald's, Papa Murphy's, Subway, Taco Bell, Tempura House Asian AmericInn, Comfort Inn, Hampton Inn city park, Copp's Foods, dsl repair, Menards, NAPA, Toyota, Verizon, vet
151	WI 54, to Waupaca, E KwikTrip/rest./dsl/scales/24hr Four Star Family Rest., Shooter's Rest. Best Western, Super 8 tires/repair
143	rd W, Bancroft, to WI Rapids, E Citgo/dsl Pop A Top Grill USPO
139	rd D, Almond
136	WI 73, Plainfield, to WI Rapids, E BP/dsl Budda's Grill service/repair, W Citgo/Subway/dsl
131	rd V, Hancock, E Citgo Smiley's Diner, W Oasis Camping
127mm	**weigh sta both lanes (exits left)**
124	WI 21, Coloma, E Mobil/A&W/dsl Red Hill Cafe, Subway Mecan Inn (4mi) Coloma Camping, W BP/Chester's/dsl Buick/Chevrolet
120mm	**sb, full facilities, litter barrels, petwalk, vending**
118mm	**nb, full facilities, litter barrels, petwalk, vending**
113	rd E, rd J, Westfield, W BP/Burger King, Cenex, Mobil/dsl McDonald's, Subway Pioneer Motel/rest. city park, Family$
106	WI 82 W, WI 23 E, Oxford, E Crossroads Motel, W Citgo/dsl
104	(from nb, no EZ return) rd D, Packwaukee
100	WI 23 W, rd P, Endeavor, E BP/dsl
92	US 51 S, Portage, E KwikTrip/dsl Asian Express, Culver's, Dino's Rest., Jimmy John's, KFC, La Tolteca Mexican, McDonald's, Papa Murphy's, Pizza Ranch, Subway, Suzy's Steaks, Taco Bell Best Western, Ridge Motel, Sunset Motel, Super 8 H, $Tree, Aldi Foods, AutoZone, Chrysler/Dodge/Jeep, Festival Foods, Ford/Lincoln, GNC, Walgreens, Walmart
89b a	WI 16, to WI 127, Portage, E BP/dsl Hitching Post Eatery
88.5mm	Wisconsin River
87	WI 33, Portage, W ski area
86mm	Baraboo River
85	Cascade Mt Rd
84	I-39, I-90 & I-94 run together sb/eb.

PORTAGE

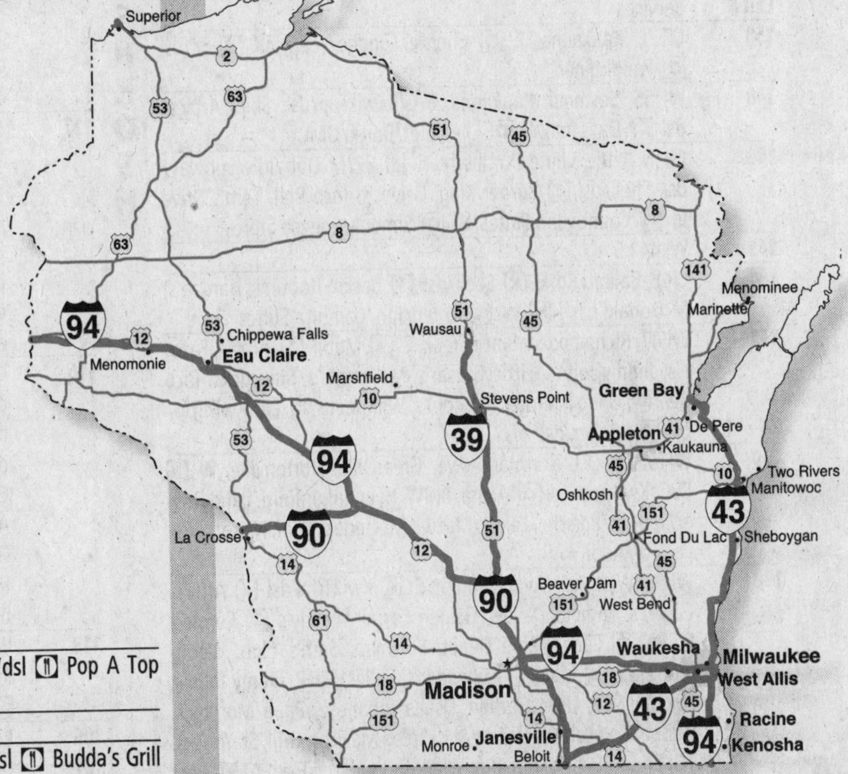

INTERSTATE 41

Exit #	Services
171	I-43 S, to Milwaukee, US 41/141 N, to Marinette
170	US 141 S, Velp Ave, E Mobil Burger King, Taco Bell, W BP/A&W/dsl, Shell/dsl Gilligan's Rest., Julie's Rest., McDonald's, River St Grill, Sunny Chinese, Watering Hole Rest.
170	Continued AmericInn Bumper Parts, CVS Drug, Family$, Harley Davidson
168c b	WI 29, WI 32, Shawano Ave, Dousman St, E KwikTrip, Tesla EVC Comfort Suites Buick/Cadillac/GMC, Meijer
168	WI 32, WI 54, Mason St, E Pizza Hut Home Depot, W Mobil, Shell/Papa John's/dsl Bon Orient Buffet, Chili's, Fazoli's, Hardee's, Little Caesar's, Los Banditos, McDonald's, Schlotsky's Festival Foods, GNC, O'Reilly Parts, Petco, Sam's Club, Walmart/Subway
167	CR VK, Lombardi Ave, Hazelwood Ln, E Shell ChuckeCheese, Margaritas, Red Lobster Cabela's, Lambeau Field, Pick'n Save
165	WI 172, to I-43
164	CR AAA, Oneida St, Waube Ln, E KwikTrip/dsl, Shell/dsl Applebee's, Cousins Subs, Culver's, Denny's, Domino's, Five Guys, Grazie's Italian, Olive Garden, Perkins, Starbucks, Subway, Wendy's Baymont Inn, Comfort Inn, Delta Hotel, EconoLodge, Fairfield Inn, Hampton Inn, Holiday Inn, Motel 6, Super 8 $Tree, Honda, Jo-Ann, W BP/dsl, KwikTrip Erbert & Gerbert's Country Inn Suites, Microtel
163b	WI 32 N, Green Bay
163a	CR G, Main Ave, E Shell/dsl, Tobacco Outlet/dsl Burger King, Dunkin', Jimmy John's, McDonald's, Papa John's, Papa Murphy's, Starbucks, Subway Aldi Foods, AutoZone, CVS Drug, Festival Foods, Peterbilt, USPO, Walgreens, W BP/A&W/Taco Bell/dsl/scales UHaul
161	CR F, Scheuring Rd, De Pete, E KwikTrip/Arby's/dsl, Shell/dsl Culver's, DQ Sleep Inn $Tree, Menard's, Verizon, Walmart/Subway, W Plank Road Rest.
157	CR S, Freedom, W KwikTrip/dsl
154	CR U, Wrightstown
153	**weigh sta nb**

GREEN BAY

WI

= gas = food = lodging = other = rest stop

INTERSTATE 41 Cont'd

WI

APPLETON

Exit #	Services
150	CR J, Kaukauna, E Chrysler/Dodge/Jeep, W BP/dsl Freightliner
148	WI 55, Seymour, Kaukauna, E KwikTrip/dsl, Shell/Arby's/dsl Days Inn, W Chevrolet/Buick/GMC
146	CR N, Little Chute, Kimberly, E BP/McDonald's/Subway/dsl, Shell/dsl Burger King, Culver's, Taco Bell, Tom's Drive In Country Inn Suites, W Simon's Cheese Store
145	WI 441 S
144	CR E, Ballard Rd, E Shell/dsl Baskin Robbins, Hardee's, McDonald's H, W AmericInn, Cambria Suites
142	WI 47, Richmond St, Black Creek, E Mobil Arby's, Fazoli's, Jimmy John's, Little Caesar's, McDonald's, Starbucks, Taco Bell Snug In Motel Kohl's, Walgreens, W KwikTrip/dsl Meijer/dsl
139	WI15, CR OO, Northland Ave, Greenville, Hortonville, W EVC, KwikTrip/dsl Acura, BMW, Hyundai, Infiniti, Land Rover/Jaguar/Porsche, Lexus, Mazda, Mercedes, Mini, Nissan, Volvo, VW/Audi
138	WI 96, Wisconsin Ave, Fremont, E KwikTrip/dsl Arby's, Culver's, Famous Dave's, Golden Corral, Wendy's Comfort Suites CarX, Home Depot, Petsmart, Sam's Club, Woodman's, W Mobil Cheddar's, Chili's, IHOP, Jimmy John's, Noodles&Co, Olive Garden, Osaka Japanese, Papa Murphy's, Qdoba, Red Lobster, Schlotsky's, Solea Mexican Grill, Starbucks, TGI Friday Holiday Inn, Wingate Inn $Tree, AT&T, Best Buy, Costco/dsl, Dick's, Discount Tire, JC Penney, Jo-Ann, Macy's, Menard's, Michael's, Petco, Scheel's, Target, Tires+, TJ Maxx, Verizon, Walgreens, Walmart/Subway
137	WI 125, College Ave, E BP/dsl, KwikTrip, Mobil Applebee's, Burger King, Chick-fil-A, Denny's, HuHot, McDonald's, Panda Express, Panera Bread, Perkins, Popeye's, Starbucks, Subway, Taco Bell, TX Roadhouse Baymont Inn, Clarion, La Quinta, Motel 6, Quality Inn, Rodeway Inn, Super 8 Big Lots, Chrysler/Dodge/Jeep, Firestone/auto, Ford, Goodyear/auto, Honda, Kia, Office Depot, Subaru, Woodman's Gas, W KwikTrip/dsl Asian Garden, Buffalo Wild Wings, Chipotle, ChuckECheese, Fazoli's, Five Guys, Machine Shed Rest., Outback Steaks, TGIFriday's AmericInn, Candlewood Suites, Country Inn Suites, DoubleTree, Fairfield Inn, GrandStay Suites, Hampton Inn, Home 2 Suites, Microtel, Residence Inn Barnes&Noble, Hobby Lobby, Old Navy, USPO, vet
136	CR BB, Prospect Ave, W BP, Mobil/Subway Van Zeeland Autocare
134	US 10 E, WI 441 N
133	CR II, Winchester Rd
132	Main St, Oak Ridge Rd (no return nb or sb), E BP/dsl, Citgo/dsl Bradke's Rest. Chevrolet/Buick/Cadillac
131	WI 114, CR JJ, Winneconne Ave, Hilbert, Sherwood, E Citgo/dsl, Fox Point, KwikTrip/dsl Cousins Subs, Ground Round, Hardee's, KFC, Little Caesar's, McDonald's, Papa Murphy's, Pizza Hut, Starbucks, Subway Best Western, Days Inn $Tree, Advance Parts, Aldi Foods, CVS Drug, Festival Foods, Firestone/auto, Ford/Lincoln, GNC, Pick'n Save, W A&W, Applebee's, Arby's, Culver's, Jimmy John's, Perkins, Qdoba, Taco Bell AT&T, Kohl's, Verizon, Walgreens, Walmart/Subway
129	Bell St, Breezewood Ln, W Mobil Solea Mexican
124	WI 76, Jackson St, E Mobil, W KwikTrip/dsl/CNG, Ole & Lena's truck repair
120	US 45, US 10 W, New London

OSHKOSH

RIPON

Exit #	Services
119	WI 21, Omro Rd, Oshkosh, E DQ La Quinta, W K Trip/dsl, Shell/McDonald's Cousins Subs, Culver's, Pa Bread, Papa Murphy's, Rocky Rococo Pizza, Subway, V dy's Holiday Inn Express Chevrolet/Buick/GMC/Cadi Dick's, Festival Foods, H, Lowe's, Menard's, Verizon, Walgre
117	9th Ave, E KwikTrip/dsl Benvenuto's Italian, Bu Wild Wings, China King, Cousins Subs, Golden Corral, IHOP, J my John's, Little Caesar's, McDonald's, Olive Garden, Pizza Potbelly, Qdoba, Red Robin, Starbucks, Taco Bell Com Suites AT&T, Best Buy, CVS Drug, Duluth Trading, Ho Lobby, Jo-Ann, Ross, TJ Maxx, Verizon, Walgreens, W B er King, Domino's, Huhot, Perkins, Pizza Ranch Goodye auto, NAPA, Walmart/Subway
116	WI 44, WI 91, S Park Ave, Ripon Rd, E BP/dsl, Mo dsl Applebee's, Arby's, Culver's, Durango's, Fazoli's, F house Subs, Friar Tuck's Rest., Hangar Grill, Hardee's, N dles&Co, Subway Cobblestone Inn, Fairfield Inn, Hil Garden, Super 8 $Tree, Advance Parts, air museum, Aldi Foods, CarX, GNC, Petco, Pick'n Save, Target, Tire W KwikTrip/dsl, Shell/dsl Johnny Rockets Ha thorn Suites Honda, Kia, Nissan, Oshkosh Outlets/famo brands, Subaru, Toyota, vet, VW
113	WI 26, CR N, Rosendale, Waupun, Pickett, E Sleepy H low Camping (2mi), W Planeview/Subway/dsl/scales/24 Cobblestone Inn
106	CR N, Van Dyne
101	CR OO, Winnebago St, E BP/Rest./dsl/scales Mack/V vo, truck wash
99	WI 23, Johnson St, Rosendale, Ripon, E 11:11 Burger, A Roma Pizza, Applebee's, Buffalo Wild Wings, Burger King, D Faro's Rest., Fazoli's, Hardee's, KFC, McDonald's, Panda Expre Panera Bread, Popeye's, Qdoba, Rocky Rococo Pizza, Schriene Rest., Starbucks Days Inn, Hampton Inn, Super 8 AT& AutoZone, Best Buy, Jo-Ann, Kohl's, Pick'n Save, Staples, Maxx, W KwikTrip/dsl, Shell/Subway/dsl Arby's, Culver Pizza Hut, Pizza Ranch $Tree, Aldi Foods, CarX, Chevrole Buick/GMC/Cadillac, Ford, Harley Davidson, Mazda, Menard Petsmart, Target, Verizon, Walmart/Subway
98	CR D, Military Rd, E McDonald's Microtel F&F/d Schiek's Campers, W BP/dsl Rolling Meadows Res Comfort Inn, Holiday Inn Express, Radisson Chrysle Dodge/Jeep, st patrol
97	CR VVV, Hickory St, E KwikTrip/dsl, Pump&Pantry/dsl, W Loves/Subway/dsl/scales/24hr Country Inn Suites
95	US 152, Madison, Manitowoc, E H
92	CR B, Oakfield, Eden, E Breezy Hill Camping (2 mi)
87	WI 49, CR KK, Brownsville, Waupun
85	WI 67, Lomira, Campbellsport, E Exxon/dsl, W BP Taco Bell/dsl, Shell/Subway/dsl Bublitz's Rest., McDonald' AmeriVu Inn $General, Ford, Piggly Wiggly
82.5mm	**both lanes, full facilities, litter barrels, petwalk**
81	WI 28, Mayville, Kewaskum
76	CR D, W fireworks
72	WI 33, CR W, West Bend, Allenton, W BP/dsl, Mobil A ma's Cafe, Subway
68	CR K, W Mobil/dsl MJ Stevens Rest.
66	WI 144, West Bend, Slinger, W Freedom RV Ctr, Held' Cheese/sausage, Slinger Speedway
64	WI 60, to Jackson, Slinger, Hartford, E Scenic RV Ctr W BP/dsl, KwikTrip/dsl Burger King, China Town, Cousins Subs, Polanco's Mexican Chevrolet, Chrysler/Dodge/Jeep, H, O'Reilly Parts, Piggly Wiggly, Schaefer's Service Ctr

 = gas = food = lodging = other = rest stop

INTERSTATE 41 Cont'd

Exit #	Services
60	CR FD, to WI 145, Richfield, E Mobil/dsl/e85 Cabela's, W BP/McDonald's/dsl/scales/24hr
59	(from nb)US 45 W
57	WI 167, Holy Hill Rd, E Mobil/Subway/dsl, W BP Sawmill Rest.
54	WI 167, CR Y, Lannon Rd, Germantown, E KwikTrip/dsl Best Western, Country Inn Suites
52	CR Q, County Line Rd, E Briscoe Co Wood Grill, W Mobil/dsl, Speedway/dsl Applebee's, Arby's, Buffalo Wild Wings, Burger King, Cracker Barrel, Jimmy John's, KFC, McDonald's, Panda Express, Pizza Hut/Taco Bell, Qdoba, Starbucks, Wendy's Holiday Inn Express, Super 8 AT&T, Best Buy, Costco/dsl, Hobby Lobby, Kohl's, Metro Mkt, Target
51b a	Pilgrim Rd, W KwikTrip Kraverz Custard, Toppers AutoZone
50b a	WI 74 W, WI 100 E, Menomonee Falls, E Buick/GMC, Ford, VW, W BP De Martinis Pizza Monro
48	WI 145, E Aldi Foods, Sam's Club/gas, Woodman's Mkt/gas
47b	CR PP, Good Hope Rd, E Broken Egg, Cousins Subs, Point Burger Bar Comfort Suites, Hilton Garden CarMax, Chevrolet, Mazda, Nissan, Toyota
47	WI 175, Appleton Ave
46	CR E, Silver Spring Dr, E Marathon/dsl, Mobil/dsl Athens Rest., Cousins Subs, KFC, McDonald's, Subway, Taco Bell, Wendy's Hampton Inn, Quality Inn Goodyear/auto, Harley Davidson, Petro Mart, W Speedway/dsl Domino's Hyatt Place
45	CR EE, Hampton Ave, E Citgo, W BP/dsl
44	WI 190, Capitol Dr, E Subway Walgreens, W Arby's, Burger King, Chick-fil-A, Chipotle, Culver's, Jimmy John's, McDonald's, Noodles&Co, Potbelly's, Qdoba, Starbucks, Taco Bell Advance Parts, GNC, Home Depot, Metro Mkt, O'Reilly Parts, Petco, Ross, Target
43	Burleigh St, E Corner Bakery Cafe, Osgood's Rest., Pizza Man Homewood Suites Dick's, H, Meijer, Old Navy, TJ Maxx, W Wendy's Cousins Subs Aldi Foods, Firestone/auto, Lowe's
42b	North Ave W, E BP Buffalo Wild Wings, Cheesecake Factory, Dave&Buster's, Denny's, Five Guys, Maggiano's, Panera Bread, PF Chang's, Potbelly, Texas de Brazil Extended Stay America, Holiday Inn Express, Radisson Barnes&Noble, Best Buy, Macy's, Nordstrom's, Walgreens, W Papa John's vet
42a	WI 100, Mayfair Rd, North Ave E (from nb), E Dave&Buster's Walgreens, W Firehouse Subs Crowne Plaza Kia, Pick'n Save, USPO
40	Watertown Plank Rd, Swan Blvd, E H, W Crowne Plaza
39	US 18, Wisconsin Ave, Bluemound Rd, E H
1b a	I-94
1d	WI 53, Greenfield Ave, E Jets Pizza, Subway CVS Drug, Family$, W Speedway/dsl DQ, Fazoli's, Las Fajitas, McDonald's, Starbucks, Wendy's O'Reilly Parts
1e	(from sb) Lincoln Ave, E same as 2 E
2a	(from sb) National Rd (wb)
2b	(from sb) Oklahoma Ave, E Citgo auto repair, H
3	Beloit Rd
4	**I-41 S runs with I-43 N/I-894 E, then I-94 E. See I-43 exits 5-9 and I-94 exits 316-347.**
0mm	Wisconsin/Illinois state line

MILWAUKEE

INTERSTATE 43

Exit #	Services
192mm	**I-43 begins/ends at Green Bay on US 41.**
192b	US 41 S, US 141 S, to Appleton, **1 mi S services on Velp Ave** BP/A&W/dsl, Express/dsl, Mobil, Shell/dsl Burger King, Gilligan's Rest., Julie's Cafe, McDonald's, Riverstreet Grill, Sunny Chinese, Taco Bell, Watering Hole Rest AmericInn Bay Parts, Bumper Parts, CVS Drug, Family$, Harley-Davidson, Trans Motive Auto
192a	US 41 N, US 141 N
189	Atkinson Dr, to Velp Ave, Port of Green Bay, W Shell/dsl
188mm	Fox River
187	East Shore Dr, Webster Ave, W Shell/dsl/24hr, Tesla EVC McDonald's, Subway, Wendy's Hampton Inn, Hyatt H
185	WI 54, WI 57, University Ave, to Algoma, E U of WI GB, W EVC, KwikTrip, Shell/A&W Domino's, Subway, Taco Bell Family$, Festival Foods, University Mkt, Walgreens
183	Mason St, rd V, E Culver's, Mackinaw's Grill Country Inn&Suites, Super 8 H, URGENT CARE, **1 mi W** BP, Mobil/dsl, Shell Applebee's, Arby's, Burger King, China Buffet, Dunkin', Fazoli's, Green Tea Chinese, KFC, Little Caesar's, McDonald's, Noodles&Co, Papa John's, Papa Murphy's, Perkins, Pizza Ranch, Qdoba, Starbucks, Taco Bell $General, $Tree, Advance Parts, Aldi Foods, AutoZone, Batteries+Bulbs, Chevrolet, Chrysler/Dodge/Jeep, Family$, Hobby Lobby, Kohl's, Mazda, Nissan, O'Reilly Parts, PetCo, Pick'n Save, Ross, Subaru, Tires+, Walgreens, Walmart/Subway
181	Eaton Rd, rd JJ, E BP/McDonald's/dsl Bellevue Cafe, Hardee's, Jimmy John's, Luigi's, Taco John's Ford/Kia, Home Depot, W Shell A&W, Ravine Grill, Subway AmericInn Farm&Fleet/gas, Festival Foods, Menards
180	WI 172 W, to US 411 exit, W BP/Taco Bell/24hr, Citgo/Country Express/dsl/scales/24hr, KwikTrip/dsl, Shell/Subway/dsl Buffalo Wild Wings, Burger King, McDonald's, Tucson's Rest. Holiday Inn Express H, AT&T, Costco/gas, Discount Tire, GNC, Pick'n Save, Target, to stadium, Verizon, Walgreens, multiple services
178	US 141, to WI 29, rd MM, Bellevue, E Shell/Arby's/dsl Little Caesar's
171	WI 96, rd KB, Denmark, E BP/dsl Blossom's Cheese, DeGrande Rest, McDonald's, Subway Shady Acres Camping
168mm	**both lanes, full facilities, litter barrels, petwalk, vending**
166mm	Devils River
164	WI 147, rd Z, Maribel, W BP/dsl
160	rd K, Kellnersville
157	rd V, Hillcrest Rd, Francis Creek, E Citgo/Subway/dsl, Marathon/diner/dsl

GREEN BAY

WI

[gas] = gas [food] = food [lodging] = lodging [other] = other [rest stop] = rest stop

WI

INTERSTATE 43 Cont'd

MANITOWOC

Exit #	Services
154	US 10 W, WI 310, Two Rivers, to Appleton, E [other] [H]
153mm	Manitowoc River
152	US 10 E, WI 42 N, rd JJ, Manitowoc, E [food] TimeOut Grill [other] [H], antiques, maritime museum
149	US 151, WI 42 S, Manitowoc, E [gas] BP, Citgo/dsl, KwikTrip/dsl, Mobil, Shell/dsl [food] A&W, Applebee's, Arby's, Buffalo Wild Wings, Burger King, Culver's, DQ, El Tequila, Fork&Knife Rest, Four Seasons Rest., Frier Tuck's Sandwiches, Hardee's, Hong Kong Buffet, Jimmy John's, KFC, Little Caesar's, McDonald's, Noodles&Co, Panda Express, Papa Murphy's, Perkins, Pizza Ranch, Qdoba, Starbucks, Taco Bell, Wendy's [lodging] Harbor Town Inn, Holiday Inn, Quality Inn [other] [H], $Tree, Advance Parts, Aldi Foods, AutoZone, Buick/Cadillac/Chevrolet/GMC, Chrysler/Dodge/Jeep, Family$, Festival Foods, GNC, Goodyear/auto, Hobby Lobby, Kohl's, Lowe's, O'Reilly Parts, PetCo, Pick'n Save, USPO, Verizon, vet, Walgreens, Walmart/Subway, W [gas] Shell/McDonald's [food] Subway [lodging] AmericInn [other] Harley-Davidson, Menards
144	rd C, Newton, E [gas] Mobil/dsl
142mm	**weigh sta sb**
137	rd XX, Cleveland, E [gas] Citgo/Subway/dsl [other] Kunes Co RV Ctr
128	WI 42, Howards Grove, E [gas] BP/dsl/24hr, KwikTrip/dsl [food] Culver's, Hardee's, Harry's Diner, Shuff's Rest., TX Roadhouse [lodging] Quality Inn [other] Pomp's Tire, W [gas] Mobil/dsl/scales [other] Menards, Walmart/Subway
126	WI 23, Sheboygan, E [gas] BP, KwikTrip/dsl, Tesla EVC [food] Applebee's, Cousins Subs, Culver's, McDonald's, New China, Noodles&Co, Panera Bread, Pizza Hut, Pizza Ranch [lodging] La Quinta, Super 8 [other] [H], Aldi Foods, Batteries+Bulbs, BigLots, Festival Foods, Ford/Kia, Goodyear/auto, Honda, Hyundai/Mazda, Kohl's, NAPA, Subaru, Toyota
123	WI 28, rd A, Sheboygan, E [gas] Citgo/dsl/24hr, Mobil/McDonald's/dsl [food] Coldstone, Jimmy John's, Perkins, Qdoba, Rocky Rococo's Pizza, Starbucks, Subway, Wendy's [lodging] AmericInn, Holiday Inn Express [other] Harley-Davidson/Cruisers Burgers, Walmart/Subway, W [food] Arby's, Buffalo Wild Wings, Chili's, Starbucks [other] $Tree, AT&T, Best Buy, GNC, Home Depot, JoAnn Fabrics, Petsmart, Target, TJ Maxx
120	rds OK, V, Sheboygan, E [gas] KwikTrip/dsl, Loves/Hardee's/Subway/dsl/scales/24hr [food] Parkside Rest. [lodging] Sleep Inn [other] camping, Nissan, to Kohler-Andrae SP, VW, 1 mi W [other] Horn's RV Ctr
116	rd AA, Foster Rd, Oostburg, 1 mi W [gas] Sunoco [food] Judi's Place Rest., Pizza Ranch, Subway [other] Piggly Wiggly/gas
113	WI 32 N, rd LL, Cedar Grove, W [gas] Citgo/dsl/repair, Mobil/dsl, Sunoco/Fueling Depot [food] Country Grove Rest. (1mi), Sunrise Rest. [lodging] Lakeview Motel
107	rd D, Belgium, E [lodging] Lake Church Inn/grill [other] Harrington Beach SP, W [gas] BP/McDonald's/dsl/24hr, How-Dea Trkstp/Hobo's Korner Kitchen/dsl/scales, Mobil/dsl/24hr [food] Kyote's Grill, Subway [lodging] Belgium Inn [other] repair, USPO
100	WI 32 S, WI 84 W, Port Washington, E [gas] BP/dsl, Mobil [food] Arby's, McDonald's, Pizza Hut, Subway [lodging] Country Inn&Suites, Holiday Inn (2mi) [other] Allen-Edmonds Shoes, Goodyear/auto, Piggly Wiggly, True Value, vet, W [lodging] Hundred Mile House Rest.
97	(from nb, exits left), WI 57, Fredonia
96	WI 33, to Saukville, E [food] Culver's (1mi) [other] Advance Parts, Best Hardware, Buick/Cadillac/Chevrolet, Camping World RV Ctr, Chrysler/Dodge/Jeep, Ford, O'Reilly Parts, Piggly Wiggly, Walgreens, Walmart, W [gas] Exxon/McDonald's, KwikTrip/dsl

MILWAUKEE

Exit #	Services
96	Continued [food] Domino's, DQ, Lam's Chinese, Papa Murphy's, Subw Taco Bell [lodging] Motel 6 [other] repair/tires
93	WI 32 N, WI 57 S, Grafton, 2 mi E [gas] BP [other] vet
92	WI 60, rd Q, Grafton, E [gas] BP/dsl [food] GhostTown Rest., Wa St Rest. [lodging] Hampton Inn, TownePlace Suites, W [gas] Cit DQ/dsl [food] Charcoal Grill, Firehouse Subs, Noodles&Co, Q ba, Starbucks, Subway [lodging] Comfort Inn [other] [H], Aldi Foo AT&T, Costco/gas, Dick's, Home Depot, Kohl's, Meijer, chael's, Petsmart, Target, Verizon
89	rd C, Cedarburg, W [gas] Mobil/dsl [other] [H]
85	WI 57 S, WI 167 W, Mequon Rd, W [gas] BP, Mobil, Shell [food] C ibou Coffee, Chancery Rest., Cousins Subs, Culver's, First Wa Cafe, Jimmy John's, Leonardo's Pizza, McDonald's, Noodles Co, Panera Bread, Papa Murphy's, Pizza Hut, Starbucks, Ta Bell [lodging] Chalet Motel [other] [H], Ace Hardware, AT&T, Marshal Metro Mkt, Sendik's Foods, Verizon, vet, Walgreens
83	rd W, Port Washington Rd (from nb only)
82b a	WI 32 S, WI 100, Brown Deer Rd, E [gas] BP, Mobil/ [food] Baskin-Robbins, Benji's Deli, Jose's Blue Sombrero, Ma field's Pancakes, McDonald's, Noodles&Co, Peking Chef, Qd ba, Starbucks, Subway, Toppers Pizza [other] Best Buy, CVS Dru GNC, Land's Inlet, Walgreens
80	Good Hope Rd, E [gas] Mobil [food] Dr Dawg, Jimmy John King's Wok, Samurai Japanese [lodging] Fairfield Inn, Residen Inn [other] Pick'n Save, to Cardinal Stritch U
78	Silver Spring Dr, E [gas] BP, Mobil [food] Arby's, Bar Louie, Bo ton Mkt, Buffalo Wild Wings, CA Pizza Kitchen, Cheesecal Factory, Cousins Subs, Devon Steaks, Fiddleheads Coffee, Fi Guys, Kopp's Custard, McDonald's, Panera Bread, Papa Mu phy's, Perkins, Potbelly, Qdoba, Taco Bell [lodging] La Quinta, M tel 6 [other] AT&T, Barnes&Noble, Batteries+Bulbs, Goodyea auto, Kohl's, Nissan, Trader Joe's, USPO, Verizon, Walgreen W [other] [H]
77b a	(from nb), E [food] Anchorage Rest., Solly's Grille [lodging] Holiday In
76b a	WI 57, WI 190, Green Bay Ave, E [other] Home Depot, W [gas] BP dsl [food] Burger King
75	Atkinson Ave, Keefe Ave, E [gas] Mobil, W [gas] BP
74	Locust St
73c	North Ave (rom sb), E [food] Wendy's, W [food] McDonald's
73b	North Ave (from nb), downtown
73a	WI 145 E, 4th St (exits left from sb), Broadway, downtown
72c	Wells St, E [lodging] Doubletree, Hilton [other] [H], Civic Ctr, museum
72b	(from sb), I-94 W, to madison
72a	(310c from nb, exits left from sb), I-794 E, I-94 W to Madison, t Lakefront, downtown
311	WI 59, National Ave, 6th St, downtown
312a	Lapham Blvd, Mitchell St, W [gas] BP, Citgo
312b	(from nb), Becher St, Lincoln Ave
314a	Holt Ave, E [gas] SP Mart/dsl [food] Applebee's, Arby's, Chin King, Jimmy John's, Little Caesar's, Rosati's Pizza, Starbucks Subway, Taco Bell, Wendy's [other] AutoZone, Family$, Home Depot, Pick'n Save Foods, Piggly Wiggly, Target, vet, W [other] [H], to Alverno Coll
314b	Howard Ave
10b	I-94 S to Chicago, E [other] [airport]
9b a	WI 241, 27th St, E [gas] Flying Eagle, Saifron/dsl [food] Arby's, Benny's Cafe, Dunkin', Famous Dave's, Sonic, Subway [lodging] Suburban Motel [other] AutoZone, Subaru, USPO, Walgreens, W [food] Buffalo Wild Wings, Chipotle Mexican, Denny's, Jimmy John's, McDonald's, New China, Omega Rest., Panda Express, Papa John's, Rich's Cakes, Starbucks, Taco Bell, Wong's Wok,

INTERSTATE 43 Cont'd

9b a	Continued Zebb's Rest Quality Inn, Rodeway Inn H, $Tree, AAA, Advance Parts/Meineke, AutoZone, Chevrolet, CVS Drug, Firestone/auto, Ford, Goodyear/auto, Kohl's, Marshall's, Michael's, Pick'n Save Foods, Ross, Walgreens, Walmart
8a	WI 36, Loomis Rd, E BP/dsl, Citgo Los Mariachi's Aldi Foods, Walgreens, W Griddler's Cafe to Alverno Coll
7	60th St, E Speedway/dsl Culver's, Subway Harley-Davidson, Meijer/dsl, W Speedway/dsl
5b	76th St (from sb, no EZ return), E Speedway/dsl Applebee's, Bakers Square, Burger King, Carrabba's Italian, Chick-fil-A, Cousins Subs, El Beso, Habaneros, Jersey Mike's, Jimmy John's, Kopp's Burgers, Kyoto Japanese, Longhorn Steaks, McDonald's, Noodles&Co, Old Country Buffet, Olive Garden, Panda Express, Panera Bread, Qdoba, Red Lobster, Red Robin, Ruby Tuesday, Starbucks, TGIFriday's, Topper's Pizza, Traditional Pancake House, Wendy's $Tree, AT&T, Barnes&Noble, Best Buy, Firestone/auto, Goodyear/auto, JC Penney, Jo-Ann Fabrics, Macy's, Midas, PetCo, Petsmart, Sendik's Food Mkt, TJ Maxx, Tuesday Morning, Verizon, Walmart, W Arby's, Pizza Hut, Subway Advance Parts, Family$, Pick'n Save Foods, USPO, Walgreens
5a	WI 24 W, Forest Home Ave, E Citgo/dsl Outback Steaks, Portillo's Boerner Botanical Gardens, Fresh Thyme Mkt, Kohl's, Marshall's, Ross, Welk's Auto
61	(4 from sb), I-894/US 45 N, I-43/US 45 S
60	US 45 S, WI 100, 108th St (exits left from sb), E BP, Citgo, Marathon, Mobil A&W, Amore Italian, Ann's Italian, Burger King, Chipotle Mexican, Confucious Chinese, Cousins Subs, Culver's, Dunkin', George Webb Rest., McDonald's, Noodles&Co, Open Flame Grill, Papa Murphy's, Starbucks, Subway, Taco Bell $Tree, AutoZone, Chevrolet, O'Reilly Parts, Pick'n Save, USPO, vet, Walgreens, W Andy's/dsl Denny's, Forum Rest., McDonald's, Organ Piper Pizza, Subway Aldi Foods, Goodyear/auto, NAPA, Nissan, vet, Walgreens, Walmart/Subway
59	WI 100, Layton Ave (from nb, exits left), same as 60, Hales Corner, W BP/Cousins Subs
57	Moorland Rd, E KwikTrip/dsl Applebee's, Stonefire Pizza Co, TX Roadhouse, Zaffiro's Pizza La Quinta Costco/dsl, W Speedway/dsl Arby's, Buffalo Wild Wings, Cocina Real, Panera Bread, Papa John's, Point Burger Holiday Inn Express Firestone/auto, GNC, Michael's, Target
54	rd Y, Racine Ave, 1-2 mi E BP/dsl, KwikTrip Cousins Subs, Culver's, McDonald's, Piggly Wiggly, Walgreens
50	WI 164, Big Bend, W KwikTrip/dsl/e85 McDonald's, Subway
44mm	Fox River
43	WI 83, Mukwonago, E BP/dsl Aldi Foods, Chevrolet, Chrysler/Dodge/Jeep, Home Depot, H, Walmart, W Citgo Boneyard Grille, Chen's Kitchen, Domino's, DQ, Starbucks, Taco Bell Baymont Inn
38	WI 20, East Troy, W Pilot/Road Ranger/Subway/dsl/24hr, Shell/McDonald's Ale Sta Rest., Cousins Subs, Dos Amigos, Genoa Pizza, LD's BBQ, Roma's Ristorante $General, Carquest
36	WI 120, East Troy, E Alpine Valley Resort, W Quality Inn Suites
33	Bowers Rd, E to Alpine Valley Music Theatre
32mm	both lanes, full facilities, litter barrels, petwalk, vending

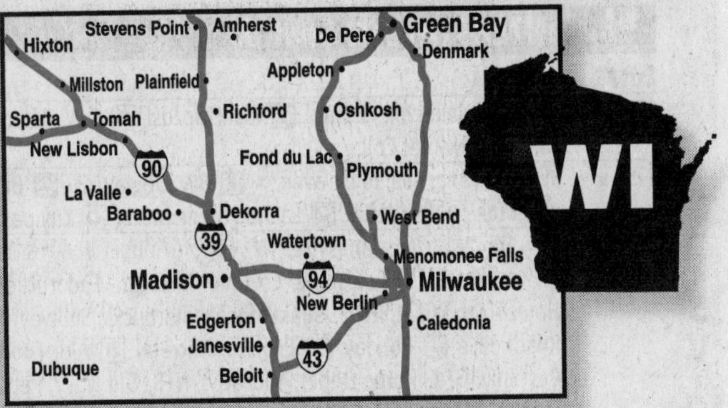

DELAVAN

29	WI 11, Elkhorn, W fairgrounds
27b a	US 12, to Lake Geneva, E H
25	WI 67, Elkhorn, E Loves/Hardee's/dsl/scales/24hr, Mobil/dsl AmericInn Buick/Chevrolet/GMC, Chrysler/Dodge/Jeep, vet, W Speedway/dsl/24hr Burger King, Subway Hampton Inn (2mi) Kunes Country RV Ctr
21	WI 50, Delavan, E Brodie's Beef, Chili's, China 1, Culver's, Domino's, Jimmy John's, Panera Bread, Papa Murphy's, Starbucks, Subway, Yoshi Japanese Aldi Foods, AT&T, F&F Tires, Kohl's, Lowe's, Petsmart, Verizon, Walmart, W Mobil/Dunkin'/dsl KFC, Little Caesar's, McDonald's, Perkins, Wendy's Comfort Suites, Super 8 $Tree, AutoZone, Cadillac/Chevrolet, Ford/Lincoln, GNC, NAPA, O'Reilly Parts, Piggly Wiggly, Walgreens
17	rd X, Delavan, Darien, W BP/dsl
15	US 14, Darien, E Mobil/dsl West Wind Diner
6	WI 140, Clinton, E Citgo/Subway/TCBY/dsl $General, Ford
2	rd X, Hart Rd, E Butterfly Fine Dining
1b a	I-90, E to Chicago, W to Madison, S Mobil/McDonald's, Pilot/Taco Bell/dsl/scales/24hr, Shell, Speedway/dsl Applebee's, Arby's, Buffalo Wild Wings, Culver's, Doc's Rest., Dunkin', Jimmy John's, Little Caesar's, Little Mexico, Noodles&Co, Qdoba, Road Dawg Rest., Starbucks, Subway, Wendy's Baymont Inn, Fairfield Inn, Hampton Inn, Holiday Inn Express, Home 2 Suites, Quality Inn, Rodeway Inn, Super 8 $Tree, Aldi Foods, AT&T, Buick/GMC, Cadillac/Chevrolet, GNC, Menards, NTB, O'Reilly Parts, Walmart

BELOIT

I-43 begins/ends on I-90, exit 185 in Beloit.

INTERSTATE 90

Exit #	Services
187mm	Wisconsin/Illinois state line, I-90 & I-39 run together nb.
187mm	Welcome Ctr wb, full facilities, info, litter barrels, petwalk, s, vending
185b	I-43 N, to Milwaukee
185a	WI 81, Beloit, S Mobil/McDonald's/dsl, Pilot/Taco Bell/dsl/scales/24hr, Shell, Speedway/dsl Applebee's, Arby's, Buffalo Wild Wings, Culver's, Doc's Rest., Dunkin', Jimmy John's, Little Caesar's, Little Mexico, Noodles&Co, Papa Murphy's, Qdoba, Road Dawg Rest., Starbucks, Subway, Wendy's Baymont Inn, Fairfield Inn, Hampton Inn, Holiday Inn Express, Home 2 Suites, Quality Inn, Rodeway Inn, Super 8 $Tree, Aldi Foods, AT&T, Buick/GMC, Cadillac/Chevrolet, GNC, Menards, NTB, O'Reilly Parts, Walmart
183	Shopiere Rd, rd S, to Shopiere, S BP/Rollette/dsl/24hr H, repair
181mm	weigh sta, wb

BELOIT

[gas] = gas [food] = food [lodging] = lodging [other] = other [RS] = rest stop

INTERSTATE 90 Cont'd

JANESVILLE

Exit #	Services
177	WI 11 W, Janesville, 2 mi S [gas] KwikTrip/dsl [other] S WI Airport, to Blackhawk Tec Coll
175b a	WI 11 E, Janesville, to Delavan, N [gas] BP/Subway/dsl [lodging] Baymont Inn [other] [H], vet, S [lodging] Lannon Stone Motel [other] city park
171c b	US 14, WI 26, Janesville, N [gas] TA/Mobil/Wendy's/dsl/scales/24hr/@ [food] Coldstone, Cozumel Mexican, Fuddruckers, HomeTown Buffet, IHOP, Quaker Steak, Starbucks, Subway, TX Roadhouse [lodging] Holiday Inn Express, Microtel [other] Aldi Foods, Best Buy, GNC, Home Depot, Michael's, NTB, Old Navy, PetCo, Staples, TJ Maxx, S [gas] Citgo, Exxon/dsl, Kwik Trip/dsl [food] Applebee's, Arby's, Buffalo Wild Wings, Burger King, Chipotle, ChuckeCheese, Culver's, Dunkin', Famous Dave's, Fazoli's, Fuji Steaks, Hacienda Real, Hardee's, Hooters, Jimmy John's, KFC, Mac's Pizza, McDonald's, Milio's Sandwiches, Milwaukee Grill, Noodles&Co, Olive Garden, Panda Express, Panera Bread, Papa Murphy's, Peking Chinese, Perkins, Pizza Hut, Prime Quarter Steaks, Qdoba Mexican, Red Robin, Road Dawg Eatery, Subway, Taco Bell, Taco John's, Toppers Pizza, World Buffet [lodging] Quality Inn, Super 8 [other] [H], $Tree, Aldi Foods, AT&T, AutoZone, Big Lots, CarQuest, CVS Drug, F&F, Festival Foods, Ford/Lincoln, Harley-Davidson, Hobby Lobby, Hyundai, JC Penney, Kohl's, Mazda, Menards, Nissan/Kia/Subaru, O'Reilly Parts, Target, Toyota, USPO, Verizon, Walgreens
171a	WI 26, N [gas] BP/dsl [food] Cracker Barrel [lodging] Hampton Inn, Motel 6, Ramada/rest. [other] Chrysler/Dodge/Jeep, Sam's Club, URGENT CARE, VW, Walgreens, Walmart, S same as 171c b
168mm	**[RS] eb, full [handicapped] facilities, litter barrels, petwalk, [phone], [picnic], vending**
163.5mm	Rock River
163	WI 59, Edgerton, to Milton, N [gas] Mobil/Subway/dsl, Shell/Dunkin'/Taco John's/dsl [food] Blue Gilly's Rest., Culver's, McDonald's, WI Cheese Store [lodging] Quality Inn [other] marina
160	US 51S, WI 73, WI 106, Oaklawn Academy, to Deerfield, S [gas] BP/dsl/scales/24hr/@ [other] [H], Creek View Camping (2mi)
156	US 51N, to Stoughton, S [lodging] Coachman's Inn/rest. [other] [H]
147	rd N, Cottage Grove, to Stoughton, S [gas] BP/Arby's/dsl, Road Ranger/[Pilot]/Subway/dsl/scales [other] Lake Kegonsa SP
146mm	**weigh sta eb**
142b a	(142a exits left from wb) US 12, US 18, Madison, to Cambridge, N [gas] BP/dsl [food] Roadhouse Rest. [lodging] Best Value Inn, Magnuson Grand Hotel [other] casino, Harley-Davidson, S [gas] Citgo/dsl, Phillips 66/Arby's/dsl, Shell/dsl [food] Denny's [lodging] Days Inn, Sleep Inn [other] [H], Menards, UWI
138a	I-94, E to Milwaukee, W to La Crosse (exits left from eb)
	I-90 W and I-94 W run together for 93 miles.
138b	WI 30, Madison, S [lodging]
135c b	US 151, Madison, N [gas] BP/dsl [food] Erin's Cafe, Happy Wok, Milio's Sandwiches, Uno Grill [lodging] Cambria Suites, Courtyard, Fairfield Inn, GrandStay Suites, Holiday Inn, Staybridge Suites [other] Buick/GMC, Chrysler/Dodge/Jeep, Ford, Honda, Hyundai, Kia, Mazda, Nissan, Subaru, Toyota
135a	US 151, Madison, S [gas] BP, Citgo, Mobil, Shell [food] Applebee's, Arby's, Buffalo Wild Wings, Chili's, Chipotle Mexican, Cracker Barrel, Culver's, Denny's, Dickey's BBQ, DoLittle's Woodfire Grill, Fazoli's, Hardee's, Hometown Buffet, Hooters, IHOP, Imperial Garden, Jimmy John's, KFC, McDonald's, Milio's, Noodles&Co, Olive Garden, Outback Steaks, Panera Bread, Perkins, Pizza Hut, Potbelly, Qdoba, Red Lobster, Red Robin, Rocky's Pizza, Starbucks, Taco Bell, Takumi Japanese, TGIFriday's, Toppers Pizza, TX Roadhouse, Wendy's [lodging] Best Western, Comfort Inn, Crowne Plaza Hotel/rest., EconoLodge, Hampton Inn, Howard

MADISON

WI

Exit #	Services
135a	Continued Johnson, Microtel, Motel 6, Red Roof Inn, Residence Inn, Ro[...]way Inn, Super 8 [other] $Tree, Aldi Foods, AT&T, Barnes&No[...] Best Buy, Burlington Coats, city park, Dick's, Firestone/au[...] Goodyear/auto, Gordman's, Hobby Lobby, Home Dep[...] Hy-Vee Foods, JC Penney, JoAnn Fabrics, Kohl's, Marsha[...] Menards, Michaels, Office Depot, Old Navy, Petsmart, Save[...] st patrol, Target, Verizon
132	US 51, Madison, De Forest, N [gas] Shell/Pinecone Rest/dsl/2[...] [other] Camping World RV Ctr, S [gas] TA/BP/Subway/Popeye's/d[...] scales/24hr/@ [other] Freightliner/GMC/Volvo/White, Goodye[...] Peterbilt, WI RV World
131	WI 19, Waunakee, N [gas] Kwik Trip/dsl, Mobil/dsl, Speedwa[...] dsl [food] A&W, McDonald's, Rodeside Grill [lodging] Days Inn, Supe[...] [other] fireworks, Kenworth, Mousehouse Cheesehaus, truckwas[...]
126	rd V, De Forest, to Dane, N [gas] BP/A&W/Rococo's/dsl, Philli[...] 66/Arby's/dsl [food] Burger King, Culver's, McDonald's, Subwa[...] Taco Bell [lodging] Holiday Inn Express [other] Cheese Chalet, KO[...] S [gas] Exxon, Shell [lodging] Comfort Inn [other] dsl repair
119	WI 60, Arlington, to Lodi, S [gas] Mobil/A&W/Cousins Sub[...] dsl [food] A&W, Rococo's Pizza [lodging] Quality Inn [other] dsl/tire repa[...]
115	rd CS, Poynette, to Lake Wisconsin, N [gas] BP/dsl [food] McDo[...]ald's, Subway [other] auto repair, dsl truck/trailer repair, Smok[...] Hollow Camping, S [gas] [Loves]/Hardee's/dsl/scales/24hr
113mm	**[RS] both lanes, full [handicapped] facilities, litter barrels, petwalk, [phone], [...] vending**
111mm	Wisconsin River
108b a	I-39 N, WI 78, to US 51 N, to Wis Dells, Portage, N [other] [H] S [gas] BP, Mobil, Petro/Iron Skillet/DQ/Subway/dsl/24hr/[...] [lodging] Comfort Suites, Days Inn [other] Blue Beacon
106mm	Baraboo River
106	WI 33, Portage, N [other] [H], S [gas] BP [other] Circus World Museu[...] Devil's Lake SP, SkyHigh Camping, to Cascade Mtn Ski Are[...] Wayside Park
92	US 12, to Baraboo, N [gas] BP/dsl, Citgo/Subway/dsl, Exxo[...] Mobil/Dunkin'/dsl/24hr [food] Buffalo Phil's Grille, Burger King[...] Cheese Factory Rest, Cracker Barrel, Culver's, Denny's, Domino'[...] Famous Dave's BBQ, Field's Steaks, Green Owl Pizza, Marley'[...] Rest., McDonald's, Milio's, Monk's Grill, Noodles&Co, Pizz[...] Ranch, Ponderosa, R Place Italian, Sarento's Italian, Starbucks[...] Taco Bell, Uno Grill, Wintergreen Grill [lodging] Alakai Hotel, Countr[...] Squire Motel, Dell Creek Motel, Glacier Canyon Lodge, Gran[...] Marquis Inn, Great Wolf Lodge, Holiday Inn Express, Kalaha[...] Resort, Ramada, Wilderness Hotel, Wintergreen Hotel [other] Mk[...] Square Cheese, Tanger Outlets Famous Brands, URGENT CARE[...] Verizon, S [lodging] Motel 6 [other] [H], Jellystone Camping, Mirror Lake SP, Red Oak Camping, Scenic Traveler RV Ctr
89	WI 23, Lake Delton, N [gas] Phillips 66, Shell/dsl [food] Brathouse Grill, Denny's Diner, Howie's Rest., KFC, Moosejaw Pizza [lodging] Hilton Garden, Kings Inn, Malibu Inn, Olympia Motel, Travelodge [other] Crystal Grand Music Theatre, Jellystone Camping, USPO, S [food] McDonald's [other] $Tree, Country Roads RV Park, Home Depot, Jo-Ann, Kohl's, Springbrook Camping, Walmart/Subway
87	WI 13, Wisconsin Dells, N [gas] Citgo/dsl, Mobil/Arby's/dsl, Shell/Dunkin' [food] Applebee's, Bunyan's Rest., Burger King, Coldstone, Culver's, Denny's, IHOP, Jimmy John's, McDonald's, Mexicali Rose Rest., Perkins, Starbucks, Taco Bell, Wei's Chinese [lodging] Ambers Resort, AmericInn, Baymont Inn, Best Western, Econolodge, Polynesian Hotel, Quality Inn, Super 8 [other] golf, info, KOA, Sherwood Forest Camping, Walgreens, waterpark

MADISON

WISCONSIN DELLS

INTERSTATE 90 Cont'd

Exit #	Services
85	US 12, WI 16, Wisconsin Dells, N Fairway Motel KOA, Sherwood Forest Camping, Standing Rock Camping, to Rocky Arbor SP, S BP Piccadilly's Arrowhead Camping, Days End Motel, Edge-O-the-Dell RV Camping, Summer Breeze Resort
79	rd HH, Lyndon Sta, S BP/Subway/dsl/24hr
76mm	**wb, full facilities, litter barrels, petwalk, , , vending**
74mm	**eb, full facilities, litter barrels, petwalk, , , vending**
69	WI 82, Mauston, N Mauston TP/BP/Taco Bell/24hr, Pilot/Wendy's/dsl/scales/24hr, Shell/24hr China Buffet, Family Rest. Best Western Oasis, Quality Inn, Super 8 Carr Valley Cheese, to Buckhorn SP, S KwikTrip/Hearty Platter Rest/dsl/scales/24hr, Mobil Culver's, Hardee's, Log Cabin Deli, McDonald's, Pizza Hut, Roman Castle Rest., Subway Alaskan Inn H, $General, Buick/Chevrolet, Family$, Festival Foods, O'Reilly Parts, Verizon, vet, Walgreens
61	WI 80, New Lisbon, to Necedah, N Mobil/A&W/Subway/dsl/scales/24hr, Shell/McDonald's/dsl Edge O' the Woods Motel, Travelers Inn Buckhorn SP, Chrysler/Dodge/Jeep, fireworks, Ford, S KwikTrip/24hr city park, Elroy-Sparta ST Tr, USPO
55	rd C, Camp Douglas, N to Camp Williams, Volk Field, wayside, S BP/dsl, Mobil/Home Front Cafe/dsl K&K Motel to Mill Bluff SP
48	rd PP, Oakdale, N Road Ranger/Pilot/Subway/dsl/scales/24hr antiques, KOA, truck/car wash, S Loves/Hardee's/dsl/scales/24hr Mill Bluff SP, repair
45	I-94 W, to St Paul
I-90 E and I-94 E run together for 93 miles.	
43	US 12, WI 16, Tomah, N BP/dsl, KwikTrip/dsl/24hr Burnstadt's Café, DQ Daybreak Inn, Rest Well Motel H, Burnstadt's Mkt, vet
41	WI 131, Tomah, to Wilton, N KwikTrip/dsl/24hr, Mobil/dsl Burnstadts Cafe Daybreak Inn vet
28	WI 16, Sparta, Ft McCoy, N BP/diner/dsl/scales Best Western H
25	WI 27, Sparta, to Melvina, N Cenex/Arby's/dsl, KwikTrip/dsl, Mobil/Taco Bell, Shell/dsl Burger King, Culver's, DQ, KFC, McDonald's, Pizza Hut, Sparta Rest., Subway Country Inn, Super 8 H, $General, $Tree, Buick/Chevrolet, Family$, Ford, Hansens IGA, O'Reilly Parts, Walgreens, Walmart/Subway
22mm	**wb, full facilities, litter barrels, petwalk, , , vending**
20mm	**eb, full facilities, litter barrels, petwalk, , , vending**
15	WI 162, Bangor, to Coon Valley, N gas
12	rd C, W Salem, N Cenex/cafe/dsl/24hr Coulee Region RV Ctr, NAPA, Neshonoc Camping, S BP/Subway/dsl AmericInn Peterbilt
10mm	**weigh sta eb**
5	WI 16, La Crosse, N Arby's, BA Burrito, Buffalo Wild Wings, Ciatti's Italian, Coldstone, Manny's Mexican, Outback Steaks Baymont Inn, Hampton Inn, Microtel $Tree, Aldi Foods, Freightliner, Home Depot, Walmart/Subway, Woodman's Foods/gas/lube, S Kwik Trip/dsl/24hr Bamboo House, Burracho's Mexican Grill, Carlos O'Kelly's, Chuckee Cheese, Culver's, Fazoli's, HuHot Grill, Jimmy John's, McDonald's, Olive Garden, Perkins, Starbucks, TGIFriday's, TX Roadhouse Holiday Inn Express H, Barnes&Noble, Best Buy, Chevrolet, Dick's, F&F, Ford/Lincoln, Hobby Lobby, JC Penney, Kohl's, Michael's, Target, Walgreens
4	US 53 N, WI 16, to WI 157, La Crosse, N Harley-Davidson, S Kwik Trip, TO Applebee's, Burger King, Caribou Coffee, China Inn, Cousins Subs, Famous Dave's BBQ, Grizzly's Rest., Ground Round, Panera Bread, Papa Murphy's, Red Lobster, Rococo's Pizza, Shogun Hibachi, Subway, Taco Bell, Wendy's Comfort Inn H, Festival Food/24hr, GNC, Goodyear/auto, La Crosse River St Trail, Office Depot, Old Navy, PetCo, Petsmart, Sam's Club, Tires+, TJ Maxx, Verizon
3	US 53 S, WI 35, to La Crosse, S Clark/dsl, Kwik Trip Hardee's, KFC, La Crosse Rest., McDonald's, North Country Steaks, Perkins, Pizza Hut, Subway Best Value Inn, Best Western, Econolodge, Motel 6, Quality Inn, Settle Inn, Super 8 to Great River St Trail, U-Haul, Viterbo Coll, Walgreens
2.5mm	Black River
2	rd B, French Island, N , S BP/dsl Days Inn/rest. Quillin's Mkt
1mm	**Welcome Ctr eb, full facilities, info, litter barrels, petwalk, , , vending**
0mm	Wisconsin/Minnesota state line, Mississippi River

TOMAH

LA CROSSE

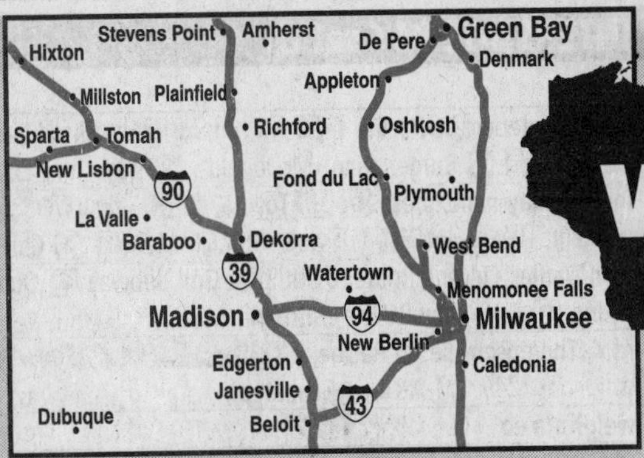

INTERSTATE 94

Exit #	Services
349mm	Wisconsin/Illinois state line, **weigh sta nb**
348.5mm	**weigh sta wb**
347	WI 165, rd Q, Lakeview Pkwy, E **Welcome Ctr nb, full facilities, , litter barrels, petwalk,** BP/dsl Chancery Rest., Culver's, McDonald's Radisson Old Navy, Premium Outlets/famous brands
345	rd C, E Holiday Inn Express (1mi)
345mm	Des Plaines River
344	WI 50, Lake Geneva, to Kenosha, 1 mi E Buffalo Wild Wings, Cheddar's, Cousins Subs, Dickey's BBQ, Famous Dave's, Mobil/dsl, Noodles&Co, Olive Garden, Panda Express, Perkins, Pizza Hut, Shell/Dunkin'/dsl, Sparti's Gyros, Starbucks, Subway, Tuscany Bistro, TX Roadhouse, White Castle, Woodman's/gas Candlewood Suites, Holiday Inn Express, La Quinta, Super 8 H, AT&T, Best Buy, Chevrolet, Dick's, GNC, JC Penney, Petsmart, Target, Verizon, Walgreens, W BP/dsl, Speedway/dsl Arby's, Birchwood Grill, Cracker Barrel, KFC, McDonald's, Phoenix Rest., Wendy's Best Western, Comfort Inn, Country Inn&Suites, Hampton Inn, Value Inn Brat-Stop Cheese Store, CarMax, Honda, Nissan, Subaru, Toyota
342	WI 158, to Kenosha, E Harley-Davidson, W antiques
340	WI 142, rd S, to Kenosha, E Kenosha TP/BP/Subway/dsl/E85/LP/scales/24hr H, W Mars Cheese Castle Rest. Oasis Inn Fun Time RV Ctr, to Bong RA
339	rd E
337	rd KR, to Mt Pleasant, W Apple Holler Rest./orchard
335	WI 11, to Mt Pleasant, Burlington, to Racine

KENOSHA

WI

[gas] = gas [food] = food [lodging] = lodging [other] = other [RS] = rest stop Copyright 2020 - The Next EX

INTERSTATE 94 Cont'd

Exit #	Services
333	WI 20, Waterford, to Racine, E [gas] KwikTrip/dsl/24hr, Shell/Cousins Subs/dsl [food] Burger King, McDonald's [lodging] Days Inn, Excel Inn, Holiday Inn Express [other] [H], Toyota, W [gas] Citgo/Wendy's/dsl/24hr, Petro/Mobil/Iron Skillet/dsl/scales/24hr/@ [food] Chicken'n Waffles, Culver's, Route 20 Outhouse Grill, Subway [lodging] Quality Inn [other] Burlington RV Ctr, visitor info
329	rd K, Thompsonville, to Racine, E [gas] Pilot/Arby's/Subway/dsl/scales/24hr [food] A&W [other] dsl repair
328mm	weigh sta eb
327	rd G, W fireworks
326	7 Mile Rd, E [gas] BP, Mobil/dsl [other] Jellystone Park, W [other] Seven Mile Fair
325	WI 241 N (from wb), to 27th St
322	WI 100, to Ryan Rd, E [gas] KwikTrip/dsl [food] McDonald's, Wendy's [other] dsl repair, W [gas] Loves/Denny's/dsl/LP/scales/RV dump/24hr, Mobil, Pilot/Subway/dsl/LP/scales/24hr, Shell/A&W/KFC/dsl [food] Arby's, Cousins Subs, Dish Bakery, Dunkin', Perkins, Starbucks, Yen Hwa Chinese [lodging] Staybridge Suites, Value Inn [other] AutoZone, Blue Beacon, Freightliner/repair, [H], Pick'n Save, vet, Walgreens
321	Drexel Ave
320	rd BB, Rawson Ave, E [gas] BP/7-11/dsl, Mobil [food] Applebee's, Burger King [lodging] La Quinta
319	rd ZZ, College Ave, E [gas] Shell/Subway, Speedway/dsl [food] Branded Steer Rest., McDonald's [lodging] Candlewood Suites, Comfort Suites, Country Inn&Suites, Crowne Plaza, Days Inn, EconoLodge, Fairfield Inn, Hampton Inn, Holiday Inn Express, MainStay Suites, Motel 6, Red Roof Inn [other] Burlington Coats, W [gas] Royal
318	WI 119, E [other] [airport]
317	I-43, I-894 (from wb)
316	I-43 S, I-894 W (I-94 exits left from eb), to Beloit, E [gas] Clark/dsl [food] Martino's Hotdogs
314b	Howard Ave, to Milwaukee, W to Alverno Coll
314a	Holt Ave, E [gas] SP Mart/dsl [food] Applebee's, Arby's, China King, Little Caesar's, Starbucks, Subway, Wendy's [other] $General, Family$, Home Depot, Pick'n Save Foods, Sentry Foods, Target, vet, W [other] [H], to Alverno Coll
312b a	Becher St, Mitchell St, Lapham Blvd, W [gas] BP, Citgo
311	WI 59, National Ave, 6th St, downtown
310a	13th St (from eb), E [other] [H]
310b	I-43 N, to Green Bay
310c	I-794 E, E [lodging] Hilton [other] Lake Michigan Port of Entry, to downtown
309b	26th St, 22nd St, Clybourn St, St Paul Ave, N [other] [H], to Marquette U
309a	35th St, N [other] URGENT CARE
308c b	US 41
308a	VA Ctr, S [other] Miller Park
307b	68th-70th St, Hawley Rd
307a	68th-70th St
306	WI 181, to 84th St, N [other] [H], S [other] Olympic Training Facility
305b	I-41 N, US 45 N, to Fond du Lac, N [other] [H]
305a	I-894 S, I-41 S, US 45 S, to Chicago, S [other] to [airport]
304b a	WI 100, N [gas] 7-11, Amstar/dsl, BP, Shell/dsl [food] Cousins Subs, Domino's, Ghengis Khan BBQ, Habanero's Mexican, HoneyBaked Cafe, Jimmy John's, Mo's Irish Grill, Peony Chinese, Qdoba, Rococo's, Starbucks, Subway, Taco Bell [lodging] Crowne Plaza, Forty Winks Inn [other] [H], zoo, S [gas] Amstar, BP/dsl, Speedway/dsl [food] Culver's, DQ, Fazoli's, McDonald's, Pallas Rest., Starbucks, Toppers Pizza, Wendy's [lodging] Days Inn [other] Aldi Foods, Midas, O'Reilly Parts, Sam's Club, U-Haul, Walgreens

MILWAUKEE

WI

Exit #	Services
301b a	Moorland Rdon US 18, N [gas] BP/dsl, Mobil [food] Bakers Squ Bravo Italiano, Buffalo Wild Wings, Chipotle, CiCi's, Coop Hawk, Culver's, Five Guys, Fleming's Rest., Food Court, F drucker's, Hooters, Jamba Juice, Jersey Mike's, Marty's Piz subs, McDonald's, Mitchell's Fish Mkt, Noodles&Co, O nal Pancake House, Qdoba, Red Robin, Starbucks, Stir Cr Subway, TGIFriday's [lodging] Courtyard, Sheraton, TowneP Suites [other] AT&T, Barnes&Noble, CVS Drug, F&F Tire, Firesto auto, Fresh Mkt Foods, Goodyear/auto, JC Penney, Jo-A Fabrics, Metro Mkt, Michael's, Office Depot, PetCo, Petsm SteinMart, TJ Maxx, Verizon, vet, Walgreens, World M S [food] Champp's Grill, Outback Steaks, Panera Bread, St bucks [lodging] Best Western Midway, Brookfield Suites, Cou Inn&Suites, Residence Inn [other] golf, Pick'n Save Foods, W greens, Walmart
297	WI 164 S, US 18, rd JJ, Blue Mound Rd, Barker Rd, 0-2 N [gas] BP, Clark [food] Applebee's, BoneFish Grill, Boston M Brookfield Rest., Bullwinkle's Rest., Carrabba's, Chili's, Chuc Cheese's, Cousins Subs, Emperors Kitchen, George Webb Re Hom Woodfired Grill, Jimmy John's, Jose's Mexican, K Kopp's Custard, Laredo's Mexican, Mama Mia's, McDonal Melting Pot, Olive Garden, Perkins, Potbelly, Starbucks, S way [lodging] DoubleTree, Extended Stay America, Hampton I La Quinta, Motel 6, Quality Inn [other] [H], $Tree, Acura, Advar Parts, Aldi Foods, Best Buy, GNC, Hobby Lobby, Lexus/Mazd VW, Meineke, Metro Mkt, S [gas] Clark, PDQ [food] Arby's, Burg King, Chancery Rest., Cousin's Subs, Culver's, Famous Dav BBQ, La Fuente Mexican, McDonald's, Meiji Chinese, New C na, Oscar's Burgers, Papa Murphy's, Sonic, Starbucks, Subw Taco Bell, Topper's Pizza, TX Roadhouse, Wendy's [lodging] Baymo Inn, Extended Stay America, Super 8 [other] AT&T, Buick/GM Cadillac, CarMax, Chevrolet, Farm&Fleet, Firestone/auto, Fo Home Depot, Honda, Hyundai, Infiniti/Maserati/Mercede Porsche, Jaguar/Land Rover/Volvo, Kia, Kohl's, Menards, M das, Nissan, Sam's Club, st patrol, Subaru, Target, Tires+, W greens, Woodman's/gas
295	rd F, to WI 74, Waukesha, N [gas] KwikTrip/dsl [food] Jimmy John [lodging] Marriott, S [other] [H], to Carroll U
294	WI 164, rd J S, to Waukesha, N [gas] Mobil/Subway/dsl [food] M chine Shed Rest., Thunder Bay Grille [lodging] Holiday Inn, Wil wood Lodge, S [other] Expo Ctr, Peterbilt
293c	WI 16 W, Pewaukee (from wb), N [other] GE Plant
293b a	rd T, Wausheka, Pewaukee, S [gas] KwikTrip/dsl, Mobil [food] A by's, Asian Fusion, Canyon City Wood Grill, Cousins Sub Culver's, Denny's, Dunkin', Feng's Kitchen, Jimmy John's, M Donald's, Mr. Wok, Papa Murphy's, Qdoba, Rococo's Pizz Spring City Rest., Subway, Taco Amigo, Topper's Pizza, Weis gerber's Gasthaus Rest., Wendy's [lodging] Best Western [other] $Tre AutoZone, CVS Drug, Firestone/auto, GNC, Goodharvest Mk Jo-Ann Fabrics, Office Depot, Pick'n Save Foods, Verizon, Wa greens
291	rd G, rd TT, N [lodging] Country Springs Inn
290	rd SS, Pewaukee
287	WI 83, Hartland, to Wales, N [food] Applebee's, Five Guys, Hard ee's, McDonald's, Noodles&Co, Panera Bread, Perkins, Qdoba Starbucks, Water St Brewery/rest. [lodging] Country Pride Inn, Holi day Inn Express [other] Albrecht's Mkt, Best Buy, GNC, Kohl's, Mar shalls, Verizon, Walgreens, S [gas] BP, PDQ/dsl/24hr [food] Burge King, Coldstone, DQ, Jimmy John's, Marty's Pizza, Pacific Asia Bistro, Pizza Hut, Rocky Rococo Pizza, StoneCreek Coffee, Sub way [lodging] La Quinta [other] $Tree, Ace Hardware, Home Depot, Pet Co, Target, Tires+, vet, Walmart/Subway

WAUKESHA

INTERSTATE 94 Cont'd

Exit #	Services
285	rd C, Delafield, N BP/dsl, Mobil/deli Delafield Hotel to St John's Military Academy, S to Kettle Moraine SF
283	rd P, to Sawyer Rd
282	WI 67, Dousman, to Oconomowoc, 0-2 mi N KwikTrip/dsl, Mobil Chili's, Cousins Subs, Culver's, Eat Smart Cafe, Feng's Kitchen, Jimmy John's, Pizza Hut, Qdoba, Quiznos, Rococo's Pizza, Rosati's Pizza, Starbucks, Stone Creek Coffee, Subway Hilton Garden, Olympia Resort Ace Hardware, Aldi Foods, AT&T, Brennan's Mkt, Ford, GNC, Pick'n Save, vet, Walgreens, S Staybridge Suites H, Harley-Davidson, Old World WI HS (13mi), to Kettle Morraine SF (8mi)
277	Willow Glen Rd (from eb, no return)
275	rd F, Ixonia, to Sullivan, N Mobil/dsl Concord Gen Store, S camping
267	WI 26, Johnson Creek, to Watertown, N BP/McDonald's/dsl, Shell/dsl/rest./scales/24hr Arby's, Hi-Way Harry's Cafe Comfort Suites, Days Inn Goodyear/auto, Johnson Creek Outlet Ctr/famous brands, Old Navy, S KwikTrip/dsl Culver's, Qdoba, Starbucks, Subway, Taco Bell H, Kohl's, Menards, to Aztalan SP
266mm	Rock River
264mm	**RS wb, full facilities, litter barrels, petwalk, , , vending**
263mm	Crawfish River
261mm	**RS eb, full facilities, litter barrels, petwalk, , , vending**
259	WI 89, Lake Mills, to Waterloo, N Mobil/rest/dsl/24hr Best Value Inn truck repair, S BP/dsl/E85, KwikTrip/dsl Jimmy John's, McDonald's, Pizza Pit, Subway Pyramid Motel/RV park Ace Hardware, Buick/Chevrolet, Country Campers, to Aztalan SP, URGENT CARE, vet, Walgreens
250	WI 73, Deerfield, to Marshall
244	rd n, Sun Prairie, Cottage Grove, N BP/dsl Subway, S BP/dsl, KwikTrip Arby's
240	I-90 E.

I-94 and I-90 run together 93 miles. See I-90, exits 48-138

Exit #	Services
147	I-90 W, to La Crosse, I-94 and I-90 run together 93 miles
143	US 12, WI 21, Tomah, N Shell/dsl A&W/LJ Silver, Perkins AmericInn, Best Western, Microtel, Super 8 Humbird Cheese/gifts, U-Haul, S BP, KwikTrip/Denny's/dsl/scales/24hr Arby's, China Buffet, Culver's, Dunkin', Ground Round, Ground Round, KFC, McDonald's, Papa Murphy's, Pizza Hut, Starbucks, Subway, Taco Bell Cranberry Lodge, EconoLodge, Hampton Inn, Quality Inn H, $Tree, Ace Hardware, Advance Parts, Aldi Foods, Burger King, Chrysler/Dodge/Jeep, Ford, GMC, NAPA, O'Reilly Parts, to Ft McCoy (9mi), Verizon, Walmart/Subway
135	rd EW, Warrens, N Cenex/dsl 3 Bears Resort Jellystone Camping, S Bog Rest.
128	rd O, Millston, N Black River SF, camping, S Cenex/dsl USPO
123mm	**RS/scenic view both lanes, full facilities, litter barrels, petwalk, , , vending**
116	WI 54, N Cenex/Subway/Taco Johns/dsl/LP Perkins AmericInn, Best Western Arrowhead/rest., Comfort Inn Black River RA, Parkland Camp, S FLYING J/Denny's/dsl/24hr/ @, KwikTrip/dsl Arby's, Burger King, Culver's, McDonald's, Oriental Kitchen, Pizza Hut Days Inn $General, Buick/Chevrolet/GMC, Walmart/Subway
115mm	Black River
115	US 12, WI 27, Black River Falls, to Merrillan, S Holiday/dsl Hardee's, KFC, Subway, Sunrise Rest. H, Ace Hardware, Gordy's Mkt, Harley-Davidson

TOMAH

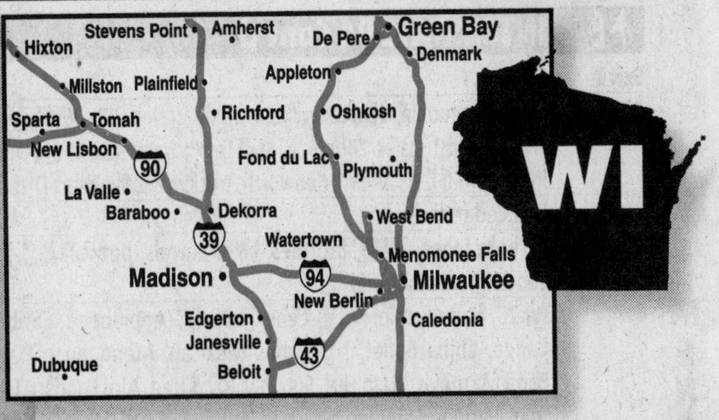

Exit #	Services
105	to WI 95, Hixton, to Alma Center, N Motel 95/camping KOA (3mi), S Cenex/dsl, Clark/dsl/24hr Timber Valley Rest. city park, USPO
98	WI 121, Northfield, Pigeon Falls, to Alma Center, S Cenex/dsl auto/truck repair
88	US 10, Osseo, to Fairchild, N BP/DQ, Exxon/Webb Rest./dsl/scales/24hr, Mobil/dsl Hardee's, Moe's Diner 10-7 Inn, Super 8 Chevrolet, Ford, Stoney Cr RV Park, S SA/dsl McDonald's, Subway, Taco John's Osseo Inn H, Family$
81	rd HH, rd KK, Foster, S Cenex/dsl/LP Foster Cheesehaus
70	US 53, Eau Claire, N **off Golf Rd** Holiday/dsl Applebee's, Asia Palace, Buffalo Wild Wings, Caribou Coffee, Chipotle, Coldstone, Culver's, Fazoli's, Fired Up Pizza, Firehouse Subs, Fuji Steaks, Grizzly's Grill, HuHot Chinese, Jade Garden, Jimmy John's, Johnny's Italian Steaks, Mancino's, Manny's Grill, McDonald's, Noodles&Co, Olive Garden, Panera Bread, Papa Murphy's, TGIFriday's, TX Roadhouse Baymont Inn, Country Inn&Suites, Grandstay, Holiday Inn $Tree, Aldi Foods, AT&T, Bam!, Best Buy, JC Penney, Jo-Ann Fabrics, Kohl's, Menards, Michael's, PetCo, Petsmart, Ross, Sam's Club, Scheel's Sports, Target, TJ Maxx, Tuesday Morning, Verizon, Walmart/Subway, S Gander Outdoors, st police
68	WI 93, to Eleva, N Holiday, KwikTrip/dsl Burger King, Cousins Subs, DQ, Famous Dave's BBQ, Great Harvest Bread Co, Hardee's, Red Robin EconoLodge BigLots, Chrysler/Dodge/Jeep, Festival Foods, Firestone/auto, Goodyear/auto, Gordy's Mkt, Kia, NAPA, Nissan, Subaru, transmissions, vet, S Holiday/dsl Metropolis Resort Audi/VW, Ford/Lincoln, Honda, Hyundai
65	WI 37, WI 85, Eau Claire, to Mondovi, N Holiday/dsl, KwikTrip/dsl Arby's, China Buffet, Godfather's Pizza, Green Mill Rest., Hardee's, Jimmy John's, Mancino's, McDonald's, Pizza Hut, Randy's Rest., Red Lobster, Starbucks, Subway, Taco Bell, Wendy's Best Value Inn, Best Western, Clarion, Hampton Inn, Motel 6, Plaza Hotel, Quality Inn, Scottish Inn, Super 8 H, Adams Automotive, Gordy's Mkt, Verizon, Walgreens, S tires
64mm	Chippewa River
59	to US 12, rd EE, to Eau Claire, N Holiday/Burger King/dsl/24hr, Holiday/Subway/dsl/24hr Dana's Grill, McDonald's, North Crossing Rest. AmericInn, Days Inn, Knights Inn H, Freightliner, Mack/Volvo Trucks, Peterbilt, S dsl repair
52	US 12, WI 29, WI 40, Elk Mound, to Chippewa Falls, S U-Fuel/e85
49mm	**weigh sta wb**

EAU CLAIRE

WI

[gas] = gas [food] = food [lodging] = lodging [other] = other [RS] = rest stop

INTERSTATE 94 Cont'd

Exit #	Services
45	rd B, Menomonie, **N** [gas] Cenex/Subway/dsl/scales/24hr, Loves/Hardee's/dsl/scales/24hr, **S** [gas] KwikTrip/dsl/scales/24hr [lodging] Quality Inn [other] [H], dsl repair, Kenworth, truckwash, Walmart Dist Ctr
44mm	Red Cedar River
43mm	[RS] **both lanes, full [handicapped] facilities, litter barrels, petwalk, [phone], [picnic], vending, weather info**
41	MENOMONIE: WI 25, Menomonie, **N** [gas] Cenex/E85 [food] Applebee's, Caribou Coffee, China Buffet, Los Cabos Mexican, Menominee Rest., Papa Murphy's, Pizza Hut, Subway [other] $Tree, Aldi Foods, AT&T, Twin Springs Camping, Walmart/Subway, **S** [gas] F&F/dsl, Holiday, SA/dsl [food] Arby's, Denny's, Dickey's BBQ, Jimmy John's, Little Caesar's, McDonald's, Perkins, Taco Bell, Taco John's, Wendy's [lodging] AmericInn, Best Western+, EconoLodge, Motel 6, Super 8 [other] [H], Advance Parts, Buick/GMC, Chevrolet, Chrysler/Dodge/Jeep, Ford, Mkt Place Foods, O'Reilly Parts, to Red Cedar St Tr, Verizon, Walgreens
32	rd Q, to Knapp
28	WI 128, Wilson, Elmwood, to Glenwood City, **N** [gas] KwikTrip/Denny's/dsl/24hr, **S** [other] camping, dsl repair, Eau Galle RA
24	rd B, to Baldwin, **N** [gas] BP [lodging] Woodville Motel, **S** [other] camping, Eau Galle RA
19	US 63, Baldwin, to Ellsworth, **N** [gas] Freedom/dsl, KwikTrip/Subway/dsl [food] A&W, Culver's, DQ, Hardee's, McDonald's [lodging] AmericInn [other] [H], **S** [lodging] Super 8 [other] fireworks
16	rd T, Hammond
10	WI 65, Roberts, to New Richmond, **N** [gas] BP/dsl (2 FLYING J/McDonald's/dsl/scales/24hr [food] Barnboard R (2mi), **S** [food] Freightliner
8mm	weigh sta eb
4	US 12, rd U, Somerset, **N** [gas] BP/dsl, TA/Country Pride/ scales/24hr/@ [lodging] Regency Inn [other] to Willow River SP, vet
3	WI 35 S, to River Falls, **S** [other] U of WI River Falls
2	HUDSON: rd F, Carmichael Rd, Hudson, **N** [gas] BP/repair, Freedo dsl, Holiday [food] Applebee's, Caribou Coffee, Culver's, Do ino's, Fiesta Loca, Jimmy John's, KFC, Papa Murphy's, T John's [lodging] Royal Inn [other] $Tree, Family Fresh Foods, GNC, pair, Target, Verizon, Walgreens, **S** [gas] F&F/dsl, Holiday/ KwikTrip/dsl, Shell [food] Arby's, Buffalo Wild Wings, Bur King, Caribou Coffee, Chipotle Mexican, Coldstone, Denn Green Mill Rest., Jersey Mike's, Kingdom Buffet, Kirin Ichib Leeann Chin, Little Caesar's, McDonald's, Noodles&Co, Pan Express, Perkins, Pita Pit, Pizza Hut, Sapporo Japanese, Sma burger, Starbucks, Subway, Taco Bell, Wendy's [lodging] Comf Suites, Fairfield Inn, Hampton Inn, Holiday Inn Express, Huds House Hotel, Quality Inn, Super 8 [other] [H], Aldi Foods, AT AutoZone, Chevrolet/GMC, Chrysler/Dodge/Jeep, County M Foods, Ford, Home Depot, Menards, NAPA, O'Reilly Parts, Ti Pros, Tires+, to Kinnickinnic SP, USPO, Verizon, Walmart
1	WI 35 N, Hudson, 1 mi **N** [gas] Freedom/dsl, Holiday [food] C bones Pizzeria, DQ
0mm	Wisconsin/Minnesota state line, St Croix River

WI

NOTES

WYOMING

INTERSTATE 25

Exit #	Services
300	I-90, E to Gillette, W to Billings. **I-25 begins/ends on I-90, exit 56.**
299	US 16, Buffalo, **E** Cenex/dsl, Exxon/dsl, Maverik/dsl Winchester Steaks Buffalo Inn, Comfort Inn, Hampton Inn, Holiday Inn Express Bighorn Tire, Deer Park Camping, KOA, vet, **W** Cenex/dsl/24hr Bozeman Tr Steaks, Dash Inn Rest., Hardee's, McDonald's, Pizza Hut, Sub Shop, Subway, Taco John's Days Inn, Quality Inn, Rodeway WYO Motel, Super 8 H, Ace Hardware, Family$, Indian RV Camp, O'Reilly Parts, to Yellowstone, Domino's
298	US 87, Buffalo, **W** Nat Hist Dist Info
291	Trabing Rd
280	Middle Fork Rd
274mm	**parking area both lanes, litter barrels**
265	Reno Rd
254	Kaycee, **E** Exxon/dsl Country Inn Diner, Invasion Rest. Cassidy Inn Motel, Siesta Motel Kaycee Gen. Store, museum, NAPA Repair, Powder River RV Park, USPO, **W both lanes, full facilities, litter barrels, petwalk,** Sinclair/pizza/subs/dsl/LP/motel KC RV Park
249	TTT Rd
246	Powder River Rd
235	Tisdale Mtn Rd
227	WY 387 N, Midwest, Edgerton, Oil Field Museum
223	no service
219mm	**parking area both lanes**
216	Ranch Rd
210	Horse Ranch Creek Rd, Midwest, Edgerton
197	Ormsby Rd
191	Wardwell Rd, to Bar Nunn, **W** Loaf'N Jug/dsl KOA
189	US 20, US 26 W, to Shoshone, **W** , Port of Entry
188b	WY 220, Poplar St, **E** McDonald's, The Fort Eatery Hampton Inn, Hilton Garden, La Quinta, Motel 6, Quality Inn, Ramkota Hotel, **W** Exxon Burger King, Casper's Rest., DQ Harley-Davidson, to Ft Casper HS
188a	Center St, Casper, **E** Conoco/dsl, Shell/dsl Taco John's National 9 Inn, Ramada, **W** La Cocina, Starbucks, Subway Days Inn, Parkway Plaza Motel/cafe USPO
187	McKinley St, Casper, **E** Ranch House Motel
186	US 20, US 26, US 87, Yellowstone St, **E** city park, dsl repair, transmissions/repair, **W** Exxon H, auto repair, Chevrolet/Subaru, Kia, O'Reilly Parts
185	WY 258, Wyoming Blvd, E Casper, **E** Kum&Go/dsl, Loaf'n Jug/dsl Applebee's, IHOP, Outback Steaks, Southern BBQ HQ, TX Roadhouse Baymont Inn, C'mon Inn, Comfort Inn, Super 8 Murdoch's Ranch Store, Smith RV Ctr, vet, **W** FLYING J/Conoco/Subway/dsl/LP/scales/24hr, Exxon/dsl Arby's, Buffalo Wild Wings, Burger King, Denny's, DQ, Five Guys, Hamburger Stand, Hardee's, KFC/LJ Silver, Koto Japanese, McDonald's, Mongolian Grill, Old Chicago Grill, Olive Garden, On The Border, Perkins, Pizza Hut, Pizza Ranch, Qdoba,

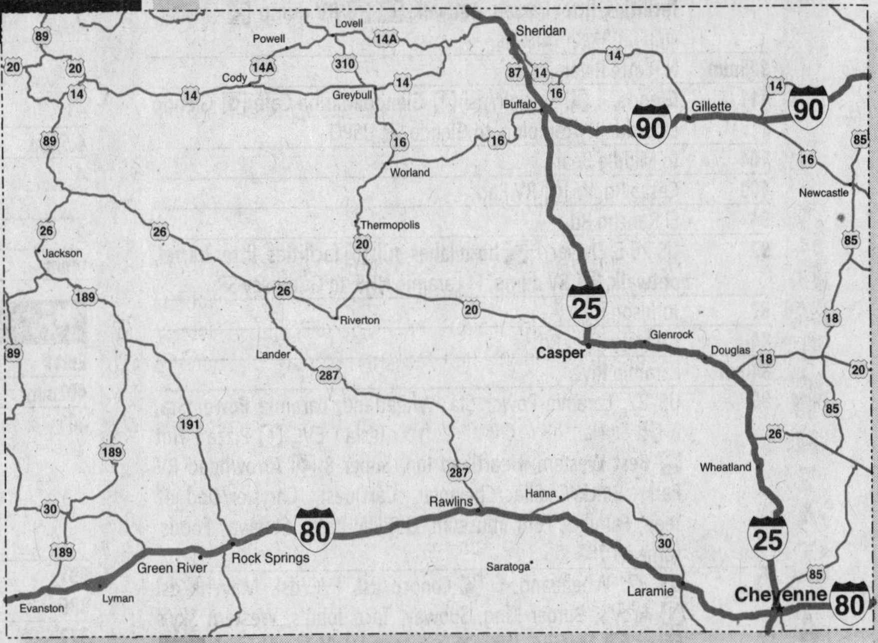

Exit #	Services
185	Continued Red Lobster, Sanford's Cafe, Starbucks, Taco Bell, Taco John's, Village Inn, Wendy's Candlewood Suites, Courtyard, Holiday Inn Express, Rodeway Inn AutoZone, Best Buy, Dick's, Home Depot, JC Penney, Macy's, Natural Grocers, Nissan, PetCo, Plains Tire, Ridley's Foods/dsl, Ross, Sam's Club/gas, Staples, Target, to Oregon Tr, Verizon, Walgreens, Walmart
182	WY 253, Brooks Rd, Hat Six Rd, **E** Sinclair/Lou's Rest/dsl Sonic Sleep Inn Rivers Edge Camping, to Wilkins SP, **W** FireRock Rest., Keg&Cork Rest., Subway, Wyo Aleworks Best Western+, Holiday Inn, Mainstay Suites H, Buick/Cadillac/GMC, Chrysler/Dodge/Jeep, Kohl's, Marshall's, Menards, Petsmart, Toyota, Verizon, VW
171mm	**parking area both lanes**
165	Glenrock, **E** dinosaur museum, same as 160
160	US 87, US 20, US 26, E Glenrock, **E** Deer Creek Village Camping, to Johnston Power Plant
156	Bixby Rd
154	Barber Rd
153mm	**parking area both lanes**
151	Natural Bridge
150	Inez Rd
146	La Prele Rd
140	WY 59, Douglas, **E** Conoco/Subway/dsl, Maverik/dsl, Shell/dsl Arby's, La Costa Mexican, McDonald's, Taco John's Douglas Inn, Hampton Inn, Holiday Inn Express, Sleep Inn, Super 8 H, city park, KOA, Lone Tree Village RV Park, Pioneer Museum, WY St Fair
135	US 20, US 26, US 87, Douglas, **E** Juanita's/dsl, Loaf'n Jug/dsl, Sinclair/rest./dsl/24hr 4 Seasons Chinese, Pizza Hut, Plains Trading Post Rest., Starbucks, Village Inn 1st Interstate Inn, 4 Winds Motel, Budget Inn Express, Plains Motel H, Douglas Hardware, Family$, O'Reilly Parts, repair, Safeway Foods/dsl, Verizon
129mm	**parking area both lanes**

= gas = food = lodging = other = rest stop Copyright 2020 - The Next EX

WY

INTERSTATE 25 Cont'd

WHEATLAND

Exit #	Services
126	US 18, US 20 E, Orin, E **Orin Jct Rest Area both lanes, full facilities, litter barrels, petwalk, RV dump** Sinclair/Orin Jct Trkstp/dsl/café
125mm	N Platte River
111	Glendo, E Sinclair/dsl Glendo Marina Café Glendo Lakeside RV camping, to Glendo SP, USPO
104	to Middle Bear
100	Cassa Rd, W RV Park
94	El Rancho Rd
92	US 26 E, Dwyer, E **both lanes, full facilities, litter barrel, petwalk, RV dump**, Ft Laramie NHS, to Guernsey SP
87	Johnson Rd
84	Laramie River Rd
84mm	Laramie River
80	US 87, Laramie Power Sta, Wheatland, Laramie Power Sta, E Sinclair/A&W/Chester's/dsl, Tesla EVC Pizza Hut Best Western, Heartland Inn, Super 8 Arrowhead RV Park, Buick/Cadillac/Chevrolet, CarQuest, Chrysler/Dodge/Jeep, Family$, Ford, museum, O'Reilly Parts, Safeway Foods, same as 78
78	US 87, Wheatland, E Conoco/dsl, FVC/dsl, Maverik/dsl Arby's, Burger King, Subway, Taco John's, Western Sky's Diner Motel 6, West Winds Motel, WY Motel H, visitors ctr, Wheatland Country Store, W Exxon/dsl, Sinclair/dsl Mtn View RV Park
73	WY 34 W, to Laramie
70	Bordeaux Rd
68	Antelope Rd
66	Hunton Rd
65.5mm	**parking area both lanes**
65	Slater Rd
64mm	Richeau Creek
57	TY Basin Rd, Chugwater
54	Lp 25, Chugwater, E **both lanes, full facilities, litter barrels, petwalk, RV dump,** Chugwater Gas&Go/dsl Buffalo Lodge/Grill RV camping
47	Bear Creek Rd
39	Little Bear Community
36mm	Little Bear Creek
34	Nimmo Rd
33mm	Horse Creek
29	Whitaker Rd
25	ranch exit
21	Ridley Rd
17	US 85 N, to Torrington, W Little Bear Rest. (2mi)
16	WY 211, Horse Creek Rd
13	Vandehei Ave, E Loaf'n Jug/Subway, Maverik/dsl Mr Jim's Pizza, Silvermine Subs, W Sinclair/dsl
12	Central Ave, Cheyenne, E **on Yellowstone Rd** Exxon/dsl, Loaf'n Jug Arby's, Godfather's, McDonald's, Pizza Hut, Starbucks, Subway, Taco John's Rodeway Inn H, Albertsons, Big O Tire, Frontier Days Park
11b	Warren AFB, Gate 1, Randall Ave, E museum, to WY St Capitol
10b d	Warren AFB, Gate 2, Missile Dr, WY 210, HappyJack Rd, W to Curt Gowdy SP
9	US 30, W Lincolnway, Cheyenne, E Exxon/Downhome Diner/dsl Outback Steaks Best Value Inn, Candlewood Suites, Days Inn, Fairfield Inn, Hampton Inn, Holiday Inn Express, La Quinta, Luxury Inn, Motel 6, My Place, Super 8, Towne Place Suites Buick/Cadillac/GMC, Chevrolet, Ford/Lincoln, Home
9	Continued Depot, Honda, Hyundai, Nissan, Subaru, Toyota, W Li America/Sinclair/dsl/rest./motel/@
8d b	I-80, E to Omaha, W to Laramie
7	WY 212, College Dr, E Loves/Wendy's/dsl/scales/2 @, Sinclair/Subway/dsl/24hr Arby's A-B RV Park (2r W FLYING J/Denny's/dsl/LP/scales/24hr/@ McDonald's Quality Inn Blue Beacon, truck repair
6.5mm	Port of Entry nb
4	High Plains Rd, **WY Welcome Ctr, both lanes, full facilit litter barrels, petwalk, rest/info ctr**
2	WY 223, Terry Ranch Rd, **2 mi** E Terry Bison Ranch RV camp
0mm	Wyoming/Colorado state line

CHEYENNE

INTERSTATE 80

Exit #	Services
402mm	Wyoming/Nebraska State line
401	WY 215, Pine Bluffs, N Exxon/Subway/dsl, Sinclair/A& dsl/24hr/@ Cafe 307, Rock Ranch Grill Gator's M tel NAPA, Pine Bluff RV Park, USPO, S **Welcome Ctr both lanes, full facilities, info, playground, nature tr litter barrels, petwalk**
391	Egbert
386	WY 213, WY 214, Burns, N Antelope Trkstp/dsl/cafe
377	WY 217, Hillsdale, N TA/Burger King/Taco Bell/dsl/scal 24hr/@ Wyo RV Camping
372mm	Port of Entry wb, **truck insp**
370	US 30 W, Archer, N Sapp Bros/T-Joe's Rest./dsl/scale 24hr/@ Rodeway Inn fireworks, repair, RV park
367	Campstool Rd, N Pilot/Subway/dsl/scales/24hr B Western+ KOA (seasonal), Volvo Trucks, S to Wyomi Hereford Ranch
364	WY 212, to E Lincolnway, Cheyenne, N Walmart/c S AB Camping (4mi), Peterbilt, **1-2 mi** N **on Lincoln w** Exxon/dsl, Kum&Go/dsl, Loaf'n Jug/Subway Burg King, KFC, McDonald's, Shari's Rest., Subway, Taco Bell, We dy's H, $Tree, AutoZone, Big O Tire, BigLots, Family$, Ha ley-Davidson, Hobby Lobby, Murdoch's Ranch Store, O'Rei Parts, Sierra Trading Post, Walgreens
362	US 85, I-180, to Central Ave, Cheyenne, Greeley, 1 N Kum&Go/dsl Arby's, Carls' Jr, Hacienda Mexica Jimmy John's, Papa John's, Village Inn H, CarQuest, Fa ily$, museum, st capitol, Verizon, S Exxon/dsl, Loaf'n Ju dsl, Sinclair/dsl Burger King, Little Caesar's, Pizza Hut, So ic, Subway, Taco John's Comfort Inn, Holiday Inn, Round Motel, SpringHill Suites AutoZone, Family$, Hideaway Village, Safeway Foods/gas, transmissions
359c a	I-25, US 87, N to Casper, S to Denver
358	US 30, W Lincolnway, Cheyenne, N Exxon/dsl/24hr, Lit America/Sinclair/dsl/motel/@ Outback Steaks Best V ue Inn, Candlewood Suites, Days Inn, Fairfield Inn, Hampt Inn, Holiday Inn Express, La Quinta, Luxury Inn, Motel 6, M Place Inn, Super 8, TownPlace Suites H, Buick/GMC/C dillac, Chevrolet, Ford/Lincoln, Home Depot, Honda, Hyund Mazda, Nissan, Subaru, Toyota
357	Wy 222, Roundtop Rd
348	Otto Rd
345	Warren Rd, N **truck parking**
342	Harriman Rd
339	Remount Rd
335	Buford, S Phin Deli/dsl
333mm	**parking area both lanes**, point of interest

INTERSTATE 80 Cont'd

Exit #	Services
329	Vedeauwoo Rd, N camping, S Nat Forest RA, to Ames Monument
323	WY 210, Happy Jack Rd, N [rest stop] **both lanes, elev. 8640, full [handicap] facilities, Lincoln Monument, litter barrels, petwalk, [phone], [picnic], to** Curt Gowdy SP
322mm	**chain up area both lanes**
316	US 30 W, Grand Ave, Laramie, **0-2 mi** N [gas] Exxon/dsl, Loaf'N Jug, USA Gas [food] Almanza's Mexican, Applebee's, Arby's, Burger King, Chili's, Dickey's BBQ, Hong Kong Buffet, Jimmy John's, Luciano's Italian, McAlister's Deli, McDonald's, Mr Jim's Pizza, Papa Murphy's, Perkins, Sonic, Starbucks, Subway, Taco Bell, Taco John's, Village Inn, Wendy's [lodging] AmericInn, Hampton Inn, Hilton Garden, Holiday Inn, Quality Inn [other] [H], $Tree, AT&T, Buick/Chevrolet/GMC, Ford/Lincoln, GNC, Ridley's Mkt, to UW, Toyota, URGENT CARE, Verizon, Walgreens, Walmart/Subway
313	US 287, to 3rd St, Laramie, Port of Entry, N [gas] Exxon, GasaMat, Loaf'N Jug, Phillips 66/dsl, Shell/dsl [food] Chuck Wagon Rest., Corona Village Mexican, Qdoba [lodging] Laramie Valley Inn, Motel 8, Sunset Inn [other] [H], Honda, Laramie Plains Museum, NAPA, Nissan, S [lodging] Motel 6, Ramada Inn [other] USPO
312mm	Laramie River
311	WY 130, WY 230, Snowy Range Rd, Laramie, N [other] WY Terr Park, S [gas] Conoco/dsl, Exxon/Chester's/Papa John's/dsl, Phillips 66/dsl [food] McDonald's, Subway [lodging] Best Value Inn [other] repair/tires, to Snowy Range Ski Area
310	Curtis St, Laramie, N [gas] Loves/Carl's Jr/Subway/dsl/scales/24hr/@, Pilot/Wendy's/dsl/scales/24hr/@ [lodging] Best Western, Days Inn, EconoLodge, Super 8 [other] [H], KOA, repair, S [gas] Blue Beacon, Petro/Iron Skillet/dsl/scales/24hr/@ [lodging] Comfort Inn, Fairfield Inn [other] Chrysler/Dodge/Jeep
307mm	**parking area both lanes**
297	WY 12, Herrick Lane
290	Quealy Dome Rd, S [gas] A&C Truckstop/dsl
279	Cooper Cove Rd
272mm	Rock Creek
272	WY 13, to Arlington, N gas, RV camping
267	**S [rest stop] both lanes, full facilities**
262mm	**parking area both lanes**
260	CR 402
259mm	E Fork Medicine Bow River
257mm	Medicine Bow River
255	WY 72, Elk Mtn, to Hanna, N [gas] Conoco/dsl, S [lodging] Elk Mtn Hotel/rest
238	Peterson Rd
235	WY 130, S US 30/87, N [gas] Shell/dsl
229mm	N Platte River
228	**N [rest stop] both lanes, [picnic], litter barrels, petwalk**
221	E Sinclair, N [gas] Sinclair/rest/dsl/24hr [other] camping, to Seminoe SP
219	W Sinclair, N [other] camping, to Seminoe SP
215	Cedar St, Rawlins, N [gas] Conoco/dsl, Sinclair/dsl [food] Asian Bistro, Burger King, KFC/Taco Bell, McDonald's, Penny's Diner, Pizza Hut, Subway, Taco John's [lodging] 1st Choice Inn, Comfort Inn, Econolodge, Fairfield Inn, Hampton Inn, Holiday Inn Express, Magnuson Inn, OakTree Inn, Rawlings Western Lodge [other] Bomgaars, Buick/Chevrolet/GMC, CarQuest, Chrysler/Dodge/Jeep, City Mkt/dsl, Do-It Hardware, Frontier Prison NHS, museum, O'Reilly Parts, to Yellowstone/Teton NP, Walmart/dsl

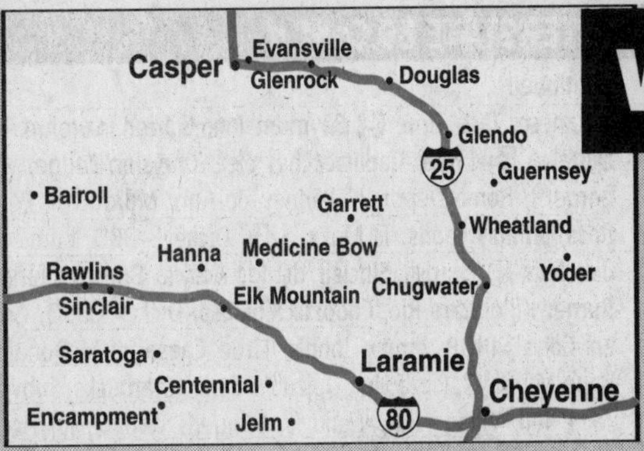

Exit #	Services
214	Higley Blvd, Rawlins, N [lodging] Microtel [other] KOA, S [gas] TA/Conoco/Subway/dsl/scales/24hr/@ [lodging] Best Value Inn
211	WY 789, to US 287 N, Spruce St, Rawlins, N [gas] Conoco/dsl, Exxon/dsl, Loaf'n Jug, Sinclair/dsl [food] Cappy's Rest., Four Season Rest. [lodging] Best Western, Express Inn, La Bella, Motel 7, Rodeway Inn, Super 8, Travelodge [other] [H], Family$, Red Desert Rose Camping, V1/LP, Verizon
209	Johnson Rd, N [gas] FLYING J/Denny's/dsl/LP/scales/24hr
206	Hadsell Rd (no return)
205.5mm	continental divide, elev 7000
204	Knobs Rd
201	Daley Rd
196	Riner Rd
190mm	**parking area wb, litter barrels**
189mm	**parking area eb, [picnic], litter barrels**
187	WY 789, Creston, Baggs Rd
184	Continental Divide Rd
173	Wamsutter, N [gas] Loves/Chester's/Subway/dsl/24hr/@, S [gas] Conoco/dsl/repair/café/24hr [food] Broadway Café, Southern Comfort Cafe [lodging] Wamsutter Motel
165	Red Desert
158	Tipton Rd, continental divide, elev 6930
156	GL Rd
154	BLM Rd
152	Bar X Rd
150	Table Rock Rd
146	Patrick Draw Rd
144mm	**[rest stop] both lanes, full [handicap] facilities, litter barrels, petwalk, [phone], [picnic]**
143mm	**parking area both lanes, litter barrels**
142	Bitter Creek Rd
139	Red Hill Rd
136	Black Butte Rd
133mm	**parking area both lanes**
130	Point of Rocks, N [gas] Conoco/dsl [other] RV Park
122	WY 371, to Superior
111	Airport Rd, Baxter Rd, S [airport]
107	Pilot Butte Ave, Rock Springs, S [gas] Kum&Go/dsl/e85, Sinclair/dsl [food] Pizza Hut [lodging] Sands Inn/cafe, Springs Motel
104	US 191 N, Elk St, Rock Springs, N [gas] FLYING J/Denny's/dsl/LP/24hr, Chevron/dsl, Conoco/dsl, Exxon, Kum&Go/dsl/e85, Mobil/dsl [food] McDonald's, Pasta Veloce, Renegade Rest., Santa Fe SW Grill, Subway, Taco Time [lodging] Best Western, EconoLodge/rest. [other] Buick/GMC, to Teton/Yellowstone Nat Parks via US 191, truck repair, S [gas] Exxon/dsl [lodging] Days Inn
103	College Dr, Rock Springs, S [gas] Loaf'n Jug/dsl [food] Domino's [other] [H], W WY Coll
102	WY 430, Dewar Dr, Rock Springs, N [gas] Exxon, Loaf'N Jug/dsl, Sinclair/dsl, Tesla EVC [food] Applebee's, KFC/LJ Silver, Sapporo

= gas = food = lodging = other = rest stop

INTERSTATE 80 Cont'd

102	Continued Japanese, Taco Time Baymont Inn, Clarion, Comfort Inn, Motel 6 $Tree, Cadillac/Chevrolet, Chrysler/Dodge, Herberger's, Home Depot, JC Penney, Jo-Ann, Murdoch's, Petco, Ross, Smith's Foods, TJ Maxx, **S** Dickey's BBQ, Kum&Go/dsl, Loaf'N Jug/dsl, Sinclair/dsl Arby's, Bonsai Chinese, Burger King, Cafe Rio, Chopstix Chinese, Dickey's BBQ, Golden Corral, IHOP, Jimmy John's, Little Caesar's, McDonald's, Papa Murphy's, Pizza Hut, Quizno's, Sonic, Starbucks, Subway, Taco Bell, Village Inn, Wendy's, Winger's, Wonderful House Chinese Hampton Inn, Holiday Inn, Holiday Inn Express, Homewood Suites, Motel 8, My Place, Quality Inn, Super 8, Western Inn H, Albertsons/Sav-on, AutoZone, Big O Tire, Family$, Ford/Lincoln, NAPA, Nissan, O'Reilly Parts, Staples, Verizon, Walgreens, Walmart/Subway
99	US 191 S, E Flaming Gorge Rd, **N** KOA (1mi), **S** Shell/A&W/dsl/24hr/@ Log Inn Rest., Ted's Rest. fireworks, truck repair
94mm	Kissing Rock
91	US 30, to WY 530, Green River, **2 mi S** Loaf'N Jug/dsl, Maverik/dsl Arctic Circle, McDonald's, Pizza Hut, Subway, Taco Time Coachman Inn, Mustang Inn, Super 8 Expedition NHS, Family$, same as 89, to Flaming Gorge NRA
89	US 30, Green River, **S** Exxon/dsl Penny's Diner, Pizza Hut, Staci Ann's Cafe Hampton Inn, OakTree Inn, Super 8, Western Inn Adam's RV Service, The Travel Camp, to Flaming Gorge NRA
87.5mm	Green River
85	Covered Wagon Rd, **S** Adams RV parts/service, The Travel Camp
83	WY 372, La Barge Rd, **N** to Fontenelle Dam
78	(from wb)
77mm	Blacks Fork River
72	Westvaco Rd
71mm	**parking area both lanes**
68	Little America, **N** Sinclair/Little America Hotel/rest./dsl/24hr/@ RV camping
66	US 30 W, to Teton, Yellowstone, Fossil Butte NM, Kemmerer
61	Cedar Mt Rd, to Granger
60mm	**parking area both lanes**
53	Church Butte Rd
49mm	**parking area wb**
48	Lp 80, Lyman, Ft Bridger, Hist Ft Bridger
45mm	Blacks Fork River
41	WY 413, Lyman, **N** **both lanes, full facilities, litter barrels, petwalk,** Gas'n Go/cafe/dsl, **S** Taco Time Gateway Inn (2mi), KOA (1mi)
39	WY 412, WY 414, to Carter, Mountain View
34	Lp 80, to Ft Bridger, **S** Wagon Wheel Motel Ft Bridger NHS, Ft Bridger RV Camp, to Flaming Gorge NRA
33.5mm	**parking area eb**
33	Union Rd
30	Bigelow Rd, **N** TA/Shell/Burger King/Taco Bell/Fork In the Road/dsl/scales/24hr/@, **S** fireworks
28	French Rd
28mm	French Rd, **parking area both lanes**
24	Leroy Rd
23	Bar Hat Rd
21	Coal Rd
18	US 189 N, to Kemmerer, to Nat Parks, Fossil Butte NM

GREEN RIVER

15	Guild Rd (from eb)
14mm	**parking area both lanes**
13	Divide Rd
10	Painter Rd, to Eagle Rock Ski Area, to Eagle Rock Ski Area
6	US 189, Bear River Dr, Evanston, **N** Pilot/Subway/scales/24hr, Shell/dsl Don Pedro's Mexican, Jody's D er Econolodge, Motel 6, Prairie Inn, Travelodge Phi RV Park, repair/tires, truck wash, Wyo Downs Racetrack (10 **S Welcome Ctr both lanes, full facilities, litter barrels, walk, , playground, RV dump (seasonal),** Bear River S
5	WY 89, Evanston, **N** Chevron/Taco Time/dsl, Maverik/dsl Arby's, Costa Vida, DragonWall Chinese, Jimmy John's, McDonald's, Papa Murphy's, Subway, Wendy's EconoLodge H, $Tree, AutoZone, Chevrolet, G Jiffy Lube, Murdoch's, NAPA, O'Reilly Parts, Verizon, Walm Subway, **S** WY St H
3	US 189, Harrison Dr, Evanston, **N** FLYING J/Subway/scales/24hr, Chevron/dsl, Shell, Sinclair, Tesla EVC J Lotty's Rest., TC's Rest., Wally's Burgers Best Western/re Comfort Inn, Days Inn, Hampton Inn, HillCrest Motel, Holi Inn Express, Howard Johnson, Quality Inn, Super 8 Ch ler/Dodge/Jeep, USPO, **S** KFC/Taco Bell H, firewor
.5mm	**Port of Entry eb, weigh sta wb**
0mm	Wyoming/Utah state line

EVANSTON

INTERSTATE 90

Exit #	Services
207mm	Wyoming/South Dakota state line
205	Beulah, **N** Sinclair/dsl/LP Buffalo Jump Rest. Beulah Campground, Sand Creek Trading Post/gas/cafe, USPO Ranch A NHP (5mi)
204.5mm	Sand Creek
199	WY 111, to Aladdin, **N** **Welcome ctr/ (both directions), facilities, , litter barrels, , petwalk,** to Devil's Tov NM, to Vore Buffalo Jump NHP (2mi)
191	Moskee Rd
189	US 14 W, Sundance, **N** Conoco/dsl/24hr Best Weste H, Mt View Camping, museum, to Devil's Tower NM, **S both lanes, full facilities, info, litter barrels, petwalk, , playground, RV dump, port of entry/weigh sta**
187	WY 585, Sundance, **N** Fresh Start/dsl, Sinclair/dsl A Rest., Higbee's Cafe, Subway Bear Lodge, Best Weste Budget Host Arrowhead, Rodeway Inn H, auto repa Decker's Foods, museum, NAPA, to Devil's Tower
185	to WY 116, to Sundance, **S** Conoco/dsl, same as 187
178	Coal Divide Rd
177mm	**parking area both lanes**
172	Inyan Kara Rd
171mm	**parking area both lanes, litter barrels**
165	Pine Ridge Rd, to Pine Haven, **N** Cedar Ridge RV Park (10mi), Keyhole SP
163mm	**parking area both lanes**
160	Wind Creek Rd
154	US 14, US 16, **S** Sinclair/dsl Donna's Diner, Subw Cozy Motel, Moorcourt Motel, Rangeland Motel/RV Pa Wyo Motel city park, Diehl's Foods/gas, museum, USPO
153	US 16 E, US 14, W Moorcroft, **N** **both lanes, full facilitie litter barrels, petwalk, , ,** **S** same as 154
152mm	Belle Fourche River
141	Rozet, **S** All Seasons RV Park (3.5mi)

SUNDANCE

WY

INTERSTATE 90 Cont'd

Exit #	Services
138mm	**parking area both lanes**
132	Wyodak Rd
129	Garner Lake Rd, S Arbuckle Lodge auto repair, Crazy Woman Camping (3mi), Harley-Davidson, High Plains Camping
128	US 14, US 16, Gillette, N Kum&Go, Maverik/dsl, MG Oil/dsl, Sinclair/Papa John's/dsl Mona's American/Mexican, Taco John's, Village Inn Howard Johnson, Mustang Motel, National 9 Inn, Quality Inn Crazy Woman Camping (2mi), East Side RV Ctr., Port of Entry, S Arbuckle Lodge High Plains Camping
126	WY 59, Gillette, N Cenex/dsl, Loaf'N Jug, Sinclair/Papa John's/dsl China King Buffet, Hardee's, Little Caesar's, McDonald's, Pizza Carrello, Pokey's BBQ, Prime Rib Rest., Starbucks, Subway Best Value Inn city park, Family$, Smith's Foods, Tire Factory, Verizon, S FLYING J/dsl/24hr, Exxon, Loaf'N Jug/dsl A&W/LJ Silver, Adriano's Italian, Applebee's, Arby's, Armando's Taco, Buffalo Wild Wings, Burger King, DQ, Goodtimes Grill/Taco John's, Great Wall Chinese, Jimmy John's, KFC, Las Margarita's Mexican, Old Chicago Grill, Papa Murphy's, Perkins, Pizza Hut, Qdoba Mexican, Quiznos, Ruby Tuesday, Smiling Moose Deli, Subway, Taco Bell, Wendy's, Wyo Rib Chophouse Candlewood Suites, Country Inn&Suites, Days Inn, Fairfield Inn, Holiday Inn Express, Home 2 Suites, La Quinta, Oak Tree Inn, Ramada Plaza, Wingate Inn $Tree, Albertson's, AT&T, AutoZone, Big O Tire, city park, GNC, Goodyear Truck Tire, Home Depot, Jo-Ann, Menards, Midas, Office Depot, O'Reilly Parts, Osco Drug, Petco, Plains Tire, Tire-O-Rama, Verizon, vet, Walgreens, Walmart/Subway
124	WY 50, Gillette, N Kum&Go/dsl, Shell/Burger King/dsl, Sinclair/Papa John's/dsl Hong Kong Rest., Los Compadres Mexican, Pizza Hut, Rooster's Rest., Subway Best Western/rest., Budget Inn, Comfort Inn, Hampton Inn, Motel 6, Super 8, TownePlace Suites H, Crazy Woman Camping, Don's Foods, Ford, S Kum&Go/dsl McDonald's Bighorn Tire, Buick/Chevrolet/GMC, Chrysler/Dodge/Jeep
116	Force Rd
113	Wild Horse Creek Rd
106	Kingsbury Rd
102	Barber Creek Rd
91	Dead Horse Creek Rd
89mm	Powder River
88	Powder River Rd, N **both lanes, full facilities, litter barrels, petwalk,** , , **RV Park**
82	Indian Creek Rd
77	Schoonover Rd
73.5mm	Crazy Woman Creek
73	Crazy Woman Creek Rd
69	Dry Creek Rd
68.5mm	**parking area wb**
65	Red Hills Rd, Tipperary Rd
60mm	**parking area both lanes,** litter barrels
58	US 16, to Ucross, Buffalo, **0-3 mi** S Cenex/dsl/24hr, Exxon/dsl, Maverik/dsl Bozeman Tr Steaks, Dash Inn Rest., Hardee's, McDonald's, Pizza Hut, Sub Shop, Subway, Taco John's, Winchester Steaks Buffalo Inn, Comfort Inn, Days Inn, Hampton Inn, Holiday Inn Express, Quality Inn, Rodeway WYO Motel, Super 8 H, Ace Hardware, Bighorn Tire, Deer Park Camping, Family$, Indian RV Camp, KOA, Nat Hist Dist, O'Reilly Parts, Verizon, vet

BUFFALO

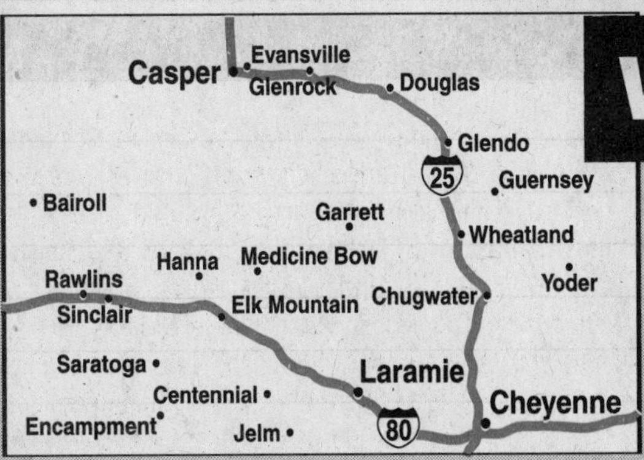

Exit #	Services
56b	I-25 S, US 87 S, to Buffalo
56a	25 Bus, 90 Bus, to Buffalo, **services 2 mi S (from eb)**
53	Rock Creek Rd
51	Lake DeSmet, **1 mi** N Lake Stop gas/motel/cafe Lake De Smet RV park
47	Shell Creek Rd
44	US 87 N, Piney Creek Rd, to Story, Banner, N Ft Phil Kearney, museum, **5 mi** S Wagon Box Cabins/Rest.
39mm	scenic turnout wb
37	Prairie Dog Creek Rd, to Story
33	Meade Creek Rd, to Big Horn
31mm	**parking area eb**
25	US 14 E, Sheridan, N Quality Inn Dalton's RV Ctr, S Cenex/dsl, Exxon/dsl, Holiday/dsl, Maverik/dsl Arby's, Burger King, Goodtimes/Taco John's, Jimmy John's, Little Caesar's, Los Agaves, McDonald's, Ole's Pizza, Papa John's, Papa Murphy's, Perkins, Qdoba, Starbucks, Subway, Taco Bell, Wendy's Candlewood Suites, Days Inn, Fairfield Inn, Holiday Inn, Holiday Lodge, Mill Inn $Tree, Ace Hardware, , Albertson's/Osco Drug, AT&T, AutoZone, Buick/GMC, Chrysler/Dodge/Jeep, Firestone/auto, Ford/Lincoln, GNC, Goodyear/auto, Home Depot, Midas, NAPA, O'Reilly Parts, Petco, Sheridan Coll, Tire-Rama, to Hist Dist, Toyota, Verizon, vet, Walgreens, Walmart/Subway
23	WY 336, 5th St, Sheridan, N **both lanes, full facilities,** , **litter barrels, petwalk, RV dump,** Rock Stop/Subway/dsl Comfort Inn, **1-2 mi** S Cenex, Holiday/dsl DQ, Powder River Pizza Alamo Motel, Best Value Inn, Best Western, Hampton Inn, Motel 6 H, city park, Honda, Peter D's RV Park, radiators, Sheridan Cty Museum
20	to Main St, Sheridan, W Common Cents/dsl, N KOA, S Cenex/dsl, Exxon/dsl/scales/24hr, Gasamat/dsl, Maverik/dsl Domino's, Kim's Rest., McDonald's, Pizza Hut Bramble Motel, Budget Inn, Rodeway Inn, Stage Stop Motel, Super 8, Super Saver Motel, Trails End Motel/rest. H, Peerless Tires, Verizon
16	to Decker, Montana, port of entry
15mm	Tongue River
14	WY 345, Acme Rd
9	US 14 W, Ranchester, **1 mi** S Conoco/dsl Conner Bfd NHS, Foothills Campground, Lazy R Campground, to Yellowstone/Teton NPs, Western Motel
1	Parkman
0mm	Wyoming/Montana state line

SHERIDAN

WY

NOTES

Assist A Fellow Traveler with...

the Next EXIT®

Published annually, the Next EXIT® provides the best USA Interstate Highway Information available. Use this form to order another copy of the Next EXIT® for yourself or for someone special.

The 2020 edition of the Next EXIT® is $19.95 plus shipping.

Please send ______ copies of the Next Exit® to the address below.

I've enclosed my check or money order for:

☐ $19.95 plus $7.00 US Shipping ($26.95) per copy.

☐ $19.95 plus $11.00 Canadian Shipping ($30.95) per copy.

Name:____

Address:____________________________ Apt./Suite #____________

City: __________________________ State: ______ Zip:____________

THREE EASY ORDER OPTIONS:

1. MAIL ORDER FORM TO: the Next EXIT®, Inc.
PO Box 888
Garden City, Utah 84028

2. ORDER ON THE WEB AT: www.theNextExit.com

3. GIVE US A CALL & USE YOUR CHARGE CARD: 1-800-NEX-EXIT or 1-800-639-3948

More digital options are available at www.theNextExit.com